ATTORNEY'S
Illustrated
MEDICAL
DICTIONARY

ATTORNEY'S
Illustrated
MEDICAL
DICTIONARY

IDA G. DOX, PH.D.
MEDICAL COMMUNICATION SPECIALIST (RETIRED)
GEORGETOWN UNIVERSITY SCHOOL OF MEDICINE
MEDICAL LEXICOGRAPHER

GILBERT M. EISNER, M.D., F.A.C.P
CLINICAL PROFESSOR OF MEDICINE
GEORGETOWN UNIVERSITY SCHOOL OF MEDICINE
CLINICAL PROFESSOR OF MEDICINE
GEORGE WASHINGTON UNIVERSITY SCHOOL OF MEDICINE
SENIOR ATTENDING PHYSICIAN
WASHINGTON HOSPITAL CENTER

JUNE L. MELLONI, PH.D.
EDUCATIONAL CONSULTANT AND EVALUATOR OF
INSTRUCTIONAL PROGRAMS IN THE MEDICAL SCIENCES
GREAT FALLS, VIRGINIA

B. JOHN MELLONI, PH.D.
EXPERT IN BIOMEDICAL COMMUNICATION (RETIRED)
NATIONAL LIBRARY OF MEDICINE, NATIONAL INSTITUTES OF HEALTH
PROFESSORIAL LECTURER IN HUMAN ANATOMY (RETIRED)
GEORGETOWN UNIVERSITY SCHOOL OF MEDICINE
CO-DIRECTOR OF THE ARCHIVES OF MEDICAL VISUAL RESOURCES
THE FRANCIS A. COUNTWAY LIBRARY OF MEDICINE
HARVARD UNIVERSITY MEDICAL SCHOOL

WEST PUBLISHING COMPANY
MINNEAPOLIS/ST. PAUL   NEW YORK   LOS ANGELES   SAN FRANCISCO

CREDITS

Composition: Carlisle Communications
Art: Electronic conversion by Publication Services
Copyeditor: Susan Ecklund
Text Design: Roslyn Stendahl, Dapper Design

WEST'S COMMITMENT TO THE ENVIRONMENT

In 1906, West Publishing Company began recycling materials left over from the production of books. This began a tradition of efficient and responsible use of resources. Today, 100% of our legal bound volumes are printed on acid-free, recycled paper consisting of 50% new fibers. West recycles nearly 27,700,000 pounds of scrap paper annually—the equivalent of 229,300 trees. Since the 1960s, West has devised ways to capture and recycle waste inks, solvents, oils, and vapors created in the printing process. We also recycle plastics of all kinds, wood, glass, corrugated cardboard, and batteries, and have eliminated the use of polystyrene book packaging. We at West are proud of the longevity and the scope of our commitment to the environment.

West pocket parts and advance sheets are printed on recyclable paper and can be collected and recycled with newspapers. Staples do not have to be removed. Bound volumes can be recycled after removing the cover.

Production, Prepress, Printing and Binding by West Publishing Company.

 TEXT IS PRINTED ON 10% POST CONSUMER RECYCLED PAPER

British Library Cataloguing-in-Publication Data. A catalogue record for this book is available from the British Library.

Published by WEST PUBLISHING COMPANY
              610 Oppermann Drive
              P.O. Box 64526
              St. Paul, MN 55164-0526

Printed in the United States of America

04 03 02 01 00 99 98 97   8 7 6 5 4 3 2 1 0

Library of Congress Cataloging-in-Publication Data

Attorney's illustrated medical dictionary / Ida G. Dox . . . [et al.].
      p.   cm.
   Includes index.
   ISBN 0-314-02895-1 (alk. paper)
   1. Medicine—Dictionaries.   2. Lawyers.   I. Dox, Ida.
R121.A88   1997
610′ .3—dc20
                                              96-41090
                                              CIP

Contents

Contents

Preface

The pursuit of legal endeavors relating to medicine and health care frequently requires consultation of a medical dictionary. A clear comprehension of the language of medicine is essential when discussing medical problems, whether in the courtroom or in discussions with clients and medical consultants. Equally important in such interactions is the proper pronunciation of medical terms. An up-to-date medical dictionary serves as a trusted aid in helping to increase understanding and facilitate proper pronunciation, thereby ensuring successful communication of medical facts.

Perusal of most professional medical dictionaries that are currently available demonstrates that a medical background is required to understand the exact meaning of many of the terms defined. Definitions are often wrought with complex technical words, many requiring additional explanation. As a result, "looking up a word" in these volumes may become a prolonged process, and understanding the meaning of the word frequently eludes the reader.

The *Attorney's Illustrated Medical Dictionary* offers an alternative for the reader in need of a working knowledge of the language of medicine and health sciences. It is designed for those in the legal fields whose work relates to medical matters. Its intended audience includes attorneys and researchers involved in such areas as personal injury, workers' compensation, medical malpractice, and social security disability; examiners of health insurance claims; social security investigators; those involved in paralegal work; and law students. It is also anticipated that this book will appeal to members of the health professions who prefer a clearly worded, visually oriented medical reference book.

The scope of the *Attorney's Illustrated Medical Dictionary* is comprehensive. The 30,000 defined terms that constitute the body of the text reflects a broad range of the medical vocabulary in current usage. Subjects covered extend from the traditional basic and clinical sciences to the newly developed technologies used in diagnosis and treatment, and to innovations in health care. Special attention with expanded definitions is given to such topics as occupational diseases and injuries, medicinal drugs and industrial chemicals, psychiatric disorders, forensic sciences, genetics, and many other medical disciplines of particular relevance to the book's intended audience.

Included also as defined entries are a number of informal terms that have been generally accepted and are frequently encountered in hospital records and reports, and in verbal and written communications. They include acronyms and the argot of newly evolving specialties and subspecialties. Although these terms are not part of the traditional, formal medical vocabulary, they are, nonetheless, integral to the language of modern medicine. Further, as a way of rounding out the scope of the book, a number of terms from the vernacular are included as entries, closely linked to their scientific equivalents by cross-references.

Developing a reference book such as a medical dictionary requires access to countless resources. Medical books and journals, scientific seminars and lectures, and one-on-one conversations with a variety of health care professionals are essential to ensure that the book's framework is on solid footing. Fortunately, all these resources were available to us and we constantly drew from them throughout the eight years of preparation of this volume. If all the resources we consulted were listed individually, they would fill many of these pages. Therefore, we herein acknowledge with appreciation their considerable contribution collectively.

Individually, we wish to express our indebtedness to a few of our colleagues for their professional contributions in specialized areas; to Brian J. Kelly, MD, neurologist and specialist in critical care medicine, for his careful review of many of the tests; to Susanne Humphrey, MLS, information specialist, for helping with some pertinent searches of the medical literature, which kept us abreast of the most up-to-date medical information; to H. Paul Melloni for his talented rendering of many of the visuals, including the finest pen and ink illustrations of blood cells, and for his valuable help in suggesting layouts of the illustrations throughout the book. Particular acknowledgment is due to Rona Eisner, PhD, who not only served as unofficial subeditor for psychiatric terms but also provided valuable stylistic advice and invaluable support. On a personal note, we thank Peter J. and Roy G. Melloni for their sustained encouragement, support, and enthusiasm for the project throughout the many years of its duration.

Our special appreciation is extended to the staff of the West Publishing Company, especially Theresa J. Lippert, JD, who as our senior editor navigated the project flawlessly and with constant enthusiasm; Kenneth Zeigler, who recognized the need for this reference book and approved its development; Shirley Qual, RN, JD, who served as a consultant to the West Publishing Company and made valuable recommendations; John M. Lindley for his astuteness in assessing the special needs for this project; Susan Ecklund, the copyeditor, for her competent work; and Deanna Quinn, who as the senior production editor, professionally managed the million and one details that go into producing a reference book of this nature.

Finally, we note also our considerable debt to the many other persons in the legal profession who suggested ways of making the dictionary a useful tool for them. We are confident that the inclusion of their suggestions will serve them well.

Suggestions for increasing the usefulness of the book are welcomed and appreciated. Such comments may be addressed to Ida G. Dox, PhD, 9308 Renshaw Drive, Bethesda, Maryland 20817.

IGD
GME
JLM
BJM

Features

To fulfill the objective of providing a practical, easy-to-use reference resource, several important features are included in the *Attorney's Illustrated Medical Dictionary*.

Illustrations

A prominent feature of the book is the liberal use of single-concept illustrations not only to help the reader grasp the meaning of a word but to enhance retention of the information. Thousands of illustrations appear throughout the book and, to correlate them with their corresponding definitions, each is placed in close proximity to the appropriate defined term. To emphasize the relationship between a definition and its illustration, important points of the illustration are highlighted in color; the corresponding entry term within the text is also printed in the same color. When appropriate, graphs and tables accompany some entries as supplementary information.

A feature of this dictionary that is expected to prove of value for its intended audience is the inclusion of full-page plates of illustrations devoted to a single topic (e.g., fractures, bursae, ligaments, and joints). Full-body systems, such as, cardiovascular, musculoskeletal and nervous systems, are depicted in the same manner. These plates, like the single illustrations, are placed near the appropriate defined terms. Similarly, all the arteries, bones, muscles, nerves, and veins of the body are organized into illustrated tables and placed within the text for easy accessibility. As used in this dictionary, illustrations, graphs and tables, in effect, complete the definitions.

Index to Illustrations

The illustrations have been indexed at the end of the book, with the page number of the most informative or pertinent illustration printed in bold type. The index will offer the reader an opportunity to examine more than one example of visuals depicting the topic under study. Some of the illustrations represent the same structures but offer different emphasis, labels, or topographical orientations or, perhaps, a close-up of a particular area. The reader, through this multiple exposure of the same entity, will gain a roadmap image that leads to better comprehension.

Vocabulary

The defining vocabulary and accuracy of the definitions are given optimum consideration. Definitions are worded simply and concisely, avoiding, whenever possible, the use of esoteric words that may require additional searching to decipher their meaning. Accuracy of the meaning of a word or phrase is rigorously maintained through extensive search of authoritative medical resources, and by consultation with experts in various fields of health care and law regarding current usage.

As a matter of convenience, the traditional practice of using the pronoun "he" is followed throughout the book in a generic sense when it is not intended to specify the gender of an individual.

Pronunciation

Pronunciation of defined main entries is indicated by a phonetic respelling placed in parenthesis after the entry, a method that is in line with accepted simplified formats. Only two diacritical marks are used: the breve (˘) and the macron (¯) to indicate the short and the long vowel sounds, respectively. An "h" is added after a vowel when an open sound of that letter is indicated. An accent is placed after the syllable to be stressed. Examples: abortion (ah-bor'tion), sonogram (so'nŏ-gram), microscope (mi'kro-skōp), tranquilizer (tran-kwĭ-līz'er).

Medical Synonyms

Mindful of the fact that medical terms usually have two or more synonyms, which can prove confusing, the definition is placed under the term most frequently used, with synonyms cited at the end of the definition. Each synonym is also listed as an entry, cross-referenced to the defined term. A few obsolete terms are included because they may appear in dated records. They are identified as obsolete and are cross-referenced to their current equivalents. When additional relevant information can be obtained by another, seemingly unrelated term, the reader is directed to it by adding "See also" at the end of the definition.

Organization of Entry Terms

With few exceptions, terms consisting of two or more words are placed under the primary single-word noun, as done in standard medical dictionaries (e.g., *avulsion fracture*, *Barton's fracture*, and *depressed skull fracture* are all listed alphabetically as subentries under *fracture*, the main entry). Words that have long lists of subentries arranged in this manner include *disease, disorder, syndrome, sign, symptom, injury, abscess, operation, test,* and others. This arrangement has the advantage of facilitating a quick review of related terms.

Abbreviations, Symbols, Laboratory Reference Values

Certain types of information are most readily accessible to a reader when placed in a handy appendix; therefore, to increase the usefulness of this dictionary, a substantial number of commonly used abbreviations and their meanings are grouped separately in Appendix A, the first of three appendices. Grouped in Appendix B are symbols frequently found in medical writings. A range of laboratory reference values is listed in Appendix C, since laboratory tests are frequently performed for diagnoses and they commonly serve as a guide in assessing the status of a patient's health.

It is hoped that the many features included in this dictionary will help answer the user's quest for the meaning of medical words as conveyed in current usage.

Guide to Dictionary Use

cross-reference to defined subentry

word element

color coordination between entry and illustration

pronunciation

ileal (il′e-al) Relating to the third and longest portion (ileum) of the small intestine.

ileitis (il-e-i′tis) Inflammation of the third and longest portion (ileum) of the small intestine.

backwash i. Inflammatory ulceration of the ileum as an extension of ulcerative colitis.

distal i. See Crohn's disease, under disease.

terminal i. See Crohn's disease, under disease.

ileo- Combining form meaning the ileum.

ileoanal (il-e-o-a′nal) Relating to the distal portion of the small intestine (the ileum) and the anus; applied to the surgical connection of the ileum and anal canal, after removal of the rectum, for the treatment of ulcerative proctitis.

ileocecal (il-e-o-se′kal) Relating to the adjacent portions of the small and large intestines (the ileum and cecum).

ileocecostomy (il-e-o-se-kos′to-me) Surgical connection of nonadjacent portions of the small and large intestines (i.e., of the ileum and cecum).

ileocecum (il-e-o-se′kum) The adjacent portions of the small and large intestines (ileum and cecum) considered as a unit.

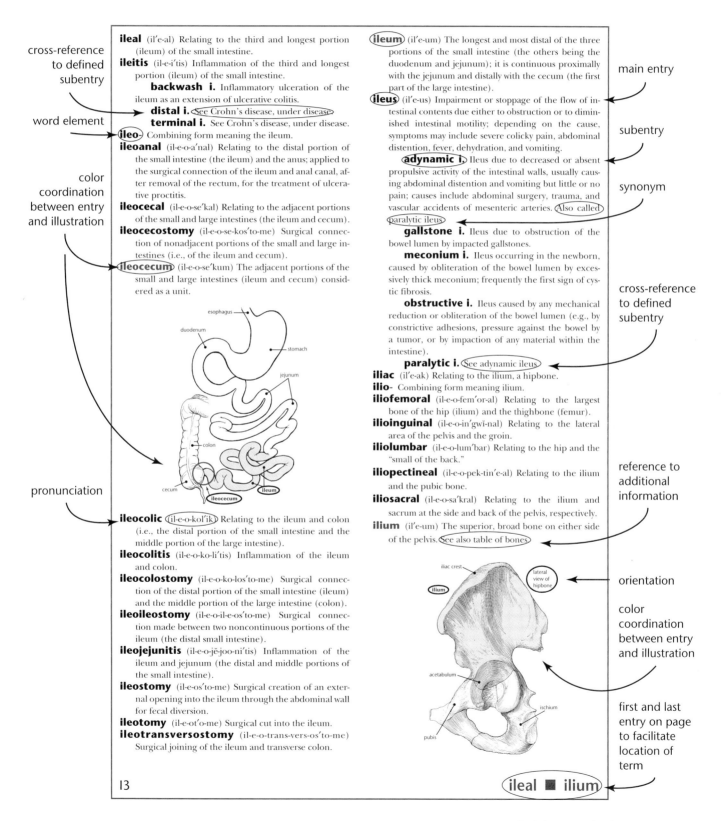

ileocolic (il-e-o-kol′ik) Relating to the ileum and colon (i.e., the distal portion of the small intestine and the middle portion of the large intestine).

ileocolitis (il-e-o-ko-li′tis) Inflammation of the ileum and colon.

ileocolostomy (il-e-o-ko-los′to-me) Surgical connection of the distal portion of the small intestine (ileum) and the middle portion of the large intestine (colon).

ileoileostomy (il-e-o-il-e-os′to-me) Surgical connection made between two noncontinuous portions of the ileum (the distal small intestine).

ileojejunitis (il-e-o-jĕ-joo-ni′tis) Inflammation of the ileum and jejunum (the distal and middle portions of the small intestine).

ileostomy (il-e-os′to-me) Surgical creation of an external opening into the ileum through the abdominal wall for fecal diversion.

ileotomy (il-e-ot′o-me) Surgical cut into the ileum.

ileotransversostomy (il-e-o-trans-vers-os′to-me) Surgical joining of the ileum and transverse colon.

ileum (il′e-um) The longest and most distal of the three portions of the small intestine (the others being the duodenum and jejunum); it is continuous proximally with the jejunum and distally with the cecum (the first part of the large intestine).

main entry

ileus (il′e-us) Impairment or stoppage of the flow of intestinal contents due either to obstruction or to diminished intestinal motility; depending on the cause, symptoms may include severe colicky pain, abdominal distention, fever, dehydration, and vomiting.

subentry

adynamic i. Ileus due to decreased or absent propulsive activity of the intestinal walls, usually causing abdominal distention and vomiting but little or no pain; causes include abdominal surgery, trauma, and vascular accidents of mesenteric arteries. Also called paralytic ileus.

synonym

gallstone i. Ileus due to obstruction of the bowel lumen by impacted gallstones.

meconium i. Ileus occurring in the newborn, caused by obliteration of the bowel lumen by excessively thick meconium; frequently the first sign of cystic fibrosis.

obstructive i. Ileus caused by any mechanical reduction or obliteration of the bowel lumen (e.g., by constrictive adhesions, pressure against the bowel by a tumor, or by impaction of any material within the intestine).

cross-reference to defined subentry

paralytic i. See adynamic ileus.

iliac (il′e-ak) Relating to the ilium, a hipbone.

ilio- Combining form meaning ilium.

iliofemoral (il-e-o-fem′or-al) Relating to the largest bone of the hip (ilium) and the thighbone (femur).

ilioinguinal (il-e-o-in′gwī-nal) Relating to the lateral area of the pelvis and the groin.

iliolumbar (il-e-o-lum′bar) Relating to the hip and the "small of the back."

iliopectineal (il-e-o-pek-tin′e-al) Relating to the ilium and the pubic bone.

reference to additional information

iliosacral (il-e-o-sa′kral) Relating to the ilium and sacrum at the side and back of the pelvis, respectively.

ilium (il′e-um) The superior, broad bone on either side of the pelvis. See also table of bones.

orientation

color coordination between entry and illustration

first and last entry on page to facilitate location of term

13

ileal ■ ilium

A

a-, an- Prefixes meaning without; not.

ab- Prefix meaning from; away from.

abampere (ab-am′pēr) Electromagnetic unit of current equal to 10 amperes.

abandonment (ă-ban′don-ment) Termination of the physician-patient relationship unilaterally by the physician under circumstances that require continuing medical care, without giving the patient reasonable time to secure the services of another physician or when alternative sources for medical care are unavailable; includes those situations where no reasonable alternatives are available for a patient regardless of reasonable amount of time to look for a replacement.

abapical (ab-ap′ĭ-kl) Opposite the apex.

abarognosis (ab-ar-og-no′sis) Loss of the ability to perceive weight.

abasia (ah-ba′zhe-ah) Inability to walk due to impaired motor coordination.

abasia-astasia (ah-ba′zhe-ah as-ta′zhe-ah) See astasia-abasia.

abasic, abatic (ah-ba′sik, ah-bat′ik) Relating to abasia.

abaxial, abaxile (ab-ak′se-al, ab-ak′sil) Located out of, or directed away from, the axis of the body or a part.

abdomen (ab′do-men, ab-do′men) The part of the body below the chest and above the pelvis, containing the largest cavity of the body; divided into nine regions by imaginary planes for the purpose of identifying location of structures contained within. Abdominal contents include nerves, blood and lymph vessels, lymph nodes, and several organs: lowest part of esophagus, stomach, intestines, liver, gallbladder, pancreas, and spleen. Also called venter; (popularly) belly; (incorrectly) stomach. See also abdominal regions, under region; abdominal cavity, under cavity.

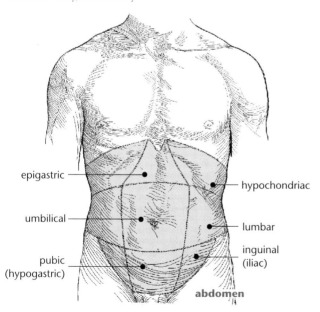

epigastric
hypochondriac
umbilical
lumbar
pubic (hypogastric)
inguinal (iliac)
abdomen

    acute a. General term denoting any intra-abdominal condition that usually requires surgical treatment. Common findings include tenderness, muscle guarding, abnormal or absent bowel sounds, and pain felt when pressure applied to the abdomen is released (rebound tenderness). Also called surgical abdomen.

    boat-shaped a. See navicular abdomen.

    carinate a. Keel-shaped prominence along the anterior midline of the abdomen.

    navicular a. A boat-shaped depression on the anterior wall of the abdomen. Also called scaphoid abdomen; boat-shaped abdomen.

    scaphoid a. See navicular abdomen.

    surgical a. See acute abdomen.

abdominal (ab-dom′ĭ-nal) Relating to the abdomen.

abdomino-, abdomin- Combining forms meaning abdomen.

abdominoanterior (ab-dom′ĭ-no-an-te′re-or) Rarely used term denoting an intrauterine position of a fetus in which the fetal abdomen faces the mother's anterior abdominal wall.

abdominocentesis (ab-dom′ĭ-no-sen-te′sis) See peritoneocentesis.

abdominocystic (ab-dom′ĭ-no-sis′tik) 1. Relating to the gallbladder. 2. See abdominovesical.

abdominoperineal (ab-dom′ĭ-no-per-ĭ-ne′al) Relating to the abdomen and perineum, used especially to indicate surgical procedures involving those areas.

abdominoplasty (ab-dom′ĭ-no-plas′te) Any operation on the abdomen for aesthetic reasons, especially to remove excess abdominal skin and underlying subcutaneous fat and, if necessary, to repair the rectus muscle. See also panniculectomy.

abdominothoracic (ab-dom′ĭ-no-tho-ras′ik) Relating to the abdomen and thorax.

abdominovesical (ab-dom′ĭ-no-ves′ĭ-kl) Relating to the abdomen and bladder. Also called abdominocystic.

abducens (ab-du′senz) Latin for abducent.

abducent (ab-du′sent) Drawing away; abducting.

abduct (ab-dukt′) To move away from the median plane.

abduction (ab-duk′shun) 1. Movement of a limb away from the median plane of the body or a digit away from the axial plane of a limb. 2. Movement of the eye toward the temple. Opposite of adduction.

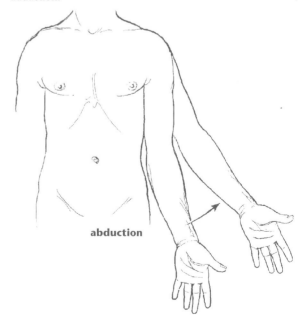

abduction

abductor (ab-duk′tor) A muscle that moves a body part away from the median plane. Opposite of adductor.

abembryonic (ab′em-bre-on′ik) Away from the region where the embryo is located.

aberrant (ab-er′ant) Differing from the normal or the usual.

aberration (ab′er-a′shun) Abnormality; deviation; imperfection.

    chromatic a. Aberration resulting from the unequal refraction of different wavelengths of light, typically manifested in a simple optical system by a fringe of color around the image. Also called color aberration; newtonian aberration.

    chromosomal a. Any irregularity in the number of chromosomes or structure of a chromosome that is discernible by microscopy. Also called chromosomal anomaly.

chromosomal aberration

    color a. See chromatic aberration.

    monochromatic a. Defect of image formation involving transmission of a single wavelength of light.

    newtonian a. See chromatic aberration.

    optical a. Failure of light rays from a source to form a perfect image after passing through an optical system.

    spherical a. Aberration occurring in simple refraction on a spherical lens surface in which the peripheral and central portions of the lens focus at different points along the axis.

    triple-X chromosomal a. The presence of three X chromosomes in a female, instead of the normal two, occurring in 1 of every 800 live female births. The frequency of mild mental retardation is slightly greater in the group of affected females than it is in the general population. Also called triple-X syndrome.

abetalipoproteinemia (a-ba′tah-lip-o-pro-ten-e′me-ah) Rare disorder of autosomal recessive inheritance that causes pigmentary degeneration of the retina (retinitis pigmentosa), presence of acanthocytes in the blood, and absence of low-density lipoproteins (LDLs) in the plasma; it may be associated with steatorrhea and progressive disease of the nervous system.

abeyance (ah-ba′ans) Temporary cessation of function or activity.

abient (ab′e-ent) Characterized by a tendency to move away from the source of a stimulus.

ability (ah-bil′ĭ-te) The physical, mental, or legal competence to function.

    impaired urinary concentrating a. Inability to concentrate solutes in the urine; measured after a period of fluid restriction. It may be caused by any disease of the kidney but is more characteristic of diseases affecting the inner portion of the kidney, including pyelonephritis, polycystic kidney disease, and sickle-cell disease.

    template a. In genetics, the capacity of the DNA molecule to code information to be replicated.

    verbal a. An adequate level of proficiency in the use of words, spoken or written, including the rapid and accurate comprehension of verbally expressed concepts.

abiosis (ab-e-o′sis) Absence of life.

abiotic (ab-e-ot′ik) Incompatible with life, such as an environment that does not support life.

abiotrophy (ab-e-ot′ro-fe) 1. Any of several degenerative processes of unknown cause affecting nerve cells in the brain or spinal cord. 2. The aging process (imprecise term).

abirritant (ab-ir′ri-tant) 1. Relieving or diminishing irritation. 2. An agent having this quality.

ablastin (ah-blas′tin) An antibody, produced by rats infected with *Trypanosoma lewisi*, that seems to inhibit reproduction of trypanosomes.

ablate (ab-lāt′) To remove, especially by surgery, or to destroy a function.

ablation (ab-la′shun) Removal or eradication of diseased tissue, usually by surgery, laser, or freezing radiotherapy.

ablepharia (ah-blef-a′rē-ah) Congenital absence of the eyelids, partial or total, unilateral or bilateral. It may be associated with other facial malformations or with malformations of the urogenital tract.

abluent (ab′lu-ent) 1. Having cleansing properties. 2. A cleansing agent.

ablution (ab-lu′shun) The act of cleansing.

ablutomania (ab-lu-to-ma′ne-ah) Rarely used term to denote abnormal concern with washing and bathing. See also obsessive-compulsive disorder, under disorder.

abneural (ab-nu′ral) Away from the central nervous system.

abnormal (ab-nor′mal) Not normal; differing substantially from the usual.

abnormality (ab-nor-mal′ĭ-te) 1. The state of being abnormal. 2. An anomaly or dysfunction.

ABO blood group International classification of human blood types according to their compatibility in transfusion, typed as A, B, AB, or O. Also called ABO factors.

abohm (ab′ōm) Electromagnetic unit of resistance equal to 1 billionth of an ohm.

aborad, aboral (ab-o′rad, ab-o′ral) Directed away from the mouth. Opposite of orad.

abort (ah-bort′) 1. To expel or to remove the products of conception before the age of viability of the fetus. 2. To arrest the usual course of a disease. 3. To cause cessation of development.

abortient (ah-bor′shent) See abortifacient.

abortifacient (ah-bor-ti-fa′shent) 1. Producing an abortion. Also called abortient; abortigenic; abortive. 2. An agent, such as a drug, that brings about an abortion.

abortigenic (ah-bor-tĭ-gen′ik) See abortifacient.

abortion (ah-bor′shun) 1. Expulsion or extraction of all or any part of the products of conception (placenta, membranes, and embryo or fetus) before the end of 20 complete weeks (139 days) of gestation calculated from the first day of the last normal menstrual period, or a fetal weight of less than 500 grams. 2. The arrest of any natural or disease process.

    accidental a. Abortion caused by injury.

    ampullar a. Abortion resulting from implantation of the fertilized ovum at the ampulla of the fallopian (uterine) tube.

    complete a. Abortion that includes the fetus (or embryo), placenta, and membranes.

    elective a. See induced abortion.

    eugenic a. See therapeutic abortion.

    habitual a. Three or more spontaneous abortions occurring in a woman's three or more consecutive pregnancies.

    incomplete a. Abortion in which some of the products of conception (usually a portion of the placenta) remain within the uterus, resulting in profuse uterine bleeding.

    induced a. Abortion deliberately carried out by means of drugs or mechanical devices or instruments. It may be therapeutic or nontherapeutic. Also called elective abortion.

    inevitable a. Condition in which the abortive process has advanced to a degree that it cannot be halted.

    infected a. Abortion accompanied by fever, purulent discharge, or an elevated white blood cell count; caused by pathogenic microorganisms.

    justifiable a. See therapeutic abortion.

    missed a. Retention of a dead fetus within the uterus for at least two months.

    natural a. See spontaneous abortion.

    nontherapeutic a. Abortion induced without a medical reason.

    septic a. Abortion accompanied by dissemination of microorganisms and toxic substances throughout the woman's blood circulation, which threatens her life.

spontaneous a. Expulsion of the products of conception due to natural causes, without deliberate mechanical or medicinal interference, occurring before the fetus can survive outside the uterus. Also called miscarriage; natural abortion.

therapeutic a. Abortion performed to preserve the physical or mental health of the pregnant woman, as when pregnancy is the result of rape or incest, or to prevent the birth of a defective child. Also called justifiable abortion; eugenic abortion.

threatened a. Slight show of blood, with or without cramplike pain, occurring during the first 20 weeks of pregnancy.

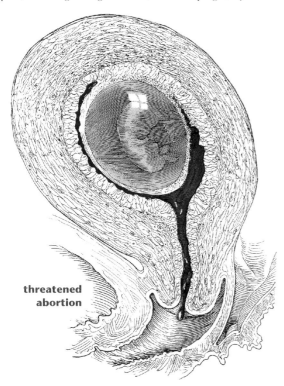

threatened
abortion

tubal a. Abortion due to an ectopic pregnancy. The embryo is expelled into the pelvic cavity, either through a rupture of the fallopian (uterine) tube at the site of implantation, or through the distal opening of the tube.

abortionist (ah-bor′shun-ist) One who induces abortion, especially illegally.

abortive (ah-bor′tiv) **1.** Cutting short the progress of a disease. **2.** Incompletely developed or formed; rudimentary. **3.** See abortifacient.

abortus (ah-bor′tus) The aborted fetus and all or part of its accompanying tissues.

abouchement (ah-boosh-maw′) The junction of a small blood vessel with a larger one.

aboulia (ah-boo′le-ah) See abulia.

abrachia (ah-bra′ke-ah) Congenital absence of the arms; may be unilateral or bilateral. Bones of the shoulder may be absent or reduced in size.

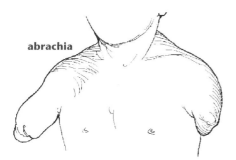

abrachia

abrade (ah-brād′) **1.** To wear off. **2.** To remove a superficial layer by mechanical means.

abrasion (ah-bra′shun) Superficial injury of the skin or mucous membrane in which the outer layers have been scraped off; a scrape.

brush burn a. See brush burn, under burn.

a. collar See abrasion collar, under collar.

corneal a. A scraping away of the anterior surface of the cornea, implying usually a superficial injury by a physical or chemical agent, causing severe pain, tearing, and blurring of vision.

dental a., tooth a. The excessive or abnormal wearing down of the tooth surface by friction, such as that caused by an abrasive dentifrice, incorrect toothbrushing methods, and grinding (bruxism).

dicing a.'s See dicing lacerations, under laceration.

gingival a. Small, circular ulcers (0.5–1.0 mm in diameter) occurring on the gingiva, usually caused by brushing with sharp-bristled, stiff toothbrushes.

marginal a. See abrasion collar, under collar.

mechanical a. See dermabrasion.

rim of a. See abrasion collar, under collar.

abrasive (ah-bra′siv) **1.** Tending to abrade. **2.** A material used for polishing teeth.

abrasiveness (ah-bra′siv-nes) The quality of being abrasive.

abreaction (ab-re-ak′shun) A form of psychotherapy, called catharsis by Freud, consisting of bringing into consciousness and reliving a previously repressed unpleasant experience, with appropriate discharge of affect.

motor a. Abreaction achieved by means of motor or muscular expression.

abrin (a′brin) A powerful protein toxin present in the seeds of *Abrus precatorius;* it is a severe irritant of mucous membranes and, when injected, may cause convulsions, stomach pain, diarrhea, nausea, and death; formerly used topically in certain eye disorders.

abruption (ah-brupt′shun) A detachment or tearing away.

abruptio placentae (ab-rup′she-o pla-sen′te) Premature detachment of the placenta from the uterine wall.

abscess (ab′ses) Localized collection of pus associated with tissue destruction; usually caused by a bacterial infection.

acute a. Abscess of short duration accompanied by fever, inflammation, and throbbing pain. Also called hot abscess.

alveolar a. Abscess in a tooth socket caused by pathogenic bacteria spreading from an infected tooth pulp (usually originating from caries or trauma to the teeth) and causing severe throbbing pain and swelling. Also called dental abscess; dentoalveolar abscess; tooth abscess; root abscess; radicular abscess; periodontal abscess.

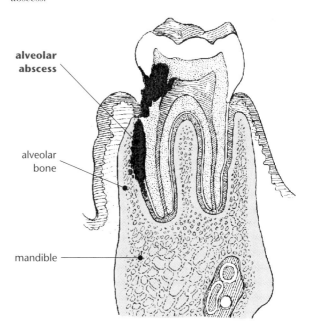

alveolar
abscess

alveolar
bone

mandible

amebic a. Abscess containing a semifluid material of degenerated tissue; associated with amebic dysentery and usually involving the right lobe of the liver. Also called tropical abscess.

anal a. Abscess (superficial and deep) occurring along the anal canal, usually originating from the folds of the anorectal junction (anal crypts); caused by bacterial infection, usually resulting from infiltration of normal rectal flora (*Bacillus coli, Bacillus proteus, Bacillus subtilis*, staphylococci, and streptococci).

apical a. (*a*) Alveolar abscess around the apex of a dental root. Also called periapical abscess; apical periodontal abscess. (*b*) An abscess located at the apex or upper tip of a lung.

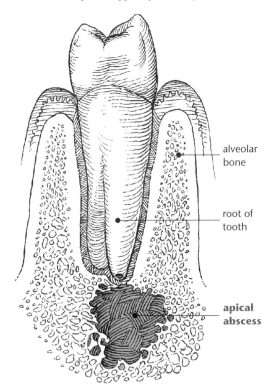

alveolar bone

root of tooth

apical abscess

apical periodontal a. See apical abscess.

appendiceal a. Abscess occurring in the vicinity of the vermiform appendix; generally formed after perforation of an inflamed appendix. Also called periappendiceal abscess; appendicular abscess.

appendicular a. See appendiceal abscess.

Bartholin's a. Abscess in a greater vestibular (Bartholin's) gland or its duct. It is sometimes, not always, a complication of a gonorrheal infection.

bone a. See osteomyelitis.

brain a. An abscess within the substance of the brain ranging in size from microscopic to a size occupying most of a cerebral hemisphere; usually caused by staphylococci although other common bacteria may be present. Organisms gain entry to the brain by extension from a nearby infection, such as from the middle ear, mastoid bone, sinuses, and infected head injuries, or from lung and heart infections via the bloodstream.

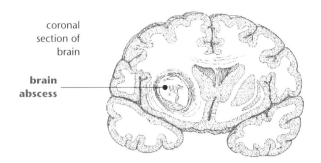

coronal section of brain

brain abscess

Brodie's a. Abscess of long bones surrounded by inflammatory fibrous tissue. It may undergo spontaneous sterilization or become an active focus of infection.

bursal a. Abscess within a membranous sac (bursa) that separates bones and tendons at a joint.

canalicular a. Abscess connected to a milk (lactiferous) duct within a breast, causing a purulent discharge from the nipple.

caseous a. Abscess containing a cheesy material.

chronic a. A long-standing, slow-developing abscess occurring without inflammation. Also called cold abscess.

cold a. See chronic abscess.

collar-button a. Two pus-containing cavities connected by a narrow channel, usually formed in the hand or foot by rupture of an abscess through a fascial layer.

crypt a. One of several minute abscesses occurring in the large intestine in and around the crypts of Lieberkühn; commonly seen in ulcerative colitis.

dental a. Popular name for an alveolar abscess.

dentoalveolar a. See alveolar abscess.

diffuse a. An abscess that is not enclosed in a capsule.

dry a. The remains of an abscess after the pus is resorbed.

gas a. Abscess containing gas due to the presence of gas-forming bacteria such as *Enterobacter aerogenes* and *Escherichia coli*.

gingival a. Abscess in the gum (gingiva) next to an infected tooth; usually formed by the rupture of an alveolar abscess, which tunnels through the alveolar bone and drains into the soft gum tissue. Also called gumboil; parulis.

gravitation a. See perforating abscess.

gummatous a. Abscess formed by the softening and breaking down of a tumor (gumma) that is characteristic of tertiary syphilis. Also called syphilitic abscess.

hot a. See acute abscess.

hypostatic a. See perforating abscess.

iliac a. See psoas abscess.

lung a. Abscess within the substance of the lung usually caused by spread of bacterial infection from other areas, such as those of the upper respiratory tract or teeth. Also called pulmonary abscess.

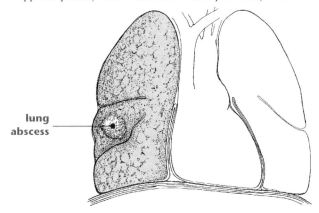

lung abscess

mammary a. Single or multiple abscesses of the breast substance, affecting usually one breast; most commonly caused by *Staphylococcus aureus*, or occasionally by streptococci. Organisms gain entry through cracks on the nipple, most frequently during lactation or in skin conditions such as eczema. Destroyed breast substance may be replaced by fibrous tissue with resulting nipple retraction, which may be mistaken for a tumor.

metastatic a. A secondary abscess caused by microorganisms carried in the bloodstream from a primary abscess.

migrating a. See perforating abscess.

miliary a. The presence of multiple minute abscesses (1–2 mm) in large areas of the body caused by the spread of a blood-borne infection.

orbital a. Abscess within the eye socket (orbit) adjacent to the eyeball, frequently resulting from direct spread of purulent sinusitis. Also called retrobulbar abscess.

abscess ■ abscess

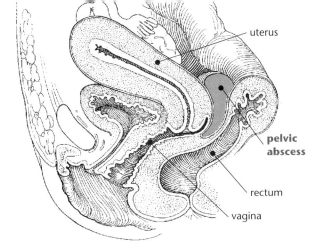

uterus

pelvic
abscess

rectum

vagina

pelvic a. Abscess in the retrouterine pouch occurring as a complication of abdominal or pelvic inflammatory disease.

perforating a. Abscess that spreads to adjacent areas through a site of least resistance. Also called gravitation abscess; hypostatic abscess; migrating abscess; wandering abscess.

periapical a. See apical abscess.

periappendiceal a. See appendiceal abscess.

perinephric a. Abscess in the tissues surrounding the kidney resulting from extension of suppurative infection of the kidney substance through the connective tissue enveloping the kidney (renal fascia).

periodontal a. See alveolar abscess.

periotonsillar a. Acute abscess formed between the palatine tonsil and its muscular bed, resulting from an extension of a tonsillar infection with streptococci and other microorganisms. Also called quinsy; retrotonsillar abscess; supratonsillar abscess.

periurethral a. Abscess involving the tissues of the urethra; associated with gonorrhea or other pyogenic infection.

psoas a. Abscess located along the sheath of the psoas muscle due to extension of infection from a tuberculous lower spine, or from regional inflammation of the intestines. Also called iliac abscess.

pulmonary a. See lung abscess.

pulp a. Abscess developed within the central soft tissues (pulp) of a tooth; caused by caries or by trauma.

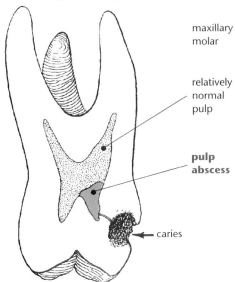

maxillary
molar

relatively
normal
pulp

pulp
abscess

caries

radicular a. See alveolar abscess.

retrobulbar a. See orbital abscess.

retropharyngeal a. An infrequent abscess occurring deep in the back of the throat, in the space between the cervical spine and the posterior lining of the throat (pharyngeal mucosa); formerly common in children as a complication of suppurative infection of the retropharyngeal lymph nodes, or from accidental perforation.

retrotonsillar a. See peritonsillar abscess.

root a. See alveolar abscess.

stitch a. A small abscess around a suture.

subdiaphragmatic a. Abscess formed between the diaphragm and liver or between the diaphragm and the spleen and stomach; it is usually a complication of abdominal surgery or diffuse peritonitis. Also called subphrenic abscess.

subphrenic a. See subdiaphragmatic abscess.

subungal a. A collection of pus beneath a fingernail or toenail.

supratonsillar a. See peritonsillar abscess.

syphilitic a. See gummatous abscess.

tooth a. Popular name for alveolar abscess.

tropical a. See amebic abscess.

tubo-ovarian a. Abscess involving both the fallopian (uterine) tube and the corresponding ovary, generally associated with inflammation of the tube.

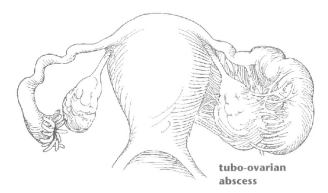

**tubo-ovarian
abscess**

verminous a. See worm abscess.

wandering a. See perforating abscess.

worm a. Abscess containing worms of any kind. Also called verminous abscess.

abscissa (ab-sis′ah) The horizontal coordinate that, together with a vertical one (ordinate), forms a frame of reference for the plotting of data.

absconsio (ab-skon′se-o) A recess, cavity, or fossa.

abscopal (ab-sko′pl) Relating to the effects of ionizing radiation of tissues distant from those directly irradiated.

absence (ab′sens) Abrupt, brief loss of consciousness without loss of postural tone or autonomic function, usually without convulsions. Also called absentia epileptica; petit mal; petit mal epilepsy; absence seizure.

absentia epileptica (ab-sen′she-ah ep-e-lep′tī-kah) See absence.

Absidia (ab-sid′e-ah) A genus of fungi (family Mucoraceae); some species may cause mucormycosis in humans.

absorb (ab-sorb′) 1. To take up by various means. 2. To assimilate or incorporate.

absorbance (ab-sor′bans) The ability of a substance to absorb radiation, expressed mathematically as the negative common logarithm of transmittance. Formerly called optical density.

absorbefacient (ab-sor′be-fa′shent) 1. Promoting absorption. 2. An agent having that quality.

absorbent (ab-sor′bent) 1. Capable of incorporating or taking up a gas, liquid, light rays, or heat. 2. Any material having such capability.

absorptiometer (ab-sorp′she-om′ĕ-ter) 1. An instrument for determining the absorption rate or solubility of a gas in a liquid. 2. Device for measuring the layer of liquid absorbed between two glass plates; used in blood analysis.

absorptiometry (ab-sorp′she-om′ĕ-tre) Any procedure for measuring absorption of waves or particles.

absorption (ab-sorp′shun) 1. The process of taking up and incorporating a substance (gas, liquid, light, heat). 2. In radiology, the uptake of radiant energy by the medium through which the radiation passes.

cutaneous a. Absorption of any substance through the intact skin.

gastrointestinal a. Absorption through the walls of the alimentary canal.

parenteral a. Absorption via any route other than the digestive tract.

absorptive (ab-sorp′tiv) Relating to absorption.

abstinence (ab′sti-nens) Voluntary refraining, especially from indulging in a craving for certain foods, alcohol, or drugs, or in sexual activity.

abstract (ab′strakt) A pharmaceutical preparation made by mixing a powdered solid extract of a substance with milk sugar (lactose).

abstraction ab-strak′shun) **1.** Removal of an ingredient from a compound. **2.** Malocclusion in which the teeth or other structures are below the normal occlusal plane.

abterminal (ab-ter′mĭ-nal) Toward the center; denoting the direction of an electrical current in a muscle.

abulia (ah-bu′le-ah) Loss of the ability to make decisions or to act independently; absence of willpower. Also spelled aboulia.

abulic (ah-bu′lik) Relating to abulia.

abuse (ah-bus′) **1.** Habitual and excessive use. **2.** Maltreatment; injurious or offensive treatment.

alcohol a. See alcoholism.

child a. An act or omission, which is not accidental, committed by a parent, caregiver, or other adult that harms, or threatens to harm, a child's physical or mental health or welfare; may occur in the following forms: *Emotional child a.*, acts or omissions usually on the part of parents or other caregivers that cause serious behavioral, cognitive, emotional, or mental disorders in the child. Emotional child abuse may involve: rejecting the child's needs, isolating the child from normal social experiences, terrorizing the child by constant verbal harassment and denigration, ignoring the child's emotional and developmental growth, corrupting the child by engagement in antisocial behavior. Emotional abuse usually accompanies other forms of abuse and neglect. Also called psychological abuse. *Physical child a.*, abuse that results in physical injury, usually perpetrated in the name of discipline or punishment and ranging from slaps to the use of belts, kitchen utensils, lit cigarettes, etc. *Psychological child a.*, see emotional child abuse. *Sexual child a.*, any sexual activity perpetrated by an adult or older child with or upon a child, or the sexual exploitation of a child for the gratification or profit of the other. It may be assaultive, which produces physical injury and severe emotional trauma, or nonassaultive, which causes little or no physical injury.

a. of children See child abuse.

drug a. See drug abuse, after drug.

elder a. Emotional, nutritional, or physical maltreatment of an elderly person, usually by family members or by institutional personnel.

substance a. See drug abuse, after drug.

abutment (ah-but′ment) A natural tooth or implanted substitute used to support a fixed or removable prosthesis. Also called abutment tooth.

abvolt (ab′volt) Electromagnetic unit of difference of potential equal to 10^{-8} volt.

acacia (ah-ka′she-ah) A gum exuded from various African trees of the genus *Acacia*, especially *Acacia senegal;* used as an emollient, as a thickening agent in food products, and in the manufacture of mucilage. Also called gum arabic.

acalculia (ah-kal-ku′le-ah) A type of aphasia marked by inability to do simple arithmetic, often associated with parietal lobe lesions.

acampsia (ah-kamp′se-ah) Rigidity of a joint for any reason.

acantha (ah-kan′thah) A spinous process.

acanthamebiasis (ah-kan′thah-me-bi′ah-sis) Infection with ameba of the genus *Acanthamoeba*.

Acanthamoeba (ah-kan′thah-me′bah) A genus of free-living amebas (family Acanthamoebidae), commonly found in moist soil and water. Some species cause disease in humans and other primates. Infections may occasionally follow injury or may occur in individuals with a weakened immunologic system. In some instances, the amebas may invade the brain with a fatal outcome.

acanthesthesia (ah-kan′thes-the′ze-ah) Abnormal sensory perception of the skin in which a simple touch gives the sensation of a pinprick.

acanthion (ah-kan′the-on) The tip of the anterior nasal spine.

acantho, acanth- Combining forms meaning spine; thorn.

Acanthocheilonema (ah-kan′tho-ki-lo-ne′mah) A genus of parasitic worms, commonly called filaria; the adults live mainly in the body cavities or the subcutaneous tissues of their host, while the larvae exist in the peripheral blood.

acanthocyte (ah-kan′tho-sit) Abnormal erythrocyte (red blood cell) having several protoplasmic projections that give it a thorny appearance.

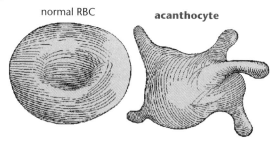

normal RBC   acanthocyte

acanthocytosis (ah-kan′tho-si-to′sis) A condition marked by the presence of numerous acanthocytes in the blood; seen in certain hereditary conditions such as abetalipoproteinemia.

acanthoid (ah-kan′thoid) Spine-shaped.

acantholysis (ak′an-thol′ĭ-sis) Disintegration of the prickle-cell layer of the epidermis, associated with formation of blisters on the skin in such conditions as pemphigus vulgaris and other skin disorders.

acanthoma (ak′an-tho′mah) A tumor of the epidermis composed of squamous cells; it may or may not be malignant.

acanthosis (ak′an-tho′sis) A thickening of the prickle-cell layer of the epidermis.

a. nigrans An eruption of velvety gray to black pigmentation of the large skin folds (axilla, groin, neck) often associated with some internal cancer in adults. A benign type occurs in children.

acapnia (ah-kap′ne-ah) Complete absence of carbon dioxide in the blood, which is incompatible with life. See also hypocapnia.

acardia (a-kar′de-ah) Absence of the heart; a rare condition sometimes occurring in one member of conjoined twins.

acardiotrophia (ah-kar′de-o-tro′fe-ah) Atrophy of the heart muscle (myocardium).

acariasis (ak-ah-ri′ah-sis) **1.** Any disease transmitted by mites. **2.** Infestation with mites. Also called acaridiasis; acarinosis.

acaricide (ah-kar′ĭ-sid) An agent that kills mites or ticks.

acarid (ak′ah-rid) A general term for any mite or tick. Also called acaridan; acarus.

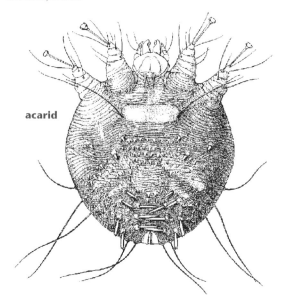

acarid

Acaridae (ah-kar'ĭ-de) A family of mites (order Acarina) consisting of exceptionally small mites (0.5 mm or less); some members infest food products, causing allergic skin rashes in humans, such as grocer's itch and vanillism.

acaridan (ah-kar'ĭ-dan) See acarid.

acaridiasis (ah-kar'ĭ-di'ah-sis) See acariasis.

acarinosis (ah-kar'ĭ-no'sis) See acariasis.

acaro-, acar- Combining forms meaning mites.

acarodermatitis (ak'ah-ro-der-mah-ti'tis) A skin rash caused by mites.

acaroid (ak'ah-roid) Resembling a mite.

acarology (ak-ah-rol'o-je) The study of mites and ticks and the diseases they transmit.

acarophobia (ak'ah-ro-fo'be-ah) Irrational fear of minute parasites and of the itch they cause.

Acarus (ak'ah-rus) A genus of mites of the family Acaridae.

> **A. scabiei** See *Sarcoptes scabiei*.

acarus (ak'ah-rus) See acarid.

acaryote (ah-kār'e-ōt) See akaryocyte.

acatalasemia (a'kat-ah-la-se'me-ah) See acatalasia.

acatalasia (a'kat-ah-la'ze-ah) Disease of autosomal recessive inheritance, found mainly in Japan and Switzerland, marked by deficiency of the enzyme catalase. Affected people often develop recurrent ulceration of the gums and related oral structures. Also called acatalasemia; Takahara's disease.

acataphasia (ah-kat'ah-fa'ze-ah) 1. Speech disability marked by difficulty with phrasing and sentence construction. 2. Inability to express thoughts coherently.

acathexis (ah'kah-thek'sis) In psychoanalysis, a person's detachment from certain memories or ideas that normally should be emotionally charged.

acaudate (ah-kaw'dāt) Without a tail.

accelerant (ak-sel'er-ant) See accelerator.

acceleration (ak-sel-er-a'shun) 1. An increase in speed. 2. The rate of change of velocity per unit time.

accelerator (ak-sel'er-a-tor) Anything (device, drug, nerve, or muscle) that increases speed of action or function. Also called accelerant.

> **linear a.** In radiation therapy, a machine that creates high-energy radiation using electricity to form a stream of fast-moving subatomic particles; used in cancer treatment. Also called megavoltage (MeV) linear accelerator; linac.

> **megavoltage (MeV) linear a.** See linear accelerator.
> **proserum prothrombin conversion a.** (PPCA) See factor VIII, under factor..
> **prothrombin a.** See accelerator globulin, under globulin.
> **serum prothrombin conversion a.** (SPCA) See factor VII, under factor..

accelerin (ak-sel'er-in) See accelerator globulin, under globulin.

accentuator (ak-sen'chu-a-tor) A substance that increases the action of a tissue stain.

acceptor (ak-sep'tor) A substance that unites with a chemical group or an ion of another substance (the donor), thus allowing a chemical reaction to proceed.

accessory (ak-ses'o-re) Supplementary; having a subordinate function to a similar but more important structure.

accident (ak'sĭ-dent) 1. An unexpected, unintended, undesirable occurrence, or an unforeseen complication in the course of a disease that causes bodily injury or death of the involved individual. 2. An unexpected sudden occurrence causing injury which is not due to negligence or misconduct on the part of the injured individual but from which he may be entitled to some legal compensation. 3. In forensic pathology, an accident is considered an immediately unpreventable event and one of the four forms of death (along with natural death, suicide, and homicide).

> **cerebrovascular a., cerebral vascular a., vascular a.,** (CVA) Occlusion or rupture of a blood vessel in the brain. See also stroke.

> **compensation a.** One for which money or services are given to an injured individual, or to his dependents or relatives, as a result of the injury.

accident-prone (ak'sĭ-dent prōn) 1. Having a number of accidents that is greater than average. 2. Having personality characteristics that predispose to accidents.

acclimatation (ah-kli'mah-ta'shun) See acclimation.

acclimation (ak'li-ma'shun) The physiologic adjustment of an organism (plant or animal) to an environmental change. Also called acclimatation.

accolé form (ako-la' form) See applique' form, under form.

accommodation (ah-kom'o-da'shun) In ophthalmology, ocular adjustment carried out for seeing at different distances; specifically, alteration of the convexity of the lens of the eye to focus the visual image upon the retina. 2. See social adaptation, under adaptation.

accommodative (ah-kom'o-da-tiv) Relating to accommodation.

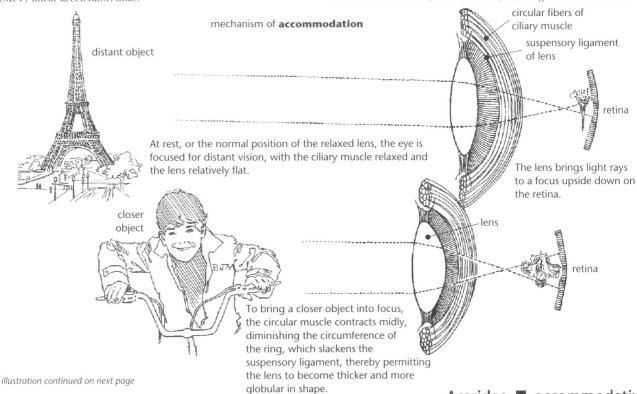

mechanism of **accommodation**

distant object

At rest, or the normal position of the relaxed lens, the eye is focused for distant vision, with the ciliary muscle relaxed and the lens relatively flat.

closer object

To bring a closer object into focus, the circular muscle contracts midly, diminishing the circumference of the ring, which slackens the suspensory ligament, thereby permitting the lens to become thicker and more globular in shape.

circular fibers of ciliary muscle

suspensory ligament of lens

retina

The lens brings light rays to a focus upside down on the retina.

lens

retina

illustration continued on next page

Acaridae ■ accommodative

A

mechanism of **accommodation** (continued)

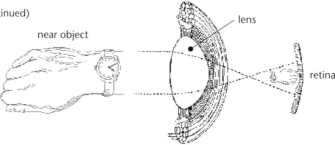

Further contraction of the circular muscle results in additional decrease of tension on the lens, which causes the lens to become more convex, resulting in a sharp focus of a near object on the retina.

accouchement (ah-kōōsh-maw′) Childbirth; labor.

accrementition (ak-re-men-tish′un) **1.** Reproduction by budding. **2.** See accretion.

accretio cordis (ah-kre′she-o kor′dis) Pathologic condition in which abnormal adhesions extend between the membranes enclosing the heart (pericardium) and adjacent structures, such as the chest wall, pleura, or diaphragm.

accretion (ah-kre′shun) **1.** Growth by addition of like material. Also called accrementition. **2.** In dentistry, accumulation of foreign material on the surface of a tooth. **3.** A growing together of parts normally separate.

acellular (a-sel′u-lar) Devoid of cells.

acenesthesia (ah-sen-es-the′ze-ah) Loss of the normal sense of one's physical existence.

acentric (ah-sen′trik) Without a center; in genetics, denoting a chromosome without a centromere.

acephalia (ah-se-fa′le-ah) See acephaly.

acephalocyst (ah-sef′ah-lo′sist) A fluid-filled cyst that is one of the developmental stages of a sterile tapeworm; it does not develop daughter cysts containing tapeworm heads (scoleces).

acephaly (ah-sef′ah-le) Congenital absence of the head. Also called acephalia.

acervuline (ah-ser′vu-lin) Occurring in clusters; said of certain glands.

acervulus (ah-ser′vu-lus), pl. acer′vuli See brain sand granules, under granule.

acetabula (as-ĕ-tab′u-lah) Plural of acetabulum.

acetabular (as-ĕ-tab′u-lah) Relating to the acetabulum.

acetabulectomy (as-ĕ-tab-u-lek′to-me) Surgical removal of the acetabulum.

acetabuloplasty (as-ĕ-tab′u-lo-plas-te) Surgical restoration of the acetabulum.

acetabulum (as-ĕ-tab′u-lum), pl. acetab′ula The cup-shaped articular depression on the lateral aspect of each hipbone into which the head of the femur fits, forming the hip joint. Also called hip socket.

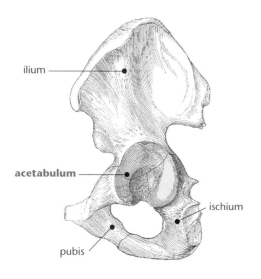

acetal (as′ĕ-tal) **1.** Any of a class of organic compounds characterized by the grouping $C(OR)_2$ and obtained by combining an aldehyde with an alcohol. **2.** A colorless, flammable liquid used as a solvent.

acetaldehyde (as-et-al′dĕ-hid) A colorless volatile liquid, used primarily in organic synthesis. It is an irritant to mucous membranes. Also called acetic aldehyde; ethanal; ethylaldehyde.

acetamide (as-et-am′id) The amide of acetic acid used in biomedical research.

acetamidofluorene (as′et-am-ĭ-do-floo′o-rēn) See acetylaminofluorene.

acetaminophen (as-et-amĭ′no-fen) A white crystalline compound, used to relieve pain and fever. It lacks anti-inflammatory properties and has been known to produce harmful effects to the liver. Also called paracetamol.

acetanilid (as-e-tan′i-lid) A white, crystalline, highly toxic substance obtained from the action of acetic acid upon aniline; formerly used to relieve pain and fever.

acetarsol (as-et-ar′sol) See acetarsone.

acetarsone (as-et-ar′sŏn) A white crystalline substance, which has been used topically to treat trench mouth (necrotizing ulcerative gingivitis) and vaginal infection with *Trichomonas vaginalis*. Formerly used to treat amebiasis and syphilis. Also called acetarsol.

acetate (as′ĕ-tāt) Any salt of acetic acid.

    active a. See acetyl coenzyme A.

acetazolamide (as′et-ah-zol′ah-mid) A diuretic that inhibits the action of carbonic anhydrase in the kidney, promoting the loss of bicarbonate and sodium; the effect is to produce a mild acidosis and to alkalinize the urine; used in glaucoma to reduce intraocular pressure and as a prevention for some forms of altitude sickness.

acetic (ah-se′tik) Relating to, or of the nature of vinegar.

acetic acid (ah-se′tik as′id) A colorless organic acid with a pungent odor, the characteristic component of vinegar. Also called ethanoic acid.

    glacial a.a. A caustic liquid containing 99.5% acetic acid; used to remove corns and warts from the skin.

acetic aldehyde (ah-se′tik al′dĕ-hid) See acetaldehyde.

acetify (ah-set′i-fi) To convert into acetic acid or vinegar.

aceto-, acet- Combining forms indicating the presence of the two-carbon fragment of acetic acid.

acetoacetic acid (as′e-to-ah-se′tik as′id) An unstable acid, one of the three substances (ketone bodies) accumulating in the blood when metabolism is impaired as in poorly controlled diabetes or starvation. Also called diacetic acid. See also ketone bodies, under body; ketoacidosis.

acetohexamide (as′ĕ-to-heks′ah-mid) A compound that stimulates insulin secretion by the pancreas and lowers the glucose content of the blood; used in the oral treatment of certain types of diabetes.

acetolysis (as-ĕ-tol′ĭ-sis) The splitting of an organic compound by introduction of the elements of acetic acid, a chemical reaction similar to hydrolysis in which acetic acid serves the role of water.

acetone (as′ĕ-tōn) A colorless, flammable liquid, found in abnormally high concentration in the blood and urine of persons with poorly controlled diabetes; a synthetic form is industrially produced as a solvent. See also ketone bodies, under body; ketoacidosis.

accouchement ■ acetone

acetonemia (as′ĕ-to-ne′me-ah) Condition marked by increased concentration of acetone in the blood due to improper fat breakdown; seen in poorly controlled diabetes, high-fat diets, and starvation.

acetonemic (as-ĕ-to-ne′mik) Relating to acetonemia.

acetophenazine maleate (as-ĕ-to-fen′ah-zēn mal′e-āt) A major tranquilizer used in the treatment of certain psychoses.

acetophenetidin (as′ĕ-to-fĕ-net′ĭ-din) Old name for phenacetin.

acetosulfone sodium (as-ĕ-to-sul′fōn so′de-um) An antibacterial compound administered orally in the treatment of Hansen's disease (leprosy).

acetrizoate sodium (as-ĕ-ri-zo′at so′de-um) An X-ray contrast medium.

acetum (ah-se′tum), pl. ace′ta Latin for vinegar.

acetyl (as′ĕ-til) The radical CH₃CO- of acetic acid; a molecule of acetic acid from which the hydroxyl group has been removed.
> **a. chloride** CH₃COCl; a colorless corrosive liquid used as a reagent. It causes severe burns.

2-acetylaminofluorene (as′ĕ-til-am′ĭ-no-floo′o-rēn) (AAF) A compound with cancer-causing properties when ingested. Also called acetamidofluorene.

acetylation (ah-set-i-la′shun) Formation of an acetyl derivative by introducing an acetyl group into the molecule of an organic compound.

acetylcholine (as-ĕ-til-ko′lēn) (ACh) The chemical transmitter of the nerve impulse across a synapse; also released by the endings of parasympathetic nerves (cholinergic nerves) upon stimulation; causes slowing of heart, dilation of blood vessels, increased gastrointestinal activity, and other effects. It is hydrolyzed and inactivated by the enzyme cholinesterase.
> **a. chloride** A compound that causes the pupil to contract; used in cataract surgery.

acetylcholinesterase (as′ĕ-til-ko′lin-es′ter-as) An enzyme present throughout body tissues that promotes the hydrolysis of acetylcholine; it acts to remove acetylcholine discharged at the neuromuscular junction, thus preventing it from reexciting the muscle.

acetylcoenzyme A, acetyl-CoA (as′ĕ-til-ko-en′zīm) An important metabolic intermediate of the tricarboxylic acid cycle; formed when an acetyl group is attached to coenzyme A by a thioester bond during oxidation of fatty acids, amino acids, or pyruvate. Also called active acetate.

acetylcysteine (as′ĕ-til-sis′te-in) A compound used to remove excessive mucus in certain bronchopulmonary disorders by reducing its viscosity.

acetylene (ah-set′ĭ-lēn) A colorless, explosive gas formerly used as an anesthetic.

acetylsalicylic acid (ah-se′til-sal-ĭ-sil′ik as′id) Chemical name for aspirin.

achalasia (ak-ah-la′ze-ah) Disorder of the motor innervation of the esophagus, causing impairment of coordinated muscular action (peristalsis) of the lower portion of the esophagus and failure of the esophageal sphincter to relax. Also called cardiospasm; esophageal aperistalsis.

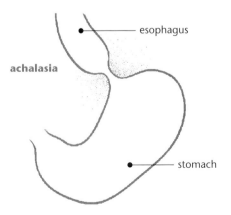

achalasia

esophagus

stomach

ache (āk) A continued pain, distinguished from a spasmodic pain.
> **bone a.** A dull pain in the bones that may become severe in certain conditions.
> **stomach a.** See stomachache.

acheilia (ah-ki′le-ah), pl. achi′lia Absence of one or both lips; a developmental defect. Also spelled achilia.

acheilous (ah-ki′lus) Relating to acheilia. Also spelled achilous.

acheiria (ah-ki′re-ah) Absence of one or both hands; a developmental defect. Also spelled achiria

acheiropodia, acheiropody (ah-ki-ro-po′de-ah, ah-ki-rop′o-de) Absence of one or both hands and feet; a developmental defect. Also spelled achiropodia, achiropody.

acheirous (ah-ki′rus) Relating to acheiria. Also spelled achirous.

achilia (ah-ki′le-ah) See acheilia.

achillobursitis (ah-kil-o-bur-si′tis) See retrocalcaneal bursitis, under bursitis.

achillodynia (ak-ĭ-lo-din′e-ah) Pain in the Achilles (calcaneal) tendon, especially at its attachment to the heel bone (calcaneus).

achillorrhaphy (ak′ĭ-lor′ah-fe) Suturing of the Achilles (calcaneal) tendon.

achillotenotomy (ah-kil-o-ten-ot′o-me) See achillotomy.

achillotomy (ak′ĭ-lot′o-me) Surgical division of the Achilles (calcaneal) tendon. Also called achillotenotomy.

achilous (ah-ki′lus) See acheilous.

achiria (ah-ki′re-ah) See acheiria.

achiropodia, achiropody (ah-ki-ro-po′de-ah, ah-ki-rop′o-de) See acheiropodia, acheiropody.

achirous (ah-ki′rus) See acheirous.

achlorhydria (ah-klor-hi′dre-ah) Absence of hydrochloric acid from stomach secretions.

acholia (ah-ko′le-ah) Absence of bile.

acholic (ah-kol′ik) Lacking bile.

acholuria (ah-ko-lu′re-ah) Lack of bile pigment in the urine.

achondrogenesis (ah-kon-dro-jen′ĕ-sis) Hereditary dwarfism characterized by underdevelopment of bone of the four limbs, resulting in markedly short arms and legs while the trunk and head are normal in size; an autosomal recessive inheritance.

achondroplasia (ah-kon-dro-pla′ze-ah) Hereditary defect in the conversion process of cartilage into bone, resulting in dwarfism and other skeletal deformities; an autosomal dominant inheritance. Also called achondroplasty; osteosclerosis congenita.

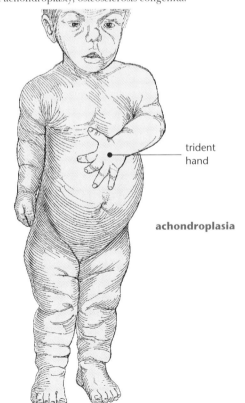

trident hand

achondroplasia

achondroplastic (ah-kon-dro-plas'tik) Relating to achondroplasia.

achondroplasty (ah-kon'dro-plas-te) See achondroplasia.

achoresis (ak-o-re'sis) A reduction in the capacity of a hollow organ (e.g., of the bladder or stomach) due to a persistent contraction.

achromasia (ak-ro-ma'se-ah) A lack of color, such as the pale complexion associated with emaciation and a debilitated state.

achromate (ah-kro'māt) A totally color-blind individual who sees colors in various shades of gray.

achromatic (ak'ro-mat'ic) 1. Devoid of color. 2. Staining poorly.

achromatin (ah-kro'mah-tin) The parts of the cell nucleus that stain only faintly with dyes.

achromatism (ah-kro'mah-tizm) 1. Freedom of an optical system from chromatic aberration. 2. The condition of being totally color-blind. 3. Colorless.

achromatophilia (ah-kro'mah-to-fil'e-ah) The quality of being resistant to the action of stains.

achromatopsia, achromatopsy (ah-kro'mah-top'se-ah, ah-kro'mah-top'se) Total color blindness.

achromatosis (ah-kro'mah-to'sis) See achromia.

achromatous (ah-kro'mah-tus) Colorless.

achromia (ah-kro'me-ah) Lack of normal pigmentation, as of the skin. Also called achromatosis.

achromic (ah-kro'mik) Colorless.

achromocyte (ah-kro'mo-sīt) An abnormal, faintly colored, crescent-shaped red blood cell; almost colorless due to losing most of its hemoglobin pigment. Also called phantom corpuscle; ghost corpuscle; shadow corpuscle.

achromoderma (ah-kro'mo-der'mah) See leukoderma.

achylia (ah-ki'le-ah) 1. Absence of intestinal digestive secretion (chyle). 2. Absence of stomach secretions.

acicular (ah-sik'u-lar) Needle-shaped.

acid (as'id) A compound that can donate a hydrogen ion (proton) to a base and combines to form a salt; any substance that turns litmus indicators red. For individual acids, see specific names.

    amino a.'s Organic compounds containing an amino group (NH_2) and a carboxyl group (COOH). Amino acids form the basic structural units of all proteins. Individual amino acid molecules are linked by chemical bonds between the amino and carboxyl groups to form chains of molecules (polypeptides). Polypeptides, in turn, link together to form a protein molecule. Those amino acids that cannot be made by the body and must be obtained from the diet to maintain health are called essential; those that can be made by the body from other amino acids are termed nonessential.

    bile a.'s Steroid acids important in digestion and absorption of fats.

    binary a. Acid made up of only two elements (e.g., hydrochloric acid).

    dibasic a. An acid containing molecules with two displaceable hydrogen ions.

    fatty a.'s A large group of organic acids, especially those present in fat, made up of molecules that contain a carboxyl group (COOH) at the end of a long hydrocarbon chain; the number of carbon atoms ranges from 2 to 34. Usually classified as *saturated* (those containing the maximum quantity of hydrogen), *unsaturated* (those whose carbon atoms contain some sites unoccupied by hydrogen), *monounsaturated* (those whose carbon atoms contain one unoccupied site), and *polyunsaturated* (those whose carbon atoms contain many unoccupied sites).

    inorganic a. An acid made up of molecules that do not contain carbon atoms.

    monobasic a. An acid containing molecules with one displaceable hydrogen ion (e.g., hydrogen chloride).

    organic a. An acid made up of molecules that contain carbon atoms.

    polybasic a. An acid containing molecules with three or more displaceable hydrogen ions.

acidemia (as-ī-de'me-ah) An increase in the hydrogen ion concentration of the blood; a fall below normal pH (7.42) of the blood. See also acidosis.

acid-fast (as'id fast) Not decolorized by acid after staining; said of certain bacteria.

acidify (ah-sid'ĭ-fi) 1. To make or convert into an acid. 2. To become acid.

acidity (ah-sid'ĭ-te) 1. The quality of being acid. 2. The acid content of a fluid.

Glycine (Gly)	Alanine (Ala)	Valine (Val)	Isoleucine (Ileu)	Leucine (Leu)

amino acids

Lysine(Lys)	Arginine (Arg)	Asparagine (Asn)	Glutamine (Gln)	Cysteine (Cys)

acidophil, acidophile (as′id-o-fil, as′id-o-fil) **1.** A cell or other tissue element that stains readily with acid dyes. **2.** An organism that thrives in a highly acid medium.

acidophilic (as′ĭ-do-fil′ik) **1.** Tending to stain readily with acid dyes. **2.** Tending to thrive in a highly acid medium.

acidosis (as′ĭ-do′sis) A process tending to produce an increase in hydrogen ion concentration in body fluids; if uncompensated, it produces a lowering of the pH. Commonly used synonymously with acidemia.

>   **carbon dioxide a.** See respiratory acidosis.

>   **compensated a.** Condition in which the pH of blood is kept within the normal range through respiratory or renal mechanisms, even though the blood bicarbonate may be out of the usual range.

>   **lactic a.** A metabolic acidosis in which lactic acid accumulates in the body, resulting in decreased bicarbonate concentration.

>   **metabolic a.** Acidosis occurring in metabolic disorders in which acid (excluding carbonic acid, H_2CO_3) accumulates in, or bicarbonate is lost from, extracellular fluids.

>   **renal tubular a.** (RTA) Acidosis secondary to kidney disorders in which there is defective elimination of acid or excessive loss of bicarbonate by the kidneys; characterized by an elevated plasma chloride and a lowered concentration of plasma bicarbonate.

>   **respiratory a.** Acidosis caused by retention of carbon dioxide (CO_2) in the blood, which yields carbonic acid (H_2CO_3); its dissociation increases the hydrogen ion concentration; seen in advanced pulmonary disease. Also called carbon dioxide acidosis.

acidotic (as-ĭ-dot′ik) Relating to or characterized by acidosis.

acidulous (ah-sid′u-lus) Sour or acid.

aciduria (as-ĭ-du′re-ah) The presence of an abnormal amount of acids in the urine.

aciduric (as-ĭ-du′rik) Capable of living in an acid environment; applied to some bacteria.

acinar (as′ĭ-nar) Relating to an acinus.

acini (as′ĭ-ni) Plural of acinus.

aciniform (ah-sin′ĭ-form) See acinous.

acinitis (as-ĭ-ni′tis) Inflammation of an acinus.

acinous (as′ĭ-nus) Resembling a grape; said of certain glands. Also called aciniform.

acinus (as′ĭ-nus), pl. ac′ini **1.** A minute grape-shaped dilatation. **2.** The smallest division of a gland.

aclasis (ah′klah-sis) Structural continuity provided by pathologic tissue that arises from, and is continuous with, normal tissue.

acleistocardia (ah-klis-to-kar′de-ah) Condition in which the foramen ovale of the heart fails to close during development.

acme (ak′me) The stage in the course of a disease marked by greatest intensity; a crisis.

acmesthesia (ak′mes-the′ze-ah) Sensation of a pinprick on the skin.

acne (ak′ne) An inflammatory condition of the sebaceous glands that open into hair follicles. When used alone, the term usually denotes acne vulgaris.

>   **chlorine a.** See chloracne.

>   **a. ciliaris** Acne along the free edges of an eyelid.

>   **common a.** See acne vulgaris.

>   **a. conglobata** A severe form of acne vulgaris characterized by the formation of cysts, abscesses, and thick scarring.

>   **a. cosmetica** Acne caused by ingredients in some cosmetics, most commonly seen on the cheeks.

>   **a. medicamentosa** An acnelike eruption caused or aggravated by a drug or chemical.

>   **a. neonatorum** Acne of the newborn infant, usually occurring as a superficial eruption on the cheeks, forehead, and chin.

>   **a. rosacea** See rosacea.

>   **steroid a.** Acne having characteristics of acne vulgaris but caused by topical or oral administration of steroids.

>   **tar a.** See chloracne.

>   **a. vulgaris** Chronic acne characterized by the formation of blackheads (comedones), pimples (pustules and papules), and scars, occurring most frequently on the face, chest, and back of adolescents and young adults. Also called common acne; acne.

acneform (ak′ne-form) Resembling acne.

acnegenic (ak-ne-jen′ik) Capable of causing acne.

acolous (ak′o-lus) Without limbs.

acomia (ah-ko′me-ah) Baldness; alopecia.

aconative (ah-kon′ah-tiv) Lacking the desire to perform volitional acts.

Serine (Ser)	Threonine (Thr)	Proline (Pro)	Aspartic acid (Asp)	Glutamic acid (Glu)

Methionine (Met)	Tryptophan (Try)	Phenylalanine (Phe)	Tyrosine (Tyr)	Histidine (His)

acorea (ah-ko-re′ah) Congenital absence of the pupil of one or both eyes.

acou- Combining form indicating a relationship to hearing.

acousma (ah-kōōs′mah) Rarely used term that denotes the hearing of imaginary diffused sounds such as hissing.

acousmatamnesia (ah-kōōs′mat-am-ne′ze-ah) Old term for auditory agnosia; see agnosia.

acoustic (ah-kōōs′tik) Relating to sound.

acoustics (ah-kōōs′tiks) The science of the physical characteristics of sound.

acoustigram (ah-koos′tĭ-gram) See acoustogram.

acoustogram (ah-koos′to-gram) The graphic representation of sounds produced by a joint in motion. Also called acoustigram.

acquired (ah-kwīrd′) Developed after birth.

acral (ak′ral) Relating to the limbs or peripheral parts of the body.

acrania (ah-kra′ne-ah) Congenital absence of a portion of the skull.

acraturesis (ah-krat-u-re′sis) Difficult urination due to impaired muscular contraction of the bladder.

acrid (ak′rid) Sharp and irritating to smell and taste.

acridine (ak′rĭ-din) A coal tar derivative occurring as colorless crystals with a strong odor; it is irritating to the skin and mucous membranes.

acritical (ah-krit′e-kal) Lacking a crisis; said of an illness.

acro- Combining form meaning extremity; tip; an extreme.

acroanesthesia (ak′ro-an-es-the′ze-ah) Lack of sensation in the limbs.

acroarthritis (ak′ro-ar-thri′tis) Arthritis of the joints of the extremities.

acroataxia (ak′ro-ah-tak′se-ah) Loss of muscular coordination of the fingers and toes.

acrocentric (ak-ro-sen′trik) Having the centromere close to one end of the chromosome.

centromere

acrocentric chromosome

acrocephalic (ak-ro-sĕ-fal′ik) See oxycephalic.

acrocephalopolysyndactyly (ak′ro-sef-ah-lo-pol-e-sin-dak′tĭ-le) (ACPS) Any of four types of inherited syndromes characterized by premature closure of the space between cranial bones (craniosynostosis), webbed fingers or toes (syndactyly), and extra digits (polydactyly). Each type has specific additional features.

acrocephalosyndactyly (ak′ro-sef-ah-lo-sin-dak′tĭ-le) Any of a group of inherited conditions occurring in varying degrees of congenital malformations of the skull and digits; characterized mainly by a high-domed or peaked head, due to premature closure of the space between cranial bones, and a partial or complete webbing of fingers or toes; an autosomal dominant inheritance.

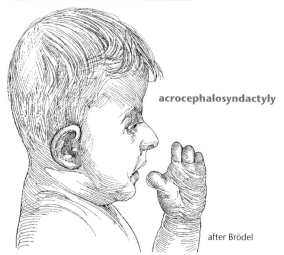

acrocephalosyndactyly

after Brödel

acrocephaly (ak-ro-sef′ah-le) See oxycephaly.

acrochordon (ak-ro-kor′don) See skin tag, under tag.

acrocyanosis (ak′ro-si-ah-no′sis) A chronic circulatory disorder marked by persistently cold, cyanotic, and profusely sweating hands and feet, with mottled blue and red skin; condition is intensified by cold or emotion.

acrodermatitis (ak′ro-der-mah-ti′tis) Cutaneous inflammation of the extremities.

    a. chronica atrophicans Progressive acrodermatitis accompanied by atrophy of the skin, which acquires a tissue-paper appearance.

    a. enteropathica An inherited disease resulting from malabsorption of zinc and affecting infants and young children; characterized by hair loss, growth retardation, diarrhea, and a rash resembling psoriasis on the limbs.

    papular a. of childhood See Gianotti-Crosti syndrome, under syndrome.

    a. vesiculosa tropica A form affecting the fingers, in which the skin becomes glossy with numerous small papules; seen in hot climates.

acrodermatosis (ak′ro-der-mah-to′sis), pl. acrodermato′ses Any cutaneous disorder of the extremities, especially the hands and feet.

acrodolichomelia (ak′ro-dol-ĕ-ko-me′le-ah) Abnormal largeness and disproportionate growth of hands and feet.

acrodynia (ak-ro-din′e-ah) Pain in peripheral parts of the body (fingers, toes, etc.) resulting from continued ingestion of mercury or exposure to mercury vapor. Seen mostly in children and chiefly characterized by redness of the extremities, ulceration of the oral cavity, excessive sweating, gastrointestinal symptoms, and weight loss. Also called pink disease; erythredema.

acroesthesia (ak-ro-es-the′ze-ah) 1. A disorder of sensation marked by increased tactile sensitiveness. 2. Pain in the extremities.

acrogeria (ak-ro-jer′e-ah) Genetic disorder characterized by premature aging of the skin of hands and feet.

acrognosis (ak-rog-no′sis) Seldom-used term denoting sensory perception of the limbs and their parts in relation to one another.

acrohyperhidrosis (ak′ro-hi-per-hi-dro′sis) Abnormally increased sweating of hands and feet.

acrokeratosis (ak′ro-ker-ah-to′sis) Any overgrowth of the horny layer of the skin of the extremities, especially the dorsal aspect of the hands and feet.

acromastitis (ak-ro-mas-ti′tis) Inflammation of the nipple.

acromegalic (ak-ro-mĕ-gal′ik) Relating to acromegaly.

acromegaly (ak-ro-meg′ah-le) Disorder characterized by gradual overgrowth of bones in the head, face, hands, and feet, with proliferation of soft tissue, especially of the hands and feet; due to overproduction of growth hormone (somatotropin) by the pituitary gland after maturity.

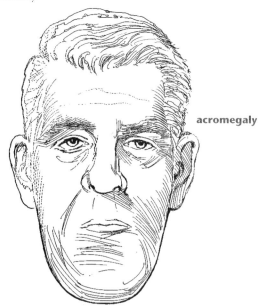

acromegaly

acrometagenesis (ak'ro-met-ah-jen'ĕ-sis) Abnormal development of the extremities.

acromial (ah-kro'me-al) Relating to the acromion.

acromicria (ak-ro-mik're-ah) Smallness of the hands, feet, and skull; the opposite of acromegaly.

acromioclavicular (ah-kro'me-o-klah-vik'u-lar) Anatomic term denoting a relationship to the acromion and the clavicle (bones of the shoulder joint).

acromiocoracoid (ah-kro'me-o-kor'ah-koid) See coracoacromial.

acromiohumeral (ah-kro'me-o-hu'mer-al) Anatomic term denoting a relationship to the acromion and the humerus (at the shoulder joint).

acromion (ah-kro'me-on) The flattened process extending laterally from the spine of the shoulder blade (scapula); it articulates with the collarbone (clavicle) and provides attachment to muscles and ligaments of the shoulder joint. Also called acromial process.

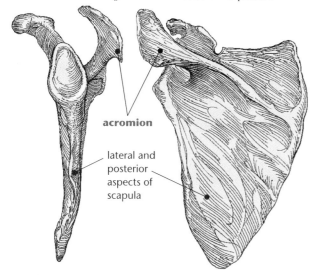

acromioscapular (ah-kro'me-o-skap'u-lar) Relating to the acromion and the body of the shoulder blade (scapula).

acromiothoracic (ah-kro'me-o-tho-ras'ik) Relating to the acromion and the thorax. Also called thoracoacromial.

acromphalus (ah-krom'fah-lus) Abnormal protrusion of the navel (umbilicus).

acromyotonia (ak-ro-mi-o-to'ne-ah) Rigidity of hands or feet, causing spasmodic deformity.

acronine (a'kro-nēn) An antineoplastic compound.

acro-osteolysis (ak'ro os-te-ol'ĭ-sis) Ulceration and bone resorption of the tips of fingers and toes; seen occasionally in workers exposed to vinyl chloride.

acropachy (ak'ro-pak-e) Clubbing of the digits due to soft-tissue thickening and bone changes associated with such disorders as hypertrophic pulmonary osteoarthropathy and hypothyroidism.

acropachyderma (ak'ro-pak-e-der'mah) Condition characterized by thickening of the skin of the face and limbs, as seen in acromegaly.

acroparesthesia (ak'ro-par-es-the'ze-ah) Abnormal sensations of numbness or tingling of the extremities.

acropathy (ah-krop'ah-the) Any disorder of the extremities.

acropetal (ah-krop'e-tal) Tending toward an apex or summit.

acrophobia (ak-ro-fo'be-ah) Abnormally exaggerated fear of heights.

acrosclerosis (ak-ro-skle-ro'sis) Stiffness of the deep layer of the skin (dermis) of the extremities, especially the hands, due to thickening and swelling of fibrous tissue; scleroderma of the hands and feet.

acrosome (ak'ro-sōm) The dense, caplike membrane-bound structure covering the anterior tip of a spermatozoon; it contains enzymes that facilitate penetration of the ovum by the sperm. Also called acrosomal cap.

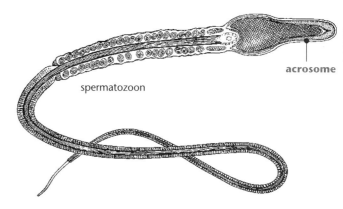

acroteric (ak'ro-ter'ik) Relating to the outermost parts of the body (e.g., ears, tip of nose, tips of fingers and toes).

acrotic (ah-krot'ik) **1.** Absence of the pulse. **2.** Old term denoting a relationship to the surface of the body.

acrotrophodynia (ak'ro-trof-o-din'e-ah) Neuritis of the extremities resulting from prolonged exposure to dampness and cold temperatures.

acrylic (ah-kril'ik) Denoting certain derivatives of acrylic acid, such as those used in construction of medical and dental prostheses. See also resin.

actin (ak'tin) A protein of muscle that, together with myosin, is responsible for muscular contraction.

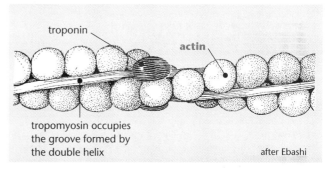

acting out The expression of an unconscious wish or conflict in action rather than words. Often used imprecisely to denote any kind of disapproved behavior.

actinic (ak-tin'ik) Relating to the rays of the light spectrum (beyond the violet range) that produce chemical effects.

actinium (ak-tin'e-um) A radioactive element; symbol Ac, atomic number 89, atomic weight 227; found in association with uranium.

actino- Combining form denoting a relation to a form of radiation.

actinodermatitis (ak'tĭ-no-der-mah-ti'tis) Inflammation of the skin due to exposure to sunlight or to any other type of radiation.

actinolite (ak-tin'o-līt) Any substance that undergoes marked changes in the presence of light.

actinometer (ak-tĭ-nom'ĕ-ter) Any of several instruments for measuring the intensity and chemical effects of light rays.

Actinomyces (ak'tĭ-no-mi'sēz) A genus of filamentous bacteria that are nonmotile and nonacid-fast (family Actinomycetaceae). Some species are responsible for pathologic infections in humans and animals.

   A. israelii An anaerobic species that is the causative agent of human actinomycosis.

   A. odontolyticus An anaerobic species that is a natural inhabitant of the human oral cavity and has been isolated from deep dental caries.

actinomycin (ak'tĭ-no-mi'sin) Any of a group of antibiotic substances obtained from various species of *Streptomyces* that are active against bacteria, fungi, and the cells of certain tumors.

actinomycosis (ak-tĭ-no-mi-ko'sis) A contagious disease characterized by multiple, painful swellings that progress to form abscesses and suppurating openings in the skin of the jaw and neck; caused by *Actinomyces israelii*. The microorganisms may inhabit the mouth, clinging to the gums, teeth, and tonsils without causing disease until they gain entrance to the tissues, as through a decayed tooth or a tooth extraction. If untreated, infection may extend via the bloodstream to the lungs and intestinal tract. Also called lumpy jaw.

actinoneuritis (ak-tĭ-no-nu-ri'tis) Obsolete term for radioneuritis.

actinophage (ak-tin'o-fāj) Any virus that destroys bacteria of the genus *Actinomyces*.

actinotherapy (ak-tĭ-no-ther'ah-pe) In dermatology, treatment with ultraviolet light.

action (ak'shun) 1. The performance of an act, movement, or function. 2. The bringing about of an effect.

ball valve a. The intermittent blockage of a tubular structure by a foreign object, which permits a flow in one direction only.

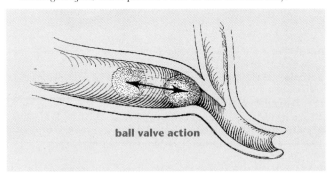

ball valve action

cumulative a. See cumulative effect, under effect.

sparing a. The lowering of the requirements for an essential food component in the diet caused by the presence of another food component that, by itself, is not essential.

specific a. The beneficial activity of a drug comprising the basis for its use.

specific dynamic a. (SDA) The increase of heat production during digestion, from 4 to 6% for carbohydrates to 30% for proteins.

synergistic a. The coordinated activity of two or more structures or drugs whereby the combined effect is greater than the sum of the effects produced by their actions alone.

activation (ak-tĭ-va'shun) 1. The process of rendering active. 2. In embryology, the stimulation of development, usually in the egg; it may be natural or artificial. 3. In chemistry, the process of increasing the reactivity of a substance. 4. The act of making radioactive.

activator (ak'tĭ-va-tor) Any substance that increases the activity of another substance, especially one that combines with an enzyme to enhance its catalytic activity.

tissue plasminogen a. (tPA) An enzyme produced by genetic engineering techniques that is capable of dissolving thrombi, such as those obstructing coronary arteries; used in the treatment of myocardial infarction. Also called tissue-type plasminogen activator.

tissue-type plasminogen a. (tPA) See tissue plasminogen activator.

active (ak'tiv) Capable of functioning, changing, or causing changes.

activity (ak-tiv'ĭ-te) 1. The quality of being active. 2. The ability to produce some effect or perform a function. 3. The release of electrical energy by nerve tissue.

plasma renin a. (PRA) Ability of the enzyme renin in a plasma sample to promote conversion of angiotensinogen (a tetradecapeptide) to angiotensin I (a decapeptide). When angiotensinogen is present in excess, this is a measure of the quantity of active renin present.

actomyosin (ak-to-mi'o-sin) A contractile protein complex with a linear molecular shape composed of actin and myosin; responsible for the contraction of muscle fibers. COMPARE actin and myosin.

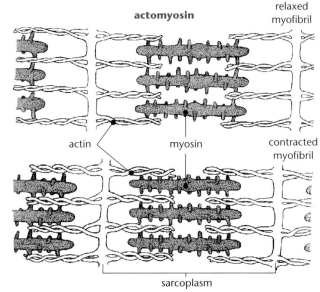

actomyosin

relaxed myofibril

actin   myosin   contracted myofibril

sarcoplasm

actual charge In medical insurance, the amount a physician or other provider or supplier actually bills a patient for a particular medical service or supply in a specific instance.

acu- Combining form meaning needle.

acuity (ah-ku'ĭ-te) Clarity; distinctness.

resolution a. See visual acuity.

visual a. (VA) The clearness of eyesight; it depends on the size and sharpness of the image on the retina, the sensitivity of the nerves, and the interpretative ability of the brain; expressed as a ratio, the first number indicates the person's distance from the test chart, usually 16 meters (20 feet), and the second number signifies the distance corresponding to the size of the letter on the test chart that the person can see. See also Snellen eye chart test, under test. Also called resolution acuity.

aculeate (ah-ku'le-āt) Pointed; covered with thorns.

acuminate (ah-ku'mĭ-nāt) Ending with a point.

acuology (ah-ku-ol'o-je) The study of certain types of needles in relation to therapy, as in acupuncture.

acupressure (ak'u-presh-er) 1. Firm, brief compression applied by the fingertip or a pointed object to a small area (acupressure point) to relieve pain in another part of the body. 2. Compression of a blood vessel by inserting needles in adjacent tissues.

acupuncture (ak-u-pungk'chūr) A form of therapy of Chinese origin whereby special needles are inserted into specific areas of the skin for certain types of anesthesia and treatment of various disorders; it is thought to work through the body's autonomic nervous system. Also called neuronixis.

acusector (ak-u-sek'tor) A needle through which a high-frequency current is passed; used in electrosurgery as a scalpel to cut tissues.

acusis (ah-ku'sis) Normal hearing.

acute (ah-kūt') Denoting a disease or symptom of sudden onset and relatively short duration; it may or may not be severe; the opposite of chronic.

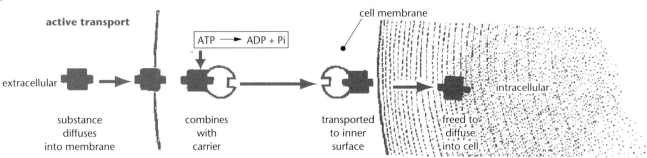

active transport

ATP → ADP + Pi

extracellular

substance diffuses into membrane

combines with carrier

transported to inner surface

cell membrane

freed to diffuse into cell

intracellular

Acute Physiology and Chronic Health Evaluation System (APACHE) A scoring system designed to assess the severity of illness of patients in intensive care units (ICUs); used for comparison of hospital ICUs to identify different standards of care and to allocate resources.

acyanotic (ah-si-ah-not′ik) Without cyanosis.

acyclic (a-si′klik) 1. Composed of molecules that have an open chain structure, said of certain chemical compounds. 2. Not occurring as part of a regularly recurring event.

acyclovir (a-si′klo-vir) An antiviral compound used chiefly in the treatment of genital herpes.

acyl (as′il) A univalent chemical group R-CO-, derived from an organic acid by removal of the hydroxyl group.

acylation (as-ĕ-la′shun) Introduction of an acyl into an organic compound.

acystia (ah-sis′te-ah) Congenital absence of the bladder.

ad- Prefix meaning to or toward; adherence; increase.

-ad Suffix used in anatomic nomenclature meaning toward the direction of (e.g., cephalad).

adactylous (a-dak′tĭ-lus) Lacking fingers or toes.

adactyly (a-dak′tĭ-le) Congenital anomaly marked by the absence of digits.

Adam's apple The subcutaneous projection at the front of the neck formed by the laryngeal prominence of the thyroid cartilage; it enlarges in males at puberty. Also called laryngeal prominence; laryngeal protuberance.

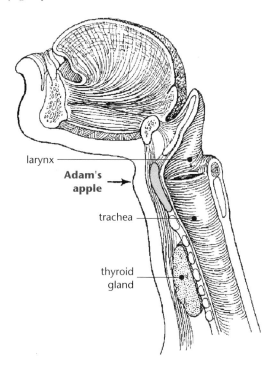

adaptation (ad-ap-ta′shun) 1. The normal adjustment of the pupil of the eye to variations in light intensity. 2. The progressive decline in response of a sense organ to a constant stimulus. 3. The advantageous changes effected by an organism in order to fit into a new environment. 4. In dentistry, the degree of molding of a restorative material necessary to attain as near a perfect fit as possible.

    dark a. Eye adjustment to reduced illumination by increasing sensitivity to light.

    light a. Eye adjustment to increased illumination by reducing sensitivity to light.

    social a. Adjustment of one's behavior to conform with social conditions and demands.

adapter, adaptor (ah-dap′ter, ah-dap′tor) A connecting part between two pieces or sections of an apparatus.

addict (ad′ikt) One who has a psychological and physiological de-

pendence upon some substance or practice that has progressed beyond voluntary control.

addiction (ah-dik′shun) Strong psychological and physiological dependence, beyond voluntary control, on a substance or practice, manifested by increased tolerance and/or severe physical and mental distress when intake is curtailed or stopped.

addictionist (ah-dik′shun-ist) A specialist in addiction medicine; a health practitioner with expertise in the diagnosis and treatment of alcoholism and other drug dependencies. Also called addictionologist.

addictionologist (ah-dik-shun-ol′o-ist) See addictionist.

additive (ad′ĭ-tiv) 1. A substance added to another to impart or increase desirable qualities. 2. The quality of two drugs that act on the same receptors; therefore, doses of one drug can substitute for those of the other, or add to the effect of the other, in proportion to their relative potency.

adducent (ah-du′sent) Bringing together; performing adduction.

adduct (ah-dukt′) 1. To draw or pull toward the median plane of the body, or the main axis of a limb (in the case of digits). 2. Rotation of the eye toward the nose.

adduction (ah-duk′shun) The act of adducting or the condition of being adducted. Opposite of abduction.

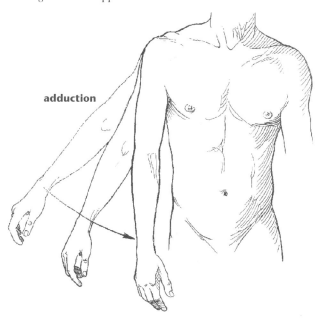

adductor (ah-duk′tor) A muscle that draws a part of the body toward the midline. Opposite of abductor.

adenalgia (ad-ĕ-nal′je-ah) Pain in a gland. Also called adenodynia.

adendritic (ah-den-drit′ik) Denoting nerve cells (neurons) without cytoplasmic branches (dendrites).

adenectomy (ad-ĕ-nek′to-me) Surgical removal of any gland.

adenectopia (ad-ĕ-nek-to′pe-ah) Presence of a gland, or glandular tissue, in other than its normal anatomic position.

adenine (ad′ĕ-nīn) A white, crystalline purine derivative, occurring in animal and vegetable tissues as one of the constituents of ribonucleic acid (RNA) and deoxyribonucleic acid (DNA).

adenitis (ad-ĕ-ni′tis) Inflammation of a gland.

adenization (ad-ĕ-ni-za′shun) A change into a glandlike structure.

adeno-, aden- Combining forms denoting a relationship to a gland.

adenoacanthoma (ad′ĕ-no-ak-an-tho′mah) A cancerous tumor, most commonly of the uterus, that is made up of malignant glandular tissue, but most of the cells exhibit benign squamous differentiation.

adenoblast (ad′ĕ-no-blast) Embryonic cell that gives origin to glandular tissue.

adenocarcinoma (ad′ĕ-no-kar-si-no′mah) Glandular cancer in which the malignant tissue is derived from epithelial cells, or arranged in a glandlike pattern.

A

clear cell a. of vagina A rare type of vaginal cancer occurring in young females, between the ages of 10 and 35 years, whose mothers were treated with diethylstilbestrol (DES) during pregnancy in cases of threatened miscarriage (spontaneous abortion).

renal a. The most common form of cancer of the kidney, especially among people over 60 years of age; may be detected by the presence of blood in the urine; often found incidentally when a sonogram of the abdomen is obtained; may spread via the bloodstream (metastasize) to the lungs, bone, liver, and brain. Also called clear cell carcinoma of kidney; hypernephroma; Grawitz' tumor; renal cell carcinoma.

adenocyte (ad'ĕ-no-sit) The secretory cell of a gland.

adenodiastasis (ad-ĕ-no-di-as'tah-sis) The presence of glands or glandular tissue in other than their normal place in the body.

adenodynia (ad-ĕ-no-din'e-ah) See adenalgia.

adenofibrosis (ad'ĕ-no-fi-bro'sis) See sclerosing adenosis, under adenosis.

adenohypophysial, adenohypophyseal (ad'ĕ-no-hi-po-fiz'e-al) Relating to the anterior, glandular portion of the pituitary (hypophysis).

adenohypophysis (ad'ĕ-no-hi-pof'ĭ-sis) The anterior, glandular lobe of the pituitary (hypophysis), including the pars intermedia and pars tuberalis; it synthesizes and secretes several important hormones, including thyroid-stimulating hormone (TSH), adrenocorticotropic hormone (ACTH), follicle-stimulating hormone (FSH), somatotropic hormone (STH), and luteinizing hormone (LH). Also called anterior lobe of pituitary; glandular lobe of pituitary.

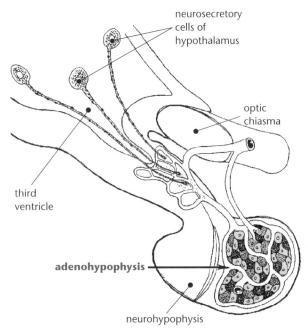

adenohypophysitis (ad'ĕ-no-hi-pof-ĭ-si'tis) An inflammatory condition of the adenohypophysis.

adenoid (ad'ĕ-noid) 1. Glandlike in form or structure. 2. Pharyngeal tonsil. See also adenoids.

adenoidectomy (ad-ĕ-noid-ek'to-me) Surgical removal of the adenoids.

adenoiditis (ad'ĕ-noid-i'tis) Inflammation of the pharyngeal tonsil.

adenoids (ad'ĕ-noidz) Popular term for enlargement (hypertrophy) of the pharyngeal tonsil.

adenolipoma (ad'ĕ-no-lĭ-po'mah) A benign (noncancerous) tumor containing both glandular and fat tissues.

adenolipomatosis (ad'ĕ-no-lip-o-mah-to'sis) Condition characterized by the presence of multiple adenolipomas.

adenolymphocele (ad'ĕ-no-lim'fo-sēl) Cystic enlargement of a lymph node.

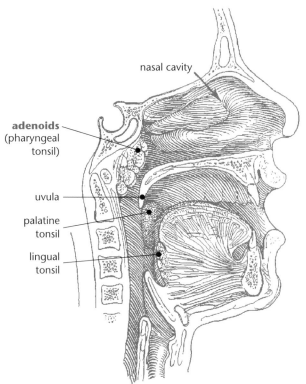

adenolymphoma (ad'ĕ-no-lim-fo'mah) A benign (noncancerous) tumor of the salivary glands, most commonly seen in the parotid gland (unilaterally); composed of cysts lined with epithelial cells and filled with retained secretions. Also called Warthin's tumor.

adenoma (ad'ĕ-no'mah) Benign (noncancerous) tumor arising from epithelial cells of glands or having a glandular structure.

bronchial a. Former term for a group of low-grade malignant tumors arising in the bronchi, including the carcinoid and mucoepidermoid tumors.

follicular a. Adenoma of the thyroid gland consisting of a single, firm nodule surrounded by a well-defined fibrous capsule, usually containing follicles of varying size; fibrosis and calcification may be present.

gonadotroph a. Any noncancerous, gonadotropin-secreting tumor arising from the anterior portion of the pituitary (hypophysis); so named because it secretes hormones targeted to the gonads (the ovaries and testes).

islet cell a. A relatively common adenoma of the pancreas derived from cells of the islet of Langerhans, capable of secreting insulin in excess. It is a firm, usually single, typically yellow-brown nodule, varying in size from microscopic to large masses weighing several kilograms, and may or may not be bound by a capsule.

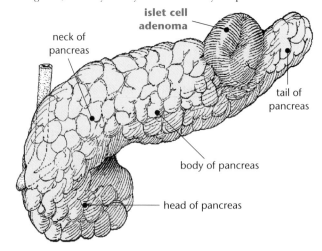

oxyphil a. See oncocytoma.

parathyroid a. A well-encapsulated, usually solitary adenoma,

adenocyte ■ adenoma

A16

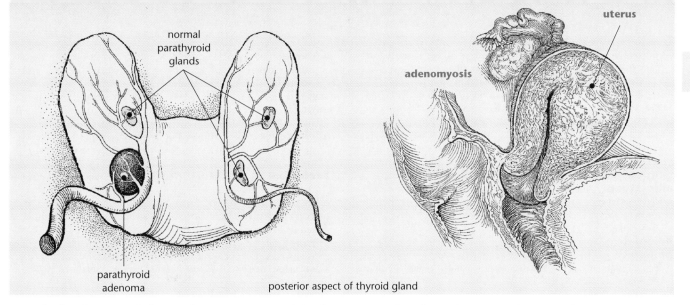

normal parathyroid glands

parathyroid adenoma

posterior aspect of thyroid gland

adenomyosis

uterus

predominantly composed of pure cell types, most commonly involving only one of the four parathyroid glands; a cause of hyperparathyroidism.

pituitary a. Any adenoma of the anterior glandular lobe of the pituitary (hypophysis), occurring most frequently in the age group between 20 and 50 years. Each is encapsulated by a thin fibrous membrane and composed mostly of one morphologic cell type that, depending on the type, may cause overproduction of specific hormones and consequent disorders (e.g., Cushing's syndrome and acromegaly).

pleomorphic a. See mixed tumor of salivary gland, under tumor.

tubular a. A benign, usually pedunculated, polyp commonly occurring in the colon mucosa; risk of its becoming cancerous correlates with size.

villous a. A potentially cancerous adenoma of the inner lining (mucosa) of the large intestine.

adenomatoid (ad'ĕ-no'mah-toid) Resembling an adenoma.

adenomatosis (ad'ĕ-no-mah-to'sis) Condition marked by multiple glandular tumors.

familial endocrine a., type I Inherited disorder marked by the occurrence of multiple noncancerous tumors (adenomas) in several endocrine glands, usually the anterior pituitary (adenohypophysis), parathyroid, and pancreas. Also called multiple endocrine neoplasia, type I; Wermer's syndrome.

familial endocrine a., type II The presence of cancerous tumors of the thyroid and the adrenal (suprarenal) glands. Also called multiple endocrine neoplasia, type II; Sipple's syndrome.

adenomatous (ad'ĕ-nom'ah-tus) Relating to an adenoma or to glandular overgrowth.

adenomyoma (ad'ĕ-no-mi-o'mah) See focal adenomyosis, under adenomyosis.

adenomyosis (ad'ĕ-no-mi-o'sis) The abnormal, but benign, ingrowth of the inner lining of the uterus (endometrium) into the uterine musculature. Also called endometriosis interna.

diffuse a. Adenomyosis involving much or all of the uterus.

focal a. Adenomyosis that concentrates in one area and forms a nodular mass resembling a fibroid. Also called adenomyoma.

adenopathy (ad'ĕ-nop'ah-the) Disease or enlargement of glands, especially the lymph nodes.

adenosarcoma (ad'ĕ-no-sar-ko'mah) A cancerous tumor containing glandular tissue.

adenose (ad'ĕ-nos) Relating to a gland.

adenosine (ah-den'o-sēn) (A, Ado) An organic compound derived from nucleic acids; composed of adenine and a pentose sugar.

a. diphosphate (ADP) The organic compound that takes up energy released during biochemical reactions forming adenosine.

a. triphosphate (ATP) Organic compound present in all cells, which, upon hydrolysis, yields the energy required by a multitude of biological processes.

adenosis (ad'ĕ-no'sis) Any disease or malformation of glands, especially one involving the lymph nodes.

sclerosing a. A benign condition of the breast, most commonly affecting young women; characterized by the formation of relatively hard nodules of glandular tissue that, occasionally, may be difficult to distinguish from cancer. Also called adenofibrosis.

adenotonsillectomy (ad'ĕ-no-ton-sil-lek'to-me) Surgical removal of the adenoids and tonsils.

Adenoviridae (ad'ĕ-no-vir'i-de) A family of viruses that contain double-stranded DNA; they attack and multiply in the cell nucleus.

adenovirus (ad'ĕ-no-vi'rus) Any virus of the family Adenoviridae.

adenyl (ad'ĕ-nil) A chemical radical, which is a component of adenine.

adenylate cyclate (ah-den'ĭ-lāt si'klāt) An enzyme, present in cell membranes, that is activated by certain hormones; the end product (cyclic AMP) is an important metabolic regulator.

adhesin (ad-he'zin) A surface structure on a microbe by means of which it attaches to the host cells.

adhesion (ad-he'zhun) 1. The sticking together of two surfaces that are normally separate, such as in inflammatory processes or injury. 2. One of the fibrous bands abnormally holding two surfaces together. 3. The attraction of two surfaces in contact, such as that of blood platelets sticking to each other or to a blood vessel wall.

abdominal a.'s Adhesions formed in the abdominal cavity, usually involving the intestines and occurring after surgery or in an inflammation of the abdominal lining (peritonitis).

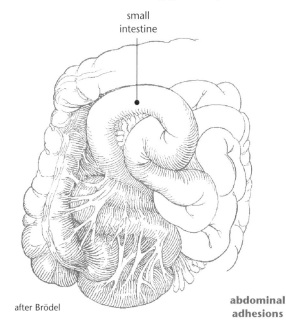

small intestine

after Brödel

abdominal adhesions

posttraumatic uterine a.'s Formation of adhesions within the uterine cavity, usually caused by scraping off of the inner uterine lining (curettage), resulting in reduced or absent menstrual flow and, frequently, infertility. Also called Asherman's syndrome.

primary a. See healing by first intention, under healing.

secondary a. See healing by second intention, under healing.

adhesiotomy (ad-he-ze-ot'o-me) The surgical division of adhesions.

adiadochokinesia, adiadochokinesis (ah-di'ah-do-ko-ki-ne'se-ah, ah-di'ah-do-ko-ki-ne'sis) Inability to carry out rapidly alternating movements of one or more of the extremities (e.g., quickly rotating the wrists) due to dysfunction of the cerebellum.

adip-, adipo- Combining forms meaning fat. See also lip-, lipo-.

adipectomy (ad-ĭ-pek'to-me) See lipectomy.

adipic acid (ah-dip'ik as'id) Acid formed by the oxidation of fats; used in the manufacture of certain chemicals that have irritant properties.

adipocele (ad'ĭ-po-sēl) See lipocele.

adipocere (ad'ĭ-po-sēr) A gray-white fatty substance of waxy consistency found on dead bodies decomposing under humid conditions. Also called grave wax; lipocere.

adipocyte (ad'ĭ-po-sīt) See fat cell, under cell.

adipogenesis (ad-ĭ-po-jen'ĕ-sis) See lipogenesis.

adipokinin (ad-ĭ-po-ki'nin) Hormone produced in the anterior pituitary (adenohypophysis); it causes mobilization of fat from the tissues.

adipometer (ad'ĭ-pom'ĕ-ter) Instrument, such as a constant-tension caliper, used to measure the thickness of a skin fold to estimate the amount of subcutaneous fat.

adiponecrosis (ad'ĭ-po-nĕ-kro'sis) See fat necrosis, under necrosis.

adipose (ad'ĭ-pōs) Denoting fat.

adiposis (ad-ĭ-po'sis) Accumulation of fat in a body area.

adiposity (ad'ĭ-pos'ĭ-te) Obesity; excessive accumulation of fat in the body.

aditus (ad'ĭ-tus) An entrance to a body cavity or tubular organ.

adjustment (ad-just'ment) **1.** In dentistry, modification made on a completed denture. **2.** In chiropractic, manipulation of the spine for restoring normal nerve function. **3.** In psychology, the adaptation of the individual to the social environment.

a. disorder See adjustment disorder, under disorder.

adjuvant (aj'ĕ-vant, ad-ju'vant) A substance that enhances the action of another; said of a substance that, when added to a vaccine, increases the production of antibodies by the immune system, thereby enhancing the vaccine's efficacy in producing immunity.

a. chemotherapy The use of anticancer drugs following removal of a tumor.

Freund's complete a. A mixture of mineral oil, plant waxes, and killed tubercle bacilli; added to antigen to increase antibody production.

Freund's incomplete a. Freund's complete antigen without the tubercle bacilli.

administrator (ad-min'is-trā'tor) **1.** The head of a health care institution responsible for managing its day-to-day affairs under the control or direction of a board of directors or trustees. **2.** One who administers, such as an officer who directs the affairs of a department, school, hospital, or foundation.

hospital a. An officer who directs or superintends the affairs of a hospital in providing medical and surgical care and treatment for the sick and the injured.

medical record a. A professional who plans, designs, develops, and manages systems of patient administration and clinical data and patient medical records in all types of health care institutions. Minimal educational requirements: baccalaureate degree in medical record science or medical record administration in a program accredited by the American Medical Association (AMA) in collaboration with the American Medical Record Association (AMRA).

admission-discharge-transfer (ADT) A procedure used in the admitting department of a hospital whereby a patient's data are collected, stored, and distributed to the various hospital departments.

adnerval (ad-ner'val) Located near, or directed toward, a nerve. Also called adneural.

adneural (ad-nu'ral) See adnerval.

adnexa (ad-nek'sah), sing. adnex'um Appendages; accessory parts.

adnexal (ad-nek'sal) Relating to accessory parts, especially the ovaries, fallopian (uterine) tubes, and ligaments of the uterus.

adolescence (ad-o-les'ens) General term meaning the period between childhood and adulthood. It overlaps puberty. See also puberty.

adolescent (ad-o-les'ent) **1.** Relating to adolescence. **2.** A person in that stage of development.

adoral (ad-o'ral) Near or directed toward the mouth.

adren-, adreno- Combining forms denoting a relationship to the adrenal (suprarenal) gland.

adrenal (ah-dre'nal) Term originally meaning near the kidney; now used in relation to the adrenal (suprarenal) glands.

adrenalectomy (ah-dre'nal-ek'to-me) Surgical removal of one or both adrenal (suprarenal) glands.

adrenaline (ah-dren'ah-lēn) See epinephrine.

adrenarche (ad'ren-ar'ke) The normal physiological change in which the function of the adrenal cortex is increased, occurring at approximately the age of nine years.

premature a. Early puberty induced by hyperactivity of the adrenal cortex, occurring most frequently in girls.

adrenergic (ad'ren-er'jik) **1.** Relating to nerve fibers of the autonomic nervous system that, upon stimulation, release norepinephrine at their endings to transmit the nerve impulse. **2.** A compound that mimics such action.

adrenocortical (ad-re'no-kor'te-kal) Relating to the cortex of the adrenal (suprarenal) glands.

adrenocorticomimetic (ad-re'no-kor'te-ko-mi-met'ik) Producing effects like those produced by hormones of the adrenal cortex.

adrenocorticotropic, adrenocorticotrophic (ad-re'no-kor'te-ko-trop'ik, ad-re'no-kor'te-ko-trof'ik) Stimulating activity of the adrenal cortex.

adrenocorticotropin (ad-re'no-kor'te-ko-trop'in) See adrenocorticotropic hormone (ACTH), under hormone.

adrenogenic, adrenogenous (ad-ren'o-jen'ik, ad'ren-oj'e-nus) Originating in the adrenal (suprarenal) glands.

adrenoleukodystrophy (ah-dre-no-loo'ko-dis'tro-fe) (ALD) Condition affecting male children inherited as an X-linked recessive trait; characterized by chronic insufficiency of adrenal cortex, skin hyperpigmentation, convulsions, mental symptoms, motor and sensory disturbances, and gradual loss of sight due to myelin degeneration in the cerebral hemispheres. Also called encephalitis periaxialis diffusa; Schilder's disease.

adrenolytic (ad-ren-o-lit'ik) Inhibiting the action of epinephrine (adrenaline) at nerve endings.

adrenomegaly (ad-ren-o-meg'ah-le) Enlargement of the adrenal (suprarenal) glands.

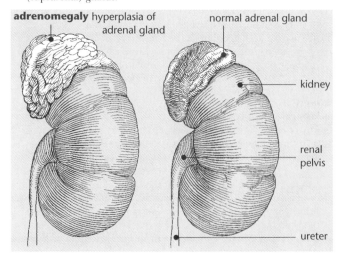

adrenomegaly hyperplasia of adrenal gland · normal adrenal gland · kidney · renal pelvis · ureter

adhesiotomy ■ **adrenomegaly**   A18

adrenomimetic (ah-dre-no-mi-met′ik) Having an action similar to that of the hormones epinephrine and norepinephrine.

adrenoprival (ad-ren′o-pri-val) Denoting loss of function of the adrenal (suprarenal) glands.

adrenosterone (ad′re-no′ster-ōn) A sex hormone (androgen) found in the adrenal cortex.

adrenotropin (ad-ren′o-trop′in) See adrenocorticotropic hormone (ACTH), under hormone.

adriamycin (a-dre-ah-mi′sin) See doxorubicin.

adsorb (ad-sorb′) To bind to a surface.

adsorbate (ad-sor′bāt) A substance that has adhered to the surface of another by adsorption.

adsorbent (ad-sor′bent) Any substance that attracts another substance and holds it to its surface.

adsorption (ad-sorp′shun) The adherence of molecules or small particles of one substance to the surface of another substance.

adsternal (ad-ster′nal) Near or toward the breastbone (sternum).

adulterant (ah-dul′ter-ant) Anything added to a pharmaceutical compound or a food, making it impure or inferior.

adulteration (ah-dul′ter-a′shun) The deliberate addition of an unnecessary or cheap ingredient to a preparation, thus rendering it below the standard specified on the label.

advanced directive A signed document (either a living will or a durable power of attorney for health care) stating a person's wishes regarding medical care in the event he becomes unable to make decisions. The document does not have to be written, reviewed, or signed by an attorney but it must be signed by two witnesses. In many states the witnesses cannot be the patient's relatives, heirs, or physicians.

advancement (ad-vans′ment) Surgical procedure whereby a muscle is detached from its normal position and sutured to a more distal point.

adventitia (ad-ven-tish′e-ah) The outermost covering of a structure, such as a blood vessel, composed of loose connective tissue that is not an integral part of the structure.

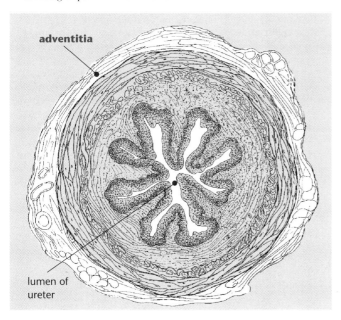

adventitial (ad-ven-tish′al) Relating to adventitia.

adynamia (ah-di-na′me-ah) Weakness; lack of strength.

Aedes aegypti (a-e′dēz a-e-gip′ti) The tiger mosquito with black and white markings; vector of yellow fever, dengue, and possibly filariasis and encephalitis.

aer-, aero- Combining forms meaning air; gas.

aerated (air′at-ed) Containing gas, carbon dioxide, or oxygen.

aeration (air-a′shun) 1. The exchange of carbon dioxide for oxygen in the lungs. 2. The saturation of a fluid with a gas.

short-term middle ear a. Surgical treatment of serous otitis media and dysfunction of the eustachian (auditory) tube; an incision is made in the eardrum (tympanic membrane), fluid accumulated in the middle ear chamber is aspirated through the incision, and a pressure-equalizing tube is placed in the eardrum and left for a period of several months to serve as an auxiliary eustachian tube. The procedure is performed with the aid of an operating microscope.

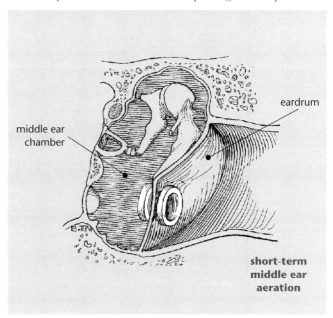

short-term middle ear aeration

aerobe (air′ōb) A microorganism that can live in the presence of air.
   facultative a. Microorganism that can grow with or without air.
   obligate a. Microorganism that needs air to survive.

aerobic (air-o′bik) 1. Relating to an aerobe. 2. Denoting an environment in which free oxygen is present. 3. Relating to a type of exercise; see under exercise.

aerobiosis (air-o-bi-o′sis) Life in an oxygen-containing environment.

aerodontalgia (air-o-don-tal′je-ah) Toothache brought on by reduction of atmospheric pressure, due to expansion of an air pocket within a tooth that irritates the nerve. Common causes are improperly fitted fillings and inflammation of the dental pulp (pulpitis).

aerogenic (air-o-jen′ik) Gas-producing; said of certain bacteria.

aeropathy (air-op′ah-te) Any pathologic condition caused by a sudden change in atmospheric pressure.

aerophagia (air-o-fa′je-ah) Excessive swallowing of air.

aerophil, aerophile (air′o-fil, air′o-fil) A microorganism that requires air for proper growth.

aerophobia (air-o-fo′be-ah) Abnormal fear of drafts or fresh air.

aerosol (air′o-sol) A suspension of liquids or solids in air, oxygen, or inert gases that can be dispersed in the form of a fine mist, usually for therapeutic purposes.

aerotitis media (air-o-ti′tis me′de-ah) See barotitis media.

aerotoxicology (air-o-tok-sī-kol′o-je) The study of the effects of inhaling airborne foreign matter upon health.

afebrile (a-feb′ril) Without fever. Also called apyretic.

affect (af′fekt) 1. Feeling or emotion. 2. External manifestations of a person's feelings.

Aedes aegypti

affective (ah-fek′tiv) Relating to affect.

afferent (af′er-ent) Conveying toward a center; said of vessels and nerves.

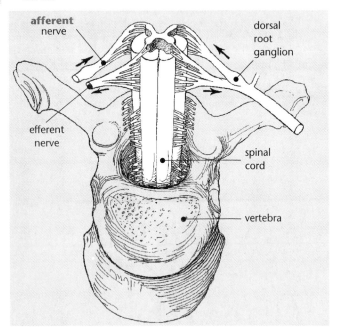

affinity (ah-fin′ĭ-te) In chemistry, the binding force between two substances.

afibrinogenemia (ah-fi′brin-o-jĕ-ne′me-ah) Marked deficiency of the blood-clotting factor fibrinogen in the blood.

aflatoxin (af′lah-tok′sin) Toxic substance produced by some strains of the fungus *Aspergillus flavus,* which grows on improperly stored grains and peanuts. It causes liver cancer in humans.

afterbirth (af′ter-berth) The placenta, umbilical cord, and fetal membranes expelled from the uterus after childbirth. Also called secundines.

aftercataract (af′ter-kat′ah-rakt) See secondary cataract, under cataract.

afterdischarge (af′ter-dis′charj) Prolongation of response from nerve elements after cessation of the stimulus.

afterimage (af′ter-im′ij) The continued visual sensation or image after cessation of the stimulus.

afterload (af′ter-lōd) In cardiac muscle, the force against which the ventricle ejects once contraction of the muscle fibers begins; for the left ventricle this is equivalent to aortic diastolic pressure.

afterpains (af′ter-pānz) The normal cramps experienced after childbirth, due to contractions of the uterus while returning to its nonpregnant size.

aftersensation (af′ter-sen-sa′shun) A sensation that persists after the sensation-causing stimulus has been removed.

agalactia (ah-gah-lak′she-ah) Absence of milk in the breasts during the lactating period.

agalactorrhea (ah-gah-lak-to-re′ah) Absence or arrest of the milk flow.

agammaglobulinemia (a-gam-ah-glob′u-lĭ-ne ′me-ah) Extremely low levels of gamma globulin in the blood, inability to form antibodies, and frequent attacks of infectious diseases.

agar (ahg′ar) A gelatinous material extracted from red algae; used as a gelling agent in media for growing bacterial cultures because it is not affected by most bacterial enzymes.

age (āj) The time elapsed since birth.

   bone a. Age as determined by x-ray studies of the degree of development in the ossification centers (epiphyses) of long bones, such as those of the extremities. Also called skeletal age.

   calendar a. See chronological age.

   chronological a. Age expressed in calendar units (days, weeks, months, years) since birth. Also called calendar age.

   a. of consent In legal medicine, the chronological age of an individual at which she or he is regarded as legally capable to assent to sexual intercourse or marriage; depending on localities, it ranges from 14 to 18 years. See also statutory rape, under rape.

   gestational a. In obstetrics, the age of an embryo or a fetus, timed in weeks beginning with the first day of the mother's last menstruation. Also called menstrual age. See also pregnancy.

   menstrual a. See gestational age.

   mental a. The age level of intellectual ability of a child, as measured by comparison, by means of standardized tests, with the ability of the average child of any given age.

   ovulational a. In embryology, age of an embryo or fetus calculated from the date of ovulation and timed in days or weeks.

   skeletal a. See bone age.

-age Combining form meaning a collection of (e.g., dosage); a result or degree of (e.g., shrinkage).

agency (a′jen-se) An administrative unit of a government.

   mandated a. A county welfare department, a unit of child protective services, police department, or a sheriff's office designed by state statutes as legally responsible for receiving and investigating reports of suspected child abuse and neglect.

agenesis (ah-jen′ĕ-sis) Absence of an organ resulting from failure of development of the primitive cells that give rise to that organ during formation of the embryo.

agenosomia (ah-jen-o-so′me-ah) Congenital absence, or abnormal development, of the genitals; usually accompanied by protrusion of the abdominal organs through an incomplete abdominal wall.

agent (a′jent) **1.** Any substance or force capable of producing a biological, chemical, or physical effect. **2.** Any microorganism, chemical substance, or form of radiation whose presence, excessive presence, or (in deficiency states) relative absence is essential for the occurrence of a disorder; a causative agent.

   adrenergic blocking a. Drug that slows the stimulating effects of sympathetic nerves, epinephrine, norepinephrine, and other adrenergic amines by blocking receptor sites of cells.

   alkylating a.'s Compounds, such as nitrogen mustard, that contain an alkyl group and that are toxic to cells (both normal and malignant); some are used in treating cancer.

   alpha-adrenergic blocking a., α-adrenergic blocking a. An agent that blocks the alpha receptors at nerve endings. Also called alpha-blocker.

   antianxiety a. Any of a group of drugs that produce muscular relaxation by acting on the central nervous system (not the muscles); usually prescribed for the temporary relief from anxiety. Also called anxiolytic; minor tranquilizer.

   antipsychotic a. Any of a group of drugs used primarily to treat mental disorders; used also to alleviate symptoms of other conditions. Also called major tranquilizer.

   beta-adrenergic blocking a., β-adrenergic blocking a. Any of a group of drugs used primarily to treat heart disorders. Adverse effects include worsening of preexisting symptoms of asthma, bronchitis, and lung disease. Also called beta-blocker.

   blocking a. A drug that selectively interferes with the function of the autonomic nervous system by preventing transmission of the impulse at a receptor site on a cell surface, a synapse, or a neuromuscular junction. Commonly called blocker.

   calcium channel-blocking a. Drug that slows muscle contraction by blocking passage of calcium across the membrane of muscle cells; also slows nerve impulses through heart muscle. Commonly called calcium channel blocker.

   delta a. See hepatitis delta virus, under virus.

   Eaton a. See *Mycoplasma pneumoniae;* under *Mycoplasma.*

   environmental a. Conditions or influences of particular surroundings.

   Norwalk a. A virus causing epidemic gastroenteritis.

   An. Orange An herbicide and defoliant containing dioxin, a toxin that causes cancer and developmental anomalies.

   sclerosing a. Any compound (e.g., sodium tetradecyl sulfate solution) used in injection sclerotherapy for the treatment of varicose veins.

toxic a. A substance that kills or injures an organism through its chemical or physical action, or by altering the organism's environment.

TWAR a. See *Chlamydia pneumoniae,* under *Chlamydia.*

ageusia (ah-gu′ze-ah) Loss or impairment of the sense of taste, usually occurring concurrently with dysfunction of the sense of smell.

agglutination (ah-gloo-tī-na′shun) The clumping of microorganisms or cells when exposed to immune serum.

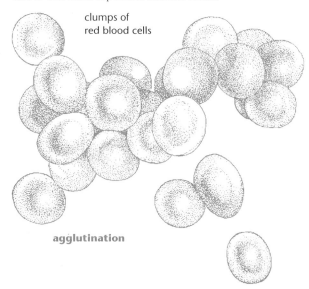

clumps of
red blood cells

agglutination

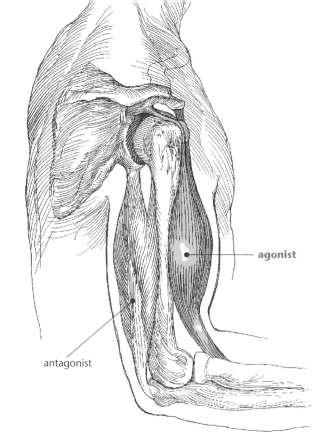

agonist

antagonist

agglutinin (ah-gloo′tī-nin) An antibody that causes particulate antigens, such as bacteria or cells, to adhere to one another and form clumps.

agglutinogenic (ah-gloo-tī-no-jen′ik) Causing the production of agglutinin.

aggravation (ag-rah-va′shun) **1.** An increase in severity. **2.** An act or circumstance that intensifies or makes worse.

    a. of preexisting condition Any occurrence, act, omission, or exposure that worsens, intensifies, or increases the severity of any physical or mental problem known to exist before the aggravating event. The doctrine applies to a broad variety of claims; e.g., in worker's compensation, exposure of an employee with known allergies to allergens in the workplace, which leads to an increase in allergic symptoms, or the worsening of a worker's mild liver damage (i.e., greater liver damage) after exposure to carbon tetrachloride; or in birth-related claims in which the infant would have had congenital problems but the obstetrician is claimed to have aggravated those by poor delivery.

aggression (ah-gresh′un) A forceful or assaultive physical, verbal, or symbolic act.

aging (aj′ing) The process of growing old; the gradual, irreversible changes occurring with the passage of time in any organism.

agitation (aj-ĭ-ta′shun) A state of chronic restlessness and motor activity, usually an expression of anxiety or mental disturbance.

agnosia (ag-no′ze-ah) Loss of the ability to identify or recognize a sensory stimulus, whether auditory, olfactory, visual, gustatory, or tactile, even though the physiologic mechanism for transmitting the stimulus to the brain is intact; believed to be caused by a disturbance of the association function of the cerebral cortex.

-agogue Combining form meaning inducing; promoting (e.g., lymphagogue).

agonist (ag′o-nist) **1.** Denoting a muscle that initiates and maintains a particular movement against another muscle (antagonist) that opposes such action. **2.** Denoting a chemical that interacts with specific receptors on the cell membrane, thereby initiating a cellular reaction.

agoraphobia (ag′o-rah-fo′be-ah) A disorder characterized by an intense and abnormal fear of being alone or in public places from which escape might be difficult or help not readily available; often prevents its victims from leaving their homes unaccompanied. Although often initially associated with recurrent panic attacks, it is the avoidance behavior that distinguishes agoraphobia from panic disorders. The diagnosis of agoraphobia is not made if the phobic symptoms result from a major depressive episode, obsessive-compulsive disorder, paranoid personality disorder, or schizophrenia.

agrammatism (ah-gram′ah-tizm) A speech impairment marked by inability to construct sentences with correct word sequence.

agranular (ah-gran′u-lar) Without granules; said of certain cells.

agranulocyte (ah-gran′u-lo-sīt) One of a group of relatively nongranular white blood cells including the lymphocyte and the monocyte; normally agranulocytes constitute about 40% of the total white blood cell population.

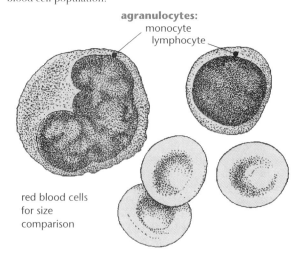

agranulocytes:
monocyte
lymphocyte

red blood cells
for size
comparison

agranulocytosis (ah-gran′u-lo-si-to′sis) Absence of granular white blood cells in the peripheral blood. Term is often used to describe a symptom complex marked by reduced polymorphonuclear leukocytes (a type of granular white blood cell), and infected ulcers of the mouth, throat, intestinal tract, and sometimes skin. The acute form

is most frequently drug-induced but may occur in leukemia; the chronic form is of unknown cause and occurs more often in women. Also called agranulocytic angina.

agraphia (ah-graf'e-ah) Loss of a previously possessed ability to write.

aide (ād) A nonlicensed individual who has received on-the-job training in routine jobs under supervision of a licensed worker.

AIDS (acquired immune deficiency syndrome) The clinical state caused by a strain of the human immunodeficiency virus (currently, HIV1 or HIV2). The HIV infection, acquired by sexual contact or from contaminated blood products or body parts, progresses as follows: *Acute stage*, viruses enter lymphocytes (helper T cells) and, from this point on, the infected person can transmit the disease to others. About three to five weeks later, symptoms may develop (fever, muscle and joint pain, rash, hives, diarrhea), lasting two to three weeks before disappearing. T cells produce antibodies to kill the virus from the beginning, but they cannot be detected in blood tests until five to six months later. *Asymptomatic stage*, the infected person may have no symptoms for several years, but the virus population increases and destroys T cells, slowly at first, rapidly later; the immune system becomes compromised. A helper T cell (T-4) population of less than 500 cells/mm^3 is a bad prognostic sign. Defenses begin to fail, and symptoms, formerly called AIDS-related complex, or ARC, begin to appear (weight loss, fatigue, fever, diarrhea, swollen lymph nodes). *Full-blown AIDS*, final stage of the disease; immune defenses break down completely and secondary (opportunistic) diseases attack the body (*Pneumocystis carinii* pneumonia; Kaposi's sarcoma; nervous system diseases; and fungal, bacterial, and parasitic infections). Death usually follows a few years later. Those at greatest risk for contacting AIDS are homosexual and bisexual men and intravenous drug users who share needles. Others include infants born to HIV-infected women and those who receive blood (in transfusion) or body parts (in transplants).

ainhum (ān'hum) Development of a constrictive fibrous band around a toe, especially the small toe, leading to spontaneous amputation of the toe; thought to be associated with the sickle-cell trait. Also called dactylolysis spontanea.

air (ār) The mixture of gases forming the earth's atmosphere, composed of nitrogen (78%), oxygen (21%), and smaller proportions of carbon dioxide, ammonia, helium, argon, neon, and organic particles.

    alveolar a. See alveolar gas under gas.

    complemental a. See inspiratory reserve volume, under volume.

    functional residual a. Obsolete term. See functional residual capacity, under capacity.

    residual a. See expiratory reserve volume, under volume.

    supplemental a. See expiratory reserve volume, under volume.

    tidal a. See tidal volume under volume.

airborne (ār'born) Denoting pathologic microorganisms and other disease-producing agents that are transported or spread through the air.

airway (ār'wa) **1.** The system through which air passes into and out of the lungs. **2.** A tube, such as an endotracheal tube or a tracheotomy tube, performing the function of a natural passageway to prevent loss of aeration during periods of unconsciousness or in case of an obstruction.

akaryocyte (ah-kar'e-o-sīt) A cell without a nucleus, such as a red blood cell (erythrocyte). Also called acaryote; akaryote.

akaryote (ah-kar'e-ōt) See akaryocyte.

akathisia (ak-ah-thiz'e-ah) Condition marked by inability to sit still or lie quietly; the person has a constant urge to move about; usually occurs as an adverse reaction to certain drugs used in treating mental disorders such as schizophrenia. It also may occur as an uncommon complication of Parkinson's disease.

akinesia (ah-ki-ne'ze-ah) **1.** Complete, or almost complete, loss of the power to move a group of muscles. **2.** Rigidity or difficulty in initiating movement even though, once started, the movement can be continued; seen in Parkinson's disease. Also called akinesis.

akinesis (ah-ki-ne'sis) See akinesia.

akinesthesia (ah-kin-es-the'zhe-ah) In neurologic testing, a lack of perception of passive movement of a body part.

akinetic (ah-ki-net'ik) Relating to akinesia.

ala (a'lah), pl. a'lae Any winglike structure.

alae (a'le) Plural of ala.

alanine (al'ah-nēn) (Ala) One of the constituents of protein; it is a major component of the cell walls of bacteria.

alar (a'lar) Relating to a winglike structure.

alastrim (ah-las'trim) A contagious eruption resembling smallpox. Also called variola minor; pseudosmallpox; milkpox.

albicans (al'bĭ-kanz) Latin for white.

albinism (al'bĭ-nizm) A group of hereditary disorders affecting all races, characterized by absence of pigment (melanin) from the skin, hair, and eyes. Affected individuals may be susceptible to skin cancer. Also called congenital leukoderma.

albino (al-bi'no) An individual affected with albinism.

albuginea (al-bu-jin'e-ah) A white fibrous layer surrounding an organ, especially the testis and ovary.

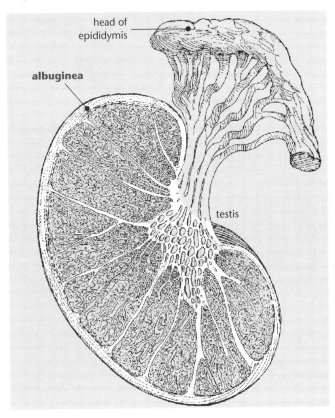

albumin (al-bu'min) A simple protein made in the liver and abundantly present in the body. It regulates movement of water between tissues and the bloodstream and helps retain substances in the circulation.

    Bence Jones a. See Bence Jones protein, under protein.

    iodinated ^{125}I serum a. A sterile human serum albumin labeled with radioactive iodine 125; used in measuring blood volume and cardiac output. Also called radioiodinated serum albumin.

    radioiodinated serum a. (RISA) See iodinated ^{125}I serum albumin.

albuminoid (al-bu'mĭ-noid) Resembling albumin.

albuminuria (al'bu-mĭ-nu're-ah) Excretion of albumin in the urine in excess of the normal daily amount.

    orthostatic a. Excessive excretion of protein in the urine occurring in healthy adolescents and young adults, appearing when the person is upright and disappearing in recumbency. Also called orthostatic proteinuria; postural proteinuria.

alcohol (al′ko-hol) **1.** Any of various compounds that are hydroxyl derivatives of hydrocarbons. **2.** A colorless, flammable liquid, obtained from fermentation of sugars and starches with yeast and produced synthetically from ethylene or acetylene. Unless modified, alcohol most commonly refers to ethyl alcohol or ethanol, which is used as a solvent, preservative, topical disinfectant, and in the preparation of drugs, and is the form of alcohol found in intoxicating beverages such as beer, wine, and spirits. Also called grain alcohol; ethyl alcohol; ethanol.

8 oz of beer, 4 oz of wine, 2 oz of sherry, and 1 oz of whiskey contain approximately equal amounts of alcohol

 ethyl a. See alcohol (2).
 grain a. See alcohol (2).
 isopropyl a. A clear, colorless, flammable, poisonous liquid, capable of mixing with water, ether, chloroform, shellac, gums, and essential oils; used as a solvent for antifreeze compounds, lotions, and cosmetics, and as a basis for isopropyl rubbing alcohol.
  isopropyl rubbing a. A preparation containing about 70% isopropyl alcohol in water; used on the skin to produce hyperemia.
 methyl a. See methanol.
 rubbing a. A mixture of about 70% absolute alcohol and varying quantities of water, denaturants, and perfumed oils.
 wood a. See methanol.
alcoholic (al-ko-hol′ik) **1.** Relating to alcohol. **2.** One who is afflicted with alcoholism.
alcoholism (al′ko-hol-ism) Pathologic condition marked by a pattern of alcohol intake accompanied by physical and psychological dependence. Regardless of the amount of alcohol consumed, alcoholism can be recognized: when it causes impairment of social or occupational functioning, by the need to increase amounts of alcohol intake to achieve desired effects (tolerance), and by severe physical (withdrawal) symptoms when alcohol intake is stopped or reduced. Also called alcohol abuse; alcohol dependence.
 paroxysmal a. See periodic drinking bouts, under bout.
aldehyde (al′dĕ-hīd) Any of a group of organic compounds containing the group CHO; obtained from oxidation of the primary alcohols.
 acetic a. See acetaldehyde.
aldosterone (al-dos′ter-ōn) A steroid hormone secreted by the outer layer (cortex) of the adrenal gland; its main function is to regulate sodium and potassium concentration; it causes retention of sodium in the body by enhancing sodium reabsorption in the kidney, the intestinal tract, and the sweat and salivary glands; sodium reabsorption is usually accompanied by increased excretion of potassium.
aldosteronism (al-dos′ter-on-izm) Condition caused by excessive production of aldosterone by the adrenal gland, usually resulting in lowered levels of potassium in the blood, muscular weakness, and high blood pressure (hypertension). Also called hyperaldosteronism.
 primary a. Excessive production of aldosterone caused by a primary disorder of the adrenal gland (e.g., an adenoma or hyperplasia). Also called Conn's syndrome.
 secondary a. Aldosteronism resulting from excessive stimulation of the adrenal gland, frequently associated with fluid-retaining disorders.

aldrin (al′drin) A chlorinated hydrocarbon used as an insecticide; found to be carcinogenic in animals.
aleukemia (ah-lu-ke′me-ah) Deficiency of white blood cells.
aleukemic (ah-lu-ke′mik) Relating to aleukemia.
alexia (ah-lek′se-ah) A type of aphasia constituting severe reading disability; characterized by inability to understand written language even though the person was previously literate; caused by damage to association pathways in the cerebral cortex. Sometimes called visual aphasia.
alexithymia (ah-leks-ī-thi′me-ah) Inability to interpret one's emotions.
alge-, algesi-, algio-, algo- Combining forms meaning pain.
algesia (al-je′ze-ah) See algesthesia.
algesimeter (al-je-sim′ĕ-ter) Instrument for measuring the threshold of perception and degree of intensity of a painful stimulus on the skin. Also called odynometer.
algesthesia (al-jes-the′ze-ah) Ability to perceive pain. Also called algesia; algesthesis.
algesthesis (al-jes-the′sis) See algesthesia.
-algia Suffix meaning pain (e.g., osteralgia).
alginate (al′jī-nāt) A salt of alginic acid, extracted from marine kelp; used as a thickening agent for food (e.g., ice cream) and for making dental impressions, especially for partial dentures.
alginic acid (al-jin′ik as′id) A colloidal polysaccharide obtained from marine kelp; used as a binder, thickening and emulsifying agent in certain drugs and food products.
algorithm (al′go-rīthm) Any structured approach to solving a problem consisting of a sequence of steps, with each subsequent step depending on the outcome of the preceding one.
alienation (āl-yen-a′shun) **1.** The state of a muscle that cannot contract fully after recovering from an acute paralytic disease such as poliomyelitis. **2.** A condition characterized by repression and isolation of one's own feelings and avoidance of emotional situations or relationships.
alignment (ah-lin′ment) **1.** In orthopedics, the arranging of fractured bones in the normal anatomic position. **2.** In dentistry, the line along which natural or artificial teeth are arranged in the dental arch.
aliment (al′ĕ-ment) Food or any material that has nutritive value.
alimentary (al-ĕ-men′tar-e) Relating to food, nutrition, or to the digestive tract.
alimentation (al-ĕ-men-ta′shun) Providing nourishment.
  enteral tube a. See nasogastric feeding, under feeding.
  total parenteral a. See total parenteral nutrition, under nutrition.
alinasal (al-e-na′sal) Relating to the flared portion of the nose.
aliquot (al′ĕ-kwot) A sample or portion (e.g., one of the equal portions into which a solution or a solid can be divided).
alkalemia (al-kah-le′me-ah) A state of increased pH or decreased hydrogen ion concentration of the blood. COMPARE alkalosis.
alkali (al′kah-li) Any of a class of basic substances that yield hydroxyl ions (OH^-) in solution.
alkaline (al′kah-lin) Relating to, or reacting as, alkali.
alkalinity (al-kah-lin′ĭ-te) The state of being alkaline.
alkaloid (al′kah-loid) Any of a group of nitrogenous substances present in certain plants (e.g., morphine, reserpine, cocaine, caffeine, nicotine) that produce strong physiologic effects.
alkalosis (al-kah-lo′sis) A pathologic process tending to decrease the hydrogen concentration in the body fluids, which, if uncompensated, leads to a rise in pH. Commonly used synonymously with alkalemia.
  metabolic a. Alkalosis stemming from loss of large amounts of stomach acid due to prolonged vomiting or stomach drainage, from taking too much bicarbonate or diuretics, or from certain metabolic disorders such as adrenocortical hormone excess.
  respiratory a. Reduction in the level of carbon dioxide (CO_2) in the blood, caused by deep, fast breathing (hyperventilation); may be due to anxiety, metabolic disorders, low oxygen pressure in the inspired air, or too high a setting on a respirator.

alkalotic (al-kah-lot′ik) Relating to alkalosis.

alkaptonuria (al-kap-to-nu′re-ah) Hereditary condition in which homogentisic acid is not broken down by the body due to a lack of the enzyme homogentisate. Homogentisic acid is excreted in the urine, which turns dark brown on exposure to air. Arthritis frequently occurs.

allachesthesia (al-ah-kes-the′ze-ah) In neurologic testing, the state in which a sensation is referred to a point other than the point to which a stimulus is applied.

allantoic (al-an-to′ik) Relating to the allantois, an embryonic sac.

allantoid (ah-lan′toid) Sausage-shaped.

allantoin (ah-lan′to-in) A nitrogenous substance present in allantoic fluid and fetal urine; also present in some plants.

allantois (ah-lan′to-is) In the early embryo, a fingerlike outpouching from the caudal wall of the yolk sac connected with the embryonic bladder (urogenital sinus); as the bladder enlarges, the allantois involutes to form the urachus.

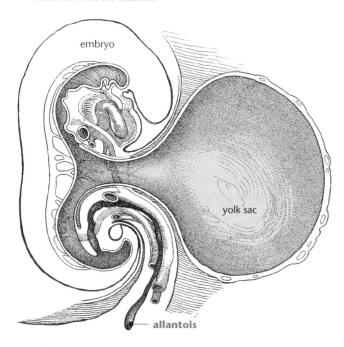

embryo

yolk sac

allantois

allel (ah-lēl′) See allele.

allele (ah-lēl′) Any one of two or more genes that occupy the same location on homologous chromosomes and determine the heredity of a particular trait. Also called allelic gene. Also spelled allel.

allelic (ah-le′lik) Relating to an allele.

allelism (al′e-lizm) The presence of alleles.

allelo- Combining form meaning reciprocally in mutual relation.

allelomorph (ah-le′lo-morf) Obsolete term for allele.

allergen (al′er-jen) Any agent that can induce an allergic reaction.

allergenic (al-er-jen′ik) Capable of inducing an allergic reaction.

allergic (ah-ler′jik) Relating to allergy.

allergic salute (ah-ler′jik sah-loot′) Rubbing of the nose in a characteristic transverse or upward movement of the hand, commonly seen in children with allergic inflammation of the nasal tissues.

allergist (al′er-jist) A physician specializing in the treatment of allergic disorders.

allergy (al′er-je) A state of abnormal hypersensitivity to a normally harmless agent (allergen), acquired by previous exposure to that particular agent. See also allergic reaction, under reaction; anaphylaxis.

 drug a. Unusual sensitivity to a drug or chemical.

 food a. An abnormal or exaggerated immunologic response to a specific allergen contained in a particular food, resulting in disease; it may or may not be mediated by immunoglobulin E; clinical manifestations occur rapidly (within one hour) and may be limited to abdominal symptoms (e.g., cramping, bloating, vomiting, or diarrhea)

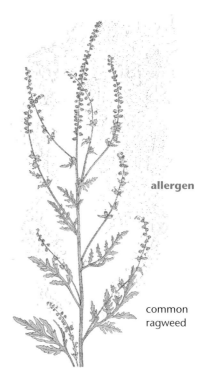

allergen

common ragweed

or may involve other body systems, producing a variety of symptoms (e.g., hives, asthma, runny nose, conjunctivitis, itchiness and swelling of the lips and tongue, itchiness and tightness of the throat, and wheezing). Also called food hypersensitivity. COMPARE food intolerance, under intolerance.

 physical a. Exaggerated response to environmental factors, such as cold, heat, or light.

allesthesia (al′es-the′ze-ah) Disorder in which a single stimulation on one side of the body is perceived in a corresponding region across the midline of the body (e.g., a stimulus applied to one arm is felt in the opposite arm). Also called allocheiria.

allethrin (al′ĕ-thrin) A synthetic compound used as an insecticide; contact or inhalation exposure may cause liver and kidney damage and lung congestion.

allo- Combining form meaning other.

alloantibody (al-o-an′tī-bod-e) An antibody, from one individual, that reacts with an antigen of another individual of the same species. Sometimes called isoantibody; isobody.

alloantigen (al-o-an′tī-jen) An antigen (such as a blood group antigen) that is present in some members of the same species and thus induces an immune response when transferred (e.g., by blood transfusion) to those who lack the antigen. Also called isoantigen; allogenic antigen; homologous antigen; isophile antigen.

allocheiria (al-o-ki′re-ah) See allesthesia.

allochezia (al-o-ke′ze-ah) 1. The passage of nonfecal matter via the anus. 2. The passage of feces through an abnormal opening such as a fistula.

allochromasia (al-o-kro-ma′ze-ah) Change of color of skin or hair.

allogeneic, allogenic (al-o-je-na′ik, al-o-jen′ik) Relating to individuals of the same species who are genetically dissimilar.

allograft (al′o-graft) A graft obtained from a genetically dissimilar individual of the same species as the recipient of the graft. Also called allogenic graft; homograft.

allolalia (al-o-la′le-ah) Speech defect that originates in the brain.

allomerism (ah-lom′er-izm) The property of having different chemical composition but the same crystalline form. COMPARE allomorphism.

allomorphism (al-o-mor′fizm) 1. The property of having different crystalline form but the same chemical composition. COMPARE allomerism. 2. A change in the shape of cells, especially due to mechanical factors.

allopathy (al-lop'ah-the) A system of alternative medicine that treats a disease by producing a second condition incompatible with the original disease being treated.

alloplasia (al-o-pla'ze-ah) See heteroplasia.

alloplast (al'o-plast) A presumably inert material, such as plastic, used for implantation into tissues.

alloploid (al'o-ploid) Denoting a hybrid cell or organism having two or more sets of chromosomes derived from different species or genera.

allopurinol (al-o-pūr'ĭ-nōl) A drug that reduces serum levels of uric acid by blocking the action of the enzyme xanthine oxidase; used in the treatment of gout. It may produce undesirable side effects such as itching, rash, and nausea.

allorhythmia (al-o-rith'me-ah) A repetitious irregularity of the heart rhythm.

all or none See Bowditch's law, under law.

allotransplantation (al-o-trans'plan-ta'shun) The transplantation of tissue from one individual to another of the same species but of a different genetic makeup (genotype). Also called homotransplantation.

alloxan (al'ok-san) A crystalline compound derived chemically by oxidizing uric acid. It is capable of destroying the insulin-producing cells in the pancreas (beta cells of the islets of Langerhans), hence it is used to induce diabetes in experimental animals for the study of the disorder.

alloy (al'loi) A material formed by the mixture of two or more metals (e.g., brass) or a metal and a nonmetal (e.g., steel) that are fused together and are mutually dissolvable in a molten state.

   amalgam a. An alloy of two or more metals, one of which is mercury.

aloe (al'o) **1.** The juice from the leaves of *Aloe vera* (family Liliaceae); a common ingredient of skin preparations due to its soothing and healing properties. **2.** The dried juice obtained from leaves of various species of the genus *Aloe*, formerly used as a purgative.

alogia (ah-lo'je-ah) Inability to speak due to dysfunction of the central nervous system. Also called aphasia.

alopecia (al-o-pe'she-ah) Baldness; partial or complete loss of hair that may be temporary or permanent, resulting from genetic factors, aging, stress, physical trauma, or trauma caused by local or systemic disease; occasionally it may be due to an adverse reaction to a drug.

   a. areata Sudden hair loss occurring in a coin-shaped pattern on the scalp and beard of individuals who have no obvious skin or systemic disorder. Also called alopecia circumscripta.

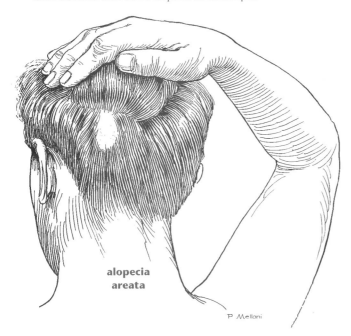

alopecia
areata

P. Melloni

   a. capitis totalis Alopecia of the entire scalp.

   cicatricial a. See scarring alopecia.

   a. circumscripta See alopecia areata.

   female-pattern a. Alopecia usually confined to thinning of the hair along the front and sides of the head.

   a. hereditaria See male-pattern alopecia.

   male-pattern a. A familial, most common, type of alopecia that requires the presence of androgens. It usually begins in the late teens or early twenties. Seen also (rarely) in postmenopausal women. Also called alopecia hereditaria.

   radiation a. Alopecia caused by exposure to ionizing radiation, as in radiation therapy.

   scarring a. Loss of hair resulting from destruction of hair follicles by injuries, inflammatory processes, or metastatic tumors, with subsequent formation of scar tissue. Also called cicatricial alopecia.

   senile a. The normal hair loss of old age.

   a. totalis, a. universalis Complete loss of hair from all parts of the body.

alpha (al'fah) (α) **1.** The first letter of the Greek alphabet. **2.** In chemistry, the position closest to the functional group of atoms in a molecule. For terms beginning with alpha, see under specific terms.

alpha-blocker (al'fah blok'er) See alpha-adrenergic blocking agent, under agent.

alpha-fetoprotein, α-fetoprotein (al'fah fe-to-pro'tēn) (AFP) A plasma protein produced in the liver and intestinal tract of the fetus. Used as a diagnostic measure in obstetrics; considerably raised levels of AFP in the amniotic fluid and maternal serum after 14 weeks of gestation may indicate developmental defects of the neural tube (spina bifida). In adults, AFP is produced in certain abnormal tissues, such as liver cancer (hepatoma) and testicular cancer; used to monitor response to antitumor therapy.

alpha-tocopherol, α-tocopherol (al'fah to-kof'er-ol) See vitamin E.

alprazolam (al-pra'zo-lam) A minor tranquilizer; member of the class of benzodiazepine drugs used for management of anxiety, panic attack, and phobias; abuse may lead to addiction.

alprostadil (al-pros'tah-dil) A prostaglandin of the E series given to newborn infants born with a heart defect (tetralogy of Fallot) to temporarily keep the ductus arteriosus open until heart surgery can be performed.

alternans (awl-ter'nanz) Latin for alternating.

   electrical a. Regular alternating variations in the wave amplitude of the electrocardiogram.

   pulsus a. See pulsus alternans, under pulsus.

Alternaria (awl-ter-na're-ah) A genus of fungus that has been implicated in skin infections and as an allergen in bronchial asthma.

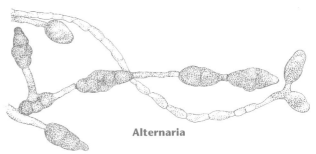

Alternaria

alternative (awl-ter'na-tiv) Either of a pair, or one of a number of objects or courses offered for choice.

   pharmaceutical a.'s Drug products that contain the identical therapeutic moiety and strength but not the same salt, ester, or dosage form, and are administered by the same route.

   therapeutic a.'s Drug products that contain different therapeutic moieties but belong to the same pharmacologic and/or therapeutic class, and can be expected to produce similar therapeutic effects when administered in equivalent doses.

alum (al'um) Any double sulfate of a trivalent metal (aluminum, chromium, iron, etc.) with a univalent metal (sodium, potassium, lithium) having astringent and hemostatic properties.

aluminosis (ah-loo-mĭ-no'sis) A dust-related disorder (pneumoconiosis) caused by deposition of aluminum particles in the lungs, as in prolonged inhalation of the offending material in the workplace.

aluminum (ah-loo'mĭ-num) A silvery white metallic element; symbol Al, atomic number 13, atomic weight 26.98; found in low concentrations in the body. Industrial processes employing aluminum aerosols (e.g., pottery making, explosives manufacturing) have been associated with various lung disorders.

    a. chloride A powder used in solution as an antiperspirant and astringent.

    a. hydroxide, a. hydrate A powder used internally as an antacid in the form of a gel and externally as a drying powder.

    a. sulfate octadecahydrate An astringent detergent used for skin ulcers. Also called cake alum.

alveolalgia (al've-o-lal'je-ah) Pain occurring in a dental alveolus. See also dry socket, under socket.

alveolar (al-ve'o-lar) Relating to an alveolus.

alveolectomy (al-ve-o-lek'to-me) See alveoloplasty.

alveoli (al-ve'o-li) Plural of alveolus.

alveolitis (al-ve-o-li'tis) Inflammation of alveoli. Also called infected alveolar socket; septic alveolar socket.

alveolo- Combining form meaning alveolus.

alveoloplasty (al-ve'o-lo-plas'te) Surgical contouring of the alveolar bone of the jaw; dental surgery consisting of smoothing out uneven alveolar ridges prior to taking an impression for dentures. Also called alveolectomy.

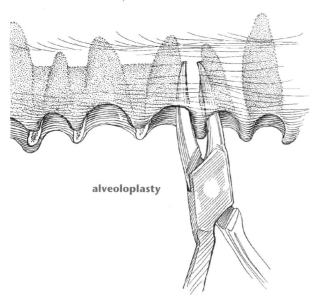

alveoloplasty

alveolotomy (al-ve-o-lot'o-me) Incision into a tooth socket to allow drainage of pus from an abscess.

alveolus (al-ve'o-lus), pl. alve'oli In anatomy, a small cavity or saclike dilatation.

    dental a. A tooth socket; one of the bony cavities into which each tooth fits.

    pulmonary a. One of the minute, balloonlike air sacs at the end of a bronchiole in the lungs. Exchange of the gases or respiration takes place through the alveolar walls.

alveus (al've-us) **1.** A channel. **2.** The layer of white fibers in the brain covering the area of the hippocampus that is adjacent to the lateral ventricle.

amalgam (ah-mal'gam) In dentistry, an alloy of mercury with other metals, primarily silver or tin, and a low concentration of copper; used to fill prepared cavities in the teeth.

amalgamate (ah-mal'gah-māt) To make an amalgam by dissolving metal in mercury.

amalgamation (ah-mal-gah-ma'shun) The process of making an amalgam.

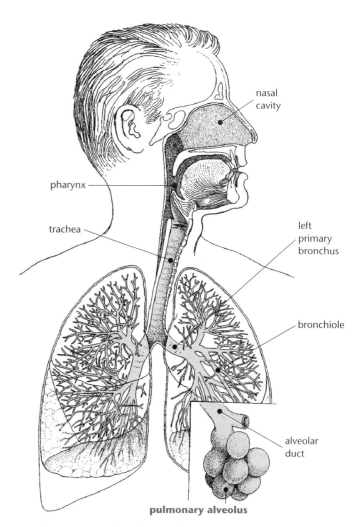

pulmonary alveolus

amalgamator (ah-mal'gah-ma'tor) In dentistry, a machine for mixing amalgam mechanically.

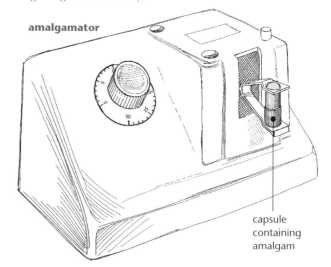

amalgamator

capsule containing amalgam

Amanita (am-ah-ni'tah) A genus of fungi.

    A. muscaria Poisonous mushroom causing rapid intoxication within a few minutes to two hours after ingestion; the symptoms include lacrimation, miosis, salivation, sweating, dyspnea, abdominal cramps, diarrhea, vomiting, and circulatory failure; it can lead to convulsions and coma. Also called fly agaric.

    A. phalloides Poisonous mushroom causing severe gastrointestinal symptoms, within 6 to 24 hours after ingestion, with subsequent damage to kidneys, liver, and central nervous system; jaundice commonly develops in two or three days; circulatory failure and coma usually follow within a week of ingestion. Also called death cup; death angel; destroying angel.

Amanita
muscaria

Amanita
phalloides

amantadine (ah-man′tah-dēn) An antiviral drug used in the prevention and treatment of influenza A infections and to relieve the symptoms of parkinsonism.

amaurosis (am-aw-ro′sis) Blindness.

 central a. Blindness caused by disease of the central nervous system.

 a. fugax Brief, unilateral blindness lasting from seconds to minutes, caused by insufficient blood supply to the eye, which may be due to temporary blockage of blood vessels or to centrifugal force (e.g., visual blackout in flight).

 toxic a. Blindness due to inflammation of the optic nerve, caused by a poisonous substance in the body, such as methyl alcohol, arsenic, lead, or other similar agents.

amaurotic (am-aw-rot′ik) Relating to amaurosis.

ambenonium chloride (am-be-no′ne-um klo′rīd) A compound that inhibits production of the enzyme cholinesterase; used in the treatment of chronic progressive muscular weakness (myasthenia gravis).

ambi- Prefix meaning both.

ambisexual (am-bī-seks′u-al) **1.** Common to both sexes. **2.** See bisexual.

ambivalence (am-biv′ah-lens) The coexistence of a feeling or emotion and its opposite, as the simultaneous love and hate of the same person.

ambly- Combining form meaning dullness.

amblyopia (am-ble-o′pe-ah) Poor or decreased vision usually involving one eye (commonly known as "lazy eye") that failed to develop normally during infancy and early childhood; caused by any condition affecting visual development and normal use of the eyes; most common cause is strabismus, whereby the misaligned eye "turns off" to avoid double vision; other causes include unequal focus of the two eyes and cloudiness in the normally clear lens.

amblyopic (am-ble-o′pik) Affected by amblyopia.

amblyoscope (am′ble-o-skōp) A device that presents separate images to each eye at different angles; used to evaluate and stimulate binocular vision.

ambo- Prefix meaning both.

ambulation (am-bu-la′shun) The act of walking.

ambulatory, ambulant (am′bu-lah-to-re, am′bu-lant) **1.** Able to walk; applied to patients who are not bedridden. **2.** Relating to ambulation.

ameba (ah-me′bah), pl. ame′bae, ame′bas Common name for any protozoan of the genus *Amoeba.*

amebiasis (am-e-bi′ah-sis) Infection with *Entamoeba histolytica;* symptoms range from mild diarrhea to dysentery. Also called entamebiasis.

amebic (ah-me′bik) Relating to amebas.

amebicide (ah-me′bī-sīd) Any drug used to combat an amebic infection; some act only on intestinal infections, others act also on other sites such as the liver.

ameboid (ah-me′boid) Resembling amebas in shape or movement.

ameboma (am-e-bo′mah) A tumorlike mass, usually occurring in the wall of the colon, associated with chronic infection with amebas (amebiasis). Also called amebic granuloma.

amelanotic (ah-mel-ah-not′ik) Lacking the pigment melanin; said of unpigmented skin growths.

amelia (ah-me′le-ah) Congenital absence of limbs.

amelioration (ah-mēl′yo-ra′shun) Lessening the severity of a disease or its symptoms.

ameloblast (ah-mel′o-blast) One of the epithelial cells in the developing tooth taking part in the formation of tooth enamel. Also called enamel cell.

ameloblastoma (ah-mel-o-blas-to′mah) Benign tumor derived from epithelial cells of a developing tooth, occurring most often in the posterior portion of the jaw; it has a tendency to recur if not properly excised.

amelogenesis (am-ĕ-lo-jen′ĕ-sis) Formation and development of tooth enamel. Also called enamelogenesis.

 a. imperfecta Hereditary defect of tooth enamel; may be deficient in quantity or defective in structure, resulting in an easily eroded enamel. Also called enamelogenesis imperfecta.

amenorrhea (ah-men-o-re′ah) Absence of menstruation.

 primary a. Failure of menstruation to begin by the age of 16 years.

 secondary a. Cessation of menstruation for at least three months in a woman who has menstruated in the past.

amenorrheal (ah-men-o-re′al) Relating to amenorrhea.

ametria (ah-me′tre-ah) Congenital absence of the uterus.

ametropia (am-ĕ-tro′pe-ah) A refractive defect in which parallel rays do not focus upon the retina; rather, they focus in front of (myopia) or behind (hyperopia) the retina.

amide (am′īd) An organic compound derived from ammonia by substituting an acyl radical for hydrogen.

amido- Combining form indicating the presence of an amide group in a molecule.

amidopyrine (am-ĭ-do-pi′rēn) See aminopyrine.

amikacin (am-ĭ-ka′sin) An antibiotic drug active against gram-negative bacterial infections. Its use is usually restricted for infections that are resistant to other antibiotics.

amiloride (ah-mil′o-rīd) A drug that acts on the distal tubules of the kidney and promotes excretion of sodium in the urine while preventing loss of potassium; used in the treatment of edema and hypertension.

amine (ah-mēn′) An organic compound derived from ammonia by substitution of one or more hydrogen atoms by hydrocarbon radicals.

-amine Combining form indicating the presence of an amino group, or substituted amino group, in a molecule (e.g., histamine).

amino- Combining form indicating the presence of the radical -NH$_2$ in a molecule.

aminoaciduria (am′ĭ-no-as-ĭ-du′re-ah) Excretion of excessive amounts of amino acids in the urine; seen in lead poisoning, as a result of damage to kidney tubules, and in other disorders.

ρ-aminobenzoic acid (par′ah ah-me-no-ben-zo′ik as′id) (PABA) See para-aminobenzoic acid.

γ-aminobutyric acid (gam′a ah-me-no-bu-ter′ik as′id) (GABA) See gamma-aminobutyric acid.

ε-aminocaproic acid (ep′sĭ-lon ah-me-no-kah-pro′ik as′id) (EACP) See epsilon-aminocaproic acid.

aminoglutethimide (ah-me′no-gloo-teth′ĭ-mīd) A drug that inhibits activity of the adrenal cortex; used in the treatment of Cushing's syndrome and some advanced cases of breast cancer.

aminoglycoside (am′ĭ-no-gli-ko′sīd) Any of a class of antibodies effective against gram-positive and gram-negative bacteria; examples include streptomycin, amikacin, and gentamicin. High dosages, especially in the presence of kidney dysfunction, may cause muscle weakness.

ρ-aminohippuric acid (par′ah ah-me-no-hip-pur′ik as′id) (PAH) See para-aminohippuric acid.

δ-**aminolevulinic acid** (del′ta ah-me-no-lev-u-lin′ik as′id) (DALA) See delta-aminolevulinic acid.

aminopeptidase (ah-me-no-pep′tĭ-dās) An intestinal enzyme that promotes the breakdown of peptides; it aids in protein digestion.

aminophylline (ah-me-no-fil′in) A compound containing theophylline and ethylenediamine that has antiasthmatic and diuretic properties; it is also a heart stimulant. Possible adverse effects include nausea, vomiting, headache, dizziness, confusion, and palpitations. Also called theophylline ethylenediamine.

aminopyrine (am-ĭ-no-pi′rin) An effective drug in reducing pain and fever but seldom used because it may cause leukocytopenia. Formerly called amidopyrine.

aminorrhexis (am-ne-o-rek′sis) Rupture of the amniotic membrane containing the fetus.

ρ-**aminosalicylic acid** (par′ah ah-me-no-sal-i-sil′ik as′id) (PAS, PASA) See para-aminosalicylic acid.

aminotransferase (ah-me-no-trans′fer-ās) Any of a group of enzymes that promote the transfer of amino groups; important in protein catabolism. Also called transaminase.

amitriptyline hydrochloride (am-ĭ-trip′tĭ-len hi-dro-klo′rĭd) An antidepressant drug with sedative properties. Possible adverse effects include dry mouth, blurred vision, dizziness, and hot flashes.

ammonia (ah-mo′ne-ah) A volatile, water-soluble gas present in small amounts in blood plasma; raised levels occur in certain conditions (liver disease, Reye's syndrome, severe congestive heart failure, gastrointestinal hemorrhage, and hemolytic disease of the newborn). In industry, ammonia is used as a refrigerant and in manufacturing plastics and explosives. It is an irritant to the skin, conjunctiva, and mucous membrane of the respiratory tract; exposure to high concentrations causes swelling and fluid retention in the lungs (pulmonary edema) and may cause death.

ammoniacal (am-o-ni′ah-kal) Relating to ammonia.

ammoniated (ah-mo′ne-āt-ed) Containing ammonia.

ammonio- Combining form denoting the group NH_3.

ammonium (ah-mo′ne-um) The chemical radical NH_4.

ammoniuria (ah-mo-ne-u′re-ah) Excessive ammonia content in the urine; ammoniacal urine.

amnesia (am-ne′ze-ah) Pathologic loss of memory; may result from brain injury, organic disease, or emotional trauma.

    anterograde a. Loss of memory for events occurring immediately after the traumatic episode that caused the amnesia; frequently associated with brain concussion. Also called posttraumatic amnesia.

    posttraumatic a. See anterograde amnesia.

    retrograde a. Loss of memory for events occurring shortly before the traumatic episode; frequently seen in brain concussion.

amnesiac (am-ne′se-ak) A person afflicted with amnesia.

amnestic (am-nes′tik) **1.** Relating to amnesia. **2.** Anything that causes amnesia.

amnio- Combining form meaning amnion.

amniocentesis (am-ne-o-sen-te′sis) Diagnostic procedure in which a few milliliters of the amniotic fluid surrounding the fetus are withdrawn with a needle and syringe through the woman's abdominal wall. The fluid and fetal cells contained in the fluid are analyzed to detect the presence of fetal abnormalities and genetic diseases.

amnion (am′ne-on) The thin, innermost layer of the membranous sac, which surrounds the embryo and fills with amniotic fluid as the pregnancy advances. Commonly called bag of waters.

amnionitis (am-ne-o-ni′tis) Inflammation of the amnion.

amniorrhea (am-ne-o-re′ah) Premature escape of amniotic fluid.

amniorrhexis (am-ne-o-rek′sis) Rupture of the amniotic membrane containing the fetus.

amniotic (am-ne-ot′ik) Relating to the amnion.

amniotome (am′ne-o-tōm) Instrument used to puncture the fetal membranes.

amniotomy (am-ne-ot′o-me) Surgical rupture of the fetal membranes.

amorphia (ah-mor′fe-ah) The state of being without definite form.

amorphous (ah-mor′fus) Lacking a definite shape or structure.

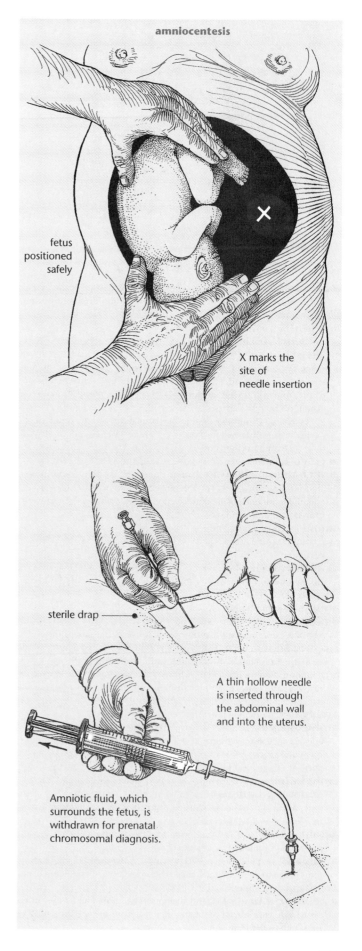

amniocentesis

fetus positioned safely

X marks the site of needle insertion

sterile drap

A thin hollow needle is inserted through the abdominal wall and into the uterus.

Amniotic fluid, which surrounds the fetus, is withdrawn for prenatal chromosomal diagnosis.

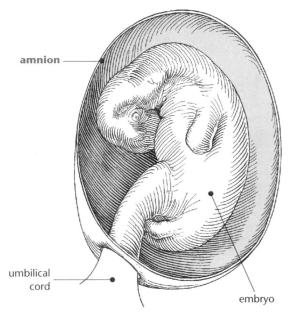

amnion

embryo

umbilical cord

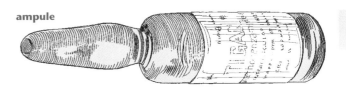

ampule

amoxicillin (ah-moks-ĭ-sil′in) A semisynthetic penicillin, active against a wide range of infections. Adverse reactions include a skin rash and, rarely, fever, itching, and breathing difficulty.

ampere (am′pēr) The unit of electrical current; commonly shortened to "amp." **1.** Scientific (SI): the current that, if maintained in two straight parallel conductors of infinite length, of negligible circular cross section, and placed 1 meter apart in a vacuum, produces between these conductors a force of 2×10^{-7} newtons per meter. **2.** Legal: the current that, flowing for one second, deposits 1.118 mg of silver from silver nitrate solution.

amphetamine (am-fet′ah-min) Any of a group of synthetic drugs that have a strong stimulant effect on the central nervous system; some are appetite suppressants and have been used to treat obesity. Abuse of the drug leads to tolerance and dependence. Adverse reactions to continued high doses include anxiety, hallucinations, intense fatigue after the stimulation phase, and prolonged depression with possible suicide.

amphi- Prefix meaning on both sides; around.

amphiarthrosis (am-fe-ar-thro′sis) See amphiarthrodial joint, under joint.

amphimixis (am-fi-mik′sis) The union of paternal and maternal nuclear elements following fertilization of the ovum.

amphixenosis (am-fiks-en-ō′sis) A transmissible disease caused by a microorganism that can inhabit either human or animal as its maintenance host.

ampho- Combining form meaning on both sides.

amphophilic (am-fo-fil′ik) Stainable with either acid or basic dyes; said of certain cells.

amphoric (am-for′ik) The quality of a sound sometimes heard on auscultation, compared to the sound produced blowing over the mouth of a bottle.

amphotericin B (am-fo-ter′ĭ-sin) An antibiotic derived from a strain of *Streptomyces nodosus;* used in the treatment of several types of fungal infections; administered by injection or topically in creams and lotions. Adverse effects are most likely to occur when amphotericin B is given by injection; these include vomiting, fever, headache, and, rarely, seizures.

ampicillin (amp-ĭ-sil′in) A semisynthetic penicillin primarily effective against certain gram-negative bacteria. It may cause skin rashes in certain individuals; the possibility of a rash is heightened when given to someone with infectious mononucleosis.

amplification (am-plĭ-fĭ-ka′shun) The act of increasing (e.g., of a sensory perception).

  gene a. The increased reduplication of a gene, especially in aberrant (often malignant) cells.

amplitude (am′plĕ-tūd) A range, breadth, or extent.

ampule, ampul (am′pūl) A small glass container that can be sealed to preserve the sterile condition of its contents. Used primarily to store solutions for injection.

ampulla (am-pul′lah), pl. ampul′lae In anatomy, a small dilatation of a canal or duct.

  anterior membranous a. The dilatation at the end of the anterior membranous semicircular duct just before it enters the utricle; it contains the ampullary crest with the nerve endings of the vestibular division of the vestibulocochlear (VIII cranial) nerve, which is surrounded by endolymph.

  anterior osseous a. A dilatation at the front of the bony anterior semicircular canal just before it enters the vestibule; it contains the anterior membranous ampulla, which is surrounded by perilymph.

  a. of deferent duct The dilatation of the deferent duct at the base of the bladder just before it combines with the duct from the seminal vesicle to form the ejaculatory duct. Also called ampulla of vas deferens.

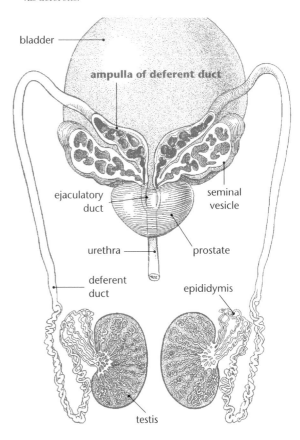

bladder

ampulla of deferent duct

ejaculatory duct

urethra

deferent duct

seminal vesicle

prostate

epididymis

testis

  hepatopancreatic a. The saclike dilatation formed by the union of the pancreatic and bile ducts just before it constricts to open into the duodenum, at the summit of the duodenal papilla. Also called ampulla of Vater.

  lateral membranous a. The dilatation at the end of the lateral (horizontal) membranous semicircular duct just before it opens into the utricle; it contains the ampullary crest with the nerve endings of the vestibular division of the vestibulocochlear (VIII cranial) nerve, which is surrounded by endolymph.

  lateral osseous a. A dilatation at the front of the bony anterior semicircular canal just before it enters the vestibule; it contains the lateral membranous ampulla surrounded by perilymph.

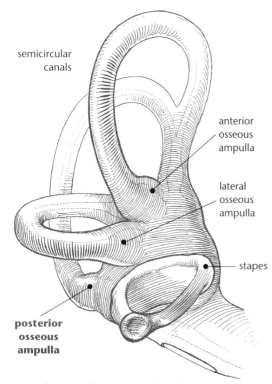

semicircular canals

anterior osseous ampulla

lateral osseous ampulla

stapes

posterior osseous ampulla

posterior membranous a. The dilatation at the end of the posterior membranous semicircular duct just before it opens into the utricle; it contains the ampullary crest with the nerve endings of the vestibular division of the vestibulocochlear (VIII cranial) nerve, which is surrounded by endolymph.

posterior osseous a. A dilatation at the front of the bony posterior semicircular canal just before it enters the vestibule; it contains the posterior membranous ampulla, which is surrounded by perilymph.

a. of uterine tube The thin-walled, tortuous portion of the fallopian (uterine) tube, forming about one-half of its length between the isthmus medially and the infundibulum laterally.

a. of vas deferens See ampulla of deferent duct.

a. of Vater See hepatopancreatic ampulla.

ampullitis (am-pul-li′tis) Inflammation of an ampulla especially of the ampulla of the deferent duct.

amputation (am-pu-ta′shun) The cutting off of any appendage or part of the body.

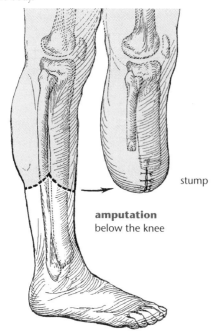

stump

amputation below the knee

Alanson's a. A circular amputation in which the remaining stump has a cone shape.

aperiosteal a. Amputation that includes the removal of periosteum at the site of the cut bone.

Carden's a. Leg amputation in which the femur is cut across the condyles.

cervical a. Surgical removal of the uterine cervix. Also called hysterotrachelectomy.

Chopart's a. Removal of the front part of the foot, through the transverse midtarsal joint, leaving the heel and adjacent bones intact.

cinematic a. See cineplastic amputation.

cineplastic a. Amputation of a limb in which muscles and tendons are arranged in the stump in such a way that they can produce motion in a specially constructed artificial limb. Also called cinematic amputation; kineplastic amputation.

circular a. The sequential division of skin, muscle, and bone of a limb, each at a higher level.

Gritti-Stokes a. Amputation of the leg above the condyles of the femur, leaving the kneecap (patella) intact to cover the end of the cut femur. Also called Gritti's operation.

hindquarter a. See hemipelvectomy.

kineplastic a. See cineplastic amputation.

Lisfranc's a. Amputation of the foot between the tarsus and metatarsus. Also called Lisfranc's operation.

root a. Surgical removal of the tip of a tooth root.

Syme's a. Amputation of the foot at the ankle (tibiotalar) joint, with removal of both malleoli. Also called Syme's operation.

traumatic a. Loss of a limb, toe, or finger through accidental injury.

amputee (am-pu-te′) A person with one or more amputated limbs.

amygdala (ah-mig′dah-lah) 1. Any almond-shaped structure of the body such as a tonsil. 2. An ovoid gray mass located in the brain, in the dorsomedial area of the temporal lobe, anterior to, and above, the inferior horn of the lateral ventricle.

amygdalin (ah-mig′dah-lin) A glycoside present in almonds and the pits of other plants of the family Rosaceae; the principal ingredient of laetrile.

amygdaline (ah-mig′dah-lin) 1. Relating to an almond. 2. Relating to a tonsil.

amygdaloid (ah-mig′dah-loid) Resembling an almond or a tonsil.

amyl (am′il) The univalent organic radical, C_5H_{11}.

a. nitrite A volatile liquid formerly administered by inhalation to relieve pain in angina pectoris.

amylase (am′ĭ-lās) An enzyme that catalyzes the splitting of starches.

salivary alpha-a. See ptyalin.

amylin (am′ĭ-lin) The insoluble component of starch.

amylo-, amyl- Combining forms meaning starch.

amylogenesis (am-ĭ-lo-jen′ĕ-sis) Starch formation.

amyloid (am′ĭ-loid) 1. Resembling starch. 2. Any of a variety of abnormal complex proteins.

amyloidosis (am-ĭ-loi-do′sis) Deposition of the abnormal protein amyloid in the tissues, usually in amounts sufficient to impair function.

acquired a. See secondary amyloidosis.

primary a. Amyloidosis occurring with no apparent cause, affecting the skin, tongue, intestinal tract, and heart.

reactive systemic a. See secondary amyloidosis.

secondary a. Amyloidosis occurring as a complication of chronic diseases, either infectious (e.g., osteomyelitis and tuberculosis) or inflammatory (e.g., rheumatoid arthritis and inflammatory bowel disease). Also called acquired amyloidosis; reactive systemic amyloidosis.

amylopectin (am-ĭ-lo-pek′tin) An insoluble component of starch that has a high molecular weight and branched structure.

amylophagia (am-ĭ-lo-fa′je-ah) Abnormal craving for starch in forms not normally used as food.

amylose am′ĭ-lōs) The soluble constituent of starch.

amyoplasia (ah-mi-o-pla′ze-ah) Deficient formation of muscle tissue.

    a. congenita See congenital multiple arthrogryposis, under arthrogryposis.

amyotonia (a-mi-o-to′ne-ah) See myatonia.

amyotrophic (ah-mi-o-trof′ik) Relating to amyotrophy.

amyotrophy (ah-mi-ot′ro-fe) Wasting of muscle tissue; usually caused by impaired blood supply or nerve innervation of the tissue, reduced use for prolonged periods (as when a limb is placed in a cast), or severe malnutrition.

    neuralgic a. See brachial plexus neuropathy, under neuropathy.

    progressive spinal a. See progressive muscular atrophy, under atrophy.

ana-, an- Prefixes meaning upward; again.

anabolic (an-ah-bol′ik) Relating to anabolism.

anabolism (ah-nab′o-lizm) The metabolic process through which living tissues build complex compounds from substances of a simple constitution (e.g., proteins from amino acids); an energy-consuming process; the opposite of catabolism.

anacidity (an-ah-sid′ĭ-te) Lack of normal acidity, as in secretions.

anaclitic (an-ah-klit′ik) Having a psychological dependence on another, as the dependence of an infant on its mother or mother substitute.

anacrotic (an-ah-krot′ik) Having an abnormal pulse, evidenced in a pulse tracing in which the ascending line of the curve has a small additional wave or shoulder (e.g., in aortic stenosis). Also called anadicrotic.

anacusis (an-ah-ku′sis) Total deafness.

anadicrotic (an-ah-di-krot′ik) See anacrotic.

anaerobe (an-a′er-ōb) A microorganism that can multiply only in the absence of air.

    facultative a. A microorganism that thrives in either the presence or the absence of air.

    obligate a. An organism unable to grow or live in the presence of air.

anaerobic (an-a-er-o′bik) Living without air.

anaerogenic (an-a-er-o-jen′ik) Producing little or no gas as a product of metabolism; said of certain bacteria.

anal (a′nal) Relating to the anus.

analeptic (an-ah-lep′tik) **1.** Strengthening, stimulating. **2.** A drug that stimulates the central nervous system, especially the breathing mechanism in the brainstem.

analgesia (an-al-je′ze-ah) Loss of pain sensation; a condition in which stimuli that normally produce pain are perceived but are not interpreted as pain; it may be induced by drugs (e.g., relief of pain without loss of consciousness during childbirth through the administration of certain inhalation anesthetics in concentrations lower than those required for surgical anesthesia); or it may result from disease interrupting pain pathways in the central or peripheral nervous system.

    a. algera Pain in a denervated or an anesthetized area. Also called analgesia dolorosa.

    a. dolorosa See analgesia algera.

    glove-and-stocking a. A characteristic finding in malingering in which a person describes loss of sensation along areas that are not demarcated by specific nerve distribution.

    patient-controlled a. (PCA) Reduction of acute pain by self-administration of narcotic drugs within limits of dose established by the physician (e.g., in a postoperative period).

analgesic (an-al-je′zik) Relating to analgesia.

analgia (an-al′je-ah) Absence of pain sensitivity.

    congenital a. Analgia present at birth.

analog, analogue (an′ah-log) **1.** An organ or part similar in function to one in another organism of a different species but different in structure or development. **2.** A chemical compound similar in structure to another but dissimilar in composition.

analogous (ah-nal′o-gus) Having a resemblance in function but a different structure or origin.

analphalipoproteinemia (an-al-fah-lip′o-pro-ten-e′me-ah) See Tangier disease, under disease.

analysand (ah-nal′ĭ-sand) A person who is being psychoanalyzed.

analysis (ah-nal′ĭ-sis), pl. anal′yses **1.** A method of study based on the separation of the object of study into smaller units. **2.** The breaking up of a chemical compound into its constituent elements. **3.** See psychoanalysis.

    bite a. See occlusal analysis.

    blood gas a. Determination of oxygen and carbon dioxide concentrations in the blood.

    decision a. In a clinical setting, the application of epidemiological information and other data on the probability of outcomes when alternative decisions can be made (e.g., drug therapy or surgical intervention for the treatment of a particular disorder).

    gastric a. Removal and study of stomach contents to aid in diagnosis of stomach disease; may be performed after a test meal, or after administration of a secretion-promoting agent.

    mixed-stain DNA a. In criminal investigation, the use of DNA typing to examine a sample of mixed semen obtained from a victim of a multiple-assailant rape, or a sample of mixed blood recovered from the scene of a homicide to determine, first, the number of individuals involved in the crime and, subsequently, to identify the culprits with virtual certainty by comparing the DNA pattern of the samples with those obtained from the suspects.

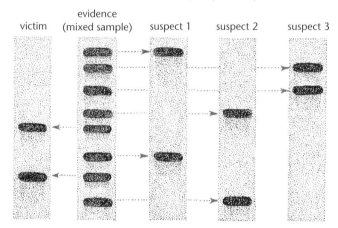

mixed stain DNA analysis (Cellmark)

Each single locus probe produces a pattern of at most two bands per person. An eight band pattern indicates the sample was from at least four individuals. Matching of the suspects' band patterns with those of the evidence confirms their involvement.

    Northern blot a. Identification of RNA fragments that have been electrophoretically separated and transferred (blotted) onto nitrocellular or other type of paper or nylon membrane. Specific RNA fragments can then be detected by radioactive probes.

    occlusal a. A study of the relations of the contact surfaces of teeth to determine the presence and degree of dysfunction. Also called bite analysis.

    qualitative a. Determination of the nature of each of the chemical elements of a substance.

    quantitative a. Determination of the amount, as well as the nature, of each chemical element of a substance.

    semen a. Examination of a semen sample to determine male fertility in an infertile marriage or to substantiate the success of vasectomy.

    Southern blot a. A procedure (first developed by E. M. Southern) for separating and identifying DNA sequences; DNA fragments are separated by electrophoresis and transferred (blotted) onto a special filter on which specific DNA fragments can then be detected by radioactive probes.

    volumetric a. Quantitative analysis by the use of graduated amounts of standard solutions of reagents.

    Western blot a. A method of identifying proteins or peptides that have been electrophoretically separated and transferred (blotted) onto nitrocellulose or nylon membrane. The blots are then detected by radiolabeled antibody probes.

analyst (an'ah-list) A psychoanalyst.

analyzer (an'ah-li-zer) In electroencephalography, a device that electronically breaks down waveforms of complex cerebral rhythms into their individual components to determine the amplitude and frequency of these components.

anamnesis (an-am-ne'sis) The history of an ailment as recalled by the patient.

anamnestic (an-am-nes'tik) **1.** Assisting the memory; mnemonic. **2.** Relating to anamnesis.

anaphase (an'ah-fāz) The stage of cell division by mitosis in which chromosomes move from the equatorial plane to the poles of the cell.

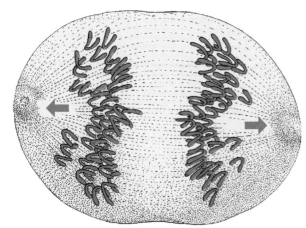

anaphase of somatic cell   46 chromosomes move toward centrioles

anaphylactic (an-ah-fī-lak'tik) Relating to anaphylaxis; having extreme sensitivity to foreign (nonself) protein.

anaphylactogenic (an-ah-fī-lak-tō-jen'ik) **1.** Producing an exaggerated or severe reaction to the presence of a foreign protein in the body. **2.** Anything that reduces immunity.

anaphylactoid (an-ah-fī-lak'toid) Resembling or having characteristics of anaphylaxis; applied to reactions occurring without a demonstrable presence of a mediating immunoglobulin (IgE), such as reactions to iodinated contrast materials and nonsteroidal anti-inflammatory drugs.

anaphylaxis (an-ah-fī-lak'sis) An immediate, severe hypersensitivity (allergic) reaction to a previously encountered antigen (allergen) to which the person was sensitized; the reaction requires the presence of IgE antibodies formed in response to a previous exposure to the same antigen; characterized by the release of histamine and other pharmacologically active substances into the bloodstream, with subsequent itchiness, hives, generalized flush, respiratory distress, and vascular collapse; occasionally accompanied by seizures, vomiting, abdominal cramps, and incontinence.

anaplasia (an-ah-pla'ze-ah) Failure of cells to differentiate and develop normal structure, characteristic of certain tumor cells.

anaplastic (an-ah-plas'tik) Relating to anaplasia.

anarthria (an-ar'thre-ah) Speechlessness; may result from brain lesion or damage to nerves innervating the muscles involved in articulating speech.

anasarca (an-ah-sar'kah) Massive swelling and accumulation of fluids in subcutaneous tissues and in body cavities.

anastomose (ah-nas'to-mōs) **1.** To open into another, said of blood vessels. **2.** To connect surgically two normally separate tubular structures.

anastomosis (ah-nas-to-mo'sis), pl. anastomo'ses **1.** The normal channel between two tubular structures. **2.** A surgical or pathologic channel opened between tubular structures or hollow organs.

    intestinal a. See enteroenterostomy.

    microvascular a. Anastomosis of minute blood vessels performed under a surgical microscope.

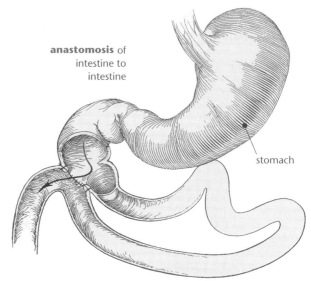

anastomosis of intestine to intestine

stomach

anastomotic (ah-nas-to-mot'ik) Relating to anastomosis.

anatomic, anatomical (an-ah-tom'ik, an-ah-tom'ĭ-kal) Relating to anatomy.

anatomic snuffbox (an-ah-tom'ik snuf'boks) A triangular depression formed on the radial side of the wrist when the thumb is fully extended and abducted.

anatomist (ah-nat'o-mist) A specialist in the field of anatomy.

anatomy (ah-nat'o-me) **1.** The science of the structure and organization of the body parts. **2.** Dissection.

    comparative a. Comparison of structures of different animal species.

    dental a. The study of teeth and their surrounding structures.

    developmental a. See embryology.

    gross a. Study of body parts as seen without the aid of a microscope. Also called macroscopic anatomy.

    macroscopic a. See gross anatomy.

    microscopic a. See histology.

    surface a. Study of the outer configuration of the body in relation to underlying and deep structures.

    surgical a. Study of anatomy with a view toward applying the knowledge to surgical techniques.

    topographical a. Study of body parts in relation to their neighboring structures.

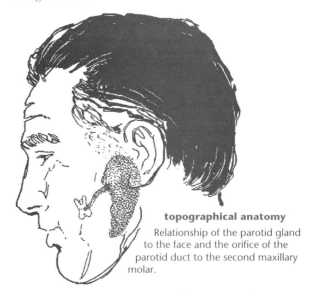

topographical anatomy
Relationship of the parotid gland to the face and the orifice of the parotid duct to the second maxillary molar.

-ance Suffix meaning action; state; condition (e.g., brilliance).

anchorage (ang'ker-ij) **1.** A tooth to which a bridge, crown, or filling is attached. **2.** The teeth used as support for an orthodontic appliance (e.g., braces).

ancillary (an′sil-lār-e) Supplementary; secondary.

anconitis (ang-ko-ni′tis) Inflammation of the elbow joint.

ancrod (an′krod) An enzyme obtained from the pit viper (*Agkistrodon rhodostoma*) that promotes the breakdown of protein; it acts specifically on fibrinogen and reduces the viscosity of blood; used as an anticoagulant of blood.

Ancylostoma (an-sī-los′to-mah) A genus of nematode parasites that includes the hookworm.

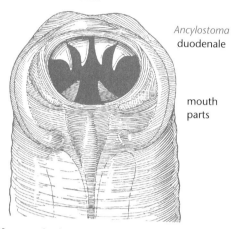

Ancylostoma duodenale

mouth parts

ancylostomiasis (an-sī-los-to-mi′ah-sis) See hookworm disease, under disease.

    cutaneous a. Small itchy vesicles and pustules on the skin at the site of entrance of *Ancylostoma* larvae; they appear just prior to intestinal manifestations.

andro- Combining form meaning male.

androblastoma (an-dro-blas-to′mah) An uncommon, benign tumor of the testis or the ovary, composed of Sertoli cells or a mixture of granulosa and Sertoli cells; on rare occasions may turn malignant. Also called Sertoli cell tumor.

androgen (an′dro-jen) General term for a substance, usually a hormone, that stimulates development of male sex characteristics.

androgenic (an-dro-jen′ik) Relating to androgen; producing male characteristics.

androgenous (an-droj′ě-nus) Tending to produce mostly males.

androgynous (an-droj′ĭ-nus) Relating to female pseudohermaphroditism (i.e., a true female with male characteristics).

android (an′droid) Resembling a man.

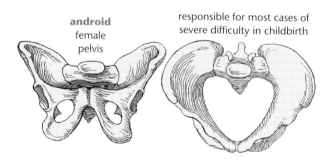

android female pelvis

responsible for most cases of severe difficulty in childbirth

andropathy (an-drop′ah-the) Any disease peculiar to males.

androstenedione (an-dro-stēn′de-ōn) An androgenic steroid produced in the testis, ovary, and adrenal cortex.

androsterone (an-dros′ter-ōn) A male sex hormone (androgen) derived from testosterone.

anechoic (an-ě-ko′ik) Echo-free. Also called sonolucent.

anemia (ah-ne′me-ah) Any condition in which concentration of blood hemoglobin decreases below normal levels for the age and sex of the person; usually there is also a decrease in the number of red blood cells per cubic mm and in the number of packed red blood cells per 100 ml of blood. Anemia decreases the oxygen-carrying capacity of the blood.

    Addison's a., addisonian a. See pernicious anemia.

    aplastic a. Anemia due to failure of bone marrow to produce the normal number of red blood cells; usually associated with decreased number of all cellular components of the blood.

    congenital hypoplastic a. Anemia occurring in infants, resulting from underdevelopment of bone marrow; minor congenital abnormalities may also occur. Also called erythrogenesis imperfecta.

    Cooley's a. See major thalassemia, under thalassemia.

    crescent-cell a. See sickle-cell anemia.

    hemolytic a. Any of a group of diseases characterized by a shortened life span of red blood cells in the bloodstream.

    hemolytic a. of newborn See hemolytic disease of the newborn, under disease.

    hemorrhagic a. Anemia resulting from loss of blood. If blood loss is chronic, it leads to iron deficiency anemia.

    hypochromic a. Anemia marked by a reduction of hemoglobin content of red blood cells (erythrocytes), as in iron deficiency anemia.

    iron deficiency a. The most common type of anemia, developed when insufficient iron is available to the bone marrow where red blood cells are formed; characterized by low concentration of hemoglobin (hypochromia) and smaller than normal red blood cells. May be caused by dietary deficiency, increased demand for iron (growing children, pregnant and lactating women); malabsorption due to other conditions; or chronic blood loss (hookworm disease, peptic ulcers, colon cancer, long-term aspirin ingestion).

    leukoerythroblastic a. See myelophthisic anemia.

    macrocytic a. of pregnancy Anemia occurring in pregnant women in which the average size of red blood cells is greater than normal, their number is reduced, and their hemoglobin content is low; usually caused by folic acid deficiency.

    Mediterranean a. Outmoded term for thalassemia.

    myelophthisic a. Condition caused by any of several space-occupying lesions in bone marrow, especially metastatic cancer, that distort and destroy the marrow architecture and its capacity for producing red blood cells; associated with reduction of all blood elements and, frequently, with the presence of immature blood cells in peripheral blood. Also called leukoerythroblastic anemia; leukoerythroblastosis.

    nutritional a. Anemia resulting from deficiency of some essential nutrient in the diet, necessary for red blood cell formation (iron, vitamins, proteins).

    pernicious a. Anemia due to vitamin B_{12} deficiency; usually caused by absence of stomach acid and intrinsic factor, which are essential for absorption of vitamin B_{12}; may also result from surgical removal of the terminal ileum where absorption occurs; it occurs predominantly after the age of 50 years and is frequently associated with neurological damage. Also called addisonian anemia; Addison's anemia.

    sickle-cell a. Hereditary anemia occurring almost exclusively among blacks; characterized by the presence of a large number of crescent-shaped red blood cells that contain an abnormal hemoglobin (hemoglobin S). Also called crescent-cell anemia; sickle-cell disease.

anemic (ah-ne′mik) Relating to anemia.

anencephaly (an-en-sef′ah-le) Developmental defect in which the top of the skull is absent and the brain is reduced to small masses lying at the base of the skull. The affected infant either is stillborn or does not survive beyond a few hours.

anephric (a-nef′rik) Without kidneys.

anergic (an-er′jik) Relating to anergy.

anergy (an′er-je) 1. A state of diminished reactivity to substances (antigens) that would ordinarily induce an immunologic or allergenic response. 2. Sluggishness.

aneroid (an′er-oid) Not requiring or containing fluids; said of certain instruments, such as the blood pressure measuring device (sphygmomanometer).

anesthekinesia (an-es-the-kī-ne′ze-ah) Combined loss of sensory perception and motor paralysis.

A

anesthesia (an-es-the′ze-ah) Loss of sensation, induced by administration of drugs, or resulting from a lesion of the nervous system.

   block a. See conduction anesthesia.

   caudal a. Anesthesia produced by injecting an anesthetic solution into the sacral canal.

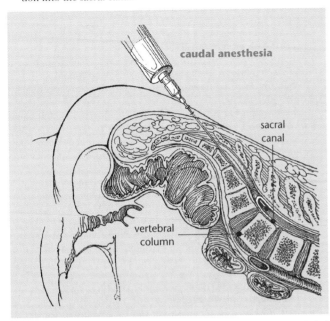

caudal anesthesia

sacral canal

vertebral column

   closed-circuit a. Inhalation anesthesia in which all exhaled gases are continuously rebreathed except carbon dioxide, which is removed by an absorption apparatus.

   conduction a. Inhibition of nerve transmission by injecting an anesthetic solution around a nerve trunk. Also called block anesthesia.

   crossed a. Anesthesia of one side of the face and the other side of the body due to a lesion of the brainstem.

   dissociated a. Loss of perception of pain and temperature while the sense of touch is retained.

   epidural a. Anesthesia produced by injection of an anesthetic solution into the epidural space.

   field block a. Anesthesia produced in a local area by multiple injections of an anesthetic solution around the circumference of the operative field.

   general a. A controlled state of unconsciousness and complete loss of sensation, accompanied by partial or complete loss of protective reflexes, including the inability to independently maintain an airway or respond purposefully to verbal command; produced by administration of intravenous or inhalation anesthetic agents. Intramuscular injection and rectal instillation are rarely used in general anesthesia. Also called surgical anesthesia.

   glove a. Loss of sensation in a hand, involving an area usually covered by a glove.

   high spinal a. Spinal anesthesia extending up to the level of the second or third thoracic dermatome.

   hyperbaric spinal a. Spinal anesthesia produced by injecting into the subarachnoid space a local anesthetic solution of greater specific gravity than that of the spinal fluid, then controlling the location of the heavy solution in the subarachnoid space by tilting the patient's body or head up or to one side.

   hypobaric spinal a. Spinal anesthesia produced by injecting into the subarachnoid space a local anesthetic solution of specific gravity lower than that of spinal fluid, then allowing the light solution to rise to the desired level of the patient's body.

   hysterical a. Loss of sensory perception occurring as a manifestation of a conversion disorder.

   local a. Anesthesia confined to one part of the body by injecting anesthetic into or adjacent to the site of surgery.

   nerve block a. Anesthesia produced by injecting a local anesthetic solution about peripheral nerves.

   paracervical block a. Anesthesia of the uterine cervix achieved by injection of a local anesthetic solution at the cervicovaginal junction.

   pudendal a. Anesthesia of the perineum produced by injection of an anesthetic solution into the areas near the pudendal nerves.

   rectal a. Anesthesia produced by instillation of a central nervous system depressant into the rectum.

   regional a. Any of four types of anesthesia: spinal, epidural, caudal, or nerve block.

   saddle block a. Anesthesia of the buttocks, perineum, and inner thighs produced by introducing the anesthetic low in the dural sac around the spinal cord.

   spinal a. *(a)* Anesthesia of the lower part of the body produced by introducing the anesthetic solution into the subarachnoid space around the spinal cord. *(b)* Anesthesia caused by disease or injury to the spinal cord.

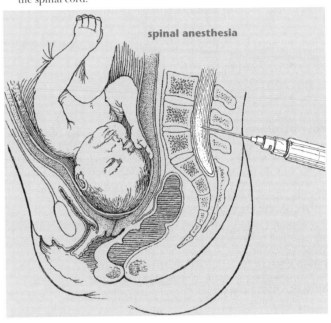

spinal anesthesia

   standby a. The use of local anesthesia by the surgeon during a surgical operation, in addition to administration of sedative-hypnotics and narcotics by the anesthesiologist.

   stocking a. Loss of sensory perception of one or both lower extremities in the areas usually covered by socks.

   surgical a. See general anesthesia.

   topical a. Superficial anesthesia of the skin or mucous membranes produced by direct application of medicated ointments, solutions, or jellies.

anesthesiologist (an-es-the-ze-ol′o-jist) A physician who specializes in anesthesiology.

anesthesiology (an-es-the-ze-ol′o-je) The study of anesthesia and its application to medical and surgical treatment.

anesthetic (an-es-thet′ik) 1. Relating to anesthesia. 2. An agent that produces anesthesia.

anesthetist (ah-nes′thĕ-tist) A person (physician, nurse, or technician) who administers anesthesia.

anesthetize (ah-nes′thĕ-tiz) To produce anesthesia.

aneuploid (an′u-ploid) Having an abnormal number of chromosomes.

aneurysm (an′u-rizm) A localized abnormal outpouching of an artery or of the heart.

   arteriosclerotic a. Aneurysm occurring in a blood vessel damaged by arteriosclerosis, most commonly seen in the abdominal portion of the aorta.

   berry a. An intracranial aneurysm in a small artery of the brain that forms part of the circle of Willis; it occurs at the site of a congenital defect of the arterial wall. Also called congenital aneurysm (a misnomer, for only the defect not the aneurysm, is present at birth).

anesthesia ■ aneurysm

A34

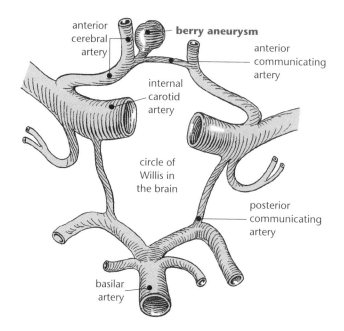

anterior cerebral artery
berry aneurysm
anterior communicating artery
internal carotid artery
circle of Willis in the brain
posterior communicating artery
basilar artery

cardiac a. See ventricular aneurysm.

congenital a. See berry aneurysm.

cylindroid a. See fusiform aneurysm.

dissecting a. Aneurysm formed by the tearing of the inner layer of the arterial wall, which allows blood flow into, within, and along the layers of the wall; it commonly occurs in the aorta.

fusiform a. A spindle-shaped dilatation of an artery. Also called cylindroid aneurysm.

intracranial a.'s Aneurysms occurring in the arterial system of the brain, usually resulting from a focal weakness in, or absence of, the middle layer of the arterial wall; a common cause of cerebral hemorrhage.

mycotic a. Aneurysm resulting from infection of the vessel wall in patients afflicted with bacterial disease.

saccular a. A large round aneurysm, sometimes reaching up to 20 cm in diameter and often containing a thrombus.

syphilitic a. Aneurysm occurring in the last stage of syphilis (tertiary stage), usually in the thoracic aorta.

traumatic a. Any aneurysm formed as a consequence of physical damage to the vascular wall.

ventricular a. An outpouching of the heart muscle, usually caused by myocardial infarction. Also called cardiac aneurysm.

aneurysmal, aneurysmatic (an-u-riz′mal, an-u-riz-mat′ik) Relating to an aneurysm.

aneurysmectomy (an-u-riz-mek′to-me) Removal of an aneurysm and insertion of a graft to reestablish vascular continuity.

aneurysmorrhaphy (an-u-riz-mor′ah-fe) The suturing of an aneurysm.

angiectasia, angiectasis (an-je-ek-ta′ze-ah, an-je-ek′ta-sis) An enlargement of a blood vessel.

angiitis (an-je-i′tis) Inflammation of a blood vessel or a lymph vessel.

allergic granulomatous a. See Churg-Strauss syndrome, under syndrome.

hypersensitivity a. Angiitis occurring as an allergic reaction to a specific substance.

necrotizing a. Fibrinoid necrosis of blood vessel walls with edema of surrounding tissues.

angina (an′ji-nah, an-ji′nah) A severe constricting pain.

abdominal a. Pain in the abdomen after eating a meal, regardless of the type of food consumed; caused by reduced circulation to the intestines. Also called intestinal angina.

agranulocytic a. See agranulocytosis.

crescendo a. See unstable angina.

intestinal a. See abdominal angina.

Ludwig's a. Bacterial infection of the floor of the mouth, causing tissues to become inflamed and hardened; it may spread to the throat and obstruct the air passages; usually develops from tooth or gum infections or may occur in association with tooth extraction, fractures of the mandible, or lacerations of the floor of the mouth.

a. pectoris Constricting pain behind the breastbone (sternum), frequently radiating to the left shoulder and arm or to the neck, due to insufficient blood supply to the heart musculature; usually caused by severe narrowing of the lumen of coronary arteries by fatty deposits within the arterial walls (atherosclerosis).

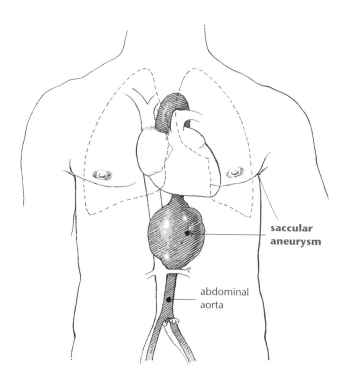

saccular aneurysm
abdominal aorta

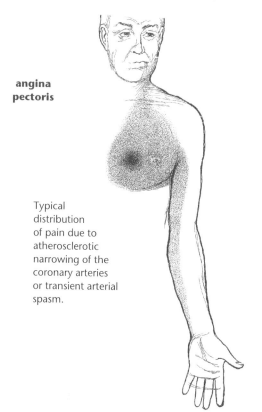

angina pectoris

Typical distribution of pain due to atherosclerotic narrowing of the coronary arteries or transient arterial spasm.

aneurysm ■ angina

Prinzmetal's a. See variant angina.

unstable a. Severe chest pain that increases in frequency or duration, starts at rest or during sleep, or recurs after myocardial infarction or bypass surgery. Also called crescendo angina.

variant a. A type of angina pectoris characterized by pain occurring at rest, believed to be caused by spasms of the coronary arteries. Also called Prinzmetal's angina.

anginal (an'ji-nal, an-ji'nal) Relating to angina.

angio-, angi- Combining forms meaning vessel, especially a blood vessel.

angioblast (an'je-o-blast) An embryonic cell that gives rise to a blood vessel.

angioblastoma (an-je-o-blas-to'mah) See hemangioblastoma.

angiocardiography (an-je-o-kar-de-og'rah-fe) Procedure that records on tape or film x-ray images of the heart and great vessels after these structures are outlined by an injected radiopaque solution.

angiocardiopathy (an-je-o-kar-de-op'ah-the) Any disease of the heart and blood vessels.

angioedema (an-je-o-e-de'mah) Allergic reaction manifested by well-demarcated, large swellings on the skin (involving superficial and deep layers) and mucous membranes. Also called angioneurotic edema; giant urticaria.

angiofibrosis (an-je-o-fi-bro'sis) Fibrosis of the blood vessel walls.

angiogenesis (an-je-o-jen'ĕ-sis) Development of blood vessels.

angiogram (an'je-o-gram) An x-ray film or tape of vessels, usually blood vessels.

angiography (an-je-og'rah-fe) The process of recording images of blood vessels on X-ray film or tape after intravenous injection of a radiopaque solution.

selective a. Introduction of the radiopaque solution through a catheter directly into vessels of the area to be studied.

angiohypertonia (an-je-o-hi-per-to'ne-ah) See vasospasm.

angioid (an'je-oid) Resembling a blood vessel.

angioinvasive (an-je-o-in-va'siv) Capable of entering or invading blood vessel walls.

angiokeratoma (an-je-o-ker-ah-to'mah) A small, dark skin lesion composed of scales over an excess of cutaneous capillaries. Also called telangiectatic wart.

angiokinesis (an-je-o-kī-ne'sis) See vasomotion.

angiology (an-je-ol'o-je) The study of blood and lymph vessels.

angioma (an-je-o'mah) A lesion of the skin or subcutaneous tissues resulting from proliferation of blood or lymph vessels. See also hemangioma; lymphangioma.

angiomatosis (an-je-o-mah-to'sis) A disease marked by the presence of multiple angiomas.

retinocerebral a. See von Hippel–Lindau disease, under disease.

angiomatous (an-je-om'ah-tus) Relating to or resembling an angioma.

angiomyolipoma (an-je-o-mi-o-li-po'mah) A benign tumor composed of adipose and muscle cells and blood vessel elements; most commonly seen in the kidney.

angiomyosarcoma (an-je-o-mi-o-sar-ko'mah) A malignant tumor (sarcoma) containing muscular elements and a large number of vascular channels.

angioneurosis (an-je-o-nu-ro'sis) A disorder or injury affecting the nerves innervating the blood vessel walls. Also called vasoneurosis.

angioneurotic (an-je-o-nu-rot'ik) Relating to angioneurosis.

angiopathy (an-je-op'ah-the) Any disease of blood or lymph vessels.

angioplasty (an'je-o-plas-te) The restructuring of a blood vessel.

balloon a. See percutaneous transluminal angioplasty.

percutaneous transluminal a. (PCTA) Procedure for enlarging the lumen of a partially occluded artery. A balloon-tipped catheter is introduced into the vessel to the site of occlusion; then the balloon is inflated to flatten the plaque or the hyperplastic area against the vessel wall and enlarge the lumen. Also called balloon angioplasty.

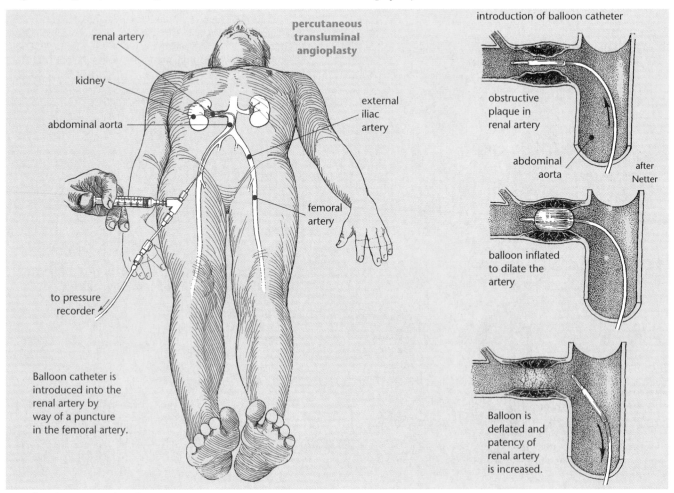

percutaneous transluminal angioplasty

renal artery

kidney

abdominal aorta

external iliac artery

femoral artery

to pressure recorder

Balloon catheter is introduced into the renal artery by way of a puncture in the femoral artery.

introduction of balloon catheter

obstructive plaque in renal artery

abdominal aorta

after Netter

balloon inflated to dilate the artery

Balloon is deflated and patency of renal artery is increased.

angiosarcoma (an-je-o-sar-ko′mah) A rare, malignant, rapidly growing fleshy mass that may occur anywhere in the body, usually in skin, breast, liver, and spleen. Also called hemangiosarcoma.

   hepatic a. Angiosarcoma of the liver; it has been linked with occupational exposure to vinyl chloride (in the manufacture of plastics) and with arsenic compounds in pesticides.

angioscopy (an-je-os′ko-pe) Visualization of small blood vessels and capillaries with a special type of microscope (angioscope).

angiospasm (an′je-o-spazm) See vasospasm.

angiostenosis (an-je-o-ste-no′sis) Constriction of a vessel.

angiostomy (an-je-os′to-me) A surgical cut into a blood vessel and insertion of a cannula.

angiotelectasis (an-je-o-tĕ-lek′tah-sis) Dilatation of the minute terminal blood vessels (venules, arterioles, and capillaries).

angiotensin (an-je-o-ten′sin) One of a family of peptides involved in regulating blood pressure. Angiotensin I, an inactive form, is split off from the precursor, angiotensinogen, by the enzyme renin and is converted to the active form, angiotensin II, by a converting enzyme. Angiotensin II causes narrowing of the blood vessels and stimulates production and release of the hormone aldosterone from the adrenal cortex. Angiotensin III is a derivative of angiotensin II and performs similar but weaker actions.

angiotensinogen (an-je-o-ten-sin′o-jen) A plasma protein from which angiotensin I is derived by the action of renin (an enzyme). Also called renin substrate.

angiotomy (an-je-ot′o-me) The surgical cutting of a blood vessel.

angiotrophic (an-je-o-trof′ik) Rarely used term. See vasotrophic.

angle (ang′gl) The figure formed by two lines or planes diverging from, or meeting at, a common point, or the space enclosed by them.

   acromial a. The angle formed where the spine of the shoulder blade (scapula) ends and the acromion begins, forming the bony prominence at the upper back of the shoulder joint.

   anterior chamber a. Angle in the eye formed by the junction of the iris and the cornea. Also called filtration angle; iridocorneal angle.

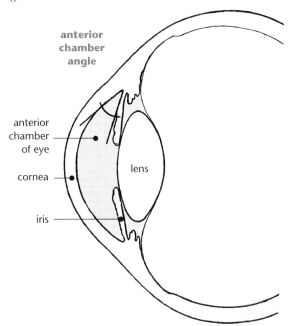

anterior chamber angle

anterior chamber of eye

cornea

iris

lens

   cerebellopontine a. Space at the junction of the cerebellum and the pons.

   filtration a. See anterior chamber angle.

   inferior a. of scapula Angle formed by the junction of the lateral and medial borders of the shoulder blade (scapula).

   iridocorneal a. See anterior chamber angle.

   a. of jaw, a. of mandible Angle formed by the lower edge of the mandibular body and the posterior edge of the mandibular ramus.

   line a. Angle formed by the junction of any two surfaces of a tooth.

   a. of Louis See sternal angle.

   lumbosacral a. Angle between the long axes of the lumbar and sacral portions of the spine (vertebral column).

   point a. Angle formed by the junction of three tooth surfaces at a point.

   sternal a. Angle formed by the articulation of the manubrium and body of the breastbone (sternum). Also called angle of Louis.

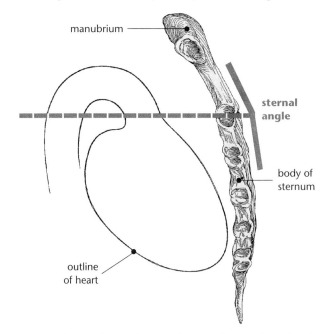

manubrium

sternal angle

body of sternum

outline of heart

   superior a. of scapula Angle between the superior and medial borders of the shoulder blade (scapula).

angstrom (ang′strom) (Å) Unit of length equal to one ten-billionth of a meter.

angulation (ang-gu-la′shun) An abnormal bend in an anatomic structure.

angulus (ang′gu-lus), pl. ang′uli Latin for angle.

anhedonia (an-he-do′ne-ah) Loss of the ability to experience pleasure.

anhidrosis (an-hĭ-dro′sis) Abnormal lack of sweat.

anhidrotic (an-hĭ-drot′ik) **1.** Relating to anhidrosis. **2.** An agent that reduces or prevents sweating.

anhydrase (an-hi′drās) An enzyme promoting removal of water from a compound.

anhydride (an-hi′drĭd) A chemical compound derived from an acid or base by the removal of water.

anhydrous (an-hi′drus) Free of water; said of a salt.

anicteric (an-ik-ter′ik) Not associated with jaundice.

anileridine (an-ĭ-ler′ĭ-dēn) A narcotic compound used for the relief of pain; it has an addiction potential similar to that of morphine.

aniline (an′ĭ-lin) An oily liquid derived from benzene; used in the preparation of dyes.

animal (an′ĭ-mal) Any organism of the animal kingdom.

   control a. In research, an animal used as a standard against which experimental observations may be evaluated; it is subjected to the same procedures as the other animals included in the research except for the one factor that is being studied.

   experimental a. An animal subjected to procedures and observations in the laboratory.

   sentinel a. In research, an animal placed in an environment that is being monitored for the presence of an infectious microorganism.

animal welfare The support of humane and responsible treatment of animals in all their uses by humans (food, clothing, research, pets, prey of the hunt). See also antivivisection.

A

anion (anʹi-on) An atom, or group of atoms, carrying one or more negative charges; indicated by a negative superscript (e.g., Clˉ). It is attracted to the positively charged anode in a solution through which current is passed.

anionic (an-i-onʹik) Relating to an anion.

aniridia (an-ī-ridʹe-ah) Developmental defect of the eye in which the iris is absent.

anisakiasis (an-is-sa-kiʹah-sis) Infection of the lining of the stomach and small intestine by larvae of *Anisakis marina*, a parasite of marine fish, causing granulomas and pain that may be mistaken for cancer, ulcers, and appendicitis. Also called herring-worm disease.

aniseikonia (an-ī-si-koʹne-ah) Defect of vision in which the images seen by the two eyes differ in size.

aniseikonic (an-ī-si-konʹik) Relating to aniseikonia.

anismus (an-isʹmus) A rare condition in which disturbance of muscular coordination (dyssynergia) of the external ani sphincter and puborectal muscles causes profound constipation.

aniso- Combining form meaning unequal.

anisochromasia (an-i-so-kro-maʹze-ah) Denoting a variable intensity of color in red blood cells due to unequal distribution of hemoglobin.

anisochromatic (an-i-so-kro-matʹik) Relating to anisochromasia.

anisocoria (an-i-so-koʹre-ah) Eye condition marked by unequal size of the two pupils.

anisocytosis (an-i-so-si-toʹsis) Condition marked by a considerable variation in the size of red blood cells.

anisometropia (an-i-so-mĕ-troʹpe-ah) A significant difference between the refractive power of the two eyes.

ankle (angʹkl) The part of the lower limb between the leg and the foot. See also talocrural joint, under joint.

ankylo- Combining form meaning bent; fused; adhered.

ankyloblepharon (ang-kī-lo-blefʹah-ron) See blepharosynechia.

ankyloglossia (ang-kī-lo-glosʹe-ah) See tongue-tie.

ankylosed (angʹkī-lōsed) Stiffened; bound by adhesions; fused.

ankylosis (ang-kī-loʹsis), pl. ankyloʹses Abnormal immobility of a joint. Popularly called frozen joint.

    artificial a. See arthrodesis.

    bony a. See synostosis.

    dental a. Bony union of a tooth to its socket as a result of ossification of the surrounding membranes.

    false a. See fibrous ankylosis.

    fibrous a. Stiffening of a joint due to proliferation of fibrous tissue which adheres to the joint structures. Also called false ankylosis; pseudankylosis.

    true a. See synostosis.

ankylotic (ang-kī-lotʹik) Relating to ankylosis.

anlage (anʹlāj), pl. anlaʹgen The earliest indication of a developing organ or structure of the body, when embryonic cells begin to group in a definite pattern; usually denoting a theoretical stage earlier than primordium.

annular (anʹu-lar) Ring-shaped.

annulus, anulus (anʹu-lus), pl. anʹnuli A ringlike structure.

    a. fibrosus The outer fibrocartilaginous ring surrounding the softer center of the pads between vertebrae (intervertebral disks).

    a. inguinalis profundus See deep inguinal ring, under ring.

    a. inguinalis superficialis See superficial inguinal ring, under ring.

    a. tendineus communis See common annular tendon, under tendon.

anodontia (an-o-donʹshe-ah) Failure of some or all teeth to develop; may involve deciduous or permanent teeth.

anodyne (anʹo-dīn) **1.** Relieving pain. **2.** A compound that relieves pain.

anogenital (a-no-jenʹi-tal) Relating to the anus and the genitals.

anomaly (ah-nomʹah-le) Deviation from what is accepted as normal of form, shape, or position of a tissue, organ, or structure.

    chromosomal a. See chromosomal aberration, under aberration.

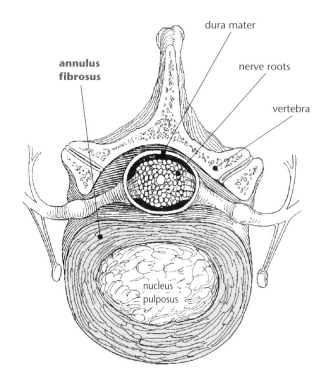

    developmental a. Anomaly occurring or originating during intrauterine life.

    Ebstein's a. Malformation of the tricuspid (right atrioventricular) valve of the heart characterized by distortion and downward displacement into the right ventricle of the heart, causing impaired function of the ventricle. Also called Ebstein's malformation.

anomia (ah-noʹme-ah) See nominal aphasia, under aphasia.

Anopheles (ah-nofʹĕ-lēz) A genus of mosquitoes (family Culicidae, subfamily Anophelinae); some members transmit the malarial parasite to humans.

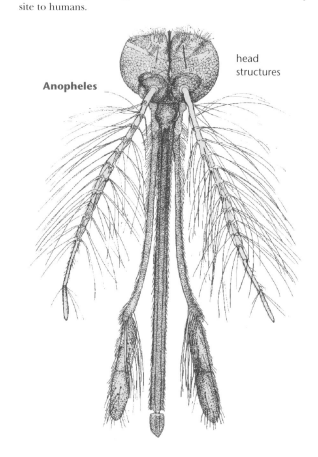

anophthalmia (an-of-thal′me-ah) Developmental defect marked by absence of a true eyeball.

anoplasty (a′no-plas-te) Plastic surgery of the anus.

anorchia (an-or′ke-ah) See anorchism.

anorchism (an-or′kizm) Congenital absence of one or both testes. Also called anorchia.

anorectal (a-no-rek′tal) Relating to the anus and rectum.

anorectic (an-o-rek′tik) **1.** Relating to anorexia nervosa. **2.** A substance that diminishes the appetite.

anorexia (an-o-rek′se-ah) Loss of appetite.

  a. nervosa An eating disorder marked by a great loss of appetite and body weight; it is accompanied by metabolic derangement and by serious neurotic symptoms centered around an abnormal fear of becoming fat, undiminished even after the patient becomes emaciated; seen most commonly in teenage girls.

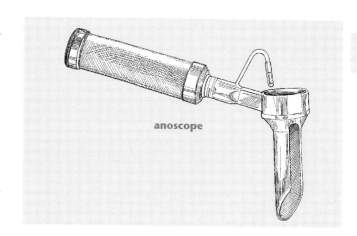

anoscope

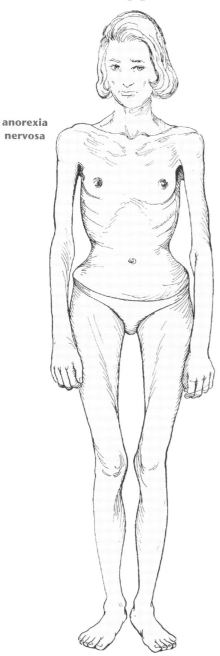

anorexia
nervosa

anoscope (a′no-skōp) An instrument for examining the anus and lower rectum.

anosigmoidoscopy (a-no-sig-moi-dos′ko-pe) Visual examination of the anus, rectum, and sigmoid colon with the aid of an instrument.

anosmia (an-oz′me-ah) Loss of the sense of smell, usually due to colds or infections of the upper respiratory tract; it may also be caused by polyps or tumors obstructing nerve impulses to the brain, or by head injuries that sever fibers of the olfactory nerve. It may be unilateral or bilateral, depending on the cause.

anosognosia (an-o-sog-no′ze-ah) The lack of awareness of, or failure to recognize, one's own disease or disability; may result from damage to the parietal lobe of the brain.

anovesical (a-no-ves′ĭ-kal) Relating to the anus and bladder.

anovular, anovulatory (an-ov′u-lar, an-ov′u-lah-to-re) Not accompanied by release of an ovum from the ovary (ovulation); said of a menstrual cycle.

anoxemia (an-ok-se′me-ah) Marked deficiency of oxygen in arterial blood.

anoxia (ah-nok′se-ah) Without oxygen.

ansa (an′sah) pl. an′sae Any anatomic structure shaped like a loop or hook.

  a. cervicalis A loop of nerves located in the neck, formed by fibers from three cervical nerves (Cl, C2, C3) and the hypoglossal nerve. Formerly called ansa hypoglossi.

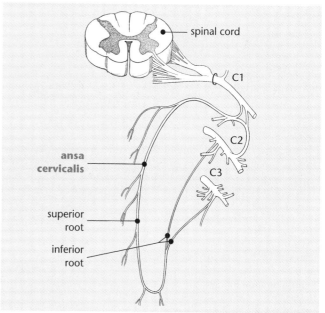

  Henle's a. See nephronic loop, under loop.
  a. hypoglossi Former name for ansa cervicalis.

anorexiant (an-o-rek′se-ant) A substance that diminishes appetite, such as a drug used to aid weight reduction.

anorexigenic (an-o-rek-sĭ-jen′ik) Having the ability to produce anorexia.

antacid (ant-as′id) **1.** Neutralizing acidity. **2.** Any agent having such properties.

A

antagonism (an-tag′o-nizm) A state of mutual opposition or competition.

    chemical a. Direct chemical interaction between an agonist and an antagonist, producing an inactive product (e.g., in counteracting the toxic effect of arsenic by dimercaprol).

    competitive a. Lessening of the action of an agonist because of competition with a nonactivating antagonist for a receptor site on a cell membrane.

    functional a. The offsetting of the effect of one agonist by the opposite effect of another agonist acting on different receptor sites (e.g., acetylcholine, which constricts the pupil, and epinephrine, which dilates it). Also called physiologic antagonism.

    physiologic a. See functional antagonism.

antagonist (an-tag′o-nist) **1.** Any structure or substance that opposes or counteracts the action of another structure or substance. **2.** In pharmacology, a chemical that occupies a receptor site on the cell membrane but does not initiate the biological reaction associated with occupation of the site by an agonist; in effect, an antagonist interferes with the formation of an agonist-receptor complex, the mechanism by which most pharmacologic effects are produced.

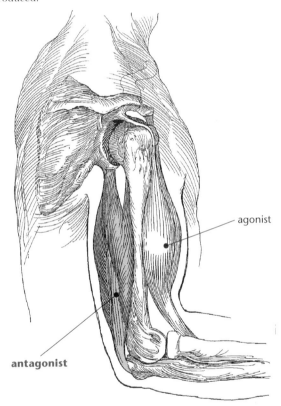
agonist

antagonist

    competitive a. A drug that interacts reversibly with the same set of receptors as the active drug (agonist) to form a complex, but the complex does not elicit a biological response and can be displaced from these receptor sites by increasing concentrations of the active drug.

ante- Prefix meaning before.

antebrachium (an-te-bra′ke-um) The forearm.

ante cibum (an′te si′bum) (a.c.) Latin for before a meal.

antecubital (an-te-ku-bī′tal) In front of the elbow.

anteflexion (an-te-flek′shun) An abnormal forward bending of an organ or anatomic structure.

antegrade (an′te-grād) See anterograde.

antemortem (an′te-mor′tem) Latin for before death, preceding death.

antenatal (an-te-na′tal) See prenatal.

antepartum (an-te-par′tum) In obstetrics, Latin for before the onset of labor.

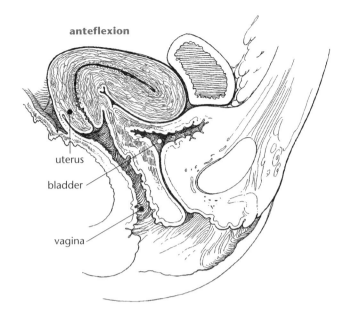
anteflexion

uterus

bladder

vagina

anterior (an-te′re-or) **1.** Located or related to the front surface of the body or limbs. **2.** Located on or near the front of an organ.

antero- Combining form meaning before; forward; anterior.

anterograde (an′ter-o-grād) Moving or extending forward. Also called antegrade.

anteroinferior (an-ter-o-in-fēr′e-or) In front and below.

anterolateral (an-ter-o-lat′er-al) In front and to one side of the midline.

anteromedial (an-ter-o-me′de-al) In front and toward the midline.

anteroposterior (an-ter-o-pos-tēr′e-or) In a direction from front to back.

anterosuperior (an-ter-o-su-pēr′e-or) In front and above.

anteversion (an-te-ver′zhun) The tilting forward of an organ.

anteverted (an-te-vert′ed) Tilted forward.

anthelix (ant′he-liks) See antihelix.

anthelmintic (ant-hel-min′tik) **1.** Capable of killing worms. **2.** Any agent that kills worms.

anthracene (an′thrah-sēn) A hydrocarbon obtained from coal tar; used in the dye industry.

anthracosilicosis (an-thrah-ko-sil-ĭ-ko′sis) Fibrous hardening of the lungs caused by long-term inhalation of coal dust.

anthracosis (an-thrah-ko′sis) See coal miner's pneumoconiosis, under pneumoconiosis.

anthracotic (an-thrah-kot′ik) Relating to anthracosis.

anthrax (an′thraks) A contagious disease caused by *Bacillus anthracis*, a bacillus infecting chiefly farm animals. The disease has a strong occupational relationship to industries dealing with animals and their products (farming, leather, and textile industries). It occurs chiefly in countries lacking disease control programs. Also called carbuncular fever.

    cutaneous a. Skin anthrax marked by the appearance of a reddish blister that, two or three days later, turns into a large bleeding pustule with a black crust resembling a piece of charcoal. Systemic involvement varies from mild to severe. Also called malignant pustule.

    pulmonary a. A rare but severe (often fatal) form of anthrax of the lungs caused by inhalation of dust containing spores of the bacillus. Also called woolsorter's disease.

anthrone (an′thron) Chemical substance that reacts with sugars in sulfuric acid; used as a reagent for detecting carbohydrates.

anthropology (an-thro-pol′o-je) The science concerned with the human species, its origin and development.

    cultural a. The study of the attributes of human groups that are acquired and transmitted by learning (e.g., language, social organizations, traditions, art).

    forensic a. The application of anthropologic methods of study to medicolegal matters, such as problems of identification.

antagonism ■ anthropology

anthropometric (an-thro-po-met′rik) Relating to anthropometry.

anthropometry (an-thro-pom′ĕ-tre) The branch of anthropology dealing with comparative measurements of the human body and its parts. It seeks to determine the range of variations in skeletal and soft-tissue dimensions.

    forensic a. Anthropometry applied to the problems of law; conducted to determine individual identity, such as that of dead bodies.

anthropophobia (an-thro-po-fo′be-ah) Abnormal dread of human association.

anthropozoonosis (an-thro-po-zo-o-no′sis) Human disease caused by microorganisms that are maintained in nature by animals.

anti- Prefix meaning opposing; against; counteracting.

antiadhesin (an-tĭ-ad-he′zin) An antibody that interacts with components of the bacterial cell surface to prevent adhesion of the bacterium to mucous membranes.

antiadrenergic (an-tĭ-ah-dren-er′jik) **1.** Blocking the adrenergic action of the sympathetic nervous system. **2.** Any drug having such properties.

antiallergic (an-tĭ-ah-ler′jik) Tending to prevent or alleviate an allergic reaction.

antiandrogen (an-tĭ-an′dro-jen) A substance that can reduce the effects of masculinizing (androgenic) hormone.

antiarrhythmic (an-tĭ-ah-rith′mik) Alleviating or preventing irregular heartbeats (arrhythmia).

antibacterial (an-tĭ-bak-te′re-al) Impairing the growth of bacteria.

antibiotic (an-tĭ-bi-ot′ik, an-tĭ-bi-ot′ik) Any of a group of drugs, derived from fungi or bacteria, that kill or inhibit the growth of other microorganisms. Antibiotics vary widely in structure and mode of action.

    broad-spectrum a. An antibiotic that has a wide range of activity; effective against both gram-positive and gram-negative bacteria.

antibody (an′tĭ-bod-e) (Ab) A protein, found in the blood and other body fluids, that can be incited by the presence of antigen (microorganisms, foreign proteins, and tissue cells); it has a destructive influence on the antigen that stimulated it. See also immunoglobin.

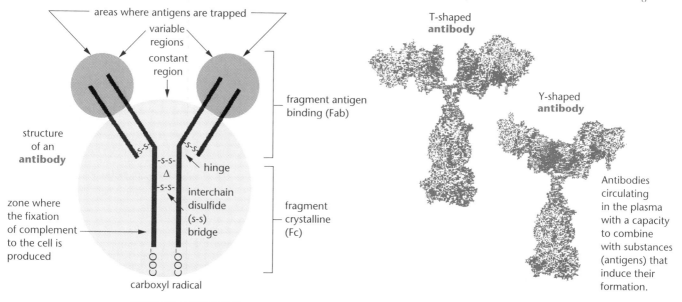

SCHEMATIC REPRESENTATION OF COMPARATIVE STRUCTURES OF 5 CLASSES OF **ANTIBODIES**

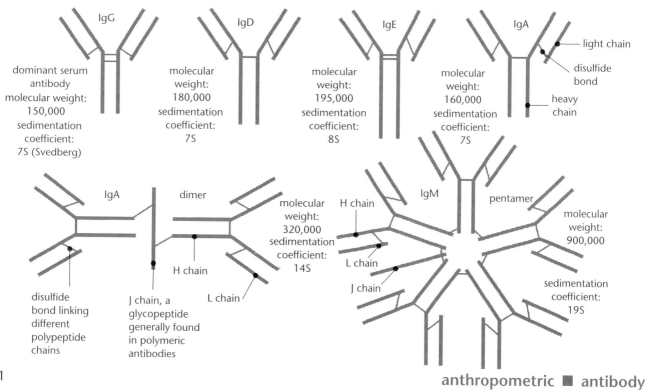

anthropometric ■ antibody

antinuclear a. (ANA) An antibody that acts on components of the cell nucleus; occurring in systemic lupus erythematosus and other connective-tissue disorders.

antisperm a.'s (ASAs) Antibodies (predominantly IgA type) that immobilize spermatozoa or interfere in any way with spermatozoan activity. They are found in the serum of both males and females and act locally (in the testicles and the vagina); level of their activity fluctuates.

autoimmune a. Older term for autoantibody.

blocking a. An antibody that, by combining with antigen, stops further activity of that antigen.

complement-fixing a. (CF antibody) An antibody that, when combined with antigen, leads to the activation of complement.

fluorescent a. Antibody to which a fluorescent dye has been attached.

monoclonal a.'s Artificially produced antibodies that are chemically and immunologically homogeneous; produced in the laboratory to react with a specific antigen; used experimentally in the treatment of some forms of cancer.

neutralizing a. An antibody that blocks a toxic site of a microorganism or a chemical toxin, either by direct reaction with the site or by interference with the chemical reaction, thereby preventing damage to the host's body.

treponema-immobilizing a. An antibody present in the serum of patients with syphilis (active or inactive); it has a specific affinity for *Treponema pallidum* and, in the presence of complement, immobilizes the organism.

anticholinergic (an-tĭ-ko-lin-er'jik) Blocking the passage of impulses through nerves of the parasympathetic system by inhibiting the action of the neurotransmitter acetylcholine.

anticholinesterase (an-tĭ-ko-lin-es'ter-ās) A drug that inhibits the action of the enzyme cholinesterase upon acetylcholine.

anticoagulant (an-tĭ-ko-ag'u-lant) Any substance that prevents blood clotting.

anticodon (an-tĭ-ko'don) In genetics, the three-base sequence in a transfer RNA (tRNA) that pairs with a specific codon in messenger RNA (mRNA) on the ribosome.

anticomplement (an-tĭ-kom'ple-ment) A substance that inactivates a complement (material in normal serum that helps to destroy pathogens).

anticonvulsant (an-tĭ-kon-vul'sant) Any drug used to prevent or control seizures.

antidepressant (an-tĭ-de-pres'sant) An agent that tends to alleviate depression.

antidiarrheal (an-tĭ-di-ah-re'al) An agent that alleviates diarrhea.

antidiuresis (an-tĭ-di-u-re'sis) Reducing urine formation.

antidiuretic (an-tĭ-di-u-ret'ik) Any agent that reduces the output of urine.

antidotal (an-tĭ-do'tal) Relating to an antidote.

antidote (an'tĭ-dōt) Any agent that neutralizes the effects of a poison.

antidromic (an-tĭ-drom'ik) Denoting the transmission of a nerve impulse in a reverse direction of the normal.

antiemetic (an-tĭ-e-met'ik) An agent that controls nausea and vomiting.

antienzyme (an-tĭ-en'zim) A substance that inhibits or neutralizes the action of an organic catalyst (enzyme).

antiestrogen (an-tĭ-es'tro-jen) 1. Capable of blocking the action of estrogens in the body. 2. Any substance that so acts.

antifebrile (an-tĭ-feb'ril) See antipyretic.

antifibrinolysin (an-tĭ-fi-brĭ-no-li'sin) A substance that inhibits the dissolution of a blood clot.

antifungal (an-tĭ-fung'gal) Destructive to fungi; said of drugs used to treat fungal infections. Also called antimycotic.

antigalactagogue (an-tĭ-gah-lak'tah-gog) Any agent that suppresses the production of milk.

antigen (an'tĭ-jen) (Ag) Any material capable of triggering in an individual the production of specific antibody or the formation of a specific population of lymphocytes (a type of white blood cell) that react with that material. Antigens may be proteins, toxins, microorganisms, or tissue cells. Whether any material is an antigen in a person depends on whether the material is foreign to the person, the genetic makeup of the person, and the dose of the material. See also CA 15-3; CA 19-9; CA 125.

allogenic a. See alloantigen.

Australia a., Au a. See hepatitis B surface antigen.

carcinoembryonic a. (CEA) A glycoprotein constituent of normal gastrointestinal tissues of the fetus; present in the adult only in certain types of cancer, such as cancer of the colon. Also called oncofetal antigen.

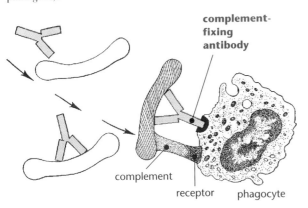

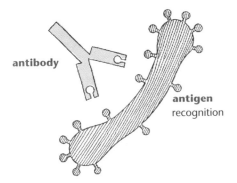

TOXIN	ANTIDOTE
cadmium	calcium disodium edetate (EDTA)
cobalt	calcium disodium edetate (EDTA)
copper	calcium disodium edetate (EDTA)
dicumarol	vitamin K
heparin	protamine
lead	calcium disodium edetate (EDTA)
morphine	naloxone
nickel	calcium disodium edetate (EDTA)
nicotene	potassium permanganate
organic phosphate in insecticides	atropine
quinine	potassium permanganate
strychnine	potassium permanganate

anticholinergic ■ antigen

CD4 a. A glycoprotein on the membrane of T-expressor cells.

CD8 a. A glycoprotein on the membrane of T-helper cells.

common acute lymphoblastic leukemia a. (CALLA) A tumor-associated antigen occurring in a high percentage (80%) of patients with acute lymphoblastic leukemia (ALL).

hepatitis-associated a. (HAA) Old term for hepatitis B surface antigen.

hepatitis B core a. (HB$_c$Ag) Antigen associated with the core of the hepatitis B virus; present in complete virons (Dane particles) and in the nuclei of infected liver cells.

hepatitis B e a. (HB$_e$Ag) A core antigen of hepatitis B virus (Dane particle) present in the blood of infected persons, associated with transmission of the infection.

hepatitis B surface a. (HB$_s$Ag) Antigen of the outer coat of the complete hepatitis virus (Dane particle) and in smaller spherical and filamentous particles. The presence of antibodies to HB$_s$AG connotes immunity; persistence of HB$_s$Ag in the blood indicates an infectious carrier state. Also called Australia antigen; Au antigen.

histocompatibility a. Any of the genetically determined antigens, present on nucleated cells of most tissues, that induce an immune response (rejection) when transplanted from the donor into a genetically different recipient.

HLA a.'s A group of histocompatibility antigens controlled by a region of chromosome 6 and its genetic sites (loci); they are polypeptides or glycoproteins responsible for rejection of tissue transplants in humans and are associated with certain diseases.

homologous a. See alloantigen.

isophile a. Old term for alloantigen.

oncofetal a. (OFA) See carcinoembryonic antigen.

prostate-specific a. (PSA) A glycoprotein secreted by the cytoplasm of epithelial prostatic cells; its normal function is to aid in the liquefaction of semen; normal values in young adults range between 0 and 4 nanograms per milliliter; it occurs in higher levels in the serum of men with benign prostatic hypertrophy. Determinations of serum PSA levels may be of value in the diagnosis and staging of prostatic cancer.

self- a. See autoantigen.

tumor-associated a. An antigen that is found on cells undergoing neoplastic transformation.

tumor-specific a. (TSA) Any antigen that can be detected only on the surface of tumor cells and not on the normal host cells.

antigenic (an-tĭ-jen′ik) Having the properties of an antigen; capable of inciting the formation of antibody. Also called immunogenic.

antigenicity (an-tĭ-jĕ-nis′ĭ-te) The state of being antigenic. Also called immunogenicity.

antihelix (an-tĭ-he′liks) The curved ridge on the external ear parallel to, and in front of, the helix. Also called anthelix.

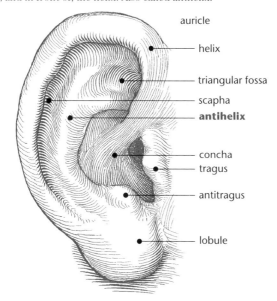

auricle
helix
triangular fossa
scapha
antihelix
concha
tragus
antitragus
lobule

antihemolysin (an-tĭ-he-mol′ĭ-sin) Any agent that inhibits the action of a hemolysin, thus reducing destruction of red blood cells.

antihemolytic (an-tĭ-he-mo-lit′ik) Preventing destruction of red blood cells.

antihidrotic (an-tĭ-hi-drot′ik) See antiperspirant.

antihistamine (an-tĭ-his′tah-min) Any drug that diminishes the action of histamine, the chemical released during an allergic reaction; used to alleviate allergic symptoms.

antihistaminic (an-tĭ-his-tah-min′ik) Tending to neutralize the action of histamine; said of certain drugs.

antihypertensive (an-tĭ-hi-per-ten′siv) Tending to reduce high blood pressure (hypertension).

anti-inflammatory (an′tĭ in-flam′ah-to-re) Relieving inflammation.

antimetabolite (an-tĭ-mĕ-tab′o-lit) Any substance that interferes with the body's utilization of another substance that is essential for normal physiologic functioning.

antimitotic (an-tĭ-mi-tot′ik) **1.** Preventing or interfering with the process of cell multiplication. **2.** Any drug having such properties (e.g., those used to treat leukemia).

antimony (an′tĭ-mo-ne) A toxic metallic element; symbol Sb, atomic number 51, atomic weight 121.75.

antimuscarinic (an-tĭ-mus′kah-rin′ik) Counteracting the neurologic effects of muscarine and similar alkaloids.

antimutagen (an-tĭ-mu′tah-jen) Any factor that reduces the rate of mutation (e.g., by interfering with the action of a mutagen, or by rendering genetic elements less susceptible to change).

antimycotic (an-tĭ-mi-kot′ik) See antifungal.

antinatriferic (an-tĭ-nah-trif′er-ik) Inhibiting the transport of sodium.

antinauseant (an-tĭ-naw′ze-ant) **1.** Relieving nausea. **2.** A drug that alleviates nausea.

antineoplastic (an-tĭ-ne-o-plas′tik) Interfering with the growth of a tumor.

antineurotoxin (an-tĭ-nu-ro-tok′sin) A substance that counteracts the action of a chemical destructive of nerve tissue.

antinuclear (an-tĭ-nu′kle-ar) Reactive with elements of the cell nucleus (e.g., an antibody); destructive to the cell nucleus.

antioxidant (an-tĭ-ok′si-dant) A substance that inhibits reactions with oxygen (oxidation).

lipid a. Any of various antioxidant substances, including fats and waxes, which (with proteins and carbohydrates) constitute the principal structural components of the living cell (e.g., vitamins A and E).

antiperistalsis (an-tĭ-per-ĭ-stal′sis) See reversed peristalsis, under peristalsis.

antiperspirant (an-tĭ-per′spĭ-rant) An agent that inhibits the secretion of sweat. Also called antihidrotic.

antiphagocytic (an-tĭ-fag-o-sit′ik) Tending to slow or prevent phagocytosis, (i.e., the process by which certain white blood cells engulf and ingest microorganisms, other cells, and foreign particles).

antiphlogistic (an-tĭ-flo-jis′tik) Preventing or reducing inflammation.

antipodal (an-tip′ŏ-dal) Situated at opposite sides (e.g., of a cell or a molecule).

antiport (an′tĭ-port) The exchange of one molecule for another across a biological membrane by means of a common carrier.

antiprogestin (an-tĭ-pro-jes′tin) A substance that inhibits the formation or action of progesterone.

antiprothrombin (an-tĭ-pro-throm′bin) An anticoagulant substance that prevents the conversion of prothrombin (plasma protein) into thrombin (enzyme), thus preventing blood clot formation.

antipruritic (an-tĭ-proo-rit′ik) An agent that alleviates itching.

antipsychotic (an-tĭ-si-kot′ik) **1.** Relieving symptoms of mental disorders. **2.** Any agent having such an effect. Also called neuroleptic.

antipyretic (an-tĭ-pi-ret′ik) **1.** Tending to reduce fever. **2.** Any agent that reduces fever. Also called antifebrile; antithermic.

antirachitic (an-tĭ-rah-kit′ik) Preventing rickets.

antirheumatic (an-tĭ-ru-mat′ik) **1.** Delaying the progression of rheumatic disorders. **2.** Any agent possessing such properties.

antiscorbutic (an-tĭ-skor-bu′tik) Preventing or curing scurvy.

antiseptic (an-tĭ-sep′tik) A compound capable of killing or inhibiting the growth of microorganisms when applied to living tissues, without significantly harming the tissues.

antiserum (an-tĭ-se′rum) Human or animal serum containing antibodies that are specific for one or more antigens.

antisialagogue (an-tĭ-si-al′ah-gog) A substance that suppresses the formation or flow of saliva.

antispasmodic (an-tĭ-spaz-mod′ik) An agent that relieves spastic contractions, especially of smooth muscle.

antistreptolysin (an-tĭ-strep-tol′ĭ-sin) An antibody that curtails the hemolytic effects of streptolysin o, a product of certain streptococci.

antisudorific (an-tĭ-su-dor-if′ik) Antiperspirant.

antithermic (an-tĭ-ther′mik) Rarely used term for antipyretic.

antithrombin (an-tĭ-throm′bin) Any substance (occurring naturally or administered therapeutically) that prevents blood clotting by inhibiting the action of thrombin.

antitoxin (an-tĭ-tok′sin) **1.** An antibody against a toxin. **2.** In general, any of several commercially prepared substances, each of which contains antibodies that can combine with, and neutralize, a specific toxin released into the bloodstream by microorganisms (such as those causing tetanus, botulism, diphtheria).

antitragus (an-tĭ-tra′gus) A prominence on the external ear just above the earlobe.

antitreponemal (an-tĭ-trep-o-ne′mal) See treponemicidal.

antitrypsin (an-tĭ-trip′sin) A substance that counteracts the action of the enzyme trypsin.

antitussive (an-tĭ-tus′iv) Relieving cough.

antivenin (an-tĭ-ven′in) An antitoxin or commercially prepared substance used to counteract or inactivate the action of specific animal poisons (such as those of snakes, scorpions, spiders).

antivivisection (an-tĭ-viv-ĭ-sek′shun) Opposition to the use of living animals for biological research, regardless of whether the animals are adequately treated and protected from misuse.

antral (an′tral) Relating to an antrum.

antrectomy (an-trek′to-me) Surgical removal of an antrum, especially of the stomach.

antro- Combining form meaning cavity.

antroduodenectomy (an-tro-du-o-de-nek′to-me) Surgical removal of the distal portion of the stomach (antrum) and the contiguous portion of the duodenum.

antronasal (an-tro-na′zal) Relating to a maxillary sinus and the nasal cavity.

antroscope (an′tro-skōp) An instrument for inspecting the interior of the maxillary sinus.

antrostomy (an-tros′to-me) The opening of a permanent opening into an antrum (e.g., into the maxillary sinus).

antrotome (an′tro-tōm) An instrument used for antrotomy.

antrotomy (an-trot′o-me) A cutting through the wall of any cavity.

antrotympanic (an-tro-tim-pan′ik) Relating to a cavity of the mastoid process (behind the ear) and the middle ear chamber.

antrum (an′trum), pl. an′tra **1.** A cavity within a bone. **2.** The normal, enlarged portion of a hollow organ.

  follicular a. The fluid-filled cavity within an ovarian follicle.

  mastoid a. An air-filled cavity within the mastoid process of the temporal bone, communicating anteriorly with the middle ear (tympanic) cavity and posteriorly with the mastoid air cells. Also called tympanic antrum; Valsalva's antrum.

  maxillary a. See maxillary sinus.

  pyloric a. The bulging of the stomach near the pylorus. Also called lesser cul-de-sac.

  tympanic a. See mastoid antrum.

  Valsalva's a. See mastoid antrum.

anulus (an′u-lus) See annulus.

anuresis (an-u-re′sis) Inability to urinate.

anuretic (an-u-ret′ik) Relating to anuresis.

anuria (ah-nu′re-ah) Inability to produce urine; in clinical use, denoting a 24-hour urine volume of less than 100 cc for an adult of average size.

anuric (ah-nu′rik) Relating to anuria.

anus (a′nus) The terminal opening of the digestive tract. Also called anal orifice.

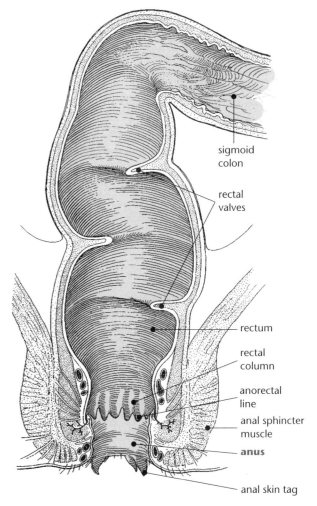

imperforate a. Congenital absence of the anus; sometimes associated with abnormal openings of the anal canal into the urethra or vagina. Also called anal atresia; proctatresia.

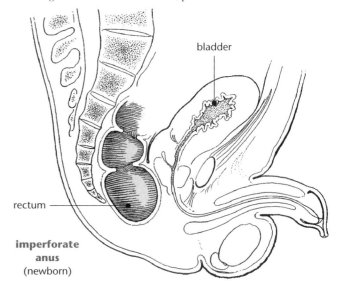

anvil (an'vil) Obsolete term for incus.

anxiety (ang-zi'ĕ-te) An affect characterized chiefly by a state of uneasiness, apprehension, and dread of impending internal or external danger, heightened vigilance, exhausting muscular tension, and autonomic hyperactivity accompanied by such physical symptoms as dizziness, profuse sweating, trembling, or rapid heartbeat.

> **castration a.** See castration complex, under complex.
> **generalized a.** See generalized disorder, under disorder.
> **a. neurosis** See anxiety neurosis, under neurosis.
> **separation a.** Exaggerated distress and apprehension upon separation from a needed person.

anxiolytic (ang-zi-o-lit'ik) See antianxiety agent, under agent.

aorta (a-or'tah), pl. aor'tas, aor'tae The largest artery of the body; the main trunk of the arterial system; it begins at the upper part of the left ventricle of the heart, from which it receives blood for delivery to all tissues except the lungs.

> **abdominal a.** The portion of the aorta from the diaphragm to the pelvis, where it divides into two branches (common iliac arteries).
> **ascending a.** The part of the aorta beginning at the top of the left ventricle and directed toward the head before it curves to form the arch of the aorta.
> **descending a.** The part of the aorta directed downward, from the arch of the aorta to its division into the two common iliac arteries; it includes the thoracic and abdominal aortas.
> **overriding a.** A developmental anomaly in which the aorta straddles the ventricular septum, thereby receiving ejected blood from both right and left ventricles of the heart.
> **thoracic a.** The portion of the descending aorta from the arch of the aorta to the diaphragm.

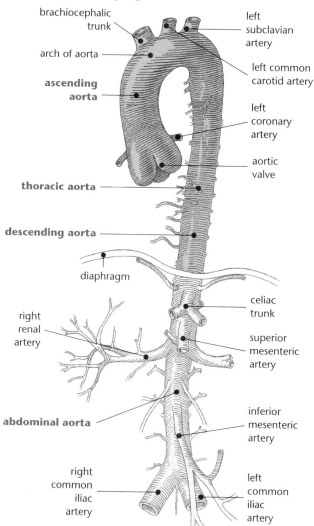

aortic (a-or'tik) Relating to the aorta.

aortitis (a-or-ti'tis) Inflammation of the aorta; may result in weakening of vessel walls and aneurysm formation.

> **syphilitic a.** A rare condition resulting from untreated syphilis and occurring in the tertiary stage of the disease, often several decades after the primary infection.

aortogram (a-or'to-gram) An x-ray image of the aorta.

aortography (a-or-tog'rah-fe) Radiographic visualization of the aorta during and after injection of a radiopaque medium into the vessel.

> **retrograde a.** Aortography performed by injecting the radiopaque medium into the aorta through one of its branches, in a direction opposite that of the bloodstream.

aortopathy (a-or-top'ah-the) Disease of the aorta.

aortoplasty (a-or-to-plas'te) Surgical repair of the aorta.

aortotomy (a-or-tot'o-me) Incision of the aorta.

apathy (ap'ah-the) Lack of emotion or feeling.

apatite (ap'ah-tīt) A calcium phosphate that is a constituent of bones and teeth.

aperiodic (ah-pe-rī-od'ik) Not occurring periodically.

aperistalsis (ah-per-ĭ-stal'sis) Absence of normal contractions of the digestive tract.

> **esophageal a.** See achalasia.

apertognathia (ah-per-tog-na'the-ah) See open bite, under bite.

aperture (ap'er-chūr) 1. An opening. 2. The diameter (usually adjustable) of an optical system such as a microscope.

> **frontal sinus a.** One of two openings in the floor of the frontal sinus leading to the nasal cavity.
> **inferior a. of minor pelvis** See pelvic plane of outlet, under plane.
> **inferior thoracic a.** See thoracic outlet, under outlet.
> **lateral a. of fourth ventricle** One of two lateral openings on the roof of the fourth ventricle of the brain; it leads to the subarachnoid cavity. Also called foramen of Luschka.
> **median a. of fourth ventricle** An opening in the midline of the roof of the fourth ventricle of the brain; it leads to the subarachnoid space. Also called foramen of Magendie.
> **sphenoid sinus a.** Opening on the anterior wall of the sphenoid sinus leading to the nasal cavity.
> **superior a. of minor pelvis** See pelvic plane of inlet, under plane.
> **superior thoracic a.** See thoracic inlet, under inlet.

apex (a'peks), pl. a'pices The tip of a conical or domed structure.

> **a. of head of fibula** See styloid process of fibula, under process.
> **a. of heart** The tip of the cone-shaped left ventricle of the heart, directed downward, anteriorly, and to the left.
> **a. of lung** The rounded upper portion of the lung extending upward to about one inch above the middle third of the collarbone (clavicle).
> **orbital a.** The posterior, conical portion of the eye socket (orbit).
> **root a.** The tip of the root of a tooth, most distal from the crown.

apexcardiography (a-peks-kar-de-og'rah-fe) The graphic recording of chest wall movement produced by pulsations of the apex of the heart.

aphagia (ah-fa'je-ah) Refusal or inability to eat.

aphakia (ah-fa'ke-ah) Absence of the lens of the eye.

aphalangia (ah-fah-lan'je-ah) Congenital absence of one or more phalanges of the fingers or toes.

aphasia (ah-fa'ze-ah) Disturbance of previously acquired language function (written or spoken) resulting from damage to the language centers of the brain, usually by a stroke or a head injury. The condition is unrelated to psychiatric disorders, diseases of the sense organs, or dysfunction of the muscles and nerves essential for speech.

> **acoustic a.** See auditory aphasia.
> **amnestic a., amnesic a.** See anomic aphasia.

anomic a. Aphasia marked by inability to find a word in the context of fluent and grammatical speech. Also called amnestic aphasia; amnesic aphasia.

auditory a. Impaired ability to comprehend spoken words, although the person has otherwise normal hearing. Also called word deafness; acoustic aphasia.

Broca's a. See expressive aphasia.

expressive a. Any of a variety of aphasias marked by impaired ability to speak or write, although comprehension of spoken and written language and ability to conceptualize are relatively intact; speech output is labored, ungrammatical, telegraphic, and poorly articulated; the patient is aware of, and visibly frustrated by, the deficit. The brain damage involves chiefly the dominant inferior frontal convolution (Broca's area). Also called motor aphasia; Broca's aphasia; nonfluent aphasia.

fluent a. See receptive aphasia.

global a. Loss of all forms of communication. Also called total aphasia.

motor a. See expressive aphasia.

nominal a. A form of expressive aphasia marked by inability to name objects or persons. Also called anomia.

nonfluent a. See expressive aphasia.

receptive a. Diminished comprehension of written and spoken language. The patient seems unaware of the deficit. Brain damage involves the area in or near the superior temporal gyrus (Wernicke's area). Also called sensory aphasia; Wernicke's aphasia; fluent aphasia.

sensory a. See receptive aphasia.

total a. See global aphasia.

visual a. See alexia.

Wernicke's a. See receptive aphasia.

aphasiac, aphasic (ah-fe′ze-ak, ah-fa′zik) Relating to aphasia.

apheresis (ah-fĕ-re′sis) Removal of blood from a donor and then infusion into the same individual after selected blood components have been removed and retained.

aphonia (ah-fo′ne-ah) Loss of the ability to produce normal speech sounds; may be due to organic or psychological causes.

conversion a. See hysterical aphonia.

functional a. See hysterical aphonia.

hysterical a. Aphonia in the absence of disease or trauma; usually due to psychological factors. Also called functional aphonia; conversion aphonia.

aphonic (ah-fon′ik) Relating to aphonia.

aphrodisiac (af-ro-diz′e-ak) **1.** Tending to enhance sexual desire. **2.** Any agent possessing such property.

aphtha (af′thah), pl. aph′thae A small, superficial ulcer of mucous membranes.

aphthous (af′thus) Relating to aphthae.

apical (ap′e-kal) Relating to an apex.

apico- Combining form meaning a summit or tip.

apicoectomy (a-pĕ-ko-ek′to-me) Surgical removal of the tip of the root of a tooth.

apicostomy (a-pĕ-kos′to-me) The surgical formation of an orifice through the alveolar bone to the tip of a tooth root.

apituitarism (ah-pī-tu′ĭ-tar-izm) A state in which the pituitary (hypophysis) has stopped functioning.

aplanatism (ah-plan′ah-tizm) Absence of spherical aberration.

aplasia (ah-pla′zhe-ah) **1.** Failure of development of an organ or tissue from its anlage (primitive cells). **2.** In hematology, failure to regenerate.

aplastic (ah-plas′tik) Relating to aplasia.

apnea (ap-ne′ah) Temporary cessation of breathing.

sleep a. Episodes of apnea occurring during sleep and lasting 10 seconds or longer; may be obstructive, due to blockage of airflow at the nose or mouth, and cause snoring, or central, associated with depression of respiratory drive, may cause excessive daytime sleepiness.

apneic (ap′ne-ik) Relating to apnea.

apneumatosis (ap-nu-mah-to′sis) An airless state of the lungs.

apo- Prefix meaning separation; derived from.

apochromatic (ap-o-kro-mat′ik) Free of spherical and chromatic aberration; said of a microscope objective.

apocrine (ap′o-krin) Relating to a type of gland that casts off some of its cellular components along with its secretory product, such as axillary sweat glands.

apodia (ah-po′de-ah) Congenital absence of feet.

apoenzyme (ap-o-en′zīm) Any protein that forms an active catalyst of biochemical reactions (holoenzyme) by combining with a nonprotein organic molecule (coenzyme).

apoferritin (ap-o-fer′ĭ-tin) A protein of the small intestine that combines with iron to form the iron-containing protein ferritin, thus beginning the process of iron absorption.

apolar (ah-po′lar) Not having poles; said of certain embryonic nerve cells.

apolipoprotein (ah-po-lip-o-pro′tēn) The protein component of a lipoprotein.

aponeurorrhaphy (ap-o-nu-ror′ah-fe) See fasciorraphy.

aponeurosis (ap-o-nu-ro′sis), pl. aponeuro′ses A broad, often thin tendinous sheet of fibrous tissue; it connects a muscle to its attachment.

epicranial a. Fibrous tissue covering the upper portion of the skull and connecting the frontal and occipital bellies of the occipitofrontal muscle. Also called galea aponeurotica.

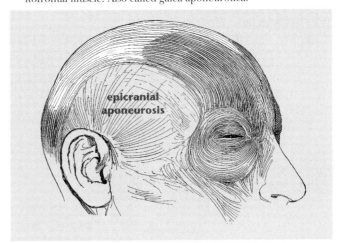

palmar a. Bundles of fibrous tissue within the palm of the hand, extending from the tendon of the long palmar (palmaris longus) muscle to the bases of the fingers. Also called palmar fascia; Dupuytren's fascia.

plantar a. The thick fibrous tissue within the sole of the foot, extending from the medial process of the calcaneal tuberosity to the bases of the toes. Also called plantar fascia.

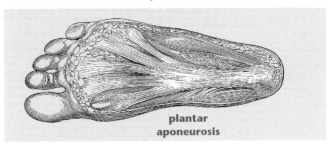

aponeurotic (ap-o-nu-rot′ik) Relating to an aponeurosis.

apophysial, apophyseal (ap-o-fiz′e-al) Relating to an apophysis.

apophysis (ah-pof′ĭ-sis), pl. apoph′yses A bony outgrowth or prominence.

apophysitis (ah-pof-ĭ-zi′tis) Inflammation of an apophysis.

apoplexy (ap′o-plek-se) **1.** Rupture of a vessel into an organ. **2.** Obsolete term for stroke.

apoptosis (ap-op-to′sis) Cell death occurring naturally from internal perturbations (unlike necrosis).

apparatus (ap-ah-ra′tus), pl. appara′tuses **1.** A group of instruments used together or in succession to perform a particular task. **2.** A group of organs or structures that collectively perform a common function.

central a. The centrosome and centrosphere of a cell.

digestive a. See digestive system, under system.

Golgi a. See Golgi complex, under complex.

juxtaglomerular a. (JGA) The juxtaglomerular body (granular epithelial cells in the terminal part of the afferent arteriole of the kidney) together with the macula densa (the thickened epithelial cells in the wall of the distal convoluted tubule where it contacts the afferent arteriole); a site of renin production. Also called juxtaglomerular complex.

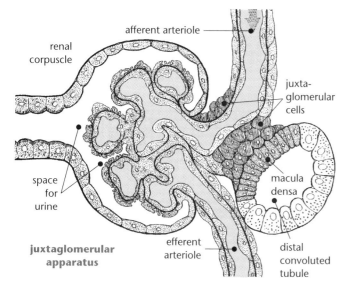

juxtaglomerular apparatus

lacrimal a. The structures involved in the secretion and transport of tears, consisting of: lacrimal gland, lacrimal lake, lacrimal canaliculi, lacrimal sac, and nasolacrimal duct.

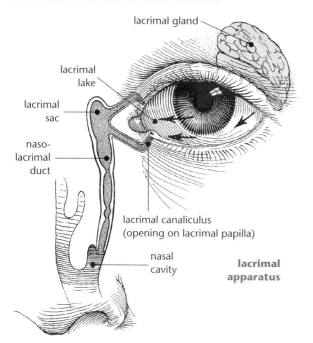

lacrimal apparatus

urogenital a. The combination of the organs concerned in the production and passage of urine, together with the organs of reproduction. Also called urogenital tract; genitourinary tract.

Warburg's a. A device for measuring oxygen consumption and the liberation of carbon dioxide by small portions of tissue.

appendage (ah-pen′dij) Any part in close but subordinate relation to a principal structure. Also called appendix.

testicular a. See appendix of testis, under appendix.

vesicular a. See vesicular appendix, under appendix.

appendectomy (ap-en-dek′to-me) The surgical removal of an appendix, especially the vermiform appendix.

appendiceal (ap-en-dis′e-al) Relating to an appendix.

appendices (ah-pen′dī-sēz) Plural of appendix.

appendicitis (ah-pen-dī-si′tis) Inflammation of the vermiform appendix.

acute a. Inflammation distal to an obstruction of the appendiceal lumen with consequent stagnation and multiplication of bacteria; associated with abdominal pain, fever, and, usually but not always, nausea and vomiting.

appendicolithiasis (ah-pen-dī-ko-lī-thi′ah-sis) The presence of concretions within the vermiform appendix.

appendicular (ap-en-dik′u-lar) **1.** Relating to an appendix. **2.** Relating to an appendage.

appendix (ah-pen′diks), pl. appen′dices **1.** An appendage or accessory part attached to a main structure. **2.** The vermiform appendix.

Morgagni's a. See vesicular appendix.

a. of testis A minute oval body situated at the upper end of the testis; a normal remnant of the embryonic paramesonephric (müllerian) duct. Also called testicular appendage.

vermiform a. A slender, finger-shaped, tubular structure branching off the blind end of the cecum (beginning part of the large intestine), about 2cm below the junction of the cecum and the ileum (terminal part of the small intestine). It has a thick wall with an ample supply of lymphoid tissue, which provides local protection against infection. Also called appendix.

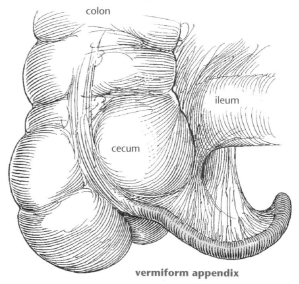

vermiform appendix

appendicitis

vesicular a. A minute fluid-filled structure attached to the open end of the fallopian (uterine) tube; a normal remnant of the embryonic mesonephric duct. Also called Morgagni's appendix; vesicular appendage.

appersonation, appersonification (ah-per-so-na′shun, ah-person-ī-fī-ka′shun) Delusion characterized by the assumption of another person's character.

applanate (ap′lah-nat) **1.** To flatten. **2.** Flattened.

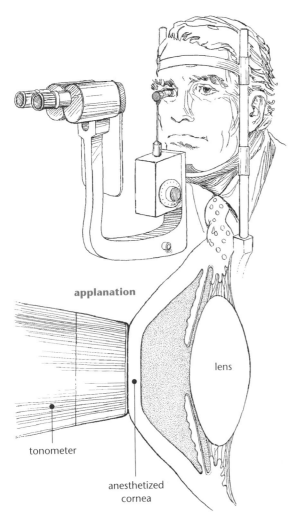

applanation

lens

tonometer

anesthetized
cornea

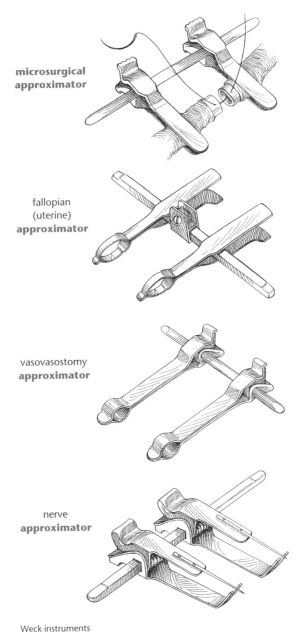

microsurgical
approximator

fallopian
(uterine)
approximator

vasovasostomy
approximator

nerve
approximator

Weck instruments

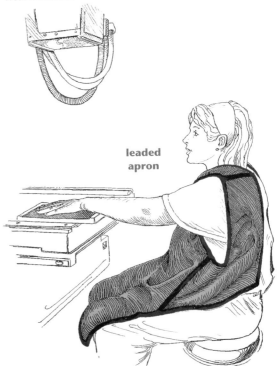

leaded
apron

applanation (ap-lah-na'shun) In ophthalmology, the flattening of the cornea with a special tonometer to measure intraocular pressure. See also applanation tonometer, under tonometer.

appliance (ah-pli'ans) **1.** Device used to provide support, perform a function, or effect a structural change. **2.** In dentistry, a general term referring to various devices employed for therapeutic purposes or to achieve aesthetic effects.

    orthodontic a. Device designed to apply force to teeth and their supporting structures; used to gradually move teeth into functional and aesthetic alignment, and in the treatment of fractures of the jaws. Also called braces.

apposition (ap-o-zish'un) The state of being in proximity.

approximator (ah-prok'sĭ-ma-tor) An instrument for bringing tissue edges into close apposition for suturing.

    microsurgical a. A noncrushing instrument designed to hold both ends of severed structures (e.g., blood vessels, nerves) for repair under magnification of a surgical microscope.

    rib a. Instrument that brings together two ribs to facilitate surgical closure of intercostal space.

apraxia (ah-prak'se-ah) Inability to carry out a requested complex movement due to brain damage in the associative motor area. Condition is not due to paralysis or comprehension deficiency.

apron (a'prun) **1.** A garment worn to protect clothing or the body. **2.** An anatomic structure resembling an apron in appearance or function, such as the omentum.

    leaded a. A shield of lead rubber that protects patients or health care workers from needless radiation exposure during radiography. Also called lead-rubber apron; protective apron.

    lead-rubber a. See leaded apron.

    protective a. See leaded apron.

aptyalia, aptyalism (ap-ti-a'le-ah, ap-ti'ah-lizm) See asialia.

APUD Acronym for amine precursor uptake and decarboxylation; denoting a system of cells, scattered throughout the body, that secrete a variety of peptide hormones and amines. Also called APUD system; neuroendocrine system.

apyretic (ah-pi-ret′ik) Without fever. Also called afebrile.

apyrexia (ah-pi-rek′se-ah) Absence of fever.

apyrexial (ah-pi-rek′se-al) Relating to apyrexia.

aqua (ah′kwah) Latin for water.

aqueduct (ak′we-dukt) A passage or canal.

    cerebral a. A small passage between the third and fourth ventricles of the brain, through which passes cerebrospinal fluid. Also called aqueduct of Sylvius; sylvian aqueduct; aqueduct of cerebrum; canal of midbrain.

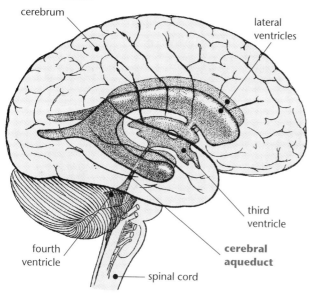

    a. of cerebrum See cerebral aqueduct.

    a. of cochlea, cochlear a. See perilymphatic duct, under duct.

    a. of Sylvius, sylvian a. See cerebral aqueduct.

    vestibular a. A canal in the internal ear extending from the medial wall of the vestibule to the posterior surface of the petrous portion of the temporal bone; it houses the endolymphatic duct.

aqueous (ā′kwe-us) Watery.

arachidonic acid (ah-rah-kī-don′ik as′id) An unsaturated fatty acid that is essential for human nutrition.

Arachnida (ah-rak′nĭ-dah) A class of arthropods that includes spiders, scorpions, ticks, and mites.

arachnidism (ah-rak′nĭ-dizm) Toxic condition caused by the bite of a spider.

arachno- Combining form meaning spider.

arachnodactyly (ah-rak-no-dak′tĭ-le) The abnormally long, slender fingers and toes characteristic of certain inherited disorders of connective tissue, such as Marfan's syndrome.

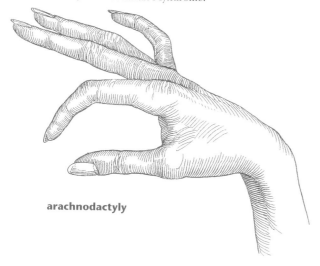

arachnodactyly

arachnoid (ah-rak′noid) **1.** Like a web. **2.** The middle of the three membranes covering the brain and spinal cord, between the dura mater and the pia mater.

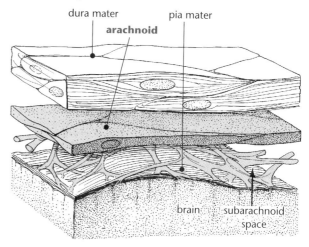

arachnoidal (ah-ak-noi′dal) Relating to the arachnoid.

arachnoiditis (ah-rak-noid-i′tis) Inflammation of the arachnoid. Signs and symptoms vary with extent of condition.

    adhesive a. Inflammation and thickening of the arachnoid and adjacent pia mater, leading to progressive obliteration of the space between them (subarachnoid space).

arachnophobia (ah-rak-no-fo′be-ah) Abnormally exaggerated fear of spiders.

arborescent (ar-bo-res′ent) Having treelike branches.

arborization (ar-bor-ĭ-za′shun) **1.** The branching termination of a nerve or blood vessel. **2.** The fern pattern sometimes formed by mucus from the uterine cervix when allowed to dry on a glass slide for inspection under the microscope. Seen in the proliferative phase of the menstrual cycle and in the presence of leaking amniotic fluid.

normal cycle

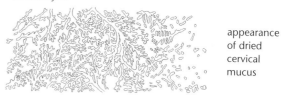

appearance of dried cervical mucus

proliferative phase of menstrual cycle

arborization (ferning)

arborize (ar′bōr-īz) To branch or ramify.

arbovirus (ar-bo-vi′rus) Any of a large group of RNA viruses that are transmitted by the bite of a vector (usually a tick or mite).

    arc (ark) A structure or a pathway shaped like an arch.

    mercury a. Ultraviolet and blue-green visible light produced by an electric discharge through mercury vapor in a glass or quartz tube; used as a source of therapeutic ultraviolet light.

    reflex a. The consistent path followed by a nerve impulse in producing an involuntary (reflex) response to a stimulus.

Arcanobacterium haemolyticum (ar-ka-no-bak-te′re-um he-mo-li′tĭ-kum) A bacterium that causes tonsillitis. Formerly called *Corynebacterium haemolyticum*.

arch (arch) Any curved structure of the body.

    a. of aorta, aortic a. The curved part of the aorta, between the ascending and descending portions.

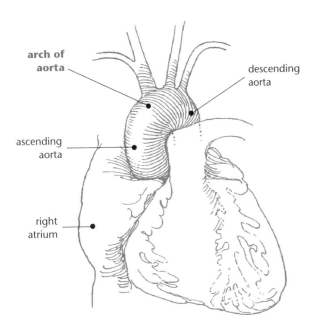

A

arch of aorta

descending aorta

ascending aorta

right atrium

aortic a.'s The six arterial channels surrounding the pharynx of the embryo; some are functional only in the very young embryo, others develop into adult arteries. They never exist all at the same time.

cortical a.'s of kidney The portion of kidney substance (cortex) situated between the bases of the pyramids and the renal capsule.

costal a. The arch at the anterior lower edge of the rib cage formed by the cartilages of ribs on both sides designated 7th through 10th.

dental a. (a) The arrangement of teeth in the maxilla or mandible. (b) The curved contour of bone left after loss of the natural teeth.

a.'s of foot The two natural arches (longitudinal and transverse) formed by the bones of the foot. Also called plantar arches.

longitudinal a. of foot The anteroposterior curvature of the foot, formed by the seven tarsal and five metatarsal bones and the ligaments and muscles that bind them together.

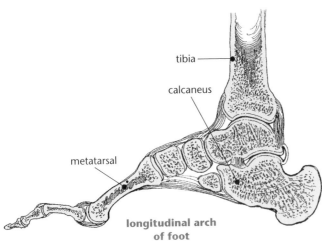

tibia

calcaneus

metatarsal

longitudinal arch of foot

neural a. See vertebral arch.

palatoglossal a. An arch on either side of the throat extending from the soft palate to the side of the tongue; formed by the palatoglossal muscle (enfolded in mucous membrane); it bounds anteriorly the recess for the palatine tonsil and plays an important role in swallowing (deglutition). Also called anterior pillar of fauces.

palatopharyngeal a. An arch on either side of the throat extending from the uvula to the side of the pharynx; formed by the

palatopharyngeal muscle (enfolded in mucous membrane); it bounds posteriorly the recess for the palatine tonsil. Also called posterior pillar of fauces.

plantar a.'s See arches of foot.

pubic a. The arch of the pelvis formed by the inferior pubic rami of both sides.

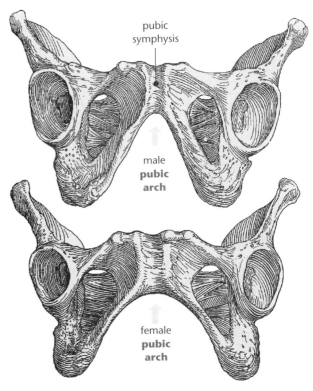

pubic symphysis

male **pubic arch**

female **pubic arch**

superciliary a. The bony ridge on the upper margin of the orbit.

transverse a. of foot The curvature of the foot formed by the proximal parts of the metatarsal bones anteriorly and the distal row of the tarsal bones posteriorly; bound together by ligaments and muscles.

vertebral a. The arch of the dorsal or posterior side of the vertebra that forms the vertebral foramen for passage of the spinal cord. Also called neural arch.

zygomatic a. The arch formed by the articulation of processes of the zygomatic and temporal bones.

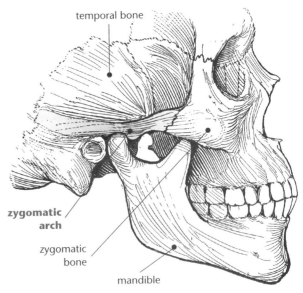

temporal bone

zygomatic arch

zygomatic bone

mandible

arch ▪ arch

A50

archenteron (ar-ken′ter-on) The primitive digestive tract of the embryo. Also called primary gut; gastrocele.

arctation (ark-ta′shun) A narrowing in a hollow tubular structure.

arcuate (ar′ku-āt) Arched or bent in the shape of a bow.

arcus (ar′kus), pl. ar′cus Any arched structure.

    a. cornealis See arcus senilis.

    a. senilis A grayish ring of fatty infiltration at the outer margin of the cornea, commonly seen in elderly persons and also in younger patients afflicted with hyperlipidemia. Also called arcus cornealis; gerontoxon.

area (a′re-ah) 1. A distinct surface or region of the body. 2. A special section of a room or building.

    aortic a. Area of the chest wall over the cartilage of the right second rib, near the breastbone (sternum).

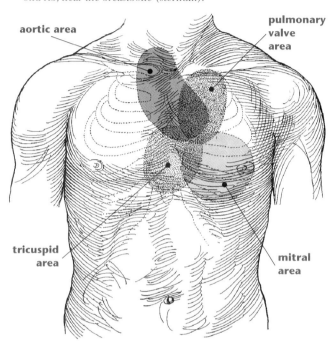

aortic area
pulmonary valve area
tricuspid area
mitral area

    apical a. Area about a dental root.

    auditory a. Area of the superficial layer of the brain (cerebral cortex) concerned with hearing. It includes portions of the anterior transverse temporal gyrus, the superior temporal gyrus, and adjacent postcentral gyrus.

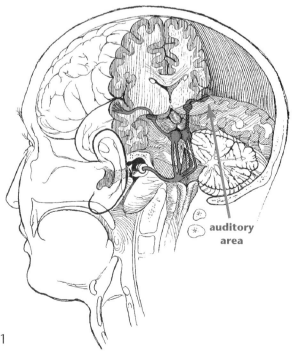

auditory area

bleeding a. of nose See Kiesselbach's area.

Broca's motor speech a. Area of the superficial layer of the brain (cerebral cortex) concerned with the motor aspects of spoken and written language; located in the triangular and opercular portions of the inferior frontal gyrus. Also called Broca's center; Broca's motor speech center; speech center.

Brodmann's a.'s The 47 areas of the superficial layer of the brain (cerebral cortex) mapped out according to the distinct arrangement of their cells.

contact a. See contact point, under point.

controlled a. In radiography, the space in a room containing the radioactive source.

Kiesselbach's a. The anterior part of the nasal septum where the mucous membrane has a rich blood supply; a frequent site of nosebleed. Also called Little's area; bleeding area of nose.

Little's a. See Kiesselbach's area.

macular a. of retina See macula lutea, under macula.

mitral a. The area of the chest wall over the apex of the heart where sounds made by the mitral (left atrioventricular) valve are heard most distinctly; usually located at the level of the left fifth intercostal space.

motor a. Area of the superficial layer of the brain (cerebral cortex) that predominantly controls voluntary movement; located in the anterior wall of the central sulcus and adjacent parts of the precentral gyrus. Also called motor cortex; motor region; rolandic region.

olfactory a. Area of the brain responsible for the subjective appreciation of smell sensations. It includes the olfactory bulb, tract, and trigone, the lateral olfactory stria, and the uncinate gyrus.

pulmonary a. Area of the chest wall overlying the lungs.

pulmonary valve a. Area of the chest wall where sounds made by the pulmonary valve of the heart are heard most distinctly; located partly behind the upper border of the left costal cartilage and partly behind the breastbone (sternum).

sensory a. Any area of the superficial layer of the brain (cerebral cortex) that is predominantly involved in perception of sensations. Also called sensory region; sensory cortex.

supporting a. Area of a toothless mandible or maxilla considered best suited to withstand the chewing pressures once the dentures are in place.

tricuspid a. Area of the chest wall where sounds made by the tricuspid (right atrioventricular) valve of the heart are heard most distinctly; located over the lower part of the breastbone (sternum).

visual a. Area of the superficial layer of the brain (cerebral cortex) concerned with vision; including the stria and peristriate portions of the occipital lobe.

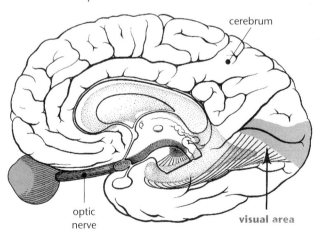

cerebrum
optic nerve
visual area

    v-shaped a. of Laimer See Laimer's triangle, under triangle.

areata, areatus (ar-e-a′tah, ar-e-a′tus) A circumscribed area.

areflexia (ah-re-flek′se-ah) Absence of reflexes.

Arenavirus (ah-re-nah-vi′rus) Genus of RNA viruses (family Arenaviridae) that includes the Lassa and lymphocytic choriomeningitis viruses.

areola (ah-re′o-lah), pl. are′olae **1.** A small space within a tissue. **2.** A circular pigmented area surrounding a central point, such as the nipple of the breast.

argasid (ar-gas′id) Any soft tick of the family Argasidae; some carry and transmit the spirochetes that cause relapsing fever.

argentaffin (ar-jen′tah-fin) Stainable by silver salts; said of certain cells.

argentaffinoma (ar-jen-taf-ĭ-no′mah) See carcinoid tumor, under tumor.

argentation (ar-jen-ta′shun) Staining specific cells with a silver salt.

argentous (ar-jen′tus) Relating to silver; denoting a compound that contains silver in its lowest valence.

argentum (ar-jen′tum) Latin for silver.

arginase (ar′jĭ-nās) An enzyme of the liver that promotes the splitting of the amino acid arginine into urea and ornithine. Also called arginine amidase.

arginine (ar′jĭ-nin) (Arg) One of the essential amino acids derived from the digestion or hydrolysis of protein.
    a. amidase See arginase.

argon (ar′gon) A gaseous chemical element comprising about 1% of the earth's atmosphere; symbol Ar, atomic number 18, atomic weight 39.95.

arm (arm) The portion of the upper limb from the shoulder to the elbow; commonly used to mean the entire upper limb.
    flail a. An arm that is paralyzed, flaccid, and anesthetic; the condition may be temporary or permanent and may be due to a variety of causes, such as avulsion of the cervical nerve roots, or compression of the brachial plexus by the head of the humerus when the arm is maintained in an abducted position for a long time.

armamentarium (ar-mah-men-tā′re-um) The therapeutic resources, considered collectively, that are available to the health professional.

armpit (arm′pit) See axilla.

arrest (ah-rest′) **1.** A state of inactivity; a cessation. **2.** To stop.
    cardiac a. (CA) Sudden stoppage of effective heart action; may be due to absence of ventricular contractions (asystole) or to ineffective, uncoordinated contractions (fibrillation).
    circulatory a. Cessation of blood circulation usually caused by cardiac arrest.
    sinus a. A temporary cessation of cardiac activity due to a brief failure of the sinoatrial (S-A) node of the heart to send impulses to the atria.
    sperm maturation a. Failure of the germinal cells in the testes to attain full maturity; may occur at any stage in the process of spermatozoon development, e.g., when the primary spermatocyte (with a diploid chromosome content) divides to form two secondary spermatocytes (each with a haploid complement of chromosomes).

arrhenoblastoma (ah-re-no-blas-to′mah) A rare benign tumor of the ovary occurring in young women. It secretes male hormones (androgens) that cause development of male characteristics (masculinization).

arrhythmia (ah-rith′me-ah) Any variation from the regular rhythm of the heartbeat; may appear in the presence or absence of heart disease. Causes range widely, but basically arrhythmias are due to a disturbance either to the site of origin of the impulse or to the conduction system of the impulse through the heart wall.

arrhythmic (ah-rith′mik) Related to arrhythmia.

arrhythmogenic (ah-rith-mo-jen′ik) Causing irregularity of the heartbeat.

arsenic (ar′se-nik) Metallic element; symbol As, atomic number 33, atomic weight 74.9. Pure arsenic and its organic compounds (found in many seafoods) are virtually nonpoisonous. Other compounds (e.g., arsenic trioxide) are potent poisons. Some arsenical compounds are used in the agricultural and pharmaceutical industries. Hazardous exposure to humans may occur in the workplace, or from smoking cigarettes made of tobacco sprayed with arsenical pesticides.

arsenical (ar-sen′ĭ-kal) **1.** Relating to arsenic. **2.** A drug containing arsenic.

arsenous (ar′sĕ-nus) Containing arsenic in a low valency.

arsine (ar′sin) A poisonous gas with a slightly garlicky odor; most occupational exposures occur in the microelectronic industry, where arsine is used to manufacture semiconductor chips; symptoms and signs of exposure include abdominal pain, nausea and vomiting, and hemolysis (in 2–24 hours). Many derivatives have been used in chemical warfare.

arsphenamine (ars-fen′ah-min) An organoarsenical compound of historical importance; its synthesis by Paul Ehrlich in 1907 represented a major advance in the treatment of syphilis. Also called salvarsan; diarsenol.

arteria (ar-te′re-ah), pl. arte′riae Latin for artery.

arterial (ar-te′re-al) Relating to an artery.

arteriectomy (ar-tĕ-re-ek′to-me) Removal of a segment of an artery.

arterio-, arteri- Combining forms meaning artery.

arteriogram (ar-te′re-o-gram) An x-ray image of an artery, obtained after injecting a radiopaque solution into it.

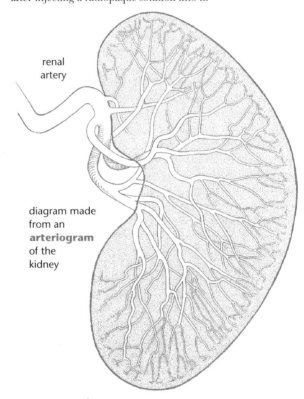

renal artery

diagram made from an **arteriogram** of the kidney

arteriography (ar-te-re-og′rah-fe) X-ray visualization of an artery after introducing a radiopaque solution into it.
    coronary a. Arteriography of the arteries supplying blood to the heart muscle.

arteriola (ar-te-re-o′lah), pl. artero′lae Latin for arteriole.
    arteriolae rectae The straight vessels arising in a group from the juxtamedullary efferent arterioles of the kidney; they extend through the renal medulla parallel to the nephronic (Henle's) loop. Also called vasa recta.

arteriolar (ar-te-re′o-lar) Relating to the arterioles.

arteriole (ar-te′re-ōl) The smallest artery (less than 0.2 mm in diameter) preceding and conveying blood to the capillaries. Arterioles have muscular walls and a rich innervation by sympathetic nerves through which they play an important role in regulating blood pressure.
    afferent glomerular a. The arteriole conveying blood toward the glomerulus of the kidney.
    efferent glomerular a. The arteriole conveying blood away from the glomerulus of the kidney.

arteriolitis (ar-tēr-ĭ-o-li′tis) Inflammation of the arterioles.
    necrotizing a. Necrosis of the walls of arterioles, seen in malignant hypertension. Also called ateriolonecrosis.

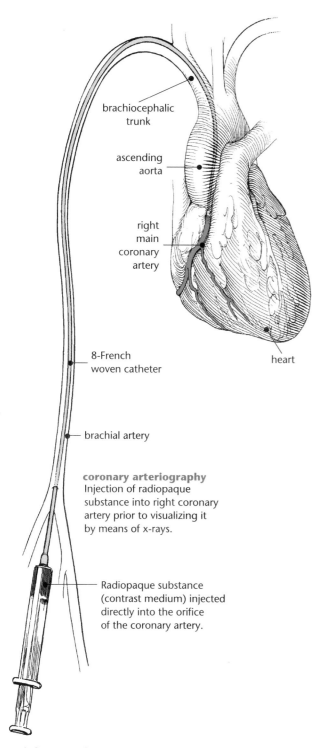

brachiocephalic trunk

ascending aorta

right main coronary artery

heart

8-French woven catheter

brachial artery

coronary arteriography
Injection of radiopaque substance into right coronary artery prior to visualizing it by means of x-rays.

Radiopaque substance (contrast medium) injected directly into the orifice of the coronary artery.

arteriolonecrosis (ar-te're-o-lo-ne-kro'sis) See necrotizing arteriolitis, under arteriolitis.

arteriolonephrosclerosis (ar-te're-o-lo-nef'ro-sklĕ-ro'sis) See arteriolar nephrosclerosis, under nephrosclerosis.

arteriolosclerosis (ar-te're-o-lo-sklĕ-ro'sis) Hardening of arterioles and small arteries associated with high blood pressure (hypertension); characterized by diffuse wall thickening, narrowing of the lumen, and resultant deficiency of blood supply to affected parts. Also called arteriolar sclerosis.

    hyaline a. A form occurring typically in elderly people, especially those with mild hypertension and mild diabetes mellitus.

    hyperplastic a. A form characteristically occurring in acute, severe elevations in blood pressure (malignant hypertension).

arteriomotor (ar-te-re-o-mo'tor) Causing dilation or contraction of arteries.

arteriomyomatosis (ar-te're-o-mi-o-mah-to's is) An overgrowth of irregular muscle fibers in an arterial wall.

arterionephrosclerosis (ar-te're-o-nef'ro-sklĕ-ro'sis) See arterial nephrosclerosis, under nephrosclerosis.

arteriopathy (ar-te-re-op'ah-the) Any disease of the arteries.

arterioplasty (ar-te-re-o-plas'te) Surgical repair of an artery.

arteriorrhaphy (ar-te-re-or'ah-fe) Suturing of an artery.

arteriorrhexis (ar-te-re-o-rek'sis) Rupture of an artery.

arteriosclerosis (ar-te-re-o-sklĕ-ro'sis) Thickening, hardening, and loss of elasticity of arterial walls from any cause (e.g., fibrosis, calcification, plaque formation). Also called arterial sclerosis; popularly known as hardening of the arteries.

    Mönckeberg's a. Degenerative change characterized by deposition of ringlike calcifications in the middle, muscular layer of the arterial wall, without narrowing of the arterial lumen. Also called Mönckeberg's sclerosis.

    a. obliterans Blockage of the arterial lumen, usually by fatty plaques on the artery's inner lining.

arteriosclerotic (ar-te-re-o-sklĕ-rot'ik) Relating to ateriosclerosis.

arteriospasm (ar-te're-o-spazm) Spasmodic contractions of arterial walls.

arteriostenosis (ar-te-re-o-ste-no'sis) Constriction of an artery.

arteriotomy (ar-te-re-ot'o-me) Surgical incision into the lumen of an artery.

arteriovenous (ar-te-re-o-ve'nus) Relating to both arteries and veins.

arteritis (ar-tĕ-ri'tis) Inflammation of an artery.

    giant cell a. See temporal arteritis.

    Takayasu's a. See Takayasu's disease, under disease.

    temporal a. Uncommon condition of unknown cause in which the inner layer of the arterial wall deteriorates; it involves middle-sized arteries, especially those of the scalp and temple, and the retina of the eye; seen in people over 50 years of age. Also called giant cell arteritis.

artery (ar'ter-e) A vessel conveying blood from the heart to all body parts. All arteries transport oxygenated blood except those from the heart to the lungs (pulmonary arteries).

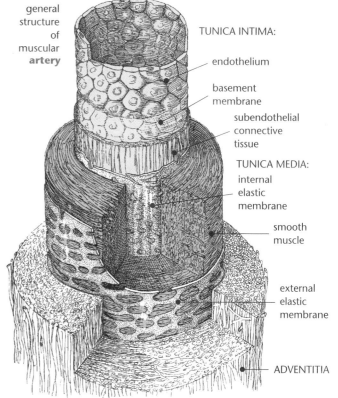

general structure of muscular **artery**

TUNICA INTIMA:
endothelium
basement membrane
subendothelial connective tissue

TUNICA MEDIA:
internal elastic membrane
smooth muscle
external elastic membrane

ADVENTITIA

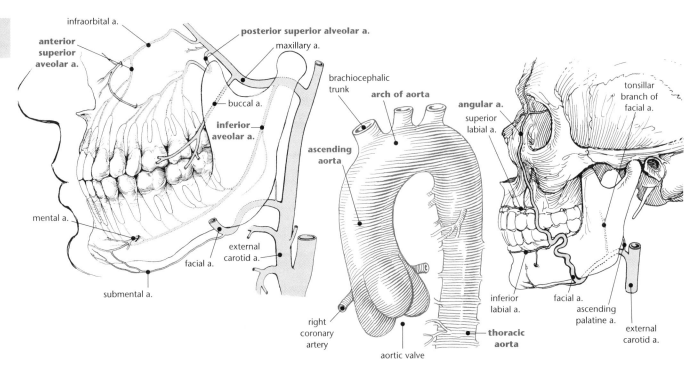

ARTERY	ORIGIN	BRANCHES	DISTRIBUTION
alveolar a., anterior superior anterior dental a. *a. alveolaris superior anterior*	infraorbital a.	dental, peridental	incisor and cuspid teeth of upper jaw, mucous membrane of maxillary sinus
alveolar a., inferior inferior dental a. mandibular a. *a. alveolaris inferior*	maxillary a.	mental, mylohyoid, dental, peridental	mandible and mandibular teeth, gums, lower lip, chin, mylohyoid muscle
alveolar a., posterior superior posterior superior dental a. *a. alveolaris superior posterior*	maxillary a.	dental, antral, alveolar, muscular	molar and bicuspid teeth of upper jaw, mucosa of maxillary sinus, gums
angular a. *a. angularis*	facial a.	muscular, lacrimal	muscles and skin of side of nose, lacrimal sac
aorta *aorta*	left ventricle at aortic valves		see specific branches
ascending aorta *aorta ascendens*	left ventricle at aortic valves	right coronary, left coronary	
arch of aorta *arcus aortae*	continuation of ascending aorta at level of the upper border of the right second sternocostal articulation	brachiocephalic trunk, left common carotid, left subclavian; continues as thoracic aorta at fourth thoracic vertebra	
thoracic aorta *aorta throacica*	continuation of arch of aorta at fourth thoracic vertebra	*visceral portion:* pericardial, bronchial, esophageal, mediastinal; *parietal portion:* posterior intercostal, subcostal, superior phrenic; continues as abdominal aorta at the aortic hiatus of diaphragm	
abdominal aorta *aorta abdominalis*	continuation of thoracic aorta at the aortic hiatus of diaphragm, usually at level of last thoracic vertebra	*visceral portion:* celiac, superior mesenteric, inferior mesenteric, middle suprarenal, renal, testicular, ovarian; *parietal portion:* inferior phrenic, lumbar, middle sacral; continues as common iliac arteries at fourth lumbar vertebra	
appendicular a. *a. appendicularis*	ileocolic a.	none	vermiform appendix
arch, deep palmar		see palmar arch, deep	
arch, plantar		see plantar arch	

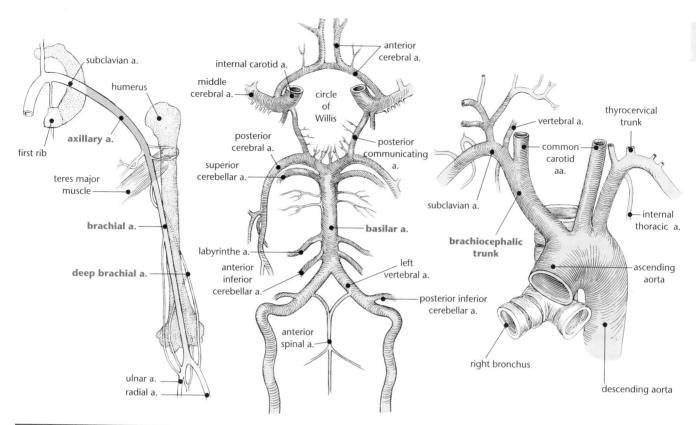

ARTERY	ORIGIN	BRANCHES	DISTRIBUTION
arch, superficial palmar		see palmar arch, superficial	
arcuate a. of foot metatarsal a. *a. arcuata pedis*	dorsal a. of foot	second, third, and fourth metatarsal arteries	foot, sides of toes
arcuate a.'s of kidney *aa. arcuatae renis*	interlobar a.	interlobular arteries	parenchyma of kidney
auditory a., internal		see labyrinthine artery	
auricular a., deep *a. auricularis profunda*	maxillary a.	temporomandibular	cuticular lining of external auditory canal, outer surface of tympanic membrane, temporomandibular joint
auricular a., posterior *a. auricularis posterior*	external carotid a.	stylomastoid, auricular, occipital, parotid	middle ear, mastoid air cells, auricle, parotid gland, digastric, stapedius, and neck muscles
axillary a. *a. axillaris*	continuation of subclavian a. beginning at outer border of first rib	*first part:* highest thoracic; *second part:* thoracoacromial, lateral thoracic; *third part:* subscapular, posterior humeral circumflex, anterior humeral circumflex	pectoral muscles, muscles of shoulder and upper arm, acromion, shoulder joint, sternoclavicular joint, breast
basilar a. *a. basilaris*	from union of right and left vertebral arteries	pontine, labyrinthine, anterior inferior cerebellar, superior cerebellar, posterior cerebral	pons, inner ear, cerebellum, pineal body, ventricles, posterior part of cerebrum
brachial a. *a.brachialis*	continuation of axillary a. at lower border of tendon of teres major muscle	deep brachial, nutrient of humerus, superior ulnar collateral, inferior ulnar collateral, muscular	muscles of shoulder, arm, forearm, and hand; elbow joint
brachial a., deep superior profunda a. *a. profunda brachii*	brachial a.	nutrient, deltoid, middle collateral, radial collateral, muscular	humerus, elbow joint, muscles of upper arm including triceps and deltoid
brachiocephalic trunk innominate a. *truncus brachiocephalicus*	beginning of arch of aorta	right common carotid, right subclavian, lowest thyroid, thymic, bronchial	right side of head, neck and upper arm, thyroid and thymus glands, and bronchus
bronchial a.'s *aa. bronchiales*	*right side:* first aortic intercostal; *left side:* thoracic aorta	none	bronchial tubes, alveolar tissue of lungs, bronchial lymph nodes, esophagus

artery ■ artery

A

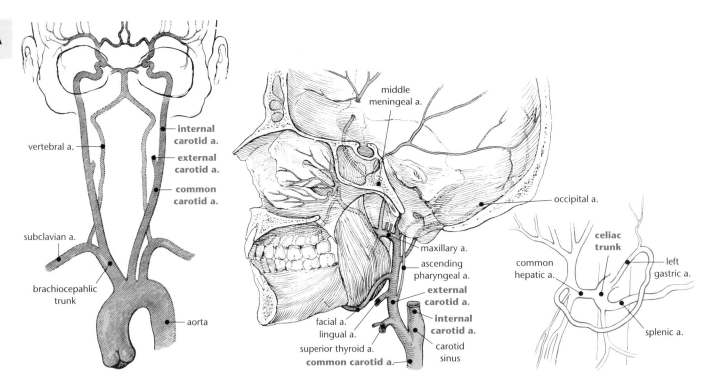

ARTERY	ORIGIN	BRANCHES	DISTRIBUTION
buccal a. buccinator a. *a. buccalis*	maxillary a.	muscular	buccinator muscle, mucosa of maxillary gums, mucosa and skin of cheeks
a. of bulb of penis *a. bulbi penis*	internal pudendal a.	bulbourethral	bulb of penis, posterior part of corpus spongiosum, bulbourethral gland
a. of bulb of vaginal vestibule *a. bulbi vestibuli vaginae*	internal pudendal a.	none	bulb of vestibule, greater vestibular glands
calcaneal a's., medial internal calcaneal a's. *rami calcanei mediales*	posterior tibial a.	none	skin and fat in back of calcaneal tendon and heel; muscles on tibial side of sole
capsular a.'s, middle		see suprarenal arteries, middle	
carotid a., common *a. carotis communis*	*right side:* bifurcation of the brachiocephalic trunk; *left side:* highest part of arch of aorta	external carotid, internal carotid	head
carotid a., external *a. carotis externa*	common carotid a.	*anterior part:* facial, superior thyroid, lingual; *posterior part:* occipital, posterior auricular; *medial part:* ascending pharyngeal; *terminal part:* superficial temporal, maxillary	anterior aspect of face and neck, side of head, skull, dura mater, posterior part of scalp
carotid a., internal *a. carotis interna*	common carotid a.	*cervical part:* carotid sinus; *petrous part:* caroticotympanic, pterygoid canal; *cavernous part:* cavernous sinus, tentorial, inferior hypophyseal, meningeal, trigeminal, and trochlear; *cerebral part:* superior hypophyseal, ophthalmic, anterior choroidal, anterior and middle cerebral, posterior communicating	middle ear, brain, hypophysis, trigeminal ganglion, meninges, orbit, choroid plexus
celiac trunk celiac artery *truncus celiacus*	abdominal aorta, just caudal to aortic hiatus of diaphragm	left gastric, common hepatic, splenic	esophagus, stomach, duodenum, spleen, pancreas, liver, gallbladder, greater omentum, common bile duct

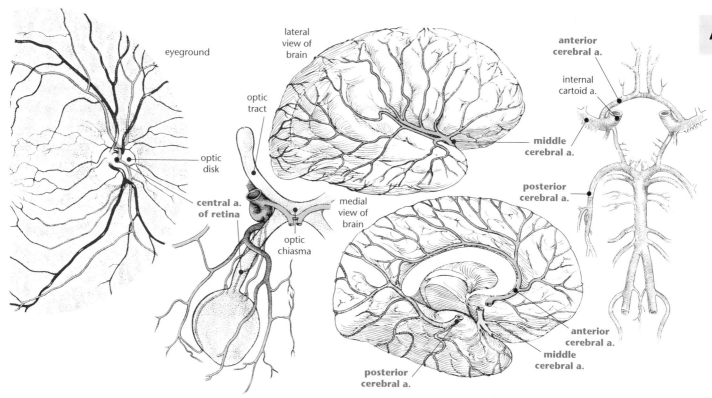

eyeground

optic disk

central a. of retina

optic tract

optic chiasma

lateral view of brain

medial view of brain

anterior cerebral a.

internal cartoid a.

middle cerebral a.

posterior cerebral a.

anterior cerebral a.

middle cerebral a.

posterior cerebral a.

ARTERY	ORIGIN	BRANCHES	DISTRIBUTION
central a. of retina *a. centralis retinae*	ophthalmic a. or lacrimal a.	superior, inferior	retina
cerebellar a., anterior inferior *a. cerebelli inferior anterior*	basilar a.	labyrinthine, posterior spinal	anterior part of inferior surface of cerebellum
cerebellar a., posterior inferior *a. cerebelli inferior posterior*	vertebral a.	medial, lateral	inferior surface of cerebellum, medulla oblongata, choroid plexus of fourth ventricle
cerebellar a., superior *a. cerebelli superior*	basilar a. near its termination	none	superior surface of cerebellum, vermis of cerebellum, pineal body, pia mater, pons, superior medullary velum, choroid plexus of third ventricle
cerebral a., anterior *a. cerebri anterior*	internal carotid a. at the medial extremity of the lateral cerebral sulcus	*precommunicating part:* anterior communicating short, long (recurrent), and anterocentral; *postcommunicating part:* medial, frontobasal, callosomarginal, paracentral, precuneal, parietooccipital	hypothalamus, caudate nucleus, internal capsule, choroid plexus, lateral ventricle, corpus striatum, corpus callosum, frontal lobe, parietal lobe
cerebral a., middle *a cerebri media*	internal carotid a.	*sphenoidal part:* anterolateral central; *insular part:* insula, lateral frontobasal, anterior, medial, and posterior temporal; *terminal part:* central, precentral, and postcentral sulcus, anterior and posterior parietal, angular gyrus	lentiform nucleus, internal capsule, caudate nucleus, corpus striatum, insula, motor, premotor, sensory, and auditory areas, lateral surface of cerebral hemisphere
cerebral a., posterior *a. cerebri posterior*	terminal bifurcation of basilar a.	*precommunicating part:* posteromedial central; *postcommunicating part:* posterolateral central, thalamus, peduncular, posteromedial, and posterolateral choroidal; *terminal part:* lateral occipital, medial occipital	thalmus, third ventricle, globus pallidus, cerebral peduncle, colliculi, pineal body, medial and lateral geniculate bodies, uncus, parahippocampal, medial and lateral occipitotemporal gyri, occipital lobe

A

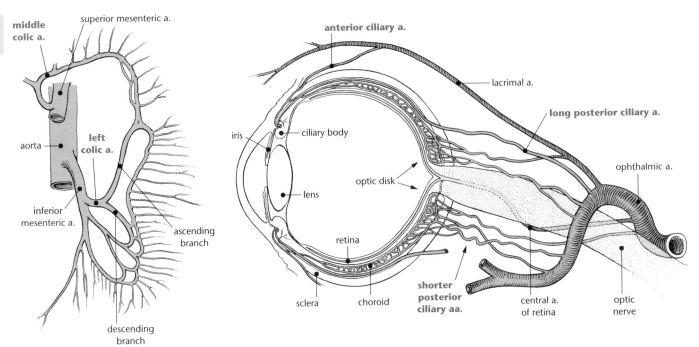

ARTERY	ORIGIN	BRANCHES	DISTRIBUTION
cervical a., ascending *a. cervicalis ascendens*	inferior thyroid a.	spinal	muscles of neck, vertebral canal, vertebrae
cervical a., deep *a. cervicalis profunda*	costocervical trunk	spinal, muscular	spinal cord, deep neck muscles
cervical a., superficial *a. cervicalis superficialis*	thyrocervical trunk	ascending, descending	trapezius and neighboring muscles
cervical a., transverse *a. transversa colli* *a. transversa cervicis*	thyrocervical trunk	superficial cervical, dorsal scapular	trapezius, levator m. of scapula, supraspinous m.
choroid a., anterior *a. choroidea anterior*	internal carotid a.	choroid plexus, optic tract, lateral geniculate body, internal capsule, cerebral peduncle, caudate nucleus, hypothalamus and surrounding area	internal capsule, choroid plexus of the inferior horn of lateral ventricle, optic tract, cerebral peduncle, base of brain, lateral geniculate body, caudate nucleus
choroid a., posterior *a. choroidea posterior*	posterior cerebral a.	medial, lateral	choroid plexuses of lateral and third ventricles
ciliary a.'s, anterior *aa. ciliares anteriores*	ophthalmic a.	episcleral, conjunctival, iridic	conjunctiva, iris
ciliary a.'s, long posterior (two in number) *aa. ciliares posteriores longae*	ophthalmic a.	iris, muscular	iris, ciliary body of eye
ciliary a.'s, short posterior (6–12 in number) *aa. ciliares posteriores breves*	ophthalmic a. or one of its branches	none	choroid layer and ciliary processes of eyeball
circumflex a., anterior humeral	see humeral circumflex artery, anterior		
circumflex a., lateral femoral	see femoral circumflex artery, lateral		
circumflex a., medial femoral	see femoral circumflex artery, medial		
circumflex a., posterior humeral	see humeral circumflex artery, posterior		
circumflex a., scapular	see scapular circumflex artery		
circumflex iliac a., deep	see iliac circumflex artery, deep		
circumflex iliac a., superficial	see iliac circumflex artery, superficial		
clitoris, deep a. of *a. profunda clitoridis*	internal pudendal a.	none	corpus cavernosum of clitoris
clitoris, dorsal a. of *a. dorsalis clitoridis*	internal pudendal a.	none	glans and prepuce of clitoris
coccygeal a.	see sacral artery, middle		
colic a., left *a. colica sinistra*	inferior mesenteric a.	ascending, descending	descending colon, left part of transverse colon

artery ■ artery

A58

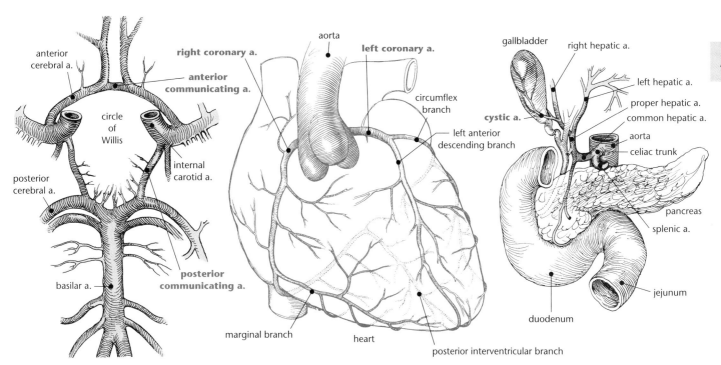

ARTERY	ORIGIN	BRANCHES	DISTRIBUTION
colic a., middle *a. colica media*	superior mesenteric a., just caudal to the pancreas	right, left	transverse colon
colic a., right *a. colica dextra*	superior mesenteric a. or ileocolic a.	descending, ascending	ascending colon
collateral a., inferior ulnar anastomotica magna a. *a. collateralis ulnaris inferior*	brachial a., about 5 cm proximal to elbow	posterior, anterior, anastomotic	triceps, elbow joint, round pronator muscle
collateral a., middle *a. collateralis media*	deep brachial a.	muscular, anastomotic	elbow joint, triceps and anconeus muscles
collateral a., radial *a. collateralis radialis*	continuation of deep brachial a.	muscular, anastomotic	triceps, elbow joint, brachioradial and brachial muscles
collateral a., superior ulnar inferior profunda a. *a. collateralis ulnaris superior*	brachial a., distal to middle of arm	muscular, articular, anastomotic	elbow joint, triceps muscle of arm
communicating a., anterior *a. communicans anterior cerebri*	anterior cerebral a. (connects the two anterior cerebral arteries)	anteromedial	anterior perforated substance of the brain
communicating a., posterior *a. communicans posterior cerebri*	connects the internal carotid a. with posterior cerebral a.	hypophyseal	base of brain between infundibulum and optic tract; internal capsule, anterior third of thalamus; third ventricle
conjunctival a.'s ,anterior *aa. conjunctivales anteriores*	anterior ciliary a.'s	none	conjunctiva
conjunctival a.'s, posterior *aa. conjunctivales posteriores*	peripheral tarsal arch	none	conjunctiva
coronary a., left *a. coronaria sinistra*	aorta at left aortic sinus	sinoatrial nodal, anterior interventricular (anterior descending), left atrial, circumflex	sinoatrial node, interventricular septum, left atrium, left and right ventricles
coronary a., right *a. coronaria dextra*	aorta at right aortic sinus	marginal, sinoatrial nodal, right atrial, posterior interventricular (posterior descending), atrioventricular nodal	sinoatrial node, atrioventricular node, right atrium, interventricular septum, right and left ventricles
costocervical trunk superior intercostal a. *truncus costocervicalis*	subclavian a.	deep cervical; continues as the highest intercostal a.	deep neck muscles, first and second intercostal spaces, vertebral column
cremasteric a. external spermatic a. *a. cremasterica*	inferior epigastric a.	none	cremaster muscle, coverings of spermatic cord
cystic a. *a. cystica*	right hepatic a.	superficial, deep	gallbladder

artery ■ artery

A

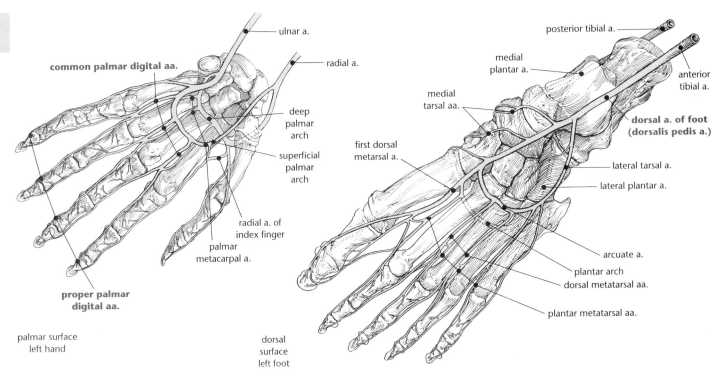

ulnar a.

common palmar digital aa.

radial a.

deep palmar arch

superficial palmar arch

radial a. of index finger

palmar metacarpal a.

proper palmar digital aa.

palmar surface left hand

posterior tibial a.

medial plantar a.

anterior tibial a.

medial tarsal aa.

dorsal a. of foot (dorsalis pedis a.)

first dorsal metarsal a.

lateral tarsal a.

lateral plantar a.

arcuate a.

plantar arch

dorsal metatarsal aa.

plantar metatarsal aa.

dorsal surface left foot

ARTERY	ORIGIN	BRANCHES	DISTRIBUTION
deep a. of clitoris		see clitoris, deep artery of	
deep a. of penis		see penis, deep artery of	
deferential a. a. of ductus deferens *a. ductus deferentis*	umbilical a. (embryonic), superior vesical a.	ureteric	ductus deferens, bladder, seminal vesicles, ureter, testicle
dental a., anterior		see alveloar artery, anterior superior	
dental a., inferior		see alveolar artery, inferior	
dental a., posterior		see alveolar artery, posterior superior	
diaphragmatic a., inferior		see phrenic artery	
digital a.'s, collateral		see digital arteries, proper palmar	
digital a.'s, common palmar (three in number) volar digital a.'s *aa. digitales palmares communes*	superficial palmar arch	proper palmar, digital	fingers
digital a.'s, common plantar *aa. digitales plantares communes*	plantar metatarsal a.'s	proper plantar, digital	toes
digital a.'s of foot, common		see metatarsal arteries, plantar	
digital a.'s, proper palmar collateral digital a.'s *aa. digitales palmares propriae*	common palmar digital a.'s	dorsal	the sides of each finger, matrix of fingernails
digital a.'s, proper plantar *aa. digitales plantares propriae*	common plantar digital a.'s	none	toes
dorsal a. of clitoris		see clitoris, dorsal artery of	
dorsal a. of foot dorsalis pedis a. dorsal pedal a. *a. dorsalis pedis* (anastomoses with lateral plantar a. to form plantar arterial arch)	continuation of anterior tibial a. at ankle joint	lateral tarsal, medial tarsal, arcuate, dorsal metatarsal, deep plantar, dorsal digital (continues to first intermetatarsal space where it divides into first dorsal metatarsal and deep plantar arteries)	foot
dorsal a. of penis		see penis, dorsal artery of	
dorsalis pedis a.		see dorsal artery of foot	
a. of ductus deferens		see deferential artery	
duodenal a.		see pancreaticoduodenal artery, inferior	
epigastric a., deep		see epigastric artery, inferior	

artery ▪ artery

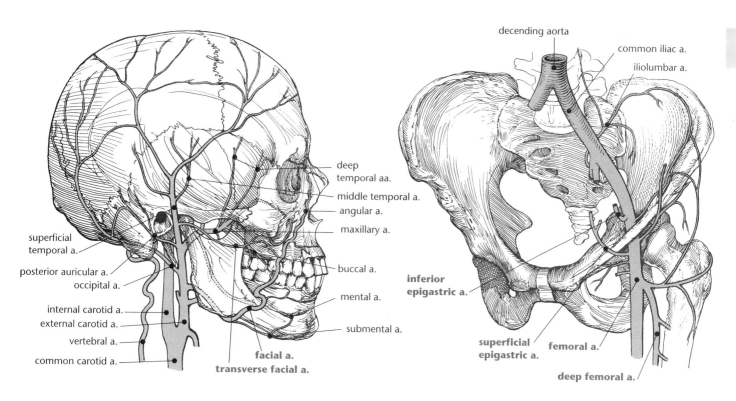

ARTERY	ORIGIN	BRANCHES	DISTRIBUTION
epigastric a., inferior deep epigastric a. *a. epigastrica inferior*	external iliac, immediately above inguinal ligament	cremasteric, pubic, muscular, round ligament of uterus	cremaster and abdominal muscles, peritoneum, skin
epigastric a., superficial *a. epigastrica superficialis*	femoral a. about 1 cm below inguinal ligament	none	lower part of abdominal wall, superficial lingual lymph nodes, skin
epigastric a., superior *a. epigastrica superior*	internal thoracic a.	cutaneous, muscular, peritoneal, phrenic, hepatic	skin, muscles, and fascia of upper part of abdominal wall; diaphragm, peritoneum, faliciform ligament of liver
episcleral a. *a. episcleralis*	anterior ciliary a.	none	iris, ciliary body, sclera, conjunctiva
esophageal a.'s (four to five in number) *aa. esophagei*	thoracic aorta; inferior thyroid and left gastric a.'s	none	esophagus
ethmoidal a., anterior *a. ethmoidalis anterior*	ophthalmic a.	meningeal, nasal	anterior and middle ethmoid air cells, frontal sinus, dura mater, nasal cavity
ethmoidal a., posterior *a. ethmoidalis posterior*	ophthalmic a.	meningeal, nasal	posterior ethmoid air cells, dura mater, nasal cavity
facial a. external maxillary a. *a. facialis*	external carotid a.	*cervical portion:* ascending palatine, tonsillar, glandular, submental; *facial portion:* inferior labial, superior labial, lateral nasal, angular, muscular	face, tonsil, palate, labial glands and muscles of lips, submandibular gland, ala and dorsum of nose, muscles of expression
facial a., deep	see maxillary artery		
facial a., transverse *a. transversa faciei*	superficial temporal a. while still in parotid gland	glandular, muscular, cutaneous	parotid gland and duct, masseter muscle, skin of face
femoral a. *a. femoralis*	continuation of external iliac a. immediately distal to inguinal ligament	superficial epigastric, superficial circumflex iliac, external pudendal, descending genicular, deep femoral, muscular	integument of abdominal wall, groin, and perineum; muscles of thigh, external genitals, inguinal lymph nodes
femoral a., deep profunda femoris a. *a. profunda femoris*	femoral a.	medial femoral circumflex, lateral femoral circumflex, perforating muscular	muscles of thigh, hip joint, head and shaft of femur, gluteal muscles

artery ■ artery

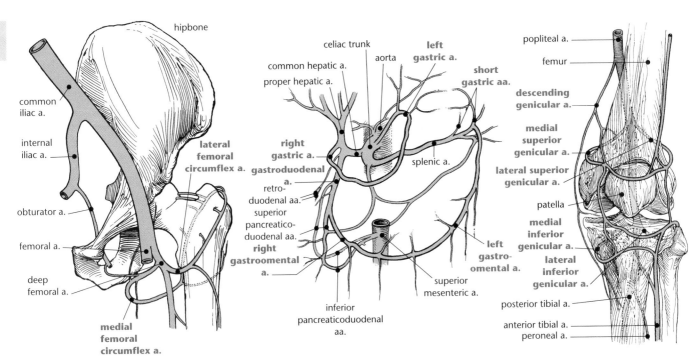

ARTERY	ORIGIN	BRANCHES	DISTRIBUTION
femoral circumflex a., lateral lateral circumflex a. of thigh *a. circumflexa femoris lateralis*	deep femoral a.	ascending, descending, transverse	hip joint, thigh muscles
femoral circumflex a., medial medial circumflex a. of thigh *a. circumflexa femoris medialis*	deep femoral a.	deep, ascending, transverse, acetabular	hip joint, thigh muscles
fibular a.		see peroneal artery	
frontal a.		see supratrochlear artery	
gastric a., left *a. gastrica sinistra*	celiac trunk	esophageal, pyloric, cardiac (stomach)	lesser curvature of stomach, abdominal part of esophagus; left lobe of liver (at times)
gastric a., right *a. gastrica dextra*	common hepatic a. or proper hepatic a.	none	pyloric end of stomach along lesser curvature
gastric a.'s, short *aa. gastricae breves*	splenic a.	none	fundus of stomach
gastroduodenal a. *a. gastroduodenalis*	common hepatic a.	right gastroepiploic, superior pancreaticoduodenal, retroduodenal, pancreatic	stomach, duodenum, pancreas, greater omentum
gastroomental a., left gastroepiploic a., left *a. gastroomentalis sinistra*	splenic a.	gastric, omental (epiploic)	stomach, greater omentum
gastoomental a., right gastroepiploic a., right *a. gastroomentalis dextra*	gastroduodenal a.	gastric, omental (epiploic)	stomach, greater omentum
genicular a., descending descending a. of the knee highest genicular a. *a. genus descendens*	femoral a.	saphenous, articular, muscular	knee joint and adjacent muscles
genicular a., highest		see genicular artery, descending	
genicular a., lateral inferior *a. genus lateralis inferior*	popliteal a.	none	knee joint, gastrocnemius muscle
genicular a., lateral superior *a. genus lateralis superior*	popliteal a.	none	lower part of femur, knee joint, patella, contiguous muscles
genicular a., medial inferior *a. genus medialis inferior*	popliteal a.	none	proximal end of tibia, knee joint
genicular a. medial superior *a. genus medialis superior*	popliteal a.	none	femur, knee joint, patella, contiguous muscles

artery ■ artery

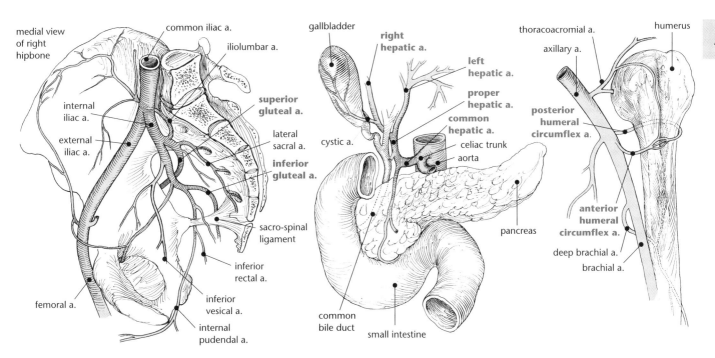

medial view of right hipbone
common iliac a.
iliolumbar a.
internal iliac a.
external iliac a.
superior gluteal a.
lateral sacral a.
inferior gluteal a.
sacro-spinal ligament
inferior rectal a.
inferior vesical a.
internal pudendal a.
femoral a.

gallbladder
right hepatic a.
left hepatic a.
proper hepatic a.
common hepatic a.
cystic a.
celiac trunk
aorta
pancreas
common bile duct
small intestine

thoracoacromial a.
humerus
axillary a.
posterior humeral circumflex a.
anterior humeral circumflex a.
deep brachial a.
brachial a.

ARTERY	ORIGIN	BRANCHES	DISTRIBUTION
genicular a., middle azygos articular a. *a. genus media*	popliteal a.	none	cruciate ligaments and synovial membrane of knee joint
gluteal a., inferior *a. glutea inferior*	internal iliac a.	sciatic, coccygeal, muscular, articular, cutaneous	muscles of the buttock and back of thigh
gluteal a., superior *a. glutea superior*	internal iliac a.	superficial, deep, nutrient, articular	muscles of hip and buttock; ilium, skin on dorsal surface of sacrum, hip joint
hemorrhoidal a., inferior		see rectal artery, inferior	
hemorrhoidal a., middle		see rectal artery, middle	
hemorrhoidal a., superior		see rectal artery, superior	
hepatic a., common *a. hepatica communis*	celiac trunk	gastroduodenal, proper hepatic, right gastric	stomach, greater omentum, pancreas, duodenum, liver, gallbladder
hepatic a., left *a. hepatica sinista*	proper hepatic a.	caudate lobe, medial segmental, lateral segmental	liver
hepatic a., proper *a. hepatica propria*	common hepatic a.	left hepatic, right hepatic, right gastric	liver, gallbladder, pyloric part of stomach
hepatic a., right *a. hepatica dextra*	proper hepatic a.	cystic, caudate lobe, anterior (left) segmental, posterior (right) segmental	liver and gallbladder
humeral circumflex a., anterior *a. circumflexa humeri anterior*	axillary a.	ascending, descending	head of humerus, shoulder joint, long head of biceps, muscle of arm, deltoid, coracobrachial, tendon of greater pectoral muscle
humeral circumflex a., posterior *a. circumflexa humeri posterior*	axillary a. at distal border of subscapular muscle	muscular, articular, nutrient, descending, acromial	shoulder joints, neck of humerus, deltoid, teres major, teres minor, and triceps muscles
hyaloid a. *a. hyaloidea* (usually disappears in the last month of intrauterine life)	central a. of retina	none	vitreous body, lens of eye
hypogastric a.		see iliac artery, internal	
ileal a.'s *aa. ilei*	superior mesenteric a.	none	ileum

A63

artery ■ artery

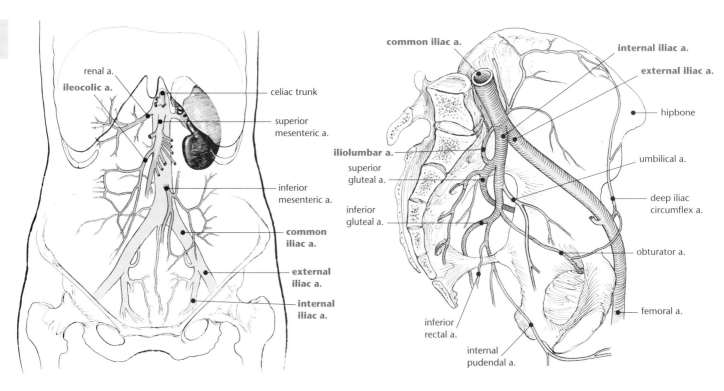

ARTERY	ORIGIN	BRANCHES	DISTRIBUTION
ileocolic a. *a. ileocolica*	superior mesenteric a.	superior (anastomoses with right colic a.), inferior (anastomoses with end of superior mesenteric a.), colic, anterior cecal, posterior cecal, appendicular, ileal	cecum, vermiform appendix, ascending colon, distal part of ileum
iliac a., common *a. iliaca communis*	abdominal aorta about the level of L4	internal and external iliac	pelvis, genital, and gluteal regions, perineum, lower abdominal wall
iliac a., external *a. iliaca externa*	continuation of common iliac a.	inferior epigastric, deep iliac circumflex, muscular	lower part of abdominal wall, external genitals, psoas major, cremaster, ductus deferens in male, round ligament of uterus in female
iliac a., internal hypogastric a. *a. iliaca interna*	common iliac a.	*anterior trunk:* obturator, superior gluteal, inferior gluteal, umbilical, inferior vesical, uterine, vaginal, middle rectal, internal pudendal: *posterior trunk:* iliolumbar, lateral sacral, superior gluteal	wall and viscera of pelvis, external genitals, region of anus, medial aspect of thigh, buttock
iliac circumflex a., deep *a. circumflexa illium profounda*	external iliac a.	ascending	psoas, iliac, sartorius, and neighboring muscles; overlying skin, oblique and transverse abdominal muscles
iliac circumflex a., superficial *a. circumflexa ilium superficialis*	femoral a.	none	skin of groin, superficial lingual lymph nodes
iliolumbar a. *a. iliolumbalis*	internal iliac a.	lumbar, iliac, spinal	greater psoas muscle, quadratus muscle of loins, gluteal and abdominal muscles; ilium, cauda equina
infraorbital a. *a. infraorbitalis*	maxillary a.	orbital, anterior superior alveolar, middle superior alveolar	orbit, maxilla, maxillary sinus and teeth, lower eyelid, extrinsic eye muscles, cheek, side of nose
innominate a.		see brachiocephalic trunk	
intercostal a.'s, anterior intercostal a.'s *aa. intercostales anteriores*	internal thoracic a.	muscular, cutaneous	first five or six intercostal spaces, pectoral muscles, skin of breast

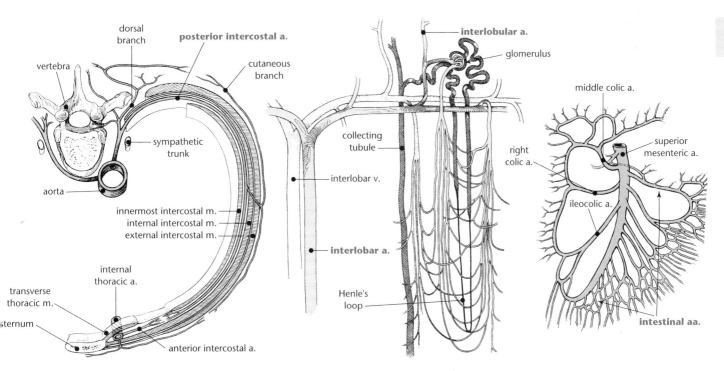

dorsal branch
posterior intercostal a.
vertebra
cutaneous branch
interlobular a.
glomerulus
middle colic a.
sympathetic trunk
collecting tubule
right colic a.
superior mesenteric a.
aorta
interlobar v.
innermost intercostal m.
internal intercostal m.
external intercostal m.
ileocolic a.
interlobar a.
internal thoracic a.
transverse thoracic m.
Henle's loop
sternum
anterior intercostal a.
intestinal aa.

ARTERY	ORIGIN	BRANCHES	DISTRIBUTION
intercostal a., highest *a. intercostalis suprema*	costocervical trunk	first and second posterior intercostal	first and second intercostal spaces, spinal cord, back muscles
intercostal a.'s I-II, posterior *aa. intercostales posteriores I-II*	highest intercostal a.	dorsal, spinal	upper part of thoracic wall
intercostal a.'s III-XI, posterior *aa. intercostales posteriores III-XI*	thoracic aorta	dorsal, collateral intercostal, lateral cutaneous, muscular	lower part of thoracic wall; mammary gland
interlobar a.'s of kidney *aa. interlobares renis*	six segmental branches of renal a.	arcuate	between pyramids of kidney
interlobular a.'s of kidney *aa. interlobulares renis*	arcuate a.'s of kidney	afferent glomeruli	renal glomeruli of kidney
interlobular a.'s of liver *aa. interlobulares hepatis*	right or left branches of proper hepatic a.	none	between lobules of liver
interosseous a., anterior volar interosseous a. *a. interossea anterior*	common interosseous a.	median, muscular, nutrient	deep muscles of front of forearm, radius, ulna
interosseous a., common *a. interossea communis*	ulnar a., immediately distal to tuberosity of radius	posterior and anterior interosseous	deep muscles of back of forearm, radius, ulna
interosseous a., posterior dorsal interosseous a. *a. interossea posterior*	common interosseous a.	recurrent interosseous	deep muscles of back of forearm
interosseous a.'s, palmar		see metacarpal arteries, palmar	
interosseous a., recurrent *a. interossea recurrens*	posterior interosseous a.	none	back of elbow joint
intestinal a.'s (12–15 in number) *aa. jejunales et ilei* *aa. intestinales*	superior mesenteric a.	none	jejunum, ileum
labial a., inferior *a. labialis inferior*	facial a. near angle of mouth	none	labial glands, mucous membrane, muscles of lower lip
labial a., superior *a. labialis superior*	facial a.	septal, alar	upper lip, nasal septum, ala of nose
labyrinthine a. internal auditory a. *a. labyrinthi*	basilar a. or anterior inferior cerebellar a.	vestibular, cochlear	inner ear
lacrimal a. *a. lacrimalis*	ophthalmic a. close to optic canal	lateral palpebral, zygomatic, recurrent meningeal, long posterior ciliary, muscular	lacrimal gland, conjunctiva, superior and lateral recti muscles, cheek, ciliary processes, eyelids

artery ■ artery

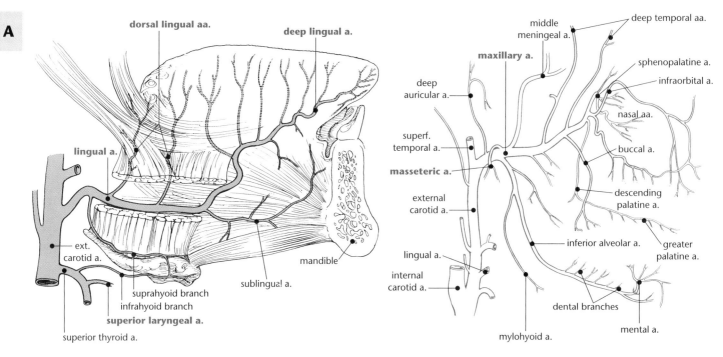

dorsal lingual aa. · deep lingual a. · lingual a. · ext. carotid a. · suprahyoid branch · infrahyoid branch · **superior laryngeal a.** · superior thyroid a. · sublingual a. · mandible

middle meningeal a. · deep temporal aa. · **maxillary a.** · deep auricular a. · superf. temporal a. · **masseteric a.** · external carotid a. · lingual a. · internal carotid a. · mylohyoid a. · sphenopalatine a. · infraorbital a. · nasal aa. · buccal a. · descending palatine a. · inferior alveolar a. · greater palatine a. · dental branches · mental a.

ARTERY	ORIGIN	BRANCHES	DISTRIBUTION
laryngeal a., inferior *a. laryngea inferior*	inferior thyroid a.	none	muscles of larynx, mucous membrane of larynx
laryngeal a., superior *a. laryngea superior*	superior thyroid a. (occasionally from external carotid a.)	none	muscles, mucous membrane, and glands of larynx
lienal a.		see splenic artery	
lingual a. *a. lingualis*	external carotid a.	suprahyoid, dorsal lingual, sublingual, deep lingual	muscles and mucosa of tongue, sublingual gland, gingiva, tonsil, epiglottis
lingual a., deep ranine a. *a. profunda liguae*	lingual a. (terminal portion)	none	intrinsic lingual muscles, lingual mucosa
lingual a.'s, dorsal *a. lingualis, rami dorsales*	lingual a.	none	mucous membrane of posterior part of tongue; palatoglossal arch, tonsil, epiglottis, soft palate
lumbar a.'s (four to five in number) *aa. lumbales*	abdominal aorta	dorsal, spinal	lumbar vertebrae, back muscles, abdominal wall
lumbar a., lowest *a. lumbalis ima*	median sacral a.	none	sacrum, iliac muscle
malleolar a., anterior lateral external malleolar a. *a. malleolaris lateralis anterior*	anterior tibial a.	none	lateral side of ankle
malleolar a., anterior medial internal malleolar a. *a. malleolaris medialis anterior*	anterior tibial a.	none	medial side of ankle
malleolar a., posterior medial internal malleolar a. *a. malleolaris medialis posterior*	posterior tibial	none	medial side of ankle
mammary a., external		see thoracic artery, lateral	
mammary a., internal		see thoracic artery, internal	
mandibular a.		see alveolar artery, inferior	
masseteric a. *a. masseterica*	maxillary a.	none	masseter muscle
maxillary a. internal maxillary a. deep facial a. *a. maxillaris*	external carotid a.	*mandibular portion:* deep auricular, anterior tympanic, inferior alveolar, middle meningeal, accessory	ear, teeth, cranial dura mater, trigeminal ganglion, temporal, masseter, buccinator, and eye muscles, lacrimal gland, palatine

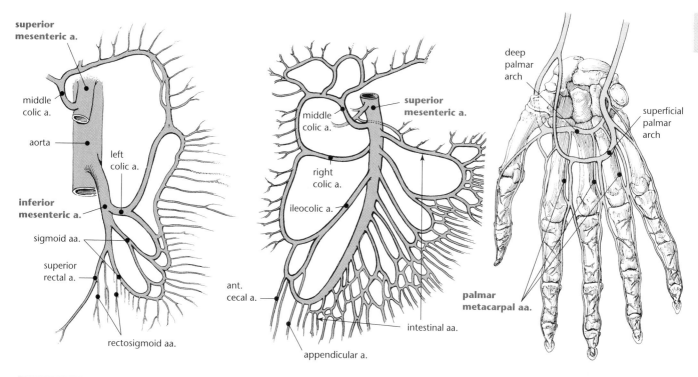

superior
mesenteric a.

middle
colic a.

aorta

left
colic a.

inferior
mesenteric a.

sigmoid aa.

superior
rectal a.

rectosigmoid aa.

middle
colic a.

superior
mesenteric a.

right
colic a.

ileocolic a.

ant.
cecal a.

intestinal aa.

appendicular a.

deep
palmar
arch

superficial
palmar
arch

palmar
metacarpal aa.

ARTERY	ORIGIN	BRANCHES	DISTRIBUTION
maxillary a. (cont'd)		meningeal; *pterygoid portion:* deep temporal, pterygoid, masseteric, buccal; *pterygopalatine portion:* posterior superior alveolar, infraorbital, descending palatine, artery of the pterygoid canal, pharyngeal, sphenopalatine	tonsil, soft palate, upper pharynx, auditory tube, nasal cavity, sinuses, mandible, maxilla, gums, temporomandibular joint
maxillary a., external		see facial artery	
maxillary a., internal		see maxillary artery	
median a. *aa. mediana*	anterior interosseous a.	none	accompanies and supplies median nerve to palm
medullary a.'s *a. medullares*	vertebral a. and its branches	none	medulla oblongata
meningeal a., anterior *a. meningea anterior*	anterior ethmoidal a. or internal carotid a.	none	dura mater of anterior cranial fossa
meningeal a., middle *a. meningea media*	maxillary a.	frontal, parietal, petrosal, superior tympanic, ganglionic, temporal	cranial bones, dura mater, tensor tympani muscle, trigeminal ganglion, orbit, tympanic cavity
meningeal a., posterior *a. meningea posterior*	ascending pharyngeal a.	none	bone and dura mater of posterior cranial fossa
mesenteric a., inferior *a. mesenterica inferior*	abdominal aorta at level of L3 or L4	left colic, sigmoid, superior rectal	transverse, descending, and sigmoid colon, upper part of rectum
mesentric a., superior *a. mesenterica superior*	abdominal aorta one cm below celiac trunk	inferior pancreaticoduodenal, intestinal, ileocolic, right colic, middle colic	small intestine, proximal half of colon
metacarpal a.'s dorsal (three in number) *aa. metacarpeae dorsales*	dorsal carpal branch or radial a.	dorsal digital	back of fingers
metacarpal a.'s, palmar palmar interosseous a.'s. *aa. metacarpeae palmares*	deep palmar arch	none	interosseous muscles, metacarpal bones, second, third, and fourth lumbrical muscles
metatarsal a., first dorsal *a. metatarsalis dorsalis I*	dorsal a. of foot	branch to medial side of great toe, branch to adjoining sides of the second and great toes	medial border of great toe and adjoining sides of great and second toes

A

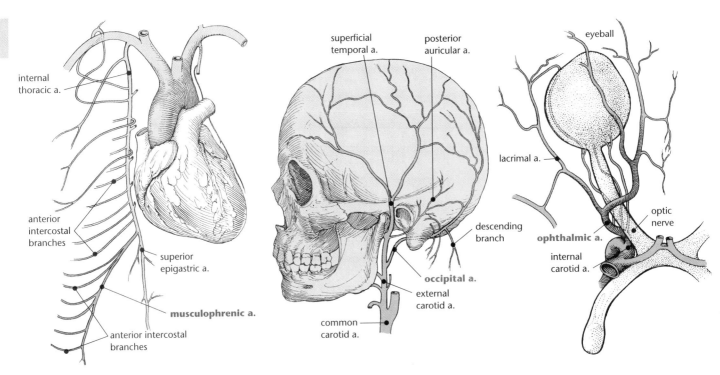

internal thoracic a.

superficial temporal a.

posterior auricular a.

eyeball

lacrimal a.

anterior intercostal branches

superior epigastric a.

descending branch

occipital a.

external carotid a.

common carotid a.

musculophrenic a.

anterior intercostal branches

optic nerve

ophthalmic a.

internal carotid a.

ARTERY	ORIGIN	BRANCHES	DISTRIBUTION
metatarsal a.'s, plantar (four in number) digital a.'s of foot, common *aa. metatarsales plantares*	plantar arch	plantar digital, anterior perforating	plantar surface and adjacent sides of toes
musculophrenic a. *a. musculophrenica*	internal thoracic a.	anterior intercostal	diaphragm, seventh, eighth, and ninth intercostal spaces, pericardium, abdominal muscles
mylohyoid a. *a. mylohyoideus*	inferior alveolar a.	none	mylohyoid muscle
nasal a., dorsal *a. dorsalis nasi*	ophthalmic a.	none	skin of nose, lacrimal sac
nasal a., lateral *a. nasalis lateralis*	facial a.	none	lateral nasal wall
nasal a., posterior lateral *a. nasalis posterioris lateralis*	sphenopalatine a.	none	frontal, ethmoidal, maxillary, and sphenoid sinuses
nasal a., posterior septal *a. nasalis posterioris septi*	sphenopalatine a.	none	nasal septum
nutrient a. of fibula *a. nutricia fibulae*	peroneal a.	none	substance of fibula
nutrient a.'s of humerus *aa. nutriciae humeri*	deep brachial a. about middle of arm	none	substance of humerus
nutrient a. of tibia (largest nutrient a. of bone in body) *a. nutricia tibiae*	posterior tibial a.	none	substance of tibia
obturator a. *a. obturatoria*	internal iliac a.	pubic, acetabular, obturator, anterior, posterior, vesical	bladder, ilium, pelvic muscles, hip joint
occipital a. *a. occipitalis*	external carotid a.	muscular, occipital, sternocleidomastoid, auricular, meningeal, descending, terminal	dura mater, diploë, mastoid air cells, muscles of neck and scalp
ophthalmic a. *a. ophthalmica*	internal carotid a.	*orbital portion:* lacrimal, supraorbital, posterior ethmoidal, anterior ethmoidal, medial palpebral supratrochlear, dorasl nasal;	orbit and surrounding parts
		ocular portion: central artery of the retina, short posterior ciliary, long posterior ciliary, anterior ciliary, muscular	muscles and bulb of the eye

artery ■ artery

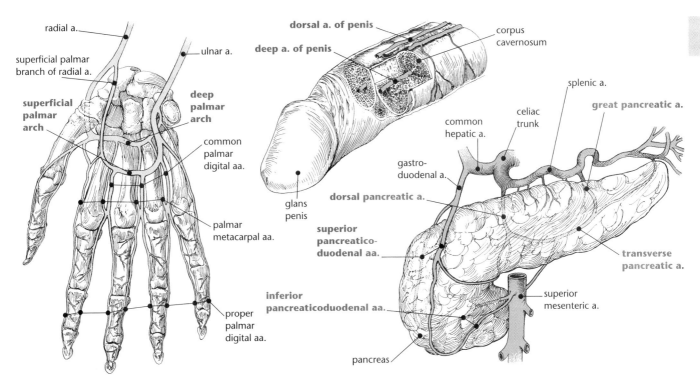

ARTERY	ORIGIN	BRANCHES	DISTRIBUTION
ovarian a.'s *aa. ovaricae*	ventral surface of abdominal aorta slightly below the renal a.'s at level of L2	ureteric, capsular, tubal; anastomoses with uterine a.	ovary, ureter, uterus, round ligament, skin of labium majus
palatine a., ascending *a. palatina ascendens*	facial a.	none	soft palate, palatine glands, auditory tube
palatine a., descending *a. palatina descendens*	maxillary a.	greater palatine, lesser palatine	soft palate, hard palate, tonsil, gums, palatine glands
palatine a., greater *a. palatina major*	descending palatine a.	none	hard palate, gums, palatine glands
palatine a.'s lesser *aa. palatina minores*	descending palatine a.	none	soft palate, palatine tonsil
palmar arch, deep *arcus palmaris profundus*	radial a.	palmar metacarpal; anastomoses with deep palmar branch of ulnar	carpal extremities of metacarpal bones, interosseous muscles
palmar arch, superficial *arcus palmaris superficialis*	ulnar a.	common palmar digital	palm, fingers
palpebral a.'s, lateral *aa. palpebrales laterales*	lacrimal a.	superior, inferior	eyelids, conjunctiva
palpebral a.'s, medial *aa. palpebrales mediales*	ophthalmic a. near the pulley of the superior oblique muscle	superior, inferior	eyelids, conjunctiva, nasolacrimal duct
pancreatic a., dorsal *a. pancreatica dorsalis*	splenic a.	right, left (inferior pancreatic)	pancreas
pancreatic a., great *a. pancreatica magna*	splenic a.	none	pancreas
pancreatic a., inferior *a. pancreatica inferior*	dorsal pancreatic a.	none	pancreas, greater omentum
pancreaticoduodenal a., inferior duodenal a. *a. pancreaticoduodenalis inferior*	superior mesenteric a. or from its first intestinal branch	anterior, posterior	head of pancreas, descending and inferior parts of duodenum
pancreaticoduodenal a., superior *a. pancreaticoduodenalis superior*	gastroduodenal a.	ventral and dorsal pancreaticoduodenal arcade	pancreas, three parts of duodenum
penis, deep a. of a. of corpus cavernosum *a. profunda penis*	internal pudendal a.	none	corpus cavernosum of penis
penis, dorsal a. of *a. dorsalis penis*	internal pudendal a.	none	glans and prepuce of penis, integument and fibrous sheath of corpus cavernosum

artery ■ artery

ARTERY	ORIGIN	BRANCHES	DISTRIBUTION
perforating a.'s *aa. perforantes*	deep femoral a.	first, second, and third perfo-rating	back of thigh, femur, buttock
pericardiacophrenic a. *a. pericardiacophrenica*	internal thoracic a.	none	diaphragm, pericardium, pleura
perineal a. superficial perineal a. *a. perinealis*	internal pudendal a.	transverse perineal, posterior scrotal/labial	perineum, external genitalia, bulbocavernous and ischio-cavernous muscles
peroneal a. fibular a. *a. peronea*	posterior tibial a.	muscular, nutrient (fibula), perforating, communicating, posterior lateral malleolar, lateral calcaneal	soleus and other deep calf muscles, lateral side and back of ankle and heel
pharyngeal a., ascending *a. pharyngea ascendens*	external carotid a.	pharyngeal, palatine, prever-tebral, inferior tympanic, posterior meningeal	wall of pharynx, soft palate, tonsil, ear, meninges, muscles of back of head and neck
phrenic a.'s phrenic a.'s, inferior diaphragmatic a., inferior *aa. phrenicae*	abdominal aorta or celiac trunk	superior suprarenal, anterior, lateral, recurrent	diaphragm, adrenal gland
phrenic a.'s, superior *aa. phrenicae superiores*	thoracic aorta	none	diaphragm
plantar a., deep communicating a. *ramus plantaris profundus*	dorsal a. foot	first plantar metatarsal; with lateral plantar a., forms plan-tar arch	undersurface and adjacent sides of first and second toes
plantar a., lateral *a. plantaris lateralis*	posterior tibial a.	calcaneal, muscular, cuta-neous; continues to form plantar arch by uniting with deep plantar branch of the dorsal artery of foot	muscles of foot, skin of toes and lateral side of foot
plantar a., medial internal plantar a. *a. plantaris medialis*	posterior tibial a.	deep, superficial	flexor muscle of toes, abduc-tor muscle of great toe, skin of inner side of sole
plantar arch *arcus plantaris*	lateral plantar a.	perforating, plantar metatarsal	interosseous muscles, toes, sole of foot
popliteal a. *a. poplitea*	continuation of femoral a. at the adductor hiatus	muscular, sural, cutaneous, medial superior genicular, lateral superior genicular, middle genicular, medial in-ferior genicular, lateral infe-rior genicular; it divides at the distal border of the popliteus and continues as anterior and posterior tibial arteries	muscles of thigh and calf in region of knee, femur, patella, and tibia
princeps pollicis a.		see principal artery of thumb	
principal a. of thumb princeps pollicis a. *a. princeps pollicis*	radial a.	radial a. of index finger, nu-trient	sides of thumb, dorsal in-terosseous muscles of hand, lateral side of index finger
profunda a., inferior		see collateral artery, superior ulnar	
profunda a., superior		see brachial artery, deep	
a. profunda brachii		see brachial artery, deep	
profunda femoris a.		see femoral artery, deep	
profunda linguae a.		see lingual artery, deep	
a. of pterygoid canal vidian a. *a. canalis pterygoidei*	maxillary a. or internal carotid a.	pharyngeal, tubal	sphenoid sinus, upper phar-ynx, auditory tube, and tym-panic cavity
pudendal a.'s, external external pudic a.'s *aa. pudendae externae*	femoral a.	anterior scrotal or anterior labial; inguinal	skin of scrotum and perineum in male; labium major and perineum in female; skin of lower abdomen
pudendal a., internal *a. pudenda interna*	internal iliac a.	muscular, inferior rectal, per-ineal, artery of the bulb, ure-thral, deep artery of the pe-nis or clitoris, dorsal artery of the penis or clitoris	muscles of perineum, anal canal, external genitalia

artery ■ artery

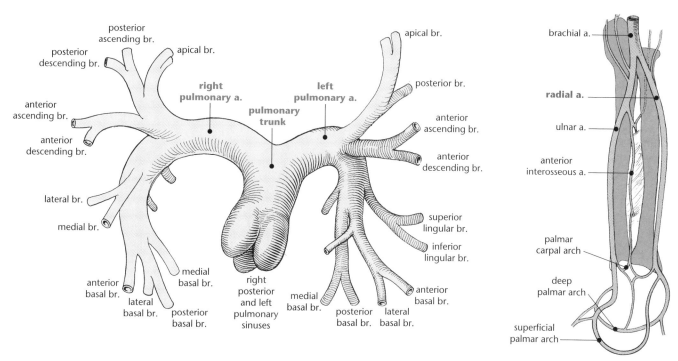

posterior ascending br. · posterior descending br. · apical br. · apical br. · right pulmonary a. · left pulmonary a. · posterior br. · anterior ascending br. · pulmonary trunk · anterior ascending br. · anterior descending br. · anterior descending br. · lateral br. · superior lingular br. · medial br. · inferior lingular br. · right posterior and left pulmonary sinuses · anterior basal br. · medial basal br. · medial basal br. · lateral basal br. · posterior basal br. · anterior basal br. · lateral basal br. · posterior basal br. · lateral basal br.

brachial a. · radial a. · ulnar a. · anterior interosseous a. · palmar carpal arch · deep palmar arch · superficial palmar arch

A

ARTERY	ORIGIN	BRANCHES	DISTRIBUTION
pulmonary a., left *a. pulmonalis sinistra*	pulmonary trunk	branches named according to the segment which they supply; e.g., apical segmental, anterior descending segmental	left lung
pulmonary a., right *a. pulmonalis dextra*	pulmonary trunk	branches named according to the segment which they supply; e.g., apical segmental, anterior descending segmental	right lung
pulmonary trunk *truncus pulmonalis*	conus of right ventricle	right and left pulmonary	lungs
radial a. *a. radialis*	brachial a.	*forearm group;* recurrent radial, muscular; *wrist group:* palmar carpal, superficial palmar, dorsal carpal; *hand group;* first dorsal metacarpal, principal a. of thumb, radial a. of index finger, deep palmar arch, palmar metacarpal, perforating, recurrent	muscles of forearm and hand, radius, skin of back of hand and palmar surface of thumb, outer aspect of index finger, intercarpal articulations
radial a. of index finger radialis indicis a. *a. radialis indicis*	radial a.	none	radial (lateral) side of index finger
radialis indicis a.		see radial artery of index finger	
ranine a.		see lingual artery, deep	
rectal a., inferior inferior hemorrhoidal a. *a. rectalis inferior*	internal pudendal a.	none	muscles and skin of anal region, rectum, external sphincter muscle
rectal a., middle middle hemorrhoidal a. *a. rectalis media*	internal iliac a.	vagina in females	rectum, prostate, seminal vesicles, vagina
rectal a., superior superior hemorrhoidal a. *a. rectalis superior*	continuation of inferior mesenteric a.	superior rectal artery branches; anastomoses with middle and inferior rectal arteries	rectum
recurrent a., anterior tibial *a. recurrens tibialis anterior*	anterior tibial a.	none	front and sides of knee joint, anterior tibial muscle
recurrent a., anterior ulnar *a. recurrens ulnaris, ramus anterior*	ulnar a., immediately distal to elbow joint	anterior, posterior	brachial and round pronator muscles
recurrent a., posterior tibial *a. recurrens tibialis posterior*	anterior tibial a.	none	tibiofibular joint, knee joint, popliteus muscle

artery ■ artery

ARTERY	ORIGIN	BRANCHES	DISTRIBUTION
recurrent a., posterior ulnar *a. recurrens ulnaris, ramus posterior*	ulnar a.	none	elbow joint and neighboring muscles and skin
recurrent a., radial *a. recurrens radialis*	radial a., immediately distal to elbow	none	elbow joint, supinator, brachioradial, and brachial muscles
recurrent a., ulnar *a. recurrens ulnaris*	ulnar a.	anterior, posterior	brachial and round pronator muscles
renal a. *a. renalis*	abdominal aorta at about the level of L1	inferior suprarenal, ureteral, anterior, posterior	kidney, adrenal gland, ureter
retroduodenal a.'s *aa. retroduodenales*	gastroduodenal a., just above level of duodenum	pancreatic, duodenal	first two parts of duodenum, head of pancreas, bile duct
sacral a.'s, lateral *aa. sacrales laterales*	internal iliac a.	superior and inferior spinal branches	muscles and skin on dorsal surface of sacrum; sacral canal
sacral a., middle coccygeal a. *a. sacralis mediana*	dorsal side of aorta, slightly above its bifurcation	middle sacral artery branches; anastomose with lumbar branch of iliolumbar and lateral sacral arteries	rectum, sacrum, coccyx
scapular circumflex a. *a. circumflexa scapulae*	subscapular a.	none	subscapular, teres major, teres minor, and deltoid muscles; shoulder joint, long head of triceps
scapular a., dorsal *a. scapularis dorsalis*	thyrocervical trunk, transverse cervical a. or subclavian a.	muscular	levator muscle of scapula, latissimus dorsi, trapezius, and rhomboid muscles
scapular a., transverse		see suprascapular artery	
sciatic a.		see gluteal artery, inferior	
sigmoid a.'s *aa. sigmoideae*	inferior mesenteric	branches of sigmoid arteries; anastomose cranially with left colic artery and caudally with superior rectal artery	caudal part of descending colon, iliac colon, sigmoid (pelvic colon)
spermatic a., external		see cremasteric artery	
spermatic a.'s internal		see testicular arteries	
sphenopalatine a. nasopalatine a. *a. sphenopalatina*	maxillary a.	posterior lateral nasal, posterior septal	frontal, maxillary, ethmoidal, and sphenoidal sinuses, nasal septum, nasopharynx
spinal a., anterior ventral spinal a. *a. spinalis anterior*	vertebral a. near termination	central	anterior side of medulla oblongata and spinal cord, filum terminale, meninges
spinal a., posterior dorsal spinal a. *a. spinalis posterior*	posterior inferior cerebellar a. or vertebral a. at side of medulla oblongata	dorsal, ventral	medulla oblongata, posterior part of spinal cord, and cauda equina, meninges, fourth ventricle
splenic a. lienal a. *a. lienalis*	celiac trunk	pancreatic, short gastric, left gastroomental, splenic, dorsal pancreatic, caudal pancreatic, great pancreatic	spleen, pancreas, stomach, greater omentum
sternocleidomastoid a. sternomastoid a. *a. sternocleidomastoidea*	occipital a. close to its commencement	none	sternocleidomastoid muscle
stylomastoid a. *a. stylomastoidea*	posterior auricular a.	mastoid, stapedial, posterior tympanic	middle ear chamber, stapes, stapedius muscle, mastoid cells, semicircular canals
subclavian a. *a. subclavia*	*right side:* brachiocephalic trunk; *left side:* arch of aorta	vertebral, thyrocervical, internal thoracic, costocervical, dorsal scapular; it becomes the axillary artery at the outer border of the first rib	neck, thoracic wall, muscles of upper arm and shoulder, spinal cord and brain
subcostal a. 12th thoracic a. *a. subcostalis*	thoracic aorta	dorsal, spinal	upper abdominal wall below twelfth rib

artery ■ artery

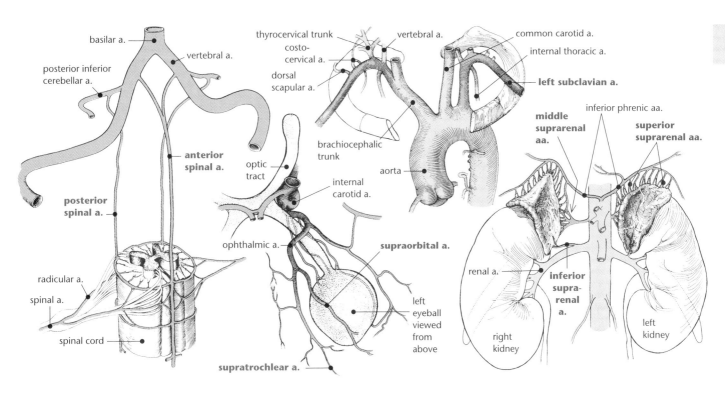

ARTERY	ORIGIN	BRANCHES	DISTRIBUTION
sublingual a. *a. sublingualis*	lingual a.	gingival, submental	sublingual gland, mylohyoid, geniohyoid, and genioglossus muscles; mucous membrane of mouth and gums
submental a. *a submentalis*	facial a. (occasionally external maxillary a.)	superficial, deep	muscles in region of chin and lower lip, submandibular gland
subscapular a. *a. subscapularis*	axillary a.	circumflex scapular, thoracodorsal	scapular region, shoulder joint
superficial perineal a.		see perineal artery	
supraorbital a. frontal a. *a. supraorbitalis*	ophthalmic a. as it crosses the optic nerve	superficial, deep	skin, muscles, and pericranium of forehead; superior rectus muscle of eyeball, levator muscle of upper eyelid, diplöe
suprarenal a., inferior *a. suprarenalis inferior*	renal a.	none	adrenal gland
suprarenal a.'s, middle middle capsular a.'s *aa. suprarenales mediae*	abdominal aorta, at level of superior mesenteric a.	anastomoses with suprarenal branches of inferior phrenic and renal arteries	adrenal gland
suprarenal a., superior *a. suprarenalis superior*	inferior phrenic a.	none	adrenal gland
suprascapular a. transverse scapular a. *a. suprascapularis*	thyrocervical trunk	acromial, suprasternal articular, nutrient, supraspinous, infraspinous	clavicle, scapula, skin of chest, skin over acromion, acromioclavicular and shoulder joints, supraspinous and intraspinous muscles
supratrochlear a. frontal a. *a. supratrochlearis* *a. frontalis*	ophthalmic a.	none	skin, muscles, and pericranium of forehead
sural a.'s inferior muscular a.'s *aa. surales*	popliteal a. opposite the knee joint	none	gastrocnemius, soleus, and plantar muscles; neighboring skin
tarsal a., lateral tarsal a. *a. tarsea lateralis*	dorsal a. of foot	none	muscles and articulations of tarsus

artery ■ artery

ARTERY	ORIGIN	BRANCHES	DISTRIBUTION
tarsal a.'s, medial *aa. tarseae mediales*	dorsal a. of foot	none	skin and joints of medial border of foot
temporal a.'s, deep (two in number) *aa. temporales profundae*	maxillary a.	none	temporal muscle
temporal a., middle *a. temporalis media*	superficial temporal a. immediately above zygomatic arch	none	temporal muscle
temporal a., superficial *a. temporalis superficialis*	external carotid a.	transverse facial, middle temporal, zygomaticoorbital, anterior auricular, frontal, parietal, parotid	temporal, masseter, frontal, and orbicular muscles; external auditory canal, auricle, skin of face and scalp, parotid gland, temporomandibular joint
testicular a.'s spermatic a.'s, internal *aa. testiculares*	ventral surface of abdominal aorta, slightly caudal to the renal a.'s	ureteral, epididymal, cremasteric (anastomose with ductus deferens a.)	epididymis, testis, ureter, cremaster muscle
thoracic a., highest *a. thoracica suprema*	axillary a. or thoracoacromial a.	none	pectoral muscles, parietes of the thorax, anterior serratus and intercostal muscles
thoracic a., internal internal mammary a. *a. thoracica interna*	subclavian a.	pericardiacophrenic, mediastinal, thymic, sternal, anterior intercostal, perforating, musculophrenic, superior epigastric	anterior thoracic wall, diaphragm, structures in mediastinum such as pericardium and thymus gland
thoracic a., lateral long thoracic a. external mammary a. *a. thoracica lateralis*	thoracoacromial, subscapular, or axillary a.	lateral mammary (in female)	pectoral, anterior serratus, and subscapular muscles; axillary lymph nodes, mammary gland (in female)
thoracic a., twelfth		see subcostal artery	
thoracoacromial a. acromiothoracic a. *a. thoracoacromialis*	axillary a.	pectoral, acromial, clavicular, deltoid	pectoral, deltoid, and subclavius muscles; mammary gland, coracoid process, sternoclavicular joint, acromion
thoracodorsal a. *a. thoracodorsalis*	subscapular a.	none	subscapular, latissimus dorsi, anterior serratus, and intercostal muscles
thyrocervical trunk *truncus thyrocervicalis*	first portion of subclavian a.	inferior thyroid, suprascapular, transverse cervical	thyroid gland, scapular region, deep neck muscles
thyroid a., inferior *a. thyroidea inferior*	thyrocervical trunk	inferior laryngeal, tracheal, pharyngeal, esophageal, ascending cervical, muscular, glandular	larynx, trachea, esophagus, pharynx, thyroid gland, neck muscles
thyroid a., lowest *a. thyroidea ima*	arch of aorta or brachiocephalic trunk	none	thyroid gland
thyroid a., superior *a. thyroidea superior*	external carotid a.	infrahyoid, sternocleidomastoid, superior laryngeal, cricothyroid	muscles and mucosa of larynx, pharynx, esophagus; thyroid gland, muscles attached to thyroid cartilage and hyoid bone; sternocleidomastoid and neighboring muscles and integument
tibial a., anterior *a. tibialis anterior*	popliteal a. at bifurcation	posterior tibial recurrent, fibular, anterior tibial recurrent, muscular, anterior medial malleolar, anterior lateral malleolar; continues as dorsal a. of foot at ankle joint	muscles of leg; knee joint, ankle, foot, skin of front of leg
tibial a., posterior *a. tibialis posterior*	popliteal a.	peroneal, nutrient (tibial), muscular, posterior medial malleolar, communicating, medial calcaneal, medial plantar, lateral plantar	muscles and bones of leg; ankle joint, foot
tibial recurrent a., anterior *a. recurrens tibialis anterior*	anterior tibial a.	none	anterior tibial muscle, knee joint, patella, long extensor muscle of toes
tibial recurrent a., posterior *a. recurrens tibialis posterior*	anterior tibial a.	none	popliteal muscle, knee joint, tibiofibular joint

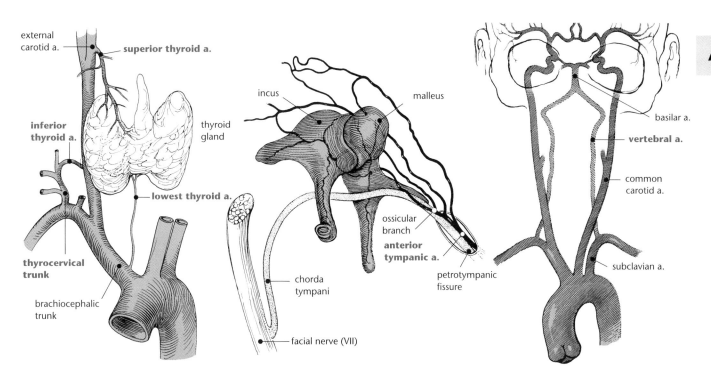

ARTERY	ORIGIN	BRANCHES	DISTRIBUTION
tympanic a., anterior tympanic a. *a. tympanica anterior*	maxillary a.	posterior, superior, ossicular	tympanic membrane, middle ear chamber, ossicles
tympanic a., inferior *a. tympanica inferior*	ascending pharyngeal a.	none	medial wall of the middle ear chamber
tympanic a., posterior *a. tympanica posterior*	stylomastoid a.	none	middle ear chamber, posterior part of tympanic membrane
tympanic a., superior *a. tympanica superior*	middle meningeal a.	none	middle ear chamber, tensor tympani muscle
ulnar a. *a. ulnaris*	brachial a., slightly distal to elbow	*forearm portion:* anterior ulnar recurrent, posterior ulnar recurrent, common interosseous, muscular; *wrist portion:* palmar carpal, dorsal carpal; *hand portion:* deep palmar, superficial palmar arch, common palmar digital	hand, wrist, forearm
umbilical a. *a. umbilicalis*	internal iliac a.	ductus deferens, superior vesical; continues as lateral umbilical ligament	urinary bladder, ureter, testes, siminal vesicles, ductus deferens
urethral a. *a. urethralis*	internal pudendal a.	none	urethra, corpus cavernosum of penis
uterine a. fallopian a. *a. uterina*	medial surface of internal iliac a.	cervical, ovarian, tubal, vaginal, ligamentous, ureteric	uterus, uterine tube, round ligament, part of vagina, ovary
vaginal a. *a. vaginalis*	internal iliac a. or uterine a.	rectal, vesical, vestibular	vagina, fundus of urinary bladder and part of rectum, vestibular bulb
vertebral a. *a. vertebralis*	subclavian a.	*cervical portion:* spinal, muscular; *cranial portion:* meningeal, posterior spinal, anterior spinal, posterior inferior cerebellar, medullary	bodies of vertebrae, deep muscles of neck, falx cerebelli, spinal cord, cerebellum, brain stem
vesical a., inferior *a. vesicalis inferior*	internal iliac a.	prostatic in males	fundus of bladder, prostate, seminal vesicles
vesical a.'s, superior *aa. vesicales superiores*	umbilical a.	ureteric	ureter, bladder, urachus
vidian a.		see pterygoid canal, artery of	
zygomaticoorbital a. *a. zygomaticoorbitalis*	superficial temporal a. (occasionally from the middle temporal a.)	none	orbicular muscle of eye, lateral portion of orbit

artery ■ artery

arthralgia (ar-thral'je-ah) Pain in a joint. Also called arthrodynia.

arthrectomy (ar-threk'to-me) Removal of a joint.

arthritic (ar-thrit'ik) Relating to arthritis.

arthritides (ar-thrit'ĭ-dēz) Plural of arthritis.

arthritis (ar-thri'tis), pl. arthrit'ides Inflammation of a joint or joints.

    degenerative a. See osteoarthritis.

    gouty a. Arthritis associated with gout.

    hypertrophic a. See osteoarthritis.

    juvenile a., juvenile rheumatoid a. (JRA) Rheumatoid arthritis of childhood affecting one or a few large joints, with enlargement of the liver, spleen, and lymph nodes; may also involve the cervical spine or cause inflammation of the iris. Complete remission may occur at puberty. Also called Still's disease.

    Lyme a. Arthritis associated with Lyme disease and affecting large joints, especially the knee; marked by swelling and pain in the joint. The condition may become chronic. See also Lyme disease, under disease.

    pyogenic a. See suppurative arthritis.

    rheumatoid a. (RA) A chronic disease of unknown cause characterized by progressive inflammation of small joints, especially those of the fingers; marked by swelling, slow thickening of connective tissues, erosion of articular cartilage, and potential deformity and disability.

    suppurative a. Bacterial infection of a single large joint (e.g., hip or knee) usually following injury to the joint; characterized by swelling, redness, local warmth, and severe pain with restriction of movement; the joint cavity becomes filled with pus; most often caused by *Staphylococcus aureus* or, less often, by *Streptococcus pyogenes*, *Streptococcus pneumoniae*, and *Neisseria gonorrhoeae*. Also called pyogenic arthritis.

arthro-, arthr- Combining forms meaning joint; articulation.

arthrocele (ar'thro-sēl) **1.** Outpouching of the synovial membrane through the capsule of a joint. **2.** A swollen joint.

arthrocentesis (ar-thro-sen-te'sis) Puncture of a joint cavity and withdrawal of fluid with needle and syringe.

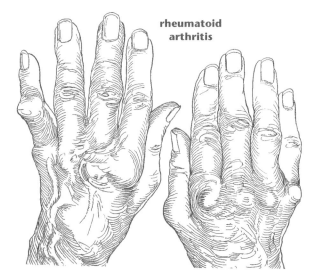

rheumatoid arthritis

arthrochondritis (ar-thro-kon-dri'tis) Inflammation of an articular cartilage.

arthrodesis (ar-thro-de'sis) Surgical fixation of a joint by obliterating the joint space and fusing the two bones so that no movement can take place. Also called artificial ankylosis.

arthrodia (ar-thro'de-ah) See plane joint, under joint.

arthrodynia (ar-thro-din'e-ah) See arthralgia.

arthrodysplasia (ar-thro-dis-pla'ze-ah) Abnormal development of one or more joints.

arthroendoscopy (ar-thro-en-dos'ko-pe) See arthroscopy.

arthrogram (ar'thro-gram) An x-ray image of a joint.

arthrography (ar-throg'rah-fe) The radiographic examination of a joint, usually the knee or shoulder, following injection of a water-soluble radiopaque material and/or air into the joint space. Arthrography outlines soft tissues (cartilage, ligaments, rotator cuff) not usually visible in ordinary x-ray images.

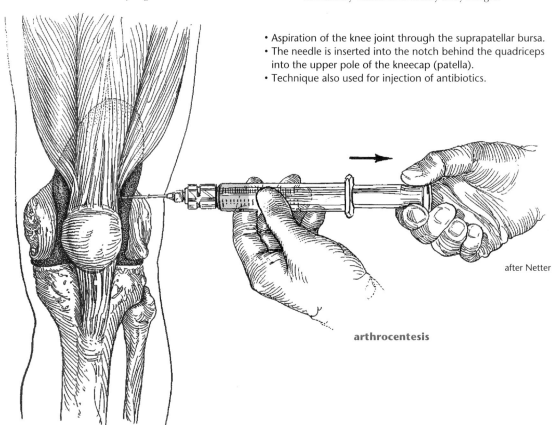

- Aspiration of the knee joint through the suprapatellar bursa.
- The needle is inserted into the notch behind the quadriceps into the upper pole of the kneecap (patella).
- Technique also used for injection of antibiotics.

after Netter

arthrocentesis

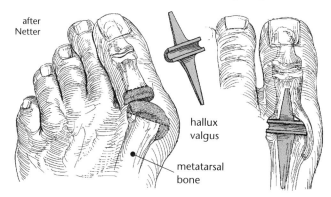

arthroplasty

after Netter

hallux valgus

metatarsal bone

arthrogryposis (ar-thro-grĭ-po'sis) Fixation of the limb joints, most often in a flexed position.

congenital multiple a. Congenital rigidity or contraction of several joints of the limbs with atrophy of associated structures. Also called amyoplasia congenita.

arthrometer (ar-throm'ĕ-ter) See goniometer.

arthropathy (ar-throp'ah-the) Any disease of a joint.

arthroplasty (ar'thro-plas-te) Surgical restoration of joint function either by repairing damaged structures or by inserting an artificial joint.

arthropod (ar'thro-pod) Any of several invertebrate animals (phylum Arthropoda), including spiders, mites, ticks, centipedes. Some transmit disease-causing microorganisms to humans.

arthropyosis (ar-thro-pi-o'sis) Pus formation within a joint.

arthroscope (ar'thro-skōp) A fiberoptic instrument especially designed and used with a light system for viewing the interior of a joint.

arthroscopy (ar-thros'ko-pe) Visual examination of the interior of a joint (most commonly the knee) with an arthroscope after injecting sterile saline solution into the joint for better visualization; used to detect and diagnose joint disease, to monitor the progression of disease, and to perform surgery in a joint. Also called arthroendoscopy.

arthrosis (ar-thro'sis) A degenerative condition of a joint.

arthrosynovitis (ar-thro-sin-o-vi'tis) Inflammation of the synovial membrane, which surrounds a joint.

arthrotomy (ar-throt'o-me) Cutting into the cavity of a joint.

articular (ar-tik'u-lar) Relating to a joint.

articulate (ar-tik'u-lāt) 1. Having joints. 2. Capable of speaking in clear language. 3. To join or connect.

articulation (ar-tik-u-la'shun) 1. A joint between bones. 2. The production of speech sounds. 3. In dentistry, the contact relationship of upper and lower (maxillary and mandibular) teeth while in action. See also joint.

artifact (ar'tĭ-fakt) Any artificially or accidentally created change or addition, as in a histologic specimen or a radiographic image.

aryepiglottic (ar-e-ep-ĭ-glot'ik) Relating to the arytenoid cartilage in the neck and the epiglottis.

arytenoid (ar-ĕ-te'noid) Shaped like a ladle or jug; said of certain cartilages and muscles of the larynx.

arytenoidectomy (ar-ĕ-te-noid-ek'to-me) Removal of an arytenoid cartilage.

asbestos (as-bes'tos) An incombustible commercial product obtained from naturally occurring silicates (amosite, crocidolite, chrysotile). It has been widely used in the manufacture of insulation, roofing and flooring products, water and sewer pipes, brake linings, and flame retardants. Major health effects of asbestos exposure include pulmonary fibrosis and cancers of the respiratory tract and lining of the lungs and abdominal organs; mesothelioma is a tumor of the lining of the lungs that is closely tied to asbestos exposure. See also asbestosis; mesothelioma; bronchogenic carcinoma.

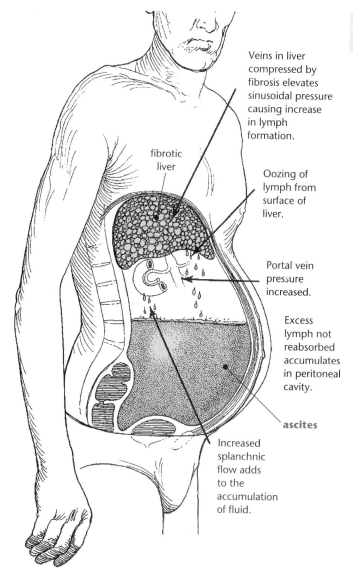

Veins in liver compressed by fibrosis elevates sinusoidal pressure causing increase in lymph formation.

fibrotic liver

Oozing of lymph from surface of liver.

Portal vein pressure increased.

Excess lymph not reabsorbed accumulates in peritoneal cavity.

ascites

Increased splanchnic flow adds to the accumulation of fluid.

asbestosis (as-bĕ-sto'sis) Disease characterized by diffuse thickening and scarring of lung tissue (pulmonary fibrosis) that is directly related to the duration and intensity of exposure to asbestos dust.

ascariasis (as-kah-ri'ah-sis) Infestation with the roundworm *Ascaris lumbricoides* involving a larval pulmonary stage and an adult intestinal stage.

ascaricide (as-kar'ĭ-sīd) An agent that kills roundworms of the genus *Ascaris*.

Ascaris (as'kah-ris) A genus of large roundworms parasitic in humans and other vertebrates.

A. lumbricoides A species parasitic in the small intestines of humans, especially children.

ascertainment (ah-ser-tān'ment) The finding and selection of families showing a tendency for some hereditary condition.

ascites (ah-si'tēz) Excessive accumulation of free serous fluid in the peritoneal cavity, causing distention of the abdomen. Also called hydroperitoneum; abdominal dropsy.

ascitic (ah-sit'ik) Relating to ascites.

asorbic acid (ah-skor'bik as'id) A white crystalline substance present in citrus fruits, green leafy vegetables, and tomatoes; used in the treatment and/or prevention of scurvy. Also called vitamin C.

-ase Suffix meaning enzyme; added to the name of the substance upon which it acts (e.g., proteinase).

asepsis (ah-sep'sis) Absence of disease-causing microorganism from a given environment.

aseptic (ah-sep'tik) Relating to asepsis. Also called sterile.

asexual (a-seks'u-al) Without sex; applied to a mode of reproduction, such as spore formation, budding, or fission.

asialia, asialism (ah-si-a'le-ah, ah-si'ah-lizm) Absence of, or diminished secretion of, saliva. Also called aptyalia; aptyalism.

asparaginase (as-par'ah-jin-ās) An enzyme that promotes the breakdown of asparagine to aspartic acid and ammonia. It has been used to treat leukemia.

asparagine (as-par'ah-jēn) (Asn) An amino acid that occurs in many plants (e.g., asparagus) and is not essential in the diet.

aspartame (ah-spar'tām) An artificial, low-calorie sweetener about 200 times sweeter than table sugar (sucrose).

aspartic acid (ah-spahr'tik as'id) One of the amino acids of proteins that is synthesized in the body and therefore not essential in the diet. It is found in sugarcane and sugar beet molasses.

aspergilloma (as-per-jil-o'mah) A mass formed in the lungs by colonization of the fungus *Aspergillus* and containing fibrin and inflammatory secretions; usually occurs in lung cavities formed by previous infections (e.g., tuberculosis) as a characteristic feature of aspergillosis. Also called fungus ball.

aspergillosis (as-per-jil-o'sis) Fungal disease caused by inhalation of aspergillus spores, especially *Aspergillus fumigatus*, a fungus found in old buildings and decaying plant material. Infection usually occurs in persons with compromised immune systems.

Aspergillus (as-per-jil'us) Genus of fungi (class Ascomycetes), some of which cause disease in humans.

aspermatogenesis (ah-sper-mah-to-jen'ĕ-sis) Absence of spermatozoa formation.

aspermatogenic (ah-sper-mah-to-jen'ik) Failing to produce spermatozoa.

aspermia (ah-sper'me-ah) Failure to produce or ejaculate sperm.

asphygmia (as-fig'me-ah) Temporary absence of the pulse.

asphyxia (as-fik'se-ah) Suffocation due to interference with the oxygen supply of the blood; may be caused by obstruction of the airway by a foreign body, a lack of oxygen in the air (e.g., within a plastic bag), or inhalation of a gas (e.g., carbon monoxide) that prevents the uptake of oxygen into the bloodstream.

    a. neonatorum Breathing failure of the newborn infant.

    perinatal a. Diminished oxygen supply to a baby at the time of birth, causing decreased fetal or newborn heart rate; it results in impaired exchange of respiratory gases, oxygen, and carbon dioxide and inadequate perfusion of the tissues and major organs; may be due to events occurring prior to delivery (maternal diabetes, preeclampsia, fetal heart abnormalities, post- or prematurity) or during labor and delivery (breech presentation, large fetal head in proportion to maternal pelvis, umbilical cord compression).

asphyxiant (as-fik'se-ant) Anything that suffocates.

asphyxiate (as-fik'se-āt) **1.** To induce suffocation. **2.** To undergo suffocation.

asphyxiation (as-fik-se-a'shun) The process of bringing about suffocation.

aspirate (as'pĭ-rāt) **1.** To withdraw (usually fluid) from a body cavity by suction. **2.** The withdrawn material.

aspiration (as-pĭ-ra'shun) **1.** Removal of material by suction. **2.** Intake of foreign material into the lungs while breathing.

    egg a. In *in vitro* fertilization, aspiration of preovulatory follicles from the ovary, performed approximately 34 hours after an injection of the hormone human chorionic gonadotropin (hCG), or 24 hours before the beginning of the natural burst of luteinizing hormone secretion (LH surge); may be performed under direct visualization with a laparoscope (laparoscopic aspiration) or under the guidance of an ultrasound scanner (ultrasound aspiration).

    endocervical a. Removal of mucus from the endocervical canal for microscopic examination of cast-off cells (exfoliative cytology) for diagnostic purposes.

    meconium a. Inhalation of meconium-contaminated amniotic fluid by an infant taking its first breath at birth, which may cause meconium blockage of the airways and lung damage.

aspirator (as-pĭ-ra'tor) Any apparatus used in removing material from body cavities by means of suction.

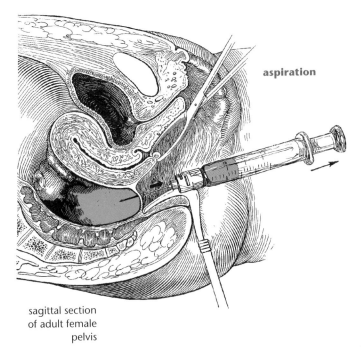

sagittal section
of adult female
pelvis

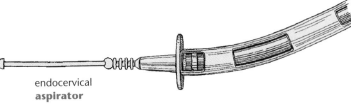

endocervical
aspirator

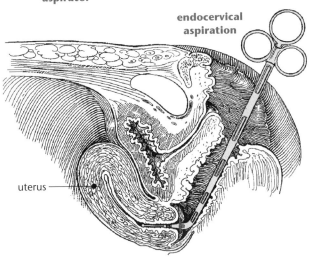

uterus

    vacuum a. Aspirator used to remove the product of conception from the uterine cavity.

aspirin (as'pĭ-rin) Acetylsalicylic acid; a widely used pharmaceutical product for reducing pain, fever, and inflammation.

asplenia (a-sple'ne-ah) Congenital absence of the spleen.

assault (ah-salt') An intentional act to make the victim apprehensive of immediate harmful or offensive bodily contact, even though contact may not actually occur.

    aggravated sexual a. See rape.

    sexual a. See rape.

assay (as-sa') Analysis to determine the presence of a substance, its quantity, or its effects on an organism.

    biological a. See bioassay.

    enzyme-linked immunosorbent a. (ELISA) A laboratory blood test employed in the diagnosis of infectious diseases (e.g., AIDS and hepatitis A and B). The antigen of interest is fixed to a solid-state immunosorbent and incubated in a medium containing a test antibody raised against the antigen; then a second incubation is conducted with an enzyme-tagged detector antibody raised against the test antibody; finally, a substrate is added, which is digested by the enzyme, producing a color that can be measured by spectrophotometry.

assessment (ah-ses′ment) Evaluation.

child abuse a. *(a)* Determination of the validity of a reported case of suspected child abuse or neglect through investigatory interviews with persons involved. *(b)* Determination of the treatment potential and treatment plan for confirmed cases of child abuse.

comprehensive geriatric a. A multidisciplinary evaluation in which the multiple problems of an older person are uncovered, described, and (if possible) explained and in which the resources and strengths of the person are cataloged, need for services determined, and a coordinated care plan developed to focus interventions on the person's problems. It includes physical, mental, social, economic, functional, and environmental evaluation. Frequently called functional assessment.

functional a. See comprehensive geriatric assessment.

assimilation (ah-sim-i-la′shun) 1. Incorporation of digested substances into the tissues. 2. The learning process in which new information is understood and absorbed into the framework of existing knowledge.

association (ah-so-se-a′shun) A relationship of persons, ideas, or emotions.

astasia (as-ta′zhe-ah) Inability to stand due to motor incoordination instead of paralysis.

astasia-abasia (as-ta′zhe-ah ah-ba′zhe-ah) Inability to stand or walk; the affected person collapses when attempting to walk, although coordinated leg movements can be performed when sitting; occurs as a symptom of a conversion disorder.

asteatosis (as-te-ah-to′sis) Deficient or arrested activity of sebaceous glands.

a. cutis Persistent dryness and scaliness of the skin, suggesting deficient sebaceous secretions.

aster (as′ter) A set of fibers (predominantly microtubules) radiating around each centriole of dividing cells.

astereognosis (ah-ster-e-og-no′sis) Inability to interpret the three-dimensional nature of objects when examined by touch, without the aid of vision. Also called stereoanesthesia.

asterion (as-te′re-on) A point on the surface of the skull (on either side) where three sutures (lambdoid, occipitomastoid, and parietomastoid) meet; used in skull measurements.

asterixis (as-ter-ik′sis) A slow flapping movement of the outstretched hands, seen in patients afflicted with metabolic disorders, especially those with impending hepatic coma. Also called flapping tremor; liver flap.

asthenia (as-the′ne-ah) Generalized loss of strength.

asthenopia (as-thĕ-no′pe-ah) General descriptive term denoting distress supposedly from prolonged use of the eyes; eyestrain.

asthenospermia (as-thĕ-no-sper′me-ah) Reduced motility of spermatozoa; one of the causes of infertility.

asthma (az′mah) A reversible respiratory condition marked by recurrent airflow obstruction, causing intermittent wheezing, breathlessness, and sometimes cough with phlegm production. When the term is used alone, it usually denotes bronchial asthma.

bronchial a. Recurrent acute narrowing of the large and small air passages within the lungs (bronchi and bronchioles), resulting in difficult breathing, intermittent wheezing, and coughing; due to spasm of bronchial smooth muscle, swelling of mucous membranes, and overproduction of thick, sticky mucus. Often simply called asthma.

cardiac a. Asthma caused by fluid collection in the lungs resulting from failure of the left ventricle of the heart.

extrinsic a. Bronchial asthma precipitated by inhalation of such allergens as pollen, mold, animal fur, dander, feathers, or house dust.

intrinsic a. Bronchial asthma due to a variety of nonspecific stimuli, including exercise (especially in cold temperatures), respiratory infections, tobacco smoke or other air pollutants, and aspirin.

occupational a. Asthma caused by inhalation of irritating particles, gases, or fumes from industrial processes. Provocative agents include wood and grain dusts; metal salts used in electroplating, jewelry manufacture, and production of fluorescent screens (e.g., platinum, nickel, chromium, cobalt, tungsten carbide): and chemical agents used in electronics, pesticides, polyurethane foams, synthetic varnishes, and as hardening agents for epoxy resins (e.g., toluene diisocyanate [TDI], trimellitic anhydride [TMA], and phthalic acid anhydride).

sulfite-induced a. (SIA) Severe respiratory distress precipitated by ingestion of chemicals (sulfites) that are commonly added to foods and drugs as preservatives and antioxidants.

astigmatic (as-tig-mat′ik) Relating to astigmatism.

astigmatism (ah-stig′mah-tizm) Faulty vision caused by defects in the curvature of the cornea, which prevent light rays entering the eye from focusing at a single point on the retina.

astigmatometer (as-tig-mah-tom′ĕ-ter) Instrument for measuring astigmatism.

astragalus (ah-strag′ah-lus) Obsolete term for talus.

astraphobia (as-trah-fo′be-ah) Abnormally exaggerated fear of lightning and thunder.

astringent (ah-strin′jent) 1. Causing contraction of tissues. 2. An agent that produces such action.

astroblast (as′tro-blast) An immature astrocyte.

astrocyte (as′tro-sīt) One of the cells constituting the supportive, nonneuronal system (neuroglia) of the brain and spinal cord; it is relatively large and has ample cytoplasm, microfilaments, and radiating processes; found in both white and gray matter.

astrocytoma (as-tro-si-to′mah) Malignant brain tumor primarily composed of white matter astrocytes; classified from I to IV depending on degree of malignancy and rate of growth.

astrocytosis (as-tro-si-to′sis) Proliferation of astrocytes adjacent to an area of injured tissue of the central nervous system.

astroglia (as-trog′le-ah) The astrocyte component of neuroglia considered as a whole.

astrokinetic (as-tro-ki-net′ik) In cytology, relating to the movements of the centrosome in a dividing cell.

asylum (ah-si′lum) Outmoded term for an institution for the care and shelter of those who are mentally ill. Now called psychiatric hospital; mental hospital.

asymptomatic (a-simp-to-mat′ik) Without symptoms (i.e., without indications of disease that are usually noticed by patients).

asynclitism (ah-sin′klĭ-tizm) In obstetrics, a situation during childbirth in which the sagittal suture of the fetal head is tilted either anteriorly or posteriorly, instead of being aligned with the pelvic planes of the mother.

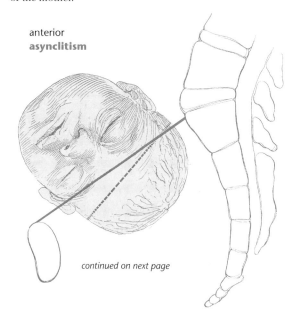

anterior
asynclitism

continued on next page

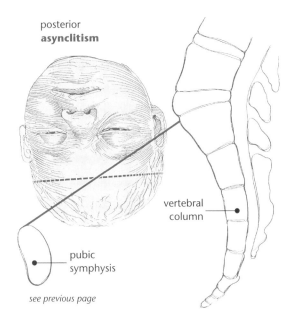

posterior
asynclitism

vertebral column

pubic symphysis

see previous page

asynergy (a-sin′er-je) Loss of coordination among parts of the body that normally work in unison.

asystole (ah-sis′to-le) Absence of a heartbeat; cardiac arrest.

atactilia (ah-tak-til′e-ah) Loss of the sense of touch.

ataractic (at-ah-rak′tik) 1. Having a tranquilizing effect. 2. A tranquilizing drug.

ataraxia (at-ah-rak′se-ah) Calmness; emotional tranquility.

atavism (at′ah-vizm) In genetics, the appearance of a heritable characteristic that was present in some remote ancestor but absent for several generations.

atavus (at′ah-vus) A characteristic or structure known to have been present in some distant ancestor but not commonly found in a contemporary organism. Also called throwback.

ataxia (ah-tak′se-ah) Loss of the coordinated muscular contractions required for the execution of smooth voluntary movement. Also called incoordination.

    cerebellar a. Ataxia caused by damage to the part of the brain concerned with coordination and equilibrium (the cerebellum), usually beginning between the ages of 30 and 50 years.

    Friedreich's a. See hereditary spinal ataxia.

    hereditary spinal a. An inherited (autosomal recessive) disorder often beginning with an unsteady gait in children between the ages of 5 and 15 years and usually progressing to speech impairment, lateral curvature of the spine, and paralysis of the lower extremities; marked by degeneration of the posterior and lateral columns of the spinal cord. Also called Friedreich's ataxia.

    locomotor a. See tabes dorsalis, under tabes.

ataxia-telangiectasia (ah-tak′se-ah tel-an-je-ek-ta′ze-ah) An inherited (autosomal recessive) multisystem disorder, marked by increasing loss of muscular coordination (cerebellar ataxia), permanent dilatation of oculocutaneous capillaries and small arteries (telangiectasia), recurrent pulmonary infection, and sometimes immunodeficiency and a propensity for developing malignant tumors of the lymph nodes.

atelectasis (at-e-lek′tah-sis) A state of airlessness and collapse or shrinkage of a lung, or of a portion of it; may be caused by obstruction of the air passages or by escape of air from the lung through a puncture of the pleura.

    primary a. Failure of the lungs to expand and establish respiration immediately after birth.

    secondary a. Collapse of the lungs occurring at any age; seen commonly in newborn infants suffering from respiratory distress syndrome and also in patients recovering from abdominal surgery.

ateliotic (ah-te-le-ot′ik) Incompletely developed.

atenolol (ah-ten′o-lōl) A beta-adrenergic blocking compound commonly used in the treatment of high blood pressure (hypertension)

and chest pain due to impaired blood supply to the heart muscle (angina pectoris).

atheroembolism (ath-er-o-em′bo-lizm) Sudden blockage of a small arterial branch by fatty debris (cholesterol embolus) released from atheromas of the larger artery.

atherogenesis (ath-er-o-jen′ĕ-sis) The formation of fatty plaques (atheromas) in the arterial wall.

atherogenic (ath-er-o-jen′ik) Capable of initiating plaque formation in the arterial walls.

atheroma (ath-er-o′mah) A fatty material deposited in the inner layer of arterial walls in atherosclerosis.

atheromatous (ath-er-o′mah-tus) Relating to atheroma.

atherosclerosis (ath-er-o-skle-ro′sis) A degenerative arterial disease characterized by deposition of complex lipids in the inner layer of the arterial wall, which results in thickening of the wall and narrowing of the vessel's lumen. Atherosclerosis causes death when it involves the blood supply of vital organs (e.g., heart, brain).

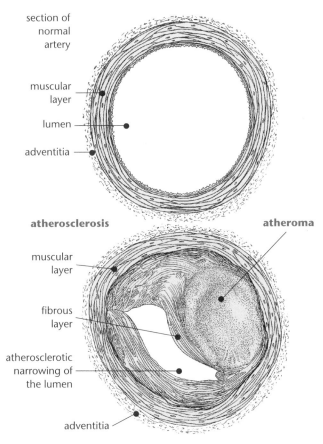

section of normal artery

muscular layer

lumen

adventitia

atherosclerosis

atheroma

muscular layer

fibrous layer

atherosclerotic narrowing of the lumen

adventitia

atherothrombosis (ath-er-o-throm-bo′sis) A blood clot formed in an atheromatous blood vessel.

athetoid (ath′ĕ-toid) Resembling athetosis.

athetosis (ath-ĕ-to′sis) Disorder of the nervous system marked by involuntary, slow, writhing movements of the upper extremities and the neck.

athlete's foot (ath′lets foot) See tinea pedis.

athymia (ah-thim′e-ah) Absence of the thymus gland.

athyroidism (ah-thi′roid-izm) Seldom-used term. See hypothyroidism.

atlantoaxial (at-lan-to-ak′se-al) Relating to the first and second cervical vertebrae (atlas and axis); e.g., the joint between two bones.

atlanto-occipital (at-lan′to ok-sip′ĭ-tal) Relating to the first cervical vertebra (atlas) and the occipital bone (of the skull).

atlanto-odontoid (at-lan′to o-don′toid) Relating to the first cervical vertebra (atlas) and the central articulating process (dens) of the second cervical vertebra (axis).

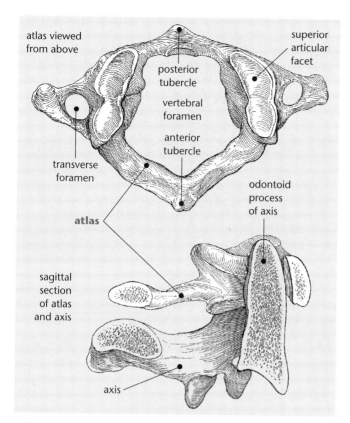

atlas viewed from above

posterior tubercle

superior articular facet

vertebral foramen

anterior tubercle

transverse foramen

atlas

odontoid process of axis

sagittal section of atlas and axis

axis

atlas (at′las) The first cervical vertebra; located next to the skull; articulates with the occipital bone above and the second cervical vertebra (axis) below.

atom (at′om) A chemical unit of an element; it consists of electrons moving around a dense nucleus composed of protons and neutrons.

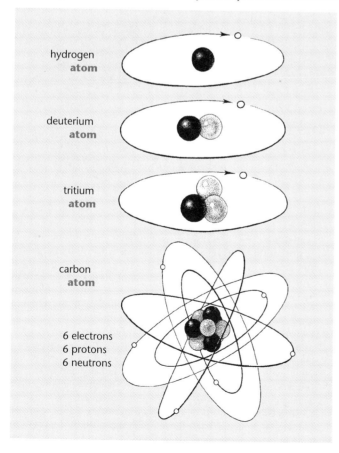

hydrogen **atom**

deuterium **atom**

tritium **atom**

carbon **atom**

6 electrons
6 protons
6 neutrons

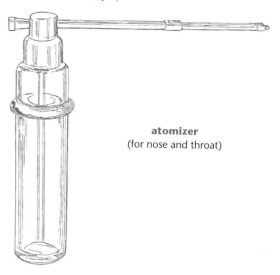

atomization (at-om-ī-za′shun) The process of turning a fluid to a jet of spray.

atomizer (at′om-i-zer) Device for delivering a fluid, such as a medication, in the form of a spray.

atomizer
(for nose and throat)

atonia (ah-to′ne-ah) See atony.

atonic (ah-ton′ik) Devoid of normal strength; said of a muscle.

atony (at′o-ne) Lack of tone or tension; flaccidity. Also called atonia.

atopic (ah-top′ik) Relating to atopy.

atopognosia, atopognosis (ah-top-og-no′ze-ah, ah-top-og-no′sis) Loss of the ability to locate a tactile stimulus.

atopy (at′o-pe) An inherited predisposition to immediate allergic reactions (type I) against common allergens (e.g., hay fever, skin rashes).

atresia (ah-tre′ze-ah) Absence of a body opening or canal resulting from failure of development during fetal life. Most require, and are usually corrected by, early surgical intervention.

    anal a. See imperforate anus, under anus.

    biliary a. Absence of one or more bile ducts; the most common cause of jaundice of newborn infants; believed to be caused by an intrauterine infection.

    esophageal a. Lack of continuity of the esophagus, usually associated with an abnormal opening into the trachea.

esophageal atresia

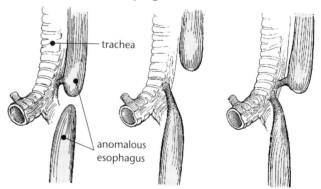

trachea

anomalous esophagus

    intestinal a. A rare anomaly consisting of absence of the lumen in one or more portions of the intestine, especially in the jejunum and ileum.

atretic (ah-tret′ik) Relating to atresia.

atria (a′tre-ah) Plural of atrium.

atrial (a′tre-al) Relating to an atrium or atria.

atrichia (ah-trik′e-ah) Absence of hair.

atriomegaly (a-tre-o-meg′ah-le) Abnormal enlargement of an atrium of the heart.

atrioseptopexy (a-tre-o-sep-to-pek′se) Surgical closure of an abnormal opening, between the two atria of the heart.

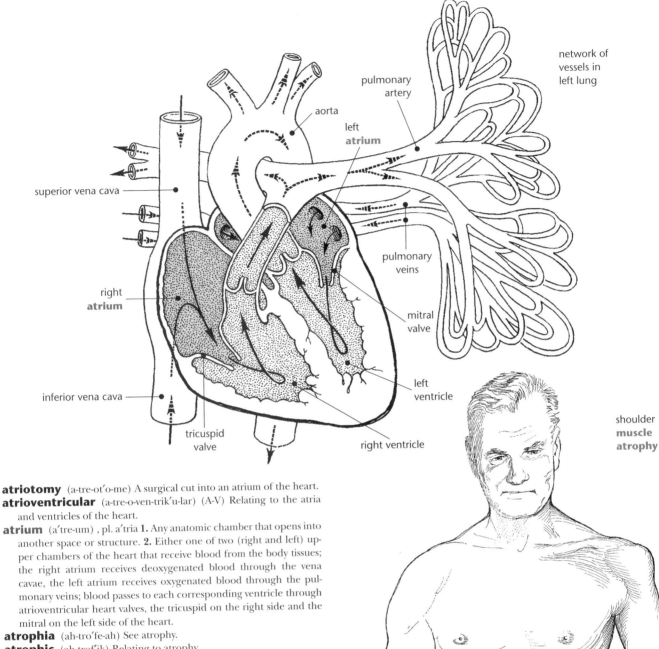

network of vessels in left lung

pulmonary artery

aorta

left **atrium**

superior vena cava

pulmonary veins

right **atrium**

mitral valve

inferior vena cava

left ventricle

tricuspid valve

right ventricle

shoulder **muscle atrophy**

atriotomy (a-tre-ot′o-me) A surgical cut into an atrium of the heart.

atrioventricular (a-tre-o-ven-trik′u-lar) (A-V) Relating to the atria and ventricles of the heart.

atrium (a′tre-um) , pl. a′tria **1.** Any anatomic chamber that opens into another space or structure. **2.** Either one of two (right and left) upper chambers of the heart that receive blood from the body tissues; the right atrium receives deoxygenated blood through the vena cavae, the left atrium receives oxygenated blood through the pulmonary veins; blood passes to each corresponding ventricle through atrioventricular heart valves, the tricuspid on the right side and the mitral on the left side of the heart.

atrophia (ah-tro′fe-ah) See atrophy.

atrophic (ah-trof′ik) Relating to atrophy.

atrophied (at′ro-fēd) Wasted; shrunk.

atrophoderma (at-ro-fo-der′mah) A thinning and wasting of the skin.

   a. pigmentosum See xeroderma pigmentosum, under xeroderma.

atrophy (at′ro-fe) A decrease in the size of any tissue or part of the body resulting from a reduction either in the size of individual cells or in the number of cells composing the tissue or part. Also called atrophia.

   infantile muscular a. See Werdnig-Hoffmann disease, under disease.

   infantile progressive spinal muscular a. See Werdnig-Hoffmann disease, under disease.

   muscular a. Atrophy of skeletal muscle, especially due to lack of use.

   neurotrophic a. Atrophy of skeletal muscle due to damage to the nerve supply of the muscle.

   peroneal muscular a. A hereditary degeneration of peripheral nerves affecting the lower two-thirds of the legs and the arms to the level of the elbows; resulting in slow, progressive wasting of corresponding muscles. Also called Charcot-Marie-Tooth disease.

   Pick's a. See Pick's disease, under disease.

   postpolio muscle a. See postpoliomyelitis syndrome, under syndrome.

   pressure a. Atrophy of tissue resulting from prolonged compression, such as from a denture base on tissues of the jaw, or from a slow-growing benign tumor upon the spinal cord within the vertebral canal. Atrophy is believed to be caused by cutting off a blood supply to the tissues rather than by compression of the cells.

   progressive muscular a. Hereditary (autosomal recessive) disease marked by degeneration of the anterior horn cells of the spinal cord, resulting in muscular wasting and paralysis of the extremities and trunk. Also called Duchenne-Aran disease; progressive spinal amyotrophy; wasting paralysis.

   Sudeck's a. Local bone loss usually occurring after fracture or minor injury and immobilization in a limb, especially the foot and ankle. Also called posttraumatic osteoporosis.

atriotomy ■ atrophy

A82

atropine (at′ro-pēn) An alkaloid derived from *Atropa belladonna* or produced synthetically; used systemically to produce relaxation of smooth muscles, and locally in the eye to dilate the pupil.

atropinism (at′ro-pin-izm) Poisoning by overdose of belladonna derivatives (atropine and scopolamine) or by ingestion of such plants as jimsonweed.

attachment (ah-tach′ment) 1. A fastening, such as muscle to bone. 2. A device for affixing a dental prosthesis, such as a cap, clasp, or retainer.

    epithelial a. A collar of epithelial cells connecting the gum to the tooth surface at the base of the gingival crevice.

attack (ah-tak′) The sudden onset of a process.

    drop a. Sudden falling without loss of consciousness, most often seen in middle-aged and elderly people; described as "giving way of the knees." Causes are not fully understood.

    heart a. Popular term for describing an episode affecting the heart, especially a myocardial infarction. See under infarction.

    panic a. A sudden episode of an overwhelming sense of impending doom and a host of physical symptoms, such as rapid heartbeat and fast breathing while gasping for air; often accompanied by sweating, weakness, and feelings of unreality. Unlike panic precipitated by simple or social phobias, which occurs in response to an anticipated encounter with the object of fear, a panic attack usually occurs unexpectedly and for no apparent reason.

    transient ischemic a. (TIA) A brief neurologic dysfunction (impairment of speech, vision, sensation, movement), usually lasting from a few seconds to a few minutes, with complete recovery within 24 hours; caused by insufficient blood supply to a specific portion of the brain. An episode lasting more than 24 hours is considered a stroke.

attending (ah-tend′ing) See attending physician, under physician.

attenuant (ah-ten′u-ant) Any agent that diminishes the virulence of a pathogen, or reduces the severity of a disease.

attenuation (ah-ten-u-a′shun) A weakening of a disease-causing microorganism or a reduction of the severity of a disease.

attenuator (ah-ten′u-a-tor) An immunoglobulin administered during the incubation period to a person exposed to an infectious disease to diminish or prevent the clinical manifestations of the infection.

attitude (at′ĭ-tōod) 1. Posture; the relative position of the body. 2. A tendency to react in a particular way toward other people, institutions, or issues.

attitudinal (at-ĭ-tōod′ĭ-nal) Relating to an attitude.

attraction (ah-trak′shun) A force that, acting between particles of matter, tends to draw them together.

    capillary a. A force that causes a fluid to move along a fine, hairlike tube.

    chemical a. The force that causes atoms of different substances to unite.

    magnetic a. The force drawing iron or steel toward a magnet.

attrition (ah-trish′un) 1. Wearing away or rubbing off by friction. 2. The wearing off of tooth surface by normal chewing or by grinding of the teeth (bruxism).

atypia (a-tip′e-ah) The condition of not being typical; different.

atypical (a-tip′ĭ-kal) Differing from the usual.

audile (aw′dil) Relating to hearing; applied to the ability to comprehend or remember most easily what has been heard, as opposed to what has been seen. COMPARE visile.

audio- Combining form meaning hearing.

audioanalgesia (au-de-o-an-al-je′ze-ah) Reduction of pain by means of music or sound delivered through earphones.

audiogenic (aw-de-o-jen′ik) Produced by sound (e.g., seizures).

audiogram (aw′de-o-gram) A graphic record or chart of the hearing threshold of a person being tested; it shows the level of loudness (intensity) at which the person can hear sounds of different pitches (frequencies).

audiologist (aw-de-ol′o-jist) A person who holds a degree and/or certificate in audiology.

audiology (aw-de-ol′o-je) The study of hearing impairment that cannot be corrected by surgery or medication; it is concerned with identification and measurement of hearing loss and rehabilitation of the hearing-impaired.

audiometer (aw-de-om′ĕ-ter) Instrument for measuring hearing acuity by producing acoustic stimuli of known pitch (frequency) and loudness (intensity) and registering hearing loss in decibels.

audiometrist (aw-de-om′ĕ-trist) A person trained in the use of the audiometer.

audiometry (aw-de-om′ĕ-tre) Measurement of hearing acuity with the audiometer.

attrition
enamel
dentin
pulp
alveolar bone

audiogram

Hertz (Hz)

x left ear
o right ear

average hearing
mild conductive hearing loss
severe hearing loss

audiometer

audit (awd′it) A methodical examination of a situation ending with a report of the findings.

>**medical a.** A detailed review and evaluation of selected clinical records by qualified professional personnel for assessing the quality of care provided.

audition (aw-dish′un) Hearing.

auditory (aw-dĭ′to-re) Relating to the sense of hearing.

aura (aw′rah) The peculiar sensations that precede, or mark the beginning of, a seizure and that are recognized as such by the patient. Seen in migraine and epilepsy.

aural (aw′ral) Relating to an aura.

auri- Combining form meaning the ear.

auriasis (aw-ri′ah-sis) See chrysiasis.

auric (aw′rik) Relating to gold.

auricle (aw′rĕ-kl) **1.** The shell-shaped part of the external ear projecting from the side of the head. Also called pinna. **2.** The pouchlike structures extending from the upper anterior part of each atrium of the heart. Formerly used as a synonym for atrium.

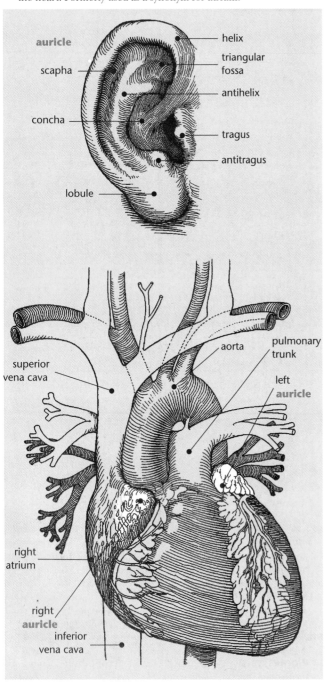

auricular (aw-rik′u-lar) Relating to the ear or to an auricle.

auris (aw′ris), pl. au′res Latin for ear.

>**a. externa** External ear.
>**a. interna** Internal ear.
>**a. media** Middle ear.

auscultate (aws′kul-tāt) To examine the chest or abdomen by listening to sounds made by the underlying organs.

auscultation (aws-kul-ta′shun) The act of listening to sounds made by a patient's organs as an aid to diagnosis.

auscultatory (aws-kul′tah-to-re) Relating to auscultation.

autism (aw′tizm) A state of mind characterized by self-absorption, disregard of external reality, daydreams, and hallucinations; characteristic in schizophrenia.

>**early infantile a.** A pervasive developmental disorder appearing during the first three years of life, characterized by self-absorption, unresponsiveness to other people, ritualistic behaviors, and a severe disturbance or failure in language development. See also Asperger's syndrome, under syndrome.

autistic (aw-tis′tik) Relating to autism.

auto-, aut- Prefixes meaning self.

autoactivation (aw-to-ak-tĭ-va′shun) See autocatalysis.

autoagglutination (aw-to-ah-gloo-tĭ-na′shun) The spontaneous clumping together (agglutination) of red blood cells in one's own plasma or serum.

autoagglutinin (aw-to-ah-gloo′tĭ-nin) An autoantibody that causes the clumping together (agglutination) of a person's own red blood cells.

autoantibody (aw-to-an′tĭ-bod-e) An antibody that is formed in response to, and reacts with, a tissue component (antigen) of the same person or animal.

autoantigen (aw-to-an′tĭ-jen) A tissue component that incites the formation of autoantibodies within the individual. Also called self-antigen.

autoblast (aw′to-blast) A unicellular organism.

autocatalysis (aw-to-kah-tal′ĭ-sis) A phenomenon whereby certain products formed during a biological process (e.g., coagulation of blood) actually promote the reactions by which they themselves were formed and at a rate that, beginning slowly, rapidly increases. Also called autoactivation.

autochthonous (aw-tok′tho-nus) Found at the site of origin.

autoclave (aw′to-klāv) An apparatus with a pressurized chamber for producing steam; the resulting high temperatures kill microorganisms; used in sterilizing surgical instruments.

autoclaving (aw-to-klāv′ing) Sterilizing in an autoclave.

autocrine (aw′to-krin) A mode of hormone action whereby the hormone affects the cell that produced it by attaching itself (binding) to the receptors of the cell.

autocytolysis (aw-to-si-tol′ĭ-sis) See autolysis.

autodigestion (aw-to-di-jes′chun) See autolysis.

autoerotism (aw-to-er′o-tizm) Self-arousal and self-gratification of sexual desire.

autogenous (aw-toj′ĕ-nus) Originating within the body.

autograft (aw′to-graft) Living tissue (skin, bone, vein) that is transplanted from one site to another in the body of the same individual. Also called autotransplant; autogeneic graft; autologous graft.

autografting (aw-to-graft′ing) See autotransplantation.

autohemolysin (aw-to-he-mol′ĭ-sin) An antibody tending to destroy the red blood cells of the individual in whose blood it was formed.

autohemolysis (aw-to-he-mol′ĭ-sis) Destruction of an individual's red blood cells at an accelerated rate by the action of an autohemolysin.

autohypnosis (aw-to-hip-no′sis) Self-induced hypnosis.

autoimmune (aw-to-ĭ-mūn′) Relating to autoimmunity.

autoimmunity (aw-to-ĭ-mu′nĭ-te) Condition in which a person's immune system subjects that person's own tissues to injurious action; the basis of autoimmune disease.

autoinoculation (aw-to-in-ok′u-la-shun) The spread of an infection from one location in the body to another.

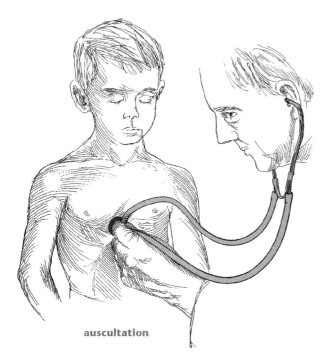

auscultation

autointoxication (aw-to-in-tok-sĭ-ka′shun) Condition resulting from absorption of waste or toxic material released within the body.

autologous (aw-tol′o-gus) Related to self, as a graft that is derived from, and transplanted into, the same individual.

autolysin (aw-tol′ĭ-sin) An antibody that causes disintegration of the cells and tissues of the individual in which the antibody was produced.

autolysis (aw-tol′ĭ-sis) Spontaneous degeneration of tissues by the action of their own enzymes, occurring immediately after death. Also called autodigestion; autocytolysis.

autolyze (aw′to-līz) To precipitate or to undergo autolysis.

automatism (aw-tom′ah-tizm) 1. Involuntary action (e.g., action of the heart). 2. Involuntary and undirected behavior of which the person is not conscious, often inappropriate to circumstances; seen in psychomotor epilepsy and certain dissociative disorders.

autonomic (aw-to-nom′ik) Relating to the autonomic nervous system.

auto-oxidation (aw′to ok-sĭ-da′shun) A substance's combination with oxygen in the presence of air at room temperature and without a catalyst.

autopepsia (aw-to-pep′se-ah) Self-digestion, as of the stomach lining by its own secretions.

autophagia (aw-to-fa′je-ah) 1. Self-biting, especially of lips or fingers, as seen in the Lesch-Nyhan syndrome. 2. The maintenance of the body's nutrition by metabolic recycling of its own tissues.

autophagy (aw-tof′ah-je) The engulfing and dissolution of deteriorating intracellular organelles by the large cytoplasmic particles (lysosomes) in the cell.

autopsy (aw′top-se) Examination of a dead body to determine the cause of death and extent of disease or injury, to study the effects of therapy, to detect crime, or to rule out a transmittable disease that may pose a threat to the public's health. Information obtained is used in research, teaching, or criminal investigations. Also called postmortem examination; necropsy.

   forensic a. See medicolegal autopsy.

   medicolegal a. Autopsy performed by a medical examiner or a county coroner in cases of unnatural death or death occurring under suspicious circumstances or in obvious homicide; it seeks determination of the cause of death, establishment of the time and manner of death, collection and preservation of evidence, discovery of preexisting diseases, and absolute identification of the deceased. The procedures and findings are documented in such a way that independent examiners may review them and reach their own conclusions. Also called forensic autopsy.

   psychological a. An investigation that seeks to determine whether a person who died a violent death was likely to have committed a particular act, such as suicide. It consists of gathering information from a variety of sources (e.g., interviews with survivors, medical records) about the deceased's habits, lifestyle, medical history, personality, character, and frame of mind just before the time of death.

autoradiograph (aw-to-ra′de-o-graf) Tissue images on photographic film obtained after injecting radioactive material into the tissue.

autoradiography (aw-to-ra-de-og′rah-fe) The process of making an autoradiograph.

autosensitize (aw-to-sen′sĭ-tīz) To develop sensitivity to the body's own tissues.

autosomal (aw-to-so′mal) Located on, or transmitted by, an autosome.

autosome (aw′to-sōm) Any chromosome that is not a sex chromosome. Autosomes normally occur in pairs in all cell nuclei except in the nuclei of the two sex cells or gametes (ovum and sperm), where they occur singly.

autosomes

Karyotype of a normal female; the chromosomes are arranged in pairs according to size. — sex chromosomes

autotopagnosis (aw′to-top-ag-no′sis) Impaired ability to recognize any part of one's own body; it may result from damage to the posteroinferior portion of the parietal lobe of the brain.

autotoxic (aw-to-tok′sik) Relating to autointoxication.

autotransfusion (aw-to-trans-fu′zhun) Transfusion of the patient's own blood or blood products.

autotransplant (aw-to-trans′plant) See autograft.

autotransplantation (aw′to-trans-plan-ta′shun) The transfer of living tissue from one location to another in the same individual. Also called autografting.

auxesis (awk-se′sis) Increase in size.

avascular (ah-vas′ku-lar) Without blood supply.

avian (a′ve-an) Relating to birds.

avirulent (a-vir′u-lent) Not virulent.

avitaminosis (a-vi-tah-mĭ-no′sis) See hypovitaminosis.

avoirdupois (av-er-dŭ-poiz′) System of weight measurements in which 16 ounces make a pound and 16 drams make an ounce.

avulsion (ah-vul′shun) A tearing away of tissue or of a body part from its point of attachment.

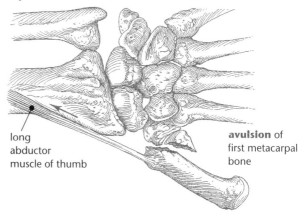

long abductor muscle of thumb

avulsion of first metacarpal bone

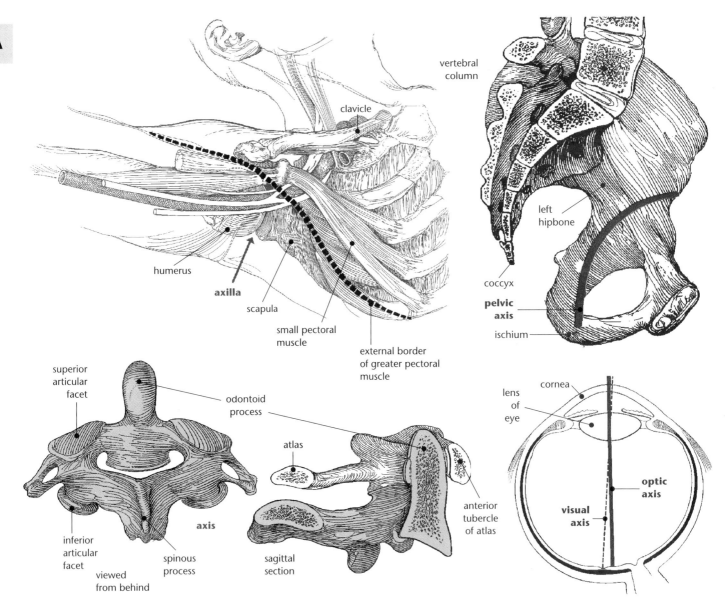

vertebral column

clavicle

humerus

axilla

scapula

small pectoral muscle

external border of greater pectoral muscle

left hipbone

coccyx

pelvic axis

ischium

superior articular facet

odontoid process

atlas

inferior articular facet

axis

spinous process

sagittal section

viewed from behind

anterior tubercle of atlas

lens of eye

cornea

optic axis

visual axis

axenic (a-zen′ik) Not contaminated by microorganisms; applied to small laboratory animals and to cultures of microorganisms.

axes (ak′sēz) Plural of axis.

axial (ak′se-al) Relating to an axis, as of a body or body part.

axifugal (ak-sif′u-gal) Directed toward the periphery or away from the axon.

axilla (ak-sil′ah) The pyramidal area at the junction of the arm and the chest; it contains the axillary blood and lymph vessels, a large number of lymph nodes, brachial plexus, and muscles. Also called armpit.

axillary (ak′sĭ-lar-e) Relating to the axilla.

axis (ak′sis) , pl. ax′es **1.** A line, real or imaginary, used as a point of reference and about which a body or body part may rotate. **2.** The second cervical vertebra. **3.** Any centrally located anatomic structure.

    celiac a. See celiac trunk, under trunk.

    electrical a. The direction of the electromotive forces originating in the heart.

    long a. A line passing lengthwise through the center of a structure.

    mandibular a .A line passing through both mandibular condyles around which the mandible rotates.

    optic a. (a)A line passing through the centers of the cornea and lens, or the closest approximation of this line. (b) In doubly refracting crystals, the direction in which light is not doubly refracted.

    pelvic a. A hypothetical curved line passing through the center point of each of the four planes of the pelvis.

    visual a. An imaginary straight line extending from the ob-

served object, through the pupil, to the central fovea of the retina (fovea centralis). Also called visual line.

axon (ak′son) The long process of a nerve cell (neuron) through which impulses travel away from the cell body.

axonal (ak′so-nal) Relating to an axon.

axoneme (ak′so-nēm) See axial filament, under filament.

axoplasm (ak′so-plazm) The cytoplasm of an axon.

azathioprine (a-zah-thi′o-prēn) A compound used to suppress the action of the immune system in order to prevent rejection of a transplant or to treat an autoimmune disorder, such as rheumatoid arthritis, in which the immune system attacks the body's own tissues.

azidothymidine (az-ĭ-do-thi′mĭ-den) (AZT) See zidovudine.

azoospermia (a-zo-o-sper′me-ah) Absence of spermatozoa in the semen; a cause of male sterility.

azotemia (az-o-te′me-ah) Elevation in blood levels of nonprotein nitrogenous waste products (mainly urea, uric acid, and creatinine), which are normally cleared by the kidney.

    prerenal a. Excess of urea nitrogen in the blood due to primary changes outside of the kidney (e.g., reduced renal blood flow due to congestive heart failure) rather than kidney disease per se. See also uremia.

azure (azh′ur) Any of a group of basic blue dyes (methylthionine or phenothiazine) used as biological stains.

azygos (az′ĭ-gos) An unpaired body structure (e.g., the azygos vein).

azygous (az′ĭ-gus) Unpaired.

B

baby (ba′be) An infant.

blue b. An infant born with a bluish (cyanotic) tint of the skin due to lack of oxygen in the blood; caused by a developmental defect, either an abnormal opening within the heart or transposition of the main arteries leaving the heart. The defect allows mixing of arterial and venous blood; some of the deoxygenated blood returning to the right side of the heart is pumped directly back into the general circulation instead of first passing through the lungs to receive oxygen.

blueberry muffin b. The occurrence of yellowish and purple patches on the skin of a newborn; it may be the result of an intrauterine viral infection transmitted from the mother through the placenta.

border b.'s Infants who are medically ready to be discharged from a hospital but are retained because they have been abandoned or because authorities have determined they would be unsafe with their parents. Such infants are usually born to drug-addicted mothers.

collodion b. A newborn infant with thick, shiny, membranous skin that cracks and peels. The condition may disappear completely or may evolve into congenital ichthyosis, especially lamellar ichthyosis, or it may cause death of the infant.

test-tube b. Popular term for an infant born from an egg fertilized *in vitro* (usually in a petri dish) and then implanted in the mother's uterus.

babygram (ba′be-gram) In neonatology, an x-ray film that includes the chest and abdomen of a newborn baby.

bacillary (bas′ĭ-la-re) **1.** Relating to bacteria. **2.** Like bacteria.

bacillemia (bas-ĭ-le′me-ah) The presence of bacilli (bacteria) in the blood.

bacilli (bah-sil′i) Plural of bacillus.

bacilliform (bah-sil′ĭ-form) Rod-shaped.

bacilluria (bas-ĭ-lu′re-ah) The presence of bacilli (bacteria) in the urine.

Bacillus (bah-sil′lus) A genus of rod-shaped, aerobic, spore-forming, gram-positive bacteria (family Bacillaceae); found usually in soil; some species cause disease.

B. anthracis Bacteria that cause anthrax in some animals and in humans.

B. cereus The species causing a diarrheal type of food poisoning.

B. histolyticus Former name for *Clostridium histolyticum*.

B. polymyxa Bacteria found in soil and water; some strains produce the antibiotic polymyxin.

B. subtilis A species found in soil and decaying organic matter; some strains produce antibiotics. Also called grass bacillus; hay bacillus.

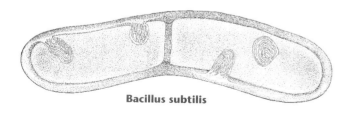

Bacillus subtilis

bacillus (bah-sil′us), pl. bacil′li **1.** General term for any microorganism of the genus *Bacillus*. **2.** Term used to denote any rod-shaped bacterium.

Bang's b. See *Brucella abortus*, under Brucella.

Calmette-Guérin b. An attenuated strain of the bacterium *Mycobacterium bovis* used in the preparation of the bacille Calmette-Guérin (BCG) vaccine.

Döderlein's b. A gram-positive bacterium occurring in normal vaginal secretions; believed to be identical to *Lactobacillus acidophilus*.

Ducrey's b. See *Haemophilus ducreyi*, under *Haemophilus*.

Friedländer's b. See *Klebsiella pneumoniae*, under *Klebsiella*.

gas b. See *Clostridium perfringens*, under *Clostridium*.

grass b. See *Bacillus subtilus*, under *Bacillus*.

Hansen's b. See *Mycobacterium leprae*, under *Mycobacterium*.

hay b. See *Bacillus subtilis*, under *Bacillus*.

Koch's b. (1) See *Mycobacterium tuberculosis*, under *Mycobacterium*. (2) See *Vibrio cholerae*, under *Vibrio*.

Koch-Weeks b. See *Haemophilus influenzae*, under *Haemophilus*.

leprosy b. See *Mycobacterium leprae*, under *Mycobacterium*.

tubercle b. See *Mycobacterium tuberculosis* (human), under *Mycobacterium*.

Welch's b. See *Clostridium perfringens*, under *Clostridium*.

bacitracin (bas-ĭ-tra′sin) An antibacterial substance primarily effective against gram-positive organisms that cause skin and eye infections, and a few gram-negative organisms. It is usually applied topically in the form of powder or ointment. Kidney damage is a possible adverse effect of systemic administration.

back (bak) The dorsum; the posterior area of the body from the shoulders to the buttocks.

poker b. See spondylitis deformans, under spondylitis.

saddle b. See lordosis.

backache (bak′āk) Any pain in the back, especially the lower (lumbosacral) portion of the back.

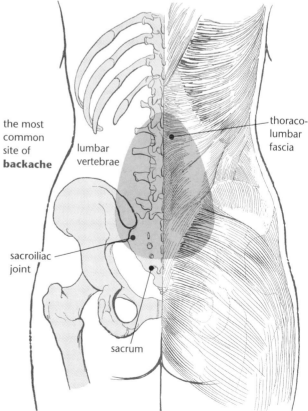

the most common site of **backache**

lumbar vertebrae

thoraco-lumbar fascia

sacroiliac joint

sacrum

backbone (bak'bōn) **1.** The vertebral column; see under column. **2.** Atoms of a polymer that are common to all its molecules. **3.** The principal chain of a polypeptide.

backscatter (bak'skat-er) In radiology, radiation deflected more than 90° from the main beam of radiation.

bacteremia (bak-ter-e'me-ah) The presence of viable bacteria in the bloodstream.

    MAC b. See Mycobacterium avium complex bacteremia.

    Mycobacterium avium complex b. Disseminated infection of the blood with a complex of bacteria that includes several strains of *Mycobacterium avium* and the closely related *Mycobacterium intracellulare;* it occurs as a common complication of advanced HIV infection, frequently as a patient's first AIDS-defining opportunistic disease, and causing a significantly increased incidence of fatigue, weight loss, fever, diarrhea, anemia, and a shortened life span. Also called MAC bacteremia; MAC disease; MAC infection.

bacteria (bak-te're-ah) Plural of bacterium.

bacterial (bak-te're-al) Relating to bacteria.

bactericidal (bak-tēr-ĭ-si'dal) Capable of destroying bacteria.

bactericide (bak-tēr'ĭ-sid) An agent that kills bacteria.

bacterid (bak'ter-id) A recurrent eruption of pus-filled blisters (pustules) localized to the palms and soles; although the primary pustule is sterile, the eruption may be aggravated by a bacterial infection; cause is unknown; previously thought to be associated with another, remote, infection. Also called pustular bacterid.

bacteriform (bak-tēr'ĕ-form) Having a bacterial form.

bacteriogenic (bak-te-re-o-jen'ik) Caused by the actions of bacteria.

bacteriologic (bak-te-re-o-loj'ik) Relating to bacteriology.

bacteriologist (bak-te-re-ol'o-jist) A specialist in bacteriology.

bacteriology (bak-te-re-ol'o-je) The branch of microbiology concerned with the study of bacteria, especially in relation to medicine and agriculture.

bacteriolysin (bak-te-re-ol'ĭ-sin) An antibody which combines with the bacterial cells (antigen) that stimulated its formation and which subsequently destroys those cells.

bacteriolytic (bac-te-re-o-lit'ik) Relating to bacteria in any way.

bacteriophage (bak-te're-o-fāj) A virus that, under certain conditions, infects and destroys bacteria; composed of a nucleic acid core (usually DNA but may also be RNA, never both) and a protein coat.

bacteriophage T4

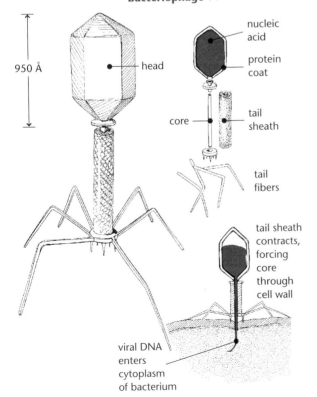

950 Å — head

nucleic acid

protein coat

core — tail sheath

tail fibers

tail sheath contracts, forcing core through cell wall

viral DNA enters cytoplasm of bacterium

Baccteriophages are named after the bacterial species or strains for which they have a specific affinity. Also called phage.

bacteriophagia (bak-te-re-o-fa'je-ah) The destruction of bacteria by a bacteriophage.

bacteriostasis (bak-te-re-os'ta-sis) The arrest or inhibition of bacterial growth.

bacteriostat (bak-te're-o-stat) Any chemical agent that inhibits bacterial growth.

bacteriostatic (bak-te-re-o-stat'ik) Inhibiting bacterial growth.

bacterium (bak-te're-um), pl. bacte'ria Any of several unicellular organisms of the plant kingdom, existing as free-living organisms or as parasites, multiplying by cell division, and having a wide range of biochemical (including pathogenic) properties. Their morphology may be rod-shaped (bacilli), spherical (cocci), spiral-shaped (spirilla), or comma-shaped (vibrios).

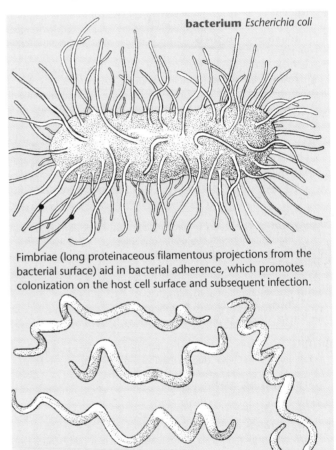

bacterium *Escherichia coli*

Fimbriae (long proteinaceous filamentous projections from the bacterial surface) aid in bacterial adherence, which promotes colonization on the host cell surface and subsequent infection.

bacterium *Treponema pallidum*

(causes syphilis)

bacteriuria (bak-te-re-u're-ah) The presence of bacteria in the urine.

bacteroid (bak'tĕ-roid) Resembling a bacterium.

Bacteroides (bak-tĕ-roi'dēz) A genus of bacteria (family Bacteroidaceae) made up of gram-negative, mostly nonmotile, strictly anaerobic, rod-shaped organisms that may normally inhabit the oral, intestinal, and urogenital cavities of humans and animals. Some species are pathogenic, constituting an important source of infection in patients with damaged tissues and weakened immune defenses.

bag (bag) A sac or pouch.

    colostomy b. A bag worn over the abdominal opening of a colostomy to collect fecal material from the intestines.

    ice b. A bag for holding crushed ice to be applied to a body part for the relief of pain or to control swelling.

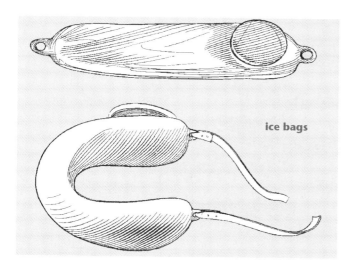

ice bags

b. of waters Popular name for the amniotic sac that encloses the fetus and the fluid in which the fetus is suspended. Also called amnion.

bagassosis (bag-ah-so'sis) Inflammation of the minute air sacs (alveoli) of the lungs; an allergic response to fungal spores in bagasse fibers (the crushed residue of sugar cane). Seen in workers who handle paper, wallboard, and other products made from bagasse that has been stored in humid high temperatures for long periods, where it becomes a breeding ground for the offending fungus.

balance (bal'ans) **1.** A state of body stability produced by the harmonious functional performance of its parts. **2.** The measured relationship between input and output of a substance by the body.

　acid-base b. The normal ratio of acid and base elements in blood plasma, expressed in the hydrogen ion concentration, or pH. Also called acid-base equilibrium.

balanitis (bal-ah-ni'tis) Inflammation of the glans penis. The term is frequently incorrectly applied to inflammation of the prepuce (posthitis).

balano-, balan- Combining forms meaning glans penis.

balanoplasty (bal'ah-no-plas-te) Plastic surgery of the glans penis.

balanoposthitis (bal-ah-no-pos-thi'tis) Inflammation of both the glans penis and the prepuce; may be due to infection with any of a wide variety of bacteria.

balanopreputial (bal-ah-no-pre-pu'she-al) Relating to the glans penis and the prepuce.

balantidiasis (bal-an-ti-di'ah-sis) A dysentery-like disease caused by the protozoan *Balantidium coli.*

Balantidium coli (bal-an-tid'e-um ko'li) A relatively large (50–80 μ long) parasitic ciliate, found in the human large intestine; causes diarrhea and ulceration of the colon.

baldness (bawld'nes) See alopecia.

ball (bawl) A round mass.

　b. of the foot The anterior portion of the sole of the foot, padded by a thick layer of fibrofatty tissue; it supports the weight of the body when the heel is raised off the ground.

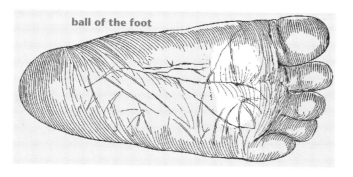

ball of the foot

fungus b. See aspergilloma.
hair b. See trichobezoar.

ballismus (bah-liz'mus) Large, flailing movements of one or more extremities caused by brain damage; specifically, to the subthalamic nucleus.

ballistocardiogram (bah-lis-to-kar'de-o-gram) A graphic record of body movements caused by ejection of blood from the ventricles with each cardiac contraction.

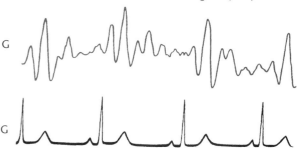

ballistocardiogram (BCG) recorded simultaneously
with an electrocardiogram (ECG)

ballistocardiograph (bah-lis-to-kar'de-o-graf) (BCG) A graphic recording system for taking a ballistocardiogram.

balloon (bah-loon') An inflatable device that can be inserted in a body cavity or tube to provide support, to maintain a catheter in place, or to increase the lumen of a tubular structure.

balloonseptostomy (bah-loon-sep-tos'to-me) The creation of an orifice in the wall between the two atria of the heart by catheterization and passing of an inflated balloon through the foramen ovale; used in the surgical treatment of transposition of the great vessels and in atresia of the tricuspid (right atrioventricular) valve.

ballottement (bah-lot'ment, bal-ot-maw') A method of physical examination to determine the size and mobility of an organ or mass in the body, especially one surrounded by fluid; the mass is pushed so as to rebound against the wall of the fluid-filled space. In obstetrics, the maneuver is used to palpate the fetus in the amniotic sac.

balm (bahm) A soothing or healing ointment.

balsam (bawl'sam) The resinous exudate of some trees and shrubs, used in pharmacological preparations.

band (band) **1.** Any cordlike anatomic structure. **2.** Any device used to encircle or connect one part of the body with another.

　A b. One of the dark-staining zones at the center of the contraction unit (sarcomere) of skeletal and cardiac muscle, composed of a collection of thick (100Å) filaments that traverse the sarcomere. Also called anisotropic band.

　　amniotic b. One of several strands of tissue that sometimes develop between the fetus and the sac in which it is contained (amnion), believed by some to cause fetal deformities.

　　anisotropic b. See A band.

　　anterior b. of colon See tenia libera, under tenia.

　　chromosome b. Portion of a chromosome distinguishable from adjacent segments by a difference in staining intensity.

　　free b. of colon See tenia libera, under tenia.

　　H b. A pale zone that bisects the A band of the contracting unit of muscle (sarcomere), representing the middle portion of the thick filaments (myosin) of the muscle fibrils; seen only in relaxed or minimally contracted muscle. Also called Hensen's line.

　　I b. One of the lightly staining zones of skeletal and cardiac muscle, composed of a collection of thin (50Å), longitudinally oriented actin filaments. Also called isotropic band.

　　isotropic b. See I band.

　　mesocolic b. See tenia mesocolica, under tenia.

　　omental b. See tenia omentalis, under tenia.

　　orthodontic b. A thin strip of metal fitted closely around the crown of a tooth, in a horizontal plane, to anchor an orthodontic appliance.

　　Z b. A dark-staining thin membrane appearing on longitudinal

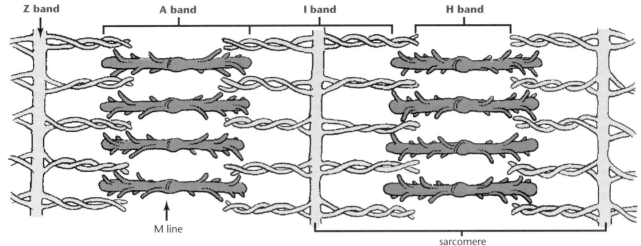

Z band   A band   I band   H band

M line

sarcomere

section of skeletal and cardiac muscle as a dark line bisecting the I bands. It represents the demarcation of the serially repeating contracting units (sarcomeres) of striated muscle fibers. Also called Z line; zwischenscheibe band.

    zwischenscheibe b. See Z band.

bandage (ban′dij) **1.** A strip of cloth, usually gauze, of varying size and shape, used to compress, prevent motion, check hemorrhage, or retain surgical dressings. **2.** To cover or wrap with gauze or other material.

    Barton's b. A figure-of-8 bandage to support the lower jaw.

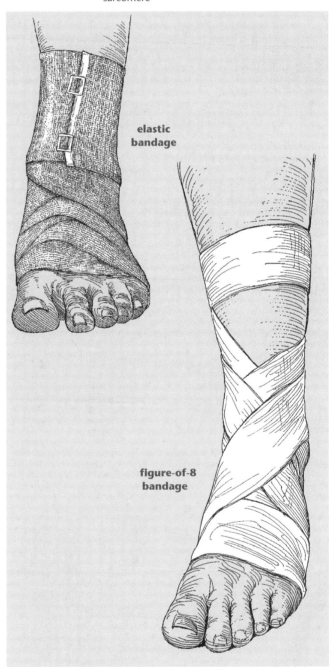

elastic bandage

figure-of-8 bandage

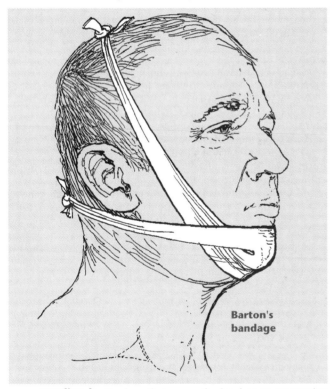

Barton's bandage

    capeline b. Bandage that covers the head or an amputation stump.

    elastic b. Bandage made of stretchable material, used to apply continuous mild pressure.

    figure-of-8 b. Roller bandage applied in such a way that the turns cross each other in a manner resembling the figure 8.

    Galen's b. A broad head bandage with the ends split into three strips; after the broad section is placed on the head, the anterior ends are tied behind the neck, the posterior ends on the forehead, and the middle ends under the chin.

    plaster b. A bandage impregnated with plaster of Paris and

bandage ■ bandage

applied moist; it provides rigid support after the plaster sets.

reverse b. Bandage applied to a limb in such a way that the roller is half twisted at each turn.

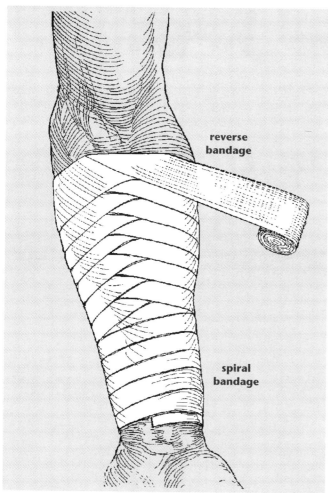

reverse bandage

spiral bandage

roller b. Bandage material rolled into a compact cylinder or disk to facilitate its application.

spica b. A figure-of-8 bandage with overlapping turns, applied to two anatomic parts of markedly different dimensions, such as the arm and thorax, thigh and pelvis, thumb and hand.

spiral b. Bandage encircling a limb; each successive turn partly overlaps the preceding one.

T b. A bandage shaped like the letter T, usually applied to the perineum.

tubular b. A gauze bandage in the shape of a tube for covering small structures, such as a finger; it is put on the structure with an applicator.

Velpeau's b. A bandage applied with the forearm positioned obliquely across the chest; it serves to immobilize the shoulder in fractures of the collarbone (clavicle).

banding (band'ing) The staining of chromosomes to make visible their characteristic cross bands to permit identification of each chromosome in a cell. The bands are consistent for all like chromosomes of an individual.

bandy-leg (ban'de-leg) See genu varum.

bank (bank) A place for obtaining and storing in a viable condition, and for future use, certain donated organs, tissues, or cells.

blood b. A place where blood is collected and typed for use in transfusions.

eye b. A facility for obtaining and distributing corneas to eye surgeons (usually within 24 hours) for use in corneal transplants.

sperm b. A place where sperm is stored in a frozen state for use in artificial insemination. Liquid nitrogen at 196°C is used to arrest molecular movement and preserve the cells' vitality.

bar (bahr) **1.** A unit of pressure equal to 1 megadyne (10^6 dyne per cm^2). **2.** A segment of tissue that bridges a gap between structures. **3.** A piece of metal connecting two or more portions of a removable partial denture.

Passavant's b. See Passavant's ridge, under ridge.

barbital (bar'bĭ-tal) A colorless or white crystalline powder, derivative of barbituric acid. It is used as a sedative and has a long-lasting effect, depressing most metabolic processes at high doses. It may induce dependence.

barbiturate (bar-bit'u-rat) Any derivative of barbituric acid (phenobarbital, amobarbital, pentobarbital, secobarbital, thiopental) that acts as an anesthetic and depressant of the central nervous system (brain and spinal cord); used primarily for sedation or the treatment of convulsive disorders. Some have a potential for abuse.

barbituric acid (bar-bĭ-tūr'ik as'id) A crystalline substance not itself a sedative, but from which sedative drugs (barbiturates) are derived.

bariatric (bar-e-at'rik) Relating to bariatrics.

bariatrician (bar-e-ah-trī'shian) A physician who specializes in treating obese patients.

bariatrics (bar-e-at'riks) The field of medicine concerned with obesity, its causes, prevention, and treatment.

baritosis (bar-ĭ-to'sis) A relatively harmless deposition of barium dust in the lungs (benign pneumoconiosis) as a result of occupational or environmental exposure; detectable in x-ray images; it produces neither symptoms nor functional impairment.

barium (ba're-um) A silvery white metallic element; symbol Ba, atomic number 56, atomic weight 137.34.

b. sulfate A barium compound of low solubility, administered orally or as an enema prior to x-ray visualization of the gastrointestinal tract.

baro- Combining form meaning pressure; weight.

baroceptor (bar-o-sep'tor) See baroreceptor.

baroreceptor (bar-o-re-sep'tor) A sensory nerve terminal that is stimulated by increased blood pressure within an artery. Also called baroceptor; pressoreceptor.

barosinusitis (bar-o-si-nu-si'tis) Inflammatory condition of paranasal sinuses caused by a sudden change in atmospheric pressure, which creates a difference between pressures within the sinuses and that of the atmosphere.

barostat (bar'o-stat) A structure (e.g., carotid sinus) that regulates pressure, as the pressure in the walls of blood vessels.

barotitis media (bar-o-ti'tis me'de-ah) Damage to the middle ear caused by the relative vacuum created in the middle ear chamber by a sudden change in atmospheric pressure (e.g., while diving or flying); usually occurs when the eustachian (auditory) tube is obstructed due to allergies or respiratory tract infection; symptoms include pain, dizziness, loss of hearing; the eardrum (tympanic membrane) may rupture. Also called aerotitis media; commonly called aviator's ear.

barotrauma (bar-o-traw'mah) Injury to tissues within a cavity (e.g., the paranasal sinuses) caused by a difference in pressure between atmospheric pressure and that within the affected cavity.

pulmonary b. The abnormal presence of air in the pleural space, resulting from injury to the pleura from therapeutically increased air pressure in the lungs; it may occur in patients with a severe case of respiratory distress syndrome who require high peak respiratory pressure or positive end-respiratory pressure.

barren (bar'en) Popular term for sterile; unable to produce offspring.

barrier (bār'e-er) An obstruction or obstacle.

blood-air b. The thin layer of tissues in the lung that separates capillary blood from alveolar air, and through which exchange of gases takes place; composed of endothelium (lining the capillaries), basal membrane, and alveolar epithelium.

blood-brain b. (BBB) The tight junction between endothelial cells of capillary walls that normally permits only a limited exchange between blood in the capillaries on the one hand and cerebrospinal fluid and extracellular fluid in the brain on the other.

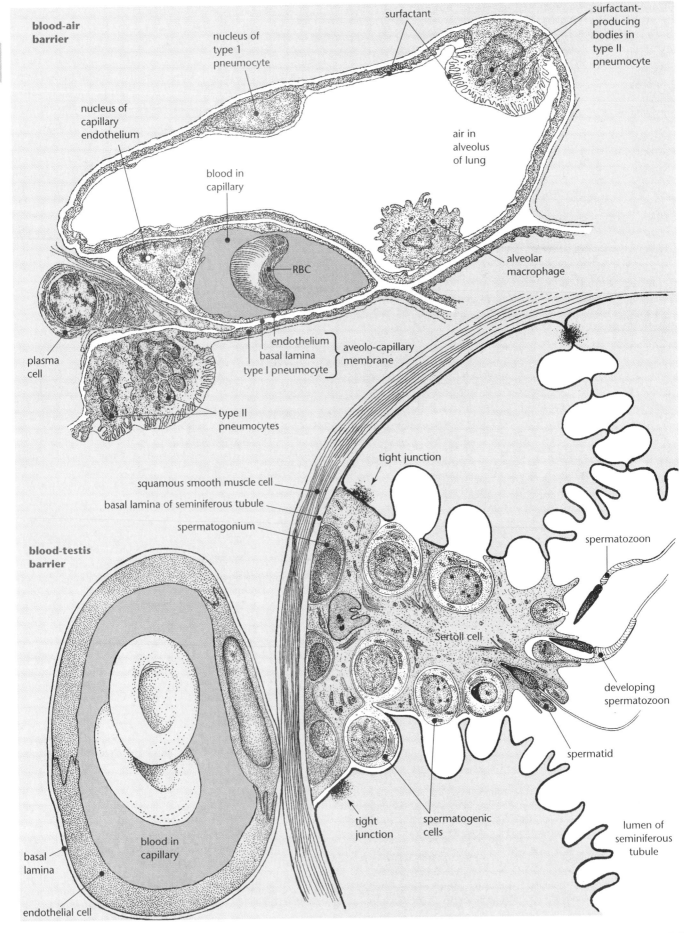

blood-air barrier

nucleus of type 1 pneumocyte

surfactant

surfactant-producing bodies in type II pneumocyte

nucleus of capillary endothelium

blood in capillary

air in alveolus of lung

RBC

alveolar macrophage

plasma cell

endothelium
basal lamina
type I pneumocyte

aveolo-capillary membrane

type II pneumocytes

tight junction

squamous smooth muscle cell

basal lamina of seminiferous tubule

spermatogonium

spermatozoon

blood-testis barrier

Sertoli cell

developing spermatozoon

spermatid

blood in capillary

tight junction

spermatogenic cells

basal lamina

lumen of seminiferous tubule

endothelial cell

barrier ■ barrier

blood-testis b. The tight junction between Sertoli cells of the seminiferous tubules that prevents substances in the circulating blood from entering the lumen of the tubules, where the spermatozoa are developing.

incest b. In psychoanalysis, the learning of parental and social prohibitions against incest.

bartholinitis (bar-tho-lin-i'tis) Inflammation of the Bartholin's glands (greater vestibular glands).

Bartonella bacilliformis (bar-to-nel'lah ba-sil-lĕ-for'mis) A species of gram-negative, rod-shaped, encapsulated bacteria that causes bartonellosis; transmitted to humans by the bite of sand flies.

bartonellosis (bar-to-nel-lo'sis) Disease occurring chiefly in the valleys of the Andes, in Peru, caused by the arthropod-borne bacillus *Bartonella bacilliformis;* transmitted by the bite of the sand fly, it is characterized by a febrile stage with severe hemolytic anemia (Oroya fever) followed several weeks later by a nodular skin eruption (verruga peruana); occasionally one stage of the disease occurs without the other. Also called Carrion's disease.

basal (ba'sal) Relating to a base.

base (bās) **1.** A supporting part of a structure. **2.** The principal ingredient of a mixture. **3.** A hydrogen ion acceptor; a substance that turns litmus indicators blue and combines with an acid to form a salt. **4.** The area opposite the apex (e.g., the base of the heart). **5.** In molecular genetics, the chemical units adenine, guanine, thymine, uracil, and cytosine, or their derivatives, as they occur bound to sugars in DNA and RNA molecules. **6.** See vehicle.

acrylic resin b. In dentistry, the supporting part of a denture, made of acrylic resin.

cement b. A layer of dental cement (sometimes medicated) placed within a tooth cavity preparation to protect the dental pulp from thermal shock and to serve as a floor for a permanent filling.

denture b. The framework of a partial denture that rests on the ridge of the gums. Also called saddle.

record b. See baseplate.

temporary b. See baseplate.

trial b. See baseplate.

baseplate (bās'plāt) In dentistry, a temporary form corresponding to the base of a denture; used for making jaw relation records and for arranging artificial teeth. Also called record base; temporary base; trial base.

basial (ba'se-al) Relating to the basion.

basic (ba'sik) **1.** Relating to a base or essence. **2.** Relating to an alkaline property or reaction.

basicranial (ba-se-kra'ne-al) Relating to the base of the skull.

basilar (bas'ĭ-lar) Relating to a base.

basilateral (ba-se-lat'er-al) Relating to the base and a side of a structure.

basion (ba'se-on) A craniometric landmark; the middle point on the anterior margin of the foramen magnum, the opening at the base of the skull where the spinal cord begins.

basis (ba'sis) Latin for base; used in anatomic nomenclature.

b. cordis The base of the heart.

b. cranii The base of the skull. The internal surface is called *basis cranii interna*, the external surface, *basis cranii externa*.

basket (bas'ket) Any basket-shaped device or anatomic structure.

stone b. An instrument for removing urinary stones.

baso-, basio-, basi- Combining forms meaning base.

basocytosis (ba-so-si-to'sis) Obsolete term for basophilic leukocytosis; see under leukocytosis.

basophil (ba'so-fil) A cell, especially a white blood cell (basophilic leukocyte), containing granules that stain easily with basic dyes.

basophilia (ba-so-fil'e-ah) **1.** Condition characterized by the presence of a large number of basophilic white blood cells (basophilic leukocytes) in the circulating blood, or an increased number of basophilic cells in organ tissues. Also called basophilic leukocytosis. **2.** The presence of basophilic red blood cells in circulating blood; seen in certain blood diseases and in lead poisoning.

basophilic (ba-so-fil'ik) Staining preferentially with basic dyes.

bath (bath) Any fluid in which the body, or any of its parts, is

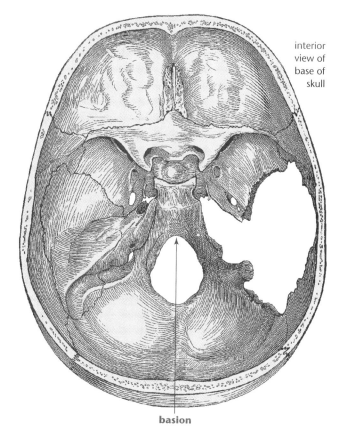

basion

immersed for therapeutic or cleansing purposes.

colloid b. A bath containing starch, sodium bicarbonate, or any other soothing material to relieve skin irritations.

contrast b. Alternating immersion of a body part (e.g., a limb) in hot and cold water, usually at half-hour intervals, to increase blood circulation to the part.

douche b. The local application of a stream of water.

sitz b. Immersion of only the hips and buttocks in a tub of water.

bathy-, batho- Combining forms meaning depth; deep.

bathyesthesia (bath-e-es-the'ze-ah) General term for the perception of subcutaneous sensations; a sensation felt beneath the skin.

battery (bat'er-e) The touching of one person by another without the consent of the person touched.

sexual b. See rape.

beaded (bēd'ed) Resembling a string of beads (e.g., some bacterial colonies).

beading (bē'ding) A row of small spherical masses.

b. of ribs See rachitic rosary, under rosary.

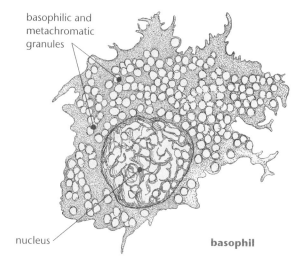

basophilic and metachromatic granules

nucleus

basophil

bearing down (bār'ing down) In obstetrics, the expulsive effort of a woman during the second stage of labor.

beat (bēt) A pulsation (e.g., of the heart or an artery).

    apex b. The beat made by the left ventricle; normally felt in the left fifth intercostal space, at the midclavicular line.

    capture b. An atrial heartbeat conducted to the ventricles or a ventricular beat conducted to the atria (i.e., a period of atrioventricular dissociation in the cardiac cycle, after which the atria regain control of the ventricles). Also called ventricular capture.

    dropped b. Absence of a single beat (i.e., a nonconducted heartbeat).

    ectopic b. A beat originating at some point in the heart other than the normal site (i.e., the sinoatrial node).

    escape b. A beat usually originating from the A-V node or ventricle following a pause longer than the normal, after the expected normal beat has defaulted.

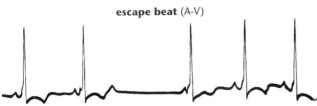

escape beat (A-V)

    fusion b. A beat triggered by two impulses from different sites in the heart.

    premature b. An ectopic beat (arising from someplace other than the sinus node) occurring before the next anticipated beat.

becquerel (bek'rel) (Bq) The SI unit of radioactivity; equal to 1 disintegration per second. It replaces the curie.

bed (bed) 1. In anatomy, a supporting tissue or matrix. 2. A piece of furniture for sleeping or resting. 3. The measure of a hospital capacity in which one bed corresponds to one patient.

    capillary b. The total mass of minute blood vessels connecting venules and arterioles and their volume capacity.

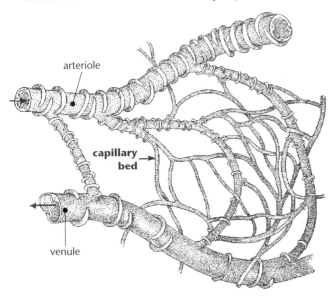

arteriole

capillary bed

venule

    Gatch b. See hospital bed.

    hospital b. Bed with a frame sectioned in three parts and hinged to permit raising the head end or the foot end as desired. Also called Gatch bed.

    nail b. The tissue upon which a fingernail or toenail rests. Also called nail matrix.

bedbug (bed'bug) A reddish brown bloodsucking insect with a disagreeable odor, *Cimex lectularius* (family Cimicidae); its bite produces itchy wheals with central hemorrhagic points. Also written bed bug.

bed conversion (bed con-ver'shun) The reallocation of beds in an inpatient health facility from one type of care service to another

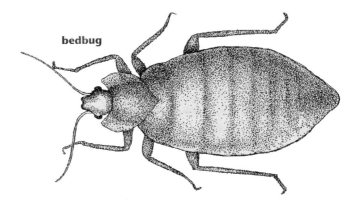

bedbug

(e.g., from acute care to long-term care).

bed occupancy (bed ok'u-pan-se) A measure of the use of an inpatient health facility, based on the average number of beds occupied for a given period of time relative to the total number of beds.

bedpan (bed'pan) A vessel used for urination and defecation by a patient who is bedridden.

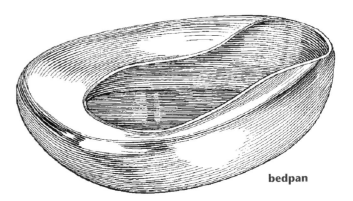

bedpan

bedsore (bed'sor) See decubitus ulcer, under ulcer.

bed-wetting (bed-wet'ing) Popular term for nocturnal enuresis; see under enuresis.

behavior (be-hāv'yor) The observable manner in which a person acts or responds.

behavioral (be-hāv'yor-al) Relating to behavior.

behaviorism (be-hāv'yor-izm) A branch of psychology that emphasizes study of the observable, objective, and tangible facts of behavior.

bejel (bej'el) Nonvenereal infection by an organism similar to *Treponema pallidum* (the causal agent of syphilis), transmitted by nonsexual body contact; characterized by a primary lesion in the mouth, followed by lesions in the axillae, inguinal regions, and rectum.

bel (bel) A unit of sound intensity.

belching (belch'ing) Popular term for eructation.

belladonna (bel-ah-don'ah) The deadly nightshade plant; highly poisonous plant *Atropa belladonna;* its leaves and roots yield atropine, scopolamine, and other alkaloids that inhibit the action of parasympathetic nerves and are used as antispasmodics to treat gastrointestinal disorders.

belle indifference (bel an-dif-er-ahns') See la belle indifference.

belly (bel'e) 1. The abdomen. 2. The fleshy part of a muscle.

belly button (bel'e but'on) Umbilicus; navel.

bends (bendz) One of the early manifestations of decompression sickness, characterized by severe joint and muscle pains, especially of the limbs, which forces the affected individual to maintain the limbs in a semiflexed position (hence the name). See also decompression sickness, under sickness.

benign (be-nīn') Essentially harmless; in regard to a tumor, one that is not invasive or metastasizing.

benoxaprofen (ben-oks-ah-pro'fen) A nonsteroidal anti-inflam-

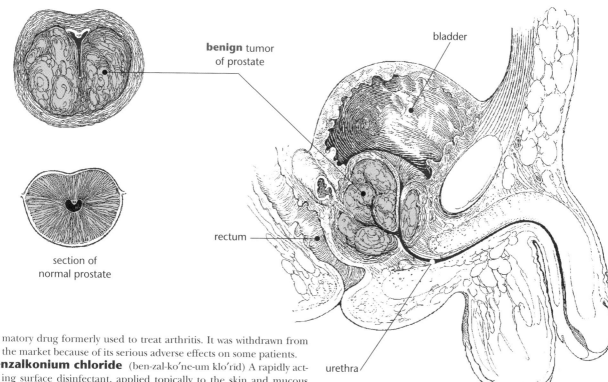

benign tumor
of prostate

section of
normal prostate

bladder

rectum

urethra

matory drug formerly used to treat arthritis. It was withdrawn from the market because of its serious adverse effects on some patients.

benzalkonium chloride (ben-zal-ko'ne-um klo'rīd) A rapidly acting surface disinfectant, applied topically to the skin and mucous membrane.

benzene (ben'zēn) A volatile, flammable, highly toxic hydrocarbon by-product of coal distillation; widely used in industry as a solvent (in paints, varnishes, gasoline); it causes acute damage to the brain and spinal cord and chronic damage to bone marrow. Also called benzol.

benzethonium chloride (ben-zĕ-tho'ne-um klo'rīd) A synthetic compound, used in solution as a disinfectant.

benzidine (ben'zĭ-din) A highly toxic industrial compound absorbed through the skin; it causes liver and kidney damage; it is known to cause bladder cancer in workers in the dye, rubber, and insulating cable industries.

benzoate (ben'zo-āt) A salt of benzoic acid.

benzocaine (ben'zo-kān) A local anesthetic that acts at nerve endings by preventing transmission of nerve impulses; used to relieve skin discomfort. It has low systemic toxicity.

benzodiazepine (ben-zo-di-az'ĕ-pēn) The parent compound of a group of widely prescribed minor tranquilizers used to treat anxiety and neuroses.

benzoic acid (ben-zo'ik as'id) A compound widely used as a food preservative for its antibacterial and antifungal properties.

benzol (ben'zol) See benzene.

benzoyl (ben'zo-il) The radical of benzoic acid.

   b. peroxide Compound used as a topical medication in the treatment of acne; it promotes peeling of the skin.

benzyl (ben'zil) A hydrocarbon radical.

   b. benzoate Compound occurring naturally in several balsams; used in topical medications to control scabies.

beriberi (ber-e-ber'e) Disease caused by deficiency of thiamine (vitamin B_1).

   dry b. Deficiency affecting nerves and skeletal muscles, especially of the lower extremities; symptoms include numbness, a burning sensation, and wasting of muscles. It may lead to emaciation and paralysis.

   infantile b. Beriberi occurring in infants, between the ages of two and four months, who are breast-fed by thiamine-deficient mothers.

   wet b. Deficiency affecting the cardiovascular system; characterized by the heart's inability to pump sufficient blood (heart failure), which leads to congestion of blood in veins of the legs and accumulation of fluid in tissues (edema) of the legs, trunk, and

sometimes the face.

berkelium (berk'le-um) A man-made radioactive element; symbol Bk, atomic number 97, atomic weight 247. Twelve isotopes have been produced.

berylliosis (ber-il-e-o'sis) An occupational disease caused by inhalation of fumes or dust from the metallic element beryllium or its soluble salts. It primarily affects the lungs; short exposure to high concentrations may result in a self-limiting episode of severe lung inflammation (pneumonitis), characterized by cough and breathlessness; exposure to small concentrations over many years may cause nodular inflammatory lesions and fibrosis (granulomatous fibrosis) of lungs and liver; less frequently, damage may involve the skin, bone marrow, and lymph nodes. Berylliosis occurs in workers in such industries as electronics, ceramics, nuclear energy, and aerospace.

beryllium (ber-il'le-um) Metallic element; symbol Be, atomic number 4, atomic weight 9.012. It has many technologic applications and constitutes a health hazard of modern industry.

bestiality (bes-te-al'ĭ-te) Sexual activities between a human and an animal.

beta (ba'tah) (β) **1.** The second letter of the Greek alphabet. **2.** The second item in a system of classification, as of chemical compounds.

beta-blocker, β-blocker (ba'tah blok'er) See beta-adrenergic blocking agent, under agent.

beta-fetoprotein, β-fetoprotein (ba'tah fe-to-pro'tēn) A liver protein normally found in the fetus; it has been found in adults with liver disease.

betamethasone (ba'tah-meth'ah-sōn) A potent anti-inflammatory glucocorticoid agent administered orally or as a topical application to the skin. Adverse effects of topical application include thinning of the skin; oral administration is associated with more serious adverse effects common to all steroids (e.g., enhanced susceptibility to infections, fluid retention, and high blood pressure).

betel (be'tl) The dried leaf and nut of an East Indian plant (Piper betle), which are chewed for their stimulant effects; associated with cancer of the mouth. The carcinogenic agent has not been identified.

bethanechol chloride (bĕ-tha'nĕ-kol klor'īd) A parasympathomimetic drug used in the treatment of constipation, paralytic ileus, and urinary retention.

bezoar (be′zōr) A concretion consisting of hair (trichobezoar) or vegetable fibers (phytobezoar) formed in the stomach or intestines.

bi- Prefix meaning two; twice.

biauricular (bi-aw-rik′u-lar) 1. Relating to both auricles. 2. Having two auricles.

bibasic (bi-ba′sik) See dibasic.

bibulous (bib′u-lus) Absorbent.

bicameral (bi-kam′er-al) Having two cavities or chambers.

bicarbonate (bi-kar′bo-nāt) The radical group HCO_3^- or any of its salts.

    standard b. The portion of bicarbonate in plasma that is derived from nonrespiratory sources; it is the bicarbonate concentration in the plasma of a whole blood sample that has been equilibrated at a 37°C temperature with a carbon dioxide pressure of 40 mm of mercury. Metabolic alkalosis and acidosis are reflected in abnormally high or low levels, respectively.

bicellular (bi-sel′u-lar) 1. Composed of two cells. 2. Having two compartments.

biceps (bi′seps) A muscle with two origins.

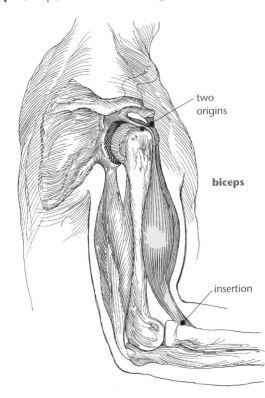

two origins

biceps

insertion

bicipital (bi-sip′i-tal) 1. Having two origins. 2. Relating to a biceps muscle.

biconcave (bi-kon′kāv) Having depressions on both sides; said of a lens.

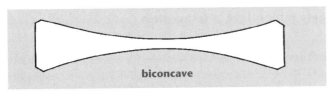

biconcave

biconvex (bi-kon′veks) Protruding on both sides.

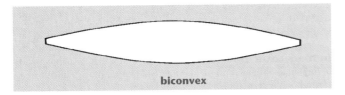

biconvex

bicornate, bicornuate (bi-kor′nāt, bi-kor′nu-āt) Having two protruding parts.

bicuspid (bi-kus′pid) Having two points or cusps; applied to a premolar tooth or a heart valve.

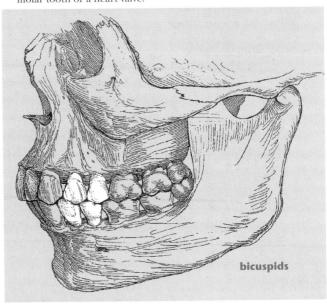

bicuspids

biduous (bid′u-us) Of two day's duration, as a fever.

bifid (bī′fid) Separated into two, usually equal, parts (e.g., a bifid uterus).

bifocal (bī-fo′kal) Having two foci.

bifurcate (bī′fur-kāt) To divide into two parts or branches.

bifurcation (bī-fur-ka′shun) 1. A separation or branching of a structure into two parts. 2. The point at which a structure branches into two parts.

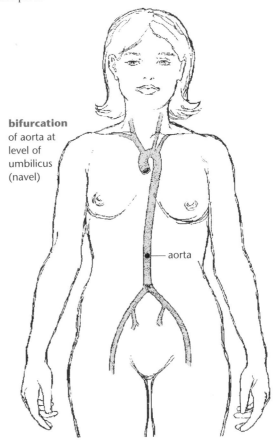

bifurcation of aorta at level of umbilicus (navel)

aorta

bigeminal (bi-jem′ĭ-nal) Paired, double.

bigemini (bī-jem′ĭ-ni) See bigeminy.

bigeminy (bī-jem′ĭ-ne) Occurring in pairs, especially two heartbeats occurring in rapid succession followed by a pause before the next two beats. Also called bigemini.

bigerminal (bī-jer′mĭ-nal) Relating to two ova.

bilateral (bī-lat′er-al) Having two sides.

bile (bil) A bitter, yellowish brown or greenish brown fluid secreted by the liver, stored in the gallbladder, and discharged into the small intestine (specifically, the duodenum); it participates in digestion chiefly by emulsifying fats. Also called gall.

bili- Combining form meaning bile.

biliary (bil′e-a-re) Relating to bile.

bilifuscin (bil-ĭ-fus′in) A dark greenish brown pigment present in bile and bile salts.

bilious (bil′yus) Relating to biliousness.

biliousness (bil′yus-ness) An imprecise term for a condition marked by nausea, digestive disturbances, excessive gas, and often constipation and headache; popularly attributed to gallbladder dysfunction.

bilirubin (bil-ĭ-roo′bin) An orange-red bile pigment formed from the normal breakdown of hemoglobin, pigment of the red blood cell (erythrocyte).

bilirubinemia (bil-ĭ-roo-bĕ-ne′me-ah) A seldom-used term denoting the presence of bilirubin in the blood, a normal condition; generally used to denote an increased level.

bilirubinuria (bil-ĭ-roo-bī-nu′re-ah) The presence of bilirubin in the urine.

biliuria (bil-ĭ-u′re-ah) The presence of bile or bile salts in the urine.

biliverdin (bil-ĭ-ver′din) A green bile pigment, a precursor of bilirubin, produced by the breakdown of hemoglobin.

bilobate, bilobed (bī-lo′bāt, bi′lobd) Having two lobes.

bilobular (bī-lob′u-lar) Having two lobules.

bilocular, biloculate (bī-lok′u-lar, bī-lok′u-lāt) Having two compartments.

bimanual (bī-man′u-al) Involving the use of both hands (e.g., bimanual palpation).

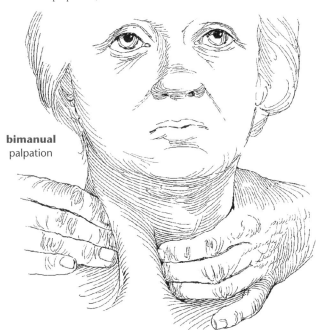

bimanual palpation

bimodal (bī-mo′dal) Having two peaks, as in a graphic curve.

binary (bī′na-re) Composed of two parts.

binaural (bī-naw′ral) Relating to both ears.

bind (bīnd) 1. To wrap, as with a bandage. 2. To take up and hold, as in a weak chemical bond. 3. Popularly, to constipate.

binocular (bin-ok′u-lar) 1. Relating to both eyes. 2. Used with both eyes (e.g., binocular microscope).

binuclear (bī-nu′kle-ar) Having two nuclei.

bio- Combining form meaning life.

bioassay (bi-o-as-sa′) The evaluation of a substance (e.g., a hormone or a vitamin) by comparing its effects on a living organism, or an *in vitro* organ preparation, with those of a standard preparation. Also called biological assay. See also biological monitoring, under monitoring.

bioastronautics (bi-o-as′tro-naw-tiks) The study of the effects of space travel on living organisms, tissues, and cells.

bioavailability (bi-o-ah-vāl-ah-bil′ĭ-te) The degree to which the active ingredient of a drug is absorbed and utilized by the target tissues of the body; it is an indication of both the relative amount of an administered drug reaching the general blood circulation and the rate at which this occurs.

biochemistry (bi-o-kem′is-tre) The study of the chemical components and processes of living organisms. Also called biological chemistry.

biodegradable (bi-o-de-gra′dah-bl) Susceptible to biodegradation.

biodegradation (bi-o-deg-rah-da′shun) The process by which living organisms (e.g., soil bacteria, plants, animals) chemically decompose or break down such materials as organic wastes, pesticides, pollutant chemicals, and implantable materials.

biodynamics (bi-o-di-nam′iks) The study of energy as it relates to living organisms and their environment.

bioenergetics (bi-o-en-er-jet′iks) The study of energy changes involved in the chemical reactions occurring within living organisms.

bioengineering (bi-o-en-jin-ēr′ing) See biomedical engineering.

bioethics (bi-o-eth′iks) The field of applied ethics concerned with the value implications (moral and social) of research and practice in the life sciences.

biofeedback (bi-o-fēd′bak) A technique for training a person to exercise some control over a normally involuntary (autonomic) body function, such as blood pressure. The patient is connected to, and receives information regarding fluctuations in the body function (feedback) from, a recording instrument.

biohazard (bi-o-haz′ard) The likelihood that potentially dangerous, biologically active, infectious agents (e.g., bacteria, viruses, recombinant DNA) will produce adverse health effects on human beings or some other target species as a result of exposure to those agents under certain conditions.

biologic, biological (bi-o-loj′ik, bi-o-loj′ĭ-kal) Relating to biology.

biologicals (bi-o-loj′ĭ-kalz) Therapeutic substances derived from living organisms (e.g., vaccine, antitoxin, serum).

biologist (bi-ol′ŏ-jist) A scientist who is trained in or specializes in biology.

biology (bi-ol′ŏ-je) The science concerned with living organisms.

  cell b. See cytology.

  molecular b. The study of biological processes in terms of the physics and chemistry of the molecular structures involved, including chemical interactions of genetic material.

  radiation b. The study of the effects of ionizing radiation on living organisms.

biomechanics (bi-o-mĕ-kan′iks) The application of the laws of mechanics to the structure of the living body.

biomedical (bi-o-med′ĭ-kal) Relating to the aspects of biological sciences that pertain to clinical medicine.

biometrician (bi-o-mĕ-trish′an) A specialist in biometry.

biometry (bi-om′ĕ-tre) The branch of statistics concerned with analysis and application of biological data.

biomicroscope (bi-o-mi′krŏ-skōp) A microscope designed for examining living tissues in the body; one equipped with a slitlike opening through which a beam of intense light is projected into the patient's eye; used in ophthalmology to examine the structure at the front of the eye under magnification. Also called slitlamp.

biomicroscopy (bi-o-mi-kros′ko-pe) Examination of the eye with a biomicroscope, especially the lids, cornea, anterior chamber, and iris; interior structures of the eye (vitreous, optic nerve, retina) are usually examined by adding a self-adhering corneal contact lens.

bion (bi′on) Any living organism.

bionics (bi-on′iks) The study of biological functions and mechanisms in order to develop electronic systems with similar organization.

bionosis (bi-o-no′sis) Any disease caused by a living organism.

biophysics (bi-o-fiz′iks) Application of the principles of physics to the study of biologic processes.

 dental b. The study of the physical properties of oral structures in relation to the mechanical forces exerted by a dental restoration.

biopsy (bi′op-se) (BX) **1.** A diagnostic procedure consisting of the removal of cells or tissues from the living body for gross and microscopic examination. **2.** A popular name for the specimen itself.

 aspiration b. See needle biopsy.

 brush b. Removal of cells with a brush-tipped instrument; the cells of interest are entrapped in the bristles by manipulating the instrument against the suspected area of disease (e.g., within a ureter).

 endoscopic b. Biopsy performed with a viewing instrument (endoscope) equipped with an attachment, either a forceps or a brush, for removing tissue or cells, respectively, from the lining of a hollow organ (e.g., the stomach, esophagus, or colon).

 excisional b. The removal of an entire lesion (e.g., a lump) and a margin of surrounding normal tissue for gross and microscopic examination.

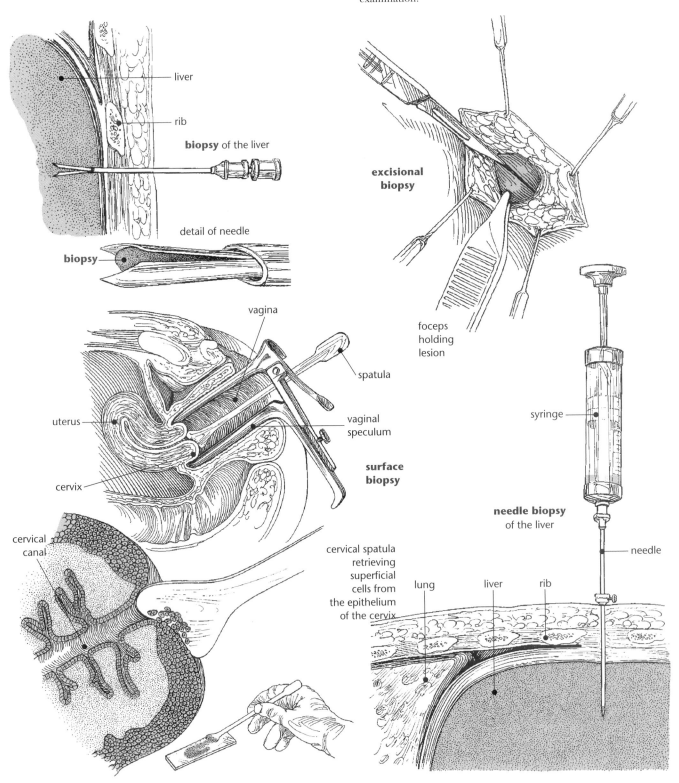

biopsy of the liver

detail of needle

biopsy

excisional biopsy

foceps holding lesion

vagina

spatula

vaginal speculum

uterus

cervix

surface biopsy

cervical canal

cervical spatula retrieving superficial cells from the epithelium of the cervix

syringe

needle biopsy of the liver

needle

lung   liver   rib

needle b. Biopsy performed with a needle attached to a syringe and inserted through the skin into the target tissue; the specimen is sucked out through the needle. Also called aspiration biopsy.

open b. Biopsy carried out during a surgical operation so that the organ may be visualized at the time of biopsy; used when there is a need to avoid dangerous nearby structures, to ascertain proper sampling, or to avoid undue bleeding.

punch b. Removal of a plug of tissue by pressing down and twisting a special cutting instrument with a cylindrical sharp end. Also called trephine biopsy.

shave b. Biopsy in which a scalpel or a razor blade is used to cut through the base of an elevated lesion in one smooth motion.

surface b. The scraping of tissue from a surface as from the opening of the uterine cervix for the detection of cancer.

timed endometrial b. In artificial insemination, a biopsy of the internal lining (endometrium) of the uterus, performed approximately in midcycle (at the time of ovulation) to determine if the endometrium is in its secretory phase, capable of participating in implantation of the fertilized egg. Also called timed uterine-wall biopsy.

timed uterine-wall b. See timed endometrial biopsy.

trephine b. See punch biopsy.

biorhythm (bi′o-rithm) A biologically determined cyclic occurrence in an organism (e.g., the sleep cycle).

biosensor (bi-o-sen′sor) Any of a variety of probes for measuring the presence or concentration of biological molecules, cells, and microorganisms; they translate a biochemical interaction at the probe surface into a quantifiable physical signal (e.g., a change in temperature).

biospectrometry (bi-o-spek-trom′ĕ-tre) Measurement of the quantity of substances in a living specimen or a specimen from a living person by means of a spectroscope.

biospectroscopy (bi-o-spek-tros′ko-pe) Examination of a living specimen or a specimen from a living person with a spectroscope.

biostatistics (bi-o-stah-tis′tiks) The application of statistical methods to the analysis and interpretation of biological and medical phenomena.

biosynthesis (bi-o-sin′thĕ-sis) The formation of chemical compounds by and within living organisms.

biotechnology (bi-o-tek-nol′o-je) The research and development concerned with the use of organisms, cells, or cell-derived constituents to develop products that are technically, scientifically, and clinically useful. The chief focus of biotechnology is the DNA molecule and the alteration of biological function at the molecular level; its laboratory methods include transfection and cloning techniques; sequence and structure analysis algorithms; computer databases; and function, analysis, and prediction of gene and protein structure. See also genetic engineering, under engineering; recombinant DNA technology, under technology; biomedical engineering, under engineering.

biotelemetry (bi-o-tel-em′ĕ-tre) The recording and measuring of vital processes of a subject located at a site remote from the measuring device; the data are transmitted without wires.

biotic (bi-ot′ik) Relating to life.

biotin (bi′o-tin) A growth factor present in minute quantities in every living cell; found abundantly in such organs as liver, kidney, and pancreas and in yeast and milk.

biotoxin (bi-o-tok′sin) Any poison formed by any living organism.

biotransformation (bi-o-trans-for-ma′shun) The interaction between a drug and a living organism, and the resulting chemical change in the drug molecules.

biparietal (bi-pah-ri′ĕ-tal) Relating to both parietal bones of the skull.

biparous (bip′ah-rus) Having borne twins.

biped (bi′ped) An animal that has two feet.

bipennate, bipenniform (bi-pen′āt, bi-pen′ĭ-form) Resembling a feather; said of a muscle with fibers arranged symmetrically along a central tendon.

bipolar (bi-po′lar) Having two poles or extremes.

birefringence (bi-re-frin′jens) See double refraction, under refraction.

birth (birth) The act of being born.

live b. The complete expulsion or extraction of a product of conception from the mother, regardless of the duration of pregnancy, and which, after such separation, breathes or shows other evidence of life (such as pulsation of the umbilical cord, beating of the heart, definite movements of involuntary muscles) whether or not the umbilical cord has been cut or the placenta has detached.

premature b. The birth of an infant after 20 weeks of gestation but before full term is achieved.

birthmark (birth′mark) Popular name for any area of discolored skin or growth present at birth (e.g., a nevus).

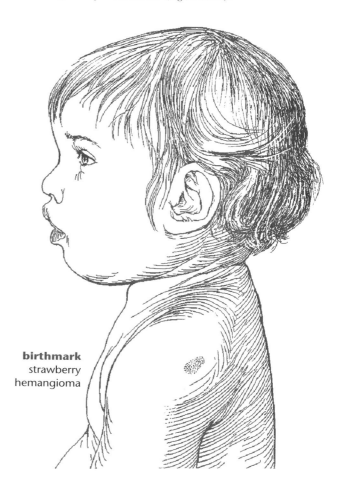

birthmark
strawberry
hemangioma

bis- Prefix meaning twice; double.

bisacodyl (bis-ak′o-dil) A laxative compound used orally or rectally.

bisexual (bi-sek′shoo-al) An individual who has sexual interests in both males and females. Also called ambisexual.

bis in die (bis in de′a) (b.i.d.) Latin for twice a day.

bismuth (biz′muth) A metallic element; symbol Bi, atomic number 83, atomic weight 209.

bite (bit) In dentistry, the contact between the upper (maxillary) and lower (mandibular) teeth in any functional relation.

closed b. See small interarch distance, under distance.

open b. Deformity marked by failure of the anterior upper and lower teeth to make contact when the jaws are fully closed. Also called apertognathia.

bitemporal (bi-tem′po-ral) Relating to both temples or temporal bones.

biteplate, biteplane (bīt′plāt, bīt′plān) A removable dental appliance that covers the palate and has either an inclined or a flat surface at the front border; designed to offer resistance to the upper incisors when they make contact.

bivalence, bivalency (bi-va′lens, bi-va′len-se) Combining power (valence) double that of a hydrogen atom. Also called divalence.

B

bivalent (bi-va′lent) **1.** Having the combining power of two hydrogen atoms. **2.** In cytogenetics, composed of two homologous chromosomes. Also called divalent.

biventer (bi′ven-ter) Having two bellies; said of certain muscles.

blackhead (blak′hed) Popular name for a comedo.

blackout (blak′owt) Momentary loss of consciousness.

black widow (blak wid′o) An extremely poisonous spider, *Lactrodectus mactans*, about 1½ inches long, with a shiny black body and an hourglass-shaped red spot on the underside of its body.

bladder (blad′der) A distensible musculomembranous sac serving as a receptacle for a fluid, especially the urinary bladder.

    atonic b. A flaccid, distended bladder that is unable to contract, usually due to paralysis of the motor nerves innervating it.

    Christmas tree b. The characteristic appearance of a spastic bladder, caused by lesions of the upper motor nerve supply of the bladder (at the 12th thoracic or 1st lumbar level).

    gall b. See gallbladder.

    ileal b. See ileal conduit, under conduit.

    nervous b. Condition in which a person has a constant desire to urinate but is unable to empty the bladder completely.

    neurogenic b. Any disturbance of bladder function originating from an impaired nerve supply to the bladder, caused by lesions either of the spinal cord or of the nerves themselves.

    urinary b. The reservoir for urine; it receives urine from the kidneys via the ureters and discharges it through the urethra. Usually called bladder.

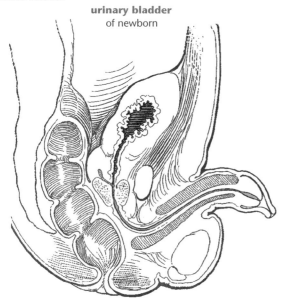

urinary bladder
of newborn

-blast Suffix meaning immature; applied to cells (e.g., erythroblast).

blasto- Combining form meaning early stage.

blastocele (blas′to-sēl) The fluid-filled cavity of a blastocyst.

blastocyst (blas′to-sist) The embryo at the time of implantation into the inner wall of the uterus. It consists of a single layer of outer cells (trophoblast), a fluid-filled cavity (blastocele), and a mass of inner cells (embryoblast). Also called blastodermic vesicle.

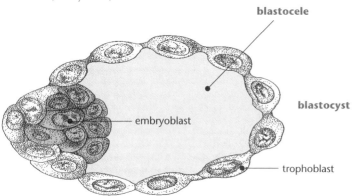

blastocele

blastocyst

embryoblast

trophoblast

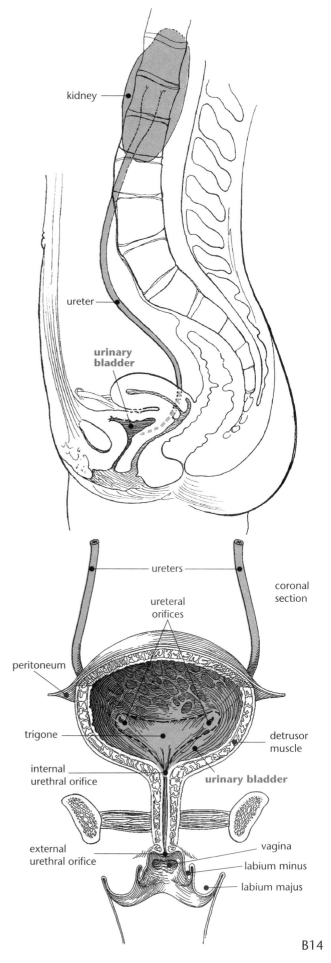

kidney

ureter

urinary bladder

ureters

coronal section

ureteral orifices

peritoneum

trigone

detrusor muscle

internal urethral orifice

urinary bladder

external urethral orifice

vagina

labium minus

labium majus

B14

Blastocystis hominis (blas-to-sis′tis hom′ĭ-nis) Protozoan found in feces; it may cause diarrhea when present in large numbers; previously considered a nonpathogenic yeast.

blastoma (blas-to′mah) Malignant tumor composed of embryonic, undifferentiated cells.

blastomere (blas′to-mēr) One of the cells into which the fertilized egg divides.

Blastomyces dermatitidis (blas-to-mi′sēz der-mah-tit′ĭ-dis) A yeastlike fungus found in wood and soil; it causes blastomycosis.

blastomycosis (blas-to-mi-ko′sis) A chronic pus–forming (suppurative) disease caused by inhaling the fungus *Blastomyces dermatitidis*. It usually begins as a lung infection and disseminates to the skin, sometimes to bone and other organs. Formerly called North American blastomycosis.

    North American b. See blastomycosis.

    South American b. See paracoccidioidomycosis.

blastula (blas′tu-lah) Early stage in the development of an embryo consisting of a spherical structure formed by a single layer of cells that encloses a fluid-filled cavity.

blastulation (blas-tu-la′shun) Formation of a blastula.

bleb (bleb) A blister.

bleeder (blēd′er) Popular name for a person afflicted with hemophilia or any other bleeding disorder.

bleeding (blēd′ing) The escape of blood.

    dysfunctional uterine b. Bleeding from the uterus due to a disturbance of endocrine glands.

    intermenstrual b. See metrorrhagia.

blennadenitis (blen-ad-ĕ-ni′tis) Inflammation of mucous glands.

blennorrhea (blen-no-re′ah) Any profuse discharge of secretions containing mucus, especially from the vagina or urethra.

    inclusion b. See inclusion conjunctivitis, under conjunctivitis.

blennorrheal (blen-no-re′al) Relating to blennorrhea.

blepharectomy (blef-ah-rek′to-me) Surgical removal of all or part of an eyelid.

blepharitis (blef-ah-ri′tis) Inflammation of one or both eyelids.

    contact b. Blepharitis caused by topically applied medication (e.g., atropine, neomycin, broad-spectrum antibiotics).

    marginal b. Chronic inflammation of the lid edges causing irritation, burning, and itching of the lid margins with redness of the eyes and scales or granulations clinging from the eyelashes. Also called granulated eyelids.

    seborrheic b. Marginal blepharitis with greasy scale formation; associated with seborrhea or dandruff of the scalp, eyebrows, and ears.

    staphylococcal b. Marginal blepharitis with dry scales, tiny ulcerations at the roots of the eyelashes, and loss of the eyelashes.

blepharo-, blephar- Combining forms meaning eyelid.

blepharochalasis (blef-ah-ro-kal′ah-sis) A redundancy of eyelid tissue that droops over the lids when the eyes are open.

blepharochalasis

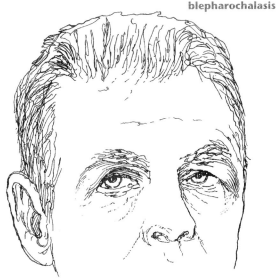

blepharoclonus (blef-ah-ro-klo′nus) A rhythmic spasm of the eyelids.

blepharoconjunctivitis (blef′ah-ro-kon-junk′ti-vi′tis) Inflammation of the eyelids and conjunctiva, the thin, transparent covering of the inner eyelids and sclera.

blepharoplasty (blef′ah-ro-plas-te) Surgical correction of a defect of the eyelids, especially removal of excess folds of skin and fat from the upper and lower eyelids to eliminate wrinkles on the upper lids and "bags" under the eye. Also called aesthetic eyelid surgery.

blepharoptosis (blef-ah-ro-to′sis) Drooping of the upper eyelid.

blepharoptosis
ptosis of left
upper eyelid

blepharospasm (blef′ah-ro-spazm) Involuntary contraction of the muscles of the eyelid, resulting in closure of the eye.

    essential b. A progressive condition affecting both eyes, marked by spasmodic, forceful closure of the eyelids, resulting in visual disability.

blepharosynechia (blef-ah-ro-sĭ-ne′ke-ah) Adhesion of the eyelids. Also called ankyloblepharon.

blepharotomy (blef-ah-rot′o-me) Incision of an eyelid.

blind (blīnd) 1. Unable to see. 2. Closed at one end; having only one opening.

blindness (blind′ness) Lack of the sense of sight.

    color b. A misnomer for a genetically transmitted condition marked by diminished ability to perceive differences in certain colors. It is not blindness as the term is generally understood.

    day b. See hemeralopia.

    eclipse b. Damage to the light-sensitive tissue within the eyeball (retina) due to destructive photochemical reactions caused by wavelengths of 440 to 500 nm (blue light), as would occur when staring at a solar eclipse. Also called solar blindness.

    flash b. Temporary loss of vision caused by bursts of high-intensity light.

    legal b. (*a*) Blindness as defined by law; in most states of the United States, it is a visual acuity of 20/200 or less in the better eye with best correction, or a total visual field of 20° or less. (*b*) Loss of vision sufficient to prevent a person from being self-supporting in an occupation, rendering that person dependent on other individuals, agencies, or devices.

    letter b. A form of aphasia in which a person can see written letters but they have no meaning.

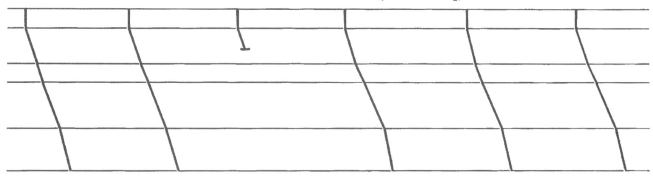

sinoatrial block (the entire P-QRS-T sequence is missing)

night b. See nyctalopia.

pure word b. A form of aphasia in which a person is unable to recognize the written word as conveyer of ideas.

river b. See ocular onchocerciasis.

snow b. Temporary blindness caused by excessive exposure to sunlight reflected from snow.

solar b. See eclipse blindness.

blister (blis'ter) General term for an elevated cutaneous lesion filled with clear fluid. See also bulla; vesicle.

fever b. See herpes febrilis, under herpes.

bloat, bloating (blōt, blōt'ing) Distention of the abdomen with gas.

bloater (blo'ter) One who is bloated.

blue b. Informal term used to describe the appearance of a patient afflicted with the lung disease emphysema. The patient appears blue-purple (cyanotic) due to oxygen deficiency in the blood and also appears bloated or swollen due to fluid collection in the tissues (edema), which is caused chiefly by heart failure. COMPARE pink puffer.

block (blok) 1. An obstruction to passage. 2. An interruption of nerve impulses.

alveolar-capillary b. Impairment of the normal passage of gases, especially oxygen, across the walls of minute blood vessels (capillaries) and air spaces (alveoli) in the lungs.

anterograde b. A block in the conduction of a cardiac impulse anywhere on its normal course from the sinoatrial node to the ventricles.

arborization b. Impaired conduction of impulses within the heart, a form of intraventricular block, thought to be due to widespread blockage in the Purkinje fibers.

atrioventricular b., A-V b. Impairment of the normal conduction of impulses between the atria and ventricles of the heart; classified in three degrees: (a) first-degree A-V block, conduction time is prolonged but all impulses from the atria reach the ventricles; (b) second-degree A-V block, some but not all atrial impulses fail to reach the ventricles; therefore, some ventricular beats are dropped; (c) third-degree A-V block, all atrial impulses are blocked.

bundle-branch b. (BBB) Impaired impulse conduction through the cardiac ventricles due to interruption at one of the main branches of the atrioventricular bundle (bundle of His).

caudal b. See caudal anesthesia, under anesthesia.

exit b. Interruption of the conduction of a cardiac impulse occurring at its point of exit.

heart b. Atrioventricular block.

intra-atrial b. Impaired impulse conduction through the atria of the heart.

intraventricular b., I-V b. Delayed conduction through the ventricles.

left bundle-branch b. (LBBB) Interruption of impulse conduction within the heart, occurring in the left branch of the atrioventricular bundle (bundle of His).

lochia b. See lochiometra.

peri-infarction b. Delayed conduction through the heart muscle (myocardium) due to an old scar, the result of deprivation of blood to that area of the muscle because of a clogged artery.

right bundle-branch b. (RBBB) Interruption of impulse conduction within the heart, occurring in the right branch of the atrioventricular bundle (bundle of His).

sinoatrial b., S-A b., sinus b. Failure of the nerve impulse to leave the sinus node.

spinal b. See spinal anesthesia, under anesthesia.

blockade (blok'ād) Temporary interruption of the function or activity of a body system, usually by a chemical substance.

adrenergic b. Chemical inhibition of the responses of effector nerve cells to sympathetic impulses and to adrenaline.

cholinergic b. Chemical interruption of nerve impulse transmission at autonomic ganglionic synapses (ganglionic blockade), at muscle-nerve junctions (myoneural blockade), and at postganglionic parasympathetic effector cells.

blocker (blok'er) See blocking agent, under agent.

blocking (blok'ing) 1. Obstructing passage or transmission. 2. A sudden interruption in flow of thinking or speaking, which is perceived as an absence of thought.

blood (blud) The fluid circulated through a closed circuit composed of the heart and blood vessels. It consists of a pale yellow fluid (plasma) in which are suspended red blood cells (erythrocytes), white blood cells (leukocytes), and platelets.

arterial b. The relatively bright red blood that has been oxygenated in the lungs and is within the left chambers of the heart and the arteries.

cord b. Blood within the umbilical cord.

occult b. Blood present in amounts too small to be seen with the naked eye.

venous b. The dark red blood within the veins; it loses oxygen and gains carbon dioxide by passing through metabolically active tissues.

whole b. Donated blood that has not been separated into its components.

blood bank (blud bangk) See blood bank, under bank.

blood banking (blud bangk'ing) See transfusion medicine, under medicine.

blood count (blud kount) See blood count, under count.

blood group (blud grōōp) Any of various immunologically distinct and genetically determined classes of human blood, identified clinically by characteristic agglutination reactions. Blood groups are used in medicolegal investigations (e.g., in excluding paternity) and in genetic and anthropological investigations. For individual blood groups, see specific names.

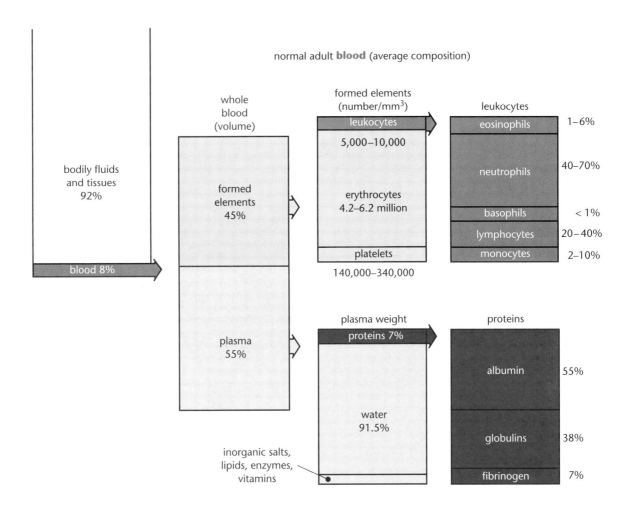

normal adult **blood** (average composition)

whole blood (volume)

bodily fluids and tissues 92%

blood 8%

formed elements 45%

plasma 55%

formed elements (number/mm³)

leukocytes 5,000–10,000

erythrocytes 4.2–6.2 million

platelets 140,000–340,000

leukocytes

eosinophils	1–6%
neutrophils	40–70%
basophils	< 1%
lymphocytes	20–40%
monocytes	2–10%

plasma weight

proteins 7%

water 91.5%

inorganic salts, lipids, enzymes, vitamins

proteins

albumin	55%
globulins	38%
fibrinogen	7%

blood grouping (blud grōōp'ing) Classification of blood samples according to their agglutinating properties. Also called blood typing.

bloodletting (blud'let-ing) The withdrawal of blood from a vein for therapeutic purposes.

bloodstream (blud'strēm) The blood circulating within the vascular component of the body, as opposed to blood that has been sequestered in a part (e.g., in a subdural hemangioma).

blood type (blud tīp) The specific reaction pattern of red blood cells of a person to the antisera of a blood group. See blood group.

blood typing (blud ti'ping) See blood grouping.

blotting (blot'ing) The process of transferring electrophoretically separated particles (such as proteins and DNA fragments) onto special filters, papers, or membranes for analysis. See also Northern, Southern, and Western blot analysis, under analysis.

blush (blush) Descriptive term for a localized density observed in x-ray examination of blood vessels, due to increased vascularity (e.g., in a tumor) or to leakage of blood.

B-mode (b-mōd) A diagnostic ultrasound presentation on a screen in which the coordinate on the X axis of an oscilloscope represents time (distance) and the strength of the echo is displayed as a dot; the dot brightness (B) indicates the echo intensity.

board certified (bord cer'tĭ-fĭd) Formally recognized as having passed an examination given by a specialty board after meeting certain specified criteria, such as prior training requirements and an examination; said of a physician or other health care professional.

bobbing (bob'ing) An up-and-down movement, such as the movement of the eyes in certain conditions.

body (bod'e) 1. The entire material structure of humans and animals. 2. The principal part of anything. 3. Any small mass of material.

acetone b.'s See ketone bodies.

alcoholic hyaline b.'s See Mallory bodies.

amyloid b.'s of prostate Small, soft masses found in the acini of the prostate, composed of prostatic secretion and epithelial cells. Also called corpora amylacea.

aortic b. One of the two small structures attached to a branch of the aorta, on either side of the aortic arch; it contains chemoreceptors that respond to reduction in blood oxygen tension.

Aschoff b.'s A collection of minute nodules consisting of cells and fibroblastic proliferation; the characteristic lesion of acute rheumatic inflammation of the heart muscle. Also called Aschoff nodules.

Auer b.'s Elongated granular structures found in the cytoplasm of immature myeloid cells in acute granulocytic leukemia.

Barr chromatin b., Barr b. See sex chromatin, under chromatin.

basal b. A thickened cellular organelle resembling the centriole, located on the subsurface of flagellate protozoa and from which the axoneme of each flagellum or cilium arises. Also called basal granule.

carotid b. A small oval structure situated at the bifurcation of each common carotid artery on either side of the neck; it contains chemoreceptors that monitor oxygen and carbon dioxide concentration in the blood; it aids in the regulation of respiration.

cell b. The portion of a cell, especially a nerve cell (neuron), that surrounds and includes the nucleus, excluding any projection.

central fibrous b. of heart See right fibrous trigone of heart, under trigone.

ciliary b. The circular, most vascular structure of the eye, connecting the vascular layer of the eyeball (choroid) with the iris; composed of six layers including the ciliary muscle and ligaments, which serve to adjust the lens for near and far vision. Also called corpus ciliare.

Councilman b.'s Oval or round, condensed globules, representing dead and shrunken liver cells (hepatocytes); formed in the liver in acute viral hepatitis. Also called Councilman's lesion.

foreign b. Any object or mass of material in the body that has been accidentally or deliberately introduced from without.

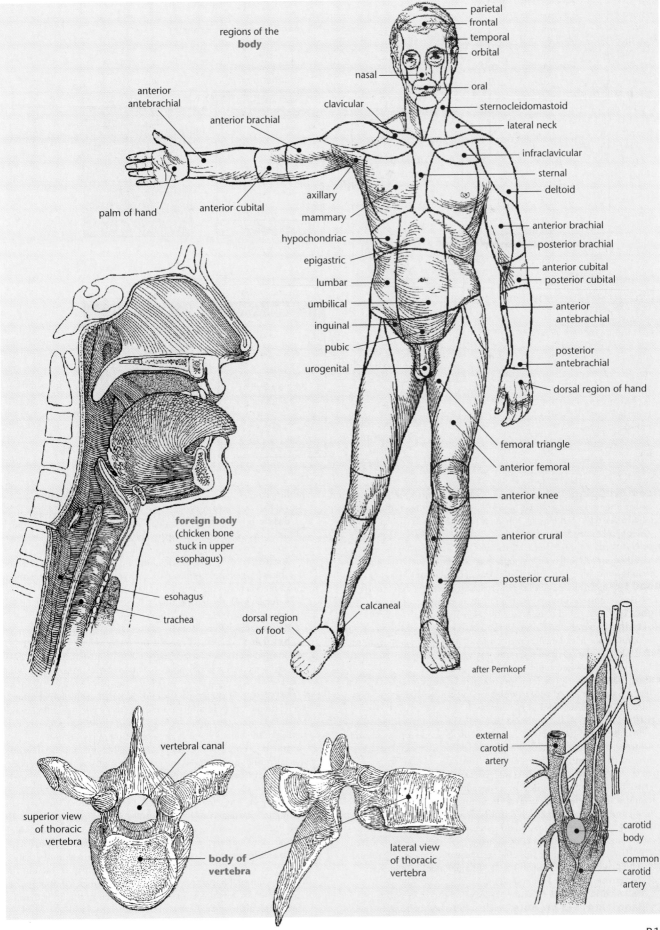

regions of the **body**

parietal
frontal
temporal
orbital
nasal
oral
sternocleidomastoid
lateral neck
infraclavicular
sternal
deltoid
anterior brachial
posterior brachial
anterior cubital
posterior cubital
anterior antebrachial
posterior antebrachial
dorsal region of hand
femoral triangle
anterior femoral
anterior knee
anterior crural
posterior crural

clavicular
anterior antebrachial
anterior brachial
palm of hand
anterior cubital
axillary
mammary
hypochondriac
epigastric
lumbar
umbilical
inguinal
pubic
urogenital

calcaneal
dorsal region of foot

after Pernkopf

foreign body
(chicken bone stuck in upper esophagus)

esohagus
trachea

vertebral canal

superior view of thoracic vertebra

body of vertebra

lateral view of thoracic vertebra

external carotid artery

carotid body

common carotid artery

B

body ■ body

B18

geniculate b.'s The four protuberances within the brain on either side of the posteroinferior aspect of the thalamus (two lateral, two medial). They contain nuclei that act as a relay in the visual and auditory pathways to the surface (cortex) of the brain.

Heinz b.'s Abnormal granules formed within red blood cells (erythrocytes) by oxidation and precipitation of the blood pigment hemoglobin. Also called Heinz granules.

hematoxylin b.'s, hematoxyphil b.'s Irregular particles found in the tissues of patients with systemic lupus erythematosus (SLE). They readily take up hematoxylin stain and are presumed to be remnants of injured cell nuclei.

Howell-Jolly b.'s Small particles found within red blood cells (erythrocytes), thought to represent degraded nucleus material; frequently found after surgical removal of the spleen and in association with hemolytic and hemoblastic anemias.

hyaline b.'s of pituitary Gelatinous material sometimes accumulating in cells of the posterior lobe of the pituitary (hypophysis).

inclusion b.'s Particles frequently observed within either the cytoplasm or the nucleus (occasionally in both) of cells infected with certain viruses; some may be infective, others may be only abnormal products elaborated by the cell in response to the virus.

juxtaglomerular b. A group of cells surrounding arterioles of the renal glomerulus; they contain granules thought to be composed of the kidney enzyme renin.

ketone b.'s Collective name for the end products of improper and excessive breakdown of stored fat in the liver. These substances are acetoacetic acid, acetone, and beta-hydroxybutyrate; they accumulate in the blood and spill over in the urine in such conditions as uncontrolled or undiagnosed diabetes and in severe starvation. Also called ketones.

Mallory's b.'s Waxy material accumulated in damaged liver cells; seen in certain diseases, especially liver disease caused by alcoholism. Also called alcoholic hyaline bodies.

malpighian b.'s of kidney See renal corpuscle, under corpuscle.

mamillary b. Either of two protuberances within the base of the brain, on each side of the interpeduncular space; it contains the mamillary nuclei of the posterior hypothalamus. Also called corpus mamillare.

melanin b. See melanosome.

Negri b.'s Particles present in the cytoplasm of nerve cells (neurons) of persons infected with the rabies virus.

Nissl b.'s Clusters of endoplasmic reticula and attached ribosomes; present in the cytoplasm of nerve cells (neurons). Also called Nissl granules.

pacchionian b.'s See arachnoid granulations, under granulation.

para-aortic b.'s See organs of Zuckerkandl, under organ.

pineal b. A small glandlike structure situated on the roof of the third ventricle of the brain. Also called pineal gland.

pituitary b. See hypophysis.

psammoma b.'s Spherical deposits of calcified material generally found in papillary cancer. Also called sand bodies.

quadrigeminal b.'s Four paired eminences forming the dorsal part of the midbrain.

restiform b. See inferior cerebellar peduncle, under peduncle.

sand b.'s See psammoma bodies.

sex chromatin b. See sex chromatin, under chromatin.

b. of stomach The major part of the stomach, extending proximally from the cardiac and fundic parts downward to where it blends imperceptibly into the more distal pyloric part of the stomach.

striate b. See corpus striatum, under corpus.

trachoma b.'s Intracellular deposits in the inner lining of the eyelids (tarsal conjunctiva), occurring characteristically in the acute stage of trachoma.

b. of uterus The upper two-thirds of the nonpregnant uterus, above the constricted lower portion (isthmus).

b. of vertebra The cylindrical anterior (ventral) portion of a vertebra, which is separated from the bodies of adjacent vertebrae by

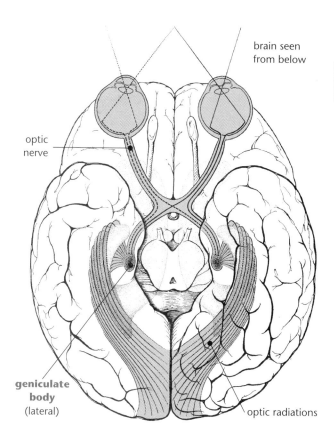

brain seen from below

optic nerve

geniculate body (lateral)

optic radiations

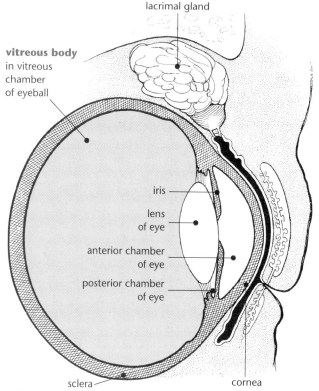

lacrimal gland

vitreous body in vitreous chamber of eyeball

iris

lens of eye

anterior chamber of eye

posterior chamber of eye

sclera

cornea

fibrocartilaginous pads (intervertebral disks).

vitreous b. The colorless, transparent gel, with a consistency slightly firmer than egg white, that occupies four-fifths of the eyeball behind the lens; composed of a watery substance contained within a delicate network of fine collagen fibrils; the periphery of the gel is condensed, forming the vitreous membrane. Also called vitreous; corpus vitreum.

wolffian b. See mesonephros.

body ■ body

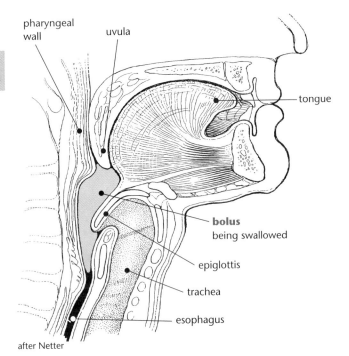

pharyngeal wall
uvula
tongue
bolus being swallowed
epiglottis
trachea
esophagus

after Netter

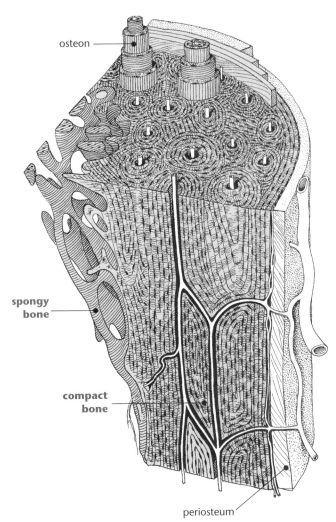

osteon
spongy bone
compact bone
periosteum

body burden (bod'e ber'den) The amount of a harmful material present in the body at any given time.

boil (boil) A swollen, pus-filled infection of a hair follicle usually caused by the bacterium *Staphylococcus aureus*. Also called furuncle.

bolus (bo'lus) **1.** A soft, round mass of food passed into the esophagus during the process of swallowing. **2.** The rapid injection into a vein of a relatively large dose of a drug.

bomb (bomb) An apparatus containing a radioactive material for therapeutic application to a circumscribed area of the body.

bombard (bom-bard') To expose to a beam of ionizing radiation.

bombesin (bom'bĕ-sin) A peptide neurotransmitter present in the inner lining of the gastrointestinal tract, thought to stimulate release of the hormone gastrin from the stomach.

bond (bond) In chemistry, any of various forces holding together atoms or ions within a molecule.

bonding (bond'ing) An emotional attachment to a person or a pet; especially the result of the process of attachment between two people, such as mother and child, whose identities are significantly affected by their mutual interaction.

bone (bōn) **1.** The special mineralized connective tissue forming the skeleton of vertebrates. **2.** Any of the units forming the skeleton. For individual bones, see table of bones.

    alveolar b. The thin plate of bone forming the tooth sockets.

    ankle b. See talus, in table of bones.

    blade b. See scapula, in table of bones.

    breast b. See sternum, in table of bones.

    brittle b.'s See osteogenesis imperfecta, under osteogenesis.

    cancellous b. See spongy bone.

    cheek b. See zygomatic bone, in table of bones.

    collar b. See clavicle, in table of bones.

    compact b. A dense, ivorylike tissue forming the outer (cortical) layer of bones; it contains minute spaces and channels. Also called dense bone; cortical substance of bone; compact substance of bone.

    cranial b.'s The 21 bones forming the skull; the paired inferior nasal concha, lacrimal, maxilla, nasal, palatine, parietal, temporal, and zygomatic; and the unpaired ethmoid, frontal, occipital, sphenoid, and vomer.

    dense b. See compact bone.

    ear b.'s See auditory ossicles, under ossicle.

    elbow b. See ulna, in table of bones.

    facial b.'s, b.'s of face The bones surrounding the mouth, nose, and part of the eye sockets (orbits); i.e., the paired maxilla, zy-gomatic, inferior nasal concha, nasal, lacrimal, and palatine; and the unpaired mandible, ethmoid, and vomer. Some authorities include the hyoid bone.

    flank b. See ilium, in table of bones.

    flat b. Any bone of slight thickness and chiefly compact structure; generally composed of two plates arranged in a parallel direction, separated by a thin layer of spongy bone.

    heel b. See calcaneus, in table of bones.

    hip b. See hipbone.

    innominate b. See hipbone.

    irregular b. Any bone of complex shape that cannot be classified as long, short, or flat.

    jaw b. See mandible, in table of bones.

    long b. Any bone having greater length than width, consisting of a tubular shaft, which contains a medullary cavity, and two expanded ends.

    marble b.'s See osteopetrosis.

    rider's b. Bone formation in the tendon of the long adductor muscle (adductor longus muscle) resulting from habitual horseback riding.

    shin b. See tibia, in table of bones.

    short b. A bone having the general appearance of a cube and a relatively large proportion of spongy bone within a layer of compact bone.

    spongy b. An inner meshwork of bony intercommunications separated by numerous large spaces filled with vascular tissue, fat, and bone marrow; it is surrounded by an outer layer of compact bone. Also called cancellous bone; spongy substance of bone.

    sutural b. See sutural bones, in table of bones.

    thigh b. See femur, in table of bones.

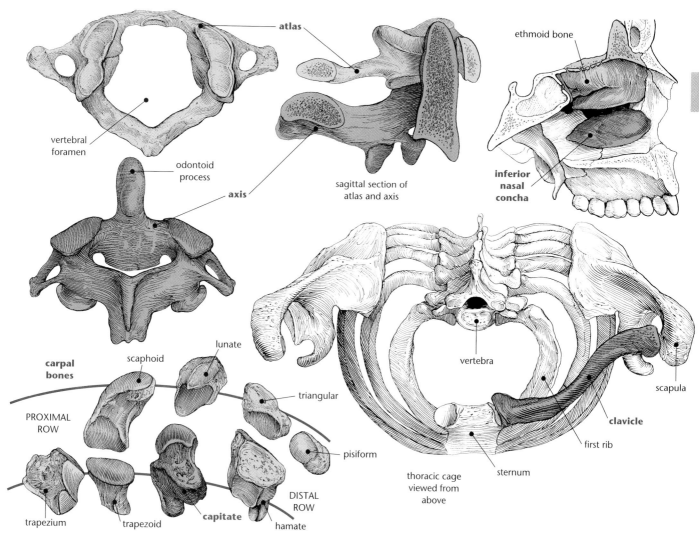

atlas

vertebral foramen

odontoid process

axis

sagittal section of atlas and axis

ethmoid bone

inferior nasal concha

B

vertebra

scapula

clavicle

first rib

sternum

thoracic cage viewed from above

carpal bones

scaphoid

lunate

triangular

pisiform

PROXIMAL ROW

DISTAL ROW

trapezium

trapezoid

capitate

hamate

BONE	LOCATION	DESCRIPTION	ARTICULATIONS
ankle b.		see talus	
anvil b.		see incus	
astragalus		see talus	
atlas *atlas*	neck	first cervical vertebra	occipital (above), axis (below)
axis epistropheus *axis*	neck	second cervical vertebra	atlas (above), third cervical vertebra (below)
backbones		see vertebrae	
calcaneus heel b. *calcaneus*	foot	largest of the tarsal b.'s situated at back of foot, forming heel; somewhat cuboidal	talus (above), cuboid (below)
capitate b. magnum b. os *capitatum*	wrist	largest of carpal b.'s, occupies center of wrist	second, third, and fourth metacarpal b.'s; lunate, trapezoid, scaphoid, hamate
carpal b.'s *ossa carpi*	wrist	eight in number, arranged in two rows: scaphoid, lunate, triangular (triquetral), and pisiform (proximal row); trapezium, trapezoid, capitate, and hamate (distal row)	
cheekbone		see zygomatic bone	
clavicle collar b. *clavicula*	shoulder	long curved b. placed nearly horizontally above first rib	sternum, scapula, cartilage of first rib
coccyx os *coccygis*	lower back	from three to five triangular rudimentary vertebrae with only the first not fused	sacrum
concha, inferior nasal inferior turbinate b. *concha nasalis inferior*	skull	thin irregular, scroll-shaped b. extending horizontally along lateral wall of nasal cavity	ethmoid, maxilla, palatine

bone ■ bone

B

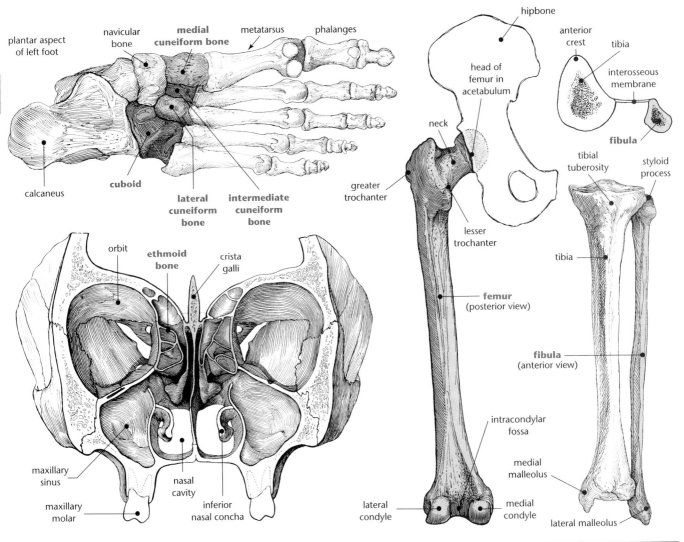

plantar aspect of left foot

navicular bone

medial cuneiform bone

metatarsus

phalanges

calcaneus

cuboid

lateral cuneiform bone

intermediate cuneiform bone

hipbone

head of femur in acetabulum

neck

greater trochanter

lesser trochanter

femur (posterior view)

intracondylar fossa

medial malleolus

lateral condyle

medial condyle

anterior crest

tibia

interosseous membrane

fibula

tibial tuberosity

styloid process

tibia

fibula (anterior view)

lateral malleolus

orbit

ethmoid bone

crista galli

maxillary sinus

maxillary molar

nasal cavity

inferior nasal concha

BONE	LOCATION	DESCRIPTION	ARTICULATIONS
cuboid *os cuboideum*	foot	pyramidal b. on lateral side of foot, proximal to fourth and fifth metatarsal b.'s	calcaneus, lateral cuneiform, fourth and fifth metatarsal b.'s, navicular
cuneiform b., intermediate second cuneiform b. *os cuneiforme intermedium*	foot	wedge-shaped; smallest of the three cuneiforms, positioned between medial and lateral ones	navicular, medial cuneiform, lateral cuneiform, second metatarsal
cuneiform b., lateral external cuneiform b. *os cuneiforme laterale*	foot	intermediate-sized cuneiform located in center of front row of tarsal b.'s	navicular, intermediate cuneiform, cuboid; second, third, and fourth metatarsals
cuneiform b., medial internal cuneiform b. *os cuneiforme mediale*	foot	largest of the three cuneiforms, at medial side of foot between the navicular and base of first metatarsal	navicular, intermediate cuneiform, first and second metatarsal
elbow b.	see ulna		
epistropheus	see axis		
ethmoid b. *os ethmoidale*	skull	unpaired, T-shaped b. forming part of nasal septum and roof of cavity; curled processes form superior and middle conchae	sphenoid, frontal, both nasal, lacrimal, and palatine b.'s; maxillae, inferior nasal conchae, vomer
fabella *fabella*	knee	sesamoid b. in lateral head of gastrocnemius muscle behind lateral condyle of femur	femur
femur thigh b. *femur*	thigh	longest and heaviest b. in the body, situated between hip and knee	hipbone, patella, tibia
fibula splint b. *fibula*	leg	lateral b. of leg	tibia, talus
flank b.	see ilium		

bone ■ bone

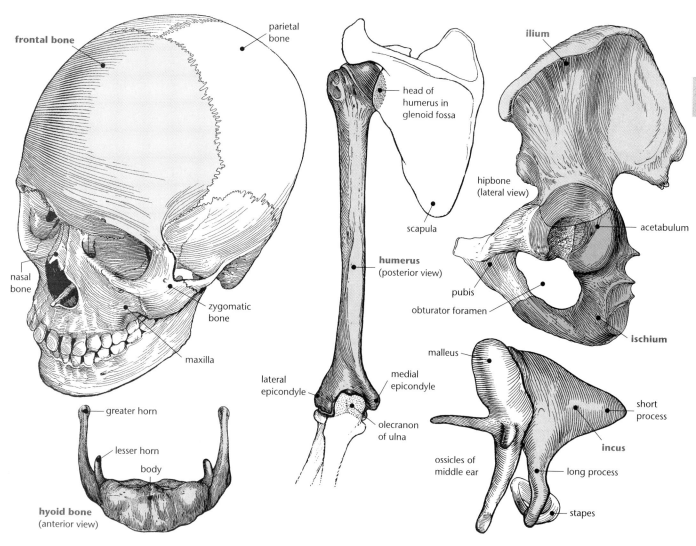

frontal bone

parietal bone

nasal bone

zygomatic bone

maxilla

greater horn

lesser horn

body

hyoid bone
(anterior view)

head of humerus in glenoid fossa

scapula

humerus
(posterior view)

lateral epicondyle

medial epicondyle

olecranon of ulna

ilium

hipbone
(lateral view)

acetabulum

pubis

obturator foramen

ischium

malleus

short process

incus

long process

ossicles of middle ear

stapes

B

BONE	LOCATION	DESCRIPTION	ARTICULATIONS
frontal b. forehead b. *os frontale*	skull	flat b. forming anterior part of skull	ethmoid, sphenoid, maxillae, and both nasal, parietal, lacrimal, and zygomatic b.'s
greater multangular b.		see trapezium bone	
hamate b. unciform b. *os hamatum*	wrist	most medial b. of distal row of carpals; distinguished by hooklike process (hamulus) that projects from its palmar surface	lunate, triquetrum, capitate, fourth and fifth metacarpals
hammer b.		see malleus	
hipbone innominate b. *os coxae*	pelvis and hip	large, broad, irregularly shaped b. that forms greater part of pelvis; consists of three parts: ilium, ischium, and pubis	femur, sacrum, with its fellow of opposite side at pubic symphysis
humerus arm b. *humerus*	arm	longest and largest b. of upper limb, situated between shoulder and elbow	scapula, radius, and ulna
hyoid b. lingual b. *os hyoideum*	neck	U-shaped b. in front of neck between mandible and larynx	suspended from tips of skull's styloid processes by ligaments
ilium flank b. *os ilium*	pelvis	broad expanded upper part of the hipbone, divisible into a body and an ala	sacrum, femur, ischium, pubis
incus anvil b. *incus*	middle ear chamber	middle b. of auditory ossicles	malleus, stapes
inferior turbinate b.		see concha, inferior nasal	
innominate b.		see hipbone	
ischium *os ischii*	pelvis	inferior and dorsal part of the hipbone, divisible into a body and a ramus	femur, ilium, pubis

bone ■ bone

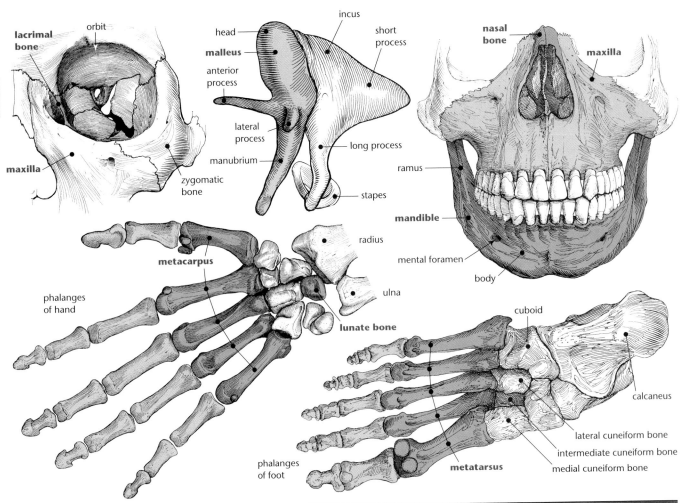

Figure labels:
- lacrimal bone, orbit, maxilla, zygomatic bone
- incus, head, malleus, anterior process, short process, lateral process, manubrium, long process, stapes
- nasal bone, maxilla, ramus, mandible, mental foramen, body
- metacarpus, phalanges of hand, radius, ulna, lunate bone
- phalanges of foot, cuboid, metatarsus, calcaneus, lateral cuneiform bone, intermediate cuneiform bone, medial cuneiform bone

BONE	LOCATION	DESCRIPTION	ARTICULATIONS
lacrimal b. *os lacrimale*	skull	smallest and most fragile b. of the face; resembles a fingernail and is situated in anterior medial wall of orbit	ethmoid, frontal, maxilla, inferior nasal concha
lesser multangular b.	see trapezoid bone		
lunate b. semilunar b. *os lunatum*	wrist	in center of proximal row of carpus between scaphoid and triangular (triquetral) b.'s	radius, capitate, hamate, triangular (triquetral), scaphoid
malar b.	see zygomatic bone		
malleus hammer b. *malleus*	middle ear chamber	most lateral b. of auditory ossicles, somewhat resembling a hammer and consisting of a head, neck, and three processes	tympanic membrane and incus
mandible inferior maxillary b. *mandibula*	lower portion of face	horseshoe-shaped b. containing the lower teeth; strongest b. of face	mandibular fossa of both temporal b.'s
maxilla maxillary b. *maxilla*	middle portion of face	largest b. of the face except the mandible; contains the upper teeth and encloses maxillary sinus	frontal, ethmoid, nasal, zygomatic, lacrimal, vomer, inferior nasal concha, other maxilla
metacarpus metacarpal b.'s *ossa metacarpalia*	hand, between wrist and fingers	five slender b.'s of the hand proper, each consisting of a body and two extremities (head and base), and numbered from 1st to 5th starting from the thumb side	base of first metacarpal with trapezium, base of other metacarpals with each other and with distal row of carpal b.'s, heads with corresponding phalanges
metatarsus metatarsal b.'s *os metatarsalia*	foot, between distal row of tarsal b.'s and first phalanges of toes	five slender b.'s of the foot proper, each consisting of a body and two extremities (head and base), and numbered from 1st to 5th starting from the great toe side	distal tarsal b.'s, bases with each other, heads with corresponding phalanges
multangular b., greater	see trapezium bone		
maltangular b., lesser	see trapezoid bone		
nasal b. *os nasale*	middle of face	one of two small oblong paired b.'s positioned side by side to form bridge of nose	frontal, ethmoid, opposite nasal, maxilla

bone ■ bone

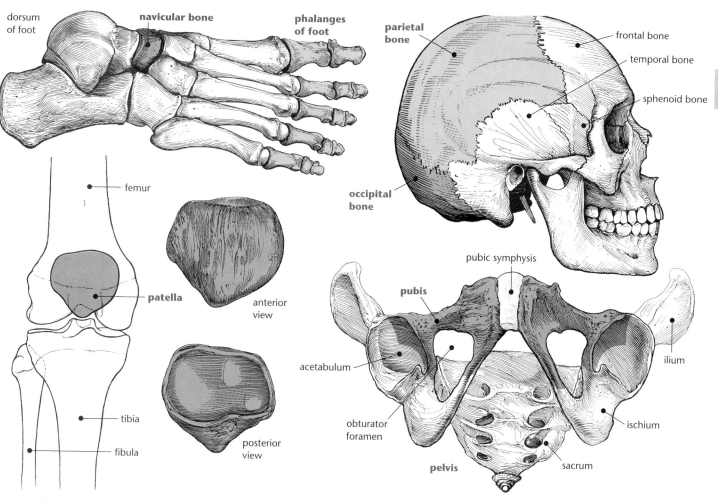

dorsum of foot • navicular bone • phalanges of foot • parietal bone • frontal bone • temporal bone • sphenoid bone • occipital bone • femur • patella • anterior view • posterior view • tibia • fibula • pubic symphysis • pubis • acetabulum • obturator foramen • ilium • ischium • sacrum • pelvis

BONE	LOCATION	DESCRIPTION	ARTICULATIONS
navicular b. scaphoid b. of foot *osnaviculare pedis*	foot	situated at medial side of tarsus between talus and cuneiform b.'s	talus, three cuneiforms, occasionally with cuboid
navicular b. of hand	see scaphoid bone		
occipital b. *os occipitale*	skull	unpaired saucer-shaped b. forming posterior part of base of cranium pierced by the foramen magnum	both parietals and temporals; sphenoid, atlas
palatine b. palate b. *os palatinum*	skull	one of two somewhat L-shaped paired b.'s, the two forming the posterior part of hard palate, part of floor and lateral wall of nasal cavity, and part of floor of the orbit	sphenoid, ethmoid, maxilla, vomer, opposite palatine, inferior nasal concha
parietal b. *os parietale*	skull	paired b.'s between frontal and occipital b.'s forming sides and roof of cranium	opposite parietal, frontal, occipital, temporal, sphenoid
patella knee cap *patella*	knee	flat, rounded, triangular b. (sesamoid), situated in front of knee joint	femur
pelvis	a body ring resembling a basin, composed of two hipbones, sacrum, and coccyx		
phalanges of foot *ossa digitorum pedis*	foot	miniature long b.'s, two in great toe and three in each of other toes	proximal row of phalanges with corresponding metatarsal b.'s and middle phalanges; middle phalanges with proximal and distal phalanges; ungualphalanges with middle phalanges
phalanges of hand *ossa digitorum manus*	hand	miniature long b.'s, two in thumb and three in each of other fingers	proximal row of phalanges with corresponding metacarpal b.'s and middle phalanges; middle phalanges with proximal and distal phalanges; ungual phalanges with middle phalanges
pisiform b. *os pisiforme*	wrist	most medial of proximal row of carpus; smallest carpal b.	triangular (triquetral)
pubis *os pubis*	pelvis	anterior lower portion of hipbone	ilium, ischium, femur

bone ■ bone

B

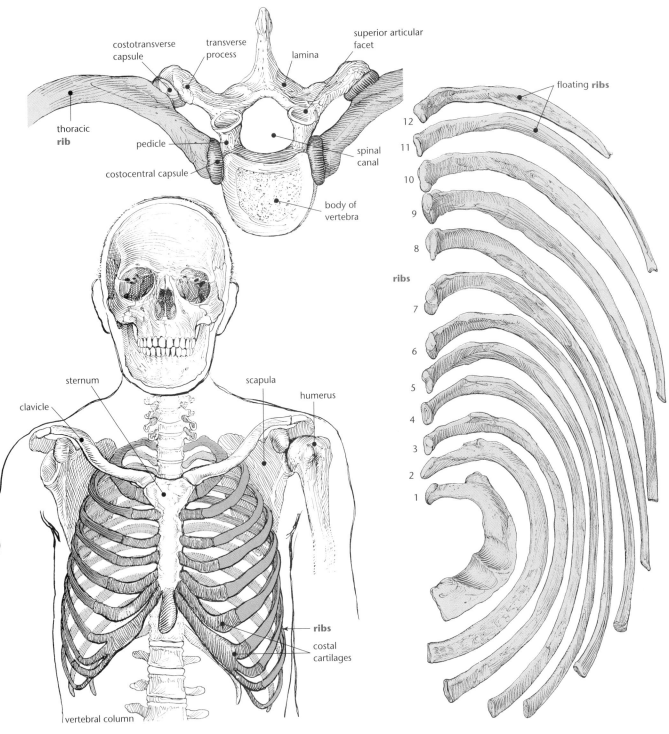

costotransverse capsule
transverse process
lamina
superior articular facet
floating **ribs**

thoracic **rib**

pedicle

costocentral capsule

spinal canal

body of vertebra

12
11
10
9
8
7
6
5
4
3
2
1

ribs

sternum
scapula
humerus
clavicle

ribs
costal cartilages

vertebral column

BONE	LOCATION	DESCRIPTION	ARTICULATIONS
pyramidal b.	see triangular bone		
radius *radius*	forearm, between elbow and wrist	lateral b. of forearm; proximal end is small and forms small part of elbow; distal end is large and forms large part of wrist joint	humerus, ulnar, lunate, scaphoid
ribs *costae*	chest	12 pairs of thin, narrow, arch-shaped b.'s forming posterior and lateral walls of chest	all posteriorly with vertebral column; upper seven pairs anteriorly with sternum, through intervention of costal cartilages; lower five pairs anteriorly with costal cartilages; lowest two pairs free at ventral extremities (floating)

bone ■ bone

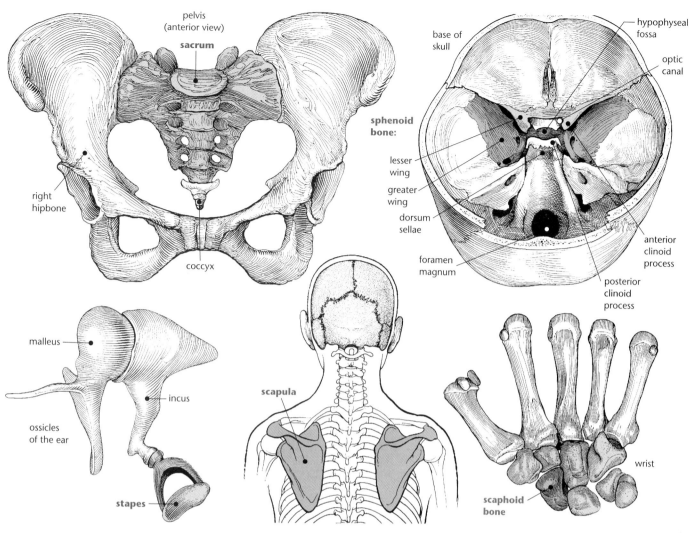

pelvis
(anterior view)
sacrum

right
hipbone

coccyx

base of
skull

hypophyseal
fossa

optic
canal

sphenoid
bone:

lesser
wing

greater
wing

dorsum
sellae

foramen
magnum

anterior
clinoid
process

posterior
clinoid
process

malleus

incus

ossicles
of the ear

scapula

stapes

wrist

**scaphoid
bone**

BONE	LOCATION	DESCRIPTION	ARTICULATIONS
sacrum *os sacrum*	lower back	large triangular b., formed by fusion of five vertebrae, and situated at dorsal part of pelvis	above with last lumbar vertebra, at each side with ilium, below with coccyx
scaphoid b. scaphoid b. of hand navicular b. of hand *os scaphoideum* *os scaphoideum manus*	wrist	largest b. of proximal row of carpus located at thumb side	radius, trapezium, trapezoid, capitate, lunate
scaphoid b. of foot		see navicular bone	
scapula shoulder blade *scapula*	shoulder	large, flat, triangular b. forming dorsal part of shoulder girdle	clavicle, humerus
semilunar b.		see lunate bone	
sesamoid b.'s *ossa sesamoidea*	extremities, usually within tendons	small rounded b.'s embedded in certain tendons; some constant ones include those in the tendons of quadriceps muscle of thigh, short flexor muscle of great toe, long peroneal muscle, anterior tibial muscle, posterior tibial muscle, and greater psoas muscle; the patella (kneecap) is the largest sesamoid bone	none
shinbone		see tibia	
sphenoid b. *os sphenoidale*	base of skull	unpaired, irregularly shaped b. forming anterior part of base of skull and portions of cranial, orbital, and nasal cavities	vomer, ethmoid, frontal, occipital, both parietals, both temporals, both zygomatics, both palatines; also articulates with tuberosity of maxilla
stapes stirrup *stapes*	middle ear chamber	most medial b. of auditory ossicles, somewhat resembling a stirrup	incus, oval window

bone ■ bone

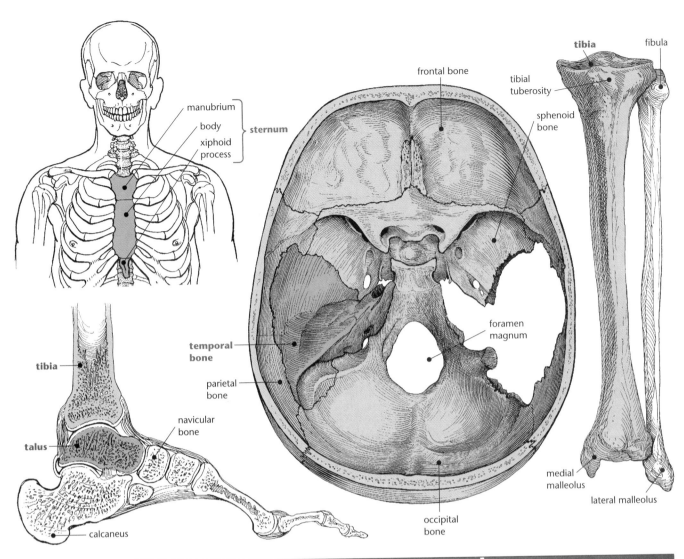

B

manubrium
body
xiphoid
process
} sternum

frontal bone

tibia · fibula

tibial
tuberosity

sphenoid
bone

temporal
bone

parietal
bone

navicular
bone

tibia

talus

calcaneus

foramen
magnum

occipital
bone

medial
malleolus

lateral malleolus

BONE	LOCATION	DESCRIPTION	ARTICULATIONS
sternum breastbone *sternum*	chest	elongated, flattened, dagger-shaped b. forming ventral wall of thorax; consists of three parts; manubrium, body, xiphoid process	both clavicles and first seven pairs of costal cartilages
stirrup b.		see stapes	
sutural b.'s wormian b.'s *ossa suturalis*	skull	irregular, isolated b.'s occasionally found along cranial sutures, especially lambdoid suture	usually occipital and parietal b.'s
talus ankle b. astragalus *talus*	ankle	second largest of the tarsal b.'s; supports tibia and rests on calcaneus	tibia, fibula, calcaneus, navicular
temporal b. *os temporale*	skull	irregularly shaped b. consisting of three parts; squamous, petrous, and tympanic, forms part of side and base of cranium	occipital, parietal, zygomatic, sphenoid, mandible
tibia shinbone *tibia*	leg	situated at medial side of leg between ankle and knee joint; second longest b. in the body	above with femur and fibula; below with fibula and talus
trapezium b. greater multangular b. *os trapezium*	wrist	most lateral of four b.'s of distal row of carpus	scaphoid, first metacarpal, trapezoid, second metacarpal
trapezoid b. lesser multangular b. *os trapezoideum*	wrist	smallest b. in distal row of carpus	scaphoid, second metacarpal, trapezium, capitate
triangular b. pyramidal b. triquetral b. *os triquetrum*	wrist	pyramidal shape; second from little finger side of proximal row of carpus	lunate, pisiform, hamate

bone ■ bone

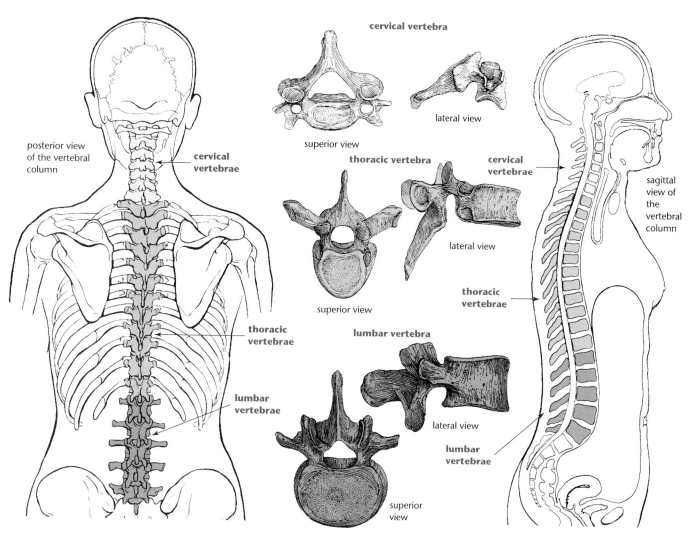

posterior view of the vertebral column

cervical vertebrae

thoracic vertebrae

lumbar vertebrae

cervical vertebra

superior view

lateral view

thoracic vertebra

superior view

lateral view

lumbar vertebra

lateral view

superior view

cervical vertebrae

thoracic vertebrae

lumbar vertebrae

sagittal view of the vertebral column

B

BONE	LOCATION	DESCRIPTION	ARTICULATIONS
triquetral b.		see triangular bone	
turbinate b., inferior		see choncha, inferior nasal	
turbinate b., middle			
turbinate b., superior		not a separate bone, see ethmoid bone	
ulna elbow b. *ulna*	forearm	medial b. of forearm; lies parallel with radius	humerus, radius
unciform b.		see hamate bone	
vertebrae, cervical backbones *vertebrae*	back of neck	seven segments of vertebral column; smallest of the true vertebrae; possess a foramen in each transverse process	first vertebra with skull, all others with adjoining vertebrae
vertebrae, lumbar backbones *vertebrae*	lower back	five segments of vertebral column; largest b.'s of movable part of vertebral column	with adjoining vertebrae; fifth vertebra with sacrum
vertebrae, thoracic backbones *vertebrae*	back	12 segments of vertebral column; possess facets on the sides of all the bodies and the first 10 also have facets on the transverse processes	with adjoining vertebrae, heads of ribs, tubercles of ribs (except 11th and 12th)
vomer *vomer*	skull	thin, flat b. forming posterior and inferior part of nasal septum	ethmoid, sphenoid, both maxillae, both palatine bones; also articulates with septal cartilage of nose
wormian b.'s		see sutural bones	
zygomatic b. malar b. cheekbone *os zygomaticum*	skull	forms prominence of cheek and lower, lateral aspects of orbit	frontal, sphenoid, temporal, maxilla

bone ■ bone

booster (boost′er) See booster dose, under dose.

borax (bo′raks) Sodium borate; used in dentistry in the casting of fluxes and to retard the setting of gypsum products.

borborygmus (bor-bo-rig′mus), pl. borboryg′mi An audible rumbling noise produced by propulsion of gas through the intestines.

border (bor′der) An edge or margin.

    brush b. A border of fine, closely packed microscopic projections (microvilli) on the cell membrane, as seen on the free surface of cuboidal cells lining the proximal convoluted tubules of the kidney. It greatly increases the surface area, thereby enhancing absorption.

    denture b. (a) The boundaries of a denture base. (b) The edge of the denture base where its polished surface meets the impression or tissue surface. Also called dental edge.

    striated b. A border of fine, closely packed microscopic projections (microvilli) on the free surface of columnar cells lining the intestinal interior; it greatly increases the surface area and absorption capability of intestines.

    vermillion b. The exterior, somewhat pink, portion of the lips.

Bordetella (bor-dĕ-tel′lah) A genus of spherical, gram-negative, aerobic, pathogenic bacteria (family Brucellaceae).

    B. pertussis A species that is the causative agent of whooping cough.

boric acid (bo′rik as′id) A white powder or crystals used as an antiseptic.

boron (bor′on) A nonmetallic element; symbol B, atomic number 5, atomic weight 10.811.

Borrelia (bŏ-rel′e-ah) A genus of gram-negative, anaerobic, screw-shaped bacteria (family Treponemataceae). Some species are pathogenic; transmitted to humans by the bites of arthropods.

    B. burgdorferi The species causing Lyme disease in humans and borreliosis in dogs and cattle; transmitted by several species of ixodid ticks.

borreliosis (bŏ-rel-e-o′sis) Any disease caused by bacteria of the genus *Borrelia*.

    Lyme b. See Lyme disease, under disease.

boss (bos) 1. A rounded protuberance. 2. A hump on the back.

bosselation (bos-ĕ-la′shun) Condition of having many rounded eminences or swellings.

botfly (bot′fli) A hairy fly (order Diptera) capable of causing larval infection (myiasis) in humans and domestic animals by depositing its eggs in open wounds.

botryoid (bot′re-oid) Resembling a bunch of grapes. Also called staphyline.

botryomycosis (bot-re-o-mi-ko′sis) A chronic bacterial infection of humans and domestic animals, characterized by formation of lesions on the skin and sometimes internal organs, containing pus and granules composed of a mass of bacteria surrounded by a capsule; usually caused by staphylococci.

bottle (bot′tl) A receptacle with a narrow neck.

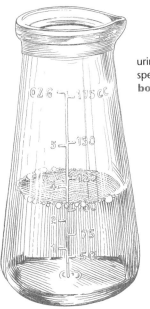

urine specimen **bottle**

wash b. (a) A fluid-containing bottle equipped with two tubes passing through its stopper, arranged in such a way that blowing through one tube forces a stream of fluid through the other. (b) A fluid-containing bottle with a tube passing to the bottom through which gases are passed in order to purify the gases.

bottom (bot′um) Popular name for the buttocks.

    tailor's b. See ischial bursitis, under bursitis.

    weaver's b. See ischial bursitis, under bursitis.

botulin (boch′u-lin) Seldom-used term for botulinum toxin; see under toxin.

botulism (boch′u-lizm) Poisoning caused by the toxin of *Clostridium botulinum* present in improperly canned or preserved food.

bougie (boo-zhe′) A slender, flexible, cylindrical instrument for insertion into tubular structures or canals of the body, such as the esophagus or urethra; used for calibration and dilatation of constricted areas and for local application of medications.

    b. à boule A bulbous bougie.

    bulbous b. A bougie with a bulb-shaped tip.

    filiform b. A very slender bougie.

bougienage (boo-zhe-nahzh′) The passage of a bougie through a tubular structure of the body for examination or treatment of a constricted area of the structure.

bouillon (boo-e-yaw′) A culture medium prepared from beef; used for cultivation of bacteria in the laboratory. Also called broth.

bound (bownd) 1. Enclosed. 2. Attached to a receptor, as on a cell membrane. 3. Denoting a substance that is present in combination with a colloid, especially a protein.

bout (bout) An episode.

    periodic drinking b.'s A form of alcoholism in which the person overindulges in alcoholic drinks continuously for days or weeks, then recovers and abstains for several weeks or months before the next episode. Also called paroxysmal alcoholism.

bouton (boo-tahn′) A small knoblike thickening.

    b. en chemise Abscesses of the intestinal lining (mucosa), occurring in amebic dysentery.

    b.'s en passage Boutons located along the length of an axon; distinguished from an axon terminal.

    b. terminaux, terminal b. See axon terminal, under terminal.

bovine (bo′vin) Relating to cattle.

bowel (bow′el) Common name for the intestine.

bowleg (bo′leg) See genu varum.

boxing (bok′sing) In dental restoration, the building up of a vertical wall at the margin of a dental impression to contain the freshly mixed plaster or dental stone.

brace (brās) 1. In orthopedics, a device for supporting or holding parts of the body in correct position. 2. (pl.) Popular name for orthodontic appliance; see under appliance.

    helicoid knee b. Brace designed to support the knee and prevent deviation from the normal helical movement of the knee joint (i.e., the normal inward rotation of the tibia when the knee flexes and outward rotation when the knee straightens); it consists of two thermoplastic U-shaped shells that fit on the thigh above the knee and on the shin below; they are connected by two stainless steel joints, lateral and medial; the lateral allows universal motion, the medial is a pin-in-slot joint, the pin being free to run along the slot as flexion and extension occur.

    Lenox-Hill b. A hinged brace designed to protect the knee joint from excessive rotation in cases of ligamentous instability caused by injury; also used to supplement surgical procedures for treating these injuries.

    metatarsal b. An elastic bandage encircling the metatarsal portion of the foot; may be combined with a plantar pad and/or toe loop; used as a mechanical aid in reducing the pain of certain foot disorders.

    Milwaukee b. An orthotic brace used in the conservative treatment of scoliosis (primarily idiopathic scoliosis) and kyphosis usually in adolescents; consists of a molded pelvic belt that fits above the upper edge of the iliac spine to an occipital hold with a throat mold; initially the brace is worn about 23 hours a day; when the radiographs

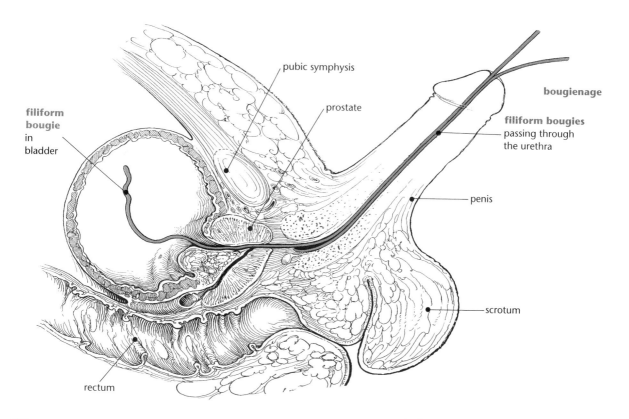

pubic symphysis

prostate

bougienage

filiform bougies
passing through
the urethra

**filiform
bougie**
in
bladder

penis

scrotum

rectum

bulbous bougie

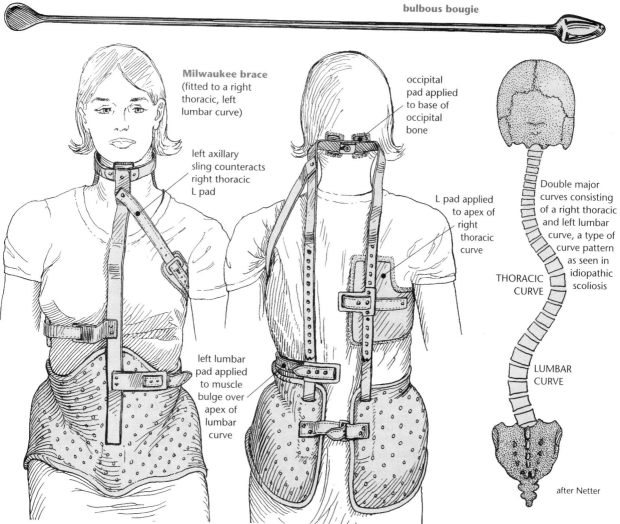

Milwaukee brace
(fitted to a right
thoracic, left
lumbar curve)

occipital
pad applied
to base of
occipital
bone

left axillary
sling counteracts
right thoracic
L pad

L pad applied
to apex of
right
thoracic
curve

left lumbar
pad applied
to muscle
bulge over
apex of
lumbar
curve

Double major
curves consisting
of a right thoracic
and left lumbar
curve, a type of
curve pattern
as seen in
idiopathic
scoliosis

THORACIC
CURVE

LUMBAR
CURVE

after Netter

B31

brace ■ brace

show that the patient is nearly mature, the patient is weaned gradually from the brace over a one- to two-year period; eventually, the brace is worn at night only until the spine is determined mature and further curve progression is unlikely to occur. Also called Moe brace.

Moe b. See Milwaukee brace.

patellar restraining b. Any brace used to reduce stress on the patellofemoral joint and to protect the kneecap (patella) from abnormal and excessive movement.

Taylor back b. See Taylor splint, under splint.

bracelet (brās′let) A band worn around the wrist.

alert b. A bracelet with an inscribed message designed to be worn by persons with a medical condition, such as diabetes. If for any reason the person becomes unconscious or disoriented, the bracelet's message makes medical personnel instantly aware of the wearer's condition, helping them to reach a correct diagnosis and to provide appropriate treatment.

identification b. A serially numbered band that, when locked into position, becomes transfer-proof; designed to provide identification for hospital patients. In obstetrics, bands are used in sets of three: for mother's wrist, baby's wrist, and baby's ankle (anklet).

brachia (bra′ke-ah) Plural of brachium.

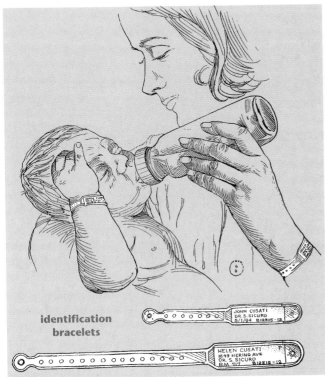

identification bracelets

brachial (bra′ke-al) Relating to the arm.

brachialgia (bra-ke-al′je-ah) Pain in one or both arms.

brachio-, brachi- Combining forms meaning arm.

brachium (bra′ke-um), pl. bra′chia **1.** The arm. **2.** Any armlike structure.

brachy- Combining form meaning short.

brachybasia (brak-e-ba′se-ah) The slow, short-stepped gait typical of disease of the pyramidal tract of the brain.

brachycephalic (brak-e-sĕ-fal′ik) Characterized by brachycephaly.

brachycephaly (brak-e-sef′ah-le) A disproportionate shortness and broadness of the head (i.e., an abnormally flattened anteroposterior plane of the skull); usually caused by a premature union of the coronal suture in infancy.

brachydactyly (brak-e-dak′tī-le) Abnormal shortness of the fingers and toes.

brachygnathia (brak-ig-na′the-ah) Abnormal shortness of the lower jaw (mandible).

brachymelia (brak-e-me′le-ah) Disproportionate shortness of the arms and legs.

brachysyndactyly (brak-e-sin-dak′tī-le) A combined shortness and webbing of fingers or toes.

brachytherapy (brak-e-ther′ah-pe) Treatment by radiation in which a small sealed (or partly sealed) radiation source is placed on or near the tissues under treatment; may be a surface application, a body cavity application (intracavitary), or placement into the tissue (interstitial). Also called internal radiation therapy.

brady- Combining form meaning slow.

bradyarrhythmia (brad-e-ah-rith′me-ah) A slow and irregular heartbeat.

bradycardia (brad-e-kar′de-ah) Excessive slowness in the action of the heart (i.e., a heart rate below 60 beats per minute).

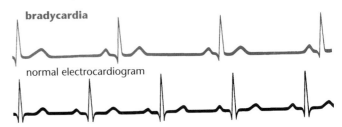

bradycardia

normal electrocardiogram

bradycrotic (brad-e-krot′ik) Relating to a slow pulse.

bradykinesia (brad-e-kī-ne′ze-ah) Abnormal slowness of movement.

bradykinin (brad-e-ki′nin) A polypeptide hormone that promotes the dilatation of blood vessels; it is produced by the action of the enzyme kallikrein on alpha$_2$-globulin.

bradypnea (brad-ip-ne′ah, brad-e-ne′ah) Abnormally slow rate of breathing.

braille (brāl) A system of writing and printing for the blind; it consists of raised dots that correspond to letters, numbers, and punctuation marks.

brain (brān) The portion of the central nervous system (CNS) located within the skull that is responsible for the coordination and control of all vital body activities; it is surrounded by cerebrospinal fluid and is continuous below with the spinal cord; composed of the forebrain (cerebrum and diencephalon), the midbrain (mesencephalon), and the hindbrain (cerebellum, pons, and medulla oblongata). The brain of the average adult weighs approximately 3 pounds. Also called encephalon.

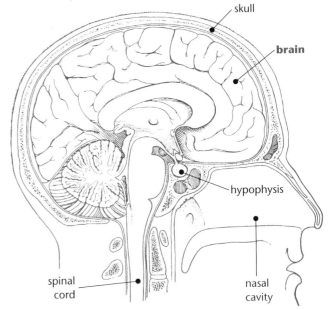

skull

brain

hypophysis

spinal cord

nasal cavity

braincase (brān′kās) The cranial part of the skull enclosing the brain; the facial bones are not included.

brainstem, brain stem (brān′stem) The portion of the brain consisting of the midbrain (mesencephalon), pons, and medulla oblongata; it connects the forebrain (prosencephalon) to the spinal cord.

brainwashing (brān'wash-ing) Inducing someone to give up basic attitudes and beliefs and adopt contrasting ones, against the person's will, through systematic pressure or torture.

bran (bran) The fibrous residue of the milling of wheat, consisting chiefly of the broken outer coat of wheat grain; eaten in breakfast cereals or in other foods; ingestion promotes bowel movements.

branchiogenic (brang-ke-o-jen'ik) Developed from branchial arches.

Branhamella catarrhalis (bran-hah-mel'ah kat-ah-ra'lis) Former name for *Moraxella catarrhalis*.

brawny (brahw'ne) Thickened and darkened; applied to a swelling.

breast (brest) 1. Mammary gland. 2. Chest.

    funnel b. See pectus excavatum.

    keel b. See pectus carinatum.

    pigeon b. See pectus carinatum.

breastbone (brest'bōn) See sternum, in table of bones.

breast-feeding (brest' fēd'ing) The nursing of a baby at the mother's breast.

breath (breth) 1. The air entering and leaving the lungs during breathing. 2. The air exhaled.

breath-holding (breth'hōld-ing) Voluntary, or involuntary, cessation of breathing on expiration; usually seen in young children. If the child faints, breathing is quickly and automatically resumed as a natural reflex. Occasionally, twitching resembling an epileptic seizure occurs.

breathing (brēth'ing) The process of taking in and expelling air from the lungs to allow blood to take up oxygen and release carbon dioxide.

    Biot's b. See ataxic respiration, under respiration.

    bronchial b. A harsh, blowing quality of the breath heard on auscultation of the chest; often heard over a consolidated lung or over a cavity in the lung.

    Cheyne-Stokes b. See Cheyne-Stokes respiration, under respiration.

    continuous positive pressure b. (CPPB) See continuous positive pressure ventilation, under ventilation.

    intermittent positive pressure b. (IPPB) See intermittent positive pressure ventilation, under ventilation.

    mouth b. Habitual breathing through the open mouth.

    mouth-to-mouth b. A stage in cardiopulmonary resuscitation (CPR) in which the rescuer places his or her mouth completely over the victim's mouth (and nose, if the victim is a child) and delivers two slow, independent breaths, while keeping the victim's airway open and allowing time for the victim to exhale before delivering the second breath; each breath lasts 1.5 to 2 seconds (1–1.5 seconds for infants and children); if after the second breath normal breathing is still absent but carotid pulse is present, then breathing is again delivered, at the rate of about 12 breaths per minute (about 20 breaths/minute for infants and children). Also called mouth-to-mouth resuscitation. See also cardiopulmonary resuscitation (CPR), under resuscitation.

    periodic b. See Cheyne-Stokes respiration, under respiration.

    pursed-lip b. A technique of breathing in which air is exhaled through pursed lips in order to slow down the outflow of air from the lungs; it relieves airway discomfort in chronic obstructive pulmonary disease.

    shallow b. A weak type of breathing, as seen in debilitated patients with acute pulmonary disease.

breech (brēch) The buttocks (nates).

bregma (breg'mah) A craniometric point situated on the upper surface of the skull at the junction of three bones: frontal and the two parietal bones.

bregmatic (breg-mat'ik) Relating to the bregma.

brei (bri) Minced tissue used in metabolic experiments.

bridge (brij) 1. A prosthesis containing one or more artificial teeth suspended from, and attached to, one or more natural teeth (abutements). 2. The upper part of the nose, between the eyes.

    fixed b. See fixed partial denture, under denture.

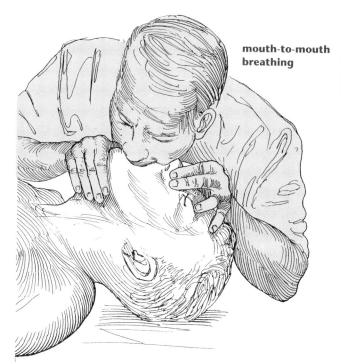

mouth-to-mouth breathing

B

brim (brim) The upper border or edge of a hollow structure.

    pelvic b. The circumference of the oblique plane dividing the major and minor pelves.

British antilewisite (brit'ish an-tī-lu'ī-sīt) (BAL) See dimercaprol.

broach (brōch) A dental instrument used for examination of the pulp of a tooth or for removal of the pulp from the root canal.

broad-spectrum (brod-spek'trum) Effective against a wide variety of bacteria; applied to certain drugs.

bromhidrosis (brom-hi-dro'sis) See bromidrosis.

bromide (bro'mīd) A binary compound containing bromine and another element or organic radical.

bromidrosis (bro-mī-dro'sis) Condition marked by a fetid odor of the sweat. Also called osmidrosis; bromhidrosis.

bromine (bro'mīn) A corrosive, volatile, nonmetallic liquid element; symbol Br, atomic number 35, atomic weight 79.9.

bromo-, brom- Combining forms meaning bromine.

bromocriptine (bro-mo-krip'tēn) An ergot derivative that suppresses secretion of the hormone prolactin from the pituitary (hypophysis). Used in the treatment of conditions caused by excessive prolactin production, such as abnormal or excessive milk production by the breasts, and to suppress lactation in women who do not wish to breast-feed.

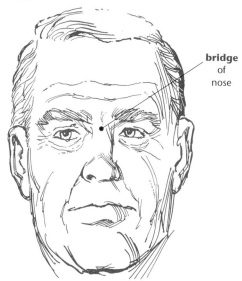

bridge of nose

brainwashing ■ bromocriptine

bronchi (brong′ki) Plural of bronchus.

bronchial (brong′ke-al) Relating to the bronchi.

bronchiectasia (brong-ke-ek-ta′ze-ah) See bronchiectasis.

bronchiectasis (brong-ke-ek′tah-sis) Abnormal and irreversible stretched condition of the main airways (bronchi) from the trachea to and within the lungs, usually resulting from chronic lung infections; it may involve the bronchus of a single lung segment or the whole bronchial tree. Also called bronchiectasia.

bronchiectatic (brong-ke-ek-tat′ik) Relating to bronchiectasis.

bronchiloquy (brong-kil′o-kwe) See bronchophony.

bronchiogenic (brong-ke-o-jen′ik) See bronchogenic.

bronchiole (brong′ke-ōl) One of the numerous smaller airways branching off the bronchi within the lungs. Also called bronchiolus.

> **terminal b.** The last portion of a bronchiole, without the final outpouchings (alveoli).

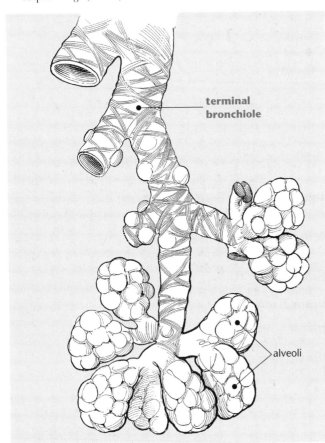

terminal bronchiole

alveoli

bronchiolectasia (brong-ke-o-lek-ta′ze-ah) See bronchiolectasis.

bronchiolectasis (brong-ke-o-lek′tah-sis) Chronic stretched condition of the bronchioles. Also called bronchiolectasia.

bronchioli (brong-ki′o-li) Plural of bronchiolus.

bronchiolitis (brong-ke-o-li′tis) Inflammation of the walls of small airways (bronchioles) that branch off the bronchi in the lungs.

> **acute b.** A viral bronchiolitis occurring most commonly in children under the age of two years; characterized by a hacking cough, difficult breathing, and wheezing resulting from damage to the bronchiole walls and formation of mucus plugs that trap air in the distal bronchioles; usually caused by a respiratory syncytial virus (RSV), but other viruses may also be responsible. Also called viral bronchiolitis.

> **b. obliterans** Inflammation of the bronchioles with obstruction caused by fibrous granulation tissue formed in the walls of the terminal bronchioles; it may be caused by inhalation of irritating gases or foreign bodies, or may occur as a complication of pneumonia.

> **viral b.** See acute bronchiolitis.

bronchiolopulmonary (brong-ke-o-lo-pul′mo-ner-e) Relating to the bronchioles and the lungs.

bronchiolus (brong-ke′o-lus), pl. bronchi′oli See bronchiole.

bronchiostenosis (brong-ke-o-sten-o′sis) Narrowing or stricture of lumen of bronchi.

bronchitis (brong-ki′tis) Inflammation of the mucous membrane lining the air passages (bronchi) from the trachea to and within the lungs; it causes persistent cough and excessive production of mucus (phlegm).

> **acute b.** A form of bronchitis that is generally self-limited, lasting only a few days, with complete recovery; it usually occurs as a complication of an upper respiratory infection.

> **allergic b.** Asthma.

> **chronic b.** Generalized narrowing and obstruction of the airways in the lungs lasting longer than three consecutive months in at least two successive years; usually resulting from cigarette smoking or from long-term exposure to air pollutants, such as irritating fumes or dusts.

> **chronic obstructive b.** Term used when chronic bronchitis is associated with extensive abnormalities and obstruction of the smaller airways.

broncho-, bronchi-, bronch- Combining forms meaning bronchus.

bronchoalveolar (brong-ko-al-ve′o-lar) Relating to the airways in the lungs (bronchi) and the terminal air sacs (alveoli).

bronchocavernous (brong-ko-kav′er-nus) Referring to both a bronchus and a pathologic cavity in the lungs.

bronchocele (brong′ko-sēl) A circumscribed abnormal outpouching of a bronchus.

bronchoconstrictor (brong-ko-kon-strik′tor) 1. Causing a narrowing of air passages in the lungs. 2. Any agent, such as histamine, having such quality.

bronchodilator (brong-ko-di-la′tor) 1. Widening the airways in the lungs by relaxing the muscles of their walls. 2. A drug possessing such quality.

bronchofiberscope (brong-ko-fi′ber-skōp) See fiberoptic bronchoscope, under bronchoscope.

bronchogenic (brong-ko-jen′ik) Of bronchial origin. Also called bronchiogenic.

bronchogram (brong′ko-gram) An x-ray image obtained by bronchography.

bronchography (brong-kog′rah-fe) Procedure for examining the air passages of the lungs; a substance, opaque to x rays, is introduced into the tracheobronchial tree prior to making x-ray images of the structures. The procedure has been largely replaced by other techniques (CT scanning, lung tomography, bronchoscopy). It is used primarily for guidance during a bronchoscopy or to provide permanent records of pathologic findings.

broncholith (brong′ko-lith) A stony, calcified concretion within a bronchus. Also called bronchial calculus.

broncholithiasis (brong-ko-li-thi′ah-sis) Condition marked by the presence of bronchial calculi (broncholiths).

bronchomalacia (brong-ko-mah-la′she-ah) A softening of the walls of respiratory air passages (trachea and bronchi).

bronchomotor (brong-ko-mo′tor) Capable of changing (either dilating or constricting) the lumen of airways in the lungs.

bronchomycosis (brong-ko-mi-ko′sis) Any disease of the respiratory airways caused by a fungus.

bronchophony (brong-kof′o-ne) The characteristic exaggerated resonance of the spoken voice heard on auscultation over an area of consolidated (solidified) lung tissue, as in pneumonia. The sound is normal when heard over a healthy bronchus. Also called bronchiloquy.

bronchoplasty (brong′ko-plas-te) Surgical repair of a bronchus.

bronchopneumonia (brong-ko-nu-mo′ne-ah) Inflammation of the lungs and airways, often resulting in widespread patches of firm, consolidated tissues; usually occurs as a secondary infection in predisposed individuals, especially those with chronic, debilitating diseases. Also called bronchial pneumonia.

bronchopulmonary (brong-ko-pul′mo-ner-e) Relating to both the lungs and the air passages within.

bronchorrhea (brong-ko-re′ah) Excessive production of mucus in the bronchi.

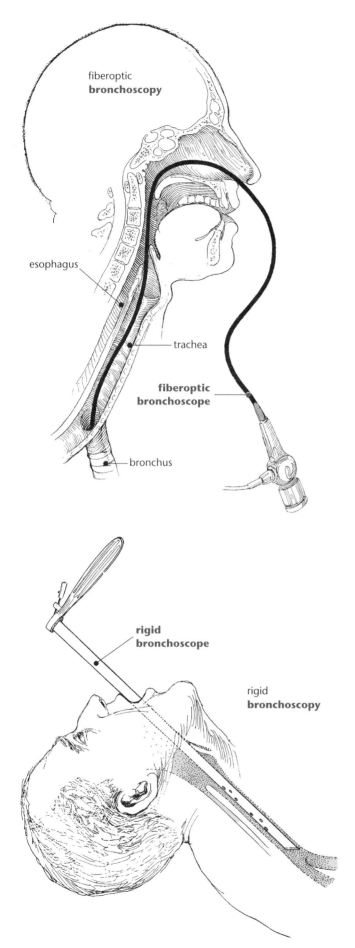

fiberoptic **bronchoscopy**

esophagus

trachea

fiberoptic bronchoscope

bronchus

rigid bronchoscope

rigid **bronchoscopy**

bronchoscope (brong′ko-scōp) A tubular instrument, inserted through the mouth or nose, for inspection or treatment of the main respiratory airways (trachea and bronchi); may be fitted with forceps, or may have attachments for performing laser surgery and cryosurgery.

    fiberoptic b. A thin, flexible tube containing light-transmitting fibers that produce a magnified image. External diameter of the tube ranges from 3 to 6 mm. Also called bronchofiberscope.

    rigid b. An open metal tube with a proximal or distal lighting device and a side channel for oxygen; used along with a suction tube (for removing secretions), forceps, and a sponge carrier.

bronchoscopy (brong-kos′ko-pe) Direct inspection of the main respiratory airways through a rigid or a fiberoptic bronchoscope.

bronchospasm (brong′ko-spazm) Spasmodic contraction of smooth muscle in the bronchial walls causing a narrowing of the lumen, as seen in asthma. Also called bronchial spasm.

bronchospirometer (brong-ko-spi-rom′ĕ-ter) An instrument for measuring separately the air capacity of each lung.

bronchospirometry (brong-ko-spi-rom′ĕ-tre) The determination of the volume and rate of gaseous exchange of a lung by means of a bronchospirometer; useful procedure for normal physiologic investigations.

bronchostenosis (brong-ko-ste-no′sis) Narrowing of the lumen of a bronchus.

bronchotome (brong′ko-tōm) Surgical instrument for cutting into a bronchus.

bronchovesicular (brong-ko-ve-sik′u-lar) Relating to the bronchi and air sacs (alveoli) in the lungs.

bronchus (brong′kus), pl. bron′chi Either of two main respiratory air passages in the lungs; it begins at the end of the trachea, subdivides into lobar, segmental, and subsegmental branches, and ends at the bronchioles.

broth (broth) See bouillon.

Brucella (broo-sel′lah) A genus of bacteria (family Brucellaceae)

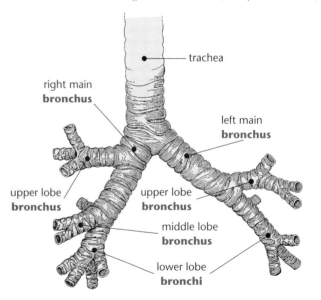

trachea

right main **bronchus**

left main **bronchus**

upper lobe **bronchus**

upper lobe **bronchus**

middle lobe **bronchus**

lower lobe **bronchi**

composed of rod-shaped to spherical (coccoid) parasitic cells; several species cause disease in some domestic animals and in humans.

    B. abortus A species that causes abortion in farm animals and brucellosis in humans. Also called Bang's bacillus.

brucellosis (broo-sel-lo′sis) An infectious disease caused by bacteria of the genus *Brucella*, marked by an acute febrile phase and a chronic one with fever, sweats, aches, and weakness; the fever has a characteristic pattern of rising in the afternoon and diminishing during the night; occurs most frequently as an occupational disease in slaughterhouse workers, veterinarians, and farmers who come in direct contact with infected animal tissues and secretions. Also called undulant fever; Malta fever.

Brugia (bruj´ĕ-ah) A genus of parasitic threadlike worms, chiefly from Southeast Asia, causing disease in humans.

B. malayi A species that causes filariasis in humans; the parasite is transmitted by the bite of several species of mosquitoes.

bruise (brooz) Popular name for contusion.

bruit (brwe, broot) An abnormal sound heard on auscultation with the stethoscope, usually caused by turbulent blood flow. Also called murmur.

abdominal b. A sound heard in the abdomen that usually can be traced to the aorta or its branches.

aneurysmal b. A blowing sound heard over an abnormal out-pouching (aneurysm) of a blood vessel.

carotid b. Sound heard over a common carotid artery, at the root of the neck.

b. de canon An abnormally loud first heart sound; heard inter-mittently when conduction of impulses from the atria to the ventri-cles is completely blocked (atrioventricular block). Also called can-non sound.

b. de Roger See Roger's murmur, under murmur.

thyroid b. Sound heard over a hyperactive thyroid gland.

bruxism (bruk´sizm) A forceful, rhythmic grinding of the teeth, es-pecially during sleep, sometimes causing extreme erosion of the oc-clusal tooth surfaces; may occur at any age, secondary to anxiety or dental problems. May cause temporomandibular joint pain. Also called odontoprisis.

bubo (bu´bo) A swollen, inflamed lymph node, especially of the groin.

tropical b. See lymphogranuloma venereum.

venereal b. Bubo associated with a venereal disease.

bubonic (bu-bon´ik) Relating to swollen lymph nodes, especially of the groin (buboes).

bucardia (bu-kar´de-ah) See cor bovinum, under cor.

bucca (buk´ah) The cheek.

buccal (buk´al) Relating to the cheek.

buccolingual (buk-o-ling´gwal) 1. Relating to the cheek and the tongue. 2. Referring to tooth surfaces and surfaces of the dental arch in contact with the cheek and/or inner aspect of the lips on one side and the tongue on the other side.

buccopharyngeal (buk-o-fah-rin´je-al) Relating to the mouth and the pharynx.

buccoversion (buk-o-ver´shun) Malposition of a tooth toward the cheek.

bud (bud) In embryology, a small mass that has the potential for growth and differentiation.

bronchial b. One of several outgrowths from the embryonic lateral and stem bronchi that become the air passages within the lungs.

limb b. A swelling on the trunk of an embryo that gives rise to an arm or leg.

metanephric b. An outgrowth from the wolffian (meso-nephric) duct that gives rise to the calyces and pelvis of the kidney, the straight collecting tubules, and the ureter. Also called ureteric bud.

taste b. One of numerous tiny organs situated on the tongue, the under surface of the soft palate, and the posterior surface of the epiglottis that transmits sensation of taste; composed of epithelial supporting cells enclosing gustatory cells and nerve fibrils from the chorda tympani and glossopharyngeal nerve. Also called taste bulb; gustatory caliculus.

tooth b. The primordial structure from which a tooth devel-ops, composed of an enamel organ, a dental papilla, and a dental sac.

ureteric b. See metanephric bud.

buffer (buf´er) 1. Any substance that maintains the relative concen-trations of hydrogen and hydroxyl ions in a solution by neutralizing added acid or alkali. 2. To add a buffer to a solution.

buffering (buf´er-ing) The process by which constant hydrogen ion concentration is maintained.

renal b. Removal of excess acid or alkali from the kidney.

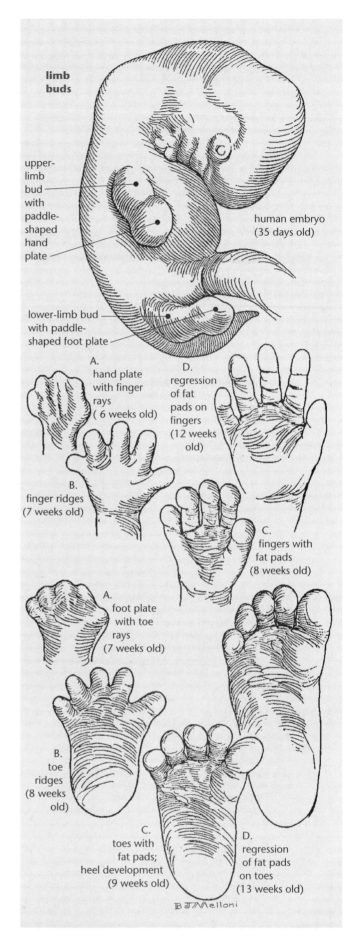

limb buds

upper-limb bud with paddle-shaped hand plate

human embryo (35 days old)

lower-limb bud with paddle-shaped foot plate

A. hand plate with finger rays (6 weeks old)

D. regression of fat pads on fingers (12 weeks old)

B. finger ridges (7 weeks old)

C. fingers with fat pads (8 weeks old)

A. foot plate with toe rays (7 weeks old)

B. toe ridges (8 weeks old)

C. toes with fat pads; heel development (9 weeks old)

D. regression of fat pads on toes (13 weeks old)

BJMelloni

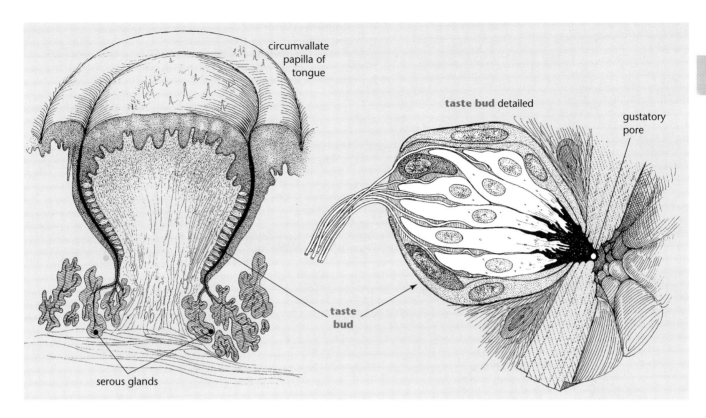

circumvallate papilla of tongue

taste bud detailed

gustatory pore

taste bud

serous glands

bug (bug) Any insect belonging to the suborder Heteroptera.

    assassin b. See kissing bug.

    bed b. See bedbug.

    cone-nose b. See kissing bug.

    kissing b. An insect (family Reduviidae) with a cone-shaped anterior end that feeds at night on the blood, usually from the lips, of sleeping people. Also called cone-nose bug; assassin bug.

    red b. See chigger.

bulb (bulb) An expanded or spherical structure or prosthesis.

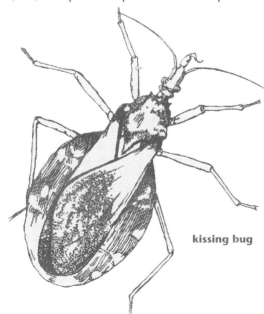

kissing bug

    aortic b. The expanded first portion of the ascending aorta containing the semilunar valves and the aortic sinuses.

    carotid b. See carotid sinus, under sinus.

    b. of corpus spongiosum See bulb of penis.

    duodenal b. See duodenal cap, under cap.

    jugular b.'s Two slight expansions of the internal jugular vein:

Superior, situated at the vein's origin just below the base of the skull. *Inferior,* near the vein's termination, just before it joins the subclavian vein to form the brachiocephalic vein, near the sternal end of the collarbone (clavicle).

    Krause's end b. A sense organ situated at the end of some sensory nerve fibers; it responds to cold stimuli. Also called Krause's corpuscle.

    olfactory b. The expanded anterior end of the olfactory tract.

    b. of penis The oval enlargement of the corpus spongiosum, at the base of the penis. Also called bulb of corpus spongiosum.

    speech b. A prosthetic device designed to close an abnormal gap (cleft) in the soft or hard palate to facilitate the production of speech.

    taste b. See taste bud, under bud.

bulbar (bul'bar) Relating to a bulb.

bulbopontine (bul-bo-pon'tin) Relating to the part of the brain composed of the pons and the portion of the medulla oblongata over it.

bulbospinal (bul-bo-spi'nal) Relating to the medulla oblongata and spinal cord; applied to nerve fibers interconnecting the two structures. Also called spinobulbar.

bulbourethral (bul-bo-u-re'thral) Relating to the bulb of the penis and the urethra.

bulimia (bu-lim'e-ah) Eating disorder occurring chiefly in young women; characterized by binge-purge cycles, i.e., episodes of overeating (binges), generally beyond voluntary control, followed by efforts to avoid weight gain by induced vomiting, laxative or diuretic abuse (purge), excessive exercise, and fasting. Bulimics usually have normal body weight. Long-term effects may include tooth decay and constant sore throat. Eventual pathologic effects are the consequences of vomiting (tears and bleeding in the esophagus and associated inflammation of the lungs) and of laxative abuse (usually resulting in alkalosis and hypokalemia, the latter sometimes severe enough to precipitate heart problems). Commonly called binge-and-purge syndrome.

bulimic (bu-lim'ik) Relating to bulimia.

bulkage (bulk'ij) Any material, such as bran, that increases the bulk of intestinal contents, thereby stimulating the intestinal propelling movements (peristalsis).

bulla (bul'ah), pl. bul'lae **1.** A fluid-or air-filled blister larger than 1 cm in diameter. **2.** An anatomic structure resembling a bubble.

   pulmonary b. An air-filled bubble on the surface of or within a lung; occurring in certain lung diseases.

bullous (bul'us) Relating to bullae.

bundle (bun'dl) A distinct collection of muscle or nerve fibers.

   atrioventricular b., A-V b. A bundle of specialized muscular fibers situated in the musculomembranous wall (interventricular septum) that divides the ventricles of the heart; it originates at the atrioventricular (A-V) node in the floor of the right atrium, extends downward within the septum, divides into right and left branches, and ends in numerous strands (Purkinje system) in the papillary and ventricular muscles. Also called bundle of His; His' bundle; fasciculus atrioventricularis; atrioventricular trunk.

   b. of His, His' b. See atrioventricular bundle.

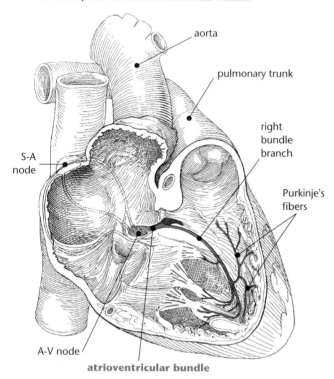

aorta
pulmonary trunk
right bundle branch
Purkinje's fibers
S-A node
A-V node
atrioventricular bundle

bunion (bun'yun) An abnormal bony protrusion at the junction of the big toe and the foot (first metatarsal head), with inflamed bursa and callosity formation; associated with an outward displacement of the big toe (hallux valgus).

   tailor's b. See bunionette.

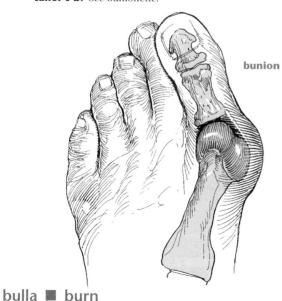

bunion

bunionectomy (bun-yun-ek'to-me) Surgical treatment of a bunion.

bunionette (bun-yun-et') Enlargement of the lateral aspect of the head of the little toe (fifth metatarsal head) with bursitis over the bony prominence. Also called tailor's bunion.

buphthalmos (buf-thal'mos) Congenital glaucoma occurring in both eyes of infants; increased fluid and pressure within the eyeball produce a larger than normal eye with milky, protruding cornea; a rare condition. Also called hydrophthalmos.

bur (ber) See burr.

buret, burette (bu-ret') A graduated glass tube with a stopcock; used in the laboratory for accurate dispensing of liquids.

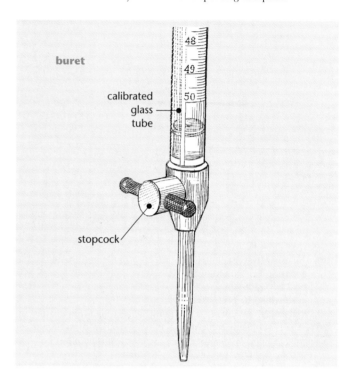

buret
calibrated glass tube
stopcock

burn (bern) **1.** To damage tissues by fire, heat, a caustic chemical, or friction. **2.** The injury thus produced.

   brush b. Burn caused by friction or rubbing with a rapidly moving object. Also called rope burn; mat burn; brush burn abrasion.

   chemical b. Burn caused by direct contact with strong caustic substances (e.g., acids and alkalies, mustard gas, and phosphorus). It produces tissue death that may continue slowly for several hours.

   electrical b. Damage caused by power line accidents and lightning strikes; skin damage is usually relatively minor, such as tiny entrance and exit sites of dead (necrotic) tissue; irregular heart rhythms may result.

   first-degree b. Reddening of the skin without blistering, involving the superficial layer (epidermis) of the skin.

   flash b. Burn caused by brief exposure to high-intensity radiant heat.

   high-voltage b. Charring of tissues over large areas of the body, with brownish discoloration apart from areas of actual burning; caused by close exposure to, or contact with, a high-tension conductor.

   mat b. See brush burn.

   radiation b. Burn caused by overexposure to x rays, radium, ultraviolet rays, or any other kind of radiant energy.

   rope b. See brush burn.

   second-degree b. Damage extending through the superficial layer of the skin (epidermis) leading to formation of blisters; usually heals without scarring, unless it covers an extensive area of the skin.

   spark b.'s Burns caused by loose or intermittent contact with an electric current; marked by dry, pitted, often tiny skin lesions usually occurring on the hands (rarely on the soles of the feet, as when electrical workers wear shoes with metal studs); a yellow, parchment-like scab may form with a surrounding pale ring around the lesion.

thermal b. Burn caused by contact with excessive heat.

third degree b. Damage and destruction that include the deep layer of the skin (dermis); may also involve subcutaneous fat, muscle, and bone.

burner (ber'ner) The source of flame in a lamp or heating equipment.

Bunsen b. A gas burner for laboratory use consisting of a metal tube with adjustable air openings at the base; it creates a hot, nearly smokeless flame.

burnisher (ber'nish-er) A dental instrument with rounded working surfaces for smoothing, polishing, or stretching the metallic surface of a tooth filling.

burnishers

burr (ber) Any of various rotary cutting tools designed to be attached to a drill and used for creating openings in bone (e.g., in the skull) or for removing carious material from a tooth and grinding the tooth surface. Also spelled bur.

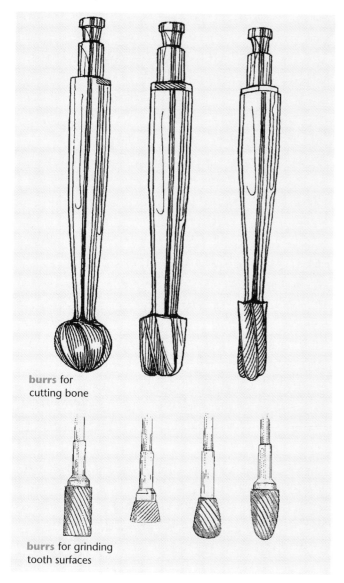
burrs for cutting bone

burrs for grinding tooth surfaces

burr hole (ber hōl) A round opening in the skull made with a bone-cutting burr that is specifically designed to prevent injury to the underlying dura.

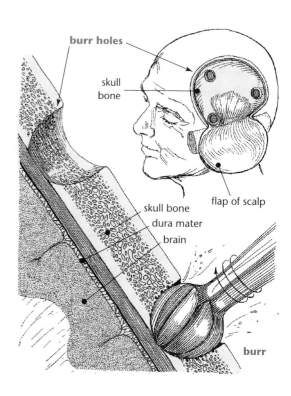
burr holes
skull bone
flap of scalp
skull bone
dura mater
brain
burr

bursa (ber'sah), pl. bur'sae A closed, flattened sac of synovial membrane containing a viscid fluid; usually present over bony prominences, between and beneath tendons, and between certain movable structures; it serves to facilitate movement by diminishing friction and by creating discontinuity between tissues, thus allowing complete freedom of movement.

Achilles b. See bursa of calcaneal tendon.

b. of acromion A small subcutaneous bursa located at the shoulder between the upper surface of the acromion and the overlying skin.

adventitious b. An abnormal bursa or cyst developed as a result of continued irritation.

anserine b. A bursa located at the medial side of the knee joint between the tibial (medial) collateral ligament and the tendon insertions of the semitendinous, gracilis, and sartorius muscles. Also called tibial intertendinous bursa.

b. of biceps brachii muscle See bicipitoradial bursa.

b. of biceps muscle of arm See bicipitoradial bursa.

b. of biceps muscle of thigh Either of two subtendinous bursae: *Lower*, a small bursa between the tendon of the biceps muscle of thigh (biceps femoris muscle) and the fibular (lateral) collateral ligament of the knee joint. *Upper*, a small bursa under the tendon of origin of the long head of the biceps muscle of thigh (biceps femoris muscle) at the ischial tuberosity of the hipbone.

bicipitoradial b. A bursa interposed between the tendon of the biceps muscle of the arm (biceps brachii muscle) and the front part of the tuberosity of the radius. Also called bursa of biceps brachii muscle; bursa of biceps muscle of arm.

b. of big toe A bursa interposed between the lateral side of the base of the first metatarsal bone of the foot and the medial side of the adjoining shaft of the second metatarsal bone.

b. of calcaneal tendon A large bursa located at the heel, between the calcaneal tendon (Achilles tendon) and the back of the heel bone (calcaneus). Also called bursa of tendo calcaneus; Achilles bursa; retrocalcaneal bursa.

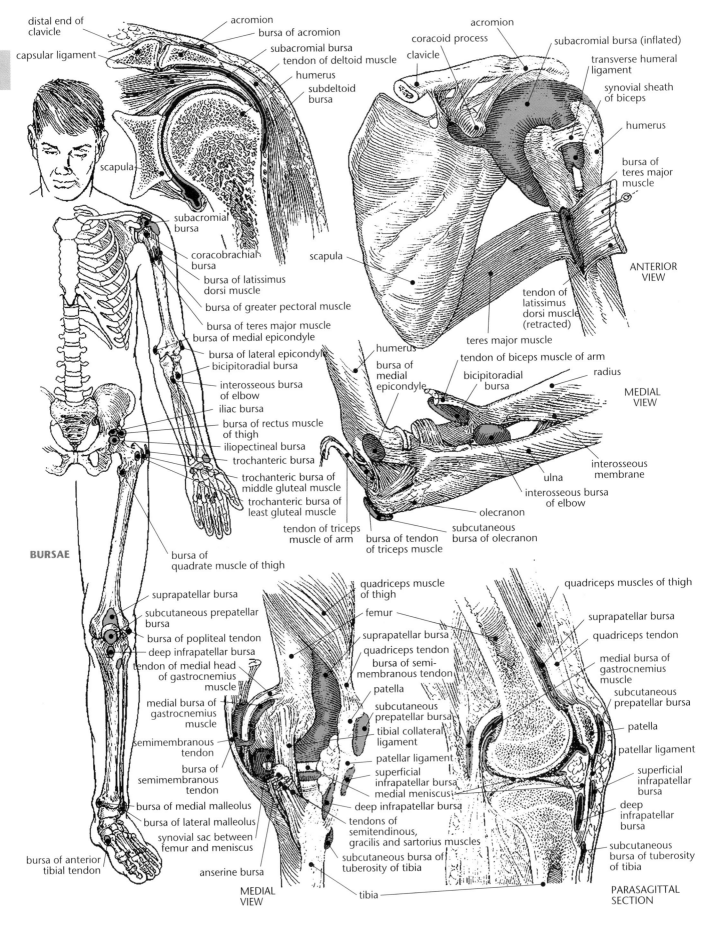

B

distal end of clavicle
capsular ligament
acromion
bursa of acromion
subacromial bursa
tendon of deltoid muscle
humerus
subdeltoid bursa
scapula
subacromial bursa
coracobrachial bursa
bursa of latissimus dorsi muscle
bursa of greater pectoral muscle
bursa of teres major muscle
bursa of medial epicondyle
bursa of lateral epicondyle
bicipitoradial bursa
interosseous bursa of elbow
iliac bursa
bursa of rectus muscle of thigh
iliopectineal bursa
trochanteric bursa
trochanteric bursa of middle gluteal muscle
trochanteric bursa of least gluteal muscle
bursa of quadrate muscle of thigh

BURSAE

acromion
coracoid process
clavicle
subacromial bursa (inflated)
transverse humeral ligament
synovial sheath of biceps
humerus
bursa of teres major muscle
scapula
ANTERIOR VIEW
tendon of latissimus dorsi muscle (retracted)
teres major muscle

humerus
bursa of medial epicondyle
tendon of biceps muscle of arm
bicipitoradial bursa
radius
MEDIAL VIEW
interosseous membrane
ulna
interosseous bursa of elbow
olecranon
subcutaneous bursa of olecranon
bursa of tendon of triceps muscle
tendon of triceps muscle of arm

suprapatellar bursa
subcutaneous prepatellar bursa
bursa of popliteal tendon
deep infrapatellar bursa
tendon of medial head of gastrocnemius muscle
medial bursa of gastrocnemius muscle
semimembranous tendon
bursa of semimembranous tendon
bursa of medial malleolus
bursa of lateral malleolus
synovial sac between femur and meniscus
bursa of anterior tibial tendon
anserine bursa
MEDIAL VIEW

quadriceps muscle of thigh
femur
suprapatellar bursa
quadriceps tendon
bursa of semi-membranous tendon
patella
subcutaneous prepatellar bursa
tibial collateral ligament
patellar ligament
superficial infrapatellar bursa
medial meniscus
deep infrapatellar bursa
tendons of semitendinous, gracilis and sartorius muscles
subcutaneous bursa of tuberosity of tibia
tibia

quadriceps muscles of thigh
suprapatellar bursa
quadriceps tendon
medial bursa of gastrocnemius muscle
subcutaneous prepatellar bursa
patella
patellar ligament
superficial infrapatellar bursa
deep infrapatellar bursa
subcutaneous bursa of tuberosity of tibia
PARASAGITTAL SECTION

bursa ■ bursa

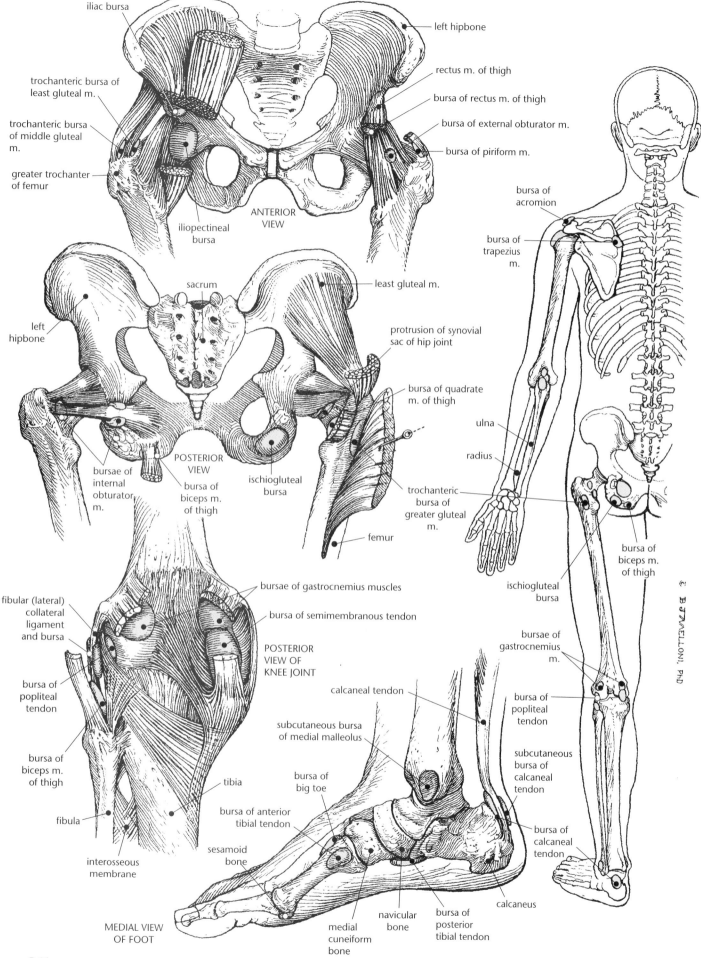

iliac bursa

trochanteric bursa of least gluteal m.

trochanteric bursa of middle gluteal m.

greater trochanter of femur

iliopectineal bursa

ANTERIOR VIEW

left hipbone

rectus m. of thigh

bursa of rectus m. of thigh

bursa of external obturator m.

bursa of piriform m.

left hipbone

sacrum

least gluteal m.

protrusion of synovial sac of hip joint

bursa of quadrate m. of thigh

bursae of internal obturator m.

POSTERIOR VIEW

bursa of biceps m. of thigh

ischiogluteal bursa

trochanteric bursa of greater gluteal m.

femur

bursae of gastrocnemius muscles

bursa of semimembranous tendon

POSTERIOR VIEW OF KNEE JOINT

fibular (lateral) collateral ligament and bursa

bursa of popliteal tendon

bursa of biceps m. of thigh

fibula

interosseous membrane

tibia

sesamoid bone

MEDIAL VIEW OF FOOT

calcaneal tendon

subcutaneous bursa of medial malleolus

bursa of big toe

bursa of anterior tibial tendon

medial cuneiform bone

navicular bone

bursa of posterior tibial tendon

calcaneus

bursa of acromion

bursa of trapezius m.

ulna

radius

ischiogluteal bursa

bursa of biceps m. of thigh

bursae of gastrocnemius m.

bursa of popliteal tendon

subcutaneous bursa of calcaneal tendon

bursa of calcaneal tendon

B

© E. TAVELLONI, PhD

B41

bursa ■ bursa

Calori's b. A bursa interposed between the aortic arch and the trachea.

communicating b. A bursa whose synovial membrane is continuous with that of the articular cavity of a joint.

b. of coracobrachial muscle An occasional bursa of the upper arm located between the tendons of the coracobrachial and subscapular muscles.

deep trochanteric b. See trochanteric bursa of greater gluteal muscle.

b. of extensor carpi radialis brevis muscle See bursa of short radial extensor muscle of wrist.

b. of fibular collateral ligament A bursa interposed between the lateral part of the knee joint capsule and the fibular (lateral) collateral ligament, which it partially envelops.

Fleischmann's b. A bursa near the frenulum of the tongue interposed between the floor of the mouth and the genioglossus muscle.

b. of gastrocnemius muscle Either of two subtendinous bursae. *Lateral*, a bursa located under the tendon of origin of the lateral head of the gastrocnemius muscle. *Medial*, a bursa located under the tendon of origin of the medial head of the gastrocnemius muscle; it is usually connected with the semimembranous bursa (of clinical importance because when distended with fluid, it is the usual cause of a popliteal cyst); it is occasionally connected to the knee joint.

gluteofemoral b. A bursa interposed between the tendon of the greater gluteal muscle (gluteus maximus muscle) and the tendon of the lateral vastus muscle (vastus lateralis muscle).

b. of greater pectoral muscle A bursa between the tendons of insertion of the greater pectoral muscle (pectoralis major muscle) and the latissimus dorsi muscle on the upper anterior aspect of the humerus. Also called bursa of pectoralis major muscle.

b. of greater psoas tendon See iliopectineal bursa.

iliac b. A large subtendinous bursa lying under the tendon of the iliac muscle just above the hip joint; sometimes in communication with the cavity of the hip joint.

iliopectineal b. A large bursa on the anterior surface of the hip joint capsule, interposed between the tendon of the iliopsoas muscle and the iliopubic eminence of the hipbone; it frequently communicates with the capsule of the hip joint. Also called bursa of greater psoas tendon; bursa of psoas major muscle.

b. of iliotibial tract A bursa interposed between the lateral part of the knee joint capsule and the iliotibial tract just above where it fuses with the patellar retinaculum and capsule.

infracardiac b. The transient embryonic peritoneal sac on the right side of the esophagus, just above the diaphragm, extending from the top of the lesser sac of the embryonic peritoneal cavity.

infrahyoid b. A small bursa between the hyoid bone and the upper part of the thyrohyoid membrane.

infrapatellar b. Either of two bursae of the knee: *Deep infrapatellar b.* a bursa located just below the kneecap (patella) between the lower part of the patellar ligament and the upper part of the front of the tibia. *Superficial infrapatellar b.* a subcutaneous bursa situated between the patellar ligament and the overlying skin.

b. of infraspinous muscle A small synovial bursa interposed between the tendon of the infraspinous muscle (infraspinatus muscle) and the capsule of the shoulder joint.

interligamentous b. A bursa located between ligaments.

interosseous b. of elbow An occasional bursa interposed between the tendon of the biceps muscle of the arm (biceps brachii muscle) and the depression of the anterior ulna between the supinator crest and tuberosity. Also called interosseous cubital bursa.

interosseous cubital b. See interosseous bursa of elbow.

ischial b. of gluteus maximus muscle See ischiogluteal bursa.

ischiogluteal b. A large bursa separating the greater gluteal muscle (gluteus maximus muscle) from the ischial tuberosity; chronic ischiogluteal bursitis is caused by prolonged sitting on hard

surfaces and is commonly known as weaver's bottom. Also called ischial bursa of gluteus maximus muscle.

b. of laryngeal prominence A small subcutaneous bursa found occasionally between the prominence of the thyroid cartilage (Adam's apple) and the overlying skin.

b. of lateral epicondyle A small subcutaneous bursa at the elbow occasionally found between the bony prominence of the lateral epicondyle of the humerus and the overlying skin.

b. of lateral malleolus A subcutaneous bursa at the ankle between the lateral malleolus of the fibula and the overlying skin.

b. of latissimus dorsi muscle An elongated bursa in front of the tendon of the latissimus dorsi muscle at the intertubecular sulcus of the humerus in the upper part of the arm.

b. of medial epicondyle A small subcutaneous bursa at the elbow found occasionally between the bony prominence of the medial epicondyle of the humerus and the overlying skin.

b. of medial malleolus A subcutaneous bursa at the ankle between the medial malleolus of the tibia and the overlying skin.

b. of obturator muscle Either of three bursae of the hip: *External*, a bursa interposed between the tendon of the external obturator muscle and the hip joint capsule and femoral neck; it communicates with the synovial cavity of the hip joint. *Internal*, (1) a well-developed sciatic bursa partially encircling the tendon of the internal obturator muscle as it emerges from the lesser sciatic notch of the hipbone; (2) a bursa between the tendon of the internal obturator muscle and the femur.

b. of olecranon A subcutaneous bursa between the olecranon process of the ulna and the overlying skin of the elbow.

omental b. See lesser sac of peritoneum, under sac.

ovarian b. A peritoneal recess between the medial surface of the ovary and the overlapping mesosalpinx.

b. of pectoralis major muscle See bursa of greater pectoral muscle.

pharyngeal b. A blind recess at the base of the pharyngeal tonsil in the posterior wall of the nasopharynx; it represents the remnant of the degenerated end of the primitive notochord.

b. of piriform muscle A small bursa under the tendons of the piriform muscle and the superior gemellus muscle at their insertion on the greater trochanter of the femur.

b. of popliteal tendon A bursal extension of the synovial cavity of the knee joint, between the lateral condyle of the femur and the tendon of the popliteal muscle. Also called subpopliteal recess.

prepatellar b. Either of three bursae of the knee: *Subcutaneous*, a large superficial bursa between the lower part of the front of the kneecap (patella) and the overlying skin; chronic irritation causes housemaid's knee (prepatellar bursitis). *Subfascial*, an occasional bursa between the deep fascia and the tendinous fibers in front of the kneecap (patella). *Subtendinous*, an occasional bursa between the kneecap (patella) and the tendinous fibers to its front.

b. of psoas major muscle See iliopectineal bursa.

b. of quadrate muscle of thigh A bursa located between the front of the quadrate muscle of thigh (quadratus femoris muscle) and the lesser trochanter of the femur. Also called bursa of quadratus femoris muscle.

quadrate b. See suprapatellar bursa.

b. of quadratus femoris muscle See bursa of quadrate muscle of thigh.

quadriceps b. See suprapatellar bursa.

radiohumeral b. A bursa located at the elbow, over the radiohumeral joint, between the extensor muscle of fingers (extensor digitorum muscle) and the supinator muscle.

b. of rectus muscle of thigh A small bursa between the tendon of origin of the rectus muscle of thigh (rectus femoris muscle) and the margin of the acetabulum.

retrocalcaneal b. See bursa of calcaneal tendon.

retrohyoid b. A bursa interposed between the back of the body of the hyoid bone and the upper part of the thyrohyoid membrane.

sciatic b. See bursa of obturator muscle, internal.

b. of semimembranous tendon A bursa located on the medial side of the knee, between the flattened tendon of the semimembranous muscle and the medial head of the gastrocnemius muscle.

b. of short radial extensor muscle of wrist A small bursa between the base of the third metacarpal bone and the tendon of the short radial extensor muscle of wrist (extensor carpi radialis brevis muscle). Also called bursa of extensor carpi radialis brevis muscle.

subacromial b. A large bursa near the capsule of the shoulder joint, between the acromion and the tendons of the supraspinous and infraspinous muscles.

subcoracoid b. See bursa of subscapular muscle.

subcutaneous b. A bursa located between the skin and an underlying superficial structure.

subdeltoid b. An extension of the subacromial bursa, which lies between the deltoid muscle and the greater tubercle of the humerus.

subfascial b. A bursa located between a layer of fascia and bone.

submuscular b. A bursa located between muscle and bone, tendon, or ligament.

b. of subscapular muscle A large subtendinous bursa located between the tendon of the subscapular muscle and the glenoid border of the scapula; it communicates with the cavity of the shoulder joint. Also called subcoracoid bursa.

subtendinous b. A bursa located between tendons and bone, tendons and ligaments, or between one tendon and another.

b. of superior oblique muscle of eyeball A synovial sheath encircling the tendon of the superior oblique muscle of the eyeball as it passes through the cartilaginous pulley (trochlea) at the superomedial angle of the orbit. Also called synovial trochlear bursa.

suprapatellar b. An anterior extension of the synovial sac of the knee joint, between the femur and the tendon of the quadriceps muscle of the thigh (quadriceps femoris muscle). Also called quadriceps bursa; quadrate bursa; suprapatellar synovial pouch.

synovial b. A closed sac formed by the synovial membrane and moistened by a small amount of viscid fluid (similar to the white part of an egg) that facilitates movement; located where structures rub together or are subject to pressure; may be subcutaneous, submuscular, subtendinous, or subfascial in location.

synovial trochlear b. See bursa of superior oblique muscle of eyeball.

b. of tendo calcaneus See bursa of calcaneal tendon.

b. of tendon of triceps muscle A bursa interposed between the tendon of the triceps muscle of the arm (triceps brachii muscle) and the olecranon process of the ulna.

b. of tensor muscle of soft palate A small bursa partly surrounding the tendon of the tensor muscle of soft palate (tensor veli palatini muscle) as it turns around the medial pterygoid hamulus of the sphenoid bone.

b. of teres major muscle A synovial sac between the tendons of the teres major and latissimus dorsi muscles.

tibial intertendinous b. See anserine bursa.

b. of tibial tendon Either of two bursae of the foot: *Anterior,* a small bursa seen under the tendon of the anterior tibial muscle, at the medial surface of the proximal part of the first metatarsal bone. *Posterior,* a small bursa interposed between the tendon of the posterior tibial muscle and the calcaneonavicular ligament on the sole of the foot.

b. of trapezius muscle A subtendinous bursa interposed between the tendinous part of the trapezius muscle and the medial end of the spine of the scapula.

trochanteric b. A subcutaneous bursa between the greater trochanter of the upper femur and the overlying skin.

trochanteric b. of gluteus medius muscle See trochanteric bursa of middle gluteal muscle.

trochanteric b. of gluteus maximus muscle See trochanteric bursa of greater gluteal muscle.

trochanteric b. of gluteus minimus muscle See trochanteric bursa of least gluteal muscle.

trochanteric b. of greater gluteal muscle A bursa, often double, that separates the tendon of the greater gluteal muscle (gluteus maximus muscle) from the posterolateral surface of the greater trochanter of the femur, over which it glides. Also called deep trochanteric bursa; trochanteric bursa of gluteus maximus muscle.

trochanteric b. of least gluteal muscle A bursa between the tendon of the least gluteal muscle (gluteal minimus muscle) and the medial part of the anterior surface of the greater trochanter of the femur. Also called trochanteric bursa of gluteus minimus muscle.

trochanteric b. of middle gluteal muscle A bursa interposed between the tendon of the middle gluteal muscle (gluteal medius muscle) and the lateral surface of the greater trochanter of the femur. Also called trochanteric bursa of gluteus medius muscle.

b. of tuberosity of tibia A subcutaneous bursa located between the tuberosity of the tibia and the overlying skin of the knee.

bursectomy (ber-sek'to-me) Surgical removal of a bursa.

bursitis (ber-si'tis) Inflammation of a thin-walled sac (bursa) surrounding muscles and tendons over bony prominences. The cause is usually unknown; may be caused by injury and repeated trauma, or be associated with a systemic disease.

Achilles b. See retrocalcaneal bursitis.

Achilles tendon b. See retrocalcaneal bursitis.

ischial b. Bursitis of the ischiogluteal bursa at the buttocks, between the greater gluteus muscle (gluteus maximus muscle) and the ischial tuberosity of the hipbone. Also called tailor's bottom; weaver's bottom.

olecranon b. Bursitis at the tip of the elbow. Also called miner's elbow; student's elbow.

prepatellar b. Inflammation of the bursa situated in front of the kneecap (patella). Also called housemaid's knee.

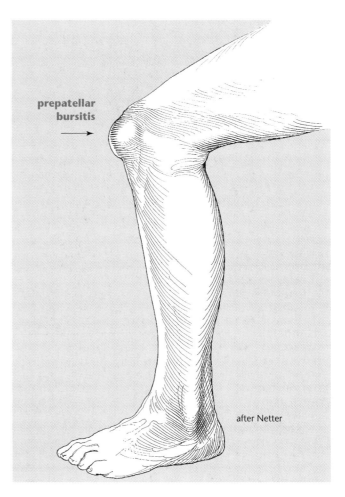

prepatellar bursitis →

after Netter

retrocalcaneal b. Inflammation of the bursa lying at the back of the heel, between the skin and the Achilles (calcaneal) tendon at the site of its insertion to the bone. Also called achillobursitis; Achilles bursitis; Achilles tendon bursitis.

subacromial b. Pain and tenderness of the shoulder caused by bursitis of the subacromial bursa at the shoulder joint, accompanied by tears and calcifications; may also involve the subdeltoid bursa (located under the deltoid muscle).

bursocentesis (ber-so-sen-te'sis) Puncture and removal of fluid from a bursa.

bursolith (ber'so-lith) A stonelike concretion formed in a bursa.

bursotomy (ber-sot'o-me) Surgical incision into a bursa.

burst (berst) **1.** A sudden, intense increase in activity. **2.** In the electroencephalogram (EEG), the occurrence of short waves against generally slower rhythms.

respiratory b. The series of enzymatic reactions employed by phagocytes after engulfing bacteria in order to convert oxygen into compounds (e.g., superoxide and hydrogen peroxide) necessary for bactericidal activity.

butacaine sulfate (bu-tah-kān' sul'fāt) A local anesthetic applied to mucous membranes (e.g., in the oral cavity).

butt (but) To place any two surfaces in contact.

butterfly (but'er-fli) **1.** Any material or device in the shape of a butterfly (e.g., a piece of tape for approximating the edges of a wound, or a wad of absorbent material used in gynecologic surgery). **2.** A butterfly-shaped rash on the cheeks and across the nose, characteristic of lupus erythematosus.

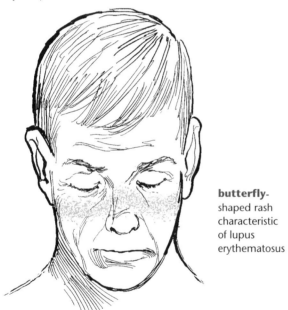

butterfly-shaped rash characteristic of lupus erythematosus

buttocks (but'oks) The protuberances formed by the gluteus muscles.

button (but'n) A knoblike structure or device.

belly b. See umbilicus.

peritoneal b. A short flanged tube for draining ascitic fluid from the peritoneum.

terminal b. See axon terminal, under terminal.

buttonhole (but'n-hōl) A small, straight surgical cut into a cavity.

butyraceous (bu-tī-ra'she-us) Having the consistency of butter.

butyric acid (bu-tir'ik as'id) A saturated fatty acid of unpleasant odor occurring in rancid butter, sweat, and other substances.

butyroid (bu'tī-roid) Resembling butter.

bypass (bi'pas) **1.** A diverted flow; a shunt. **2.** To create a new flow from one site of the body to another.

cardiopulmonary b. Diversion of the blood flow from the heart and lungs to a circuit outside the body (heart-lung machine), where it passes through an oxygenator for gas exchanges, and then returns to the arterial side of the circulation. The procedure is used in open-heart surgery.

coronary b., coronary artery b. graft (CABG) The suturing of a graft to the aorta and to a coronary artery, circumventing a clogged portion of the coronary artery, to restore circulation.

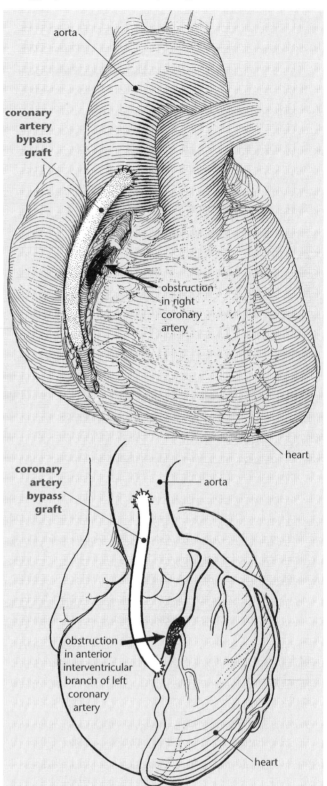

byssinosis (bis-ĭ-no'sis) An occupational respiratory disease occurring in textile workers (at cotton, flax, and hemp mills); marked by chest tightening, wheezing, labored breathing, and cough; characteristically, symptoms are worse the first day of work after a weekend or vacation. Long exposure, beyond 10 years, may cause permanent respiratory disability. Also called cotton-mill fever; mill fever.

C

CA 15-3 An antigen found in the serum of a high percentage of patients with metastatic cancer.

CA 19-9 An antigen found in the serum of a high percentage of patients with metastatic pancreatic cancer.

CA 125 An antigen found in the serum of a high percentage of patients with metastatic ovarian cancer.

cachectic (kah-kek′tik) Relating to cachexia.

cachet (kah-sha′) A wafer capsule formerly used by pharmacists to enclose a dose of unpalatable medication.

cachexia (kah-kek′se-ah) Condition characterized by extreme weight loss, anemia, wasting of muscles, and weakness; associated with a long-term disease or severe malnutrition.

cacosmia (kak-oz′me-ah) A subjective sensation of unpleasant odors that do not exist; an olfactory hallucination.

cadaver (kah-dav′er) A dead body; in common medical use, the term refers to a human corpse that has been embalmed for teaching and research purposes.

cadaverine (kah-dav′er-in) A nitrogenous substance of disagreeable odor formed in decomposing animal tissue.

cadaverous (kah-dav′er-us) Resembling a corpse.

cadherin (kad′her-in) One of a family of receptors that bind cells together.

cadmium (kad′me-um) A toxic metallic element; symbol Cd, atomic number 48, atomic weight 112.41. Cadmium and its compounds are used in numerous industries; long-term industrial exposure of workers constitutes a health hazard unless adequate safeguards are adopted. See also cadmium poisoning, under poisoning.

caduceus (kah-doo′se-us) A winged staff with two oppositely entwined serpents; emblem of the U.S. Army Medical Corps.

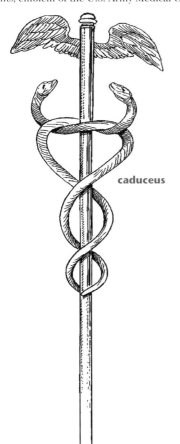

caduceus

caffeine (kah-fēn′) A bitter crystalline substance present in various plants, e.g., tea (*Thea sinensis*), coffee (*Coffea arabica*), kola (*Cola nitida*), cacao (*Theobroma cacao*), maté (*Ilex paraguayensis*); it stimulates the central nervous system, promotes an increased discharge of urine (diuresis), and stimulates dilatation of blood vessels (vasodilatation). Caffeine has been administered in combination with other drugs to treat migraine.

caffeinism (kaf′ēn-izm) Condition resulting from ingesting excessive amounts of caffeine; marked by increased rate of the heartbeat (tachycardia), insomnia, and irritability.

CAGE (kāj) See CAGE test, under test.

cage (kāj) **1.** Any box or enclosure. **2.** An anatomic structure resembling a box.

    rib c. See thoracic cage.

    thoracic c. The bones and musculature of the chest; it contains the thoracic organs and functions during respiration. Commonly called rib cage.

calamine (kal′ah-mīn) A powder composed of zinc oxide and a small amount of ferric oxide (about 0.5%); used in the form of lotions and ointments to relieve itching in certain skin disorders.

calcaneal, calcanean (kal-ka-ne-al, kal-ka-ne-an) Relating to the heel bone (calcaneus).

calcaneonavicular (kal-ka-ne-o-nah-vik′u-lar) Relating to the calcaneus and the navicular bone of the foot.

calcaneus (kal-ka-ne-us) See table of bones.

calcar (kal′kar) A bony projection; a spur.

calcareous (kal-ka′re-us) Chalky; relating to calcium or lime.

calces (kal′sēz) Plural of calx.

calcicosis (kal-sĭ-ko′sis) A lung disorder (pneumoconiosis) caused by inhalation of limestone dust. Formerly called marble cutter's phthisis.

calcidiol (kal-sĭ-di′ol) The first product in the conversion of vitamin D₃ to the more active form, calcitriol (1,25-dihydroxycholecalciferol); it is formed in the liver and converted to calcitriol by the kidney. Calcidiol serves as a good indicator of the amount of vitamin D stored in the body. Also called calcifediol; 25-hydroxycholecalciferol.

calcifediol (kal-sif-ĕ-di′ōl) See calcidiol.

calciferol (kal-sif′er-ol) See vitamin D₂.

calciferous (kal-sif′er-us) Producing or containing calcium or calcium carbonate.

calcific (kal-sif′ik) Caused by calcification.

calcification (kal-sĭ-fĭ-ka′shun) The process by which calcium salts are deposited in organic tissue.

    dystrophic c. Focal deposition of calcium salts in previously damaged tissues (e.g., heart valves, blood vessel walls) of persons whose plasma levels of calcium and phosphate are normal.

    metastatic c. Deposition of calcium salts in tissues resulting from increased plasma levels of calcium or phosphate, as seen in kidney disease.

    pathologic c. Calcification occurring in tissues other than bones and teeth.

    physiologic c. Deposition of mineral salts in bone and tooth tissues occurring as a normal process of hardening and maturation of these structures.

    rail-track c. The characteristic linear calcifications in cerebral blood tumors (angiomas) of the Sturge-Weber syndrome; visible in x-ray images.

calcination (kal-sĭ-na′shun) The process of turning a substance (e.g., gypsum) into a powder (e.g., plaster of Paris) by means of heating under high temperature.

calcine (kal'sin) To cause loss of water, oxidation, or reduction by means of high temperatures.

calcinosis (kal-sĭ-no'sis) Pathologic deposition of calcium salts in the tissues, usually associated with another disease.

   c. circumscripta Areas of focal, white deposits of calcium salts in the skin and subcutaneous tissues.

   c. cutis A calcium deposit in the skin, usually occurring in tissue damaged by other conditions such as scleroderma.

   renal c. See nephrocalcinosis.

   c. universalis A widespread deposition of calcium in the skin and subcutaneous tissues, frequently involving tendons and muscles, as seen in patients with dermatomyositis.

calcipenia (kal-sĭ-pe'ne-ah) Calcium deficiency.

calciphilia (kal-sĭ-fil'e-ah) Condition in which the tissues have a tendency to absorb calcium salts circulating in the blood and become hardened.

calcitonin (kal-sĭ-to'nin) A hormone produced by the thyroid gland and secreted in response to high levels of calcium in the blood; it lowers the level by inhibiting bone resorption. Also called thyrocalcitonin.

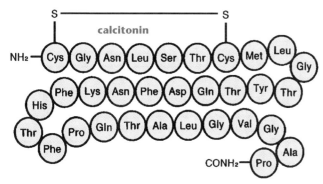

calcitriol (kal-sĭ-tri'ol) The physiologically active form of vitamin D; it increases intestinal absorption of calcium and phosphorus and increases bone resorption. Its production is stimulated by parathyroid hormone in response to low levels of calcium in the blood; formed from calcidiol by the addition of a hydroxy group by the kidney. In kidney disease, calcitriol levels tend to be low and calcium levels in the blood tend to fall.

calcium (kal'se-um) Metallic element; symbol Ca, atomic number 20, atomic weight 40.08; component of bones and teeth; essential in regulating blood coagulation, muscle contraction, conduction of nerve impulses from nerve endings to muscle fibers, function of cell membranes, activity of enzymes, and maintaining rhythmicity of the heartbeat.

   c. carbonate A calcium salt used as an antacid.

   c. chloride A calcium salt used in the treatment of calcium deficiencies.

   c. gluconate A calcium salt of gluconic acid used as a calcium supplement and in the treatment of low-calcium tetany.

   c. hydroxide Slaked lime used topically in dentistry as a stimulant for production of secondary dentin to reseal a pulp cavity.

   c. lactate The calcium salt of lactic acid, used as a calcium supplement.

   c. oxalate A white, insoluble calcium salt of oxalic acid found in acid urine as crystals and as a constituent of urinary stones.

calcium 45 A radioactive isotope of calcium; symbol ^{45}Ca, physical half-life 165 days; used in mineral metabolism research.

calcium channel-blocker See calcium channel-blocking agent, under agent.

calciuria (kal-sĭ-u're-ah) The presence of calcium in the urine.

calcodynia (kal-ko-din'e-ah) Pain in the heel.

calculi (kal'ku-li) Plural of calculus.

calculous (kal'ku-lus) Relating to calculus.

calculus (kal'ku-lus), pl. cal'culi An abnormal concretion in the body, usually in the lumen of ducts or hollow organs, formed by accumulation of mineral salts. See also stone.

   articular c. Calculus formed within a joint.

   biliary c. See gallstone.

   bronchial c. See broncholith.

   dental c. A yellowish to brown concretion adhering to the surface of a tooth or its root, composed of calcium salts, microorganisms, and other organic material. Also called tartar.

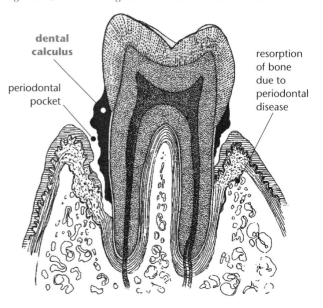

   mulberry c. Calculus resembling a mulberry, composed chiefly of calcium oxalate and formed in the bladder.

   renal c. See kidney stone, under stone.

   salivary c. A calculus in a salivary gland or duct.

   staghorn c. A large kidney stone with many branches filling the pelvis and calices of the kidney.

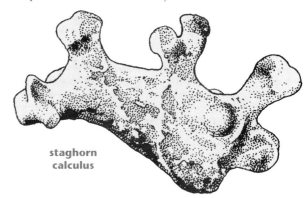

staghorn calculus

   subgingival c. Dental calculus formed below the gum margin.

   supragingival c. Dental calculus adhering to the tooth surface above the gum margin.

   urinary c. See urinary stone, under stone.

   vesical c. See vesical stone, under stone.

calefacient (kal-e-fa'shent) An agent that produces a localized sensation of heat.

calf (kaf), pl. calves The fleshy mass at the back of the human leg, formed by the bellies of the gastrocnemius and soleus muscles.

caliber (kal'ĭ-ber) The internal diameter of a tube or a tubular structure.

calibrate (kal'ĭ-brāt) **1.** To graduate or adjust a measuring instrument by comparing it with a known standard. **2.** To measure the lumen of a tubular structure.

caliceal (kal-ĭ-se'al) Relating to a calix.

calicectasis (kal-ĭ-sek'tah-sis) See caliectasis.

calices (ka'lĭ-sēz) Plural of calix.

caliculus (kah-lik'u-lus), pl. calic'uli A small cup-shaped structure or bud. Also called calycle.

gustatory c. See taste bud, under bud.

caliectasis (ka-lĭ-ek′tah-sis) Abnormal distention of the calices of the kidney. Also called calycectasis; calicectasis; pyelocaliectasis.

californium (kal-ĭ-for′ne-um) A man-made radioactive element; symbol Cf, atomic number 98, atomic weight 249. It has 12 known isotopes with half-lives ranging from 3.7 minutes to 900 years.

calipers (kal′ĭ-perz) An instrument for measuring diameters, such as the pelvic diameters.

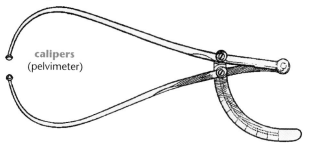

calipers (pelvimeter)

calisthenics (kal-is-then′iks) A system of light exercises for improving muscle tone and posture.

calix (ka′liks), pl. cal′ices A cup-shaped cavity in an organ. Also written calyx.

    major renal c. One of two or three primary divisions of the kidney pelvis.

    minor renal c. One of several subdivisions of each of the major renal calices.

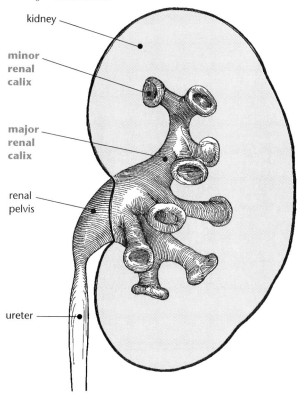

kidney

minor renal calix

major renal calix

renal pelvis

ureter

callosal (kah-lo′sal) Relating to the corpus callosum.

callosity (kah-los′ĭ-te) See callus (1).

callous (kal′us) Relating to a callus or a callosity.

callus (kal′us) **1.** A circumscribed area of toughened skin, usually due to friction. Also called callosity. **2.** A hard, bonelike substance formed between and around the fragments of broken bone; it begins as a collection of fibrous tissue to establish continuity between the bone fragments and eventual repair of the bone.

    central c. Provisional callus formed within the central portion of a bone that contains bone marrow.

    definitive c. The fibrous secretion that changes into and becomes permanent true bone.

provisional c. The original fibrous tissue that keeps bone fragments in apposition and that becomes absorbed when repair is completed.

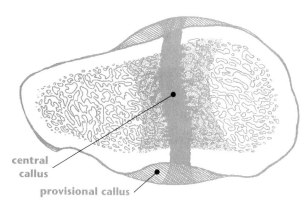

central callus

provisional callus

calor (ka′lor) Latin for heat.

caloric (kah-lo′rik) **1.** Relating to calories. **2.** Relating to heat.

calorie (kal′o-re) A unit of heat content.

    gram c. See small calorie.

    large c. (C, Cal) The calorie used in metabolic studies as a measurement of the energy-producing value of a food according to the amount of heat it produces when oxidized in the body; specifically, it is the amount of heat required to raise the temperature of 1 kg of water 1°C under specified conditions. Also called kilocalorie (Kcal).

    small c. (c, cal) The quantity of heat required to raise the temperature of 1 gr of water 1°C under specified conditions. Also called gram calorie.

calorific (kal-o-rif′ik) Relating to the production of heat.

calorigenic (kah-lor-ĭ-jen′ik) Generating or stimulating heat production.

calorimeter (kal-o-rim′ĕ-ter) Any of several apparatuses for measuring the quantity of heat liberated in a chemical or metabolic process.

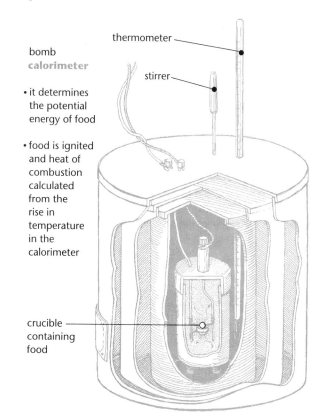

thermometer

bomb calorimeter

stirrer

• it determines the potential energy of food

• food is ignited and heat of combustion calculated from the rise in temperature in the calorimeter

crucible containing food

calorimetry (kal-o-rim′ĕ-tre) The measurement of heat production.

calvaria (kal-va′re-ah), pl. calva′riae The upper, domelike part of the skull. Popularly called skullcap; roof of skull.

calvarium (kal-va′re-um) Term used incorrectly for calvaria.

calx (kalks), pl. cal′ces The heel.

calyceal (kal-ĭ-se′al) See caliceal.

calycectasis (kal-ĭ-sek′tah-sis) See caliectasis.

calycle, calyculus (kal′ĭ-kl, kah-lik′u-lus) See caliculus.

calyx (ka′liks), pl. cal′yces See calix.

camera (kam′er-ah) **1.** An apparatus for recording images, either photographically or electronically. **2.** In anatomy, any cavity or enclosed space.

   gamma c. An electronic instrument that produces images of the gamma-ray emissions from organs containing radionuclide tracers. Also called scintillation camera.

   scintillation c. See gamma camera.

camisole (kam′ĭ-sol) Straightjacket.

camphor (kam′for) A crystalline substance obtained primarily from the evergreen tree *Cinnamonum camphora;* used in certain pharmaceutical preparations. Ingestion of large amounts of camphor by children may induce convulsions.

Campylobacter (kam-pĭ-lo-bak′ter) See *Helicobacter.*

   C. jejuni See *Helicobacter jejuni,* under *Helicobacter.*

   C. pylori See *Helicobacter pylori,* under *Helicobacter.*

canal (kah-nal′) A tubular structure; a channel; a relatively narrow passage or conduit.

   adductor c. A tunnel through the aponeurosis of the great adductor muscle (adductor magnus muscle) in the middle third of the thigh; it communicates with the popliteal fossa situated at the back of the knee; it transmits the femoral vessels and the saphenous nerve. Also called Hunter's canal; subsartorial canal.

   Alcock's c. See pudendal canal.

   alimentary c. A canal, lined with mucous membrane, formed by the esophagus, stomach, and small and large intestines.

   anal c. A canal, about 3.8 cm long in the adult, that begins at the lower end of the rectum and passes downward and backward to the end of the anus; sphincter muscles normally keep the canal closed.

   atrioventricular c. The canal in the embryonic heart through which the common atrium communicates with the primitive ventricle.

   auditory c. Either of two canals of the ear: *External,* see external auditory canal. *Internal,* see internal auditory canal.

   birth c. The channel through which the fetus passes at birth; consists of the uterine cervix, vagina, and vulva. Also called parturient canal; obstetric canal.

   bony semicircular c.'s See semicircular canals.

   carotid c. A curved passage through the petrous part of the temporal bone of the skull, occupied by the internal carotid artery and its plexus of sympathetic nerves and veins; it opens into the cranial cavity.

   caudal c. See sacral canal.

   central c. A cerebrospinal canal present in the lower half of the medulla oblongata (where it opens into the fourth ventricle of the brain) and extending throughout the entire length of the spinal cord. After the age of approximately 40 years, the lower canal tends to obliterate.

   cervical c. See canal of the cervix.

   c. of the cervix A normally closed, flattened canal within the cervix of the uterus, approximately 2.5 cm in length, connecting the vagina to the cavity within the body of the uterus. Also called cervical canal.

   cochlear c. See cochlear duct, under duct.

   diploetic c. See diploic canal.

   diploic c. A channel in the spongy (diploë) tissue of certain cranial bones providing passage for the diploic veins; absent at birth, it begins to develop at the age of about two years. Also called diploetic canal.

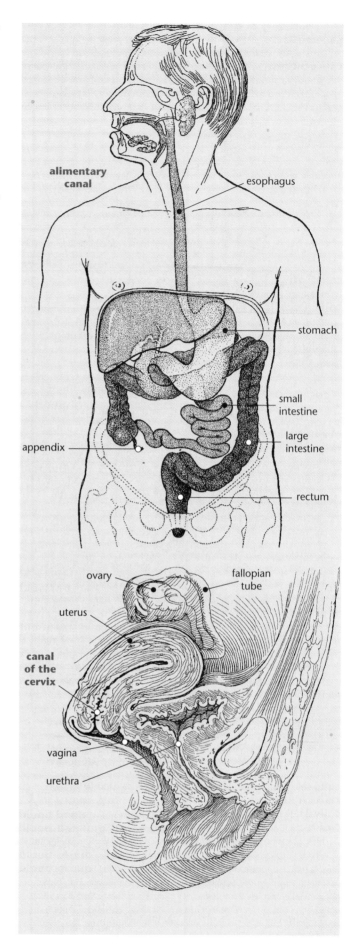

alimentary canal · esophagus · stomach · small intestine · large intestine · appendix · rectum

ovary · fallopian tube · uterus · canal of the cervix · vagina · urethra

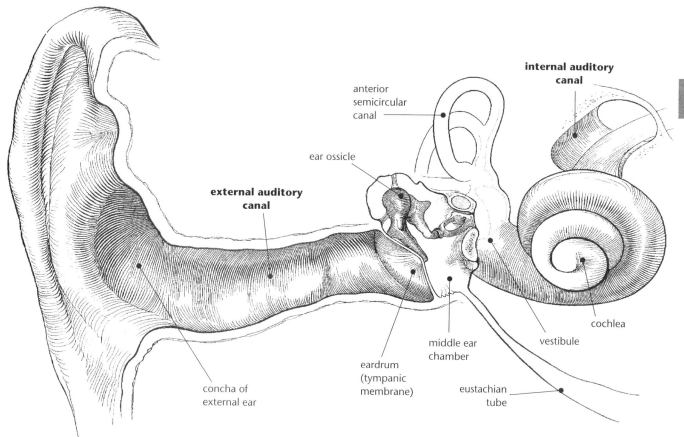

anterior semicircular canal

internal auditory canal

ear ossicle

external auditory canal

cochlea

vestibule

middle ear chamber

eardrum (tympanic membrane)

eustachian tube

concha of external ear

external acoustic c. See external auditory canal.

external auditory c. The passage that extends from the concha of the external ear (auricle) to the eardrum (tympanic membrane); in the adult, it is approximately 25 mm in length on its superoposterior wall and 6 mm longer on its anteroinferior wall, due to the obliquely directed eardrum. Also called external auditory meatus; external acoustic meatus; external acoustic canal; meatus acusticus externus.

facial c. The bony canal in the temporal bone of the skull through which passes the facial nerve; it begins at the internal auditory canal and ends at the stylomandibular foramen as it reaches the exterior of the skull.

femoral c. The medial and smallest of the three compartments of the femoral sheath underlying the inguinal ligament at the groin; it is bounded posteriorly by the pectineus muscle, medially by the lacunar ligament, and laterally by the femoral vein; it is cone-shaped and contains extraperitoneal fatty and lymphoid tissue, which cushions any expansion of the femoral vein or artery as it traverses the intermediate and lateral compartments of the femoral sheath.

haversian c.'s Canals at the center of concentrically arranged thin plates of bony tissue (osteons) in compact bone; the canals contain nerves, capillaries, and postcapillary venules.

Hunter's c. See adductor canal.

hyaloid c. A narrow canal that runs through the vitreous body of the eye from the optic disk to the center of the posterior surface of the lens; in the fetus, the canal was occupied by the hyaloid artery, which normally disappears several weeks before birth.

incisive c. of maxilla One of two canals leading from the nasal cavity, on either side of the midline, and opening through the hard palate, just behind the central incisor tooth; through it pass the terminal branches of the descending palatine artery and the nasopalatine nerve.

inferior dental c. See mandibular canal.

inguinal c. An obliquely directed passage through the layers of the lower abdominal wall on either side, through which pass the spermatic cord in the male and the round ligament of the uterus in the female.

internal acoustic c. See internal auditory canal.

internal auditory c. A transverse canal through the petrous part of the temporal bone of the skull, about 1 cm in length, extending from the cranial cavity to the medial wall of the internal ear; it provides passage for the vestibulocochlear (8th cranial) nerve, the motor and sensory roots of the facial (7th cranial) nerve, and the labyrinthine blood vessels. Also called internal auditory meatus; internal acoustic meatus; internal acoustic canal; meatus acusticus internus.

mandibular c. A canal that traverses the ramus and body of the mandible, from the mandibular foramen to the mental foramen; it runs horizontally below the tooth sockets with which it communicates by small canals; it contains the inferior alveolar vessels and nerves, from which terminal branches reach the mandibular teeth. Also called inferior dental canal.

c. of midbrain See cerebral aqueduct, under aqueduct.

nasolacrimal c. A 1-cm-long canal, just medial to the maxillary sinus, leading from the eye socket (orbit) to the inferior meatus of the nasal cavity; it contains the nasolacrimal duct.

obstetric c. See birth canal.

optic c. A short canal through the sphenoid bone at the apex of the orbit through which pass the optic nerve and ophthalmic artery from the cranial cavity to the orbit. Also called optic foramen.

parturient c. See birth canal.

pudendal c. A fibrous tunnel formed by the splitting of the obturator fascia that lines the lateral wall of the ischiorectal fossa; it transmits the internal pudendal vessels and nerves. Also called Alcock's canal.

pulp c. See root canal.

root c. The portion of the pulp cavity within a tooth, leading from the pulp chamber to the apical foramen at the tip of the root; it transmits blood vessels and sensory nerves into the pulp chamber. Also called pulp canal.

sacral c. The part of the spinal canal from the first sacral vertebra to the inferior end of the sacrum (sacral hiatus); it contains a collection of spinal roots (cauda equina), the terminal filament (filum terminale) of the spinal cord, and the spinal membranes (meninges). Also called caudal canal.

canal ■ canal

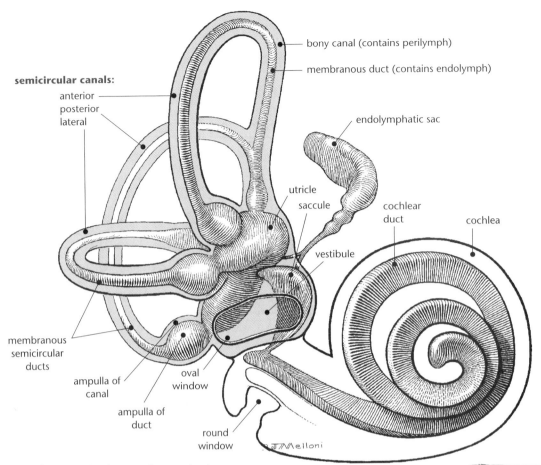

semicircular canals:
anterior
posterior
lateral

bony canal (contains perilymph)
membranous duct (contains endolymph)

endolymphatic sac

utricle
saccule

cochlear
duct

cochlea

vestibule

membranous
semicircular
ducts

ampulla of
canal

ampulla of
duct

oval
window

round
window

J. Melloni

Schlemm's c. See scleral venous sinus, under sinus.

semicircular c.'s Three canals (anterior, lateral, posterior) of the bony labyrinth of the internal ear in which the membranous semicircular ducts are enclosed; each canal, 0.8 mm in diameter, presents a dilatation at one end (ampulla) while the other end opens into an oval cavity (vestibule) within the temporal bone. Also called bony semicircular canals.

spinal c. The canal formed by the foramina of successive vertebrae; it is large and triangular in the cervical and lumbar regions, small and circular in the thoracic region, and small and triangular in the sacral region; it encloses the spinal cord and its membranes (meninges). Also called vertebral canal.

subsartorial c. See adductor canal.

tarsal c. See tarsal sinus, under sinus.

tympanic c. of cochlea See scala tympani, under scala.

vaginal c. The space within the vagina that leads from the vulva to the cervix of the uterus.

vertebral c. See spinal canal.

vestibular c. of cochlea See scala vestibuli, under scala.

Volkmann's c.'s Small oblique and transverse channels in compact bone linking the larger haversian canals with each other and with the medullary cavity, spaces in spongy bone, and the surface of the bone; they permit the transmission of blood vessels and nerves throughout the bone.

canalicular (kan-ah-lik'u-lar) Relating to a small canal (canaliculus).

canaliculi (kan-ah-lik'u-li) Plural of canaliculus.

canaliculization (kan-ah-lik-u-li-za'shun) The formation of small channels (canaliculi) in a tissue.

canaliculus (kan-ah-lik'u-lus), pl. canalic'uli A small channel or canal.

bile canaliculi The numerous fine channels forming a network between liver cells. Also called bile capillaries.

dental c. See dental tubule, under tubule.

lacrimal c. One of two channels (superior and inferior) leading from the medial margin of each eyelid to the lacrimal sac at the bridge of the nose. Also called lacrimal duct.

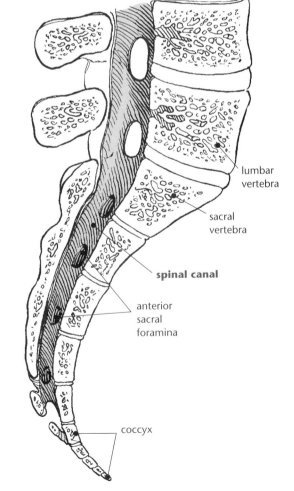

lumbar
vertebra

sacral
vertebra

spinal canal

anterior
sacral
foramina

coccyx

canalicular ■ canaliculus

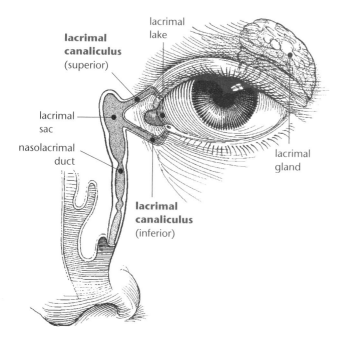

lacrimal lake

lacrimal canaliculus (superior)

lacrimal sac

lacrimal canaliculus (inferior)

nasolacrimal duct

lacrimal gland

canalization (kan-al-i-za'shun) The formation of channels through tissues or through an obstructing blood clot.

cancellated (kan'sel-lāt-ed) See cancellous.

cancellous (kan'sĕ-lus) Spongelike; like a honeycomb. Also called cancellated.

cancer (kan'ser) (CA) General term for any of a group of diseases in which symptoms are due to unrestrained proliferation of abnormal, malignant cells in the body's organs or tissues. Unlike noncancerous (benign) tumors, this new growth (neoplasm) is (1) invasive, i.e., it infiltrates and destroys adjacent tissues and/or it spreads (metastasizes) via blood vessels and lymphatic channels to other sites of the body, creating new satellite tumors that grow independently; (2) it has a tendency to recur after treatment; (3) unless adequately treated, it causes death. See also CA 15-3; CA 19-9; CA 125.

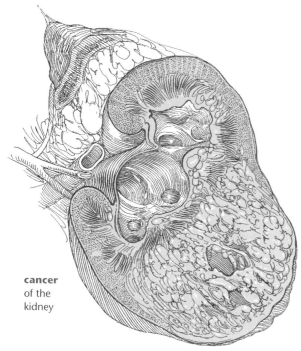

cancer of the kidney

chimney-sweep's c. Squamous cell carcinoma on the skin of the scrotum occurring as an occupational disease in chimney sweeps; caused by prolonged exposure to tar products.

epithelial c. Any malignant growth originating from the superficial layer (epithelium) of the skin.

glandular c. See adenocarcinoma.

lung c. Popular term for any cancer of the lungs, most commonly referring to bronchogenic carcinoma; see under carcinoma.

mule-spinner's c. Squamous cell carcinoma on the skin of the scrotum and adjacent areas; it has a high incidence in cotton industry workers from long-term contact with petroleum distillates used in oiling the spindles at cotton-spinning mills.

pipe-smoker's c. Squamous cell carcinoma of the lips occurring in pipe smokers.

cancericidal (kan-ser-ī-si'dal) See carcinolytic.

Cancer Information Service (CIS) A nationwide telephone service supported by the National Cancer Institute (NCI) that responds to inquiries from cancer patients and their families, health care professionals, and the general public.

CANCERLIT Cancer Literature. An on-line database on the MED-LARS system of the National Library of Medicine; sponsored by the National Cancer Institute of the National Institutes of Health (NIH). The database contains more than 600,000 references dealing with various aspects of cancer. It may be accessed by universities, medical schools, hospitals, government agencies, commercial and nonprofit organizations, and private individuals.

cancerous (kan'ser-us) Relating to malignant growths.

cancerphobia (kan-ser-fo'be-ah) An abnormally intense fear of developing malignant growths, out of proportion to actual risks.

cancroid (kang'kroid) Resembling a malignant growth.

cancrum (kang'krum), pl. can'cra A rapidly spreading ulcer, usually in the mucous membrane of the mouth or nose.

candela (kan-del'ah) (cd) The SI unit of luminous intensity equal to the luminous intensity of 5 mm² of platinum at its solidification point (1973.5°C). Also called candle.

Candida (kan'dĭ-dah) A genus of yeastlike fungi.

C. albicans A species that normally inhabits the intestinal tract of humans but may cause disease under certain conditions (e.g., in debilitated individuals). Also called thrush fungus.

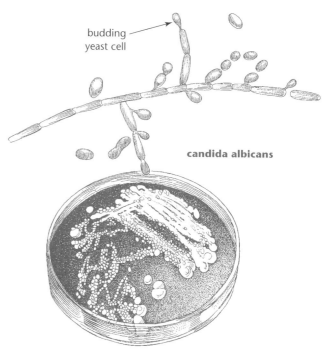

budding yeast cell

candida albicans

candidal (kan'dĭ-dal) Relating to or caused by *Candida*. Also called (incorrectly) monilial.

candidemia (kan-dĭ-de'me-ah) The presence of *Candida* fungus in the blood, usually due to systemic candidiasis.

candidiasis (kan-dĭ-di'ah-sis) Infection with fungi of the genus *Candida*.

candidosis (kan-dī-do′sis) See candidiasis.

candle (kan′dl) See candela.

canine (ka′nīn) **1.** Relating to a dog. **2.** Relating to a cuspid, the third tooth from the midline.

canister (kan′is-ter) See absorber head, under head.

canker (kang′ker) See aphthous stomatitis, under stomatitis.

cannabinoid (kan-ab′ĭ-noid) Any of the substances present in the cannabis plants.

cannabis (kan′ah-bis) A plant of the species *Cannabis sativa* (family Moraceae) from which marijuana and hashish are prepared.

cannabis

flower cluster

cannula (kan′u-lah) A tube for withdrawing fluid from a body cavity; used in conjunction with a metal rod (trocar) fitted into its lumen to puncture the wall of the cavity and then withdrawn, leaving the cannula in place.

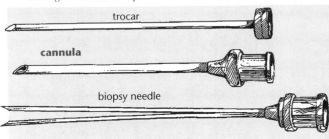

trocar

cannula

biopsy needle

cannulation, cannulization (kan-u-la′shun, kan-u-li-za′shun) Insertion of a cannula into a body cavity.

cantharis (kan′thar-is), pl. canthar′ides The dried beetle *Lytta (Cantharis) vesicatoria*, formerly used as a counterirritant and to promote blister formation. Also called Spanish fly.

canthectomy (kan-thek′to-me) Surgical removal of a corner (canthus) of an eyelid.

canthitis (kan-thi′tis) Inflammation of a canthus or corner of the eyelids.

canthoplasty (kan′tho-plas-te) Surgical procedure for changing the shape of or repairing a canthus or corner of the eyelids.

canthorrhaphy (kan-thor′ah-fe) Partial suturing of the eyelids, usually at the outer corner (canthus), to shorten the palpebral fissure.

canthotomy (kan-thot′o-me) A horizontal cut through the lateral corner (canthus) of the eyelids, made to widen the space between the eyelids.

canthus (kan′thus), pl. can′thi The two angles formed by the junction of the upper and lower eyelids; named medial or nasal and lateral or temporal.

cap (kap) **1.** Any structure that resembles or serves as a cover. **2.** Popular name for an artificial dental crown.

acrosomal c. See acrosome.

bishop's c. See duodenal cap.

cervical c. A thimble-shaped contraceptive device smaller than a diaphragm. See also contraceptive cap.

contraceptive c. Any of three latex devices (cervical, vault, and vimule caps) used to prevent pregnancy; designed to fit snugly over the neck (cervix) of the uterus, where it is held in place by suction; often used by women who cannot use a diaphragm due to anatomic changes (e.g., prolapse of the uterus, cystocele).

cradle c. A matted, crusted scale of the scalp occurring in infants, usually during the first three months of life; a seborrheic dermatitis of the scalp.

duodenal c. The first 4 to 5 cm of the duodenum, the portion of small intestine adjacent to the stomach. Also called bishop's cap; duodenal bulb.

enamel c. In embryology, the caplike structure covering the enamel organ of a developing tooth.

knee c. Kneecap; see patella.

vault c. A bowl-shaped contraceptive device smaller than a diaphragm. See also contraceptive cap.

vimule c. Contraceptive cap, smaller than a diaphragm, that includes features of both cervical and vault caps. See also contraceptive cap.

capacitation (kah-pas-ĭ-ta′shun) The physiologic and chemical events that spermatozoa go through when coming in contact with fluids in the uterus and fallopian (uterine) tubes, which render them capable of penetrating and thereby fertilizing an ovum. The process can also be accomplished *in vitro* in suitable tissue culture medium.

capacity (kah-pas′ĭ-te) **1.** The ability to hold or retain. **2.** A measure of such ability. **3.** A legal qualification, competence, or fitness. **4.** The ability to do something.

cranial c. The amount of space within the skull.

forced vital c. (FVC) The volume of air that is forcefully and rapidly expired from full inspiration. In testing, the patient inhales maximally to full lung capacity, then exhales into an apparatus (spirometer) as forcefully, as rapidly, and as completely as possible.

functional c. The assessed ability of an individual to perform basic work activities.

functional residual c. (FRC) The volume of air remaining in the lungs at the end of exhaling during normal breathing. Formerly called functional residual air.

heat c. The amount of heat required to raise the temperature of a body or substance 1°C.

inspiratory c. (IC) The maximum volume of air that can be inhaled into the lungs after a normal expiration.

iron-binding c. (IBC) The maximum ability of plasma proteins to combine with iron. Total iron-binding capacity (TIBC) is a quantitative measure of the content of transferrin, the iron-binding protein, in serum.

maximum breathing c. (MBC) See maximum voluntary ventilation (MVV), under ventilation.

residual c. See residual volume (RV), under volume.

testamentary c. The state of mental competence established by law as necessary for making a will (i.e., the person is aware of making a will, of the property involved and its approximate monetary value, and to whom the property will pass at death).

total iron-binding c. (TIBC) See iron-binding capacity.

total lung c. (TLC) The volume of air contained in the lungs at full inflation (i.e., following maximum inspiration).

vital c. (VC) The maximum volume of air that can be exhaled from the lungs after a maximal inspiration.

capillariasis (kap-ĭ-lah-ri′ah-sis) Disease caused by intestinal infection with worms of the genus *Capillaria*, especially *Capillaria philippinensis*.

capillariomotor (kap-ĭ-lār-e-o-mo′tor) Relating to dilatation or constriction of minute blood vessels (capillaries).

capillarity (kap-ĭ-lār′ĭ-te) The surface forces that cause liquids to move along fine, hairlike tubes.

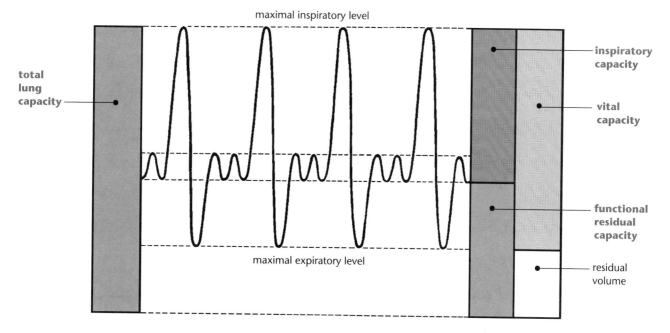

maximal inspiratory level

total lung capacity

inspiratory capacity

vital capacity

functional residual capacity

residual volume

maximal expiratory level

capillary (kap'ĭ-lar-e) The minute blood vessels connecting venules and arterioles; their thin walls, which consist of a single layer of cells, permit passage of oxygen and chemicals in capillary blood into the tissues, and metabolic wastes from tissues into the capillary blood.

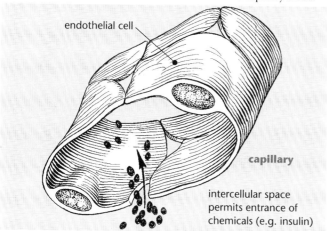

endothelial cell

capillary

intercellular space permits entrance of chemicals (e.g. insulin)

bile c.'s See bile canaliculi, under canaliculus.

capitulum (kah-pit'u-lum) A small rounded eminence or articular end of a bone.

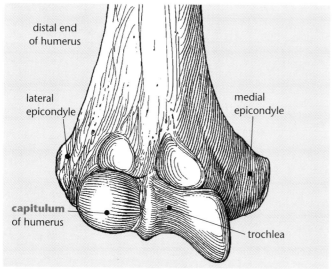

distal end of humerus

lateral epicondyle

medial epicondyle

capitulum of humerus

trochlea

Capnocytophaga (kap-no-si-tof'ah-gah) A genus of gram-negative bacteria; some species cause generalized infection (sepsis) following dog bites, especially in immunocompromised individuals.

capnogram (kap'no-gram) A graphic record of the carbon dioxide content in exhaled air.

capnographer (kap-no'grah-fer) A type of monitor used in anesthetized patients to detect carbon dioxide in exhaled air.

capping (kap'ing) Covering.

    pulp c. The covering of an exposed tooth pulp.

capsid (kap'sid) The shell or protein coat of a virus.

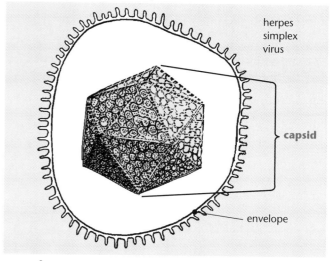

herpes simplex virus

capsid

envelope

capsule (kap'sūl) **1.** A soluble, gelatinous container enclosing a dose of a drug. **2.** A saclike structure enveloping an organ, a part, or a tumor. **3.** In radiotherapy, a small, sealed metallic tube containing a radioactive material (e.g., radium), applied to a body surface or within a cavity. **4.** A mucopolysaccharide substance surrounding certain bacteria; it is secreted by the organisms and remains in intimate contact with them.

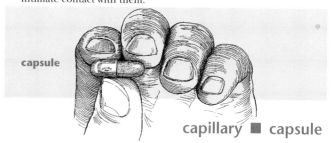

capsule

capillary ■ capsule

articular c. See joint capsule.

bacterial c. A loose gelatinous envelope surrounding a bacterial cell, associated with the virulence of pathogenic bacteria; most consist of simple polysaccharides, some are made of polypeptides.

Bowman's c. See glomerular capsule.

Crosby c. An attachment at the end of a flexible tube, which is introduced into the small intestine through the mouth for obtaining a sample of intestinal lining (mucosa) for biopsy.

Glisson's c. Former name for perivascular fibrous capsule.

glomerular c. A double-walled, spherical, pouchlike structure enveloping a tuft of capillaries (glomerulus) in the kidney; it constitutes the beginning of a renal tubule.

internal c. A broad band of white fibers located in each cerebral hemisphere, between the caudate nucleus and thalamus on the medial side and the lentiform nucleus on the lateral side; generally divided into an anterior limb, a genu, a posterior limb, a retrolentiform part, and a sublentiform part; along with the caudate and lentiform nuclei, it forms the corpus striatum, an important unit of the extrapyramidal system.

joint c. A double-layered sac enclosing the cavity of a synovial joint; it permits movements of the joint. Also called articular capsule.

lens c. The transparent elastic membrane surrounding the lens of the eye.

perivascular fibrous c. A fibrous sheath surrounding the bile duct, hepatic artery, and portal vein and their branches within the liver. Also called Glisson's capsule.

c. of Tenon See fascial sheath of eyeball, under sheath.

capsulitis (kap-su-li′tis) Inflammation of an enveloping sheath of an organ or part.

capsulolenticular (kap-su-lo-len-tik′u-lar) Relating to the lens of the eye and its capsule.

capsuloplasty (kap′su-lo-plas-te) Reparative operation on the fibrous membrane (capsule) enclosing a joint.

capsulorrhaphy (kap-su-lor′ah-fe) Suture of a tear in the enveloping membrane (capsule) of a joint.

capsulotomy (kap-su-lot′o-me) The procedure of cutting into a capsule, as of the lens capsule in a cataract operation.

captopril (kap′to-pril) A member of a group of drugs known as ACE inhibitors (angiotensin-converting enzyme inhibitors); it acts to prevent the formation of angiotensin II and to lower blood pressure.

capture (kap′chur) A catching and holding, as of particles or nerve impulses originating elsewhere.

atrial c. Control of the atria by the retrograde impulse after an interval of independent beating.

ventricular c. See capture beat, under beat.

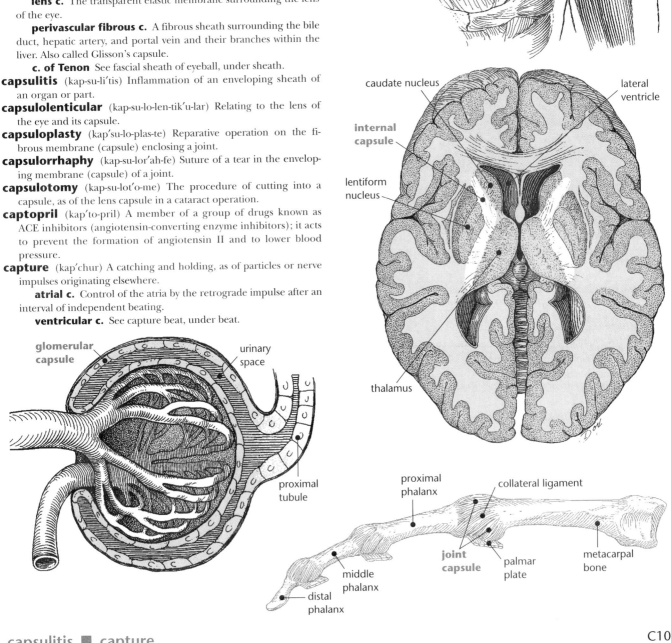

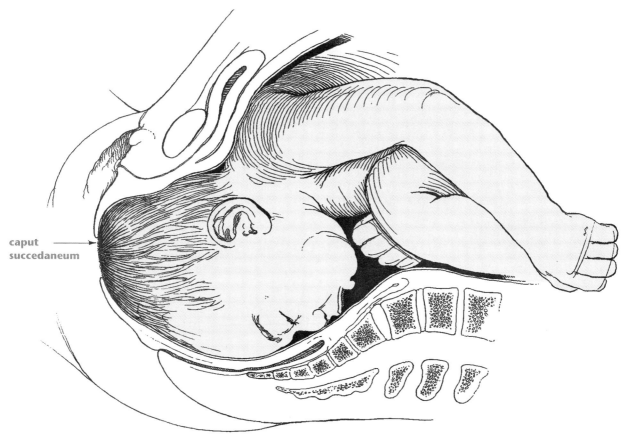

caput
succedaneum

caput (kap'ut), pl. cap'ita **1.** Latin for head. **2.** Any headlike or rounded prominence of an organ or structure.

   c. medusae Medusa head; a venous rosette around the navel formed by tortuous distention of the paraumbilical veins; seen in the Cruveilhier-Baumgarten syndrome.

   c. succedaneum A subcutaneous soft swelling on the presenting area (usually one side) of the head of a newborn infant, due to collection of fluid just beneath the scalp between the membrane covering the skull (periosteum) and the scalp; the swelling occurs as a result of mild trauma as the head presses against the uterine cervix; it is most obvious after prolonged labor and usually disappears within two or three days. Removal of fluid predisposes to infection and is not necessary. COMPARE cephalhematoma.

carbachol (kar'bah-kol) A stimulant of the parasympathetic nervous system; used chiefly as eyedrops to treat glaucoma.

carbamazepine (kar-bah-maz'ĕ-pēn) An anticonvulsant drug.

carbamide (kar'-bă-mīd) Obsolete term. See urea.

carbaminohemoglobin (kar-bam-ĭ-no-he-mo-glo'bin) Carbon dioxide bound to the blood pigment hemoglobin; the normal mode of transport of carbon dioxide in the blood.

carbamoyl (kar'bah-moil) The organic group NH$_2$CO. Also called carbamyl.

carbamyl (kar'bah-mil) See carbamoyl.

carbinol (kar'bĭ-nol) See methanol.

carbohydrate (kar-bo-hi'drāt) Any of a group of organic compounds that are typically composed of carbon, hydrogen, and oxygen (e.g., sugars, starches, cellulose).

carbolic (kar-bol'ik) Relating to phenol.

carbolic acid (kar-bol'ik as-'id) See phenol.

carbon (kar'bon) An organic element; symbol C, atomic number 6, atomic weight 12.011.

   c. dioxide (CO$_2$) A colorless and odorless heavier-than-air gas present in body tissues as a by-product of normal breakdown of such substances as carbohydrates and fats; it is carried by the blood to the lungs, where it is released and exhaled.

   c. monoxide (CO) A colorless, odorless, highly poisonous gas; a normal by-product of incomplete combustion of carbon-containing substances; it is a major air pollutant. Harmful effects commonly occur through long-term exposure to inefficient burning of coal, gas, oil, or propane in home appliances, or to the exhaust

plasma

lung
alveolus

CO$_2$ O$_2$

red blood
cell containing
**carbamino-
hemolglobin**

red blood
cell containing
oxyhemoglobin

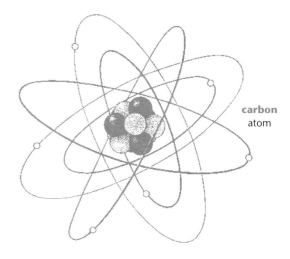

carbon
atom

fumes of gasoline-powered engines. Its toxic action is due to its strong affinity for hemoglobin (the oxygen-carrying molecule of red blood cells), to which it binds, thus preventing oxygen transport to the tissues.

c. tet See carbon tetrachloride.

c. tetrachloride (CCl₄) A clear liquid used as a refrigerant, solvent, in fire extinguishers, and as a grain fumigant; it depresses brain and spinal cord activity and causes damage to liver and kidneys. Popularly called carbon tet.

carbonic (kar-bon'ik) Relating to carbon.

carboxyhemoglobin (kar-bok'se-he-mo-glo'bin) (HbCO) Carbon monoxide bound to the blood pigment hemoglobin; present in the blood in carbon monoxide poisoning. Also called carbon monoxide hemoglobin.

carboxyhemoglobinemia (kar-bok'se-he-mo-glo-bin-e'me-ah) The presence of carboxyhemoglobin in the blood, as in carbon monoxide poisoning.

carboxyl (kar-bok'sil) The monovalent group -COOH present in organic acids.

carbuncle (kar'bung-kl) A large inflammatory mass beginning as a cluster of pimples or boils and spreading deeply and laterally in the skin and subcutaneous tissues, with interconnected clusters of suppuration; usually caused by *Staphylococcus aureus*.

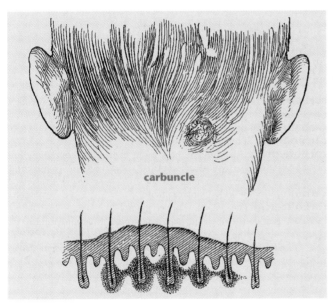

carbuncle

renal c., kidney c. An abscess in the superficial area (cortex) of the kidney substance usually resulting from the union of several small abscesses; occasionally it ruptures into the collecting tubules or to the surrounding area of the kidney.

carbuncular (kar-bung'ku-lar) Relating to a carbuncle.

carcinoembryonic (kar-sin-o-em-bre-on'ik) Relating to substances that are present normally in embryonic tissues and are associated with cancer in the adult, e.g., carcinoembryonic antigen (CEA) and alpha-fetoprotein (AFP).

carcinogen (kar-sin'o-jen) Any cancer-causing agent.

direct-contact c. See proximate carcinogen.

proximate c. An industrial, agricultural, or household chemical that acts locally at the site of contact without having to undergo metabolic changes in the body. Also called direct-contact carcinogen.

ultimate c. Chemicals that are metabolically converted in the body into active cancer-causing agents.

carcinogenesis (kar-si-no-jen'ĕ-sis) Production of cancer.

transplacental c. The passage of cancer-producing substances from the mother to the unborn child through the placental circulation; e.g., the intrauterine exposure to diethylstilbestrol (DES), which causes cancer of the cervix and vagina in the adult offspring.

carcinogenic (kar-si-no-jen'ik) Causing cancer.

carcinogenicity (kar-si-no-gĕ-nis'ĭ-te) The ability to produce or incite cancer.

carcinoid (kar'si-noid) **1.** See carcinoid tumor, under tumor **2.** See carcinoid syndrome, under syndrome.

carcinolytic (kar-si-no-lit'ik) Destructive to cancerous cells.

carcinoma (kar-si-no'mah), pl. carcino'mas, carcino'mata (CA) Any of various malignant tumors derived from epithelial cells (which form the surface layers and lining membranes of organs); characteristically carcinomas invade adjacent tissues, spread to distant sites of the body via the bloodstream (metastasize), and tend to recur and cause death.

alveolar cell c. See bronchiolar carcinoma.

basal cell c. (BCC) A slow-growing carcinoma of the skin that only rarely spreads to distant sites of the body; derived from the basal layer of the epidermis; it may develop anywhere in the body except the palms and soles; most commonly seen in sun-exposed areas, especially the face; typically begins as a small shiny nodule that enlarges and develops a central punched-out ulcer surrounded by a raised border with a pearly appearance. Also called basal cell epithelioma; popularly called rodent ulcer.

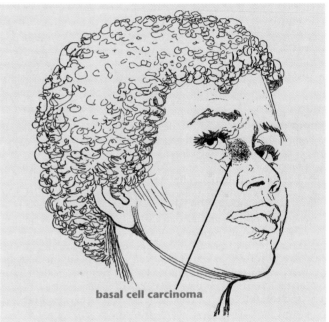

basal cell carcinoma

bronchiolar c. A rare type of carcinoma located primarily in the walls of the air sacs (alveoli) of the lungs; thought to originate in the terminal bronchioles and then spread to the alveoli. Also called terminal bronchiolar carcinoma; alveolar cell carcinoma; bronchioloalveolar carcinoma.

bronchioloalveolar c. See bronchiolar carcinoma.

bronchogenic c. The most common cancer of the lung, originating from the inner lining of major air passages (bronchi); most commonly caused by cigarette smoking; may also be caused by industrial agents, radiation, and urban pollution. Commonly called lung cancer.

clear cell c. of kidney See renal adenocarcinoma, under adenocarcinoma.

colloid c. See mucinous carcinoma.

ductal c. *in situ* (DCIS) A preinvasive cancer developed within one or more milk-transporting ducts of the breast; it does not invade other breast tissues as long as it remains within the duct.

embryonal c. of testis A highly malignant tumor of the testis composed of undifferentiated cells, appearing as a nodule, sometimes associated with bleeding.

epidermoid c. See squamous cell carcinoma.

hepatocellular c. (HCC) See hepatoma.

infiltrating breast c. Cancer of the breast that begins as a small and movable painless mass that enlarges, sometimes rapidly, and in later stages becomes fixed to the chest wall and skin and ulcerates through the skin.

c. in situ Carcinoma that is confined to transformation of cells to abnormal patterns (typical of invasive cancer) within its original location and has not spread into surrounding tissues. Also called intraepithelial carcinoma.

intraductal c. Carcinoma derived from the lining membrane of a duct, especially in the breast, forming masses that obliterate the duct's lumen.

intraepithelial c. See carcinoma *in situ*.

oat cell c. A rapidly spreading carcinoma composed of small, round-to-oval, undifferentiated cells with scant cytoplasm, typically occurring in the lungs and originating in the major air passages (bronchi); it may occur in other parts of the body. Also called small cell carcinoma.

papillary c. A finger-shaped carcinoma.

primary c. Carcinoma at the site of origin.

renal cell c. See renal adenocarcinoma, under adenocarcinoma.

scirrhous c. A hard nodule containing a large amount of fibrous tissue, usually developing in the breast. Also called fibrocarcinoma.

small cell c. See oat cell carcinoma.

squamous cell c. (SCC) Carcinoma derived from the superficial flattened cells of epithelium, appearing as thickened plaques that progress to nodules, ulcer formation, and eventual invasion of surrounding tissues and spread to distant sites (metastasis); may develop from normal tissue that has been made susceptible by long-term exposure to certain agents commonly found in the lungs; seen in the oral cavity (from cigarette and pipe smoking, tobacco chewing); sinuses (from dust in textile and shoe industries); skin (from excessive exposure to sun, petroleum distillates, tar products); may also develop in the uterine cervix. Also called epidermoid carcinoma.

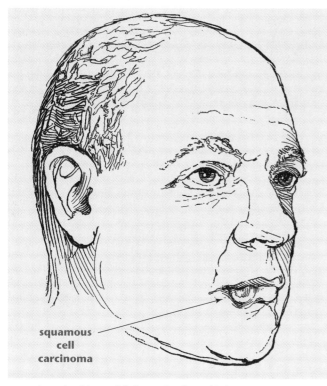

squamous
cell
carcinoma

terminal bronchiolar c. See bronchiolar carcinoma.

transitional cell c. Carcinoma derived from transitional cells of the urinary tract; most frequently occurring in the bladder and is especially associated with cigarette smoking; also seen in workers in the dye, rubber, and insulating cable industries who work with products containing benzidine.

verrucous c. See giant condyloma, under condyloma.

carcinomata (kar-sī-no′mah-tah) Plural of carcinoma.

carcinomatoid (kar-sī-nom′ah-toid) Resembling carcinoma.

carcinomatosis (kar-sī-no-mah-to′sis) The presence in the body of widely disseminated cancer.

carcinomatous (kar-sī-nom′ah-tus) Relating to carcinoma.

cardia (kar′de-ah) The area of the stomach nearest the opening between the stomach and the esophagus.

cardiac (kar′de-ak) 1. Relating to the heart. 2. Relating to the area of the stomach nearest the esophagus.

cardiatelia (kar-de-ah-te′le-ah) Incomplete development of the heart.

cardiectasia (kar-de-ek-ta′ze-ah) Dilatation of the heart.

cardiectomy (kar-de-ek′tŏ me) Surgical removal of the upper part of the stomach, adjacent to the esophagus.

cardiectopia (kar-de-ek-to′pe-ah) Congenital development of the heart in a position other than the normal.

cardio-, cardi- Combining forms meaning the heart; the orifice between the esophagus and the stomach; the area of the stomach adjacent to the esophagus.

cardioaccelerator (kar-de-o-ak-sel′er-a-tor) Anything that hastens the heart's action.

cardioactive (kar-de-o-ak′tiv) Affecting the heart; said especially of drugs.

cardiocele (kar′de-o-sēl) Protrusion of the heart through an abnormal opening (e.g., a wound or a fissure through the diaphragm).

cardiocentesis (kar-de-o-sen-te′sis) Surgical puncture of the heart.

cardiodynamics (kar-de-o-di-nam′iks) The movements and forces involved in the activity of the heart.

cardiodynia (kar-de-o-din′e-ah) Pain in the heart.

cardioesophageal (kar-de-o-ĕ-sof-ah-je′al) Relating to the esophagus and adjacent area of the stomach.

cardiogenesis (kar-de-o-jen′ĕ-sis) The formation of the heart in the embryo.

cardiogenic (kar-de-o-jen′ik) Originating in the heart.

cardiogram (kar′de-o-gram) A graphic record of the movements of the heart obtained with a cardiograph. The term is frequently used instead of electrocardiogram.

cardiograph (kar′de-o-graf) Instrument used in making graphic records of the movements of the heart.

cardiography (kar-de-og′rah-fe) Any technique of graphically recording the action of the heart.

cardioinhibitory (kar-de-o-in-hib′ĭ-to-re) Slowing the action of the heart.

cardiokinetic (kar-de-o-kĭ-net′ik) Influencing the activity of the heart.

cardiolipin (kar-de-o-lip′in) A substance obtained from beef heart muscle that is used as an antigen to test for syphilis.

cardiologist (kar-de-ol′o-jist) A specialist in cardiology.

cardiology (kar-de-ol′o-je) The medical specialty concerned with the diagnosis and treatment of heart disease.

cardiomegaly (kar-de-o-meg′ah-le) Pathologic enlargement of the heart. Also called megalocardia.

cardiomyoliposis (kar-de-o-mi′o-li-po′sis) Fatty degeneration of the heart muscle (myocardium).

cardiomyopathy (kar-de-o-mi-op′ah-the) Primary disease of the muscular wall of the heart, characterized by ventricular enlargement occurring in the absence of congenital, hypertensive, valvular, or ischemic heart disease. Also called myocardiopathy.

alcoholic c. Cardiomyopathy occurring in chronic alcoholics, resulting either from the toxic effect of alcohol or from thiamine deficiency due to malnutrition (frequently occurring in alcoholics); it usually leads to heart failure.

beer drinker's c. Cardiomyopathy occurring in individuals who consume large quantities of beer, caused by the toxic effects of cobalt (added to beer to enhance its foamy quality).

familial hypertrophic c. (FHCM) See hypertrophic cardiomyopathy.

hypertrophic c. (HCM) Inherited disease that is the most common cause of sudden death in the young (especially young athletes participating in strenuous sports); characterized by enlargement of the heart due to hypertrophy of the ventricles, involving the left ventricle more than the right one, resulting in poor diastolic relaxation, inadequate filling, and rapid emptying of the ventricle. The disease is an autosomal dominant inheritance, linked to a mutation of the beta-myosin heavy-chain gene located on chromosome 14; mutations involving the amino acid arginine are predictors of sudden death. Also called familial hypertrophic cardiomyopathy (FHCM). See also sudden death, under death.

idiopathic dilated c. One of a group of diseases of unknown cause that lead to dilatation of the ventricle(s) of the heart; the left ventricle is affected more commonly than the right; cardiac output is low and the prognosis is poor. The most common presenting symptom is shortness of breath.

cardiomyotomy (kar-de-o-mi-ot′ŏ me) See esophagomyotomy.

cardionephric (kar-de-o-nef′rik) See cardiorenal.

cardioneurosis (kar-de-o-nu-ro′sis) See cardiac neurosis, under neurosis.

cardiopathy (kar-de-op′ah-the) Heart disease.

cardiopericardiopexy (kar′de-o-per-ī-kar′de-o-pek-se) An operative procedure for stimulating adhesion formation between the heart and its enveloping sac (pericardium); formerly used to increase collateral blood flow to the heart muscle.

cardiophone (kar′de-o-fōn) A special stethoscope for listening to heart sounds.

cardioplasty (kar′de-o-plas-te) See esophagogastroplasty.

cardioplegia (kar-de-o-ple′je-ah) Temporary interruption of the heart's activity with cold or chemical agents to allow performance of heart surgery.

cardiopulmonary (kar-de-o-pul′mo-ner-e) Relating to the heart and lungs.

cardiorenal (kar′de-o-re′nal) Relating to the heart and kidneys. Also called cardionephric; nephrocardiac.

cardiorrhaphy (kar-de-or′ah-fe) Suturing of the heart wall (e.g., to close a penetrating heart wound).

cardiorrhexis (kar-de-o-rek′sis) Rupture of the heart wall.

cardioselectivity (kar-de-o-sĕ-lek-tiv′e-te) Having a greater effect on heart tissue than on other muscular tissue; a property of certain drugs.

cardiospasm (kar′de-o-spazm) See achalasia.

cardiotomy (kar-de-ot′ŏ me) **1.** A surgical cut into the heart wall. **2.** A surgical cut into the junction of the esophagus and the stomach.

cardiotonic (kar-de-o-ton′ik) Enhancing the action of the heart.

cardiotoxic (kar-de-o-tok′sik) Having a deleterious effect on the function of the heart.

cardiovascular (kar-de-o-vas′ku-lar) Relating to the heart and blood vessels.

cardiovasculorenal (kar-de-o-vas′ku-lo-re′nal) Relating to the heart, arteries, and kidneys.

cardioversion (kar-de-o-ver′shun) See defibrillation.

cardioverter (kar-de-o-ver′ter) See defibrillator.

carditis (kar-di′tis) Inflammation of any part of the heart.

care (kār) General term used in medicine and public health to denote the application of knowledge to the benefit of an individual person or a community.

ambulatory c. See outpatient care.

comprehensive medical c. Medical care that includes prevention of disease and rehabilitation of disabled persons in addition to traditional treatment of acutely and chronically ill patients.

critical c. Health care given to a critically ill patient during a medical emergency or crisis.

custodial c. Personal assistance services, excluding medical care, generally provided on a long-term basis.

inpatient c. Medical treatment given to a patient who has been admitted to a hospital.

intensive c. The constant monitoring and immediate treatment of seriously ill patients by specially trained personnel using advanced technology at a hospital.

long-term c. Health services provided over an extended period of time (e.g., to persons who are chronically ill, disabled, or retarded).

managed c. In general, health care plans containing features to control health care costs. Specifically, a group of health care plans (e.g., Health Maintenance Organization, Point of Service Plan, Preferred Provider Organization) that (a) use specific criteria for selecting network providers, i.e., physicians, hospitals, and other health care providers who agree to cooperate with some form of cost control (utilization management), and offer financial incentives for patients to use the services of these network providers; (b) employ the concept of gatekeepers to channel patients to primary care providers (limiting referrals to specialists), and require preauthorization for hospital care and other services to keep costs down.

medical c. The application of medical knowledge to the identification, treatment, and prevention of illness.

ordinary c. In medical practice, the degree of care that a reasonable practitioner exercises to prevent risk of unreasonable harm to the patient; failure to exercise such care when under duty to do so constitutes negligence. Also called reasonable care.

outpatient c. Treatment provided by a clinic or facility that does not require the patient to stay overnight. Also called ambulatory care.

preconception c. A comprehensive program of health care that aims to identify and reduce a woman's reproductive risks before conception takes place (e.g., genetic counseling and testing, financial and family planning, medical assessment, and nutritional guidance); may include the male partner in providing counseling and educational information in preparation for fatherhood. Distinguished from prenatal care.

prenatal c. Comprehensive care provided the pregnant woman and her unborn child throughout pregnancy to enhance the health and well-being of the woman and fetus, to prevent complications at delivery, and to decrease the incidence of disease and mortality of both; may include tests of both woman and fetus to detect disease, defects, or potential hazards, and guidance regarding diet and exercise.

primary medical c. Care given by the first member of the health professions approached by the patient. In general use, the term refers to care provided by a family physician, internal medicine specialist, or pediatrician, who may refer out for special care needs.

reasonable c. See ordinary care.

secondary medical c. Care given by a medical specialist at the request of the professional who administered primary care.

standard of c. See under standard.

tertiary medical c. Consultative care given by a specialist at a medical center (e.g., in specialized surgical procedures, intensive care support).

uncompensated c. The charges for services rendered by providers for which the recipient cannot or is unwilling to pay and for which there is usually charity care or bad debt.

caregiver (kār′giv-er) Any person involved in the prevention, identification, and treatment of illness and in the rehabilitation of the patient, including community and social workers, family members, friends, members of the clergy, etc.

caries (kar′ēz) The localized, gradual destruction of teeth by inorganic acids and bacteria; if untreated, it often extends to the pulp.

carina (kah-ri′nah), pl. cari′nae In anatomy, any ridgelike projection.

carinate (kar′ĭ-nāt) Having a keel-shaped ridge or process.

cario- Combining form meaning caries.

cariogenesis (kār-e-o-jen′ĕ-sis) The process of caries formation.

cariogenic (kār-e-o-jen′ik) Causing caries.

cariostatic (kār-e-os-tat′ik) Arresting the progression of caries.

carious (ka′re-us) Relating to caries.

carisoprodol (kar-i-so-pro′dol) A muscle-relaxant drug used to treat muscle spasm.

carneous (kar′ne-us) Fleshy.

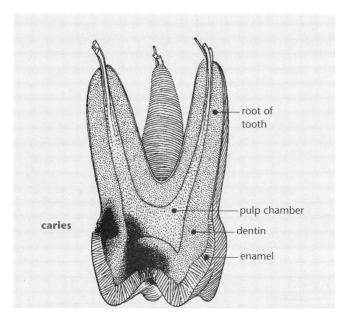

caries

root of tooth

pulp chamber

dentin

enamel

carnosine (kar′no-sēn) A dipeptide found in skeletal muscle. Its function is not known.

carotene (kar′o-tēn) General term for a group of fat-soluble pigments present in green, yellow, and leafy vegetables and yellow fruits; they are provitamins, converted to vitamin A in the intestines. Also spelled carotin.

carotenemia (kar-o-te-ne′me-ah) Increased concentration of carotene in the blood, frequently causing a yellow pigmentation of the skin; it often results from excessive consumption of carrots. Also spelled carotinemia; also called xanthemia.

carotid (kah-rot′id) Relating to the principal blood vessels of the neck; often used alone to denote either of the carotid arteries (in the neck). See also table of arteries.

carotidynia (kah-rot-ĭ-din′e-ah) See carotodynia.

carotin (kar′o-tin) See carotene.

carotinemia (kar-o-tin-e′me-ah) See carotenemia.

carotodynia (kah-rot-o-din′e-ah) Pain along the carotid artery, usually caused by pressure. Also called carotidynia.

carpal (kar′pal) Relating to the wrist bones (carpus).

carpometacarpal (kar-po-met-ah-kar′pal) Relating to the bones of the wrist and the hand.

carpopedal (kar-po-pe′dal) Relating to the wrist and the foot.

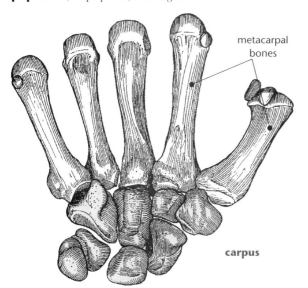

metacarpal bones

carpus

carpus (kar′pus) The wrist; the eight bones of the wrist and associated structures. See also carpal bones, in table of bones.

carrier (kar′e-er) **1.** An individual who shows no signs of a disease but harbors infective microorganisms that cause disease in those to whom they are transmitted. **2.** In genetics, an individual who carries an abnormal gene in a recessive state; that is, the person does not show signs of carrying the abnormality but can transmit it to an off-spring who, when inheriting the same gene from the other parent, may develop the disease or abnormality of the gene. The abnormal gene may be detected by appropriate laboratory tests. **3.** A substance in a cell that is capable of accepting an atom or a subatomic particle, thus facilitating transport of organic solutes. **4.** In immunology, a molecule, or part of a molecule, capable of inducing an immune response that is recognized by T cells in an antibody response.

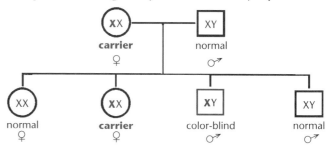

A possible expression of the X-linked recessive trait for color blindness

cartilage (kar′tĭ-lij) A firm, slightly elastic connective tissue present throughout the body; e.g., in articular surfaces of bones, in the ear, eustachian (auditory) tube, nose, larynx, air passages (trachea and bronchi); it consists of specialized cells (chondrocytes) embedded in a ground substance (matrix), which is permeated by collagenous fibers; it has no nerve or blood supply of its own. Cartilage constitutes the major portion of the fetal skeleton.

   accessory c.'s of nose See lesser alar cartilages.

   articular c. A type of hyaline cartilage covering the articulating surfaces of synovial joints.

   arytenoid c. One of two triangular cartilages in the posterior larynx, between the cricoid and corniculate cartilages.

   c. of auditory tube A cartilaginous tube about 24 mm in length (in the average adult), constituting the inner two-thirds of the auditory (eustachian) tube, which connects the middle ear chamber with the nasal part of the pharynx; it is shaped like an inverted gutter and consists of a broad medial lamina and a narrow lateral lamina. Also called cartilage of pharyngotympanic tube; cartilage of eustachian tube.

   auricular c. A single plate of elastic fibrocartilage forming the framework of the ear (auricle), except for the lobe; it is continuous with the cartilage of external auditory canal.

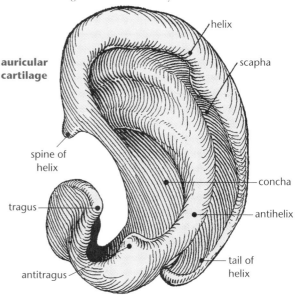

auricular cartilage

helix

scapha

spine of helix

concha

antihelix

tragus

tail of helix

antitragus

bronchial c.'s Incomplete rings of hyaline cartilage in the walls of the main air passages of the lungs (bronchi); they become irregular plates as the bronchi approach the lungs; in the intrapulmonary bronchi, the plates diminish in size and number, forming less and less of the bronchial wall, until they disappear at the beginning of the bronchioles.

corniculate c. One of two small, conical elastic cartilages in the posterior larynx, immediately above the apex of each arytenoid cartilage.

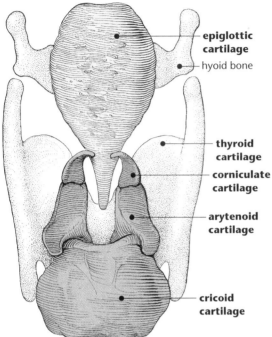

costal c. One of 24 bars of hyaline cartilage at the anterior end of each rib, serving to extend the ribs anteriorly and contributing to the elasticity of the chest wall.

cricoid c. The ring-shaped and lowermost of the cartilages of the larynx.

cuneiform c. One of two small rod-shaped laryngeal cartilages on either side of the aryepiglottic fold.

elastic c. Cartilage composed of matrix permeated with elastic fibers, as in the cartilage of ear (auricle), the eustachian (auditory) tube, and the epiglottis. Also called yellow elastic cartilage; yellow fibrocartilage.

epiglottic c. A thin, leaflike lamina of elastic cartilage located behind the root of the tongue and in front of the entrance to the larynx; its function is to fold back and close the entrance of the larynx, thereby preventing food or fluid from passing into the larynx or trachea during the process of swallowing.

epiphyseal c. The layer of cartilage between the shaft and the epiphysis of a long bone; present during bone development, after which it ossifies as growth in length ceases. Also called growth cartilage; epiphyseal plate; growth plate.

c. of eustachian tube See cartilage of auditory tube.

c. of external auditory canal The fibrocartilage of the lateral third of the external auditory canal, about 8 mm long and continuous with the auricular cartilage.

fibrous c. See fibrocartilage.

greater alar c.'s Two thin cartilaginous plates curling around and supporting the nostrils; they possess a septal process and an outer part. Also called lower nasal cartilages.

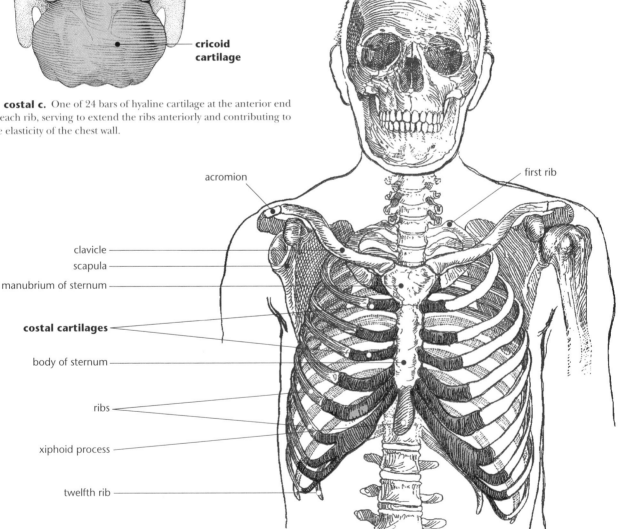

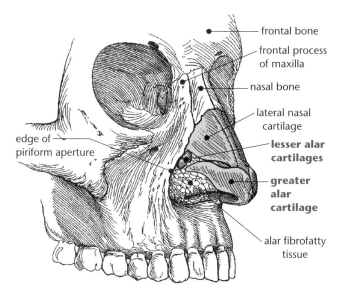

frontal bone
frontal process of maxilla
nasal bone
lateral nasal cartilage
lesser alar cartilages
greater alar cartilage
edge of piriform aperture
alar fibrofatty tissue

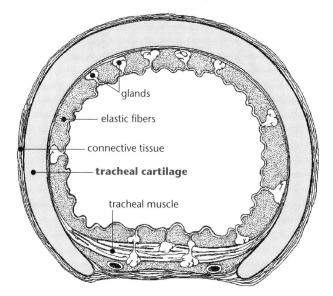

glands
elastic fibers
connective tissue
tracheal cartilage
tracheal muscle

growth c. See epiphyseal cartilage.

hyaline c. A semielastic, bluish white, transparent cartilage with a homogeneous glassy appearance; it is usually covered with a membrane (perichondrium) except when coating the articular ends of bones.

intervertebral c.'s See intervertebral disks, under disk.

c. of the larynx The major constituent of the framework of the larynx, consisting of the single thyroid, cricoid, and epiglottis, and the paired arytenoid, corniculate, and cuneiform cartilages.

lesser alar c.'s Two to four small cartilaginous plates in the fibrous membrane that join the back of the greater alar cartilage to the frontal process of the maxilla. Also called accessory cartilages of nose.

loose c. A cartilage that has been damaged and torn; a common athletic injury, usually involving the semilunar cartilages of knee (menisci).

lower nasal c.'s See greater alar cartilages.

c. of nasal septum A flat, quadrilateral plate of cartilage at the lower anterior part of the nasal septum; it completes the separation of the nasal cavities.

c. of pharyngotympanic tube See cartilage of auditory tube.

semilunar c.'s of knee See lateral meniscus and medial meniscus, under meniscus.

thyroid c. The largest of the cartilages of the larynx, consisting of two flat laminae or plates that fuse anteriorly, forming the Adam's apple (laryngeal prominence).

tracheal c.'s The 16 to 20 hyaline cartilages extending the length of the trachea; they are horseshoe-shaped and form approximately two-thirds of the anterior circumference of the trachea; behind, a fibrous membrane joins the free ends of each cartilage, forming a ring. Also called tracheal rings.

xiphoid c. See xiphoid process, under process.

yellow elastic c. See elastic cartilage.

cartilaginous (kar-tĭ-laj′ĭ-nus) Relating to cartilage.

caruncle (kar′ung-kl) A small, soft nodule.

lacrimal c. A reddish mass at the medial junction of the eyelids.

urethral c. A small protrusion just within the opening of the female urethra, usually representing varicosities of the veins within the lining tissue (mucosa).

cascade (kas-kād′) A series of sequential events (e.g., a physiologic process) that, once initiated, continues to the final state, with each event being activated by the preceding one.

cascara sagrada (kas′kar-ah sag-ra′dah) The dried bark of the buckhorn tree *Rhamnus purshiana;* used as a laxative. Often simply called cascara.

case (kās) **1.** An instance of disease. **2.** A person having such disease; a patient. Although in common usage, this connotation is regarded by some as objectionable.

index c. See proband.

caseation (ka-se-a′shun) Degeneration and change of tissue into a substance resembling cheese, as seen in the lungs of patients with tuberculosis.

casein (ka′sēn) The most nutritive protein of milk.

caseinogen (ka-se-in′o-jen) A substance present in milk that is converted into casein by the enzyme renin.

caseous (ka′se-us) Cheeselike; relating to caseation.

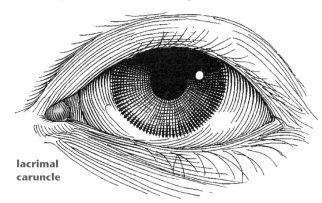

lacrimal caruncle

cast (kast) **1.** A rigid dressing usually made by impregnating a gauze bandage with wet plaster of Paris, used to immobilize a body part. **2.** A cylindrical hardened material formed within tubular structures of the body as a product of certain disease processes; it is molded in the shape of the structure in which discharges accumulated.

blood c. Cast composed of blood elements, usually occurring in kidney tubules or in the smallest air passages in the lungs (bronchioles) as a result of bleeding into these structures; a characteristic finding of glomerulonephritis. Also called red blood cast.

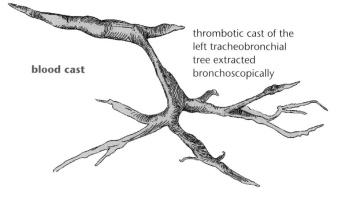

blood cast

thrombotic cast of the left tracheobronchial tree extracted bronchoscopically

epithelial c. Cast containing cells from the inner lining (epithelium) of the tubular structure in which it was formed.

false c. See cylindroid.

fatty c. Urinary cast containing fat globules with cholesterol esters.

granular c. Urinary cast containing particles of cellular debris from the kidney tubules.

hanging c. A plaster cast applied to the arm for immobilizing a fractured bone while applying traction force via the weight of the cast; commonly used in fractures of the lower portion of the humerus.

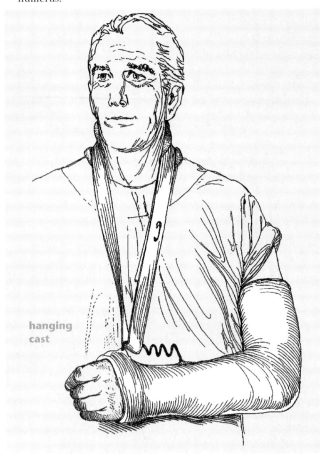

hanging cast

hyaline c. A clear urinary cast composed chiefly of protein.

mucous c. See cylindroid.

red blood cell c. See blood cast.

renal c. See urinary cast.

urinary c. Any cast formed in the kidney and discharged in the urine; most are usually indicative of kidney disease but occasionally some occur in healthy people. Also called renal cast.

waxy c. A light yellow urinary cast associated with oliguria or anuria.

white blood cell c. A urinary cast composed of white blood cells; found in interstitial nephritis.

castrate (kas′trāt) To remove the ovaries or testes by surgical means.

castration (kas-tra′shun) The removal of the testes (orchiectomy) or ovaries (oophorectomy), usually performed when these organs are diseased or in the treatment of cancer of the prostate or breast.

functional c. Destruction of the hormonal function of the gonads by prolonged use of sex hormones.

catabolic (kat-ah-bol′ik) Relating to catabolism.

catabolism (kah-tab′o-lizm) The biological process through which the body breaks down complex chemical molecules into simpler ones; the opposite of anabolism.

catabolite (kah-tab′o-līt) One of the products of catabolism.

catacrotism (kah-tak′ro-tizm) An anomalous pulse with one or more secondary expansions of the artery after the main heartbeat;

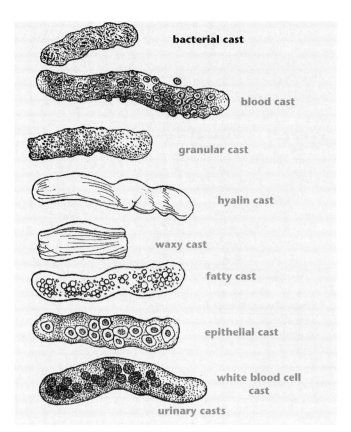

bacterial cast
blood cast
granular cast
hyalin cast
waxy cast
fatty cast
epithelial cast
white blood cell cast

urinary casts

represented in a pulse tracing by one or more small notches on the downstroke of the wave.

catalepsy (kat′ah-lep-se) The assumption of rigid posturing, especially of the limbs, for prolonged periods; the person appears to be in a trancelike state, unresponsive to any stimuli.

catalyst (kat′ah-list) A substance that influences the rate of a chemical reaction without being changed in the process.

negative c. A catalyst that retards a reaction.

organic c. See enzyme.

positive c. A catalyst that accelerates a reaction.

catalyze (kat′ah-līz) To act as a catalyst.

catamenia (kat-ah-me′ne-ah) The menses.

catamnesis (kat-am-ne′sis) Seldom-used term denoting the "follow-up" medical history of a patient after an illness or discharge from the hospital.

cataphasia (kat-ah-fa′ze-ah) Involuntary repetition of the same word.

cataplexy (kat′ah-plek-se) Brief episodes of muscular paralysis, causing the person to collapse without loss of consciousness; usually associated with narcolepsy and other sleep disorders; often precipitated by emotional events.

Catapres-TTS (kat′ah-pres) Trade name for the transdermal clonidine patch; see under patch.

cataract (kat′ah-rakt) A cloudy or opaque area in the normally transparent lens of the eye, or its capsule, that obstructs passage of light rays and diminishes vision.

cerulean c. A nonprogressive collection of light blue spots distributed throughout the lens, apparently congenital and of little or no significance.

concussion c. Traumatic cataract resulting from a blow to the eye, with or without rupture of the capsule that envelops the lens.

congenital c. Cataract present at birth due to faulty development of the fetus; may be caused by a maternal infection (especially rubella) during early pregnancy, or it may be associated with chromosomal abnormalities (e.g., Down's syndrome).

cortical c. Cataract beginning as wedges around the periphery of the lens, directed toward the center. Also called peripheral cataract; cuneiform cataract.

cuneiform c. See cortical cataract.

glassblower's c., glassworker's c. See infrared cataract.

hard c. See nuclear cataract.

immature c. An early stage of cataract development.

infrared c. A traumatic cataract caused by exposure to wavelengths greater than 750 mm in the infrared spectrum; once common among workers who were required to watch masses of molten glass without eye protection.

juvenile c., early-onset c. Cataract occurring in a child or young adult; may result from a variety of conditions (e.g., from congenital syphilis, congenital rubella, galactosemia).

mature c. A cataract that is completely opaque. It may cause the lens to swell and eventually disintegrate.

membranous c. A flattened, densely opaque cataract usually formed after perforating injuries through the lens capsule.

morgagnian c. A mature cataract that has progressed to liquefaction of the lens, which is retained within the capsule as a milky fluid; the freely movable lens nucleus sinks to the bottom.

nuclear c. A form of senile cataract involving the lens center or nucleus. Also called hard cataract.

peripheral c. See cortical cataract.

posterior subcapsular c. A type of senile cataract involving the interior aspect of the lens periphery.

radiation c. Cataract caused by intense or prolonged exposure to any form of radiation (x rays, gamma rays, ultraviolet rays, heat rays, microwaves, laser), which may occur in the workplace.

secondary c. *(a)* Cataract associated with a systemic disease (diabetes, hyperthyroidism, myotonic dystrophy). *(b)* Cataract related to a local eye disease (intraocular tumor, uveitis). *(c)* Cataract occurring postoperatively in the retained (posterior) portion of the lens capsule after an extracapsular cataract extraction. Also called aftercataract.

senescent c. See senile cataract.

senile c. An age-related cataract of slow progression. It may occur in the periphery of the lens (cortical), its center (nuclear), or its posterior surface (posterior subcapsular). Also called senescent cataract.

stationary c. A cataract that does not progress.

toxic c. Cataract caused by exposure to or ingestion of chemical agents (steroids, ergot, chlorpromazine).

traumatic c. Cataract caused by injury to the lens, most commonly by a direct perforating wound (e.g., with BB shots, rocks), less commonly by a blow to the eyeball, overexposure to heat, x rays, and radioactive material.

cataractous (kat-ah-rak′tus) Relating to cataracts.

catarrh (kah-tahr′) Inflammation of mucous membranes of the upper respiratory tract accompanied by a discharge.

catarrhal (kah-tahr′al) Relating to catarrh.

catatonia (kat-ah-to′ne-ah) Marked motor anomalies, usually seen in schizophrenia, that may be either a *withdrawn type*, characterized by general inhibition, negativism, mutism, stupor, and waxy flexibility; or an *excited type*, characterized by excitement and excessive (sometimes violent) motor activity.

catching (kach′ing) Popular term for contagious.

catecholamine (kat-ĕ-kol′ah-mēn) Any of a group of amine compounds, some of which (e.g., epinephrine, norepinephrine, dopamine) are important neurotransmitters and have an important influence on many metabolic processes.

catgut (kat′gut) A suture material obtained from connective tissue of healthy animals and sterilized; frequently impregnated with chromium trioxide to increase its strength. Also called catgut suture; surgical gut.

catharsis (kah-thar′sis) **1.** The promotion of vigorous bowel evacuation. Also called purgation. **2.** Therapeutic release of emotional tension by recalling and talking about past events.

cathartic (kah-thar′tik) An orally administered agent that promotes intense motor activity of the intestines and a fluid evacuation of intestinal contents. A reduced dose may produce only a laxative effect. COMPARE laxative.

cathepsin (kah-thep′sin) An enzyme, widely distributed in animal tissues, that promotes the breakdown of proteins.

catheter (kath′ĕ-ter) A thin tube, usually flexible, that is inserted into a body cavity (e.g., bladder) to drain fluids or to introduce diagnostic or therapeutic agents.

acorn-tipped c. A catheter with a cone-shaped tip used to occlude the distal opening of the ureter during x-ray examination of the ureter and kidney pelvis. Also called cone-tipped catheter.

balloon-tip c. A catheter with a balloon at its tip that can be inflated and deflated after insertion, usually into a blood vessel; used in diagnostic procedures and in angioplasty.

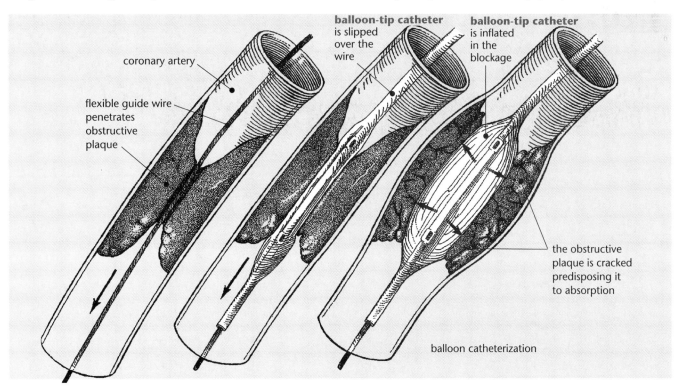

coronary artery

flexible guide wire penetrates obstructive plaque

balloon-tip catheter is slipped over the wire

balloon-tip catheter is inflated in the blockage

the obstructive plaque is cracked predisposing it to absorption

balloon catheterization

cone-tipped c. See acorn-tipped catheter.

Coude c. See elbowed catheter.

double-channel c. A catheter with two lumens, which permit irrigation and aspiration. Also called two-way catheter.

elbowed c. A catheter with a curved tip, which allows great mobility of the tip by simply twisting the catheter. Also called Coude catheter.

Fogarty c. A catheter equipped with a balloon near its tip for removing blood clots from large veins or stones from bile ducts.

Foley c. A catheter held in place by an inflated balloon.

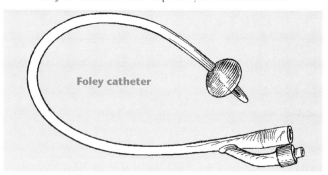

Foley catheter

indwelling c. Catheter designed to be left within a body cavity or passage for an extended period of time.

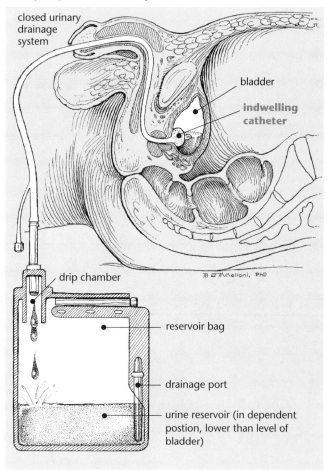

closed urinary drainage system

bladder

indwelling catheter

drip chamber

reservoir bag

drainage port

urine reservoir (in dependent postion, lower than level of bladder)

B. J. Melloni, PhD

pacing c. A catheter equipped with electrodes at the tip; when positioned in the right atrium or ventricle and connected to a pulse generator, it functions as a heart pacer.

Swan-Ganz c. A multilumen, flow-directed catheter, used with or without a balloon at its tip, for diagnosis and for hemodynamic and therapeutic monitoring (e.g., cardiopulmonary procedures) to measure pulmonary arterial pressure.

two-way c. See double-channel catheter.

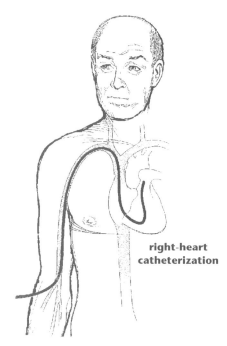

right-heart catheterization

catheterization (kath'ĕ-ter-ĭ-za'shun) Introduction of a catheter into a body cavity to obtain data for diagnosis or for therapeutic purposes (e.g., to maintain patency).

cardiac c. The passage of a long flexible catheter into the heart via a blood vessel, usually performed to obtain diagnostic information and to assess the extent of a congenital heart disease or defects of the heart valves.

left-heart c. Introduction of a radiopaque catheter into a brachial or femoral artery and passage in a retrograde direction through the artery to the aorta and, frequently, across the aortic valve into the left ventricle.

right-heart c. Introduction of a radiopaque catheter into a vein, usually the basilic vein, through the venous system into the right atrium and eventually the right ventricle and pulmonary artery.

urinary c. Insertion of a catheter into the bladder to drain urine.

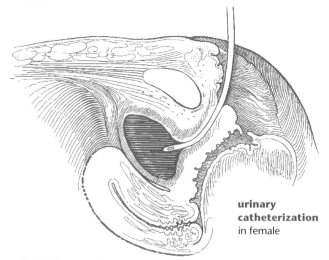

urinary catheterization in female

catheterize (kath'ĕ-ter-īz) To introduce a catheter into a body cavity.

cathexis (kah-thek'sis) Attachment, conscious or unconscious, of emotional energy and significance to an object, an idea, or a person.

CATLINE (catalog on line) A computerized system of on-line references to books and serials catalogued at the National Library of Medicine, available at medical libraries in the MEDLARS network for immediate access to authoritative cataloguing information; also used as a source of information for ordering books and journals and to provide reference and interlibrary loan services. See also MEDLARS.

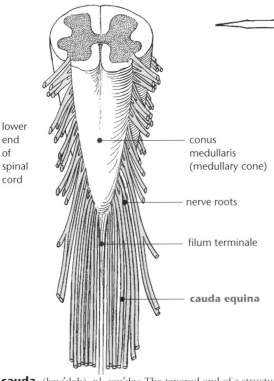

lower end of spinal cord — conus medullaris (medullary cone)

— nerve roots

— filum terminale

— **cauda equina**

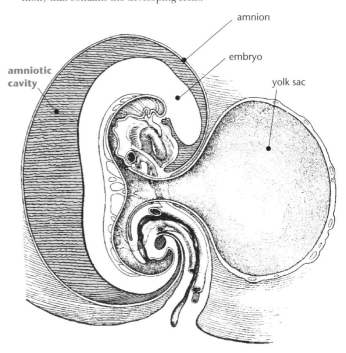

cautery

cauda (kaw′dah), pl. cau′dae The tapered end of a structure.

   c. equina A group of nerves from the lumbar, sacral, and coccygeal segments of the spinal cord; it extends beyond the end of the spinal cord and occupies the lower third of the vertebral canal.

caudad (kaw′dad) Directed toward the tail.

caudal (kaw′dal) Relating to the tail or the part of the body opposite the head.

caudate (kaw′dāt) Having a tail or a taillike appearance.

caul (kawl) A portion of the fetal membrane (amnion) that sometimes envelops the child's head at birth. Popularly called veil.

causalgia (kaw-zal′je-ah) A painful condition of an arm or a leg usually caused by injury to a nerve by a gunshot wound, a fracture, or a deep cut; characterized by severe burning pain, with glossy skin, redness, and sweating of the area overlying the injured nerve. Symptoms may not appear until several weeks after the injury and may be aggravated by the slightest jarring or any normal exposure such as touch or a cold breeze.

cause (kawz) Something that produces an effect or change.

   constitutional c. An inherent cause acting through systemic processes.

   exciting c. The direct provocation of a particular result or condition.

   immediate c. In a succession of multiple causes, the final cause producing the ultimate result (e.g., the immediate cause of death is the final concluding event that actually produces death).

   legal c. See proximate cause.

   proximate c. A cause that directly, without any other intervening cause, produces an effect and without which the effect would not have occurred. Also called legal cause.

   specific c. A cause that produces one condition.

   underlying c. of death. An internationally recognized equivalent of proximate cause of death.

caustic (kaws′tik) 1. Having a corrosive or burning action on body tissues. 2. An agent having such property.

cauterization (kaw-ter-ī-za′shun) Destruction or searing of body tissues with heat, electricity, or a caustic chemical to stop bleeding or to promote healing.

cauterize (kaw′ter-īz) To apply a cautery.

cautery (kaw′ter-e) An agent used to destroy body tissues by scarring or burning.

caval (ka′val) Relating to the vena cava, the largest vein in the body.

caveola (ka-ve-o′lah), pl. caveo′lae Minute indentations or pits on the cell membrane; they usually pinch off and form free vesicles within the cell in the process of cell ingestion.

cavern (kav′ern) A cavity, especially one formed in a diseased organ (e.g., a tuberculous lung).

cavernitis (kav-er-ni′tis) Inflammation of one or both columns of erectile tissue (corpus cavernosum) in the penis.

   fibrous c. See Peyronie's disease, under disease.

cavernous (kav′er-nus) 1. Containing cavities or having the characteristics of a cavity. 2. Resulting from the presence of cavities.

cavitary (kav′ĭ-tar-e) Relating to a cavity.

cavitation (kav-ĭ-ta′shun) Formation of a cavity or cavities.

cavity (kav′ĭ-te) 1. A hollow space within the body, often designating a potential space between layers of tissue or membranes. 2. Popular term for loss of tooth structure (caries).

   abdominal c. The body cavity between the diaphragm above and the pelvis below.

   amniotic c. The fluid-filled space inside the membrane (amnion) that contains the developing fetus.

amnion

embryo

amniotic cavity

yolk sac

   axillary c. The armpit.

   buccal c. The space between the lips and teeth.

   cranial c. The space within the skull.

   glenoid c. See glenoid fossa, under fossa.

   greater peritoneal c. See greater sac of peritoneum, under sac.

   lesser peritoneal c. See lesser sac of peritoneum, under sac.

   medullary c. The narrow, elongated cavity within a long bone.

   middle ear c. See tympanic cavity.

   nasal c. The space extending from the nostrils to the base of the cranium above and the roof of the mouth below; divided in two by a thin plate of bone and cartilage (nasal septum). It communicates with the pharynx and paranasal sinuses.

   oral c. The cavity of the mouth.

   pelvic c. The short, wide, curved space within the bony framework of the minor pelvis, between the pelvic brim and the pelvic floor (pelvic diaphragm); it contains the pelvic colon, rectum, bladder, and some of the organs of reproduction.

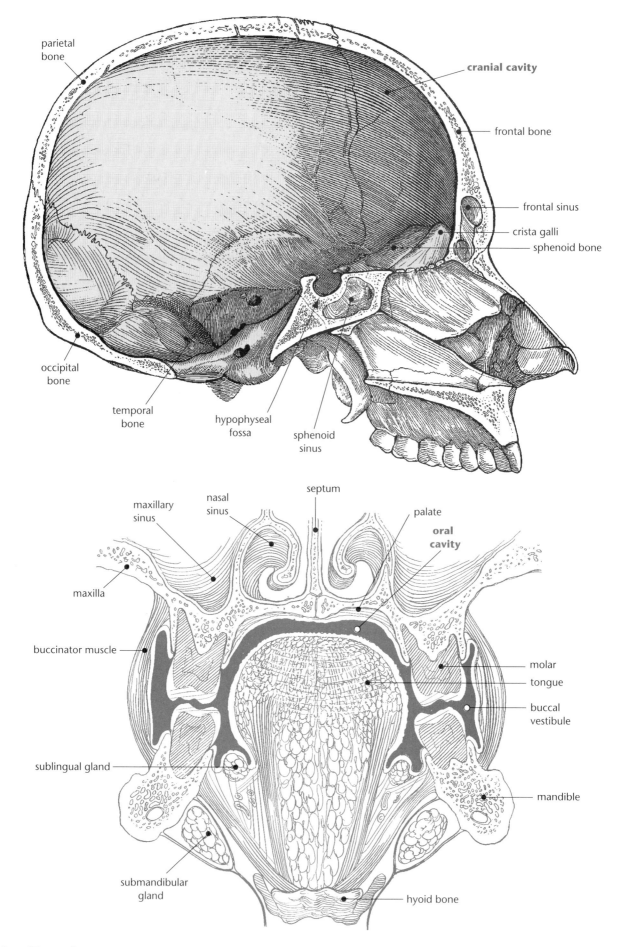

parietal
bone

cranial cavity

frontal bone

frontal sinus

crista galli

sphenoid bone

occipital
bone

temporal
bone

hypophyseal
fossa

sphenoid
sinus

maxillary
sinus

nasal
sinus

septum

palate

oral
cavity

maxilla

molar

buccinator muscle

tongue

buccal
vestibule

sublingual gland

mandible

submandibular
gland

hyoid bone

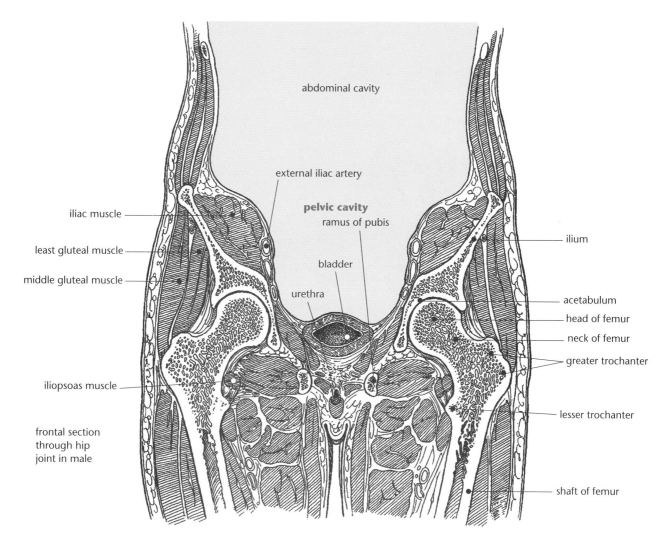

abdominal cavity

external iliac artery

pelvic cavity

ramus of pubis

iliac muscle

least gluteal muscle

middle gluteal muscle

bladder

urethra

ilium

acetabulum

head of femur

neck of femur

greater trochanter

iliopsoas muscle

lesser trochanter

frontal section
through hip
joint in male

shaft of femur

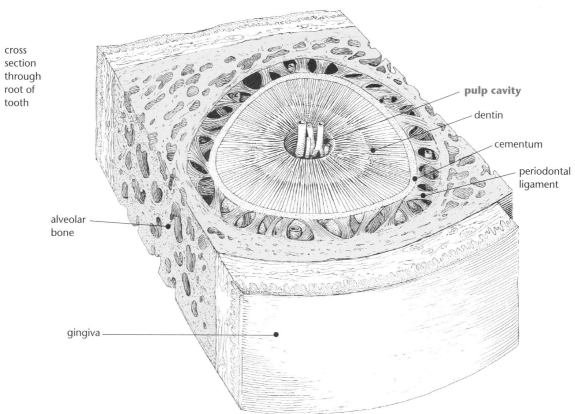

cross
section
through
root of
tooth

pulp cavity

dentin

cementum

periodontal
ligament

alveolar
bone

gingiva

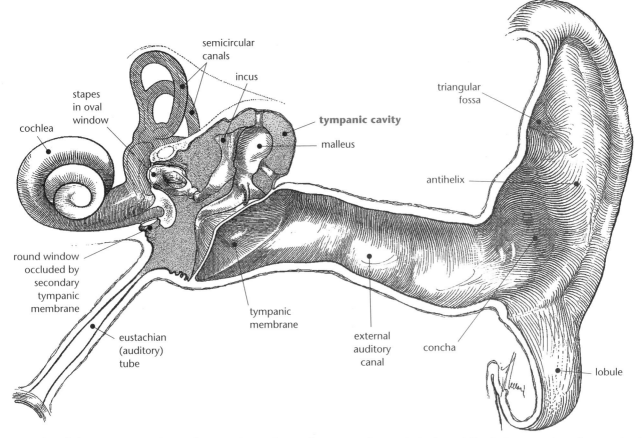

pericardial c. The potential space between the two layers of membrane (pericardium) that enclose the heart.

pleural c. The potential space between the two layers of membrane (pleura) that enclose each lung.

prepared c. In dentistry, a dental excavation made by removal of caries and other procedures for enhancing retention of a restoration.

pulp c. The central space within a tooth, including the space within its crown (crown cavity) and its root (root canal); it contains pulp, blood and lymphatic vessels, and nerves.

thoracic c. The space between the neck and the respiratory diaphragm.

tympanic c. A small irregular space of the middle ear in the temporal bone of the skull; it communicates anteriorly with the nasopharynx through the eustachian (auditory) tube and posteriorly with air cells of the mastoid bone of the skull. It contains a chain of tiny articulated bones (ossicles) for transmission of sound vibrations across the cavity. Also called middle ear cavity; middle ear chamber. See also middle ear, under ear.

visceral c. One of the three major cavities of the body: cranial, thoracic, and abdominal.

cavogram (ka′vo-gram) An x-ray image of the vena cava made possible by injecting a radiopaque substance into the vessel.

cavosurface (ka-vo-sur′fis) **1.** The surface of a prepared cavity of a tooth. **2.** Relating to a prepared cavity and the tooth surface.

cavum (ka′vum), pl. ca′va Latin for cavity or hollow.

cavus (kāv′us) See talipes cavus, under talipes.

CCRIS Acronym for Chemical Carcinogenesis Research Information System. An on-line database on the MEDLARS system of the National Library of Medicine; sponsored by the National Cancer Institute of the National Institutes of Health (NIH). The database contains evaluated data and information derived from both short- and long-term bioassays on more than 1200 chemical substances. Studies include cancer- and mutant-causing substances, as well as cancer inhibitors.

cecal (se′kal) **1.** Relating to the widest, saclike portion of the large intestine (cecum) to which the appendix is attached. **2.** Ending in a saclike structure.

cecostomy (se-kos′to-me) Surgical construction of an opening into the cecum through the abdominal wall, either with a tube or by suturing the cecum directly to the surrounding peritoneum; performed in cases of colonic obstruction.

cecotomy (se-kot′o-me) A surgical cut into the cecum.

cecum (se′kum) The widest, saclike portion of the large intestine to which the vermiform appendix is attached.

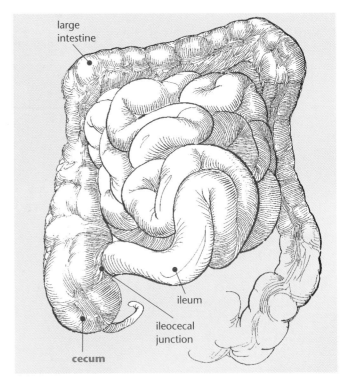

cefaclor (sef'ah-klor) A semisynthetic, broad-spectrum antibiotic used orally.

cefotaxime (sef-o-tak'sem) A broad-spectrum semisynthetic antibiotic; a third-generation derivative of cephalosporin; it has been used to treat pneumococcal meningitis.

cefoxitin (sĕ-foks'ĭ-tin) A semisynthetic antibiotic effective against aerobic and anaerobic infections; used also to prevent infection in abdominal surgery.

ceftizoxime (sef-tī-zoks'em) A semisynthetic antibiotic; a third-generation derivative of cephalosporin used against gram-negative infections including meningitis; considered safe for use in aged patients and those with blood disorders.

ceftriaxone (sef-tri'ah-zōn) A semisynthetic antibiotic; a third-generation derivative of cephalosporin; it has high penetrability to usually inaccessible infections, including those of the brain membranes (meninges), inner ear, eyes, and urinary tract.

celiac (se'le-ak) Relating to the abdominal cavity.

celioenterotomy (se-le-o-en-ter-ot'o-me) Cutting into the intestine through an incision on the abdominal wall.

celiohysterectomy (se'le-o-his-ter-ek'to-me) See abdominal hysterectomy.

celiorrhaphy (se-le-or'ah-fe) Suture of a wound or an incision on the abdominal wall.

celioscopy (se-le-os'ko-pe) See laparoscopy.

cell (sel) **1.** The smallest unit of living organisms capable of independent functioning, composed of a nucleus and organelle-containing cyplasm enclosed within a semipermeable plasma membrane. **2.** In anatomy, any small hollow cavity or somewhat closed compartment. **3.** In crystallography, the element of a crystal's structure. **4.** A receptacle.

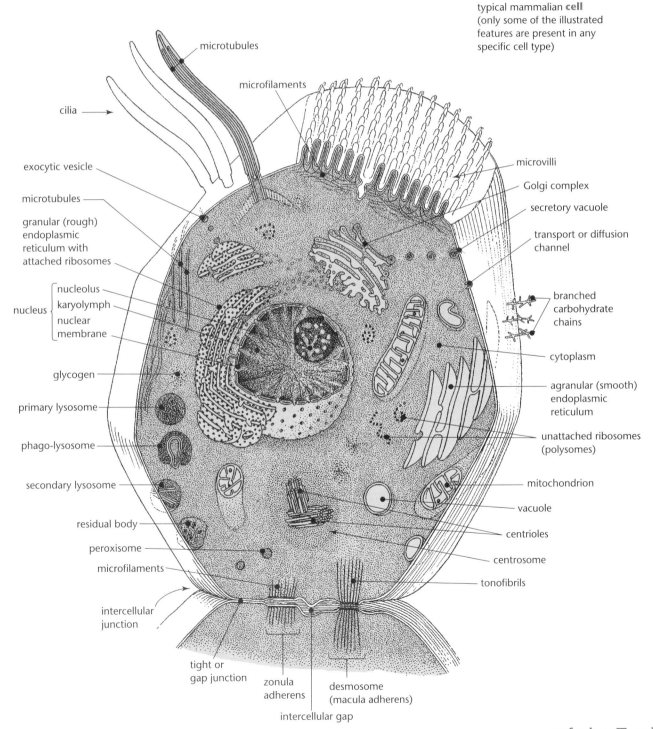

typical mammalian **cell**
(only some of the illustrated features are present in any specific cell type)

microtubules · microfilaments · cilia · exocytic vesicle · microtubules · granular (rough) endoplasmic reticulum with attached ribosomes · nucleus { nucleolus · karyolymph · nuclear membrane } · glycogen · primary lysosome · phago-lysosome · secondary lysosome · residual body · peroxisome · microfilaments · intercellular junction · tight or gap junction · zonula adherens · desmosome (macula adherens) · intercellular gap · microvilli · Golgi complex · secretory vacuole · transport or diffusion channel · branched carbohydrate chains · cytoplasm · agranular (smooth) endoplasmic reticulum · unattached ribosomes (polysomes) · mitochondrion · vacuole · centrioles · centrosome · tonofibrils

C

A c.'s of pancreas See alpha cells of pancreas.

acidophilic c. A cell whose cytoplasm or its granules stain strongly with acidic dyes, such as eosin.

acinar c. One of the secreting cells lining an acinus or alveolus of a compound acinous gland, such as the pancreas. Also called acinous cell.

acinous c. See acinar cell.

adipose c. See fat cell.

air c. An air-containing space, such as an alveolus of the lungs or a sinus of the skull.

alpha c.'s of hypophysis The acidophilic cells of the anterior pituitary gland (adenohypophysis); they secrete growth hormones, prolactin, and adrenocorticotrophic hormone (ACTH).

alpha c.'s of pancreas Cells in the pancreatic islets (of Langerhans) that synthesize, store, and secrete glucagon (hyperglycemic-glycogenolytic factor) directly into perforated (fenestrated) capillaries; the cells are generally arranged toward the periphery of the islets. Also called A cells of pancreas.

alveolar c. See type I pneumocyte, under pneumocyte.

anaplastic c. An undifferentiated cell characteristic of carcinoma.

antigen-presenting c. (APC) A cell in the body that helps to initiate an immune response by capturing antigen and carrying it on its cell membrane in a form that is recognized by T lymphocytes, thereby stimulating the lymphocyte's immune activity.

antigen-sensitive c. See immunocyte.

argentaffin c. See neuroendocrine cell.

B c.'s One of two main classes of lymphocytes. See B lymphocyte, under lymphocyte.

B c.'s of pancreas See beta cells of pancreas.

balloon c. A large, degenerated cell, as seen in the vesicles of herpes zoster.

band c. A granulocytic white blood cell (leukocyte) recently released from the bone marrow, characterized by a simple, unsegmented nucleus resembling a continuous band; it represents a normal stage prior to the development of a mature white blood cell. Also called stab cell.

basal c. A cell appearing in the deepest (basal) layer of a stratified epithelium; an early keratinocyte.

basophilic c. A cell whose cytoplasm or its granules stain strongly with basic dyes, such as aldehyde fuchsin.

beta c.'s of hypophysis The basophilic cells of the anterior pituitary (adenohypophysis); they secrete thyroid-stimulating hormone (TSH), follicle-stimulating hormone (FSH) and luteinizing hormone (LH).

beta c.'s of pancreas Cells in the pancreatic islets (of Langerhans) that synthesize, store, and secrete insulin directly into perforated (fenestrated) capillaries; the cells normally constitute about 80% of the cells in the pancreatic islets and are generally centrally located. Also called B cells of pancreas.

blast c. *(a)* An immature precursor cell (e.g., erythroblast, lymphoblast, neuroblast); a primitive cell, the least differentiated of a line of blood-forming elements. *(b)* A leukemic cell of indeterminable type.

blood c. One of the formed elements of the blood, such as a red blood cell (erythrocyte) or a white blood cell (leukocyte).

bristle c.'s See hair cells.

bronchiolar c.'s Unciliated cells located at the boundary where alveolar ducts branch from the bronchioles. Also called Clara cells.

burr c. See echinocyte.

cartilage c. See chondrocyte.

chief c.'s of parathyroid gland The principal cells of the parathyroid gland that synthesize and secrete parathyroid hormone (parathormone) directly into the sinusoidal capillaries, from which it circulates throughout the body. Also called principal cells of parathyroid gland.

chief c. of stomach An enzyme-producing cell of a gastric gland in the stomach. Also called peptic cell.

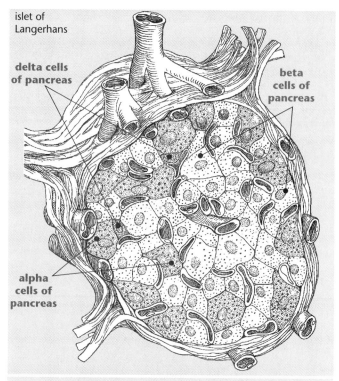

islet of Langerhans
delta cells of pancreas
beta cells of pancreas
alpha cells of pancreas

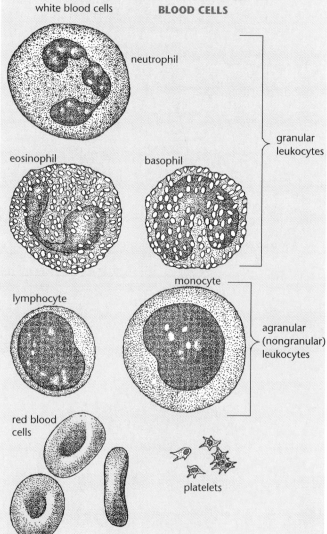

white blood cells   **BLOOD CELLS**

neutrophil
eosinophil
basophil
granular leukocytes
lymphocyte
monocyte
agranular (nongranular) leukocytes
red blood cells
platelets

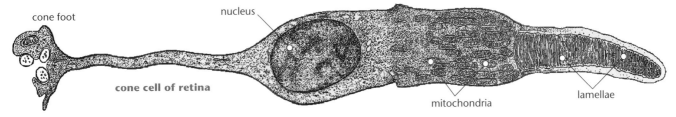

cone foot

nucleus

cone cell of retina

mitochondria

lamellae

Clara c.'s See bronchiolar cells.

columnar c. An elongated epithelial cell; one in which the height is significantly greater than the width; it may be a tall columnar or low columnar cell.

committed c. A lymphocyte (white blood cell) that, after the initial immune response to antigen, becomes committed to differentiate into either a cell producing antibodies or a memory B cell; the latter form retains the ability to proliferate and differentiate when encountering the same antigen at a later time.

cone c. of retina One of the cone-shaped visual receptor cells in the retina of the eyeball, most numerous in the central area (macula), and associated with fine perception of contours and color vision; different cone cells respond to different wavelengths of light; the total number of cone cells in the human retina is estimated at about 6.5 million.

cuboid c. An epithelial cell in which all its diameters are approximately the same, somewhat resembling a cube.

D c.'s of pancreas See delta cells of pancreas.

daughter c. Any cell resulting from the division of another (parent) cell.

delta c.'s of pancreas Cells in the pancreatic islets (of Langerhans) that synthesize, store, and secrete somatostatin, thought to inhibit glucagon release of neighboring alpha cells of pancreas in which they share a peripheral location in the islets. Also called D cells of pancreas.

dendritic c.'s Antigen-presenting cells that stimulate T cells; found in lymph nodes, spleen, and at low levels in blood.

dust c. Alveolar macrophage; see under macrophage.

effector c. In immunology, a lymphocyte or phagocyte that has been activated by exposure to antigen and produces the end effect (direct mediator of the immune response).

enamel c. See ameloblast.

endothelial c. One of the thin, flat (squamous) cells lining the blood and lymph vessels as well as the chambers of the heart.

ependymal c.'s The cells constituting the lining membrane of the ventricles of the brain and of the central canal of the spinal cord (ependyma).

epithelial c. One of the numerous varieties of cells that form the surface epithelium of the skin and the alimentary, respiratory, and genitourinary passages, and their associated glands; it covers all free surfaces of the body except the synovial membranes and the bursae of joints.

fat c. A large connective tissue cell (60–80 microns in diameter), capable of synthesizing and storing a great amount of fat; such cells are generally bloated with a fat droplet compressing the cell cytoplasm into a thin envelope, with the nucleus at one point in the periphery of the cell. Also called adipose cell; adipocyte; lipocyte.

fibroblast c. A spindle-shaped connective tissue cell responsible for producing (elaborating) collagen and reticular fibers; the most common cell type found in connective tissue.

follicular c.'s See granulosa cells.

follicular lutein c.'s See granulosa lutein cells.

germ c. An ovum or spermatozoon, or one of their precursors (immature stages). Also called reproductive cell; germinal cell.

germinal c.'s (a) See germ cell. (b) Cells from which other cells are derived, especially the dividing cells in the embryonic neural tube from which the nerve cells are derived by proliferation and migration.

giant c. A large, multinucleated cell that has its nuclei scattered throughout the cytoplasm; thought to result from fusion of macrophages; sometimes seen in granulomatous reactions.

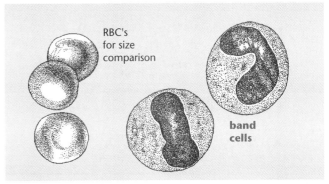

RBC's for size comparison

band cells

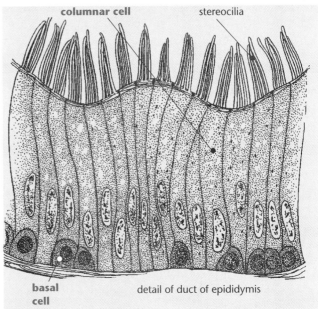

columnar cell

stereocilia

basal cell

detail of duct of epididymis

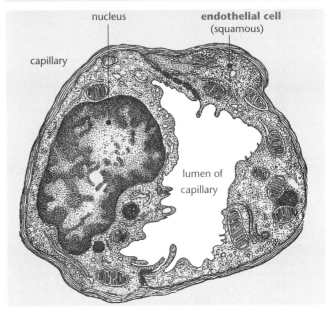

nucleus

endothelial cell (squamous)

capillary

lumen of capillary

glial c. See neuroglial cell.

goblet c. A unicellular mucous gland in which the distal cytoplasm is distended by a large globule of clear mucus, giving the appearance of a goblet or chalice; found in the epithelium of certain mucous membranes, especially of the respiratory and intestinal tracts.

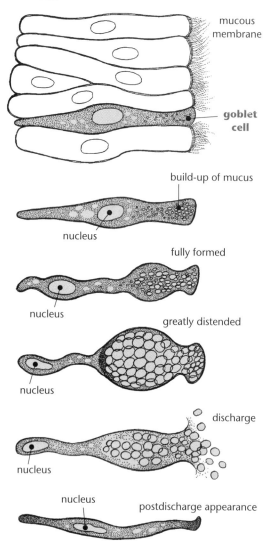

granulosa c.'s Special epithelial cells surrounding the ovum within developing ovarian follicles. Also called follicular cells.

granulosa lutein c.'s Giant glandular cells that constitute the major part of the wall of a ruptured vesicular follicle (corpus luteum) in the ovary; formed by hypertrophy of the granulosa cells of the old vesicular follicle; they produce the sex steroid progesterone. Also called follicular lutein cells.

great alveolar c. See type II pneumocyte, under pneumocyte.

hair c.'s Either of two types of cells serving as a sensory transducer in the membranous labyrinth of the internal ear; located in the cristae and maculae of the semicircular ducts and in the spiral organ of Corti of the cochlear duct; the apical ends of both types of hair cells have a tuft of about 50 sensory hairs (stereocilia) and a single kinocilium; in the cristae, the hairs are embedded in the gelatinous cupula; in the maculae, they are embedded in the gelatinous otolithic membrane containing crystals of calcium carbonate (otoconia); in the cochlear duct, they are embedded in the tectorial membrane; the stimulus for the hair cells is a shearing force that bends its sensory hairs. *Type I,* A sensitive hair cell characterized by a large goblet-shaped nerve calix. *Type II,* A less sensitive hair cell characterized by small, budlike axon terminals (synaptic boutons). Also called bristle cells.

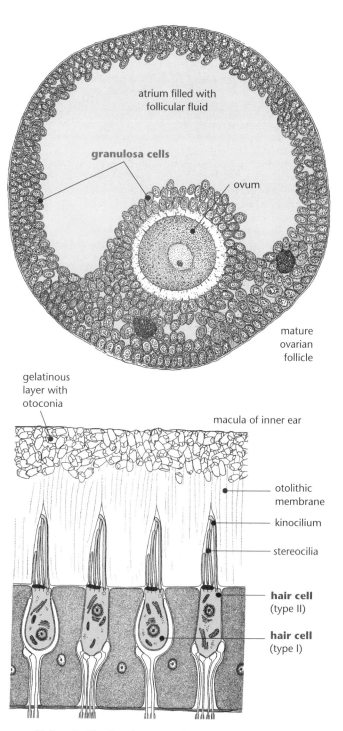

HeLa c.'s The first documented, continuously cultured human malignant cells, derived from a squamous cell carcinoma of the uterine cervix; often used in the culture of viruses.

helmet c. See shistocyte.

helper c. Any of a subtype of T lymphocytes that facilitate an immune response by stimulating conversion of B lymphocytes into antibody-producing cells. Also called helper T-lymphocyte.

hematogenous mast c.'s Basophilic white blood cells (leukocytes) circulating in the blood.

I c. See immunocyte.

immunocompetent c. See immunocyte.

immunologic memory c. See memory B cell.

inducible c. An unprimed cell that can become a primed cell or an antibody-producing cell when stimulated by an antigen.

interstitial c.'s of testis See Leydig's cells.

islet c.'s Any of the cells in their pancreatic islets (of Langerhans).

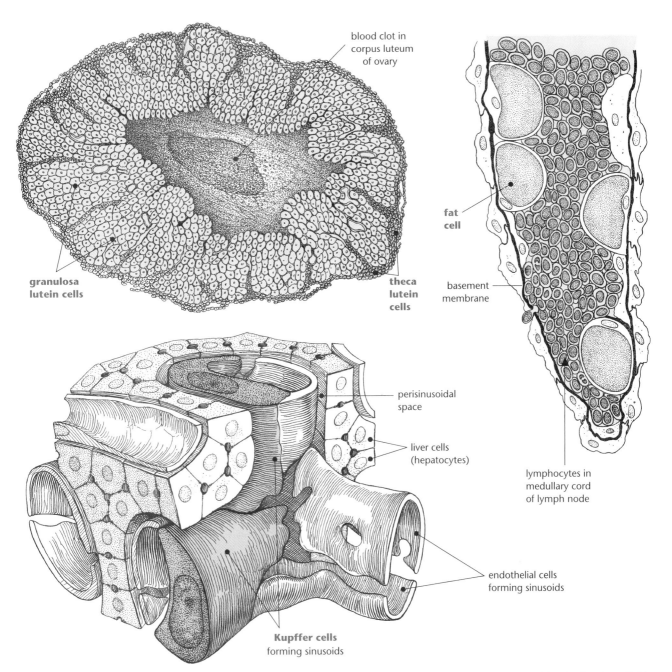

blood clot in
corpus luteum
of ovary

granulosa
lutein cells

theca
lutein
cells

fat
cell

basement
membrane

lymphocytes in
medullary cord
of lymph node

perisinusoidal
space

liver cells
(hepatocytes)

endothelial cells
forming sinusoids

Kupffer cells
forming sinusoids

C

juxtaglomerular c.'s Modified smooth muscle cells seen in the middle layer of the wall of the afferent arteriole of the kidney just before it enters the glomerulus; they secrete the hormone renin and form part of the juxtaglomerular apparatus.

Kupffer c.'s The cells of the mononuclear phagocyte system that line the sinusoids of the liver; a major function is the removal of circulating immune complexes from the blood.

Langerhans' c. A specialized macrophage-type cell of the epidermis; an antigen-presenting cell in skin that migrates to neighboring lymph nodes to become dendritic cells, active in stimulating T cells.

Langhans' giant c.'s Multinucleated macrophages that have their nuclei arranged in the form of an arc (arciform) at the periphery of the cells; typically seen in epithelioid cell granulomas or tuberculosis.

L.E. c. Lupus erythematosus cell; a white blood cell (leukocyte) containing an amorphous round body; the amorphous material is a phagocytosed nucleus from another cell that has been traumatized and exposed to serum antinuclear globulin; a large, purple-red, homogenous inclusion body is seen occupying most of the cytoplasm of the phagocytosing cell. L.E. cells are formed *in vitro* in the blood of individuals with systemic lupus erythematosus, or by the action of the individual's serum on normal white blood cells. Also called lupus erythematosus cell.

Leydig's c.'s The endocrine interstitial cells of the testis that secrete androgens (chiefly testosterone); situated between the seminiferous tubules. Also called interstitial cells of testis.

lupus erythematosus c. See L.E. cell.

lymph c., lymphoid c. See lymphocyte.

mast c.'s Large cells with coarse cytoplasmic granules containing heparin (anticoagulant) and histamine (vasodilator), occurring in most loose connective tissue, especially along the path of blood vessels; the cells act as mediators of inflammation on contact with antigen. Also called tissue mast cells; mastocytes.

memory B c. B cell that has already encountered antigen, undergone class switching, and returned to a resting state to be reactivated by a second challenge from the antigen it recognizes; during the second challenge, the cell mounts a more sustained response. Also called immunologic memory cell.

mesenchymal c. A nonepithelial cell present in the mesenchyme and capable of differentiating into any of the special types of connective tissue or supporting tissues, smooth muscle, vascular endothelium, or blood cells.

cell ■ cell

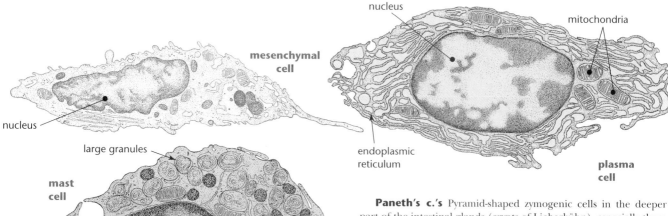

mesenchymal cell

nucleus

nucleus

mitochondria

endoplasmic reticulum

plasma cell

large granules

mast cell

mesothelial c. A cell of mesodermal origin; one of the flat cells of the simple squamous epithelium (mesothelium) lining the pleural, pericardial, peritoneal, and scrotal cavities.

mother c. See parent cell.

myeloid c. Any young white blood cell (leukocyte) that develops into a mature granulocyte.

myoepithelial c. One of the smooth muscle cells of ectodermal origin, with processes that spiral around some of the epithelial cells of sweat, mammary, lacrimal, and salivary glands; their contraction forces the secretion of the glands toward the ducts.

natural killer c.'s Large lymphocytes that do not mark as either B or T lymphocytes; they constitute a small percentage of lymphocytes of normal blood; they are cytotoxic against target cells without being specifically sensitized against them.

nerve c. *(a)* See neuron. *(b)* The cell body of a neuron.

neuroendocrine c.'s Cells of the diffuse endocrine system of the body that release hormones into the bloodstream that signal distant targets; they include the polypeptide hormone-secreting cells of the gastrointestinal tract, the endocrine pancreas, the parafollicular cells of the thyroid gland, the adrenocorticotrophs and melanotrophs of the anterior pituitary (adenohypophysis), the chromaffin cells of the adrenal medulla, the paraganglia, and the carotid body, as well as the small-granule cells in the respiratory tract. Formerly called argentaffin cells.

neuroepithelial c. A cell in a specialized sensory epithelium, between the environment and a nerve ending, sensitive to specific external stimuli, such as the cells of a taste bud. Also called neuroepithelium.

neuroglial c. Any of the nonneuronal cells of the supportive tissue of the central nervous system, including oligodendroglia, astrocytes, microglia, and ependymal cells. Also called glial cell.

null c. A lymphocyte devoid of surface immunoglobulin (neither T nor B markers). Also called NUL lymphocyte.

olfactory c. One of the sensory nerve cells surmounted by sensitive hairs, present in the olfactory mucous membrane at the roof of the nose; the receptor for the sense of smell.

osteochondrogenic c. A young cell of the inner layer of periosteum, capable of developing into a bone or a cartilage cell.

oxyntic c. See parietal cell.

oxyphil c.'s Acidophilic cells in the parathyroid glands; the cells contain an abundance of mitochondria that account for the granular character of the cytoplasm; they increase in number with age.

Paneth's c.'s Pyramid-shaped zymogenic cells in the deeper part of the intestinal glands (crypts of Lieberkühn), especially those of the duodenum; they are the source of the digestive enzymes produced by the walls of the small intestine.

parent c. A cell that undergoes division and gives rise to a new generation of daughter cells. Also called mother cell.

parietal c. The hydrochloric acid–secreting cell of the stomach (gastric) glands. Also called oxyntic cell.

peptic c. See chief cell of stomach.

permanent c. A fetal cell that is unable to divide mitotically in postnatal life.

plasma c. A cell characterized by RNA-rich cytoplasm and an eccentrically placed nucleus; the cytoplasm contains an extensive system of endoplasmic reticulum studded with ribosomes. The cell arises from the antigen-induced, terminal transformation of a B lymphocyte. It produces specific antibody against the antigen that induced its formation. Also called plasmacyte.

prickle c. One of the cells from the inner layer (stratum spinosum) of the epidermis that possesses radiating protoplasmic processes or spines connecting it with similar neighboring cells.

primed c. A cell that has been primed by antigen for antibody production.

principal c.'s of parathyroid gland See chief cells of parathyroid gland.

red blood c. (RBC) See erythrocyte.

Renshaw c. An inhibitory interneuron.

reproductive c. See germ cell.

rod c. of retina One of the rod-shaped visual receptor cells in the eye, located mostly in the area encircling the central retina and slowly diminishing in frequency to the periphery; associated with perception of black-and-white vision in reduced light and with shades of dark and light; the total number of rod cells in the human retina is estimated at about 115 million.

Schwann's c. A special cell that surrounds a peripheral axon forming a myelin sheath.

septal c. See type II pneumocyte, under pneumocyte.

Sertoli's c.'s The elaborate nonspermatogenic supporting cells in the seminiferous tubules of male gonads (testes) extending from the basal lamina to the lumen; they house the developing spermatogenic cells in deep recesses and produce sex hormone–binding globulin and androgens.

sickle c. An abnormal crescent-shaped red blood cell (erythrocyte); the shape is caused by the presence of varying proportions of hemoglobin S; seen in the hereditary form of anemia (sickle-cell anemia). Also called meniscocyte.

sperm c. See spermatozoon.

squamous c. A flat, scalelike cell that is usually arranged in layers to form a lining (e.g., epithelium, endothelium, and mesothelium) of certain structures.

squamous alveolar c. See type I pneumocyte, under pneumocyte.

stab c. See band cell.

stable c. A cell that does not divide unless stimulated to regenerate; it generally has a long life span.

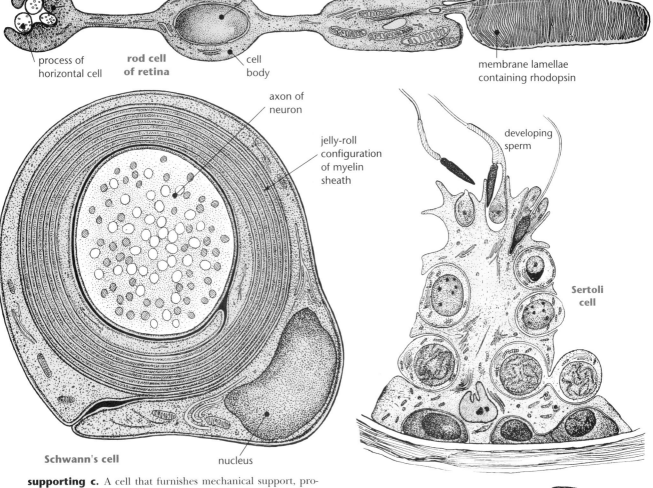

rod spherule

nucleus

process of
horizontal cell

**rod cell
of retina**

cell
body

membrane lamellae
containing rhodopsin

axon of
neuron

jelly-roll
configuration
of myelin
sheath

developing
sperm

**Sertoli
cell**

Schwann's cell

nucleus

supporting c. A cell that furnishes mechanical support, protection, and nutritive assistance to more highly differentiated adjacent cells, as seen in the spiral organ of Corti, taste bud, and olfactory epithelium. Also called sustentacular cell.

sustentacular c. See supporting cell.

T c.'s One of two main classes of lymphocytes; they play an important role in the body's immune system. See T lymphocyte, under lymphocyte.

target c. *(a)* An abnormal erythrocyte that when stained shows a dark center surrounded by a light band encircled by a darker ring, resembling a bull's-eye target; found in a variety of anemias, including thalassemia and other hemoglobinopathies. Also called Mexican hat cell. *(b)* A cell displaying a foreign (nonself) antigen recognized by an effector T lymphocyte. *(c)* A cell containing specific receptors for circulating messengers such as hormones.

taste c. A neuroepithelial cell that perceives gustatory stimuli, situated at the center of a taste bud.

teardrop-shaped c. An abnormally shaped red blood cell associated with myelofibrosis and other infiltrative processes of bone marrow, such as carcinoma.

theca lutein c.'s Lutein cells located within the folds of the glandular corpus luteum of the ovary and derived from the theca interna; they produce estrogens.

tissue mast c.'s See mast cells.

thyroid follicular c.'s The cells of the thyroid follicle responsible for the production of the hormones triiodothyronine (T_3) and thyroxine (T_4).

thyroid parafollicular C c.'s The cells in the parenchyma of the thyroid gland responsible for the production of the hormone calcitonin.

transitional c. Any cell thought to represent a phase of devel-

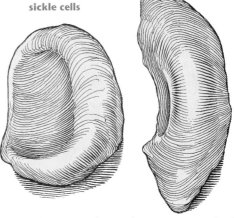

sickle cells

opment from one form to another, such as a monocyte (a phase between promonocyte and macrophage).

type I c.'s See type I pneumocyte, under pneumocyte.

type II c.'s See type II pneumocyte, under pneumocyte.

Tzanck c. A degenerated epithelial cell that has lost its connections with neighboring cells in the epidermis, as seen in pemphigus.

Warthin-Finkeldey c. A giant cell with many nuclei; seen in tissue infected with the measles virus.

white blood c.'s (WBC) Formed elements in the blood that include granular leukocytes (neutrophils, eosinophils, and basophils), lymphocytes (small and large), and monocytes.

zymogenic c. An enzyme-secreting cell as seen in the salivary glands, pancreas, and intestinal glands (crypts of Lieberkühn).

cellular (sel′u-lar) **1.** Relating to cells. **2.** Having numerous compartments.

cellularity (sel-u-lār′ĭ-te) The state of being cellular.

cellule (sel′ul) In gross anatomy, a small space or compartment.

cellulite (sel′u-lit) Popular term for fat deposits beneath the skin.

cellulitis (sel-u-li′tis) A rapidly spreading acute inflammation of subcutaneous tissue occurring as a complication of wound infection; the infective organism is usually *Streptococcus pyogenes*.

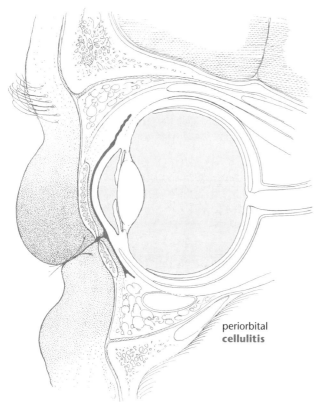

periorbital
cellulitis

cellulose (sel′u-lōs) A polysaccharide that is the main constituent of the cell walls of plants; it is an abundant source of dietary fibers.

celom (se′lom) The body cavity of the embryo, formed between the two layers of mesoderm after one unites with the ectoderm and the other with the endoderm.

celomic (se-lom′ik) Relating to the celom.

Celsius (sel′se-us) (C) See Celsius scale, under scale.

cement (se-ment′) **1.** Any of several materials used in orthopedics as a luting agent (e.g., in fracture or prosthesis fixation) and in dentistry as an adherent sealer (e.g., for attaching restorations or orthodontic bands to teeth). **2.** See cementum.

cementation (se-men-ta′shun) The process of attaching body parts or dental restorations by means of cement.

cementoblast (se-men′to-blast) One of the large cells active in forming the bonelike substance (cementum) of a tooth root.

cementoclast (se-men′to-klast) The bone cell involved with the progressive resorption of the cementum on the root of a tooth, as seen during the replacement of the deciduous dentition.

cementocyte (se-men′to-sit) One of the cells lying in spaces (lacunae) within the bonelike substance (cementum) of a tooth root.

cementoma (se-men-to′mah) A benign tumor made up largely of cementum and fibrous connective tissue, usually formed around a tooth root, especially at its apex.

cementum (se-men′tum) A specialized, bonelike tissue surrounding the root of a tooth; it offers attachment to the periodontal ligament.

censor (sen′sor) In psychoanalytical theory, the mechanism that prevents unconscious thoughts from surfacing into consciousness, unless disguised (e.g., in dreams).

center (sen′ter) **1.** The middle of an organ or structure. **2.** A point or region at which a process begins. **3.** A collection of nerve cells

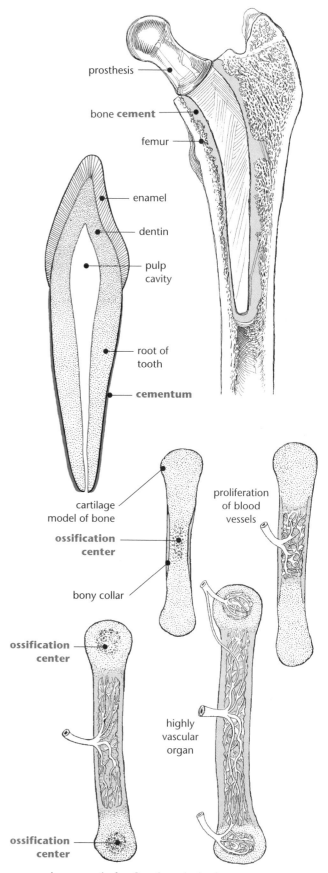

prosthesis
bone **cement**
femur
enamel
dentin
pulp cavity
root of tooth
cementum
cartilage model of bone
ossification center
bony collar
proliferation of blood vessels
ossification center
highly vascular organ
ossification center

governing a particular function. **4.** A place, agency, or group designated to serve the community.

    ambulatory surgical c. An outpatient center equipped for performing surgical procedures in cases that do not require hospitalization. The center must be licensed by the state in which it is located, surgical care must be provided by licensed professionals, and there must be a written agreement with local hospitals to immediately accept patients who develop complications.

birth c. An institution that provides prenatal, childbirth, and postnatal care and usually includes family-oriented maternity care concepts and practice.

Broca's c. See Broca's motor speech area, under area.

Broca's motor speech center See Broca's motor speech area, under area.

germinal c. The area of antibody formation within a lymph nodule containing a large number of antibody-producing white blood cells (lymphocytes). Also called germinal follicle.

motor speech c. See Broca's motor speech area, under area.

ossification c. Any region in a tissue or structure where bone begins to form.

respiratory c.'s Regions of the medulla oblongata and pons that regulate breathing activities.

speech c. See Broca's motor speech area, under area.

Center for Devices and Radiological Health (CDRH) A unit of the Food and Drug Administration (FDA) in charge of ensuring the safety and effectiveness of medical devices, ranging from breast implants to heart valves and x-ray machines.

Centers for Disease Control (CDC) and Prevention A federal agency of the Public Health Service (headquartered in Atlanta, Georgia) that conducts and supports programs for the prevention and control of disease and provides consultation and assistance to health departments in the United States and in other countries; composed of six centers: Center for Infectious Diseases, Center for Environmental Health, Center for Health Promotion and Education, Center for Prevention Services, Center for Professional Development and Training, and Center for Occupational Safety and Health. Formerly called Communicable Disease Center; Centers for Disease Control.

centesis (sen-te'sis) Perforating or puncturing a cavity.

centi- Combining form meaning one-hundredth.

centigrade (sen'tĭ-grād) (C) **1.** Divided into 100 gradations. **2.** See Celsius scale, under scale.

centigram (sen'tĭ-gram) (cg) One-hundredth of a gram.

centiliter (sen'tĭ-le-ter) (cl) One-hundredth of a liter.

centimeter (sen'tĭ-me-ter) (cm) A unit of length; one-hundredth of a meter.

centimorgan (sen'tĭ-mor-gan) (cM) One-hundredth of a morgan; used in genetics. Also called map unit.

centrad (sen'trad) **1.** Toward the middle or center. **2.** (∇) A unit of ophthalmic prism strength.

centrage (sen'trāj) A state of perfect alignment of the refracting and reflecting surfaces of an optical system.

centralis (sen-tra'lis) Latin for central; in the center.

centrencephalic (sen-tren-sĕ-fal'ik) Relating to the middle of the brain, especially the brainstem.

centric (sen'trik) Relating to a center.

centrifugal (sen-trif'u-gal) **1.** Tending to move away from a center, especially in a circular path. **2.** Directed away from any center or axis, such as the central nervous system; efferent.

centrifuge (sen'trĭ-fūj) An apparatus that, by means of centrifugal force, separates suspended particles or mixed fluids according to their relative densities.

centrilobular (sen-trĭ-lob'u-lar) Situated at or near the middle of a lobule.

centriole (sen'trĭ-ōl) Either of two short, hollow, cylindrical bodies in the cytoplasm of animal cells and lower plant cells; its wall is composed of nine sets of microtubules. Centrioles are responsible for organizing the spindle apparatus during cell division (mitosis).

centripetal (sen-trip'e-tal) **1.** Tending to move toward a center, especially in a circular path. **2.** Directed toward a central axis, such as the central nervous system; afferent.

centromere (sen'tro-mēr) The constricted part of the chromosome to which spindle fibers attach during cell division (mitosis). Chromosome movement occurs about the centromere.

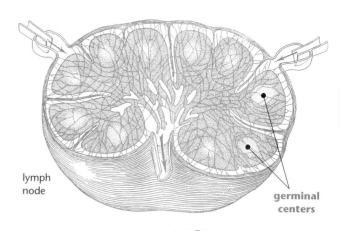

lymph node

germinal centers

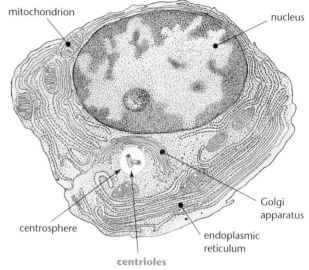

mitochondrion

nucleus

Golgi apparatus

endoplasmic reticulum

centrosphere

centrioles

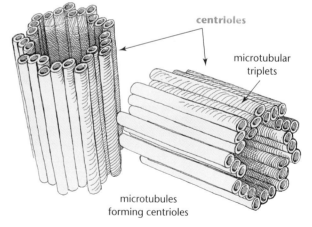

centrioles

microtubular triplets

microtubules forming centrioles

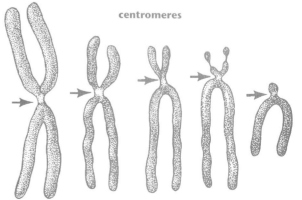

centromeres

centrosome (sen'tro-sōm) A specialized area of cytoplasm, situated near the cell nucleus, that plays an important role in cell division (mitosis). Also called cytocentrum.

centrosphere (sen'tro-sfēr) A clear specialized area of a cell containing the centrosome.

centrum (sen'trum), pl. cen'tra The center of any anatomic structure.

cephalad (sef'ă-lad) Directed toward the head.

cephalalgia (sef-ah-lal'je-ah) Headache.

cephalhematoma (sef-al-he-mah-to'mah) A blood cyst often occurring in newborn infants after normal delivery with no apparent trauma; blood accumulates between a single cranial bone and its lining membrane (periosteum). It is gradually absorbed, becomes firmer and smaller, and disappears by three months. On rare occasions it calcifies, forming a bony protuberance that takes over a year to absorb. COMPARE caput succedaneum, under caput.

cephalic (sĕ-fal'ik) Relating to the head.

cephalization (sef-al-ī-za'shun) The development or embryologic growth of structures and function of the head.

cephalo-, cephal- Combining forms meaning head.

cephalocentesis (sef'ah-lo-sen-te'sis) The draining of fluid from the brain with a hollow needle or with a trocar and cannula.

cephalogyric (sef-ah-lo-ji'rik) Relating to turning movements of the head.

cephalomegaly (sef-ah-lo-meg'ah-le) Abnormal enlargement of the head.

cephalometry (sef-ah-lom'ē-tre) Measurement of the head.
    ultrasonic c. Measurement of the fetal head by means of ultrasonography.

cephalosporin (sef-ah-lo-spōr'in) Any of a group of antibiotics derived from *Cephalosporium acremonium* and other fungi; cephalosporins are effective against a wide range of bacteria, including those resistant to penicillin. Adverse reactions, such as venous inflammation with blood clot formation at site of intravenous injection, may follow administration.

-ceptor Suffix meaning receiver (e.g., proprioceptor).

ceramide (ser'ah-mīd) Any of a group of amides found in small amounts in plant and animal tissues; formed by linking a fatty acid to sphingosine.

cercaria (ser-ka're-ah), pl. cerca'riae The free-swimming larva of a trematode parasite; it may penetrate human skin directly (as in *Schistosoma*), or infect aquatic vegetation and fish.

cerclage (sār-klahzh') Encircling with a ring or loop (e.g., in the treatment of bone fractures, a detached retina, or an incompetent cervix).

cerea flexibilitas (sēr'e-ah flek-sĭ-bil'ĭ-tas) The fixed bizarre posturing assumed by patients with catatonia. Also called flepibilitas cerea.

cerebellar (ser-ĕ-bel'ar) Relating to the cerebellum.

cerebellitis (ser-ĕ-bel-li'tis) Inflammation of the cerebellum.

cerebellopontine (ser-ĕ-bel-o-pon'tēn) Relating to the cerebellum and the pons.

cerebellorubral (ser-ĕ-bel-o-ru'bral) Relating to the cerebellum and the red nucleus.

cerebellum (ser-ĕ-bel'um) The part of the central nervous system situated within the back portion of the skull, below and posterior to the cerebrum and above the pons and medulla oblongata; it serves to maintain equilibrium and coordination.

cerebral (se-rĕ'bral) Relating to the brain.

cerebration (ser-ĕ-bra'shun) Mental activity.

cerebriform (sĕ-reb'rĭ-form) Resembling the brain or brain tissue.

cerebritis (ser-ĕ-bri'tis) Diffuse inflammation of the brain without suppuration.

cerebro-, cerebri-, cerebr- Combining forms meaning cerebrum or brain.

cerebrogalactoside (ser-ĕ-bro-gah-lak'to-sīd) See cerebroside.

cerebromeningitis (ser-ĕ-bro-men-in-ji'tis) See meningoencephalitis.

cerebron (ser'ĕ-bron) See phrenosin.

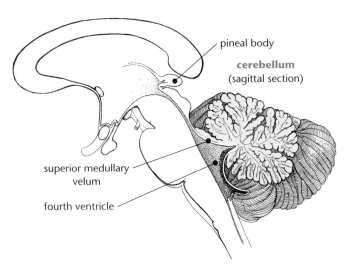

pineal body
cerebellum
(sagittal section)
superior medullary velum
fourth ventricle

cerebrosclerosis (ser-ĕ-bro-skle-ro'sis) Sclerosis of the brain substance.

cerebroside (ser'ĕ-bro-sīd) A phosphorus-free glycolipid containing a fatty acid, an unsaturated amino-alcohol, and galactose (or occasionally glucose). Found in myelin sheaths and cell coats in nervous tissue. Also called cerebrogalactoside.

cerebrosidosis (ser-ĕ-bro-si-do'sis) See Gaucher's disease, under disease.

cerebrospinal (ser-ĕ-bro-spi'nal) Relating to the brain and spinal cord.

cerebrotomy (ser-ĕ-brot'o-me) A surgical cut into the brain substance.

cerebrovascular (ser-ĕ-bro-vas'ku-lar) Relating to the blood vessels or circulation of the brain.

cerebrum (sĕ-re'brum) The brain, excluding the cerebellum, midbrain, pons, and medulla oblongata.

cerium (se're-um) Metallic element; symbol Ce, atomic number 58, atomic weight 140.12.

certifiable (ser-tĭ-fi'ah-bl) **1.** Denoting a disease that by law must be reported to health authorities whenever it occurs. **2.** Denoting a person whose behavior is sufficiently psychotic to warrant confinement.

certification (ser-tĭ-fĭ-ka'shun) **1.** The reporting of a contagious disease to health authorities as required by law. **2.** The process of completing the necessary legal procedures for detention and treatment in a mental hospital. **3.** The formal signing of a statement of cause of death by a medical practitioner. **4.** The formal written statement by which an agency or organization evaluates and recognizes an individual or an institution as meeting certain predetermined standards.

ceruloplasmin (sĕ-roo-lo-plaz'min) A protein of blood plasma active in the transport of copper through the tissues. A deficiency of ceruloplasmin is found in Wilson's disease (hepatolenticular degeneration).

cerumen (sĕ-roo'men) The yellowish brown secretion of glands of the external ear canal. Also called earwax.

ceruminolytic (sĕ-roo-mĭ-no-lit'ik) Denoting any substance that softens or dissolves earwax in the external ear canal.

ceruminosis (sĕ-roo-mĭ-no'sis) Excessive secretion of cerumen.

cervical (ser'vĭ-kal) **1.** Relating to the neck. **2.** Relating to the uterine cervix.

cervicectomy (ser-vĭ-sek'to-me) Amputation of the uterine cervix. Also called trachelectomy.

cervicitis (ser-vĭ-si'tis) Inflammation of the uterine cervix, often caused by a sexually transmitted disease (e.g., gonorrhea, herpes, chlamydial infection) or by trauma (e.g., during childbirth). Also called trachelitis.

cervico- Combining form meaning neck; cervix.

cervicobrachial (ser-vĭ-ko-bra'ke-al) Relating to the neck and the arm.

cervicodynia (ser-vĭ-ko-din'e-ah) Neck pain. Also called trachelodynia.

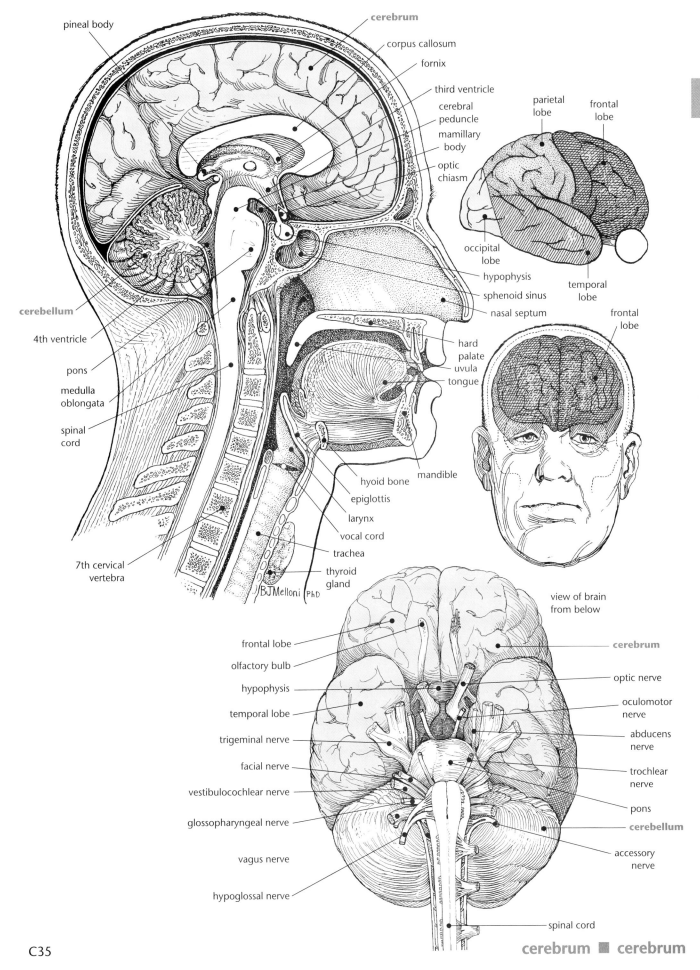

pineal body

cerebrum

corpus callosum

fornix

third ventricle

cerebral peduncle

mamillary body

optic chiasm

parietal lobe

frontal lobe

occipital lobe

temporal lobe

frontal lobe

hypophysis

sphenoid sinus

nasal septum

cerebellum

4th ventricle

pons

medulla oblongata

spinal cord

hard palate

uvula

tongue

mandible

hyoid bone

epiglottis

larynx

vocal cord

trachea

thyroid gland

7th cervical vertebra

BJMelloni PhD

view of brain from below

frontal lobe

olfactory bulb

hypophysis

temporal lobe

trigeminal nerve

facial nerve

vestibulocochlear nerve

glossopharyngeal nerve

vagus nerve

hypoglossal nerve

cerebrum

optic nerve

oculomotor nerve

abducens nerve

trochlear nerve

pons

cerebellum

accessory nerve

spinal cord

C35

cerebrum ∎ cerebrum

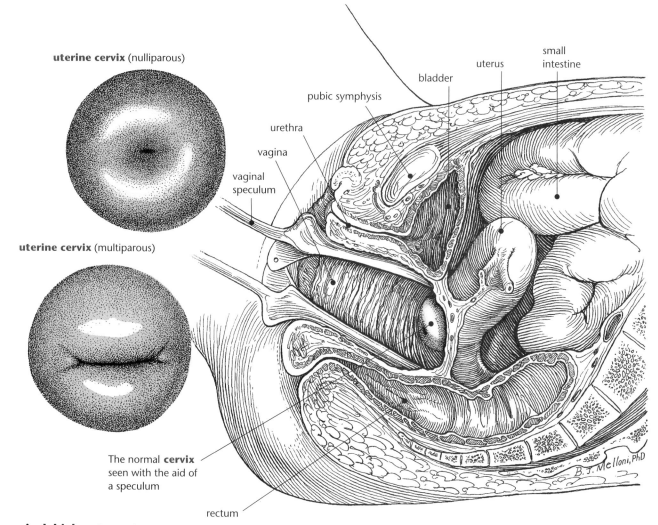

uterine cervix (nulliparous)

uterine cervix (multiparous)

The normal **cervix** seen with the aid of a speculum

cervicolabial (ser'vĭ-ko-la'be-al) Relating to the labial side of the neck of a tooth, specifically of an incisor or a cuspid.

cervicolingual (ser'vĭ-ko-ling'gwal) Relating to the lingual side of the neck of a tooth.

cervico-occipital (ser'vĭ-ko ok-sip'ĭ-tal) Relating to the neck and the lower back of the head.

cervicovesical (ser'vĭ-ko-ves'ĭ-kal) Relating to the uterine cervix and the bladder.

cervix (ser'viks), pl. cer'vices Any constricted, necklike part of an organ or structure. The term is frequently used alone to denote the uterine cervix.

  uterine c. The neck of the uterus; the cylindrical, lower portion of the uterus extending from the isthmus into the vagina; it contains a spindle-shaped canal or passage that is continuous with the interior of the uterus above and the vagina below. Frequently called cervix; popularly called neck of womb.

cesarean (se-se're-an) See cesarean section, under section.

cesium (se'ze-um) Metallic element; symbol Cs, atomic number 55, atomic weight 132.91.

Cestoda (ses-to'dah) A subclass of parasitic flatworms that includes the tapeworms.

cestode (ses'tōd) A tapeworm.

cetomacrogol (se-to-ma'cro-gol) A surfactant of the polyethylene family; used in emulsifying foods, in cosmetics, and in pharmaceuticals as an ointment base.

chafe (chāf) To irritate the skin by friction.

chain (chān) **1.** In chemistry, a sequence of atoms bonded together in a linear fashion. **2.** In bacteriology, a group of microorganisms that have divided and remained attached in a linear arrangement.

  heavy c., H c. The larger of the two pairs of polypeptide chains that constitute the immunoglobulin (Ig) molecule.

  J c. A polypeptide chain that makes possible the formation of immunoglobulin polymers in IgM and certain IgA molecules.

  light c., L c. The smaller of the two pairs of polypeptide chains that constitute the immunoglobulin (Ig) molecule.

  sympathetic c.'s See sympathetic trunks, under trunk.

chalasia, chalasis (kah-la'ze-ah, kah-la'sis) The relaxation of a group of muscles from sustained contraction.

chalazion (kah-la'ze-on), pl. chala'zia An indurated mass in an eyelid resulting from chronic inflammation of a meibomian gland at the edge of the eyelid; believed to be caused by obstruction of the gland duct with retention of secretions. The mass may be mistaken for a tumor. A fully developed chalazion can be distinguished from a hordeolum by the absence of acute inflammatory signs. Also called meibomian cyst; tarsal cyst.

chalone (kal'ōn) A chemical substance released by a cell that inhibits cellular proliferation.

chamber (chām'ber) An enclosed space or cavity.

  Abbe-Zeiss counting c. See Thoma-Zeiss counting chamber.

  anterior c. of eye The space at the front of the eye, between the cornea and the iris, filled with a clear fluid (aqueous humor).

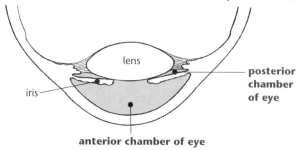

cervicolabial ■ **chamber**

hyperbaric c. An airtight chamber in which air pressure may be raised above atmospheric pressure; used in the treatment of decompression sickness and to provide oxygen in the treatment of carbon monoxide poisoning.

ionization c. A gas-filled chamber containing a charged electrode that attracts ions generated in the gas when radiation enters the chamber; used to measure the intensity of ionizing radiation.

middle ear c. See tympanic cavity, under cavity.

posterior c. of eye The space at the front of the eye, between the iris and the lens, filled with clear fluid (aqueous humor).

pulp c. The portion of the pulp cavity of a tooth above the gum line.

Thoma-Zeiss counting c. A device with a receptacle 0.1 mm in depth and a surface divided into 0.05 mm squares; used for counting blood cells. Also called Abbe-Zeiss counting chamber.

vitreous c. of eye The cavity of the eyeball, behind the lens, containing a transparent, gelatinous mass (the vitreous body).

chancre (shang′ker) An ulcer formed at the site of initial invasion by the sexually transmitted *Treponema pallidum,* marking the beginning of the first stage of syphilis (primary syphilis). It first appears, 14 to 30 days after infection, as a dull red spot that develops into a painless ulcer with an indurated base; usual sites are the penis (head or shaft) and the vulva; other sites include the uterine cervix, scrotum, anus, rectum, and the lips or throat. Also called hard chancre; hard sore.

hard c. See chancre.

soft c. See chancroid.

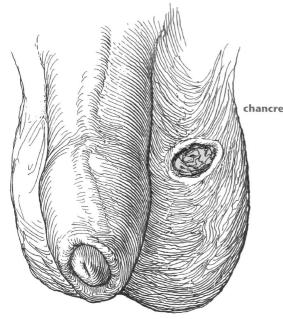

chancre

chancroid (shang′kroid) A sexually transmitted disease caused by *Haemophilus ducreyi,* a gram-negative bacillus; characterized by one or more painful ulcers on the genitals, with acute inflammation of lymph nodes of the groin. Also called soft chancre; soft sore; venereal ulcer.

change (chānj) A modification.

fatty c. Accumulation of fats (lipids) within cells; it occurs in all organs, most frequently in the liver in cases of cirrhosis.

c. of life Popular term for menopause.

channel (chan′el) A passageway; a canal.

CHAP Acronym for cyclophosphamide, hexamethylmelamine, doxorubicin, and cisplatin; a chemotherapy for ovarian cancer.

chapped (chapt) Denoting skin that is dry, scaly, and cracked.

character (kar′ak-ter) 1. A distinctive trait or feature; an attribute. 2. The totality of a person's relatively stable personality traits and habitual modes of response.

charcoal (char′kōl) Carbon obtained by burning wood or other organic material in an airless environment.

activated c. A fine charcoal powder used as an antidote and as an antacid. It adsorbs many toxins and is used as an adsorbent in hemoperfusion to remove poisons from the bloodstream.

charlatan (shar′lah-tan) See quack.

charley horse (char′le hors) Popular name for painful stiffness of muscles, especially of the leg, following injury or excessive activity.

chart (chart) 1. The graphic or tabular presentation of data. 2. A record of the course of a patient's illness, including temperature, pulse, blood pressure, respiratory rate, urinary and fecal output, and comments from physicians and nurses. 3. To enter data into a patient's health record or to present data in graphic form.

charting (chart′ing) The process of recording data in a tabular or graphic form.

basal temperature c. (BTC) A method of detecting the time of ovulation in the menstrual cycle by recording body temperature daily.

cheek (chēk) The side of the face.

cheekbone (chēk′bōn) See zygomatic bone, in table of bones.

cheilectomy (ki-lek′to-me) 1. Surgical removal of a portion of a lip. 2. In orthopedics, cutting away irregular bony edges of a joint cavity.

cheilectropion, chilectropion (ki-lek-tro′pe-on) Eversion of the lips.

cheilion (ki-le′on) The angle or corner of the mouth.

cheilitis (ki-li′tis) Inflammation of the lips.

actinic c. See solar cheilitis.

angular c. See cheilosis.

solar c. Inflammation, cracking, and dryness of the lips, usually caused by overexposure to sunlight. Also called actinic cheilitis.

cheilo-, cheil- Combining forms meaning lips.

cheilognathouranoschisis (ki′lo-na′tho-u-rah-nos′ki-sis) Developmental malformation consisting of a cleft that extends from the palate, through the gum, to the upper lip.

cheiloplasty (ki′lo-plas′te) Plastic or reparative surgery of the lip.

cheilorrhaphy (ki-lor′ah-fe) Suturing of a lip.

cheiloschisis (ki-los′ki-sis) Cleft lip; see under lip.

cheilosis (ki-lo′sis) A noninflammatory chronic condition of the lips, marked by fissuring and dry scaling, especially at the angles of the mouth, indicative of riboflavin deficiency.

cheiro-, cheir- Combining forms meaning hand.

cheiroplasty (ki′ro-plas-te) Plastic surgery of the hand.

chelate (ke′lāt) A compound with a chemical ring structure that contains a metal ion held by coordinate bonds.

chelation (ke-la′shun) The binding (by coordinate bond) between a metal ion and two or more nonmetal ions in the same molecule.

chemabrasion (kem-ah-bra′shun) The combined use of chemical peel and mechanical removal (dermabrasion) of the superficial layers of the skin to remove facial wrinkles.

chemical (kem′ĭ-kal) 1. Relating to chemistry. 2. A product of a chemical process.

chemise (shem-ez′) Surgical dressing consisting of a square piece of gauze fastened to a catheter that has been placed in the wound.

chemistry (kem′is-tre) The science concerned with the structure of matter (molecules, atoms, and particles) and of the laws that govern reactions between different types of matter.

analytical c. The breaking up of compounds to determine the nature of their elements.

clinical c. Analytical chemistry applied to the study of physiologically important substances found in biological samples (e.g., blood, urine, tissues) for diagnosis or therapeutic purposes.

forensic c. The specialized application of chemistry to the solution of legal problems, especially criminal problems.

organic c. The chemistry of substances containing carbon.

physiologic c. See biochemistry.

chemo-, chem- Combining forms meaning chemistry.

chemoattractant (ke-mo-aw-trak′tant) A chemical substance that stimulates migration of cells toward it.

chemobiotic (ke-mo-bi-ot′ik) Denoting a compound that contains an antibiotic and another therapeutic chemical.

chemocautery (kem′o-kaw′ter-e) Destruction of tissues with a caustic agent.

chemoceptor (kem′mo-sep-tor) See chemoreceptor.

chemodectoma (ke-mo-dek-to′mah) Any benign tumor of the chemoreceptor system (i.e., carotid body, glomus jugulare, aortic arch bodies).

chemodectomatosis (ke-mo-dek-to-mah-to′sis) Condition marked by the presence of several minute tumors of the chemoreceptor type in the lungs.

chemodifferentiation (ke′mo-dif′er-en-she-a′shun) Differentiation of cells at the molecular level in the developing embryo; it precedes and controls morphologic differentiation.

chemokinesis (ke-mo-kĭ-ne′sis) Stimulation of increased activity or random movement of cells by a diffusible chemical substance.

chemolysis (kem-ol′ĭ-sis) Chemical decomposition.

chemonucleolysis (ke-mo-nu-kle-ol′ĭ-sis) Injection of an enzyme into the center of a herniated intervertebral disk; an alternative procedure to surgical removal of the disk.

chemopallidectomy (ke-mo-pal-ĭ-dek′to-me) Destruction of the globus pallidus in the brain by injection of a chemical substance; procedure has been performed to relieve the rigidity of parkinsonism.

chemopallidothalamectomy (ke-mo-pal′ĭ-do-thal-ah-mek′to-me) Destruction of two central brain portions (globus pallidus and thalamus) by injection of a chemical substance.

chemoprophylaxis (ke-mo-pro-fĭ-lak′sis) Prevention of a specific disease by administration of a chemical agent.

chemoreceptor (ke-mo-re-sep′tor) An end organ (e.g., taste bud) or a sense organ (e.g., carotid body) that is sensitive to chemical stimuli. Also called chemoceptor.

chemoreflex (ke-mo-re′fleks) A reflex resulting from stimulation of a chemoreceptor.

chemosensitive (ke-mo-sen′sĭ-tiv) Responsive or sensitive to chemical changes in the environment.

chemosis (ke-mo′sis) Swelling of the membrane (conjunctiva) covering the front of the eyeball around the cornea; may have a variety of causes.

chemosurgery (ke-mo-sur′jer-e) Destruction of abnormal or diseased tissue with a chemical agent.

chemotaxis (ke-mo-tak′sis) Directed movement of cells (e.g., white blood cells) or an organism in response to a diffusible chemical stimulus.

chemotherapeutic (ke-mo-ther-ah-pu′tik) Relating to chemotherapy.

chemotherapy (ke-mo-ther′ah-pe) Treatment of disease with any drug (e.g., antimicrobial, antibiotic, and antitumor drugs).

chenodeoxycholic acid (ke-no-de-ok-se-kol′ic as′id) A bile acid that dissolves fats for intestinal absorption. It is prescribed to dissolve cholesterol gallstones. Also called chenodiol.

chenodiol (ke-no-di′ol) See chenodeoxycholic acid.

cherubism (cher′ū-bizm) An uncommon hereditary disease of the jaws, usually only the lower jaw (mandible); manifested in childhood as painless bilateral swelling with upward turning of the eyes, which gives the child's face a characteristic cherubic appearance.

chest (chest) The thorax.

    barrel c. A short, rounded chest with expanded, almost horizontal ribs; seen in persons with advanced emphysema.

    flail c. Condition in which part of the chest moves independently, usually caused by fractures of the breastbone (sternum) or the ribs, or both.

    foveated c. See pectus excavatum.

    funnel c. See pectus excavatum.

    keel c. See pectus carinatum.

    phthinoid c. A long, narrow chest with ribs directed in a more oblique direction than normal.

chestpiece (chest′pēs) The part of a stethoscope placed on the patient.

chiasma, chiasm (ki-as′mah, ki′azm) **1.** In anatomy, the crossing of two structures, such as nerves. **2.** In cytogenetics, the cross configuration at the region of contact between homologous chromosomes during meiosis.

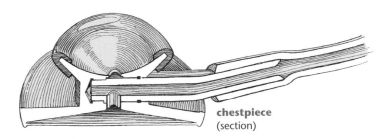

chestpiece
(section)

    optic c. The flattened X-shaped structure formed by the crossing of optic nerve fibers, adjacent to the anterior pituitary gland.

chickenpox (chik′en-poks) A contagious disease, mostly of childhood, caused by the varicella-zoster virus; characterized by skin eruption, fever, and mild constitutional symptoms. Complications may include corneal lesions, causing visual impairment; pneumonia; and encephalitis. Also called varicella.

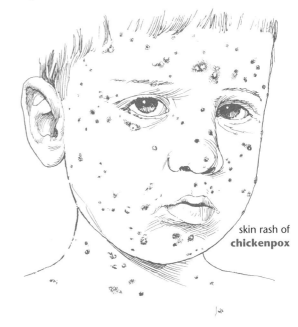

skin rash of
chickenpox

chigger (chig′er) Any of various six-legged, bloodsucking larvae of mites (family Trombiculidae). Also called red bug; harvest mite.

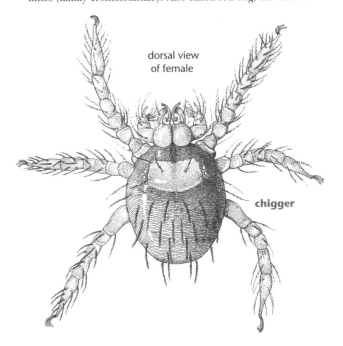

dorsal view
of female

chigger

chigoe (chig'o) The sand flea *Tunga penetrans*. The female burrows within the skin of humans, causing intense itching. Also called jigger; sand flea.

chilblains (chil'blānz) Inflammatory swelling of the fingers and toes with purplish, itchy skin that may progress to ulceration and bleeding; caused by prolonged exposure to extreme cold temperature. May be an occupational condition of both indoor and outdoor workers (e.g., meat packers, construction workers, warehouse personnel). Also called pernio.

child (chīld) 1. From the medical standpoint, a person between the age of infancy and puberty. 2. From the legal standpoint, a person from birth to the age of majority; a minor.

    battered c. A child who has been subjected to physical or sexual abuse, or both, by an adult. See also battered child syndrome, under syndrome.

    exceptional c. A child who deviates from the average in mental, physical, or social characteristics to the extent that modified services are required to develop the child's maximum potential.

    hyperactive c. A child who, for his age, shows poor impulse control, poor modulation of emotions and behavior, and excessive fidgeting, talking, or motor activity; usually associated with attention deficit. See also attention-deficit hyperactivity disorder (ADHD), under disorder.

childbearing (chīld'bār-ing) Pregnancy and parturition.

childbirth (chīld'birth) The process of giving birth to a child.

childhood (chīld'hood) Period of life from two years to puberty.

    early c. Period from two to five years.

    late c. Period between five years and puberty.

chill (chil) 1. A mild sensation of coldness. 2. A feeling of coldness accompanied by paleness, shivering, and fever.

chilo-, chil- Combining forms meaning lips.

Chilomastix (ki-lo-mas'tiks) A genus of protozoans parasitic in the intestines of vertebrates. One species, *Chilomastix mesnili*, is suspected of causing diarrhea in children.

chimera (ki-me'rah) 1. A person who has received genetically and immunologically different cell types, as in a graft or a bone marrow transplant. 2. In experimental genetics, an organism developed from cells or tissues from two different species.

chin (chin) The prominence below the mouth; the mentum.

    double c. The fatty flesh under the chin.

chiro-, chir- Combining forms meaning hand.

chiropodist (ki-rop'o-dist) See podiatrist.

chiropody (ki-rop'o-de) See podiatry.

chiropractic (ki-ro-prak'tik) A system of therapeutics based on the principle that the nervous system determines to a large extent the health of a person and that disease results from abnormal nerve function. Treatment consists primarily of manipulation of parts of the body, especially the vertebral column. Also called chiropractic medicine.

chiropractor (ki-ro-prak'tor) A licensed and certified practitioner of chiropractic.

Chlamydia (klah-mid'e-ah) A genus of bacteria (family Chlamydiaceae) consisting of gram-negative, intracellular parasites; formerly considered viruses.

    C. pneumoniae A species causing 10% of pneumonia and 5% of bronchitis in young adults. Formerly called TWAR agent.

    C. psittaci A species causing infection (ornithosis) in a wide variety of birds; also causes lung infections in humans through contact with feces of infected birds (e.g., parakeets, parrots, pigeons) People most at risk are bird handlers, pet shop workers, zoo attendants, and poultry workers.

    C. trachomatis A species causing infectious diseases in humans. Some strains cause eye infections (trachoma, conjunctivitis); other strains cause sexually transmitted diseases and infections of the genitourinary tract (lymphogranuloma venereum, nongonococcal urethritis, epididymitis, cervicitis, salpingitis, proctitis).

chlamydia (klah-mid'e-ah), pl. chlamyd'iae Any bacterium of the genus *Chlamydia*.

chloasma (klo-az'mah) See melasma.

chloro-, chlor- Combining forms meaning chlorine.

chloracne (klor-ak'ne) A skin eruption resembling acne occurring after exposure to certain chlorinated hydrocarbons (e.g., dioxin, chlorinated naphthalenes, azobenzenes). Exposure is usually occupational, as in the manufacture and repair of transformers containing polychlorinated biphenyls (PCBs). Exposure has also occurred in residential communities as a result of accidental contamination of the environment. Also called chlorine acne; tar acne.

chloral (klo'ral) A colorless, oily liquid produced by the action of chlorine gas on alcohol.

    c. hydrate A depressant of the central nervous system; used as a sedative to treat insomnia; can cause addiction.

chloralism (klor'ah-lizm) Habitual and excessive use of chloral compounds.

chlorambucil (klor-am'bu-sil) Drug prescribed to treat certain types of cancer, such as chronic lymphocytic leukemia and Hodgkin's disease. Adverse effects may include nausea, vomiting, cataracts, and secondary cancer.

chloramphenicol (klo-ram-fen'ĭ-kol) An antibiotic drug used selectively because it carries the risk of causing aplastic anemia; often prescribed in the form of eyedrops or ointment to treat bacterial conjunctivitis.

chlordane (klor'dān) A poisonous chlorinated hydrocarbon effective as an insecticide; human poisoning occurs by absorption through the skin, inhalation, or ingestion.

chlordiazepoxide (klor'di-az'ē-pok'sīd) A tranquilizer used mainly to treat anxiety; may cause dependence.

chloremia (klo-re'me-ah) 1. See chlorosis. 2. See hyperchloremia.

chlorhydria (klor-hi'dre-ah) See hyperchlorhydria.

chloric (klo'rik) Containing pentavalent chlorine.

chloric acid (klo'rik as'id) An acid of pentavalent chlorine.

chloride (klo'rīd) A compound containing chlorine.

    carbonyl c. See phosgene.

chlorinate (klo'rī-nāt) 1. To cause to combine with chlorine. 2. A chlorine compound.

chlorinated (klo'rī-nāt-ed) Containing chlorine.

chlorine (klor'ēn) A gaseous element; symbol Cl, atomic number 17, atomic weight 34.45; used as a disinfectant and bleaching agent.

chloroethane (klo-ro-eth'ān) See ethyl chloride.

chloroform (klor'o-form) A colorless, volatile liquid formerly used as an anesthetic; now used chiefly as a solvent and a reagent in organic synthesis. Chloroform is toxic to inhale, causing liver and kidney damage.

chloroma (klo-ro'mah) A collection of pale green masses arising from myeloid tissue, most frequently around the head and neck, and occurring in association with acute myeloblastic leukemia.

chloropsia (klo-rop'se-ah) Condition in which everything appears green, as may occur in digitalis poisoning.

chloroquine (klo'ro-kwin) A drug used in the treatment of malaria and amebiasis.

chlorosis (klo-ro'sis) A rarely used term for a type of iron deficiency anemia that is characterized by a moderate decrease in the number of red blood cells (erythrocytes) and a large decrease of the blood pigment hemoglobin.

chlorothiazide (klor-o-thi'ah-zīd) A diuretic drug widely used to reduce fluid retention (edema) and as an adjunct in the management of high blood pressure (hypertension).

chlorotic (klo-rot'ik) Relating to chlorosis.

chlorpheniramine (klor-fen-ir'ah-mēn) A potent antihistamine with a duration of three to six hours; used in the treatment of allergies.

chlorpromazine (klor-pro'mah-zēn) One of the first antipsychotic drugs; used as a tranquilizer and to treat nausea and vomiting caused by chemotherapy, radiation therapy, and anesthesia.

chlorpropamide (klor-pro'pah-mīd) An oral hypoglycemic agent used to reduce blood sugar levels (hyperglycemia) in persons with non-insulin-dependent diabetes. It may cause adverse reactions.

chlortetracycline (klor-tet-rah-si'klēn) A broad-spectrum antibiotic; it has been supplanted by other antibiotic drugs that have fewer adverse effects.

chloruresis (klor-u-re′sis) The excretion of chloride in the urine.

chloruretic (klor-u-ret′ik) Any condition or drug that increases urinary excretion of chloride.

choana (ko′a-nah), pl. cho′anae The posterior opening of the nasal cavity into the nasopharynx on either side. Also called posterior naris.

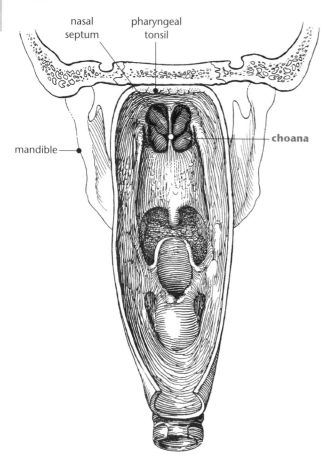

choanal (ko′ah-nal) Relating to a choana.

chokes (chōks) Popular term for a group of symptoms occurring in decompression sickness, which may include chest pain beneath the breastbone (sternum), chest tightness, severe coughing, shallow breathing, and dizziness.

cholagogue (ko′lah-gog) An agent that stimulates the flow of bile into the intestine.

cholangiectasis (ko-lan-je-ek′tah-sis) Dilatation of the bile duct.

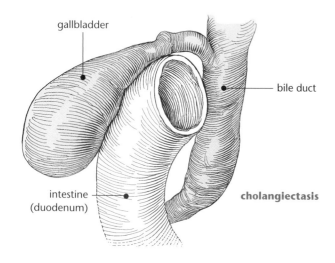

cholangiectasis

cholangiocarcinoma (ko-lan′je-o-kar-sī-no′mah) Cancer arising from the bile ductules within the liver, frequently occurring in the Far East, where infection with the liver fluke, *Clonorchis sinensis,* is believed to constitute a predisposing factor.

cholangioenterostomy (ko-lan′je-o-en-ter-os′to-me) Surgical suturing of the bile duct to the small intestine.

cholangiofibrosis (ko-lan′je-o-fi-bro′sis) Fibrosis of the bile ducts.

cholangiogram (ko-lan′je-o-gram) An x-ray picture of the biliary ducts obtained in cholangiography.

cholangiography (ko-lan-je-og′rah-fe) Radiologic visualization of the biliary ducts after injection of a radiopaque substance; performed to distinguish between obstructive and nonobstructive jaundice, to determine the location and extent of an obstruction, and to detect fistulas and bile leaks.

  operative c. A test performed during gallbladder surgery. The contrast substance is injected directly into the common bile duct and cystic duct to detect the presence of stones or small tumors within the ducts.

  percutaneous c. See transhepatic cholangiography.

  percutaneous transhepatic c. See transhepatic cholangiography.

  transhepatic c. (THC) Cholangiography in which the contrast medium is introduced into the biliary ducts with a thin, flexible needle inserted through the skin and the liver; usually performed when ultrasonography has failed to provide a diagnosis. Potential complications include bleeding, infection, and bile peritonitis. Also called percutaneous transhepatic cholangiography; percutaneous cholangiography.

cholangiole (ko-lan′je-ōl) One of the minute terminal branches of the bile duct.

cholangiolitis (ko-lan′je-o-li′tis) Inflammation of the terminal branches of the bile duct.

cholangiopancreatography (ko-lan′je-o-pan′kre-ah-tog′rah-fe) Radiologic visualization of the bile and pancreatic ducts after infusion of a radiopaque substance.

  endoscopic retrograde c. (ERCP) Procedure in which the radiopaque substance is introduced into the bile and pancreatic ducts through the hepatopancreatic ampulla (ampulla of Vater) in the duodenum, about 8 to 10 cm distal to the end of the stomach (pylorus).

cholangioscopy (ko-lan-je-os′ko-pe) Visual examination of the bile ducts with an endoscope.

cholangiostomy (ko-lan-je-os′to-me) Surgical procedure that creates an opening into the bile duct for drainage purposes.

cholangiotomy (ko-lan-je-ot′o-me) Incision into a bile duct.

cholangitis (ko-lan-ji′tis) Inflammation of the biliary ducts, usually associated with stone formation.

  sclerosing c. Cholangitis usually associated with ulcerative colitis; characterized by irregular fibrosis and narrowing of the biliary ducts both within and outside the liver, leading to obstructive jaundice; the cause is unknown.

cholanopoiesis (ko′lah-no-poi-e′sis) The formation of bile acids or their conjugates and salts by the liver.

chole-, chol- Combining forms meaning bile.

cholecalciferol (ko-le-kal-sif′er-ol) See vitamin D₃, under vitamin.

cholechromopoiesis (ko′le-kro-mo-poi-e′sis) The formation of bile pigment by the liver.

cholecyst (ko′le-sist) Gallbladder.

cholecystagogic (ko-le-sis-tah-goj′ik) Tending to stimulate contraction of the gallbladder.

cholecystagogue (ko-le-sis′tah-gog) A substance that stimulates contraction of the gallbladder.

cholecystectasia (ko′le-sis-tek-ta′ze-ah) Dilatation of the gallbladder.

cholecystectomy (ko-le-sis-tek′to-me) Surgical removal of the gallbladder.

  laparoscopic c. Removal of the gallbladder through a tiny abdominal incision using a laparoscope with the aid of a miniaturized camera; images of the gallbladder are projected onto a screen in the operating room to serve as a guide for the surgeon.

cholecystenterostomy (ko'le-sis-ten-ter-os'to-me) Surgical procedure in which the gallbladder is connected directly to the small intestine.

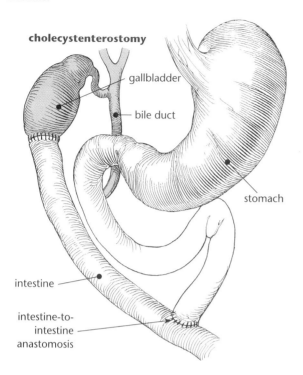

cholecystenterostomy
- gallbladder
- bile duct
- stomach
- intestine
- intestine-to-intestine anastomosis

cholecystic (ko-le-sis'tik) Relating to the gallbladder.

cholecystis (ko-le-sis'tis) Gallbladder.

cholecystitis (ko-le-sis-ti'tis) Inflammation of the gallbladder, causing severe pain in the upper right area of the abdomen; usually caused by obstruction of the outlet of the gallbladder (cystic duct or bile duct); may be acute or chronic.

cholecystoduodenostomy (ko-le-sis'to-du-o-dĕ-nos'to-me) Surgical establishment of a direct communication between the gallbladder and the duodenum.

cholecystogram (ko-le-sis'to-gram) An x-ray image of the gallbladder.

cholecystography (ko-le-sis-tog'rah-fe) Radiologic visualization of the gallbladder after administration of a radiopaque substance; usually performed to detect gallstones after an ultrasound test has failed to provide a diagnosis.

cholecystojejunostomy (ko-le-sis-to-jĕ-ju-nos'to-me) Surgical establishment of a direct connection between the gallbladder and the jejunum.

cholecystokinase (ko-le-sis-to-ki'nās) An enzyme that stimulates the breakdown (hydrolysis) of the hormone cholecystokinin.

cholecystokinetic (ko-le-sis-to-ki-net'ik) Causing release of bile from the gallbladder.

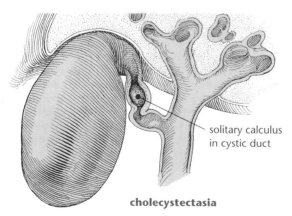

- solitary calculus in cystic duct

cholecystectasia

cholecystokinin (ko-le-sis-to-ki'nin) (CCK) A polypeptide hormone secreted by the inner lining of the upper intestinal tract upon contact with stomach contents; also found in the brain; it stimulates gallbladder contraction (therefore, release of bile) and release of digestive enzymes from the pancreas; it may participate in the regulation of the appetite. Also called pancreozymin.

cholecystolithiasis (ko-le-sis'to-lī-thi'ah-sis) See cholelithiasis.

cholecystorrhaphy (ko-le-sis-tor'ah-fe) Suturing of the gallbladder.

cholecystostomy (ko-le-sis-tos'to-me) Establishment of an opening into the gallbladder for placement of a tube to effect external drainage; usually performed when the patient cannot tolerate removal of the gallbladder (cholecystectomy).

cholecystotomy (ko-le-sis-tot'o-me) Surgical incision into the gallbladder. Opening into the gallbladder may also result from inflammatory or traumatic causes.

choledochal (kol'ĕ-dok-al) Relating to the common bile duct.

choledochectomy (kol-ĕ-do-kek'to-me) A surgical procedure in which all or part of the common bile duct is removed.

choledochitis (kol-ĕ-do-ki'tis) Inflammation of the common bile duct.

choledocho-, choledoch- Combining forms meaning the common bile duct.

choledochoduodenostomy (ko-led'o-ko-du'o-dĕ-nos'to-me) Surgical creation of a communication between the common bile duct and the duodenum; performed when the natural duct opening into the duodenum is obliterated by disease.

choledocholith (ko-led'ŏ ko-lith) Stone in the common bile duct.

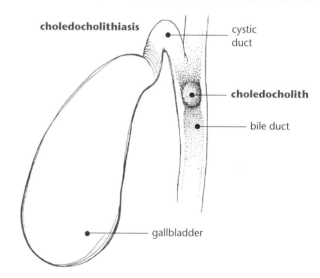

choledocholithiasis
- cystic duct
- choledocholith
- bile duct
- gallbladder

choledocholithiasis (ko-led-ŏ -ko-li-thi'ah-sis) The presence of a stone in the bile duct; usually a stone in the duct has originated in the gallbladder; only rarely is a stone formed in a duct.

choledocholithotomy (ko-led-ŏ-ko-lī-thot'o-me) Incision of the common bile duct for the removal of a stone.

choledochoplasty (ko-led-o-ko-plas'te) Surgical procedure performed on the common bile duct to restore patency in an area of stricture.

choledochorrhaphy (ko-led-o-kor'ah-fe) Suturing of the common bile duct.

choledochoscope (ko-led'o-ko-skōp') A flexible fiberoptic instrument for inspecting the interior of the common bile duct to detect stones or tumors.

choledochoscopy (ko-led-o-kos'ko-pe) Surgical operation for direct inspection of the interior of the common bile duct with the aid of a choledochoscope.

choledochotomy (ko-led-o-kot'o-me) The opening of the common bile duct to remove stones.

choledochous (ko-led'o-kus) Conveying bile.

cholelith (ko'le-lith) Gallstone.

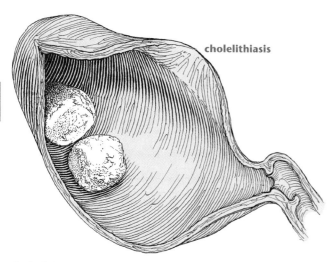
cholelithiasis

cholelithiasis (ko-le-li-thi′ah-sis) The presence of stones in the gallbladder. Also called cholecystolithiasis.

cholelithotomy (ko-le-lĭ-thot′o-me) Surgical removal of a gallstone.

cholemesis (ko-lem′ĕ-sis) Vomiting of bile.

cholemia (ko-le′me-ah) The presence of bile in the blood.

choleperitonitis (ko-le-per-ĭ-to-ni′tis) See bile peritonitis, under peritonitis.

cholepoiesis (ko-le-poi-e′sis) Formation of bile.

cholera (kol′er-ah) An acute infectious disease caused by the bacterium *Vibrio cholerae;* marked by severe watery diarrhea, cramps, vomiting, dehydration, and collapse. It is commonly transmitted by contaminated drinking water.

choleresis (ko-ler′ĕ-sis) Bile secretion by the liver; distinguished from the bile expulsion from the gallbladder.

cholerrhagia (ko′lĕ-ra′je-ah) Excessive secretion of bile.

cholestasia (ko-le-sta′ze-ah) Seldom used term for cholestasis.

cholestasis (ko-le-sta′sis) Suppression of bile flow; may occur at any level, from the canaliculus in the liver to the duodenum; causes may include use of oral contraceptives, anabolic steroids, and oral antidiabetic drugs.

cholestatic (ko-le-stat′ik) Tending to suppress bile flow.

cholesteatoma (ko-le-ste-ah-to′mah) A tumorlike mass formed in the middle ear chamber in association with long-standing middle ear infection (otitis media); composed of proliferating skin cells, from the external ear (auditory) canal, that enter the middle ear chamber through a ruptured eardrum (tympanic membrane). If untreated, cholesteomas may continue to grow and destroy the ear ossicles and other bone.

cholesteremia (ko-les-ter-e′me-ah) Increased amounts of cholesterol in the blood.

cholesterol (ko-les′ter-ol) A white, waxy, organic alcohol; present in all animal fats and oils, in bile, brain tissue, blood, and egg yolk; it constitutes a large portion of the most common type of gallstones and is found in plaques within blood vessel walls in atherosclerosis.

cholesterol

cholesterologenesis (ko-les′ter-ol-o-jen′ĕ-sis) The formation of cholesterol.

cholesterolosis (ko-les-ter-ol-o′sis) Condition marked by abnormal deposition of cholesterol in body tissues.

cholic (ko′lik) Relating to bile.

cholic acid (ko′lik as′id) Digestive acid present in bile.

choline (ko′lin) A compound present in most animal tissues; important in fat metabolism.

cholinergic (ko-lin-er′jik) Relating to nerve cell fibers that use acetylcholine to transmit impulses.

cholinester (ko-lin-es′ter) An ester of choline.

cholinesterase (ko-lin-es′ter-ās) Any of several enzymes that promote the hydrolysis of acetylcholine.

cholinomimetic (ko′lĭ-no-mi-met′ik) Having actions similar to those of the neurotransmitter acetylcholine.

chondral (kon′dral) Relating to cartilage.

chondralgia (kon-dral′je-ah) Pain in a cartilage.

chondrectomy (kon-drec′to-me) Surgical removal of a cartilage.

chondrification (kon-drĭ-fi-ka′shun) The process of turning into cartilage.

chondritis (kon-dri′tis) Inflammation of cartilage.
  costal c. See costochondritis.

chondrio-, chondro- Combining forms meaning cartilage.

chondroblast (kon′dro-blast) A cell that produces cartilage.

chondroblastoma (kon-dro-blas-to′mah) An uncommon, benign tumor of long bones, composed of cartilage-like tissue; seen chiefly in persons under the age of 20 years; sites most commonly affected are the femur and tibia, near the knee joint, and the humerus, near the shoulder joint.

chondrocalcinosis (kon-dro-kal-sĭ-no′sis) A degenerative joint disease characterized by deposition of calcium pyrophosphate in the articular cartilages of one or more joints and attacks of self-limiting acute arthritis (lasting one to four weeks); seen most commonly in people over 50 years of age.

chondroclast (kon′dro-klast) A cell concerned with cartilage absorption.

chondrocostal (kon-dro-kos′tal) Relating to the cartilage of the ribs.

chondrocranium (kon-dro-kra′ne-um) The fetal skull.

chondrocyte (kon′dro-sit) A mature cartilage cell occupying a small space (lacuna) within the cartilage matrix; it is occasionally multinucleated and generally increases in size with age. Also called cartilage cell.

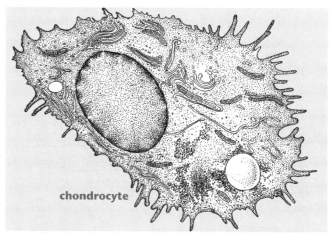
chondrocyte

chondrodynia (kon-dro-din′e-ah) Pain in the cartilage.

chondrodysplasia (kon-dro-dis-pla′ze-ah) See chondrodystrophy.

chondrodystrophia (kon-dro-dis-tro′fe-ah) See chondrodystrophy.

chondrodystrophy (kon-dro-dis′tro-fe) Abnormal development of cartilage, especially at the epiphyses of long bones, resulting in stunted growth of the limbs and short stature (chondrodystrophic dwarfism), while the head and vertebral column develop normally. Also called chondrodystrophia; chondrodysplasia.

chondroectodermal (kon-dro-ek-to-der′mal) Relating to cartilage that is derived from the ectoderm.

chondrogenesis (kon-dro-jen′ĕ-sis) Cartilage formation.

chondrolysis (kon-drol′ĭ-sis) Dissolution of cartilage, especially articular cartilage.

chondroma (kon-dro′mah) A relatively common benign tumor of the hands and feet, composed of cells that normally give rise to cartilage.

chondromalacia (kon-dro-mah-la′she-ah) Abnormal softening of articular cartilage, especially of the kneecap (patella).

chondromatosis (kon-dro-mah-to′sis) Condition marked by the presence of multiple cartilaginous growths (chondromas).

chondromyxoma (kon-dro-mik-so′mah) See chondromyxoid fibroma, under fibroma.

chondro-osseous (kon′dro os′e-us) Composed of both cartilage and bone.

chondro-osteodystrophy (kon′dro os-te-o-dis′tro-fe) General term for a group of disorders affecting bone and cartilage (e.g., Morquio's syndrome). Also called osteochondrodystrophy.

chondropathy (kon-drop′ah-the) Any disease of cartilage.

chondrophyte (kon′dro-fit) An abnormal cartilaginous growth developed at the articular end of a bone.

chondroplasty (kon′dro-plas-te) Reparative operation on cartilage.

chondroporosis (kon-dro-po-ro′sis) The formation of spaces within cartilage; may be a normal occurrence during the process of ossification, or may be pathologic.

chondrosarcoma (kon-dro-sar-ko′mah) A cancerous growth within a bone, derived from cartilage cells; it occurs most frequently in the pelvis, ribs, shoulder girdle, and long bones of middle-aged and old people.

chondrosternal (kon-dro-ster′nal) Relating to the rib cartilages and the breastbone (sternum).

chondrotome (kon′dro-tōm) Surgical knife for cutting cartilage.

chondrotomy (kon-drot′o-me) A surgical cut into a cartilage.

CHOP A term for a chemotherapy regimen that includes cyclophosphamide, doxorubicin, vincristine (Oncovin), and prednisone.

chorda (kor′dah) pl. chor′dae A cordlike structure.

 cordae tendineae The fibrous cords in the heart ventricles attaching the leaflets of the atrioventricular valves to the papillary muscles of the heart wall.

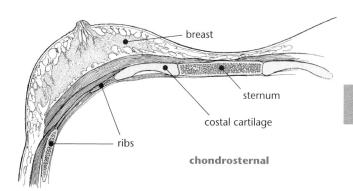

chondrosternal

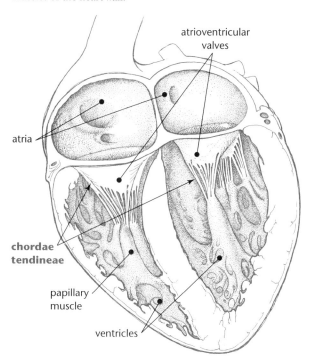

 c. tympani A branch of the facial nerve that innervates the submandibular and sublingual glands and the anterior two-thirds of the tongue.

Chordata (kor-da′tah) The phylum of animals that have a notochord at some stage of their development.

chordate (kor′dāt) An animal of the phylum Chordata.

chordee (kor-de′) An abnormal downward curvature of the penis resulting from a congenital anomaly (hypospadias) or from other conditions (e.g., Peyronie's disease, gonorrhea).

chorditis (kor-di′tis) Inflammation of a cord.

chordoma (kor-do′mah) A slow-growing malignant tumor derived from remnants of notochordal tissue. It arises in bone and protrudes inward, either at the base of the skull (where it compresses the brain) or in the lower part of the vertebral canal (where it compresses lumbosacral nerve roots).

chorea (kor-e′ah) Irregular, rapid, jerky, involuntary movements of the face and limbs; they disappear during sleep.

 chronic progressive c. See Huntington's disease, under disease.

 hereditary c. See Huntington's disease, under disease.

 Huntington's c. See Huntington's disease, under disease.

 Sydenham's c. Condition seen most commonly in children, characterized by an acute onset of emotional instability, involuntary movements, muscular weakness, incoordination, and slurred speech usually following (by many months) an epidsode of rheumatic fever. The individual attack of chorea is self-limited but may last up to three months. Formerly called St. Vitus' dance.

choreic (kŏ-re′ik) Relating to chorea.

choreiform (kŏ-re′ĭ-form) Resembling the spastic movements of chorea.

choreo- Combining form meaning chorea.

choreoathetoid (ko′re-o-ath′ĕ-toid) Relating to choreoathetosis.

choreoathetosis (ko′re-o-ath-ĕ-to′sis) Combined involuntary movements typical of chorea and athetosis (i.e., rapid twitching and slower writhing, contortions of face, bizarre posturing).

choreophrasia (ko′re-o-fra′ze-ah) A repetition of meaningless phrases.

chorio- Combining form meaning membrane.

chorioadenocarcinoma (ko-re-o-ad-ĕ-no′kar-sĭ-no′mah) See invasive mole, under mole.

chorioadenoma destruens (ko-re-o-ad-ĕ-no′mah des-tru′ens) See invasive mole, under mole.

chorioamnionitis (ko-re-o-am-ne-on-i′tis) Inflammation of the fetal membranes, usually due to infection with microorganisms from the vagina (e.g., when delivery does not follow shortly after rupture of the membranes).

choriocarcinoma (ko-re-o-kar-sĭ-no′mah) An uncommon but highly malignant tumor of the uterus occurring after any type of pregnancy (normal or ectopic), most frequently as a complication of a hydatidiform mole; occasionally it occurs after an abortion or may develop months after the pregnancy; the tumor is derived from cells of the original placental tissues (trophoblast). Also called chorioepithelioma; chorionic epithelioma; trophoblastoma; invasive mole.

chorioepithelioma (ko′re-o-ep-ĭ-the-le-o′mah) See choriocarcinoma.

choriomeningitis (ko-re-o-men-in-ji′tis) Inflammation of the membranes (meninges) covering the brain and of the choroid plexuses, especially of the third and fourth ventricles.

 lymphocytic c. (LCM) A disease affecting mice and hamsters, sometimes transmitted to humans; caused by an arenavirus.

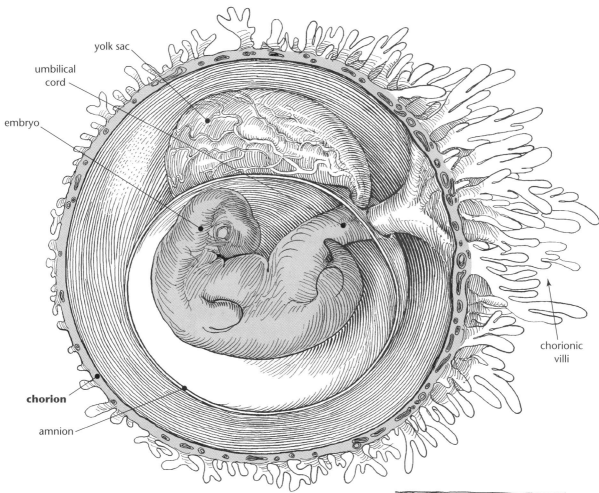

yolk sac

umbilical
cord

embryo

chorionic
villi

chorion

amnion

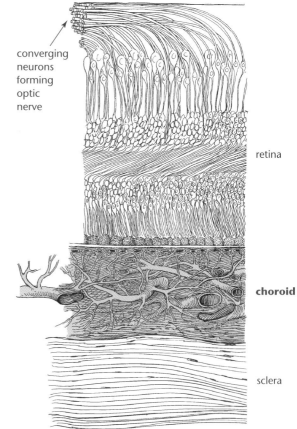

converging
neurons
forming
optic
nerve

retina

choroid

sclera

chorion (ko′re-on) The outermost membrane enclosing the fetus.

chorionic (ko-re-on′ik) Relating to the chorion.

chorioretinitis (ko-re-o-ret-ĭ-ni′tis) Inflammation of two layers of tissue investing the eyeball, the vascular layer (choroid) and the light-sensitive layer (retina). Also called retinochoroiditis; Jensen's disease.

choristoma (ko-ris-to′mah) A mass composed of normal tissue growing in abnormal locations; a developmental anomaly, not a true neoplasm.

choroid (ko′roid) **1.** The middle layer of the eyeball between the retina and the sclera containing a network of minute blood vessels. **2.** Resembling the outermost membrane (chorion) enclosing the fetus.

choroideremia (ko-roi-der-e′me-ah) A hereditary condition marked by progressive degeneration of the vascular layer (choroid) of the eye, beginning as night blindness and ending in total blindness.

choroiditis (ko-roi-di′tis) Inflammation of the vascular layer (choroid) of the eyeball.

choroidocyclitis (ko-roi-do-sik-li′tis) See uveitis.

chromato-, chromat-, chromo-, chrom- Combining forms meaning color.

chromaffin (kro′maf-in) Having an affinity for chromium salts; said of certain cells and tissues characterized by a dark brown color when oxidized by chromate salts; a feature of cells of the adrenal medulla and paraganglia related to the presence of epinephrine.

chromaffinoma (kro-maf-ĭ-no′mah) See pheochromocytoma.

chromaffinopathy (kro-maf-ĭ-nop′ah-the) Any disease of chromaffin tissue (e.g., of the adrenal medulla).

chromate (kro′măt) A salt of chromic acid.

chromatic (kro-mat′ik) Relating to colors.

chromatid (kro′mah-tid) One of two strands in the cell nucleus (joined by a single centromere) formed by longitudinal splitting of a

chorion ■ chromatid

chromosome during mitosis or meiosis. Eventually, each chromatid becomes a chromosome.

chromatin (kro'mah-tin) The irregular clumps of DNA proteins in a cell nucleus that are readily stainable by basic dyes (due to their DNA contents) and of which chromosomes are made.

sex c. The chromatin mass situated just inside the nuclear membrane in somatic (body) cells of the normal female. Its presence or absence in cells obtained from a smear of the inside of the cheek (buccal mucosa) has been used as an indicator of the sexual genotype of an individual. Also called Barr chromatin body; Barr body; sex chromatin body.

chromatism (kro'mah-tizm) Abnormal pigmentation.

chromatogenous (kro-mah-toj'ĕ-nus) Producing or causing pigmentation.

chromatogram (kro-mat'o-gram) The graphic record obtained in chromatography.

chromatography (kro-mah-tog'rah-fe) An analytical technique for the separation and identification of chemical substances in a mixture; effected by their differential movement through a two-phase system.

chromatolysis (kro-mah-tol'ĭ-sis) Disintegration of chromophil substance (Nissl bodies) in a nerve cell following injury to the cell body or to its axon.

chromatophilic (kro-mah-to-fil'ik) See chromophilic.

chromatopsia (kro-mah-top'se-ah) An abnormal perception of color.

chromesthesia (kro-mes-the'ze-ah) Condition in which the perception of color elicits other sensations (e.g., smell, taste).

chromium (kro'me-um) A metallic element; symbol Cr, atomic number 24, atomic weight 51.996. Exposure to chromium compounds constitutes an occupational hazard, causing disorders of the skin and the respiratory tract, including lung cancer. Workers at risk include those involved in the production of stainless steel, in electroplating, lithography, printing, and photography, and in the paint, textile, leather, glass, and rubber industries.

Chromobacterium (kro-mo-bak-te're-um) A genus of gram-negative bacteria; present in soil and water; some species are pathogenic to humans.

chromoblast (kro'mo-blast) An embryonic pigment cell.

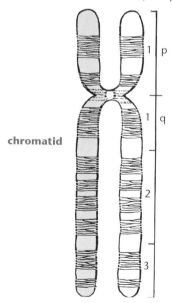

chromatid

chromoblastomycosis (kro-mo-blas-to-mi-ko'sis) A localized skin disease caused by certain soil fungi and characterized by chronic warty outgrowths and minor swelling; the fungi enter the skin through punctures or cuts, especially in the lower extremity. Also called chromomycosis.

chromocyte (kro'mo-sīt) Any pigmented cell.

chromogen (kro'mo-jen) **1.** A substance that can be chemically transformed into a pigment, or that can yield a pigmented derivative. **2.** A pigment-producing cell or microorganism.

chromogranins (kro-mo-gran'ins) A group of soluble proteins present in neurosecretory granules; they serve as markers for certain types of tumors (e.g., small cell carcinoma).

chromomycosis (kro-mo-mi-ko'sis) See chromoblastomycosis.

chromonema (kro-mo-ne'mah), pl. chromone'mata In genetics, the coiled central filament, extending the length of the chromosome, that contains the genes.

chromophil, chromophile (kro'mo-fil, kro'mo-fil) A cell that stains readily with appropriate dyes.

chromophilia (kro-mo-fil'e-ah) The property of staining easily; applied to certain cells.

chromophilic, chromophilous (kro-mo-fil'ik, kro-mof'ĭ-lus) Tending to stain easily; denoting certain cells. Also called chromatophilic.

chromophobe (kro'mo-fōb) Staining slightly or not at all; said of certain cells.

chromophobia (kro-mo-fo'be-ah) **1.** Resistance to staining. **2.** Abnormal, intense dislike of colors.

chromophore (kro'mo-fōr) The molecular group that is responsible for the color of a substance.

chromoprotein (kro-mo-pro'tēn) A substance (e.g., hemoglobin) composed of a pigment and a simple protein.

chromosome (kro'mo-sōm) In any cell, one of a group of threadlike structures that are located within the cell nucleus and contain DNA (deoxyribonucleic acid) encoding genetic information (hereditary material) from both parents. Normally, human cells contain 46 chromosomes.

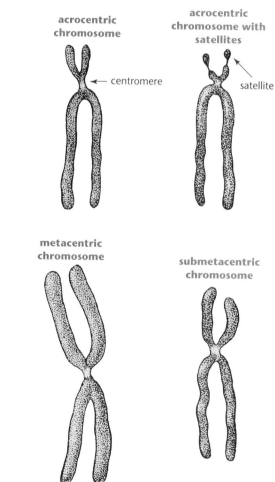

acrocentric c. A chromosome in which the centromere is situated near one end so that the chromosome has a very short arm, often with a satellite.

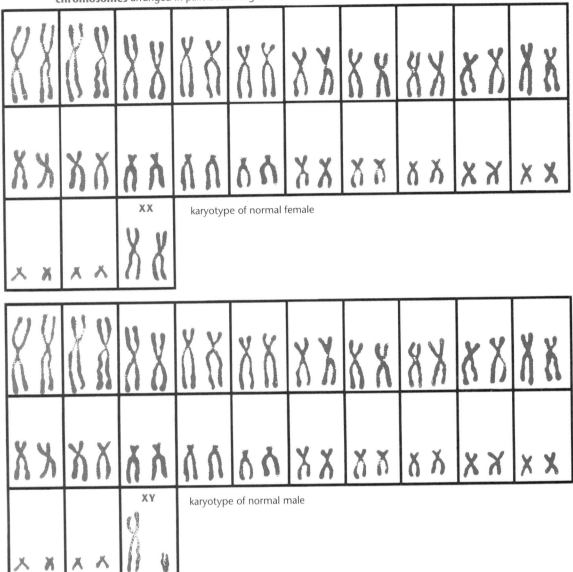

chromosomes arranged in pairs according to size

karyotype of normal female

karyotype of normal male

fragile X c. An abnormal X chromosome that causes mental retardation. It has an area associated with chromosome breakage, discernible under special culture medium as a nonstaining band. Male carriers of the fragile X chromosome are not afflicted with mental retardation but they can transmit the condition through their daughters (some of whom may also be affected) to their grandchildren.

metacentric c. A chromosome with the centromere situated at its middle, creating nearly equal lengths of the arms.

Philadelphia c. (Ph[1]) An abnormal chromosome (of group 22) that is small, acrocentric, and lacking parts of its long arm. It has been found in dividing nuclei of precursors of white blood cells and red blood cells of patients with chronic granulocytic leukemia.

sex c. A chromosome that has a major role in determining the sex of an individual; in humans and most animals, they are designated X or Y. Normally females have two X chromosomes (no Ys); males have one X and one Y chromosome.

submetacentric c. A chromosome with its centromere so placed that two arms, which ordinarily would be equal, have unequal lengths.

X c. In humans, a large metacentric sex chromosome.

Y c. In humans, a small acrocentric sex chromosome.

chronaxia, chronaxy (kro-nak'se-ah, kro-nak'se) See chronaxie.

chronaxie (kro-nak'se) The minimum length of time required for excitation of nerve or muscle tissue by a constant electric current of twice the threshold voltage. Also called chronaxia, chronaxy.

chronic (kron'ik) Of slow development and long duration; said of diseases; the opposite of acute.

chrono- Combining form meaning time.

chronobiology (kron-o-bi-ol'ŏ -je) The study of the timing of biological rhythms in individual organisms.

chronognosis (kron-og-no'sis) Subjective perception of the passage of time.

chronograph (kron'o-graf) A device for graphically recording the passage of short time intervals.

chronotaraxis (kron-o-tar-ak'sis) Disorientation relating to time passage.

chronotropism (kro-not'ro-pizm) Interference with the rate of a regular or recurrent phenomenon (e.g., the heartbeat).

chryso-, chrys- Combining forms meaning gold.

chrysiasis (krī-si'ah-sis) Deposition of gold in the skin and sclera of the eyeball following therapy with gold salts. Also called chrysoderma; auriasis.

chrysoderma (kris-o-der'mah) See chrysiasis.

chrysotherapy (kris-o-ther'ah-pe) Treatment of disease with gold salts.

chyle (kīl) The milky fluid composed of lymph and digested fat, taken up by the lymphatic capillaries during digestion and transported to the circulating blood by the thoracic duct and right lymphatic duct to the left subclavian vein and right subclavian vein, respectively.

chylemia (ki-le´me-ah) The presence of chyle in the circulating blood.

chylo-, chyl- Combining forms meaning chyle.

chylomediastinum (ki-lo-me-de-as-ti´num) Abnormal presence of chyle in the middle compartment of the chest cavity.

chylomicron (ki-lo-mi´kron) A minute fat globule composed mainly of triglyceride and cholesterol; formed in the epithelial cells of the small intestine and carried in the lymph to the bloodstream.

chylomicronemia (ki-lo-mi-kron-e´me-ah) Increased number of chylomicrons in the blood.

chylopoiesis (ki-lo-poi-e´sis) The formation of chyle.

chylothorax (ki-lo-tho´raks) Accumulation of a milky lymph fluid in the pleural space, indicating an abnormal communication between the thoracic duct and the pleura, as would result from injuries to the thoracic duct (in trauma or surgery) or from infiltration of the thoracic duct by a malignant tumor.

chylous (ki´lus) Relating to chyle.

chyluria (ki-lu´re-ah) The presence of chyle or lymph in the urine, which gives urine a white, turbid appearance.

chyme (kīm) The semifluid mass of food that is moved along the upper gastrointestinal tract.

chymopapain (ki-mo-pah-pa´in) An enzyme used to shrink the tissues of a herniated disk.

chymopoiesis (ki-mo-poi-e´sis) The formation of chyme.

chymotrypsin (ki-mo-trip´sin) A digestive enzyme of pancreatic origin.

chymotrypsinogen (ki-mo-trip-sin´o-jen) A substance, secreted by the pancreas, that gives rise to the digestive enzyme chymotrypsin.

cicatrectomy (sik-ah-trek´to-me) Surgical removal of a scar.

cicatricial (sik-ah-trish´al) Relating to a scar.

cicatricotomy, cicatrisotomy (sik-ah-tri-kot´o-me, sik-ah-tris-ot´o-me) Incision of a scar.

cicatrix (sik-a´triks), pl. cica´trices A scar.

cicatrization (sik-ah-tri-za´shun) The formation of scar tissue.

ciguatera (se-guah-ter´ah) A rare type of food poisoning resulting from eating reef fish (e.g., snapper, grouper, amberjack) that have ingested a toxin (ciguatoxin) found in specific tropical reefs and island waters; characterized by nausea, vomiting, diarrhea, and abdominal pain (3–5 hours after eating the fish). Neurologic symptoms (12–18 hours later) include muscular aches; dizziness; numbness and tingling of the lips, tongue, and mouth; metallic taste; and hot-cold inversion (i.e., hot foods feel cold, cold foods feel hot).

ciguatoxic (se-guah-tok´sik) Relating to ciguatoxin.

ciguatoxin (se-guah-tok´sin) A toxin produced by certain algae that grow on tropical reefs.

cilia (sil´e-ah) Plural of cilium.

ciliarotomy (sil-e-ar-ot´o-me) An incision in the eye at the periphery of the anterior surface of the iris (ciliary zone).

ciliary (sil´e-er-e) **1.** Relating to the eyelashes or any hairlike process. **2.** Relating to structures of the eye socket (orbit).

ciliated (sil´e-ā-ted) Having hairlike processes.

cilioretinal (sil-e-o-ret´ī-nal) Relating to the ciliary body and the retina.

cilium (sil´e-um), pl. cil´ia **1.** A microscopic hairlike process on a cell surface capable of rhythmic motion. **2.** An eyelash.

cillosis (sil-lo´sis) Twitching of an eyelid.

cimetidine (si-met´ī-dēn) A drug that inhibits stomach secretion of hydrochloric acid; used to promote healing of stomach and duodenal ulcers. Adverse effects may include headache, dizziness, and confusion.

cinchona (sin-ko´nah) Any tree of the genus *Cinchona;* the bark contains a variety of alkaloids, including quinine.

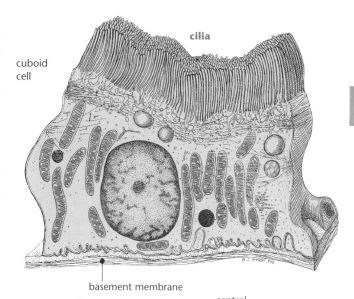

cilia
cuboid cell
basement membrane

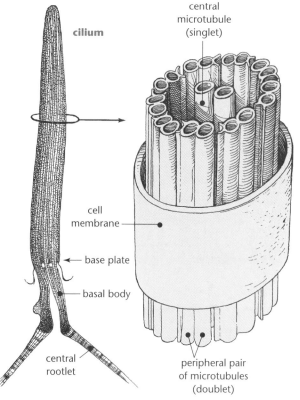

cilium
central microtubule (singlet)
cell membrane
base plate
basal body
central rootlet
peripheral pair of microtubules (doublet)

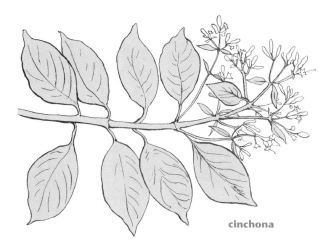

cinchona

cinchonism (sin′ko-nizm) Toxic condition caused by overuse of cinchona or its alkaloids, such as quinine; symptoms include giddiness, headache, ringing in the ears, and deafness. Also called quininism.

cine-, cin- Combining forms meaning movement.

cineangiocardiography (sin-ĕ-an′je-o-kar-de-og′rah-fe) The production of motion picture films showing, fluoroscopically, a radiopaque substance passing (with the bloodstream) through the heart chambers and great vessels.

cineangiography (sin-ĕ-an-je-og′rah-fe) The making of motion picture films of a radiopaque substance passing through blood vessels.

cine-esophagoscopy (sin-ĕ ĕ-sof-ah-gos′ko-pe) Motion pictures of the action of the esophagus.

cinegastroscopy (sin-ĕ-gas-tros′ko-pe) Recording of gastroscopy with motion pictures of the interior of the stomach.

cineradiography (sin-ĕ-ra-de-og′rah-fe) The production of motion picture films of sequential fluoroscopic images. Also called cineroentgenography.

cineroentgenography (sin-ĕ-rent-gen-og′rah-fe) See cineradiography.

cineurography (sin-ĕ-u-rog′rah-fe) Motion pictures of the bladder in action.

cingulotomy (sing-gu-lot′o-me) Operation on the brain consisting of the electrolytic destruction of portions of the congulate gyrus and corpus callosum; usually performed for the relief of severe chronic pain, addiction, or certain intractable psychoses.

cingulum (sin′gu-lum), pl. cin′gula **1.** A band of fibers in the brain that partly encircles the corpus callosum. **2.** The V- or W-shaped enamel ridge on the lingual surface of incisor teeth.

circadian (ser-ka′de-an) Relating to the rhythm of biologic phenomena that recurs approximately every 24 hours. Blood pressure, body temperature, and many other functions normally show circadian variations. Also called circadian rhythm.

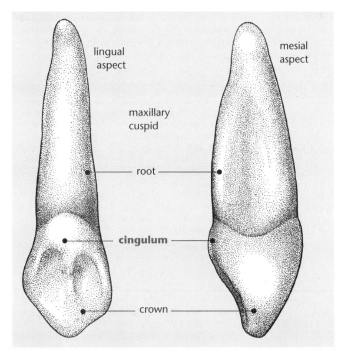

circinate (ser′sĭ-nāt) Ring-shaped.

circle (ser′kl) A ring-shaped anatomic structure.

    arterial c. A ring of arteries formed by connecting (anastomosing) branches of the carotid and basilar arteries at the base of the brain; it is a common site of aneurysms. Commonly called circle of Willis.

    c. of Willis See arterial circle.

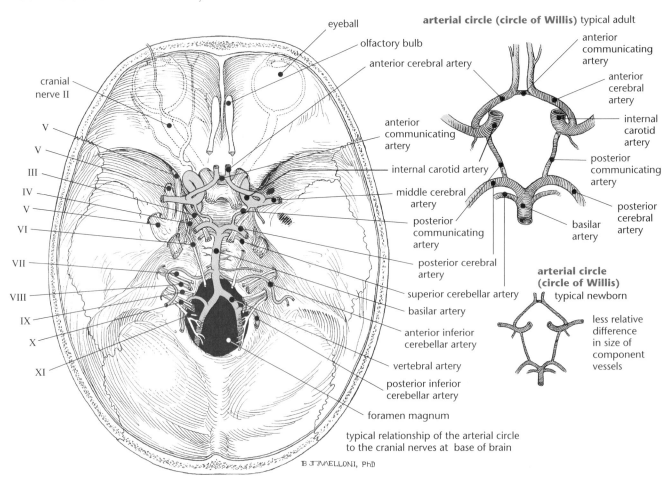

typical relationship of the arterial circle
to the cranial nerves at base of brain

circulation (ser-ku-la'shun) Movement through a circular course; unless otherwise specified, the term refers to blood circulation.

cerebrospinal fluid c. The circulation of the fluid that surrounds the brain and spinal cord; it is secreted by the choroid plexus within the ventricles of the brain; from there it passes through the median and lateral apertures of the fourth ventricle into the subarachnoid space, where it bathes the brain and spinal cord; when it reaches the arachnoid villi at the superior sagittal space above the brain, it drains into the blood, which then circulates to the choroid plexus, as well as throughout the body.

collateral c. Alternate circulation through small connecting blood vessels when the normally larger vessels are obstructed.

coronary c. The blood flow through the vessels supplying the heart muscle.

enterohepatic c. Normal passage of substances through the liver, into the bile, through the intestines, and back to the liver.

extracorporeal c. Temporary diversion of blood through a special machine that performs the function of an organ (e.g., through a heart-lung machine for oxygen–carbon dioxide exchange, or through an artificial kidney for dialysis).

fetal c. The blood circulating through the blood vessels of the fetus, carried to the placenta (by two arteries in the umbilical cord) and returned from the placenta to the fetus (by a vein in the umbilical cord).

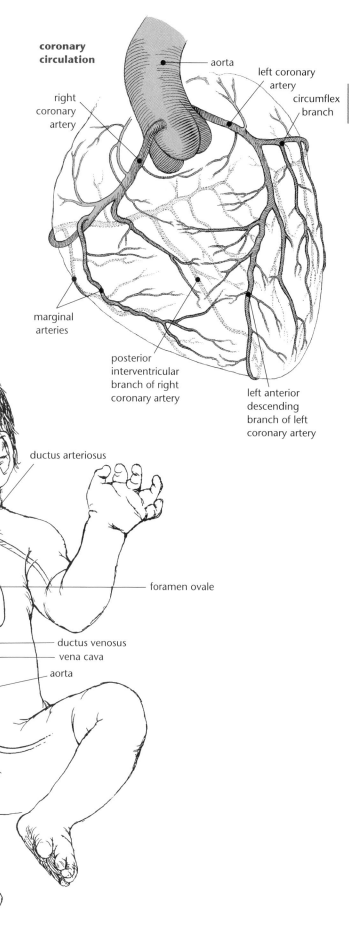

coronary circulation

aorta

left coronary artery

circumflex branch

right coronary artery

marginal arteries

posterior interventricular branch of right coronary artery

left anterior descending branch of left coronary artery

fetal circulation

ductus arteriosus

placenta

foramen ovale

umbilical vein

liver

ductus venosus

vena cava

aorta

umbilical arteries

near-term fetus

lymphatic c. The circulation of lymph from the tissue spaces to the circulating blood; it commences in minute blind channels in the spaces of many tissues of the body; contraction of surrounding muscles compresses the lymphatic channels, moving the lymph in the direction of the lymph nodes; from the lymph nodes, the lymph eventually reaches either the thoracic duct, which empties the lymph into the left subclavian vein, or the right lymphatic duct, which empties the lymph into the right subclavian vein; the greater part of the lymph is conveyed to the circulating blood by the thoracic duct, which drains from the entire body except the right thoracic cavity, right upper limb, and right side of the head and neck.

placental c. The flow of blood through the placenta which transfers oxygen and nutritive materials from mother to fetus and carbon dioxide and waste products from fetus to mother.

portal c. (a) The blood flow through the spleen, pancreas, stomach, and intestines, carried to the liver via the portal vein. (b) In general, any blood circulation between the capillary beds of two organs before the blood returns to the heart, as between the hypothalamus and pituitary (hypophysis) in the brain.

pulmonary c. The flow of blood from the heart, through the pulmonary artery and lungs, and back to the heart through the pulmonary veins.

systemic c. Blood circulation through the whole body.

third c. See twin-twin transfusion syndrome, under syndrome.

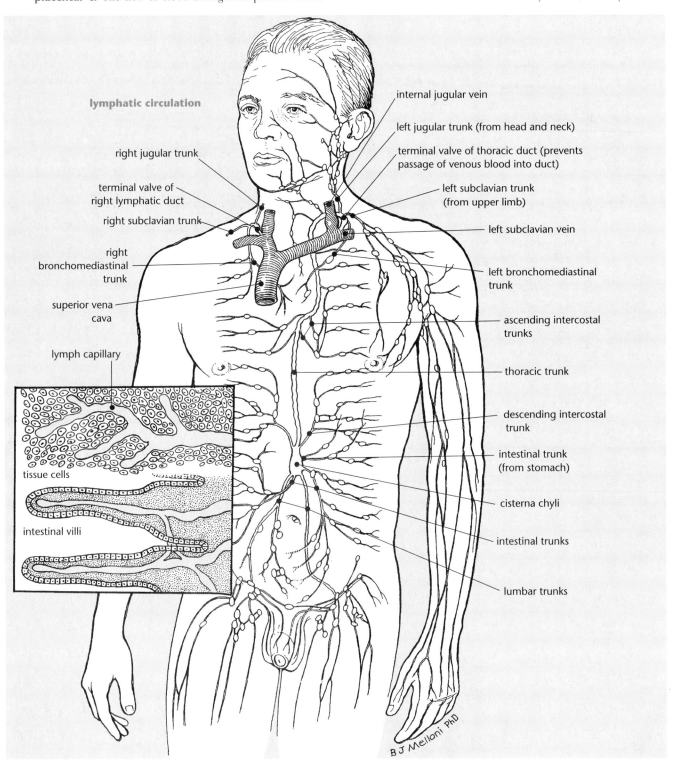

lymphatic circulation

internal jugular vein

left jugular trunk (from head and neck)

terminal valve of thoracic duct (prevents passage of venous blood into duct)

right jugular trunk

left subclavian trunk (from upper limb)

terminal valve of right lymphatic duct

left subclavian vein

right subclavian trunk

right bronchomediastinal trunk

left bronchomediastinal trunk

superior vena cava

ascending intercostal trunks

lymph capillary

thoracic trunk

descending intercostal trunk

tissue cells

intestinal trunk (from stomach)

cisterna chyli

intestinal villi

intestinal trunks

lumbar trunks

B J Melloni PhD

circulation ■ circulation

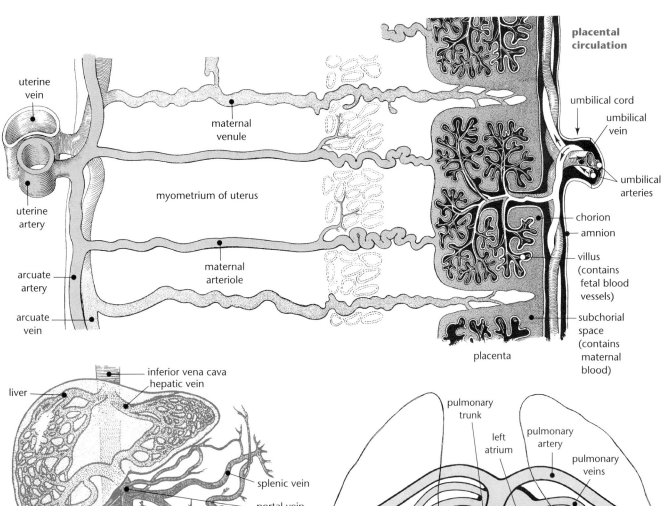

uterine vein

maternal venule

myometrium of uterus

uterine artery

arcuate artery

arcuate vein

maternal arteriole

placental circulation

umbilical cord

umbilical vein

umbilical arteries

chorion

amnion

villus (contains fetal blood vessels)

subchorial space (contains maternal blood)

placenta

liver

inferior vena cava
hepatic vein

splenic vein

portal vein

inferior mesenteric vein

superior mesenteric vein

portal circulation

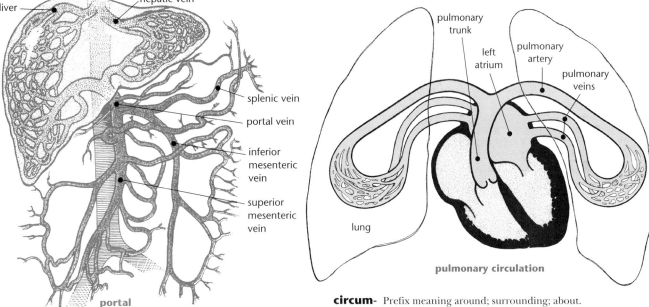

pulmonary trunk

left atrium

pulmonary artery

pulmonary veins

lung

pulmonary circulation

Yellin bell

dorsal incision of foreskin

circumcision

Yellin bell is placed over glans penis before tissue is

excised with a scalpel against the bell

foreskin

glans penis

circum- Prefix meaning around; surrounding; about.

circumanal (ser-kum-a'nal) See perianal.

circumcision (ser-kum-sizh'un) The cutting away of a circular portion of the foreskin of the penis.

circumduction (ser-kum-duk'shun) A circular movement, as of an eye or a limb.

circumflex (ser'kum-fleks) Arched.

circumnuclear (ser-kum-nu'kle-ar) Around a nucleus.

circumocular (ser-kum-ok'u-lar) Around an eye.

circumoral (ser-kum-o'ral) Around the mouth.

circumscribed (ser'kum-skrībd) Confined within boundaries or to a limited area.

circumstantiality (ser-kum-stan'she-al'ĭ-te) An indirect pattern of speech characterized by interpolation of excessive, tedious details (circumstances) and parenthetical remarks that delay reaching the point; observed in persons with obsessive-compulsive disorders.

circumvallate (ser-kum-val'āt) Surrounded by a ridge (e.g., a taste bud).

circumvolute (ser-kum-vo'lūt) Twisted around a central axis.

cirrhosis (sir-ro'sis) General term for any liver disease characterized by loss of the lobular architecture of the liver with formation of fibrous scars, nodules, and abnormal interconnections between arteries and veins; these abnormalities interfere with liver function and circulation. Symptoms may include appetite and weight loss, weakness, fatigue, diarrhea, and vomiting.

    alcoholic c. Cirrhosis characterized in its early stage by liver enlargement and fatty changes of liver cells throughout the entire organ; it slowly progresses to fat resorption, regeneration of small nodules, and scarring (Laennec's cirrhosis) with a fatal outcome; caused by long-term alcohol abuse.

    biliary c. Cirrhosis associated with long-standing obstruction of bile flow, which may occur within or outside the liver in the biliary ducts, resulting in an enlarged, firm, finely granular liver with a greenish color.

    cardiac c. Fibrosis of the central veins of the liver, without nodule formation, as seen in prolonged passive congestion of the liver from any cause.

    cryptogenic c. Cirrhosis usually of unknown cause, but may result from chronic viral hepatitis or from autoimmune liver disease.

    Laennec's c. See alcoholic cirrhosis.

    postnecrotic c. Cirrhosis of varied and sometimes unknown causes, most commonly resulting from viral or toxic hepatitis; characterized by large irregular nodules of regenerated or residual liver tissue, separated by broad scars.

    primary biliary c. (PBC) Cirrhosis of unknown cause, believed to be an autoimmune disease; characterized by fibrosis of bile ducts, progressive obstructive jaundice, high levels of blood cholesterol, hyperpigmentation of skin, and itching; it chiefly affects middle-aged women.

cirrhotic (sir-rot'ik) Relating to cirrhosis.

cis- **1.** Prefix meaning on this side. **2.** In genetics, prefix denoting the location of two genes on the same chromosome of a homologous pair.

cisapride (sis'ah-prīd) A drug used in the treatment of heartburn caused by esophageal reflux.

cisplatin (sis'plah-tin) A compound used in the treatment of cancer, especially of the testis and ovary; it may cause kidney damage.

cistern (sis'tern) In anatomy, an enclosed space, or a normal dilatation in a channel, containing fluids.

    cerebellomedullary c. The largest subarachnoid cistern, situated between the underside of the cerebellum and the medulla oblongata. Also called cisterna magna; cisterna cerebellomedullaris.

    chyle c. See cisterna chyli.

    subarachnoid c.'s The several enlargements of the space between two of the membranes covering the brain, the pia mater and arachnoid (subarachnoid space); formed where the arachnoid, crossing over prominences of the brain surface, diverges from the pia mater, which adheres to the brain contours. Also called cisternae subarachnoideales.

cisterna (sis-ter'nah), pl. cister'nae Latin for cistern.

    c. cerebellomedullaris See cerebellomedullary cistern, under cistern.

    c. chyli The saccular dilatation at the beginning of the thoracic duct, situated in front of the second lumbar vertebra, to the right of the abdominal aorta; it receives the right and left lumbar and intestinal lymphatic trunks. Also called chyle cistern; receptaculum chyli; lymphatic sac.

    c. magna See cerebellomedullary cistern, under cistern.

    cisternae subarachnoideales See subarachnoid cisterns, under cistern.

cisternal (sis-ter'nal) Relating to a cistern.

cisternogram (sis-ter'no-gram) A radiographic image obtained in cisternography.

cisternography (sis-ter-nog'rah-fe) The making of radiographic images of the ventricles of the brain for detection of certain types of hydrocephalus (e.g., normal pressure hydrocephalus) and to rule out cerebrospinal fluid leak; conducted by injecting a radioactive tracer substance into the subarachnoid space of the lower spine (in the lumbar region), then scanning the substance's flow into the cisterna of the brain.

cistron (sis'tron) The smallest hereditary unit of function (i.e., the portion of the DNA molecule that specifies a particular biochemical function).

citrate (sit'rāt) A salt of citric acid.

citrated (sit'rāt-ed) Containing a salt of citric acid.

citric acid (sit'rik as'id) The acid of citrus fruits; an important intermediate in the tricarboxylic acid (Kreb's) cycle.

Citrobacter (sit-ro-bak'ter) A genus of gram-negative bacteria (family Enterobacteriaceae); a variety of species cause infections of the alimentary and urinary tracts, neonatal meningitis, and opportunistic infections in debilitated persons.

clamp (klamp) An instrument for compressing a part or tissue.

    bulldog c. A small cross-action clamp for occluding cut blood vessels; the jaws are frequently covered with rubber tubing to prevent injury to the vascular wall. Also called bulldog forceps.

    Cope's c. Clamp used in the surgical removal of the colon and rectum.

clan (klăn) See kindred.

clap (klap) Slang for gonorrhea.

-clasia, -clasis Combining forms meaning disintegration; breaking up (e.g., osteoclasis).

clarificant (klar-if'i-kant) An agent that clears a liquid of turbidity.

clasp (klasp) In dentistry, one of the metal components of a partial denture, consisting of two elongated projections for encircling a natural tooth and stabilizing the denture.

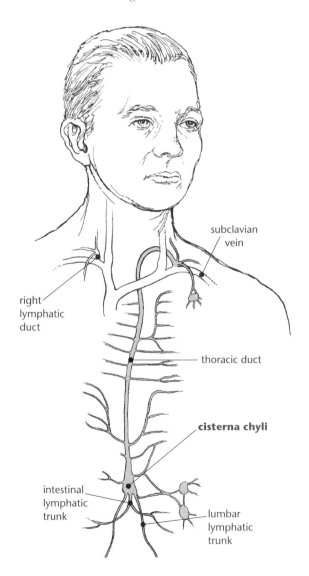

subclavian vein

right lymphatic duct

thoracic duct

cisterna chyli

intestinal lymphatic trunk

lumbar lymphatic trunk

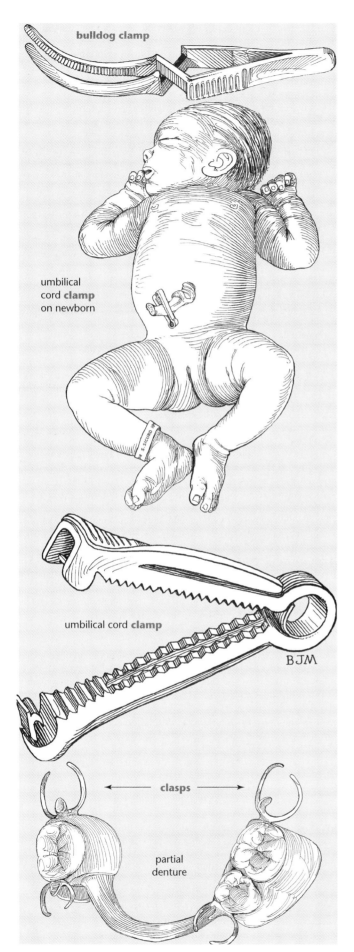

bulldog clamp

umbilical
cord **clamp**
on newborn

umbilical cord **clamp**

BJM

← **clasps** →

partial
denture

class (klas) A category of biological taxonomy ranking below phylum and above order.

classification (klas-sĭ-fĭ-ka'shun) A systematic grouping according to established criteria.

    Angle's c. Classification of dental malocclusion based on the anteroposterior (mesiodistal) position of upper and lower permanent molars.

    Ann Arbor staging c. A staging classification of Hodgkin's disease: *state I*, involvement of one lymph node region (I) or one extralymphatic site (I_E); *stage II*, involvement of two or more lymph node regions on the same side of the diaphragm (II), or one extralymphatic site and one or more lymph node regions on the same side of the diaphragm (II_E); *stage III*, involvement of lymph node regions on both sides of the diaphragm (III), which may be accompanied by localized involvement of one extralymphatic site (III_E), or the spleen (III_S), or both (III_{SE}); *stage IV*, diffused involvement of extralymphatic organs or tissues with or without lymph node enlargement. Each stage may be designated A or B, depending on presence or absence (respectively) of unexplained fever, night sweats, and loss of 10% body weight.

    Bethesda system of c. See Bethesda system of classification, under system.

    Caldwell-Moloy c. Classification of the female pelvis based on anteroposterior and transverse dimensions of the pelvic inlet.

    Duke's c. A classification of the degree of spread of colon carcinoma; modifications to the original have been made. Also called Duke's staging system.

    International C. of Disease–Clinical Modifications (ICD-CM) The standard designation for diseases used in record keeping and reporting; updated periodically.

    Lancefield c. Immunologic classification of streptococci into groups A through O, based on specific precipitin reactions. "Strep throats" are usually caused by group A streptococci.

    Lukes-Collins c. An immunologically based classification of non-Hodgkin's lymphomas according to the cell of origin (e.g., T cell, B cell, or histiocyte), and the correlation between the pattern of tumor cells and the appearance of normal lymphocytes after antigen challenge.

    Rappaport c. A morphologic classification of non-Hodgkin's lymphomas based on cytologic criteria (i.e., degree of differentiation of tumor cells and similarity between tumor cells and those of normal lymphoid tissues), and the growth pattern of tumor cells.

    Rye c. Classification of Hodgkin's disease into four subtypes, according to histologic features: lymphocyte predominant (LP), mixed cellularity (MC), lymphocyte depleted (LD), and nodular sclerosis (NS).

    Salter-Harris c. Classification of fractures through the end of a growing bone involving the growth plate; grouped into: *Type I*, transverse fracture of the growth plate; *Type II*, fracture of the growth plate and adjacent portion (metaphysis) of the bone shaft; *Type III*, fracture of the growth plate and the end (epiphysis) of the bone; *Type IV*, fracture along the long axis of the bone and crossing the growth plate; *Type V*, a crush or compacting fracture of the growth plate.

    working formulation c. Classification of non-Hodgkin's lymphomas into four major prognostic groups, based on survival statistics. *Low grade:* includes small lymphocytic cell lymphoma; follicular, small cleaved cell lymphoma; follicular, mixed small cleaved and large cell lymphoma. *Intermediate grade:* includes follicular, large cell lymphoma; diffuse, small cleaved cell lymphoma; diffuse, mixed small and large cell lymphoma; diffuse large cell lymphoma. *High grade:* includes large cell, immunoblastic lymphoma; lymphoblastic cell lymphoma; small noncleaved cell (Burkitt's) lymphoma. A miscellaneous group includes histiocytic lymphoma, some T-lymphomatous disorders involving the skin, and others.

    wrist fracture c. Classification of fractures of the distal ends of the radius and ulna, at the wrist; grouped into: *I*, fracture pattern; *II*, fracture extent; *III*, angulation; *IV*, displacement.

-clast Combining form meaning something that destroys (e.g., osteoclast).

clastic (klas′tik) Having a tendency to separate or divide into parts.

claudication (klaw-di-ka′shun) Limping, often accompanied by pain.

> **intermittent c.** Cramplike pain of the leg muscles, usually of the calf, brought on by walking and disappearing with rest; caused by insufficient blood to muscles due to narrowing of the arteries.

claustra (klaws′trah) Plural of claustrum.

claustrophobia (klaws-tro-fo′be-ah) Abnormal, exaggerated fear of being in a confined space.

claustrum (klaws′trum), pl. claus′tra A thin layer of gray matter in the brain, between the insula and lentiform nucleus; it is reciprocally connected with the cerebral cortex.

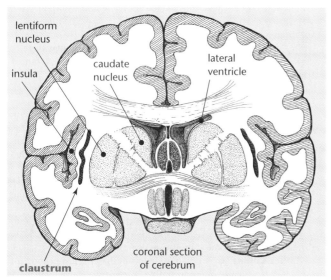

lentiform nucleus
insula
caudate nucleus
lateral ventricle
claustrum
coronal section of cerebrum

clava (kla′vah) See gracile tubercle, under tubercle.

clavicle (klav′ĭ-kl) See table of bones.

clavicotomy (klav-ĭ-kot′o-me) The cutting of a collarbone (clavicle), usually for gaining access to deeper structures.

clavicular (klah-vik′u-lar) Relating to the collarbone (clavicle).

clavus (kla′vus), pl. cla′vi Latin for corn.

clawfoot (klaw′fut) A foot deformity marked by an abnormally high longitudinal arch and a turning under of the toes. Also called pes cavus.

clawhand (klaw′hand) Permanent backward bending of the metacarpophalangeal joints connecting the base of the fingers to the hand, with curling of the fingers. Also called main en griffe.

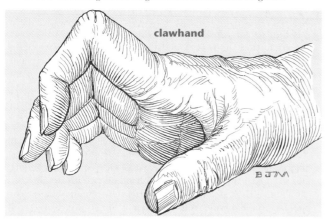

clawhand

clearance (klēr′ans) **1.** Removal of a substance from the body by an excretory organ (e.g., the kidney). **2.** The space between apposed structures (e.g., teeth). **3.** In toxicology, the rate at which a toxic agent is excreted, divided by the average concentration of the agent in the plasma. It is a measure of the volume of fluid that is freed of a toxic agent per unit time, rather than the amount of toxic substance removed.

cleavage (klēv′ij) **1.** The series of cell divisions immediately after fertilization of the egg and formation of the zygote; one of these divisions. **2.** The splitting of a molecule into simpler ones.

cleft (kleft) A groove or slit.

> **branchial c.'s** In mammalian embryology, a term loosely applied to bilateral ectodermal grooves (the equivalent of gills in aquatic animals); on rare occasions, they persist in the adult form as fistulas, sinus tracts, or cysts in the neck area.

> **synaptic c.** The extracellular space (usually between 200 and 300Å) between the pre- and postsynaptic surfaces of two nerve cells.

> **vulvar c.** The cleft between the major lips (labia majora) of the vulva. Also called rima pudendi; pudendal fissure; urogenital fissure.

cleidal (kli′dal) Relating to the collarbone (clavicle).

cleidocostal (kli-do-kos′tal) Relating to the collarbone (clavicle) and the ribs. Also spelled clidocostal.

-cleisis Suffix meaning closure (e.g., otocleisis).

click (klik) A sharp sound heard on auscultation of the heart.

> **ejection c.** A high-pitched sound occurring at the beginning of contraction of the heart chambers (systole); heard over the aorta or pulmonary trunk when these vessels are dilated.

> **mitral c.** The opening snap of the mitral (left atrioventricular) valve.

> **systolic c.** A sharp sound heard during contraction of the heart chambers (systole) due to a variety of reasons, including prolapse of the mitral (left atrioventricular) valve.

clidal (kli′dal) Relating to the collarbone (clavicle).

clido-, clid- Combining forms meaning collarbone (clavicle).

clidocostal (kli-do-kos′tal) See cleidocostal.

client (kli′ent) A person utilizing the services of a social agency.

> **involuntary c.** A person, such as an abusive or neglectful parent, who has been referred or court-ordered for services but who has not asked for help; such a client often denies that there is a problem and may resist assistance.

climacteric (kli-mak′ter-ik) A critical period in life when physiologic changes take place; known as menopause for women and male climacteric for men. Also called climacterium.

climacterium (kli-mak-te′re-um) See climacteric.

climatology (kli-mah-tol′o-je) The study of climate as it relates to disease.

climatotherapy (kli-mah-to-ther′ah-pe) The inclusion of favorable climate conditions in the treatment of disease.

climax (kli′maks) **1.** The stage of greatest severity in the course of a disease. **2.** Orgasm.

clinic (klin′ik) **1.** An institution, building, or part of a building where treatment is given to patients not requiring hospitalization. **2.** Medical instruction given to students in which patients are examined and treated in their presence. **3.** An establishment run by medical specialists working cooperatively.

> **pain c.** A clinic for the multidisciplinary or integrated approach to the management of pain.

clinical (klin′e-kl) **1.** Relating to the bedside observation of the course and symptoms of a disease. **2.** Relating to a clinic.

clinician (klĭ-nish′an) A practicing physician.

clinicopathologic (klin′e-ko-path-o-loj′ik) Relating to the symptoms and signs of a disease and the results of laboratory study of specimens obtained through biopsy or autopsy.

clinicopathologic conference A teaching conference during which a patient's disease is discussed; then the pathologic data are presented.

clinocephaly (kli-no-sef′ah-le) Congenital deformity in which the top of the skull is flat.

clinodactyly (kli-no-dak′tĭ-le) Permanent deflection (lateral or medial) of one or more fingers, usually the little finger.

clinoid (kli′noid) Resembling a bed; said of certain anatomic structures (e.g., the clinoid process of the sphenoid bone).

clinoscope (kli'no-skōp) Instrument for measuring the degree to which an eye tends to deviate (cyclophoria).

clip (klip) **1.** A device used in surgical procedures to approximate cut skin edges or to stop or prevent bleeding. **2.** A clasp.

   aneurysm c. Any of several noncrushing clips used in the surgical treatment of cerebral aneurysms; they usually have a spring mechanism that allows their removal, repositioning, and reapplication.

   towel c. A forceps for clipping towels to the skin at the edge of the operative field. Also called towel forceps.

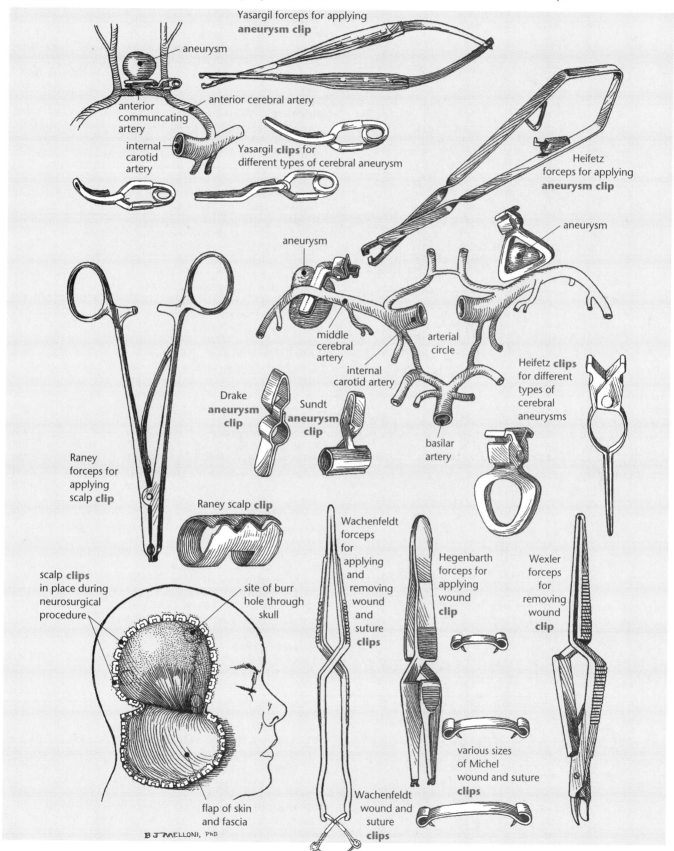

Yasargil forceps for applying **aneurysm clip**

aneurysm

anterior cerebral artery

anterior communcating artery

internal carotid artery

Yasargil **clips** for different types of cerebral aneurysm

Heifetz forceps for applying **aneurysm clip**

aneurysm

aneurysm

middle cerebral artery

internal carotid artery

arterial circle

basilar artery

Heifetz **clips** for different types of cerebral aneurysms

Raney forceps for applying scalp **clip**

Drake **aneurysm clip**

Sundt **aneurysm clip**

Raney scalp **clip**

scalp **clips** in place during neurosurgical procedure

site of burr hole through skull

flap of skin and fascia

Wachenfeldt forceps for applying and removing wound and suture **clips**

Wachenfeldt wound and suture **clips**

Hegenbarth forceps for applying wound **clip**

various sizes of Michel wound and suture **clips**

Wexler forceps for removing wound **clip**

B J MELLONI, PhD

clitoral (klit'o-ral) Relating to the clitoris.

clitoridectomy (klit-o-rĭ-dek'to-me) Surgical removal of the clitoris.

clitoris (klit'o-ris) An erectile organ of the female genitalia, partially enclosed between the anterior ends of the labia minora, just below the pubic symphysis; its free extremity (glans clitoris) is a small, rounded tubercle with a high degree of cutaneous sensitivity; it is homologous with the penis of the male.

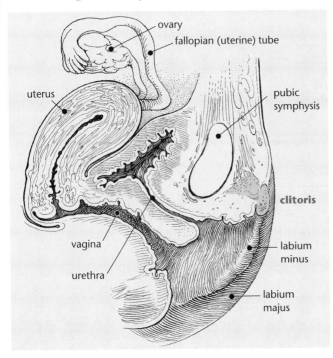

clitoromegaly (klit-o-ro-meg'ah-le) Enlargement of the clitoris.

clivus (kli'vus) The sloped area within the base of the skull, from the front of the foramen magnum to the dorsum sellae, formed by portions of the occipital and sphenoid bones; it supports the pons and medulla oblongata.

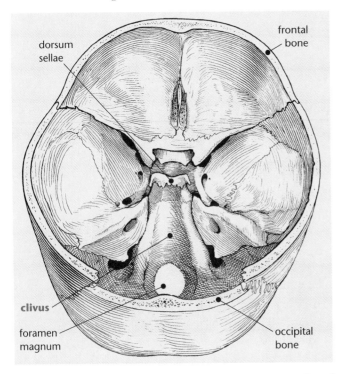

cloaca (klo-a'kah) In mammalian embryology, the common ending of the intestinal and genitourinary tracts of an early embryo.

clofibrate (klo-fi'brāt) A drug, administered orally, for the treatment of hypercholesterolemia and atherosclerosis to reduce high levels of fats in the blood.

clomiphene citrate (klo'mĭ-fēn ci'trāt) A nonsteroid compound that stimulates ovulation; used to treat infertility in women who fail to produce eggs (ova) and inadequate sperm formation in men; treatment of a woman may result in multiple births.

clonal (klōn'al) Relating to a clone.

clone (klōn) A group of cells, derived by mitosis from a single ancestral cell; all members of the clone have the same genetic information and are, therefore, nearly identical with the parental cell.

clonic (klon'ik) Relating to a clone.

clonicotonic (klon-e-ko-ton'ik) Denoting certain muscular spasms that alternate between rapid contractions and relaxations (clonic feature) and prolonged tension (tonic feature).

cloning (klōn'ing) **1.** The asexual development of a colony of genetically identical cells from a single cell (common ancestor) by repeated mitosis. **2.** Transportation of the nucleus of a somatic (body) cell to an ovum for the purpose of developing an embryo through sexual reproduction.

    gene c. The process of isolating a gene and making copies of it by inserting it into cells and allowing it to multiply.

clonorchiasis (klo-nor-ki'ah-sis) Disease caused by infection of the bile ducts with the liver fluke *Clonorchis sinensis;* transmitted to humans by ingestion of raw or undercooked freshwater fish infected with the fluke's larvae. Also called clonorchiosis.

clonorchiosis (klo-nor-ke-o'sis) See clonorchiasis.

Clonorchis sinensis (klo-nor'kis si-nen'sis) The Chinese or Oriental liver fluke; a species of trematodes (family Opisthorchiidae) that infect the bile ducts of humans and fish-eating animals.

clonus (klo'nus) Repeated reflex movements (i.e., alternating muscular contractions and relaxations occurring in rapid succession).

Clostridium (klo-strid'e-um) A genus of bacteria (family Bacillaceae) composed of gram-positive, anaerobic or aerotolerant, rod-shaped organisms commonly found in soil; some species cause putrefaction of proteins.

    C. bifermentans A species found in feces, sewage, and soil; some strains cause disease.

    C. botulinum A species that produces the botulinum toxin, the cause of food poisoning (botulism); there are six main types (A to F), each of which elaborates an immunologically distinct toxin; all but types C and D cause human illness.

    C. difficile A species found in the feces of human infants; it has been associated with pseudomembranous enterocolitis in patients receiving antibiotic therapy.

    C. histolyticum Species invading wounds and causing tissue necrosis. Formerly called *Bacillus histolyticus.*

    C. novyi A species associated with certain liver diseases.

    C. perfringens A species found in soil and milk; the causative agent of gas gangrene; may also cause intestinal conditions (enteritis, appendicitis) and infection in women within the first 24 hours after childbirth (puerperal fever) or after an abortion. Also called gas bacillus; Welch bacillus.

    C. septicum A species found in wound infections and sometimes in association with appendicitis.

    C. tetani A strictly anaerobic species that produces a toxin with affinity for motor nerve centers; the cause of tetanus or lockjaw.

closure (klo'shur) **1.** The act of closing or the state of being closed. **2.** The conclusion of a reflex pathway.

clot (klot) **1.** A thrombus or semisolid mass formed from a liquid. **2.** To form such a mass.

    blood c. An elastic mass containing fibrin, platelets, red blood cells (erythrocytes), and white blood cells; the product of whole blood coagulation.

clotrimazole (klo-trim'ah-zol) A compound used topically to treat fungal and yeast infections, especially candidiasis.

cloxacillin (kloks-ah-sil'in) A penicillin-type antibiotic used primarily to treat infections with certain types of staphylococcal bacteria.

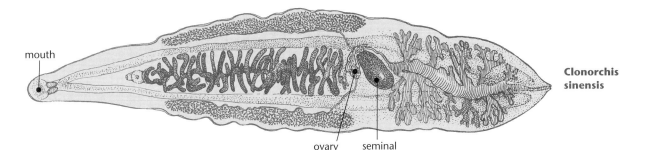

mouth

Clonorchis sinensis

ovary   seminal vesicle

clubbing (klub'ing) Enlargement of the terminal phalanx of the fingers or toes due to thickening of the base of the nail and loss of the angle between nail and nail bed; may be a sign of low oxygen levels in the blood; most common causes include such conditions as bronchiectasis, subacute bacterial endocarditis, atrial septal defect, right heart failure, pulmonary emphysema, and regional enteritis.

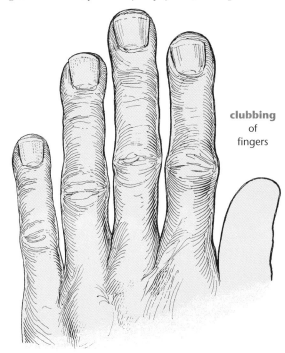

clubbing of fingers

clubfoot (klub'foot) See talipes equinovarus.
clump (klump) **1.** To form into clusters or a mass of individual entities. **2.** A mass so formed.
clumping (klump'ing) The clustering of bacteria or other cells suspended in a liquid.
-clysis Combining form meaning injection (e.g., phleboclysis).
clysis (kli'sis) Infusion of a fluid into the body, usually subcutaneously.
coaglutinin (ko-ah-gloo'tĭ-nin) A substance that causes aggregation or clumping of antigenic particles only in the presence of univalent antibody; by itself it does not cause aggregation.
coagulable (ko-ag'u-lah-bl) Susceptible to clotting.
coagulant (ko-ag'u-lant) **1.** Causing clotting. **2.** Any substance that causes clotting.
coagulate (ko-ag'u-lāt) To undergo or cause clotting.
coagulation (ko-ag-u-la'shun) **1.** The process of clot formation; clotting, especially of blood. **2.** A clot.
   disseminated intravascular c. (DIC) The presence of numerous widespread blood clots in minute blood vessels throughout the body, occurring as a complication of a variety of disorders; e.g., obstetric conditions (abruptio placentae, retained dead fetus in the uterus, septic abortion, amniotic fluid embolism), cancers, infectious diseases, massive trauma, extensive surgery and burns. Symptoms vary depending on the underlying disorder; may be acute (as in amniotic fluid embolism and major trauma) or chronic (as in retention of dead fetus and cancer); outcome also varies.

coagulative (ko-ag'u-la-tiv) Capable of causing clotting.
coagulopathy (ko-ag-u-lop'ah-the) Any disease that affects the blood-clotting mechanism.
   consumption c. A marked reduction of platelets and certain blood-clotting factors in the blood, resulting from utilization of platelets in excessive blood clotting throughout the body.
coagulum (ko-ag'u-lum), pl. coag'ula A blood clot.
coal tar (kōl' tar) A black, semisolid, sticky substance; a by-product of the destructive distillation of bituminous coal; used in ointments and shampoos to treat certain skin and scalp conditions.
coapt (ko-apt') To approximate two surfaces.
coaptation (ko-ap-ta'shun) The approximation of two surfaces, such as those of a broken bone.
coarct (ko-arkt') To constrict.
coarctation (ko-ark-ta'shun) A constriction, as of a blood vessel.
   adult c. of aorta Coarctation of the aorta in which the constricted segment of the vessel is just beyond the insertion of a normal, closed ductus arteriosus (ligamentum arteriosus); the condition occurs more frequently in males than in females. Also called postductal coarctation of aorta.
   c. of aorta A congenital defect of the large artery (aorta) leaving the left atrium of the heart; characterized by a localized narrowing of the vessel's lumen just beyond the point where the left subclavian artery branches off the aorta.

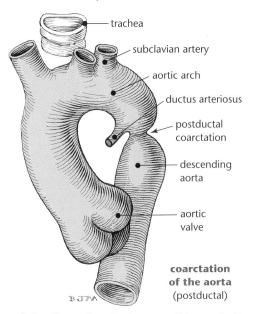

trachea
subclavian artery
aortic arch
ductus arteriosus
postductal coarctation
descending aorta
aortic valve

coarctation of the aorta (postductal)

   infantile c. of aorta A rare condition marked by extreme narrowing of a segment of the aorta just beyond the insertion of an abnormal (patent) ductus arteriosus. Also called preductal coarctation of aorta.
   postductal c. of aorta See adult coarctation of aorta.
   preductal c. of aorta See infantile coarctation of aorta.
coat (kōt) **1.** An enveloping sheath. **2.** A layer in the wall of a tubular structure.
   buffy c. (a) A cream-colored layer composed of white blood cells

and platelets covering the packed red blood cells (erythrocytes) of centrifuged blood. (*b*) A layer of similar composition plus fibrin, formed on a blood clot when coagulation is delayed so that red blood cells had time to settle.

cobalamin (ko-bal'ah-min) A cobalt-containing complex molecule of vitamin B_{12}.

cobalt (ko'bawlt) Metallic element; symbol Co, atomic number 27, atomic weight 58.94.

cobalt 60 A radioactive isotope of cobalt used as a source of gamma rays in place of radium in the treatment of cancer and in radiography.

coca (ko'kah) A shrub of the genus *Erythroxylon;* the source of cocaine and other alkaloids.

cocaine (ko'kān) A narcotic alkaloid extracted from coca leaves or synthesized from ergomine or its derivatives; when used habitually or in excess, it causes functional changes of the cardiovascular system, the central nervous system, the autonomic nervous system, and the gastrointestinal system, as well as psychosocial changes.

    crack c. The purified, potent form of cocaine; it is usually smoked (free-based), injected intravenously, or taken orally. Popularly called crack.

cocarcinogen (ko-kar-sin'o-jen) An agent that increases the activity of a cancer-producing substance.

cocci (kok'si) Plural of coccus.

Coccidia (kok-sid'e-ah) A subclass of protozoans (class Sporozoa); some are parasitic in the intestinal lining.

Coccidioides (kok-sid-e-oi'dēz) A genus of fungi occurring in soil of dry areas; one species, *Coccidioides immitis,* causes coccidioidomycosis.

coccidioidin (kok-sid-e-oi'din) A test solution containing the fungus *Coccidioides immitis,* used in intracutaneous skin testing for coccidioidomycosis.

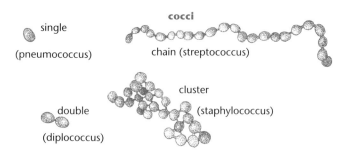

single (pneumococcus)

cocci

chain (streptococcus)

cluster (staphylococcus)

double (diplococcus)

coccidioidomycosis (kok-sid-e-oi-do-mi-ko'sis) Disease usually caused by inhalation of spores of the fungus *Coccidioides immitis;* it primarily affects the upper respiratory tract and the lungs. Also called desert fever; San Joaquin fever.

coccidiosis (kok-sid-e-o'sis) General term for diseases caused by any species of coccidium, a protozoan parasite.

coccobacillus (kok-o-bah-sil'us), pl. coccobacil'li An oval bacterium.

coccoid (kok'oid) Resembling a spherical bacterium (coccus).

coccus (kok'us), pl. coc'ci A spherical bacterium.

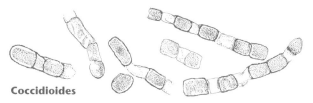

Coccidioides

coccyalgia (kok-se-al'je-ah) See coccygodynia.

coccydynia (kok-sĕ-din'e-ah) See coccygodynia.

coccygeal (kok-sij'e-al) Relating to the coccyx.

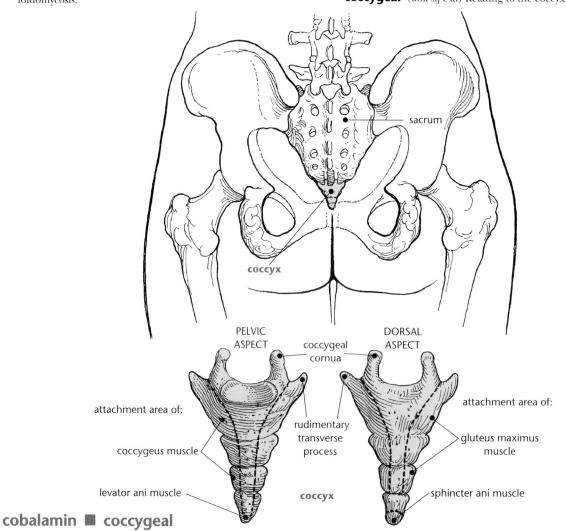

sacrum

coccyx

PELVIC ASPECT

coccygeal cornua

DORSAL ASPECT

attachment area of:

rudimentary transverse process

attachment area of:

coccygeus muscle

gluteus maximus muscle

levator ani muscle

coccyx

sphincter ani muscle

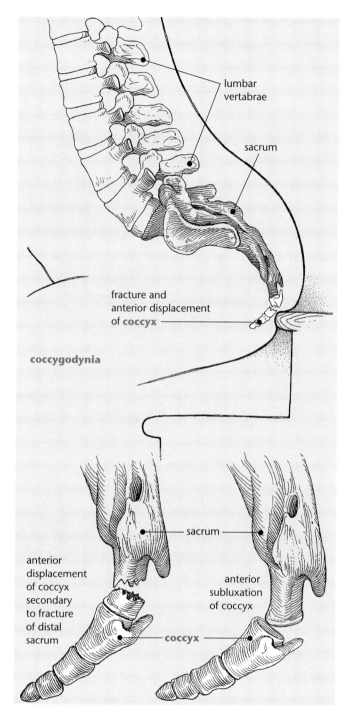

lumbar vertebrae

sacrum

fracture and anterior displacement of **coccyx**

coccygodynia

anterior displacement of coccyx secondary to fracture of distal sacrum

sacrum

coccyx

anterior subluxation of coccyx

coccyx

coccygectomy (kok-se-jek′to-me) Surgical removal of the coccyx.

coccygodynia (kok-se-go-din′e-ah) Pain at the tip of the spine (coccyx) usually caused by a fall upon the buttocks. Also called coccyalgia; coccydynia.

coccyx (kok′siks), pl. coc′cyges The three or four fused rudimentary vertebrae that form the lower end of the vertebral column. See also table of bones.

cochlea (kok′le-ah) The spiral channel of the internal ear that turns 2 3/4 times through dense bone at the base of the skull; it is divided lengthwise into three fluid-filled spaces: the scala vestibuli and scala tympani (filled with perilymph) and, between them, the cochlear duct (filled with endolymph), which contains the essential organ of hearing (spiral organ of Corti) and the terminal fibers of the cochlear nerve. The cochlea measures about 5 mm from base to apex; its base is about 9 mm wide. See also spiral organ of Corti, under organ.

cochlear (kok′le-ar) Relating to the cochlea.

cochleare magnum (kok-le-a′re mag′num) (coch. mag.) Latin for tablespoon.

cochleitis (kok-le-i′tis) See cochlitis.

cochleovestibular (kok′le-o-ves-tib′u-lar) Relating to the cochlea and the vestibule of the ear.

cochlitis (kok-li′tis) Inflammation of the cochlea. Also called cochleitis.

cocktail (kok′tāl) A fluid mixture of several ingredients.

    Brompton c. A drink containing cocaine hydrochloride and morphine hydrochloride, given orally as a pain reliever to patients who are dying of cancer. Also called Brompton mixture.

code (kōd) **1.** A system of symbols or characters devised to transmit information. **2.** A set of rules establishing a standard. **3.** To assign a standard designation (e.g., a number) to a disease or a medical procedure; the use of numbers for standard nomenclature facilitates epidemiologic surveys; the numerical coding for procedures is the basis of billing third parties for the services performed.

    c. blue A commonly used designation for the hospital resuscitation team or for the resuscitation procedure.

    genetic c. The pattern of three adjacent nucleotides in a DNA molecule that controls protein synthesis.

    c. red A commonly used emergency call designating a fire threat or alarm in an area of the hospital.

codeine (ko′dēn) A drug derived from opium; used to relieve mild to moderate pain and as a cough suppressant; adverse effects include dizziness, drowsiness, and dependence.

codominant (ko-dom′ĭ-nant) Of equal dominance; relating to the dominance of two genes that are equally expressed in the phenotype of an individual.

codon (ko′don) The set of three adjacent nucleotides in DNA or RNA that codes the insertion of one specific amino acid in the synthesis of a protein chain; the term is also used for the corresponding (and complementary) sequences of three nucleotides in messenger RNA into which the original DNA sequence is transcribed.

coefficient (ko-ĕ-fish′ent) The numerical expression of the change produced by variations of specified conditions, or of the ratio between two quantities.

coeno- Combining form meaning shared in common.

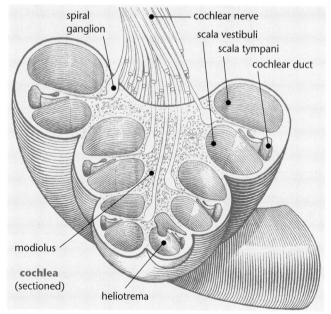

spiral ganglion

cochlear nerve

scala vestibuli

scala tympani

cochlear duct

modiolus

cochlea (sectioned)

heliotrema

coenzyme (ko-en′zīm) A nonprotein organic substance, produced by living cells, that plays an intimate role in the activation of enzymes.

    c. A (CoA) A widely distributed coenzyme containing adenine, ribose, pantothenic acid, and thioethanolamine; it plays an essential role in various metabolic reactions.

C

coeur (ker) French for heart.

    c. en sabot The characteristic x-ray appearance of the heart in tetralogy of Fallot; it resembles a wooden shoe.

cofactor (ko'fak-tor) An atom or molecule necessary to bring about the action of a large molecule.

cognition (kog-nish'un) **1.** The mental or intellectual process of obtaining knowledge, as contrasted with emotional processes. **2.** The product of this process. Also called comprehension; perception.

cohesion (ko-he'zhun) The force that holds molecules or particles together.

cohort (ko'hort) In epidemiology, a group of persons who share a designated characteristic and who are traced over an extended period of time. See also cohort study, under study.

coil (koil) Term commonly used for a type of intrauterine contraceptive device.

coin-counting (koin'kownt'ing) See pill-rolling tremor, under tremor.

coinsurance In medical insurance, a cost-sharing requirement of a health program that requires the enrollee to pay a percentage of the cost of specified covered services.

coital (ko'ĭ-tal) Relating to vaginal sexual intercourse.

coitus (ko'ĭ-tus) Vaginal sexual intercourse between man and woman.

    c. interruptus Withdrawal of the penis from the vagina just prior to ejaculation; used as a method of birth control. Also called onanism.

    c. reservatus Coitus in which ejaculation is intentionally delayed or suppressed.

cola (ko'lah) See kola nut.

colchicine (kol'chĭ-sīn) An alkaloid extracted from the autumn crocus (*Colchicum autumnale*); used in the treatment of gout and Mediterranean fever.

cold (kōld) The common cold; a contagious infection of the upper respiratory tract caused by any of several viruses; characterized by inflammation of the mucous membranes of the nose and throat, nasal discharge, sneezing, cough, and general malaise.

colectomy (ko-lek'to-me) Surgical removal of the colon, or of a portion of it.

coleo- Combining form meaning sheath or vagina.

colic (kol'ik) **1.** Relating to the colon. **2.** An acute abdominal pain.

    biliary c. Intense pain in the upper right area of the abdomen, usually caused by an impacted gallstone. Also called hepatic colic; gallstone colic.

    hepatic c. See biliary colic.

    gallstone c. See biliary colic.

    infantile c. Symptom complex of early infancy that tends to occur in the evenings; characterized by episodes of irritability, paroxysmal crying or screaming, and drawing up of the legs with apparent abdominal pain; during the episodes the infant does not respond to usual means of comforting.

    lead c. Abdominal pain occurring with lead poisoning.

    renal c. Severe pain caused by the impaction or passage of a kidney stone along the kidney pelvis or the slender tube (ureter) leading from the kidney to the bladder; the pain may be in the back, the flank, or the lower part of the abdomen.

coliform (ko'lĭ-form) General term denoting any bacteria inhabiting the intestinal tract or the large intestine, specifically the colon.

colitis (ko-li'tis) Inflammation of the colon, a part of the large intestine.

    granulomatous c. Colitis producing lesions in the wall of the colon similar to those seen in the small intestine in cases of regional enteritis.

    mucous c. See irritable bowel syndrome, under syndrome.

    pseudomembranous c. An acute form of colitis characterized by formation of a membrane-like substance (composed of gray-yellow inflammatory debris, fibrin, and mucosal elements) that cover eroded areas of intestinal lining; usually caused by toxin of the bacterium *Clostridium difficile*, especially in patients undergoing long-term antibiotic therapy; may also be caused by other infections.

    ulcerative c. A recurrent, chronic disease of uncertain cause, affecting primarily the rectum and adjacent colon; characterized by ulceration of the mucosa and submucosa; it causes lower abdominal pain and diarrhea with passage of blood and mucus in the stool.

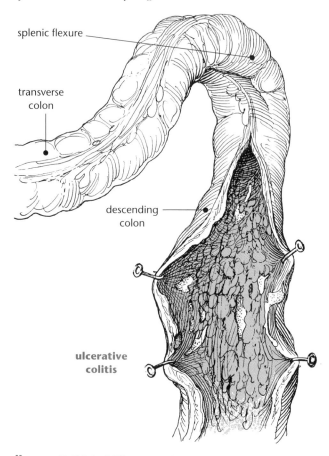

splenic flexure

transverse colon

descending colon

ulcerative colitis

collagen (kol'ah-jen) The supportive protein constituent of connective tissue.

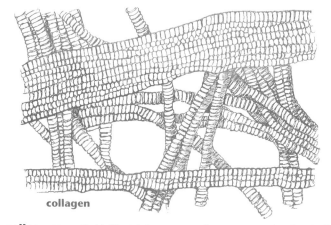

collagen

collagenase (kol-laj'ĕ-nās) Any enzyme that promotes the chemical breakdown of collagen.

collagenosis (kol-laj-ĕ-no'sis) See connective tissue diseases, under disease.

collapse (kŏ laps') **1.** A state of extreme prostration from physical or psychological cause. **2.** Abnormal falling in or caving in.

collar (kol'ăr) **1.** An encircling band. **2.** An anatomic structure that surrounds another. **3.** An encircling device.

    abrasion c. A reddish brown parchment surrounding the margin of a gunshot entrance wound; produced by the entering

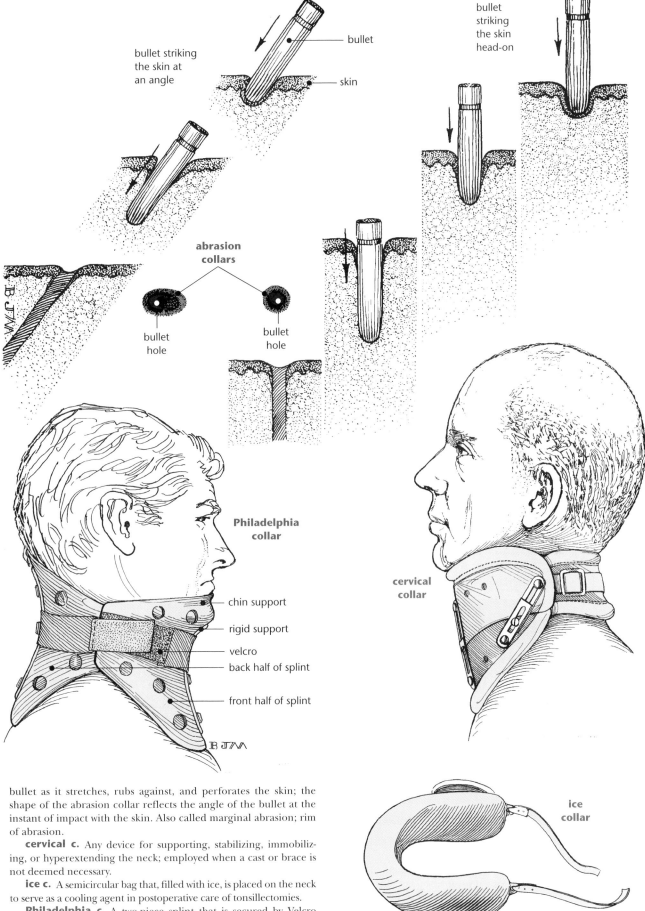

bullet striking the skin at an angle

bullet — bullet

skin

bullet striking the skin head-on

abrasion collars

bullet hole — bullet hole

Philadelphia collar

chin support

rigid support

velcro

back half of splint

front half of splint

cervical collar

ice collar

bullet as it stretches, rubs against, and perforates the skin; the shape of the abrasion collar reflects the angle of the bullet at the instant of impact with the skin. Also called marginal abrasion; rim of abrasion.

cervical c. Any device for supporting, stabilizing, immobilizing, or hyperextending the neck; employed when a cast or brace is not deemed necessary.

ice c. A semicircular bag that, filled with ice, is placed on the neck to serve as a cooling agent in postoperative care of tonsillectomies.

Philadelphia c. A two-piece splint that is secured by Velcro straps; used for rigid immobilization of the cervical spine.

collarbone (kol′ăr-bōn) See clavicle, in table of bones.

collateral (kŏ-lat′er-al) Secondary or alternate.

colliculitis (kŏ-lik-u-li′tis) See verumontanitis.

colliculus (kŏ-lik′u-lus), pl. collic′uli In anatomy, a small elevation.

    colliculi of midbrain Four rounded elevations behind the third ventricle, forming the roof (tectum) of the midbrain; designated as two superior and two inferior colliculi; they serve as reflex centers for auditory, visual, tactile, thermal, and pain impulses. Also called quadrigeminal bodies; corpora quadrigemina.

    c. seminalis See verumontanum.

colligative (kol′ĭ-ga-tiv) A term denoting properties of solutions that depend on the number of particles present and not on the nature of those particles.

collimation (kol-lĭ-ma′shun) In radiology, restricting the peripheral spread of the x-ray beam; in nuclear medicine, restricting detection of emitted radiation from a given area.

collimator (kol-ĭ-ma′tor) A device (e.g., a cone or lead shutters) attached to an x-ray tube to limit the width of the x-ray beam to the area of interest.

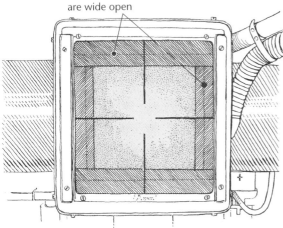

The shutters of the **collimator** are wide open

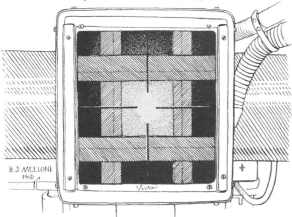

The shutters of the **collimator** are adjusted to restrict the x-ray beam to the area of diagnostic interest

colliquation (kol-ĭ-kwa′shun) Disease process in which tissue degenerates into a liquid or semiliquid form.

colliquative (kŏ lik′wah-tiv) **1.** Characterized by excessive fluid discharge. **2.** Characterized by liquid degeneration of tissues.

collodion (ko-lo′de-on) A flammable solution of pyroxylin in ether and alcohol, which dries to a thin transparent film; useful in sealing the edge of a dressing. Also called collodium.

collodium (ko-lo′de-um) Collodion.

colloid (kol′oid) **1.** A substance (e.g., gelatin) consisting of a fine dispersion of submicroscopic particles throughout a continuous medium. **2.** A translucent, yellowish, gelatinous material found in tissues in a state of degeneration. Also called colloidin. **3.** The substance stored within follicles of the thyroid gland.

colloidin (ko-loi′din) See colloid (2).

collum (kol′lum), pl. col′la In anatomy, any necklike structure.

colo- Combining form meaning colon.

coloboma (kol-o-bo′mah) Any abnormal cleft, notch, or indentation in any structure, especially structures of the eye, occurring as a developmental defect.

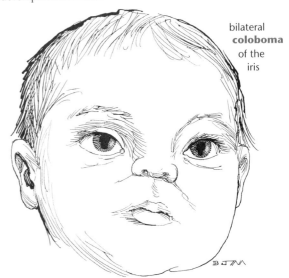

bilateral **coloboma** of the iris

colocolic (ko-lo-kol′ik) Relating to two separate parts of the colon; said of a surgical joining, or an abnormal fistular connection.

cololysis (ko-lol′ĭ-sis) Surgical freeing of the colon from abnormal adhesions that fix it to the abdominal wall or to other organs.

colon (ko′lon) The part of the large intestine between the cecum and the rectum.

    ascending c. The part of the colon extending upward toward the liver on the right side of the abdomen, from the cecum to the right colic flexure.

    descending c. The part of the colon extending downward on the left side of the abdomen, from the left colic flexure to the pelvic brim.

    irritable c. See irritable bowel syndrome, under syndrome.

    lead pipe c. The x-ray appearance of the colon in ulcerative colitis (i.e., contracted, rigid, and scarred).

    sigmoid c. The S-shaped, terminal portion of the colon, situated in the pelvis between the descending colon and the rectum.

    spastic c. See irritable bowel syndrome, under syndrome.

    transverse c. The relatively horizontal portion of the colon, crossing the abdomen between the right and left colic flexures.

colonic (ko-lon′ik) Relating to the colon.

colonization (kol-ŏ nī-za′shun) The establishment of a compact group of the same type of microorganisms at a site of implantation.

colonorrhagia (ko-lon-o-ra′je-ah) See colorrhea.

colonorrhea (ko-lon-o-re′ah) See colorrhea.

colonoscopy (ko-lon-os′ko-pe) Visual examination of the interior of the colon by means of a long, flexible fiberoptic instrument (colonoscope).

colony (kol′o-ne) A compact mass of microorganisms growing in a solid medium, presumably arising from a single microorganism.

    M c. See mucoid colony.

    mucoid c. A colony (usually virulent) with a well-developed sticky carbohydrate capsule that may act as a defense mechanism. Also called M colony.

    R c. See rough colony.

    rough c. A nonvirulent, or slightly virulent, granular colony with a wrinkled, flat surface and irregular margins. Also called R colony.

    S c. See smooth colony.

    smooth c. A colony with a round, glistening, even surface; some capsule-forming species have some degree of virulence. Also called S colony.

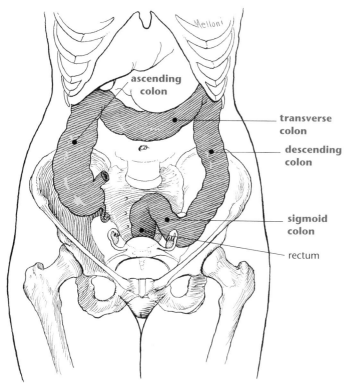

ascending colon

transverse colon

descending colon

sigmoid colon

rectum

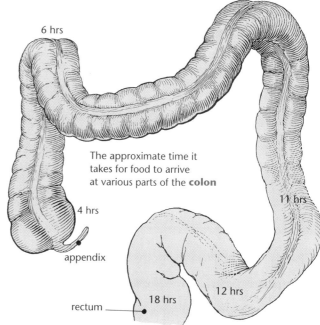

6 hrs

The approximate time it takes for food to arrive at various parts of the **colon**

4 hrs

appendix

11 hrs

12 hrs

rectum

18 hrs

coloproctitis (ko-lo-prok-ti'tis) Inflammation of the colon and rectum. Also called proctocolitis; colorectitis; rectocolitis.

color (kul'or) Visual perception characterized by the attributes of hue, saturation, and brightness, arising from stimulation of the retina by light.

colorectal (kol-o-rek'tal) Relating to the colon and rectum.

colorectitis (ko-lo-rek-ti'tis) See coloproctitis.

colorimetry (kul-or-im'ĕ-tre) The quantitative chemical analysis of a solution by color comparison with a standard solution.

colorrhagia (ko-lo-ra'je-ah) Abnormal discharge originating from the colon. Also called colonorrhagia.

colorrhea (ko-lo-re'ah) Diarrhea thought to originate in the colon. Also called colonorrhea.

colostomy (ko-los'to-me) The surgical establishment of an opening (stoma) into the colon through the abdominal wall to allow evacuation of intestinal contents.

colostrorrhea (ko-los-tro-re'ah) A copious discharge of colostrum.

colostrum (kŏ-los'trum) A sticky yellowish fluid produced by the breasts during late pregnancy and the first few days after delivery; it contains less fat and sugar, and more minerals and proteins, than milk; it is rich in a certain type of white blood cells (lymphocytes) and antibodies (immunoglobulins), which help protect the newborn from infection. Popularly called foremilk.

colotomy (ko-lot'o-me) A surgical cut into the colon.

colpatresia (kol-pah-tre'se-ah) Occlusion of the vagina.

colpectomy (kol-pek'to-me) Surgical removal of the vagina.

colpo-, colp- Combining forms meaning vagina.

colpocele (kol'po-sel) 1. A hernia protruding into the vagina. Also called vaginocele. 2. See colpoptosis.

colpocleisis (kol-po-kli'sis) Suturing of the vaginal canal to obliterate its lumen.

colpocystocele (kol-po-sis'to-sēl) See cystocele.

colpodynia (kol-po-din'e-ah) See vaginodynia.

colpohysterectomy (kol-po-his-ter-ek'to-me) See vaginal hysterectomy, under hysterectomy.

colpomicroscope (kol-po-mi'kro-skōp) A high-powered microscope, especially designed for insertion into the vagina, for direct examination of cells and tissues of the cervix *in situ*.

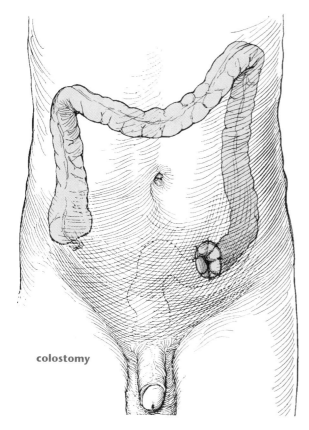

colostomy

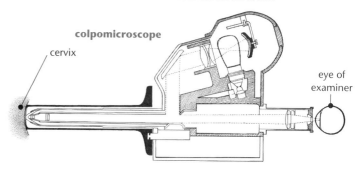

colpomicroscope

cervix

eye of examiner

coloproctitis ■ colpomicroscope

colpomicroscopy (kol-po-mi-kros′ko-pe) Examination of cells of the cervix by means of a colpomicroscope.

colpoperineorrhaphy (kol-po-per-ĭ-ne-or′ah-fe) Surgical repair and reinforcement of a lacerated vagina and musculature of the pelvic floor. Also called vaginoperineorrhaphy.

colpopexy (kol′po-pek-se) See vaginopexy.

colpoplasty (kol′po-plas-te) See vaginoplasty.

colpopoiesis (kol-po-poi-e′sis) Surgical construction of a vagina, when none exists, by dissection and insertion of a split-thickness graft.

colpoptosis (kol-po-to′sis) Prolapse of the vagina. Also called colpocele.

colporrhaphy (kol-por′ah-fe) The suturing of a vaginal tear.

colporrhexis (kol-po-rek′sis) Laceration or tearing of the vagina.

colposcope (kol′po-skōp) A low-powered microscope with a built-in light source for examination of the vagina and cervix under magnification.

colposcopy (kol-pos′ko-pe) Visualization of the cervical and vaginal tissues under magnification by means of a colposcope; performed after obtaining a positive Pap test or to evaluate suspicious lesions.

colpospasm (kol′po-spazm) See vaginismus.

colpostat (kol′po-stat) An intracavitary applicator containing radioactive material used in local irradiation of a gynecologic cancer.

colpostenosis (kol′po-stĕ-no′sis) Abnormal narrowing of the vaginal lumen.

colpotomy (kol-pot′o-me) Incision through the vaginal wall (e.g., to drain a pelvic abscess). Also called vaginotomy.

colpoxerosis (kol-po-ze-ro′sis) Abnormal dryness of the vaginal lining (mucous membrane).

columella (kol-u-mel′lah), pl. columel′lae In anatomy, a small column.

column (kol′um) A cylindrical, pillar-shaped structure.

anterior gray c. of spinal cord The anterior (ventral) column of gray matter extending along either side of the anterior median fissure of the spinal cord; it is broad and short and does not reach the surface of the spinal cord; it consists of cell bodies and dendrites of spinal neurons and the axons and axon terminals emerging from them or ending upon them; it contains motor neurons that innervate the skeletal muscles and the infrafusal muscle fibers of neuromuscular spindles of the neck, trunk, and limbs. Also called ventral gray column of spinal cord.

dorsal gray c. of spinal cord See posterior gray column of spinal cord.

lateral gray c. of spinal cord The column of gray matter between the anterior and posterior columns of the spinal cord on either side; it is a small, angular projection that extends only from the second thoracic to the first lumbar segments of the spinal cord.

posterior gray c. of spinal cord The posterior (dorsal) column of gray matter extending along either side of the spinal cord; it is transversely narrow and extends almost to the surface of the spinal cord near the posterolateral sulcus; it is composed of groups of motor neurons extending the entire length of the spinal cord, as well as some limited to the thoracic and upper lumbar segments. Also called dorsal gray column of spinal cord.

spinal c. See vertebral column.

ventral gray c. of spinal cord See anterior gray column of spinal cord.

vertebral c. The arrangement of vertebrae, from just below the skull through the coccyx, that encloses and provides flexible support to the spinal cord. Also called backbone; spinal column; spine.

coma (ko′mah) A state of deep, sustained pathologic unconsciousness resulting from dysfunction of the ascending reticular activating (arousal) system in either the brainstem or both cerebral hemispheres; the patient cannot be aroused; the eyes remain closed. The condition must persist for at least an hour to be clearly distinguished from syncope, concussion, or other states of transient unconsciousness. See also stupor; persistent vegetative state.

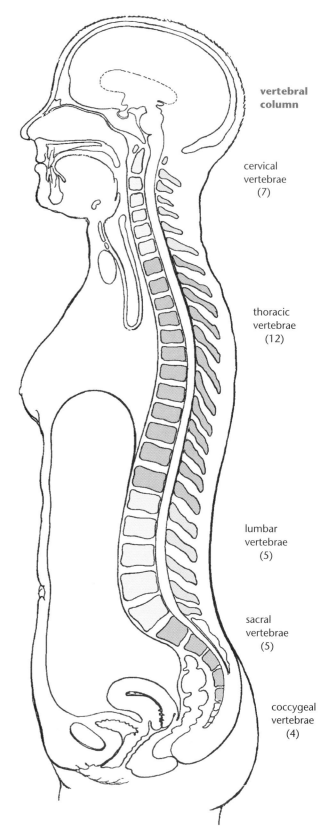

vertebral column

cervical vertebrae (7)

thoracic vertebrae (12)

lumbar vertebrae (5)

sacral vertebrae (5)

coccygeal vertebrae (4)

diabetic c. Coma occurring almost exclusively in type I (insulin-dependent) diabetes as a result of severe diabetic ketoacidosis. See also hyperosmolar nonketotic coma; hypoglycemic coma.

hepatic c. Coma occurring in the final stages of cirrhosis of the liver, hepatitis, poisoning, or other liver disease; may be preceded by confusion or delirium and accompanied by jaundice.

hyperosmolar nonketotic c. Coma occurring in diabetic persons with a high concentration of sugar (glucose) in the blood (but without formation of ketone bodies); it is a complication of therapy that results chiefly from dehydration of brain cells due to sustained excessive urination and insufficient water intake, which does not keep up with urinary fluid losses. Commonly occurs in elderly persons with uncontrolled diabetes who develop a stroke or an infection and in whom fluid intake may be inadequate. Other causes include tube feedings of high-protein formulas, peritoneal dialysis, and high carbohydrate intake. It is associated with a high mortality rate.

hypoglycemic c. Coma occurring in persons with type I (insulin-dependent) diabetes mellitus when the blood sugar (glucose) level becomes excessively low; it occurs most frequently when the usual daily schedule of insulin injections is given and one or more meals is missed or lost by vomiting.

comatose (ko′mah-tōs) In a state of coma.

combustion (kom-bust′yun) Burning; a chemical change with emission of heat.

comedo (kom′ĕ-do), pl. com′edos, comedo′nes A plug of oxidized sebaceous material obstructing the opening of a hair follicle. Also called blackhead.

comedocarcinoma (kŏ-me-do-kar-sĭ-no′mah) Carcinoma of the breast, filling and plugging the milk (lactiferous) ducts with a necrotic substance that can be expressed with slight pressure.

comes (ko′mēz), pl. com′ites A blood vessel (artery or vein) accompanying another blood vessel or nerve.

commensal (kŏ-men′sal) Denoting two organisms living together, one benefitting from the association, the other being neither benefitted nor harmed.

commensalism (kŏ-men′sal-izm) A relationship between two living organisms in which one benefits from the association while the other remains unaffected.

comminuted (kom′ĭ-nūt-ed) Broken into several small pieces, such as a type of bone fracture.

comminution (kom-ĭ-nu′shun) 1. The process of breaking into small pieces. 2. The condition of being broken into small pieces.

commissure (kom′ĭ-shūr) 1. A bundle of nerve fibers, in the brain or spinal cord, that pass from one side to the other across the midline. 2. An angle formed by the eyelids, the lips, or the labia.

anterior c. of brain. A bundle of white fibers crossing the midline of the brain in front of the ventricles.

posterior c. of brain A bundle of white fibers crossing the midline of the brain posterior to the third ventricle, at its junction with the cerebral aqueduct.

commissurotomy (kom-ĭ-shūr-ot′o-me) Surgical division of a commissure.

mitral c. Surgical separation of an abnormally fused leaflet of a mitral (left atrioventricular) valve of the heart; performed for the relief of mitral stenosis.

commitment (kŏ-mit′ment) The legal process of placing or the placement of a person found to be suffering from a severe mental disorder into a mental health facility or under another form of protective custody.

commotio retinae (kŏ-mo′she-o ret′ĭ-ne) See Berlin's traumatic edema, under edema.

communicable (kŏ-mu′nĭ-kah-bl) Capable of being transmitted from one organism to another; said of diseases.

Communicable Disease Center Former name of the Centers for Disease Control and Prevention.

communicans (kŏ-mu′nĕ-kanz), pl. communican′tes A structure, such as a nerve, that connects two others.

communication (kŏ-mu-nĭ-ka′shun) 1. The transmission of ideas, attitudes, or beliefs between individuals or groups by any means, including speech, sign language, gestures, facial expressions, touching, writing, etc. 2. The information transmitted. 3. In anatomy, an access or connecting passage between two structures.

confidential c. Personal and private information received in the course of a confidential relationship (e.g., psychotherapist-patient and physician-patient relationships) that the recipient cannot be forced to divulge (e.g., to employer, insurance company, attorney, or in judicial proceedings) without the consent of the client or patient, except as defined by the applicable laws of the jurisdiction. Most legal systems require physicians to override confidentiality in certain cases (e.g., certain infectious and sexually transmitted diseases and suspected cases of child abuse or neglect).

comorbidity (ko-mor-bid′ĭ-te) The simultaneous presence of more than one pathologic condition in one individual.

compatible (kom-pat′ĭ-bl) 1. Denoting two drugs that can be administered simultaneously without nullifying the effects of either. 2. Denoting two samples of blood in which the serum of each does not clump (agglutinate) the red blood cells of the other.

compensation (kom-pen-sa′shun) 1. The process of offsetting a structural or functional defect. 2. A defense mechanism by which a person, consciously or unconsciously, attempts to make up for real or imagined deficiencies. 3. Payment that is intended to amend for, or offset, the damage suffered by a claimant; indemnification; to restore the claimant to former position.

compensatory (kom-pen′sah-to-re) Serving to make up for a deficiency or loss.

competence (kom′pĕ-tens) 1. The ability of an organ or part to perform a required function (e.g., the ability of a heart valve to close so as to prevent leakage of blood from one heart chamber to another). 2. The ability of embryonic cells to respond in a characteristic manner to the stimulus of an organizer. 3. The ability of a bacterial cell to take up DNA. 4. In psychiatry, the state of being capable of adult functioning and rational decision making.

competency (kom′pĕ-ten-se) The condition of being legally qualified or eligible to participate in a judicial proceeding (e.g., participating as a witness and supplying testimony, including written evidence).

c. to stand trial The ability of a defendant to understand the nature of the charges against him, to distinguish between pleas of guilty and not guilty, to understand consequences that may result from his conviction, to assist and instruct counsel in preparing a defense, and to challenge a witness.

competition (kom-pĕ-tish′un) The process by which a substance inhibits the activity of another, structurally similar, substance.

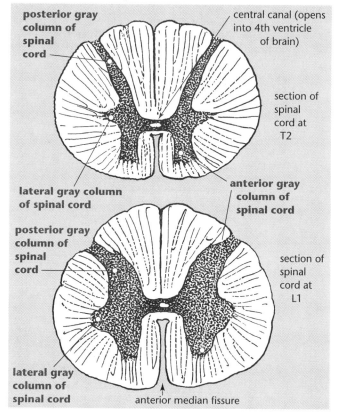

posterior gray column of spinal cord

central canal (opens into 4th ventricle of brain)

section of spinal cord at T2

lateral gray column of spinal cord

anterior gray column of spinal cord

posterior gray column of spinal cord

section of spinal cord at L1

lateral gray column of spinal cord

anterior median fissure

complaint (kom-plānt') A symptom or discomfort as reported by a patient.

chief c. (C.C.) The symptom that prompted the patient to seek medical treatment; the presenting symptom.

complement (kom'plĕ-ment) (C) A group of proteins present in normal serum that become involved in the control of inflammation, the activation of phagocytes (cells that engulf nonself particles, bacteria, and other cells), and the destructive attack on cell membranes; the reaction of the complement system can be activated by the immune system.

c. component In immunology, any of the nine proteins participating in the sequential activities of complement (complement cascade); each complement component takes its turn in the precise chain steps set in motion (like a domino effect) when the first protein in the complement series is activated; complement components are named on the basis of functional activity by the symbols C1 through C9.

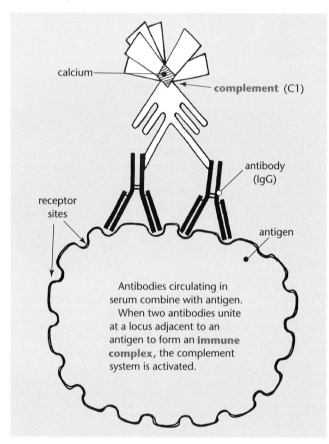

Antibodies circulating in serum combine with antigen. When two antibodies unite at a locus adjacent to an antigen to form an **immune complex**, the complement system is activated.

complex (kom'pleks) **1.** A collection of interrelated parts or factors. **2.** In psychiatry, a group of associated ideas that have a strong emotional tone, the core of which are unconscious, and which powerfully influence the personality. **3.** In electrocardiography, a group of deflections corresponding to a part of the heart cycle.

AIDS-related c., ARC A group of symptoms and signs representing a stage in the course of AIDS (i.e., manifestation of AIDS before the body is attacked by the pathogens of such opportunistic diseases as *Pneumocystis carinii* pneumonia, Kaposi's sarcoma, and others). See also AIDS.

atrial c. The portion of the electrocardiogram (ECG) representing electrical activation of the atria; the P wave.

brain wave c. A combination of fast and slow electrical activities of the brain that recur often enough to be recognized as a discrete phenomenon.

castration c. Fear of injury to the genitals as punishment for forbidden sexual desires. Also called castration anxiety.

Eisenmenger's c. The combination of a developmental heart defect in which there is a hole in the wall separating the two ventricles of the heart (septal defect) and the resulting right-to-left shunt of blood causing high blood pressure in the pulmonary arteries (pulmonary hypertension).

Ghon c. See primary complex.

Golgi c. A cytoplasmic organelle composed of an assembly of vesicles and folded membranes near the cell nucleus, involved in the intracellular transport of secretory products (such as enzymes and hormones) and in formation of the cell wall. Also called Golgi apparatus.

immune c. A complex composed of antigen and antibody molecules bound together in a lattice; it may also contain proteins of the complement system.

inferiority c. A feeling of personal inferiority due to real or imagined physical or social inadequacies; manifested by extreme shyness or timidity or by overcompensation through excessive ambition or aggressiveness.

juxtaglomerular c., j-g c. See juxtaglomerular apparatus, under apparatus.

major histocompatibility c. (MHC) A cluster of closely linked genetic regions (loci) on chromosome 6 coding for cell proteins that contain the major histocompatibility antigens; it is the chief determinant of tissue type and transplant compatibility.

membrane attack c. In immunology, the complex of complement components C5 through C9 that creates a hole in the membrane of cells or bacteria, allowing passage of water and small solutes and causing the cell to swell and burst. See also complement component, under complement.

Mycobacterium avium c. (MAC) See *Mycobacterium avium* complex, under *Mycobacterium*.

Oedipus c. The natural strong attachment of a child to the parent of the opposite sex, accompanied by aggressive feelings toward

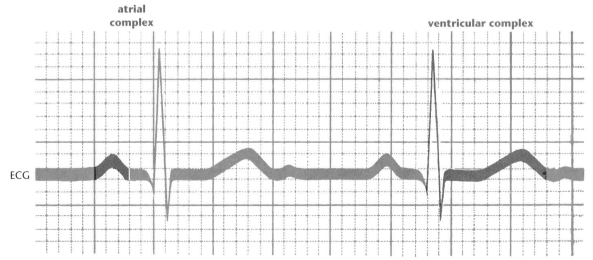

atrial complex

ventricular complex

ECG

the parent of the same sex, usually occurring between three and six years of age; the feelings are largely repressed because of fear of punishment by the parent of the same sex, who is regarded as a rival.

oocyte-cumulus-corona c. (OCCC) In *in vitro* fertilization, the entirety of the egg and its accompanying coverings harvested from the ovary.

persecution c. A feeling that one's well-being is being threatened, without any basis in reality.

primary c. The combination of lung and lymph node granulomatous inflammation, occurring in primary childhood tuberculosis, in a child who has not been previously exposed to the *Mycobacterium tuberculosis*. Also called Ghon complex.

QRS c. The deflection in the electrocardiogram (ECG) representing ventricular contraction of the heart.

spike and wave c. A complex in the electroencephalogram (EEG) consisting of a dart and a dome wave, usually occurring in petit mal seizures.

superiority c. Exaggerated self-assertion and aggressiveness representing an overcompensation for feelings of inferiority.

ventricular c. The QRS wave in the electrocardiogram (ECG) representing depolarization of the ventricles.

complexion (kom-plek'shun) The general appearance of the skin of the face.

compliance (kom-pli'ans) **1.** The quality of yielding to pressure. **2.** A measure of the ease with which an air- or fluid-filled organ may be distended. **3.** A patient's disposition to follow a specific regimen prescribed by a physician or any other health professional.

lung c. Distensibility of the lung, measured as the pressure required per unit increase of lung volume.

component (kom-po'nent) A constituent part of the whole. See also complement component, under complement.

composition (kom-po-zish'un) In chemistry, the groups of atoms forming the molecule of a substance.

compos mentis (kom'pos men'tis) Latin term meaning sound mind.

compound (kom'pownd) **1.** A substance composed of two or more chemical elements. **2.** A pharmaceutical preparation containing a mixture of drugs.

acyclic c. An organic compound in which the chain of atoms does not form a ring. Also called open-chain compound.

aromatic c. A cyclic compound.

closed-chain c. See cyclic compound.

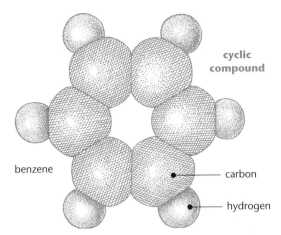

cyclic compound

benzene — carbon — hydrogen

cyclic c. Any compound that has atoms linked in the form of a ring. Also called ring compound; closed-chain compound.

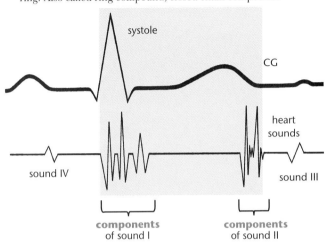

systole
CG
heart sounds
sound IV
sound III
components of sound I
components of sound II

composition of living cells (major elements)

element	O	C	H	N	Ca	P	K	Total
composition by weight (%)	65	18	10	3	1.5	1.0	0.35	98.85

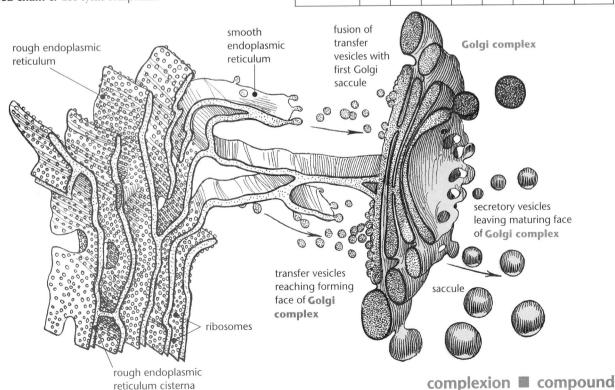

rough endoplasmic reticulum

smooth endoplasmic reticulum

fusion of transfer vesicles with first Golgi saccule

Golgi complex

secretory vesicles leaving maturing face of **Golgi complex**

transfer vesicles reaching forming face of **Golgi complex**

saccule

ribosomes

rough endoplasmic reticulum cisterna

complexion ■ **compound**

heterocyclic c. A cyclic compound.

impression c. A thermoplastic material used in dentistry to make a negative imprint of oral structures. Also called *modeling compound.*

inorganic c. Compound with atoms that are held together by electrostatic forces rather than by covalent bonds, as is the case in organic compounds.

modeling c. See impression compound.

nonpolar c. Compound in which atoms forming a bond share electrons equally, so that no positive or negative poles exist.

open-chain c. See acyclic compound.

organic c. A compound containing carbon atoms.

ring c. See cyclic compound.

comprehension (kom-pre-hen′shun) See cognition (2).

compress (kom′pres) A pad of gauze or any soft material used to apply pressure to a part; it may be wet or dry, hot or cold, or medicated (e.g., with an antiseptic solution).

graduated c. Compress made of several layers of cloth, thickest in the center, thinner toward the periphery.

compression (kom-presh′un) Pressing or squeezing together.

cerebral c. Abnormal pressure on the brain by any means (e.g., tumor, hemorrhage, blood clot, depressed fracture of the skull, abscess).

digital c. Pressure applied with the fingers over a cut blood vessel to stop bleeding.

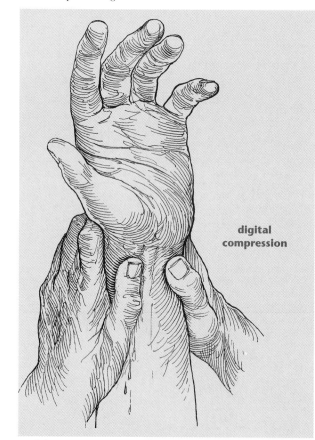

digital
compression

compulsion (kom-pul′shun) An insistent, irresistible, and unwanted urge to so something that is contrary to one's standards or wishes; failure to perform the compulsive act produces overt anxiety; performing the act may afford some relief of tension.

con- Prefix meaning with; together; in association.

conation (ko-na′shun) The volitional or active part of behavior, which includes drive, impulse, and purposive striving; it is one of three parts of behavior, the other two being cognition (thinking) and affect (feeling).

concameration (kon-kam-er-a′shun) A group of interconnecting cavities.

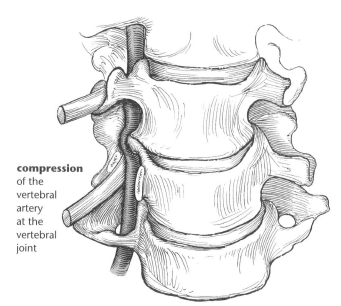

compression
of the
vertebral
artery
at the
vertebral
joint

concatenate (kon-kat′e-nāt) Connected in a chainlike series.

concave (kon′kāv) Having a depressed surface.

concavity (kon-kav′ĭ-te) A depression.

concavoconcave (kon-ka′vo-kon′kav) Concave on both sides; said of an optical lens.

concavoconvex (kon-ka′vo-kon′veks) Concave on one side and convex on the opposite side; said of an optical lens.

concentration (kon-sen-tra′shun) **1.** The quantity of a substance in a unit (of volume or weight) of another substance. **2.** A pharmaceutical preparation that has had its strength increased by evaporation (e.g., by evaporating the solvent of a solution).

spermatozoa c. The number of spermatozoa in 1 ml of semen; normal values range from 20 to 200 million sperms per 1 ml of semen; in most *in vitro* fertilization (IVF) programs, a semen specimen containing up to 40 million sperms may be considered inadequate (hypofertile).

concentric (kon-sen′trik) Having a common center.

conception (kon-sep′shun) The fertilization of an ovum by a spermatozoon.

wrongful c. In medical negligence, *(a)* an unwanted pregnancy resulting from the physician's failure to inform the parents that a sterilization procedure might be unsuccessful, or a promise that the procedure would be successful; *(b)* development of a genetically defective fetus resulting from the physician's failure to inform the parents of the genetic risk.

conceptus (kon-sep′tus) The product of conception from the time the ovum and sperm unite and form a zygote until birth; it includes the placenta, membranes, and fetus.

concha (kon′kah), pl. con′chae A shell-shaped structure.

c. of ear The deep hollow of the external ear between the antihelix, posteriorly, and the tragus, anteriorly.

inferior c. *(a)* A thin, curved bony plate on the lateral wall of the nasal cavity; it articulates with the maxilla and the ethmoid, palatine, and lacrimal bones; its lacrimal process helps to form the canal for the nasolacrimal duct. *(b)* The thick, highly vascular mucoperiosteum covering the above bone. Also called inferior turbinate.

middle c. *(a)* A thin, curved bony plate projecting on the lateral wall of the nasal cavity; it is part of the ethmoid bone and separates the superior meatus from the middle meatus. *(b)* The thick, highly vascular mucoperiosteum covering the above bone. Also called middle turbinate.

sphenoidal c. A paired, thin, cone-shaped bony plate forming part of the roof of the nasal cavity.

superior c. *(a)* The upper, thin, bony plate projecting from the medial surface of the ethmoidal labyrinth into the nasal cavity above and behind the middle concha. *(b)* The mucoperiosteum covering the above bone. Also called superior turbinate.

conchoidal (kon-koi′dal) Shaped like a shell.

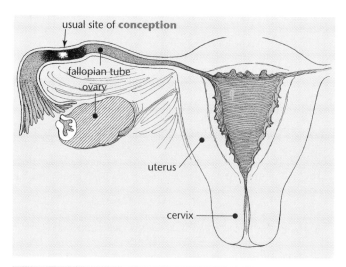

usual site of **conception**

fallopian tube
ovary
uterus
cervix

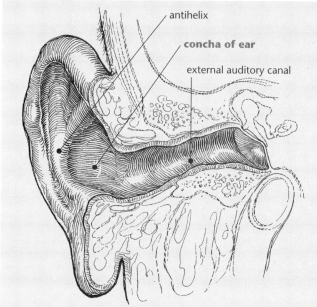

antihelix
concha of ear
external auditory canal

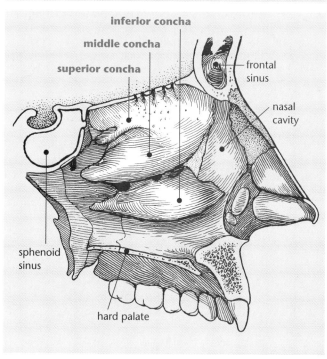

inferior concha
middle concha
superior concha
frontal sinus
nasal cavity
sphenoid sinus
hard palate

concrement (kon′kre-ment) A concretion.

concrescence (kon-kres′ens) Any mass of inorganic material; a calculus or stone, such as a kidney stone.

concussion (kon-kush′un) **1.** A sudden and violent jarring of the body. **2.** The condition resulting from such a jarring.

 brain c. Temporary brain dysfunction that is most severe immediately after a head injury and clears within 24 hours; symptoms include variable degrees of drowsiness, irritability, and memory dysfunction, usually with amnesia for the event that caused the injury; it may be accompanied by slowing of the heartbeat (bradycardia), lowering of blood pressure (hypotension), and sweating; often but not always it is accompanied by loss of consciousness; no anatomic changes are detected.

condensation (kon-den-sa′shun) **1.** The act of rendering a material more compact by applying pressure (e.g., condensing a dental amalgam). **2.** The process of changing a gas into a liquid, or a liquid into a solid. **3.** The fusion of several ideas into a single symbol or dream image representing the multiple concepts, or the process whereby one idea or memory contains all the emotion pertaining to a wider network of ideas or memories.

condense (kon-dens′) To compress or pack firmly, such as the restorative material into the prepared cavity of a tooth.

condenser (kon-den′ser) **1.** A device for lowering the temperature of a material, as in converting a gas or vapor into a liquid or a liquid into a solid. **2.** A system of lenses for focusing light upon an object subjected to microscopic examination. **3.** A dental instrument for compressing restorative material into a prepared tooth cavity.

 dark-field c. An optical system in a microscope that throws reflected light upon the specimen, which appears brilliantly light against a dark background.

condition (kon-dish′un) **1.** State of health. **2.** An ailment or disease. **3.** In psychology, to train a person to respond to a specified stimulus in a particular way.

 preexisting c. In health insurance, a physical or mental condition that exists prior to the effective date of coverage of a health insurance policy or health care service contract, and for which treatment under the policy or contract may be limited or may be excluded for a set period of time.

conditioning (kon-dish′un-ing) The process of training or establishing new responses to a specified stimulus.

 instrument c. See operant conditioning.

 operant c. Conditioning in which a response to a stimulus is instrumental in producing a reward or preventing punishment; thereafter, the particular stimulus is more likely to evoke that response. Also called instrumental conditioning.

condom (kon′dum) A sheath, usually made of thin latex rubber or plastic; placed over the penis before intercourse, it provides a barrier against conception and provides both partners with protection against sexual transmission of disease. Also called contraceptive sheath; prophylactic.

 female c. A polyurethane, prelubricated sheath (the same length of a male condom, but wider), inserted into the vagina, and covering the vaginal wall and labia; it functions as a contraceptive sheath and as protection against minute abrasions and transmission of disease during sexual intercourse. Also called vaginal pouch.

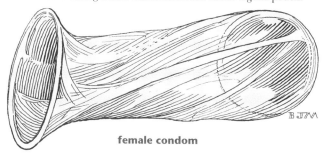

female condom

conduct (kon-dukt′) The manner in which a person acts.
 criminal sexual c. See rape.

conductance (kon-duk'tans) A measure of a material's ability to allow an electrical charge to pass through it.

conduction (kon-duk'shun) The transmission of nervous impulses, sound waves, heat, or electricity.

 aberrant ventricular c. Abnormal pathway of the excitatory impulse in the ventricle of the heart; caused by delayed activation of a branch of the atrioventricular bundle.

 accelerated c. Abnormally rapid rate of travel of the excitatory impulse of the heart from atrium to ventricle; it results in early activation of the ventricular muscle.

 air c. Transmission of sound waves to the inner ear through the external auditory canal and structures in the middle ear (tympanic) cavity.

 antidromic c. Propagation of an action potential in a direction opposite to the normal (e.g., conduction of impulses toward the spinal cord along motor nerves, which normally conduct impulses away from it). Opposite of orthodromic conduction.

 bone c. Transmission of sound waves to the inner ear through the bones of the skull. Also called osteophony.

 concealed c. Transmission of an excitatory impulse through only part of the conducting tissue of the heart; so called because the electrocardiogram (ECG) shows no direct evidence of its presence, only its effect on the next impulse.

 delayed c. First-degree atrioventricular block. See atrioventricular block, under block.

 intraventricular c. Conduction of the activating impulse of the heart through the ventricular muscle. Also called ventricular conduction.

 nerve c. Propagation of an impulse along a nerve fiber.

 orthodromic c. Propagation of an action potential in the normal direction (e.g., conduction of impulses away from the spinal cord via motor nerves). Opposite of antidromic conduction.

 retrograde c. Transmission of an activating impulse of the heart in a direction opposite to normal (i.e., from ventricles to atria). Also called ventriculoatrial conduction; retroconduction.

 saltatory c. The jumping of a nerve impulse from one node of Ranvier to the next, rather than along the entire nerve fiber.

 synaptic c. Transmission of a nerve impulse across a synapse.

 ventricular c. See intraventricular conduction.

 ventriculoatrial c., V-A c. See retrograde conduction.

conductivity (kon-duk-tiv'i-te) The ability of a material to transmit heat, electricity, or sound.

conductor (kon-duk'tor) 1. Any material that can transmit sound, heat, or electricity. 2. A grooved probe for guiding a surgical knife.

conduit (kon'doo-it) A channel.

 ileal c. A surgically created channel made for discharging urine through the abdominal wall when the bladder has been removed; it consists of a detached segment of small intestine (ileum) to which the ureters are attached (anastomosed) at one end; the other end of the segment opens to the exterior through a permanent opening (stoma). Also called ileal bladder.

condylar (kon'di-lar) Relating to a condyle.

condylarthrosis (kon-dil-ar-thro'sis) A joint composed of an ovoid surface (condyle) fitting into an elliptical cavity.

condyle (kon'dil) A knoblike prominence at the end of a bone by means of which it articulates with another bone.

condylectomy (kon-dil-ek'to-me) Surgical removal of a condyle.

condyloma (kon-di-lo'mah), pl. condylo'mata A wartlike growth.

 c. acuminatum A soft, pointed, warty growth, or collection of growths, usually occurring around the anus and on the external genitalia of males or females, and in the uterine cervix; when numerous, they become confluent, resembling a cauliflower; caused by infection with human papillomavirus and transmitted through sexual contact; although almost always benign, cancerous transformations, especially in the cervix, have been reported. Also called anorectal wart; genital wart; venereal wart; moist wart; pointed wart; fig wart; verruca acuminata; papilloma venereum; pointed condyloma.

 giant c. A single, large, locally invasive, and recurrent infection

of the penis. Also called Buschke-Lowenstein tumor; verrucous carcinoma.

 c. latum The highly infectious lesion of the secondary stage of syphilis, appearing as multiple, slightly elevated, disk-shaped or oval growths with a moist surface; occurring on the genitalia, around the anus, and on the inner thighs and buttocks. Also called moist papule.

 pointed c. See condyloma acuminatum.

condylomatous (kon-di-lo'mah-tus) Relating to a condyloma.

condylotomy (kon-di-lot'o-me) Incision or surgical division of a condyle.

-cone Suffix meaning the cusp of a tooth in the upper jaw (maxilla).

cone (kōn) A figure or structure tapering to a point from a broad or circular base.

 arterial c. See conus arteriosus, under conus.

 c. cell of retina See cone cell of retina, under cell.

 c. of light A triangular area at the anteroinferior part of the eardrum (tympanic membrane), which is seen as a bright reflection of light. Also called pyramid of light.

 medullary c. The tapered end of the spinal cord. Also called conus medullaris.

confabulation (kon-fab-u-la'shun) The filling of memory gaps with detailed stories of imaginary experiences; may result from organic disorders that affect intellectual functioning.

confectio (kon-fek'she-o) See confection.

confection (kon-fek'shun) A sweetened medicinal preparation. Also called confectio; electuary.

confidentiality (kon-fi-den-she-al'i-te) Privilege of a patient to limit access to information disclosed in the course of a professional relationship with a health professional; the laws affecting this privilege vary among jurisdictions.

configuration (kon-fig-u-ra'shun) The arrangement of parts that form a whole structure (e.g., the spatial arrangement of atoms in a molecule).

confinement (kon-fin'ment) The period of childbirth.

conflict (kon'flikt) The struggle between incompatible or opposing thoughts, drives, needs, or emotions.

confluence of sinuses The joining of the five channels of the dura mater (superior sagittal, straight, occipital, and two transverse), which drain venous blood from the brain; located in the back of the head, at the internal protuberance of the occipital bone.

conformation (kon-for-ma'shun) The spatial arrangement of atoms in a molecule produced by rotations around single covalent bonds.

conformer (kon-for'mer) A mold inserted into a body cavity to preserve its shape after surgery, as in the eye socket after removal of the eye and before inserting an artificial eye.

confrontation (kon-frun-ta'shun) Bringing to a patient's attention his or her attitudes and feelings by a therapist or by members of a therapy group.

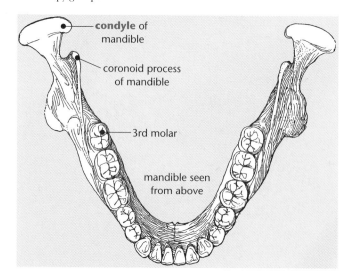

condyle of mandible

coronoid process of mandible

3rd molar

mandible seen from above

confusion (kon-fu′zhun) A state of perceptual disorientation, inattentiveness, and impaired ability to think clearly and with customary speed.

congener (kon′jĕ-ner) **1.** A drug that is a member of a group sharing the same parent compound. **2.** A member of a group of muscles having the same function.

congenic (kon-jen′ik) Relating to inbred animals.

congenital (kon-jen′ĭ-tal) Present at birth; denoting a condition manifested, or occurring, at the time of birth.

congested (kon-jest′ed) Containing an abnormally increased amount of blood.

congestion (kon-jest′yun) Abnormal accumulation of blood in a body part resulting from impaired drainage of venous blood and distention of veins, venules, and capillaries; it may be localized, caused by obstruction of a vein, or generalized (systemic) as seen in heart failure; the affected part appears reddish blue and, often, swollen. Sometimes called passive hyperemia.

   hyperemic c. Congestion due in great part to capillary and arteriolar dilatation.

   hypostatic c. See venous stasis, under stasis.

   nasal c. Congestion of the lining of air passages in the nose, resulting in obstruction; usually caused by infection or allergy.

   pulmonary c. Congestion characterized by prominence of pulmonary veins and smaller venous vessels (venules) seen in left heart failure or mitral stenosis.

conglutination (kon-gloo-tī-na′shun) **1.** Abnormal adhesion of tissues. **2.** The clumping of sensitized cells or of antigen-antibody complexes that have absorbed complement, occurring in the presence of bovine serum that contains the protein conglutinin.

conglutinin (kon-gloo′tī-nin) Protein of normal bovine serum that is capable of combining with the carbohydrate portion of complement, thus causing clumping (agglutinating) of particles covered with the complement.

-conid Suffix meaning the cusp of a tooth in the lower jaw (mandible).

coniofibrosis (ko-ne-o-fi-bro′sis) Abnormal formation of fibrous tissue, as in the lungs, due to exposure to dust.

coniosis (ko-ne-o′sis) Any disease caused by dust.

Conium maculatum (ko-ne′um mah-cu-la′tum) A large, poisonous herb (family Umbelliferae). Commonly called poison hemlock.

conization (kon-ī-za′shun) Surgical removal of a conical portion of tissue, as from the uterine cervix.

conjugate (kon′ju-gāt) Coupled, paired.

conjugation (kon-ju-ga′shun) **1.** In biochemistry, the combination of different products of metabolism with certain molecules that favor

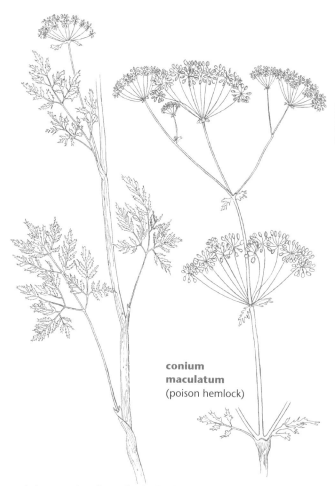

conium
maculatum
(poison hemlock)

their excretion from the body. **2.** The union of two unicellular microorganisms and the exchange of genetic material between them.

conjunctiva (kon-junk-ti′vah), pl. conjuncti′vae The thin, transparent, mucous membrane lining the outer surface of the eyeball, up to the edge of the cornea, and the inner surface of the eyelids; it contains blood vessels that are invisible to the naked eye.

   bulbar c. The part of the conjunctiva lining the eyeball, over the white of the eye (sclera).

   palpebral c. The part of the conjunctiva lining the inside of the eyelids.

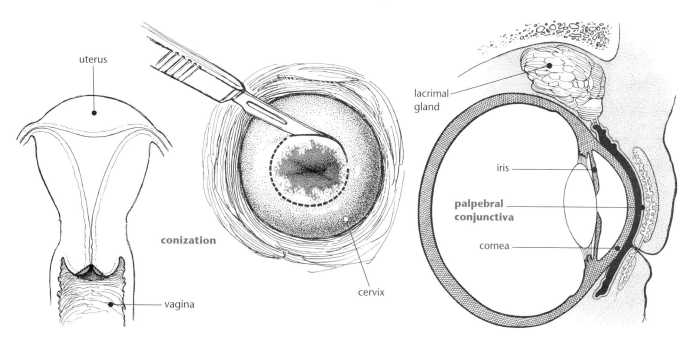

conjunctivitis (kon-junk-tī-vi'tis) Inflammation of the conjunctiva.

   acute contagious c. Bacterial conjunctivitis caused by *Haemophilus influenza*, causing redness of the eye and a mucopurulent discharge. Also called pinkeye; acute epidemic conjunctivitis.

   acute epidemic c. See acute contagious conjunctivitis.

   acute follicular c. Conjunctivitis associated with formation of round cellular masses (follicles) in the inner aspect of the eyelids, especially at the inner fold (fornix) of the lower eyelids; usually caused by inclusion conjunctivitis.

   adult inclusion c. See inclusion conjunctivitis.

   chronic c. Conjunctivitis characterized by exacerbations and remissions occurring over months or years.

   eczematous c. See phlyctenular conjunctivitis.

   gonococcal c. Acute conjunctivitis characterized by a profuse purulent discharge and edematous eyelids; caused by *Neisseria gonorrhea*, the bacterium causing gonorrhea.

   inclusion c. Acute chlamydial conjunctivitis caused by *Chlamydia oculogenitalis*, occurring most frequently in sexually active people exposed to infected genital secretions; indirect transmission in inadequately chlorinated swimming pools has occasionally been reported; newborn infants usually acquire the infection by direct contact with secretions from an infected birth canal. Also called inclusion blennorrhea; swimming pool conjunctivitis; adult inclusion conjunctivitis.

   neonatal c. See ophthalmia neonatorum.

   occupational c. Conjunctivitis caused by chemicals and irritants, such as fertilizers, hair sprays, soaps, cosmetics, and various acids and alkali.

   phlyctenular c. Localized conjunctivitis characterized by formation of elevated, hard plaques, which may involve the cornea; usually associated with tuberculosis. Also called eczematous conjunctivitis.

   swimming pool c. See inclusion conjunctivitis.

connector (kŏ-nek'tor) In dentistry, a part of a fixed partial denture that unites its components.

consanguineous (kŏn-san-gwin'e-us) Genetically related; of the same blood.

consanguinity (kon-san-gwin'ĭ-te) Genetic relationship between individuals that is attributable to a common ancestor; blood relationship.

conscious (kon'shus) Being aware of having perception of one's existence, actions, and surroundings.

consciousness (kon'shus-nes) A state of awareness of, and responsiveness to, one's environment.

consensual (kon-sen'shu-al) Relating to a reflex response of one organ in response to sensory stimulation of another (e.g., the eyes).

consent (kon-sent') Voluntary agreement to medical care or treatment by one with the capacity to do so.

   informed c. Voluntary permission given by a patient or patient's legal representative for medical, surgical, or experimental treatment, based on full discussion between physician and patient (or patient's representative) of the purpose and potential benefits of the treatment, the risks involved, the possible complications and adverse effects (e.g., of drugs), the consequences of withholding permission, and alternative methods of treatment; the physician is legally obligated to disclose fully to the patient (or patient's representative) all information necessary for a reasoned decision except in a medical emergency; the informed consent obtained from the patient is usually documented in the medical record.

conservative (kon-ser'vah-tiv) Denoting therapeutic practice that is based on cautious methods.

conservator (kon-ser'vah-tor) A person who is appointed to manage another person's business affairs but who has not been granted any authority over the person's body or health care decisions (e.g., with regard to giving consent for therapeutic or experimental procedures).

consolidation (kon-sol-ĭ-da'shun) The act of becoming solid (e.g., induration of the normally air-filled spaces of the lungs due to accumulation of inflammatory secretions of pneumonia).

constant (kon'stant) A quantity that, under specified conditions, does not change.

   decay c. The mathematical expression for the number of atoms in a nuclide that will disintegrate in a unit of time.

   dissociation c. (K) A constant that depends on the equilibrium of the dissociated and undissociated forms of a molecule in a solution.

   gas c. (R) The constant of proportionality in the ideal gas law, equal to the pressure of the gas times its volume divided by its temperature.

   Michaelis c. (Km) A constant that expresses the concentration of a substrate at which half the maximum velocity of a reaction is achieved.

   Planck's c. (h) A constant that expresses the ratio of the energy of a quantum of radiation to its frequency.

constellation (kon-stel-a'shun) In psychiatry, a set of related ideas.

constipate (kon'stĭ-pāt) To cause constipation.

constipation (kon-stĭ-pā'shun) Infrequent, or prolonged and difficult, bowel movements.

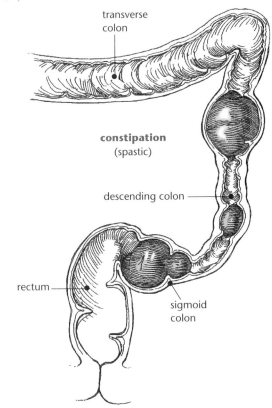

transverse colon

constipation (spastic)

descending colon

rectum

sigmoid colon

constitution (kon-stĭ-tu'shun) The physical makeup and health status of the body.

constriction (kon-strik'shun) **1.** A narrowing. **2.** Subjective sensation of being squeezed.

   secondary c. A narrowed section of a chromosome not associated with the centromere; often the site of attachment of a satellite.

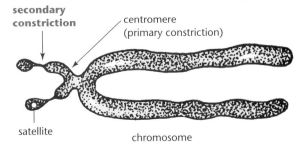

secondary constriction

centromere (primary constriction)

satellite

chromosome

constrictor (kon-strik'tor) Anything that binds or squeezes a part, such as a muscle that narrows an opening.

consult (kon-sult′) To seek advice from.

consultand (kon-sul′tand) The person seeking, or referred for, genetic counseling; one whose genetic constitution is in question. COMPARE proband.

consultant (kon-sul′tant) person called upon for expert or professional advice.

    medical c. A physician who is called upon to give advice regarding diagnosis or treatment of a patient. A medical consultant may or may not be called upon to perform a physical examination or advise about a future course of action; an assessment of data, sometimes within the context of legal policies and regulations may be done (e.g., Social Security entitlement assessments, or worker compensation evaluations).

consultation (kon-sul-ta′shun) A meeting of two or more physicians to determine or evaluate a diagnosis or therapy of a patient's condition.

consumption (kon-sump′shun) Obsolete term for a wasting of tissue by disease, usually by tuberculosis.

contact (kon′takt) **1.** The point or area at which two adjacent structures touch (e.g., two adjacent teeth in the same dental arch). **2.** A person who has been exposed to the causative agent of an infectious disease.

contact tracing Identification of persons or animals who have had an association with an infected person, animal, or contaminated environment and who, through such an association, have had the opportunity to acquire the infection; contact tracing is an accepted method of controlling sexually transmitted diseases.

contagion (kon-ta′jun) The direct or indirect transmission of an infectious disease.

contagious (kon-ta′jus) Transmissible by direct or indirect means. Popularly called catching.

contagium (kon-ta′je-um) The causative agent of a disease.

containment of biohazards (kon-tain′ment bio-haz′ards) Provision of physical and biological barriers to the spread of potentially hazardous, biologically active agents; physical barriers include the use of special areas, equipment, and procedures to prevent the escape of the agent; biological barriers involve such provisions as the use of immune personnel to minimize the risk should the agent escape the containment.

contaminant (kon-tam′ĭ-nant) An impurity.

contamination (kon-tam-ĭ-na′shun) **1.** The process of rendering impure or unhealthy. **2.** The material involved in such a process.

content (kon′tent) Material or substance contained.

contiguity (kon-tĭ-gyōō ′ĭ-te) The state of being contiguous (sharing a boundary, touching).

continence (kon′tĭ-nens) Self-control (e.g., ability to delay urination or defecation).

contour (kon′toor) **1.** An outline or shape. **2.** To shape into a desired form, such as a denture.

contraception (kon-trah-sep′shun) The use of pharmaceutical preparations, devices, methods, or procedures that diminish the likelihood of, or prevent, conception.

contraceptive (kon-trah-sep′tiv) **1.** Preventing conception. **2.** Anything that prevents conception.

    oral c. Any drug taken orally by regular doses to prevent conception; it alters the woman's hormonal balance, thereby blocking ovulation and preventing pregnancy. Also called birth-control pill; popularly called the pill.

    postcoital c. Oral contraceptive taken within 72 hours after sexual intercourse (coitus); usually a combination of hormones (a progestogen and an estrogen). Also called morning-after pill.

contract (kon-tract′) **1.** To compress or shorten, as a muscle. **2.** To acquire, as a disease.

contractile (kon-trac′til) Capable of contracting.

contractility (kon-trac-til′ĭ-te) The ability to shorten, said of a muscle.

contraction (kon-trak′shun) (C) **1.** A shortening or increase of tension, as a functioning muscle. **2.** A shrinkage. **3.** A heartbeat.

    Braxton Hicks c.'s Short, relatively painless contractions of

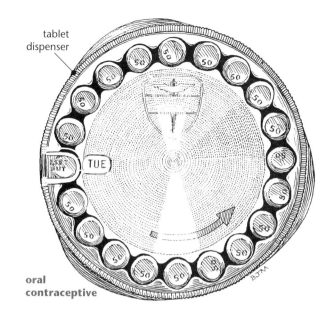

tablet dispenser

oral contraceptive

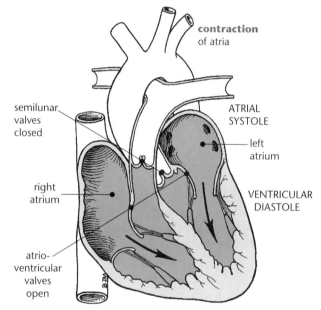

contraction of atria

semilunar valves closed

right atrium

atrio-ventricular valves open

ATRIAL SYSTOLE

left atrium

VENTRICULAR DIASTOLE

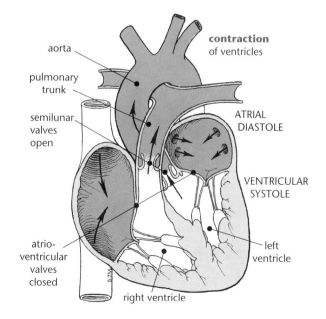

aorta

pulmonary trunk

semilunar valves open

atrio-ventricular valves closed

right ventricle

contraction of ventricles

ATRIAL DIASTOLE

VENTRICULAR SYSTOLE

left ventricle

the pregnant uterus, usually beginning at irregular intervals during early pregnancy and becoming more frequent and rhythmic as pregnancy advances, especially during the last two weeks of gestation, when they may be mistaken for labor pains; they occasionally occur without pregnancy, as in the presence of soft tumors of the uterine wall.

hourglass c. Narrowing of a hollow organ (e.g., uterus) around its middle area.

premature c. A premature heartbeat.

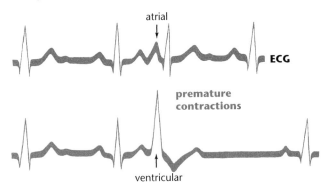

contracture (kon-trak'tur) Permanent contraction of a muscle due to tonic spasm, atrophy, or development of fibrous tissue within the muscle or its tendon.

Dupuytren's c. Nodular thickening and shortening of fascia on the palmar aspect of the hand, resulting in rigid, permanent flexion of one or more fingers; of unknown cause, it is seen most commonly in white males over age 50; a higher incidence is noted in alcoholics and in patients with chronic diseases.

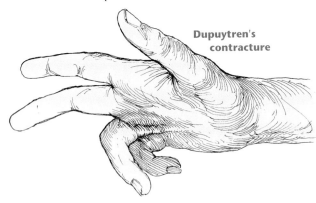

Dupuytren's contracture

ischemic c. of left ventricle Irreversible contracture of the muscular wall of the left ventricle of the heart, occurring as a complication of cardiopulmonary bypass. Also called stony heart; myocardial rigor mortis.

Volkmann's c. Tissue degeneration and contracture of muscle due to deprivation of blood supply, usually occurring in the finger following a severe injury or improper use of a tourniquet.

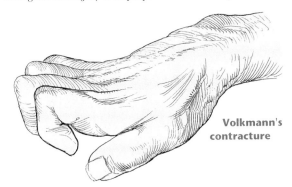

Volkmann's contracture

contraindication (kon-trah-in-di-ka'shun) Any factor in a patient's condition that renders a particular course of treatment undesirable or unwise.

contralateral (kon-trah-lat'er-al) Relating to the opposite side.

contrastimulant (kon-trah-stim'u-lant) **1.** Counteracting the effects of a stimulant. **2.** Any drug or agent having such an effect; a sedative.

contrecoup (kon-tr-koo') Occurring on the opposite side (e.g., injury to the brain on the opposite side of a blow to the head).

control (kon-trol') **1.** A subject or a group used in an experiment or study as a standard against which observations are evaluated. **2.** To verify or evaluate results of an experiment or study against a standard. **3.** Limitation of certain events.

birth c. Deliberate use of contraceptive measures to limit the number of children conceived.

Controlled Substances Act An act passed by the U.S. Congress that codifies the regulations covering drugs subject to abuse.

contusion (kon-tu'zhun) A bluish black discoloration generally caused by blunt trauma; characterized by bleeding into the tissues without significant tissue disruption; most commonly occurs in the skin but may also occur in internal organs. Commonly called bruise.

cardiac c. A focal area of bleeding usually originating in the inner layer (endocardium) of the heart wall, ranging from minute spots (petechiae) to frank hemorrhage spreading across all three layers of the heart wall, causing extensive damage; most common cause is impact with a steering wheel in automobile accidents; may also occur in falls from heights, from high-velocity bullets striking the abdomen or chest, or in blast explosions in the air or water.

brain c. Superficial focal bruising of the brain surface without rupture of the pia mater, accompanied by bleeding and local swelling; bruising may occur immediately underneath the site of impact (coup injury), at a point opposite (contrecoup injury), or on the inferior surfaces of the frontal and temporal lobes where the brain in motion strikes protuberances of the skull's interior.

c. of spinal cord Bruising and rapid swelling of the spinal cord and increased pressure within its outer covering (dura), caused by physical injury.

wind c. See windage.

conus (ko'nus), co'ni A cone-shaped structure.

c. arteriosus The upper, anterior portion of the right ventricle of the heart, ending where the pulmonary trunk begins. Also called arterial cone.

c. medullaris See medullary cone, under cone.

convalescence (kon-vah-les'ens) A stage in the process of recovery between abatement of a disease or injury and full restoration of health.

convection (kon-vek'shun) Transport of heat in liquids or gases by the movement of heated particles within.

convergence (kon-ver'jens) **1.** The act of approaching a common point. **2.** The process of directing both eyes to a near point.

negative c. See divergence.

positive c. An increase in the degree to which the eyes turn toward the midline.

convergent (kon-ver'jent) Moving toward a common point.

conversion (kon-ver'shun) **1.** The process of changing. **2.** In psychiatry, somatic symptoms (e.g., paralysis, pain, loss of sensation) occurring as the symbolic physical expression of a psychic conflict or painful emotion.

convertin (kon-ver'tin) See factor VII.

convex (kon'veks) An outwardly curved surface; said of a lens.

convexoconcave (kon-vek-so-kon'kav) Convex on one side, concave on the opposite side.

convoluted (kon'vo-lut-ed) Coiled or rolled.

convolution (kon-vo-lu'shun) The tortuous elevations characteristic of the brain.

convulsant (kon-vul'sant) Causing convulsions.

convulsion (kon-vul'shun) A violent spasm of voluntary muscles; a seizure; it may be a series of discontinuous contractions, either a long contraction interrupted by intervals of muscular relaxation or brief ones repeated at short intervals.

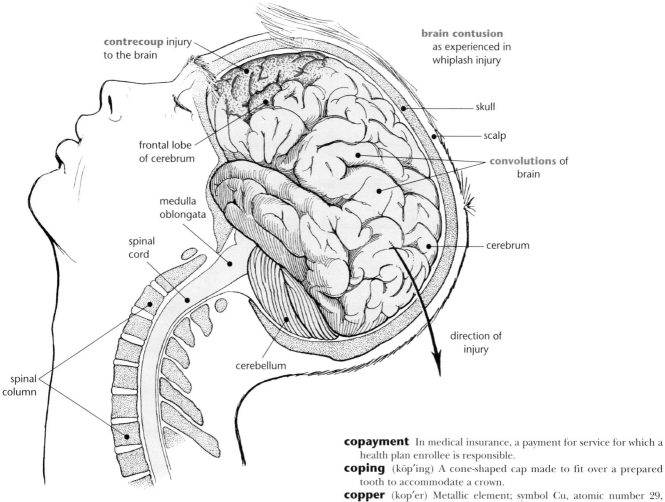

contrecoup injury to the brain

brain contusion as experienced in whiplash injury

skull

scalp

frontal lobe of cerebrum

convolutions of brain

medulla oblongata

spinal cord

cerebrum

spinal column

cerebellum

direction of injury

hyperextension of neck (beyond the normal limit)

copayment In medical insurance, a payment for service for which a health plan enrollee is responsible.

coping (kōp′ing) A cone-shaped cap made to fit over a prepared tooth to accommodate a crown.

copper (kop′er) Metallic element; symbol Cu, atomic number 29, atomic weight 63.54.

coproantibody (kop-ro-an′tī-bod-e) An antibody found in the feces.

coprolalia (kop-ro-la′le-ah) Involuntary uttering of obscene words, as seen in Gilles de la Tourette's syndrome.

axon of neuron

dendrite

cell body of neuron

axon hillock

direction of impulse

convergence of four axons to one cell body

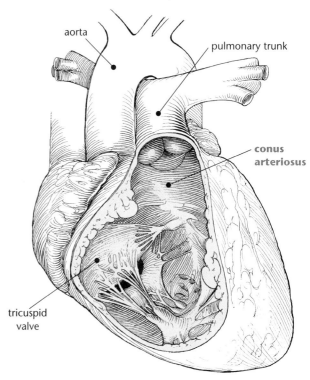

aorta

pulmonary trunk

conus arteriosus

tricuspid valve

U.S. Customary Units to Metric Units
inches to centimeters . . . . multiply by 10, then divide by 4
yards to meters . . . . multiply by 9, then divide by 10
pounds to kilograms. . . . . multiply by 5, then divide by 11
gallons to liters. . . multiply by 4, then subtract 1/5 of the number of gallons

Temperature Units
degrees Fahrenheit to degrees Centigrade . . . . subtract 32, then multiply by 5/9
degrees Centigrade to degrees Fahrenheit . . . . multiply by 9/5, then add 32
degrees Kelvin to degrees Centigrade . . . . add 273

coprolith (kop′ro-lith) See fecalith.

coproporphyrin (kop-ro-por′fir-in) A porphyrin, formed as a decomposition product of bilirubin, normally found in the feces.

coptosis (kop-to′sis) Constant fatigue.

copulation (kop-u-la′shun) Coitus; sexual intercourse.

cor (kor) Latin for heart.

    c. biloculare A defective heart in which the walls (septa) separating the atria and the ventricles are absent.

    c. bovinum Massive enlargement (hypertrophy) of the heart, as seen in the third stage of syphilis (tertiary syphilis). Also called bucardia.

    c. pulmonale Dilatation of the right ventricle of the heart progressing to enlargement (hypertrophy) of the ventricular wall and eventual failure of the ventricle's ability to function; it occurs secondary to disease of lungs leading to an increase in the resistance against which the ventricles must work; symptoms depend on underlying disease but generally include difficult breathing, cough, and fatigue.

    c. triloculare A defective heart that has only three, instead of four, chambers due to absence of the wall between the atria (interatrial septum) or of the wall between the ventricles (interventricular septum).

coracoacromial (kor-ah-ko-ah-kro′me-al) Relating to the coracoid and acrominal processes of the shoulder blade (scapula). Also called acromiocoracoid.

coracobrachial (kor-ah-ko-bra′ke-al) Relating to the coracoid process of the shoulder blade (scapula) and the arm.

coracoclavicular (kor-ah-ko-klah-vik′u-lar) Relating to the coracoid process of the shoulder blade (scapula) and the collarbone (clavicle).

coracohumeral (kor-ah-ko-hu′mer-al) Relating to the coracoid process of the shoulder blade (scapula) and the long bone of the arm (humerus).

coracoid (ko′rah-koid) Shaped like a crow's beak, denoting the thick, curved process at the upper border of the shoulder blade (scapula).

cord (kord) Any stringlike structure.

    false vocal c.'s See vestibular folds, under fold.

    medullary c.'s Strands of dense lymphoid tissue in the medulla of a lymph node, between the nodal sinuses.

    spermatic c. The cord extending from the deep inguinal ring to the testis within the scrotum; it is composed of arteries, veins, nerves, lymphatic vessels, and the deferent duct held together by loose connective tissue.

    spinal c. The elongated portion of the central nervous system enclosed by the vertebral column.

    true vocal c.'s See vocal folds, under fold.

    umbilical c. The slender structure connecting the navel (umbilicus) of the fetus with the placenta; it contains two arteries and one vein and measures about 55 cm in length and 1 cm in diameter.

    vocal c.'s See vocal folds, under fold.

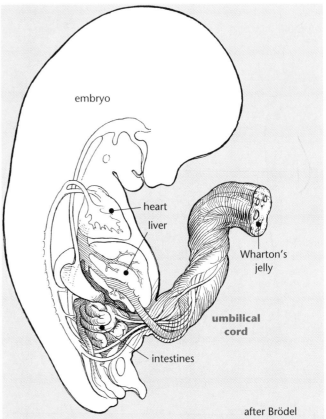

after Brödel

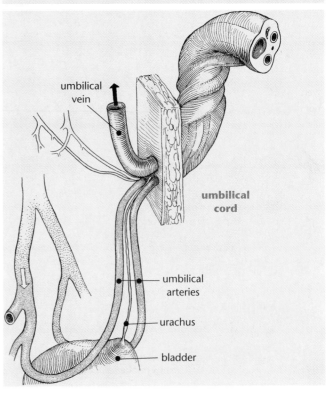

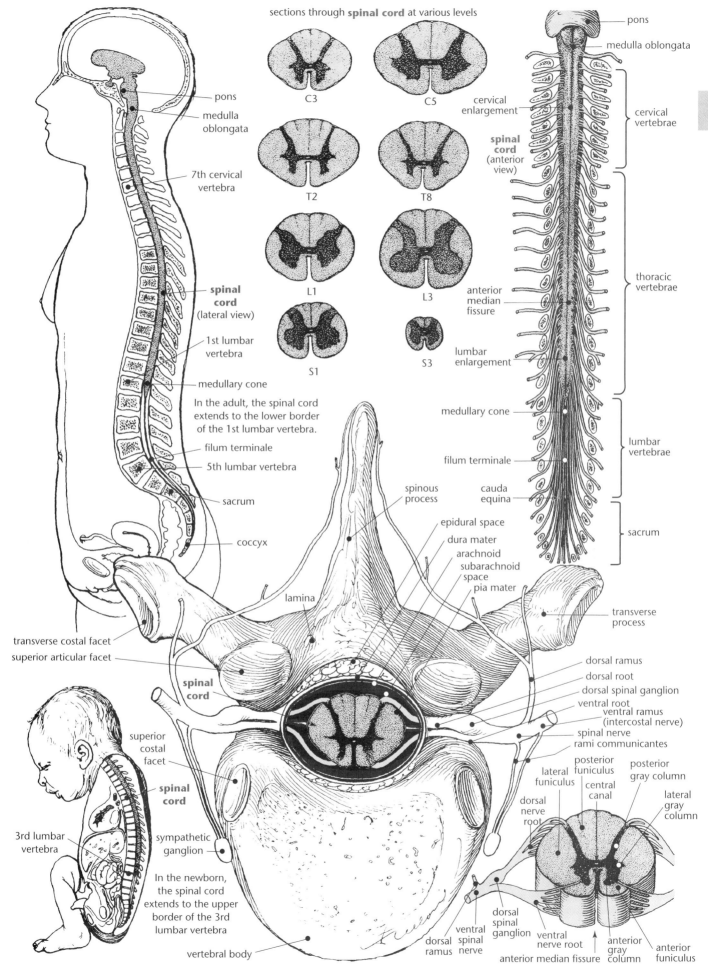

sections through **spinal cord** at various levels

C3

C5

T2

T8

L1

L3

S1

S3

pons

medulla oblongata

7th cervical vertebra

spinal cord (lateral view)

1st lumbar vertebra

medullary cone

In the adult, the spinal cord extends to the lower border of the 1st lumbar vertebra.

filum terminale

5th lumbar vertebra

sacrum

coccyx

transverse costal facet

superior articular facet

spinal cord

spinal cord

3rd lumbar vertebra

superior costal facet

sympathetic ganglion

In the newborn, the spinal cord extends to the upper border of the 3rd lumbar vertebra

vertebral body

spinous process

epidural space

dura mater

arachnoid

subarachnoid space

pia mater

lamina

dorsal ramus

ventral spinal nerve

dorsal spinal ganglion

ventral nerve root

anterior median fissure

pons

medulla oblongata

cervical enlargement

spinal cord (anterior view)

cervical vertebrae

thoracic vertebrae

anterior median fissure

lumbar enlargement

medullary cone

filum terminale

cauda equina

lumbar vertebrae

sacrum

transverse process

dorsal ramus

dorsal root

dorsal spinal ganglion

ventral root

ventral ramus (intercostal nerve)

spinal nerve

rami communicantes

posterior funiculus

posterior gray column

lateral funiculus

central canal

lateral gray column

dorsal nerve root

anterior gray column

anterior funiculus

C

cordate (kor'dāt) Heart-shaped.

cordectomy (kor-dek'to-me) Surgical removal of a cord such as a vocal cord.

cordopexy (kor'do-pek'se) The suturing of an anatomic cord in a permanent position.

cordotomy (kor-dot'o-me) Surgical division of bundles of nerve fibers of the spinal cord, usually for relief of persistent pain that has not responded to therapy with strong painkillers (analgesics) or with transcutaneous electrical nerve stimulation (TENS).

core (kōr) 1. The central part of an entity, such as the central mass of necrotic material in a boil. 2. A section of a mold for recording and maintaining the relationship of parts such as teeth or metallic restorations.

coreo-, core-, coro- Combining forms meaning pupil.

coreclisis (kōr-e-kli'sis) Occlusion of the pupil of the eye.

corectasis (kōr-ek'tah-sis) An abnormally dilated state of the pupil.

corectopia (kōr-ek-to'pe-ah) Abnormal, off-center position of the pupil.

corepressor (ko-re-pres'sor) A metabolite that, when combined with an inactive repressor protein, blocks the transcription of messenger ribonucleic acid (mRNA). Individually, neither the repressor protein nor the metabolite corepressor can block transcription.

corestenoma (ko-re-ste-no'mah) An abnormally constricted state of the pupil.

corium (ko're-um) See dermis.

corn (korn) A localized induration or callosity of the skin.

    hard c. Corn over a toe joint caused by ill-fitting shoes.

    seed c. Popular name for a wart on the sole of the foot; caused by a virus.

    soft c. Corn formed on the side of a toe caused by pressure and friction from an adjacent toe.

cornea (kor'ne-ah) The transparent anterior part of the outer coat of the eyeball that serves as the major refracting medium and through which the iris and pupil are seen; it consists of five layers: the epithelium (continuous with that of the conjunctiva), the anterior limiting (Bowman's) membrane, the substantia propria (stroma), the posterior limiting (Descemet's) membrane, and the endothelium.

    conical c. See keratoconus.

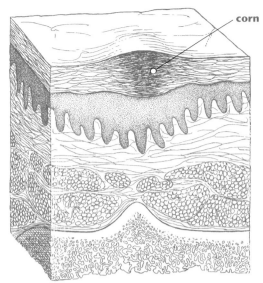

corneal (kor'ne-al) Relating to the cornea.

corneitis (kor-ne-i'tis) See keratitis.

corneoscleral (kor-ne-o-skle'ral) Relating to the cornea and the white of the eye (sclera).

corneous (kor'ne-us) Composed of hornlike material or keratin.

corneum (kor'ne-um) 1. The superficial layer of the epidermis. 2. The nail plate; a fingernail or toenail.

corniculate (kor-nik'u-lāt) 1. Having the shape of a small horn. 2. Having a horn or hornlike processes.

cornification (kor-nĭ-fĭ-ka'shun) Conversion into hornlike material or keratin.

cornu (kor'nu), pl. cor'nua 1. Any horn-shaped anatomic structure. Also called horn. 2. Any structure composed of hornlike material or tissue.

    c. anterius ventriculi lateralis See anterior horn of lateral ventricle, under horn.

    coccygeal cornua Bilateral extensions from the back of the upper part of the first coccygeal vertebra; they articulate with the cornua of the sacrum. Also called coccygeal horns.

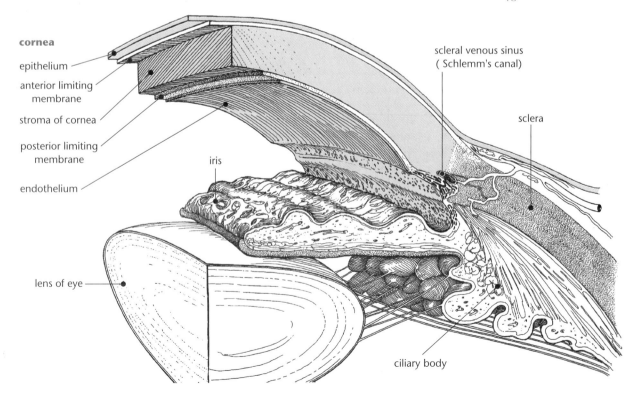

greater c. of hyoid bone Either of the two slender bony projections passing backward and upward from each end of the body of the hyoid bone; it ends in a tubercle and can be felt when the throat is grasped between finger and thumb just above the thyroid cartilage. Also called greater horn of hyoid bone.

inferior c. of thyroid cartilage The short, downward extension of the posterior border of the thyroid cartilage containing a facet on its medial surface for articulation with the side of the cricoid cartilage (cricothyroid joint). Also called inferior horn of thyroid cartilage.

c. inferius ventriculi lateralis See inferior horn of lateral ventricle, under horn.

lesser c. of hyoid bone Either of two small conical eminences connected by fibrous tissue to both sides of the hyoid bone at the angle of junction between the body and greater cornua. Also called lesser horn of hyoid bone.

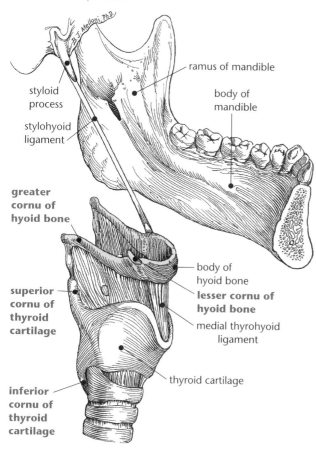

c. posterius ventriculi lateralis See posterior horn of lateral ventricle, under horn.

sacral cornua Bilateral processes extending downward from the arch of the fifth or last sacral vertebra; they articulate with the cornua of the coccyx. Also called sacral horns.

superior c. of thyroid cartilage The long, upward extension of the posterior border of the thyroid cartilage, ending in a conical extremity, to which is attached the lateral thyrohyoid ligament. Also called superior horn of thyroid cartilage.

uterine cornua See lateral horn of uterus, under horn.

corona (ko-ro′nah), pl. coro′nas or coro′nae Any anatomic structure resembling a crown or a wreath.

coronal (ko-ro′nal) 1. Relating to the crown of the head. 2. Relating to the side-to-side plane of the head or any vertical plane parallel to it.

coronary (kor′ŏ-na-re) 1. Encircling like a crown or wreath; said of certain structures (e.g., blood vessels supplying the heart muscle). 2. Popular term for (a) coronary thrombosis; (b) myocardial infarction.

Coronaviridae (kor-o-nah-vir′ĭ-de) A family of RNA viruses re-

sembling the myxoviruses; some species cause respiratory tract infections in humans.

coronavirus (kor-o-nah-vi′rus) Any virus of the family Coronaviridae.

coroner (kor′o-ner) A county official empowered to investigate any death occurring within his or her jurisdiction thought to be of other than natural causes; qualifications for the position vary with the jurisdiction. In some communities, medical examiners have replaced coroners.

coronion (ko-ro′ne-on) A craniometric point situated at the tip of the coronoid process of the lower jaw (mandible).

coronoid (kor′o-noid) 1. Shaped like a crow's beak; said of certain bones. 2. Crown-shaped.

corpora (kor′po-rah) Plural of corpus.

corporeal (kor-po′re-al) 1. Relating to the body. 2. Relating to a corpus.

corpulence (kor′pu-lens) Obesity.

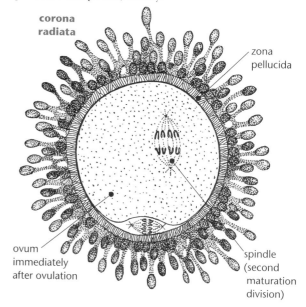

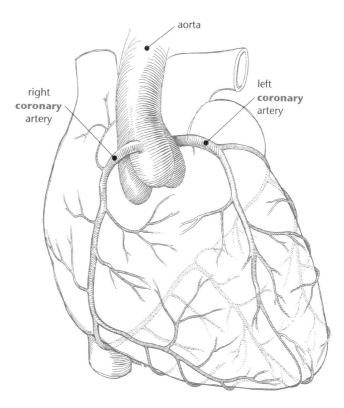

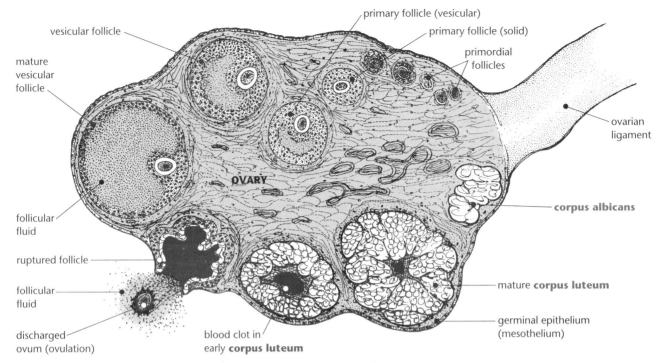

vesicular follicle

mature vesicular follicle

follicular fluid

ruptured follicle

follicular fluid

discharged ovum (ovulation)

blood clot in early **corpus luteum**

primary follicle (vesicular)

primary follicle (solid)

primordial follicles

OVARY

ovarian ligament

corpus albicans

mature **corpus luteum**

germinal epithelium (mesothelium)

corpus (kor′pus), pl. cor′pora **1.** The body. **2.** The principal portion of a structure, especially if it can be delimited from its surroundings.

c. albicans The shrunken convolutions of hyalinized material (yellowish white scar tissue) that was formerly the corpus luteum; when conception failed to occur, the lutein cells degenerated into amorphous hyaline masses united by strands of connective tissue; the decrease of estrogen and progesterone (during this regressive phase) prompts a new ovulatory growth cycle.

corpora amylacea See amyloid bodies of prostate, under body.

corpora arenaces See brain sand granules, under granule.

c. atreticum A follicle of the ovary that was unable to mature.

c. callosum The mass of transverse fibers (commissure) connecting the two hemispheres of the brain (cerebrum); it is the largest of the cerebral commissures, and its fibers diverge to all parts of the cerebral cortex.

c. cavernosum One of two columns of erectile tissue forming the greater part of the body of the penis (and clitoris); posteriorly, it is continuous with the crus and anteriorly, it inserts into an acorn-shaped cap formed by the glans.

c. ciliare See ciliary body, under body.

c. hemorrhagicum A blood clot in the ovary formed in the cavity left by ovulation, the normal rupture of a vesicular ovarian follicle.

c. luteum A secretory structure in the ovary formed at the site of a ruptured vesicular ovarian follicle after it has discharged its ovum; it consists of a large mass of cells containing a yellow pigment (lutein), which is derived from the follicular (granulosa) and theca cells; it produces the hormone progesterone that causes thickening of the uterine lining in preparation for the implantation of the fertilized ovum; if pregnancy fails to occur, the corpus luteum regresses to a mass of scar tissue (corpus albicans), which eventually vanishes; if pregnancy occurs, it continues to grow for 13 weeks before slowly regressing.

c. mamillare, c. mamillaria See mamillary body, under body.

corpora para-aortica See organs of Zuckerkandl, under organ.

corpora quadrigemina See colliculi of midbrain, under colliculus.

c. spongiosum The median cylindrical mass of erectile tissue of the penis, situated between and inferior to the corpora cavernosa and surrounding the urethra; it is continuous with the bulb of the penis posteriorly and the glans penis anteriorly.

c. striatum The caudate and lentiform nuclei and the internal capsule considered as a whole, situated in front of and lateral to the thalamus in each hemisphere of the brain. Also called striate body.

c. vitreum See vitreous body, under body.

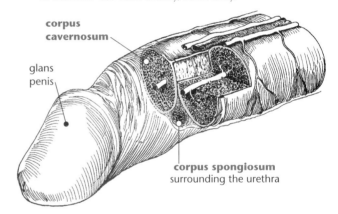

corpus cavernosum

glans penis

corpus spongiosum surrounding the urethra

corpuscle (kor′pus-l) **1.** A small, discrete anatomic structure, such as a microscopic encapsulated nerve ending. **2.** A cell in the body, either one capable of moving freely or one restricted to a particular structure. **3.** A primary particle such as a photon or an electron.

blood c. Any blood cell.

bone c. A bone cell (osteocyte).

cartilage c. A cartilage cell (chondrocyte).

colostral c. A large, round cellular body containing cytoplasmic fat globules, present in breast secretion occurring in the later stages of pregnancy and for a few days after childbirth (parturition); thought to be a phagocytic cell of the mammary gland. Also called galactoblast.

concentric c. of Hassall See concentric corpuscle of thymus.

concentric c. of thymus A corpuscle, from 30 to 100 μm in diameter, found in the medulla of the thymus; formed by concentric layers of epithelial cells around a central nerve fiber; it increases in size and number during episodes of intense lympholysis. Also called concentric corpuscle of Hassall.

end c. See terminal corpuscle.

genital c. A specialized sensory nerve ending enveloped by a capsule, found in the skin of the external genitalia and of the nipple.

ghost c. See achromocyte.

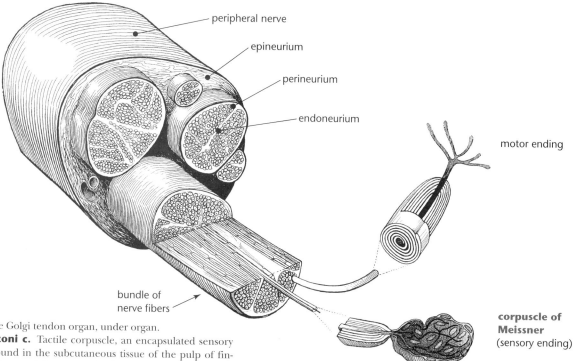

peripheral nerve
epineurium
perineurium
endoneurium

motor ending

bundle of
nerve fibers

corpuscle of
Meissner
(sensory ending)

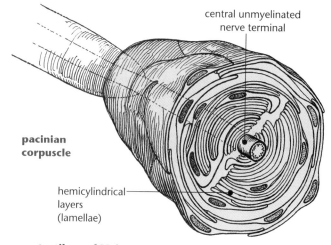

central unmyelinated
nerve terminal

pacinian
corpuscle

hemicylindrical
layers
(lamellae)

Golgi c. See Golgi tendon organ, under organ.

Golgi-Mazzoni c. Tactile corpuscle, an encapsulated sensory nerve ending found in the subcutaneous tissue of the pulp of fingertips; similar to a pacinian corpuscle, but with a thinner capsule and with a nerve fiber that ramifies more extensively.

Krause's c. A small, encapsulated, bulbous nerve ending found at the termination of some sensory nerve fibers in the skin, mucous membranes, conjunctiva, and the heart; it responds to the sensation of cold. Also called Krause's end-bulb.

lamellated c.'s Encapsulated nerve endings (receptor terminals) that possess circumferential, concentric layers of connective tissue around the terminal part of a nerve; examples include the pacinian corpuscle, Krause's corpuscle, and genital corpuscle.

malpighian c. See renal corpuscle.

c. of Meissner A small, oval, encapsulated nerve ending with a central core, seen in the dermal papillae of the skin of the hand and foot, in the lips, palpebral conjunctiva, and the mucous membrane of the most anterior part of the tongue; functions as low-threshold receptors for the sensation of discriminative touch. Also called oval corpuscle; tactile corpuscle of Meissner; corpuscle of touch.

oval c. See corpuscle of Meissner.

pacinian c. A relatively large (up to 2 mm in length) receptor nerve ending composed of a capsule with approximately 25 to 35 concentrically arranged lamellae of flattened cells and a core consisting of approximately 50 to 60 closely packed lamellae positioned on both sides of a central unmyelinated nerve terminal; it responds to pressure stimuli from touch or vibrations and is present in subcutaneous tissue, fascial planes around joints and tendons, and in the mesentery about the pancreas; especially numerous in the palm of the hand, sole of the foot, and genital organs; occasionally seen in the outer coat of the aorta. Also called lamellated corpuscle; Vater-Pacini corpuscle.

phantom c. See achromocyte.

red blood c. See erythrocyte.

renal c. The most proximal part of the nephron formed by a central tuft of capillaries (glomerulus) encased in Bowman's (glomcrular) capsule, about 0.2 mm in diameter; there are approximately 1 to 2 million renal corpuscles in each kidney, serving as a filter of constituents from plasma. Also called malpighian body; malpighian corpuscle.

c. of Ruffini Encapsulated nerve ending concerned with the perception of pressure and of warmth; found in the dermis of hairy skin and in the superficial layers of the articular capsules of joints. Also called Ruffini's nerve ending.

salivary c. A large oval cell containing granules of various sizes, found in normal saliva.

shadow c. See achromocyte.

tactile c. of Meissner See corpuscle of Meissner.

terminal c. Any encapsulated sensory nerve ending, such as the pacinian corpuscle. Also called end corpuscle.

c. of touch See corpuscle of Meissner.

Vater-Pacini c. See pacinian corpuscle.

white blood c. See leukocyte.

correspondence (kor-e-spon'dens) The condition of being in harmony or agreement.

corrosive (kŏ-ro'siv) Causing a gradual wearing away or disintegration of a substance or tissues by chemical action; caustic.

cortex (kor'teks), pl. cor'tices The outer layer of an organ (e.g., of the brain, kidney, or adrenal gland); distinguished from the inner medullary substance.

motor c. See motor area, under area.

sensory c. See sensory area, under area.

cortical (kor'tĭ-kal) Relating to the cortex.

corticifugal (kor-tĭ-sif'u-gal) Conveying impulses away from the cerebral cortex; said of certain nerve fibers.

corticipetal (kor-tĭ-sip'e-tal) Conveying impulses toward the cerebral cortex; said of certain nerve fibers.

corticoid (kor'tĭ-koid) See corticosteroid.

corticosteroid (kor-tĭ-ko-ste'roid) Any of the hormones produced by the cortex of the adrenal (suprarenal) gland, or a synthetic substitute. Also called corticoid.

corticosterone (kor-tĭ-kos'ter-on) A hormone produced in the adrenal cortex that induces deposition of the simple sugar glycogen in the liver, some retention of sodium, and excretion of potassium.

corticothalamic (kor-tĭ-ko-thah-lam'ik) Relating to the cerebral cortex and the thalamus.

corticotropin (kor-tĭ-ko-tro'pin) See adrenocorticotropic hormone (ACTH), under hormone.

cortisol (kor'tĭ-sol) See hydrocortisone.

cortisone (kor'tĭ-son) A hormone produced in minute amounts by the adrenal cortex in response to the action of a pituitary hormone (adrenocorticotropic hormone); also produced synthetically.

Corynebacterium (ko-ri'ne-bak-te're-um) A genus of gram-positive, club-shaped bacteria; a cause of disease in plants, animals, and humans.

    C. diphtheriae A species causing diphtheria in humans; some strains produce a potent toxin that causes degeneration of heart muscle in humans and experimental animals.

    C. equi Former name for *Rhodococcus equi*.

    C. haemolyticum Former name for Arcanobacterium haemolyticum.

    C. jeikeium A species infecting the blood (bacteremia) of patients afflicted with an abnormally low neutrophil count (neutropenia).

coryza (kŏ-ri'zah) See acute rhinitis, under rhinitis.

cosmesis (koz-me'sis) Concern for the physical appearance of the patient, especially during surgical operations.

cosmetic (koz-met'ik) Denoting a preparation or procedure designed to improve the appearance of a person.

costa (kos'tah), pl. cos'tae Latin for rib.

costal (kos'tal) Relating to a rib.

costectomy (kos-tek'to-me) Surgical removal of a rib, or a portion of one.

costive (kos'tiv) **1.** Relating to constipation. **2.** Any agent that causes constipation.

costo- Combining form meaning rib.

costochondral (kos-to-kon'dral) Relating to the rib cartilage.

costochondritis (kos-to-kon-dri'tis) Inflammation of one or more cartilages of the ribs, causing pain of the anterior chest wall; pain is usually sharply localized and may be brief and darting or a continuous dull ache. Also called costal chondritis.

costoclavicular (kos-to-klah-vik'u-lar) Relating to the ribs and the collarbone (clavicle).

costoscapular (kos-to-skap'u-lar) Relating to the ribs and the shoulder blade (scapula).

costosternal (kos-to-ster'nal) Relating to the ribs and the breastbone (sternum).

costosternoplasty (kos-to-ster'no-plas-te) Surgical repair of a malformation of the chest wall.

costotome (kos'to-tom) A surgical instrument used in cutting through a rib.

costotome

costotomy (kos-tot'o-me) Surgical cutting into, or division of, a rib.

costovertebral (kos-to-ver'tĕ-bral) Relating to the ribs and the thoracic vertebrae.

cothromboplastin (ko-throm-bo-plas'tin) See factor VII, under factor.

cotinine (ko'tĭ-nēn) A major by-product of nicotine; it is rapidly eliminated by the kidneys and excreted in the urine; thought to be an indicator of the amount of tobacco smoke a person has inhaled; has been found also in the urine of nonsmokers exposed to tobacco smoke.

cotransport (ko-trans'port) The simultaneous transmission of two substances across a membrane and in the same direction.

cotton (kot'n) The white fibers covering the seeds of the cotton plant.

    absorbent c. Cotton from which cottonseed oil and impurities have been removed.

cotyle (kot'ĭ-le) **1.** Any cup-shaped anatomic structure. **2.** See acetabulum.

cotyledon (kot-ĭ-le'don) One of the 15 to 20 subdivisions of the placenta, on the maternal side (i.e., the side that is attached to the uterine wall).

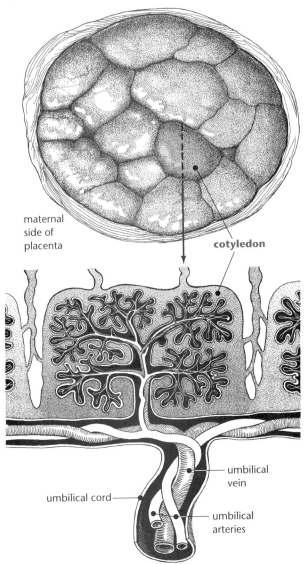

maternal side of placenta

cotyledon

umbilical vein

umbilical cord

umbilical arteries

cough (kawf) A sudden expulsion of air from the lungs.

    whooping c. Popular term for pertussis.

coulomb (koo'lom) (Q) The unit of the quantity of electrical transport in one second by a current of one ampere.

counseling (kown'sel-ing) A type of professional service that includes guidance in psychosocial situations and gives a person an understanding of his or her problems and potentialities.

    genetic c. A professional service that provides individuals and families having a genetic disorder, or at risk of such a disorder, with information about their condition; it also provides information that would allow couples at risk to make informed decisions about having children.

count (kownt) **1.** The total number of items in a sample (e.g., of blood cells or pollutant particles). **2.** The process of obtaining such a number.

    Arneth c. The distribution of polymorphonuclear neutrophils (PMNs), when classified by the number of lobes in their nuclei.

    blood c. The determination of the number of red (RBC) or white (WBC) blood cells in a cubic millimeter of blood.

coliform c. The number of coliform bacteria (*Escherichia coli*) in a sample of water; used as a measure of suitability of water for drinking.

complete blood c. (CBC) A combination of laboratory tests including red blood cell count, white blood cell count, differential white cell count, hemoglobin concentration, hematocrit, and stained red cell examination; may also include platelet count.

differential white cell c. Determination of the percentage of various types of white blood cells that make up the total white blood cell count.

sharp c.'s A counting procedure usually performed before, during, and after a surgical operation to ensure that none of the sharp items taken into the operating room is misplaced (e.g., needles, scalpel blades, electrosurgical blades, or any other sharp objects).

sperm c. The total number of sperms (spermatozoa) in the ejaculate; the human ejaculate generally measures 3 to 5 ml with about 50 to 150 million sperms per milliliter. If the ejaculate has fewer than 20 million sperms per milliliter, the male is likely to be infertile.

sponge c.'s The counting of all soft goods (e.g., sponges and tapes) taken into an operating room to be used in a surgical procedure; items are usually counted before, during, and after the procedure to ensure that none is misplaced.

counter- Combining form meaning opposite.

counter (kown'ter) Any device used for counting.

Geiger c. See Geiger-Müller counter.

Geiger-Müller c. An instrument for detecting and measuring radioactivity; it consists of a negatively charged metallic cylinder in a vacuum tube containing a positively charged wire. Also called Geiger counter.

scintillation c. Device used for detecting radioactive particles by using fluorescent materials and photomultiplier tubes.

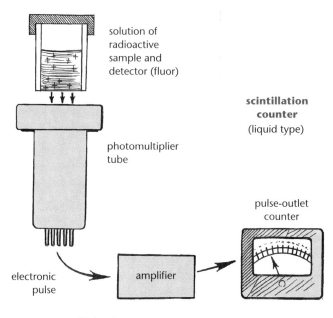

solution of radioactive sample and detector (fluor)

scintillation counter (liquid type)

photomultiplier tube

pulse-outlet counter

electronic pulse

amplifier

counterconditioning (kown'ter-kon-dish'un-ing) In behavior therapy, establishment of a second conditioned response to nullify a previously learned response.

countercurrent (kown'ter-ker-ent) Flowing in an opposite direction.

counterdepressant (kown-ter-de-pres'ant) **1.** Preventing the depressant effects of a drug. **2.** Anything having such an effect.

counterextension (kown-ter-eks-ten'shun) See countertraction.

counterirritant (kown-ter-ir'ĭ-tant) A substance applied locally to produce a mild superficial irritation in order to alleviate an underlying inflammation (e.g., poultice).

counteropening (kown-ter-o'pen-ing) A second opening or puncture made opposite to an earlier one to promote better drainage (as of an abscess). Also called counterpuncture.

counterpulsation (kown-ter-pul-sa'shun) A procedure used to increase an impaired circulation (e.g., in acute myocardial infarction) by means of a pump that is synchronized with the heartbeat.

counterpuncture (kown-ter-pun'chur) See counteropening.

countershock (kown'ter-shok) An electric shock applied to the heart to stop an abnormal rhythm of the heartbeat, such as fibrillation.

counterstain (kown'ter-stān) A dye used in microscopy to stain tissue elements that remained unaffected by a previously used dye of another color (which was taken up only by the tissue elements under study). The counterstain renders the target elements more visible. Also called contrast stain.

countertraction (kown-ter-trak'shun) A traction that is antagonistic to another; a back-pull. Also called counterextension.

countertransference (kown-ter-trans-fer'ens) The emotional reaction of a psychotherapist to the patient based both on the unconscious needs and conflicts of the therapist and on reactions induced by the patient; it is a necessary aspect of psychoanalytic therapy. See also transference.

countertransport (kown-ter-trans'port) The passage of two substances across a cell membrane simultaneously but in opposite directions.

coupling (kup'ling) A regular succession of paired heartbeats, a normal beat followed by a premature beat.

constant c. See fixed coupling.

fixed c. Coupling in which the premature heartbeats constantly follow the normal ones at regular intervals. Also called constant coupling.

variable c. Coupling in which the premature heartbeats follow the normal ones at irregular intervals.

covalence (ko-vāl'ens) The number of electron pairs an atom can share with its neighbor.

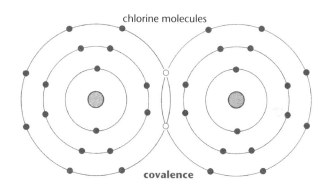

chlorine molecules

covalence

coverslip (kov'er-slip) See cover glass, under glass.

cowpox (kow'poks) A mild eruptive skin disease affecting the teats and udders of cattle, caused by a poxvirus; the virus can be transmitted to humans by skin contact with infected animals. See also vaccinia.

coxalgia (kok-sal'je-ah) See coxodynia.

Coxiella burnetii (kok-se-el'ah bur-net'i) A species of bacteria (genus *Coxiella*) that causes Q fever in humans.

coxodynia (kok-so-din'e-ah) Pain in the hip. Also called coxalgia.

coxsackievirus (kok-sak'e-vi'rus) Any of a group of RNA viruses (genus *Enterovirus*, family Picornaviridae); two types, A and B, have been identified, with a number of serotypes in each; they are the cause of aseptic meningitis and other diseases affecting muscles, heart, and skin. Also written Coxsackie virus.

crack (krak) See crack cocaine, under cocaine.

cramp (kramp) A painful muscular contraction.

heat c.'s Slow, painful muscle contractions and severe muscle spasms that last from one to three minutes; they occur in persons doing strenuous work in extreme hot temperatures; they usually occur in the muscles employed in the work.

occupational c. Any painful spasm associated with the movements and activities required by a particular occupation, or with the environment where the work is performed, which renders work performance increasingly difficult. Also called professional cramp; fatigue spasm; functional spasm; occupational spasm; professional spasm.

painter's c. Severe contraction of smooth muscles of the intestinal wall causing intense colicky pain and rigidity of the abdomen, which may mimic a surgical emergency; caused by toxic exposure to lead; persons at risk include workers in industries that process and manufacture lead, batteries, paints, and gasoline, as well as young children.

professional c. See occupational cramp.

tailor's c. Muscle spasm and neuralgic pain of the forearm and hand. Also called tailor's spasm.

writer's c. Painful spasm or neuralgic pain of the muscles of the hand employed in writing, especially of the thumb and two adjacent fingers; caused by excessive writing. Also called graphospasm; writer's spasm; mogigraphia.

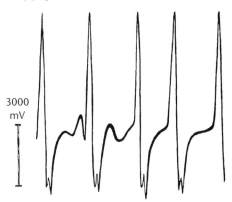

electromyogram of **muscle cramp**

cranial (kra′ne-al) **1.** Relating to the cranium (i.e., the part of the skull containing the brain). **2.** Relating to the head.

craniectomy (kra-ne-ek′to-me) Surgical removal of a portion of the skull.

cranio-, crani- Combining forms meaning the cranium.

craniocele (kra′ne-o-sēl) See encephalocele.

craniofacial (kra-ne-o-fa′shal) Relating to the skull and the face.

craniology (kra-ne-ol′o-je) The scientific study of skulls in all their aspects.

craniomalacia (kra-ne-o-mah-la′she-ah) A softening of the bones of the skull.

craniometer (kra-ne-om′e-ter) An instrument for measuring skulls.

craniometric (kra-ne-o-met′rik) Relating to craniometry.

craniometry (kra-ne-om′ĕ-tre) Measurement of the distances between standard (craniometric) points on the skull, and the study of their proportions.

craniopagus (kra-ne-op′ah-gus) Conjoined twins with fused skulls.

craniopathy (kra-ne-op′ah-the) Any disease of the skull.

craniopharyngioma (kra-ne-o-fah-rin-je-o′mah) A noncancerous, encapsulated tumor of the brain, with solid and cystic components and calcium deposits; believed to be derived from remnants of the embryonic adenohypophysis (Rathke's pouch); tumor may encroach on certain brain structures (pituitary, third ventricle, optic chiasm), causing resulting symptoms.

craniopuncture (kra′ne-o-punk-tūr) Puncture of the skull.

craniorachischisis (kra′ne-o-rah-kĭs′kĭ-sis) Congenital defect marked by the presence of a fissure or open slit in the skull and vertebral column.

cranioschisis (kra′ne-os′kĭ-sis) The presence of a congenital fissure or open slit in the skull.

craniosclerosis (kra-ne-o-skle-ro′sis) Thickening of the bones of the skull.

craniostosis (kra-ne-os-to′sis) See craniosynostosis.

craniosynostosis (kra-ne-o-sin-os-to′sis) Condition characterized by early union of one or more of the joints between the bones of the skull,

resulting in a deformed head; it may occur in an infant with other bone defects or in an otherwise healthy body. Also called craniostosis.

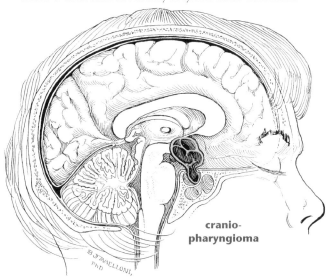

cranio-
pharyngioma

craniotabes (kra-ne-o-ta′bēz) Localized softening of the skull, usually occurring in children afflicted with rickets.

craniotome (kra′ne-o-tōm) Instrument formerly used to perforate and crush a fetal head.

craniotomy (kra-ne-ot′ō-me) **1.** A cut or incision into the skull. **2.** A formerly used procedure in which the head of a dead fetus was punctured and its contents evacuated to allow a vaginal delivery.

cranium (kra′ne-um), pl. cra′nia The skull; in general, the bones of the head; in particular, the bones enclosing the brain, excluding the bones of the face.

crater (kra′ter) A depressed, usually central, area (as of an ulcer).

crateriform (kra-ter′ĭ-form) Depressed or hollowed; shaped like a bowl.

crazing (kra′zing) The formation of fine, minute cracks on the surface of a structure (e.g., natural or artificial teeth).

crease (krēs) A slight linear depression.

simian c. A major flexion crease across the entire palm of the hand; formed by fusion of the proximal and distal palmar creases; occasionally occurs in normal individuals; most frequently seen in persons afflicted with Down's syndrome. Also called simian line.

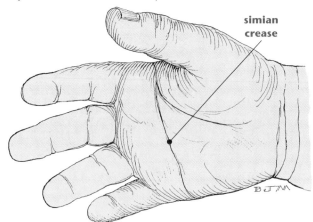

simian
crease

creatine (kre′ah-tin) A product of protein metabolism in muscles, it combines with phosphate to form a high-energy compound (phosphocreatine); increased amounts of creatine are released into the bloodstream in certain muscular diseases (e.g., muscular dystrophy); metabolized to creatinine.

c. kinase An essential enzyme for muscle contraction; it promotes the formation of adenosine triphosphate (ATP) from phosphocreatine and adenosine diphosphate (ADP). Increased amounts are released into the bloodstream after acute muscle damage, as in myocardial infarction; different forms, or isoenzymes, are found in skeletal muscle, heart muscle, and brain tissue; formerly called creatine phosphokinase (CPK).

c. phosphate See phosphocreatine.

c. phosphokinase (CPK) Former name for creatine kinase.

creatinine (kre-at′ĭ-nin) (Cr) A product of creatine metabolism and a normal metabolic waste; it is removed from the blood by glomerular filtration in the kidneys and excreted in the urine. Since creatinine is usually produced at a constant rate, the clearance rate and the serum level are used as an index of kidney function. See also creatinine test, under test.

creatinuria (kre-at-ĭ-nu′re-ah) An increased amount of creatine in the urine.

cremaster (kre-mas′ter) See table of muscles.

crenate, crenated (kre′nāt, kre′nāt-ed) Notched.

crenocyte (kre′no-sīt) An abnormal red blood cell (erythrocyte) with notched edges.

crepitant (krep′ĭ-tant) Crackling or grating.

crepitation (krep-ĭ-ta′shun) A crepitus.

crepitus (krep′ĭ-tus) 1. The grating sound elicited by friction of the ends of a broken bone or the motion of arthritic joints. 2. The sensation felt over an area containing subcutaneous gas, as in gas gangrene.

crescent (kres′ent) Any structure shaped like a sickle.

c. of Giannuzzi See serous demilunes, under demilune.

malarial c. The gametocyte of *Plasmodium falciparum*, the parasite causing falciparum malaria. Also called sickle form.

cresol (kre′sol) A poisonous compound derived from coal tar; used as a disinfectant.

CREST Acronym for a syndrome: Calcinosis, Raynaud's phenomenon,

Esophageal involvement, Sclerodactyly, and Telangiectasia. See also CREST syndrome, under syndrome.

crest (krest) A bony ridge or linear elevation.

alveolar c. The margin of the alveolar bone socket surrounding a tooth.

ampullary c. See crista ampullaris, under crista.

conchal c. A horizontal ridge just above the inferior meatus of the nasal cavity; it articulates with the inferior nasal concha.

ethmoidal c. of maxilla A horizontal ridge located on the medial side of the frontal process of the maxilla; it articulates with the middle nasal concha of the ethmoid bone.

frontal c. The median sagittal ridge on the internal surface of the frontal bone projecting inward to the anterior cranial fossa; it extends from the foramen cecum to the sulcus for the superior sagittal sinus.

ganglionic c. See neural crests.

gingival c. The margin of the free gingiva separating the gingival sulcus from the external gingiva.

c. of head of rib The transverse ridge between the two articulating facets on the head of the rib.

iliac c. The long, curved upper and outer border of the ilium.

incisor c. The front part of the nasal crest of maxilla that rises as it passes forward to form a sharp spine (anterior nasal spine).

infundibuloventricular c. See supraventricular crest.

intertrochanteric c. See trochanteric crest.

nasal c. of maxilla The ridge along the middle of the nasal cavity floor, which, along with the ridge of the opposite maxilla, forms a groove for the articulation of the vomer; it makes a minor contribution to the formation of the nasal septum.

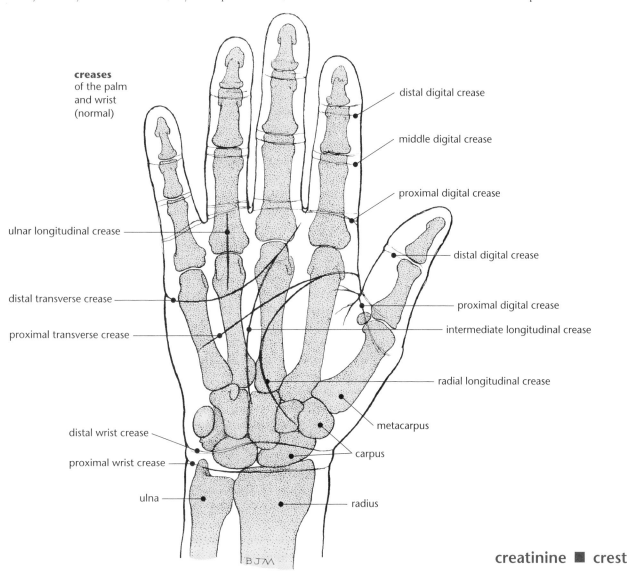

creases
of the palm
and wrist
(normal)

distal digital crease

middle digital crease

proximal digital crease

distal digital crease

proximal digital crease

ulnar longitudinal crease

intermediate longitudinal crease

distal transverse crease

proximal transverse crease

radial longitudinal crease

metacarpus

distal wrist crease

carpus

proximal wrist crease

ulna

radius

BJM

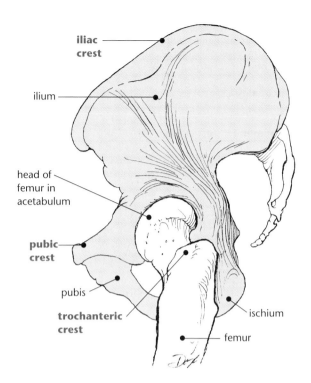

nasal c. of palatine bone A thick ridge along the medial border of the horizontal plate of the palatine bone; it articulates with the back portion of the vomer and makes a minor contribution to the nasal septum.

neural c.'s The two bands of ectodermal cells flanking the neural plate of the early embryo; eventually they give rise to the nerve cells of sensory and autonomic ganglia. Also called ganglionic crests.

occipital c.'s *External*, a vertical ridge on the external occipital bone extending from the external occipital protuberance toward the foramen magnum; it accommodates the attachment of the nuchal ligament. *Internal*, the cross-shaped bony elevation on the internal surface of the occipital bone of the skull, at the intersection of sinus ridges; it accommodates the attachment of the falx cerebelli.

pubic c. The roughened, free, upper anterior border of the body of the pubic bone.

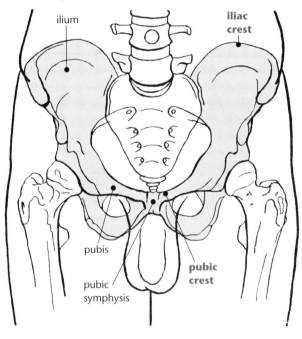

c. of spine of scapula The posterior border of the spine of the shoulder blade (scapula); it continues laterally to the acromion and provides attachment to the supraspinous, infraspinous, deltoid, and trapezius muscles.

spiral c. The serrated edge of the delicate bony spiral lamina of the cochlea, which winds around a central core approximately 2 3/4 turns.

supraventricular c. A massive muscular ridge between the atrioventricular and pulmonary orifices of the right ventricle of the heart, separating the conus arteriosus from the remaining chamber of the right ventricle. Also called infundibuloventricular crest.

trochanteric c. A prominent ridge between the greater and lesser trochanters of the femur, marking the junction of the neck and shaft of the bone. Also called intertrochanteric crest.

urethral c. *Female*, a longitudinal fold of mucous membrane on the posterior wall of the urethral canal; the site where many small mucous urethral glands open. *Male*, a narrow median longitudinal elevation on the posterior wall of the urethral canal passing vertically through the prostate; the site where the two ejaculatory ducts open.

cretin (kre′tin) A person afflicted with cretinism.

cretinism (kre′tin-izm) An uncommon disease of childhood due to lack of thyroid hormone; characterized in early stages by feeding problems, lethargy, failure to thrive, coarse skin, and a hoarse cry; later manifestions include stunted growth, a large protruding tongue, and mental retardation; it may be caused by failure of development of the thyroid gland, by dietary iodine deficiency of both the mother during pregnancy and the baby after birth, or by a defect in hormone synthesis. Also called hypothyroid dwarfism.

cretinoid (kre′tin-oid) Having symptoms like those of cretinism.

crevice (krev′is) A crack.

gingival c. The space between a tooth and the margin of the gums.

cribriform (krib′rĭ-form) Having many small perforations; sievelike.

cricoarytenoid (kri-ko-ar-ĭ-te′noid) Relating to the cricoid and arytenoid cartilages of the larynx.

cricoid (kri′koid) **1.** Ringlike. **2.** See cricoid cartilage, under cartilage.

cricoidectomy (kri-koi-dek′to-me) Surgical removal of the lowermost component (the cricoid cartilage) of the larynx.

cricothyroid (kri-ko-thi′roid) Relating to two components of the larynx, the cricoid and thyroid cartilages.

cricothyroidostomy (kri-ko-thi′roi-dos′to-me) An emergency measure for the relief of upper airway obstruction by way of a midline incision through the skin and cricothyroid membrane, followed by insertion of a tracheostomy tube through the opening; it is a temporary expedient pending establishment of a tracheostomy.

cricotomy (kri-kot′o-me) Division of the lowermost component (the cricoid cartilage) of the larynx.

criminalist (krim′in-ah-list) One who practices criminalistics.

criminalistics (krim-in-ah-lis′tiks) The application of scientific techniques to the problems of criminal investigation and apprehension. It involves collecting evidence at the crime scene; documenting, packaging, sealing, and preserving the evidence in a non-contaminated state; and maintaining chain of custody of the evidence.

criminology (krim-ĭ-nol′o-je) The scientific study of crime as a social phenomenon, of criminal behavior in all its aspects, and of all characteristics of criminals; with special emphasis on the personality factors and social conditions leading toward or away from crime.

crinogenic (krin-o-jen′ik) Causing or stimulating increased glandular secretion.

cripple (krip′l) **1.** To cause a disability. **2.** A person who is partially or completely disabled.

crisis (kri′sis), pl. cri′ses **1.** A sudden change, for better or worse, in the course of a disease. **2.** An abrupt paroxysmal attack of pain or distress.

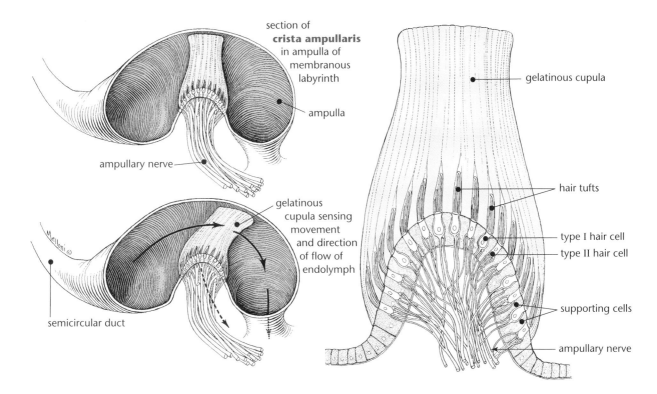

section of **crista ampullaris** in ampulla of membranous labyrinth

ampulla

ampullary nerve

gelatinous cupula sensing movement and direction of flow of endolymph

semicircular duct

gelatinous cupula

hair tufts

type I hair cell

type II hair cell

supporting cells

ampullary nerve

addisonian c. See acute adrenocortical insufficiency, under insufficiency.

adrenal c. See adrenocortical insufficiency, under insufficiency.

Dietl's c. Excruciating pain in the lumbar or abdominal areas, usually caused by a kinked ureter.

oculogyric c. An attack of spastic, upward movement of both eyes, frequently accompanied by a backward head tilt; attacks may occur sporadically or frequently, often followed by sleep; seen in certain types of encephalitis and as a toxic effect of the drug phenothiazine.

thyroid c. See thyrotoxic crisis.

thyrotoxic c. A life-threatening flare of thyrotoxicosis, characterized by high fever, rapid pulse, a rise in basic metabolic rate, nausea, vomiting, diarrhea, agitation, delirium, coma, and occasionally, heart failure. The crisis occurs in patients afflicted with thyrotoxicosis, precipitated by events that cause marked release of thyroid hormone such as thyroid surgery, radioactive thyroid therapy, childbirth, or during a severe illness. Also called thyroid storm; thyroid crisis.

crista (kris'ta), pl. cris'tae A ridge or a protruding structure.

c. ampullaris An elevation on the inner surface of the ampulla of each semicircular duct of the internal ear; it contains innervated hair cells whose hairlike stereocilia and kinocilia are embedded in an overlying gelatinous cupula that extends almost to the opposite wall of the ampulla; it serves as a detector of body movements. Also called ampullary crest.

c. galli A perpendicular bony ridge on the upper surface of the ethmoid bone in the midline of the anterior cranial fossa at the base of the skull, projecting above the level of the cribriform plate; it serves as a point of attachment for the fold of cranial dura mater (the falx cerebri) that separates the cerebral hemispheres.

c. terminalis A muscular band in the wall of the right atrium of the heart; it separates the atrium proper from the sinus (sinus venarum) that receives blood from the superior vena cava and the inferior vena cava.

c. tuberculi majoris See spine of greater tubercle of humerus, under spine.

c. tuberculi minoris See spine of smaller tubercle of humerus, under spine.

cristobalite (kris-to'bah-līt) A crystalline silica, stable at high temperatures, used in dental casting investments to increase thermal expansion.

criterion (kri-te're-on), pl. crite'ria **1.** A standard against which something can be judged. **2.** A list of symptoms and/or signs of a disorder that should be present (in totality or in sufficient numbers) to warrant diagnosis of the disorder.

Rome criteria Symptom criteria for diagnosis of irritable bowel syndrome, consisting of at least three months of continuous or recurrent abdominal pain or discomfort, relieved by defecation, and/or associated with a change in frequency or consistency of stool, plus two or more of the following (at least 25% of the time): altered stool frequency, altered stool form (lumpy/hard or loose/watery), altered stool passage (straining, urgency, or feeling of incomplete evacuation), passage of mucus, bloating, or feeling of abdominal distention.

critical (krit'ĭ-kl) **1.** Relating to a crisis. **2.** Denoting the state of a patient's illness in which death is possible or imminent.

critical-case individual A person applying for disability benefits (e.g., a Social Security claimant) who is identified as having a terminal illness; identifying the person in this way facilitates handling the application on a priority basis and speeds the processing of the steps necessary before payments can begin.

crossbite (kros'bīt) Condition in which the normal relationship between a group of teeth of the upper and lower jaws is reversed (i.e., the lower teeth are anterior and/or buccal to the upper teeth).

cross-dressing (kros' dres'ing) See transvestism.

cross-eye (kros'ī) See esotropia.

crossfoot (kros'foot) See talipes varus, under talipes.

crossing-over (kros'ing o'ver) Reciprocal exchange of DNA segments between two homologous chromosomes at corresponding sites; it occurs during meiosis through the formation of a chiasm.

cross-matching (kros mach'ing) A test using cells from a recipient and serum from a donor to detect the presence of antibodies directed at the recipient's cells.

crossway (kros'wā) The crossing of two nerve paths (e.g., sensory pathways in the brain).

croup (krōōp) Popular term for any type of laryngitis, usually affecting children and including any or all of the following symptoms: laryngeal spasm, a brassy barking cough, and a shrill respiratory sound.

croupy (krōōp'e) Relating to croup.

crown (krown) The top of a structure, as of the head or a tooth.

anatomic c. The area of a tooth covered by enamel.

artificial c. A restoration of the crown of a tooth; it may be partial (covering three or more surfaces) or complete (covering all surfaces) and can be made of gold or other metal, porcelain, or acrylic resin.

clinical c. The part of a tooth visible over the gums. Also called physiologic crown.

dowel c. A complete artificial crown replacing the natural crown and supported by means of a post fitted into the filled root canal of a nonviable tooth.

face c. An artificial crown that has all or part of its surfaces covered with a veneer of porcelain or acrylic resin for aesthetic purposes.

crown and bridge The branch of prosthodontics that deals with crown restorations and with the fixed type of tooth-borne dentures.

crowning (krown´ing) In obstetrics, the end of the second stage of labor when the head of the baby is visible, its largest diameter encircled by the stretched vulva.

cruciate (kroo´she-āt) Resembling a cross.

crucible (kroo´sĭ-bl) A special heat-resistant receptacle used for melting materials at high temperatures.

crucible former (kroo´si-bl for´mer) A stand for holding the sprued wax pattern of a dental restoration; it forms the base for the casting ring.

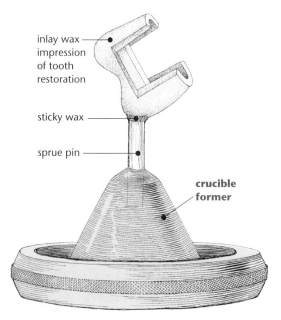

inlay wax impression of tooth restoration

sticky wax

sprue pin

crucible former

crura (kroo´rah) Plural of crus.

crural (kroor´al) Relating to the leg or thigh.

crus (krus), pl. cru´ra **1.** In anatomic nomenclature, the leg; the region between the knee joint and the ankle joint. **2.** Any elongated process or leglike structure.

crura of antihelix Two crura of the auricle of the ear into which the antihelix divides, between which is enclosed the triangular fossa.

crura of clitoris Two elongated, inward extensions of the corpora cavernosa of the clitoris, attached to the pubic and ischial rami; they converge anteriorly to form the greater part of the body of the clitoris.

common membranous c. A short membranous duct of the internal ear (in adults, about 4 mm in length), formed by the union of the upper end of the posterior semicircular duct with the anterior semicircular duct, opening into the medial part of the vestibule.

common osseous c. The short bony canal of the internal ear formed by the union of the upper end of the posterior semicircular canal with the anterior semicircular canal; it accommodates the common membranous crus, which is about one-fourth the diameter of the canal. Also called crus commune.

c. commune See common osseous crus.

crura of diaphragm Two fibromuscular bands that encircle the aorta and connect the respiratory diaphragm to the lumbar vertebrae: *Left,* the fibromuscular origin of the left side of the respiratory diaphragm arising from the upper two or three lumbar vertebral bodies. *Right,* the fibromuscular origin of the right side of the respiratory diaphragm arising from the first three or four lumbar vertebral bodies; during its course, it separates to accommodate the passage of the esophagus from the thoracic cavity to the abdominal cavity.

c. of incus Either of two crura of the incus (middle ear ossicle): *Long,* the process coming off the body of the incus, directed downward; at its lower end it articulates with the head of the stapes. *Short,* a conical process coming off the body of the incus, directed backward; it is attached by a ligament to the posterior wall of the middle ear (tympanic) cavity.

c. of inguinal ring Either of two bands forming the margins of the superficial inguinal ring: *Lateral (inferior),* a curved band forming the lateral (inferior) margin of the superficial inguinal ring; composed of fibers of the inguinal ligament. *Medial (superior),* a thin, flat band forming the medial (superior) margin of the superficial inguinal ring; composed of the aponeurosis of the external abdominal oblique muscle.

crura of penis Two elongated, inward extensions of the corpora cavernosa of the penis, attached to the pubic arch, just in front of the ischial tuberosity; they converge anteriorly to form the greater part of the body of the penis.

c. of stapes Either of two crura of the stapes (innermost ear ossicle): *Anterior,* the anterior crus that extends from the neck of the stapes to the baseplate; it is the shorter and less curved of the two crura. *Posterior,* the posterior crus that extends from the neck of the stapes to the baseplate; it is the longer, larger, and more curved of the two crura.

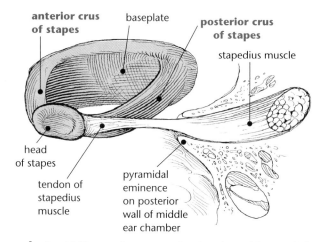

anterior crus of stapes

baseplate

posterior crus of stapes

stapedius muscle

head of stapes

tendon of stapedius muscle

pyramidal eminence on posterior wall of middle ear chamber

crush (krush) To press between two hard surfaces with enough force to cause injury. See also crush injury, under injury.

crust (krust) **1.** The hardened secretion of a lesion; a scab. **2.** Any hard outer layer.

crutch (kruch) A supporting device used singly or in pairs as an aid to walking.

crux (kruks) Latin for cross.

c. of heart The walls, in the shape of a cross, at the intersection of the four chambers of the heart.

cry (kri) **1.** A loud utterance of distress. **2.** A warning sign.

epileptic c. A harsh vocal utterance sometimes made by a person at the start of an epileptic seizure.

c. for help Communicative gestures, actions, or behavior that are messages manifesting a state of extreme distress (e.g., a person contemplating suicide may place notes in conspicuous places; parent may take a battered child to an emergency room three or four times a week; an isolated new mother may take her healthy infant to an emergency room with multiple complaints).

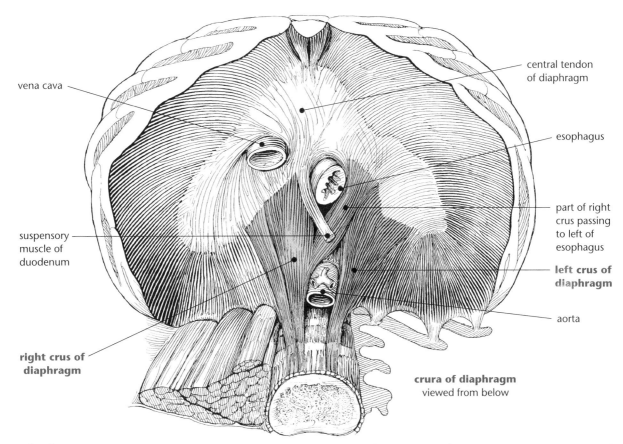

vena cava

central tendon
of diaphragm

esophagus

suspensory
muscle of
duodenum

part of right
crus passing
to left of
esophagus

**left crus of
diaphragm**

aorta

**right crus of
diaphragm**

crura of diaphragm
viewed from below

C

cryanesthesia (kri-an-es-the′ze-ah) Loss of the ability to perceive cold.

cryesthesia (kri-es-the′ze-ah) Abnormal sensitivity to cold.

cryo-, cry- Combining forms meaning cold.

cryobiology (kri-o-bi-ol′o-je) The study of low temperature effects on living organisms.

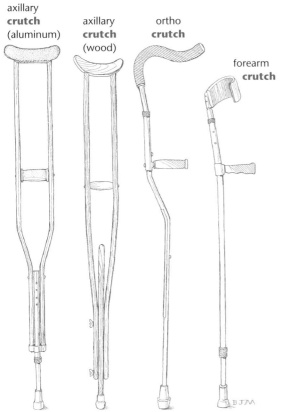

axillary
crutch
(aluminum)

axillary
crutch
(wood)

ortho
crutch

forearm
crutch

cryocautery (kri-o-kaw′ter-e) Destruction of tissue by application of extreme cold.

cryoconization (kri-o-kon-i-za′shun) Removal of a cone of tissue from the wall of the lower cervical canal with a freezing instrument (cryoprobe).

cryoextraction (kri-o-eks-trak′shun) Removal of a cataract by means of adhesion of the cataractous lens of the eye to the frozen tip of a special instrument (cryoextractor).

cryoextractor (kri-o-eks-trak′tor) Instrument consisting of a probe with a fine point that, by freezing, can create a small ice ball to which tissues can adhere; used in cryoextraction.

cryogenic (kri-o-gen′ik) Relating to the production of low temperatures.

cryogenics (kri-o-jen′iks) The branch of physics concerned with the production and effects of very low temperatures.

cryoglobulinemia (kri-o-glob-u-lin-e′me-ah) The presence of cryoglobulins in the blood; on exposure to cold, they solidify in the tiny blood vessels and cause restricted blood flow in exposed areas of the body; associated with a variety of abnormal conditions.

cryoglobulins (kri-o-glob′u-lins) Abnormal immunoglobulins in blood plasma that aggregate and solidify when exposed to low temperatures, usually below 37° C.

cryometer (kri-om′ĕ-ter) A device for measuring very low temperatures.

cryopathy (kri-op′ah-the) Any illness caused by cold.

cryopexy (kri′o-pek-se) Surgical reattachment of a detached retina by means of a freezing probe.

cryoprecipitate (kri-o-pre-sip′i-tāt) Any substance in solution that solidifies when exposed to cold (e.g., cryoglobulin).

cryopreservation (kri-o-prez-er-va′shun) The preservation of viable cells by freezing.

   c. of embryos The freezing of *in vitro* fertilized embryos in liquid nitrogen to allow their implantation at a later date.

cryoprobe (kri′o-prōb) A blunt surgical instrument with a tip that can be maintained at below freezing temperatures; used in cryosurgery for destroying tissue or to cause tissue to adhere to the instrument for removal.

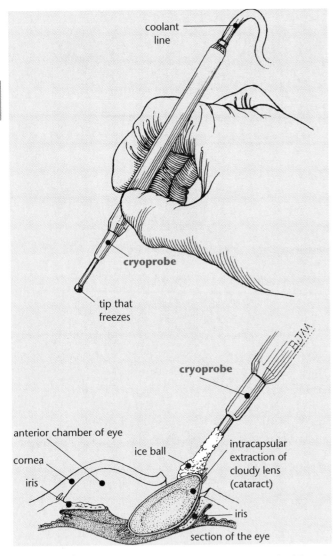

coolant line

cryoprobe

tip that freezes

cryoprobe

anterior chamber of eye

cornea

iris

ice ball

intracapsular extraction of cloudy lens (cataract)

iris

section of the eye

cryoprotein (kri-o-pro'tēn) A protein, present in dissolved form in the blood, that solidifies when cooled and redissolves when warmed.

cryoscope (kri'o-skōp) An instrument for determining the freezing point of solutions.

cryoscopy (kri-os'ko-pe) The determination of the freezing point of a solution compared with that of distilled water.

cryospasm (kri'o-spazm) Painful muscle contraction induced by cold.

cryostat (kri'o-stat) Device for maintaining a low temperature environment to carry out certain procedures, such as sectioning frozen tissue for microscopy.

cryosurgery (kri-o-sur'jer-e) Surgical technique in which freezing temperature is used to destroy or remove tissue.

cryothalamectomy (kri-o-thal-ah-mek'to-me) Destruction of the thalamus, within the brain, by application of temperatures below freezing.

cryotherapy (kri-o-ther'ah-pe) Treatment of disease with cold temperatures.

crypt (kript) A pitlike depression on a surface.

    anal c. See anal sinus, under sinus.

    dental c. A space in the jaws occupied by a developing tooth.

    c.'s of Lieberkühn See intestinal glands, under glands.

    tonsillar c. One of 10 to 15 pits on the surface of the palatine tonsils.

crypta (krip'tah), pl. cryp'tae A crypt.

cryptitis (krip-ti'tis) Inflammation of a glandular recess (e.g., in the rectum).

crypto-, crypt- Combining forms meaning crypt; obscured; without apparent cause; concealed; disguised.

cryptococcosis (krip-to-kok-o'sis) A disease caused by inhalation of the yeast *Cryptococcus neoformans;* it causes lung infection that may spread to other parts of the body, especially the central nervous system, where it causes meningitis; it is one of several opportunistic diseases attacking AIDS patients.

Cryptococcus (krip-to-kok'us) A genus of yeastlike fungi (family Cryptococcaceae).

    C. neoformans A species usually found in pigeon droppings and causing cryptococcosis in humans.

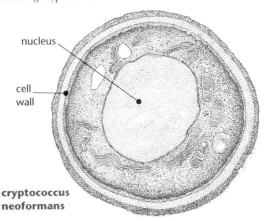

nucleus

cell wall

cryptococcus neoformans

cryptogenic (krip-to-jen'ik) Of obscure origin.

cryptolith (krip'to-lith) A concretion present in a crypt or follicle.

cryptomenorrhea (krip-to-men-o-re'ah) The monthly occurrence of menstruation symptoms without a flow of blood, as seen in imperforate hymen and cervical obstruction.

cryptomerorachischisis (krip-to-me-ro-rah-kis'kĭ-sis) See spina bifida occulta, under spina.

cryptophthalmos (krip-tof-thal'mos) A developmental anomaly in which the typical structure of eyelids is replaced by uninterrupted skin covering a small or rudimentary eyeball.

cryptorchid (krip-tor'kid) Relating to an undescended testis.

cryptorchidectomy (krip-tor-kid-ek'to-me) Surgical removal of an undescended testis.

cryptorchidism (krip-tor'kĭ-dizm) Failure of one or both testes to descend normally from the abdominal cavity into the scrotum during the last three months of intrauterine life; normally the process is completed by the time of birth; distinguished from ectopic testis. Also called undescended testicle; undescended testis; retained testis; cryptorchism.

cryptorchism (krip-tor'kizm) See cryptorchidism.

cryptosporidiosis (krip-to-spo-rid-e-o'sis) Infection with protozoan parasites of the genus *Cryptosporidium*, causing diarrhea, usually self-limited except in immunocompromised patients.

Cryptosporidium (krip-to-spo-rid'e-um) A genus of pathogenic protozoans (family Cryptosporidae) parasitic in the intestinal tract of humans and domestic animals; the cause of watery diarrhea in AIDS patients and other persons with compromised immune function.

crystal (kris'tal) A solid substance composed of regular units arranged systematically in a characteristic geometric form.

    asthma c.'s See Charcot-Leyden crystals.

    Charcot-Leyden c.'s Elongated, diamond-shaped structures associated with eosinophil fragmentation; found in the mucous secretions of bronchial asthma. Also called asthma crystals; Charcot-Neumann crystals.

    Charcot-Neumann c.'s See Charcot-Leyden crystals.

crystalline (kris'tah-lin) 1. Transparent. 2. Relating to crystals.

crystallization (kris-tah-lĭ-za'shun) The process of crystal formation, as when a dissolved substance solidifies (precipitates) from solution.

cryoprotein ■ crystallization

crystallography (kris-tah-log′rah-fe) The study of crystals.

crystalloid (kris′tah-loid) **1.** Resembling a crystal. **2.** A substance that, when in solution, can pass through a semipermeable membrane, unlike a colloid, which cannot.

crystalluria (kris-tah-lu′re-ah) The presence of crystals in the urine.

cubital (ku′bĭ-tal) Relating to the forearm, the ulna, or the elbow.

cubitus (ku′bĭ-tus) The elbow.

cuboid (ku′boid) Shaped like a cube.

cuboidal (ku-boi′dal) Relating to the cuboid bone of the foot.

cue (kyu) A stimulus to which a person has learned to respond.

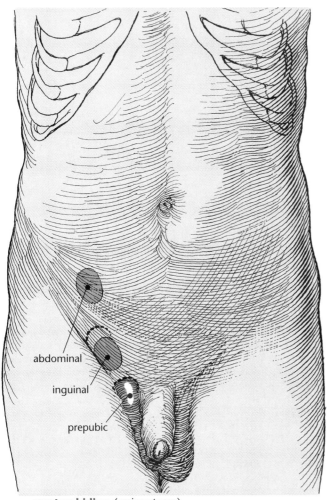

cryptorchidism (various types)

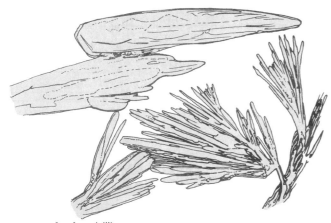

crystals of penicillin

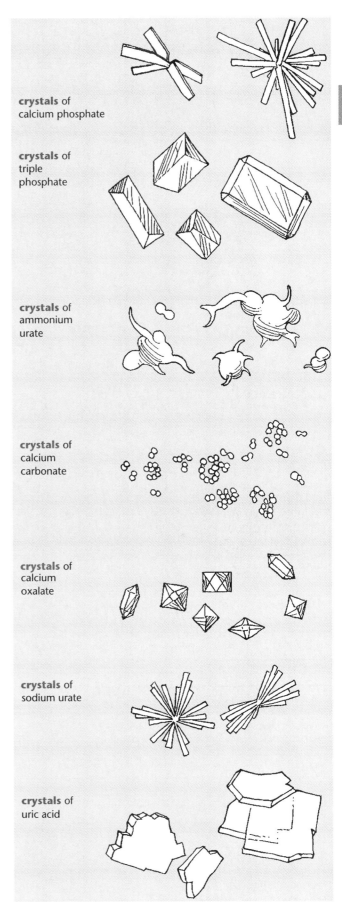

crystals of
calcium phosphate

crystals of
triple
phosphate

crystals of
ammonium
urate

crystals of
calcium
carbonate

crystals of
calcium
oxalate

crystals of
sodium urate

crystals of
uric acid

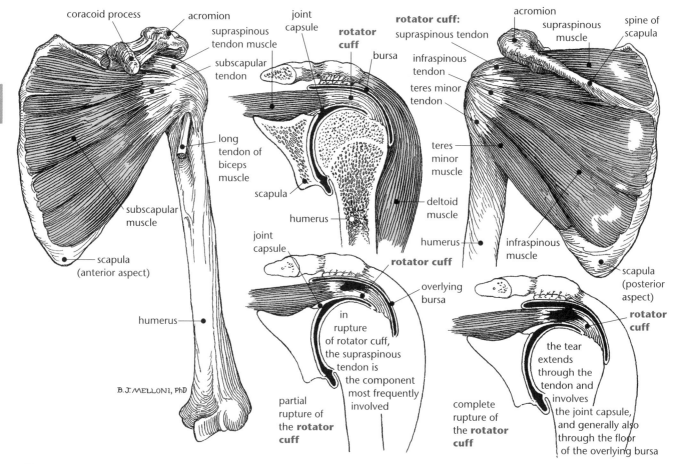

coracoid process
acromion
supraspinous tendon muscle
subscapular tendon
long tendon of biceps muscle
subscapular muscle
scapula (anterior aspect)
humerus

joint capsule
rotator cuff
bursa
scapula
humerus

rotator cuff:
supraspinous tendon
infraspinous tendon
teres minor tendon
teres minor muscle
deltoid muscle
humerus
infraspinous muscle
scapula (posterior aspect)
rotator cuff

joint capsule
rotator cuff
overlying bursa
in rupture of rotator cuff, the supraspinous tendon is the component most frequently involved
partial rupture of the **rotator cuff**

rotator cuff
the tear extends through the tendon and involves the joint capsule, and generally also through the floor of the overlying bursa
complete rupture of the **rotator cuff**

acromion
supraspinous muscle
spine of scapula

B.J. MELLONI, PhD

cuff (kuf) A bandlike structure encircling a part of the body.
  musculotendinous c. See rotator cuff.
  rotator c. A structure reinforcing the shoulder joint, formed by the tendons of four muscles (supraspinous, infraspinous, teres minor, subscapular); it covers, and blends with, the upper portion of the joint capsule and provides active support for the joint in motion. Also called musculotendinous cuff.
cul-de-sac (kul-de-sahk'), pl. culs-de-sac' A pouch or saclike space.
  conjunctival c. See fornix of conjunctiva, under fornix.
  Douglas' c. See rectouterine pouch, under pouch.
  lesser c. See pyloric antrum, under antrum.
culdocentesis (kul-do-sen-te'sis) A needle aspiration of fluid from the retrouterine pouch through the posterior vaginal wall.
culdoscope (kul'do-skōp) Instrument for viewing the pelvic cavity and its contents.
culdoscopy (kul-dos'ko-pe) Visual examination of the uterus, ovaries, and fallopian (uterine) tubes with a culdoscope, introduced into the pelvic cavity through the posterior vaginal wall.
Culex (ku'leks) A genus of mosquitos, many of which are vectors for disease-causing organisms.
culicide (ku'li-sīd) Any agent that kills mosquitoes.
culicifuge (ku-lis'i-fūj) A repellent of mosquitoes.
culture (kul'chūr) A colony of microorganisms or cells, or of tissues grown in a suitable nutrient medium in the laboratory.
  blood c. A nutrient medium that has been inoculated with a sample of blood thought to be infected, to identify disease-causing organisms.
  pure c. A culture containing microorganisms of only one species.
  tissue c. The *in vitro* growth of tissues.

cumulus oophorus (ku'mu-lus ooph'orus) In reproductive biology, the mass of cells surrounding the egg in the vesicular ovarian follicle; when the follicle ruptures and releases the egg during ovulation, the cells of the cumulus, now termed corona radiata, still surround the egg. The cumulus oophorus remains attached when the egg is harvested for *in vitro* fertilization (IVF); its presence and appearance are important criteria in the evaluation of harvested eggs for IVF.
cuneate (ku'ne-āt) Wedge-shaped.
cuneiform (ku-ne'ĭ-form) Wedge-shaped.
cuneus (ku'ne-us), pl. cu'nei The wedge-shaped portion of cerebral cortex on the medial surface of each occipital lobe.
cuniculus (ku-nik'u-lus) The burrow made in the skin by the itch mite (*Sarcoptes scabiei*).
cunnilingus (kun-ĭ-ling'gus) Oral stimulation of the female genitals.
cunnus (kun'us) Latin for vulva.
cup (kup) Any anatomic or pathologic hollow space.
  glaucomatous c. A deep depression of the optic disk caused by increased intraocular pressure in glaucoma.
  optic c. See physiologic cup.
  physiologic c. The normal slight depression of the optic disk. Also called optic cup.

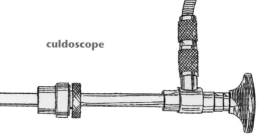

culdoscope

cupola (ku′po-lah) See cupula.

cupping (kup′ing) Formation of a cup-shaped depression.

cupric (ku′prik) Relating to copper.

cupula (ku′pu-lah), pl. cu′pulae An overlying dome-shaped cap or structure. Also spelled cupola.

    c. of ampullary crest See cupula of crista ampullaris.

    c. of cochlea The conical apex of the bony cochlea of the internal ear.

    c. of crista ampullaris A gelatinous mass overlying the crista within each ampulla (crista ampullaris) of the internal ear; from each crista, about 40 sensory hairs (stereocilia) and a single kinocilium extend and embed into the gelatinous cupula that stretches from the crista almost to the opposite wall of the ampulla; body movements cause the circulating endolymph within the ampulla to distort the cupula and its sensory hairs, thus registering the movements. Also called cupula of ampullary crest.

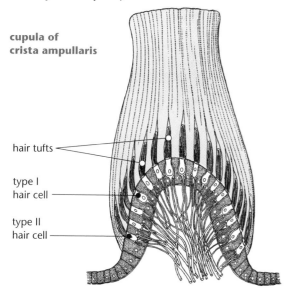

cupula of
crista ampullaris

hair tufts

type I
hair cell

type II
hair cell

    c. of pleura The domelike roof of the pleural cavity on either side, extending up through the inlet of the chest cavity.

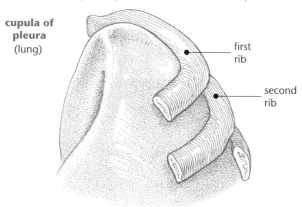

cupula of
pleura
(lung)

first
rib

second
rib

cupular (ku′pu-lar) 1. Relating to a cupula. 2. Dome-shaped.

curare (koo-rah′re) An extract of alkaloids from the bark of several plants, especially *Strychnos toxifera;* the principal active ingredient is tubocurarine, which inhibits muscle contraction by interfering with the action of the neurotransmitter acetylcholine; used as a muscle relaxant.

curarization (koo-rah-re-za′shun) Therapeutic administration of curare or of related compounds.

curative (kūr′ah-tiv) Tending to heal.

cure (kŭr) 1. To restore to normal health. 2. A remedy or therapeutic measure. 3. In dentistry, a method of hardening a plastic material, such as that of a denture base.

curet (ku-ret′) See curette.

curettage (ku-rĕ-tahzh′) The use of a sharp-edged, spoon-shaped instrument to scrape tissue from the lining of a cavity (e.g., uterus); may be used to remove abnormal tissue or to obtain a specimen for analysis and diagnosis.

    periapical c. The scraping and removal of diseased tissue adjoining the root of a tooth.

    subgingival c. Removal of inflammatory material from pockets formed in the gums.

curette (ku-ret′) A sharp-edged, spoon-shaped instrument for scraping the inner wall or lining of a body cavity. Also spelled curet.

curie (ku′re) (Ci) A unit of radioactivity equal to 3.7×10^{10} disintegrations per second.

curium (ku′re-um) An artificially created radioactive element; symbol Cm, atomic number 96, atomic weight 247.

current (kur′ent) A steady flow, as of electricity, air, or a fluid.

    alternating c. (AC) An electric current that changes direction at regular intervals.

    demarcation c. See current of injury.

    direct c. (DC) A current that flows in one direction only.

    high–frequency c. An alternating current that has a frequency of at least 10,000 cycles per second.

    c. of injury The current that passes between a depolarized area of injured heart muscle and the normally polarized noninjured part. It produces a shift (elevation) of the ST segment in the electrocardiogram; may also occur in nerve tissue. Also called demarcation current.

Current Procedure Terminology (CPT) A standardized nomenclature with modifiers to provide to a third party (health insurance company) for reimbursement of medical procedures.

curvature (kur′vah-tūr) A bending.

    greater c. of stomach The left concave side of the stomach.

    lesser c. of stomach The right concave side of the stomach.

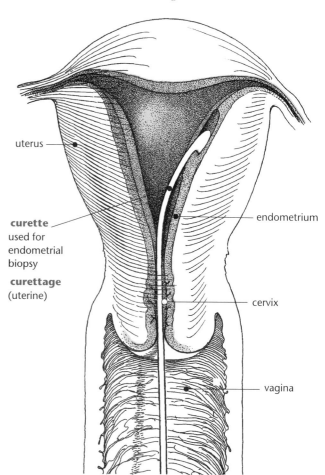

uterus

curette
used for
endometrial
biopsy

curettage
(uterine)

endometrium

cervix

vagina

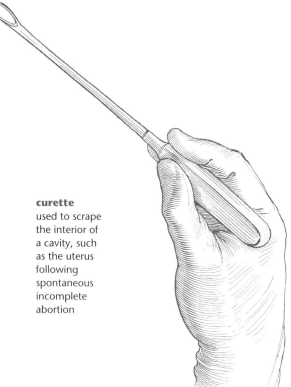

curette
used to scrape
the interior of
a cavity, such
as the uterus
following
spontaneous
incomplete
abortion

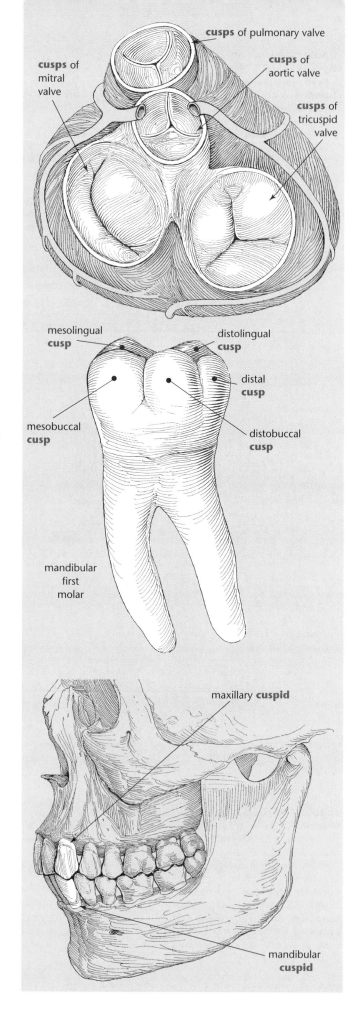

cusps of pulmonary valve

cusps of
mitral
valve

cusps of
aortic valve

cusps of
tricuspid
valve

mesolingual
cusp

distolingual
cusp

distal
cusp

mesobuccal
cusp

distobuccal
cusp

mandibular
first
molar

maxillary **cuspid**

mandibular
cuspid

spinal c. Abnormal deviation of the vertebral column. See kyphosis; lordosis; scoliosis.

curve (kurv) **1.** A deviation from a straight line. **2.** Representation of plotted data on a graph.

    dose-response c., dose-effect c. A curve showing the relationship between a dose of a chemical or radiation and its influence on a biological process.

    dye-dilution c. A curve showing the concentrations of a dye at a specified point in the circulation, measured over a period of time, after the dye is quickly injected into the bloodstream; used in studies of cardiac output, in detection of cardiovalvular incompetence, and for diagnosis of congenital cardiac shunts.

    Price-Jones c. A curve representing variations in the diameter of red blood cells.

cushingoid (koosh'ing-oid) Having the characteristics of Cushing's syndrome or disease. See also Cushing's disease, under disease; Cushing's syndrome, under syndrome.

cushion (koosh'un) In anatomy, any padlike structure.

    eustachian c. See torus tubarius, under torus.

    Passavant's c. See Passavant's ridge, under ridge.

cusp (kusp) **1.** A conical projection on the crown of a tooth. **2.** One of the triangular leaflets forming a heart valve.

    c. of Carabelli A normal fifth cusp on the lingual surface of the permanent maxillary first molar. Also called Carabelli's tubercle.

cuspid (kus'pid) One of four single-cusped teeth. Also called canine tooth; dog tooth; eye tooth (an upper cuspid).

cut (kut) **1.** To incise. **2.** To dilute. **3.** In forensic medicine, a wound, made with a sharp instrument, that has a surface length greater than its penetration depth.

cutaneous (ku-ta'ne-us) Relating to the skin.

cutdown (kut'down) A small incision made over a vein to gain access into the vessel for introduction of intravenous fluids.

cuticle (ku'te-kl) **1.** The thin fold of tissue overlying the base of a nail. **2.** The shinglelike layer of cells covering a hair. **3.** The shinglelike layer of cells lining a hair follicle.

cuticularization (ku-tik-u-lar-ĭ-za'shun) Development of skin over an abraded area.

cutis (ku'tis) The skin.

    c. laxa An abnormally loose condition of the skin.

    c. marmorata A transient marbleized appearance of the skin, sometimes occurring in normal newborns when exposed to cold temperature; a persistent form may be associated with certain syndromes.

c. vera The dermis, or deep layer, of the skin.

cuvet, cuvette (ku-vet′) A glass container in which solutions are placed for photometric study.

cyanide (si′ah-nīd) Any of several highly reactive, poisonous compounds containing a carbon atom linked to a nitrogen atom; some are used as pesticides; occupational exposure may occur in such industries as electroplating and synthetic rubber manufacturing, and in photographic laboratories; exposure may also occur in fires, especially of aircraft and high-rise buildings.

cyanmethemoglobin (si-an-met-he-mo-glo′bin) A relatively nontoxic compound of hydrogen cyanide and hemoglobin.

cyano-, cyan- 1. Combining forms meaning blue. 2. Prefix denoting the cyanide group CN.

cyanocobalamin (si-ah-no-ko-bal′ah-min) Vitamin B$_{12}$.

cyanophil (si-an′o-fil) Any cell readily stainable with blue dyes.

cyanopsia (si-ah-nop′se-ah) Condition in which everything is perceived as having a bluish color.

cyanosed (si′ah-nōsd) See cyanotic.

cyanose tardive (si′ah-nōs tahr′div) A congenital heart disease characterized by an abnormal communication between systemic and pulmonary circulation, causing cyanosis when there is a right-to-left shunt; cyanosis is absent while the shunt is from left to right. Also called delayed cyanosis.

cyanosis (si-ah-no′sis) A bluish discoloration of the skin, mucous membranes, and nail beds seen when there is insufficient oxygen in the blood; caused by the presence of 5 gm reduced (deoxygenated) hemoglobin or more per 100 ml blood; seen in certain malformations of the heart (e.g., tetralogy of Fallot) and in respiratory disease.

    delayed c. See cyanose tardive.

cyanotic (si-ah-not′ik) Relating to cyanosis. Also called cyanosed.

cyclacillin (si-klah-sil′in) A penicillin-type antibiotic.

cyclarthrodial (si-klar-thro′de-al) Relating to a rotary joint.

cyclarthrosis (si-klar-thro′sis) A rotary joint.

cycle (si′kl) A recurrent series of phenomena usually occurring at regular intervals.

    anovulatory c. Failure of ovulation to take place even though menstruation occurs.

    brain wave c. The complete set of changes in the wave of an electroencephalogram (EEG), before repetition occurs.

    carbon c. The natural process through which living organisms take carbon from the atmosphere in the form of carbon dioxide, metabolize it, and return it to the atmosphere, again as carbon dioxide.

    cardiac c. The complete course of events occurring in the heart with each beat.

    exogenous c. The stage of a parasite's development spent outside the host.

CARDIAC CYCLE

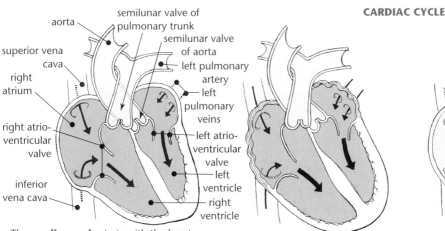

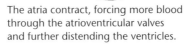

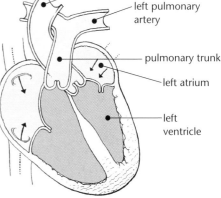

The **cardiac cycle** starts with the heart relaxed; blood streams into the atria from the venae cavae and pulmonary veins and flows through the open atrioventricular valves to the ventricles.

The atria contract, forcing more blood through the atrioventricular valves and further distending the ventricles.

Immediately after the atria contract, the ventricles start contracting and the increase in ventricular pressure closes the atrioventricular valves.

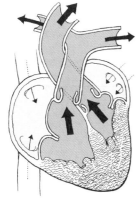

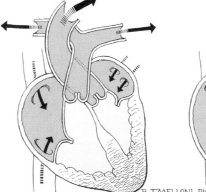

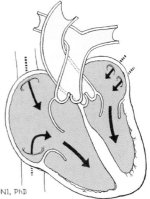

Once the ventricular pressure overcomes the residual pressure of the aorta and pulmonary trunk, it forces the semilunar valves of those vessels to open, permitting blood to be pumped out of the heart. In contracting, the ventricles force most, but not all, of the contents into the great vessels.

Ventricular pressure lessens when the ventricles begin to relax; pressure in the aorta and pulmonary trunk remains high and the semilunar valves close, thereby forcing blood throughout the body; at this stage of the **cardiac cycle**, all the valves are closed.

With the complete relaxation of the ventricles, the atrioventricular valves are forced open by the blood streaming in from the atria and begins a new **cardiac cycle**. This period of relaxation is the longest phase of the **cardiac cycle**.

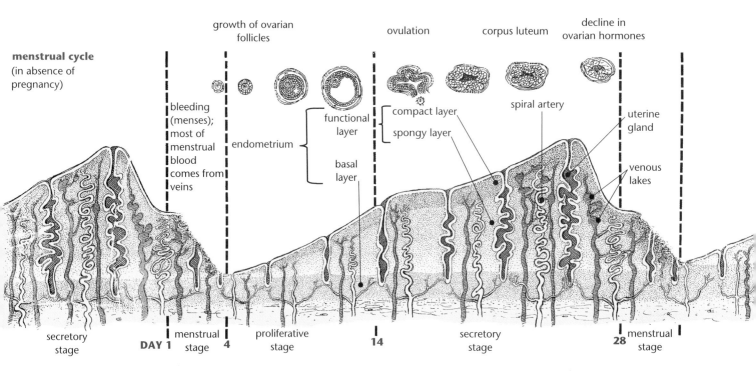

menstrual cycle (in absence of pregnancy)

growth of ovarian follicles

ovulation

corpus luteum

decline in ovarian hormones

bleeding (menses); most of menstrual blood comes from veins

endometrium

functional layer

basal layer

compact layer

spongy layer

spiral artery

uterine gland

venous lakes

secretory stage

DAY 1

menstrual stage

4

proliferative stage

14

secretory stage

28

menstrual stage

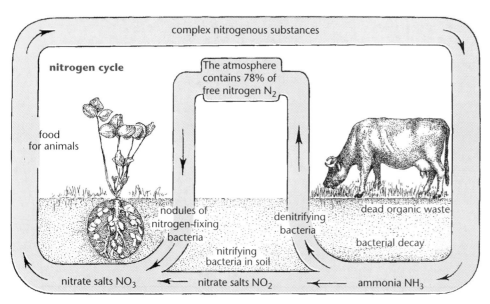

complex nitrogenous substances

nitrogen cycle

The atmosphere contains 78% of free nitrogen N_2

food for animals

nodules of nitrogen-fixing bacteria

denitrifying bacteria

nitrifying bacteria in soil

dead organic waste

bacterial decay

nitrate salts NO_3 ← nitrate salts NO_2 ← ammonia NH_3

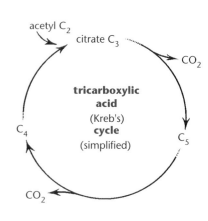

acetyl C_2

citrate C_3

CO_2

tricarboxylic acid (Kreb's) cycle (simplified)

C_4

C_5

CO_2

Kreb's c. See tricarboxylic acid cycle.

life c. The complete life of an organism.

menstrual c. The sequence of normal changes taking place (about every 28 days) in the inner lining of the uterus, culminating with shedding of uterine mucosa and bleeding (menstruation); the changes correspond to changes in the ovary (ovarian cycle) and occur in response to hormonal activity; in popular usage, the term encompasses all ovarian and uterine changes.

nitrogen c. The continuous process whereby nitrogen is deposited in the soil, taken up by bacteria and plants, transferred to animals, and returned to the soil.

ovarian c. The recurrent sequence of events taking place in the ovary, including production and release of the egg (ovum), in response to hormonal activity.

tricarboxylic acid c. The enzymatic reactions that provide the body with its chief source of energy, taking place mostly during respiration. Also called Kreb's cycle.

urea c. The sequence of chemical reactions in the liver culminating in production of urea, a major end product of protein metabolism.

cyclectomy (sik-lek'to-me) Eye surgery consisting of removal of a portion of the ciliary body.

cyclitis (sik-li'tis) Inflammation of the ciliary body, beneath the border of the iris.

plastic c. Cyclitis causing accumulation of fibrinous secretion in the anterior chamber of the eye.

cyclizine hydrochloride (si'kli-zēn hi-dro-klo'rīd) An antihistamine used to treat motion sickness.

cyclo-, cycl- Combining forms meaning round; recurring.

cyclobenzaprine hydrochloride (si'klo-ben'zah-prēn hi-dro-klo'rīd) A muscle-relaxant drug used in the short-term treatment of spasms.

cyclochoroiditis (si'klo-ko-roid-i'tis) Inflammation of the ciliary body and adjoining choroid, beneath the peripheral border of the iris.

cyclocryotherapy (si'klo-kri-o-ther'ah-pe) Destruction of the ciliary processes by freezing, applied through the sclera to reduce secretion of aqueous humor in glaucoma.

cyclodialysis (si'klo-di-al'ĭ-sis) Surgical detachment of a portion of the ciliary body from the sclera for the treatment of glaucoma; the ciliary body atrophies in the region of the separation, thus reducing production of aqueous humor with resultant decrease in intraocular pressure.

cyclodiathermy (si′klo-di-ah-ther′me) Electrical destruction of the ciliary processes to reduce secretion of aqueous humor in glaucoma.

cycloid (si′kloid) Denoting a person who has swings of mood but within normal ranges.

cyclophosphamide (si′klo-fos′fah-mid) A compound with antitumor properties, used to treat autoimmune diseases.

cycloplegia (si′klo-ple′je-ah) Paralysis of the ciliary muscle, which controls the shape of the lens during focusing of the eye.

cycloplegic (si′klo-ple′jik) **1.** Acting to put the ciliary muscle at rest, dilate the pupil, and block the process of accommodation of the lens. **2.** A drug with such properties.

cyclopropane (si′klo-pro′pān) A colorless gas used as an inhalant in anesthesia.

cyclosporin A (si′klo-spōr′in) See cyclosporine.

cyclosporine (si′klo-spōr′in) An immunosuppressive drug used in organ transplantation to inhibit rejection; it selectively inhibits T lymphocytes. Formerly called cyclosporin A.

cyclothymia (si′klo-thi′me-ah) Cyclic fluctuations of mood between elation and mild depression.

cyclotomy (si′klot′o-me) Incision of the ciliary muscle of the eye.

cylinder (sil′in-der) (cyl.) A rod-shaped urinary cast.

cylindroid (sil′in-droid) A ribbonlike mucous mass resembling a urinary cast. Also called false cast; mucous cast.

cylindroma (sil-in-dro′mah) Multiple coalescing nodules, usually benign, occurring on the scalp and forehead.

cylindruria (sil-in-droo′re-ah) Excretion of casts in the urine.

cynophobia (si-no-fo′be-ah) Irrational fear of dogs.

cypridophobia (si-prĭ-do-fo′be-ah) Abnormal fear of venereal disease or sexual intercourse.

cyst (sist) **1.** An abnormal saclike, epithelium-lined cavity within the body containing fluid or gas. **2.** A bladder.

    allantoic c. See urachal cyst.

    Baker's c. A swelling behind the knee due to a synovial-sac herniation from the knee joint.

    Bartholin's c. A common cyst of the vulva, containing secretions from a Bartholin's (greater vestibular) gland; caused by obstruction of a major duct of the gland.

    bronchogenic c. Cyst arising from a developmental defect in which an accessory bronchial bud loses communication with the main respiratory airway (trachea) but remains attached to it.

    bursal c. Cyst formed within a bursa.

    chocolate c. Ovarian cyst containing a thick, dark brown fluid typically occurring in endometriosis. Also called endometrioma.

    corpus luteum c. Ovarian cyst developed when the corpus luteum does not regress normally during the ovarian cycle.

    dermoid c. A common ovarian cyst, often bilateral, lined with skin and containing displaced skin elements, including hair and sebaceous glands, well-formed teeth, and mandibular bone. Also called mature benign teratoma; benign cystic teratoma; dermoid.

    distention c. See retention cyst.

    ependymal c. A demarcated distention of a ventricle of the brain or of the central canal of the spinal cord. Also called neural cyst.

    lacteal c. See milk-retention cyst.

    meibomian c. See chalazion.

    milk-retention c., milk c. A cystic dilatation of one or more milk ducts in the breast, caused by occlusion of these ducts during lactation. Also called lacteal cyst; galactocele; lactocele.

    mucous c. Retention cyst resulting from an obstructed duct of a mucous gland.

    nabothian c.'s Cysts on the uterine cervix due to compression of the ducts of nabothian glands, frequently occurring in chronic cervicitis. Also called nabothian follicle.

    neural c. See ependymal cyst.

    ovarian c. Any cyst of the ovary, usually implying a noncancerous condition.

    periapical c. Cyst at the tip of a tooth root, usually a nonviable tooth. Also called radicular cyst.

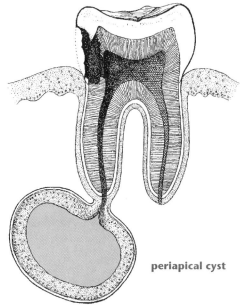

periapical cyst

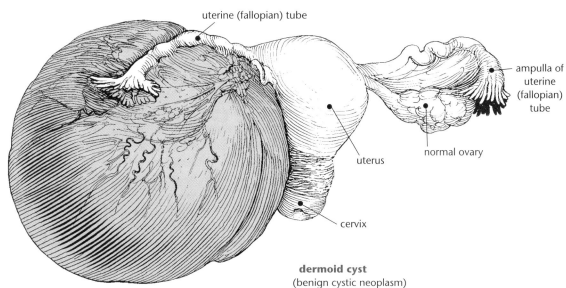

uterine (fallopian) tube

ampulla of uterine (fallopian) tube

normal ovary

uterus

cervix

dermoid cyst
(benign cystic neoplasm)

piliferous c. A dermoid cyst containing hair.

pilonidal c. A superficial cyst connected to the skin surface by a narrow sinus tract; it contains hair follicles and is usually located in the sacrococcygeal area.

radicular c. See periapical cyst.

retention c. Cyst caused by obstruction or compression of a duct draining a gland. Also called distention cyst; secretory cyst.

sebaceous c. Cyst of the skin or scalp containing sebum and keratin, caused by obstruction of the duct of a sebaceous gland.

secretory c. See retention cyst.

serous c. Cyst containing a clear or translucent fluid.

solitary bone c. Cyst occurring in the shaft (metaphysis) of a long bone of children, within the medullary cavity of the bone. Also called unicameral cyst; osteocystoma.

sublingual c. See ranula.

tarsal c. See chalazion.

thyroglossal duct c., thyrolingual c. A cyst between the base of the tongue and the thyroid gland; may be congenital or develop later in life, usually in young children; it is a dilatation of a remnant of the embryonic thyroglossal duct that failed to obliterate during development.

unicameral c. A cyst contained within a single cavity. See solitary bone cyst.

urachal c. An abdominal cyst, which may communicate with the bladder or with the umbilicus, resulting from persistent patency of a segment of the urachus, which failed to obliterate completely during intrauterine life. Also called allantoic cyst.

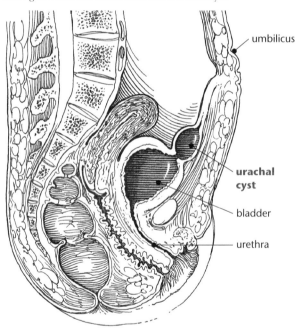

umbilicus

urachal cyst

bladder

urethra

cystadenocarcinoma (sis-tad-e-no-kar′sī-no′mah) A malignant tumor composed of cystic cavities filled with a combination of secretions and solid masses; found most frequently in the ovary.

cystadenoma (sis-tad-e-no′mah) Benign tumor containing large cystic masses lined with epithelium; typically found in the ovary and pancreas.

cystalgia (sis-tal′je-ah) Pain in the bladder.

cystathioninuria (sis-tah-thi-o-ne-nu′re-ah) An inherited disorder of amino acid metabolism marked by excessive excretion of cystathionine in the urine.

cystectomy (sis-tec′to-me) Removal of a portion of the bladder.

cysteine (sis-te′in) (Cys) An amino acid present in most proteins.

cystic (sis′tik) **1.** Relating to cysts. **2.** Relating to the urinary bladder or the gallbladder.

cysticercosis (sis-tī-ser-ko′sis) Infection with larvae of the pork tapeworm *Taenia solium.*

cysticercus (sis-tī-sĕr′kus) The larval stage of tapeworms consisting of a fluid-filled cystic sac containing the head (scolex).

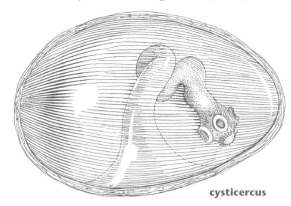

cysticercus

cystiform (sis′tī-form) Resembling a cyst.

cystine (sis′tēn) An amino acid present in many proteins; it is a frequent component of kidney stones; may also be present in the urine (cystinuria).

cystinosis (sis-tī-no′sis) Condition marked by accumulation of the amino acid cystine in several tissues, including bone marrow and epithelium of kidney tubules; caused by faulty cystine metabolism due to enzyme deficiency.

cystinuria (sis-tī-nu′re-ah) A persistent excessive excretion of cystine in the urine.

cystitis (sis-ti′tis) Inflammation of the urinary bladder.

acute c. Cystitis caused by a bacterial infection; onset in women frequently follows sexual intercourse.

chronic c. Cystitis that may be unresolved or persistent, or that occurs in separate but frequent bouts (e.g., three episodes in one year).

hemorrhagic c. Cystitis and bleeding from the urinary bladder; caused by radiation treatment (e.g., for cancers of the bladder and cervix), by treatment with antitumor drugs excreted via the urine (e.g., cyclophosphamide), or occasionally by bacterial infection.

interstitial c. Cystitis of unknown cause involving the lining and musculature of the lower urinary bladder, causing suprapubic pain brought on by bladder distention and relieved upon urination. Also called Hunner's ulcer.

radiation c. Cystitis occurring as a complication of radiation treatment (e.g., for cancer of the cervix); symptoms may develop months after termination of treatment.

papillary **cystadenoma** as seen through a peritoneoscope

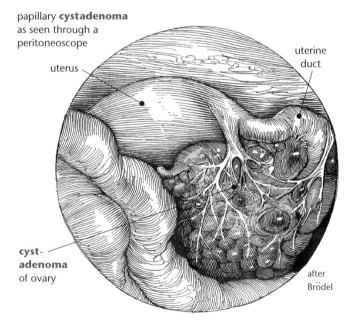

uterus

uterine duct

cyst-adenoma of ovary

after Brödel

cysto-, cyst- Combining forms meaning bladder; cyst.

cystocele (sis'to-sēl) Prolapse of the urinary bladder wall into the vagina due to weakening of the supporting pelvic musculature. Also called colpocystocele; vesicocele.

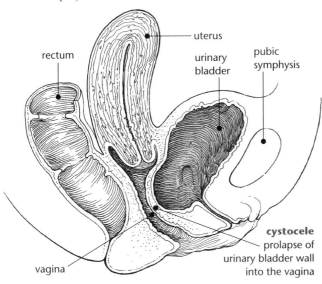

rectum
uterus
urinary bladder
pubic symphysis
cystocele prolapse of urinary bladder wall into the vagina
vagina

cystogram (sis'to-gram) X-ray picture of the urinary bladder filled with a radiopaque solution.

cystography (sis-tog'rah-fe) Roentgenography of the urinary bladder after instilling a radiopaque solution into the organ.

cystoid (sis'toid) Having the shape and consistency of a cyst but lacking an enclosed wall.

cystolith (sis'to-lith) See vesical stone, under stone.

cystolithectomy (sis-to-li-thek'to-me) See cystolithotomy.

cystolithiasis (sis-to-li-thi'ah-sis) The presence of one or more stones in the bladder. Also called vesicolithiasis.

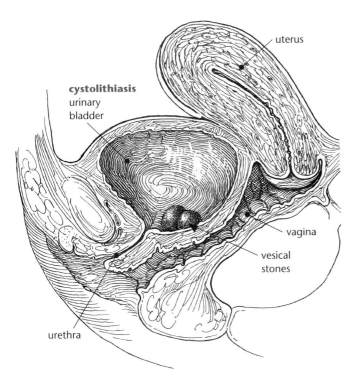

uterus
cystolithiasis urinary bladder
vagina
vesical stones
urethra

cystolithic (sis-to-lith'ik) Relating to bladder stones.

cystolithotomy (sis-to-li-thot'o-me) Surgical removal of bladder stones. Also called cystolithectomy; vesicolithotomy.

cystoma (sis-to'mah) A tumor containing cysts.

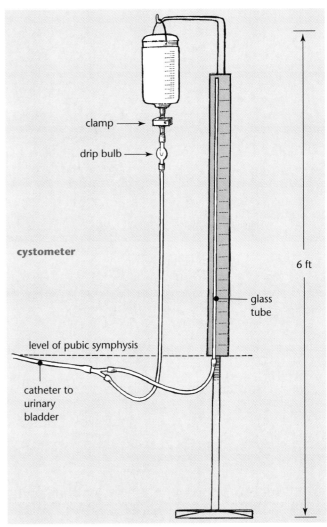

clamp
drip bulb
cystometer
glass tube
level of pubic symphysis
catheter to urinary bladder
6 ft

cystometer (sis-tom'ĕ-ter) Device used to measure the tone of the bladder musculature in relation to the volume of fluid in the bladder.

cystometrogram (sis-to-met'ro-gram) A graphic recording made by a cystometer.

cystometry (sis-tom'ĕ-tre) A method of evaluating bladder function by means of a cystometer; it includes measurements of total bladder capacity, of the pressure changes within the bladder during filling and voiding, and of the amount of residual urine after voiding.

cystoplasty (sis'to-plas-te) Any reconstructive operation on the bladder.

cystoplegia (sis-to-ple'je-ah) Paralysis of the bladder.

cystoptosis (sis-top-to'sis) Prolapse of the inner lining of the bladder into the urethra.

cystorrhagia (sis-to-ra'je-ah) Bleeding from the bladder.

cystorrhea (sis-to-re'ah) Mucous discharge from the bladder.

cystoscope (sis'to-skōp) A tubular instrument, equipped with a light, for visual examination of the interior of the bladder. See illustration on next page.

cystoscopy (sis-tos'ko-pe) Visual examination of the interior of the bladder with the aid of a cystoscope.

cystospasm (sis'to-spazm) Spasmodic contraction of the bladder muscles.

cystostomy (sis-tos'to-me) Creation of an opening into the bladder through the abdominal wall for the purpose of draining the bladder when drainage with a catheter via the urethra is not possible or advisable. Also called vesicostomy.

cystotomy (sis-tot'o-me) Surgical cutting or opening into the bladder. Also called vesicotomy.

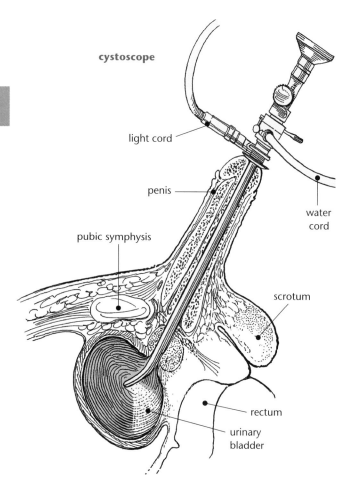

cystoscope

light cord

penis

pubic symphysis

water cord

scrotum

rectum

urinary bladder

cystoureteritis (sis-to-u-re-ter-i′tis) Inflammation of the bladder and one or both tubes (ureters) leading from the kidneys to the bladder.

cystourethritis (sis-to-u-re-thri′tis) Inflammation of the bladder and the urethra.

cystourethrocele (sis-to-u-re′thro-sēl) Prolapse of the neck of the bladder and urethra toward the vagina.

-cyte Combining form meaning cell (e.g., lymphocyte).

cytidine (si′tĭ-dēn) (C, Cyd) A major constituent of ribonucleic acid (RNA); contains the pyrimidine cytosine.

cyto-, cyt- Combining forms meaning cell.

cytoanalyzer (si-to-an′ah-li′zer) A device for screening samples of cells suspected of malignancy.

cytoarchitecture (si-to-ar′kĭ-tek-tūr) The manner in which cells are arranged in a tissue.

cytobiology (si-to-bi-ol′o-je) See cytology.

cytocentrum (si-to-sen′trum) See centrosome.

cytochemistry (si-to-kem′is-tre) The study of chemical activities within cells.

cytochrome (si′to-krōm) A respiratory enzyme capable of undergoing alternate reduction and oxidation; it is chemically related to hemoglobin.

cytocidal (si-to-si′dal) Destructive to cells.

cytocide (si′to-sīd) Any agent that destroys cells.

cytoclasis (si-tok′lah-sis) Disintegration of cells.

cytodiagnosis (si-to-di-ag-no′sis) Diagnosis of disease by examination of cells in a sample of tissue, secretions, or fluid from a patient.

cytogenesis (si-to-jen′ĕ-sis) Origin of cells.

cytogeneticist (si-to-je-net′ĭ-sist) A specialist in cytogenetics.

cytogenetics (si-to-jĕ-net′iks) The field of science derived from both genetics and cytology concerned with the study of physical components of heredity; it concentrates on the chromosome, especially its structure, replication, and recombination.

clinical c. The study of the relationship between aberrations of chromosome structure and abnormal or pathologic conditions.

cytokine (si′to-kīn) A soluble, nonantibody protein molecule that mediates interactions between cells, as in the production of immune responses.

cytology (si-tol′o-je) The science concerned with the study and identification of cells. Also called cell biology; cytobiology.

cytolysin (si-tol′ĭ-sin) A substance capable of causing dissolution of cells.

cytolysis (si-tol′ĭ-sis) The dissolution of cells.

cytomegalic (si-to-meg-al′ik) Relating to marked enlargement of cells.

cytomegalovirus (si-to-meg′ah-lo-vi′rus) (CMV) Any of a group of herpesviruses infecting humans, rodents, and other mammals; they cause enlargement of cells and development of characteristic inclusions in the cytoplasm or nucleus of the cell; they cause a variety of disorders in humans, including cytomegalovirus mononucleosis (a mononucleosis-like disease), hepatitis, pneumonia, and cytomegalic inclusion disease (in the newborn); the species causing human diseases is also called human herpesvirus 5 (HHV-5). See also herpesvirus.

cytometer (si-tom′ĕ-ter) A standardized device for counting and measuring cells, particularly blood cells.

cytometry (si-tom′ĕ-tre) A method of separating and enumerating cells suspended in a fluid (e.g., blood cells).

flow c. A high-speed procedure perfomed with an instrument (flow cytometer) in which a laser beam rapidly scans a large number of fluorescently labeled cells suspended in a stream; the instrument automatically sorts and counts the different types of cells as they flow individually through an aperture and cross the laser beam. The technique can analyze cell size, DNA content, viability, enzyme content, and surface characteristics; it is employed for diagnosis of malignancy in difficult cases by establishing the presence of an aneuploid cell population. The procedure is being investigated for detecting fetal abnormalities by examining the few fetal cells present in the mother's blood (as opposed to amniocentesis, in which the fetal cells examined are obtained from the amniotic fluid surrounding the fetus).

cytomorphology (si-to-mor-fol′o-je) The study of cell structure.

cytopathic (si-to-path′ik) Denoting a diseased condition of cells.

cytopathogenic (si-to-path-o-jen′ik) Denoting an agent that is capable of producing pathologic changes in cells.

cytopathology (si-to-pah-thol′o-je) The study and interpretation of cellular changes in disease.

cytopenia (si-to-pe′ne-ah) A diminished number of the cellular components of the blood.

cytophagy (si-tof′ah-je) The engulfing and ingestion of a cell by another cell.

cytophilic (si-to-fil′ik) See cytotropic.

cytophotometry (si-to-fo-tom′ĕ-tre) The measuring of light absorbed by, or emitted from, stained cells or intracellular structures.

flow c. Enumeration and separation of cells on the basis of their size and fluorescence intensity.

cytoplasm (si′to-plazm) The aqueous content of the cell (excluding that of the nucleus) and the organelles suspended in it, where most of the cell's chemical activities occur.

cytopoiesis (si-to-poi-e′sis) Formation of a cell or cells.

cytosine (si′to-sēn) (Cyt) A chemical of the pyrimidine type; a component of DNA.

cytosmear (si′to-smēr) See cytologic smear, under smear.

cytostatic (si-to-stat′ik) Capable of stopping cell growth.

cytotoxic (si-to-tok′sik) Capable of killing cells.

cytotoxin (si-to-tok′sin) A substance that destroys cells.

cytotropic (si-to-trop′ik) Having a propensity to bind to cells. Also called cytophilic.

cytozoic (si-to-zo′ik) Living within cells, such as certain microorganisms.

cytozoon (si-to-zo′on) A cell parasite.

D

dacryadenitis (dak-re-ad-ĕ-ni′tis) See dacryoadenitis.

dacryagogue (dak′re-ah-gog) **1.** Inducing the flow of tears. **2.** Any agent that stimulates the lacrimal glands to secrete tears.

dacryo-, dacry- Combining forms meaning tears; the lacrimal apparatus.

dacryoadenalgia (dak-re-o-ad-ĕ-nal′je-ah) Pain or discomfort in a lacrimal gland.

dacryoadenitis (dak-re-o-ad-ĕ-ni′tis) Inflammation of a lacrimal gland; may be associated with systemic conditions (e.g., mumps or sarcoidosis). Also called dacryadenitis.

dacryoblennorrhea (dak-re-o-blen-o-re′ah) A chronic discharge of mucus from the tear ducts, as seen in dacryocystitis.

dacryocele (dak′re-o-sēl) See dacryocystocele.

dacryocyst (dak′re-o-sist) A lacrimal sac.

dacryocystalgia (dak-re-o-sis-tal′je-ah) Pain or discomfort in a lacrimal sac.

dacryocystectasia (dak-re-o-sis-tek-ta′ze-ah) Dilatation of a lacrimal sac.

dacryocystectomy (dak-re-o-sis-tek′to-me) Surgical removal of a lacrimal sac.

dacryocystitis (dak-re-o-sis-ti′tis) Inflammation of the lacrimal sac, usually caused by obstruction of the nasolacrimal duct; most often seen in infants and in persons over 40 years old.

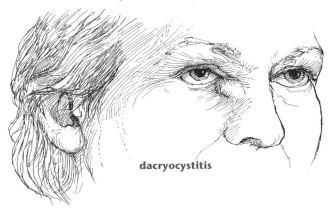
dacryocystitis

dacryocystocele (dak-re-o-sis′to-sēl) Abnormal enlargement of a lacrimal sac with fluid, usually due to obstruction of the nasolacrimal duct. Also called dacryocele.

dacryocystogram (dak-re-o-sis′to-gram) An x-ray picture of the lacrimal apparatus obtained after injection of a radiopaque substance, usually performed to locate the site of an obstruction.

dacryocystorhinostenosis (dak-re-o-sis-to-ri-no-stĕ-no′sis) Narrowing of a nasolacrimal duct with resulting obstruction of the normal flow of tears into the nasal cavity.

dacryocystorhinostomy (dak-re-o-sis-to-ri-nos′to-me) Surgical creation of a passage between the lacrimal sac and the nose to effect drainage of tears when the nasolacrimal duct is occluded.

dacryocystotomy (dak-re-o-sis-tot′o-me) A surgical cut into a lacrimal gland.

dacryohemorrhea (dak-re-o-hem-o-re′ah) The shedding of tears tinged with blood.

dacryolith (dak′re-o-lith) A stone found in the tear-forming or the tear-conducting structures. Also called tear stone.

dacryolithiasis (dak-re-o-lĭ-thi′ah-sis) The presence of stony concretions in the tear passages.

dacryoma (dak-re-o′mah) **1.** A cyst caused by obstruction of the lacrimal duct. **2.** A tumor of the lacrimal apparatus.

dacryon (dak′re-on) A cranial point where the lacrimal, frontal, and maxillary bones meet on the medial aspect of the ocular orbit.

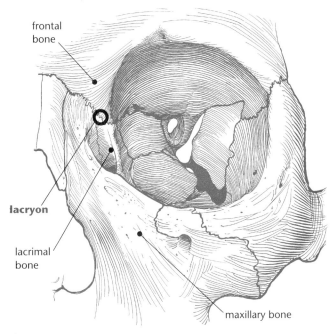
frontal bone
lacryon
lacrimal bone
maxillary bone

dacryops (dak′re-ops) **1.** Persistent tearing due to poor drainage caused by constriction of the lacrimal punctum at the inner corner of the eye. **2.** Cystic dilatation of a lacrimal duct.

dacryopyorrhea (dak-re-o-pi-o-re′ah) Purulent discharge from the lacrimal apparatus.

dacryopyosis (dak-re-o-pi-o′sis) Formation of pus in a lacrimal sac or duct.

dacryorrhea (dak-re-o-re′ah) Excessive flow of tears.

dacryosolenitis (dak-re-o-so-lĕ-ni′tis) Inflammation of a lacrimal duct.

dacryostenosis (dak-re-o-stĕ-no′sis) Stricture or obstruction of a lacrimal duct; in the newborn infant, it may be due to failure of the lacrimal duct to canalize completely at birth, usually at the nasal end of the duct, causing persistent tearing and often a mucoid discharge in the inner corner of the eye.

dactyl (dak′til) A finger or toe; a digit.

dactylalgia (dak-tĭ-lal′je-ah) Pain in a finger or toe. Also called dactylodynia.

dactyledema (dak-til-ĕ-de′mah) Swelling of a digit.

dactylitis (dak-tĭ-li′tis) Inflammation of a digit.

dactylo-, dactyl- Combining forms meaning digit, usually a finger.

dactylocampsis (dak-tĭ-lo-kamp′sis) Permanent flexion of a digit.

dactylodynia (dak-tĭ-lo-din′e-ah) See dactylalgia.

dactylogryposis (dak-tĭ-lo-grĭ-po′sis) Contraction of the fingers.

dactylology (dak-til-ol′o-je) The use of the fingers in sign language; finger spelling.

dactylolysis (dak-tĭ-lol′ĭ-sis) Loss of a finger or toe.

    d. spontanea See ainhum.

dactylomegaly (dak-tĭ-lo-meg′ah-le) See macrodactyly.

dactyloscopy (dak-tĭ-los′ko-pe) Inspection of fingerprint impressions for purposes of personal identification.

dactylospasm (dak'ĭ-lo-spazm) A spasm of a digit.

dactylus (dak'tĭ-lus) A digit.

dalton (dawl'ton) A unit of molecular weight equivalent to the weight of a hydrogen atom.

dam (dam) In dentistry, a thin rubber sheet for isolating the operative field from oral fluids. Also called rubber dam.

dance (dans) In medical parlance, abnormal movements, especially of the extremities, associated with brain lesions.

    hilar d. Strong pulsations of the pulmonary arteries seen on fluoroscopic examination in patients with congenital left-to-right shunt.

    St. Vitus' d. See Sydenham's chorea, under chorea.

D and C See dilatation and curettage.

D and E See dilatation and evacuation.

dander (dan'der) Dry skin shed by animals (e.g., dogs and cats); a common source of allergy in susceptible people.

dandruff (dan'druf) Popular name for the mild form of seborrheic dermatitis.

dapsone (dap'sōn) A compound with antibacterial properties, especially against *Mycobacterium tuberculosis* and *Mycobacterium leprae*, the organisms causing tuberculosis and leprosy (Hansen's disease), respectively.

Datura stramonium (da-tu'rah strah-mo'ne-um) A tropical herb containing alkaloids that block the action of parasympathetic nerves; has been used as an inhalant in the treatment of asthma. Also called jimsonweed; thorn apple.

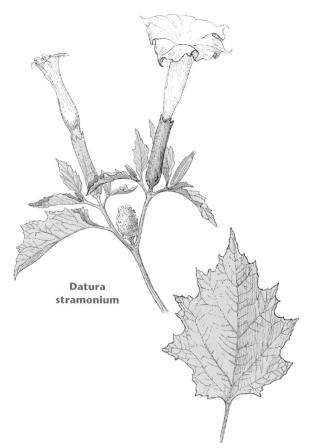

**Datura
stramonium**

deacidification (de-ah-sid-ĭ-fĭ-ka'shun) The process of reducing acidity; neutralizing an acid.

deactivation (de-ak-tĭ-va'shun) The process of making ineffective; reducing activity (e.g., chemical activity).

dead (ded) Lifeless.

deaf (def) Unable to hear.

deafferentation (de-af-er-en-ta'shun) The suppression or loss of sensory nerve conduction.

deaf-mute (def mūt') A person who cannot hear and does not speak; the deafness is usually congenital or is acquired before the child has learned to speak.

deafmutism (def-mūt'izm) The state of being deaf-mute.

deafness (def'nes) Inability to hear, partial or complete. See also hearing loss.

    acoustic trauma d. See noise-induced hearing loss.

    conductive d. See conductive hearing loss, under hearing loss.

    congenital d. Any type of deafness that is present at birth; may be due to a chromosomal abnormality or to a variety of nongenetic causes (e.g., maternal intake of ototoxic drugs, viral infections, irradiation in the first trimester, fetal distress, Rh incompatibility).

    functional d. See psychogenic deafness.

    genetic d. Deafness (usually congenital) caused by a chromosomal abnormality.

    hysterical d. See psychogenic deafness.

    industrial d. See noise-induced hearing loss, under hearing loss.

    nerve d., neural d. See sensorineural hearing loss, under hearing loss.

    occupational d. See occupational hearing loss, under hearing loss.

    postlingual d. Deafness developing after the person has learned to speak.

    prelingual d. Deafness occurring before the person has learned to speak.

    psychogenic d. Deafness in the absence of any organic cause and not faked for the purpose of secondary gain (malingering). Also called functional deafness; hysterical deafness.

    pure word d. Condition in which the person can hear but cannot comprehend spoken language, while comprehension of written words and ability to speak are relatively preserved; has been attributed to a lesion in or near the primary auditory cortex (Heschl's gyrus) in the temporal lobe of the brain.

    sensorineural d. See sensorineural hearing loss, under hearing loss.

    sudden d. Deafness (usually unilateral) resulting from a variety of causes, most commonly a viral infection of the inner ear or a blood clot in the internal auditory (labyrinthine) artery; may also be caused by a sudden loud noise (e.g., explosion or firecracker) or by a tumor in the vestibulocochlear (8th cranial) nerve.

    word d. See auditory aphasia, under aphasia.

dealbation (de-al-ba'shun) Whitening; bleaching.

dealcoholization (de-al-ko-hol-i-za'shun) Removal of alcohol from a substance or from a histologic specimen.

deamidation, deamidization (de-am-ĭ-da'shun, de-am-ĭ-di-za'shun) Removal of an amide group from a compound.

deaminase (de-am'ĭ-nās) An enzyme that promotes removal of the amino group from compounds such as amino acids.

deamination, deaminization (de-am-ĭ-na'shun, de-am-ĭ-ni-za'shun) Removal of an amino group from a compound.

death (deth) The Uniform Determination of Death Act passed by the U.S. Congress (1981) states that an individual is dead if there is *(1)* irreversible cessation of circulatory and respiratory functions or *(2)* irreversible cessation of all functions of the entire brain, including the brainstem.

    black d. The worldwide epidemic of the fourteenth century, believed to be pneumonic plague.

    brain d. An irreversible state persisting after a specified length of time (usually 6–24 hours) in which there is total cessation of brain function (i.e., complete unresponsiveness to all stimuli, including painful stimuli such as hard pinching), absence of brainstem reflexes (e.g., pupils are dilated and unresponsive to light), and disappearance of the electroencephalogram pattern (electrocerebral silence; i.e., a "flat" electroencephalogram); heartbeat and breathing may continue only with the aid of a respirator. Two conditions are excluded: hypothermia and depression of the central nervous system by drugs (e.g., barbiturates or alcohol). Although the use of confirmatory tests makes it possible to shorten the observation period in adults, in the case of infants and young children a full 24-hour observation period is recommended. Also called cerebral death.

cell d. The termination of a cell's ability to carry out such vital functions as metabolism, growth, reproduction, and adaptability.

cerebral d. See brain death.

clinically unexplained d. (a) Death of a patient whose prolonged, complex illness was extensively studied but a satisfactory diagnosis was not established. (b) Death following an illness of such brief duration that there was little or no opportunity for medical observation or studies to provide a reasonable explanation of the events.

crib d. See sudden infant death syndrome, under syndrome.

fetal d. Death of a fetus in the uterus; in early pregnancy, the first sign is absence of uterine enlargement; in later pregnancy, the first sign is absence of fetal movement.

infant d. Death of a baby under the age of one year.

maternal d. Death of a woman from any cause while pregnant or during the puerperium (i.e., within 42 days of termination of pregnancy).

neonatal d. Death of an infant during the first 28 days of life; usually designated *early* when it occurs during the first 7 days and *late* thereafter.

perinatal d. Death occurring during the perinatal period (i.e., from completion of 20 weeks of gestation through the first 28 days after delivery).

sudden cardiac d. (SCD) Unexpected cessation of cardiac contraction occurring within one hour of the onset of symptoms; most commonly caused by obstruction of one or more coronary arteries; other causes include constriction of the aortic valve, abnormalities of the conduction system in the heart muscle, and prolapse of the mitral (left atrioventricular) valve. In the young (especially young athletes participating in strenuous sports), it may be caused by familial hypertrophic cardiomyopathy (FHCM) due to a genetic defect (a mutation in the myosin gene). See also hypertrophic cardiomyopathy, under cardiomyopathy.

death rattle (deth rat′l) A gurgling sound often heard in end-stage lung disease, when secretions in the airways cannot be cleared and the air merely moves back and forth in the bronchi; it often indicates imminent death.

debilitant (de-bil′ĭ-tant) Causing debility.

debilitate (de-bil′ĭ-tāt) To make weak.

debility (de-bil′ĭ-te) A lack of strength; a weakened state.

debouch (dĭ-boo͞ sh′) To empty into a cavity or similar part of the body.

débridement (da-brēd-maw′) The surgical cleansing of wounds by removing dead tissue and foreign debris to accelerate the healing process. Also called revivification.

debt (det) Deficit.

oxygen d. The extra oxygen consumed by the body, above its resting needs, to satisfy demands caused by intensive exercise.

debulking (de-bulk′ing) Operative removal of portions of a large malignant tumor to (1) reduce its size, (2) oxygenate the tumor tissues (oxygen is often toxic to malignant cells), and (3) provide space to encourage proliferation of malignant cells, thus rendering the tumor more susceptible to destruction by chemotherapy (quiescent cells are not as susceptible).

deca- Prefix used in the SI system meaning 10.

decagram (dek′ah-gram) Ten grams.

decalcification (de-kal-sĭ-fĭ-ka′shun) 1. The loss of calcium from bones and/or teeth. 2. The removal of calcium ions from blood to prevent or delay clotting.

decaliter (dek′ah-le-ter) Ten liters.

decapitate (de-kap′ĭ-tāt) To remove the head.

decapsulation (de-kap-su-la′shun) Removal of an enveloping tissue or capsule.

decarboxylase (de-kar-bok′sĭ-lās) Any enzyme that accelerates removal of carbon dioxide from a compound.

decay (de-ka′) 1. To decompose. 2. The spontaneous progressive decrease in the number of atoms from a radioactive nucleus.

deceleration (de-sel-er-a′shun) Decrease in velocity.

decerebrate (de-ser′ĕ-brāt) 1. To eliminate brain-stem control over certain body functions in an experimental animal by dividing or removing a portion of brain tissue above the pons at the level of the red nucleus. Also called decerebrize. 2. See decerebrate rigidity, under rigidity.

decerebration (de-ser-ĕ-bra′shun) The process of decerebrating.

decerebrize (de-ser′ĕ-brīz) See decerebrate.

deci- Prefix used in the SI system meaning one-tenth (10^{-1}).

decibel (des′ĭ-bel) (dB, db) A unit for measuring the ratio of two powers or intensities (e.g., electric or acoustic powers); in measurement of acoustic intensities, it is equal to 10 times the common logarithm of the ratio of two levels of intensity, or to the smallest degree of loudness that is ordinarily heard by the human ear; at a distance of about four feet, an ordinary conversation produces a level of approximately 60 dB (on a scale from 1 to 130).

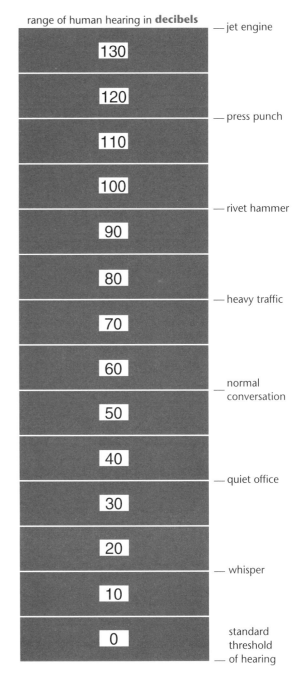

range of human hearing in **decibels**

130 — jet engine
120 — press punch
110
100 — rivet hammer
90
80 — heavy traffic
70
60 — normal conversation
50
40 — quiet office
30
20 — whisper
10
0 — standard threshold of hearing

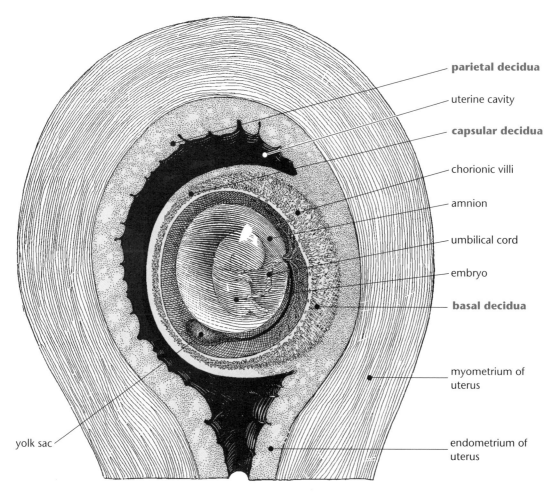

parietal decidua
uterine cavity
capsular decidua
chorionic villi
amnion
umbilical cord
embryo
basal decidua
myometrium of uterus
endometrium of uterus
yolk sac

D

decidua (de-sid'u-ah) The inner lining of the pregnant uterus, which has become thick and vascular, forming a receptive nidus for the product of conception (conceptus). It is shed at childbirth except the deepest layer. Also called decidual membrane; decidua of pregnancy.

basal d. The area of the endometrium to which the developing ovum is attached, i.e., between the implanted conceptus and the uterine muscular wall (myometrium); it develops into the maternal part of the placenta. Also called decidua basalis; decidua serotina.

capsular d. The part of the endometrium that seals the implanted conceptus from the uterine cavity; it stretches as the ovum grows and undergoes rapid regression from about the fourth month of pregnancy, thereby allowing the nonvillous part of the chorion to make direct contact with the parietal decidua. Also called decidua capsularis; reflex decidua.

menstrual d. The engorged (hyperemic) endothelial mucosa of the nonpregnant uterus that is shed during the menstrual period. Also called decidua menstrualis.

parietal d. The entire endometrium lining the cavity of the pregnant uterus except at the site of attachment of the conceptus. Also called decidua parietalis; decidua vera; true decidua.

d. polyposa Hyperplasia of the uterine decidua with projections on its surface resembling polyps.

reflex d. See capsular decidua.

d. serotina See basal decidua.

true d. See parietal decidua.

d. vera See parietal decidua.

decidual (de-sid'u-al) Relating to decidua.

deciduation (de-sid-u-a'shun) The casting off of endometrial tissue after giving birth.

deciduoma (de-sid-u-o'mah) A mass of decidual tissue in the uterus.

deciduous (de-sid'u-us) Temporary; not permanent (e.g., the primary dentition).

deciliter (des'i-le-ter) One-tenth (10^{-1}) of a liter.

decimeter (des'i-me'ter) (dm) One-tenth (10^{-1}) of a meter.

decinormal (des'i-nor-mal) (0.1N) One-tenth of normal; applied to a solution that has one-tenth of the normal strength.

Declaration of Geneva A code of medical ethics that is pledged by new doctors of medicine during graduation ceremonies at several schools of medicine worldwide. The code adheres to the basic tenets of the centuries-old Hippocratic oath but restates its archaic language and formulation.

Declaration of Geneva At the time of being admitted as a Member of the Medical Profession, I solemnly pledge myself to consecrate my life to the service of humanity;

I will give to my teachers the respect and gratitude which is their due;

I will practice my profession with conscience and dignity;

I will respect the secrets which are confided in me;

I will maintain by all the means in my power the honor and the noble traditions of the medical profession;

My colleagues will be my brothers;

I will not permit considerations of religion, nationality, race, party politics or social standing to intervene between my duty and my patient;

I will maintain the utmost respect for human life from the time of conception; even under threat, I will not use my medical knowledge contrary to the laws of humanity;

I make these promises solemnly, freely and upon my honor.

declination (dek-li-na'shun) Deviation from the vertical, such as rotation of the eye about the anteroposterior plane.

declive (de-klīv′) The sloping portion of the vermis of the cerebellum (in its middle lobe); bounded anteriorly by the primary fissure and posteriorly by the postclival fissure.

decoction (de-kok′shun) 1. The process of concentrating by boiling; a boiling down. 2. A medicine prepared by boiling.

decompensation (de-kom-pen-sa′shun) 1. Failure of the heart to maintain adequate circulation, occurring in certain cardiac and circulation disorders. 2. Failure of usual defenses or coping mechanisms, resulting in personality disintegration or aggravation of pathologic behavior.

decomposition (de-kom-po-zish′un) 1. The process of breaking down into constituent components. 2. Organic decay or disintegration.

decompression (de-kom-presh′un) A reduction or relief of pressure.

   cardiac d. Surgical cut into the sac (pericardium) enveloping the heart to release accumulated fluid, which exerts pressure upon the heart. Also called pericardial decompression.

   cerebral d. Removal of a portion of the skull and puncture of the dura mater to reduce intracranial pressure; usually employed when other measures have failed.

   pericardial d. See cardiac decompression.

decongestant (de-kon-jes′tant) Any agent that reduces congestion, especially of the nasal lining.

decongestive (de-kon-jes′tiv) Reducing congestion.

decontamination (de-kon-tam-i-na′shun) The process of eliminating or inactivating harmful agents from a person or from the environment.

decorticate (de-kor′tĭ-kat) 1. To remove the outer layer of an organ (e.g., of the brain or kidney). 2. See decorticate posture, under posture.

decortication (de-kor-tĭ-ka′shun) The act of decorticating.

decrudescence (de-kroo-des′ens) A decrease (e.g., of symptoms or of their intensity).

decubital (de-ku′bĭ-tal) Relating to decubitus.

decubitus (de-ku′bĭ-tus) The position assumed while lying down, often modified by a term indicating the part of the body in contact with the resting surface (e.g., dorsal decubitus means lying on the back). See also decubitus ulcer, under ulcer.

decussate (de-kus′āt) To intersect at an angle so as to form the letter X.

decussation (de-kŭ-sa′shun) A crossing (e.g., of nerve tracts) in the form of an X; commonly applied to the crossing of the right and left optic nerves.

dedifferentiation (de-dif-er-en-she-a′shun) The reversion of specialized cellular forms to a more homogeneous state.

defecation (def-ĕ-ka′shun) The discharge of feces through the anus. Also called bowel movement.

defect (de′fekt) Malformation; mutation.

   atrial septal d. (ASD) An abnormal hole in the septum dividing the two atria of the heart.

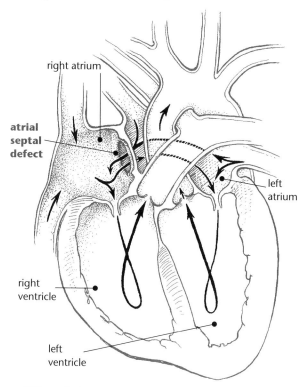

right atrium

atrial septal defect

left atrium

right ventricle

left ventricle

   filling d. An abnormality seen in x-ray pictures of certain structures (e.g., gastrointestinal tract or gallbladder) filled with radiopaque medium; gaps in the continuity of the medium suggest the presence of masses, such as tumors, polyps, or stones.

   ventricular septal d. (VSD) An abnormal hole in the septum between the two ventricles of the heart.

defective (de-fek′tiv) Having a defect; applied to persons deficient in some physical or mental attribute.

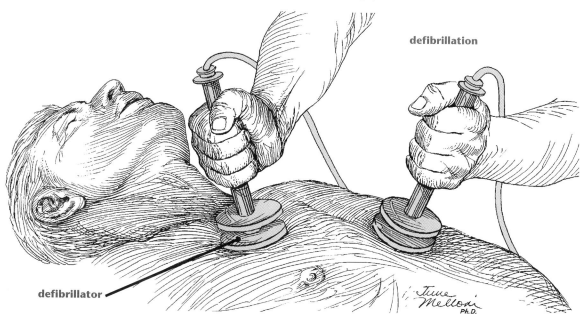

defibrillation

defibrillator

defeminization (de-fem-ĭ-nĭ-za'shun) The loss or decrease of female characteristics.

defensins (de-fen'sins) Family of peptides found in liposomal granules or neutrophils. They have bactericidal, fungicidal, and cytotoxic properties and can neutralize certain viruses.

deferent (def'er-ent) Conveying away.

deferentectomy (def-er-en-tek'to-me) See vasectomy.

deferentitis (def-er-en-ti'tis) Inflammation of the deferent duct. Also called vasitis.

defervescence (def-er-ves'ens) The lowering of fever.

defibrillation (de-fib-rĭ-la'shun) The arrest of quivering movements (fibrillation) of the heart muscle. Also called cardioversion.

defibrillator (de-fib-rĭ-la'tor) **1.** A device for delivering an electric current to stop fibrillation of the heart muscle. **2.** Any agent that stops fibrillation. Also called cardioverter.

defibrination (de-fi-brĭ-na'shun) The removal of fibrin from the blood to prevent clot formation.

deficiency (de-fish'en-se) An insufficient state; a lack.

alpha1-antitrypsin (α1-AT) d. An autosomal recessive inheritance that frequently leads to chronic obstructive lung disease and cirrhosis of the liver.

familial high-density lipoprotein d. See Tangier disease, under disease.

immune d. See immunodeficiency.

mental d. See mental retardation, under retardation.

ornithine transcarbamoylase (OTC) d. A dominantly inherited deficiency of OTC (an enzyme important in urea synthesis in the liver); it affects mostly males, most of whom die in infancy; those who survive (usually females) may be physically and mentally retarded, may display a gradual developmental regression, or may have only mild symptoms; deficits are related to the degree of deficiency.

pseudocholinesterase (PChe) d. An autosomal recessive inheritance resulting in reduced PChe (an enzyme present in the liver and plasma); usually no clinical manifestations are evident, but a protracted reaction occurs when a muscle relaxant such as succinylcholine is administered.

pyruvate kinase d. Chronic hemolytic anemia resulting from deficiency of pyruvate kinase in red blood cells; an autosomal recessive inheritance.

deficit (def'ĭ-sit) A deficiency, usually temporary.

pulse d. The difference between the number of heartbeats (greater) and the number of beats counted at the wrist (fewer) due to failure of a very early ventricular contraction to propel sufficient blood to produce a palpable pulse.

deflection (de-flek'shun) **1.** A turning aside. **2.** A wave of the electrocardiogram.

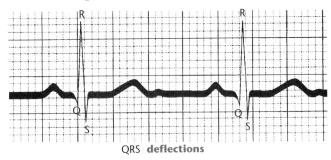

QRS **deflections**

deflorescence (def-lo-res'ens) Disappearance of a rash or skin lesions of an eruptive disease.

defluvium (de-floo've-um) Hair loss.

deformation (de-for-ma'shun) **1.** An alteration in structure or shape of a body part that was previously normally formed. **2.** In dysmorphology, a congenital defect of form or position of any body part that may result from an abnormal mechanical constraint in the uterus or from an intrinsic defect of the fetus. **3.** In rheology, the process of changing shape in order to adapt to a particular stress (e.g., the change in shape of red blood cells as they pass through the narrow lumen of a capillary).

deformity (de-for'mĭ-te) Any malformation.

bayonete d. See Colles' fracture, under fracture.

bone d. Any deformity resulting from abnormal growth, improperly healed fractures, or softening of bone tissues.

boutonnière d. Hyperextension of the distal interphalangeal joint and flexion of the proximal joint, with splitting of the dorsal hood so that the head of the proximal phalanx protrudes through the resulting "buttonhole"; usually develops slowly (sometimes suddenly) after trauma over the joint. Also called buttonhole deformity.

buttonhole d. See boutonnière deformity.

gunstock d. Displacement of the forearm to one side resulting from fracture of a condyle at the elbow.

lobster-claw d. A hand or foot that has the middle digits fused or missing.

open-bite d. See apertognathia.

silver fork d. See Colles' fracture, under fracture.

swan-neck d. Finger deformity occurring as a frequent complication of mallet finger, but also seen associated with other conditions; consists of hyperextension of the proximal interphalangeal joint and flexion of the distal interphalangeal joint.

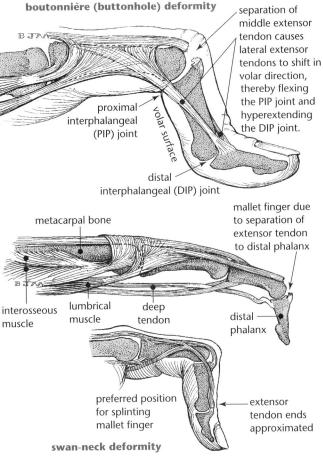

boutonnière (buttonhole) deformity

swan-neck deformity

defurfuration (de-fur-fu-ra'shun) The scalelike shedding of the superficial layer of skin.

degeneracy (de-jen'er-ah-se) **1.** The process of degenerating. **2.** The condition of being degenerate.

degeneration (de-jen-er-a'shun) **1.** Any deterioration or process of worsening. **2.** The process of deterioration of tissues with corresponding functional impairment as a result of injury or disease; the process may advance to an irreversible stage and eventually cause death of the tissues (necrosis).

adipose d. See fatty degeneration.

amyloid d. Deposition of an abnormal protein-polysaccharide substance (amyloid) in the extracellular spaces of tissues, occurring in certain diseases.

atheromatous d. A localized accumulation of lipid material (atheroma) in the inner layer of an arterial wall.

ballooning d. Liquefaction of cell protoplasm leading to swelling and softening of the cells; seen in certain viral infections.

colloid d. Conversion of tissues into a gumlike inspissated material.

fatty d. Any abnormal accumulation of fat within cells forming the substance of an organ. Also called adipose degeneration.

fibrinoid d. The formation of a dense, homogeneous acidophilic substance in tissues, usually in blood vessel walls and connective tissues.

hepatolenticular d. See Wilson's disease, under disease.

heredomacular d. See macular degeneration.

hyaline d. A cellular change in which the cytoplasm becomes glossy and homogeneous; may be due to viral inclusions or to injury that causes coagulation of proteins.

hydropic d. A reversible swollen state of cells due to accumulation of water.

macular d. Any genetically determined disorder of the eye resulting in degenerative changes of the macula; may be an autosomal dominant or autosomal recessive disease. Also called heredomacular degeneration.

mucoid medial d. See cystic medial necrosis, under necrosis.

secondary d. See wallerian degeneration.

senile d. The normal degeneration of tissues characteristic of old age.

vitelliform d., vitelliruptive d. An autosomal dominant disease of the eye detectable at or shortly after birth; characterized by an abnormality of the retinal pigment epithelium which, although diffuse, is visible only in the macular area as a yellow deposit resembling a "sunny-side up" fried egg; may lead to scarring and loss of central vision by the second decade of life. Also called Best's disease.

wallerian d. Dissolution and resorption of the distal stump of a sectioned peripheral nerve. Also called secondary degeneration.

Zenker's d. A severe form of hyaline degeneration affecting the cytoplasm of striated muscle cells, which becomes clumped, homogeneous, and waxy; seen in severe infections.

degloving (de-gluv'ing) **1.** In dentistry, an operation in which intra-oral bone is exposed in preparation for another procedure. **2.** See degloving injury, under injury.

deglutition (deg-loo-tish'un) The act of swallowing.

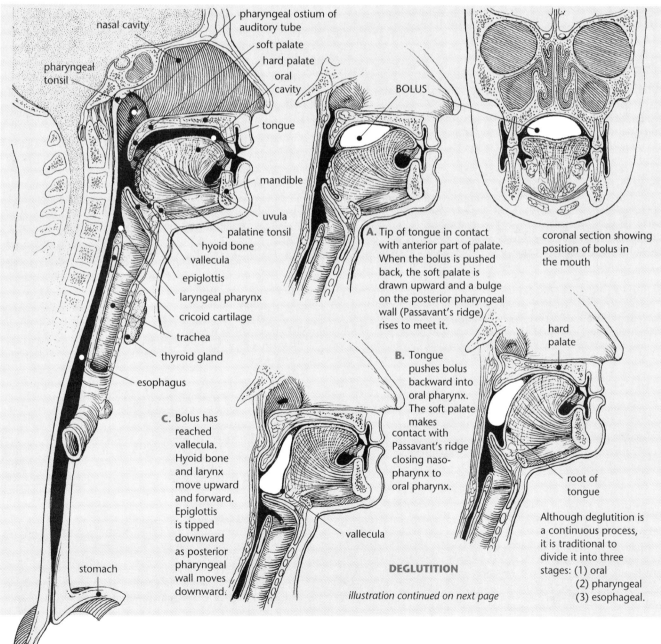

nasal cavity
pharyngeal ostium of auditory tube
soft palate
hard palate
oral cavity
pharyngeal tonsil
tongue
mandible
uvula
palatine tonsil
hyoid bone
vallecula
epiglottis
laryngeal pharynx
cricoid cartilage
trachea
thyroid gland
esophagus
stomach

BOLUS

coronal section showing position of bolus in the mouth

A. Tip of tongue in contact with anterior part of palate. When the bolus is pushed back, the soft palate is drawn upward and a bulge on the posterior pharyngeal wall (Passavant's ridge) rises to meet it.

B. Tongue pushes bolus backward into oral pharynx. The soft palate makes contact with Passavant's ridge closing nasopharynx to oral pharynx.

hard palate
root of tongue

C. Bolus has reached vallecula. Hyoid bone and larynx move upward and forward. Epiglottis is tipped downward as posterior pharyngeal wall moves downward.

vallecula

DEGLUTITION

illustration continued on next page

Although deglutition is a continuous process, it is traditional to divide it into three stages: (1) oral (2) pharyngeal (3) esophageal.

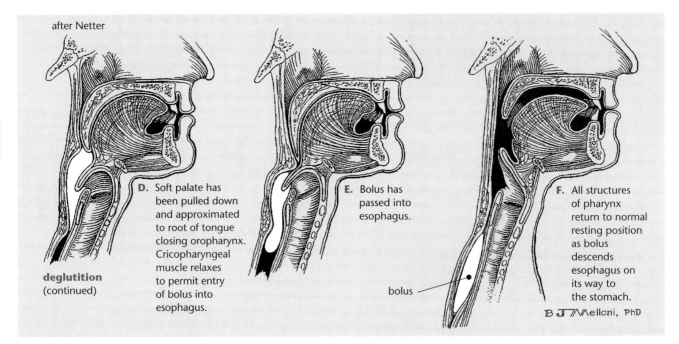

after Netter

D. Soft palate has been pulled down and approximated to root of tongue closing oropharynx. Cricopharyngeal muscle relaxes to permit entry of bolus into esophagus.

deglutition (continued)

E. Bolus has passed into esophagus.

F. All structures of pharynx return to normal resting position as bolus descends esophagus on its way to the stomach.

bolus

B J Melloni, PhD

deglutitory (de-gloo′tĭ-to-re) Relating to swallowing.

degranulation (de-gran-u-la′shun) The loss of granules; applied to certain white blood cells.

degree (de-gre′) **1.** A unit of a temperature scale. **2.** A unit of angular measure.

degustation (de-gus-ta′shun) The act of tasting.

dehiscence (de-his′ens) A splitting, rupturing, or bursting.

uterine d. An uncommon postoperative complication of cesarean section, associated with adhesions between the abdominal wall and the uterus; symptoms include spiking temperatures, pain, and intestinal obstruction.

wound d. The partial or complete disruption of any or all layers of an operative wound at any stage of healing.

dehydrate (de-hi′drāt) To lose or extract water from the body or from any substance.

dehydration (de-hi-dra′shun) **1.** The process of removing water from a substance or tissue. **2.** The state resulting from excessive loss of body water.

dehydrocholic acid (de-hi-dro-ko′lik as′id) A synthetic bile acid that stimulates secretion of bile; used in states of deficient bile formation.

dehydroepiandrosterone (de-hi-dro-ep-ĭ-an-dros′ter-ōn) (DHEA) A steroid hormone of weak physiologic activity, produced primarily by the adrenal cortex of both males and females; it plays a role in the formation of such sex hormones as testosterone and estrogen; production of DHEA begins during fetal life and usually declines at about age 25. Its role in the process of aging is being currently investigated.

dehydrogenase (de-hi-droj′ĕ-nās) Any enzyme that promotes the removal of hydrogen from a compound.

dehydrogenation (de-hi-dro-jĕ-na′shun) The process of removing hydrogen from a compound.

dehypnotize (de-hip′no-tīz) To awaken from a hypnotic state.

déjà vu (da-zhah′ voo′) The feeling that a new situation or event has been experienced before.

dejection (de-jek′shun) A state of mental depression.

delamination (de-lam-ĭ-na′shun) A division or separation into separate layers.

de-lead (de-led′) To remove lead from body tissues.

deleterious (del-ĕ-te′re-us) Harmful.

deletion (de-le′shun) In genetics, a chromosomal abnormality marked by the spontaneous loss of a segment of DNA from the chromosome; the deleted segment may be of any length and from any part of the chromosome.

delimitation (de-lim-ĭ-ta′shun) The process of placing limits; preventing the spread of disease.

deliquesce (del-ĕ-kwes′) To become damp; to become liquid.

deliquescent (del-ĕ-kwes′ent) Liquefied; applied to a solid substance (e.g., table salt) that becomes liquefied by absorbing moisture from the atmosphere.

delirious (de-lēr′e-us) In a state of mental confusion and excitement.

delirium (dĕ-lir′e-um) A state of acute confusion accompanied by changes in levels of attentiveness and consciousness that worsen at night; may include hallucinations, delusions, anxiety, and incoherence; caused by an organic factor (e.g., drug toxicity, infections, heart and respiratory diseases).

d. tremens (DT) A state of increasing confusion, severe trembling, vivid auditory and visual hallucinations, agitated and wild behavior, and, eventually, convulsions; caused by sudden cessation of alcohol consumption, typically occurring in long-term alcoholics.

deliver (de-liv′er) **1.** To assist a woman in childbirth. **2.** To remove or extract (e.g., a tumor or a cataract).

delivery (de-liv′er-e) The mode of actual expulsion of the infant and placenta from the uterus.

abdominal d. See cesarean section, under section.

breech d. Vaginal delivery of a baby whose pelvis or a lower extremity is the presenting part.

forceps d. The use of forceps for delivery of a fetus in vertex presentation (when the top-back of the skull is foremost within the birth canal).

high forceps d. Forceps delivery in which the instrument is applied to the fetal head before its foremost part is aligned with the ischial spines of the mother's pelvis.

low forceps d. Forceps delivery in which the instrument is applied to the fetal head when the head has reached the perineal floor and the scalp is visible without separating the labia, and only when the sagittal suture of the fetal head is in the anteroposterior diameter of the birth canal outlet. Also called outlet forceps delivery.

midforceps d. Forceps delivery in which the instrument is applied before the criteria for low forceps are met, but after the fetal head has begun to move toward the birth canal and the lowermost part of the skull has reached the level of the ischial spines of the maternal pelvis.

postmortem d. Delivery of a fetus after death of its mother.

premature d. The birth of a fetus before 34 weeks of gestation.

vaginal d. Delivery of an infant through the birth canal and vaginal orifice.

delta (del′tah) (Δ,δ) **1.** The fourth letter of the Greek alphabet.

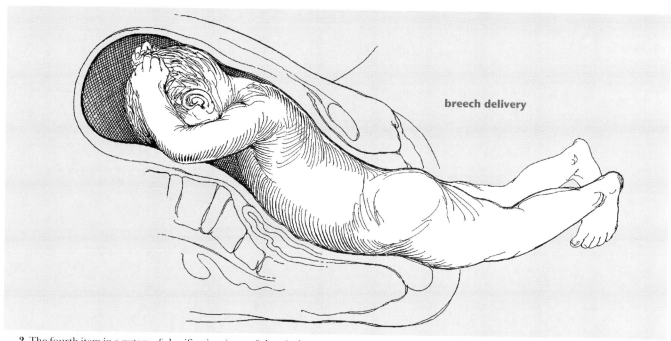

breech delivery

2. The fourth item in a system of classification (e.g., of chemical compounds). **3.** Any triangular anatomic space.

    Galton's d. The middle triangular pattern of the lines of a fingerprint.

delta-aminolevulinic acid (del'ta ah-me-no-lev-u-lin'ik as'id) (ALA) δ-aminolevulinic acid; an important intermediate in the synthesis of heme; increased levels of ALA in the blood and urine occur in lead poisoning.

deltoid (del'toid) Triangular. See table of muscles.

delusion (de-lu'zhun) A false belief firmly maintained even against contradictory evidence or logical argument.

    d. of grandeur, grandiose d. Exaggerated belief in one's importance.

    d. of persecution A false belief that one has been singled out for persecution or harassment.

demarcation (de-mar-ka'shun) The marking of distinct boundaries.

    surface d. See line of demarcation, under line.

demasculinization (de-mas-ku-lin-ĭ-za'shun) Loss of male characteristics.

demented (de-ment'ed) Afflicted with dementia.

dementia (de-men'she-ah) Condition caused by organic factors affecting the brain; characterized by a progressive, multidimensional loss of intellectual abilities, such as abstract thinking and judgment, and failure of memory; mechanisms of arousal from natural sleep are usually normal; self-awareness is present but lost in late stages; motor function becomes limited with progression of the condition. Advanced stages can progress until self-awareness and all evidence of learned behavior are lost; at this point, the condition is considered a vegetative state.

    Alzheimer's d. See Alzheimer's disease, under disease.

    d. praecox Obsolete term for schizophrenia.

    presenile d. *(a)* Dementia occurring before the age of 65 years. *(b)* See Alzheimer's disease, under disease.

    senile d. A slowly progressive mental deterioration associated with generalized atrophy of the brain; cause is unknown.

    toxic d. Dementia caused by chemical poisoning.

demi- Prefix meaning half; lesser.

demifacet (dem-e-fas'et) A part, usually one half, of an articular surface of a bone (e.g., on a thoracic vertebra for articulation with a rib).

demilune (dem'e-lūn) A crescent-shaped cell.

    serous d.'s A group of five to ten crescent-shaped cells capping the end of a secretory unit of mixed salivary glands (e.g., submandibular gland). Also called crescent of Giannuzzi.

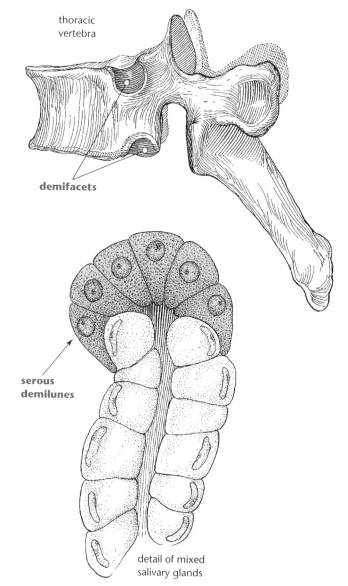

thoracic vertebra

demifacets

serous demilunes

detail of mixed salivary glands

demineralization (de-min-er-al-ī-za'shun) A reduction of the mineral component of tissues; applied especially to calcium depletion of bones.

demipenniform (dem-e-pen'ĭ-form) See unipennate.

demography (de-mog'rah-fe) The study of human populations, especially with reference to their size, density, growth, geographical distribution, and vital statistics.

demonstrator (dem'on-stra-tor) A person who supplements the teachings of a professor (e.g., by instructing small groups, preparing dissections).

demulcent (de-mul'sent) **1.** Soothing. **2.** A substance that alleviates irritation of the skin and mucous membranes, especially abraded surfaces.

demyelination, demyelinization (de-mi-ĕ-li-na'shun, de-mi-ĕ-lin-i-za'shun) A pathologic loss or breakdown of the fatty sheath (myelin) that envelops and electrically insulates nerve fibers; may occur in the brain or spinal cord or in the peripheral nerves, causing disruption of nerve functioning.

denaturation (de-na-chur-a'shun) **1.** Change of the nature of a substance, such as the loss of characteristic biologic activity of protein when submitted to extremes of pH or temperature. **2.** Alteration of a substance to make it unfit for consumption.

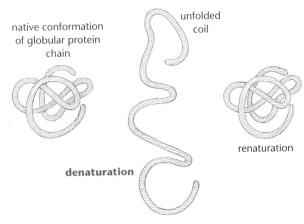

native conformation of globular protein chain

unfolded coil

denaturation

renaturation

denatured (de-na'tūrd) Changed in nature; adulterated.

dendriform (den'drĭ-form) Having branches like a tree. Also called dendroid.

dendrite (den'drīt) One of several protoplasmic extensions from the body of a nerve cell conducting impulses toward the cell body.

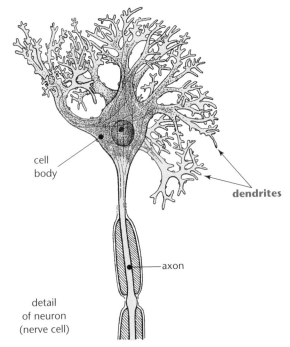

cell body

dendrites

axon

detail of neuron (nerve cell)

dendritic (den-drit'ik) Relating to dendrites.

dendroid (den'droid) See dendriform.

denervate (de-ner'vāt) To deprive a body part of its nerve supply.

dengue (deng'e) Disease of tropical and subtropical areas caused by a dengue virus, transmitted by *Aedes* mosquitoes; symptoms appear after an incubation period of three to eight days; they include severe headache, fever, ocular pain and tenderness on pressure, muscle and bone pain, and a skin rash.

denial (dĕ-ni'al) An unconscious psychological defense mechanism by means of which a person rejects or blocks out thoughts, wishes, feelings, or needs that on a conscious level are intolerable to that person.

denidation (den-ĭ-da'shun) Disintegration and discharge of the superficial layer of the uterine lining.

denitrify (de-ni'trī-fī) To remove nitrogen from a substance.

dens (dens), pl. **den'tes 1.** Latin for tooth. **2.** See odontoid process, under process.

densimeter (den-sim'ĕ-ter) See densitometer.

densitometer (den-sĭ-tom'ĕ-ter) **1.** A device for determining the density of a liquid. **2.** A device for determining the degree of bacterial growth in a medium. **3.** A device for determining the optical density of a material, such as x-ray film, by way of a photocell that measures light transmission through given areas of the film.

densitometry (den-sĭ-tom'ĕ-tre) Measurement of variations in density.

density (den'sĭ-te) **1.** The state of compactness; the quantity of matter per unit volume, expressed in grams per cubic centimeter. **2.** A measure of the degree of resistance to the speed of transmission of light.

    bone d. In clinical practice, the amount of mineral per square centimeter of bone; usually measured by photon absorptiometry or by x-ray computed tomography; actual bone density is expressed in grams per milliliter.

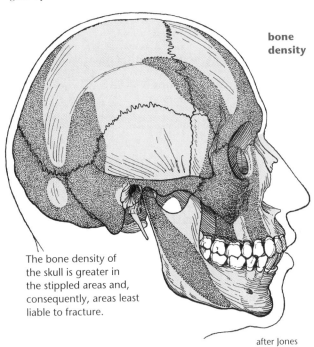

bone density

The bone density of the skull is greater in the stippled areas and, consequently, areas least liable to fracture.

after Jones

    optical d. See absorbance.

    photon d. In radioisotope scanning, the number of counted events per square centimeter of imaged area.

dental (den'tal) Relating to teeth.

dentalgia (den-tal'je-ah) Toothache.

dentate (den'tāt) Having toothlike projections.

denticle (den'tĭ-kl) **1.** See pulp stone, under stone. **2.** A toothlike projection.

denticulated (den-tik'u-lāt-ed) Having minute projections.

dentiform (den'tĭ-form) Shaped like a tooth.

dentigerous (den-tij′er-us) Containing teeth; applied to certain cysts (e.g., a dermoid cyst).

dentin (den′tin) The hard tissue forming the main substance of teeth; it surrounds the tooth pulp and is covered by enamel in the crown and by cementum in the root; permeated by tubules that contain odontoblast processes; it is softer than enamel but harder than bone. Also spelled dentine.

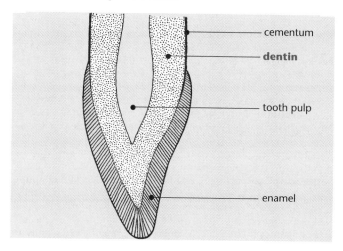

  functional d. See secondary regular dentin.

  hypoplastic d. Poorly calcified dentin marked by many interglobular spaces that are prone to caries; usually associated with deficiency diseases during calcification.

  mantle d. The outer part of the dentin abutting the enamel or cementum; it consists of mostly coarse fibers.

  primary d. Dentin formed during the physiologic development of the tooth, before its eruption; it is separated from the secondary dentin by a line of demarcation.

  reparative d. See secondary irregular dentin.

  sclerotic d. See transparent dentin.

  secondary irregular d. Highly irregular protective barrier of dentin formed by the cells of the pulp in response to severe pulp irritation from expanding caries, cavity preparation, or injury. Also called reparative dentin.

  secondary regular d. Dentin formed by the cells of the pulp in response to the normal wearing down (attrition) of the tooth. Also called functional dentin.

  transparent d. Dentin that appears translucent, usually resulting from abrasion or normal aging processes. Also called sclerotic dentin.

dentinal (den′tĭ-nal) Relating to dentin.

dentine (den′tēn) Dentin.

dentinogenesis (den-tĭ-no-jen′ĕ-sis) The development of dentin.

dentinoma (den-tĭ-no′mah) An uncommon encapsulated tumor composed of connective tissue and dentin.

dentist (den′tist) One who is trained and licensed to practice dentistry.

dentistry (den′tis-tre) The science and art of preventing, diagnosing, and treating the teeth, oral cavity, and associated structures, and of providing restorations and prostheses. Also called odontology.

  cosmetic d. Any procedure or treatment for improving the appearance of teeth.

  forensic d. Application of dental science to legal investigations or problems (e.g., dental identification of dead bodies, analysis of bite marks, evaluation of alleged dental malpractice). Also called legal dentistry; dental jurisprudence; forensic odontology.

  legal d. See forensic dentistry.

  pediatric d. See pedodontics.

dentition (den-tish′un) **1.** The arrangement of the natural teeth in the mouth; the teeth, considered collectively, in the dental arch. **2.** The process of teething.

  artificial d. See denture.

  deciduous d. The set of 20 teeth that erupts between 6 and 26 months of age and is replaced by permanent dentition from 6 to 12 years of age. Also called primary dentition.

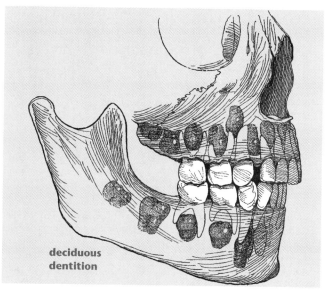

deciduous dentition

  delayed d. Eruption of the first deciduous tooth after 13 months of age or eruption of the first permanent tooth after 7 years of age. Also called retarded dentition.

  mandibular d. Dentition of the lower jaw.

  maxillary d. Dentition of the upper jaw.

  mixed d. Dentition composed of erupted permanent and deciduous teeth, as seen in children between 6 and 12 years of age. Also called transitional dentition.

  permanent d. The set of 32 teeth that begins to appear at about 6 years of age, when the first permanent molars erupt, to about 18 years of age, when the third molars erupt. Also called secondary dentition.

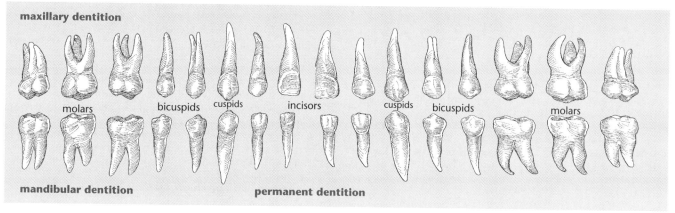

maxillary dentition

molars   bicuspids   cuspids   incisors   cuspids   bicuspids   molars

mandibular dentition   permanent dentition

primary d. See deciduous dentition.

retarded d. See delayed dentition.

secondary d. See permanent dentition.

transitional d. See mixed dentition.

dento-, denti-, dent- Combining forms meaning tooth.

dentoid (den'toid) See odontoid.

dentolegal (den-to-le'gal) Relating to both dentistry and legal matters. See forensic dentistry, under dentistry.

dentulous (den'tu-lus) Having natural teeth, deciduous or permanent.

denture (den'chur) An artificial replacement for missing natural teeth and surrounding tissues. Also called artificial dentition.

    complete d. A denture replacing all the natural teeth and associated structures in one jaw.

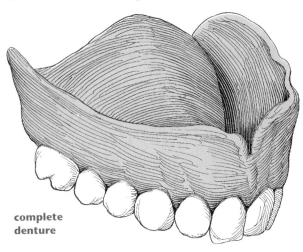

complete
denture

    fixed partial d. A partial denture attached to natural teeth or roots; it cannot be readily removed. Also called fixed bridge.

    immediate d. A denture made prior to extraction of the front teeth and inserted immediately after extraction for cosmetic purposes.

    partial d. A removable denture supported entirely by the natural teeth.

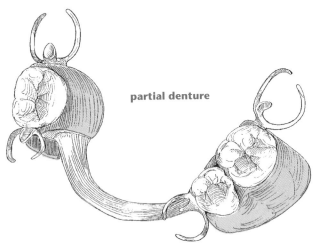

partial denture

denturist (den'chūr-ist) A person, usually a dental technician, who provides dentures for patients. The practice is illegal in some jurisdictions.

denucleated (de-nu'kle-āt-ed) Deprived of a nucleus.

denudation (den-u-da'shun) Removal of surface epithelium and exposure of subepithelial tissues.

deossification (de-os-ĭ-fĭ-ka'shun) Removal of the mineral components of bone.

deoxidation (de-ok'sĭ-da'shun) Removal of oxygen from a chemical compound.

deoxycholic acid (de-ok'se-ko'lik as'id) A digestive bile acid formed in the small intestine by the action of intestinal bacteria on cholic acid.

deoxycorticosterone, desoxycorticosterone (de-ok'se-kor-tĭ-kos'ter-ōn, des-ok'se-kor-tĭ-kos'ter-ōn) (DOC) A steroid hormone with mineralocorticoid activity formed in the cortex of the adrenal (suprarenal) gland.

deoxyribonuclease (de-ok'se-ri-bo-nu'kle-ās) (DNAase) An enzyme that promotes the breakdown of DNA to nucleotides.

deoxyribonucleic acid (de-ok'se-ri-bo-nu-kle'ik as'id) (DNA) The molecular basis of heredity. See DNA.

deoxyribose (de-ok'se-ri'bōs) The pentose sugar constituent of DNA.

dependence (de-pen'dens) A psychologic and/or physical need for a person, object, or substance. See also drug dependence.

    alcohol d. See alcoholism.

Dependovirus (de-pen-do-vi'rus) A genus of viruses (family Parvoviridae) that require the presence of adenovirus to replicate. Also called adeno-associated virus; adeno-pharyngeal-conjunctival virus; A-P-C virus; adenosatellite virus.

depersonalization (de-per-sun-al-ĭ-za'shun) Loss of one's sense of personal identity, or the feeling that one's mind or body is unreal. COMPARE dissociative disorders, under disorder. See also derealization.

dephosphorylation (de-fos-for-ĭ-la'shun) Removal of a phosphate group from a compound by the action of an enzyme.

depigmentation (de-pig-men-ta'shun) Loss of pigment, partial or complete.

depilate (dep'ĭ-lāt) To remove hair.

depilatory (de-pil'ah-to-re) A chemical hair remover.

depletion (de-ple'shun) 1. The act of emptying. 2. Excessive loss of body constituents that are necessary for body functioning. 3. The condition resulting from such process.

depolarization (de-po-lar-ĭ-za'shun) The neutralization of polarity.

deposit (de-poz'it) Sediment.

depot (de'po) An organ or tissue in which drugs or biologic substances are deposited and stored by the body.

depraved (de-prāvd') The condition of being corrupt or degenerate.

depressant (de-pres'ant) 1. Reducing functional activity. 2. An agent that has such property.

depressed (de-prest') 1. Pressed down or sunk below the level of a surrounding surface. 2. Below the normal functional level. 3. Dejected; afflicted by depression.

depression (de-presh'un) 1. Emotional dejection and reduction of functioning; a morbid sadness accompanied by lack of interest in surroundings and reduced energy; may range from mild to major. 2. A pressed-down area, lower than the surrounding level.

    agitated d. Depression accompanied by a state of restlessness and apprehension.

    anaclitic d. A state of listlessness, loss of appetite, weight loss, and withdrawal from social interactions displayed by an infant separated from its mother or mother substitute; may persist or recur later in life.

    endogenous d. Depressive disorder occurring without predominant psychosocial causative factors and thus presumed to be somatic in origin; symptoms include disturbances of sleep, appetite, sexual interest, and motor regulation as well as depressed mood.

    major d. A syndrome that, every day for at least two weeks, includes at least four of the following symptoms: *(a)* decreased or increased appetite with corresponding change in weight; *(b)* insomnia (especially very early awakening) or sleeping for excessively long periods; *(c)* motor retardation, or agitation; *(d)* loss of interest and pleasure in surroundings and decreased sexual drive; *(e)* feelings of excessive guilt, self-reproach, or worthlessness; *(f)* decreased ability to make decisions; *(g)* fatigue; and *(h)* recurrent suicidal thinking or attempts.

    major d. with psychotic features See psychotic depression.

psychotic d. Depression accompanied by delusions and hallucinations, mutism, or stupor; usually referred to as major depression with psychotic features. See also affective disorders, under disorder.

reactive d. Depression caused by some external factor and relieved once that factor is removed.

depressomotor (de-pres-o-mo′tor) **1.** Reducing motor activity. **2.** Anything that causes such an effect.

depressor (de-pres′or) **1.** Anything that reduces or retards activity. **2.** Any device or instrument that presses down or pushes aside a structure during an examination or operation. **3.** Any muscle that pulls down or depresses a body part. See table of muscles.

tongue d. A broad wooden blade for pushing the tongue against the floor of the mouth during examination of the mouth and throat.

deprivation (dep-rĭ-va′shun) A lack of something needed or the condition evoked by such a lack.

emotional d. A lack of psychologic support provided by adequate and appropriate interpersonal and environmental relationships, usually in the early developmental years.

sensory d. The condition evoked, either accidentally or experimentally, by a marked reduction of the usual range of sensory stimulation (e.g., restlessness, disorganized thinking, delusions, panic, or depression stemming from the loss of sight or hearing, a hospital confinement, or some other physical isolation).

depth (depth) A dimension downward or inward.

anesthetic d. The degree of depression of the central nervous system caused by an anesthetic drug; it is an indication of the potency of the anesthetic.

d. of focus The range of distance between object and lens without causing objectionable blurring.

depulization (de-pu-lĭ-za′shun) Elimination or destruction of fleas, especially those carrying the plague bacillus; the term is generally used with reference to antiplague measures.

depurant (dep′u-rant) **1.** Capable of purifying. **2.** Any substance that cleans or purifies.

depurative (dep′u-ra-tiv) Tending to cleanse or purify.

derangement (de-rānj′ment) **1.** See mental disorder, under disorder. **2.** A disorganized configuration or loss of organization or functioning; disorder.

derealization (de-re-al-ĭ-za′shun) A feeling of detachment from the external world; may be accompanied by feelings of loss of personal identity and feelings of being unreal or strange. COMPARE dissociative disorders, under disorder. See also depersonalization.

dereism (de′re-izm) A type of thinking that is not concordant with reality, logic, or experience.

dereistic (de-re-is′tik) Relating to dereism.

derivative (de-riv′ah-tiv) **1.** In chemistry, a compound obtained from another compound and which retains some of the elements of the original one. **2.** Resulting from modification of something else.

-derm Combining form meaning layer (e.g., ectoderm).

dermabrader (der-mah-brād′er) Any device used in dermabrasion.

dermabrasion (der-mah-bra′shun) Surgical removal of the superficial layer of the skin with a rapidly turning wire brush or gritty paper or cloth; employed in removing scars, tattoos, and superficially embedded foreign particles (from road or industrial accidents). Also called mechanical abrasion; planing.

Dermacentor (der-mah-sen′tor) A genus of ticks (family Ixodidae); some species are vectors of disease-causing microorganisms.

D. andersoni The wood tick; a reddish brown tick, transmitter of Rocky Mountain spotted fever and tularemia and the cause of tick paralysis.

D. variabilis The American dog tick; a dark brown tick, the principal vector of Rocky Mountain spotted fever.

dermal (der′mal) Relating to the skin.

dermalaxia (der-mah-lak′se-ah) Softening of the skin.

dermametropathism (der-mah-mĕ-trop′ah-thizm) A technique of diagnosing certain skin disorders by observing the markings made when a blunt instrument is drawn across the skin.

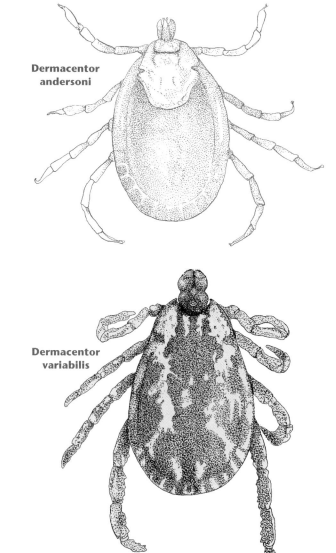

Dermacentor andersoni

Dermacentor variabilis

dermatitis (der-mah-ti′tis), pl. dermatit′ides Inflammation of the skin.

actinic d. Dermatitis produced by exposure to sunlight; a sensitivity reaction of the skin, distinguished from sunburn.

allergic contact d. Localized dermatitis characterized by a sharply demarcated area of redness and itchiness, often with an eruption of blisters; it results from contact with any of a variety of natural or manufactured substances (allergens) to which the skin has already been exposed and sensitized; it occurs as a delayed cutaneous hypersensitivity reaction to the substance. Some of the most common allergens include cosmetics, deodorants, depilatories, hair products, topical medications, clothing, and jewelry; industrial products include epoxy resins, formaldehyde, dyes, metals (chromium, nickel, cobalt, platinum), and acrylic monomers.

allergic contact dermatitis

d. artifacta See factitial dermatitis.

artifactual d. See factitial dermatitis.

atopic d. A form of dermatitis that is usually seen in people susceptible to asthma and hay fever; characterized by eruptions of scaly red patches, blistering, crusting, fissuring, and severe itching; occurs most predominantly in front of the elbow and behind the knee. Also called atopic eczema.

berloque d., berlock d. A phototoxic contact dermatitis characterized by deep brown pigmentation of the skin after initial redness, produced by exposure to sunlight after application of perfumes containing bergamot oil.

chemical d. Contact dermatitis produced by any natural or manufactured chemical substance.

contact d. Dermatitis resulting from contact with any of a variety of natural or manufactured substances and occurring as a delayed allergic reaction to the substance.

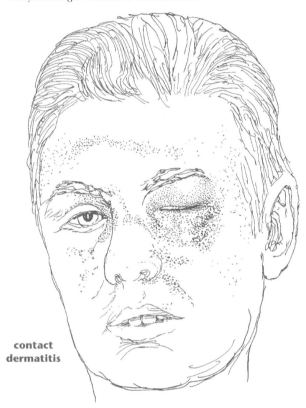

contact
dermatitis

exfoliative d. Generalized severe scaliness and redness of the skin with constitutional symptoms.

factitial d. Dermatitis caused by self-inflicted trauma (e.g., by intentionally dabbing acid on the skin or by self-injecting any of a variety of substances). Also called artifactual dermatitis; dermatitis artifacta.

d. herpetiformis (DH) An eruption of highly itchy plaques and vesicles occurring mostly on the extensor surfaces of the extremities, the upper back, and buttocks; affects mostly the 30 to 40-year age group, males more frequently than females. The disease is strongly associated with the presence of specific types of HLAs (human lymphocyte antigens) and with sensitivity to dietary gluten. The cause is unknown but it is presumed that it originates in the gastrointestinal tract. Also called Duhring's disease.

irritant contact d. Dermatitis developed at the site of contact with an irritating substance; may be *Acute*, a severe, precisely delineated skin burn with redness and blistering followed by sloughing of damaged tissue; caused by contact with strong chemicals such as acids, alkalis, and solvents; or *Chronic*, a poorly delineated area of redness, scaling, fissuring, and itching caused by cumulative exposure to any of a wide variety of mildly irritating chemicals. It is the most common occupational skin disease.

d. medicamentosa See drug eruption, under eruption.

phototoxic contact d. Chemical burn (frequently occurring as an occupational condition) in which the offending substance is capable of injuring the skin only when it is activated by exposure to sunlight; characterized by immediate swelling and redness, often with blistering of the skin and usually resolving within 48 to 72 hours, leaving a brown discoloration that may persist for months or years. Workers usually exposed are those handling such products as tars and creosote (e.g., construction workers, roofers, railway workers); wild carrots (e.g., forestry and utility workers); psoralens and sulfonamides (e.g., pharmaceutical workers).

rhus d. A delayed hypersensitivity reaction marked by an eruption of weeping, crusting vesicles; caused by contact with urushiol from species of the genus *Rhus* (poison ivy, poison oak, or poison sumac).

seborrheic s. A condition of the skin characterized by red patches with greasy yellowish scales; occurs chiefly on the scalp, eyebrows, armpits, and chest.

solar d. Dermatitis occurring in persons who are allergic to the sun's rays.

stasis d. Dermatitis of the legs associated with varicose veins, marked by swelling and purplish discoloration of the skin; caused by increased pressure within veins with consequent leakage of blood out of capillaries and deposition in the skin.

dermato-, dermo-, derm- Combining forms meaning skin.

Dermatobia (der-mah-to′be-ah) A genus of flies (family Oestridae) that includes the parasitic botflies.

dermatocele (der′mah-to-sēl) A localized loose condition of the skin.

dermatofibroma (der-mah-to-fi-bro′mah) A noncancerous skin tumor; a form of benign histiocytoma characterized by a firm, sometimes tender, mass in the deep layer of the skin; believed to be caused by a previous injury with aberrant healing.

dermatofibrosarcoma protuberans (der-mah-to-fi-bro-sar-ko′ mah pro-tu′ber-ans) A slow-growing cancerous tumor of the skin that may invade adjacent tissues but rarely spreads to other sites; composed of several small nodules covered with thin, dark, red-blue skin; it tends to recur after removal.

dermatoglyphics (der-mah-to-glif′iks) **1.** The ridge patterns on the volar surface of fingers, toes, palms, and soles and their configurational arrangements; useful in diagnosing Down's syndrome and other genetic disorders. **2.** The study of these configurations as they relate to other scientific disciplines (e.g., anthropology, genetics, and criminology).

dermatoglyphics

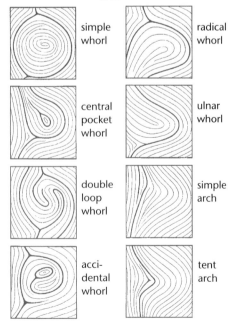

simple whorl | radical whorl
central pocket whorl | ulnar whorl
double loop whorl | simple arch
accidental whorl | tent arch

dermatographia (der-mah-to-graf'e-ah) See dermatographism.

dermatographism (der-mah-tog'rah-fizm) Formation of wheals after stroking the skin with a pencil or blunt instrument. Also called dermatographia; dermographism; dermographia; skin writing.

dermatoid (der'mah-toid) Resembling hair.

dermatologist (der-mah-tol'o-jist) A specialist in disorders of the skin and related systematic diseases. Popularly called skin specialist.

dermatology (der-mah-tol'o-je) The medical specialty concerned with the diagnosis and treatment of diseases of the skin and its appendages.

dermatome (der'mah-tōm) **1.** Surgical instrument for cutting thin slices of skin for grafting. **2.** A skin area supplied by sensory fibers of a single spinal nerve. **3.** In embryology, the dorsolateral portion of the somite from which the skin is derived.

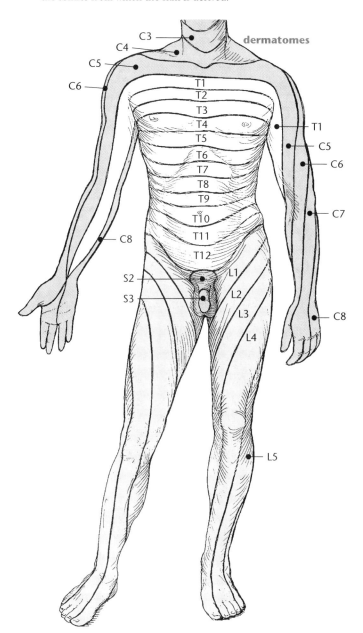

dermatomes

dermatomegaly (der-mah-to-meg'ah-le) Congenital defect consisting of excessive development, thickening, and folding of the skin.

dermatomycosis (der-mah-to-mi-ko'sis) Any fungal infection of the skin.

dermatomyositis (der-mah-to-mi-o-si'tis) A disorder of skin and muscle characterized by a blue-violet rash on the face (especially around the eyes) and on the back of the hands and fingers, with muscle weakness especially on the shoulder and pelvic areas; two varieties are known, affecting children or adults; the adult form is sometimes associated with an occult internal cancer.

dermatonosology (der-mah-to-no-sol'o-je) The classification of skin diseases. Also called dermonosology.

dermatopathology (der-mah-to-pah-thol'o-je) The study of skin diseases.

dermatopathy (der-mah-top'ah-the) Any skin disease.

Dermatophagoides (der-mah-tof-ah-goi'dēs) Genus of mites; some species, especially *Dermatophagoides farinae* and *Dermatophagoides pteronyssinus*, provide the principal source of allergic material of house dust; the mites feed on human dander and encase their feces within a coating that contains the primary allergen.

dermatophobia (der-mah-to-fo'be-ah) An exaggerated, abnormal fear of acquiring a skin disease.

dermatophylaxis (der-mah-to-fī-lak'sis) Protective measures that guard against skin diseases.

dermatophyte (der'mah-to-fīt) Any fungus, such as species of the genera *Trichophyton*, *Microsporum*, and *Epidermophyton*, that grows in keratin and causes infections of the skin, hair, or nails.

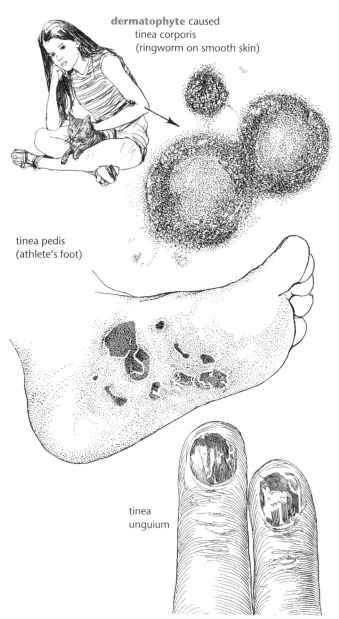

dermatophyte caused tinea corporis (ringworm on smooth skin)

tinea pedis (athlete's foot)

tinea unguium

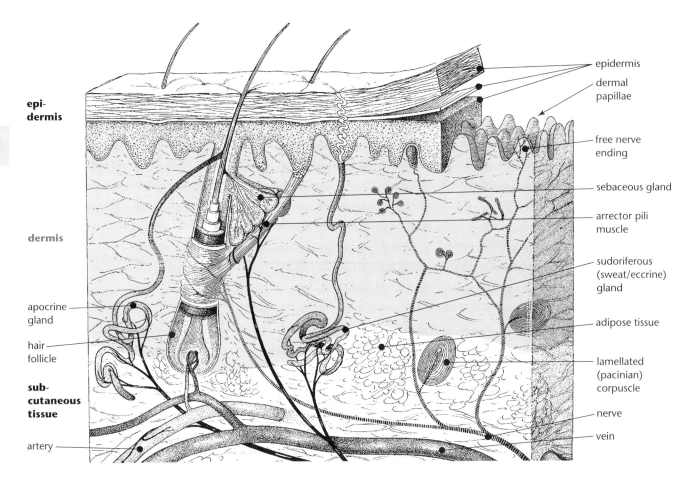

epidermis

dermal papillae

free nerve ending

sebaceous gland

arrector pili muscle

sudoriferous (sweat/eccrine) gland

adipose tissue

lamellated (pacinian) corpuscle

nerve

vein

epi-dermis

dermis

apocrine gland

hair follicle

sub-cutaneous tissue

artery

dermatophytid (der-mah-tof′ĭ-tid) Secondary skin eruption, usually on the fingers and hands, following sensitization to fungi. Often called id. See also id reaction, under id.

dermatophytosis (der-mah-to-fi-to′sis) Any superficial fungal infection of the skin, such as athlete's foot (tinea pedis) and ringworm (tinea corporis).

dermatoplasty (der′mah-to-plas-te) Skin grafting.

dermatosis (der-mah-to′sis), pl. dermato′ses General term for any disease of the skin.

  progressive pigmented d. Benign chronic condition characterized by repeated crops of minute purplish hemorrhagic spots (petechiae) on the legs and feet, especially of men. Also called Schamberg's disease.

dermatotherapy (der-mah-to-ther′ah-pe) Treatment of skin diseases.

dermatotropic (der-mah-to-trop′ik) Tending to act only on the skin. Also called dermotropic.

dermic (der′mik) Relating to the skin.

dermis (der′mis) The connective tissue layer of the skin, just below the epidermis; composed of a thin superficial layer and a deeper thick, dense, reticular layer; it contains blood vessels, nerves and nerve endings, glands, lymphatic channels, and hair follicles. Also called corium; cutis vera.

dermo- Combining form meaning skin.

dermoblast (der′mo-blast) One of the mesodermal cells of the embryo that develops into the true skin (dermis).

dermographia (der-mo-graf′e-ah) See dermatographism.

dermographism (der-mog′rah-fizm) See dermatographism.

dermoid (der′moid) 1. Resembling skin. 2. See dermoid cyst, under cyst.

dermonosology (der-mo-no-sol′o-je) See dermatonosology.

dermostosis (der-mo-sto′sis) Bony formations on the skin.

dermotoxin (der-mo-tok′sin) Any substance that is capable of causing pathologic changes in the skin.

dermotropic (der-mo-trop′ik) See dermatotropic.

dermovascular (der-mo-vas′ku-lar) Relating to the blood supply of the skin.

desaturation (de-sach-er-a′shun) The chemical process of transforming a saturated compound into an unsaturated one.

descemetitis (des-ĕ-mĕ-ti′tis) Inflammation of Descemet's (posterior lining) membrane of the cornea.

descensus (de-sen′sus) The process of moving downward; a descent.

  d. testis Descent of the testes from the abdominal cavity into the scrotum shortly before birth.

desensitization (de-sen-sĭ-ti′za-shun) 1. Treatment of allergic disease in which the patient is deliberately exposed to low doses of the offending substance (allergen) in order to reduce (or possibly eliminate) the allergic response; the allergen is administered in increasing amounts by a series of injections until the patient develops increased tolerance to the specific allergen on natural exposure. Also called allergen immunotherapy; hyposensitization; allergy injection therapy. 2. A method of treating an emotional disorder (e.g., behavior therapy).

  systematic d. Procedure used in behavior modification, especially to modify behaviors associated with phobias, in which the patient is introduced to gradually increasing anxiety-producing stimuli until they no longer produce anxiety.

desensitize (de-sen′sĭ-tiz) 1. To subject a person to desensitization. 2. To reduce or eliminate sensation.

desiccant (des′ĭ-kant) 1. Absorbing moisture and causing dryness. 2. A drying agent (e.g., dusting powder). Also called exsiccant.

desiccate (des′ĭ-kāt) To dry.

desiccator (des′ĭ-ka-tor) A closed vessel for placing a substance or apparatus for drying or to be kept free of moisture; it contains a dehydrating agent (e.g., calcium chloride, sulfuric acid).

designation (dez-ig-na′shun) A distinguishing name.

  cluster d. (CD) A numerical nomenclature for cell surface molecules (markers) that are typical of different cell lineages and that are recognized by specific monoclonal antibodies.

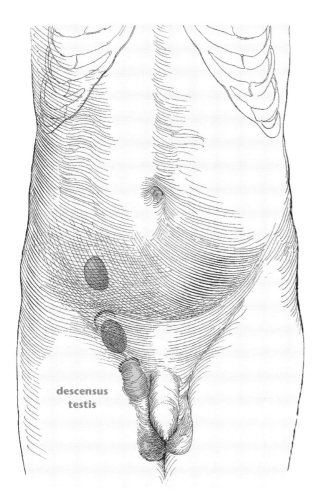

descensus
testis

desmitis (des-mi′tis) Inflammation of a ligament.

desmo-, desm- Combining forms meaning ligament.

desmoid (des′moid) A locally aggressive nodule formed by proliferation of fibrous tissue of muscle sheaths; most common site is the abdominal rectus muscle, especially in women after pregnancy; it does not spread to other sites but tends to recur after surgical removal unless a wide margin of healthy tissue is included in the resection. Also called aggressive fibromatosis.

desmoplasia (des-mo-pla′ze-ah) Proliferation of fibrous tissue, particularly in a tumor.

desmoplastic (des-mo-plas′tik) 1. Relating to desmoplasia. 2. Causing adhesions.

desmopressin acetate (des-mo-pres′in as′ĕ-tāt) (DDAVP) A synthetic analog of vasopressin used as an antidiuretic.

desmosome (des′mo-sōm) The specialized area of contact and adhesion between two adjacent cells, especially epithelial cells. Also called macula adherens.

desquamate (des′kwah-mat) To cast off or shed; the process of desquamation.

desquamation (des-kwah-ma′shun) Shedding the outer layer of a surface (e.g., of the skin).

detachment (de-tach′ment) 1. The state of being separated (e.g., of the retina from its normal attachment to the choroid). 2. In psychiatry, the condition of being free from emotional involvement.

deterioration (de-ter-e-er-a′shun) Any worsening condition or progressive impairment.

determinant (de-ter′mĭ-nant) Some factor that establishes the characteristics or occurrence of an event.

    antigenic d. The exact site on the surface of an antigen molecule or a hapten (smaller molecule) to which attaches a specific antibody produced by the host's immune system; a single antigen molecule may have several determinants recognized separately and specifically by the host's immune system. Also called epitope.

determination (de-ter-mĭ-na′shun) 1. The process of measuring a quantity in scientific, laboratory, or forensic investigations. 2. A conclusion reached after deliberation as to the nature of a disease or of the cause of death.

    paternity d. The process of establishing whether a man has a biological relationship to a child.

paternity determination (DNA bands)

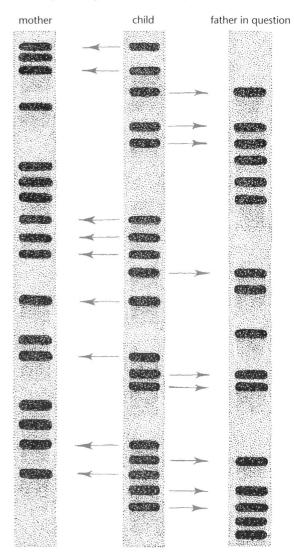

mother   child   father in question

The paternal DNA bands show a biologic relationship to the child.

    toxicity d. The process of establishing the presence of a toxic substance in the body; may include emergency tests to evaluate the type and quantity of drugs (legal or illegal) taken in accidental or intentional overdoses. Usually, blood and urine are examined; appropriate specimens also include stomach contents or lavage fluid (if test is performed soon after ingestion).

determinism (de-ter′min-izm) The doctrine that any event, including human behavior, is the inevitable consequence of prior influences.

detersive (de-ter′siv) Detergent.

detoxicate (de-tok′sĭ-kāt) See detoxify.

detoxification, detoxication (de-tok-sĭ-fi-ka′shun, de-tok-sĭ-ka′shun) 1. The process of neutralizing the toxic effects of a substance. 2. The recovery from the toxic effects of a substance.

detoxify (de-tok′sĭ-fi) The act or process of detoxification.

detritus (de-tri′tus) Any residue remaining after deterioration of organic matter; organic debris.

detrusor (de-troo'sor) Denoting a muscle that effects an expulsion or pushing out of something (e.g., the detrusor muscle of the bladder).

detubation (de-tu-ba'shun) Removal of a tube from the body (e.g., of a tracheostomy tube).

detumescence (de-tu-mes'ens) The return of a swollen or turgid part or organ to its original size.

deuteranopia (doo-ter-ah-no'pe-ah) A form of color blindness in which there is difficulty distinguishing colors except blue and yellow; a sex-linked hereditary defect occurring almost exclusively in males.

deuterium (doo-ter'e-um) (D) See hydrogen 2.

deutero-, deuto- Combining forms meaning secondary; two.

devascularization (de-vas-ku-lar-ĭ-za'shun) Removal of blood vessels from a part.

deviance (de've-ans) See deviation.

deviation (de-ve-a'shun) **1.** A turning aside. **2.** Departure from a norm, rule, or accepted course of behavior.

    axis d. Deviation of the electrical axis of the heart to the right or to the left. Also called axis shift.

    parallel conjugate d. (*a*) The normal joint and equal movement of the two eyes in the same direction when shifted from one object to another. (*b*) Pathologic condition marked by failure of both eyes to turn to one side; the person compensates by rotating or tilting the head.

    primary d. In strabismus, deviation of the defective eye measured with the normal eye fixed on an object.

    secondary d. In strabismus, deviation of the normal eye measured when the defective eye is made to fixate on an object.

    skew d. Movement of both eyes in opposite directions.

    standard d. (SD) In statistics, a measure of dispersion in a distribution.

device (dĕ-vis') Something constructed for a particular purpose.

    contraceptive d. Any device for preventing conception.

    intrauterine d. (IUD) A device made of plastic or metal inserted into the uterus to prevent conception. IUDs are no longer made in the United States. Also called intrauterine contraceptive device.

    intrauterine contraceptive d. (IUCD) See intrauterine device.

devitalization (de-vi-tal-ĭ-za'shun) In dentistry, the act of destroying the pulp of a tooth.

devolution (dev-o-lu'shun) The slow, systematic changes of observable genetic characteristics (phenotype) toward less complexity; the opposite of evolution.

devolutive (dev-o-lu'tiv) Relating to devolution.

dexter (dek'ster) (D) Latin for right.

dextrad (deks'trad) Toward the right.

dextral (deks'tral) **1.** Relating to the right side. **2.** Right-handed.

dextran (dek'stran) Any of various large polymers of glucose, widely used in solution as a plasma substitute.

dextrin (deks'trin) A water-soluble carbohydrate resulting from the breakdown of starch by hydrolysis; used in pharmaceutical preparations and in solution, as an adhesive.

dextroamphetamine sulfate (deks-tro-am-fet'ah-mēn sul'fāt) A stimulant of the central nervous system and an appetite depressant. It is one of the drugs of abuse popularly known as "uppers."

dextrocardia (deks-tro-kar'de-ah) **1.** Abnormal congenital position of the heart on the right side of the chest with or without mirror-image transposition of the right and left heart chambers. **2.** An acquired condition in which the major portion of the heart is displaced to the right side, as may occur in collapse of the right lung.

dextrocular (deks-trok'u-lar) Relating to the right eye.

dextromethorphan hydrobromide (dek-stro-meth'or-fan hi-dro-bro'mīd) Pharmaceutical preparation taken orally as a cough suppressant.

dextroposition (deks-tro-po-zish'un) Abnormal right-sided location of an organ normally located on the left side.

    d. of heart See dextrocardia.

dextrose (deks'trōs) See glucose.

dextroversion (deks-tro-ver'shun) A displacement toward the right.

di- Prefix meaning two.

dia- Prefix meaning through.

diabetes (di-ah-be'tēz) General term for metabolic disorders characterized by excessive excretion of urine (polyuria); when used alone, the term refers to diabetes mellitus.

    d. I See insulin-dependent diabetes mellitus (IDDM).

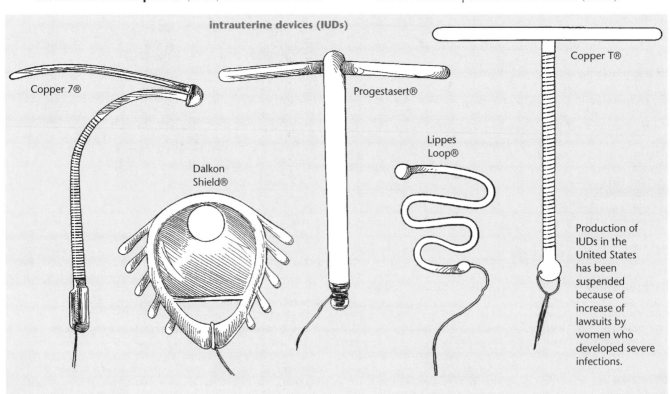

intrauterine devices (IUDs)

Copper 7®

Dalkon Shield®

Progestasert®

Lippes Loop®

Copper T®

Production of IUDs in the United States has been suspended because of increase of lawsuits by women who developed severe infections.

Classification of **DIABETES MELLITUS** and other categories of glucose intolerance

	CLASS	FORMER TERMINOLOGY	CLINICAL CHARACTERISTICS
DIABETES MELLITUS (DM)	Insulin-dependent type (IDDM) type I	juvenile diabetes juvenile-onset diabetes juvenile-onset-type diabetes JOD Ketosis-prone diabetes brittle diabetes	Persons in this subclass are dependent on injected insulin to prevent ketosis, acidosis, and hyperglycemia; in the preponderance of cases, onset is in youth, but insulin dependent diabetes mellitus (IDDM) may occur at any age; characterized by insulinopenia.
	Non-insulin-dependent type (NIDDM) type II	adult-onset diabetes maturity-onset diabetes	Persons in this subclass are not insulin-dependent or ketosis-prone, although they may use insulin for correction of symptomatic or persistent hyperglcemia and they can develop ketosis under special circumstances; serum insulin levels may be normal, elevated or depressed; in the preponderance of cases, onset is after age 40, but noninsulin dependent diabetes mellitus (NIDDM) is known to occur at all ages; about 60–90% of NIDDM subjects are obese and constitute a subtype of NIDDM; in these individuals, glucose tolerance is often improved by weight loss; hyperinsulinemia and insulin resistance characterize some individuals in this subtype.
	other types, including diabetes mellitus associated with certain conditions and syndromes: 1) pancreatic disease 2) hormonal 3) drug or chemical induced 4) insulin receptor abnormalities 5) certain genetic syndromes 6) other types	secondary diabetes	In addition to the presence of the specific condition or syndrome, diabetes mellitus is also present.
IMPAIRED GLUCOSE TOLERANCE (IGT)	Nonobese **IGT** Obese **IGT** IGT associated with certain syndromes, which may be 1) pancreatic disease 2) hormonal 3) drug or chemical induced 4) insulin receptor abnormalities 5) genetic syndromes	asymptomatic diabetes chemical diabetes subclinical diabetes borderline diabetes latent diabetes	Mild glucose intolerance of subjects in this class may be attributable to normal variation of glucose tolerance within a population; in some subjects, impaired glucose tolerance (IGT) may represent a stage in the development of NIDDM or IDDM although the majority of persons with IGT remain in this class for many years or return to normal glucose tolerance.
GESTATIONAL DIABETES (GDM)	Gestational diabetes	same	Glucose intolerance that has its onset or recognition during pregnancy thus, diabetics who become pregnant are not included in this class; associated with increased perinatal complications and with increased risk for progression to diabetes within 5–10 years after parturition; usually requires treatment with insulin; necessitates reclassification after pregnancy terminates.

adapted from the National Diabetes Association |

d. II See non-insulin-dependent diabetes mellitus (NIDDM).

adult-onset d. See non-insulin-dependent diabetes mellitus (NIDDM).

alloxan d. The production of diabetes mellitus in experimental animals (animal models) by the administration of alloxan, an agent that selectively destroys the insulin-producing (beta) cells of the pancreas.

brittle d. Term formerly used for insulin-dependent diabetes mellitus that is difficult to control, with unpredictable and frequent episodes of hyper- and hypoglycemia.

bronzed d. See hemochromatosis.

chemical d. mellitus See latent diabetes mellitus.

class A d. mellitus See gestational diabetes mellitus.

gestational d. mellitus (GDM) Pregnancy-induced glucose intolerance limited to the pregnant condition. Also called class A diabetes mellitus; pregnancy-induced glucose intolerance.

d. insipidus A comparatively rare form of diabetes marked by excessive thirst and the passage of large amounts of dilute urine (of low specific gravity), due to an inadequate production of antidiuretic hormone (vasopressin) by the posterior lobe of the pituitary; normally, the antidiuretic hormone curtails the amount of water the kidney releases in the urine. COMPARE nephrogenic diabetes insipidus.

insulin-dependent d. mellitus (IDDM) An often severe type of diabetes mellitus characterized by a sudden onset of insulin deficiency, with a tendency to develop ketoacidosis; may occur at any age, but is most common in childhood and adolescence (peak age of onset is 11–15 years); the disorder is due to destruction of the beta cells of the islets of Langerhans in the pancreas, possibly by a viral infection and autoimmune reactions; symptoms and signs include elevated blood glucose levels (hyperglycemia), excessive urination (polyuria), chronic excessive thirst (polydipsia), excessive eating (polyphagia), weight loss, and irritability; affected persons must have injections of insulin to survive. Formerly called juvenile diabetes; juvenile-onset diabetes mellitus; brittle diabetes mellitus. Also called type I diabetes mellitus; diabetes I.

juvenile d., juvenile-onset d.. Former terms for insulin-dependent diabetes mellitus.

latent d. mellitus Asymptomatic diabetes mellitus detected by an abnormal oral glucose tolerance test, although the abnormality is not sufficient to be diagnostic of diabetes mellitus. Also called impaired glucose tolerance; chemical diabetes mellitus; preclinical diabetes mellitus; subclinical diabetes mellitus.

maturity-onset d. mellitus See non-insulin-dependent diabetes mellitus (NIDDM).

maturity-onset d. of youth (MODY) A subtype of non-insulin dependent diabetes mellitus characterized by a gradual onset during late adolescence or early adulthood.

d. mellitus (DM) A chronic systemic disease of disordered metabolism of carbohydrate, protein, and fat; its primary feature is abnormally high levels of sugar (glucose) in the blood (hyperglycemia), from which the term *mellitus* (Latin for "honeyed") was derived. The condition has been classified into two major categories (insulin-dependent diabetes mellitus and non-insulin-dependent diabetes mellitus).

nephrogenic d. insipidus A rare familial form of diabetes insipidus due to severely diminished ability of the kidney tubules to reabsorb water; it does not respond to the administration of antidiuretic hormone. Also called vasopressin-resistant diabetes.

non-insulin-dependent d. mellitus (NIDDM) A relatively mild form of diabetes mellitus characterized by a gradual onset that may occur at any age but is most common in adults over the age of 40 years, especially those with a tendency to obesity (peak age of onset is 50–60 years); may be due to a delayed insulin release from the pancreas in response to glucose intake, or to a tissue insensitivity to insulin; a genetic predisposition is noted when it occurs in young people. Formerly called adult-onset diabetes mellitus; maturity-onset diabetes mellitus. Also called type II diabetes mellitus; diabetes II.

preclinical d. mellitus See latent diabetes mellitus.

subclinical d. mellitus See latent diabetes mellitus.

type I d. mellitus See insulin-dependent diabetes mellitus (IDDM).

type II d. mellitus See non-insulin-dependent diabetes mellitus (NIDDM).

vasopressin-resistant d. See nephrogenic diabetes insipidus.

diabetic (di-ah-bet′ik) Relating to diabetes.

diabetogenic (di-ah-bet-o-jen′ik) Causing diabetes.

diabetologist (di-ah-be-tol′o-jist) A physician who specializes in the treatment of diabetic patients.

diabetology (di-ah-be-tol′o-je) The field of medicine concerned with the study and treatment of diabetes.

diacetic acid (di-ah-se′tik as′id) See acetoacidic acid.

diacetylmorphine (di-ah-se-til-mor′fen) See heroin.

diaclasis (di-ak′lah-sis) See osteoclasis.

diadochokinesia, diadochokinesis (di-ad-ō-ko-ki-ne′se-ah, di-ad-ō-ko-ki-ne′sis) The normal ability to alternately perform coordinated, opposite movements (e.g., extension and flexion of a limb).

diagnose (di′ag-nōs) To identify the nature of a disease.

diagnosis (di-ag-no′sis) The determination of the nature of a disease.

antenatal d. See prenatal diagnosis.

clinical d. Diagnosis based on the signs and symptoms produced by the disease.

differential d. Diagnosis made by comparing and contrasting available information of diseases (e.g., symptoms, signs, physical findings, and laboratory data) that are possibly responsible for the patient's illness.

d. by exclusion Diagnosis made by excluding all but one of the diseases thought to be possible causes of the symptoms being presented.

laboratory d. Diagnosis based on laboratory study of blood, tissues, discharges, or secretions.

neonatal d. Diagnosis of disease or malformation of the newborn reached after systematic evaluation.

pathologic d. *(a)* Diagnosis made from the study of lesions present in the body. *(b)* Diagnosis of the pathologic conditions present, made by a study and comparison of the symptoms.

physical d. Diagnosis based on information obtained through inspection, palpation, percussion, or auscultation.

prenatal d. Diagnosis of disorders (e.g., chromosome abnormalities, neural tube defects, inborn errors of metabolism) made by examining fetal cells obtained by amniocentesis (from amniotic fluid), chorionic villous sampling (from placenta), or fetal blood sampling (from umbilical cord). Also called antenatal diagnosis.

radioisotope d. Diagnosis made by the use of radioactive materials.

diagnostic (di-ag-nos′tik) See pathognomonic.

diagnostician (di-ag-nos-tish′an) One who is experienced in determining the nature of diseases; formerly used to describe physicians

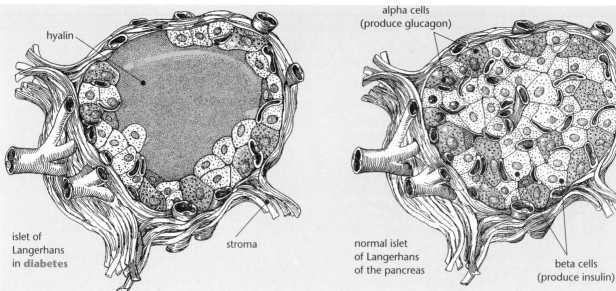

hyalin

islet of Langerhans in **diabetes**

stroma

alpha cells (produce glucagon)

normal islet of Langerhans of the pancreas

beta cells (produce insulin)

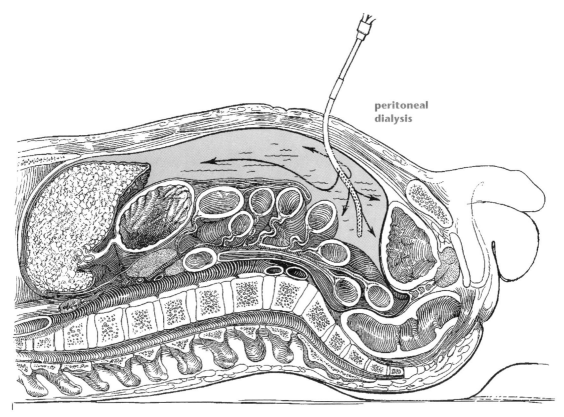

peritoneal
dialysis

with extensive training and experience in medicine, comparable to current specialists in internal medicine.

diakinesis (di-ah-kī-ne′sis) The last stage of prophase I of meiosis during which the chromosomes reach maximal condensation.

dialysance (di-ah-li′sans) The amount of blood (measured in milliliters) which, if completely cleared of a substance, would yield the amount removed by a dialyzing membrane in one minute.

dialysate (di-al′ĭ-sāt) Fluid used in dialysis.

dialysis (di-al′ĭ-sis) Separation of large molecules from low-molecular-weight molecules in a fluid by means of a semipermeable membrane.

   chronic ambulatory peritoneal d. (CAPD) A treatment modality in which the patient exchanges the dialyzing fluid three to five times daily through a permanently placed catheter.

   chronic cyclical peritoneal d. (CCPD) Peritoneal dialysis in which automated equipment (cycler) is set each night at bedtime to make several exchanges of fluid while the patient sleeps.

   peritoneal d. A treatment modality for removing toxic substances from the blood by placing a sterile dialyzing fluid in the abdominal cavity for several hours and then drawing it off; the lining membrane (peritoneum) of the abdominal cavity acts as the semipermeable membrane.

dialyze (di′ah-līz) To perform dialysis.

dialyzer (di′ah-līz-er) A semipermeable membrane serving as a filter in dialysis.

diameter (di-am′e-ter) **1.** A straight line passing through the center of any circular anatomic structure or space; fequently used to specify certain dimensions of the female pelvis and fetal head. **2.** The distance along such a line. **3.** The thickness or width of any structure or opening.

   anteroposterior d. The distance between two points located on the anterior and posterior aspects of the structure measured.

   anteroposterior d. of pelvic inlet The distance between the midpoints of the upper rim of the pubic symphysis and the sacral promontory.

   anteroposterior d. of pelvic outlet The distance between the midpoint of the lower rim of the pubic symphysis and the tip of the coccyx. Sometimes the sacrococcygeal junction is used for the posterior point.

   biparietal d. The transverse distance between the two parietal eminences of the skull, representing the maximal cranial breadth.

   bispinous d. See interspinous diameter.

   bitemporal d. The distance between the two temporal sutures of the fetal skull at term, usually around 8.0 cm.

   bituberous d. See transverse diameter of pelvic outlet.

   fronto-occipital d. See occipitofrontal diameter.

   interspinous d. The transverse pelvic diameter between the two ischial spines. Also called bispinous diameter.

   intertuberous d. See transverse diameter of pelvic outlet.

   mento-occipital d. See occipitomental diameter.

   oblique d.'s of pelvis *(a)* Of the inlet: the distance from one sacroiliac joint to the opposite junction of the ischial and pubic rami (iliopubic eminence); *(b)* of the outlet: the distance from the midpoint of the sacrotuberous ligament to the opposite junction of the ischial and pubic rami (iliopubic eminence).

   occipitofrontal d. The diameter of the skull from the frontal bone between the eyebrows (glabella) to the external occipital protuberance (furthest point at occiput); it represents the maximal cranial diameter. The greatest circumference of the head corresponds to the plane of the occipitofrontal diameter. Also called fronto-occipital diameter.

   occipitomental d. The distance of a skull from the chin to the most prominent portion of the occipital bone (external occipital protuberance). Also called mento-occipital diameter.

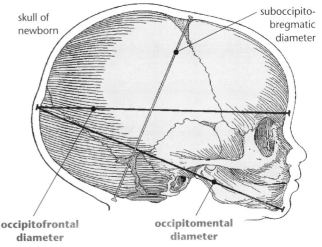

skull of newborn

suboccipito-bregmatic diameter

occipitofrontal diameter

occipitomental diameter

diakinesis ■ **diameter**

posterior sagittal d. of midpelvis A right-angled diameter extending posteriorly from the midpoint on the interspinous diameter and a point on the sacrum on the same plane.

posterior sagittal d. of pelvic outlet A right-angled diameter extending posteriorly from the midpoint on the transverse diameter of the pelvic outlet to the sacrococcygeal junction.

suboccipitobregmatic d. The diameter of a fetal skull at term from the middle of the anterior fontanel to the under surface of the occipital bone, just where it joins the neck. The smallest circumference of the fetal head corresponds to the plane of the suboccipitobregmatic diameter.

d. transversa pelvis See transverse diameter of pelvic inlet.

transverse d. of pelvic inlet The maximum distance between opposite sides of the pelvic brim, i.e., between the terminal lines (lineae terminales) of the pelvis. Also called diameter transversa pelvis.

transverse d. of pelvic outlet The distance between the two ischial tuberosities. Also called bituberous diameter; intertuberous diameter.

diapedesis (di-ah-pĕ-de′sis) **1.** The outward passage of blood cells through the pores of blood and lymph vessels. **2.** The process by which phagocytic white blood cells leave the blood vessels and accumulate outside the vessels at sites of tissue injury.

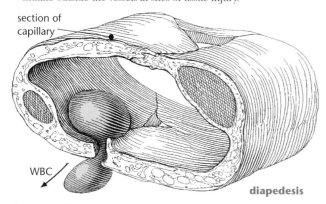

section of capillary

WBC

diapedesis

diaphoresis (di-ah-fo-re′sis) Sweating.

diaphoretic (di-ah-fo-ret′ik) **1.** An agent that causes sweating, especially profuse sweating. **2.** Sweaty.

diaphragm (di′ah-fram) **1.** A dome-shaped, musculofibrous partition separating the thoracic from the abdominal cavity, and functioning in such activities as respiration, defecation, and parturition; its periphery consists of muscular fibers attached to the circumference of the thoracic outlet, namely, to the back of the xiphoid process, to the internal surface of the lower six ribs and their cartilages, to the arcuate ligaments, and to the lumbar vertebrae; they converge into a central tendon, a thin but strong aponeurosis situated near the center of the dome, immediately below the pericardium of the heart, with which it is partly blended. A number of apertures appear in the diaphragm, including the aortic, the esophageal, and the vena caval, plus a number of smaller openings. The elevation of the diaphragm on the right side is positioned noticeably higher than on the left side. Also called thoracoabdominal diaphragm. **2.** Any membranous partition that divides or separates structures. **3.** A device with a variable aperture that controls the amount of light illuminating a specimen on a light microscope. **4.** The adjustable grid of lead strips used for minimizing radiation exposure to patients when taking x-ray pictures.

contraceptive d. A flexible ring, usually covered with thin rubber coated with a spermicidal agent, fitted over the cervix of the uterus to prevent pregnancy. Also called diaphragmatic pessary.

pelvic d. The part of the pelvic floor formed by the paired levator ani and coccygeus muscles and their fasciae.

thoracoabdominal d. See diaphragm (1).

urogenital d. A deep and strong musculomembranous partition stretched across the anterior half of the pelvic outlet between the ischiopubic rami; it is composed of the sphincter muscle of the membranous urethra, the right and left deep transverse muscle of the perineum (transversus perinei profundus) and fascia. In the female, it is primarily pierced by the urethra and vagina; in the male, by the membranous urethra and the ducts of the Cowper's (bulbourethral) glands.

diaphysis (di-af′ĭ-sis), pl. diaph′yses The shaft of a long bone.

diaphysitis (di-ah-fiz-i′tis) Inflammation of the shaft of a long bone.

diaplacental (di-ah-plah-sen′tal) Through the placenta.

diapophysis (di-ah-pof′ĭ-sis) The upper articular surface of a transverse vertebral process.

diarrhea (di-ah-re′ah) An increase in the looseness or fluidity and frequency of bowel movements beyond what is normal for the person.

nocturnal d. Diarrhea occurring primarily at night, seen in diabetes mellitus when neurologic complications are present.

traveler's d. Diarrhea occurring in a person who lives in an industrialized country and travels to a developing country, usually in tropical or semitropical areas; caused by a variety of bacterial and vi-

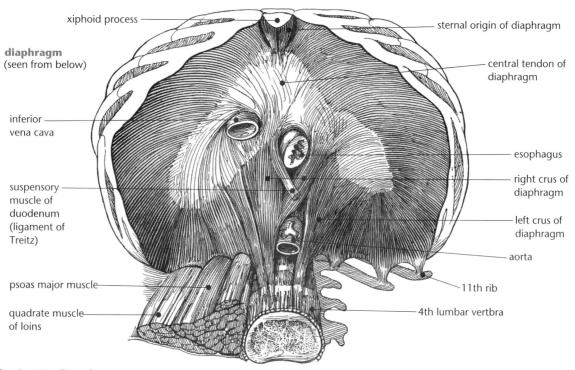

xiphoid process

sternal origin of diaphragm

diaphragm (seen from below)

central tendon of diaphragm

inferior vena cava

esophagus

right crus of diaphragm

suspensory muscle of duodenum (ligament of Treitz)

left crus of diaphragm

aorta

psoas major muscle

11th rib

quadrate muscle of loins

4th lumbar vertbra

diapedesis ■ diarrhea

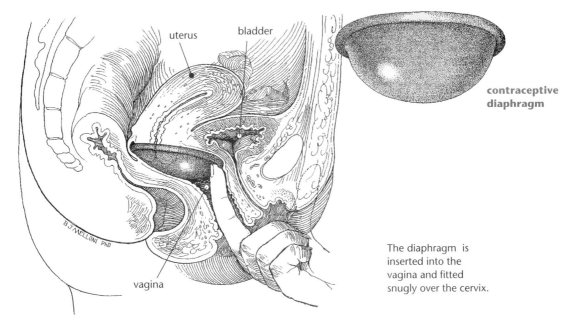

uterus

bladder

contraceptive diaphragm

vagina

The diaphragm is inserted into the vagina and fitted snugly over the cervix.

ral microorganisms; may occur suddenly while traveling, lasting 1 to 3 days and causing the passage of at least three unformed stools in a 24-hour period, accompanied by nausea, vomiting, abdominal cramps, fecal urgency, or the passage of bloody or mucoid stools; or it may occur during the first 7 to 10 days after returning home, causing the passage of 3 to 10 unformed stools daily for 3 to 5 days, usually accompanied by abdominal cramps and, sometimes, fever, vomiting, and bloody stools. Colloquially called turista.

diarrheogenic (di-ah-re-o-jen'ik) Causing diarrhea.

diarsenol (di-ar-sen'ol) See arsphenamine.

diarthric (di-ar'thrik) Relating to two joints.

diarthrosis (di-ar-thro'sis) See synovial joint, under joint.

diaschisis (di-as'kĭ-sis) A sudden functional disorder caused by a focal disturbance of the brain.

diastase (di'ah-stās) A mixture of starch-splitting enzymes that convert starch into dextrin and maltose.

diastasis (di-as'tah-sis) Abnormal separation of two normally joined structures.

    d. recti Separation of the two abdominal rectus muscles along the midline, sometimes occurring in pregnancy or abdominal surgery.

diastema (di-ah-ste'mah) Abnormally wide space between two adjacent teeth, usually the upper central incisors.

diastole (di-as'to-le) The resting period of the heart muscle during which time the heart chambers fill with blood.

diastolic (di-ah-stol'ik) Relating to a diastole.

diataxia (di-ah-tak'se-ah) Loss of muscular coordination on both sides of the body.

diathermy (di'ah-ther-me) Local generation of heat in body tissues by a high frequency electric current.

    medical d. Production of sufficient heat to warm tissues without destroying them.

    short wave d. Heating of tissues with an oscillating high frequency current; used in physical therapy to relieve pain.

    surgical d. High frequency diathermy used for destroying diseased tissue, arresting bleeding, or to separate tissues without causing bleeding.

diathesis (di-ath'ĕ-sis) An inherited predisposition to a disease or abnormality; a constitutional susceptibility.

    cystic d. A susceptibility to formation of cysts in an organ.

    gouty d. A susceptibility to gout.

    hemorrhagic d. Susceptibility to spontaneous bleeding or bleeding from slight trauma.

diatomic (di-ah-tom'ik) Consisting of two atoms.

diatrizoate sodium (di-ah-tri-zo'āt so'de-um) See under sodium.

diazepam (di-az'ĕ-pam) A benzodiazepine derivative used primarily as an antianxiety agent and as an adjunct in the treatment of muscle spasms; also used in the treatment of alcohol withdrawal. Trade name: Valium.

diazoxide (di-az-ok'sīd) A nondiuretic thiazide derivative used intravenously to lower blood pressure in the management of a hypertensive crisis.

dibasic (di-bā'sic) In chemistry, having two hydrogen atoms capable of reacting with bases.

dibenzothiazine (di-ben-zo-thi'ah-zēn) See phenothiazine.

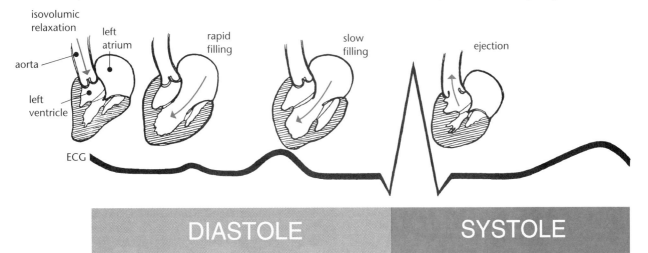

isovolumic relaxation
left atrium
rapid filling
slow filling
ejection
aorta
left ventricle
ECG

DIASTOLE	SYSTOLE

dicelous (di-se'lus) Having two cavities; the state of being concave on both sides.

dicentric (di-sen'trik) Having two centers; applied to certain abnormal chromosomes.

dichloride (di-klo'rīd) A chemical compound containing two chloride atoms per molecule.

dichotomy (di-kot'o-me) Cutting into two parts.

dichromatic (di-kro-mat'ik) **1.** Having two colors. **2.** Relating to dichromatism.

dichromatism (di-kro'mah-tism) A defective color perception in which the spectrum is seen as composed of only two colors separated by a colorless band. Also called dichromatopsia; dyschromatopsia.

dichromatopsia (di-kro-mah-top'se-ah) See dichromatism.

dichromophil, dichromophile (di-kro'mo-fil, di-kro'mo-fil) Denoting cells or tissues that take up both acid and basic histologic dyes, but in different areas.

dicing (dis'ing) See dicing lacerations, under laceration.

dicrotic (di-krot'ik) Double beat; applied to a pulse with two beats for each heartbeat.

dictyoma (dik-te-o'mah) Tumor of the retina.

didactic (di-dak'tik) Relating to lecture and textbook instruction rather than clinical demonstrations with patients and laboratory work.

didactylism (di-dak'til-izm) The condition of having only two fingers on a hand or two toes on a foot.

didanosine (di-dan-o'sin) A drug used for patients with advanced HIV infection who are intolerant to AZT (zidovudine) therapy or who had shown significant deterioration during AZT therapy.

-didymis Combining form meaning testis (e.g., epididymis).

didymo-, didym- Combining forms meaning testis.

didymus (did'ĭ-mus) Greek for testis.

die (di) A specialized model; in dentistry, a replica of a prepared tooth, made of metal or specially prepared dental stone; used for making a wax pattern for a cast restoration.

diencephalon (di-en-sef'ah-lon) The portion of the embryonic brain containing the third ventricle; it gives rise to the epithalamus, thalamus, and hypothalamus. Also called interbrain.

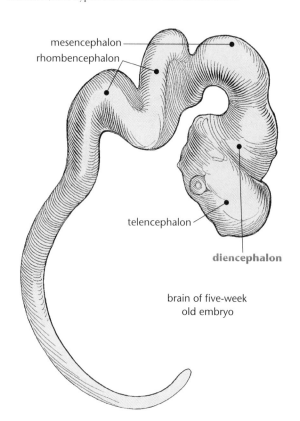

mesencephalon
rhombencephalon
telencephalon
diencephalon

brain of five-week
old embryo

diener (de'ner) A laboratory assistant.

diet (di'et) **1.** Bodily nourishment; daily sustenance. **2.** Regulated nourishment, including or excluding certain items of food, especially as prescribed for health reasons. **3.** To follow a specific dietary plan, especially for reduction of body weight by limitation of caloric intake. **4.** Anything taken regularly.

　　absolute d. Fasting.

　　acid-ash d. A diet planned to acidify the urine, consisting of acidic foods (e.g., fish, eggs and cereals) with little or no alkali-producing foods, such as fruits, vegetables, milk, and cheese; used in prophylaxis in some types of urolithiasis.

　　adequate d. See balanced diet.

　　balanced d. A diet containing all the essential dietary ingredients, including the vitamins, in the proper proportions for adequate nutrition. Also called adequate diet; optimal diet.

　　bland d.'s Regular diets modified to be free from roughage or spicy, irritating foods; progressive regimen (bland 1, 2, 3, or 4), generally used in treatment of upper gastrointestinal disorders (e.g., peptic ulcers, gastritis, irritable bowel syndrome). Also called Sippy diets; smooth diets.

　　cholesterol-lowering d. See low saturated fat diet.

　　clear liquid d. One used postoperatively for patients unable to tolerate full liquids or solid food.

　　diabetic d.'s Diets prescribed in the treatment of diabetes mellitus; any of nine balanced diets recommended by the American Diabetes Association that are limited in the amount of sugar or high carbohydrate foods and have caloric levels from about 1200 to 3500; they are commonly divided in fifths, generally consisting of three meals and two snacks.

　　elimination d. A diet that sequentially omits foods suspected of causing allergic reactions, in order to detect those responsible for symptoms; commonly eliminated are eggs, milk, and wheat, less frequently, nuts, chocolate, and fish.

　　full liquid d. A diet composed of foods that are in liquid form at body temperature; it basically serves as a pre- or postoperative diet, and as a transition to a more liberal soft regimen.

　　Giordano-Giovannetti d. A low-protein diet recommended to patients having symptoms of chronic renal failure. Also called Giovannetti diet.

　　Giovannetti d. See Giordano-Giovannetti diet.

　　gluten-free d. A diet free of the cereal protein gluten (present in wheat, oats, rye, barley, and other similar grains); used in the treatment of some celiac disorders such as gluten enteropathy.

　　high calorie d. One furnishing more calories than required to maintain body weight, often more than 3500 to 4000 calories per day.

　　high fiber d. A diet high in dietary fibers to relieve inadequate bowel movements.

　　high potassium d.'s Diets for individuals undergoing vigorous diuretic therapy; they provide approximately 100 mEq of potassium per day.

　　Kempner rice-fruit d. A diet consisting chiefly of rice and fruits with the addition of iron and vitamins and restrictions on salt; recommended to patients with hypertension or chronic kidney disease.

　　low calcium d. A daily diet of from 100 to 200 mg of calcium; recommended in the treatment of hyperparathyroidism and urinary calcium stones, or as a test diet to determine urinary calcium excretion; diets of 250 mg of calcium may be used in the treatment of certain patients with hypercalcemia and/or hypercalciuria.

　　low calorie d. One furnishing fewer calories than required to maintain body weight, often less than 1000 to 1200 calories per day.

　　low cholesterol d. See low saturated fat diet.

　　low fat d. A diet containing limited amounts of fats, no more than 50 g per day; it may include lean meat, fish, skim milk, cottage cheese, and cereal products; the caloric level may be varied through changes in protein and carbohydrate levels.

　　low oxalate d. A diet that excludes fiber vegetables, potatoes, beans, tea, chocolate, sweets, and sweet fruits; used for minimizing the formation of oxalate stones in the urinary tract.

low residue d. A diet low in cellulose content, as gelatin, broth, hard-boiled eggs, rice, cottage cheese, fruits, vegetables, and unrefined cereals; vegetables are pureed to change the consistency of the cellulose; it results in the least amount of fecal residue.

low salt d.'s See low sodium diets.

low saturated fat d. One high in polyunsaturated fatty acids of vegetable origin, with restrictions on food high in cholesterol and fatty acids, such as eggs, butter, and meat. Also called low cholesterol diet; cholesterol-lowering diet.

low sodium d.'s Diets containing very little salt (sodium chloride); recommended to patients with hypertension, congestive heart failure, and other conditions associated with edema; four levels of low sodium diets are commonly used: 250 mg, 500 mg, 1000 mg, and 2000 mg of sodium (a regular diet without added salt provides about 4000 mg of sodium). Also called low salt diets; salt-free diets.

optimal d. See balanced diet.

reduction d.'s Diets for weight reduction with caloric levels of 800, 1000, 1200, 1500, and 1800, that are adequate in protein and restricted in carbohydrate and fat.

renal d.'s, kidney d.'s Diets low in protein, sodium, and potassium; used in the treatment of kidney failure. COMPARE Giordano-Giovannetti diet.

salt-free d.'s See low sodium diets.

Sippy d.'s See bland diets.

smooth d.'s See bland diets.

subsistence d. A minimum diet providing sufficient nourishment on which one can be sustained.

dietetic (di-ĕ-tet'ik) Relating to diet; in food labeling, it denotes that one or more ingredients usually found in a food has been changed or replaced.

dietetics (di-ĕ-tet'iks) The study of nutrition and diets relative to health and disease.

diethyl ether (di-eth'il e'ther) A flammable volatile liquid obtained from distillation of ethyl alcohol and sulfuric acid; used for general inhalation anesthesia. Also called ethyl ether.

diethylstilbestrol (di-eth-il-stil-bes'trol) (DES) A synthetic compound with estrogenic properties effective in the treatment of atrophic vaginitis; formerly used to treat threatened miscarriage, a practice now abandoned because of the drug's carcinogenic tendency in the daughters of women who took it while pregnant. Also called stilbestrol.

dietician (di-ĕ-tish'an) A specialist in dietetics.

dietogenetics (di-ĕ-to-jĕ-net'iks) The relationship between the genetic makeup and nutrition requirements of a person.

difference (dif'er-ens) **1.** A particular variation. **2.** The amount by which one quantity varies from another.

arteriovenous oxygen d. The difference in the oxygen content of arterial blood entering and the venous blood leaving a specified area or organ.

differential (dif-er-en'shal) Relating to a difference or distinction.

differentiation (dif-er-en-she-a'shun) **1.** In biology, the process of developing into specialized tissues or organs. **2.** See differential diagnosis, under diagnosis.

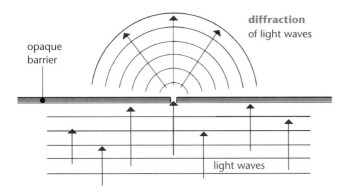

opaque barrier

diffraction of light waves

light waves

cell d. In embryology, the progressive restriction of developmental potential and the increasing specialization of function occurring during development of the embryo, leading to formation of tissues and organs.

diffraction (dī-frak'shun) The interaction of solid matter with any waveform (i.e., light, sound, or electronic waves), especially the tendency of light rays to bend or deflect from a straight line when passing by the edge of an opaque barrier.

diffusion (dī-fu'zhun) **1.** The tendency of a gas or substance in solution to pass from a point of higher pressure or concentration to an area of lower pressure or concentration and to distribute itself uniformly throughout; it is the principal mechanism of biologic transport. **2.** See dialysis.

digastric (di-gas'trik) Having two bellies; applied to certain muscles.

Digenea (di-je'ne-ah) Subclass of flatworms (class Trematode) that includes all the parasitic flukes of humans and other mammals.

digest (di-jest') To break down food into simpler, assimilable compounds by chemical action.

digestant (di-jes'tant) An agent that promotes the process of digestion in the gastrointestinal tract.

digestion (di-jest'yun) The process of breaking down ingested food into chemical substances that can be absorbed by the intestines.

digestive (di-jes'tiv) Relating to digestion.

digit (dij'it) A finger or a toe.

clubbed d. See clubbing.

digitalis (dij-ĭ-tal'is) Foxglove; a plant of the genus *Digitalis* and the main source of steroid glycosides, which have an effect on the activity of the heart muscle.

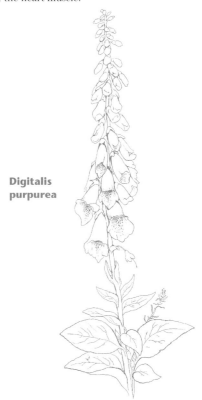

Digitalis purpurea

digitalism (dij'ĭ-tal-ism) The symptoms (e.g., headache, loss of appetite, nausea, and vomiting) produced by toxic levels of digitalis drugs.

digitalization (dij-ĭ-tal-ĭ-za'shun) Administration of a digitalis drug until the desired therapeutic level is reached.

digitate (dij'ĭ-tāt) Having fingerlike processes.

digitation (dij-ĭ-ta'shun) A fingerlike process.

digitoxin (dij-ĭ-tok'sin) A glycoside obtained from *Digitalis purpurea*, used in the treatment of heart failure.

digoxin (di-goks'in) A glycoside obtained from *Digitalis lanata*, used widely in the treatment of heart failure and rapid irregular heartbeat (atrial fibrillation).

dihydrate (di-hi'drāt) A compound having two molecules of water.

dihydroergotamine (di-hi-dro-er-got'ah-mēn) Compound produced by the hydrogenation of ergotamine; used in the treatment of migraine.

dilatation (dil-ah-ta'shun) The condition of being enlarged or stretched, by normal or artificial processes or as a result of disease; applied to a tubular structure, a cavity, or an opening. Also called dilation.

dilatation and curettage (dil-ah-ta'shun ku-rĕ-tahzh') (D and C) Dilatation of the uterine cervix and scraping of the lining of the uterus (endometrium) with a curette; performed as a diagnostic procedure to ascertain the cause of irregular menstrual bleeding and after an early spontaneous abortion to remove any residual placenta.

dilatation and evacuation (dil-ah-ta'shun e-vak-u-a'shun) (D and E) Induced abortion performed by dilatation of the uterine cervix and removal of the products of conception with a blunt curette and forceps.

dilate (di-lat') To enlarge; to stretch.

dilation (di-la'shun) See dilatation.

dilator (di-la'tor) Instrument for enlarging a passage, cavity, or opening.

   pneumatic d. An inflatable tube used for stretching a muscular constriction (achalasia) of the esophagus.

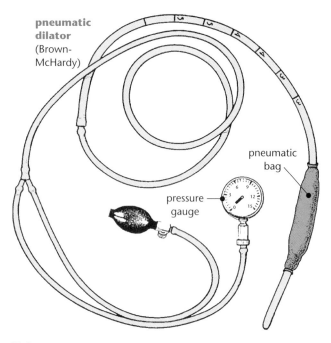

pneumatic dilator (Brown-McHardy)

pressure gauge

pneumatic bag

diltiazem (dil-ti'ah-zem) A calcium channel blocking agent of the benzothiazepine class used in the treatment of angina pectoris and hypertension; adverse effects include swelling of the ankles, headache, and constipation.

diluent (dil'u-ent) A substance that reduces the concentration of a solution.

dilution (di-lu'shun) **1.** The process of reducing the concentration of a solution or substance. **2.** A weakened solution or substance.

dimenhydrinate (di-men-hi'drĭ-nāt) An antihistamine drug used in the prevention and treatment of motion sickness. Trade name: Dramamine.

dimension (dī-men'shun) Any measurable distance expressed numerically.

   occlusal vertical d. See vertical dimension.

   rest vertical d. See vertical dimension.

   vertical d. In prosthodontics, the distance between two points on the face, one above and one below the mouth, usually in the midline; it may be measured when the opposing occlusal surfaces of the teeth are in maximum contact (occlusal vertical dimension) or in rest position, when the upper and lower teeth are not in contact (rest vertical dimension).

dimercaprol (di-mer-kap'rol) Compound developed as an antidote for lewisite (a war gas) and other arsenical poisons; also used as an antidote for poisoning by other metals (mercury, antimony, nickel, bismuth, and chromium). Also called British antilewisite (BAL).

dimethyl sulfoxide (di-meth'il sul-fok'sīd) (DMSO) An industrial solvent occasionally used as a skin penetrant to enhance absorption of medications from the skin.

dimorphism (di-mor'fizm) The property of occurring in two structural forms.

dimple (dim'pl) A small, usually circular depression; may be congenital or the result of trauma.

   coccygeal d. See foveola of coccyx, under foveola.

diopter (di-op'ter) (D) Unit of the refractive power of a lens.

dioptrics (di-op'triks) The science of the refraction of light.

dioxide (di-ok'sīd) Compound containing two atoms of oxygen per molecule.

dioxin (di-ok'sin) A toxic chlorinated hydrocarbon, a herbicide contaminant; also formed at incineration sites; causes birth defects and cancer in laboratory animals and possibly in humans.

dipeptidase (di-pep'tī-dās) A protein-splitting enzyme; promotes the breakdown of dipeptides into two amino acids.

dipeptide (di-pep'tīd) Two amino acids linked by a peptide bond.

diphenhydramine hydrochloride (di-fen-hi'drah-mēn hi-dro-klo'rīd) An antihistamine drug used in the treatment of allergies; adverse effects include drowsiness and dry mouth. Trade name: Benadryl.

diphtheria (dif-the're-ah) An acute contagious disease caused by the bacillus *Cornebacterium diphtheriae;* characterized by severe inflammation of the upper respiratory tract, fibrin formation (false membrane) of the mucous membranes of the throat and nose, and degeneration of heart and nerve tissues.

diphtheroid (dif'ther-oid) Resembling diphtheria.

diphyllobothriasis (di-fil-o-both-ri'ah-sis) Infestation with tapeworms of the genus *Diphyllobothrium latum,* acquired by eating inadequately cooked infected fish.

Diphyllobothrium (di-fil-o-both're-um) A genus of tapeworms that are intestinal parasites of fish, birds, and mammals including humans.

   D. latum Intestinal parasite transmitted to humans by ingestion of undercooked infected fish. Also called fish tapeworm.

diplacusis (dip-lah-ku'sis) Different perception of one sound by the two ears, giving the impression of hearing two sounds instead of one.

diplegia (di-ple'je-ah) Symmetrical paralysis (i.e., on corresponding parts on both sides of the body).

   congenital facial d. See Möbius syndrome, under syndrome.

diplo- Combining form meaning double.

diplobacteria (dip-lo-bak-te're-ah) Bacteria that occur linked in pairs.

Diplococcus (dip-lo-kok'us) See *Streptococcus*.

   D. pneumoniae See *Streptococcus pneumoniae,* under *Streptococcus*.

diplococcus (dip-lo-kok'us), pl. diplococ'ci Spherical bacteria joined together in pairs.

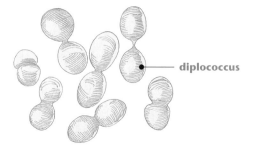

diplococcus

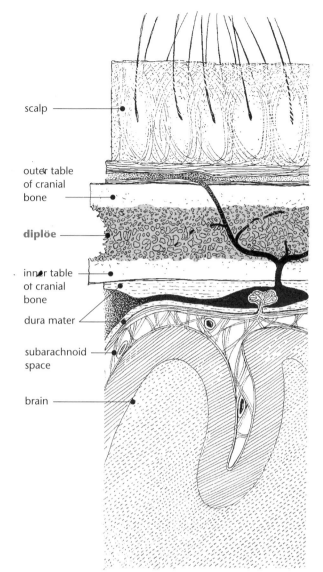

scalp

outer table
of cranial
bone

diplöe

inner table
of cranial
bone

dura mater

subarachnoid
space

brain

diploë (dip'lo-e) The spongy bone substance that lies between the outer and inner tables of most cranial bones; it contains red bone marrow in its interspaces.

diploid (dip'loid) Having two complete sets of homologous chromosomes; the normal state of all somatic cells and of the progenitors of sperm and egg.

diplomate (dip'lo-māt) A board-certified physician.

diplopia (dī-plo'pe-ah) The condition of seeing one object as two. Also called double vision.

diplotene (dip'lo-tēn) The fourth stage of the meiotic prophase in which the paired homologous chromosomes begin to separate but remain attached in an X configuration; at this stage blocks of genes are exchanged between the chromosomes.

dipsesis (dip-se'sis) Abnormal thirst for unusual drinks. Also called dipsosis.

dipsomania (dip-so-ma'ne-ah) A periodic compulsion to drink alcoholic beverages excessively.

dipsosis (dip-so'sis) See dipsesis.

dipstick (dip'stik) A cellulose strip impregnated with any of various chemicals that undergo a color change when in contact with certain substances (e.g., glucose, protein); used to detect the presence of these substances in a sample of urine.

dipyridamole (di-pi-rid'ah-mōl) A compound that reduces the stickiness of platelets in the blood, thereby helping to prevent formation of clots within blood vessels.

director (di-rek'tor) 1. The head of a service or an organized group. 2. A grooved instrument for guiding and limiting the motion of a surgical knife.

    medical d. A physician employed by a hospital or clinic to serve in a medical and administrative capacity as head of the medical staff; may also serve as liaison for the medical staff with the administration and governing board.

Directory of Rare Analyses (DORA) Book published by the American Chemical Society listing clinical tests that are not commonly ordered and the laboratories performing them.

dirigation (dir-ĭ-ga'shun) The process of developing voluntary control over usually involuntary body functions.

dirigomotor (dir-ĭ-go-mo'tor) Anything that controls muscular activity.

dirt-eating (durt ēt'ing) See geophagia.

dis- Prefix meaning opposite of; not; apart.

disability (dis-ah-bil'ĭ-te) 1. Medically, any defect or loss of function of one or more organs or parts of the body resulting from an impairment. 2. Legally, limitation on one's full enjoyment of ordinary legal rights; may be due to mental capacity, age, imprisonment, etc. See also impairment; handicap.

    developmental d. The presence of cognitive, emotional or physical conditions that prevent a child from progressing through expected developmental milestones.

    learning d. (LD) (a) A cognitive disorder resulting in difficulty in mastering one or more basic cognitive skills (speaking, reading, writing, calculation). (b) See attention-deficit hyperactivity disorder, under disorder.

    permanent d. A disability that is reasonably expected to last forever. In Social Security context, disability that, when maximum improvement is achieved, still prevents gainful employment in capacity prior to disability.

    presumptive d. An apparent disability. An impairment demonstrated by a claimant of Social Security disability of such severity that a temporary decision is made to allow the claim before the case is fully investigated.

    temporary d. A disability that has not yet stabilized or from which recovery is expected; disability occurring during the healing period of an injured worker, lasting as long as treatment can reasonably be expected to eliminate the disability, or until a decision is reached that further treatment will probably not change the disability status.

    total d. Permanent disability that precludes any substantial gainful employment for a sustained period of time.

    work-related d. A disability that arises out of and in the course of employment.

disaccharide (di-sak'ah-rīd) Any of a class of sugars (including sucrose, maltose, and lactose) that yield two monosaccharides when subjected to hydrolysis.

disarticulation (dis-ar-tik-u-la'shun) Amputation of a limb by separating the bones at the joint.

disc (disk) See disk.

discectomy (dis-kek'to-me) See diskectomy.

discharge (dis-charj') 1. A substance that is released or evacuated as from a body orifice or wound. 2. To pour forth; to emit. 3. The activation of a nerve cell.

disciform (dis'ĭ-form) Disk-shaped.

discission (dis-sizh'un) A fine surgical cutting, such as the puncturing or cutting into the capsule of the lens of the eye to remove a cataract.

discitis (dis-ki'tis) See diskitis.

discogenic (dis-ko-jen'ik) Originating in an intervertebral disk; applied to certain disorders.

discography (dis-kog'rah-fe) See diskography.

discoid (dis'koid) 1. Having the shape of a disk. 2. In dentistry, an instrument with a disk-shaped blade used for carving dental restorations.

discopathy (dis-kop'ah-the) See diskopathy.

discrete (dis-kret') Separate, not confluent; applied to certain lesions of the skin.

discrimination (dis-krim-ĭ-na'shun) Process of distinguishing among several stimuli (e.g., speech sounds).

discus (dis'kus), pl. dis'ci Latin for disk.

discutient (dis-ku'she-ent) Causing a dispersal, as of a pathologic or abnormal accumulation.

disease (dĭ-zēz') Any abnormal condition that affects either the whole body or any of its parts, is manifested by a characteristic set of symptoms and signs, and impairs normal functioning.

Adams-Stokes d. See Stokes-Adams syndrome, under syndrome.

Addison's d. Chronic deficiency of the hormones concerned with mineral and glucose metabolism due to destruction of the adrenal cortex; findings include a bronzelike pigmentation of skin and mucous membranes and scars, anemia, and low blood pressure, with low concentration of sodium in the blood. Also called primary chronic adrenocortical insufficiency.

adult polycystic kidney d. (PCKD) An inherited disease (autosomal dominant inheritance) with the PCKD gene in chromosome 6 characterized by the presence of multiple cysts in each kidney; gradually the cysts enlarge and compress the normal tissue, leading to renal insufficiency; often causes blood in the urine (hematuria), and high blood pressure (hypertension); may be accompanied by minute aneurysms in the brain.

Albers-Schönberg d. See osteopetrosis.

alcoholic liver d. Liver damage occurring with a history of excessive alcohol consumption; may occur in one or more of three forms: fatty liver, alcoholic hepatitis, or cirrhosis.

some forms of **alcoholic liver disease**

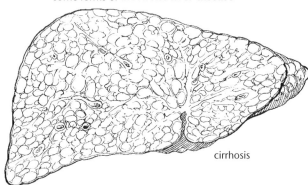

cirrhosis

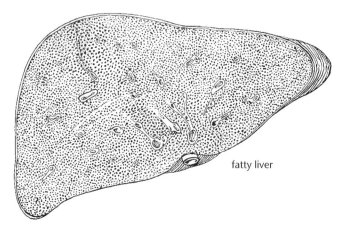

fatty liver

Alzheimer's d. Disease manifested by impairment of higher intellectual function that progresses to profound dementia over a 5- to 10-year period; it rarely begins before the age of 50, but thereafter increases steadily with advancing age. Early clinical symptoms and signs include memory loss (particularly of recent events), decreased ability to concentrate and solve problems, and mild emotional instability, progressing to disorientation, confusion, hallucinations, paranoid delusions, and eventual inability to carry out daily activities and personal care. The brain undergoes gross and microscopic changes. Also called Alzheimer's dementia.

aortoiliac occlusive d. Gradual obstruction of the lowest portion of the aorta and its two branches (common iliac arteries) by deposition of fatty-fibrous plaques (atherosclerosis); associated with pain in the legs when walking (which disappears at rest), low back pain, atrophy of the legs, and, sometimes, impotence. Also called Leriche's syndrome.

autoimmune d. Any disease resulting from the breakdown of natural tolerance and the subsequent severe reaction (specific humoral or cell-mediated) against the body's own antigens; reaction may be organ-specific (i.e., against the tissues of one organ), as in Hashimoto's thyroiditis and insulin-dependent diabetes mellitus (IDDM), or may be systemic (i.e., against many if not all tissues in the body), as in systemic lupus erythematosus, rheumatoid arthritis, and scleroderma.

Baastrup's d. See kissing spines, under spine.

Batten-Mayou d. See cerebral sphingolipidosis, under sphingolipidosis.

Bechterew's d. See spondylitis deformans, under spondylitis.

Behçet's d. Recurrent ulceration of the genitals, oral cavity, and structures of the eye (iris, ciliary body, and choroid) and accumulation of a puslike fluid in the anterior chamber of the eye; cause is unknown. Also called Behçet's syndrome.

Berger's d. See IgA nephropathy, under nephropathy.

Best's d. See vitelliform degeneration, under degeneration.

Bielschowsky's d. See cerebral sphingolipidosis, under sphingolipidosis.

black lung d. See coal miner's pneumoconiosis, under pneumoconiosis.

blinding d. See onchocerciasis.

Blount's d. A severe bowing of the legs (often unilateral) caused by a growth disturbance of the tibia, at the medial side of the growth centers closest to the knees.

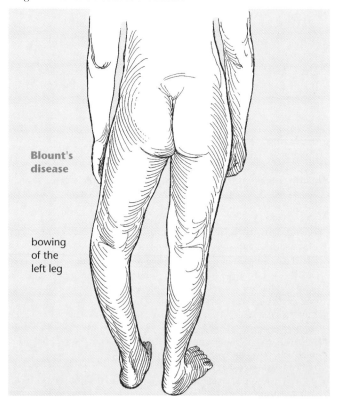

Blount's disease

bowing of the left leg

Bornholm d. See epidemic pleurodynia, under pleurodynia.

Bourneville's d. See tuberous sclerosis, under sclerosis.

Bowen's d. Noninvasive squamous cell carcinoma of the skin involving only the superficial layer (epidermis), appearing as reddish papules or plaques covered with gray-white encrustations; may occur in sun-exposed areas of the body and in the genitals of both males and females over age 35; associated with increased (25%) incidence of cancer of internal organs.

Bright's d. Outmoded term formerly applied to a variety of acute and chronic kidney diseases, especially those thought to be forms of glomerulonephritis.

Brill's d. See Brill-Zinsser disease.

Brill-Zinsser d. The recurrence of typhus in a person who suffered an infection of primary epidemic typhus years before and who is believed to have remained in a carrier state during the intervening period; caused by *Rickettsia prowazekii*. Also called Brill's disease; recrudescent typhus.

brittle bone d. See osteogenesis imperfecta, under osteogenesis.

Buerger's d. See thromboangiitis obliterans, under thromboangiitis.

Caffey's d. See infantile cortical hyperostosis, under hyperostosis.

caisson d. See decompression sickness, under sickness.

calcium pyrophosphate deposition d. (CPDD) See pseudogout.

cardiovascular d.'s Disorders of the heart, blood vessels, and blood circulation.

Caroli's d. A familial disease characterized by saccular dilatations of the biliary ducts and predisposition to stone formation.

Carrion's d. See bartonellosis.

cat-scratch d. A disease of unknown cause characterized by local inflammation of lymph nodes occurring about 3 to 10 days after the bite or scratch of a cat. Also called cat-scratch fever.

celiac d. Disorder characterized by intolerance to gluten, a protein present in wheat and other cereals; gluten alters the inner lining of the small intestine, resulting in malnutrition. Also called nontropical sprue; celiac sprue; gluten-induced enteropathy.

cerebrovascular d. Any brain dysfunction due to a disruption of the blood supply to the brain.

Chagas' d. Infection with the protozoan parasite *Trypanosoma cruzi*, transmitted when reduviid bug feces contaminate skin abrasions or the inner lining (conjunctiva) of the eyelids, or by transfusion of contaminated blood. Initially, the infection most often causes unilateral swelling of the face and enlargement of regional lymph nodes; later, systemic spread may cause encephalitis and damage to the heart and intestines. Also called American trypanosomiasis.

Charcot-Marie-Tooth d. See peroneal muscular atrophy, under atrophy.

childhood polycystic kidney d. Childhood PCKD; an autosomal recessive inheritance characterized by the presence of multiple cysts of both kidneys with renal impairment appearing early in life (perinatal, neonatal, infantile, and juvenile ages); the liver almost always contains cysts and proliferating bile ducts, leading to fibrosis.

Christmas d. See hemophilia B.

chronic granulomatous d. Condition that becomes evident during the first few years of life, chiefly in males, inherited as an X-linked recessive trait; characterized by susceptibility to severe infection due to inability of white blood cells to destroy bacteria. Affected persons may die of infection by organisms of low virulence.

chronic obstructive lung d. (COLD) See chronic obstructive pulmonary disease.

chronic obstructive pulmonary d. (COPD) The combination of chronic bronchitis and emphysema in which there is increased resistance to airflow in the lungs. Also called chronic obstructive lung disease (COLD).

collagen d.'s See connective tissue diseases.

collagen-vascular d.'s See connective tissue diseases.

communicable d. See contagious disease.

connective tissue d.'s A group of diseases that share certain features, including inflammatory damage of structures rich in connective tissue, inflammation of blood vessel walls with deposition of fibrinoid material, evidence of an autoimmune cause, and abnormalities of cell-mediated immunity. The group includes such conditions as systemic lupus erythematosus, scleroderma, rheumatoid arthritis, and polyarteritis nodosa. Also called collagen diseases; collagen-vascular diseases; collagenosis.

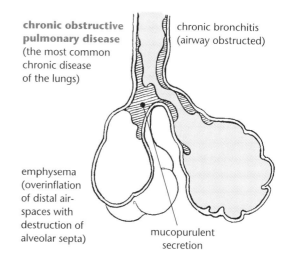

chronic obstructive pulmonary disease (the most common chronic disease of the lungs)

chronic bronchitis (airway obstructed)

emphysema (overinflation of distal airspaces with destruction of alveolar septa)

mucopurulent secretion

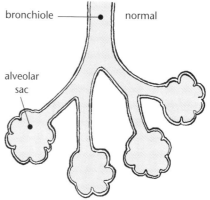

bronchiole — normal

alveolar sac

contagious d. Any disease transmissible through direct contact or through a vector of a disease-causing microorganism. Also called communicable disease.

coronary artery d. (CAD) Any disease of the coronary arteries which supply blood to the heart muscle (e.g., angina pectoris). Also called coronary heart disease (CHD).

coronary heart d. (CHD) See coronary artery disease.

Creutzfeldt-Jakob d. Disease usually affecting people over 50 years of age, marked by rapidly progressive mental deterioration, disturbances of gait, impaired vision and balance, jerky movements, and confusion; the brain undergoes minor atrophy; death occurs within a year; caused by proteinaceous infectious particles (prions). There has been transmission secondary to corneal transplantation, intracranial implantation of electroencephalogram (EEG) electrodes, and administration of human growth hormone from a cadaveric pituitary. Also called subacute spongiform encephalopathy.

rheumatoid arthritis, a **connective tissue disease**

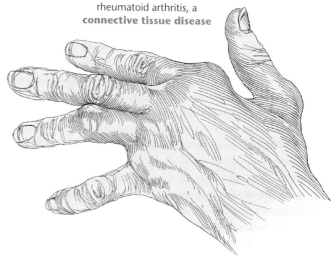

Crigler-Najjar d. See Crigler-Najjar syndrome, under syndrome.

Crohn's d. Chronic inflammation of the gastrointestinal tract; it most commonly affects the ileum but may involve the entire gut from mouth to anus; characterized by formation of sharply demarcated deep ulcers separated by normal (skip) areas, with thickening of the walls, narrowing of the lumen, and perforations with connections into adjacent structures (e.g., other bowel segments, bladder, vagina) or abdominal skin; symptoms may be precipitated by periods of emotional or physical stress and include diarrhea, fever, and pain in the lower right area of the abdomen. Also called regional enteritis; terminal ileitis; distal ileitis.

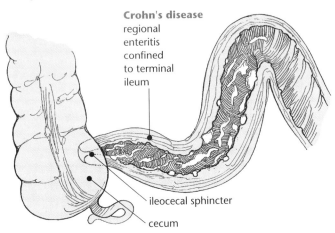

Crohn's disease
regional enteritis confined to terminal ileum

ileocecal sphincter

cecum

Crouzon's d. See craniofacial dysostosis, under dysostosis.

Cushing's d. Overactivity of the adrenal cortex caused by excessive secretion of adrenocorticotropic hormone (ACTH) from the pituitary (hypophysis) in the brain. Also called hypercortisolism. See also Cushing's syndrome, under syndrome.

cystic d. of the breast See fibrocystic disease of the breast.

cystic d. of renal medulla The presence of multiple cysts in the medulla of the kidney, seen mainly in two clinical syndromes: uremic cystic disease and medullary sponge kidney (nonuremic medullary cystic disease); the former is associated with glomerulosclerosis, interstitial fibrosis, and kidney failure, often appears in childhood, and is inherited as an autosomal recessive trait; the latter is a relatively benign condition of adults, is inherited as an autosomal dominant trait, and may be associated with stones in the cysts (usually diagnosed by intravenous pyelography) or with infection.

cytomegalic inclusion d. Disease caused by infection with cytomegalovirus (CMV), a herpesvirus that remains dormant indefinitely in the tissues of the infected person and may be reactivated. Symptoms depend on the organs affected or may be asymptomatic. It may be acquired through sexual contact, transfusion of infected blood, or transplantation of an infected organ. An infected pregnant woman can transmit the disease to her fetus through the placenta, or during childbirth as the infant passes through the birth canal, or via breast milk. The infected infant may develop enlargement of the liver and spleen, jaundice, superficial hemorrhages (purpura), central nervous system involvement, and mental retardation. Individuals undergoing immunosuppressive therapy and those afflicted with acquired immune deficiency syndrome (AIDS) are susceptible to infection with the virus or its reactivation.

decompression d. See decompression sickness, under sickness.

deficiency d. Disease resulting from prolonged lack of vitamins, minerals, or any other essential dietary nutrient.

degenerative d.'s of central nervous system Diseases of the brain or spinal cord that have the following characteristics: *(a)* they begin insidiously and follow a slowly progressive course; *(b)* they tend to depend on genetic factors or occur in various members of the same family; *(c)* there is a gradual, often selective, loss of nerve cells; *(d)* once the disease is established, the resulting atrophy tends to be symmetrical.

degenerative joint d. (DJD) See osteoarthritis (OA).

demyelinating d., demyelinative d. Any of several diseases of unknown cause that affect the myelin sheaths of nerve fibers, leaving axons and their cells of origin unaffected; multiple sclerosis is the most common of these disorders.

Deutschländer's d. See fatigue fracture, under fracture.

Devic's d. See neuromyelitis optica, under neuromyelitis.

diverticular d. of colon Condition occurring most commonly in people over 60 years old; characterized by formation of outpouchings of the mucous lining of the colon, which protrude through defects in the muscular wall of the bowel at points of blood vessel entry; may be asymptomatic or may cause intermittent cramping pain and bleeding; occasionally may undergo inflammatory changes and infection. Also called diverticulosis. See also diverticulitis.

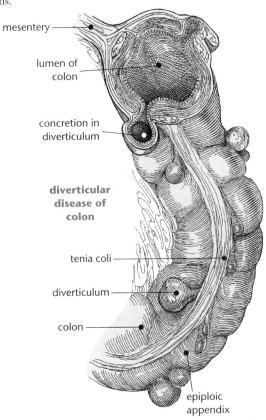

mesenterey

lumen of colon

concretion in diverticulum

diverticular disease of colon

tenia coli

diverticulum

colon

epiploic appendix

Duchenne-Aran d. See progressive muscular atrophy, under atrophy.

Duhring's d. See dermatitis herpetiformis, under dermatitis.

Duncan's d. See X-linked lymphoproliferative disease.

emotional d. See mental disorder, under disorder.

endemic d. A disease present in a particular locality more or less continuously.

end-stage renal d. (ESRD) Insufficiency of kidney function to the extent that dialysis or kidney transplantation is required for survival.

extramammary Paget's d. A red, crusted, maplike area restricted to the superficial layer of the skin; it occurs most predominantly on the major lips (labia majora) of the vulva; may be associated with underlying cancer of vulvar glands; seen mostly in elderly women.

Fabry's d. Inherited lysosomal storage disease resulting from deficiency of the X-linked enzyme alpha-galactosidase; marked by accumulation of neutral glycolipids in many tissues (especially in the kidneys and central nervous system), hemangiomas, and disturbances of the cardiovascular and central nervous systems; death usually occurs from progressive kidney failure.

fibrocystic d. (FCD) of the breast Benign condition of the female breast characterized by formation of cysts, overgrowth of connective tissue and intraductal epithelium, and sclerosing of gland tissue. Also called cystic disease of the breast; cystic hyperplasia of the breast; chronic cystic mastitis; mammary dysplasia.

fibrocystic d. (FCD) of pancreas See cystic fibrosis, under fibrosis.

fifth d. See erythema infectiosum, under erythema.

Fordyce's d. See Fordyce's spots, under spot.

Forrestier's d. See diffuse idiopathic skeletal hyperostosis (DISH), under hyperostosis.

Fox-Fordyce d. An uncommon disorder affecting mainly women, characterized by eruptions of dry, intensely itchy papules in the breasts, armpits, and pubic area.

Freiberg's d. See epiphyseal aseptic necrosis, under necrosis.

functional d. See functional disorder, under disorder.

Gaucher's d. An autosomal, recessively inherited disease; characterized by deficiency of the enzyme glucocerebrosidase, with resulting accumulation of glucocerebroside in mononuclear phagocytic cells and, in some forms, in the central nervous system; manifestations include enlargement of the liver, spleen, and lymph nodes, and erosion of bone tissue; three types have been distinguished on the basis of clinical signs and symptoms: *type 1*, nonneuronopathic; *type 2*, acute neuronopathic; *type 3*, subacute neuronopathic. Also called cerebrosidosis.

genetic d. General term for any inherited disease caused by a defective gene.

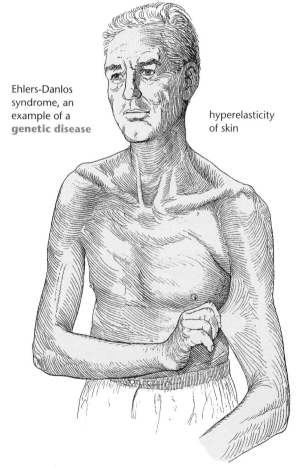

Ehlers-Danlos syndrome, an example of a **genetic disease**

hyperelasticity of skin

gestational trophoblastic d. Any of a group of tumors or tumorlike conditions that have a progressive potential of becoming cancerous; characterized by proliferation of trophoblastic tissue; the lesions include invasive mole, hydatidiform mole, and choriocarcinoma.

Gilbert's d. See Gilbert's syndrome, under syndrome.

Gilles de la Tourette's d. See Gilles de la Tourette's syndrome, under syndrome.

Glanzmann's d. See thrombasthenia.

glycogen storage d. See glycogenosis.

graft-versus-host d. (GVHD) A type of incompatibility reaction in which the T lymphocytes of the graft react against the host tissues; it is the major cause of mortality in bone marrow transplantation.

Grave's d. Disorder resulting from excessive production of thyroid hormone; symptoms include generalized enlargement of the thyroid gland, bulging eyeballs, muscular tremors, rapid pulse rate, and weight loss.

H d. See Hartnup's disease.

hand-foot-and-mouth d. A contagious disease of children characterized by ulcerations on the tongue and lining of the oral cavity and a vesicular eruption on the palms and soles; caused by coxsackieviruses A5, A10, and A16.

Hand-Schüller-Christian d. See multifocal Langerhans-cell histiocytosis, under histiocytosis.

Hansen's d. See leprosy.

Hartnup's d. Hereditary disorder of amino acid transport, characterized by eruption of a reddish, peeling rash upon exposure to sunlight, temporary muscular incoordination, and excretion of excessive amounts of amino acid in the urine. Also called H disease.

Hashimoto's d. See Hashimoto's thyroiditis, under thyroiditis.

hearing d. A disorder of impaired hearing sensitivity of the physiologic auditory system; classified according to difficulties in detection, recognition, discrimination, comprehension, or perception of auditory information.

heavy-chain d. Any of a group of malignant diseases characterized by overproduction of a specific immunoglobulin fragment that is detected in the blood or urine, and proliferation of lymphoid tissue; varieties include alpha-chain disease, gamma-chain disease, and mu-chain disease.

hemoglobin H d. See alpha thalassemia, under thalassemia.

hemolytic d. of the newborn Destruction of fetal red blood cells by maternal antibodies (IgGs) entering the fetal circulation through the placenta; usually associated with Rh-factor incompatibility between mother and child; often accompanied by enlargement of liver and spleen and jaundice in the newborn. Also called erythroblastosis fetalis; fetal erythroblastosis; hemolytic anemia of the newborn.

hemorrhagic d. of newborn Deficiency of vitamin K-dependent clotting factors (II, VII, IX, X), causing bleeding in an infant in the first days of life; sites of bleeding usually include the gastrointestinal tract, umbilical stump, circumcision site, and nose.

hereditary d. Disease transmitted genetically from parent to offspring.

Herlitz d. See junctional epidermolysis bullosa, under epidermolysis bullosa.

herring-worm d. See anisakiasis.

Hippel-Lindau d. See von Hippel–Lindau disease.

Hippel's d. See von Hippel-Lindau disease.

Hirschsprung's d. See congenital megacolon, under megacolon.

Hodgkin's d. A malignant disease of unknown cause, characterized by painless enlargement of lymph nodes (most commonly those in the neck and armpits) with or without systemic symptoms such as fever, sweats, and weight loss; if untreated, it progresses to involve the spleen and other organs. Also called Hodgkin's lymphoma.

hookworm d. Infestation with hookworms, either *Ancylostoma duodenale* (ancylostomiasis) or *Necator americanus* (necatoriasis); the parasites enter the body in their threadlike larval stage through skin penetration, causing a rash at the site of entrance; eventually they migrate through the lungs to the upper small intestine, where they attach by their mouths to the intestinal lining and suck blood. Severe infections may cause iron deficiency anemia and hypoalbuminemia. Chronic ancylostomiasis in childhood may cause physical and mental retardation. Also called necatoriasis.

Huntington's d. (HD) A rare disease, inherited as an autosomal dominant trait, occurring in people between the ages of 20 and 50 years; marked by involuntary, jerky movements of the face and limbs, depression, and progressive intellectual deterioration. Also called chronic progressive chorea; hereditary chorea; Huntington's chorea.

hyaline membrane d. See respiratory distress syndrome of the newborn, under syndrome.

hydatid d. See echinococcosis.

Iceland d. See epidemic neuromyasthenia, under neuromyesthenia.

idiopathic Parkinson's d. See Parkinson's disease.

immune complex d. (ICD) Any of various diseases caused by circulating immune complexes (i.e., antibody and antigen molecules tightly bound together and sometimes including protein), which become trapped within the walls of small blood vessels, especially within the filtering units (glomeruli) of the kidney, thereby triggering a hypersensitivity reaction.

infectious d., infective d. Disease caused by the presence of a pathologic microorganism or its toxins.

iron storage d. Accumulation of excess iron in the tissues of many organs, especially the liver and pancreas, leading to fibrosis and functional insufficiency.

Jansky-Bielschowsky d. See cerebral sphingolipidosis, under sphingolipidosis.

Jensen's d. See chorioretinitis.

Kawasaki's d. See mucocutaneous lymph node syndrome, under syndrome.

Kienböck's d. See epiphyseal aseptic necrosis, under necrosis.

Kikuchi's d. Disease primarily affecting young women, characterized by unilateral, usually painless enlargement of lymph nodes in the neck; cause is unknown. Also called histiocytic necrotizing lymphadenitis.

kissing d. Popular name for infectious mononucleosis; see under mononucleosis.

Köhler's d. See epiphyseal aseptic necrosis, under necrosis.

Krabbe's d. See globoid cell leukodystrophy, under leukodystrophy.

Kufs' d. See cerebral sphingolipidosis, under sphingolipidosis.

Leber's d. Inherited loss of central vision in both eyes due to optic nerve death, occurring predominantly in young males 20 to 30 years old; patients are always related on the maternal line; however, the exact mode of transmission is still in doubt.

Legg-Calvé-Perthes d. See avascular necrosis of proximal femur, under necrosis.

legionnaire's d. Infectious bacterial disease caused by *Legionella pneumophila*, an aerobic bacterium that thrives in hot-water distribution systems of buildings, transmitted via respiratory inhalation; incubation period of 2 to 10 days; symptoms include high fever, headache, abdominal pain, and pneumonia; the liver, kidneys, and nervous system may also be affected.

Letterer-Siwe d. See acute disseminated Langerhans-cell histiocytosis, under histiocytosis.

Lewandawski-Lutz d. See epidermodysplasia verruciformis.

Lindau's d. See von Hippel–Lindau disease.

Löffler's d. See Löffler's endocarditis, under endocarditis.

Lou Gehrig's d. See amyotropic lateral sclerosis, under sclerosis.

Lyell's d. See staphylococcal scalded skin syndrome, under syndrome.

Lyme d. A multisystem disease involving the skin, heart, nervous system, and joints caused by a corkscrew-shaped microorganism *(Borrelia burgdorferi)*. Field mice and white-tailed deer are common reservoirs of the microorganisms, which are transmitted to humans by the bite of infected ixodid ticks (especially *Ixodes dammini*). In most cases the disease begins one to four weeks after the bite of an infected tick as a raised dot that expands into a reddened area several inches across, sometimes accompanied by flulike symptoms; the redness disappears after four weeks. Several weeks later other symptoms occur, and may include fever, headache, neuritis, meningitis, lethargy, muscle and joint pains, irregular heartbeat, dizziness, and fainting. Arthritis of one or more large joints, especially the knee, is a predominant feature of the last stage, appearing months to years later; it may become chronic, lasting weeks or months with recurrences. Also called Lyme borreliosis. Formerly called Lyme arthritis.

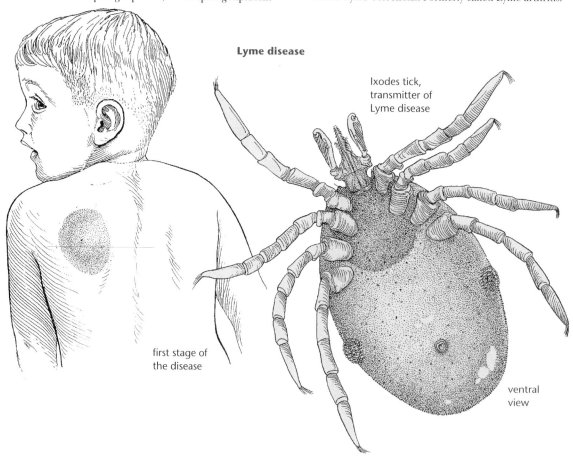

Lyme disease

first stage of the disease

Ixodes tick, transmitter of Lyme disease

ventral view

MAC d. See *Mycobacterium avium* complex bacteremia, under bacteremia.

McArdle's d. See type V glycogenosis, under glycogenosis.

Majocchi's d. See annular telangiectatic purpura, under purpura.

maple syrup urine d. Disorder of newborn infants due to deficient oxidative decarboxylation of alpha-keto acids, which produces a characteristic urine odor resembling maple syrup or burned sugar, neurologic dysfunction, lethargy, and hypoglycemia; it is inherited as an autosomal recessive trait and becomes apparent during the first week of life. Also called branched-chain ketoaciduria.

marble bone d. See osteopetrosis.

Marburg d. A severe hemorrhagic fever disease reported in laboratory workers handling animal tissues infected with the Marburg virus (family Filoviridae). Also called Marburg virus disease.

Marburg virus d. See Marburg disease.

Marie-Strümpell d. See ankylosing spondylitis, under spondylitis.

Ménétrier's d. Uncommon disease of the gastrointestinal tract, characterized by greatly increased size of rugal folds and the presence of pseudopolyps; may be associated with ulcerlike symptoms, bleeding, or loss of protein via the intestines; cause is unknown. Also called Ménétrier's syndrome. See also hypertrophic gastritis.

Ménière's d. Disease of the inner ear characterized clinically by episodes of vertigo, a feeling of fullness and ringing in the ears, and progressive deafness; due to an excessive accumulation of endolymphatic fluid; cause is unknown. Also called endolymphatic hydrops; hydrops of labyrinth; Ménière's syndrome.

mental d. See mental disorder, under disorder.

Milroy's d. Hereditary disease present at birth characterized by swelling with subcutaneous accumulation of lymph, typically in the legs; thought to be due to defective development of the lymphatic system, weak vessels, and valve incompetence.

minimal change d. (MCD) Kidney condition in which biopsy shows minimal or no glomerular abnormalities by light microscopy and the major abnormality noted on electron microscopy is fusion of the foot processes of visceral epithelial cells. It is the major cause of nephrotic syndrome in children. Also called lipoid nephrosis; nil (nothing in light microscopy) disease.

mixed connective tissue d. (MCTD) Disease combining features suggestive of other systemic connective tissue diseases, such as those of systemic lupus erythematosus (SLE), polymyositis, and progressive systemic sclerosis (PSS); characterized by a speckled pattern of antinuclear antibody reaction.

Mondor's d. Inflammation of the superficial veins of the chest and breasts, occurring in both males and females.

motor neuron d. General term applied to any disease of the nervous system that involves motor neurons (e.g., amyotrophic lateral sclerosis [ALS]).

myeloproliferative d.'s Disorders characterized by abnormal proliferation of one or more types of bone marrow cells; they include polycythemia vera, myelofibrosis, idiopathic thrombocytosis, and chronic myelogenous leukemia. Also called myeloproliferative syndrome.

Newcastle d. An acute contagious disease of poultry caused by a paramyxovirus; transmissible to humans, causing severe conjunctivitis; occupational infections occur in poultry handlers, veterinarians, and laboratory workers.

Niemann-Pick d. A genetic disorder of lipid metabolism transmitted as an autosomal recessive inheritance; characterized by accumulation of foam cells in the reticuloendothelial system, causing enlargement of the liver and spleen; the pancreas and kidneys may be also involved; at a late stage, deposits of sphingomyelin, gangliosides, and cholesterol may be found in the brain and spinal cord.

nil (nothing in light microscopy) d. See minimal change disease.

notifiable d. A disease that, by statutory requirements, must be reported to public health officials of the proper jurisdiction (federal, state, or local) when diagnosis is made and is deemed important to human health. Also called reportable disease.

occupational d. Any disease identified as arising out of exposure to some condition peculiar to a given occupation. The cause may be a physical, chemical, or biological agent and may include such factors as risks a worker must bear that are greater than those of the general public, psychosocial factors, or those aggravating an underlying disease process.

occupational lung d. Any disease of the lungs directly related to inhalation of materials present in the work environment.

oculoglandular d. Any of a group of diseases affecting the inner lining (conjunctiva) of a lower eyelid, characterized by one or more granulomas, inflammation of lymph nodes around the ear, and low-grade fever; caused by bacterial infections, especially with *Leptotrichia buccalis*.

Ollier's d. See enchondromatosis.

organic d. Disease involving structural changes in body tissues.

Osgood-Schlatter d. See traumatic tibial epiphysitis, under epiphysitis.

Osler's d. See hereditary hemorrhagic telangiectasia, under telangiectasia.

Osler-Weber-Rendu d. See hereditary hemorrhagic telangiectasia, under telangiectasia.

Paget's d. (a) Generalized bone disease of unknown cause, marked by areas of bone destruction and replacement with overdeveloped, soft, porous new growth, and bending of weight-bearing long bones. Also called osteitis deformans. (b) Cancer of the breast arising within large excretory ducts and extending to involve the skin of the nipple and areola. See also extramammary Paget's disease.

Panner's d. See epiphyseal aseptic necrosis, under necrosis.

Parkinson's d. A slowly progressing disease with onset usually after the age of 50 years in which pigmented cells of the brain stem deteriorate and there is a deficiency of the neurotransmitter dopamine; characterized by increased rigidity of muscles, resting tremors, slowness of movement, stooped walking posture, and a quick shuffling gait; cause is unknown. Also called idiopathic Parkinson's disease; paralysis agitans.

pelvic inflammatory d. (PID) Acute or chronic inflammation of the female reproductive organs and associated structures; may not have obvious causes; often caused by sexually transmitted diseases (e.g., gonorrhea, chlamydia infection); may also occur after abortion, miscarriage, or childbirth.

periodic d. Any disease that recurs regularly.

periodontal d. Any condition affecting the surrounding and supporting tissues of the teeth; may involve the gums only (gingivitis) or include the deeper structures (periodontitis).

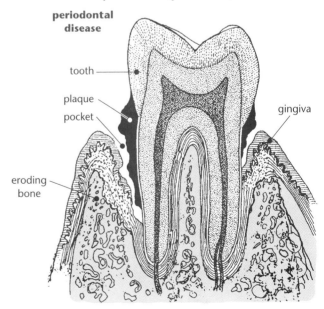

periodontal disease

tooth

plaque

pocket

gingiva

eroding bone

peripheral vascular d. Any disorder of the arteries, veins, or lymphatics of the extremities.

Peyronie's d. A disorder characterized by dense thickening of the fibrous sheath of the penis with eventual involvement of erectile tissue (corpus cavernosum), causing painful erections; may be associated with sclerosis of other parts of the body. Also called fibrous cavernitis.

Pick's d. A rare disease of the brain, occurring in the age group from 40 to 65 years; characterized by degeneration and atrophy of circumscribed areas of the frontal and temporal lobes, which cause clinical manifestations similar to those of Alzheimer's disease. Also called Pick's atrophy.

pink d. See acrodynia.

Plummer's d. Term sometimes applied to hyperthyroidism resulting from toxic adenoma of the thyroid gland.

polycystic kidney d. (PKD, PCKD) Inherited disease characterized by formation of numerous enlarging, fluid-filled cysts in the kidney, which over time destroy the structure and function of the kidney. The adult-onset form is usually inherited in an autosomal dominant fashion; a less common form appears in infancy or early childhood and is of autosomal recessive inheritance. See also adult polycystic kidney disease; childhood polycystic kidney disease.

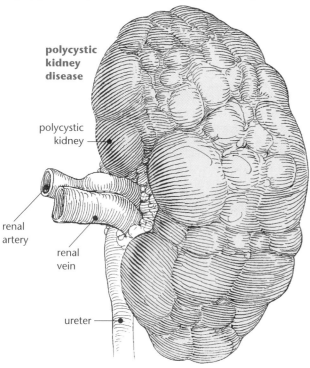

polycystic kidney disease

polycystic kidney
renal artery
renal vein
ureter

polycystic liver d. Condition marked by development of multiple cysts in the liver, frequently associated with polycystic kidney disease (PKD). Also called polycystic liver.

polygenic d. Any disease resulting from the interaction of multiple genes that alone produce relatively minor effects.

Pompe's d. See type II glycogenosis, under glycogenosis.

Pott's d. See tuberculous spondylitis, under spondylitis.

proliferative breast d. (PBD) Condition marked by a benign but excessive multiplication of cells in mammary tissue; the cells do not lose their distinctive characteristics or invade other tissues as do cancerous cells. The condition occurs as an inherited trait in families that have a high prevalence of either premenopausal or postmenopausal breast cancer.

pulseless d. See Takayasu's disease.

Raynaud's d. See Raynaud's phenomenon, under phenomenon.

Recklinghausen's d. See neurofibromatosis I, under neurofibromatosis.

Recklinghausen's d. of bone See osteitis fibrosa cystica, under osteitis.

Rendu-Osler-Weber d. See hereditary hemorrhagic telangiectasia, under telangiectasia.

reportable d. See notifiable disease.

rheumatic heart d. (RHD) A manifestation of rheumatic fever consisting of inflammatory changes of the heart wall (carditis) and/or damaged heart valves.

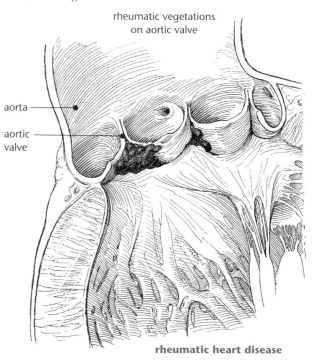

rheumatic vegetations on aortic valve
aorta
aortic valve

rheumatic heart disease

Ritter's d. See staphylococcal scalded skin syndrome, under syndrome.

Robles' d. See ocular onchocerciasis, under onchocerciasis.

Roger's d. Congenital anomaly of the heart in which there is a single small hole (interventricular defect) in the wall separating the two ventricles.

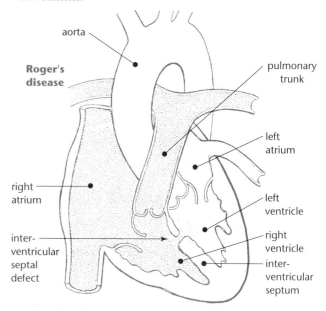

aorta
Roger's disease
pulmonary trunk
left atrium
right atrium
left ventricle
right ventricle
interventricular septal defect
interventricular septum

Romberg's d. See facial hemiatrophy, under hemiatrophy.

Schamberg's d. See progressive pigmented dermatosis, under dermatosis.

Schilder's d. See adrenoleukodystrophy.

Schönlein's d. See Henoch-Schönlein purpura, under purpura.

Schuller's d. See multifocal Langerhans-cell histiocytosis, under histiocytosis.

Senear-Usher d. See pemphigus erythematosus, under pemphigus.

severe combined immunodeficiency d. (SCID) A severe form of congenital immunodeficiency characterized by failure of T and B lymphocyte functions and deficiency of lymphoid tissue; development of the thymus gland is typically arrested in fetal life; caused by a defect of the lymphoid stem cells; inherited in a variable pattern, either as an autosomal recessive or an X-linked recessive inheritance. Death usually occurs from opportunistic infections within the first year of life.

sexually transmitted d.'s (STDs) Disorders spread by intimate contact (including sexual intercourse, kissing, cunnilingus, anilingus, fellatio, mouth-breast contact, and anal intercourse); many can be acquired transplacentally by the fetus or through contact with maternal secretions by the newborn; causative microorganisms include herpesvirus 1 and 2, cytomegalovirus, *Chlamydia*, group B *Streptococcus*, molluscum contagiosum virus, *Sarcoptes scabiei*, hepatitis viruses, and human immunodeficiency virus (HIV). Also called venereal diseases.

short bowel d. See short bowel syndrome, under syndrome.

sickle-cell d. See sickle-cell anemia, under anemia.

sickle cell–hemoglobin C d. Disease characterized by anemia, blood vessel occlusion, chronic leg ulcers, and bone deformities; caused by a genetically determined abnormality of red blood cells, which contain hemoglobin S and hemoglobin C.

Simmonds' d. See panhypopituitarism.

sixth d. See exanthem subitum, under exanthem.

slim d. Popular designation for AIDS in some countries of Africa in reference to the extreme weight loss caused by the disease.

social d. Obsolete term for any sexually transmitted disease.

Spielmeyer-Vogt d. See cerebral sphingolipidosis, under sphingolipidosis.

Still's d. See juvenile arthritis, under arthritis.

storage d. Abnormal or excessive accumulation of a specific substance in tissue due to congenital deficiency or absence of an enzyme needed for the chemical breakdown of the substance.

Strümpell's d. See spondylitis deformans, under spondylitis.

Sturge-Weber d. See Sturge-Weber syndrome, under syndrome.

systemic d. Any disease affecting several organs of the body.

Takahara's d. See acatalasia.

Takayasu's d. Progressive inflammation of the aorta (especially the aortic arch) and its major branches, causing neurologic and ocular disturbances, loss of pulses in the arms and neck, anorexia, weight loss, and fever; most commonly seen in young women in the Far East. Also called pulseless disease; Takayasu's arteritis; Takayasu's syndrome. See also aortic arch syndrome.

Tangier d. Disease in which there is absence of alpha-lipoprotein in the circulation, deficiency of high-density lipoprotein (HDL), and deposition of cholesterol esters in the tissues, occurring as an autosomal recessive inheritance; symptoms and signs include enlargement of liver, spleen, and tonsils, with orange spots in pharyngeal and rectal mucosa. Also called analphalipoproteinemia; familial high-density lipoprotein (HDL) deficiency; hypoalphalipoproteinemia.

Tay-Sachs d. See cerebral sphingolipidosis, under sphingolipidosis.

Thiemann's d. See epiphyseal aseptic necrosis, under necrosis.

Thomsen's d. See myotonia congenita, under myotonia.

Tourette's d. See Gilles de la Tourette's syndrome, under syndrome.

tsutsugamushi d. Infectious disease occurring in Southeast Asia, caused by *Rickettsia tsutsugamushi* and transmitted by mites; marked by painful swelling of lymphatic glands, fever, headache, and an eruption of dark red blisters with blackish scabs on the genitals. Also called mite-borne typhus; scrub typhus; island fever; tsutsugamushi fever.

venereal d.'s See sexually transmitted diseases.

vibration-induced white finger d. Popular name for an occupational form of Raynaud's phenomenon occurring in the absence of vascular occlusive disease or autoimmune disease; characterized by reversible blanching, numbness, and exaggerated fall in temperature of fingers upon exposure to cold temperature; after exposure (when blood flow returns) the fingers throb and become red and then bluish; in severe cases ulceration of the fingers may occur. The condition is caused by damage to minute blood vessels of the hands when exposed to long periods of vibratory energy (e.g., in the use of chain saws, pneumatic tools, grinding wheels, and handheld hard rock drills). Occupational exposure includes those workers involved in demolition, road construction, foundry work, lumbering, and mining.

Vincent's d. See necrotizing ulcerative gingivitis, under gingivitis.

von Gierke's d. See type I glycogenosis, under glycogenosis.

von Hippel–Lindau d. An inherited disease characterized by the formation of several benign and malignant tumors in several organs; may include multiple hemangiomas in the retina and brain, accompanied by hemangioblastomas of the cerebellum and cysts in the kidneys and pancreas; clinical features depend on the organs affected. Also called Lindau's disease; Hippel–Lindau disease; Hippel's disease; retinocerebral angiomatosis; von Hippel–Lindau syndrome.

von Recklinghausen's d. See neurofibromatosis I, under neurofibromatosis.

von Willebrand's d. Hemorrhagic disease transmitted as an autosomal inheritance, characterized by spontaneous bleeding from mucous membranes (especially the gums and gastrointestinal tract), excessive bleeding from wounds, and profuse or prolonged menstrual flow; the abnormal bleeding occurs in the presence of normal platelet count and normal clot retraction; caused by partial and variable deficiency of factor VIII, a blood-clotting factor.

Weber-Christian d. See relapsing febrile nodular panniculitis, under panniculitis.

Weil's d. A severe form of leptospirosis, caused by *Leptospira icterohemorrhagiae* transmitted to humans by rats; characterized primarily by persistent fever and liver disturbances, associated with jaundice, kidney manifestations, and congestion of the conjunctiva.

Werdnig-Hoffmann d. A rare disease of newborns inherited as an autosomal trait; it affects the motor nerve cells of the spinal cord, causing floppiness and paralysis of muscle (including those involved in breathing and feeding). Death usually occurs before the child is three years old. Cause is unknown. The infant's mother sometimes recalls being aware of reduced fetal movements during pregnancy. Also called infantile progressive spinal muscular atrophy; infantile muscular atrophy; (colloquially) floppy infant.

Whipple's d. An uncommon systemic disorder characterized by episodes of arthritis preceding steatorrhea and other signs of malabsorption; associated with anemia and increased skin pigmentation; the intestinal walls and lymphatics are infiltrated by macrophages filled with glycoproteins; it occurs predominantly in middle-aged men. Also called intestinal lipodystrophy; lipophagic intestinal granulomatosis.

Wilson's d. An autosomal recessive disorder marked by a defect in copper metabolism, resulting in accumulation of copper deposits primarily in the liver, the lenticular nucleus of the brain, and around the cornea, which acquires a green–brown discoloration (Kayser-Fleischer ring); eventually may cause cirrhosis of the liver and degenerative changes in the brain. Also called hepatolenticular degeneration.

woolsorter's d. See pulmonary anthrax, under anthrax.

X-linked lymphoproliferative d. A recessive inherited disease characterized by a marked impairment in production of antibodies to the Epstein-Barr (EB) virus, which renders the affected person susceptible to severe and overwhelming infections with the virus (e.g., infectious mononucleosis becomes potentially fatal). Also called Duncan's disease.

disengagement (dis-en-gāj′ment) In obstetrics, the emergence of the presenting part of the fetus through the vulva.

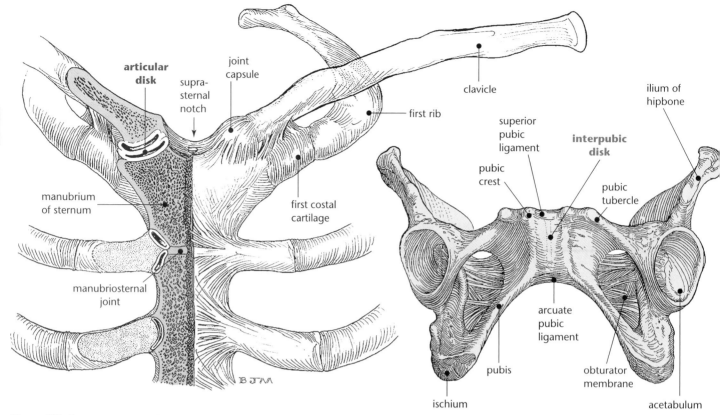

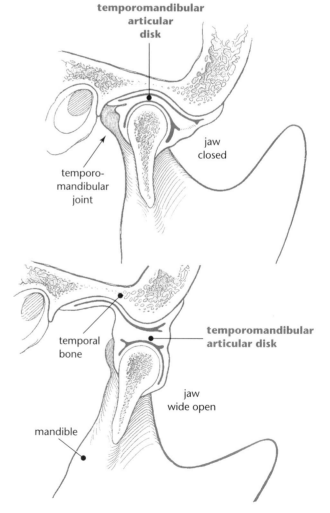

disequilibrium (dis-e-kwĭ-lib′re-um) Lack of balance or stability.

    dialysis d. Acute changes in mental function associated with rapid, marked changes in chemical composition of the blood by hemodialysis.

DISH Acronym for Diffuse Idiopathic Skeletal Hyperostosis; see under hyperostosis.

disimpaction (dis-im-pak′shun) **1.** Separation of an impacted bone fracture. **2.** The breaking down of a fecal impaction.

disinfectant (dis-in-fek′tant) Any agent that kills disease-causing microorganisms.

disinfection (dis-in-fek′shun) Destruction of disease-causing microorganisms on a surface or material by chemical or physical means.

disintegration (dis-in-tĕ-gra′shun) **1.** The process of breaking down into component parts. **2.** Disorganization of mental processes.

disk (disk) Any platelike structure, usually circular in form. Also spelled disc.

    abrasive d. See dental disk.

    articular d. A circular fibrocartilaginous pad present in some synovial joints and attached to the joint capsule; it serves to reduce friction between the articulating surfaces of the bones.

    choked d. See papilledema.

    cloth d. See rag wheel, under wheel.

    dental d. A small disk of paper or plastic, coated with abrasive material (emery, garnet, silica); used in dentistry to cut, grind, smooth, or polish teeth and dental restorations. Also called abrasive disk.

    ectodermal d. In the embryo, an elongated mass of epithelial cells developed from the inner cell mass about a week after fertilization.

    epiphyseal d. See epiphyseal plate, under plate.

    herniated d. Posterior rupture of the inner portion of an intervertebral disk, causing pressure on the nerve roots with resulting pain; occurring most commonly in the lower back. Also called ruptured disk; prolapsed disk; slipped disk.

    intercalated d. Dense double membrane separating cells of cardiac muscle fibers, while retaining points of cell contact through desmosomes and gap junctions.

    interpubic d. A midline plate of fibrocartilage interposed

disequilibrium ■ disk

D36

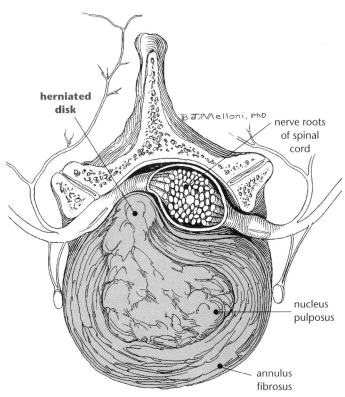

herniated disk

B.J.Melloni, PhD

nerve roots of spinal cord

nucleus pulposus

annulus fibrosus

between the pubic bones at the symphysis; it connects the pubic bones (along with the superior pubic and arcuate pubic ligaments) at the anterior median plane of the pelvis.

intervertebral d.'s The fibrocartilaginous pads interposed between the bodies of adjacent vertebrae, from the axis (second cervical vertebra) to the sacrum, consisting of a jellylike center (nucleus pulposus) surrounded by a fibrous ring (annulus fibrosus). They act as elastic buffers to absorb the daily mechanical shocks sustained by the spinal column. The disks are lacking between the atlas (first cervical vertebra) and the axis, and between the atlas and the lower part of the skull (occiput). Also called intervertebral cartilages.

optic d. The portion of the optic nerve in the eyeball formed by retinal nerve fibers converging to a central area; it appears as an elevated pinkish white oval or circular disk; it is the blind spot in the visual field.

Placido's d. See keratoscope.

prolapsed d. See herniated disk.

ruptured d. See herniated disk.

slipped d. Popular name for herniated disk.

stenopeic d. In ophthalmology, an opaque disk with a narrow slit used in testing for astigmatism.

tactile d. The saucer-shaped termination of specialized sensory nerve fibers in contact with a single, modified epithelial cell in the deep layer of the epidermis, in hair follicles, and in the hard palate; it functions as a touch receptor. Also called meniscus tactus.

temporomandibular articular d. The articular disk of the temporomandibular joint; it separates the joint cavity into two compartments. Also called temporomandibular meniscus.

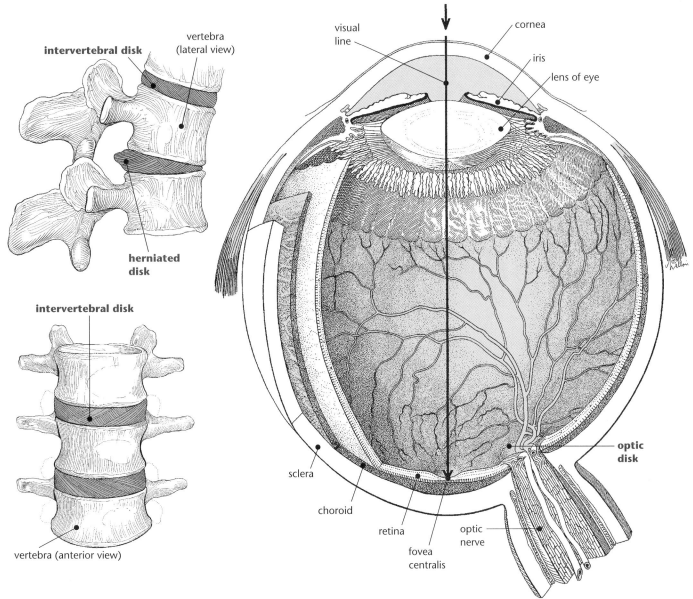

intervertebral disk

vertebra (lateral view)

herniated disk

intervertebral disk

vertebra (anterior view)

visual line

cornea

iris

lens of eye

sclera

choroid

retina

fovea centralis

optic nerve

optic disk

D

diskectomy (dis-kek′to-me) Removal, in part or whole, of an intervertebral disk. Also spelled discectomy.

diskitis (dis-ki′tis) Inflammation of a disk, especially one between two vertebrae. Also spelled discitis.

diskography (dis-kog′rah-fe) The making of x-ray pictures of an intervertebral disk after injection of a radiopaque substance into the disk. Also spelled discography.

diskopathy (dis-kop′ah-the) Any disease of the intervertebral disks. Also spelled discopathy.

dislocate (dis′lo-kāt) To shift from the usual or normal position, especially to displace a bone from its socket; to luxate.

dislocation (dis-lo-ka′shun) Displacement of a body part from its normal location, especially of a bone from its socket or joint.

   closed d. Dislocation of a bone occurring without an external wound. Also called simple dislocation.

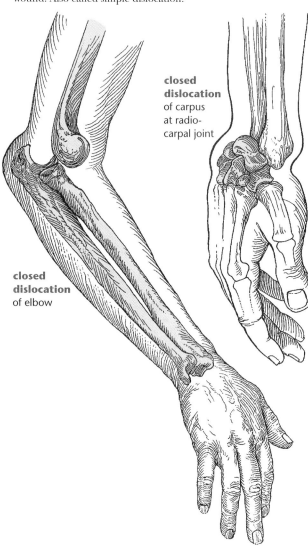

closed dislocation of carpus at radio-carpal joint

closed dislocation of elbow

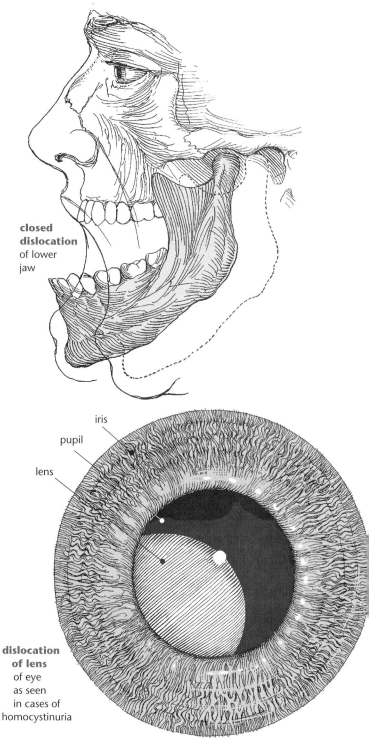

closed dislocation of lower jaw

iris
pupil
lens

dislocation of lens of eye as seen in cases of homocystinuria

   compound d. See open dislocation.

   d. of lens Partial or complete displacement of the lens of the eye; may be *hereditary,* a usually bilateral dislocation occurring as part of a syndrome or disorder (e.g., Marfan's syndrome, homocystinuria); or may be *traumatic,* a dislocation following a contusion injury (e.g., a blow to the eye with a fist). Also called ectopia lentis.

   open d. Dislocation of a bone occurring in conjunction with an open wound. Also called compound dislocation.

   simple d. See closed dislocation.

disorder (dis-or′der) An abnormality of function.

   adjustment d. A maladaptive or unusually prolonged reaction to stressful events or situations; may be severe but is often relatively limited in scope, generally reversible, and usually resolved by therapeutic intervention or by the passage of time as the person adapts to the stress.

   affective d.'s A group of disorders characterized principally by a disturbance of mood, either elation or depression, expressed as an increase or decrease of activity and thought, and not due to any other physical or mental disorder.

   antisocial personality d. A personality disorder beginning before the age of 15, characterized by a life pattern of repeated conflict with society and its rules, lack of remorse or shame, and inability to sustain meaningful interpersonal relationships; in childhood, it is characterized by truancy, lying, running away from home, promiscuity, vandalism, etc.; persisting difficulties in adulthood include disregard for others and others' property, irresponsibility, an inconsistent work record, and a tendency to blame others or give plausible rationalizations for deviant behavior. Formerly called psychopathic personality; psychopathy.

anxiety d.'s A group of disorders characterized by persistent apprehension and worry as the predominant disturbance or where anxiety is experienced if the person attempts to confront his symptoms. See also anxiety.

attention-deficit hyperactive d. (ADHD) Disorder with onset before seven years of age, characterized by age-inappropriate short attention span and impulsiveness, poor modulation of emotions and behavior, and difficulty screening out extraneous stimuli; symptoms are especially noticeable in group settings; may or may not have hyperactivity as a prominent component; some difficulties often persist into adulthood. Formerly called minimal brain dysfunction; hyperkinetic reaction of childhood; learning disability; hyperactive child.

avoidant personality d. Personality disorder characterized by a pervasive timidity, social discomfort, and fear of criticism.

behavior d. of childhood A childhood disorder characterized by persistent behavior patterns that violate either the basic rights of others or age-appropriate societal norms; if severe, may predispose to antisocial personality disorder. Also called conduct disorder.

bipolar d. An affective disorder characterized by extreme swings of mood, from euphoric (manic) to depressive. Formerly called manic-depressive psychosis; manic-depressive illness; manic-depressive disorder.

bleeding d. Popular name for any disorder associated with spontaneous bleeding or with abnormally prolonged or excessive bleeding after injury.

borderline personality d. Personality disorder characterized by unstable, intense interpersonal relationships and impulsive, unpredictable, often self-damaging, behavior; frequently includes disturbances in identity.

character d. See personality disorder.

conduct d. See behavior disorder of childhood.

conversion d. A somatoform disorder in which unconscious or repressed emotional conflict finds expression as aberrant body functioning, either of the special senses or of the motor nervous system (e.g., blindness, deafness, paralysis, pain). Also called hysteria; conversion hysteria; hysterical neurosis; conversion reaction.

cumulative trauma d. Any disorder resulting from damage to tissues due to repetitive minor injuries, such as those affecting the musculoskeletal system when performing repetitive-motion activities, including those performed in the workplace or in certain sports and hobbies.

cyclothymic d. Affective disorder characterized by a chronic mood disturbance that is not of sufficient severity or duration to be classified as major depression or mania but in which there are both depressive and manic episodes.

dependent personality d. Personality disorder characterized by a pervasive pattern of dependent and submissive behavior.

depersonalization d. A dissociation disorder characterized by one or more episodes of alteration in the experience of the self wherein the usual sense of one's own reality is lost or changed temporarily (depersonalization); it causes social or occupational impairment.

developmental d.'s Disorders of childhood characterized by a substantial impairment or delay in development of one or more psychological function.

dissociative d. A group of disorders characterized chiefly by a sudden, temporary change in the normal functioning of consciousness, identity, or motor behavior; includes psychogenic amnesia and psychogenic fugue.

dysthymic d. An affective disorder characterized by chronic depressed mood, loss of interest or pleasure but not of the severity of a major depression.

eating d. Any of a group of disorders characterized by abnormalities of appetite, food intake, or both, including bulimia, anorexia nervosa, and pica.

ecogenetic d. Disorder caused by the interaction of a common environmental factor with a specific genetic predisposition to the disease.

factitious d.'s A group of disorders characterized by physical or psychological symptoms that are produced under voluntary control and used to pursue goals that are involuntarily adopted; often the goal is to assume the patient role; distinguished from malingering, where the goal is obvious from a knowledge of the environmental circumstances.

formal thought d. Thought disorder characterized by an abnormality in the structure, as opposed to the content, of thought.

functional d. Any of a broad class of physical or mental impairments that cannot be traced to organic causes.

generalized anxiety d. Anxiety disorder characterized by generalized, persistent anxiety of at least one month's duration without the specific symptoms of phobias, panic attacks, or obsessions or compulsions; symptoms include motor tension, autonomic hyperactivity, apprehensive expectation, vigilance, and scanning.

genetic d. Any disorder due entirely or in part to a defective gene; distinguished from congenital, although a disorder may be genetic and congenital.

histrionic personality d. Personality disorder characterized by a pervasive pattern of excessive emotionality and attention seeking.

immunoproliferative d. Proliferation of cells of the lymphoreticular system associated with autoallergic disturbances or gamma-globulin abnormalities.

impulse control d.'s A group of disorders in which there is a failure to resist an impulse, drive, or temptation to do something harmful, with an increase in tension before committing the act and the experience of relief, pleasure, or gratification at the time of the act; includes pathological gambling, kleptomania, pyromania, and explosive disorders.

manic-depressive d. See bipolar disorder.

mental d. A disorder characterized by clinically significant psychological or behavioral symptoms and/or impairment of functioning; in general, a mental disorder is any psychiatric disorder listed in the *Standard Nomenclature of Diseases and Operations* of the American Medical Association (AMA), or in the *Diagnostic and Statistical Manual for Mental Disorders* of the American Psychiatric Association (APA). Also called mental illness; emotional illness; mental disease; emotional disturbance; emotional disease; mental disturbance.

multiple personality d. A dissociative disorder characterized by the existence within the individual of two or more distinct personalities, each of which is dominant at a particular time.

narcissistic personality d. Personality disorder characterized by a pervasive pattern of grandiosity, lack of empathy, and hypersensitivity to the evaluation of others.

obsessive-compulsive d. (OCD) Anxiety disorder characterized by obsessions (recurrent egodystonic ideas, thoughts, or impulses) and compulsions (repetitive behaviors designed to produce or prevent some future situation or event) that are experienced as distressful and interfere with social or role functioning.

organic mental d.'s A group of disorders characterized by psychological or behavioral abnormalities associated with transient or permanent dysfunction of the brain; includes delirium, dementia, and amnestic syndromes, secondary to such factors as age, physical illness or injury, alcohol or drug use.

panic d. Anxiety disorder characterized by recurrent episodes of panic attacks. See also panic attack, under attack.

papulosquamous d. Any of a group of skin conditions that have a characteristic primary lesion (usually a reddish papule) with a variable amount of scale on the surface, and from which plaques develop (e.g., pityriasis rosea, lichen planus, psoriasis, seborrheic dermatitis, drug eruptions, and tinea corporis).

paranoid d.'s A group of disorders characterized by persistent persecutory delusions or delusional jealousy not due to any other mental disorder.

paranoid personality d. Personality disorder characterized by a pervasive and unwarranted suspiciousness and mistrust of others.

passive-aggressive personality d. A personality disorder in which resistance to demands for adequate performance is expressed indirectly, leading to social and occupational ineffectiveness.

personality d.'s Any of a group of disorders, often recognizable by adolescence or earlier, characterized by persistent, long-standing, inflexible maladaptive patterns of relating, perceiving, and thinking; the patterns are typical of the person and not limited to discrete episodes. Also called character disorders.

pervasive developmental d. A developmental disorder characterized by distortion in the development of multiple basic psychological functions involved in social skills and language; usually begins in early childhood; includes early infantile autism. See also early infantile autism, under autism.

phobic d.'s Anxiety disorders in which the primary characteristic is irrational and persistent fear of a particular object, activity, or situation that the person feels compelled to avoid. The person recognizes the fear as excessive and unreasonable. See also phobia.

posttraumatic stress d. (PTSD) Anxiety disorder occurring as a result of having experienced an overwhelming stress or trauma (e.g., rape, assault, disasters, or military combat), characterized by recurrent nightmares, flashbacks, intrusive recollections, general blunting of affect or detachment from others, excessive startle response, and dysfunctional responsiveness to stimuli that recall the event. Also called posttraumatic neurosis; posttraumatic stress syndrome.

psychophysiologic d., psychosomatic d. Disturbances of visceral functioning secondary to long-continued emotional attitudes or stress.

psychosexual d.'s A group of disorders of sexual functioning caused primarily by psychological factors; includes gender identity disorders such as transsexualism, the paraphilias (e.g., fetishes, voyeurism, exhibitionism, sexual sadism, sexual masochism), and psychosexual dysfunctions.

reactive attachment d. A disorder of early infancy (onset before eight months) due to lack of adequate caretaking wherein the infant is apathetic, lacks age-appropriate signs of social responsiveness, and shows evidence of failure to thrive; the condition is reversible with adequate care.

seasonal affective d. (SAD) An affective disorder characterized by recurrent episodes of major depression occurring in fall and winter with remission through spring and summer.

separation anxiety d. An anxiety disorder of childhood characterized by excessive anxiety concerning separation from those to whom the child is attached, persisting at least two weeks; may include reluctance or refusal to go to school or to go to sleep unaccompanied, or unrealistic worry about attachment figure.

schizoid personality d. A personality disorder in which there is a deficit in the capacity to form social relationships as shown by withdrawal, aloofness, and lack of humor.

schizophrenic d. See schizophrenia.

sleep d. Any disturbance of the sleep-wake cycle (e.g., insomnia, narcolepsy, jet-lag and work-shift syndromes, somnambulism, night terrors, sleep paralysis).

somatization d. A somatoform disorder characterized by multiple recurrent somatic complaints of several years' duration for which medical attention has been sought, often from several doctors simultaneously, and apparently not due to any physical disorder; usually anxiety and depressed mood are associated features; usually begins in adolescence; rarely found in males. Also called Briquet's syndrome.

somatoform d.'s Any of a group of disorders with symptoms suggesting a physical ailment but without demonstrable organic cause or known physiological mechanism; usually involves frequent taking of medicines and/or seeking medical treatment and alteration of lifestyle patterns; a psychological cause is strongly presumed. The affected person does not consciously or intentionally manifest the symptoms (as is the case in malingering or the factitious disor-

ders). Symptoms range from vague complaints to severe impairment (e.g., paralysis). Included are somatization disorder, conversion disorder, and hypochondriasis.

substance use d.'s Disorders characterized by the maladaptive behavior associated with substance abuse or dependence as distinguished from the substance-induced organic mental disorders, which constitute the effects of the substance on the brain.

thought d. Any abnormality of thinking that affects thought process, thought content, and communication.

disorganization (dis-or-gan-i-za'shun) A marked change in tissues with loss of characteristics and associated impairment of function.

disorientation (dis-o-re-en-ta'shun) Loss of the sense of direction, position, or location.

dispensary (dis-pen'sah-re) **1.** An office in any institution (e.g., hospital, school) from which medical supplies and medicines are distributed. **2.** An outpatient department of a hospital.

dispensatory (dis-pen'sah-to-re) A book describing the sources, preparation, components, and uses of medicines.

dispense (dis-pens') To fill out prescriptions and to distribute medicines.

disperse (dis-pers') To scatter.

dispersion (dis-per'shun) **1.** The process of dispersing or the state of being dispersed. **2.** A suspension of solid, liquid, or gaseous particles in another medium.

displacement (dis-plās'ment) An unconscious psychological defense mechanism in which emotions are transferred from an anxiety-provoking idea, wish, or object to a more tolerable one.

disruption (dis-rup'shun) Deformity of a body part resulting from breakdown of, or interference with, an originally normal developmental process.

dissect (dĭ-sekt', dis-sekt') To cut apart, especially in the study of anatomy.

dissection (dĭ-sek'shun, dis-sek'shun) The act of dissecting.

disseminated (dis-sem'ĭ-nāt'ed) Widely distributed; widespread.

dissimulation (dis-sim-yu-la'shun) The feigning of health by a sick person.

dissociation (dis-so-she-a'shun) **1.** Separation. **2.** Change of a complex chemical compound into a simpler one. **3.** An unconscious psychological defense mechanism in which there is the disconnection of various mental processes from each other so that there is an alteration in the normal integration of consciousness, identity, or motor behavior (e.g., automatic writing, psychogenic amnesia, depersonalization, derealization, multiple personality). See also dissociative disorders, under disorder.

albuminocytologic d. Abnormal increase of protein in the cerebrospinal fluid with no increase in cells; the characteristic finding in Guillain-Barré syndrome.

atrioventricular d. Abnormal independent action of the atria and ventricles of the heart.

complete A-V d. Complete heart (atrioventricular) block; independent contraction of atria and ventricles caused by failure of impulses to reach the ventricles.

electromechanical d. Continuing transmission of impulses within the heart without causing contractions of the heart muscle; often caused by cardiac rupture; may also be caused by drugs.

incomplete A-V d. Atrioventricular dissociation interrupted occasionally by atrial control of the ventricles.

dissolve (diz-zolv') To cause a substance to change from a solid to a dispersed state by placing it in contact with a solvent fluid.

distad (dis'tad) Toward the periphery.

distal (dis'tal) **1.** Farthest from a point of reference. **2.** In dentistry, farthest from the median line of the jaw.

distance (dis'tans) The space between two points.

interocclusal d. The space between chewing (occlusal) surfaces of the upper and lower teeth when the mandible is in the physiologic rest position. Also called freeway space.

map d. The distance between two gene loci in a chromosome; measured in centimorgans.

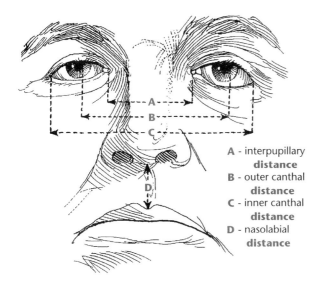

A - interpupillary **distance**
B - outer canthal **distance**
C - inner canthal **distance**
D - nasolabial **distance**

reduced interarch d. Condition in which the mandible rises too high before the upper and lower teeth make contact.

small interarch d. A small space between the upper (maxillary) and lower (mandibular) dental arches. Also called close bite.

distension (dis-ten'shun) See distention.

distention (dis-ten'shun) The state of being stretched as from internal pressure. Also spelled distension.

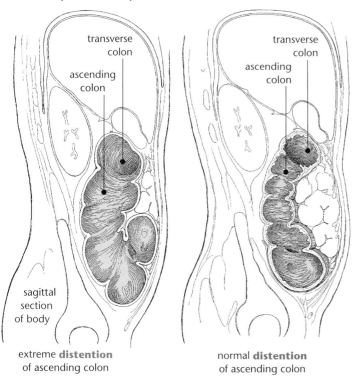

extreme **distention** of ascending colon

normal **distention** of ascending colon

sagittal section of body

transverse colon

ascending colon

distill (dis-til') To subject a liquid mixture to distillation. Also spelled distil.

distillation (dis-til-la'shun) Vaporization of a liquid mixture by heat followed by separation of its components by condensation of the vapor.

distobucco-occlusal (dis-to-buk-o ŏ-kloo'zal) Relating to the point angle formed by three surfaces of a posterior tooth: the one farthest from the midline of the jaw, the one in contact with the cheek, and the chewing (occlusal) surface.

distolinguo-occlusal (dis-to-ling-gwo ŏ-kloo'zal) Relating to the point angle formed by three surfaces of a posterior tooth: the one farthest from the midline of the jaw, the one in contact with the tongue, and the chewing (occlusal) surface.

disto-occlusal (dis-to ŏ-kloo'zal) Relating to the line angle formed by two surfaces of a posterior tooth: the one farthest from the midline and the chewing (occlusal) surface.

distortion (dis-tor'shun) 1. An apparent curvature at the periphery of an image seen through a lens, due to a difference in magnification as the light rays approach the edge of the lens. 2. A mechanism aiding in the disguising or repression of unacceptable thoughts.

distraction (dī-strak'shun) 1. Mental or emotional disturbance. 2. Separation of bone segments after surgical division.

distress (dī-stres') Physical or mental anguish or pain.

fetal d. In obstetrics, an adverse or threatening condition of the fetus resulting from inadequate oxygen supply and removal of carbon dioxide (asphyxia); usually caused by decreased amount of oxygen in the blood entering the fetal circulation (as in maternal respiratory depression), or by insufficient blood flow to the fetus (as in compression of umbilical cord).

distribution (dis-trī-bu'shun) 1. The arrangement of terminal branches of vessels and nerves in various body parts and organs. 2. The areas of the body supplied by such structures.

disturbance (dis-tur'bans) Any deviation from a normal condition or function.

emotional d. See mental disorder, under disorder.

mental d. See mental disorder, under disorder.

disulfiram (di-sul'fi-ram) A counterdrug used to produce an aversion to alcohol in the treatment of alcoholism; it interferes with the normal metabolism of alcohol, causing accumulation of a metabolite (acetaldehyde), which produces an unpleasant reaction in the individual. Ingestion of large amounts of alcohol in the presence of disulfiram may lead to very serious reactions. Trade name: Antabuse.

diuresis (di-u-re'sis) Discharge of increased amounts of urine.

alcohol d. Diuresis induced by consumption of alcoholic beverages.

osmotic d. Diuresis caused by filtration into the kidney tubules of substances that limit water reabsorption.

water d. Diuresis caused by a reduced release of antidiuretic hormone from the pituitary (hypophysis) in response to lower osmotic pressure in the blood after administration of water.

diuretic (di-u-ret'ik) An agent that increases the volume flow of urine.

divalence, divalency (di-va'lens, di-va'len-sē) See bivalence.

divalent (di-va'lent) See bivalent.

divergence (di-ver'jens) Spreading apart or moving in different directions (e.g., a condition in which the eyes turn outward). Also called negative convergence.

diverticula (di-ver-tik'u-lah) Plural of diverticulum.

diverticular (di-ver-tik'u-lar) Relating to a diverticulum.

diverticulectomy (di-ver-tik-u-lek'to-me) Removal of a diverticulum or of diverticula.

diverticulitis (di-ver-tik-u-li'tis) Inflammatory changes occurring in diverticular disease of the colon; the saccular outpouchings protruding through the intestinal wall become impacted with feces and infected; bowel perforation, abscess formation, or peritonitis may also occur; most common symptoms include acute abdominal pain and tenderness, fever, and nausea. See also diverticular disease of colon, under disease.

diverticulosis (di-ver-tik-u-lo'sis) See diverticular disease of colon, under disease.

diverticulum (di-ver-tik'u-lum), pl. divertic'ula A saccular dilatation of variable size protruding from the wall of a tubular organ or structure; it occurs normally or is created by herniation through the muscular coat of a tubular organ.

esophageal d. Diverticulum through a weak spot in the wall of the esophagus, usually caused by abnormal contractions of the esophageal muscles. It may become large enough to trap food and may cause chest pain, difficult swallowing, or regurgitation of undigested food into the back of the throat.

hypopharyngeal d. A diverticulum originating from the lower part of the pharynx (hypopharynx) between the inferior constrictor muscle and the cricopharyngeal muscle.

intestinal d. A herniation of the mucous membrane through a defect in the muscular layer of the intestinal wall.

Meckel's d. A congenital sacculation or appendage of the distal part of the small intestine (ileum); it is derived from the yolk stalk (omphalomesenteric duct) that failed to normally obliterate.

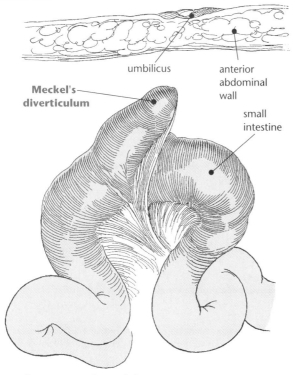

pharyngoesophageal d. A diverticulum located between the pharynx and esophagus. Also called Zenker's diverticulum.

urethral d. An outpouching of the urethral lumen.

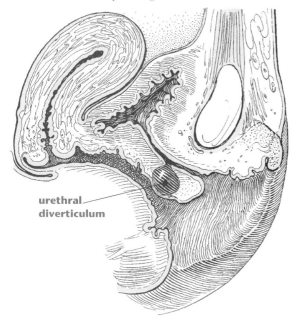

Zenker's d. See pharyngoesophageal diverticulum.

divulse (dī-vuls′) To separate by pulling or tearing.

divulsion (dī-vul′shun) The act of pulling apart.

dizygotic (di-zi-got′ik) (DZ) Derived from two separate ova; applied to fraternal twins.

dizziness (diz′ĭ-nes) An abnormal sensation of unsteadiness characterized by a sensation of movement within the head, without actual motion.

DNA Deoxyribonucleic acid; the double-helix molecule present in the chromosomes of cells; it encodes the genes responsible for the structure and function of living organisms and allows transmission of genetic information from one generation to the next.

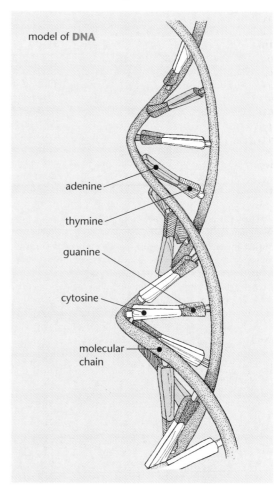

model of **DNA**

DNA fingerprinting See DNA typing, under typing.

recombinant DNA (rDNA) Biologically active DNA produced by the *in vitro* joining of segments of DNA from different sources.

DNA typing See DNA typing, under typing.

Z DNA A form of DNA that is twisted in the opposite direction from the usual DNA spiral.

doctor (dok′tor) **1.** A person holding a doctorate degree awarded by a college or university in any specialized field (e.g., music). **2.** A person trained in and licensed to practice the healing arts (e.g., physician, dentist, veterinarian). **3.** To treat medically.

dol (dōl) A unit of measure of pain intensity.

dolicho- Combining form meaning long.

dolichocephalic, dolichocephalous (dol-ĭ-ko-se-fal′ik, dol-ĭ-ko-sef′ah-lus) Having an abnormally long head; denoting a skull with a cephalic index below 80.

dolichocolon (dol-ĭ-ko-ko′lon) An abnormally long colon.

dolichopelvic (dol-ĭ-ko-pel′vik) Having a long, narrow pelvis.

dolorific (do-lor-if′ik) Producing pain.

domain (do-mān′) One of the regions of a peptide molecule having a coherent structure or functional significance that distinguishes it from other regions of the same molecule.

dominant (dom′ĭ-nant) In genetics, denoting a characteristic that is apparent even when the gene for it is inherited from only one parent.

donor (do′nor) **1.** One who contributes or provides blood for transfusion, organs for transplantation, or spermatozoa for artificial insemination. **2.** In chemistry, a substance that yields part of itself to another substance.

dopa, DOPA (do'pah) 3,4-Dihydroxyphenylalanine; a crystalline amino acid that is the precursor of norepinephrine, epinephrine, and melanin.

dopamine (do'pah-mēn) The precursor of the hormone norepinephrine; found primarily in the adrenal medulla, brain (in high concentrations), sympathetic ganglia, and carotid body (where it acts as a neurotransmitter).

dopaminergic (do-pah-mēn-er'jik) Relating to the physiologic activities or influences of dopamine; applied to nerve cells or cell receptors.

dope (dōp) Any narcotic or habit-forming drug taken for pleasure or to maintain an addiction.

dornase (dor'nās) See streptodornase.

pancreatic d. A deoxyribonuclease preparation made from beef pancreas, used as an inhalant medication to reduce the tenacity of respiratory secretions.

dorsal (dor'sal) Relating to the back of the body or to the posterior part of an anatomic structure.

dorsiflexion (dor-sĭ-flek'shun) Flexion or bending upward, as of the foot or toes.

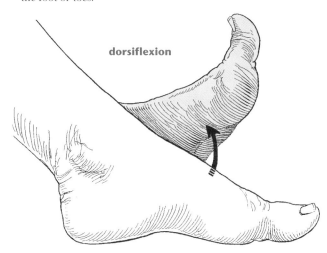

dorsiflexion

dorsolumbar (dor-so-lum'bar) Relating to the back of the body between the upper lumbar and lower thoracic regions.

dorsum (dor'sum) The back of the body; the upper or posterior surface of a part (e.g., the top of the foot or the back of a hand).

d. sellae The part of the sphenoid bone in the skull forming the posterior boundary of the sella turcica.

dosage (do'sij) 1. The determination and formulation of doses (e.g., of medications or radioactivity). 2. In genetics, the number of copies of a particular gene present in a chromosome.

dose (dōs) (D) The specified amount given at one time or at stated intervals.

absorbed d. The amount of ionizing radiation absorbed by the tissues at one time.

booster d. A supplementary dose of an immunizing agent given to maintain immunity.

curative d. The amount of any therapeutic substance required to cure a disease or correct a deficiency.

daily d. The total amount of a medication taken during a 24-hour period.

divided d. A portion of the dose of a drug given repeatedly at short intervals to add up to the full dose within a specified period of time.

erythema d. The minimal safe amount of radiation required to produce redness of the skin within 10 days to two weeks.

initial d. A relatively large dose administered at the beginning of a treatment. Also called loading dose.

loading d. See initial dose.

maintenance d. The amount of medication administered to keep the patient under the influence of the drug after larger amounts have been given previously.

maximal permissible d. (MPD) The greatest amount of radiation to which a person may be exposed without causing harmful effects.

minimal infective d. (MID) The smallest amount of infective material that produces disease.

minimal lethal d. (MLD, mld) The smallest amount of a toxin required to kill an experimental animal.

minimal reacting d. (MRD, mrd) The smallest amount of a toxic substance required to cause a reliable level of reaction in a susceptible test animal.

sensitizing d. The first dose of an allergen administered to an experimental animal, which renders the animal susceptible to a hypersensitivity reaction upon a subsequent exposure to the same allergen.

skin d. (SD) The amount of radiation received on the skin surface.

dosimetry (do-sim'ĕ-tre) Determination of correct dosages.

dosimetrist (do-sim'ĕ-trist) A person who plans and calculates the proper radiation dose necessary for treatment in radiation therapy.

dot (dot) A small mark or spot.

Maurer's d.'s Red-staining granules sometimes seen in the cytoplasm of red blood cells infected with the malarial parasite *Plasmodium falciparum*.

Schüffner's d.'s The characteristic small, dark granules seen in red blood cells infected with malarial parasites (particularly *Plasmodium vivax*), giving the cells a dotted or stippled appearance. Also called Schüffner's granules.

dotage (do'tij) The mental weakness common in old age.

doublet (dub'let) 1. A close continuation of two similar structures (e.g., two joined microtubules in a flagellum). 2. Two lenses mounted together to form a single lens system.

douche (dōōsh) A stream of liquid, vapor, or gas directed into a cavity of the body, especially the rinsing of the vagina with a liquid.

dovetail (dŭv'tāl) In dentistry, a fanned-out prepared cavity made purposely to prevent displacement of the restoration or filling.

dowel (dow'l) A metal pin fitted into the root canal of a natural tooth to provide support to an artificial crown.

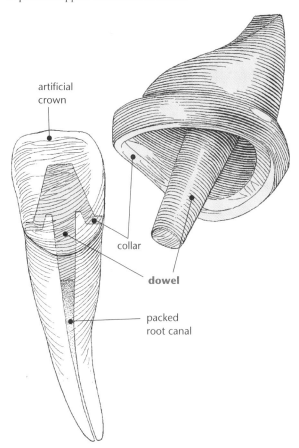

artificial crown

collar

dowel

packed root canal

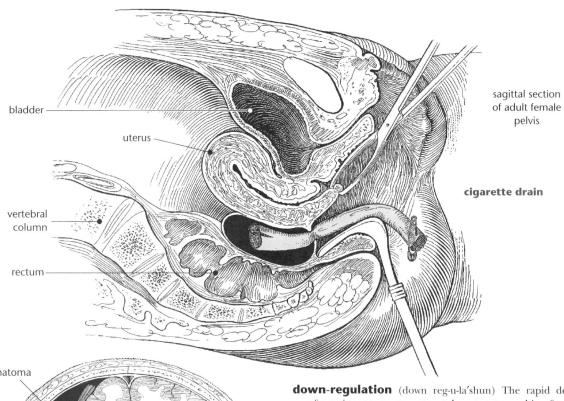

bladder

uterus

sagittal section
of adult female
pelvis

cigarette drain

vertebral
column

rectum

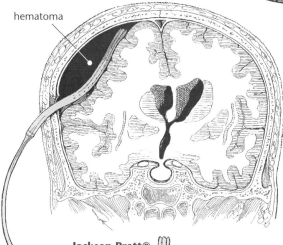

hematoma

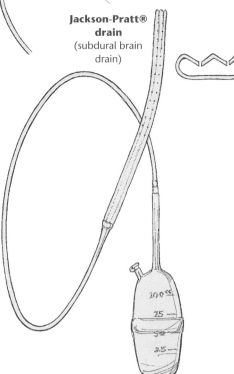

**Jackson-Pratt®
drain**
(subdural brain
drain)

down-regulation (down reg-u-la'shun) The rapid development of a resistant-to-treatment or tolerant state resulting from repeated administration of a pharmaceutically or physiologically active agent.

drain (drān) **1.** To draw fluid from a cavity. **2.** Device for removing fluid from a cavity.

  cigarette d. A gauze wick enclosed in a thin-walled rubber tube. Also called Penrose drain.

  Jackson-Pratt® d. A flexible suction drain that has small intraluminal ridges to prevent collapse of its lumen and a radiopaque marker; used to drain the subdural space after removal of a subdural hematoma. Also called subdural brain drain.

  Penrose d. A cigarette drain.

  stab d. A surgical drain introduced through a puncture made some distance away from the operative incision.

  subdural brain d. See Jackson-Pratt® drain.

  sump d. A drain composed of two tubes, the larger one containing a slender tube that is attached to a suction pump.

drainage (drān'ij) **1.** The continuous draining of fluid from a body cavity or wound. **2.** The fluid drained off.

  capillary d. Drainage effected by means of a wick of gauze or other material.

  closed d. Drainage of a cavity (e.g., of the chest) carried out with protection against entrance of outside air into the cavity.

  open d. Drainage of a cavity without sealing off the wound against entrance of outside air.

  postural d. A gravitational method of draining accumulated secretions in the airways of the lungs; the patient lies on an inclined surface with head downward in alternating positions (on the back, side, and abdomen); each position clears a different section of the lungs; sessions may last 15 to 20 minutes and may be done in conjunction with forceful expiration, clapping of the chest, mechanical vibrators, etc.; employed in the treatment of bronchopulmonary diseases in which there is a copious secretion of mucus (e.g., chronic bronchitis, cystic fibrosis, bronchiectasis).

  tidal d. Drainage of a paralyzed bladder by means of an irrigation apparatus.

dram (dram) (dr) A unit of weight equal to 1/8 oz or 60 grams (apothecary system) and 1/16 oz (avoirdupois system).

drawsheet (draw'shēt) A narrow sheet stretched crosswise under a patient in bed; used as an aid in moving or turning the patient.

dream (drēm) A series of images experienced during sleep.

  wet d. See nocturnal emission, under emission.

D

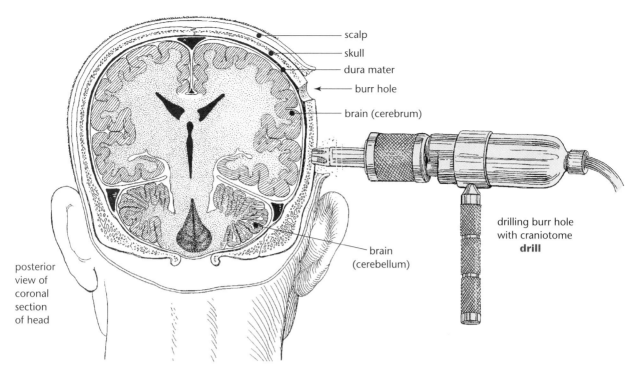

scalp
skull
dura mater
burr hole
brain (cerebrum)

drilling burr hole
with craniotome
drill

brain
(cerebellum)

posterior
view of
coronal
section
of head

dress (dres) To apply a dressing.

dressing (dres'ing) Any material or preparation applied to a wound for protection from infection or for absorbing discharges.

    occlusive d. A dressing that completely seals off a wound.

    pressure d. A dressing usually consisting of abundant resilient material held in place with elastic bandage; used for exerting pressure on tissues to prevent pooling of serum or blood.

dribble (drĭb'bl) **1.** To drool. **2.** To flow gradually in drops (e.g., leakage of urine in urinary incontinence).

drift (drift) A gradual movement or change.

    genetic d. Random fluctuations in the genetic composition of small populations.

drill (dril) A cutting instrument for boring holes in bones or teeth by rotary motion.

drip (drip) **1.** A drop-by-drop flow. **2.** Colloquial term for the purulent discharge from the penis occurring in gonorrhea, usually beginning about two to four days after infection with *Neisseria gonorrhoeae* bacterium.

    intravenous d. The slow, continuous injection of a substance into a vein, a drop at a time.

    postnasal d. Colloquial term for an excessive discharge of mucus from the back of the nasal cavity (posterior nares).

dromic (dro'mik) Relating to nerve impulses that flow in a normal direction.

dromotropic (drom-o-trop'ik) Affecting nerve conduction of impulses.

drop (drop) The quantity of fluid that falls in one pear-shaped globule.

    foot d. See footdrop.

    hanging d. A drop of fluid adhering by surface tension to the undersurface of a slide; used for microscopic examination.

    toe d. See footdrop.

    wrist d. See wristdrop.

droplet (drop'let) A tiny spherical mass or drop of fluid.

    lipid d. A droplet of lipid in the cytoplasm of cells, often a renal tubular cell; may result from defective metabolism of lipids.

drops (drops) Common name for any medicine administered in doses measured by drops (e.g., eyedrops).

    knockout d. Popular name for chloral alcoholate; made by mixing chloral hydrate with any alcoholic beverage and given with criminal intent to produce rapid unconsciousness.

dropsy (drop'se) Old term for describing generalized swelling (edema).

    abdominal d. See ascites.

Drosophila melanogaster (dro-sof'i-lah mel-ah-no-gas'ter) A fruit fly used in genetic studies because of the large size of its chromosomes.

drowning (drown'ing) Death occurring as a result of aspiration of fluids into the respiratory tract.

    freshwater d. Death occurring when a massive absorption of freshwater enters the circulation via the alveolar membranes in the lungs (with ensuing increase in blood volume and electrolyte and osmotic imbalance), resulting in cardiac failure.

    seawater d., saltwater d. Death occurring as a result of pulmonary edema and a frothy fluid in the air passages after immersion in seawater; if immersion is sustained for more than a few minutes, anoxic changes then supervene. There is no massive absorption of water into the circulation since seawater is hypertonic compared with plasma.

drowsiness (drou'ze-nes) A state of impaired consciousness and marked desire to sleep.

drug (drug) Any chemical agent capable of affecting living processes.

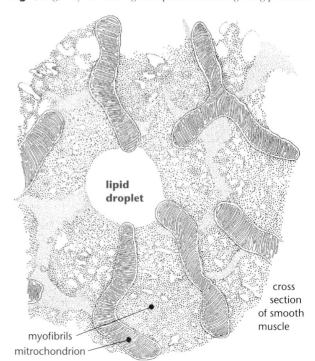

lipid
droplet

cross
section
of smooth
muscle

myofibrils
mitochondrion

d.'s of abuse A group of substances most frequently taken for the effects they produce on the brain and spinal cord; usually they are the psychoactive group of drugs, including alcohol, sedative-hypnotics, opiates and opioids, stimulants, and hallucinogenics.

backdrop d. A drug of pharmacologic equivalent to another.

crude d. Any medicinal material, usually of plant origin, before refining.

designer d.'s A group of highly potent drugs of abuse produced in clandestine laboratories; they are either analogs of such narcotic analgesics and stimulants as meperidine, fentanyl, and amphetamines, or are variants of phencyclidine (PCP); they are manufactured in such a way that their chemical structures do not fall within the federal laws controlling manufacture and distribution of drugs listed under Controlled Substances Act.

ethical d. See prescription drug.

generic d. A drug whose name is not protected by a trademark; it may be manufactured by any pharmaceutical company.

nonprescription d. A pharmaceutical that does not require a prescription to purchase. Commonly called over-the-counter drug.

orphan d. See orphan product, under product.

over-the-counter d. See nonprescription drug.

prescription d. One that requires the approval of a licensed health professional to purchase. Also called ethical drug.

psychedelic d. See hallucinogenic.

psychoactive d.'s A group of substances that exert a direct action on the brain and spinal cord (central nervous system) and produce profound effects on mood, feeling, and behavior.

recreational d. A drug, usually with euphoric effects, taken for self-gratification rather than for medical reasons.

stimulant d. Any drug that increases the excitability of the central nervous system (CNS), either as its principal action or as a side or adverse effect.

sulfa d.'s See sulfonamides.

drug abuse (drug ah-būs′) The excessive and persistent use (usually by self-administration) of any drug without due regard for accepted medical practice. Also called substance abuse.

drug addiction (drug ah-dik′shun) See drug dependence.

drug dependence (drug de-pen′dens) General term for a condition in which the user of a drug has a compelling desire to continue taking the drug either to experience its effects or to avoid the discomfort that occurs when it is not taken. The dependence may be: *psychologic,* characterized by an emotional drive to continue taking a drug, which the user believes is necessary to maintain a sense of optimal well-being; *physical,* characterized by an adaptive physiologic state resulting from the repeated use of a drug (i.e., the body has adapted to the presence of the drug). Formerly called drug addiction; drug habituation.

drug-fast (drug′ fast) See drug resistance.

drug habituation (drug′ hah-bit-u-a′shun) See drug dependence.

drug misuse (drug′ mis-yoos′) **1.** The occasional nonmedical use of a drug. **2.** The inappropriate medical use of drugs (i.e., for conditions for which they are not suited). **3.** The appropriate medical use of a drug but in inappropriate dosages.

drug resistance (drug′ re-zis′tans) The state (of cells or microorganisms) of diminished response, or total lack of response, to drugs that ordinarily inhibit growth of or kill the target cells or organisms. Formerly called drug-fast. COMPARE drug tolerance.

drug tolerance (drug′ tol′er-ans) A condition of decreased responsiveness to a drug acquired by repeated intake of the drug; characterized by the necessity to increase the size of successive doses in order to produce effects of equal magnitude or duration; it is the inability of the same dose to be as effective as the preceding one. COMPARE drug resistance.

drunkenness (drunk′en-nes) See alcoholism.

drusen (droo′zen) Multiple, tiny, yellowish deposits located within the eye, especially around the macula and optic disk, as a result of degenerative changes of the retinal pigment epithelium; usually occurs in the aging process but may also occur in certain diseases.

duct (dukt) A channel or tube, usually for conveying fluid, such as secretions from a gland to another part of the body.

accessory pancreatic d. The smaller of the two pancreatic ducts which enter the small intestine; it is occasionally connected to the main pancreatic duct. Also called duct of Santorini.

adipose d. See sebaceous duct.

alveolar d.'s The two or three thin-walled ducts leading from each terminal bronchiole to the alveoli of the lungs.

arterial d. See ductus arteriosus, under ductus.

bile d. The duct formed by the union of the common hepatic duct and the cystic duct; it conveys bile and is usually joined by the main pancreatic duct before emptying into the small intestine; in the adult, it is approximately 8 cm long and 6 mm in diameter.

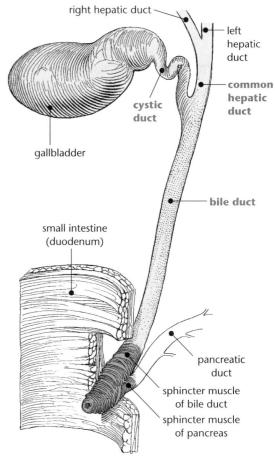

right hepatic duct
left hepatic duct
common hepatic duct
cystic duct
gallblatter
bile duct
small intestine (duodenum)
pancreatic duct
sphincter muscle of bile duct
sphincter muscle of pancreas

cochlear d. A spirally arranged membranous tube (2 3/4 turns in humans) within the bony canal of the cochlea of the internal ear; it is triangular in transverse section, houses the spiral organ of Corti, and is filled with endolymph; its apex is closed and its base communicates with the saccule by way of the ductus reuniens. Also called scala media; cochlear canal.

collecting d.'s The ducts of the kidney that convey urine from the nephron to the pelvis of the kidney. They include the cortical collecting duct, which receives the connecting tubules of the nephron and which is situated in the cortex of the kidney; the medullary collecting duct, situated lower in the medulla of the kidney; and papillary duct of Bellini, which empties the urine into the pelvis of the kidney. Formerly called collecting tubules.

common hepatic d. The duct formed by the junction of the right and left hepatic ducts (two main ducts issued from the liver); it lies in front of the portal vein and is approximately 3 cm long.

cortical (straight) collecting d. One of many ducts originating in the cortical part of the kidney, receiving the contents of the connecting tubules of the nephron, and joining other collecting ducts in the medullary part of the kidney to form the duct of Bellini (papillary duct).

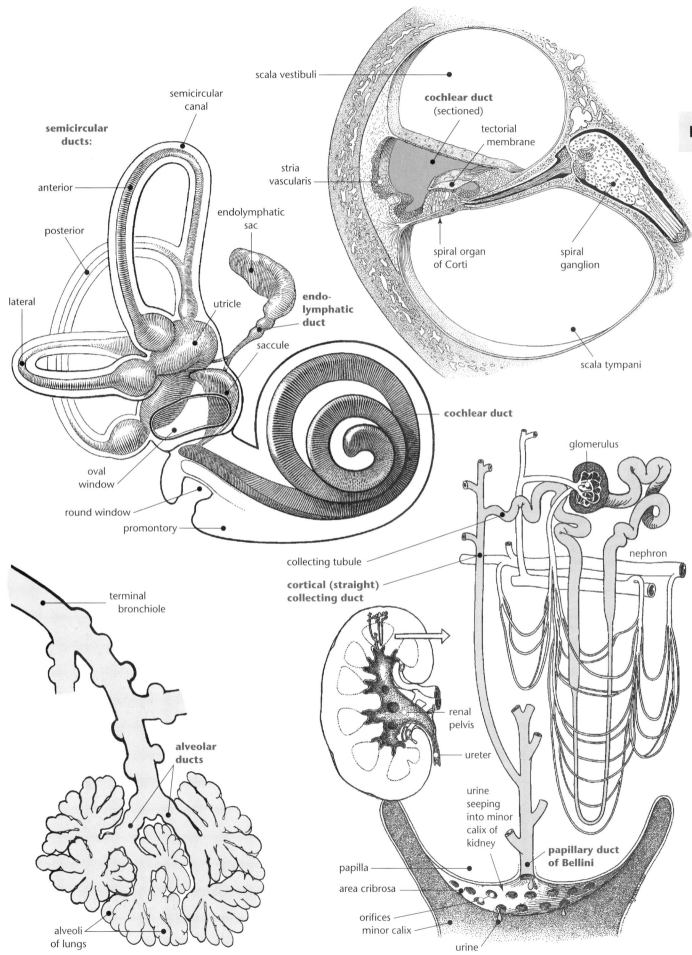

scala vestibuli

cochlear duct (sectioned)

tectorial membrane

stria vascularis

spiral organ of Corti

spiral ganglion

scala tympani

D

semicircular ducts:

semicircular canal

anterior

posterior

lateral

endolymphatic sac

utricle

endo-lymphatic duct

saccule

oval window

round window

promontory

cochlear duct

terminal bronchiole

alveolar ducts

alveoli of lungs

glomerulus

collecting tubule

nephron

cortical (straight) collecting duct

renal pelvis

ureter

urine seeping into minor calix of kidney

papillary duct of Bellini

papilla

area cribrosa

orifices minor calix

urine

cystic d. The duct coming off the neck of the gallbladder and joining the common hepatic duct to form the bile duct; it is about 3.5 cm long.

deferent d. The muscular duct that conveys sperm from the tail of the epididymis in the testis to the base of the prostate gland, where it is joined by the seminal vesicle duct to form the ejaculatory duct; the terminal part of the deferent duct (ampulla) is dilated; in the average adult male the deferent duct is approximately 46 cm in length. Also called vas deferens; ductus deferens; spermatic duct.

ejaculatory d. One of two tubes formed by the union of the terminal part of the deferent duct with the seminal vesicle duct; it is approximately 2 cm long and after passing through the prostate gland opens into the prostatic urethra.

endolymphatic d. A duct in the labyrinth of the ear that connects the endolymphatic sac with the utricle and saccule.

lacrimal d. See lacrimal canaliculus, under canaliculus.

lactiferous d.'s About 20 to 25 main ducts of the breast that drain milk from the lobes of the mammary gland and open on the nipple. Also called milk ducts.

lymphatic d.'s The main lymph channels conveying lymph and emptying it into the bloodstream; they include the thoracic duct and the right lymphatic duct. Also called ductus lymphaticus.

main pancreatic d. A duct that, after traversing the entire length of the pancreas, joins the bile duct and passes obliquely into the lumen of the small intestine. Also called pancreatic duct.

mesonephric d. An embryonic duct that develops, in the male, into the deferent duct; in the female it is obliterated. Also called Wolffian duct.

milk d.'s See lactiferous ducts.

müllerian d. See paramesonephric duct.

nasolacrimal d. A duct conveying tears from the lacrimal sac to the nasal cavity; in the average adult it is approximately 2 cm in length.

pancreatic d. See main pancreatic duct.

papillary d.'s of Bellini Numerous ducts in the upper part of the renal medulla, each formed by a succession of junctions of several medullary (straight) collecting ducts; they open into the summit of a papilla, where they convey urine to the pelvis of the kidney.

paramesonephric d. In the female, either of the two embryonic tubes that develop into the uterine tubes, vagina, and uterus; it disappears in the male. Also called müllerian duct.

paraurethral d. In the female, a duct formed from the union of minute excretory channels leaving the many small mucous urethral (Skene's) glands; it opens into the lateral margin of the external urethral orifice.

parotid d. The duct that conveys saliva from the parotid gland to the vestibule of the mouth, opposite the upper second molar.

perilymphatic d. A minute canal connecting the perilymphatic space of the cochlea with the subarachnoid space. Also called aqueduct of cochlea; cochlear aqueduct.

right lymphatic d. The smaller of two terminal lymphatic channels (about 1 cm long); it conveys lymph from the right side of the head and neck, the right upper limb, and the right side of the chest and ends by opening into the junction of the right subclavian and internal jugular veins.

d. of Santorini See accessory pancreatic duct.

sebaceous d. A duct that emerges from a sebaceous gland and opens most frequently into the distal part of the hair follicle, but occurs in most parts of the dermis, especially around the apertures of the anus, mouth, nose, and ear; it does not appear in the palms of the hand and soles of the feet; it conveys an oily secretion (sebum). Also called adipose duct.

semicircular d.'s Three membranous ducts (filled with perilymphatic fluid) within the bony semicircular canals of the inner ear; each contains an ampulla that contributes to balance and orientation.

seminal vesicle d. The short, narrow, straight tube at the lower end of the seminal vesicle that joins the deferent duct to form the ejaculatory duct.

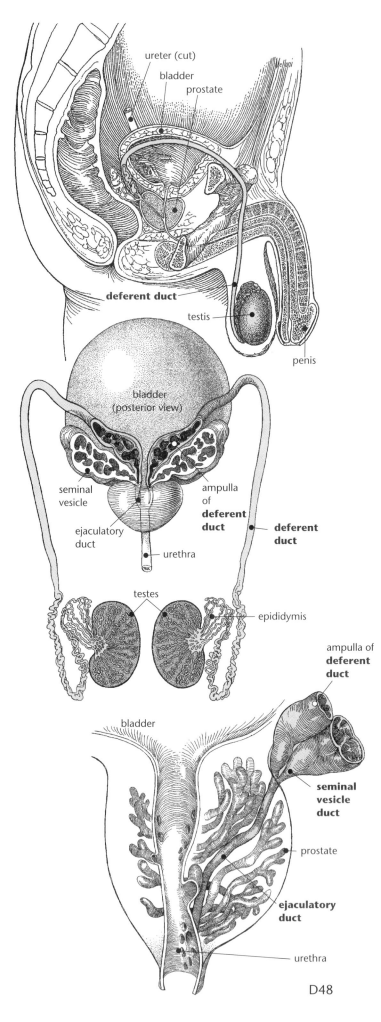

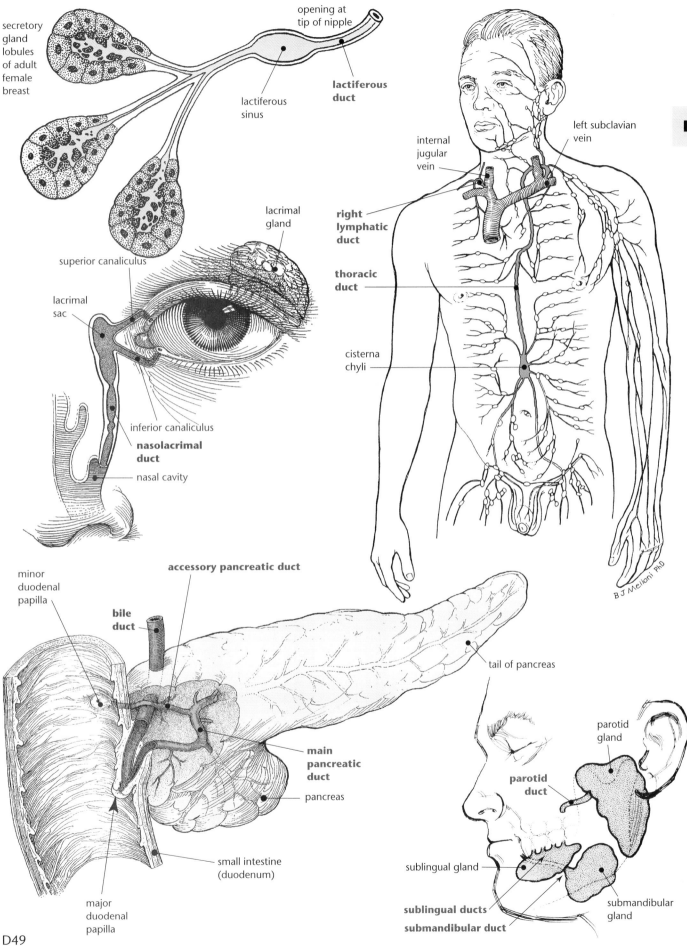

secretory
gland
lobules
of adult
female
breast

opening at
tip of nipple

**lactiferous
duct**

lactiferous
sinus

lacrimal
gland

superior canaliculus

lacrimal
sac

inferior canaliculus

**nasolacrimal
duct**

nasal cavity

D

internal
jugular
vein

left subclavian
vein

**right
lymphatic
duct**

**thoracic
duct**

cisterna
chyli

B J Melloni PhD

minor
duodenal
papilla

accessory pancreatic duct

**bile
duct**

tail of pancreas

**main
pancreatic
duct**

pancreas

small intestine
(duodenum)

major
duodenal
papilla

parotid
gland

**parotid
duct**

sublingual gland

submandibular
gland

sublingual ducts

submandibular duct

D49

spermatic d. See deferent duct.

sublingual d.'s A group of 8 to 20 excretory channels conveying saliva from the sublingual gland to the floor of the mouth; most are small channels that open on the summit of the sublingual fold; those from the anterior part of the gland occasionally join to form a larger channel that opens at or near the sublingual papilla adjacent to the frenulum of the tongue.

submandibular d. A duct about 5 cm long that conveys saliva from the submandibular gland to the floor of the mouth, opening at the tip of the sublingual papilla next to the frenulum of the tongue. Also called Wharton's duct.

sudoriferous d. See sweat duct.

sweat d. The duct leading from the body of a sweat gland to the surface of the skin; it affects body temperature by surface evaporation of sweat. Also called sudoriferous duct.

thoracic d. The larger of two terminal lymphatic channels in the body; it conveys the greater part of the lymph into the circulating blood; it arises from the saccular dilatation (cisterna chyli) in the abdomen and empties into the left subclavian vein near its junction with the internal jugular vein.

thyroglossal d. An embryonic duct extending along the midline of the neck; its lower part gives rise to the isthmus of the thyroid gland; normally the remainder disappears but occasionally it persists in the adult and forms a cyst or a fistula.

urogenital d.'s The mesonephric (wolffian) and the paramesonephric (müllerian) ducts.

utriculosaccular d. A duct located in the internal ear extending from the utricle and joining the endolymphatic duct.

Wharton's d. See submandibular duct.

wolffian d. See mesonephric duct.

ductal (duk′tal) Relating to a duct.

ductile (duk′til) Capable of being made into a wire (e.g., certain metals and plastics).

duction (duk′shun) The movement of an eye by the extrinsic muscles.

ductular (duk′tu-lar) Relating to a ductule.

ductule (dukt′ūl) A small duct.

ductus (duk′tus), pl. duc′tus Latin for duct, a tubular structure. Also called duct.

d. arteriosus A communicating channel between the pulmonary artery and the beginning of the descending aorta in the fetus, directing the major output of the right ventricle into the aorta; it

closes spontaneously in normal term infants by four days of age and remains as a fibrous remnant, the ligamentum arteriosum. Also called arterial duct.

d. deferens See deferent duct, under duct.

d. lymphaticus See lymphatic ducts, under duct.

patent d. arteriosus (PDA) A ductus arteriosus that abnormally remains open (patent) beyond a few weeks after birth, with the flow of blood from the aorta to the pulmonary artery, resulting in recirculation of oxygenated blood through the lungs; the signs of PDA include an active precordium, increased peripheral pulses, and a widened pulse pressure, with or without asystolic heart murmur; the abnormal condition can be confirmed by echocardiography; seen in some children born to mothers who had German measles (rubella) during the first trimester of pregnancy and in a high percentage of premature infants weighing less then 1500 grams. Also called persistent ductus arteriosus.

persistent d. arteriosus See patent ductus arteriosus.

d. reuniens A small tube uniting the lower part of the saccule to the basal end of the cochlear duct.

reversed d. arteriosus Patent ductus arteriosus accompanied by obstruction of the small vessels of the lungs, resulting in reversed blood flow from the pulmonary artery to the aorta.

d. venosus A major blood channel in the liver of the fetus created by the union of the left umbilical vein (from the umbilical cord) and the left branch of the portal vein in the liver; it is later joined by the left hepatic vein immediately before the ductus venosus terminates by opening into the inferior vena cava, below the right atrium of the heart. At birth, when the umbilical cord is severed, the ductus venosus becomes obliterated and its fibrous remnant is termed the ligamentum venosum of the liver; the umbilical vein also becomes obliterated, and its fibrous remnant is termed the ligamentum teres of the liver.

dull (dul) 1. Not sharp, acute, or resonant; applied to an instrument, pain, or sound. 2. Lacking mental alertness.

dullness, dulness (dul′nes) The quality of diminished resonance, such as the characteristic sound elicited by percussion over a solid part or organ.

shifting d. Dull sound produced by percussion, usually of the abdominal cavity, that shifts location as the patient is moved; indicative of the presence of free fluid.

duodenal (du-o′de-nal, du-o-de′nal) Relating to the duodenum.

duodenectomy (du-od′ĕ-nek′to-me, du-o-dĕ-nek′to-me) Removal of the duodenal portion of the small intestine, partial or total.

duodenitis (du-od-ĕ-ni′tis) Inflammation of the duodenum.

duodenocholecystostomy (du-od′e-no-ko′le-sis-tos′to-me) Surgical formation of a passage between the gallbladder and the duodenum.

duodenocholedochotomy (du-od′ĕ-no-ko′led-o-kot′o-me) A surgical cut into the common bile duct and the adjoining portion of the duodenum.

duodenoenterostomy (du-od′ĕ-no-en-ter-os′to-me) Surgical formation of a passage between the duodenum and another portion of the small intestine.

duodenojejunostomy (du-od′ĕ-no-jĕ-joo-nos′to-me) Surgical formation of a passage between two portions of the small intestine, the duodenum and the jejunum.

duodenolysis (du-o-dĕ-nol′ĭ-sis) The operation of freeing the duodenum from adhesions.

duodenoplasty (du-od′ĕ-no-plas′te) Reparative operation upon the duodenum, usually performed to repair damage caused by an obstruction at the junction of the stomach and the duodenum.

duodenorrhaphy (du-od′ĕ-nor′ah-fe) Suturing of the duodenum.

duodenoscopy (du-od′ĕ-nos′ko-pe) Examination of the interior of the duodenum by means of a flexible instrument (endoscope) equipped with fiberoptic illumination.

duodenostomy (du-od′ĕ-nos′to-me) Surgical formation of an orifice or direct passage through the abdominal wall into the duodenum.

duodenotomy (du-od-ĕ-not′o-me) A surgical cut into the duodenum.

duodenum (du-od′ĕ-num, du-o-de′num) The first portion of the small intestine, extending from the lower end of the stomach to the

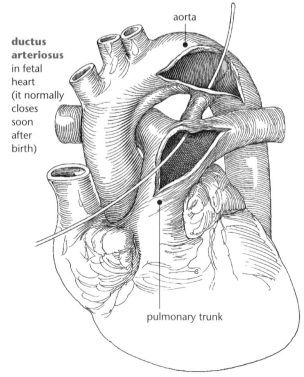

ductus
arteriosus
in fetal
heart
(it normally
closes
soon
after
birth)

aorta

pulmonary trunk

jejunum; it measures approximately 20 to 25 cm in length and forms a constant C-shaped curve surrounding the head of the pancreas; it lies entirely above the level of the umbilicus.

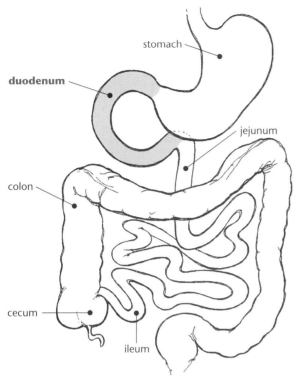

duplication of chromosomes (doo-pli-ka′shun kro′mo-sōms) A chromosome aberration characterized by the presence of an extra, distinct portion of chromosome, usually resulting from unequal exchange of fragments between homologous chromosomes (unequal crossing over).

dura (du′rah) See dura mater.

dural (du′ral) Relating to the dura mater.

dura mater (du′rah ma′ter) The fibrous, outermost of the three membranes covering the brain and spinal cord. Also called dura.

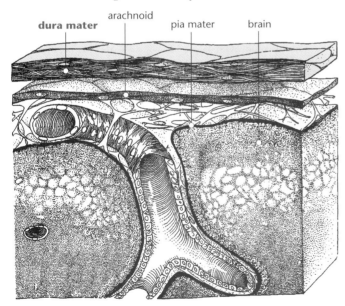

dwarf (dwarf′) A very small person for whom there is no expectation of reaching the size in the range typical for people of like race and sex. Also called nanus; person of short stature.

dwarfism (dwarf′izm) In a broad sense, failure to achieve full growth potential; an abnormal condition of being very undersized, due to arrested growth; may be induced by ecological factors (e.g.,

dietary intake, systemic disease), by genetic factors, or by endocrine factors; diminished height is only one of the resulting features. Also called nanosomia.

achondroplastic d. Dwarfism caused by congenital abnormality in the ossification process of cartilage at the ends of long bones; affected individuals have a relatively elongated trunk, short extremities, and a large head.

acromelic d. Dwarfism characterized by extremely short distal segments of the limbs.

hypothyroid d. See cretinism.

Laron-type d. Dwarfism associated with ineffectiveness of growth hormone (somatotropin) due to deficiency or absence of somatomedin, a peptide that mediates the action of growth hormone on cartilage; plasma contains high or normal levels of the growth hormone.

pituitary d. Dwarfism accompanied by sexual infantilism and decreased function of the thyroid and adrenal glands; caused by lesions of the anterior portion of the pituitary (adenohypophysis) early in childhood.

primordial d. Inadequate term designating a condition characterized by insufficient growth with normal functional development.

dyad (di′ad) **1.** A pair. **2.** One pair of chromosomes formed after disjunction of a tetrad in the first meiotic division.

dynamics (di-nam′iks) **1.** The physical science dealing with the relationship between motion and the forces causing it. **2.** The emotional forces influencing patterns of behavior.

dynamo- Combining form meaning force; strength; movement.

dynamograph (di-nam′o-graf) See ergograph.

dynamometer (di-nah-mom′ĕ-ter) See ergometer.

dyne (din) A unit of force equal to the force required to give a mass of 1 gram an acceleration of 1 cm per second squared.

dys- Combining form meaning defective; bad; difficult.

dysacusis, dysacusia (dis-ah-koo′sis, dis-ah-koo′ze-ah) **1.** Inability to distinguish between sounds. **2.** Discomfort or pain in the ear caused by sound.

dysarthria (dis-ar′thre-ah) Impaired ability to articulate clear speech sounds due to muscular dysfunction secondary to disease of the nervous system (central or peripheral).

dysarthric (dis-ar′thrik) Relating to dysarthrosis.

dysarthrosis (dis-ar-thro′sis) **1.** Malformation of a joint. **2.** A false joint.

dysautonomia (dis-aw-to-no′me-ah) Dysfunction of the autonomic nervous system.

familial d. Autosomal recessive disorder affecting infants and children; symptoms include excessive sweating, deficiency of tears, poor motor coordination, and indifference to pain. Also called Riley-Day syndrome.

dysautonomic (dis-aw-to-nom′ik) Relating to dysautonomia.

dysbarism (dis′bar-izm) Imbalance between air pressure in the atmosphere and the pressure of gases or free air within the body; caused by a sudden shift in ambient pressure, e.g., in rapid ascension to the surface from deep-sea diving (decompression) or with loss of cabin pressure while flying at high altitudes (compression).

dysbasia (dis-ba′ze-ah) Difficult or distorted walking; it may be organically or psychically determined.

dyscephaly (dis-sef′ah-le) Malformation of the head and face.

dyschezia (dis-ke′ze-ah) Difficult or painful defecation.

dyschiria (dis-ki′re-ah) Disorder in which the person is unable to tell which side of the body has been touched.

dyschondrogenesis (dis-kon-dro-jen′ĕ-sis) Defective formation of cartilage.

dyschondroplasia (dis-kon-dro-pla′ze-ah) See enchondromatosis.

dyschromatopsia (dis-kro-mah-top′se-ah) See dichromatism.

dyschromia (dis-kro′me-ah) Any abnormality of pigmentation of skin or hair.

dyscoria (dis-ko′re-ah) An irregularity in the shape of the pupil.

dyscrasia (dis-kra′ze-ah) A general abnormal condition, especially of blood cells or platelets.

plasma cell d.'s A group of disorders (e.g., multiple myeloma, primary amyloidosis) characterized by proliferation of a single clone of immunoglobulin-secreting cells and increased levels of a single homogeneous immunoglobulin in serum or urine. Also called monoclonal gammopathy.

dysdiadochokinesia (dis-di-ad-ŏ-ko-ki-ne′se-ah) Inability to make alternating movements in rapid succession (e.g., extending and flexing a limb).

dyseneia (dis-e-ne′ah) Defective articulation of speech resulting from impaired hearing.

dysenteric (dis-en-ter′ik) Relating to dysentery.

dysentery (dis′en-ter-e) Intestinal disease characterized by frequent watery stools containing blood and mucus, abdominal pain, and sometimes fever; when severe, it may cause dehydration.

    amebic d. Dysentery caused by infection with the protozoan parasite *Entamoeba histolytica;* symptoms vary from mild to severe; may cause ulceration of the colon.

    bacillary d. Dysentery caused by bacteria of the genus *Shigella;* it has a relatively gradual onset and tends to run a chronic course.

dyserethism (dis-er′e-thizm) A slow response to stimuli.

dysergia (dis-er′je-ah) Motor incoordination.

dysesthesia (dis-es-the′ze-ah) An abnormal spontaneous, usually unpleasant sensation (e.g., a burning pain, a sensation of an electric shock) which may be an indication of sensory pathway dysfunction, but is not in itself diagnostic.

dysfluency (dis-flu′en-se) An interruption in the flow of speaking marked by hesitations, prolongations, and repetitions of syllables, words, or phrases; may be accompanied by excessive tension, struggle, and secondary mannerisms.

dysfunction (dis-funk′shun) An impaired or disordered functioning of an organ or body system.

    erectile d. Term suggested as more precise than impotence for describing the inability to attain and/or maintain erection of the penis sufficient for satisfactory sexual intercourse; it is considered part of the overall multifaceted process of male sexual function; causes may be organic (from the nervous or vascular systems) or psychological, but they most commonly appear to derive from problems in all three areas acting in concert; assessment and treatment of the dysfunction may require a multidisciplinary approach. Also called impotence.

    minimal brain d. (MBD) See attention-deficit hyperactivity disorder, under disorder.

dysgammaglobulinemia (dis-gam-mah-glob-u-li-ne′me-ah) An abnormal percentage distribution of gamma globulins in the body.

dysgenic (dis-jen′ik) Relating to dysgenesis.

dysgenesis (dis-jen′ĕ-sis) Abnormal differentiation of the mass of embryonic cells (anlage) leading to the formation of structurally abnormal organs.

    gonadal d. Defective or deficient development of the ovaries or testes.

    seminiferous tubule d. See Klinefelter's syndrome, under syndrome.

dysgerminoma (dis-jer-mĭ-no′mah) An uncommon malignant tumor of the ovary composed of undifferentiated germinal epithelium; it occurs usually in the young (20–30) age group, occasionally in children.

dysgeusia (dis-gu′ze-ah) A distortion of the sense of taste.

dysgnathia (dis-na′the-ah) Any abnormality of the jaws.

dysgnosia (dis-no′se-ah) Any disorder of the intellect.

dysgonic (dis-gon′ik) Denoting a slow and relatively poor growth; applied to bacteria.

dysgraphia (dis-gra′fe-ah) Difficulty in writing; may be due to ataxia, tremor, or motor neurosis.

dyshematopoiesis (dis-hem-ah-to-poi-e′sis) Defective or imperfect blood formation.

dyshidrosis (dis-hi-dro′sis) The presence of recurrent, tiny, itchy vesicles on the sides of fingers, palms of hands, and soles of feet; vesicles may dry up and become crusts or become enlarged and susceptible to fungal or bacterial infection. Also called pompholyx.

dyskeratoma (dis-ker-ah-to′mah) Skin tumor formed from abnormal keratinization of the epidermis.

    warty d. A benign skin tumor containing a keratin plug, occurring on the scalp, face, or neck.

dyskinesia (dis-ki-ne′ze-ah) Any abnormality of involuntary movement.

    orofacial d. See oromandibular dystonia, under dystonia.

dyslalia (dis-la′le-ah) Impairment of speech caused by defective speech structures.

dyslexia (dis-lek′se-ah) Difficulty in reading due to impaired ability to identify and understand written symbols, and a tendency to reverse certain letters and words.

dyslexic (dis-lek′sik) Relating to dyslexia.

dyslogia (dis-lo′je-ah) Impairment of thought processes and speech.

dysmegalopsia (dis-meg-ah-lop′se-ah) Abnormal visual perception in which objects appear larger than they actually are.

dysmelia (dis-me′le-ah) Congenital absence of a portion of one or more extremities.

dysmenorrhea (dis-men-o-re′ah) Painful menstrual periods.

    functional d. See primary dysmenorrhea.

    primary d. Dysmenorrhea occurring in the absence of organic disease. Also called functional dysmenorrhea.

    secondary d. Dysmenorrhea caused by inflammation, tumor, infection, or anatomic factors.

dysmetria (dis-me′tre-ah) Inability to place an extremity at an exact point in space (e.g., to place a finger on the nose); usually caused by a cerebellar lesion.

dysmorphism (dis-mor′fizm) Abnormalities of shape, as seen in syndromes of genetic and environmental origin.

dysmorphology (dis-mor-fol′o-je) The area of clinical genetics dealing with the diagnosis and interpretation of abnormal development of body structures.

dysnystaxis (dis-nis-tak′sis) A state of half wakefulness or light sleep.

dysontogenesis (dis-on-to-jen′ĕ-sis) Abnormal development.

dysosmia (dis-oz′me-ah) A distortion of the sense of smell.

dysostosis (dis-os-to′sis) Defective formation of bone.

    cleidocranial d. An autosomal dominant inheritance marked by partial or complete absence of the collarbones (clavicles) and delay in ossification of the skull, often with underdeveloped facial bones, and defective teeth.

    craniofacial d. An autosomal dominant inheritance characterized by a wide skull, widely separated eyes, undersized upper jaw, beaked nose, and exophthalmos. Also called Crouzon's disease.

    mandibulofacial d. Abnormalities of the palpebral fissures, lower jaw, cheek (zygomatic) bones, and lower lids, associated with malposition of teeth, low-set malformed ears, and high cleft palate; called Franceschetti's syndrome when total, and Treacher Collins syndrome when partial.

dyspareunia (dis-pah-roo′ne-ah) Painful intercourse.

dyspepsia (dis-pep′se-ah) Indigestion.

dysphagia (dis-fa′je-ah) Difficulty in swallowing.

    d. lusoria Dysphagia due to compression of the esophagus by a congenital abnormality of a blood vessel, usually the right subclavian artery when it abnormally comes off the thoracic aorta.

    sideropenic d. See Plummer-Vinson syndrome, under syndrome.

dysphasia (dis-fa′ze-ah) Loss of ability to produce or comprehend spoken or written language, or both, due to disease of the brain.

dysphonia (dis-fo′ne-ah) A disturbance or impairment of voice.

    abductor spasmodic d. Difficulty in speaking caused by forceful, involuntary separation of the vocal folds, which produces breathy speech interruptions.

    adductor spasmodic d. Difficulty in speaking caused by forceful, involuntary approximation of the vocal folds, which interrupts the air stream and produces a strained, hoarse, choppy voice.

dysphoria (dis-fo′re-ah) An emotional state characterized by depression, restlessness, and malaise, usually associated with poor self-esteem.

dysplasia (dis-pla′se-ah) **1.** In pathology, abnormality of cell growth in which some cells in a tissue have some of the characteristics of malignancy but not enough for a diagnosis of an early cancer; unlike cancer (which is irreversible), dysplastic tissue may sometimes reverse spontaneously to normal. **2.** In embryology, abnormal or altered development of a body part.

atriodigital d. See Holt-Oram syndrome, under syndrome.

cervical d. Dysplasia involving the superficial layer (epithelium) of the uterine cervix; it is considered a precancerous lesion; depending on degree of involvement, it is graded as mild, moderate, or severe; the severe form is most likely to progress to carcinoma *in situ*. The human papillomavirus (HPV) has been implicated as a causative agent, especially types 16, 18, and 31. Also called cervical intraepithelial neoplasia (CIN).

chondroectodermal d. A disorder inherited as an autosomal recessive trait characterized by short limbs with normal trunk, more than 10 fingers (polydactyly), and abnormal development of teeth and nails; frequently associated with heart defects. Also called Ellis–van Creveld syndrome.

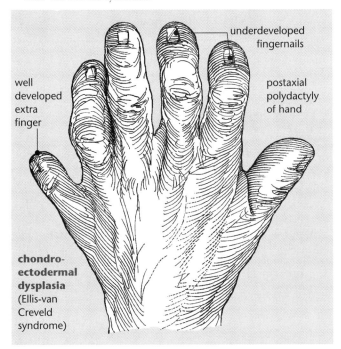

underdeveloped
fingernails

well
developed
extra
finger

postaxial
polydactyly
of hand

**chondro-
ectodermal
dysplasia**
(Ellis-van
Creveld
syndrome)

congenital acetabular d. Congenital dislocation of the hip; a complete or partial displacement of the femoral head out of the acetabulum; not related to trauma or to other musculoskeletal disease.

dentin d. Hereditary abnormality of dentin formation marked by disarrangement of dentin tubules by masses of collagenous matrix; tooth roots are poorly developed with varying amounts of pulpal obliteration; the pulp chamber is filled with an abnormal dentin; inherited as an autosomal dominant trait.

fibromuscular d. Nonatherosclerotic disease of arteries, especially renal arteries, causing constriction.

fibrous d. of bone A benign, progressive condition marked by localized replacement of bone by proliferating fibrous tissue.

hereditary renal-retinal d. Inherited disorder characterized by retinitis pigmentosa, diabetes insipidus, and progressive uremia.

mammary d. See fibrocystic disease of the breast, under disease.

vulvar d. Dysplasia of the vulva characterized as multicentric mucosal lesions; graded as mild, moderate, or severe, depending on the degree of involvement; it is associated with the presence of human papillomavirus (HPV), especially types 16 and 18 (in 80–90% of cases). Also called vulvar intraepithelial neoplasia (VIN). See also Bowen's disease, under disease.

dysplastic (dis-plas′tik) Relating to dysplasia.

dyspnea (disp′ne-ah) Difficult or labored breathing usually occurring in association with serious disease of the heart or lungs.

paroxysmal nocturnal d. (PND) Acute dyspnea occurring suddenly at night; caused by pulmonary congestion and edema, usually due to congestive heart failure.

dyspneic (disp-ne′ik) Relating to dyspnea.

dyspraxia (dis-prak′se-ah) Impaired ability to perform learned patterns of movement, usually due to a brain lesion.

dysproteinemia (dis-pro-tēn-e′me-ah) Any abnormality in blood proteins, especially immunoglobulins.

dysrhythmia (dis-rith′me-ah) A disturbance of the heart rhythm.

dyssomnia (dis-som′ne-ah) Any of a group of sleep disorders included in the International Classification of Sleep Disorders as *intrinsic* (e.g., narcolepsy, sleep apnea, restless leg syndrome), *extrinsic* (e.g., altitude insomnia, drug- or alcohol-dependent sleep disorders), and *circadian rhythm* sleep disorder (e.g., shift-work sleep disorder, jet-lag syndrome).

dysstasia (dis-sta′se-ah) Difficulty in standing.

dysstatic (dis-stat′ik) Relating to dysstasia.

dyssynergia (dis-sin-er′je-ah) Disturbance of muscular coordination.

detrusor-sphincter d. Disturbance of the normal coordination between bladder muscles during voiding efforts (i.e., between

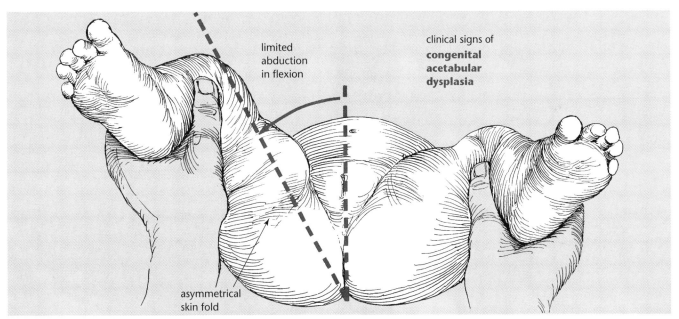

limited
abduction
in flexion

clinical signs of
**congenital
acetabular
dysplasia**

asymmetrical
skin fold

contraction of the detrusor muscle and relaxation of the urinary sphincter; instead, sphincter spasm occurs simultaneously with bladder contraction).

dystaxia (dis-tak′se-ah) A mild degree of ataxia.

dysthymia (dis-thi′me-ah) Chronic mild depression.

dystocia (dis-to′se-ah) Difficult childbirth.

fetal d. Difficult labor due to excessive fetal size, malposition, or multiple fetuses.

maternal d. Difficult labor caused by a variety of factors, including aberrations of pelvic architecture, soft-tissue abnormalities of the birth canal, tumors, aberrant location of the placenta, and ineffective uterine activity.

dystonia (dis-to′ne-ah) Abnormality of muscle tone.

cervical d. Asymmetric muscle spasms of the neck, causing turning or tilting movements and sustained abnormal postures of the head; may be accompanied by moderate head tremor and musculoskeletal pain. Spontaneous remission may occur. Also called spasmodic torticollis.

focal d. Dystonia usually affecting one area of the body; it occasionally affects two contiguous ones.

generalized d. A rare disorder that usually begins in childhood with a gait abnormality or with torticollis (wryneck), resulting in sustained, often bizarre postures. Also called torsion dystonia; dystonia musculorum deformans.

d. musculorum deformans See generalized dystonia.

occupational d. A focal dystonia marked by spasm of limited muscles precipitated by voluntary muscle contractions while performing skilled movements, such as writing or playing a musical instrument (writer′s cramp, musician′s cramp).

oromandibular d. Neurological disorder marked by continuous, bilateral, asynchronous spasms of muscles of the face, lower jaw, pharynx, tongue, and, in some severe cases, the neck, larynx, and respiratory system. Also called orofacial dyskinesia.

torsion d. See generalized dystonia.

dystonic (dis-ton′ik) Relating to dystonia.

dystopia (dis-to′pĕ-ah) Malposition; faulty position.

dystopic (dis-top′ik) Out of place.

dystrophin (dis-tro′fin) Protein present in normal muscle bound to the muscle membrane; it helps to maintain the integrity of the muscle fiber; in its absence, the muscle fiber degenerates. It is absent in muscles of people afflicted with Duchenne′s muscular dystrophy.

dystrophy (dis′tro-fe) Disorder caused by faulty nutrition or by lesions of the pituitary (hypophysis) and/or other parts of the brain.

adiposogenital d. Condition caused by lesions in the pituitary (hypophysis) and hypothalamus, characterized by increased body fat, especially about the abdomen, hips, and thighs, with underdeveloped genital organs and hair loss; often mistaken for obesity. Also called adiposogenital syndrome; Frohlich′s syndrome.

Becker′s muscular d. (BMD) Genetic disorder similar to Duchenne′s muscular dystrophy but much milder, occurring later in childhood and progressing at a much slower rate; some patients may remain ambulatory for many years; caused by mutations in the structural gene for the protein dystrophin; an X-linked recessive inheritance.

childhood muscular d. See Duchenne′s muscular dystrophy.

Duchenne′s muscular d. (DMD) Genetic disorder occurring as an X-linked recessive inheritance and affecting males almost exclusively; characterized by progressive muscle weakness that starts in the pelvic girdle and spreads rapidly, a swaying gait, frequent falls, and difficulty arising from the floor (the child usually "climbs up his legs"); deposits of fibrofatty tissue replace muscle fibers and may occupy a greater volume than the normal muscle (pseudohypertrophy); may also involve the heart muscle; manifestations of the disorder begin between three and five years of age; death usually occurs by the end of the second decade. The defective gene is in the short arm of the X chromosome. Also called childhood muscular dystrophy; pseudohypertrophic muscular dystrophy; Duchenne′s paralysis.

Fuchs′ endothelial d. An eye disorder secondary to spontaneous loss of endothelium of the central cornea; characterized by formation of epithelial blisters, reduced vision, and pain.

muscular d. (MD) Any of several genetic disorders that are characterized primarily by progressive deterioration of muscle fibers.

myotonic d. Genetic disorder, occurring as an autosomal dominant inheritance (genetic defect on chromosome 19); it typically becomes evident in the second to third decades of life with varying degrees of muscular involvement and severity; symptoms include stiffness and eventual atrophy of muscles, especially of the face and neck, associated with slurred speech and cataracts. Also called myotonia atrophica.

pseudohypertrophic muscular d. See Duchenne′s muscular dystrophy.

dysuria (dis-u′re-ah) Painful or difficult urination.

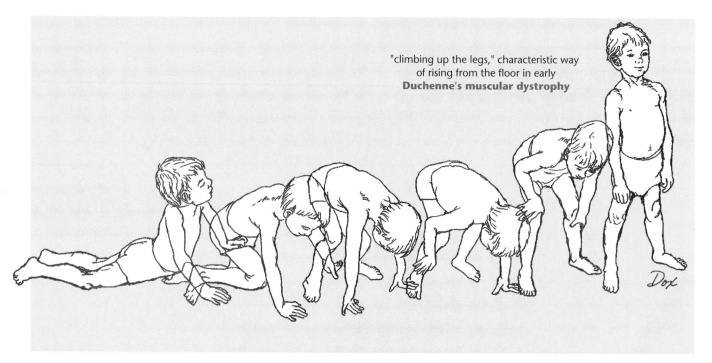

"climbing up the legs," characteristic way of rising from the floor in early **Duchenne's muscular dystrophy**

dystaxia ▪ dysuria

E

ear (ēr) The compound organ of hearing and equilibrium; it is sensitive to sound waves, to the effects of gravity, and to motion. The organ consists of the external ear, which includes the auricle (serves to collect the air vibrations) and the external auditory canal (serves to transmit the air vibrations to the eardrum); the middle ear cavity (serves to transmit the vibrations from the eardrum across the cavity to the inner ear by means of a chain of three movable bones known as ossicles); and the inner ear, which includes the cochlea, semicircular canals, and vestibule (serve to transmit the impulses to the brain via the vestibulocochlear nerve for interpretation).

aviator's e. See barotitis media.

bat e. See lop ear.

Blainville e.'s Auricles of the two external ears that are not symmetrical.

boxer's e. See cauliflower ear.

Cagot e. An external ear devoid of a lobe.

cat e. A deformed auricle that is folded downward on itself.

cauliflower e. A thickened auricle somewhat resembling a cauliflower, deformed by extravasation of blood and subsequent perichondritis due to repeated injuries. Also called boxer's ear.

Darwin's e. An auricle in which the upper border of the helix is not rolled over, but has an angular contour similar to those of some monkeys; some may also possess an eminence on the edge of the helix.

dead e. A thoroughly traumatized ear devoid of audiometric and caloric responses.

external e. The outer portion of the ear, composed of the auricle and the external auditory canal; it collects and transmits air vibrations to the eardrum (tympanic membrane). Also called outer ear.

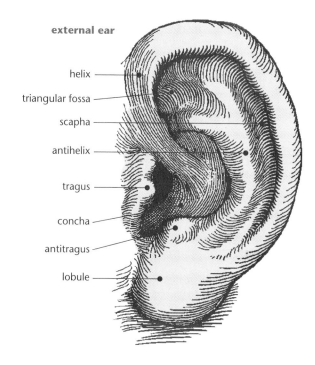

external ear

helix

triangular fossa

scapha

antihelix

tragus

concha

antitragus

lobule

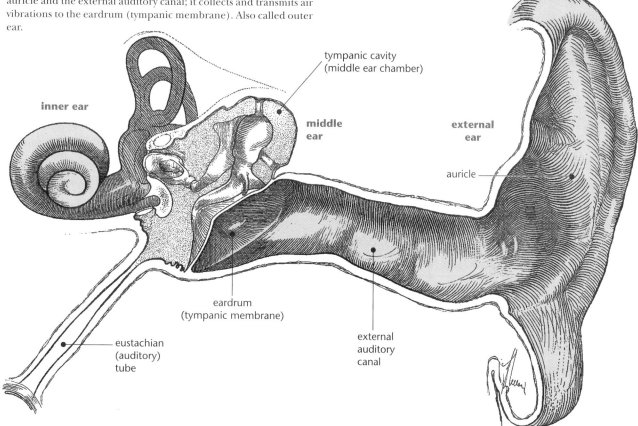

inner ear

middle ear

tympanic cavity (middle ear chamber)

external ear

auricle

eardrum (tympanic membrane)

external auditory canal

eustachian (auditory) tube

inner e. The innermost portion of the ear situated within the petrous portion of the temporal bone; it consists of the bony and membranous labyrinths of the cochlea, vestibule, and semicircular channels (canals and ducts) with the neurosensory apparatus for conduction of impulses to the brain. Also called internal ear.

internal e. See inner ear.

lop e. A developmental deformity of the ear in which the conchal portion of the auricle projects from the head at a right angle. Also called bat ear.

middle e. The air-filled chamber in the temporal bone extending from the eardrum (tympanic membrane) to the lateral wall of the inner ear and composed of the tympanic cavity, the bony chain of three ossicles, and mastoid appendages; the eustachian (auditory) tube opens into the chamber.

Morel e. An abnormally large auricle marked by diminished folds and grooves of the external ear with edges that are noticeably thinner than normal.

Mozart e. A congenitally abnormal auricle marked by fusion of the crura of the helix and antihelix, resulting in an outward bulging appearance of the top part of the auricle.

outer e. See external ear.

swimmer's e. See otitis externa.

Wildermuth's e. A congenitally abnormal auricle in which the antihelix forms the most prominent part of the external ear while the helix is deficient and turned back.

earache (ēr'āk) Pain in the ear. Also called otalgia.

eardrum (ēr'drum) See tympanic membrane, under membrane.

earth (erth) **1.** Soil. **2.** Any of the metallic elements characterized by easy oxidation.

diatomaceous e. A powder containing mostly silica (96%) obtained from the siliceous remains of aquatic plants (diatoms); used as a filtering agent and as an inert filler in many dental materials and as a mild abrasive and polishing agent.

fuller's e. A naturally occurring clay used in powder form as a dusting powder, or moistened with water as a poultice.

earth-eating (erth ēt'ing) See geophagia.

earwax (ēr'waks) See cerumen.

ebonation (e-bo-na'shun) Removal of loose bone fragments from an injury.

ebullism (eb'yu-lizm) Formation of water vapor in the tissues due to extreme reduction of barometric pressure, as occurs at altitudes above 60,000 feet.

ebur (e'bur) Ivory; applied to tissues resembling ivory superficially.

eburnation (e-bur-na'shun) Tranformation of bone into a shiny ivory-like substance; seen in certain diseases (e.g., osteoarthritis).

eburneous (e-bur'ne-us) Resembling ivory.

ec- Prefix meaning out of; away from.

eccentric (ek-sen'trik) **1.** Situated away from or proceeding from a center. **2.** Deviating from the established norm. **3.** A person who in any way deviates markedly from conventional conduct or speech, or who shows abnormal emotional reactions but has no intellectual defect.

eccentrochondroplasia (ek-sen-tro-kon-dro-pla'se-ah) Formation of bone tissue, especially of long bones, in areas other than the normal epiphyseal cartilage.

ecchondroma (ek-kon-dro'mah) A benign outgrowth of normally situated cartilage through the shaft of a bone.

ecchondrosis (ek-kon-dro'sis) Multiple ecchondromas.

ecchymoma (ek-ī-mo'mah) A slight blood-containing swelling caused by a bruise.

ecchymosis (ek-ī-mo'sis), pl. ecchymo'ses Bleeding within the skin, causing an area of bluish black discoloration.

e. of eyelid Injury commonly called black eye.

ecchymotic (ek-ī-mot'ik) Relating to ecchymosis.

eccrine (ek'rin) See exocrine.

eccrinology (ek-ri-nol'ŏ-je) The study of secretions and excretions.

eccrisis (ek'rī-sis) **1.** Excretion of waste products. **2.** Any waste product.

eccritic (ek-krit'ik) Any agent that promotes excretion of waste products.

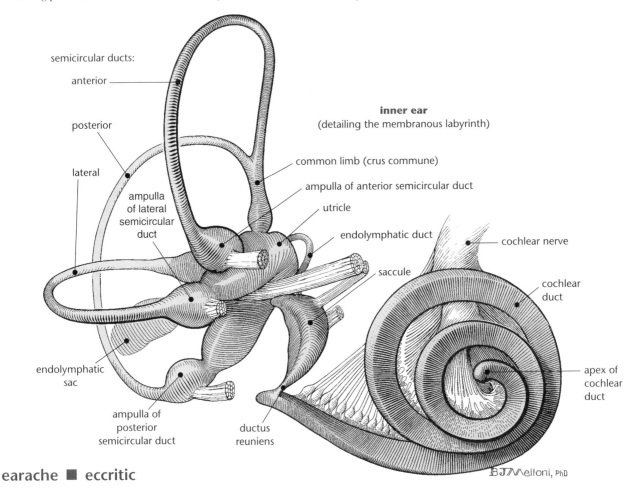

semicircular ducts:
anterior
posterior
lateral
ampulla of lateral semicircular duct
endolymphatic sac
ampulla of posterior semicircular duct
ductus reuniens
common limb (crus commune)
ampulla of anterior semicircular duct
utricle
endolymphatic duct
saccule
cochlear nerve
cochlear duct
apex of cochlear duct

inner ear
(detailing the membranous labyrinth)

BJMelloni, PhD

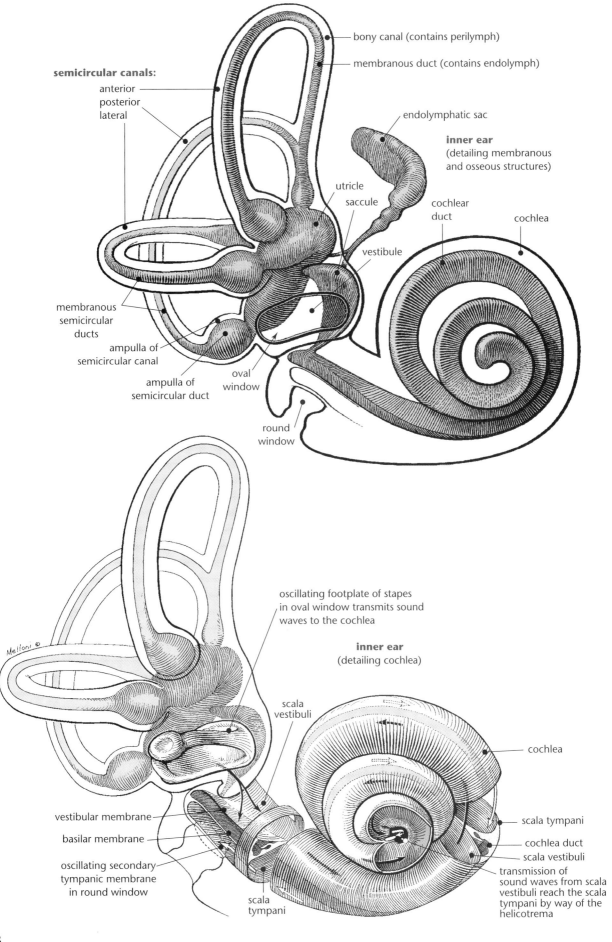

semicircular canals:
anterior
posterior
lateral

bony canal (contains perilymph)

membranous duct (contains endolymph)

endolymphatic sac

inner ear
(detailing membranous
and osseous structures)

utricle
saccule

cochlear
duct

cochlea

vestibule

membranous
semicircular
ducts

ampulla of
semicircular canal

ampulla of
semicircular duct

oval
window

round
window

Melloni ©

oscillating footplate of stapes
in oval window transmits sound
waves to the cochlea

inner ear
(detailing cochlea)

scala
vestibuli

cochlea

vestibular membrane

basilar membrane

scala tympani

cochlea duct

scala vestibuli

oscillating secondary
tympanic membrane
in round window

transmission of
sound waves from scala
vestibuli reach the scala
tympani by way of the
helicotrema

scala
tympani

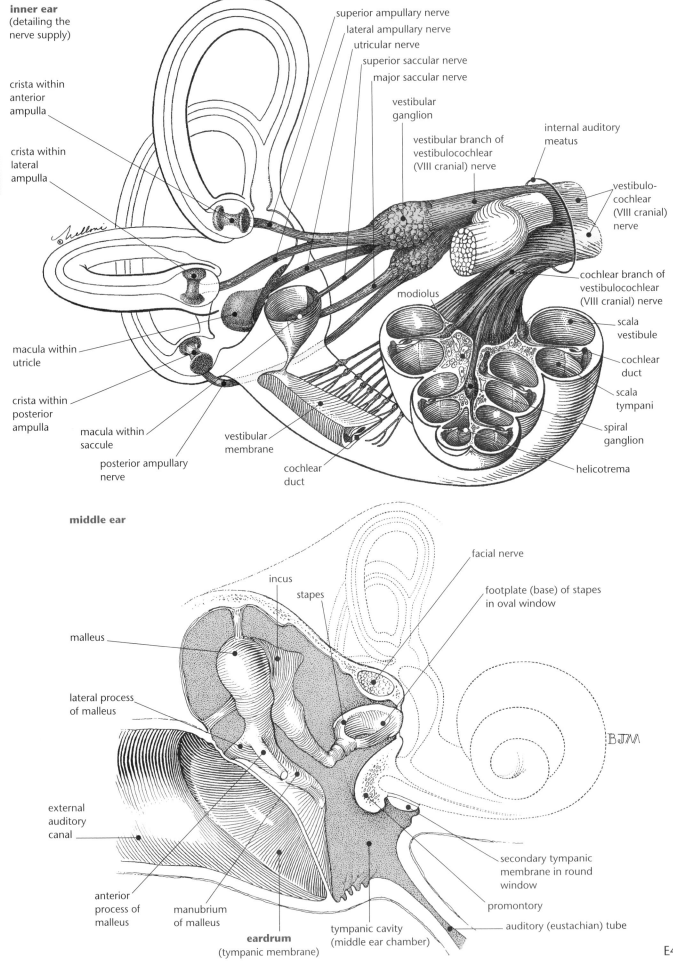

inner ear
(detailing the nerve supply)

crista within anterior ampulla

crista within lateral ampulla

macula within utricle

crista within posterior ampulla

macula within saccule

posterior ampullary nerve

vestibular membrane

cochlear duct

superior ampullary nerve

lateral ampullary nerve

utricular nerve

superior saccular nerve

major saccular nerve

vestibular ganglion

vestibular branch of vestibulocochlear (VIII cranial) nerve

internal auditory meatus

vestibulo-cochlear (VIII cranial) nerve

cochlear branch of vestibulocochlear (VIII cranial) nerve

modiolus

scala vestibule

cochlear duct

scala tympani

spiral ganglion

helicotrema

middle ear

incus

stapes

facial nerve

footplate (base) of stapes in oval window

malleus

lateral process of malleus

external auditory canal

anterior process of malleus

manubrium of malleus

eardrum
(tympanic membrane)

tympanic cavity (middle ear chamber)

secondary tympanic membrane in round window

promontory

auditory (eustachian) tube

E

E4

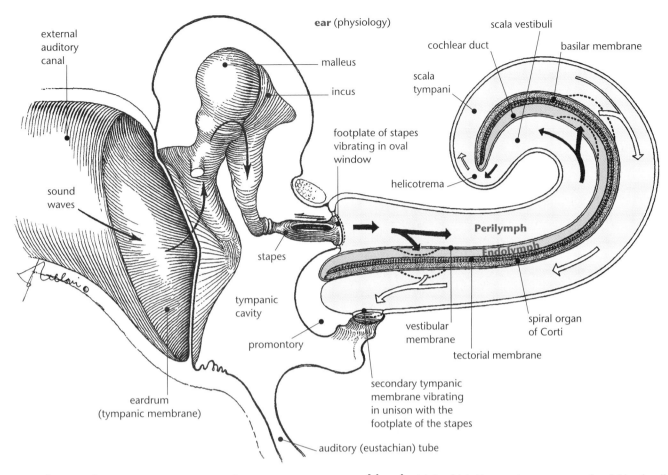

ear (physiology)

external auditory canal
malleus
incus
sound waves
footplate of stapes vibrating in oval window
stapes
helicotrema
scala tympani
scala vestibuli
cochlear duct
basilar membrane
Perilymph
Endolymph
tympanic cavity
promontory
vestibular membrane
tectorial membrane
spiral organ of Corti
eardrum (tympanic membrane)
secondary tympanic membrane vibrating in unison with the footplate of the stapes
auditory (eustachian) tube

eccyesis (ek-si-e′sis) See ectopic pregnancy, under pregnancy.

ecdemic (ek-dem′ik) Denoting a disease that is brought in from another region; not endemic.

echidnine (e-kid′nin) The toxic principle in viper venom.

echino-, echin- Combining forms meaning prickly; spiny.

echinococcosis (e-ki-no-kok-o′sis) Infection with larva of the tapeworm *Echinococcus granulosus,* or *Echinococcus multilocularis,* which produces expanding cysts especially in the liver and lungs; anaphylactic reaction may occur when cysts rupture and fluid escapes into the peritoneal cavity or pleura. Also called hydatid disease.

Echinococcus (e-ki-no-kok′us) A genus of small tapeworms; the adult forms live in the intestines of dogs and other mammals; the larvae infect humans, forming hydatid cysts in the liver and other organs.

echinocyte (e-ki′no-sīt) An abnormally shaped red blood cell with evenly distributed, regularly shaped spiny projections; seen in uremia. Also called burr cell.

echinosis (ek-ī-no′sis) Abnormal appearance of red blood cells; they resemble sea urchins.

Echinostoma (ek-ī-nos′to-mah) A genus of flukes with a characteristic collar of spines, widely distributed in Southeast Asia; some species cause diarrhea in humans.

echinulate (e-kin′u-lāt) Having small spines; applied to certain bacterial colonies.

echocardiogram (ek-o-kar′de-o-gram) A graphic display produced by recording the echoes returned from the heart after the application of ultrasonic impulses; the ultrasound image of the heart.

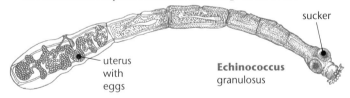

sucker
uterus with eggs
Echinococcus granulosus

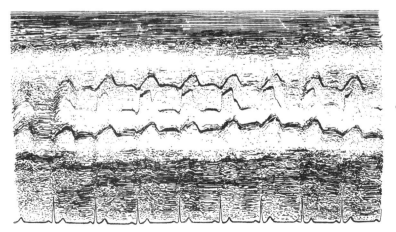

echocardiogram

echocardiography (ek-o-kar-de-og′rah-fe) The placing of an ultrasonic device on the chest wall to send sound impulses toward the walls of the heart, which in turn bounce or echo the sounds back; the patterns produced are graphically displayed for interpretation; used for determining the movement patterns of the heart and its valves, chamber size, wall thickness, and the presence of pericardial fluid.

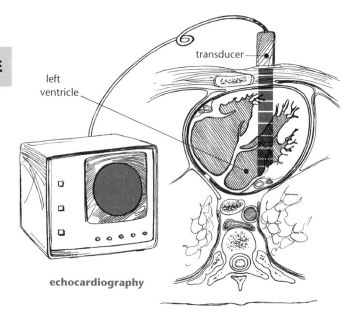

echocardiography

   cross-sectional e. See two-dimensional echocardiography.
   Doppler e. Measurement of blood flow within the heart using a motion-mode (M-mode) and two-dimensional echocardiogram while simultaneously recording the audible Doppler signals (e.g., direction, velocity, intensity, amplitude) reflected from the moving column of red blood cells.
   two-dimensional e. Technique in which the ultrasound beam rapidly moves through an arc, producing a cross-sectional or fan-shaped image of heart structures. Also called cross-sectional echocardiography.
echoencephalogram (ek-o-en-sef′ah-lo-gram) The record produced by echoencephalography.
echoencephalography (ek-o-en-sef′ah-log′rah-fe) A method of examining the brain by recording reflections (echoes) of ultrasound waves; used for estimating the position of the midline of the third ventricle; useful in evaluating patients with suspected subdural or epidural hemorrhage or other conditions that might cause the brain to shift its position. It has been superseded by computerized tomography scan (CT) and by magnetic resonance imaging (MRI).
echogenic (ek-o-jen′ik) Generating reflections (echoes) of ultrasound waves.
echogram (ek′o-gram) See ultrasonogram.
echograph (ek′o-graf) See ultrasonograph.
echography (ĕ-kog′rah-fe) See ultrasonography.
echokinesis (ek-o-ki-ne′sis) See echopraxia.
echolalia (ek-o-la′le-ah) A meaningless, echolike repetition of words or phrases, often uttered with a mumbling or staccato intonation; distinct from habitual repetition of questions before formulating an answer. Also called echophrasia.
echopathy (ĕ-kop′ah-the) A syndrome marked by the senseless repetition of speech (echolalia) or initiation of gestures or postures (echopraxia) of others; may occur during the catatonic phase of schizophrenia.
echophrasia (ek-o-fra′se-ah) See echolalia.
echopraxia (ek-o-prak′se-ah) The senseless imitation of the gestures and postures of another, sometimes seen in catatonic schizophrenia. Also called echokinesis.

echovirus (ek-o-vi′rus) Any of a group of viruses isolated from humans and originally thought not to be associated with disease; now several serotypes have been found to cause meningitis, diarrhea, and respiratory disease. Also written ECHO (acronym of original name, enteric cytopathic human orphan) virus.
   e. 6 An echovirus that has caused outbreaks of aseptic meningitis in children and adults.
   e. 9 A strain associated with outbreaks of aseptic meningitis.
eclampsia (ĕ-klamp′se-ah) An acute disorder occurring in pregnant and puerperal women, representing a progression of preeclampsia; characterized by one or more convulsions (seizures); there are no warning signs (aura). Seizure-induced complications may include pulmonary edema and retinal detachment. Fever is a bad prognostic sign. Eclamptic seizures occur most commonly before delivery, usually after the 20th week of gestation; most postpartum episodes occur in the first 48 hours after delivery, but may occur as late as 6 weeks.
   puerperal e. Eclampsia occurring after childbirth.
eclamptic (ĕ-klamp′tik) Relating to eclampsia.
eclamptogenic (ĕ-klamp-to-jen′ik) Causing eclampsia.
ecmnesia (ek-ne′ze-ah) Forgetfulness.
eco- Combining form meaning environment.
ecology (e-kol′o-je) The study of the relationship between living organisms and their environment.
econazole (ĕ-kon′ah-zōl) An antifungal agent effective against athlete's foot (tinea pedis) and other similar infections.
economy (e-kon′o-me) The functional arrangement of body structures.
Eco RI A bacterial enzyme that helps to protect genetic material against viral attack. It is used by genetic engineers to slice chromosomes at precise locations.
ecosystem (ek-o-sis′tem) A community of living organisms and its physical environment considered together as an entity.
ecotaxis (ek′o-tak-sis) Migration of lymphocytes from the thymus and bone marrow to other tissues that provide an appropriate microenvironment.
ecstasy, MDMA (ek′stah-se) Popular name for 3,4-methylenedioxy-methamphetamine, a hallucinogenic drug of abuse; it produces euphoria followed by depression and difficulty in concentration.
ectad (ek′tad) Directed outward; from the inside toward the periphery.
ectal (ek′tal) Outer; superficial.
-ectasia, -ectasis Combining forms meaning a stretching out (e.g., dacryocystectasia, desmectasis).

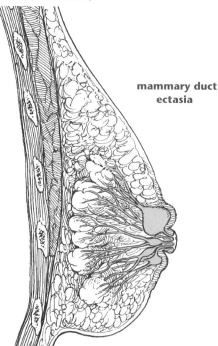

mammary duct ectasia

ectasia, ectasis (ek-ta′ze-ah, ek′tah-sis) Dilatation of a tubular structure.

　corneal e. See keratectasia.

　mammary duct e. A breast condition affecting multiparous women 50 to 60 years of age; characterized by thickening (inspissation) of secretions within major excretory ducts, duct dilatation, and periductal inflammation; the condition may superficially resemble cancer of the breast.

　vascular e. A collection of abnormally prominent capillaries, arterioles, or venules in skin or mucous membranes.

ectatic (ek-tat′ik) Relating to ectasia.

ecthyma (ek-thi′mah) A pus-forming skin infection characterized by an eruption of pustules with superficial crusting and underlying ulcerations, which leave scars upon healing; caused by staphylococci.

　contagious e. See orf.

ectiris (ek-ti′ris) The outer layer of the iris.

ecto- Prefix meaning on the outside.

ectoantigen (ek-to-an′te-jen) Any molecule inciting antibody production that is separate or separable from its source. Also called exoantigen.

ectoblast (ek′to-blast) See ectoderm.

ectocardia (ek-to-kar′de-ah) Abnormal position of the heart.

ectocervical (ek-to-ser′vĭ-kal) Relating to the vaginal portion of the uterine cervix.

ectocervix (ek-to-ser′viks) The lowest portion of the uterine cervix that extends into the lumen of the vagina.

ectochoroidea (ek-to-ko-roi′de-ah) The outer part of the choroid layer of the eyeball.

ectocornea (ek-to-kor′ne-ah) The anterior or outer epithelium of the cornea.

ectocyst (ek′to-sist) The outer membrane of a hydatid cyst.

ectoderm (ek′to-derm) The outermost of three germ layers of the embryo; it gives rise mainly to the nervous system and to the skin and its derivatives (e.g., hair, lens of the eye). Sometimes called ectoblast.

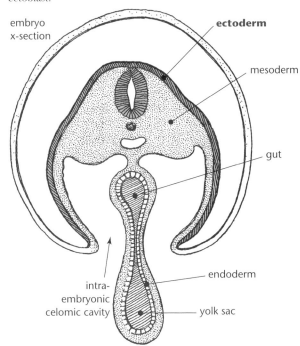

embryo x-section

ectoderm

mesoderm

gut

endoderm

intra-embryonic celomic cavity

yolk sac

ectodermal, ectodermic (ek-to-der′mal, ek-to-der′mik) Relating to the ectoderm.

ectodermatosis (ek-to-der-mah-to′sis) See ectodermosis.

ectodermosis (ek-to-der-mo′sis) Any disorder of a tissue derived from the ectoderm (e.g., skin, neural tissues). Also called ectodermatosis.

ectogenous (ek-toj′ĕ-nus) See exogenous.

ectohormone (ek-to-hor′mōn) A substance that is secreted by an organism (mostly an invertebrate) into its immediate environment and which modifies the functional activity of some distant organism; it is a chemical mediator of ecological importance.

ectomere (ek′to-mēr) Any of the cells derived from division of the fertilized ovum that participates in the formation of the ectoderm.

ectomorph (ek′to-morf) A person with a body-type configuration in which the limbs predominate over the trunk and muscles and body are thin.

ectomorphic (ek-to-mor′fik) Relating to the body type of an ectomorph.

-ectomy Combining form meaning removal (appendectomy).

ectoparasite (ek-to-par′ah-sit) A parasite inhabiting the surface of the host body.

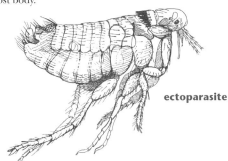

ectoparasite

ectopia (ek-to′pe-ah) **1.** Congenital displacement of a body part. Also called ectopy. **2.** In cardiology, a state in which heartbeats originate at some point in the heart other than the sinoatrial node (ectopic heartbeats).

　e. cordis Protrusion of the heart through an abnormal opening in the breastbone (sternum).

　e. lentis See dislocation of lens, under dislocation.

　e. testis See ectopic testis, under testis.

　e. vesicae See exstrophy of bladder, under exstrophy.

ectopic (ek-top′ik) **1.** The occurrence of a structurally normal tissue or organ in an abnormal location. Also called heterotopic. **2.** Arising from a site other than normal (e.g., a heartbeat).

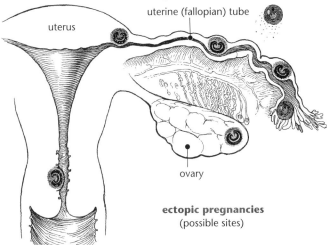

uterine (fallopian) tube

uterus

ovary

ectopic pregnancies (possible sites)

ectoplacental (ek-to-plah-sen′tal) Outside of, or adjacent to, the placenta.

ectoplasm (ek′to-plazm) The clear, thin cytoplasm at the periphery of a cell.

ectopy (ek′to-pe) Ectopia.

ectostosis (ek-to-sto′sis) Formation of bone beneath the perichondrium or the periosteum.

ectothrix (ek′to-thriks) A fungus that infests hair and produces spores on the surface of the hair shaft (e.g., *Microsporum audouinii*).

ectotoxin (ek-to-tok′sin) See exotoxin.

ectozoon (ek-to-zo′on) Any parasitic animal living on the surface of a host.

ectro- Combining form meaning congenital absence.

ectrodactyly (ek-tro-dak′tĭ-le) Congenital absence of fingers and toes.

ectrogeny (ek-troj′ĕ-ne) Congenital absence of a body part.

ectromelia (ek-tro-me′le-ah) Congenital absence of one or more limbs.

ectropion (ek-tro′pe-on) Eversion of an eyelid.

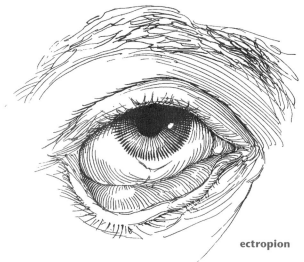

ectropion

ectrosyndactyly (ek-tro-sin-dak′tĭ-le) Congenital absence of one or more digits and the fusion of the rest.

eczema (ek′zĕ-mah) General term for a group of acute or chronic, noncontagious skin conditions characterized by redness and thickening of the skin, sometimes accompanied by itching and formation of papules, vesicles, and crusts.

    allergic e. Eczema occurring as an allergic reaction, sometimes seen as an occupational condition.

    atopic e. See atopic dermatitis, under dermatitis.

    e. herpeticum A widespread viral eruption of ulcerating vesicles accompanied by fever, occurring five to seven days after exposure to the herpesvirus 1 (HSV-1); most commonly acquired by people with atopic dermatitis (particularly during flare-ups) and those with suppressed or deficient immune systems (including AIDS patients). Complications may include secondary skin infection, pneumonia, and central nervous system infection.

    e. madidans A moist eruption. Commonly called weeping eczema.

    e. marginatum See tinea cruris.

    nummular e. A coin-shaped vesicular eruption usually affecting the extensor surfaces of the hands, arms, and legs.

    pustular e. A secondary infection of a vesicular eruption, usually caused by staphylococci.

    e. rubrum An eruption of red, excoriated, oozing lesions.

    stasis e. Eczema of the legs, frequently with ulceration, caused by impaired circulation.

    e. vaccinatum A vesicular eruption caused by the vaccinia virus, frequently occurring as a superimposed infection in patients with atopic dermatitis.

    weeping e. See eczema madidans.

    winter e. Dry scaling of the skin caused by evaporation of surface moisture.

eczematous (ek-zem′ah-tus) Marked by or resembling eczema.

edema (ĕ-de′mah) Soft tissue swelling due to collection of fluid in the intercellular spaces.

    angioneurotic e. See angioedema.

    Berlin's traumatic e. Edema of the macular area of the retina at the back of the eye, caused by a severe blow to the front of the eye. Also called concussion edema; commotio retinae.

    cardiac e. Edema caused by heart disease with resulting increase in venous pressures.

    cerebral e. Edema of the brain; may be caused by tumors,

infarction, abscesses, concussions, certain toxic conditions, or an obstruction in the cerebrospinal fluid circulation.

    concussion e. See Berlin's traumatic edema.

    dependent e. Subcutaneous edema localized in dependent areas, especially the feet, ankles, and lower legs (when the person is upright).

    generalized e. Edema of most or all regions of the body usually caused by heart, kidney, or liver disease; may also be caused by drugs (e.g., steroids, estrogen, vasodilators), pregnancy, or starvation.

    hereditary angioneurotic e. (HANE) A condition inherited as an autosomal dominant trait, characterized by recurrent attacks of angioedema with involvement of the gastrointestinal tract and the larynx; due to deficiency of C1 esterase inhibitor or to an inactive form of the inhibitor.

    high-altitude pulmonary e. (HAPE) A form of mountain sickness manifested by pulmonary edema appearing within 48 hours after rapid ascent to a high altitude (over 8000 feet).

    menstrual e. Water retention during or just prior to menstruation.

    nutritional e. Edema caused by prolonged dietary deficiency, at least in part by low levels of protein in the blood.

    pitting e. Edema characterized by prolonged persistence of indentations made by finger pressure on the edematous part.

    pulmonary e. Escape of fluid into the air sacs (alveoli) and intercellular spaces of the lungs; causes include left ventricular failure (left-sided heart failure), narrowing of the mitral valve (mitral stenosis), and chemicals that are pulmonary toxins.

edematous (ĕ-dem′ah-tus) Characterized by edema.

edentulous, edentate (e-den′tu-lus, e-den′tāt) Toothless.

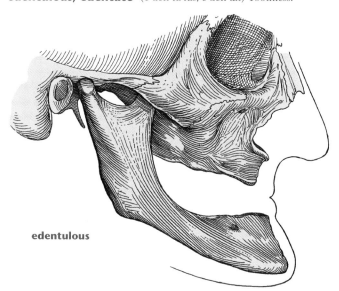

edentulous

edge (ej) A margin or border.

    denture e. See denture border, under border.

educt (e′dukt) An extract.

effect (e-fekt′) The result of an action.

    additive e. The combined effects of two or more drugs, acting simultaneously, which elicit the same overt response by the same mechanism of action, the total being equal to that expended by simple addition.

    adverse e. A deleterious secondary response or side effect to the normal dose of a drug.

    Bohr e. The lowering of blood affinity for oxygen evoked by carbon dioxide (CO_2); i.e., CO_2 in the tissues facilitates release of oxygen from the blood pigment hemoglobin, resulting in a greater availability of oxygen to tissues.

    ceiling e. The maximum intensity of a specific effect that can be produced in the body by a given drug, regardless of how large a dose is administered.

clasp-knife e. See clasp-knife spasticity, under spasticity.

Compton e. The scattering of an x-ray or gamma-ray photon upon impact with a peripheral electron within an atom, with resulting transfer of the photon's energy to the electron.

cumulative e. Increased intensity of a drug apparent only after a number of doses have been given and the rate of intake is greater than the rate of elimination. Also called cumulative action.

cytopathic e. A degenerative change in cells, such as that produced by a virus infection.

Doppler e. The apparent change in frequency of sound or light waves when the observer and the source are in relative motion; the frequency increases when they approach one another and decreases when they move away. Also called Doppler phenomenon.

Haldane e. Hemoglobin's affinity for carbon dioxide diminishes with its oxygenation.

Pasteur e. The slowing down of fermentation by oxygen.

rebound e. A reaction to a drug frequently experienced by substance abusers; it is the opposite of the original drug effect and occurs when the sought-after effect wears off (e.g., stimulant drugs produce lethargy and fatigue; depressant drugs produce anxiety, irritability, and nervousness). Although rebound effects eventually subside, in some instances drug users react to the rebound experience by taking more of the drug to reverse the discomfort; the rebound effect is thus relieved to some extent, but this effect also wears off, and the subsequent rebound is usually more severe than the previous one. A similar effect may be seen in persons taking topical decongestants (nose drops) for several days; the duration of decongestant effect becomes increasingly shorter and the tissue becomes quite engorged when the effect wears off.

side e. A result or consequence other than that for which a drug or therapy is administered; the term applies to an additional or secondary effect and usually (although not always) refers to an undesirable or adverse result. It is not applied to the toxic consequences of a drug overdose.

toxic e. An effect of a drug on a living organism that is harmful to the well-being or life of the organism.

effectiveness (ĕ-fek′tiv-nes) The extent to which a drug, procedure, regimen, or specific intervention does what it is intended to do for a defined population.

effector (ef-fek′tor) A tissue that reacts to a nerve impulse (e.g., a muscular contraction or a glandular secretion).

efferent (ef′er-ent) Conveying something away from a center (e.g., a nerve impulse, blood, or lymph).

effervesce (ef-er-ves′) To produce gas in a liquid in the form of small bubbles.

effervescent (ef-er-ves′ent) Bubbling; producing effervescence.

efficacy (ef′ĭ-kah-se) The extent to which a drug, procedure, regimen, or specific intervention produces a beneficial effect.

efficiency (e-fish′en-se) The ability to achieve a desired effect or end result with a minimum of unnecessary effort; competency.

visual e. A rating used in determining compensation for eye injuries based on measurable functions of central acuity, field vision, and eye motility.

effloresce (ef-lo-res′) To lose water and become powdery upon exposure to dry air.

efflorescent (ef-lo-res′ent) Having a tendency to effloresce.

effluvium (ef-floo′ve-um) A shedding (e.g., of hair).

effuse (ĕ-fūs′) Thinly spread; applied to a bacterial culture.

effusion (ĕ-fu′zhun) **1.** Escape of fluid into a body space or cavity (e.g., pleural, pericardial, or joint cavities). **2.** The fluid effused.

chronic middle ear e. Persistent accumulation of fluid in the middle ear chamber, usually seen in children, often accompanied by enlarged adenoids.

pleural e. Fluid appearing in the space surrounding the lung; if large it may impede respiration; causes include congestive heart failure (which more commonly begins first as a right-sided effusion), infection (e.g., pneumonia, tuberculosis), or tumor involving the pleural surface. An infected effusion may develop into empyema.

egg (eg) See ovum.

fertilized e. See zygote.

ego (e′go) In psychoanalytic theory, the part of the psychic apparatus that serves an executive function, mediates among the id, the superego, and external reality, and enables self-awareness, adaptation to reality, and motor control.

egocentric (e-go-sen′trik) Marked by constant or extreme concern for one's own interests; self-centered.

ego-dystonic (e-go dis-ton′ik) Denoting ideas or impulses that are unacceptable to the ego; ego-alien; the opposite of ego-syntonic.

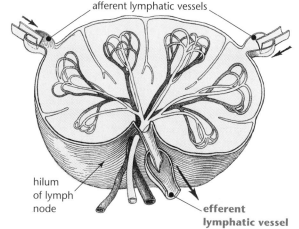

afferent lymphatic vessels

hilum of lymph node

efferent lymphatic vessel

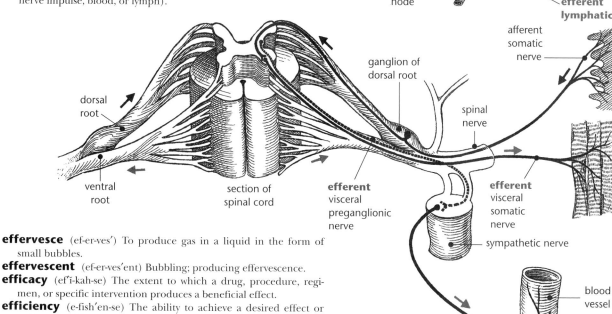

dorsal root

ventral root

section of spinal cord

ganglion of dorsal root

spinal nerve

efferent visceral preganglionic nerve

sympathetic nerve

afferent somatic nerve

efferent visceral somatic nerve

blood vessel

egomania (e-go-ma′ne-ah) Pathologic preoccupation with one's self.

egophony (e-gof′o-ne) An abnormal bleating, nasal quality of the voice heard on auscultation over an area of pleural effusion or an area of lung consolidation.

ego-syntonic (e-go-sin-ton′ik) Denoting ideas or impulses that are acceptable to the ego; the opposite of ego-dystonic.

Ehrlichia (ār-lik′e-ah) A genus of small, round or ovoid bacteria (family Rickettsiaceae) transmitted by ticks and causing diseases in humans and some domestic mammals.

    E. canis A species infecting dogs.

    E. chaffeensis The species causing human ehrlichiosis.

    E. sennetsu A species infecting humans.

ehrlichiosis (ār-lik-e-o′sis) A tick-borne rickettsial disease, caused by *Ehrlichia chaffeensis;* it shares features with other rickettsial diseases, such as Rocky Mountain spotted fever, and is most frequently seen in southeastern and southwestern regions of the United States; usually it is an acute, self-limited febrile illness, characterized by fever, chills, malaise, headache, muscle pain, and a rash, without evidence of shock or multisystem organ failure. Occasionally, ehrlichiosis can occur as a severe, life-threatening illness that may resemble toxic shock syndrome, involving at least three organ systems.

eicosanoid (i-ko′sah-noid) Any of the unsaturated fatty acids derived from arachidonic acid; the physiologically important compounds include the prostaglandins, leukotrienes, and thromboxanes.

eikonometer (i-ko-nom′ĕ-ter) Instrument for measuring the difference in sizes of the images seen by the two eyes in aniseikonia.

einsteinium (īn-sti′ne-um) A synthetic radioactive element; symbol Es, atomic number 99, atomic weight (of the longest-lived isotope) 254.

ejaculate (e-jak′u-lāt) **1.** To discharge suddenly, especially semen. **2.** The material so discharged. Also called ejaculum.

ejaculation (e-jak-u-la′shun) The propulsion of semen out of the urethra at orgasm.

    inhibited e. A rare condition in which erection is normal (or prolonged) but ejaculation does not occur.

    premature e. Discharge of the semen prior to or immediately upon engaging in sexual intercourse.

    retrograde e. Condition in which semen is forced backward into the bladder due to failure of the sphincter muscle of the bladder to close at orgasm; may result from neurological disease, a surgical operation upon the neck of the bladder and prostatic urethra, or certain antihypertensive medications.

ejaculatory (e-jak′u-lah-to-re) Relating to ejaculation.

ejaculum (e-jak′u-lum) See ejaculate.

ejector (e-jek′tor) Any device for removing any substance forcefully.

    saliva e. A perforated tube used in dentistry for suctioning fluids from the mouth. Also called dental suction pump.

elastance (e-las′tans) A measure of the ability of a structure (e.g., bladder, lungs) to return to its original dimensions after the deforming factor (i.e., urine or air) is removed.

elastic (e-las′tik) **1.** Capable of being stretched, bent, or deformed in any way and then returned to original form. **2.** A rubber or plastic band used in orthodontics to apply pressure to the teeth.

    intermaxillary e. Material, such as a rubber band, connecting orthodontic appliances on the upper and lower jaws to apply traction and thereby causing tooth movement as the jaws open and close.

elastica (e-las′tĭ-kah) General term for elastic tissues (e.g., in the wall of an artery).

elasticin (e-las′tĭ-sin) See elastin.

elasticity (e-las-tis′ĭ-te) The condition of being elastic.

elastin (e-las′tin) A yellow scleroprotein that is the major component of elastic fibers, which allows them to stretch about 1 1/2 times their original length. Also called elasticin.

elastoma (e-las-to′mah) See pseudoxanthoma elasticum.

elastometer (e-las-tom′ĕ-ter) Device for measuring the elasticity of body tissues.

elastosis (e-las-to′sis) **1.** Degeneration of elastic tissue. **2.** Degeneration of collagen fibers.

    e. dystrophica A manifestation of pseudoxanthoma elasticum characterized by streaking of the retina due to degeneration of the basal lamina of the choroid.

elbow (el′bo) The joint between the arm and the forearm.

    bend of the e. See cubital fossa, under fossa.

    miner's e. See olecranon bursitis, under bursitis.

    nursemaid's e. Popular term for a partial dislocation (subluxation) of the head of the radius in which the radial head slips under the annular ligament at the elbow joint, with the ligament remaining intact; it is a common injury of infants and young children (under four years old) as a result of being suddenly pulled or lifted by the arm or hand. The injury is difficult or impossible to see in x-ray pictures because the radial head may not be ossified. Also called pulled elbow.

    point of the e. See olecranon.

    pulled e. See nursemaid's elbow.

    student's e. See olecranon bursitis, under bursitis.

    tennis e. See lateral humeral epicondylitis, under epicondylitis.

    tip of the e. See olecranon.

elective (e-lek′tiv) Nonurgent; applied especially to surgical procedures that, although advisable, do not pose imminent problems to the health of the patient.

electroacupuncture (e-lek-tro-ak-u-pung′cher) A type of acupuncture using low-frequency electrically stimulated needles to produce analgesia or anesthesia.

electroanesthesia (e-lek-tro-an-es-the′ze-ah) Anesthesia brought about by an electric current.

electrocardiogram (e-lek-tro-kar′de-o-gram) (ECG, EKG) A graphic record of the variations in voltage produced by the heart muscle during the different phases of the cardiac cycle, made with an electrocardiograph.

electrocardiogram (ECG)

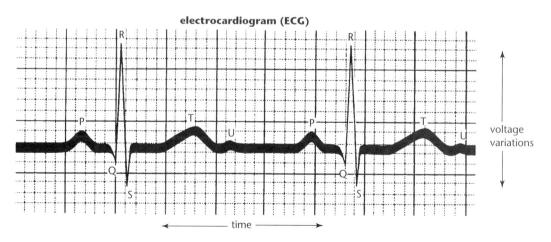

voltage variations

time

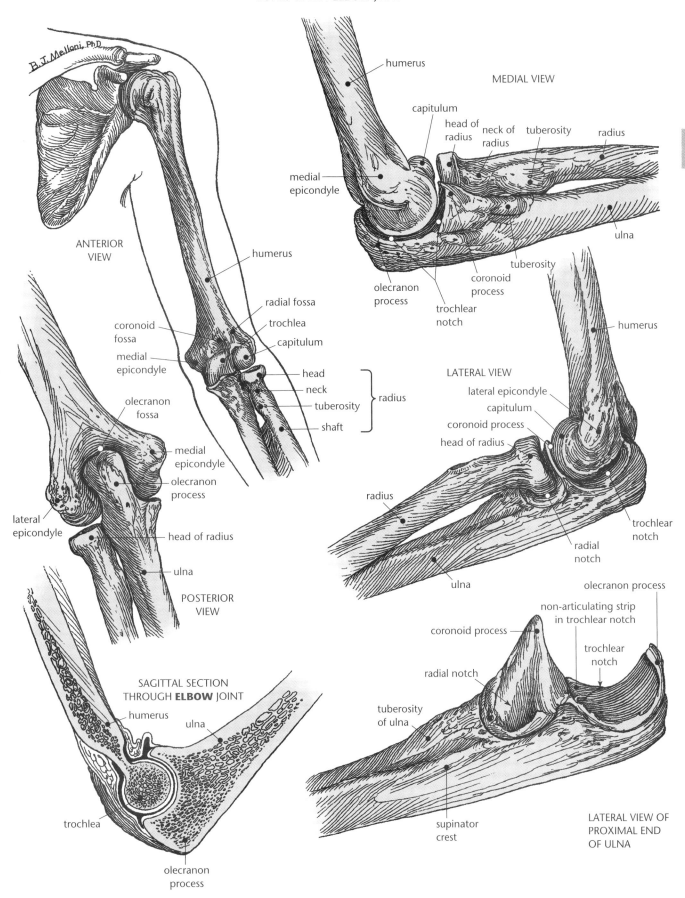

B.J. Melloni, Ph.D.

E

MEDIAL VIEW

humerus

capitulum

head of radius

neck of radius

tuberosity

radius

medial epicondyle

ulna

olecranon process

coronoid process

tuberosity

trochlear notch

ANTERIOR VIEW

humerus

radial fossa

trochlea

capitulum

coronoid fossa

head

medial epicondyle

neck

tuberosity

radius

shaft

olecranon fossa

LATERAL VIEW

lateral epicondyle

capitulum

coronoid process

head of radius

radius

medial epicondyle

olecranon process

head of radius

lateral epicondyle

trochlear notch

radial notch

ulna

POSTERIOR VIEW

ulna

olecranon process

non-articulating strip in trochlear notch

coronoid process

trochlear notch

SAGITTAL SECTION THROUGH **ELBOW** JOINT

humerus

ulna

radial notch

tuberosity of ulna

trochlea

supinator crest

LATERAL VIEW OF PROXIMAL END OF ULNA

olecranon process

electrocardiograph (e-lek-tro-kar′de-o-graf) Instrument for making an electrocardiogram.

electrocardiography (e-lek-tro-kar′de-og′rah-fe) A method of recording the conduction, magnitude, and duration of the electric current generated by the activity of the heart muscle.

    fetal e. Electrocardiography of a fetus while in the uterus.

electrocauterization (e-lek-tro-kaw′ter-ī-za′shun) See electrocoagulation.

electrocautery (e-lek-tro-kaw′ter-e) See electrocoagulation.

electrochemistry (e-lek-tro-kem′is-tre) The science of chemical reactions produced by electricity.

electrocoagulation (e-lek-tro-ko-ag-u-la′shun) The delivery of high-frequency electric current to a tissue through a fine needle, wire, or cutting instrument; may be used to seal blood vessels (thereby stop bleeding), to eradicate spider nevi and other cutaneous abnormalities of blood vessels, or to remove tumors and other diseased tissue. Also called electrocauterization; electrocautery.

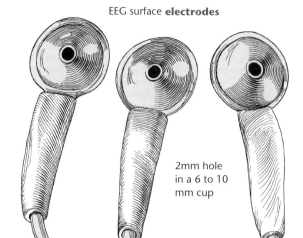

EEG surface **electrodes**

2mm hole in a 6 to 10 mm cup

electrocoagulation
(bipolar)

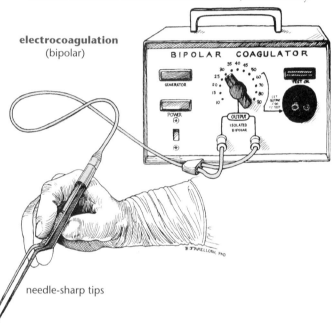

needle-sharp tips

ECG wrist-clip **electrode** placed on patient's wrist to record ECG signals, usually during electroencephalographic (EEG) testing

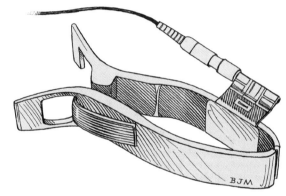

electrocontractility (e-lek-tro-kon-trak-til′ĭ-te) The capacity of muscle to contract in response to an electric stimulus.

electroconvulsive (e-lek-tro-kon-vul′siv) Inducing convulsions by means of electric current.

electrocorticogram (e-lek-tro-kor′tĭ-ko-gram) A record of electrical activity of the brain during surgery, obtained by applying electrodes directly on the cerebral cortex.

electrocute (e-lek′tro-kūt) To cause death by passing a high-voltage electric current through the body.

electrode (e-lek′trōd) A conductor of electricity through which a current enters or leaves a medium.

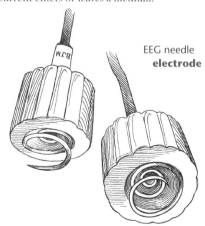

EEG needle **electrode**

stainless steel helical needle penetrates the scalp and becomes self-retained during surgical procedure

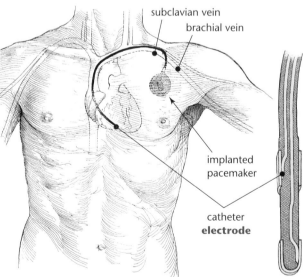

subclavian vein

brachial vein

implanted pacemaker

catheter **electrode**

    central terminal e. In electrocardiography, one in which wire connections from the two arms and left leg are fastened together and connected to the electroencephalogram to form the indifferent electrode.

    exploring e. In electroencephalography, an electrode that is placed on the chest near the heart area and paired with an indifferent electrode.

    glass e. A thin-walled glass bulb containing a platinum wire, a standard buffer solution, and quinhydrone; used in determining hydrogen ion (pH) concentrations.

indifferent e. In electrocardiography, an electrode that has multiple terminals.

electrodesiccation (e-lek-tro-des-ĭ-ka′shun) Destruction of tissue by dehydration with an electric current passed through a needle electrode; used in the treatment of cervical erosion, early cervical cancer, and warts.

electrodiagnosis (e-lek-tro-di-ag-no′sis) Diagnosis of certain disorders by recording the spontaneous electrical activity of tissues, or by the response to stimulation of electrically excitable tissues.

electrodialysis (e-lek-tro-di-al′ĭ-sis) Dialysis in which an electric field is applied across the semipermeable dialysis membrane, used especially to separate electrolytes.

electroejaculation (e-lek-tro-e-jak-u-la′shun) A method of treating male infertility in men with spinal cord injuries or those who have had retroperitoneal lymph node surgery; a semen sample is obtained for artificial insemination by stimulating the postganglionic sympathetic nerves (supplying the prostate and seminal vesicles) with an electric current delivered through a rectal probe.

electroencephalogram (e-lek-tro-en-sef′ah-lo-gram) (EEG) A graphic record of the electrical activity of the brain obtained with an electroencephalograph.

electroencephalograms (EEGs)

frontal-central

central-occipital

frontal-temporal

temporal-occipital

50 μV
1 second

electroencephalograph (e-lek-tro-en-sef′ah-lo-graf) An instrument used in electroencephalography; it receives, amplifies, and records graphically as brain waves the electrical events beneath and between two electrodes placed on the scalp.

electroencephalography (e-lek-tro-en-sef′ah-log′rah-fe) The recording of the electric currents generated by the activity of the brain, especially the cerebral cortex, by means of the electroencephalograph.

electroexcision (e-lek-tro-ek-sĭ′zhun) Surgical removal of tissue by electrical means.

electrogram (e-lek′tro-gram) Any electrically produced graph or tracing (e.g., of the heart or brain).

His bundle e. An electrogram usually made by placing a catheter electrode in the right ventricle of the heart; it records the electrical activity of the bundle of His (atrioventricular bundle).

electrokymogram (e-lek-tro-ki′mo-gram) (EKY) Graphic record of the heart movements obtained during electrokymography.

electrokymography (e-lek-tro-ki-mog′rah-fe) A radiographic procedure that combines a photoelectric recording system with fluoroscopy; used especially with electrocardiography in studies of heart motion.

electrolysis (e-lek-trol′ĭ-sis) 1. Chemical decomposition of a substance in solution by passage of an electric current. 2. Destruction of hair follicles by electric means.

electrolyte (e-lek′tro-lit) A substance that, when in solution, splits (dissociates) into constituent ions, thereby becoming capable of transmitting electricity.

electrolytic (e-lek-tro-lit′ik) 1. Relating to electrolytes. 2. Relating to electrolysis.

electrolyze (e-lek′tro-liz) To cause disintegration with an electric current.

electromyogram (e-lek-tro-mi′o-gram) (EMG) A graphic record of electric discharges generated by muscular activity.

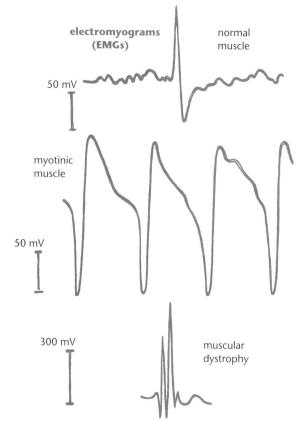

electromyograms (EMGs)   normal muscle

50 mV

myotinic muscle

50 mV

300 mV   muscular dystrophy

electromyography (e-lek-tro-mi-og′rah-fe) Recording of electric discharges generated by muscular activity with the use of surface or needle electrodes; useful primarily for differentiating diseases of neuromuscular junctions from those of muscles or nerves.

electron (e-lek′tron) A subatomic particle with the smallest known

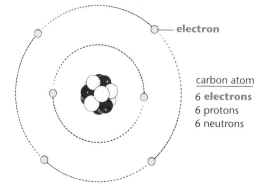

electron

carbon atom
6 **electrons**
6 protons
6 neutrons

negative charge; present in all elements. When emitted from the nucleus of a radioactive substance (as a by-product of nuclear decay), it is called a beta particle.

number of **electrons** in some atoms

element	symbol	atomic number	K	L	M	N	O	P	Q
hydrogen	H	1	1						
lithium	Li	3	2	1					
carbon	C	6	2	4					
nitrogen	N	7	2	5					
oxygen	O	8	2	6					
sodium	Na	11	2	8	1				
chlorine	Cl	17	2	8	7				
potassium	K	19	2	8	8	1			
calcium	Ca	20	2	8	8	2			
mercury	Hg	80	2	8	18	32	18	2	
radium	Ra	88	2	8	18	32	18	18	2

The "shell" header spans columns K, L, M, N, O, P, Q.

valence e. An electron in an atom's outermost shell that is shared or exchanged in chemical reactions.

electronarcosis (e-lek-tro-nar-ko′sis) A state of profound stupor created by passing an electric current through two electrodes placed on the head.

electroneurography (e-lek-tro-nu-rog′rah-fe) Measurement of nerve-conduction velocity along peripheral nerves.

electronic (e-lek-tron′ik) **1.** Relating to electrons. **2.** Relating to the conduction of electricity through solids, gases, or a vacuum; applied to certain devices.

electron volt (e-lek′tron vōlt) (eV, ev) The energy imparted to an electron by a potential of 1 volt.

electronystagmography (e-lek-tro-nis′tag-mog′rah-fe) (ENG) Electronic registering of the abnormal eye movements of nystagmus (spontaneous or induced); applied to the testing of vestibular function. It registers changes in electrical potential by eye movements between two skin electrodes placed on either side of each eye (for horizontal nystagmus) or above and below each eye (for vertical nystagmus).

electro-oculogram (e-lek′tro ok′u-lo-gram) (EOG) A record obtained in electro-oculography.

electro-oculography (e-lek′tro ok-u-log′rah-fe) Recording of the amplitude of electrical potential arising between the front and back of the eyeball (cornea and retina) as the eyes move a constant distance between two points to the right and the left; used to detect dysfunction of the retinal pigment epithelium.

electro-olfactogram (e-lek′tro ol-fak′to-gram) (EOG) A recording of the changes in electrical potential occurring in the olfactory mucosa in response to stimulation by an odor; detected by an electrode placed on the mucosa.

electrophoresis (e-lek-tro-fo-re′sis) A process in which particles with an electric charge in a solution migrate under the influence of an applied electric current; used as a means of separating substances in a diffusing medium. Also called phoresis; ionophoresis.

paper e. Electrophoresis in which paper is used as the diffusion medium, usually employing relatively high voltages; confined almost exclusively to separation of small molecules (e.g., amino acids, peptides).

thin-layer e. (TLE) The movement of electrically charged particles through a thin layer of cellulose or other inert material.

electrophoretic (e-lek-tro-fo-ret′ik) Relating to electrophoresis. Also called ionophoretic.

electrophysiology (e-lek-tro-fiz-e-ol′o-je) The study of electrical phenomena that are associated with physiologic processes.

electroporation (e-lek-tro-por-a′shun) The application of a high-voltage electric pulse to cells in the presence of DNA to permit DNA to enter the cells.

electropositive (e-lek-tro-poz′ĭ-tiv) Denoting an element whose atoms tend to release electrons (e.g., sodium, calcium, potassium), leaving the element positively charged.

electropuncture (e-lek-tro-pungk′chur) Passage of an electric charge through a needle electrode.

electroresection (e-lek-tro-re-sek′shun) Surgical removal of tissue by electrical means (e.g., with an electrical loop).

electroretinogram (e-lek-tro-ret′ĭ-no-gram) (ERG) The recorded difference in electrical potential between an electrode placed in a corneal contact lens and an electrode placed on the forehead.

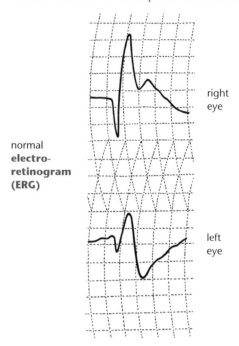

normal **electro-retinogram (ERG)**

right eye

left eye

electroretinography (e-lek-tro-ret-ĭ-nog′rah-fe) Measurement of changes in electrical potential in the retina under the influence of light; usually performed under both light-adapted (photopic) and dark-adapted (scotopic) conditions; it depicts the integrity of the neuroepithelium of the retina.

electroshock (e-lek′tro-shok) See electroconvulsive therapy, under therapy.

electrostethograph (e-lek-tro-steth′o-graf) Electrical instrument for amplifying or recording the respiratory and cardiac sounds in the chest.

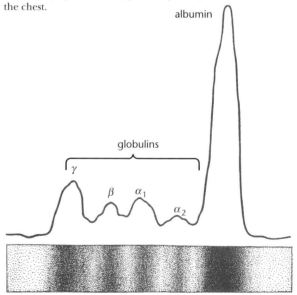

paper electrophoresis

electrosurgery (e-lek-tro-sur'jer-e) The surgical use of high-frequency current delivered by needles, wire loops, or blades.

electrotherapy, electrotherapeutics (e-lek-tro-ther'ah-pe, e-lek-tro-ther-ah-pu'tiks) Any therapeutic use of electricty.

electuary (e-lek'tu-a-re) See confection.

element (el'ĕ-ment) **1.** A substance made up of atoms with the same number of protons in each nucleus. **2.** An irreducible substance or an indivisible constituent of a composite entity.

> **trace e.** Any of a group of minerals (e.g., copper, selenium, zinc) required only in minute amounts by the body to maintain health; important in metabolism or to form essential compounds. Also called trace mineral.

eleo- Combining form meaning oil.

eleotherapy (el-e-o-ther'ah-pe) See oleotherapy.

elephantiasis (el-ĕ-fan-ti'ah-sis) Inflammation and thickening of the skin and subcutaneous tissues, especially of the legs and genitalia, due to a long-term obstruction of the lymphatic circulation from any cause.

> **filarial e.** Elephantiasis caused by parasitic infestation of the lymphatic system by the nematode worms *Wuchereria bancrofti* or *Brugia malayi*. Also called lymphatic filariasis.

elevator (el'ĕ-va-tor) **1.** Instrument used as a lever to pry up and reposition a depressed bone fragment. **2.** A dental instrument for extracting teeth and roots that cannot be grasped with a forceps. **3.** Instrument for detaching a membrane from the surface of bone.

elevator

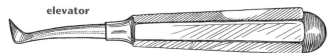

eliminant (e-lim'ĭ-nant) Any agent that promotes the excretion of waste products from the body.

elimination (e-lim-ĭ-na'shun) Excretion or removal of waste products from the body.

ELISA Acronym for enzyme-linked immunosorbent assay; see under assay.

elixir (e-lik'ser) A sweetened solution of alcohol and water used as a vehicle for certain oral medications (e.g., liquid cough medicines).

ellipsoid (e-lip'soid) Having an oval shape; applied especially to certain anatomic structures such as the oval masses of cells surrounding the second part of the penicillate artery of the spleen, and the outer portion of the inner rod segment of the retina.

ellipticines (e-lip'tĭ-sins) A group of antileukemic compounds with immunosuppressive properties; they inhibit both DNA and RNA synthesis.

elliptocyte (e-lip'to-sīt) A red blood cell that has an abnormal oval shape. Also called ovalocyte.

elliptocytosis (e-lip-to-si-to'sis) Disorder of autosomal dominant inheritance in which a large number of red blood cells (50–90%) have an oval or rod shape. Also called ovalocytosis.

elongate (e-long'gāt) **1.** To increase or grow in length. **2.** Long in proportion to width.

eluate (el'u-āt) The material separated by elution.

eluent (e-lu'ent) The liquid used in elution.

elution (e-lu'shun) Separation of substances by washing.

elutriation (e-lu-tre-a'shun) **1.** The process of purifying, separating, or removing by decanting and settling. **2.** Elution.

emaciation (e-ma-se-a'shun) Excessive wasting of the body.

emaculation (e-mak-u-la'shun) Removal of blemishes from the skin.

emanation (em-ah-na'shun) **1.** The act of giving off. **2.** The substance given off. **3.** The radiation from a radioactive material.

emancipation (e-man-sĭ-pa'shun) In embryology, the gradual separation of specific areas of the embryo into relatively autonomous or specialized development, as in organ formation.

emasculation (e-mas-ku-la'shun) Castration.

embalm (em-bahm') To treat a corpse with preservatives to retard its decay.

embed (em-bed') To surround a tissue specimen with a firm substance (e.g., wax) to facilitate the cutting into thin slices for study under the microscope.

embolectomy (em-bo-lek'to-me) Surgical removal of an embolus.

emboli (em'bo-li) Plural of embolus.

embolic (em-bol'ik) Relating to an embolus or to embolism.

emboliform (em-bol'ĭ-form) Resembling an embolus or a wedge.

embolism (em'bo-lizm) Blockage of a blood vessel by an abnormal solid or gaseous mass (embolus) that is transported by the bloodstream to that site from another location in the body.

PATHOGENESIS OF **EMBOLISM**

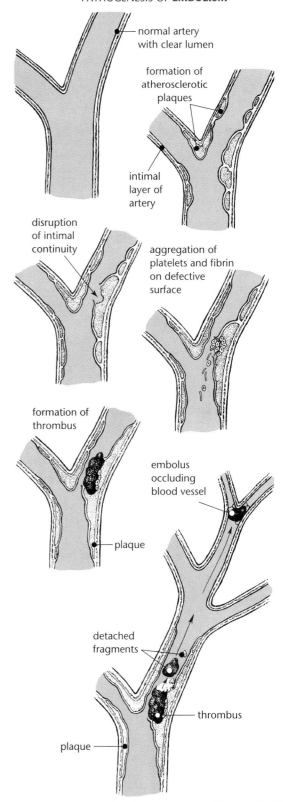

electrosurgery ■ embolism

air e. Obstruction of a blood vessel by bubbles of air, occurring as a result of entry of air into the veins during injury, surgery, or faulty administration of an intravenous fluid. Also called gas embolism.

amniotic fluid e. (AFE) A rare complication of childbirth in which amniotic fluid (usually containing particulate matter) enters the blood circulation of the woman in labor through ruptured uterine veins, causing hemorrhage, shock, pulmonary embolism, and, frequently, maternal death, principal predisposing factors include tumultuous uterine contractions, premature detachment of the placenta, and a dead fetus; other precipitating factors may include trauma due to abdominal injuries, operative delivery of the infant, and introduction of an intrauterine catheter for monitoring uterine contractions.

crossed e. See paradoxical embolism.

fat e. The presence of fat globules in the blood, usually occurring after fractures of arm and leg bones or after corticosteroid therapy; seen also in burns and in association with fatty degeneration of the liver. Also called oil embolism.

gas e. See air embolism.

oil e. See fat embolism.

paradoxical e. The presence in an artery of an embolus that was formed in a vein, having passed directly to the arterial circulation through a septal defect in the heart. Also called crossed embolism.

pulmonary e. (PE) Clogging of one or more arteries supplying blood to the lungs by detached fragments of a blood clot (thrombus), most frequently located in a deep vein of a leg or the pelvis and carried in the bloodstream through the heart to the lung vessels; it occurs as a complication of surgery and childbirth, and in patients who are immobilized for any reason.

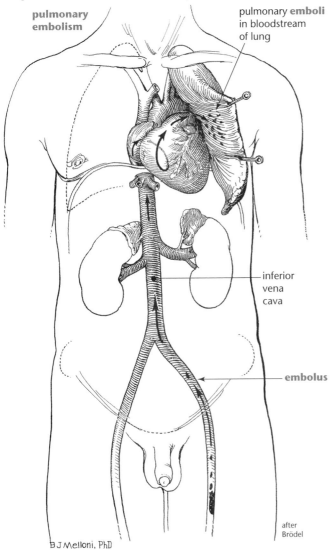

pulmonary embolism

pulmonary **emboli** in bloodstream of lung

inferior vena cava

embolus

B J Melloni, PhD

saddle e. See straddling embolism.

straddling e. Embolism lodged at the bifurcation of an artery. Also called saddle embolism.

embolization (em-bo-lĭ-za′shun) The deliberate obstruction of a blood vessel with any of a variety of materials; usually performed to stop uncontrollable internal bleeding or to cut off the blood supply of a difficult to remove, vascular tumor (thereby shrinking the tumor).

embolalia (em-bo-lŏ-la′le-ah) Involuntary insertion of meaningless words in a sentence.

embolus (em′bo-lus) A plug within a vessel (e.g., a blood clot, air bubble, fat, or tumor mass) that is carried in the bloodstream from another site until it lodges and becomes an obstruction to the blood circulation.

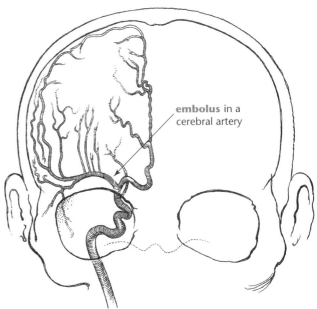

embolus in a cerebral artery

embrasure (em-bra′zhur) A space produced by the diverging surfaces of two adjacent teeth.

embrocation (em-bro-ka′shun) **1.** The act of rubbing the body with a liquid medication. **2.** The liquid so used.

embryo (em′bre-o) An organism in its earliest stage of development; in humans, from conception to the end of the eighth week, at which time it is 2.1 to 2.5 cm. long and weighs 1 gram; the head constitutes about half the bulk; the lobes of the liver may be recognized; the kidneys are forming; red blood cells containing hemoglobin are forming in the yolk sac and liver; the heart is functionally complete, with a rate of over 80 beats per minute; the hands and feet are formed and distinctly human.

embryoblast (em′bre-o-blast) An aggregation of cells forming the portion of the blastocyst from which the embryo itself develops (i.e., excluding the placenta and other extraembryonic structures). Also called inner cell mass.

embryogenesis (em-bre-o-jen′ĕ-sis) The development of the embryo from the fertilized egg.

embryogenic (em-bre-o-jen′ik) **1.** Relating to the development of an embryo. **2.** Producing an embryo.

embryogeny (em-bre-oj′ĕ-ne) The formation of the embryo.

embryologist (em-bre-ol′o-jist) A specialist in embryology.

embryology (em-bre-ol′o-je) The science concerned with living organisms from fertilization of the ovum until birth; the study of the development of the ovum. Also called developmental anatomy.

embryoma (em-bre-o′mah) See embryomal tumor, under tumor.

e. of kidney See Wilms' tumor, under tumor.

embryomorphous (em-bre-o-mor′fus) Resembling an embryo or embryonic tissue in form or development; applied to certain abnormal adult tissues or cells.

embryonal (em′bre-o-nal) Relating to an embryo.

embryonate (em′bre-o-nāt) Containing an embryo.

after Brödel

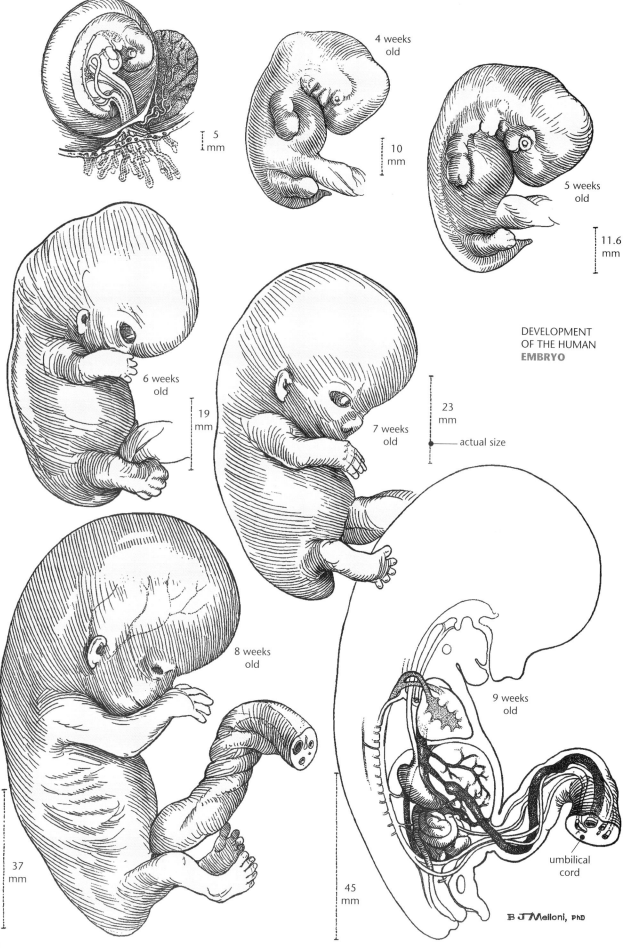

5
mm

4 weeks
old

10
mm

5 weeks
old

11.6
mm

E

DEVELOPMENT
OF THE HUMAN
EMBRYO

6 weeks
old

19
mm

7 weeks
old

23
mm

← actual size

8 weeks
old

37
mm

9 weeks
old

45
mm

umbilical
cord

B. J. Melloni, PhD

E17

embryonic (em-bre-on′ik) Relating to an embryo.

embryonization (em-bre-o-nĭ-za′shun) The reversion of cells or tissues to a primitive form.

embryopathy (em-bre-op′ah-the) An abnormal condition in an embryo.

embryotomy (em-bre-ot′o-me) The mechanical destruction of a fetus to facilitate its removal through the birth canal when delivery is not otherwise possible.

embryotoxon (em-bre-o-tok′son) A congenital opacity of the cornea involving the deep layers of the periphery.

embryotroph (em′bre-o-trōf) The nutriment supplied to the embryo.

emedullate (e-med′u-lāt) To extract bone marrow.

emergency (e-mer′jen-se) A condition that requires immediate intervention to prevent death or serious complications.

emergent (e-mer′jent) **1.** Occurring suddenly. **2.** Becoming apparent through successive developmental stages.

emery (em′er-e) An abrasive composed of aluminum oxide combined with iron, magnesia, or silica.

emesis (em′ĕ-sis) Vomiting.

emetic (ĕ-met′ik) **1.** Relating to vomiting. **2.** Any agent that induces vomiting.

emetine (em′ĕ-tin) An alkaloid effective against amebas.

emetocathartic (em-ĕ-to-kah-thar′tik) Denoting an agent that induces both vomiting and bowel evacuation (catharsis).

-emia Suffix meaning blood (e.g., leukemia).

emigration (em-ĭ-gra′shun) The active outward passage of white blood cells through the intact walls of minute blood vessels (i.e., through intercellular spaces of vessel walls) to surrounding tissues and toward a site of injury.

eminence (em′ĭ-nens) A rounded prominence; a raised area, especially on the surface of a bone.

   arcuate e. The bulge on the upper surface of the petrous part of the temporal bone at the base of the skull that accommodates the underlying anterior (superior) semicircular canal.

   canine e. A prominent ridge on the surface of the maxilla that corresponds to the root of the canine (cuspid) tooth. Also called cuspid prominence; canine prominence.

   cuspid e. See canine eminence.

   frontal e. The rounded elevation on the frontal bone of the skull on either side, just above the eye; it indicates the site where ossification of the frontal bone first occurred. Also called frontal protuberance.

   hypothenar e. The elongated prominence on the medial border of the palm of the hand, produced mostly by the three intrinsic short muscles of the little finger.

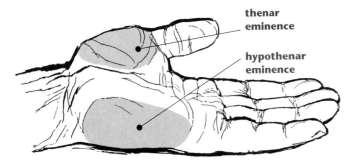

thenar eminence

hypothenar eminence

   iliopectineal e. See iliopubic eminence.

   iliopubic e. The rounded elevation on the medial border of the hipbone that marks the union of the superior ramus of the pubic bone with the body of the ilium. Also called iliopectineal eminence.

   intercondylar e. A pointed elevation on the upper surface of the front of the tibia between the articular surfaces of the two condyles. Also called tibial spine.

   parietal e. The most prominent part of the parietal bone of the skull on either side, just above the superior temporal line; it

indicates the site where ossification of the parietal bone first occurred. Also called parietal protuberance.

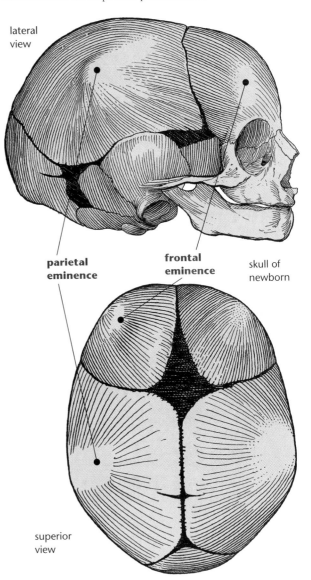

lateral view

parietal eminence

frontal eminence

skull of newborn

superior view

   pyramidal e. A small, hollow, conical bony projection on the posterior wall of the middle ear (tympanic) cavity, immediately behind the oval window (fenestra vestibuli); it houses the stapedius muscle, whose tendon leaves by a small apical aperture to attach to the posterior surface of the neck of the stapes. Also called pyramid of tympanum.

   thenar e. The bulging prominence at the base of the thumb on the lateral aspect of the palm of the hand; it is created mainly by the three intrinsic muscles that flex, abduct, and oppose the thumb.

emiocytosis (e-me-o-si-to′sis) See exocytosis.

emissary (em′ĭ-sar-e) Providing drainage; applied to certain veins.

emission (e-mish′un) A discharge.

   nocturnal e. Ejaculation of semen during sleep, generally occurring among adolescent males during an erotic dream. Commonly called wet dream.

emmenagogue (ĕ-men′ah-gog) Denoting an agent that induces or produces menstruation.

emmenia (ĕ-me′ne-ah) Menses.

emmetropia (em-ĕ-tro′pe-ah) The normal state of the refractory system of the eye in which light rays entering the eyeball focus clearly on the retina when the eye is at rest.

emollient (e-mol′e-ent) **1.** Soothing. **2.** Any agent that softens skin or mucous membranes.

emotion (e-mo'shun) Any strong feeling.

emotional (e-mo'shun-al) Relating to emotion.

empathic (em-path'ik) Relating to empathy.

empathy (em'pah-the) The insightful understanding of, and identification with, the feelings of another person.

emphysema (em-fĭ-se'mah) **1.** Abnormal accumulation of air within a tissue. **2.** Abnormal and permanent enlargement of air spaces (alveoli) distal to the terminal bronchioles in the lungs; the alveoli burst and blend to form fewer and larger air spaces. Also called pulmonary emphysema.

    centriacinar e. See centrilobular emphysema.

    centrilobular e. Destruction of air spaces occupying the central portion of the respiratory unit (acinus) and predominantly involving the upper lobes of the lungs; commonly seen in chronic bronchitis; severe lesions are seen in heavy smokers and in coal miner's pneumoconiosis. Also called centriacinar emphysema.

    compensatory e., compensating e. Dilatation of a portion of the lung when another portion is unable to function properly.

    interstitial e. Rupture of overdistended alveoli or terminal airways, causing escape of air into perivascular tissues of the lungs and into the connective tissue planes; trapped air may expand into the mediastinum or subcutaneous tissues; rarely, it may be caused by trauma; it may occur in newborns, almost exclusively in the very low birth weight infant on ventilatory support. Also called pulmonary interstitial emphysema (PIE).

    irregular e. A usually asymptomatic form of emphysema in which the affected respiratory units (acini) are not uniformly involved; it is associated with scarring.

    mediastinal e. The presence of air in the mediastinum.

    panacinar e. Emphysema characterized by uniform destruction and enlargement of the whole respiratory unit (acinus), with predominance in the lower basal zones of the lungs; there is a strong association with hereditary deficiency of alpha$_1$-antitrypsin.

    paraseptal e. Emphysema in which the lesions occur primarily on the superficial regions of the lung, usually near its covering membrane (pleura) and adjacent to scars; often causes escape of air into the pleural space (pneumothorax).

    pulmonary e. See emphysema (2).

    pulmonary interstitial e. (PIE) See interstitial emphysema.

    subcutaneous e. The presence of air in tissues underlying the skin.

    surgical e. Subcutaneous emphysema resulting from surgical operation or injury.

emphysematous (em-fĭ-sem'ah-tus) Affected with, or of the nature of, emphysema.

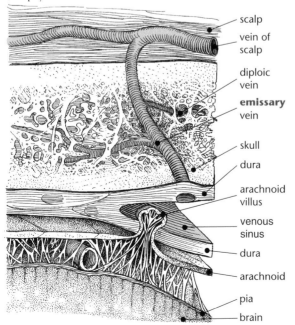

scalp
vein of scalp
diploic vein
emissary vein
skull
dura
arachnoid villus
venous sinus
dura
arachnoid
pia
brain

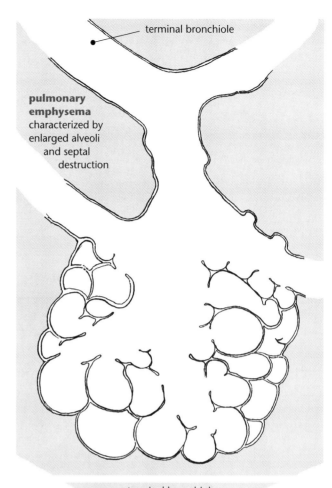

terminal bronchiole

pulmonary emphysema characterized by enlarged alveoli and septal destruction

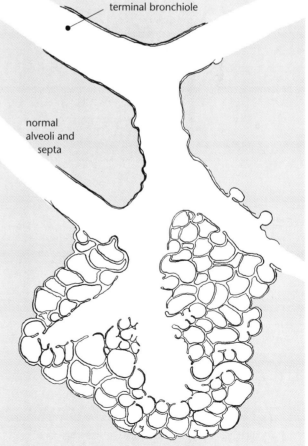

terminal bronchiole

normal alveoli and septa

empirical, empiric (em-pir′e-kal, em-pir′ik) **1.** Based on practical experience. **2.** Relating to empiricism.

empiricism (em-pir′ĭ-sizm) The view that experience serves as a guide to medical practice; reliance on experience as the only source of knowledge.

empyema (em-pi-e′mah) Accumulation of pus in a body cavity, especially the pleural space.

subdural e. Collection of pus within the skull, beneath the dura mater.

empyocele (em′pi-o-sēl) Accumulation of pus in the scrotum. Also called suppurating hydrocele.

emulgent (e-mul′jent) Purifying, straining; applied to a process.

emulsify (e-mul′sĭ-fi) To convert into an emulsion.

emulsion (e-mul′shun) A preparation containing two liquids that do not mix, one being dispersed in the other in the form of small globules.

emulsive (e-mul′siv) **1.** Susceptible to being emulsified. **2.** Capable of emulsifying.

emulsoid (e-mul′soid) A colloidal dispersion in which the dispersed particles absorb some of the liquid in which they are suspended.

en- Prefix meaning in.

enalapril maleate (e-nal′ah-pril mal′e-āt) A drug that inhibits the action of angiotensin-converting enzyme (ACE); it produces dilatation of kidney vessels with an increase in sodium excretion; effective for the treatment of essential hypertension and has beneficial effects on the decreased pumping efficiency of the failing heart (heart failure).

enamel (en-am′el) The hard substance covering the anatomic crowns of teeth.

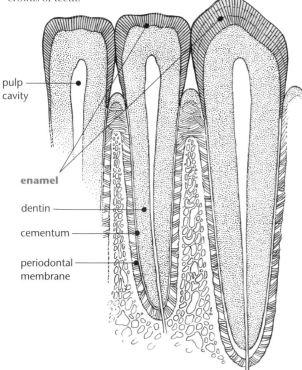

mottled e. Enamel with white, yellow, or brown, sometimes pitted, spots; when several teeth are affected, it may be due to excessive fluoride intake during tooth formation.

enamelogenesis (en-am-el-o-jen′ĕ-sis) See amelogenesis.

e. imperfecta See amelogenesis imperfecta, under amelogenesis.

enameloma (en-am-el-o′mah) An abnormal spherical nodule of enamel attached to a tooth, usually on the root. Also called enamel pearl.

enanthema (en-an-the′ma) An eruption on a mucous membrane.

enarthrodial (en-ar-thro′de-al) Relating to a ball-and-socket joint.

enarthrosis (en-ar-thro′sis) See ball-and-socket joint, under joint.

encanthis (en-kan′this) Obsolete term for a small tumor at the inner angle of the eye.

encapsulated (en-kap′su-lāt-ed) Encased in a capsule.

enceinte (aw-sawt′) Pregnant.

encephalemia (en-sef-ah-le′me-ah) Congestion of the brain.

encephalic (en-se-fal′ik) **1.** Relating to the brain. **2.** In the skull.

encephalitic (en-sef-ah-lit′ik) Relating to encephalitis.

encephalitis (en-sef-ah-li′tis), pl. encephalit′ides Inflammation of the brain; may result from bacterial, viral, or fungal infection; initial symptoms include headache, nausea, vomiting, fever, and lethargy.

acute necrotizing e. Encephalitis with tissue destruction affecting chiefly the temporal lobes; usually caused by herpes simplex virus.

arbovirus e. Encephalitis caused by a variety of viruses (families Bunyaviridae, Togaviridae, Reoviridae, Rabdoviridae), transmitted by bloodsucking arthropods and occurring in epidemics designated by their geographic distribution. Also called arthropod-borne encephalitis.

arthropod-borne e. See arbovirus encephalitis.

e. periaxialis diffusa See adrenoleukodystrophy.

encephalo-, encephal- Combining forms meaning brain.

encephalocele (en-sef-ah-lo-sēl) Protrusion of brain substance through a congenital or traumatic opening in the skull. Also called craniocele.

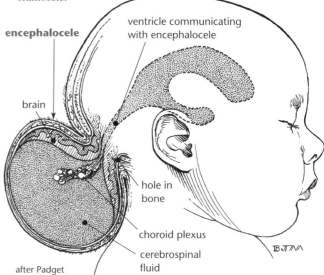

encephalocele
ventricle communicating with encephalocele
brain
hole in bone
choroid plexus
cerebrospinal fluid
after Padget

encephalodynia (en-sef-ah-lo-din′e-ah) Headache.

encephalogram (en-sef′ah-lo-gram) An x-ray picture of the head.

encephalography (en-sef-ah-log′rah-fe) Roentgenography of the brain.

encephalolith (en-sef′ah-lo-lith) A concretion in the brain.

encephalomalacia (en-sef-ah-lo-mah-la′she-ah) Localized softening of brain tissue, usually due to lack of blood supply to the area.

encephalomeningitis (en-sef-ah-lo-men-in-ji′tis) See meningoencephalitis.

encephalomyelitis (en-sef-ah-lo-mi-ĕ-li′tis) Acute inflammation of the brain and spinal cord.

acute disseminated e. A rapidly progressive illness usually following a viral infection, vaccination, or a vague respiratory illness; considered a perivascular hypersensitivity response.

benign myalgic e. See epidemic neuromyasthenia, under neuromyasthenia.

encephalomyelocele (en-sef-ah-lo-mi-el′o-sēl) Protrusion of the medulla, spinal cord, and membranes through a congenital bone defect in the occipital region of the skull.

encephalomyelopathy (en-sef-ah-lo-mi-ĕ-lop′ah-the) Any disease of the brain and spinal cord.

encephalomyeloradiculopathy (en-sef-ah-lo-mi′ĕ-lo-rah-dik-u-lop′ah-the) Disease involving the brain, spinal cord, and roots of spinal nerves.

encephalon (en-sef'ah-lon) See brain.

encephalopathy (en-sef-ah-lop'ah-the) Any disease or dysfunction of the brain.

  anoxic-ischemic e. Brain dysfunction occurring after injury severe enough to cause loss of consciousness (e.g., in cardiorespiratory failure, carbon monoxide poisoning, asphyxia, drowning); clinical expression of brain damage ranges from transient confusion to coma, depending on the degree of injury. Occasionally, delayed degeneration of brain function occurs weeks after apparent recovery from original episode.

  hepatic e. A metabolic disorder of the nervous and neuromuscular systems causing edema of the brain with flapping tremor (asterixis), musty breath odor (fetor hepaticus), and disturbances of consciousness that may progress to deep coma and even death; associated with advanced liver disease or with passage of toxic substances from the portal to the systemic circulation via a portocaval shunt.

  hypertensive e. Encephalopathy associated with severe arterial hypertension; marked by headache, vomiting, convulsions, drowsiness progressing to coma, and sometimes edema of the optic disk (papilledema) and retinal hemorrhage.

  hypoxic e. See ischemic encephalopathy.

  ischemic e. Encephalopathy resulting from oxygen deficiency (hypoxia), severe anemia, hypoglycemia, or reduced perfusion of brain tissues; effects range from mild, transient brain dysfunction to severe brain damage and coma or vegetative state reflecting the degree of pathologic severity. Also called hypoxic encephalopathy.

  lead e. Inflammation of the brain, with vomiting, convulsions, stupor, and coma caused by ingestion or absorption of lead compounds.

  metabolic e. Generalized disruption of brain function occurring in patients with serious physical illness; usually begins with drowsiness, followed by agitation, confusion, delirium, or psychosis; it may progress to stupor and coma. The condition may also result from a jejunal bypass for obesity.

  nutritional e. Brain dysfunction caused by deficiency of vitamin B_{12}, thiamine, niacin, pyridoxine, or nicotinic acid. The symptoms associated with vitamin B_{12} deficiency are occasionally mistaken for those of Alzheimer's dementia.

  subacute spongiform e. See Creutzfeldt-Jakob disease, under disease.

encephalosclerosis (en-sef-ah-lo-skle-ro'sis) Hardening of brain tissue.

enchondroma (en-kon-dro'mah) A benign growth composed of mature cartilage developed within a bone; it is usually asymptomatic but may cause pain, bone deformity, and fracture.

enchondromatosis (en-kon-dro-mah-to'sis) A nonhereditary condition characterized by the presence of multiple enchondromas in a long bone, resulting in shortening of the limb. Also called Ollier's disease; dyschondroplasia.

enchondrosarcoma (en-kon-dro-sar-ko'mah) Malignant tumor within a bone, arising from a preexisting cartilaginous growth (enchondroma).

enclave (en'klāv) A mass of tissue totally enclosed within a tissue of a different type.

encoding (en-kod'ing) A mental modification of stimuli received through the senses; the first stage in the memory process. It is followed by storage and retrieval.

encopresis (en-ko-pre'sis) Unintentional passage of feces.

encysted (en-sist'ed) Enclosed within a membranous sac.

endarterectomy (end-ar-ter-ek'to-me) Removal of a cholesterol-containing plaque (atheroma) and the diseased inner layer of arterial wall to which it is attached.

endarterial (end-ar-te're-al) 1. Within an artery. 2. Relating to the inner layer (intima) of the arterial wall.

endarteritis (end-ar-ter-i'tis) Inflammation of the inner layer of the arterial wall (intima). Also called endoarteritis.

  e. obliterans, obliterating e. The severe narrowing of small arteries resulting from cellular proliferation of the arterial inner layer.

endaural (end-aw'ral) 1. Within the ear. 2. Through the ear canal.

end-bulb (end'bulb) One of the minute rounded bodies located at the termination of a sensory nerve fiber; present in certain parts of the skin, mucous membranes, muscles, joints, and connective tissue of internal organs.

  Krause's e-b. See Krause's corpuscle, under corpuscle.

end-diastolic (end di-ah-stol'ik) Relating to, or occurring at the end of the resting period of the heart muscle (diastole), just prior to the beginning of the next contraction (systole) (e.g., end-diastolic pressure).

endemic (en-dem'ik) Relating to any disease present continuously in a given locality or population.

endergonic (end-er-gon'ik) Relating to a chemical reaction that is accompanied by uptake of free energy.

endermic (en-der'mik) Absorbed through the skin.

end-foot (end'foot) See axon terminal, under terminal.

ending (end'ing) A termination, as of a nerve.

  annulospiral nerve e. The principal sensory nerve terminal in a muscle (neuromuscular) spindle, consisting of branches that coil around the intrafusal voluntary muscle fiber at its central point (nuclear region); sensitive to stretch of muscle length. Also called primary nerve ending.

  calyciform nerve e. The terminal part of a nerve that is goblet-shaped, as the nerve calyx of type I hair cells in the membranous labyrinth of the ear.

  encapsulated nerve e.'s Specialized fibrous capsules enveloping the terminal parts of sensory nerves; they vary widely in size and shape; examples include the pacinian corpuscle, the corpuscle of Meissner, the corpuscle of Ruffini, and the Golgi-Mazzoni corpuscle.

  flower-spray nerve e. A sensory nerve terminal in a muscle (neuromuscular) spindle, composed of spraylike beaded configurations on the intrafusal voluntary muscle fiber at the sides away from the central point (nuclear region); sensitive to increased muscle tension. Also called secondary nerve ending.

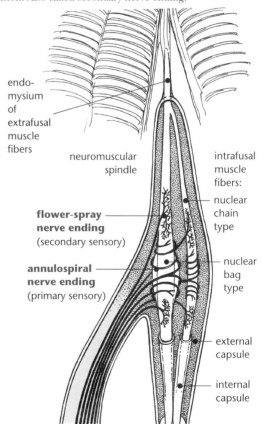

endo-
mysium
of
extrafusal
muscle
fibers

neuromuscular
spindle

intrafusal
muscle
fibers:

nuclear
chain
type

**flower-spray
nerve ending**
(secondary sensory)

**annulospiral
nerve ending**
(primary sensory)

nuclear
bag
type

external
capsule

internal
capsule

free nerve e.'s Unmyelinated nerve endings that branch repeatedly to form networks, found in many different sites throughout the body, including the skin, mucous membranes, fascia, joint capsules, ligaments, tendons, blood vessels, meninges, bones, and muscles; they are usually of small diameter and low conduction speed and respond to different stimuli, including pain, light touch, tickle, and itch sensations. Also called nonencapsulated nerve endings.

nonencapsulated nerve e.'s See free nerve endings.
primary nerve e. See annulospiral nerve ending.
Ruffini's nerve e. See corpuscle of Ruffini, under corpuscle.
secondary nerve e. See flower-spray nerve ending.
synaptic e. The knoblike terminal part of an axon where chemical transmitter substances are released from synaptic vesicles to adjoining neurons for the chemical transmission of impulses.

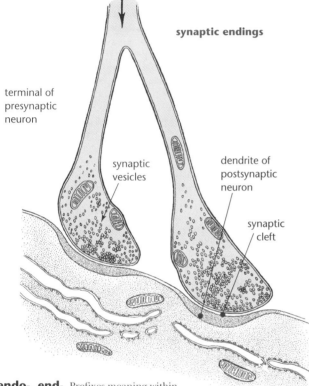

synaptic endings

terminal of presynaptic neuron

synaptic vesicles

dendrite of postsynaptic neuron

synaptic cleft

endo-, end- Prefixes meaning within.
endoarteritis (en-do-ar-ter-i'tis) See endarteritis.
endoauscultation (en-do-aws-kul-ta'shun) Auscultation of the stomach by passing a stethoscopic tube or electronic amplifier into the stomach.
endobronchial (en-do-brong'ke-al) See intrabronchial.
endocardial (en-do-kar'de-al) 1. Relating to, or situated within, the inner lining of the heart chambers (endocardium). 2. Within the heart.
endocardiography (en-do-kar-de-og'rah-fe) Recording of the electric current traversing the heart muscle, prior to a heartbeat, with the exploring electrode placed within the heart chambers.
endocarditic (en-do-kar-dit'ik) Relating to endocarditis.
endocarditis (en-do-kar-di'tis) Inflammation of the lining membrane (endocardium) of the heart chambers.
abacterial thrombotic e. See nonbacterial thrombotic endocarditis.
acute infective e., acute IE A necrotizing, ulcerative, and invasive infection of previously normal heart valves by a highly virulent organism, causing abrupt onset of high fever, chills, malaise, and weakness.
atypical verrucous e. See Libman-Sacks endocarditis.
bacterial e. See infective endocarditis.
infective e. (IE) Endocarditis due to colonization of the heart valves with microorganisms, leading to the formation of fragile, infected vegetations and deformation of the valve leaflets; may be acute or subacute. Also called bacterial endocarditis.
Libman-Sacks e. A nonbacterial endocarditis associated with systemic lupus erythematosus (SLE). Also called atypical verrucous endocarditis.
Löffler's e. An uncommon condition characterized by fibrosis and large thrombi of the heart wall, frequently associated with eosinophilia, congestive heart failure, and a rapidly fatal outcome. Also called Löffler's disease.
marantic e. See nonbacterial thrombotic endocarditis.
nonbacterial thrombotic e. (NBTE) Endocarditis often seen in the last stages of prolonged or debilitating illnesses (e.g., kidney failure, cancer). Also called abacterial thrombotic endocarditis; marantic endocarditis; terminal endocarditis.
rheumatic e. Endocarditis with involvement of the heart valves associated with rheumatic fever.
subacute infective e. Endocarditis with insidious onset of symptoms, caused by an organism of moderate to low virulence; symptoms include nondescript malaise, low-grade fever without chills, weight loss, and flulike symptoms.
terminal e. See nonbacterial thrombotic endocarditis.
vegetative e., verrucous e. Endocarditis associated with the formation of fibrinous clots on the ulcerated valves of the heart.
endocardium (en-do-kar'de-um) The serous membrane lining the heart chambers.

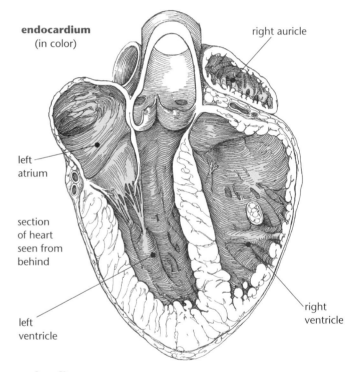

endocardium (in color)

right auricle

left atrium

section of heart seen from behind

left ventricle

right ventricle

endoceliac (en-do-se'le-ak) Within a body cavity. Also called intraceliac.
endocervical (en-do-ser'vĭ-kal) Within the uterine cervix. Also called intracervical.
endocervicitis (en-do-ser-vĭ-si'tis) Inflammation of the lining of the uterine cervix.
endochondral (en-do-kon'dral) See intracartilaginous.
endocranial (en-do-kra'ne-al) Within the braincase (cranium).
endocrine (en'do-krin) Secreting internally; applied to a gland that secretes a hormone directly into the blood or lymph.
endocrinologist (en-do-krĭ-nol'o-jist) A specialist in endocrinology.
endocrinology (en-do-krĭ-nol'o-je) A subspecialty of internal medicine concerned with the metabolism, physiology, and disorders of endocrine glands and their secretions (hormones); includes such disorders as diabetes mellitus, hypo- and hyperthyroidism, hypo- and hyperadrenalism, etc.

endocrinopathy (en-do-krī-nop'ah-the) Any disease of the endocrine glands; characterized in general by the underproduction or overproduction of hormones, with the clinical picture of a hypo- or hyperfunctional state.

endocrinotherapy (en-do-krī-no-ther'ah-pe) Treatment of disease with hormones (e.g., hormone replacement therapy). Also called hormonotherapy.

endocytosis (en-do-si-to'sis) The uptake of particles by a cell through invagination of its plasma membrane.

endoderm (en'do-derm) The innermost of the three germ layers of the embryo; it gives rise to the lining of the gastrointestinal tract from the pharynx to the rectum and to neighboring glands (e.g., liver, pancreas, thyroid). Also called entoderm.

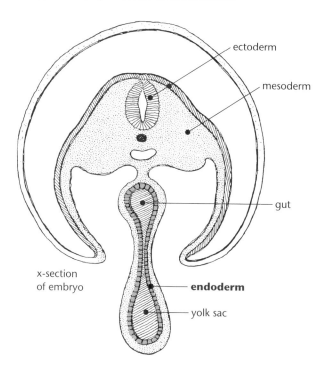

x-section of embryo

ectoderm
mesoderm
gut
endoderm
yolk sac

endodontics (en-do-don'tiks) The branch of dentistry concerned with the tooth pulp, pulp chamber, root canal, and tissues surrounding the root of the tooth.

endodontist (en-do-don'tist) A specialist in endodontics.

endoenzyme (en-do-en'zīm) See intracellular enzyme.

endogastric (en-do-gas'trik) Within the stomach.

endogenous (en-doj'ĕ-nus) Originating within the body.

endointoxication (en-do-in-tok-sī-ka'shun) Poisoning by a toxin produced within the organism.

endolaryngeal (en-do-lah-rin'je-al) Within the larynx.

endolith (en'do-lith) See pulp stone, under stone.

endolymph (en'do-limf) The fluid contained within the membranous labyrinth of the inner ear.

endolymphatic (en-do-lim-fat'ik) Relating to the endolymph.

endometrial (en-do-me'tre-al) Relating to the inner lining of the uterus (endometrium).

endometrioid (en-do-me'tre-oid) Microscopically resembling the lining (endometrium) of the uterus.

endometrioma (en-do-me-tre-o'mah) See chocolate cyst, under cyst.

endometriosis (en-do-me-tre-o'sis) Disorder in which abnormal growths of tissue, microscopically resembling the uterine lining membrane (endometrium), are present in locations other than the uterine lining, most commonly over pelvic organs; growths vary from microscopic to large masses invading underlying organs; may be asymptomatic or cause intense pain and infertility; seen almost exclusively in women of reproductive age but occasionally may occur in postmenopausal women.

E23

e. interna See adenomyosis.

endometritis (en-do-mĕ-tri'tis) Inflammation of the uterine lining (endometrium).

endometrium (en-do-me'tre-um) The mucous membrane lining the interior of the uterus; its structure changes with age and with the menstrual cycle. Also called tunica mucosa of uterus.

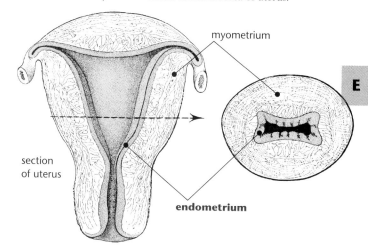

myometrium

section of uterus

endometrium

endomorph (en'do-morf) A body type in which, from a morphologic standpoint, the trunk predominates over the limbs.

endomysium (en-do-mis'e-um) The delicate connective tissue surrounding individual muscle fibers.

endoneurium (en-do-nu're-um) The delicate connective tissue surrounding individual nerve fibers. Also called Henle's sheath; sheath of Retzius; endoneurial sheath.

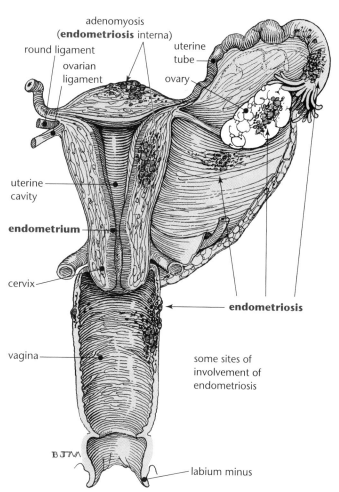

adenomyosis (**endometriosis** interna)
round ligament
ovarian ligament
uterine tube
ovary
uterine cavity
endometrium
cervix
endometriosis
vagina
some sites of involvement of endometriosis
labium minus

endonuclease (en-do-nu'kle-ās) Any enzyme that promotes the breaking of interior chemical bonds of DNA and RNA chains, producing fragments of short (oligo-) or long (poly-) nucleotides.

> **restrictive e.** One of many endonucleases isolated from bacteria that act as molecular scissors to cut DNA molecules at specific locations, thus inactivating a foreign DNA (e.g., from a virus) and restricting its activity; used extensively as a laboratorty tool. Also called restrictive enzyme; commonly called chemical knife.

endoparasite (en-do-par'ah-sit) Parasite that lives within the body of its host.

endopeptidase (en-do-pep'tĭ-dās) An enzyme that splits peptide linkages at points remote from the ends of the molecule chain.

endophlebitis (en-do-fle-bi'tis) Inflammation of the inner layer of a vein.

endophthalmitis (en-dof-thal-mi'tis) Extensive intraocular infection.

endoplasm (en'do-plazm) The inner portion of the cytoplasm, containing most of the cell's solid structures.

end-organ (end' or-gan) See end organ, under organ.

endorphin (en-dor'fin) One of a group of peptides normally found in the brain and other body parts, capable of producing effects similar to those of opiates.

endoscope (en'do-skōp) A tubular instrument with lenses and a light source attached for viewing the interior of a hollow organ, tubular structure, or body cavity; may be used with a camera or video recorder.

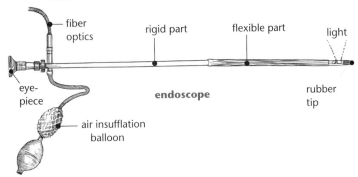

fiber optics — rigid part — flexible part — light
eye-piece
endoscope
rubber tip
air insufflation balloon

endoscopist (en-dos-ko'pist) A person trained in the use of endoscopes.

endoscopy (en-dos'ko-pe) Inspection of a body cavity or organ with an endoscope.

> **peritoneal e.** See laparoscopy.

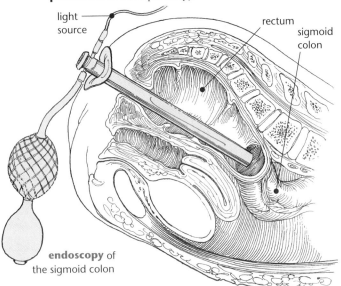

light source
rectum
sigmoid colon
endoscopy of the sigmoid colon

endoskeleton (en-do-skel'ĕ-ton) The internal bony structures (skeleton) of vertebrates.

endosonoscopy (en-do-son-os'kŏ-pe) Ultrasonic scanning conducted by introducing transducers, serving as miniature probes, into hollow or tubular structures (e.g., gastrointestinal tract, bladder).

endosseous (en-dos'e-us) Within bone.

endosteal (en-dos'te-al) Relating to the vascular membrane lining the interior cavity of bones.

endosteitis (en-dos-te-i'tis) Inflammation of the membrane lining the inner cavities of bones.

endosteoma (en-dos-te-o'mah) Benign tumor in the internal, medullary cavity of a bone.

endosteum (en-dos'te-um) The vascular membrane lining bone cavities.

endothelin (en-do-the'lin) A peptide, derived from the inner lining of blood vessels, that is a powerful constrictor of blood vessels.

endothelioma (en-do-the-le-o'mah) A tumor derived from the endothelial tissue of blood vessels, lymphatic vessels, or serous membranes; may be benign or malignant.

endothelium (en-do-the'le-um) A thin membrane lining body cavities, lymphatic channels, and blood vessels.

endothermic (en-do-ther'mik) Accompanied by heat absorption; applied to certain chemical reactions.

endothrix (en'do-thriks) Within the hair shaft; applied to certain fungal infections of the hair.

endotoxemia (en-do-toks-e'me-ah) Presence of endotoxins in the blood; it may cause shock.

endotoxin (en-do-tok'sin) A toxic component of the walls of gram-negative bacteria, released only by destruction or death of the organisms; in small amounts endotoxins cause fever and leukopenia, in larger amounts diarrhea and shock. Also called intracellular toxin.

endotracheal (en-do-tra'ke-al) Within the trachea.

endoxin (en-dok'sin) See natriuretic hormone, under hormone.

endplate, end-plate (end'plāt) The terminal part of a motor nerve fiber that transmits nerve impulses to muscle.

> **motor e.** See neuromuscular junction, under junction.

end-tidal (end ti'dal) At the completion of a normal expiration.

enema (en'ĕ-mah) 1. Infusion of a fluid into the rectum for therapeutic or diagnostic purposes. 2. The liquid so infused.

> **barium e.** Instillation of the radiopaque medium barium sulfate in solution prior to x-ray examination of the bowel.

> **contrast e.** Enema using any radiopaque medium.

> **double contrast e.** Instillation and evacuation of a radiopaque medium followed by instillation of air prior to x-ray examination of the bowel. Distention of the bowel with air provides a clear image of the intestinal lining.

> **high e.** Enema instilled high into the colon, usually with the aid of a tube. Also called enteroclysis.

energy (en'er-je) (W) The exertion of power to effect physical change.

enervation (en-er-va'shun) Condition marked by lack of energy and vigor.

enflurane (en'floo-rān) An inhalation anesthetic that is neither flammable nor explosive; used in obstetrics in subanesthetic concentrations for normal vaginal deliveries with no detectable toxicity in mothers or newborns.

engagement (en-gāj'ment) The stage of childbirth when the fetal head no longer simply lies in the pelvis but begins its descent and its lowermost part reaches the level of the ischial spines of the maternal pelvis.

engineering (en-jin-er'ing) 1. The practical application of the principles of mathematics and the physical sciences. 2. Work performed by an engineer.

> **biomedical e.** Application of engineering principles to solve medical problems in research and practice; it includes development of such devices as prostheses (e.g., artificial limbs and heart valves) and electrical devices (e.g., pacemakers). Also called bioengineering. See also biotechnology.

> **genetic e.** Directed alteration of the genetic material of a

living organism to study genetic processes, to modify heredity, to produce hormones or proteins, and potentially to correct genetic defects. Genetic engineering is a tool of biotechnology; its potential applicability extends to agriculture, industry, and the environment. See also recombinant DNA technology, under technology.

human factor e. See ergonomics.

engorgement (en-gorj′ment) The condition of being distended or filled to excess with fluid.

enhancement (en-hans′ment) **1.** Augmentation. **2.** In immunology, prolongation of a process by suppressing opposing factors (e.g., prolongation of graft survival by therapy with antibodies directed toward the graft allogens). **3.** Improvement of the definition of an x-ray or computer image.

enkephalins (en-kef′ah-linz) A group of pentapeptides, or synthetic derivatives of these substances, that mimic the action of morphine in the nervous system; found in the brain, the pituitary (hypophysis), and in nerve endings elsewhere in the body.

enophthalmos (en-of-thal′mos) Retraction of the eye into the orbit, most commonly caused by trauma (e.g., fracture of orbital floor); also occurs normally in elderly people due to age-related atrophy of orbital fat.

enostosis (en-os-to′sis) An abnormal bony growth within a bone.

ensiform (en′sĭ-form) Shaped like a sword; xiphoid.

entamebiasis (en-tah-me-bi′ah-sis) See amebiasis; *Entamoeba histolytica*, under *Entamoeba*.

Entamoeba (en-tah-me′bah) A genus of amebas; most species are harmless parasites of the intestinal tract.

E. histolytica A species causing amebic dysentery in humans; may ulcerate the walls of the large intestine and reach the liver via the portal circulation, causing liver abscesses; occasionally it spreads to the lungs, brain, and skin.

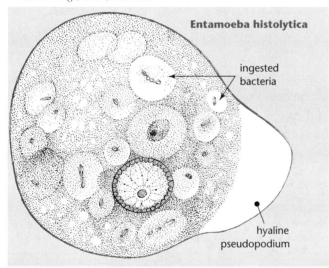

Entamoeba histolytica
ingested bacteria
hyaline pseudopodium

enteral (en′ter-al) Within the intestine or by way of the gastrointestinal tract (e.g., administration of drugs or nutrients).

enterectomy (en-ter-ek′to-me) Removal of an intestinal segment.

enteric (en-ter′ik) Relating to the intestines.

enteritis (en-ter-i′tis) Inflammation of the intestines.

regional e. See Crohn's disease, under disease.

enteroanastomosis (en-ter-o-ah-nas-to-mo′sis) See enteroenterostomy.

Enterobacter (en-ter-o-bak′ter) Genus of gram-negative, rod-shaped, gas-producing bacteria found in soil, sewage, feces, and dairy products.

E. cloacae A species found in hospital environments.

Enterobacteriaceae (en-ter-o-bak-te-re-a′se-e) A family of gram-negative, rod-shaped bacteria that includes the genus *Escherichia*.

enterobiasis (en-ter-o-bi′ah-sis) Intestinal infection with *Enterobius vermicularis*, a short roundworm commonly called pinworm.

Enterobius (en-ter-o′be-us) A genus of roundworms found in the large intestines of humans and other primates.

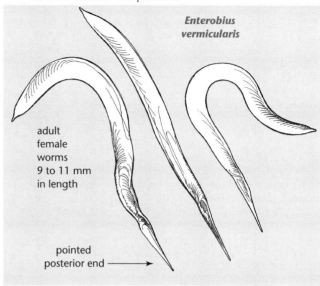

E. vermicularis The pinworm.

Enterobius vermicularis

adult female worms 9 to 11 mm in length

pointed posterior end →

enterocele (en′ter-o-sēl) A herniation of Douglas' pouch (rectouterine pouch) that may protrude *(a)* anteriorly into the rectovaginal septum, forming a bulge in the posterior vaginal wall, *(b)* posteriorly into the anal canal, simulating a prolapsed rectum, or *(c)* (rarely) in both directions, out through the vagina and through the anal canal as a "saddle hernia"; usually seen in menopausal or postmenopausal women who have borne more than one child; it is almost always associated with other musculofascial weakness (e.g., cystocele, rectocele, uterine prolapse). Also called posterior vaginal hernia; cul-de-sac hernia; Douglas' pouch hernia; rectovaginal hernia.

enterocleisis (en-ter-o-kli′sis) Occlusion of the intestinal tract.

omental e. The operative use of omentum to close an opening in the intestinal wall.

enteroclysis (en-ter-ok′lĭ-sis) See high enema, under enema.

Enterococcus (en-ter-o-kok′us) A genus of gram-positive, round bacteria; its species were previously thought to be members of the genus *Streptococcus*.

E. faecalis A species isolated from clinical specimens of the human intestinal tract; it is a cause of subacute bacterial endocarditis. Formerly called *Streptococcus faecalis*.

E. faecium A species normally inhabitating the human intestinal tract. Formerly called *Streptococcus faecium*.

enterococcus (en-ter-o-kok′us) Any bacterium of the genus *Enterococcus*.

enterocolitis (en-ter-o-ko-li′tis) Inflammation of the intestinal mucous membrane.

necrotizing e. (NEC) An acquired disease of newborn infants, resulting from vascular and mucosal damage of the intestinal wall, which allows bacterial-viral invasion and gangrenous deterioration of the bowel; it usually occurs in premature infants within the first week of life and three to seven days after institution of feeding through a tube inserted into the stomach (enteral nutrition). Several bacteria and viruses have been implicated (e.g., *Escherichia coli*, enterobacter, salmonella, coronoviruses, rotaviruses, enteroviruses).

pseudomembranous e. A severe form of colitis with formation, and passage in the feces, of a membrane-resembling material or plaques containing bits of intestinal lining (mucosa); associated with prolonged antibiotic therapy.

enterocolostomy (en-ter-o-ko-los′to-me) Operative creation of an opening between the small intestine and any part of the colon.

enterocyst (en′ter-o-sist) A cyst within the peritoneal lining of the intestine.

enteroenterostomy (en′ter-o-en-ter-os′to-me) The suturing together of two segments of the intestine. Also called intestinal anastomosis; enteroanastomosis.

E

enterogastrone (en-ter-o-gas′trōn) A gastrointestinal hormone secreted by the duodenum in the presence of fats; it inhibits both the motility and the acid secretion of the stomach.

enterokinase (en-ter-o-ki′nās) See enteropeptidase.

enterokinetic (en-ter-o-ki-net′ik) Stimulating contraction of the gastrointestinal tract.

enterolith (en′ter-o-lith) A concretion in the intestine.

enterology (en-ter-ol′o-je) The study of the intestinal tract.

enteroparesis (en-ter-o-par-e′sis) A relaxed, weak state of the intestinal walls.

enteropathogenic (en-ter-o-path-o-jen′ik) Causing intestinal disease.

enteropathy (en-ter-op′ah-the) Any intestinal disease.

    gluten-induced e. See celiac disease, under disease.

    protein-losing e. Excessive excretion of serum protein, especially albumin, resulting in hypoproteinemia.

enteropeptidase (en-ter-o-pep′tī-dās) Enzyme secreted by the duodenal mucosa that converts the pancreatic protein trypsinogen into the protein-splitting enzyme trypsin. Also called enterokinase.

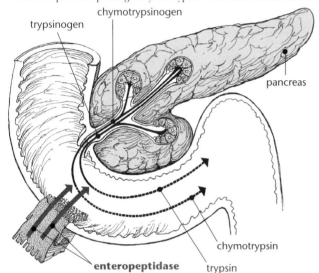

enteropexy (en′ter-o-pek-se) Suturing of a portion of the intestine to the abdominal wall.

enteroptosis (en-ter-op-to′sis) Downward displacement of the intestines upon assuming upright posture.

enterosorption (en-ter-o-sorp′shun) Adsorption of toxins, or biologically active substances, from the gastrointestinal tract onto an orally administered sorbent medium (e.g., activated charcoal).

enterospasm (en′ter-o-spazm) Intestinal spasm.

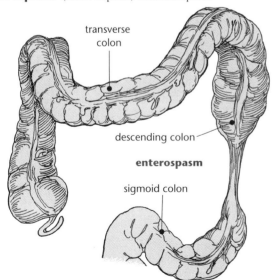

enterostenosis (en-ter-o-stĕ-no′sis) Narrowing of the intestinal lumen.

enterostomy (en-ter-os′to-me) Creation of an artificial opening into the intestine, permanent or temporary, through the abdominal wall.

enterotomy (en-ter-ot′o-me) A surgical cut into the intestine.

enterotoxin (en-ter-o-tok′sin) A substance produced by bacteria that has an adverse effect on the cells of the intestinal mucosa, causing such symptoms as vomiting and diarrhea.

Enterovirus (en-ter-o-vi′rus) Genus of viruses (family Picornaviridae) preferentially inhabiting the intestinal tract but also multiplying in nerves, muscles, and other tissues.

enterovirus (en-ter-o-vi′rus) Any member of the genus *Enterovirus*. Also called enteric virus.

enterozoon (en-ter-o-zo′on) Parasite in the intestines.

enthesitis (en-the-si′tis) Irritation of muscular attachments to bones.

ento-, ent- Prefixes meaning inside.

entoderm (en′to-derm) See endoderm.

entomology (en-to-mol′o-je) The branch of zoology concerned with the study of insects.

    forensic e. The application of entomologic knowledge to medicolegal investigations (e.g., examination of the type of insects, larvae, or maggots present in a decomposing body may help establish the approximate time of death, the season of the year in which death occurred, the presence of toxic substances, and whether the victim was killed indoors and then moved outdoors). See also insect.

    medical e. The study of insects that affect human health in any way (i.e., by inflicting harm themselves or by transporting disease-causing microorganisms).

entomophobia (en-to-mo-fo′be-ah) Abnormally exaggerated fear of insects.

entopic (en-top′ik) Situated or occurring in the normal site; opposed to ectopic.

entoptic (en-top′tik) Within the eyeball.

entozoon (en-to-zo′on), pl. entozo′a An animal parasite of internal organs.

entropion (en-tro′pe-on) A turning inward of the margin of an eyelid.

enucleate (e-nu′kle-āt) **1.** To remove whole. **2.** To remove the nucleus (e.g., from a cell).

enucleation (e-nu-kle-a′shun) Surgical removal of an organ (e.g., an eyeball) or a tumor in its entirety.

enuresis (en-u-re′sis) Involuntary release of urine.

    nocturnal e. Involuntary and repeated release of urine while asleep occurring in children beyond the age of toilet training; may be of nervous or emotional origin, or may be caused by infection or inflammation of the urinary tract. Commonly called bed-wetting.

envelope (en′vĕ-lōp) Any enclosing covering or membrane.

    nuclear e. A flattened double membrane, with its individual membranes about 150 Å apart, that envelops the cell nucleus, separating it from the cytoplasm; the outer membrane is part of the endoplasmic reticulum and is studded with ribosomes that synthesize proteins between the double membrane; the inner membrane, somewhat thinner than the outer one, is in direct contact with the nucleus and at some stages of division, some chromosomes may attach to its inner surface; the double membranes are fused at intervals to form nuclear pores, which are passageways between the nucleus and the cytoplasm.

environment (en-vi′ron-ment) The aggregate of the external conditions affecting the growth, development, and health of organisms; includes physical, biological, social, and cultural factors.

    minimal acceptable e. The emotional climate and physical surroundings necessary for children to grow physically, mentally, socially, and emotionally.

envy (en′ve) A feeling of ill will or resentment toward another who has characteristics, advantages, or possessions that one desires for oneself.

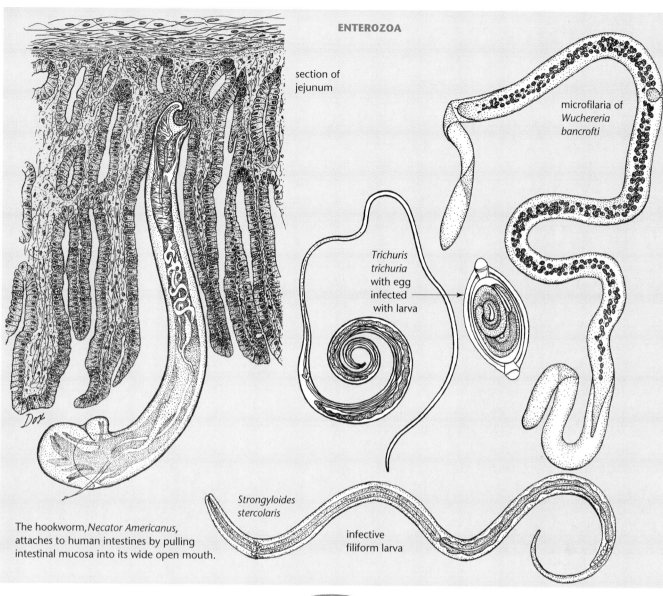

section of jejunum

microfilaria of *Wuchereria bancrofti*

Trichuris trichuria with egg infected with larva

Strongyloides stercolaris

infective filiform larva

The hookworm, *Necator Americanus*, attaches to human intestines by pulling intestinal mucosa into its wide open mouth.

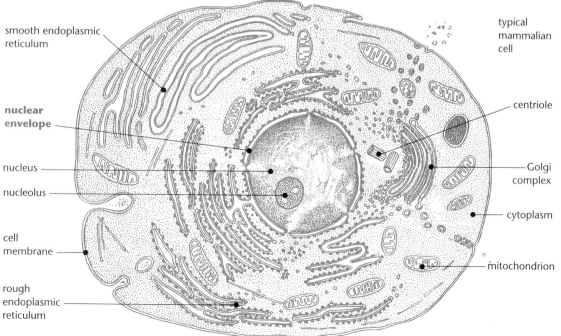

typical mammalian cell

smooth endoplasmic reticulum

nuclear envelope

nucleus

nucleolus

cell membrane

rough endoplasmic reticulum

centriole

Golgi complex

cytoplasm

mitochondrion

penis e. A psychoanalytic concept in which a woman has a generalized envy of men.

enzymatic (en-zi-mat′ik) Relating to an enzyme. Also called enzymic.

enzyme (en′zīm) A protein that acts as a catalyst, regulating the rate of chemical reactions of other body substances while remaining unchanged in the process. Also called organic catalyst.

    autolytic e. Enzyme capable of digesting the cell that produced it.

    extracellular e. An enzyme that functions outside a cell. Also called exoenzyme.

    induced e. Enzyme formed only in the presence of a specific inducer, i.e., the specific substance upon which the enzyme acts (substrate) or an analog thereof.

    intracellular e. Enzyme that acts upon the cell that produces it. Also called endoenzyme.

    respiratory e. Enzyme that takes part in oxidation-reduction processes; it transfers electrons from the substance that produced it (substrate) to molecular oxygen.

    restrictive e. See restrictive endonuclease, under endonuclease.

enzymic (en-zim′ik) See enzymatic.

enzymology (en-zi-mol′o-je) The study of enzymes, their structure and function.

enzymolysis (en-zi-mol′ĭ-sis) Chemical decomposition brought about by an enzyme.

eosin (e′o-sin) Product of coal tar, used in solution to stain cells for microscopic study. Cells that take up eosin acquire a red color.

eosinopenia (e-o-sin-o-pe′ne-ah) Deficiency of eosinophils, white blood cells that stain readily with eosin dye.

eosinophil (e-o-sin′o-fil) See eosinophilic leukocyte, under leukocyte.

eosinophilia (e-o-sin-o-fil′e-ah) Presence of an abnormally high number of eosinophilic leukocytes in the circulating blood; characteristic of such conditions as allergic drug reactions, parasitic infections, bronchial asthma, hay fever, collagen-vascular diseases, and malignant tumors. Also called eosinophilic leukocytosis.

    simple pulmonary e. The presence of benign, transient infiltrates in the lungs accompanied by prominent eosinophilia in peripheral blood; may be asymptomatic or may cause cough and fever; most frequent causes are roundworm infestation and administration of certain drugs. Also called Löffler's syndrome.

eosinophilic (e-o-sin-o-fil′ik) Stained readily with the acid dye eosin.

ependyma (ĕ-pen′dĭ-mah) The lining membrane of the cerebral ventricles and central canal of the spinal cord.

ependymal (ĕ-pen′dĭ-mal) Relating to or composed of ependyma.

ependymoma (ĕ-pen-dĭ-mo′mah) Tumor derived from the lining membrane of the cerebral ventricles and spinal canal; most frequently seen in the fourth ventricle up to the age of 20 years, and in the spine in older adults; although benign, it tends to recur after removal.

ephedrine (ĕ-fed′rin) Drug that stimulates release of the neurotransmitter norepinephrine; used in eyedrops to narrow dilated blood vessels and reduce redness of the eye, to dilate bronchi in the treatment of asthma, and as a decongestant.

ephelides (ĕ-fel′ĭ-dēz) Freckles.

ephelis (ĕ-fe′lis), pl. ephel′ides A freckle.

epi- Prefix meaning upon.

epibulbar (ep-ī-bul′bar) Over the eyeball.

epicanthus (ep-ī-kan′thus) A semilunar skin fold of the upper eyelid, extending from its medial surface downward to cover the medial corner (inner canthus) of the eye and caruncle; normal characteristic of many individuals, including Native Americans, Chinese, Japanese, Malayans, Mongolians, Siberians, Koreans, and Eskimos; may also occur in others as a congenital anomaly, as in Down's syndrome. Also called epicanthal fold; palpebronasal fold; plica palpebronasalis.

epicardia (ep-ī-kar′de-ah) The portion of the esophagus from the diaphragm to the stomach.

epicardium (ep-ī-kar′de-um) The inner layer of the membrane enclosing the heart (pericardium); it is in contact with the heart.

epicondyle (ep-ī-kon′dīl) Any bony protuberance on or above the smooth articular eminence of a long bone (condyle).

    external e. of femur See lateral epicondyle of femur.

    external e. of humerus See lateral epicondyle of humerus.

    internal e. of femur See medial epicondyle of femur.

    internal e. of humerus See medial epicondyle of humerus.

    lateral e. of femur The short, most lateral prominence of the lower femur, just above the lateral condyle; it gives attachment to the fibular collateral ligament of the knee joint. Also called external epicondyle of femur.

    lateral e. of humerus The blunt, most lateral prominence of the lower humerus, just above the capitulum; it gives attachment anterolaterally to the radial collateral ligament of the elbow joint, and to the tendon common to the origin of the supinator and some of the extensor muscles of the forearm; posteriorly, it gives attachment to the anconeus muscle.

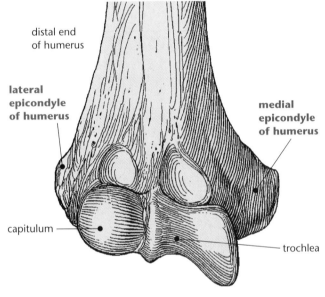

distal end of humerus

lateral epicondyle of humerus

medial epicondyle of humerus

capitulum

trochlea

    medial e. of femur A large medial convex prominence of the lower femur just above the medial condyle; it gives attachment to the tibial collateral ligament of the knee joint. Also called internal epicondyle of femur.

    medial e. of humerus A conspicuous prominence of the lower humerus, just above and medial to the trochlea; it gives attachment to the ulnar collateral ligament of the elbow joint below, to the round pronator (pronator teres) muscle above, and to a common tendon of origin of most of the forearm's flexor muscles in the middle. Also called internal epicondyle of humerus.

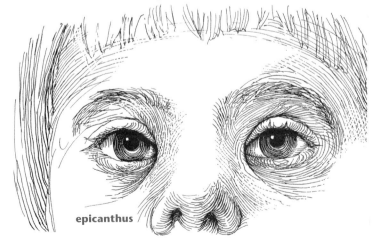

epicanthus

E

epicondylitis (ep′ĭ-kon-dī-li′tis) Inflammation of tissues surrounding a bony prominence (epicondyle) at a joint.

    lateral humeral e. Chronic pain and tenderness of tendons on the outer side of the elbow, near the lateral epicondyle of the humerus, usually due to repetitive strenuous rotatory motion of the wrist against resistance (as in manual screwdriving) or forceful extension of the wrist with the hand in a pronated position (as in playing tennis). Also called tennis elbow.

epicranium (ep-ĭ-kra′ne-um) The scalp, including muscle, aponeurosis, and skin covering the cranium.

epicrisis (ep-ĭ-kri′sis) Secondary crisis occurring after the first, primary crisis of a disease.

epicritic (ep-ĭ-krit′ik) Denoting sensory nerve fibers in skin and mucous membranes that perceive fine variations in touch and temperature.

epidemic (ep-ĭ-dem′ik) **1.** An outbreak of a disease, specific health-related behavior, or other health-related event affecting people of one community at the same time, in excess of normal expectancy, and during a specified time period. **2.** Relating to epidemics.

    common source e. Short-term epidemic, lasting a few days or hours, occurring in a group of persons or animals exposed to the same source of infection. Also called point epidemic; point source epidemic.

      point e. See common source epidemic.

      point source e. See common source epidemic.

epidemiography (ep-ĭ-de-me-og′rah-fe) Treatise on one or several epidemic diseases.

epidemiologist (ep-ĭ-de-me-ol′o-jist) A specialist in epidemiology.

epidemiology (ep-ĭ-de-me-ol′o-je) The study of the distribution and determinants of disease and health-related conditions in specified populations; knowledge gained in such a study is used to develop programs to prevent and control the spread of disease.

    chronic disease e. Epidemiology conducted to determine the possible causes of diseases that may have a prolonged latency or dormant period before they are clinically identifiable.

epidermal (ep-ĭ-der′mal) Relating to the superficial layer of skin (epidermis).

epidermatoplasty (ep-ĭ-der-mat′o-plas-te) Skin grafting.

epidermis (ep-ĭ-der′mis), pl. epider′mides The outer of the two layers of the skin, varying in thickness from 0.05 to 1.5 mm; it is devoid of blood vessels (receives nutrition through diffusion from capillaries of the deeper layer of the skin) and contains a limited distribution of nerve endings; it is composed of five layers: *(1)* an outer horny layer (stratum corneum), which is highly impermeable to water; *(2)* a clear layer (stratum lucidum), composed of several layers of clear, transparent cells; *(3)* a granular layer (stratum granulosum), composed of flattened granular cells; *(4)* a prickle-cell layer (stratum spinosum), composed of polyhedral cells with short spines (processes); and *(5)* a basal layer (stratum basale), composed of columnar cells arranged perpendicularly and in contact with the dermis. In some areas of the body, the clear layer may be absent. See also skin.

epidermodysplasia verruciformis (ep-ĭ-der-mo-dis-pla′se-ah vĕ-roo-sĭ-for′mis) Development of numerous flat warts, especially on the hands and feet, some of which tend to become cancerous. Also called Lewandowski-Lutz disease.

epidermolysis bullosa (ep-ĭ-der-mol′ĭ-sis bul-lo′sa) (EB) A group of inherited disorders characterized by a loose state of the superficial layer of the skin (epidermis), which tends to form large blisters at various levels of the epidermis as a result of pressure or minor trauma.

    dystrophic e.b., e.b. dystrophica A scarring type of epidermolysis bullosa with onset at birth; the epidermis as a whole separates from the deep layer of the skin (dermis) to form blisters; occurs in two variants: *autosomal dominant*, a relatively mild form; and *autosomal recessive*, a severe form marked by deforming blistering of the hands and feet in a mitten pattern with webbing of fingers and damage of nails, teeth, and hair; the mouth and esophagus may be also involved.

    junctional e.b. A progressive, potentially fatal form with onset at birth; characterized by severe widespread, unscarring blisters. Also called Herlitz disease; formerly called epidermolysis bullosa letalis.

    e.b. simplex A form inherited as an autosomal dominant trait and occurring in both children and adults; blisters develop on sites of friction only and heal rapidly without scarring.

Epidermophyton (ep-ĭ-der-mof′ĭ-ton) Genus of fungi causing skin diseases.

epididymectomy (ep-ĭ-did-ĭ-mek′to-me) Removal of the epididymis.

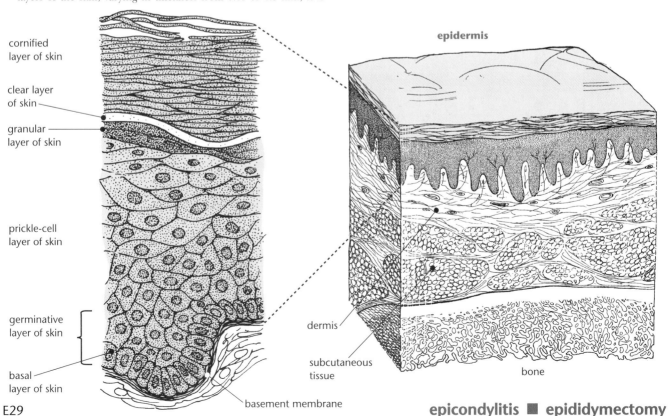

cornified layer of skin

clear layer of skin

granular layer of skin

prickle-cell layer of skin

germinative layer of skin

basal layer of skin

basement membrane

epidermis

dermis

subcutaneous tissue

bone

epicondylitis ■ epididymectomy

epididymis (ep-ĭ-did′ĭ-mis) The tortuous, cordlike excretory duct connected to the posterior border of the testis that provides storage, transit, and maturation of the spermatozoa; it consists of a head (15–20 coiled tubules), a body, and a tail (single convoluted duct continuous with the deferent duct).

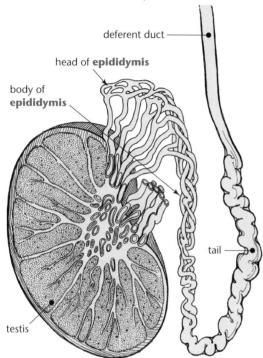

deferent duct

head of **epididymis**

body of **epididymis**

tail

testis

epididymitis (ep-ĭ-did-ĭ-mi′tis) Inflammation of the epididymis; the causes vary, depending on age of patient.

epididymo-orchitis (ep-ĭ-did′ĭ-mo or-ki′tis) Inflammation of both epididymis and testis.

epididymotomy (ep-ĭ-did-ĭ-mot′o-me) A surgical cut into the epididymis.

epididymovasostomy (ep-ĭ-did-ĭ-mo-vaz-os′to-me) Surgical joining of the epididymis and the deferent duct (vas deferens) to bypass an obstruction in the duct, thereby allowing the sperm to pass up the duct from the epididymis.

epidural (ep-ĭ-du′ral) Outside or upon the dura mater.

epigastrium (ep-ĭ-gas′tre-um) The upper central area of the abdomen; the pit of the stomach.

epiglottis (ep-ĭ-glot′is) The leaf-shaped cartilage that covers the opening of the larynx during swallowing to prevent food from entering the airways.

epiglottitis (ep-ĭ-glot-ti′tis) Inflammation of the epiglottis; may cause respiratory obstruction.

　　acute e. Condition, seen usually in children, necessitating emergency treatment (e.g., tracheal intubation); characterized by sudden onset of fever, difficult swallowing, drooling, muffled voice, and a shrill respiratory sound; almost always caused by *Haemophilus influenzae* type B; *Streptococcus pneumoniae* has also been implicated.

epikeratophakia (ep-ĭ-ker-ah-to-fa′ke-ah) Eye operation in which a section of cornea from a donor is sutured onto the anterior surface of the patient's cornea from which the transparent covering (epithelium) has been removed; performed for the correction of refractive errors (e.g., hyperopia); it can also be used after cataract extraction.

epikeratophakic (ep-ĭ-ker-ah-to-fa′kik) Relating to epikeratophakia.

epilation (ep-ĭ-la′shun) Removal of hair in its entirety.

epilepsy (ep′ĭ-lep-se) A chronic disorder, or group of disorders, characterized by recurrent, unpredictable seizures occurring spontaneously without consistent provoking factors; the seizures reflect a temporary physiologic dysfunction of the brain in which nerve cells (neurons) in the cerebral cortex produce excessive electrical discharges.

focal e. Epilepsy characterized by minor seizures restricted to isolated areas of the body, arising in a localized area of a cerebral hemisphere. Also called partial epilepsy; local epilepsy.

generalized e. Epilepsy characterized by seizures that result from involvement of both cerebral hemispheres; may range from minor (absence seizures) to major (tonic-clonic seizures).

generalized tonic-clonic e. Epilepsy marked by loss of consciousness and stiffness of the entire body, i.e., sustained (tonic) muscular contractions, followed by jerking (clonic) movements. Also called grand mal epilepsy; major epilepsy; grand mal; falling sickness. See also status epilepticus.

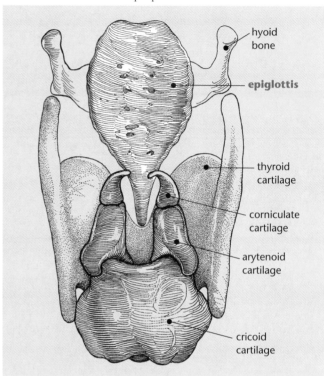

hyoid bone

epiglottis

thyroid cartilage

corniculate cartilage

arytenoid cartilage

cricoid cartilage

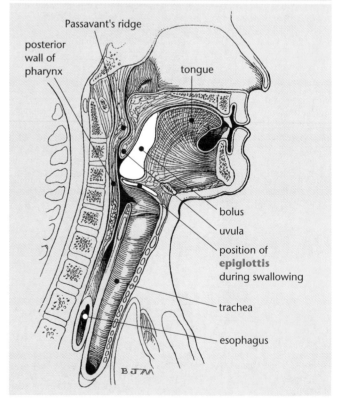

Passavant's ridge

posterior wall of pharynx

tongue

bolus

uvula

position of **epiglottis** during swallowing

trachea

esophagus

B JM

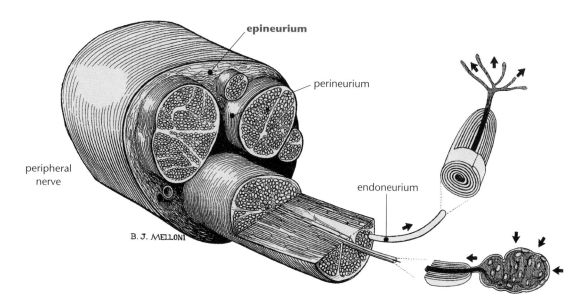

epineurium

perineurium

peripheral nerve

endoneurium

B. J. MELLONI

grand mal e. See generalized tonic-clonic epilepsy.

jacksonian e. Focal epilepsy in which the seizure arises in a localized area of the motor cortex and spreads to adjacent areas, manifested by a twitching beginning at the periphery of a structure and progressing to involve the entire musculature of one side.

local e. See focal epilepsy.

major e. See generalized tonic-clonic epilepsy.

nocturnal e. Epilepsy in which the attacks occur mainly at night, while the person sleeps.

partial e. See focal epilepsy.

petit mal e. See absence.

posttraumatic e. Epilepsy caused by brain damage incurred in a head injury; most frequently seen in penetrating brain injuries and in depressed skull fractures with injury to underlying brain; it also occurs in closed head trauma.

psychomotor e. Obsolete term. See temporal lobe epilepsy.

sleep e. See narcolepsy.

temporal lobe e. A type of focal epilepsy in which the seizure arises from all or part of the temporal lobe, often producing auditory, olfactory, or gustatory hallucinations, as well as bizarre activity and behavior; it often arises after injury to the temporal lobe. Formerly called psychomotor epilepsy.

uncinate e. A type of temporal lobe epilepsy in which the seizure arises from the anteromedial aspect of the temporal lobe, causing impairment of consciousness and a dreamy state with hallucinations of smell and taste; usually caused by a medial temporal lesion.

epileptic (ep-ĭ-lep′tik) **1.** Relating to epilepsy. **2.** A person who has epilepsy.

epileptoid (ep-ĭ-lep′toid) Resembling epilepsy.

epiloia (ep-ĭ-loi′ah) See tuberous sclerosis, under sclerosis.

epimandibular (ep-ĭ-man-dib′u-lar) On the lower jaw.

epimenorrhea (ep-ĭ-men-o-re′ah) Menstruation occurring at excessively short intervals.

epimicroscope (ep-ĭ-mi′kro-skōp) Opaque microscope; microscope equipped with a condenser around the objective for illuminating the specimen.

epimysium (ep-ĭ-mis′e-um) Connective tissue surrounding a skeletal muscle.

epinephrine (ep-ĭ-nef′rin) **1.** Hormone produced by the medulla of the adrenal gland; it is released into the circulation in response to stress, exercise, or emotions; it stimulates the sympathetic nervous system. Also called adrenaline. **2.** A synthetic drug that produces heart stimulation, constriction or dilation of blood vessels, and bronchial relaxation; used as a heart stimulant and in the treatment of bronchial asthma.

epineural (ep-ĭ-nu′ral) Overlying the neural arch of a vertebra.

epineurial (ep-ĭ-nu′re-al) Relating to the connective tissue surrounding a nerve trunk (epineurium).

epineurium (ep-ĭ-nu′re-um) Connective tissue covering a peripheral nerve.

epipharynx (ep-ĭ-far′inks) See nasopharynx.

epiphenomenon (ep-ĭ-fĕ-nom′ĕ-non) Any symptom that occurs during the course of a disease but is not necessarily associated with it.

epiphora (ĕ-pif′o-rah) Persistent overflow of tears onto the cheek; may be due to injury disrupting the tear-conveying passages to the nose (e.g., in avulsion of the medial canthal ligament at the inner corner of the eye), to eversion of the margin of the lower eyelid, or to excessive tear secretion.

epiphysiodesis (ep-ĭ-fiz-e-od′ĕ-sis) **1.** Premature fusion of the end (epiphysis) of a long bone and its shaft (diaphysis), resulting in arrest of growth. **2.** Surgical destruction of the epiphyseal plate of a long bone to arrest growth of the bone shaft prematurely (e.g., to equalize the length of the legs).

epiphysis (ĕ-pif′ĭ-sis), pl. epiph′yses The end of a long bone, developed and ossified separately from the shaft (diaphysis) and initially separated from the latter by a plate of cartilage (the "growth plate").

epiphysitis (ĕ-pif-ĭ-si′tis) Inflammation of an epiphysis.

traumatic tibial e. A knee injury most commonly seen in adolescents active in sports; produced when the powerful vastus muscle complex, which inserts into a small area of the tibial tuberosity, exerts a sufficiently forceful contraction to separate a small portion of bone in an area of developmental bone formation; symptoms include a "knee knob" or protrusion below the kneecap (patella), tenderness elicited by pressure, and pain when the knee is extended against resistance. Also called Osgood-Schlatter disease; Osgood-Schlatter syndrome.

epiplo- A combining form meaning omentum.

epiploic (ep-ĭ-plo′ik) See omental.

epiploitis (ĕ-pip-lo-i′tis) See omentitis.

epiplopexy (ĕ-pip′lo-pek-se) See omentopexy.

episclera (ep-ĭ-skle′rah) The loose connective tissue over the white of the eye (sclera) and under the transparent cover of the eye (conjunctiva); it contains a large number of minute blood vessels.

episcleritis (ep-ĭ-skle-ri′tis) Inflammation of the episclera.

episio- Combining form meaning vulva.

episioperineorrhaphy (ĕ-piz-e-o-per-ĭ-ne-or′ah-fe) Surgical repair of a lacerated vulva and adjoining musculofibrous tissues (perineum).

episioplasty (ĕ-piz′e-o-plas′te) Surgical repair of a defect of the vulva.

episiotomy (ĕ-piz-e-ot′o-me) Incision of the posterior vaginal wall for controlled enlargement of the vaginal opening at the time of childbirth; performed to prevent vaginal, vulvar, or perineal tear; to shorten the second stage of labor; and to prevent undue pressure on the fetal skull during childbirth. The two most common incisions are median and mediolateral. Also called perineotomy.

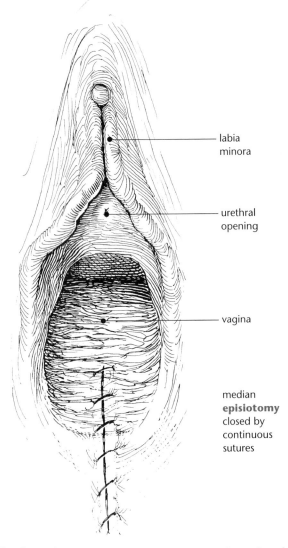

labia
minora

urethral
opening

vagina

median
episiotomy
closed by
continuous
sutures

episode (epʹĭ-sōd) A distinct occurrence or event (e.g., of an abnormal condition or disease).
    e. of care An interval of care provided by a health care facility or professional for a specific medical condition.
episome (epʹĭ-sōm) Genetic material of bacteria that can replicate either independently or as segments of the bacterial chromosome.
epispadias (ep-ĭ-spaʹde-as) Developmental defect in the male in which the urethral opening is on the dorsal surface of the penis; lso a similar defect in the female in which a fissure is present in the upper wall of the urethra.
epispastic (ep-ĭ-spasʹtik) See vesicant.
epispinal (ep-ĭ-spiʹnal) On the vertebral column.
episplenitis (ep-ĭ-splĕ-niʹtis) Inflammation of the fibrous covering of the spleen.
epistasis (ĕ-pisʹtah-sis) **1.** The suppressive action of one gene over another. **2.** A surface film formed on standing urine.
epistaxis (ep-ĭ-stakʹsis) Nosebleed.
episternal (ep-ĭ-sterʹnal) Over the breastbone (sternum).
epithelial (ep-ĭ-theʹle-al) Relating to the outermost layer (epithelium) covering all body surfaces.
epithelialization (ep-ĭ-the-le-al-ĭ-zaʹshun) Final stage in the healing of superficial injuries during which the denuded area is covered with epithelium. Also called epithelization.
epithelioid (ep-ĭ-theʹle-oid) Resembling the outermost layer (epithelium) of skin or mucous membranes.

epithelioma (ep-ĭ-the-le-oʹmah) Malignant tumor of the skin or mucous membrane.
    basal cell e. See basal cell carcinoma, under carcinoma.
    chorionic e. See choriocarcinoma.
    Malherbe's calcifying e. See pilomatrixoma.

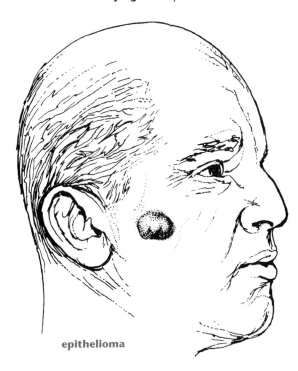

epithelioma

epithelium (ep-ĭ-theʹle-um) The nonvascular, closely packed cellular layer that covers the external surface and the mucous membrane of the entire body; functions as a selective barrier, capable of facilitating or preventing the passage of substances across the surfaces which it covers; classified as simple (one-layered) and stratified (multilayered). Also called epithelial tissue.
    ciliated e. Any epithelium bearing fine hairlike strands (cilia) on the free surface; it facilitates the movement of matter (e.g., of the ovum in the uterine tube or of inhaled particles in the respiratory tract).
    columnar e. Epithelium composed of tall (columnar) cells.
    cuboidal e. Epithelium composed of cube-shaped cells.

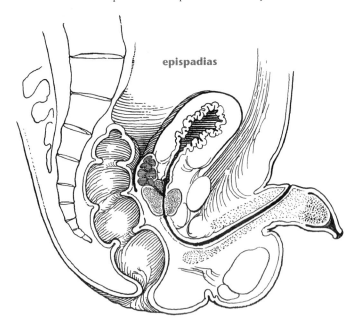

epispadias

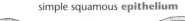

simple squamous **epithelium**

simple cuboidal **epithelium**

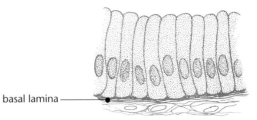

simple columnar **epithelium**

basal lamina

stratified squamous **epithelium**

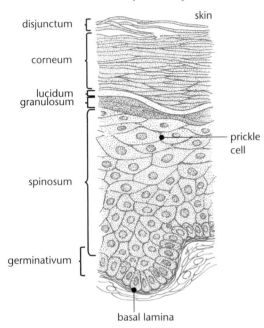

disjunctum
corneum
lucidum
granulosum
spinosum
germinativum

skin

prickle cell

basal lamina

ciliated pseudostratified columnar **epithelium**

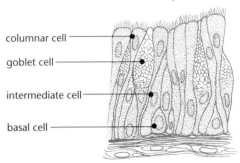

columnar cell
goblet cell
intermediate cell
basal cell

transitional **epithelium**

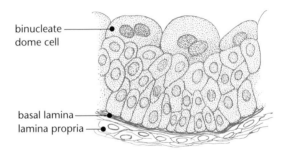

binucleate dome cell

basal lamina
lamina propria

germinal e. Specialized covering of the free surface of the ovary; in the young female it is composed of cuboidal cells; in older adults the cells are flattened.

gingival e. The epithelium of the gums (gingiva); it is composed of stratified squamous cells.

junctional e. A collarlike band of stratified epithelium that provides attachment for the free gingival margin to a tooth surface.

olfactory e. The pseudostratified epithelium lining the olfactory area of the nasal cavity; it is composed of olfactory receptor cells, supporting (sustentacular) cells, and basal cells.

pseudostratified columnar e. Epithelium in which all the cells are in contact with the basement membrane, but their nuclei lie at different levels in a vertical section, giving the false impression of more than one layer of cells.

respiratory e. Epithelium composed of columnar or pseudostratified ciliated cells, goblet cells, nonciliated columnar cells (with microvilli), and basal cells; it lines most of the respiratory tract.

sensory e. Epithelium containing sensory cells, as those restricted to the special sense organ of the olfactory system.

simple e. Unilayered epithelium; may be divided according to the shape of the constituent cells into squamous, cuboidal, and columnar types.

squamous e. Epithelium composed of flattened, polygonal cells, as seen lining the alveoli of the lungs.

stratified e. Multilayered epithelium.

transitional e. The stratified columnar epithelium of the urinary passage, extending from the ends of the collecting ducts of the kidneys, through the ureters and bladder to the distal end of the urethra. The transitional epithelium is capable of being greatly stretched without losing its integrity by modifying the arrangement of its constituent cells.

visceral e. A unicellular layer of squamous mesothelial cells that covers various organs.

epithelization (ep-ĭ-the-lĭ-za′shun) See epithelialization.

epitope (ep′ĭ-top) See antigenic determinant, under determinant.

epizoic (ep-ĭ-zo′ik) Living as a parasite on the body surface of the host.

epizoon (ep-ĭ-zo′on), pl. epizo′a An animal that is parasitic on the surface of its host's body.

Epoetin alfa (e-pō-e′tin al′fah) A genetically engineered form of the kidney protein erythropoietin that stimulates the production of red blood cells (erythrocytes); used mainly to treat the anemia associated with end-stage renal disease; also administered to AIDS patients to counteract the anemia caused by zidovudine (AZT) therapy and to patients on dialysis. Also called Epoin alfa. Trade names include Epogen; Procrit.

Epogen (e′pō-jen) Trade name for a preparation of Epoetin alfa.

Epoin alfa (e′pō-in al′fah) See Epoetin alfa.

eponychia (ep-o-nik′e-ah) Infection of the eponychium.

eponychium (ep-o-nik′e-um) **1.** The narrow fold of skin extending over the root of the nail; its free cornified margin forms the cuticle (cuticular fold). **2.** The horny epidermis at the site of the future nail of the embryo.

eponym (ep′o-nim) The name of a disease, structure, or surgical procedure that includes the name of a person (e.g., Barrett's esophagus).

eponymic (ep-o-nim′ik) Named after a person.

epoophoron (ep-o-of′o-ron) Vestiges of the embryonic mesone-

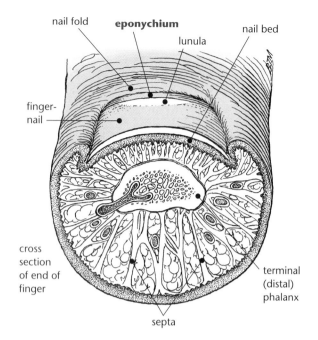

nail fold | **eponychium** | nail bed | lunula | finger-nail | cross section of end of finger | terminal (distal) phalanx | septa

phros (wolffian body) consisting of rudimentary tubules located in the mesosalpinx between the ovary and ovarian tube.

epsilon-aminocaproic acid (ep'-si-lon ah-me-no-kah-pro'ik as'id) (EACP) A compound that inhibits dissolutiion of fibrin in the blood; used to prevent bleeding. Also written ξ-aminocaproic acid.

epulis (ĕ-pu'lis) A tumor of the gums.

 e. gravidarum Tumor of the gums typically occurring during pregnancy and regressing after childbirth.

equation (e-kwa'zhun) A statement representing the equality of two entities.

equicaloric (e-kwi-kah-lōr'ik) Having the same heat value.

equilibration (e-kwĭ-lĭ-bra'shun) **1.** The act of bringing about or maintaining balance. **2.** In dentistry, adjustment of contact (occlusal) surfaces of upper and lower teeth to equalize pressure.

equilibrium (e-kwĭ-lib're-um) **1.** In chemistry, a stable condition created by two reactions occurring at equal speed in opposite directions. **2.** Mental or emotional stability. **3.** A state of bodily balance. **4.** Maintenance of body position or orientation.

 acid-base e. See acid-base balance, under balance.

equivalence (e-kwiv'ah-lens) **1.** In immunology, the concentrations of antigen and antibody that result in maximum immune complexes. **2.** In chemistry, the relative combining power of a set of atoms or radicals.

equivalent (e-kwiv'ah-lent) **1.** Equal in any way. **2.** Having similar or equal effects.

 biological e.'s Drug products that are chemical equivalents and that, when administered in the same amounts, provide the same biologic or physiologic availability, as measured by blood levels or urine levels. See also chemical equivalents.

 chemical e. See gram equivalent.

 chemical e.'s Drug products that contain identical amounts of the identical active ingredients in identical dosage forms (but not necessarily the same inactive ingredients), and that meet existing physical-chemical standards in the official compendium (*US Pharmacopeia-National Formulary*).

 gram e. (*a*) The weight of a substance that can combine with, or displace, a unit weight of hydrogen from a compound or its equivalent of another substance. (*b*) The atomic or molecular weight of an atom or group of atoms involved in a chemical reaction divided by the number of electrons shared, donated, or taken up by the atom or group of atoms during that reaction. (*c*) The weight of a substance contained in 1 liter of 1 normal solution. Also called chemical equivalent.

 nitrogen e. The nitrogen content of protein.

 therapeutic e.'s Drug products that are chemical equivalents and that, when administered in the same amounts, provide the same therapeutic results, as measured by the control of a symptom or disease. See also chemical equivalents.

 toxic e. A measure of toxicity of a poison or toxin expressed as the amount of the substance per kilogram of body weight necessary to kill a test animal.

erbium (er'be-um) Rare-earth element; symbol Er, atomic number 68, atomic weight 167.26.

erectile (ĕ-rek'tĭl) Capable of becoming turgid.

erection (ĕ-rek'shun) Firmness, swelling, and elevation of the penis.

erector (ĕ-rek'tor) A structure (e.g., a muscle) that raises and holds up a part.

erethism (er'ĕ-thizm) A heightened degree of irritability and excitability accompanied by mental and emotional changes; may be associated with inorganic mercury poisoning.

erg (erg) Unit of work equal to 1 dyne moving a weight of 1 gram a distance of 1 cm. In the SI system = 10^{-7} joule.

ergastoplasm (er-gas'to-plazm) See granular endoplasmic reticulum, under reticulum.

ergo- Combining form meaning work.

ergocalciferol (er-go-kal-sif'er-ol) See vitamin D_2, under vitamin.

ergograph (er'go-graf) Instrument for recording the amount of work performed by a muscular contraction, or the amplitude of the contraction. Also called dynamograph.

ergometer (er-gom'ĕ-ter) An instrument for measuring the amount of physical work performed and the body's response to a controlled amount of exercise. It records continuously (during and immediately after activity) the heart rate and rhythm, blood pressure, rate of breathing, and amount of oxygen taken up from ambient air. The exercise is performed on a stationary bicycle, treadmill, or rowing machine. Also called dynamometer.

ergometry (er-gom'ĕ-tre) Any method of measuring (*a*) the amount of physical work done by an organism; (*b*) the power of a muscle or a group of muscles.

ergonomics (er-go-nom'iks) The study of activities and behavior of people working with mechanical and electronic equipment, in the office or on the factory floor, taking into account the variable anatomic, physiologic, and psychologic attributes of the people working in the given environment. Also called human factor engineering.

equivalent measures and weights

US Customary Unit (Avoirdupois)	US Equivalents	Metric Equivalents
LENGTH		
inch	0.083 foot	2.54 centimeters
foot	1/3 yard or 12 inches	0.3048 meters
yard	3 feet or 36 inches	0.9144 meters
CAPACITY		
fluid ounce	8 fluid ounces	29.573 milliliters
pint	16 fluid ounces	0.473 liter
quart	2 pints	0.946 liter
gallon	4 quarts	3.785 liters
WEIGHT		
grain	0.036 dram	64.798 milligrams
dram	27.344 grains	1.772 grams
ounce	16 drams	28.350 grams
pound	16 ounces	453.592 grams

Apothecary Weight Unit	US Customary Equivalents	Metric Equivalents
scruple	20 grains	1.296 grams
dram	60 grains	3.888 grams
ounce	480 grains	31.103 grams

ergonomist (er-gon′o-mist) A specialist in ergonomics, concerned with designing or improving the environment of the workplace; the aim is to ensure the safe, healthy, and efficient attainment of personal and organizational goals.

ergonovine (er-go-no′vin) Drug derived from ergot that causes muscular contractions; effective in control of bleeding after childbirth caused by atony of the uterus. Occasional adverse effects include an allergic reaction (sometimes leading to shock), and extreme elevation of blood pressure.

ergosterol (er-gos′tĕ-rol) Sterol present in plant and animal tissues; converted to vitamin D₂ under ultraviolet irradiation.

ergot (er′got) Any fungus of the genus *Claviceps* that infests cereal plants; it has muscle-contracting and blood vessel–constricting properties and yields drugs of clinical usefulness.

ergotamine (er-got′ah-min) Drug derived from ergot; it stimulates muscular contraction, especially of the uterus and blood vessels; it may cause exacerbation of angina pectoris.

ergotism (er′got-izm) Poisoning by ergot-infested grain or from excessive use of medicinal ergot; constriction of arterioles leads to pain and, if allowed to persist, gangrene of the extremities.

ERISA Acronym for the Employee Retirement Income Security Act, which exempts self-insured health plans from state laws governing health insurance, including risk pools, prohibitions against disease discrimination, and other state health reforms.

erogenous (ĕ-roj′ĕ-nus) Producing sexual desire. Also called erotogenic.

erosion (e-ro′zhun) 1. Gradual wearing away. 2. Progressive loss of tooth substance by a chemical or abrasive process without bacterial action, resulting in a hard, polished, smooth depression on the tooth surface.

erotic (ĕ-rot′ik) Relating to sexual arousal.

eroticism (e-rot′ĭ-sizm) A state of sexual excitement.

erotogenic (ĕ-ro-to-jen′ik) See erogenous.

erratic (ĕ-rat′ik) 1. Denoting symptoms that do not follow the usual pattern. 2. Unconventional.

error (er′or) Defect.

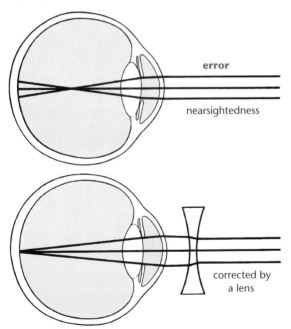

inborn e.'s of metabolism Inherited disorders caused by a gene-determined defect; each involves a single enzyme; manifestations may be the result of accumulation of the substance upon which the enzyme acts (substrate), of a deficiency of the product of the enzyme, or of forcing metabolism through an auxiliary path.

erubescence (er-u-bes′ens) Flushing of the skin; a blush.

eructation (ĕ-ruk-ta′shun) The expulsion of stomach gas or air through the mouth. Commonly called belching.

eruption (e-rup′shun) 1. The process of breaking out with skin lesions. 2. Skin lesions; a rash. 3. Cutting a tooth; piercing of the gums by an erupting tooth.

drug e. Skin rash occurring as an allergic reaction to a drug taken internally. Also called dermatitis medicamentosa.

eruption of deciduous teeth

central incisors	6–8 months
lateral incisors	7–9 months
cuspids	16–18 months
first molars	12–14 months
second molars	20–24 months

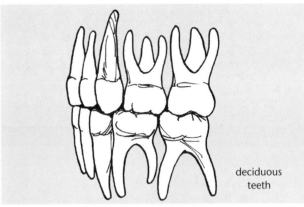

deciduous teeth

eruption of permanent teeth

central incisors	6–8 years
lateral incisors	7–9 years
cuspids	9–12 years
first bicuspids	10–12 years
second bicuspids	10–12 years
first molars	6–7 years
second molars	11–13 years
third molars	17–21 years

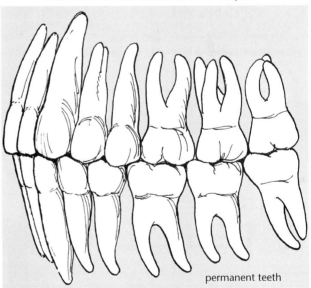

permanent teeth

erysipelas (er-ĭ-sip′ĕ-las) Acute, contagious skin disease with involvement of cutaneous lymphatic vessels; caused by group A streptococcus organisms; marked by a rapidly spreading reddish rash with sharp borders, chiefly on the face, with fever, chills, and vomiting.

coastal e. See onchocerciasis.

erysipeloid (er-ĭ-sip′ĕ-loid) Infection of the hands with the bacillus *Erysipelothrix rhusiopathiae;* marked by a self-limiting reddish eruption at a site of injury; seen in animal handlers (butchers, fishermen, veterinarians).

erysipelotoxin (er-ĭ-sip-ĕ-lo-tok′sin) Toxin produced by group A hemolytic streptococci bacteria; present in erysipelas.

erythema (er-ĭ-the′mah) Redness of the skin.

e. chronicum migrans The characteristic lesion of Lyme disease; an oval, peripherally expanding red eruption, with a central clearing at the site of a tick bite (*Ixodes dammini*).

e. induratum Inflammation of subcutaneous fat (panniculitis) typically affecting adolescents and menopausal women; marked by formation of nodules, especially on the legs, which eventually ulcerate. Cause is unknown.

e. infectiosum A mild viral infection, most commonly seen in school-aged children, marked by a lacelike skin rash; caused by human parvovirus B19. Also called fifth disease.

e. marginatum A rash of macular lesions with reddish borders and central clearing, usually occurring on the trunk with a "bathing suit distribution"; sometimes seen in children in association with rheumatic fever.

e. migrans An oval or round, slowly spreading ring around a central tick bite; often associated with Lyme disease.

e. multiforme Eruption of skin lesions occurring in a variety of forms, most commonly red papules and vesicles, often circular with a dark necrotizing center (target or iris lesion); most common causes include reactions to drugs or to concurrent infections (e.g., herpes simplex, *Mycoplasma*).

e. multiforme bollusom See Stevens-Johnson syndrome, under syndrome.

e. nodosum Inflammation of subcutaneous fat (panniculitis) typically of abrupt onset, occurring as a hypersensitive reaction to a drug (e.g., birth control pills) or in association with infections, inflammatory bowel disease, sarcoidosis, or internal organ cancer; characterized by bright red, painful nodules on the shins, frequently on the anterior thighs and extensor surfaces of the forearms. Also called nodal fever.

e. toxicum Diffuse skin rash occurring as an allergic reaction to a toxic substance. A form frequently seen in newborn infants (50%), usually at 24 to 48 hours of age, is characterized by blotches of reddish macules 2 to 3 cm in diameter anywhere on the body but most prominently on the chest; lesions usually fade within 48 hours.

erythermalgia (er-ĭ-ther-mal′je-ah) Painful reddening of hands and feet occurring on exposure to warmth (e.g., warm water and when "coming in from the cold"); usually of unknown cause but may be associated with other conditions (e.g., connective tissue diseases).

erythrasma (er-ĭ-thraz′mah) Contagious skin eruption of reddish brown patches in the armpit and groin; caused by the bacterium *Corynebacterium minutissimum*.

erythredema (ĕ-rith-rĕ-de′mah) See acrodynia.

erythremia (er-ĭ-thre′me-ah) See polycythemia vera.

erythrityl tetranitrate (ĕ-rith′rĭ-til tet-rah-ni′trāt) Drug used in the treatment of angina pectoris for its coronary artery vasodilating effect.

erythro-, erythr- Combining forms meaning red.

erythroblast (ĕ-rith′ro-blast) A young red blood cell in its immature, nucleated stage from which a mature red blood cell (erythrocyte) develops.

acidophilic e. See orthochromatic normoblast, under normoblast.

basophilic e. See basophilic normoblast, under normoblast.

early e. See basophilic normoblast, under normoblast.

eosinophilic e. See orthochromatic normoblast, under normoblast.

intermediate e. See polychromatic normoblast, under normoblast.

late e. See orthochromatic normoblast, under normoblast.

orthochromatic e. See orthochromatic normoblast, under normoblast.

oxyphilic e. See orthochromatic normoblast, under normoblast.

polychromatic e. See polychromatic normoblast, under normoblast.

erythroblastemia (ĕ-rith′ro-blas-te′me-ah) The presence of immature nucleated red blood cells (erythroblasts) in the peripheral blood; may occur in a variety of diseases.

erythroblastopenia (ĕ-rith′ro-blas-to-pe′ne-ah) Primary deficiency of young red blood cells (erythroblasts) in bone marrow; seen in aplastic anemia.

erythroblastosis (ĕ-rith′ro-blas-to′sis) Abnormally large number of immature red blood cells (erythroblasts) in the blood.

e. fetalis, fetal e. See hemolytic disease of the newborn, under disease.

erythrochromia (ĕ-rith-ro-kro′me-ah) A red coloration.

erythroclasis (er-ĕ-throk′lah-sis) Fragmentation of red blood cells.

erythrocyanosis (ĕ-rith-ro-si-ah-no′sis) Purplish discoloration in areas with significant subcutaneous fat (e.g., thighs and buttocks), which produces intense burning sensations especially upon exposure to cold temperatures; seen mainly in overweight young women.

erythrocyte (ĕ-rith′ro-sīt) A mature red blood cell; it has a life span of about 120 days.

erythrocythemia (ĕ-rith-ro-si-the′me-ah) See polycythemia.

erythrocytic (ĕ-rith-ro-sit′ik) Relating to red blood cells.

erythrocytolysin (ĕ-rith-ro-si-tol′ĭ-sin) See hemolysin.

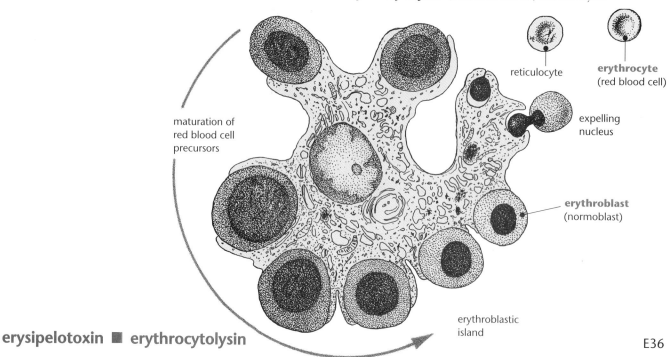

reticulocyte

erythrocyte (red blood cell)

maturation of red blood cell precursors

expelling nucleus

erythroblast (normoblast)

erythroblastic island

erythrocytolysis (ĕ-rith-ro-si-tol′ĭ-sis) See hemolysis.

erythrocytometer (ĕ-rith-ro-si-tom′ĕ-ter) See hemocytometer.

erythrocytopenia (ĕ-rith-ro-si-to-pe′ne-ah) See erythropenia.

erythrocytorrhexis (ĕ-rith-ro-si-to-rek′sis) Partial destruction of red blood cells, which allows escape of protoplasm and consequent alteration of the cells' appearance. Also called erythrorrhexis.

erythrocytosis (ĕ-rith-ro-si-to′sis) See polycythemia.

erythrocyturia (ĕ-rith-ro-si-tu′re-ah) Presence of red blood cells in the urine.

erythroderma (ĕ-rith-ro-der′mah) Widespread redness of the skin usually associated with a moist, oozing scaling and shedding; in adults, it may be due to a drug reaction, aggravation of an underlying skin condition, or an underlying malignancy (especially lymphoma).

erythrodontia (ĕ-rith-ro-don′she-ah) Reddish discoloration of the teeth.

erythrogenesis imperfecta (ĕ-rith-ro-jen′ĕ-sis im-per-fek′tah) See congenital hypoplastic anemia, under anemia.

erythrogenic (ĕ-rith-ro-jen′ik) 1. Causing a red color or a red skin rash. 2. Producing red blood cells (seldom-used term).

erythroid (er′ĭ-throid) Reddish.

erythrokinetics (ĕ-rith-ro-ki-net′iks) The rate of red blood cell formation in relation to the rate of red blood cell destruction (i.e., the mechanism of maintaining a steady number of circulating red blood cells in the normal individual).

erythroleukemia (ĕ-rith-ro-lu-ke′me-ah) Proliferation of immature red and white blood cells.

erythrolysin (er-ĭ-throl′ĭ-sin) See hemolysin.

erythromelalgia (ĕ-rith-ro-mel-al′je-ah) Disorder of blood circulation causing a burning sensation of the hands and/or feet, sometimes involving the whole limb and lasting from minutes to hours.

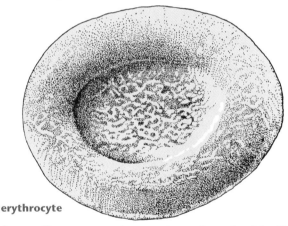

erythrocyte

erythromelia (ĕ-rith-ro-me′le-ah) Widespread atrophy of the skin.

erythromycin (ĕ-rith-ro-mi′sin) Antibiotic drug effective against a variety of infections, especially those of the skin, throat, chest, and ears caused by streptococci, staphylococci, mycoplasma, or *Legionella* organisms.

erythron (er′ĭ-thron) The total mass of red blood cells and the tissues producing them, viewed as a functional, though dispersed, organ.

erythropenia (ĕ-rith-ro-pe′ne-ah) Deficiency of red blood cells. Also called erythrocytopenia.

erythrophagia (ĕ-rith-ro-fa′je-ah) See erythrophagocytosis.

erythrophagocytosis (ĕ-rith-ro-fag′o-si-to′sis) Engulfment and digestion of red blood cells by other cells, such as monocytes and polymorphonuclear leukocytes.

erythroplasia of Queyrat (ĕ-rith-ro-pla′ze-ah of ka-rahz′) A squamous cell carcinoma *in situ* on the head of the penis, appearing as a localized chronic, velvety, red plaque.

erythropoiesis (ĕ-rith-ro-poi-e′sis) The formation of red blood cells.

    ineffective e. Condition in which red blood cells are produced normally but do not last to maturity.

erythropoietic (ĕ-rith-ro-poi-et′ik) Relating to the formation of red blood cells.

erythropoietin (ĕ-rith-ro-poi′ĕ-tin) A hormone produced mainly by the kidneys in response to a reduced concentration of red blood cells (erythrocytes); it stimulates the bone marrow to produce red blood cells, and thereby enhances the oxygen-carrying capacity of the blood. Also called hemopoietin.

erythroprosopalgia (ĕ-rith-ro-pros-o-pal′je-ah) Burning pain and redness of the face, believed to indicate organic disease of the nervous system.

erythropyknosis (ĕ-rith-ro-pik-no′sis) A degenerated condition of red blood cells, which become dark and shrunken (brassy bodies); caused by malarial parasites.

erythrorrhexis (ĕ-rith-ro-rek′sis) See erythrocytorrhexis.

erythruria (er-ĭ-throo′re-ah) Passing urine of a red color.

escape (es-kāp′) The emergence of a lower, suppressed, cardiac pacemaker to initiate ventricular contraction when the normal, higher, pacemaker defaults, or when atrioventricular conduction of impulses fails.

    nodal e. Escape with the atrioventricular (A-V) node as pacemaker.

    ventricular e. Escape with an ectopic ventricular focus as pacemaker.

eschar (es′kar) A scab.

escharotic (es-kah-rot′ik) Caustic.

Escherichia (esh-er-ik′e-a) A genus of gram-negative bacteria (family Enterobacteriaceae) present in feces; some may cause disease in humans.

    E. coli A motile species normally inhabiting human intestines.

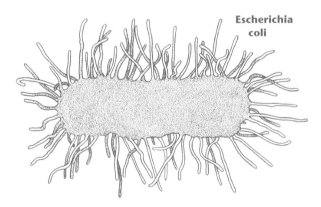

Escherichia coli

escutcheon (es-kuch′an) A shield-shaped area (e.g., the pattern of pubic hair).

eserine (es′er-in) See physostigmine.

-esis Suffix meaning a process (e.g., amniocentesis).

esodeviation (e-so-de-ve-a′shun) 1. Esophoria. 2. Esotropia.

esodic (e-sod′ik) See afferent.

esophagalgia (ĕ-sof-ah-gal′je-ah) Pain in the esophagus. Also called esophagodynia.

esophageal (ĕ-sof-ah-je′al) Relating to the esophagus.

esophagectasia, esophagectasis (ĕ-sof-ah-jek-ta′se-ah, ĕ-sof-ah-jek′tah-sis) Abnormal dilatation of the esophagus.

esophagectomy (ĕ-sof-ah-jek′to-me) Removal of a portion of the esophagus.

esophagitis (ĕ-sof-ah-ji′tis) Inflammation of the esophagus; may be acute or chronic, and caused by bacteria, viruses, chemicals, or trauma.

    Candida e. Esophagitis caused by infection with *Candida* organisms; predisposing factors include deficiency of immune system (e.g., in AIDS), diabetes, malignancy, and corrosive injuries; symptoms include painful, difficult swallowing and oral thrush.

    corrosive e. Acute esophagitis caused by swallowing a corrosive chemical, accidentally or in an attempted suicide; symptoms include swelling, severe pain, and shock.

    herpes e. Esophagitis caused by herpes I or II, varicella-zoster virus, or cytomegalovirus, which produces painful, difficult swallowing, fever, and bleeding.

  peptic e. See reflux esophagitis.

  pill-related e. Esophagitis with a tendency to form strictures caused by habitual lying down after swallowing pills with small sips of fluid or by swallowing pills with insufficient fluid to sweep them into the stomach.

  reflux e. Diffuse esophagitis of the distal esophagus caused by habitual regurgitation of gastric juice and/or other stomach contents through an incompetent lower esophageal sphincter muscle; frequently associated with a hiatal hernia or a duodenal ulcer. Also called peptic esophagitis.

esophagocardioplasty (ĕ-sof-ah-go-kar′de-o-plas-te) Reparative operation on the lower esophagus and adjacent cardiac portion of the stomach.

esophagocele (ĕ-sof′ah-go-sēl) Herniation of the mucous membrane of the esophagus through a tear in the esophageal muscular layer.

esophagodynia (ĕ-sof-ah-go-din′e-ah) See esophagalgia.

esophagoenterostomy (ĕ-sof-ah-go-en-ter-os′to-me) Surgical connection of the esophagus and small intestine after removal of the stomach.

esophagogastrectomy (ĕ-sof-ah-go-gas-trek′to-me) Removal of a portion of the lower esophagus and adjacent portion of the stomach; usually performed for eradication of a cancerous tumor.

esophagogastroduodenoscopy (ĕ-sof-ah-go-gas′tro-du′od-ĕ-nos′ko-pe) Inspection of the interior of the esophagus, stomach, and duodenum with an endoscope.

esophagogastroplasty (ĕ-sof-ah-go-gas′tro-plas-te) Surgical procedure on the muscular junction of the esophagus and stomach (e.g., for relief of spasm). Also called cardioplasty.

esophagogastrostomy (ĕ-sof-ah-go-gas-tros′to-me) Surgical creation of an artificial communication between the esophagus and the stomach. Also called gastroesophagostomy.

esophagogram (ĕ-sof′ah-go-gram) An x-ray picture of the esophagus.

esophagojejunostomy (ĕ-sof-ah-go-jĕ′ju-nos′to-me) Surgical creation of alimentary continuity after total removal of the stomach by connecting the lower esophagus to the jejunum.

esophagomalacia (ĕ-sof-ah-go-mah-la′she-ah) Abnormal softening of the walls of the esophagus.

esophagomyotomy (ĕ-sof-ah-go-mi-ot′o-me) Operation for the relief of sustained muscular contraction (achalasia) at the junction of the esophagus and the stomach; consists of a longitudinal cut through the sphincter muscle down to, but not including, the mucosa. Also called cardiomyotomy.

esophagoplasty (ĕ-sof′ah-go-plas-te) Reparative operation upon the esophagus.

esophagoplication (ĕ-sof-ah-go-pli-ka′shun) The suturing of longitudinal folds in the walls of a stretched esophagus to reduce the size of its lumen.

esophagoscope (ĕ-sof′ah-go-skōp) Any of various instruments designed for inspecting the interior of the esophagus.

esophagoscopy (ĕ-sof-ah-gos′ko-pe) Examination of the interior of the esophagus with an esophagoscope; may be used to locate, identify, and photograph pathologic changes, to obtain biopsy material or perform other surgical procedures, or to introduce medication.

esophagostenosis (ĕ-sof-ah-go-stĕ-no′sis) Abnormal narrowing of the esophagus.

esophagostomy (ĕ-sof-ah-gos′to-me) An external opening (stoma) made directly into the esophagus from without.

esophagotomy (ĕ-sof-ah-got′o-me) A surgical cut into the esophagus.

esophagus (ĕ-sof′ah-gus) The part of the digestive tract consisting of a musculomembranous tube that extends downward from the pharynx to the cardia of the stomach, just below the diaphragm. It is about 25 cm long in the adult.

  Barrett's e. Abnormal cellular changes in the lining of the

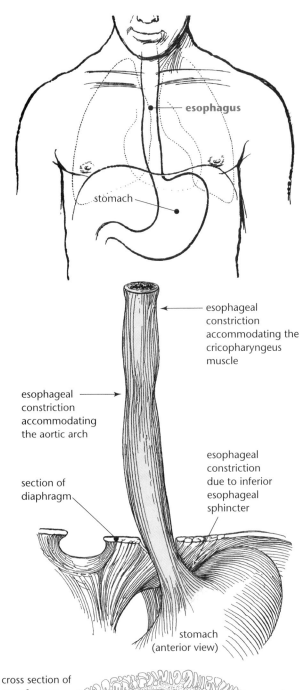

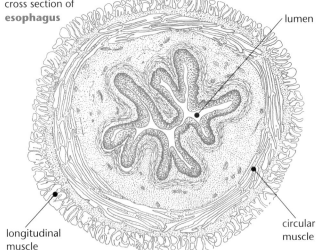

lower esophagus in which the normal cells are replaced by a mixture of gastric and intestinal cell types; seen in persons with long-standing reflux of stomach contents into the esophagus, most commonly in adults but may occur in children and infants. It is associated with an increased risk of developing ulceration (Barrett's ulcer), stricture, and adenocarcinoma of the esophagus. Also called Barrett's syndrome.

esophoria (es-o-fo're-ah) A tendency of the eyes to turn inward, toward the nose.

esophoric (es-o-for'ik) Relating to esophoria.

esotropia (es-o-tro'pe-ah) Strabismus in which one or both eyes deviate inward, toward the nose. Also called convergent strabismus; convergent squint; cross-eye.

esotropic (es-o-trop'ik) Relating to esotropia.

essential (ĕ-sen'shal) **1.** Necessary to life or health. **2.** Having no apparent external cause; idiopathic; applied to a disease (e.g., essential hypertension).

ester (es'ter) Organic compound formed by condensation of alcohol and carboxylic acid.

esterase (es'ter-ās) Enzyme that promotes the breakdown of esters.

esthesia (es-the'ze-ah) Perception of sense impressions.

esthesiogenic (es-the-ze-o-jen'ik) Producing a reaction in a sensory zone.

esthesiography (es-the-ze-og'ra-fe) **1.** Mapping out on the skin the areas of sensation. **2.** A description of the mechanisms of sensation.

esthesiometer (es-the-ze-om'ĕ-ter) Instrument for determining the state of the sense of touch. Also called tactometer.

estival (es'tĭ-val) Occurring in the summer.

estivoautumnal (es-tĭ-vo-aw-tum'nal) Occurring during the summer and autumn seasons.

Estraderm (es-trah'derm) Trade name for the transdermal estradiol patch; see under patch.

estradiol (es-trah-di'ol) An estrogenic hormone essential for the development and functioning of female reproductive organs; a synthetic preparation is used in estrogen replacement therapy.

estriol (es'tre-ol) An abundant but relatively weak estrogenic hormone; a major metabolic product of the hormones estradiol and estrone; found in urine.

estrogen (es'tro-jen) General term for the group of female sex hormones, responsible for stimulating the development and maintenance of female secondary sex characteristics; formed in the ovary, placenta, testis, adrenal cortex, and some plants; therapeutic uses (with natural or synthetic preparations) include the relief of menopausal symptoms and amelioration of cancer of the prostate.

conjugated e.'s A buff-colored powder, a mixture of the sodium salts of the sulfate esters of estrogenic hormones (chiefly estrone and equilin).

nonsteroidal e.'s Nonsteroidal compounds that act as estrogens.

estrone (es'trōn) An estrogenic hormone found in the ovary and in the urine of pregnant mammals.

ethacrynic acid (eth-ah-krin'ik as'id) A rapid-acting diuretic drug derived from aryloxyacetic acid.

ethambutol (ĕ-tham'bu-tōl) An antibacterial drug effective against the organism causing tuberculosis *(Mycobacterium tuberculosis)*; adverse effects may include transient swelling of the optic nerve and blurred vision.

ethamoxytriphetol (eth-ah-moks'e-tri-fe'tol) A nonsteroidal estrogen antagonist.

ethanal (eth'ah-nal) See acetaldehyde.

ethanoic acid (eth-ah-no'ik as'id) See acetic acid.

ethanol (eth'ah-nol) See alcohol.

ethchlorvynol (eth-klōr'vĭ-nol) Drug with anticonvulsant and sedative properties.

ether (e'ther) **1.** Any organic compound having two hydrocarbon groups linked by an oxygen atom. **2.** Term generally used for the anesthetic diethyl ether.

anesthetic e. See diethyl ether.

ethereal (e-the're-al) **1.** Relating to ether. **2.** Evanescent.

ethical (eth'ĭ-kal) **1.** Relating to ethics. **2.** In conformity with professionally accepted principles.

ethics (eth'iks) Standards of conduct governing an individual or a profession.

medical e. A code of behavior that governs professional relationships between physician and patient and the patient's family, and among physicians.

ethinyl estradiol (eth'ĭ-nil es-trah-di'ol) Synthetic estradiol, the female sex hormone; most commonly used as an ingredient of oral contraceptives.

ethmoid (eth'moid) Resembling a sieve (e.g., the ethmoid bone).

ethmoidectomy (eth-moi-dek'to-me) Removal of portions of the ethmoid bone.

ethmoiditis (eth-moi-di'tis) Inflammation of the mucous membrane lining the ethmoid bone.

ethmosphenoid (eth-mo-sfe'noid) Relating to both the ethmoid and sphenoid bones.

ethosuximide (eth-o-suk'sĭ-mīd) Anticonvulsive drug used in the management of petit mal epilepsy (absence attacks); adverse effects may include nausea, vomiting, and, on rare occasions, aplastic anemia.

ethylaldehyde (eth'il-al'dĕ-hīd) See acetaldehyde.

ethyl chloride (eth'il klo'rīd) A gas at ordinary temperatures, a volatile liquid under pressure; once used as an anesthetic, now used as a local anesthetic before minor surgery (e.g., lancing a boil) or to ameliorate muscle ache. Also called chloroethane.

ethylene (eth'ĭ-lēn) An explosive gas formerly used as an inhalation anesthetic.

ethylene dibromide (eth'ĭ-lēn di-bro'mīd) (EDB) Chemical pesticide widely used as a fumigant of foodstuffs; has been incriminated as a carcinogen.

ethylene glycol (eth'ĭ-lēn gli'kol) Common ingredient of antifreeze products that can be absorbed through skin, mucous membranes, and digestive tract; acts as depressant of central nervous system and is metabolized to calcium oxalate, which, deposited as crystals in the kidney, causes acute kidney failure; chronic exposure in the workplace causes cracking and scaling of the skin; ingestion seen on occasion in alcoholics causes vomiting, a sweet breath odor, slurred speech, staggering gait, pulmonary edema, coma, and death.

ethylenediamine tetra-acetic acid (eth-il-ēn-di'ah-mēn-tet'rah-ah-se'tik as'id) (EDTA) A heavy metal antagonist (chelating agent) that forms complexes (chelates) with divalent and trivalent metals; used in the treatment of lead poisoning.

estrogens
estrone
estriol
estradiol

esophoria ■ **ethylenediamine tetra-acetic acid**

etio- Combining form meaning cause.

etiocholanolone (e-te-o-ko-lan'o-lōn) Product of metabolism of hormones from the adrenal cortex and the testis; excreted in the urine.

etiolation (e-te-o-la'shun) **1.** Paleness of the skin from deprivation of sunshine. **2.** Blanching.

etiologic (e-te-o-loj'ik) Relating to etiology.

etiology (e-te-ol'o-je) Study of the causes of disease and their mechanism of action.

etoposide (e-to-po'sid) A semisynthetic derivative of podophyllotoxin that inhibits cell division (mitosis), decreases DNA production, and is effective against certain tumors; adverse effects may include nausea and vomiting, fever and chills, bone marrow depression, and kidney damage.

Eubacterium (u-bak-te're-um) Genus of anaerobic bacteria; some species may cause disease.

eubiotics (u-bi-ot'iks) The science concerned with healthy living.

eucaine (u'kān) Compound used as a local anesthetic.

eucaryote (u-kar'e-ōt) See eukaryote.

eucholia (u-ko'le-ah) The normal condition of bile.

euchromatin (u-kro'mah-tin) The lightly stainable portion of the cell nucleus containing genetically active DNA.

eugenics (u-jen'iks) Improvement of a population by selective breeding.

eugenol (u'jen-ol) Eugenic acid; a light yellow, oily liquid used in dentistry as an antiseptic and local anesthetic.

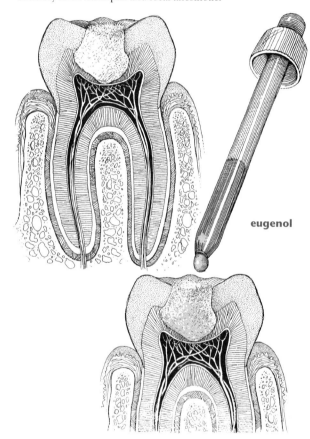

eugenol

euglobulin (u-glob'u-lin) A simple protein soluble in saline solutions; insoluble in pure water.

euglycemia (u-gli-se'me-ah) The condition of having a sugar (glucose) level in the blood within the normal range. Also called normoglycemia.

euglycemic (u-gli-se'mik) Relating to euglycemia. Also called normoglycemic.

eugonic (u-gon'ik) Growing rapidly on an artificial medium; applied to certain bacterial cultures (e.g., the human tubercle bacillus, *Mycobacterium tuberculosis*).

eukaryote (u-kar'e-ōt) Organism that has cells with a well-defined nucleus (containing chromosomes and enclosed by a nuclear membrane) and a mitotic cycle. Also written eucaryote.

eunuch (u'nuk) A male whose testes have been removed by castration or failed to develop.

eunuchoid (u'nŭ-koid) Having the characteristics of a eunuch, especially the body habitus of a male whose testicular function was absent during puberty.

eunuchoidism (u'nŭ-koi-dizm) Condition in which testes fail to function.

euosmia (u-os'me-ah) A normal state of the sense of smell.

eupepsia (u-pep'se-ah) Good, normal digestion.

euphoria (u-fo're-ah) **1.** A feeling of well-being. **2.** An exaggerated feeling of happiness not consonant with a stimulus of any kind, seen in drug-induced states and in certain mental disorders.

euplasia (u-pla'ze-ah) Normal condition of cells or tissues.

euplastic (u-plas'tik) **1.** Relating to euplasia. **2.** Able to heal quickly.

euploidy (u-ploi'de) The state of having a complete normal set of chromosomes.

eupnea (ŭp-ne'ah) Normal breathing.

europium (u-ro'pe-um) Rare-earth element; symbol Eu, atomic number 63, atomic weight 151.96.

eury- Combining form meaning wide.

eurygnathic (u-rig-nath'ik) Having a wide jaw.

euryon (u're-on) A point on the right and the left sides of the head (on each parietal bone) marking the longest transverse diameter of the head.

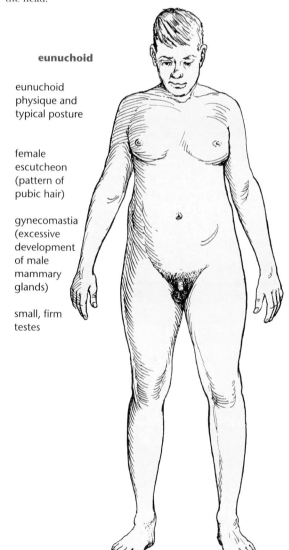

eunuchoid

eunuchoid physique and typical posture

female escutcheon (pattern of pubic hair)

gynecomastia (excessive development of male mammary glands)

small, firm testes

eustachitis (u-sta-ki′tis) Inflammation of the lining membrane of the eustachian (auditory) tube.

eutectic (u-tek′tik) **1.** Easily melted; applied to a mixture with a melting point lower than that of any of its constituent substances. **2.** Having a fixed melting point.

euthanasia (u-thah-na′zhe-ah) An easy, quiet death.

    active e. Deliberate actions, such as disconnecting life-support systems or giving a lethal overdose of a drug, that serve to cause or hasten death. Also called mercy killing; positive euthanasia.

    negative e. See passive euthanasia.

    passive e. The withholding of therapy or measures that prolong life, allowing nature to take its course; the patient is kept as comfortable and as pain-free as possible. Also called negative euthanasia; nonintervention.

    positive e. See active euthanasia.

euthyroid (u-thi′roid) Having a normally functioning thyroid gland and normal levels of thyroid hormone.

euthyroidism (u-thi′roid-ism) A normal condition of the thyroid gland.

eutonic (u-ton′ik) See normotonic.

eutrophia (u-tro′fe-ah) Healthy nutrition.

evacuant (e-vak′u-ant) **1.** Inducing a bowel movement. **2.** An agent having such an effect.

evacuate (e-vak′u-āt) To accomplish evacuation.

evacuation (e-vak-u-a′shun) **1.** The process of emptying, as of the bowels. **2.** The material discharged from the bowels. **3.** The creation of a vacuum by removing gas or air from a closed vessel.

evagination (e-vaj-ī-na′shun) Outpouching or protrusion of a part or organ.

evaluation (e-val-u-a′shun) Examination and judgment of the significance of something.

    clinical e. Evaluation based on direct observation of a patient.

evanescent (ev-ah-nes′ent) Of brief duration.

Evans blue (ev′ans blu) A dye used to measure blood volume; following intravenous injection, it binds to plasma protein so that its concentration in the blood can be used to calculate the volume of blood in which it is distributed.

evaporation (e-vap-o-ra′shun) Process by which a liquid becomes a vapor.

event (e-vent′) An occurrence.

    adverse e. (AE) In forensic medicine, an injury or complication caused by a medical intervention (rather than by the disease), which prolongs hospitalization, produces a disability, or both; examples include drug reactions and wound infections.

eventration (e-ven-tra′shun) **1.** Protrusion of the bowels through an opening on the abdominal wall. **2.** Removal of the abdominal organs.

    e. of diaphragm Elevation of part or all of the diaphragm into the thoracic cavity due to incomplete or defective development of the diaphragmatic muscle. It may also occur as a direct injury to the phrenic nerve associated with trauma to the brachial or cervical plexuses during birth.

    total abdominal e. (TAE) A technique for removing transplant organs from a dead donor in which several organs are removed en block, rather than individually, to reduce incidence of function loss.

eversion (e-ver′zhun) A turning outward (e.g., a foot) or inside out (e.g., an eyelid).

evert (e-vert′) To turn outward.

evidence (ev′ī-dens) All testimony, documents, objects, material substances, and displays presented to a court of law to either prove or disprove an alleged fact.

    trace e. Physical, often microscopic evidence (e.g., blood and seminal stains, hairs, fibers, fingerprints, paint chips, soil samples, glass fragments), that is recovered from a crime scene, from the body of a victim or assailant, or from an object involved in a crime; used to establish a connection between the crime and its perpetrator or victim.

evisceration (e-vis-er-a′shun) Removal of internal organs.

evulsion (e-vul′shun) A forcible extraction.

ex- Prefix meaning out of; from.

exacerbation (eg-zas-er-ba′shun) Increase in severity; applied to a disease or its symptoms.

examination (eg-zam-ī-na′shun) Inspection as a means of arriving at a diagnosis or assessing a therapy.

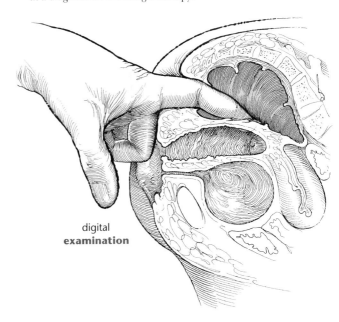

digital **examination**

    cytologic e. Microscopic examination of cells.

    Papanicolaou e. See Papanicolaou test, under test.

    physical e. The second stage of most medical examinations (after history taking), consisting of inspection, palpation, percussion, and auscultation; may be generalized to all or several parts of the body or restricted to specific areas of concern (e.g., of the ears, nose, and throat, or the pelvis).

    postmortem e. See autopsy.

    well-baby e. Periodic medical examinations of a baby to ensure continuing good health; usually conducted by physicians, sometimes by specially trained nurses; generally includes check on the child's growth and development, appropriate timely immunizations, guidance to parents in areas of nutrition.

examiner (eg-zam′in-er) A person who conducts examinations.

    medical e. (a) An appointed medical officer with training and/or expertise in forensic pathology who is empowered to investigate sudden, violent, or unexplained deaths, or any other category of death as defined by law. In many jurisdictions, medical examiners have replaced elected coroners. (b) A physician who is employed by public or private enterprise and whose duties are defined by the employer (e.g., examination of applicants for worker's compensation, or of prospective purchasers of life insurance). Also called forensic physician.

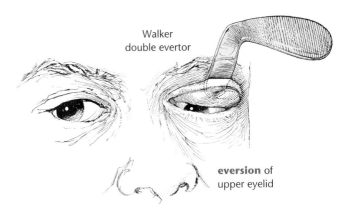

Walker double evertor

eversion of upper eyelid

exanthem (ek-san'them) Any disease accompanied by a skin eruption.

e. subitum Viral disease of sudden onset in children within 3 years of age, most commonly between 6 and 18 months; after two to four days of fever, the temperature falls and a skin rash appears; caused by human herpesvirus 6 (HHV6). Also called roseola infantum; sixth disease.

exanthema (ek-san-the'mah) See exanthem.

exanthematous (eg-san-them'ah-tus) Of the nature of exanthem.

excavation (eks-kah-va'shun) **1.** Any natural or pathologic cavity or recess. **2.** The process of hollowing out a space (e.g., in a tooth).

atrophic e. An abnormal degree of depression of the optic disk caused by atrophy of the optic nerve.

glaucomatous e. See glaucomatous cup, under cup.

physiologic c. See physiologic cup, under cup.

excavator (eks'kah-va-tor) A spoon-shaped instrument for scraping or scooping out diseased tissue or for removing carious material from a tooth.

exchange (eks-chānj') The substitution of one thing for another.

plasma e. Removal of plasma and replacement with any of various fluids; e.g., saline or dextran solutions, albumin preparations, fresh-frozen plasma (FFP), plasma protein fractions (PPF); used in the treatment of such conditions as autoimmune diseases and diseases of excess plasma factors.

excipient (ek-sip'e-ent) Inert substance used to give a pharmaceutical preparation a suitable consistency or form.

excise (ek-sīz') To remove surgically.

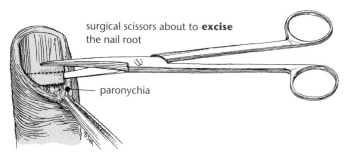

surgical scissors about to **excise** the nail root

paronychia

excision (ek-sizh'un) The surgical removal of tissues or organs.

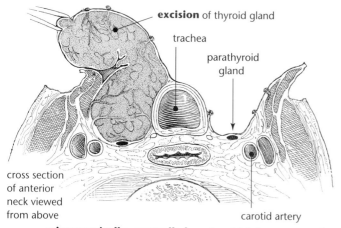

excision of thyroid gland

trachea

parathyroid gland

cross section of anterior neck viewed from above

carotid artery

microscopically controlled e. See Mohs' surgery, under surgery.

shave e. Removal of a benign, superficial skin lesion (e.g., seborrheic and actinic keratoses and dome-shaped nevi) by cutting across the base of the lesion with a scalpel or double-edged razor blade.

wide e. Complete removal of a lesion or tumor, including a margin of healthy tissue.

excitability (ek-sit-ah-bil'ĭ-te) The quality of being capable of quick response to a stimulus.

excitation (ek-si-ta'shun) **1.** Stimulation; agitation. **2.** Response to a stimulus.

excitement (ek-sit'ment) The state of being agitated.

excitoglandular (ek-si-to-glan'du-lar) Increasing the activity of a gland.

excoriate (eks-ko're-āt) To scratch the skin deeply.

excoriation (eks-ko-re-a'shun) Loss of the superficial layer of skin (epidermis) and part of the deep layer (dermis) through minor trauma, chemical damage, or breakage of blisters.

neurotic e. Skin lesions self-inflicted by emotionally disturbed persons, usually by scratching forcibly.

excrement (eks'krĕ-ment) Feces.

excrescence (eks-kres'ens) An abnormal outgrowth from a surface.

excreta (eks-kre'tah) Natural wastes discharged from the body (e.g., feces, urine).

excrete (eks-krēt') To discharge waste material from the body.

excretion (eks-kre'shun) **1.** Process by which waste products of metabolism are discharged from the body. **2.** The material so discharged.

excretory (eks'krĕ-to-re) Relating to excretion.

excursion (eks-kur'zhun) An oscillating motion; a movement implying a return to the original position (e.g., of the mandible, or of the chest wall or diaphragm).

exenteration (eks-en-ter-a'shun) Removal of an organ, especially the intestines.

orbital e. Removal of the entire contents of the orbit, including the eyeball and eyelids.

exercise (ek'ser-sīz) Repetitive activity that has, or is intended to have, a long-range effect in improving, maintaining, or restoring health or skill, or that is used for diagnosis.

aerobic e. A cardiopulmonary exercise that increases the body's ability to utilize oxygen while conditioning the heart, lungs, and blood vessels; it reduces body fat and builds endurance.

some types of **aerobic exercise**

vigorous walking
jogging
swimming
biking
rowing
jumping rope
skating
dancing

Kegel e. Contraction of the levator ani and perineal muscles for treatment of urinary stress incontinence or to strengthen the pelvic floor in the perinatal and postpartum periods.

muscle-setting e. Exercise of a muscle whose contraction does not result in joint motion (e.g., contraction of the quadriceps muscle of the thigh when the leg is fixed in full extension by a cast). Also called static exercise.

progressive-resistant e. A weight training exercise designed to tone the skeletal muscles of the body.

static e. See muscle-setting exercise.

stump e. Exercise of muscles of an amputation stump and adjacent parts.

exergonic (ek-ser-gon'ik) Releasing energy; applied to certain chemical reactions.

exertion (ek-ser'shun) Expenditure of energy by skeletal muscle, measured by rate of oxygen consumed, heat produced, or heart rate.

exfoliation (eks-fo-le-a'shun) **1.** Peeling or shedding of skin. Also called desquamation. **2.** The casting off of deciduous teeth.

exfoliative (eks-fo'le-a-tiv) Characterized by peeling.

exhalation (eks-hah-la'shun) **1.** The act of breathing out. **2.** Exhaled gas or vapor.

exhale (eks-hāl') **1.** To breathe out. **2.** To emit gas or vapor.

exhaustion (eg-zaws'chun) **1.** Extreme fatigue. **2.** Removal or depletion of active ingredients of a drug.

heat e. Condition of sudden onset and usually brief duration, characterized by intense thirst, weakness, nausea, fatigue, headache, confusion, and cold, clammy skin but normal body temperature;

may progress to heat stroke; caused by prolonged exposure to hot temperatures. COMPARE heatstroke.

exhibitionism (ek-sĭ-bish'ŭ-nizm) Morbid compulsion to expose the genitalia.

exhumation (eks-hu-ma'shun) The process of taking a dead body out of its place of burial after obtaining legal authorization.

ex modo prescripto (eks mo'do pre-skrip'to) (e.m.p.) Latin for in the manner prescribed.

exo- Prefix meaning outside.

exoantigen (ek-so-an'te-jen) See ectoantigen.

exocrine (ek'so-krin) **1.** Denoting a gland that discharges its secretions through a duct. **2.** Denoting the secretion of such a gland.

exocytosis (eks-o-si-to'sis) Mechanism for releasing substances out of a cell by fusion with the cell membrane; the membrane ruptures at the site of fusion, thereby ejecting the substance. Also called emiocytosis.

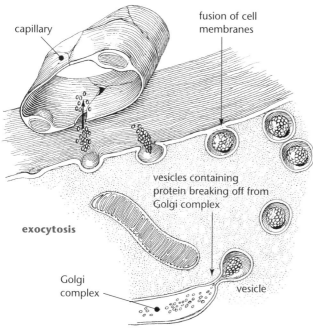

exocytosis

exodeviation (ek-so-de-ve-a'shun) **1.** Exophoria. **2.** Exotropia.

exodontics, exodontia (ek-so-don'tiks, ek-so-don'she-ah) The branch of dentistry concerned with extraction of teeth.

exoenzyme (ek-so-en'zīm) See extracellular enzyme, under enzyme.

exogenous (eks-oj'ĕ-nus) Produced or originating outside the body. Also called ectogenous.

exomphalos (eks-om'fah-los) See omphalocele.

exonuclease (ek-so-nu'kle-ās) Enzyme that removes DNA from the ends of a polynucleotide chain.

exophoria (ek-so-fo're-ah) Tendency of the eyes to turn outward.

exophthalmic (ek-sof-thal'mik) Relating to exophthalmos.

exophthalmometer (ek-sof-thal-mom'ĕ-ter) Instrument for measuring the degree of protrusion of the eyeball. Also called proptometer.

exophthalmos (ek-sof-thal'mos) Abnormal protrusion of the eyeball. May be due to hyperthyroidism or a mass behind the eye.

   malignant e. Severe exophthalmos that is usually bilateral and may be unresponsive to treatment, leading to blindness; mostly seen in middle-age people.

   pulsating e. Exophthalmos caused by a penetrating or contusion injury to the eye that has produced a shunt between arterial and venous channels, transmitting the pulse into the orbital tissues.

exostosis (ek-sos-to'sis), pl. exosto'ses Benign, mushroom-shaped outgrowth on the surface of a bone, often along bone.

   hereditary multiple e. Condition inherited as an autosomal dominant trait, marked by the formation of numerous exostoses in long bones of children due to a defect in ossification in cartilage; it causes stunted growth. Also called multiple exostosis; osteochondromatosis.

multiple e. See hereditary multiple exostosis.

exoteric (ek-so-ter'ik) Relating to external factors.

exothermic (ek-so-ther'mik) **1.** Releasing heat; applied to certain chemical reactions. **2.** Relating to the external temperature of the body.

exotoxin (ek-so-tok'sin) An injurious protein complex produced by bacteria and secreted into the environment. Also called ectotoxin; extracellular toxin.

exotoxins produced by some bacteria pathogenic to man

TOXIN	DISEASE	SPECIES	ACTION
tetanospasmin	tetanus	*Clostridium tetani*	spastic hemolytic cardiotoxin
diphtheritic toxin	diphtheria	*Corynebacterium diphtheriae*	necrotizing
α-toxin	pyogenic infection	*Staphylococcus aureus*	necrotizing, hemolytic, leukocidic
whooping cough toxin	whooping cough	*Bordetella pertussis*	necrotizing
neurotoxin	dysentery	*Shigella dysenteriae*	hemorrhagic paralytic
neurotoxin	botulism	*Clostridium botulinum*	paralytic

exotropia (ek-so-tro'pe-ah) Strabismus in which the eyes deviate outward, toward the temples. Also called divergent strabismus; divergent squint; walleye.

expansiveness (ek-span'siv-nes) An exaggerated sense of one's importance.

expectorant (ek-spek'to-rant) **1.** Promoting the coughing up or expulsion of mucus or other matter from the air passages. **2.** Any medication having such an effect.

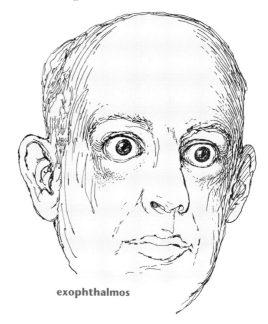

exophthalmos

expectoration (ek-spek-to-ra'shun) **1.** The process of coughing up mucus and other matter from the air passages. **2.** The matter so expelled.

experiment (ek-sper'ĭ-ment) A test, trial, or study.

   blind e. See blind trial, under trial.

   control e. Experiment for checking the results of other experiments by keeping the same conditions but omitting the particular intervention being tested.

   double-blind e. See double-blind trial, under trial.

expiration (eks-pĭ-ra'shun) **1.** The act of breathing out. **2.** Death.

expiratory (eks-pi'rah-to-re) Relating to expiration.

expire (ek-spīr') **1.** To breathe out; to exhale. **2.** To die.

explant (eks'plant) Living tissue that has been taken from its original site and placed in an artificial culture medium for growth.

exploration (eks-plo-ra'shun) A diagnostic search; may be a digital, instrumental, or surgical examination of tissues or organs.

explorer (eks-plōr'er) A sharp probe for examining teeth.

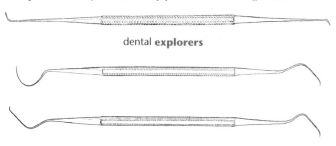

dental **explorers**

express (eks-pres') **1.** To show; to give form. **2.** To extract by squeezing.

expression (eks-presh'un) The act of expressing.

   gene e. The manifestation of the genetic material of an organism as specific traits.

expressivity (eks-pres-siv'ĭ-te) In genetics, the degree to which a heritable trait is manifested by an individual carrying the gene for the trait.

exquisite (eks-kwiz'it) Extremely intense; applied to pain or tenderness (e.g., of an inflamed organ).

exsanguinate (eks-sang'gwĭ-nāt) To drain the blood from the body or a part; may lead to death.

exsiccant (ek-sik'ant) See desiccant.

exsiccate (ek'sĭ-kāt) To remove moisture.

exsiccation (ek-sĭ-ka'shun) The process of removing moisture.

exstrophy (ek'stro-fe) Congenital turning inside out of a hollow organ.

   e. of bladder Malformation consisting of a gap in the lower abdominal wall and absence of the anterior bladder wall; the posterior bladder wall may extrude through the opening or lie exposed as an open sac; defect occurs in varying degrees of severity. Also called ectopia vesicae.

extension (eks-sten'shun) **1.** The process of straightening a limb. **2.** The condition of being straightened.

   Buck's e. A method of applying longitudinal tension to a leg; adhesive tape, applied to the leg, is attached to a cord, which in turn is passed over a pulley and connected to weights, with the foot of the bed raised so that the body acts as a counterweight. Also called Buck's traction.

   ridge e. In oral surgery, a method of increasing the relative height of a toothless alveolar bone by surgically deepening the adjacent sulci; performed to improve denture retention.

extensor (eks-ten'sor) In general, any muscle that, by contracting, extends a part.

exteriorize (eks-te're-or-īz) To direct a patient's interests toward others rather than himself.

extern (eks'tern) A medical student or recent graduate who assists in the care of hospital patients; formerly, one who lived outside the hospital.

external (eks-ter'nal) Situated on the outer surface.

exteroceptor (eks-ter-o-sep'tor) A sensory nerve ending in the skin and mucous membranes that responds primarily to stimuli from the adjacent environment.

extinction (eks-ting'shun) **1.** In behavior modification, the breaking of the stimulus-response bond; that is, the procedure of presenting the conditioned stimulus without reinforcement to a previously conditioned individual. **2.** The disappearance of a conditioned response as a result of nonreinforcement.

extirpation (ek-stir-pa'shun) Complete removal of a part or of a tumor.

extorsion (eks-tor'shun) The act of rotating outward; applied to a limb or an organ (e.g., the eye).

extra- Prefix meaning beyond; outside of; in addition.

extra-articular (eks'trah ar-tik'u-lar) Outside a joint.

extracapsular (eks-trah-kap'su-lar) Outside the capsule of a joint.

extracellular (eks-trah-sel'u-lar) Outside the cells.

extracorporeal (eks-trah-kor-po're-al) Outside the body.

extracorpuscular (eks-trah-kor-pus'ku-lar) Outside the blood corpuscles.

extracranial (eks-trah-kra'ne-al) Outside the skull.

extract (ek'strakt/ek-strakt') **1.** A semiliquid, solid, or dry powder that is the concentrated preparation of a drug. **2.** To take out or pull out forcibly.

extraction (eks-trak'shun) The act of moving or drawing out.

   breech e. In obstetrics, extraction of the baby by its buttocks.

   extracapsular e. Removal of an opaque lens (cataract), leaving the posterior portion of the lens capsule in place.

exteroceptors

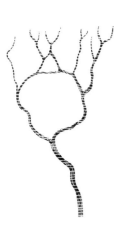

free
nerve endings
(pain)

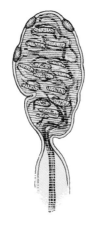

corpuscle
of Meissner
(touch)

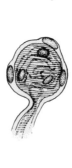

Krause's
end-bulb
(cold)

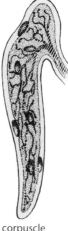

corpuscle
of Ruffini
(heat)

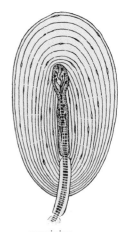

paccinian
corpuscle
(pressure)

intracapsular e. Removal of an entire opaque lens (cataract), including its capsule.

tooth e. The removal of a tooth as part of dental treatment.

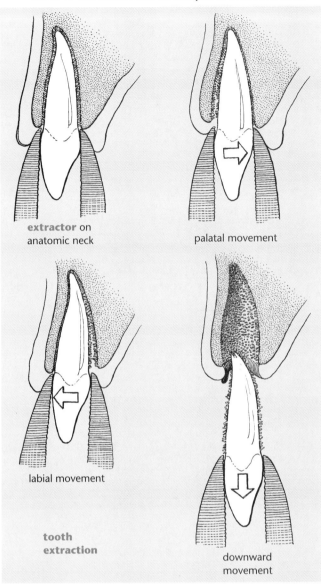

extractor on anatomic neck

palatal movement

labial movement

tooth extraction

downward movement

extractor (eks-trak′tor) Any instrument used in drawing out or removing a bodily part or foreign material, especially forceps for extracting teeth.

extractor for superior molars

extradural (eks-trah-du′ral) Situated outside the dura mater.

extrahepatic (eks-trah-hĕ-pat′ik) Outside the liver.

extramedullary (eks-trah-med′u-la-re) Outside any medulla, especially the medulla oblongata.

extramural (eks-trah-mu′ral) Outside the wall of an organ or structure (e.g., of the heart or blood vessels.)

extraneous (eks-tra′ne-us) Occurring outside an organism, or not belonging to it.

extranuclear (eks-trah-nu′kle-ar) Outside a nucleus.

extraocular (eks-trah-ok′u-lar) External to the eye.

extraperitoneal (eks-trah-per-ĭ-to-ne′al) Outside the peritoneal cavity.

extrapulmonary (eks-trah-pul′mo-na-re) Outside the lungs.

extrapyramidal (eks-trah-pĭ-ram′ĭ-dal) Outside the pyramidal tracts; applied to descending nerve tracts that are not part of the pyramids of the medulla oblongata.

extrasensory (eks-trah-sen′so-re) Not perceptible by the ordinary senses (e.g., telepathy).

extrasystole (eks-trah-sis′to-le) Premature contraction of the heart occurring in response to a stimulus from a site other than the sinoatrial (S-A) node.

ventricular **extrasystole** (premature contraction)

extrauterine (eks-trah-u′ter-in) Outside the uterus.

extravasate (eks-trav′ah-sāt) To leak out of a blood vessel or lymphatic vessel into the tissues.

extravasation (eks-trav-ah-sa′shun) **1.** Leakage of fluid from a vessel. **2.** The fluid that has leaked into the surrounding tissues.

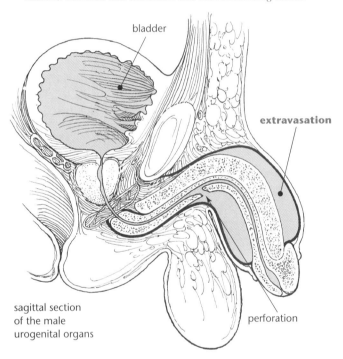

bladder

extravasation

sagittal section of the male urogenital organs

perforation

extravascular (eks-trah-vas′ku-lar) Outside blood vessels or lymphatics.

extraversion (eks-trah-ver′zhun) See extroversion.

extremity (eks-trem′ĭ-te) An arm or a leg; a limb.

extrinsic (eks-trin′sik) Originating outside the organ or part served; applied to anatomic structures (e.g., extrinsic muscles of the eye).

extroversion (eks-tro-ver′zhun) **1.** A turning inside out of a hollow organ (e.g., of the uterus). **2.** Personality trait in which a person's interests lie in the environment and other people rather than in himself.

extrude (eks-trood′) To push out.

extrusion (eks-troo′zhun) The process of pushing out, such as the migration of a tooth beyond it normal position.

extubate (eks-tu′bāt) To withdraw a tube (e.g., an endotracheal tube) that has been introduced into a body cavity.

extubation (eks-tu-ba′shun) The process of withdrawing a tube from a cavity of the body.

exuberant (eg-zu′ber-ant) Plentiful; denoting excessive growth or proliferation of tissue or granulation.

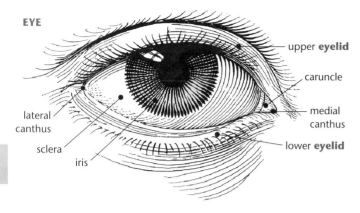

EYE

- upper **eyelid**
- caruncle
- medial canthus
- lower **eyelid**
- lateral canthus
- sclera
- iris

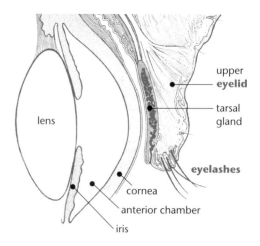

- upper **eyelid**
- tarsal gland
- **eyelashes**
- cornea
- anterior chamber
- iris
- lens

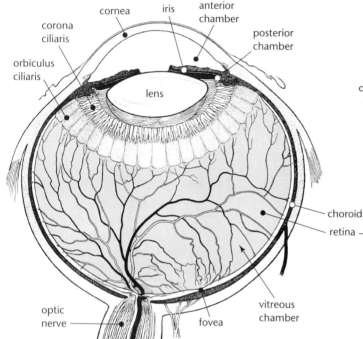

- cornea
- iris
- anterior chamber
- posterior chamber
- corona ciliaris
- orbiculus ciliaris
- lens
- choroid
- retina
- optic nerve
- fovea
- vitreous chamber

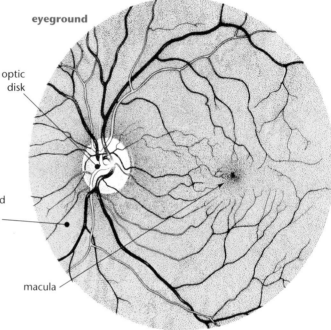

eyeground

- optic disk
- retina
- macula

exudate (eks'u-dāt) Material that has been gradually discharged and deposited in a tissue, space, or cavity, usually as a result of inflammation.

   cotton-wool e.'s See cotton-wool patches, under patch.

exudation (eks-u-da'shun) The oozing out of fluid containing white blood cells and protein from minute blood vessels into tissue spaces, due to increased permeability of the walls of the vessels, usually caused by inflammation.

exudative (eks-oo'dah-tiv) Relating to exudation.

exude (ek-zud') To ooze; to pass gradually through tissues or through an opening.

ex vivo (eks ve'vo) Outside the living body.

eye (i) The organ of vision; in humans, it is a nearly spherical structure consisting of three concentric coats: (1) the outermost, fibrous, protective coat made up of an opaque white part called the sclera (which surrounds most of the eyeball) and a transparent part called the cornea; (2) the middle, vascular, nutritive coat made up (from behind forward) of choroid, ciliary body, and iris; and (3) the innermost, nervous coat called the retina. Within the eye are the anterior and posterior chambers, filled with a clear liquid (aqueous humor), the lens, and the gelatinous vitreous body (which fills most of the eyeball).

   artificial e. See ocular prosthesis, under prosthesis.

   black e. Purplish discoloration (ecchymosis) of the eyelids due to extravasation of blood.

   dancing e.'s See opsoclonus.

   fixating e. In strabismus, the eye that is directed toward the object of regard.

   lazy e. See amblyopia.

   pink e. See pinkeye.

   shipyard e. See epidemic keratoconjunctivitis, under kerato-conjunctivitis.

   squinting e. In strabismus, the eye that is not directed toward the object of regard; the deviating eye.

   white of the e. The visible portion of the sclera.

eyeball (i'bawl) The globe of the eye.

eyebrow (i'brow) The row of hairs over the eye.

eyeground (i'ground) The inner surface of the eye as seen through the pupil with the ophthalmoscope.

eyelash (i'lash) A hair on the margin of the eyelids. Also called cilium.

eyelid (i'lid) One of two folds (upper and lower) that cover the anterior portion of the eyeball.

   granulated e.'s See marginal blepharitis, under blepharitis.

eyepiece (i'pēs) The lens or lens system in an optical instrument (e.g., a microscope) that is closest to the eye of the observer.

eyestrain (i'strān) Popular term for asthenopia; denoting fatigue or discomfort associated with the use of the eyes; may be due to uncorrected errors of refraction, imbalance of the eye muscles, or prolonged use of the eyes.

eyewash (i'wosh) A medicated solution for irrigating the eyes.

exudate ■ **eyewash**

E46

F

fabella (fah-bel′ah) A small sesamoid bone sometimes found in the tendon of the lateral head of the gastrocnemius muscle, behind the knee joint.

fabrication (fab-rĭ-ka′shun) See confabulation.

face (fās) The anterior aspect of the head, from forehead to chin and from ear to ear.

> **hippocratic f.** See hippocratic facies, under facies.
>
> **masklike f.** See Parkinson's facies, under facies.
>
> **moon f.** The rounded face characteristic of Cushing's disease.

face-bow (fās′ bo) A caliper-like instrument for recording the relationship of the jaws to the temporomandibular joints.

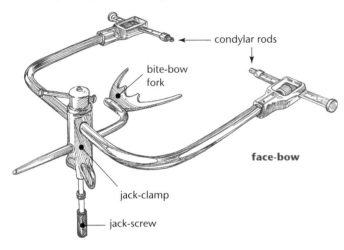

facelift (fās′lift) See rhytidectomy.

facet (fas′et) A small, highly smooth surface, such as an articulating surface on a bone or a worn area on a tooth.

> **articular f.** A flat or rounded facet on a bone at the site of articulation with another bone.

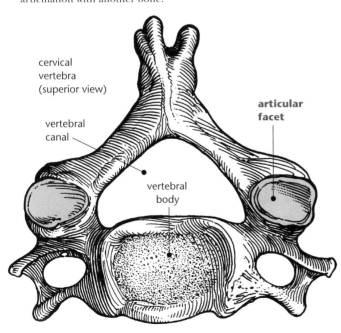

facetectomy (fas-ĕ-tek′to-me) Surgical removal of an articular facet (e.g., of a vertebra).

facial (fa′shal) Relating to the face.

facies (fa′she-ēz), pl. fa′cies **1.** The outward appearance or expression of the face characteristic of a particular condition. **2.** A surface of a body part, especially an articular surface.

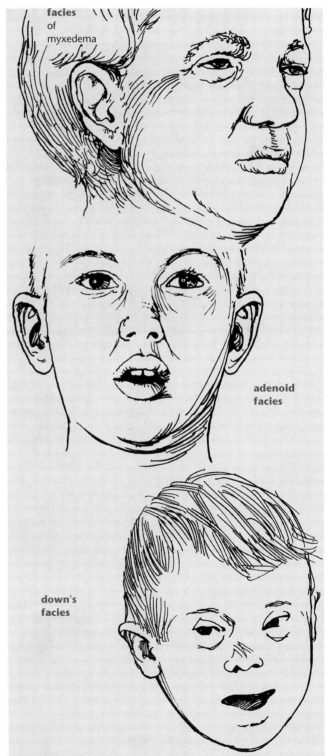

adenoid f. The open-mouth facial characteristic of children with adenoid growths obstructing breathing.

Down's f. The open-mouth, often with protruding tongue, characteristic eye and nose features of persons afflicted with Down's syndrome.

hippocratic f. The dull expression with a hollow, drawn facial appearance observed in a dying person after an exhausting illness. Also called hippocratic face.

Parkinson's f. Absence of facial expression characteristic of parkinsonism. Also called masklike face.

facilitation (fah-sil-ĭ-ta'shun) Enhancement of a natural process, such as the reinforcement of the activity of nerve tissue by additional impulses.

facility (fah-sil'ĭ-te) An institution where services are provided.

skilled nursing f. An institution that operates under the law that, in addition to room and board, *(a)* provides nursing care under the direction of a physician; *(b)* has 24-hour-a-day nursing service under the supervision of a graduate registered nurse (RN) or a licensed practical nurse (LPN); and *(c)* keeps a daily record of each patient. It may be a separate institution or part of another (e.g., of a hospital).

facing (fās'ing) In dentistry, the visible (labial or buccal) part of a combined metal-nonmetal crown; made of plastic or porcelain.

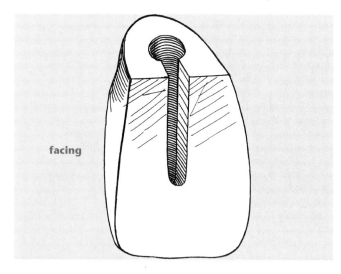

facing

facio- Combining form meaning face.

facioplegia (fa-she-o-ple'je-ah) See Bell's palsy, under palsy.

factitious (fak-tish'us) Artificial; contrived. See factitious disorders, under disorder.

factor (fak'tor) (F) A substance, circumstance, or influence that contributes to an action, process, or result such as blood clotting or the growth process. The term is generally used when the nature or mechanism of action of a substance is unknown; when those properties become known, factors are redesignated, frequently as hormones.

f. I See fibrinogen.

f. II See prothrombin.

f. III See thromboplastin.

f. IV Calcium ions present in plasma.

f. V See accelerator globulin, under globulin.

f. VI The original designation for a factor previously thought to be an activated form of a blood-coagulating protein (the accelerator globulin). The term is no longer used.

f. VII A substance that acts as an intermediate in the coagulation of blood. Its deficiency is associated with hemorrhagic disease of the newborn and purpura in the adult. Also called convertin; proconvertin; serum prothrombin conversion accelerator (SPCA); stable factor; cothromboplastin.

f. VIII An antihemophilic globulin present in plasma, essential in the first phase of blood clotting; deficiency causes the hereditary disease hemophilia A. Also called thromboplastinogen; proserum prothrombin conversion accelerator (PPCA).

f. IX Factor essential in the first phase of clotting; deficiency is inherited, causing hemophilia B.

f. X A factor essential in the second stage of blood clotting; it is required for conversion of the plasma protein prothrombin into the enzyme thrombin; deficiency of factor X may be congenital, but it also occurs in hemorrhagic disease of the newborn, liver disease, and deficiency of vitamin K.

f. XI A factor essential in the first phase of clotting; deficiency is most commonly congenital, producing a mild bleeding tendency.

f. XII Factor present in normal blood; it initiates the clotting process when plasma contacts collagen or a foreign surface. Deficiency of factor XII does not cause a bleeding tendency.

f. XIII An enzyme of blood plasma that cross-links strands of fibrin monomers, thereby creating a mesh that stabilizes the blood clot.

ABO f.'s See ABO blood group.

angiogenesis f. Substance, secreted by a white blood cell (macrophage), which stimulates growth of new blood vessels, as in cancers and in healing of wounds.

clotting f., coagulation f. Any of the substances in the blood that are essential for blood clotting; some are designated by Roman numerals, others by Arabic numerals.

coronary risk f. Any of several factors that increase the likelihood of suffering occlusion of coronary arteries (e.g., high blood pressure, smoking, elevated blood lipids, diabetes mellitus, and heredity).

corticotropin-releasing f. (CRF) See corticotropin-releasing hormone, under hormone.

epidemiologic f. Any event, characteristic, or other definable entity having the potential to bring about a change in a health state or in any other defined outcome.

fibroblast growth f. (FGF) A growth factor that plays a role in wound healing, blood vessel formation, and proliferation of arterial walls. It also facilitates entry of herpes simplex virus (HSV-1) into vertebrate cells that normally have FGF receptors on their membranes.

follicle-stimulating hormone-releasing f. (FRF; FSH-RF) See follicle-stimulating hormone-releasing hormone, under hormone.

growth hormone–releasing f. (GRF; GH-RF) See growth hormone–releasing hormone, under hormone.

intrinsic f. (IF) A mucoprotein secreted by the parietal cells of gastric glands, essential for absorption of vitamin B_{12} in the ileum; deficiency causes pernicious anemia.

luteinizing hormone–releasing f. (LHF) See luteinizing hormone–releasing hormone, under hormone.

platelet-activating f., platelet-aggregating f. (PAF) Substance released from basophilic white blood cells that induces aggregation of blood platelets and is involved in immune responses.

prolactin-inhibiting f. (PIF) A substance produced in the hypothalamus that inhibits release of the milk hormone prolactin from the anterior pituitary (adenohypophysis).

prolactin-releasing f. (PRF) A substance produced in the hypothalamus that stimulates release of the milk hormone prolactin from the anterior pituitary (adenohypophysis).

rheumatoid f. (RF) An immunoglobulin commonly found in the blood of persons with rheumatoid arthritis.

risk f. *(a)* In epidemiology, an attribute or exposure that is associated with increased probability (but not necessarily the cause) of a specified outcome, such as developing or dying from a disease. *(b)* In health insurance, a characteristic of a person that is correlated with higher probability of health care expenses (e.g., health status, age, gender).

somatotropin release-inhibiting f. See somatostatin.

stable f. See factor VII.

sun-protection f. (SPF) The increased amount of ultraviolet radiation required to produce redness of the skin in the presence of a sunscreen.

thyrotropin-releasing f. (TRF) See thyrotropin.

transfer f. (TF) *(a)* A genetic particle in bacterial cells that is transferred from one bacterium to another. *(b)* A substance, free of nucleic acid and antibody, capable of transferring antigen-specific cell-mediated immunity from donor to recipient.

tumor-angiogenesis f. (TAF) A substance that stimulates rapid formation of new blood vessels; secreted by malignant tumors and not found in normal tissues except the placenta.

facultative (fak'ul-ta-tiv) Capable of adapting to, or living under, varying environmental conditions; opposite of obligate.

failure (fāl'yer) **1.** The state of being insufficient. **2.** A cessation of normal functioning.

acute renal f. (ARF) Condition in which the filtration rate within the kidneys is abruptly diminished, causing a sudden retention of metabolism products (e.g., urea, potassium, phosphate, sulfate, creatinine) that are normally cleared by the kidneys.

backward heart f. A theory maintaining that congestive heart failure results in engorgement of the veins responsible for raising blood pressure proximal to the failing heart chambers.

cardiac f. See heart failure.

chronic renal f. (CRF) Permanent loss of kidney function, which, when advanced, produces the signs and symptoms termed uremia; commonly caused by uncontrolled diabetes mellitus, high blood pressure (hypertension), glomerulonephritis, and polycystic kidney disease.

congestive heart f. (CHF) See heart failure.

end-stage renal f. (ESRF) Irreversible failure of kidney function.

forward heart f. A theory maintaining that congestive heart failure results from inadequate cardiac output, which results in inadequate blood flow in the kidneys and retention of sodium and water.

heart f. Inability of the heart to pump enough oxygenated blood to satisfy the needs of body tissues, or ability to do so only from an abnormally elevated filling pressure in the ventricles. Also called cardiac insufficiency.

high-output f. Condition in which the cardiac output, although at normal levels or higher, is inadequate to meet the demands of the body; seen in states such as marked anemia, Paget's disease, and arteriovenous fistulas.

left ventricular f., left ventricle f. Heart failure manifested by congestion of the lungs.

low-output f. An inadequate cardiac output seen in heart failure, usually due to coronary or valvular disease or to high blood pressure (hypertension).

pacemaker f. Failure of an artificial pacemaker to stimulate the heart muscle.

power f. See pump failure.

pump f. Failure of the heart as a mechanical pump rather than disturbance of electrical impulse (arrhythmia). Also called power failure.

renal f. Failure or diminution of kidney function.

respiratory f. Failure of the respiratory system to maintain normal gas tensions of oxygen, carbon dioxide, or both, in the arterial circulation.

right ventricular f., right ventricle f. Heart failure manifested by distention of the neck veins, fluid retention and swelling, and enlargement of the liver.

thermal regulatory f. A state in which the balance between body heat production and heat loss is disturbed, the main feature of such conditions as heat stroke, heat cramps, heat syncope, and heat exhaustion; symptoms range from weakness, dizziness, nausea, vomiting, confusion, delirium, and visual disturbances to convulsions, collapse, and unconsciousness.

f. to thrive See failure-to-thrive syndrome, under syndrome.

faint (fānt) Popular name for syncope.

faintness (fānt'nes) A feeling that one is about to faint.

falces (fal'sez) Plural of falx.

falciform, falcate (fal'sĭ-form, fal'kāt) Sickle-shaped.

false-negative (fawls' neg'ă-tiv) Denoting a test result that wrongly indicates that a person does not have the attribute or disease for which the test is conducted.

false-positive (fawls' pos'ĭ-tiv) Denoting a test result that wrongly indicates that a person has the attribute or disease for which the test is conducted.

falx (falks), pl. fal'ces A sickle-shaped structure, especially of folds of fascia.

f. cerebelli A sickle-shaped cranial dura mater separating the posterosuperior portions of the two cerebellar hemispheres; it extends from the posterior part of the undersurface of the tentorium cerebelli and the internal occipital protuberance at the back of the inner skull to the foramen magnum below; it encloses the occipital sinus.

f. cerebri The midline fold of the sickle-shaped cranial dura mater between the two cerebral hemispheres, extending from the crista galli, to the tentorium cerebelli. The upper convex margin is fixed to the roof of the skull, and encloses the superior sagittal sinus; the lower free concave margin lies just above the corpus callosum, and encloses the inferior sagittal sinus.

inguinal f. See conjoined tendon, under tendon.

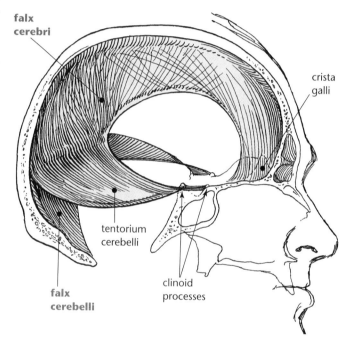

falx cerebri

crista galli

tentorium cerebelli

falx cerebelli

clinoid processes

familial (fah-mil'e-al) Denoting any trait that is more common among relatives of an affected person than in the general population; could be due to genetic or environmental causes, or both.

family (fam'ĭ-le) **1.** Strictly, a group comprising parents and their offspring. **2.** In biologic classification, a category ranking above a genus and below an order.

CEPH f.'s In genetics, a reference group of 40 Caucasian families from whom cell lines have been collected and distributed to researchers collaborating with the *Centre d'Etude du Polymorphisme Humain* for the mapping of the human genome.

farad (far'ad) (F) A unit of electrical capacity, equal to the capacity of a condenser having a charge of 1 coulomb under an electromotive force of 1 volt.

faradic (fah-rad'ik) Relating to the alternating asymmetric current used in faradism.

faradism, faradization (far'ah-dizm, far-ah-dī-za'shun) The therapeutic application of a direct current abruptly interrupted 80 to 100 times per second (faradic current); used primarily to stimulate a muscle through its nerve.

farinaceous (far-ĭ-na'shus) Of the nature of or containing starch.

farsightedness (far-sīt'ed-nes) See hyperopia.

F

fascia (fash'e-ah) An aggregation of connective tissue that lies just under the skin or forms an investment for muscles and various organs.

f. of abdominal wall A thick subcutaneous fascia composed of a thick superficial fatty layer (Camper's fascia) and a deeper membranous layer (Scarpa's fascia), between which are superficial lymph nodes, vessels, and nerves; it is continuous with the superficial fascia of the perineum and the superficial fascia of the thigh; in the male, it is continuous with the fascia in the penis and scrotum; in the female, it is continuous with the fascia in the labia majora.

antebrachial f. The deep dense fascia of the forearm investing the muscles and sending septa between them to attach on bone. Two thickenings of the fascial sheath occur near the wrist to help retain the digital tendons in their proper position, namely the extensor retinaculum posteriorly and the flexor retinaculum anteriorly.

axillary f. A thick layer of fascia conforming to the concavity of the armpit; it extends from the lower border of the greater pectoral (pectoralis major) muscle in front, to the lower border of the latissimus dorsi muscle behind.

brachial f. The deep fascia investing the muscles of the arm and epicondyles of the humerus; continuous with the axillary fascia proximally and the antebrachial fascia distally.

Buck's f. See fascia of penis, deep.

bulbar f. Connective tissue sheath enveloping the eyeball with the exception of the cornea; attached to the sclera at the sclerocorneal junction. Also called Tenon's capsule; Tenon's fascia; fascial sheath of eyeball.

Camper's f. The thick subcutaneous fatty layer of the superficial fascia of the lower part of the anterior abdominal wall; it is continuous with the superficial fascia of the thigh and perineum; in the male, it is continuous with the penis and scrotum; in the female, it is continuous with the fascia of the labia majora.

f. of clitoris A dense fibrous sheath that encases the two corpora cavernosa of the clitoris; it is continuous with the suspensory ligament of the clitoris.

Colles' f. The deep membranous layer of the superficial fascia of the perineum; it is of considerable strength and is continuous with the fascia of the penis and the membranous layer of the superficial fascia of the anterior abdominal wall.

coracoclavicular f. A strong, thickened fascia situated under the clavicular portion of the greater pectoral (pectoralis major) muscle; it occupies the interval between the smaller pectoral (pectoralis minor) and subclavius muscles, protecting the axillary vessels and nerves. Above, it divides to enclose the subclavius muscle and the collarbone (clavicle).

cremasteric f. The part of the fascia of the cremasteric muscle that invests the spermatic cord and testis; it contains discrete strands of muscle, which, when contracted, elevate the testis toward the body.

deep f. A compact fascia composed mostly of collagen fibers that lies beneath the superficial fascia and invests the trunk, neck, limbs, and parts of the head; it also covers and holds the muscles and other structures in their proper positions, separating them or joining them for independent or integrated function.

Denonvilliers' f. Fascia located between the rectum behind and the prostate in front.

Dupuytren's f. See palmar aponeurosis, under aponeurosis.

endothoracic f. The thin fascial sheet that lines the internal surface of the chest (thoracic) cavity, between the parietal pleura and the periosteum of the ribs and sternum.

f. lata The deep, broad fascia investing the muscles of the thigh and hip; on the lateral side of the thigh, it forms the strong, thick iliotibial tract.

nuchal f. Fascia of the back of the neck.

palmar f. See palmar aponeurosis, under aponeurosis.

parotid f. Strong fascia that extends from the deep cervical fascia and invests the parotid gland, covers the masseter muscle, and is attached to the zygomatic arch.

pectoral f. Fascia that invests the greater pectoral (pectoralis major) muscle; it is attached to the breastbone (sternum) and collarbone (clavicle), and is continuous with neighboring fascia.

pelvic f. Fascia of the pelvis, composed of two layers: *Parietal pelvic f.,* fascial sheaths of the pelvic muscles, above the level of origin of the levator ani muscle. *Visceral pelvic f.,* fascial sheaths from around the pelvic organs and their blood vessels and nerves to the upper surface of the levator ani muscle.

f. of penis Connective tissue enveloping the penis, composed of two layers: *Deep f. of penis,* a deep fascial sheath of the penis, continuous with Scarpa's fascia of the abdomen and Colles' fascia of

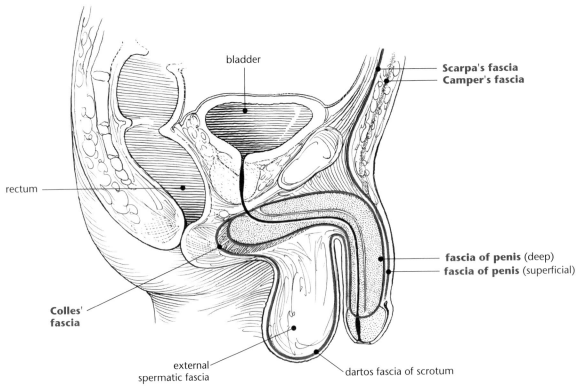

bladder

Scarpa's fascia
Camper's fascia

rectum

fascia of penis (deep)
fascia of penis (superficial)

Colles'
fascia

external
spermatic fascia

dartos fascia of scrotum

fascia ■ fascia

the perineum. Also called Buck's fascia. *Superficial f. of penis,* the shallow, loose areolar tissue enveloping the penis, continuous with the superficial fascia of the abdominal wall (Camper's fascia).

plantar f. See plantar aponeurosis, under aponeurosis.

renal f. A sheath of fascia that surrounds the kidney and perirenal fat; formed from retroperitoneal connective tissue; connected to the fibrous capsule of the kidney by minute trabeculae.

Scarpa's f. The deep membranous or fibrous layer of the superficial fascia of the lower part of the anterior abdominal wall; it is continuous with the deep membranous layer of the superficial fascia of the perineum (Colles' fascia).

subcutaneous f. See superficial fascia.

superficial f. A loose collection or layer of connective tissue just below the skin; composed mostly of collagen fibers, it allows the skin freedom of movement and acts as a thermal insulator. Also called subcutaneous fascia; hypodermis; hypoderm.

temporal f. A fibrous, fan-shaped investment (aponeurosis) covering the temporal muscle on the side of the head, attached above to the superior temporal line of the cranium, and below to the zygomatic arch.

Tenon's f. See bulbar fascia.

transversalis f. The fascial lining of the abdominal cavity between the deep or inner surface of the abdominal musculature and the peritoneum.

triangular f. See reflex inguinal ligament, under ligament.

fascial (fash'e-al) Relating to fascia.

fascicle (fas'ĭ-kl) A small bundle of fibers; a fasciculus.

fascicular (fah-sik'u-lar) **1.** Relating to a fascicle (fasciculus). **2.** Arranged in bundles.

fasciculation (fah-sik-u-la'shun) Independent random contraction or twitching of all or most of the fibers of a motor unit of a muscle; a coarser form of muscular contraction than fibrillation.

fasciculus (fah-sik'u-lus), pl. fascic'uli A bundle of fibers all with the same orientation, especially applicable to nerve fibers or tracts, but also includes the specialized impulse-conveying muscular fibers of the heart.

f. atrioventricularis See atrioventricular bundle, under bundle.

cuneate f. of spinal cord A fasciculus that derives its fibers from the dorsal (posterior) roots of the upper thoracic and cervical nerves and directs them to the cuneate nucleus of the medulla oblongata; it is situated in the posterior spinal cord, lateral to the fasciculus gracilis.

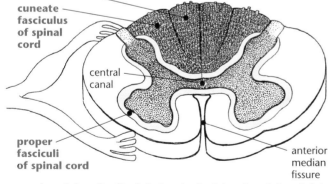

fasciculus gracilis of spinal cord
cuneate fasciculus of spinal cord
central canal
proper fasciculi of spinal cord
anterior median fissure

dorsal longitudinal f. Longitudinal bundle of fine, lightly myelinated fibers of the midbrain, near the medial longitudinal fasciculus, extending from the hypothalamus and thalamus to the central gray matter of the midbrain, pons, and the medulla oblongata.

f. gracilis of spinal cord A fasciculus that contains fibers from the coccygeal, sacral, lumbar, and lower thoracic spinal cord segments; it occupies the medial part of the posterior spinal cord.

lenticular f. The bundle of myelinated nerve fibers that interconnects the globus pallidus with the lateral thalamus, after passing through the internal capsule.

longitudinal f. of cerebrum Bundle of arcuate (association) nerve fibers interconnecting cortical areas of the same hemisphere:

Inferior longitudinal f. of cerebrum, the bundle of association fibers coursing along the posterior horn of the lateral ventricle, connecting the cortex of the occipital and temporal lobes of the cerebrum and consisting mostly of the geniculocalcarine tract; it is crossed by the superior longitudinal fasciculus of cerebrum. *Superior longitudinal f. of cerebrum,* the largest of all the association bundles, it arches over the insula in connecting the cortex of the frontal lobe with the cortex of the occipital and temporal lobes, constantly giving off and receiving fibers from adjoining cortex.

mamillothalamic f. The bundle of myelinated nerve fibers that extends from the mamillary body of the hypothalamus to the thalamus.

medial longitudinal f. A bundle of fibers running under the fourth ventricle from the midbrain to the upper cervical levels of the spinal cord; it interconnects the vestibular nuclei with motor nuclei, chiefly those of the oculomotor (3rd), trochlear (4th), abducent (6th), and accessory (11th) cranial nerves.

proper fasciculi of spinal cord Intersegmental tracts of ascending and descending association fibers surrounding the gray columns of the spinal cord; the fibers travel for a short distance of only a few segments of the spinal cord.

subthalamic f. The bundle of myelinated nerve fibers that interconnects the globus pallidus with the subthalamic nucleus, after passing through the internal capsule.

thalamic f. The complex bundle of myelinated nerve fibers that extends from the globus pallidus (internal and external), putamen, dentate, and red nuclei to terminate principally in the lateral thalamus.

fasciectomy (fas-e-ek'to-me) Surgical removal of part of a fascia.

fasciitis (fas-e-i'tis) Inflammation of a fascia.

eosinophilic f. Inflammatory reaction producing a hard, thickened skin of the extremities suggestive of scleroderma, associated primarily with increased numbers of eosinophils in the blood.

necrotizing f. A serious, rapidly spreading bacterial infection of superficial fascia with extensive necrosis; usually caused by group A streptococcus; may occur after trauma, surgery, or inadequate care of abscesses.

nodular f. A benign, rapid proliferation of fibroblasts forming palpable nodules in soft tissues, most often in the extremities; it is sometimes mistaken for malignant tumors. Also called pseudosarcomatous fasciitis.

pseudosarcomatous f. See nodular fasciitis.

Fasciola (fah-si'o-lah) A genus of liver flukes (family Fasciolidae).

F. hepatica The liver fluke of sheep and cattle, transmitted to humans by eating undercooked infested liver.

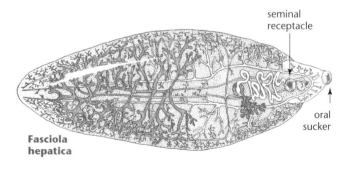

seminal receptacle
oral sucker
Fasciola hepatica

fascioliasis (fas-e-o-li'ah-sis) Infection of the liver with flukes of the genus *Fasciola.*

fascioplasty (fash'e-o-plas-te) Reparative surgery on a fascia.

fasciorrhaphy (fash-e-or'ah-fe) Suture of a fascia. Also called aponeurorrhaphy.

fasciotomy (fash-e-ot'o-me) Surgical cut through a fascia.

fast (fast) Resistant to change.

fastidious (fas-tid'e-us) Having special or highly specific growth requirements; applied to bacteria that grow poorly or not at all in the usual culture media, under ordinary laboratory conditions.

fastigium (fas-tij'e-um) **1.** The highest point in the roof of the fourth ventricle of the brain. **2.** The height of a fever or any acute state.

fat (fat) Any of several organic compounds composed mostly of fatty acids combined with glycerol; they are stored in cells and tissues.

    brown f. A mass of brown tissue composed of cells filled with fat globules; found in the space between the shoulder blades of hibernating mammals and newborn human infants. Also called interscapular gland.

    saturated f. See fatty acid, under acid.

    unsaturated f. See fatty acid, under acid.

    wool f. See anhydrous lanolin, under lanolin.

fatal (fa'tal) Causing death.

fatality (fa-tal'ĭ-te) Anything resulting in death.

fatigability (fat-ĭ-gah-bil'ĭ-te) Susceptibility to fatigue.

fatigue (fah-tēg') A feeling of exhaustion; may result from physical or mental exertion.

    battle f. Severe anxiety resulting from the stresses of battle; marked by loss of effectiveness, poor judgment, physical complaints, and/or feeling of imminent death.

fatty acids (fat'te as'ids) See fatty acids, under acid.

fauces (faw'sēz) The constricted passage between the mouth (oral cavity) and the oral part of the pharynx, including the lumen bounded by the soft palate superiorly, the dorsum of the tongue in the region of the sulcus terminalis inferiorly, and the right and left palatoglossal folds (anterior pillars of fauces), which arise archlike on each side on the posterior limit of the oral cavity; it is the aperture by which the mouth communicates with the pharynx (i.e., the dividing line between the oral cavity and the oral pharynx.)

faucial (faw'shal) Relating to the fauces.

faveolate (fa-ve'o-lāt) Pitted.

faveolus (fa-ve'o-lus), pl. fave'oli A tiny depression.

favism (fa'vism) Acute hemolytic anemia resulting from ingestion of the fava bean *(Vicia faba)*; it occurs in persons who have inherited a deficiency of the enzyme glucose-6-phosphate dehydrogenase (G6PD deficiency); the defect renders red blood cells susceptible to destruction by chemicals in the bean.

favus (fa'vus) A chronic fungal infection, usually of the scalp, caused primarily by *Trichophyton schoenleini*.

fear (fēr) A feeling of alarm or apprehension in response to an external source of danger; distinguished from anxiety.

    morbid f. See phobia.

features (fe'churz) The external appearance of the face or any of its parts.

febrifacient (feb-rĭ-fa'shent) **1.** Causing fever. **2.** Any agent that produces fever.

febrile (feb'ril) Relating to fever.

fecal (fe'kal) Relating to feces.

fecalith (fe'kah-lith) A small, stonelike mass of dried feces, usually formed in outpouchings (diverticuli) of the large intestine; they are usually harmless unless they become infected. Also called coprolith; stercolith.

fecaluria (fe-kah-lu're-ah) The passage of fecal matter with the urine; occurs when there is an abnormal connecting channel (fistula) between the rectum and the bladder.

feces (fe'sēz) The waste material discharged from the bowel.

feculent (fek'u-lent) Fecal; fowl.

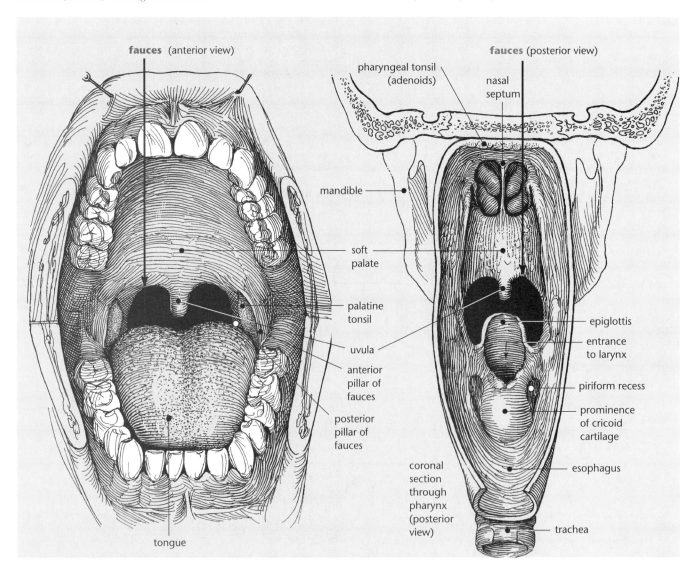

fauces (anterior view)

fauces (posterior view)

pharyngeal tonsil (adenoids)

nasal septum

mandible

soft palate

palatine tonsil

uvula

anterior pillar of fauces

posterior pillar of fauces

tongue

epiglottis

entrance to larynx

piriform recess

prominence of cricoid cartilage

esophagus

coronal section through pharynx (posterior view)

trachea

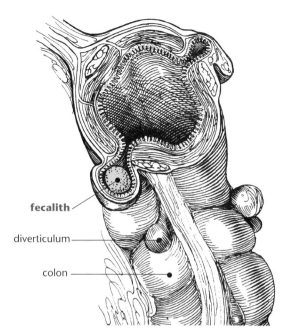

fecalith

diverticulum

colon

fecundate (fe'kun-dāt) To fertilize; to impregnate.

fecundation (fe-kun-da'shun) Fertilization.

fecundity (fĕ-kun'dĭ-te) In demography, a reproductive potential as distinguished from reproductive performance or fertility.

feedback (fēd'bak) 1. A process whereby a portion of a system's output is returned to the input. 2. The portion of the output so returned. 3. The feeling created by another person's reaction to oneself.

    negative f. A signal or information returning from the output to the control system and resulting in reduced output.

    positive f. A signal or information returning to the control system from the output and resulting in increased output.

feeding (fēd'ing) The giving or taking of nourishment.

    bolus f. A method of tube feeding in which a set amount of nutrients is administered at intermittent periods throughout the day.

    intravenous f. Introduction of liquid nutrient preparations directly into the blood circulation through a vein; used only when tube feeding is impractical or ineffective.

    nasogastric f. Administration of nutrients through a small, flexible tube that is passed through the nose down the esophagus and into the stomach; employed in patients with a functional gastrointestinal tract who are unable or unwilling to eat. Also called enteral tube alimentation.

    tube f. Administration of nutrient solutions (usually as a continuous drip) via a flexible narrow tube passed through the nose and into the stomach or duodenum; the rate of flow can be controlled by a pump.

feeling (fēl'ing) 1. Any sensation perceived by the sense of touch. 2. Emotional or affective state or process. 3. A vague belief.

fellatio (fĕ-la'she-o) Oral stimulation of the penis.

felon (fel'on) An acute staphylococcal infection of the nail bed or nail fold in a finger or a toe, causing localized swelling and intense throbbing pain; it results from trauma, either from an ingrown toenail or from manipulation of the cuticle for cosmetic reasons; typically the suppurative lesion, instead of bursting, spreads inward along anatomic compartments. Also called whitlow.

female (fe'māl) In zoology, relating to the sex that produces eggs or bears the young.

feminization (fem-ĭ-ni-za'shun) The development of female characteristics in the male.

femoral (fem'or-al) Relating to the femur or to the thigh.

femur (fe'mur) The thighbone; the longest bone in the body. See table of bones.

fenestra (fĕ-nes'trah), pl. fenes'trae 1. A small windowlike opening in the body, especially, either of two openings in the medial wall of the middle ear chamber. 2. An opening in a plaster cast, surgical drapes, or instruments (blade of forceps or side of endoscope).

    f. of cochlea A round opening in the medial wall of the middle ear chamber leading to the scala tympani of the cochlea; it is covered by the secondary tympanic membrane. Also called round window; fenestra rotunda; fenestra cochleae; cochlear window.

    f. cochleae See fenestra of cochlea.

    f. ovalis See fenestra of vestibule.

    f. rotunda See fenestra of cochlea.

    f. of vestibule An oval opening between the middle ear chamber and the vestibule of the inner ear; it is covered by the footplate (base) of the stapes and fixed to the margin of the opening by the annular ligament. Also called oval window; fenestra ovalis; fenestra vestibuli; vestibular window.

    f. vestibuli See fenestra of vestibule.

fenestrated (fen'es-trāt-ed) Having one or more small openings.

fenestration (fen-es-tra'shun) 1. In dentistry, the creation of a circumscribed opening through the alveolar bone to the tip of a tooth root; performed to allow drainage. 2. See fenestration operation, under operation.

fentanyl citrate (fen'tah-nil sit'rāt) A narcotic analgesic that acts

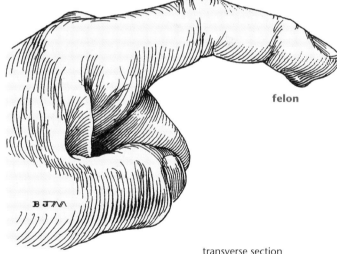

felon

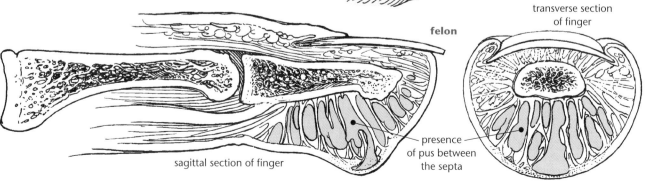

felon

sagittal section of finger

transverse section of finger

presence of pus between the septa

similarly to morphine and meperidine; used as a supplementary analgesic in general anesthesia. See also fentanyl transdermal patch, under patch.

ferment (fer-ment′) To induce or to undergo fermentation.

fermentation (fer-men-ta′shun) Chemical decomposition of an organic compound induced by an enzyme.

fermium (fer′me-um) Radioactive element; symbol Fm, atomic number 100.

ferning (fern′ing) The typical palm-leaf pattern of dry endocervical mucus formed upon crystallization as a result of electrolyte action on protein; observed under the light microscope; it is a normal physiologic phenomenon occurring at midmenstrual cycle, from days 7 to 18 peaking on day 14.

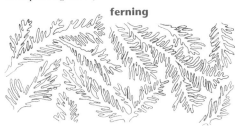
ferning

ferric (fer′ik) Relating to iron, especially a salt containing iron in its highest valence (3).

ferritin (fer′ĭ-tin) An iron-rich protein found mainly in the liver, spleen, and intestinal inner lining. See also ferritin test, under test.

ferroprotoporphyrin (fer′o-pro-to-por′fĭ-rin) See heme.

ferrous (fer′us) Relating to iron, especially a salt containing iron in its lowest valence (2).

    f. sulfate Compound widely used in treating uncomplicated iron deficiency anemia. Also called green vitriol.

ferruginous (fer-u′jĭ-nus) Containing iron.

fertile (fer′til) Capable of reproducing.

fertility (fer-til′ĭ-te) **1.** The capacity to conceive and bear offspring. **2.** In demography, reproductive performance as distinguished from fecundity, the potential capacity to reproduce.

    impaired f. See infertility (2).

fertilization (fer′tĭ-lĭ-za′shun) The union of a spermatozoon with an ovum.

    in vitro f. The process of placing several ova in a petri dish containing blood serum and nutrients and adding sperm. Once an egg is fertilized, it is transferred to another dish where it is allowed to grow for three to six days and then placed in the uterus, where it attaches to the wall and normal development proceeds. Commonly called test-tube fertilization.

    test-tube f. See *in vitro* fertilization.

fervescence (fer-ves′ens) Increase of body temperature.

fester (fes′ter) To form pus.

festinant (fes′tĭ-nant) Accelerating.

festination (fes-tĭ-na′shun) The involuntary acceleration of walking that occurs when the center of gravity is displaced; usually the trunk is bent forward, legs stiff and slightly flexed at the knees, steps shuffling and short; seen in parkinsonism and other neurologic disorders. Also called festinating gait.

festoon (fes-toon′) In dentistry, a simulation of the curved margin of the natural gingiva in a denture.

    gingival f. Swelling or thickening of the marginal gingiva usually due to inflammation.

festooning (fes-toon′ing) The process of cutting, carving, or grinding material to accommodate the contours of natural tissue.

fetal (fe′tal) Relating to the fetus.

feticide (fe′tĭ-sid) Intentional destruction of the embryo or fetus in the uterus.

fetid (fe′tid) Having a disagreeable odor.

fetish (fet′ish) An object to which reverence or excessive attention is devoted; often a source of sexual stimulation or gratification.

fetishism (fet′ish-izm) Excessive emotional attachment to an inanimate object or body part.

feto- Combining form meaning fetus.

fetography (fe-tog′rah-fe) Radiography of the fetus in the uterus.

fetology (fe-tol′o-je) The study of the fetus and its diseases.

fetomaternal (fe-to-mah-ter′nal) Relating to both the fetus and its mother (e.g., hemorrhage).

fetometry (fe-tom′ĕ-tre) Estimation of the size of the fetal head before delivery.

fetopelvic (fe-to-pel′vik) Relating to the fetus and the maternal pelvis (e.g., disproportion).

fetoplacental (fe-to-plah-sen′tal) Relating to the fetus and the placenta.

α-fetoprotein (al′fah fe-to-pro′tēn) See alpha-fetoprotein.

fetor (fe′tor) An offensive odor.

    f. hepaticus A musty odor of the breath occurring in persons with severe liver disease.

    f. oris Halitosis.

fetoscope (fe′to-skōp) **1.** Instrument for listening to the fetal heartbeat. **2.** Endoscope for viewing a fetus in the uterus.

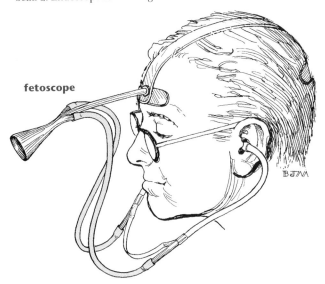
fetoscope

fetotoxicity (fe-to-tok-sis′ĭ-te) Injurious alteration of the developmental processes of the fetus caused by maternal exposure to such agents as radiation, viruses, gases, and drugs; effects may include malformations, intrauterine growth retardation, or death.

fetus (fe′tus) The developing young in the uterus, from about the second month of pregnancy to birth. During the first two months, it is called embryo.

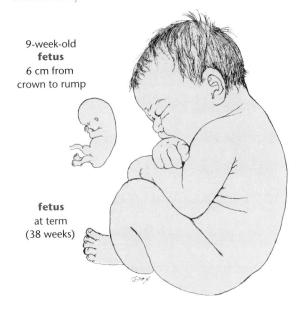
9-week-old **fetus** 6 cm from crown to rump

fetus at term (38 weeks)

FERTILIZATION

The penetration of sperm through the corona radiata and the zona pellucida is accomplished by the release of acrosomal enzymes (acid phosphatase and acrosomase) by many sperms.

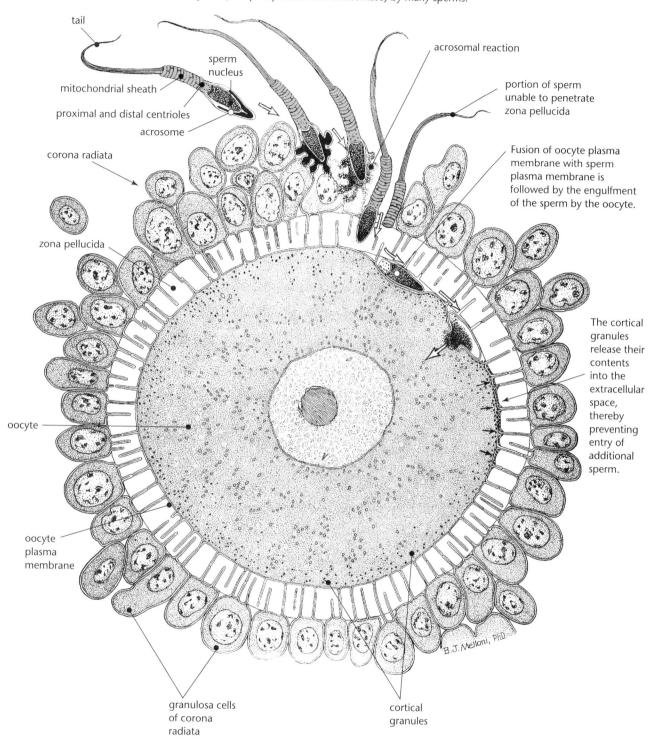

tail

sperm nucleus

mitochondrial sheath

proximal and distal centrioles

acrosome

corona radiata

zona pellucida

oocyte

oocyte plasma membrane

granulosa cells of corona radiata

cortical granules

acrosomal reaction

portion of sperm unable to penetrate zona pellucida

Fusion of oocyte plasma membrane with sperm plasma membrane is followed by the engulfment of the sperm by the oocyte.

The cortical granules release their contents into the extracellular space, thereby preventing entry of additional sperm.

B.J. Melloni, PhD.

f. compressus See fetus papyraceus.

f. papyraceus A flattened, partly mummified twin fetus that dies early in pregnancy and remains in the uterus until completion of term, compressed between the uterine wall and the membranes (amniotic sac) of the living twin; its portion of the placenta becomes pale and atrophic. Also called fetus compressus.

fever (fe'ver) **1.** A rise in body temperature above the normal range (an early morning temperature of 99.0°F (32.2°C) or greater, or an evening temperature of 100°F (37.8°C) or greater). **2.** Condition in which the body temperature is above the normal. Also called pyrexia.

carbuncular f. See anthrax.

cat-scratch f. See cat-scratch disease, under disease.

childbed f. Popular name for puerperal fever.

Colorado tick f. Viral disease similar to Rocky Mountain spotted fever but without the rash, marked by fever and low levels of white blood cells (leukopenia); spread by a hard-shelled tick (*Dermacentor andersoni*).

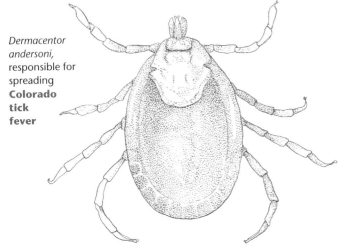

Dermacentor andersoni, responsible for spreading **Colorado tick fever**

cotton-mill f. See byssinosis.

deer-fly f. See tularemia.

desert f. See coccidioidomycosis.

familial Mediterranean f. (FMF) Recurrent attacks of abdominal pain and inflammation of the peritoneum, pleura, and pericardium; the condition is asymptomatic between attacks.

glandular f. See infectious mononucleosis, under mononucleosis.

Haverhill f. Disorder caused by infection with *Streptobacillus moniliformis;* marked by fever, rash, and arthritis (usually of large joints and spine), lasting two to three weeks. Although the same organism causes rat-bite fever, Haverhill fever is not transmitted by the bite of a rat.

hay f. Seasonal inflammation of the mucous membranes of the nose characterized by sneezing, watery nasal discharge, stuffiness and obstruction of the nasal passages, and itching of the eyes, nose, and palate; occurs as an allergic reaction to pollens. Also called seasonal allergic rhinitis.

hemorrhagic f. Any disease of viral origin in which the primary symptoms are fever, capillary hemorrhages, and shock.

island f. See tsutsugamushi disease, under disease.

jungle yellow f. A form of yellow fever transmitted by various forest mosquitoes (rather than by the domestic *Aedes aegypti*).

Lassa f. A highly contagious, often fatal disease characterized by fever, chills, muscle aches, rashes, nausea, severe sore throat, bleeding gums, and oral ulcerations; caused by the Lassa virus, an arenavirus, transmitted by a rat (*Mastomys natalensis*).

Malta f. See brucellosis.

Mediterranean f. (a) Old term for brucellosis. (b) See familial Mediterranean fever.

mill f. See byssinosis.

nodal f. See erythema nodosum.

Oroya f. See bartonellosis.

paratyphoid f. Infectious intestinal disease resembling a mild form of typhoid fever, caused by strains of *Salmonella* enterobacteria, especially *Salmonella paratyphi, Salmonella schotmulleri,* and *Salmonella hirschfeldii.*

pharyngoconjunctival f. Infectious disease characterized by fever, sore throat, and acute inflammation of the transparent covering membrane of the eye (conjunctiva) with follicle formation; caused by a virus, usually type 3 adenovirus; seen most frequently in children.

phlebotomus f. An influenza-like febrile disease of short duration, caused by a virus of the Bunyaviridae family and transmitted mostly by the bloodsucking sandfly *Phlebotomus papatasii.*

polymer fume f. Occupational condition occurring in plastics workers, characterized by fever, chills, malaise, and respiratory impairment, occurring 12 to 24 hours after inhaling fumes produced by overheating of certain plastics (such as fluoropolymers), or where transmitted from a worker's hands to cigarettes.

Pontiac f. A self-limiting, influenza-like illness of sudden onset that lasts two to five days; characterized by fever, chills, headache, muscle pains (myalgias), and, sometimes, cough and sore throat; it is a building-associated illness caused by *Legionella* bacteria transmitted through air-conditioning systems.

pretibial f. A form of leptospirosis characterized by mild fever, enlargement of the spleen, and a rash on the anterior part of the legs; caused by a strain of the bacterium *Leptospira interrogans.*

psychogenic f. Habitual low-grade fever associated with a neurosis, seen especially in young women.

puerperal f. Fever occurring after childbirth; may be due to infection. Popularly called childbed fever.

Q f. An occupational infectious disease caused by the bacterium *Coxiella burnetii,* transmitted to humans through contact with tissues and excreta from infected cattle, sheep, and goats, and by inhalation of contaminated dust; characterized by sudden onset of fever, headache, cough, and difficult breathing due to inflammation of the lungs. Persons at risk include laboratory workers, workers in rendering plants and slaughterhouses, and ranchers.

rabbit's f. See tularemia.

rat-bite f. Disease marked by inflammation of the lymph nodes and lymphatic vessels, joint pains, and a rash on the legs; caused by infection with *Spirillum minor* or *Streptobacillus moniliformis;* transmitted by rat bites. Also called sodoku.

recurrent f. See relapsing fever.

relapsing f. Acute infectious bacterial disease characterized by recurrent attacks of fever each lasting about six days; caused by species of *Borrelia,* transmitted by a louse or a soft tick.

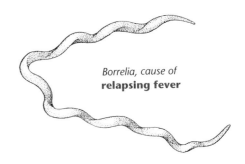

Borrelia, cause of **relapsing fever**

rheumatic f. (RF) An acute recurrent inflammatory disease mainly of children and young adults (peak incidence between ages of 5 and 15 years); it typically occurs one to five weeks after a throat infection with a group A streptococcus; diagnosis depends on the presence of two of the following five major criteria (Jones criteria): skin rash, typically in a bathing suit distribution (erythema marginatum); inflammation of large joints; abnormal involuntary movements (Sydenham's chorea); inflammation of the heart wall (carditis) with involvement of the heart valves; and subcutaneous nodules.

Rocky Mountain spotted f. (RMSF) Acute infectious disease characterized by severe fever, bone and muscle pain, headache, prostration, and a generalized rash; caused by the bacterium *Rickettsia rickettsii;* transmitted by several varieties of hard ticks.

sandfly f. See phlebotomus fever.

San Joaquin f. See coccidioidomycosis.

scarlet f. An acute contagious disease usually originating in the throat; characterized by sore throat, fever, and a rash, which erupts one to three days after onset of throat symptoms; caused by beta-hemolytic streptococci. Also called scarlatina.

splenic f. See anthrax.

tick f. Any infectious disease transmitted by the bite of a tick.

trench f. A relapsing type of fever caused by *Rochalimaea quintana*, transmitted by infected lice.

tsutsugamushi f. See tsutsugamushi disease, under disease.

typhoid f. Acute infectious disease caused by *Salmonella typhi*, characterized mainly by fever, skin rash on the abdomen and chest, intestinal distention with gas, and enlargement of the liver and spleen; infection is acquired by eating or drinking contaminated food or water; may be transmitted by a person who is a symptomless carrier of the organism.

typhus f. See typhus.

undulant f. See brucellosis.

West Nile f. Acute illness caused by the mosquito-borne West Nile virus; characterized by fever, headache, a papular rash, inflammation of lymph nodes, and decreased number of white blood cells.

yellow f. An acute infectious disease caused by a flavivirus (family Togaviridae), transmitted by a mosquito *(Aedes aegypti);* characterized by fever, degeneration of the liver (producing jaundice), and intestinal disturbances.

fiber (fi′ber) Any slender threadlike process, structure, or material; a filament.

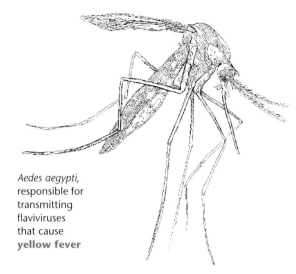

Aedes aegypti, responsible for transmitting flaviviruses that cause **yellow fever**

asbestos f.'s Long, smooth, flexible fibers composed of either of two incombustible chemical-resistant forms of magnesium silicate; exposure to significant concentrations of asbestos fibers can produce a lung fibrosis (asbestosis), as well as increase the risk of cancer to the lungs, stomach, and colon; it can also cause certain skin disorders.

association f.'s Nerve fibers in the brain that either connect mostly different areas of the cortex of the cerebrum in the same hemisphere or interconnect adjacent cortical folia of the cerebellum in the same hemisphere.

augmentor f.'s See accelerator fibers.

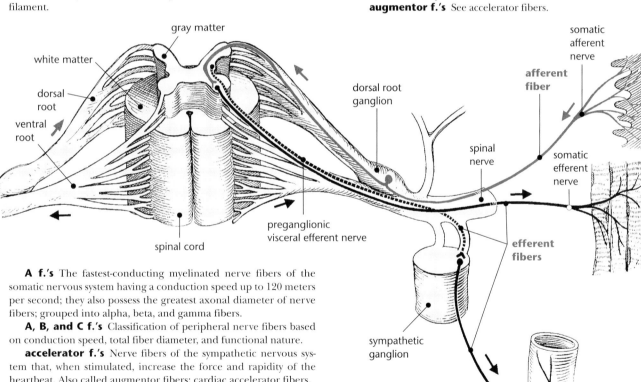

A f.'s The fastest-conducting myelinated nerve fibers of the somatic nervous system having a conduction speed up to 120 meters per second; they also possess the greatest axonal diameter of nerve fibers; grouped into alpha, beta, and gamma fibers.

A, B, and C f.'s Classification of peripheral nerve fibers based on conduction speed, total fiber diameter, and functional nature.

accelerator f.'s Nerve fibers of the sympathetic nervous system that, when stimulated, increase the force and rapidity of the heartbeat. Also called augmentor fibers; cardiac accelerator fibers.

adrenergic f.'s Any group of nerve fibers that release norepinephrine or epinephrine at their synapse (e.g., postganglionic sympathetic nerve fibers).

afferent f.'s Nerve fibers that conduct impulses to a nerve center in the brain or spinal cord. Also called sensory fibers.

alpha f.'s Large-caliber myelinated motor neurons or proprioceptive fibers exclusively innervating extrafusal muscle fibers and having a rapid conduction speed; one of the three subgroups of A fibers.

argentaffin f.'s See reticular fibers.

fiber ■ fiber

B f.'s Small myelinated nerve fibers of the autonomic nervous system having a conduction speed of up to 30 meters per second; found primarily in the autonomic nervous system (ANS) as preganglionic autonomic efferent fibers.

beta f.'s One of the three subgroups of the A fibers; it supplies motor endplates to extrafusal and intrafusal muscle fibers; the conduction speed is rated from 40 to 60 meters per second. Also called beta-efferent fibers.

beta-efferent f.'s See beta fibers.

bone f.'s See Sharpey's fibers.

bulbospiral f.'s A group of heart muscle fibers that form part of the spiral musculature of the atrial and ventricular walls of the heart.

C f.'s Unmyelinated nerve fibers that have a slow conduction speed, under 4 meters per second; they constitute the majority of the autonomic axons, and also innervate some sense organs, such as nociceptors.

cardiac accelerator f.'s See accelerator fibers.

cardiac depressor f.'s See depressor fibers.

cardiac muscle f.'s A network of branching and anastomosing muscle fibers of the heart marked by striations similar to those of skeletal muscle fibers; their ends display conspicuous cross striations (intercalated disks).

cardiac pressor f.'s See pressor fibers.

chief f.'s The principal radial fibers of the eye that attach the margin of the lens capsule to the ciliary region.

cholinergic f. Any nerve fiber that releases the neurotransmitter acetylcholine at its synapses.

chromosomal f. See chromosomal spindle fiber.

chromosomal spindle f. A spindle fiber that is attached to a chromosome and draws it toward the pole (aster) during cell division. Also called chromosomal fiber; discontinuous spindle fiber.

collagen f.'s, collagenous f.'s The white and inelastic fibers making up the principal constituent of connective tissue, the predominant component of ligaments, tendons, and fascia, as well as an essential part of bone and cartilage.

continuous spindle f. A spindle fiber in mitosis and meiosis that extends from one pole (aster) to the other, without interruption.

depressor f.'s Sensory (afferent) nerve fibers with endings in some arterial walls, which, when stimulated, diminish vascular tone and lower blood pressure. Also called cardiac depressor fibers.

dietary f. Elongated, thick-walled fiber of plant tissue that, when eaten, is not digested by the body; prevalent in grains, fruits, vegetables, nuts, and legumes; an essential part of a healthy diet.

discontinuous spindle f. See chromosomal spindle fiber.

EF f. See extrafusal muscle fiber.

efferent f.'s Nerve fibers that convey impulses from a nerve center in the brain or spinal cord outward to the organs. Also called motor fibers.

elastic f.'s Yellowish fibers that stretch easily, forming a network in the substance of loose connective tissue, elastic cartilage, the dermis of the skin, and the walls of large blood vessels; composed mostly of the protein elastin along with other constituents, including traces of collagen. Also called elastin fibers.

elastin f.'s See elastic fibers.

extrafusal muscle f. Any skeletal muscle fiber excluding the intrafusal fibers in muscle (neuromuscular) spindles. Also called EF fiber.

gamma f.'s Myelinated afferent or efferent nerve fibers having a conduction speed of less than 20 meters per second; they constitute the slowest of the three subgroups of the A fibers; they innervate one or more intrafusal fibers in a muscle (neuromuscular) spindle.

gray f.'s See unmyelinated fibers.

IF f. See intrafusal muscle fiber.

inhibitory f.'s Nerve fibers that transmit impulses that slow down the action of an organ.

intrafusal muscle f. One of 6 to 14 fine, small, specialized

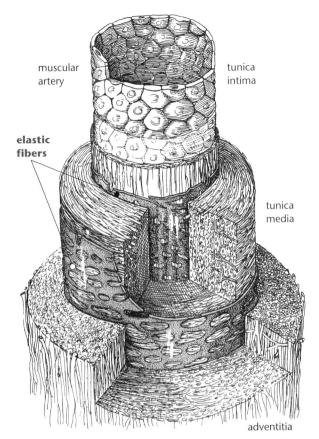

muscle fibers composing a muscle (neuromuscular) spindle; innervated by both motor and sensory nerve endings. Also called IF fiber.

itinerant f.'s See projection fibers.

motor f.'s See efferent fibers.

muscle f.'s Fibers composed of contractile elements of striate, cardiac, and smooth muscular tissue.

myelinated f.'s Nerve fibers possessing a myelin sheath.

nerve f. One of the slender units of a nerve trunk; the long axon of a nerve cell (neuron).

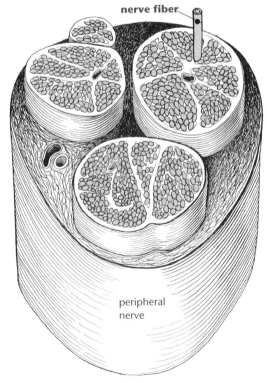

nonmyelinated f.'s See unmyelinated fibers.

nonstriated muscle f. See smooth muscle fiber.

postganglionic f. An axon of the autonomic nervous system that emerges from the peripheral sympathetic and parasympathetic ganglia and passes to viscera, nonstriated muscles, blood vessels, and glands; more numerous than preganglionic fibers.

preganglionic f. An axon of the autonomic nervous system that originates from the spinal cord or brainstem and passes to peripheral sympathetic and parasympathetic ganglia; one preganglionic fiber is known to synapse with up to 20 postganglionic fibers.

pressor f.'s Sympathetic nerve fibers that, upon stimulation, produce an increase in cardiac output and contraction of the arterioles (vasoconstriction), with a corresponding increase in blood pressure. Also called cardiac pressor fibers.

projection f.'s Fibers connecting the cerebral cortex with distant structures in the brain, such as the thalamus. Also called itinerant fibers.

Purkinje's f.'s Specialized fibers formed of modified heart muscle cells, located beneath the endocardium, that are capable of transmitting excitatory impulses from the atrioventricular (A-V) node to the muscles of the ventricles.

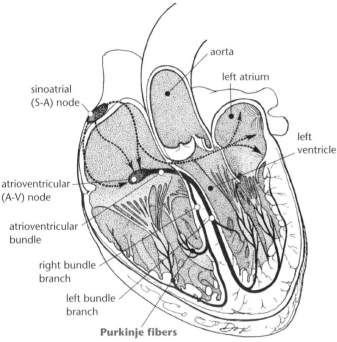

red f. See type I muscle fiber.

red muscle f. See type I muscle fiber.

reticular f.'s Fine immature fibers of connective tissue; found also in the papillary layer of the skin and the interstitial tissue of glands. Also called argentaffin fibers.

sensory f.'s See afferent fibers.

Sharpey's f.'s Thick perforating collagenous or fibroelastic bundles that attach tendons, ligaments, fascia, or periosteum to the underlying bone; they pierce the bone obliquely or at right angles to the long axis. Also called bone fibers.

skeletal muscle f.'s Long, parallel muscle fibers with cross-sectional dimensions of about 10 to 100 μm; marked by transverse striations and nuclei positioned just under the cell membrane (sarcolemma).

smooth muscle f.'s Narrow and tapering muscle fibers ranging in length from 20 μm in small blood vessels to 500 μm in the pregnant uterus; unlike the striated muscle fibers, the smooth muscle fibers contain no transverse striations. Also called nonstriated muscle fibers.

spindle f.'s Microtubules extending between the poles of a dividing cell during mitosis and meiosis, forming a spindle-shaped structure.

type I muscle f. Small skeletal muscle fiber that is rich in large mitochondria, myoglobin, and oxidative enzymes; it is reddish in color. Also called red muscle fiber; red fiber.

type II muscle f. Large skeletal muscle fiber that is low in mitochondrial content and oxidative enzymes, but relatively rich in glycogen and phosphatase enzyme; it is whitish in color. Also called white muscle fiber; white fiber.

unmyelinated f.'s A group of small axons lacking a myelin sheath but associated with a longitudinal chain of Schwann cells that extend cytoplasm between the individual axons. Approximately 75 percent of axons of cutaneous nerves and dorsal spinal nerve roots are unmyelinated, whereas only 30 percent of ventral spinal nerve roots are unmyelinated. Also called gray fibers; nonmyelinated fibers.

varicose f. An axon exhibiting varicosities along its length; usually the result of postmortem degenerative changes.

vasconstrictor f.'s Nerve fibers, usually of the sympathetic nervous system, which transmit impulses that result in constriction of blood vessels, usually of the arterioles and capillaries.

vasodilator f.'s Nerve fibers, of the autonomic nervous system (both sympathetic and parasympathetic), which transmit impulses that result in dilatation of blood vessels, especially of the arterioles.

white f. See type II muscle fiber.

white muscle f. See type II muscle fiber.

fiberoptic (fi-ber-op′tik) Relating to fiberoptics.

fiberoptics (fi-ber-op′tiks) The transmission of images along a bundle of fine, parallel, flexible fibers of plastic or glass.

fiberscope (fi′ber-skōp) An optical instrument with fine flexible plastic or glass rods, used for viewing internal structures of the body.

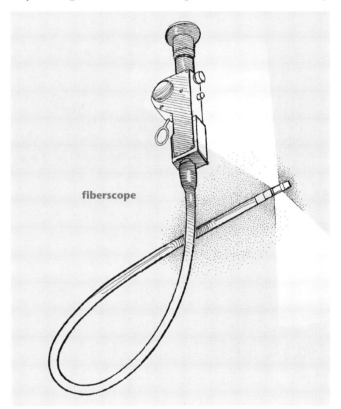

fiberscope

fibril (fi′bril) A delicate thin fiber or filament.

fibrillar, fibrillary (fi′brĭ-lar, fi′brĭ-lār-e) **1.** Relating to a fibril. **2.** Relating to a twitching of small muscle fibrils.

fibrillate (fi′brĭ-lāt) To undergo fibrillation.

fibrillated (fi′brĭ-lāt-ed) Composed of fibrils.

fibrillation (fi-brĭ-la′shun) The rapid, uncoordinated, and ineffective contraction of single muscle fibers, not of the muscle as a whole.

atrial f. A cardiac arrhythmia in which the normal rhythmic contractions of the muscular wall of the atria are replaced by rapid

fiberoptic ■ fibrillation

uncoordinated quivers; not all of the impulses pass through the A-V node.

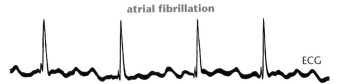

atrial fibrillation

ECG

ventricular f. A cardiac arrhythmia in which rapid, irregular twitching of the muscular wall of the ventricles replaces the normal rhythmic contractions; the rhythm does not permit effective ventricular contraction.

fibrillin (fi'brĭ-lin) One of the protein components of connective tissue; it is markedly reduced in certain disorders (e.g., Marfan's syndrome).

fibrillogenesis (fi-bril-o-jen'ĕ-sis) The development of minute fibrils, as occurs normally in collagenous fibers of connective tissue.

fibrin (fi'brin) A fibrous, insoluble protein derived from fibrinogen by the action of the enzyme thrombin; it is the basic component of a blood clot.

fibrino- Combining form meaning fibrin.

fibrinogen (fi-brin'o-jen) A protein, present in dissolved form in blood plasma, that is converted into a network of delicate elastic filaments by the action of the enzyme thrombin; during blood clot formation, blood cells become entangled in the fibrin network; a blood coagulation factor. Also called factor I.

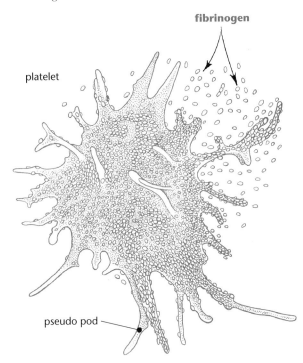

fibrinogen

platelet

pseudo pod

fibrinogenopenia (fi-brin-o-jen-o-pe'ne-ah) Deficiency of fibrinogen in the blood.

fibrinoid (fi'brĭ-noid) 1. Resembling fibrin. 2. A homogeneous substance, with the staining properties of fibrin, that accumulates in degenerating connective tissues.

fibrinolysis (fi-brĭ-nol'ĭ-sis) Dissolution of fibrin resulting from activation of the enzyme plasmin in the bloodstream.

fibrinopeptide (fi-brĭ-no-pep'tid) A peptide thought to be the product of fibrinolysis; elevated levels are found in the blood after a stroke.

fibrinopurulent (fi-brĭ-no-pu'roo-lent) Containing pus and a large amount of fibrin; applied to a discharge.

fibrinous (fi'brĭ-nus) Containing fibrin.

fibro-, fibr- Combining forms meaning fiber.

fibroadenoma (fi-bro-ad-ĕ-no'mah) A noncancerous tumor derived from glandular epithelium.
   f. of breast A single, freely movable nodule 1 to 10 cm in diameter; it is the most common noncancerous tumor of the female breast, usually occurring during the reproductive years.

fibroadipose (fi-bro-ad'ĭ-pōs) Containing both fibrous and fatty elements. Also called fibrofatty.

fibroblast (fi'bro-blast) A flattened spindle-shaped cell with a flat oval nucleus and one or two nucleoli; one of the most common cell types found in growing connective tissue.

fibrocarcinoma (fi-bro-kar-sĭ-no'mah) See scirrhous carcinoma, under carcinoma.

fibrocartilage (fi-bro-kar'tĭ-lij) A type of cartilage containing collagen fibers; found in such structures as intervertebral disks.
   yellow f. See elastic cartilage, under cartilage.

fibrochondritis (fi-bro-kon-dri'tis) Inflammation of fibrocartilage.

fibrochondroma (fi-bro-kon-dro'mah) A benign tumor composed primarily of cartilage and abundant fibrous tissue.

fibrocyst (fi'bro-sist) A lesion consisting of a cyst within a fibrous network.

fibrocystadenoma (fi-bro-sis-tad-ĕ-no'mah) See fibrocystoma.

fibrocystic (fi-bro-sis'tik) Having fibrous and cystic components.

fibrocystoma (fi-bro-sis-to'mah) A benign tumor containing cysts within a predominant fibrous network. Also called fibrocystadenoma.

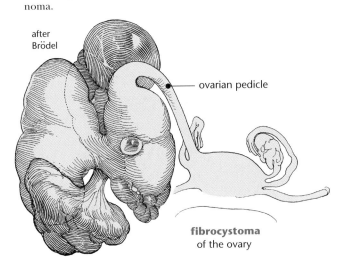

after Brödel

ovarian pedicle

fibrocystoma
of the ovary

fibrocyte (fi'bro-sīt) A quiescent or resting fibroblast.

fibroelastic (fi-bro-e-las'tik) Consisting of elastic fibers and collagen.

fibroelastosis (fi-bro-e-las-to'sis) Overgrowth of fibroelastic tissue.
   endocardial f., endomyocardial f. Uncommon congenital heart disease characterized by a milky white thickening of the inner lining of the heart chambers, especially of the left ventricle, with hardening and disorganization of heart muscle fibers; the other chambers of the heart and the atrioventricular valves may also be involved; cause is unknown; a fetal infection has been suggested, possibly with the mumps virus. Also called endocardial sclerosis.

fibroenchondroma (fi-bro-en-kon-dro'mah) A benign tumor within a bone, composed of cartilage and abundant fibrous tissue.

fibroepithelioma (fi-bro-ep-ĭ-the-le-o'mah) A benign skin tumor composed of fibrous tissue and elements of the superficial layer of the skin; it may be transformed into a basal cell carcinoma. Also called premalignant fibroepithelioma.
   premalignant f. See fibroepithelioma.

fibrofatty (fi-bro-fat'e) See fibroadipose.

fibroid (fi'broid) 1. Commonly used term for a tumor more properly called leiomyoma, since the tumor mass is primarily composed of smooth muscle rather than fibrous tissue. See leiomyoma. 2. Composed of or resembling fibrous tissue.

fibrolamellar (fi-bro-lah-mel'ar) Containing compartments or layers separated by fibrous bands or walls; seen in certain tumors (e.g., hepatoma).

fibrolipoma (fi-bro-lĭ-po'mah) A benign tumor composed primarily of fat cells but containing abundant fibrous tissue.

fibroma (fi-bro'mah) A benign tumor derived from fibrous tissue.

chondromyxoid f. An uncommon benign tumor composed of chondroid, myxoid, and fibrous tissues; occurs in long bones, especially about the knee, of young adults. Also called chondromyxoma.

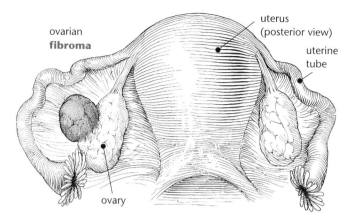

ovarian
fibroma

uterus
(posterior view)

uterine
tube

ovary

fibromatosis (fi-bro-mah-to'sis), pl. fibromato'ses **1.** Any of a group of conditions with abnormal proliferation of fibrous tissue as the common feature (e.g., Dupuytren's contracture, Peyronie's disease). **2.** Condition marked by formation of multiple fibromas.

aggressive f. A large, locally aggressive mass resulting from the proliferation of fibrous tissues of muscle sheaths; it is intermediate between a benign and malignant growth, tending to recur after surgical removal but rarely spreading to other areas of the body; occurs most commonly in the abdominal muscles, especially of women after pregnancy. Also called desmoid; desmoid tumor.

retroperitoneal f. See sclerosing retroperitonitis, under retroperitonitis.

fibromuscular (fi-bro-mus'ku-lar) Denoting tissues with both fibrous and muscular components.

fibromyoma (fi-bro-mi-o'mah) See leiomyoma.

fibromyositis (fi-bro-mi-o-si'tis) Chronic inflammation of a muscle with overgrowth of its connective tissue.

fibromyxoma (fi-bro-mik-so'mah) Connective-tissue tumor that is predominantly fibrous but contains abundant acellular elements.

fibronectin (fi-bro-nek'tin) An adhesive glycoprotein present in plasma, where it participates in phagocytosis of bacteria and other cells, or on the cell surface, where it mediates cellular adhesive interactions.

fibroplasia (fi-bro-pla'se-ah) Abnormal production of fibrous tissue.

retrolental f. See retinopathy of prematurity, under retinopathy.

fibroplastic (fi-bro-plas'tik) Relating to fibroplasia.

fibrosarcoma (fi-bro-sar-ko'mah) Malignant tumor composed of fibrous connective tissue.

fibrosis (fi-bro'sis) The formation of fibrous tissue, denoting particularly an abnormal degenerative process.

cystic f. (CF) Genetic disorder affecting the mucus-secreting glands and sweat glands throughout the body, leading to the prduction of abnormally sticky secretions and formation of mucus plugs in the pancreatic and bile ducts and in the lung airways; manifestations range from mild to severe, usually including the passage of fatty stools, recurring lung infections, and the presence of excessive sodium and chloride in the sweat; the defective gene is located in chromosome 7 and is transmitted as an autosomal recessive inheritance. Also called mucoviscidosis; fibrocystic disease of pancreas.

endomyocardial f. Fibrous thickening of the muscular wall of the cardiac ventricles.

idiopathic pulmonary f. A poorly understood condition of the lungs characterized by progressive fibrosis of lung tissue that results in deficient concentration of oxygen in arterial blood; cause is unknown.

idiopathic retroperitoneal f. See sclerosing retroperitonitis, under retroperitonitis.

perimuscular f. Fibrosis involving the arteries of the kidneys. Also called subadventitial fibrosis.

retroperitoneal f. See sclerosing retroperitonitis, under retroperitonitis.

subadventitial f. See perimuscular fibrosis.

fibrositis (fi-bro-si'tis) Inflammatory proliferation of fibrous or connective tissue in the muscles.

fibrous (fi'brus) Composed of fibers.

fibula (fib'u-lah) The lateral and smaller of the two bones of the leg, between the knee and the ankle. See table of bones.

fibular (fib'u-lar) Relating to the fibula. Also called peroneal.

fibulocalcaneal (fib-u-lo-kal-ka'ne-al) Relating to the fibula and the heel bone (calcaneus).

field (fēld) A limited area or space.

auditory f. The area within which a sound is perceived.

magnetic f. The space around a magnet within which magnetic force is perceptible.

visual f. (F) The area of physical space visible to the eye in a fixed position.

filament (fil'ah-ment) A thin, threadlike structure.

acrosomal f. A stiff filament extruded by the acrosomal cap at the head of the spermatozoon, when it contacts the surface of a targeted ovum.

actin f. The smaller of the two contractile elements in muscle fibers, measuring about 50 Å in width; in skeletal and cardiac muscles, one end is attached to the Z line, a transverse septum that gives the muscle a characteristic striated appearance; the other free end interdigitates with the myosin filament in the contraction and relaxation of muscle.

axial f. The central filament of the tail of a spermatozoon, consisting of a central pair of fibrils within a symmetrical set of nine doublet fibrils, enveloped by an outer ring of nine larger dense fibers. Also called axoneme.

myosin f. The thicker of the two contractile elements in all muscle fibers; in skeletal and cardiac muscles, it measures about 100 Å in width, and traverses the central portion of each sarcomere, producing a dense A band; when interdigitating with the free ends of actin filaments, it is responsible for the contraction and relaxation of muscle.

root f.'s of spinal nerves Threadlike root filaments or rootlets of the spinal nerves emerging from the spinal cord along its anterolateral and posterolateral regions; the ventral (anterior) filaments emerge in two or three irregular rows; the dorsal (posterior) filaments are attached in a regular series along a shallow groove, the posterolateral sulcus.

spermatic f. The short naked fragment at the terminal part of the tail of a spermatozoon.

filamentous (fil-ah-men'tus) Threadlike.

filaria (fĭ-la're-ah) Common name for threadworms of the family Onchocercidae.

filariasis (fil-ah-ri'ah-sis) The presence of parasitic threadworms in the body.

lymphatic f. See filarial elephantiasis, under elephantiasis.

filaricide (fĭ-lār'ĭ-sīd) Any agent that kills threadworms.

filariform (fĭ-lār'ĭ-form) Resembling threadworms.

file (fīl) A device used for cutting, smoothing, or grinding.

filial (fil'e-al) Relating to a son or daughter.

filiform (fil'ĭ-form) Threadlike.

fillet (fil'et) **1.** A thin strip of bandage or tape for making traction. **2.** A band of fibers.

bone **file**

filling (fil′ing) **1.** Any substance used to fill a space or cavity (e.g., amalgam placed into a tooth cavity, after removal of the carious tissue, to restore the missing portion of the tooth). **2.** The procedure of inserting, condensing, shaping, and polishing a filling in a prepared cavity or root canal of a tooth.

    acrylic resin f. A material used for restoration of teeth when aesthetic properties are required.

    combination f. A filling usually made of two distinct components placed one on top of the other in a tooth cavity.

    complex f. See compound filling.

    composite f. One consisting of a resin of distinct components, usually a setting resin and silicious particles.

    compound f. A filling that involves more than one surface of a tooth (e.g., disto-occlusal filling). Also called complex filling.

    contour f. A filling that restores the original contour of the tooth.

    direct f. A filling formed and finished directly in the tooth cavity.

    indirect f. A filling, usually of gold, cast from an accurate model of the tooth cavity and then cemented into the tooth.

    interim f. See temporary filling.

    nonleaking f. A filling with perfect contact with the walls of the tooth cavity that prevents the penetration of moisture or microorganisms.

    overhang f. A poorly finished filling with excessive material overhanging at the junction of the prepared tooth cavity.

    permanent f. A filling intended to be functional for as long as possible.

    root-canal f. A filling placed in the root canal of a nonvital tooth to seal the space once occupied by the dental pulp; the canal is filled from the apical end of the root canal to the surface.

    silicate f. A filling of lost tooth structure made with silicate cement, essentially acid-soluble glass.

    temporary f. A filling, usually of temporary cement or gutta-percha, intended to remain in place for a limited time; it is used to allay sensitive dentin prior to final restoration. Also called interim filling; treatment filling.

    treatment f. See temporary filling.

    zinc oxide–eugenol f. A temporary filling material, often referred to as ZOE.

film (film) **1.** Any thin layer of a substance. **2.** A thin cellulose sheet coated with an emulsion sensitive to light or x-rays.

    bite-wing f. Dental x-ray film with an appendage that is held between the occlusal surfaces of teeth.

film badge (film baj) A small device containing x-ray-sensitive film, worn by personnel exposed to ionizing radiation to monitor their exposure; approximate exposure is determined by the degree of darkening of the film.

film fault (film fawlt) A defect in an x-ray film due either to physical or chemical causes or to electrical errors in its production.

    fogged f.f. Hazy appearance of a roentgenogram; may be caused by exposure of the film to light or stray radiation, subjection to unusual temperatures or chemical actions, or use of outdated film.

filter (fil′ter) **1.** A porous material for trapping particles suspended in a gas or liquid. **2.** A device that permits passage of rays of certain wavelengths only; used in radiologic diagnosis or treatment. **3.** To pass a substance or rays through such devices.

filtrable, filterable (fil′trah-bl, fil′ter-ah-bl) Small enough to pass through a filter; applied to certain viruses.

filtrate (fil′trāt) Fluid that has passed through a filter.

filtration (fil-tra′shun) The process of filtering.

filum (fi′lum), pl. fi′la A filamentous or threadlike structure or part; Latin for thread.

    external f. terminale See filum of spinal dura mater.

    internal f. terminale See filum terminale.

    fila radicularia nervorum spinalium See root filaments of spinal nerves, under filament.

    f. of spinal dura mater The extension of the dura mater

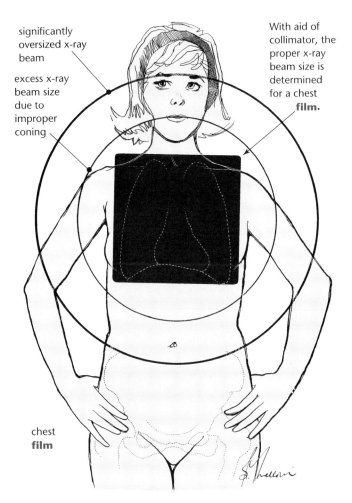

significantly oversized x-ray beam

excess x-ray beam size due to improper coning

With aid of collimator, the proper x-ray beam size is determined for a chest **film.**

chest **film**

surrounding the spinal cord; it starts from the apex of the dural sac and descends for about 5 cm, and then fuses with the filum terminale before attaching to the periosteum of the coccyx. Also called external filum terminale.

    f. terminale The slender threadlike prolongation of the spinal cord, about 20 cm long, consisting mainly of filaments of connective tissue (continuous with the pia mater of the spinal cord); it extends from the conus medullaris of the spinal cord to the apex of the dural sac, where it unites with the filum of spinal dura mater before attaching to the periosteum of the coccyx; usually seen from the

No. Name

x-ray sensitive film

film badge

level of the second lumbar vertebra to the coccyx. Also called internal filum terminale.

fimbria (fim′bre-ah), pl. fim′briae **1.** Any fringelike structure. **2.** See pilus (2).

f. of fornix See hippocampal fimbria.

hippocampal f. A narrow band of white nerve fibers that forms a fringe along the medial concave border of the hippocampus of the brain; it receives fibers from the hippocampus. Also called fimbria of fornix.

ovarian f. The longest and most deeply grooved fimbria of the fallopian (uterine) tube that runs along the lateral border of the mesosalpinx to attach to the tubal extremity of the ovary.

fimbriae of uterine tube The numerous diverging fringelike processes on the margins of the distal end of the fallopian (uterine) tube; they are closely applied to the surface of the ovary during ovulation.

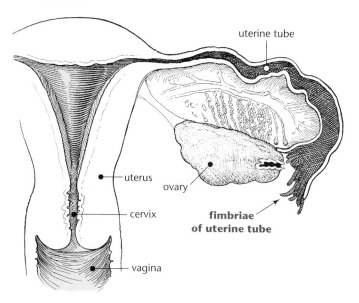

fimbriated (fim′bre-āt-ed) Having fimbria.

fimbriectomy (fim-bre-ek′to-me) Surgical removal of fimbria, especially of the fallopian (uterine) tubes for the purpose of sterilization.

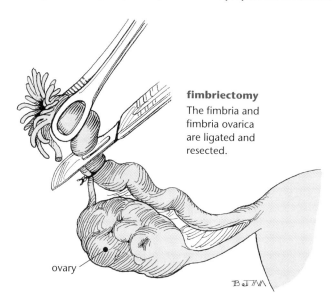

fimbriectomy
The fimbria and fimbria ovarica are ligated and resected.

ovary

fimbrioplasty (fim-bre-o-plas′te) Reconstruction of existing fimbria in a partially or totally occluded fallopian (uterine) tube.

finger (fing′ger) One of the digits of the hand.

baseball f. See mallet finger.

clubbed f.'s See clubbing.

drop f. See mallet finger.

drumstick f.'s See clubbing.

fifth f. The fifth digit of the hand. Also called little finger.

first f. The first digit of the hand. Also called thumb.

fourth f. The fourth digit of the hand. Also called ring finger.

hammer f. See mallet finger.

index f. See second finger.

little f. See fifth finger.

lock f. See trigger finger.

mallet f. Involuntary flexion of the bone at the end of the finger while the rest of the digit is held in rigid extension; the sudden bending causes the extensor tendon either to tear or to pull off a fragment of bone. Also called baseball finger; drop finger; hammer finger.

middle f. See third finger.

ring f. See fourth finger.

second f. The second digit of the hand. Also called index finger; forefinger.

snapping f. See trigger finger.

third f. The third digit of the hand. Also called middle finger.

trigger f. A finger that is temporarily "locked" in a flexed position, producing an audible click upon forcible extension; results from localized inflammation of the tendon and inflammation of the fibrous sheath enclosing the tendon; when the finger is flexed, the inflamed portion of the tendon is forced out of the narrowed mouth of the enclosing sheath and then is unable to reenter it; frequently caused by repetitive finger action (e.g., excessive use of the index finger for operating the triggers of hand tools). Also called snapping finger; lock finger.

webbed f.'s Congenital abnormality in which two or more fingers are united in various degrees by a fold of skin.

white f.'s Occupational disorder occurring on exposure to cold, characterized by blanching of the fingers, loss of sensation, and reduction in skin temperature; usually mild, but severe cases may lead to tissue injury; the condition is vibration-induced and may occur in workers operating chain saws (lumberers), grinding wheels (foundry workers), pneumatic tools (demolition and road construction workers), Jack leg drills (miners and surveyors).

finger cot (fing′ger kot) A protective rubber covering for the finger; used in digital examinations.

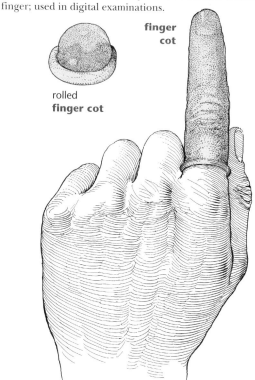

finger cot

rolled
finger cot

fingernail (fing′ger-nāl) The horny plate on the dorsal surface of the tip of each finger. See also nail.

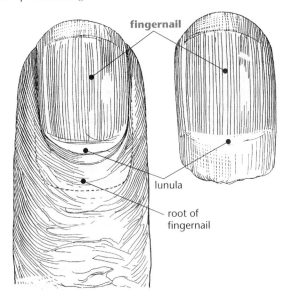

fingernail
lunula
root of fingernail

fingerprint (fing′ger-print) An impression of the configuration of ridges (dermatographic pattern) on the volar surface of a fingertip; usually used as a means of identification; the patterns are sometimes of clinical importance.

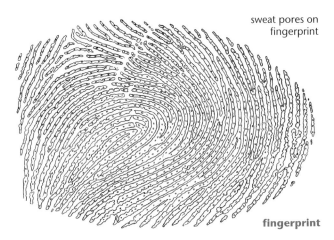

sweat pores on fingerprint

fingerprint

Galton's system of classification of f.'s The arch-loop-whorl system of classifying variations in the dermatographic patterns.

record f.'s Fingerprints obtained by applying ink to the fingertips and rolling each one on an assigned space of a white card; preserved for future identification and comparison.

fingerprinting (fing′ger-prin′ting) **1.** To take a fingerprint. **2.** A visual form, especially one used as a means of specific identification.

DNA f. See DNA typing, under typing.

first aid (ferst ād) Emergency assistance provided to an injured or sick person before the availability of professional medical care.

fission (fish′un) The act of splitting, such as a cell or an atom.

fissiparous (fi-sip′ah-rus) Propagating by fission.

fissura (fis-su′rah) Latin for fissure; cleft.

fissural (fish′u-ral) Relating to a fissure.

fissuration (fish-u-ra′shun) The formation of a fissure.

fissure (fish′ūr) A cleft, groove, depression, or slit; a sulcus or deep fold.

　　anal f. A painful, difficult-to-heal slit in the mucous membrane at the margin of the anus.

　　anterior median f. of spinal cord A deep midline groove, extending the entire length of the front of the spinal cord; along

with the shallow posterior median sulcus and the median septum, it divides the spinal cord into symmetrical halves.

　　antitragohelicine f. A deep slitlike fissure in the cartilage of the ear (auricle) between the tail of the helix (cauda helicis) posteriorly and the antihelix anteriorly.

　　calcarine f. See calcarine sulcus, under sulcus.

　　cerebellar horizontal f. A deep fissure encircling the circumference of the superior surface of the cerebellar hemispheres of the brain. Also called cerebellar horizontal sulcus.

　　cerebral f.'s See cerebral sulci, under sulcus.

　　cerebral central f. See cerebral central sulcus, under sulcus.

　　cerebral longitudinal f. The deep midline groove that divides the cerebrum into right and left hemispheres; it extends down to the mass of white matter (corpus callosum) that connects the hemispheres across the median plane.

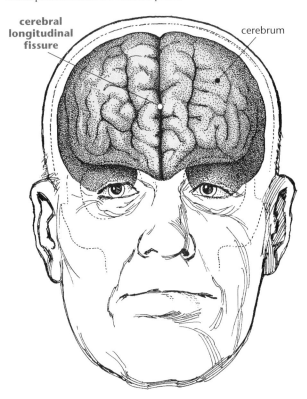

cerebral longitudinal fissure
cerebrum

　　cerebral transverse f. A cleft between the large mass of transverse fibers connecting the two hemispheres of the brain (corpus callosum) and the roof of the third ventricle and thalami.

　　decidual f. A cleft in the decidua basalis of the placenta, as seen toward the end of pregancy.

　　f. of false glottis The interval between the false vocal folds (vestibular folds) of the larynx. Also called rima vestibuli.

　　f. of glottis The elongated opening between the true vocal folds in the larynx; situated at the narrowest part of the laryngeal cavity. Also called rima glottidis.

　　inferior orbital f. A large fissure separating the lateral wall and floor of the orbit, opening posteriorly into the pterygopalatine and infratemporal fossae; it transmits the maxillary nerve, filaments from the pterygopalatine ganglion, and blood channels between the orbital and pterygoid venous plexuses.

　　intercotyledonal f.'s Grooves that separate some 15 to 30 lobules (cotyledons) on the maternal side of the placenta.

　　lateral cerebral f. See cerebral lateral sulcus, under sulcus.

　　f.'s of lungs Fissures separating the lobes of the lungs; they divide the left lung into two lobes (superior and inferior), and the right lung into three lobes (superior, middle, and inferior).

　　palpebral f. The longitudinal slit between the eyelids. Also called rima palpebrarum.

　　parietooccipital f. See parietooccipital sulcus, under sulcus.

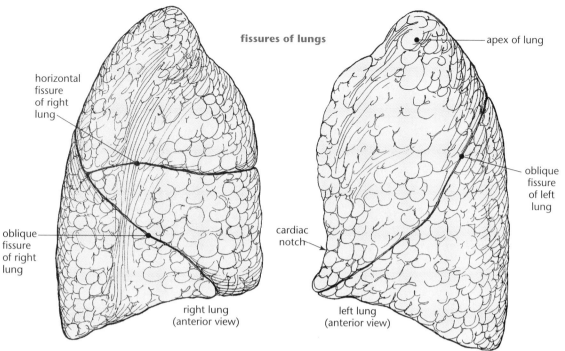

fissures of lungs

horizontal fissure of right lung

oblique fissure of right lung

right lung (anterior view)

apex of lung

oblique fissure of left lung

cardiac notch

left lung (anterior view)

posterior median f. of spinal cord See posterior median sulcus of spinal cord, under sulcus.

pudendal f. See vulval cleft, under cleft.

f. of Rolando See cerebral central sulcus, under sulcus.

superior orbital f. A large irregular fissure between the roof of the orbit (lesser wing of sphenoid bone) and its lateral wall (greater wing of sphenoid bone); it connects the orbit and the middle cranial fossa and transmits the oculomotor (3rd cranial), trochlear (4th cranial), and abducent (6th cranial) nerves, as well as branches of the ophthalmic nerve, the ophthalmic veins, and some meningeal vessels.

f. of Sylvius See cerebral lateral sulcus, under sulcus.

urogenital f. See vulval cleft, under cleft.

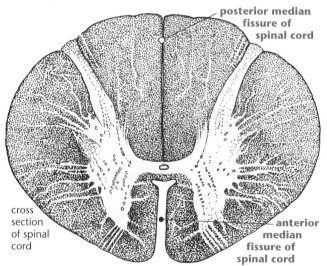

posterior median fissure of spinal cord

cross section of spinal cord

anterior median fissure of spinal cord

fistula (fis'tu-lah), pl. fis'tulas An unnatural passage between one organ and another, or between an organ and the surface of the body; usually designated according to the organ with which it communicates.

anal f. An open channel in the region of the anus, invariably the result of an abscess; the port of entry is generally an anal crypt and from there it could course submucously, subcutaneously, or transsphincterally to the surrounding tissue, exiting to the skin near the anal opening or ascending to open in the rectum.

arteriovenous f. An abnormal direct communication (congenital or traumatic) between an artery and a vein; it may develop into an arteriovenous aneurysm.

branchial f. A congenital defect consisting of a narrow channel between the pharynx and the lateral surface of the neck, in front of the sternocleidomastoid muscle; it results from the failure of the fetal branchial cleft to close completely. Also called cervical fistula.

bronchoesophageal f. A congenital passage between a bronchus and the esophagus, permitting the possible aspiration of esophageal contents into the lungs.

bronchopleural f. A fistula connecting a bronchus to the pleural cavity, where pus may have accumulated.

carotid-cavernous f. Arteriovenous connection formed by rupture of the internal carotid artery while traveling through the cavernous venous sinus, permitting arterial blood to mix with venous blood in the sinus; usually due to a rupture of an aneurysm on the intracavernous portion of the internal carotid artery.

cervical f. See branchial fistula.

colovesical f. See vesicocolonic fistula.

enterovaginal f. A fistula between the vagina and neighboring intestine, usually associated with intestinal disease, especially diverticulitis.

gastrocolic f. A fistulous passage between the stomach and the colon; usually resulting from invasive carcinoma.

gastrointestinal f. An abnormal passage between the stomach and adjacent intestine.

pilonidal f. See pilonidal sinus, under sinus.

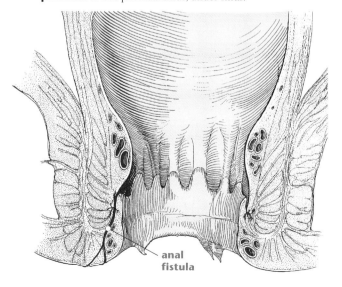

anal fistula

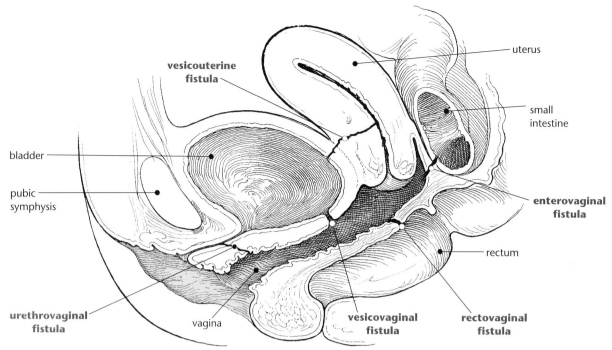

vesicouterine fistula

uterus

small intestine

bladder

pubic symphysis

enterovaginal fistula

rectum

urethrovaginal fistula

vagina

vesicovaginal fistula

rectovaginal fistula

rectovaginal f. A fistulous passage between the rectum and the vagina, usually caused by direct surgical trauma, disease of the rectum, or obstetrical injury.

tracheoesophageal f. Congenital fistula between the trachea and the esophagus; frequently associated with failure of the full esophageal lumen to develop (atresia).

urachal f. A fistula between the bladder and the navel (umbilicus); a congenital abnormality that occurs when the lumen of the embryonic urachus (which extends from the bladder to the umbilicus) fails to obliterate during intrauterine life and persists over the entire length, allowing urine to seep through the umbilicus. Also called patent urachus; vesicoumbilical fistula.

urethrovaginal f. A fistula between the urethra and the vagina; may be due to obstetrical injury or may be congenital.

vesicocolonic f. An abnormal passage between the bladder and the colon. Also called colovesical fistula.

vesicoumbilical f. See urachal fistula.

vesicouterine f. A fistula between the bladder and the uterus, usually caused by cancer of the cervix or by surgical injury to the bladder.

vesicovaginal f. A fistula between the bladder and the vagina, often the result of traumatic delivery or advanced cancer; almost invariably causes urinary incontinence.

fistulation (fis-tu-la'shun) The formation of a fistula.

fistulatome (fis'tu-lah-tōm) A thin-bladed long knife for cutting open a fistula.

fistulectomy (fis-tu-lek'to-me) Surgical obliteration of a fistula by removal of its walls, thus creating an open wound that heals from within outward.

fistulotomy (fis-tu-lot'o-me) A surgical incision into a fistula. Also called syringotomy.

fistulous (fis'tu-lus) Containing a fistula.

fitness (fit'nes) **1.** Well-being. **2.** (f) In genetics, the probability that the genes of an individual will be passed to the next generation and that they will survive in that generation to be passed to the next, in relation to the average probability for the population.

physical f. A state of physical well-being that enables a person to perform daily work without undue fatigue.

fixation (fik-sa'shun) **1.** The process of making stationary. **2.** In ophthalmology, the act of directing the eye toward an object, causing its image to fall on the fovea of the retina. **3.** In psychiatry, the persistence of immature patterns of behavior; a stopping of psychosocial development. **4.** In histology, the preservation of tissue elements with minimal alteration of the normal state.

bifoveal f. Fixation in which the images of the observed object center simultaneously on the foveae of both eyes, as occurs in normal vision. Also called binocular fixation.

binocular f. See bifoveal fixation.

complement f. (CF) Fixation that occurs when an antigen is allowed to combine with its specific antibody in the presence of complement; used in the detection of antibodies in serum.

external f. The holding together in alignment the fragments of a broken bone by means of a plaster cast or a plaster splint until successful healing occurs.

internal f. Surgical application of pins, wires, screws, or plates directly onto a fractured bone to keep the fragments in proper alignment.

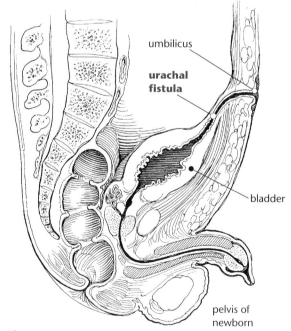

umbilicus

urachal fistula

bladder

pelvis of newborn

fixative (fik'sah-tiv) A substance used in the preservation of histologic specimens.

flaccid (flak'sid) Limp; flabby.

flagellate (flaj'ĕ-lāt) A microorganism equipped with one or more whiplike processes for locomotion.

flagellosis (flaj-e-lo'sis) Infection with flagellates.

flagellum (flah-jel′um), pl. flagel′la A hairlike protoplasmic structure, present on the free surface of some microorganisms and used for locomotion.

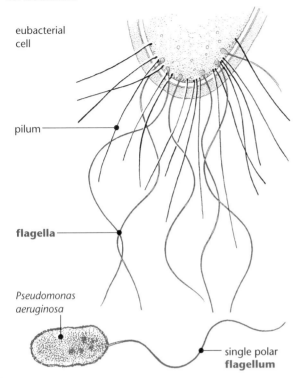

eubacterial cell

pilum

flagella

Pseudomonas aeruginosa

single polar **flagellum**

flange (flanj) A protruding rim or edge.

denture f. The nearly vertical extension from the body of a denture into one of the spaces of the mouth adjoining the lips or cheeks (labial or buccal vestibules) or into the space adjacent to the tongue (alveololingual sulcus).

flank (flank) The side of the body between the ribs and the pelvis.

flap (flap) Any tissue that is raised and moved to a new location but remains temporarily attached by a base and a pedicle through which all or part of its original blood supply enters and exits; used for reconstruction or closure of a wound. Also called pedicle graft.

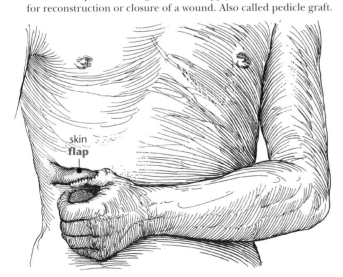

skin **flap**

axial pattern f. A flap that has a well-defined pattern of arteries and veins running along its long axis.

bone f. A section of bone cut from the skull and reflected on a hinge of muscle and/or other tissue.

fasciocutaneous f. A flap consisting of skin and the vascular rich fascia covering certain muscles (e.g., rectus abdominus, gastrocnemius, quadriceps).

liver f. See asterixis.

musculocutaneous f. Flap consisting of skin and underlying muscle.

random pattern f. Flap consisting of skin and subcutaneous tissues obtained from any area of the body, with no distinct pattern of the blood supply to the skin.

sliding f. A flap used to either lengthen or shorten a localized area of tissue.

flare (flār) Diffuse redness of the skin around an injured joint.

flash (flash) **1.** An intense burst of light or heat. **2.** In dentistry, the surplus material squeezed out of a two-section mold.

hot f. Popular term for a sudden sensation of heat; a vasomotor symptom of menopause.

welder's f. See photokeratoconjunctivitis.

flashback (flash′bak) The spontaneous and unpredictable recurrence of distorted visual perceptions stemming from having previously taken psychedelic drugs.

flask (flask) **1.** A bottle with a narrow neck and expanded lower portion used in laboratory work. **2.** A metal case or tube used in investing procedures, as when making artificial dentures.

crown f. A small dental flask.

dental f. A metal case in which a sectional gypsum mold is made for shaping and curing resinous structures, such as dentures or other resinous restorations.

Erlenmeyer f. A flask with a conical body, broad base, and narrow neck.

Florence f. A globular long-necked bottle of thin glass used for holding water or other liquid in laboratory work.

volumetric f. A flask calibrated to indicate exact amounts of liquid contained within.

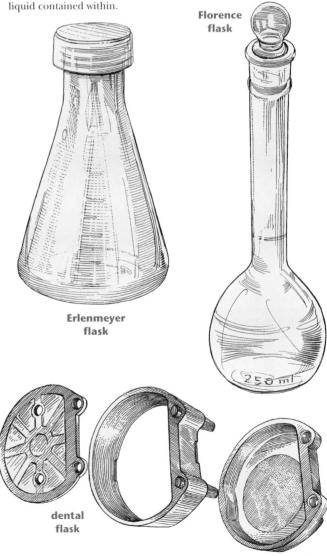

Florence flask

Erlenmeyer flask

250 ml

dental flask

flasking (flask′ing) In dentistry, the investing of the cast and a wax denture prior to molding the denture-base material into the form of a denture.

flatfoot (flat′foot) Condition marked by varying degrees of depression of the longitudinal arch of the foot, resulting in the body's weight being borne over the entire sole; it may be congenital or acquired. Also called pes planus; talipes planus; splayfoot.

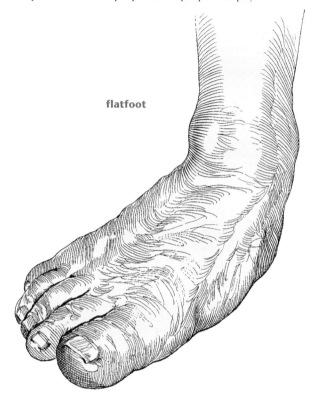

flatfoot

flatulence (flat′u-lens) Excessive gas in the stomach and intestines causing distention.

flatulent (flat′u-lent) Relating to flatulence.

flatus (fla′tus) Intestinal gas expelled through the anus.

flatworm (flat′werm) Any member of the phylum Platyhelminthes (e.g., flukes, tapeworms).

flavin (fla′vin) Any of various nitrogenous yellow pigments found in animal and plant tissue.

    f. adenine dinucleotide (FAD) A nucleotide containing riboflavin; it participates as a coenzyme in oxidation-reduction reactions.

    f. mononucleotide (FMN) A cofactor containing riboflavin in cellular oxidation-reduction systems.

Flavivirus (fla-ve-vi′rus) A genus of viruses (family Togaviridae) that includes those causing yellow fever, encephalitis, and dengue.

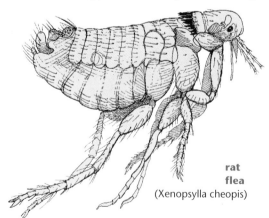

rat
flea
(Xenopsylla cheopis)

flavobacterium (fla-vo-bak-te′re-um) A genus of gram-negative bacteria that produce yellow, orange, red, or yellow-brown pigments; some species cause disease.

flavoenzyme (fla-vo-en′zīm) Any enzyme that needs a flavin nucleotide as coenzyme.

flavor (fla′vor) **1.** The distinctive taste of a substance. **2.** An inert substance added to a pharmaceutical preparation to give it a pleasant taste.

flea (fle) A bloodsucking insect of the order Siphonaptera; about 1500 species are known to be parasites on warm-blooded animals; some are vectors of disease-causing microorganisms.

    rat f. General term for any of several species of fleas that are parasitic on rats, including *Pulex fasciatus, Typhlopsylla musculi,* and *Xenopsylla cheopis;* some are vectors of bubonic plague.

    sand f. See chigoe.

flesh (flesh) **1.** Muscular tissue. **2.** The meat of animals.

    proud f. Excessive granulation on the surface of a wound or ulcer.

flex (fleks) To approximate two parts connected by a joint.

flexibilitas cerea (flek-sī-bil′ī-tas sēr′e-ah) See cerea flexibilitas.

fleximeter (fleks-im′ĕ-ter) See goniometer.

flexion (flek′shun) **1.** The act of approximating two parts connected by a joint (e.g., of a limb) or of bending forward (e.g., of the spine). **2.** The condition of being bent.

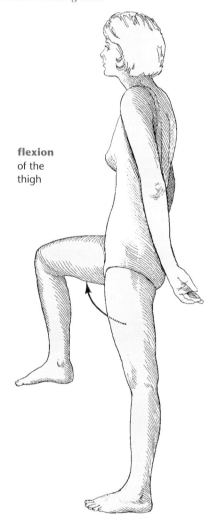

flexion
of the
thigh

    palmar f. Flexion at the wrist, causing the hand to be bent toward the anterior surface of the forearm.

    plantar f. Flexion at the ankle joint, causing the foot to be bent downward.

flexor (flek′sor) A muscle that flexes a joint.

flexura (flek-shoo′rah) Latin for a bend.

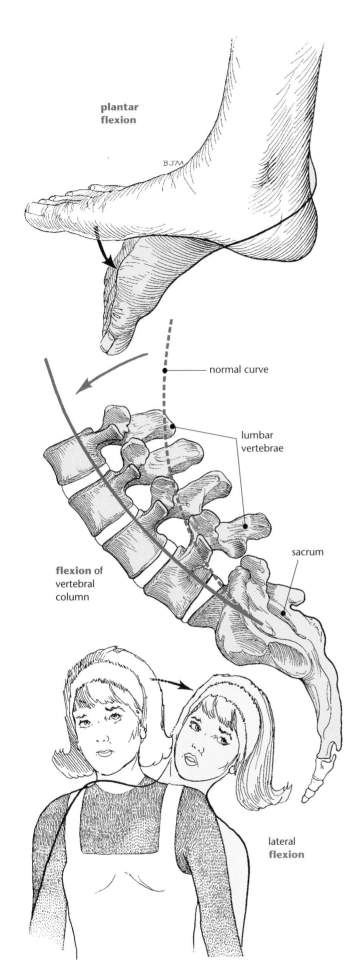

plantar flexion

normal curve

lumbar vertebrae

flexion of vertebral column

sacrum

lateral **flexion**

flexure (flek′sher) A bend, turn, or curve, usually of an anatomic structure or organ.

   caudal f. The bend at the caudal end of the embryo. Also called sacral flexure.

   cephalic f. The bend at the cephalic region of the embryo. Also called cranial flexure.

   cervical f. The bend at the junction of the embryonic brain and spinal cord. Also called nuchal flexure.

   cranial f. See cephalic flexure.

   dorsal f. The dorsal convexity of the spine in the thoracic region.

   duodenal f.'s Angulations of the duodenum: *Inferior duodenal f.,* the sharp curve formed by the angulation between the second (descending) and third (horizontal) parts of the duodenum. *Superior duodenal f.,* the sharp curve formed by the first (superior) and second (descending) parts of the duodenum; generally situated in the region just below the neck of the gallbladder.

   duodenojejunal f. The acute bend in the small intestine at the junction of the fourth (ascending) part of the duodenum and the beginning of the jejunum, about 1 inch from the median plane;

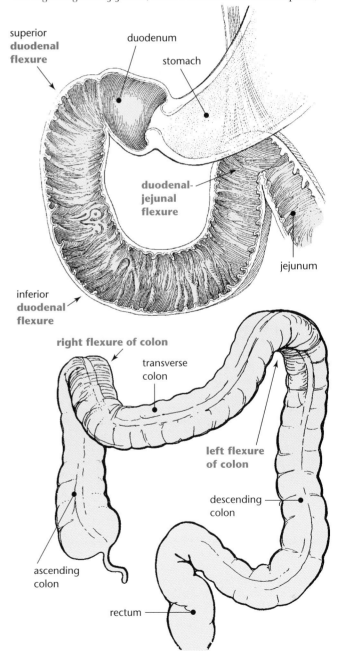

superior **duodenal flexure**

duodenum

stomach

duodenal-jejunal flexure

jejunum

inferior **duodenal flexure**

right flexure of colon

transverse colon

left flexure of colon

descending colon

ascending colon

rectum

it is fixed to the right crus of the diaphragm (near the esophageal hiatus) by the suspensory ligament of the duodenum.

hepatic f. See right flexure of colon.

left colic f. See left flexure of colon.

left f. of colon The acute bend between the transverse colon and the descending colon, near the lower part of the spleen and tail of the pancreas; it is anchored to the diaphragm by a peritoneal fold (phrenicocolic ligament); the left flexure of colon is more acute than the right flexure of colon and lies at a higher level in the body. Also called splenic flexure; left colic flexure.

lumbar f. The dorsal concavity of the spine in the lumbar region.

nuchal f. See cervical flexure.

right colic f. See right flexure of colon.

right f. of colon The acute bend between the terminal part of the ascending colon and the beginning of the transverse colon, near the right lobe of the liver (hepar). Also called hepatic flexure; right colic flexure.

sacral f. See caudal flexure.

splenic f. See left flexure of colon.

floaters (flo′ters) Small dark spots in the vitreous body of the eye that can stimulate the retina by casting a shadow upon it; they appear to drift away when an attempt is made to focus on them; when abundant, may result from any of various degenerative changes. Formerly called muscae volitantes.

floating (flo′ting) Unduly movable.

flocculation (flok-u-la′shun) The formation of fluffy masses or lumps in a solution being tested, such as occurs in the reaction between antigen and certain antibodies in solution (antisera).

flocculent (flok′u-lent) **1.** A fluid containing small fluffy masses. **2.** In bacteriology, denoting a liquid culture containing small adherent masses of bacteria.

flocculus (flok′u-lus) Latin for small tuft; in anatomy, the small lobule of the posterior lobe of the cerebellum, adjoining the middle cerebellar peduncle.

flood (flud) Colloquial term for profuse bleeding from the uterus, e.g., after childbirth (postpartum hemorrhage) or during menstruation (menorrhagia).

floor (flor) The lowest part or surface of a hollow structure or cavity.

f. of pelvis The broad hammock of muscle sweeping down from the pelvic brim, attaching posteriorly to the sacrum and coccyx; in the female, it invests the urethra, vagina, and rectum; in the male, it invests the urethra and rectum.

flora (flo′rah) Plant life, especially of localized areas.

intestinal f. The bacteria normally inhabiting the bowel.

florid (flor′id) A flushed appearance of the skin or a bright red coloration of a skin lesion.

floss (flos) **1.** To use thread (dental floss) or ribbon (dental tape) to remove particles from spaces between teeth. **2.** Dental floss.

flow (flo) **1.** To move freely. **2.** Popular term for the menstrual discharge.

effective renal plasma f. (ERPF) The amount of plasma passing through the kidneys as measured by clearance of para-aminohippuric acid (PAH).

gene f. The gradual diffusion of genes from one population to another by migration and mating rather than by mutation.

laminar f. (*a*) The directional flow of air created in a controlled environment (as with a fan and filter) to reduce airborne contamination. (*b*) The relative movement of constituents of a fluid along parallel paths.

flowers (flow′erz) In chemistry, a powdery mineral substance produced by condensation and sublimation.

f. of zinc See zinc oxide.

flowmeter (flo′me-ter) Device for measuring the rate at which a liquid or gas moves within a closed system (e.g., within blood vessels).

floxuridine (floks-ur′ĭ-dēn) (5-FUDR) A derivative of fluorouracil used in the treatment of gastrointestinal cancer.

flu (floo) Popular term for influenza and, sometimes, for a variety of

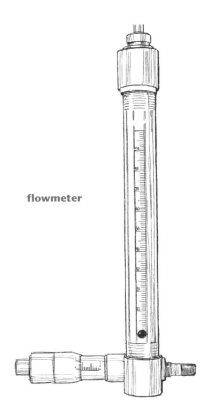

flowmeter

brief illnesses (e.g., intestinal disturbances) presumed to be caused by a virus.

fluctuation (fluk-tu-a′shun) **1.** A change, especially an irregular or subtle change. **2.** The wavelike motion of a fluid in a body cavity produced by palpation.

fluid (floo′id) **1.** Any nonsolid substance, either liquid or gas. **2.** Capable of flowing.

amniotic f. Fluid within the amnion, the membrane in which the fetus floats; it begins to accumulate from the 12th day of gestation.

cerebrospinal f. (CSF) The clear fluid circulating within the four ventricles of the brain, the subarachnoid space surrounding the brain and spinal cord, and the central canal of the spinal cord. Also called neurolymph.

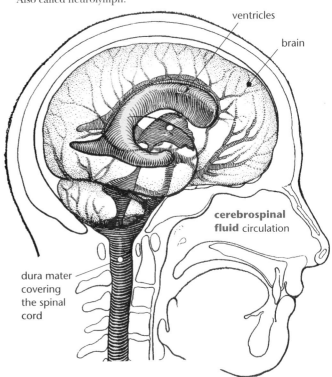

ventricles

brain

cerebrospinal **fluid** circulation

dura mater covering the spinal cord

floaters ▪ fluid

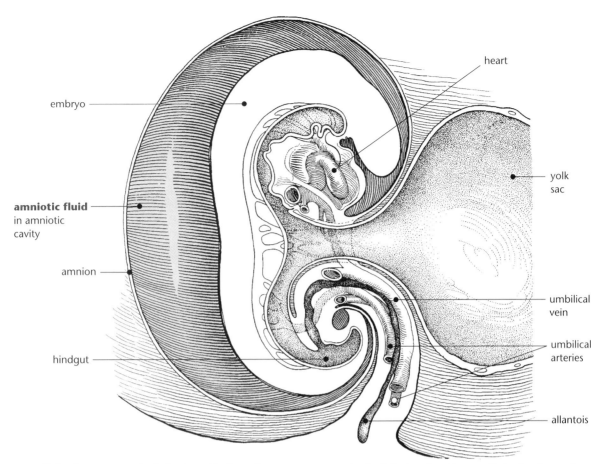

embryo

heart

amniotic fluid
in amniotic
cavity

yolk
sac

amnion

hindgut

umbilical
vein

umbilical
arteries

allantois

extracellular f. (ECF) The body fluid outside the cells; sometimes the term is restricted to the interstitial fluid and blood plasma.

follicular f. An albuminous fluid secreted by the granulosa (follicular) cells in a developing follicle of the ovary.

infranatant f. The clear fluid settled at the bottom of a container after separating from an insoluble liquid or solid.

interstitial f. Tissue fluid in spaces between cells.

intracellular f. Fluid within cells.

intraocular f. Clear fluid within the anterior and posterior chambers at the front of the eye.

seminal f. See semen.

supernatant f. The clear fluid at the top of a container after separating from an insoluble liquid or solid.

fluidextract (floo-id-ek′strakt) An alcohol solution of a vegetable drug in which 1 ml of the solution contains the active ingredients of 1g of the standard solution it represents.

fluidram (floo-id-ram′) A measure of capacity equal to one-eighth of a fluid ounce; a teaspoonful.

fluke (flook) Common name for parasitic flatworms of the class Trematoda, including the blood, intestinal, liver, and lung flukes. See *Clonorchis; Fasciola; Fasciolopsis; Paragonimus; Schistosoma.*

flumina pilorum (floo-mī′na pi′lor-um) The lined pattern along which hair grows on the scalp and throughout the body. Also called hair streams.

fluocinolone acetonide (floo-ŏ-sin′ŏ-lon as′ĕ-to-nīd) A fluorinated corticosteroid used as an ointment to relieve itching and redness caused by certain skin disorders.

fluorescein (floo-res′e-in) A harmless, fluorescent, orange-red dye used in studies of blood circulation, especially of the eye, and to detect lesions of the cornea.

fluorescence (floo-res′ens) The emission of visible light by a substance resulting from, and only during, the absorption of radiation (especially ultraviolet rays) from another source.

fluoridation (floor-ī-da′shun) The addition of fluoride to the public water supply to prevent tooth decay.

fluoride (floor-īd) A compound containing fluorine.

topical f. Any fluoride, usually in the form of paste or gel, applied on the teeth to reduce the incidence of caries.

fluorine (floo′ŏ-rēn) Gaseous chemical element; symbol F, atomic number 9, atomic weight 19.

fluorometer (floo-or-om′ĕ-ter) Device for the detection and analysis of fluorescence.

fluoroscope (floo′ŏ-ro-skōp) A type of x-ray apparatus, used in medical diagnosis, in which x-rays passing through the body strike upon a fluorescent screen, which absorbs the radiation and produces a visible image of various densities.

fluoroscopic (floor-o-skop′ic) Relating to fluoroscopy.

fluoroscopy (floo-or-os′ko-pe) Examination of internal structures of the body with a fluoroscope. Also called radioscopy; roentgenoscopy.

fluorosis (floo-ro′sis) Condition characterized by mottling of tooth enamel, caused by excessive intake of fluorides during tooth formation.

fluorouracil (floor-o-ūr′ah-sil) (5-FU) A pyrimidine analog used in the treatment of gastrointestinal cancer and, topically, in the treatment of multiple premalignant skin lesions; adverse effects may include nausea, diarrhea, hair loss, and anemia.

flush (flush) 1. To wash with a brisk gush of water. 2. Sudden redness of the skin.

hot f. Hot flash.

flutter (flut′er) Quick vibrations or pulsations.

atrial f. An arrhythmia marked by quick, regular contractions of the cardiac atria, at the rate of 240 to 300 per minute.

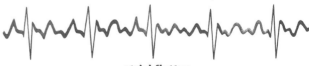

atrial flutter

diaphragmatic f. Rapid contractions of all or part of the diaphragm.

ventricular f. A flutter of the ventricles of the heart.

flutter-fibrillation (flut′er fi-brī-la′shun) An arrhythmia that is a combination of flutter and fibrillation of the atria.

fluidextract ■ flutter-fibrillation

flux (fluks) **1.** Excessive discharge of a body secretion. **2.** In dentistry, a substance that increases fluidity of molten metal, thereby enhancing fusion. **3.** Denoting the movement of ions or molecules through a membrane.

fly (fli) Any of numerous winged insects of the order Diptera; many are vectors of disease. See also *Drosophila; Glossina; Lutzomyia; Phlebotomus; Simulium.*

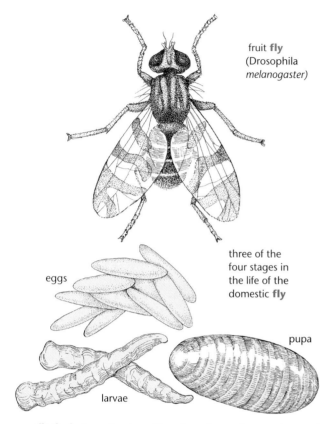

fruit **fly** (Drosophila *melanogaster*)

three of the four stages in the life of the domestic **fly**

eggs

pupa

larvae

    flesh f. Any of various flies whose larvae (maggots) grow in putrefying tissues or open wounds.

    Spanish f. See cantharis.

foam (fōm) A frothy substance.

    contraceptive f. See spermicidal preparation, under preparation.

focal (fo'kal) **1.** Relating to a focus. **2.** Localized.

foci (fo'si) Plural of focus.

focimeter (fo-sim'ĕ-ter) See lensometer.

focus (fo'kus), pl. fo'ci **1.** The point in an optical system where light rays meet. **2.** To adjust a lens system to produce a clear image. **3.** The principal site or starting point of a disease process.

    Ghon's f. See Ghon's primary lesion, under lesion.

    principal f. The real or virtual axial meeting point of rays passing into a lens parallel to its optical axis.

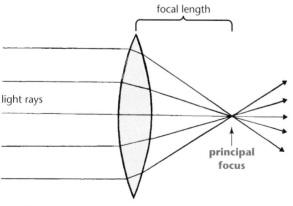

focal length

light rays

principal focus

real f. The point at which convergent light rays meet and form a real image.

    virtual f. The point at which the backward extensions of diverging light rays intersect and form a virtual image.

fog (fog) In radiology, the dense appearance of an x-ray image caused by stray radiation, accidental exposure to light, subjection to unusual temperatures or chemical actions, or the use of outdated film.

fogging (fog'ing) In ophthalmology, the deliberate undercorrection of nearsightedness (myopia) or the overcorrection of farsightedness (hyperopia); a procedure for preventing unconscious accommodation of the eye during testing for astigmatism.

folate (fo'lāt) A salt of folic acid.

fold (fōld) **1.** The doubling of a part upon itself. **2.** A thin ridge or margin in soft tissue, usually of the external surface of the body.

    alar f.'s of knee Two fringelike folds of synovial membrane projecting into the knee joint from the lateral and medial borders of the articular surface of the kneecap (patella). They converge at the intercondylar fossa of the femur.

    aryepiglottic f.'s Folds of mucous membrane in the larynx, which arch downward and backward from the epiglottis to the arytenoid cartilages.

    axillary f. One of the musculocutaneous ridges bounding the armpit (axilla) anteriorly and posteriorly, and containing respectively the greater pectoral (pectoralis major) muscle and the latissimus dorsi muscle.

    cecal f. A mesenteric sheet of peritoneum that passes from the cecum and adjoins the ascending colon to the posterior abdominal wall. Also called parietocolic fold.

    ciliary f.'s A number of minor or low ridges in the furrows between the 70 to 80 ciliary processes of the eyeball. Also called plicae ciliares.

    circular f.'s Permanent transverse folds of mucous membrane that project partly or totally into the lumen of the small intestine; they are most abundant in the proximal half of the jejunum; they considerably augment the absorption surface of the intestine. Also called Kerckring's folds of small intestine; plicae circularis; Kerckring's valves.

    conjunctival f. The cul-de-sac formed where the conjunctiva is reflected from the sclera of the eyeball to the inner surface of the upper and lower eyelids. Also called palpebral fold.

    cuticular f. See eponychium.

    Douglas' f.'s See rectouterine folds.

    duodenojejunal f. See superior duodenal fold.

    duodenomesocolic f. See inferior duodenal fold.

    epicanthal f. See epicanthus.

    false vocal f.'s See vestibular folds.

    fimbriated f. of tongue See plica fimbriata, under plica.

    gastric f.'s See villous folds of stomach.

    glossoepiglottic f.'s Three folds of mucous membrane (one median, two lateral) connecting the back of the tongue to the front of the epiglottis.

    gluteal f. The horizontal fold marking the lower margin of the buttock at its junction with the upper limit of the thigh. Also called gluteal sulcus.

    horizontal f.'s of rectum See transverse folds of rectum.

    ileocecal f. A peritoneal fold adherent to the cecum and extending from the end of the ileum to the front of the appendix.

    inferior duodenal f. A nonvascular, triangular peritoneal fold, which has a sharp upper free margin and extends from the lower part of the ascending duodenum to the posterior abdominal wall. Also called duodenomesocolic fold.

    infrapatellar f. Fold of synovial membrane situated at the intercondylar fossa of the femur and formed by the union of the two alar folds of the knee.

    Kerckring's f.'s of small intestine See circular folds.

    lacrimal f. A valvelike fold of mucous membrane in the nasal cavity at the lower end of the nasolacrimal duct; it keeps air from entering the lacrimal sac when the nose is blown. Also called Bianchi's valve.

malleolar f.'s of tympanic membrane Two folds, anterior and posterior, extending from the upper part of the incomplete fibrocartilaginous ring around the eardrum (tympanic membrane) to the lateral process of the malleus; they divide the eardrum into an upper, small triangular part that is lax and thin (pars flaccida) and a lower, taut, larger part (pars tensa).

medial umbilical f. One of two folds of peritoneum on the inner surface of the abdominal wall that cover the obliterated umbilical arteries as they ascend from the pelvis toward the navel (umbilicus).

median umbilical f. The fold of peritoneum on the inner surface of the anterior abdominal wall that covers the median umbilical ligament; it extends from the apex of the urinary bladder to the navel (umbilicus). Also called fold of urachus.

mesoappendix f. A triangular fold of the peritoneum (mesentery) extending from the area of the ileocecal junction to the vermiform appendix. It encloses the blood vessels and nerves that supply the vermiform appendix as well as the lymph vessels and lymph nodes that drain it.

nail f. The fold of skin overlapping the root of the nail; it is prolonged distally as a thin cuticular fold (eponychium).

neural f. A fold of ectoderm forming the edges of the neural plate of the early embryo, just before the formation of the neural tube.

palatine f.'s Four to six transverse corrugations in the dense mucoperiosteum (mucous membrane and periosteum fused together) of the hard palate.

palpebral f. See conjunctival fold.

paraduodenal f. A falciform peritoneal fold extending from the ascending portion of the duodenum to the posterior abdominal wall; the fold forms a mesentery and its right-free edge contains the inferior mesenteric vein and the ascending branch of the left colic artery.

parietocolic f. See cecal fold.

peritoneal f.'s Folds of peritoneum collectively called mesenteries; they include the peritoneal folds of the small intestine, the mesoappendix, the transverse mesocolon, and the sigmoid mesocolon.

rectouterine f.'s Folds of peritoneum that extend from the neck of the uterus (uterine cervix) on either side of the rectum, to the posterior wall of the pelvis. Also called Douglas' folds.

rectovaginal f. A fold of peritoneum extending from the front of the rectum to the back of the posterior fornix of the vagina; it forms the floor of the deep rectovaginal pouch. Also called posterior ligament of uterus.

rectovesical f. See sacrogenital fold.

sacrogenital f. A peritoneal fold, in the male, that extends from the sides of the urinary bladder posteriorly, on either side of the rectum, to the front of the sacrum; it bounds the rectovesical pouch. Also called rectovesical fold.

salpingopalatine f. A small vertical fold of mucous membrane on the lateral wall of the nasopharynx, passing from the orifice of the eustachian (auditory) tube to the soft palate.

salpingopharyngeal f. A vertical fold of mucous membrane on the lateral wall of the nasopharynx passing downward from the bottom of the posterior margin of the pharyngeal opening of the eustachian (auditory) tube to the wall of the pharynx; it covers the salpingopharyngeal muscle.

f.'s of scrotum Transverse corrugated folds (rugae) of thin skin across the scrotum; formed by a thin layer of smooth (nonstriated) muscular fibers (dartos muscle) which is closely united to the skin, along with the external spermatic, cremasteric, and internal spermatic fasciae.

semilunar f.'s of colon Crescent-shaped transverse folds of the colon consisting of mucosa, submucosa, and a layer of circular muscle. Also called plicae semilunares coli.

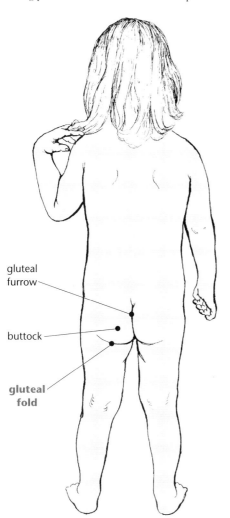

gluteal
furrow

buttock

**gluteal
fold**

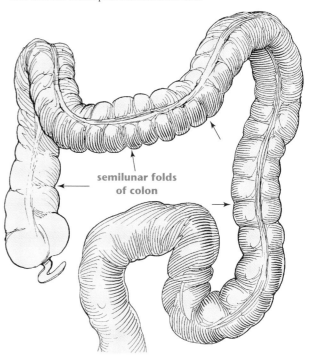

semilunar folds
of colon

semilunar f. of conjunctiva The crescent-shaped fold of conjunctiva at the inner (medial) angle of the eye, lateral to and partially obscured by the caruncle. It contains numerous goblet cells. Also called plica semilunaris conjunctivae.

sigmoid mesocolon f. A fold of peritoneum (mesentery) that attaches the sigmoid colon to the pelvic wall.

F

small intestine f. A broad, fan-shaped fold of peritoneum (mesentery) connecting the coils of the jejunal and ileal parts of the small intestine to the posterior abdominal wall.

sublingual f. A mucous membrane fold formed just under the tongue on the floor of the mouth by the underlying sublingual gland; it extends from the region of the molars to the sublingual caruncle near the base of the frenulum of the tongue; the minute multiple ducts of the gland open on the edge of the fold.

superior duodenal f. A fold of peritoneum with a semilunar free lower margin extending from the upper portion of the ascending part of the duodenum to the posterior abdominal wall; it merges with the peritoneum covering the front of the left kidney. Also called duodenojejunal fold.

transverse mesocolon f. A broad fold of peritoneum (mesentery) that connects the transverse colon to the posterior abdominal wall.

transverse f.'s of rectum Permanent semilunar, horizontal folds (usually three) of the rectal mucosa; the middle fold is the most prominent and divides the rectum into an upper part (reservoir for feces) and a lower part (normally empty). Also called horizontal folds of rectum; rectal valves.

triangular f. of tonsil See plica triangularis of tonsil, under plica.

tubal f.'s of uterine tube A series of major plicated folds of mucous membrane projecting into the lumen of the fallopian (uterine) tube; especially well developed in the ampulla of the tube.

f. of urachus See median umbilical fold.

uterovesical f. A fold of peritoneum extending from the front of the uterus to the upper surface of the urinary bladder. Also called anterior ligament of uterus.

vaginal f.'s See rugae of vagina, under ruga.

vascular cecal f. The fold of peritoneum that arches over the branches of the ileocolic artery and vein to attach to the end of the ileum and the medial wall of the cecum, forming the superior ileocecal recess.

ventricular f.'s See vestibular folds.

vestibular f.'s The false vocal folds in the voice box (larynx);

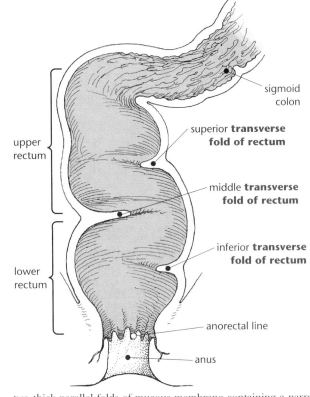

superior **transverse fold of rectum**

middle **transverse fold of rectum**

inferior **transverse fold of rectum**

upper rectum

lower rectum

sigmoid colon

anorectal line

anus

two thick parallel folds of mucous membrane containing a narrow band of fibrous tissue, situated above the true vocal folds; they do not participate in phonation. Also called ventricular folds; plicae vestibulares; false vocal folds; false vocal cords.

villous f.'s of stomach Smooth, soft, convoluted folds (rugae) of mucous membrane on the interior surface of the stomach wall, which for the most part have a longitudinal direction and subdivide

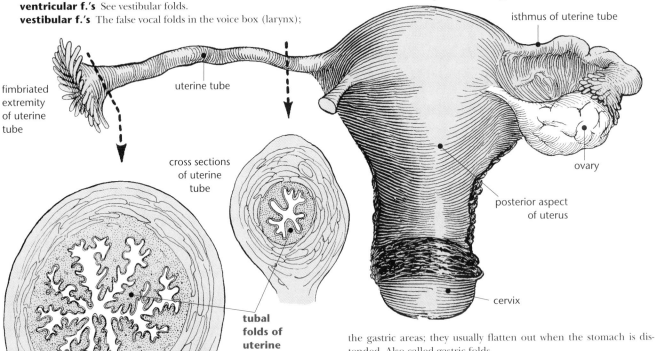

fimbriated extremity of uterine tube

uterine tube

cross sections of uterine tube

tubal folds of uterine tube

isthmus of uterine tube

ovary

posterior aspect of uterus

cervix

the gastric areas; they usually flatten out when the stomach is distended. Also called gastric folds.

vocal f.'s The true vocal folds in the voice box (larynx); the vocal ligament and vocal muscle covered with mucous membrane that stretch from the inside of the thyroid cartilage to the base of the arytenoid cartilages; responsible for producing vocal sounds when air is passed up from the lungs and allowed to escape in little rhythmic puffs. Also called vocal cords; true vocal cords; plicae vocales.

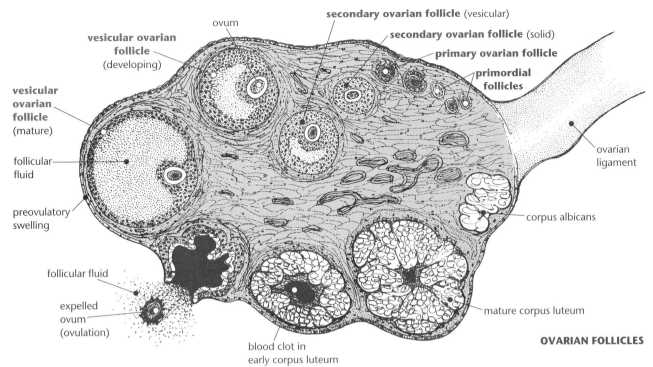

Labels on diagram:

ovum

vesicular ovarian follicle (developing)

secondary ovarian follicle (vesicular)

secondary ovarian follicle (solid)

primary ovarian follicle

primordial follicles

vesicular ovarian follicle (mature)

follicular fluid

preovulatory swelling

follicular fluid

expelled ovum (ovulation)

blood clot in early corpus luteum

ovarian ligament

corpus albicans

mature corpus luteum

OVARIAN FOLLICLES

foliate, foliaceous (fo'le-āt, fo-le-a'shus) Resembling a leaf.

folic acid (fo'lik as'id) A constituent of the vitamin B complex; essential for production of red blood cells in bone marrow; deficiency may occur in malnourished people, in alcoholics, and in malabsorption states, and may result in megaloblastic anemia. Also called pteroylglutamic acid.

folie (fo-le') French for psychosis.

   f. à deux Psychosis affecting two closely associated persons in which they have the same delusions.

   f. gemellaire The simultaneous occurrence of a psychosis in twins who are not necessarily closely associated at the time.

folinic acid (fo-lin'ik as'id) A reduced form of folic acid. Also called leucovorin.

folium (fo'le-um), pl. fo'lia A leaflike anatomic structure.

   folia of cerebellum The numerous parallel infoldings of the cerebellar surface.

follicle (fol'le-kl) 1. A somewhat spherical mass of cells usually containing a cavity. 2. A small crypt, such as the depression in the skin from which the hair emerges. 3. A small circumscribed body.

   atretic ovarian f. A follicle in the ovary that degenerates before reaching maturity, or one that enlarges but fails to ovulate.

   germinal f. See germinal center, under center.

   graafian f. See vesicular ovarian follicle.

   hair f. An invagination of the epidermis and superficial portion of the dermis that serves as a receptacle for the hair; it dilates at its deepest part to accommodate the hair bulb.

   lingual f.'s The individual nodules of lymphoid tissue at the base of the tongue constituting the lingual tonsil.

   lymph f. See lymphatic follicle.

   lymphatic f. A densely packed mass of lymphocytes and lymphoblasts embedded in a reticular meshwork of lymphatic tissue, located in lymph nodes, tonsils, spleen, and in the mucosa of the gut. Also called lymph follicle.

   mature ovarian f. See vesicular ovarian follicle.

   multilaminar primary ovarian f. A primary ovarian follicle in which the flattened follicular cells of a single layer become cuboidal and proliferate to form a stratified epithelium; it has a distinct basement membrane.

   nabothian f. See nabothian cyst, under cyst.

   ovarian f. The ovum together with its surrounding cells, at any stage of development.

   primary ovarian f. A developing follicle in the ovary before

the appearance of a fluid-filled antrum; it is composed of a growing oocyte and a single layer of flattened follicular cells surrounded by a sheath of stroma (theca); it usually develops during adolescence. Also called unilaminar primary ovarian follicle.

   primordial f. The earliest and most immature ovarian follicle consisting of the original primordial germ cell, the oogonium, and a thin single layer of squamous (flattened) follicular cells; at birth, there are about 400,000 primordial follicles in each ovary; most undergo atresia, and at the time of puberty there are about 200,000 left; they continue to decline in number throughout reproductive life. Also called unilaminar follicle.

   sebaceous f. An oil (sabaceous) gland of the skin; it opens into a hair follicle just below the opening on the surface of the skin.

   secondary ovarian f. A growing ovarian follicle in which the follicular cells have proliferated into 7 to 12 layers, surrounded by developing follicular theca cells; small lakes of follicular fluid appear in the follicle. Also called solid secondary ovarian follicle.

   solid secondary ovarian f. See secondary ovarian follicle.

   tertiary ovarian f. See vesicular ovarian follicle.

   thyroid f.'s Aggregates of minute secretory vesicles of the thyroid gland lined with follicular epithelial cells that surround a space filled with a jellylike colloid substance, which is the stored precursor (iodinated thyroglobulin) of the thyroid hormones T_3 (triiodothyronine) and T_4 (thyroxine); there are about 30 follicles in each thyroid lobule. Unlike T_3 and T_4, the thyroid hormone calcitonin is not secreted by the follicular epithelial cells, but by the parafollicular C cells located in the parenchyma of the thyroid gland.

   tooth f. The fibrous layer of mesenchyme surrounding a developing tooth and from which the periodontal membrane and the cementum are formed. Also called dental sac.

   unilaminar f. See primordial follicle.

   unilaminar primary ovarian f. See primary ovarian follicle.

   vesicular ovarian f. A large mature follicle in the ovary in which the accumulation of lakes of follicular fluid enlarges and coalesces to form a fluid-filled cavity (antrum); the fluid, liquor folliculi, is rich in hyaluronic acid; when the cavity is completely formed, the eccentric ovum (oocyte) attains full size (about four times that of the primordial germ cell, from 120 to 150 μm in humans); at this stage of development, the follicle migrates toward the surface of the ovary, causing a preovulatory swelling. Also called graafian follicle; mature ovarian follicle; tertiary ovarian follicle.

follicular (fo-lik'u-lar) Relating to a follicle.

folliculi (fo-lik′u-li) Plural of folliculus.

folliculitis (fo-lik-u-li′tis) Inflammation of hair follicles.

    f. barbae See tinea barbae.

folliculoma (fo-lik-u-lo′mah) See granulosa cell tumor, under tumor.

folliculosis (fo-lik-u-lo′sis) Abnormal overdevelopment of follicles in the eyelids, especially the lower eyelids; a benign self-limited condition most commonly seen in children.

folliculus (fo-lik′u-lus), pl. follic′uli Latin for follicle.

fomentation (fo-men-ta′shun) The therapeutic application of warmth and moisture to a body part.

fomes (fo′mēz), pl. fo′mites Any object or fabric (e.g., toys, clothing, linen) capable of harboring and transmitting disease-causing microorganisms.

fontanel, fontanelle (fon-tah-nel′) Any of the normally six unossified spaces in the fetal and infant skull, covered by fibrous tissue membrane. Commonly called soft spot.

    anterior f. The largest of the six fontanels; it is diamond-shaped and located at the junction of the frontal, sagittal, and coronal sutures; it normally ossifies within 18 months of birth. Also called frontal fontanel; bregmatic fontanel.

    anterolateral f. See sphenoidal fontanel.

    bregmatic f. See anterior fontanel.

    frontal f. See anterior fontanel.

    lateral f.'s The mastoid and sphenoidal fontanels.

    mastoid f. An irregularly shaped, small fontanel on either side of the fetal and infant skull, between the adjacent edges of the parietal, temporal, and occipital bones; ossification generally occurs by the first year of birth. Also called posterolateral fontanel.

    occipital f. See posterior fontanel.

    posterior f. A triangular fontanel located at the junction of the sagittal and lambdoid sutures; it generally ossifies within 2 or 3 months of birth. Also called occipital fontanel.

    posterolateral f. See mastoid fontanel.

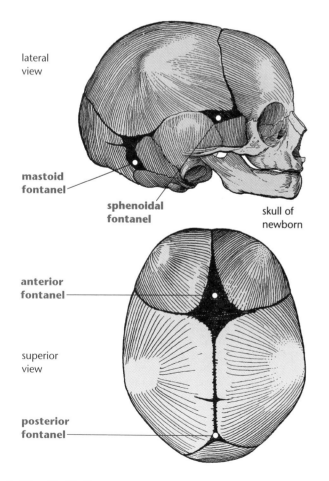

lateral view

mastoid fontanel

sphenoidal fontanel

skull of newborn

anterior fontanel

superior view

posterior fontanel

    sphenoidal f. An irregularly shaped, small fontanel located on either side of the fetal and newborn skull at the junction of the frontal, parietal, temporal, and sphenoid bones; it generally ossifies within two or three months of birth. Also called anterolateral fontanel.

food (fōōd) Any nourishing substance, usually of plant or animal origin.

    enriched f., fortified f. Food to which vitamins and iron have been added within specified limits.

foot (foot) **1.** The distal end of the lower limb. Also called pes. **2.** (ft) A unit of length equal to 12 inches (0.3048 meters).

    athlete's f. See tinea pedis, under tinea.

    claw f. See clawfoot.

    club f. See talipes equinovarus, under talipes.

    drop f. See footdrop.

    end f. See axon terminal, under terminal.

    flat f. See flatfoot.

    fungus f. See mycetoma.

    immersion f. A nonfreezing injury to the feet caused by prolonged exposure to cold (not freezing) water or mud; usually includes three clinical stages: *ischemic immersion f.,* initially the feet become cold, numb, swollen, and whitish or purplish; *hyperemic immersion f.,* a few (two to three) days after removal from cold, feet become hot, red, painful, blistered, and (in severe cases) bleed and become gangrenous; *posthyperemic immersion f.,* abnormal sensations frequently occur, which may last for years. Also called trench foot.

    Madura f. See mycetoma.

    tip f. See talipes equinus, under talipes.

    trench f. See immersion foot.

footcandle (foot-kan′dl) Unit of illumination on a surface 1 foot distant from a uniform point source of light of 1 candela, equal to 1 lumen per square foot; a candela in the International System of Units.

footdrop (foot′drop) Weakness or paralysis of the dorsiflexor muscles of the foot and ankle (in the anterior portion of the leg), causing the foot to drop and the toes to drag on the floor while walking; usually a result of injury to the peroneal nerve. Also called drop foot; toe drop.

footplate (foot′plāt) The base of the stapes, the smallest bone in the middle ear chamber.

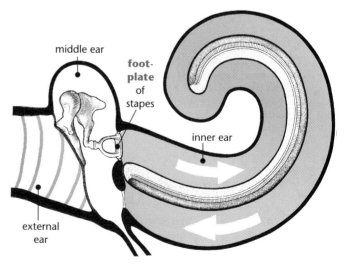

middle ear

foot-plate of stapes

inner ear

external ear

foramen (fo-ra′men), pl. foram′ina An aperture; a natural opening through a bone or a membranous structure; a short passage.

    aortic f. See aortic hiatus, under hiatus.

    apical dental f. The opening at the tip of the root of a tooth through which pass the nerves and blood vessels supplying the pulp.

    f. cecum A pit or blind foramen.

    f. cecum of frontal bone In the anterior cranial fossa of the skull, the depression or opening between the front of the crista galli of the ethmoid bone, and the crest of the frontal bone; occasionally an emissary vein may pass through to connect the superior sagittal sinus with veins in the nasal cavity.

f. cecum of medulla oblongata A small triangular pit at the cranial end of the anteromedian fissure at the lower border of the pons.

f. cecum of tongue The median pit on the dorsal surface of the tongue at the apex of the sulcus terminalis, between the anterior and posterior parts of the tongue; it marks the remains of the upper end of the outgrowth of the thyroid diverticulum in the embryo.

epiploic f. The short, vertically flattened passage, about 3 cm long, connecting the two sacs of the peritoneum, namely the greater sac and the lesser sac (omental bursa). Also called Winslow's foramen.

ethmoidal foramina Two openings (anterior and posterior) in the orbit that lead into minute bony canals passing through the orbital plate of the ethmoid bone; they transmit the ethmoidal nerves and vessels.

great f. See foramen magnum.

greater palatine f. A foramen in the vascular groove situated in the posterolateral part of the hard palate; it transmits the greater palatine nerve and vessels.

greater sciatic f. The large opening bounded by the sacrum, the greater sciatic notch of the hipbone, and the sacrotuberous and sacrospinous ligaments; the structures that pass through it when exiting the pelvis include: the piriform muscle, sciatic nerve, pudendal nerve, posterior femoral cutaneous nerves, nerves to the internal obturator muscle and quadrate muscle of thigh, superior gluteal nerve and vessels, and the internal pudendal vessels.

incisive foramina Openings in the incisive fossa of the hard palate. *Lateral incisive foramina*, openings of the incisive canals leading to the lateral wall of the nasal cavity. *Median incisive foramina*, openings of the incisive canals leading to the anterior and posterior walls of the nasal cavity.

inferior dental f. See mandibular foramen.

inferior vena caval f. See vena caval hiatus, under hiatus.

interatrial f. primum *(a)* The temporary valvelike opening of the embryonic heart between the right and left atria. Also called ostium primum; foramen primum; foramen ovale. *(b)* The abnormal persistence of such an opening in the adult heart.

interatrial f. secundum A secondary opening appearing in the embryonic heart between the right and left atria, just prior to the closure of the interatrial foramen primum. Also called ostium secundum; foramen secundum.

interventricular f. An oval communication between the lateral and third ventricles of the brain, permitting circulation of cerebrospinal fluid. Also called foramen of Monro.

intervertebral foramina Openings into the spinal (vertebral) canal between adjacent vertebrae, formed by notches on the superior and inferior borders of the vertebral pedicles; they transmit spinal vessels and nerves.

jugular f. The opening at the base of the skull between the lateral part of the occipital bone and the petrous part of the temporal bone; it transmits the vagus (10th cranial), glossopharyngeal (9th cranial), and accessory (11th cranial) nerves as well as the posterior meningeal artery.

lacerated f. See foramen lacerum.

f. lacerum The irregular aperture located at the base of the skull between the apex of the petrous part of the temporal bone and the body of the sphenoid bone; gives passage to the small nerve of the pterygoid canal and a small meningeal branch of the ascending pharyngeal artery. Also called lacerated foramen.

lesser palatine foramina Foramina, usually two on each side of the hard palate, situated just behind the greater palatine foramen; they transmit the lesser palatine nerves and vessels.

lesser sciatic f. The opening bounded by the lesser sciatic notch of the hipbone and the sacrotuberous and sacrospinous ligaments; it transmits the tendon of the internal obturator muscle, the nerve to the internal obturator muscle, the pudendal nerve, and the internal pudendal vessels.

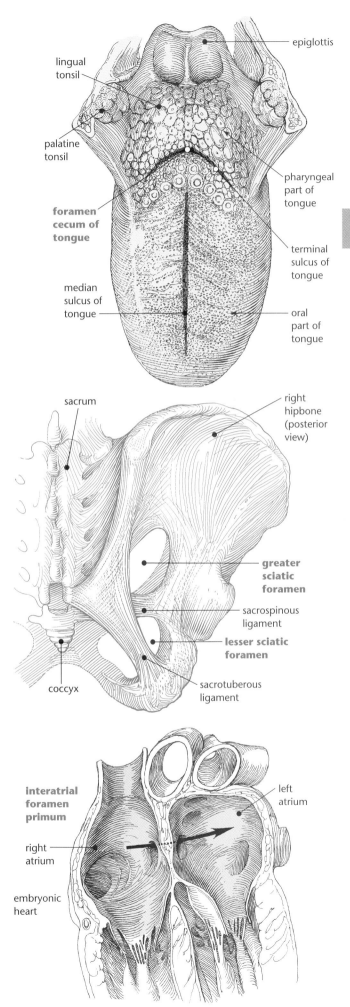

epiglottis

lingual tonsil

palatine tonsil

foramen cecum of tongue

pharyngeal part of tongue

terminal sulcus of tongue

median sulcus of tongue

oral part of tongue

sacrum

right hipbone (posterior view)

greater sciatic foramen

sacrospinous ligament

lesser sciatic foramen

sacrotuberous ligament

coccyx

interatrial foramen primum

left atrium

right atrium

embryonic heart

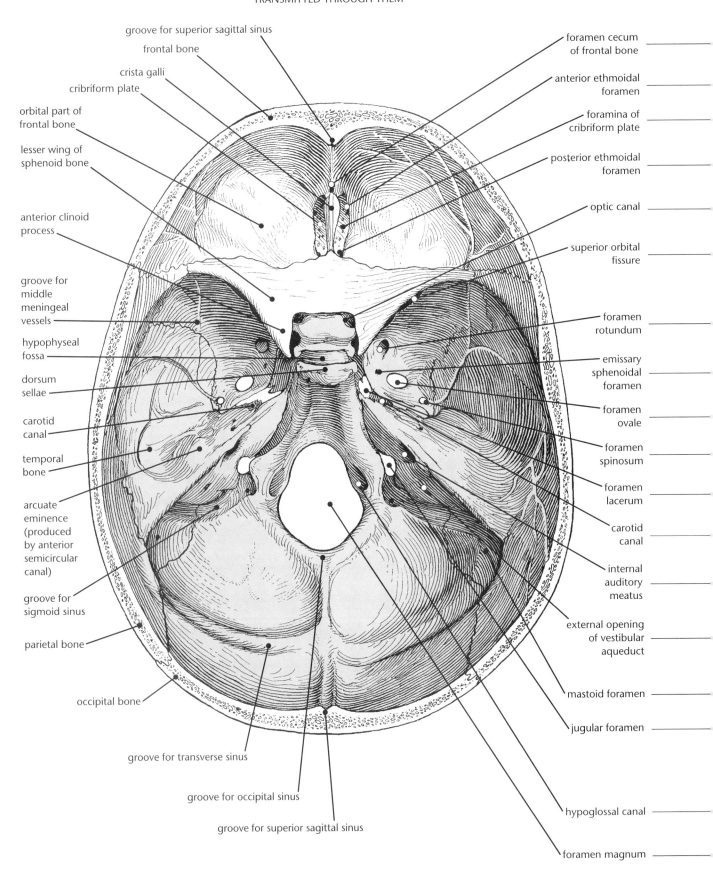

groove for superior sagittal sinus

frontal bone

crista galli

cribriform plate

orbital part of
frontal bone

lesser wing of
sphenoid bone

anterior clinoid
process

groove for
middle
meningeal
vessels

hypophyseal
fossa

dorsum
sellae

carotid
canal

temporal
bone

arcuate
eminence
(produced
by anterior
semicircular
canal)

groove for
sigmoid sinus

parietal bone

occipital bone

groove for transverse sinus

groove for occipital sinus

groove for superior sagittal sinus

foramen cecum
of frontal bone

anterior ethmoidal
foramen

foramina of
cribriform plate

posterior ethmoidal
foramen

optic canal

superior orbital
fissure

foramen
rotundum

emissary
sphenoidal
foramen

foramen
ovale

foramen
spinosum

foramen
lacerum

carotid
canal

internal
auditory
meatus

external opening
of vestibular
aqueduct

mastoid foramen

jugular foramen

hypoglossal canal

foramen magnum

STRUCTURES TRANSMITTED

emissary vein to superior sagittal sinus

anterior ethmoidal artery, vein, and nerve

olfactory nerve

posterior ethmoidal artery, vein, and nerve

optic (2nd cranial) nerve, ophthalmic artery, meninges

oculomotor (3rd cranial) nerve, trochlear (4th cranial) nerve, terminal branches of ophthalmic nerve, abducent (6th cranial) nerve, ophthalmic veins)

maxillary nerve

emissary vein from cavernous sinus

mandibular nerve, accessory meningeal artery, lesser petrosal nerve (inconstant)

middle meningeal artery and vein, meningeal branch of mandibular nerve

internal carotid artery and accompanying sympathetic and venous plexus

internal carotid artery

facial (7th cranial) nerve, vestibulocochlear (8th cranial) nerve, nervus intermedius, labyrinthine vessels

endolymphatic duct

emissary vein from sigmoid sinus

glossopharyngeal (9th cranial) nerve, vagus (10th cranial) nerve, accessory (11th cranial) nerve, sigmoid sinus, inferior petrosal sinus, posterior meningeal artery

hypoglossal (12th cranial) nerve, meningeal branch of ascending pharyngeal artery

medulla oblongata, spinal roots of accessory (11th cranial) nerve, meningeal branches of vertebral arteries, meninges

f. of Luschka See lateral aperture of fourth ventricle, under aperture.

f. of Magendie See medial aperture of fourth ventricle, under aperture.

f. magnum The large median opening penetrating the occipital bone at the base of the skull, the point at which the medulla oblongata extends caudally as the spinal cord; it also transmits the vertebral arteries and the spinal roots of the accessory (11th cranial) nerves. Also called great foramen.

mandibular f. An opening located on the medial aspect of each ramus of the mandible; it transmits the inferior dental nerve and vessels, from which branches enter the roots of the teeth. Also called inferior dental foramen.

mental f. One of two lateral openings on the body of the lower jaw (mandible), usually beneath the second bicuspid tooth; it transmits the mental branch of the inferior dental nerve and vessels.

f. of Monro See interventricular foramen.

obturator f. The large opening in the hipbone bounded by the pubis and ischium (large and oval in the male and smaller and nearly triangular in the female); it is almost completely covered by a fibrous sheet (obturator membrane) except the upper area, where a small gap (obturator canal) permits direct communication between the pelvis and the thigh; it transmits the obturator nerve and vessels.

optic f. See optic canal, under canal.

f. ovale *(a)* See interatrial foramen primum *(a)*. *(b)* A large opening in the greater wing of the sphenoid bone at the base of the skull, through which pass the mandibular division of the trigeminal nerve and the small meningeal artery.

f. primum See interatrial foramen primum.

f. rotundum A circular opening in the base of the skull located in the greater wing of the sphenoid bone; the maxillary nerve passes through it on its way to the pterygopalatine fossa.

f. secundum See interatrial foramen secundum.

f. spinosum An opening in the greater wing of the sphenoid bone, at the base of the skull, posterolateral to the foramen ovale; it transmits the middle meningeal artery and veins and the meningeal branch of the mandibular nerve.

stylomastoid f. An opening on the inferior surface of the skull between the styloid and mastoid processes; it is at the lower end of the facial canal and transmits the facial (7th cranial) nerve and the stylomastoid branch of the posterior auricular artery.

vertebral f. The large enclosed space within a vertebra, between the neural arch (posterior aspect) and the body (anterior aspect); it is occupied by the spinal cord, filaments of dorsal and ventral roots, associated vessels, and adipose tissue.

Winslow's f. See epiploic foramen.

foramina (fo-ram′ĭ-nah) Plural of foramen.

force (fōrs) (F) Capacity to produce work, motion, or physical change.

electromotive f. (EMF) Force causing electricity to flow from one point to another, giving rise to an electric current.

f. of mastication Force applied by the muscles during chewing. Also called masticatory force.

masticatory f. See force of mastication.

forceps (fōr′seps) An instrument resembling a pair of tongs or pincers, whose blades are used for grasping, compressing, manipulating, applying traction, cutting, crushing, extracting, or grasping a structure, tissue, or object.

alligator f. A long, slender, strong-toothed forceps with small jaws (double bite), the lower of which is stationary.

Allis tissue f. A forceps with serrated jaws for grasping tissue; a fine-toothed tissue forceps widely used in surgery.

aneurysm clip–applying f. A forceps for applying aneurysm clips to various types of cerebral aneurysms; two commonly used are the Yasargil and Heifetz.

axis-traction f. Specially jointed obstetrical forceps by which traction on the head of a fetus can be exerted in the axis corresponding to that of the birth canal.

Babcock tissue f. Forceps with a curved flanged tip, designed for use in surgery on the ureters but also used widely in many operations, including the removal of lymph nodes and surgical procedures on the uterine tube and deferent duct. Also called Babcock ureteral forceps.

Babcock ureteral f. See Babcock tissue forceps.

bayonet f. Thumb forceps with blades offset from the axis of the handle, resembling a bayonet; commonly used for dressing wounds, or in ear, nose, and throat operative procedures. The design allows the fingers holding the forceps to be kept out of the line of vision.

biopsy f. Any forceps used to remove living tissue from the body for examination under the microscope.

bone cutting f. A strong, plierlike forceps with a sharp edge, for cutting bone or cartilage.

bone holding f. A strong, clamplike forceps, usually with serrated jaws, used for grasping bone during a surgical orthopedic procedure; some have an adjustable joint and a ratchet catch.

bulldog f. See bulldog clamp, under clamp.

bullet f. Forceps with serrated grasping surfaces, for extracting bullets from wounds.

capsule f. A tweezerlike forceps used for grasping and removing the capsule of the lens of the eye in membranous cataract.

catheter introducing f. Forceps used to place a catheter into a body cavity for the purpose of drainage.

chalazion f. A thumb forceps with a flattened plate at the end of one arm and a ring on the other; used for the removal of a cyst (chalazion) in a meibomian gland of an eyelid.

clip-applying f. Any forceps designed to clamp clips to specific areas, such as cerebral aneurysms or skin wounds.

coagulation f. Forceps that coagulate tissue with bipolar current; primarily used to clot bleeding blood vessels during surgery.

Collin T-f. Forceps with a T-bar at the tip of each blade, used in vaginal hysterectomy for providing tension on the vaginal mucosa, thus facilitating dissection of the vesicovaginal and rectovaginal fascias.

dental extracting f. A forceps used for grasping a tooth in order to dislocate (luxate) and extract it from the tooth socket (alveolus).

double-action f. A multiple-action cutting forceps, with two joints between the blades and handles for increased force.

dressing f. A hinged, straight or bayonet forceps, commonly used in dressing wounds.

fine f. See mosquito forceps.

fixation f. One of a range of forceps for steadying or holding a part during an operation.

hemostatic f. A forceps used to control bleeding by compressing the cut end of a blood vessel; it generally has a multiple-lock catch (ratchet) to provide varying degrees of pressure, and jaw serrations that mesh well to ensure a closure of the severed blood vessel and to minimize trauma.

intubation f. Forceps used to guide a tracheal tube into the larynx under direct vision.

Kocher-Ochsner f. A commonly used sponge forceps.

mosquito f. A small hemostatic forceps with fine points, usually used for grasping delicate tissue; its jaws are either straight, curved, or angular. Also called fine forceps.

needle f. See needle holder, under holder.

obstetrical f. A forceps consisting of two blades, introduced separately in the vaginal canal, to grasp and apply traction to the fetal head during a difficult labor.

punch f. A forceps with blades which, when closed, cut out a small piece of tissue (biopsy) for examination under the microscope.

ring f. A forceps with ring jaws at the tip of the blades.

rongeur f. See rongeur.

scalp clip–applying f. Any forceps for applying scalp clips on skin flap procedures during a neurosurgical operation, such as the Ramey.

sponge holding f. A hemostat-like forceps with straight, curved, or ringed blades, with tips that are either smooth or serrated; has multiple uses in addition to facilitating the operative use of sponges, such as securing the ovary during surgery.

suture f. See needle holder, under holder.

tenaculum f. Forceps having a sharp hook at the end of each blade.

throat f. A long, slender, angled forceps commonly used to remove foreign bodies from the throat or larynx.

thumb f. A spring forceps with two fine-toothed blades, used by compression with thumb and forefinger, for manipulating delicate tissue with minimum of trauma; in surgery, used especially during suturing.

tongue seizing f. A forceps with serrated rings at the end of each blade for drawing the tongue forward.

tonsil seizing f. Angulated locking forceps with fine teeth at the tips of the handles, used for grasping the palatine tonsil securely in tonsillectomy.

toothed f. Thumb forceps with teeth at the tip of the blades; used when stretching tissue to facilitate dissection.

towel f. See towel clip, under clip.

uterine f. Any forceps designed for surgery on the uterus, including single-toothed tenaculum, double-toothed tenaculum, and quadruple-toothed tenaculum; the selected forceps depends upon the size of the uterus and the available exposure of the operative field.

vulsellum f. A forceps with interlocking teeth on the end of each hinged blade, for grasping tissue and applying traction.

wound clip–applying f. Any forceps for applying wound or suture clips, such as the Hegenbarth and Wachenfeldt.

wound clip–removing f. Any forceps for removing wound or suture clips from the body, such as the Wexler.

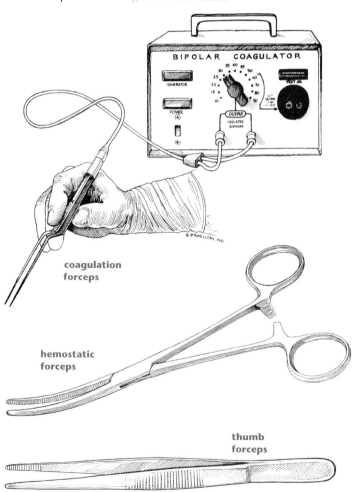

coagulation forceps

hemostatic forceps

thumb forceps

FORCEPS

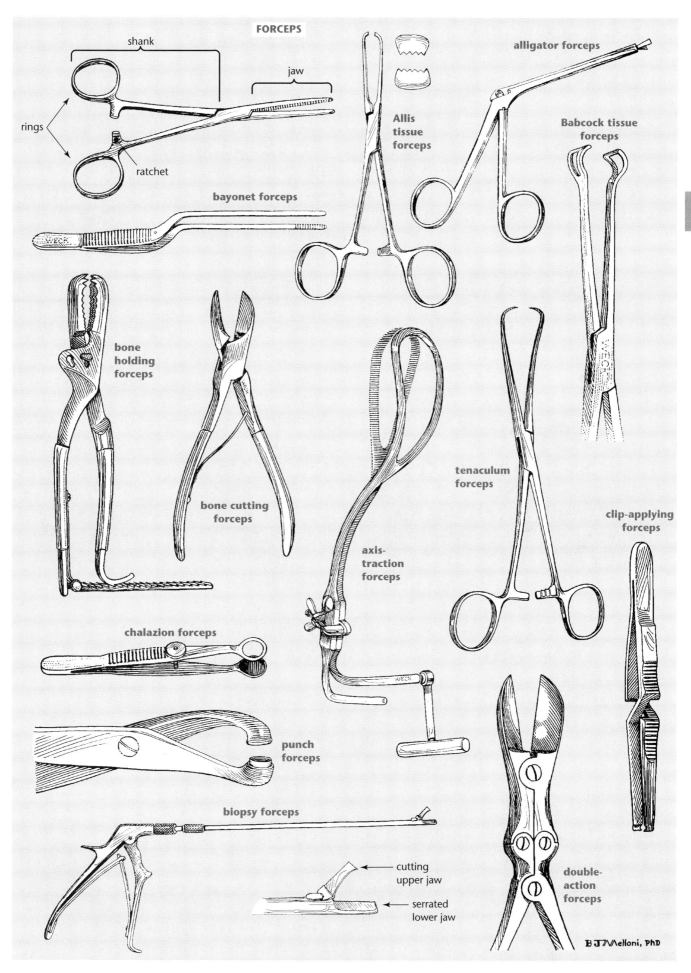

shank

jaw

rings

ratchet

bayonet forceps

WECK

Allis tissue forceps

alligator forceps

Babcock tissue forceps

bone holding forceps

bone cutting forceps

tenaculum forceps

clip-applying forceps

axis-traction forceps

WECK

chalazion forceps

punch forceps

biopsy forceps

cutting upper jaw

serrated lower jaw

double-action forceps

B J Melloni, PhD

F

forearm (fōr′arm) The part of the upper limb between the elbow and the wrist. Also called antebrachium.

forebrain (fōr′brān) See prosencephalon.

foregut (fōr′gut) The cephalic portion of the primitive digestive tract of the embryo. Also called headgut.

forehead (fahr′id, fōr′hed) The part of the face above the eyebrows.

foremilk (fōr′milk) Popular name for colostrum.

forensic (fo-ren′zik) Relating to or employed in legal proceedings or argumentation. See also under medicine, pathology, psychiatry, psychology, dentistry, toxicology, and entomology.

foreplay (fōr′plā) Sexual stimulation leading to sexual intercourse.

forepleasure (fōr-plezh′er) Pleasurable excitement preceding orgasm.

foreskin (fōr′skin) See prepuce.

forewaters (fōr′waht-erz) In obstetrics, the portion of the fluid-filled amniotic sac that bulges into the cervical canal in front of the fetal head or any other presenting part of the fetus.

fork (fork) A pronged device.

    tuning f. A device made of metal, such as steel or magnesium, with two prongs (tines) which, when struck, vibrate, producing a sound of fixed pitch; used in testing of hearing.

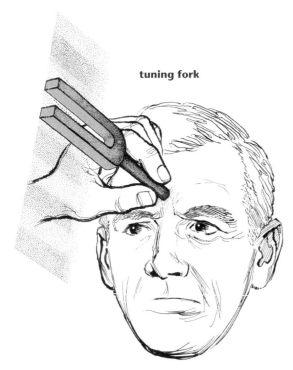

tuning fork

form (form) A configuration.

    accolé f. See appliqué form.

    appliqué f. A ring of young malarial parasites (of *Plasmodium falciparum*) within the marginal areas of red blood cells. Also called eccolé form.

    convenience f. In dentistry, a form modified beyond the basic to allow access of instruments for preparation of a cavity and insertion of restorative materials.

    L f. See L-phase variant, under variant.

    resistance f. In dentistry, the configuration given to the prepared cavity of a tooth so that the restoration will withstand the stress of chewing.

    retention f. In dentistry, the configuration given to the prepared cavity of a tooth to prevent displacement of the restoration by lateral forces as well as the forces of chewing.

    sickle f. See malarial crescent, under crescent.

formaldehyde (fōr-mal′dĕ-hīd) A pungent gaseous aldehyde used in solution as a preservative and disinfectant.

formation (for-ma′shun) 1. The process of developing or forming. 2. The result of such process.

personality f. The development or structure of the personality components.

    reaction f. An unconscious defense mechanism wherein the individual adopts conscious attitudes, ideas, affects, or behaviors that are the opposites of unacceptable impulses the person harbors consciously or unconsciously.

    reticular f. A diffusely organized tissue in the central nervous system (brainstem, medulla oblongata, and cervical spinal cord), consisting of intermingled fibers of white and gray matter. Also called reticular substance.

    rouleaux f. Red blood cells positioned like stacks of coins.

forme fruste (fōrm froost), pl. formes frustes French expression for a partial or atypical form of a disease.

formic (for′mik) Relating to ants.

formic acid (for′mik as′id) A colorless caustic liquid used in solution as an astringent; it occurs naturally in ants and other insects.

formication (for-mi-ka′shun) The abnormal sensation that ants or other insects are crawling on one's skin.

formiminoglutamic acid (for-mim-ĭ-no-gloo′tam′ik as′id) (FIGLU) An intermediate in the breakdown (catabolism) of histidine; may be present in the urine of patients with folic acid deficiency.

formula (fōr′mu-lah) 1. A symbolic representation of the structure or composition of a chemical substance. 2. An established group of symbols for expressing a concept. 3. A recipe of ingredients in fixed proportions (e.g., a milk mixture for feeding an infant). 4. A prescription containing instructions for the preparation of a medicine.

    Bernhardt's f. A formula for determining the ideal weight, in kilograms, for an adult: the height in cm $\times$ the chest circumference in cm $\div$ 240.

    DuBois' f. Formula for determining the body's surface area from its weight and height; $A = W^{0.425} \times H^{0.725} \times 71.84$.

    empirical f. Chemical formula depicting the number of atoms of each element in the molecules of a substance but not their interrelationships in the structure of the molecule. Also called molecular formula.

(methadone) $C_{21}H_{27}NO$ **empirical formula**

    Mall's f. Formula for calculating the age (in days) of an embryo; equal to the square root of its length (crown-to-rump) in mm $\times$ 100.

    molecular f. See empirical formula.

    stereochemical f. A formula showing a spatial representation of the relative positions of linked atoms, and the number of atoms of each element present in a molecule of a substance.

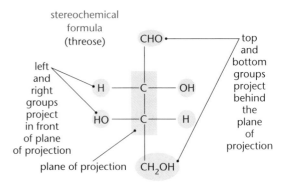

stereochemical formula (threose)

    structural f. Chemical formula showing the linkage of atoms and groups of atoms as well as their number.

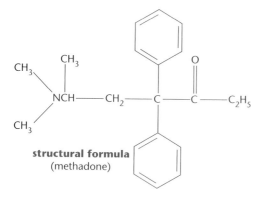

structural formula
(methadone)

formulary (fōr′mu-lar-e) A collection of formulas for the preparation of medicines.

fornix (for′niks), pl. for′nices **1.** Any arched structure. **2.** Any space created by such a structure.

    f. of cerebrum A harp-shaped, bilateral structure in the brain, composed of two pillars (crura of the fornix), the body, and two anterior pillars (columns of the fornix); it is situated under the corpus callosum and is made up mainly of white efferent fibers arising from the hippocampus and terminating in the mamillary bodies.

    f. of conjunctiva The recess formed by the reflection of the conjunctiva from the inner surface of the upper eyelid to the bulb of the eye (superior fornix) and from the inner surface of the lower eyelid to the bulb of the eye (inferior fornix). Also called conjunctival cul-de-sac.

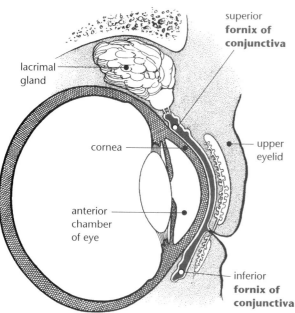

    f. of lacrimal sac The upper dome-shaped, blind extremity of the lacrimal sac, just above the opening of the superior and inferior lacrimal canaliculi.

    f. of vagina The space at the upper end of the vagina between the vaginal wall and the uterine cervix; it extends higher on the posterior than the anterior surface of the cervix. Also called fundus of vagina.

fossa (fos′ah), pl. fos′sae A pit, hollow, or depression.

    acetabular f. A roughened, circular depression forming the floor of the acetabulum; it is devoid of cartilage and lodges a fibroelastic mass of fat largely covered with a synovial membrane.

    f. of antihelix See triangular fossa of auricle.

    articular f. A cartilage-lined depression at the end of a bone for articulation with the extremity of another bone to form a joint.

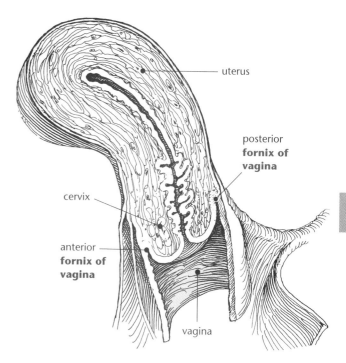

    axillary f. The armpit; the axilla.

    canine f. See cuspid fossa.

    coronoid f. A hollow on the front of the lower end of the humerus which accommodates the coronoid process of the ulna during flexion of the elbow.

    cranial f. Any of three depressions (anterior, middle, and posterior) of the internal surface of the base of the skull; each accommodates a different portion of the brain; the dura mater is firmly attached to it.

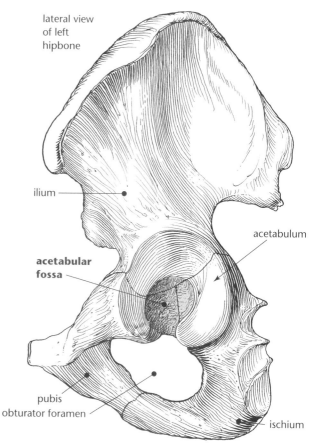

formulary ■ fossa

cubital f. The triangular hollow of the skin in front of the elbow joint, bounded medially by the round pronator (pronator teres) muscle, laterally by the brachioradial (brachioradialis) muscle, and above by a line joining the lateral and medial epicondyles of the humerus; it contains the median nerve and the termination and division of the brachial artery. Also called antecubital space; triangle of elbow; popularly called bend of the elbow.

cuspid f. A shallow depression on the front of the maxilla, lateral to the ridge formed by the root of the cuspid tooth. Also called canine fossa; maxillary fossa.

epigastric f. The depression on the mediastinal surface of the left lung where it comes into contact with the left ventricle of the heart. Also called cardiac fovea.

glenoid f. The depression on the lateral angle of the shoulder blade (scapula) for articulation with the head of the humerus forming the shoulder joint. Also called glenoid cavity.

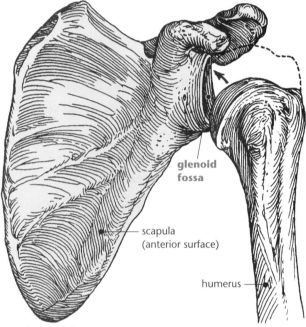

glenoid fossa

scapula (anterior surface)

humerus

hyaloid f. The deep concavity on the anterior aspect of the vitreous body adjacent to the lens of the eye. Also called lenticular fossa.

hypophyseal f. A deep depression in the sphenoid bone accommodating the pituitary (hypophysis). Sometimes written hypophyseal fossa. Also called pituitary fossa.

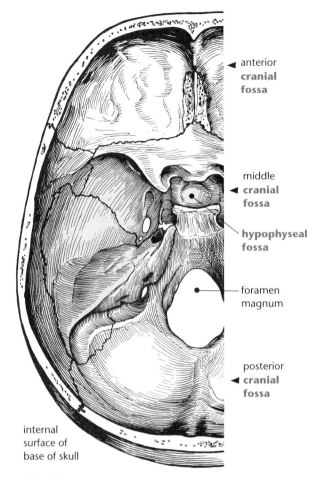

anterior **cranial fossa**

middle **cranial fossa**

hypophyseal fossa

foramen magnum

posterior **cranial fossa**

internal surface of base of skull

iliac f. The smooth, concave hollow on the inner surface of the anterior and upper part of the iliac bone; it forms the posterolateral wall of the greater pelvis.

infraclavicular f. The triangular depression on the skin just below the clavicle, between the greater pectoral (pectoralis major) muscle and the deltoid muscle.

intercondylar f. See intercondylar notch, under notch.

jugular f. A fossa on the temporal bone at the base of the skull that accommodates the bulb of the internal jugular vein.

lacrimal f. A deep fossa in the medial wall of the orbit, formed by the lacrimal bone and the frontal process of the maxilla; it

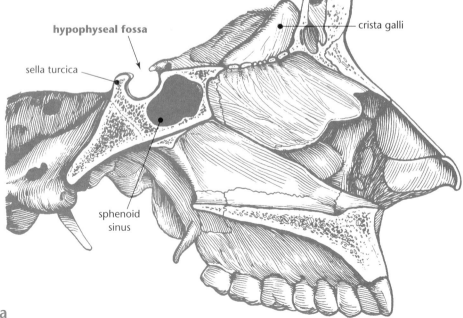

hypophyseal fossa

sella turcica

sphenoid sinus

crista galli

communicates with the nasal cavity and houses the lacrimal sac and the upper part of the nasolacrimal duct. Also called fossa of lacrimal sac.

f. of lacrimal sac See lacrimal fossa.

lenticular f. See hyaloid fossa.

lingual f. See tonsillar fossa.

mandibular f. One of two transversely disposed depressions on the temporal bone at the base of the skull that accommodates the condyle of the lower jaw (mandible).

maxillary f. See cuspid fossa.

navicular f. A dilatation at the end of the penile urethra.

olecranon f. A deep hollow on the back of the lower end of the humerus that accommodates the tip of the olecranon of the ulna when the elbow is extended.

f. ovalis (a) A depression on the septal wall of the right atrium representing the site of the foramen ovale of the fetal heart. (b) The saphenous opening in the upper thigh, about 38 mm below and lateral to the pubic tubercle, giving passage to the great saphenous vein.

pituitary f. See hypophysial fossa.

popliteal f. The diamond-shaped area on the skin situated at the back of the knee joint.

radial f. A shallow depression on the anterior aspect of the lower end of the humerus, just above the capitulum and lateral to the coronoid fossa; it accommodates the rim of the head of the radius during full flexion of the forearm.

scaphoid f. The narrow longitudinal depression between the helix and the antihelix of the auricle. Also called scapha.

submandibular f. A shallow depression on the inner surface of the lower jaw (mandible), below the mylohyoid line, which accommodates the submandibular gland. Also called submandibular fovea.

supraclavicular f. Either of two depressions on the surface of the body just above the clavicle. *Major supraclavicular f.*, the depression above the clavicle and lateral to the tendon of the sternocleidomastoid muscle. *Minor supraclavicular f.*, the depression above the clavicle between the clavicular and sternal heads of the sternocleidomastoid muscle.

tonsillar f. The depression between the palatoglossal and palatopharyngeal arches on either side at the end of the oral cavity; it houses the palatine tonsil. Also called tonsillar sinus; lingual fossa.

triangular f. of auricle The depression between the two ridges (crura) into which the antihelix divides superiorly. Also called fossa of antihelix.

fossette (fos-et′) A small, deep ulcer of the cornea.

fossula (fos′u-lah), pl. fos′sulae A small depression on the surface of a structure or organ, such as the tonsils.

fossulate (fos′u-lāt) Containing many small depressions.

fouling (foul′ing) In forensic medicine, the solid black zone of soot surrounding the edges of skin or clothing left by the passage of a projectile, fired at close range.

foundation (foun-da′shun) A base, especially one that provides support to a structure.

denture b. The natural oral structures supporting a denture.

fovea (fo′ve-ah), pl. fo′veae A small depression.

cardiac f. See epigastric fossa.

central f. An area approximately 1.5 mm in diamter in the macula lutea of the retina; it is the area of greatest visual acuity. Also called fovea centralis.

f. centralis See central fovea.

f. of femoral head The small depression on the head of the femur below and behind its center; it affords attachment to the round ligament of the femur.

f. of radial head The shallow saucer-shaped surface of the proximal head of the radius for articulation with the capitulum of the humerus.

submandibular f. See submandibular fossa, under fossa.

foveate, foveated (fo′ve-āt, fo-ve-a′ted) Having small depressions; pitted.

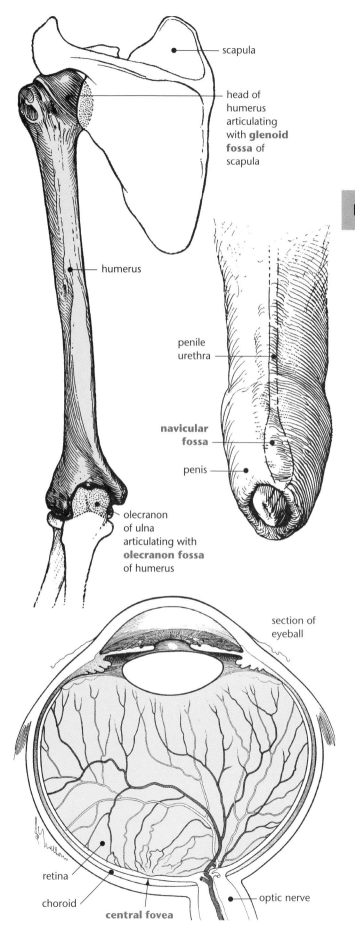

scapula

head of humerus articulating with **glenoid fossa** of scapula

humerus

penile urethra

navicular fossa

penis

olecranon of ulna articulating with **olecranon fossa** of humerus

section of eyeball

retina

choroid

central fovea

optic nerve

foveation (fo-ve-a'shun) The formation of a pit (e.g., the pitted scar of smallpox).

foveola (fo-ve'o-lah), pl. fove'olae A minute depression, fovea, or pit.

f. of coccyx A small, shallow dimple often present in the skin at the tip of the coccyx; it represents the site of attachment of the embryonic neural tube to the skin. Also called coccygeal dimple.

gastric foveolae The numerous small pits between the folds of the gastric mucosa, at the bottom of which open the gastric glands. Also called gastric pits.

granular foveolae Irregular small depressions on the internal surface of the cranial bones on each side of the sagittal sulcus; they accommodate the arachnoid granulations and become more numerous with age. Also called granular foveolae of Pacchioni.

granular foveolae of Pacchioni See granular faveolae.

foveolar (fo-ve'o-lar) Relating to a minute pit.

foveolate (fo-ve'o-lāt) Having minute pits.

foxglove (foks'glov) Any of various plants of the genus *Digitalis*.

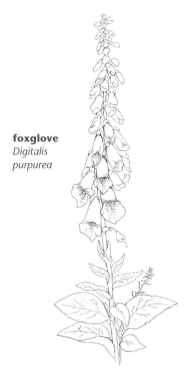

foxglove
*Digitalis
purpurea*

fraction (frak'shun) **1.** A quotient of two quantities. **2.** A component of a substance separated by crystallization or distillation.

blood plasma f. The separated constituents of plasma.

ejection f. The fraction of blood contained in the left ventricle of the heart that is expelled when the ventricle contracts; it is a measure of the ventricle's ability to expel blood.

filtration f. (FF) The fraction of plasma entering the kidney that filters into the renal tubules; the glomerular filtration rate divided by the renal plasma flow; generally ranges about 20%.

fractionation (frak-shun-a'shun) In radiation therapy, division of the total dose of a therapeutic dose of radiation into small doses of low intensity administered over a period of time, usually at daily or alternate-day intervals.

fracture (frak'chur) (fx) The breaking of a bone or cartilage.

articular f. Fracture of the joint (articular) surface of a bone.

avulsion f. The tearing off of a small fragment of bone at the attachment site of a tendon or ligament, caused by a sudden forceful pull on the tendon or ligament (e.g., when the ankle is twisted or when a strong muscle contracts forcefully and suddenly). Also called sprain fracture.

Bankart f. A fracture of the shoulder blade (scapula) at the shoulder joint in which a bone fragment is detached from the

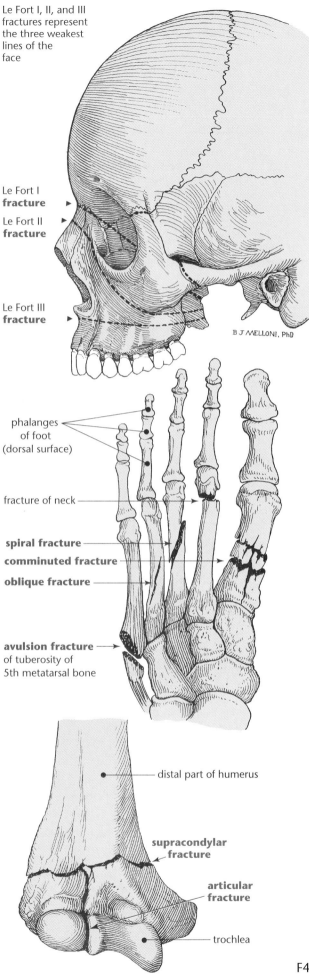

Le Fort I, II, and III fractures represent the three weakest lines of the face

Le Fort I fracture ▶

Le Fort II fracture ▶

Le Fort III fracture ▶

B J MELLONI, PhD

phalanges of foot (dorsal surface)

fracture of neck

spiral fracture

comminuted fracture

oblique fracture

avulsion fracture of tuberosity of 5th metatarsal bone

distal part of humerus

supracondylar fracture

articular fracture

trochlea

foveation ■ fracture

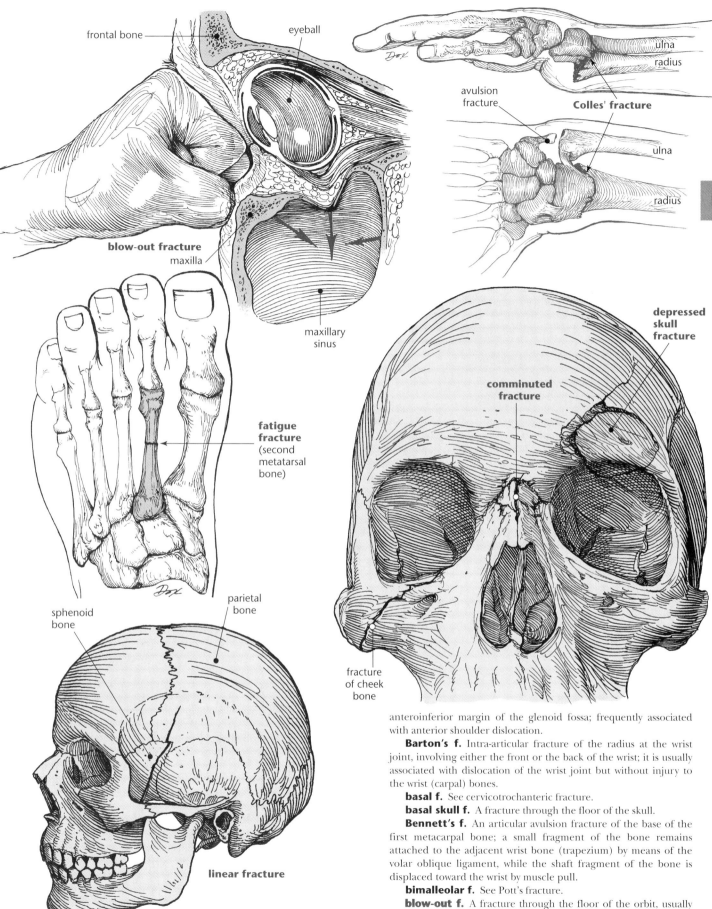

frontal bone

eyeball

ulna

radius

avulsion fracture

Colles' fracture

ulna

radius

blow-out fracture

maxilla

maxillary sinus

depressed skull fracture

comminuted fracture

fatigue fracture (second metatarsal bone)

parietal bone

sphenoid bone

fracture of cheek bone

linear fracture

anteroinferior margin of the glenoid fossa; frequently associated with anterior shoulder dislocation.

   Barton's f. Intra-articular fracture of the radius at the wrist joint, involving either the front or the back of the wrist; it is usually associated with dislocation of the wrist joint but without injury to the wrist (carpal) bones.

   basal f. See cervicotrochanteric fracture.

   basal skull f. A fracture through the floor of the skull.

   Bennett's f. An articular avulsion fracture of the base of the first metacarpal bone; a small fragment of the bone remains attached to the adjacent wrist bone (trapezium) by means of the volar oblique ligament, while the shaft fragment of the bone is displaced toward the wrist by muscle pull.

   bimalleolar f. See Pott's fracture.

   blow-out f. A fracture through the floor of the orbit, usually caused by a blow to the eye. Also called orbital floor fracture.

fracture ■ fracture

boot-top f. Fracture of the tibia and fibula in the lower one-third of the leg, caused by violent stress against the rim of a ski boot.

boxer f. Fracture of the neck of the fifth metacarpal bone (on the side of the little finger), with displacement of the bone head toward the palm and protrusion of the shaft toward the back of the hand.

buckle f. See torus fracture.

bumper f. Compression fracture of the lateral articular area of the tibia at the knee, often associated with avulsion of the medial (tibial) collateral ligament of the knee joint. Also called fender fracture.

capillary f. A hairline fracture.

cervicotrochanteric f. A fracture across the base of the femoral neck, at the hip joint. Also called basal fracture.

Chance f. A horizontal splitting of the body of a lumbar vertebra and its posterior arch, frequently caused by a lap seat belt of an automobile in a traffic accident victim. Also called seat-belt fracture. See also seat-belt syndrome, under syndrome.

closed f. Fracture in which the overlying skin remains intact. Formerly called simple fracture.

Colles' f. Fracture of the end of the radius (at the wrist) with dorsal displacement of the distal fragment, producing the "silver fork" or "bayonet" deformity.

comminuted f. Fracture in which the bone is broken in several small pieces.

compound f. Former name for open fracture.

compression f. Fracture in which the hard shaft of a long bone (e.g., femur) is driven through the porous lower end of the bone, giving rise to a T- or V-shaped fracture.

crush f. Fracture accompanied by extensive soft-tissue damage; the bone may be broken transversely or it may be extensively broken into small fragments (comminuted); when occurring in the leg or forearm, both bones (i.e., tibia and fibula or radius and ulna) are fractured at the same level.

dashboard f. Common name for a shear fracture with dislocation of the hipbone; it occurs when an automobile passenger seated in the front seat is thrown forward; the knee strikes the dashboard, transmitting axial force to the flexed and adducted thighbone (femur) and dislocating the hip either through a rent in the posterior joint capsule, or where the posterior acetabular rim is sheared by the head of the femur.

depressed skull f. Fracture of the skull with inward displacement of the fragment.

deQuervain's f. A fraction-dislocation of the wrist; specifically, fracture of the scaphoid bone with dislocation of the lunate bone.

displaced f. Fracture in which the main bone fragments are relatively widely separated.

Dupuytren's f. Fracture of the lower end of the fibula or lateral malleolus with dislocation of the ankle joint.

epiphyseal f. Traumatic separation and/or fracture of the growth (epiphyseal) plate of a long bone; it may or may not involve fracture of the adjoining bone. Displacement of the bone is the only obvious indicator of a plate disruption in the x-ray image due to the radiotransluscent nature of the cartilagenous plate. Also called growth plate fracture; epiphysial separation.

extracapsular f. Fracture of a bone near but outside of the joint capsule.

fatigue f. Fracture of a metatarsal shaft, usually the second or third, associated with prolonged weightbearing activities as in walking for long periods (e.g., during basic military training), ballet dancing, and athletics; believed to be due to muscle fatigue, when the muscle action is no longer optimal and allows increased loading of the bone. Also called march fracture; stress fracture; Deutschländer's disease.

fender f. See bumper fracture.

fissured f. See linear fracture.

folding f. See torus fracture.

greenstick f. An incomplete fracture in which the compres-

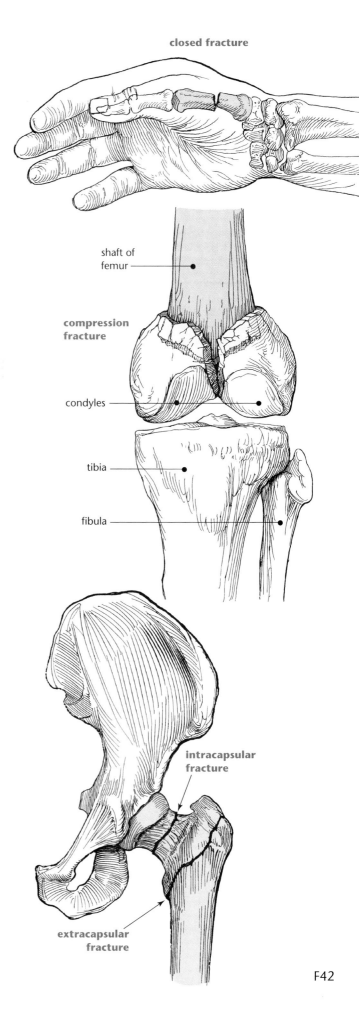

closed fracture

shaft of femur

compression fracture

condyles

tibia

fibula

intracapsular fracture

extracapsular fracture

sion side of the bone is only bent, with cortex and periosteum remaining intact; seen most frequently in children.

growth plate f. See epiphyseal fracture.

hairline f. A small fracture without separation of bone fragments. Also called capillary fracture.

hangman's f. Dislocation and fracture through the pedicles or lamina of the second cervical vertebra (C2) secondary to a traumatic forceful separation and extension of the joint surfaces.

impacted f. Fracture in which one of the bone fragments is driven into the substance of the other and is fixed in that position.

incomplete f. A fracture that involves the bone only partly, not its whole thickness or length.

intracapsular f. A fracture within a joint capsule.

linear f. A fracture running parallel with the long axis of the bone. Also called fissured fracture.

longitudinal f. One in which the direction of the fracture line is along the axis of the bone.

march f. See fatigue fracture.

Monteggia's f. Injury of the forearm at the elbow, characterized by fracture of the shaft of one bone (ulna) with dislocation of the head of the other bone (radius) within the elbow joint.

nightstick f. An undisplaced, or minimally displaced, fracture of the ulnar shaft alone without disruption of the interosseous membrane between ulna and radius; results most frequently from a direct blow to the forearm.

oblique f. Fracture running obliquely to the axis of the bone.

occult f. Condition in which originally there is no evidence of a fracture but after three or four weeks an x-ray image shows new bone formation, indicating a healed fracture.

open f. Fracture occurring with an open wound through which the broken bone may protrude. Formerly called compound fracture.

open-book f. Fracture of the anterior portion of the pelvic ring; may range from a simple separation of the pubic symphysis to a wide separation and forward protrusion of one side of the pelvis (resembling an open book), with severe injury to the pelvic floor and genitourinary structures; caused by anteroposterior compression, due either to direct violence or to a force transmitted through the legs.

orbital floor f. See blow-out fracture.

paratrooper f. Fracture of the lower shafts of the two bones of the leg (tibia and fibula).

pathologic f. Bone fracture through an area of bone weakened by preexisting disease (e.g., malignant tumor or osteoporosis) and inflicted by relatively minor trauma, or occurring with no trauma at all.

periosteal f. Fracture occurring beneath the bone-covering membrane (periosteum), without displacement of fragments.

pertrochanteric f. Fracture of the thighbone (femur) at the hip joint, between the femoral neck and the greater trochanter.

Pott's f. A fracture-dislocation of the ankle joint; specifically, fracture of the lower end of the fibula (medial malleolus), associated with fracture of the lower end of the tibia (lateral malleolus) and dislocation of the ankle joint. Also called bimalleolar fracture.

reverse Colles' f. See Smith's fracture.

seat-belt f. See Chance fracture.

Segond f. A small avulsion-type fracture of the lateral condyle of the tibia (at the knee) associated with major ligamentous damage to the meniscus-synovial portion of the capsule on the lateral side of the knee joint.

simple f. Former name for closed fracture.

Smith's f. A fracture of the distal end of the radius (at the wrist) similar to a Colles' fracture, but the end piece is displaced toward the palm, making a deformity that resembles a horizontal silver fork with its tines pointing upward. Also called reverse Colles' fracture.

spiral f. Breakage in which the fracture line is relatively spiral in direction, seen in the shaft of a long bone; caused by a twisting force.

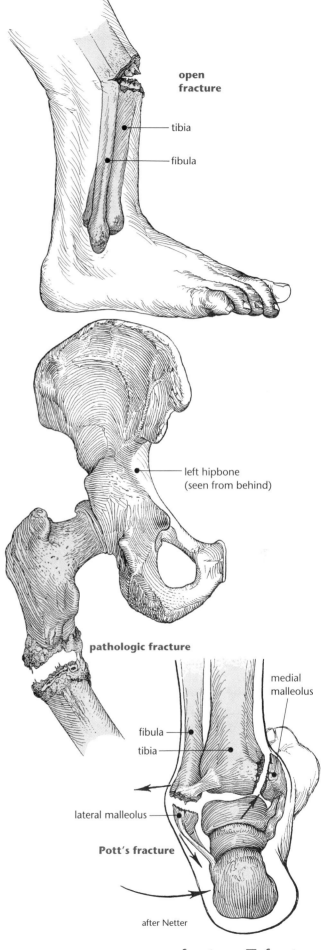

open fracture

tibia

fibula

left hipbone (seen from behind)

pathologic fracture

medial malleolus

fibula

tibia

lateral malleolus

Pott's fracture

after Netter

fracture ■ fracture

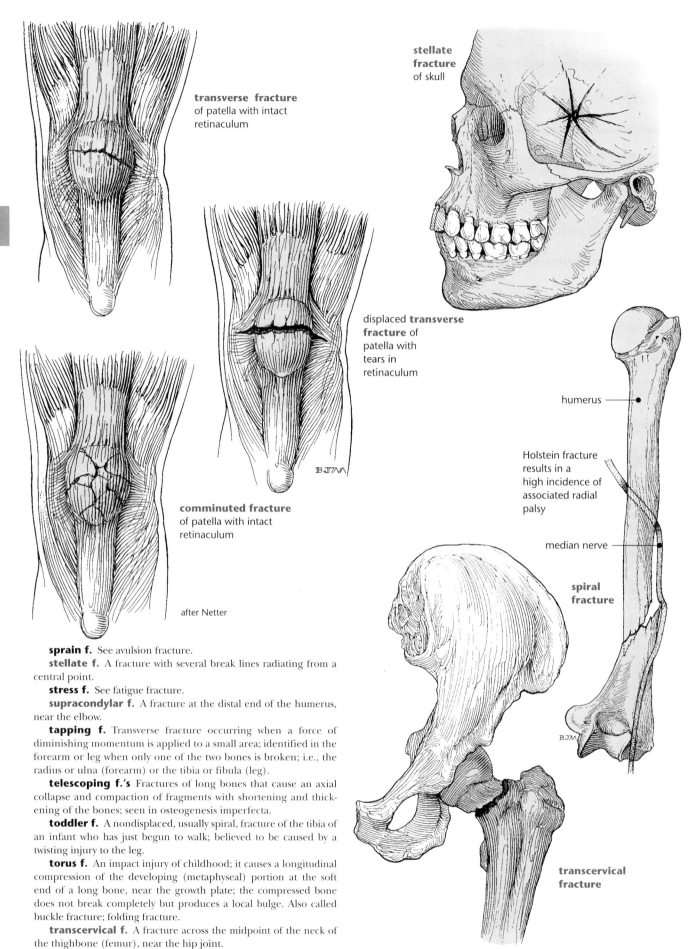

transverse fracture of patella with intact retinaculum

stellate fracture of skull

displaced **transverse fracture** of patella with tears in retinaculum

comminuted fracture of patella with intact retinaculum

after Netter

humerus

Holstein fracture results in a high incidence of associated radial palsy

median nerve

spiral fracture

transcervical fracture

sprain f. See avulsion fracture.

stellate f. A fracture with several break lines radiating from a central point.

stress f. See fatigue fracture.

supracondylar f. A fracture at the distal end of the humerus, near the elbow.

tapping f. Transverse fracture occurring when a force of diminishing momentum is applied to a small area; identified in the forearm or leg when only one of the two bones is broken; i.e., the radius or ulna (forearm) or the tibia or fibula (leg).

telescoping f.'s Fractures of long bones that cause an axial collapse and compaction of fragments with shortening and thickening of the bones; seen in osteogenesis imperfecta.

toddler f. A nondisplaced, usually spiral, fracture of the tibia of an infant who has just begun to walk; believed to be caused by a twisting injury to the leg.

torus f. An impact injury of childhood; it causes a longitudinal compression of the developing (metaphyseal) portion at the soft end of a long bone, near the growth plate; the compressed bone does not break completely but produces a local bulge. Also called buckle fracture; folding fracture.

transcervical f. A fracture across the midpoint of the neck of the thighbone (femur), near the hip joint.

transcondylar f. A fracture through the condyles of the humerus, at the elbow.

transepiphyseal f. A traumatic separation of a previously normal epiphysis, at the end of a long bone.

transverse f. A fracture in which the break line runs perpendicular with the axis of the bone.

unstable f. A fracture with a high likelihood of slipping after it has been reduced, producing further deformity.

fragility (frah-jil′ĭ-te) A tendency to break or disintegrate.

capillary f. Increased susceptibility of capillary walls to rupture.

erythrocyte f. Fragility of red blood cells due to mechanical trauma or when the saline content of the blood is altered.

fragment (frag′ment) A small detached piece from a larger entity.

Fab f.'s The two fragments of the immunoglobulin (antibody) molecule, each containing an antigen-binding site, derived by the enzymatic action of papain.

Fc f. The crystallizable fragment of the immunoglobulin (antibody) molecule, derived by the enzymatic action of pepsin.

frambesia (fram-be′ze-ah) See yaws.

frame (frām) A structure for immobilizing or giving support to a body part.

Balkan f. An overhead bar supported from the floor or bedposts to suspend a fractured limb. Also called Balkan splint.

Stryker f. A rigid stretcher-type device that allows turning of the patient without individual motion of parts.

framework (frām′werk) **1.** See stroma. **2.** The portion of a partial denture to which the remaining parts of the prosthesis are attached.

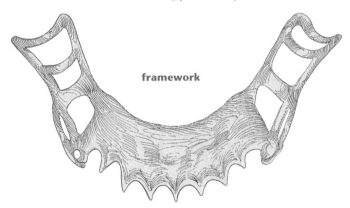

framework

Francisella tularensis (fran-sĭ-sel′ah too-lah-ren′sis) A gram-negative, aerobic bacterium (genus *Francisella*) that causes tularemia in humans; transmitted from wild animals by bloodsucking insects or by drinking contaminated water.

francium (fran′se-um) An unstable radioactive element; symbol Fr, atomic number 87, with atomic weight 223; the most stable of its isotopes has a half-life of 21 minutes.

frank (frank) Clinically evident.

fraternal (frah-tur′nal) **1.** Having a sibling relationship. **2.** Derived from two ova that were fertilized separately; applied to twins.

fratricide (frat′rĭ-sīd) The killing of one's brother or sister.

freckle (frek′l) A brownish spot on the skin. Also called ephelid.

freeze-drying (frēz dri′ing) A method of tissue preparation in which the specimen is instantly frozen and then the ice in the specimen is sublimed away in a high vacuum.

freezing (frēz′ing) Hardening from exposure to low temperatures.

gastric f. Freezing of secretory cells of the stomach to reduce the secretion of gastric acid used in the treatment of peptic ulcer.

fremitus (frem′ĭ-tus) A vibration usually produced in the chest and felt on palpation.

pleural f. Abnormal vibration of the chest produced by the rubbing together of the roughened surfaces of the pleural membranes, as in pleurisy.

tactile f. A palpable vibration.

vocal f. Vibration in the chest produced by the spoken voice.

frenectomy (fre-nek′to-me) The surgical removal of a frenulum.

frenotomy (fre-not′o-me) Surgical division of a frenulum.

frenulum (fren′u-lum) A small fold of mucous membrane that restrains the movements of an organ or movable part. Also called frenum.

f. of clitoris A suspensory fold connecting the undersurface of the clitoris with the labia minora; homologous with the frenulum of the prepuce.

f. of foreskin See frenulum of prepuce of penis.

f. of ileocecal valve The frenulum formed by the two semilunar lips of the ileocecal "valve" that coalesce and project into the lumen of the large intestine as a narrow membranous ridge; it is at the junction of the ileum and the large intestine. Also called frenulum of Morgagni.

f. of labia The posterior union of the two labia minora.

labial f. See frenulum of lips.

f. of lips A midline fold of mucous membrane extending from each lip to the adjacent gums, that of the upper lip being larger. Also called labial frenulum.

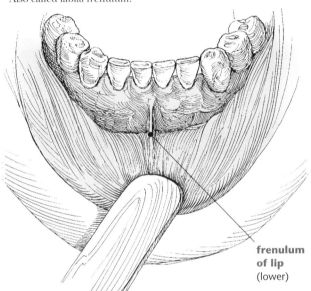

frenulum
of lip
(lower)

f. of Morgagni See frenulum of ileocecal valve.

f. of prepuce of penis A small median fold of mucous membrane that unites the foreskin (prepuce) to the undersurface of the glans penis. Also called frenulum of foreskin.

f. of tongue A crescentic fold extending from the midline of the undersurface of the anterior part of the tongue to the floor of the mouth.

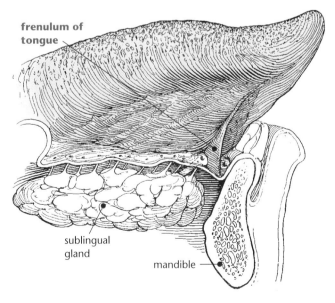

frenulum of tongue

sublingual gland

mandible

fragility ■ frenulum

frenum (fre'num) See frenulum.

frequency (fre'kwen-se) The number of recurrences of an event per unit time.

critical flicker fusion f. The minimal number of intermittent or discontinuous visual stimuli per second that gives rise to a continuous visual sensation obliterating the flicker.

dominant f. The particular frequency appearing most often in an electroencephalogram (EEG).

urinary f. The condition of urinating more frequently than usual for a given person; in severe cases, the desire to urinate may become constant, with each voiding producing only a few cubic centimeters of urine; causes are varied; they include infection or inflammation of the bladder, stones, tumors, radiation cystitis, tuberculosis, and schistomiasis. It is a natural condition in pregnancy due to blood vessel engorgement, hormonal changes that alter bladder function, and, in late pregnancy, decreased bladder capacity due to pressure from the enlarging uterus.

freshening (frĕsh'en-ing) Removal of granulation and early scar tissues from a partially healed wound to hasten healing.

fretum (fre'tum) A constriction.

friable (fri'ah-bl) Crumbly; easily damaged.

fricative (frik'ah-tiv) In phonetics, a sound produced by the forcing of air through a narrow opening (e.g., the sounds of the letters *f, v, s, z*).

frigid (frĭj'id) **1.** Very cold. **2.** Abnormally lacking the desire for sexual intercourse or unable to achieve orgasm during intercourse; applied chiefly to women.

frigidity (frĭ-jid'ĭ-te) The state of being frigid.

fringe (frĭnj) See fimbria.

frons (fronz) Latin for forehead.

frontad (frun'tad) Toward the front.

frontal (frunt'l) **1.** Relating to the forehead. **2.** Relating to the anterior aspect of the body.

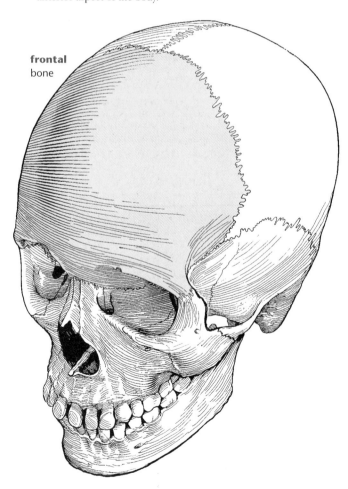

frontal bone

frontomalar (frun-to-ma'lar) See frontozygomatic.

frontomaxillary (frun-to-mak'sĭ-lār-e) Relating to the frontal and maxillary bones.

frontonasal (frun-to-na'zal) Relating to the frontal and nasal bones.

fronto-occipital (frun-to ok-sip'ĭ-tal) Relating to the frontal and occipital bones at the front and back of the head.

frontoparietal (frun-to-pah-ri'e-tal) Relating to the frontal and parietal bones of the head.

frontotemporal (frun-to-tem'po-ral) Relating to the frontal and temporal bones of the head.

frontozygomatic (frun-to-zi-go-mat'ik) Relating to the frontal and cheek (zygomatic) bones. Also called frontomalar.

frost (frost) A covering resembling minute ice crystals.

urea f., uremic f. Tiny flakes of urea sometimes seen on the skin of patients with uremia.

frostbite (frost'bīt) Local condition of varying degrees of severity caused by freezing of tissues upon exposure to extreme cold temperatures, affecting usually the fingers, toes, ears, and nose; may lead to gangrene. COMPARE chilblain.

froth of drowning (froth drown'ing) A profuse foamy fluid from the mouth and nostrils of corpses retrieved from water, composed of mucus, protein, and inhaled water; it is a classic sign of drowning by immersion.

fructokinase (fruk-to-ki'nās) A liver enzyme that promotes the reaction of adenosine triphosphate (ATP) and D-fructose to form fructose 6-phosphate.

fructosan (fruk'to-san) A polyfructose (e.g., inulin) present in certain tubers. Also called levan; levulin; levulan.

fructose (fruk'tos) (Fru) The sweetest of the simple sugars (monosaccharides) present in honey and fruits; formed in the body as one of two products of the breakdown of sucrose; used intravenously as a nutrient replenisher. Also called fruit sugar; levulose.

fructosemia (fruk-to-se'me-ah) The presence of fructose in the blood; seen in hereditary fructose intolerance.

fructosuria (fruk-to-su're-ah) The presence of fructose in the urine due to a disorder of metabolism in which blood fructose levels are excessive.

frusemide (frus'ĕ-mīd) See furosemide.

frustration (frus-tra'shun) In psychology, the denial of gratification by reality.

fugue (fūg) A form of dissociation in which there is physical flight from an environment the person finds disturbing; when the usual mental state returns, the individual has no recollection of his actions during this period.

fulgurant (ful'gu-rant) Piercing; applied to the nature of a pain.

fulguration (ful-gu-ra'shun) Destruction of tissues with a high-frequency electric current (e.g., of a short section of the fallopian tubes for the purpose of sterilization).

fulminant, fulminating (ful'mĭ-nant, ful-mĭ-nat'ing) Of sudden, violent onset and rapid course; applied to pains.

fumigant (fu'mĭ-gant) Any chemical used in the form of gas or aerosol to kill insects, insect eggs, and microorganisms; used widely in agriculture; one (ethylene oxide) is used primarily to sterilize medical instruments. Exposure to some may cause acute effects (e.g., burning eyes, nose, and throat, cough, headache, nausea, vomiting, dizziness, slurred speech, disorientation, loss of consciousness); others may cause chronic effects (e.g., anorexia, abdominal pain, jaundice, abnormal liver function tests).

fumigation (fu-mĭ-ga'shun) Disinfection by exposure to the fumes of a germicide.

fuming (fūm'ing) Releasing a visible vapor.

function (funk'shun) **1.** The natural or special type of activity that is proper for an organ or body part. **2.** To perform such an action. **3.** The general properties of any substance.

functional (funk'shun-al) **1.** Relating to a function. **2.** Nonorganic.

fundal (fun'dal) Relating to a fundus.

fundiform (fun'dĭ-form) Like a sling.

fundoplication (fun-do-plĭ-ka'shun) Suturing of the fundus of the stomach, as in the treatment of hiatal hernia.

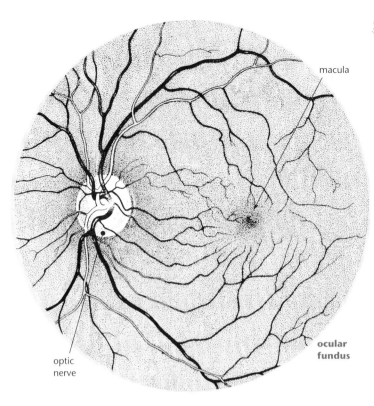

optic nerve

macula

ocular fundus

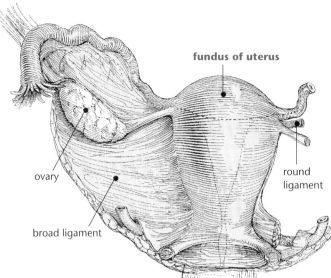

fundus of uterus

ovary

broad ligament

round ligament

fundus (fun′dus), pl. fun′di The portion of a hollow organ that is farthest from, or opposite, its opening.

   ocular f. posterior portion of the interior of the eye. See also eyeground.

   f. of stomach The dome-shaped portion of the stomach, above its junction with the esophagus.

   f. of uterus The rounded portion of the uterus, above the orifices of the fallopian (uterine) tubes.

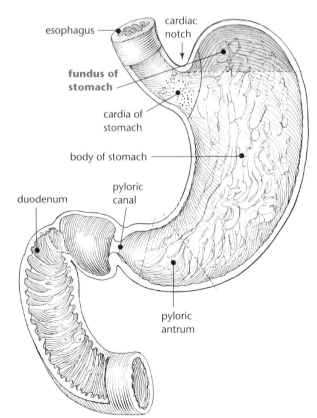

esophagus

cardiac notch

fundus of stomach

cardia of stomach

body of stomach

duodenum

pyloric canal

pyloric antrum

fungal (fung′gal) Relating to a fungus.

fungate (fung′gāt) To grow rapidly or to assume a funguslike form.

fungemia (fun-je′me-ah) The presence of viable fungi in the circulating blood, usually occurring as an opportunistic infection in immunosuppressed patients, or in postoperative patients with intravenous catheters, usually after prolonged antibiotic therapy.

fungi (fun′ji) Plural of fungus.

fungicide (fun′ji-sīd) Any substance that destroys fungi.

fungiform (fun′ji-form) Shaped like a fungus.

fungistat (fun′ji-stat) Inhibiting the growth of fungi.

fungoid (fung′goid) Resembling fungus.

fungosity (fun-gos′i-te) A fungal growth.

fungous (fung′gus) Relating to fungus.

funguria (fung-u′re-ah) Urinary tract infection with a funguslike yeast (e.g., *Candida albicans* and *Torulopsis glabrata);* usually seen in patients with indwelling urinary catheters, and those undergoing anticancer and immunosuppressive therapy.

fungus (fung′gus), pl. fun′gi General term for a large group of spore-bearing forms of the kingdom Protista; characterized by lack of chlorophyll, asexual reproduction, and parasitic qualities; some cause disease in humans.

   thrush f. See *Candida albicans,* under Candida.

funic (fu′nik) Relating to the umbilical cord.

funicle (fu′nī-kl) A small cordlike structure.

funicular (fu-nik′u-lar) 1. Relating to, or having the characteristics of, a funiculus. 2. Relating to the umbilical cord.

funiculitis (fu-nik-u-li′tis) 1. Inflammation of the spermatic cord. 2. Inflammation of the portion of the spinal nerve located within the spinal (vertebral) canal.

funiculus (fu-nik′u-lus), pl. funic′uli 1. A cordlike structure. 2. One of three main divisions or columns of white matter on either side of the spinal cord, designated anterior, lateral, and posterior. 3. The spermatic cord from the abdominal inguinal ring to the testis. 4. The umbilical cord.

   f. separans A narrow translucent ridge covered by a strip of thickened ependyma on the floor of the fourth ventricle of the brain; the usual blood-brain barrier is thought to be altered in this area.

funiform (fu′nī-form) Cordlike.

funis (fu′nis) 1. The umbilical cord. 2. Any cordlike structure.

funnel (fun′el) 1. A conical, hollow vessel with a tube extending from its apex. 2. In anatomy, a conical structure; an infundibulum.

furcal (fur′kal) Forked; divided into branches.

furcation (fur-ka′shun) A branching, such as the area of a multirooted tooth where the roots arise.

furfur (fur′fur), pl. fur′fures A dry scale.

furfuraceous (fur-fu-ra′shus) Scaly; brawny; a fine scaling.

furosemide (fu-ro′sĕ-mīd) A powerful diuretic used orally or intravenously; possible adverse effects include deafness and inflammation

F

of the kidneys or pancreas. Also called frusemide.

furrow (fur'o) **1.** A groove, generally long, narrow, and shallow. **2.** A wrinkle in the skin.

   atrioventricular f. The transverse groove on the outside of the heart indicating where the atria meet the ventricles.

   cleavage f. During the anaphase stage of cell division, a deep infolding of the cell equator that constricts the cell and eventually divides it into two.

   digital f. One of the grooves across the joints on the palmar surface of the fingers.

   gluteal f. The groove between the buttocks.

   mentolabial f. See mentolabial sulcus, under sulcus.

   nasolabial f. A furrow from each side of the nose to each side of the upper lip.

   nuchal f. The median groove at the back of the neck, just below the base of the skull.

   nympholabial f. The groove separating the labium majora from the labium minora.

   palpebral f. The groove of the upper eyelid extending from the inner to outer corners of the eye.

   scleral f. See scleral sulcus, under sulcus.

   Sibson's f. The groove representing the lower margin of the greater pectoral (pectoralis major) muscle.

furuncle (fu'rung-kl) See boil.

furuncular (fu-rung'ku-lar) Relating to a boil (furuncle).

furunculoid (fu-rung'ku-loid) Boil-like.

furunculosis (fu-rung-ku-lo'sis) Condition characterized by the eruption of numerous boils.

fusiform (fu'zĭ-form) Tapering at both ends.

fusion (fu'zhun) **1.** A surgical joining together or formation of an ankylosis, as of two vertebrae. **2.** The integration into one perfect image of the images seen simultaneously by the two eyes. **3.** An abnormal union of two anatomic structures.

   renal f. The abnormal fusion of the kidneys; may occur in different degrees; named according to either the shape or the location (e.g., horseshoe kidney, cake kidney, lump kidney, sigmoid kidney), the most common being the horseshoe kidney.

   spinal f. The permanent operative fusion of two or more vertebrae to eliminate motion between them.

fusospirochetal (fu-so-spi-ro-ke'tal) Relating to a mixed infection with fusiform and spirochetal microorganisms.

-fy Suffix meaning to make or form into (e.g., humidify)

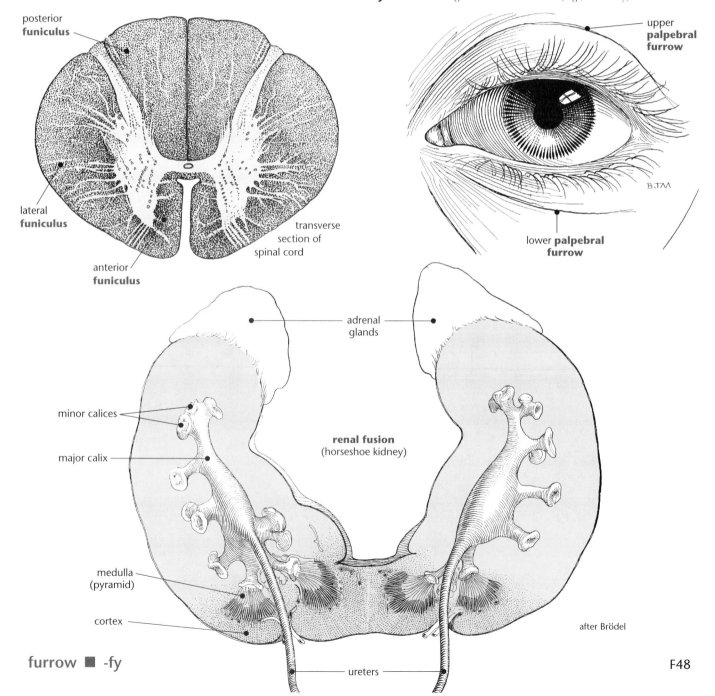

posterior **funiculus**

lateral **funiculus**

anterior **funiculus**

transverse section of spinal cord

upper **palpebral furrow**

lower **palpebral furrow**

adrenal glands

minor calices

major calix

renal fusion (horseshoe kidney)

medulla (pyramid)

cortex

after Brödel

ureters

furrow ■ **-fy**   F48

G

gadolinium (gad-o-lin'e-um) Metallic element; symbol Gd, atomic number 64, atomic weight 157.25. Gadolinium compounds are used to enhance contrast in magnetic resonance imaging.

gag (gag) **1.** To retch. **2.** An instrument placed between the upper and lower teeth to keep the mouth open during operations on the tongue and throat.

gain (gān) An advantage; an increase.

    primary g. The relief of anxiety and emotional conflict provided by defense mechanisms.

    secondary g. The additional indirect satisfaction or advantage derived from an illness or symptom (e.g., extra attention or protective attitudes from relatives or friends).

gait (gāt) A way of walking or running.

    antalgic g. A self-protective limp due to pain.

    cerebellar g. A wide-base gait with erratic placement of feet and veering toward one side (due to a unilateral lesion on the same side of the cerebellum); causes include multiple sclerosis, cerebellar tumor, and cerebellar degeneration (hereditary and acquired).

    choreoathetotic g. A gait in which the legs advance slowly and awkwardly, and which may include plantar flexion, dorsiflexion, or inversion of the foot; the patient suspends the leg in the air, twisting the trunk or pelvis; seen in a variety of choreic, athetotic, and dystonic states (e.g., Sydenham's chorea, Huntington's disease, or reactions to certain drugs).

    drunken g. See staggering gait.

    equine g. See steppage gait.

    festinating g. See festination.

    hemiplegic g. Gait in which the affected leg is held stiffly (unflexed at the hip, knee, and ankle) and may be swung outward in a semicircle, with the foot turned down and inward; caused most often by cerebral infarction or trauma. Also called spastic gait.

    hysterical g. Any of various gaits that are not due to organic causes; the patient may drag a leg or push it in front, or walk as though on stilts, or lurch in different directions.

    sensory ataxic g. Gait characterized by leg movements that are brusque and irregular in length and height of step; often the foot is dropped to the floor with a slapping sound; the patient displays a loss of position sense of the legs and feet and watches the ground for cues; usual causes include tabes dorsalis, compression of spinal cord (especially posterior column), subacute degeneration of spinal cord (e.g., in vitamin B_{12} deficiency), and degenerative disorders of the cerebellum or spinal cord (e.g., hereditary spinal ataxia). Also called tabetic gait.

    spastic g. See hemiplegic gait.

    staggering g. The characteristic gait of intoxication with alcohol or other sedative drugs. Also called drunken gait.

    steppage g. Gait characterized by regular, even steps with the advancing foot hanging and toes pointing down; the leg is lifted high so that the foot clears the floor, and a slapping noise is made as the foot hits the floor. If unilateral, it is usually due to compression of the common peroneal nerve; if bilateral, it may be due to a hereditary nerve disease or to certain types of muscular dystrophy. Also called equine gait.

    tabetic g. See sensory ataxic gait.

    toppling g. An unsteady, hesitant gait with wobbling, sudden lurches and unexpected falls in the absence of ataxia, loss of deep sensation, and weakness; seen in advanced stages of Parkinson's disease and in posterior inferior cerebellar artery syndrome.

    waddling g. Exaggerated lateral movements or leaning of the trunk with each step taken; common causes include progressive muscular dystrophy and congenital dislocation of the hips.

galactacrasia (gal-ak-tah-kra'se-ah) Abnormal composition of human milk.

galactagogue (gah-lak'tah-gog) Any agent that promotes the flow of milk.

galactan (gah-lak'tan) Any of several carbohydrates that yield the simple sugar galactose on hydrolysis.

galactic (gah-lak'tik) Relating to milk.

galacto-, galact- Combining forms meaning milk.

galactoblast (gah-lak'to-blast) See colostral corpuscle, under corpuscle.

galactocele (gah-lak'to-sēl) See milk-retention cyst, under cyst.

galactokinase (gah-lak-to-ki'nās) An enzyme that, in the presence of adenosine triphosphate (ATP), promotes the phosphorylation of the sugar galactose to galactose 1-phosphate.

galactophore (gah-lak'to-for) A milk duct.

galactophorous (gal-ak-tof'o-rus) Conveying milk.

galactopoiesis (gah-lak-to-poi-e'sis) Secretion of milk.

galactopoietic (gah-lak-to-poi-et'ik) Relating to milk secretion.

galactorrhea (gah-lak-to-re'ah) **1.** Profuse discharge of milk from the mother's breasts after the child has been weaned. Also called lactorrhea. **2.** A milky discharge from the breasts due to a pathologic condition unrelated to pregnancy.

galactosamine (gah-lak-to-sam'in) An amino sugar derived from galactose.

galactose (gah-lak'tōs) (Gal) A crystalline simple sugar not found free in foods; produced in the body by the breakdown of lactose (milk sugar) and then converted into glucose for energy. Also called brain sugar.

galactosemia (gah-lak-to-se'me-ah) Defect of galactose metabolism in which the conversion of galactose to glucose is deficient; characterized (in its most severe form) by mental and physical retardation, enlargement of liver and spleen, and elevated blood and urine galactose levels; the disorder usually becomes evident soon after birth by feeding problems.

galactosidase (gah-lak-to-si'dās) Any enzyme that promotes the hydrolysis of galactosides.

galactoside (gah-lak'to-sid) A glycoside containing galactose.

galactosis (gal-ak-to'sis) The formation of milk.

galactosuria (gah-lak-to-su're-ah) Presence of galactose in the urine.

galactotherapy (gah-lak-to-ther'ah-pe) Treatment with a milk diet.

galea (ga'le-ah) **1.** A helmetlike structure. **2.** A type of bandage.

    g. aponeurotica See epicranial aponeurosis, under aponeurosis.

galeatomy (gal-e-a'to-me) Surgical cut into the epicranial aponeurosis (galea aponeurotica).

galena (gah-len'ah) See lead sulfide.

galenical (gah-len'ĭ-kal) A medicine prepared by extracting the active constituents of a plant.

galeophobia (gal-e-o-fo'be-ah) Abnormally exaggerated fear of cats.

gall (gawl) See bile.

gallamine triethiodide (gal'ah-mīn tri-ĕ-thi'o-dīd) A compound used as a muscle relaxant.

gallbladder (gawl'blad-der) A pear-shaped sac situated in a depression under the liver; it stores bile until it is needed in the duodenum for digestion.

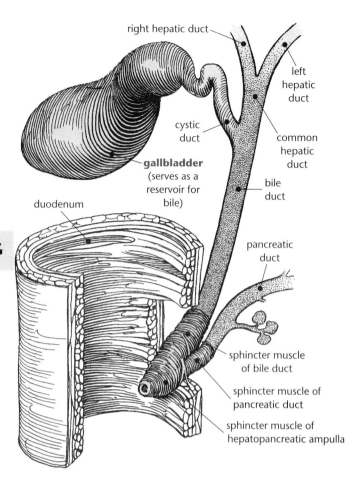

right hepatic duct

left hepatic duct

cystic duct

common hepatic duct

gallbladder
(serves as a reservoir for bile)

bile duct

duodenum

pancreatic duct

sphincter muscle of bile duct

sphincter muscle of pancreatic duct

sphincter muscle of hepatopancreatic ampulla

porcelain g. Extensive calcification within the gallbladder wall occurring in chronic inflammation of the organ (chronic cholecystitis).

strawberry g. Gallbladder with an inner lining that is red, congested, and dotted with yellowish deposits of cholesterol.

gallium (gal′e-um) Metallic element; symbol Ga, atomic number 31, atomic weight 69.72.

gallium 67 (^{67}Ga) A radioactive isotope of gallium used as a tracer to detect inflammatory lesions or metastatic tumors; can also be used to locate a number of primary tumors.

gallop (gal′op) A triple or quadruple cadence of heart sounds resembling the canter of a horse, heard on auscultation. Also called gallop rhythm; cantering rhythm.

atrial g. Presystolic sound related to atrial contraction, occurring in late diastole and designated as a fourth sound. Also called presystolic gallop.

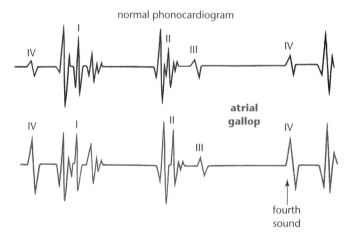

normal phonocardiogram

IV   I   II   III   IV

atrial gallop

IV   I   II   III   IV

fourth sound

presystolic g. See atrial gallop.

protodiastolic g. See ventricular gallop.

summation g. Atrial and ventricular gallop sounds occurring simultaneously.

ventricular g. Third heart sound occurring in early diastole (0.14–0.16 seconds after the second heart sound). Also called protodiastolic gallop.

gallstone (gawl′ston) A stone formed in the gallbladder or (rarely) in the bile duct. Also called biliary stone; biliary calculus; gallbladder stone.

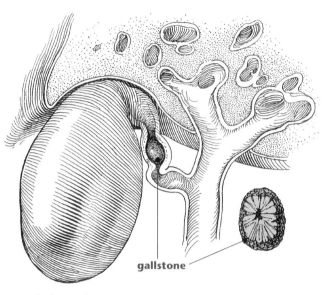

gallstone

cholesterol g. A solitary pale yellow radiolucent stone, spherical (when small) or oval (when large) and reaching a size up to 5 cm in diameter.

mixed g. The most common type of gallstone, typically multiple, multifaceted, and 1 to 3 cm in diameter; composed of varying proportions of cholesterol, calcium carbonate, phosphates, and bilirubin.

pigmented g. A small, jet-black stone occurring in great numbers; composed of the bile pigment bilirubin.

silent g. A gallstone that produces no symptoms.

galvanic (gal-van′ik) Relating to galvanism.

galvanism (gal′vah-nizm) **1.** Direct current electricity, especially when produced by chemical activity. **2.** Treatment with direct current electricity. Also called galvanotherapy.

dental g. Direct current electricity created in the oral cavity when dental restorations of metals with different electrical potentials are placed within, causing pain and white patches in the tissues.

galvano- Combining form meaning electrical, especially a direct current.

galvanocautery (gal-vah-no-kaw′ter-e) See electrocoagulation.

galvanocontractility (gal-vah-no-kon-trak-til′ĭ-te) The ability of a muscle to contract under a direct electrical current.

galvanofaradization (gal-vah-no-far-ah-dĭ-za′shun) The simultaneous application of continuous and interrupted electrical currents.

galvanometer (gal-vah-nom′ĕ-ter) Instrument for measuring a current of electricity.

galvanopalpation (gal-vah-no-pal-pa′shun) The testing of cutaneous nerve responses by stimulation of the nerve endings on the skin with a weak electric current.

galvanosurgery (gal-vah-no-sur′jer-e) The use of direct electrical current in an operative procedure.

galvanotherapy (gal-vah-no-ther′ah-pe) See galvanism (2).

galvanotonus (gal-vah-not′o-nus) Tonic muscular response to stimulation with a direct electrical current.

gamete (gam′ēt) In embryology, either of the two reproductive cells (ovum or spermatozoon); it contains only one member of each chromosome pair (haploid chromosome number) and combines with the other reproductive cell to form a zygote, from which a new organism develops. See also GIFT.

gameto- Combining form meaning gamete.

gametocide (gah-me′to-sīd) Any agent destructive to gametes.

gametocyte (gah-me′to-sīt) A cell (either spermatocyte or oocyte) from which gametes are produced by cell division.

gametogenesis (gam-ĕ-to-jen′ĕ-sis) The production of gametes (ova or spermatozoa).

gamma (gam′ah) (γ) **1.** The third letter of the Greek alphabet. **2.** The third item in a series of classification, as of chemical compounds. See also gamma ray, under ray.

gamma-aminobutyric acid (gam′ah ah-me-no-bu-tir′ik as′id) (GABA, γ Abu) An amino acid neurotransmitter present in brain tissue that inhibits nerve impulses. Also written γ-aminobutyric acid.

gamma globulin (gam′ah glob′ u-lin) See under globulin.

gammagram (gam′ah-gram) See scintiscan.

gammopathy (gam-op′ah-the) General term for any disorder characterized by an abnormal proliferation of antibody-forming cells and the presence of abnormally high levels of immunoglobulins (or any of their constituents) in the plasma and/or the urine; most of these disorders are malignant (e.g., multiple myeloma and heavy-chain disease).

    benign monoclonal g. See monoclonal gammopathy of undetermined significance.

    monoclonal g.'s See plasma cell dyscrasias, under dyscrasia.

    monoclonal g. of undetermined significance (MGUS) Condition marked by elevated levels of M protein in the serum but without symptoms of any immunoglobulin-producing disease; usually follows a benign course but in some cases (about l8%) a plasma cell dyscrasia develops. Also called benign monoclonal gammopathy.

gamogenesis (gam-o-jen′ĕ-sis) Sexual reproduction.

ganciclovir (gan-si′klō-vir) Antiviral agent used in the treatment of cytomegalovirus (CMV) infections.

ganglia (gang′gle-ah) Plural of ganglion.

ganglial (gang′gle-al) Relating to a ganglion.

gangliated, gangliate (gang′gle-āt-ed, gang′gle-āt) See ganglionated.

gangliectomy (gang-gle-ek′to-me) See ganglionectomy.

gangliform (gang′glī-form) Resembling a ganglion. Also called ganglioform.

ganglioblast (gang′gle-o-blast) An embryonic cell from which ganglion cells develop.

gangliocytoma (gang′gle-o-si-to′mah) See ganglioneuroma.

ganglioform (gang′gle-o-form) See gangliform.

ganglioglioma (gang′gle-o-gli-o′mah) A tumor composed of mature cells resembling nerve cells.

ganglioma (gang′gle-o′mah) See ganglioneuroma.

ganglion (gang′gle-on), pl. gang′lia, gang′lions **1.** A collection of nerve cell bodies located outside the brain and spinal cord. **2.** A cystic swelling resembling a tumor, occurring on a tendon sheath or joint capsule.

    aorticorenal g. The lower extension of each celiac ganglion which receives the lesser splanchnic nerve and gives off the greater part of the renal plexus; its location varies but is generally situated where the renal artery branches off the abdominal aorta.

    autonomic g. Any ganglion of the sympathetic and parasympathetic nervous systems.

    basal ganglia See basal nuclei, under nucleus.

    cardiac g. One of several ganglia in the superficial cardiac plexus situated between the arch of the aorta and the bifurcation of the pulmonary artery.

    celiac ganglia Two large, irregularly shaped sympathetic ganglia situated between the adrenal glands in the upper abdominal cavity; they receive the greater splanchnic nerves which innervate the liver, gallbladder, spleen, stomach, and intestines. Also called solar ganglia.

    cervical ganglia Three sympathetic ganglia in the neck: *Superior cervical g.,* the largest cervical ganglion situated just below the base of the skull. *Middle cervical g.,* the smallest cervical ganglion

situated opposite the sixth cervical vertebra. *Inferior cervical g.,* the lowest cervical ganglion; when fused with the first thoracic ganglion, it is called the cervicothoracic ganglion.

    cervicothoracic g. A large ganglion of irregular shape, formed by the fusion of the inferior cervical and first thoracic ganglia. Also called stellate ganglion.

    ciliary g. One of four parasympathetic ganglia associated with cranial nerves of the head; it lies behind the orbit between the optic nerve and the lateral rectus muscle.

    dorsal root g. See spinal ganglion.

    g. of facial nerve A sensory ganglion of the facial (7th cranial) nerve, situated in the facial canal in the medial wall of the middle ear. Also called genicular ganglion.

    ganglia of glossopharyngeal nerve The two sensory ganglia (superior and inferior) situated on the glossopharyngeal nerve as it passes through the jugular foramen at the base of the skull.

    gasserian g. See trigeminal ganglion.

    genicular g. See ganglion of facial nerve.

    otic g. One of four parasympathetic ganglia located just below the foramen ovale medial to the mandibular nerve; its pregan-

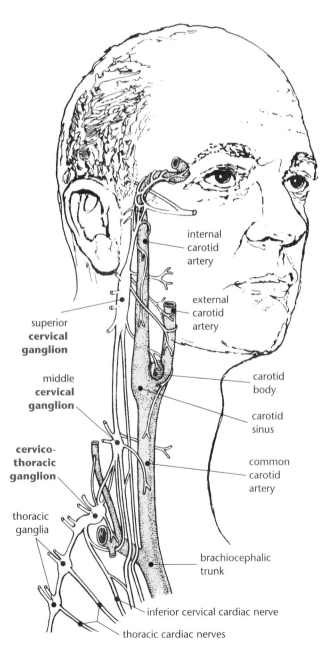

internal carotid artery

external carotid artery

superior **cervical ganglion**

middle **cervical ganglion**

cervico-thoracic ganglion

thoracic ganglia

carotid body

carotid sinus

common carotid artery

brachiocephalic trunk

inferior cervical cardiac nerve

thoracic cardiac nerves

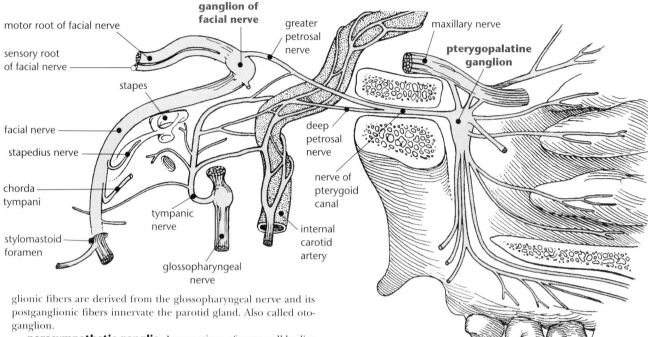

motor root of facial nerve
sensory root of facial nerve
stapes
facial nerve
stapedius nerve
chorda tympani
stylomastoid foramen
glossopharyngeal nerve
tympanic nerve
ganglion of facial nerve
greater petrosal nerve
deep petrosal nerve
nerve of pterygoid canal
internal carotid artery
maxillary nerve
pterygopalatine ganglion

glionic fibers are derived from the glossopharyngeal nerve and its postganglionic fibers innervate the parotid gland. Also called oto-ganglion.

parasympathetic ganglia Aggregations of nerve cell bodies of the parasympathetic nervous system; they include the ciliary, pterygopalatine, otic, and submandibular ganglia of the head as well as several others located near the organs of the thorax, abdomen, and pelvis.

paravertebral ganglia Sympathetic ganglia located at intervals on each sympathetic trunk along the side of the vertebral column; generally there are 3 cervical, 11 thoracic, 4 lumbar, and 4 sacral. Also called ganglia of sympathetic trunk.

prevertebral ganglia The sympathetic ganglia situated in front of the vertebral column and contributing to the plexuses of the thorax and abdomen; distinguished from the paravertebral ganglia, which lie along each side of the vertebral column.

pterygopalatine g. The largest of the four parasympathetic ganglia associated with cranial nerves of the head; it is located in the pterygopalatine fossa just posterior to the middle nasal concha; it sends postganglionic parasympathetic fibers to the lacrimal gland, nose, oral cavity, and the uppermost part of the pharynx. Also called sphenopalatine ganglion.

g. of Scarpa See vestibular ganglion.

semilunar g. See trigeminal ganglion.

sensory g. of dorsal root of spinal nerve See spinal ganglion.

solar ganglia See celiac ganglia.

sphenopalatine g. See pterygopalatine ganglion.

spinal g. An ovoid ganglion found on each dorsal spinal root situated in the intervertebral foramen; composed mostly of unipolar nerve cell bodies of the sensory neurons. Also called dorsal root ganglion; sensory ganglion of dorsal root of spinal nerve.

spiral g. of cochlea The ganglion of bipolar nerve cell bodies located within the modiolus of the internal ear; it sends fibers peripherally to the spiral organ of Corti and centrally to the cochlear nucleus of the brain stem.

stellate g. See cervicothoracic ganglion.

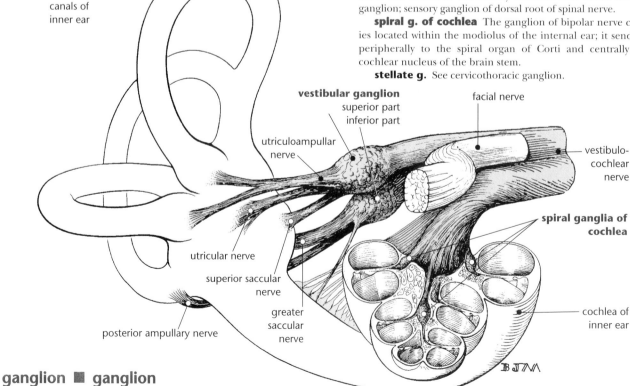

semicircular canals of inner ear
vestibular ganglion
superior part
inferior part
facial nerve
utriculoampullar nerve
vestibulo-cochlear nerve
spiral ganglia of cochlea
utricular nerve
superior saccular nerve
greater saccular nerve
posterior ampullary nerve
cochlea of inner ear

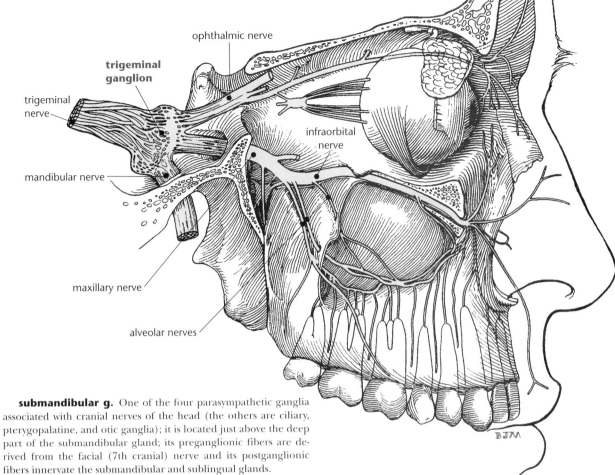

ophthalmic nerve

**trigeminal
ganglion**

trigeminal
nerve

infraorbital
nerve

mandibular nerve

maxillary nerve

alveolar nerves

BJM

G

submandibular g. One of the four parasympathetic ganglia associated with cranial nerves of the head (the others are ciliary, pterygopalatine, and otic ganglia); it is located just above the deep part of the submandibular gland; its preganglionic fibers are derived from the facial (7th cranial) nerve and its postganglionic fibers innervate the submandibular and sublingual glands.

ganglia of sympathetic trunk See paravertebral ganglia.

thoracic g. One of about 11 ganglia on the thoracic segment of the sympathetic trunk.

trigeminal g. The large flattened ganglion containing the cells of origin of the sensory fibers of the trigeminal (5th cranial) nerve; situated in the back of the middle cranial fossa near the cavernous sinus. Also called semilunar ganglion; gasserian ganglion.

ganglia of vagus nerve Either of two ganglia situated on the vagus nerve at the base of the skull: *Superior ganglia of vagus nerve,* the small, spherical sensory ganglion, about 4 mm in diameter, situated in the jugular foramen; it is joined by several filaments, including one from the superior cervical ganglion of the sympathetic trunk. *Inferior ganglia of vagus nerve,* the main sensory ganglion of the vagus nerve, about 2.5 cm long, situated in the carotid sheath just below the base of the skull; it is connected to the superior cervical ganglion of the sympathetic trunk, as well as other nerves.

vertebral g. A small ganglion situated at the site where the vertebral artery branches off the subclavian artery; generally regarded as a detached part of the cervicothoracic ganglion.

vestibular g. A collection of bipolar nerve cell bodies forming a swelling of the vestibulocochlear (8th cranial) nerve in the internal auditory canal; it is subdivided into superior and inferior parts. Also called ganglion of Scarpa.

ganglionated (gang´gle-o-nāt-ed) Having ganglia. Also called gangliated; gangliate.

ganglionectomy (gang´gle-o-nek´to-me) Removal of a ganglion. Also called gangliectomy.

stellate g. See stellectomy.

ganglioneuroma (gang´gle-o-nu-ro´mah) A small, encapsulated, slow-growing tumor, composed of mature ganglion cells and nerve fibers. Also called ganglioma; gangliocytoma; neurocytoma.

ganglionic (gang´gle-on´ik) Relating to a ganglion.

ganglionitis (gang´gle-on-i´tis) Inflammation of any ganglion.

ganglioplegia (gang´gle-o-ple´je-ah) Any agent that blocks transmission of nerve impulses (usually for a short period of time) through an autonomic ganglion.

ganglioside (gang´gle-o-sid) One of a class of sphingoglycolipids present in neural tissue containing *N*-acetylneuraminic acid (NANA).

gangliosidosis (gang´gle-o-si-do´sis) Any disease involving an abnormal accumulation of specific gangliosides in the nervous system. Also called ganglioside lipidosis.

G_{M2} g. See cerebral sphingolipidosis, infantile type, under sphingolipidosis.

gangosa (gang-go´sah) Ulceration of the roof of the mouth, the nose, and the back of the nose; a sequel to yaws. Also called rhinopharyngitis mutilans.

gangrene (gang´grēn) Death and decomposition of body tissue due to inadequate blood supply; a form of necrosis combined with putrefaction.

diabetic g. Gangrene due to arteriosclerosis occurring as a complication of diabetes.

dry g. Gangrene not preceded by inflammation. Also called mummification.

gas g. Gangrene occurring in extensively traumatized wounds, infected with soil bacteria of the genus *Clostridium;* characterized by the presence of gas in affected tissues.

moist g. A soft and moist gangrene due to the action of putrefactive bacteria.

gangrenous (gang´grĕ-nus) Affected by gangrene.

gap (gap) An interval or an opening.

air-bone g. The difference between hearing acuity by air conduction and by bone conduction.

auscultatory g. A silent interval sometimes noticed during the determination of blood pressure. Also called silent gap.

silent g. See auscultatory gap.

Gardnerella vaginalis (gard-ner-el´ah vaj´ĭ-na´lis) A nonmotile, gram-staining bacterium (genus *Gardnerella*) that invades the human genital tract; it is a major cause of vaginitis, transmitted by

ganglionated ■ Gardnerella vaginalis

sexual contact; may occasionally cause bacteremia in women after childbirth or in men after transurethral resection of the prostate.

gargle (gar'gl) **1.** To rinse or medicate the throat by forcing exhaled air through a solution held in the back of the mouth while the head is tilted back. **2.** A medicated solution used for gargling.

gargoylism (gar'goil-izm) Obsolete term denoting the gargoylelike facies of some forms of mucopolysaccharidosis.

gas (gas) **1.** An airlike state of matter with freely moving molecules, capable of expanding and contracting with changes in temperature and pressure. **2.** Popular name for inhalation anesthesia.

    alveolar g. The gas in the air sacs (alveoli) of the lungs. Also called alveolar air.

    asphyxiant noxious g.'s Gases that may cause sudden death by displacing oxygen from inspired air (e.g., carbon monoxide, nitrogen, methane).

    inert g. Any of the atmospheric gases (helium, neon, argon, krypton, xenon, radon) that exhibit no chemical activity.

    irritant noxious g.'s Gases that may pose injury to the lungs by direct effect on the respiratory lining, by causing acute spasm of the airways, or by inducing inflammation of lining membranes in the airways; may also injure the larynx.

    laughing g. See nitrous oxide.

    marsh g. See methane.

    tear g. Any of several gases, such as chloroacetophenone (CAP), which irritate the eyes, causing profuse tearing.

gaseous (gash'us) Of the nature of a gas.

gasometer (gas-om'ĕ-ter) A calibrated apparatus for measuring the volume of gases; generally used for measuring respiratory gases.

gasometry (gas-om'ĕ-tre) The measurement of a gas in a mixture.

gastrectomy (gas-trek'to-me) Removal of the stomach or, most frequently, a portion of it. Also called gastric resection.

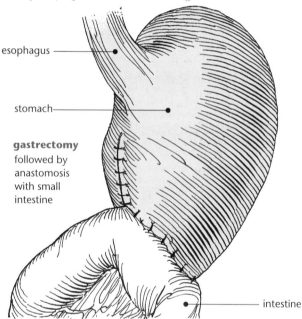

esophagus

stomach

gastrectomy followed by anastomosis with small intestine

intestine

gastric (gas'trik) Relating to the stomach.

gastrin (gas'trin) One of the gastrointestinal hormones released during digestion; it is secreted by the mucosa of the pyloric region of the stomach upon contact with food; it increases secretion of hydrochloric acid and, to a lesser degree, of pepsinogen.

gastrinoma (gas-trin-o'mah) A gastrin-producing tumor, usually of (non-beta) cells in the pancreas, associated with the Zollinger-Ellison syndrome.

gastritis (gas-tri'tis) Inflammation of the stomach lining (mucosa).

    antral g. See type B gastritis.

    atrophic g. A chronic form of gastritis characterized by inflammation and degeneration of the stomach lining with flattening of the rugal folds.

    erosive g. Gastritis with erosions of the stomach lining; may be asymptomatic or associated with nausea, discomfort of the upper abdomen, and slow oozing of blood into the intestines; or may induce vomiting of blood; may be caused by irritation (e.g., by aspirin or alcohol consumption) or by severe stress (e.g., head injuries, burns, surgery, or liver failure). Also called hemorrhagic gastritis.

    fundal g. See type A gastritis.

    hemorrhagic g. See erosive gastritis.

    hypertrophic g. Gastritis characterized mainly by abnormally large rugal folds due to an increased number of cells (hyperplasia) of the stomach lining; may involve the superficial cells (as in Ménétrièr's disease), or the chief mucosal cells (as in hypersecretory gastropathy), or may be secondary to excessive gastrin secretion by a tumor (as in Zollinger-Ellison syndrome).

    interstitial g. Gastritis involving the muscular layer of the stomach wall in addition to the mucosal lining.

    phlegmonous g. Severe gastritis with purulent involvement of the stomach wall.

    pseudomembranous g. Inflammation of the stomach marked by the formation of a false membrane.

    type A g. Chronic gastritis generally involving the uppermost region (fundus) and body of the stomach; usually asymptomatic and most common in elderly people; may be associated with pernicious anemia, Hashimoto's thyroiditis, and Addison's disease; long-standing disease has an increased risk of becoming cancerous. Also called fundal gastritis.

    type B g. A common form of chronic gastritis primarily affecting the lower portion (antrum) of the stomach; believed to be caused by infection with a bacterium (*Helicobacter pylori*); occurs in all age groups and may be asymptomatic or cause upset stomach, burning pain, and belching. Also called antral gastritis.

    type II g. Disorder seen in newborn infants resulting from defective breakdown of glycogen molecules in the body due to lack of the enzyme alpha-glucosidase; glycogen accumulates in many tissues, especially the heart muscle; the heart becomes massively enlarged; death occurs from heart failure by two years of age.

gastro-, gastr- Combining forms meaning stomach.

gastroanastomosis (gas-tro-ah-nas-to-mo'sis) Surgical connection of the cardiac and pyloric ends of the stomach after resection of the middle portion. Also called gastrogastrostomy.

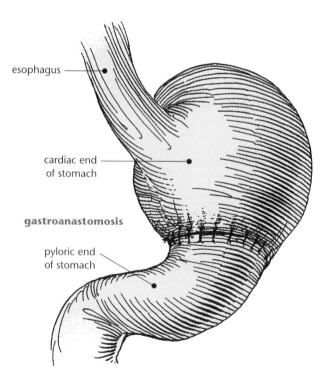

esophagus

cardiac end of stomach

gastroanastomosis

pyloric end of stomach

gastroblenorrhea (gas-tro-blen-no-re'ah) Excessive secretion of mucus by the stomach.

gastrocele (gas'tro-sēl) 1. See archenteron. 2. A herniation of the stomach wall.

gastrocnemius (gas-trok-ne'me-us) See table of muscles.

gastrocolic (gas-tro-kol'ik) Relating to the stomach and colon.

gastrocolitis (gas-tro-ko-li'tis) Inflammation of the stomach and colon.

gastrocoloptosis (gas-tro-ko-lop-to'sis) Downward displacement of stomach and colon.

gastrocolostomy (gas-tro-ko-los'to-me) Surgical construction of a passage between the stomach and the colon.

gastrodiscoides hominis (gas-tro-dis-koi'dēz hom'ĭ-nis) A species of trematode worms parasitic in the intestines of pigs and humans.

gastroduodenal (gas-tro-du-od'ĕ-nal) Relating to the stomach and duodenum.

gastroduodenoscopy (gas-tro-du-od-ĕ-nos'ko-pe) Visualization of the interior of the stomach and duodenum with a gastroscope.

gastroduodenostomy (gas-tro-du-od-ĕ-nos'to-me) Surgical construction of an artificial passage between the stomach and a noncontinuous portion of the duodenum.

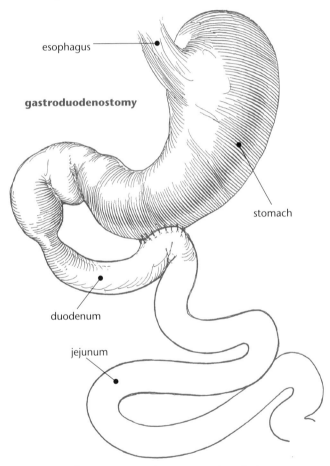

esophagus

gastroduodenostomy

stomach

duodenum

jejunum

gastroenteric (gas-tro-en-ter'ik) See gastrointestinal.

gastroenteritis (gas-tro-en-ter-i'tis) Inflammation of the mucous lining of the stomach and intestines.

gastroenteroanastomosis (gas-tro-en-ter-o-ah-nas-to-mo'sis) See gastroenterostomy.

gastroenterologist (gas-tro-en-ter-ol'o-jist) A specialist in gastroenterology.

gastroenterology (gas-tro-en-ter-ol'o-je) The branch of medicine concerned with disorders of the digestive system, including the esophagus, stomach, intestines, liver, gallbladder, and pancreas.

gastroenteropathy (gas-tro-en-ter-op'ah-the) Any disease of the digestive tract.

gastroenteroptosis (gas-tro-en-ter-op-to'sis) The downward displacement or prolapse of the stomach and a portion of intestine.

gastroentostomy (gas-tro-en-ter-os'to-me) Surgical construction of an artificial passage between the stomach and a portion of the intestine. Also called gastroenteroanastomosis.

gastroenterotomy (gas-tro-en-ter-ot'o-me) A surgical cut into the stomach and the intestine.

gastroepiploic (gas-tro-ep-ĭ-plo'ik) Relating to the stomach and the greater omentum.

gastroesophageal (gas-tro-ĕ-sof-ah-je'al) Relating to the stomach and esophagus.

gastroesophagitis (gas-tro-ĕ-sof-ah-ji'tis) Inflammation of the stomach and esophagus.

gastroesophagostomy (gas-tro-ĕ-sof-ah-gos'to-me) See esophagogastrostomy.

gastrogastrostomy (gas-tro-gas-tros'to-me) See gastroanastomosis.

gastrogavage (gas-tro-gah-vazh') The passage of nutrients into the stomach via a tube introduced through the stomach wall.

gastrogenic (gas-tro-jen'ik) Originating in the stomach.

gastrograph (gas'tro-graf) Instrument for recording stomach movements.

gastrohepatic (gas-tro-hĕ-pat'ik) Relating to the stomach and liver.

gastrohydrorrhea (gas-tro-hi-dro-re'ah) Excessive production of a watery secretion by the stomach.

gastrointestinal (gas-tro-in-tes'tī-nal) (GI) Relating to the stomach and intestines. Also called gastroenteric.

gastrojejunocolic (gas-tro-jĕ-ju-no-kol'ik) Relating to the stomach, the middle portion of the small intestine (jejunum), and the colon; applied to an abnormal channel (fistula) through the three structures.

gastrojejunostomy (gas-tro-jĕ-ju-nos'to-me) Surgical construction of an artificial passage between the stomach and the middle portion of the small intestine (jejunum).

gastrolith (gas'tro-lith) A stony concretion in the stomach; a gastric calculus or stone.

gastrolithiasis (gas-tro-lī-thi'ah-sis) The presence of one or more gastroliths in the stomach.

gastromalacia (gas-tro-mah-la'she-ah) Abnormal softening of the stomach wall.

gastromegaly (gas-tro-meg'ah-le) Abnormal enlargement of the stomach.

gastropathy (gas-trop'ah-the) Any disease of the stomach.

    hypersecretory g. Thickening of the stomach lining with excessive acid secretion, frequently with ulceration; it is not associated with a gastrin-secreting tumor. See also hypertrophic gastritis, under gastritis.

gastropexy (gas'tro-pek-se) Surgical attachment of the stomach to the abdominal wall.

    anterior g. Suturing of the stomach to the posterior sheath of rectus abdominis muscle in the operative repair of a paraesophageal hiatal hernia.

gastrophrenic (gas-tro-fren'ik) Relating to the stomach and the diaphragm.

gastroplasty (gas'tro-plas-te) Operative correction of a defect of the stomach.

    vertical banded g. Surgical technique for the treatment of obesity whereby two vertical rows of plastic staples are placed along the lesser curvature of the stomach to create a small stomach pouch with a restricted outlet. The intent is to reduce the amount of food intake. Also called gastric stapling; stomach stapling.

gastroplication (gas-tro-pli-ka'shun) An operative procedure for reducing the size of the stomach, usually by suturing a fold along its length.

gastroptosis (gas-trop-to'sis) Downward displacement of the stomach.

gastropyloric (gas-tro-pi-lor'ik) Relating to the stomach as a whole and to the pylorus.

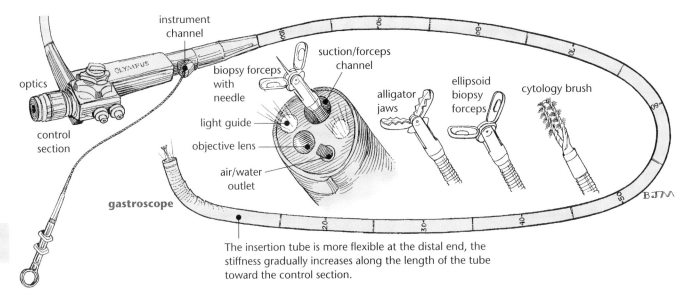

gastroscope

The insertion tube is more flexible at the distal end, the stiffness gradually increases along the length of the tube toward the control section.

gastrorrhagia (gas-tro-ra′je-ah) Copious bleeding from the stomach.

gastrorrhaphy (gas-tror′ah-fe) Any suturing of the stomach.

gastrorrhexis (gas-tro-rek′sis) A rupture of the stomach.

gastroschisis (gas-tros′ki-sis) In newborn infants, a full-thickness defect of the abdominal wall located just to the right of the intact umbilical cord; consists of an opening 2 to 4 cm in diameter through which protrudes an exposed loop of intestine (without a protective covering sac).

gastroscope (gas′tro-skōp) Endoscope consisting basically of a flexible insertion tube, an instrument channel, and an optical system; used for inspection and treatment of the stomach's interior.

gastroscopy (gas-tros′ko-pe) Direct inspection of the interior of the stomach with a gastroscope.

gastrospasm (gas′tro-spazm) Spasmodic contraction of the stomach.

gastrosplenic (gas-tro-splen′ik) Relating to the stomach and spleen.

gastrostaxis (gas-tro-stak′sis) Chronic slight bleeding from the mucosal lining of the stomach; occurs in certain types of chronic gastritis.

gastrostenosis (gas-tro-stĕ-no′sis) Abnormal constriction of the stomach.

gastrostomy (gas-tros′to-me) Surgical construction of a passage into the stomach through the abdominal wall.

gastrotomy (gas-trot′o-me) Surgical cut into the stomach.

gastrotropic (gas-tro-trop′ik) Having an effect on the stomach.

gastrula (gas′troo-lah) An embryo at the stage of development following the blastula.

gastrulation (gas-troo-la′shun) In embryology, the formation of a gastrula; the stage of development when the three germ layers (ectoderm, mesoderm, endoderm) begin to form.

gathering (gath′er-ing) Colloquial term for the maturing of a boil or abscess when it swells and fills with pus.

gauge (gāj) A measuring instrument.
 bite g. See gnathodynamometer.
 Boley g. A caliper-type instrument used in dentistry for taking measurements necessary for dental prostheses.
 catheter g. A metal plate with perforations of different sizes for determining the size of catheters.

gauntlet (gawnt′let) A glovelike bandage for protecting the hand and fingers.

gauss (gous) (G) A unit of magnetic field intensity, equal to 10^{-4} **tesla.**

gauze (gawz) A thin, open-weave surgical dressing or bandage material.

gavage (gah-vahzh′) The passage of material through a tube (nasogastric tube) introduced into the stomach via the nose; forced feeding via a tube.

gaze (gāz) To look steadily.

gel (jel) **1.** The semisolid state of a coagulated colloid. **2.** To become a gel.

gelate (jel′āt) See gel.

gelatin (jel′ah-tin) A colorless protein obtained by boiling collagen in water; used for nutritional purposes and as an inactive agent in certain pharmaceutical preparations.
 zinc g. A medicinal jelly containing zinc oxide, gelatin, glycerin, and water; used between layers of bandage as a protecting agent.

gelatinize (jĕ-lat′ĭ-nīz) **1.** To convert to gelatin. **2.** To coat with gelatin.

gelatinoid (jĕ-lat′ĭ-noid) Like gelatin.

gelatinous (jĕ-lat′ĭ-nus) Relating to or containing gelatin.

gelation (jĕ-la′shun) The conversion into a gel of a colloid suspended in a liquid.

gelosis (jĕ-lo′sis) A hard mass in a tissue, especially a muscle.

gemellology (jem-el-ol′o-je) The study of twins and twinning.

gemfibrozil (jem-fi′bro-zil) A lipid-lowering preparation used in the treatment of certain types of hyperlipidemia; it chiefly reduces the liver production of fats combined with proteins (lipoproteins).

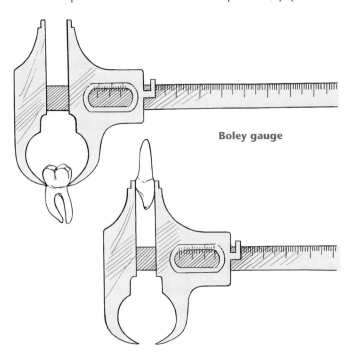

Boley gauge

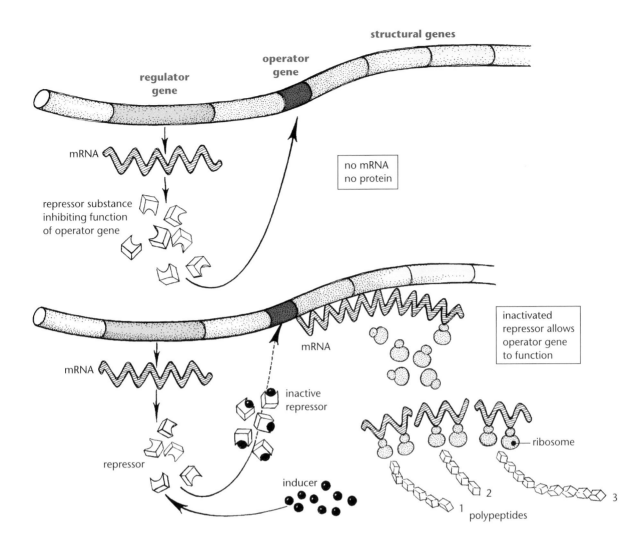

regulator gene

operator gene

structural genes

mRNA

repressor substance inhibiting function of operator gene

no mRNA no protein

mRNA

mRNA

inactive repressor

repressor

inducer

inactivated repressor allows operator gene to function

ribosome

1   2   3
polypeptides

geminate (jem′ĭ-nāt) Occurring in pairs.

gemma (jem′ah) Any budlike structure (e.g., a taste bud).

gemmules (jem′ūls) See dendritic spines, under spine.

-gen Combining form meaning something that produces; something produced (e.g., pathogen, chromogen).

gender (jen′der) (g) Sex category.

gene (jēn) The hereditary unit occupying a fixed position (locus) in the chromosome, capable of reproducing itself at each cell division and of managing the formation of proteins. In molecular terms, it is a segment of the DNA molecule containing the code for a specific function.

    allelic g. See allele.

    g. amplification See under amplification.

    autosomal g. A gene that is present in any chromosome other than a sex (X or Y) chromosome.

    codominant g.'s In clinical genetics, two or more alleles of a gene that express a recognizable effect on a heterozygous individual.

    g.'s in common Those genes inherited by two individuals from a common ancestor.

    dominant g. A gene that produces a recognizable effect in the organism whether paired with an identical or a dissimilar gene.

    g. expression See under expression.

    g. flow See under flow.

    holandric g. A gene occurring only in the male of the species, located on the nonhomologous portion of a Y (male) chromosome. Also called Y-linked gene.

    g. library See under library.

    g. map See chromosome map, under map.

    operator g. A gene that activates messenger-RNA production.

    g. pool See under pool.

    g. product See under product.

    recessive g. A gene that is expressed only when homozygous (i.e., the individual inherits it from both parents); it does not produce a detectable effect in the organism when occurring in combination with a dominant gene (i.e., the individual inherits it only from one parent).

    regulator g. A gene that controls the rate of protein formation or suppression.

    sex-linked g. A gene located on a sex (X or Y) chromosome.

    structural g. A gene that specifies the formation of a particular polypeptide chain required for the functions of cells.

    g. therapy See under therapy.

    X-linked g. A gene carried on an X (female) chromosome.

    Y-linked g. See holandric gene.

genera (jen′er-ah) Plural of genus.

generalist (jen′er-al-ist) A physician who treats a broad range of diseases; a family or general physician, or an internist who does not subspecialize.

generalize (jen′er-al-īz) To advance from local to general (e.g., a local lesion that spreads and becomes systemic).

generation (jen-ĕ-ra′shun) One full cycle of sexual reproduction, from parent to offspring.

    filial g. Offspring produced from a genetically specified mating: *first filial g.* (F_1), offspring of the first mating of two individuals; *second filial g.* (F_2), offspring of the mating of two F_1 individuals; F_3, F_4, etc., are filial generations of succeeding inbreeding.

generative (jen′ĕ-ra-tiv) Relating to reproduction.

generator (jen′er-a-tor) **1.** An apparatus for producing electrical energy from some other form of energy. **2.** A device for producing vapor or gas from a liquid or solid substance.

    aerosol g. Device for producing airborne suspension of particles, usually for inhalation therapy.

    asynchronous pulse g. A cardiac generator that produces pulses at a fixed rate, unaffected by the natural activity of the heart. Also called fixed rate pulse generator.

    atrial synchronous g. A ventricular stimulating generator with a rate of discharge that is determined by the atrial rate. Also called atrial triggered pulse generator.

    atrial triggered pulse g. See atrial synchronous pulse generator.

    demand pulse g. See ventricular inhibited pulse generator.

    fixed rate pulse g. See asynchronous pulse generator.

    pulse g. An apparatus serving as the electromotive source for an artificial pacemaker assembly; it generates and discharges electrical impulses to stimulate the heart.

    standby pulse g. See ventricular inhibited pulse generator.

    ventricular inhibited pulse g. A generator that suppresses its electrical output in response to natural activity of the ventricles but which, in the absence of such activity, functions as an asynchronous pulse. Also called demand pulse generator; standby pulse generator.

    ventricular synchronous pulse g. A generator that delivers its output synchronously with natural ventricular activity but which, in the absence of such activity, functions as an asynchronous pulse. Also called ventricular triggered pulse generator.

    ventricular triggered pulse g. See ventricular synchronous pulse generator.

generic (jĕ-ner′ik) **1.** Relating to a genus. **2.** See generic name, under name.

genesial, genesic (jĕ-ne′ze-al, jĕ-nes′ik) **1.** Relating to origin. **2.** Relating to generation.

genesiology (jĕ-ne-ze-ol′o-je) The study of generation and reproduction.

genesis (jen′ĕ-sis) Origin; creation.

genetic (jĕ-net′ik) **1.** Relating to the study of heredity. **2.** Determined by genes (distinguished from congenital).

    g. code See under code.

    g. disorder See under disorder.

    g. drift See under drift.

    g. engineering See under engineering.

    g. imprinting See under imprinting.

    g. marker See under marker.

    g. probe See probe (2).

    g. screening See under screening.

geneticist (jĕ-net′ĭ-sist) A scientist who specializes in genetics.

genetics (jĕ-net′iks) The science of heredity; the study of the way in which particular qualities or traits are transmitted from parents to offspring.

    medical g. The study of the causes, symptoms, treatment, and prevention of genetic disorders.

genetotrophic (jĕ-net-o-trof′ik) Denoting inherited nutritional factors; applied especially to certain hereditary deficiency disorders.

genial, genian (jĕ-ni′al, jĕ-ni′an) Relating to the chin.

-genic Combining form meaning producing; formed by (e.g., oncogenic).

genic (jen′ik) Relating to genes.

geniculate, geniculated (jĕ-nik′u-lāt, jĕ-nik′u-lā-ted) Shaped like a bent knee.

geniculum (jĕ-nik′u-lum), pl. genic′ula Latin for small knee; applied to a sharp kneelike bend of a small structure.

    g. of facial nerve The right-angled bend of the horizontal portion of the facial nerve in the medial wall of the middle ear chamber; it is marked by the presence of the geniculate ganglion (sensory ganglion of the facial nerve).

genio- Combining form meaning chin.

genioglossus (je-ne-o-glos′us) See table of muscles.

geniohyoid (je-ne-o-hi′oid) See table of muscles.

genioplasty (jĕ′ne-o-plas-te) Reparative or plastic surgery of the chin.

genital (jen′ĭ-tal) **1.** Relating to the genitals. **2.** Relating to reproduction.

genitalia (jen-ĭ-ta′le-ah) The genitals.

genitality (jen-ĭ-tal′ĭ-te) In psychoanalysis, a general term denoting the genital constituents of sexuality.

genitals (jen′ĭ-tals) The organs of reproduction, male and female.

genitourinary (jen-ĭ-to-u′rĭ-nar-e) (GU) Relating to the organs of reproduction and the genitals. Also called urogenital.

genodermatosis (jen-o-der-mah-to′sis) A genetically determined condition of the skin.

genome (je′nōm) The total genetic information packed in a chromosome.

genotype (jen′o-tīp) The full set of genes carried by an individual, including those that are not obviously expressed.

genotypical (jen-o-ti′pik-al) Relating to a genotype.

gentamicin sulfate (jen-tah-mi′sin sul′fāt) A broad-spectrum aminoglycoside antibiotic that inhibits the growth of bacteria.

genu (je′nu) **1.** Latin for knee. **2.** Any structure resembling a bent knee.

    g. of corpus callosum The kneelike bend at the anterior extremity of the corpus callosum of the brain.

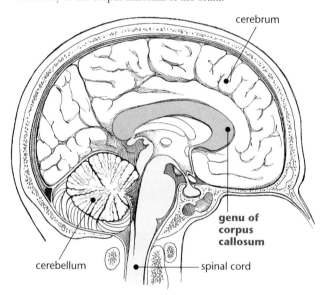

cerebrum

genu of corpus callosum

cerebellum — spinal cord

    g. impressum A deformity of the leg in which the knee is angulated to one side, with a displaced patella facing upward and to the affected side.

    g. recurvatum Abnormal backward bending of the knee joint; back knee.

    g. valgum A deformity of the leg, usually bilateral, in which the knees converge toward the midline while the ankles remain separated. Also called knock-knee.

    g. varum A congenital deformity, usually bilateral, in which the leg has an outward curvature in the region of the knee, resulting in an abnormally large distance between the knees when standing with the feet close together. Also called bowleg; bandy-leg.

genual (jen′u-al) Relating to the knee.

genus (je′nus), pl. gen′era The biological category ranking below a family and above a species.

geomedicine (je-o-med′ĭ-sin) The study of environmental influences on health and disease.

geopathology (je-o-pah-thol′o-je) The study of disease as it relates to the environment.

geo- Combining form meaning soil; earth.

geophagia (je-o-fa′je-ah) The eating of clay or dirt. Also called earth-eating; dirt-eating.

geotrichosis (je-o-tri-ko′sis) Condition attributed to infection with the fungus *Geotrichum candidum;* characterized by formation of

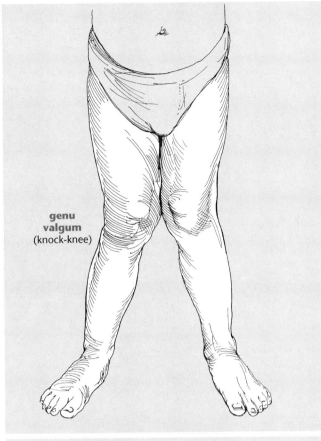

genu valgum (knock-knee)

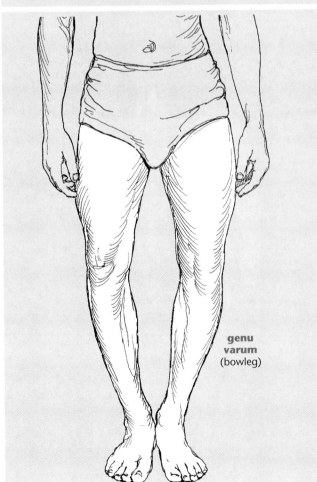

genu varum (bowleg)

lesions in the mouth and the lungs and bronchi.

geriatric (jer-e-at′rik) Relating to old age.

geriatrician (jer-e-ah-trish′an) A physician who specializes in the treatment of elderly patients and the special conditions related to aging.

geriatrics (jer-e-at′riks) See geriatric medicine, under medicine.

germ (jerm) **1.** A disease-causing microorganism; a pathogen. **2.** An embryonic structure; a primordium.

   wheat g. The vitamin-rich embryonic or germinating wheat kernel; used as a cereal or a dietary supplement.

germanium (jer-ma′ne-um) Metallic element; symbol Ge, atomic number 32, atomic weight 72.6.

germicidal (jer-mĭ-si′dal) Destructive to disease-causing microorganisms.

germicide (jer′mĭ-sīd) Any agent that kills germs.

germinal (jer′mĭ-nal) **1.** Relating to germination. **2.** Relating to a germ.

germinoma (jer-mĭ-no′mah) A tumor arising from germinal tissue, as of the ovaries or testes (e.g., seminoma).

geroderma (jer-o-der′mah) Atrophy of the skin.

gerodontics, gerodontology (jer-o-don′tiks, jer-o-don-tol′o-je) The diagnosis and treatment of dental disorders related to advancing age.

geromarasmus (jer-o-mah-raz′mus) Atrophy or wasting of tissues associated with old age.

gerontal (jer-on′tal) Relating to old age.

geronto-, gero-, geront- Combining forms meaning old age.

gerontology (jer-on-tol′o-je) The study of medical and social problems associated with aging.

gerontophobia (jer-on-to-fo′be-ah) Abnormal fear of old people.

gerontopia (jer-on-to′pe-ah) See second sight, under sight.

gerontotherapeutics (jer-on-to-ther-ah-pu′tiks) Treatment of diseases of elderly people.

gerontoxon (jer-on-tok′son) See arcus senilis, under arcus.

gestagen (jes′tah-jen) General term for hormones that induce progestational changes in the uterus, including progesterone.

gestagenic (jes-tah-jen′ik) Inducing prostagenic changes in the uterus.

gestalt (gĕ-stawlt′) A unified system of physical, psychological, or symbolic phenomena having properties that cannot be derived solely from its individual components.

gestation (jes-ta′shun) See pregnancy.

giantism (ji′ant-izm) See gigantism.

giardiasis (je-ar-di′ah-sis) Infection of the small intestine with the protozoon *Giardia lamblia*, frequently causing outbreaks of diarrhea lasting one to three weeks; transmitted via the fecal-oral route, mostly through contaminated water supplies and through direct person-to-person contact (e.g., children in day care centers and male homosexuals).

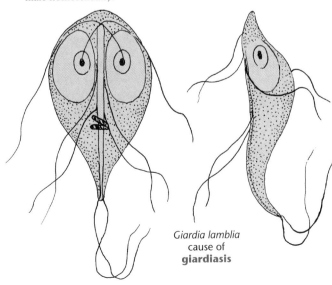

Giardia lamblia
cause of
giardiasis

G

gibbous (gib'us) Humpbacked.

gibbus (gib'us) A hump or kyphos.

GIFT Acronym for gamete intrafallopian transfer; the placing of sperm and unfertilized ova together in a fallopian (uterine) tube to enhance the possibility of fertilization.

gigantism (ji-gan'tizm) An abnormal condition of excessive growth of the body, especially height, which greatly surpasses the average for the person's race; caused by excessive production of growth hormone during childhood or adolescence. Also called giantism.

gingiva (jin-ji'vah) (G) The gum; the mucous membrane and fibrous tissue covering the alveolar processes of the jaws and surrounding the necks of the teeth (cervical margins); in the healthy mouth it is pale pink and stippled.

 attached g. The portion of gingiva attached to the tooth and alveolar bone beyond the gingival crevice.

 buccal g. The portion of gingiva facing the cheek.

 free g. The unattached margin of gingiva closely surrounding the tooth.

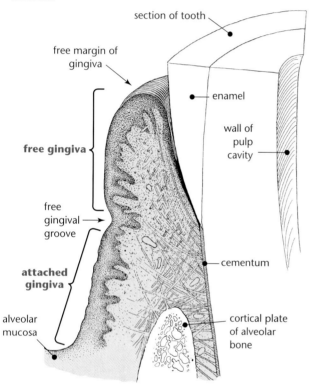

section of tooth

free margin of gingiva

free gingiva

free gingival groove

attached gingiva

alveolar mucosa

enamel

wall of pulp cavity

cementum

cortical plate of alveolar bone

 labial g. The portion of gingiva facing the lips.

 lingual g. The portion of gingiva facing the tongue.

gingival (jin-ji'val) Relating to the gums.

gingivectomy (jin-ji-vek'to-me) Surgical removal of diseased gum tissue.

gingivitis (jin-ji-vi'tis) Inflammation of the gums.

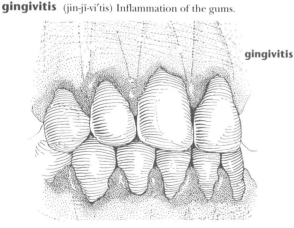

gingivitis

 chronic desquamative g. An uncommon form of gingivitis characterized by localized patches of tissue atrophy and shedding of epithelium associated with burning sensation. Cause is unknown. Also called gingivosis.

 necrotizing ulcerative g. (NUG) A recurrent bacterial (fuso-spirochetal) infection, usually of sudden onset, characterized by tender, bleeding gums with ulcer formation, a gray exudate, and fetid breath; most commonly occurs in people with poor oral hygiene. Also called Vincent's disease; Vincent's infection; trench mouth.

gingivo- Combining form meaning gingiva.

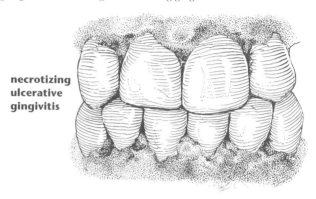

necrotizing ulcerative gingivitis

gingivoplasty (jin'ji-vo-plas-te) Surgical contouring of the gums.

gingivosis (jin-ji-vo'sis) See chronic desquamative gingivitis, under gingivitis.

gingivostomatitis (jin-ji-vo-sto-mah-ti'tis) Inflammation of the gums and oral mucosa.

ginglymus (jin'gli-mus) See hinge joint, under joint.

girdle (ger'dl) An encircling band, structure, region, or zone.

 pectoral g. See shoulder girdle.

 pelvic g. The bony ring formed by the sacrum and two hipbones.

 shoulder g. A girdle formed by the two collarbones (clavicles), the two shoulder blades (scapulas), and the upper portion of the breastbone (manubrium of sternum). Also called pectoral girdle.

glabella (glah-bel'ah) The smooth area of the frontal bone, between the eyebrows.

glabrous (gla'brus) Hairless, smooth, or bare; applied to areas of the body that are normally devoid of hair.

gland (gland) An organized aggregation of epithelial cells that elaborate secretions or excretions.

 accessory g. A small detached remnant of glandular tissue located near a principal gland or similar structure.

 accessory adrenal g.'s Adrenocortical bodies occurring in areolar tissue around the adrenal gland or in the spermatic cord, epididymis, and broad ligament of uterus, as well as in or near the ovary and kidney and along the ureter.

 acinous g. A gland made up of one or several saclike structures that encompass a central lumen. Also called alveolar gland.

 adrenal g.'s A pair of flattened endocrine glands positioned at the upper pole of each kidney; the shape of the right adrenal gland is somewhat triangular, while the left one is crescent-shaped; their cortex produces steroid hormones (aldosterone, androgens, glucocorticoids, progestins, and estrogens) while their medulla produces epinephrine and norepinephrine. Also called suprarenal glands.

 alveolar g. See acinous gland.

 apocrine g. A gland producing a secretion that contains part of the secretory cells, as in some sweat glands and mammary glands.

 Bartholin's g.'s See greater vestibular glands.

 Brunner's g.'s See duodenal glands.

 buccal g.'s Small salivary glands positioned between the buccinator muscle and the mucous membrane of the cheek; they discharge mucus into the mouth (oral cavity).

 bulbocavernous g.'s See bulbourethral glands.

 bulbourethral g.'s Two pea-shaped glands situated in the

gibbous ■ gland

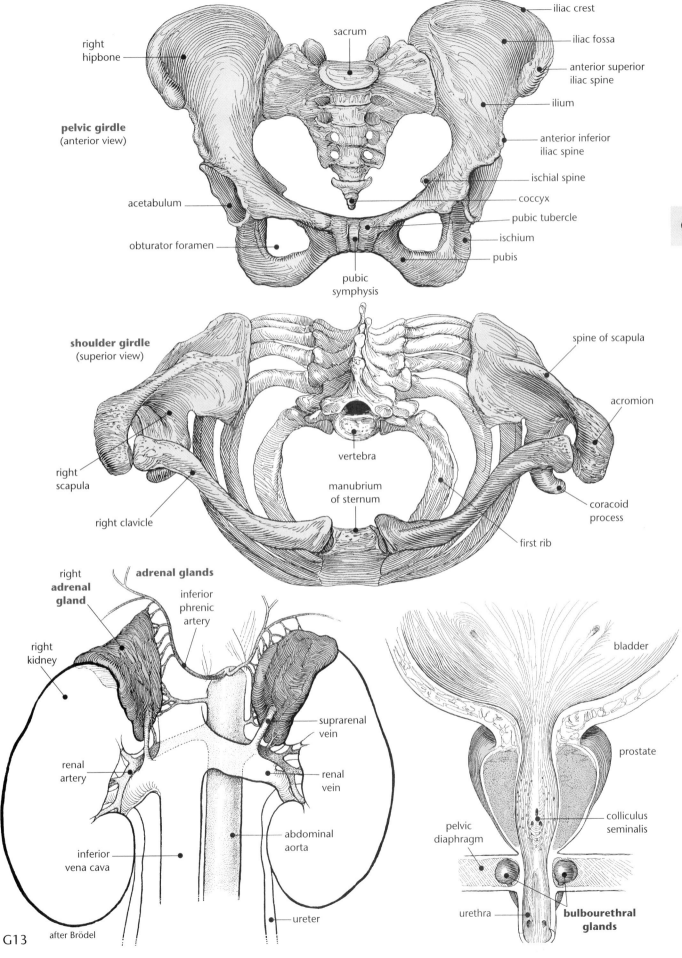

pelvic girdle
(anterior view)

right
hipbone

sacrum

iliac crest

iliac fossa

anterior superior
iliac spine

ilium

anterior inferior
iliac spine

ischial spine

acetabulum

coccyx

pubic tubercle

obturator foramen

ischium

pubis

pubic
symphysis

G

shoulder girdle
(superior view)

spine of scapula

acromion

right
scapula

vertebra

manubrium
of sternum

coracoid
process

right clavicle

first rib

right
**adrenal
gland**

adrenal glands

inferior
phrenic
artery

bladder

right
kidney

suprarenal
vein

prostate

renal
artery

renal
vein

colliculus
seminalis

abdominal
aorta

pelvic
diaphragm

inferior
vena cava

urethra

bulbourethral
glands

ureter

after Brödel

G13

urogenital diaphragm on each side of the membranous portion of the male urethra, just above the bulb of the corpus spongiosum; the excretory ducts, about 1 inch long, pass obliquely downward to open in the spongy (bulbous) portion of the urethra; during sexual stimulation, the glands secrete a mucuslike substance into the urethra that serves as a lubricant for the urethral epithelium. Also called Cowper's glands; bulbocavernous glands.

cardiac g.'s The tubular, branched, slightly coiled, predominantly mucus-secreting glands located in the transition zone between the esophagus and the cardiac orifice of the stomach; they also secrete electrolytes.

ceruminous g.'s Modified apocrine sweat glands in the thick subcutaneous tissue of the outer part of the external auditory canal; the ducts open onto the epithelial surface of the canal or into a neighboring sebaceous gland of a hair follicle; they secrete ear wax (cerumen), which prevents maceration of the canal's lining.

ciliary g.'s See Moll's glands.

compound g. An exocrine gland composed of numerous small sacs (acini) whose excretory ducts combine to form larger ones, as seen in the pancreas and salivary glands.

Cowper's g.'s See bulbourethral glands.

ductless g. A gland with no excretory duct; an endocrine gland.

duodenal g.'s Small, branched, compound tubular glands in the submucosa of the duodenum, principally the first (superior) part; they secrete an alkaline mucoid substance into the intestinal glands (crypts of Lieberkühn) or directly to the surface of the lumen between the duodenal villi. Also called Brunner's glands.

Ebner's g. See gustatory gland.

eccrine g. A gland that delivers its secretion onto the surface of the skin, via a single duct; found in almost every part of the skin, being especially large in regions where perspiration is profuse, as in the armpit (axilla) and in the groin.

endocrine g.'s A group of ductless glands or portions of a gland, whose secretion (hormone) is discharged directly into the bloodstream and transported to distant effector cells; the secretion has an important influence on body functions.

endoexocrine g. A gland that produces both internal and external secretions (e.g., the pancreas, which secretes hormones internally into the bloodstream, and enzymes externally into the duodenum).

exocrine g. A gland that discharges its secretion through a duct or series of ducts onto the internal or external surface of the body (e.g., salivary and sweat glands); it may be a simple gland or compound gland.

gastric g.'s, proper Numerous straight, sometimes branched, tubular glands in the mucosa of the fundus and body of the stomach that open into the bottom of the gastric pits (absent in the cardiac and pyloric regions of the stomach); they contain cells that produce digestive enzymes of the stomach. Also called peptic glands.

greater vestibular g.'s Two small mucus-secreting glands on either side of the vaginal orifice, with their ducts opening between the hymen and the labia minus; their major function is the production of lubrication of the introitus. Also called Bartholin's glands; vulvovaginal glands.

gustatory g. One of the specialized mucin-secreting glands in the tongue near the taste buds. Also called von Ebner's gland; Ebner's gland.

holocrine g. An exocrine gland whose secretion includes a portion of the disintegrated cells of the gland itself (e.g., the sebaceous gland).

interscapular g. See brown fat, under fat.

intestinal g.'s Numerous simple tubular glands in the mucous membrane throughout the small and large intestines, concerned with the secretion of digestive enzymes and some hormones; the intestinal glands in the epithelium of the large intestine are especially rich in goblet cells. Also called crypts of Lieberkühn.

labial g.'s of mouth Small salivary glands embedded in the lips between the mucous membrane and the orbicular muscle of mouth; they secrete mucus into the vestibule of the mouth.

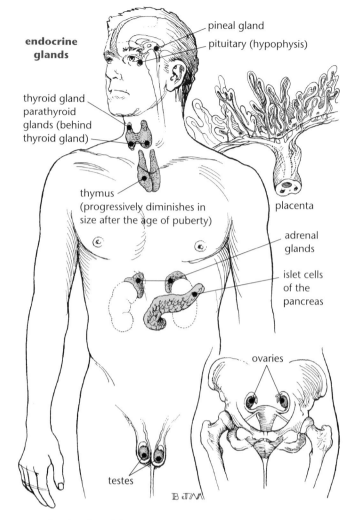

endocrine glands

pineal gland
pituitary (hypophysis)
thyroid gland
parathyroid glands (behind thyroid gland)
thymus (progressively diminishes in size after the age of puberty)
placenta
adrenal glands
islet cells of the pancreas
ovaries
testes

lacrimal g. A lobulated tubuloacinar gland (the size and shape of an almond) situated in the upper lateral corner of each orbit; consists of a larger upper orbital part and a lower palpebral part. It secretes tears into the superior fornix of the conjunctiva through 10 to 12 fine excretory ducts.

Littre's g.'s See urethral glands of male urethra.

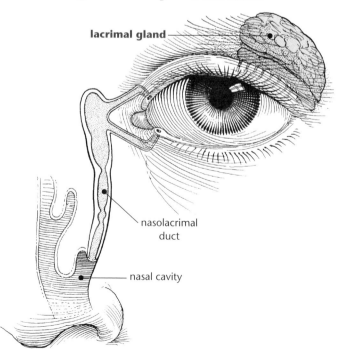

lacrimal gland
nasolacrimal duct
nasal cavity

gland ■ gland

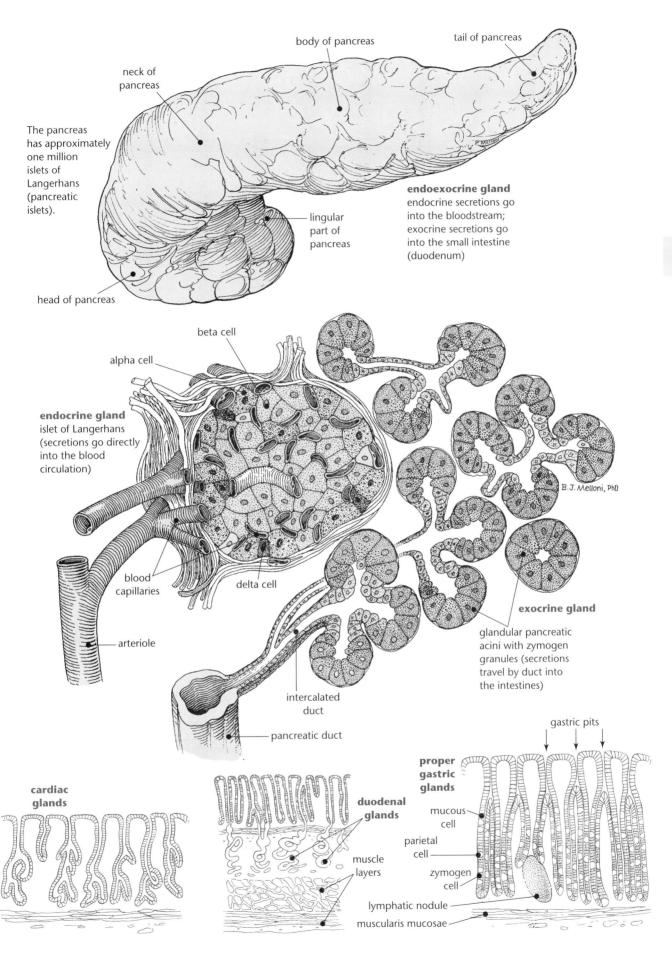

body of pancreas

tail of pancreas

neck of pancreas

The pancreas has approximately one million islets of Langerhans (pancreatic islets).

lingular part of pancreas

endoexocrine gland
endocrine secretions go into the bloodstream; exocrine secretions go into the small intestine (duodenum)

head of pancreas

beta cell

alpha cell

endocrine gland
islet of Langerhans (secretions go directly into the blood circulation)

blood capillaries

delta cell

arteriole

exocrine gland

glandular pancreatic acini with zymogen granules (secretions travel by duct into the intestines)

intercalated duct

pancreatic duct

gastric pits

proper gastric glands

cardiac glands

duodenal glands

muscle layers

mucous cell

parietal cell

zymogen cell

lymphatic nodule

muscularis mucosae

gland ■ gland

G

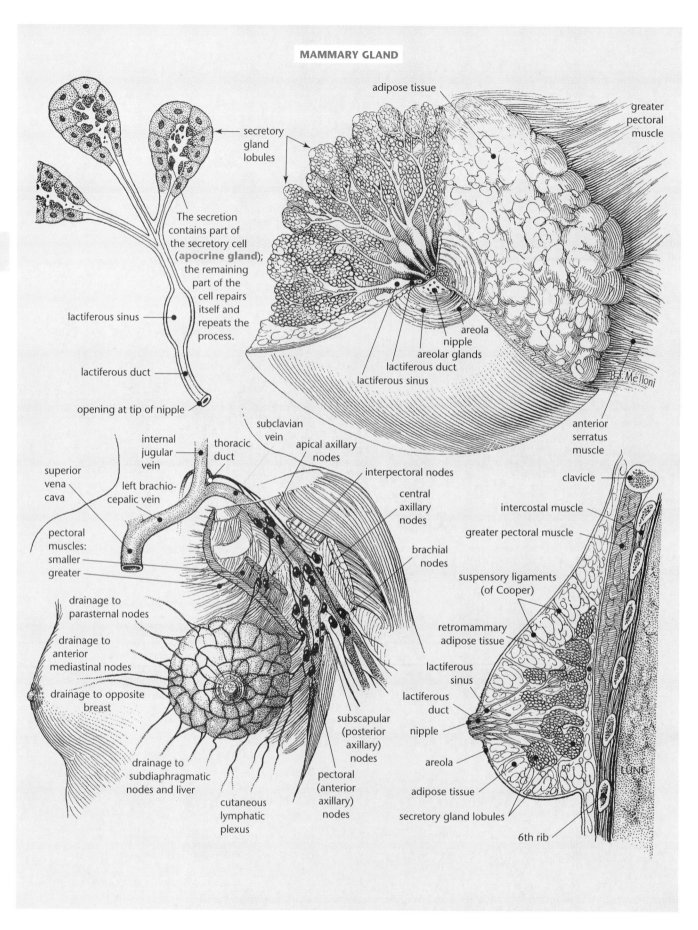

secretory gland lobules

The secretion contains part of the secretory cell (**apocrine gland**); the remaining part of the cell repairs itself and repeats the process.

lactiferous sinus

lactiferous duct

opening at tip of nipple

adipose tissue

greater pectoral muscle

areola
nipple
areolar glands
lactiferous duct
lactiferous sinus

anterior serratus muscle

B.J. Melloni

subclavian vein

internal jugular vein

thoracic duct

apical axillary nodes

interpectoral nodes

central axillary nodes

brachial nodes

superior vena cava

left brachio-cepalic vein

pectoral muscles:
smaller
greater

drainage to parasternal nodes

drainage to anterior mediastinal nodes

drainage to opposite breast

drainage to subdiaphragmatic nodes and liver

cutaneous lymphatic plexus

subscapular (posterior axillary) nodes

pectoral (anterior axillary) nodes

clavicle

intercostal muscle

greater pectoral muscle

suspensory ligaments (of Cooper)

retromammary adipose tissue

lactiferous sinus

lactiferous duct

nipple

areola

adipose tissue

secretory gland lobules

6th rib

LUNG

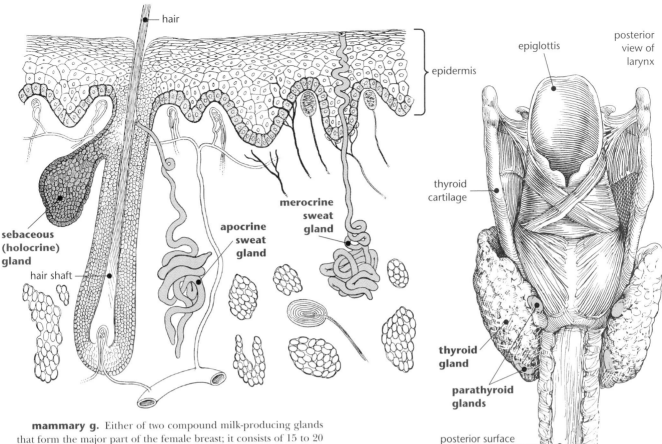

hair

epidermis

sebaceous (holocrine) gland

hair shaft

apocrine sweat gland

merocrine sweat gland

epiglottis

posterior view of larynx

thyroid cartilage

thyroid gland

parathyroid glands

posterior surface of trachea

mammary g. Either of two compound milk-producing glands that form the major part of the female breast; it consists of 15 to 20 lobes, each of which has a separate lactiferous duct opening at the apex of the nipple (papilla); it reaches functional maturity after pregnancy. In the male, the mammary gland is rudimentary.

meibomian g.'s See tarsal glands of eyelid.

merocrine g. A gland whose secretory cells remain intact while forming and discharging the secretory product, as those in the salivary glands and some sweat glands.

mixed g. An exocrine gland in which some secretory units contain both serous and mucous cells (e.g., the submandibular gland). Also called seromucous gland.

Moll's g.'s Rows of rudimentary sweat glands near the free margin of the eyelid, with ducts that usually open into the follicles of the eyelashes. Also called ciliary glands.

mucous g. A gland that secretes fluid rich in mucin, such as those of the intestines, larynx, lips, nose, palate, and tongue.

palatine g.'s Numerous small mucus-secreting salivary glands, positioned in the mucous membrane of the oral and nasopharyngeal surfaces of the soft palate, and between the mucous membrane and the periosteum of the posterior half of the hard palate.

palpebral g.'s See tarsal glands of eyelid.

parathyroid g.'s The smallest of the endocrine glands, situated between the posterior surface of the thyroid gland and its capsule; usually four in number (two superior and two inferior), each the approximate size of an apple seed; they produce parathyroid hormone (parathormone), which regulates the calcium and phosphate metabolism of the body.

paraurethral g.'s The glands in the lining of the lower end of the female urethra that convey mucus just within the external urethral orifice by way of the paraurethral ducts on each side. Also called Skene's glands.

parotid g. The largest of the salivary glands (average weight in adults, 25 grams), located below and in front of each ear; it secretes saliva directly into the mouth by way of the parotid duct.

peptic g.'s See gastric glands proper.

perspiratory g.'s See sweat glands.

pineal g. See pineal body, under body.

pituitary g. See hypophysis.

preputial g.'s Numerous small glands on the glans and the

neck of the penis that secrete a sebaceous material, smegma.

pyloric g. One of the simple, coiled tubular glands that open into a conical pit in the pyloric part of the stomach; the cells are predominantly mucus in type with occasional parietal (oxyntic) cells; it also secretes some gastrin, an enteric hormone that increases stomach motility and secretory activity.

racemose g. An exocrine gland whose acini are arranged like grapes on a stem (e.g., parotid gland).

salivary g. Any of two groups of glands that discharge saliva into the mouth: *Major salivary g.'s*, the three large paired glands (parotid, submandibular, and sublingual) that secrete saliva into the mouth by way of extraglandular ducts to assist the process of digestion. *Minor salivary g.'s*, the many small glands that lie in the mucosa and submucosa of the mouth (lingual, labial, buccal, palatine, and gustatory) and whose secretions provide lubrication for swallowing and speech; also secrete digestive enzymes.

sebaceous g. A simple branched holocrine gland in the dermis of the skin that usually opens into the distal part of the hair follicle and secretes an oily substance (sebum); some sebaceous glands open directly onto the skin surface, such as on the vermilion border of the lips.

sebaceous g.'s of conjunctiva See glands of Zeis.

seromucous g. See mixed gland.

serous g. A gland with granular cytoplasm that secretes a thin watery fluid containing proteins, such as lysozyme or digestive enzymes.

simple g. An exocrine gland that discharges directly into a nonbranching duct; the type of gland can be tubular, tubuloalveolar, or alveolar.

Skene's g.'s See paraurethral glands.

sublingual g. One of two salivary glands located beneath the mucous membrane of the floor of the mouth, where it forms the sublingual fold; the majority of its 12 excretory ducts leave the superior surface of the gland and, for the most part, open individually into the floor of the mouth on the summit of the sublingual fold; some of the ducts arising from the anterior part of the gland usually combine to form a major sublingual duct that generally opens at the sublingual

section through shoulder and neck

scapula · vertebra · spinal cord · 1st rib · scapula · head of humerus · deltoid muscle · platysma · clavicle · sternocleido-mastoid muscle · THYROID GLAND · trachea · esophagus · sterno-thyroid muscle · parathyroid gland · internal jugular vein · anterior scalene muscle · common carotid artery

lesser horn of hyoid bone · greater horn of hyoid bone · epiglottis · hyoid bone · medial thyro-hyoid ligament · thyroid cartilage · cricoid cartilage · THYROID GLAND · trachea · esophagus · anterior view

epiglottis · foramen for superior laryngeal vessels and internal laryngeal nerve · middle pharyngeal constrictor muscle · superior parathyroid gland · inferior parathyroid gland · posterior view

follicles of thyroid gland · colloidal iodinated thyroglobulin · iodine · thyroglobulin secretion · thyroid follicle cell · iodide · amino acid radicals · hormone · fenestrated blood capillary · T_3, T_4 · T_3, T_4 · lymph capillary

T_3 (tri-iodothyroine)
T_4 (tetra-iodothyroine)

B.J.Melloni, PhD

caruncle near the frenulum of the tongue; most of the secretory units are mucus-secreting with some serous demilunes; it is the smallest of the three paired salivary glands.

submandibular g. One of the three paired salivary glands, which lies under cover of the ramus of the mandible (submandibular fossa) and partly extending into the upper neck; its long excretory duct runs forward to open in the floor of the mouth beneath the tongue on each side of the frenulum.

sudoriferous g.'s See sweat glands.

suprarenal g.'s See adrenal glands.

sweat g.'s Coiled tubular glands located deep in the skin; they secrete sweat, which is rich in sodium and chloride. Also called sudoriferous glands; perspiratory glands.

tarsal g.'s of eyelid Twenty to 30 modified sebaceous glands embedded in vertical grooves in the tarsus of each eyelid; their ducts open on the inner free margin of the eyelid by minute foramina; the oily secretion of the glands reduces evaporation of the tear film on the eye and also forms a barrier on the margin of the eyelid that tends to prevent or delay tears from overflowing onto the cheek. Also called meibomian glands; palpebral glands.

thymus g. See thymus.

thyroid g. The largest endocrine gland in humans, with an average weight of 25 grams in the adult male; slightly heavier in the female; situated in front of the lower part of the neck, and

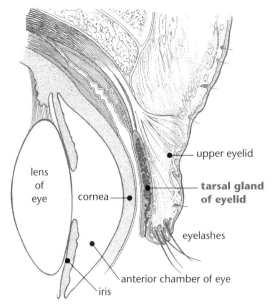

lens of eye

cornea

upper eyelid

tarsal gland of eyelid

eyelashes

anterior chamber of eye

iris

consisting of right and left lobes, on either side of the trachea, joined by a connecting isthmus; it secretes the iodine-rich hormones thyroxine (T_4) and triiodothyronine (T_3), which are concerned with regulating the rate of metabolism; also secretes thyrocalcitonin, important in calcium metabolism.

   tubular g. An exocrine gland consisting of cells around one or more tubules closed at one end.

   urethral g.'s of female urethra Many small mucous glands that open into the proximal part of the female urethra; considered to be the homologue of the male prostate.

   urethral g.'s of male urethra Numerous small mucous glands located in the lining of the proximal two-thirds of the spongy part of the male urethra. Also called Littre's glands.

   von Ebner's g. See gustatory gland.

   vulvovaginal g.'s See greater vestibular glands.

   g.'s of Zeis Modified rudimentary sebaceous glands with ducts that open into the follicles of eyelashes. Also called sebaceous glands of conjunctiva.

glanders (glan'derz) An infectious disease of horses, mules, and donkeys, caused by the gram-negative bacillus *Pseudomonas mallei;* occasionally transmitted to humans, causing skin lesions, pneumonia, or blood poisoning (septicemia); the cutaneous form is called farcy.

glandilemma (glan-dĭ-lem'ah) The enveloping membrane of a gland.

glandula (glan'du-lah) A small gland; a glandule.

glandular (glan'du-lar) Relating to a gland.

glandule (glan'dūl) A small gland.

glans (glanz), pl. glan'des A small glandlike structure.

   g. clitoridis, g. of clitoris The small rounded tip of the body of the clitoris.

   g. penis The caplike extension of the corpus spongiosum at the tip of the penis. Commonly called head of penis.

glass (glas) A hard, transparent or transluscent material composed of sand fused with any of a variety of oxides.

   cover g. A thin glass placed over a histologic specimen for examination under a microscope. Also called coverslip.

   crown g. Compound of lime, potash, alumina, and silica; used in ophthalmic lenses.

   quartz g. Glass made by fusing pure quartz sand; it transmits ultraviolet rays.

   Wood's g. A nickle oxide glass used with ultraviolet light to filter out visible light in order to detect fluorescence; used for diagnostic purposes (e.g., ringworm of the scalp), and for visualizing abrasions of the cornea.

glaucoma (glaw-ko'mah) Abnormally increased pressure within the eye.

   acute g. See angle-closure glaucoma.

   angle-closure g. Glaucoma of sudden onset occurring when the outermost part of the iris is pushed against the inner periphery of the cornea, closing the anterior chamber angle and preventing the outflow of aqueous humor from the anterior chamber of the eye; the condition may be precipitated by drugs used to dilate the pupil, or may result from hemorrhage or swelling of the iris or of the ciliary body; symptoms include pain, loss of vision, dilatation of pupil, and redness of the eye. Also called acute glaucoma; narrow-angle glaucoma.

   congenital g. See buphthalmos.

   narrow-angle g. See angle-closure glaucoma.

   open-angle g. A chronic, slowly progressive, bilateral glaucoma due to some defect in the trabecular meshwork of the anterior

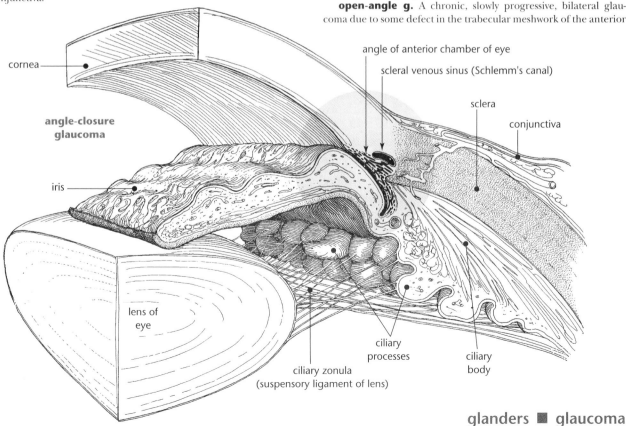

cornea

angle-closure glaucoma

iris

lens of eye

ciliary zonula (suspensory ligament of lens)

ciliary processes

ciliary body

angle of anterior chamber of eye

scleral venous sinus (Schlemm's canal)

sclera

conjunctiva

chamber, which prevents adequate drainage of aqueous humor; the condition is asymptomatic until late in its course when visual loss occurs due to optic nerve damage by the persistent elevated ocular pressure.

phacolytic g. Glaucoma occurring as a complication of cataract; fluid from the liquefied cortex of the lens seeps into the anterior chamber of the eye, causing swelling of the uvea, which obstructs the outflow system and prevents adequate escape of aqueous humor from the anterior chamber.

secondary g. Increased ocular pressure occurring as a manifestation of another, preexisting, intraocular disease.

glenohumeral (gle-no-hu′mer-al) Relating to the glenoid fossa of the shoulder blade (scapula) and the articulating humerus.

glenoid (gle′noid) Resembling a socket; applied to an articular depression on a bone.

glia (gli′ah) See neuroglia.

gliacyte (gli′ah-sit) A cell of the nonnervous components of brain and spinal cord tissues.

gliadin (gli′ah-din) Any of various simple proteins obtained from wheat and rye glutens. Also called glutin.

glial (gli′al) Relating to the nonnervous components of brain and spinal cord tissues.

glide (glid) An effortless movement.

mandibular g. Lateral and protrusive movements of the lower jaw when the occluding surfaces of the teeth are in contact.

glioblastoma (gli-o-blas-to′mah) General term for malignant growths containing neuroglial cells. See also astrocytoma.

g. multiforme The most malignant and rapidly growing tumor of the brain, composed of undifferentiated cells. Now called grade IV astrocytoma.

glioma (gli-o′mah) In general, any tumor derived from various types of cells that make up brain tissue (e.g., astrocytoma, oligodendroglioma, ependymoma, choroid plexus papilloma).

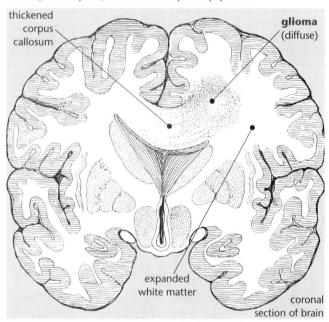

coronal section of brain

gliomatosis (gli-o-mah-to′sis) The presence of gliomas in the brain. Also called neurogliomatosis.

gliomatous (gli-o′mah-tus) Relating to a glioma.

gliosis (gli-o′sis) Overgrowth of the nonnervous cellular elements of the brain and spinal cord.

globin (glo′bin) A simple protein constituent of the blood pigment hemoglobin.

globule (glob′ul) A minute spherical body.

Morgagni's g.'s Minute opaque globules of fluid beneath the capsule and lens fibers of the eye, sometimes seen in cataract formation.

globulin (glob′u-lin) Any of a category of simple proteins that are insoluble in water, soluble in saline solutions, and coagulable by heat; found in blood and cerebrospinal fluid; human serum globulin is divided into alpha, beta, and gamma fractions on the basis of electrophoretic mobility.

accelerator g. (AcG, ac-g) A blood-coagulating factor of plasma that speeds the conversion of prothrombin to thrombin in the presence of thromboplastin and ionized calcium. Also called accelerin; factor V.

gamma g.'s Serum proteins that constitute the majority of immunoglobulins and antibodies; used in the prevention of numerous diseases, including measles and certain types of hepatitis. Also written γ-globulins.

Total **Gamma Globulin** Levels in Serum of Normal Subjects

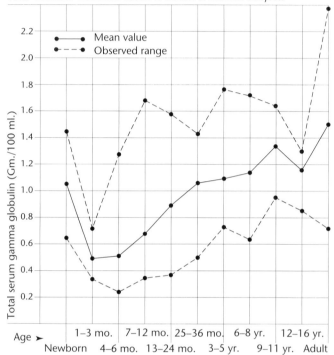

immune serum g. A sterile preparation containing a number of antibodies normally present in adult human blood; used as an immunizing agent.

thyroxin-binding g. (TBG) An alpha globulin with a strong affinity for the hormone thyroxin; it acts as a carrier of thyroxin in the blood; significant changes in the levels of TBG may alter measured T_4 levels.

globulinuria (glob-u-lin-u′re-ah) The presence of globulin in the urine.

globus (glo′bus) A globular structure or ball.

g. hystericus A hysterical sensation of having a lump or ball in the throat.

g. pallidus The inner gray portion of the lentiform nucleus in the brain.

glomangioma (glo-man-je-o′mah) See glomus tumor, under tumor.

glomerular (glo-mer′u-lar) Relating to a glomerulus.

glomeruli (glo-mer′u-li) Plural of glomerulus.

glomerulitis (glo-mer-u-li′tis) Inflammation of the glomeruli of the kidney.

glomerulonephritis (glo-mer-u-lo-ně-fri′tis) (GN) Kidney disease characterized by changes in the structure of the filtering units (glomeruli) within the kidney; may be acute, subacute, or chronic.

acute crescentic g. See rapidly progressive glomerulonephritis.

acute proliferative g. Disorder occurring chiefly in children and sometimes in young adults, most often following streptococcal infections; characterized by development (over days) of high blood pressure, swelling around the eyes, fluid retention, presence of blood and protein in the urine, red blood cell casts, and sometimes diminished urine output. Also called acute nephritis; proliferative glomerulonephritis.

chronic g. Glomerulonephritis of insidious onset or occurring as a sequel to acute glomerulonephritis; characterized by excretion of protein in the urine, slow progressive impairment of kidney function, and eventual kidney failure; high blood pressure is common; kidneys become symmetrically shrunken and granular. Also called chronic nephritis.

diffuse g. Glomerulonephritis involving most of the kidney glomeruli.

focal embolic g. A complication of subacute bacterial endocarditis.

focal proliferative g. A glomerular proliferation and/or damage restricted to segments of some glomeruli; may be a mild condition or a manifestation of a more serious progressive disease (e.g., lupus erythematosus, polyarteritis nodosa, Goodpasture's syndrome).

global g. Complete involvement of the affected glomerulus, as opposed to involvement of restricted segments or segmental glomerulonephritis.

hypocomplementemic g. See membranoproliferative glomerulonephritis.

lobular g. See membranoproliferative glomerulonephritis.

membranoproliferative g. (MPGN) Disease of children and young adults characterized primarily by a combination of thickening of the capillary loops and proliferation of glomerular cells, causing symptoms suggesting either acute glomerulonephritis or a nephrotic syndrome, with excretion of microscopic blood in the urine; some types involve the immune system, with complement depression ranging from intermittent to persistent. Two distinct patterns are recognized: *type I*, associated with the presence of immunoglobulins; *type II*, with characteristic dense, ribbonlike deposits in capillary walls. Also called mesangiocapillary glomerulonephritis; hypocomplementemic glomerulonephritis; lobular glomerulonephritis.

membranous g. (MGN) Disease of the glomerulus characterized by immunoglobulin-containing deposits in the capillary walls and thickening of the basement membrane; manifested by generalized swelling and excretion of protein in the urine and other features of the nephrotic syndrome; may be due to an underlying disease (e.g., hepatitis B, tumors, systemic lupus erythematosus) or exposure to certain drugs.

mesangiocapillary g. See membranoproliferative glomerulonephritis.

proliferative g. See acute proliferative glomerulonephritis.

rapidly progressive g. Disease of the glomerulus characterized by accumulation of cells in the form of crescents in the Bowman's (glomerular) capsule, within the urinary space; characterized by a gradual onset and progressing rapidly to kidney failure and death within weeks to months; may occur as a complication of other types of glomerulonephritis, or in the course of an underlying systemic disease. Also called acute crescentic glomerulonephritis.

subacute g. A term used variously to describe rapidly progressive glomerulonephritis, or a type with a nephrotic syndrome and a prolonged course.

glomerulopathy (glo-mer-u-lop'ah-the) Any disease of the filtering units (glomeruli) of the kidney.

glomerulosclerosis (glo-mer-u-lo-skle-ro'sis) Scarring and degeneration of the structures within the filtering units (glomeruli) of the kidney. Seen in diabetes, in remnant kidneys, and in focal sclerosing glomerulonephritis (FSGN).

diabetic g. Glomerulosclerosis in which scarring occurs in a nodular pattern at the periphery of the glomeruli; occurs as a complication of diabetes mellitus, predominantly the insulin-dependent type; associated with excretion of protein in the urine, swelling of soft tissues, and high blood pressure.

glomerulus (glo-mer'u-lus), pl. glomer'uli **1.** A small cluster of nerves or minute blood vessels (capillaries); when used alone the term refers to the filtering unit of the kidney, a tuft of capillaries at the beginning of each uriniferous tubule within the kidney. Also called glomerular tuft. **2.** The coiled secretory portion of a sweat gland.

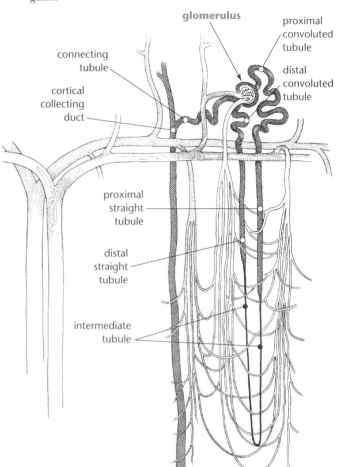

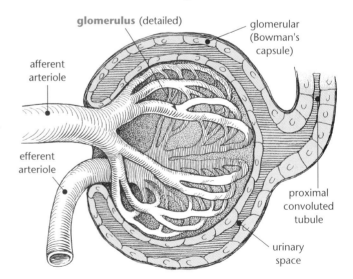

glomus (glo'mus) A small round nodule composed of connected (anastomosed) minute arteries and veins and provided with a rich nerve supply.

g. jugular A glomus in the connective tissue surrounding a jugular bulb; serves as a chemoreceptor.

glossal (glos'al) Relating to the tongue; lingual.

glossalgia (glos-sal'je-ah) Pain in the tongue. Also called glossodynia.

glossectomy (glos-sek'to-me) Removal of the tongue, or a portion of it.

Glossina (glos-si'nah) Genus of bloodsucking flies, the tsetse flies, which are the vectors of microorganisms causing African sleeping sickness (trypanosomiasis).

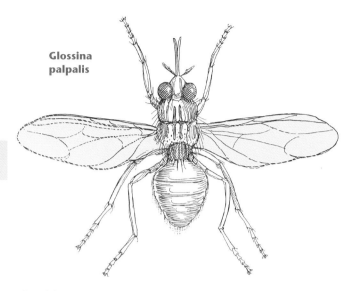

Glossina
palpalis

glossitis (glos-si'tis) Inflammation of the tongue.
   benign migratory g. See geographic tongue, under tongue.
glosso-, gloss- Combining forms meaning tongue.
glossodynia (glos-o-din'e-ah) See glossalgia.
glossograph (glos'o-graf) Instrument for recording the tongue movements while speaking.
glossolalia (glos-o-la'le-ah) Meaningless speech; nonsensical, rapid chatter; gibberish.
glossolysis (glos-ol'ĭ-sis) See glossoplegia.
glossopharyngeal (glos-o-fah-rin'je-al) Relating to the tongue and the space behind it (pharynx).
glossoplasty (glos'o-plas-te) Reparative surgery of the tongue.
glossoplegia (glos-o-ple'je-ah) Paralysis of the tongue. Also called glossolysis.
glossoptosis (glos-op-to'sis) A downward and backward displacement of the tongue, usually of an abnormally small tongue.
glossorrhaphy (glŏ-sor'ah-fe) Suturing of the tongue.
glossospasm (glos'o-spazm) Spasmodic contraction of the tongue.
glossotomy (glŏ-sot'o-me) A surgical cut into the tongue.
glossotrichia (glos-o-trik'e-ah) See black tongue, under tongue.
glottic (glot'ik) 1. Relating to the tongue. 2. Relating to the glottis.
glottides (glot'ĭ-dēz) Plural of glottis.
glottis (glot'is), pl. glot'tides The vocal apparatus located in the larynx; consists of a fold of mucous membrane (vocal fold) covering the vocal ligament and muscle (vocal cord) on each side and the opening between them.
glottitis (glŏ-ti'tis) Inflammation of the vocal apparatus of the larynx.
glucagon (gloo'kah-gon) A polypeptide hormone, normally produced by alpha cells of the islets of Langerhans in the pancreas when the blood sugar level gets too low; it aids in the breakdown of the sugar glycogen in the liver, thus elevating the blood sugar concentration.
glucagonoma (gloo-kah-gon-o'mah) A glucagon-secreting tumor of the alpha cells in the pancreas, associated with a distinctive skin rash, weight loss, formation of canker sores in the oral mucosa, mild diabetes, and anemia.
glucan (gloo'kan) Any polyglucose (e.g., starch amylose, glycogen amylose).
gluco- Combining form meaning glucose.
glucocorticoid (gloo-ko-kor'tĭ-koid) Any of a class of steroid hormones produced by the adrenal cortex (or synthetically) that stimulate gluconeogenesis and glycogen formation in the liver and

tend to raise blood glucose levels; other properties include anti-inflammatory activity and ability to suppress the synthesis of adrenocorticotropic hormone (ACTH) and melanocyte-stimulating hormone (MSH). The major natural glucocorticoid in humans is cortisol.
glucokinetic (gloo-ko-kĭ-net'ik) Tending to mobilize the sugar glucose in the body (e.g., in the maintenance of sugar level).
gluconeogenesis (gloo-ko-ne-o-jen'ĕ-sis) See glyconeogenesis.
glucosamine (gloo-kōs'ah-mēn) An amino sugar present in many mucopolysaccharides (as in cell membranes and bacterial cell walls).
glucose (gloo'kōs) A simple sugar (monosaccharide) present in plant and animal tissues and obtained synthetically from starch; it is the body's chief source of energy for cell metabolism; its concentration in the blood is regulated by several hormones (especially insulin and glucagon); normal human blood levels range from 70 to 120 mg per 100 ml; an excess of 180 mg is excreted in the urine. Also called dextrose; blood sugar.
glucose 6-phosphatase (gloo'kōs fos'fah-tās) (G6P) Enzyme that promotes the hydrolysis of glucose 6-phosphate to glucose and inorganic phosphate; present in liver, kidney, intestinal lining, and the lining of the uterus (endometrium); it enables the liver to regulate blood sugar (glucose) concentration. Inherited deficiency of the enzyme results in a glycogen storage disease, type I glycogenosis.
glucose 6-phosphate dehydrogenase (gloo'kōs fos'fāt de-hi'dro-jen-ās) (G6PD) An enzyme that promotes the oxidation of glucose 6-phosphate to 6-phosphogluconolactone; abnormally low levels in red blood cells (genetically determined) may make the red blood cells unusually susceptible to destruction by certain drugs.
glucosuria (gloo-ko-su're-ah) The presence of sugar (glucose) in the urine.
glucuronic acid (gloo-ku-ron'ik as'id) The uronic acid of glucose; it inactivates various substances (e.g., benzoic acid and the female hormones); the glucuronides so formed are excreted in the urine.
glucuronide (gloo-ku-ron'īd) Any glycoside of glucuronic acid. Many substances (e.g., steroid metabolites) are excreted in the urine as glucuronides.
glue-sniffing (gloo snif'ing) The practice of inhaling the fumes given off by plastic cement to experience its intoxicating effect; it produces stimulation of the central nervous system followed by depression. It is a potentially fatal form of substance abuse.
glutamic acid (gloo-tam'ik as'id) (Glu) An amino acid present in protein; involved in ammonia production in the kidney.
glutamine (gloo'tah-min) (Gln) An amino acid found as a constituent of proteins and in free form in the blood; it yields glutamic acid ammonia on hydrolysis.
glutaraldehyde (gloo-tah-ral'dĕ-hīd) A chemical commonly used as a fixative in tissue preservation for electron microscopy; it is a frequent cause of occupational allergic contact dermatitis.
gluteal (gloo'te-al) Relating to the buttocks.
gluteus (gloo'te-us) Any of the three muscles of the buttock. See table of muscles.
glutin (gloo'tin) See gliadin.
glutinous (gloo'tĭ-nus) Sticky.
glutitis (gloo-ti'tis) Inflammation of the gluteus muscles of the buttocks.
glycemia (gli-se'me-ah) The presence of sugar (glucose) in the blood.
glycerin (glis'er-in) A syrupy sweet liquid used as a sweetener, a lubricant, and a solvent in various pharmaceutical preparations. See also glycerol.
glycerol (glis'er-ol) A syrupy alcohol produced by the fermentation of sugar; pharmaceutical preparations are known as glycerin.
glycine (gli'sēn) (Gly) The principal amino acid present in sugarcane and a major component of gelatin; it is the simplest amino acid in protein.
glycinuria (gli-si-nu're-ah) The presence of glycine in the urine.
glyco- Combining form meaning sugar.

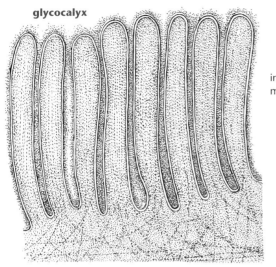

glycocalyx

intestinal microvilli

glycocalyx (gli-ko-kal'iks) A fuzzy coating of certain epithelial cells that is rich in mucoid components.

glycocholic acid (gli-ko-ko'lik as'id) The principal acid of bile.

glycogen (gli'ko-jen) The form in which carbohydrate is stored in the body, especially in the liver and muscles; it is broken down to glucose as needed.

glycogenase (gli'ko-jĕ-nās) Enzyme that promotes the breakdown of glycogen to glucose.

glycogenesis (gli-ko-jen'ĕ-sis) The formation of glycogen from glucose or other monosaccharides.

glycogenolysis (gli-ko-jĕ-nol'ĭ-sis) The breakdown of glycogen to simpler products.

glycogenosis (gli-ko-jĕ-no'sis), pl. glycogeno'ses Abnormal accumulation of glycogen in the tissues; caused by deficiency of an enzyme involved in glycogen metabolism. Also called glycogen storage disease.

    type I g. Disorder caused by deficiency of the liver enzyme glucose 6-phosphatase, resulting in excessive accumulation of glycogen in the liver and kidneys (because it cannot be broken down to free glucose) and low blood glucose levels (hypoglycemia). Also called von Gierke's disease.

    type II g. Disease of infancy caused by deficiency of an enzyme, lysosomal alpha-1,4-glucosidase, resulting in accumulation of glycogen in several organs, particularly in the heart muscle; newborn infants have massive enlargement of the heart; death results from cardiac failure by two years of age. Also called Pompe's disease.

    type V g. Disease caused by deficiency of phosphorylase, an enzyme that fuels the breakdown of glycogen, an energy-producing process in skeletal muscles; results in accumulation of glycogen in the muscles, with weakness and muscle cramps induced by exercise. Also called McArdle's disease.

glycogeusia (gli-ko-ju'se-ah) A subjective sweet taste in the mouth.

glycolysis (gli-kol'ĭ-sis) The energy-producing process occurring in the body, especially in muscles, in which sugar is broken down into lactic acid; since oxygen is not consumed, it is frequently termed anaerobic glycolysis.

glycolytic (gli-ko-lit'ik) Causing the digestion of sugar.

glyconeogenesis (gli-ko-ne-o-jen'ĕ-sis) The new formation of sugar; the formation of glucose or glycogen from substances other than carbohydrates, such as protein or fat. Also called gluconeogenesis.

glycoprotein (gli-ko-pro'tēn) Any of several protein-carbohydrate compounds (conjugated proteins); they include the mucins, the mucoids, and the chondroproteins.

glycoside (gli'ko-sīd) Any of a group of compounds containing a carbohydrate and a noncarbohydrate residue in the same molecule; on hydrolysis they produce sugars and related compounds; found in animal tissues and in many drugs and spices.

glycosphingolipid (gli-ko-sfing-o-lip'id) A ceramide linked to one or more sugars by the terminal OH group.

glycostatic (gli-ko-stat'ik) Tending to maintain a constant glycogen level in the tissues.

glycosuria (gli-ko-su're-ah) Excessive excretion of sugar in the urine; frequently a sign of diabetes mellitus.

    renal g. Glycosuria occurring with normal blood sugar levels, due to failure of the kidney tubules to reabsorb filtered glucose to the normal degree.

glycosylation (gli-ko-sī-la'shun) Formation, by nonenzymatic means, of linkages with glycosyl groups (e.g., between glucose and the hemoglobin chain to form an electrophoretically fast-moving hemoglobin, the level of which rises in association with elevated blood glucose concentration in poorly controlled diabetes mellitus).

glycyrrhiza (glis-ĭ-ri'zah) The dried roots of the plant *Glycyrrhiza glabra*, used in extracts as a demulcent, and in flavoring some drugs. Also called licorice; licorice root.

gnat (nat) One of several small, winged biting insects; a midge.

    buffalo g. *Simulium pecuarium;* a black gnat, vector of microorganisms causing onchocerciasis.

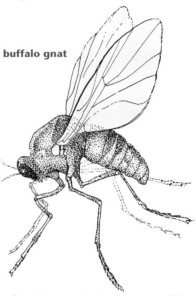

buffalo gnat

gnathic (nath'ik) Relating to the lower jaw (mandible).

gnathion (nath'e-on) The lowest point of the middle of the lower jaw (mandible); a craniometric point.

gnatho-, gnath- Combining forms meaning jaw.

gnathodynamometer (nath'o-di-nah-mom'ĕ-ter) In dentistry, instrument for measuring the biting pressure. Also called bite gauge; occlusometer.

gnathoplasty (nath'o-plas-te) Plastic or reparative surgery of a jaw.

gnathostatics (nath'o-stat'iks) In orthodontic diagnosis, a technique based on relationships between the teeth and certain skull landmarks.

Gnathostoma spinigerum (nath-os'to-mah spin-ig'er-um) A species of parasitic worms frequently transmitted to humans by eating the larvae in undercooked infected fish; it causes migratory swelling of the subcutaneous tissues or abscesses in the intestinal wall; the wandering larvae may also invade the eyes and brain.

gnathostomiasis (nath'o-sto-mi'ah-sis) Infection with *Gnathostoma spinigerum*.

gnotobiotic (no-to-bi-ot'ik) Denoting a laboratory animal that is germ-free or contains only known microorganisms.

goiter (goi'ter) Enlargement of the thyroid gland, causing visible swelling in front of the neck.

    adenomatous g. Goiter due to the presence of a benign tumor composed of glandular tissue.

    colloid g. A marked, soft enlargement of the thyroid gland secondary to massive accumulation of colloid in the follicles.

cystic g. An enlarged thyroid gland containing one or more cysts.

diffuse nontoxic g. A generalized moderate enlargement of the thyroid gland with no evidence of hyper- or hypothyroidism; may progress to colloid goiter or to multinodular goiter. Also called simple goiter.

exophthalmic g. Goiter associated with protrusion of the eyeballs, as seen in Graves' disease.

multinodular g. Enlargement and nodularity of the thyroid gland associated with focal hemorrhage, cyst formation, and scarring; occasionally the gland may extend behind the breastbone, trachea, and esophagus, causing difficult swallowing; may be nontoxic or associated with hyperthyroidism.

simple g. See diffuse nontoxic goiter.

toxic g. A goiter due to overactivity of the thyroid gland, with excessive production of thyroid hormones.

goitrogen (goi′tro-jen) Any agent that produces goiter.

goitrogenic (goi-tro-jen′ik) Causing goiter.

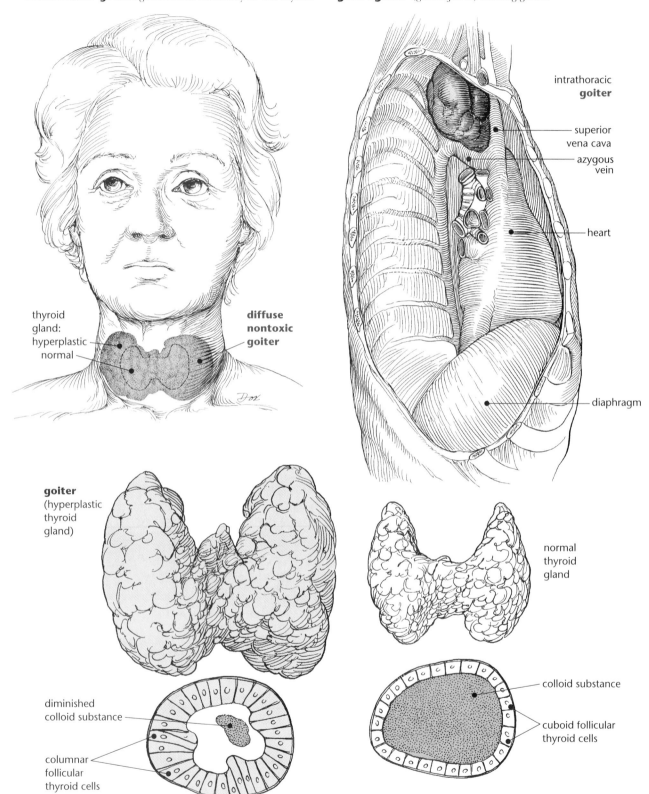

intrathoracic **goiter**

superior vena cava

azygous vein

heart

diaphragm

thyroid gland: hyperplastic normal

diffuse nontoxic goiter

goiter (hyperplastic thyroid gland)

normal thyroid gland

diminished colloid substance

columnar follicular thyroid cells

colloid substance

cuboid follicular thyroid cells

goiter ■ goitrogenic

gold (gōld) A corrosion-resistant element; symbol Au, atomic number 79, atomic weight 196.97.

gomphosis (gom-fo'sis) A type of fibrous articulation in which a bony process fits into a depression of another bone (e.g., a tooth and its socket).

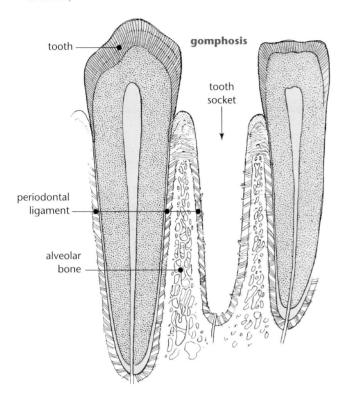

gonad (go'nad) A sexual gland.
  female g. Ovary.
  male g. Testis.

gonadal (go-nad'al) Relating to the ovaries or the testes.

gonadectomy (go-nah-dek'to-me) Removal of an ovary or a testis.

gonado-, gonad- Combining forms relating to the ovaries or testes.

gonadotrophic (gon-ah-do-tro'fik) See gonadotropic.

gonadotropic (gon-ah-do-trōp'ik) Influencing the gonads (e.g., hormones produced by the adenohypophysis, which stimulate the ovaries or testes). Also called gonadotrophic.

gonadotropin (gon-ah-do-tro'pin) Any hormone that stimulates the ovaries or testes.
  chorionic g. (CG) See human chorionic gonadotropin.
  human chorionic g. (hCG) A protein hormone produced by trophoblastic cells that enter into formation of the early placenta (i.e., the syncytiotrophoblast); its secretion begins soon after implantation of the fertilized ovum, with concentration peaking at 60 to 95 days; also produced by abnormal chorionic epithelial tissue such as hydatiform moles, chorioadenoma destruens, and choriocarcinoma; used in diagnostic tests.

gonalgia (go-nal'je-ah) Pain in the knee.

goniometer (go-ne-om'ĕ-ter) **1.** Device for measuring angles. **2.** Device for testing disorders of the inner ear labyrinth. **3.** Device for measuring the range of motion in joints. Also called fleximeter; pronometer; arthrometer.

gonion (go'ne-on) The most posterior, inferior, and lateral point of the external mandibular angle.

gonioscope (go'ne-o-skōp) A combination of a contact lens, magnifying device, and light source for direct viewing of the anterior chamber angle.

gonioscopy (go-ne-os'ko-pe) Examination of the anterior chamber angle of the eye with a gonioscope.

goniosynechia (go'ne-o-sī-nek'e-ah) Adhesion of the iris to the inner surface of the cornea, at its periphery; seen in angle-closure glaucoma.

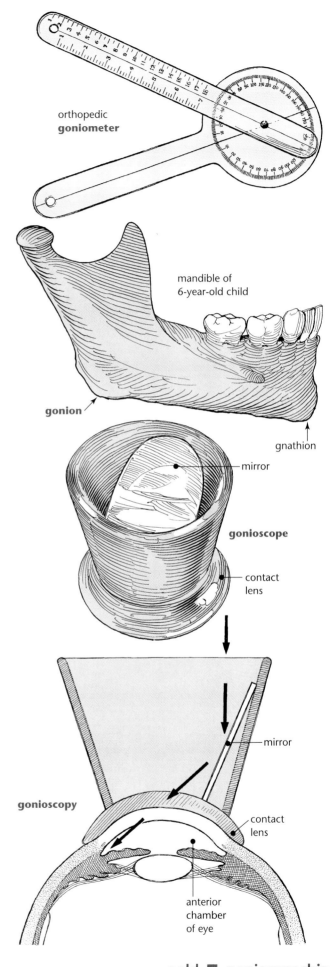

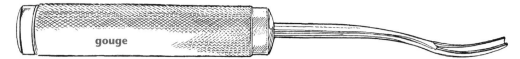

gouge

goniotomy (go-ne-ot′o-me) An eye operation for the management of infantile glaucoma, and sometimes juvenile glaucoma, in which a cut is made through one-third of the trabecular meshwork of the eye; the goniotomy knife is introduced via a puncture made in the opposite area and passed across the anterior chamber; the aqueous humor can then drain into Schlemm's canal (scleral venous sinus).

gonococcal (gon-o-kok′al) Relating to gonococci.

gonococcemia (gon-o-kok-se′me-ah) The presence of gonococci in the blood.

gonococcus (gon-o-kok′us), pl. gonococ′ci The bacterium that causes gonorrhea, *Neisseria gonorrhoeae*.

gonocyte (gon′o-sit) A primitive reproductive cell.

gonorrhea (gon-o-re′ah) A common contagious disease caused by *Neisseria gonorrhoeae*, transmitted chiefly by sexual intercourse; incubation period is two to five days; characterized by inflammation of the mucous membrane of the genital tract, purulent discharge, and painful, frequent urination; if untreated may lead to complications such as epididymitis, prostatitis, tenosynovitis, arthritis, and endocarditis; in females it may lead to sterility, and in males to urethral stricture.

   pharyngeal g. See gonococcal pharyngitis, under pharyngitis.

   rectal g. Gonorrhea of the rectum; may be asymptomatic or cause a purulent discharge, swelling, and pain.

gonorrheal (gon-o-re′al) Relating to gonorrhea.

gonycampsis (gon-ĭ-kamp′sis) Any abnormal curvature of the knee.

gouge (gowj) A strong surgical chisel with a troughlike blade, usually used for cutting and removing bone.

goundou (goon′doo) Endemic disease of West Africa associated with yaws; characterized by egg-shaped bony outgrowths of the maxillae on either side of the nose.

gout (gowt) A group of metabolic disorders that share the following features (which may occur singly or combined): an excess of uric acid in the blood, recurrent painful inflammation of joints, especially of the big toes, and deposits of sodium biurate in the cartilages of affected joints and in the kidneys.

   saturnine g. Gout accompanying lead poisoning.

   secondary g. Gout occurring as a result of increased nucleoprotein metabolism and uric acid production.

   tophaceous g. Gout marked by the presence of deposits of sodium urate (tophi) about the joints and cartilaginous structures.

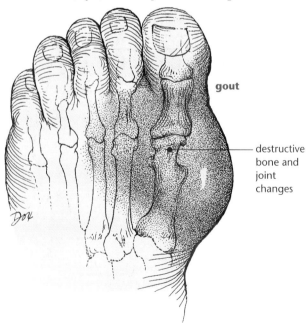

gout

destructive bone and joint changes

gouty (gow′te) Relating to gout.

gradient (gra′de-ent) Change in the value of a variable (e.g., temperature or pressure) per unit distance, time, or other continuously changing influence.

   density g. In a solution, the continuous increase in concentration (density) of a solute from top to bottom of the container.

   mitral g. The difference in diastolic pressure between the left atrium and left ventricle of the heart.

   systolic g. The difference in pressure during systole between two communicating chambers of the heart.

   ventricular g. In electrocardiography, the algebraic sum of the areas within the QRS complex and the T wave of the electrocardiogram.

grading (grād′ing) A histologic method of providing an estimate of the gravity of a cancerous tumor, based on the degree of cell differentiation and the number of cell divisions within the tumor.

graduate (grad′u-āt) A laboratory vessel marked off in units of fluid volume.

graduated (grad′u-āt-ed) Marked by a series of lines to indicate capacity, degrees, percentages, etc.

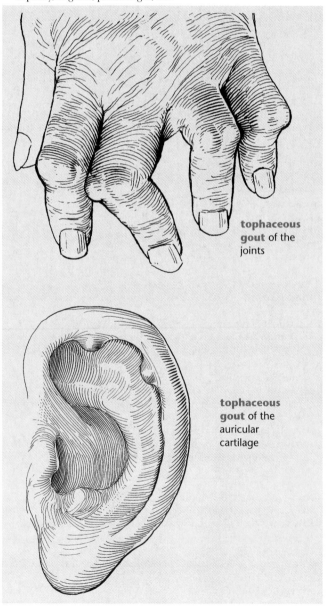

tophaceous gout of the joints

tophaceous gout of the auricular cartilage

graft (graft) **1.** Any tissue transplanted into a body. **2.** To insert such a tissue.

   accordion g. See mesh graft.

   allogenic g. See allograft.

   autogeneic g. See autograft.

   autologous g. See autograft.

   composite g. A type of skin graft that includes deeper tissues such as subcutaneous tissue and/or cartilage; it is small and generally used on the face.

   corneal g. See keratoplasty.

   coronary artery bypass g. (CABG) See coronary bypass, under bypass.

   cutis g. A piece of skin from which the superficial layer (epidermis) and subcutaneous tissue have been removed.

   delayed g. Grafting postponed until infection has been eliminated.

   full-thickness g. A skin graft consisting of both superficial and deep layers of the skin (i.e., epidermis and dermis).

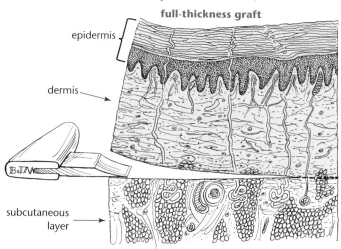

full-thickness graft

epidermis

dermis

subcutaneous layer

   isogeneic g. See isograft.

   isologous g. See isograft.

   isoplastic g. See isograft.

   mesh g. A graft that has been passed under a special cutting machine to create a mesh pattern; the perforations allow expansion of the graft from about 1 1/2 to 9 times its original size; useful for covering irregularly shaped wounds. Also called accordion graft.

   partial-thickness g. See split-thickness graft.

   pedicle g. See flap.

   pinch g.'s Small circular bits of skin a few millimeters in diameter.

   skin g. A piece of skin completely removed from one area of the body (or from another person) and placed in a new bed of blood supply in a denuded area of the body.

   split-skin g. See split-thickness graft.

   split-thickness g. *(a)* A skin graft consisting of the epidermis and part of the thickness of the dermis. *(b)* A graft of a mucous membrane that does not include all the layers of the membrane. Also called partial-thickness graft; split-skin graft.

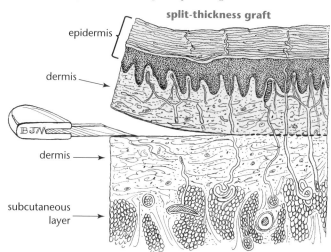

split-thickness graft

epidermis

dermis

dermis

subcutaneous layer

   syngeneic g. See isograft.

   synthetic g. A synthetic fabric graft (e.g., of Dacron™) used to replace a diseased or damaged segment of a blood vessel (e.g., an aneurysm).

   xenogeneic g. See xenograft.

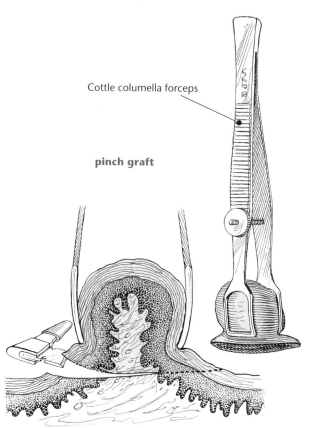

Cottle columella forceps

pinch graft

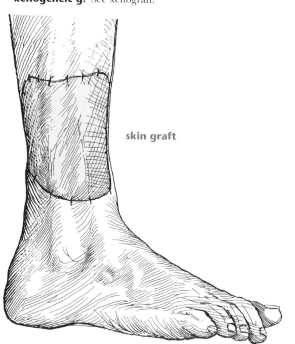

skin graft

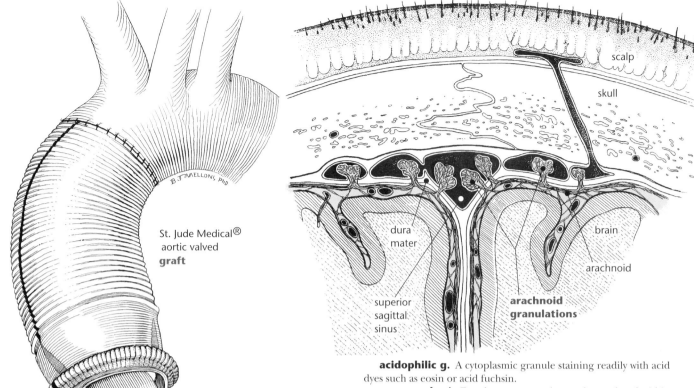

St. Jude Medical® aortic valved **graft**

grafting (graft′ing) The act of transplanting tissues.

grain (grān) Unit of mass or weight equal to 0.065 gram.

gram (gram) (g) Metric unit of mass or weight equal to 0.001 kilogram.

-gram Combining form meaning something written (e.g., electrocardiogram).

gramicidin (gram-ĭ-sĭ′din) An antibioic compound used in combination with other drugs of the same class, and in the form of eyedrops or ointments, for the topical treatment of bacterial infection of the eyes and skin.

gram-meter (gram me′ter) A unit of energy equal to the force required to raise a weight of 1 gram to a height of 1 meter.

gram-molecule (gram mol′ĕ-kŭl) The quantity of a substance that has a weight in grams numerically equal to the molecular weight of the substance (e.g., a gram-molecule of hydrogen weighs 2 grams).

gram-negative (gram neg′ah-tiv) See Gram's stain, under stain.

gram-positive (gram poz′ĭ-tiv) See Gram's stain, under stain.

grandiose (gran′dĭ-ōs) In psychiatry, an exaggerated belief of self-importance, often manifested by delusions of having great fame or power.

grand mal (grahn mahl) See generalized tonic-clonic epilepsy, under epilepsy.

granular (gran′u-lar) Composed of or having the texture of grains or granules.

granulation (gran-u-la′shun) 1. The formation of small red, moist masses on the surface of an ulcer or wound during the healing process. 2. The masses so formed. 3. A mass of numerous tiny blood vessels.

 arachnoid g.'s The numerous protrusions of the arachnoid into the venous sinuses of the brain; they constitute the main site of resorption of cerebrospinal fluid into the bloodstream. Some become calcified with increasing age and indent the inner surface of the skull. Also called pacchionian bodies; meningeal granules; arachnoid villi.

granule (gran′ul) 1. A small, free-flowing particle, as the insoluble nonmembranous particles found in cytoplasm. 2. A small pill, usually sugar coated or gelatin coated. 3. A minute membrane-bound vesicle in the cytoplasm of many cells containing various secretory or storage products.

 acidophilic g. A cytoplasmic granule staining readily with acid dyes such as eosin or acid fuchsin.

 acrosomal g.'s Fused proacrosomal granules enclosed within the bilaminar cap (acrosome) covering the anterior two-thirds of the head of a spermatozoon.

 alpha g.'s (a) Large granules in the alpha cells of the pancreatic islets of Langerhans that contain glucagon. (b) Granules of mostly platelet-derived growth factor, found in platelets.

 amphophilic g.'s Cytoplasmic granules with an affinity for both acid and basic dyes.

 azurophilic g.'s, azure g.'s Cytoplasmic granules staining readily with azure dyes; commonly found in lymphocytes, especially natural killer lymphocytes.

 basal g. See basal body, under body.

 basophilic g. A cytoplasmic granule staining readily with basic

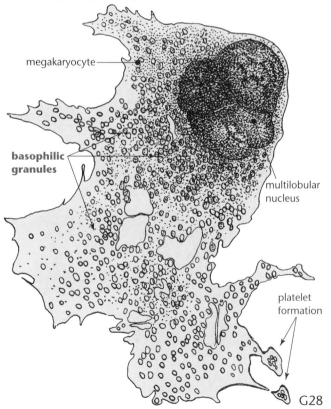

dyes such as azure A; seen in the beta cells of the anterior pituitary (adenohypophysis).

beta g.'s *(a)* Cytoplasmic granules in the beta cells of the pancreatic islets of Langerhans that contain proinsulin (insulin and C-peptide). *(b)* Cytoplasmic granules in the beta cells of the anterior pituitary (adenohypophysis), containing various hormones.

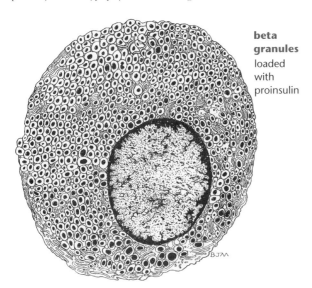

beta granules loaded with proinsulin

Bollinger's g.'s Small masses of yellowish white granules seen in the granulation tissue of cutaneous lesions of botryomycosis; usually composed of aggregates of staphylococci.

brain sand g.'s A mass of gritty matter usually seen in later life in the brain (within the pineal body and choroid plexus); it consists of concretions of phosphate and carbonate. Also called acervuli; corpora arenaces; brain sand.

chromophobe g. A cytoplasmic granule that stains poorly or not at all with either acid or basic dyes.

compound g.'s See mast-cell granules.

cone g. The nucleus of a retinal cone cell.

cortical g.'s Membrane-bound granules visible in oocytes prior to fertilization. As a consequence of fertilization, the mucopolysaccharide contents are released (cortical reaction) to form a barrier that prevents additional sperm penetration.

Crooke's g.'s Masses of basophilic material in the basophilic cells of the anterior pituitary (adenohypophysis); seen in Cushing's disease or after the administration of adrenocorticotropic hormone (ACTH).

cytoplasmic g. A granule found in the cytoplasm of a cell.

delta g.'s Cytoplasmic granules in the delta cells of the pancreatic islets of Langerhans that contain somatostatin.

eosinophilic g.'s Granules with an affinity for the acid dye eosin, seen especially in the cytoplasm of eosinophilic leukocytes.

Fordyce's g.'s See Fordyce's spots, under spot.

glycogen g.'s Clusters of glycogen, not bound by membranes, lying within the more fluid, finely granular, part of the cytoplasm of cells (hyaloplasm).

Heinz g.'s See Heinz bodies, under body.

juxtaglomerular g.'s Granules present in the juxtaglomerular cells that represent stored renin prior to secretion.

keratohyaline g.'s Conspicuous cytoplasmic granules in the granular layer of the skin (between the prickle cell layer and the clear layer); thought to be the precursor of keratin (the principal constituent of epidermis, hair, nails, and the organic matrix of tooth enamel).

lamellated g.'s See membrane-coating granules.

g.'s of Langerhans Rodlike granules about 0.1 μm long and 0.01 μm wide, with a regular granular interior, lying within the Langerhans cells of the deeper part of the germinative layer of the epidermis.

lipofuscin g.'s Minute cytoplasmic granules of the yellowish pigment lipofuscin (senility pigment); as cells age, they tend to accumulate these granules, thus providing a marker for roughly estimating the age of an organism; seen especially in the cells of the spinal ganglia.

mast-cell g.'s Large metachromatic granules or vesicles of varying size and shape found in the cytoplasm of mast cells; they contain three active substances: histamine and serotonin (agents in inflammatory change) and heparin (which prevents clotting of plasma); the substances may coexist in the same granule and as a result are sometimes referred to as compound granules.

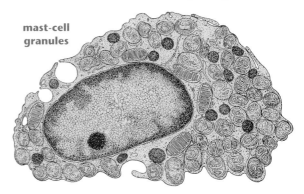

mast-cell granules

matrix g.'s Highly electron-dense intramitochondrial granules, about 500 Å in diameter; thought to be the binding sites for calcium ions.

melanin g. See melanosome.

membrane-coating g.'s One of several ovoid cytoplasmic granules in the spinous cells of the epidermis about 300 nm in diameter, bound by a double-layered membrane and filled with lamellae; considered by some to be a specialized epidermal lysosome. Also called keratinosomes; lamellated granules.

meningeal g.'s See arachnoid granulations, under granulation.

mucinogen g.'s Cytoplasmic granules in mucous secretory cells that contain the glycoprotein, mucinogen; they fuse with the surface of the cell before being secreted.

neurosecretory g. A cytoplasmic granule in nerve cells containing neurosecretory substances such as releasing hormones, vasopressin, neurotransmitters, etc.

neutrophilic g.'s Membrane-bound lysosome granules of neutrophil polymorphonuclear leukocytes (white blood cells); they contain hydrolytic enzymes capable of phagocytic activity and have an affinity for both acid and basic dyes.

Nissl g.'s See Nissl bodies, under body.

nonspecific g.'s Large cytoplasmic granules or primary lysosomes seen in developing neutrophils (polymorphonuclear leukocytes), containing lysozyme, peroxidase, acid phosphatase, and other enzymes. Also called primary granules.

osmophilic g. A granule that flourishes in the environment of high osmotic pressure.

primary g.'s See nonspecific granules.

rod g. The nucleus of a rod cell in the retina.

Schüffner's g.'s See Schüffner's dots, under dot.

secondary g.'s See specific granules.

secretory g.'s Membrane-lined synthesized substances stored in secretory cells; they are released by the process of exocytosis. Also called secretory vacuoles.

seminal g.'s Small granules or granular bodies seen in semen, containing a number of proteolytic enzymes.

specific g.'s Small cytoplasmic granules or secondary lysosomes seen in mature neutrophils (polymorphonuclear leukocytes), containing alkaline phosphatase, collagenase, lysozyme, and aminopeptidase. Also called secondary granules.

sulfur g.'s Characteristic yellow granules of the pus from actinomycotic lesions.

granule ■ granule

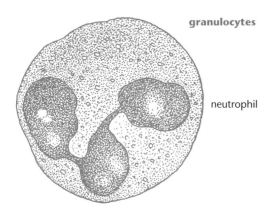
granulocytes

neutrophil

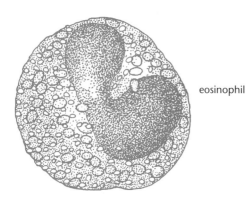
eosinophil

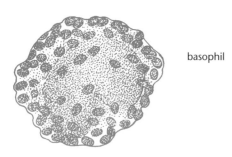
basophil

toxic g.'s Small dark-staining basophilic granules representing phagosomes or autophagic vacuoles; seen in the cytoplasm of neutrophils (polymorphonuclear leukocytes) when they contend with infections.

zymogen g. One of several secretory granules containing zymogenic material present in the cytoplasm of enzyme-secreting cells (e.g., those of salivary glands).

granuloblast (gran'u-lo-blast) See myeloblast.

granulocyte (gran'u-lo-sit) A mature granular white blood cell (leukocyte) developed in bone marrow; may be neutrophilic, eosinophilic, or basophilic depending on the stainable properties of the granules it contains.

granulocytopenia (gran-u-lo-si-to-pe'ne-ah) Deficiency of granular white blood cells (granulocytes) in the blood. Also called granulopenia.

granulocytopoiesis (gran-u-lo-si-to-poi-e'sis) See granulopoiesis.

granulocytosis (gran-u-lo-si-to'sis) The presence of an excessive number of granulocytes in the blood or tissues.

granuloma (gran-u-lo'mah) A tumor composed chiefly of granulation tissue; characteristic of certain diseases that may be caused either by infectious microorganisms (e.g., tuberculosis) or by mineral dust (e.g., silicosis), or may be due to unknown causes (e.g., sarcoidosis).

amebic g. See ameboma.

dental g. See periapical granuloma.

eosinophilic g. See unifocal Langerhans-cell histiocytosis, under histiocytosis.

foreign-body g. Granuloma incited by the presence of relatively inert particulate matter in a tissue.

giant cell g. A tumorlike mass protruding from the gums (gingiva), believed to be of inflammatory origin.

g. gravidatum A suppurating granuloma of the gums (gingiva) occurring during pregnancy; thought to be due to hormonal activity.

g. inguinale A sexually transmitted chronic infection of the skin and subcutaneous tissues, characterized by ulcerations in the groin, perineum, and the genitals; caused by infection with the bacterium *Calymmatum granulomatis;* incubation period is two to three months; may cause lymphatic obstruction and elephantiasis.

periapical g. A mass of chronic inflammatory tissue, usually asymptomatic, occurring at the tip of a dental root, usually a dead tooth.

pyogenic g. A small, red, benign overgrowth of granulation tissue on the skin or oral mucosa often arising as a result of trauma.

sperm g. Granuloma of the spermatic cord; may be formed at the site of a vasectomy or after vasography.

swimming pool g. A chronic warty growth, which may ulcerate, arising on abrasions, resulting from infection with *Mycobacterium marinum* in swimming pools, aquariums, or any body of water.

granulomatosis (gran-u-lo-mah-to'sis) Any disease characterized by the presence of multiple granulomas.

allergic g. See Churg-Strauss syndrome, under syndrome.

lipoid g., lipid g. See xanthomatosis.

lipophagic intestinal g. See Whipple's disease, under disease.

Wegener's g. An uncommon, often fatal, disease characterized by ulceration of the upper respiratory tract progressing to involvement of the lungs, acute necrotizing vasculitis, and glomerulonephritis; affects males predominantly, with peak incidence in the fifth decade.

granulomatous (gran-u-lom'ah-tus) Resembling a granuloma.

granulopenia (gran-u-lo-pe'ne-ah) See granulocytopenia.

granuloplastic (gran-u-lo-plas'tik) Tending to form granules.

granulopoiesis (gran-u-lo-poi-e'sis) The formation of granulocytes. Also called granulocytopoiesis.

granulosis, granulocity (gran-u-lo'sis, gran-u-los'ĭ-te) A mass of granules.

-graph Combining form meaning instrument for recording; a written or pictorial record (e.g., electrocardiograph, monograph, radiograph).

graph (graf) Any pictorial device depicting a relationship of values.

graphology (graf-ol'o-je) The analysis of handwriting to assess the character of the writer.

graphospasm (graf'o-spazm) See writer's cramp, under cramp.

GRAS Acronym for Generally Regarded As Safe; applied to a food additive.

grave (grāv) Very serious or severe; applied to a disorder or symptoms.

gravel (grav'el) Minute mineral concretions usually in the kidneys or bladder.

gravid (grav'id) See pregnant.

gravida (grav'ĭ-dah) A pregnant woman. A Roman numeral designates the number of pregnancies (e.g., gravida I is a woman in her first pregnancy, gravida II in her second, etc.).

gravidity (grah-vid'ĭ-te) The total number of pregnancies including abortions, ectopic pregnancies, hydatidiform moles, and normal intrauterine pregnancies.

gravimeter (grah-vim'ĕ-ter) See hydrometer.

gravimetric (grav-ĭ-met'rik) Determined by weight.

gravity (grav'ĭ-te) The gravitational force.

specific g. The weight of any substance compared to the weight of another substance of equal volume regarded as a unit.

gray (gra) (Gy) An SI unit of absorbed radiation dosage equal to 100 rad.

grid (grid) In radiology, an instrument composed of alternate strips of lead and radiolucent material, placed in apposition to a film to prevent scattered x rays from reaching the film.

Wetzel g. A chart for evaluating the growth and physical fitness of young and adolescent children.

grinding (grīnd'ing) In dentistry, the shaping of a tooth with abrasive tools.

selective g. The grinding of selective spots on the occlusal surfaces of teeth marked with articulating paper to equalize occlusal stress.

grip, grippe (grip) See influenza.

devil's g. See epidemic pleurodynia, under pleurodynia.

griseofulvin (gris-e-o-ful'vin) An oral antifungal preparation prescribed for the treatment of tinea infections; long-term treatment may cause liver and bone marrow damage.

gristle (gris'l) Cartilage.

groin (groin) The inguinal region; the area around the crease formed at the junction of the thigh and trunk.

groove (groōv) A narrow, elongated depression; a sulcus; a furrow; a niche.

arterial g.'s See arterial sulci, under sulcus.

atrioventricular g. See coronary sulcus, under sulcus.

bicipital g. of humerus See intertubercular sulcus of humerus, under sulcus.

carotid g. of sphenoid bone A shallow groove on the floor of the skull that accommodates the internal carotid artery immediately upon emerging through the foramen lacerum; it also supports the cavernous sinus. Also called carotid sulcus of sphenoid bone.

costal g. A groove on the lower border of the internal surface of ribs (except the first ribs) that houses the intercostal vessels and nerves. Also called costal sulcus.

deltopectoral g. The long groove between the deltoid muscle and the greater pectoral (pectoralis major) muscle; it accommodates the cephalic vein.

developmental g. A groove in the enamel of a tooth marking the fusion of the embryonic tooth lobes of the crown during tooth development.

infraorbital g. A groove on the floor of the orbit that passes forward and ends at the infraorbital canal; it transmits the infraorbital nerve and vessels.

interventricular g. Any of two linear depressions on the surface of the heart separating the right from the left ventricles: *Anterior interventricular g.,* the groove on the sternocostal surface of the heart separating the ventricles; it extends from the coronary sulcus to a notch just to the right of the apex of the heart; the groove is occupied by the anterior interventricular branch of the left coronary artery. Also called anterior interventricular sulcus. *Posterior interventricular g.,* the oblique groove on the diaphragmatic surface of the heart separating the ventricles; it is continuous with the anterior interventricular groove; the groove is occupied by the posterior interventricular branch of the right coronary artery. Also called posterior interventricular sulcus.

lacrimal g. See lacrimal fossa, under fossa.

malleolar g. See malleolar sulcus, under sulcus.

meningeal g.'s Grooves on the inner surface of the cranial vault (calva) that transmit meningeal vessels; the deeper grooves appear in the parietal and sphenoid bones, while the smaller ones are present in the frontal, temporal and occipital bones.

mylohyoid g. See mylohyoid sulcus of mandible, under sulcus.

nail g. See sulcus of nail, under sulcus.

nasolabial g. See nasolabial sulcus, under sulcus.

neural g. The transitory groove on the dorsal surface of the young embryo produced by the thickened ectoderm (neural plate) as it begins to close to form a tubular structure (neural tube).

paracolic g.'s Shallow longitudinal peritoneal furrows between the colon (ascending and descending) and the posterolateral abdominal wall. Also called paracolic sulci.

g. of sigmoid sinus The broad S-shaped groove in the posterior cranial fossa that is a continuation of the lateral extremity of the groove for transverse sinus; it ends at the jugular notch of the occipital bone and accommodates the sigmoid sinus. Also called sulcus of sigmoid sinus.

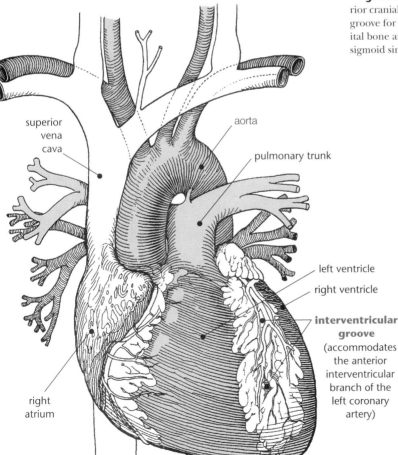

superior vena cava

aorta

pulmonary trunk

left ventricle

right ventricle

interventricular groove (accommodates the anterior interventricular branch of the left coronary artery)

right atrium

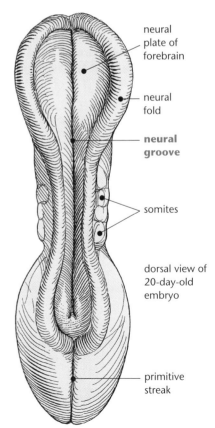

neural plate of forebrain

neural fold

neural groove

somites

dorsal view of 20-day-old embryo

primitive streak

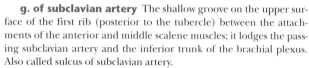

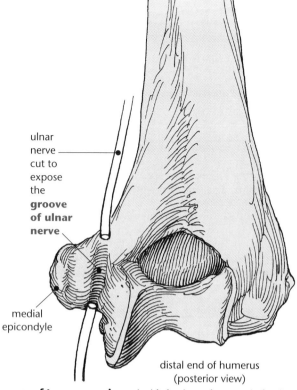

G

skull

middle and anterior scalene muscles

anterior scalene muscle

groove of subclavian artery

groove of subclavian vein

1st rib

ulnar nerve cut to expose the **groove of ulnar nerve**

medial epicondyle

distal end of humerus (posterior view)

g. of subclavian artery The shallow groove on the upper surface of the first rib (posterior to the tubercle) between the attachments of the anterior and middle scalene muscles; it lodges the passing subclavian artery and the inferior trunk of the brachial plexus. Also called sulcus of subclavian artery.

g. of subclavian vein The shallow groove on the upper surface of the first rib (anterior to the tubercle) between the attachments of the costoclavicular ligament and the anterior scalene muscle; it lodges the passing subclavian vein. Also called sulcus of subclavian vein.

g. of superior sagittal sinus The midline groove on the internal surface of the cranial vault that accommodates the superior sagittal sinus. Also called sulcus of superior sagittal sinus.

g. of tendon of long flexor muscle of big toe An oblique groove on the posterior surface of the ankle bone (talus) and the medial surface of the heel bone (calcaneus) that accommodates the tendon of the long flexor muscle of the big toe (flexor hallucis longus muscle). Also called sulcus of tendon of long flexor muscle of big toe.

g. of transverse sinus A wide horizontal groove (sulcus) on either side of the internal surface of the back of the cranium that accommodates the transverse sinus; it extends laterally from the internal occipital protuberance; the groove of the right transverse sinus is usually continuous with the groove of the superior sagittal sinus. Also called sulcus of transverse sinus.

g. of ulnar nerve A shallow vertical groove on the back surface of the medial epicondyle of the humerus; it accommodates the ulnar nerve. When the nerve is sharply pressed against the bony groove (popularly known as hitting the funny bone), a tingling sensation is generally felt. Also called sulcus of ulnar nerve.

gross (grōs) Visible to the naked eye, without the aid of a microscope; macroscopic.

group (grōop) **1.** A collection or assemblage of related entities. **2.** In chemistry, mutually bonded atoms in a molecule that constitute an identifiable part of that molecule; a radical.

　family g. See kindred.

　symptom g. See syndrome.

growth (grōth) **1.** A progressive development or increase in size of an organism. **2.** A tumor.

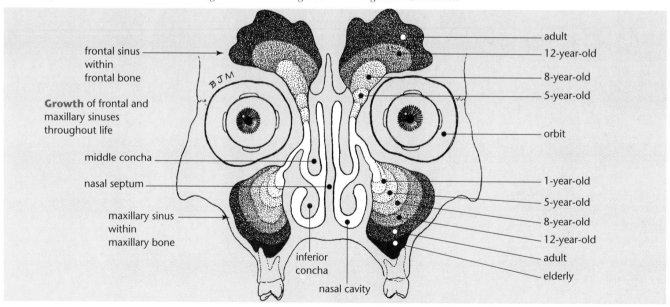

frontal sinus within frontal bone

Growth of frontal and maxillary sinuses throughout life

middle concha

nasal septum

maxillary sinus within maxillary bone

inferior concha

nasal cavity

BJM

adult
12-year-old
8-year-old
5-year-old
orbit
1-year-old
5-year-old
8-year-old
12-year-old
adult
elderly

gross ■ growth

appositional g. Growth by addition of layers.

differential g. The growth rates of related tissues, as in embryonic structures, with resulting change in proportions.

interstitial g. Growth by formation of new tissue throughout the structure.

grub (grub) The larva of certain insects.

gruel (groo'el) Any semiliquid food (e.g., cereal boiled in water).

grumous (groo'mus) Thick; semisolid; clotted.

grunt (grunt) A guttural sound heard in the chest of patients afflicted with pneumonia and in newborn infants with respiratory distress syndrome or hyaline membrane disease.

expiratory g. A laryngeal sound sometimes heard during surgical manipulation of the area below the diaphragm.

gryposis (grĭ-po'sis) An abnormal curvature.

guaifenesin (gwi-fen'ĕ-sin) An expectorant preparation used to reduce the stickiness of mucus in the respiratory tract.

guanethidine sulfate (gwan-eth'ĭ-dēn sul'fāt) A potent antihypertensive agent that works by blocking transmission of nervous impulses at the adrenergic ganglia.

guanine (gwan'in) One of the two purine bases of DNA and RNA.

guarding (gahrd'ing) Spasm of muscles at the site of injury or disease occurring as the body's protection against further injury.

abdominal g. A sign of acute peritonitis marked by involuntary rigid contraction of the abdominal rectus muscles, occurring when the examiner gently depresses the abdomen with both hands; the muscles contract, remaining taut, rigid, and boardlike throughout deep respiration.

gubernaculum (gu-ber-nak'u-lum) A fibrous cord between two structures.

g. dentis The fibrous band connecting the permanent tooth follicle to the gums.

g. testis A cord extending from the lower end of the fetal testis through the inguinal canal to the floor of the developing scrotum; it guides the normal descent of the testis from the abdomen into the scrotum.

guide (gīd) A device that directs the course of something by preceding it (e.g., a guide wire) or by confining its motion (e.g., by means of grooves).

guideline (gīd'lin) A line serving as an indicator or a guide.

clasp g. See survey line (b).

guillotine (gil'o-tēn) A surgical cutting instrument that slides in the grooves of a guide.

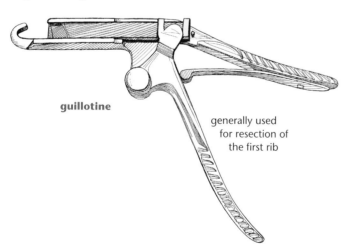

guillotine

generally used for resection of the first rib

guilt (gilt) An affect of self-reproach that results from doing or thinking something that violates an ethical, moral, or religious principle; associated with lowered self-esteem and the need for punishment.

guinea pig (gin'e pig) Any of several small rodents of the genus *Cavia* used extensively for experimental work.

gullet (gul'et) The passage leading from the mouth to the stomach (i.e., the pharynx and esophagus).

gum (gum) **1.** The gingiva. **2.** The dried viscous sap from certain plants; it is water-soluble, noncrystalline, and brittle.

g. arabic See acacia.

gumboil (gum'boil) Popular term for a gingival abscess. See under abscess.

gumma (gum'ah), pl. gum'mas, gum'mata A soft, gummy, infectious tumor usually seen in the third stage of syphilis.

gummatous (gum'ah-tus) Relating to a gumma.

gurney (gŭr'nē) A wheeled stretcher or cot for transporting patients, usually within a hospital.

gustation (gus-ta'shun) **1.** The sense of taste. **2.** The act of tasting.

gustatory (gus'tah-to-re) Relating to the sense of taste.

gut (gut) **1.** The intestine. **2.** The digestive tube of the embryo.

primary g. See archenteron.

surgical g. See catgut.

gutta (gut'ah) (gt.) Latin for a drop.

gutta-percha (gut'ah per'chah) A milky latex sap of a group of tropical trees (family Sapotaceae); used in the manufacture of splints, as a sealer of wounds, and, in dentistry, as a temporary filling.

guttate (gut'āt) Having the shape of a drop; applied to certain skin lesions.

guttural (gut'ur-al) Relating to the throat.

gymnocyte (jim'no-sīt) A cell without an outer limiting membrane.

gymnophobia (jim-no-fo'be-ah) Abnormal fear of the sight of the naked body.

gynandroid (jī-nan'droid) A female pseudohermaphrodite.

gynandromorphous (jī-nan-dro-mor'fus) Having both male and female characteristics.

gynatresia (jin-ah-tre'ze-ah) Occlusion of a portion of the female genital tract.

gynecic (jī-nes'ik) Relating to women.

gynecoid (jin'ĕ-koid) Resembling a female.

gynecologic (gi-nĕ-ko-loj'ik) Relating to gynecology.

gynecologist (gi-nĕ-kol'o-jist) A specialist in gynecology.

gynecology (gi-nĕ-kol'o-je) (GYN) The medical-surgical specialty concerned with disorders of female endocrinology and reproductive physiology; for the most part it is not concerned with the pregnant state.

gynecomania (gīn-ĕ-ko-ma'ne-ah) Insatiable sexual desire for women.

gynecomastia (gīn-ĕ-ko-mas'te-ah) Abnormal overdevelopment of the mammary glands in the male.

gynecophobia (gin-ĕ-ko-fo'be-ah) Abnormal fear of or aversion to women.

gynecoplasty (gin-ĕ-ko-plas'te) Reparative surgery of the female genitals.

gynopathy (gin-op'ah-te) Any disease of the female organs.

gypsum (jip'sum) The dehydrate of calcium sulfate from which dental stone and plaster of Paris are derived.

gyration (ji-ra'shun) In anatomy, a group of gyri in the brain.

gyri (ji'ri) Plural of gyrus.

guinea pig

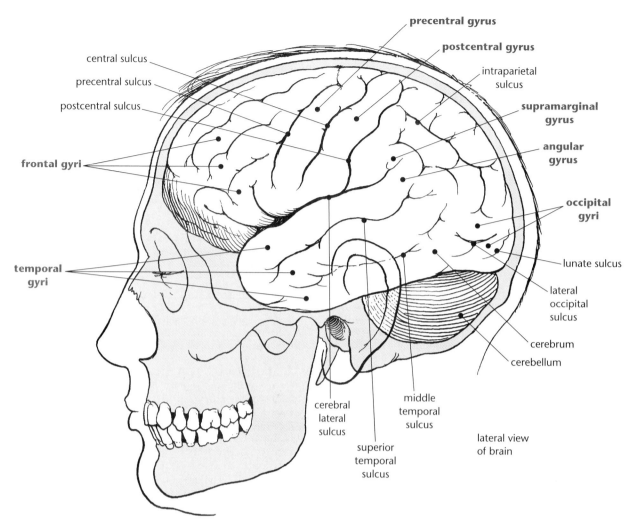

central sulcus
precentral sulcus
postcentral sulcus
frontal gyri
temporal gyri

precentral gyrus
postcentral gyrus
intraparietal sulcus
supramarginal gyrus
angular gyrus
occipital gyri
lunate sulcus
lateral occipital sulcus
cerebrum
cerebellum

cerebral lateral sulcus
superior temporal sulcus
middle temporal sulcus
lateral view of brain

gyrus (ji′rus), pl. gy′ri An irregular eminence or convolution on the surface of the brain, separated by furrows (sulci); each sulcus corresponds to an infolding of brain tissue that greatly increases the surface area of the cerebral cortex by about three times.

angular g. A convolution on the lateral surface of the cerebrum, arching over the slightly upturned end of the superior temporal sulcus; it represents the middle part of the inferior parietal lobule as it joins the caudal part of the superior and middle temporal gyri.

cingulate g. The long curved convolution on the medial surface of the cerebral hemisphere overlying the corpus callosum; it is continuous posteriorly with the isthmus.

cuneolingual gyri The convolutions on the medial surface of the cerebral hemisphere adjoining the calcarine sulcus; it contains the visual cortex.

dentate g. A crenated fringe of cortex occupying the narrow space between the fimbria of the hippocampus and the parahippocampal gyrus; it continues posteriorly under the splenium of the corpus callosum.

frontal gyri The three gyri (superior, middle, and inferior) on the superolateral surface of the frontal lobe of the cerebral hemisphere.

gyri of insula Two convolutions (short and long) on the surface of the insula, the central lobe of the cerebral hemisphere, lying deep within the lateral sulcus; the short and long convolutions are divided by the central sulcus of insula.

lingual g. An occipitotemporal convolution on the medial surface of the cerebral hemisphere, between the calcarine sulcus and collateral sulcus; it contains portions of the visual cortex.

occipital gyri Two convolutions (superior and inferior) on the lateral surface of the occipital lobe of the cerebral hemisphere, divided by the lateral occipital sulcus.

occipitotemporal gyri Two convolutions (lateral and medial) on the tentorial surface of the cerebral hemisphere, divided by the occipitotemporal sulcus; the lateral occipitotemporal gyrus is continuous with the inferior temporal gyrus of the lateral surface of the cerebral hemisphere.

parahippocampal g. A convolution that lies between the collateral sulcus and the hippocampal sulcus, on the inferior surface of each cerebral hemisphere; posteriorly, it is continuous above with the cingulate gyrus through the isthmus, and below with the lingual gyrus.

postcentral g. The anterior convolution of the parietal lobe, bounded in front by the central (rolandic) sulcus of the cerebrum and posteriorly by the postcentral sulcus.

precentral g. The posterior convolution of the frontal lobe, bounded posteriorly by the central (rolandic) sulcus of the cerebrum and anteriorly by the precentral sulcus.

g. rectus See straight gyrus.

straight g. The convolution on the orbital surface of the frontal lobe of the cerebral hemisphere, medial to the olfactory sulcus. Also called gyrus rectus.

supramarginal g. The convolution (gyrus) on the lateral side of the cerebral hemisphere that arches over the upturned end of the lateral sulcus; it is the anterior part of the inferior parietal lobule.

temporal gyri The three gyri (superior, middle, and inferior) on the lateral surface of the temporal lobe of the cerebral hemisphere, located below the lateral sulcus.

transverse temporal gyri Two or three transverse convolutions marking the posterior extremity of the superior temporal gyrus, extending deeply into the lateral sulcus; it houses the primary auditory cortex.

gyrus ■ gyrus

habena (hah-be′nah) **1.** A restricting fibrous band. **2.** A restrictive bandage.

habenula (hah-ben′u-lah) A cell mass within the brain situated in the dorsomedial part of the thalamus bordering the third ventricle.

habit (hab′it) **1.** A fixed or established practice, or a learned response acquired through repetition. **2.** Colloquial term for addiction.

habituation (hah-bit-u-a′shun) **1.** The process of establishing a habit. **2.** Method by which the nervous system gradually reduces its response to a repeated stimulus.

habitus (hab′ĭ-tus) Physical and constitutional characteristics of a person, especially in relation to susceptibility to disease.

    eunuchoid h. Infantile genitalia and sexual characteristics in an older male; seen in certain disorders.

Haemodipsus ventricosus (he-mah-dip′sus ven-trĭ-ko̅′sus) The rabbit louse; it transmits the causative bacterium of tularemia (Francisella tularensis) to humans.

Haemophilus (he-mof′ĭ-lus) A genus of gram-negative bacteria that require blood components for growth; some cause disease in humans. Also spelled Hemophilus.

    H. aegyptius A species that causes subacute catarrhal conjunctivitis in warm climates.

    H. ducreyi A species that causes chancroid (soft chancre) on the genitals of humans. Also called Ducrey's bacillus.

    H. influenzae A species containing strains that are normally found in the nasopharynx of adult humans; in children some strains cause acute meningitis, others may cause pneumonia, middle ear infections, sinusitis, and subacute catarrhal conjunctivitis. Also called Koch-Weeks bacillus.

    H. parahaemolyticus A species found in the upper respiratory tract; frequently associated with pharyngitis.

hafnium (haf′ne-um) Chemical element; symbol Hf, atomic number 72, atomic weight 178.5.

hagiotherapy (hag′e-o-ther′ah-pe) Treatment of disease by placing the patient in contact with religious relics or by participating in religious observances.

hair (hār) Pilus; a long threadlike skin appendage covering almost the entire surface of the human body except the palms of the hands, the soles of the feet, the dorsal surface of the distal phalanges, the umbilicus, the glans penis, the inner surface of the prepuce of the penis, the clitoris, and the major and minor labia; consists of a portion implanted in the skin (root), in a flasklike pit in the skin (hair follicle), and a portion projecting from the surface (shaft). Hair on the normal scalp grows approximately half an inch per month. The analysis of hair can be used as a biologic marker to determine the extent of exposure to some drugs or chemicals, such as nicotine, cocaine, and methyl mercury.

    auditory h.'s Hairlike stereocilia emanating from the hair cells of the cochlear receptor of the inner ear; each cell is capped with 50 to 100 stereocilia.

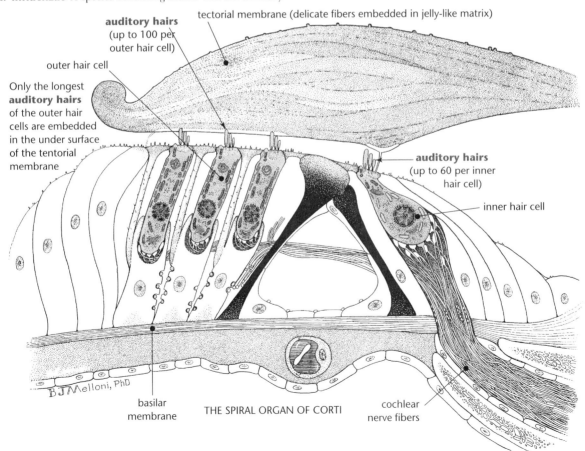

THE SPIRAL ORGAN OF CORTI

tectorial membrane (delicate fibers embedded in jelly-like matrix)

auditory hairs (up to 100 per outer hair cell)

outer hair cell

Only the longest **auditory hairs** of the outer hair cells are embedded in the under surface of the tentorial membrane

auditory hairs (up to 60 per inner hair cell)

inner hair cell

basilar membrane

cochlear nerve fibers

B.J.Melloni, PhD

burrowing h. Hair that continues to grow but fails to emerge from the flesh, generally forming a small cicumscribed, superficial elevation of the skin (papule), which may become infected; most commonly occurs on the neck. Also called pilus cuniculatus. COMPARE ingrown hair.

gustatory h. See taste hair.

ingrown h. Hair that emerges from the skin but then curves and reenters it, generally causing a papule, which may become infected; commonly seen in closely-shaved hair. Also called pilus incarnatus. COMPARE burrowing hair.

lanugo h. See lanugo.

olfactory h.'s Nonmotile modified cilia that project from the surface of receptor cells into the film of liquid overlying the olfactory epithelium.

primary h. See lanugo.

pubic h.'s Terminal hairs of the pubic region that are thick and their development and growth are under hormonal control.

secondary h. See vellus.

sensory h.'s Hairlike structures on the surface of sensory epithelial cells.

split h. Hair split at the free (distal) end. Also called stellate hair.

stellate h. See split hair.

tactile h.'s The whiskers (vibrissae) of certain animals that are sensitive to touch.

taste h. One of the short hairlike processes projecting into the lumen of a taste bud; each hair is actually composed of groups of fine microvilli. Also called gustatory hair.

terminal h. Coarse hair that replaces secondary hair (vellus) in various areas of the body during adult years, including eyebrows, axillary, scalp, and pubic hairs, as well as those hairs in the nose and ears and on the face and front of the chest in the male.

vellus h. See vellus.

vestibular h.'s Sensory hairs (stereocilia) emerging from type I and II hair cells of the vestibular receptors (cristae and maculae) of the inner ear; the apical ends of both types of hair cells bear a tuft of 40 or more stereocilia and a single kinocilium (motile cilium).

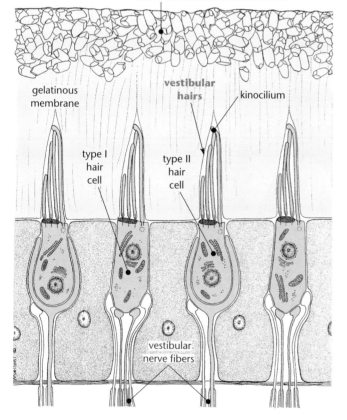

statoconia embedded in the gelatinous membrane of the macula within the utricle end saccule of the inner ear

gelatinous membrane

vestibular hairs

kinocilium

type I hair cell

type II hair cell

vestibular nerve fibers

hair stream (hār strēm) See flumina pilorum.

halazone (hal'ah-zōn) Antibacterial chemical used in the sterilization of water supplies.

half-life (haf'līf) (HL) The time required for half of the radioactivity originally associated with a radioactive substance to disintegrate (radioactive decay).

biological h-l. ($T_{1/2}$) (a) The time required for an administered radioactive substance to lose half of its activity within the body; it depends both on the natural half-life of the substance and on the rate of excretion from the body. (b) The time it takes for the body to eliminate 50% of a drug.

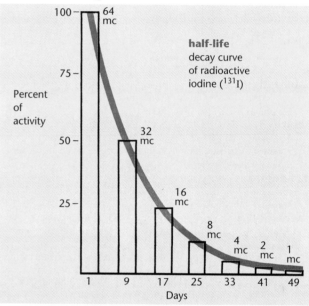

half-life decay curve of radioactive iodine (^{131}I)

Percent of activity

Days

halide (hal'īd) A salt of a halogen (e.g., bromide, chlorine, fluorine, iodine).

halitosis (hal-ī-to'sis) Unpleasant breath; some causes include poor oral hygiene; infection of the sinuses, nasal passages, or throat; and lung abscess.

halitus (hal'ī-tus) **1.** Latin for breath. **2.** An exhalation.

hallucal (hal'u-kal) Relating to the big toe.

hallucination (hah-loo-sī-na'shun) Perception of objects or events that are not actually present.

hypnagogic h. Vivid sensory, dreamlike perception occurring in the transitional state between wakefulness and sleep.

hallucinatory (hah-loo'sī-nah-to-re) Characterized by hallucinations.

hallucinogen (hah-loo'sī-no-jen) Any chemical agent capable of inducing hallucinations.

hallucinosis (hah-loo-sī-no'sis) A psychotic condition in which a person experiences hallucinations while in a state of consciousness.

hallux (hal'uks), pl. hal'luces The big toe; the first or inner digit of the foot.

h. dolorosa A painful condition, usually associated with flatfoot, in which walking causes severe discomfort in the metatarsophalangeal joint of the big toe.

h. malleus Hammer toe of the hallux; a big toe that is congenitally bent downward.

h. rigidus Stiff toe; painful flexion of the big toe due to stiffness in the metatarsophalangeal joint.

h. valgus The most common of the painful conditions of the toes, marked by an abnormal fixed displacement (angulation) of the big toe toward the other toes of the same foot (away from the midline of the body); the big toe may ride over or under the other toes; the condition is generally attributed to the wearing of narrow or pointed shoes; predisposing congenital and familial factors may exist. COMPARE bunion.

h. varus Abnormal fixed displacement (angulation) of the big toe away from the other toes of the same foot (toward the midline of the body).

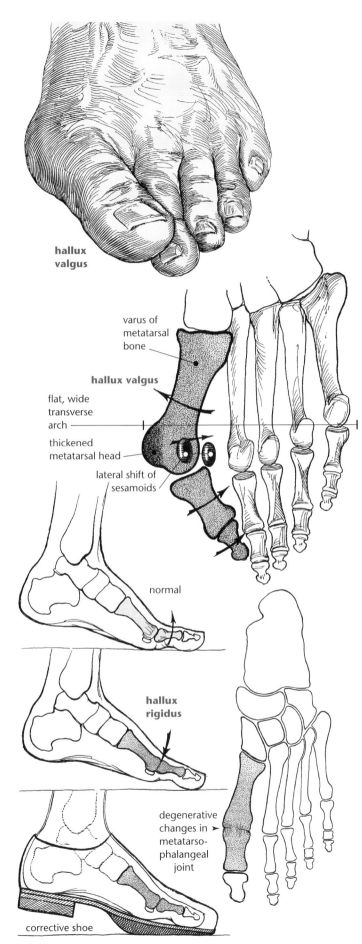

hallux valgus

varus of metatarsal bone

hallux valgus

flat, wide transverse arch

thickened metatarsal head

lateral shift of sesamoids

normal

hallux rigidus

degenerative changes in metatarsophalangeal joint

corrective shoe

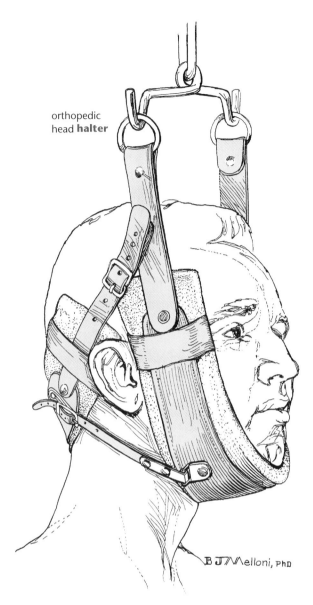

orthopedic head **halter**

B J Melloni, PhD

halo (ha′lo) **1.** A circular configuration around a focus. **2.** Colored rings seen around lights or bright objects by patients afflicted with any process involving edema of the cornea (e.g., glaucoma).

halogen (hal′o-jen) Any of a group of chemically related nonmetallic elements that form similar saltlike compounds in combination with sodium; they include bromine, chlorine, fluorine, iodine, and the radioactive element astatine.

haloperidol (hah-lo-per′ĭ-dol) An antipsychotic drug used especially in the management of Gilles de la Tourette's syndrome and Alzheimer's disease.

halophil (hal′o-fil) A microorganism that thrives in a salty environment.

halothane (hal′o-thān) A liquid hydrocarbon used as a vapor in general anesthesia; on rare occasions it may cause irregular heartbeat or liver damage.

halter (haul′ter) In orthopedics, a device for holding the head in traction.

hamartoblastoma (ham-ar-to-blas-to′mah) Malignant tumor that is thought to be derived from a hamartoma.

hamartoma (ham-ar-to′mah) Tumorlike, nonmalignant growth formed from disordered proliferation of tissues that are normally present in the site where it occurs.

hammertoe (ham′er-to) See hammer toe, under toe.

hamstring (ham′string) See hamstring tendon, under tendon.

hamular (ham′u-lar) Shaped like a hook.

hamulus (ham'u-lus), pl. ham'uli Any small hook-shaped process, as seen at the end of a bone; a little hook.

h. of hamate bone A hooklike process of the hamate bone of the wrist, which projects from the distal part of the palmar surface; the flexor retinaculum attaches to its tip in the formation of the carpal tunnel.

lacrimal h. The hooklike process on the orbital surface of the lacrimal bone articulating with the maxilla and forming the upper aperture of the bony nasolacrimal canal.

pterygoid h. The hooklike process at the bottom of the medial pterygoid plate of the sphenoid bone of the skull; the tensor muscle of the soft palate (tensor veli palatini muscle) bends around it in passing from the sphenoid fossa to the soft palate.

h. of spiral lamina The small hooklike termination at the apex of the bony spiral lamina of the cochlea, in the inner ear.

hand (hand) The terminal part of the upper extremity below the forearm, composed of the carpus, metacarpus, and digits.

accoucheur's h. The characteristic position of the hand produced by spasm in tetany; the hand is flexed at the wrist, the fingers are flexed at the metacarpophalangeal joints and extended at the interphalangeal joints, with the thumb tightly flexed into the palm; so called because it resembles the posture of the obstetrician's hand when examining the vagina. Also called obstetrician's hand; main d'accoucheur.

claw h. See clawhand.

dead h. A dark bluish hand caused by a multitude of concussions; seen sometimes as an occupational disorder in those who use vibratory tools.

drop h. See wristdrop.

obstetrician's h. See accoucheur's hand.

opera-glass h. The characteristic contracted hand of advanced rheumatoid arthritis; marked by erosion and compressive collapse of the proximal phalanges at the base of the fingers, with consequent overriding of bones and dislocation of the metacarpophalangeal joints. May also occur in other conditions (e.g., osteoarthritis, chronic infection, and leprosy). Also called main en lorgnette.

spade h. The characteristic coarse, thick, square hand of acromegaly or myxedema.

trident h. The characteristic hand of achondroplasia; a hand in which the fingers are short and thick and nearly equal in length, with a deflection (at the second phalangeal joint) of the index and middle fingers toward the radial side and the ring and little fingers toward the ulnar side, and so with the thumb form the three elements of a trident.

handicap (han'dĭ-kap) According to the International Classification of Impairments, Disabilities, and Handicaps (ICIDH): a disadvantage for a person, resulting from an impairment or a disability, that limits or prevents the fulfillment of a role that is normal for that person (depending on sex, age, and social and cultural practice). The term reflects interaction with, and adaptation to, the person's surroundings. See also impairment; disability.

handpiece (hand'pēs) In dentistry, the part of a mechanized, hand-held device that holds rotary instruments such as burs and mandrels during operative procedures.

high-speed h. One that operates at rotational speeds in excess of 12,000 revolutions per minute.

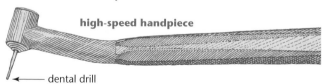

high-speed handpiece

← dental drill

ultra-high-speed h. One that operates at rotational speeds of 100,000 to 300,000 revolutions per minute.

ultrasonic h. One that vibrates at a frequency of 29,000 cycles per second (above audible range).

water-turbine h. One with a turbine powered by water under great pressure.

hamulus ▪ handpiece

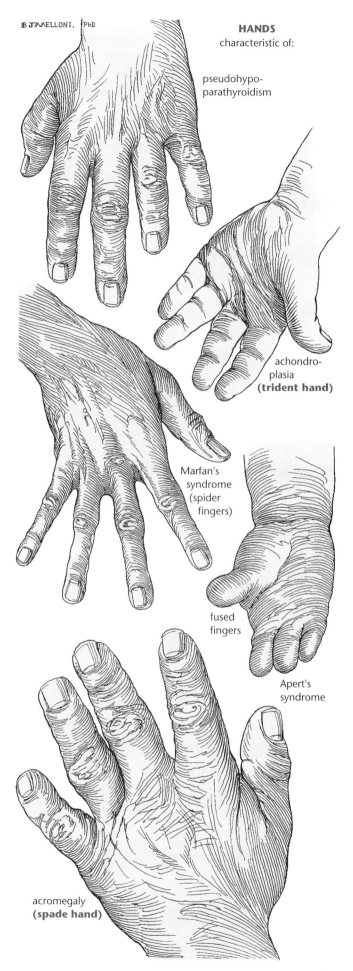

B. J. MELLONI, PhD

HANDS
characteristic of:

pseudohypo-parathyroidism

achondro-plasia
(trident hand)

Marfan's syndrome (spider fingers)

fused fingers

Apert's syndrome

acromegaly
(spade hand)

hangnail (hang′nāl) A partly detached piece of skin at the base or side of a nail.

hapalonychia (hap-ah-lo-nik′e-ah) A soft condition of fingernails or toenails; may be normal for the person, or may be acquired as a result of malnutrition.

haplodont (hap′lo-dont) Having peglike molar teeth, that is, molar teeth without cusps or ridges.

haploid (hap′loid) The chromosome number contained in a normal sex cell (sperm or egg cell); it is half the usual number of chromosomes, that is, with only one member of each chromosome pair contained in the rest of the body cells. In humans, the haploid number is 23.

hapten (hap′ten) Small molecules (lipids, carbohydrates, nucleic acids, and various drugs) that develop antigenic capabilities and evoke the production of antibodies only when combined with larger antigen molecules.

haptoglobin (hap-to-glo′bin) A protein present in human blood serum, capable of combining with hemoglobin; a low level of haptoglobin indicates a recent destruction of red blood cells (hemolysis).

haptometer (hap-tom′ĕ-ter) Instrument for determining degree of sensitivity to touch.

hardening (hard′en-ing) The process of making hard or firm.

    h. of the arteries See arteriosclerosis.

harelip (hār′lip) See cleft lip, under lip.

harpoon (har-poon′) Instrument with a barbed head for removing small pieces of tissue for microscopic examination.

hasamiyami (has-ah-me-yah′me) A fever occurring in Japan in the autumn, caused by the bacterium *Leptospira autumnalis*.

hashish (hash′ēsh) A resin containing a high concentration of cannabinols; obtained from the hemp plant *Cannabis sativa* and smoked or ingested to induce euphoria.

Cannabis sativa, the female hemp plant from which a resin is extracted to produce **hashish**

hatchet (hach′it) An angled hand instrument used in dentistry to cut and remove enamel and dentin.

haunch (hawnch) The region of the upper thigh, hip, and buttocks considered as a unit.

haustra (haws′trah) Plural of haustrum.

haustration (haws-tra′shun) Increase in size of the normally small sacculations of the colon.

haustrum (haws′trum), pl. haus′tra One of the natural pouchlike expansions present throughout the length of the colon.

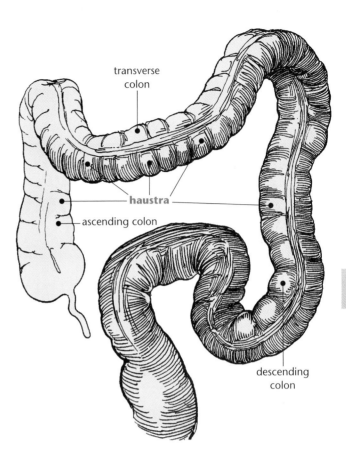

hazard (haz′erd) **1.** Any circumstance that increases the probability of loss or injury. **2.** The chance that injury will result from exposure to a substance or physical agent under certain conditions.

head (hed) **1.** The upper or anterior end of the body. **2.** The end of a bone or organ (e.g., pancreas) that is nearest the vertebral column; the proximal end. **3.** The part of a muscle attached to the less movable of its two attachments. **4.** The part of an apparatus that performs an important function. **5.** Slang expression applied to one who frequently uses illegal narcotics.

    absorber h. In anesthesiology, the part of the apparatus containing an absorber of carbon dioxide. Commonly called canister.

headache (hed′āk) Pain in the head. Also called cephalalgia.

    blind h. See migraine.

    cluster h. Recurrent unilateral headache in the orbitotemporal area; usually of brief duration, often severe, generally occurring at regular intervals of six-week cycles; usually accompanied by stuffiness of the nose and tearing of the eye on the same side as the pain; can be precipitated by the use of histamine, alcohol, or nitroglycerin; more prevalent among males who smoke heavily. Also called histaminic headache; Horton's headache.

    histaminic h. See cluster headache.

    Horton's h. See cluster headache.

    migraine h. See migraine.

    organic h. Headache caused by disease occurring within the skull.

    powder h. Popular name for headache associated with occupational exposure to nitroglycerin during manufacturing and handling of explosives, munitions, and pharmaceuticals; it frequently begins in the forehead and migrates to the back (occipital) region of the head, where it remains for hours or days; associated symptoms include restlessness, insomnia, and depression. Alcohol ingestion sometimes worsens the headache.

    sick h. See migraine.

    tension h. Headache caused by sustained contraction of muscles about the scalp, face, and neck.

    vascular h. See migraine.

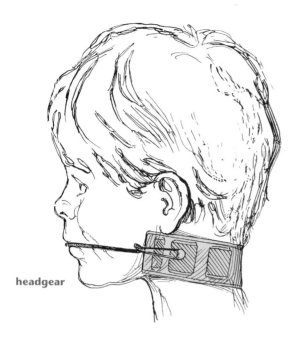

headgear

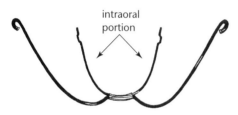

intraoral portion

headgear (hed′gēr) **1.** In orthodontics, a device encircling the head or neck to provide external support for an intraoral appliance. **2.** In radiology, a device for protecting the head from radiation injury.

headgut (hed′gut) See foregut.

heal (hēl) **1.** To close or unite naturally; applied to an incision, wound, or ulcer. **2.** To restore to health.

healer (hēl′er) One who heals or cures.

healing (hēl′ing) The process of restoring to health.

    faith h. Psychotherapeutic treatment based on a deep belief in divine intervention.

    h. by first intention A relatively rapid healing of wounds when the edges are in close apposition and there is no suppuration; new connective tissue may form an almost imperceptible, temporary scar. Also called primary adhesion; primary union.

    h. by second intention A delayed process occurring when the edges of a wound are not in close approximation; granulation tissue develops to unite the wound edges, after some suppuration has occurred, generally leaving a visible scar. Also called secondary adhesions; secondary union.

    h. by third intention The slow process of filling the gap of a wound or ulcer with granulations, which leaves a scar of tough fibrous tissue.

health (helth) A state of physical, mental, and social well-being, characterized by optimal functioning without disorders of any nature.

    public h. The organized programs, services, and institutions concerned with the prevention and control of disease of the population on the international, national, state, or municipal level.

Health maintenance organization (HMO) An organized system for providing comprehensive prepaid health care, designed to deliver a set of agreed-upon basic, supplemental, and treatment services to a voluntarily enrolled group of people in a defined geographic area; it requires that its enrollees use the services of designated physicians, hospitals, and other providers of medical care; it receives reimbursement through a predetermined, fixed, periodic prepayment made by (or in behalf of) each individual or family unit regardless of the number of services provided.

healthy (hel′the) In good health; free from disease.

hear (hēr) To perceive sound.

hearing (hēr′ing) The ability to perceive sound.

    color h. A subjective color sensation produced by certain sound waves.

hearing aid (hēr′ing ād) A small electronic device that amplifies sound; consists of a microphone, amplifier, and receiver; used to compensate for a hearing loss.

    air-conduction h.a. A hearing aid designed to utilize the normal air-conduction pathways.

    bone-conduction h.a. A hearing aid designed to utilize the normal bone-conduction mechanism; the amplified sound waves are transmitted to a bone-conductor vibrator located on the mastoid process behind the ear.

hearing loss (hēr′ing los′) Reduced or complete loss of hearing ability. See also deafness.

    conductive h.l. Hearing loss developed from any disease or injury preventing sound waves from reaching the fluids within the cochlea of the inner ear; causes include complete occlusion of the ear canal (between the auricle and eardrum), perforation of the

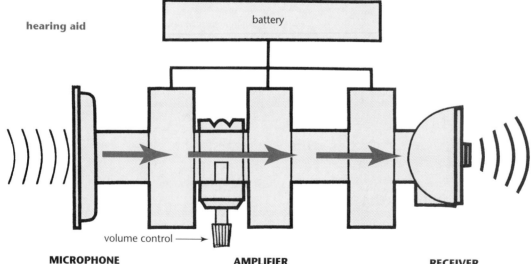

hearing aid

battery

volume control

MICROPHONE
Microphone collects sound waves (just as the ear does) and converts them into electrical impulses.

AMPLIFIER
Amplifier, powered by a battery, increases the intensity of the electrical impulses several thousand times; loudness can be adjusted by the volume control.

RECEIVER
Receiver or speaker changes the amplified electrical impulses back to sound waves which is delivered many times louder into the ear.

eardrum, the presence of fluid in the middle ear chamber, and dislocation or fixation of the ear ossicles. Also called conductive deafness.

noise-induced h.l. Hearing loss caused by high intensity noise levels in which the acoustically generated shearing forces entering the inner ear damage the sensory cells of the cochlea, hence disrupting transmission of sound energy. Also called industrial deafness; acoustic trauma deafness.

occupational h.l. Hearing loss associated with a person's occupation; may be partial or total, unilateral or bilateral, conductive or sensorineural; and may result from a wide variety of causative factors (e.g., blunt or penetrating head injuries, prolonged exposure to noise in excess of 85 decibels, exposure to ototoxic substances, ther-

mal injuries). Also called occupational deafness.

ototoxic h.l. Hearing loss caused by the intake of certain medications or exposure to heavy metals, industrial solvents, dyes, and other toxic substances.

sensorineural h.l. Hearing loss due to any abnormality, disease, or trauma that brings about dysfunction, deterioration, or destruction of the inner ear or of the cochlear fibers of the vestibulo-cochlear (eighth cranial) nerve. Also called nerve deafness; neural deafness; sensorineural deafness.

heart (hart) The hollow, muscular, four-chambered organ covered by a membranous sac (pericardium), lying between the lungs; it receives blood from the veins and pumps it into the arteries, thus maintaining blood circulation throughout the body.

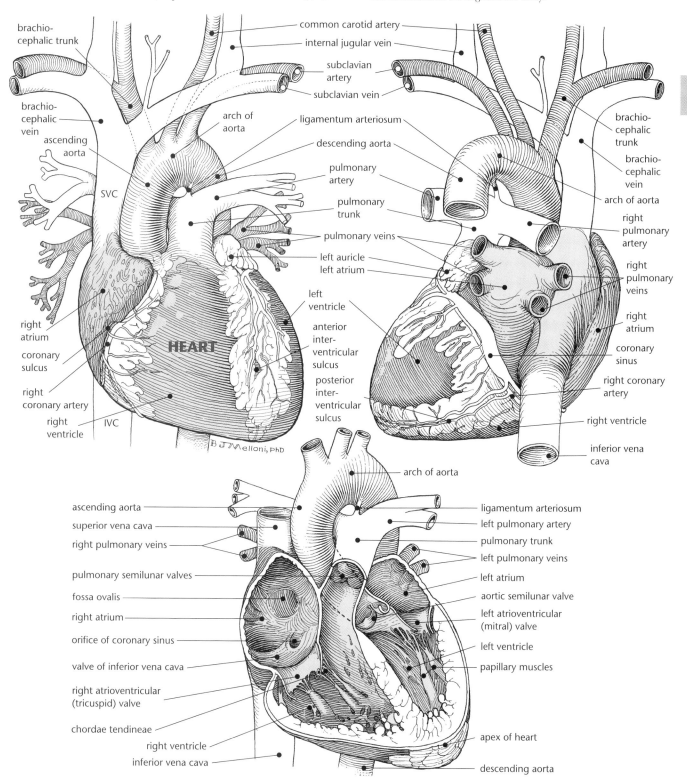

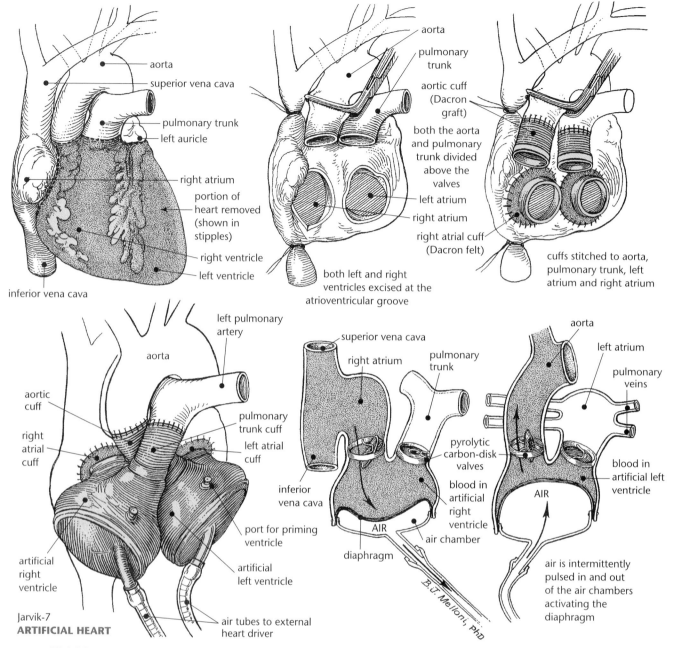

aorta
superior vena cava
pulmonary trunk
left auricle
right atrium
portion of heart removed (shown in stipples)
right ventricle
left ventricle
inferior vena cava

aorta
pulmonary trunk
aortic cuff (Dacron graft)
both the aorta and pulmonary trunk divided above the valves
left atrium
right atrium
right atrial cuff (Dacron felt)
both left and right ventricles excised at the atrioventricular groove

cuffs stitched to aorta, pulmonary trunk, left atrium and right atrium

left pulmonary artery
aorta
aortic cuff
right atrial cuff
pulmonary trunk cuff
left atrial cuff
port for priming ventricle
artificial right ventricle
artificial left ventricle
air tubes to external heart driver
Jarvik-7
ARTIFICIAL HEART

superior vena cava
right atrium
pulmonary trunk
inferior vena cava
blood in artificial right ventricle
AIR
diaphragm
air chamber

aorta
left atrium
pulmonary veins
pyrolytic carbon-disk valves
blood in artificial left ventricle
AIR
air is intermittently pulsed in and out of the air chambers activating the diaphragm

B. J. Melloni, PhD

artificial h. A mechanical device that partially or completely replaces the function of the natural heart.

left h. The left atrium and left ventricle considered together.

right h. The right atrium and right ventricle considered together.

stony h. See ischemic contracture of left ventricle, under contracture.

heartbeat (hart'bēt) One single complete cardiac cycle; one set of contraction and dilatation of the heart muscle.

heartburn (hart'bern) A burning sensation felt in the lower chest, which may extend from the tip of the breastbone to the throat, caused by irritation of the esophagus; occurs when stomach acid flows back (acid reflux) into the esophagus due to an incompetent esophageal sphincter muscle (which fails to close completely). Also called pyrosis.

heartworm (hart'werm) A parasitic worm, *Dirofilaria immitis*, infecting the heart of dogs, rarely of humans.

heat (hēt) A state of elevated temperature.

h. of combustion The quantity of heat released by complete

oxidation of 1 mole of a substance at constant pressure.

prickly h. A common skin condition of hot humid climates, characterized by blockage of sweat pores, retention of sweat, and formation of tiny vesicular papules that itch and burn. Also called miliaria rubra; heat rash.

heat-labile (hēt' la'bl) Susceptible to being destroyed by a rise in temperature.

heat stroke (hēt'strōk) Failure of the body's thermal regulatory mechanism, a life-threatening emergency, characterized chiefly by dizziness, confusion, visual disturbances, high body temperature (approaching 106°F), hot and dry skin, cessation of sweating, rapid pulse, and low blood pressure; caused by prolonged exposure to hot environments; persons at risk include chronically ill patients, those taking diuretics or other medications, and nonacclimatized workers performing strenuous tasks. Also called thermoplegia. COMPARE heat exhaustion.

hebephrenia (heb-ĕ-fre'ne-ah) See schizophrenia, disorganized type, under schizophrenia.

hectic (hek'tik) **1.** Relating to daily fever, as occurs in certain diseases (e.g., tuberculosis). **2.** Feverish.

hectogram (hek′to-gram) One hundred grams.

hectoliter (hek′to-le-ter) One hundred liters, the equivalent of 26.4 American gallons.

heel (hēl) **1.** The rounded posterior portion of the foot. **2.** The part of a shoe that supports the heel bone area.

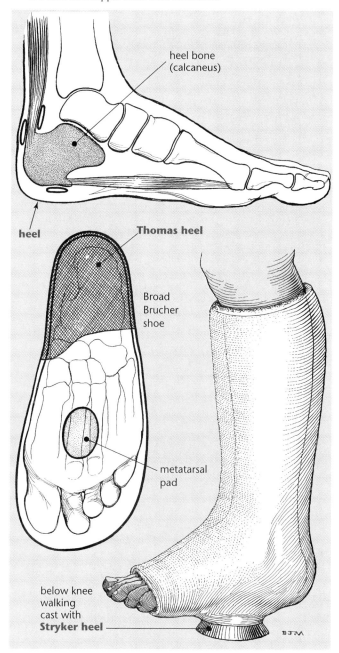

Thomas h. A shoe modification consisting of a piece of leather that is thicker on the medial side of the shoe and built out anteriorly under the instep; it supports the waist of the shoe against excessive pressure (e.g., in some forms of flatfoot).

Stryker h. A solid rubber device attached to the bottom of a walking cast to facilitate walking.

heelstick (hēl′stik) In neonatology, a capillary blood sampling procedure consisting of puncturing the side of the heel with a lancet and collecting the blood with a tube through capillary action; performed on newborn infants when only a small quantity of blood is needed; may also be performed to obtain a capillary blood gas sample.

helicine (hel′ĭ-sīn) **1.** Relating to a spiral or helix. **2.** Coiled.

Helicobacter (hel-ĭ-ko-bak′ter) Genus of motile, spiral, gram-negative bacteria found in the intestinal tract and reproductive organs of animals and the intestinal tract of humans. Formerly called *Campylobacter.*

　H. jejuni Species that is the major cause of enterocolitis ranging from self-limited mild intestinal disturbances to severe recurrent diarrhea with inflammatory changes resembling those of ulcerative colitis or Crohn's disease. Formerly called *Campylobacter jejuni.*

　H. pylori A species causing active chronic gastritis (type B gastritis); found in more than 90% of patients with duodenal ulcers and believed to play a central role in development of this condition. The organism has been implicated as a cause of stomach cancer. Formerly called *Campylobacter pyloris.*

helicoid (hel′ĭ-koid) Spiral.

helicotrema (hel-ĭ-ko-tre′mah) The narrow opening within the tip of the cochlea of the inner ear connecting the scala tympani with the scala vestibuli.

helio- Combining form meaning the sun.

heliopathy (he-le-op′ah-the) Any injury caused by exposure to sunlight.

heliosis (he-le-o′sis) See sunstroke.

heliotaxis (he-le-o-tak′sis) The tendency of a microorganism to move either toward or away from a light source.

helium (he′le-um) A gaseous element; symbol He, atomic number 2, atomic weight 4.003.

helix (he′liks) **1.** The folded skin-covered cartilage forming the margin of the outer ear (auricle). **2.** A coiled structure.

　DNA h. See double helix.

　double h. The spiral structure formed by two strands of deoxyribonucleic acid (DNA) held together by hydrogen bonds between pairs of bases projecting from each strand. Also called DNA helix; twin helix; Watson-Crick helix.

　twin h. See double helix.

　Watson-Crick h. See double helix.

helminth (hel′minth) **1.** A parasitic intestinal worm. **2.** A wormlike parasite.

helminthemesis (hel-min-them′ĕ-sis) The vomiting of parasitic worms.

helminthiasis (hel-min-thi′ah-sis) Infestation with intestinal worms.

helminthic (hel-min′thik) Relating to worms, especially intestinal worms.

helminthoid (hel-min′thoid) Resembling a worm.

helminthology (hel-min-thol′o-je) The study of worms, especially the parasitic intestinal worms.

heloma (he-lo′mah) Latin for corn.

　h. durum See hard corn, under corn.

　h. molle See soft corn, under corn.

helotomy (he-lot′o-me) Surgical removal or paring of corns or calluses.

hemacytometer (he-mă-si-tom′ĕ-ter) See hemocytometer.

hemacytozoon (he-mă-si-to-zo′on) See hemocytozoon.

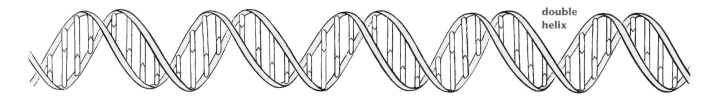

double helix

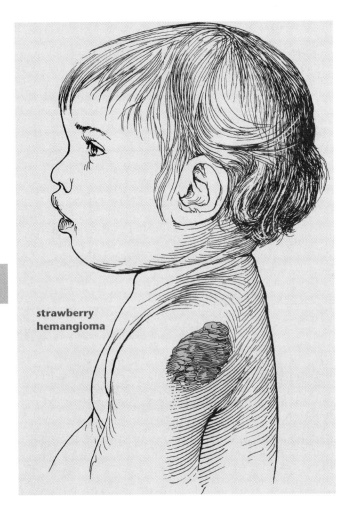

strawberry hemangioma

minute, closely packed blood vessels; occurs in many tissues, especially the skin and the mucous membrane of the oral cavity.

    cavernous h. Hemangioma composed of thin-walled channels forming a spongy mass, usually 1 to 2 cm in diameter; may occur in many tissues and organs, including the central nervous system and liver.

    port-wine h. See nevus flammeus, under nevus.

    senile h. A bright red capillary hemangioma varying in size from pinhead to several centimeters in diameter; may be flat or slightly raised; seen most frequently in elderly persons.

    strawberry h. A well-demarcated capillary hemangioma present at birth and growing rapidly into a red, rough, elevated lesion; it usually peaks in one to three years and gradually disappears without treatment by age five to seven. Also called nevus vasculosus; nevus vascularis.

hemangiomatosis (he-man′je-o-mah-to′sis) The presence of several hemangiomas.

hemangiopericytoma (he-man′je-o-per-ĭ-si-to′mah) Malignant tumor, usually small but may get as large as 8 cm, most commonly arising in the lower extremities or in the retroperitoneum; composed of numerous tiny blood channels encased in masses of connective-tissue cells (pericytes). Also called perithelioma.

hemangiosarcoma (he-man′je-o-sar-ko′mah) See angiosarcoma.

hemapheresis (he-mă-fĕ-re′sis) The process of separating freshly drawn blood into its components, retaining the desired components and returning the rest to the donor.

hemarthrosis (he-mar-thro′sis) Bleeding into a joint.

hematemesis (he-mă-tem′ĕ-sis) Vomiting of blood.

hematic (he-mat′ik) Relating to blood.

hematin (hem′ah-tin) The hydroxide of heme.

hematinic (he-mă-tin′ik) An agent that improves the condition of the blood.

hemato- Combining form meaning blood.

hematoblast (hem-at′o-blast) A primitive blood cell from which develop immature blood cells (e.g., erythroblasts, lymphoblasts, myeloblasts).

hematocele (hem-at′o-sēl) Collection of blood in a structure, especially under the serous covering of a testis.

hematochezia (hem′ah-to-ke′ze-ah) The passage of bloody feces.

hematocolpometra (hem′ah-to-kol′po-me′trah) Accumulation of blood in the uterus and vagina resulting from an obstruction (e.g., an imperforate hymen).

hematocolpos (hem′ah-to-kol′pos) Collection of menstrual blood in the vagina, usually due to an imperforate hymen.

hematocrit (he-mat′o-krit) (HCT) **1.** The volume percentage of packed red blood cells in a whole blood sample. **2.** A small centrifuge for separating the cellular constituents of blood from the plasma.

hematocystis (hem′ah-to-sis′tis) An escape of blood into the bladder.

hematocyte (hem′ah-to-sīt) See hemocyte.

hematocytometer (hem′ah-to-si-tom′ĕ-ter) See hemocytometer.

hematocytozoon (hem′ah-to-si′to-zo′on) See hemocytozoon.

hematocyturia (hem′ah-to-si-tu′re-ah) The presence of red blood cells in the urine.

hematogenesis (hem′ah-to-jen′ĕ-sis) See hemopoiesis.

hematogenic, hematogenous (hem′ah-to-jen′ik, hem′ah-toj′ĕ-nus) Derived from or transported by the blood.

hematohistioblast (hem-ah-to-his′te-o-blast) See hemohistioblast.

hematoid (he′mă-toid) Resembling blood.

hematoidin (he-mă-toid′in) A golden yellow pigment derived from the breakdown of hemoglobin; formed in the tissues as a result of hemorrhage.

hematologist (he-mă-tol′o-jist) A specialist in hematology.

hematology (he-mă-tol′o-je) The medical specialty concerned with the diagnosis and treatment of diseases of the blood and blood-forming tissues.

hematolysis (he-mă-tol′ĭ-sis) See hemolysis.

hematolytic (he-mă-to-lit′ik) See hemolytic.

hemadsorption (he-mad-sorp′shun) Phenomenon in which a substance adheres to the surface of a red blood cell.

hemagglutination (he-mă-gloo′tĭ-na′shun) Clumping (agglutination) of red blood cells.

hemagglutinin (he-mă-gloo′tĭ-nin) A protein present in blood serum that causes clumping (agglutination) of red blood cells; also present in surface projections of some viruses.

hemagogic (he-mă-goj′ik) Stimulating flow of blood.

hemagogue, hemagog (he′mă-gog) Any agent that stimulates blood flow, particularly during menstruation.

hemal (he′mal) **1.** Relating to blood. **2.** Relating to the part of the body in front of the spinal column; ventral.

hemangiectasis, hemangiectasia (he-man-je-ek′tah-sis, he-man-je-ek-ta′se-ah) Dilatation of blood vessels.

hemangioblast (hē-man′je-o-blast) One of the embryonic precursor cells eventually giving rise to blood cells and the inner lining of blood vessels.

hemangioblastoma (he-man-je-o-blas-to′mah) A benign, slowly growing tumor of the cerebellum containing cysts and solid masses and originating from capillary-forming cells. Also called angioblastoma.

hemangioendothelioblastoma (he-man′je-o-en′do-the′le-o-blas-to′mah) A tumor originating in blood cells composed predominantly of immature endothelial cells.

hemangioendothelioma (he-man′je-o-en′do-the′le-o′mah) A tumor originating in blood vessels, composed chiefly of endothelial cells.

hemangioma (he-man-je-o′mah) A benign lesion formed of blood vessels, usually present at birth and occurring in the skin, mucous membranes, or some organs (e.g., brain and liver); composed of small superficial capillaries or deeper thin-walled channels, or both.

    capillary h. A bright red to purple hemangioma composed of

hematoma (he-mă-to'mah) A mass of blood accumulated outside a blood vessel, often found in a partly clotted state.

 epidural h. Localized collection of blood between the dura mater and skull due to rupture of a meningeal artery (occasionally a vein) that runs between the dura and skull; the blood vessel is torn by a skull fracture, usually of a temporal or parietal bone; the patient may or may not have suffered a brain concussion and may have regained consciousness from the initial trauma, only to slip into a coma hours later as the clot expands.

 subdural h. Collection of blood between the dura and arachnoid membranes of the brain resulting from rupture of a bridging vein as it passes from the arachnoid to the dura. It may be *acute subdural h.,* seen in major brain injury; or *chronic subdural h.,* developed from a slow leakage after a trivial, often forgotten or unnoticed, head trauma; seen most commonly in the elderly, in alcoholics, and in patients taking anticoagulant drugs; it causes such symptoms as drowsiness, confusion, inattentiveness, and decreased pain and touch sensations.

hematomanometer (hem'ah-to-mah-nom'e-ter) See hemomanometer.

hematomediastinum (hem-ah-to-me-de-as-ti'num) See hemomediastinum.

hematometra (hem'ah-to-me'trah) Cystic enlargement of the uterus due to accumulation of blood in the uterine cavity, usually caused by an imperforate hymen. Also called hemometra.

hematometry (he-mă-tom'ĕ-tre) Measurement of hemoglobin and percentage of formed elements in the blood. Also called hemometry.

hematomyelia (hem-ah-to-mi-e'le-ah) Effusion of blood into the substance of the spinal cord. Also called myelorrhagia.

hematopathology (hem'ah-to-pah-thol'o-je) A division of pathology concerned with diseases of the blood, blood-forming tissues, and lymphoid tissues. Also called hemopathology.

hematopathy (hem-ah-top'ah-the) See hemopathy.

hematopenia (hem'ah-to-pe'ne-ah) Blood deficiency.

hematopoiesis (hem'ah-to-poi-e'sis) See hemopoiesis.

hematoporphyrin (hem'ah-to-por'fi-rin) A dark red substance formed by the decomposition of hemoglobin. Also called hemoporphyrin.

hematosalpinx (hem'ah-to-sal'pinks) Distention of a fallopian (uterine) tube with accumulated blood. Also called hemosalpinx.

hematosepsis (hem'ah-to-sep'sis) See septicemia.

hematospermia (hem'ah-to-sper'me-ah) The presence of blood in the seminal fluid; most commonly seen in middle-aged men. Also called hemospermia.

hematostaxis (hem'ah-to-stak'sis) Abnormal spontaneous bleeding.

hematotrachelos (hem'ah-to-trah-ke'los) Distention of the uterine cervix with accumulated blood.

hematoxylin (he-mă-tok'si-lin) A crystalline compound used as a histologic stain.

hematozoon (hem'ah-to-zo'on) See hemozoon.

hematuria (hem'ah-tu're-ah) Discharge of red blood cells in the urine.

heme (hēm) The nonprotein, iron-containing porphyrin molecule forming the oxygen-binding element of hemoglobin. Also called ferroprotoporphyrin.

hemeralopia (hem-er-ah-lo'pe-ah) Dimness of vision in a bright light. Also called day blindness; night sight.

hemiageusia (hem-e-ah-gu'ze-ah) Loss of the sense of taste from one side of the tongue. Also called hemiageustia.

hemiageustia (hem-e-ah-gūs'te-ah) See hemiageusia.

hemialgia (hem-e-al'je-ah) Pain on one side of the body only.

hemianalgesia (hem-e-an-al-je'ze-ah) Loss of pain sensation on one side of the body.

hemianesthesia (hem-e-an-es-the'ze-ah) Loss of touch sensation on one side of the body.

 alternate h. Anesthesia on one side of the head and the opposite side of the body and extremities. Also called crossed hemianesthesia.

 crossed h. See alternate hemianesthesia.

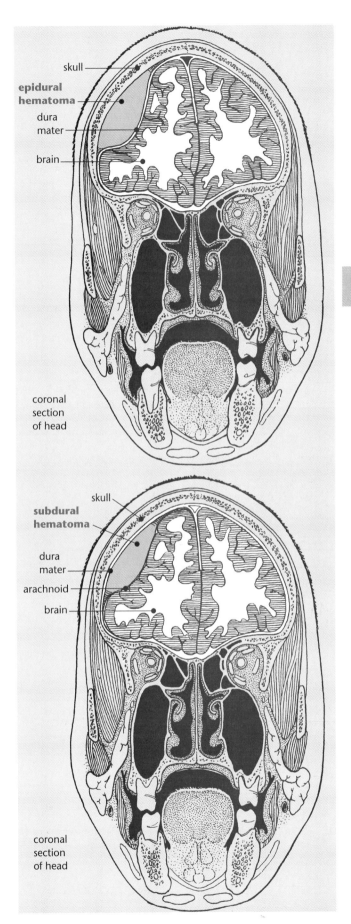

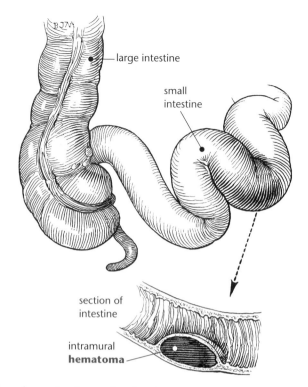

large intestine

small intestine

section of intestine

intramural **hematoma**

hemianopia (hem-e-ah-no′pe-ah) Loss of, or defective, vision in one-half the field of vision of one or both eyes. Also called hemianopsia.

absolute h. No perception of light, color, and form, in one-half the field of vision.

altitudinal h. Hemianopia in the upper or lower half of the field of vision in each eye.

bilateral h. Hemianopia affecting the visual fields of both eyes. Also called binocular hemianopia.

binasal h. Bilateral hemianopia affecting the nasal halves of the visual fields of both eyes.

binocular h. See bilateral hemianopia.

bitemporal h. Bilateral hemianopia affecting the temporal halves of the visual fields of both eyes.

complete h. Hemianopia of the entire half of the visual field of each eye.

congruous h. A homonymous hemianopia in which the defects in the field of vision in each eye are identical in position, size, shape, and degree and are superimposable, resulting in a single defect of the binocular field.

crossed h. Bilateral hemianopia affecting the upper half of one visual field and the lower half of the other.

heteronymous h. Bilateral hemianopia affecting either both nasal halves of the field of vision or both temporal halves.

homonymous h. Bilateral hemianopia affecting the nasal half of one field of vision and the temporal half of the other, making the loss on the same side of each eye.

incomplete h. Hemianopia affecting less than an entire half of the field of vision.

quadrant h., quadrantic h. See quadrantanopia.

hemianopsia (hem-e-an-op′se-ah) See hemianopia.

hemianosmia (hem-e-an-oz′me-ah) Loss of the sense of smell on one side only.

hemiarthroplasty (hem-e-ar′thro-plas-te) Replacement of only part of a joint with artificial material (e.g., of the shoulder joint or the hip joint).

hemiatrophy (hem-e-at′ro-fe) Atrophy confined to one side of the body or an organ.

facial h. Atrophy, usually progressive, affecting one side of the face. Also called Romberg's disease.

hemiballismus (hem-e-bal-iz′mus) Large, flinging, and unusually violent involuntary movements of the arm and leg on one side of the body, caused by disease of the subthalamic nucleus in the brain; the movements cease during sleep.

hemiblock (hem′ĭ-blok) Arrest of nerve impulses in either of the two main divisions of the left branch of the atrioventricular (A-V) bundle in the heart.

hemic (hem′ik) Relating to the blood.

hemicentrum (hem-e-sen′trum) Either lateral half of the body of a vertebra.

hemichorea (hem-e-ko-re′ah) Chorea in which the uncontrollable, quick, and irregular movements are confined to one side of the body.

hemicolectomy (hem-e-ko-lek′to-me) Removal of a portion of the colon.

hemicrania (hem-e-kra′ne-ah) Pain on one side of the head.

hemidiaphoresis (hem-e-di-ah-fo-re′sis) Sweating on one side of the body.

hemifacial (hem-e-fa′shal) Relating to one side of the face.

hemigastrectomy (hem-e-gas-trek′to-me) Removal of one half of the stomach, usually the lowest (pyloric) end.

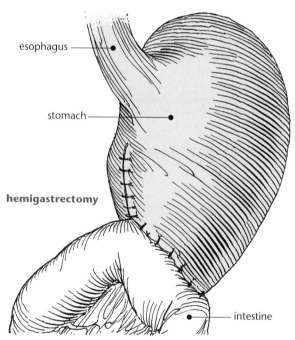

esophagus

stomach

hemigastrectomy

intestine

hemihypertrophy (hem-e-hi-per′tro-fe) Congenital overgrowth of one side of the body.

hemikaryon (hem-e-kar′e-on) A cell nucleus containing half the usual (diploid) number of chromosomes.

hemilaminectomy (hem-e-lam-ĭ-nek′to-me) Removal of one side of the vertebral arch, performed to gain access to a nerve root or intervertebral disk.

hemiparesis (hem-e-par-e′sis) Muscular weakness or mild paralysis of one side of the body.

hemipelvectomy (hem-e-pel-vek′to-me) Removal of the entire leg and varying portions of the hipbone, usually performed when

binasal hemianopia

bitemporal hemianopia

congruous hemianopia

crossed hemianopia

incomplete hemianopia

malignant tumors of the pelvis or leg cannot be removed by lesser procedures. Also called hindquarter amputation.

hemiplegia (hem-e-ple'je-ah) Paralysis of one side of the body.

> **h. alternans** See alternating hemiplegia.

> **alternating h.** Paralysis of one or more cranial nerves on the same side of a brainstem lesion and paralysis of the arm and leg on the opposite side. Also called crossed hemiplegia; hemiplegia alternans.

> **crossed h.** See alternating hemiplegia.

hemiplegic (hem-e-ple'jik) One whose body is paralyzed on one side only.

Hemiptera (he-mip'ter-ah) A large order of insects, including the common bedbug and other bloodsucking species of medical importance.

hemisphere (hem'ĭ-sfēr) Half of a symmetric, approximately spherical object; a half sphere.

> **cerebellar h.** Either one of the two lateral halves of the cerebellum; the portion lateral to the narrow median part (vermis) of the cerebellum.

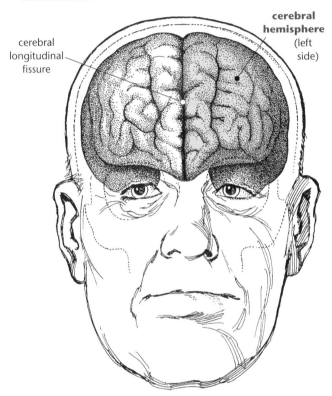

cerebral longitudinal fissure

cerebral hemisphere (left side)

> **cerebral h.** Either one of the lateral halves of the cerebrum.

> **dominant h.** The left cerebral hemisphere in a right-handed individual; the right cerebral hemisphere in a left-handed one; there is usually a close association between speech and the left cerebral hemisphere, except in a small proportion of left-handed individuals.

hemithorax (hem-e-tho'raks) One side of the torso.

hemizygosity (hem-e-zi-gos'ĭ-te) The state of having only one representative of a chromosome or chromosome segment, instead of the usual two.

hemizygote (hem-e-zi'gōt) A cell, tissue, or organism characterized by hemizygosity; the human male is a hemizygote with reference to X and Y chromosomes.

hemizygous, hemizygotic (hem-e-zi'gus, hem-e-zi-got'ik) Relating to hemizygosity or to a hemizygote; the term refers especially to X-linked genes in the male but is also used in reference to genes in any chromosome segment that is deleted on the homologous chromosome.

hemlock (hem'lok) Any of several poisonous plants (genus *Conium*)

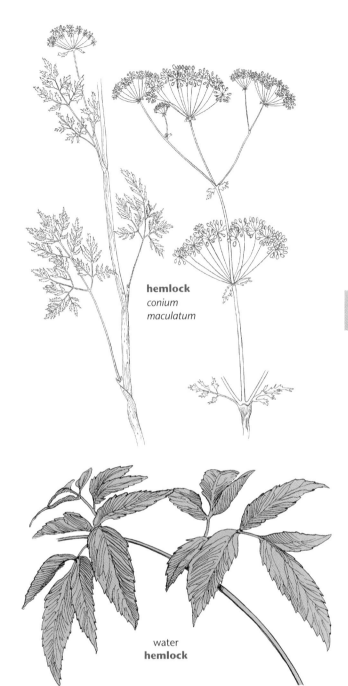

hemlock
*conium
maculatum*

water
hemlock

capable of producing motor paralysis. Commonly called poison hemlock.

hemoagglutinin (he-mo-ah-gloo'tĭ-nin) An antibody present in serum that causes clumping (agglutination) of red blood cells.

hemobilia (he-mo-bil'e-ah) Bleeding into the biliary passages.

hemochromatosis (he-mo-kro-mah-to'sis) Disorder of iron metabolism resulting in accumulation of iron in many tissues, especially the skin, liver, and pancreas, leading to fibrosis and functional deficiency of organs that are severely affected; the heart and other muscles and endocrine glands are also affected; deposition of iron in the skin causes a bronzed pigmentation; deposits in the pancreas lead to a form of diabetes (bronzed diabetes).

hemoclasis, hemoclasia (he-mok'lah-sis, he-mo-kla'se-ah) Destruction of red blood cells.

hemoconcentration (he-mo-kon-sen-tra'shun) Increased concentration of the formed elements of circulating blood, usually as a consequence of loss of plasma from the bloodstream.

hemocyte (he'mo-sīt) Any formed element of the blood. Also called hematocyte.

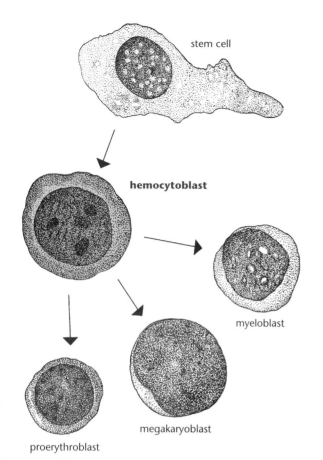

stem cell

hemocytoblast

myeloblast

megakaryoblast

proerythroblast

hemocytoblast (he-mo-si'to-blast) A primitive cell from which granulocytes, red blood cell precursors, and megakaryocytes are derived.

hemocytometer (he-mo-si-tom'ĕ-ter) Instrument for estimating the red blood cell count in a measured volume of blood. Also called erythrocytometer; hemacytometer; hematocytometer.

hemocytotripsis (he-mo-si-to-trip'sis) Destruction of blood cells by mechanical means.

hemocytozoon (he-mo-si-to-zo'on) An animal parasite of blood cells. Also called hemacytozoon; hematocytozoon.

hemodialysis (he-mo-di-al'ĭ-sis) Removal of waste matter or poisons from the blood by means of an artificial kidney (hemodialyzer).

hemodialyzer (he-mo-di'ah-līz-er) An apparatus used as a substitute for the kidneys to purify the blood in acute or chronic kidney failure and in certain types of poisoning or drug overdose; toxic elements are removed by passing the blood through a semipermeable membrane lying in a bathing solution, then returning it to the body. Commonly called artificial kidney; kidney machine.

hemodilution (he-mo-di-lu'shun) Increased plasma content of the blood with consequent decreased concentration of red blood cells.

hemodynamic (he-mo-di-nam'ik) Relating to blood circulation.

hemodynamics (he-mo-di-nam'iks) The science concerned with blood circulation.

hemofiltration (he-mo-fil-tra'shun) Technique for purifying the blood by filtering out blood components that are smaller than albumin and replacing a similar quantity of a balanced electrolyte solution; by this process, unwanted solutes (e.g., urea, creatinine, and other nitrogenous wastes) are removed from the body.

hemoflagellate (he-mo-flaj'ĕ-lāt) Any blood parasite that moves by means of a hairlike structure (flagellum).

hemofuscin (he-mo-fūs'in) A brown pigment derived from hemoglobin; sometimes found in urine along with hemosiderin, indicating increased red blood cell destruction.

hemogenesis (he-mo-jen'ĕ-sis) See hemopoiesis.

hemoglobin (he'mo-glo-bin) (Hb, HgB) The oxygen-bearing protein of red blood cells; it is bright red when saturated with oxygen, purplish when it is not carrying oxygen. Also called blood pigment.

    h. A (Hgb A) The predominant form of hemoglobin of human adults.

    h. A₂ (Hgb A₂) Hemoglobin making up about 1.5 to 3% of the total hemoglobin concentration. An elevated proportion is usually indicative of beta-thalassemia.

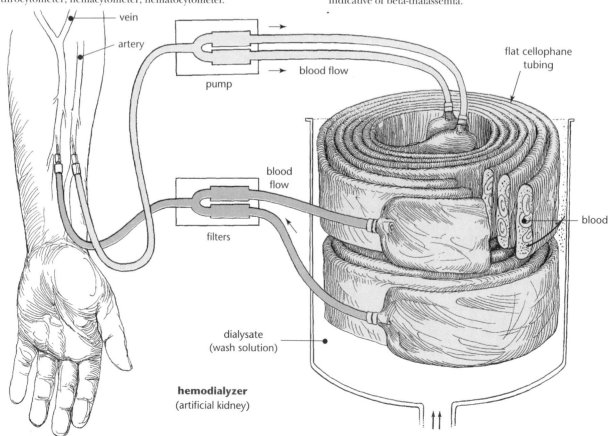

vein

artery

pump

blood flow

blood flow

filters

flat cellophane tubing

blood

dialysate (wash solution)

hemodialyzer
(artificial kidney)

hemocytoblast ■ **hemoglobin**

h. C (Hgb C) An abnormal hemoglobin characterized by an amino acid substitution (lysine for glutamic acid at position 6 of the beta chain); it reduces the normal plasticity of red blood cells. When present, target cells are seen. When homozygous, it is associated with chronic hemolytic anemia.

carbon monoxide h. See carboxyhemoglobin.

h. F (Hgb F) Hemoglobin of a normal fetus; it is the major hemoglobin component during intrauterine life. Also called fetal hemoglobin.

glycated h. A fraction of hemoglobin A to which glucose binds; high concentrations occur in patients with elevated blood sugar levels (as in diabetes). Also called glycosylated hemoglobin.

glycosylated h. See glycated hemoglobin.

h. H (Hgb H) An abnormal hemoglobin composed of four beta chains with a marked affinity for oxygen. It is associated with a variant of alpha-thalassemia.

oxygenated h. See oxyhemoglobin.

reduced h. Hemoglobin after it has released its oxygen in the tissues; the hemoglobin of venous blood.

h. S (Hgb S) Abnormal hemoglobin characterized by an amino acid substitution (valine for glutamic acid at position 6 of the beta chain). An individual with hemoglobin S and hemoglobin A has sickle-cell trait. An individual homozygous for hemoglobin S has sickle-cell anemia. Also called sickle-cell hemoglobin.

sickle-cell h. See hemoglobin S.

hemoglobinemia (he-mo-glo-bī-ne′me-ah) The presence of free hemoglobin in the plasma, resulting from significant mechanical injury to the circulating red blood cells.

hemoglobinopathy (he-mo-glo-bī-nop′ah-the) Any blood disorder due to abnormality of the hemoglobin molecule or to the amounts in which hemoglobin is produced.

hemoglobinuria (he-mo-glo-bī-nu′re-ah) The presence of free hemoglobin in the urine, an indication of recent injury or destruction of red blood cells of at least moderate severity.

malarial h. Uncommon condition caused by infection with the malarial parasite *Plasmodium falciparum*.

march h. Episodes of hemoglobinuria caused by prolonged, intense physical activity (e.g., in marathon running).

paroxysmal nocturnal h. (PNH) An uncommon, acquired disease of circulating red blood cells characterized by increased sensitivity of the cells' membrane to complement with resulting destruction of the cells. Also called Marchiafava-Micheli syndrome.

hemogram (he′mo-gram) A record of the number, proportion, and morphologic features of the cellular elements of blood.

hemohistioblast (he-mo-his′te-o-blast) An undifferentiated cell of the reticuloendothelial system believed to be capable of developing into any of the blood cells. Also called hematohistioblast.

hemolith (he′mo-lith) A stony concretion within the wall of a blood vessel.

hemolysin (he-mol′ĭ-sin) Any substance that destroys blood cells (e.g., toxins, enzymes, antibodies). Also called erythrocytolysin; erythrolysin.

immune h. Hemolysin made by injecting an animal with red blood cells or whole blood from another species.

hemolysinogen (he-mo-lī-sin′o-jen) Antigenic substance in red blood cells capable of stimulating formation of a hemolysin.

hemolysis (he-mol′ĭ-sis) Destruction of red blood cells. Also called erythrocytolysis; hematolysis.

hemolytic (he-mo-lit′ik) Causing disintegration of red blood cells. Also called hematolytic.

hemolyze (he′mo-liz) To cause injury or destruction of red blood cells, with liberation of hemoglobin.

hemomanometer (he-mo-mah-nom′ĕ-ter) Instrument for measuring blood pressure. Also called hematomanometer.

hemomediastinum (he-mo-me-de-as-ti′num) A leaking of blood into the middle compartment of the chest cavity. Also called hematomediastinum.

hemometra (he-mo-me′trah) See hematometra.

hemometry (he-mom′ĕ-tre) See hematometry.

hemopathology (he-mo-pah-thol′o-je) See hematopathology.

hemopathy (he-mop′ah-the) Any disorder of blood and blood-forming tissues. Also called hematopathy.

hemoperfusion (he-mo-per-fu′zhun) Removal of poisons or waste products from the circulation by passing the blood over semipermeable microcapsules containing adsorbents (e.g., activated charcoal) or enzymes within an extracorporeal circuit.

hemopericardium (he-mo-per-ī-kar′de-um) Accumulation of pure blood in the pericardium, the membranous sac surrounding the heart; usually caused by traumatic perforation of the heart, rupture of the heart wall due to disease (e.g., transmural myocardial infarction), or hemorrhage from an abscess or tumor.

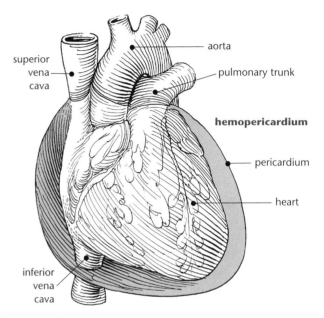

superior vena cava · inferior vena cava · aorta · pulmonary trunk · **hemopericardium** · pericardium · heart

hemoperitoneum (he-mo-per-ī-to-ne′um) Accumulation of blood in the peritoneal cavity; causes include abdominal surgery, bleeding disorders, or trauma.

hemopexin (he-mo-pek′sin) A serum protein of human plasma produced in the liver; important in binding heme.

hemophagocytosis (he-mo-fag-o-si-to′sis) The engulfing of red blood cells by phagocytic cells.

hemophil (he′mo-fil) A microorganism that thrives in blood-containing medium.

hemophilia (he-mo-fil′e-ah) Inherited disorder caused by deficiency of a specific blood-clotting factor; occurs in two main forms, hemophilia A and hemophilia B.

h. A The most common form of hemophilia, transmitted as an X-linked recessive inheritance; characterized by prolonged clotting time, easy bruising, and bleeding into joints and muscles; caused by a reduced amount or activity of factor VIII, a component of the blood-clotting process. The defective gene is transmitted from an affected male to his grandsons through his daughters, who (except in rare occasions) are asymptomatic. Also called classic hemophilia. See also factor VIII, under factor.

h. B A form of hemophilia, caused by deficiency of factor IX, that has clinical and laboratory features similar to those of hemophilia A; transmitted as an X-linked recessive inheritance. Also called Christmas disease (after a man named Christmas, the first patient in whom the disease was shown to be distinct from hemophilia A). See also factor IX, under factor.

classic h. See hemophilia A.

hemophiliac (he-mo-fil′e-ak) A person afflicted with hemophilia. Popularly called bleeder.

hemophilic (he-mo-fil′ik) Relating to hemophilia.

Hemophilus (he-mof′ĭ-lus) See Haemophilus.

hemophobia (he-mo-fo′be-ah) Abnormally exaggerated fear of the sight of blood.

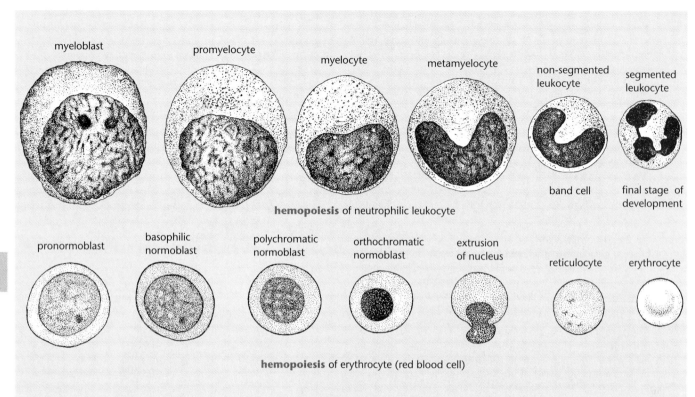

myeloblast promyelocyte myelocyte metamyelocyte non-segmented leukocyte segmented leukocyte

band cell final stage of development

hemopoiesis of neutrophilic leukocyte

pronormoblast basophilic normoblast polychromatic normoblast orthochromatic normoblast extrusion of nucleus reticulocyte erythrocyte

hemopoiesis of erythrocyte (red blood cell)

hemophthalmia (he-mof-thal′me-ah) Bleeding into the eyeball.

hemopneumopericardium (he-mo-nu-mo-per-ĭ-kar′de-um) Accumulation of blood and air in the pericardium, the sac that envelops the heart. Also called pneumohemopericardium.

hemopneumothorax (he-mo-nu-mo-tho′raks) Accumulation of blood and air in the pleural space (i.e., between the two layers of the membrane enveloping a lung). Also called pneumohemothorax.

hemopoiesis (he-mo-poi-e′sis) The formation of blood cells. Also called hematopoiesis; hematogenesis; hemogenesis.

hemopoietic (he-mo-poi-et′ik) Relating to the formation of blood cells.

hemopoietin (he-mo-poi-e′tin) See erythropoietin.

hemoporphyrin (he-mo-por′fĭ-rin) See hematoporphyrin.

hemoprotein (he-mo-pro′tēn) Any protein that is linked to heme (e.g., hemoglobin).

hemoptysis (he-mop′tĭ-sis) Spitting of blood, usually from the larynx, trachea, or lower respiratory tract.

hemopyelectasis (he-mo-pi-ĕ-lek′tah-sis) Distention of the kidney pelvis with blood.

hemorrhage (hem′or-ij) Bleeding, especially profuse.

   antepartum h. In obstetrics, excessive bleeding occurring at the onset of labor, as seen in premature separation of a placenta previa.

   cerebral h. Bleeding from blood vessels within the brain; usually causes include hypertension and trauma. Also called intracerebral hemorrhage.

   duret h.'s Linear hemorrhages of the midbrain and upper portion of the pons, occurring as a result of downward movement of the midbrain due to brain swelling.

   dysfunctional uterine h. Abnormal bleeding from the uterus in the absence of organic disease or lesion.

   internal h. Bleeding into a body cavity or an organ.

   intracerebral h. See cerebral hemorrhage.

   intracranial h. Bleeding occurring anywhere within the skull.

   postpartum h. Excessive bleeding (in excess of 500 ml) following vaginal delivery; designated *early* when it occurs within 24

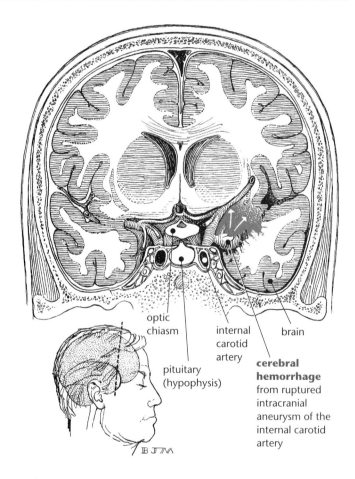

optic chiasm

internal carotid artery

brain

pituitary (hypophysis)

cerebral hemorrhage from ruptured intracranial aneurysm of the internal carotid artery

hours after delivery, and *late* when it occurs between 24 hours and 6 weeks after delivery.

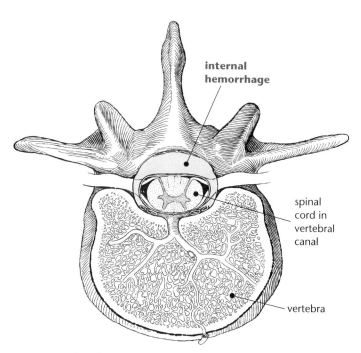

internal hemorrhage

spinal cord in vertebral canal

vertebra

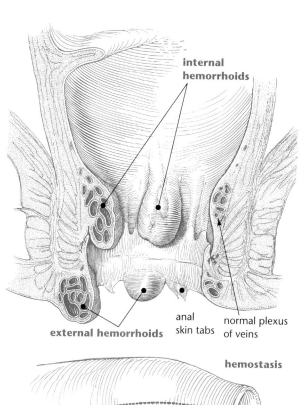

internal hemorrhoids

external hemorrhoids

anal skin tabs

normal plexus of veins

H

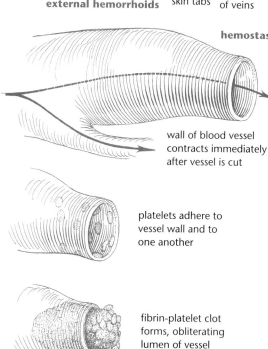

hemostasis

wall of blood vessel contracts immediately after vessel is cut

platelets adhere to vessel wall and to one another

fibrin-platelet clot forms, obliterating lumen of vessel

clot shrinks further constricting vessel wall

secondary h. Bleeding occurring at an interval after an injury or operation.

subdural h. Bleeding into the subdural space, between the dural and arachnoidal membranes of the brain, usually resulting from head injuries that rupture veins traversing the space.

vitreous h. Bleeding into the vitreous body (within the eyeball); may be caused by rupture of adjacent vessels by trauma (e.g., contusion, concussion, penetrating injuries) or acute vitreous collapse; or by systemic disease (e.g., diabetes, hypertension, leukemia).

hemorrhagenic (hem-o-rah-jen'ik) Causing hemorrhage.

hemorrhagic (hem-o-raj'ik) Relating to hemorrhage.

hemorrhagin (hem-o-ra'jin) Any of a group of toxins that destroy the endothelial cells in capillaries, causing hemorrhage throughout the tissues; found in certain poisonous substances (e.g., rattlesnake venom and castor oil seeds).

hemorrheology (he-mo-re-ol'o-je) The study of the effects of blood flow in blood vessels and the formed elements of blood.

hemorrhoidal (hem-o-roi'dal) **1.** Relating to hemorrhoids. **2.** Relating to blood vessels of the rectum and anus.

hemorrhoidectomy (hem-o-roid-ek'to-me) Surgical removal of hemorrhoids.

hemorrhoids (hem'o-roids) A varicose distention of superficial veins at or within the anus; may become strangulated, ulcerated, or fissured; generally associated with recurrent constipation, pregnancy (due to pressure against the veins), or, occasionally, portal hypertension. Also called piles.

external h. Hemorrhoids at the anal opening involving the inferior rectal (hemorrhoidal) veins.

internal h. Hemorrhoids within the anal canal, at the anorectal junction, involving the superior rectal (hemorrhoidal) veins.

hemosalpinx (he-mo-sal'pinks) See hematosalpinx.

hemosiderin (he-mo-sid'er-in) A granular, iron-containing yellow pigment formed during decomposition of hemoglobin; found in a variety of tissues upon breakdown of red blood cells.

hemosiderosis (he-mo-sid-er-o'sis) Deposition of hemosiderin in tissues.

idiopathic pulmonary h. Recurrent hemorrhage of the lungs; cause is unknown.

hemospermia (he-mo-sper'me-ah) See hematospermia.

hemostasis (he-mo-sta'sis) The arrest of bleeding.

hemostat (he'mo-stat) Instrument for compressing a blood vessel to stop bleeding.

hemostatic (he-mo-stat'ik) **1.** Tending to stop bleeding. **2.** Any agent having such property.

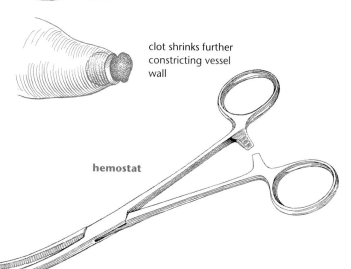

hemostat

H17

hemorrhagenic ■ hemostatic

hemostyptic (he-mo-stip′tik) A chemical hemostatic; any agent that stops bleeding by constricting tissues (i.e., by astringent action).

hemothorax (he-mo-tho′raks) Accumulation of blood between the two layers of the pleura, the membrane enveloping a lung; may be caused by trauma, pulmonary infarction, tumors, tuberculosis, diagnostic procedures, or surgery.

hemotoxic (he-mo-tok′sik) Injurious to blood cells.

hemotoxin (he-mo-tok′sin) Any toxin capable of injuring or destroying red blood cells.

hemotympanum (he-mo-tim′pah-num) Collection of blood in the middle ear chamber.

hemozoon (he-mo-zo′on) Any parasitic microorganism that thrives in the circulating blood of its host. Also called hematozoon.

henry (hen′re) (H) Unit of electric inductance.

Hepadnaviridae (he-pad-nah-vir′ĭ-de) A family of DNA viruses that includes the hepatitis B and D viruses.

hepar (he′par) Latin for liver.

heparin (hep′ah-rin) An anticoagulant compound used in the prevention and treatment of abnormal blood clot formation (thrombosis).

heparinize (hep′er-ĭ-nīz) To administer heparin in order to delay blood clotting.

hepatalgia (hep-ah-tal′je-ah) Pain in the liver. Also called hepatodynia.

hepatectomy (hep-ah-tek′to-me) Surgical removal of a portion of the liver.

hepatic (hĕ-pat′ik) Relating to the liver.

hepaticoduodenostomy (hĕ-pat-ĭ-ko-du-o-de-nos′to-me) Surgical creation of a passage between the hepatic duct and the duodenum.

hepaticojejunostomy (hĕ-pat-ĭ-ko-je-ju-nos′to-me) Surgical creation of a passage between the hepatic duct and the jejunum.

hepatitis (hep-ah-ti′tis) Inflammation of the liver.

   h. A Hepatitis caused by the hepatitis A virus (HAV), transmitted through fecal contamination of food and water (fecal-oral route), with a 15- to 45-day incubation period; may occur sporadically or in epidemics; it does not produce a chronic disease or a carrier state; passive immunization can be induced by administration of immune globulin. Formerly called infectious hepatitis.

   alcoholic h. Inflammatory liver damage caused by excessive alcohol ingestion; symptoms and signs may include focal destruction of liver cells, progressive fibrosis, obstruction of bile ducts, jaundice, and tender enlargement of the liver. See also alcoholic liver disease, under disease.

   anicteric h. Hepatitis in which hyperbilirubinemia is mild, serum transaminase levels are elevated, and liver biopsy resembles icteric forms.

   h. B Hepatitis caused by hepatitis B virus (HBV), present in body fluids such as saliva, semen, and vaginal fluid; spread by transfusion of infected blood, the use of contaminated needles, needle-prick accidents, the sexual route, or from mother to child (vertical transmission); incubation period is 4 to 26 weeks (typically 6–8 weeks); produces an asymptomatic carrier state and plays a significant role in development of cancer of the liver (hepatocellular carcinoma). Prevention and treatment: administration of hepatitis B immune globulin (to induce passive immunity), recombinant HBsAg vaccine, and alpha interferon therapy. Formerly called serum hepatitis.

   h. C Hepatitis caused by hepatitis C virus (HCV); transmitted via transfusion of infected blood or blood products, the use of contaminated needles, needle-prick accidents, the sexual route, and from mother to newborn (predominantly with HIV coinfection); often causes chronic hepatitis, possibly with highest incidence in newborns, leading to cirrhosis; incubation period is 8 to l2 weeks. It is treated with alpha interferon. Formerly called transfusion-associated non-A, non-B hepatitis.

   cholestatic h. Hepatitis in which the signs of bile duct obstruction are more prominent than those of liver cell necrosis; may be seen occasionally in viral hepatitis or may be drug-induced; must be differentiated from extrahepatic obstruction.

   chronic h. Condition in which there is biochemical or serologic evidence of continuing inflammatory liver disease for more than six months, producing symptoms and without steady improvement.

   chronic active h. Progressive destruction of the liver architecture characterized by piecemeal necrosis and formation of intralobular septa leading eventually to cirrhosis and liver failure; usually associated with hepatitis B and C viruses (HBV and HCV), especially in newborn infants; nonviral causes include metabolic disorders and drug-induced hepatitis. Also called chronic aggressive hepatitis.

   chronic aggressive h. See chronic active hepatitis.

   chronic persistent h. (CPH) A usually benign, self-limited condition, considered a delayed recovery from an acute infection with hepatitis viruses A, B, or C or combined B and D viruses, and lasting up to several years; symptoms are usually minor, and liver function tests show only mild abnormalities. The patients may be carriers of the viruses, often asymptomatic.

   h. D Hepatitis caused by hepatitis D virus (HDV), developed in the presence of hepatitis B virus (HBV); may occur when transfused blood contains both viruses (coinfection), or as an additional infection of a chronic HBV carrier (superinfection); incubation period is 30 to 120 days (typically 60 days). Prevention: vaccination against HBsAG; currently there is no vaccine for chronic carriers. Also called delta hepatitis; delta agent hepatitis.

   delta h., delta agent h. See hepatitis D.

   drug-induced h., toxic h. Acute hepatitis occurring as a complication of ingesting certain drugs (e.g., phenytoin or salicylates), or from occupational exposure to chemicals (e.g., polypropylene chloride).

   h. E Self-limited hepatitis (with a high mortality rate in pregnant women) caused by hepatitis E virus (HEV), transmitted through fecally contaminated food and water (fecal-oral route); may occur in waterborne epidemics; incubation period is 14 to 60 days (typically 40 days); it does not produce a chronic state. Formerly called non-A, non-B hepatitis.

   infectious h. See hepatitis A.

   neonatal h. General term for a variety of disorders of newborn infants, involving injury to liver cells and tissues and causing hyperbilirubinemia and jaundice; cause is unknown; may be associated with hepatitis B.

   non-A, non-B (NANB) h. See hepatitis C and E.

   serum h. (SH) See hepatitis B.

   viral h. Hepatitis caused by a virus; unless otherwise specified, the term refers to infection of the liver by a small group of viruses (A, B, C, D, and E viruses) that have an affinity for the liver and produce similar patterns of clinical and morphologic acute hepatitis, but vary in their potential to induce chronic or fulminant hepatitis or the carrier state of the disease.

hepatization (hep-ah-ti-za′shun) The consolidation of normally loose tissue into a mass resembling liver.

hepatobiliary (hep-ah-to-bil′e-ār-e) Relating to the liver and bile ducts.

hepato-, hepat- Combining forms meaning liver.

hepatoblastoma (hep-ah-to-blas-to′mah) A malignant tumor of infancy composed of primitive cells resembling liver.

hepatocellular (hep-ah-to-sel′u-lar) Relating to the liver cells.

hepatocyte (hep′ah-to-sīt) A cell forming the characteristic tissue (parenchyma) of the liver.

hepatoduodenal (hep-ah-to-du-od′ĕ-nal) Relating to the liver and the duodenum, the portion of small intestine adjoining the stomach.

hepatodynia (hep-ah-to-din′e-ah) See hepatalgia.

hepatoenteric (hep-ah-to-en-ter′ik) Relating to the liver and the intestine.

hepatogastric (hep-ah-to-gas′trik) Relating to the liver and the stomach.

hepatogenic, hepatogenous (hep-ah-to-jen′ik, hep-ah-toj′ĕ-nus) Formed in the liver; originating from the liver.

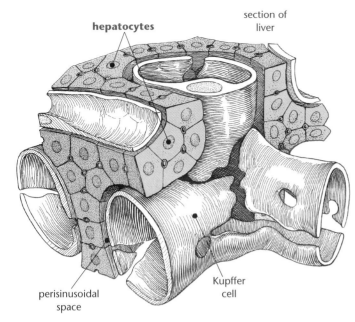

hepatocytes
section of liver
perisinusoidal space
Kupffer cell

hepatography (hep-ah-tog'rah-fe) Radiography of the liver.

hepatojugular (hep-ah-to-jug'u-lar) Relating to the liver and a jugular vein.

hepatolienal (hep-ah-to-li'e-nal) Relating to the liver and spleen.

hepatolienography (hep-ah-to-li-ĕ-nog'rah-fe) See hepatosplenography.

hepatolith (hep'ah-to-lith) A stony concretion in the liver.

hepatolithiasis (hep-ah-to-lī-thi'ah-sis) The presence of stones in the liver.

hepatologist (hep-ah-tol'o-jist) A specialist in diseases of the liver.

hepatology (hep-ah-tol'o-je) The study of the liver and its diseases.

hepatolysin (hep-ah-tol'ĭ-sin) Any agent injurious to liver tissue.

hepatoma (hep-ah-to'mah) Malignant tumor of the liver originating in the parenchymal cells; commonly arises in the presence of chronic hepatitis often associated with an increase in the blood level of alpha fetoprotein. Also called hepatocellular carcinoma.

hepatomegaly (hep-ah-to-meg'ah-le) Abnormal enlargement of the liver.

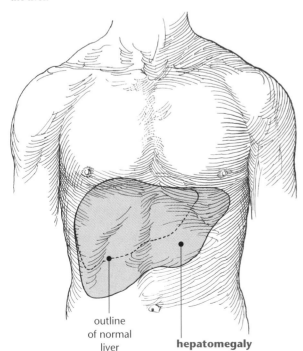

outline of normal liver

hepatomegaly

hepatonecrosis (hep-ah-to-nĕ-kro'sis) Death of liver tissue.

hepatopathy (hep-ah-top'ah-the) Any disease of the liver.

hepatopetal (hep-ah-top'ĕ-tal) Toward the liver; applied to the flow of the portal circulation.

hepatorenal (hep-ah-to-re'nal) Relating to the liver and kidney. See also hepatorenal syndrome, under syndrome.

hepatorrhaphy (hep-ah-tor'ah-fe) Suturing of a cut or wound of the liver.

hepatosplenography (hep-ah-to-splĕ-nog'rah-fe) X-ray imaging of the liver and spleen after infusion of a radiopaque medium. Also called hepatolienography.

hepatosplenomegaly (hep-ah-to-sple-no-meg'ah-le) Abnormal enlargement of the liver and spleen.

hepatotherapy (hep-ah-to-ther'ah-pe) **1.** Treatment of liver disease. **2.** Administration of liver extract.

hepatotoxic (hep-ah-to-tok'sik) Injurious to the liver.

hepatotoxin (hep-ah-to-tok'sin) Any agent destructive to liver cells.

herbivorous (her-biv'o-rus) Feeding on plants.

hereditary (he-red'ĭ-ter-e) Genetically transmitted from parent to offspring. COMPARE heritable.

heredity (he-red'ĭ-te) **1.** The genetic transmission of a specific characteristic from parent to offspring. **2.** The totality of physical and mental characteristics and potentialities so transmitted to the offspring.

heredity linked to chromosome X (colorblindness)

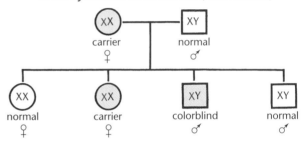

XX carrier ♀   XY normal ♂
XX normal ♀   XX carrier ♀   XY colorblind ♂   XY normal ♂

heredo- Combining form meaning heredity.

heritability (her-ĭ-tah-bil'ĭ-te) A statistical measure of the degree to which a trait is genetically determined.

heritable (her'ĭ-tah-bl) Capable of being inherited (e.g., a trait), provided its determining gene is present in the sex cell (egg or sperm) of one of the parents. COMPARE hereditary.

hermaphrodism (her-maf'ro-dizm) See hermaphroditism.

hermaphrodite (her-maf'ro-dīt) An individual who has genital tissues of both sexes. Also called intersex.

hermaphroditism (her-maf'ro-di-tizm) The presence in one individual of both ovaries and testes, either combined (ovotestes) or with a different gonad on each side; true hermaphroditism. Also called hermaphrodism; intersexuality.

hermetic (her-met'ik) Completely sealed; airtight.

hernia (her'ne-ah) Protrusion of part of an organ through an abnormal opening in the tissues containing it.

    abdominal h. Hernia protruding through any part of the abdominal wall.

    complete h. An indirect inguinal hernia that passes fully into the scrotum.

    concealed h. Hernia that is not detected on palpation.

    congenital diaphragmatic h. Protrusion of abdominal organs into the chest cavity through a developmental defect in the diaphragm, usually a large posterolateral opening (foramen of Bochdalek) or through an enlarged foramen of Morgagni, behind the breastbone. Also called diaphragmatic hernia.

    cul-de-sac h. See enterocele.

    diaphragmatic h. See congenital diaphragmatic hernia.

    direct inguinal h. Inguinal hernia in which a peritoneal sac (which usually contains a loop of intestine) protrudes through a weakened part of the inguinal triangle (area bounded inferiorly by the inguinal ligament, medially by the lateral border of the abdomi-

hepatography ■ **hernia**

nal rectus muscle, and laterally by the inferior epigastric artery); the hernial protrusion enters the inguinal canal on the medial side of the spermatic cord and may emerge from the superficial inguinal ring and lie over the body of the pubic bone; seen more often in men than in women.

dorsal h. See lumbar hernia.

Douglas' pouch h. See enterocele.

epigastric h. Hernia through the linea alba above the navel.

fascial h. See fatty hernia.

fatty h. Hernia in which a mass of adipose tissue protrudes through a gap or tear in a fibrous layer of tissue (fascia or aponeurosis). Also called pannicular hernia; fascial hernia.

femoral h. Protrusion of a sac-enclosed loop of intestine through the femoral ring and into the femoral canal. The hernia may be one of two types: *Incomplete femoral h.,* if it remains in the canal as far as the saphenous opening; or *Complete femoral h.,* if it passes through the opening and into the loose tissues of the groin; seen most frequently in women, especially those who have borne several children.

gastroesophageal h. See hiatal hernia.

hiatal h., hiatus h. (HH) A saclike protrusion of the upper portion of the stomach into the chest cavity, above the diaphragm, through the esophageal opening of the diaphragm. See also paraesophageal hiatal hernia; sliding hiatal hernia.

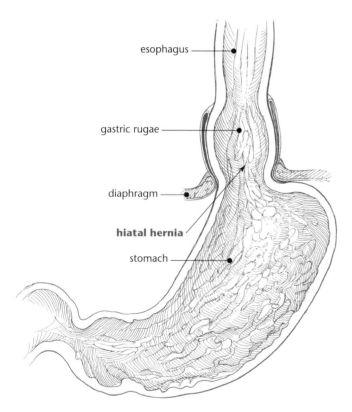

esophagus

gastric rugae

diaphragm

hiatal hernia

stomach

incarcerated h. See irreducible hernia.

incisional h. Hernia through a surgical incision, occurring almost exclusively in the abdominal wall; factors most commonly responsible include poor suturing technique, type of incision made, postoperative wound infection, failure to use nonabsorbable suture material, placement of drains in the primary incision, postoperative pulmonary complications that produce forceful coughing, obesity, advanced age, and general debility of the patient. Also called ventral hernia.

indirect inguinal h. Inguinal hernia in which a peritoneal sac (which usually contains a loop of intestine) protrudes through the deep inguinal ring and passes down obliquely into the inguinal canal in front of the spermatic cord; it may descend farther and emerge from the canal through the superficial inguinal ring, and

even descend into the scrotum. Also called oblique inguinal hernia. See also sliding inguinal hernia.

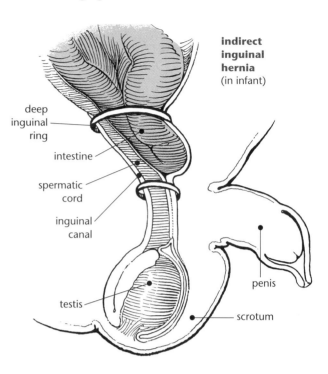

indirect inguinal hernia (in infant)

deep inguinal ring

intestine

spermatic cord

inguinal canal

testis

penis

scrotum

inguinal h. Hernia in the area of the groin. See also direct inguinal hernia; indirect inguinal hernia.

internal h. Any hernia occurring in large cavities (e.g., protrusion of an intestinal loop through a narrow opening created by a peritoneal adhesion).

irreducible h. Hernia which, as a result of adhesions or for any other reason, cannot be pushed back into the original position without surgical intervention. Also called incarcerated hernia.

lumbar h. A hernia in the lower back, between the last rib and iliac crest, frequently described by patients as "a lump in the flank"; may be caused by severe direct trauma, penetrating wounds, abscesses, or poor healing of surgical incisions; or it may be congenital. Also called dorsal hernia.

oblique inguinal h. See indirect inguinal hernia.

pannicular h. See fatty hernia.

paraesophageal hiatal h. A type of hiatal hernia characterized by displacement of the upper portion of the stomach into the chest cavity (alongside the undisplaced esophagus) through an abnormally enlarged esophageal opening (hiatus) of the diaphragm.

posterior vaginal h. See enterocele.

rectovaginal h. See enterocele.

reducible h. Hernia that can be reduced (i.e., its contents can be pushed back to their original position with manual pressure).

scrotal h. An inguinal hernia that extends into the scrotum. Also called scrotocele.

sliding esophageal hiatal h. A bell-like dilatation of the stomach protruding through the diaphragm into the chest cavity, continuous with an abnormally short esophagus, which ends above the diaphragm; may be caused by a congenitally short esophagus or by scarring of the esophagus with traction on the stomach. Also called sliding hiatal hernia.

sliding hiatal h. See sliding esophageal hiatal hernia.

sliding inguinal h. A type of indirect inguinal hernia in which the wall of the intestine forms part of the wall of the hernial sac; the cecum is most commonly involved on the right side and the sigmoid colon on the left side.

strangulated h. An irreducible hernia with obstructed blood circulation and contents that have become, or are likely to become, gangrenous.

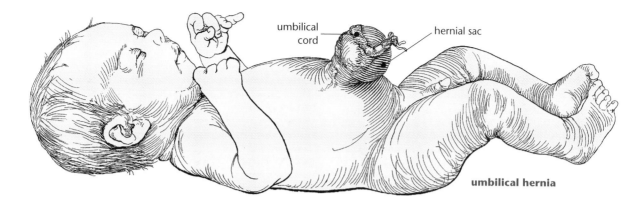

umbilical cord

hernial sac

umbilical hernia

umbilical h. Hernia in which part of the intestine protrudes through the umbilical ring; it usually results from a fascial and muscular defect with failure of the umbilical ring to close.

    ventral h. See incisional hernia.

herniated (her′ne-āt-ed) Protruding through a defect or abnormal opening.

herniation (her-ne-a′shun) Formation of an abnormal protrusion.

    cerebellar tonsillar h. Protrusion of the cerebellar tonsils through the foramen magnum, at the base of the skull. Also called tonsillar herniation; foraminal herniation.

    cerebral h. Any protrusion of brain tissue under the dural partitions within the skull due to increased intracranial pressure.

    cingulate h. Herniation of the cingulate gyrus under the falx.

    foraminal h. See cerebellar tonsillar herniation.

    subfalcial h. Displacement of a portion of the brain under the falx.

    tonsillar h. See cerebellar tonsillar herniation.

    transtentorial h. Protrusion of a portion of the brain through the free margin of the tentorium; may be downward (uncal) or upward (rostral).

herniorrhaphy (her-ne-or′ah-fe) Surgical repair of a hernia.

heroic (her-o′ik) Involving a high degree of risk; applied to certain procedures and therapies.

heroin (her′o-in) A highly addictive narcotic compound prepared from morphine by acetylation. Also called diacetylmorphine.

herpangina (herp-an-ji′nah) Infection of the oral mucous membrane with coxsackievirus A; marked primarily by severe sore throat, sudden onset of fever, loss of appetite, and a grayish vesicular eruption around the tonsils; may be accompanied by lesions in the hands and feet; seen most often in young children.

herpes (her′pēz) Inflammatory eruption of a cluster of deep-seated vesicles caused by a herpesvirus.

    corneal h. See herpetic keratitis, under keratitis.

    h. febrilis Herpes simplex caused by herpesvirus 1, transmitted primarily by oral secretions; characterized by recurrent blisters and ulcers usually on the lips (herpes labialis), nostrils, and/or lining membrane of the oral cavity. Also called cold sore; fever blister.

    genital h., h. genitalis Sexually transmitted herpes simplex of the genital organs, usually caused by human herpesvirus 2 (HHV-2); blisters appear from 2 to 12 days after contact with a person who has active lesions; ulcerations heal within two weeks; initial (primary) infection in a pregnant woman may be transmitted to the fetus through the placenta; if the mother has an active eruption at the time of delivery, the newborn may become infected during its passage through the birth canal.

    h. gestationis An eruption of reddish plaques and vesicles, usually in the arm and legs, occurring during the second or third trimester of pregnancy; despite its name, the condition is not caused by a herpesvirus; cause is unknown. Also called hydroa gestationis.

    h. gladiatorum Infection with herpesvirus 1, causing lesions of the eyes, scalp, and skin of the face, neck, trunk, or limbs, accompanied by fever, chills, sore throat and inflammation of lymph nodes; seen primarily in wrestlers and rugby players.

    h. labialis See herpes febrilis.

    neonatal h. Infection of the newborn with human herpesvirus 2 (HHV-2); a potentially fatal infection acquired during one of three periods: intrauterine (through the placenta); during birth (as an ascending infection through ruptured membranes [80%], or by delivery through infected cervix and vagina); or after birth. The infant appears healthy at birth, becoming symptomatic at 1 to 4 weeks of age; infection may be localized (causing lesions in the skin, eyes, or oral cavity); may involve the brain (causing encephalitis, seizures, lethargy, tremors, temperature instability, a bulging fontanel); or may be disseminated (producing a variety of symptoms and signs, such as jaundice, low blood pressure, disseminated intravascular coagulation, respiratory distress, bleeding, shock).

    h. simplex An acute eruption of painful blisters caused by human herpesvirus 1 and 2 (HHV-1, HHV-2); once established, the infection remains in the body and recurs at intervals with complete healing of the eruption between episodes; reappearance may be precipitated by emotional stress, febrile disease, local trauma, or menstruation.

    h. zoster A painful, itchy eruption of vesicles, usually on one side of the body along the course of one or more cutaneous nerves; caused by human herpesvirus 3 (HHV-3), which infects ganglia of the sensory (posterior) roots of spinal nerves, or of the fifth cranial nerve. The condition is considered a reactivation of the virus, which remains latent in the ganglia following the primary infection (chickenpox); may be precipitated by physical or emotional stress or by malignancies (e.g., lymphoma, Hodgkin's disease). Also called shingles.

herpesvirus (her-pēz-vi′rus) Any of a group of viruses that share the following features: they contain double-stranded DNA, replicate in the cell nucleus, accumulate between inner and outer layers of nuclear membrane and in the cisterna of endoplasmic reticulum, are transported to the cell surface through modified endoplasmic reticulum, and may remain latent in their host for several years or the lifetime of the host.

    human h. 1 (HHV1) Herpes simplex 1; the virus causing herpes simplex 1, responsible for most cases of nongenital herpes. The organism enters the cell through the fibroblast growth factor receptor on the cell membrane.

    human h. 2 (HHV2) Herpes simplex 2; the herpesvirus infecting primarily the genital organs of both male and female (including the cervix and vagina), and the anal and perianal areas of homosexual men; the organism has been recovered from the urethra and prostate of asymptomatic men; extragenital involvement (e.g., of the eyes and fingers) usually occurs through self-infection; infection of the newborn is associated with a high mortality rate (about 60%), and about half of the survivors have serious neurological or eye complications. An HHV2 infection is frequently associated with other sexually transmitted diseases.

    human h. 3 (HHV3) Herpes varicella-zoster virus; the organism causing two clinical forms of infection: acute HHV3 (varicella, commonly called chickenpox) and chronic HHV3 (herpes zoster, commonly called shingles).

H

human h. 4 (HHV4) The Epstein-Barr virus (EBV), with specificity for B cells (B lymphocytes); the cause of infectious mononucleosis, transmitted by saliva; associated with malignancies such as Burkitt's lymphoma, anaplastic nasopharyngeal cancer, and B-cell lymphomas in immunosuppressed patients (e.g., organ transplants and AIDS).

human h. 5 (HHV5) See cytomegalovirus.

human h. 6 (HHV6) A herpesvirus with affinity for B cells (B lymphocytes), occurring frequently as a coinfection with human immunodeficiency virus (HIV). An initial (primary) infection with HHV6 is a frequent cause of exanthem subitum, an acute febrile illness in infants and young children, usually associated with a variety of clinical manifestations; it is also associated with syndromes resembling infectious mononucleosis.

human h. 7 (HHV7) A herpesvirus isolated from activated, CD4-positive T lymphocytes obtained from the blood of healthy people.

herpetic (her-pet′ik) Relating to herpes or herpesvirus.

herpetiform (her-pet′ĭ-form) Resembling herpes.

hersage (ār-sahzh′) The surgical separation of fibers of an injured nerve.

hertz (hertz) (Hz) Unit of frequency of a periodic process equivalent to 1 cycle per second.

hesitancy (hez′ĭ-tan-sē) An abnormal delay in starting the urinary stream.

heterecious (het-er-e′shus) Having more than one host; applied to parasites that spend parts of their life cycle in different animals and plants (e.g., flukes, tapeworms). Also called metoxenous.

hetero- Combining form meaning other; different.

heterochromatin (het-er-o-kro′mah-tin) The electron-dense part of the cell nucleus that contains clumped, highly extended filaments of chromosomes that stain deeply; associated with low degree of metabolic activity.

heterochromia (het-er-o-kro′me-ah) Difference in color of body parts that are normally of the same color.

heteroerotic (het-er-o-er-ot′ik) Denoting sexual feelings for another person.

heterogametic (het-er-o-gah-met′ik) Having sex cells (gametes) of different types with respect to the sex chromosomes (i.e., X and Y chromosomes), as in human males.

heterogamy (het-er-og′ah-me) The union of two gametes of different size, structure, and function.

heterogeneity (het-er-o-jĕ-ne′ĭ-te) In genetics, production of the same observable characteristic either from mutations at different loci in the chromosome, or the same locus, or from different genetic mechanisms.

heterogeneous (het-er-o-je′ne-us) Composed of dissimilar elements; not homogeneous.

heterogenic, heterogenous (het-er-o-jen′ik, het-er-oj′ĕ-nus) Relating to heterogeneity.

heterograft (het′er-o-graft) See xenograft.

heterolalia (het-er-o-la′le-ah) The involuntary substitution of inappropriate words for those intended. Also called heterophasia.

heterologous (het-er-ol′o-gus) 1. Composed of tissues not normal to the region. 2. See xenogeneic.

heterolysis (het-er-ol′ĭ-sis) Dissolution of cells by the enzymatic action of lysosomes from other cells (leukocytes), rather than from the dead cells themselves.

heteromeric (het-er-o-mer′ik) 1. Having processes that cross the midline; applied to certain nerve cells. 2. Of different chemical composition.

heteromorphism (het-er-o-morf′izm) A variation in shape or size between homologous chromosomes.

heteronymous (het-er-on′ĭ-mus) 1. Relating to different sides of the two visual fields (e.g., the right side of one field and the left side of the other). 2. Having different but correlated names.

heterophagy (het-er-of′ah-je) The uptake of materials from the immediate surroundings; may be accomplished through phagocytosis (e.g., engulfing and degradation of bacteria by leukocytes or removal of necrotic debris by macrophages), or through absorption (e.g., reabsorption of protein by the proximal tubules in the kidney).

heterophasia (het-er-o-fa′ze-ah) See heterolalia.

heterophid (het′er-o-fid) Any fluke of the genus *Heterophyes*.

heterophonia (het-er-o-fo′ne-ah) The change of voice in the male at puberty.

heterophoria (het-er-o-fo′re-ah) The tendency of the eyes to deviate toward or away from each other and held in check when the individual "focuses" the gaze on something (i.e., by the fusion mechanism).

heterophthalmus (het-er-of-thal′mus) A different appearance of the two eyes.

Heterophyes (het-er-of′ĭ-ēz) A genus of small (1- 3-mm) flukes parasitic in human intestines.

heterophyiasis (het-er-o-fi-i′ah-sis) Infection with a heterophid fluke.

heteroplasia (het-er-o-pla′ze-ah) The presence of cells, tissues, or parts in a location where they do not normally occur. Also called alloplasia.

heteroplastic (het-er-o-plas′tik) Relating to heteroplasia.

heteroploidy (het′er-o-ploi-de) The state of having a chromosome number other than the normal for the particular cell or organism.

heterosexual (het-er-o-sek′shoo-al) 1. Relating to heterosexuality. 2. One who is characterized by heterosexuality.

heterosexuality (het-er-o-sek-shoo-al′ĭ-te) The state of having one's sexual interests directed toward a member of the opposite sex; opposite of homosexuality.

heterotaxia (het-er-o-tak′se-ah) Abnormal arrangement of organs or body parts; anomalous structural arrangement.

heterotaxic (het-er-o-tak′sik) Occurring in an abnormal place of the body.

heterotopic (het-er-o-top′ik) See ectopic.

heterotransplant (het-er-o-trans′plant) See xenograft.

heterotropia (het-er-o-tro′pe-ah) See strabismus.

heterotypic (het-er-o-tip′ik) Not typical.

heterozygosity (het-er-o-zi-gos′ĭ-te) The state of being heterozygous.

heterozygote (het-er-o-zi′gōt) A heterozygous individual.

heterozygous (het-er-o-zi′gus) Term applied to two corresponding genes that are not identical; the characteristic of having different alleles at one or more loci in homologous chromosome segments.

hexa- Combining form meaning six.

hexacanth (hek′sah-kanth) The motile, first-stage larva of a tapeworm. Also called oncosphere.

hexachlorophene (hek-sah-klo′ro-fēn) An antibacterial compound used as a local antiseptic in soaps and detergents; associated with toxicity of the nervous system, especially in newborns.

hexadecanoic acid (hek-sah-dek-ah-no′ik as′id) See palmitic acid.

hexokinase (hek-so-ki′nās) Enzyme precipitating the transfer of a phosphate group from adenosine triphosphate (ATP) to glucose to yield glucose 6-phosphate; present in yeast, muscle, and other tissues.

hexosan (hek′so-san) Any of several polysaccharides that yield a hexose on hydrolysis.

hexose (hek′sōs) A simple sugar (monosaccharide) that has six carbon atoms in the molecule (e.g., glucose and fructose).

hiatal (hi-a′tal) Relating to a hiatus.

hiatus (hi-a′tus) An opening or gap.

adductor h. See tendinous hiatus.

aortic h. The opening between the diaphragm and the vertebra through which pass the descending aorta, azygos vein, and thoracic duct; located at the level of the 12th thoracic vertebra. Also called aortic foramen.

esophageal h. The opening in the diaphragm through which pass the esophagus, the right and left vagus nerves, and small esophageal arteries and veins; located at the level of the 10th thoracic vertebra.

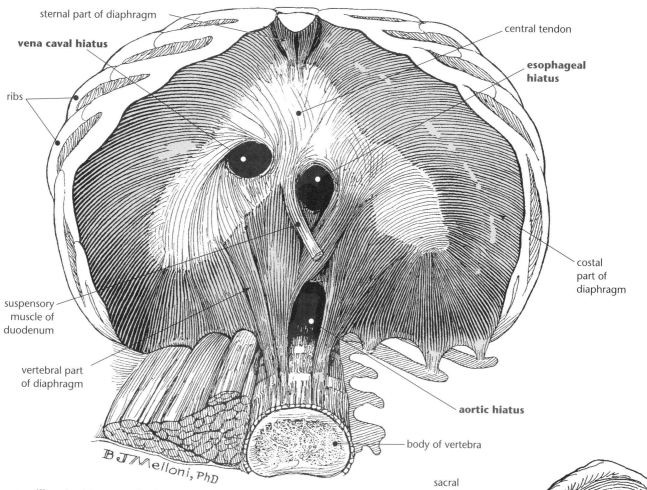

sternal part of diaphragm

vena caval hiatus

ribs

suspensory
muscle of
duodenum

vertebral part
of diaphragm

B.J.Melloni, PhD

central tendon

esophageal
hiatus

costal
part of
diaphragm

aortic hiatus

body of vertebra

maxillary h. A large opening between the upper medial side of the maxillary sinus and the middle meatus of the nasal cavity. Also called orifice of maxillary sinus.

sacral h. The opening on the dorsal aspect of the fifth segment of the sacrum, leading into the vertebral canal, and through which the terminal filament (filum terminale) passes out to become attached to the coccyx; the sacral hiatus is a site for injection of epidural anesthesia.

tendinous h. The opening between the tendon of the great adductor (adductor magnus) muscle and the lower part of the medial surface of the femur; it transmits the femoral artery to, and the femoral vein from, the popliteal space in back of the knee joint. Also called adductor hiatus.

vena caval h. The opening in the diaphragm through which pass the inferior vena cava and some branches of the right phrenic nerve; located at the level between the eighth and ninth thoracic vertebrae. Also called inferior vena caval foramen.

hibernation (hi-ber-na′shun) The dormant state, with reduced metabolic activity, in which certain animals pass the cold months.

artificial h. A drug-induced state resembling the natural hibernation of certain animals.

hiccup (hik′up) A spasm of the diaphragm followed by sudden closing of the vocal folds, which produces the characteristic sound.

hidradenitis (hi-drad-ĕ-ni′tis) Inflammation of a sweat gland.

h. suppurativa A chronic staphylococcal infection of apocrine sweat glands, characterized by formation of pea-sized nodules that become abscessed; occurs most frequently in the armpits, groin, and perianal area.

hidradenoma (hi-drad-ĕ-no′mah) A mobile, benign tumor of sweat gland origin; may be solid or cystic, usually found in the subcutaneous tissues of the labia or perianal region.

hidro-, hidr- Combining forms meaning sweat.

hidroa (hid-ro′ah) See hydroa.

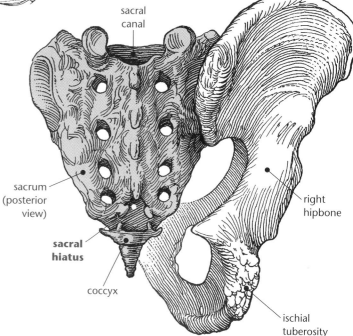

sacral
canal

sacrum
(posterior
view)

sacral
hiatus

coccyx

right
hipbone

ischial
tuberosity

hidrocystoma (hid-ro-sis-to′mah) A cystic deformation of a sweat gland.

hidropoiesis (hid-ro-poi-e′sis) The formation of sweat.

hidrosis (hi-dro′sis) **1.** Excessive sweating. **2.** Any sweat gland disorder.

high (hi) Colloquial term for a state of drug-induced intoxication, as from a narcotic, alcohol, or hallucinogenic agent.

hilar (hi′lar) Relating to a hilum.

hilum (hi′lum), pl. hi′la The point or depression at which nerves, vessels, or ducts enter and leave an organ. Also called hilus.

H

h. of adrenal (suprarenal) gland The narrow vertical depression on the anterior surface of the adrenal gland from where the suprarenal vein emerges to join the renal vein.

h. of kidney A deep vertical notch on the central part of the medial border of each kidney that contains the renal vessels and nerves and the renal pelvis (the upper expanded end of the ureter).

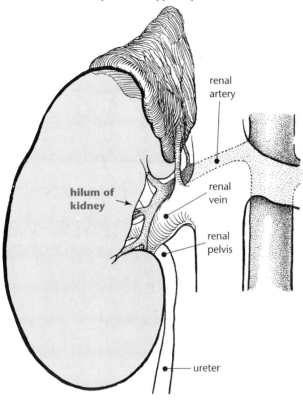

h. lienis See hilum of spleen.

h. of lung The depression on the mediastinal surface of the lung where several structures enter and leave the organ (principal bronchus, pulmonary artery, the two pulmonary veins, the pulmonary plexus of nerves, and lymph vessels) and where brochopulmonary lymph nodes and areolar tissue are located. It generally lies opposite the bodies of the fifth, sixth, and seventh thoracic vertebrae; the hilum of the left lung usually lies in front of the descending thoracic aorta, just below the aortic arch; the hilum of the right lung lies in back of the superior vena cava and part of the right atrium of the heart.

h. of lymph node A slight depression on one side of a lymph node through which the arteries enter and the veins and an efferent lymph vessel emerge from the node.

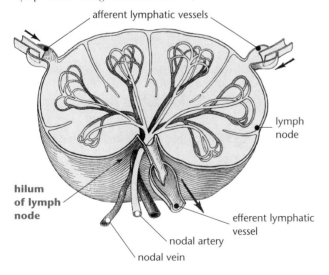

h. of ovary The slight indentation on the straight mesovarian border of the ovary where the blood vessels and nerves enter and leave.

h. of spleen A long fissure near the lower border of the gastric surface of the spleen through which blood vessels and nerves enter and leave the organ. Also called hilum lienis.

hilus (hi′lus) See hilum.

hindfoot (hīnd′foot) The back part of the foot that contains the ankle bone (talus) and the heel bone (calcaneus); it is separated from the midfoot by the transverse midtarsal joint.

hindgut (hīnd′gut) The back portion of the embryonic alimentary canal.

hip (hip) The lateral area of the body from the waist to the thigh.

hipbone (hip′bōn) The large, flattened bone enclosing the pelvic cavity; formed by the fusion of three bones (ilium, ischium, pubis). Formerly called innominate bone; also written hip bone.

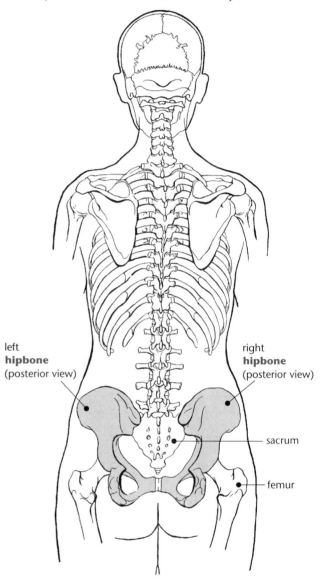

hippocampus (hip-o-kam′pus) An infolded, specialized portion of cerebral cortex forming an elevation in the floor of each lateral ventricle of the brain.

Hippocrates (hip-pok′rah-tēz) A Greek physician known as the Father of Medicine.

Hippocratic Oath (hip-o-krat′ik ōth′) A code of ethical conduct for the medical profession attributed to Hippocrates.

hippus (hip′us) An abnormal, spasmodic, and rhythmic contraction and dilatation of the pupil.

HIPBONE

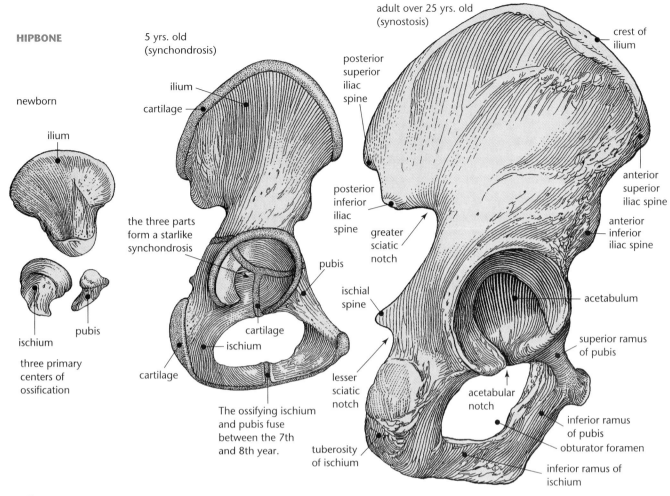

newborn

ilium

ischium

pubis

three primary centers of ossification

5 yrs. old (synchondrosis)

ilium

cartilage

the three parts form a starlike synchondrosis

cartilage

ischium

pubis

cartilage

The ossifying ischium and pubis fuse between the 7th and 8th year.

adult over 25 yrs. old (synostosis)

crest of ilium

posterior superior iliac spine

posterior inferior iliac spine

greater sciatic notch

ischial spine

lesser sciatic notch

tuberosity of ischium

anterior superior iliac spine

anterior inferior iliac spine

acetabulum

superior ramus of pubis

acetabular notch

inferior ramus of pubis

obturator foramen

inferior ramus of ischium

H

THE OATH OF HIPPOCRATES

I SWEAR BY APOLLO, THE PHYSICIAN, AND ÆSCULAPIUS AND HEALTH, AND ALL-HEAL AND ALL THE GODS AND GODDESSES, THAT, ACCORDING TO MY ABILITY AND JUDGMENT, I WILL KEEP THIS OATH AND STIPULATION:

TO RECKON him who taught me this art equally dear to me as my parents, to share my substance with him, and relieve his necessities if required; to regard his offspring as on the same footing with my own brothers, and to teach them this art, if they should wish to learn it, without fee or stipulation; and that by precept, lecture and every other mode of instruction, I will impart a knowledge of the art to my own sons, and to those of my teachers and to disciples bound by a stipulation and oath, according to the law of medicine, but to none others.

I WILL FOLLOW that method of treatment which, according to my ability and judgment, I consider for the benefit of my patients, and abstain from whatever is deleterious and mischievous. I will give no deadly medicine to anyone if asked, nor suggest any such counsel; furthermore, I will not give to a woman an instrument to produce abortion.

WITH PURITY AND WITH HOLINESS I will pass my life and practice my art. I will not cut a person who is suffering with a stone, but will leave this to be done by practitioners of this work. Into whatever houses I enter I will go into them for the benefit of the sick and will abstain from every voluntary act of mischief and corruption; and further, from the seduction of females or males, bond or free.

WHATEVER, in connection with my professional practice, or not in connection with it, I may see or hear in the lives of men which ought not to be spoken abroad, I will not divulge, as reckoning that all such should be kept secret.

WHILE I CONTINUE to keep this oath unviolated, may it be granted to me to enjoy life and the practice of the art, respected by all men at all times, but should I trespass and violate this oath, may the reverse be my lot.

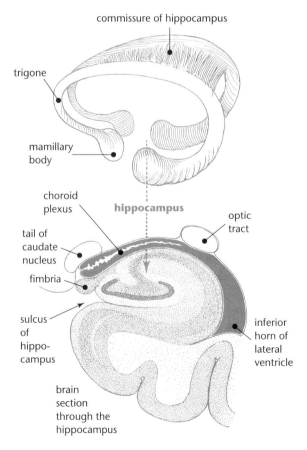

commissure of hippocampus

trigone

mamillary body

choroid plexus

tail of caudate nucleus

fimbria

sulcus of hippocampus

hippocampus

optic tract

inferior horn of lateral ventricle

brain section through the hippocampus

hirsute (her'soot) 1. Relating to hair or to hirsutism. 2. Hairy.

hirsutism (her-soot'izm) Excessive hair on the face and chest, especially in women. Also called pilosis.

hirudin (hǐ-roo'din) A substance secreted by the salivary glands of a leech that prevents clotting of the blood while the leech is sucking.

histamine (his'tah-mēn) A bioactive amine occurring in all animal and plant tissue; it causes contraction of the smooth muscles forming the walls of bronchioles and small blood vessels, increased permeability of capillaries, increased secretion of nasal and bronchial mucous glands, and a fall in blood pressure.

histidine (his'tĭ-dēn) (His) One of the basic amino acids forming the protein molecule.

histiocyte (his'te-o-sīt) A large mononuclear phagocyte or macrophage; a tissue cell capable of engulfing and digesting particulate organic materials such as bacteria and other foreign bodies.

histiocytoma (his-te-o-si-to'mah) Any of various tumors composed predominantly of histiocytes; some are benign, others malignant.

histiocytosis (his-te-o-si-to'sis), pl. histiocyto'ses Abnormal proliferation of histiocytes.

  acute disseminated Langerhans-cell h. An acute progressive disease most commonly affecting infants and children under three years of age; characterized by proliferation of histiocytes in almost all organs and tissues, including the skin, lymph nodes, spleen, liver, and particularly bone marrow; accompanied by enlargement of the spleen and liver and, frequently, a purpuric rash, anemia, and chronic inflammation of the middle ear chamber. Formerly called Letterer-Siwe disease.

  Langerhans-cell h. General term for a group of histiocytoses that are distinct clinicopathologic entities but have in common one predominant feature: the proliferating cell is the Langerhans cell. Formerly called histiocytosis X.

  multifocal Langerhans-cell h. Disease of childhood, usually in children under five years of age; characterized by diffuse eruptions (especially of the scalp and in the ear canals), frequent bouts of upper respiratory infections, otitis media, exophthalmos (unilateral or bilateral), diabetes insipidus, and destruction of bone (especially of the skull). Formerly called Hand-Schüller-Christian disease; Schüller disease.

  sinus h. Disease of the lymph nodes in which the lymphatic sinusoids become distended due to hypertrophy of cells within the sinusoid lining and infiltration with histiocytes; frequently seen in cancers involving the lymph nodes.

  unifocal Langerhans-cell h. A relatively benign disorder affecting children and young adults, especially males; characterized by a single lesion involving one or several bones; may cause no symptoms or may produce pain and tenderness and, sometimes, pathologic fractures; it may heal spontaneously. Formerly called eosinophilic granuloma.

  h. X See Langerhans-cell histiocytosis.

histo- Combining form meaning tissue.

histochemistry (his-to-kem'is-tre) The study of intracellular distribution and action of chemicals and enzymes by any of a variety of methods.

histocompatibility (his-to-kom-pat-ĭ-bil'ĭ-te) The state of being histocompatible.

histocompatible (his-to-kom-pat'ĭ-bl) Relating to the ability of a tissue or organ to be accepted upon transplantation; related to similarity of human leukocyte antigens (HLAs) between graft and host.

histofluorescence (his-to-floo-o-res'ens) Fluorescence of tissues produced by exposure to ultraviolet rays after injection of a fluorescent substance.

histogenesis (his-to-jen'ĕ-sis) Development of a tissue from primitive, undifferentiated cells.

histogram (his'to-gram) A visual representation of statistical data consisting of a series of rectangles, the areas of each representing the frequency of values within the range covered by their bases; a bar graph.

histoincompatibility (his-to-in-kom-pat-ĭ-bil'ĭ-te) The state of being histoincompatible.

histoincompatible (his-to-in-kom-pat'ĭ-bl) Relating to the condition of two individuals who have sufficient antigenic differences for inducing an immune response leading to rejection of tissue transplants from one of the individuals to the other.

histologic (his-to-log'ik) Relating to histology.

histologist (his-tol'o-jist) A specialist in histology.

histology (his-tol'o-je) The branch of anatomy concerned with the microscopic structure and function of tissues. Also called microscopic anatomy; microanatomy.

histolysis (his-tol'ĭ-sis) The breakdown of tissue.

histone (his'tōn) A small chromosomal protein attached to DNA in the nucleus of a cell.

histophysiology (his-to-fiz-e-ol'o-je) The study of the microscopic structure of tissues in relation to their function.

Histoplasma capsulatum (his-to-plaz'mah kap-su-la'tum) A yeast-like fungus present in soil contaminated with fowl droppings; the cause of histoplasmosis.

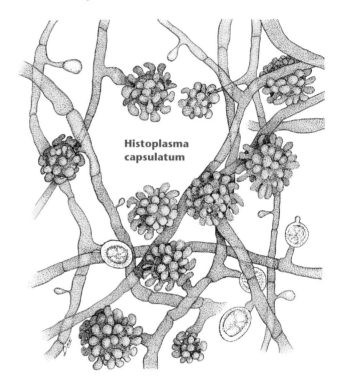

Histoplasma capsulatum

histoplasmin (his-to-plaz'min) An antigenic concentrate obtained from cultures of *Histoplasma capsulatum;* used in immunologic testing for histoplasmosis.

histoplasmosis (his-to-plaz-mo'sis) A fungal disease caused by inhalation of dust contaminated with *Histoplasma capsulatum;* may occur as an asymptomatic or mild lung illness; or may become an acute disseminated disease involving several organs and causing fever, enlargement of the spleen and liver, jaundice, anemia, nodules in the lungs, and ulcers of the nose, mouth and throat; often occurs as an occupational infection affecting poultry producers, farmers, and rural demolition workers.

history (his'to-rē) A chronologic account of related events.

  medical h. A record of a patient's previous health care, illnesses, treatments, etc., that becomes part of that patient's medical record.

  occupational medical h. A medical history that includes a variety of information not always considered pertinent to a general medical history (e.g., a chronologic list of the patient's employment, types of equipment used in the workplace, exposure to hazardous chemicals or radioactive materials, noise levels in the workplace).

hives (hivz) Popular name for urticaria.

HMO See health maintenance organization.

hoarseness (hōrs'nes) A harsh, grating quality of the voice.

hirsute ■ hoarseness

H26

holandric (hol-an′drik) Relating to males only or to a gene on the Y chromosome (e.g., a pattern of inheritance of genes on the Y chromosome from a father to his sons, not to his daughters).

holarthritis (hol-ar-thri′tis) Inflammation of most or all joints.

holder (hōld′er) A device by which something is grasped.

    needle h. Instrument for grasping a needle during surgery. Also called needle forceps; suture forceps.

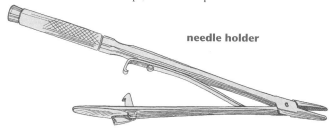

needle holder

hole in the heart Popular term for a septal defect. See atrial septal defect or ventricular septal defect, under defect.

holo- Combining form meaning whole; undivided.

holoblastic (hol-o-blas′tik) Denoting the division of the entire ovum into individual blastomeres.

holocrine (ho′lo-krin) Wholly secretory; applied to a gland that includes its own disintegrated cells in its secretion (e.g., sebaceous glands).

holodiastolic (hol-o-di-ah-stol′ik) In cardiology, relating to or occupying all of diastole from the second heart sound to the succeeding first heart sound.

hologram (hol′o-gram) A three-dimensional pattern recorded on photographic film by exposing it to a laser beam reflected by the object under study.

holography (hol-og′raf-e) The process of making a hologram.

hologynic (hol-o-jin′ik) In genetics, relating to or occurring in females only.

holosystolic (hol-o-sis-tol′ik) In cardiology, relating to or occupying all of systole.

homeo- Combining form meaning the same; alike.

homeomorphous (ho-me-o-mor′fus) Of similar shape.

homeopath (ho′me-o-path) See homeopathist.

homeopathic (ho-me-o-path′ik) Relating to homeopathy.

homeopathist (ho-me-op′ah-thist) One who practices homeopathy. Also called homeopath.

homeopathy (ho-me-op′ah-the) A system of alternative medicine in which treatment of disease is based on the administration of drugs that would, in larger doses, produce symptoms of the disease being treated (e.g., diarrhea would be treated with a minute amount of laxative).

homeoplasia (ho-me-o-pla′ze-ah) The formation of new tissue similar to that already existing in, and normal to, the part.

homeostasis (ho-me-o-sta′sis) A state of physiologic stability within the living body (i.e., temperature, blood pressure, chemical content) maintained under variations in the external environment.

homeotherapy (ho-me-o-ther′ah-pe) Treatment of disease according to the principles of homeopathy.

homeothermal (ho-me-o-ther′mal) See homeothermic.

homeothermic (ho-me-o-ther′mik) Having a relatively constant body temperature despite variations in ambient temperature. Also called homeothermal; homothermal; homothermic.

homicidal (hom-ĭ-si′dal) Having a tendency to kill another human being.

homicide (hom′ĭ-sīd) The killing of one person by another.

Homo (ho′mo) A genus of primates that includes the extinct and existing species of man.

    H. sapiens The present-day human species.

homo- Combining form meaning the same; alike.

homoblastic (ho-mo-blas′tik) Originating from only one type of tissue.

homocentric (ho-mo-sen′trik) Having the same center.

homocysteine (ho-mo-sis-te′in) A sulfur-containing amino acid.

homocystine (ho-mo-sis′tin) A sulfur-containing amino acid derived from the oxidation of homocysteine.

homocystinuria (ho-mo-sis-tin-u′re-ah) A genetically determined disorder of metabolism in which there is a deficiency of the enzyme cystathionine synthase; characterized primarily by elevated levels of homocystine in blood and urine, mental retardation, skeletal abnormalities, and episodes of thromboembolism.

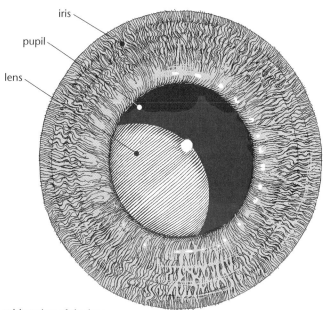

iris

pupil

lens

subluxation of the lens
downward as seen in some cases of **homocystinuria**

homoeroticism (ho-mo-ĕ-rot′ĭ-sizm) Homosexuality.

homogametic (ho-mo-gah-met′ik) Producing only one kind of germ cell in terms of the sex chromosomes it contains, such as the human female, whose ova contain only X chromosomes. Also called monogametic.

homogenate (ho-moj′ĕ-nāt) 1. A substance that has been homogenized. 2. In biochemistry, tissue that has been reduced to a uniform creamy consistency.

homogeneous (ho-mo-je′ne-us) Composed of similar elements throughout.

homogenization (ho-moj-ĕ-ni-za′shun) The process of blending diverse elements into a mixture that is uniform in structure or consistency throughout.

homogenize (ho-moj′ĕ-nīz) To render homogeneous.

homogenous (ho-moj′ĕ-nus) In biology, having a similarity of parts because of common ancestry.

homogentisic acid (ho-mo-jen-tis′ik as′id) An intermediate in the metabolism of the amino acid tyrosine; excreted in the urine of people afflicted with alkaptonuria.

homograft (ho′mo-graft) See allograft.

homolateral (ho-mo-lat′er-al) See ipsilateral.

homologous (ho-mol′o-gus) Corresponding in position, structure, function, origin, or development.

homologue, homolog (hom′o-log) Any organ or structure homologous to another.

homology (ho-mol′o-je) The state of being homologous.

homolysis (ho-mol′ĭ-sis) See isohemolysis.

homomorphic (ho-mo-mor′fik) Having similar size and form; applied to certain chromosomes and to anatomic structures.

homonomous (ho-mon′o-mus) Denoting body parts that are similar in function and structure (e.g., fingers and toes).

homonymous (ho-mon′ĭ-mus) 1. Having the same name. 2. Relating to the same right or left side of the two visual fields (e.g., the nasal half of one visual field and the temporal half of the other).

homoplasty (ho′mo-plas-te) Surgical repair of a defect with a graft

H

from another member of the same species.

homopolymer (ho-mo-pol′ĭ-mer) A polymer composed of only one type of monomer.

homosexual (ho-mo-sek′shoo-al) **1.** Relating to homosexuality. **2.** Characterized by homosexuality.

homosexuality (ho-mo-sek-shoo-al′ĭ-te) Sexual interest in, or sexual relationship with, members of one's own sex.

homothermal (ho-mo-ther′mal) See homeothermic.

homothermic (ho-mo-ther′mik) See homeothermic.

homotransplantation (ho′mo-trans-plan-ta′shun) See allotransplantation.

homotype (hom′o-tīp) Any body part of the same structure or function as another (e.g., a hand, a kidney).

homozoic (ho-mo-zo′ik) Relating to the same animal species.

homozygosis (ho-mo-zi-go′sis) The formation of a zygote by the union of genetically identical gametes.

homozygosity (ho-mo-zi-gos′ĭ-te) The state of being homozygous.

homozygote (ho-mo-zi′gōt) A homozygous individual.

homozygous (ho-mo-zi′gus) Characterized by having two corresponding genes that are identical (i.e., having identical genes at a given locus of homologous chromosomes).

homunculus (ho-munk′u-lus) **1.** The proportional representation of various parts of the body in the motor or sensory areas or the cerebral cortex. **2.** A minute body imagined by sixteenth- and seventeenth-century biologists to be present in the sperm, from which the human body was supposed to be developed.

honk (hongk) Term used in medical parlance to describe sounds resembling the call of a goose.

systolic h. A loud, vibratory, often musical heart murmur of relatively clear pitch, usually occurring in late systole; believed to originate in the mitral (left atrioventricular) valve. Also called systolic whoop.

hook (hook) **1.** A metal instrument with a curved or sharply bent tip, used for traction or fixation on a tissue or a part. **2.** A sharply angled anatomic structure.

blunt h. Hook used to make traction upon the groin of a dead

infant during a difficult breech presentation.

h. of hamate bone A hooklike process (hamulus), which projects from the distal part of the palmar surface of the hamate bone; it provides attachment to the flexor retinaculum.

palate h. A retractor used to draw the soft palate forward to facilitate posterior rhinoscopy.

tracheotomy h. A stout right-angled hook designed for holding the trachea steady at tracheotomy.

hooklets (hook′lets) Small horny residues from infestation with tapeworm larvae (genus *Echinococcus*); found in the walls of *Echinococcus* cysts.

hookworm (hook′werm) Any parasitic, bloodsucking roundworm, especially of the genera *Ancylostoma* (the Old World hookworm), and *Necator* (the American hookworm).

hora decubitus (or′ah de-ku′bĭ-tus) (h.d., hor. decub.) Latin for at bedtime.

hordeolum (hor-de′o-lum) An abscess of any of the eyelid glands characterized by a localized red, swollen, and acutely tender area of the lid, with pus formation within the lumen of the affected gland; it is a bacterial infection usually caused by *Staphylococcus aureus*.

external h. A superficial hordeolum involving a sebaceous gland of an eyelash (gland of Zeis) or a modified sweat gland of an eyelash (Moll's gland). Also called sty.

internal h. A relatively large, deep abscess involving a meibomian gland of the eyelid; distinguished from a chalazion.

hormonal (hor′mo-nal) Relating to a hormone.

hormone (hor′mōn) Any chemical substance secreted into the bloodstream by specialized cells in endocrine glands or certain other tissues (e.g., gastrointestinal tract); they are carried by the blood to specific target organs or tissues elsewhere in the body, where they produce a particular effect (either stimulate or retard function).

adrenocortical h.'s Hormones (steroids) secreted by the human adrenal cortex; the principal ones are cortisol, aldosterone, and corticosterone.

adrenocorticotropic h. (ACTH) Hormone produced by the

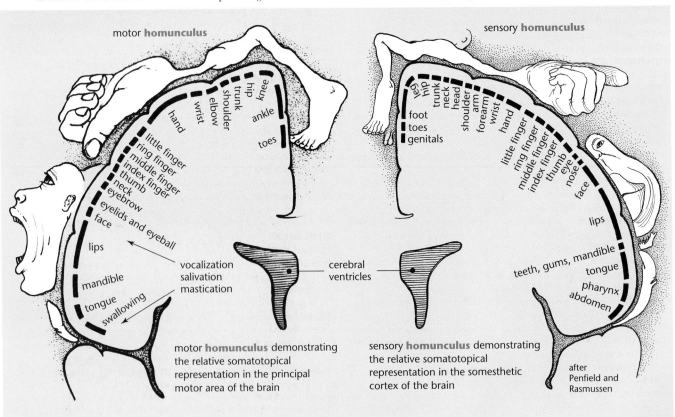

motor **homunculus** demonstrating the relative somatotopical representation in the principal motor area of the brain

sensory **homunculus** demonstrating the relative somatotopical representation in the somesthetic cortex of the brain

after Penfield and Rasmussen

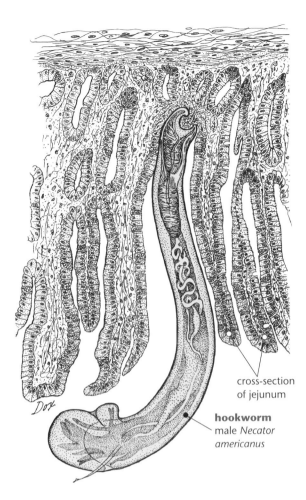

cross-section
of jejunum

hookworm
male *Necator
americanus*

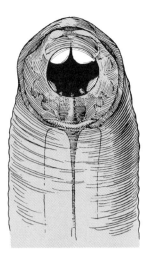

American **hookworm**
Necator americanus

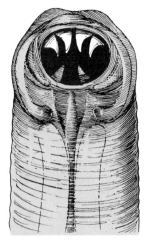

Old World **hookworm**
Ancylostoma duodenale

The hookworm attaches to human intestine by pulling the intestinal mucosa into its wide mouth and securing it with strong teeth.

anterior lobe of the pituitary; its primary action is to stimulate the adrenal cortex to functional activity (i.e., production and secretion of corticosteroids and androgens). Also called corticotropin; corticotropic hormone; adrenotropin; adrenocorticotropin.

adrenomedullary h.'s Any of the hormones formed by the adrenal medulla (e.g., epinephrine, norepinephrine).

androgenic h. Any of the masculinizing hormones including testosterone, the most potent one.

antidiuretic h. (ADH) One produced by the posterior lobe of the pituitary, having a potent antidiuretic action and some vasoconstrictive action on the visceral circulation; it makes the collecting duct of the kidney tubule permeable to water and allows concentration of urine. Also called vasopressin.

bovine growth h. (bGH) See recombinant bovine somatotropin (rBST), under somatotropin.

corticotropic h. See adrenocorticotropic hormone.

corticotropin-releasing h. (CRH) Hormone of hypothalamic origin capable of accelerating pituitary secretion of corticotropin (adrenocorticotropic hormone). Formerly called corticotropin-releasing factor.

follicle-stimulating h. (FSH) A glycoprotein hormone of the anterior lobe of the pituitary that stimulates normal cyclic growth of the ovarian follicle in females and stimulates the seminiferous tubules to produce spermatozoa in males.

follicle-stimulating hormone-releasing h. (FSH-RH) A hypothalamic hormone capable of accelerating pituitary secretion of follicle-stimulating hormone.

gastrointestinal h. Any secretion of the gastrointestinal mucosa (e.g., secretin) affecting the timing of various digestive secretions.

gonadotropin-releasing h. (GnRH, GRH) A decapeptide secreted by the hypothalamus that stimulates the pituitary to produce luteinizing hormone and follicle-stimulating hormone.

growth h. (GH) Hormone secreted by the anterior lobe of the pituitary of the brain; it promotes fat mobilization, affects the rate of skeletal growth, and inhibits utilization of sugar (glucose); can produce diabetes when present in excess. Also called somatotropin; somatotrophic hormone.

growth hormone–releasing h. (GH-RH) A hormone from the hypothalamus that stimulates release of growth hormone by the anterior lobe of the pituitary. Formerly called growth hormone–releasing factor.

interstitial cell–stimulating h. (ICSH) An anterior pituitary secretion that stimulates testicular interstitial cells to produce androgen; ICSH in the male is identical to luteinizing hormone (LH) in the female, which is essential for ovulation and formation of the corpus luteum in the ovary.

luteinizing h. (LH) A glycoprotein hormone of the anterior pituitary that stimulates secretion of estrogen and progesterone from the ovary; it promotes maturation of an ovarian follicle and its rupture to release the egg, followed by the conversion of the ruptured follicle into the corpus luteum; continued release of LH stimulates secretion of progesterone. Also called lutein-stimulating hormone (LSH).

luteinizing hormone–releasing h. (LH-RH, LRH) Hypothalamic hormone capable of accelerating pituitary secretion of luteinizing hormone. Formerly called luteinizing hormone–releasing factor.

lutein-stimulating h. (LSH) See luteinizing hormone.

melanocyte-stimulating h. (MSH) A secretion of the pituitary that increases deposition of melanin by the melanocytes. It arises from the intermediate zone in animals, but in humans, where the intermediate zone is poorly developed, it derives from the anterior lobe.

natriuretic h. A nonpeptide substance of less than 500 daltons, isolated from plasma after volume expansion, and thought to be released from the brain; it inhibits sodium-potassium ATPase throughout the body and is both natriuretic and vasoconstrictive; considered a possible cause of essential hypertension. Also called endoxin because it binds to digoxin antibodies.

ovarian h.'s Hormones secreted by the human ovary including estradiol, estrone, estriol, and progesterone.

parathyroid h. (PTH) A protein biosynthesized and secreted into the bloodstream by the four parathyroid glands, which are

H

located in the neck behind the thyroid gland; it acts on the cells of bone, kidney, and the intestinal tract to maintain a constant con-

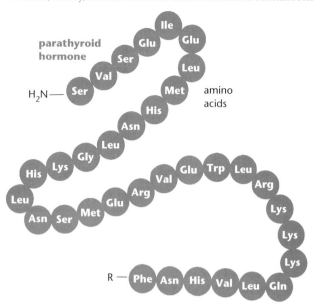

parathyroid
hormone

amino
acids

centration of calcium in the blood. Also called parathormone.

pituitary growth h. (PGH) The growth hormone of the anterior lobe of the pituitary.

placental h. Any of the hormones secreted by the placenta, namely, human chorionic gonadotropin, estrogen, progesterone, and human placental lactogen.

progestational h. Progesterone.

prolactin-releasing h. A hypothalamic hormone that stimulates pituitary secretion of prolactin.

sex h.'s Estrogens (female sex hormones) and androgens (male sex hormones) formed by ovarian, testicular, and adrenocortical tissues.

somatotrophic h. See growth hormone.

testicular h.'s The hormones elaborated by the human testis, especially testosterone.

thyroid h. A term that commonly refers to thyroxine, but may also include triiodothyronine.

thyroid-stimulating h. (TSH) See thyrotropin.

thyrotrophic h. See thyrotropin.

thyrotropic h. See thyrotropin.

thyrotropin-releasing h. (TRH) A tripeptide hormone from the hypothalamus that stimulates pituitary secretion of thyrotropin.

hormonogenic (hor-mo-no-jen'ik) Relating to the production of a hormone.

hormonotherapy (hor-mo-no-ther'ah-pe) See endocrinotherapy.

horn (horn) 1. Any anatomic structure projecting from a base and suggestive of a horn. 2. One of the hard protuberances projecting from the head of certain mammals.

anterior h. of lateral ventricle The part of a lateral ventricle of the brain that extends anteriorly into the frontal lobe. Also called cornu anterius ventriculi lateralis.

anterior h.'s of spinal cord The two anterior columns of the spinal cord appearing in cross section as two horn-shaped portions of gray matter projecting anteriorly within the spinal cord; the anterior columns of the spinal cord seen on cross section.

coccygeal h.'s See coccygeal cornua, under cornu.

cutaneous h. A horny growth of skin.

greater h. of hyoid bone See greater cornu of hyoid bone, under cornu.

inferior h. of falciform margin The hornlike distal end of the falciform margin forming the lower boundary of the saphenous opening, in the deep fascia of the upper thigh; the great saphenous vein and some smaller vessels pass through the opening. Also called

inferior horn of saphenous opening.

inferior h. of lateral ventricle The part of the lateral ventricle of the brain that extends forward into the temporal lobe. Also called cornu inferius ventriculi lateralis.

inferior h. of saphenous opening See inferior horn of falciform margin.

inferior h. of thyroid cartilage See inferior cornu of thyroid cartilage, under cornu.

lateral h.'s of spinal cord The two horn-shaped portions of gray matter projecting laterally within the spinal cord; the lateral columns of the spinal cord seen on cross section.

lateral h.'s of uterus The hornlike extensions of the body of the uterus to the upper right and left lateral borders where the fallopian (uterine) tubes join the uterus. Also called uterine horns; uterine cornua.

lesser h. of hyoid bone See lesser cornu of hyoid bone, under cornu.

posterior h. of lateral ventricle The part of the lateral ventricle of the brain that extends posteriorly into the occipital lobe. Also called cornu posterius ventriculi lateralis.

posterior h.'s of spinal cord The two posterior columns of the spinal cord appearing in cross section as two horn-shaped portions of gray matter projecting posteriorly.

pulp h. The extension of the tooth's pulp chamber toward a

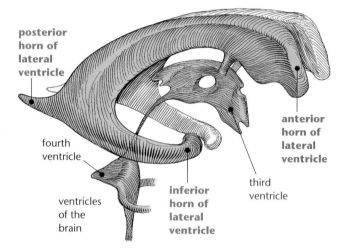

posterior
horn of
lateral
ventricle

fourth
ventricle

ventricles
of the
brain

inferior
horn of
lateral
ventricle

third
ventricle

anterior
horn of
lateral
ventricle

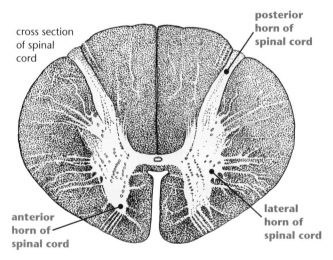

cross section
of spinal
cord

posterior
horn of
spinal cord

anterior
horn of
spinal cord

lateral
horn of
spinal cord

cusp.

sacral h.'s See sacral cornua, under cornu.

superior h. of falciform margin The hornlike proximal end of the falciform margin, which forms the upper boundary of the saphenous opening in the deep fascia, through which pass the great saphenous vein and some smaller vessels. Also called superior horn of saphenous opening; Scarpa's ligament.

superior h. of thyroid cartilage See superior cornu of thyroid cartilage, under cornu.

uterine h.'s See lateral h.'s of uterus.

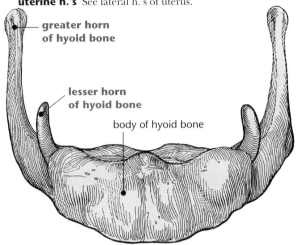

greater horn
of hyoid bone

lesser horn
of hyoid bone

body of hyoid bone

hornet (hor′nit) Any of several stinging wasps, chiefly of the genera *Vespa* and *Vespula;* antigens responsible for hypersensitivity reactions are present in both the venom sac and the body of the insect.

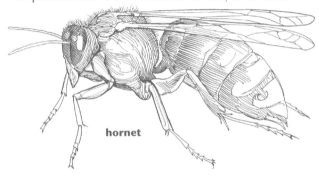

hornet

horny (hor′ne) Having the structure of horn; keratinous.

horripilation (hor-ĭ-pĭ-la′shun) Erection of the fine hairs on the skin.

hospice (hos′pis) An institution or program designed to provide care for dying patients who voluntarily select to forgo treatment for their illnesses but still require nursing care and pain medication; care may also include psychological, social, and spiritual support from professionals and volunteers.

hospital (hos′pĭ-tl) An institution that is licensed (if required by state laws) to operate, under the law, for admission, care, and treatment of injured or sick persons as inpatients; has a 24-hour-a-day nursing service by or under the supervision of a graduate registered nurse (RN) or a licensed practical nurse (LPN); has a staff of one or more licensed physicians available at all times; and provides organized facilities for diagnosis and surgery.

civil defense emergency h. See packaged hospital.

closed h. Hospital in which only members of its attending and consulting staff may admit and treat patients.

community h. A full-range hospital providing services primarily to a neighboring area, and funded by community-generated contributions.

convalescent h. Hospital providing care for patients immediately after an acute illness and until health is restored.

county h. One controlled by the county government.

day h. Hospital providing treatment during the day and enabling patients to return home at night; it may be a special facility within a large hospital.

federal h. One controlled by an agency or department of the U.S. federal government.

general h. Any large hospital with a resident medical staff for continuous or short-term care of medical, surgical, and maternity patients.

group practice h. Hospital organized and controlled by a group of physicians who practice with mutual cooperation and support.

investor-owned h. See proprietary hospital.

maternity h. A hospital for the care of women immediately before, during, and shortly after childbirth and for the care of newborn infants.

mental h. See psychiatric hospital.

military h. Hospital for the care of military personnel and their dependents.

municipal h. Hospital controlled by a city government.

packaged h. The hospital equipment and supplies, placed in boxes for long-term storage, that are adequate to set up a general hospital in an emergency. Formerly called civil defense emergency hospital.

private h. Any hospital (including profit and not-for-profit) controlled by a legal entity other than an agency of a government.

proprietary h. A hospital owned and operated for profit by a single individual or by a corporation. Also called investor-owned hospital.

psychiatric h. Special hospital for the care and treatment of persons afflicted with mental disorders. Also called mental hospital.

public h. Any hospital administered by a government agency (city, county, state, or federal).

satellite h. A relatively small hospital that is an extension of a larger main hospital, and which is administered by that institution (wholly or partly).

special h. Any hospital for the treatment of a special type of disorder; it is equipped and staffed for specific services.

state h. Hospital administered by a state agency.

teaching h. A hospital that, in addition to providing patient care, is engaged in educational and research programs and has a close affiliation with a medical school or university.

Veterans Administration h. Hospital funded by the federal government for the treatment of veterans of U.S. wars and retired military personnel.

hospital auxiliary An organization whose members perform services at a hospital without compensation.

hospital chaplaincy service A hospital department for administering any religious activity within the hospital (e.g., religious services, pastoral care).

hospital communication system The transmission of messages within a hospital (e.g., to staff or to patients).

hospital department One of several major administrative divisions of a hospital.

hospital distribution system The method of delivering hospital supplies, food, laundry, etc., to the different patient care areas.

hospital information system (HIS) An integrated, computer-assisted scheme designed to store and retrieve information relating to the administrative and clinical aspects of hospital services.

hospital shared services Cooperation among hospitals with regard to sharing services of various departments (e.g., data processing, pharmacy, laundry).

hospital unit A defined area in a hospital equipped to provide specialized patient care (e.g., an intensive care unit).

hospitalization (hos-pĭ-tl-ĭ-za′shun) The period of confinement in a hospital, beginning with the patient's admission and ending with his discharge.

hospital-physician joint venture A financial agreement between one or more physicians and a hospital to provide ambulatory alternative care to patients who do not need hospitalization.

host (hōst) 1. Any organism that serves as nourishment or means of transport for a parasite. 2. The recipient of a graft or organ transplant from a donor. 3. In molecular cloning, the organism (e.g., the bacterium *Escherichia coli* or the yeast *Saccharomyces cerevisiae*) used to

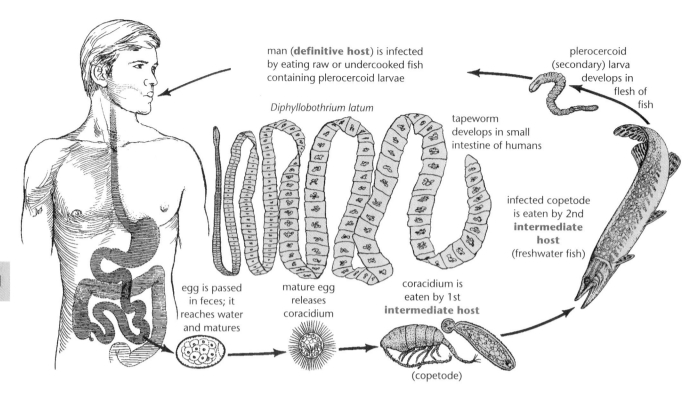

man (**definitive host**) is infected by eating raw or undercooked fish containing plerocercoid larvae

Diphyllobothrium latum

tapeworm develops in small intestine of humans

plerocercoid (secondary) larva develops in flesh of fish

infected copetode is eaten by 2nd **intermediate host** (freshwater fish)

egg is passed in feces; it reaches water and matures

mature egg releases coracidium

coracidium is eaten by 1st **intermediate host**

(copetode)

propagate a recombinant DNA molecule.

    definitive h. The organism in which a parasite lives during its adult and sexual phase.

    intermediate h. The organism in which a parasite lives during its larval phase. Also called secondary host.

    reservoir h. An animal that serves as a host to species of parasites that are also parasitic in humans and from which humans may be infected, either directly through ingestion or indirectly through a carrier, such as a mosquito.

    secondary h. See intermediate host.

housefly (hows′fli) A widely distributed flying insect, *Musca domestica*, vector of a variety of disease-causing microorganisms.

house officer A member of the house staff of a hospital.

house staff The physicians training in a graduate medical education program at a hospital; composed of the hospital's interns, residents, and fellows. Occasionally the term includes physicians who are salaried by a hospital but not receiving graduate training.

hum (hum) Descriptive term used in medical parlance for a continuous low-pitched sound usually caused by altered patterns of blood flow within veins.

    venous h. A hum heard on auscultation over the internal jugular veins at the base of the neck; intensified when the patient is in a sitting position and abolished by light pressure; caused by high-velocity blood flow in the veins; commonly heard in association with a goiter. The hum is frequently mistaken for an intracardiac murmur. Also called humming–top murmur.

humectant (hu-mek′tant) A substance that helps to retain moisture.

humeral (hu′mer-al) Relating to the humerus.

humerus (hu′mer-us) The long bone of the arm, extending from the shoulder to the elbow; it has a rounded end for articulation with the shoulder blade (scapula), a shaft, and a lower end adapted for articulation with the radius and ulna at the elbow. See also table of bones.

humidity (hu-mid′ĭ-te) Dampness.

    absolute h. The amount of water vapor present in the air when saturated at a given temperature, expressed in grains per cubic foot.

    relative h. (RH) The percentage of water vapor present in the atmosphere, as compared with the amount necessary to cause saturation at a specific temperature.

humor (hu′mor) Any fluid or semifluid occurring normally in the body.

    aqueous h. The clear, watery fluid filling the anterior and posterior chambers of the eye (i.e., in front of and behind the iris); it provides nutrients to the avascular lens and cornea, serves as a refractive medium, and maintains intraocular pressure. It is formed in the ciliary body, released into the posterior chamber, passed through the pupil into the anterior chamber, and drained into the venous circulation by way of the venous sinus of the sclera at the junction of the iris and cornea (iridocorneal angle). Obstruction of the free flow of aqueous humor at the drainage point (the iridocorneal angle) results in an increase in intraocular pressure that causes glaucoma. See also glaucoma.

    vitreous h. The soft, transparent, gelatinous substance within the largest chamber of the eyeball behind the lens of the eye; it fills the spaces of a loose network of collagen fibrils; the humor and fibril network, together, form the vitreous body. See also vitreous body, under body.

humoral (hu′mor-al) In immunology, relating to molecules that are in solution in a body fluid, especially antibody and complement (i.e., proteins mediating antigen-antibody reactions).

humpback (hump′bak) See kyphosis.

Humulin® (hyoo′mu-lin) A biosynthetic human insulin.

hunchback (hunch′bak) See kyphosis.

hunger (hung′ger) 1. A desire for nourishment. 2. A strong craving for anything.

hyalin (hi′ah-lin) 1. A transparent substance formed in certain degenerative diseases. 2. The homogeneous matrix of hyaline cartilage.

hyaline (hi′ah-lin) Translucent; glassy.

hyalitis (hi-ah-li′tis) Inflammation of the hyaloid membrane, the outer surface of the vitreous body.

hyalo-, hyal- Combining forms meaning glassy; vitreous body; vitreous humor.

hyaloid (hi′ah-loid) 1. See hyaline. 2. Relating to the vitreous body.

hyalomere (hi′ah-lo-mēr) The pale, homogeneous, peripheral por-

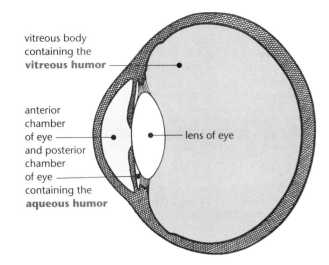

vitreous body containing the **vitreous humor**

anterior chamber of eye and posterior chamber of eye containing the **aqueous humor**

lens of eye

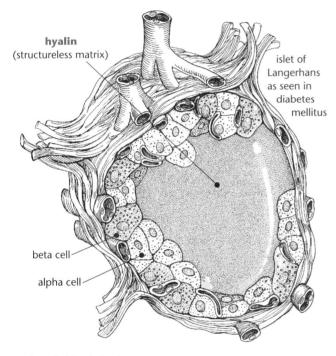

hyalin (structureless matrix)

islet of Langerhans as seen in diabetes mellitus

beta cell

alpha cell

tion of a blood platelet.

hyalosis (hi-ah-lo'sis) An eye condition marked by degenerative changes of the vitreous body.

 asteroid h. An uncommon eye condition occurring in elderly people, characterized by formation of hundreds of tiny white spheres composed of calcium soaps and deposited among the collagen fibers of the vitreous body; they move when the eye moves but always return to their original position; they are not associated with systemic disease and have little or no effect upon vision.

hyaluronic acid (hi-ah-lu-ron'ik as'id) (HA) A gelatinous mucopolysaccharide present in tissue spaces, binding cells together and holding water in the tissues; it serves in the lubricating and shock-absorbing system of joints.

hyaluronidase (hi-ah-lu-ron'ĭ-dās) **1.** Any of three enzymes present in sperm, snake and bee venom, and certain disease-causing bacteria; they cause the breakdown of hyaluronic acid in tissue spaces, thus enabling the invading agent to enter cells and tissues. **2.** A pharmaceutical preparation from mammalian testes, used to increase absorption of medicinal agents.

hybaroxia (hi-bār-ok'se-ah) See hyperbaric oxygen therapy, under therapy.

hybrid (hi'brid) **1.** The offspring (plant or animal) of parents who are genetically dissimilar. **2.** In experimental genetics, a cell formed from the fusion of two cells of different origin, with their nuclei merging into one; the resulting cell can be cloned to generate a hybrid cell line.

hybridization (hi-brid-ĭ-za'shun) **1.** The production of a hybrid by any method of fusing or mating. **2.** In molecular biology, the placement of complementary single strands of nucleic acids together (i.e., DNA or DNA and RNA) so that they will stick and form a double helix; used in conjunction with DNA and RNA probes to detect the presence or absence of specific complementary nucleic acid sequences.

hybridoma (hi-brĭ-do'mah) A cell culture composed of fused cells of different types, cloned to produce antibody of a single specificity.

hydantoins (hi-dan'to-ins) A group of anticonvulsant drugs used in the treatment of certain seizure disorders; maternal use during pregnancy causes fetal hydantoin syndrome.

hydatid (hi'dah-tid) **1.** A cystic structure containing the embryo of the tapeworm *Taenia echinococcus;* a hydatid cyst. **2.** Any structure resembling a cyst.

hydatidiform (hi-dah-tid'ĭ-form) Resembling a hydatid.

hydralazine hydrochloride (hi-dral'ah-zēn hi-dro-klo'rīd) An adrenergic blocking agent that lowers blood pressure by acting directly on arteriolar smooth muscle; it may be administered by mouth or intramuscularly. Trade name: Apresoline.

hydramnios, hydramnion (hi-dram'ne-os, hi-dram'ne-on) See polyhydramnios.

hydranencephaly (hi-dran-en-sef'ah-le) Congenital absence of most of the cerebral hemispheres, the space being filled with cerebrospinal fluid; the skull is intact and usually enlarged, but often of normal size and shape; initially the newborn infant sucks without difficulty and abnormal neurological signs are not originally obvious.

hydrargyrism, hydrargyria (hi-drar'jĭ-rizm, hi-drar-jir'e-ah) See mercury poisoning, under poisoning.

hydrarthrodial (hi-drar-thro'de-al) Relating to hydrarthrosis.

hydrarthrosis (hi-drar-thro'sis) Collection of fluid in a joint cavity.

hydratase (hi'drah-tās) An enzyme that promotes the addition of water to, or its removal from, a molecule.

hydrate (hi'drāt) Any compound containing water, which is retained in its molecule.

hydrated (hi'drāt-ed) Combined with water.

hydration (hi-dra'shun) The combination of a substance with water.

hydriatric (hi-dre-at'rik) Relating to hydrotherapy. Also called hydrotherapeutic.

hydric (hi'drik) Relating to or combined with hydrogen.

hydride (hi'drīd) Any compound of hydrogen with an element or group.

hydro-, hydr- Combining forms meaning water; hydrogen.

hydroa (hi-dro'ah) Any eruption of vesicles on the skin. Also spelled hidroa.

 h. estivale See hydroa vacciniforme.

 h. febrile See herpes simplex, under herpes.

 h. gestationis See herpes gestationis, under herpes.

 h. puerorum See hydroa vacciniforme.

 h. vacciniforme Blisters formed on the face and arms of children under the age of 10 upon exposure to sunlight; seen most commonly in the summer months; the blisters heal, leaving necrotic scars. Also called hydroa estivale; hydroa puerorum.

hydroappendix (hi-dro-ah-pen'diks) Abnormal accumulation of a serous fluid in the vermiform appendix.

hydroblepharon (hi-dro-blef'ah-ron) Edema of an eyelid.

hydrocarbon (hi'dro-kar'bon) A vast group of compounds containing only carbon and hydrogen in various combinations; found especially in fossil fuels such as coal, petroleum, and natural gas; some are major air pollutants, others contribute to smog; some may cause cancers.

 paraffin h. See paraffin (2).

hydrocele (hi'dro-sēl) Abnormal accumulation of fluid in a body cavity, especially under the serous covering of the testis or alongside

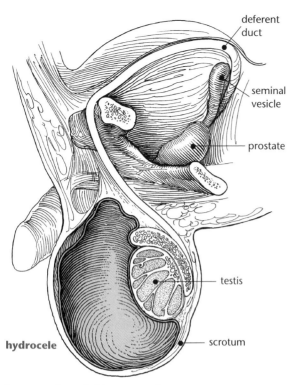

deferent
duct

seminal
vesicle

prostate

testis

scrotum

hydrocele

the spermatic cord either as a result of generalized edema or due to incomplete closure of the tunica vaginalis.

hernia h. The presence of a hernia and hydrocele in which the hernial sac is filled with a fluid.

suppurating h. See empyocele.

hydrocelectomy (hi-dro-se-lek′to-me) Surgical removal of a hydrocele.

hydrocephalic (hi-dro-sĕ-fal′ik) Relating to hydrocephalus.

hydrocephalus (hi-dro-sef′ah-lus) An abnormal increase in the amount of cerebrospinal fluid (CSF) in the ventricles of the brain due to blockage of the CSF flow, causing compression of brain tissue. The head enlarges in infants and children under two years of age (whose cranial sutures have not fully closed) as a result of increased intracranial pressure.

communicating h. Hydrocephalus occurring when the cerebrospinal fluid flows freely through the openings between ventricles but is improperly drained at the subarachnoid space or at the arachnoid granulations. Also called external hydrocephalus.

external h. See communicating hydrocephalus.

h. ex vacuo Term applied to a condition occurring even though the flow and absorption of cerebrospinal fluid are normal; the condition is actually hydrocephalus by default, i.e., the ventricles enlarge "passively" as a compensatory mechanism to restore intracranial volume, as when the brain atrophies (e.g., in Alzheimer's disease).

internal h. Hydrocephalus confined to the ventricles.

noncommunicating h. See obstructive hydrocephalus.

obstructive h. Hydrocephalus occurring as a result of a block within the ventricular system, i.e., at any of the openings (foramina) of the ventricles. Also called noncommunicating hydrocephalus.

hydrochloric acid (hi-dro-klor′ik as′id) An aqueous compound of hydrogen chloride; it is the acid secreted by the stomach during digestion; produced commercially for use in electroplating, leather tanning, and in the photographic and textile industries; used also in the production of fertilizers, paint pigments, dyes, and soap. Hydrochloric acid may be released in the thermal degradation of polyvinyl chloride, presenting a health hazard to firefighters.

hydrochloride (hi-dro-klo′rĭd) Compound formed by the reaction of hydrochloric acid with an organic base.

hydrochlorothiazide (hi-dro-klor-o-thi′ah-zīd) A thiazide compound used as an oral diuretic; possible adverse effects include leg cramps, dizziness, lethargy, skin rash, and impotence.

hydrocolloid (hi-dro-kol′loid) A gelatinous compound used in dentistry as an impression material.

irreversible h. A hydrocolloid (e.g., alginate) formed by mixing a powder with water, used in dentistry to make permanent diagnostic casts of teeth and partial denture impressions.

reversible h. A solid hydrocolloid of agar-agar base that can be changed to a liquid by heating and then to an elastic gel by cooling.

hydrocolpocele, hydrocolpos (hi-dro-kol′-po-sēl, hi-dro-kol′pos) Accumulation of fluid in the vagina.

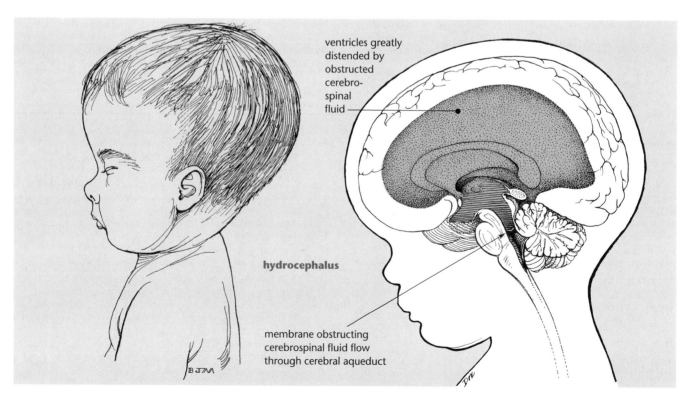

ventricles greatly
distended by
obstructed
cerebro-
spinal
fluid

hydrocephalus

membrane obstructing
cerebrospinal fluid flow
through cerebral aqueduct

hydrocortisone (hi-dro-kor'tĭ-sōn) A potent steroid hormone secreted by the cortex of the adrenal (suprarenal) glands; also produced synthetically; it provides resistance to stress and maintains a number of enzymatic systems. Also called cortisol.

hydrocyanic acid (hi-dro-si-an'ik as'id) See hydrogen cyanide, under hydrogen.

hydrodynamics (hi-dro-di-nam'iks) The branch of physics concerned with fluids in motion and the forces affecting the motion.

hydrogel (hi'dro-jel) A gel that has water as its dispersion medium. COMPARE hydrosol.

hydrogen (hi'dro-jen) A colorless, flammable, gaseous element; symbol H, atomic number 1, atomic weight 1.0079.

> **activated h.** Hydrogen removed from a compound (donor) by an enzyme (dehydrogenase).

> **h. cyanide** A colorless, highly poisonous compound with an almond odor, used as a fumigant. Also called hydrocyanic acid.

> **h. fluoride** Compound that is a potent irritant of the respiratory tract, causing edema of the lungs; occupational exposure occurs in the glass, ceramic, and silicon chip industries that use the compound to etch microcircuits and markers.

> **heavy h.** See hydrogen 2.

> **h. sulfide** A poisonous gas with a rotten–egg odor, released in geothermal energy (by decaying organic matter) and in drilling for oil and natural gas; occupational exposure occurs in the tannery, coal mining, rubber manufacturing, and petroleum refining industries. Exposure may occur in either of two forms: *Acute exposure,* in which massive inhalation causes sudden severe eye and respiratory irritation and possibly pulmonary injury and death; or *Chronic exposure,* which causes eye irritation (leading to inflammation of the cornea) and worsening of existing lung disease. Also called sulfurated hydrogen.

> **sulfurated h.** See hydrogen sulfide.

hydrogen 1 (hi'dro-jen) (^{1}H) The hydrogen isotope making up about 99% of hydrogen atoms occurring in nature. Also called protium.

hydrogen 2 (hi'dro-jen) (^{2}H) An isotope of hydrogen that has one proton and one neutron in its nucleus; atomic weight 2.0141. Also called deuterium; heavy hydrogen.

hydrogen 3 (hi'dro-jen) (^{3}H) The heaviest of the three isotopes of hydrogen; weakly radioactive, half-life 12.4 years; mass number 3. Also called tritium.

hydrogenation (hi-dro-jĕ-nā'shun) The chemical combination of an unsaturated compound with hydrogen.

hydrogymnastics (hi-dro-jim-nas'tiks) Therapeutic exercises conducted in the water.

hydrokinetics (hi-dro-kĭ-net'iks) The study of fluids in motion.

hydrolabyrinth (hi-dro-lab'ĭ-rinth) Abnormal increase of endolymph in the membranous canals of the inner ear; thought to be the cause of aural vertigo.

hydrolase (hi'dro-lās) Enzyme that precipitates the breakdown of compounds by hydrolysis.

hydrolysate (hi-drol'ĭ-zāt) Any product of hydrolysis.

hydrolysis (hi-drol'ĭ-sis) The splitting of a compound into simpler substances by the addition of the elements of water.

hydrolytic (hi-dro-lit'ik) Relating to hydrolysis.

hydrolyze (hi'dro-liz) To subject to hydrolysis.

hydromassage (hi-dro-mah-sahzh') Massage conducted by a whirlpool or any other form of water in motion.

hydrometer (hi-drom'ĕ-ter) Instrument for measuring the specific gravity of a liquid (e.g., urine). Also called gravimeter.

hydrometra (hi-dro-me'trah) Abnormal accumulation of a fluid in the uterus.

hydrometrocolpos (hi-dro-me-tro-kol'pos) Abnormal accumulation of a fluid in the uterus and vagina.

hydrometry (hi-drom'ĕ-tre) Measuring of the specific gravity of a fluid.

hydromphalus (hi-drom'fah-lus) A cystlike tumor of the navel.

hydromyelia (hi-dro-mi-e'le-ah) Distention of the central canal of the spinal cord with accumulated cerebrospinal fluid.

hydromyelocele (hi-dro-mi'el-o-sēl) A fluid-filled saclike protrusion of the spinal cord through a spina bifida.

hydronephrosis (hi-dro-nĕ-fro'sis) Distention of the pelvis and calices of one or both kidneys with urine, associated with progressive atrophy of the kidney, caused by obstruction to the outflow of urine.

hydronephrotic (hi-dro-nĕ-frot'ik) Relating to hydronephrosis.

hydropenia (hi-dro-pe'ne-ah) Condition characterized by less than normal water content in the body.

hydropericardium (hi-dro-per-ĭ-kar'de-um) Abnormal accumulation of serous fluid in the pericardium, the membrane around the heart.

hydroperitoneum (hi-dro-per-ĭ-to-ne'um) See ascites.

hydrophilia (hi-dro-fil'e-ah) Tendency to absorb water; affinity for water.

hydrophilic (hi-dro-fil'ik) Characterized by hydrophilia.

hydrophobia (hi-dro-fo'be-ah) See rabies.

hydrophthalmos (hi-drof-thal'mos) See buphthalmos.

hydropneumopericardium (hi-dro-nu-mo-per-ĭ-kar'de-um) Accumulation of serous effusion and gas within the pericardium, the membrane that envelops the heart.

hydropneumothorax (hi-dro-nu-mo-thor'aks) Accumulation of fluid and air in the pleural space (i.e., between the two layers of the pleura). Also called pneumohydrothorax.

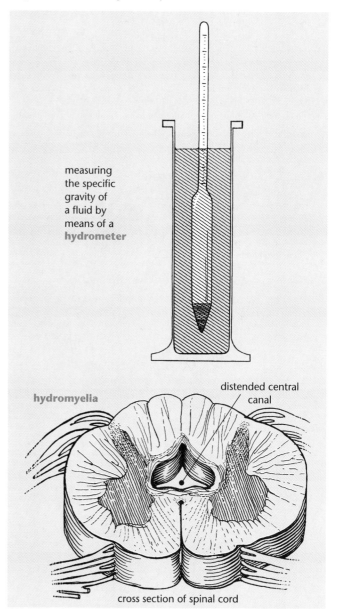

measuring the specific gravity of a fluid by means of a **hydrometer**

hydromyelia

distended central canal

cross section of spinal cord

hydrops (hi'drops) Abnormal accumulation of clear fluid in body cavities or tissues. Formerly called dropsy.

    endolymphatic h. See Ménière's disease, under disease.

    h. fetalis, fetal h. Hydrops of the fetus, as seen in severe hemolytic disease.

    h. of gallbladder Distention of the gallbladder with a watery, mucinous fluid due to obstruction of the neck of the gallbladder or the cystic duct, usually by a stone.

    h. of labyrinth See Ménière's disease, under disease.

hydropyonephrosis (hi-dro-pi-o-nĕ-fro'sis) Collection of urine and pus in the pelvis and calices of the kidney, usually caused by obstruction to urine outflow in the ureter.

hydrorchis (hi-dro-or'kis) Abnormal accumulation of fluid around the testis, within its serous covering.

hydrorrhea (hi-dro-re'ah) A profuse watery secretion.

    h. gravidarum An uncommon condition in which a pregnant woman passes a clear fluid from the vagina; usually a scant amount throughout the pregnancy, occasionally as much as 500 ml as a onetime occurrence; cause is not known.

hydrosalpinx (hi-dro-sal'pinks) Accumulation of serous fluid in a fallopian (uterine) tube.

hydrosol (hi'dro-sol) A sol in which the dispersing medium is water. COMPARE hydrogel.

hydrostatic (hi-dro-stat'ik) Relating to the pressures exerted by liquids at rest; the opposite of hydrokinetic.

hydrotherapeutic (hi-dro-ther-ah-pu'tik) See hydriatic.

hydrotherapy (hi-dro-ther'ah-pe) Treatment by the external application of water (e.g., in whirlpool baths, exercise pools, and showers); used for some patients who lack motility and those recovering from injuries.

hydrothermal (hi-dro-ther'mal) Relating to hot water.

hydrothorax (hi-dro-tho'raks) Abnormal accumulation of fluid in the pleural space (i.e., between the two layers of the pleura).

hydroureter (hi-dro-u-re'ter) Abnormal distention of the ureter with urine due to obstruction to the urine outflow.

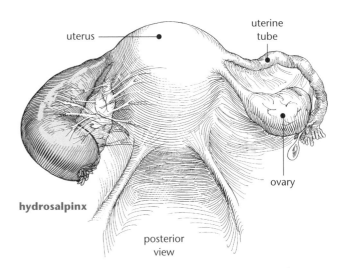

hydrosalpinx

uterus — uterine tube — ovary

posterior view

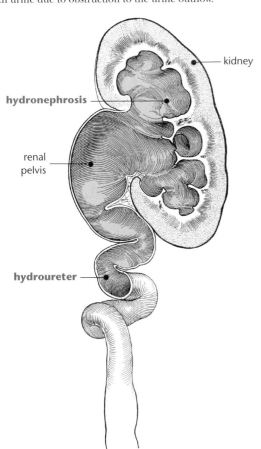

kidney

hydronephrosis

renal pelvis

hydroureter

hydrous (hi'drus) Containing water.

hydroxide (hi-drok'sīd) Any chemical compound of hydroxyl with another element or radical.

hydroxocobalamin (hi-drok'so-ko-bal'ah-min) A long-acting synthetic compound of vitamin B$_{12}$.

hydroxyapatite (hi-drok'se-ap'ah-tīt) A mineral compound used in chromatography of nucleic acids.

25-hydroxycholecalciferol (hi-drok'se-ko-le-kal-sif'ĕ-rol) See calcidiol.

hydroxyphenyluria (hi-drok'se-phen-il-u're-ah) Excretion of the amino acids tyrosine and phenylalanine in the urine, usually resulting from vitamin C deficiency.

hydroxyproline (hi-drok'se-pro'lin) A nutritionally nonessential amino acid found among the breakdown products of collagen; not found in proteins other than those of connective tissue.

hydroxyprolinemia (hi-drok'se-pro-len-e'me-ah) Metabolic disorder occurring as an autosomal recessive inheritance, characterized by increased blood level and urinary excretion of hydroxyproline, associated with severe mental retardation.

hygiene (hi'jēn) The science concerned with the methods of achieving and maintaining good health.

    industrial h. The recognition, evaluation, and control of occupational health hazards.

    oral h. The care of the mouth and teeth as a measure for preventing disease.

hygienic (hi-je-en'ik) Relating to hygiene.

hygienist (hi-je'nist) One who is skilled in the application of the principles of hygiene.

    dental h. One who has been trained in the techniques of removing plaque from teeth and other preventive treatments, including instructing patients in the proper care of their teeth.

    industrial h. A person having either a baccalaureate degree in engineering, chemistry, or physics, or a baccalaureate degree in a related biological or physical science, from an accredited college or university and, in addition, a minimum of three years of industrial hygiene experience. A completed PhD or ScD degree in a related physical or biological science or an MD degree can be substituted for two years of the three-year requirement. The American Industrial Hygiene Association suggests that all industrial hygienists consulted be certified by the American Board of Industrial Hygiene.

hygric (hi'grik) Relating to moisture.

hygro-, hygr- Combining forms meaning moist; moisture.

hygroma (hi-gro'mah) A fluid-filled swelling or tumor.

    cystic h. See cavernous lymphangioma, under lymphangioma.

    subdural h. Collection of fluid beneath the dura mater, in the subdural space.

hygrometer (hi-grom'ĕ-ter) Any device for measuring atmospheric moisture.

hygroscopic (hi-gro-skop'ik) Capable of absorbing moisture.

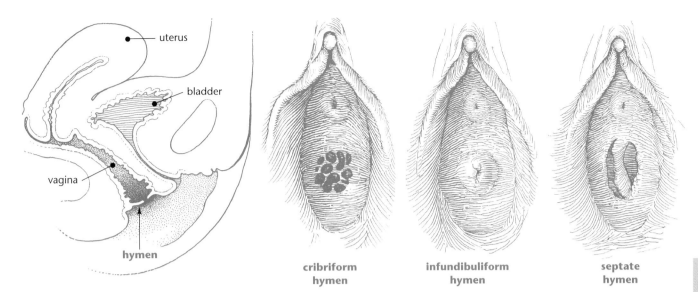

uterus

bladder

vagina

hymen

cribriform hymen

infundibuliform hymen

septate hymen

hymen (hi′men) The thin fold of mucous membrane that partially or entirely closes the vaginal orifice in the virgin; it varies much in shape and extent, and occasionally may be absent. Also called virginal membrane.

    circular h. A hymen with a small round opening.

    cribriform h. A hymen with a number of small perforations. Also called fenestrated hymen.

    denticular h. A hymen in which the opening has serrated edges.

    falciform h. A crescent-shaped hymen.

    fenestrated h. See cribriform hymen.

    imperforate h. A hymen which completely closes the vaginal orifice.

    infundibuliform h. A protruding hymen with a central opening.

    ruptured h. A hymen that has been forcibly disrupted as a result of injury or coitus.

    septate h. A hymen in which the opening is divided by a narrow band of tissue (septum).

hymenal (hi′men-al) Relating to the hymen.

hymenectomy (hi-men-ek′to-me) Excision of the hymen.

hymenolepiasis (hi-mĕ-no-lep-i′ah-sis). Infestation with tapeworms of the genus *Hymenolepis.*

Hymenolepis (hi-mĕ-nol′ĕ-pis) A genus of tapeworms (family Hymenolepididae).

    H. nana A small tapeworm (averaging 20–30 mm in length) parasitic in the intestines of rats, mice, and children. Also called dwarf tapeworm; dwarf mouse tapeworm.

Hymenoptera (hi-men-op′ter-ah) An order of winged insects that includes many stinging species (e.g., wasps, yellow jackets, hornets, honeybees, and fire ants); the venom-carrying stings may cause severe reactions and even death in hypersensitive people.

hymenopteran (hi-men-op′ter-an) Any member of the order Hymenoptera.

hymenorrhaphy (hi-men-or′ah-fe) **1.** Closing of the vagina by suturing the hymen. **2.** Suture of any membrane.

hymenotomy (hi-men-ot′o-me) Surgical cut through the hymen, especially an imperforate hymen.

hyo- Combining form meaning U-shaped.

hyoepiglottic (hi-o-ep-ĭ-glot′ik) Relating to the hyoid bone and the epiglottis.

hyoglossal (hi-o-glos′al) Relating to the hyoid bone and the tongue.

hyoid (hi′oid) U-shaped; applied to the horseshoe-shaped bone in the throat between the thyroid cartilage and the root of the tongue. See table of bones.

hyoscyamine (hi-o-si′ah-min) An alkaloid occurring in certain plants (e.g., belladonna and *Datura stramonium)* which blocks the action of parasympathetic nerves.

hypacusia (hi-pah-ku′ze-ah) See hypacusis.

hypacusis (hi-pah-ku′sis) Impaired hearing; usually attributable to conductive or neurosensory deficiency in the peripheral organs of hearing. Also called hypoacusis; hypacusia.

hypalgesia (hi-pal-je′ze-ah) Decreased pain perception.

hypamnios, hypamnion (hi-pam′ne-os, hi-pam′ne-on) The presence of a smaller than usual amount of amniotic fluid in the amniotic sac.

hypencephalon (hi-pen-sef′ah-lon) The midbrain, pons, and medulla considered together.

hyper- Prefix meaning over; above; excessive; increased; above normal.

hyperacidity (hi-per-ah-sid′ĭ-te) The presence of an excessive amount of acid.

    gastric h. Excessive secretion of hydrochloric acid by the parietal cells of the stomach.

hyperactivity (hi-per-ak-tiv′ĭ-te) (HA) **1.** Excessive activity. **2.** Excessive motion and general restlessness (e.g., in children with attention deficit disorder). See also hyperactive child, under child.

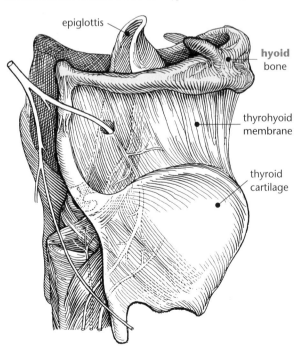

epiglottis

hyoid bone

thyrohyoid membrane

thyroid cartilage

hyperacusis, hyperacusia (hi-per-ah-ku´sis, hi-per-ah-ku´ze-ah) A grossly exaggerated sensitivity to sound.

hyperadrenalism (hi-per-ah-dre´nal-izm) Abnormally increased function of the adrenal cortex, with excessive output of steroid hormones. Also called hyperadrenocorticism; hypercorticism.

hyperadrenocorticism (hi-per-ah-dre-no-kor´tĭ-sizm) See hyperadrenalism.

hyperal (hi-per´al) A shortened version of the term hyperalimentation.

hyperaldosteronism (hi-per-al´do-ster´ŏn-izm) See aldosteronism.

hyperalgesia (hi-per-al-je´ze-ah) Excessive sensitivity or response to painful stimulus.

hyperalimentation (hi-per-al-ĭ-men-ta´shun) Administration of nutrients beyond requirements for therapeutic purposes.

    parenteral h. The continuous administration of fluids containing nutrients (particularly a solution of amino acids and sugar) into the superior vena cava through a catheter.

hyperalphalipoproteinemia (hi-per-al-fah-lip´o-pro-tēn-e´me-ah) Elevated levels of high-density lipoprotein (HDL) in blood serum; it is not associated with any disease process.

hyperbaric (hi-per-bār´ik) Relating to pressures greater than atmospheric pressure.

hyperbarism (hi-per-bar´izm) Any condition resulting from exposure to ambient gases in excess of that within the body.

hyperbetalipoproteinemia (hi-per-ba´tah-lip´o-pro-tēn-e´me-ah) Increased accumulation of betalipoprotein in the blood.

hyperbilirubinemia (hi-per-bil-ĭ-roo-bĭ-ne´me-ah) The presence of abnormally high levels of bilirubin in the blood.

    drug-induced h. A form produced by intake of certain substances (e.g., vitamin K_2 and sulfonamides).

    hereditary h. Any of a group of inherited metabolic disorders in which the excessive bilirubin in the circulating blood is due either to increased bilirubin production or to delayed clearance of bilirubin from the blood.

hypercalcemia (hi-per-kal-se´me-ah) An abnormally high concentration of calcium in the blood; symptoms of severe hypercalcemia include headache, constipation, and renal impairment; causes include hyperparathyroidism, sarcoidosis, bone tumors, and vitamin D intoxication.

    idiopathic h. of infancy An uncommon disorder of unknown cause occurring in infants; symptoms include distinctive facial features, failure to thrive, mental and motor retardation, hypertension, osteosclerosis, and kidney disease.

hypercalcinuria (hi-per-kal-sĭ-nu´re-ah) See hypercalciuria.

hypercalciuria (hi-per-kal-sĭ-u´re-ah) Abnormally elevated level of calcium in the urine; may result from increased calcium levels in the blood, as seen in disorders of the parathyroid glands, bone tumors, and vitamin D intoxication. Also called hypercalcuria; hypercalcinuria.

hypercalcuria (hi-per-kal-ku´re-ah) See hypercalciuria.

hypercapnia, hypercarbia (hi-per-kap´ne-ah, hi-per-kar´be-ah) Abnormally high concentration of carbon dioxide in the blood.

hypercapnic, hypercapneic (hi-per-kap´nik, hi-per-kap´ne-ik) Relating to hypercapnia.

hypercellularity (hi-per-sel-u-lār´ĭ-te) Abnormal increase in the number of cells of a structure (e.g., in bone marrow or in kidney glomeruli).

hypercementosis (hi-per-se-men-to´sis) Overdevelopment of cementum over the root surface of teeth.

hyperchloremia (hi-per-klo-re´me-ah) An abnormally high concentration of chloride ions in the blood.

hyperchlorhydria (hi-per-klōr-hi´dre-ah) Excessive hydrochloric acid in the stomach. Also called chlorhydria.

hypercholesterolemia (hi-per-ko-les´ter-ol-e´me-ah) The presence of excessive amounts of cholesterol in the blood.

    familial h. (FH) Genetic disorder occurring as an autosomal inheritance, one of several disorders grouped as type II familial hyperlipoproteinemia; characterized by increased concentration of plasma cholesterol carried in low-density lipoprotein (LDL), the principal cholesterol transport in plasma. The disorder is due to defects in the cell surface receptors that are responsible for binding LDL and delivering it to the cell's interior; clinical findings include cholesterol deposits (xanthomas) in the skin or in the patella and Achilles tendons at the knees and heels, cholesterol accumulation around the periphery of the cornea (arcus senilis), and premature atherosclerosis of coronary arteries.

hypercholia (hi-per-ko´le-ah) Excessive secretion of bile by the liver.

hyperchromasia (hi-per-kro-ma´se-ah) See hyperchromatism.

hyperchromatic (hi-per-kro-mat´ik) Relating to excessive pigmentation; applied especially to cells that stain deeply. Also called hyperchromic.

hyperchromatism (hi-per-kro´mah-tizm) Excessive pigmentation, especially the increased staining capacity of certain degenerated cell nuclei.

hyperchromia (hi-per-kro´me-ah) Abnormal increase in the hemoglobin content of red blood cells.

hyperchromic (hi-per-kro´mik) See hyperchromatic.

hyperchylia (hi-per-ki´le-ah) Abnormal increase in gastric juice.

hypercorticism (hi-per-kor´tĭ-sizm) See hyperadrenalism.

hypercortisolism (hi-per-kor´tĭ-sōl-izm) See Cushing's disease, under disease.

hypercryalgesia, hypercryesthesia (hi-per-kri-al-je´ze-ah, hi-per-kri-es-the´ze-ah) Excessive sensitivity to cold.

hypercupremia (hi-per-ku-pre´me-ah) Abnormally high copper content in the blood. Seen in Wilson's disease.

hypercythemia (hi-per-si-the´me-ah) Excessive number of red blood cells in the circulating blood.

hypercytosis (hi-per-si-to´sis) Any condition in which there is an abnormal increase in the number of blood cells, especially white blood cells. Infrequently used term.

hyperdipsia (hi-per-dip´se-ah) An abnormally intense thirst.

hyperdistention (hi-per-dis-ten´shun) Excessive distention.

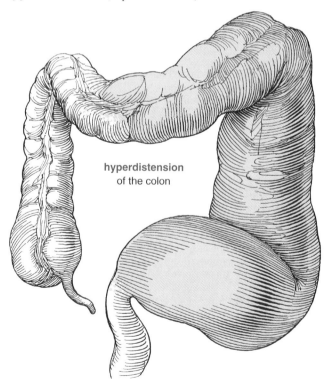

hyperdistension
of the colon

hyperdynamia (hi-per-di-na´me-ah) Extreme muscular activity; exaggeration of function.

hyperechoic (hi-per-ĕ-kō´ik) Producing echoes of a greater amplitude or density than those produced by the surrounding medium or tissues.

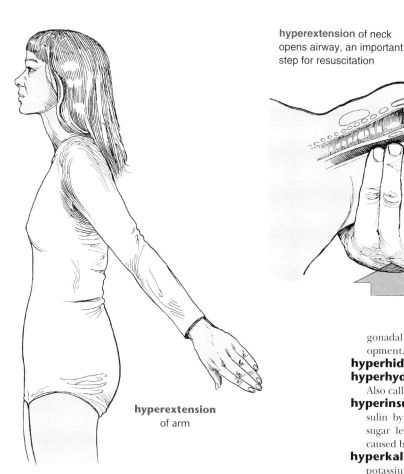

hyperextension of neck opens airway, an important step for resuscitation

hyperextension of arm

gonadal hormones, marked by growth and precocious sexual development.

hyperhidrosis (hi-per-hi-dro'sis) Excessive sweating.

hyperhydration (hi-per-hi-dra'shun) Excess of fluids in the body. Also called overhydration.

hyperinsulinism (hi-per-in'su-lin-izm) **1.** Excessive secretion of insulin by the islets of Langerhans of the pancreas, causing blood sugar level to fall considerably (hypoglycemia). **2.** Insulin shock caused by excess dosage of insulin.

hyperkalemia (hi-per-kah-le'me-ah) An abnormally elevated potassium concentration in the blood; may cause changes in cardiac function, leading to cardiac arrest. Sometimes called hyperpotassemia.

hyperkeratosis (hi-per-ker-ah-to'sis) Overgrowth of the horny layer of the epidermis resulting in elevations on the skin (e.g., calluses).

hyperkinesis, hyperkinesia (hi-per-kĭ-ne'sis, hi-per-kĭ-ne'ze-ah) Abnormally increased motor activity; seen in some psychiatric disorders, especially in children.

hyperkinetic (hi-per-ki-net'ik) Relating to hyperkinesis.

hyperlactation (hi-per-lak-ta'shun) Excessive or prolonged secretion of milk.

hyperflexion of the uterus

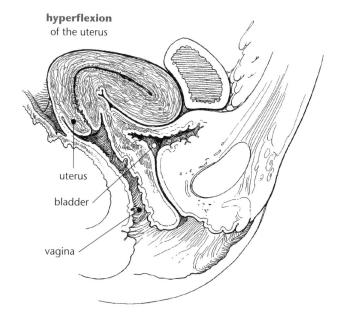

uterus

bladder

vagina

hyperemesis (hi-per-em'ĕ-sis) Excessive vomiting.

    h. gravidarum Severe and prolonged vomiting occurring in pregnancy, usually associated with dehydration and ketonuria.

hyperemia (hi-per-ĕ'me-ah) Excess of blood in a body part; congestion.

    active h. Hyperemia due to increased inflow of arterial blood resulting in dilatation of arterioles and capillaries, as seen normally in the skin and muscles after exercise or in acute inflammation.

    collateral h. Increased blood flow through smaller auxiliary blood vessels due to obstruction of the larger, main vessel.

    passive h. See congestion.

hyperesthesia (hi-per-es-the'ze-ah) Abnormally exaggerated sensitivity or response to sensory stimuli.

hyperextension (hi-per-ek-sten'shun) Extension of a joint beyond its neutral position; it is normal in some joints (e.g., the shoulder joint) but not in others (e.g., the knee joint). Also called overextension.

hyperflexion (hi-per-flek'shun) Flexion of a body part beyond its normal limit.

hypergammaglobulinemia (hi-per-gam'ah-glob'u-lĭ-ne'me-ah) An excess of gamma globulin in the blood.

hypergenitalism (hi-per-jen'i-tal-izm) Overdeveloped genital organs for age of the individual.

hyperglobulinemia (hi-per-glob'u-lĭ-ne'me-ah) Excess of globulin in the circulating blood.

hyperglycemia (hi-per-gli-se'me-ah) Abnormally high level of sugar (glucose) in the blood.

hyperglycorrhachia (hi-per-gli-ko-ra'ke-ah) Excessive content of sugar (glucose) in the cerebrospinal fluid (CSF).

hypergonadism (hi-per-go'nad-izm) Abnormally increased physiologic activity of the gonads (testes or ovaries), with secretion of

Type and prevalence	I RARE	II COMMON	III FAIRLY COMMON	IV COMMON	V UNCOMMON
Appearance of plasma	creamy layer over clear infranatant on standing	clear or only slightly turbid	clear, cloudy, or milky	clear to grossly turbid	creamy layer over turbid infranatant on standing
Cholesterol level	↑	↑	↑	↑	↑
Triglyceride level	↑	↑	↑	↑	↑
Signs and symptoms	abdominal pain hepatosplenomegaly lipemia retinalis eruptive xanthomas	tendon xanthomas tuberous xanthomas corneal arcus accelerated atheroclerosis	tendon, tuboeruptive, and planar xanthomas accelerated atheroclerosis	accelerated coronary atherosclerosis abnormal glucose tolerance	abdominal pain hepatosplenomegaly lipemia retinalis eruptive xanthomas abnormal glucose tolerance

hyperlipemia (hi-per-li-pe′me-ah) High levels of any of the triglyceride-rich lipoproteins in blood plasma.

    mixed h. See type V familial hyperlipoproteinemia, under hyperlipoproteinemia.

hyperlipidemia (hi-per-lip-i-de′me-ah) High levels of any kind of lipoprotein in blood plasma. Also called lipemia; lipidemia.

hyperlipoproteinemia (hi-per-lip-o-pro-tēn-e′me-ah) A group of disorders of fat metabolism characterized by concentrations of lipoproteins in blood and causing increased risk of heart disease.

    type I familial h. Uncommon disorder characterized by accumulation of chylomicrons in the blood (proportional to intake of dietary fat) and increase of cholesterol and triglyceride levels; causes fatty nodules (xanthomas) in skin, abdominal pain, and inflammation of pancreas; occurs as an autosomal recessive inheritance.

    type II familial h. A group of disorders of autosomal inheritance characterized by increased plasma concentration of low-density (beta) lipoprotein (LDL), cholesterol, and phospholipids, with normal to slightly elevated levels of triglyceride; associated with fatty nodules (xanthomas) in the Achilles, patellar, and digital extensor tendons, and susceptibility to atherosclerosis; manifestations are usually detected in infants and young children.

    type III familial h. An uncommon form considered an autosomal recessive inheritance, characterized by increased plasma levels of very-low-density (pre-beta) lipoprotein (VLDL) and cholesterol; associated with flat, yellow-orange fat deposits (usually on the palmar and digital creases), glucose intolerance, and premature atherosclerosis; usually detected in young adults.

    type IV familial h. A common disorder, usually detected in middle age, probably an autosomal recessive inheritance; characterized by increased levels of plasma triglyceride of hepatic origin and very-low-density (pre-beta) lipoprotein (VLDL) with normal cholesterol levels, and by a predisposition to atherosclerosis.

    type V familial h. An uncommon form with characteristics of both type I and type IV, which include increased plasma levels of chylomicrons, very-low-density (pre-beta) lipoprotein (VLDL), and triglycerides while on ordinary diets, with skin eruption of fatty nodules (xanthomas) and recurrent acute inflammation of the pancreas; occurs chiefly during adolescence and middle age, probably as an autosomal recessive inheritance. Also called mixed hyperlipemia.

hyperlysinemia (hi-per-li-se-ne′me-ah) Metabolic disorder transmitted as an autosomal recessive inheritance, characterized by abnormally high levels of the amino acid lysine in circulating blood; associated with physical and mental retardation, anemia, weak muscles, convulsions, and impaired sexual development.

hyperlysinuria (hi-per-li-se-nu′re-ah) Abnormally high concentration of the amino acid lysine in the urine.

hypermagnesemia (hi-per-mag-nĕ-se′me-ah) Abnormally high levels of magnesium in blood serum, seen in patients with renal failure who have ingested magnesium-containing antacids. In the newborn, it is most commonly caused by therapeutic administration of magnesium sulfate to the mother during pregnancy.

hypermastia (hi-per-mas′te-ah) Overdevelopment of the mammary glands.

hypermenorrhea (hi-per-men-o-re′ah) See menorrhagia.

hypermetabolism (hi-per-mĕ-tab′o-lizm) An unusually high metabolic rate.

hypermetria (hi-per-me′tre-ah) A manifestation of ataxia characterized by voluntary muscular movement overreaching the intended goal.

hypermetropia (hi-per-me-tro′pe-ah) See hyperopia.

hypermobility (hi-per-mo-bil′i-te) A wide or increased range of motion in a joint.

hypermorph (hi′per-morf) A tall, usually slender person whose standing height is disproportionately greater than the sitting height due to excessively long legs.

hypermotility (hi-per-mo-til′i-te) In fertilization, the exaggerated vigorous movements of the spermatozoon, especially in the vicinity of the ovum, which cause it to move in circles rather than in the usual forward direction; considered part of the fertilization process.

hypermyotonia (hi-per-mi-o-to′ne-ah) Excessive tone of muscle.

hypermyotrophy (hi-per-mi-ot′ro-fe) See muscular hypertrophy, under hypertrophy.

hypernatremia (hi-per-nah-tre′me-ah) Abnormally high concentration of sodium in the blood.

hypernephroma (hi-per-nĕ-fro′mah) See renal adenocarcinoma, under adenocarcinoma.

hyperoncotic (hi-per-ong-kot′ik) Denoting an oncotic pressure (e.g., of blood) that is higher than normal.

hyperonychia (hi-per-o-nik′e-ah) Hypertrophy of the nails.

hyperope (hi′per-ōp) A person afflicted with hyperopia.

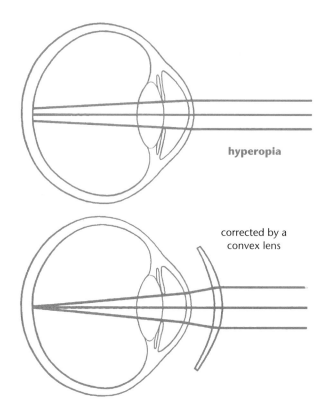

hyperopia

corrected by a
convex lens

hyperopia (hi-per-o'pe-ah) (H) Refractive error in which parallel light rays entering the eyeball do not converge enough to focus on the retina; may be caused by shortness of the eyeball, or weakness of the refractive power of the lens of the eye or of the cornea. Also called hypermetropia; farsightedness; far sight.

latent h. (Hl) The portion of total hyperopia that is not revealed because it is compensated by the tonicity of the ciliary muscles; the effort required for accommodation is minor, and near vision may not be impaired.

manifest h. (Hm) The portion of total hyperopia that may be measured by the relaxation of accommodation.

total h. (Ht) The sum of latent and manifest hyperopia.

hyperopic (hi-per-o'pik) Relating to hyperopia.

hyperosmia (hi-per-oz'me-ah) An abnormally heightened sense of smell.

hyperosmotic (hi-per-os-mot'ik) Having a relatively high concentration of osmotically active solutes, i.e., higher than a comparative (standard) solution.

hyperostosis (hi-per-os-to'sis) Abnormal increase in the mass of bone.

ankylosing h. See diffuse idiopathic skeletal hyperostosis.

diffuse idiopathic skeletal h. (DISH) A variant of osteoarthritis occurring most commonly in elderly men, characterized by development of large bony outgrowth bridging the vertebrae and ossification of tendon insertions and ligaments (especially along the anterior aspect of the vertebral column). Also called Forrestier's disease; ankylosing hyperostosis.

h. frontalis interna Abnormal deposition of bone in the skull, on the inner surface of the frontal bone.

infantile cortical h. A self-limited, benign condition of unknown cause that has its onset before the age of six months and persists for many weeks or months; characterized by bone formation on the surface of bones, typically the mandible and collarbones (clavicles), but may involve any bone, especially the shafts of ribs and bones of the arm; causes irritability, fever, and tender, painful swellings. Also called Caffey's syndrome; Caffey's disease.

sternoclavicular h. Uncommon benign condition characterized by hyperostosis and ossification of soft tissues between the collarbones (clavicles) and anterior portion of ribs; often associated with eruption of vesicles on the palms and soles (bacterid); a bone infection has been suggested as a possible cause.

hyperovarianism (hi-per-o-va're-an-izm) Abnormally increased functional activity of the ovaries, usually leading to sexual precocity in young girls.

hyperoxaluria (hi-per-ok-sah-lu're-ah) The presence of an unusually large amount of oxalic acid and oxalates in the urine.

primary h. Hyperoxaluria due to a genetic defect affecting the metabolism of glycoxylic acid and becoming evident during the first 10 years of age; causes kidney stones and scattered calcifications in the kidneys; an autosomal recessive inheritance.

hyperoxia (hi-per-ok'se-ah) Excessive oxygen in tissues.

hyperparathyroidism (hi-per-par-ah-thi'roid-izm) Abnormally elevated serum level of parathyroid hormone (PTH) due to increased secretion by the parathyroid glands. It may cause osteitis fibrosa cystica (von Rechlinghausen's disease of bone).

primary p. Hyperparathyroidism resulting from an intrinsic abnormality of one or more glands, usually a single benign glandular tumor (adenoma) in one parathyroid gland or, less often, diffuse hyperplasia of all four parathyroid glands. The classic laboratory findings are high serum calcium and low serum phosphate. May produce bone disease and kidney stones.

secondary h. Hyperparathyroidism occurring as a compensatory process carried out by slightly enlarged but otherwise normal parathyroid glands to correct a lowered serum level of calcium (as in chronic kidney disease, vitamin D deficiency, and intestinal malabsorption).

hyperpathia (hi-per-path'e-ah) General term for an exaggerated reaction to painful stimuli.

hyperpepsinia (hi-per-pep-sin'e-ah) Excessive secretion of the enzyme pepsin in the stomach.

hyperperistalsis (hi-per-per-ĭ-stal'sis) Increase in the rate of propelling (peristaltic) movements of the gastrointestinal tract, resulting in excessively rapid passage of food through the stomach and intestines.

hyperphagia (hi-per-fa'je-ah) Overeating.

hyperphoria (hi-per-fo're-ah) Tendency of one eye to deviate upward.

hyperphosphatemia (hi-per-fos-fah-te'me-ah) Abnormally high amount of phosphates in the blood.

hyperphosphaturia (hi-per-fos-fah-tu're-ah) Abnormally high amount of phosphates in the urine.

hyperpigmentation (hi-per-pig-men-ta'shun) Excessive pigmentation in a tissue.

hyperpituitarism (hi-per-pĭ-tu'ĭ-tah-rizm) Excessive production of pituitary hormones, usually caused by a benign glandular tumor (adenoma) in the anterior pituitary (adenohypophysis) or, less commonly, by primary disorders of the hypothalamus.

hyperplasia (hi-per-pla'ze-ah) Excessive but regulated increase in the number of cells of an organ or body part, usually accompanied by increase in size.

benign prostatic h. (BPH) See nodular hyperplasia of prostate.

congenital adrenal h. (CAH) Inherited condition characterized by hyperplasia of the adrenal cortex and excessive secretion of androgens resulting from enzymatic defects in the biosynthesis of corticosteroids; there are four major types: a virilizing form; a sodium-losing form; one causing high blood pressure; and a 3-beta-hydroxysteroid dehydrogenase defect that may produce feminization of male genitals.

cystic h. of the breast See fibrocystic disease of the breast, under disease.

endocervical h. The development of small groups of benign, proliferating submucosal glands in the uterine cervix, usually occurring in women taking progesterone-containing oral contraceptives.

endometrial h. Hyperplasia of the uterine lining (endometrium) usually due to estrogen stimulation, especially when not opposed by progesterone secretion, causing abnormal uterine bleeding; the condition is benign except when it involves atypical

H

changes in the cells (cellular atypia); then it is considered precancerous.

fibromuscular h. Fibrosis and hyperplasia of the arterial muscular layer, usually involving the renal arteries.

gingival h. Cellular proliferation of the gingiva to the extent that the gums overgrow the teeth; may be caused by certain medicinal drugs or certain types of leukemia.

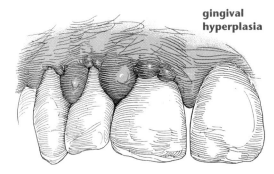

gingival hyperplasia

nodular h. of prostate Enlargement of the prostate with formation of large nodules that may press against the urethra and produce obstruction to urinary outflow; a common disorder of men over 50 years of age. Also called benign prostatic hyperplasia; benign prostatic hypertrophy (a misnomer).

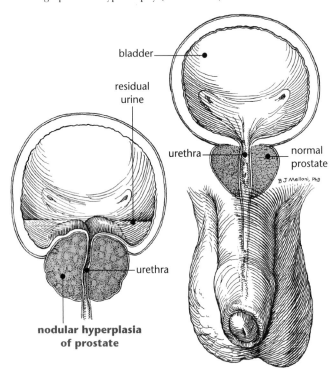

bladder

residual urine

urethra

normal prostate

B J Melloni, PhD

urethra

nodular hyperplasia of prostate

hyperplastic (hi-per-plas′tik) Relating to hyperplasia.

hyperpnea (hi-perp-ne′ah) Abnormally rapid and deep breathing.

hyperpolarization (hi-per-po-lar-ĭ-za′shun) An increase in the positive charges normally present at the surface of a nerve cell membrane.

hyperpotassemia (hi-per-po-tah-se′me-ah) See hyperkalemia.

hyperprolactinemia (hi-per-pro-lak-tin-e′me-ah) Increased amounts of the hormone prolactin in the blood; normal only during lactation; may be caused by certain medicinal drugs or by a pituitary tumor.

hyperprolinemia (hi-per-pro-lī-ne′me-ah) An inherited disorder of amino acid metabolism characterized by an increased level of proline in plasma; an autosomal recessive inheritance.

hyperproteinemia (hi-per-pro-tēn-e′me-ah) The presence of excessive protein in blood.

hyperpyretic (hi-per-pi-ret′ik) Relating to high fever. Also called hyperpyrexial.

hyperpyrexia (hi-per-pi-rek′se-ah) An extremely high fever, usually 105.0°F or higher.

hyperpyrexial (hi-per-pi-rek′se-al) See hyperpyretic.

hyperreflexia (hi-per-re-flek′se-ah) Increased tendon reflexes; usually an indication of upper motor neuron disease.

hyperresonance (hi-per-rez′o-nans) An exaggerated degree of resonance on percussion, as heard in pulmonary emphysema.

hypersalivation (hi-per-sal-ĭ-va′shun) Excessive saliva secretion.

hypersecretion (hi-per-se-kre′shun) Excessive secretion.

hypersensitive (hi-per-sen′sĭ-tiv) Overreactive to a stimulus.

hypersensitivity (hi-per-sen′sĭ-tiv-ĭ-te) An exaggerated immune response evoked by a particular substance (antigen) and manifested on subsequent contacts with that particular antigen. The response is actually no more than an expression of the beneficial immune response acting inappropriately, sometimes causing tissue damage.

delayed-type h. (DTH) T cell–mediated immune reactivity to an antigen applied topically or injected subcutaneously; cellular infiltration and swelling are maximal at about 48 hours. Also called delayed reaction.

food h. See food allergy, under allergy.

hypersensitization (hi-per-sen-sĭ-tĭ-za′shun) The process of creating an abnormally sensitive state.

hypersomatotropism (hi-per-so-mat-ah-trop′izm) Abnormally increased secretion of growth hormone (GH) from the pituitary.

hypersomia (hi-per-so′me-ah) Gigantism.

hypersomnia (hi-per-som′ne-ah) Abnormal state of excessive need to sleep, or of sleeping for excessive periods of time.

hyperspermia (hi-per-sper′me-ah) A high sperm count, more than 200 million per millimeter of semen; sometimes paradoxically associated with (not necessarily the cause of) male infertility.

hypersplenism (hi-per-splen′izm) Disorder characterized by enlargement of the spleen and destruction of cellular elements of blood by increased activity of the spleen; it may result in anemia, thrombocytopenia, or a combination of these states.

hypersteatosis (hi-per-ste-ah-to′sis) Excessive secretion of sebum by sebaceous glands.

hypertelorism (hi-per-te′lor-izm) Excessive distance between paired body parts.

ocular h. Developmental malformation of the skull, marked by an enlarged sphenoid bone, causing extreme distance between the eyes; seen in craniofacial dysostosis.

hypertensin (hi-per-ten′sin) Former name for angiotensin.

hypertensinogen (hi-per-ten-sin′o-jen) Former name for angiotensinogen.

hypertension (hi-per-ten′shun) High blood pressure, usually described as a blood pressure greater than two standard deviations above normal values for age and weight of the individual. In general, blood pressure exceeding 140 mm Hg systolic and 90 mm Hg diastolic pressure (140/90 mm Hg).

essential h. Hypertension occurring without a known cause. Also called idiopathic hypertension; primary hypertension.

idiopathic h. See essential hypertension.

isolated systolic h. Elevation of the systolic blood pressure with a normal or low diastolic blood pressure.

malignant h. Severe hypertension causing degenerative changes in the walls of blood vessels throughout the body; hemorrhages in the retina, kidney, and other areas; and altered cerebral function.

portal h. Increased pressure in the portal venous system; most cases result from obstruction to outflow of blood from the portal system; causes may be grouped into: intrahepatic (e.g., cirrhosis of the liver), suprahepatic (e.g., heart failure), and infrahepatic (e.g., formation of blood clots in the portal vein).

primary h. See essential hypertension.

pulmonary h. Hypertension in the blood circulation of the lungs resulting from primary lung disease (e.g., pulmonary fibrosis) or from heart disease (e.g., mitral stenosis).

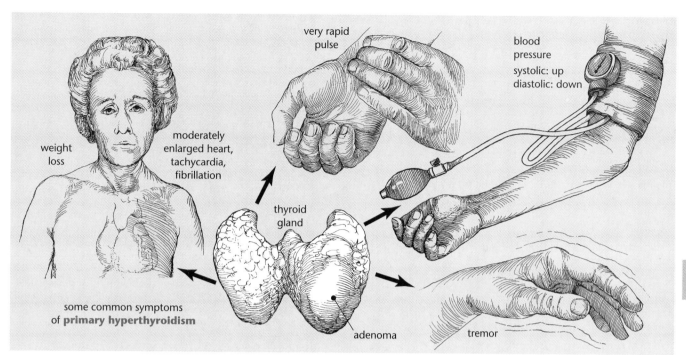

weight loss

moderately enlarged heart, tachycardia, fibrillation

very rapid pulse

blood pressure
systolic: up
diastolic: down

thyroid gland

adenoma

tremor

some common symptoms of **primary hyperthyroidism**

H

renal h. Hypertension resulting from kidney disease, especially chronic parenchymal disease.

renovascular h. Hypertension resulting from obstruction in one or both renal arteries (e.g., renal artery stenosis).

hypertensive (hi-per-ten′siv) **1.** Relating to hypertension. **2.** Denoting a person afflicted with hypertension.

hyperthecosis (hi-per-the-ko′sis) Hyperplasia of the theca cells of the vesicular ovarian follicles.

hyperthelia (hi-per-the′le-ah) See polythelia.

hyperthermia (hi-per-ther′me-ah) Extremely high body temperature.

malignant h. A rapid rise in body temperature to potentially fatal levels accompanied by muscular rigidity, brought on by general anesthesia; occurs in genetically susceptible individuals (either as an autosomal dominant or recessive inheritance) and, occasionally, in some people afflicted with certain muscular disorders.

hyperthrombinemia (hi-per-throm-bī-ne′me-ah) Excessive levels of the enzyme thrombin in the blood.

hyperthymia (hi-per-thi′me-ah) State of increased emotivity or overactivity.

hyperthyroid (hi-per-thi′roid) Having higher than normal levels of thyroid hormone.

hyperthyroidism (hi-per-thi′roi-dizm) Condition caused by excessive production or administration of thyroid hormone; most common symptoms include weight loss, increased appetite, rapid heart rate, tremor, and fatigue; when protrusion of the eyeballs (exophthalmos) is present, the disease is called exophthalmic goiter.

congenital h. Excessive thyroid hormone present at birth; affected infants usually are born to mothers afflicted with Graves' disease during pregnancy.

primary h. A form originating from a disorder of the thyroid gland itself.

secondary h. A form caused by abnormal stimulation of thyroid gland activity by pituitary hormones due to a disorder of the pituitary.

hypertonia (hi-per-to′ne-ah) Excessive tension of muscles.

hypertonic (hi-per-ton′ik) **1.** Characterized by excessive tension. **2.** See hypertonic solution, under solution.

hypertonicity (hi-per-to-nis′i-te) The state of being hypertonic.

hypertrichosis, hypertrichiasis (hi-per-tri-ko′sis, hi-per-tri-ki′ah-sis) Growth of hair in excess of normal for that particular area of the body; distinguished from hirsutism.

hypertriglyceridemia (hi-per-tri-glis-er-i-de′me-ah) Excessive concentration of triglycerides in the blood.

hypertrophic (hi-per-trof′ik) Relating to hypertrophy.

hypertrophy (hi-per′tro-fe) The enlargement of an organ or part due to the increase in size of the cells composing it; the overgrowth meets a demand for increased functional activity (e.g., in muscle-building exercises or in the heart muscle due to heart disease), or it responds to hormonal stimulation (e.g., in the pregnant uterus). COMPARE hyperplasia.

adaptive h. Thickening of the walls of a hollow organ (e.g., the bladder) when the outflow of its contents is obstructed.

asymmetric septal h. (ASH) See idiopathic hypertrophic subaortic stenosis, under stenosis.

benign prostatic h. (BPH) See nodular hyperplasia of prostate, under hyperplasia.

compensatory h. of the heart Thickening of the heart walls occurring in response to increased work load, i.e., when a chamber must pump against increased resistance (e.g., in hypertension or in disease of the valves), thus the power of the heart to maintain output is increased to compensate for the increased resistance.

concentric h. Thickening of the walls of a hollow organ with little or no change in the size of its cavity; seen in the left ventricle of the heart in association with hypertension or with aortic stenosis.

eccentric h. Enlargement of the walls of a hollow organ as well as its cavity, seen in the left ventricle of the heart due to volume overload (e.g., in aortic or mitral regurgitation).

muscular h. Marked development of muscle tissue. Also called hypermyotrophy.

physiologic h. Temporary hypertrophy of an organ in order to meet the demand of a natural increase in functional activity (e.g., in the female breast during pregnancy and lactation).

rugal h. See Ménétrièr's disease, under disease.

vicarious h. Hypertrophy of an organ due to dysfunction of another organ of allied activity.

hypertropia (hi-per-tro′pe-ah) An uncontrollable manifest deviation of one eye in an upward direction; unlike hyperphoria, the condition is not relieved when the other eye is fixating; may be due to traumatic paralysis of a vertically acting muscle, complications of systemic disease, or unknown causes.

hyperuricemia (hi-per-u-rī-se′me-ah) Excessive uric acid in the blood.

hyperuricemic (hi-per-u-rĭ-se′mik) Relating to hyperuricemia.

hyperuricosuria, hyperuricuria (hi-per-u-rik-os-u′re-ah, hi-per-u-rik-u′re-ah) Excretion of excessive amounts of uric acid in the urine.

hyperventilation (hi-per-ven-tĭ-la′shun) Rapid deep breathing, which tends to remove increased amounts of carbon dioxide from the body and lower the partial pressure of the gas; may cause buzzing in the ears, tingling of the lips and fingers, and sometimes fainting. Also called overventilation.

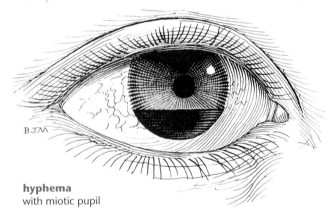

patterns of respiration

normal

central neural

hyper-ventilation ⊢———— one minute ————⊣

hypervitaminosis (hi-per-vi-tah-mĭ-no′sis) Condition caused by consumption of excessive amounts of a vitamin.

hypervolemia (hi-per-vo-le′me-ah) Abnormal increase in the volume of blood, as seen in pregnancy and in some cases of hydatidiform mole.

hypervolemic (hi-per-vo-le′mik) Relating to hypervolemia.

hypesthesia (hĭp-es-the′ze-ah) See hypoesthesia.

hyphema (hi-fe′mah) Hemorrhage into the anterior chamber of the eye.

hyphema
with miotic pupil

hyphidrosis (hĭp-hid-ro′sis) See hypohydrosis.

hypnagogic (hĭp-nah-goj′ik) Relating to the transitional, partially conscious state immediately preceding sleep.

hypnagogue (hĭp′nah-gog) Any agent that induces sleep; a hypnotic.

hypno-, hypn- Combining forms meaning sleep; hypnosis.

hypnoanalysis (hĭp-no-ah-nal′ĭ-sis) Psychoanalysis conducted while the patient is under hypnosis.

hypnogenesis (hĭp-no-jen′ĕ-sis) The process of inducing sleep or a hypnotic state.

hypnology (hĭp-nol′o-je) The study of sleep or hypnosis.

hypnophobia (hĭp-no-fo′be-ah) Abnormal fear of falling asleep.

hypnopompic (hĭp-no-pom′pik) Relating to the transitional, partially conscious state immediately before awakening.

hypnosis (hĭp-no′sis) An artificial state, usually induced by another person, in which the individual becomes receptive to the hypnotist's suggestion; it may vary in degree from mild suggestibility to a deep sleeplike state with total anesthesia.

hypnotherapy (hĭp-no-ther′ah-pe) Treatment with hypnosis.

hypnotic (hĭp-not′ik) 1. A drug that depresses the central nervous system (CNS), inducing a state that resembles natural sleep. COMPARE sedative. 2. Relating to hypnosis.

hypnotism (hĭp′no-tizm) 1. The practice of inducing hypnosis. 2. Hypnosis.

hypnotist (hĭp′no-tist) One who induces hypnosis.

hypnotize (hĭp′no-tiz) To induce hypnosis.

hypo- Prefix meaning below normal; deficient; diminished; under.

hypo (hi′po) Colloquial term for subcutaneous (hypodermic) injection.

hypoacidity (hi-po-ah-sid′ĭ-te) Deficiency of acid (e.g., in gastric juice).

hypoacusis (hi-po-ah-ku′sis) See hypacusis.

hypoadrenalism (hi-po-ah-dre′nal-izm) Deficient function of the adrenal cortex, with diminished production of steroid hormones.

hypoalbuminemia (hi-po-al-bu-mĭn-e′me-ah) Reduced concentration of albumin in the blood.

hypoaldosteronism (hi-po-al-do-stēr′ōn-izm) Deficiency of aldosterone, a hormone produced by the adrenal cortex.
   hyporeninemic h. Deficiency of aldosterone with metabolic acidosis, a tendency toward hyperkalemia, and low plasma levels of the enzyme renin.

hypoalimentation (hi-po-al-ĭ-men-ta′shun) See subalimentation.

hypoalphalipoproteinemia (hi-po-al-fah-lip′o-pro-tēn-e′me-ah) See Tangier disease, under disease.

hypobaric (hi-po-bār′ik) Relating to pressures lower than atmospheric pressure.

hypobaropathy (hi-po-bār-op′ah-the) Condition caused by greatly reduced air pressure and decreased oxygen intake.

hypocalcemia (hi-po-kal-se′me-ah) Abnormally low serum calcium levels.

hypocalcification (hi-po-kal-sĭ-fĭ-ka′shun) A deficient calcification process; diminished calcification.
   enamel h. A defect in the formation of tooth enamel, resulting in breakage of the enamel soon after tooth eruption, leaving the dentin exposed, which gives the teeth a yellow appearance.

hypocapnia (hi-po-kap′ne-ah) Deficiency of carbon dioxide in the blood.

hypocellularity (hi-po-sel-u-lār′ĭ-te) An abnormally low content of cells (e.g., in bone marrow disease and in chemotherapy).

hypochloremia (hi-po-klo-re′me-ah) A marked reduction of chloride in the blood.

hypochlorhydria (hi-po-klor-hi′dre-ah) Abnormally low concentration of hydrochloric acid in gastric juice.

hypochlorite (hi-po-klo′rīt) A salt of hypochlorous acid.

hypochlorous acid (hi-po-klor′us as′id) An unstable acid used as a bleach and disinfectant.

hypocholesterolemia (hi-po-ko-les-ter-o-le′me-ah) An abnormally low level of cholesterol in the blood.

hypochondria (hi-po-kon′dre-ah) See hypochondriasis.

hypochondriac (hi-po-kon′dre-ak) A person afflicted with hypochondriasis.

hypochondriasis (hi-po-kon-dri′ah-sis) The persistent neurotic preoccupation with one's health and fear of presumed diseases that persist despite reassurances; an exaggerated concern over one's physical health in absence of organic disease. Also called hypochondria.

hypochondrium (hi-po-kon′dre-um) Any of two regions on either side of the upper abdomen.

hypochondroplasia (hi-po-kon-dro-pla′ze-ah) A genetic condition of autosomal dominant inheritance, similar to achondroplasia but milder and without involvement of the head and face; the individual has short limbs, but with an average height slightly above the mean for achondroplasia.

hypochromatic (hi-po-kro-mat′ik) Characterized by abnormally deficient pigmentation.

hypochromia (hi-po-kro′me-ah) A decrease in the hemoglobin content of red blood cells so that they appear paler than normal when stained with certain histologic dyes.

hypochromic (hi-po-kro′mik) Characterized by hypochromia.

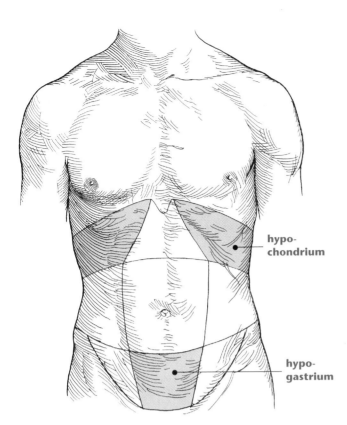

hypo-chondrium

hypo-gastrium

hypochylia (hi-po-ki′le-ah) Abnormally low amount of chyle.

hypocitraturia, hypocitruria (hi-po-sī-tra-tur′e-ah, hi-po-sī-troo′re-ah) Abnormally low excretion of citrate in the urine; has been implicated as a contributing factor in the formation of kidney stones.

hypocomplementemia (hi-po-kom′plĕ-men-te′me-ah) A condition of the blood characterized by a lack, or decreased activity, of complement or any of the complement components of blood; may be hereditary or acquired. The condition has been postulated to be a factor in increased susceptibility to certain infections.

hypocomplementemic (hi-po-kom′plĕ-men-te′mik) Relating to hypocomplementemia.

hypocorticism (hi-po-kor′tĭ-sizm) See adrenocortical insufficiency, under insufficiency.

hypocorticoidism (hi-po-kor′tĭ-koid-izm) See adrenocortical insufficiency, under insufficiency.

hypocupremia (hi-po-ku-pre′me-ah) Abnormally low concentration of copper in the blood.

hypodactylia, hypodactyly (hi-po-dak-til′e-ah, hi-po-dak′tĭ-le) The presence of fewer than 10 fingers or toes.

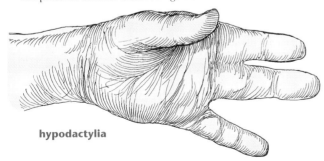

hypodactylia

hypodermic (hi-po-der′mik) Subcutaneous.

hypodermis, hypoderm (hi-po-der′mis, hi′po-derm) See superficial fascia, under fascia.

hypodermoclysis (hi-po-der-mok′lĭ-sis) The infusion of fluid (e.g., saline solution) into the subcutaneous space.

hypodontia (hi-po-don′she-ah) Congenital absence of one or more teeth. Also called oligodontia.

hypodynamic (hi-po-di-nam′ik) Characterized by markedly reduced force, as of muscular contraction.

hypoechoic (hi-po-ĕ-kō′ik) Producing echoes of a lower amplitude or density than those produced by the surrounding medium or tissues.

hypoesophoria (hi-po-es-o-fo′re-ah) Combined downward and inward deviation of the eyeball.

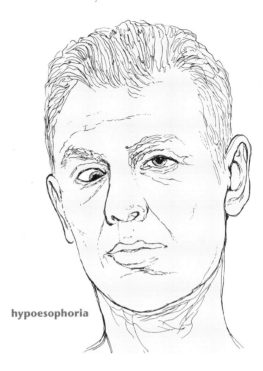

hypoesophoria

hypoesthesia (hi-po-es-the′ze-ah) Abnormally decreased response to sensory stimuli. Also called hypesthesia.

hypofibrinogenemia (hi-po-fi-brin′o-jĕ-ne′me-ah) Deficiency of the protein fibrinogen in the blood; seen in pregnant women with a retained dead fetus, four to five weeks after intrauterine fetal death; may also occur in amniotic fluid embolism, abruptio placenta, and, occasionally, in intra-amniotic instillation of hypertonic saline.

hypofunction (hi-po-funk′shun) Diminished or inadequate function of an organ or part.

hypogalactia (hi-po-gah-lak′she-ah) Insufficient production of milk.

hypogammaglobulinemia (hi-po-gam-ah-glob-u-lī-ne′me-ah) Lack of gamma globulin in the blood, manifested by recurrent infections; primary forms result from diminished rates of synthesis; secondary forms result from increased catabolism. The term is sometimes used to describe a deficiency of all major classes of serum immunoglobulins.

hypogastrium (hi-po-gas′tre-um) The middle region of the lower abdomen; the pubic region.

hypogenitalism (hi-po-jen′ĭ-tal-izm) Underdevelopment of the genitals.

hypogeusia (hi-po-gu′ze-ah) Decreased sense of taste.

hypoglossal (hi-po-glos′al) Beneath the tongue.

hypoglottis (hi-po-glot′is) The undersurface of the tongue.

hypoglycemia (hi-po-gli-se′me-ah) A lower than normal level of sugar (glucose) in the blood; may cause one or several of the following symptoms: sweating, trembling, palpitation, hunger, weakness, lightheadedness, or double vision; symptoms may vary in duration and often disappear after eating a sweet snack. The condition may result from excessive production of insulin by the pancreas (e.g., due to the presence of a tumor); or it may occur in a diabetic person who has taken too large a dose of insulin or an oral hypoglycemic drug, who misses a meal or fails to eat enough after taking an insulin dose, or who exercises too much without taking precautionary measures.

   nonfasting h. Hypoglycemia occurring two to three hours after a meal (e.g., when carbohydrates are discharged too rapidly into the small intestine, as in the dumping syndrome), or three to five hours later (e.g., when insulin is discharged excessively by the pancreas). Also called reactive hypoglycemia.

   reactive h. See nonfasting hypoglycemia.

hypognathous (hi-pog′nah-thus) Having an underdeveloped lower jaw.

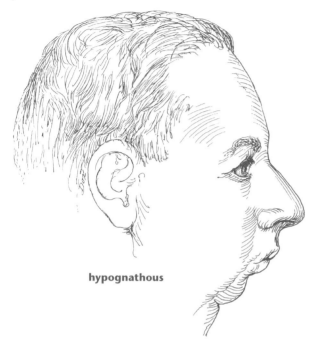

hypognathous

hypogonadism (hi-po-go′nad-izm) Decreased physical development of an individual's sexual characteristics, resulting from insufficient hormone secretion or from defective response to hormonal activity by the target tissues.

   hypogonadotropic h. See Kallmann's syndrome, under syndrome.

hypohydrosis (hi-po-hi-dro′sis) Abnormally reduced sweating. Also called hyphidrosis.

hypokalemia (hi-po-ka-le′me-ah) Abnormally low concentration of potassium in the circulating blood; depletion may be due to excessive loss of potassium from the gastrointestinal tract or kidneys. Also called hypopotassemia.

hypokinemia (hi-po-ki-ne′me-ah) Abnormally reduced cardiac output; reduced circulation rate.

hypokinesis, hypokinesia (hi-po-ki-ne′sis, hi-po-ki-ne′ze-ah) Diminished movement. Also called hypomotility.

hypomagnesemia (hi-po-mag-ně-se′me-ah) Abnormally low concentration of magnesium in the blood.

hypomania (hi-po-ma′ne-ah) A moderate form of manic activity, usually characterized by slightly abnormal elation and overactivity.

hypomastia (hi-po-mas′te-ah) Abnormally small size of the female breasts.

hypomenorrhea (hi-po-men-o-re′ah) Scanty menstrual flow, sometimes consisting only of "spotting." See also cryptomenorrhea.

hypometabolism (hi-po-mě-tab′o-lizm) Reduced metabolism.

hypometria (hi-po-me′tre-ah) A decreased range of voluntary movements.

hypomorph (hi′po-morf) A person who has short legs.

hypomotility (hi-po-mo-til′ĭ-te) See hypokinesis.

hyponatremia (hi-po-nah-tre′me-ah) Low blood concentration of sodium.

hyponychial (hi-po-nik′e-al) Relating to hyponychium.

hyponychium (hi-po-nik′e-um) The thickened portion of the epidermis beneath the free border of the nail.

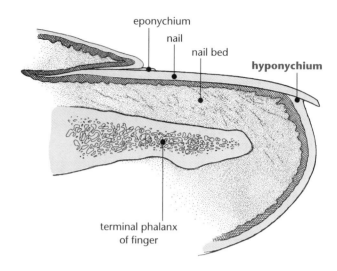

eponychium

nail

nail bed

hyponychium

terminal phalanx of finger

hypo-ovarianism (hi-po o-va′re-an-izm) Insufficient secretion of hormones from the ovaries.

hypoparathyroidism (hi-po-par-ah-thi′roid-izm) Condition resulting either from lack of hormone secretion by the parathyroid glands, from secretion of an inactive form of the hormone, or from target-organ resistance to the hormone; signs and symptoms include reduced plasma calcium level and increased plasma phosphate level, neuromuscular excitability, high intracranial pressure, abnormalities in the conduction system of the heart, and cataracts.

hypophalangism (hi-po-fah-lan′jizm) Congenital lack of a phalanx on a finger or toe.

hypophoria (hi-po-fo′re-ah) Tendency of one eye to deviate downward.

hypophosphatasia (hi-po-fos-fah-ta′ze-ah) Lack of alkaline phosphatase in the blood.

hypophosphatemia (hi-po-fos-fah-te′me-ah) A decreased amount of phosphates in the blood.

hypophyseal (hi-po-fiz′e-al) Relating to the hypophysis. Also called hypophysial; pituitary.

hypophysectomize (hi-po-fiz-ek′to-mīz) To remove or destroy the hypophysis for therapeutic purposes.

hypophysectomy (hi-pof-ĭ-sek′to-me) Removal or destruction of the hypophysis by surgical, chemical, or radioactive means.

hypophysial (hi-po-fiz′e-al) See hypophyseal.

hypophysis (hi-pof′ĭ-sis) A reddish gray, ovoid structure located at the base of the skull in the hypophyseal fossa of the sphenoid bone, attached to the brain by a short stalk (infundibulum); it consists of two main parts: an anterior part composed of the adenohypophysis and a slender portion of the infundibulum, and a posterior part composed of the neurohypophysis and the major portion of the infundibulum; between them there is a narrow, relatively avascular intermediate zone containing granules of endorphin. The adenohypophysis is glandular and highly vascular; it constitutes the major portion of the hypophysis (about 75% of its weight), and secretes many important hormones; the neurohypophysis contains axon terminations of neurons whose cell bodies are located in the hypothalamus; it serves as a reservoir for the chief hormones produced by the hypothalamus, releasing them when needed by the body. Also called pituitary gland; pituitary body; pituitary; master gland.

hypopituitarism (hi-po-pĭ-tu′ĭ-tah-rizm) A condition due to abnormally diminished production of anterior pituitary hormones, caused by any disease that results in destruction of the hypophysis; it leads to atrophy of the thyroid and adrenal glands and the gonads (ovaries and testes).

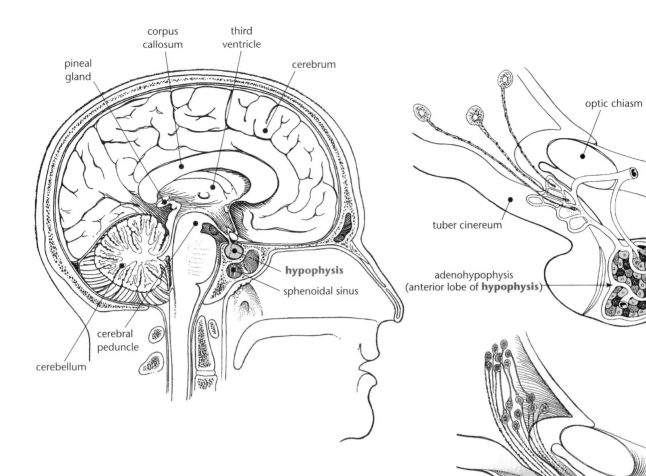

hypoplasia (hi-po-pla′ze-ah) Defective or incomplete development of a body part.

hypoplastic (hi-po-plas′tik) Relating to hypoplasia.

hypopnea (hi-po-ne′ah) Abnormally shallow breathing.

hypopotassemia (hi-po-po-tah-se′me-ah) See hypokalemia.

hypoproteinemia (hi-po-pro-tĭ-ne′me-ah) Abnormally low levels of protein in the blood.

hypoproteinosis (hi-po-pro-tĭ-no′sis) Dietary protein deficiency.

hypoprothrombinemia (hi-po-pro-throm-bĭ-ne′me-ah) Deficiency of the blood-clotting factor prothrombin in the blood.

hypoptyalism (hi-po-ti′al-izm) See hyposalivation.

hypopyon (hi-po′pe-on) Accumulation of pus in the anterior chamber of the eye, secondary to inflammation of the cornea, iris, or ciliary body.

hyporeflexia (hi-po-re-flek′se-ah) A state of weakened reflexes.

hyporeninemia (hi-po-re-nin-e′me-ah) A low level of the enzyme renin in the blood.

hyporeninemic (hi-po-re-nin-e′mik) Relating to hyporeninemia.

hyposalivation (hi-po-sal-ĭ-va′shun) Diminished flow of saliva. Also called hypoptyalism.

hyposensitivity (hi-po-sen-sĭ-tiv′ĭ-te) A state of diminished or delayed response to a stimulus.

hyposensitization (hi-po-sen-sĭ-tĭ-za′shun) See desensitization (1).

hyposialadenitis (hi-po-si-al-ad-ĕ-ni′tis) Inflammation of a salivary gland.

hyposmia (hi-poz′me-ah) Reduced sense of smell.

hypospadia (hi-po-spa′de-ah) See hypospadias.

hypospadias (hi-po-spa′de-as) A congenital defect in which the urethra abnormally opens on the undersurface of the penis in the male or in the vagina in the female. Also called hypospadia.

hypospermatogenesis (hi-po-sper′mah-to-jen′ĕ-sis) Insufficient production of spermatozoa in the seminiferous tubules; the number of spermatozoa is so low, it is extremely difficult to find them in the ejaculate, frequently leading to the diagnosis of azospermia.

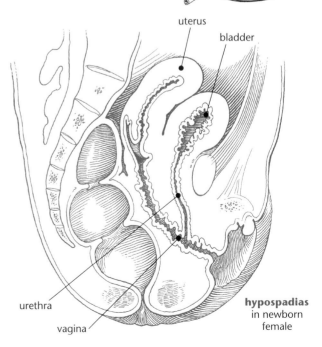

hypospadias in newborn female

hypoplasia ■ hypospermatogenesis

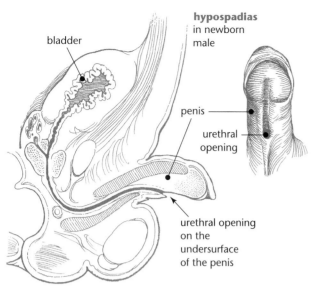

hypospadias in newborn male

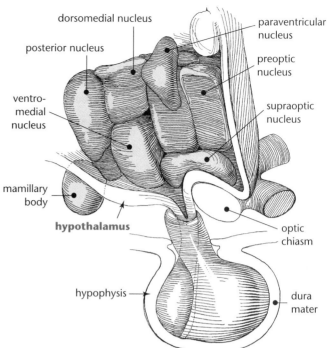

hypostasis (hi-pos′tah-sis) **1.** A sediment. **2.** Blood congestion or pooling of blood in a part.

   postmortem h. See livor mortis, under livor.

hyposthenia (hi-pos-the′ne-ah) Decreased strength; a weakened state.

hyposthenuria (hi-pos-thĕ-nu′re-ah) Inability to concentrate urine.

hypostosis (hip-os-to′sis) Inadequate bone development.

hypostyptic (hi-po-stip′tik) Mildly astringent.

hypotaxia (hi-po-tak′se-ah) Imperfect or diminished muscular coordination.

hypotelorism (hi-po-tel′o-rizm) Abnormally small distance between paired organs or body parts (e.g., the eyes).

hypotension (hi-po-ten′shun) Abnormally low blood pressure.

   orthostatic h. A fall of blood pressure when arising from a recumbent position or when standing still. Also called postural hypotension.

   postural h. See orthostatic hypotension.

hypotensive (hi-po-ten′siv) Relating to hypotension.

hypothalamic (hi-po-thah-lam′ik) Relating to, produced by, or originating in the hypothalamus.

hypothalamus (hi-po-thal′ah-mus) A small, deep-lying part of the brain composed of more than a dozen cell clusters (hypothalamic nuclei); it lies between the thalamus above, the pituitary below, and the optic chiasma in front. The hypothalamus serves as the key neuroendocrine effector mechanism of the central nervous system; it produces the hormones vasopressin and oxytocin, which are transported to and stored in the posterior pituitary (neurohypophysis) and released when needed by the body; also produces many other hormones that exert control over functions of the anterior pituitary (adenohypophysis). By controlling and integrating the autonomic nervous system, the hypothalamus regulates vital bodily functions, such as heart rate, movement of food through the digestive tract, body temperature, sensation of hunger and thirst, sleep pattern, regulation of water balance, contraction of the urinary bladder, and many biologic rhythms.

hypothenar (hi-poth′ĕ-nar) The fleshy part of the palm of the hand, on the side of the thumb.

hypothermal (hi-po-ther′mal) Relating to a below-average body temperature.

hypothermia (hi-po-ther′me-ah) Reduction of the body's core temperature below 95°F (35°C).

hypothesis (hi-poth′ĕ-sis) A tentative theory subject to verification.

   sequence h. The concept that the amino acid sequence of a protein is determined by a particular sequence of nucleotides in a definite portion of the DNA of the organism producing the protein.

   Starling's h. The rate of fluid exchange between extracapillary and capillary tissue depends on the hydrostatic and osmotic pressures on both sides of the capillary wall, considering the wall as a semipermeable membrane.

hypothrombinemia (hi-po-throm-bĭ-ne′me-ah) Abnormally low content of the clotting factor thrombin in the blood.

hypothyroid (hi-po-thi′roid) Having lower than normal levels of thyroid hormone.

hypothyroidism (hi-po-thi′roid-izm) Condition caused by deficiency of thyroid hormone, characterized by a lessened metabolic rate; chemical features may include cold intolerance, dry skin, hair loss, puffy face, constipation, slow speech, slow heart rate, and retarded mentality; when present at birth it is called cretinism; the severe form in adults is called myxedema.

hypotonia (hi-po-to′ne-ah) Lack of muscle tone.

hypotonic (hi-po-ton′ik) Having an abnormally reduced tension.

hypotoxicity (hi-po-tok-sis′ĭ-te) Reduced toxicity.

hypotrichosis (hi-po-trĭ-ko′sis) Scanty hair on the head and body. Also called oligotrichosis.

hypotropia (hi-po-tro′pe-ah) A constant downward deviation of one eye.

hypoventilation (hi-po-ven-tĭ-la′shun) A reduced quantity of air entering the lungs, with consequent retention of carbon dioxide.

hypovitaminosis (hi-po-vi-tah-min-o′sis) Any state caused by deficiency of one or more essential vitamins. Also called avitaminosis.

hypovolemia (hi-po-vo-le′me-ah) Marked reduction of blood volume.

hypoxanthine (hi-po-zan′thēn) An intermediate product in the synthesis of uric acid; present in muscles and other tissues.

hypoxemia (hi-pok-se′me-ah) Abnormally low oxygen content in arterial blood.

hypoxia (hi-pok′se-ah) Reduction of oxygen in the tissues below normal levels.

   cell h. Decreased oxygen content at the cellular level.

hypsarrhythmia (hip-sah-rith′me-ah) An abnormal, chaotic pattern of the encephalogram sometimes observed in infants with spasms.

hypsi-, hypso- Combining forms meaning height.

hysteralgia (his-tĕ-ral′je-ah) Pain or discomfort in the uterus. Also called hysterodynia.

hysteratresia (his-ter-ah-tre′ze-ah) Abnormal closure of the uterine cavity.

hysterectomy (his-tĕ-rek′to-me) Removal of the uterus.

    abdominal h. Removal of the uterus through an incision in the abdominal wall. Also called laparohysterectomy; celiohysterectomy.

    cesarean h. Delivery of a baby through an abdominal and uterine incision, followed by removal of the uterus through the same abdominal incision.

    subtotal h. See supracervical hysterectomy.

    supracervical h. An infrequently performed operation in which the main body of the uterus (the fundus) is removed, to the level of the internal os, leaving the cervix in place. Also called subtotal hysterectomy.

    total h. Removal of the entire uterus, including the cervix. Usually simply called hysterectomy.

    vaginal h. Removal of the uterus through the vagina; usually performed in benign conditions when the uterus is not greatly enlarged, or when other repairs are also performed (e.g., for a cystocele or a rectocele). Also called colpohysterectomy; vaginohysterectomy.

hysteresis (his-tĕ-re′sis) A failure of coincidence (e.g., a time lag) of two usually associated phenomena.

hysteria (his-ter′e-ah) See conversion disorder, under disorder.

    conversion h. See conversion disorder, under disorder.

hysterical (his-ter′ĭ-kal) **1.** Relating to hysterics. **2.** Relating to a conversion disorder.

hysterics (his-ter′iks) Colloquial term for an uncontrollable emotional outburst.

hystero- Combining form meaning uterus; hysteria.

hysterocolposcope (his-ter-o-kol′po-skōp) Instrument for inspecting the uterine cavity and vagina.

hysterodynia (his-ter-o-din′e-ah) See hysteralgia.

hysterogram (his′ter-o-gram) An x-ray picture of the uterus obtained after filling its cavity with a radiopaque material.

hysterography (his-tĕ-rog′rah-fe) The making of a hysterogram.

hysterolith (his′ter-o-lith) A concretion or calculus in the uterus.

hysterometer (his-tĕ-rom′ĕ-ter) A graduated instrument for measuring the depth of the uterine cavity.

hysteromyoma (his-ter-o-mi-o′mah) A benign tumor of the uterine wall.

hysteromyomectomy (his-ter-o-mi-o-mek′to-me) Surgical removal of a myoma from the uterus.

hysteromyotomy (his-ter-o-mi-ot′o-me) A surgical cut into the muscular wall of the uterus.

hystero-oophorectomy (his-ter-o o-of-o-rek′to-me) Removal of the uterus and ovaries.

hysteropathy (his-tĕ-rop′ah-the) Any disease of the uterus.

hysteropexy (his′ter-o-pek-se) The suturing of a displaced uterus (e.g., to the abdominal wall); an operation no longer performed.

hysterorrhaphy (his-ter-or′ah-fe) Surgical repair of a lacerated or ruptured uterus.

hysterorrhexis (his-ter-o-rek′sis) Rupture of the uterus. Also called metrorrhexis.

hysterosalpingectomy (his-ter-o-sal-pin-jek′to-me) Removal of the uterus and at least one fallopian (uterine) tube.

hysterosalpingography (his′ter-o-sal′ping-gog′rah-fe) The radiopaque visualization of the cavities of the uterus and fallopian (uterine) tubes after instilling a radiopaque substance via the cervix. Performed as part of an infertility study and as a follow-up to surgery, especially tubal reunification (reanastomosis). Perforation of the uterine wall is a possible complication.

hysterosalpingo-oophorectomy (his-ter-o-sal-ping′go o-of-o-rek′to-me) Removal of the uterus, fallopian (uterine) tubes, and ovaries.

hysterosalpingostomy (his-ter-o-sal-ping-gos′to-me) Operation to restore the patency of an obstructed fallopian (uterine) tube.

hysteroscope (his′ter-o-skōp) An endoscope that permits direct viewing of the uterus; consists of a rigid rod equipped with a fiberoptic light source, a channel to introduce a medium to distend the uterus, and a channel through which instruments (e.g., probes,

forceps, electrocautery, or laser) may be visually manipulated in the uterine cavity. Also called metroscope.

hysterostomatomy (his-ter-o-sto-mat′o-me) See Dührssen's incisions, under incision.

hysterotomy (his-ter-ot′o-me) A surgical cut into the uterus. Also called metrotomy; uterotomy; laparohysterotomy.

hysterotrachelectomy (his-ter-o-tra-kel-ek′to-me) See cervical amputation, under amputation.

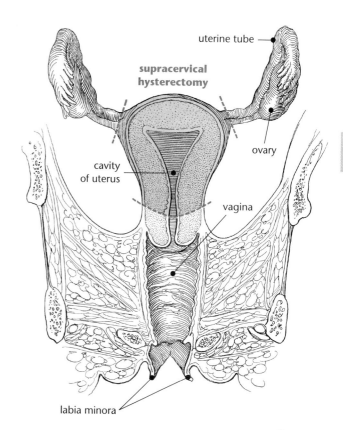

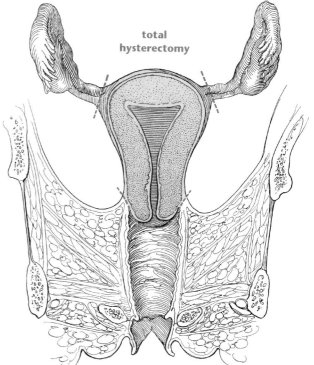

hysterectomy ■ **hysterotrachelectomy**

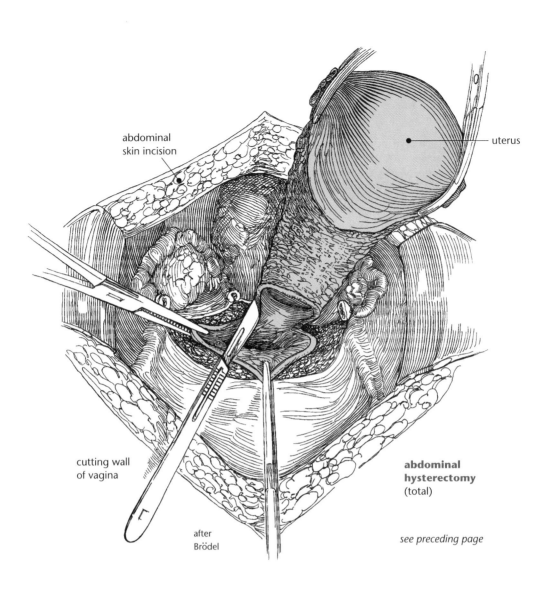

abdominal
skin incision

uterus

cutting wall
of vagina

after
Brödel

**abdominal
hysterectomy**
(total)

see preceding page

H

hysterectomy ■ hysterectomy

I

-ia Suffix meaning a state; a condition (e.g., melancholia).

-iasis Suffix meaning disease; infection (e.g., amebiasis).

-iatrics Combining form meaning medical care (e.g., pediatrics).

iatrogenic (i-at-ro-jen′ik) Caused by a physician; originally applied to an illness unwittingly induced in a patient by the physician's attitude, treatment, or comments; currently applied to any unfavorable effect resulting from medical diagnosis and treatment, regardless of whether the condition occurs as a known risk of a procedure or through errors of omission or commission.

iatrotechnique (i-at-ro-tek-nēk′) Medical and surgical techniques.

ibuprofen (i-bu′pro-fen) A nonsteroid anti-inflammatory compound: inhibitor of prostaglandin synthetase.

-ic Suffix meaning relating to (e.g., hypodermic).

ichor (i′kor) A watery discharge from a wound or ulcer.

ichthyism (ik′the-izm) Poisoning resulting from eating spoiled fish.

ichthyo-, ichthy- Combining forms meaning fish.

ichthyohemotoxin (ik-the-o-he-mo-tok′sin) A poisonous substance present in the blood of certain fish.

ichthyoid (ik′the-oid) Fishlike.

ichthyosarcotoxin (ik-the-o-sar-ko-tok′sin) A poisonous substance present in the flesh of certain fishes.

ichthyosis (ik-the-o′sis) Inherited disorder characterized by formation of dry, rough, and thick scales on the skin, caused by a defect of the horny layer of the skin; may affect the eyelids, conjunctiva, and cornea. Also called alligator skin; fish skin; sauriasis.

    acquired i. A dry thickening and scaling of the skin that may herald the occurrence of a cancerous disease or may be associated with severe nutritional deficiencies.

    lamellar i. A condition of autosomal recessive inheritance with onset at birth, characterized by large, coarse scales over the body with severe involvement of the palms and soles.

    i. vulgaris Condition of autosomal dominant inheritance with onset in childhood, characterized by fine scales over the trunk and especially the limbs, sparing the flexural areas, and by deep creases on the palms and soles.

    X-linked i. Condition of X-linked recessive inheritance affecting males with onset at birth, characterized by thick scales that darken with age, sparing the soles and palms; the mother is carrier of the defective gene; both mother and offspring have small cataracts; most patients lack the enzyme steroid sulfatase.

ichthyotic (ik-the-ot′ik) Relating to ichthyosis.

ichthyotoxin (ik-the-o-tok′sin) Any poisonous substance present in or derived from fish.

ictal (ik′tal) Relating to convulsion.

icteric (ik-ter′ik) Relating to jaundice.

icterogenic (ik-ter-o-jen′ik) Causing jaundice.

icterus (ik′ter-us) See jaundice.

    benign familial i. See Gilbert's syndrome, under syndrome.

    neonatal i. See physiologic jaundice, under jaundice.

    i. neonatorum See physiologic jaundice, under jaundice.

    physiologic i. See physiologic jaundice, under jaundice.

ictus (ik′tus) A sudden attack or convulsion.

    i. epilepticus An epileptic convulsion.

id (id) **1.** In psychoanalytic theory, the part of the psychic apparatus associated with the unconscious instinctive impulses and primitive needs of a person. **2.** See id reaction, under reaction.

idea (i-de′ah) A conception existing in the mind as the product of mental activity.

    compulsive i. An inappropriate idea that recurs and persists despite reason.

    fixed i. A loosely used term for describing an obsessive idea, a compulsive drive, or a delusion. Also called idée fixe.

ideal (i-de′al) A conception regarded as a standard of perfection.

    ego i. The part of the personality structure comprising the goals of the self; it develops from the emulation of significant individuals with whom the person has identified.

ideation (i-de-a′shun) The formation of ideas or conceptions, indicative of a person's ability to think.

ideational (i-de-a′shun-al) Relating to ideation.

idée fixe (e-da′ fēks′) French for fixed idea. See fixed idea, under idea.

identification (i-den-tī-fi-ka′shun) An unconscious psychological defense mechanism in which a person tries to pattern himself after another; distinguished from imitation, which is a conscious process.

identity (i-den′tī-te) The role of a person in society and his perception of it.

    ego i. A unified sense of one's own self, distinct from the external world.

    gender i. The anatomic-sexual identity of an individual.

ideo- Combining form meaning ideas.

ideology (i-de-ol′o-je) The body of intellectual-moral ideas reflecting the needs and aspirations of an individual or a group.

idio- Combining form meaning distinctive; personal; originating from within.

idioagglutinin (id-e-o-ah-gloo′tī-nin) An agglutinin that is formed naturally in the blood of an individual.

idiogenesis (id-e-o-jen′ĕ-sis) A development without a known cause; applied to development of an idiopathic disease (i.e., one without an apparent cause).

idiogram (id′e-o-gram) A diagrammatic representation of the set of chromosomes of an individual, or of a single representative chromosome, using standard conventions.

idiolysin (id-e-ol′ī-sin) An antibody occurring naturally in the blood of an individual.

idionodal (id-e-o-no′dal) Originating in the atrioventricular (A-V) node of the heart; applied to a heartbeat.

idiopathic (id-e-o-path′ik) Of unknown cause; applied to certain diseases.

idiophrenic (id-e-o-fren′ik) Relating to the brain or the mind exclusively.

idiosyncrasy (id-e-o-sin′krah-se) **1.** A characteristic (physical or behavioral) that is particular to an individual. **2.** In pharmacology, a genetically determined abnormal response to a drug.

idiosyncratic (id-e-o-sin-krat′ik) Relating to idiosyncracies.

idiotope (id′i-o-tōp) One of several antigenic determinants in the variable region of an antibody molecule. It can be recognized as antigen by the combining site (receptor) of another antibody in the same species.

idiot-savant (e′dyo sah-vahn′) A mentally retarded person capable of performing remarkable tasks (e.g., solving difficult mathematical problems almost instantly, playing a classical composition on the piano after hearing it only once).

idiotype (id′i-o-tīp) The collection of idiotopes in the variable region of an antibody molecule (immunoglobulin); it provides the variable region with its individual antigenic characteristics.

idioventricular (id-e-o-ven-trik′u-lar) Relating to the ventricles of the heart alone (i.e., excluding the atria).

idoxuridine (i-doks′ur′ī-dēn) (IDU) An antiviral preparation used locally for the treatment of herpes simplex infections of the eye.

ileal (il′e-al) Relating to the third and longest portion (ileum) of the small intestine.

ileitis (il-e-i′tis) Inflammation of the third and longest portion (ileum) of the small intestine.

    backwash i. Inflammatory ulceration of the ileum as an extension of ulcerative colitis.

    distal i. See Crohn's disease, under disease.

    terminal i. See Crohn's disease, under disease.

ileo- Combining form meaning the ileum.

ileoanal (il-e-o-a′nal) Relating to the distal portion of the small intestine (the ileum) and the anus; applied to the surgical connection of the ileum and anal canal, after removal of the rectum, for the treatment of ulcerative proctitis.

ileocecal (il-e-o-se′kal) Relating to the adjacent portions of the small and large intestines (the ileum and cecum).

ileocecostomy (il-e-o-se-kos′to-me) Surgical connection of nonadjacent portions of the small and large intestines (i.e., of the ileum and cecum).

ileocecum (il-e-o-se′kum) The adjacent portions of the small and large intestines (ileum and cecum) considered as a unit.

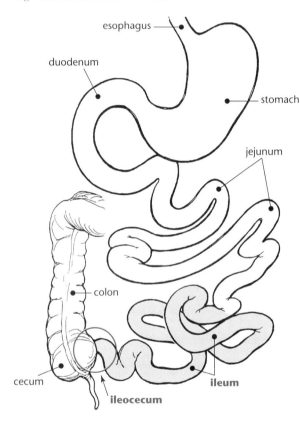

ileocolic (il-e-o-kol′ik) Relating to the ileum and colon (i.e., the distal portion of the small intestine and the middle portion of the large intestine).

ileocolitis (il-e-o-ko-li′tis) Inflammation of the ileum and colon.

ileocolostomy (il-e-o-ko-los′to-me) Surgical connection of the distal portion of the small intestine (ileum) and the middle portion of the large intestine (colon).

ileoileostomy (il-e-o-il-e-os′to-me) Surgical connection made between two noncontinuous portions of the ileum (the distal small intestine).

ileojejunitis (il-e-o-jĕ-joo-ni′tis) Inflammation of the ileum and jejunum (the distal and middle portions of the small intestine).

ileostomy (il-e-os′to-me) Surgical creation of an external opening into the ileum through the abdominal wall for fecal diversion.

ileotomy (il-e-ot′o-me) Surgical cut into the ileum.

ileotransversostomy (il-e-o-trans-vers-os′to-me) Surgical joining

of the ileum and transverse colon.

ileum (il′e-um) The longest and most distal of the three portions of the small intestine (the others being the duodenum and jejunum); it is continuous proximally with the jejunum and distally with the cecum (the first part of the large intestine).

ileus (il′e-us) Impairment or stoppage of the flow of intestinal contents due either to obstruction or to diminished intestinal motility; depending on the cause, symptoms may include severe colicky pain, abdominal distention, fever, dehydration, and vomiting.

    adynamic i. Ileus due to decreased or absent propulsive activity of the intestinal walls, usually causing abdominal distention and vomiting but little or no pain; causes include abdominal surgery, trauma, and vascular accidents of mesenteric arteries. Also called paralytic ileus.

    gallstone i. Ileus due to obstruction of the bowel lumen by impacted gallstones.

    meconium i. Ileus occurring in the newborn, caused by obliteration of the bowel lumen by excessively thick meconium; frequently the first sign of cystic fibrosis.

    obstructive i. Ileus caused by any mechanical reduction or obliteration of the bowel lumen (e.g., by constrictive adhesions, pressure against the bowel by a tumor, or by impaction of any material within the intestine).

    paralytic i. See adynamic ileus.

iliac (il′e-ak) Relating to the ilium, a hipbone.

ilio- Combining form meaning ilium.

iliofemoral (il-e-o-fem′or-al) Relating to the largest bone of the hip (ilium) and the thighbone (femur).

ilioinguinal (il-e-o-in′gwĭ-nal) Relating to the lateral area of the pelvis and the groin.

iliolumbar (il-e-o-lum′bar) Relating to the hip and the "small of the back."

iliopectineal (il-e-o-pek-tin′e-al) Relating to the ilium and the pubic bone.

iliosacral (il-e-o-sa′kral) Relating to the ilium and sacrum at the side and back of the pelvis, respectively.

ilium (il′e-um) The superior, broad bone on either side of the pelvis. See also table of bones.

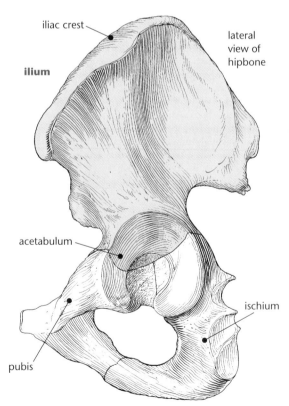

illinition (il-ĭ-nish′un) Friction of the skin while applying an ointment to facilitate absorption.

illness (il′nes) Disease.

    building-associated i.'s Outbreaks of illnesses acquired in indoor air (e.g., hypersensitivity pneumonitis, Q fever, Legionnaires' disease, Pontiac fever); may result from bacterial or fungal contamination of organic dusts, aerosols from cooling towers, evaporative condensers, and air-conditioning systems.

    catastrophic i. An acute or prolonged illness usually threatening to cause death or a serious residual disability.

    critical i. One in which death is imminent or possible.

    emotional i. See mental disorder, under disorder.

    functional i. See functional disorder, under disorder.

    manic-depressive i. See bipolar disorder, under disorder.

    mass psychogenic i. A building-associated illness of psychophysiologic origin occurring simultaneously in a group of individuals; the cause is unknown but it appears to be triggered by the occurrence of an appropriate stimulus (e.g., an irritating odor) in a psychologically susceptible population; has been reported in workers involved in low-paying repetitive work, which they consider stressful; symptoms vary with different members of the group and occur when the group is together; they include headaches, light-headedness, dizziness, ear, nose, and throat irritation, chest pains, and weakness; usually few or no physical or laboratory findings are noted.

    mental i. See mental disorder, under disorder.

illumination (ĭ-lu-mĭ-na′shun) **1.** The process by which light is made to fall on a surface or object, generally for inspection. **2.** In microscopy, the light cast upon the specimen to be examined.

    contact i. Illumination from a source of light placed directly on the cornea and conjunctiva of the eyeball.

    critical i. In microscopy, the focusing of the light source directly on the specimen, creating a narrow, intense light beam.

    dark-field i. Illumination of a microscopic specimen by a hollow cone of light from the condenser; the vertically directed light rays are blocked by a black circular shield, and only the peripheral rays are directed toward the specimen, thereby making the object appear bright on a dark background. Also called dark-ground illumination.

    dark-ground i. See dark-field illumination.

    direct i. In microscopy, illumination by a beam of light from above the microscope stage falling almost perpendicularly upon the specimen. Also called vertical illumination; surface illumination.

    focal i. Illumination of an object by light focused upon it through an optical system.

    surface i. See direct illumination.

    vertical i. See direct illumination.

illusion (ĭ-lu′zhun) A false perception of reality.

    optical i. An erroneous interpretation of a visual sensation.

illusional (ĭ-lu′zhun-al) Relating to an illusion.

image (im′ij) **1.** A facsimile of the appearance of an object formed by the rays of light emanating or reflected from it. **2.** A representation or picture of someone or something not present, formed in the mind from memory. Also called mental image. **3.** The concept of an institution or character of a person that is held by the public.

    after i. See afterimage.

    double i. Two images of a single object, as formed perceptually in diplopia.

    false i. An image formed by the squinting or deviating eye in strabismus; it is less defined than the true image since it does not focus on the macula area of the retina.

    hypnopompic i. Imagery occurring after the sleeping state but before complete awakening, as when a dream figure momentarily persists in waking life.

    inverted i. See real image.

    mental i. See image (2).

    mirror i. *(a)* An image with right and left parts reversed, as the relationship of an object in a mirror. *(b)* The image of the light source from the reflecting surface of the cornea and lens of the eye when illuminated through the slit lamp.

    real i. An image formed by converging light rays, which can be seen by inserting a ground glass into the optical system, or which can be recorded on a photographic plate; the opposite of virtual image; the pictured object is always seen inverted. Also called inverted image.

    retinal i. The image formed on the surface of the retina of an object seen by the refracting system of the eye.

    true i. In strabismus, the image that falls on the macula from the undeviated eye; it is more defined than the false image of the deviated eye.

optical illusions

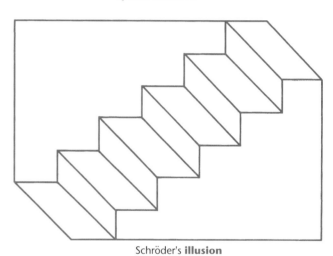

Schröder's **illusion** of reversible staircase

Müller-Lyer **illusion**   the line on the right appears shorter than the equal line on the left

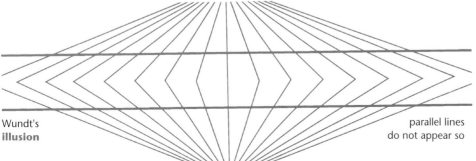

Wundt's **illusion**   parallel lines do not appear so

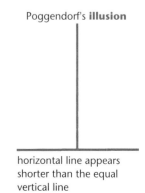

Poggendorf's **illusion**

horizontal line appears shorter than the equal vertical line

virtual i. An image in which light, originating from a point on the object, and having traversed an optical system, appears to be diverging; it cannot be demonstrated on a screen or recorded on a photographic plate as in the case of a real image; the image has the same orientation as the object.

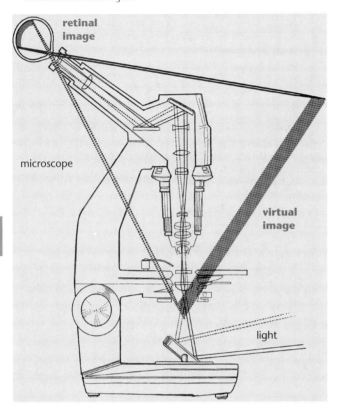

retinal image

microscope

virtual image

light

imaging (im′ah-jing) The process of producing a visual representation.

functional magnetic resonance i. High-speed magnetic resonance imaging techniques that measure changes in blood volume and flow, thereby producing functional MRI maps of brain activity.

magnetic resonance i. (MRI) A high-resolution *in vivo* diagnostic procedure that provides sectional images of internal structures without the use of radioactive material. The patient is placed in a magnetic field within a cyclindrical hollow magnet. Under this magnetic influence, the nuclei (protons) of the body's hydrogen atoms (which normally point in different directions) line up parallel to each other, like rows of minute magnets. Brief pulses of radio waves are then applied to knock the nuclei out of alignment. As they fall back into alignment, the nuclei produce detectable radio signals, which vary in strength depending on the hydrogen content of the tissue. The signals are then translated into images by a computer. Also called nuclear magnetic resonance.

nuclear magnetic resonance (NMR) i. See magnetic resonance imaging.

SPECT i. See single proton emission computed tomography, under tomography.

imbalance (im-bal′ans) Lack of equality (e.g., in the activities of the sympathetic and parasympathetic nervous systems) or a change in the normal levels of chemicals in the blood (e.g., sodium, potassium bircarbonate).

imbibition (im-bĭ-bish′un) Absorption of a fluid (e.g., the taking up of water by a gel).

imbrication (im-brĭ-ka′shun) **1.** The turning in of the edges of a surgical wound. **2.** Overcrowding and overlapping of anterior teeth.

imino acid (ĭ-me′no as′id) A compound containing both an acid group and an imino group.

imipramine hydrochloride (ĭ-mip′rah-mēn hi-dro-klo′rĭd) Compound used in the treatment of depression; also used for nocturnal enuresis.

immersion (ĭ-mer′shun) **1.** The placing of an object, a body part, or the body in a liquid. **2.** In microscopy, the placing of oil or water between the specimen and objective to allow high-power magnification for better visibility.

immiscible (ĭ-mis′ĭ-bl) Incapable of mixing (e.g., oil and water).

immobilization (im-mo-bil-ĭ-za′shun) The act of impeding movement.

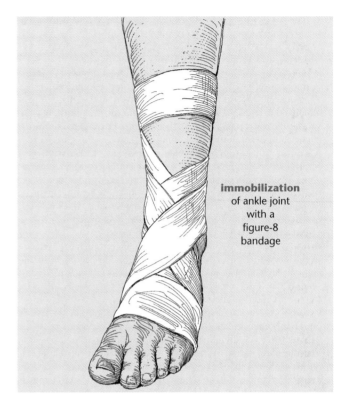

immobilization of ankle joint with a figure-8 bandage

immobilize (im-mo′bil-īz) To render incapable of motion; to fix in one position.

immortalization (im-mor-tal-ĭ-za′shun) The conferring of a virtually infinite life span to an *in vitro* cell culture by artificial means (e.g., exposure to viral infection or cancer-causing chemicals).

immotile (ĭ-mot′l, im-mo′til) Incapable of moving.

immune (ĭ-mun′) **1.** Characterized by a state of being secure against harmful effects from disease-causing agents or influences; having immunity. **2.** Relating to immunity.

immunity (ĭ-mu′nĭ-te) **1.** The physiologic state that enables the body to recognize materials that are not of itself and to neutralize, eliminate, or metabolize them with or without injury to its own tissue. **2.** An inherited or acquired (naturally or artificially) conditioning to a specific pathogen.

acquired i. Immunity acquired after birth; may be active or passive.

active i. Immunity resulting from an acquired infection or from vaccination, which triggers the individual's own immune system to produce blood-circulating antibodies directed against the microorganism or its toxins, or it may initiate responses mediated by specifically reactive white blood cells (lymphocytes or macrophages).

cell-mediated i. (CMI) Immunity in which the participation of certain white blood cells (lymphocytes and macrophages) is predominant.

humoral i. Immunity in which the involvement of blood-circulating antibodies (immunoglobulins) is predominant.

innate i. Resistance to certain infections that has not been acquired through vaccination or previous infection; it includes species-determined immunity (e.g., resistance of humans to the virus of canine distemper). Also called natural immunity.

natural i. See innate immunity.

neonatal passive i. Passive immunity in a newborn infant acquired as a fetus through transplacental transfer from its mother; it protects the infant from many common infections and lasts about six months.

passive i. Immunity acquired in either of two forms: by means of transferred antibodies either naturally (e.g., from immune mother to fetus), or artificially (e.g., by intentional innoculation with serum); or by means of transferred lymphoid cells from an immune donor.

immunization (ĭm′u-nĭ-za′shun) The act of rendering a person resistant to a specific disease.

active i. Administration of antigens (i.e., modified or killed infectious microorganism or its toxins) to stimulate the person's immune system into producing a high level of antibodies. The principle is used in many childhood vaccines to provide long-term protection.

combined passive-active i. A simultaneous passive and active immunization undertaken to produce an immediate, transient protection and a slowly durable protection against such diseases as rabies and tetanus.

occupational preexposure i. See prophylactic immunization.

passive i. Immunization for immediate short-term protection by administration of preformed antibody to a person who has been exposed to an infectious disease. Antibody could be serum from a person who has had the disease (e.g., rubella) or serum from an animal specifically immunized against an antigen (e.g., tetanus toxin).

prophylactic i. *(a)* Immunization of travelers to regions where endemic diseases are prevalent. *(b)* Immunization of laboratory workers or anyone at risk of contact with live pathogenic organisms. Also called occupational preexposure immunization.

immunize (im′u-niz) To render a person immune.

immunoagglutination (im-u-no-ah-gloo-tĭ-na′shun) A clumping (agglutination) of cells brought about by antibody.

immunoassay (im-u-no-as′a) Any of a group of laboratory techniques, such as enzyme-linked immunosorbent assay (ELISA) and radioimmunoassay (RIA) that employ antigen-antibody reactions to detect specific proteins in a person's blood. The proteins detected are antigens (e.g., an infectious microorganism) or an antibody formed by the body to combat the organism.

immunobead (im-u-no-bēd′) One of several minute plastic spheres coated with antibody or antigen used in determining immune reactions by agglutination or binding of cells (e.g., in male infertility studies to determine whether spermatozoa are bound to sperm-reactive antibody).

immunochemistry (im-u-no-kem′is-tre) The chemistry of immunologic processes.

immunocompetence (im-u-no-kom′pĕ-tens) Ability to produce antibodies or cell-mediated immunity when exposed to an antigen (i.e., any substance recognized by the body as being nonself).

immunocompromised (im-u-no-kom′pro-mizd) Reduced immune response resulting from immunosuppressive drugs, chemotherapy, irradiation, disease, or malnutrition.

immunocyte (im-u-no-sīt′) Any lymphoid cell that can form antibodies or elaborate cells that form antibodies when reacting with antigens (e.g., an inducer cell). Also called I cell; immunocompetent cell; antigen-sensitive cell.

immunocytochemistry (im-u-no-si-to-kem′is-tre) Any technique (e.g., the use of fluorescent antibodies) for analyzing cells and tissues to identify particulate antigens; useful in detecting certain cancerous tumors (e.g., sarcomas and gliomas).

immunodeficiency (im-u-no-dĕ-fish′en-se) Any congenital or acquired impairment of the immune response; may involve the cell-mediated (T-cell) portion of the immune system or the antibody-mediated (B-cell) portion, or both; it may be secondary to a developmental defect, or due to an enzymatic defect, or to unknown causes; symptoms and signs, in general, are related to the degree of deficiency and the specific body organs that are deficient in function; characteristically, affected persons have a susceptibility to infections. Also called immune deficiency.

common variable i. (CVI) General term for a group of disorders (hereditary or acquired) with onset at any age; characterized by low levels of all or some of the immunoglobulin classes, but with the number of B lymphocytes in peripheral blood usually within normal range; the deficiency leads to recurrent bacterial infections and an increased incidence of autoimmune disease.

severe combined i. (SCI) A group of congenital diseases of autosomal recessive or X-linked inheritance, characterized by dysfunction of both antibody formation and cellular immunity; affected infants seldom survive beyond the first year of life.

immunodiffusion (im-u-no-dĭ-fu′zhun) A technique for the study of immune reactions that involves diffusion of antibody or antigen through a semisolid substance (e.g., a gel).

immunoelectrophoresis (im-u-no-e-lek-tro-fo-re′sis) (IE, IEP) A form of electrophoresis in which an antigen-antibody reaction (immune precipitation) is additionally employed.

immunofluorescence (im-u-no-floo-o-res′ens) The microscopic identification of particular antigens by using specific antibodies labeled with a fluorescent dye.

immunogen (im′u-no-jen) An antigen stimulating specific immunity.

immunogenetics (im-u-no-jĕ-net′iks) The branch of genetics concerned with all factors controlling immune reactions and the transmission of antigenic specificities from generation to generation.

immunogenic (im-u-no-jen′ik) See antigenic.

immunogenicity (im-u-no-jĕ-nis′ĭ-te) See antigenicity.

immunoglobulin (im-u-no-glob′u-lin) (Ig) Any of a group of proteins present in serum and tissue fluids of all mammals; essentially, the immunoglobulin molecule has two main functions: one region of the molecule is concerned with binding to antigen (e.g., bacterial cells), another with mediating the binding of the molecule to host tissues (including cells of the immune system and phagocytic cells). Five classes of immunoglobulins have been recognized (IgA, IgD, IgE, IgG, IgM), each differing from the others in size, amino acid composition, and carbohydrate content. All antibodies are immunoglobulins; probably all immunoglobulins have antibody activity. See also antibody.

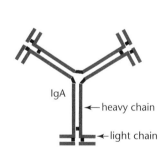
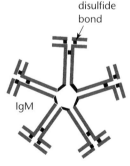

schematic representation of the comparative structures of **immunoglobulins**

IgG   IgE

disulfide bond

IgA   IgM

heavy chain

light chain

monoclonal i. Immunoglobulin derived from a single clone of plasma cells proliferating abnormally.

immunohematology (im-u-no-hem-ah-tol′o-je) The branch of hematology involved with antigen-antibody reactions and their effect on the blood.

immunologist (im-u-nol′o-jist) A specialist in immunology.

immunology (im-u-nol′o-je) The study of specific processes by which the body maintains constancy of its internal environment when confronted by substances which it recognizes as foreign (nonself), whether generated from within or introduced from the outside.

immunomodulation (im-u-no-mod-u-la′shun) Any of various

methods for therapeutic manipulation of the body's immune response to an antigen.

immunopathic (im-u-no-path′ik) Relating to damage inflicted upon cells, tissues, or organs by reactions of immunity.

immunoreaction (im-u-no-re-ak′shun) See immune response, under response.

immunoscintigraphy (im-u-no-sin-tig′rah-fe) The making of a two-dimensional image of a radiolabeled monoclonal antibody (Mab) that has bound to a preselected antigen at a target tissue; used to detect specific tumors.

immunoselection (im-u-no-sĕ-lek′shun) The survival of certain cell lines able to escape the actions of antibody or lymphocytes.

immunosuppression (im-u-no-sŭ-presh′un) Diminution of the body's immune response, either by infection or carried out by any of several means (e.g., drugs, radiation, lymphocyte depletion) as a way to prevent rejection of a transplant.

immunosuppressive (im-u-no-sŭ-pres′iv) Capable of inducing immunosuppression.

immunotherapy (im-u-no-ther′ah-pe) **1.** Passive immunization through the use of serum or gamma globulin. **2.** Transplantation of immunocompetent tissues (e.g., bone marrow, fetal thymus) into an immunodeficient patient. **3.** A therapeutic modality intended to non-specifically induce the immune system of a cancer patient to destroy malignant cells. **4.** Treatment with immunosuppressive drugs or biological products.

    allergen i. See desensitization.

immunotolerance (im-u-no-tol′er-ans) See immunologic tolerance, under tolerance.

impact (im′pakt) The sudden striking of one body against another; a collision.

impact (im-pakt′) **1.** To press firmly together. **2.** To act upon another body.

impaction (im-pak′shun) Tightly wedged together or firmly lodged so as to be immovable.

    ceruminal i. Accumulation of earwax (cerumen) in the external auditory canal.

    dental i. Condition in which a tooth is so positioned in its socket as to be incapable of complete eruption.

    fecal i. A mass of compressed, hardened feces retained in some part of the bowel, usually the sigmoid colon or rectum.

    food i. The forcible crowding of food into the spaces between adjoining teeth during mastication; the food becomes lodged like a wedge and may contribute to the formation of gingival and periodontal pockets.

    mucoid i. Mucuslike impaction of a bronchus in the lung.

impairment (im-pār′ment) A deficiency resulting from injury or disease measured by anatomic or functional loss, which may produce disability. See also disability; handicap.

    mental i. Intellectual defect as manifested by psychologic tests and diminished social and work effectiveness.

    physician i. A physician's diminished ability to practice medicine within accepted standards of medical practice as a result of impairment; causes may include alcohol and drug abuse, mental illness, physical handicaps, and senility.

impatent (im-pa′tent) Closed; applied especially to tubular structures.

impedance (im-pēd′ans) **1.** Total opposition to flow; pertains to electric current and also to pulsatile blood flow. **2.** Opposition to the flow of sound in a mechanical system (e.g., the eardrum and chain of ossicles in the middle ear chamber).

imperforate (im-per′fo-rāt) Abnormally closed.

impermeable (im-per′me-ah-bl) Unable to be penetrated; not allowing passage of any substance.

impermeant (im-per′me-ant) Unable to penetrate or pass through a membrane.

impetigo (im-pĕ-ti′go) Contagious bacterial skin infection usually caused by staphylococci, occurring mainly in children; characterized by development of pustules that form a characteristic yellowish crust upon bursting.

implant (im-plant′) To graft or place something in the body.

implant (im′plant) Any material, object, or device inserted or placed within the body.

    breast i. A silicone bag filled with silicone gel, saline, air, or a combination thereof, placed either behind the breast or behind the pectoral muscle to increase breast size (augmentation mammoplasty) or to reconstruct the breast after mastectomy.

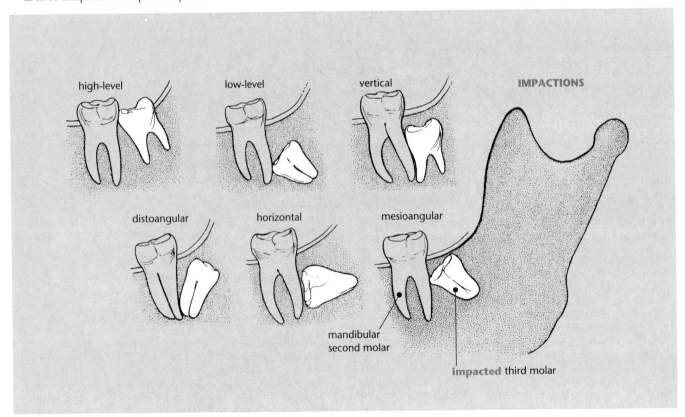

high-level   low-level   vertical   **IMPACTIONS**

distoangular   horizontal   mesioangular

mandibular second molar

impacted third molar

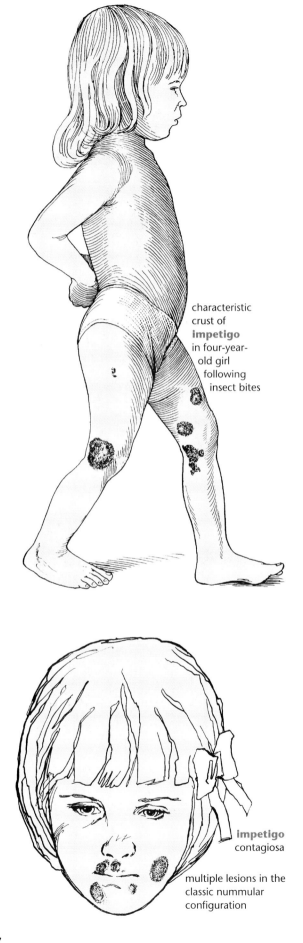

characteristic crust of **impetigo** in four-year-old girl following insect bites

impetigo contagiosa

multiple lesions in the classic nummular configuration

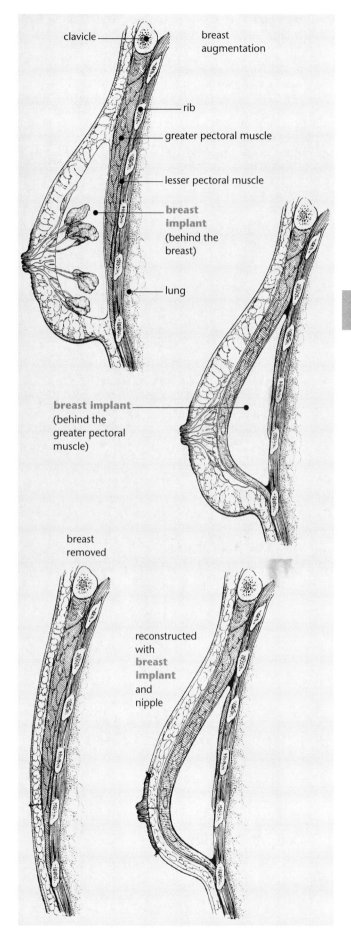

breast augmentation

clavicle

rib

greater pectoral muscle

lesser pectoral muscle

breast implant (behind the breast)

lung

breast implant (behind the greater pectoral muscle)

breast removed

reconstructed with **breast implant** and nipple

I

cochlear i. A device inserted through the skin adjacent to the ear of persons with total sensory deafness, and positioned either within or outside the cochlea; electrodes of the device leading to the cochlear nerve create sensation of sound.

dental i. See endosseous dental implant.

endosseous dental i. An implant made of biocompatible materials for insertion into the socket of a missing tooth, where it becomes directly attached to the jawbone; it functions as the tooth root, providing support for a subsequently inserted post bearing the artificial tooth or teeth.

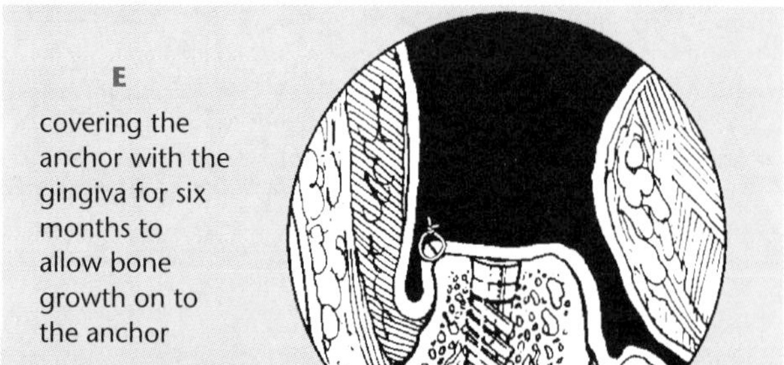

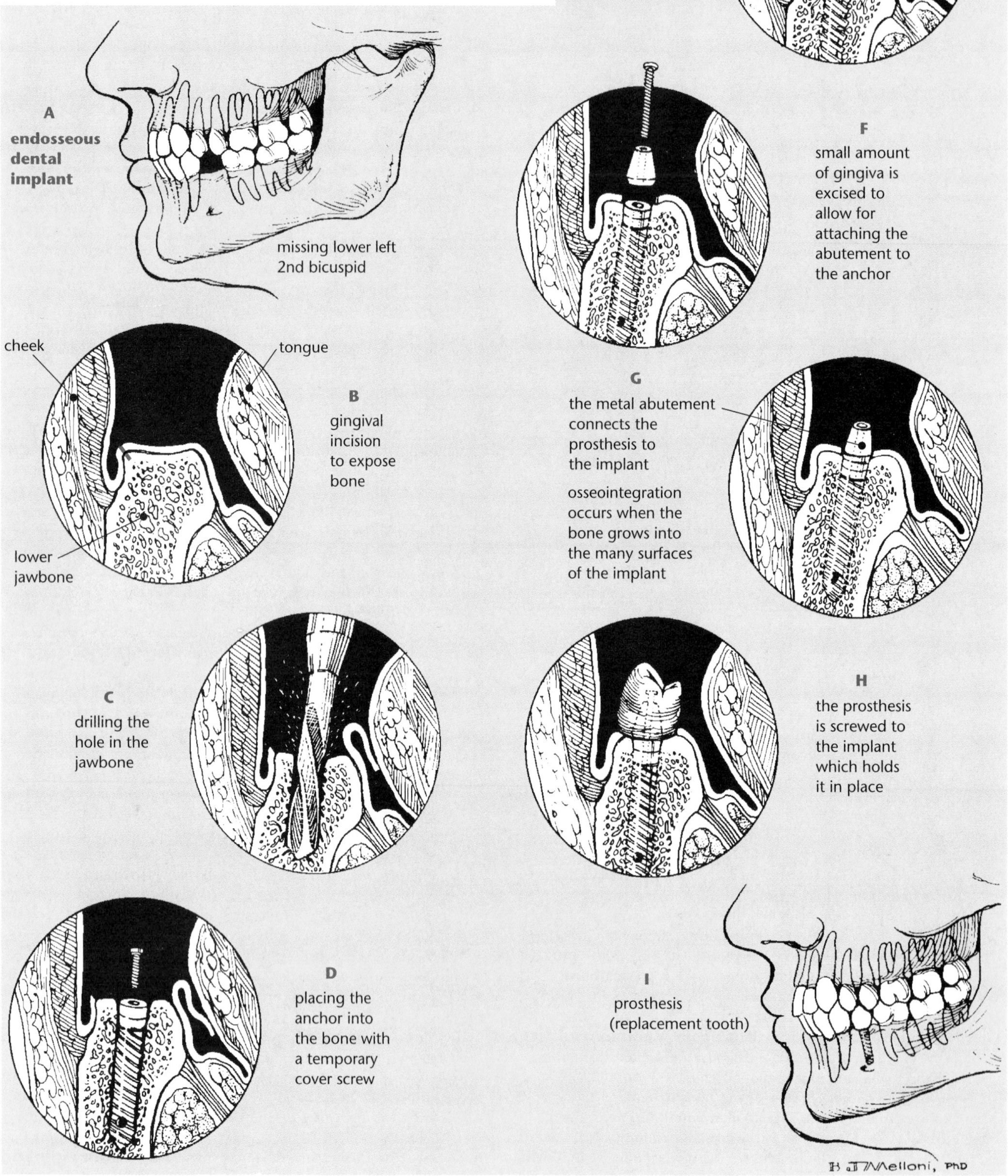

A endosseous dental implant

missing lower left 2nd bicuspid

cheek
tongue
B gingival incision to expose bone
lower jawbone

C drilling the hole in the jawbone

D placing the anchor into the bone with a temporary cover screw

E covering the anchor with the gingiva for six months to allow bone growth on to the anchor

F small amount of gingiva is excised to allow for attaching the abutement to the anchor

G the metal abutement connects the prosthesis to the implant

osseointegration occurs when the bone grows into the many surfaces of the implant

H the prosthesis is screwed to the implant which holds it in place

I prosthesis (replacement tooth)

B. J. Melloni, PhD

implant ■ implant

hair i. See hair transplant, under transplant.

interstitial i. In radiation therapy, a radioactive material placed directly into the tissue (not in a body cavity).

intracavitary i. In radiation therapy, a radioactive material placed in a body cavity (e.g., vagina, chest cavity).

intraocular i. Plastic lens inserted in the eye to replace a diseased natural lens removed in a cataract operation.

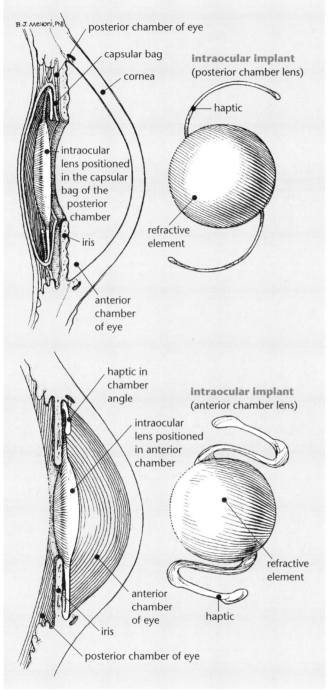

B. J. Melloni, PhD
posterior chamber of eye
capsular bag
cornea
intraocular implant
(posterior chamber lens)
haptic
intraocular lens positioned in the capsular bag of the posterior chamber
refractive element
iris
anterior chamber of eye

haptic in chamber angle
intraocular implant
(anterior chamber lens)
intraocular lens positioned in anterior chamber
anterior chamber of eye
refractive element
haptic
iris
posterior chamber of eye

penile i. See penile prosthesis, under prosthesis.

subdermal contraceptive i. A reversible female contraceptive implanted under the skin; effective for an extended period of time (usually five years). Trade name: Norplant.

implantation (im-plan-ta′shun) **1.** The embedding of a fertilized ovum, normally to the inner wall of the uterus. **2.** The surgical placing or insertion of an implant.

impotence (im′po-tens) Term traditionally used to describe the inability to attain and maintain erection of the penis sufficiently to per-

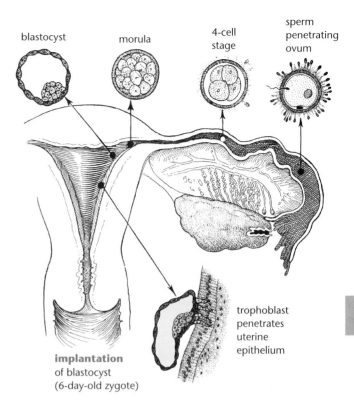

blastocyst   morula   4-cell stage   sperm penetrating ovum

trophoblast penetrates uterine epithelium

implantation of blastocyst (6-day-old zygote)

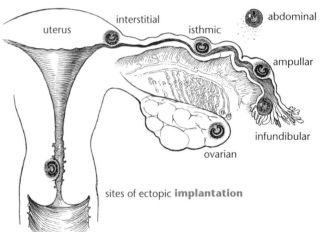

uterus   interstitial   isthmic   abdominal   ampullar   infundibular   ovarian

sites of ectopic **implantation**

mit satisfactory sexual intercourse. Currently, the term *"erectile dysfunction"* has been suggested as a more precise description of the condition. See erectile dysfunction, under dysfunction.

physical i. Impotence occurring when certain nerves or blood vessels are damaged, or the body's balance of hormones is upset by surgery, an accident, or disease (e.g., diabetes, high blood pressure, kidney disease).

psychic i. See psychological impotence.

psychological i. Impotence caused by emotional problems (e.g., depression, worry, anger, tension, fear, stress). Also called psychic impotence.

impregnate (im-preg′nāt) **1.** To render pregnant. **2.** To saturate.

impression (im-presh′un) **1.** An imprint made on a surface by pressure, such as a mold taken of the mouth by a dentist. **2.** A feeling acquired as a consequence of experience.

complete denture i. An impression of the dental arch for the purpose of making a complete denture.

dental i. A negative likeness of the teeth or other structures of the oral cavity, made of a plastic material that, when hardened, is filled with plaster of Paris or dental stone, thus producing an exact copy (study model) of the structures.

esophageal i. A concavity on the posterior surface of the left lobe of the liver, lodging the abdominal part of the esophagus.

final i. In dentistry, the impression used for making the master cast. Also called secondary impression.

secondary i. See final impression.

imprinting (im′print-ing) **1.** A distinguishing manifestation (e.g., a genetic trait). **2.** A mode of rapid learning during the first few hours of animal life, which determines species recognition. The extent to which imprinting occurs in humans has not been established.

genetic i. Process in which gene expression is influenced by the sex of the parent from whom the gene is inherited.

improvement (im-proov′ment) A betterment.

medical i. (MI) Any decrease in the severity of a medical impairment as determined by changes in symptoms, signs, and/or laboratory findings.

impulse (im′puls) **1.** The brief action potential of nerve fibers; the energy that is transferred along a nerve fiber. **2.** A sudden, forceful urge to act.

cardiac i. The movement of the chest wall produced by contraction of the heart.

in- Prefix meaning in; into; toward; causing to become; becoming; emphasis.

inactivate (in-ak′tĭ-vāt) To make inert (e.g., to make bacteria biologically inert).

inanimate (in-an′ĭ-māt) Without life.

inanition (in-ah-nish′un) Weakness, as from lack of food or from defective absorption of nutrients.

inapparent (in-ah-par′ent) Not recognizable.

inarticulate (in-ar-tik′u-lāt) **1.** Unable to produce intelligible speech sounds. **2.** Unable to express one's thoughts easily with words.

inattention (in-ah-ten′shun) Lack of attention.

selective i. Failure to pay attention to a part of a perceived situation, especially one that generates anxiety.

inborn (in′born) Ambiguous term generally meaning acquired genetically; inherited.

i. errors of metabolism See under error.

inbreeding (in′brēd-ing) The mating of closely related individuals, occurring naturally or as a deliberate process to preserve desirable characteristics.

incarcerated (in-kar′ser-āt-ed) Trapped; held fast and confined, as may occur in certain cases of irreducible hernias.

incest (in′sest) Sexual intercourse or sexual activity between persons closely related by blood (e.g., parents and offspring, brothers and sisters).

incestuous (in-ses′chū-ŭs) Relating to incest.

incidence (in′sĭ-dens) The frequency at which new events (e.g., new cases of a disease) occur in a given population in a specified period of time (usually one year).

incident (in′sĭ-dent) **1.** A distinct occurrence. **2.** Falling upon; applied to light rays (incident rays).

incipient (in-sip′e-ent) Beginning to appear or occur (e.g., a disease in an initial stage).

incisal (in-si′zal) Cutting.

incise (in′siz) To cut with a knife.

incision (in-sizh′un) **1.** A surgical cut into tissue made by a sharp instrument. **2.** The act of cutting.

Battle's i. A vertical incision along the outer border of the abdominal rectus muscle, with division of the rectus sheath and retraction of the rectus muscle inward. Also called lateral rectus incision.

bikini i. A horizontal skin incision near the pubic hairline; made to approach the uterus for a cesarean section.

bucket-handle i. A subcostal incision extending just below the lower margin of the rib cage on both sides.

buttonhole i. A small drainage incision made by the removal of some skin.

celiotomy i. An incision through the abdominal wall to access the peritoneal cavity.

cesarean i.'s Any incision through the anterior abdominal wall and the uterus; made to approach the fetus or fetuses for delivery.

cruciate i. A cross-shaped surgical incision usually performed for drainage purposes.

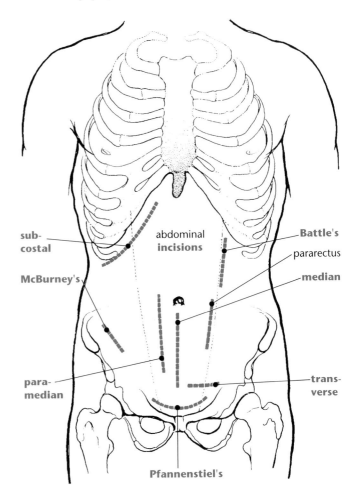

Dührssen's i.'s In obstetrics, two or three longitudinal incisions made in the partially dilated uterine cervix to facilitate vaginal delivery of the fetal head in a breech presentation. Also called hysterostomatomy.

gridiron i. See McBurney's incision.

Kocher's i. A subcostal incision on the right side of the abdominal wall just below and parallel to the costal margin; it provides surgical exposure to the common bile duct, cystic duct, and gallbladder. When transposed to the left side, it provides surgical exposure to the spleen.

lateral rectus i. See Battle's incision.

Maylard i. A lower abdominal incision that provides surgical exposure to the reproductive organs of women.

McBurney's i. An oblique abdominal incision, in the right lower quadrant, parallel to the fibers of the external oblique muscle; located approximately one-third the distance along a line between the anterior superior iliac spine and the navel (umbilicus); commonly used in appendectomy. Also called gridiron incision.

McLaughlin's i. A skin incision extending forward from the acromion in line with the shoulder strap; an approach to the subacromial bursa, between the acromion and the insertion tendon of the supraspinatus muscle.

median i. A surgical incision in the midline of the anterior abdominal wall; designated *lower median i.,* when made below the umbilicus to expose the pelvic organs; or *upper median i.,* when made above the umbilicus to expose the stomach and transverse colon. Also called midline incision.

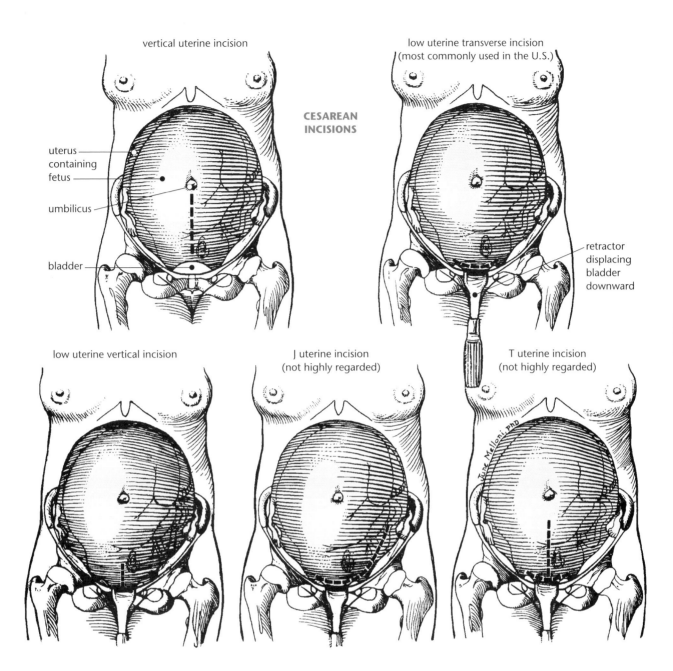

vertical uterine incision

low uterine transverse incision
(most commonly used in the U.S.)

CESAREAN
INCISIONS

uterus
containing
fetus

umbilicus

bladder

retractor
displacing
bladder
downward

low uterine vertical incision

J uterine incision
(not highly regarded)

T uterine incision
(not highly regarded)

median sternotomy i. A vertical incision through the midline of the breastbone (sternum) from the manubrium to the xiphoid process; performed for most heart operations and for access to mediastinal lesions.

midline i. See median incision.

paramedian i. A vertical incision about an inch from the midline of the anterior abdominal wall that permits the retraction of the abdominal rectus muscle laterally.

Pfannenstiel's i. A curved, transverse abdominal incision through the skin, just above the pubic symphysis; generally followed by a vertical midline incision of the fascia and peritoneum.

relief i. A skin incision made away from a wound to relax the tension of the skin so that it can be stretched to cover the wound.

stab i. A puncture incision made for drainage.

subcostal i. An incision of the abdominal wall just below and parallel to the costal margin.

suprapubic i. Any skin incision between the pubis and the umbilicus.

transverse abdominal i. A transverse incision through the abdominal wall.

incisor (in-si′zer) 1. Any of the eight front cutting teeth, four in each jaw. 2. Anything adapted for cutting.

central i. The tooth closest to and on either side of the midline of the head, on either jaw.

lateral i. The second tooth, upper or lower, on either side of the midline of the head, situated distal to the central incisor and mesial to the cuspid.

incisura (in-si-su′rah) Latin for incisure.

incisure (in-si′zhūr) A notch or indentation on an anatomic structure.

Schmidt-Lanterman i.'s A series of funnel-shaped indentations in the myelin sheaths covering nerve fibers.

inclination (in-klĭ-na′shun) 1. A leaning or sloping (e.g., the leaning of the long axis of a tooth away from the vertical). 2. A disposition or trend toward a particular condition.

inclusion (in-klu′zhun) 1. The state of being enclosed. 2. Anything that is enclosed.

cell i. Transient substance in a cell that does not participate in the cell's activity (e.g., lipids, pigment granules).

fetal i. A small, incompletely developed conjoined twin enclosed within the body of the other.

incoherent (in-ko-hēr′ent) Disoriented and confused; unable to speak logically.

incompatible (in-kom-pat′ĭ-bl) **1.** Incapable of being mixed or used simultaneously without producing undesirable effects or undergoing chemical changes (e.g., blood which, when administered to someone whose own blood is of a different type, triggers harmful immune reactions; or certain drugs whose interactions render them injurious or ineffective). **2.** The nature of two or more people who are unable to interact without attendant conflict and anxiety.

incompetence (in-kom′pe-tens) **1.** The state of being insufficient; inability of an organ or part to perform its required function adequately. **2.** In psychiatry, the state of lacking the qualities necessary for adequate independent functioning. **3.** The condition of lacking the legal qualification or fitness to perform adequately (e.g., to drive an automobile due to intoxication).

    aortic i. Failure of the aortic valve to close tightly, allowing regurgitation of blood from the aorta into the left ventricle of the heart during diastole.

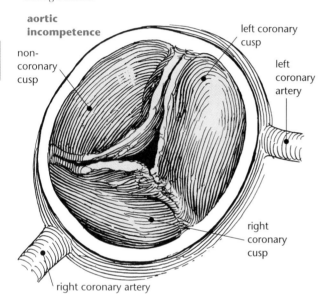

aortic incompetence; non-coronary cusp; left coronary cusp; left coronary artery; right coronary cusp; right coronary artery

    cervical i. Failure of the cervical opening to remain closed during pregnancy due to either an anatomic or a functional defect, a frequent cause of second-trimester abortion.

    mitral i. Inadequate closure of a mitral (left atrioventricular) valve in the heart, allowing regurgitation of blood into the left atrium, from the left ventricle, during systole.

    muscular i. Inadequate action of the papillary muscles of the heart, resulting in imperfect closure of a normal valve.

    pulmonic i. Imperfect closure of a pulmonic valve, allowing regurgitation of blood from the pulmonary trunk into the right ventricle of the heart during diastole.

    pyloric i. A relaxed state of the circular muscle (pylorus) between the stomach and small intestine, allowing food to pass into the intestine before gastric digestion is completed.

    tricuspid i. Imperfect closure of a tricuspid (right atrioventricular) valve in the heart, allowing regurgitation of blood into the right atrium, from the right ventricle, during systole.

    valvular i. Failure of a valve in the heart to close completely, allowing leakage of blood through it.

incompetency (in-kom′pe-ten-se) The state of lacking the legal qualifications to participate in a legal proceeding (e.g., to legally give consent, make a contract, stand trial, make a will, testify as a witness).

incompetent (in-kom′pe-tent) **1.** Characterized by incompetence. **2.** Held to be legally unqualified to participate in a judicial proceeding or to make certain kinds of decisions independently.

inconstant (in-kon′stant) **1.** Variable. **2.** In anatomy, denoting a structure that may or may not be present, may have a tendency to change, or is given to change of location.

incontinence (in-kon′tĭ-nens) Inability to control the passage of urine or feces.

    mechanical i. Incontinence stemming from congenital abnormalities (e.g., ectopic urethral openings) or from prostate or pelvic surgery or irradiation.

    overflow i. Leakage of urine when the bladder is overextended and its sphincters are overcome.

    stress i. Involuntary passage of urine occurring with physical stress (e.g., coughing, sneezing, or straining).

    urge i. Inability to postpone voiding because the urge to urinate is abrupt and uncontrollable.

incontinent (in-kon′tĭ-nent) Characterized by incontinence.

incoordination (in-ko-or-dĭ-na′shun) See ataxia.

incrustation (in-krus-ta′shun) **1.** The formation of a scab. **2.** A scab.

incubation (in-ku-ba′shun) **1.** The phase of an infectious disease from the time the infectious agent enters the body to the appearance of the first symptoms. **2.** The maintenance of optimal condition of an environment with regard to temperature, humidity, and gas content (e.g., for the care of a premature infant, for maintenance of bacterial cultures, for the preparation of biological and chemical materials).

incubator (in′ku-ba-ter) An apparatus in which a controlled environment can be maintained for the care of premature or sick newborn infants; also used for bacterial cultures.

incurable (in-ku′rah-bl) Not curable.

incus (ing′kus) The middle of the three ossicles of the middle ear, between the malleus and the stapes, involved in transmitting sound vibrations from the eardrum (tympanic membrane) to the inner ear; it resembles an anvil and is sometimes called by that name. See also table of bones.

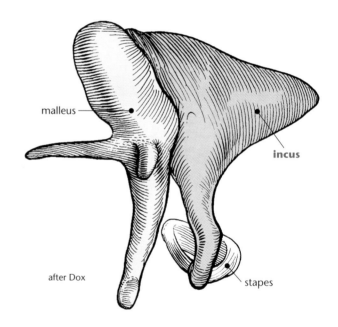

malleus; incus; after Dox; stapes

indentation (in-den-ta′shun) **1.** A notch, dent, or impression. **2.** The act of notching or indenting.

index (in′deks), pl. in′dexes, in′dices **1.** The forefinger; the second finger of the hand. **2.** A value expressing the ratio of one measurement to another. **3.** A mold for recording or maintaining the relative position of teeth to one another and/or to a cast. **4.** A guide for repositioning teeth, casts, or parts.

    addiction severity i. (ASI) A structured clinical research interview that assesses problem severity in several areas that would render a person vulnerable to substance abuse: it includes physical condition, employment, drug use, alcohol use, illegal activity, family relations, and psychiatric condition.

    cardiac i. The quantity of blood ejected by the heart in a given

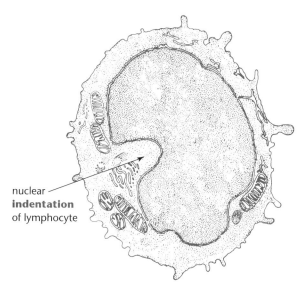

nuclear **indentation** of lymphocyte

time (expressed in minutes), divided by the body surface (expressed in square meters).

cardiothoracic i. The ratio of the maximal transverse diameter of the heart shadow on an x-ray image to the maximal transverse diameter of the chest, normally less than one-half.

cephalic i. The ratio of the maximal breadth to the maximal length of the head of a living subject; (breadth $\times$ 100/length) Also called length-breadth index.

chemotherapeutic i. The ratio of the minimal effective dose of a drug to the maximal tolerated dose.

chest i. See thoracic index.

color i. The ratio of the quantity of hemoglobin to the number of red blood cells. Also called blood quotient; globular value.

cranial i. The breadth/length ratio of a dried skull.

glycemic i. A blood-sugar (glucose) index for assessing and classifying carbohydrate foods on the basis of their effects on blood glucose levels; it indicates the response of a given food compared with the response of pure glucose (with glucose having a value of 100); the lower the glycemic index, the slower the food is in releasing its glucose content into the bloodstream.

icterus i. A value indicating the relative amount of bilirubin in the blood.

length-breadth i. See cephalic index.

maturation i. An index for detecting estrogenic activity by determining the percentage of mature cells exfoliated from the vagina; the action of estrogen matures the vaginal lining, therefore, the higher percentage of mature cells exfoliated suggests increased estrogenic activity.

nasal i. A ratio of the greatest width of the nose to its length.

orbital i. The ratio of the height of the eye socket (orbit) to its width.

penetrating abdominal trauma i. (PATI) A way of scoring abdominal trauma by taking into account the number of abdominal organs injured.

periodontal disease i. (PDI) An index for determining disease of tissues surrounding and supporting the teeth (periodontal disease), based on condition of representative teeth regarding gum inflammation, pockets, plaques, lack of contact, and mobility.

refractive i. (n) The ratio of the speed of light in a given medium to the speed in a medium of reference (e.g., air or vacuum).

therapeutic i. The ratio of the dose fatal to 50% of test animals (LD_{50}) to the dose producing the desired effect in 50% of test animals (ED_{50}); used in quantitative comparison of drugs.

thoracic i. The ratio of the anteroposterior to the transverse diameter of the chest. Also called chest index.

vital i. The ratio of births to deaths in a given population at a given time.

indican (in′dĭ-kan) **1.** A water-soluble glucoside, present in plants, that yields the blue dye indigo. **2.** A substance present in urine and blood as the normal breakdown product of the amino acid tryptophan; increased urinary excretion of indican occurs in certain diseases (e.g., Hartnup disease) due to intestinal bacterial degradation of unabsorbed tryptophan.

indicant (in′dĭ-kant) Serving to indicate (e.g., a symptom that indicates a form of treatment).

indicanuria (in-dĭ-kan-u′re-ah) The presence of increased amounts of indican in the urine; a sign of protein putrefaction, mainly in the intestines.

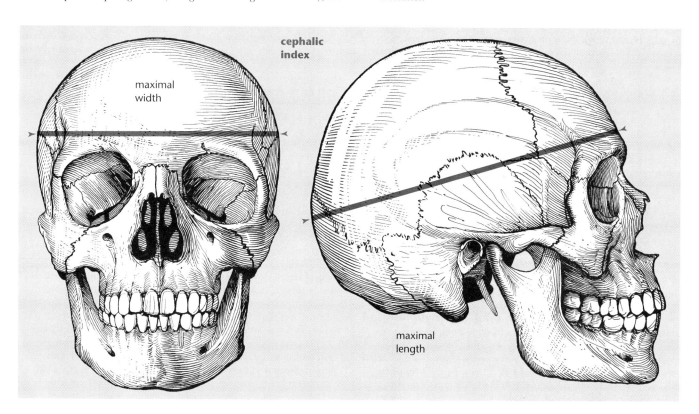

cephalic index

maximal width

maximal length

indication (in-dī-ka′shun) Anything (e.g., a sign or a symptom) that suggests the proper treatment of a disease.

indicator (in′dĭ-ka-ter) In chemistry, any of various substances (e.g., litmus) that by changing color indicate the presence, absence, or concentration of a substance, or the degree of completion of a chemical reaction between two substances.

indigenous (in-dij′ĕ-nus) Native or occurring naturally in a particular area.

indigestible (in-di-jes′tĭ-bl) Not susceptible to being digested.

indigestion (in-di-jes′chun) General term for discomfort caused by a temporary inability or failure to digest food properly.

    nervous i. Indigestion caused by emotional disturbances.

indigo (in′dĭ-go) A blue dye originally obtained from plants of the genus *Indigofera,* now produced synthetically; used in histologic and cytologic techniques as a counterstain.

indigo carmine (in′dĭ-go kar′min) A blue dye, sodium indigotindisulfonate; a reagent for the detection of nitrates and chlorates.

indisposition (in-dis-po-zish′un) Malaise; a slight, general ill feeling.

indium (in′de-um) Metallic element; symbol In, atomic number 49, atomic weight 114.82.

indium-111 (^{111}In) A gamma-emitting radionuclide, used primarily as a tag for labeling white blood cells for locating occult abscesses.

individuation (in-dĭ-vid-u-a′shun) The process of becoming a separate person differentiated from the family or community.

indocyanine green (in-do-si′ah-nēn grēn) A dye used in a variety of blood flow, volume, and function studies; used most commonly in measuring the quantity of blood pumped by the heart per unit of time (cardiac output).

indole (in′dōl) A normal product of protein decomposition in the large intestine. Also called ketole.

indolent (in′do-lent) **1.** Sluggish; slow; applied to the progression of a disease process or the development and growth of a tumor. **2.** Causing little or no pain.

indolic acids (in-dol′ik as′ids) Products of the metabolic breakdown of the amino acid tryptophan.

indomethacin (in-do-meth′ah-sin) A nonsteroidal anti-inflammatory compound, used in the treatment of rheumatoid arthritis, osteoarthritis, acute gout, and other musculoskeletal disorders. Trade name: Indocin.

induce (in-doos′) **1.** To bring about or to effect by stimulation; to cause. **2.** In psychology, to arouse by indirect influence.

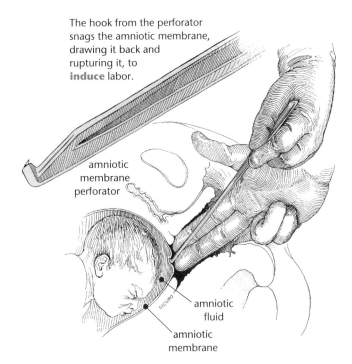

The hook from the perforator snags the amniotic membrane, drawing it back and rupturing it, to **induce** labor.

amniotic membrane perforator

amniotic fluid

amniotic membrane

inducer (in-doos′er) In molecular genetics, a small molecule that accelerates the transcription of a particular gene by combining with a regulatory gene.

inductance (in-duk′tans) (L) The property of an electric circuit by which a changing current can produce in it (or in a neighboring circuit) an electromotive force proportional to the change of the current. The unit of inductance is the henry (H).

induction (in-duk′shun) Causing to occur (e.g., morphologic changes in the embryo, differentiation of cells, anesthesia).

    enzyme i. Stimulation of the production of an enzyme from amino acids programmed by a structural gene in the presence of a small inducer molecule.

inductor (in-duk′ter) Anything that stimulates or brings about induction (e.g., a chemical substance, a coil of wire).

indurated (in′du-rāt-ed) Hardened; applied especially to normally soft tissues that have become abnormally firm.

induration (in-du-ra′shun) **1.** The hardening of a tissue. **2.** An abnormally hard area.

    brown i. of lung Term applied to a brown pigmentation and hardening of lung tissue due to long-standing congestion of the lungs resulting from heart disease.

    cyanotic i. Induration and bluish tint of an organ caused by chronic venous congestion and fibrotic changes of the veins.

indurative (in′du-ra-tiv) Relating to induration.

indwelling (in-dwel′ing) Remaining in place; applied to a catheter or drainage tube that is fixed and held in position for a period of time.

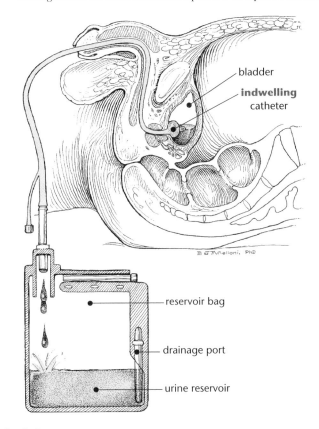

bladder

indwelling catheter

reservoir bag

drainage port

urine reservoir

inebriant (in-e′bre-ant) An intoxicating substance.

inebriation (in-e-bre-a′shun) The condition of being intoxicated.

inert (in-ert′) **1.** Resisting action. **2.** Devoid of chemical activity; applied to a gas and to compounds or drugs that have no therapeutic activity.

inertia (in-er′she-ah) **1.** Resistance offered by a physical mass to a change in its position of rest or motion. **2.** Inability to move unless stimulated by an external force.

    colonic i. Sluggish muscular activity of the colon.

    uterine i. Absence of effective contractions of the uterus during labor.

in extremis (in ek-stre′mis) Latin for at the point of death.

infancy (in′fan-se) The period from birth through the first year (to about the second year) of life; babyhood.

infant (in′fant) An individual from the moment of birth to the end of one year of life.

    appropriate for gestational age (AGA) i. An infant whose weight is between the 10th and 90th percentiles when compared with other infants of the same gestational age.

    excessive-size i. An infant who at the time of birth weighs over 4500 grams (9.9 lbs).

    floppy i. See Werdnig-Hoffmann disease, under disease.

    immature i. An infant born between the ages of 20 and 28 weeks of gestation, weighing 500 to 1000 grams (1.1–2.2 lbs).

    large for gestational age (LGA) i. An infant whose weight is greater than the 90th percentile of that particular gestational age.

    live-born i. An infant who, after being expelled or extracted from the mother, breathes or shows other evidence of life (such as beating of the heart, pulsation of the umbilical cord, and definite movements of involuntary muscles) whether or not the umbilical cord has been cut or the placenta has detached.

    low birth weight i. An infant weighing 2500 grams (5.5 lbs) or less at birth.

    oversize i. Infant weighing over 4000 grams (8.8 lbs).

    postterm i., postmature i. An infant who has completed 42 or more weeks of gestation.

    premature i. An infant born between 28 and 38 weeks of gestation, weighing 1000 to 2500 grams (2.2–5.5 lbs). Popularly called preemie.

    preterm i. General term for an infant born at any time through the 37th week of gestation (259 days).

    small for gestational age (SGA) i. An infant whose weight is less than the 10th percentile for all infants at that particular gestational age.

    stillborn i. An infant who shows no signs of life at birth.

    term i., mature i. An infant born between 38 and 42 weeks of gestation and usually weighing over 2500 grams (5.5 lbs).

    very low birth weight (VLBW) i. An infant weighing less than 1000 grams (2.2 lbs) at birth.

infanticide (in-fan′tĭ-sīd) The killing of an infant by a willful act of commission or omission. The period of infancy as defined in such cases may vary slightly from jurisdiction to jurisdiction.

infantile (in′fan-tīl) Relating to an infant.

infantilism (in′fan-tĭ-lizm) Abnormally slow development of mind or body, or both.

infarct (in′farkt) An area of dead tissue caused most often by obstruction of its arterial supply or, rarely, by obstruction of venous drainage.

    anemic i. See pale infarct.

    bland i. A sterile infarct (i.e., one that is not infected).

    hemorrhagic i. A red and swollen infarct due to infiltration or extravasation of blood. Also called red infarct.

    pale i. Infarct resulting from obstruction of a terminal artery; seen in solid organs (e.g., kidney, spleen) that lack collateral circulation. Also called anemic infarct; white infarct.

    red i. See hemorrhagic infarct.

    septic i. Infarct into which a bacterial infection has spread, occurring usually when microorganisms are present in the occluding embolus and frequently transforming the infarct into an abscess.

    white i. See pale infarct.

infarction (in-fark′shun) 1. The formation of an infarct. 2. An infarct.

    myocardial i. (MI) Deterioration and/or death of a portion of the heart muscle as a result of deprivation of its blood supply, usually due to occlusion of a coronary artery supplying blood to the area; the occlusion may or may not be due to a blood clot (thrombus). Popularly called heart attack; coronary.

    silent myocardial i. Myocardial infarction occurring without producing the characteristic symptoms.

    subendocardial myocardial i. Infarction limited to the inner

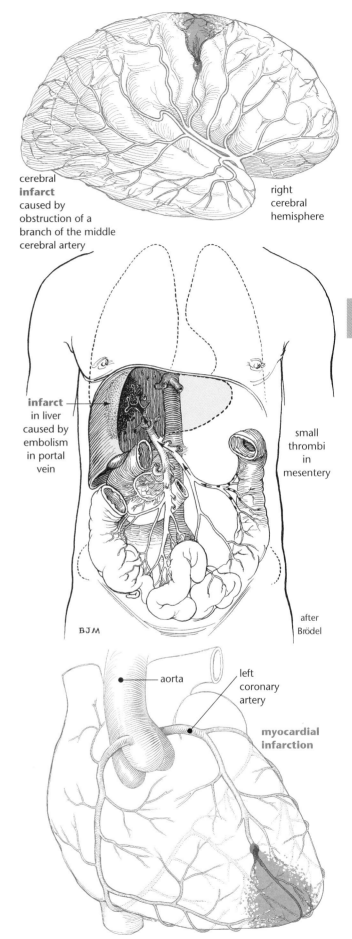

cerebral **infarct** caused by obstruction of a branch of the middle cerebral artery

right cerebral hemisphere

infarct in liver caused by embolism in portal vein

small thrombi in mesentery

BJM

after Brödel

aorta

left coronary artery

myocardial infarction

(subendocardium) one-third to one-half of the ventricular wall of the heart.

   transmural myocardial i. Infarction involving the full thickness of the ventricular wall of the heart.

infect (in-fekt') **1.** To invade and become established in the body; applied to microorganisms. **2.** To contaminate with harmful agents. COMPARE infest.

infectibility (in-fek-tĭ-bil'ĭ-te) The characteristic or the state of an individual that renders him or her capable of being infected.

infection (in-fek'shun) A phenomenon characterized by an inflammatory response to the presence of living microorganisms or their invasion of normally sterile tissue. COMPARE infestation.

   hospital-acquired i. See nosocomial infection.

   inapparent i. The presence of an infection in a person without the occurrence of recognizable clinical manifestations; it is of epidemiological significance because people so infected serve as carriers and spread the infective agent. Also called subclinical infection.

   latent i. A persistent inapparent infection in which the causative organism cannot be detected by currently available methods; it may flare up from time to time under certain conditions. Also called subclinical infection.

   MAC i. See *Mycobacterium avium* complex bacteremia, under bacteremia.

   nosocomial i. An infection acquired as a result of hospitalization or treatment received at a hospital and that was not present or incubating at the time of exposure to the hospital environment; usually caused by exposure to bacteria or fungi either through diagnostic or therapeutic procedures, or from the natural hospital environment (which harbors a multitude of microorganisms from other patient's infectious diseases), or from the hospital staff; predisposing factors include a patient's susceptible state. Common nosocomial infections include those of the genitourinary tract (e.g., from indwelling catheters), lungs (e.g., from respiratory tract instrumentation), surgical wounds, and newborn infants (e.g., epidemic diarrhea in the nursery). Also called hospital-acquired infection.

   perinatal i. Any infection occurring during the time of life between the completion of 20 weeks of gestation and the first 28 days after birth (i.e., during the perinatal period).

   pyogenic i. A pus-producing infection caused by certain bacteria (e.g., *Staphylococcus aureus* and *Streptococcus pyogenes*).

   retrograde i. An infection of a tubular structure that spreads in a direction opposite the natural flow of secretions.

   secondary i. An infection, usually bacterial, occurring in a person already afflicted with an infection due to another microorganism.

   subclinical i. See latent infection.

   terminal i. An acute infection occurring toward the end of another disease (usually chronic) and generally causing death.

   Vincent's i. See necrotizing ulcerative gingivitis, under gingivitis.

infectious (in-fek'shus) Capable of being transmitted with or without direct contact.

infectiousness (in-fek'shus-nes) The state of being infectious.

infective (in-fek'tiv) **1.** Capable of producing infection. **2.** Relating to infection.

infecundity (in-fe-kun'dĭ-te) A woman's inability to bear children.

inferior (in-fēr'e-or) Located in a lower position relative to a point of reference.

infertility (in-fer-til'ĭ-te) **1.** Inability to produce offspring. In males, inability to fertilize the ovum; in females, inability to conceive after one year of regular intercourse without use of contraceptives. Infertility may or may not be reversible. COMPARE sterility. **2.** Inability of a woman to carry a pregnancy to term. Also called impaired fertility.

infest (in-fest') To invade and live as a parasite, usually on the body surface of the host organism (e.g., lice). COMPARE infect.

infestation (in-fes-ta'shun) The presence of parasites, usually on the surface of the body (e.g., lice). The term is sometimes used synonymously with infection. COMPARE infection.

infiltrate (in-fil'trāt) **1.** To pass into the tissue spaces. **2.** Material accumulated in the tissues (e.g., in a lung, detected in x-ray pictures).

infiltration (in-fil-tra'shun) **1.** Accumulation in a tissue of substances that are not ordinarily present in that tissue, or the invasion by cells that are not normal to the location. **2.** Injection of a solution into a tissue (e.g., in local anesthesia).

   fatty i. Abnormal accumulation of fat globules in a cell.

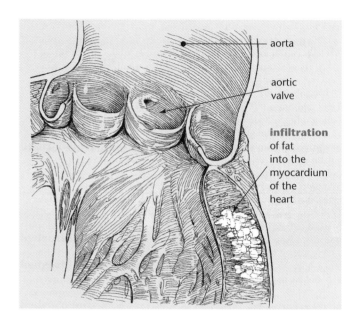

aorta

aortic valve

infiltration of fat into the myocardium of the heart

infirm (in-firm') A weak condition of the body due to disease or old age.

infirmary (in-fir'mah-re) A space in an institution allocated for the short-term care of the sick or injured, especially in a school or camp.

infirmity (in-fir'mĭ-te) A disabling state of the mind or body.

inflammation (in-flah-ma'shun) A protective response of tissues to injury by a physical, chemical, bacterial, or viral agent. The response includes: dilatation of local blood vessels with increased blood flow; exudation of fluid from blood vessels into tissues; and removal or destruction of the injurious material by white blood cells (leukocytes).

   acute i. Inflammation that has a relatively rapid onset and a fairly distinct termination. It demonstrates four cardinal signs: redness, swelling, pain, and increased temperature (in Latin, rubor, tumor, dolor, calor).

   chronic i. The sum of responses mounted by the tissues against a persistent injurious agent. It may follow an acute inflammatory response that failed to destroy the injuring agent, or it may occur without an apparent acute phase. Its duration is long enough to cause insidious but progressive and, often extensive, necrosis of tissue and continuous formation of new blood vessels and deposition of collagen (fibrosis) in the tissues.

inflammatory (in-flam'ah-to-re) Characterized by, resulting from, or causing inflammation.

inflation (in-fla'shun) The act of distending, or the state of being distended by a gas or liquid.

inflection, inflexion (in-flek'shun) The act of bending inward, or the state of being inwardly bent.

influenza (in-flu-en'zah) An acute infectious disease caused by infection with an influenza virus, usually type A or B, often occurring in epidemic outbreaks; marked by headache, fever, chills, sore throat, coughs, and muscle aches. Popularly called the flu; formerly called grippe (grip).

Influenzavirus (in-flu-en'zah-vi'rus) A genus of viruses (family Orthomyxoviridae) that includes serotypes A and B (and probably C), and several subgroups or strains, classified on the basis of their

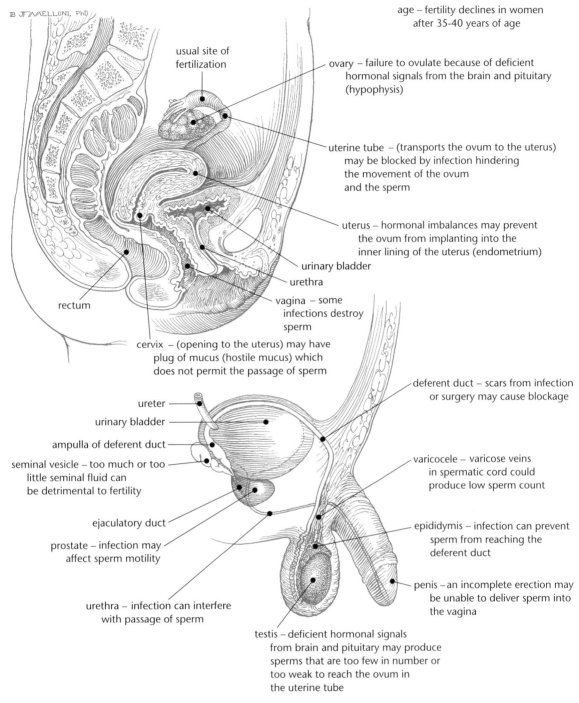

B J TAMELLONI, PhD

usual site of
fertilization

age – fertility declines in women
after 35-40 years of age

ovary – failure to ovulate because of deficient
hormonal signals from the brain and pituitary
(hypophysis)

uterine tube – (transports the ovum to the uterus)
may be blocked by infection hindering
the movement of the ovum
and the sperm

uterus – hormonal imbalances may prevent
the ovum from implanting into the
inner lining of the uterus (endometrium)

urinary bladder

urethra

vagina – some
infections destroy
sperm

rectum

cervix – (opening to the uterus) may have
plug of mucus (hostile mucus) which
does not permit the passage of sperm

deferent duct – scars from infection
or surgery may cause blockage

ureter

urinary bladder

ampulla of deferent duct

seminal vesicle – too much or too
little seminal fluid can
be detrimental to fertility

varicocele – varicose veins
in spermatic cord could
produce low sperm count

epididymis – infection can prevent
sperm from reaching the
deferent duct

ejaculatory duct

prostate – infection may
affect sperm motility

penis – an incomplete erection may
be unable to deliver sperm into
the vagina

urethra – infection can interfere
with passage of sperm

testis – deficient hormonal signals
from brain and pituitary may produce
sperms that are too few in number or
too weak to reach the ovum in
the uterine tube

surface antigens; the cause of respiratory disease in humans and other vertebrates.

infold (in-fōld′) To fold inward, either surgically or as a developmental process of a structure.

information (in-for-ma′shun) **1.** The communication of knowledge. **2.** Knowledge derived from experience, study, or instruction.

    genetic i. See genetic code, under code.

informed consent (in-form′ed kon-sent′) See under consent.

infra- Prefix meaning below; beneath.

infraclavicular (in-frah-klah-vik′u-lar) Below a collarbone (clavicle).

infraclusion (in-frah-kloo′zhun) Condition in which a tooth fails to erupt. Also called infraocclusion.

infradian (in-fra′de-an) Relating to biorhythms occurring in cycles less frequent than 24 hours. Also called infradian rhythm.

infraglottic (in-frah-glot′ik) See subglottic.

infrahyoid (in-frah-hi′oid) Below the hyoid bone, in the neck.

inframandibular (in-frah-man-dib′u-lar) Below the lower jaw.

infraocclusion (in-frah-o-kloo′zhun) See infraclusion.

infraorbital (in-frah-or′bi-tal) Beneath or below the eye socket (orbit). Also called suborbital.

infrapatellar (in-frah-pah-tel′ar) Below the kneecap (patella).

infrared (in-frah-red′) The electromagnetic radiation beyond the red end of the spectrum with wavelengths between 770 and 1000 nm, too long to be seen by the human eye; usually felt as heat.

infrascapular (in-frah-skap′u-lar) Below the shoulder blade (scapula).

infraspinous (in-frah-spi′nus) Below a spinous process.

infrasplenic (in-frah-splen′ik) Below or beneath the spleen.

infrasternal (in-frah-ster′nal) Below the breastbone (sternum).

infratrochlear (in-frah-trok′le-ar) Located below the pulley (trochlea) of the superior oblique muscle of the eye.

infraumbilical (in-frah-um-bil′ĭ-kal) Below the navel (umbilicus).

infrazygomatic (in-frah-zi-go-mat′ik) Below the cheekbone (zygoma).

infundibuliform (in-fun-dib′u-li-form) Shaped like a funnel.

infundibulum (in-fun-dib′u-lum), pl. infundib′ula Any funnel-shaped structure or passage; when used alone, the term refers to the infundibulum of the pituitary (hypophysis).

    ethmoidal i. The long, curved, funnel-shaped passage connecting the anterior ethmoidal air cells and the frontal sinus with the nasal cavity, usually at the lateral wall of the middle meatus.

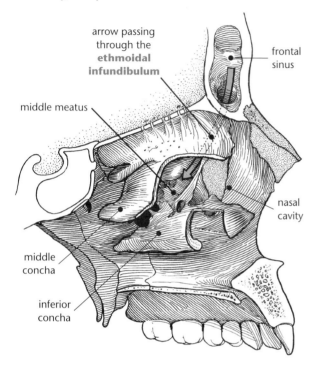

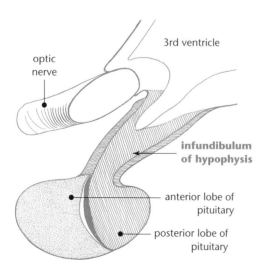

    i. of heart The upper portion of the right ventricle from which the pulmonary trunk arises; the conus arteriosus.

    i. of hypophysis The infundibulum of the pituitary (hypophysis); it consists of two parts: a neural core (infundibular stem) containing the neural connections of the posterior lobe of the pituitary (neurohypophysis) and an extension of the anterior lobe of the pituitary (adenohypophysis) that surrounds most of the infundibular stem. Also called hypophyseal stalk; pituitary stalk; infundibular stalk.

    i. of lung In the embryo, the minute expanded termination of bronchioles from which the air sacs (pulmonary alveoli) develop after the fifth to sixth month of development.

    i. of uterine tube The lateral, funnel-shaped opening of the fallopian (uterine) tube.

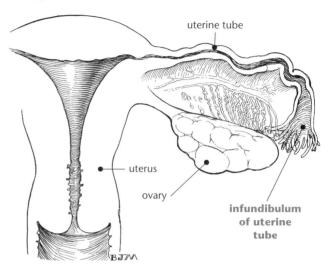

infusible (in-fu′zĭ-bl) **1.** Resistant to changes by heat. **2.** Capable of being infused.

infusion (in-fu′zhun) **1.** The introduction of a fluid (other than blood) into a blood vessel or body cavity for therapeutic or diagnostic purposes. **2.** The soaking or steeping of a substance in water in order to extract its soluble constituents. **3.** The resulting liquid.

ingesta (in-jes′tah) Any material that has been swallowed or is intended to be swallowed.

ingestion (in-jes′chun) The swallowing of food, drink, or medicines.

ingestive (in-jes′tiv) Relating to ingestion.

inguen (ing′gwen) The area of the body between the abdomen and thigh; the groin.

inguinal (ing′gwĭ-nal) Relating to the groin (inguen).

inhalant (in-ha′lant) Any therapeutic agent taken by inhalation.

inhalation (in-hah-la′shun) The act of breathing in.

inhale (in-hāl′) To breathe in; to inspire.

inhaler (in-ha′ler) A device for introducing medicinal substances into the respiratory tract by inhalation.

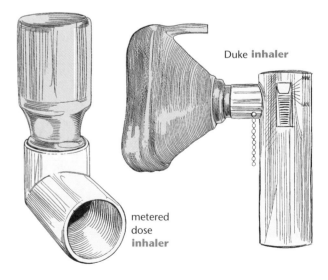

inherent (in-hēr′ent) Belonging naturally; intrinsic.

inheritance (in-her′ĭ-tans) **1.** In genetics, the process of transmitting characters from parent to offspring. **2.** The characters so transmitted.

autosomal i. The transmission of a character determined by a gene located in any chromosome in the body other than those of the sex cells (sperm and ovum).

dominant i. An inheritance that is manifest when the individual is heterozygous for the mutant gene (i.e., the individual has one copy of the mutant gene from one parent and one copy of the normal gene from the other parent).

holandric i. Transmission of a character determined by a gene on the Y chromosome (i.e., occurring only in males).

hologynic i. Transmission of a character from a mother to all her daughters but not to her sons (i.e., occurring only in females).

mosaic i. Inheritance characterized by the dominance of paternal influence in one group of cells and the dominance of the maternal influence in another.

recessive i. An inheritance that is manifest only when an individual is homozygous for the mutant gene (i.e., the individual carries a double dose of the mutant gene, one from each parent).

sex-linked i. See sex linkage, under linkage.

inherited (in-her′it-ed) Acquired through a genetic determination; inborn.

inhibition (in-hĭ-bish′un) **1.** Restriction or suppression of a function or activity. **2.** An unconscious suppression or restraint of instinctual drives or impulses; may interfere with carrying out specific activities.

inhibitor (in-hib′ĭ-tor) Any agent or nerve that represses or diminishes a physiologic activity.

ACE i. See angiotensin-converting enzyme inhibitor.

angiotensin-converting enzyme i. (ACEI) Any of a class of drugs that inhibit the action of the enzyme kininase II, which converts angiotensin I to angiotensin II; used in the treatment of high blood pressure (hypertension) and congestive heart failure. Also called ACE inhibitor.

monoamine oxidase i. (MAOI) Any of a group of drugs used in the treatment of depression and high blood pressure (hypertension).

inion (in′e-on) The most protruding point of the external occipital protuberance (at the back of the skull); used as a fixed craniometric point.

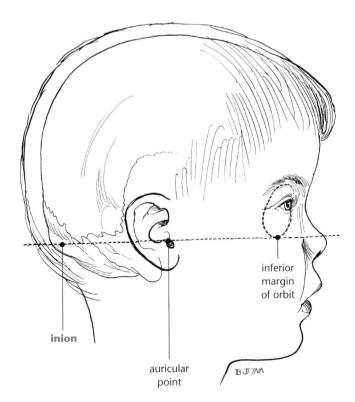

inion

auricular point

inferior margin of orbit

BJTN

initiation (ĭ-nish-e-a′shun) In chemical carcinogenesis, the first stage in the process leading to the development of a cancerous tumor; characterized by irreversible mutagenic changes inflicted upon the DNA of cells by a chemical agent. Affected (initiated) cells do not, at this time, grow and proliferate abnormally; unlike normal cells, however, they give rise to a tumor when subsequently exposed to an appropriate chemical (the promoter). See also promotion.

inject (in-jekt′) To drive a fluid into a body part.

injectable (in-jek′ta-bl) Any substance that may be injected.

injection (in-jek′shun) **1.** The act of introducing a fluid into a tissue or body cavity. **2.** The fluid injected. **3.** Popular term for a state of visible congestion or hyperemia, as of the eye blood vessels.

hypodermic i. See subcutaneous injection.

intra-articular i. An injection into the cavity of a joint.

intramuscular (IM) i. Injection into a muscle.

intrathecal i. Injection into the subarachnoid space (e.g., of an anesthetic solution to induce spinal anesthesia).

intravenous (IV) i. Injection into a vein.

subcutaneous i. Injection into the loose tissue just beneath the skin. Also called hypodermic injection; popularly called hypo.

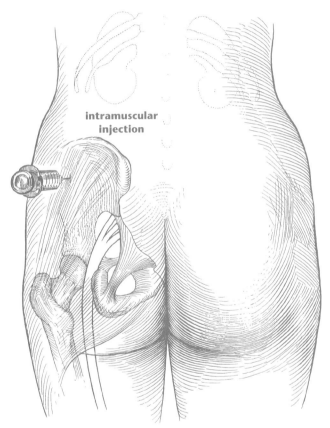

intramuscular injection

injector (in-jek′tor) Device for administering injection (e.g., a syringe).

jet i. A machine that, through high pressure, forces a liquid through a small orifice.

injure (in′jur) To damage, wound, or hurt.

injury (in′ju-re) Damage to any part of the body by any of a wide variety of external means (mechanical, chemical, radiant, electrical, or thermal) and which may or may not cause a disability.

birth i. Damage sustained by an infant during labor and delivery. Usual predisposing conditions include prematurity, prolonged pregnancy, breech birth, an abnormally large fetus, a small maternal pelvic opening, and the use of forceps to pull the infant from the birth canal.

blast i. Injury caused by sudden changes in atmospheric pressure, as occurs in munitions explosions or in explosive home and industrial accidents; pressure waves may suddenly increase the pressure in the body's air-filled cavities (e.g., within the lungs and intestines), causing a burst and hemorrhage; or they may compress the body surface and exert internal pressure on solid organs (e.g., liver and spleen), causing laceration and rupture of these organs.

blunt i. Injury to superficial and/or internal structures caused by the sudden impact of a blunt object that lacerates, tears, or crushes as opposed to the slashing of a sharp instrument; seen frequently in traffic accidents, criminal assaults, and certain sports (e.g., the injuries to the lungs or heart sustained by a football player when hit forcefully on the chest by the helmet of another player).

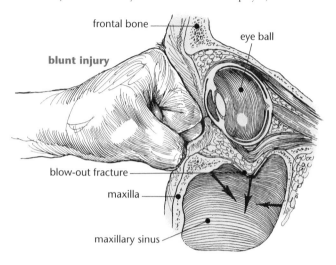

cell i. Any adverse influence that deranges the cell's ability to maintain a constant physiologic equilibrium in the living body; they range from external physical violence to genetic deficiency of a vital substance (e.g., an enzyme).

closed head i. Brain damage produced by nonpenetrating trauma and occurring in several degrees of severity, i.e., concussion (with transient loss of brain function, including loss of consciousness), contusion (with rupture of blood vessels near the brain surface and bleeding into its substance), or laceration (with tearing of brain tissue, profound dysfunction, and possible death).

cold i. Localized tissue damage caused by prolonged exposure to cold (not necessarily freezing) temperatures. See also immersion foot, under foot; frostbite.

countercoup i. Rupture of superficial small blood vessels in the brain and bleeding into the deeper brain substance, caused by a blow to the head and occurring on the side opposite the point of impact. The momentum of the brain in motion, propelled by the blow, is suddenly stopped by the skull on the opposite side, causing the damage.

crush i. Injury that results from severe muscle damage and release of muscle cell constituents which may cause systemic reactions (e.g., kidney failure, shock, heart irregularities).

cumulative i. See cumulative trauma, under trauma.

degloving i. Avulsion of the skin and subcutaneous fat usually of the upper extremity, sometimes the foot, as might occur when the limb is caught in machine-driven rollers, a common industrial accident; vessels, nerves, and muscles may also be avulsed. Also called wringer injury.

diffuse axonal i. (DAI) Brain injury involving a shearing and widespread tearing of axons in the white matter just beneath the outer gray layer (cortex) of the brain.

immersion blast i. A blast injury to anyone in the water caused by the shock waves of an underwater explosion.

injection i. Injury caused by forceful and sudden introduction of a material through the skin under high pressure (hundreds of pounds per square inch); usually occurs as an industrial accident; the material may be gas, water, paint, oil, etc.; the point or points of entrance may be occasionally undetectable.

occupational i. Any injury resulting from and in the course of work.

open head i. Brain damage associated with skull fractures, penetration of brain substance, and a high incidence of infection. Severity depends on extent and area of damage.

physeal i., physial i. Colloquial term for any injury involving the ends (epiphyses) of long bones.

repetitive motion i. (RMI) Damage to muscles, nerves, or bones from performing activities for prolonged periods.

scalping i. Traumatic avulsion of the scalp (e.g., when hair becomes entangled in a hay baler).

soft-tissue i. Damage to skin, muscle, fascia, ligament, tendon, fat, or any other tissue of the body that is not bone or cartilage.

whiplash i. Injury to muscles and ligaments of the neck by forcible and sudden bending backward and then forward (hyperextension and hyperflexion) of the neck, as seen in rear-end automobile collision, caused by acceleration-deceleration forces of the collision. Also called whiplash.

wringer i. See degloving injury.

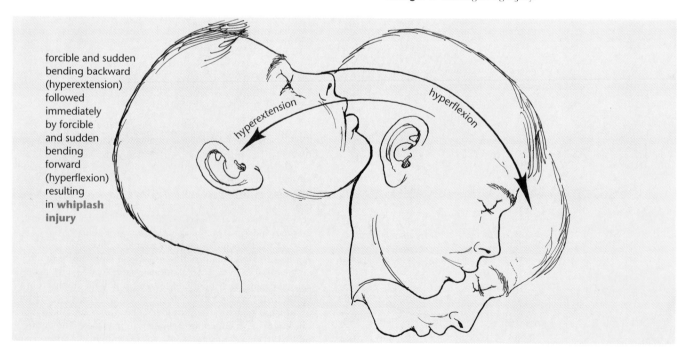

forcible and sudden bending backward (hyperextension) followed immediately by forcible and sudden bending forward (hyperflexion) resulting in **whiplash injury**

inlay (in'la) A restorative material (e.g., gold, plastic, porcelain) that is fitted and cemented into the cavity preparation of a tooth.

inlet (in'let) A passage leading into a cavity.

pelvic i. The upper opening of the minor (true) pelvis; the space within the pelvic brim.

thoracic i. The kidney-shaped inlet of the chest cavity bounded in back by the first thoracic vertebra, at the sides by the first ribs, and in front by the upper border of the breastbone (sternum). Also called superior thoracic aperture.

innate (in'nāt) Present at birth.

innervation (in-er-va'shun) The nerve supply of a given body structure or area.

innidiation (ĭ-nid-e-a'shun) Multiplication of cells in a location where they have been carried by the lymph or by the bloodstream.

innocent (in'o-sent) Benign; not pathologic; applied to certain heart murmurs.

innocuous (ĭ-nok'u-us) Harmless.

innominate (ĭ-nom'ĭ-nāt) Unnamed; formerly applied to certain anatomic structures, such as the innominate bone (hipbone) and the innominate artery (brachiocephalic trunk).

innoxious (ĭ-nok'shus) Harmless; not injurious.

inoculable (ĭ-nok'u-lah-bl) Susceptible to transmission by innoculation.

inoculate (ĭ-nok'u-lāt) 1. To introduce an infective agent or antigenic material into the body for preventive, therapeutic or experimental purposes. 2. In microbiology, to introduce any material into a culture medium for study purposes.

inoculation (ĭ-nok-u-la'shun) The act or process of inoculating.

inoculum (ĭ-nok'u-lum) Material introduced by inoculation.

inoperable (in-op'er-ah-bl) Not suitable for any surgical procedure.

inorganic (in-or-gan'ik) Neither composed of, nor derived from, vegetable or animal material.

inosculate (in-os'ku-lāt) To make continuous or unite by small openings or anastomosis.

inosculation (in-os-ku-la'shun) See anastomosis.

inositol (in-o'sī-tol) A substance classified as a member of the vitamin B complex; formed in plant and animal tissue.

inotropic (in-o-trop'ik) Affecting muscular contraction.

negatively i. Inhibiting muscular contraction.

positively i. Enhancing muscular contraction.

inpatient (in-pa'shent) A person admitted into a hospital or any health care institution for a period of at least one overnight for observation, diagnosis, or treatment.

insalivation (in-sal-ī-va'shun) The mixing of food with saliva during chewing (mastication).

insane (in-sān') In legal contexts, relating to insanity, or to one who is of unsound mind. The term is no longer used in psychiatry.

insanity (in-san'ĭ-te) Term used in a legal context to indicate a mental state in which one is legally nonresponsible or incompetent for some or all purposes. Originally a medical term referring to loss of reason, by the end of the nineteenth century it came to include diseases of the intellect, the will, or the emotions; since the 1920s, the term has not been used in the United States for medical purposes but continues to have multiple legal meanings, all of which involve some degree of nonresponsibility or incompetence for legal purposes. The law defines different kinds or degrees of insanity (e.g., for making a will, making a business contract, committing criminal acts, or reasonable likelihood of imminent danger to oneself or others); insanity for one act does not necessarily mean insanity for other kinds of acts.

inscription (in-skrip'shun) The part of a pharmaceutical prescription stipulating the names and amounts of ingredients to be used by the pharmacist.

insect (in'sekt) Any member of the class Insecta; important in forensic investigations. See also forensic entomology, under entomology.

necrophagous i. An insect that feeds on tissues of a dead body; it is the first type of insect invading a corpse.

omnivorous i. An insect feeding on dead tissues and any other type of insect.

predatory i. A type that feeds on necrophagous insects; it is the second type of insect invading a corpse, after enough time has elapsed for necrophagous insects to accumulate.

insectarium (in-sek-ta're-um) A place in which living insects are kept and bred for scientific purposes.

insecticide (in-sek'tī-sīd) Any agent that kills insects.

insectifuge (in-sek'tī-fūj) Any agent that repels insects.

insemination (in-sem-ī-na'shun) 1. Introduction of seminal fluid into the vagina. Also called semination. 2. Fertilization of an ovum.

artificial i. Deposit of sperm in the vagina, cervix, or within the uterine cavity by means other than sexual intercourse.

heterologous i., (artificial insemination, donor) (AID) Artificial insemination with sperm from a donor other than the woman's husband.

homologous i., (artificial insemination, husband) (AIH) Artificial insemination with sperm from the woman's husband.

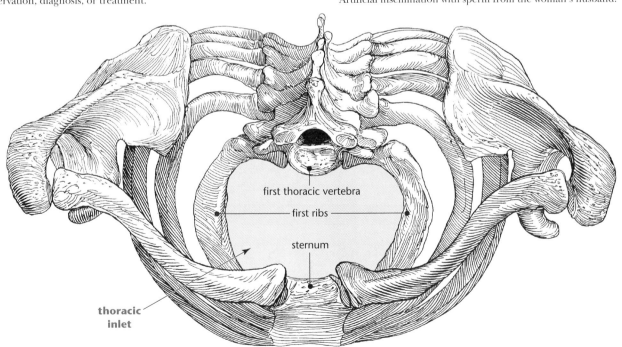

first thoracic vertebra
first ribs
sternum
thoracic inlet

intrauterine i. (IUI) The direct placement of sperm in the intrauterine cavity using a washed and concentrated specimen (i.e., sperm that has been diluted and centrifuged to remove the prostaglandin-containing seminal fluid); usually performed when infertility is due to a cervical condition (i.e., to bypass the uterine cervix when there are problems with this structure or its secretions).

therapeutic i. Procedure in which fresh sperm, either husband's (TIH) or donor's (TID), is placed in a woman's vagina, cervix, or uterus; performed in the periovulatory part of the menstrual cycle.

insensible (in-sen′sĭ-bl) **1.** Imperceptible by the senses. **2.** Unconscious.

insert (in′sert) In molecular cloning, a fragment of DNA cloned into a DNA molecule (the vector) for replication in a particular host.

insertion (in-ser′shun) **1.** The site of attachment of a muscle to a bone that is most movable during the action of that muscle. **2.** A chromosomal abnormality in which part of the material from one chromosome is interposed into a dissimilar chromosome.

insidious (in-sid′e-us) Developing or spreading harmfully in an imperceptible way.

insight (in′sit) **1.** The ability to understand the real meaning of a situation. **2.** Self-understanding. **3.** In psychiatry, the extent to which a person is aware of the reasons for certain actions or thoughts.

in situ (in si′tu) Latin for in place; in its original or normal position. The term is applied especially to an early stage in cancerous tumor development in which abnormal cells are still restricted to the site of origin (i.e., they have not invaded tissues beyond their original confines). Sometimes used synonymously with precancerous.

insoluble (in-sol′u-bl) Not capable of entering into solution.

insomnia (in-som′ne-ah) Inability to sleep under normal conditions; three varieties are recognized: inability to fall asleep upon retiring; intermittent waking after falling asleep; unusually early awakening (e.g., two hours before one's usual waking time) and inability to return to sleep.

insomniac (in-som′ne-ak) A person affected by insomnia.

inspiration (in-spĭ-ra′shun) Inhalation; breathing in.

inspiratory (in-spi′rah-to-re) Relating to inspiration.

inspire (in-spīr′) To breathe in; to inhale.

inspissate (in-spis′āt) **1.** To thicken or bring about inspissation. **2.** To undergo inspissation.

inspissation (in-spis-sa′shun) The process of thickening or decreasing the liquidity of a fluid (e.g., by evaporation).

inspissator (in-spis′a-tor) Device for air-drying fluids.

instability (in-stah-bil′ĭ-te) A lack of physical or emotional stability.

posttraumatic nervous i. See posttraumatic syndrome, under syndrome.

instep (in′step) The arched middle part of the dorsum of the foot.

instillate (in′stil-āt) Any liquid agent used in instillation.

instillation (in-stil-la′shun) The gradual, drop-by-drop delivery of a liquid into a body part or cavity. Unlike irrigation, in which the liquid is removed within minutes, the instillate is left in place.

instinct (in′stinkt) An inherent drive or tendency to act or respond in a certain way without the aid of reason.

institutionalization (in-stĭ-tu′shun-al-ĭ-za′shun) **1.** The commitment of an individual to a health care or custodial institution (e.g., mental hospital, state-run nursing home, prison). **2.** The adaptation of an institutionalized individual to the routines of the institutional environment, and/or loss of ability to live outside the institution.

instrumentation (in-stroo-men-ta′shun) The use of instruments in any therapeutic procedure.

insuccation (in-sŭ-ka′shun) The thorough soaking of a crude drug prior to, or in the process of, extracting its principle.

insudate (in′su-dāt) Fluid passed into blood vessels through the blood vessel walls.

insufficiency (in-sŭ-fish′en-se) Inability to perform a normal function.

acute adrenocortical i. Inadequate secretion of adrenocortical hormone by the outer layer (cortex) of the adrenal glands; it may result from lesions in the adrenal cortex; most commonly occurs as a

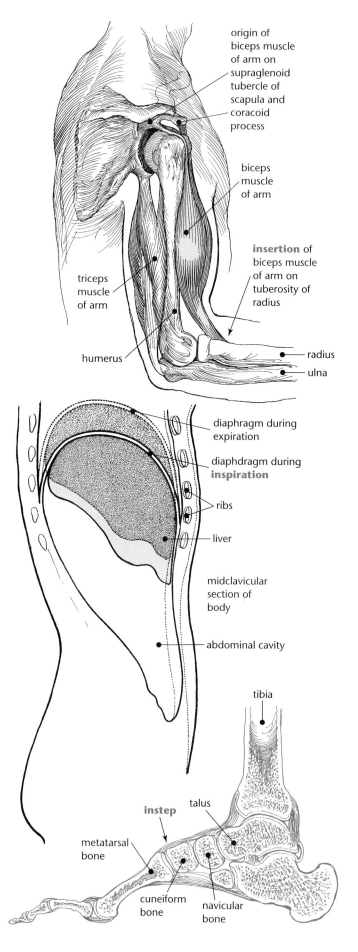

origin of biceps muscle of arm on supraglenoid tubercle of scapula and coracoid process

biceps muscle of arm

insertion of biceps muscle of arm on tuberosity of radius

triceps muscle of arm

humerus

radius

ulna

diaphragm during expiration

diaphdragm during **inspiration**

ribs

liver

midclavicular section of body

abdominal cavity

tibia

instep

talus

metatarsal bone

cuneiform bone

navicular bone

complication of corticosteroid therapy, e.g., in patients being treated with high doses of synthetic glucocorticoids (such as prednisone) who are suddenly subjected to trauma or develop an infection, or if the therapy is withdrawn rapidly; the condition may also occur in massive adrenal hemorrhage, as in the Waterhouse-Friderichsen syndrome; manifestations include nausea, vomiting, hypotension, and collapse. Also called addisonian crisis; adrenal crisis.

adrenocortical i. Reduced function of the adrenal cortex. Also called hypocorticoidism; hypocorticism.

aortic i. See valvular insufficiency.

cardiac i. See heart failure, under failure.

chronic adrenocortical i. See Addison's disease, under disease.

coronary i. Insufficient blood flow (ischemia) through the coronary arteries to the heart muscle, leading to prolonged pain or discomfort (angina).

mitral i. See valvular insufficiency.

posttraumatic pulmonary i. See adult respiratory distress syndrome, under syndrome.

primary chronic adrenocortical i. See Addison's disease, under disease.

pulmonary i. See valvular insufficiency.

pyloric i. A flaccid condition of the sphincter muscle closing the lowest portion of the stomach, allowing regurgitation of intestinal contents from the duodenum into the stomach.

renal i. Defective kidney function, especially decreased glomerular filtration and consequent increase in blood levels of urea and creatinine.

tricuspid i. See valvular insufficiency.

valvular i. Failure of a heart valve to close tightly after blood has passed through it, thus allowing regurgitation of blood; named according to the valve involved (e.g., aortic, mitral, pulmonary, or tricuspid).

venous i. Inadequate drainage of blood from a part resulting from a swollen condition of that part.

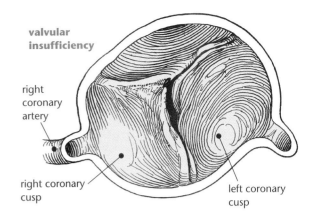

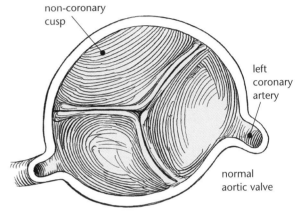

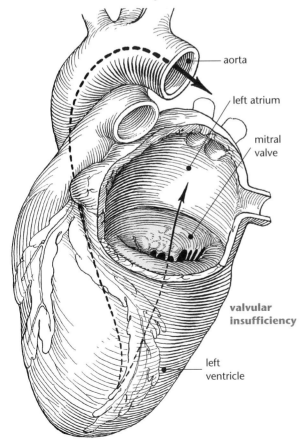

insufflate (in-sŭf'lāt) **1.** To blow into (e.g., in artificial respiration). **2.** To blow a gas, medicated vapor, powder, or anesthetic into a body cavity.

insufflation (in-sŭ-fla'shun) The act of blowing a gas, medicated vapor, powder, or anesthetic into a body cavity.

perirenal i. Injection of air or carbon dioxide in the area around the kidneys for x-ray visualization of the adrenal (suprarenal) glands.

tubal i. The transvaginal introduction of a gas, usually carbon dioxide, into the uterus to determine whether the fallopian (uterine) tubes are free of obstruction. Also called tubal insufflation test; Rubin's test.

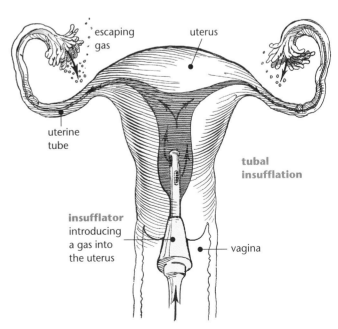

insufflator (in'sŭ-fla-tor) Instrument used in insufflation.

insula (in'su-lah) The portion of cerebral cortex located deep in the lateral sulcus of each hemisphere of the cerebrum. Also called island of Reil.

insular (in'su-lar) **1.** Relating to the insula. **2.** Relating to the islets of Langerhans.

insulate (in'sŭ-lāt) To prevent passage of heat, sound, electricity, or radioactivity by interposing a material with nonconductive properties.

insulation (in-sŭ-la'shun) **1.** The act of insulating. **2.** The material used to insulate. **3.** The state of being insulated.

insulator (in'su-la-tor) Any material or substance used to effect insulation.

insulin (in'su-lin) A hormone produced by the beta cells of the islets of Langerhans in the pancreas and secreted in response to increased blood sugar (glucose) levels, vagus nerve stimulation, and other factors; it is concerned with regulating carbohydrate, lipid, and protein metabolism. Deficiency of insulin results in diabetes mellitus.

human i. A protein prepared either by recombinant DNA techniques or by semisynthetic processes from porcine insulin; the resulting product has the normal structure of the human form.

intermediate-acting i. Any insulin preparation that has a 2 to 4 hour onset of action after injection, lasting 18 to 24 hours, with 8 to 10 hours of peak action (e.g., NPH insulin; lente insulin).

isophane i. See NPH insulin.

lente i. A preparation of intermediate action, consisting of a mixture of 30% semilente and 70% ultralente insulin.

long-acting i. Any insulin preparation that has a 4 to 5 hour onset of action after injection, lasting 25 to 36 hours, with 8 to 14 hours of peak action (e.g., ultralente insulin; protamine zinc insulin).

NPH i. An intermediate-acting suspension of insulin, protamine and zinc. N denotes a neutral solution; P, the protamine zinc insulin content; H, its developer, Hans C. Hagedorn, M.D. Also called isophane insulin.

premixed i. A preparation containing both a short-acting (regular) and an intermediate-acting (NPH) insulin. The preparation has a 15 to 30 minute onset of action after injection lasting 18 to 24 hours, with 10 to 12 hours of peak action.

protamine zinc i. (PZI) A long-acting preparation consisting of a suspension of insulin, protamine, and zinc chloride. A seldom-used preparation in the United States.

regular i. A short-acting aqueous solution of crystalline zinc insulin; its action begins within 15 minutes after subcutaneous injection, peaking at l to 3 hours, and lasting 5 to 7 hours; can be injected intravenously or used in continuous subcutaneous pumps.

semilente i. A short-acting preparation consisting of an amorphous form of insulin and zinc in acetate buffer.

short-acting i., rapid-acting i. Any insulin preparation that begins to act 15 to 30 minutes after injection, lasting 5 to 7 hours, with 1 to 3 hours of peak action (e.g., regular insulin; semilente insulin).

ultralente i. A long-acting preparation containing a suspension of large insulin crystals.

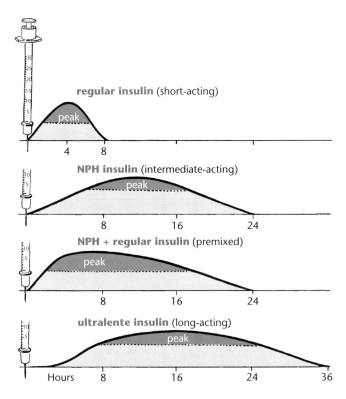

insulinoma, insuloma (in-su-lin-o'mah, in-su-lo'mah) An insulin-producing tumor of the islet cells of the pancreas.

insulitis (in-su-li'tis) Destruction of beta cells of the pancreas by cellular infiltration of the patient's own immune system (autoimmunity), as occurs in insulin-dependent diabetes (type I diabetes); believed to be related to a genetic mechanism or triggered by an environmental agent (e.g., virus or unknown toxin).

insult (in'sult) An injury or irritation.

integration (in-tĕ-gra'shun) **1.** The process of bringing all parts together to form a whole (e.g., the building of living substance by

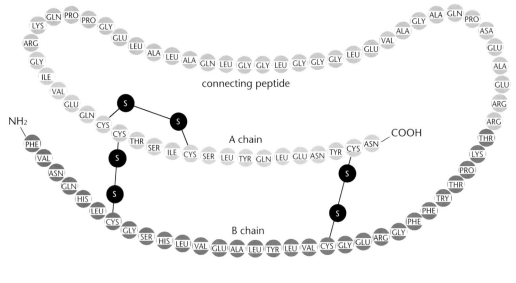

The amino acid sequence of proinsulin; it converts to **insulin** when the connecting peptide detaches from the A chain and B chain before it is released into the bloodstream.

assimilation of nutritive material). **2.** In psychiatry, the organization of new and old experiences and individual characteristics and capacities into the personality. **3.** The condition of being combined.

integrin (in′te-grin) Any of a family of glycoproteins bound to the cell membrane that promote cell adhesion and participate in many important processes, including embryological development, wound healing, and immune and nonimmune defense activities.

integument (in-teg′u-ment) A covering tissue (e.g., skin or a membranous cover or capsule of organs).

intelligence (in-tel′ĭ-jens) **1.** The faculty of thought, reason, and understanding. **2.** The ability to acquire and apply knowledge.

   abstract i. The capacity to understand and manipulate symbols and abstract ideas (e.g., in problem solving).

   artificial i. (AI) Computer programming that includes certain features usually associated with human intelligence.

   mechanical i. Ability to acquire knowledge and understanding of technical mechanisms.

   social i. An aptitude for understanding and coping reasonably with human relationships.

intensity (in-ten′sĭ-te) A magnitude of activity, tension, strength, etc. (e.g., of sound, radiation, brightness).

intensive (in-ten′siv) relating to or characterized by intensity (e.g., an exhaustive and concentrated form of treatment).

intensivist (in-ten′sĭ-vist) A physician who specializes in intensive care.

intention (in-ten′shun) **1.** A process. **2.** Objective.

   healing by first i. See under healing.

   healing by second i. See under healing.

   healing by third i. See under healing.

inter- Prefix meaning between; among.

interacinous (in-ter-as′ĭ-nus) Between the glandular units (acini) of a gland.

interaction (in-ter-ak′shun) Reciprocal action.

   cognate i. In immunology, direct interaction between a processed antigen on the surface of a B lymphocyte and T lymphocyte receptor and eventual antibody production.

interalveolar (in-ter-al-ve′o-lar) Between the air sacs (alveoli) of the lungs.

interarticular (in-ter-ar-tik′u-lar) Between two joints or joint surfaces.

interatrial (in-ter-a′tre-al) Between the two upper chambers (atria) of the heart.

interbrain (in′ter-brān) The midline structure of the brain with symmetrical right and left halves that forms the greater part of the median slit-like third ventricle; it contains the thalamus and hypothalamus on each side and narrows caudally to continue into the aqueduct of the midbrain. Also called diencephalon.

intercadence (in-ter-kād′ens) The occurrence of an extra pulse beat, between two regular beats.

intercalary (in-ter′kah-ler-e) Interposed between two others. Also called intercalated.

intercalated (in-ter′kah-la-ted) See intercalary.

intercalative (in-ter-kah-la′tiv) Capable of inserting itself between two original or existing parts; applied to certain chemicals capable of inserting themselves between successive bases in the DNA molecule and preventing its proper functioning.

interclavicular (in-ter-klah-vik′u-lar) Between the collarbones (clavicles).

intercondylar, intercondylic (in-ter-kon′dĭ-lar, in-ter-kon-dil′ik) Between two condyles.

intercostal (in-ter-kos′tal) Between two successive ribs.

intercourse (in′ter-kōrs) **1.** Interchange or interactions between or among people. **2.** Coitus.

   sexual i. Coitus.

intercristal (in-ter-kris′tal) Between two crests of a bone.

intercurrent (in-ter-kur′ent) Occurring during the course of a pre-existing disease.

interdental (in-ter-den′tal) Between adjacent teeth of the same dental arch.

interdentium (in-ter-den′she-um) The space between two adjacent teeth.

interdigital (in-ter-dij′ĭ-tal) Between fingers or toes.

interdigitation (in-ter-dij-ĭ-ta′shun) **1.** Interlocking of structures by means of fingerlike processes. **2.** The processes so interlocked.

interdisciplinary (in-ter-dis′ĭ-pli-ner′e) Drawing from, contributing to, or cooperating with two or more fields of study.

interface (in′ter-fās) A common boundary between two different materials or bodies or between two electronic devices.

interfacial (in-ter-fa′shal) Relating to an interface.

interference (in-ter-fēr′ens) **1.** A hampering of an action or effect. **2.** In atrioventricular (A-V) dissociation, the interruption of the regular rhythm of the heart ventricles by activation derived from the atria.

interferon (in-ter-fēr′on) (INF) Any of a family of proteins produced by certain body cells in response to invasion by viruses and other intracellular parasites; it interferes with proliferation of the virus and is effective against such protozoan infections as malaria; may also inhibit growth of cancerous tumors.

interictal (in-ter-ik′tal) Denoting the interval between convulsions.

interleukin (in-ter-loo′kin) (IL) Any of a group of molecules (IL-1 through IL-7) produced by a variety of cells; they mediate cellular activities by acting as messengers transmitting signals between cells.

interleukin-1 (in-ter-loo′kin) (IL-1) A hormonelike molecule (cytokine) with multiple biological activities (metabolic, endocrine, immunologic, hematologic), including the ability to induce fever during inflammatory reactions; in the immune system, it acts upon macrophages and monocytes, enhancing their antitumor activities by inducing its own production and the production of other hormonelike substances such as tumor-necrosis factor (TNF) and interleukin-6 (IL-6).

interleukin-2 (in-ter-loo′kin) (IL-2) A glycoprotein that induces proliferation of responsive T lymphocytes; released by certain activated cells.

interlobar (in-ter-lo′bar) Between two lobes.

interlobular (in-ter-lob′u-lar) Between two lobules.

intermediate (in-ter-me′de-it) **1.** Between two extremes. **2.** A substance formed in a stage of a chemical reaction, and necessary for the eventual formation of the final product.

intermenstrual (in-ter-men′stroo-al) Denoting the interval between two consecutive menstrual periods.

intermittence, intermittency (in-ter-mit′ens, in-ter-mit′en-se) The characteristic of being recurrent (often at regular intervals); not continuous.

intermuscular (in-ter-mus′ku-lar) Between muscles or muscle groups.

intern (in′tern) **1.** A recent medical school graduate who receives supervised practical training by assisting in the medical and surgical care of patients at a hospital, or one in the first year of specialized postgraduate training. **2.** A predoctoral clinical psychology student who receives supervised practical training in the diagnosis and treatment of patients with psychiatric disorders.

internal (in-ter′nal) Located within or inside; away from the surface.

internalization (in-ter-nal-ĭ-za′shun) In psychiatry, the unconscious process of taking into one's sense of self aspects of significant persons.

International Agency for Research on Cancer (IARC) A scientific institution within the World Health Organization (WHO) concerned with investigating potential human carcinogens; it supports experimental studies on animals.

International Classification of Impairments, Disabilities, and Handicaps (ICIDH) A systematic taxonomy of the consequences of injury and disease; first attempted and published by the World Health Organization (WHO) in 1980.

International System of Units (SI) A complete system of units, based on the metric system, to which has been added units of time, electric current, temperature, and luminous intensity; the abbreviation SI is from the French equivalent, *Système International.*

INTERNATIONAL SYSTEM OF UNITS (SI)

Quantity	Name	Symbol
SI base units:		
length	meter	m
mass	kilogram	kg
time	second	s
electric current	ampere	A
thermodynamic temperature	kelvin	K
amount of substance	mole	mol
luminous intensity	candela	cd
SI supplementary units:		
plane angle	radian	rad
solid angle	steradian	sr

PREFIXES AND THEIR SYMBOLS USED TO DESIGNATE DECIMAL MULTIPLES AND SUBMULTIPLES

Prefix	Symbol	Factor
tera	T	$10^{12} =$
giga	G	$10^{9} = 1\,000\,000\,000$
mega	M	$10^{6} = 1\,000\,000$
kilo	k	$10^{3} = 1\,000$
hecto	h	$10^{2} = 100$
deka	da	$10^{1} = 10$
deci	d	$10^{-1} = 0.1$
centi	c	$10^{-2} = 0.01$
milli	m	$10^{-3} = 0.001$
micro	μ	$10^{-6} = 0.000\,001$
nano	n	$10^{-9} = 0.000\,000\,001$
pico	p	$10^{-12} = 0.000\,000\,000\,001$
femto	f	$10^{-15} = 0.000\,000\,000\,000\,001$
atto	a	$10^{-18} = 0.000\,000\,000\,000\,000\,001$

EXAMPLES OF SI DERIVED UNITS EXPRESSED IN TERMS OF BASE UNITS

Quantity	SI unit	Unit Symbol
area	square meter	m^2
volume	cubic meter	m^3
speed, velocity	meter per second	m/s
acceleration	meter per second squared	m/s^2
wave number	1 per meter	m^{-1}
density, mass density	kilogram per cubic meter	kg/m^3
current density	ampere per square meter	A/m^2
magnetic field strength	ampere per meter	A/m
concentration (of amount of substance)	mole per cubic meter	$mol/^3$
specific volume	cubic meter per kilogram	m^3/kg
luminance	candela per square meter	cd/m^2

SI DERIVED UNITS WITH SPECIAL NAMES

Quantity	Name	Symbol	Expression in terms of other units
frequency	hertz	Hz	s^{-1}
force	newton	N	$kg \cdot m/s^2$
pressure, stress	pascal	Pa	N/m^2
energy, work, quantity of heat	joule	J	$N \cdot m$
power, radiant flux	watt	W	J/s
quantity of electricity, electric charge	coulomb	C	$A \cdot s$
electric potential, potential difference, electromotive force	volt	V	W/A
capacitance	farad	F	C/V
electric resistance	ohm	Ω	V/A
conductance	siemens	S	A/V
magnetic flux	weber	Wb	$V \cdot$
magnetic flux density	tesla	T	Wb/m^2
inductance	henry	H	Wb/A
luminous flux	lumen	lm	$cd \cdot sr$
illuminance	lux	lx	lm/m^2
activity (of a radionuclide)	becquerel	Bq	s^{-1}
absorbed dose	gray	Gy	J/kg

RECOMMENDED UNITS

Quantity	Symbol	Dimension	Unit	Unit symbol	Recommended sub-units	Not recommended units
Length	l	L	meter	m	mm, μm, nm	cm, μ, u, mμ, mu, A
Area	A	L^2	square meter	m^2	mm^2, μm^2	cm^2, μ^2
Volume	V	L^3	cubic meter / liter	m^3 / l	dm^3, cm^3, mm^3, μm^3 / ml, μl, nl, pl, fl	cc, ccm, μ^3, u^3 / L, λ, ul, $\mu\mu$l, uul
Mass	m	M	kilogram	kg	g, mg, μg, ng, pg	Kg, gr, γ, ug, mμg, mug, $\gamma\gamma$, $\mu\mu$g, uug
Number	N	I	one	1	10^9, 10^6, 10^3, 10^{-3}	all other factors
Amount of substance	n	N	mol	mol	mmol, μmol, nmol	M, eq, val, g-mol, mM, meq, mval, μM μeq, μval, nM, neq, nval
Mass concentration		$L^{-3}m$	kilogram per liter	kg/l	g/l, mg/l, μg/l, ng/l	g/ml, %, g%, % (w/v), g/100 ml, g/dl, ‰, ‰ (w/v), mg%, mg% (w/v), mg/100 ml, mg/dl, ppm, ppm (w/v), μg%, μg% (w/v), μg/100 ml, μ/dl, γ%, ppb, ppb (w/v), $\mu\mu$g/ml, uug/ml
Substance concentration	c	L^{-3} N	mol per liter	mol/l	mmol/l, μmol/l, nmol/l	M, eq/l, val/l, N, n, mM, meq/l, mval/l, μM, uM, μeq/l, nM, neq/l
Molality	m	M^{-1} N	mol per kilogram	mol/kg	mmol/kg, μmol/kg	m, mmol/g, μmol/mg, mm, μm, mm

interneuron (in-ter-nu'ron) An excitatory or inhibitory nerve cell in the central nervous system, between the primary afferent and final motor nerve cells; it usually has a short range of action. Also called internuncial neuron.

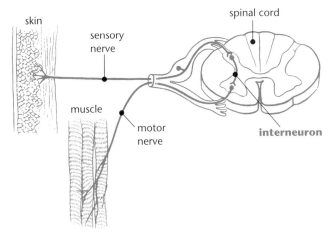

internist (in-ter'nist) A specialist in internal medicine, trained in the diagnosis and nonsurgical treatment of diseases and disorders.

internodal (in-ter-no'dal) Between two nodes; applied to the segment of a nerve fiber between two successive nodes of Ranvier.

internode (in'ter-nōd) Any of the myelinated segments of nerve fibers between the regularly spaced nodes of Ranvier; the unmyelinated gaps.

internuncial (in-ter-nun'she-al) Serving as a connecting part or a means of communication (e.g., a nerve cell connecting two other nerve cells).

interoceptor (in-ter-o-sep'tor) Any specialized sensory nerve ending within the walls of organs, glands, and blood vessels.

interosseous (in-ter-os'e-us) Between bones; applied especially to ligaments and muscles.

interphalangeal (in-ter-fah-lan'je-al) Between two contiguous bones of fingers or toes (i.e., between two phalanges).

interphase (in'ter-fāz) The interval between two mitotic divisions of a cell, when it is not dividing but is actively synthesizing DNA. Formerly called resting stage.

interpretation (in-ter-prĕ-ta'shun) In psychoanalysis, the process by which the therapist explains to the patient the meaning of a particular aspect of the patient's problem.

interproximal (in-ter-prok'sĭ-mal) Between adjacent surfaces (e.g., the space between adjacent teeth in the same dental arch).

interscapular (in-ter-skap'u-lar) Between the shoulder blades (scapulas).

interseptal (in-ter-sep'tal) Between two tissue partitions (septa).

intersex (in'ter-seks) See hermaphrodite.

intersexuality (in-ter-seks-u-al'ĭ-te) See hermaphroditism.

interspace (in'ter-spās) Space between two similar structures.

interspinal (in-ter-spi'nal) Between the spinous processes of the vertebrae.

interstice (in-ter'stis) A minute space within a tissue.

interstitial (in-ter-stish'al) Relating to, occurring, or located within the minute spaces within a tissue.

intertriginous (in-ter-trij'ĭ-nus) Relating to intertrigo.

intertrigo (in-ter-tri'go) Skin eruption occurring between two adjacent surfaces (e.g., between scrotum and thigh).

intertrochanteric (in-ter-tro-kan-ter'ik) Between the greater and lesser trochanters of the femur, at the hip.

interval (in'ter-val) **1.** A gap in a continuous process. **2.** A distance between two objects. **3.** The lapse of time between two events or between the recurrence of similar episodes of a disease.

    birth i. *(a)* The lapse of time between the time of sexual intercourse by a woman and the birth of her first child; *(b)* the lapse of time between successive births.

    coupling i. The interval between an abnormal, premature heartbeat and the normal beat preceding it.

    lucid i. A period of normal brain function occurring immediately after a head injury in which a ruptured artery produces slow bleeding into the space between skull and dura mater; no neurological signs or clouding of consciousness occurs until blood begins to accumulate outside the dura and compresses the brain. *(b)* In forensic medicine, a period of psychosis remission during which restoration of reason enables a person to comprehend and perform an action with enough memory, perception, and judgment to be held legally responsible for the action.

    P-P i. The distance between corresponding points on two consecutive P waves of the electrocardiogram.

    P-R i. The conduction time from the atria to the ventricles of the heart (usually between 0.12 and 0.20 second), measured from the beginning of the P wave to the beginning of the QRS complex of the electrocardiogram.

    Q-R i. The interval from the beginning of the QRS complex to the peak of the R wave of the electrocardiogram.

    QRS i. The duration of the QRS complex, representing the measurement of total depolarization of the ventricles.

    Q-T i. The interval between the onset of the Q wave and the end of the T wave of the electrocardiogram; it measures the total duration of electrical activity of the ventricles.

    R-R i. The interval between two consecutive QRS complexes of the electrocardiogram.

    S-T i. The interval from the S wave to the end of the T wave.

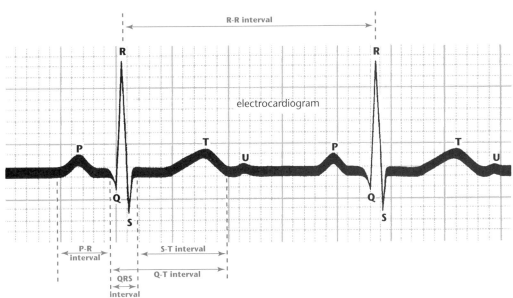

electrocardiogram

intervertebral (in-ter-ver′tĕ-bral) Between two vertebrae.

intervillous (in-ter-vil′us) Among the minute hairlike projections (villi) on the surface of certain tissues.

intestinal (in-tes′tĭ-nal) Relating to the bowel.

intestine (in-tes′tin) The portion of the digestive tract from the end of the stomach to the anus.

> **large i.** The sacculated portion of the intestine, extending from the end of the ileum to the anus and measuring approximately 1.5 m in length in the adult; composed of three parts: cecum (including appendix), colon, and rectum; its function is primarily the absorption of fluid and solutes and the passage of fecal matter out of the body.

> **small i.** The convoluted portion of the intestine, extending from the end of the stomach to the cecum, where it joins the large intestine; in the adult, it is approximately 5 to 6 m in length, lies in the central and lower parts of the abdominal cavity, and is composed of three parts: duodenum, jejunum, and ileum.

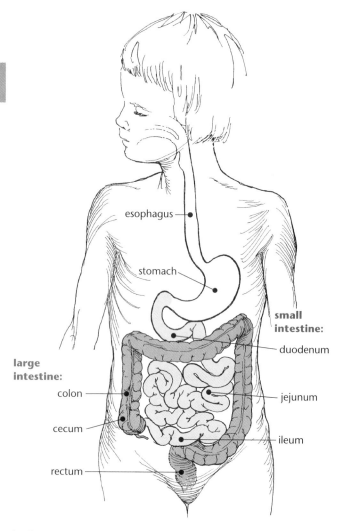

esophagus

stomach

large intestine:

colon

cecum

rectum

small intestine:

duodenum

jejunum

ileum

intima (in′tĭ-mah) The inner layer of a blood vessel wall.

intimal (in′tĭ-mal) Relating to the intima.

intoe (in′to) The turning in of the feet on walking; it may be a minor self-correcting condition of toddlers, or may be a physical sign of other disorders such as metatarsus adductus, medial torsion of the tibia, bowlegs, or congenital contraction of the internal rotators of the hip. Popularly called pigeon toe.

intolerance (in-tol′er-ans) Unfavorable reaction to a substance.

> **food i.** Abnormal physiologic response to an ingested food or food additive, which is not immunologic in nature and which may be idiosyncratic, metabolic, pharmacologic, or toxic. COMPARE food allergy, under allergy.

> **hereditary fructose i.** Metabolic defect due to an autosomal recessive inheritance; characterized by deficiency of the enzyme fructose-1-phosphate aldolase, causing vomiting and low blood sugar levels upon ingestion of fructose; repeated ingestion of fructose by infants with this disorder may result in severe disease.

> **lactose i.** Intolerance to the milk sugar lactose due to deficiency of the enzyme lactase; characterized by abdominal cramps and diarrhea upon ingestion of milk and milk products.

> **pregnancy-induced glucose i.** See gestational diabetes mellitus, under diabetes.

intorsion (in-tor′shun) The real or apparent inward turning of one or both eyes.

intortor (in′tor-tor) A medial or inward rotator; applied to a muscle (e.g., an extraocular muscle) that turns a part inward.

intoxicant (in-tok′sĭ-kant) An intoxicating agent (e.g., alcohol).

intoxication (in-tok-sĭ-ka′shun) A poisoning or abnormal state produced by certain substances.

> **alcohol i.** Drunkenness due to excessive intake of alcoholic beverages in a relatively short period of time. Most states in the United States define intoxication as a blood alcohol concentration of at least 80 to 100 mg of alcohol per deciliter of blood (mg/dl, or 0.1%).

> **water i.** Excessive water content of the body resulting in salt depletion and a variety of associated symptoms. Also called water poisoning.

intra- Prefix meaning within.

intra-abdominal (in′trah ab-dom′ĭ-nal) Within the abdomen.

intra-articular (in′trah ar-tik′u-lar) Within a joint cavity.

intrabronchial (in-trah-brong′ke-al) Within the bronchi. Also called endobronchial.

intracapsular (in-trah-kap′su-lar) Within a capsule, especially a joint capsule.

intracardiac (in-trah-kar′de-ak) Within the heart.

intracartilaginous (in-trah-kar-tĭ-laj′ĭ-nus) Within a cartilage. Also called endochondral.

intracatheter (in-trah-kath′ĕ-ter) A slender plastic tube inserted into a vein for injection or infusion, or for monitoring of venous pressure.

intracelial (in-trah-se′le-al) See endoceliac.

intracellular (in-trah-sel′u-lar) Within a cell or cells.

intracerebellar (in-trah-ser-ĕ-bel′ar) Within the cerebellum.

intracerebral (in-trah-ser′ĕ-bral) Within the cerebrum.

intracervical (in-trah-ser′vĕ-kal) See endocervical.

intracisternal (in-trah-sis-ter′nal) Within an enclosed space (cisterna), especially the large subarachnoid space between the medulla oblongata and the inferior surface of the cerebellum.

intracostal (in-trah-kos′tal) On the inner surface of a rib or ribs.

intracranial (in-trah-kra′ne-al) Within the skull (cranium).

intractable (in-trak′tah-bl) Resistant to therapy.

intradermal (in-trah-der′mal) (I.D., i.d.) Within the deep layer (dermis) of the skin.

intraductal (in-trah-duk′tal) Within a duct.

intradural (in-trah-du′ral) Within the outermost membrane (dura mater) covering the brain and spinal cord.

intraepithelial (in-trah-ep-ĭ-the′le-al) Within the epithelium (i.e., cells forming the outermost layer of a lining membrane).

intrafusal (in-trah-fu′zal) Within a muscle spindle; applied to muscle fibers.

intrahepatic (in-trah-hĕ-pat′ik) Within the liver.

intraictal (in-trah-ik′tal) Occurring during a convulsion or seizure.

intralobar (in-trah-lo′bar) Within a lobe of an organ.

intraluminal (in-trah-lu′mĭ-nal) Within the lumen of a tubular structure.

intramedullary (in-trah-med′u-lār-e) Within the bone marrow, the medulla oblongata, or the spinal cord.

intramembranous (in-trah-mem′brah-nus) Between layers of a membrane.

intramolecular (in-trah-mo-lek′u-lar) Occurring or located within the molecule.

intramural (in-trah-mu´ral) Within the walls of an organ, cavity, or any tubular structure.

intramuscular (in-trah-mus´ku-lar) (I.M., i.m.) Within muscle tissue.

intranasal (in-trah-na´zal) Within the nasal cavity.

intraneural (in-trah-nu´ral) Within a nerve.

intraocular (in-trah-ok´u-lar) Within the eyeball.

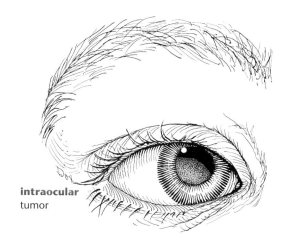

intraocular tumor

intraoperative (in-trah-op´er-ah-tiv) Occurring or performed during the actual surgical operation (e.g., ancillary care or procedures; complications).

intraoral (in-trah-o´ral) Within the mouth.

intraorbital (in-trah-or´bĭ-tal) Within the eye socket (orbit).

intraosseous (in-trah-os´e-us) Within bone tissue.

intrapartum (in-trah-par´tum) In obstetrics, relating to labor and delivery; distinguished from antepartum and postpartum.

intraperitoneal (in-trah-per-ĭ-to-ne´al) (I.P., i.p.) Within the cavity lined with peritoneum (i.e., the abdominopelvic cavity).

intrapsychic (in-trah-si´kik) Taking place within the mind.

intrapulmonary (in-trah-pul´mo-ner-e) Within the lung.

intrarenal (in-trah-re´nal) Within the kidney.

intrasellar (in-trah-sel´ar) Within the bony cavity (sella turcica) in the skull that houses the pituitary.

intrasplenic (in-trah-sple´nik) Within the spleen.

intrastromal (in-trah-stro´mal) Within the tissues (e.g., connective tissue) forming the framework of an organ.

intrasynovial (in-trah-sĭ-no´ve-al) Within the sac in a joint that contains synovial fluid.

intrathecal (in-trah-the´kal) Within a sheath.

intrathoracic (in-trah-tho-ras´ik) Within the chest cavity.

intratympanic (in-trah-tim-pan´ik) Within the middle ear chamber.

intrauterine (in-trah-u´ter-in) Within the uterus.

intravascular (in-trah-vas´ku-lar) Within any blood vessel (vein or artery) or lymphatic vessel.

intravenous (in-trah-ve´nus) (I.V., i.v.) Within a vein.

intraventricular (in-trah-ven-trik´u-lar) (I-V) Within a ventricle of the heart or brain.

intravesical (in-trah-ves´e-kal) Within a bladder, especially the urinary bladder.

intra vitam (in´trah vi´tam) Latin for during life.

intravitreous (in-trah-vit´re-us) Within the vitreous body (in the back portion of the eyeball's interior).

intrinsic (in-trin´sik) Situated entirely within, and forming an integral part of, an organ or structure.

intro- Prefix meaning into; directed inward.

introducer (in-tro-du´ser) Instrument for facilitating the passing of another instrument (e.g., an endotracheal tube) into the body.

introitus (in-tro´ĭ-tus) Entrance into a body cavity or hollow organ.

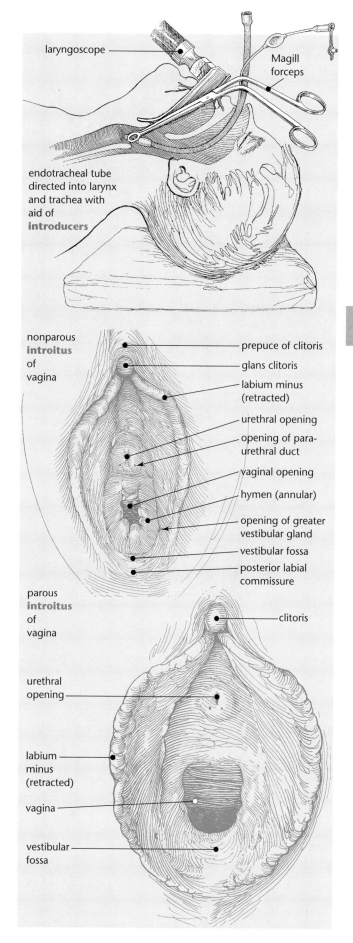

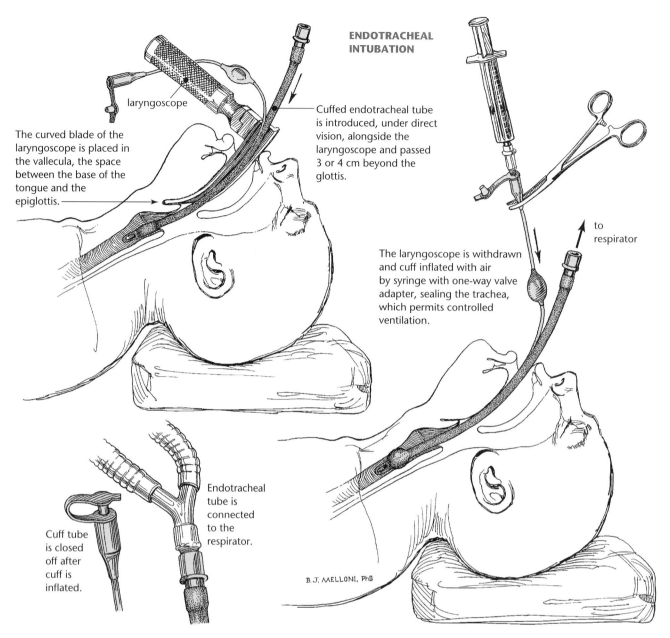

ENDOTRACHEAL INTUBATION

laryngoscope

The curved blade of the laryngoscope is placed in the vallecula, the space between the base of the tongue and the epiglottis.

Cuffed endotracheal tube is introduced, under direct vision, alongside the laryngoscope and passed 3 or 4 cm beyond the glottis.

The laryngoscope is withdrawn and cuff inflated with air by syringe with one-way valve adapter, sealing the trachea, which permits controlled ventilation.

to respirator

Endotracheal tube is connected to the respirator.

Cuff tube is closed off after cuff is inflated.

B.J. MELLONI, PhD

introjection (in-tro-jek'shun) An unconscious psychological defense mechanism in which there is symbolic assimilation of a loved or hated object, making it a part of the self; the complement of projection. See also projection.

intromission (in-tro-mish'un) Insertion; introduction.

intron (in'tron) One of the noncoding regions of the DNA molecule in a gene, situated between coding segments (exons).

introspection (in-tro-spek'shun) Examination of one's own mental processes.

introversion (in-tro-ver'zhun) **1.** Preoccupation with one's own interests and experiences and concomitant reduction of outside interests. **2.** The process of turning an organ or part inward.

introvert (in'tro-vert) One whose thoughts are predominantly about himself or herself.

introvert (in-tro-vert') To turn inward.

intubate (in'tu-bāt) To perform intubation.

intubation (in-tu-ba'shun) Introduction of a tube into a body cavity, canal, or any other tubular structure. Distinguished from catherization.

　　endotracheal i. The passage of a tube via the mouth into the trachea to allow air to enter the lungs (e.g., during administration of

anesthesia).

intubator (in'tu-ba-tor) Instrument used in intubation.

intumesce (in-tu-mes') To swell.

intumescence (in-tu-mes'ens) A swelling.

intumescent (in-tu-mes'ent) Characterized by swelling; becoming swollen.

intussusception (in-tus-sus-sep'shun) An infolding; especially applied to the abnormal infolding of one portion of intestine into the lumen of a contiguous portion; occurs usually at the junction of the small and large intestines (the iliocecal junction), causing acute abdominal symptoms; seen most commonly in children.

intussusceptum (in-tus-sus-sep'tum) The inner portion of intestine in an intussusception.

intussuscipiens (in-tus-sus-sip'e-ens) The outer portion of intestine surrounding the inner segment in an intussusception.

inulin (in'u-lin) A fructose polysaccharide used in kidney function tests as a measure of glomerular filtration rate since it is filtered at the glomerulus and is neither secreted nor reabsorbed by the kidney tubules.

inunction (in-ungk'shun) **1.** The rubbing of therapeutic ointment on the skin. **2.** An ointment.

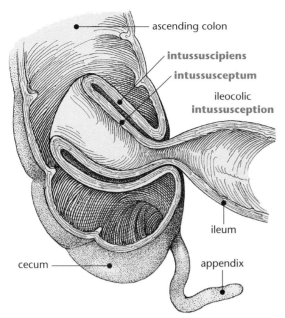

ascending colon

intussuscipiens

intussusceptum

ileocolic
intussusception

ileum

cecum

appendix

in utero (in u'ter-o) Latin for within the uterus.

in vacuo (in vak'u-o) Latin for in a vacuum.

invaginate (in-vaj'ĭ-nāt) To infold; to turn within; to ensheath.

invagination (in-vaj-ĭ-na'shun) 1. The process of invaginating. 2. The state of being invaginated.

invalid (in'vah-lid) A person disabled by chronic illness, injury, or infirmity.

invalidism (in'vah-lid-izm) The condition of being an invalid.

invasion (in-va'zhun) 1. The spread of a tumor, usually cancerous, to neighboring tissues. 2. The beginning of a disease process.

invasive (in-va'siv) 1. Tending to spread to healthy tissues. 2. Involving penetration of the skin or any body tissue; applied to certain procedures.

inventory (in'ven-tor-e) In psychology, a list of questions.

    personality i. A psychological test for evaluating personal characteristics; usually a checklist about, and answered by, the patient.

inversion (in-ver'zhun) 1. A turning inside out. 2. Any reversal of the normal relation of two organs or structures. 3. In genetics, a structural abnormality of a chromosome resulting from fragmentation of the chromosome by two breaks, followed by a turning end for end of the fragment and reunification in the same place, so that the gene sequence for the fragment is reversed with regard to the rest of the chromosome.

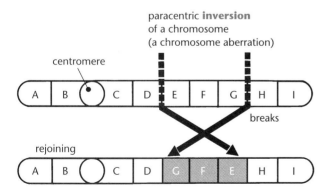

paracentric **inversion**
of a chromosome
(a chromosome aberration)

centromere

| A | B | C | D | E | F | G | H | I |

breaks

rejoining

| A | B | C | D | G | F | E | H | I |

    i. of nipple Failure of the nipple to protrude from the breast; it may be a benign congenital anomaly or it may be caused by a cancerous growth within the breast.

    i. of uterus Abnormal turning of the uterus inside out, exposing the inner lining (endometrium).

invert (in-vert') To turn inside out or upside down.

invertase (in-ver'tās) β-fructofuranosidase; an enzyme of the small intestine that converts sucrose into glucose and fructose.

invertebrate (in-ver'tĕ-brāt) Any animal that does not have a spinal column.

invertor (in-ver'tor) Any muscle that turns a part inward.

investing (in-vest'ing) In dentistry, the covering of a wax pattern of a tooth restoration or a denture with a setting material to make a mold.

    vacuum i. Forming a mold around a pattern in a vacuum to prevent formation of air bubbles in the investment material.

investment (in-vest'ment) 1. An outer covering. 2. In dentistry, a setting material used in investing, especially a refractory material.

inviscation (in-vis-ka'shun) The mixing of food with secretions in the mouth during chewing.

in vitro (in ve'tro) In an environment outside of the body, usually a test tube, Petri dish, or similar artificial environment.

in vivo (in ve'vo) Occurring, or performed, in the living body; applied to biological events, reactions, or procedures.

involucrum (in-vo-lu'krum) An enveloping sheath, such as the sheath of new bone formed around a necrosed area (sequestrum) of the bone.

involuntary (in-vol'un-ter-e) 1. Performed, or occurring, independently of one's own free will. 2. Not performed willingly.

involution (in-vo-lu'shun) A retrograde process resulting in lessening in the size of a tissue (e.g., return to normal size of the uterus after childbirth; the shrinking of organs and tissues in old age).

involutional (in-vo-lu'shun-al) Relating to involution.

iodate (i'o-dāt) 1. A salt of iodic acid. 2. To iodize.

iodic acid (i-o'dik as'id) A water-soluble powder used as an antiseptic and deodorant.

iodide (i'o-dīd) A compound of iodine with another element, especially with potassium or sodium.

iodimetry (i-o-dim'ĕ-tre) See iodometry.

iodinate (i-o'dĭ-nāt) To add iodine, or to combine with iodine.

iodine (i'o-dīn) A nonmetallic element; symbol I, atomic number 53, atomic weight 126.90; used as an antiseptic and in the diagnosis and treatment of thyroid disease.

    protein-bound i. (PBI) Iodine present in blood serum firmly bound to one or more proteins.

iodine-131 (^{131}I) A beta-emitting radioactive iodine isotope with a half-life of 8.05 days; used primarily to deliver therapeutic doses of radiation to the thyroid gland and to certain tumors (e.g., pheochromocytomas); it has limited use in imaging the thyroid gland and the cortex and medulla of the adrenal (suprarenal) gland.

iodism (i'o-dizm) Poisoning from prolonged use of iodine or an iodide; symptoms include acute inflammation of the nasal passages, nasal discharge, headache, salivation, and a skin eruption.

iodize (i'o-dīz) To treat or combine with iodine.

iodoform (i-o'do-form) A lemon yellow iodine compound used as a topical antiseptic.

iodohippurate sodium (i-o-do-hip'u-rāt so'de-um) A radiopaque compound used in x-ray examination of the urinary tract.

iodometry (i-o-dom'ĕ-tre) The volumetric determination of the amount of iodine in a compound. Also called iodimetry.

iodophilia (i-o-do-fil'e-ah) Affinity for iodine; applied to certain white blood cells.

iodopsin (i-o-dop'sin) A violet pigment composed of a vitamin A derivative and a protein, present in the cone cells of the retina and important in color vision. Also called visual violet.

ion (i'on) An atom or group of atoms that has acquired an electric charge; the form in which certain substances, such as ammonium, calcium, sodium, phosphate, potassium, hydrogen, move across cell membranes to perform important biologic functions (e.g., acid-base balance, conduction of nerve impulses, muscle contraction, bone and tooth formation).

ionic (i-on'ik) Relating to ions.

ionization (i-on-ī-za'shun) 1. Production of ions, i.e., electrically charged atoms or molecules (e.g., by irradiation). 2. See iontophoresis.

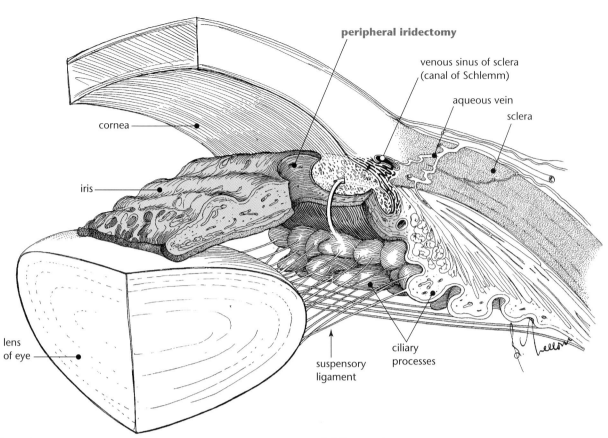

peripheral iridectomy

venous sinus of sclera
(canal of Schlemm)

aqueous vein

sclera

cornea

iris

lens
of eye

suspensory
ligament

ciliary
processes

ionize (i′on-īz) To separate into ions.

ionophore (i′o-no-fōr) A molecule (e.g., of an antibiotic drug) that increases the permeability of cell membranes (e.g., of bacterial cells).

ionophoresis (i-on-o-fo-re′sis) See electrophoresis.

ionophoretic (i-on-o-fo-ret′ik) See electrophoretic.

iontophoresis (i-on-to-fo-re′sis) Introduction of ions of soluble salts into tissues by means of electric current; especially applied to the process of increasing penetration of a medication through intact skin by means of an electric current. Also called ionic medication; ionization; iontotherapy.

iontotherapy (i-on-to-ther′ah-pe) See iontophoresis.

iopanoic acid (i-o-pah-no′ik as′id) A radiopaque iodine compound used as a contrast medium in x-ray examination of the gallbladder and ducts.

ipecac, ipecacuanha (ip′ĕ-kak, ip′ĕ-kak-yu-an′ah) The dried roots of a tropical shrub (*Cephaelis ipecacuanha*), containing substances with emetic, expectorant, and antidysentery properties. Possible adverse effects include heart and kidney damage.

    i. syrup Preparation used to induce vomiting (e.g., in the management of certain poisonings).

ipsilateral (ip-sĭ-lat′er-al) Occurring or located on the same side (e.g., symptoms occurring on the same side as a brain lesion). Also called homolateral.

iridectomy (ir-ĭ-dek′to-me) Eye surgery in which a portion of the iris is removed.

    peripheral i. Removal of a minute portion of the edge of the iris, under the periphery of the cornea (e.g., in the treatment of glaucoma).

iridemia (ir-ĭ-de′me-ah) Bleeding from the iris.

iridencleisis (ir-ĭ-den-kli′sis) An eye operation for the treatment of glaucoma in which a portion of the iris is cut and trapped (incarcerated) in an incision on the border of the cornea; thus a channel is created for draining the fluid (aqueous humor) from the anterior and posterior chambers of the eye.

irides (i′rĭ-dēz) Plural of iris.

iridic (i-rid′ik) Relating to the iris.

iridium (ĭ-rid′e-um) A metallic element; symbol Ir, atomic number 77, atomic weight 192.2.

irido-, irid- Combining forms relating to the iris.

iridocele (i-rid′o-sēl) Protrusion of a portion of the iris through a wound or defect in the cornea.

iridochoroiditis (ir-ĭ-do-ko-roi-di′tis) Inflammation of the iris and the vascular layer of the eyeball.

iridocoloboma (ir-ĭ-do-kol-o-bo′mah) Developmental defect in which a portion of the iris is absent.

iridoconstrictor (ir-ĭ-do-kon-strik′tor) Stimulating constriction of the circular muscle (sphincter) of the iris, thereby reducing the size of the pupil; applied to the nerve supplying the muscle or to a chemical substance.

iridocorneal (ir-ĭ-do-kor′ne-al) Relating to the iris and cornea.

iridocyclectomy (ir-ĭ-do-si-klek′to-me) Surgical removal of the iris and ciliary body.

iridocyclitis (ir-ĭ-do-si-kli′tis) Inflammation of the iris and the ciliary body; signs and symptoms include the oozing of exudates into the anterior chamber of the eye, discoloration of the iris, constriction of the pupil, radiating pain, and excessive tearing.

iridodilator (ir-ĭ-do-di-la′tor) Stimulating constriction of the dilator muscle of the pupil, thereby enlarging the size of the pupil; applied to the nerve supplying the muscle or to a chemical substance.

iridodialysis (ir-ĭ-do-di-al′ĭ-sis) Separation or rupture of a portion of the iris from its attachment to the ciliary body; may result from a contusion injury of the eyeball caused by traumatic contact with a blunt object.

iridodonesis (ir-ĭ-do-do-ne′sis) Abnormal quivering of the iris upon movement of the eye, as may occur in partial dislocation of the lens.

iridokinesis, iridokinesia (ir-ĭ-do-ki-ne′sis, ir-ĭ-do-ki-ne′ze-ah) The natural movement of the iris resulting in dilatation and contraction of the pupil.

iridokinetic (ir-ĭ-do-ki-net′ik) Relating to the movements of the iris.

iridomalacia (ir-ī-do-mah-la′she-ah) Abnormal degenerative softening of the iris due to disease.

iridoplegia (ir-ī-do-ple′je-ah) Paralysis of the iris.

iridosclerotomy (ir-ī-do-skle-rot′o-me) A surgical cut into the white of the eye (sclera) and the margin of the iris.

iridotomy (ir-ī-dot′o-me) Surgical cut into the iris.

iris (i′ris), pl. i′rides The delicate and adjustable diaphragm of the eye that surrounds the pupil and controls the amount of light entering the eye; it is situated between the cornea and the lens; it is immersed in the aqueous humor, partially separating the anterior and posterior chambers of the eye; the concentration of pigment cells (melanocytes) is the predominant factor that determines the color of the iris.

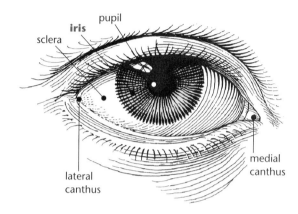

i. bombé An abnormal bulging forward of the iris; it is caused by pressure from accumulated aqueous humor in the posterior chamber of the eye, due to obstruction of the aqueous circulation by adhesion of the pupillary border of the iris to the anterior surface of the lens.

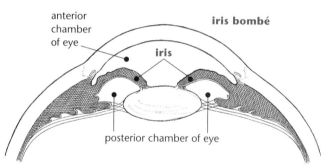

iris bombé

i. tuck The entrapment of a portion of peripheral iris due to misplacement of the haptic arm of an intraocular prosthetic lens; the entrapment of the iris distorts the pupil.

iritic (i-rit′ik) Relating to the iris.

iritides (i-rit′ĭ-dez) Plural of iritis.

iritis (i-ri′tis) Inflammation of the iris, causing redness around the cornea, discoloration of the iris, and a constricted, sluggish pupil.

iron (i′ern) Metallic element; symbol Fe, atomic number 26, atomic weight 55.85; present in the body as a component of hemoglobin, myoglobin, cytochrome, and of the enzymes catalase and peroxidase; its role in the body is predominantly concerned with cellular respiration.

iron-59 (i′ern) (^{59}Fe) A radioactive beta-emitter iron isotope with a half-life of 45 days; used as a tracer in studies of iron metabolism.

irradiate (ĭ-ra′de-āt) To treat with or to expose to radiation.

irradiation (ĭ-ra-de-a′shun) **1.** Exposure to the action of rays. **2.** The condition resulting from having been subjected to radiation. **3.** Therapy by exposure to radiation.

irrational (ĭ-rash′un-al) Contrary to reason or to the principles of logic.

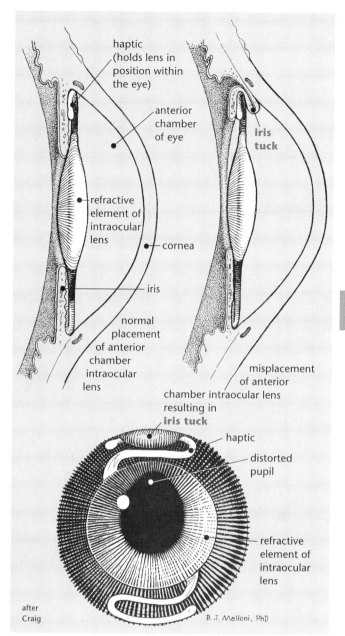

after Craig

B. J. Melloni, PhD

irreducible (ir-re-dūs′ĭ-bl) Incapable of being made simpler or smaller.

irresponsibility (ir-re-spon′sĭ-bil′ĭ-te) The state of not being responsible.

criminal i. The state of not being responsible for one's own criminal conduct due to a mental defect or disorder.

irreversible (ir-re-ver′sĭ-bl) Permanent; incapable of returning to its original state.

irrigant (ir′ĭ-gant) Any fluid used to flush or wash out a wound or body cavity.

irrigate (ir′ĭ-gāt) To wash out a wound or body cavity with a stream of liquid; the liquid, which is commonly normal saline, may be medicated.

irrigation (ir-ĭ-ga′shun) The act of irrigating.

irritability (ir-ĭ-tah-bil′ĭ-te) **1.** Responsiveness of excitable tissue to stimulation; excitability. **2.** Exaggerated response to stimuli; hypersensitivity to any stimulation.

irritable (ir′ĭ-tah-bl) **1.** Capable of reacting to a stimulus. **2.** The state of being hypersensitive to, or tending to overreact, to a stimulus.

irritant (ir′ĭ-tant) **1.** Causing irritation. **2.** Any chemical agent or drug acting locally on the skin or mucous membranes to produce inflammation. **3.** A stimulus.

irritation (ir-ĭ-ta′shun) **1.** Incipient inflammation of a tissue. **2.** The act of eliciting a reaction (normal or exaggerated) in the tissues.

ischemia (is-ke′me-ah) Lack of blood in a circumscribed area of the body due to mechanical obstruction or functional constriction of a blood vessel.

   myocardial i. Ischemia of the heart muscle, usually due to disease of the coronary arteries, which supply blood to the muscle.

   silent i. The occurrence of transient episodes of myocardial ischemia without accompanying symptoms; evident in the electrocardiogram by ST-segment depressions.

ischia (is′ke-ah) Plural of ischium.

ischial (is′ke-al) Relating to the ischium.

ischialgia (is-ke-al′je-ah) Pain in the hip, especially the posterior area. Also called ischiodynia.

ischio- Combining form meaning ischium.

ischiodynia (is-ke-o-din′e-ah) See ischialgia.

ischium (is′ke-um), pl. is′chia The lower, posterior portion of the hipbone; the bone on which the body rests when sitting; it is surrounded by cartilage in early life and eventually ossifies, fusing with the ilium and pubis in the adult to form the hipbone. See also table of bones.

ischuria (is-ku′re-ah) Suppression of urine.

island (i′land) An isolated structure or cluster of cells. See also islet.

   erythroblastic i. One or two central reticulum cells of the bone marrow surrounded by normoblasts at various stages of development; the reticulum cells phagocytize the ejected nuclei of the developing normoblasts just prior to their release into the marrow capillaries as erythrocytes; they also ingest worn out or damaged red blood cells, conserving their iron as ferritin.

   i.'s of Langerhans See islets of Langerhans, under islet.

   pancreatic i.'s See islets of Langerhans, under islet.

   i. of Reil See insula.

islet (i′let) An isolated cluster of cells.

   i.'s of Langerhans Cluster of cells in the pancreas that produce and secrete insulin, glucagon, and somatostatin directly into the bloodstream. Also called islets of the pancreas; islands of Langerhans; pancreatic islands.

   i.'s of the pancreas See islets of Langerhans.

-ism Suffix meaning act or process (e.g., plagiarism); state or condition (e.g., hypothyroidism); a practice (e.g., hypnotism).

iso- Prefix meaning equal; sameness (with respect to immunologic species); sameness (with respect to genetic constitution).

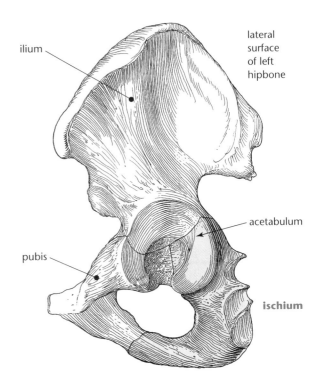

lateral surface of left hipbone

ilium

acetabulum

pubis

ischium

isoagglutinin (i-so-ah-gloo′tĭ-nin) An antibody capable of clumping cells of individuals different from the individual from whom it originated, but of the same species. Also called isohemagglutinin.

isoantibody (i-so-an′tĭ-bod-e) See alloantibody.

isoantigen (i-so-an′tĭ-jen) See alloantigen.

isobody (i′so-bod-e) See alloantibody.

isocellular (i-so-sel′u-lar) Composed of similar cells.

isochromatic (i-so-kro-mat′ik) Of uniform or equal color.

isochromosome (i-so-kro′mo-sōm) Chromosomal aberration occurring during meiosis in which two daughter chromosomes are formed, each lacking a chromosome arm but with the other (homologous) arm duplicated; probably results from a transverse (rather than the normal longitudinal) division of the centromere.

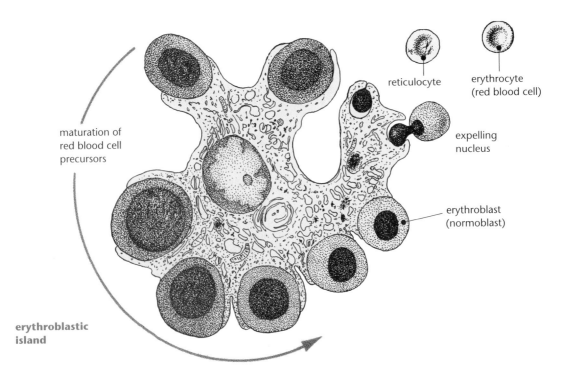

maturation of red blood cell precursors

reticulocyte

erythrocyte (red blood cell)

expelling nucleus

erythroblast (normoblast)

erythroblastic island

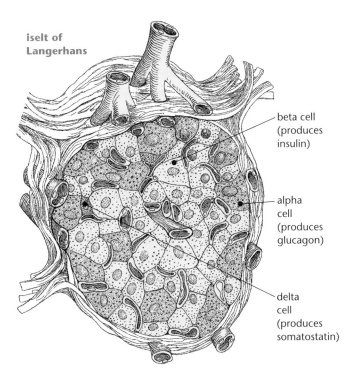

iselt of
Langerhans

beta cell
(produces
insulin)

alpha
cell
(produces
glucagon)

delta
cell
(produces
somatostatin)

isocoria (i-so-ko're-ah) Equal size of the two pupils.

isodynamic (i-so-di-nam'ik) Of equal strength.

isoelectric (i-so-e-lek'trik) Having the same electric potential.

isoenzyme (i-so-en'zīm) One of a group of enzymes that facilitates the same chemical reaction but have different physical properties. Also called isozyme.

isogeneic (i-so-jĕ-ne'ik) Genetically identical or nearly identical; applied to identical (monozygous) twins or to animals so highly inbred that they have complete compatibility of genes. Also called isogenic; isologous; isoplastic; syngeneic.

isogenic (i-so-jen'ik) See isogeneic.

isograft (i'so-graft) A tissue transplant involving two genetically identical or near-identical individuals (e.g., identical twins or animals so highly inbred that they have complete compatibility). Also called isogeneic graft; isologous graft; isoplastic graft; syngeneic graft; syngraft; isotransplant.

isohemagglutinin (i-so-hem-ah-gloo'tī-nin) See isoagglutinin.

isohemolysin (i-so-he-mol'ĭ-sin) A specific antibody from one individual that reacts with antigen in red blood cells of another individual of the same species, causing cell destruction.

isohemolysis (i-so-he-mol'ĭ-sis) Dissolution of red blood cells caused by reaction between specific antigens present in the cells and antibodies from another individual of the same species. Also called homolysis.

isohydric (i-so-hi'drik) Having the same pH.

isoimmunization (i-so-im-u-ni-za'shun) The development of specific antibody following exposure to, and against, an antigen originating in a genetically different individual of the same species.

isolation (i-so-la'shun) **1.** Separation from a group, such as the placing of a patient in quarantine and segregation of his body fluids and clotting to prevent transmission of infection. **2.** In microbiology, the identification and separation of a pure strain of microorganisms from a mixed source such as a clinical specimen. **3.** A psychological defense mechanism in which experiences or memories are dissociated from the affects pertaining to them, so as to render them a matter of indifference; an unconscious psychological defense mechanism against anxiety. **4.** Psychological or social isolation; the aversion to making interpersonal contact.

Isolette (i-so'let) Trademark for an incubator designed for the care of premature and low birth weight newborns; it provides controlled temperature and humidity; if handled properly, relative sterility of the microenvironment is assured.

isoleucine (i-so-lu'sin) (Ile) An essential amino acid.

isologous (i-sol'o-gus) See isogeneic.

isomer (i'so-mer) Any one of two or more compounds that have the same percentage composition and molecular weight but different physical or chemical properties due to a different arrangement of atoms in the molecule.

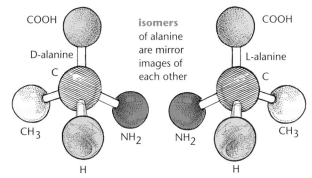

COOH

D-alanine

C

CH₃   NH₂

H

isomers of alanine are mirror images of each other

COOH

L-alanine

C

NH₂   CH₃

H

isomerase (i-som'er-ās) An enzyme that promotes the conversion of a substance to an isomeric form.

isomeric (i-so-mer'ik) Having the characteristics of isomers.

isomerization (i-som-er-ĭ-za'shun) The conversion of one isomer into another.

isometric (i-so-met'rik) Having the same dimensions; denoting a muscle contraction in which the tension of the muscle is increased while its length remains the same.

isometropia (i-so-mĕ-tro'pe-ah) Equality in the refractive power of both eyes.

isomorph (i'so-morf) Old term for allele.

isomorphism (i-so-mor'fizm) Similarity of form.

isoniazid (i-so-ni'ah-zid) An antibacterial drug used in the treatment of tuberculosis.

isoplastic (i-so-plas'tik) See isogeneic.

isoproterenol (i-so-pro-tĕ-re'nol) Synthetic drug similar to epinephrine, used mainly in the treatment of such lung diseases as asthma, emphysema, and chronic bronchitis, and in advanced life support as a heart stimulator. Adverse effects may include dry mouth, dizziness, and palpitations.

isopter (i-sop'ter) A curved or contour line on a visual field passing through points of visual acuity.

isosexual (i-so-seks'u-al) Having the characteristics of the sex to which the individual belongs.

isosmotic (i-sos-mot'ik) Of equal osmotic pressure; applied to two liquids.

isosorbide dinitrate (i-so-sor'bīd di-ni'trāt) Compound used to relieve the chest pain (angina pectoris) caused by impaired blood circulation to the heart muscle. Adverse effects include headache, hot flashes, dizziness, and fainting.

Isospora belli (i-sos'po-rah bel'e) A species of bacteria (family Eimeriidae) that is parasitic in human small intestines, sometimes causing mucous diarrhea, especially in children, and an unresponsive-to-treatment type of diarrhea in people with immunosuppressed conditions (e.g., AIDS).

isosporiasis (i-sos-po-ri'ah-sis) Infection with a species of *Isospora*.

isosthenuria (i-sos-thĕ-nu're-ah) A sign of advanced kidney failure characterized by excretion of urine with a fixed density of about 1.010 regardless of the quantity of fluid consumed, due to inability of the kidneys to concentrate or dilute the urine.

isothermal (i-so-ther'mal) Relating to the same termperature.

isotonic (i-so-ton'ik) **1.** Of equal tension; usually applied to two solutions. **2.** Denoting a muscle contraction in which the muscular fibers are markedly shortened but without corresponding increase in the force of the contraction.

isotonicity (i-so-to-nis'ĭ-te) The state of being isotonic.

isotope (i'so-tōp) One of two or more chemical elements in which all atoms have the same atomic number but varying atomic weights; many are radioactive.

isotransplant (i-so-trans'plant) See isograft.

isotransplantation (i-so-trans-plan-ta′shun) The transfer of an isograft.

isotropic, isotropous (i-so-trop′ik, i-so-trop′us) Equal in all directions.

isovalericacidemia (i-so-vah-ler′ik-as-ĭ-de′me-ah) A disorder of metabolism of the amino acid leucine inherited as an autosomal recessive trait; characterized by elevated serum levels of isovaleric acid upon protein ingestion or during infections; associated with recurrent episodes of coma, acidosis, and malodorous sweat.

isovolumic (i-so-vol-u′mik) Unchanged volume; occurring without an associated alteration in volume.

isozyme (i′so-zīm) See isoenzyme.

isthmus (is′mus), pl. isth′mi **1.** A narrow band of tissue connecting two larger parts. **2.** A narrow passage between two larger cavities or tubular structures.

    i. of aorta In the fetus, a slight constriction of the aorta between the origin of the left subclavian artery and the attachment of the ductus arteriosus; the constriction becomes less noticeable after birth, when the ductus arteriosus obliterates and becomes the fibrous ligamentum arteriosum.

    i. of auditory tube The narrowest part of the eustachian (auditory) tube, at the junction of the bony and cartilaginous portions. Also called isthmus of eustachian tube.

    i. of cingulate gyrus A narrow posterior connection in the brain, between the cingulate gyrus and the parahippocampal gyrus. Also called isthmus of limbic lobe.

    i. of eustachian tube See isthmus of auditory tube.

    i. of external auditory canal A narrow segment of the external auditory canal near the junction of the bony and cartilaginous portions.

    i. of fallopian tube See isthmus of uterine tube.

    i. of fauces See isthmus of oropharynx.

    i. of limbic lobe See isthmus of cingulate gyrus.

    i. of oropharynx The slight constriction between the mouth and pharynx, at the palatoglossal arches. Also called isthmus of fauces.

    i. of prostate A band of fibromuscular tissue, ventral to the urethra, that connects the right and left lateral lobes of the prostate; considered by some to be an anterior lobe.

    i. of thyroid gland The narrow, central portion of the thyroid gland that connects the lower parts of the two lateral lobes; it lies in front of the upper trachea.

    i. of uterine tube The narrowest part of the fallopian (uterine) tube, at its attachment to the uterus. Also called isthmus of fallopian tube.

    i. of uterus The constricted upper third of the uterine cervix, contiguous with the body of the uterus.

itch (ich) **1.** A skin sensation and/or irritation causing a desire to scratch. **2.** Popular name for scabies.

    barber's i. See tinea barbae, under tinea.

    jock i. See tinea cruris, under tinea.

    swimmer's i. An itchy rash caused by penetration of the skin by the larvae of the worm *Schistosoma mansoni* during immersion in contaminated fresh water.

-ite Suffix meaning a substance derived from some specified process (e.g., metabolite); a part of the body, especially in a developmental stage (e.g., somite).

iter (i′ter) A passageway from one anatomic part to another.

-ites Plural of -itis.

-itides Plural of -itis

-itis pl. -itises, -itides, -ites Suffix meaning inflammation of a specified organ or part (e.g., appendicitis).

-ity Suffix meaning a state or condition (e.g., immunity).

Ixodes (iks-o′dĕz) Genus of parasitic ticks (family Ixodidae); some species are vectors of organisms causing human infections.

    I. dammini The deer tick; the chief vector of *Borrelia burgdorferi*, the spirochete causing Lyme disease.

    I. holocyclus A species prevalent in Australia and South Africa; vector of tick paralysis in sheep, cattle, dogs, and occasionally humans.

    I. pacificus The black-legged tick of California; it infests cattle and deer; may bite humans, causing severe reactions.

    I. ricinus The castor bean tick; a species infecting cattle, sheep, and wild animals; it transmits a variety of organisms, including those causing tularemia and infectious encephalomyelitis.

ixodiasis (iks-o-di′ah-sis) Skin lesions and fever caused by the bite of ticks, especially the hard-bodied ticks of the family Ixodidae.

ixodic (ik-sod′ik) Relating to ticks.

Ixodidae (iks-od′ĭ-de) A family of hard-bodied ticks (order Acarina); vectors of a variety of disease-causing microorganisms. Also called hard ticks.

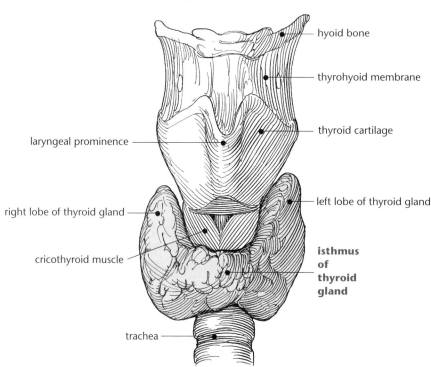

hyoid bone

thyrohyoid membrane

thyroid cartilage

laryngeal prominence

left lobe of thyroid gland

right lobe of thyroid gland

isthmus of thyroid gland

cricothyroid muscle

trachea

J

jacket (jak'et) **1.** A covering or garment, usually enveloping the upper part of the body. **2.** A material surrounding certain structures.

> **Minerva j.** A plaster of Paris cast immobilizing the upper body, from the chin to the hips, for fractures in the lower cervical or upper thoracic spine.

> **porcelain j.** In dentistry, a porcelain crown.

> **Sayre's j.** A plaster of Paris covering used to immobilize the vertebral column.

> **strait j.** See straightjacket.

jackscrew (jak'skroo) A device incorporated into a removable orthodontic appliance; used in orthodontics *(a)* to slowly widen the midpalatine suture at the roof of the mouth, thus expanding the upper dental arch; *(b)* to slowly bring together or separate teeth of the upper or lower jaw.

jactitation (jak-tĭ-ta'shun) Restless tossing of a distressed patient in bed.

jaundice (jawn'dis) Yellow coloring of the skin and white of the eye (sclera) resulting from high levels of the bile pigment bilirubin. Also called icterus.

> **breast milk j.** Jaundice occurring in some full-term newborn infants who are breast-fed, resulting from elevated unconjugated bilirubin.

> **chronic idiopathic j.** See Dubin-Johnson syndrome, under syndrome.

> **familial nonhemolytic j.** See Gilbert's syndrome, under syndrome.

> **hemolytic j.** Jaundice caused by increased production of bilirubin resulting from an excessive breakdown of red blood cells (hemolysis).

RESULTS OF LABORATORY TESTS IN COMMON JAUNDICE DISORDERS

DISORDER	SERUM TRANSAMINASES		ALKALINE PHOSPHATASE	ALBUMIN-GLOBULIN RATIO	PROTHROMBIN TIME	OTHER
	SGOT*	SGPT*				
Viral hepatitis	Moderate or great increase	Moderate or great increase	Slight or moderate increase	Usually normal	Decreased	Cephalin-cholesterol flocculation positive, dark urine, pale stool
Cirrhosis	Slight increase	Normal, occasional slight increase	Slight or moderate increase	Albumin decreased, globulin increased	Decreased	Cephalin-cholesterol flocculation positive, dark urine, pigmented stool
Carcinoma of pancreas and ampulla of Vater	Normal or slight increase	Normal or slight increase	Moderate or great increase	Normal	Normal or decreased	Prothrombin increases after vitamin K, pale stool
Choledocholithiasis	Normal, slight or moderate increase	Normal or slight increase	Slight to great increase	Normal	Normal or decreased	Fever, leukocytosis, intermittent pale stool
Drug cholestasis	Slight or moderate increase	Normal or slight increase	Moderate or great increase	Normal	Normal or slightly decreased	Cholesterol increased, eosinophilia, pale stool
Drug necrosis	Moderate or great increase	Moderate or great increase	Slight increase	Normal or slight albumin decrease	Decreased	Cephalin-cholesterol flocculation positive, dark urine, pale stool
Billiary cirrhosis	Slight or moderate increase	Slight or moderate increase	Moderate or great increase	Normal	Normal or decreased	Cholesterol and phospholipids increased, steatorrhea
Hemolytic jaundice	Normal	Normal	Normal	Normal	Normal	Anemia, reticulocytosis, acholuria, stool pigment increase

*Slight increase: 40-200; moderate: 200-1,000; great: over 1,000 units

American Family Physician

jacket ■ jaundice

hepatocellular j. Jaundice caused by diseased liver cells that do not function properly, usually because of liver inflammation.

neonatal j. See physiologic jaundice.

obstructive j. Jaundice resulting from the blockage of bile from the liver cells to the upper part of the small intestine (duodenum).

physiologic j. Slight jaundice of the newborn that disappears within one week after birth. Also called icterus neonatorum; neonatal icterus; neonatal jaundice; physiologic icterus.

jaw (jaw) Either of two bones of the face that support the teeth; the upper one is formed by the two maxillae and the lower one is the mandible.

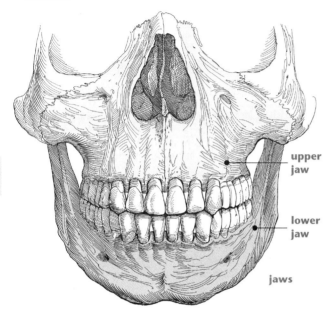

jaws

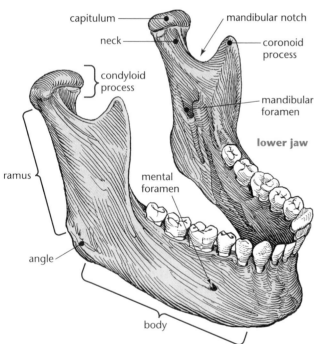

capitulum
neck
condyloid process
ramus
mental foramen
angle
body

mandibular notch
coronoid process
mandibular foramen

lower jaw

lower j. See mandible.
lumpy j. See actinomycosis.
upper j. See maxilla.

jawbone (jaw′bōn) See mandible.
jejunal (jĕ-joo′nal) Relating to the jejunum.
jejunectomy (jĕ-joo-nek′to-me) Surgical removal of all or a portion of the jejunum.

jejunitis (jĕ-joo-ni′tis) Inflammation of the jejunum.
jejuno-, jejun- Combining forms meaning jejunum.
jejunocolostomy (jĕ-joo-no-ko-los′to-me) Surgical procedure that connects and creates an opening between the jejunum and the colon.
jejunoileitis (jĕ-joo-no-il-e-i′tis) Inflammation of both the jejunum and the ileum.
jejunoileostomy (jĕ-joo-no-il-e-os′to-me) Surgical procedure that connects and creates an opening between the jejunum and a noncontiguous part of the ileum.
jejunojejunostomy (jĕ-joo-no-jĕ-joo-nos′to-me) Surgical procedure that connects and creates an opening between two noncontiguous parts of the jejunum.
jejunoplasty (jĕ-joo′no-plas-te) Surgical repair of the jejunum.
jejunostomy (jĕ-joo-nos′to-me) Surgical procedure that creates a permanent opening through the abdominal wall into the midportion of the small intestine (jejunum).
jejunotomy (jĕ-joo-not′o-me) Surgical cut into the jejunum.
jejunum (jĕ-joo′num) The middle part of the small intestine, located between the duodenum and the ileum; in the adult, it is approximately 8 feet long.

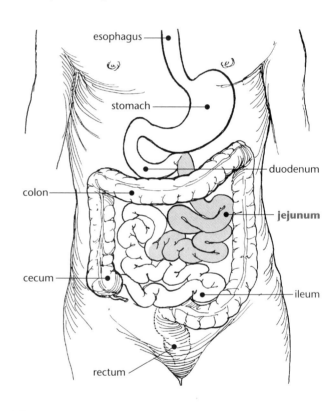

esophagus
stomach
colon
cecum
duodenum
jejunum
ileum
rectum

jelly (jel′e) A semisolid, gelatinous substance; translucent in appearance.

contraceptive j. A jelly used alone or with another contraceptive device to prevent conception.

petroleum j. See petrolatum.

Wharton's j. The soft, mucous substance of the umbilical cord that supports the umbilical vessels.

jerk (jerk) A sudden reflex or movement.

ankle j. See Achilles reflex, under reflex.

crossed j. See crossed reflex, under reflex.

crossed knee j. See crossed knee reflex, under reflex.

elbow j. See triceps reflex, under reflex.

knee j. See patellar reflex, under reflex.

jigger (jig′ger) See chigoe.

jimsonweed (jim′son-wēd) *Datura stramonium;* a poisonous plant with white or purple flowers and prickly fruit. Also called thorn apple.

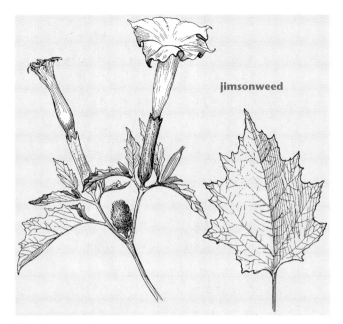

jimsonweed

jitteriness (jit′er-e-nes) Condition similar to seizure activity observed in some newborn infants; characterized by abnormal, tremorlike movements of the extremities; unlike the coarse, jerky movements of seizures, those of a jittery infant are finer, will cease if the child's hands are grasped, and are not accompanied by abnormal eye movements.

jitters (jit′ers) **1.** Slight but rapid movements caused by nervousness. **2.** Abrupt movement in the limbs due to cerebral irritation, hypoglycemia, or hypocalcemia.

joint (joint) The skeletal site at which two or more bones meet; an articulation.

   acromioclavicular j. The articulation between the lateral end of the collarbone (clavicle) and the acromion of the shoulder blade (scapula).

   amphiarthrodial j. A joint in which the surfaces of two bones are connected by intervening cartilage, enabling slight movement, as in the articulation between two vertebrae. Also called cartilaginous joint; amphiarthrosis.

ankle j. See talocrural joint.
anterior talocalcanean j. See talocalcaneonavicular joint.
arthrodial j. See plane joint.
atlantoaxial j. Either of two articulations between the first and second cervical vertebrae (atlas and axis).
atlantoepistrophic j. Either of two joints at the neck: *Lateral atlantoepistrophic j.,* the junction between the inferior articular processes of the atlas and the superior articular processes of the axis. *Median atlantoepistrophic j.,* the junction between the dens of the axis and the anterior arch and transverse ligament of the atlas.
   atlanto-occipital j.'s The ellipsoid joints between the two superior articular facets of the first cervical vertebra (atlas) and the condyles of the occipital bone on each side of the foramen magnum.

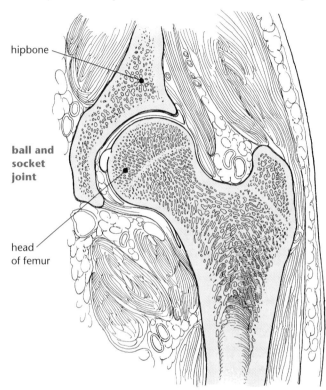

hipbone

ball and socket joint

head of femur

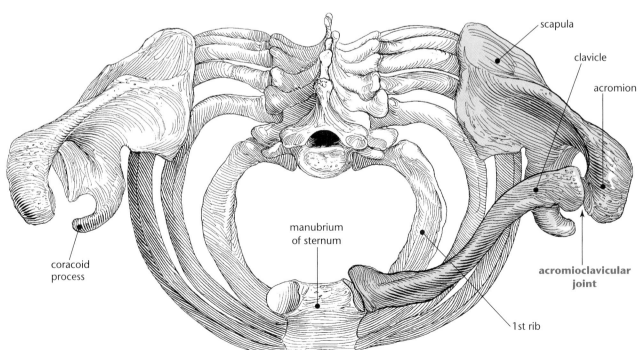

scapula

clavicle

acromion

coracoid process

manubrium of sternum

acromioclavicular joint

1st rib

ball-and-socket j. A synovial joint in which a rounded head (ball) of one bone fits into a cuplike cavity (socket) of another bone, permitting a wide range of movement in any direction (e.g., in the shoulder and hip joints). Also called spheroidal joint; enarthrosis.

bicondylar j. A synovial joint in which two rounded condyles of one bone fit into two shallow cavities of another bone, as in the knee or temporomandibular joints, allowing all movement except rotation. Also called condyloid joint; condylar joint.

calcaneocuboid j. A saddle-shaped joint in the posterior portion of the foot between the front surface of the heel bone (calcaneus) and the back surface of the cuboid bone.

capitular j. An articulation between the head of a rib and the bodies of two adjacent thoracic vertebrae.

carpometacarpal j.'s The plane joints between the carpal bones of the wrist and the second, third, fourth, and fifth metacarpal bones of the hand.

carpometacarpal j. of thumb The joint between the trapezium of the wrist and the first metacarpal bone of the hand.

cartilaginous j. See amphiarthrodial joint.

Charcot's j. A swollen, unstable but painless joint, frequently with destruction of intra-articular ligaments and consequent abnormally increased range of motion; caused by loss of sensory innervation; the lack of sensation deprives the joint of protective reactions to undue stresses; considered a complication of a neurologic disorder (e.g., tabes dorsalis or diabetic neuropathy). Also called neuropathic joint.

Chopart's j. See transverse tarsal joint.

coccygeal j. See sacrococcygeal joint.

condylar j. See bicondylar joint.

condyloid j. See bicondylar joint.

costochondral j. The cartilaginous articulation between the anterior end of a rib and the lateral end of a costal cartilage.

cricothyroid j. The synovial joint between the side of the cricoid cartilage and the inferior horn of the thyroid cartilage, permitting gliding and rotational movements.

cuneometatarsal j.'s See tarsometatarsal joints.

cuneonavicular j. An articulation in the posterior portion of the foot between the front surface of the navicular bone and the back surfaces of the three cuneiform bones.

diarthrodial j. See synovial joint.

ellipsoidal j. A joint shaped like a ball and socket, but with the articulating surfaces more closely resembling an oval; an oval-shaped part fits into an elliptic cavity, permitting all types of movement except pivotal.

false j. See pseudarthrosis.

femoropatellar j. The part of the knee joint formed by the articulation between the back surface of the kneecap (patella) and corresponding anterior surface of the femur.

fibrous j. A joint in which fibrous tissue unites two bones, permitting only slight movement, such as in the joints between the bones of the skull; the types of fibrous joints are syndesmosis, suture, and gomphosis. Also called synarthrodial joint; synarthrosis; immovable joint.

frozen j. See ankylosis.

ginglymoid j. See hinge joint.

gliding j. See plane joint.

hinge j. A synovial joint that permits only a forward and backward movement similar to that of a door hinge (e.g., the bending and straightening of the fingers). Also called ginglymus; ginglymoid joint.

hip j. The ball-and-socket joint between the head of the femur and the acetabulum of the hipbone.

humeroradial j. The joint at the elbow between the humerus and the head of the radius.

humeroulnar j. The joint at the elbow between the trochlea of the humerus and the trochlear notch of the ulna.

immovable j. See fibrous joint.

intercarpal j.'s The joints between the carpal bones of the wrist.

interchondral j.'s The joints between the contiguous surfaces of the 5th through 10th costal cartilages.

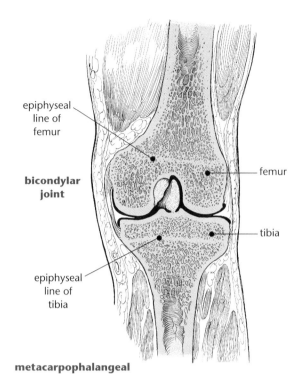

epiphyseal line of femur

bicondylar joint

femur

tibia

epiphyseal line of tibia

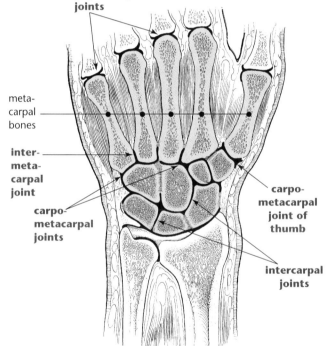

metacarpophalangeal joints

meta-carpal bones

inter-meta-carpal joint

carpo-metacarpal joints

carpo-metacarpal joint of thumb

intercarpal joints

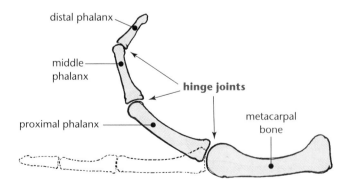

distal phalanx

middle phalanx

hinge joints

proximal phalanx

metacarpal bone

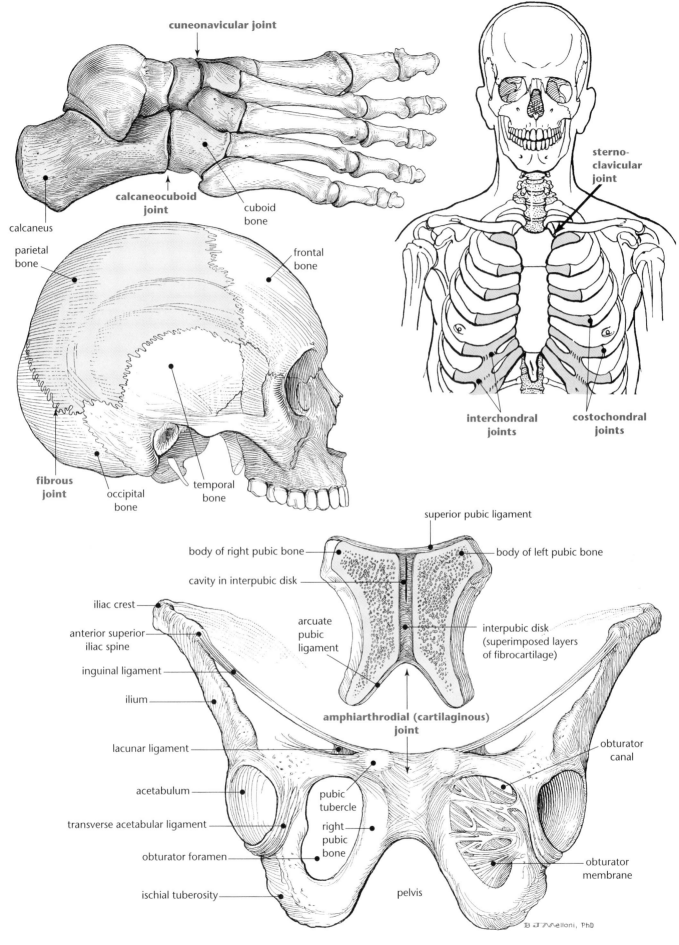

cuneonavicular joint

calcaneocuboid joint

calcaneus

cuboid bone

parietal bone

frontal bone

fibrous joint

occipital bone

temporal bone

sterno-clavicular joint

interchondral joints

costochondral joints

superior pubic ligament

body of right pubic bone

body of left pubic bone

cavity in interpubic disk

arcuate pubic ligament

interpubic disk (superimposed layers of fibrocartilage)

iliac crest

anterior superior iliac spine

inguinal ligament

ilium

amphiarthrodial (cartilaginous) joint

obturator canal

lacunar ligament

acetabulum

transverse acetabular ligament

obturator foramen

ischial tuberosity

pubic tubercle

right pubic bone

pelvis

obturator membrane

B.J. Melloni, PhD

joint ■ joint

intermetacarpal j.'s The plane joints between the adjoining bases of the second through fifth metacarpal bones of the hand.

intermetatarsal j.'s The plane joints between the adjoining bases of the five metatarsal bones of the foot.

interphalangeal j.'s The hinge joints between the phalanges of each finger and toe.

intertarsal j.'s The joints between the tarsal bones in the posterior portion of the foot. Also called tarsal joints.

jaw j. See temporomandibular joint.

knee j. A compound condylar joint formed by the two condyles and patellar surface of the femur, the posterior surface of the kneecap (patella), and the superior articular surface of the tibia.

Lisfranc's j.'s See tarsometatarsal joints.

lumbosacral j. The joint between the fifth lumbar vertebra and the sacrum.

mandibular j. See temporomandibular joint.

metacarpophalangeal j.'s The ellipsoidal joints between the shallow concave bases of the five proximal phalanges and the convex heads of the corresponding metacarpal bones.

metatarsophalangeal j.'s The ellipsoid joints at the front of the foot between the heads of the five metatarsal bones and the concave bases of the corresponding proximal phalanges.

midtarsal j. See transverse tarsal joint.

movable j. See synovial joint.

neuropathic j. See Charcot's joint.

pivot j. See rotary joint.

plane j. A synovial joint in which the opposing articular surfaces are either flat planes or slightly curved; it allows gliding movements, as in the intermetacarpal joints. Also called gliding joint; arthrodial joint.

radiocarpal j. The ellipsoid joint at the wrist between the radius and its articular disk, and the scaphoid, lunate, and triangular bones. Also called wrist joint.

radioulnar j.'s The two articulations between the radius and the ulna: *Distal radioulnar j.*, the joint between the rounded head of the ulna and the ulnar notch of the radius at the distal end of the forearm, near the wrist; also called inferior radioulnar joint. *Proximal radioulnar j.*, the joint between the head of the radius and the radial notch of the ulna within the annular ligament of the radius at the proximal end of the forearm, near the elbow. Also called superior radioulnar joint.

rotary j. A joint in which a central bony projection rotates within a ring, or a ring pivots around the bony projection as in the joint between the first and second vertebrae; movement is limited to one plane. Also called trochoid joint; pivot joint.

sacrococcygeal j. The joint between the sacrum and the tailbone (coccyx). Also called coccygeal joint.

sacroiliac j. The joint between the vertebral column and the pelvis, specifically between the two auricular surfaces on the upper part of the sacrum and each ilium on the posterior part of the pelvis.

saddle j. A synovial joint in which the opposing surfaces of two bones are reciprocally concave on one side and convex on the other as in the carpometacarpal joint of the thumb; movement is effected by the two bony surfaces opposing each other. Also called sellar joint; saddle-shaped joint.

saddle-shaped j. See saddle joint.

sellar j. See saddle joint.

spheroidal j. See ball-and-socket joint.

sternoclavicular j. The joint formed by the medial end of the collarbone (clavicle), the manubrium of the breastbone (sternum), and the cartilage of the first rib.

subtalar j. The joint between the inferior surface of the ankle bone (talus) and the superior surface of the heel bone (calcaneus). Also called talocalcanean joint.

synarthrodial j. See fibrous joint.

synovial j. A joint that usually permits free movement, characterized by a layer of hyaline cartilage or fibrocartilage and a synovial

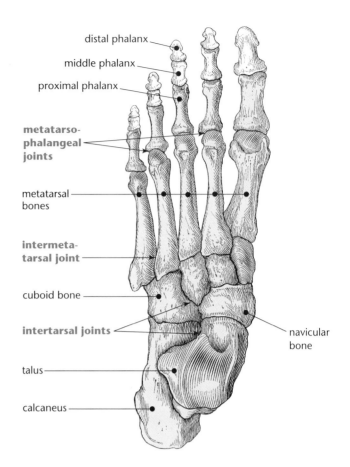

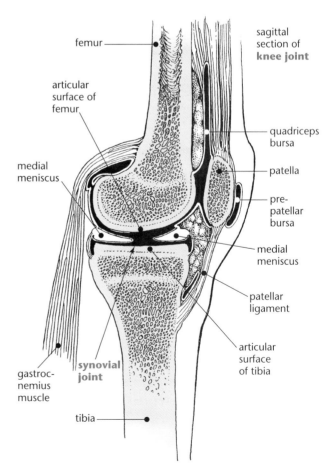

J

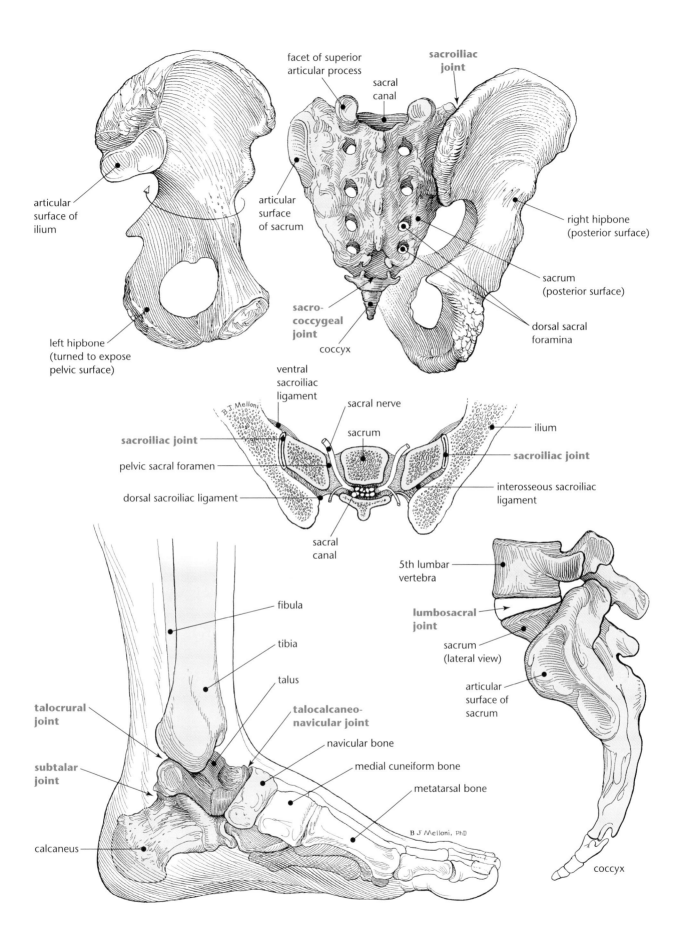

facet of superior
articular process

sacral
canal

**sacroiliac
joint**

articular
surface of
ilium

articular
surface
of sacrum

right hipbone
(posterior surface)

left hipbone
(turned to expose
pelvic surface)

**sacro-
coccygeal
joint**

coccyx

sacrum
(posterior surface)

dorsal sacral
foramina

ventral
sacroiliac
ligament

sacral nerve

sacrum

ilium

B.J. Melloni

sacroiliac joint

sacroiliac joint

pelvic sacral foramen

dorsal sacroiliac ligament

interosseous sacroiliac
ligament

sacral
canal

5th lumbar
vertebra

**lumbosacral
joint**

sacrum
(lateral view)

articular
surface of
sacrum

fibula

tibia

talus

**talocrural
joint**

**talocalcaneo-
navicular joint**

navicular bone

medial cuneiform bone

metatarsal bone

**subtalar
joint**

B.J. Melloni, PhD

calcaneus

coccyx

joint ■ joint

cavity between the bones (i.e., a cavity lined by a synovial membrane and containing synovial fluid); it includes most of the joints of the body. Also called diarthrosis; diarthrodial joint; movable joint.

talocalcanean j. See subtalar joint.

talocalcaneonavicular j. A joint formed by the rounded head of the ankle bone (talus), the concave surface of the navicular bone, the upper surface of the heel bone (calcaneus), and the plantar calcaneonavicular ligament. Also called anterior talocalcanean joint.

talocrural j. A hinge joint formed by the tibia and fibula and the ankle bone (talus). Also called ankle joint.

tarsal j.'s See intertarsal joints.

tarsometatarsal j.'s The three joints between the tarsal and metatarsal bones of the foot, involving a medial joint between the first metatarsal bone and the medial cuneiform bone; an intermediate joint between the second and third metatarsal bones and the intermediate and lateral cuneiform bones; and a lateral joint between the fourth and fifth metatarsal bones and the cuboid bone. Also called Lisfranc's joints; cuneometatarsal joints.

temporomandibular j. (TMJ) The synovial joint between the condyle of the mandible inferiorly and the mandibular fossa and articular tubercle of the temporal bone superiorly; separated by a thin articular disk into two cavities, each of which is lined by a synovial membrane. Also called jaw joint; mandibular joint.

tibiofibular j., superior The plane joint between the lateral condyle of the tibia and the head of the fibula, near the knee.

transverse tarsal j. The joint between the heel bone (calcaneus) and cuboid bone, and the ankle bone (talus) and navicular bone of the foot. Also called Chopart's joint; midtarsal joint.

trochoid j. See rotary joint.

wrist j. See radiocarpal joint.

joule (jool) (J) A unit of energy equal to that consumed when a current of 1 ampere passes through a resistance of 1 ohm for 1 second.

judgment (juj′ment) An authoritative opinion or evaluation.

mere medical j. In Social Security disability, judgment of a medical impairment that is based on insufficient objective data and that tends to rely on subjectivity.

substantial medical j. In Social Security disability, judgment of a medical impairment that is well grounded on a preponderance of objective data.

jugal (joo′gal) **1.** Uniting. **2.** Relating to the cheek.

jugular (jug′u-lar) Relating to the neck.

jugum (joo′ gum), pl. ju′ga A ridge or depression connecting two structures.

juga alveolaria Eminences on the front of the upper and lower jaws (maxilla and mandible) produced by the roots of incisors and cuspids within.

j. sphenoidale The raised smooth front part of the body of the sphenoid bone that connects the lesser wings of the bone; it separates the anterior cranial fossa from the sphenoidal sinus.

juice (joos′) Any fluid from plant or animal tissues, such as intestinal

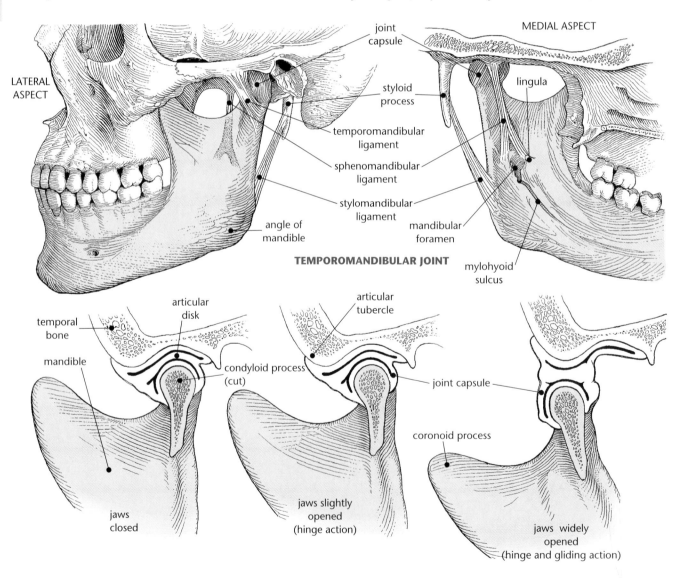

TEMPOROMANDIBULAR JOINT

LATERAL ASPECT

MEDIAL ASPECT

joint capsule
styloid process
temporomandibular ligament
sphenomandibular ligament
stylomandibular ligament
angle of mandible
lingula
mandibular foramen
mylohyoid sulcus

temporal bone
mandible
articular disk
condyloid process (cut)
jaws closed

articular tubercle
joint capsule
coronoid process
jaws slightly opened (hinge action)

jaws widely opened (hinge and gliding action)

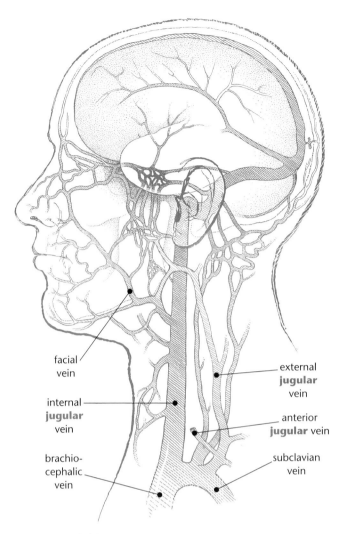

facial vein

internal **jugular** vein

brachio-cephalic vein

external **jugular** vein

anterior **jugular** vein

subclavian vein

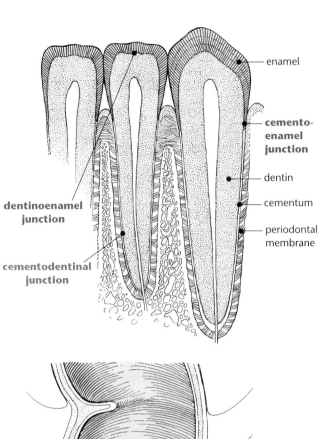

enamel

cemento-enamel junction

dentin

cementum

periodontal membrane

dentinoenamel junction

cementodentinal junction

J

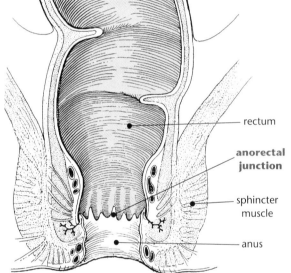

rectum

anorectal junction

sphincter muscle

anus

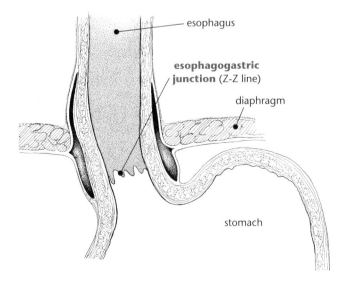

esophagus

esophagogastric junction (Z-Z line)

diaphragm

stomach

or pancreatic juice.

junction (junk'shun) The point where two structures or parts unite.

   amelodentinal j. See dentinoenamel junction.

   anorectal j. The region where the rectum ends and the anal canal begins, in front of and slightly below the tip of the coccyx.

   cementodentinal j. The boundary between the dentin and the cementum of the root of a tooth. Also called dentinocemental junction.

   cementoenamel j. The boundary between the cementum of the root of a tooth and the enamel of its crown.

   communicating j. See gap junction.

   costochondral j. The site of articulation between a rib and its cartilage.

   dentinocemental j. See cementodentinal junction.

   dentinoenamel j. The boundary between the dentin and enamel of the crown of a tooth. Also called amelodentinal junction.

   electrical j. See gap junction.

   esophagogastric j. The line at which the esophagus joins the stomach; it is situated on the left of the median plane at the approximate level of the 11th thoracic vertebra.

   gap j. The space (about 3 nm wide) between certain nerve cells and cells of smooth and cardiac muscles that mediate communication by allowing passage of molecules from one cell to the next; also present in the liver, epidermis, and connective tissues; it forms an electric synapse between some neurons in the brain. Also called communicating junction; electrical junction.

   mucocutaneous j. The region where the mucous membrane adjoins the superficial layer of the skin.

   myoneural j. See neuromuscular junction.

myotendinal j. The junctional region between the end of the muscle fibers and the tendinous attachment.

neuromuscular j. The point of contact between the end-plate of a motor nerve and a muscle fiber; specialized junctional area involved in nerve-muscle transmission. Also called myoneural junction; motor end-plate.

occluding j. See tight junction.

sclerocorneal j. See limbus of cornea, under limbus.

tight j. An annular junction around the apices of epithelial cells, present at sites requiring a barrier to diffusion through the intercellular space; at the junction, the membranes are in firm contact, obliterating the space between them and thereby creating a barrier to the movement of molecules. Also called occluding junction; zonula occludens.

jurisprudence (joor′is-proo′dens) The science or philosophy of a particular system of law.

dental j. See forensic dentistry.

medical j. See forensic medicine.

juvenile (joo′vĕ-nīl) **1.** Relating to youth. **2.** Not fully developed; a young person; child.

juxtaepiphyseal (juks-tah-ep-ĭ-fiz′e-al) Near or next to an end (epiphysis) of a long bone.

juxtaglomerular (juks-tah-glo-mer′u-lar) Near or next to a filtration unit (glomerulus) of the kidney.

juxtapose (juks-tah-pōz′) To place in a side-by-side position.

juxtaposition (juks-tah-po-zish′un) The state of being side by side; apposition.

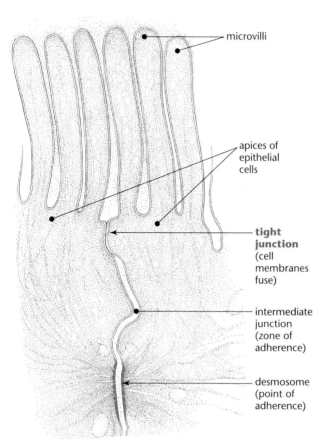

microvilli

apices of epithelial cells

tight junction (cell membranes fuse)

intermediate junction (zone of adherence)

desmosome (point of adherence)

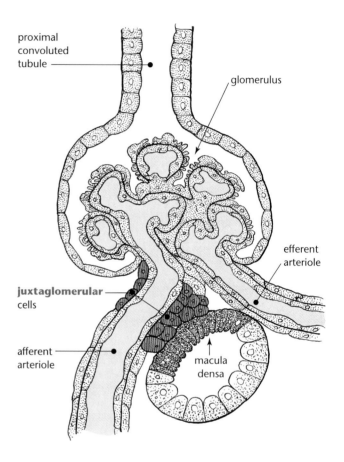

proximal convoluted tubule

glomerulus

efferent arteriole

juxtaglomerular cells

afferent arteriole

macula densa

K

kala-azar (kah′lah ah-zar′) See visceral leishmaniasis, under leishmaniasis.

kaliopenia (ka-le-o-pe′ne-ah) Deficiency of potassium.

kaliopenic (ka-le-o-pe′nik) Deficient in potassium.

kalium (ka′le-um) Latin for potassium.

kaliuresis (ka-le-u-re′sis) Increased levels of potassium excretion in the urine. Also called kaluresis.

kaliuretic (ka-le-u-ret′ik) 1. Relating to kaliuresis. 2. An agent that increases potassium excretion in the urine.

kallikrein (kal-ĭ-kre′in) An enzyme that can convert the globulin kininogen to produce kinins; found in plasma, saliva, urine, pancreatic digestive juices, and other exocrine secretions.

kaluresis (kal-u-re′sis) See kaliuresis.

kaolin (ka′o-lin) A whitish powder found in natural deposits, used as a demulcent and absorbent. Also called fuller's earth; terra alba.

karyochrome (kar′e-o-krōm) A nerve cell with a nucleus that stains intensely.

karyocyte (kar′e-o-sīt) A nucleated cell.

karyogamy (kar-e-og′ah-me) Fusion of the nuclei of two cells during fertilization in cell conjugation.

karyogenesis (kar-e-o-jen′ĕ-sis) The development of a cell nucleus.

karyogram (kar′e-o-gram) See karyotype.

karyokinesis (kar-e-o-kī-ne′sis) The division of the nucleus during mitosis. See also mitosis.

karyolymph (kar′e-o-limf) The clear fluid substance in the cell nucleus.

karyolysis (kar-e-ol′ĭ-sis) The destruction or dissolution of the nucleus of a cell from swelling.

karyomorphism (kar-e-o-mor′fizm) 1. Development of a cell nucleus. 2. The shape of a cell nucleus, particularly of a white blood cell (leukocyte).

karyon (kar′e-on) The nucleus of a cell.

karyoplasm (kar′e-o-plazm) The protoplasm of the nucleus of a cell. Also called nucleoplasm.

karyopyknosis (kar-e-o-pik-no′sis) Shrinkage of cell nuclei and condensation of the chromatin into formless masses.

karyorrhexis (kar-e-o-rek′sis) Fragmentation of the nucleus of a cell; the chromatin is distributed throughout the cytoplasm.

karyosome (kar′e-o-sōm) A mass of chromatin, knotlike in appearance, found in the cell nucleus during the interphase stage of mitosis; often confused with the nucleolus. Also called net knot; chromatin nucleolus; false nucleolus.

karyotype (kar′e-o-tīp) 1. The chromosome constitution of an individual. 2. A systematized graphic arrangement of individual chromosomes in the nucleus of a single cell, presented in the standard classification (i.e., in pairs according to size); the chromosomes are photomicrographed during the metaphase stage of mitosis. Also called karyogram. 3. The process of making such an arrangement.

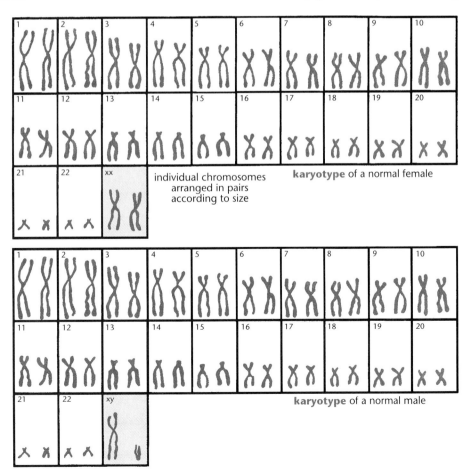

individual chromosomes arranged in pairs according to size

karyotype of a normal female

karyotype of a normal male

Kell blood group (kel blud groop) A blood group of clinical importance because of its immunogenicity; consists of a series of codominant antigens determined by alleles at a site that is thought to be on the short arm of chromosome 2; first detected through antiserum produced by a Mrs. Kell.

keloid (ke′loid) A firm, nodular mass of hyperplastic scar tissue; usually formed in people with dark complexions.

keloidosis (ke-loi-do′sis) The occurrence of multiple keloids.

keloplasty (ke′lo-plas-te) Surgical removal of a keloid or scar.

kelvin (kel′vin) (K) A unit of thermodynamic temperature. See Kelvin scale, under scale.

keratectasia (ker-ah-tek-ta′ze-ah) Protrusion of the cornea due to thinning of corneal tissue. Also called corneal ectasia.

keratectomy (ker-ah-tek′to-me) Surgical removal of part of the cornea affected by scarring or degeneration.

keratic (ker-at′ik) 1. Relating to keratin. 2. Relating to the cornea.

keratin (ker′ah-tin) A protein found in epidermal structures such as hair, nails, feathers, scales, and horns; it is insoluble in water and gastric juices, and has a high sulfur content. Also spelled ceratin.

keratinization (ker-ah-tin-ĭ-za′shun) The development of keratin or a horny layer of tissue.

keratinize (ker′ah-tin-iz) 1. To develop keratin. 2. To become keratin-like.

keratinized (ker′ah-tin-izd) Covered with hornlike processes.

keratinosome (kĕ-rat′ĭ-no-sōm) See membrane-coating granules, under granule.

keratinous (ke-rat′ĭ-nus) Relating to or containing keratin.

keratitis (ker-ah-ti′tis) Inflammation of the cornea. Also called corneitis. See also keratopathy.

    disciform k. Formation of a round lesion on the cornea associated with moderate to severe edema; usually self-limited, lasting weeks to months. It is the most common complication of a herpes simplex infection.

    exposure k. Keratitis caused by dryness of the cornea and exposure to minor trauma due to failure of the eyelids to close properly; may occur in a variety of conditions (e.g., exophthalmos, eversion of the lower eyelid, eyelid paralysis). Also called lagophthalmic keratitis.

    fascicular k. Progressive corneal ulcer that migrates from the periphery to the center of the cornea while accompanied by a band of blood vessels from the conjunctiva.

    herpes simplex k. Keratitis caused by the herpes simplex virus (HSV).

    herpetic k. Recurrent ulceration of the cornea, usually in a branchlike pattern, caused by herpesvirus 1 and 2; attacks may be precipitated by overexposure to sunshine, trauma, or menstruation. Also called corneal herpes.

    interstitial k. Inflammatory disease of the deep substance of the cornea; found in children and young adults between the ages of 5 and 20 years as a late manifestation of congenital syphilis. Also called parenchymatous keratitis.

    lagophthalmic k. See exposure keratitis.

    neuroparalytic k. Corneal damage resulting from loss of function of the sensory nerve to the cornea due to injury to the trigeminal (5th cranial) nerve.

    parenchymatous k. See interstitial keratitis.

    sicca k. See keratoconjunctivitis sicca.

    superficial punctate k. Multiple round or oval erosions of the corneal epithelium; suspected to be caused by a virus.

kerato-, kerat- Combining forms meaning the cornea; horny tissue; hornlike.

keratoacanthoma (ker-ah-to-ak-an-tho′mah) A rapidly growing benign skin lesion, often with a central depression, occurring predominantly on exposed areas of the skin; it resembles squamous cell carcinoma and is associated with sun exposure.

keratocele (ker′ah-to-sēl) Hernia of the innermost layer of the cornea (Descemet's membrane), occurring through a flaw in the outer layer of the cornea.

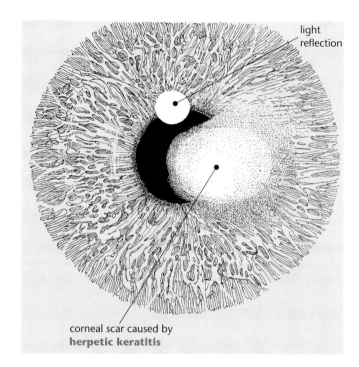

corneal scar caused by
herpetic keratitis

keratoconjunctivitis (ker′ah-to–kon–junk′tĭ–vi′tis) Inflammation of both the cornea and the transparent membrane (conjunctiva) covering the eyeball and inner eyelid.

    epidemic k. A highly contagious form of keratoconjunctivitis caused by adenovirus types 8 and 19, characterized by swelling of eyelids and conjunctiva around the cornea and conjunctival hyperemia; often caused by improperly sterilized ophthalmic instruments, contaminated solutions, or dust and trauma in industry. Also called shipyard eye.

    phlyctenular k. A delayed hypersensitivity to proteins from microorganisms, including those from tubercle bacillus, *Candida albicans, Chlamydia lymphogranulomatis,* and especially *Staphylococcus aureus;* characterized by formation of minute, ulcerating nodules (phlyctenules) primarily on the conjunctiva and the cornea, especially around its periphery. Those occurring on the cornea may cause scarring.

    k. sicca (KCS) A condition associated with diminished tears; occurs principally in women at the time of menopause. Also called sicca keratitis; dry eye syndrome. See also Sjögren's syndrome.

keratoconus (ker-ah-to-ko′nus) An uncommon inherited condition characterized by a central degeneration and thinning of the cornea, resulting in a cone-shaped deformity. Also called conical cornea.

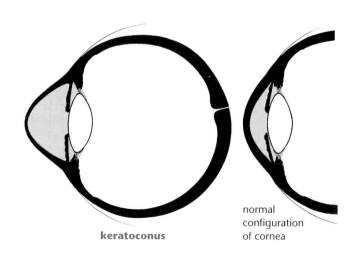

keratoconus

normal
configuration
of cornea

keratome

keratocyte (ker′ah-to-sit) **1.** An abnormally shaped red blood cell, sometimes caused by drugs. **2.** A flattened cell between lamellae of the cornea.

keratoderma (ker-ah-to-der′mah) **1.** A horny superficial covering. **2.** A thickening of the horny layer of the skin. Also called keratodermia.

    k. blennorrhagica See keratosis blennorrhagica.

    k. palmaris et plantaris See palmoplantar keratoderma.

    palmoplantar k. A patchy thickening of the skin in symmetrical areas of the palms and soles. Also called keratoderma palmaris et plantaris; keratoderma symmetrica.

    k. symmetrica See palmoplantar keratoderma.

keratodermia (ker-ah-to-der′me-ah) See keratoderma (2).

keratogenesis (ker-ah-to-jen′ĕ-sis) The production of horny tissue (e.g., nails, feathers, scales).

keratogenous (ker-ah-toj′ĕ-nus) Causing the production of horny tissue.

keratoid (ker′ah-toid) **1.** Horny. **2.** Resembling the cornea. Also called keroid.

keratoleptynsis (ker-ah-to-lep-tin′sis) An operation involving plastic surgery of the eye in which the anterior surface of the cornea is removed and replaced with bulbar conjunctiva.

keratolysis (ker-ah-tol′ĭ-sis) The loosening and peeling of the epidermis.

keratolytic (ker-ah-to-lit′ik) Relating to keratolysis.

keratomalacia (ker-ah-to-mah-la′she-ah) A dryness and softening of the cornea, usually in both eyes, associated with severe vitamin A deficiency.

keratome (ker′ah-tōm) A surgical knife for cutting the cornea. Also called keratotome.

keratometer (ker-ah-tom′ĕ-ter) An instrument for measuring the anterior curvature of the cornea. Also called ophthalmometer.

keratometry (ker-ah-tom′ĕ-tre) The measuring of the anterior curvature of the cornea with a keratometer. Also called ophthalmometry.

keratomycosis (ker-ah-to-mi-ko′sis) A fungus infection of the cornea.

keratopathy (ker-ah-top′ah-the) A noninflammatory disease of the cornea.

    bullous k. A condition caused by an excessive accumulation of fluid in the cornea; occurs occasionally after intraocular operations (e.g., in cataract procedures).

    calcific band k. Condition of the eye characterized by the presence of a gray, horizontal, opaque band across the cornea; it is formed by deposition of calcium salts in the anterior layers of the cornea that begins at its periphery and progresses toward its center; symptoms include eye irritation and redness, and blurring of vision; seen in certain inflammatory, metabolic, and degenerative conditions (e.g., chronic iridocyclitis, hypercalcemia, and juvenile rheumatoid arthritis).

    climatic k. A symmetrical and bilateral degeneration of the cornea (believed to be caused by prolonged exposure to ultraviolet rays or extreme heat or cold). Also called Labrador keratopathy; pearl-diver's keratopathy.

    Labrador k. See climatic keratopathy.

    pearl-diver's k. See climatic keratopathy.

keratoplasty (ker′ah-to-plas-te) An operation in which all, or part of a defective cornea is removed and replaced with a normal cornea (corneal graft). Also called corneal transplantation; corneal graft.

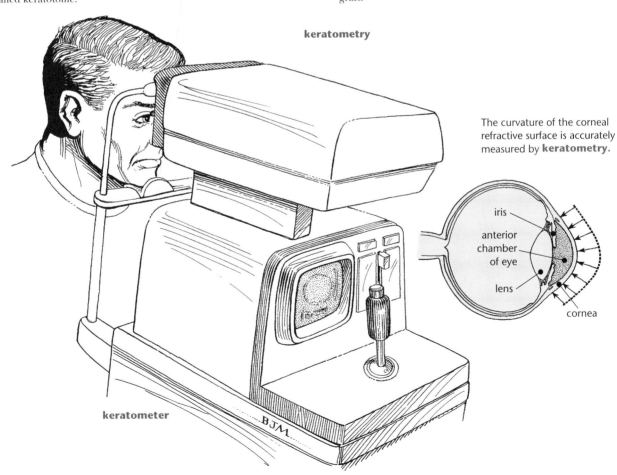
keratometry

The curvature of the corneal refractive surface is accurately measured by **keratometry.**

iris
anterior chamber of eye
lens
cornea

keratometer

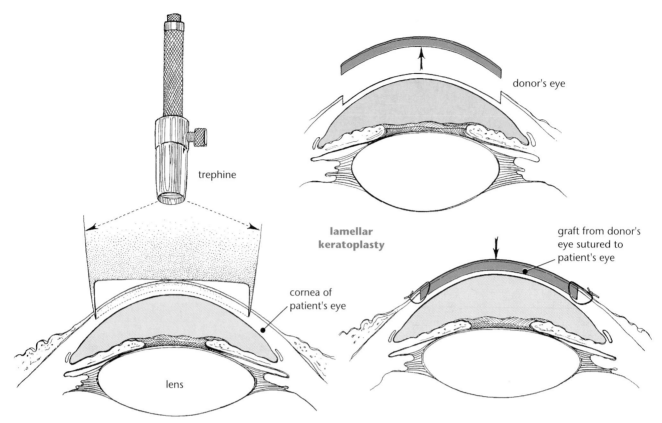

trephine

donor's eye

lamellar
keratoplasty

graft from donor's
eye sutured to
patient's eye

cornea of
patient's eye

lens

appearance of
completed
operation

lamellar k. A procedure in which only the superficial layer of the cornea is removed and replaced with healthy corneal tissue. Also called nonpenetrating keratoplasty.

    nonpenetrating k. See lamellar keratoplasty.

    penetrating k. A procedure in which the full thickness of the cornea is removed and replaced with healthy corneal tissue.

keratoprosthesis (ker-ah-to-pros-the′sis) Replacement of a diseased portion of the cornea with a plastic implant.

keratorhexis (ker-ah-to-rek′sis) Rupture of the cornea due to a perforating ulcer or an injury sustained in an accident. Also spelled keratorrhexis.

keratorrhexis (ker-ah-to-rek′sis) See keratorhexis.

keratoscleritis (ker-ah-to-skle-ri′tis) Inflammation of both the cornea and the sclera.

keratoscope (ker′ah-to-skōp) An instrument containing a disk with black and white concentric rings, used to examine the curvature of the cornea. Also called Placido's disk.

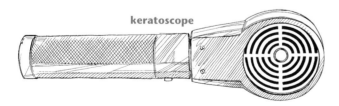

keratoscope

keratoscopy (ker-ah-tos′ko-pe) Examination of the reflections of light from the anterior surface of the cornea to determine the state and degree of corneal curvature.

keratose (ker′ah-tōs) **1.** Relating to keratosis. **2.** Horny; applied to certain types of skin lesions.

keratosis (ker-ah-to′sis) A benign lesion on the epidermis consisting of a circumscribed overgrowth of the horny layer of the skin.

    actinic k. See solar keratosis.

    arsenical k. Discrete papules on the skin, located primarily on the palms and soles, resulting from chronic exposure to arsenic; may become malignant.

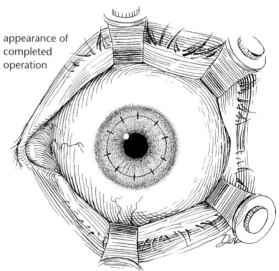

    k. blennorrhagica Pustules and crusts that develop most often on the palms, soles, toes, and glans penis; associated with Reiter's syndrome; formerly believed to be associated with gonorrhea. Also called keratoderma blennorrhagica.

    k. pilaris Multiple small keratotic papules, limited to the hair follicles, occurring chiefly on the lateral regions of the upper arms, thighs, and buttocks; the condition is recurrent and most prominent in cold weather.

    seborrheic k. (SK) Superficial, dark, warty plaques occurring most often on the trunk and extremities of persons after the third decade of life.

    senile k. See solar keratosis.

    solar k. A premalignant warty lesion that usually affects the elderly and is caused by prolonged exposure to the sun. Also called actinic keratosis; senile keratosis.

keratotome (ker-at′o-tōm) See keratome.

keratotomy (ker-ah-tot′o-me) Surgical incision through the cornea.

keraunophobia (kĕ-raw-no-fo'be-ah) Abnormally exaggerated fear of lightning and thunder.

kerion (ke're-on) A large, highly inflammatory, hairless mass on the scalp, occurring as a reaction to infection with a fungus that usually infects animals only (e.g., *Microsporum canis);* it tends to heal spontaneously, but if severe may leave scars.

kernicterus (ker-nik'ter-us) Bilirubin pigmentation of the gray matter of the central nervous system; a complication of hemolytic disease of the newborn and accompanied by severe neurological deficits or death.

keroid (ker'oid) See keratoid.

ketamine (kĕt'ah-mēn) A rapid-acting general anesthetic, administered intravenously and intramuscularly; causes analgesia and increased sympathetic activity; a cyclohexanone derivative.

keto acid (ke'to as'id) An acid containing both a carbonyl group and an acidic group and having the general formula R-CO-COOH.

ketoacidosis (ke-to-ah-sĭ-do'sis) The presence of an excessive amount of ketone bodies (acetoacetic acid, beta-hydroxybutyrate, and acetone) in the tissues and body fluids; it occurs in such conditions as diabetes and starvation.

ketoaciduria (ke-to-as-ĭ-du're-ah) An elevated amount of ketonic acids in the urine.

    branched-chain k. See maple syrup urine disease, under disease.

ketoconazole (ke-to-kon'ah-zol) A broad-spectrum antifungal agent, administered orally or topically for the treatment of fungal infections.

ketogenesis (ke-to-jen'ĕ-sis) The production of ketone bodies.

ketole (ke'tol) See indole.

ketone (ke'tōn) Any of a group of compounds that have a carbonyl group (CO) linked to hydrocarbon groups.

ketonemia (ke-to-ne'me-ah) The presence of ketone bodies in the blood.

ketones (ke'tōns) See ketone bodies, under body.

ketonization (ke-to-nĭ-za'shun) The process of being converted into a ketone.

ketonuria (ke-to-nu're-ah) The presence of ketone bodies (acetoacetic acid, beta-hydroxybutyrate, and acetone) in the urine.

ketorolac tromethamine (ke-to-ro'lak tro-meth'ah-mĭn) A potent nonopioid pain reliever (analgesic) for limited-duration use in managing pain; it provides pain relief comparable to that of narcotic analgesics without narcotic-like side effects such as potential for addiction, respiratory depression, nausea, and constipation. Trade name: Toradol.

ketose (ke'tōs) A carbohydrate that contains a ketone group in its molecule.

ketosis (ke-to'sis) An abnormally increased production of ketone bodies in the tissues and fluids of the body, as occurs in starvation and diabetes mellitus.

17-ketosteroid (ke-to'ste-roid) A steroid hormone derived from the gonads or adrenal glands; found in the urine of adults and in excess in certain tumors of the adrenal cortex; normal values in the urine are 6 to 18 mg/24 hr in the male and 4 to 13 mg/24 hr in the female.

ketosuccinic acid (ke-to-suk'sĭ-nik as'id) See oxaloacetic acid.

kick (kik) A quick and forceful thrust.

    atrial k. A forceful contraction of the cardiac atrium that helps deliver blood into the ventricle when the ventricular wall has become stiffened (e.g., in hypertension).

Kidd blood group (kid blud grōōp) A blood group consisting of red blood cell antigens, determined by the JK gene, that react with the anti-JKa and anti-JKb antibodies; named after a Mrs. Kidd, in whom the antibodies were first found.

kidney (kid'ne) One of two bean-shaped organs located in the back on either side of the spine and behind the peritoneum; it serves to filter the blood, excrete metabolic wastes in the form of urine, and regulate acid-base concentration and water balance in the tissues. The adult kidney is approximately 4 in. long, 2 in. wide and 1 in. thick.

    artificial k. See hemodialyzer.

    Ask-Upmark k. An anomalous kidney that failed to develop fully, with deep transverse grooving on its superficial layer and a

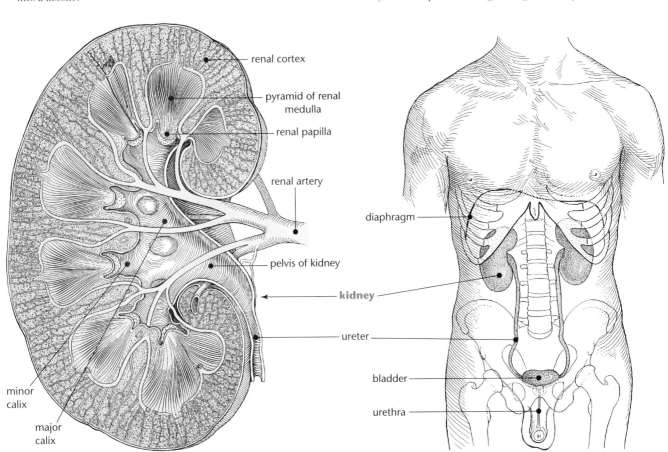

renal cortex

pyramid of renal medulla

renal papilla

renal artery

pelvis of kidney

kidney

ureter

minor calix

major calix

diaphragm

kidney

ureter

bladder

urethra

keraunophobia ■ **kidney**

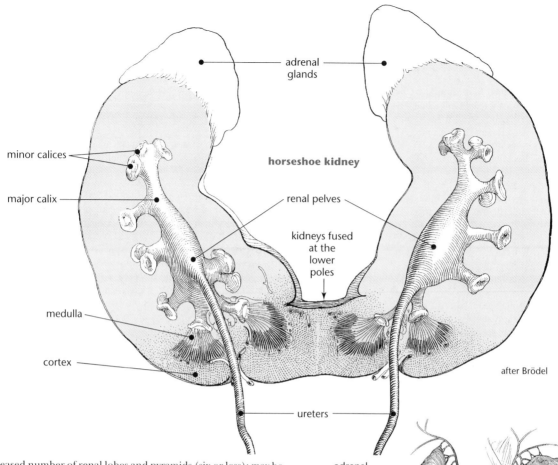

adrenal glands

horseshoe kidney

minor calices

major calix

renal pelves

kidneys fused
at the
lower
poles

medulla

cortex

after Brödel

ureters

K

decreased number of renal lobes and pyramids (six or less); may be the result of reflux nephropathy early in life.

contracted k. A shrunken scarred kidney due to the presence of an abnormally large amount of fibrous tissue, such as in arteriolar nephrosclerosis.

crush k. Degeneration of the renal tubule epithelium due to a crushing injury of muscles.

ectopic k. A kidney sited in an abnormal location (e.g., on the pelvic brim, in the pelvis, or on the same side of the normally placed kidney).

floating k. The excessively mobile kidney seen in nephroptosia. Also called wandering kidney; movable kidney.

Goldblatt k. A kidney with deficient arterial blood supply due to a narrowed renal artery, resulting in arterial hypertension.

horseshoe k. A horseshoe-shaped structure resulting from an anomalous fusion of the upper or lower poles of the two kidneys across the midline, in front of the aorta and vena cava.

medullary sponge k. A congenital defect characterized by the development of cysts of the pyramids of the kidney; occasionally associated with dilatation of the collecting tubules and formation of stones; it is usually asymptomatic and not a cause of kidney failure. See also cystic disease of renal medulla.

movable k. See floating kidney.

polycystic k. A kidney in which multiple cysts of varying size, resembling a bunch of grapes, have replaced most of the kidney substance. See also polycystic disease of kidney, under disease.

wandering k. See floating kidney.

killing (kil′ing) Producing death.

mercy k. See active euthanasia, under euthanasia.

kilobase (kil′o-bās) (kb) One thousand base pairs in a DNA sequence.

kilocalorie (kil-o-kal′o-re) (Kcal) See large calorie, under calorie.

kilocycle (kil′o-sī-kl) A thousand cycles per second.

kilogauss (kil′o-gows) (Kg) In magnetic resonance imaging (MRI), the unit of magnetic field strength equal to 10^3 gauss.

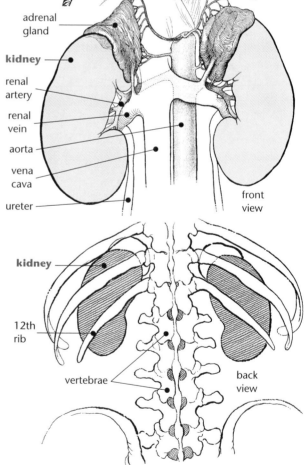

adrenal gland

kidney

renal artery

renal vein

aorta

vena cava

ureter

front view

kidney

12th rib

vertebrae

back view

killing ■ kilogauss

kilogram (kil'o-gram) (kg) One thousand grams, or 2.2046 pounds.

kilovolt (kil'o-vōlt) (kv) A thousand volts.

kinanesthesia (kin-an-es-the'ze-ah) Inability to perceive the sensation of movement, resulting in ataxia.

kinase (ki'nās) An enzyme that catalyzes the phosphorylation of an acceptor molecule by ATP.

kindling (kind'ling) A phenomenon of the central nervous system characterized by the enduring reduction in threshold needed to activate a repeated stimulus (e.g., repetition of a perturbation, such as stress, will elicit the same response at a later date even though the level of stress may not be as high as in the earlier occurrence). Posttraumatic stress disorder is a clinical example of this phenomenon.

kindred (kin'dred) A group of genetically related persons. Also called clan; tribe; family group.

kine-, kin- Combining forms meaning movement.

kinematics (kin-ĕ-mat'iks) The science of motion, especially of the body parts, exclusive of the influences of mass or force.

kinesalgia (kin-ĕ-sal'je-ah) Pain evoked by muscular movement.

kinesia (kĭ-ne'se-ah) Motion sickness.

kinesiatrics (ki-ne-se-at'riks) See kinesitherapy.

kinesics (ki-ne'siks) The study of nonverbal body motion as a form of communication (e.g., crossing arms and shrugging).

kinesio-, kineso-, kinesi- Combining forms meaning motion.

kinesiology (kĭ-ne-se-ol'o-je) The study of movement of the human body and its parts, particularly as it applies to treatment.

kinesiotherapy (kĭ-ne-se-o-ther'ah-pe) See kinesitherapy.

kinesitherapy (kĭ-ne-sĕ-ther'ah-pe) Treatment using movement or exercise and massage as the mode of therapy; the term is frequently used to mean physical therapy in general. Also called kinesiatrics; kinesiotherapy; kinesotherapy; kinetotherapy.

kinesotherapy (kĭ-ne-so-ther'ah-pe) See kinesitherapy.

kinesthesia (kin-es-the'ze-ah) The perception or sensation of one's own muscular movement.

kinesthetic (kin-es-thet'ik) Relating to kinesthesia.

kinetic (kĭ-net'ik) Relating to or producing motion.

kinetics (kĭ-net'iks) The study of all characteristics of motion (e.g., rate of change, acceleration, deceleration) and the forces that affect motion.

  chemical k. The study of the rates and velocities of chemical reactions.

kineto- Combining form meaning movement.

kinetocardiogram (kĭ-ne-to-kar'de-o-gram) Graphic representation of low-frequency vibrations of the chest wall produced by heart activity.

kinetocardiograph (kĭ-ne-to-kar'de-o-graf) An apparatus used to produce graphic representations of low-frequency motion of the chest wall in the region of the heart.

kinetochore (ki-ne'to-kōr) See centromere.

kinetoplasm (kĭ-ne'to-plazm) **1.** The most contractile part of the cell cytoplasm. **2.** The part of the cytoplasm of nerve cells that contains chromophil.

kinetotherapy (kĭ-ne-to-ther'ah-pe) See kinesitherapy.

kinin (ki'nin) Any of various small peptides (e.g., bradykinin) that have proinflammatory properties, such as increasing blood flow or permeability of blood vessel walls.

kink (kink) **1.** A sharp twist or bend. **2.** A muscle spasm, often painful.

Klebsiella (kleb-se-el'lah) A genus of bacteria (family Enterobacteriaceae) composed of gram-negative, nonmotile microorganisms; found in the intestinal, respiratory, and urogenital tracts of the human body. Some species cause disease.

  K. pneumoniae A species commonly found in soil, water, and the intestinal tract of healthy humans; may cause bacterial pneumonia and is frequently present as a secondary invader in the lungs of persons with chronic pulmonary diseases. Also called Friedländer's bacillus.

  K. rhinoscleromatis A species found in persons afflicted with rhinoscleroma.

kleptomania (klep-to-ma'ne-ah) A disorder characterized by an uncontrollable impulse to steal, without having a desire or need for the stolen object.

knee (ne) The articulation of the lower limb between the femur and the tibia.

  dashboard k. Term applied to a knee injury caused by a blow to the front of the knee; the extent of the injury depends on the force of the impact and position of the knee when struck and may involve

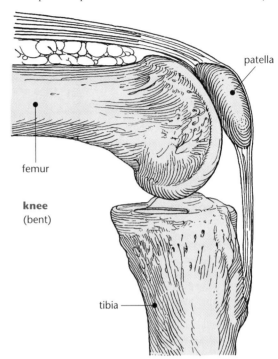

patella
femur
knee (bent)
tibia

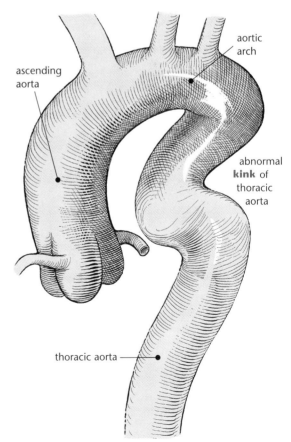

aortic arch
ascending aorta
abnormal **kink** of thoracic aorta
thoracic aorta

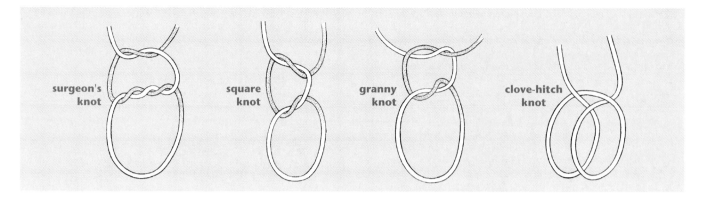

surgeon's knot   square knot   granny knot   clove-hitch knot

all or some of the following structures: patellar ligament, infrapatellar fat pad, anterior horns of the two semilunar cartilages, and articular surfaces of the femoral condyles. The injury is usually seen in a passenger of the front seat of an automobile involved in a collision; the passenger is thrown forward, striking the flexed knee on the dashboard.

housemaid's k. See prepatellar bursitis, under bursitis.

jumper's k. Inflammation of the patellar or quadriceps tendons, causing discomfort, tenderness, or pain, especially at the tendon's attachment to the kneecap (patella); may occur in athletes after jumping, kicking, climbing, or running.

knock k. See genu valgum.

locked k. A condition in which the flexion and extension motion of the leg is limited, due to the presence of torn cartilage in the knee joint.

runner's k. Condition of the knee characterized by anterior knee pain or discomfort around the kneecap (patella) experienced after running or jogging a predictable distance, or when sitting with the knee flexed for long periods; it also occurs when walking up or down stairs; seen most commonly (not exclusively) in recreational joggers and long-distance runners. The condition is considered to be caused by prolonged, excessive pronation of the subtalar joint of the foot, which may occur as a compensatory mechanism for any of a variety of anatomical abnormalities of the leg.

kneecap (ne′cap) See patella.

knife (nif) A cutting instrument, of different sizes and shapes, with a sharp blade.

Bard-Parker k. A surgical knife with a disposable blade.

Blair k. A knife with a long sharp blade and a straight edge, designed to cut skin grafts.

buck k. A periodontal knife with a spearlike point, used for cutting the gums between teeth.

cautery k. A knife connected to an electric battery that sears tissue to control bleeding while cutting.

chemical k. See restrictive endonuclease.

Merrifield k. A periodontal knife with a long, triangular, narrow blade; used in gingivectomy.

needle k. A fine pointed knife used in surgical procedures of the eye (e.g., in cataract removal). Also called discission needle.

knitting (nit′ing) The union of the fragments of a broken bone in the healing process.

knob (nob) A protuberance; a mass.

knee k. See traumatic tibial epiphysitis, under epiphysitis.

knock (nok) A short, sharp sound.

pericardial k. A clicking heart sound heard early during diastole, after the second heart sound but before the normal third sound; often present in patients with constrictive pericarditis.

knot (not) 1. An intertwining of the two ends of one or two threads, sutures, ropes, cords, or other similar object, so that they cannot easily separate. 2. A node or knoblike swelling resembling a knot.

clove-hitch k. A knot that consists of two continuous loops around an object; often used to create traction on the object for the reduction of dislocations.

flat k. See square knot.

granny k. An insecure double knot in which the two pieces of thread or cord are separated by the loop and do not pass together under it.

net k. See karyosome.

reef k. See square knot.

square k. A double knot in which the free ends of the second knot are parallel to the ends of the first knot, thereby resembling a square and preventing slippage. Also called flat knot; reef knot.

surgeon's k. Knot in which the thread or cord is passed through the loop of the first knot two times to prevent slippage and then passed through only once for the second knot.

knuckle (nuk′l) A protuberance on the dorsal surface of a clenched hand formed by a joint of the finger, especially the metacarpophalangeal joint.

koilonychia (koi-lo-nik′e-ah) An uncommon condition, usually associated with iron deficiency anemia, in which the nails are spoon-shaped or concave.

kola nut (ko′lah nut) The seed of the *Cola acuminata* tree that contains caffeine; its extract is used in beverages.

kraurosis vulvae (kraw-ro′sis vul′vah) Drying and atrophy of the vagina and vulva accompanied by itchiness, pain, inflammation, and leukoplakic patches on the mucosa; occurs most often in older women.

krypton (krip′ton) An inert gas found in the atmosphere; symbol Kr, atomic number 36, atomic weight 83.80.

krypton 85 (^{85}Kr) A radioactive form of krypton, used as a tracer (e.g., in studies of regional blood flow).

kwashiorkor (kwash-e-or′kor) A nutritional disorder due to severe protein deficiency; characterized by anemia, edema, delayed growth, diarrhea, changes in hair and skin color, skin lesions on the limbs and back, apathy, atrophy of the pancreas, fatty changes in the liver cells, and low serum albumin; first seen in Africa, especially in young children; presently reported in different parts of the world, mainly in tropical countries.

kymograph (ki′mo-graf) An instrument that graphically records variations in pressure or motion.

kymoscope (ki′mo-skōp) A device used to measure pulse waves or variations in blood pressure.

kynurenic acid (ki-nu-ren′ik as′id) A product of tryptophan metabolism; may appear in human urine in some hereditary disorders of metabolism.

kyphos (ki′fos) Greek for hump.

kyphoscoliosis (ki-fo-sko-le-o′sis) A deformity of the spine characterized by a backward and lateral curvature, usually progressive, leading to failure of lung function and congestive heart failure.

kyphosis (ki-fo′sis) Excessive backward curvature of the spine, affecting most frequently the upper thoracic and lower cervical vertebrae; may be caused by any of a variety of spinal disorders (e.g., fracture or tumor of the vertebrae); seen frequently in older people, especially women, affected with osteoporosis, in which case the vertebral bodies collapse upon each other. Popularly called hunchback; humpback; dowager's hump (in older women).

L

lab (lab) Common shortened version of the term laboratory.

label (la'bl) See marker; tag (2).

labeling (la'bl-ing) See tagging.

la belle indifference (la bel' ahn-de-fer-ahns') French term meaning a constant unjustified state of complacency and indifference, often seen in patients with a conversion disorder.

labia (la'be-ah) Plural of labium.

labial (la'be-al) Relating to lips.

labile (la'bĭl) **1.** Unstable or easily changed (e.g., drugs that are readily altered when exposed to heat). **2.** In psychiatry, emotionally unstable.

lability (lah-bil'ĭ-te) Instability; the condition of being unstable.

labio- Combining form meaning lips.

labiochorea (la-be-o-ko-re'ah) Spasm and stiffening of the lips during speech.

labiogingival (la-be-o-jin'jĭ-val) Relating to the junction of the lips and gums.

labiograph (la'be-o-graf) Device for recording movement of the lips in speech.

labiomental (la-be-o-men'tal) Relating to the lower lip and chin.

labionasal (la-be-o-na'zal) Relating to the lips and nose.

labioplacement (la-be-o-plās'ment) Abnormal position of a tooth or teeth toward the lips.

labioplasty (la'be-o-plas'te) Plastic surgery of the lips.

labioversion (la-be-o-ver'zhun) Deviation of teeth toward the lips.

labium (la'be-um), pl. la'bia A lip or liplike structure.

    l. anterius The anterior portion of the uterine cervix; it is shorter and thicker than the posterior portion (l. posterius). Also called anterior lip. See also labia uteri.

    labia majora The two prominent mounds of tissue forming the lateral boundaries of the vulva and extending from the mons pubis anteriorly to the perineum posteriorly; embryologically, they correspond to the scrotum of the male. Also called greater lips of pudendum; commonly called major lips.

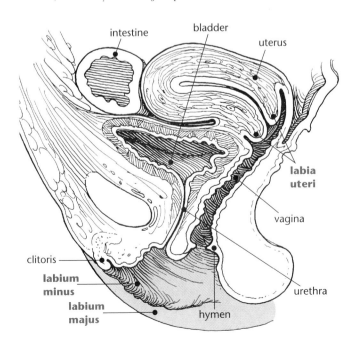

labia minora The two narrow folds situated between the labia majora, on either side of the urethral and vaginal openings. Anteriorly, each labium minus splits into two folds, the upper ones meet over the free end of the clitoris (forming the prepuce of the clitoris), the lower ones meet under the clitoris (forming the frenulum of the clitoris). Posteriorly, each labium minus either blends with its corresponding major lip or, in the virginal state, they join across the midline via a fold of skin (frenulum of labia minora). Also called lesser lips of pudendum; nymphae; commonly called minor lips.

    l. posterius The posterior portion of the uterine cervix; it is longer and thinner than the anterior portion (l. anterius). Also called posterior lip. See also labia uteri.

    labia uteri The portions of the uterine cervix surrounding its vaginal opening (exterior os); most prominently seen in women who have borne children, in whom the originally round opening becomes a transverse slit. See labium anterius; labium posterius.

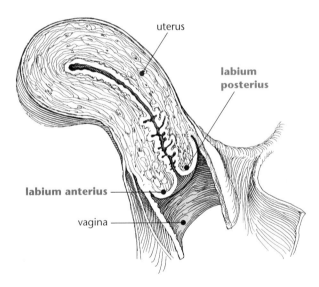

labor (la'bor) The coordinated sequence of involuntary contractions of the uterus that increase in regularity, intensity, and duration, resulting in effacement and dilatation of the cervix and voluntary bearing-down efforts leading to expulsion of the fetus and placenta via the vagina; commonly divided into three stages: *first stage of l.,* begins with the onset of labor to full dilatation of the cervix (10 cm); *second stage of l.,* begins with full dilatation of the cervix and ends with complete delivery (birth) of the baby; *third stage, placental stage of l.,* the period from delivery of the infant through delivery of the placenta. Also called true labor.

    dry l. Labor occurring after premature rupture of the fetal membranes with loss of amniotic fluid. Also called xerotocia.

    false l. Irregular brief uterine contractions occurring in late pregnancy; they are inconsistent in interval, duration, and strength; they cause no change in the status of the cervix; and they evoke abdominal and/or back pain.

    induced l. Labor brought on by medical or surgical means, usually performed under specific indications (e.g., prolonged pregnancy, premature rupture of membranes, preeclampsia, suspected intrauterine growth retardation).

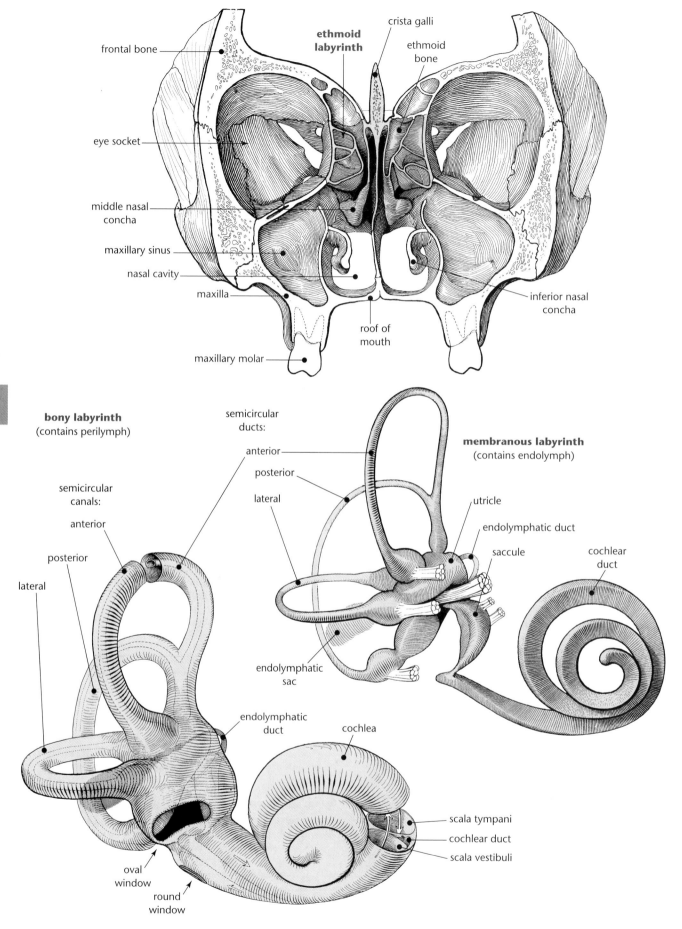

frontal bone

ethmoid labyrinth

crista galli

ethmoid bone

eye socket

middle nasal concha

maxillary sinus

nasal cavity

maxilla

roof of mouth

inferior nasal concha

maxillary molar

L

bony labyrinth
(contains perilymph)

semicircular ducts:

anterior

posterior

lateral

membranous labyrinth
(contains endolymph)

utricle

endolymphatic duct

saccule

cochlear duct

semicircular canals:

anterior

posterior

lateral

endolymphatic sac

endolymphatic duct

cochlea

scala tympani

cochlear duct

scala vestibuli

oval window

round window

labyrinth ■ labyrinth

L2

precipitate l. Labor of unusually short duration, frequently due to abnormally low resistance of maternal soft tissues or abnormally strong contractions of uterine and abdominal muscles.

premature l. Labor occurring before term.

prolonged l. Labor that, for any of various causes, lasts longer than 20 hours in first pregnancies and 14 hours in women who have had children.

true l. See labor.

laboratory (lab'o-rah-to-re) A place equipped with scientific equipment for conducting experiments, tests, and manufacture of drugs and chemicals. Commonly called lab.

labrum (la'brum), pl. la'bra Any liplike structure or edge.

labyrinth (lab'ĭ-rinth) A group of interconnecting channels.

bony l. The connecting cavities and canals of the inner ear, located in the petrous portion of the temporal bone; it houses the membranous labyrinth.

ethmoid l. The aggregation of thin-walled cavities within the ethmoid bone, near the nasal cavity and eye socket.

membranous l. A system of communicating membranous ducts and sacs of the inner ear, situated within the bony labyrinth.

labyrinthine (lab-ĭ-rin'thĭn) Relating to a labyrinth, especially of the inner ear.

labyrinthitis (lab-ĭ-rin-thi'tis) Inflammation of the inner ear. Also called otitis interna.

labyrinthotomy (lab-ĭ-rin-thot'o-me) Surgical cut into the labyrinth of the inner ear.

lac (lak), pl. lac'ta Any whitish, milky fluid.

laceration (las-er-a'shun) A superficial tearing of tissue.

cerebral l., brain l. A tear of brain tissue that, after healing, leaves a yellowish brown scar penetrating the gray cortex and into the subcortical white matter.

dicing l.'s The multiple angular skin lacerations occurring on the face, upper torso, and upper arms of victims of motor vehicle accidents; caused by fragmentation of the tempered safety glass of the side windows into small angular and cubelike pieces that strike the victims. Also called dicing; dicing abrasions; dicing pattern.

esophageal l.'s See Mallory-Weiss syndrome, under syndrome.

obstetric l.'s Lacerations that may occur during the process of vaginal delivery, designated by four degrees: *first-degree l.,* involves only the vaginal lining (mucous membrane) or the skin (or both); *second-degree l.,* involves the above tissues plus disruption of the underlying superficial connective tissue (fascia) and transverse perineal muscle (excluding the anal sphincter); *third-degree l.,* involves all the above structures plus the anal sphincter muscle; *fourth-degree l.,* lacerations include all the above structures and extend into the lumen of the rectum, causing profuse bleeding and fecal soiling.

lacinia (lah-sin'e-ah) Fringe; fimbria.

lacrimal (lak'rĭ-mal) Relating to tears.

lacrimation (lak-rĭ-ma'shun) Secretion of tears.

lacrimatory (lak'rĭ-mah-to-re) Causing secretion of tears.

lacrimotome (lak'rĭ-mo-tōm) A fine knife used in lacrimotomy.

lacrimotomy (lak-rĭ-mot'o-me) A surgical cut into the lacrimal sac or duct.

lactacidemia (lak-tas-ĭ-de'me-ah) See lacticacidemia.

lactagogue (lak'tah-gog) See galactagogue.

lactalbumin (lak-tal-bu'min) An albumin of milk.

lactase (lak'tās) Intestinal, sugar-splitting enzyme that promotes conversion of the milk sugar lactose into glucose and galactose; lactase deficiency may cause bloating, flatulence, and diarrhea after ingestion of milk or milk products.

lactate (lak'tāt) 1. To secrete milk. 2. Any salt or ester of lactic acid.

lactate dehydrogenase (lak'tāt de-hi'dro-jĕ-nās) (LDH) An enzyme present in the cytoplasm of cells; it may be measured in serum for diagnosis of certain diseases (e.g., myocardial infarction and liver disease).

lactation (lak-ta'shun) The production of milk.

lacteal (lak'te-al) An intestinal lymphatic vessel transporting chyle from the intestines.

lactescent (lak-tes'ent) Resembling milk; milky.

lactic (lak'tik) Relating to milk.

lactic acid (lak'tik as'id) A colorless syrupy substance formed by the fermentation of milk sugar (lactose); it is an end product of anaerobic glycolysis in the body.

lacticacidemia (lak-tik-as-ĭ-de'me-ah) The presence of lactic acid in the circulating blood. Also called lactacidemia.

lactiferous (lak-tif'er-us) Conveying milk (e.g., ducts).

lactifuge (lak'tĭ-fūj) An agent that arrests milk secretion.

lactigenous (lak-tij'ĕ-nus) Producing milk.

lactinated (lak'tĭ-nāt-ed) Containing lactose.

lacto-, lacti-, lact- Combining forms meaning milk.

Lactobacillus (lak-to-bah-sil'lus) A genus of gram-positive bacteria that produce lactic acid in the fermentation of milk; found in the human mouth, intestines, and vagina.

L. acidophilus Species occurring in the feces of infants and individuals on a high-lactose or dextrin-containing diet.

lactocele (lak'to-sēl) See milk-retention cyst, under cyst.

lactoflavin (lak'to-fla-vin) The original name of riboflavin.

lactogen (lak'to-jen) Any agent that stimulates milk production.

human placental l. (hPL, HPL) A polypeptide hormone that appears in the blood of pregnant women at about the sixth week of gestation, rises steadily thereafter, and disappears from the blood within 48 hours after childbirth; it is secreted by the placenta and is intimately involved in carbohydrate metabolism of both mother and fetus. It occurs in high concentration in molar pregnancy and in choriocarcinoma. Also called somatomammotropin.

lactogenic (lak-to-jen'ik) Inducing milk production.

lactoglobulin (lak-to-glob'u-lin) A simple protein present in milk.

lactoprotein (lak-to-pro'tēn) Any protein normally present in milk.

lactorrhea (lak-to-re'ah) See galactorrhea.

lactose (lak'tōs) A sugar present in milk; it yields glucose and galactose on hydrolysis. Also called milk sugar.

lactosuria (lak-to-su're-ah) The presence of lactose in the urine, sometimes occurring in premature newborn infants.

lactovegetarian (lak-to-vej-ĕ-ta're-an) A person who lives on a diet of vegetables, milk, and milk products.

lactulose (lak'tū-lōs) Synthetic compound used in the treatment of constipation and hepatic coma.

lacuna (lah-ku'nah), pl. lacu'nae 1. A small anatomic cavity or depression. 2. A defect or gap.

Howship's l. A depression in bone caused by resorption of bone tissue by osteoclasts. Also called resorption lacuna.

resorption l. See Howship's lacuna.

lacunar (lah-ku'nar) Relating to a lacuna.

lacus (la'kus) Latin for a small collection of fluid (lake).

lag (lag) 1. A slowness. 2. The time interval between a change and its effect (e.g., of a stimulus or action).

lid l. See Graefe's sign, under sign.

lagophthalmia, lagophthalmos (lag-of-thal'me-ah, lag-of-thal'mos) Condition in which the eyelids cannot be closed completely.

lake (lāk) A small accumulation of fluid.

lacrimal l. The pool of tears normally present in the triangular space at the medial angle of the eye.

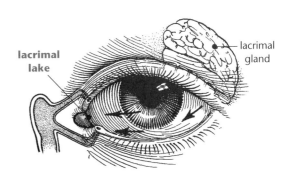

lacrimal lake — lacrimal gland

lalling (lal′ing) **1.** Disorder of speech articulation characterized by errors on sounds involving elevation of the tip of the tongue (e.g., of the letters *l, t, d*). **2.** The babbling of infants.

laloplegia (lal-o-ple′je-ah) Paralysis of muscles involved in production of speech.

lambda (lam′dah) (λ) **1.** The eleventh letter of the Greek alphabet. **2.** A craniometric point on the back of the skull, at the junction of the sagittal and lambdoid sutures. **3.** Designation for one of the two low molecular weight polypeptide chains constituting the light chain of an immunoglobulin; may be present in the urine as a constituent of Bence Jones protein in multiple myeloma.

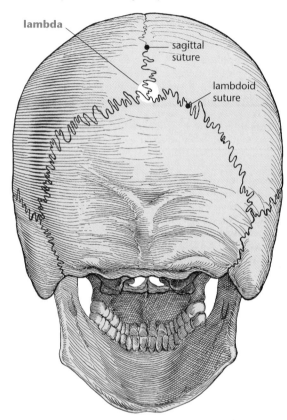

lambda
sagittal
suture
lambdoid
suture

lambdoid (lam′doid) Resembling the Greek letter lambda (λ).

lambert (lam′bert) (L) The unit of brightness equal to one lumen per square centimeter.

lamella (lah-mel′ah), pl. lamel′lae **1.** A thin plate, as of bone. **2.** A small medicated gelatin disk for insertion under the eyelid in place of solutions.

lamellar (lah-mel′ar) **1.** Scaly. **2.** Relating to lamellae.

lamina (lam′ĭ-nah), pl. lam′inae A thin layer of cells or soft tissue or a thin bony plate.

  anterior elastic l. of cornea See Bowman's membrane, under membrane.

  anterior limiting l. See Bowman's membrane, under membrane.

  basal l. of choroid The thin, transparent, inner layer of the choroid of the eye, firmly attached to the pigmented layer of the retina. Also called membrane of Bruch; lamina vitrea; Bruch's membrane.

  basal l. of epithelium A relatively thin layer, about 300 to 1,200 Å in thickness, composed of slender filamentous material enmeshed in a mucopolysaccharide matrix; present at the base of epithelial cells, where it blends with the reticular lamina to form the basement membrane. Also called boundary membrane; basement lamina.

  basement l. See basal lamina of epithelium.

  bony spiral l. A delicate flange of bone projecting from the spiral-shaped modiolus of the inner ear into the cochlear canal, and par-

tially dividing it into an upper scala vestibuli and a lower scala tympani. Also called osseous spiral lamina.

  choroidocapillary l. See intermediate capillary choroidal lamina.

  cribriform l. of ethmoid bone See cribriform plate of ethmoid bone, under plate.

  l. cribrosa sclerae The sievelike portion of the posterior sclera that is traversed by the nerve fibers of the optic nerve.

  external cranial l. The outer plate of a flat cranial bone.

  external elastic l. of artery The outer of the two layers of elastic fibers in the wall of an artery, situated between the tunica media and tunica adventitia.

  external vascular choroidal l. The layer of the choroid of the eye containing the larger blood vessels in loose supporting connective tissue; suffused by many branches of the short posterior ciliary arteries and drained by larger veins that converge in whorls upon a small number of vorticose veins, which exit through the sclera to empty into the ophthalmic veins; it is encircled by the suprachoroid lamina.

  l. fusca of sclera See suprachoroid lamina.

  intermediate capillary choroidal l. The middle layer of the choroid of the eyeball, composed of minute blood vessels; it is separated from the retina by the basal lamina of choroid and from the sclera by the external vascular choroidal lamina. Also called choroidocapillary lamina; formerly called choriocapillary layer.

  internal cranial l. The inner plate of a flat cranial bone.

  internal elastic l. of artery The inner of the two layers of elastic fibers in the wall of an artery, situated between the tunica intima and tunica media.

  interpubic fibrocartilaginous l. The fibrocartilaginous disk uniting the articular surfaces of the pubic bones at the symphysis.

  lateral l. of pterygoid process The broad, thin, and everted plate of the lateral pterygoid process of the sphenoid bone of the skull; its lateral surface forms part of the medial wall of the infratemporal fossa; its medial surface forms part of the pterygoid fossa.

  medial l. of pterygoid process A narrow, long plate of the medial pterygoid process of the sphenoid bone of the skull; it curves laterally at its inferior extremity into a hooklike process, the pterygoid hamulus.

  osseous spiral l. See bony spiral lamina.

  posterior elastic l. of cornea See Descemet's membrane, under membrane.

  posterior limiting l. See Descemet's membrane, under membrane.

  reticular l. A relatively thin layer of reticular and collagenous fibers embedded in a mucopolysaccharide matrix; together with the basal lamina, it makes up the basement membrane that holds the basal cells of the epithelium firmly to the underlying connective tissue; it also encloses fat cells, muscle cells, and Schwann cells of peripheral nerves.

  laminae of septum pellucidum A partition consisting of two thin vertical sheets that separate the lateral ventricles of the brain.

  laminae of spinal cord Nine layers that extend throughout the length of the spinal cord, differentiated by specific features of nerve cells (neurons) as well as their size, shape, and packing density.

  suprachoroid l. The delicate, nonvascular layer of loose connective tissue, about 30 μm thick, forming the outer layer of the choroid of the eye; it is in direct contact with the inner surface of the sclera. Also called lamina fusca of sclera.

  l. terminalis The thin anterior wall of the third ventricle of the brain, extending from the superior surface of the optic chiasma to the rostrum of the corpus callosum.

  laminae of vertebral arch Two broad plates directed dorsally and medially from the right and left pedicles of a vertebra; their posterior midline fusion forms the vertebral arch and completes the vertebral foramen.

  l. vitrea See basal lamina of choroid.

L

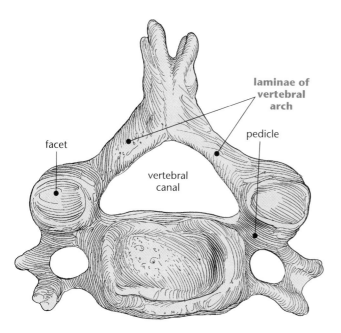

laminae of vertebral arch

pedicle

facet

vertebral canal

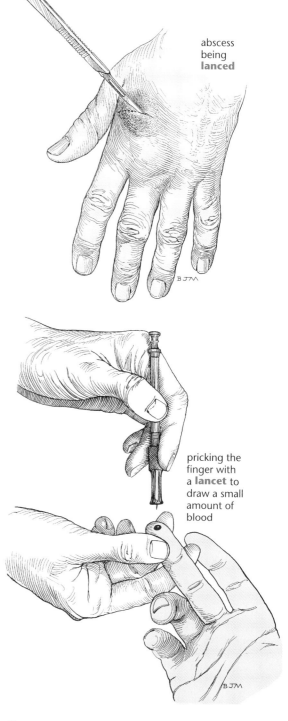

abscess being **lanced**

pricking the finger with a **lancet** to draw a small amount of blood

laminagraphy (lam-ī-nag′rah-fe) See tomography.

laminar (lam′ī-nar) **1.** Arranged in layers. **2.** Relating to a bony plate.

Laminaria digitata (lam-ī-na′re-ah dij-ī-tah′tah) A species of seaweed from which tents are made by drying and sterilizing the stems; the dry stem is capable of expanding to about five times its original diameter; used for atraumatic dilatation of the uterine cervix (e.g., as a preoperative procedure in abortion and prior to induction of labor at or near term). See also laminaria tent, under tent.

lamination (lam-ī-na′shun) An arrangement in layers.

laminectomy (lam-ī-nek′to-me) Surgical removal of the posterior arch of a vertebra. Also called rachiotomy; rachitomy.

laminin (lam′ī-nin) Glycoprotein of extracellular matrix; important in developing and maintaining cellular organization.

laminotomy (lam-ī-not′o-me) Surgical division of the lamina of a vertebra.

lamp (lamp) Any device for producing light, heat, or therapeutic radiation.

    Eldridge-Green l. Lamp used in color-vision testing by means of special filters mounted in rotating disks.

    Kromayer's l. A U-shaped quartz lamp of mercury vapor that generates ultraviolet rays, used in the treatment of certain skin ulcers.

    mignon l. A tiny electric lamp used with a variety of endoscopic instruments.

    slit l. See slitlamp.

    uviol l. An electric lamp with a globe of uviol glass producing light with a high content of ultraviolet rays; used in phototherapy.

    Wood's l. A lamp that produces ultraviolet rays (Wood's light) passed through a nickel oxide filter; used to demonstrate *Microsporum, Pseudomonas,* and other infections of skin and hair.

lance (lans) To cut into (e.g., a boil or abscess).

lancet (lan′set) A small, pointed surgical knife or a small disposable blade for piercing the skin.

lancinating (lan′sī-nāt-ing) Denoting a piercing, transient pain.

language (lang′gwij) **1.** The use of vocal sounds in articulate, meaningful patterns as a form of communication. **2.** The transmission of meaning by act or manner.

    body l. Expression of one's thoughts and feelings through body movements and gestures.

languor (lang′er) A loss of the sense of well-being in an otherwise healthy person.

lanolin (lan′o-lin) Fatlike substance obtained from sheep's wool containing 25 to 30% water; used in the preparation of ointments.

    anhydrous l. Lanolin containing less than 25% water. Also called wool fat.

lanthanum (lan′thah-num) Metallic element; symbol La, atomic number 57, atomic weight 138.91.

lanuginous (lah-nu′jī-nus) Covered with fine, downlike hair (lanugo).

lanugo (lah-nu′go) The fine soft hairs covering the body of the fetus from the fourth month of pregnancy; they are shed after birth and are replaced by fine vellus hairs. Also called lanugo hairs; primary hairs.

laparo- Combining form meaning flank or loin; abdominal wall.

laparohysterectomy (lap-ah-ro-his-ter-ek′to-me) See abdominal hysterectomy, under hysterectomy.

laparohysterotomy (lap-ah-ro-his-ter-ot'o-me) See hysterotomy.

laparoscope (lap'ah-ro-skōp) An endoscopic instrument used in laparoscopy. Also called peritoneoscope.

laparoscopy (lap-ah-ros'ko-pe) Visual examination of contents of the abdominal or pelvic cavity by means of a laparoscope introduced through a small incision in the abdominal wall. Also called peritoneoscopy; peritoneal endoscopy; celioscopy. See also laparoscopic surgery, under surgery.

laparotomy (lap-ah-rot'o-me) A surgical cut into the flank or through any part of the abdominal wall. Also called abdominal section; peritoneotomy.

lardaceous (lar-da'shus) 1. Resembling lard. 2. Producing amyloid.

larva (lar'vah), pl. lar'vae The wormlike early stage in the life cycle of certain animals, bearing little or no resemblance to the adult form.

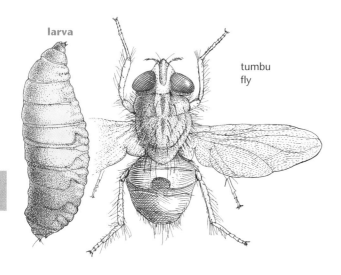

larva

tumbu fly

larva migrans (lar'vah mi'grans) Larval worms existing temporarily in the tissues of a host other than the one to which they are adapted.

   cutaneous l.m. A subcutaneous creeping eruption of the skin caused by wandering larvae of domestic animal hookworms; acquired through contact with soil contaminated by dog or cat feces.

   visceral l.m. Disease caused by the larvae of *Toxocara canis,* intestinal parasite of dogs that penetrates the wall of the intestine and wanders through organs, especially the liver; acquired through consumption of raw vegetables contaminated with eggs of the parasite.

larvicide (lar'vĭ-sīd) An agent destructive to larvae.

laryngeal (lah-rin'je-al) Relating to the larynx.

laryngectomy (lar-in-jek'to-me) Surgical removal of the larynx.

laryngismus (lar-in-jiz'mus) Spasmodic contraction of the larynx.

   l. stridulus A condition occurring in children, characterized by sudden attacks of spasm of the larynx lasting a few seconds; it produces a crowing noise on inspiration and cyanosis. Also called pseudocroup.

laryngitis (lar-in-ji'tis) Inflammation of the larynx.

laryngocele (lah-ring'go-sēl) A congenital anomaly of the larynx consisting of an outpouching of the laryngeal lining; it may reach upward between the true and false vocal folds, or may extend outward through the thyrohyoid membrane and produce a bulge in the neck.

laryngofissure (lah-ring-go-fish'ūr) Surgical incision of the larynx, usually through the midline. Also called median laryngotomy.

laryngograph (lah-ring'go-graf) Device for making tracings of the movements of the larynx.

laryngology (lar-ing-gol'o-je) The study of the larynx and treatment of its diseases.

laryngoparalysis (lah-ring-go-pah-ral'ĭ-sis) Paralysis of the muscles of the larynx.

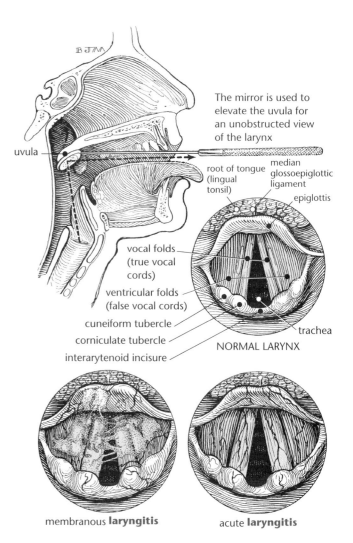

The mirror is used to elevate the uvula for an unobstructed view of the larynx

uvula

root of tongue (lingual tonsil)

median glossoepiglottic ligament

epiglottis

vocal folds (true vocal cords)

ventricular folds (false vocal cords)

cuneiform tubercle

corniculate tubercle

interarytenoid incisure

trachea

NORMAL LARYNX

membranous **laryngitis**

acute **laryngitis**

laryngopharyngeal (lah-ring-go-fah-rin'je-al) Relating to the larynx and pharynx.

laryngopharyngectomy (lah-ring-go-far-in-jek'to-me) Removal of the laryngopharynx.

laryngopharynx (lah-ring-go-far'inks) The lower portion of the pharynx (behind the larynx) from the level of the hyoid bone to the esophagus, with which it is continuous.

laryngoplasty (lah-ring'go-plas-te) Reparative surgery of the larynx.

laryngoscope (lah-ring'go-skōp) An endoscope designed for inspection of the larynx.

laryngoscopy (lar-ing-gos'ko-pe) Examination of the larynx with a laryngoscope.

laryngospasm (lah-ring'go-spazm) An abnormal reflex contraction of the muscles of the larynx.

laryngostenosis (lah-ring-go-stě-no'sis) Abnormal narrowing of the laryngeal lumen.

laryngostomy (lar-ing-gos'to-me) Creation of a permanent opening into the larynx through the neck.

laryngotome (lah-ring'go-tōm) Surgical instrument for cutting into the larynx.

laryngotomy (lar-ing-got'o-me) A surgical cut into the larynx.

   median l. See laryngofissure.

laryngotracheobronchitis (lah-ring'go-tra'ke-o-bron-ki'tis) Inflammation of the upper respiratory tract; may occur as a primary infection or accompany a systemic disease, such as diphtheria or whooping cough.

larynx (lar'inks) The organ of voice production at the upper end of the trachea; it is composed of a cartilaginous and muscular frame,

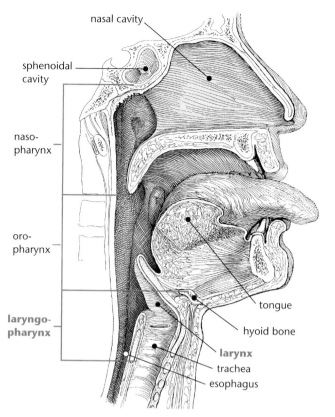

nasal cavity

sphenoidal cavity

naso-pharynx

oro-pharynx

laryngo-pharynx

tongue

hyoid bone

larynx
trachea
esophagus

lined with mucous membrane, and contains the vocal folds. Popularly called voice box.

lase (lās) Acronym for laser-assisted spinal endoscopy; a technique for performing percutaneous diskectomy in which laser fibers are inserted through 18- or 20-gauge needles for vaporization of intervertebral disk material, usually in the lumbar area of the vertebral column.

laser (la'zer) Acronym for light amplification by stimulated emission of radiation; a device that transforms high energies into a concentrated narrow beam of monochromatic light (electromagnetic radiation). Electrons of any of various media (solid, liquid, gas) are stimulated with electricity to reach a high energy state, which is released in the form of photons (light particles); the photons collide within the laser chamber between mirrors, thus creating more energy,

which is then emitted in a controlled manner as the laser beam. The laser beam is used as a tool in a variety of surgical and medical procedures.

argon l. A laser employing argon as the medium; used in eye surgery to repair tears and stop bleeding of the retina and in plastic surgery to remove certain types of birthmarks.

carbon dioxide l. Laser with carbon dioxide (CO_2) as the medium; usually employed in cutting and coalescing of certain tissues, such as vascular anastomoses.

excimer l. A laser with an intense beam of ultraviolet light used to vaporize arterial fatty deposits (atheromas) and unclog the artery, while the remaining tissue remains cool.

krypton l. A laser using krypton as the medium; usually used to stop minute spots of bleeding (photocoagulation) of the retina.

neodymium: yttrium-aluminum-garnet (Nd:YAG) l. A laser using as a medium a crystal of yttrium, aluminum, and garnet doped with neodymium ions; the beam can be transmitted by a flexible probe through an endoscope to coagulate bleeding sites in deep tissues such as those of gastrointestinal, urinary, and respiratory tracts.

lassitude (las'ĭ-tūd) A sense of weariness or loss of a sense of well-being in a person who is healthy in mind and body.

latah (lah'tah) Condition characterized by imitative behavior and extreme response to suggestion.

latent (la'tent) Present but not manifest; concealed.

lateral (lat'er-al) On the side; away from the midline, toward the right or left.

laterality (lat-er-al'ĭ-te) A tendency to use either the right or the left side of the body; right or left dominance of the brain.

latero- Combining form meaning a side.

laterodeviation (lat-er-o-de-ve-a'shun) Displacement to one side.

lateroduction (lat-er-o-duk'shun) Movement of a body part (e.g., a limb) to one side of the body.

lateroflexion (lat-er-o-flek'shun) A bending or angulation of an organ (e.g., the uterus) to one side.

lateropulsion (lat-er-o-pul'shun) Involuntary movement to one side seen in certain nervous disorders.

laterotorsion (lat-er-o-tor'shun) Rotation of the eyeball on its anteroposterior axis.

lateroversion (lat-er-o-ver'shun) Tilting of an organ (e.g., the uterus) to one side.

latissimus (lah-tis'ĭ-mus) Latin for broadest; widest.

latus (la'tus) 1. Latin for broad. 2. The side of the body between the ribs and the pelvis; the flank.

laudanum (law'dah-num) A tincture of opium.

L

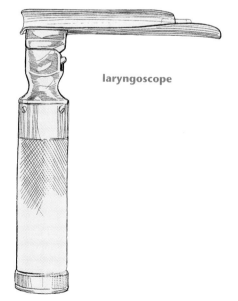

laryngoscope

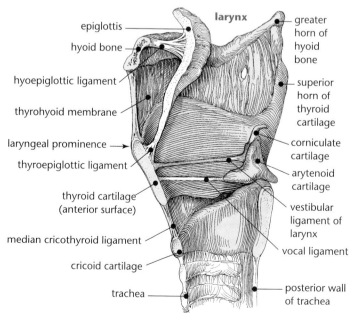

larynx

epiglottis

hyoid bone

hyoepiglottic ligament

thyrohyoid membrane

laryngeal prominence

thyroepiglottic ligament

thyroid cartilage (anterior surface)

median cricothyroid ligament

cricoid cartilage

trachea

greater horn of hyoid bone

superior horn of thyroid cartilage

corniculate cartilage

arytenoid cartilage

vestibular ligament of larynx

vocal ligament

posterior wall of trachea

lavage (lah-vahzh′) The washing out of a body cavity or hollow organ.

bronchoalveolar l. Lavage of the small, distal airways and pulmonary air spaces for the collection of diagnostic cells and fluids; used as an adjunct to visual examination with the fiberoptic bronchoscope (bronchoscopy); also used for treatment of alveolar proteinosis.

gastric l. Irrigation of the stomach cavity to remove ingested toxic substances.

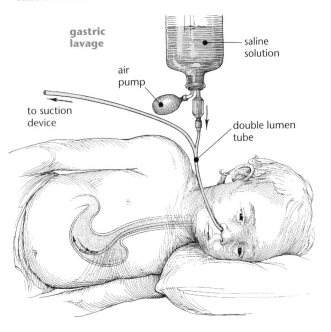

gastric lavage

saline solution

air pump

to suction device

double lumen tube

peritoneal l. Lavage of the peritoneal cavity as a means of removing infectious, irritating, or cancerous material.

law (law) A principle, rule, or formula expressing a fact based on observed recurrence, order, relationship, or interactions of natural processes or actions.

all-or-none l. See Bowditch's law.

Beer's l. The intensity of a light ray is inversely proportional to the depth of liquid through which it is transmitted (the absorption is dependent upon the number of molecules in the ray's path).

Bowditch's l. The heart muscle will contract to the fullest extent, even if the stimulus is weak, or it will not contract at all. Also called all-or-none law; all-or-none.

Courvoisier's l. Jaundice accompanied by enlargement of the gallbladder is likely to be caused by cancer of the head of the pancreas, not from gallstones, since the latter condition produces a scarred gallbladder that does not distend. Also called Courvoisier's sign.

Henry's l. The amount of gas that can be dissolved in a liquid solution is proportional to the partial pressure of the gas; when the pressure is doubled, twice as much gas passes into solution.

l. of independent assortment See Mendel's law (b).

Koch's l. See Koch's postulate, under postulate.

mendelian l.'s See Mendel's law.

Mendel's l. The principles of heredity summarized in two laws and expressed in modern times as: *First law or law of segregation,* paired hereditary units (genes) in the offspring, one from each parent, do not mix or alter one another, therefore they are able to separate during the formation of sex cells (gametes) in meiosis and are transmitted independently from generation to generation. *Second law or law of independent assortment,* the corresponding hereditary units in a pair of gametes unite in the offsping to form new combinations and recombinations according to the laws of chance, provided that the two pairs of genes do not lie on the same chromosome. Also called mendelian laws.

l. of segregation See Mendel's law (a).

lawrencium (law-ren′se-um) Synthetic element; symbols Lw, Lr, atomic number 103, atomic weight 257.

laxative (lak′sah-tiv) An orally administered agent that promotes intestinal evacuation in formed, soft stools, either by increasing motor activity in the intestine or by changing the water content of the stool. COMPARE cathartic.

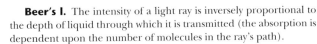

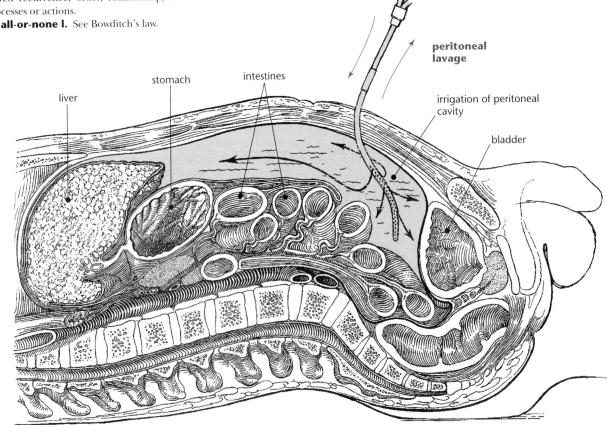

peritoneal lavage

stomach

intestines

irrigation of peritoneal cavity

liver

bladder

layer (la′er) **1.** A band of cells or tissue of relatively uniform thickness, especially when part of a larger structure, as in the retina, cornea, or skin. **2.** A sheetlike coating; a single thickness of tissue covering a surface. Also called lamina.

    ameloblastic l. A layer of cells derived from the inner enamel epithelium that produces the enamel of the tooth. Also called enamel layer.

    bacillary l. See layer of rods and cones.

    basal l. of endometrium The deepest layer of the uterine mucosa (endometrium); it accommodates the blind ends of the tubelike uterine glands, which are not shed during menstruation or at parturition and from which the endometrium regenerates.

    basal l. of epidermis See basal layer of skin.

    basal l. of skin The single layer of the epidermis situated adjacent to the basement membrane from which all other cells of the skin are derived by mitotic division of its cells. Also called basal layer of epidermis; malpighian layer.

    l.'s of cerebellar cortex Three distinct layers of the cerebellar cortex that, from the surface inward, are: the outer molecular layer, the middle Purkinje cell layer, and the inner granular layer. The granular layer abuts the cerebellar white matter.

    l.'s of cerebral cortex Six not too obvious layers of the cerebral cortex that tend to blend into each other; from the surface inward, they are: molecular (zonal) layer, outer granular layer, pyramidal cell layer, inner granular layer, ganglionic layer, and multiform layer.

    cerebral l. of retina The multilayered neural part of the retina.

    choriocapillary l. See intermediate capillary choroidal lamina, under lamina.

    circular l. of muscles of colon The strong, inner layer of circular muscle fibers of the colon.

    circular l. of muscles of rectum The thick, inner layer of circular muscle fibers of the rectum.

    circular l. of muscles of small intestine The relatively thick inner circular layer of the muscular coat (tunic) of the small intestine.

    circular l. of muscles of stomach The strongest of three muscular layers of the stomach, consisting of a middle circular layer of smooth muscle fibers that covers the entire stomach wall (the other two layers, the superficial longitudinal and the deeper oblique layers, are incomplete coats); it begins as a continuation of the circular esophageal muscle and becomes markedly thickened as it approaches the pylorus, where it forms the pyloric sphincter. Also called circular stratum of muscular tunic of stomach.

    clear l. of skin A narrow homogeneous layer of the skin between the cornified layer and the granular layer; it consists of a few rows of clear, flat, dead cells containing a refractile substance (eleidin) that eventually is transformed to keratin; nuclei and cell boundaries are not visible; generally seen only in the thick skin of palms and soles. Also called stratum lucidum.

    compact l. of endometrium The layer of the uterine endometrium nearest the surface, above the spongy layer; it contains the neck of the uterine glands and is shed during menstruation and at parturition.

    cornified l. of skin The outermost horny keratinized layer of skin (epidermis), composed of flat, dead, nonnucleated epithelial cells filled with keratin; it is very thick in the palms and soles; the cells shed and are continuously replaced; the layer serves as a barrier against light and heat waves, bacteria, and chemicals. Also called stratum corneum.

    eighth l. of retina See ganglion cell layer of retina.

    enamel l. See ameloblastic layer.

    epithelial l. of granulosa cells Granulosa (follicular) cells that form the wall of a developing ovarian follicle, located between the zona pellucida surrounding the ovum and the glassy membrane.

    fifth l. of retina See outer plexiform layer of retina.

    first l. of retina See pigment layer of retina.

    fourth l. of retina See outer nuclear layer of retina.

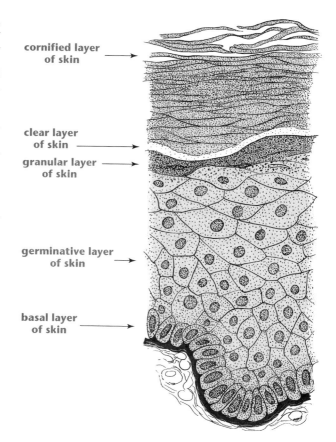

cornified layer of skin

clear layer of skin

granular layer of skin

germinative layer of skin

basal layer of skin

L

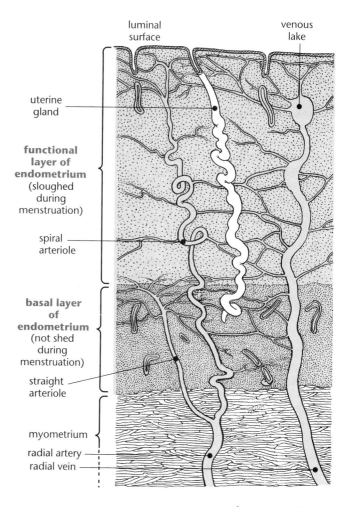

luminal surface

venous lake

uterine gland

functional layer of endometrium (sloughed during menstruation)

spiral arteriole

basal layer of endometrium (not shed during menstruation)

straight arteriole

myometrium

radial artery

radial vein

functional l. of endometrium The compact layer of the uterine endometrium along with the spongy layer; during the secretory phase of the endometrial cycle, it becomes tremendously engorged; it is shed during menstration.

ganglion cell l. of retina The eighth layer of the retina of the eye, composed of multipolar nerve cells positioned between the innermost layer of optic nerve fibers and the inner plexiform layer.

germ l. Any of the three primary layers of cells constituting the early embryo, the ectoderm (outer layer), the mesoderm (middle layer), or the endoderm (inner layer), which give rise to specific tissues of the body.

germinative l. of skin The growing part of the skin (epidermis) containing several rows of cells undergoing active mitosis; composed of a deep row of columnar cells (basal layer) and a superficial layer of variable thickness composed of polyhedral cells (prickle-cell layer).

granular l. of skin The layer just below the clear layer of skin (stratum lucidum), composed of flattened cells with pyknotic nuclei; surrounded by conspicuous granules of keratohyalin and associated with keratinization.

inner nuclear l. of retina The sixth layer of the retina, composed of the cell bodies of the retinal bipolar, horizontal, and amacrine neurons, as well as the retinal gliocytes; positioned between the outer plexiform layer and the layer of ganglion cells. Also called internal nuclear lamina of retina.

inner plexiform l. of retina The seventh layer of the retina, composed of the interconnecting neurites of bipolar, amacrine, and ganglionic neurons; positioned between the inner nuclear layer and the ganglion cell layer.

longitudinal l. of muscles of colon The outer longitudinal layer of the muscular coat of the colon, being relatively thick in the areas of the teniae coli.

longitudinal l. of muscles of rectum The outer longitudinal layer of muscles of rectum.

longitudinal l. of muscles of small intestine The outer longitudinal layer of the muscular coat of the small intestine.

longitudinal l. of muscles of stomach The incomplete, outer longitudinal layer of the stomach that is continuous with the longitudinal muscle layer of the esophagus; it divides at the cardia of the stomach into two bands: the stronger band follows the lesser curvature of the stomach; the thinner band follows along the greater curvature of the stomach; both bands converge at the pyloric area to form a uniform layer.

malpighian l. See basal layer of skin.

nerve fiber l. of retina The ninth layer of the retina, composed of the axons of ganglion cells converging toward the optic disk from all parts of the retina. Also called stratum opticum.

neuroepithelial l. of retina See layer of rods and cones.

ninth l. of retina See nerve fiber layer of retina.

oblique l. of muscles of stomach The incomplete, innermost oblique muscular layer of the stomach that is strongly developed in the fundal region and becomes progressively thinner as it approaches the pylorus; totally absent at the lesser curvature of the stomach and quite sparse at the greater curvature.

odontoblastic l. The layer of odontoblast cells lining the pulpal surface of the dentin of teeth; it extends protoplasmic processes into the dentin.

outer nuclear l. of retina The fourth layer of the retina, composed of the parts of the rod and cone cells that are internal to the external limiting membrane; positioned between the membrane and the outer plexiform layer. Also called external nuclear lamina of retina.

outer plexiform l. of retina The fifth layer of the retina, composed of an intricate zone of multiple synapses of the rod and cone cells with the dendrites and axons of the bipolar and horizontal neurons. Also called external plexiform lamina of retina.

papillary l. of skin The most superficial or outermost layer of the dermis, marked by ridges (papillae) that interdigitate with the epidermis.

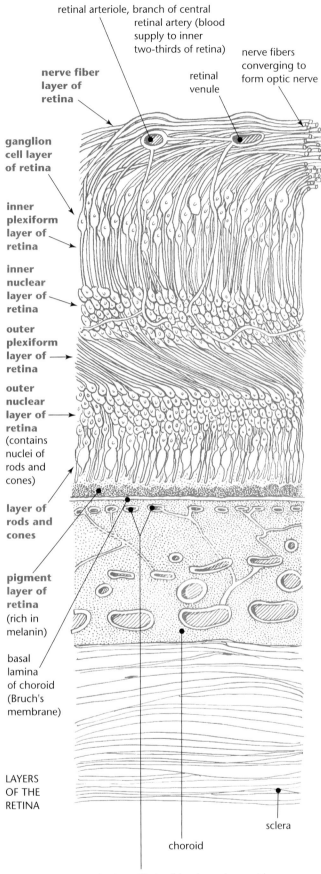

retinal arteriole, branch of central retinal artery (blood supply to inner two-thirds of retina)

nerve fibers converging to form optic nerve

retinal venule

nerve fiber layer of retina

ganglion cell layer of retina

inner plexiform layer of retina

inner nuclear layer of retina

outer plexiform layer of retina

outer nuclear layer of retina (contains nuclei of rods and cones)

layer of rods and cones

pigment layer of retina (rich in melanin)

basal lamina of choroid (Bruch's membrane)

LAYERS OF THE RETINA

sclera

choroid

choriocapillaries (blood supply nourishes avascular outer third of the retina)

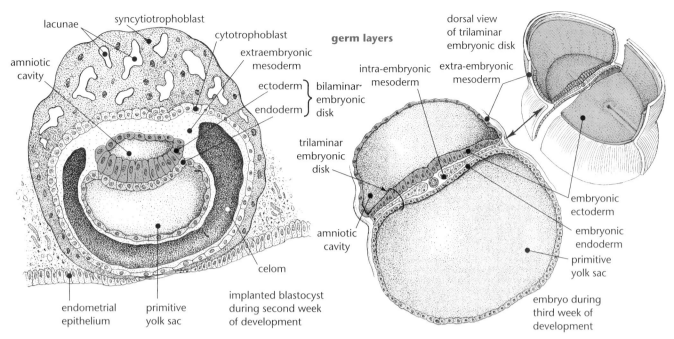

germ layers

Labels on left illustration: lacunae, syncytiotrophoblast, cytotrophoblast, amniotic cavity, extraembryonic mesoderm, ectoderm } bilaminar embryonic disk, endoderm } bilaminar embryonic disk, trilaminar embryonic disk, amniotic cavity, celom, endometrial epithelium, primitive yolk sac, implanted blastocyst during second week of development

Labels on right illustration: dorsal view of trilaminar embryonic disk, intra-embryonic mesoderm, extra-embryonic mesoderm, embryonic ectoderm, embryonic endoderm, primitive yolk sac, embryo during third week of development

pigment l. of retina A single layer of flat cells that constitutes the outermost (first) layer of the retina; it serves as a mechanism for preventing reflections by absorbing light, as well as for mechanical support for the retinal photoreceptor cells (rods and cones).

prickle-cell l. of skin The thick layer of the skin (epidermis) between the basal layer and the granular layer, composed of several rows of flattened rhombic cells with their long axis parallel with the skin; thought to represent the transitional stage in the formation of soft keratin; the cells contain conspicuous granules of keratohyalin; the prickle-cell layer provides most of the mechanical coherence of the skin. Also called stratum spinosum.

Purkinje's l. The middle of the three layers of the cerebellar cortex, consisting of large flask-shaped Purkinje nerve cell bodies that have a vertical diameter of about 60 μm and a transverse diameter of about 30 μm; the cells are characteristically found only in the cerebellar cortex.

l. of rods and cones The second layer of the retina of the eye that contains the photoreceptors (rod and cone cells); it serves as the neural sensory layer of the eyeball. Also called bacillary layer; neuroepithelial layer of rods and cones.

second l. of retina See layer of rods and cones.

seventh l. of retina See inner plexiform layer of retina.

sixth l. of retina See inner nuclear layer of retina.

spinous l. of skin See prickle-cell layer of skin.

spongy l. of endometrium The midportion of the uterine endometrium, lying between the compact layer on the luminal surface and the basal layer on the myometrial side; seen especially during the late proliferative stage of the endometrial cycle, marked by growth of the stroma and engorged corkscrew convolutions of glands; it reflects heightened regenerative activity and coincides with the maturing follicle in the ovary.

subendothelial l. The thin layer of connective tissue located between the endothelium and elastic lamina of the intima of large and medium-sized blood vessels, as well as under the endothelial lining of the heart (endocardium).

tenth l. of retina See internal limiting lamina of retina, under lamina.

third l. of retina See external limiting lamina of retina, under lamina.

leaching (lēch′ing) The process of washing out soluble matter from a substance by a percolating liquid. Also called lixiviation.

lead (led) Metallic element extracted chiefly from lead sulfide; symbol Pb, atomic number 82, atomic weight 207.19. See also lead poisoning, under poisoning.

l. carbonate Poisonous white powder used in manufacture of paints.

l. chromate Poisonous lemon-white powder used as a paint pigment.

l. sulfide The natural form in which lead is usually found. Also called galena.

L

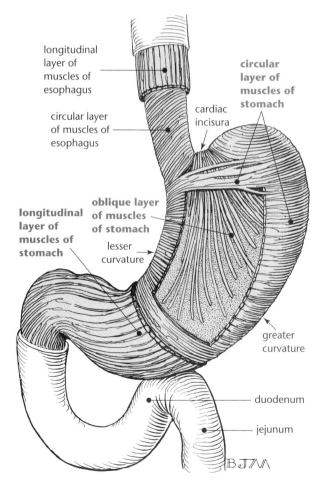

Labels: longitudinal layer of muscles of esophagus, circular layer of muscles of esophagus, circular layer of muscles of stomach, cardiac incisura, longitudinal layer of muscles of stomach, oblique layer of muscles of stomach, lesser curvature, greater curvature, duodenum, jejunum

BJM

lead (lēd) An array of electrodes connected to the electrocardiograph used in recording the electrical potential created by a functioning organ such as the heart (electrocardiography).

    bipolar l. A lead in which the electrodes detect electric variations at two sites and record the difference.

    chest l. See precordial lead.

    esophageal l. An exploring electrode introduced into the lumen of the esophagus to improve visualization of atrial deflections on the electrocardiogram; useful in the recognition of irregular heartbeats (arrhythmia).

    intracardiac l. A lead in which the exploring electrode is placed in one of the heart's chambers, usually by means of cardiac catherization.

    limb l. One of the three standard leads or one of the three unipolar augmented leads (aVR, aVL, aVF).

    precordial l. A lead in which the exploring electrode is placed on the chest overlying the heart or its vicinity.

    standard l. One of the original bipolar limb leads, designated I, II, and III.

    unipolar l. A lead in which one electrode registers variations in electrical potential at one point with respect to another point that does not vary significantly during cardiac contraction.

    V l. A precordial lead with the central terminal as the indifferent electrode.

lecithin (les'ĭ-thin) One of a group of waxy phospholipids present in nerve tissue and egg yolk.

lecithinase (les'ĭ-thin-ās) See phospholipase.

lectin (lek'tin) Protein present predominantly in seeds, especially those of legumes; it binds to specific carbohydrate-containing receptor sites on the red blood cell surface and can cause the cells to clump together.

leech (lēch) Any of various worms of the class Hirudinea; the blood-sucking species, *Hirudo medicinalis,* was formerly used extensively for therapeutic drawing of blood.

leg (leg) The lower limb, between the knee and ankle.

    milk l. See puerperal thrombophlebitis, under thrombophlebitis.

    painful white l. See puerperal thrombophlebitis, under thrombophlebitis.

    tennis l. Rupture of the calf muscles (gastrocnemius and soleus muscles) caused by activities in which the rapidly moving body abruptly changes directions (e.g., in tennis or soccer playing, downhill skiing); causes severe pain and accumulation of extravasated blood (hematoma); a snapping sound may be heard in the popliteal space (behind the knee).

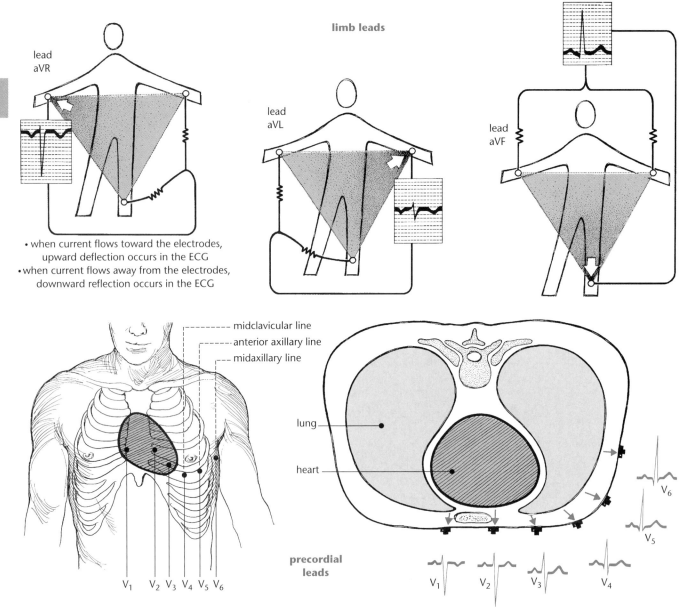

limb leads

lead aVR

lead aVL

lead aVF

• when current flows toward the electrodes, upward deflection occurs in the ECG
• when current flows away from the electrodes, downward reflection occurs in the ECG

midclavicular line
anterior axillary line
midaxillary line

V_1 V_2 V_3 V_4 V_5 V_6

precordial leads

lung

heart

V_6

V_5

V_1 V_2 V_3 V_4

Legionella pneumophila (le-jun-el'ah nu-mo'fil-ah) A gram-negative, rod-shaped bacterium that thrives in hot-water distribution systems of buildings; the cause of legionnaires' disease.

legumin (lĕ-gu'min) Protein found in peas and beans.

leiomyofibroma (li-o-mi-o-fi-bro'mah) See leiomyoma.

leiomyoma (li-o-mi-o'mah) A benign grayish-white mass composed mostly of smooth muscle cells and varying degrees of collagen; although it may occur in any tissue that has an abundant smooth muscle component, the tumor is seen most frequently in the uterus; may be single or multiple and occur anywhere in the uterine wall; it tends to grow rapidly during pregnancy, often undergoing necrosis with severe abdominal pain; it usually regresses after the menopause. Commonly called fibroid; also called fibroid tumor; myoma; fibromyoma; leiomyofibroma.

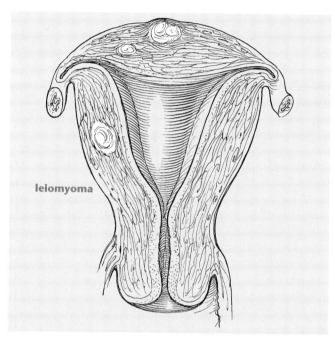

leiomyoma

leiomyomatosis (li-o-mi-o-mah-to'sis) The state of having multiple leiomyomas.

leiomyosarcoma (li-o-mi-o-sar-ko'mah) Malignant tumor of smooth muscle occurring predominantly in the female genital tract, especially the uterus; may occur also in other tissues containing abundant smooth muscle (e.g., intestinal wall, scrotum, nipple).

Leishmania (lēsh-ma'ne-ah) A genus of flagellated parasitic protozoa (family Trypanosomatidae) transmitted to humans by the bite of infected sandflies; several species cause leishmaniasis.

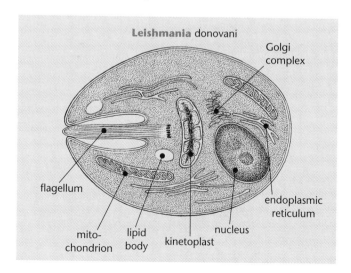

Leishmania donovani

Golgi complex

flagellum

mito-chondrion | lipid body | kinetoplast | nucleus

endoplasmic reticulum

leishmaniasis (lēsh-mah-ni'ah-sis) Infection with any of various species of *Leishmania*.

American l. See mucocutaneous leishmaniasis.

cutaneous l. Chronic ulcer on the skin beginning as a papule that develops into a necrotic ulcer, leaving a hypopigmented scar, usually on the face and legs; caused by *Leishmania tropica* and *Leishmania major;* incubation period is 2 to 24 months. Also called oriental sore; Old World leishmaniasis.

diffuse cutaneous l. Masses of nonnecrotizing skin lesions covering wide areas of the body; seen in immunosuppressed individuals; caused by New and Old World species of *Leishmania*.

mucocutaneous l. Nodular or ulcerative skin lesions, usually healing after a period of time but may appear months to years later as ulcers in the nose, mouth, and pharynx; caused by *Leishmania braziliens* and *Leishmania mexicana*. Also called American leishmaniasis; New World leishmaniasis.

New World l. See mucocutaneous leishmaniasis.

Old World l. See cutaneous leishmaniasis.

visceral l. Disease characterized by chronic fever, enlargement of the spleen, reduced number of white blood cells, and excess of globulin in the blood; caused by the protozoan parasite *Leishmania donovani*, transmitted by the bite of a sandfly. Also called kala-azar; tropical splenomegaly.

lema (le'mah) The normal sebaceous secretion of the meibomian glands in the eyelids, collected at the inner angle of the eye.

lemic (lem'ik) Relating to any epidemic disease.

lemniscus (lem-nis'kus), pl. lemnis'ci A band or bundle of nerve fibers in the central nervous system.

lateral l. The major auditory pathway to the brain stem; it consists of longitudinal ascending nerve fibers that pass through the pons to the level of the midbrain, where most of the fibers terminate in the inferior colliculus with a few fibers projecting directly to the medial geniculate body; from these nuclei, impulses are relayed to the auditory cortex.

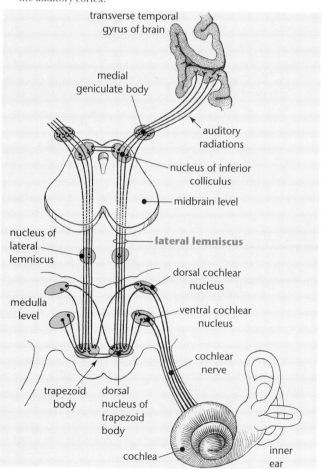

transverse temporal gyrus of brain

medial geniculate body

auditory radiations

nucleus of inferior colliculus

midbrain level

nucleus of lateral lemniscus

lateral lemniscus

dorsal cochlear nucleus

medulla level

ventral cochlear nucleus

cochlear nerve

trapezoid body | dorsal nucleus of trapezoid body

cochlea

inner ear

medial l. A bundle of ascending fibers that originates in the nuclei of the lower brainstem and terminates in the ventral posterior portion of the thalamus. Each leminiscus carries sensory impulses from the opposite side of the body.

trigeminal l. A band of fibers in the brainstem conveying sensory impulses from the trigeminal nuclei to the ventral posterior portion of the thalamus.

length (lengkth) Distance between two points.

crown-heel l., C-H l. The length of an embryo from the top of the head to the heel.

crown-rump l., C-R l. The length of an embryo from the top of the head to the bottom of the buttocks.

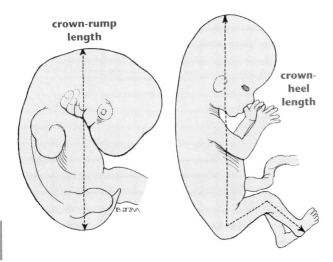

crown-rump length

crown-heel length

lenitive (len′ĭ-tiv) **1.** Soothing. **2.** Any soothing agent.

lens (lenz) **1.** An object made of polished glass, plastic, or other transparent substance that has at least one curved surface. **2.** The lens of the eye; the biconvex transparent structure situated in front of the vitreous body and behind the iris; it serves as a refractive medium to focus images on the retina and adjusts its shape in accommodation for near and far vision. Also called crystalline lens.

achromatic l. A compound lens that eliminates or reduces chromatic aberration; made of two kinds of glass with different dispersive powers.

acrylic l. A lens made of acrylic material; used to replace a cataractous lens.

aplanatic l. A lens that corrects spherical aberration.

apochromatic l. A lens that corrects both spherical and chromatic aberrations.

bifocal l. Lens having one portion (usually the upper and larger portion) suited for distant vision and the other suited for near vision.

compound l. Optical system having two or more lenses.

concave l. A lens that disperses light rays. Also called minus, diverging, myoptic, negative, or reducing lens.

concavoconvex l. Lens having one concave and one convex surface. Also called positive meniscus lens.

contact l. A small, thin plastic disk designed to fit directly on the cornea of the eye. It adheres to a film of tears covering the front of the eye through surface tension (the force that causes a drop of water to cling to the side of a glass). Contact lenses are used primarily to correct conditions in which images focus improperly on the retina, such as nearsightedness (myopia), farsightedness (hyperopia), and refractive errors (astigmatism).

convexoconcave l. Lens having one convex and one concave surface. Also called negative meniscus lens.

crystalline l. See lens (2).

cylindrical l. A lens in which one or both surfaces have the curve of a cylinder, either concave or convex; used to correct astigmatism.

gas-permeable l. A hard contact lens that allows atmospheric

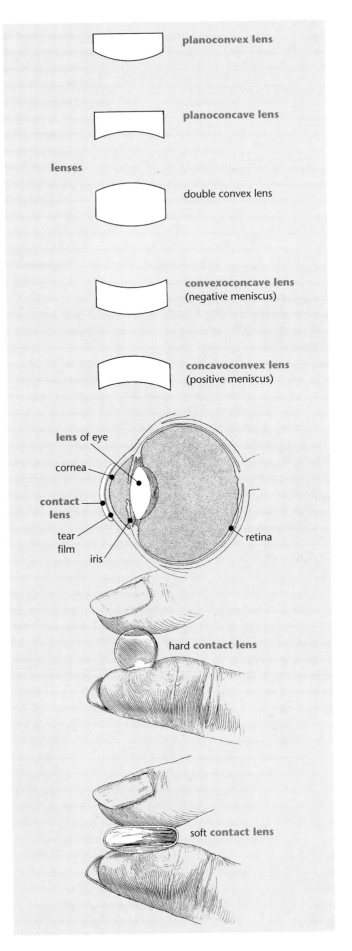

planoconvex lens

planoconcave lens

lenses

double convex lens

convexoconcave lens (negative meniscus)

concavoconvex lens (positive meniscus)

lens of eye

cornea

contact lens

tear film

iris

retina

hard **contact lens**

soft **contact lens**

oxygen to pass directly through to reach the cornea, which renders the lens comfortable to wear for long periods of time.

hard contact l. A contact lens made of a substance that absorbs little or no water, thus the lens remains rigid when worn. Also called hydrophobic contact lens; rigid contact lens.

hydrophilic contact l. See soft contact lens.

hydrophobic contact l. See hard contact lens.

immersion l. The lens in a microscope nearest the histologic specimen, designed so that it can be lowered into contact with a fluid that is placed on the cover glass.

meniscus l. A crescent-shaped lens; one that is concave on one surface and convex on the other.

minus l. See concave lens.

myoptic l. See concave lens.

negative l. See concave lens.

negative meniscus l. See convexoconcave lens.

non-gas-permeable l. A hard contact lens that, as it moves up and down with each blink of the eyelid, allows oxygen-carrying tears to bathe the cornea.

planoconcave l. A lens that is flat on one surface and concave on the other.

planoconvex l. A lens that is flat on one surface and convex on the other.

plus l. See convex lens.

reducing l. See concave lens.

rigid contact l. See hard contact lens.

soft contact l. A flexible contact lens made of a water-absorbing substance. Also called hydrophilic contact lens.

spherical l. A lens in which all refractive surfaces are spherical.

sphericocylindrical l. A lens in which one surface is spherical and the other is cylindrical.

trifocal l. A lens having three portions with different focal powers serving for distant, intermediate, and near vision.

lensometer (lenz-om′ĕ-ter) An optical instrument for determining the refractive power, optical center, cylinder axis, and prismatic effect of ophthalmic lenses. Also called focimeter.

lenticonus (len-tī-ko′nus) Abnormal conical protrusion on either the anterior or posterior surface of the lens of the eye, usually affecting one eye only.

lenticular (len-tik′u-lar) **1.** Relating to a lens. **2.** Shaped like a lens. Also called lentiform.

lentiform (len′tī-form) Shaped like a lens or a lentil.

lentigo (len-ti′go), pl. lentig′ines A flat, tan or brown spot on the skin; distinguished from a freckle, which darkens with sun exposure.

l. maligna, malignant l. See melanoma *in situ*, under melanoma.

senile l. A brown discoloration on the exposed area of the skin occurring in elderly people. It is not a premalignant lesion. Also called liver spot.

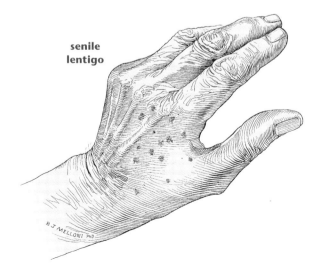

senile lentigo

Lentivirinae (len-tī-vir′i-ne) A subfamily of nononcogenic retroviruses (family Retroviridae) that cause multiorgan diseases of long incubation periods.

lentivirus (len-tī-vi′rus) Any virus of the subfamily Lentivirinae.

leontiasis (le-on-ti′ah-sis) The lionlike appearance of some patients with advanced leprosy, characterized by ridges and furrows on the forehead and cheeks.

LEOPARD Acronym for Lentigines, Electrographic disturbances, Ocular hypertelorism, Pulmonary stenosis, Abnormalities of genitalia, Retarded growth, neural Deafness.

leper (lep′er) A person afflicted with leprosy.

lepidosis (lep-ī-do′sis) A scaly eruption on the skin.

lepothrix (lep′o-thriks) See trichomycosis axillaris.

leprid (lep′rid) The early skin lesion of leprosy.

leprology (lep-rol′o-je) The study of leprosy.

leproma (lep-ro′mah) The characteristic lesion of the focus of infection with *Mycobacterium leprae*, the bacillus causing leprosy.

lepromatous (lep-ro′mah-tus) Relating to a leproma.

lepromin (lep′ro-min) Extract from tissue containing the leprosy bacillus *(Mycobacterium leprae),* used in skin tests to determine resistance to leprosy.

leprosarium (lep-ro-sa′re-um) A special hospital for the care and treatment of those afflicted with leprosy.

leprosary (lep′ro-sar-e) A leper colony.

leprostatic (lep-ro-stat′ik) **1.** Inhibiting the growth of the leprosy bacillus *(Mycobacterium leprae).* **2.** A drug having such an effect.

leprosy (lep′ro-se) A chronic infectious disease caused by the bacillus *Mycobacterium leprae* with a patient-to-patient transmission; it produces granulomatous lesions of the skin and mucous membranes, with involvement of the peripheral nervous system. Its severity can range from benign forms (tuberculoid leprosy) to highly contagious malignant forms (lepromatous leprosy) marked by mutilation. Also called Hansen's disease.

leprous (lep′rus) Relating to leprosy.

-lepsy Combining form meaning seizure (e.g., epilepsy).

lepto- Combining form meaning thin; delicate; fine.

leptocyte (lep′to-sit) An abnormal, thin red blood cell.

leptocytosis (lep-to-si-to′sis) The presence of leptocytes in the blood; seen in certain disorders.

leptodermic (lep-to-der′mik) Thin-skinned.

leptomeningeal (lep-to-mĕ-nin′je-al) Relating to the pia mater and arachnoid collectively.

leptomeninges (lep-to-mĕ-nin′jēz) Collective term for the pia mater and arachnoid, two of the three membranes covering the brain and spinal cord (the third one being the dura mater). Also called piaarachnoid; piarachnoid.

leptomeninx (lep-to-men′inks) Singular of leptomeninges.

Leptospira (lep-to-spi′rah) A genus of spiral, hook-ended spirochetes, bacteria of the order Spirochaetales; some cause human diseases.

L. interrogans A species that is parasitic in rodents and domestic animals; rats and dogs are special reservoirs; can be transmitted to humans, causing diseases ranging from subclinical to severe.

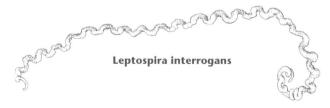

Leptospira interrogans

leptospire (lep′to-spir) Any organism belonging to the genus *Leptospira.*

leptospirosis (lep-to-spi-ro′sis) Infection with bacteria of the genus *Leptospira;* acquired by contact with urine or tissues of infected animals, rodent excreta, or contaminated water through skin abrasions; the clinical picture may vary from a mild fever to a fulminating toxic illness with jaundice, liver damage, and kidney failure; specific syndromes include aseptic meningitis and pretibial fever. Persons at risk of occupational exposure include agricultural workers, farmers, sewer workers, veterinarians, laboratory workers, and fishermen.

Leptotrichia (lep-to-trik'e-ah) Genus of anaerobic, gram-negative bacteria indigenous to the oral cavity of humans.

Leptotrombidium (lep-to-trom-bid'e-um) A genus of mites that includes the *Leptotrombidium akamushi,* vector of scrub typhus (tsutsugamushi disease).

lesbian (lez'be-an) **1.** A homosexual female. **2.** Relating to lesbianism.

lesbianism (lez'be-ah-nizm) Female homosexuality.

lesion (le'zhun) General term for any morbid change in the structure or function of tissues due to injury or disease.

    coin l. A round shadow the size of a small coin in x-ray pictures of the lungs; may indicate tuberculosis, cancer, or other diseases.

    Councilman l. See Councilman bodies, under body.

    focal cerebral l.'s Lesions of specific regions of the brain, causing localized symptoms and signs by disrupting functional centers of the brain or pathways that connect them.

    Ghon's primary l. The calcified lesion formed in a lung at the initial focus of infection in primary pulmonary tuberculosis. Also called Ghon's tubercle; Ghon's focus.

    Janeway l. A small hemorrhagic lesion on the palm or sole, occurring in some cases of bacterial endocarditis.

    polypoid l. Inflammatory mass arising from the submucosa or muscle layer of a hollow organ and protruding into the lumen.

let-down (let' down) Popular term for the passage of milk from the alveoli of the breasts into the lactiferous ducts in lactating women.

lethal (le'thal) (L) Deadly.

lethargy (leth'ar-je) Drowsiness due to a condition other than normal sleep.

leucine (loo'sin) (Leu) An essential amino acid of protein, present in many tissues, especially the pancreas and spleen.

leucovorin (loo-ko-vo'rin) See folinic acid.

leukapheresis (loo-kah-fĕ-re'sis) The process of separating and retaining leukocytes from withdrawn blood and returning the remaining blood to the donor.

leukemia (loo-ke'me-ah) Disease characterized by proliferation of large numbers of immature and abnormal white blood cells in bone marrow, where they impair production of normal white blood cells, red blood cells, and platelets; in most cases these malignant cells are also present in peripheral blood and may also infiltrate other tissues and organs. Leukemia is classified as acute or chronic depending (in part) on the rapidity of its course and (primarily) on the degree of immaturity of predominant cells; may also be classified on the basis of the dominant cell involved (e.g., granulocytic, lymphocytic, monocytic).

    acute l. Leukemia of abrupt onset and rapid course leading to death if untreated; characterized by proliferation of primitive undifferentiated cells ("blasts") that mature little, if at all; bone marrow is the primary site of the disease; clinical features include: rapidly developing anemia (often severe), fatigue, fever, susceptibility to infections, abnormal bleeding (of gums, nose, and subcutaneous tissues), enlargement of lymph nodes (usually) and organs (sometimes), and bone pain and tenderness; may involve the central nervous system, causing associated symptoms (e.g., headache, stiff neck, vomiting, lethargy, swelling of optic disks).

    acute granulocytic l. (AGL) See acute myeloblastic leukemia.

    acute lymphoblastic l. (ALL) Leukemia occurring predominantly in children, with peak incidence at three to four years of age; it constitutes 80% of childhood acute leukemias. Most of the blood cells involved are B lymphocytes (80%), others are T lymphocytes. Also called acute lymphocytic leukemia.

    acute lymphocytic l. See acute lymphoblastic leukemia.

    acute myeloblastic l. (AML) Leukemia originating from any white blood cell of the granulocyte series. Also called acute granulocytic leukemia (AGL); acute myelocytic leukemia; acute myeloid leukemia.

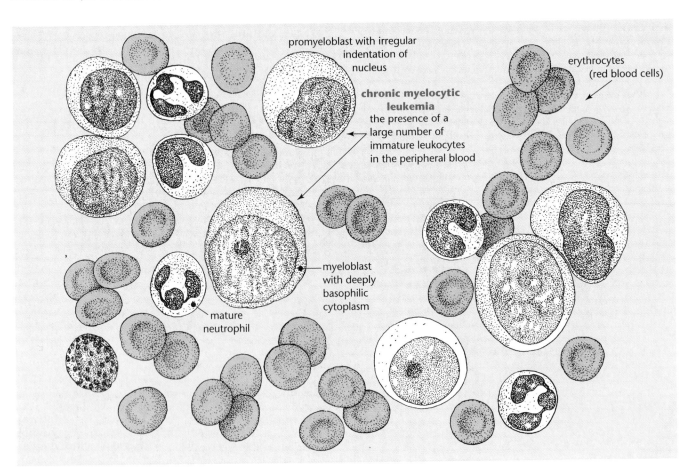

promyeloblast with irregular indentation of nucleus

erythrocytes (red blood cells)

chronic myelocytic leukemia the presence of a large number of immature leukocytes in the peripheral blood

myeloblast with deeply basophilic cytoplasm

mature neutrophil

acute myelocytic l. See acute myeloblastic leukemia.

acute myeloid l. See acute myeloblastic leukemia.

chronic l. Leukemia characterized by an insidious onset and a slow clinical course; patients often survive several years, sometimes without treatment; characterized by proliferation of immature cells that are more mature than those of acute leukemia; white blood cell counts in peripheral blood are usually very high; clinical features include a slowly developing anemia (sometimes over years), generalized lymph node enlargement (in some types) and massive enlargement of spleen and liver (in others). The condition is frequently discovered accidently.

chronic granulocytic l. (CGL) See chronic myelocytic leukemia.

chronic lymphocytic l. (CLL) Leukemia occurring primarily in persons over the age of 50 years; men are affected more often than women; cells involved are B lymphcytes; clinical features include: fatigability, weight loss, and anorexia, with generalized lymph node and liver enlargement. Median survival rate after onset is usually 4 to 5 years.

chronic myelocytic l. (CML) Leukemia primarily affecting adults 25 to 60 years old, with peak incidence in the fourth and fifth decades of life; dominant cells involved are myelocytes, metamyelocytes, and granulocytes; symptoms include fatigability, weakness, weight loss, and anorexia, with a typical dragging sensation in the abdomen caused by massive enlargement of the spleen. Some patients develop an accelerated phase (blast crisis) for which all forms of treatment are ineffective. Also called chronic granulocytic leukemia; chronic myeloid leukemia.

hairy-cell l. A rare form of chronic B lymphocyte leukemia in which the abnormal cells have fine, hairlike projections; affects primarily males over 50 years of age; most prominent symptom is massive enlargement of the spleen. Median survival is 4 years.

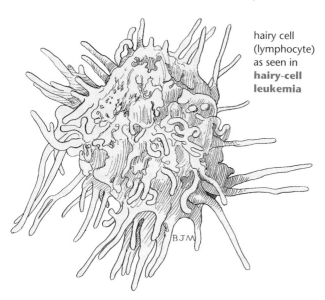

hairy cell
(lymphocyte)
as seen in
**hairy-cell
leukemia**

leukemic (loo-ke′mik) Relating to leukemia.

leukemogen (loo-ke′mo-jen) Anything considered to cause leukemia.

leukemogenesis (loo-ke-mo-jen′ĕ-sis) Development of leukemia.

leukemoid (loo-ke′moid) Resembling the blood changes of leukemia.

leuko- Combining form meaning white.

leukoagglutinin (loo-ko-ah-gloo′tĭ-nin) Antibody that causes white blood cells to clump together.

leukoblast (loo′ko-blast) An immature white blood cell.

leukocoria (loo-ko-ko′re-ah) A white appearance of the pupil caused by conditions such as cataract, retrolental fibroplasia, persistence of the embryonic tunica vasculosa lentis. Also spelled leukokoria.

leukocytactic (loo-ko-si-tak′tik) See leukocytotactic.

leukocytaxia, leukocytaxis (loo-ko-si-tak′se-ah, loo-ko-si-tak′sis) See leukocytotaxia.

leukocyte (loo′ko-sīt) Any of the colorless cells of the blood generally called white blood cells; may be granular (which has readily stainable cytoplasmic granules and lobulated nuclei) or nongranular (which has minute granules, not detectable by ordinary methods).

basophilic l. Leukocyte containing large granules that stain readily with basic dyes (e.g., methylene blue); constitutes about 0.5% of total white blood cell count. Also called basophil; mast leukocyte.

eosinophilic l. Phagocytic white blood cell with a bilobar nucleus and numerous large granules that stain readily with acid dyes (e.g., eosin) and are rich in protein highly toxic to parasites; constitutes 2 to 5% of total white blood cell count and increases in number during parasitic infestations and allergic states. Also called eosinophil; acidophil; oxyphil.

neutrophilic l. A mature phagocytic leukocyte with a nucleus of three to five distinct lobes and granules that stain with either basic or acid dyes; constitutes about 50 to 75% of total white blood cell count; its main function is to ingest and digest particulate matter, especially virulent bacteria. Also called neutrophil; neutrophilic granulocyte.

polymorphonuclear (PMN) l., polynuclear l. Any granular leukocyte, especially a neutrophilic leukocyte. Also called neutrophil; polymorph; poly.

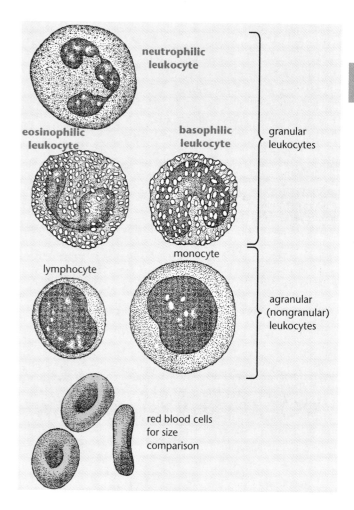

leukocytoblast (loo-ko-si′to-blast) General term for any immature white blood cell.

leukocytogenesis (loo-ko-si-to-jen′ĕ-sis) The formation of white blood cells.

leukocytolysin (loo-ko-si-tol′ĭ-sin) Any agent causing dissolution of white blood cells.

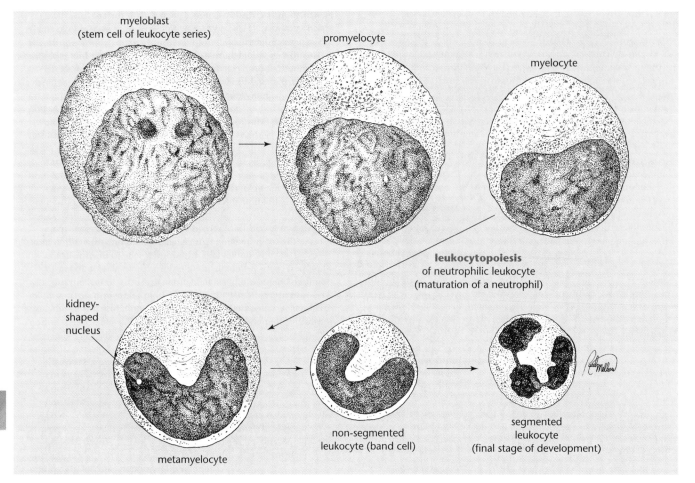

myeloblast
(stem cell of leukocyte series)

promyelocyte

myelocyte

leukocytopoiesis
of neutrophilic leukocyte
(maturation of a neutrophil)

kidney-
shaped
nucleus

metamyelocyte

non-segmented
leukocyte (band cell)

segmented
leukocyte
(final stage of development)

leukocytolysis (loo-ko-si-tol′ĭ-sis) Dissolution of white blood cells. Also called leukolysis.

leukocytometer (loo-ko-si-tom′ĕ-ter) A standardized glass slide for counting white blood cells.

leukocytopenia (loo-ko-si-to-pe′ne-ah) See leukopenia.

leukocytopoiesis (loo-ko-si-to-poi-e′sis) The formation of white blood cells.

leukocytosis (lu-ko-si-to′sis) Abnormal increase in the number of white blood cells in the blood.

   basophilic l. See basophilia.
   eosinophilic l. See eosinophilia.
   lymphocytic l. See lymphocytosis.
   monocytic l. See monocytosis.
   neutrophilic l. See neutrophilia.

leukocytotactic (loo-ko-si-to-tak′tic) Relating to leukocytotaxia. Also called leukocytactic; leukotactic.

leukocytotaxia, leukocytotaxis (loo-ko-si-to-tak′se-ah, loo-ko-si-to-tak′sis) The tendency of white blood cells to move either toward or away from certain microorganisms or substances formed in inflamed tissue. Also called leukocytaxia; leukotaxis.

leukocytoxin (loo-ko-si-tok′sin) Any agent that causes degeneration of white blood cells.

leukoderma (loo-ko-der′mah) Absence of pigment of the skin. Also called achromoderma.

   acquired l. See vitiligo.
   congenital l. See albinism.

leukodystrophy (loo-ko-dis′tro-fe) A group of familial diseases affecting primarily the white matter of the brain, especially the cerebral hemispheres, usually beginning in infancy and childhood.

   globoid cell l. A disease of late infancy characterized by progressive loss of myelin and massive infiltration of large globoid phagocytic cells in the white matter of the brain and spinal cord, resulting in early death; an autosomal recessive inheritance. Also called Krabbe's disease.

   metachromatic l. A progressive disorder of sphingolipid metabolism in which sulfatide accumulates in the tissues; it affects both the central and peripheral nervous systems, causing blindness, deafness, mutism, and quadriplegia; death usually occurs a few years after onset; seen most commonly in young children and infants; an autosomal recessive inheritance. Also called sulfatide lipidosis.

leukoencephalitis (loo-ko-en-sef-ah-li′tis) Inflammation of the white matter of the brain.

   acute necrotizing hemorrhagic l. A rare, rapidly progressing illness usually following a nonspecific respiratory infection; characterized by severe brain swelling, necrosis of blood vessels, and hemorrhages into the brain tissue; leads to coma and usually death.

leukoencephalopathic (loo-ko-en-sef-ah-lo-path′ik) Relating to leukoencephalopathy.

leukoencephalopathy (loo-ko-en-sef-ah-lop′ah-the) Disease of the brain involving the white matter.

   progressive multifocal l. (PML) Disease of insidious onset and fatal outcome affecting immunocompromised patients, especially those with AIDS or undergoing chemotherapy for cancer; characterized by widespread but focal disintegration of myelin in the brain; clinical features include organic brain dysfunction, hemiplegia, partial loss of vision, and language difficulties; caused by infection with JC virus (a polyomavirus).

   subtotal l. Diffuse loss of white matter, axons, and myelin deep in the cerebral hemispheres, occurring with marked hardening (sclerosis) of minute branches of the penetrating arteries of the brain; often associated with arteriosclerosis and/or infarcts in other regions of the brain; may be associated with progressive dementia.

leukoerythroblastosis (loo′ko-ĕ-rith′ro-blas-to′sis) See myelophthisic anemia, under anemia.

leukokoria (loo-ko-ko′re-ah) See leukocoria.

leukolysis (loo-kol′ĭ-sis) See leukocytolysis.

leukoma (loo-ko′mah) An opaque white spot on the cornea.

leukomyelopathy (loo-ko-mi-ĕ-lop′ah-the) Any disease involving the white nerve tracts of the spinal cord.

leukonychia (loo-ko-nik′e-ah) Unusually white nails, especially white spots or patches under the nail.

leukopathia, leukopathy (loo-ko-path′e-ah, loo-kop′ah-the) See leukoderma.

    congenital l. See albinism.

leukopedesis (loo-ko-pĕ-de′sis) Movement of white blood cells through the capillary walls into the tissues.

leukopenia (loo-ko-pe′ne-ah) Abnormal reduction of any of the various types of white blood cells in the blood. Also called leukocytopenia.

    monocytic l. See monocytopenia.

leukoplakia (loo-ko-pla′ke-ah) A visible white, flat lesion occurring in mucous membranes, most commonly of the lips, oral cavity, and genitals; may be simply an increased thickness of the keratin layer of tissues due to chronic irritation, or it may be precancerous. When it occurs on the lips, it is popularly called smoker's patch.

leukopoiesis (loo-ko-poi-e′sis) The formation of white blood cells.

leukoprotease (loo-ko-pro′te-ās) Enzyme causing liquefaction of dead tissue, produced by certain white blood cells in an area of inflammation.

leukorrhea (loo-ko-re′ah) An abnormal white or yellowish discharge from the vagina containing mucus and pus. Popularly called whites.

leukosis (loo-ko′sis) Abnormal proliferation of the tissues forming white blood cells.

leukostasis (loo-ko-sta′sis) Occlusion of blood vessels mediated by the excessive accumulation of immature white blood cells, as seen in certain types of leukemia, which may result in cerebral or pulmonary infarcts or hemorrhage.

leukotactic (loo-ko-tak′tik) See leukocytotactic.

leukotaxine (loo-ko-tak′sin) A crystalline nitrogenous substance formed when tissue is injured; it promotes capillary permeability and escape of white blood cells into the tissues; it can be recovered from inflammatory exudates.

leukotaxis (loo-ko-tak′sis) See leukocytotaxia.

leukotomy (loo-kot′o-me) A surgical cut into the white matter of the brain.

    prefrontal l. See prefrontal lobotomy, under lobotomy.

    transorbital l. See transorbital lobotomy, under lobotomy.

leukotriene (loo-ko-tri′ēn) Any 20-carbon unsaturated fatty acid from arachidonic acid; members of this group increase vascular permeability, trigger smooth muscle contraction (e.g., in asthma), and have important roles in the inflammatory response; some cause marked increase in mucus secretion.

levallorphan tartrate (lev-al-lor′fan tahr′trāt) A bitter, crystalline antianalgesic compound; used in the treatment of narcotics overdose.

levan (lev′an) See fructosan.

levator (le-va′tor) 1. Any muscle that raises a part. 2. Surgical instrument used to lift a structure or a depressed segment of a fractured skull.

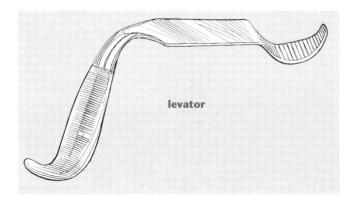

levator

level (lev′el) A standard.

    hearing l. The measure of hearing ability as read on the hearing loss scale of the audiometer.

    l. of significance The probability that an observed difference is due to some factor or factors other than chance.

levo- Combining form meaning left; to the left.

levodopa, L-dopa (le-vo-do′pah, el do′pah) A compound used in the treatment of Parkinson's disease.

levorotation (le-vo-ro-ta′shun) A turning to the left; applied to polarized light.

levorotatory (le-vo-ro′tah-to′re) Turning the plane of polarized light to the left or counterclockwise; applied to certain substances.

levulan (lev′u-lan) See fructosan.

levulin (lev′u-lin) See fructosan.

levulose (lev′u-lōs) See fructose.

levulosuria (lev-u-lo-su′re-ah) See fructosuria.

Lewis blood group (Le) Antigens of red blood cells, saliva, and other body fluids; they are specified by the Le gene and react with the antibodies designated anti-Le[a] and anti-Le[b]; named after a Mrs. Lewis, in whose blood the antibodies were discovered.

lewisite (lu′ĭ-sīt) An oily liquid used to manufacture a highly poisonous war gas.

libido (lĭ-be′do) 1. The emotional energy associated with primitive biologic impulses. 2. In psychoanalysis, the term applied to the motive force of the sexual instinct.

library (li′brĕ-re) 1. A collection of materials organized and kept for information, study, reference, etc. 2. A building or space where such a collection is kept. 3. A systematically arranged collection of substances.

    chromosome-specific l. A type of gene library that contains only clones from a specific human chromosome; constructed by the cloning of DNA from chromosomes separated on the basis of size from all other chromosomes; used for screening or isolating a particular gene of interest from a chromosome (e.g., in the study and diagnosis of genetic disease).

    gene l. A set of independently cloned DNA fragments that contains the gene of interest and, theoretically, one copy of all the genes of the original source from which the DNA was obtained.

lice (līs) Plural of louse.

    diver's l. Popular name for the bluish mottling on the skin of divers with decompression sickness. See also decompression sickness, under sickness.

lichen (li′ken) See liken.

lichenification (li-ken-ĭ-fi-ka′shun) Hardening and thickening of the skin resulting from long-continued irritation.

lichenoid (li′ken-oid) Resembling lichen planus.

licorice (lik′o-ris) See glycyrrhiza.

lid (lid) See eyelid.

lidocaine hydrochloride (li′do-kān hi-dro-klo′rīd) An anesthetic drug, used locally as a cream or ointment to relieve pain and irritation or intravenously as a liquid injection to prevent irregular heartbeats (ventricular fibrillation) after a heart attack (myocardial infarction).

lie (li) The relation that the long axis of the fetus bears to that of the mother.

    longitudinal l. Relationship in which the long axis of the fetus is approximately parallel to the long axis of the mother; noted in about 99% of all labors at term.

    transverse l. Relationship in which the long axis of the fetus is at right angles to that of the mother.

lien (li′en) Latin for spleen.

lienorenal (li-e-no-re′nal) See splenorenal.

life (līf) The state of an organism manifested by active metabolism.

ligament (lig′ah-ment) 1. Any band of thickened white fibrous tissue that connects bones and forms the capsule of joints. 2. A fold of peritoneum, a fascial condensation, or a cordlike fibrous band that holds an organ in position.

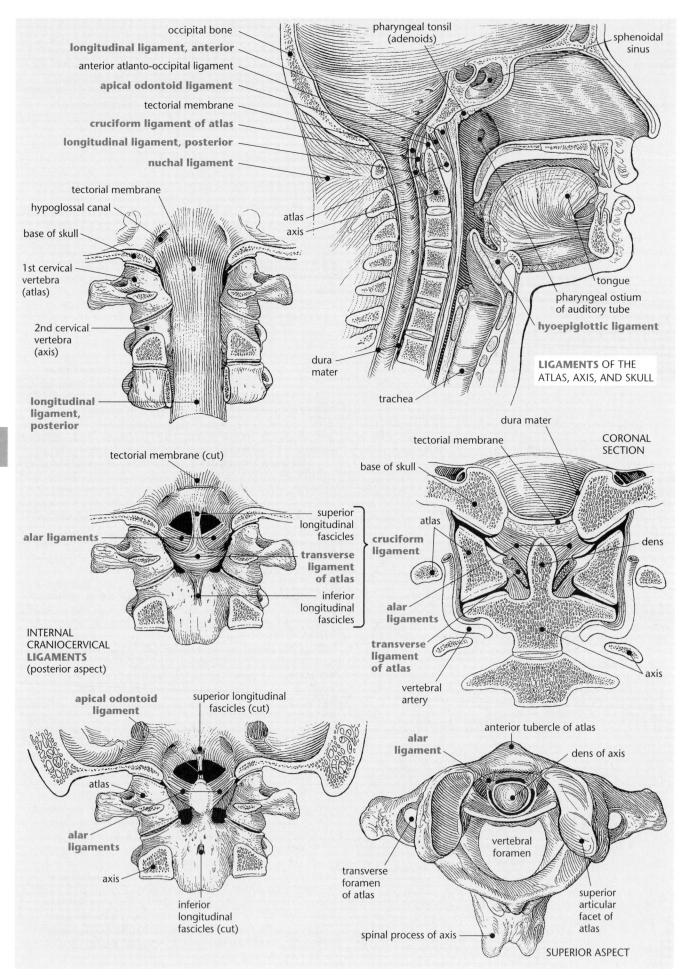

occipital bone

longitudinal ligament, anterior

anterior atlanto-occipital ligament

apical odontoid ligament

tectorial membrane

cruciform ligament of atlas

longitudinal ligament, posterior

nuchal ligament

pharyngeal tonsil (adenoids)

sphenoidal sinus

tectorial membrane

hypoglossal canal

base of skull

1st cervical vertebra (atlas)

2nd cervical vertebra (axis)

longitudinal ligament, posterior

atlas

axis

tongue

pharyngeal ostium of auditory tube

hyoepiglottic ligament

dura mater

trachea

LIGAMENTS OF THE ATLAS, AXIS, AND SKULL

tectorial membrane (cut)

alar ligaments

superior longitudinal fascicles

transverse ligament of atlas

inferior longitudinal fascicles

INTERNAL CRANIOCERVICAL **LIGAMENTS** (posterior aspect)

dura mater

tectorial membrane

base of skull

CORONAL SECTION

atlas

cruciform ligament

alar ligaments

transverse ligament of atlas

vertebral artery

dens

alar ligaments

transverse ligament of atlas

axis

apical odontoid ligament

superior longitudinal fascicles (cut)

atlas

alar ligaments

axis

inferior longitudinal fascicles (cut)

alar ligament

anterior tubercle of atlas

dens of axis

vertebral foramen

transverse foramen of atlas

superior articular facet of atlas

spinal process of axis

SUPERIOR ASPECT

ligament ■ ligament

L20

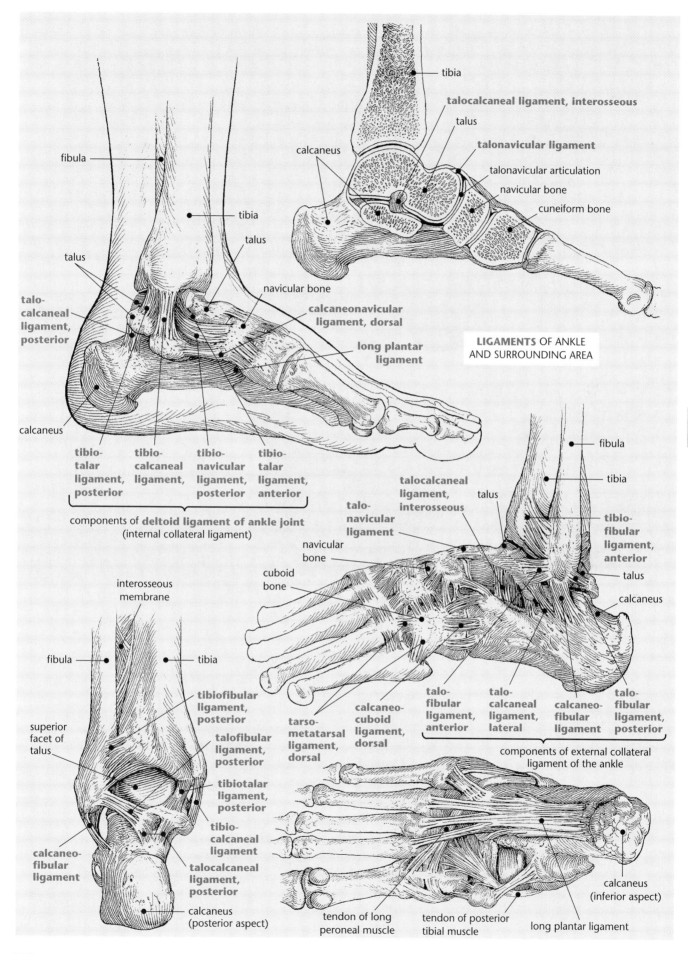

fibula

tibia

talus

talo-
calcaneal
ligament,
posterior

calcaneus

navicular bone

**calcaneonavicular
ligament, dorsal**

**long plantar
ligament**

tibia

talocalcaneal ligament, interosseous

talus

talonavicular ligament

talonavicular articulation

calcaneus

navicular bone

cuneiform bone

LIGAMENTS OF ANKLE
AND SURROUNDING AREA

tibio-
talar
ligament,
posterior

tibio-
calcaneal
ligament,

tibio-
navicular
ligament,
posterior

tibio-
talar
ligament,
anterior

components of **deltoid ligament of ankle joint**
(internal collateral ligament)

interosseous
membrane

fibula

tibia

fibula

tibia

**tibiofibular
ligament,
anterior**

talus

talus

calcaneus

**talocalcaneal
ligament,
interosseous**

talus

**talo-
navicular
ligament**

navicular
bone

cuboid
bone

superior
facet of
talus

**tibiofibular
ligament,
posterior**

**talofibular
ligament,
posterior**

**tibiotalar
ligament,
posterior**

**tibio-
calcaneal
ligament**

**talocalcaneal
ligament,
posterior**

calcaneus
(posterior aspect)

**calcaneo-
fibular
ligament**

**tarso-
metatarsal
ligament,
dorsal**

**calcaneo-
cuboid
ligament,
dorsal**

**talo-
fibular
ligament,
anterior**

**talo-
calcaneal
ligament,
lateral**

**calcaneo-
fibular
ligament**

**talo-
fibular
ligament,
posterior**

components of external collateral
ligament of the ankle

tendon of long
peroneal muscle

tendon of posterior
tibial muscle

calcaneus
(inferior aspect)

long plantar ligament

L

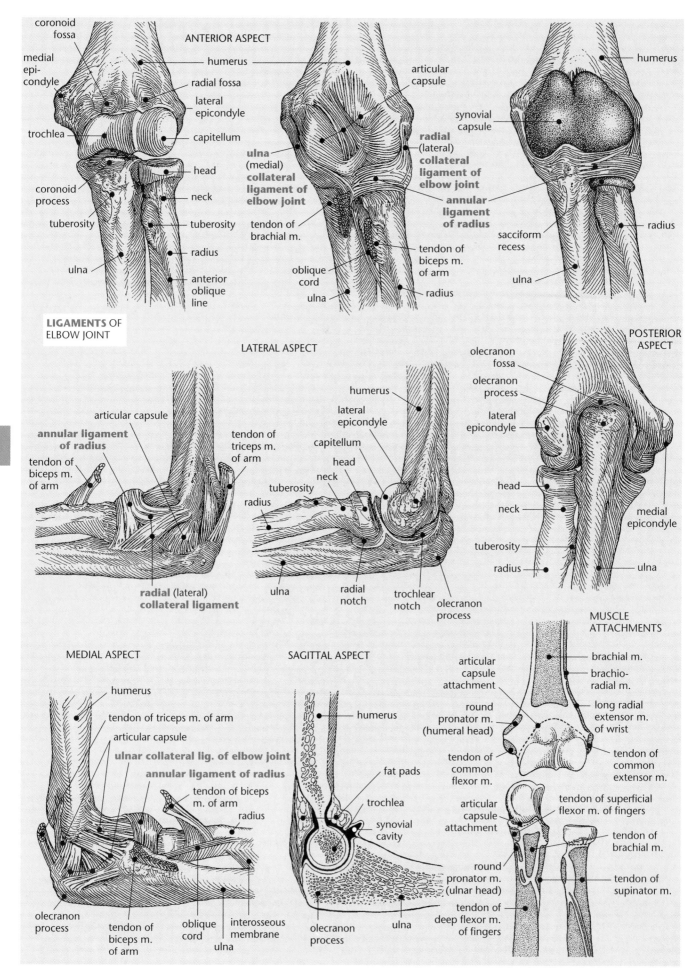

ANTERIOR ASPECT

coronoid fossa
medial epi-condyle
trochlea
coronoid process
tuberosity
ulna

humerus
radial fossa
lateral epicondyle
capitellum
head
neck
tuberosity
radius
anterior oblique line

articular capsule
radial (lateral) collateral ligament of elbow joint
ulna (medial) collateral ligament of elbow joint
annular ligament of radius
tendon of brachial m.
tendon of biceps m. of arm
oblique cord
ulna
radius

humerus
synovial capsule
radial (lateral) collateral ligament of elbow joint
annular ligament of radius
radius
sacciform recess
ulna

LIGAMENTS OF ELBOW JOINT

LATERAL ASPECT

articular capsule
annular ligament of radius
tendon of biceps m. of arm
tendon of triceps m. of arm
radial (lateral) collateral ligament

humerus
lateral epicondyle
capitellum
head
neck
tuberosity
radius
ulna
radial notch
trochlear notch
olecranon process

POSTERIOR ASPECT

olecranon fossa
olecranon process
lateral epicondyle
head
neck
tuberosity
radius
medial epicondyle
ulna

MEDIAL ASPECT

humerus
tendon of triceps m. of arm
articular capsule
ulnar collateral lig. of elbow joint
annular ligament of radius
tendon of biceps m. of arm
radius
olecranon process
tendon of biceps m. of arm
oblique cord
ulna
interosseous membrane

SAGITTAL ASPECT

humerus
fat pads
trochlea
synovial cavity
olecranon process
ulna

MUSCLE ATTACHMENTS

articular capsule attachment
round pronator m. (humeral head)
tendon of common flexor m.
articular capsule attachment
round pronator m. (ulnar head)
tendon of deep flexor m. of fingers
brachial m.
brachio-radial m.
long radial extensor m. of wrist
tendon of common extensor m.
tendon of superficial flexor m. of fingers
tendon of brachial m.
tendon of supinator m.

L

ligament ■ ligament

L22

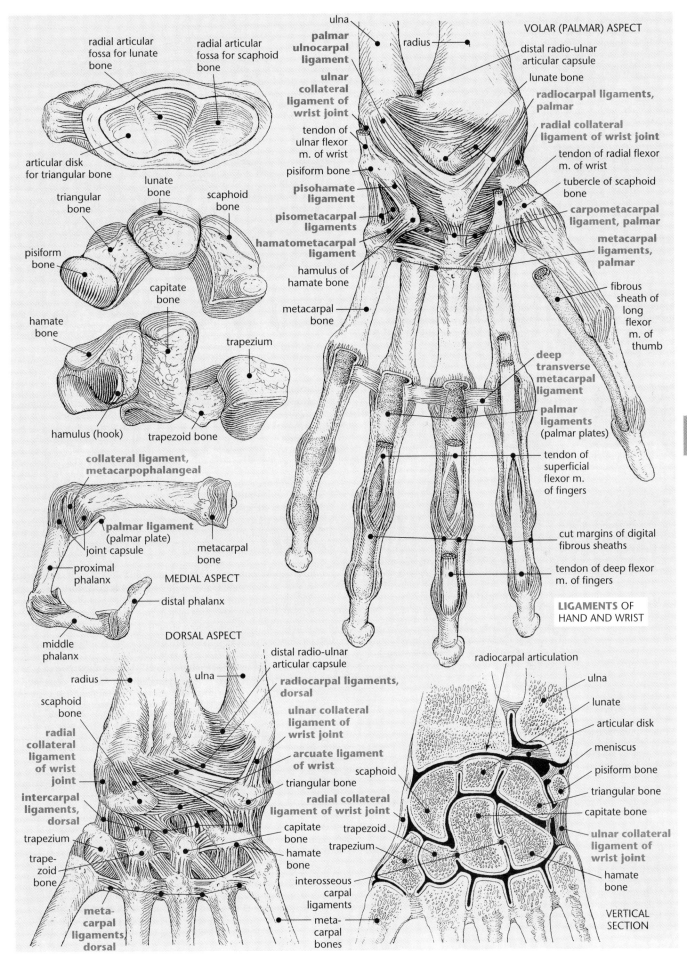

ulna
radius
VOLAR (PALMAR) ASPECT

radial articular
fossa for lunate
bone

radial articular
fossa for scaphoid
bone

palmar
ulnocarpal
ligament

distal radio-ulnar
articular capsule

lunate bone

radiocarpal ligaments,
palmar

ulnar
collateral
ligament of
wrist joint

radial collateral
ligament of wrist joint

tendon of
ulnar flexor
m. of wrist

tendon of radial flexor
m. of wrist

articular disk
for triangular bone

pisiform bone

tubercle of scaphoid
bone

pisohamate
ligament

carpometacarpal
ligament, palmar

triangular
bone

lunate
bone

scaphoid
bone

pisiform
bone

pisometacarpal
ligaments

metacarpal
ligaments,
palmar

hamatometacarpal
ligament

capitate
bone

hamulus of
hamate bone

fibrous
sheath of
long
flexor
m. of
thumb

hamate
bone

trapezium

metacarpal
bone

deep
transverse
metacarpal
ligament

palmar
ligaments
(palmar plates)

hamulus (hook)

trapezoid bone

tendon of
superficial
flexor m.
of fingers

collateral ligament,
metacarpophalangeal

palmar ligament
(palmar plate)

cut margins of digital
fibrous sheaths

joint capsule

metacarpal
bone

tendon of deep flexor
m. of fingers

proximal
phalanx

MEDIAL ASPECT

distal phalanx

LIGAMENTS OF
HAND AND WRIST

middle
phalanx

DORSAL ASPECT

radius

ulna

distal radio-ulnar
articular capsule

radiocarpal articulation

ulna

scaphoid
bone

radiocarpal ligaments,
dorsal

lunate

articular disk

radial
collateral
ligament
of wrist
joint

ulnar collateral
ligament of
wrist joint

meniscus

arcuate ligament
of wrist

scaphoid

pisiform bone

triangular bone

triangular bone

intercarpal
ligaments,
dorsal

radial collateral
ligament of wrist joint

capitate bone

ulnar collateral
ligament of
wrist joint

capitate
bone

trapezoid

trapezium

trapezium

hamate
bone

trapezoid

hamate
bone

trape-
zoid
bone

interosseous
carpal
ligaments

meta-
carpal
ligaments,
dorsal

meta-
carpal
bones

VERTICAL
SECTION

L23

ligament ■ ligament

L

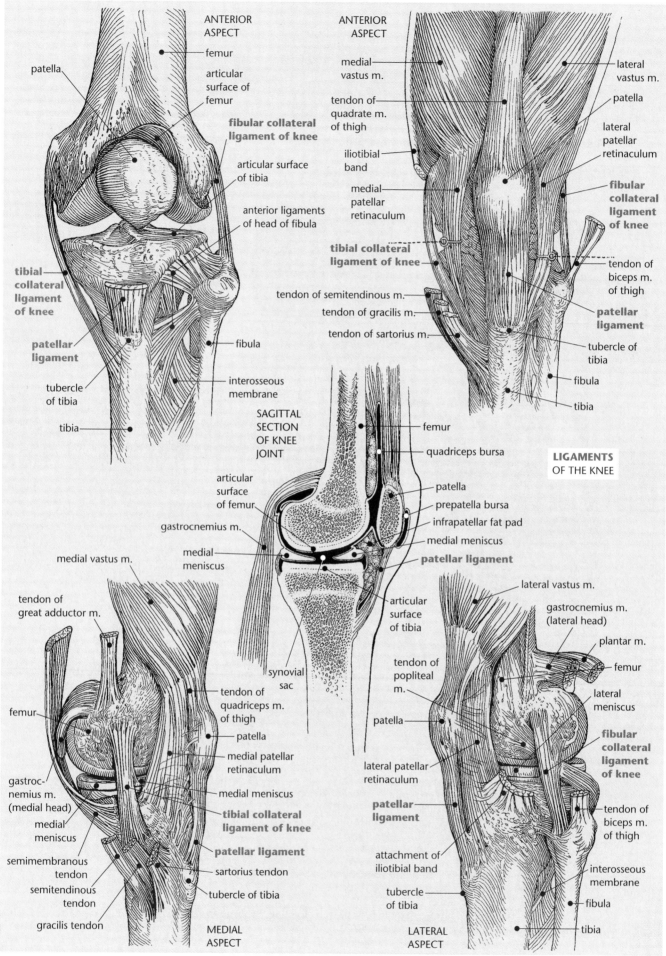

ANTERIOR
ASPECT

patella

femur

articular
surface of
femur

**fibular collateral
ligament of knee**

articular surface
of tibia

anterior ligaments
of head of fibula

**tibial
collateral
ligament
of knee**

**patellar
ligament**

tubercle
of tibia

tibia

fibula

interosseous
membrane

ANTERIOR
ASPECT

medial
vastus m.

tendon of
quadrate m.
of thigh

iliotibial
band

medial
patellar
retinaculum

**tibial collateral
ligament of knee**

tendon of semitendinous m.

tendon of gracilis m.

tendon of sartorius m.

lateral
vastus m.

patella

lateral
patellar
retinaculum

**fibular
collateral
ligament
of knee**

tendon of
biceps m.
of thigh

**patellar
ligament**

tubercle of
tibia

fibula

tibia

SAGITTAL
SECTION
OF KNEE
JOINT

articular
surface
of femur

gastrocnemius m.

medial
meniscus

synovial
sac

femur

quadriceps bursa

patella

prepatella bursa

infrapatellar fat pad

medial meniscus

patellar ligament

articular
surface of
tibia

LIGAMENTS
OF THE KNEE

medial vastus m.

tendon of
great adductor m.

femur

gastroc-
nemius m.
(medial head)

medial
meniscus

semimembranous
tendon

semitendinous
tendon

gracilis tendon

tendon of
quadriceps m.
of thigh

patella

medial patellar
retinaculum

medial meniscus

**tibial collateral
ligament of knee**

patellar ligament

sartorius tendon

tubercle of tibia

MEDIAL
ASPECT

lateral vastus m.

gastrocnemius m.
(lateral head)

plantar m.

femur

lateral
meniscus

**fibular
collateral
ligament
of knee**

tendon of
biceps m.
of thigh

interosseous
membrane

fibula

tibia

tendon of
popliteal
m.

patella

lateral patellar
retinaculum

**patellar
ligament**

attachment of
iliotibial band

tubercle
of tibia

LATERAL
ASPECT

ligament ■ ligament

L24

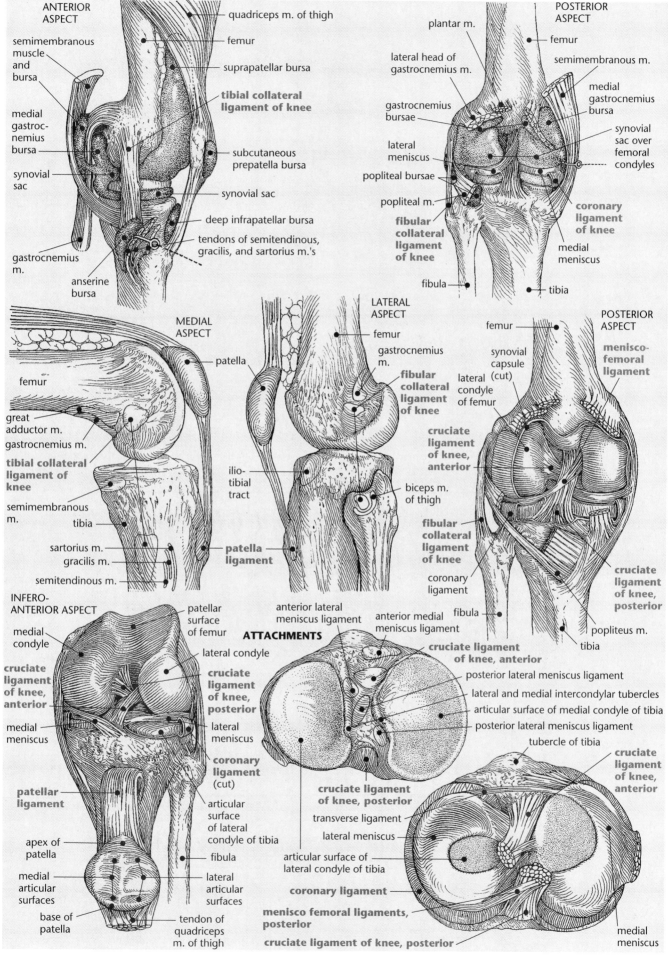

ANTERIOR ASPECT

quadriceps m. of thigh
femur
suprapatellar bursa
semimembranous muscle and bursa
medial gastrocnemius bursa
synovial sac
gastrocnemius m.
anserine bursa
tibial collateral ligament of knee
subcutaneous prepatella bursa
synovial sac
deep infrapatellar bursa
tendons of semitendinous, gracilis, and sartorius m.'s

POSTERIOR ASPECT

plantar m.
femur
lateral head of gastrocnemius m.
semimembranous m.
gastrocnemius bursae
medial gastrocnemius bursa
lateral meniscus
popliteal bursae
popliteal m.
synovial sac over femoral condyles
fibular collateral ligament of knee
coronary ligament of knee
medial meniscus
fibula
tibia

MEDIAL ASPECT

patella
femur
great adductor m.
gastrocnemius m.
tibial collateral ligament of knee
semimembranous m.
tibia
sartorius m.
gracilis m.
semitendinous m.

LATERAL ASPECT

femur
gastrocnemius m.
fibular collateral ligament of knee
ilio-tibial tract
patella ligament
biceps m. of thigh

POSTERIOR ASPECT

femur
synovial capsule (cut)
lateral condyle of femur
menisco-femoral ligament
cruciate ligament of knee, anterior
fibular collateral ligament of knee
coronary ligament
fibula
cruciate ligament of knee, posterior
popliteus m.
tibia

INFERO-ANTERIOR ASPECT

patellar surface of femur
medial condyle
lateral condyle
cruciate ligament of knee, anterior
cruciate ligament of knee, posterior
medial meniscus
lateral meniscus
coronary ligament (cut)
patellar ligament
articular surface of lateral condyle of tibia
apex of patella
fibula
medial articular surfaces
lateral articular surfaces
base of patella
tendon of quadriceps m. of thigh

ATTACHMENTS

anterior lateral meniscus ligament
anterior medial meniscus ligament
cruciate ligament of knee, anterior
posterior lateral meniscus ligament
lateral and medial intercondylar tubercles
articular surface of medial condyle of tibia
posterior lateral meniscus ligament
cruciate ligament of knee, posterior
transverse ligament
lateral meniscus
articular surface of lateral condyle of tibia
coronary ligament
menisco femoral ligaments, posterior
cruciate ligament of knee, posterior
tubercle of tibia
cruciate ligament of knee, anterior
medial meniscus

ligament ■ ligament

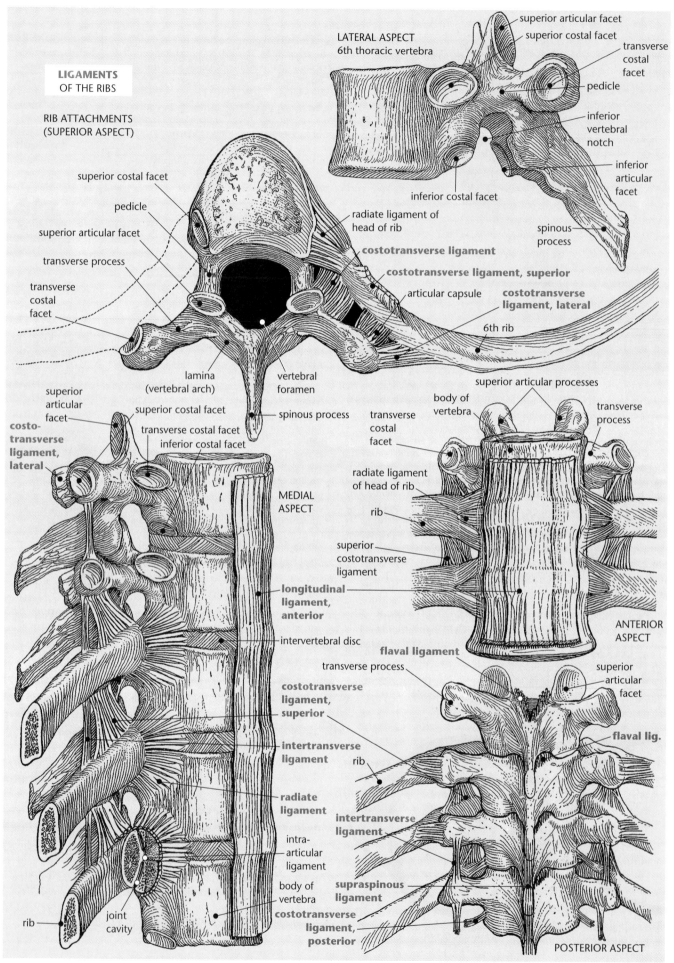

LIGAMENTS OF THE RIBS

RIB ATTACHMENTS (SUPERIOR ASPECT)

LATERAL ASPECT
6th thoracic vertebra

superior articular facet
superior costal facet
transverse costal facet
pedicle
inferior vertebral notch
inferior articular facet
spinous process
inferior costal facet

superior costal facet
pedicle
superior articular facet
transverse process
transverse costal facet
radiate ligament of head of rib
costotransverse ligament
costotransverse ligament, superior
articular capsule
costotransverse ligament, lateral
6th rib
lamina (vertebral arch)
vertebral foramen
spinous process

superior articular facet
costo-transverse ligament, lateral
superior costal facet
transverse costal facet
inferior costal facet
MEDIAL ASPECT
transverse costal facet
radiate ligament of head of rib
rib
superior costotransverse ligament
longitudinal ligament, anterior
intervertebral disc
costotransverse ligament, superior
intertransverse ligament
rib
radiate ligament
intra-articular ligament
body of vertebra
costotransverse ligament, posterior
rib
joint cavity

superior articular processes
body of vertebra
transverse process
ANTERIOR ASPECT

flaval ligament
transverse process
superior articular facet
flaval lig.
intertransverse ligament
supraspinous ligament
POSTERIOR ASPECT

L

ligament ■ ligament

L26

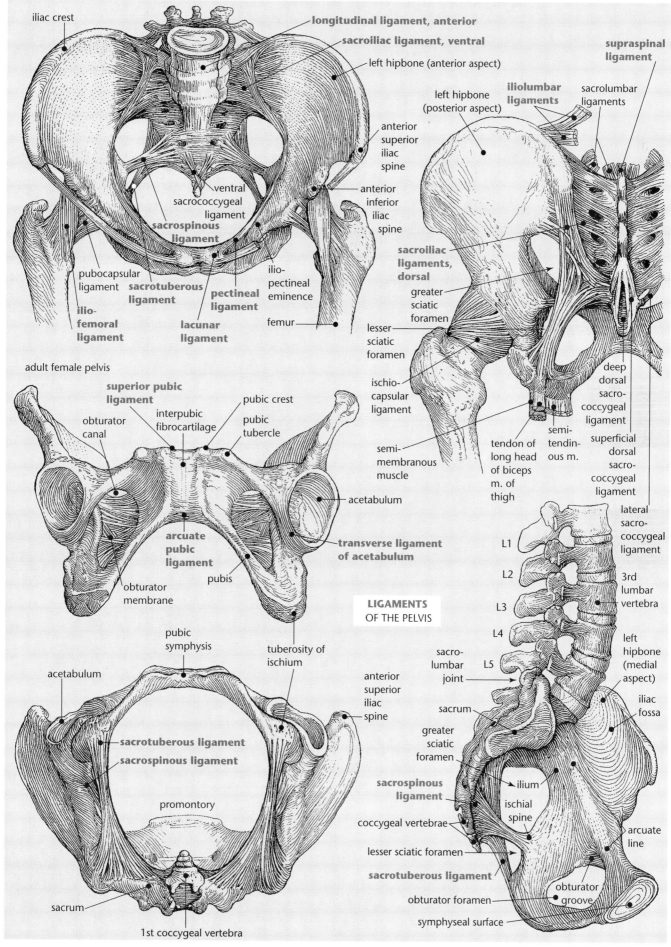

iliac crest

longitudinal ligament, anterior

sacroiliac ligament, ventral

left hipbone (anterior aspect)

supraspinal ligament

left hipbone (posterior aspect)

iliolumbar ligaments

sacrolumbar ligaments

anterior superior iliac spine

anterior inferior iliac spine

ventral sacrococcygeal ligament

sacrospinous ligament

pubocapsular ligament

sacrotuberous ligament

pectineal ligament

ilio-pectineal eminence

ilio-femoral ligament

lacunar ligament

femur

sacroiliac ligaments, dorsal

greater sciatic foramen

lesser sciatic foramen

ischio-capsular ligament

semi-membranous muscle

tendon of long head of biceps m. of thigh

semi-tendin-ous m.

deep dorsal sacro-coccygeal ligament

superficial dorsal sacro-coccygeal ligament

lateral sacro-coccygeal ligament

adult female pelvis

superior pubic ligament

obturator canal

interpubic fibrocartilage

pubic crest

pubic tubercle

arcuate pubic ligament

obturator membrane

pubis

acetabulum

transverse ligament of acetabulum

L1
L2
L3
L4
L5

3rd lumbar vertebra

left hipbone (medial aspect)

iliac fossa

sacro-lumbar joint

anterior superior iliac spine

sacrum

greater sciatic foramen

sacrospinous ligament

ilium

ischial spine

coccygeal vertebrae

lesser sciatic foramen

sacrotuberous ligament

obturator foramen

obturator groove

symphyseal surface

arcuate line

LIGAMENTS OF THE PELVIS

acetabulum

pubic symphysis

tuberosity of ischium

sacrotuberous ligament

sacrospinous ligament

promontory

sacrum

1st coccygeal vertebra

L

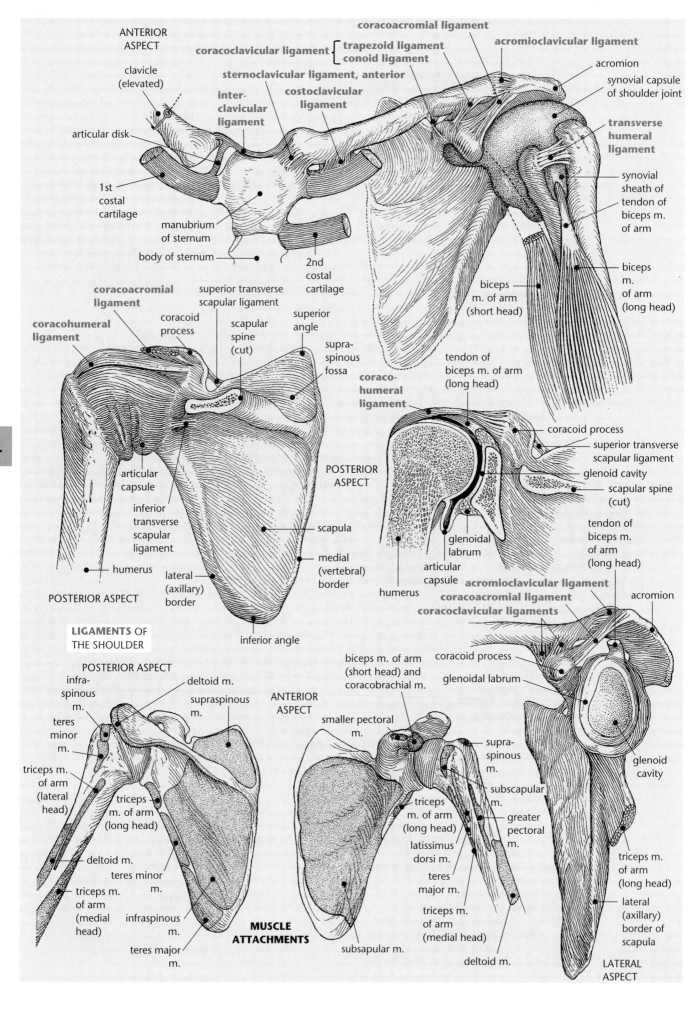

ANTERIOR ASPECT

clavicle (elevated)

articular disk

1st costal cartilage

manubrium of sternum

body of sternum

coracoclavicular ligament { **trapezoid ligament** **conoid ligament** }

coracoacromial ligament

sternoclavicular ligament, anterior

inter-clavicular ligament

costoclavicular ligament

2nd costal cartilage

acromioclavicular ligament

acromion

synovial capsule of shoulder joint

transverse humeral ligament

synovial sheath of tendon of biceps m. of arm

biceps m. of arm (long head)

biceps m. of arm (short head)

coracoacromial ligament

coracohumeral ligament

coracoid process

superior transverse scapular ligament

scapular spine (cut)

superior angle

supra-spinous fossa

coraco-humeral ligament

tendon of biceps m. of arm (long head)

articular capsule

inferior transverse scapular ligament

humerus

lateral (axillary) border

scapula

medial (vertebral) border

POSTERIOR ASPECT

inferior angle

coracoid process

superior transverse scapular ligament

glenoid cavity

scapular spine (cut)

glenoidal labrum

articular capsule

humerus

tendon of biceps m. of arm (long head)

acromioclavicular ligament
coracoacromial ligament
coracoclavicular ligaments

coracoid process

glenoidal labrum

acromion

glenoid cavity

triceps m. of arm (long head)

lateral (axillary) border of scapula

LATERAL ASPECT

POSTERIOR ASPECT

LIGAMENTS OF THE SHOULDER

POSTERIOR ASPECT

infra-spinous m.

teres minor m.

triceps m. of arm (lateral head)

triceps m. of arm (long head)

deltoid m.

teres minor m.

triceps m. of arm (medial head)

infraspinous m.

teres major m.

deltoid m.

supraspinous m.

ANTERIOR ASPECT

biceps m. of arm (short head) and coracobrachial m.

smaller pectoral m.

supra-spinous m.

subscapular m.

triceps m. of arm (long head)

latissimus dorsi m.

teres major m.

triceps m. of arm (medial head)

greater pectoral m.

subsapular m.

deltoid m.

MUSCLE ATTACHMENTS

L

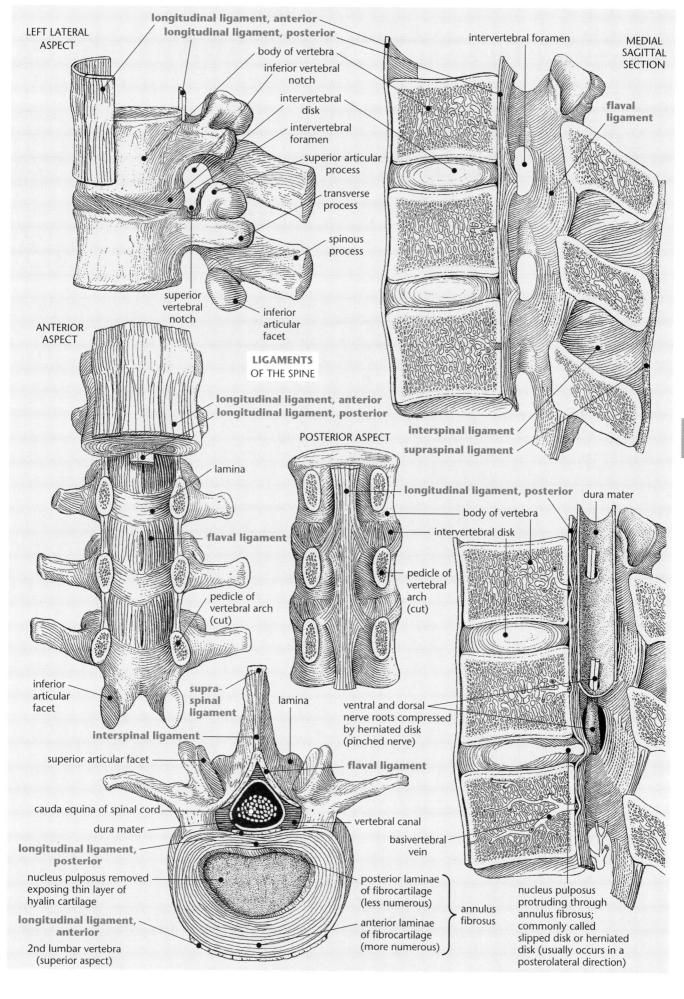

LEFT LATERAL ASPECT

longitudinal ligament, anterior
longitudinal ligament, posterior
body of vertebra
inferior vertebral notch
intervertebral disk
intervertebral foramen
superior articular process
transverse process
spinous process
superior vertebral notch
inferior articular facet

intervertebral foramen

MEDIAL SAGITTAL SECTION

flaval ligament

ANTERIOR ASPECT

LIGAMENTS OF THE SPINE

longitudinal ligament, anterior
longitudinal ligament, posterior

lamina
flaval ligament
pedicle of vertebral arch (cut)

inferior articular facet
supra-spinal ligament
interspinal ligament
superior articular facet
cauda equina of spinal cord
dura mater
longitudinal ligament, posterior
nucleus pulposus removed exposing thin layer of hyalin cartilage
longitudinal ligament, anterior
2nd lumbar vertebra (superior aspect)

POSTERIOR ASPECT

longitudinal ligament, posterior
body of vertebra
intervertebral disk
pedicle of vertebral arch (cut)

lamina
flaval ligament
vertebral canal
basivertebral vein

interspinal ligament
supraspinal ligament

dura mater

ventral and dorsal nerve roots compressed by herniated disk (pinched nerve)

posterior laminae of fibrocartilage (less numerous)
anterior laminae of fibrocartilage (more numerous)
annulus fibrosus

nucleus pulposus protruding through annulus fibrosus; commonly called slipped disk or herniated disk (usually occurs in a posterolateral direction)

L

acromioclavicular l. A broad fibrous band extending from the acromion, a process of the shoulder blade (scapula), to the lateral end of the collarbone (clavicle); it covers the upper part of the capsule of the acromioclavicular joint at the shoulder.

alar l.'s Two short, rounded cords connecting the dens (odontoid process) of the axis (second cervical vertebra) to the occipital bone at the back of the skull. Also called odontoid ligaments.

alveolodental l. See periodontal ligament.

annular l. of base of stapes A ring of elastic fibers encircling the base of the innermost ear ossicle (stapes), attaching it to the circumference of the oval window (fenestra vestibuli); it permits movement of the ossicle during the transmission of sound vibrations from the eardrum (tympanic membrane) to the inner ear; it also serves as a hinge in response to the contraction of the stapedius muscle.

annular l. of radius Four fifths of an osseofibrous band that encircles the head of the radius at the elbow and retains it in contact with the radial notch of the ulna; it blends with surrounding tissues.

anococcygeal l. A mass of fibrous and muscular tissue situated between the anal canal and the tip of the coccyx to which some of the fibers of the levator ani muscle are attached.

anterior l. of uterus See uterovesical fold, under fold.

apical l. of dens. See apical odontoid ligament.

apical odontoid l. A ligament that extends from the tip of the dens (odontoid process) of the axis (second cervical vertebra) to the anterior margin of the foramen magnum of the skull. Also called apical ligament of dens.

arcuate l.'s Two arched ligaments (lateral and medial) that attach the diaphragm to the first lumbar vertebra and the 12th rib on either side, serving as the origin of the diaphragm.

arcuate l. of knee See arcuate popliteal ligament.

arcuate popliteal l. Y-shaped capsular fibers, with the stem attached to the head of the fibula, and with the posterior limb arched medially over the tendon of the popliteus muscle and the anterior limb extending to the lateral epicondyle of the femur. Also called arcuate ligament of knee.

arcuate pubic l. A thick arch of ligamentous fibers connecting the lower border of the pubic symphysis, where it intermingles with the interpubic disk of the symphysis; it forms the upper border of the pubic arch.

arcuate l. of wrist A band stretching transversely from the triangular (triquetral) bone to the scaphoid bone on the dorsal aspect of the wrist.

atlantoaxial l. The ligament extending from the anteroinferior margin of the atlas (first cervical vertebra) down to the anterosuperior margin of the axis (second cervical vertebra).

auricular l.'s Ligaments of the auricular cartilage: *Extrinsic auricular l.*, three ligaments (anterior, posterior, and superior) connecting the auricular cartilage to the side of the head, *Intrinsic auricular l.*, fibrous bands connecting various parts of the auricular cartilage (e.g., one stretching from the tragus to the helix).

bifurcate l. See bifurcated ligament.

bifurcated l. A strong band attached to the front of the upper surface of the heel bone (calcaneus) that divides (bifurcates) as it extends anteriorly to form the calcaneonavicular and calcaneocuboid ligaments, attached respectively to the navicular and cuboid bones of the foot. Also called bifurcate ligament.

broad l. of uterus One of the two fibrous folds covered with peritoneum and extending from the lateral surface of the uterus to the lateral pelvic wall, on both sides, and containing the ovary, fallopian (uterine) tube, ligaments, nerves and vessels.

calcaneocuboid l. The medial part of the bifurcated ligament that connects the anterior part of the upper surface of the heel bone (calcaneus) to the dorsal part of the cuboid bone of the foot.

calcaneofibular l. A long cordlike band extending from the tip of the lateral malleolus of the fibula downward to the lateral side of the heel bone (calcaneus).

calcaneonavicular l. The lateral part of the bifurcated ligament that connects the heel bone (calcaneus) to the navicular bone of the foot: *Dorsal calcaneonavicular l.*, a band connecting the dorsal

aspects of the calcaneus and cuboid bones of the foot.

calcaneotibial l. See tibiocalcaneal ligament.

capsular l. Fibrous layer of ligamentous thickenings investing synovial joints.

carpometacarpal l. A series of ligaments in the hand reinforcing the joints between the distal row of carpal bones and the second to fifth metacarpal bones: *Dorsal carpometacarpal l.*, strong bands extending from the carpal to the metacarpal bones on their dorsal surfaces. *Interosseous carpometacarpal l.*, short, thick fibers connecting the capitate and hamate bones (distal row of carpus) to the adjacent surfaces of the third and fourth metacarpal bones. *Palmar carpometacarpal l.*, bands extending from the carpal to the metacarpal bones on their palmar surfaces.

collateral l.'s Collateral ligaments of the hand and foot: *Interphalangeal collateral l.*, strong, obliquely running bands along the sides of the phalangeal joints of both hand and foot. *Metacarpophalangeal collateral l.*, strong, obliquely running bands along the sides of the joint between the metacarpus and adjoining phalanx of the hand. *Metatarsophalangeal collateral l.*, strong, obliquely running bands along the sides of the joint between the metatarsus and adjoining phalanx of the foot.

conoid l. Part of the coracoclavicular ligament extending from the root of the coracoid process of the scapula (adjacent to the scapular notch) upward to the undersurface of the lateral end of the collarbone (clavicle).

Cooper's l.'s *(a)* See suspensory ligaments of breast. *(b)* See pectineal ligament.

coracoacromial l. A strong triangular band on the shoulder blade (scapula) extending from the tip of the acromion to the lateral edge of the coracoid process; it forms a protective arch over the shoulder joint.

coracoclavicular l. A strong band that connects the coracoid process of the shoulder blade (scapula) with the overlying undersurface of the lateral end of the collarbone (clavicle); composed of two parts: the conoid and trapezoid ligaments.

coracohumeral l. A band of fibers extending from the root of the coracoid process to the front of the greater tuberosity of the humerus; it blends with the capsule of the shoulder joint.

coronary l. of knee The part of the fibrous capsule of the knee joint that extends downward to the peripheral margins of the condyle of the tibia and firmly encapsulates the periphery of each meniscus.

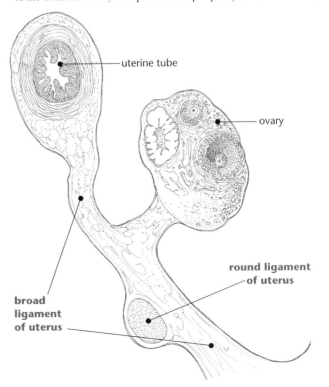

uterine tube

ovary

round ligament of uterus

broad ligament of uterus

coronary l. of liver A ligament formed by the peritoneal reflection from the diaphragm to the superior and posterior surfaces of the right lobe of the liver; it consists of an upper and lower layer enclosing the bare area of the liver that is not covered with peritoneum.

costoclavicular l. A strong, short, flattened band extending downward from the bottom of the medial end of the collarbone (clavicle) to the upper surface of the first costal cartilage and adjoining rib.

costocoracoid l. The thickened band extending from the first rib to the coracoid process of the shoulder blade (scapula); it blends with the coracoclavicular ligament.

costotransverse l.'s Ligaments that reinforce the joints between the ribs and the vertebrae: *Lateral costotransverse l.,* the strong ligament extending from the nonarticular part of the tubercle of each rib (costal tubercle) to the tip of the thoracic transverse process of the corresponding vertebra. *Superior costotransverse l.,* the ligament extending from the neck of each rib to the transverse process of the vertebra above.

costoxiphoid l.'s Ligaments binding the sixth and seventh costal cartilages to the front and back of the xiphoid process of the breastbone (sternum).

cricothyroid l. The median part of the cricothyroid membrane; a well-defined band of elastic tissue that extends in the midline from the lower border of the thyroid cartilage down to the upper border of the cricoid cartilage. Also called cricovocal membrane.

cricotracheal l. A fibrous ligament that unites the lower part of the cricoid cartilage with the first ring of the trachea.

cruciate l.'s of knee Two ligaments (anterior and posterior) of considerable strength in the middle of the knee joint; they cross each other like the letter X and stabilize the tibia and femur in their anteroposterior glide upon one another; they are frequently deranged by trauma: *Anterior cruciate l. of knee,* a strong band attached below to the front of the intercondylar area of the tibia and above to the back of the medial surface of the lateral condyle of the femur; it partly blends with the anterior end of the lateral meniscus; it is tight on extension and limits excessive anterior mobility of the tibia against the femur. Rupture of the ligament is indicated if there is increased anterior mobility of the tibia when tested in flexion. *Posterior cruciate l. of knee,* a strong band (stronger, shorter, and less oblique than the anterior ligament) attached below to the back of the intercondylar area of the tibia and above to the lateral surface of the medial condyle of the femur; it partly blends with the posterior end of the lateral meniscus; it limits posterior mobility and is tight on flexion. Rupture of the ligament is indicated if the tibia assumes a position of posterior displacement against the flexed femur.

cruciform l. of atlas A cross-shaped ligament consisting of two parts: *(a)* A thick, strong transverse band that arches within the ring of the first cervical vertebra and divides the vertebral foramen into two unequal parts. The spinal cord passes through the posterior and larger part; the dens of the second cervical vertebra passes through the anterior and smaller part. Also called transverse ligament of atlas. *(b)* A vertical band (frequently called the superior longitudinal fascicles of the cruciform ligament) that extends upward from the transverse band to the anterior margin of the foramen magnum and a vertical band (frequently called the inferior longitudinal fascicles of the cruciform ligament) that extends downward from the transverse band to the back of the body of the second cervical vertebra.

cuboideonavicular l.'s Ligaments that reinforce the articulation between the cuboid and navicular bones of the foot: *Dorsal cuboideonavicular l.,* ligament extending from the dorsal surface of the navicular bone, obliquely forward and laterally to the cuboid bone. *Interosseous cuboideonavicular l.,* strong transverse fibers connecting the navicular bone to the cuboid bone. *Plantar cuboideonavicular l.,* ligament extending from the plantar surface of the navicular bone, transversely to the cuboid bone.

cuneocuboid l.'s Ligaments that reinforce the articulation of the cuboid bone with the lateral cuneiform bone of the foot: *Dorsal cuneocuboid l.,* a transverse band that extends from the dorsal surface of the cuboid bone to the lateral cuneiform bone. *Interosseous cuneocuboid l.,* a strong ligament that connects the nonarticular surfaces of the cuboid bone and adjoining lateral cuneiform bone. *Plantar cuneocuboid l.,* a transverse band that extends from the plantar surface of the cuboid bone to the lateral cuneiform bone.

cuneonavicular l.'s Ligaments that bind the articulation of the navicular bone with the three adjoining cuneiform bones of the foot: *Dorsal cuneonavicular l.,* three small fasciculi extending from the dorsal surface of the navicular bone to each of the three adjoining cuneiform bones. *Plantar cuneonavicular l.,* three small fasciculi extending from the ventral surface of the navicular bone to each of the three adjoining cuneiform bones.

deep transverse metacarpal l.'s Three short, wide, flattened bands in the hand that connect transversely the palmar ligaments (plates) of the second, third, fourth, and fifth metacarpophalangeal joints to one another.

deep transverse metatarsal l.'s Four short, wide, flattened bands in the foot that connect the plantar ligaments (plates) of the first, second, third, fourth, and fifth metatarsophalangeal joints to one another.

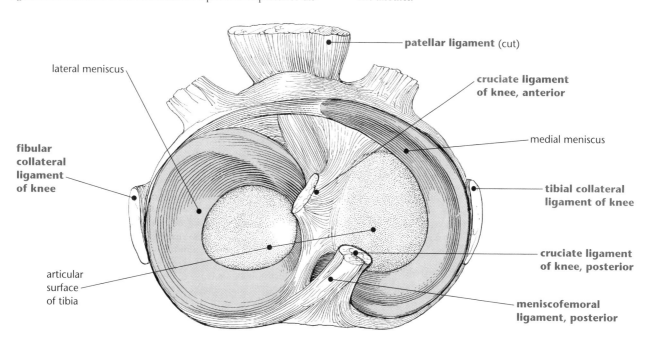

patellar ligament (cut)

cruciate ligament of knee, anterior

lateral meniscus

medial meniscus

fibular collateral ligament of knee

tibial collateral ligament of knee

articular surface of tibia

cruciate ligament of knee, posterior

meniscofemoral ligament, posterior

deltoid l. of ankle joint The medial reinforcing ligament of the ankle joint, composed of the tibiocalcaneal, anterior tibiotalar, posterior tibiotalar, and tibionavicular ligaments; they pass downward from the medial malleolus of the tibia to the navicular bone, calcaneus, and talus, respectively. Also called internal collateral ligament of ankle; medial collateral ligament of ankle.

dorsal basal metacarpal l.'s See metacarpal ligaments, dorsal.

external collateral l. of ankle See lateral collateral ligament of ankle.

falciform l. of liver A median sickle-shaped ligament composed of two layers of peritoneum connecting the liver to the diaphragm and anterior abdominal wall as low as the level of the navel (umbilicus); it contains the round ligament of liver between its layers.

fibular collateral l. of knee. A strong, round, fibrous cord, situated on the lateral side of the knee joint, extending from the lateral epicondyle of the femur to the lateral side of the head of the fibula. Also called lateral collateral ligament of knee.

flaval l.'s A series of yellow elastic bands that bind together the laminae of adjacent vertebrae from the first cervical vertebra to the first sacral vertebra; they serve to maintain the body in an upright position. Also called ligamentum flavum; yellow ligament.

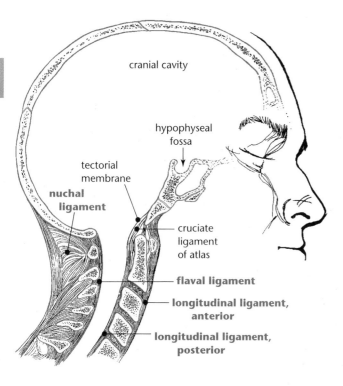

fundiform l. of penis A thickened fibroelastic tissue that is intimately adherent to the lower part of the linea alba and the top of the pubic symphysis and extends to the dorsum of the penis.

glenohumeral l.'s Three thick fibrous bands (superior, middle, and inferior) overlying the anterior portion of the shoulder joint capsule, extending from the anterior border of the glenoid cavity to the lesser tuberosity and neck of the humerus.

l. of head of femur A flattened intracapsular band at the hip joint originating from the head of the femur and attaching by two bands to the acetabulum, one on each side of the acetabular notch; it blends with the transverse ligament of acetabulum and relaxes when the thigh is abducted. Also called round ligament of femur.

hamatometacarpal l. A ligament that passes from the palmar aspect of the hook of the hamate bone to the base of the fifth metacarpal bone of the wrist.

hyoepiglottic l. A short triangular elastic band that unites the anterior surface of the upper epiglottic cartilage to the upper part of the hyoid bone.

iliofemoral l. A strong triangular ligament overlying the hip joint and blending with its capsule; it extends from the bottom of the anterior inferior iliac spine, broadening out as it descends to the trochanteric line of the femur. Also called Y-shaped ligament.

iliolumbar l.'s Strong bands extending from the transverse processes of the fourth and fifth lumbar vetebrae to the inner lip of the posterior iliac crest and the lateral side of the upper sacrum; they blend below with the ventral sacroiliac ligament.

inguinal l. The thickened upturned lower margin of the aponeurosis of the external oblique muscle, extending from the anterior superior spine of the ilium to the tubercle of the pubic bone. Also called Poupart's ligament.

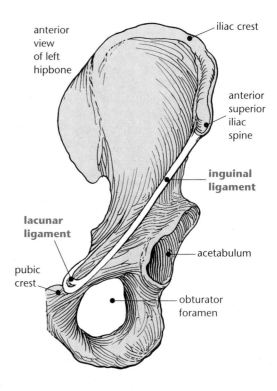

intercarpal l.'s A series of dorsal, interosseous, and palmar ligaments that unite the wrist (carpal) bones with one another.

interclavicular l. A strong band of curved fibers connecting the medial (sternal) ends of the two collarbones (clavicles) across the clavicular notch of the breastbone (sternum).

intercuneiform l.'s Ligamentous bands between the intermediate cuneiform bone and both the medial and lateral cuneiform bones; they are reinforced by slips from the tendon of the posterior tibial muscle.

interfoveolar l. A ligamentous band that connects the lower margin of the transverse abdominal muscle to the superior ramus of the pubic bone; it is inconstant.

intermetacarpal l.'s Ligamentous bands reinforcing the bases of the four medial metacarpal bones: *Dorsal intermetacarpal l.'s,* bands passing transversely on the dorsal surface of the bases of the second, third, fourth, and fifth metacarpal bones. *Interosseous intermetacarpal l.'s,* bands connecting the contiguous surfaces of the metacarpal bones. *Palmar intermetacarpal l.'s,* bands passing transversely on the palmar surfaces of the bases of the second, third, fourth, and fifth metacarpal bones.

internal collateral l. of ankle See deltoid ligament of ankle joint.

interspinal l.'s A series of short ligaments connecting the spinous processes of adjoining vertebrae; they abut the flaval ligament in front and the supraspinal ligament behind.

intertarsal l.'s A series of dorsal, interosseous, and plantar ligaments that unite the ankle (tarsal) bones with one another.

intertransverse l.'s A series of weak ligaments connecting the tips of adjacent transverse processes of vertebrae, mainly in the lumbar region.

ischiofemoral l. A spiral ligament overlying the back of the hip joint capsule; it extends from the ischium (below and behind the acetabulum) to the back of the neck of the femur.

lacunar l. A triangular band extending from the medial end of the inguinal ligament to the iliopectineal line of the hipbone.

lateral atlanto-occipital l.'s The lateral thickening of the articular capsule surrounding the joints between the occipital condyles of the skull and the superior facets of the first cervical vertebra; they limit lateral tilting of the head.

lateral collateral l. of ankle The lateral reinforcing ligament of the ankle joint, consisting of the posterior talofibular ligament, the calcaneofibular ligament, and the anterior talofibular ligament. Also called external collateral ligament of ankle.

lateral collateral l. of elbow See radial collateral ligament of elbow joint.

lateral collateral l. of knee See fibular collateral ligament of knee.

lateral collateral l. of wrist See radial collateral ligament of wrist joint.

lateral temporomandibular l. See temporomandibular ligament.

longitudinal l.'s Long, broad, flat bands of fibers that reinforce the articulations of the vertebral bodies: *Anterior longitudinal l.,* a band of fibers that extends along the anterior surface of the vertebral bodies from the base of the skull to the upper part of the sacrum; it is firmly fixed to the intervertebral disks and is thickest in the thoracic area. *Posterior longitudinal l.,* a band of fibers on the posterior surface of the vertebral canal, extending from the second cervical vertebra to the upper part of the sacrum; it is attached to the intervertebral disks.

long plantar l. A strong thick band (the longest of the tarsal ligaments) extending from the plantar surface of the calcaneus and dividing into deep fibers, which attach to the plantar surface of the cuboid bone, and superficial fibers, which attach to the proximal ends of the second, third, fourth, and occasionally the fifth metatarsal bones; it limits the flattening of the lateral longitudinal arch of the foot.

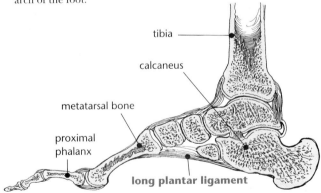

tibia
calcaneus
metatarsal bone
proximal phalanx
long plantar ligament

long posterior sacroiliac l. See sacroiliac ligament, dorsal.

medial collateral l. of ankle See deltoid ligament of ankle joint.

medial collateral l. of elbow See ulnar collateral ligament of the elbow joint.

medial collateral l. of knee See tibial collateral ligament of knee.

medial collateral l. of wrist See ulnar collateral ligament of wrist joint.

meniscofemoral l. Meniscus ligaments of the knee joint: *Anterior meniscofemoral l.,* an inconstant oblique band passing from the posterior end of the lateral meniscus in the knee joint to the medial condyle of the femur; it passes anterior to the posterior cruciate ligament. *Posterior meniscofemoral l.,* a strong band that passes upward and medially from the posterior end of the lateral meniscus in the knee to the medial condyle of the femur; it passes behind the posterior cruciate ligament.

meniscofibular l. An inconstant bundle of fibers extending from the posterior end of the lateral meniscus of the knee to the fibula.

metacarpal l.'s Ligaments that strengthen the proximal metacarpal articulations of the hand: *Dorsal metacarpal l.'s,* short transverse bands uniting the dorsal surface of the bases of the second, third, fourth, and fifth metacarpal bones with one another. Also called dorsal basal metacarpal ligaments. *Interosseous metacarpal l.'s,* short bands connecting the contiguous surfaces of the metacarpal bones of the hand. *Palmar metacarpal l.'s,* short transverse bands uniting the palmar surface of the bases of the second to fifth metacarpal bones with one another. Also called ventral basal metacarpal ligaments.

metatarsal l.'s Ligaments that strengthen the proximal intermetatarsal articulations of the foot: *Dorsal metatarsal l.'s,* short, thin transverse bands uniting the dorsal surface of the bases of the second, third, fourth, and fifth metatarsal bones of the foot. *Interosseous metatarsal l.'s,* strong, transverse bands uniting the nonarticular parts of the adjacent metatarsal bones of the foot. *Plantar metatarsal l.'s,* four transverse bands uniting the plantar surface of the bases of the metatarsal bones of the foot.

nuchal l. A broad, somewhat triangular fibroelastic septum in the back of the neck, stretching from the base of the skull to the posterior tubercle of the first cervical vertebra and the spinous processes of all the other cervical vertebrae; it forms a midline septum for attachment of muscles on either side of the neck. Also called ligamentum nuchae.

L

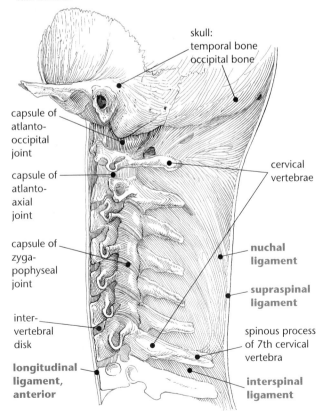

skull:
temporal bone
occipital bone
capsule of atlanto-occipital joint
capsule of atlanto-axial joint
capsule of zyga-pophyseal joint
inter-vertebral disk
longitudinal ligament, anterior
cervical vertebrae
nuchal ligament
supraspinal ligament
spinous process of 7th cervical vertebra
interspinal ligament

oblique popliteal l. See oblique posterior ligament of knee.

oblique posterior l. of knee A ligament from the tendon of the semimembranous muscle (near its insertion), extending obliquely to the posterior part of the knee joint capsule. Also called oblique popliteal ligament.

odontoid l.'s See alar ligaments.

ovarian l. A cordlike bundle of fibers between the layers of the broad ligament of uterus, joining the uterine end of the ovary to the lateral margin of the uterus, immediately behind the attachment of the fallopian (uterine) tube.

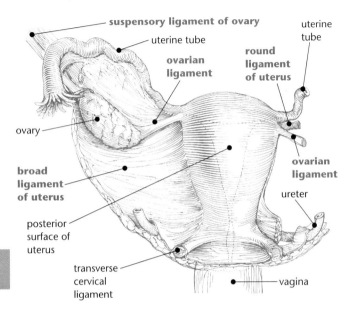

suspensory ligament of ovary
uterine tube
ovarian ligament
uterine tube
round ligament of uterus
ovary
ovarian ligament
broad ligament of uterus
ureter
posterior surface of uterus
transverse cervical ligament
vagina

palmar l.'s Thick fibrocartilaginous plates on the palmar surfaces of the metacarpophalangeal joints, firmly united to the bases of the proximal phalanges and loosely connected to the metacarpal bones.

palmar ulnocarpal l.'s A rounded fibrous band passing downward and laterally from the base of the styloid process of the ulna and the front of the articular disk of the distal radioulnar joint to the palmar surface of the lunate and triangular (triquetral) bones (proximal row of wrist bones).

palpebral l.'s Ligaments of the eyelids (palpebrae): *Lateral palpebral l.,* a thin band that connects the lateral ends of the tarsal plates of the eyelids to the zygomatic bone, just within the orbital margin. *Medial palpebral l.,* a strong tendinous band that connects the medial ends of the tarsal plates of the eyelids to the frontal process of the maxilla, in front of the nasolacrimal groove.

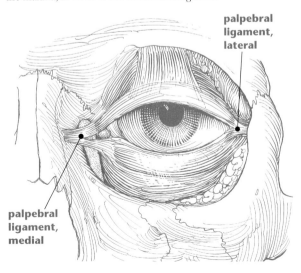

palpebral ligament, lateral
palpebral ligament, medial

patellar l. The continuation of the strong, flattened common tendon of the quadriceps muscle of thigh (quadriceps femoris) from the kneecap (patella) downward to the tuberosity of the tibia.

pectineal l. A strong fibrous band that extends from the upper border of the pectineal surface of the hipbone to the medial end of the lacunar ligament at the groin, with which it is continuous. Also called Cooper's ligament.

periodontal l. Connective tissue fibers that attach the root of a tooth to the bone of its socket. Also called periodontal membrane; alveolodental ligament.

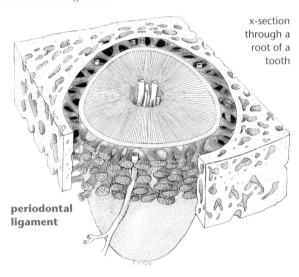

x-section through a root of a tooth
periodontal ligament

pisohamate l. A ligament that passes from the pisiform bone to the hook of the hamate bone at the wrist; basically it is a ligamentous extension from the tendon of insertion of the ulnar flexor muscle of wrist (flexor carpi ulnaris muscle).

pisometacarpal l. A ligament that passes from the pisiform bone to the base of the fifth metacarpal bone of the wrist; basically it is a ligamentous extension from the tendon of insertion of the ulnar flexor muscle of wrist (flexor carpi ulnaris muscle).

plantar l.'s Thick, dense fibrocartilaginous plates on the plantar surfaces of the metatarsophalangeal joints, firmly united to the bases of the proximal phalanges and loosely connected to the metatarsal bones.

plantar calcaneocuboid l. The strong, short band, extending from the plantar surface of the heel bone (calcaneus) to the contiguous plantar surface of the cuboid bone. It limits flattening of the lateral longitudinal arch of the foot. Also called short plantar ligament.

plantar calcaneonavicular l. The broad, thick fibrocartilaginous band connecting the anterior margin of the heel bone (calcaneus) to the plantar surface of the navicular bone; it limits flattening of the medial longitudinal arch of the foot. Also called spring ligament.

plantar metatarsal l.'s Transverse bands over the capsules of the intermetatarsal joints and connecting the plantar surfaces of the bases of the four lateral metatarsal bones of the foot.

posterior l. of uterus See rectovaginal fold, under fold.

Poupart's l. See inguinal ligament.

pubic l.'s See superior pubic ligament; arcuate pubic ligament.

pubofemoral l. A triangular ligament overlying the capsule of the hip joint on its inferior aspect; it extends from the iliopubic eminence and adjacent superior pubic ramus to blend with the hip joint capsule and iliofemoral ligament.

radial collateral l. of elbow joint A fan-shaped ligament extending from the bottom part of the lateral epicondyle of the humerus to the annular ligament of radius and the upper end of the supinator crest of the ulna. Also called lateral collateral ligament of elbow.

radial collateral l. of wrist joint Poorly developed fibrous band extending downward from the styloid process of the radius to the scaphoid bone of the wrist. Also called lateral collateral ligament of wrist.

radiate l. A fan-shaped band that extends from the side of the bodies of two adjoining vertebrae to the head of the rib with which it articulates. Also called radiate ligament of head of rib.

radiate l. of head of rib See radiate ligament.

radiate sternocostal l.'s See sternocostal ligaments.

radiocarpal l.'s Ligaments of the wrist joint: *Dorsal radiocarpal l.*, a thin sheath of ligamentous tissue overlying the wrist joint extending from the distal end of the radius to the dorsal surface of the proximal row of wrist bones (triangular, lunate, and scaphoid bones); it blends with the underlying articular disk of the inferior radioulnar articulation. *Palmar radiocarpal l.*, a broad membranous band extending from the anterior aspects of the lower end of the radius and its styloid process to the anterior surface of the proximal row of wrist bones (triangular, lunate, and scaphoid bones), and occasionally to the capitate bone.

reflex inguinal l. The part of the inguinal ligament that extends from the lateral side of the superficial inguinal ring, passes upward and medially to interlace at the linea alba with is counterpart from the other side of the body. Also called triangular fascia; reflected part of inguinal ligament.

round l. of femur See ligament of head of femur.

round l. of liver A fibrous cord (the remains of the umbilical vein of the fetus) extending from the anterior abdominal wall at the level of the navel (umbilicus) to the inferior surface of the liver (in the free edge of the falciform ligament of liver). Also called ligamentum teres of liver.

round l. of uterus A fibromuscular ligamentous cord extending from the lateral margin of the uterus, on either side, passing between the two layers of the broad ligament of uterus, it traverses the inguinal canal to become attached to the connective tissue of the labium majus.

sacroiliac l.'s Ligaments that bind the sacrum with the ilium of the hipbone: *Dorsal sacroiliac l.*, a set of thick fibrous bands overlying the interosseous sacroiliac ligament, consisting of a lower, superficial group (long posterior sacroiliac ligament) that extends from the posterior superior iliac spine of the hipbone to the transverse tubercles of the third and fourth segments of the sacrum (the bands blend with the sacrotuberous ligament); and an upper, deep group (short posterior sacroiliac ligament) that extends from the posterior inferior iliac spine and adjacent part of the ilium to the back of the sacrum. *Interosseous sacroiliac l.*, short, thick bundles of fibers interconnecting the sacral and iliac tuberosities, posterior to their articular surfaces; one of the strongest ligaments in the body, it serves as the principal bond between the sacrum and ilium. *Ventral sacroiliac l.*, a thin, wide, fibrous layer reinforcing the anterior part of the articular capsule of the sacroiliac joint and stretching from the ala and pelvic surface of the sacrum to the adjoining parts of the ilium.

sacrospinous l. A strong triangular ligament attached by its apex to the spine of the ischium of the hipbone and by its base to the lateral part of the lower sacrum and coccyx.

sacrotuberous l. A long, strong triangular ligament extending from the tuberosity of the ischium of the hipbone to the lateral part of the sacrum and coccyx and to the superior and inferior posterior iliac spines.

Scarpa's l. See superior horn of falciform margin, under horn.

short plantar l. See plantar calcaneocuboid ligament.

short posterior sacroiliac l. See sacroiliac ligament, dorsal.

sphenomandibular l. A flat, thin fibrous band that extends from the spine of the sphenoid bone, becoming broader as it descends to the lingula of the mandibular foramen.

spring l. See plantar calcaneonavicular ligament.

sternoclavicular l.'s Ligaments that reinforce the sternoclavicular joint: *Anterior sternoclavicular l.*, a short, broad band overlying the front of the sternoclavicular joint, extending from the medial end of the collarbone (clavicle) to the front of the upper breastbone (sternum) and adjoining cartilage of the first rib (costal cartilage);

Posterior sternoclavicular l., a short, broad band overlying the back of the sternoclavicular joint, extending from the medial end of the clavicle to the back of the upper sternum and adjoining cartilage of the first rib (costal cartilage).

sternocostal l.'s Thin, wide bands radiating from the sternal ends of the cartilages of the true ribs to the front and back surfaces of the breastbone (sternum). Also called radiate sternocostal ligaments.

stylomandibular l. A condensed band of deep cervical fascia extending from the tip of the styloid process, downward to the posterior margin of the angle of the lower jaw (mandible).

superior pubic l. A transverse band that binds the two pubic bones superiorly, and extends as far as the pubic tubercles; it is firmly attached to the interpubic disk at the midline.

superior transverse l. of scapula See suprascapular ligament.

suprascapular l. A flat ligament extending from the medial end of the scapular notch to the coracoid process, thus converting the notch into a foramen. Also called superior transverse ligament of scapula.

supraspinal l. A strong fibrous band that connects the tips of the spinous processes from the seventh cervical vertebra to the sacrum; it blends with the interspinous ligament. From the seventh cervical vertebra to the base of the skull, it expands to form the nuchal ligament.

suspensory l.'s of breast Coarse connective-tissue bands distributed between the lobes of the female breast (mammary gland), extending from the overlying skin to the underlying pectoral fascia. Also called Cooper's ligaments; suspensory ligaments of mammary gland.

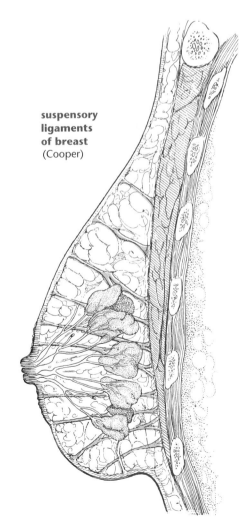

suspensory ligaments of breast (Cooper)

suspensory l. of duodenum See suspensory muscle of duodenum in the table of muscles.

suspensory l. of lens See ciliary zonula, under zonula.

suspensory l.'s of mammary gland See suspensory ligaments of breast.

suspensory l. of ovary The part of the broad ligament of uterus arising from the tubal side of the ovary and extending upward toward the lateral wall of the pelvis; it contains the ovarian blood vessels, lymphatic vessels, and nerves.

talocalcaneal l.'s Fibrous bands that reinforce the two articulations between the ankle bone (talus) and the heel bone (calcaneus): *Anterior talocalcaneal l.,* a band extending from the upper anterior part of the neck of the talus to the upper surface of the calcaneus. *Interosseous talocalcaneal l.,* a strong, broad, flattened band extending obliquely from the deep groove of the talus to the deep groove of the calcaneus. *Lateral talocalcaneal l.,* a short, flattened band extending from the lateral process of the talus and passing downward and backward to the lateral surface of the calcaneus. *Medial talocalcaneal l.,* a band extending from the medial tubercle of the talus to the medial surface of the calcaneus; it blends with the deltoid ligament. *Posterior talocalcaneal l.,* a short, wide band extending from the posterior process of the talus, downward to the adjacent calcaneus.

talofibular l.'s Ligaments of the ankle joint: *Anterior talofibular l.,* a ligament that stretches from the anterior margin of the lateral malleolus of the fibula to the lateral aspect of the neck of the talus. *Posterior talofibular l.,* a ligament that stretches from the posterior margin of the lateral malleolus of the fibula to the posterior process of the talus.

L

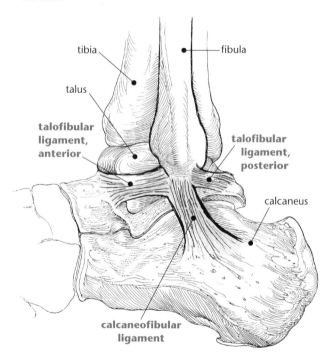

talonavicular l. A broad, thin band extending from the neck of the ankle bone (talus) to the dorsal surface of the adjoining navicular bone of the foot. Also called dorsal talonavicular ligament.

talotibial l.'s See tibiotalar ligaments.

tarsometatarsal l.'s Ligaments reinforcing the joints between the tarsus and the metatarsal bones of the foot: *Dorsal tarsometatarsal l.'s,* strong, flat bands connecting the dorsal surface of the proximal metatarsal bones to the distal tarsus (cuboid and three cuneiform bones). *Interosseous tarsometatarsal l.'s,* bands from the first and third cuneiform bones to the second and fourth metatarsal bones, respectively. *Plantar tarsometatarsal l.'s,* oblique bands connecting the plantar surface of the proximal metatarsal bones to the distal tarsus (cuboid and three cuneiform bones).

temporomandibular l. An oblique band that reinforces the temporomandibular joint, extending downward and backward from the lower surface of the zygomatic process to the posterolateral surface margin of the neck of the lower jaw (mandible). Also called lateral temporomandibular ligament.

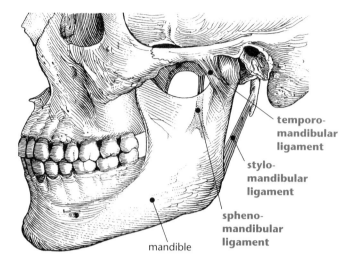

thyroepiglottic l. An elastic ligament that attaches the stalk (petiole) of the lower end of the epiglottic cartilage to the back of the thyroid cartilage just below the notch.

tibial collateral l. of knee A broad, flat, membranous band, posteromedial to the knee joint, extending from the medial epicondyle of the femur to the medial condyle and medial surface of the tibia; consists of two parts: a short, deep, thick posterior band, and a longer anterior band, extending from the femoral epicondyle and fanning out into a broad expansion on the anteromedial surface of the tibia; the latter one is the most frequently injured ligament of the knee. Also called medial collateral ligament of knee.

tibiocalcaneal l. The widest part of the deltoid ligament of the ankle joint extending from the medial malleolus of the tibia to the median projection (sustentaculum tali) of the heel bone (calcaneus). Also called calcaneotibial ligament.

tibiofibular l.'s Ligaments connecting the tibia and fibula at the proximal and distal ends: *Anterior (superior) tibiofibular l.,* flat bands that extend from the front of the head of the fibula to the front of the lateral condyle of the tibia. *Anterior (inferior) tibiofibular l.,* a flattened oblique band extending downward and laterally from the distal end of the front of the tibia to the adjoining fibula. *Posterior (superior) tibiofibular l.,* thick band that extends from the back of the head of the fibula to the back of the lateral condyle of the tibia. *Posterior (inferior) tibiofibular l.,* a strong, oblique band extending downward and laterally from the distal end of the back of the tibia to the adjoining fibula; its lowest part extends transversely from the fibula to the ankle bone (talus).

tibionavicular l. The part of the deltoid ligament of the ankle joint extending from the medial malleolus of the tibia to the tubercle on the dorsal side of the navicular bone.

tibiotalar l.'s Parts of the deltoid ligament of the ankle joint: *Anterior tibiotalar l.,* the deep part extending from the medial malleolus of the tibia to the medial surface of the talus. Also called anterior talotibial ligament. *Posterior tibiotalar l.,* the part that extends from the medial malleolus of the tibia, posteriorly to the medial side of the ankle bone (talus) and its tubercle. Also called posterior talotibial ligament.

tracheal annular l. The fibroelastic membrane that posteriorly encloses and connects the ends of the incomplete tracheal rings.

transverse l. of acetabulum A strong, flattened ligament that is attached to the margin of the acetabulum and crosses the acetabular notch, forming a foramen at the hip joint for the passage of nerves and vessels.

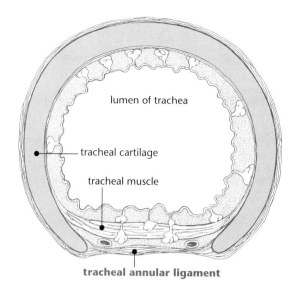

lumen of trachea

tracheal cartilage

tracheal muscle

tracheal annular ligament

transverse l. of atlas See cruciform ligament of atlas *(a)*.

transverse carpal l. A broad ligament bridging over the carpal tunnel of the wrist extending from the pisiform and hamate bones to the scaphoid and trapezium bones of the wrist.

transverse humeral l. The lowest part of the capsule of the shoulder joint, extending from the lesser to the greater tubercle of the humerus; it serves as a retinaculum for the tendon of the long head of the biceps muscle of arm (biceps brachii) as it emerges from the capsule to enter the occipital groove.

transverse l. of knee An inconstant bundle of fibers extending between the anterior extremities of the menisci of the knee joint by connecting the anterior convex margin of the lateral meniscus to the anterior end of the medial meniscus. Also called transverse ligament of menisci.

transverse l. of menisci See transverse ligament of knee.

trapezoid l. Part of the coracoclavicular ligament extending from the upper surface of the coracoid process upward to the undersurface of the lateral end of the collarbone (clavicle).

l. of Treitz See suspensory muscle of duodenum, in table of muscles.

ulnar collateral l. of elbow joint A strong, triangular ligament on the medial side of the elbow joint, composed of anterior and posterior bands united by a thin oblique band; the anterior band extends from the front of the medial epicondyle of the humerus to the medial margin of the coronoid process of the ulna; the posterior band extends from the lower part of the medial epicondyle to the medial surface of the olecranon; the oblique band stretches from the olecranon to the coronoid process. Also called medial collateral ligament of elbow.

ulnar collateral l. of wrist joint A fibrous band extending downward from the styloid process of the ulna to the wrist; it divides into two parts, one attached to the triangular (triquetral) bone and the other to the pisiform bone of the wrist. Also called medial collateral ligament of wrist.

uterosacral l. Fibromuscular band that extends backward on either side from the uterine cervix, along the lateral wall of the pelvis to the front of the sacrum. It passes by the sides of the rectum and can be palpated on rectal examination.

venous l. of liver A thin fibrous cord, the remains of the obliterated ductus venosus of the fetus, lying in a fossa on the posterior part of the diaphragmatic surface of the liver. Also called ligamentum venosum.

ventral basal metacarpal l.'s See metacarpal ligaments, ventral.

vestibular l. of larynx A thin fibrous band in the ventricular fold of the larynx that extends from the thyroid cartilage, anteriorly, to the arytenoid cartilage, posteriorly. Also called vestibular ligament.

vocal l. The elastic tissue band that extends on either side from the thyroid cartilage in front, to the vocal process of the arytenoid cartilage behind; it is situated within the vocal fold, just below the vestibular ligament.

yellow l. See flaval ligament.

Y-shaped l. See iliofemoral ligament.

l. of Zinn See common annular tendon, under tendon.

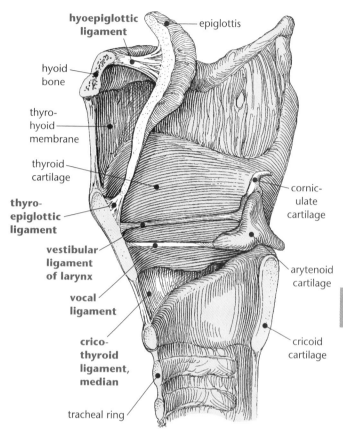

hyoepiglottic ligament — epiglottis

hyoid bone

thyro-hyoid membrane

thyroid cartilage

thyro-epiglottic ligament

vestibular ligament of larynx

vocal ligament

crico-thyroid ligament, median

tracheal ring

cornic-ulate cartilage

arytenoid cartilage

cricoid cartilage

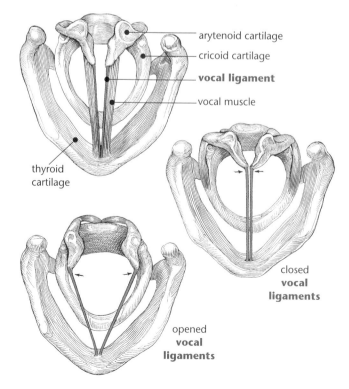

arytenoid cartilage

cricoid cartilage

vocal ligament

vocal muscle

thyroid cartilage

closed vocal ligaments

opened vocal ligaments

L37

ligamentous (lig-ah-men'tus) Of the nature of a ligament.

ligamentum (lig-ah-men'tum) Latin for ligament.

    l. flavum See flaval ligament, under ligament.

    l. nuchae See nuchal ligament, under ligament.

ligand (li'gand) **1.** Any linking (binding) molecule. **2.** An organic molecule attached to a central metal ion (e.g., the oxygen molecule attached to the central iron atom of hemoglobin). **3.** An organic molecule attached to a radioactive tracer element; used in such diagnostic tests as ELISA.

ligase (li'gās) An enzyme that promotes the forming of a specific substance concomitant with the breakdown of ATP or some other nucleoside triphosphate.

ligate (li'gāt) To constrict a blood vessel, duct, pedicle of a tumor, etc., with a tightly tied thread (ligature).

ligation (li-ga'shun) **1.** The act of ligating. **2.** In genetic engineering, the joining of two double-stranded DNA molecules with the enzyme DNA ligase; step in constructing recombinant DNA.

    tubal l. A surgical method of tubal sterilization by interrupting the continuity of the fallopian (uterine) tubes through either the abdominal wall or the vagina. See also Irving's, Madlener's, and Pomeroy's operations, under operation; tubal sterilization, under sterilization; fimbriectomy.

ligator (li'ga-tor) Surgical instrument used to facilitate ligation of deep, difficult-to-reach blood vessels.

ligature (lig'ah-chūr) Any thread made of synthetic or natural material used in ligation.

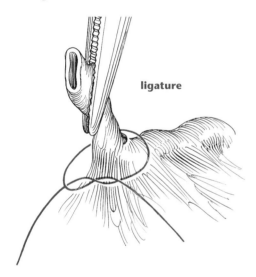

ligature

light (līt) Electromagnetic radiation perceived by the retina in the eye.

    coherent l. Light that has rays traveling in parallel, or nearly parallel, paths, with little divergence.

    Wood's l. Ultraviolet light produced by the Wood's lamp; uses include diagnosis and treatment of certain skin diseases and detection of corneal abrasions.

lightening (līt'en-ing) In obstetrics, the sinking of the fetal head into the pelvic inlet, causing the uterus to descend to a lower level and fall forward, thus relieving pressure on the diaphragm, making breathing easier and imparting a feeling of "lightness."

liken (li'ken) An aggregation of small firm papules occurring on the skin or mucous membranes. Also spelled lichen.

    l. planus (LP) Chronic disorder of unknown cause, characterized by an eruption of flat, polygonal papules with depressed purplish centers; the extremities are most commonly involved; may occur also in the oral mucosa as whitish lesions.

    l. sclerosis (LS) Chronic disorder of the lining of the vulva, usually occurring in postmenopausal women; characterized by formation of yellowish blue papules or macules that eventually coalesce to form whitish plaques of thin, glistening parchmentlike patches. The condition is not precancerous; cause is unknown.

    l. simplex chronicus Chronic condition marked by patches of thickened, itchy, sometimes discolored skin, usually on the neck, abdomen, and ankles; caused by constant scratching or rubbing, which aggravates the condition.

limb (lim) **1.** An extremity; an arm or a leg. **2.** Any appendage projecting from a main structure.

    artificial l. A prosthesis that replaces a natural arm or leg.

    phantom l. A phenomenon often experienced by a person who has had a limb amputated in which sensations, sometimes painful, seem to originate from the amputated limb.

    thick ascending l. See distall straight tubule, under tubule.

    thick decending l. See proximal straight tubule, under tubule.

limbic (lim'bik) **1.** Relating to a border. **2.** Relating to the limbic system of the brain.

limbus (lim'bus), pl. lim'bi A border.

    l. of cornea The highly vascular area of the eye around the cornea at the junction of the cornea and sclera. Also called sclerocorneal junction; corneal margin.

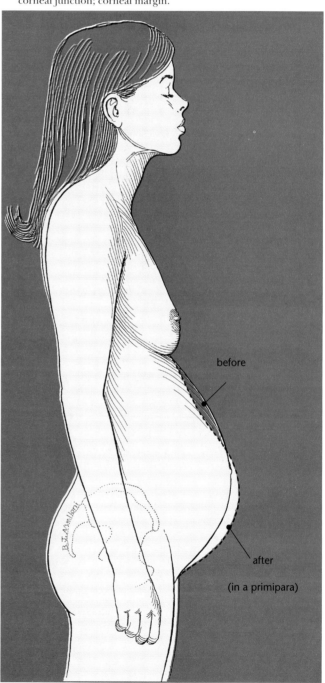

before

after

(in a primipara)

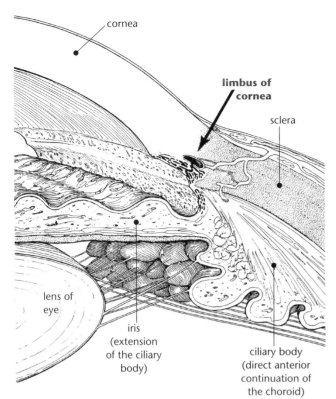

cornea

limbus of cornea

sclera

lens of eye

iris (extension of the ciliary body)

ciliary body (direct anterior continuation of the choroid)

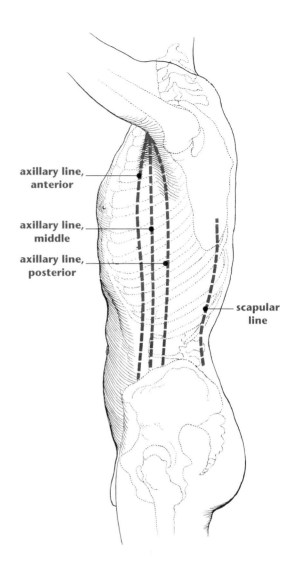

axillary line, anterior

axillary line, middle

axillary line, posterior

scapular line

lime (līm) Calcium oxide; a white caustic powder used in waste treatment, insecticides, and in several industries.

limen (li′men), pl. lim′ina A threshold or boundary.

l. insulae An area on the inferior surface of a cerebral hemisphere, between the cortex of the insula and the perforated substance of the frontal lobe.

l. nasi The ridge demarcating the boundary between the vestibule of the nose and the nasal cavity proper, where the mucous membrane and the skin meet.

liminal (lim′ĭ-nal) Relating to a threshold (e.g., a stimulus that is just strong enough to elicit a response).

liminometer (lim-ĭ-nom′ĕ-ter) Instrument for measuring the strength of a stimulus to determine a reflex threshold (e.g., of a tendon or muscle).

limit (lim′it) A boundary; a value regarded as an end.

ceiling l. The maximum level (e.g., of a toxin at the workplace) that should not be exceeded for any period of time. The Occupational Safety and Health Administration (OSHA) has some exceptions to this rule.

limp (limp) **1.** To walk unevenly, favoring one leg. **2.** An uneven, yielding gait. **3.** Flaccid.

linac (lin′ak) See linear accelerator, under accelerator.

lincomycin (lin-ko-mi′sin) An antibiotic compound used to treat bacterial infections that are resistant to penicillin or other commonly prescribed drugs.

lindane (lin′dān) A drug used as a lotion, cream, or shampoo to treat scabies and infestation with lice.

line (līn) **1.** A thin area of demarcation designating the junction of two structures. **2.** A thin, continuous strip, mark, or ridge. **3.** A skin crease; a wrinkle. **4.** An imaginary mark connecting two points or landmarks on the body or passing through them. **5.** A boundary.

l. of accommodation The linear extent to which an object can be moved closer to, or away from, the eye in a given state of refraction without causing noticeable blurriness.

anatomic anorectal l. See pectinate line.

axillary l. One of three imaginary vertical lines associated with the armpit (axilla): *Anterior axillary l.,* the line that passes through the anterior fold of the axilla. *Middle axillary l.,* the line that passes through the middle of the axilla; also called midaxillary line. *Posterior axillary l.,* the line that passes through the posterior fold of the axilla.

B l.'s of Kerley Horizontal lines in the chest x-ray film (above the costophrenic angle) of individuals with pulmonary hypertension secondary to mitral stenosis.

blue l. See lead line.

Brödel's l. A relatively avascular longitudinal linear zone along the convex lateral border of the kidney, where the minute terminal distributions of the anterior and posterior branches of the renal artery partially overlap. Once thought to be bloodless and therefore a preferred approach for surgically entering the kidney; current approaches favor the radial and intersegmental incisions. Also called Brödel's white line.

cervical l. The undulating line around the neck of a tooth marking the junction between the enamel of the crown and the cementum of the root.

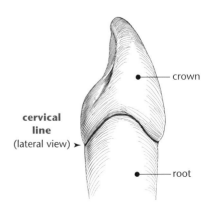

crown

cervical line (lateral view)

root

L

cleavage l.'s Definite linear clefts in the skin indicative of the direction of the underlying parallel subcutaneous collagen fibers; they represent choice sites for incisions. Also called Langer's lines.

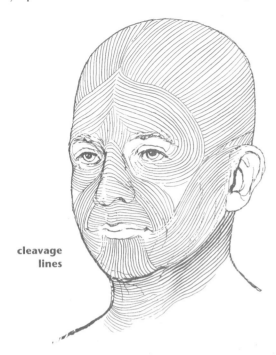

cleavage lines

Conradi's l. A line from the base of the xiphoid process of the breastbone (sternum) to the apex of the heart, indicating the upper limits of percussion of the liver's left lobe.

l. of demarcation An inflamed area separating granulomatous tissue from healthy tissue. Also called surface demarcation.

dentate l. See pectinate line.

epiphyseal l. The line of the cartilaginous plate formed in the adult long bone by the junction of the epiphysis and diaphysis.

Fleischner l.'s Linear shadows on a chest x-ray film, indicating foci of atelectasis.

flexure l.'s Furrows on the external surface of the skin that correspond to habitual joint movements, seen especially on the surface of the palms, soles, and digits.

gingival l. The position of the margin of the gums (gingiva) as it extends onto the neck of a tooth. Also called gum line.

gluteal l. One of three rough curved lines on the outer surface of the iliac part of the hipbone: *Anterior gluteal l.,* the gluteal line that provides attachment to the middle gluteal muscle. *Inferior gluteal l.,* the gluteal line that provides attachment to the least gluteal muscle. *Posterior gluteal l.,* the gluteal line that provides attachment to the greater gluteal muscle.

gravidic's l. See striae atrophicae, under stria.

gum l. See gingival line.

Hampton l. In radiography, a line of decreased density surrounding a typical benign stomach ulcer in profile.

Hensen's l. See H band, under band.

Holden's l. A flexure line of the groin, below the inguinal fold, crossing the capsule of the hip joint.

iliopectineal l. An oblique ridge on the surface of the ilium and continued on the pelvis, which forms the lower boundary of the iliac fossa; it separates the true from the false pelvis; it is a posterior continuation of the pectineal line. Also called linea terminalis.

interspinal l. A horizontal line across the abdomen connecting the two anterior superior iliac spines of the hipbones.

intertrochanteric l. An oblique, rough ridge on the anterior surface of the upper femur, between the neck and the shaft of the bone.

K l.'s A group of lines emitted in an x-ray spectrum with characteristic wavelengths, designated K, L, M, N, O, and P lines.

Langer's l. See cleavage line.

lead l. A dark bluish line coursing along the gingival margin, usually about 1 mm from the gingival crest; a symptom of lead absorption. Also called blue line.

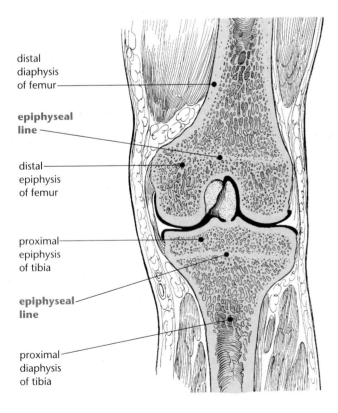

distal diaphysis of femur

epiphyseal line

distal epiphysis of femur

proximal epiphysis of tibia

epiphyseal line

proximal diaphysis of tibia

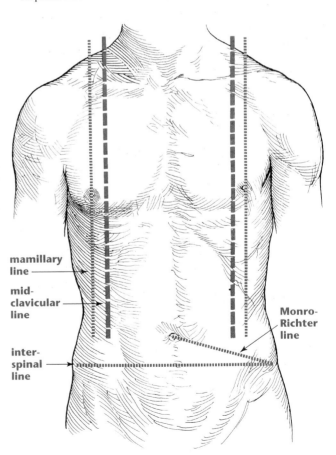

mamillary line

mid-clavicular line

interspinal line

Monro-Richter line

line ■ line

L40

M l. (a) A line formed by the nodular thickening of the myofilament (myosin) bisecting the H central zone of striated muscle myofibrils (sarcomere). (b) See K lines.

mamillary l. An imaginary vertical line on the anterior surface of the body, passing through the nipple of either breast; it corresponds roughly to the vertical line passing through the middle of the collarbone (clavicle). Also called nipple line.

median l. An imaginary vertical line dividing the surface of the body equally into right and left sides.

Mees' l.'s White lines across fingernails occurring in arsenic poisoning. Also called Mees' stripes.

mercurial l. A linear discoloration of the gingival tissues associated with absorption of mercurial salts and seen along the gingival margin; the color can range from bluish brown to purplish red.

midaxillary l. See axillary line.

midclavicular l. An imaginary vertical line on the anterior surface of the body, passing through the midpoint of the collarbone (clavicle) on either side; it corresponds roughly to the vertical line passing through the nipple.

midsternal l. A vertical line passing through the center of the breastbone (sternum), from the cricoid cartilage in the neck to the xiphoid process, at the tip of the sternum.

Monro-Richter l. A line from the navel (umbilicus) to the left anterior superior iliac spine of the hipbone.

mylohyoid l. An oblique ridge on the inner surface of the body of the mandible, extending from the area of the third molar socket to the digastric fossa at the base of the mental symphysis; it provides attachment to the mylohyoid muscle. Above the line lies the sublingual salivary gland, and below the line lies the submandibular salivary gland.

nasolabial l. A line extending from the ala of the nose, obliquely downward toward the corner of the mouth.

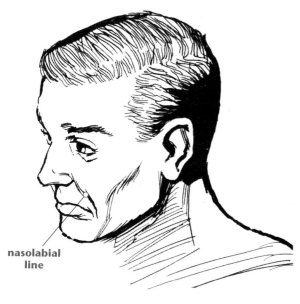

nasolabial
line

nipple l. See mamillary line.

nuchal l.'s Three lines or ridges on the exterior surface of the occipital bone of the skull: *Highest nuchal l.*, the higher of the two transverse curved lines on the back of the skull, extending laterally, on both sides, from the external occipital protuberance. *Superior nuchal l.*, the lower of the two transverse curved lines on the back of the skull, extending laterally, on both sides, from the external occipital protuberance. *Inferior nuchal l.*, the transverse curved line coursing on the back of the skull between the external occipital protuberance and the posterior margin of the foramen magnum.

l. of occlusion The horizontal line formed by maxillary and mandibular teeth that are in normal occlusion.

Pastia's l.'s A linear confluence of minute subcutaneous hemorrhages (petechiae) along skin folds; seen in scarlet fever.

pectinate l. The undulating horizontal line following the bulges of the rectal columns and the depressions of the rectal sinuses, between the rectal mucosa and the skin lining the anus. Also called dentate line; anatomic anorectal line.

pectineal l. The sharp edge on the superior ramus of the pubic bone extending from the pubic tubercle anteriorly, to the iliopubic eminence posteriorly. Also called pecten pubis.

rough l. See linea aspera, under linea.

scapular l. An imaginary vertical line on the posterior surface of the body, passing through the lower angle of the scapula on either side.

Schwalbe's annular l. See anterior limiting ring of eye, under ring.

semilunar l. See linea semilunaris, under linea.

simian l. See simian crease, under crease.

survey l. (a) A line inscribed on a cast of a tooth by a surveyor scriber; it marks the greatest height of contour in relation to the chosen path of insertion of the restoration. (b) The line denoting the height of contour of a tooth after the cast has been positioned according to the chosen path of insertion. Also called clasp guideline.

sutural l. A line formed by cut tissue edges approximated by sutures.

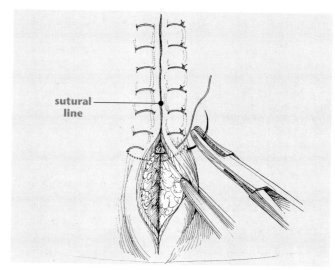

sutural
line

temporal l.'s The two curved, transverse lines on the outer surface of the parietal bones of the skull on either side: *Inferior temporal l.*, the lower temporal line that provides attachment to the temporal muscle. *Superior temporal l.*, the upper temporal line that provides attachment to the temporal fascia.

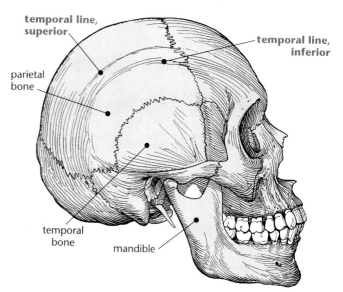

temporal line,
superior

temporal line,
inferior

parietal
bone

temporal
bone

mandible

visual l. See visual axis, under axis.

Z l. See Z band, under band.

zigzag l. See Z-Z line.

Z-Z l. An irregular dentate or zigzag line between the esophagus and the stomach; it represents the transition from esophageal to gastric mucosa, easily recognized by a color change. Also called zigzag line.

linea (lin′e-ah), pl. lin′eae A line, strip, or narrow ridge, usually on the surface of a structure; a thin, continuous mark.

l. alba The narrow portion of the anterior aponeurosis extending from the midline of the xiphoid process stretching down to the pubic symphysis, formed by the interlacing aponeurotic fibers of the flat abdominal muscles; the navel (umbilicus) is situated slightly below its midpoint.

lineae albicantes See striae atrophicae, under stria.

l. aspera A broad, rough longitudinal ridge with crestlike lateral and medial lips, located on the posterior middle third surface of the shaft of the femur; it provides attachment to the short head of the biceps, long adductor, great adductor, and pectineal muscles, along with the intermuscular septa of the thigh. Also called rough line.

l. gravidarum See striae atrophicae, under stria.

l. nigra A dark streak on the abdomen of some women during the later months of pregnancy, extending from the region of the navel (umbilicus) to the pubic symphysis; it is the pigmented linea alba of pregnancy.

l. semilunaris The lateral edge of the abdominal rectus muscle, extending from the pubic tubercle to the tip of the ninth costal cartilage. Also called semilunar line.

l. terminalis See iliopectineal line, under line.

lingua (ling′gwah) Latin for tongue.

lingual (ling′gwal) Relating to the tongue or any tonguelike anatomic structure.

lingula (ling′gu-lah) Any tongue-shaped process.

l. of cerebellum The most anterior portion of the vermis of the cerebellum.

l. of left lung A projection from the upper lobe of the left lung, just beneath the cardiac notch.

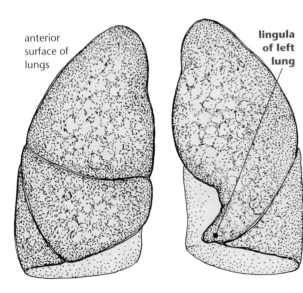

anterior surface of lungs

lingula of left lung

l. of mandible A small triangular spur of bone projecting partly over the mandibular foramen on the medial surface of the ramus of the mandible; it provides attachment to the sphenomandibular ligament. Also called spine of Spix.

lingular (ling′gu-lar) Relating to any lingula.

lingulectomy (ling-gu-lek′to-me) Removal of the lingular portion of the left lung.

linguoclusion (ling-gwo-kloo′zhun) Displacement of teeth toward the tongue. Also called lingual occlusion.

linguo-occlusal (ling′gwo ŏ-kloo′zal) Relating to the lingual and occlusal surfaces of the posterior teeth; applied to the line angle at the junction of these two surfaces.

linguopapillitis (ling-gwo-pap-ĭ-li′tis) Inflammation and/or ulceration of the papillae of the tongue.

linguoversion (ling-gwo-ver′zhun) Malposition of a tooth toward the tongue.

liniment (lin′ĭ-ment) An oily medicinal liquid applied to the skin by friction as a counterirritant.

linin (li′nin) The fine, threadlike, clear substance of the cell nucleus interconnecting the chromatin granules.

lining (lin′ing) A cement coating, such as zinc-oxide eugenol (ZOE), applied under a dental filling to prevent irritation.

linitis (lī-ni′tis) Inflammation of the stomach wall.

l. plastica Diffuse thickening and rigidity of the stomach walls caused by infiltration from a cancerous tumor. Formerly thought to be due to inflammation. Also called leather-bottle stomach; sclerotic stomach.

linkage (lingk′ij) 1. In genetics, the relationship between two or more genes on a chromosome whereby they function together as a unit to direct some activity; usually, they are inherited together. 2. In chemistry, the force that holds together the atoms in a compound.

medical record l. The systematic assemblage of all items of information pertaining to a person's long-term vital and medical histories, derived from multiple sources, to provide a cumulative up-to-date record of significant health events.

sex l. Old term for X linkage.

X l. Linkage associated with a gene on the X chromosome.

Y l. Linkage associated with a gene on the Y chromosome.

linoleic acid (lin-o-le′ik as′id) A polyunsaturated fatty acid essential in the human diet; it is a necessary precursor for the biosynthesis of prostaglandins; it strengthens capillary walls, lowers serum cholesterol, and prolongs clotting time.

liothyronine (li-o-thi′ro-nēn) See triiodothyronine.

lip (lip) 1. One of the two fleshy folds forming the anterior boundary of the mouth. 2. Any liplike structure.

anterior l. See labium anterius, under labium.

cleft l. A developmental defect of the upper lip; it ranges from a scarlike groove, or a notch on the lip, to a complete cleft extending through the lip into the nasal cavity. Also called cheiloschisis; harelip.

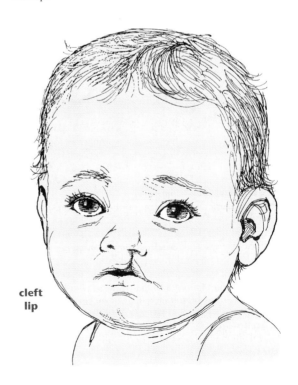

cleft lip

greater l.'s of pudendum See labia majora, under labium.

lesser l.'s of pudendum See labia minora, under labium.

major l.'s See labia majora, under labium.

minor l.'s See labia minora, under labium.

posterior l. See labium posterius, under labium.

lipase (lip′ās, li′pās) Any enzyme promoting the breakdown of fat molecules; present in pancreatic juice, blood, and many tissues.

lipectomy (lĭ-pek′to-me) Surgical removal of subcutaneous fat, usually from the abdominal wall. Formerly called adipectomy.

suction l. See liposuction.

lipedema (lip-ĕ-de′mah) Chronic swelling of the legs, occurring most frequently in middle-aged women.

lipemia (lĭ-pe′me-ah) See hyperlipidemia.

lipid (lip′id) **1.** In general, any fat, oil, or wax, or any derivative of these materials; soluble in organic compounds like alcohol and insoluble in water. **2.** Specifically, the fat and fatlike substances that, together with carbohydrates and proteins, constitute the main structural substance in the living cell. See also lipoprotein.

lipidemia (lip-ĭ-de′me-ah) See hyperlipidemia.

lipidosis (lip-ĭ-do′sis) General term applied to disorders characterized by accumulation of lipids in tissues.

ganglioside l. See gangliosidosis.

sulfatide l. See metachromatic leukodystrophy, under leukodystrophy.

lipo-, lip- Combining forms meaning fat.

lipoatrophy, lipoatrophia (li-po-at′ro-fe, li-po-ah-tro′fe-ah) Atrophy or loss of subcutaneous body fat.

insulin l. Circumscribed loss of subcutaneous body fat after repeated injections of insulin into the same spot, occurring in persons afflicted with insulin-dependent diabetes.

lipocele (lip′o-sēl) A hernia containing fat. Also called adipocele.

lipocere (lip′o-sēr) See adipocere.

lipochondrodystrophy (lip-o-kon-dro-dis′tro-fe) See Hurler's syndrome, under syndrome.

lipochrome (lip′o-krōm) Any of various naturally occurring fatty pigments (e.g., carotene and lipofuscin).

lipocyte (lip′o-sīt) See fat cell, under cell.

lipodystrophy (lip-o-dis′tro-fe) Faulty metabolism of fat.

intestinal l. See Whipple's disease, under disease.

lipofibroma (lip-o-fi-bro′mah) A noncancerous tumor composed of fibrous and fatty tissues.

lipofuscin (lip-o-fu′sin) A golden brown lipid-containing pigment, the indigestible residue of lysosomal activity in cells; associated with normal wear and tear of tissues.

lipogenesis (lip-o-jen′ĕ-sis) The production of fat. Also called adipogenesis.

lipogenic (lip-o-jen′ik) Fat-producing.

lipoid (lip′oid) Fatlike.

lipoidosis (lip-oi-do′sis) Deposition of fatty material in various organs.

lipolysis (lĭ-pol′ĭ-sis) Chemical dissolution or hydrolysis of fat.

lipoma (lĭ-po′mah) A noncancerous, usually small, tumor composed of mature fat cells; it occurs in subcutaneous tissues anywhere in the body, most commonly on the neck, back, and shoulders. Also called adipose tumor.

lipomatoid (lĭ-po′mah-toid) Resembling a lipoma.

lipomatosis (lip-o-mah-to′sis) Deposition of fat, either local or general. Also called liposis.

lipomatous (lĭ-po′mah-tus) **1.** Of the nature of a lipoma. **2.** Having lipomas.

lipophage (lip′o-fāj) A fat-absorbing cell.

lipophagic (lip-o-fa′jik) Ingesting or absorbing fat; applied to certain cells.

lipophil (lip′o-fil) A substance having an affinity for lipids.

lipoprotein (lip-o-pro′tēn) (LP) Any of a family of lipid-containing proteins circulating in the blood.

high-density l. (HDL) A plasma protein of relatively small molecular weight containing proportionately more protein and less cholesterol and triglycerides; thought to be protective against

atherosclerosis.

low-density l. (LDL) A plasma protein of relatively large molecular weight containing proportionately less protein and more cholesterol and triglycerides; involved in the formation of atheromas.

very-low-density l. (VLDL) A large plasma protein containing a relatively high percentage of triglycerides.

l. X An abnormal lipoprotein associated with obstructive jaundice.

lipoprotein lipase (lip-o-pro′tēn lip′ās) Enzyme promoting the breakdown of fat to fatty acid and glycerol.

liposarcoma (lip-o-sar-ko′mah) An uncommon, usually bulky, aggressive cancerous tumor of elderly people; it arises anywhere in the body, most frequently in retroperitoneal tissues and the thighs.

liposis (lĭ-po′sis) See lipomatosis.

liposuction (lip-o-suk′shun) Removal of subcutaneous fat deposits with a high-pressure vacuum-suctioning device. Also called suction lipectomy.

lipotropic (lip-o-trop′ik) Relating to lipotrophy.

lipotrophy (lĭ-pot′ro-fe) **1.** Prevention of excessive accumulation of fat in the liver. **2.** Affinity of basic dyes for fatty tissue.

lipoxygenase (lĭ-pok′se-jĕ-nās) Enzyme that promotes oxidation of polyunsaturated fatty acids.

lipping (lip′ing) Formation of a liplike border at the articular end of a bone occurring in degenerative disease of bone.

lipuria (lĭ-pu′re-ah) The presence of fat in the urine.

liquefacient (lik-wĕ-fa′shent) Any agent that causes a solid to become liquid.

liquefaction (lik-wĕ-fak′shun) The process of changing from a solid to a liquid form.

liquescent (lik-wes′ent) Tending to liquefy.

liquid (lik′wid) Being in a fluid state, neither gaseous nor solid.

liquor (lik′er) **1.** Any fluid. **2.** A body secretion produced by certain tissues (e.g., the antrum of an ovarian follicle). **3.** In pharmacy, a solution of a nonvolatile substance in water.

Listeria (lis-te′re-ah) Genus of gram-positive bacteria (family Corynebacteriaceae); found in feces, sewage, and vegetation.

L. monocytogenes A species causing meningitis, septicemia, and abscesses.

listeriosis (lis-ter-e-o′sis) An uncommon but serious food-borne infection caused by bacteria of the genus *Listeria;* acquired by ingesting raw or undercooked contaminated food, such as poultry, meat, fish, eggs, and cheese; it is often fatal for persons with weakened immune systems (e.g., by cancer, kidney disease, diabetes, and HIV infection).

listlessness (list′lis-nes) Weariness; a loss of the sense of well-being.

liter (le′ter) (L, l) A metric unit of capacity equal to 1000 cubic centimeters; equivalent to 1.056 quarts.

lithagogue (lith′ah-gog) An agent causing dislodgment of a stone (calculus), especially a urinary stone.

lithiasis (lĭ-thi′ah-sis) The presence of stones in the body, especially urinary or gallbladder stones.

lithium (lith′e-um) Metallic element; symbol Li, atomic number 3, atomic weight 6.9. Some of its compounds are used in the treatment of mental disorders, especially manic-depressive disorders.

litho-, lith- Combining forms meaning stone or calculus.

lithocystotomy (lith-o-sis-tot′o-me) Surgical removal of stones from the bladder.

lithodialysis (lith-o-di-al′ĭ-sis) The dissolving of a stone in the bladder.

lithogenesis (lith-o-jen′ĕ-sis) Formation of stones within the body.

lithogenic (lith-o-jen′ik) Causing formation of stones in the body.

lithogenous (lĭ-thoj′ĕ-nus) Forming stones.

litholapaxy (lĭ-thol′ah-pak-se) See lithotripsy.

litholysis (lĭ-thol′ĭ-sis) Dissolution of stones.

lithopedion (lith-o-pe′de-on) A calcified fetus retained in the uterus or outside the uterus (e.g., in the abdominal cavity).

lithotomy (lĭ-thot′o-me) Operation for the removal of a stone (e.g., from the bladder).

L

lithotresis (lith-o-tre′sis) The boring of holes in a large calculus to facilitate its removal.

lithotripsy (lith′o-trip-se) The operation of crushing a stone in the urinary bladder by means of a lithotrite and then washing out the fragments through a wide transurethral catheter. Also called litholapaxy.

   extracorporeal shock-wave l. (ESWL) Breaking up kidney stones by shock waves generated outside the body and focused on the stones electronically; applied mostly to the urinary tract but can also be used on gallstones.

lithotriptic (lith-o-trip′tik) 1. Relating to lithotripsy. 2. An agent that dissolves a calculus.

lithotriptor (lith′o-trip-tor) Device for breaking up urinary stones by extracorporeal shock-wave lithotripsy.

lithotrite (lith′o-trit) Surgical instrument for crushing bladder stones.

lithuresis (lith-u-re′sis) The passage of sand or minute stones in the urine.

lithuria (lith-u′re-ah) The presence of excessive uric acid or urates in the urine.

litmus (lit′mus) A blue pigment that is turned red by acids and blue again by alkalies; used as a pH indicator.

litter (lit′er) A stretcher.

littritis (lit-tri′tis) Inflammation of the urethral (Littre's) glands in the penile portion of the male urethra.

liver (liv′er) The largest glandular organ in the body, situated in the right upper abdomen, beneath the right dome of the diaphragm and approximately one third of the left dome; it secretes bile and plays an important role in the metabolism of fats, carbohydrates, protein, minerals, and vitamins.

   cirrhotic l. See cirrhosis.

   fatty l. An enlarged, yellowish, greasy liver due to fatty degeneration and infiltration (fatty metamorphosis); may occur as a complication of any disease in which protein malnutrition is present; other causes include alcohol abuse, diabetes mellitus, hepatotoxins, drugs, and obesity. Also called hepatic steatosis.

   nutmeg l. A liver characterized by a mottled appearance when sectioned.

   polycystic l. See polycystic liver disease, under disease.

livid (liv′id) Having a black-and-blue, bluish, or ash gray coloration, as from the effects of congestion or bruising.

lividity (li-vid′i-te) 1. The quality of being livid. 2. See livor mortis, under livor.

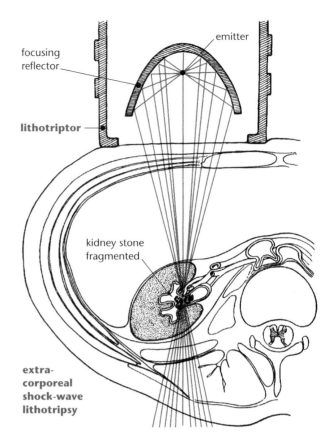

emitter

focusing reflector

lithotriptor

kidney stone fragmented

extracorporeal shock-wave lithotripsy

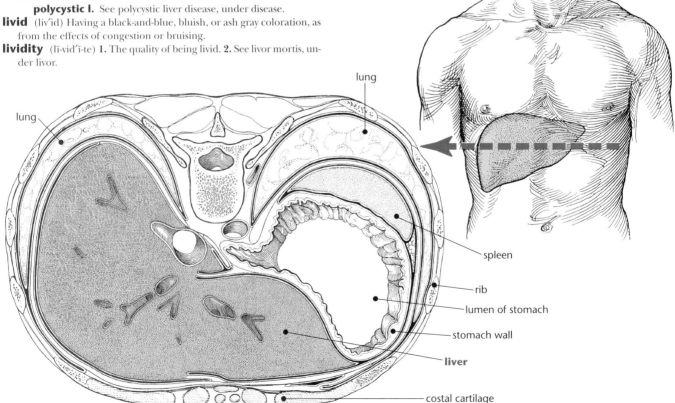

lung

lung

spleen

rib

lumen of stomach

stomach wall

liver

costal cartilage

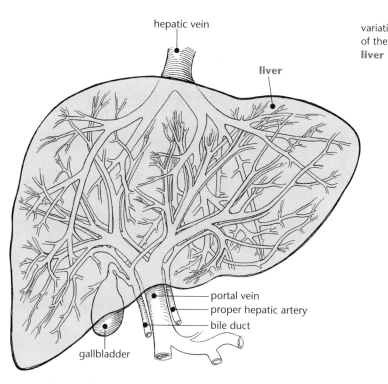

hepatic vein

liver

portal vein
proper hepatic artery
bile duct
gallbladder

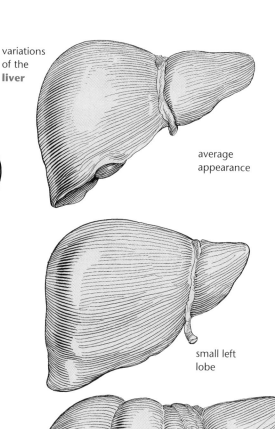

variations of the **liver**

average appearance

small left lobe

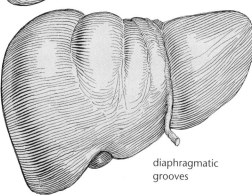

diaphragmatic grooves

cadaveric l. See livor mortis, under livor.

postmortem l. See livor mortis, under livor.

livor (li'vor), pl. livo'res **1.** See lividity. **2.** See livor mortis.

l. mortis A reddish blue to purple coloration of the dependent, noncompressed skin surfaces of a corpse; caused by cessation of circulation and resulting gravitational settling of blood in the minute blood vessels (capillaries) just below the skin. The coloration is occasionally misinterpreted as bruising (contusion) by those unfamiliar with the phenomenon. The process begins immediately after death and usually becomes evident within two hours after death. Those areas of the body that have been in contact with a hard surface appear blanched, an important factor in determining whether the body was moved after death. Also called livor; lividity; postmortem lividity; cadaveric lividity; postmortem hypostasis.

lixiviation (liks-iv-e-a'shun) See leaching.

lixivium (liks-iv'e-um) See lye.

load (lōd) **1.** A quantity or force. **2.** A deviation from the normal body contents (e.g., of water, salt); usually referring to a greater-than-normal amount. **3.** To administer a defined quantity of a substance to a patient for some test purpose (e.g., for testing metabolic function) or to achieve a desired blood level.

compressile l. In orthopedics, any force that compresses bones, joints, tendons, or ligaments.

functional l. In orthopedics, the normal forces acting on bones, joints, tendons, or ligaments.

tensile l. In orthopedics, a load that distracts (i.e., separates) the fragments of a broken bone, or the articular surfaces of a joint.

loading (lōd'ing) Administration of a substance to test the body's ability to metabolize it.

Loa loa (lo'ah lo'ah) The African eyeworm; a threadlike roundworm that infests subcutaneous tissues, causing tumefactions; the worms migrate rapidly, usually being noticed when passing through the conjunctiva across the eyeball. See also loiasis.

lobar (lo'bar) Relating to a lobe.

lobate (lo'bāt) Composed of or divided into lobes; lobed.

lobe (lōb) **1.** A fairly well defined portion of an organ or gland bounded by structural borders such as fissures, sulci, grooves, or septa. **2.** A rounded projecting part, as the fatty lobule of the human ear. **3.** A cusp on the crown of a tooth, formed from a distinct point of calcification.

anterior l. of cerebellum The anterior part of the upper portion of the cerebellum lying in front of the primary fissure (fissura prima); it consists of the lingula, central lobule, culmen, alae of the central lobules, and quadrangular lobules.

anterior l. of pituitary See adenohypophysis.

anterior l. of prostate The prostate lobe in front of the prostatic urethra, which joins the right and left lateral lobes together; composed of a band of fibromuscular tissue with a spattering of glands. Also called ventral lobe of prostate.

caudate l. of liver A small, elongated part of the left lobe (not the right lobe as originally thought) of the liver located on the inferior and posterior diaphragmatic surface, bounded on the right side by the inferior vena cava, and on the left side by the fissure for the venous ligament of the liver (ligamentum venosum).

dorsal l. of prostate See posterior lobe of prostate.

ear l. The lower fleshy part of the ear (auricle).

flocculonodular l. See posterior lobe of cerebellum.

frontal l. of cerebrum The anterior part of the cerebral hemisphere; it is bounded behind by the cerebral central sulcus and below by the cerebral lateral sulcus.

glandular l. of pituitary See adenohypophysis.

hepatic l.'s, l.'s of liver The lobes of the liver divided according to markings on its surface; designated left and right lobes, with the right lobe further subdivided into the caudate and quadrate lobes. More current determination, based on distribution of hepatic ducts, places the caudate and quadrate lobes as subdivisions of the left lobe of the liver.

inferior l. of lung See lower lobe of lung.

l. of kidney A part of the kidney that includes a pyramid, capped by cortical substance, marked by an apex that projects into the interior of a minor calix; the number of lobes in the average kidney ranges from 5 to 15. Also called renal lobe.

lateral l.'s of prostate The main mass of the prostate, partially separated by a median sulcus into left and right lateral lobes; they develop from 30 to 50 lateral tubules evaginating from the left and right lateral walls of the primitive prostatic urethra.

left l. of liver The smaller of the two major lobes of the liver, defined by the area of distribution of the left hepatic duct; it includes the quadrate and caudate lobes (except the caudate process).

limbic l. A general term that usually denotes the cingulate and parahippocampal gyri along with the olfactory bulb and stalk and the parolfactory and olfactory gyri.

lower l. of lung Either of two lobes of the lungs located below the oblique fissure. Also called inferior lobe of lung.

l. of mammary gland Either one of 15 to 20 milk-producing lobes of the female breast; each lobe is drained by a lactiferous duct that opens at the nipple (papilla).

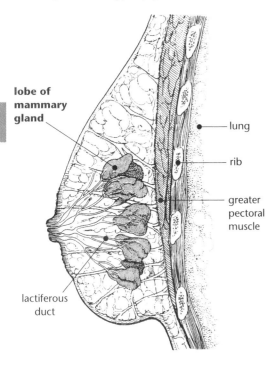

lobe of mammary gland

lung

rib

greater pectoral muscle

lactiferous duct

median l. of prostate The prostate lobe immediately behind the prostatic urethra that develops from an independent group of 7 to 12 tubules, arising from the floor of the urethra proximal to the ejaculatory ducts. Also called middle lobe of prostate.

middle l. of cerebellum The major part of the body of the cerebellum lying in back of the primary fissure (fissura prima), between the anterior and posterior (flocculonodular) lobes; it consists of the declive, folium vermis, tuber vermis, pyramid, uvula, lobuli simplices, biventral lobules, semilunar lobules, and cerebellar tonsils.

middle l. of lung The small wedge-shaped lobe of the right lung, between the horizontal and oblique fissures.

middle l. of prostate See median lobe of prostate.

milk l. One of two ridges on either side of the ventral surface of the embryo's trunk, extending from the axillary to the inguinal region; the upper intermediate portion of the ridge thickens to form the mammary primordium, while the rest of the ridge disappears before the end of the embryonic period.

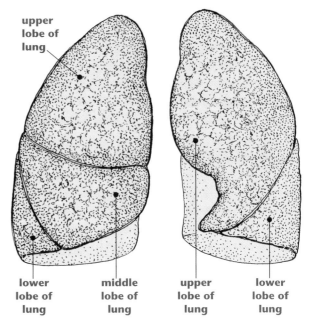

upper lobe of lung

lower lobe of lung

middle lobe of lung

upper lobe of lung

lower lobe of lung

Muercke's l.'s Parallel, transverse white lines in fingernails and toenails; associated with chronic hypoalbuminemia.

neural l. of pituitary See neurohypophysis.

occipital l. The posterior portion of the cerebral hemisphere behind the line joining the preoccipital notch to the parietooccipital sulcus; it contains the calcarine sulcus and associated visual cortex; it merges anteriorly with the temporal lobe.

olfactory l. A general term that usually denotes the olfactory bulb, tract, and trigone plus the anterior perforated substance.

parietal l. of cerebrum The lobe of the cerebral hemisphere situated between the frontal, occipital, and temporal lobes; it is separated from the frontal lobe anteriorly by the cerebral central sulcus, from the occipital lobe behind by the parieto-occipital sulcus (on the medial surface), and from the temporal lobe below by the cerebral lateral sulcus.

posterior l. of cerebellum The lobe of the cerebellum that includes the two flocculi and the nodule. Also called flocculonodular lobe.

posterior l. of pituitary See neurohypophysis.

posterior l. of prostate The prostate lobe situated behind the ejaculatory ducts; it is separated from the median and lateral lobes and the ejaculatory ducts by fibromuscular tissue. Also called dorsal lobe of prostate.

pyramidal l. of thyroid An inconstant cone-shaped lobe of the thyroid gland usually arising from the upper part of the isthmus; sometimes it is attached to the hyoid bone by a fibromuscular band; present in about one third of thyroid glands. Also called pyramid of thyroid gland.

quadrate l. of liver A small quadrilateral lobe on the inferior surface of the left lobe of the liver between the gallbladder and the round ligament of the liver (ligamentum teres); it is in physical contact with the pylorus and the first portion of the duodenum; formerly considered part of the right lobe.

renal l. See lobe of kidney.

Riedel's l. An anomalous tongue-shaped mass of tissue occasionally extending downward from the right lobe of the liver.

right l. of liver The larger of the two major lobes of the liver, formerly determined by superficial features (attachment of the falciform fold and the fissures for the round ligament and venous ligament of liver), but currently determined by the distribution of the right hepatic ducts; it includes the caudate process.

superior l. of lung See upper lobe of lung.

temporal l. The long lobe on the outer side and undersurface of each cerebral hemisphere; it is bounded above by the cerebral lat-

L

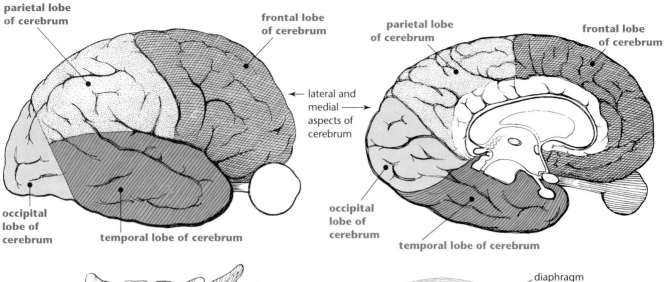

parietal lobe of cerebrum

frontal lobe of cerebrum

← lateral and medial aspects of cerebrum →

occipital lobe of cerebrum

temporal lobe of cerebrum

parietal lobe of cerebrum

frontal lobe of cerebrum

occipital lobe of cerebrum

temporal lobe of cerebrum

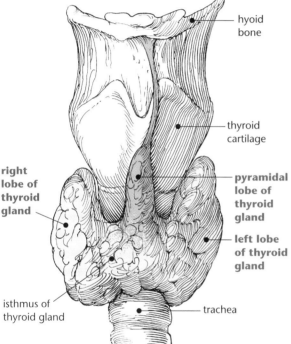

hyoid bone

thyroid cartilage

right lobe of thyroid gland

pyramidal lobe of thyroid gland

left lobe of thyroid gland

isthmus of thyroid gland

trachea

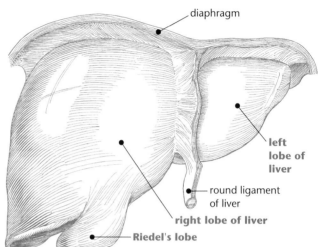

diaphragm

left lobe of liver

round ligament of liver

right lobe of liver

Riedel's lobe

lobectomy (lo-bek′to-me) Surgical removal of a lobe.

lobeline (lo′bĕ-lēn) A mixture of alkaloids derived from plants of the genus Lobelia; it has actions similar to those of nicotine but less potent.

lobotomy (lo-bot′o-me) A surgical cut into a lobe.

prefrontal l. A psychosurgical procedure in which the fibers connecting the prefrontal and frontal lobes with the thalamus are divided. The procedure is no longer performed because of its disabling effects on the patient. Also called prefrontal leukotomy.

transorbital l. Lobotomy approached through the roof of the eye socket; a no-longer-performed procedure. Also called transorbital leukotomy.

lobulated (lob′u-lāt-ed) Consisting of or divided into lobules.

lobule (lob′ūl) A small lobe.

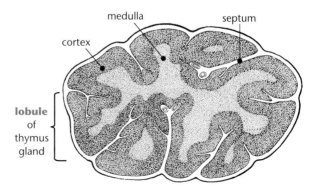

medulla

septum

cortex

lobule of thymus gland

eral sulcus and behind by the preoccipital notch. The lateral surface is marked by two parallel sulci dividing the lobe into three parallel gyri (superior, middle, and inferior temporal gyri).

l. of testis One of the subdivisions of the testis surrounded by septa and containing from one to four convoluted seminiferous tubules (where the spermatozoa are produced); there are about 250 lobes in each testis containing approximately 500 tubules.

l. of thymus Either of two unequally sized, pyramidal lobes of the thymus, connected by areolar tissue; it varies in size with age, but generally is located from just below the larynx, downward to the fourth costal cartilage; it is the primary central organ of the lymphatic system.

l.'s of thyroid gland Two lobes of the thyroid gland on either side of the larynx, connected near their bases by a narrow band of tissue (isthmus) that lies across the upper anterior trachea.

upper l. of lung Either of two superior lobes of the lungs: *Left upper l. of lung*, the part above the oblique fissure; it includes the cardiac notch and its projection (lingula). *Right upper l. of lung*, the part above the oblique and horizontal fissures. Also called superior lobe of lungs.

ventral l. of prostate See anterior lobe of prostate.

L

lobulet, lobulette (lob'u-let') A tiny lobule or a subdivision of a lobule.

lobulus (lob'u-lus) Latin for lobule.

lobus (lo'bus) Latin for lobe.

local (lo'kal) Confined to an area of the body; not systemic or general.

localization (lo-kah-lī-za'shun) **1.** Confinement of a process to a limited area. **2.** Determination of the confines of a process or the site of a lesion or foreign body.

localized (lo'kal-izd) Limited or confined to a particular part or region of the body; not general.

locator (lo'ka-ter) Any instrument used in determining the location of a foreign body within a tissue or organ.

lochia (lo'ke-ah) The discharge from the uterus following childbirth. Initially, it is blood-tinged and includes shreds of tissue (lochia rubra); a few days later, it becomes serous and paler (lochia serosa); during the second week, it becomes thicker, yellowish white, and mucoid (lochia alba) and ceases by the fifth postpartum week when the placental site heals.

lochiometra (lo-ke-o-me'trah) Distention of the uterus with retained lochia following childbirth due to blocking of the cervical canal with debris from the uterus; associated with inflammation of the uterine lining. Commonly called lochia block.

lochiorrhea (lo-ke-o-re'ah) Excessive flow of discharges after childbirth.

loci (lo'si) Plural of locus.

lockjaw (lok'jaw) A symptom of tetanus; see trismus.

locomotor (lo-ko-mo'tor) Relating to motion; applied to certain parts of the nervous system and their impulses.

locular (lok'u-lar) Relating to a loculus.

loculate (lok'u-lāt) Divided into several small cavities.

loculation (lok-u-la'shun) **1.** The state of being loculate. **2.** The process of forming small cavities.

loculus (lok'u-lus), pl. loc'uli A small cavity or space.

locum tenens (lo'kum ten'inz) One who temporarily assumes the place of another (e.g., a practitioner assuming someone else's practice during an illness or vacation).

locus (lo'kus), pl. lo'ci **1.** In anatomy, a specific site in the body. **2.** In genetics, the site on a chromosome where a gene is located.

logo- Combining form meaning word; speech.

logopathy (log-op'ah-the) Any disorder of speech.

logoplegia (log-o-ple'je-ah) Paralysis of the speech organs.

logorrhea (log-o-re'ah) Excessive, uncontrollable talking.

log roll (log' rōl) Colloquialism for a procedure using a drawsheet to turn a patient in bed (as if the patient were a rigid log) to prevent injury to the spine; it usually involves three persons, two on one side of the bed, the other on the opposite side.

-logy Combining form meaning the science or study of (e.g., bacteriology).

loiasis (lo-i'ah-sis) Parasitic infection with the African eyeworm *Loa loa*, transmitted by the bite of an infected horsefly or deerfly. See also Loa loa.

loin (loin) The region of the back between the lowest rib and the upper rim of the pelvis (iliac crest), on either side of the spine.

loop (lōōp) **1.** A bend in a cord or cordlike structure. **2.** A platinum wire attached to a handle at one end and bent into a circle at the other; used to transfer bacterial cultures.

   Henle's l. See nephronic loop.

   nephronic l. The part of the renal tubule situated between the proximal and distal convoluted tubules; composed of the straight part of the proximal tubule, the thin U-shaped descending and ascending limbs, and the thick ascending limb. Also called Henle's loop.

lordoscoliosis (lor-do-sko-le-o'sis) Abnormal backward and lateral curvature of the spine.

lordosis (lor-do'sis) An abnormally exaggerated inward curvature of the lower spine. Also called swayback; saddle back.

lordotic (lor-dot'ik) Relating to lordosis.

lotion (lo'shun) **1.** Any of various liquids for external use, especially those containing one or more insoluble substances in suspension. **2.** Any liquid preparation used for cosmetic purposes.

   calamine l. A preparation of mineral oil with zinc oxide, ferric oxide, glycerin, bentonite magma, and calcium hydroxide solution; used for inflamed and pruritic skin lesions.

loupe (lōōp) A small magnifying lens, usually set in an eyepiece.

louse (lows), pl. lice Any of various wingless parasitic insects, including the sucking lice (of the order Anoplura) and the biting lice (of the order Mallophaga); some species are vectors of human diseases (e.g., relapsing fever, typhus, and trench fever). Human parasites include: the body or clothes louse (*Pediculus humanus corporis*); the pubic louse, popularly called crab and crab louse (*Phthirus pubis*), which infests pubic hair; and the head louse (*Pediculus humanus capitis*), which infests scalp hair and attaches its eggs (nits) firmly on the hair shaft.

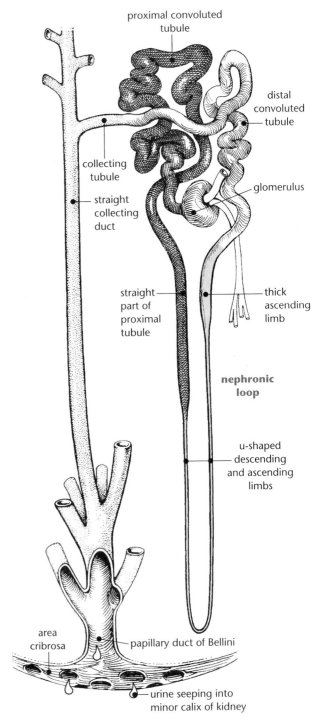

proximal convoluted tubule

distal convoluted tubule

collecting tubule

glomerulus

straight collecting duct

straight part of proximal tubule

thick ascending limb

nephronic loop

u-shaped descending and ascending limbs

area cribrosa

papillary duct of Bellini

urine seeping into minor calix of kidney

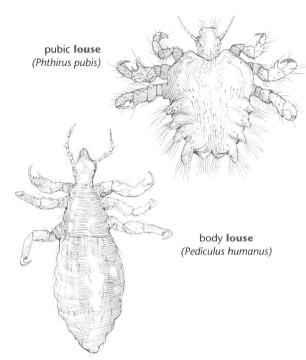

pubic **louse**
(Phthirus pubis)

body **louse**
(Pediculus humanus)

Loxosceles reclusa (loks-os′sĕ-lēz re-kloo′sah) The highly poisonous North American brown recluse spider, found primarily in the South and Southwest of the United States. It has a violin-shaped marking on its back. See also loxoscelism.

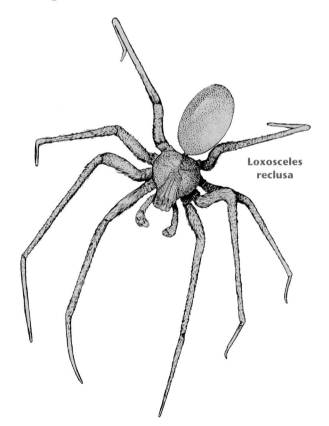

Loxosceles reclusa

loxoscelism (lok-sos′sĕ-lizm) Condition caused by the bite of the North American brown recluse spider and other species of the genus Loxosceles; characterized by formation of a painful gangrenous slough at the site of the bite; the loss of tissue usually leaves a permanent scar. Some people experience muscle weakness, fever, malaise, nausea, and vomiting.

lozenge (loz′enj) A medicated tablet for local treatment of the mouth or throat. Also called troche.

lub-dub (lub dub′) Commonly used term to describe the normal sounds made by the closing heart valves.

lucifugal (loo-sif′u-gal) Avoiding light.

lues (loo′ez) Syphilis.

luetic (loo-et′ik) Syphilitic.

lumbago (lum-ba′go) Pain in the loins (lumbar region).

lumbar (lum′bar) Relating to the loins (i.e., the part of the back between the lowest rib and the pelvic bone on either side of the spine).

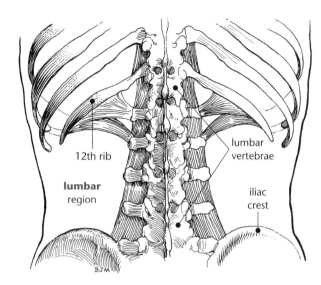

12th rib

lumbar region

lumbar vertebrae

iliac crest

BJM

lumbarization (lum-ber-ĭ-za′shun) Fusion between the transverse processes of the lowest lumbar and adjacent sacral vertebrae.

lumbo- Combining form meaning loins.

lumbosacral (lum-bo-sa′kral) Relating to the lumbar portion of the vertebral column and the sacrum.

lumbrical (lum′brĭ-kal) **1.** Relating to or resembling an earthworm. **2.** See table of muscles.

lumbricoid (lum′brĭ-koid) Resembling an earthworm.

lumen (loo′men), pl. lu′mina **1.** Space within a tubular structure (e.g., of a blood vessel). **2.** Unit of emitted light equal to 0.001946 watts.

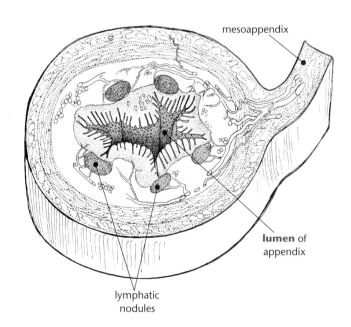

mesoappendix

lumen of appendix

lymphatic nodules

lumina (loo'min-ah) Plural of lumen.

luminal (loo'mĭ-nal) Relating to the space within tubular structures such as blood vessels or intestines.

lumirhodopsin (loo-mĭ-ro-dop'sin) An intermediate product formed in the retina during the process of light perception, triggered by the action of light upon rhodopsin (a retinal pigment).

lumpectomy (lum-pek'to-me) Surgical removal of a hard mass and a margin of surrounding tissue, especially from the breast.

lunacy (loo'nah-se) Obsolete term for a major mental disorder.

lung (lung) The paired organ of respiration situated in the chest cavity and enveloped by the pleura; generally the right lung is slightly larger than the left and is divided into three lobes, while the left has but two. The primary purpose of the lungs is the uptake of oxygen and the elimination of carbon dioxide; it is accomplished by the following processes: ventilation (inspired air reaches the air sacs [alveoli] in the lungs), diffusion (oxygen and carbon dioxide pass across the alveolar capillary membranes), and pulmonary capillary blood flow (flow is distributed evenly to all the ventilated alveoli).

bird-breeder's l., bird-fancier's l. An allergic reaction caused by inhalation of particulate matter from bird excreta, characterized by inflammation of the air sacs (alveoli) in the lungs.

black l. A form of pneumoconiosis characterized by heavy deposit of carbon dust in the lungs; may be associated with chronic bronchitis and emphysema; commonly seen in coal miners. Also called coal miner's lung.

coal miner's l. See black lung.

farmer's l. Allergic reaction to inhalation of moldy hay dust containing spores of thermophilic actinomycetes; usually occurs in people handling grains, particularly in threshing; may cause fever, chills,

difficult breathing, and cough four to eight hours after exposure (acute form), or may cause fibrosis of lung tissue after low-intensity, long-term exposure (chronic form). Also called thresher's lung.

honeycomb l. A lung with a spongy or honeycomb appearance due to the presence of numerous cysts; results from diffuse fibrosis and cystic dilatation of the minute air passages (bronchioles). Cause is unknown.

iron l. See Drinker respirator, under respirator.

mason's l. Silicosis resulting from inhalation of silica particles, usually seen in stone masons. See also silicosis.

miner's l. See black lung.

pump l. See adult respiratory distress syndrome, under syndrome.

shock l. See adult respiratory distress syndrome, under syndrome.

thresher's l. See farmer's lung.

wet l. (a) See adult respiratory distress syndrome, under syndrome. (b) See transient tachypnea of the newborn, under tachypnea.

lunula (loo'nu-lah) The half-moon of the nail; the pale semicircle at the base of the nail plate.

lupoid (loo'poid) Resembling lupus.

lupous (loo'pus) Relating to lupus.

lupus (loo'pus) General term used with a qualifying adjective for any of several diseases manifested by characteristic skin lesions.

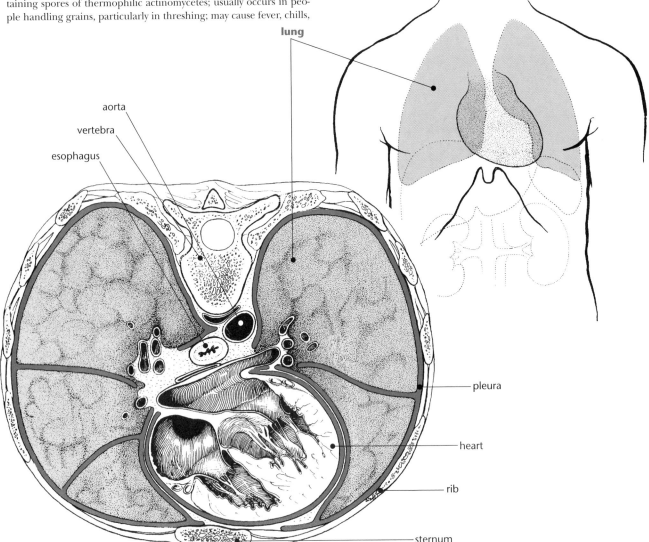

lung

aorta

vertebra

esophagus

pleura

heart

rib

sternum

discoid l. erythematosus (DLE) Disease of the skin characterized by a scaly rash, usually in a butterfly pattern over the nose and cheeks, sometimes extending to the scalp and causing baldness.

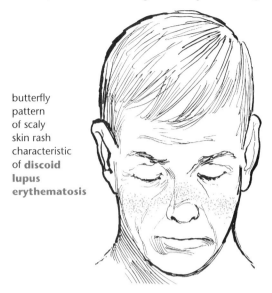

butterfly pattern of scaly skin rash characteristic of **discoid lupus erythematosis**

drug-induced l. Systemic lupus erythematosus, including the presence of antinuclear antibodies but only rarely involving the kidneys, precipitated by drugs used to lower high blood pressure (e.g., hydralazine), or to control cardiac arrhythmias (e.g., procainamide). Withdrawal of the drug reverses the condition.

l. pernio Lesions of the hands, ears, and nose resembling frostbite.

systemic l. erythematosus (SLE) A progressive, often severe, condition involving multiple systems (including skin, blood vessels, joints, heart, nervous system, and kidneys); thought to be of autoimmune origin. It is characterized by the presence of antinuclear antibodies (ANA) and other autoantibodies, including rheumatoid factor; antibodies producing false-positive VDRL (syphilis) tests; antibodies against plasma-coagulating protein; and antibodies against antigens on red and white blood cells and platelets, leading to immune destruction of these cells. Clinical features of the disease are diverse, depending on the location of the immune injury.

l. vulgaris Bacterial infection of the skin with the tuberculosis bacillus (*Mycobacterium tuberculosis*), causing reddish brown patches, most frequently on the face.

lusitrophy (lu-sit′ro-fe) Relaxation of heart muscle.

luteal (loo′te-al) Relating to the corpus luteum of the ovary.

lutein (loo′tēn) Yellow pigment present in egg yolk, fat cells, and corpus luteum.

luteinization (loo-tēn-ĭ-za′shun) Formation of luteal tissue and the corpus luteum in the ovary after discharge of the ovum.

luteogenic (loo-te-o-jen′ik) Inducing development of corpora lutea (e.g., a hormone).

luteoma (loo-te-o′mah) An uncommon ovarian enlargement, usually occurring during pregnancy and regressing after childbirth.

luteotropic (loo-te-o-trop′ik) Having a stimulating action on the development and function of the corpus luteum.

lutetium (loo-te′she-um) Rare-earth element; symbol Lu, atomic number 71, atomic weight 174.97.

Lutheran blood group Antigens of red blood cells, specified by the Lu gene, that react with antibodies designated anti-Lu^a and anti-Lu^b; first detected in the serum of an individual who had received many transfusions.

lutzomyia (loot-zo-mi′ah) Genus of sandflies or bloodsucking midges that transmit microorganisms causing leishmaniasis and bartonellosis.

lux (luks) A unit of illumination equal to 1 lumen per square meter.

luxation (luk-sa′shun) Dislocation.

lye (li) The liquid resulting from leaching wood ashes. Household lye is a mixture of sodium hydroxide and sodium carbonate. Also called lixivium.

lying-in (li-ing in′) Popular term for the period from childbirth through the first few weeks afterward.

lymph (limf) The tissue fluids collected by the lymphatic vessels and conveyed to the blood circulation after passing through a filtering system (lymph nodes); composed of a liquid, a number of white blood cells (especially lymphocytes), and a few red blood cells.

inflammatory l. The slightly yellow fluid collecting on the surface of an acutely inflamed surface wound or membrane.

lymphadenectomy (lim-fad-ĕ-nek′to-me) Removal of lymph nodes.

lymphadenitis (lim-fad′ĕ-ni-tis) Inflammation of lymph nodes.

histiocytic necrotizing l. See Kikuchi's disease, under disease.

lymphadeno-, lymphaden- Combining forms meaning lymph node.

lymphadenography (lim-fad-ĕ-nog′rah-fe) X-ray examination of a lymph node after injection of a radiopaque substance.

lymphadenopathy (lim-fad-ĕ-nop′ah-the) Enlargement of lymph nodes; may be localized, affecting one lymph node group anywhere in the body; or may be generalized to multiple lymph node groups throughout the body, in which case lymphoid tissues (e.g., the spleen) may also be involved.

lymphadenosis (lim-fad-ĕ-no′sis) Generalized enlargement of lymph nodes and lymphoid tissues.

benign l. See infectious mononucleosis, under mononucleosis.

malignant l. Obsolete term. See lymphoma.

lymphagogue (lim′fah-gog) An agent that stimulates production and flow of lymph.

lymphangiectasis, lymphangiectasia (lim-fan-je-ek′tah-sis, lim-fan-je-ek-ta′ze-ah) Abnormal dilatation of lymphatic vessels. Also called lymphectasia.

lymphangiectomy (lim-fan-je-ek′to-me) Surgical removal of a lymphatic vessel.

lymphangio-, lymphangi- Combining forms meaning lymphatic vessels.

lymphangioendothelioma (lim-fan-je-o-en′do-the-le-o′mah) A tumor composed primarily of small masses of endothelial cells and aggregations of tubular structures thought to be lymphatic vessels.

lymphangiography (lim-fan-je-og′rah-fe) Radiographic examination of the lymphatic system following injection of an oil-based contrast medium into a lymphatic vessel in each foot or, less frequently, in each hand. X-ray films are taken twice, immediately after injection to visualize the lymphatic vessels and 24 hours later to visualize the lymph nodes. Also called lymphography.

lymphangiology (lim-fan-je-ol′o-je) The study of lymphatic vessels. Also called lymphology.

lymphangioma (lim-fan-je-o′mah) A noncancerous tumor-like mass of dilated lymphatic vessels.

capillary l. See simple lymphangioma.

cavernous l. A poorly demarcated mass observed at birth or shortly thereafter, usually in the area of the parotid gland, at the neck, or in the armpit (axilla), and often reaching considerable size (up to 15 cm in diameter); may also occur in the tongue. It is a common feature of Turner's syndrome. Also called cystic hygroma.

simple l. A lymphangioma occurring anywhere in the body, typically in the head and neck as a rubbery cutaneous nodule 1 to 2 cm in diameter; may also occur within connective tissue of any organ as a well-demarcated mass. Also called capillary lymphangioma.

lymphangiosarcoma (lim-fan-je-o-sar-ko′mah) A rarely occurring cancerous tumor arising from the inner lining of lymphatic vessels.

lymphangitis (lim-fan-ji′tis) Inflammation of the lymphatic vessels; a common manifestation of a bacterial infection, frequently (but not exclusively) caused by the hemolytic streptococcus; occurs as a cluster of painful reddish streaks just below the skin.

lymphatic (lim-fat′ik) Relating to lymph, lymph nodes, or lymph vessels.

lymphectasia (lim-fek-ta′ze-ah) See lymphangiectasis.

lymphedema (lim-fe-de′mah) Chronic swelling, usually of the extremities; caused by any obstruction of lymph flow, either in the lymphatic vessels or the lymph nodes, and consequent accumulation of lymph in tissue spaces.

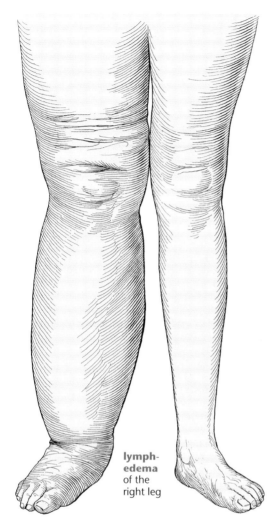

lymph-
edema
of the
right leg

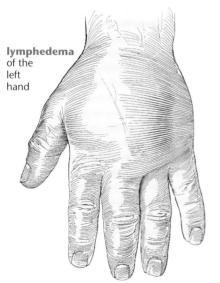

lymphedema
of the
left
hand

lymphoblast (lim′fo-blast) An immature cell that is the precursor of the lymphocyte. Also called lymphocytoblast.

lymphoblastic (lim-fo-blas′tik) Relating to lymphoblasts.

lymphoblastoma (lim-fo-blas-to′mah) Cancerous tumor arising from lymphoblasts.

lymphoblastosis (lim-fo-blas-to′sis) Excess of lymphoblasts in peripheral blood.

lymphocele (lim′fo-sēl) A cystic mass containing lymph. Also called lymphocyst.

lymphocyst (lim′fo-sist) See lymphocele.

lymphocyte (lim′fo-sit) A white blood cell formed in lymphoid tissues; normally constitutes 25 to 33% of all white blood cells in adult peripheral blood. Also called lymph cell; lymphoid cell.

    B l.'s Lymphocytes, derived from bone marrow, that play an important role in immune regulatory functions; they interact chiefly with the humoral immune system, which involves substances such as antibodies, antigens, and serum complement enzymes in the blood. Also called B cells.

    cytotoxic T l. Lymphocyte that kills target cells (e.g., tumor cells) by releasing a protein (perforin) to perforate the target cell membrane after antibodies have reacted with an antigen on the target cell.

    helper T l. See helper cell, under cell.

    NUL l. See null cell, under cell.

    T l.'s Lymphocytes, derived from the thymus, that play an important role in the cellular immune system by responding to antigens and triggering reactions in other cells, such as macrophages. Also called T cells.

lymphocytic (lim-fo-sit′ik) Relating to lymphocytes.

lymphocytoblast (lim-fo-si′to-blast) See lymphoblast.

lymphocytoma (lim-fo-si-to′mah) A tumorlike mass in a lymph node, chiefly made up of mature lymphocytes.

lymphocytopenia (lim-fo-si-to-pe′ne-ah) See lymphopenia.

lymphocytopoiesis (lim-fo-si-to-poi-e′sis) Formation of lymphocytes.

lymphocytosis (lim-fo-si-to′sis) Excess of lymphocytes in the blood. Also called lymphocytic leukocytosis.

lymphoepithelioma (lim-fo-ep-ī-the-le-o′mah) Cancerous tumor derived from the lining membrane around the tonsils and nasopharynx and containing abundant lymphoid tissue.

lymphogenesis (lim-fo-jen′ĕ-sis) Production of lymph.

lymphogenous (lim-foj′ĕ-nus) **1.** Originating from lymph. **2.** Forming lymph.

lymphogranuloma venereum, venereal lymphogranuloma (lim-fo-gran-u-lo′mah ve-ne′re-um, ve-ne′re-al lim-fo-gran-u-lo′mah) A sexually transmitted disease caused by *Chlamydia trachomatis;* characterized by a genital blister or ulcer that heals and disappears in a few days without leaving a scar; may be accompanied by fever, headache, muscle and joint pains, and a rash; lymph nodes in the groin become inflamed and swollen. In females, lymph nodes around the rectum may become involved, causing a stricture. Also called tropical bubo.

lymphography (lim-fog′rah-fe) See lymphangiography.

lymphoid (lim′foid) **1.** Relating to tissues of the lymphatic system. **2.** Resembling lymphatic tissue.

lymphoidectomy (lim-foi-dek′to-me) Removal of lymphoid tissue (e.g., adenoids).

lymphokines (lim′fo-kīns) Soluble products of lymphocytes that act as intercellular messengers to regulate immunologic and respiratory responses.

lymphokinesis (lim-fo-kī-ne′sis) **1.** Circulation of lymph through lymphatic vessels and lymph nodes. **2.** The movement of endolymph in the membranous labyrinth of the inner ear.

lymphology (lim-fol′o-je) See lymphangiology.

lymphoma (lim-fo′mah) Any of a group of malignant diseases originating in the lymphoreticular system, usually in the lymph nodes. Formerly called malignant lymphadenosis.

    Burkitt's l. A malignant tumor usually affecting children and young adults of the middle African regions and occurring sporati-

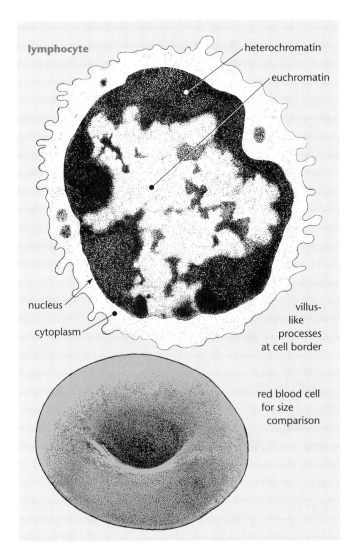

lymphocyte

heterochromatin

euchromatin

nucleus

cytoplasm

villus-
like
processes
at cell border

red blood cell
for size
comparison

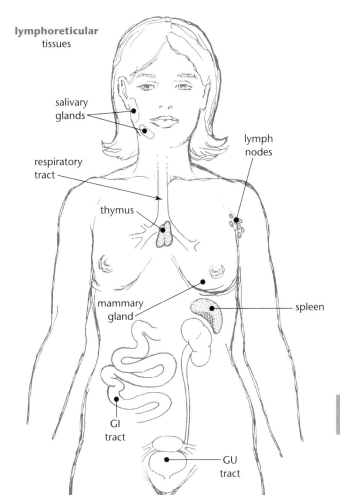

lymphoreticular
tissues

salivary
glands

respiratory
tract

thymus

mammary
gland

GI
tract

lymph
nodes

spleen

GU
tract

cally in other areas of the world; the African form involves the jaw initially; in the United States the abdominal area is affected first.

    histiocytic l. Malignant lymphoma in which the abnormal cells are a mixture of large histiocytes and smaller cells resembling lymphocytes.

    Hodgkin's l. See Hodgkin's disease, under disease.

    nodular l. A type of non-Hodgkin's lymphoma characterized by a growth pattern in which the tumor cells aggregate and form nodules.

    non-Hodgkin's l. (NHL) A group of malignant lymphomas that characteristically begin as painless enlargement of a lymph node that tends to spread to other lymph nodes; some eventually involve the spleen, liver, and bone marrow; others, after becoming widespread, disseminate to the circulating blood, creating a leukemia-like condition in the peripheral blood. Non-Hodgkin's lymphomas are classified by the Working Formulation for clinical use into three prognostic groups, based on survival statistics, as low-grade, intermediate-grade, and high-grade.

lymphomatosis (lim-fo-mah-to'sis) Any disease characterized by the presence of multiple malignant tumors of lymphoid tissue.

lymphopathy (lim-fop'ah-the) Any disease of the lymphatic system.

lymphopenia (lim-fo-pe'ne-ah) A reduced number of lymphocytes in the blood. Also called lymphocytopenia.

lymphopoiesis (lim-fo-poi-e'sis) The formation of lymphocytes.

lymphoreticular (lim-fo-rě-tik'u-lar) Relating to lymphoid tissues and their associated reticuloendothelial framework.

lymphostasis (lim-fos'tah-sis) Obstruction to lymph flow.

lyo- Combining form meaning dissolution.

lyophilic (li-o-fil'ik) Dissolving easily due to having an affinity for the dissolving medium (solvent); applied to colloids.

lyophilization (li-of-ĭ-li-za'shun) The process of freeze-drying.

lyophobic (li-o-fo'bik) Lack of affinity for the solvent; applied to colloids.

lyotropic (li-o-trop'ik) Readily soluble.

lyse (līz) To cause disintegration of cells.

lysergic acid (li-sur'jik as'id) A crystalline compound derived from ergot.

    l.a. diethylamide (LSD) A hallucinogenic drug derived from lysergic acid.

lysin (li'sin) 1. An antibody that destroys cells by dissolving them. 2. Any substance capable of causing damage and dissolution of cells.

lysine (li'sēn) (Lys) One of the essential amino acids.

lysis (li'sis) 1. Destruction of cells by a specific lysin. 2. The gradual recovery from an acute disease.

lysogen (li'so-jen) An antigen (e.g., a bacterial cell) that stimulates formation of a lysin (e.g., antibody) specific to that antigen.

lysogenesis (li-so-jen'ĕ-sis) The production of lysins (i.e., antibodies that cause dissolution of cells).

lysogeny (li-soj'e-ne) A form of viral parasitism whereby viral DNA that has entered a bacterial cell does not replicate as usual; instead, it attaches to a specific site of a chromosome in the bacterial cell, thus becoming part of the cell's genetic makeup; it is then reproduced along with the chromosome and transmitted to daughter cells with each cell division.

lysosomal (li-so-so'mal) Relating to lysosomes.

lysosome (li'so-sōm) A large cytoplasmic particle in a cell containing digestive fluid (hydrolytic enzyme); particularly large and abundant in white blood cells.

    primary l. A lysosome that has not engaged in any digestive activity.

    secondary l. A vacuolated lysosome that is the site of current or previous digestive activity.

lysozyme (li'so-zīm) An antibacterial enzyme naturally present in tears, sweat, saliva, and nasal secretions. Also called mucopeptide glucohydrolase.

lytic (lit'ik) Relating to lysis.

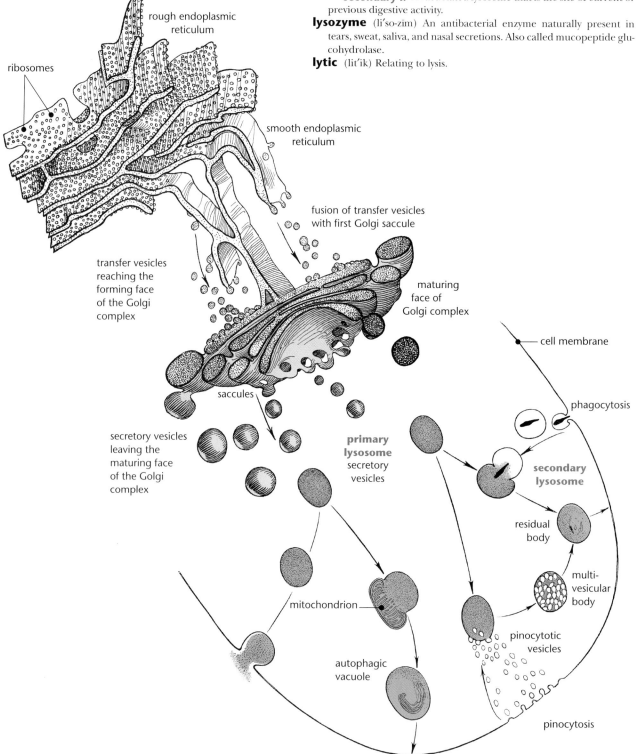

rough endoplasmic reticulum

ribosomes

smooth endoplasmic reticulum

fusion of transfer vesicles with first Golgi saccule

transfer vesicles reaching the forming face of the Golgi complex

maturing face of Golgi complex

cell membrane

saccules

phagocytosis

secretory vesicles leaving the maturing face of the Golgi complex

primary lysosome secretory vesicles

secondary lysosome

residual body

multi-vesicular body

mitochondrion

pinocytotic vesicles

autophagic vacuole

pinocytosis

L

M

Macaca mulatta (mah-kak′ah mu-lat′tah) The rhesus monkey (genus *Macaca,* family Cercopithecidae); used extensively in biomedical research.

Mace, MACE (mās) Trademark for a form of tear gas used in aerosol form as a defensive weapon; it causes intense eye pain and respiratory distress.

macerate (mas′er-āt) To soften by soaking in a liquid.

maceration (mas-er-a′shun) **1.** The process of softening a tissue or other solid or the separation of its constituents by soaking it in a liquid. **2.** In obstetrics, the softening and disintegration (without putrefaction) of a dead fetus remaining in the uterus.

machine (mah-shēn′) Any mechanical apparatus.

　anesthesia m. In inhalation anesthesia, apparatus for delivering quantified volumes of anesthetic gases and oxygen to the patient's breathing circuit for inducement of general anesthesia; it includes vaporizers, flowmeters, and sources of compressed gases.

　heart-lung m. Machine consisting of a blood pump (artificial heart) and an oxygenator (artificial lung); used to support the circulation with oxygenated blood while keeping the heart essentially free of blood and permitting surgery within the heart, coronary arteries, and ascending arch of the aorta.

　kidney m. See hemodialyzer.

　panoramic rotating m. An x-ray machine capable of radiographing all the teeth and surrounding structures by using extraoral film and a reciprocating motion of the x-ray tube.

macrencephaly, macrencephalia (mak-ren-sef′ah-le, mak-ren-sĕ-fa′le-ah) The state of having an oversized brain.

macro-, macr- Combining forms meaning large.

macroadenoma (mak-ro-ad-ĕ-no′mah) Benign glandular tumor of the anterior portion of the pituitary (hypophysis) measuring more than 10 mm in diameter.

macroamylase (mak-ro-am′ĭ-lās) A starch-splitting enzyme present in serum bound to a globulin.

macrobiote (mak-ro-bi′ōt) Long-lived; denoting an organism capable of surviving in a dormant state.

macrobiotic (mak-ro-bi-ot′ik) Tending to prolong life.

macrobiotics (mak-ro-bi-ot′iks) In alternative medicine, a diet based on ancient Oriental philosophy, arbitrarily assigning foods either positive (yin) or negative (yang) energy. The diet consists mainly of whole grains, vegetables, and enough food of animal source to prevent malnutrition; advocates believe macrobiotics can prevent cancer; some erroneously conclude that it is also an appropriate treatment for cancer.

macrobrachia (mak-ro-bra′ke-ah) The condition of having long arms.

macrocephalic (mak-ro-se-fal′ik) Relating to macrocephaly. Also called megacephalic.

macrocephalous (mak-ro-sef′ah-lus) Having an abnormally large head. Also called megacephalous.

macrocephaly (mak-ro-sef′ah-le) An abnormally large head circumference of an infant, i.e., two or more standard deviations (SDs) above the mean for its age and sex; it may or may not be associated with hydrocephalus; other causes include slow subdural effusions (usually from trauma) and large cystic defects.

macrocheilia (mak-ro-ki′le-ah) **1.** Abnormally large lips. **2.** Permanent swelling of a lip due to enlarged lymph nodes.

macrocheiria (mak-ro-ki′re-ah) Abnormally large hands. Also called megalocheiria.

macrochemistry (mak-ro-kem′is-tre) Denoting chemical reactions that can be seen with the naked eye.

macrocornea (mak-ro-kor′ne-ah) See megalocornea.

macrocranium (mak-ro-kra′ne-um) Enlargement of the cranium.

macrocryoglobulinemia (mak-ro-kri′o-glob′u-lin-e′me-ah) The presence of cold-precipitating globulins in the blood.

macrocyte (mak′ro-sīt) A large red blood cell (at least 2 μm larger than normal) with decreased life span; seen in the blood of people with pernicious anemia, folic acid deficiency, and other anemias. Also called macroerythrocyte.

macrodactyly (mak-ro-dak′tĭ-le) Abnormal largeness of one or more digits. Also called megalodactyly; dactylomegaly; megadactyly.

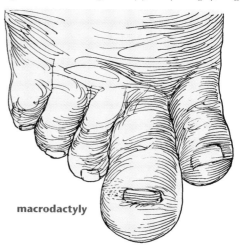

macrodactyly

macrodont (mak′ro-dont) An abnormally large tooth.

macrodontia (mak-ro-don′she-ah) The condition of having abnormally large teeth.

macroerythrocyte (mak-ro-ĕ-rith′ro-sīt) See macrocyte.

macrogenitosomia (mak-ro-jen-ĭ-to-so′me-ah) Disorder of the cortex of the adrenal gland, most commonly affecting male children; characterized by excessive and early development of sexual organs associated with rapid maturation of the musculoskeletal system, resulting in short stature.

macroglia (mak-rog′le-ah) The two neuroglial elements of ectodermal origin, the astrocyte and oligodendrocyte.

macroglobulin (mak-ro-glob′u-lin) An unusually large plasma globulin (protein); molecular weight is often about 1 million.

macroglobulinemia (mak-ro-glob-u-lin-e′me-ah) The presence of macroglobulins in the circulating blood.

　Waldenstrom's m. A malignancy predominantly seen in people over 60 years old, characterized by diffuse infiltration of bone marrow by certain cells (lymphocytes, plasma cells, and lymphocytoid plasma cells) that secrete an abnormal protein (M component, a monoclonal immunoglobulin); cells may also infiltrate lymph nodes, spleen, and liver; symptoms include weakness, weight loss, visual impairment, dizziness, and deafness. Also called Waldenström's syndrome.

macroglossia (mak-ro-glos′e-ah) Abnormally large size of the tongue.

macrognathia (mak-ro-na′the-ah) Abnormal largeness of the jaw.

macrogyria (mak-ro-ji′re-ah) Abnormality of the superficial layer of the brain (cerebral cortex) in which the convolutions are larger than normal due to a reduction in the number of sulci.

macrolides (mak′ro-līds) A group of broad-spectrum antibiotics with molecules made up of large-ring lactones; they inhibit protein

M

synthesis in target bacteria. The group includes erythromycin, clarithromycin, and azithromycin.

macromastia, macromazia (mak-ro-mas′te-ah, mak-ro-ma′ze-ah) Abnormally large size of the breasts.

macromelia (mak-ro-me′le-ah) Abnormally large size of one or more limbs. Also called megalomelia.

macromolecule (mak-ro-mol′ĕ-kūl) Any long-chain molecule (e.g., proteins, polysaccharides, nucleic acids).

macronodular (mak-ro-nod′u-lar) Containing nodules larger than 3 mm in diameter.

macronucleus (mak-ro-nu′kle-us) **1.** Any nucleus that occupies a large area of the cell. **2.** The larger of the two nuclei of ciliated protozoa.

macroparasite (mak-ro-par′ah-sīt) Parasite visible to the unaided eye (e.g., a louse).

macropathology (mak-ro-pah-thol′o-je) The gross anatomic changes caused by disease.

macrophage (mak′ro-fāj) A large mononuclear cell formed in bone marrow and found in large numbers throughout the body, with greatest accumulation in the spleen; its function is to remove degenerated cells and blood tissue from the circulation, and it is also involved in the production of antibodies and in cell-mediated immune response.

    alveolar m. A white blood cell that moves about on the alveolar surface of the lungs engulfing inhaled airborne particles that have reached the alveolus. Also called dust cell; alveolar phagocyte.

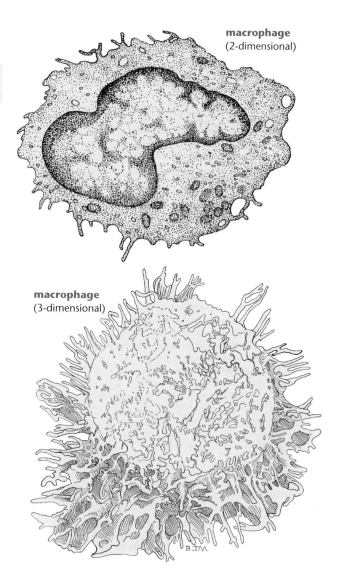

macrophage
(2-dimensional)

macrophage
(3-dimensional)

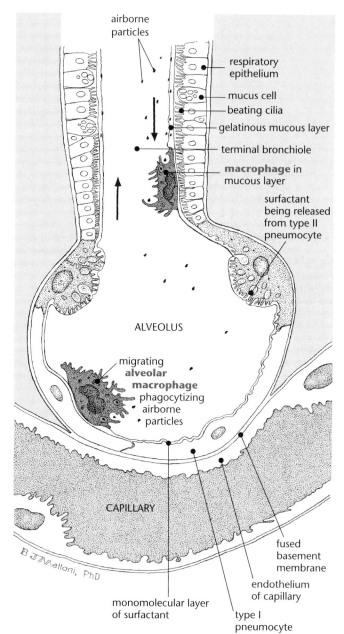

- airborne particles
- respiratory epithelium
- mucus cell
- beating cilia
- gelatinous mucous layer
- terminal bronchiole
- **macrophage** in mucous layer
- surfactant being released from type II pneumocyte
- ALVEOLUS
- migrating **alveolar macrophage** phagocytizing airborne particles
- CAPILLARY
- fused basement membrane
- endothelium of capillary
- monomolecular layer of surfactant
- type I pneumocyte

B.J.Melloni, PhD

macropolycyte (mak-ro-pol′e-sīt) An extremely large white blood cell (polymorphonuclear leukocyte) with a highly segmented nucleus; a cellular characteristic that precedes pernicious anemia.

macropsia (mah-krop′se-ah) The condition of seeing objects larger than their actual sizes.

macrorhinia (mak-ro-rin′e-ah) An abnormally large size of the nose.

macroscopic (mak-ro-skop′ik) Visible with the naked eye.

macrosomia (mak-ro-so′me-ah) Abnormally large size of the body, such as that of a newborn infant of a diabetic mother.

macrosomic (mak-ro-som′ik) Relating to macrosomia.

macrostomia (mak-ro-sto′me-ah) Developmental malformation in which the mouth extends toward the ear; may be unilateral or bilateral.

macrotia (mak-ro′she-ah) Abnormal largeness of the ears.

macula (mak′u-lah), pl. mac′ulae A small area differing in appearance from the surrounding tissue; a circumscribed spot, stain, or thickening.

    m. adherens See desmosome.

    m. area of retina See macula lutea.

    m. densa The cell plaque located within the final portion of the distal straight tubule (thick ascending limb) abutting the wall of the

M

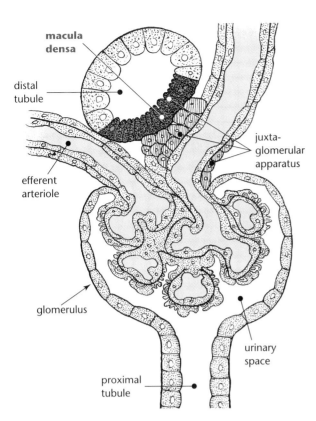

macula densa

distal tubule

efferent arteriole

juxta-glomerular apparatus

glomerulus

urinary space

proximal tubule

afferent arteriole of its own renal corpuscle; it is part of the juxta-glomerular apparatus and is composed of heavily nucleated cells that are narrow and slightly taller than surrounding cells; the specialized cells produce renin.

m. of follicle A relatively avascular area on the surface of an ovary at which a vesicular ovarian follicle ruptures, forcing the enclosed egg (ovum), cumulus, some detached follicular (granulosa) cells, and follicular fluid out into the peritoneal cavity; usually the rupture point is rapidly sealed off.

m. of gonorrhea The red, inflamed orifice of the duct of the greater vestibular gland, seen in gonorrheal vulvitis.

m. lutea The small oval, yellowish area on the posterior part of the retina, lateral to and slightly below the optic nerve; it has a central depression (fovea centralis) that houses only cone cells responsible for visual resolution of the highest order. Also called macula retinae; yellow spot; macular area of retina.

m. retinae See macula lutea.

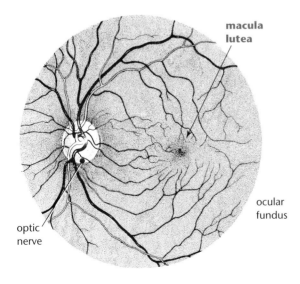

macula lutea

optic nerve

ocular fundus

m. of saccule The oval thickening of the epithelium on the anterior wall of the saccule of the inner ear, which lies in a plane at right angles to the macula of the utricle; it receives the saccular fibers of the vestibulocochlear (8th cranial) nerve and serves as the special end organ concerned with equilibratory vestibular reflexes.

m. of utricle The 2-by-3-mm thickening of the epithelium on the inferolateral wall of the utricle of the inner ear; it receives the utricular fibers of the vestibulocochlear (8th cranial) nerve and serves as the special end organ concerned with equilibratory vestibular reflexes.

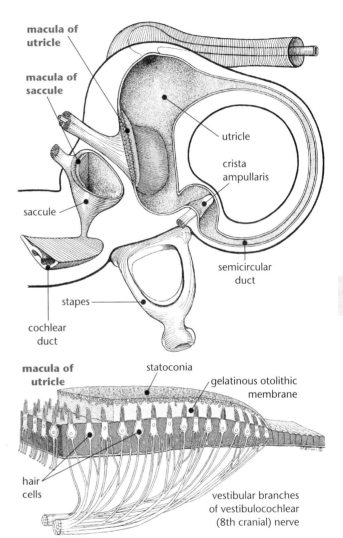

macula of utricle

macula of saccule

utricle

crista ampullaris

saccule

semicircular duct

stapes

cochlear duct

macula of utricle

statoconia

gelatinous otolithic membrane

hair cells

vestibular branches of vestibulocochlear (8th cranial) nerve

macular (mak'u-lar) **1.** Relating to a macula (e.g., of the retina). **2.** Relating to a spot or discoloration (macule) on the skin.

maculation (mak-u-la'shun) The presence of spots on the skin.

macule (mak'ūl) A nonpalpable spot on the skin, level with the surface, less than 1 cm in diameter, and identified only by a difference in color from surrounding skin.

maculocerebral (mak-u-lo-ser'e-bral) Relating to the brain and the macula lutea of the retina; applied to certain diseases involving both structures.

maculoerythematous (mak-u-lo-er-ĭ-them'ah-tus) Both spotty and reddish; applied to certain skin eruptions.

maculopapular (mak-u-lo-pap'u-lar) Containing or composed of both spots (macules) and raised lesions of any color (papules); applied to certain skin eruptions.

maculopathy (mak-u-lop'ah-the) Any disease of the macula lutea of the retina.

M

mad (mad) Colloquial term for one suffering from a mental disorder.

madarosis (mad-ah-ro'sis) Loss of eyebrows or eyelashes.

maggot (mag'ot) The larva of various insects; most thrive in dead organic matter, others in live tissues.

maggots

magma (mag'mah) A paste or salve.

magnesia (mag-ne'zhe-ah) Magnesium oxide.

   citrate of m. See magnesium citrate, under magnesium.

   m. magma See milk of magnesia.

   milk of m. (MOM) An aqueous suspension of magnesium peroxide; used as a laxative and antacid. Also called magnesia magma.

magnesium (mag-ne'ze-um) Metallic element; symbol Mg, atomic number 12, atomic weight 24.31. Magnesium plays several vital roles in body functions, such as bone and tooth formation, muscle contraction, transmission of nerve impulses, transportation of sodium and potassium across cell membranes, and activation of many substances (enzymes) that promote biochemical reactions in the body. Many of its compounds are used as antacids and laxatives (e.g., magnesium citrate, magnesium oxide, magnesium sulfate).

   m. citrate A white powder, used in solution as a mild cathartic. Also called citrate of magnesia.

   m. oxide Calcinated magnesia; used primarily as a gastric antacid. Also called magnesia.

   m. peroxide See milk of magnesia, under magnesia.

magnetic moment (mag-net'ik mo'ment) The force exerted in a magnetic field of given strength when the axis of the magnet is at right angles to the field.

magnetism (mag'ně-tizm) 1. The property of mutual attraction or repulsion produced by a magnet or by an electric current. 2. The force exhibited by a magnetic field.

magnetoencephalography (mag-ne'to-en-sef'ah-log'rah-fe) The use of instruments by which evoked potentials and evoked magnetic fields are measured simultaneously to examine those structures beneath the cortex of the brain, and to study and diagnose functional areas of the brain.

magneton (mag'ně-ton) A unit of measure of the magnetic movement of an atomic or subatomic particle.

magnification (mag-ni-fi-ka'shun) The apparent increase in the size of an object as seen through an optical instrument.

main (mān) French for hand.

   m. d'accoucheur See accoucheur's hand, under hand.

   m. en crochet Permanent flexure of the fourth and fifth fingers, resembling the position of a person's hand while crocheting.

   m. en griffe See clawhand.

   m. en lorgnette See opera-glass hand, under hand.

mainlining (mān'lin-ing) Common name for the habit of injecting illegal drugs intravenously.

mainstreaming (mān'strēm-ing) 1. The placement of children with physical or mental disabilities in the same classroom as other children, while supplementing their learning with an appropriate educational program. 2. Any effort to integrate a person with an affliction (e.g., mental disorder) into society; a deinstitutionalization.

mal- Combining form meaning bad; ill.

mal (mahl) French and Spanish for disease.

   grand m. See generalized tonic-clonic epilepsy, under epilepsy.

   petit m. See absence.

malabsorption (mal-ab-sorp'shun) Impaired absorption of dietary nutrients by the intestinal lining (mucosa).

malacia (mah-la'she-ah) Abnormal softening of tissues.

malaco- Combining form meaning soft; softening.

malacoplakia (mal-ah-ko-pla'ke-ah) The formation of soft, fungus-like growths on the interior lining of a hollow organ, especially the bladder.

maladjustment (mal-ad-just'ment) Failed attempts to adapt one's inner needs to the environment.

malady (mal'ah-de) Illness; disease.

malaise (mal-āz') A vague general discomfort or feeling of illness.

malalignment (mal-ah-lin'ment) Displacement of one or more teeth from normal position.

malar (ma'lar) Relating to the cheek; the cheekbone (zygomatic bone).

malaria (mah-la're-ah) Infectious disease caused by any of four species of a protozoan parasite (*Plasmodium falciparum, Plasmodium vivax, Plasmodium ovale,* or *Plasmodium malariae*), transmitted by the bite of an infected female mosquito of the genus *Anopheles;* usual symptoms include extreme exhaustion, paroxysms of high fever, sweating, shaking chills, anemia, and enlargement of the spleen.

malarial (mah-la're-al) Relating to malaria.

Malassezia furfur (mal-ah-se'ze-ah fur'fer) A fungus that causes tinea versicolor.

malathion (mal-ah-thi'on) A widely used insecticide.

male (māl) One who produces spermatozoa.

   genetic m. An individual with a normal male karyotype, one X and one Y chromosome.

malemission (mal-e-mish'un) Failure of semen to be discharged through the penis.

malformation (mal-for-ma'shun) A primary structural defect of a body part that results from a localized developmental error (e.g., cleft lip).

   Ebstein's m. See Ebstein's anomaly, under anomaly.

malfunction (mal-funk'shun) Inadequate or abnormal function.

malignancy (mah-lig'nan-se) The state of being malignant.

malignant (mah-lig'nant) 1. Tending to become worse and cause death; applied to any disease. 2. Denoting a tumor that infiltrates adjacent tissues and spreads to other parts of the body with potentially life-threatening results.

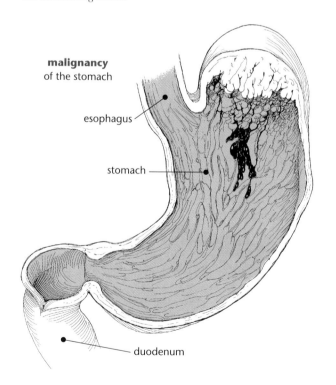

malignancy of the stomach

esophagus

stomach

duodenum

malinger (mah-ling′ger) To engage in malingering.

malingerer (mah-ling′ger-er) A person who engages in malingering.

malingering (mah-ling′ger-ing) A faking of illness or voluntary production of symptoms for a rationally determined gain (e.g., monetary compensation, avoidance of responsibility).

malleable (mal′e-ah-bl) Capable of being shaped into thin sheets; applied to certain metals.

malleation (mal-e-a′shun) A sharp spasmodic twitching of the hands.

malleolar (mal-e′o-lar) Relating to one or both bony projections on either side of the ankle.

malleolus (mal-le′o-lus), pl. malle′oli One of two bony prominences (one on the tibia, one on the fibula) on either side of the ankle.

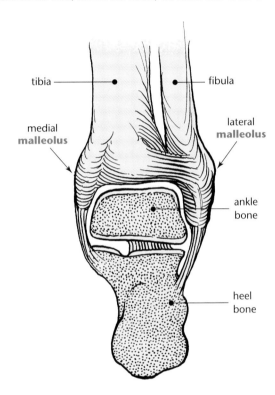

malleus (mal′e-us) The club-shaped and most lateral of the three ossicles in the middle ear chamber; it is attached to the eardrum (tympanic membrane) and articulates with the incus; it resembles a hammer and is sometimes called by that name. See also table of bones.

malnutrition (mal-nu-trish′un) Faulty nutrition due to inadequate diet (e.g., consuming inadequate amounts or the wrong proportions of nutrients), or to a metabolic abnormality.

　　protein-calorie m. Any disorder resulting from insufficient supply of protein and calories to the body.

malocclusion (mal-o-kloo′zhun) Any deviation from the normal contact of upper and lower (maxillary and mandibular) teeth. It may result from a variety of causes and is the cardinal sign of both mandibular and maxillary fractures. Also called abnormal occlusion.

malposition (mal-po-zish′un) An abnormal position.

malpractice (mal-prak′tis) Negligence by a professional (e.g., physician, attorney, accountant).

　　medical m. Negligence by a medical professional; medical care provided to a patient that falls below the accepted standards of medical practice, thereby exposing the patient to an unreasonable risk of harm. A legal claim for medical malpractice requires that the patient prove the health care professional owed the patient a duty to provide medical care within the accepted standards of medical practice, that the duty was breached, and that the breach caused injury to the patient. The injury claimed by the patient must be recognized by law as compensable.

malpresentation (mal-prez-en-ta′shun) Any position of the baby at the time of birth that differs from the usual facedown headfirst position.

malrotation (mal-ro-ta′shun) Failure of a structure (e.g., of all or a portion of the intestines) to undergo normal rotation during embryonic development.

maltase (mawl′tās) Digestive enzyme that promotes the conversion of maltose into a simpler sugar, glucose.

maltose (mawl′tōs) A sugar formed by the action of amylase (a digestive enzyme) on starch. Also called malt sugar.

malunion (mal-ūn′yon) The healing of a fractured bone in a faulty alignment or position.

mamelon, mammelon (mam′ĕ-lon) One of the three small rounded projections on the cutting edge of an erupting (or newly erupted) incisor tooth.

mamilla (mah-mil′ah), pl. mamil′lae 1. A nipple. 2. Any nipplelike protrusion.

mamillary (mam′ĭ-ler-e) Relating to a nipple.

mamillated (mam-ĭ-lāt′ed) Having nipplelike projections.

mamma (mam′ah), pl. mam′mae A mammary gland; a breast, male or female.

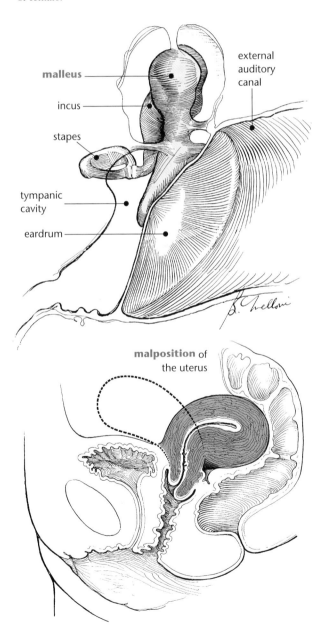

mammal (mam′al) Relating to the class Mammalia.

Mammalia (mah-ma′le-ah) A class of vertebrates that nourish their young with milk.

mammaplasty (mam′ah-plas-te) See mammoplasty.

mammary (mam′er-e) Relating to the breasts.

mammectomy (mah-mek′to-me) See mastectomy.

mammilliplasty (mah-mil′ĭ-plas-te) Reparative or aesthetic surgery of the nipple. Also called mammiloplasty; theleplasty.

mammillitis (mam-ĭ-li′tis) Inflammation of a nipple.

mammitis (mam-i′tis) See mastitis.

mammilliplasty (mah-mil′ĭ-plas-te) See mammilaplasty.

mammo- Combining form meaning breast.

mammogram (mam′o-gram) An x-ray picture of a breast produced by mammography.

mammography (mam-og′rah-fe) A soft-tissue x-ray technique for detecting nonpalpable breast growths and identifying palpable lesions.

mammoplasty (mam′o-plas-te) Plastic surgery of the breast. Also called mammaplasty; mastoplasty.

  augmentation m. Enlargement of the breasts by implantation of a prosthesis, usually a silcone bag filled with silicone gel, saline, or air, or a combination of the three; implant may be placed beneath the breast tissue or beneath the greater pectoral (pectoralis major) muscle.

reconstructive m. Introduction of an implant to replace a breast that has been removed partly or completely; may be performed at the time the breast is removed or at a later date.

  reduction m. Any of various techniques for reducing breast size, generally by removing a portion of breast tissue from the center and lower areas of the breast; the nipple and areola are retained in a skin pedicle and repositioned.

mammotroph (mam′o-trōf) A cell of the anterior portion of the pituitary (hypophysis) that produces the hormone prolactin; a prolactin cell.

mammotrophic (mam-o-trof′ik) Stimulating the development, growth, and function of the mammary glands.

mandelate (man′del-āt) A salt of mandelic acid.

mandelic acid (man-del′ik as′id) A water-soluble substance used as a urinary antibacterial agent.

mandible (man′dĭ-bl) The horseshoe-shaped bone of the lower jaw articulating with both sides of the skull at the temporomandibular joints (TMJs); it holds the lower teeth. Also called lower jaw; jawbone. See also table of bones.

  prognathous m. See protruded mandible.

  protruded m. A mandible in an anterior or forward projection relative to the rest of the facial skeleton. Also called prognathous mandible.

  retrognathous m. See retruded mandible.

  retruded m. A mandible in a posterior or backward position relative to the rest of the facial skeleton. Also called retrognathous mandible.

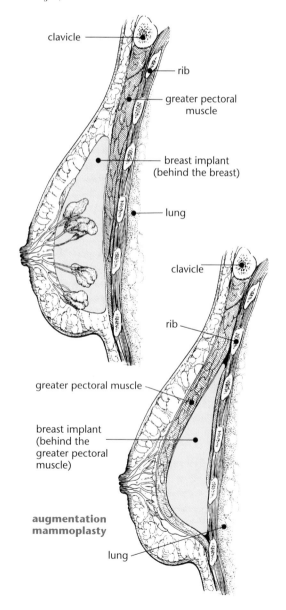

clavicle

rib

greater pectoral muscle

breast implant (behind the breast)

lung

clavicle

rib

greater pectoral muscle

breast implant (behind the greater pectoral muscle)

augmentation mammoplasty

lung

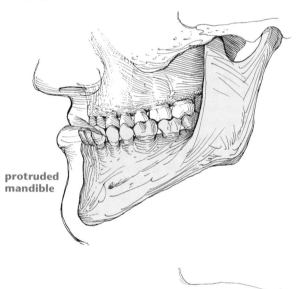

protruded mandible

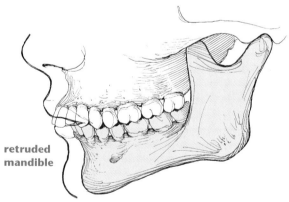

retruded mandible

mandibular (man-dib′u-lar) Relating to the lower jaw.

mandibulectomy (man-dib-u-lek′to-me) Removal of the lower jaw or a portion of it.

mandibulopharyngeal (man-dib-u-lo-fah-rin′je-al) Relating to the lower jaw (mandible) and the back of the oral cavity (pharynx).

mandragora (man-drag′o-rah) A poisonous European herb that has sedative, hypnotic, and anesthetic properties. Also called mandrake.

M

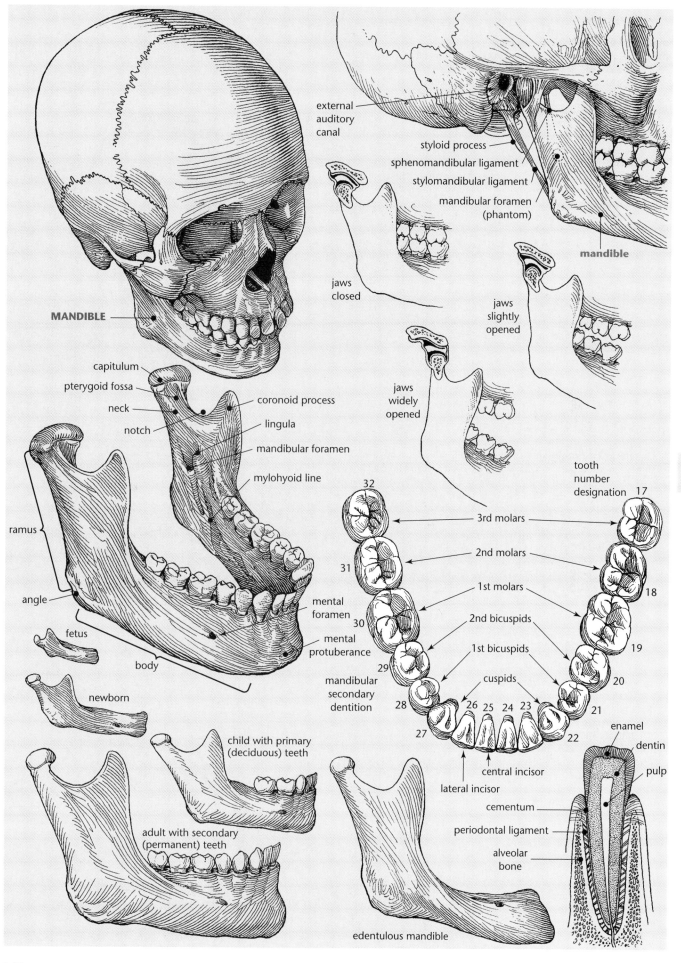

MANDIBLE

external auditory canal

styloid process

sphenomandibular ligament

stylomandibular ligament

mandibular foramen (phantom)

mandible

jaws closed

jaws slightly opened

jaws widely opened

capitulum

pterygoid fossa

neck

notch

coronoid process

lingula

mandibular foramen

mylohyoid line

ramus

angle

fetus

body

newborn

mental foramen

mental protuberance

mandibular secondary dentition

child with primary (deciduous) teeth

adult with secondary (permanent) teeth

edentulous mandible

tooth number designation

3rd molars

2nd molars

1st molars

2nd bicuspids

1st bicuspids

cuspids

central incisor

lateral incisor

32
31
30
29
28
27
26 25 24 23
22
21
20
19
18
17

enamel

dentin

pulp

cementum

periodontal ligament

alveolar bone

M

mandrake (man′drāk) See mandragora.

maneuver (mah-noo′ver) A procedure requiring skill and dexterity.

    Adson's m. See Adson's test, under test.

    Bracht's m. In obstetrics, a maneuver used in breech delivery in which the breech is allowed to deliver spontaneously up to the navel, then the baby's body is held against the mother's symphysis and moderate suprapubic pressure is applied by an assistant.

    Brandt-Andrews m. A method of delivering the placenta during the last stage of childbirth; pressure is applied with the fingers of one hand just above the symphysis to elevate the uterus into the abdomen and at the same time express the placenta into the vagina; gentle cord traction with the other hand is used to guide the placenta into the birth canal.

    Credés m. See Credés method, under method.

    Heimlich m. A method of expelling an obstruction, such as food, from the throat of a choking person by wrapping one's arms around the victim from behind and placing a fist just above the navel, grasping the fist with the other hand and forcefully thrusting it inward and upward. The sudden pressure forces air up the trachea, which usually dislodges the obstruction.

    Leopold's m.'s In obstetrics, abdominal examination consisting of four steps to determine: 1) fetal position in uterine fundus; 2) location of fetal back and limbs; 3) engagement of presenting part; 4) direction and degree of flexion of head.

    Mauriceau m. A method of extracting the fetal head in partial breech presentation when the chin is directed posteriorly; the baby's body straddles the forearm of the operator, the index and middle fingers are placed over the maxilla to maintain flexion of the head, and two fingers of the operator's other hand are placed forklike over the baby's shoulders to exert gentle traction.

    McDonald m. See McDonald technique, under technique.

    modified Prague m. A method of delivering the fetal head in breech presentation when the back of the head remains directed posteriorly and the rest of the body has been delivered; one hand of the operator supports the shoulders from below while the other hand gently elevates the baby's body upward toward the maternal abdomen, thus flexing the head within the birth canal, which results in delivery of the back of the head over the perineum.

    modified Ritgen m. Maneuver for facilitating a slow, gradual delivery of the baby's head in vertex presentation to prevent injuries to the infant's nervous system and to the mother's perineal musculature; gentle forward pressure is applied on the infant's chin through the maternal perineum with one hand while applying pressure on the back of the head with the other hand; performed between contractions.

    Pinard's m. A method of extracting a fetal foot in frank breech presentation; two fingers are passed along the fetal thigh to the knee to push it away from the midline and flex the leg; the foot is then readily grasped and brought down and out.

    Scanzoni m. Rotation of the fetal head with forceps followed by removal and reapplication of the instrument for delivery to avoid injury to the maternal soft parts.

    Valsalva's m. *(a)* Forced expiration with closed mouth and pinched nose to clear the eustachian (auditory) tube. *(b)* Forced expiration against the closed vocal folds to increase pressure within the lungs; it decreases venous blood return to the right atrium of the heart; used in cardiovascular studies.

manganese (man′gah-nēs) Metallic element; symbol Mn, atomic number 25, atomic weight 54.94; some of its compounds are used in medicine.

mange (mānj) A skin disease of animals caused by burrowing itch mites, usually *Sarcoptes chorioptes;* in humans, the disease is called scabies.

-mania Combining form meaning a morbid preoccupation with an idea (e.g., megalomania); a compulsive need to behave in some deviant way (e.g., kleptomania).

mania (ma′ne-ah) Mental state characterized by episodes of excessive elation, hyperactivity, and profuse and rapidly changing ideas; occurs as an affective disorder and in certain mental disorders of organic origin.

M

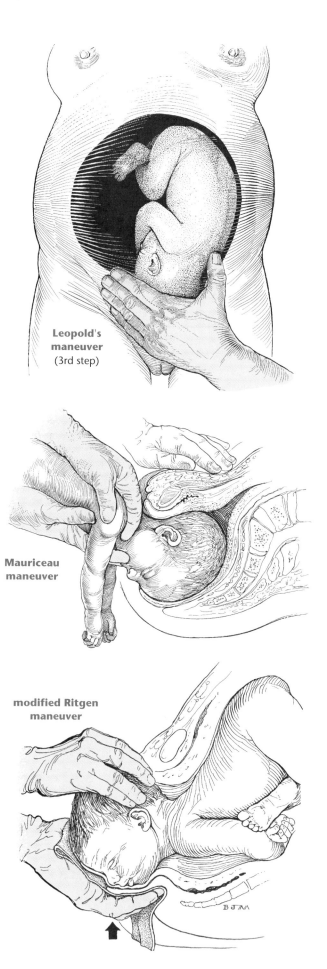

Leopold's maneuver (3rd step)

Mauriceau maneuver

modified Ritgen maneuver

mandrake ■ **mania**

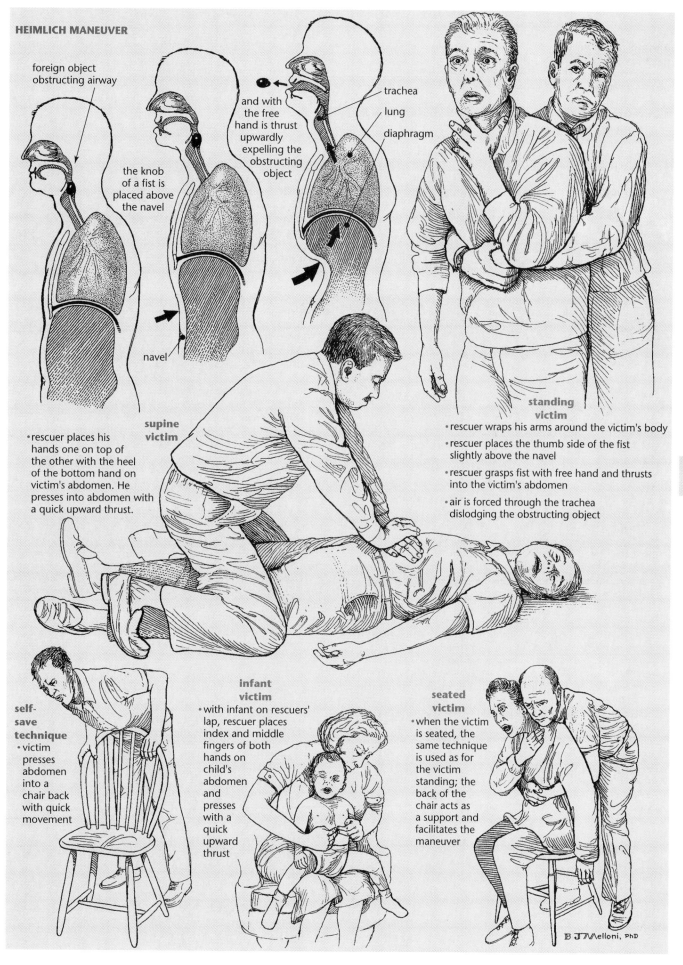

foreign object obstructing airway

the knob of a fist is placed above the navel

and with the free hand is thrust upwardly expelling the obstructing object

trachea

lung

diaphragm

navel

standing victim
- rescuer wraps his arms around the victim's body
- rescuer places the thumb side of the fist slightly above the navel
- rescuer grasps fist with free hand and thrusts into the victim's abdomen
- air is forced through the trachea dislodging the obstructing object

supine victim
- rescuer places his hands one on top of the other with the heel of the bottom hand on victim's abdomen. He presses into abdomen with a quick upward thrust.

self-save technique
- victim presses abdomen into a chair back with quick movement

infant victim
- with infant on rescuers' lap, rescuer places index and middle fingers of both hands on child's abdomen and presses with a quick upward thrust

seated victim
- when the victim is seated, the same technique is used as for the victim standing; the back of the chair acts as a support and facilitates the maneuver

B J Melloni, PhD

M

maniac (ma'ne-ak) Common imprecise and misleading term for a mentally disturbed (especially violent) person.

manic, maniacal (man'ik, mah-ni'ah-kal) Relating to mania.

manic-depressive (man'ik de-pres'iv) Relating to bipolar disorder; see under disorder.

manifestation (man-ĭ-fes-tā'shun) An observable sign or symptom.

   neurotic m. Defense mechanisms that handicap a person's daily living activities; they are used in an attempt to handle anxiety (e.g., phobias, dissociation, displacement, conversion).

   psychophysiologic m. Symptoms that are primarily physical with a partial emotional origin.

   psychotic m. The loss of contact with reality, impairing the person's ability to function in society; they indicate personality disintegration.

manikin (man'ĭ-kin) An anatomic model of the human body designed for practicing certain procedures.

maniphalanx (man-ĭ-fa'lanks) One of the bones (phalanges) of the fingers.

manipulation (mah-nip-u-la'shun) Therapy by the skillful use of the hands as practiced by orthopedists, physical therapists, osteopaths, and chiropractors (e.g., in aligning bones displaced by a fracture, reducing a dislocation, stretching a shortened muscle or tendon).

manner of death (man'ner of deth) In forensic pathology, a means by which death occurred; may be natural, suicide, homicide, accident, or (in cases where an unequivocal determination cannot be made) undetermined.

mannerism (man'er-izm) A distinguishing characteristic or behavior.

mannitol (man'ĭ-tol) A drug used intravenously as a short-term diuretic. Adverse effects include headache, dizziness, and confusion.

manometer (mah-nom'ĕ-ter) Instrument for measuring the pressure of gases and liquids.

manometric (man-o-met'rik) Relating to a manometer.

manometry (mah-nom'ĕ-tre) Measurement of the pressures of liquids and gases by means of a manometer.

   esophageal m. Measurement of the pressures within the esophagus and its ability to contract normally at one or more sites. Used in diagnosing achalasia and other disorders of the esophagus.

manslaughter (man'slot-er) The unjustifiable killing of one human being by another under circumstances devoid of deliberation, premeditation, and malice.

   involuntary m. *(a)* The unintentional killing of a person by an individual committing an unlawful but not felonious act (e.g., striking and killing a pedestrian while driving through a stop sign). *(b)* The unintentional killing of a person by committing a lawful act but without the requisite precautions associated with the act (e.g., a surgeon causing the death of a patient by performing surgery while intoxicated or under the influence of another drug, when no extenuating circumstances exist).

   voluntary m. The unpremeditated killing of another in a sudden heat of anger.

Mansonia (man-so'ne-ah) A widely distributed genus of mosquitoes, vectors of such disease-causing organisms as *Brugia malayi* and *Wuchereria bancrofti.*

manubrial (mah-nu'bre-al) Relating to the upper portion of the breastbone (sternum).

manubrium (mah-nu'bre-um) A body structure resembling a handle. When used alone, the term usually refers to the manubrium of the breastbone (sternum).

   m. of malleus The bony process of the largest of the auditory ossicles (malleus) in the middle ear chamber, attached to the inner surface of the eardrum (tympanic membrane).

   m. of sternum The upper portion of the breastbone (sternum), articulating with the collarbones (clavicles) and the cartilages of the first and second ribs on each side.

manus (ma'nus) Latin for hand.

   m. extensa Backward deviation of the hand.

   m. flexa Forward deviation of the hand.

   m. valga Deviation of the hand toward the side of the little finger (ulnar side).

   m. vara Deviation of the hand toward the side of the thumb (radial side).

map (map) A graphic representation of the relative positions of any parts or units.

   chromosome m. The specific linear arrangement of genes along the chromosomes. Also called gene map.

   gene m. See chromosome map.

mapping (map'ing) In genetics, the process of determining the relative locations of different genes on chromosomes.

marantic (mah-ran'tik) **1.** Marasmic. **2.** See nonbacterial thrombotic endocarditis, under endocarditis.

marasmic (mah-raz'mik) Relating to marasmus.

marasmus (mah-raz'mus) Gradual wasting of the body, caused by protein and calorie depletion and seen mostly in children.

marbling (mar'bling) In forensic pathology, the formation of a network of greenish black coloration on the skin of a corpse, along its superficial blood vessels; it occurs at a particular stage during the process of decomposition.

margin (mar'jin) **1.** The border or edge of a structure, such as the boundary of an organ and the area just adjacent to it. **2.** A quantity beyond that which is needed.

   anterior m. of fibula The crest on the anterior border of the fibula; the anterior intermuscular septum of the leg is secured to its upper three-fourths, and the superior retinaculum to the lower part.

   anterior pulmonary m. The ventral border of each lung that separates the costal and mediastinal surfaces.

   anterior m. of tibia The prominent subcutaneous ridge on the front surface of the tibia extending from the tuberosity (proximal end) to the medial malleolus (distal end); its entire length, except for the lower fourth quarter, forms a sharp crest that is popularly known as the shin.

   cervical m. An undulating line at the neck of a tooth representing the junction of enamel and cementum; it is covered by the gum (gingiva), which is attached near the cervical margin of the tooth by the epithelial attachment.

   ciliary m. of iris The outer border of the iris contiguous with the ciliary body.

   corneal m. See limbus of cornea, under limbus.

   falciform m. An arched fascial margin that forms the superior, lateral, and inferior boundaries of the saphenous opening (an aper-

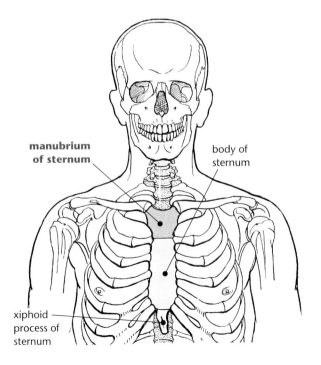

manubrium of sternum

body of sternum

xiphoid process of sternum

M

ture in the deep fascia at the front of the upper thigh, through which pass the great saphenous vein and other smaller vessels).

free gingival m. The edge of the gum tissue that is not directly attached to the tooth. Also called free gum margin.

free gum m. See free gingival margin.

infraorbital m. The lower border of the orbit formed by the maxillary and zygomatic bones.

lateral orbital m. The lateral edge of the orbit formed by the frontal process of the zygomatic bone (almost entirely) and the zygomatic process of the frontal bone.

medial orbital m. The medial edge of the orbit formed above by the frontal bone and below by the frontal process of the maxilla.

pupillary m. of iris The inner border of the iris, which surrounds the pupil of the eye.

right m. of heart The indefinite curved border of the right side of the heart between the sternocostal and diaphragmatic surfaces.

m. of safety A standard of drug safety predicated upon the margin between the therapeutic dose and the toxic dose.

supraorbital m. The superior edge of the orbit formed entirely by the frontal bone; it contains the supraorbital notch (or foramen), which transmits the supraorbital vessels and nerves.

m. of tongue The free lateral border on either side of the body of the tongue that separates the dorsum from the undersurface of the tongue.

margination (mar-jĭ-na′shun) Adhesion of white blood cells (leukocytes) to the interior of the capillary walls during early stages of inflammation.

marginoplasty (mar-jin′o-plas-te) Surgical procedure to repair the border of any structure (e.g., of the eyelid).

marijuana (mar-ĭ-hwan′ah) The dried, chopped leaves, flowers, and stems of the hemp plant *Cannabis sativa;* smoked or mixed into food to induce euphoria.

mark (mark) A skin blemish.

hesitation m.'s See hesitation scars, under scar.

port-wine m. See nevus flammeus, under nevus.

stretch m. See striae atrophicae, under stria.

marker (mark′er) A characteristic or factor by which a cell or molecule can be identified or a disease can be recognized.

cutaneous m. Any of various skin changes that serve as a sign of an internal (frequently malignant) disease.

genetic m. Any character that serves as a signpost of the presence or location of a gene in an individual in a given population.

tumor m. A substance secreted by a tumor and released into the blood and other body fluids; detection of its presence aids diagnosis of the tumor; examples include alpha-fetoprotein (AFP) for hepatoma and chorionic embryonic antigen (CEA) for colon cancer.

marmot (mar′mot) A rodent vector of ticks that transmit Rocky Mountain spotted fever. Also called groundhog; woodchuck.

marrow (mar′o) A medulla, especially of bone.

bone m. The soft tissue occupying the cavities of bones; it produces most of the cells that circulate in the blood (erythrocytes, leukocytes, and megakaryocytes). Also called marrow; medulla of bone; medulla ossium.

red m. The marrow found mainly within the spongy tissues of ribs, breastbone, and the ends of the long bones; it is the site of production of red blood cells and granular white blood cells.

yellow m. The material located mainly within the large cavities of large bones; consists mainly of fat cells and a few immature blood cells.

marsupialization (mar-su-pe-al-ĭ-za′shun) Surgical procedure for eradicating a cyst, whereby the cystic sac is opened and emptied, its anterior wall removed, and its edges sutured to the margins of the skin incision.

masculine (mas′ku-lin) Relating to the male sex.

masculinization (mas-ku-lin-ĭ-za′shun) 1. See virilization. 2. The normal attainment of secondary male characteristics.

mask (mask) **1.** A shield designed to cover the nose and mouth to preserve antiseptic conditions (i.e., in operating rooms), or to prevent the spread of an infectious disease when caring for patients. **2.** A device for administration of inhalation anesthesia. **3.** An expressionless facial appearance of people afflicted with certain diseases (e.g., Parkinson's disease; depression).

m. of pregnancy Popular term for melasma gravidarum; see under melasma.

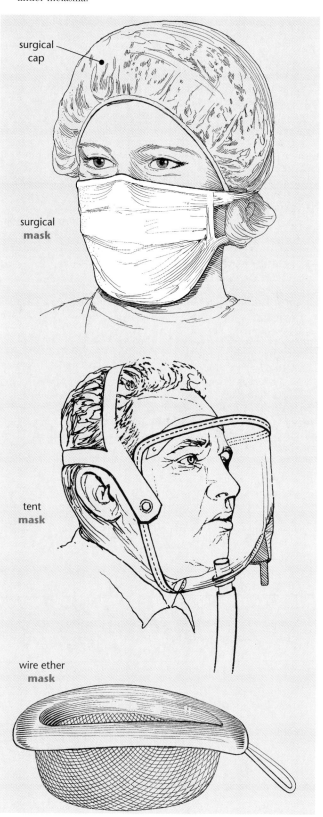

surgical cap

surgical **mask**

tent **mask**

wire ether **mask**

M11

margination ■ mask

masking (mask'ing) **1.** In audiology, the introduction of a noise in one ear to prevent that ear from hearing the test given to the other ear. **2.** In dentistry, the placing of an opaque material over the metal part or any other part of a denture.

masochism (mas'o-kizm) The derivation of pleasure from being subjected to physical or psychological pain or abuse either by one-self or by others; may be sought for sexual gratification or to relieve guilt.

masochist (mas'o-kist) One who derives pleasure (often sexual pleasure) from being subjected to physically or psychologically painful or humiliating experiences by others or by the self.

mass (mas) **1.** A body of coherent material. **2.** In pharmacy, a soft mix-ture of drugs suitable for rolling into pills.

  inner cell m. See embryoblast.

  lateral m. of atlas The solid parts of the first cervical vertebra on either side, articulating above with the occipital condyles of the skull and below with the second cervical vertebra.

massage (mah-sahzh') The therapeutic rubbing, kneading, tapping, etc., of areas of the body (e.g., to relieve painful muscle spasms, re-duce swelling due to water retention in tissues, and increase blood circulation).

  cardiac m. The manual rhythmic pressure to the ventricles of the heart to restore circulation. Also called open chest massage.

  closed chest m. The rhythmic compression of the heart be-tween the breastbone (sternum) and the spine (vertebral column) by applying pressure on the breastbone approximately 60 times per minute to restore circulation. Also called external cardiac massage.

  external cardiac m. See closed chest massage.

  gingival m. Stimulation of the gums by rubbing or pressing.

  open chest m. See cardiac massage.

  prostatic m. Pressing of the prostate with the pad of the index finger to express secretions into the urethra for diagnostic and ther-apeutic purposes.

masseter (mas-se'ter) See table of muscles.

massotherapy (mas-o-ther'ah-pe) The therapeutic use of massage.

Mastadenovirus (mast-ad'ĕ-no-vi'rus) Genus of viruses (family Adenoviridae) that infect humans, causing respiratory diseases and eye disorders (conjunctivitis and epidemic keratoconjunctivitis).

mastalgia (mas-tal'je-ah) See mastodynia.

mastatrophy, mastatrophia (mas-tat'ro-fe, mas-tah-tro'fe-ah) Atrophy of the breasts.

mastectomy (mas-tek'to-me) Removal of the breast. Also called mammectomy.

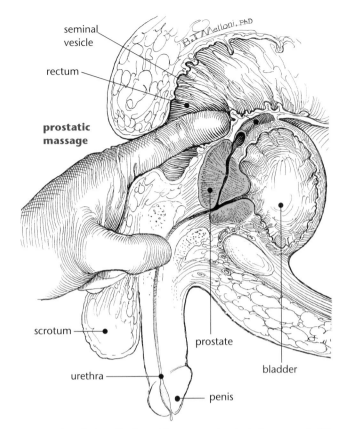

seminal vesicle
rectum
prostatic massage
scrotum
urethra
prostate
bladder
penis

  extended radical m. Mastectomy that includes removal of the underlying chest muscles, the axillary lymph nodes, and the internal mammary nodes.

  modified radical m. Removal of the breast, the connective tis-sue covering the greater pectoral (pectoralis major) muscle (but not the muscle), and the axillary lymph nodes.

  partial m. See segmental mastectomy.

  radical m. Removal of the breast, the underlying pectoral mus-cles, the axillary lymph nodes, and the associated skin and subcuta-neous tissue. Also called Halsted's operation.

  segmental m. Removal of part of the breast, or of a growth (e.g., quadrantectomy, lumpectomy) along with only enough breast

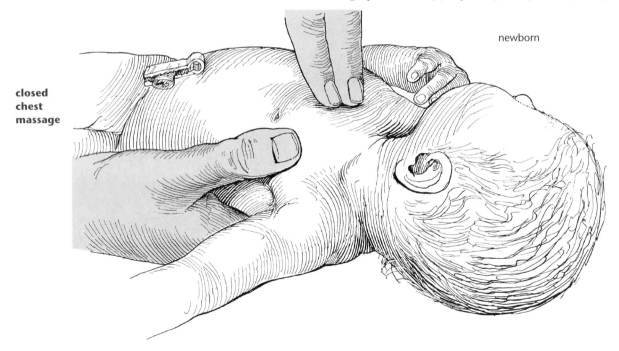

closed chest massage

newborn

tissue to ensure that the margins of the removed specimen are free of tumor. Also called partial mastectomy.

   simple m. Removal of the whole breast only. Also called total mastectomy.

   subcutaneous m. Removal of breast with preservation of overlying skin, areola, and nipple in order to reconstruct breast form.

   total m. See simple mastectomy.

masticate (mas′tĭ-kāt) To chew.

mastication (mas-tĭ-ka′shun) The process of chewing.

mastitis (mas-ti′tis) Inflammation of breast tissue. Also called mammitis.

   chronic cystic m. See fibrocystic disease of the breast, under disease.

   infectious m. Acute condition in which one breast (often only one quadrant) becomes tender, reddened, swollen, and hot; the patient develops fever and appears ill; occurs as a complication of breast-feeding usually affecting first-time mothers; caused by a microorganism, especially *Staphylococcus aureus,* which gains entry through cracks in the nipple. Also called puerperal mastitis; postpartum mastitis; lactational mastitis.

   interstitial m. Inflammation of connective tissue within the breast.

   lactational m. See infectious mastitis.

   phlegmonous m. Diffuse breast inflammation, sometimes accompanied by abscess formation.

   plasma cell m. A chronic noncancerous condition characterized mainly by dilatation and obstruction of lactiferous ducts with masses of dried secretions and plasma cells; usually seen in perimenopausal women; may cause nipple retraction resembling breast cancer.

   postpartum m. See infectious mastitis.

   puerperal m. See infectious mastitis.

masto-, mast- Combining forms meaning breast.

mastocyte (mas′to-sit) See mast cell, under cell.

mastocytogenesis (mas-to-si′to-jen′ĕ-sis) The formation of mast cells.

mastocytoma (mas-to-si-to′mah) A benign nodule resembling a tumor, composed chiefly of mast cells.

mastocytosis (mas-to-si-to′sis) A group of diseases characterized by proliferation of mast cells.

mastodynia (mas-to-din′e-ah) Pain in the breast. Also called mastalgia.

mastoid (mas′toid) The downward projection of the temporal bone, behind the ear.

mastoidectomy (mas-toi-dek′to-me) Any operation entailing removal of a portion of the mastoid bone or hollowing out of the mastoid air cells, especially as a treatment for mastoiditis or otitis; rarely indicated since the advent of antibiotics.

mastoideocentesis (mas-toi′de-o-sen-te′sis) Surgical creation of an opening into the mastoid air cells.

mastoiditis (mas-toi-di′tis) Inflammation of the mastoid process of the temporal bone (behind the ear).

mastopathy (mas-top′ah-the) Any disease of the breast.

mastopexy (mas′to-pek-se) Procedure for correction of sagging breasts; it involves repositioning of the areola and nipple in a higher location, above the level of the inferior fold of the breast (inframammary fold), and tightening of the skin for support.

mastoplasty (mas′to-plas-te) See mammoplasty.

mastoptosis (mas-to-to′sis) Sagging breasts.

mastotomy (mas-tot′o-me) A surgical cut into a breast.

masturbation (mas-tur-ba′shun) Self-manipulation of the genitals for sexual excitement.

matching (mach′ing) In epidemiology, the process of making a group under study and a comparison group comparable regarding extraneous factors.

materia (mah-te′re-ah) Latin for matter; substance.

   m. alba Whitish deposit on teeth composed mainly of food debris.

   m. medica The branch of science concerned with the study of medicinal drugs in all their aspects.

material (mah-te′re-al) The substance of which something is made.

   radiopaque m. See contrast medium, under medium.

maternal (mah-ter′nal) Relating to a mother.

maternity (mah-ter′nĭ-te) **1.** The state of being a mother or pregnant. **2.** Relating to childbirth (e.g., a section of the hospital).

matricide (mat′rĭ-sīd) The killing of one's mother.

matrilineal (ma-trī-lin′e-al) In genetics, inherited through the maternal line.

matrix (ma′triks), pl. ma′trices **1.** The intercellular substance of any tissue. **2.** A mold from which a dental restoration is made.

   nail m. See nail bed, under bed.

matter (mat′er) Substance.

   gray m. The gray portion of the brain and spinal cord consisting primarily of cell bodies of neurons along with dendritic trees, initial axon segments, and the terminal segments and synaptic endings of axons associated with them, together with glial cells and blood vessels. Also called gray substance; substantia grisea.

   white m. The pinkish white opalescent portion of the brain and spinal cord consisting primarily of nerve fibers covered by a laminated lipoprotein sheath of myelin that is derived from neighboring glial cells. Also called white substance; substantia alba.

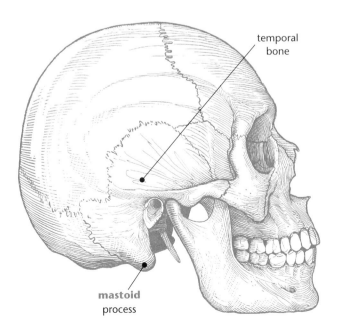

temporal bone

mastoid process

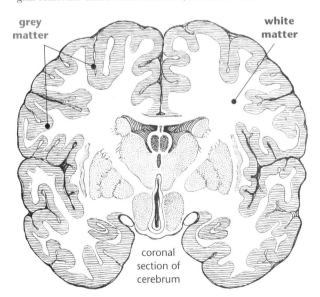

grey matter

white matter

coronal section of cerebrum

masticate ■ matter

matting (mat'ing) A cohesive, enlarged state, as of lymph nodes in certain infections (e.g., tuberculosis).

maturate (mat'u-rāt) To bring to maturity; to cause to ripen.

maturation (mat-u-ra'shun) 1. The process of attaining full development. 2. The process by which a primitive cell reaches its final structure and functional capacity. 3. A stage in cell division in which the number of chromosomes in the sex cells (spermatozoon and ovum) is reduced to one-half the number characteristic of the species.

mature (mah-tūr') 1. Fully developed. 2. To attain full development.

maturity (mah-tu'rĭ-te) The state of being mature.

maxilla (mak-sil'ah), pl. maxil'lae One of a pair of bones forming the upper jaw; it holds the upper teeth. See also table of bones.

maxillary (mak'sĭ-ler-e) Relating to the upper jaw (maxillae).

maxillectomy (mak-sĭ-lek'to-me) Removal of a portion of the upper jaw.

maxillofacial (mak-sil-o-fa'shal) Relating to the upper jaw and the face.

maximum (mak'sĭ-mum) The most.

   glucose transport m. (glucose Tm) The maximum rate at which the kidneys can reabsorb glucose (about 300 mg per minute).

   transport m., tubular m. (Tm) The maximum ability of the renal tubules to reabsorb or to secrete a substance.

maxwell (maks'wel) An electromagnetic unit of the CGS system of units; replaced in the SI system by the weber.

maze (māz) An intricate pattern of walled pathways for studying the learning process of experimental animals.

meal (mēl) Food.

   Boyden m. Meal for testing the evacuation time of the gallbladder; consists of four egg yolks and milk mixed with sugar or port wine.

   test m. Any bland food (e.g., toast and tea) given before analysis of stomach secretions.

mean (mēn) The numerical average. Without qualification, the term refers to the arithmetic mean.

   arithmetic m. An average; the sum of all individual values divided by the number of values in the group.

measle (me'zel) The larva of the tapeworm.

measles (me'zelz) A highly contagious disease marked by high fever, cough, inflammation of respiratory tract, eruption of white (Koplik's) spots in the mouth, and a reddish skin rash; caused by a paramyxovirus; incubation period is about 10 days; complications that may sometimes occur include pneumonia and encephalitis. Also called rubeola.

   German m. See rubella.

measly (me'zle) Containing tapeworm larvae.

measurement (mezh'er-ment) The dimensions, quantity, or capacity of something determined by measuring.

meatal (me-a'tal) Relating to a body opening (meatus).

meato- Combining form meaning a body opening.

meatometer (me-ah-tom'ĕ-ter) A device for measuring a body opening (e.g., an orifice of the urethra).

meatoplasty (me'ah-to-plas-te) Reconstructive surgery of the external auditory canal or the urethral meatus.

meatoscope (me-at'o-skōp) Instrument for visual examination of the internal urethral orifice.

meatoscopy (me-ah-tos'ko-pe) Examination of the internal urethral orifice with a meatoscope.

meatotome (me-at'o-tōm) Knife used in meatotomy.

meatotomy (me-ah-tot'o-me) A cut made into a urethral orifice to enlarge its diameter.

meatus (me-a'tus), pl. mea'tuses or mea'tus A passageway in the body, or its external opening.

   m. acusticus externus See external auditory canal, under canal.

   m. acusticus internus See internal auditory canal, under canal.

   external acoustic m. See external auditory canal, under canal.

   external auditory m. See external auditory canal, under canal.

   external m. of female urethra See external orifice of female urethra, under orifice.

   external m. of male urethra See external orifice of male urethra, under orifice.

   inferior nasal m. The part of the nasal cavity below and lateral to the inferior nasal concha; it allows the nasolacrimal duct to communicate with the nasal cavity. Also called inferior meatus of nose.

   inferior m. of nose See inferior nasal meatus.

   internal acoustic m. See internal auditory canal, under canal.

   internal auditory m. See internal auditory canal, under canal.

   internal m. of urethra See internal orifice of urethra, under orifice.

   middle nasal m. The part of the nasal cavity below and lateral to the middle nasal concha; it serves as the passageway from which the anterior ethmoidal cells and the frontal and maxillary sinuses communicate with the nasal cavity. Also called middle meatus of nose.

   middle m. of nose See middle nasal meatus.

   nasopharyngeal m. The passage in the posterior part of the nasal cavity from the back part of the turbinates to the choanae.

   superior nasal m. The part of the nasal cavity below and lateral to the superior nasal concha; it serves as the passageway from which the posterior ethmoidal cells communicate with the nasal cavity. Also called superior meatus of nose.

   superior m. of nose See superior nasal meatus.

   urethral m. See external orifice of female urethra; external orifice of male urethra; and internal urethral orifice, all under orifice.

mechanics (mĭ-kan'iks) The science dealing with energy and forces acting on solids, liquids, or gases either in motion or at rest.

   body m. Muscular action in relation to body movement and posture.

mechanism (mek'ah-nizm) 1. An aggregation of parts that interact to perform a common function. 2. The means by which some result is obtained.

   m. of action The process through which a substance (e.g., drug, hormone) produces its effects.

   association m. Mental process through which past experiences may be related to current ones.

   coping m. Any of various ways (conscious or unconscious) that people use to adjust to their surroundings.

   countercurrent m. A mechanism essential to the production of osmotically concentrated urine; it involves two basic processes: countercurrent multiplication of the nephronic (Henle's) loop and countercurrent exchange in the medullary blood vessels (vasa recta). Similar mechanisms are used in heat exchanges.

   defense m. (a) Any of the various, usually unconscious techniques (e.g., denial, repression, projection) used by the mind as a means of coping with unpleasant or unwelcome experiences, events, emotions, or impulses; they serve as a protection against awareness of conflicts and the experiences of anxiety. (b) The immune system.

   immunologic m. The immune system.

   pressoreceptive m. Process through which certain areas of the body (especially the carotid sinuses and aortic arch) react to a stimulus such as a rise in blood pressure.

   proprioceptive m. Process by which the body regulates its muscular movements and maintains its equilibrium.

mechanocardiography (mek'ah-no-kar'de-og'rah-fe) The use of tracings representing the mechanical effects of the heartbeat.

mechanoreceptor (mek'ah-no-re-sep'tor) Any receptor that responds to mechanical pressure (e.g., touch receptors in the skin).

meclizine hydrochloride (mek'lĭ-zēn hi-dro-klo'rĭd) Antihistamine drug used in the prevention and treatment of motion sickness and nausea caused by vestibular disorders of the ear (e.g., Ménière's disease) and chemotherapy. Probable adverse effects include drowsiness, dry mouth, and blurred vision.

M

meclofenamate (mĕ-klo-fen-am′āt) A nonsteroidal anti-inflammatory drug (NSAID); used to reduce stiffness and pain of osteoarthritis and rheumatoid arthritis. Adverse effects include nausea and diarrhea.

mecometer (mē-kom′ĕ-ter) Instrument for measuring the newborn infant.

meconiorrhea (mĕ-ko-ne-o-re′ah) Passage of an abnormally large amount of meconium by the newborn infant.

meconium (mĕ-ko′ne-um) The dark green intestinal contents formed before birth and present in a newborn infant.

media (me′de-ah) 1. The middle layer of blood vessel walls. 2. Plural of medium.

mediad (me′de-ad) Toward the midline.

medial (me′de-al) 1. Relating to the middle. 2. Situated near the median plane of the body or an organ. 3. Relating to the middle layer of a blood vessel wall.

median (me′de-an) 1. Situated in the middle or midline; central. 2. In statistics, denoting the middle value (i.e., the point at which half of the plotted values are on one side and half on the other).

mediastinal (me-de-as-ti′nal) Relating to the mediastinum.

mediastinitis (me-de-as-tĭ-ni′tis) Inflammation of tissues in the central compartment of the chest cavity (mediastinum), usually resulting from infection introduced through a perforation of the esophagus or of the trachea by trauma (e.g., penetrating wounds, ingestion of corrosives, excessive forceful vomiting, surgical procedures); by instrumentation (e.g., endoscopy, dilatation, introduction of endotracheal tubes); or by invading cancer and spread of chronic diseases (e.g., actinomycosis, tuberculosis, histoplasmosis).

mediastinography (me-de-as-tĭ-nog′rah-fe) X-ray examination of the central compartment of the chest cavity (mediastinum).

mediastinopericarditis (me-de-as-tĭ-no-per-ĭ-kar-di′tis) Inflammation of the central compartment of the chest cavity (mediastinum) and the sac enveloping the heart (pericardium).

mediastinoscope (me-de-ah-sti′no-skōp) Instrument consisting of a tube equipped with a light and lens used in mediastinoscopy.

mediastinoscopy (me-de-as-tĭ-nos′ko-pe) A diagnostic exploration of the mediastinum, under anesthesia, through a transverse incision at the base of the neck (usually 2 cm above the suprasternal notch); it permits access to the lymph nodes overlying the trachea for biopsy.

mediastinotomy (me-de-as-ti-not′o-me) Surgical cut into the mediastinum.

mediastinum (me-de-as-ti′num), pl. mediasti′na 1. The central space in the chest bounded anteriorly by the breastbone (sternum), posteriorly by the spine (vertebral column), and laterally by the pleural sacs. Also called interpleural space. 2. A septum between two parts of an organ.

   anterior m. The portion of the lower mediastinum bounded behind by the pericardium, in front by the body of the sternum, and on each side by the pleura; it contains, among other structures, part of the thymus gland, a few lymph nodes, and loose areolar tissue.

   inferior m. See lower mediastinum.

   lower m. The three lower portions of the mediastinum (below the plane that extends from the manubriosternal joint to the lower border of the fourth vertebra); it is subdivided into anterior, middle, and posterior mediastina. Also called inferior mediastinum.

   middle m. The broadest portion of the lower mediastinum; it contains, among other structures, the bifurcation of the trachea into two bronchi, a large part of the roots of the lungs, some tracheobronchial lymph nodes, the heart enclosed in the pericardium, and adjacent parts of the great vessels.

   posterior m. The portion of the lower mediastinum behind the heart, in front of the vertebral column, and between the pleurae of the lungs; it contains, among other structures, the esophagus, descending thoracic aorta, thoracic duct, vagus nerves, and many lymph nodes.

   superior m. See upper mediastinum.

   m. testis A thick, incomplete vertical septum extending along the upper two-thirds of the posterior border of the testis; it is continuous with the tunica albuginea and gives off septa, which divide the organ into a number of cone-shaped lobules containing the seminiferous tubules; it conveys blood and lymphatic vessels of the testis.

   upper m. The portion of the mediastinum from the level of the manubriosternal joint to the root of the neck (plane of thoracic inlet); it contains, among other structures, the aortic arch (with its branches), brachiocephalic veins, upper half of the superior vena cava, vagus nerves, trachea, esophagus, thoracic duct, thymus gland, and some lymph nodes. Also called superior mediastinum.

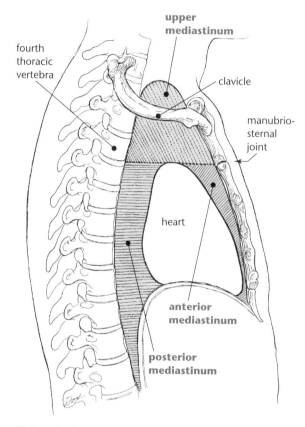

mediator (me′de-a-tor) Anything that functions in an intermediary capacity (e.g., a chemical substance).

medicable (med′ĭ-kah-bl) Potentially curable by drug therapy.

medical (med′ĭ-kal) 1. Relating to medicine. 2. Medicinal.

medicament (med′ĭ-kah-ment) A remedy.

medicamentous (med-ĭ-kah-men′tus) Relating to a drug.

medicate (med′ĭ-kāt) 1. To treat disease with drugs. 2. To permeate with a medicinal substance.

medicated (med′ĭ-kāt-ed) 1. Treated medicinally. 2. Impregnated with a medicinal substance.

medication (med-ĭ-ka′shun) 1. A drug. 2. The administration of drugs.

   ionic m. See iontophoresis.

medicinal (me-dis′ĭ-nal) Having curative properties.

medicine (med′ĭ-sin) 1. The science concerned with diagnosing and treating disease and the maintenance of health. 2. Any substance used in the treatment of disease.

   addiction m. A subspecialty concerned with evaluation and treatment of patients with drug use disorders; it includes such topics as risk factors for developing substance abuse disorders, transmission of human immunodeficiency virus (HIV), and the presence of coexisting (comorbid) psychiatric disorders.

   adolescent m. The branch of medicine concerned with individuals in the approximate age-group between the onset of puberty and 20 years.

M

alternative m. Any therapeutic system that usually has no satisfactory scientific explanation for its effectiveness. The term does not refer to therapies of unknown or unproven value.

chiropractic m. See chiropractic.

clinical m. The study and practice of medicine at the bedside (i.e., by direct examination and observation of patients as opposed to theoretical, classroom, or laboratory study).

community m. Health care focused on the needs of the community rather than of the individual (e.g., public health services, preventive measures). Also called population medicine.

critical care m. Medical subspecialty concerned with the care of medical and surgical patients whose conditions are life-threatening and require comprehensive care and constant monitoring; it involves relevant areas of anesthesiology, surgery, internal medicine, and pediatrics. Also called intensive care medicine.

defensive m. The performance of diagnostic tests and procedures primarily as protection against any charge of malpractice.

emergency m. The branch of medicine concerned with the acutely (often suddenly) ill or injured person.

experimental m. Medical research based on experimentation with animals and on clinical studies.

family m. The branch of medicine concerned with provision of primary care for all members of the family unit.

folk m. Treatment of ailments by using home remedies and measures handed down from generation to generation.

forensic m. The branch of medicine concerned with the application and practice of medical knowledge to the solution of problems associated with the administration of justice. It includes the medical information and testimony to be presented in judicial or quasi-judicial settings (e.g., before trials and hearings) as well as formal legal investigations. Also called legal medicine; medical jurisprudence.

geriatric m. Medical specialty concerned with the diagnosis, treatment, and prevention of disease in the elderly. Also called geriatrics.

holistic m. Medical care provided from the perspective that organisms function as complete integrated units instead of aggregates of separate parts.

industrial m. Obsolete term for occupational medicine.

intensive care m. See critical care medicine.

internal m. The branch of medicine that deals with nonsurgical treatment of disease of the adult.

laboratory m. The branch of medicine concerned with performance of laboratory procedures used in clinical diagnosis or for monitoring therapy.

legal m. See forensic medicine.

mail-order m. Derogatory term commonly used in reference to the practice of relying heavily on test results in making therapeutic decisions.

neonatal m. See neonatology.

nuclear m. The branch of medicine concerned with the use of radioactive substances (radionuclides) to diagnose and treat certain types of disease.

occupational m. A branch of medicine concerned with the effects of the work environment on workers' health and with preventing disease and injury at the workplace. Formerly called industrial medicine. Also called occupational and environmental medicine.

occupational and environmental m. See occupational medicine.

osteopathic m. See osteopathy.

perinatal m. See perinatology.

physical m. See physical medicine and rehabilitation.

physical m. and rehabilitation (PMR) The branch of medicine that predominantly uses mechanical methods and physical agents (heat, light, electricity, mechanical devices) for the diagnosis, treatment, and prevention of disease; it includes restorative therapies to overcome disabilities or impairments and the establishment of re-

habilitation programs. Also called physiatrics; physical medicine; rehabilitation medicine.

podiatric m. See podiatry.

population m. See community medicine.

preventive m. The branch of medicine concerned with preventing disease and disability of individuals and of whole populations; e.g., by public health measures (purification of water supplies), treatment (immunization), screening programs to detect diseases such as glaucoma and genetic conditions.

primary care m. Medical service provided by a physician who offers a wide range of diagnostic and therapeutic procedures and, especially in nonemergent situations, is the physician to whom the patient reports. Primary care medicine is practiced by generalists in internal medicine, family practice, and pediatrics.

proprietary m. A medicinal preparation that is the property of the maker and, by patent or trademark, is protected against imitation.

pulmonary m. Medical specialty concerned with diagnosis and treatment of lung diseases.

rehabilitation m. See physical medicine and rehabilitation.

socialized m. A medical care system regulated by a government agency in which practitioners receive standardized compensation and to which the public contributes through taxation.

space m. The field of medicine concerned with the effects of space travel on the body.

sports m. The field of medicine concerned with the diagnosis, care, and prevention of injuries sustained in any athletic activity.

transfusion m. A subspecialty of either clinical pathology or internal medicine that is concerned with the therapeutic administration of blood or blood products; it involves relevant areas of hematology, immunology, and infectious diseases. Legal issues of transfusion medicine center around the purity of the transfused product (i.e., whether it is free of infectious material, especially hepatitis and human immunodeficiency virus), or whether a person has the right to refuse a medically appropriate and potentially lifesaving transfusion. Also called blood banking.

tropical m. Medical specialty concerned with diseases characteristic of hot or warm climates.

veterinary m. The field concerned with diagnosis and treatment of diseases of animals.

medicolegal (med-ĭ-ko-le′gal) Relating to overlapping aspects of the health professions and the law, especially those medical matters called before a court of law; applied to matters concerning damages, which may include injuries due to medical negligence or malpractice, medical evidence of injury in a civil action, mental competence of people who have drawn legal documents, commitment of the mentally ill to mental institutions, and the use of tests for determining paternity; may also relate to such matters as a person's right to die, sterilization, artificial insemination, *in vitro* fertilization, surrogacy, and the right to confidentiality (particularly in the context of AIDS). For medical aspects of criminal law, see forensic medicine, under medicine.

mediocarpal (me-de-o-kar′pal) See midcarpal.

medionecrosis (me-de-o-ne-kro′sis) Tissue death in the middle layer of arterial walls.

m. of the aorta See cystic medial necrosis, under necrosis.

meditation (med-ĭ-ta′shun) Concentration on one thing (e.g., an object, word, or idea) with the intention of inducing an altered state of mind.

transcendental m. (TM) An exercise of contemplation that induces a temporary feeling of complete relaxation, a sense of well-being, and a state associated with changes in physiologic function (including a reduction of oxygen consumption, decrease in cardiac output, and altered brain wave activity).

medium (me′de-um), pl. me′dia or me′diums **1.** A substance through which something is transmitted. **2.** A substance in which interactions take place. **3.** An intervening substance. **4.** See culture medium.

clearing m. Substance used in histology to make tissues or cells transparent.

contrast m. In radiology, a substance (e.g., barium) that blocks the passage of x rays or any other form of radiation; introduced into or around a structure to provide contrast with surrounding tissues and allow visualization of the structure in x-ray or fluoroscopic examinations; those materials used intravenously or intra-arterially (e.g., in intravenous pyelography angiography) usually consist of iodinated compounds. Also called radiopaque medium; radiopaque substance; radiopaque material.

culture m. Any substance used for the cultivation of bacteria. Frequently called medium.

radiopaque m. See contrast medium.

selective m. Culture medium that limits growth to only one type of bacteria.

separating m. In dentistry, substance for coating impressions to facilitate removal of the cast.

MEDLARS Acronym for Medical Literature Analysis and Retrieval System; a computerized system of databases operated by the National Library of Medicine (in Bethesda, Maryland), containing citations of the world's biomedical literature; may be accessed by anyone.

MEDLINE (MEDLARS–on-line) One of the on-line databases of MEDLARS, extending from 1966 to the present; it is updated monthly.

medroxyprogesterone acetate (med-rok-se-pro-jes'ter-ōn as'e-tāt) Preparation used in combination with ethynyl estradiol as an oral contraceptive.

medulla (me-dul'ah), pl. medul'lae **1.** Any centrally located soft tissue. **2.** The marrow of bone or any similar structure. **3.** Any part of an organ situated more centrally than the cortex.

adrenal m. The inner, reddish brown portion of the adrenal (suprarenal) gland containing masses of granular chromaffin cells permeated by venous sinusoids; the cells elaborate epinephrine and norepinephrine, which are released directly into the sinusoids by such stimuli as anger, fright, or stress; the sinusoids open into the suprarenal vein at the hilum of the gland.

m. of bone See bone marrow, under marrow.

m. of hair shaft The innermost core of the shaft of coarse hair, surrounded by the cortex and the cuticle.

m. of kidney The inner portion of the kidney that lies deep to the cortex; it contains very few glomeruli and consists of a number of striated conical masses (renal pyramids) with bases extending toward the periphery as far as the arcuate vessels, while the apices converge toward the renal sinus, where they form prominent papillae projecting into the interior of the calices.

m. of lymph node The inner, darker portion of the lymph node, composed of a stroma of reticular fibers containing cordlike masses of lymphocytes, plasma cells, and macrophages separated by lymph sinuses; it reaches the surface of the node at the hilum, where it directly contributes to the single efferent lymphatic vessel leaving the node.

m. oblongata The oblong, caudal portion of the brain stem extending from the lower margin of the pons to the beginning of the spinal cord at the level of the upper border of the first cervical vertebra; it contains the involuntary centers that control the heart, the blood vessels, and the respiratory organs.

m. ossium See bone marrow, under marrow.

m. of ovary The inner core of the ovary, composed of loose fibroelastic tissue containing smooth muscles, lymphatics, nerves, and a mass of large contorted blood vessels; it is surrounded by a thick cortex containing the ovarian follicles and corpora lutea.

medullary (med'u-lār-e) **1.** Relating to a medulla. **2.** Resembling bone marrow.

medullated (med'u-lāt-ed) Containing, or covered with, a soft marrowlike substance.

medullation (med-u-la'shun) The formation of marrow or a medulla.

medullization (med-u-lī-za'shun) Abnormal enlargement of bone marrow spaces (e.g., in rarefying osteosis).

medulloblastoma (mĕ-dul-o-blas-to'mah) A rapidly growing tumor of the cerebellum occurring in the first two decades of life and causing progressive cerebellar dysfunction.

mefenamic acid (mef-ĕ-nam'ik as'id) A nonsteroidal antiinflammatory drug (NSAID) with analgesic properties; useful in relieving pain of endometriosis and arthritis. Adverse effects may include nausea, vomiting, and, after prolonged use, peptic ulcer and hemolytic anemia.

mega- Combining form meaning large.

megacephalic (meg-ah-sĕ-fal'ik) See macrocephalic.

megacephalous (meg-ah-sef'ah-lus) See macrocephalous.

megacephaly (meg-ah-sef'ah-le) See macrocephaly.

megacolon (meg-ah-ko'lon) Abnormally large colon.

congenital m. Condition resulting from absence of ganglion (nerve) cells at the junction of the rectum and colon; the aganglionic area of the intestine is unable to relax during normal intestinal movements, producing constriction, constipation, and distention of the colon; eventually the entire colon (including the appendix) may become dilated; in the newborn infant, symptoms include a distended abdomen, failure to pass meconium, and vomiting of a bilious

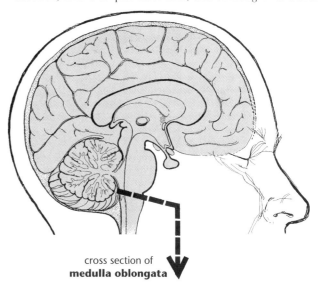

cross section of
medulla oblongata

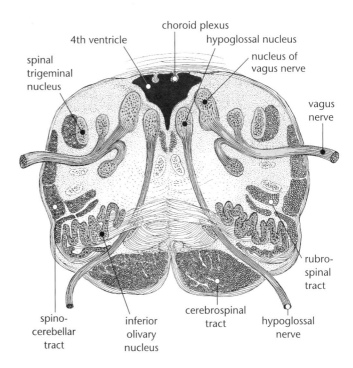

spinal trigeminal nucleus — 4th ventricle — choroid plexus — hypoglossal nucleus — nucleus of vagus nerve — vagus nerve — rubrospinal tract — hypoglossal nerve — cerebrospinal tract — inferior olivary nucleus — spinocerebellar tract

material. Also called Hirschsprung's disease; congenital aganglionic megacolon.

congenital aganglionic m. See congenital megacolon.

idiopathic m., acquired m. Megacolon that is not due to absence of ganglion cells but in which the bowel walls are distended and thin; seen in both children and adults.

toxic m. Megacolon occurring in acute ulcerative colitis; at that degree of dilatation there is marked risk of perforation of the colon.

megadactyly (meg-ah-dak′tĭ-le) See macrodactyly.

megadyne (meg′ah-dīn) Unit of force equal to 1 million dynes.

megaesophagus (meg-ah-ĕ-sof′ah-gus) A grossly distended lower portion of the esophagus (close to the stomach); seen in patients with achalasia.

megakaryoblast (meg-ah-kar′e-o-blast) The precursor cell of a megakaryocyte.

megakaryocyte (meg-ah-kar′e-o-sīt) The largest cell in bone marrow; it gives rise to the blood platelet.

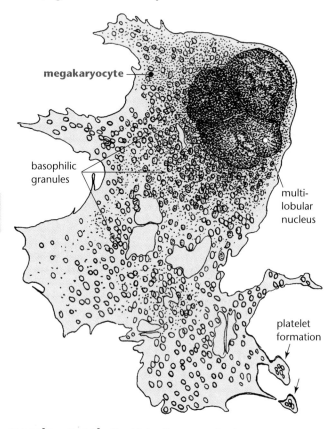

megalo-, megal- Combining forms meaning large.

megaloblast (meg′ah-lo-blast) Large embryonic red blood cell found in bone marrow in pernicious anemia and in folic acid deficiency states.

megalocardia (meg-ah-lo-kar′de-ah) See cardiomegaly.

megalocheiria (meg-ah-lo-ki′re-ah) See macrocheiria.

megalocornea (meg-ah-lo-kor′ne-ah) Developmental eye anomaly in which an otherwise normal cornea is abnormally large at birth and continues to grow in diameter; the pressure within the eye remains normal, a feature that distinguishes this condition from buphthalmos. Also called macrocornea.

megalodactyly (meg-ah-lo-dak′tĭ-le) See macrodactyly.

megalogastria (meg-ah-lo-gas′tre-ah) Abnormally large size of the stomach.

megalomania (meg-ah-lo-ma′ne-ah) A psychopathologic condition characterized by unfounded conviction of one's own great importance and power.

megalomelia (meg-ah-lo-me′le-ah) See macromelia.

megalopenis (meg-ah-lo-pe′nis) Abnormally large penis.

megalosplenia (meg-ah-lo-sple′ne-ah) See splenomegaly.

megaloureter (meg-ah-lo-u-re′ter) Excessive dilatation of a ureter without obstruction. Also called megaureter.

megarectum (meg-ah-rek′tum) Abnormally dilated rectum.

megasigmoid (meg-ah-sig′moid) Abnormally dilated sigmoid colon.

-megaly Suffix meaning enlargement (e.g., acromegaly).

megaureter (meg-ah-u-re′ter) See megaloureter.

megavolt (meg′ah-vōlt) (MV) One million volts; a unit of electromotive force.

megavoltage (meg-ah-vol′tij) Electromotive force in excess of 1 million volts; used in radiation therapy.

megestrol (mĕ-jes′trōl) A progesterone drug with anticancer properties, used when other anticancer drugs and radiation therapy are ineffective. Possible adverse effects include dizziness, skin rash, swollen ankles, and elevation of blood calcium levels.

meglumine diatrizoate (meg′lu-mēn di-ah-tri-zo′āt) Radiopaque compound used as a contrast medium in the making of x-ray pictures. Also called methylglucamine diatrizoate.

megohm (meg′ōm) One million ohms; a unit of electric resistance.

meibomianitis (mi-bo-me-ah-ni′tis) Inflammation of the meibomian (tarsal) glands of the eyelid.

meiosis (mi-o′sis) A special type of cell division that occurs only in the ovaries and testes during maturation of the germ cells (the forerunners of eggs and sperm cells); two cell divisions occur in rapid succession, forming four daughter cells, each containing half the number of chromosomes found in the general body cells.

meiotic (mi-ot′ik) Relating to meiosis.

mel (mel) Honey, especially the refined form used in pharmaceutical preparations.

melalgia (mel-al′je-ah) Pain in the leg.

melancholia (mel-an-ko′le-ah) A severe form of depression characterized by loss of pleasure in almost all usual activities; symptoms include excessive or inappropriate guilt, psychomotor retardation, anorexia, and disordered sleep usually with early morning wakening and worsening of the depression in the morning. See also major depression, under depression; affective disorders, under disorder.

melancholic (mel-an-kol′ik) Relating to melancholia.

melaniferous (mel-ah-nif′er-us) Containing the pigment melanin.

melanin (mel′ah-nin) The dark natural pigment of the skin and hair; also present in other tissues of the body. Also called melanotic pigment.

melanism (mel′ah-nizm) See melanosis.

melano-, melan- Combining forms meaning black.

melanoameloblastoma (mel′ah-no-ah-mel′o-blas-to′mah) See melanotic neuroectodermal tumor, under tumor.

melanoblast (mel′ah-no-blast) A precursor of the melanocyte.

melanocyte (mel′ah-no-sit) Mature pigment cell of the skin that produces melanin.

melanoderma (mel-ah-no-der′mah) Excessive melanin pigmentation of the skin.

melanodermatitis (mel-ah-no-der-mah-ti′tis) Dermatitis associated with excessive melanin pigmentation of the skin.

melanogen (mĕ-lan′o-jen) Colorless substance that, under certain conditions, may be converted to melanin.

melanogenemia (mel-ah-no-je-ne′me-ah) The presence of melanin precursors in the blood; may occur in disseminated malignant melanoma.

melanogenesis (mel-ah-no-jen′ĕ-sis) The formation of melanin.

melanoma (mel-ah-no′ma) A malignant tumor derived from pigment-producing cells (melanocytes), occurring usually in the skin and (less commonly) the eye, oral cavity, genitalia, and other sites that contain melanocytes. Melanomas vary in appearance and rate of growth and metastasis but generally they grow and spread rapidly and have four distinguishing features known as the ABCD of melanoma: *Asymmetry,* one half of the tumor is unlike the other half; *Border* is irregular, scalloped, and poorly circumscribed; *Color* varies from one area of the tumor to another; *Diameter* is, as a rule, larger than 6 mm (diameter of a pencil eraser). The tumor's pigment ranges from light brown and white to red and bluish black. Also called malignant melanoma.

megakaryocyte

basophilic granules

multi-lobular nucleus

platelet formation

M

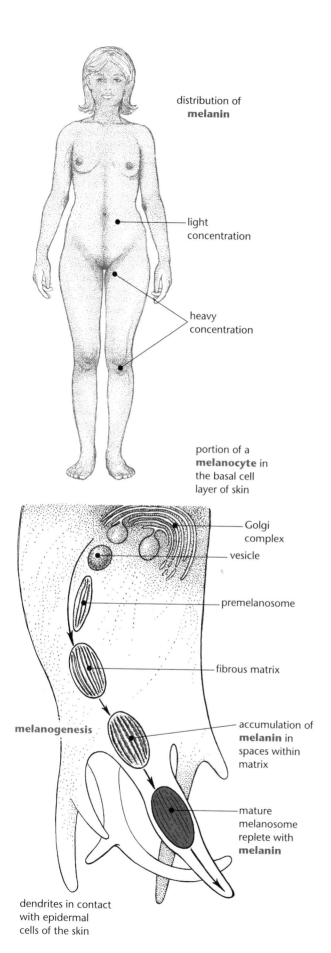

distribution of **melanin**

light concentration

heavy concentration

portion of a **melanocyte** in the basal cell layer of skin

Golgi complex

vesicle

premelanosome

fibrous matrix

accumulation of **melanin** in spaces within matrix

mature melanosome replete with **melanin**

melanogenesis

dendrites in contact with epidermal cells of the skin

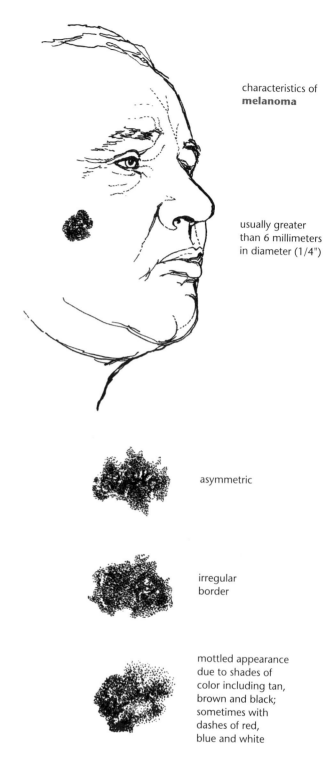

characteristics of **melanoma**

usually greater than 6 millimeters in diameter (1/4")

asymmetric

irregular border

mottled appearance due to shades of color including tan, brown and black; sometimes with dashes of red, blue and white

M

acral lentiginous m. (ALM) A subtype of melanoma occurring as a darkly pigmented, flat to nodular lesion on palms, soles, and beneath nails (subungual). Also called melanotic whitlow.

early m. Either melanoma *in situ* or a thin invasive melanoma less than 1 mm in depth.

m. in situ Subtype of early melanoma characterized by flat or elevated lesions with histologic features identical to those of melanoma but confined to the full thickness of the superficial layer of the skin (epidermis) and its surrounding outermost layer (epithelium). Has been called malignant lentigo; lentigo maligna; atypical melanotic proliferation; pagetoid melanotic proliferation.

melanoma ■ melanoma

lentigo maligna m. (LMM) A subtype of early melanoma occurring as a flat, nonpalpable pigmentation less than 1 cm in diameter (macule), on sun-exposed skin (head, neck); often seen in elderly persons.

malignant m. Term used interchangeably with melanoma.

nodular m. (NM) A subtype of early melanoma consisting of an elevated or polypoid lesion on any anatomic site; may be uniform in pigmentation and frequently shows ulceration when advanced.

superficial spreading m. (SSM) The most common subtype of early melanoma, occurring on any anatomic site, and with typical asymmetry, border irregularity, color variegation, and diameter greater than 6 mm (the ABCDs of melanoma).

melanomatosis (mel-ah-no-mah-to'sis) The occurrence of numerous melanomas.

melanonychia (mel-ah-no-nik'e-ah) Black pigmentation of the nails.

melanopathy (mel-ah-nop'ah-the) Any disease that is characterized by dark skin discoloration.

melanophage (mel'ah-no-fāj) A phagocytic cell that engulfs melanin particles.

melanoplakia (mel-ah-no-pla'ke-ah) Pigmented patches on the tongue and oral mucous membrane.

melanorrhagia, melanorrhea (mel-ah-no-ra'je-ah, mel-ah-no-re'ah) See melena.

melanosis (mel-ah-no'sis) Abnormal deposits of dark pigments in various organs or tissues.

m. coli Blackening of the mucosal surface of the colon; associated with heavy and prolonged laxative use.

melanosome (mel'an-o-sōm) Any of the granules within the melanocytes that contain the synthesized pigment melanin. Also called melanin granule; melanin body.

melanotic (mel-ah-not'ik) 1. Relating to melanin. 2. Relating to melanosis.

melanuria (mel-an-u're-ah) The presence of melanin or any other dark pigment in the urine.

melasma (mĕ-laz'mah) Areas of brown patches on the skin, most commonly of the face and neck; caused by hormonal action, as in pregnancy and the use of oral contraceptives. Also called chloasma.

m. gravidarum Increased pigmentation on the forehead and across the cheeks and nose occurring sometimes during pregnancy. Commonly called mask of pregnancy.

melatonin (mel-ah-to'nin) A hormone chiefly produced and secreted by the pineal body, near the center of the brain; it is released into the circulation and its level is dependent on light; it is higher in darkness. The function of melatonin relative to the inducement of sleep is currently being investigated.

melena (me-le'nah) Passage of black, tarry feces; caused by bleeding, usually in the esophagus, stomach, or duodenum (the blood being darkened by the action of digestive secretions). Also called melanorrhagia; melanorrhea.

m. spuria Melena caused by swallowed blood; seen in infants who swallowed blood while nursing from a fissured, cracked nipple.

melicera, meliceris (mel-ĭ-se'rah, mel-ĭ-se'ris) A cyst containing a semisolid sticky material.

melioidosis (me-le-oi-do'sis) Infectious glanderslike disease of rodents of Southeast Asia, caused by the bacillus *Pseudomonas pseudomallei;* may be transmitted to humans, often causing fever, cough, and abscess formation.

melitis (mĕ-li'tis) Inflammation of the cheek.

melito-, melit-, meli- Combining forms meaning honey; sugar.

melitten (mĕ-li'ten) A polypeptide present in the venom of honeybees; it contains 62 amino acids, is destructive to cells, releases histamine, and causes muscle contraction. Also spelled melliten; melittin.

mellitum (mĕ-li'tum) Any pharmaceutical preparation containing honey.

melo-, mel Combining forms meaning limb; cheek.

meloplasty (mel'o-plas-te) Plastic surgery of the cheek.

melphalan (mel'fah-lan) An anticancer drug derivative of nitrogen mustard sometimes used in the management of multple myeloma. Adverse effects include hemolytic anemia.

membrane (mem'brān) 1. A thin, pliable layer of tissue that covers a surface, lines a cavity, connects two structures, or divides a space or organ. 2. A limiting protoplasmic surface.

abdominal m. See peritoneum.

alveolocapillary m. The thin blood-air barrier in the lung through which respiratory exchange of gases occurs between the alveolar air and the capillary blood; it consists of the surfactant-covered alveolar epithelium, basal lamina, and capillary endothelium. Also called respiratory membrane.

anterior limiting m. See Bowman's membrane.

atlantooccipital m. Any of two membranes (anterior and posterior) extending from the margin of the foramen magnum of the skull to the upper margin of the arch of the atlas (first cervical vertebra); the anterior fibers correspond below with the anterior longitudinal ligament, and the posterior fibers correspond below with the flaval ligament.

basement m. A thin, transparent, noncellular layer on the basal surface of epithelium; a composite structure consisting of a basal lamina (a thin, amorphous, collagen-containing sheet) and a reticular lamina (which varies in composition and appearance according to location); generally, the basement membrane serves to stabilize tissue shapes, but may have specialized functions in select areas, such as in the glomerulus of the kidney, where it serves as a selective permeability barrier for ultrafiltration of plasma in forming urine; it also invests muscle, fat, and Schwann cells.

basilar m. of cochlear duct The fibrous membrane that forms the greater part of the floor of the cochlear duct and the roof of the scala tympani, extending from the tip of the bony spiral lamina to the spiral ligament on the lateral wall of the duct; it is about 35 mm in length and accommodates the spiral organ of Corti within the cochlear. duct

boundary m. See basal lamina of epithelium, under lamina.

Bowman's m. The second of the five layers forming the cornea of the eye; it is situated just under the outer epithelial layer and consists of fine, closely interwoven fibrils. Also called anterior limiting lamina; anterior elastic lamina of cornea; anterior limiting membrane.

Bruch's m. See basal lamina of choroid, under lamina.

cell m. A delicate structure about 90 Å in thickness that envelops the cell, separating the contents of the cell from the surrounding environment; it consists of lipids and proteins with associated glycoproteins on the outer surface; it regulates the passage of substances into and out of the cell. Also called plasma membrane; plasmalemma; unit membrane.

cricovocal m. See cricothyroid ligament, under ligament.

crural interosseous m. See interosseous membrane of leg.

decidual m. The layers of the altered mucous lining (endometrium) of the pregnant uterus that are continuous with the placenta and are expelled (deciduated) after parturition. Also called deciduous membrane; decidua.

deciduous m. See decidual membrane.

Descemet's m. The fourth of the five layers forming the cornea of the eye; it is situated between the corneal stroma (substantia propria) and the endothelial layer of the anterior chamber; it is a thin, transparent, homogeneous membrane; at the margin of the cornea, it forms the trabecular tissue on the inner surface of Schlemm's canal (sinus venous sclerae), thereby permitting passage of aqueous humor from the anterior chamber to the canal. Also called posterior limiting lamina; posterior elastic lamina of cornea; posterior limiting membrane.

dialysis m. A semipermeable membrane in an artificial kidney (hemodialyzer) that separates the patient's blood from the wash solution (dialysate); the blood flows along one side of the membrane, while a wash solution flows countercurrent on the other side; depending on the concentration of the solutes in the blood and wash solution, there is an exchange through the membrane, thereby purifying the blood before returning it to the patient's body.

diphtheritic m. See false membrane.

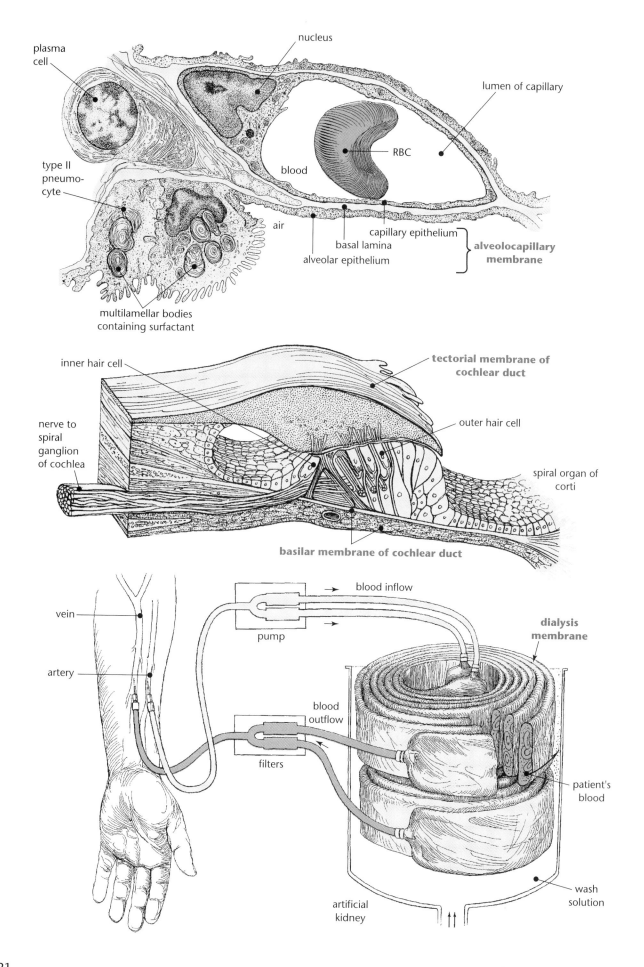

plasma cell

nucleus

lumen of capillary

RBC

blood

type II pneumo-cyte

air

capillary epithelium

basal lamina

alveolar epithelium

alveolocapillary membrane

multilamellar bodies containing surfactant

inner hair cell

tectorial membrane of cochlear duct

nerve to spiral ganglion of cochlea

outer hair cell

spiral organ of corti

basilar membrane of cochlear duct

vein

blood inflow

dialysis membrane

pump

artery

blood outflow

filters

patient's blood

artificial kidney

wash solution

M

membrane ■ membrane

external elastic m. A thin, fenestrated, discontinuous elastic membrane that constitutes the innermost component of the tunica adventitia of arteries; it separates the tunica adventitia from the muscular layer (tunica media) and is characterized by the presence of loosely packed collagen and elastic fibers.

external limiting m. The third of 10 layers of the retina; it is poorly defined and profusely fenestrated to allow the passage of rod and cone photoreceptor cells; it is composed of a row of junctional complexes consisting of adhering zones (zonulae adherentes) uniting the adjacent photoreceptor processes as well as adjoining glial fibers.

false m. A skinlike layer of fibrous exudate composed of sloughed necrotic epithelium, bacteria, coagulated fibrin, and white blood cells (leukocytes), as seen on the mucous membrane of the pharynx of patients with diphtheria. Also called pseudomembrane; diphtheritic membrane; neomembrane.

fetal m.'s The extraembryonic structures that protect the developing embryo or fetus and provide for its nourishment, respiration, excretion, and hormonal secretions; they include the amnion, chorion, allantois, yolk sac, decidua, and all structures of the placenta.

glomerular filtration m. The capillary wall of the renal corpuscle; it allows ultrafiltration of the blood by delivering the plasma to the urinary space within the nephronic (Bowman's) capsule; it does not allow the formed elements and large protein molecules to pass through.

hyaline-like m. The eosinophilic, homogeneous, transparent membrane lining the alveoli and air passages of newborn infants (particularly premature) who are afflicted with respiratory distress syndrome of the newborn.

internal elastic m. A well-developed fenestrated elastic membrane that constitutes the outermost component of the tunica intima of arteries; it is wavy in cross section, with occasional emanating strands that merge with the muscular layer (tunica media).

internal limiting m. The innermost of the 10 layers of the retina; it separates the retinal nerve fiber layer from the vitreous body of the eyeball and plays a role in the mechanism of fluid exchange between the vitreous body and the retina.

interosseous m. of forearm A broad, thin sheet of fibers connecting the shafts of the radius and ulna of the forearm, running downward and medially from the interosseous border of the radius to that of the ulna. Also called radioulnar interosseous membrane.

interosseous m. of leg A dense membrane connecting the shafts of the tibia and fibula, running downward and laterally for the most part, from the interosseous borders of the tibia and fibula; it divides the front muscles from those on the back of the leg. Also called crural interosseous membrane.

mucous m. A membrane whose surface is moistened by mucous glands; it lines tubular structures, such as the eustachian and fallopian tubes, as well as the alimentary, respiratory, and urogenital tracts.

Nasmyth's m. The primary enamel cuticle; an extremely thin membrane covering the entire enamel of recently erupted teeth; it is soon abraded by mastication.

nuclear m. The membrane in direct contact with the nucleus of a cell; the innermost membrane of the nuclear envelope. See nuclear envelope, under envelope.

obturator m. The thin interlacing membrane of white fibers that almost completely closes the obturator foramen of the hipbone; it leaves a small canal for the passage of the obturator nerve and vessels.

otolithic m. A gelatinous mass in the inner ear overlying the sensory cells of the utricular and saccular maculae; it contains numerous crystals of calcium carbonate (statoconia), as well as the embedded hairs (stereocilia and kinocilia) of the sensory cells.

perineal m. The lower layer of fascia of the urogenital diaphragm stretched across the anterior half of the pelvic outlet, filling the gap of the pubic arch; it is situated between the ischiopubic rami and covers the underside of the urethral sphincter and deep transverse perineal muscles; in the male, it is penetrated by the urethra

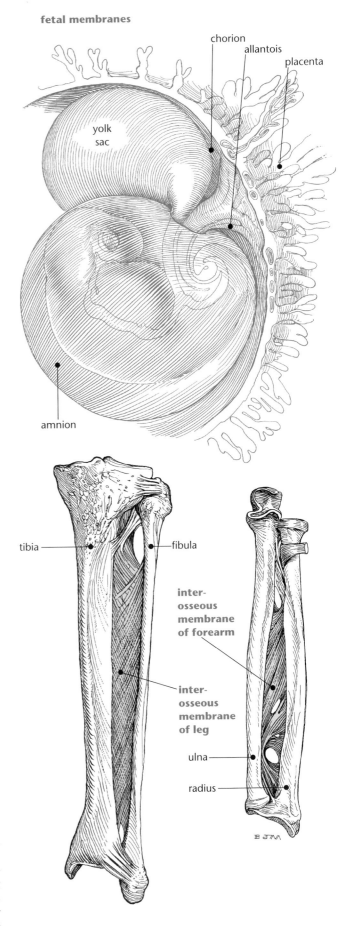

fetal membranes

chorion
allantois
placenta
yolk sac
amnion

tibia
fibula
inter-osseous membrane of forearm
inter-osseous membrane of leg
ulna
radius

and the ducts of the bulbourethral glands; in the female, by the urethra and the vagina.

periodontal m. See periodontal ligament, under ligament.

plasma m. See cell membrane.

posterior limiting m. See Descemet's membrane.

postjunctional m. See postsynaptic membrane.

postsynaptic m. The specialized portion of the cell membrane of a target structure, such as the motor neuron or muscle fiber, which is sensitive to chemical neurotransmitter substances. Also called postjunctional membrane.

prejunctional m. See presynaptic membrane.

presynaptic m. The specialized cell membrane of an axon terminal (i.e., of the knoblike terminal expansion of an axonal branch at the site of a synapse); it directly faces (across the synaptic gap) either another nerve cell, a muscle fiber, or cells of a gland. Also called prejunctional membrane.

radioulnar interosseous m. See interosseous membrane of forearm.

Reissner's m. See vestibular membrane of cochlear duct.

respiratory m. See alveolocapillary membrane.

secondary tympanic m. The membrane that closes the round window (fenestra cochleae) between the blind end of the scala tympani of the internal ear and the medial wall of the middle ear (tympanic) cavity; the membrane normally bulges slightly into the scala tympani.

semipermeable m. A membrane that permits the passage of water or other solvent, but prevents the passage of the dissolved substance (solute) or colloidal matter.

serous m. A membrane whose surface is covered with a film of thin serouslike fluid; it lines the pleural, peritoneal, and pericardial cavities of the body, and exposed surfaces of protruding organs. Also called serosa.

spiral m. of cochlear duct See vestibular membrane of cochlear duct.

suprapleural m. The thickened domelike expansion of the endothoracic fascia that strengthens the cervical pleura over the apex of the lung; it extends from the medial border of the first rib anteri-

orly, to the transverse process of the seventh cervical vertebra posteriorly; it helps to close the thoracic inlet.

synaptic m. See presynaptic membrane and postsynaptic membrane.

synovial m. The smooth connective-tissue membrane that lines the cavity of a synovial joint, except the articular cartilages of bones; it produces a pale yellow viscous (synovial) fluid as a lubricant that increases joint efficiency and reduces erosion of surfaces.

tectorial m. A broad, strong membrane that lies within the vertebral column; it is a cranial prolongation of the posterior longitudinal ligament upward from the posterior surface of the bodies of the second and third cervical vertebrae, to the anterior and anterolateral margins of the foramen magnum of the skull, where it blends with the dura mater.

tectorial m. of cochlear duct A delicate gelatinous membrane in the cochlear duct of the inner ear; it is attached to the limbus of the bony spiral lamina, and its free end extends over the sensory part of the spiral organ of Corti, where it embeds the underlying stereocilia, about 250,000 extending from the inner hair cells and about 900,000 extending from the outer hair cells.

thyrohyoid m. A broad fibroelastic membrane that fills the interval between the hyoid bone and the thyroid cartilage.

tympanic m. The thin, oblique, semitransparent membrane separating the external auditory canal from the middle ear (tympanic) cavity; it is kept taut for better reception of sound vibrations by the tensor muscle of the tympanum (tensor tympani); an ear ossicle (the malleus) is attached to its depressed center on its inner surface. Also called eardrum.

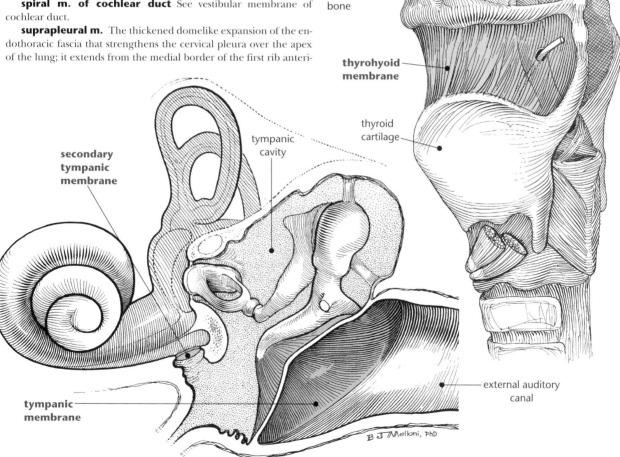

secondary tympanic membrane

tympanic cavity

tympanic membrane

epiglottis

hyoid bone

thyrohyoid membrane

thyroid cartilage

external auditory canal

B J Melloni, PhD

undulating m. A wavy, protoplasmic membrane or organelle of locomotion of certain flagellate parasites, such as the trypanosomes; it consists of a finlike extension of the limiting membrane with a wavelike flagellar sheath.

  unit m. See cell membrane.

  vestibular m. See vestibular membrane of cochlear duct.

  vestibular m. of cochlear duct The delicate membrane of the inner ear separating the endolymph-filled cochlear duct from the perilymph-filled scala vestibuli; it consists of a basal lamina with flattened epithelial cells on both sides. Also called Reissner's membrane; vestibular membrane; spiral membrane of cochlear duct.

  virginal m. See hymen.

  vitreous m. The condensed periphery of the vitreous body. See vitreous body, under body.

  Zinn's m. The outermost layer of the iris, consisting of flattened endothelial cells.

membranectomy (mem'brah-nek'to-me) Removal of a membrane, or a portion of it.

membranocartilaginous (mem'brah-no-kar'ti-laj'ĭ-nus) Composed of or derived from both membrane and cartilage.

membranous (mem'brah-nus) Relating to membrane.

memory (mem'o-re) **1.** General term for recollection of past experiences. **2.** The mental process by which information is received, modified (encoded), stored, and retrieved.

  immunologic m. The capacity of the immune system to respond more quickly and strongly to a subsequent exposure to a particular antigen (e.g., microorganism) than to the first exposure; produced by proliferation of special white blood cells (memory cells), which can recognize the antigen when encountered again.

  long-term m. (LTM) Memory that is stored and retained for long periods of time.

  short-term m. (STM) Memory of short duration unless reinforced; seen in certain neurologic disorders.

menacme (mĕ-nak'me) The time in a woman's life between onset of menstruation (menarche) and menopause.

menadione (men-ah-di'ōn) Synthetic preparation that has vitamin K properties.

menarche (mĕ-nar'ke) The onset of cyclic menstruation in the adolescent female.

mendelevium (men-dĕ-le've-um) Radioactive element; symbol Md, atomic number 101, atomic weight 256.

meningeal (mĕ-nin'je-al) Relating to the meninges.

meningeorrhaphy (mĕ-nin-je-or'ah-fe) Surgical repair of a membrane, especially those covering the brain and spinal cord (meninges).

meninges (mĕ-nin'jēz) Specifically, the membranes covering the brain and spinal cord (pia mater, arachnoid, dura mater).

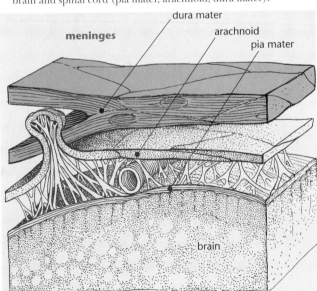

meningioma (mĕ-nin-je-o'mah) A benign intracranial tumor arising from the arachnoid, one of the membranes covering the brain; usually occurs in people over 30 years of age.

meningism (mĕ-nin'jizm) Irritation of the brain or spinal cord producing symptoms suggestive of meningitis, but without inflammation of the membranes (meninges).

meningitis (men-in-ji'tis) Inflammation of the membranes covering the brain and spinal cord. Routes of infection include cerebrospinal fluid and bloodstream pathways, skull fractures and penetrating wounds, lumbar punctures, and brain surgery.

  acute bacterial m. Meningitis generally characterized by headache, irritability, fever, lethargy, neck stiffness, presence of large numbers of polymorphonuclear leukocytes in a cloudy (normally clear) cerebrospinal fluid; caused by a variety of bacteria, especially *Escherichia coli* (affecting chiefly newborn infants), *Haemophilus influenzae*, *Neisseria meningitidis* (the cause of epidemics), and *Streptococcus pneumoniae* (affecting most frequently infants and old people and those with head injuries). If untreated, the disease may be fatal. Also called acute pyogenic meningitis.

  acute chemical m. Meningitis caused by irritating substances introduced or released into the cerebrospinal fluid (e.g., certain spinal anesthetics or contents of intradural cysts).

  acute lymphocytic m. See aseptic meningitis.

  acute nonpyogenic m. See aseptic meningitis.

  acute pyogenic m. See acute bacterial meningitis.

  aseptic m. Meningitis characterized by intense headache, nausea, vomiting, neck stiffness, an increase of lymphocytes in the cerebrospinal fluid, normal glucose levels, and an absence of bacteria; usually caused by viruses, most frequently by coxsackieviruses, echoviruses, and the genital herpes (herpes simplex II) virus. Also called acute lymphocytic meningitis; acute nonpyogenic meningitis.

  chronic m. Meningitis characterized by a progression of headache, malaise, mental confusion, and vomiting; caused by bacteria, especially those of tuberculosis *(Mycobacterium tuberculosis)*, and by fungi (e.g., species of *Candida* and *Coccidioides*); most common site of infection is the base of the brain, causing obstruction of cerebrospinal fluid circulation and (in children) hydrocephalus.

meningocele (mĕ-ning'go-sēl) A congenital saclike, skin-covered bulge of the membranes covering the brain or spinal cord through an abnormal gap in the skull or in the vertebrae; most frequent sites are the back (occipital) area of the skull and the lower back area of the spine.

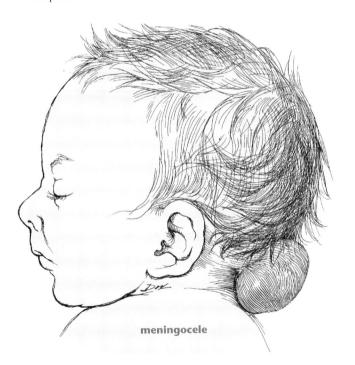

meningocele

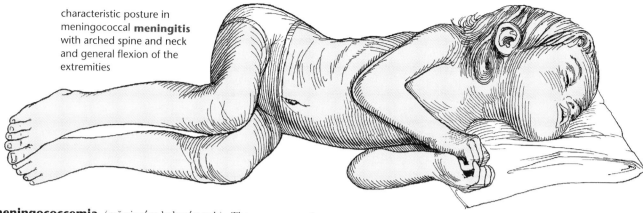
characteristic posture in meningococcal **meningitis** with arched spine and neck and general flexion of the extremities

meningococcemia (mě-ning′go-kok-se′me-ah) The presence of *Neisseria meningitidis* in the blood; may be associated with tiny subcutaneous purplish spots (petechiae), cardiovascular collapse, and/or meningitis.

meningococcus (mě-ning′go-kok′us) The *Neisseria meningitidis* bacterium.

meningocortical (mě-ning′go-kor′tĭ-kal) Relating to the membranes (meninges) and superficial layer of the brain (cortex).

meningoencephalitis (mě-ning′go-en-sef′ah-li′tis) Inflammation of the brain and its covering membranes. Also called encephalomeningitis; cerebromeningitis.

    primary amebic m. Invasive infection with the ameba *Naegleria fowleri;* symptoms include cough, nausea, fever, and neck rigidity; the amebae enter the brain through the nasal cavity, frequently from swimming in infested waters. Death occurs within a few days after onset.

meningoencephalocele (mě-ning′go-en-sef′ah-lo-sel) Congenital defect consisting of an outpouching of the brain and its membranes (meninges) through a large gap in the skull, usually in the back (occipital) area.

meningoencephalomyelitis (mě-ning′go-en-sef′ah-lo-mi-ě-li′tis) Inflammation of the brain and spinal cord and their covering membranes (meninges).

meningoencephalopathy (mě-ning′go-en-sef′ah-lop′ah-the) Any disease of the brain and its covering membranes (meninges).

meningomyelitis (mě-ning′go-mi-ě-li′tis) Inflammation of the spinal cord and its covering membranes (meninges), most commonly the arachnoid and pia mater.

meningomyelocele (mě-ning′go-mi′ě-lo-sēl) Outpouching of the membranes covering the spinal cord through an abnormal gap (spina bifida) in the vertebral column; the protrusion is devoid of a skin covering and contains spinal cord tissue and/or nerve roots. Also called myelomeningocele.

meningoradiculitis (mě-ning′go-rah-dik′u-li′tis) Inflammation of the meninges and nerve roots.

meningovascular (mě-ning′go-vas′ku-lar) Relating to the meninges and adjacent blood vessels.

meninx (me′ninks), pl. menin′ges A membrane, especially one of the three membranes covering the brain and spinal cord.

meniscectomy (men-ĭ-sek′to-me) Removal of an interarticular cartilage, especially from the knee joint.

menisci (men-is′si) Plural of meniscus.

meniscitis (men-ĭ-si′tis) Inflammation of cartilage within a joint.

meniscocyte (mě-nis′ko-sīt) See sickle cell, under cell.

meniscus (mě-nis′kus), pl. menis′ci A crescent-shaped structure, such as a fibrocartilage serving as a cushion between two bones meeting at a joint.

    lateral m. of knee joint A nearly circular, crescent-shaped fibrocartilage attached to the lateral articular surface of the superior end of the tibia. Also called lateral semilunar cartilage of knee.

    medial m. of knee joint A crescent-shaped fibrocartilage attached to the medial articular surface of the superior end of the tibia. Also called medial semilunar cartilage of knee.

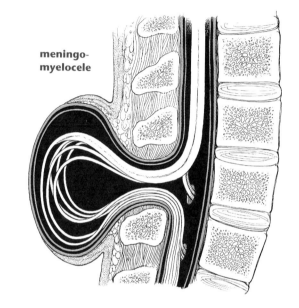
meningo-myelocele

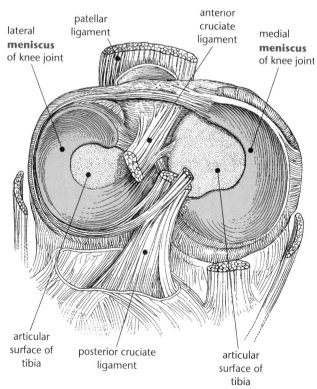
lateral **meniscus** of knee joint
patellar ligament
anterior cruciate ligament
medial **meniscus** of knee joint
articular surface of tibia
posterior cruciate ligament
articular surface of tibia

m. tactus See tactile disk, under disk.

temporomandibular m. See temporomandibular articular disk, under disk.

meno- Combining form meaning the menses.

menometrorrhagia (men-o-met-ro-ra′je-ah) Uterine bleeding occurring at irregular intervals and in varying amount and duration of flow.

menopausal (men-o-paw′zal) Relating to the menopause.

menopause (men′o-pawz) The normal termination of the menses, occurring usually between the ages of 45 and 50; symptoms correlate with the diminution of ovarian function and hormone production and may include hot flushes, headache, vulvar discomfort, painful sexual intercourse, and mental depression. Commonly called "the change in life." Also called physiologic menopause.

artificial m. Permanent cessation of ovarian function brought about by surgical removal of the ovaries or by radiation therapy before the age at which menopause normally occurs.

physiologic m. See menopause.

premature m. Cessation of ovarian function at an abnormally early age.

menorrhagia (men-o-ra′je-ah) Excessive or prolonged menstrual flow. Also called hypermenorrhea.

menoschesis (mĕ-nos′kĕ-sis) Suppression of the menses.

menses (men′sēz) The cyclic discharge of blood from the uterus; a menstrual period. See also menstruation.

menstrual (men′stroo-al) Relating to menstruation.

menstruation (men-stroo-a′shun) The cyclic bleeding and shedding of the uterine lining (endometrium); it is normally preceded by discharge of an ovum from the ovary and occurs at approximately four-week intervals, lasting three to five days.

anovular m., anovulatory m. Menstruation without ovulation.

vicarious m. Bleeding from sites other than the uterus (e.g., the nose), occurring at the time when normal menstruation takes place.

mensual (men′su-al) Monthly.

mensuration (men-su-ra′shun) The process of measuring.

mental (men′tal) **1.** Relating to the mind. **2.** Relating to the chin.

mentation (men-ta′shun) Mental activity.

menthol (men′thol) Organic compound derived from peppermint oil or prepared synthetically; used as a nasal decongestant, minor local anesthetic, and to relieve itching.

menton (men′ton) A craniometric point on the lower jaw, at the lowermost point of its median plane.

mentoplasty (men′to-plas-te) Plastic surgery on the chin.

mentum (men′tum) Latin for chin.

meperidine hydrochloride (mĕ-per′ĭ-dēn hi-dro-klo′rīd) An analgesic drug similar to but less powerful than morphine; may produce a physical and psychological dependence.

meprobamate (mĕ-pro′bah-māt) A minor tranquilizer used to treat anxiety.

meralgia (me-ral′je-ah) Pain in the thigh.

m. paresthetica Abnormal sensations (e.g., burning, tingling, numbness) of the lateral area of the thigh due to compression of the lateral femoral cutaneous nerve.

merbromin (mer-bro′min) Compound of organic mercury used as a topical antiseptic.

mercaptopurine (mer-kap-to-pu′rēn) An anticancer drug. Adverse effects include nausea, vomiting, mouth ulcers, and appetite loss.

mercurial (mer-ku′re-al) Relating to mercury.

mercurialism (mer-ku′re-al-izm) Mercury poisoning; see under poisoning.

mercuric (mer-ku′ric) Containing divalent mercury.

mercurous (mer′ku-rus) Containing monovalent mercury.

mercury (mer′ku-re) Heavy metallic element, liquid at room temperature; symbol Hg, atomic number 80, atomic weight 200.59, specific gravity 13.54; uses include the manufacture of thermometers, barometers, manometers, vapor lamps, and batteries and in the preparation of pharmaceuticals and dental amalgams. Also called quicksilver; hydrargyrum. See also mercury poisoning, under poisoning.

meridian (mĕ-rid′e-an) An imaginary line surrounding a globular structure passing through both poles.

m. of eye A meridian encircling the eyeball, passing through the anterior and posterior poles.

mero-, mere- Combining forms meaning part.

merocrine (mer′o-krīn) Releasing secretions without disintegration of secretory cells; applied to the type of gland using such method of releasing its secretion (e.g., a sweat gland) and to the secretory method or process

meromelia (mer-o-me′le-ah) The congenital absence of any part of a limb.

merotomy (mĕ-rot′o-me) Cutting into parts.

mesad (me′sad) Toward the middle.

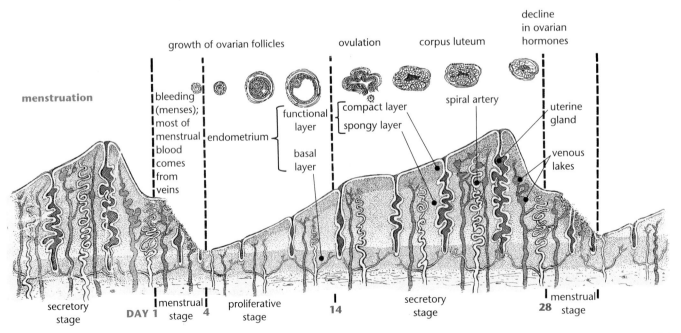

mesangial (mes-an'je-al) Relating to the mesangium.

mesangium (mes-an'je-um) The thin specialized connective tissue supporting the loops in a renal glomerulus, composed of a few cells and a small amount of matrix produced by the cells.

mesaortitis (mes-a-or-ti'tis) Inflammation of the middle, muscular layer of the aortic wall.

mesarteritis (mes-ar-ter-i'tis) Inflammation of the middle, muscular layer of an arterial wall.

mescaline (mes'kah-lin) A hallucinogenic addictive alkaloid present in the peyote cactus.

mesencephalon (mes-en-sef'ah-lon) The embryonic midbrain.

mesenchymal (mĕ-seng'kĭ-mal) Relating to the mesenchyme (e.g., a tumor).

mesenchyme (mes'eng-kīm) Embryonic connective tissue; an aggregation of widely separated stellate cells surrounded by ground substance. Also called mesenchymal tissue.

mesenteric (mes-en-ter'ik) Relating to the mesentery.

mesenteritis (mes-en-tĕ-ri'tis) Inflammation of the mesentery.

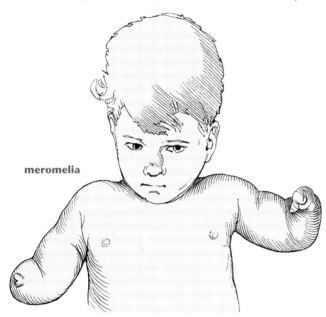

meromelia

mesentery (mes'en-ter-e) The double layer of peritoneum attaching various organs to the body wall and conveying to them their blood vessels and nerves. The term is commonly used in reference to the peritoneal fold attaching the small intestine to the posterior abdominal wall.

meshwork (mesh'werk) See network.

mesial (me'ze-al) Toward the median plane (e.g., of the dental arch).

mesio- Combining form meaning toward the median plane.

mesiodens (me'ze-o-denz) An accessory tooth located in the upper jaw, between the two front teeth (central incisors).

mesiodistocclusal (me-ze-o-dist-o-kloo'zal) In dentistry, denoting a three-surface cavity preparation or restoration in the back teeth (premolars and molars).

mesioversion (me-ze-o-ver'zhun) Inclination of a tooth in the direction of the tooth in front of it in the dental arch.

mesmerism (mes'mer-izm) Early name for hypnosis.

meso-, mes- Prefixes meaning intermediate; connecting.

mesoappendix (mes-o-ah-pen'diks) The small, double-layered fold of peritoneum attaching the appendix to the mesentery of the lower ileum.

mesoblast (mes'o-blast) In embryology, a cell of the early mesoderm.

mesocardium (mes-o-kar'de-um) In embryology, the double layer of mesoderm attaching the developing heart to the wall of the pericardial cavity.

mesocecum (mes-o-se'kum) The mesentery of the cecum; it is often absent.

mesocephalic (mes-o-sĕ-fal'ik) Denoting a skull with an intermediate breadth-length proportion (i.e., a cephalic index between 75 and 80). Also called normocephalic.

mesocolic (mes-o-kol'ik) Relating to the mesocolon.

mesocolon (mes-o-ko'lon) The double layer of peritoneum attaching the colon to the posterior abdominal wall.

mesoderm (mes'o-derm) In embryology, the middle layer of embryonic cells (between the ectoderm and endoderm); gives rise to the deep layer of the skin, connective tissues, vascular and genitourinary systems, and most skeletal and smooth muscles.

mesogaster (mes-o-gas'ter) See mesogastrium.

mesogastrium (mes-o-gas'tre-um) In embryology, the primitive mesentery enveloping the embryonic stomach (enteric canal); from it develops the greater omentum. Also called mesogaster.

mesognathion (mes-o-na'the-on) The segment of the upper jaw (maxilla) bearing the lateral incisor tooth.

mesometrium (mes-o-me'tre-um) The portion of the broad ligament of the uterus, below the attachment of the ovary, and extending to the lateral wall of the pelvis.

mesomorph (mes'o-morf) A body type with prominent musculature and heavy bone structure.

meson (mes'on) Any of various subatomic particles that may be positively or negatively charged or neutral and have a mass between that of an electron and a proton; found in cosmic radiation or produced from nuclear disintegration; some have been proposed for cancer radiation therapy because they produce powerful but short-lived secondary radiation.

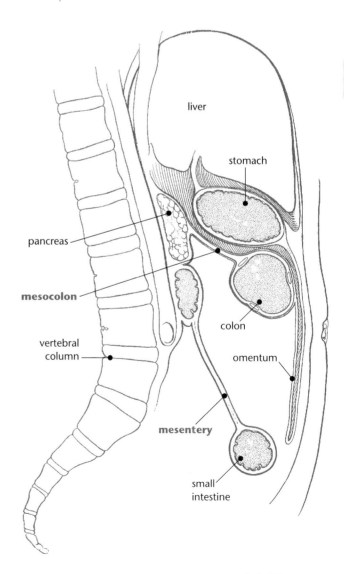

liver

stomach

pancreas

mesocolon

colon

vertebral column

omentum

mesentery

small intestine

mesonephric (mes-o-nef′rik) Relating to the mesonephros.

mesonephroma (mes-o-ne-fro′mah) Uncommon ovarian tumor derived from displaced embryonic tissues (mesonephros).

mesonephros (mes-o-nef′ros) An intermediate excretory organ of the embryo, eventually replaced by the kidney; in the male, its duct system is retained as the epididymis and the vas deferens (deferent duct). Also called wolffian body.

mesorchial (mě-sor′ke-al) Relating to the mesorchium.

mesorchium (mes-or′ke-um) 1. In the fetus, the fold of peritoneum attaching the developing testis to the developing urinary system (mesonephros). 2. In the adult, the fold of peritoneum between the testis and the epididymis.

mesorectum (mes-o-rek′tum) The short peritoneal fold investing the upper part of the rectum and attaching it to the back wall of the body cavity, in front of the sacrum.

mesorrhine (mes′o-rin) Denoting a nose of moderate width with a nasal index between 47 and 51 on the skull.

mesosalpinx (mes-o-sal′pinks) The upper free portion of the broad ligament of the uterus, above the attachment of the ovary and investing the fallopian (uterine) tube.

mesosigmoid (mes-o-sig′moid) The portion of the mesocolon relating to the sigmoid colon.

mesotendon, mesotendineum (mes-o-ten′don, mes-o-ten-din′e-um) Connective tissue covered by synovial membrane; it extends between a tendon and the wall of its tendon sheath; it conveys blood vessels and nerve fibers.

mesothelioma (mes-o-the-le-o′mah) Tumor composed of spindle cells or fibrous tissue, occurring most frequently on the lining of the lung (pleura).

  benign m. A well-defined, solitary, fibrous growth on the pleura, often attached to the lung by a pedicle; it does not invade other tissues.

  malignant m. A cancerous growth arising from the pleura and spreading diffusely over the surface of the lung, forming a firm grayish sheath over it, and frequently invading both lungs and the chest wall; symptoms include cough, chest pain, and breathing difficulty; occurs in people occupationally exposed to asbestos, with a latency period of 20 to 40 years, and with incidence increasing when the person is a smoker; few patients survive beyond two years. Tumor occurs less frequently in the peritoneum and other organs.

mesothelium (mes-o-the′le-um) The single layer of flattened cells derived from the mesoderm and lining the inner walls of body cavities.

mesovarium (mes-o-va′re-um) The short fold of peritoneum attaching the ovary to the posterior layer of the broad ligament.

messenger (mes′en-jer) A conveyor of information.

  first m. A hormone that interacts with a mediator (second messenger) at or near the cell membrane.

  second m. Cyclic adenosine monophosphate or cyclic guanosine monophosphate; it functions as mediators of enzyme action; found on cell membranes.

messenger RNA (mes′en-jer) See under ribonucleic acid.

mestranol (mes′trah-nōl) Estrogen used in various oral contraceptive preparations.

meta- Prefix meaning changed in position or form; following; beyond.

meta-analysis (met-ah ah-nal′ĭ-sis) A method of statistically examining the findings of two or more studies, often used when there are conflicting data between independent trials and when effects from single studies are too small to be statistically significant.

metabolism (mě-tab′o-lizm) The sum of the chemical changes occurring in the living body by which energy is provided for vital processes and by which new substances are produced and assimilated for growth and maintenance. See also anabolism; catabolism.

  basal m. The minimum amount of energy required to maintain vital functions in an individual at complete physical and mental rest. Also called basal metabolic rate (BMR).

  inborn errors of m. See under error.

  protein m. The breakdown and manufacture of proteins in the tissues. Also called proteometabolism.

metabolite (mě-tab′o-līt) Any substance taking part in, or resulting from metabolism.

  essential m. A substance necessary for a metabolic process to occur.

metacarpal (met-ah-kar′pal) Relating to the metacarpus.

metacarpophalangeal (met′ah-kar′po-fah-lan′je-al) Relating to the bones in the broad part of the hand (metacarpus) and those of the fingers (phalanges); applied to their articulations.

metacarpus (met-ah-kar′pus) The five bones of the hand between those of the wrist (carpus) and of the fingers (phalanges).

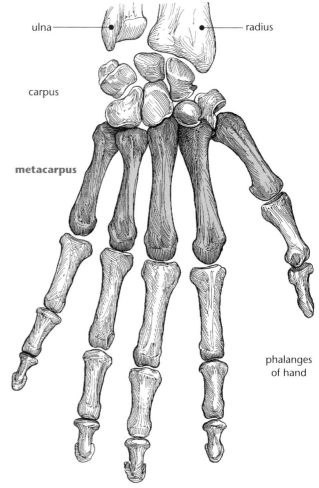

ulna — radius — carpus — metacarpus — phalanges of hand

metacentric (met-ah-sen′trik) Having the centromere in the center; applied to a chromosome.

metachromasia (met-ah-kro-ma′ze-ah) The property of certain tissues that causes them to stain a different color from the color of the histologic dye used.

metachromatic (met-ah-kro-mat′ik) Relating to metachromasia.

metacyesis (met-ah-si-e′sis) See ectopic pregnancy, under pregnancy.

Metagonimus yokogawai (met-ah-gon′i-mus yo-ko-ga′wa-e) One of the smallest intestinal flukes (1–2.5 mm long) infecting humans; transmitted by eating raw or undercooked infected fish; prevalent in the Far East and the Balkan States.

metainfective (met-ah-in-fek′tiv) Occurring after an infection.

metakinesis (met-ah-ki-ne′sis) Moving apart; applied to the separation of the two chromatids of a chromosome during cell division.

metalloenzyme (mě-tal-o-en′zim) Enzyme that has metal atoms as an integral part of its structure.

metallophilia (mě-tal-o-fil′e-ah) Affinity for metal salts; applied to certain cells (e.g., those of the reticuloendothelial system).

metalloporphyrin (mě-tal-o-por′fĭ-rin) Compound containing a porphyrin and a metal (e.g., chlorophyll and hematin).

metalloprotein (mě-tal-o-pro′tēn) Protein containing a tightly bound metal ion or ions (e.g., hemoglobin).

metamere (met'ah-mēr) One of a series of similarly constructed body segments.

metamerism (me-tam'er-ism) The state of having a series of similar structures arranged in a repetitive pattern (e.g., ribs, vertebrae).

metamorphosis (met-ah-mor'fo-sis) A change in form and/or function.

metamyelocyte (met-ah-mi'ĕ-lo-sit) An immature cell, precursor of the granular white blood cell granulocyte, usually confined to the bone marrow.

metanephrine (met-ah-nef'rin) A normal breakdown product of epinephrine; it is excreted in the urine.

metanephros (met-ah-nef'ros) The tubular excretory system of the embryo representing the permanent embryonic kidney; its formation follows the regression of the mesonephros.

metaneutrophil (met-ah-nu'tro-fil) Not staining normally with neutral histologic dyes.

metaphase (met'ah-fāz) Second stage of cell division in which the contracted chromosomes, each consisting of two chromatids, are aligned along the equatorial plane of the cell prior to separation of the chromatids.

metaphysis (me-taf'ĭ-sis), pl. metaph'yses The growth area of a long bone at the junction of the epiphysis with the shaft.

metaplasia (met-ah-pla'ze-ah) The development of adult tissue from cells that normally produce a different type of tissue.

metapsychology (met-ah-si-kol'o-je) The theoretical attempt to describe what lies beyond the empirical facts of psychology.

metaraminol bitartrate (met-ah-ram'ĭ-nol bi-tar'trāt) A sympathomimetic drug used to elevate and maintain blood pressure in acute hypotensive conditions.

metastable (met'ah-sta-bl) Unstable; transient from a thermodynamic perspective.

metastasis (mĕ-tas'tah-sis), pl. metas'tases **1.** The process by which cancerous cells form secondary tumors that are discontinuous with the primary tumor, in parts of the body distant from the original site; it is the most important feature distinguishing malignant from benign tumors. **2.** The secondary cancerous tumor thus formed.

metastasize (mĕ-tas'tah-siz) To spread by metastasis.

metatarsal (met-ah-tar'sal) Relating to the metatarsus.

metatarsalgia (met-ah-tar-sal'je-ah) Pain over the ball of the foot.

metatarsophalangeal (met-ah-tar-so-fah-lan'je-al) Relating to the metatarsus and the bones of the toes.

metatarsus (met-ah-tar'sus) The five bones in the anterior part of the foot between the tarsus, at the back of the foot, and the bones of the toes (phalanges).

  m. adductus Foot deformity in which only the front part of the foot (at the tarsometatarsal joints) is drawn toward the midline. Also called metatarsus varus.

  m. varus See metatarsus adductus.

metathalamus (met-ah-thal'ah-mus) The posterior portion of the thalamus (in the brain), composed of the medial and lateral geniculate bodies.

metencephalon (met-en-sef'ah-lon) The portion of the embryonic brain from which develop the pons and cerebellum.

meteorism (me'te-ŏ-rizm) See tympanites.

meter (me'ter) (m) **1.** Unit of length, equal to 39.37 inches. **2.** A measuring instrument.

  dose-rate m. In radiology, an instrument that displays the rate of a radiation dose.

  rate m. Instrument that continuously displays the magnitude of some phenomenon (e.g., a radiation detector that continuously shows radiation intensity).

meth (meth) Slang name for methamphetamine hydrochloride.

methadone (meth'ah-dōn) Synthetic narcotic compound resembling morphine, used to relieve pain and to relieve withdrawal symptoms in the detoxification treatment of heroin and morphine addiction. Withdrawal symptoms may also appear upon discontinuing methadone. Possible adverse effects include nausea, constipation, dizziness, dryness of the mouth, and impotence.

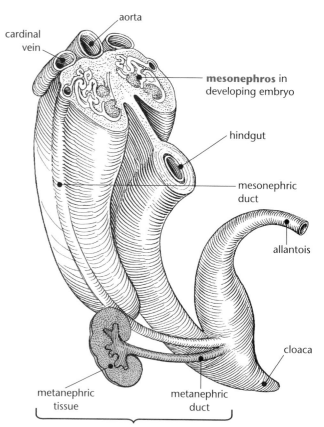

aorta
cardinal vein
mesonephros in developing embryo
hindgut
mesonephric duct
allantois
cloaca
metanephric tissue
metanephric duct
metanephros

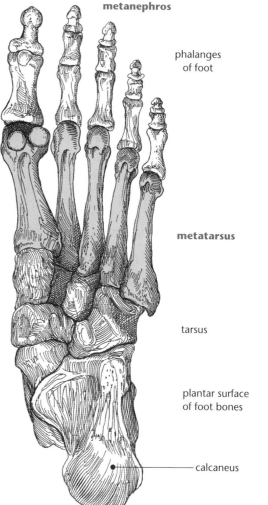

phalanges of foot
metatarsus
tarsus
plantar surface of foot bones
calcaneus

metamere ■ **methadone**

methamphetamine hydrochloride (meth-am-fet'ah-mēn hi-dro-klo'rīd) A sympathomimetic drug that stimulates the central nervous system and depresses intestinal motility, thus allaying hunger. Drug abusers take it orally or intravenously; it produces psychological dependence. Effects of abuse during pregnancy include prematurity, placental abruption, fetal distress, low birth weight, and postpartum hemorrhage. Also known by the slang terms meth; speed.

methane (meth'ān) Odorless, colorless, highly flammable gas produced by decomposition of organic matter; present in natural gas; also a component of intestinal gas. Also called marsh gas.

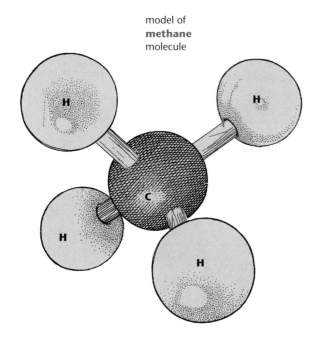

model of
methane
molecule

methanol (meth'ah-nol) A flammable toxic liquid widely used as an industrial solvent, an antifreeze, and in the production of formaldehyde. Ingestion may cause blurred vision and blindness. Also called methyl alcohol; wood alcohol; carbinol.

methaqualone (mĕ-thah'kwah-lōn) A short-acting sedative; a drug of abuse that causes psychological and physical dependence.

methemalbumin (met-hēm-al-bu'min) Abnormal compound found in the blood of individuals with such conditions as malarial hemoglobinuria or paroxysmal nocturnal hemoglobinuria.

methemoglobin (met-he'mo-glo'bin) (metHb) A dark brown compound sometimes formed in red blood cells by the action of certain drugs or chemicals on the blood pigment hemoglobin. Unlike oxygenated hemoglobin, it is unable to transport oxygen.

methemoglobinemia (met-he-mo-glo'bī-ne'me-ah) Condition resulting from excessive amounts of methemoglobin in the blood, producing a bluish skin coloration (cyanosis); may be caused by exposure to oxidizing agents including nitrites, nitroglycerin, paints, varnishes, and aniline dyes.

methenamine (meth-en-am'in) A urinary antiseptic that acts by releasing formaldehyde in an acid medium.

methicillin sodium (meth-ī-sil'in so'de-um) A semisynthetic penicillin derivative used as an antibiotic in staphylococcal infections resistant to penicillin.

methimazole (meth-im'ah-zōl) A drug that suppresses production of thyroid hormones by the thyroid gland.

methionine (mĕ-thi'o-nin) (Met) An essential amino acid present in such proteins as egg albumin.

method (meth'ud) A manner of performing an act, especially a systematic way of performing an examination, operation, or test. See also technique; procedure.

Abbott's m. Treatment of scoliosis by means of a plaster jacket after partial correction of the spine curvature has been made by application of external force.

activated sludge m. A method of treating sewage waste with 15% bacterially active liquid sludge, which causes the colloidal material in the sewage to coagulate and undergo sedimentation.

confrontation m. Procedure used to determine the extent of a patient's visual field; with one eye covered, the patient fixes the other eye on the corresponding (confronting) eye of the examiner, as the examiner slowly moves a finger out of and back into the line of vision, noting when the finger is just seen by the patient.

copper sulfate m. Determination of the specific gravity of blood or plasma; solutions of copper sulfate graded in specific gravity by increments of 0.004 are placed in small containers; a drop of blood or plasma is placed in each container; the specific gravity of the copper sulfate solution, in which the drop of blood or plasma remains suspended indefinitely, indicates the specific gravity of the sample.

Credé's m.'s (a) A method of expressing the placenta, after the infant has been delivered, by squeezing or kneading the body of the uterus to produce placental separation; it usually traumatizes the placental site, and therefore is not generally recommended. Also called Credé's maneuver. (b) The application of one drop of a 2% solution of silver nitrate onto each eye of the newborn infant to prevent gonococcal conjunctivitis; may cause inflammation and eye discharge within the first 24 hours of life. (c) The use of manual pressure on the bladder, especially a paralyzed bladder, to express urine.

cross-sectional m. In developmental psychology, comparison of groups of individuals at different age levels in terms of observations made about a given characteristic.

direct m. In dentistry, a method of making a wax pattern of lost tooth structure directly in the prepared cavity of the tooth; an inlay technique.

disk sensitivity m. A method of determining the relative effectiveness of various antibiotic drugs against a specific microorganism; small disks of paper are impregnated with known antibiotics and placed on the surface of a medium containing the microorganism being tested in a Petri dish; after an incubation period, the lack of microbial growth in the areas around the various disks indicates the relative effectiveness of the drugs.

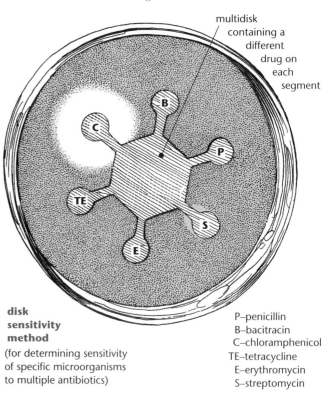

multidisk
containing a
different
drug on
each
segment

disk sensitivity method
(for determining sensitivity of specific microorganisms to multiple antibiotics)

P–penicillin
B–bacitracin
C–chloramphenicol
TE–tetracycline
E–erythromycin
S–streptomycin

experimental m. In experimental psychology, the control of a subject's environmental, physiologic, or attitudinal factors to observe behavioral changes dependent on those factors.

flash m. A method of pasteurizing milk by quickly heating it to a temperature of 178°F, holding it there for a short time, and then reducing it rapidly to 40°F.

flotation m. Any laboratory procedure for separating eggs and cysts of parasites from fecal components of the specimen by using a solution intermediate in density between the lighter eggs and cysts (which float) and the heavier fecal material (which remains as sediment).

immunofluorescence m. A method of determining the presence or location of an antigen by using a corresponding antibody labeled with a fluorescent substance.

indirect m. In dentistry, the making of an inlay entirely on a cast made from an impression of the prepared tooth cavity.

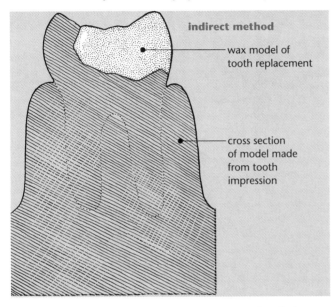

indirect method
wax model of tooth replacement
cross section of model made from tooth impression

Lamaze m. In obstetrics, a method of psychophysiologic preparation for the birth process; it involves educating the pregnant woman about her body functions and the physiology of labor, emphasizing exercise, breathing techniques, and relaxation; usually includes the assistance of a partner or "coach."

Lee-White m. A method of determining the coagulation time of venous blood by placing the blood in tubes of standard bore at body temperature.

Nissl's m. A histologic technique using basic dyes to demonstrate the presence of Nissl bodies or aggregated RNA in the cytoplasm of nerve cells. Also called Nissl's stain.

Pavlov's m. A method of studying conditioned reflex activity by observing such response indicators as saliva secretion.

reference m. An analytic procedure that is used as a standard against which other procedures are validated because of its relatively high degree of accuracy.

rhythm m. Birth control by avoiding sexual intercourse for a few days before and after the expected day of ovulation.

Schick m. See Schick test, under test.

seroepidemiologic m. Any method of detecting latent subclinical infections and carrier states as well as clinically overt states; based on the serologic testing of characteristic changes in the serum level of specific antibodies.

split-cast m. A method of indexing dental casts on an articulator by cutting grooves on the base of the casts to facilitate their removal and replacement on the same articulator.

Westergren m. Procedure for measuring the sedimentation rate of red blood cells in fluid blood; venous blood mixed with an aqueous solution of sodium citrate is placed and allowed to stand in a standard pipet (300 mm long, 2 mm internal diameter, and graduated at 1-mm intervals from 0 through 200); the pipet is filled to the 0 mark and kept in an upright position; in one hour the fall of the red blood cells is recorded. The normal sedimentation rate for men is 0 to 15 mm/hr, for women 0 to 20 mm/hr.

methotrexate (meth-o-trek′sāt) A drug with antineoplastic properties. Adverse effects include nausea, vomiting, mouth sores, and, if taken during pregnancy, fetal defects and low birth weight.

methoxsalen (mĕ-thok′sah-len) Compound that increases melanin production in the skin when exposed to ultraviolet light; used in the treatment of vitiligo to enhance repigmentation and in the treatment of psoriasis to precipitate a phototoxic response.

methoxyflurane (mĕ-thok-se-floo′rān) A clear colorless liquid with a fruity odor; it is nonflammable and nonexplosive; used as a slow inhalation anesthetic.

methyl (meth′il) (Me) The univalent chemical group -CH$_3$.
   m. alcohol See methanol.
   m. methacrylate An acrylic resin used for denture bases.
   m. salicylate A volatile oil used in ointments for the relief of muscle pain. Also called oil of wintergreen.

methylate (meth′ĭ-lāt) 1. To combine with the chemical group methyl or with methanol. 2. A compound of methanol and a metal.

methylbenzene (meth-il-ben′zēn) See toluene.

methylcellulose (meth-il-sel′u-lōs) Compound used as a bulk-forming laxative and in the formulation of contact lens solution and eyedrops to relieve dryness of the eyes.

methylcholanthrene (meth-il-ko-lan′thrēn) A cancer-causing polycyclic hydrocarbon present in coal tar.

methyldopa (meth-il-do′pah) Drug used in the treatment of high blood pressure (hypertension). Adverse effects include drowsiness, depression, rashes, impotence, and a flulike syndrome.

methylglucamine diatrizoate (meth-il-gloo′kah-mĭn di-ah-tri-zo′āt) See meglumine diatrizoate.

methylmalonic acid (meth-il-mah-lon′ik as′id) (MMA) An important intermediary in the metabolism of fatty acids.

methylmalonic aciduria (meth-il-mah-lon′ik as-ĭ-du′re-ah) Excretion of excessive amounts of methylmalonic acid in urine; it results either from a congenital metabolic disorder, from an autosomal recessive inheritance causing severe ketoacidosis in infancy, or from vitamin B^{12} deficiency.

methylparaben (meth-il-par′ah-ben) An antifungal preservative.

methylphenidate hydrochloride (meth-il-fen′ĭ-dāt hi-dro-klo′rĭd) A mild central nervous system stimulant similar to amphetamine; used in the management of hyperkinetic syndrome in children.

methylprednisolone (meth-il-pred′nĭ-so-lōn) A corticosteroid drug used in the treatment of asthma and in replacement therapy for pituitary and adrenal hormone deficiencies. Adverse effects include weight gain and high blood pressure (hypertension).

methysergide (meth-ĭ-ser′jīd) Drug used in the preventive treatment of migraine and cluster headaches, usually when other treatments are ineffective. Long-term use may cause adverse effects, including abnormal tissue growth around blood vessels and ureters.

metoclopramine (met-o-klo′prah-mēn) Drug used to relieve nausea and vomiting associated with anticancer drugs and radiation therapy. Adverse effects may include dryness of mouth, irritability, and agitation.

metolazone (mĕ-tōl′ah-zōn) Diuretic drug used in the treatment of high blood pressure (hypertension) and to reduce fluid retention (edema) in such conditions as kidney disorders, heart failure, and premenstrual syndrome. Possible side effects include weakness and lethargy.

metopic (me-top′ik) Relating to the forehead.

metopion (mĕ-to′pe-on) Craniometric point on the sagittal plane between the two frontal eminences.

metopism (met′o-pizm) Persistence of the frontal suture in the adult skull.

metopoplasty (met′o-po-plas-te) Plastic or reconstructive surgery of the skin of the forehead and/or underlying bone.

M

metoprolol (mĕ-to′pro-lōl) A beta-blocker drug used in the treatment of angina pectoris and high blood pressure (hypertension). Possible adverse effects include skin rash, cold hands and feet, and lethargy.

Metorchis (met-or′kis) A genus of flukes; some species are parasitic in dogs, cats, and, occasionally, humans.

metoxenous (mĕ-tok′sĕ-nus) See heterecious.

metra (me′trah) Greek for uterus.

metria (me′tre-ah) Inflammatory condition of the uterus after childbirth.

metric (met′rik) Relating to or based on the meter as a standard of measurement.

metritis (mĕ-tri′tis) Inflammation of the uterus.

metrodynamometer (me-tro-di-nah-mom′ĕ-ter) Instrument for measuring the force of uterine contractions.

metromalacia (me-tro-mah-la′she-ah) Abnormal softening of the uterus.

metronidazole (mĕ-tro-ni′dah-zōl) Antibiotic drug effective against anaerobic bacteria (e.g., in tooth abscesses and peritonitis) and protozoan infections (e.g., amebiasis, giardiasis, and trichomoniasis). Adverse effects include loss of appetite, abdominal pain, dark urine, and taste disturbance.

metropathia hemorrhagica (me-tro-path′e-ah hem-o-raj′ik-ah) Abnormal, profuse, and prolonged uterine bleeding associated with cyst formation in the inner lining (endometrium).

metropathic (me-tro-path′ik) Relating to disease of the uterus.

metropathy (mĕ-trop′ah-the) Any disease of the uterus.

metrophlebitis (me-tro-flĕ-bi′tis) Inflammation of the uterine veins occurring only during pregnancy and immediately after childbirth.

metrorrhagia (me-tro-ra′je-ah) Bleeding from the uterus occurring anytime between menstrual periods; causes include acute inflammation of the cervix, a benign tumor, and endometrial or cervical cancer; at midcycle, may be due to ovulation. Also called intermenstrual bleeding.

metrorrhea (me-tro-re′ah) Discharge of mucus or pus from the uterus.

metrorrhexis (me-tro-rek′sis) See hysterorrhexis.

metrosalpingitis (me-tro-sal-pin-ji′tis) Inflammation of the uterus and one or both fallopian (uterine) tubes.

metroscope (me′tro-skōp) See hysteroscope.

metrostaxis (mĕ-tro-stak´sis) A slight continuous bleeding from the uterus.

metrostenosis (me-tro-ste-no′sis) Constriction of the uterine cavity.

metrotomy (mĕ-trot′o-me) Hysterotomy.

-metry Combining form meaning measuring (e.g., thermometry).

miconazole (mī-kon′ah-zōl) An antifungal drug used to treat such fungal infections as vaginal candidiasis, ringworm, and athlete's foot.

micro-, micr- Combining forms meaning minute; small size.

microabscess (mi-kro-ab′ses) One of numerous microscopic aggregations of white blood cells occurring in such conditions as psoriasis (Munro's microabscess) and mycosis fungoides (Pautrier's microabscess).

microadenoma (mi-kro-ad-ĕ-no′mah) A noncancerous glandular tumor, smaller than 10 mm in diameter, such as those occurring in the anterior pituitary (adenohypophysis).

microaerophil (mi-kro-a′er-o-fil) A microorganism that requires very little free oxygen.

microanatomy (mi-kro-ah-nat′o-me) See histology.

microaneurysm (mi-kro-an′u-rizm) Small areas of vessel distention seen in conditions such as chronic high blood pressure (hypertension) and visible in the retina in diabetes mellitus.

microangiography (mi-kro-an′je-og′rah-fe) The making of x-ray pictures of the smallest blood vessels after the injection of a radiopaque medium.

microangiopathic (mi-kro-an′je-o-path′ik) Relating to any disease of small blood vessels.

microangiopathy (mi-kro-an′je-op′ah-the) Disease of the small blood vessels, especially of the capillaries.

diabetic m. Diffuse thickening of vascular basement membrane, especially of capillaries of the skin and medulla of the kidney.

thrombotic m. A combination of arteriolar and capillary wall thickening resulting in a narrow lumen.

microbe (mi′krōb) A microorganism, especially a one-celled animal or plant that causes disease.

microbial (mi-kro′be-al) Relating to a microbe.

microbicide (mi-kro′bĭ-sid) Anything that destroys microorganisms.

microbiologic (mi-kro-bi-o-loj′ik) Relating to microbiology.

microbiologist (mi-kro-bi-ol′o-jist) A specialist in microbiology.

microbiology (mi-kro-bi-ol′o-je) The study of microorganisms, especially of those causing disease.

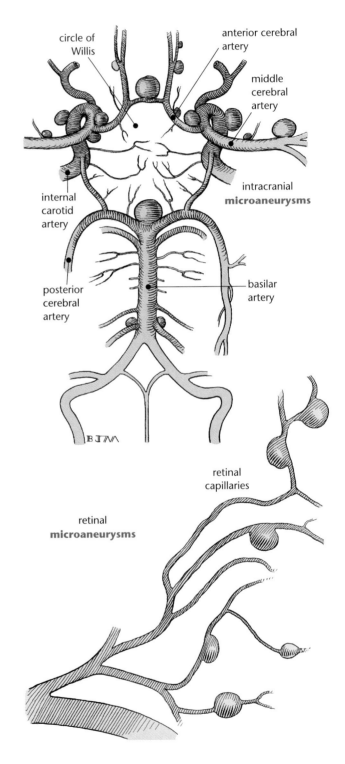

circle of Willis

anterior cerebral artery

middle cerebral artery

internal carotid artery

intracranial **microaneurysms**

posterior cerebral artery

basilar artery

retinal capillaries

retinal **microaneurysms**

industrial m. Microbiology concerned with the utilization and manipulation of microorganisms capable of economically producing desirable substances, and the control of undesirable microorganisms.

microblast (mi′kro-blast) A small nucleated red blood cell.

microbody (mi-kro-bod′e) See peroxisome.

microbrachia (mi-kro-bra′ke-ah) Abnormal smallness of the arms.

microcardia (mi-kro-kar′de-ah) Abnormal smallness of the heart.

microcephaly (mi-kro-sef′ah-le) Abnormal smallness of the head. Also called nanocephaly.

microcheiria (mi-kro-ki′re-ah) Abnormal smallness of the hands.

microcirculation (mi-kro-sir-ku-la′shun) Blood circulation in small vessels (arterioles, capillaries, and venules).

micrococci (mi-kro-kok′si) Plural of micrococcus.

Micrococcus (mi-kro-kok′us) Genus of gram-positive bacteria that occur in irregular masses and resemble staphylococci but do not cause disease.

micrococcus (mi-kro-kok′us), pl. micrococ′ci Any member of the genus *Micrococcus.*

microcoria (mi-kro-ko′re-ah) Congenital smallness of the pupil.

microcornea (mi-kro-kor′ne-ah) Abnormal smallness of the cornea.

microcoulomb (mi-kro-koo′lom) (μC) A microunit of electric quantity; one-millionth (10^{-6}) of a coulomb.

microcurie (mi-kro-ku′re) (μCi) A measure of activity of a radioactive source; one-millionth (10^{-6}) of a curie.

microcyst (mi′kro-sist) A minute cyst, usually undetectable by the naked eye.

microcyte (mi′kro-sīt) A red blood cell with a decreased corpuscular volume; occurs in iron deficiency anemia.

microcythemia (mi-kro-si-the′me-ah) The presence of many abnormally small red blood cells in the blood.

microdactylous (mi-kro-dak′tĭ-lus) Having abnormally small or short fingers or toes.

microdactyly (mi-kro-dak′tĭ-le) Abnormal smallness of fingers or toes.

microdissection (mi-kro-di-sek′shun) Dissection of tissues with the aid of a microscope or magnifying lens.

microdontia (mi-kro-don′she-ah) The presence of abnormally small teeth, most commonly affecting one or two lateral incisors or third molars.

microelectrode (mi-kro-e-lek′trōd) A fine-caliber electrode used in physiologic experiments.

microfilament (mi-kro-fil′ah-ment) Any of several rodlike structures (4–6 nm in diameter) within cells composed of the proteins actin and myosin; involved in movement of cellular elements within the cell and movement of the cell itself.

microfilaremia (mi-kro-fil-ah-re′me-ah) Presence of microfilariae in the blood.

microfilaria (mi-kro-fi-la′re-ah), pl. microfila′riae The prelarval or embryonic forms of filarial worms (e.g., of *Wuchereria bancrofti).*

microgenia (mi-kro-jen′e-ah) Abnormal smallness of the chin.

microgenitalism (mi-kro-jen′ĭ-tal-izm) Abnormal smallness of the external genital organs.

microglia (mi-krog′le-ah) The smallest neuroglial cells; they are phagocytic and help remove cellular debri in areas of inflammation in the brain and spinal cord.

microglossia (mi-kro-glos′e-ah) Abnormal smallness of the tongue.

micrognathia (mi-kro-na′the-ah) Abnormal smallness of the jaws, especially the lower jaw (mandible).

microgram (mi′kro-gram) (mcg, μg) A unit of weight; one-millionth (10^{-6}) of a gram.

microgyria (mi-kro-jir′e-ah) Abnormal smallness of the convolutions of the brain.

microhm (mi′krōm) A unit of electrical resistance; one-millionth (10^{-6}) of an ohm.

microincineration (mi-kro-in-sin-er-a′shun) The combustion of a tissue section in order to examine the remaining mineral ashes under a darkfield microscope. Also called spodography.

microincision (mi-kro-in-sizh′un) Incision made with the aid of a microscope.

microinvasion (mi-kro-in-va′zhun) The earliest, limited stage in the spread of a cancerous tumor to adjacent tissues.

microkymatotherapy (mi-kro-ki-mat′o-ther′ah-pe) Treatment of disease with high-frequency radiation. Also called microwave therapy.

microliter (mi′kro-le-ter) (μl) Unit of volume or capacity; one-millionth (10^{-6}) of a liter.

microlith (mi′kro-lith) A minute concretion or stone (calculus).

microlithiasis (mi-kro-lĭ-thi′ah-sis) The presence of many minute sandlike concretions.

micromanipulation (mi-kro-mah-nip-u-la′shun) The performance of dissection, surgery, injection, etc., of microscopic structures with the aid of a microscope and micromanipulators.

micromanipulator (mi-kro-mah-nip′u-la-tor) An attachment to a microscope used to maneuver tiny instruments while performing micromanipulations.

micromelia (mi-kro-me′le-ah) Abnormal smallness of the limbs. Also called nanomelia.

micrometer (mi′kro-me-ter) (μm) A unit of length; one-millionth (10^{-6}) of a meter. Formerly called micron.

micrometer (mi-krom′ĕ-ter) Instrument for measuring microscopic objects.

micrometry (mi-krom′e-tre) Measuring with a micrometer.

micromicrogram (mi′kro-mi′kro-gram) (μμg) Former term for picogram (pg).

micromicron (mi′kro-mi′kron) (μμ) Former term for picometer (pm).

micromole (mi′kro-mōl) (μmol) Unit of concentration; one-millionth (10^{-6}) of a mole.

micromyelia (mi-kro-mi-e′le-ah) Congenital smallness or shortness of the spinal cord.

micron (mi′kron) (μ) Former term for micrometer.

micronutrients (mi-kro-nu′tre-ents) Essential dietary substances (e.g., vitamins and trace elements) required by the body only in small quantities.

microorganism (mi-kro-or′gan-izm) A microscopic animal or plant.

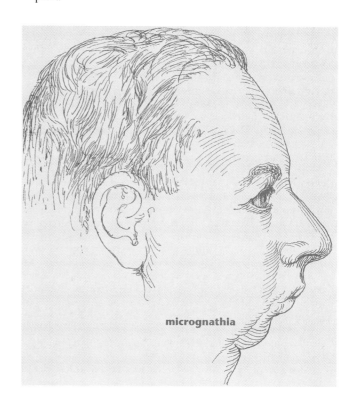

micrognathia

micropathology (mi-kro-pah-thol′o-je) Microscopic study of disease-caused changes in body tissues.

micropenis (mi-kro-pe′nis) An abnormally small penis; in the newborn, one less than 2 cm in length from the pubis to the tip.

microphage (mi′kro-fāj) A small white blood cell that leaves the bloodstream to engulf bacteria and small particles.

microphobia (mi-kro-fo′be-ah) Exaggerated, irrational fear of microorganisms.

microphthalmia, microphthalmos (mi-krof-thal′me-ah, mi-krof-thal′mus) Abnormal smallness of the eyeballs.

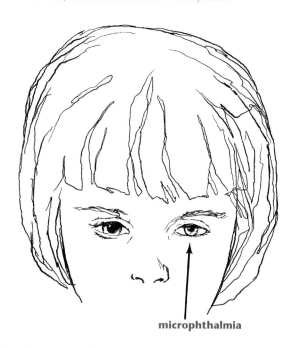

microphthalmia

micropipette, micropipet (mi-kro-pi-pet′) A calibrated glass tube for transferring minute quantities of fluid.

microplasia (mi-kro-pla′ze-ah) Stunted growth.

microplethysmography (mi-kro-pleth-is-mog′rah-fe) Recording of minute changes in the volume of an organ that result from the flow of blood into and out of the organ.

microprobe (mi′kro-prōb) An ultrafine probe used in microsurgery.

    laser m. See laser microscope, under microscope.

micropsia (mi-krop′se-ah) The condition of seeing objects as smaller than their actual size.

micropuncture (mi′kro-punk′chūr) Procedure for studying the function of the kidney; a micropipette is placed within a tubule and/or blood vessel of the kidney of an experimental animal to sample the composition of fluid, measure the pressure, or determine electrical potential at various sites.

microscope (mi′kro-skōp) Instrument equipped with a combination of lenses for viewing small objects under magnification.

    atomic force m. (AFM) A microscope that allows examination of cellular structures under physiologic (aqueous) conditions (unlike the electron microscope, which uses a vacuum).

    binocular m. Microscope with two eyepiece tubes, allowing observation with both eyes simultaneously.

    comparison m. A microscope designed to allow the similarity, or dissimilarity, of individual identifying characteristics of two objects (e.g., two bullets) to be observed at the same time.

    compound m. Microscope with two or more lenses.

    darkfield m. Microscope that permits illumination of the object from the side; details of the object appear light against a dark background.

    electron m. (EM) Microscope that uses a beam of electrons instead of visible light, thereby allowing a much greater magnification than a light microscope. The image may be seen on a fluorescent

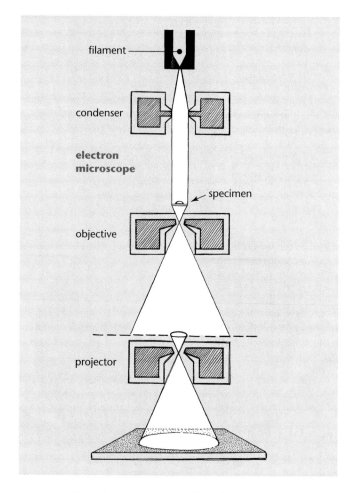

filament

condenser

electron microscope

specimen

objective

projector

screen or it may be photographed. Also called transmission electron microscope.

    fluorescence m. See fluorescence microscopy, under microscopy.

    interference m. Microscope that uses two separate beams of light that are passed through the specimen and combined with each other on the image plane, thereby making transparent and refractile details visible; useful for examining living and unstained cells.

    laser m. Microscope that uses a fine laser beam to vaporize a portion of the specimen; the resulting vapor is then analyzed by means of a microspectrometer. Also called laser microprobe.

    operating m., surgical m. Microscope used to magnify the surgical field while performing microsurgery; it provides adequate working distance between objective lens and surgical field, ease of adjustment, and bright illumination; magnification minimizes traumatic manipulation of tissues (e.g., permits precise control of bleeding with pinpoint electrocoagulation).

    phase-contrast m., phase m. Microscope that makes use of two paths of light so that the refraction differences within the specimen become visible as variations of intensity; useful for examining transparent specimens (e.g., living cells).

    polarizing m. Microscope especially equipped to illuminate the specimen with polarized light and a means to analyze and measure the alterations of the polarized light by the specimen; useful in the identification of crystals.

    scanning electron m. (SEM) A microscope in which a beam of electrons scans over the specimen point by point, giving the surface image a three-dimensional quality.

    stereoscopic m. A microscope with double eyepieces and objectives, designed to give a three-dimensional view of the specimen; magnifying power is usually limited.

    surgical m. See operating microscope.

    transmission electron m. (TEM) See electron microscope.

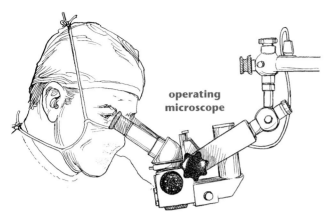

operating microscope

ultraviolet m. Microscope in which the image is formed by ultraviolet radiation and visualized by ultraviolet-transmitting lenses.

x-ray m. A microscope that produces images by recording the differences in the specimen's absorption or emission of x-rays; the image is usually recorded on film.

microscopic (mi-kro-skop'ik) **1.** Visible only through a microscope. **2.** Relating to a microscope.

microscopy (mi-kros'ko-pe) The application of microscope magnification to the study of materials that cannot be seen with the unaided eye.

fluorescence m. Microscopy in which specimens are stained with a fluorescent dye (usually fluorescein isothiocyanate) and then illuminated with ultraviolet rays or blue light, which makes the stained elements glow; useful in studying the chemical composition of cells.

microsome (mi'kro-sōm) Any of a group of lipoprotein-rich vesicles formed from ruptured endoplasmic reticulum after disruption and centrifugation of cells.

microsomia (mi-kro-so'me-ah) Abnormal smallness of the body. Also called nanocormia.

hemifacial m. Developmental defect characterized by unilateral underdevelopment of the facial skeleton and soft tissues.

microspherocytosis (mi-kro-sfe-ro-si-to'sis) Presence of numerous small spherical erythrocytes in the blood; associated with hemolysis.

Microsporum (mi-kros'po-rum) Genus of fungi that cause skin infections.

M. audouini Species causing ringworm, especially of the scalp.

microsurgery (mi'kro-ser-jer-e) Surgery performed under magnification of an operating microscope and with the use of minute instruments and sutures; used in such procedures as cataract removal, corneal transplantation, removal of a middle ear ossicle (stapes) for the treatment of deafness, unblocking obstructed fallopian (uterine) tubes, and rejoining cut blood vessels and nerve fibers.

microsuture (mi-kro-su'chur) Suture material 40 μm or less in diameter; used in microsurgery.

microsyringe (mi-kro-sēr-inj') Syringe designed to measure accurately minute amounts of fluid for injection.

microtia (mi-kro'she-ah) Abnormal smallness of the auricle of the ear, sometimes associated with an incompletely developed or absent ear canal.

microtome (mi'kro-tōm) Instrument for slicing thin sections of tissue for microscopic examination.

microtomy (mi-krot'o-me) The slicing of tissue into thin sections with a microtome.

microtonometer (mi-kro-to-nom'ĕ-ter) Instrument for measuring the tensions of oxygen and carbon dioxide in arterial blood.

microtubule (mi-kro-tu'būl) One of many hollow cylindrical structures found in the cytoplasm of nearly all cells, composed of protein and measuring about 250 Å in diameter; important in intracellular activities (e.g., cell division, transport of intracellular elements) and in maintaining cell shape.

M

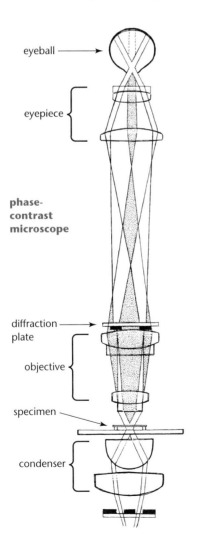

eyeball

eyepiece

phase-contrast microscope

diffraction plate

objective

specimen

condenser

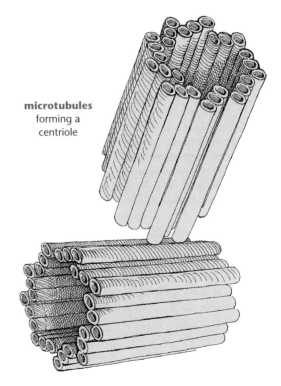

microtubules forming a centriole

microvascular (mi-kro-vas′ku-lar) Relating to the microvasculature.

microvasculature (mi-kro-vas′ku-lah-chūr) The arterioles, capillaries, and venules considered as a whole.

microvilli (mi-kro-vil′i) Submicroscopic fingerlike projections on the free surface of a cell, which greatly increase the surface area of the cell.

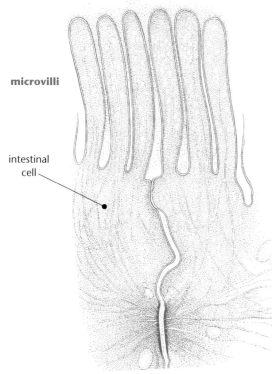

microvilli

intestinal cell

microvolt (mi′kro-volt) (μV) One-millionth (10^{-6}) of a volt.

microwave (mi′kro-wāv) Any electromagnetic radiation with a wavelength between 1 mm and 30 cm. Wavelengths shorter than 1 mm are heat (infrared) waves, those above 30 cm are radio waves. Also called microelectric wave.

microwelding (mi-kro-weld′ing) A way of fastening stainless steel sutures.

micrurgic (mi-krur′jik) Relating to micrurgy.

micrurgy (mi′krur-je) Any manipulation of tissues performed under magnification of a microscope. See also micromanipulation.

micturate (mik′tu-rāt) To urinate.

micturition (mik-tu-rish′un) The act of urinating. Also called urination.

mid- Combining form meaning middle.

midazolam hydrochloride (mi-daz′ō-lam hi-dro-klo′rīd) A short-acting depressant of the central nervous system, used as a preoperative sedative. It rapidly crosses the placenta into the fetus.

midbrain (mid′brān) The 2-cm-long upper portion of the brainstem, connecting the pons and cerebellum with the hypothalamus; through it passes the cerebral aqueduct.

midcarpal (mid-kar′pal) Between the two rows of bones forming the wrist. Also called mediocarpal.

midclavicular (mid-klah-vik′u-lar) Relating to the middle of the collarbone (clavicle).

midgut (mid′gut) **1.** The middle portion of the embryonic digestive tract between the foregut and the hindgut from which develop the ileum and jejunum. **2.** The small intestine.

midmenstrual (mid-men′stroo-al) Midway between two menstrual periods.

midoccipital (mid-ok-sip′ĭ-tal) Relating to the central portion of the back of the head.

midpain (mid′pān) See intermenstrual pain, under pain.

midsection (mid-sek′shun) A cut through the middle of an organ.

midsternum (mid-ster′num) The middle, largest portion of the breastbone (sternum).

midwife (mid′wīf) A formally trained person, usually a registered nurse, who provides care to a woman during pregnancy and childbirth and cares for both mother and infant immediately following childbirth, usually with physician backup in case of emergencies or complications.

midwifery (mid′wif′e-re) The care provided by a midwife in a hospital, birthing center, or home.

mifepristone (mif-pris′tōn) A synthetic steroid with potent antiprogestational and antiglucocorticoid properties that provides an effective medical method of inducing abortion in early pregnancy; administered orally. Adverse effects may include slight pelvic pain, nausea, fatigue, and headache. Trade name: RU486.

migraine (mi′grān) Recurrent, intense headache of unknown cause and tending to occur in families, most commonly in females; traditionally thought to be of vascular origin; most recent hypotheses emphasize the role of sensitized nerve endings in the blood vessels, or a disturbance of the hypothalamus or limbic system of the brain. Also called migraine headache; blind headache; vascular headache.

  classic m. Migraine characterized by episodes of visual disturbances (aura) consisting of a slowly expanding blind spot surrounded by a brilliant zigzag edge and sparkles, lasting about 20 minutes, followed by a throbbing pain that may last two to six hours; at its maximal intensity, the headache is associated with nausea and vomiting. Less often, a sensory aura occurs, manifested as numbness or weakness of the extremities; occasionally visual and sensory auras occur consecutively or simultaneously.

  common m. Migraine in which visual and sensory disturbances are absent; the headache develops slowly and increases to a throbbing pain, which may last from four hours to several days, and is made worse by slight movement or noise; the headache is often but not always limited to one side of the head and is accompanied by nausea, seldom by vomiting.

migration (mi-gra′shun) Passing from one part of the body to another; applied to cells, parasitic organisms, molecules, and pathologic processes.

miliaria (mil-e-a′re-ah) A skin eruption of minute vesicles due to retention of sweat in the sweat follicles.

  m. rubra See prickly heat, under heat.

miliary (mil′e-a-re) Having a dimension of about 2 mm in diameter, similar to that of a millet seed (e.g., the nodules of miliary tuberculosis).

milium (mil′e-um), pl. mil′ia A minute whitish papule or cyst in the skin caused by retention of fatty material. Also called whitehead.

milk (milk) **1.** The secretion of the mammary glands for nourishment of the young; contains protein, a sugar (lactose), and fats. **2.** An aqueous suspension.

  certified m. Cow's milk containing no more than the maximum permissible limit of bacteria (10,000/ml) at any time prior to delivery to the consumer.

  certified pasteurized m. Cow's milk in which the maximum permissible limit for bacteria does not exceed 10,000/ml before pasteurization and 500/ml after pasteurization.

  m. of magnesia See under magnesia.

  uterine m. Secretion produced by uterine glands that nourishes the implanted fertilized ovum.

  witch's m. Milklike fluid sometimes secreted by the breasts of newborn infants of either sex.

milking (milk′ing) A technique for removing the contents of a tubular structure by gently running a finger along its length.

milkpox (milk′poks) See alastrim.

milli- Prefix meaning one-thousandth.

milliampere (mil-e-am′pēr) (ma, mA) One-thousandth (10^{-3}) of an ampere.

millicurie (mil-ī-ku′re) (mCi) One-thousandth (10^{-3}) of a curie.

milliequivalent (mil-ī-e-kwiv′ah-lent) (mEq, meq) A quantity equal to one-thousandth (10^{-3}) of the equivalent weight of an element or compound.

M

milligram (mil′ĭ-gram) (mg) One-thousandth (10^{-3}) of a gram.

milliliter (mil′ĭ-le-ter) (ml, mL) One-thousandth (10^{-3}) of a liter.

millimeter (mil′ĭ-me-ter) (mm) One-thousandth (10^{-3}) of a meter.

millimicron (mil-ĭ-mi′kron) (mμ) Former term for nanometer.

millimole (mil′ĭ-mōl) (mmol) One-thousandth (10^{-3}) of a gram-molecule.

milling-in (mil′ing in) In dentistry, the placing of abrasives between the occlusal surfaces of dentures and rubbing them together in the mouth or on the articulator; used to perfect the occlusion.

milliosmole (mil-ĭ-os′mōl) (mOsm) One-thousandth (10^{-3}) of an osmole.

millisecond (mil-ĭ-sek′ond) (ms) One-thousandth (10^{-3}) of a second.

millivolt (mil′ĭ-vōlt) (mV) One-thousandth (10^{-3}) of a volt.

mimesis (mi-me′sis) Condition in which one disease presents the symptoms of another disease.

mind (mīnd) The totality of conscious and unconscious processes serving to adjust the individual to the demands of the environment. Also called psyche.

mineral (min′er-al) Any naturally occurring inorganic substance.

    trace m. See trace element, under element.

mineralocorticoid (min-er-al-o-kor′tĭ-koid) One of the steroids in the superficial layer of the adrenal gland that controls salt metabolism.

minilaparotomy (min-e-lap-ah-rot′o-me) Technique for gaining access into the abdominopelvic cavity through a minute incision in the abdominal wall (e.g., to ligate the uterine tubes for female sterilization).

minoxidil (mĭ-noks′ĭ-dil) A very potent vasodilator used to lower blood pressure; also applied topically to increase hair growth.

mio- Combining form meaning less.

miosis (mi-o′sis) **1.** Reduction in the size of the pupil. **2.** Stage of a disease in which the severity of symptoms begins to subside. Rarely used term.

miotic (mi-ot′ik) **1.** Relating to contraction of the pupil. **2.** An agent that causes contraction of the pupil.

miracidium (mi-rah-sid′e-um), pl. miracid′ia A free-swimming first-stage larva of a trematode that penetrates a small intermediate host (e.g., snail), where it develops into the second-stage parasite (sporocyst).

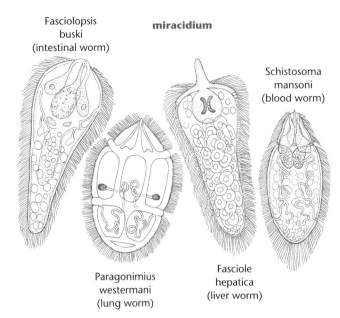

Fasciolopsis buski (intestinal worm)

miracidium

Schistosoma mansoni (blood worm)

Paragonimius westermani (lung worm)

Fasciole hepatica (liver worm)

mire (mēr) One of the luminous objects in an instrument (ophthalmometer) used to measure the curvature of the cornea.

mirror (mir′or) A polished surface that forms images by reflection.

    head m. Mirror attached to a headband; used to illuminate a body cavity.

    laryngeal m. Circular mirror about 2 cm in diameter mounted on a slender handle at an angle of 120°; used to examine the interior of the larynx and pharynx.

misandry (mis-an′dre) Hatred of men.

misanthropy (mis-an′thro-pe) Aversion to people.

miscarriage (mis-kar′ij) Popular term for spontaneous abortion. See under abortion.

miscarry (mis-kar′e) To give birth to a nonviable fetus.

miscible (mis′ĭ-bl) Capable of being mixed.

misconduct (mis-kon′dukt) Intentional wrongdoing.

    research m. Fraudulent behavior that directly affects the integrity of research (i.e., the deliberate falsification or fabrication of data, research procedures, or data analysis; plagiarism; and other

COMPOSITION OF MILK (per 100 g)		HUMAN	COW'S
	protein	2 g	3.5 g
	carbohydrate	7 g	5 g
	fat	4 g	3.5 g
	calcium	25 mg	120 mg
	phosphorus	16 mg	95 mg
	iron	0.1 mg	0.1 mg
	thiamine	17 μg	40 μg
	riboflavin	30 μg	150 μg
	nicotinic acid	170 μg	80 μg
	ascorbic acid	3.5 μg	2.0 μg
	vitamin A	170 IU	150 IU
	vitamin D	1.0 IU	1.5 IU
	calories	70	66

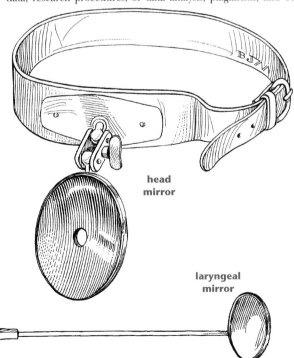

head mirror

laryngeal mirror

M

intentional misrepresentation in proposing, conducting, reporting, or reviewing the results of research).

misdiagnosis (mis-di-ag-no′sis) A wrong diagnosis.

misogyny (mĭ-soj′ĭ-ne) Hatred of women.

missile dust (mis′l dust) Colloquialism for the x-ray appearance of multiple tiny metal fragments deposited in tissues along the course of a bullet tract.

mite (mīt) Any of various minute, often parasitic, arthropods; they may infest food and carry disease.

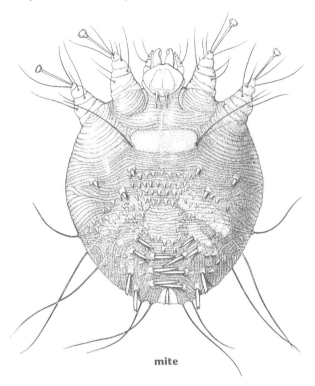

mite

    harvest m. See chigger.

    hay itch m., grain itch m. See *Pyemotes tritici.*

    itch m. See *Sarcoptes scabiei.*

    northern fowl m. See *Ornithonyssus sylviarum.*

mithridatism (mith′rĭ-da-tizm) The acquisition of immunity to a poison by ingesting gradually increased doses of it.

miticide (mi′tĭ-sīd) An agent that kills mites.

mitochondria (mi-to-kon′dre-ah) Plural of mitochondrion.

mitochondrion (mi-to-kon′dre-on) One of numerous compartmentalized organelles present in the cytoplasm of most cells, responsible for generating usable energy by the formation of adenosine triphosphate (ATP). The average cell usually contains several hundred mitochondria.

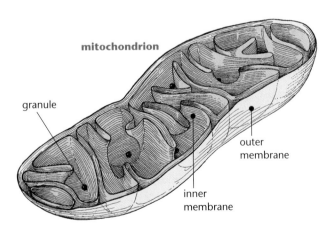

mitochondrion

granule

inner membrane

outer membrane

mitogen (mi′to-jen) A substance derived from plants or microorganisms that causes cells (particularly lymphocytes) to undergo cell division.

    pokeweed m. (PWM) A mitogen for B lymphocytes, derived from the plant *Phytolacca americana.*

mitogenesis (mi-to-jen′ĕ-sis) The initiation of cell division (mitosis).

mitogenic (mi-to-jen′ik) Inducing cell division (mitosis).

mitosis (mi-to′sis) Process whereby a cell divides and forms two daughter cells, each normally receiving the same chromosome and DNA content as that of the original cell.

mitotic (mi-tot′ik) Relating to cell division (mitosis).

mitral (mi′tral) **1.** Relating to the mitral (left atrioventricular) valve of the heart. **2.** Shaped like a bishop's miter or a turban.

mitralization (mi-tral-i-za′shun) The straightened appearance of the left border of the heart seen in an x-ray image, due to protrusion of the left atrial appendage and/or the pulmonary trunk and its left main branch.

mittelschmerz (mit′el-shmārts) A dull, fleeting abdominal pain occurring between two menstrual periods, at the time of ovulation.

mixture (miks′tūr) **1.** An aggregation of two or more substances that are not chemically combined. **2.** A pharmaceutical preparation containing an insoluble substance suspended in a liquid by means of a viscid material (e.g., glycerol or sugar).

    Brompton m. See Brompton cocktail, under cocktail.

    Ringer's m. See Ringer's solution, under solution.

M-mode (m mōd) In ultrasonography, a presentation of echo changes in which a B-mode tracing is moved to indicate the pattern of echomotion (M) as a function of time (T). Also called TM-mode.

mnemonic (ne-mon′ik) Assisting the memory.

mnemonics (ne-mon′iks) A system of techniques for assisting the memory.

mobilization (mo-bĭ-lĭ-za′shun) **1.** Making a part of the body movable. **2.** Initiating a sequence of physiologic activity.

    stapes m. Surgical procedure through which the footplate of the stapes is freed from overlapping bone tissue or adhesions caused by otosclerosis or middle ear infection.

mobilize (mo′bĭ-līz) To cause the release of substances stored in the body for participation in physiologic activities.

modality (mo-dal′ĭ-te) Any of several forms of therapy.

mode (mōd) In statistics, the value occurring most frequently.

model (mod′el) **1.** Something that represents something else and serves as a basis for study or experimentation. **2.** A dental cast.

modeling (mod′el-ing) The acquisition of new skills by observing and imitating the behavior of others.

ball and stick **model**

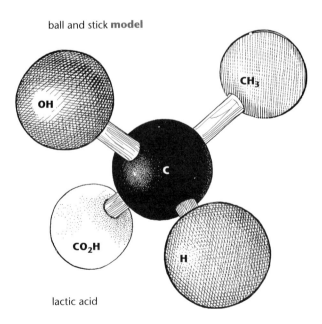

OH

CH₃

C

CO₂H

H

lactic acid

M

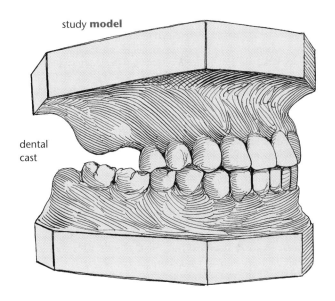

study **model**

dental
cast

modification (mod-ĭ-fi-ka'shun) A change in an organism that is acquired, not inherited.

    behavior m. The systematic use of techniques, such as desensitization and biofeedback, to modify or eliminate selected undesirable behaviors, attitudes, or phobias. Also called behavior modification therapy.

modiolus (mo-di'o-lus) The spongy bone around which the spiral canals of the cochlea turn.

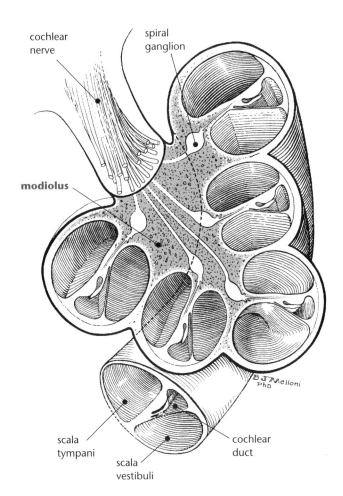

cochlear
nerve

spiral
ganglion

modiolus

scala
tympani

scala
vestibuli

cochlear
duct

modulation (mod-u-la'shun) A cell's changes in shape and/or function in response to changes in its environment.

mogigraphia (moj-e-graf'e-ah) See writer's cramp, under cramp.

moiety (moi'ĕ-te) **1.** A portion of indefinite size. **2.** Formerly, one of two more or less equal parts.

molal (mo'lal) Containing 1 mole of a solute per 1,000 grams of solvent.

molality (mo-lal'ĭ-te) Moles of solute per kilogram of solvent.

molar (mo'lar) **1.** (M) One of the 8 back teeth in the deciduous dentition, or one of the 12 back teeth in the permanent dentition. **2.** Containing 1 mole of solute per liter of solution. **3.** Relating to a body of matter; not molecular.

    deciduous m. One of the eight back teeth in the deciduous (primary) dentition.

    first permanent m. The largest permanent tooth in the mouth; first permanent tooth to erupt, usually at the age of six years. Also called six-year molar.

    impacted m. A molar that fails to erupt or erupt fully because of an obstruction.

    permanent m. One of the 12 back teeth in the permanent (secondary) dentition.

    second permanent m. A permanent molar immediately distal to the first molar; it usually erupts at the age of 12 years. Also called 12-year molar.

    six-year m. See first permanent molar.

    third permanent m. Last permanent back tooth in the mouth; it generally erupts between the ages of 17 and 21 years. Also called wisdom tooth.

    12-year m. See second permanent molar.

molarity (mol-ar'ĭ-te) Moles of solute per liter of solution.

mold (mōld) **1.** Any fungus usually growing on decaying organic material. **2.** A receptacle in which a cast material is shaped. **3.** To shape.

molding (mōld'ing) **1.** The process of shaping, as with a mold. **2.** The temporary change in shape of the fetal head as it passes through the birth canal.

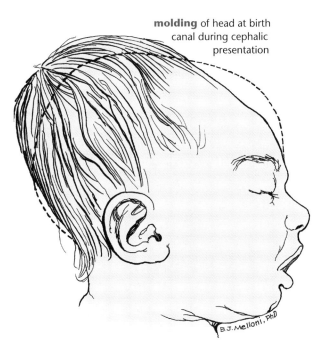

molding of head at birth canal during cephalic presentation

mole (mōl) **1.** Popular term for a nevocellular nevus. See nevocellular nevus, under nevus. **2.** An intrauterine mass. **3.** (mol) The amount of a substance containing as many elementary entities (ions, atoms, molecules, or radicals) as there are carbon atoms in 12 grams of carbon 12.

    atypical m. An acquired pigmented lesion of the skin that has clinical and histologic characteristics different from a typical common mole (nevocellular nevus); may have macular and/or papular components; has well-defined irregular borders; is typically larger than most acquired common moles (over 6 mm) with pigment variegation, ranging from tan to dark brown; and occurs on both sun-exposed and nonexposed areas of the body, especially on the trunk. Also called dysplastic nevus. See also familial atypical mole and melanoma syndrome, under syndrome.

hydatid m. See hydatidiform mole.

hydatidiform m. An abnormal pregnancy in which a mass of clear vesicles resembling a bunch of grapes grows within the uterus from proliferation of placental tissues; initial symptoms are usually those of early pregnancy, including a positive pregnancy test and vomiting (often severe); characteristic symptoms include bleeding, passage of vesicles, absence of fetal heart tones, a uterus too large for the estimated time of gestation, and absence of an intact fetus. There is no embryo present. Also called hydatid mole; molar pregnancy.

invasive m. A hydatidiform mole that invades the uterine wall; it may completely penetrate the wall and be associated with uterine rupture. Also called chorioadenoma destruens; chorioadenocarcinoma; choriocarcinoma.

molecular (mo-lek′u-lar) Relating to molecules.

molecule (mol′ĕ-kūl) The smallest unit of a substance that can exist in a free state and still retain the chemical properties of the substance; composed of two or more linked atoms.

molluscum contagiosum (mŏ-lus′kum kon-ta-je-o′sum) Infectious skin eruption of small, white wartlike lesions containing a cheesy substance; caused by a poxvirus, transmitted by direct contact; typically seen on the trunk and the genital and anal areas.

molybdenum (mo-lib′dĕ-num) Metallic element; symbol Mo, atomic number 42, atomic weight 95.94.

monad (mon′ad) **1.** A one-cell organism. **2.** A single chromosome formed after the second division in meiosis.

monarthritis (mon-ar-thri′tis) Arthritis of one joint.

monarticular (mon-ar-tik′u-lar) Relating to one joint.

monaural (mon-aw′ral) Relating to one ear.

mongolism (mon′go-lizm) See Down's syndrome, under syndrome.

mongoloid, mongolian (mon′go-loid, mon-go′le-an) Having characteristics that resemble those of Down's syndrome.

monilial (mo-nil′e-al) Relating to the fruit molds; frequently used incorrectly with reference to *Candida*.

moniliasis (mon-ī-li′ah-sis) Candidiasis.

moniliasis (candidiasis) of the uterine cervix

moliform (mo-nil′ĭ-form) Shaped like a string of pearls.

monitor (mon′ĭ-tor) **1.** To maintain a close, constant watch on a patient's condition. **2.** In laboratory medicine, a part of an instrument for detecting physical or chemical changes in electromagnetic radiation. **3.** Any device used in monitoring.

apnea m. An alarm system for alerting attendants when a patient (e.g., a premature infant) has stopped breathing.

blood pressure m. A device for continuously measuring and displaying a patient's arterial blood pressure.

cardiac m. An electronic device that displays a patient's electrocardiogram on a screen and signals the heartbeat both visually and audibly.

monitoring (mon′ĭ-tor-ing) **1.** A close, sometimes continuous, watch, observation, or supervision (as of a patient considered at risk). **2.** Periodic or continuous surveillance or testing to provide early warning of adverse effects (e.g., exposure to toxic substances or radioactivity).

auscultatory fetal m. Assessment of the fetal heart tones with a head stethoscope (fetoscope) during labor.

biologic m. In occupational medicine, the measuring of a pollutant (either a chemical or its metabolite) in a biologic specimen to assess the extent of exposure and the effect of that exposure on a worker; typically, specimens are blood, urine, or exhaled air. Total exposure is measured instead of just workplace exposure. The measurement indicates the quantity of a chemical absorbed regardless of the route of absorption (skin contact, inhalation, ingestion). Accurate interpretation of data depends on correct timing of the specimen collection because some chemicals are rapidly cleared from the blood.

electronic fetal m. Monitoring of the fetal heart rate during labor; may be *external* (indirect), with an electrode attached to the maternal abdomen, or *internal* (direct), with an electrode attached directly on the presenting part of the fetus.

environmental m. In occupational medicine, measuring of the external (ambient) exposure of a chemical in the workplace by examining samples taken from the air or from workplace surfaces. Measurements provide information about potential exposure, primarily from one route of exposure (e.g., air, surfaces).

mono-, mon- Combining forms meaning one.

mono (mon′o) Popular term for infectious mononucleosis; see under mononucleosis.

monoamniotic (mon′o-am-ne-ot′ik) Sharing one amniotic sac in the uterus; applied to twins.

monoblast (mon′o-blast) An immature cell, precursor of a monocyte.

monochromatic (mon-o-kro-mat′ik) Having one color.

monoclonal (mon-o-klōn′al) Derived from a group of cells or microorganisms that have an identical genetic composition (a clone).

monoclinic (mon-o-klin′ik) Denoting crystals with one oblique inclination.

monocrotic (mon-o-krot′ik) Forming a smooth single crest on the downward line of a curve; applied to a pulse.

monocular (mon-ok′u-lar) Relating to one eye.

monocyte (mon′o-sīt) A large white blood cell with a single kidney-shaped or lobulated nucleus; it is the largest cell (15–25 µm) in the blood; it has the ability to develop into an infection-fighting phagocyte.

monocytic (mon-o-sit′ik) Relating to monocytes.

monocytopenia (mon-o-si-to-pe′ne-ah) Reduced number of monocytes in the blood. Also called monocytic leukopenia.

monocytosis (mon-o-si-to′sis) An increase in the number of monocytes in the blood; a common reaction to inflammatory states. Also called monocytic leukocytosis.

monodactylism (mon-o-dak′til-izm) The presence of only one finger or toe on a hand or foot, respectively.

monogametic (mon-o-gah-met′ik) See homogametic.

monogenic (mon-o-jen′ik) Relating to an inherited characteristic or process that is determined by a single gene.

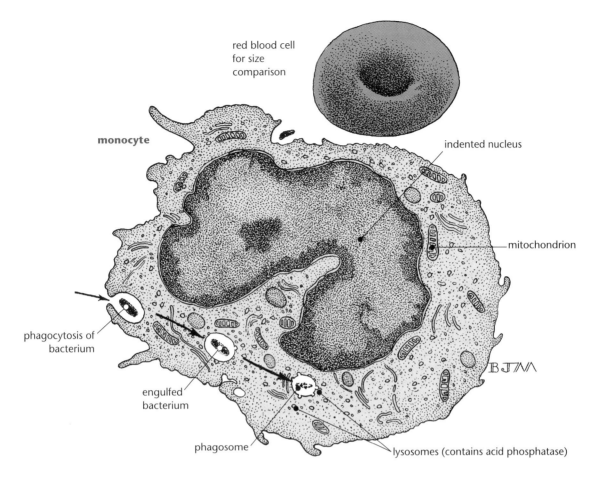

red blood cell for size comparison

monocyte

indented nucleus

mitochondrion

phagocytosis of bacterium

engulfed bacterium

phagosome

lysosomes (contains acid phosphatase)

B JⓂ

monograph (mon′o-graf) A detailed written account of one particular subject, one class of subjects, or a small area or special field of learning.

monoinfection (mon-o-in-fek′shun) Infection with a single species of microorganism.

monolocular (mon-o-lok′u-lar) Having a single chamber. Also called unicameral.

monomania (mon-o-ma′ne-ah) Pathologic preoccupation with a single idea.

monomer (mon′o-mer) **1.** A single molecule that, when repeated in a chain, forms a polymer (e.g., ethylene is the monomer of polyethylene). **2.** The protein structural unit of the covering (capsid) of a virus particle (virion).

monomorphic (mon-o-mor′fik) Having but one size and form.

mononeuritis (mon-o-nu-ri′tis) Inflammation of a single nerve trunk or some of its fibers.

   m. multiplex Simultaneous inflammation of single noncontinuous nerves at several distant sites.

mononeuropathy (mon-o-nu-rop′ah-the) Dysfunction of a single peripheral nerve due to a variety of causes (e.g., entrapment, diabetes mellitus, carcinoma).

mononuclear (mon-o-nu′kle-ar) Having but one nucleus; applied especially to blood cells.

mononucleosis (mon-o-nu-kle-o′sis) Abnormal increase of mononuclear white blood cells (monocytes) in circulating blood.

   cytomegalovirus (CMV) m. Infectious disease resembling infectious mononucleosis but caused by CMV, a herpesvirus classified as human herpesvirus 5 (HHV-5); incubation period is 20 to 60 days; characterized by prolonged high fevers, headache, malaise, profound fatigue, muscle pains, and enlargement of the spleen; in contrast to infectious mononucleosis, throat and cervical node involvement is uncommon; it is a common problem in transplant recipients receiving organs from donors with prior CMV infections.

   infectious m. Infectious disease caused by the Epstein-Barr virus (EBV), a herpesvirus classified as human herpesvirus 4 (HHV-4); symptoms occur after an incubation period of one to two months; they include fever, sore throat, and enlargement of the spleen and lymph nodes; blood contains a large number of atypical lymphocytes (i.e., infected lymphocytes that resemble monocytes). The virus can be carried in the throat and saliva of afflicted persons for several months after disappearance of clinical symptoms; occurs mostly in adolescents and young adults. Sometimes called glandular fever; benign lymphadenosis; popularly called mono; kissing disease.

monophasia (mon-o-fa′ze-ah) Disorder in which the individual's vocabulary is limited to a single word or sentence.

monophasic (mon-o-fa′zik) Relating to monophasia.

monophenol monooxygenase (mon-o-fe′nol mon-o-ok′sĭ-jĕ-nās) A copper-containing enzyme that promotes the oxidation of phenols such as tyrosine; it is involved in the eventual conversion of tyrosine to melanin; its absence in the body tissues is linked to albinism. Also called tyrosinase.

monophobia (mon-o-fo′be-ah) Abnormally exaggerated fear of being left alone.

monoplegia (mon-o-ple′je-ah) Paralysis of a single limb.

monorchid (mon-or′kid) Having only one testicle.

monorchidic (mon-or-kid′ik) Relating to monorchism.

monorchism (mon′or-kizm) The state of having only one testicle. Distinguished from the condition of having one undescended testicle.

monosaccharide (mon-o-sak′ah-rīd) A carbohydrate that is not further broken down by hydrolysis; a simple sugar.

monosodium glutamate (mon-o-so′de-um glu′tah-māt) (MSG) A food additive used as a flavor enhancer; in large doses it may be a contributing cause of "Chinese restaurant" syndrome in some individuals.

monosome (mon′o-sōm) A chromosome without its homologous chromosome.

monosomic (mon-o-so′mik) Characterized by monosomy.

monosomy (mon′o-so-me) Condition in which 1 chromsome of a pair is missing so that there are 45 instead of the normal 46 chromosomes; seen in certain genetic disorders (e.g., Turner's syndrome).

monovalent (mon-o-va′lent) Having the combining power of one hydrogen atom. Also called univalent.

monozygotic (mon-o-zi-got′ik) Derived from a single fertilized ovum; applied to identical twins.

mons (monz), pl. mon′tes A slight anatomic prominence.

m. pubis The pad of fatty tissue over the pubic symphysis in the female.

m. ureteris A slight prominence on the wall of the bladder at the entrance of each ureter.

mood (mood) A prevailing emotional state of mind or feeling-tone.

Moraxella (mo-rak-sel′ah) A genus of aerobic parasitic bacteria (family Neisseriaceae); found on the mucous membranes of humans.

M. catarrhalis A species of bacteria (genus *Moraxella*) that are normal inhabitants of the nasal cavity and nasopharynx, causing respiratory disease and otitis media. Formerly called *Branhamella catarrhalis; Neisseria catarrhalis.*

morbid (mor′bid) Relating to disease; pathologic.

morbidity (mor-bid′ĭ-te) 1. A diseased (pathologic) condition. 2. The proportion of patients with a particular disease during a given time period in a given unit of population.

morbilli (mor-bil′i) Measles.

morbilliform (mor-bil′ĭ-form) Resembling measles.

Morbillivirus (mor-bil-ĭ-vi′rus) A genus of viruses (family Paramyxoviridae) that includes the measles and canine distemper viruses.

morbillous (mor-bil′us) Relating to measles.

morbus (mor′bus) Latin for disease.

morgan (mor′gan) (M) The unit of map distance on a chromosome.

morgue (morg) 1. A building where unidentified dead bodies are held pending identification before burial. 2. A building or place in a hospital where the dead are placed pending autopsy, burial, or cremation.

moribund (mor′ĭ-bund) Dying.

morphea (mor-fe′ah) Skin condition characterized by the presence of indurated yellowish plaques surrounded by a violet ring, occurring mainly on the chest, neck, or face. Also called localized scleroderma.

morphine (mor′fēn) An alkaloid compound extracted from opium, used in medicine as an analgesic (e.g., to relieve pain of myocardial infarction, major surgery or injury, and cancer). Commonly administered as morphine sulfate (m.s.). Adverse effects include dizziness, confusion, nausea, vomiting, and constipation; long-term use produces physical and psychologic dependence. Also called diacetylmorphine.

morpho-, morph- Combining forms meaning form; shape; structure.

morphogenesis (mor-fo-jen′ĕ-sis) The embryonic differentiation of cells leading to the characteristic structure and form of the organism or its parts.

morphologic (mor-fo-loj′ik) Relating to morphology.

morphology (mor-fol′o-je) The study of the configuration or structure of living plants or animals.

mors (morz) Latin for death.

mortal (mor′tal) 1. Subject to death. 2. Deadly.

mortality (mor-tal′ĭ-te) The condition of being mortal.

mortar (mor′tar) Small receptacle in which substances (e.g., crude drugs) are crushed with a pestle.

mortise (mor′tis) The articular surface for the talus at the ankle joint, formed by the union of the lower (distal) ends of the tibia and fibula.

morula (mor′u-lah) A cluster of cells (blastomeres) resulting from the early division of the zygote; an early stage in the development of the embryo.

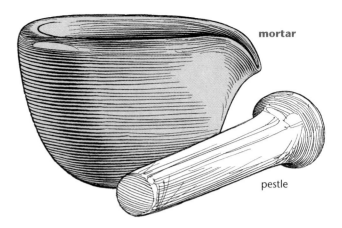

mortar

pestle

morulation (mor-u-la′shun) The formation of the morula.

mosaic (mo-za′ik) A person or tissue affected with mosaicism.

mosaicism (mo-sa′ĭ-sizm) The presence within one person of two or more populations of cells, some with a normal set of chromosomes, others with extra or missing chromosomes; caused by errors of cell division in the fertilized egg (zygote). Predominance of abnormal cells gives rise to chromosomal abnormality syndromes (e.g., Down's syndrome, Turner's syndrome).

mosquito (mos-ke′to) Any flying insect of the family Culicidae; some bloodsucking species transmit disease-causing parasites, especially those of the genera *Aedes, Anopheles, Culex,* and *Mansonia.*

tiger m. See *Aedes aegypti.*

mother (muth′er) 1. A female parent. 2. In obstetrics, a pregnant woman, distinct from the fetus. 3. Any cell or structure that gives rise to other similar cells or structures.

surrogate m. A woman who agrees to become pregnant (usually through artificial means) and to carry the pregnancy to term with the understanding that she will relinquish the infant to the contractual parent or parents.

m. surrogate See under surrogate.

motile (mo′til) Capable of self-generated motion.

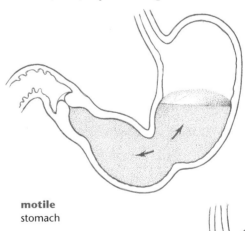

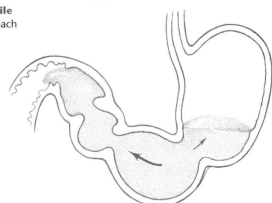

motile
stomach

motilin (mo-til′in) A polypeptide hormone of 22 amino acids produced in the mucosa of the lower stomach, duodenum, and upper jejunum; it stimulates motility of the stomach and intestines.

motor (mo′tor) **1.** Producing movement; applied to nerves carrying impulses from nerve centers to effector organs or parts. **2.** A mechanism or device that produces movement.

plastic m. An artificial point of attachment on an amputation stump through which motion is provided to an artificial limb.

mottling (mot′ling) Skin eruption containing various colors and shades.

moulage (moo-lahzh′) A mold of a body structure or lesion used especially for identification, prosthetic, or teaching purposes.

mounding (mownd′ing) See myoedema.

mount (mownt) To prepare tissues for microscopic examination.

mounting (mownt′ing) In dentistry, a laboratory procedure in which a cast of one or both jaws is attached to an articulator.

mouse (mows) Any small rodent of the genus *Mus*. Many species are used extensively in laboratory research, for which strains have also been developed.

New Zealand black (NZB) m. An inbred strain of mice used to study autoimmune diseases.

nude m. A genetically athymic mouse that lacks T cells and also carries a gene that produces a defect in hair production.

transgenic m. A mouse that is the product of bioengineering (i.e., one produced to mimic human diseases by *in vitro* transfer of genes of interest into the mouse embryo); it serves as a model for studying such diseases as cancer. Harvard University received the first patent in the United States for the transgenic mouse it developed in 1988; it was named Harvard I mouse.

mouth (mowth) **1.** The oral cavity and related parts, including the lips. **2.** An orifice or opening of a tubular structure or cavity.

dry m. Popular name for xerostomia.

trench m. See necrotizing ulcerative gingivitis, under gingivitis.

movement (moov′ment) **1.** A change of place or position. **2.** Popular name for defecation; bowel movement.

associated contralateral m. An involuntary movement occurring on the affected side of a hemiplegic patient, induced by a voluntary movement on the normal side.

athetoid m.'s Movements resembling the slow, writhing movements characteristic of athetosis.

bowel m. (BM) See defecation.

brownian m. Erratic motion of microscopic particles suspended in a liquid or gas, resulting from collision with molecules in the suspending medium.

cardinal ocular m.'s The six principal eye movements: to the right and left, upward to the right and left, and downward to the right and left; used in diagnosis of certain neurologic disorders.

choreic m. An involuntary jerking involving groups of muscles.

circus m. Activation of part of the heart muscle occurring over a circular pathway. Also called circus rhythm.

conjugate m. of eyes Coordinated movement of the two eyes in one direction.

non–rapid eye m. (NREM) The slow, oscillating movement of the eyes during sleep.

passive m. Movement of the body or any of its parts produced by an external force.

rapid eye m.'s (REMs) The short, quick, jerky movements occurring during deep sleep and lasting 5 to 60 minutes; associated with dreaming.

saccadic m. A quick, abrupt movement of the eyes occurring normally when changing fixation from one point to another.

streaming m. The characteristic movement of protoplasm involved in the locomotion of certain white blood cells and unicellular organisms.

mover (moo′ver) One that sets something in motion.

prime m. See agonistic muscle, under muscle.

moxa (mok′sah) A small mass of combustible herbal material (e.g., wormwood leaves) placed near the skin or on an acupuncture needle and ignited to produce a counterirritation; used in traditional Chinese and Japanese medicine.

moxibustion (mok-sĭ-bust′yun) Counterirritation by means of a moxa.

mu (mu) (μ) **1.** Twelfth letter of the Greek alphabet. **2.** A micron.

muci- Combining form meaning mucus; mucin.

muciferous (mu-sif′er-us) See muciparous.

muciform (mu′sĭ-form) Resembling mucus.

mucigenous (mu-sij′ĕ-nus) See muciparous.

mucilage (mu′sĭ-lij) **1.** A thick gumlike substance. **2.** A water solution of a gum used in pharmaceutical preparations.

mucin (mu′sin) A viscous fluid composed of glycoproteins, secreted by mucous glands (e.g., salivary glands and those of the intestinal lining).

mucinase (mu′sĭ-nās) Enzyme that promotes the breakdown of mucin.

mucinoid (mu′sĭ-noid) Resembling mucin.

mucinosis (mu-sĭ-no′sis) A condition in which mucin is present in excessive amounts.

mucinous (mu′sĭ-nus) Containing mucin.

muciparous (mu-sip′ah-rus) Secreting mucus. Also called muciferous; mucigenous.

muco- Combining form meaning mucus.

mucocele (mu′ko-sēl) **1.** A retention cyst of a mucous gland. **2.** Distention of a hollow organ or part (e.g., gallbladder, appendix) with mucin-containing secretions.

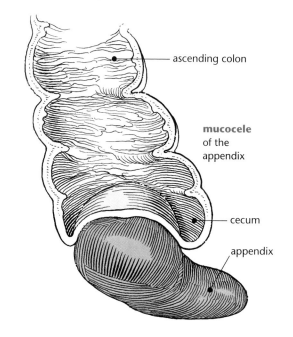

ascending colon

mucocele of the appendix

cecum

appendix

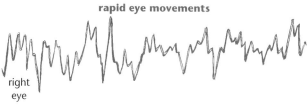

rapid eye movements

right eye

electro-oculogram

left eye

mucocutaneous (mu-ko-ku-ta′ne-us) Relating to mucous membrane and skin.

mucoenteritis (mu-ko-en-ter-i′tis) Inflammation of the interior lining of the intestines.

mucoid (mu′koid) Resembling mucus.

mucolipidosis (mu-ko-lip-ĭ-do′sis) Any of a group of inherited metabolic diseases characterized by accumulation of mucopolysaccharides and lipids in the tissues; an autosomal recessive inheritance.

mucolytic (mu-ko-lit′ik) Capable of dissolving mucus.

mucomembranous (mu-ko-mem′brah-nus) Relating to mucous membrane.

mucoperiosteum (mu-ko-per-e-os′te-um) Mucous membrane and periosteum that are closely adhered, as seen in the nasal cavity and sinuses.

mucopolysaccharide (mu-ko-pol-e-sak′ah-rīd) General term for polysaccharide components (e.g., hyaluronic acid and chondroitin sulfate) attached to a polypeptide component by weak chemical bonding.

mucopolysaccharidosis (mu-ko-pol-e-sak′ah-rĭ-do′sis) (MPS) A group of disorders resulting from inherited deficiencies of enzymes involved in the breakdown of mucopolysaccharides, causing accumulation of these substances in the cells.

> **type I m.** See Hurler's syndrome, under syndrome.
> **type IS m.** See Scheie's syndrome, under syndrome.
> **type II m.** See Hunter's syndrome, under syndrome.
> **type III m.** See Sanfilippo's syndrome, under syndrome.
> **type IV m.** See Morquio's syndrome, under syndrome.
> **type V m.** Former name for Scheie's syndrome.
> **type VI m.** See Maroteaux-Lamy syndrome, under syndrome.
> **type VII m.** A type caused by beta-glucuronidase deficiency; it resembles a mild form of Hurler's syndrome.

mucoprotein (mu-ko-pro′tēn) Any of a group of organic compounds containing proteins and mucopolysaccharides.

mucopurulent (mu-ko-pu′roo-lent) Containing mucus and pus; applied especially to discharges.

mucopus (mu′ko-pus) A discharge composed of mucus and pus.

Mucor (mu′kor) Genus of fungi (class Zygomycetes); some species cause human diseases.

mucormycosis (mu-kor-mi-ko′sis) See phycomycosis.

mucosa (mu-ko′sah) A mucous membrane; the inner lining of a cavity or tubular structure.

mucosanguineous (mu-ko-sang-gwin′e-us) Containing mucus and blood; applied to a discharge.

mucoserous (mu-ko-se′rus) Relating to or containing mucus and serum or plasma.

mucous (mu′kus) Relating to mucus.

mucoviscidosis (mu-ko-vis-ĭ-do′sis) See cystic fibrosis, under fibrosis.

mucus (mu′kus) The slippery suspension of mucin, desquamated cells, inorganic salts, and water secreted by glands in mucous membranes and serving to moisten and protect the membrane.

MUDDLES Acronym for Miosis, Urination, Diarrhea, Defecation, Lacrimation, Excitation, and Salivation; the signs and symptoms of acute intoxication with certain pesticides (organophosphates, carbamates).

muliebria (mu-le-eb′re-ah) The female genital organs.

muliebris (mu-le-eb′ris) Relating to a female.

multangular (mul-tang′gu-lar) Having several angles.

multi- Combining form meaning more than one; many.

multiarticular (mul-te-ar-tik′u-lar) Relating to several joints.

multicellular (mul-tĭ-sel′u-lar) Composed of many cells.

multifid (mul′tĭ-fid) Divided into many segments.

multifocal (mul-tĭ-fo′kal) Arising from many sites.

multiform (mul′tĭ-form) See polymorphic.

multiglandular (mul-tĭ-glan′du-lar) See pluriglandular.

multigravida (mul-tĭ-grav′ĭ-dah) A woman who has been pregnant more than once.

multi-infarct (mul′ti in′farkt) Several areas of cell death resulting from lack of blood supply.

multilobar (mul-tĭ-lo′bar) Having several lobes.

multilobular (mul-tĭ-lob′u-lar) Having several lobules.

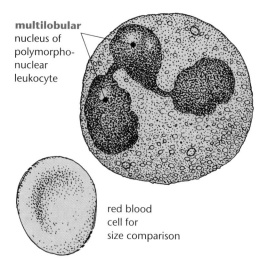

multilobular nucleus of polymorpho-nuclear leukocyte

red blood cell for size comparison

multilocular (mul-tĭ-lok′u-lar) Having several compartments.

multimammae (mul-tĭ-mam′e) See polymastia.

multinuclear, multinucleate (mul-tĭ-nu′kle-ar, mul-tĭ-nu′kle-āt) Having more than one nucleus. Also called polynuclear.

multipara (mul-tip′ah-rah) A woman who has completed two or more pregnancies in which the fetuses reached the stage of viability, regardless of whether the infants were live or stillborn.

multiparity (mul-tĭ-par′ĭ-te) The condition of being a multipara.

multiparous (mul-tip′ah-rus) Relating to a multipara.

multiple (mul′tĭ-pl) 1. Having more than one component. 2. Occurring in several sites at the same time.

multipolar (mul-tĭ-po′lar) Having more than two poles (e.g., certain cells).

multivalence (mul-tĭ-va′lens) The state of being multivalent.

multivalent (mul-tĭ-va′lent) In chemistry, having the combining power of two or more hydrogen atoms.

mummification (mum-ĭ-fi-ka′shun) 1. See dry gangrene, under gangrene. 2. The drying and compression of a fetus that has died and remained in the uterus.

mumps (mumps) Contagious viral disease with an incubation period of 18 to 22 days, marked by inflammation and pain of the parotid glands, fever, malaise, and headache; occasionally other salivary glands are involved; complications include orchitis in postpubertal males and, rarely, meningoencephalitis; caused by a paramyxovirus, transmitted by infected salivary secretions and urine. Also called epidemic parotitis.

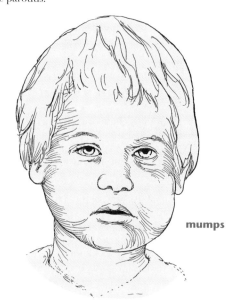

mumps

M

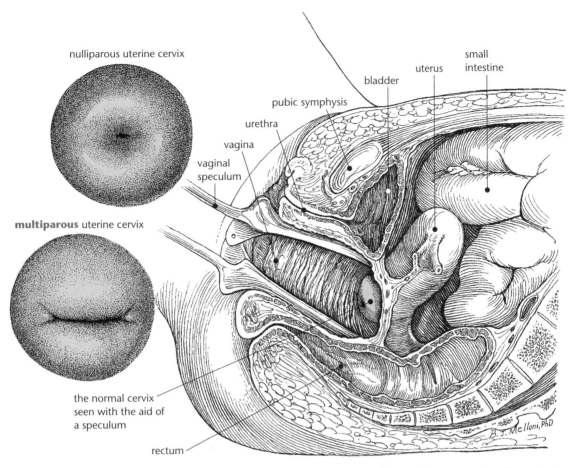

nulliparous uterine cervix

multiparous uterine cervix

the normal cervix
seen with the aid of
a speculum

vaginal speculum

vaginal

vagina

urethra

pubic symphysis

bladder

uterus

small intestine

rectum

B.J. Melloni, PhD

M

mural (mu'ral) Relating to the wall of a cavity or hollow organ.

muramic acid (mu-ram'ik as'id) A component of the murein molecules in bacterial cell walls.

murein (mu're-in) The rigid layer of a bacterial cell wall.

murine (mu'rin) Relating to animals of the family Muridae, especially rats and mice.

murmur (mur'mur) An abnormal, relatively prolonged, series of auditory vibrations, heard on auscultation and resulting from turbulent blood flow in the cardiovascular system.

aortic m. Murmur arising from the aortic orifice.

Austin Flint's m. See Flint's murmur.

cardiac m. Murmur arising from the heart.

continuous m. Murmur that starts in systole and continues without interruption into all or part of the diastole.

crescendo m. Murmur that increases in loudness and then stops abruptly.

Cruveilhier-Baumgarten m. Venous murmur heard over the abdominal wall when there are veins connecting the portal and caval venous systems.

diamond-shaped m. Murmur that increases in loudness and then decreases in such a manner as to produce a diamond-shaped curve on the phonocardiogram.

diastolic m. Murmur that starts with or after the second heart sound and ends before the first heart sound (e.g., during diastole).

Duroziez' m. A double or to-and-fro murmur heard over the femoral artery in cases of aortic insufficiency. Also called Duroziez' symptom.

dynamic m. Murmur caused by a condition other than heart valve disease.

early diastolic m. Murmur that starts with the second heart sound (i.e., at the time of aortic valve closure); the typical murmur of aortic incompetence.

ejection m. A diamond-shaped murmur occurring when blood is ejected across the aortic or pulmonary valves, from the left or right ventricles into the aorta or pulmonary trunk.

extracardiac m. Any murmur heard over the heart area but arising from another structure.

Flint's m. A mid-diastolic or presystolic rumble that appears to originate at the anterior leaflet of the mitral (left atrioventricular) valve when normal and abnormal streams of blood enter the left ventricle; heard in some cases of aortic incompetence. Also called Austin Flint's murmur.

functional m. Murmur due to causes other than heart disorders. Also called inorganic murmur; innocent murmur.

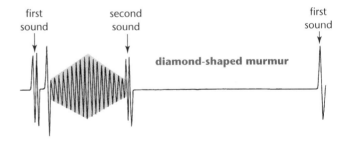

first sound

second sound

first sound

diamond-shaped murmur

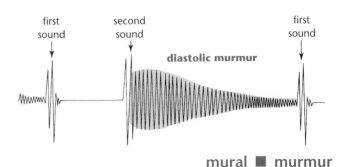

first sound

second sound

first sound

diastolic murmur

M45

mural ■ murmur

Graham Steell's m. An early diastolic, high-pitched murmur; caused by pulmonary incompetence due to pulmonary hypertension.

hemic m. Murmur occurring in anemic persons without heart disease.

holosystolic m. See pansystolic murmur.

humming-top m. See venous hum, under hum.

innocent m. See functional murmur.

inorganic m. See functional murmur.

late diastolic m. See presystolic murmur.

machinery m. The continuous murmur typical of patent ductus arteriosus.

mid-diastolic m. Murmur beginning soon, but at a clear interval, after the second heart sound; arises at the atrioventricular heart valves, usually due either to constriction of the valve orifices or to abnormal patterns of atrioventricular blood flow.

mitral valve m. Murmur produced at the mitral (left atrioventricular) valve; caused by constriction of the valve orifice or backward blood flow through the valve.

musical m. A heart murmur with a musical quality.

organic m. Murmur caused by organic disease (e.g., valvular deformity or septal defect) in contrast to a functional murmur.

pansystolic m. Murmur lasting throughout systole, from the first to the second heart sound. Also called holosystolic murmur.

presystolic m. A short, usually crescendo murmur, occurring immediately before the first heart sound (i.e., during atrial systole), due most often to obstruction of one of the atrioventricular orifices. Also called late diastolic murmur.

pulmonary m., pulmonic m. Murmur heard at the orifice of the pulmonary trunk.

regurgitant m. Murmur originating at the valvular orifices of the heart due to leakage or backward blood flow.

Roger's m. A loud pansystolic murmur with maximal intensity at the left border of the breastbone (sternum) caused by the presence of a small hole in the wall dividing the ventricles (ventricular septal defect). Also called bruit de Roger.

sea gull m. A musical murmur similar to the cry of a sea gull.

seesaw m. See to-and-fro murmur.

systolic m. Murmur beginning with or after the first heart sound and ending at or before the second sound (i.e., during systole).

to-and-fro m. Murmur heard in both systole and diastole. Also called seesaw murmur.

tricuspid m. Murmur originating at the orifice of the tricuspid (right atrioventricular) valve of the heart.

muscae volitantes (mus′ke vol-ī-tan′tes) Former name for floaters.

muscarine (mus′kah-rin) Poisonous alkaloid present in certain mushrooms; it stimulates postganglionic nerve fibers of the parasympathetic nervous system, causing several effects (e.g., inhibition of the heart action, constriction of air passages, and overactivity of stomach and intestines).

muscarinic (mus-kah-rin′ik) 1. Producing an effect similar to that of muscarine. 2. Denoting an agent producing such an effect.

muscarinism (mus′kar-in-izm) See mycetism.

muscle (mus′el) Tissue that serves to produce movement by its contraction; composed primarily of contractile cells. See table of muscles for individual muscles.

abductor m. A muscle that draws a part away from the median plane, or in the fingers and toes, away from the axial line of the limb.

adductor m. A muscle that draws a part toward the median plane, or in the fingers and toes, toward the axial line of the limb.

agonistic m. A muscle that is constantly active in both the initiation and maintenance of a particular movement of an anatomic part, such as the brachial muscle in flexion of the forearm at the elbow joint; the action of the agonistic muscle can be opposed by that of another muscle called antagonistic. Also called prime mover.

antagonistic m. A muscle with opposing force that counteracts the action of another muscle, called the agonistic muscle, or that initiates and maintains a movement opposite to that of the agonist.

antigravity m.'s Muscles maintaining the normal posture of the body characteristic of a given species by resisting the constant pull of gravity.

bipennate m. Muscle with a central tendon in which the muscle fibers converge in barblike fashion (e.g., the rectus muscle of the thigh).

cardiac m. Muscle of the heart (myocardium), composed of striated fibers identical in organization with those of skeletal muscle but with conspicuous cross striations (intercalated disks) marking the junctions between the ends of the cells.

congenerous m.'s Muscles that perform the same action or function.

constrictor m. A muscle that makes a passage smaller or narrower by contracting (e.g., the constrictor muscles of the pharynx).

depressor m. A muscle that serves to depress the structure into which it is inserted.

dilator m. A muscle that dilates an opening, such as the pupil of the eye.

emergency m.'s Muscles that assist agonistic muscles when considerable force is required.

extensor m. A muscle that straightens out to full length (extends) a joint.

extrinsic m. A muscle that does not originate in the same part or limb to which it is inserted (e.g., superior rectus muscle of eyeball).

facial m.'s Muscles of facial expression that affect movements of the skin, eyelids, eyebrows, nose, lips, and scalp.

fixation m.'s See fixator muscles.

fixator m.'s Agonistic and antagonistic muscles collaborating in stabilizing the position of a joint or part; they contract together to hold the joint in position when powerful external forces are encountered. Also called fixation muscles.

flexor m. A muscle that bends (flexes) a joint.

fusiform m. A muscle with a fleshy belly tapering upon a tendon at either end. Also called spindle-shaped muscle.

hamstring m.'s The three muscles at the back of the thigh: the biceps muscle of the thigh (biceps femoris), the semitendinous muscle, and the semimembranous muscle; they flex the leg and rotate it medially and laterally at the knee joint, and extend the thigh at the hip joint. Also called posterior femoral muscles.

intrinsic m. A muscle in which both origin and insertion are lying wholly within the same part or limb (e.g., ciliary muscle of eyeball).

involuntary m. See smooth muscle.

levator m. A muscle that elevates a structure into which it is inserted.

longitudinal m. A muscle in which the fiber bundles are lengthwise (i.e., parallel to the long axis of the body or part).

multipennate m. A muscle in which the fiber bundles converge to several tendons (e.g., deltoid muscle).

nonstriated m. See smooth muscle.

papillary m.'s The fleshy columns of muscles arising from the inner walls of the cardiac ventricles, attached to the triangular cusps of the atrioventricular valves by the chordae tendinae; there are two major papillary muscles in each ventricle.

posterior femoral m.'s See hamstring muscles.

red m. Skeletal muscle of dark reddish color, due to the presence of large amounts of the protein pigment myoglobin; characterized by slow contractibility (with a twitch duration of 75 msec) and resistance to fatigue; well suited to a repetitive type of contraction (e.g., muscles that sustain posture). Also called type I muscle; slow twitch muscle. COMPARE white muscle.

skeletal m. A striated voluntary muscle that is attached to bones, usually crossing at least one joint on which it acts; when viewed microscopically, the muscle fibers exhibit regularly spaced transverse bands. Also called voluntary muscle.

smooth m. Nonstriated muscle that is not under voluntary control, but responds to the autonomic nervous system; mainly concerned with movements and contractions of blood vessels, the alimentary canal, the respiratory, and urogenital systems, and glands. Also called nonstriated muscle; unstriated muscle; involuntary muscle.

sphincter m. A circular band of muscle arranged around an orifice or tube (e.g., sphincter muscle of the anus; the sphincter muscle of the bile duct).

spindle-shaped m. See fusiform muscle.

strap m. Any flat muscle, especially those of the neck associated with the hyoid bone and thyroid cartilage.

striated m. Skeletal and cardiac muscle in which cross striations occur in the fibers; with the exception of the cardiac muscle, striated muscles are voluntary, as opposed to the smooth muscles under control of the autonomic nervous system.

synergistic m. A muscle that acts in conjunction with the agonistic muscle (prime mover) to maximize a mutually helpful action.

type I m. See red muscle.

type II m. See white muscle.

unipennate m. Muscle with a tendon attached to one side only (e.g., extensor muscle of the little finger).

unstriated m. See smooth muscle.

voluntary m. See skeletal muscle.

white m. Skeletal muscle of pale color, due to the presence of relatively small amounts of the protein pigment myoglobin; characterized by fast contractibility (with a twitch duration of 25 msec) and rapid onset of fatigue; generally involved in large-scale movements of body segments. Also called type II muscle; fast twitch muscle. COMPARE red muscle.

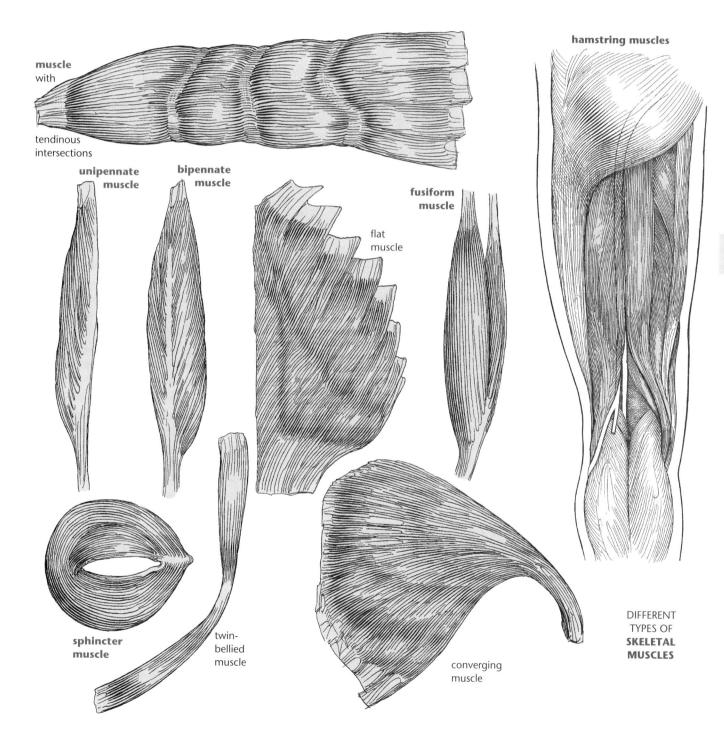

muscle with tendinous intersections

unipennate muscle

bipennate muscle

flat muscle

fusiform muscle

hamstring muscles

sphincter muscle

twin-bellied muscle

converging muscle

DIFFERENT TYPES OF **SKELETAL MUSCLES**

M

muscle ■ muscle

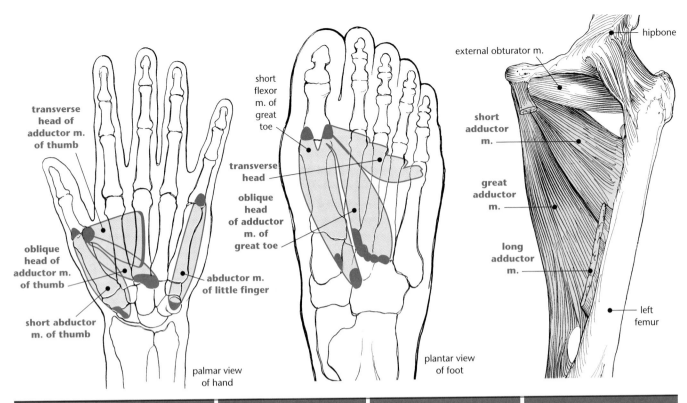

transverse head of adductor m. of thumb

oblique head of adductor m. of thumb

short abductor m. of thumb

abductor m. of little finger

palmar view of hand

short flexor m. of great toe

transverse head

oblique head of adductor m. of great toe

plantar view of foot

external obturator m.

hipbone

short adductor m.

great adductor m.

long adductor m.

left femur

MUSCLE	ORIGIN	INSERTION	ACTION
abductor m. of great toe *m. abductor hallucis*	calcaneus, plantar aponeurosis	proximal phalanx of great toe (joined by short flexor muscle of great toe)	abducts and aids in flexion of great toe
abductor m. of little finger *m. abductor digiti minimi manus*	pisiform bone, tendon of ulnar flexor muscle of wrist	proximal phalanx of fifth digit	abducts little finger
abductor m. of little toe *m. abductor digiti minimi pedis*	lateral tubercle of calcaneus, plantar aponeurosis	proximal phalanx of little toe	abducts and flexes little toe
abductor m. of thumb, long *m. abductor pollicis longus*	posterior surface of ulna, middle third of radius	first metacarpal bone	abducts and extends thumb
abductor m. of thumb, short *m. abductor pollicis brevis*	flexor retinaculum of hand, scaphoid and trapezium	proximal phalanx of thumb	abducts and aids in flexion of thumb
adductor m., great *m. adductor magnus*	*adductor part:* inferior ramus of pubis, ramus of ischium; *extensor part:* ischial tuberosity	*adductor part:* linea aspera of femur; *extensor part:* adductor tubercle of femur	adducts, flexes, and rotates thigh medially
adductor m., long *m. adductor longus*	pubis, below pubic crest	linea aspera of femur	adducts, flexes, and rotates thigh medially
adductor m., short *m. adductor brevis*	pubis, below origin of the long adductor m.	upper part of linea aspera of femur	adducts, flexes, and rotates thigh laterally
adductor m., smallest *m. adductor minimus*	the proximal portion of the great adductor m. when it forms a distinct muscle		
adductor m. of great toe *m. adductor hallucis*	*oblique head:* bases of middle three metatarsal bones; *transverse head:* metatarsophalangeal ligaments of lateral three toes	proximal phalanx of great toe (joined by flexor m. of great toe)	*oblique head:* adducts and flexes great toe; *transverse head:* supports transverse arch, adducts great toe
adductor m. of thumb *m. adductor pollicis*	*oblique head:* capitate, second, and third metacarpal bones; *transverse head:* third metacarpal bone	proximal phalanx of thumb; medial sesamoid bone	adducts and aids in apposition of thumb
anconeus m. *m. anconeus*	back of lateral epicondyle of humerus	olecranon process, posterior surface of ulna	extends forearm, abducts ulna in pronation of wrist
antitragus m. *m. antitragicus*	outer surface of antitragus of ear	caudate process of helix and antihelix	thought to be vestigial
arrector m.'s of hair *mm. arrectores pilorum*	dermis	hair follicles	elevate hairs of skin; aid in discharging sebum
articular m. of elbow *m. articularis cubiti*	lower part of triceps m. of arm	posterior aspect of elbow joint capsule	elevates capsule in extension of elbow joint
articular m. of knee *m. articularis genus*	lower part of anterior surface of femur	upper part of synovial membrane of knee joint	elevates capsule of knee joint during extension of leg

muscle ■ muscle

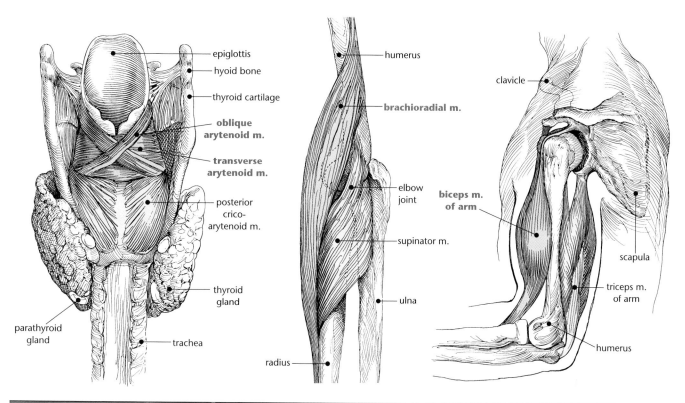

Labels on illustrations:

epiglottis
hyoid bone
thyroid cartilage
oblique arytenoid m.
transverse arytenoid m.
posterior crico-arytenoid m.
thyroid gland
parathyroid gland
trachea

humerus
brachioradial m.
elbow joint
supinator m.
ulna
radius

clavicle
biceps m. of arm
scapula
triceps m. of arm
humerus

MUSCLE	ORIGIN	INSERTION	ACTION
aryepiglottic m. *m. aryepiglotticus*	apex of arytenoid cartilage	lateral margin of epiglottis	narrows inlet of larynx by lowering epiglottis
arytenoid m., oblique *m. arytenoideus obliquus*	muscular process of arytenoid cartilage	apex of opposite arytenoid cartilage, prolonged as aryepiglottic muscle	helps to close inlet of larynx by approximating arytenoid cartilages
arytenoid m., transverse (only unpaired muscle of the larynx) *m. arytenoideus transversus*	posterior surface of arytenoid cartilage	posterior surface of opposite arytenoid cartilage	approximates arytenoid cartilages; constricts entrance to larynx during swallowing
auricular m., anterior *m. auricularis anterior*	superficial temporal fascia	cartilage of ear	feeble forward movement of auricle
auricular m., posterior *m. auricularis posterior*	mastoid process	cartilage of ear	feeble backward movement of auricle
auricular m., superior *m. auricularis superior*	temporal fascia, epicranial aponeurosis	cartilage of ear	feeble elevation of auricle
auricular m., transverse *m. auricularis transversus*	upper surface of auricle	circumference of auricle	retracts helix
biceps m. of arm *m. biceps brachii*	*long head:* supraglenoid tubercle of scapula; *short head:* apex of coracoid process	tuberosity of radius; posterior border of ulna through bicipital aponeurosis	flexes forearm and arm, supinates hand
biceps m. of thigh *m. biceps femoris*	*long head:* ischial tuberosity; *short head:* linea aspera and second supracondylar ridge of femur	head of fibula, lateral condyle of tibia	flexes knee, rotates leg laterally; long head extends thigh
brachial m. *m. brachialis*	anterior surface of distal two-thirds of humerus	coronoid process of ulna	flexes forearm
brachioradial m. *m. brachioradialis*	lateral supracondylar ridge and intermuscular septum of humerus	lower end of radius	flexes forearm
bronchoesophageal m. *m. bronchoesophageus*	muscle fibers arising from wall of left bronchus	musculature of esophagus	reinforces esophagus
buccinator m. *m. buccinator*	pterygomandibular raphe, alveolar processes of jaws	orbicular m. (orbicularis oris) at angle of mouth	retracts angle of mouth by compressing cheek; accessory muscle of mastication
bulbocavernous m. *m. bulbospongiosus*	*female:* central tendon of perineum; *male:* median raphe over bulb of penis, central tendon of perineum	*female:* dorsum of clitoris, urogenital diaphragm; *male:* corpus spongiosum, root of penis	*female:* compresses vaginal orifice; *male:* compresses urethra; assists in ejaculation

M

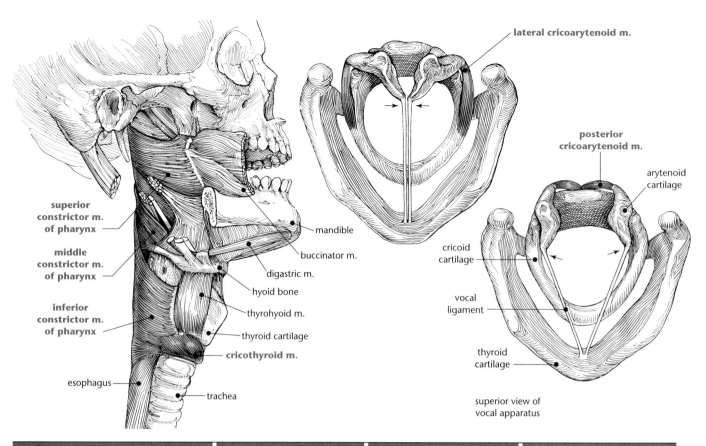

superior constrictor m. of pharynx

middle constrictor m. of pharynx

inferior constrictor m. of pharynx

esophagus

mandible

buccinator m.

digastric m.

hyoid bone

thyrohyoid m.

thyroid cartilage

cricothyroid m.

trachea

lateral cricoarytenoid m.

posterior cricoarytenoid m.

arytenoid cartilage

cricoid cartilage

vocal ligament

thyroid cartilage

superior view of vocal apparatus

MUSCLE	ORIGIN	INSERTION	ACTION
canine m. *caninus m.*	see levator m. of angle of mouth		
ceratocricoid m. *m. ceratocricoideus*	lower margin of cricoid cartilage	inferior horn (cornu) of thyroid cartilage	helps posterior cricoarytenoid muscle separate vocal cords
chin m. *m. mentalis*	incisive fossa of mandible	skin of chin	raises and protrudes lower lip
chondroglossus m. *m. chondroglossus*	lesser horn (cornu) and body of hyoid bone	side of tongue	depresses tongue
ciliary m. *m. ciliaris*	*meridional part:* scleral spur; *circular part:* sphincter of ciliary body	ciliary process	makes lens more convex in accommodation for near vision
coccygeal m. ischiococcygeus m. *m. coccygeus*	ischial spine and sacrospinous ligament	coccyx, lower part of lateral border of sacrum	aids in raising and supporting pelvic floor
constrictor M. of pharynx, inferior *m. constrictor pharyngis inferior*	cricoid cartilage, oblique line of thyroid cartilage, inferior horn of thyroid cartilage	median raphe of posterior wall of pharynx	narrows lower part of pharynx in swallowing
constrictor m. of pharynx, middle *m. constrictor pharyngis medius*	stylohyoid ligament and horns of hyoid bone	median raphe of posterior wall of pharynx	narrows pharynx in swallowing
constrictor m. of pharynx, superior *m. constrictor pharyngis superior*	medial pterygoid plate, pterygoid hamulus, pterygomandibular raphe, mandible, side of tongue	median raphe of posterior wall of pharynx; pharyngeal tubercle of skull	narrows pharynx in swallowing
coracobrachial m. *m. coracobrachialis*	coracoid process of scapula (shoulder blade)	midway along inner side of humerus	flexes, adducts arm
corrugator m. *m. corrugator*	brow ridge of frontal bone	skin of eyebrow	draws eyebrows together, wrinkles forehead
cremaster m. *m. cremaster*	inferior border of internal oblique abdominal m.	spermatic cord	elevates testis in male, encircles round ligament in female
cricoarytenoid m., lateral *m. cricoarytenoideus lateralis*	upper margin of arch of cricoid cartilage	muscular process of arytenoid cartilage	approximates vocal cords so they meet in midline for phonation
cricoarytenoid m., posterior *m. cricoarytenoideus posterior*	posterior surface of lamina of cricoid cartilage	muscular process of arytenoid cartilage	separates vocal cords, opening the glottis
cricothyroid m. *m. cricothyroideus*	anterior surface of arch of cricoid cartilage	lamina and inferior horn of thyroid cartilage	lengthens, stretches, and tenses vocal cords

M

muscle ■ muscle

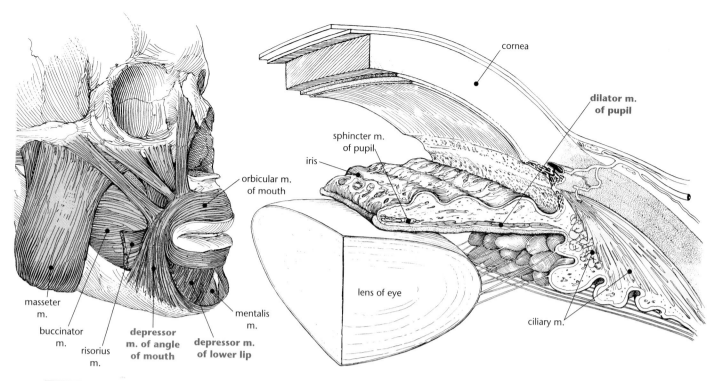

masseter m.

buccinator m.

risorius m.

depressor m. of angle of mouth

depressor m. of lower lip

mentalis m.

orbicular m. of mouth

cornea

dilator m. of pupil

sphincter m. of pupil

iris

lens of eye

ciliary m.

MUSCLE	ORIGIN	INSERTION	ACTION
deltoid m. *m. deltoideus*	lateral third of clavicle, acromion, and spine of scapula	deltoid tuberosity of shaft of humerus	abductor of arm; aids in flexion, extension, and lateral rotation of arm
depressor m., superciliary *m. depressor supercilii*	orbicular fibers of eye; medial palpebral ligament	skin of eyebrow	pulls eyebrow downward
depressor m. of angle of mouth triangular m. *m. depressor anguli oris*	oblique line of mandible	angle of mouth	pulls corner of mouth downward
depressor m. of lower lip quadrate m. of lower lip *m. depressor labii inferioris*	mandible adjacent to mental foramen	skin of lower lip	draws lower lip downward and slightly laterally
depressor m. of nasal septum *m. depressor septi nasi*	incisive fossa of maxilla (over roots of incisor teeth)	ala and septum of nose	widens the nostrils in deep inspiration
detrusor m. of urinary bladder *m. detrusor vesicae*	in wall of urinary bladder, consisting of three layers of nonstriated m. fibers		empties urinary bladder
detrusor urinae m.	see detrusor m. of urinary bladder		
diaphragm diaphragmatic m. *diaphragma*	xiphoid process, six lower costal cartilages, four lower ribs, lumbar vertebrae, arcuate ligaments	central tendon of diaphragm	increases capacity of thorax in inspiration (main m. of inhalation)
diaphragm m., pelvic	composed of the coccygeal and levator ani m.'s sheathed in a superior and inferior layer of fascia		forms floor to support pelvic viscera
digastric m. *m. digastricus*	digastric notch at mastoid process; mandible near symphysis	tendon bound to hyoid bone by fascia	raises hyoid bone and base of tongue, lowers mandible
dilator m. of nose *m. dilator naris*	nasal notch of maxilla	ala cartilage at margin of nostril	widens nostril
dilator m. of pupil *m. dilator pupillae*	ciliary margin	near margin of pupil	dilates pupil
epicranial m. *m. epicranius*	the muscular and tendinous layer of the scalp composed of the occipitofrontal and temporoparietal muscles connected by the epicranial aponeurosis (galea aponeurotica)		elevates eyebrows, draw scalp forward and backward, tightens scalp
erector m. of penis	see ischiocavernous m.		
erector m. of spine *m. erector spinae*	deep m. arising from the broad and thick tendon attached to the middle crest of sacrum, spinous processes of lumbar and 11th and 12th thoracic vertebrae, and back part of the iliac crest; it splits in the upper lumbar region into three columns of m.'s.; iliocostal (lateral division), longissimus (intermediate division), and spinal (medial division)		
extensor m. of fingers *m. extensor digitorum*	lateral epicondyle of humerus	phalanges of digits 2 to 5, via dorsal digital expansion	extends fingers, hand, and forearm
extensor m. of great toe, long *m. extensor hallucis longus*	middle of fibula, interosseous membrane	distal phalanx of great toe	extends great toe, dorsiflexes foot

M

muscle ■ muscle

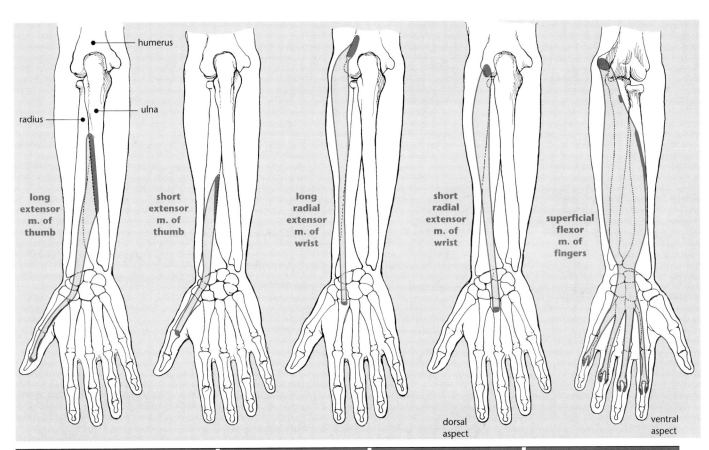

long extensor m. of thumb

short extensor m. of thumb

long radial extensor m. of wrist

short radial extensor m. of wrist

superficial flexor m. of fingers

humerus

radius

ulna

dorsal aspect

ventral aspect

M

MUSCLE	ORIGIN	INSERTION	ACTION
extensor m. of great toe, short *m. extensor hallucis brevis*	dorsal surface of calcaneus	base of proximal phalanx of great toe	dorsiflexes great toe
extensor m. of index finger *m. extensor indicis*	posterior surface of ulna, interosseous membrane	extensor expansion of index finger	extends index finger and hand
extensor m. of little finger *m. extensor digiti minimi manus*	lateral epicondyle of humerus	extensor expansion of little finger	extends little finger
extensor m. of thumb, long *m. extensor pollicis longus*	middle third of ulna, adjacent interosseous membrane	distal phalanx of thumb	extends distal phalanx of thumb, abducts hand
extensor m. of thumb, short *m. extensor pollicis brevis*	middle third of radius, interosseous membrane	proximal phalanx of thumb	extends thumb and abducts hand
extensor m. of toes, long *m. extensor digitorum longus pedis*	lateral condyle of tibia, upper three-fourths of fibula, interosseous membrane	extensor expansion of four lateral toes (by four slips)	extends toes and dorsiflexes foot
extensor m. of toes, short *m. extensor digitorum brevis pedis*	dorsal surface of calcaneus	extensor tendons of second, third, and fourth toes	extends toes
extensor m. of wrist, radial, long *m. extensor carpi radialis longus*	lateral supracondylar ridge of humerus	second metacarpal bone	extends wrist, abducts hand
extensor m. of wrist, radial, short *m. extensor carpi radialis brevis*	lateral epicondyle of humerus, radial collateral ligament of elbow joint	third metacarpal bone	extends wrist, abducts hand
extensor m. of wrist, ulnar *m. extensor carpi ulnaris*	*humeral head:* lateral epicondyle of humerus; *ulnar head:* posterior border of ulna	fifth metacarpal bone	extends wrist, adducts hand
fibular m.	see peroneal muscle		
flexor m. of fingers, deep *m. flexor digitorum profundus manus*	proximal three-fourths of ulna and adjacent interosseous membrane	distal phalanges of fingers	flexes terminal phalanges of lateral four digits; aids in flexing wrist
flexor m. of fingers, superficial *m. flexor digitorum superficialis manus*	*humeroulnar head:* medial epicondyle of humerus, coronoid process of ulna; *radial head:* anterior border of radius	middle phalanges of fingers	flexes phalanges and wrist
flexor m. of great toe, long *m. flexor hallucis longus*	lower two-thirds of posterior surface of fibula, intermuscular septum, interosseous membrane	distal phalanx of great toe	flexes great toe and plantarflexes foot

muscle ■ muscle

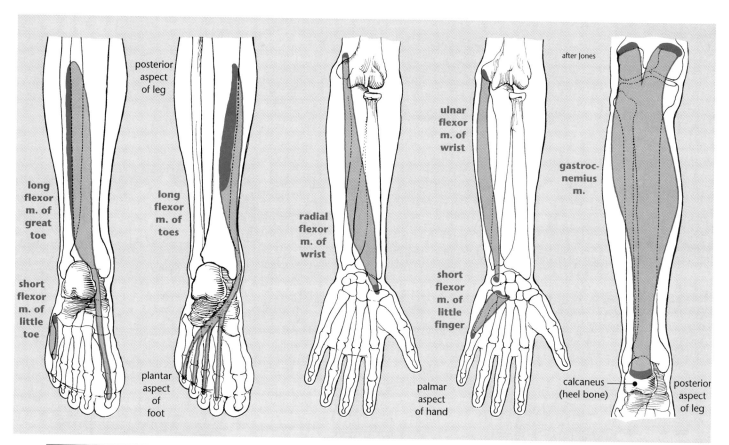

posterior aspect of leg

long flexor m. of great toe

short flexor m. of little toe

plantar aspect of foot

long flexor m. of toes

radial flexor m. of wrist

ulnar flexor m. of wrist

short flexor m. of little finger

palmar aspect of hand

after Jones

gastroc-nemius m.

calcaneus (heel bone)

posterior aspect of leg

MUSCLE	ORIGIN	INSERTION	ACTION
flexor m. of great toe, short *m. flexor hallucis brevis*	cuboid and lateral cuneiform bones	both sides of proximal phalanx of great toe	flexes great toe
flexor m. of little finger, short *m. flexor digiti minimi brevis manus*	hook of hamate, flexor retinaculum	proximal phalanx of little finger	flexes proximal phalanx of little finger
flexor m. of little toe, short *m. flexor digiti minimi brevis pedis*	base of fifth metatarsal and plantar fascia	lateral surface of proximal phalanx of little toe	flexes little toe
flexor m. of thumb, long *m. flexor pollicis longus*	radius, adjacent interosseous membrane, coronoid process of ulna	distal phalanx of thumb	flexes thumb
flexor m. of thumb, short *m. flexor pollicis brevis*	trapezium, trapezoid, and capitate bones of wrist	proximal phalanx of thumb	flexes thumb
flexor m. of toes, long *m. flexor digitorum longus pedis*	middle half of tibia	distal phalanges of lateral four toes (by four tendons)	flexes second to fifth toes and plantarflexes foot
flexor m. of toes, short *m. flexor digitorum brevis pedis*	tuberosity of calcaneus and plantar fascia	middle phalanges of four lateral toes	flexes four lateral toes
flexor m. of wrist, radial *m. flexor carpi radialis*	medial epicondyle of humerus; antibrachial fascia	bases of second and third metacarpal bones	flexes wrist; aids in pronation and abduction of hand
flexor m. of wrist, ulnar *m. flexor carpi ulnaris*	*humeral head:* medial epicondyle of humerus; *ulnar head:* olecranon and posterior border of ulna	pisiform, hamate, and fifth metacarpal bones; flexor retinaculum	flexes wrist; adducts hand
frontal m.	see occipitofrontal muscle		
gastrocnemius m. *m. gastrocnemius*	*medial head:* popliteal surface of femur, upper part of medial condyle of femur; *lateral head:* lateral condyle of femur	calcaneus via calcaneal tendon (tendo calcaneus) (in common with soleus muscle)	flexes leg and plantarflexes foot
gemellus m., inferior *m. gemellus inferior*	lower margin of lesser sciatic notch	greater trochanter via internal obturator tendon	rotates thigh laterally
gemellus m., superior *m. gemellus superior*	spine if ischium	greater trochanter via internal obturator tendon	rotates thigh laterally; abducts flexed thigh
genioglossus m. *m. genioglossus*	mental spine of the mandible	ventral surface of tongue and body of hyoid bone	protrudes, retracts, and depresses tongue, elevates hyoid bone
geniohyoid m. *m. geniohyoideus*	mental spine (genial tubercle) of the mandible	body of hyoid bone	elevates hyoid bone and draws it forward

muscle ■ muscle

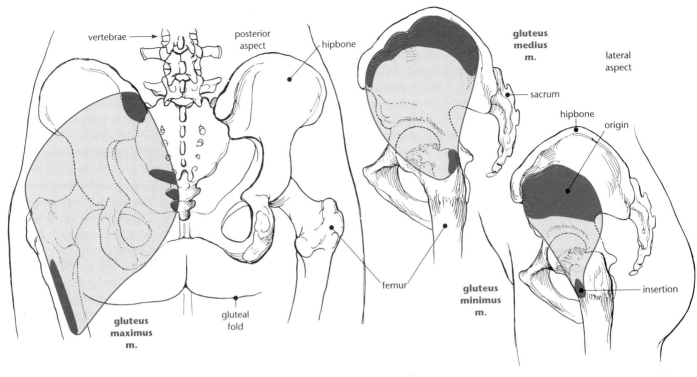

MUSCLE	ORIGIN	INSERTION	ACTION
glossopalatine m.	see palatoglossus muscle		
gluteus maximus m. greatest gluteal m. *m. gluteus maximus*	upper portion of ilium, sacrum and coccyx, sacro-tuberous ligament, gluteus aponeurosis	gluteal tuberosity of femur, iliotibial tract (band of fascia lata)	chief extensor, powerful lateral rotator of thigh
gluteus medius m. middle gluteal m. *m. gluteus medius*	midportion of outer surface of ilium	greater trochanter and oblique ridge of femur	abducts, rotates thigh medially; tilts pelvis to raise opposite foot from floor
gluteus minimus m. least gluteal m. *m. gluteus minimus*	lower portion of outer surface of ilium	greater trochanter of femur, capsule of hip joint	abducts, rotates thigh medially
gracilis m. *m. gracilis*	lower half of pubis	medial side of upper part of tibia	adducts thigh, flexes and rotates leg medially
helix m., larger *m. helicis major*	spine of helix	anterior border of helix	thought to be vestigial
helix m., smaller *m. helicis minor*	anterior rim of helix	crux of helix	thought to be vestigial
hyoglossus m. hyoglossal m. *m. hyoglossus*	body and greater horn (cornu) of hyoid bone	side of tongue	retracts, depresses tongue
iliac m. *m. iliacus*	iliac fossa, lateral aspect of sacrum	greater psoas tendon, lesser trochanter of femur	flexes thigh
iliococcygeal m. *m. iliococcygeal*	ischial spine and arching tendon over internal obturator muscle	coccyx and perineal body between tip of coccyx and anal canal	supports pelvic viscera
iliocostal m. *m. iliocostalis*	the lateral division of erector m. of spine composed of three parts: iliocostal m. of loins, iliocostal m. of neck, iliocostal m. of thorax		extends vertebral column and assists in lateral movements of trunk
iliocostal m. of loins *m. iliocostalis lumborum*	iliac crest and thoracolumbar fascia	transverse processes of lumbar vertebrae, angles of lower seven ribs	extends lumbar vertebral column and flexes it laterally
iliocostal m. of neck *m. iliocostalis cervicis*	angles of third, fourth, fifth, and sixth ribs	transverse processes of fourth, fifth, and sixth cervical vertebrae	extends cervical vertebral column and flexes it laterally
iliocostal m. of thorax *m. iliocostalis thoracis*	lower six ribs, medial to angles of the ribs	angles of upper six ribs, transverse process of seventh cervical vertebra	extends thoracic vertebral column and flexes it laterally
iliopsoas m. *m. iliopsoas*	a compound muscle consisting of the iliac and greater psoas muscles, which join to form the iliopsoas tendon and insert to the lesser trochanter of femur		
incisive m.'s of lower lip *mm. incisivi labii inferioris*	portion of orbicular muscle of mouth (orbicularis oris)	angle of mouth	make vestibule of mouth shallow; aid in articulation

M

muscle ■ muscle

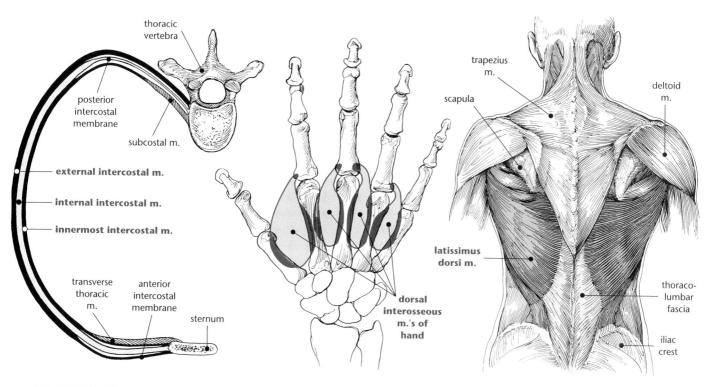

thoracic vertebra

posterior intercostal membrane

subcostal m.

external intercostal m.

internal intercostal m.

innermost intercostal m.

transverse thoracic m.

anterior intercostal membrane

sternum

dorsal interosseous m.'s of hand

trapezius m.

scapula

deltoid m.

latissimus dorsi m.

thoraco-lumbar fascia

iliac crest

MUSCLE	ORIGIN	INSERTION	ACTION
incisive m.'s of upper lip *mm. incisivi labii superioris*	portion of orbicular muscle of mouth (*orbicularis oris*)	angle of mouth	make vestibule of mouth shallow; aid in articulation
infrahyoid m.'s *mm. infrahyoidei*	the ribbonlike muscles below the hyoid bone including the omohyoid, sternohyoid, sternothyroid, and thyrohyoid muscles		
infraspinous m. *m. infraspinatus*	infraspinous fossa of scapula	midportion of greater tubercle of humerus	rotates arm laterally
intercostal m.'s, external *mm. intercostales externi*	inferior border of rib	superior border of rib below origin	draw ribs together
intercostal m.'s, innermost *mm. intercostales intimi*	superior border of rib	inferior border of rib above origin	draw ribs together
intercostal m.'s, internal *mm. intercostales interni*	inferior border of rib, costal cartilage	superior border of rib below origin, costal cartilage	draw ribs together
interosseous m.'s, palmar (three in number) *mm. interossei palmares*	medial side of second, lateral side of fourth and fifth metacarpals	base of proximal phalanx in line with its origin	adduct second, fourth, and fifth fingers; aid in flexing proximal phalanges
interosseous m.'s, plantar (three in number) *mm. innterossei plantares*	medial side of third, fourth, and fifth metatarsal bones	medial side of proximal phalanges of third, fourth, and fifth toes	adduct three lateral toes toward second toe; flex toes
interosseous m.'s of foot, dorsal (four in number) *mm. interossei dorsales pedis*	adjacent sides of metatarsal bones	proximal phalanges of both sides of second toe, lateral side of third and fourth toes	abduct lateral toes, move second toe from side to side; flex proximal phalanges
interosseous m.'s of hand, dorsal (four in number) *mm. interossei dorsales manus*	adjacent sides of metacarpal bones	extensor tendons of second, third, and fourth fingers	abduct second, third, and fourth fingers, spread fingers; flex phalanges
interspinal m.'s *mm. interspinales*	short muscles between the spinous processes of contiguous vertebrae on either side of the interspinous ligament		extend vertebral column
intertransverse m.'s *mm. intertransversarii*	small paired muscles between the transverse processes of contiguous vertebrae		aid in maintaining erect posture by extension, lateral flexion, and rotation of the body
ischiocavernous m. erector m. of penis *m. ischiocavernosus*	ramus of ischium adjacent to crus of penis or clitoris	crus near pubic symphysis	maintains erection of penis or clitoris
ischiococcygeal m.	see coccygeal muscle		
latissimus dorsi m. *m. latissimus dorsi*	spinous processes of vertebrae T7 to S3; thoracolumbar fascia; iliac crest; lower four ribs; inferior angle of scapula	floor or intertubercular groove of humerus	adducts, extends, and medially rotates arm

muscle ■ muscle

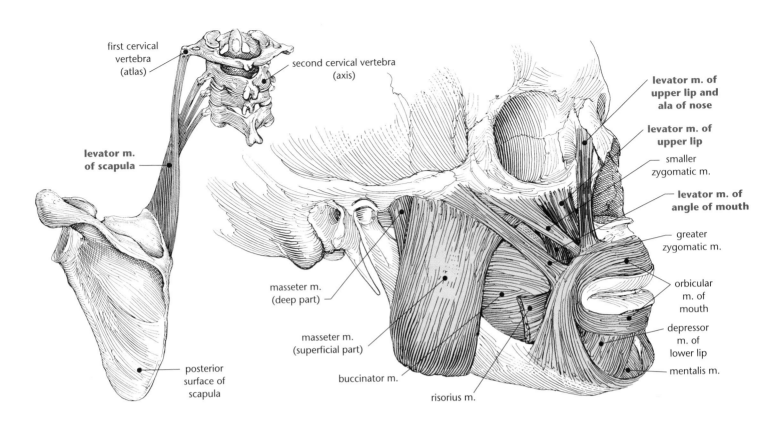

first cervical vertebra (atlas)

second cervical vertebra (axis)

levator m. of scapula

posterior surface of scapula

masseter m. (deep part)

masseter m. (superficial part)

buccinator m.

risorius m.

levator m. of upper lip and ala of nose

levator m. of upper lip

smaller zygomatic m.

levator m. of angle of mouth

greater zygomatic m.

orbicular m. of mouth

depressor m. of lower lip

mentalis m.

MUSCLE	ORIGIN	INSERTION	ACTION
levator ani m. *m. levator ani*	the main m. of the pelvic floor within the lesser pelvis; composed of pubococcygeal, iliococcygeal, and puborectal m.´s as well as the levator m. of prostate in the male		supports pelvic viscera and separates it from the perineum; constricts lower end of rectum and vagina
levator m. of angle of mouth caninus m. canine m. *m. levator anguli oris*	maxilla next to cuspid fossa, just below infraorbital foramen	corner of mouth	raises angle of mouth
levator m. of soft palate *m. levator veli palatini*	apex of petrous part of temporal bone and undersurface of cartilaginous part of auditory tube	aponeurosis of soft palate	raises soft palate in swallowing; aids in opening orifice of auditory tube
levator m. of prostate *m. levator prostatae*	pubic symphysis	fascia of prostate gland	elevates and compresses prostate gland
levator m.'s of ribs *mm. levatores costarum*	transverse processes of seventh cervical and first 11 thoracic vertebrae	angle of rib below	aid in raising ribs; extend vertebral column
levator m. of scapula *m. levator scapulae*	transverse processes of first four cervical vertebrae	vertebral (medial) border of scapula	raises scapula; aids in rotating the neck
levator m. of thyroid gland (inconstant muscle) *m. levator glandulae thyroideae*	isthmus or pyramidal lobe of thyroid gland	body of hyoid bone	stabilizes thyroid gland
levator m. of upper eyelid *m. levator palpebrae superior*	roof of orbital cavity above optic canal	skin and tarsal plate of upper eyelid, and superior fornix of conjunctiva	raises upper eyelid
levator m. of upper lip quadrate m. of upper lip *m. levator labii superioris*	maxilla and zygomatic bone above level of infraorbital foramen	muscular substance of upper lip and margin of nostril	raises upper lip, dilates nostril
levator m. of upper lip and ala of nose *m. levator labii superioris alaeque nasi*	frontal process of maxilla	skin of upper lip, ala of nose	raises upper lip, dilates nostril (muscle of facial expression)
long m. of head *m. longus capitis*	transverse processes of third to sixth cervical vertebrae	basal part of occipital bone	flexes head
long m. of neck *m. longus colli*	*superior oblique part:* anterior tubercle of transverse processes of third, fourth, and fifth cervical vertebrae;	*superior oblique part:* anterolateral surface of tubercle on anterior arch of first vertebra (atlas);	bends neck forward and slightly rotates cervical portion of vertebral column

M

muscle ■ muscle

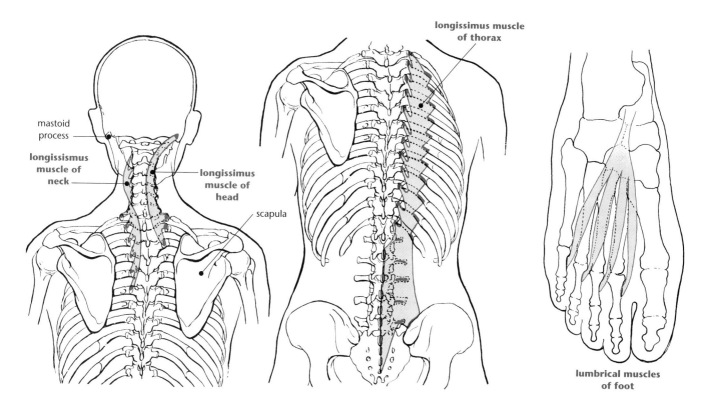

mastoid process

longissimus muscle of neck

longissimus muscle of head

scapula

longissimus muscle of thorax

lumbrical muscles of foot

MUSCLE	ORIGIN	INSERTION	ACTION
long m. of neck (cont'd)	*inferior oblique part:* front of bodies of first two or three thoracic vertebrae; *vertical part:* front of bodies of first three thoracic and last three cervical vertebrae	*inferior oblique part:* anterior tubercle of transverse processes of fifth and sixth cervical vertebrae; *vertical part:* front of bodies of second, third, and fourth cervical vertebrae	
longissimus m. of head trachelomastoid m. *m. longissimus capitis*	transverse processes of cervical and thoracic vertebrae C3 to T4	mastoid process of temporal bone	draws head backward, rotates head
longissimus m. of neck m. longissimus cervicis	transverse processes of upper six thoracic vertebrae	transverse processes of second through sixth cervical vertebrae	bends vertebral column backward and laterally
longissimus m. of thorax longissimus dorsi m. *m. longissimus thoracis*	thoracolumbar fascia, transverse processes of lower six thoracic and first two lumbar vertebrae	transverse processes of lumbar and thoracic vertebrae, inferior borders of lower 9 or 10 ribs	bends vertebral column backward and laterally
longitudinal m. of tongue, inferior m. longitudinalis inferior linguae	undersurface of tongue at base	tip of tongue	acts to alter shape of tongue
longitudinal m. of tongue, superior m. longitudinalis superior linguae	submucosa and median septum of tongue	margins of tongue	acts to alter shape of tongue
lumbrical m.'s of foot mm. lumbricales pedis	tendons of long flexor muscles of toes	medial side of proximal phalanges and extensor tendon of four lateral toes	flex proximal, extend middle and distal phalanges
lumbical m.'s of hand (four in number) mm. lumbricales manus	tendons of deep flexor muscles of fingers	extensor tendons of four lateral fingers	flex proximal, extend middle and distal phalanges
masseter m. m. masseter	*superficial part:* zygomatic process and arch; *deep part:* zygomatic arch	*superficial part:* ramus and angle of lower jaw; *deep part:* upper half of ramus, coronoid process of lower jaw	closes mouth, clenches teeth (m. mastication)
mentalis m. m. levator menti	incisor fossa of mandible	skin of chin	raises and protrudes lower lip
multifidus m. m. multifidus	sacrum and transverse processes of lumbar, thoracic, and lower cervical vertebrae	spinous processes of lumbar, thoracic, and lower cervical vertebrae	extends, rotates vertebral column; maintains posture

M

muscle ■ muscle

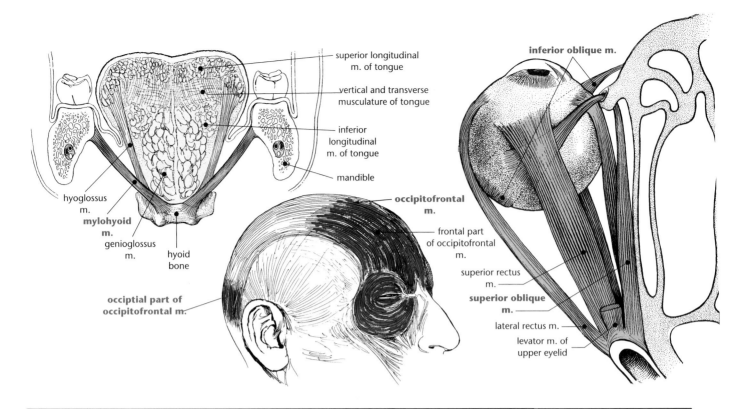

superior longitudinal m. of tongue

vertical and transverse musculature of tongue

inferior longitudinal m. of tongue

mandible

hyoglossus m.

mylohyoid m.

genioglossus m.

hyoid bone

occiptial part of occipitofrontal m.

occipitofrontal m.

frontal part of occipitofrontal m.

inferior oblique m.

superior rectus m.

superior oblique m.

lateral rectus m.

levator m. of upper eyelid

MUSCLE	ORIGIN	INSERTION	ACTION
m. of Treitz	see suspensory muscle of duodenum		
mylohyoid m. *m. mylohyoideus*	mylohyoid line of mandible	median raphe and hyoid bone	elevates floor of mouth and tongue; elevates hyoid bone and larynx; depresses mandible
nasal m. *m. nasalis*	maxilla adjacent to cuspid and incisor teeth	side of nose above nostril	draws margin of nostril toward septum
oblique m. of abdomen, external *m. obliquus externus abdominis*	inferior borders of lower eight ribs	anterior half of crest of ilium, linea alba through rectus sheath, inguinal ligament	flexes and rotates vertebral column, tenses abdominal wall; aids in defecation and micturition
oblique m. of abdomen, internal *m. obliquus internus abdominis*	iliac crest, thoracolumbar fascia, inguinal ligament	lower three or four costal cartilages, linea alba by conjoint tendon to pubis	flexes and rotates vertebral column, tenses abdominal wall
oblique m. of auricle *m. obliquus auriculae*	eminence of concha (media surface)	convexity of the helix (medial surface)	thought to be vestigial
oblique m. of eyeball, inferior *m. obliquus inferior bulbi*	floor of orbital cavity at anterior margin	between insertion of superior and lateral recti	rotates eyeball upward and outward
oblique m. of eyeball, superior *m. obliquus superior bulbi*	lesser wing of sphenoid above the optic canal	after passing through a fibrous pulley, reverses direction to insert on sclera deep to superior rectus muscle	rotates eyeball downward and outward
oblique m. of head, inferior *m. obliquus capitis inferior*	spine of second vertebra (axis)	transverse process of first vertebra (atlas)	rotates head laterally
oblique m. of head, superior *m. obliquus capitis superior*	transverse process of first vertebra (atlas)	outer third of inferior curved line of occipital bone	rotates head laterally; bends head backward
obturator m., external *m. obturatorius externus*	external margin of obturator foramen of pelvis, obturator membrane	trochanteric fossa of femur	flexes and rotates thigh laterally
obturator m., internal *m. obturatorius internus*	pelvic surface of hipbone and internal margin of obturator foramen, obturator membrane	greater trochanter of femur	abducts and rotates thigh laterally
occipital m.	see occipitofrontal muscle		
occipitofrontal m. *m. occipitofrontalis*	*frontal part:* epicranial aponeurosis; *occipital part:* highest nuchal line of occipital bone; mastoid process	*frontal part:* skin of eyebrow, root of nose; *occipital part:* epicranial aponeurosis	*frontal part:* elevates eyebrows, wrinkles forehead; *occipital part:* draws scalp backward

M

muscle ■ muscle

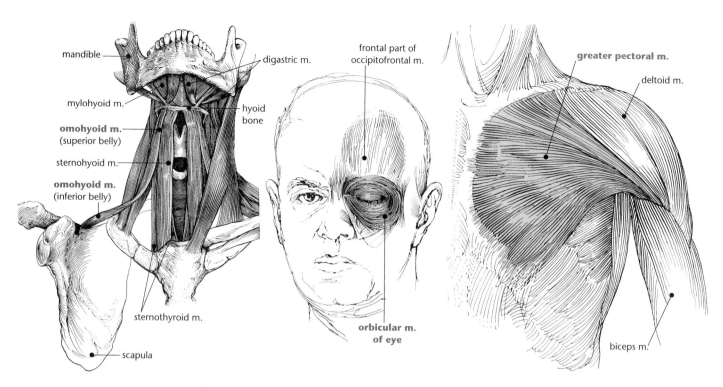

Labels in figure:
- mandible
- mylohyoid m.
- **omohyoid m.** (superior belly)
- sternohyoid m.
- **omohyoid m.** (inferior belly)
- sternothyroid m.
- scapula
- digastric m.
- hyoid bone
- frontal part of occipitofrontal m.
- **orbicular m. of eye**
- **greater pectoral m.**
- deltoid m.
- biceps m.

MUSCLE	ORIGIN	INSERTION	ACTION
omohyoid m. *m. omohyoideus*	medial tip of suprascapular notch on upper scapula	lower border of body of hyoid bone	depresses and retracts hyoid bone
opposing m. of little finger *m. opponens digiti minimi manus*	hook of hamate bone, flexor retinaculum	fifth metacarpal	draws fifth metacarpal bone toward palm, opposes thumb
opposing m. of thumb *m. opponens pollicis*	tubercle of trapezium, flexor retinaculum	lateral border of first metacarpal bone	draws first metacarpal bone toward palm
orbicular m. of eye *m. orbicularis oculi*	*orbital part:* frontal process of maxilla, adjacent portion of frontal bone; *palpebral part:* medial palpebral ligament; *lacrimal part:* posterior lacrimal ridge of lacrimal bone	near origin after encircling orbit; lateral palpebral raphe; superior and inferior tarsi	closes eyelids, tightens skin of forehead, compresses lacrimal sac
orbicular m. of mouth *m. orbicularis oris*	muscle adjacent to mouth	muscles interlace to encircle mouth	closes and purses lips
orbital m. *m. orbitalis*	bridges inferior orbital groove and sphenomaxillary fissure		thought to be rudimentary; may feebly protrude the eyeball
palatoglossus m. glossopalatine m. *m. palatoglossus*	undersurface of soft palate	dorsum and side of tongue	elevates back of tongue and narrows fauces
palatopharyngeal m. *m. palatopharyngeus*	soft palate; back of hard palate	posterior wall of thyroid cartilage and wall of pharynx	elevates pharynx and shortens it during swallowing; narrows fauces
palmar m., long *m. palmaris longus*	medial epicondyle of humerus	flexor retinaculum, palmar aponeurosis	flexes hand
palmar m., short *m. palmaris brevis*	flexor retinaculum; medial side of palmar aponeurosis	skin of palm over hypothenar eminence	aids in deepening hollow of palm, wrinkles skin of palm
pectinate m.'s *mm. pectinati*	a number of muscular columns projecting from the inner walls of the atria of the heart		contract the atria of the heart during systole
pectineal m. *m. pectineus*	pectineal line of pubis	pectineal line of femur between lesser trochanter and linea aspera	adducts and aids in flexion of thigh
pectoral m., greater *m. pectoralis major*	medial half of clavicle, sternum, and costal cartilages; aponeurosis of external oblique muscle of abdomen; sixth rib	lateral lip of intertubercular groove of humerus	flexes, adducts, and rotates arm medially

M

muscle ■ muscle

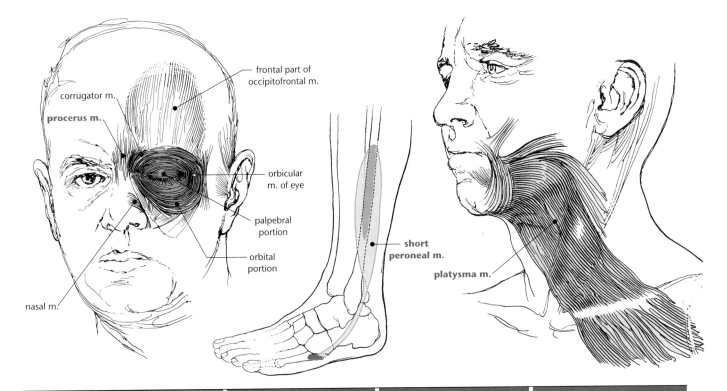

frontal part of
occipitofrontal m.

corrugator m.

procerus m.

orbicular
m. of eye

palpebral
portion

orbital
portion

nasal m.

short
peroneal m.

platysma m.

MUSCLE	ORIGIN	INSERTION	ACTION
pectoral, m., smaller *m. pectoralis minor*	anterior aspect of third through fifth ribs, near costal cartilages	coracoid process of scapula	draws scapula downward, elevates ribs
pectoralis major m.	see pectoral m. greater		
pectoralis minor m.	see pectoral m. smaller		
peroneal m., long fibular m., long *m. peroneus longus*	upper two-thirds of fibula; crural septum	first metatarsal bone, medial cuneiform bone	aids in plantar flexion and everts foot; helps maintain transverse arch of foot
peroneal m., short fibular m., short *m. peroneus brevis*	lower two-thirds of fibula; crural septum	tuberosity of fifth metatarsal bone	aids in plantar flexion; everts foot; aids in preventing over-inversion of foot
peroneal m., third *m. peroneus tertius*	distal third of fibula; crural fascia	fascia of fifth metatarsal bone on dorsum of foot	dorsiflexes and everts foot
piriform m. *m. piriformis*	internal aspect of sacrum, sacrotuberous ligament	upper portion of greater trochanter of femur	rotates thigh laterally
plantar m. *m. plantaris*	supracondylar line just above lateral condyle of femur; oblique popliteal ligament	posterior part of calcaneus (along with calcaneal tendon)	plantar flexion of foot
platysma m. *m. platysma*	superficial fascia of upper chest	skin over mandible and neck	depresses lower jaw and lower lip, wrinkles skin of neck and upper part of chest; draws down angle of mouth
pleuroesophageal m. *m. pleuroesophageus*			reinforces musculature of esophagus
popliteal m. *m. popliteus*	popliteal groove of lateral condyle of femur; arcuate popliteal ligament	upper part of posterior surface of tibia	flexes and rotates leg medially
procerus m. *m. procerus*	fascia covering bridge of nose	skin between eyebrows	wrinkles skin over bridge of nose (assists frontal muscle)
pronator m., quadrate *m. pronator quadratus*	distal fourth of shaft of ulna	distal fourth of shaft of radius	pronates forearm
pronator m., round *m. pronator teres*	humeral part: medial epicondyle of humerus; ulnar part: coronoid process of ulna	lateral aspect of radius bone at point of maximum convexity	pronates and flexes forearm
psoas m., greater *m. psoas major*	transverse processes and bodies of lumbar vertebrae; body of 12th thoracic vertebra	lesser trochanter of femur	flexes and medially rotates thigh
psoas m., smaller *m. psoas minor*	bodies of last thoracic and first lumbar vertebrae	pectineal line of hipbone	flexes vertebral column

M

muscle ■ muscle

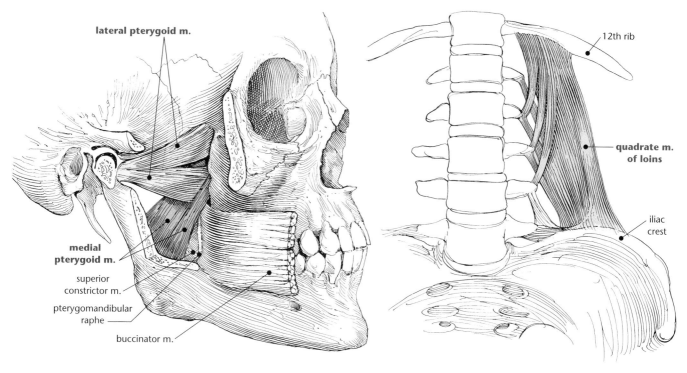

lateral pterygoid m.

12th rib

quadrate m. of loins

medial pterygoid m.

superior constrictor m.

pterygomandibular raphe

buccinator m.

iliac crest

MUSCLE	ORIGIN	INSERTION	ACTION
pterygoid m., lateral external pterygoid m. *m. pterygoideus lateralis*	lateral pterygoid plate and greater wing of sphenoid	condyle of mandible, capsule of temporomandibular joint	opens and protrudes mandible
pterygoid m., medial internal pterygoid m. *m. pterygoideus medialis*	maxillary tuberosity and lateral pterygoid plate, tubercle of palatine bone	medial surface of ramus and angle of mandible	closes and protrudes mandible and moves it side to side
pubococcygeal m. *m. pubococcygeus*	back of pubis and obturator fascia	coccyx and perineal body	supports pelvic floor
puborectal m. *m. puborectalis*	back of pubis and pubic symphysis	interdigitates to form a sling which passes behind the rectum	holds anal canal at right angle to rectum
pubovaginal m. *m. pubovaginalis*	part of levator ani m. in the female		
pubovesical m. *m. pubovesicalis*	posterior surface of body of pubis	*female:* around fundus of bladder to front of vagina; *male:* around fundus of bladder to prostate gland	strengthens musculature of urinary bladder; secures base of bladder
pyramidal m. *m. pyramidalis*	pubis and pubic symphysis	linea alba	tenses abdominal wall
quadrate m. of loins *m. quadratus lumborum*	iliac crest, transverse processes of lumbar vertebrae, iliolumbar ligament	12th rib, transverse processes of upper lumbar vertebrae	draws rib cage inferiorly, bends vertebral column laterally
quadrate m. of lower lip *m. quadratus labli inferioris*	see depressor m. of lower lip		
quadrate m. of sole accessory flexor m. *m. quadratus plantae*	calcaneus and plantar fascia	tendons of long flexor muscle of toes (*m. flexor digitorum longus*)	aids in flexing all toes except the big toe
quadrate m. of thigh *m. quadratus femoris*	proximal part of external border of tuberosity of ischium	proximal part of linea quadrata (line extending vertically and distally from intertrochanteric crest of femur)	rotates thigh laterally
quadrate m. of upper lip *m. quadratus labii superioris*	see levator m. of upper lip		
quadratus lumborum m.	see quadrate m. of loins		
quadriceps m. of thigh *m. quadriceps femoris*	the large four-headed fleshy mass that covers the front and sides of the femur, consisting of the rectus muscle of thigh (*m. rectus femoris*), lateral vastus (*m. vastus lateralis*), medial vastus m. (*m. vastus medialis*), and intermediate vastus m. (*m. vastus intermedius*)		great extensor muscle of leg

M

muscle ■ muscle

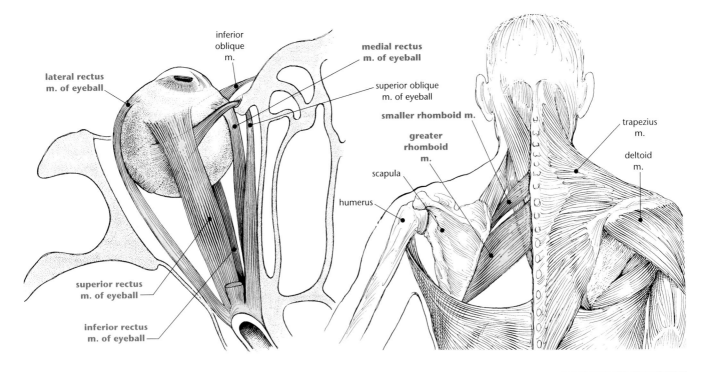

Labels on illustration:
- inferior oblique m.
- lateral rectus m. of eyeball
- medial rectus m. of eyeball
- superior oblique m. of eyeball
- smaller rhomboid m.
- greater rhomboid m.
- scapula
- humerus
- trapezius m.
- deltoid m.
- superior rectus m. of eyeball
- inferior rectus m. of eyeball

M

MUSCLE	ORIGIN	INSERTION	ACTION
rectococcygeal m. *m. rectococcygeus*	smooth muscle fibers in the pelvic fascia between the coccyx and rectum		secures rectum
rectourethral m. *m. rectourethralis*	smooth muscle fibers in the pelvic fascia between the rectum and membranous urethra of male		secures urethra
rectouterine m. *m. rectouterinus*	bundle of smooth muscle fibers in pelvic fascia between rectum and cervix of uterus		secures uterus
rectus m. of abdomen *m. rectus abdominis*	pubic crest, pubic symphysis	xiphoid process, fifth to seventh costal cartilages	tenses abdominal wall, draws thorax downward, flexes vertebral column
rectus m. of eyeball, inferior *m. rectus inferior bulbi*	common tendon ring around the optic canal	lower part of sclera just posterior to corneoscleral junction	rotates eyeball downward and somewhat medially
rectus m. of eyeball, lateral *m. rectus lateralis bulbi*	common tendon ring around the optic canal	lateral part of sclera just posterior to corneoscleral junction	rotates eyeball laterally
rectus m. of eyeball, medial *m. rectus medialis bulbi*	common tendon ring around the optic canal	medial part of sclera just posterior to corneoscleral junction	rotates eyeball medially
rectus m. of eyeball, superior *m. rectus superior bulbi*	common tendon ring around the optic canal	top part of sclera just posterior to corneoscleral junction	rotates eyeball upward and somewhat medially
rectus m. of head, anterior *m. rectus capitis anterior*	lateral portion of first vertebra (atlas)	basilar portion of occipital bone, in front of foramen magnum	flexes and supports head
rectus m. of head, lateral *m. rectus capitis lateralis*	transverse process of first vertebra (atlas)	jugular process of occipital bone	aids in lateral movements of head, supports head
rectus m. of head, posterior, greater *m. rectus capitis posterior major*	spinous process of second vertebra (axis)	occipital bone	extends head
rectus m. of head, posterior smaller *m. rectus capitis posterior minor*	posterior tubercle of first vertebra (atlas)	occipital bone	extends head
rectus m. of thigh *m. rectus femoris*	anterior inferior iliac spine, rim of acetabulum	base of patella (kneecap)	extends leg and flexes thigh
rhomboid m., greater *m. rhomboideus major*	spinous processes of second through fifth thoracic vertebrae	lower two-thirds of vertebral margin of scapula	adducts and laterally rotates scapula
rhomboid m., smaller *m. rhomboideus minor*	spinous processes of seventh cervical and first thoracic vertebrae and lower part of nuchal ligament	vertebral margin of scapula above spine	adducts and laterally rotates scapula
risorius m. *m. risorius*	fascia over masseter muscle; platysma muscle	skin at angle of mouth	retracts angle of mouth

muscle ■ muscle

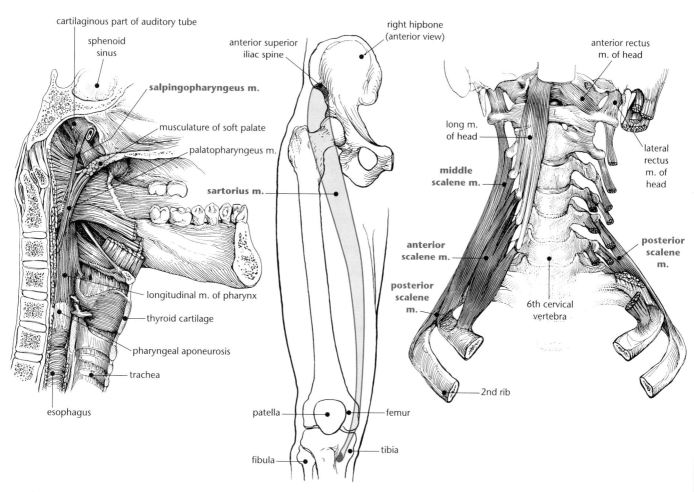

cartilaginous part of auditory tube
sphenoid sinus
salpingopharyngeus m.
musculature of soft palate
palatopharyngeus m.
longitudinal m. of pharynx
thyroid cartilage
pharyngeal aponeurosis
trachea
esophagus

anterior superior iliac spine
right hipbone (anterior view)
sartorius m.
patella
fibula
femur
tibia

anterior rectus m. of head
long m. of head
middle scalene m.
lateral rectus m. of head
anterior scalene m.
posterior scalene m.
6th cervical vertebra
posterior scalene m.
2nd rib

M

MUSCLE	ORIGIN	INSERTION	ACTION
rotator m.'s *mm. rotatores*	transverse process of all vertebrae below second cervical	lamina above vertebra of origin	extend and rotate the vertebral column toward opposite side
sacrococcygeal m., dorsal *m. sacrococcygeus dorsalis*	a muscular slip from the dorsal aspect of the sacrum to the coccyx		feebly protects sacrococcygeal joint
sacrococcygeal m., ventral *m. sacrococcygeus ventralis*	a muscular slip from the ventral aspect of the sacrum		feebly protects sacrococcygeal joint
sacrospinal m.		see erector m. of spine	
salpingopharyngeal m. *m. salpingopharyngeus*	cartilage of auditory tube near nasopharyngeal orifice	wall of pharynx	elevates nasopharynx
sartorius m. *m. sartorius*	anterior superior iliac spine	upper medial surface of tibia	flexes thigh and leg; rotates thigh laterally
scalene m., anterior *m. scalenus anterior*	transverse processes of third to sixth cervical vertebrae	scalene tubercle of first rib	raises first rib, stabilizes or inclines neck to the side
scalene m., middle *m. scalenus medius*	transverse processes of first six cervical vertebrae	upper surface of first rib	raises first rib, stabilizes or inclines neck to the side
scalene m., posterior *m. scalenus posterior*	transverse processes of fifth to seventh cervical vertebrae	outer surface of upper border of second rib	raises second rib, stabilizes or inclines neck to the side
scalene m., smallest *m. scalenus minimus*	occasional extra muscle fibers or slip of posterior scalene m.		tenses dome of pleura
semimembranous m. *m. semimembranosus*	tuberosity of ischium	medial condyle of tibia; oblique popliteal ligament	extends thigh, flexes and rotates leg medially
semispinal m. of head *m. semispinalis capitis*	transverse processes of six upper thoracic and four lower cervical vertebrae	occipital bone between superior and inferior nuchal lines	rotates head and draws it backward
semispinal m. of neck *m. semispinalis cervicis*	transverse processes of upper six thoracic vertebrae	spinous processes of second through sixth cervical vertebrae	extends and rotates vertebral column
semispinal m. of thorax *m. semispinalis thoracis*	transverse processes of lower six thoracic vertebrae	spinous processes of upper six thoracic and lower two cervical vertebrae	extends and rotates vertebral column

muscle ■ muscle

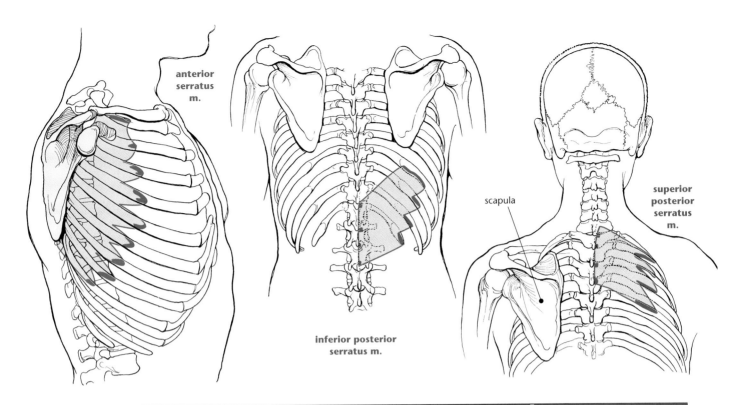

anterior
serratus
m.

inferior posterior
serratus m.

scapula

superior
posterior
serratus
m.

MUSCLE	ORIGIN	INSERTION	ACTION
semitendinous m. *m. semitendinosus*	tuberosity of ischium (in common with biceps muscle of thigh)	upper part of tibia near tibial tuberosity	flexes and rotates leg medially, extends thigh
serratus m., anterior *m. serratus anterior*	lateral surface of eight or nine uppermost ribs	anterior surface of vertebral border of scapula	draws scapula forward and laterally, rotates scapula in raising arm
serratus m., posterior, inferior *m. serratus posterior inferior*	spinous processes of last two thoracic and first two or three lumbar vertebrae, supraspinal ligament	inferior borders of the last four ribs, slightly beyond their angles	draws the ribs outward and downward (counteracting the inward pull of the diaphragm)
serratus m. posterior, superior *m. serratus posterior superior*	caudal part of nuchal ligament, spinous processes of the seventh cervical and first two or three thoracic vertebrae, supraspinal ligament	upper borders of the second, third, fourth, and fifth ribs, slightly beyond their angles	raises the ribs
soleus m. *m. soleus*	upper third of fibula, soleal line of tibia, tendinous arch	calcaneus by calcaneal tendon (*tendo calcaneus*)	plantarflexes foot
sphincter m. of anus, external *m. sphincter ani externus*	tip of coccyx, anococcygeal ligament	central tendon of perineum, skin	closes anal canal and anus
sphincter m. of anus, internal *m. sphincter ani internus*	1-cm-thick muscular ring surrounding approximately 2.5 cm of the upper part of the anal canal, about 6.0 mm from the orifice of the anus		aids in occlusion of anal aperture and expulsion of feces
sphincter m. of bile duct *m. sphincter choledochi*	a circular m. around lower part of the bile duct within the wall of the duodenum (part of the sphincter muscle of hepatopancreatic ampulla)		constricts lower part of the common bile duct
sphincter m. of hepatopancreatic ampulla sphincter of Oddi *m. sphincter ampullae hepatopancreaticae*	circular muscle around terminal part of main pancreatic duct and common bile duct, including the duodenal ampulla (papilla of Vater)		constricts both lower part of common bile duct and main pancreatic duct
sphincter m. of pupil *m. sphincter pupillae*	circular fibers of iris arranged in a narrow band about 1 mm in width		constricts pupil
sphincter m. of pylorus *m. sphincter pylori*	thick muscular ring at the end of the stomach, near opening of the duodenum		acts as valve to close lumen
sphincter m. of urethra external urethral sphincter m. *m. sphincter urethrae*	ramus of pubis	fibers interdigitate around urethra	compresses urethra
sphincter m. of urinary bladder *m. sphincter vesicae urinariae*			acts as valve to close internal urethral orifice

muscle ■ muscle

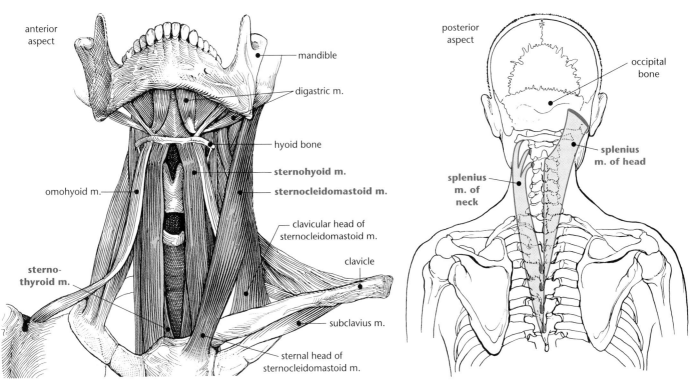

anterior aspect

- mandible
- digastric m.
- hyoid bone
- **sternohyoid m.**
- **sternocleidomastoid m.**
- clavicular head of sternocleidomastoid m.
- clavicle
- subclavius m.
- sternal head of sternocleidomastoid m.

omohyoid m.

sterno-thyroid m.

posterior aspect

- occipital bone
- **splenius m. of head**

splenius m. of neck

MUSCLE	ORIGIN	INSERTION	ACTION
sphincter m. of vagina *m. sphincter vaginae*	pubic symphysis	interdigitates around and interlaces into vaginal barrel	constricts vaginal orifice
sphincter of Oddi	see sphincter muscle of hepatopancreatic ampulla		
spinal m. of head biventer cervicis m. *m. spinalis capitis*	spinous processes of vertebrae C6 to T2	occipital bone between superior and inferior nuchal lines	extends head
spinal m. of neck *m. spinalis cervicis*	spinous processes of vertebrae C7 to T2	spinous processes of second, third, and fourth cervical vertebrae	extends vertebral column
spinal m. of thorax *m. spinalis thoracis*	spinous processes of upper two lumbar and lower two thoracic vertebrae, nuchal ligament	spinous processes of second through seventh thoracic vertebrae	extends vertebral column
splenius m. of head *m. splenius capitis*	spinous processes of upper thoracic vertebrae	mastoid process and superior nuchal line	inclines and rotates head
splenius m. of neck splenius colli m. *m. splenius cervicis*	nuchal ligament, spinous processes of third to sixth thoracic vertebrae	posterior tubercles of the transverse processes of upper two or three cervical vertebrae	extends head and neck, turns head toward the same side
stapedius m. *m. stapedius*	bony canal in pyramidal eminence on posterior wall of middle ear chamber	posterior surface of neck of stapes	dampens excessive vibrations of stapes by tilting the baseplate
sternal m. *m. sternalis*	small superficial muscular band at sternal end of greater pectoral m. (*m. pectoralis major*) parallel with the margin of sternum		protects sternum
sternocleidomastoid m. *m. sternocleidomastoideus*	*sternal head:* anterior surface of manubrium; *clavicular head:* medial third of clavicle	mastoid process, superior nuchal line of occipital bone	rotates and extends head, flexes vertebral column
sternocostal m.	see transverse muscle of thorax		
sternohyoid m. *m. sternohyoideus*	medial end of clavicle, posterior surface of manubrium, first costal cartilage	lower border of body of hyoid bone	depresses hyoid bone and larynx from elevated position during swallowing
sternothyroid m. *m. sternothyroideus*	dorsal surface of upper part of sternum and medial edge of first costal cartilage	oblique line on lamina of thyroid cartilage	draws thyroid cartilage downward from elevated position during swallowing
styloglossus m. *m. styloglossus*	lower end of styloid process, upper end of stylomandibular ligament	*longitudinal part:* side of tongue near dorsal surface; *oblique part:* over hyoglossus muscle	raises and retracts tongue

muscle ■ muscle

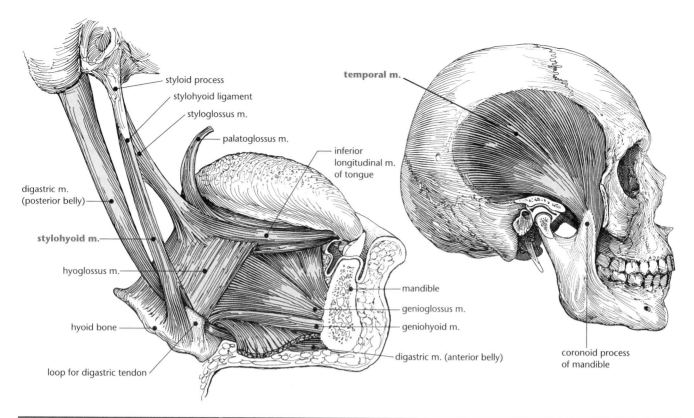

styloid process
stylohyoid ligament
styloglossus m.
palatoglossus m.
inferior longitudinal m. of tongue
digastric m. (posterior belly)
stylohyoid m.
hyoglossus m.
hyoid bone
loop for digastric tendon
mandible
genioglossus m.
geniohyoid m.
digastric m. (anterior belly)
temporal m.
coronoid process of mandible

MUSCLE	ORIGIN	INSERTION	ACTION
stylohyoid m. *m. stylohyoideus*	posterior and lateral surfaces of the styloid process near the base	hyoid bone at junction of greater horn and body	draws hyoid bone upward and backward
stylopharyngeal m. *m. stylopharyngeus*	root of styloid process of temporal bone	borders of thyroid cartilage, wall of pharynx	elevates and opens pharynx
subclavius m. *m. subclavius*	junction of first rib and costal cartilages	lower surface of clavicle	depresses lateral end of clavicle
subcostal m.'s *mm. subcostales*	inner surface of lower ribs near their angles	lower inner surface of second or third rib below rib of origin	draw adjacent ribs together; depresse lower ribs
subscapular m. *m. subscapularis*	subscapular fossa	lesser tubercle of humerus	rotates arm medially
supinator m. *m. supinator*	lateral epicondyle of humerus, supinator crest of ulna	upper third of radius	supinates the forearm by rotating radius
suprahyoid m.'s *mm. suprahyoidei*	the group of muscles attached to the upper part of the hyoid bone from the skull; includes the digastric, stylohyoid, mylohyoid, and geniohyoid m.'s		elevates hyoid bone
supraspinous m. *m. supraspinatus*	supraspinous fossa	superior aspect of greater tubercle of humerus	abducts arm
suspensory m. of duodenum ligament of Treitz suspensory ligament of duodenum m. of Treitz *m. suspensorius duodeni*	connective tissue around celiac artery and right crus of diaphragm	superior border of duodenojejunal junction, part of ascending duodenum	acts as suspensory ligament of the duodenum
tarsal m., inferior *m. tarsalis inferior*	aponeurosis of inferior rectus muscle of eyeball	lower border of tarsal plate of lower eyelid	widens palpebral fissure by depressing lower eyelid
tarsal m., superior lamina profundus m. *m. tarsalis superior*	aponeurosis of levator muscle of upper eyelid	upper border of tarsus plate of upper eyelid	widens palpebral fissure by raising upper eyelid
temporal m. *m. temporalis*	temporal fossa on side of cranium	coronoid process of mandible	closes mouth, clenches teeth, retracts lower jaw
temporoparietal m. *m. temporoparietalis*	temporal fascia above ear	frontal part of epicranial aponeurosis	tightens scalp
tensor m. of fascia lata *m. tensor fasciae latae*	iliac crest, anterior superior iliac spine, fascia lata	iliotibial tract of fascia lata	extends knee with lateral rotation of leg
tensor m. of soft palate *m. tensor veli palatini*	spine of sphenoid, scaphoid fossa of pterygoid process, cartilage and membrane of the auditory tube	midline of aponeurosis of soft palate, wall of auditory tube	elevates palate and opens auditory tube

M

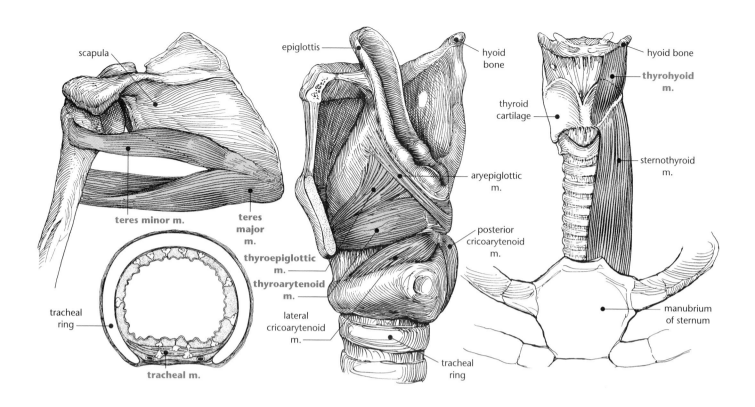

scapula

teres minor m.

teres major m.

tracheal ring

tracheal m.

epiglottis

hyoid bone

aryepiglottic m.

posterior cricoarytenoid m.

thyroepiglottic m.

thyroarytenoid m.

lateral cricoarytenoid m.

tracheal ring

hyoid bone

thyrohyoid m.

thyroid cartilage

sternothyroid m.

manubrium of sternum

MUSCLE	ORIGIN	INSERTION	ACTION
tensor m. of tympanum tensor m. of tympanic membrane (eardrum) *m. tensor tympani*	cartilaginous portion of auditory (eustachian) tube and adjoining part of great wing of sphenoid bone	manubrium of malleus near its root	draws tympanic membrane medially, thus increasing its tension
teres major m. *m. teres major*	inferior axillary border of scapula	crest of lesser tubercle of humerus	adducts and rotates arm medially
teres minor m. *m. teres minor*	axillary border of scapula	inferior aspect of greater tubercle of humerus	rotates arm laterally, and weakly adducts it
thyroarytenoid m. *m. thyroarytneoideus*	inside of thyroid cartilage	lateral surface of arytenoid cartilage	aids in closure of laryngeal inlet, relaxes vocal ligament
thyroepiglottic m. *m. thyroepiglotticus*	inside of thyroid cartilage	margin of epiglottis	depresses the epiglottis, widens inlet of larynx
thyrohyoid m. *m. thyrohyoideus*	oblique line of thyroid cartilage	greater horn (cornu) of hyoid bone	elevates larynx, depresses hyoid bone
tibial m., anterior *m. tibialis anterior*	upper two-thirds of tibia, interosseous membrane	first metatarsal bone, medial cuneiform bone	dorsiflexes and inverts foot
tibial m., posterior *m. tibialis posterior*	tibia, fibula, and interosseous membrane	navicular, with slips to three cuneiform bones; cuboid, second, third, and fourth metatarsals	principal inverter of foot, aids in plantarflexion of foot
tracheal m. *m. trachealis*	anastomosing transverse muscular bands connecting the ends of the tracheal rings		reduces size of tracheal lumen
trachelomastoid m.	see longissimus m. of head		
tragus m. *m. tragicus*	a short band of vertical muscular fibers on the outer surface of the tragus of the ear		slightly alters shape of ear
transverse m. of abdomen *m. transversus abdominis*	7th through 12th costal cartilages, thoracolumbar fascia, iliac crest, inguinal ligament	xiphoid process, linea alba, conjoint tendon to pubis	supports abdominal viscera; tenses abdominal wall
transverse m. of auricle *m. transversus auriculae*	see auricular m., transverse		
transverse m. of chin *m. transversus menti*	superficial muscular fibers of depressor m. of angle of mouth (triangular m.) which turn back and cross to the opposite side below the chin		aids in drawing angle of mouth downward
transverse m. of nape *m. transversus nuchae*	an occasional muscle passing between the tendons of the trapezius and sternocleidomastoid m.'s		moves scalp feebly
transverse m. of perineum, deep *m. transverse perinei profundus*	inferior ramus of ischium	central tendon of perineum, external anal sphincter	supports pelvic viscera

muscle ■ muscle

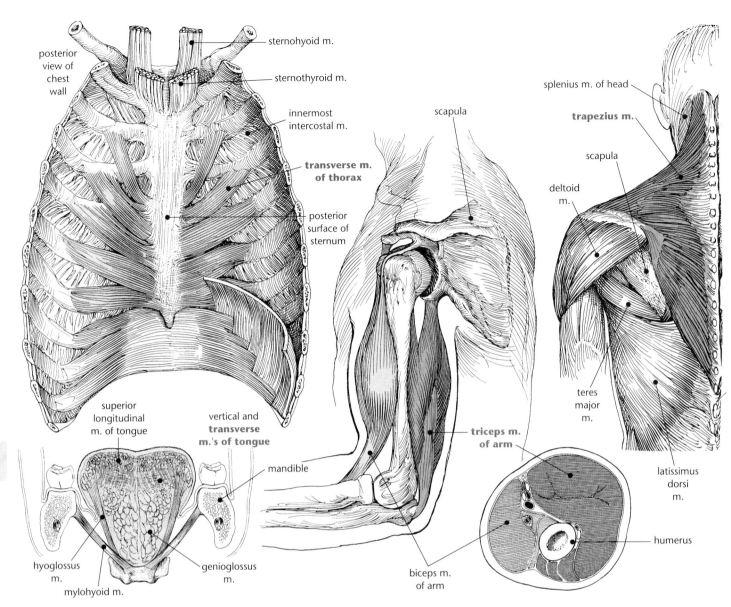

posterior view of chest wall

sternohyoid m.

sternothyroid m.

innermost intercostal m.

transverse m. of thorax

posterior surface of sternum

superior longitudinal m. of tongue

vertical and **transverse m.'s of tongue**

mandible

hyoglossus m.

mylohyoid m.

genioglossus m.

scapula

triceps m. of arm

biceps m. of arm

splenius m. of head

trapezius m.

scapula

deltoid m.

teres major m.

latissimus dorsi m.

humerus

MUSCLE	ORIGIN	INSERTION	ACTION
transverse m. of perineum, superficial *m. transversus perinei superficialis*	ramus of ischium near tuberosity	central tendon of perineum	supports pelvic viscera
transverse m. of thorax sternocostal m. *m. transversus thoracis*	xiphoid process, posterior surface of lower part of sternum, adjacent costal cartilages	second to sixth costal cartilages (inner surface)	narrows chest, draws costal cartilages downward
transverse m. of tongue *m. transversus linguae*	median fibrous septum of tongue	submucous fibrous tissue at sides of tongue	narrows and elongates tongue
trapezius m. *m. trapezius*	superior nuchal line of occipital bone, nuchal ligament, spinous processes of seventh cervical and all thoracic vertebrae, external occipital protuberance	*superior part:* posterior border of lateral third of clavicle; *middle part:* medial margin of acromion, superior lip of posterior border of scapular spine; *inferior part:* tubercle at apex of medial end of scapular spine	elevates, rotates, and retracts scapula (shoulder blade)
triangular m.	see depressor muscle of angle of		
triceps m. of arm *m. triceps brachii*	*long head:* infraglenoid tubercle of scapula; *lateral head:* proximal portion of humerus; *medial head:* distal half of humerus	posterior part of superior surface of olecranon process of ulna; adjacent deep fascia; articular capsule of elbow joint	main extensor of forearm

muscle ■ muscle

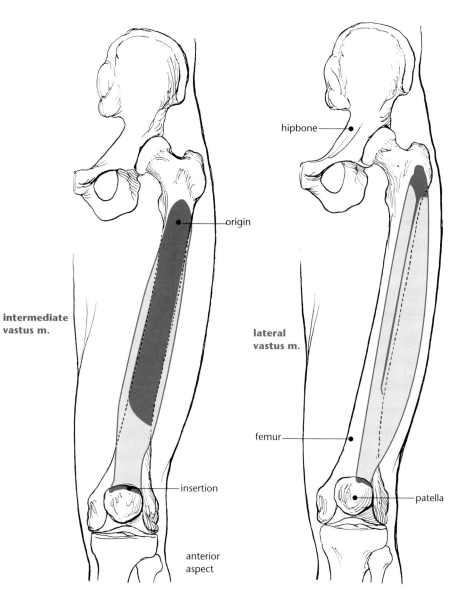

intermediate vastus m.

origin

insertion

anterior aspect

lateral vastus m.

hipbone

femur

patella

medial vastus m.

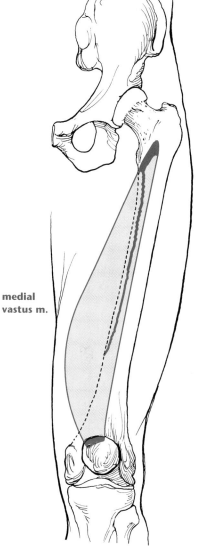

MUSCLE	ORIGIN	INSERTION	ACTION
triceps m. of calf *m. triceps surae*	combined gastrocnemius and soleus m.'s; its tendon of insertion is the calcaneal tendon		plantar flexes foot
uvula m. *m. uvulae*	palatine aponeurosis and posterior nasal spine of palatine bone	mucous membrane and connective tissue of uvula	elevates uvula
vastus m., intermediate *m. vastus intermedius*	anterior and lateral surface of the upper two-thirds of femur	common tendon of quadriceps m. of thigh, patella	extends leg
vastus m., lateral *m. vastus lateralis*	lateral aspect of upper part of femur	common tendon of quadriceps m. of thigh, patella	extends leg
vastus m., medial *m. vastus medialis*	medial aspect of femur	common tendon of quadriceps m. of thigh, patella	extends leg
vertical m. of tongue *m. verticalis linguae*	dorsal fascia of tongue	undersurface of tongue	aids in mastication, swallowing, and speech by altering shape of tongue
vocal m. *m. vocalis*	inner surface of thyroid cartilage near midline	vocal process of arytenoid cartilage	adjusts tension of vocal cords
zygomatic m., greater *m. zygomaticus major*	zygomatic arch	angle of mouth	draws upper lip upward and laterally
zygomatic m., smaller *m. zygomaticus minor*	malar surface of zygomatic bone	upper lip	aids in forming nasolabial furrow (muscle of facial expression)

muscle ■ muscle

muscular (mus′ku-lar) 1. Relating to muscles. 2. Having well-developed muscles.

muscularis (mus-ku-la′ris) Latin for muscular; applied especially to the muscular layer of the wall of a hollow or tubular structure.

musculature (mus′ku-lah-chur) The system of muscles in the body or a body part.

musculoaponeurotic (mus′ku-lo-ap-o-nu-rot′ik) Relating to a muscle and its sheet of connective tissue (aponeurosis).

musculocutaneous (mus′ku-lo-ku-ta′ne-us) Relating to muscle and skin.

musculomembranous (mus′ku-lo-mem′brah-nus) Relating to or composed of muscular and membranous tissues.

musculophrenic (mus′ku-lo-fren′ik) Relating to the muscular portion of the diaphragm.

musculoskeletal (mus′ku-lo-skel′e-tal) Relating to muscles and bones.

musculospiral (mus′ku-lo-spi′ral) Denoting the form of distribution of certain nerves (e.g., the radial nerve, which crosses obliquely across the back of the humerus, then spirals around the bone to enter the anterior compartment of the arm).

musculotropic (mus′ku-lo-trop′ik) Acting upon muscular tissue.

mussitation (mus-ĭ-ta′shun) Movement of the lips without uttering sounds; observed in certain neurologic conditions.

mutagen (mu′tah-jen) Any agent that causes a permanent, heritable change in the genetic material of a cell (e.g., radioactive substances, certain chemicals).

mutagenesis (mu-tah-jen′ĕ-sis) Production of a mutation.

    insertional m. Mutation resulting from insertion of different material into a normal gene, especially the slow transformation induced by certain cancer-causing retroviruses.

mutagenic (mu-tah-jen′ik) Causing mutations.

mutagenicity (mu-tah-jĕ-nis′ĭ-te) The ability to induce basic and transmissible changes in the genetic material (chromosomes and genes).

mutant (mu′tant) An organism or cell that differs from the parental strain as a result of having a gene that has undergone structural change.

mutase (mu′tās) Any enzyme that promotes the apparent migration of a chemical group within a molecule.

mutation (mu-ta′shun) A permanent, heritable structural change in the genetic material of a cell.

    point m. Mutation involving a minute section of a single gene, as seen in sickle-cell anemia.

mute (mūt) A person who is unable to speak, or one who refuses to speak for conscious or unconscious reasons.

mutilate (mu′tĭ-lāt) 1. To damage, destroy, or remove a part of the body. 2. To subject to such extreme injury or deformity as to render unidentifiable in death.

mutism (mu′tizm) The state of being unable or unwilling to speak.

    akinetic m. An uncommon condition characterized by pathologically slowed or nearly absent body movements, loss of speech, and reduced level of mental function; wakefulness and self-awareness may be preserved; the condition characteristically accompanies a gradually developing, or subacute, damage to the brain (i.e., bilateral damage to the paramedian part of the midbrain, basal part of the interbrain, or inferior frontal lobes).

myalgia (mi-al′je-ah) Muscle pain.

myasthenia (mi-as-the′ne-ah) Weakness of muscle.

    m. gravis (MG) Neuromuscular disorder of autoimmune origin characterized by varying degrees of weakness and fatigability of certain muscle groups, which may progress to paralysis; it frequently begins in the eyelids, often associated with abnormalities of the thymus. There is evidence that specific antibodies interfere with the action of the neurotransmitter acetylcholine (Ach) in passing nerve impulses to muscles at the neuromuscular junctions.

myasthenic (mi-as-then′ik) Relating to myasthenia.

myatonia, myatony (mi-ah-to′ne-ah, mi-at′o-ne) Absence of muscle tone. Also called amyotonia.

myatrophy (mi-at′ro-fe) See myoatrophy.

mycet- Combining form meaning fungus.

mycete (mi′sēt) A fungus.

mycetism, mycetismus (mi′sĕ-tizm, mi-sĕ-tiz′mus) Mushroom poisoning. Also called muscarinism.

mycetogenic (mi-sĕ-to-jen′ik) Caused by fungi.

mycetoma (mi-sĕ-to′mah) Chronic pus-forming inflammation of the skin characterized by indurated abscess, extensive local tissue destruction, and multiple draining orifices on the overlying skin; caused by a variety of microorganisms, including bacteria of the genera *Actinomyces* and *Nocardia* and several fungi, especially *Allescheria boydii*. Also called Madura foot; fungus foot.

mycid (mi′sid) A secondary lesion occurring in certain mycotic infections.

myco- Combining form meaning fungus.

mycobacteria (mi-ko-bak-te′re-ah) Microorganisms of the genus *Mycobacterium.*

    group I m. A group of organisms that produce a bright yellow pigment when grown in the presence of light; some cause a tuberculosis-like disease. Also called photochromogens.

    group II m. Mycobacteria that produce a yellow to orange pigment and grow in dead animal or plant tissues. Also called scotochromogens.

    group III m. Mycobacteria that either are colorless or produce a light yellow pigment when grown in the presence of light. Also called nonchromogens.

mycobacteriosis (mi-ko-bak-te-re-o′sis) Infection with any species of mycobacteria.

Mycobacterium (mi-ko-bak-te′re-um) Genus of gram-positive aerobic bacteria (family Mycobacteriaceae); the principal habitat of some species is diseased or dead tissues.

    M. avium complex (MAC) A bacterial complex that includes several strains of *Mycobacterium avium* and the immunologically related *Mycobacterium intracellulare;* most frequently found in respiratory secretions from persons with a tuberculous-like lung disease; it is the cause of a disseminated blood infection (MAC bacteremia) in AIDS patients. Distinguished from *Mycobacterium avium,* which causes disease primarily in birds. See also *Mycobacterium avium* complex bacteremia, under bacteremia.

    M. avium-intracellulare (MAI) Species causing a nontuberculous lung disease in humans, similar to tuberculosis; occurs primarily in persons with underlying lung disease and as an opportunistic infection in AIDS patients.

    M. fortuitum Species causing postoperative and posttraumatic wound infections.

    M. kansasii Species causing a lung disease similar to tuberculosis but milder.

    M. leprae The causative agent of Hansen's disease. Also called Hansen's bacillus; leprosy bacillus.

    M. marinum Species causing warty skin nodules (granulomas) that may ulcerate; transmitted through contaminated aquariums, swimming pools, or natural bodies of water.

    M. scrofulaceum Species associated with inflammation of the lymph nodes of the neck in children.

    M. tuberculosis The causative agent of tuberculosis in humans. Also called Koch's bacillus; tubercle bacillus (human).

mycodermatitis (mi-ko-der-mah-ti′tis) Any fungal infection of the skin.

mycogastritis (mi-ko-gas-tri′tis) Inflammation of the stomach caused by a fungus.

mycologist (mi-kol′o-jist) A specialist in fungi and fungal diseases.

mycology (mi-kol′o-je) The study of fungi.

Mycoplasma (mi-ko-plaz′mah) A genus of bacteria that are the smallest free-living organisms presently known (about the same size as viruses); like viruses, they lack a rigid cell wall but, unlike viruses, they can reproduce outside living cells; some species cause disease.

    M. pneumoniae Species causing mycoplasmal pneumonia primarily in school-age children and young adults. Also called Eaton agent.

mycoplasma (mi-ko-plaz′mah) Any bacterium of the genus *Mycoplasma.*

mycosis (mi-ko′sis), pl. myco′ses Any disease caused by a fungus.

mycosis fungoides (mi-ko′sis fung-goi′dez) (MF) A type of T cell tumor of the skin (cutaneous T cell lymphoma) that begins with an inflammatory rash phase and progresses through a scaly plaque phase to a nodular tumor phase; affects primarily the skin of the buttocks, back or shoulders but may occur at other sites; the most severe cases may include ulceration, enlargement of lymph nodes and involvement of internal organs. Cause is unknown.

mycotic (mi-kot′ik) Relating to fungi.

mydriasis (mī-dri′ah-sis) Enlargement of the pupil; may be induced normally by emotion and changes in accommodation and in light intensity, or by certain drugs (mydriastics).

mydriatic (mid-re-at′ik) **1.** Capable of enlarging the pupil. **2.** Any agent having such property.

myectomy (mi-ek′to-me) Removal of a portion of a muscle.

myelencephalon (mi-ĕ-len-sef′ah-lon) The part of an embryonic brain from which develop the most posterior portion of the brainstem (i.e., portion composed of medulla oblongata and the caudal part of the fourth ventricle).

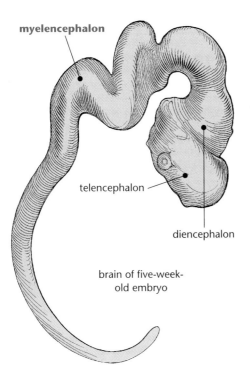

brain of five-week-old embryo

myelic (mi-el′ik) **1.** Relating to the spinal cord. **2.** Relating to bone marrow.

myelin (mi′ĕ-lin) A fatty substance that is a major constituent of the sheath surrounding and insulating the axon of some nerve cells.

myelinated (mi′ĕ-li-nāt-ed) Having a myelin sheath.

myelination (mi-ĕ-li-na′shun) The formation of a medullary sheath around a nerve fiber.

myelinic (mi-ĕ-lin′ik) Relating to myelin.

myelinization (mi-e-li-ni-za′shun) See myelination.

myelinolysis (mi-ĕ-lin-ol′i-sis) Demyelination; destruction of the myelin sheath of nerve fibers.

    central pontine m. Demyelination distributed about the mid-base of the pons.

myelitis (mi-ĕ-li′tis) **1.** Inflammation of the spinal cord. **2.** Inflammation of bone marrow.

    concussion m. Inflammation following concussion of the spinal cord (e.g., in a fracture dislocation of a vertebra). Also called traumatic myelitis.

    transverse m. Inflammation involving the whole thickness of the spinal cord.

    traumatic m. See concussion myelitis.

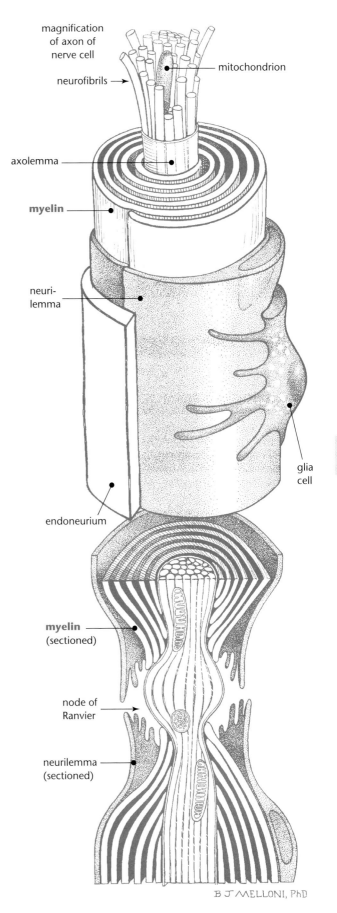

B J MELLONI, PhD

myelo-, myel- Combining forms meaning spinal cord; bone marrow.

myeloarchitectonics (mi-ĕ-lo-ar′ke-tek-ton′iks) The study of the organization of nerve fibers and fiber tracts in the brain.

myeloblast (mi′ĕ-lo-blast) A white blood cell in its earliest stages of development, occurring normally in bone marrow; it can differentiate into a neutrophilic, eosinophilic, or basophilic granulocyte. Also called granuloblast.

myeloblastemia (mi-ĕ-lo-blas-te′me-ah) The presence of myeloblasts in the circulating blood, as seen in myeloblastic leukemia.

myeloblastoma (mi-ĕ-lo-blas-to′mah) A nodular accumulation of myeloblasts.

myeloblastosis (mi-ĕ-lo-blas-to′sis) The presence of a large number of myeloblasts in the circulating blood.

myelocele (mi′ĕ-lo-sēl) Developmental defect of the vertebral column in which the vertebral arches are absent, leaving an open groove lined with imperfect spinal cord tissue through which cerebrospinal fluid drains.

myelocyst (mi′ĕ-lo-sist) A cyst originating from a rudimentary medullary canal in the central nervous system.

myelocystic (mi-ĕ-lo-sis′tik) Relating to a myelocyst.

myelocystocele (mi-ĕ-lo-sis′to-sēl) Hernial protrusion of spinal cord substance through an abnormal gap in the vertebral column.

myelocyte (mi′ĕ-lo-sit) A white blood cell in an early stage of development, present normally in bone marrow.

myelocytic (mi-ĕ-lo-sit′ik) Relating to myelocytes.

myelocytosis (mi-ĕ-lo-si-to′sis) The presence of abnormally large numbers of myelocytes in the circulating blood.

myelodysplasia (mi-ĕ-lo-dis-pla′se-ah) Abnormal changes in formation of blood cell precursors in bone marrow.

myelodysplastic (mi-ĕ-lo-dis-plas′tic) Relating to myelodysplasia.

myelofibrosis (mi-ĕ-lo-fi-bro′sis) Abnormal increase in the reticular fibers of bone marrow; may occur as a primary disease or secondary to other conditions (e.g., to chronic myelocytic leukemia or polycythemia vera). Also called myelosclerosis; osteomyelofibrotic syndrome.

myelogenesis (mi-ĕ-lo-jen′ĕ-sis) Development of bone marrow.

myelogenic (mi-ĕ-lo-jen′ik) Relating to myelogenesis.

myelogenous (mi-ĕ-loj′ĕ-nus) Produced in bone marrow.

myelography (mi-ĕ-log′rah-fe) Procedure that combines fluoroscopy and radiography to visually examine the spinal subarachnoid space after injection of a radiopaque substance; used to demonstrate such conditions as herniated intervertebral disks, tumors of the spinal cord, or damage to nerve roots. The procedure is being replaced by newer imaging techniques (e.g., CT scanning, MRI).

myeloid (mi′ĕ-loid) **1.** Resembling or relating to the spinal cord. **2.** Resembling or relating to bone marrow. **3.** Relating to myelocytes.

myelolysis (mi-ĕ-lol′ĭ-sis) Dissolution of the fatty sheath (myelin) covering certain nerve fibers.

myeloma (mi-ĕ-lo′mah) A tumor composed of cell types normally formed in bone marrow. See multiple myeloma.

    giant cell m. See giant cell tumor of bone, under tumor.

    multiple m. An uncommon malignant proliferation of plasma cells forming numerous nodules, chiefly within the bone marrow but occasionally occurring in other parts of the body; may also occur as a single tumor (plasmacytoma); seen most commonly in men over 40 years of age. Also called myeloma; plasma cell myeloma; multiple plasmacytoma; myelomatosis.

    plasma cell m. See multiple myeloma.

myelomalacia (mi-ĕ-lo-mah-la′she-ah) Pathologic softening of the spinal cord.

myelomatosis (mi-ĕ-lo-mah-to′sis) See multiple myeloma, under myeloma.

myelomeningocele (mi-ĕ-lo-mĕ-ning′go-sēl) See meningomyelocele.

myeloneuritis (mi-ĕ-lo-nu-ri′tis) See neuromyelitis.

myelonic (mi-ĕ-lon′ik) Relating to the spinal cord.

myelopathy (mi-ĕ-lop′ah-the) Any disease of the spinal cord.

myelophthisis (mi-ĕ-lof′thĭ-sis) **1.** A wasting of the spinal cord. **2.** Insufficiency of the cell-forming activity of bone marrow.

myeloplast (mi′ĕ-lo-plast) A white blood cell of bone marrow.

myelopoiesis (mi-ĕ-lo-poi-e′sis) The formation of bone marrow or the blood cells derived from it.

myeloproliferative (mi-ĕ-lo-pro-lif′er-ah-tiv) Relating to the increased formation of blood cells in bone marrow.

myeloradiculitis (mi-ĕ-lo-rah-dik′u-li′tis) Inflammation of the spinal cord and spinal nerve roots.

myeloradiculodysplasia (mi-ĕ-lo-rah-dik′u-lo-dis-pla′ze-ah) Abnormal development of the spinal cord and spinal nerve roots.

myeloradiculopathy (mi-ĕ-lo-rah-dik′u-lop′ah-the) Any disease involving both the spinal cord and spinal nerve roots. Also called radiculomyelopathy.

myelorrhagia (mi-ĕ-lo-ra′je-ah) See hematomyelia.

myelosarcoma (mi-ĕ-lo-sar-ko′mah) Malignant tumor derived from bone marrow cells.

myelosclerosis (mi-ĕ-lo-skle-ro′sis) See myelofibrosis.

myelosis (mi-ĕ-lo′sis) Condition characterized by abnormal proliferation of blood-forming cells in bone marrow and other organs.

    chronic nonleukemic m. Condition characterized primarily by abnormal proliferation of elements that give rise to white blood cells, while the total count remains within the normal range.

    erythremic m. Neoplastic abnormality of the red cell–forming process (erythropoiesis); characterized by anemia, hemorrhagic disorders, immature red cells in the circulating blood, and enlargement of the spleen and liver. Also called Di Guglielmo's syndrome.

myelotomy (mi-ĕ-lot′o-me) The cutting of nerve fibers in the spinal cord.

myelotoxic (mi-ĕ-lo-tok′sik) **1.** Destructive to bone marrow. **2.** Any agent having such an effect.

myenteric (mi-en-ter′ik) Relating to the muscular layer (myenteron) of the intestines.

myenteron (mi-en′ter-on) The muscular layer of the intestinal wall.

myesthesia (mi-es-the′ze-ah) Sensation felt in a muscle.

myiasis (mi′yah-sis) Infestation of human tissue by fly maggots, usually by deposition of eggs in open skin lacerations.

mylohyoid (mi-lo-hi′oid) Relating to the inner part of the lower jaw (mandible) and the hyoid bone situated in the neck.

myo- Combining form meaning muscle.

myoarchitectonic (mi-o-ar-ke-tek-ton′ik) Relating to the inner structure of muscle.

myoatrophy (mi-o-at′ro-fe) Wasting away of muscle. Also called myatrophy.

myoblast (mi′o-blast) An embryonic cell that becomes a muscle cell.

myoblastoma (mi-o-blas-to′mah) Tumor composed of immature muscle cells.

    granular cell m. See granular cell tumor, under tumor.

myocardial (mi-o-kar′de-al) Relating to the heart muscle (myocardium).

myocardial hibernation (mi-o-kar′de-al hi-ber-na′shun) Heart condition characterized by a chronic reduction of blood supply to a portion of the heart muscle, producing reduced function of the affected muscle. The muscle remains viable and can regain full function rapidly upon perfusion.

myocardial infarction (mi-o-kar′de-al in-fark′shun) See under infarction.

myocardial stunning (mi-o-kar′de-al stun′ing) Heart condition characterized by brief severe reduction of blood supply to the muscular wall of the left ventricle (often involving the wall's full thickness), lasting from minutes to hours, and resulting in prolonged (hours to days or weeks) dysfunction of the ventricle.

myocardiograph (mi-o-kar′de-o-graf) Instrument for graphically recording the action of the heart muscle.

myocardiopathy (mi-o-kar-de-op′ah-the) See cardiomyopathy.

myocardiorrhaphy (mi-o-kar-de-or′ah-fe) Suture of the muscular wall of the heart.

myocarditis (mi-o-kar-di′tis) Inflammation of the heart muscle, most commonly caused by acute viral infection.

acute isolated m. Acute pericarditis of unknown cause. Also called Fiedler's myocarditis.

Fiedler's m. See acute isolated myocarditis.

myocardium (mi-o-kar′de-um) The middle and thickest layer of the heart wall, composed of specialized striated muscle cells and intervening connective tissue.

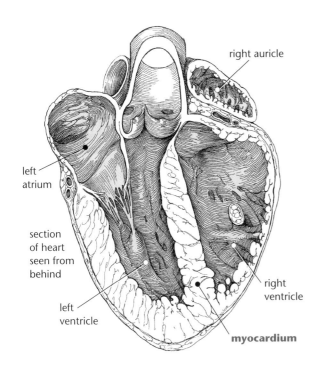

section of heart seen from behind

left atrium

right auricle

left ventricle

right ventricle

myocardium

myocele (mi′o-sēl) Herniation of a muscle through a gap in its connective-tissue covering.

myocelitis (mi-o-se-li′tis) Inflammation of muscles forming the abdominal wall.

myocellulitis (mi-o-sel-u-li′tis) Inflammation of muscle and subcutaneous tissue.

myoclonia (mi-o-klo′ne-ah) Any disorder characterized by twitching or spasmodic contraction of muscles.

myoclonic (mi-o-klon′ik) Relating to myoclonus.

myoclonus (mi-ok′lo-nus) A sudden rapid contraction of a single muscle or a muscle group.

myocyte (mi′o-sit) A muscle cell.

myodegeneration (mi-o-de-jen-er-a′shun) Degeneration of muscle; may be due to primary disease or to interruption of nerve supply.

myodynamometer (mi-o-di-nah-mom′ĕ-ter) Instrument for measuring muscular strength.

myodystony (mi-o-dis′to-ne) Any abnormality of muscular tone.

myoedema (mi-o-ĕ-de′mah) **1.** Swelling of a muscle. **2.** The localized contraction (forming a lump) of a degenerating muscle when struck. Also called mounding.

myoelectric (mi-o-e-lek′trik) Relating to the electrical attributes of muscle tissue.

myoendocarditis (mi-o-en-do-kar-di′tis) Inflammation of the muscular layer and inner lining of the heart wall (myocardium and endocardium, respectively).

myoepithelial (mi-o-ep-ĭ-the′le-al) Relating to myoepithelium.

myoepithelium (mi-o-ep-ĭ-the′le-um) Tissue composed of contractile epithelial cells that resemble smooth muscle cells.

myofibril (mi-o-fi′bril) One of numerous fine fibrils present in a muscle fiber; each is divided into a series of repeating units (sarcomeres), which are the fundamental structural and functional units of muscle contraction.

myofibroma (mi-o-fi-bro′mah) A noncancerous tumor containing muscular and fibrous tissues.

myofibrosis (mi-o-fi-bro′sis) Chronic inflammation of a muscle and excessive formation of connective tissue, with resulting atrophy of the muscle.

myofilament (mi-o-fil′ah-ment) One of the numerous microscopic structures that make up the fibrils of striated muscle.

myogen (mi′o-jen) A mixture of proteins, extractable from skeletal muscle with cold water; it consists primarily of glycolytic enzymes.

myogenic (mi-o-jen′ik) Of muscular origin.

myoglobin (mi-o-glo′bin) (Mb) An oxygen-transporting protein found in muscle fibers, functionally similar to the blood pigment hemoglobin.

myoglobinuria (mi-o-glo-bin-u′re-ah) Excretion of myoglobin in the urine originating from release of this protein into the bloodstream from an injured muscle; usually occurs after a crush injury or occasionally after very vigorous exercise. Also called myoglobulinuria.

myoglobulin (mi-o-glob′u-lin) A globulin present in muscle tissue.

myoglobulinuria (mi-o-glob-u-lin-u′re-ah) See myoglobinuria.

myogram (mi′o-gram) A tracing made in myography.

myograph (mi′o-graf) Instrument for graphically recording muscular contractions.

myography (mi-og′rah-fe) Technique used for making graphic records (myograms) of muscular activity.

myoid (mi′oid) Like muscle.

myoischemia (mi-o-is-ke′me-ah) Lack of blood supply to localized areas of muscle tissue.

myokymia (mi-o-kim′e-ah) A benign condition characterized by tremors of individual bundles of fibers (fasciculi) of a muscle.

myolipoma (mi-o-li-po′mah) Benign tumor mainly composed of adipose and muscle tissues.

myology (mi-ol′o-je) The study of muscles.

myolysis (mi-ol′ĭ-sis) Disintegration and dissolution of muscle tissue.

myoma (mi-o′mah) See leiomyoma.

myomalacia (mi-o-mah-la′she-ah) Abnormal softening and degeneration of muscle.

myomatous (mi-o′mah-tus) Of the nature of a myoma.

myomectomy (mi-o-mek′to-me) Surgical removal of a myoma, especially of the uterus.

myometer (mi-om′ĕ-ter) Instrument for measuring the strength of a muscular contraction.

myometritis (mi-o-mĕ-tri′tis) Inflammation of the muscular layer (myometrium) of the uterine wall.

myometrium (mi-o-me′tre-um) The smooth muscle forming the middle layer of the uterine wall.

myon (mi′on) An individual functional unit of muscle composed of a muscle fiber with its basal membrane, together with the associated blood capillaries and nerves.

myonecrosis (mi-o-nĕ-kro′sis) Death of muscle tissue.

myoneural (mi-o-nu′ral) Relating to muscle and nerve.

myopathy (mi-op′ah-the) Any disease of muscle from any cause.

myopericarditis (mi-o-per-ĭ-kar-di′tis) Inflammation of the heart muscle (myocardium) and its enveloping membrane (pericardium).

myopia (mi-o′pe-ah) (M, My) Condition in which only those rays of light entering the eyeball from a short distance focus on the retina. Also called shortsightedness; short sight; nearsightedness; near sight.

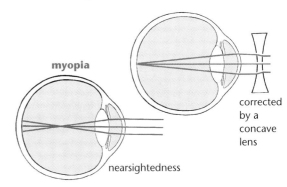

myopia

corrected by a concave lens

nearsightedness

myopic (mi-op′ik) Relating to myopia.

myoplasm (mi′o-plazm) The contractile portion of a muscle cell.

myoplasty (mi′o-plas-te) Surgical repair of a muscle.

myorrhaphy (mi-or′ah-fe) Suture of a muscle cut or tear.

myorrhexis (mi-o-rek′sis) A tearing or rupturing of a muscle.

myosalpinx (mi-o-sal′pinks) The muscular layer of a fallopian (uterine) tube.

myosarcoma (mi-o-sar-ko′mah) General term for a cancerous tumor derived from muscle tissue.

myosclerosis (mi-o-skle-ro′sis) Chronic inflammation of a muscle with overgrowth of interstitial connective tissue and consequent hardening of the muscle.

myoseism (mi′o-sīzm) Condition characterized by nonrhythmic contractions of muscle.

myosin (mi′o-sin) A globulin present in muscle tissue; a type of protein that, combined with actin, forms actomyosin.

myositis (mi-o-si′tis) Inflammation of muscle tissue causing pain and tenderness.

    m. ossificans Formation of bone within muscle tissues; it may be localized secondary to an injury (e.g., after a blow or a tear, especially in a thigh or arm muscle) or, rarely, may be generalized, beginning in childhood and due to unknown causes.

myospasm (mi′o-spazm) Spasmodic contraction of a muscle or group of muscles.

myotactic (mi-o-tak′tik) Relating to the muscular proprioceptive sense; denoting any reflex elicited by tapping the belly or tendon of a muscle.

myotasis (mi-ot′ah-sis) The stretching of muscle.

myotatic (mi-o-tat′ik) Relating to the stretching of a muscle.

myotomy (mi-ot′o-me) Surgical division of a muscle (e.g., of the lower esophageal sphincter in the treatment of achalasia).

myotonia (mi-o-to′ne-ah) Delayed relaxation of a muscle after voluntary contraction, electrical stimulation, or tapping (percussion) of the muscle.

    m. atrophica See myotonic dystrophy, under dystrophy.

    m. congenita Hereditary condition present at birth, characterized by temporary myotonia whenever a voluntary movement is attempted, often interfering with feeding and causing a "strangled" cry.

    myotonic (mi-o-ton′ik) Relating to myotonia.

myotrophic (mi′o-tro-fik) Relating to nutrition of muscle tissue.

myotropic (mi-o-trop′ik) Acting upon muscle tissue.

myringitis (mir-in-ji′tis) Inflammation of the eardrum (tympanic membrane).

myringo-, myring- Combining forms denoting the eardrum (tympanic membrane).

myringoplasty (mī-ring′go-plas-te) Surgical repair of a perforated eardrum (tympanic membrane) by means of a graft; the graft material usually is fibrous tissue (fascia) taken from the patient's temple or thigh.

myringotome (mī-ring′go-tōm) The fine surgical knife used for cutting into the eardrum (tympanic membrane) in myringotomy.

myringotomy (mir-in-got′o-me) Surgical opening through the eardrum (tympanic membrane) made for inserting a ventilation tube; usually performed on children to treat persistent middle ear effusion when other forms of treatment have failed. Also called ototomy; tympanotomy.

mysophobia (mi-so-fo′be-ah) Abnormal fear of dirt or contamination.

myxadenoma (miks-ad-ĕ-no′mah) Noncancerous tumor derived from glandular epithelial tissue.

myxedema (mik-sĕ-de′mah) A severe form of hypothyroidism caused by deficiency of thyroid hormone; symptoms and signs include slowing of physical and mental activity, apathy, cold intolerance, puffy eyes, dry skin, brittle hair, and coarsening of skin and facial features.

    pretibial m. A swelling over the lateral aspect of the lower leg above the lateral malleolus, due to localized mucoid (mucopolysaccharide) deposits in the subcutaneous tissues; usually associated with Graves' disease.

myxedematoid (mik-sĕ-dem′ah-toid) Resembling myxedema.

myxedematous (mik-sĕ-dem′ah-tus) Relating to myxedema.

myxo-, myx- Combining forms meaning mucus.

myxochondrofibrosarcoma (mik-so-kon′dro-fi′bro-sar-ko′mah) Cancerous tumor derived from fibrous connective tissue.

myxochondroma (mik-so-kon-dro′mah) Benign tumor composed mainly of cartilaginous tissue; occurs frequently in the chest wall, and around the breastbone (sternum) and rib margin areas.

myxocyte (mik′so-sit) One of the stellate cells found in mucous tissue.

myxoid (mik′soid) Resembling mucus or containing mucus.

myxolipoma (mik-so-li-po′mah) Benign tumor with mucoid components.

myxoma (mik-so′mah) Benign tumor composed of fibrous strands embedded in a soft, jellylike material; typically grows in subcutaneous tissues, especially of the limbs and neck, but may occur at other sites.

    atrial m. A benign primary tumor of the heart, arising from the lining of the atria and resembling a polyp; it may cause heart murmurs that change with shifts in body position, or simulate obstruction of the atrioventricular valves (e.g., mitral or tricuspid stenosis).

myxomatous (mik-so′mah-tus) Having the characteristics of a myxoma.

myxopoiesis (mik-so-poi-e′sis) The production of mucus.

myxosarcoma (mik-so-sar-ko′mah) Cancerous tumor derived from connective tissue.

myxovirus (mik-so-vi′rus) General term for a group of viruses that include the influenza, mumps, and Newcastle disease viruses.

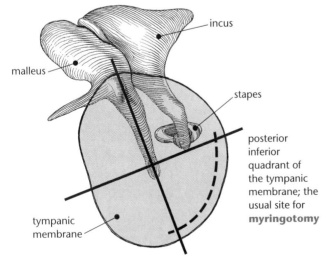

incus

malleus

stapes

tympanic membrane

posterior inferior quadrant of the tympanic membrane; the usual site for **myringotomy**

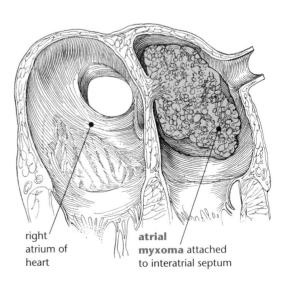

right atrium of heart

atrial myxoma attached to interatrial septum

M

N

Naegleria (na-gle′re-ah) Genus of free-living amebae (family Vahlkamfiidae); some species have been implicated in swimming pool-transmitted meningoencephalitis and in building-associated hypersensitivity pneumonitis.

nail (nāl) **1.** The curved keratinous structure on the end of a digit, composed of several layers of flat, clear cells. See also nail bed, under bed; nail root, under root. **2.** A rigid piece of metal or other hard material used for holding together the segments of a fractured bone. Also called bone nail.

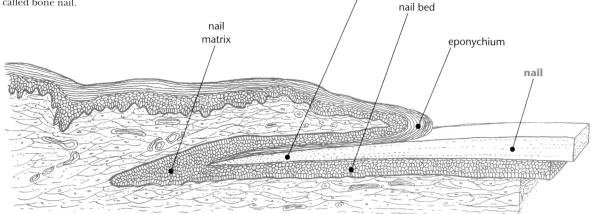

nail matrix — nail root — nail bed — eponychium — nail

bone n. See nail (2).

hippocratic n.'s Deformed curved nails overhanging the fingertips; associated with clubbed fingers characteristic of certain pulmonary and cardiac conditions.

ingrown n. A toenail with edges growing into the soft tissues. Also called onychocryptosis.

Jewett n. A pointed metal rod generally used for internally holding together a fractured femur at the hip in which the head and neck of the bone separate from its shaft.

Plummer's n.'s Abnormal condition of the nails, which separate from their nail beds; seen in thyrotoxicosis.

nailing (nāl′ing) The fastening of the fractured ends of a bone by means of nails.

naloxone (nal-oks′ōn) A compound that blocks the action of narcotics; usually employed in treating respiratory depression in cases of a narcotic drug overdose (by drug abusers), in patients who have received high doses of a narcotic during surgery, and in newborn infants affected by the anesthetic administered to the mother during childbirth.

name (nām) A word designating and distinguishing one entity from another.

brand n. See trade name.

chemical n. A scientific name indicating a precise chemical constitution and the arrangement of atoms or atomic groups; e.g., 2-(diphenylmethoxy)-N,N-dimethylethylamine hydrochorlide (Benadryl®). Also called systematic name.

generic n. Strictly defined, a name designating a family relationship among drugs; e.g., antihistamine, barbiturate; often used as a synonym for nonproprietary name, e.g., diphenhydramine (Benadryl®).

nonproprietary n. In pharmaceutical nomenclature, a name assigned to a drug by the United States Adopted Name (USAN) Council when it is found to have therapeutic value; it indicates the chemical composition of the drug and it is not protected by trademark registration; e.g., diphenhydramine (Benadryl®). Also called official name.

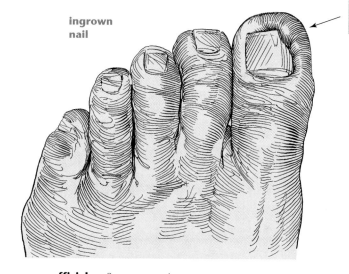

ingrown nail

official n. See nonproprietary name.

proprietary n. See trade name.

semisystematic n., semitrivial n. A name used in the sciences, especially chemistry, composed of two parts, one of which relates to a scientific (systematic) name, the other to a common (trivial) name.

systematic n. See chemical name.

trade n. Name selected for a product by the company manufacturing and selling it; it is registered and protected by a trademark and is usually followed by an encircled superscript R; e.g., Benedryl®. One product may have several trade names, each selected by the company manufacturing it. Also called brand name; proprietary name.

trivial n. A common name that tells nothing about the chemical structure of the product it designates; e.g., caffeine, nicotine, water.

nano- **1.** (n) Prefix meaning one-billionth (10^{-9}). **2.** Combining form meaning dwarf.

nanocephaly (nan-o-sef'ah-le) See microcephaly.

nanocormia (nan-o-kor'me-ah) See microsomia.

nanogram (nan'o-gram) (ng) A unit of weight equal to one-billionth (10^{-9}) of a gram.

nanoid (nan'oid) Dwarfish.

nanomelia (nan-o-me'le-ah) See micromelia.

nanometer (nan-o'me-ter) (nm) A unit of linear measure equal to one-billionth (10^{-9}) of a meter. Formerly called millimicron.

nanosomia (nan-o-so'me-ah) See dwarfism.

nanus (nan'us) See dwarf.

nape (nāp) The back of the neck. Also called nucha.

naphthalene (naf'thah-lēn) Tar camphor, a crystalline hydrocarbon derived from coal tar; it is soluble in alcohol, insoluble in water; used in the plastics, chemical, and dye industries, as a moth repellant, and as an air freshener. Acute inhalation exposure may cause headache, nausea, and vomiting; repeated skin contact may cause irritation and rash.

naphthol (naf'thol) A derivative of naphthalene used as an antiseptic.

naproxen (nah-proks'en) Nonsteroidal, anti-inflammatory drug used to treat the signs and symptoms of arthritis, (inflammation and pain). Trade name: Naprosyn.

narcissism (nar'sĭ-sizm) Self-love as opposed to love of another person (object love). See also narcissistic personality disorder, under disorder.

narco- Combining form meaning stupor.

narcoanalysis (nar-ko-ah-nal'ĭ-sis) Psychotherapeutic treatment conducted under light anesthesia. Also called narcosynthesis.

narcolepsy (nar'ko-lep-se) Condition characterized by paroxysmal episodes of sleep lasting from minutes to hours; frequently accompanied by muscular weakness and sleep paralysis. Also called paroxysmal sleep; sleep epilepsy.

narcosis (nar-ko'sis) A deep stuporous state produced by certain chemicals and physical agents.

narcosynthesis (nar-ko-sin'thě-sis) See narcoanalysis.

narcotherapy (nar-ko-ther'ah-pe) Psychotherapy conducted after a state of complete relaxation is induced by intravenous injection of a barbiturate drug (either sodium amytal or sodium pentothal). Under this therapy some people have the capacity to communicate thoughts previously repressed.

narcotic (nar-kot'ik) **1.** Producing narcosis. **2.** In medicine, a drug (natural or synthetic) intended for the relief of pain that also tends to produce insensibility, stupor, and sleep (i.e., it has both analgesic and sedative actions); it has morphine-like pharmacologic activities and, with prolonged use, it may become addictive. In legal parlance, the term also includes marijuana and cocaine although these substances are pharmacologically unrelated to morphine and produce entirely different states of dependence.

narcotism (nar'ko-tizm) Addiction to a narcotic drug.

naris (na'ris), pl. na'res See nostril.

    posterior n. See choana.

nasal (na'zal) Relating to the nose. Also called rhinal.

nasion (na'ze-on) A craniometric point on the middle of the nasofrontal suture. Also called nasal point.

nasoantral (na-zo-an'tral) Relating to the nose and the maxillary sinus.

nasofrontal (na-zo-frun'tal) Relating to the nose (or nasal bone) and the frontal bone.

nasogastric (na-zo-gas'trik) Relating to the nasal passages and the stomach.

nasolabial (na-zo-la'be-al) Relating to the nose and lip.

nasolacrimal (na-zo-lak'rĭ-mal) **1.** Relating to the nasal and lacrimal bones. **2.** Relating to the nose and the structures producing and conveying tears.

naso-oral (na'zo o'ral) Relating to the nose and the mouth.

nasopalatine (na-zo-pal'ah-tin) Relating to the nose and the palate.

nasopharyngeal (na-zo-fah-rin'je-al) Relating to the upper portion of the pharynx (nasopharynx).

nasopharyngitis (na-zo-far-in-ji'tis) Inflammation of the back of the nasal cavity and upper pharynx behind the soft palate.

nasopharyngoscope (na-zo-fah-rin'go-skōp) Instrument equipped with a light for examining the nasopharynx.

nasopharynx (na-zo-far'inks) The nasal part of the pharynx; the uppermost part of the pharynx, located above the level of the soft palate, immediately behind the nasal cavity and above the oral pharynx. Also called rhinopharynx; postnasal space; epipharynx.

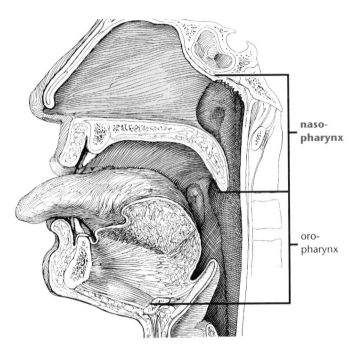

nasoscope (na'zo-skōp) See rhinoscope.

nasosinusitis (na-zo-si-nu-si'tis) Inflammation of the lining membranes of the nasal passages and adjoining sinuses.

nasus (na'sus) Latin for nose.

natal (na'tal) **1.** Relating to birth. **2.** Relating to the buttocks (nates).

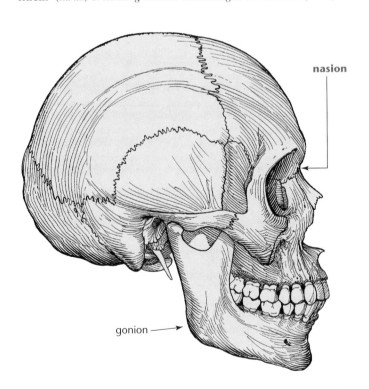

natality (na-tal′ĭ-te) The birth rate.

nates (na′tēz) The buttocks.

natimortality (na-tĭ-mor-tal′ĭ-te) The proportion of stillbirths and newborn deaths to the birth rate.

National Acid Precipitation Assessment Program (NA-PAP) An interagency body created by Congress in 1980 to settle the debate over the effects of acid rain on the environment caused by industrial pollution.

National Formulary (NF) An official publication of the American Pharmaceutical Association that provides authoritative information on drugs.

National Institute for Occupational Safety and Health (NIOSH) The federal research agency that conducts studies to develop safety and health standards. Its officers have authority to conduct inspections and to question employers and employees and, when necessary, to use warrants to gain information on workplace conditions. The agency does not have the legal authority to adopt or enforce regulations; it simply recommends standards to the Occupational Safety and Health Administration (OSHA).

National Institutes of Health (NIH) An agency of the United States Public Health Service, consisting of a number of health institutes (e.g., National Cancer Institute) that support integrated programs of research, clinical trials, and demonstrations relating to cause, diagnosis, and treatment of disease.

natrium (na′tre-um) (Na) Latin for sodium. The symbol Na is used in chemical formulas.

natriuresis (na-tre-u-re′sis) Increased excretion of sodium in the urine.

natriuretic (na-tre-u-ret′ik) **1.** Excretion of sodium in the urine. **2.** Any agent that promotes urine excretion of sodium.

naturopath (na′tūr-o-path) A person who practices naturopathy.

naturopathy (na-tūr-op′ah-the) An alternative treatment of disease by means of the forces of nature (e.g., light, heat, water, cold) supplemented with massage and water.

nausea (naw′ze-ah) The imminent desire to vomit, often preceding or accompanying vomiting.

n. gravidarum The nausea experienced by some pregnant women.

nauseant (naw′ze-ant) **1.** Inducing a desire to vomit. **2.** Any agent that induces nausea.

nauseate (naw′ze-āt) To cause a desire to vomit.

nauseous (naw′shus) Relating to nausea.

navel (na′vel) The umbilicus.

navicular (nah-vik′u-lar) Boat-shaped; applied to certain bones. See table of bones.

nearsightedness (nēr-sīt′ed-nes) See myopia.

nebula (neb′u-lah) A slightly opaque appearance of the cornea.

nebulization (neb-u-lĭ-za′shun) The process of converting a liquid into a fine spray.

nebulize (neb′u-līz) **1.** To produce a fine spray. **2.** To medicate through a fine spray.

nebulizer (neb′u-līz-er) A device for dispersing a liquid in the form of a fine spray.

Necator (ne-ka′tor) A genus of parasitic hookworms (family Ancylostomatidae).

N. americanus Species causing the human hookworm disease (necatoriasis). Also called American hookworm.

necatoriasis (ne-ka-to-ri′ah-sis) See hookworm disease, under disease.

neck (nek) **1.** The part of the body between the head and trunk. **2.** Any relatively narrow area of a structure or organ (e.g., tooth, bladder). **3.** The germinative portion of an adult tapeworm, adjacent to the scolex.

stiff n. See torticollis.

webbed n. A neck with a fold on each side, extending from the head to the collarbones (clavicles), giving it a broad and short appearance; seen in certain inherited conditions (e.g., Turner's syndrome).

n. of womb See uterine cervix, under cervix.

wry n. See torticollis.

necro-, necr- Combining forms meaning death; necrosis.

necrobiosis (nek-ro-bi-o′sis) The natural death of tissues with the concurrent replacement thereof.

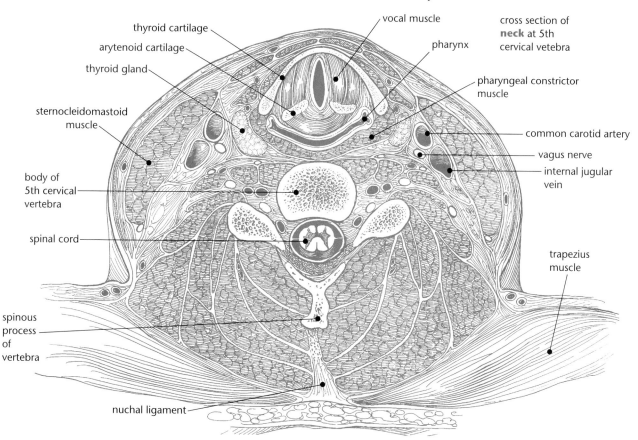

vocal muscle
cross section of **neck** at 5th cervical vetebra
pharynx
thyroid cartilage
arytenoid cartilage
thyroid gland
pharyngeal constrictor muscle
sternocleidomastoid muscle
common carotid artery
vagus nerve
internal jugular vein
body of 5th cervical vertebra
spinal cord
trapezius muscle
spinous process of vertebra
nuchal ligament

natality ■ necrobiosis

n. diabeticorum Condition characterized by patchy degeneration of the skin in which fat tissue is excessively involved in the concurrent degeneration and reparative process; usually, not exclusively, associated with diabetes mellitus.

necrocytosis (nek-ro-si-to′sis) Abnormal degeneration and death of cells.

necrogenic (nek-ro-jen′ik) Originating in dead matter.

necrology (nĕ-krol′o-je) 1. A record of people who have died, especially during a specified time span. 2. The study of death statistics.

necrolysis (nĕ-krol′ĭ-sis) Disintegration of tissues due to death and decay of cells.

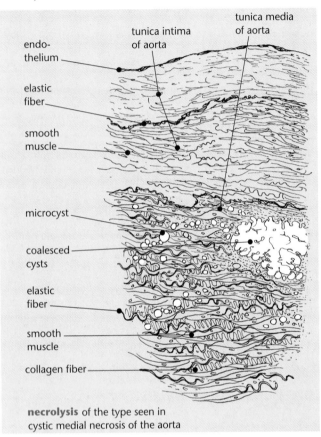

endo-
thelium

elastic
fiber

smooth
muscle

tunica intima
of aorta

tunica media
of aorta

microcyst

coalesced
cysts

elastic
fiber

smooth
muscle

collagen fiber

necrolysis of the type seen in
cystic medial necrosis of the aorta

toxic epidermal n. (TEN) An acute desquamative condition characterized by formation of large blisters and/or loss of diffuse sheets of skin; may occur as a reaction to systemic drugs, most commonly barbiturates and antibiotics; it may also be due to unknown causes; the patient's life may be threatened by fluid loss, abnormal temperature control, and other disturbances, or by infection.

necromania (nek-ro-ma′ne-ah) Abnormal interest in death or dead bodies.

necroparasite (nek-ro-par′ah-sit) See saprophyte.

necrophilia (nek-ro-fil′e-ah) An abnormal fascination with the dead; especially erotic attraction for contact with dead bodies.

necrophilic (nek-ro-fil′ik) Relating to necrophilia.

necrophilous (nĕ-krof′ĭ-lus) Feeding and growing in dead tissue; applied to certain bacteria.

necrophobia (nek-ro-fo′be-ah) Abnormally exaggerated fear of death or dead bodies.

necropsy (nek′rop-se) See autopsy.

necrose (nek′rōs) To undergo irreversible damage, decomposition, and death; applied to cells, tissues, and organs.

necrosis (nĕ-kro′sis) The total morphologic changes that follow irreversible injury and death of cells in a circumscribed area of living tissues and organs.

acute tubular n. (ATN) A form of acute kidney failure usually caused by a toxic agent or occurring in association with a period of low blood pressure (hypotension), especially from shock, crush injury, burns, or sepsis; characterized by absent or scanty urination for hours or several days followed by a gradually increasing flow of dilute urine, often reaching very large amounts. Formerly called lower nephron nephrosis.

aseptic n. Necrosis occurring without infection.

avascular n. (AVN) Necrosis caused by deficient blood supply; may occur anywhere in the body.

avascular n. of proximal femur Condition affecting the growth plate of the femur, near the hip joint, occurring most frequently in young children four to eight years old; characterized by death of bone tissue followed by replacement and healing; caused by loss of blood supply to the growth plate; symptoms include persistent pain and limping or limitation of motion. The condition usually follows trauma (e.g., hip dislocation) in which arteries supplying blood to the bone and the ligament conveying the arteries are torn. Also called Legg-Calvé-Perthes disease.

caseous n. Necrosis in which the tissues become soft, dry, and cheeselike (e.g., in the lesions of tuberculosis).

central n. Necrosis involving the inner portion of a part (e.g., in cells surrounding the central veins of the liver).

coagulation n. Necrosis induced by loss of arterial blood supply to a tissue, leading to denaturation and coagulation of cell protein; occurs typically in heart muscle, kidneys, liver, and adrenal (suprarenal) glands. Also called ischemic necrosis.

colliquative n. See liquefactive necrosis.

cystic medial n. (CMN) Focal accumulation of mucopolysaccharide in the middle layer of the aortic wall with fragmentation of the connective tissue, predisposing to dissecting aneurysms; seen in Marfan's syndrome. Also called medionecrosis of the aorta; mucoid medial degeneration.

epiphyseal aseptic n. Avascular necrosis affecting the ends (epiphyses) of bones, most commonly occurring in the head of the femur; may also occur in the second metatarsal head (Freiberg's disease), in the lunate bone of the wrist (Kienböck's disease), in the navicular bone of the foot and sometimes the kneecap (Köhler's disease), in the head of the humerus (Panner's disease), or in the proximal phalanges of fingers and toes (Thiemann's disease); may be associated with systemic corticosteroid therapy, sickle-cell disease, alcoholism, and other disorders.

fat n. Destruction of fatty tissue, as seen in acute inflammation of the pancreas and in the female breast as a result of trauma. When occurring in the breast, it is usually followed by inflammation and fibrosis, forming a benign hard mass superficially resembling a cancerous growth. Also called steatonecrosis; adiponecrosis.

fibrinoid n. A type of necrosis affecting particularly the middle layer of blood vessel walls; characterized by degeneration of normal structure and replacement by a material resembling fibrin; seen in autoimmune diseases (e.g., rheumatic fever, serum sickness, systemic lupus erythematosus).

ischemic n. See coagulation necrosis.

liquefactive n. Complete and rapid dissolution of cells (including cell membranes) by enzymes, forming circumscribed areas of softened tissue with a semifluid exudate; characteristic of brain infarcts and localized bacterial infections (abscesses). Also called colliquative necrosis.

postpartum n. of pituitary See Sheehan's syndrome, under syndrome.

renal papillary n. Necrosis of the renal papilla resulting from deprivation of blood supply; usually occurs in patients with diabetes and pyelonephritis, in people who have habitually ingested large quantities of painkillers (analgesics), in sickle-cell disease, and in obstructive disease and infection of the urinary tract. Also called necrotizing papillitis.

subcutaneous fat n. of newborn A collection of sharply circumscribed reddish or purple firm nodules on the cheeks, arms, thighs, and buttocks of newborn infants, appearing between days 1

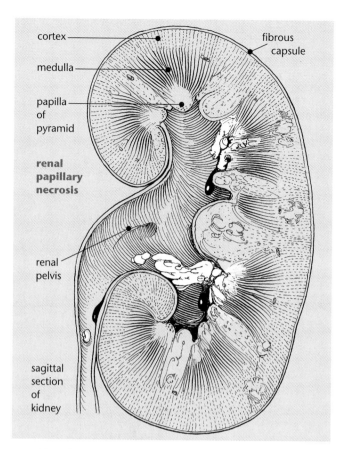

cortex

medulla

papilla
of
pyramid

**renal
papillary
necrosis**

fibrous
capsule

renal
pelvis

sagittal
section
of
kidney

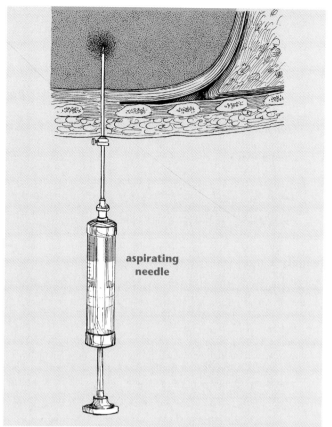

**aspirating
needle**

and 7, and usually resolving within a few weeks; may also calcify; cause is unknown, but a cold injury is thought to play a role.

necrospermia (nek-ro-sper′me-ah) Condition in which semen contains a high percentage of nonmotile spermatozoa.

necrotic (nĕ-krot′ik) Relating to dead cells or tissues.

necrotomy (nĕ-krot′o-me) Surgical removal of a sequestrum (i.e., dead bone tissue within a bone).

needle (ne′dl) **1.** Any of various slender, sharp, solid or hollow implements for stitching, puncturing, injection, or aspiration. **2.** To punc-

ture the lens capsule to allow aspiration of the lens substance; a surgical procedure for the treatment of soft cataract.

    acupuncture n. A fine needle, usually 76.2 to 127.0 mm in length, employed in performing acupuncture.

    aneurysm n. A needle with a large blunt end for passing a ligature around a blood vessel.

    aspirating n. A long, hollow needle for withdrawing fluid from a cavity.

    atraumatic n. A surgical needle of small diameter that minimizes damage to tissue.

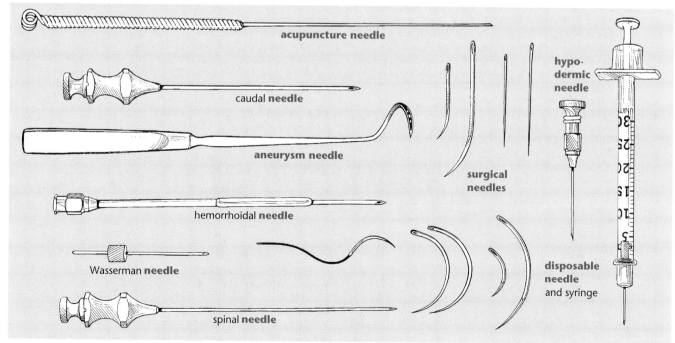

acupuncture needle

caudal **needle**

aneurysm needle

**surgical
needles**

hypo-
dermic
needle

hemorrhoidal **needle**

Wasserman **needle**

spinal **needle**

**disposable
needle**
and syringe

biopsy n. A hollow needle employed in obtaining tissue for microscopic examination.

discission n. See needle knife, under knife.

disposable n. A needle intended to be thrown away after a single use.

exploring n. A needle with a longitudinal groove for determining the presence of fluid in a cavity or a tumor.

hypodermic n. A short, hollow needle for injecting fluids beneath the skin.

lumbar puncture n. A needle designed for entering the spinal canal to remove cerebrospinal fluid or to introduce medication.

Menghini n. A long, hollow needle designed to obtain tissue, especially from the liver, for biopsy; the tissue core is obtained and held with the aid of suction applied to the end of the needle.

stop n. A needle designed with a shoulder to permit insertion up to a predetermined depth.

surgical n. Any needle used in a surgical procedure.

needling (nēd′ling) In cataract surgery, puncturing of the lens capsule with a needle knife to permit absorption of a soft cataract.

negative (neg′ah-tiv) Denoting absence of a condition, or microorganism, or failure of a response to occur, especially one being tested.

negativism (neg′ah-tiv-izm) Persistent opposition to suggestions or advice, occurring as a symptom of certain psychiatric disorders; it occurs normally in late infancy.

negatron (neg′ah-tron) An electron.

neglect (nĭ-glekt′, ne′glekt) 1. To fail to care for or to give sufficient or proper attention to (e.g., a responsibility). 2. The act of neglecting something; a failure. 3. The condition of being neglected.

child n. Failure of a parent, or other person legally responsible for a child's welfare, to provide for the child's basic needs and proper level of care.

educational child n. Failure to provide for a child's cognitive development, which may include nonconformance to state legal requirements regarding school attendance.

emotional child n. Failure to provide the nurturing necessary for the child's psychological growth and development; the parents or caregivers usually display lack of concern for, and unresponsiveness to, the child; the child may exhibit lack of attachment and inappropriate social responses to the parents or caregivers and to others. Since it is usually difficult to prove a cause-and-effect relationship, many states do not include emotional neglect in their reporting laws. Also called psychological child neglect.

medical child n. Failure to seek medical or dental treatment for a child's disease or condition that, if untreated, could become severe enough to pose a danger to the child. Withholding treatment for religious reasons under some circumstances may not be included.

physical child n. Failure to provide for a child's basic survival needs (e.g., food, shelter, clothing, supervision) to the extent of posing a hazard to the child's health or safety.

psychological child n. See emotional child neglect.

negligence (neg′lĭ-jens) Failure to use care that a reasonably prudent person would exercise under similar circumstances, thereby exposing another to an unreasonable risk of harm. In order to have a legal claim against another for a negligent act, one must prove that a duty to exercise reasonable care was owed to the claimant, that the duty was breached, and that the breach of duty caused a legally compensable injury to the claimant. See also assumption of risk, under risk.

comparative n. The apportioning of the negligence of all parties, including the claimant, when determining responsibility for the claimant's losses. The award is reduced by the percent of negligence, if any, allocated to the claimant.

contributory n. An affirmative defense in a negligence claim wherein the claimant is proven to have contributed to his own loss by his own acts of negligence. In medical malpractice, failure of the patient to exercise reasonable care in following the physician's instructions concurrent with the physician's negligent conduct, and constituting a part of the proximate cause of the injury or loss for which compensation is being sought.

Neisseria (nīs-se′re-ah) Genus of bacteria (family Neisseriaceae) composed of gram-negative microorganisms that occur in pairs and are parasitic in humans; some species cause disease.

N. catarrhalis See *Moraxella catarrhalis*.

N. gonorrhoeae A species causing gonorrhea and, in newborns, ophthalmia neonatorum.

N. meningitidis A species causing meningococcal meningitis.

nematocide (nem′ah-to-sīd) An agent that kills roundworms.

Nematoda (nem-ah-to′dah) A phylum of roundworms, including species that are parasitic in humans.

nematode (nem′ah-tōd) A roundworm.

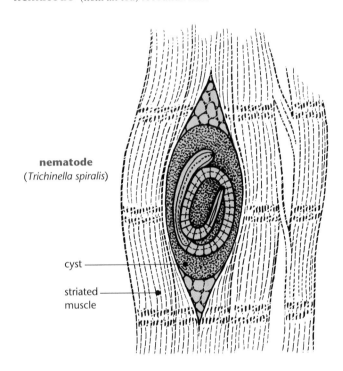

nematode
(*Trichinella spiralis*)

cyst

striated
muscle

nematodiasis (nem-ah-to-di′ah-sis) Infestation with roundworm parasites.

nematoid (nem′ah-toid) 1. Relating to a roundworm. 2. Resembling a thread.

nematology (nem-ah-tol′o-je) The study of roundworms.

neoarthrosis (ne-o-ar-thro′sis) See pseudarthrosis.

neoblastic (ne-o-blas′tik) Relating to new tissue.

neocerebellum (ne-o-ser-ĕ-bel′um) The posterior lobes of the cerebellum consisting of the middle portions of the vermis and their lateral extensions; concerned primarily with coordination of those skilled movements that are initiated in the cerebral cortex.

neocystostomy (ne-o-sis-tos′to-me) Surgical creation of a new connection between a ureter and the bladder to facilitate urine flow, either by inserting a ureter into a new site or by using a segment of defunctionalized ileum.

neodymium (ne-o-dim′e-um) Metallic element; symbol Nd, atomic number 60, atomic weight 144.24.

neogenesis (ne-o-jen′ĕ-sis) See regeneration.

neokinetic (ne-o-kĭ-net′ik) Denoting the area of the cerebral cortex that controls relatively specialized voluntary movements.

neolalism (ne-o-lal′izm) Abnormal use of neologisms.

neologism (ne-ol′o-jizm) Any new word or phrase or old word used in a new way; the coining of bizarre neologisms is a common symptom of certain psychoses.

neomembrane (ne-o-mem′brān) See false membrane, under membrane.

neomorph (ne′o-morf) A part or organ that is relatively new in the process of evolution.

neomycin (ne′o-mi-sin) An antibacterial substance produced by the bacteria *Streptomyces fradiae*.

neon (ne'on) An inert, gaseous element present in the atmosphere; symbol Ne, atomic number 10, atomic weight 20.183.

neonatal (ne-o-na'tal) Relating to the first four weeks of life.

neonate (ne'o-nāt) A baby from birth through the first 28 days of life. Also called newborn.

neonatologist (ne-o-na-tol'o-jist) A specialist in neonatology.

neonatology (ne-o-na-tol'o-je) The branch of medicine concerned with disorders of the newborn infant from birth through the first 28 days of life. Also called neonatal medicine.

neoplasia (ne-o-pla'ze-ah) The abnormal process that results in the formation and growth of a tumor (neoplasm).

   cervical intraepithelial n. (CIN) Abnormal cell growth in the inner lining of the uterine cervix that may progress and develop into

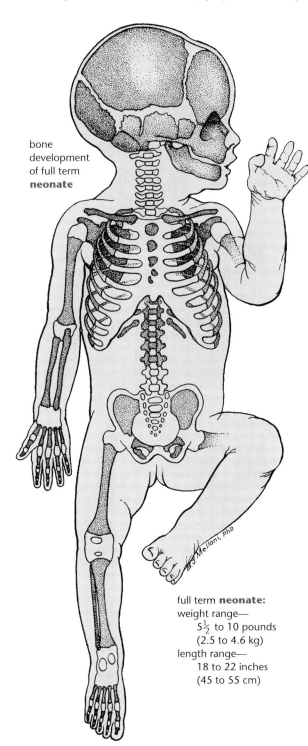

bone development of full term **neonate**

full term **neonate**:
weight range—
$5\frac{1}{2}$ to 10 pounds
(2.5 to 4.6 kg)
length range—
18 to 22 inches
(45 to 55 cm)

cancer depending on degree of involvement: CIN I (mild), CIN II (moderate), CIN III (severe).

   multiple endocrine n., type I See familial endocrine adenomatosis, type I, under adenomatosis.

   multiple endocrine n., type II See familial endocrine adenomatosis, type II, under adenomatosis.

   vulvar intraepithelial n. (VIN) See vulvar dysplasia, under dysplasia.

neoplasm (ne'o-plazm) An abnormal mass of tissue characterized by excessive growth that is uncoordinated with that of the surrounding normal tissues and persists in the same excessive manner after cessation of the stimuli that initiated the change. Also called tumor.

neostomy (ne-os'to-me) Surgical construction of a new artificial opening in a structure or organ.

neovascularization (ne-o-vas-ku-lar-ī-za'shun) Abnormal formation of new blood vessels in any tissue.

neoxanthoendothelioma (ne-o-zan-tho-en-do-the-le-o'mah) See juvenile xanthogranuloma, under xanthogranuloma.

nephelometer (nef-ĕ-lom'ĕ-ter) Instrument used in nephelometry.

nephelometry (nef-ĕ-lom'ĕ-tre) Estimation of the degree of turbidity of a solution by measuring reflected or transmitted light passing through the solution.

nephrectasis, nephrectasia (nĕ-frek'tah-sis, nef-rek-ta'ze-ah) Abnormal distention of the kidney pelvis.

nephrectomy (nĕ-frek'to-me) Removal of a kidney.

nephric (nef'rik) See renal.

nephritic (nĕ-frit'ik) Relating to nephritis.

nephritis (nĕ-fri'tis), pl. nephrit'ides Inflammation of one or both kidneys; a nonspecific term often used to indicate glomerulonephritis.

   acute n. See acute proliferative glomerulonephritis, under glomerulonephritis.

   acute interstitial n. Acute inflammation of the supporting (interstitial) tissues of the kidney, generally with involvement of the tubules and relative sparing of the filtration units (glomeruli); commonly caused by a reaction to a drug.

   analgesic n. Necrosis of the kidney papilla and inflammation of the tubules and supporting tissues, caused by long-term intake of large amounts of nonsteroidal analgesics and anti-inflammatory drugs; symptoms include passage of blood in the urine, hemolytic anemia, gastrointestinal disturbances, and high blood pressure. Also called analgesic abuse nephropathy.

   chronic n. See chronic glomerulonephritis, under glomerulonephritis.

   hereditary n. A group of hereditary kidney diseases progressing to chronic kidney failure, affecting males most severely, and becoming evident in childhood by variable episodes of blood excretion in the urine. In some families, the kidney disease is associated with nerve deafness, cataracts, lens dislocation, and dystrophy of the cornea (Alport's syndrome).

   salt-losing n. A tendency of some people with chronic kidney disease to excrete a high percentage of filtered sodium in the urine; it is most likely to occur with chronic pyelonephritis, polycystic kidneys, or analgesic nephropathy.

nephritogenic (nĕ-frit-o-jen'ik) Causing nephritis.

nephro-, nephr- Combining forms meaning kidney.

nephroblastoma (nef-ro-blas-to'mah) See Wilms' tumor, under tumor.

nephrocalcinosis (nef-ro-kal-si-no'sis) Condition characterized by the presence of calcium deposits scattered throughout the kidneys. Also called renal calcinosis.

nephrocardiac (nef-ro-kar'de-ak) See cardiorenal.

nephrogenic (nef-ro-jen'ik) Developing into or forming kidney tissue.

nephrogram (nef'ro-gram) An x-ray picture of the kidney structures made after infusion of a radiopaque substance.

nephrography (nĕ-frog'rah-fe) The process of making a nephrogram.

nephroid (nef'roid) Resembling a kidney.

nephrolith (nef'ro-lith) See kidney stone, under stone.

nephrolithiasis (nef-ro-lĭ-thi'ah-sis) Condition characterized by the presence of stones in the kidney.

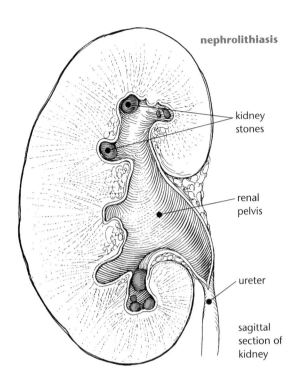

nephrolithiasis

kidney stones

renal pelvis

ureter

sagittal section of kidney

nephrolithotomy (nef-ro-lĭ-thot'o-me) Cutting into the kidney for the removal of stones.

nephrologist (nĕ-frol'o-jist) A specialist in nephrology.

nephrology (nĕ-frol'o-je) The study of the kidney and its diseases.

nephrolysin (ne-frol'ĭ-sin) An antibody that causes specific destruction of kidney cells.

nephromalacia (nef-ro-mah-la'she-ah) Abnormal softening of the kidneys.

nephron (nef'ron) The functional unit of the kidney; it consists of the filtering unit (glomerulus), convoluted tubules (proximal and distal), connecting tubule, and Henle's (nephronic) loop. There are approximately 1 million nephrons in each kidney, the number declining with increasing age; three processes work together in each nephron to carry out the excretory and regulatory functions of the kidney, namely: filtration at the glomerulus; selective resorption of many materials (e.g., water, glucose, amino acids, phosphate, chloride, sodium, calcium, bicarbonate) from the filtrate as it passes along the nephron; and secretion of various substances (e.g., hydrogen ions, ammonium, organic acids) into the filtrate by the cells of the tubules.

nephropathy (nĕ-frop'ah-the) Any disease of the kidney.

　　analgesic abuse n. See analgesic nephritis, under nephritis.

　　IgA n. Condition marked by deposition of immunoglobulin A (IgA) in the central portions of the filtering units of the kidney (glomeruli) and recurrent excretion of blood in the urine. Also called Berger's disease.

nephropexy (nef'ro-pek-se) Surgical fixation of a displaced kidney.

nephrophthisis (nĕ-frof'thĭ-sis) Suppurative inflammation of the kidney with wasting of kidney substance.

nephroptosis, nephroptosia (nef-rop-to'sis, nef-rop-to'se-ah) Downward displacement of the kidney.

nephropyelitis (nef-ro-pi-ĕ-li'tis) Inflammation of the kidney pelvis.

nephropyeloplasty (nef-ro-pi'ĕ-lo-plas-te) Reparative operation on the pelvis of a kidney.

nephropyosis (nef-ro-pi-o'sis) Suppuration of a kidney.

nephrorrhagia (nef-ro-ra'je-ah) Bleeding from or into the kidney.

nephrorrhaphy (nef-ror'ah-fe) Suturing of a kidney.

nephrosclerosis (nef-ro-skle-ro'sis) Impairment of kidney function secondary to arteriosclerosis or high blood pressure.

　　arterial n. Atrophy and scarring of the kidney due to arteriosclerotic thickening of the walls of large branches of the renal artery, with narrowing of their lumina; may cause hypertension. Also called arterionephrosclerosis.

　　arteriolar n. Kidney changes associated with high blood pressure; the arterioles thicken and the areas of the kidney to which they supply blood undergo ischemic atrophy and interstitial fibrosis. Also called arteriolonephrosclerosis; benign nephrosclerosis.

　　benign n. See arteriolar nephrosclerosis.

　　malignant n. Rapid deterioration of kidney function caused by inflammation of the arterioles; it accompanies malignant hypertension.

nephrosclerotic (nef-ro-skle-rot'ik) Relating to nephrosclerosis.

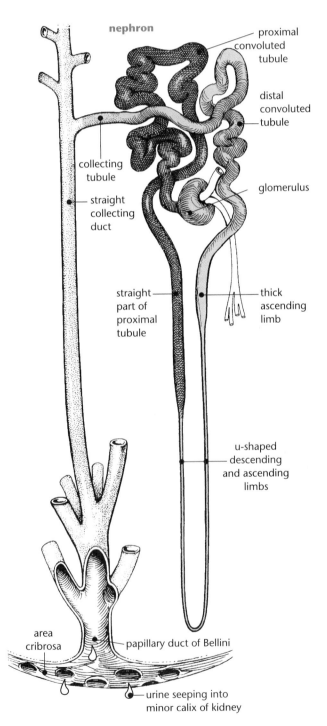

nephron

proximal convoluted tubule

distal convoluted tubule

collecting tubule

straight collecting duct

glomerulus

straight part of proximal tubule

thick ascending limb

u-shaped descending and ascending limbs

area cribrosa

papillary duct of Bellini

urine seeping into minor calix of kidney

nephrosis (nĕ-fro′sis), pl. nephro′ses **1.** General term denoting a noninflammatory disease of the kidney. **2.** See nephrotic syndrome, under syndrome.

    lipoid n. See minimal change disease, under disease.

    lower nephron n. Obsolete term for acute tubular necrosis.

nephrostomy (nĕ-fros′to-me) Surgical construction of an opening into the kidney pelvis for insertion of an external drainage tube.

nephrotic (nĕ-frot′ik) Relating to nephrosis.

nephrotome (nef′ro-tōm) The plate of embryonic tissue from which the kidneys develop.

nephrotomogram (nef-ro-to′mo-gram) Sectional x-ray picture of the kidney following introduction of a radiopaque substance.

nephrotomography (nef-ro-to-mog′rah-fe) X-ray examination of the kidney by means of tomography.

nephrotomy (nĕ-frot′o-me) A surgical cut into the kidney.

nephrotoxic (nef-ro-tok′sik) Destructive to the cells of the kidney.

nephrotoxin (nef-ro-tok′sin) A substance (cytotoxin) that is destructive to kidney cells.

nephrotropic (nef-ro-trop′ik) See renotrophic.

nephrotuberculosis (nef-ro-too-ber-ku-lo′sis) Tuberculosis of the kidney.

nephroureterectomy (nef-ro-u-re-ter-ek′to-me) Removal of a kidney and partial or complete removal of its ureter.

neptunium (nep-tu′ne-um) Radioactive element; symbol Np, atomic number 93, atomic weight 237.

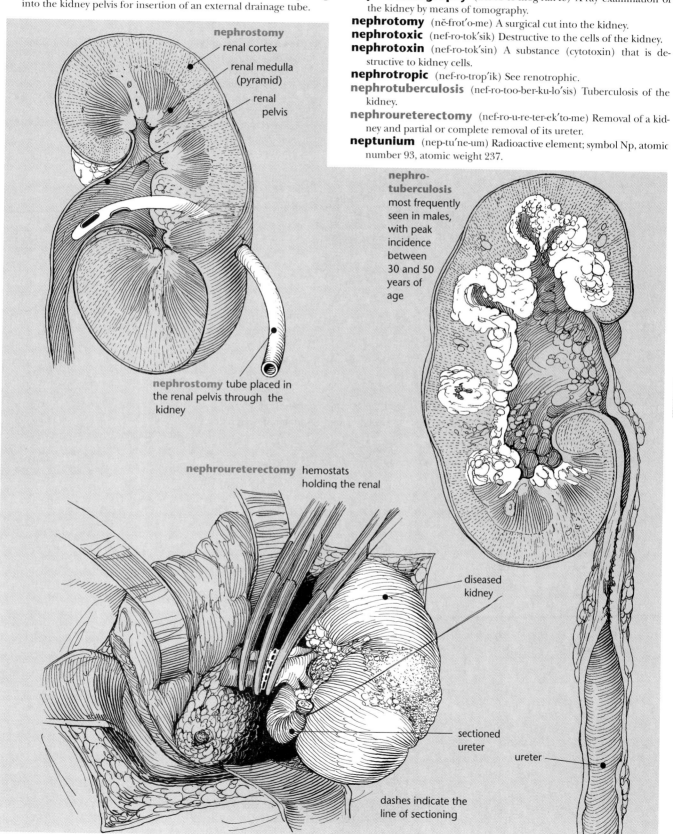

nephrostomy
renal cortex
renal medulla (pyramid)
renal pelvis

nephrostomy tube placed in the renal pelvis through the kidney

nephro-tuberculosis most frequently seen in males, with peak incidence between 30 and 50 years of age

nephroureterectomy hemostats holding the renal

diseased kidney

sectioned ureter

ureter

dashes indicate the line of sectioning

nerve (nerv) A cordlike structure composed of nerve fascicles that carries impulses between a part of the central nervous system (brain and spinal cord) and some other part of the body. For specific nerves, see table of nerves.

accelerator n.'s Nerves serving to increase the rate of the heart contraction; they originate from the sympathetic trunk and innervate the heart muscle.

afferent n. Any nerve that transmits impulses from the periphery of the body to the brain or spinal cord.

aortic n. A branch of the vagus (10th cranial) nerve supplying the aortic arch and base of the heart; its stimulation produces a slowing of the heart, dilatation of peripheral blood vessels, and a lowering of blood pressure. Also called depressor nerve of Ludwig.

augmentor n.'s Nerves of sympathetic origin that increase the force as well as the rate of the heart contraction.

autonomic n. Any nerve from either of the two divisions of the autonomic nervous system (i.e., the sympathetic or parasympathetic trunks).

cranial n. Any of the 12 pairs of nerves connected directly with the brain.

dead n. Misnomer for a nonfunctioning dental pulp.

depressor n. of Ludwig See aortic nerve.

efferent n. Any nerve that transmits impulses from the brain or spinal cord to the periphery of the body.

mixed n. A nerve containing both afferent and efferent fibers.

motor n. An efferent nerve conveying impulses to skeletal muscles, inciting contraction.

parasympathetic n. Any nerve of the parasympathetic trunk (a division of the autonomic nervous system).

pressor n. An afferent nerve that produces constriction of blood vessels, thereby increasing blood pressure.

sensory n. An afferent nerve that conducts impulses from a sense organ in the periphery of the body to the central nervous system.

spinal n. Any of the 31 paired nerves connected directly with the spinal cord. See table of nerves.

sympathetic n. Any nerve of the sympathetic trunk (a division of the autonomic nervous system).

vasomotor n. An efferent nerve of the autonomic nervous system conducting impulses to blood vessel walls, causing the vessels either to dilate or to constrict.

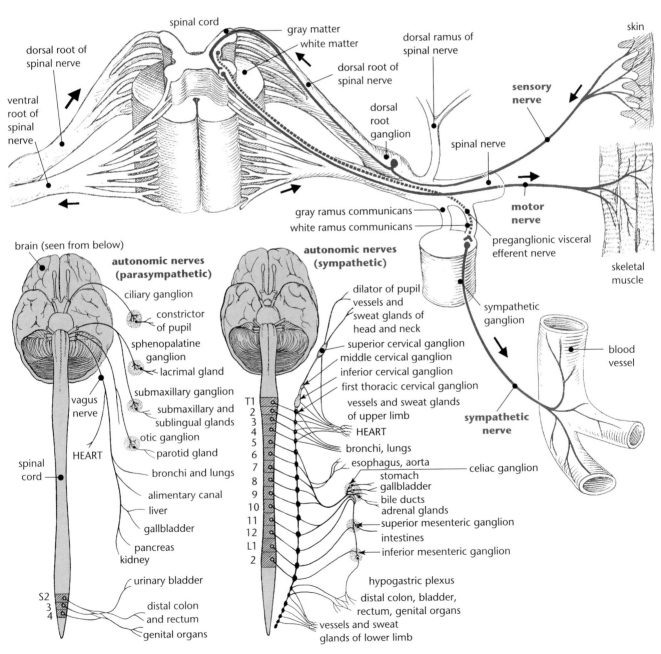

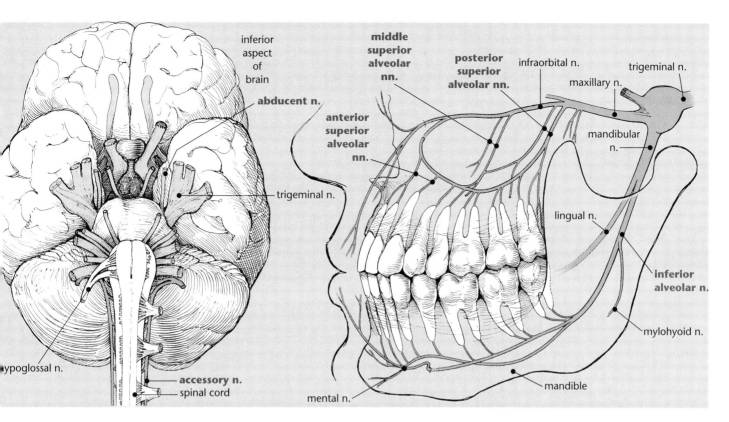

inferior aspect of brain

abducent n.

trigeminal n.

hypoglossal n.

accessory n.
spinal cord

middle superior alveolar nn.

posterior superior alveolar nn.

infraorbital n.

trigeminal n.

maxillary n.

mandibular n.

anterior superior alveolar nn.

lingual n.

inferior alveolar n.

mylohyoid n.

mental n.

mandible

NERVE	ORIGIN	BRANCHES	DISTRIBUTION
abducent n. sixth cranial n. *n. abducens*	brainstem at inferior border of pons located in floor of fourth ventricle	filaments	lateral rectus muscle of eyeball
accessory n. spinal accessory n. eleventh cranial n. *n. accessorius*	*cranial part:* side of medulla oblongata; *spinal part:* first five cervical segments of spinal cord	internal branch external branch	striate muscles of larynx, pharynx, and soft palate; sternocleidomastoid and trapezius muscles
acoustic n.	see vestibulocochlear n.		
acoustic meatus n., external *n. meatus acustici externi*	auriculotemporal n.	filaments	external acoutic meatus
alveolar n.'s, anterior superior anterior superior dental n.'s *nn. alveolares anterior superior*	infraorbital n.	filaments, nasal, superior alveolar	anterior teeth (incisors and cuspids), mucous membrane of anterior walls and floor of nasal cavity; nasal septum
alveolar n., inferior inferior dental n. *n. alveolaris inferior*	mandibular n.	mylohyoid, inferior alveolar, incisive, mental	mylohyoid and anterior belly of digastric muscles, lower teeth, skin of chin, mucous membrane of lower lip
alveolar n., middle superior middle superior dental n. *n. alveolaris superior medius*	infraorbital n.	filaments, superior alveolar	maxillary sinus, superior dental plexus, maxillary bicuspid teeth
alveolar n., posterior superior posterior superior dental n. *n. alveolaris superior posterior*	maxillary n.	filaments, superior alveolar	maxillary sinus, cheek, gums, molar and bicuspid teeth, superior dental plexus
ampullary n., anterior	see ampullary n., superior		
ampullary n., lateral *n. ampullaris lateralis*	utriculoampullar n.	none	ampulla of lateral semicircular duct
ampullary n., posterior inferior ampullary n. *n. ampullaris posterior*	vestibular ganglion	none	ampulla of posterior semicircular duct
ampullary n., superior anterior ampullary n. *n. ampullaris superior*	utriculoampullar n.	none	ampulla of superior semicircular duct
anococcygeal n.'s *nn. anococcygei*	coccygeal plexus	filaments	skin over coccyx
ansa cervicalis ansa hypoglossi *ansa cervicalis*	branch from first cervical uniting with branches from second and third cervical segments of spinal cord (forming a loop)	filaments	omohyoid, sternohyoid, and sternothyroid muscles.

N

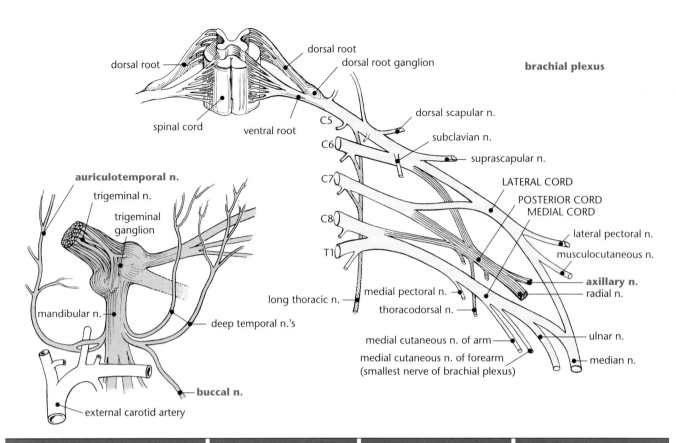

Diagram labels:

dorsal root
dorsal root
dorsal root ganglion
spinal cord
ventral root
C5
C6
C7
C8
T1
dorsal scapular n.
subclavian n.
suprascapular n.
LATERAL CORD
POSTERIOR CORD
MEDIAL CORD
lateral pectoral n.
musculocutaneous n.
axillary n.
radial n.
long thoracic n.
medial pectoral n.
thoracodorsal n.
medial cutaneous n. of arm
medial cutaneous n. of forearm
(smallest nerve of brachial plexus)
ulnar n.
median n.

auriculotemporal n.
trigeminal n.
trigeminal ganglion
mandibular n.
deep temporal n.'s
buccal n.
external carotid artery

NERVE	ORIGIN	BRANCHES	DISTRIBUTION
auditory n.	see vestibulocochlear nerve		
auricular n.'s, anterior (usually two in number) *nn. auriculares anteriores*	auriculotemporal n.	filaments	skin of anteriosuperior part of external ear, principally helix and tragus
auricular n., great *n. auricularis magnus*	second and third cervical n.'s	anterior, posterior	skin over ear, mastoid process and parotid gland
auricular n., posterior *n. auricularis posterior*	facial n.	auricular, occipital	posterior auricular and occipital muscles, skin of external ear
auriculotemporal n. *n. auriculotemporalis*	mandibular division of trigeminal n.	anterior auricular, external, acoustic meatus, articular, parotid, superficial temporal, branches communicating with otic ganglion and facial n.	external meatus and skin of anterior superior part of auricle, temporomandibular joint, parotid gland, skin of temporal region
axillary n. circumflex n. *n. axillaris*	posterior cord of brachial plexus	posterior, anterior, cutaneous, articular	deltoid and teres minor muscles, and neighboring skin
brachial plexus *plexus brachialis*	ventral rami of fifth to eight cervical and first thoracic n.'s	*from cervical nerves:* phrenic, muscular, accessory phrenic; *from roots:* dorsal scapular, long thoracic; *from trunks:* subclavius, suprascapular; *from cords:* pectoral, subscapular, thoracodorsal, axillary, medial cutaneous of forearm, medial cutaneous of arm; *terminal nerves:* musculocutaneous, median, ulnar, radial	upper limb
buccal n. buccinator n. long buccal n. *n. buccalis*	mandibular division of trigeminal n.	filaments, branches communicating with buccal branches of facial n.	skin of cheek, mucous membranes of mouth and gums
buccinator n.	see buccal nerve		
cardiac n., inferior cervical *n. cardiacus cervicalis inferior*	inferior cervical ganglion, first thoracic ganglion, stellate ganglion, or ansa subclavia	filaments	heart

N

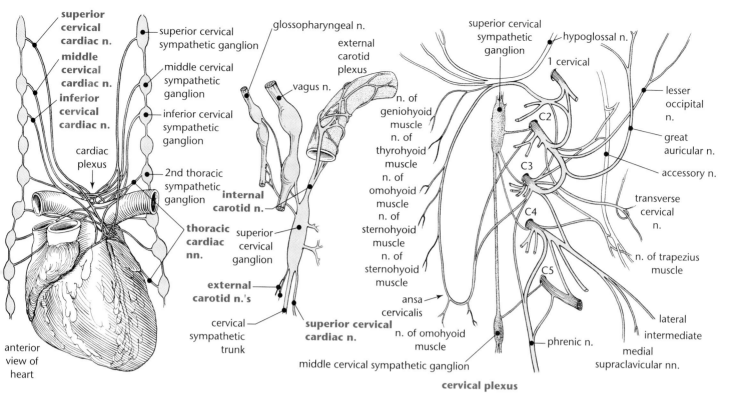

anterior view of heart

cervical plexus

NERVE	ORIGIN	BRANCHES	DISTRIBUTION
cardian n., middle cervical great cardiac n. *n. cardiacus cervicalis medius*	middle cervical ganglion	filaments	heart
cardiac n., superior cervical *n. cardiacus cervicalis superior*	lower part of superior cervical ganglion	filaments	heart
cardiac n.'s, thoracic *nn. cardiaci thoracici*	second to fifth thoracic ganglion of sympathetic trunk	filaments	heart
caroticotympanic n.'s *nn. caroticotympanici*	superior cervical sympathetic ganglion	superior, inferior	middle ear chamber, auditory tube
carotid n.'s, external *nn. carotici externi*	superior cervical ganglion	filaments	external carotid plexus, cranial blood vessels, smooth muscles and glands of head
carotid n., internal *n. caroticus internus*	cephalic end of superior cervical ganglion	medial, lateral	internal carotid plexus, cranial blood vessels, smooth muscle, glands of head, cavernous plexus
carotid sinus n. carotid n. *n. caroticus*	glossopharyngeal n. just beyond its emergence from jugular foramen	filaments	carotid sinus, carotid body
cavernous n. of clitoris, greater *n. cavernosus clitoridis major*	uterovaginal plexus	filaments	corpus cavernosum of clitoris
cavernous n.'s of clitoris, lesser *nn. cavernosi clitorides minor*	uterovaginal plexus	filaments	erectile tissue of clitoris
cavernous n. of penis, greater *n. cavernosus penis major*	prostatic plexus	filaments	corpus cavernosum of penis
cavernous n.'s of penis, lesser *nn. cavernosi penis minor*	prostatic plexus	filaments	corpus spongiosum of penis and penile urethra
cervical n.'s (eight pairs of spinal nerves) *nn. cervicales*	cervical segments of spinal cord	filaments	cervical plexus and brachial plexus
cervical plexus *plexus cervicalis*	ventral rami of first to fourth cervical nerves	*cutaneous branches:* lesser occipital, great auricular, anterior cutaneous, supraclavicular; *muscular branches:* anterior and lateral rectae of head, long muscles of head and neck, geniohyoid, thyrohyoid, and omohyoid (superior belly), sternohyoid, and omohyoid	muscles and skin of neck, upper back and parts of head and chest; diaphragm

N13

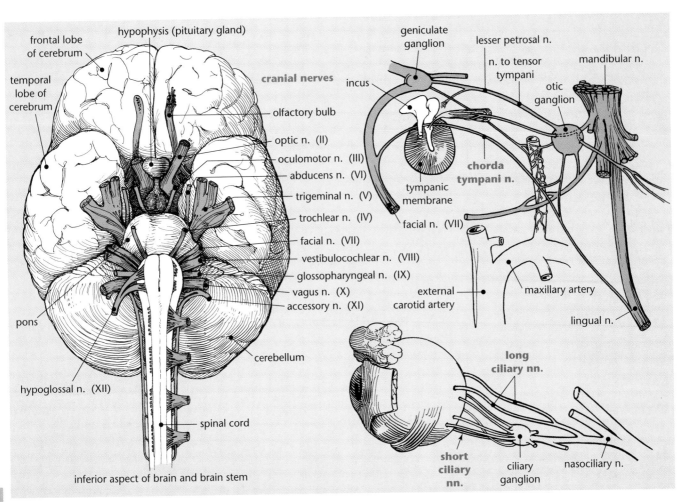

frontal lobe of cerebrum
hypophysis (pituitary gland)
temporal lobe of cerebrum
cranial nerves
olfactory bulb
optic n. (II)
oculomotor n. (III)
abducens n. (VI)
trigeminal n. (V)
trochlear n. (IV)
facial n. (VII)
vestibulocochlear n. (VIII)
glossopharyngeal n. (IX)
vagus n. (X)
accessory n. (XI)
pons
cerebellum
hypoglossal n. (XII)
spinal cord
inferior aspect of brain and brain stem

geniculate ganglion
lesser petrosal n.
n. to tensor tympani
mandibular n.
incus
otic ganglion
chorda tympani n.
tympanic membrane
facial n. (VII)
external carotid artery
maxillary artery
lingual n.
long ciliary nn.
short ciliary nn.
ciliary ganglion
nasociliary n.

NERVE	ORIGIN	BRANCHES	DISTRIBUTION
cervical plexus (cont'd)		(inferior belly), phrenic, sternocleidomastoid, trapezius, levator muscle of scapula, middle scalene	
chorda tympani n. *n. chorda tympani*	facial n. (intermediate) just above stylomastoid foramen	filaments	anterior two-thirds of tongue, submandibular and sublingual glands
ciliary n.'s, long (two or three in number) *nn. ciliares longi*	nasociliary n. as it crosses optic n.	filaments	iris, cornea, ciliary body
ciliary n.'s, short (6–10 in number) *nn. ciliares breves*	ciliary ganglion from oculomotor n.	filaments	ciliary body, iris, cornea, and choroid layer of eyeball
circumflex n.		see axiliary n.	
clunial n.'s, inferior *nn. clunium inferiores*	posterior cutaneous n. of thigh	filaments	skin of lower and lateral gluteal region
clunial n.'s, middle *nn. clunium medii*	first, second, and third sacral n.'s	filaments	skin of medial gluteal region
clunial n.'s, superior *nn. clunium superiores*	first, second, and third lumbar n.'s	filaments	skin of upper gluteal region
coccygeal n. *n. coccygeus*	coccygeal segments of spinal cord	filaments	coccygeal plexus
coccygeal plexus *plexus coccygeus*	fourth and fifth sacral n.'s and coccygeal n.'s	anococcygeal, filaments	skin of region of the coccyx
cochlear n. n. of hearing *n. cochlearis*	vestibulocochlear n.	vestibular, filaments	through spiral ganglion of cochlea to spiral organ of Corti of internal ear
common peroneal n.		see peroneal nerve, common	
cranial n.'s cerebral n.'s *nn. craniales*	12 pairs of nerves attached to the base of the brain; they include the following: (I) olfactory; (II) optic; (III) oculomotor; (IV) trochlear; (V) trigeminal; (VI) abducent; (VII) facial; (VIII) vestibulocochlear; (IX) glossopharyngeal; (X) vagus; (XI) accessory; (XII) hypoglossal		

nerve ■ nerve

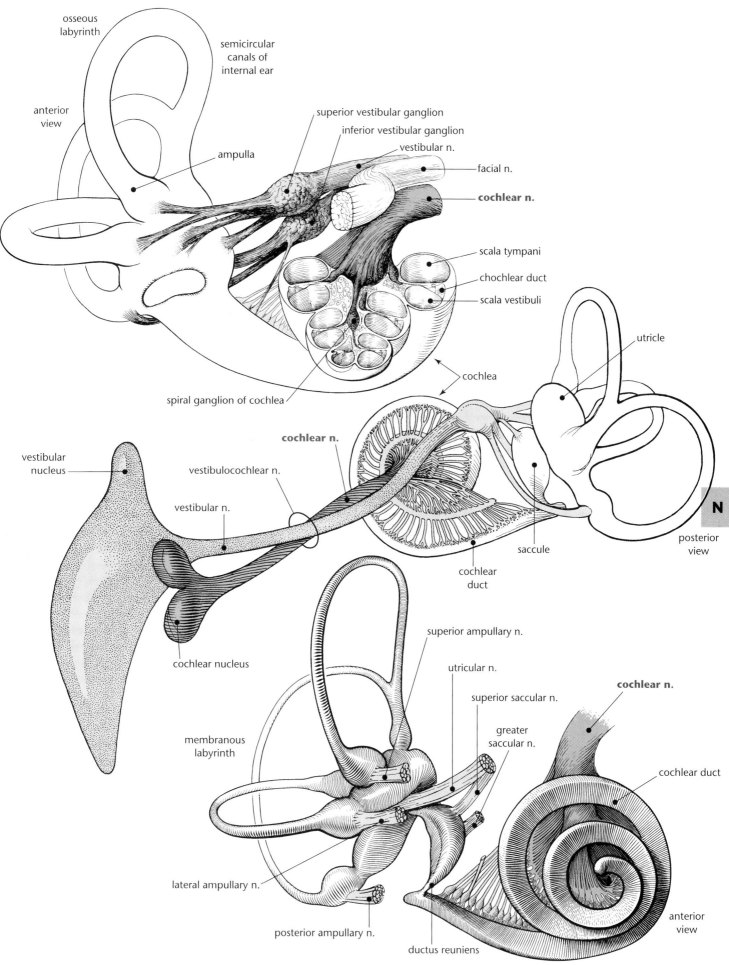

osseous labyrinth

semicircular canals of internal ear

anterior view

ampulla

superior vestibular ganglion

inferior vestibular ganglion

vestibular n.

facial n.

cochlear n.

scala tympani

chochlear duct

scala vestibuli

cochlea

spiral ganglion of cochlea

utricle

cochlear n.

vestibulocochlear n.

vestibular n.

vestibular nucleus

cochlear nucleus

saccule

cochlear duct

N

posterior view

superior ampullary n.

utricular n.

superior saccular n.

greater saccular n.

membranous labyrinth

cochlear n.

cochlear duct

lateral ampullary n.

posterior ampullary n.

ductus reuniens

anterior view

N15

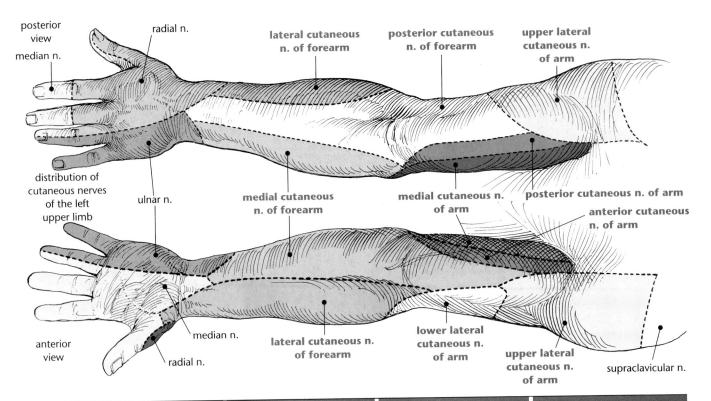

posterior view

median n.

radial n.

lateral cutaneous n. of forearm

posterior cutaneous n. of forearm

upper lateral cutaneous n. of arm

distribution of cutaneous nerves of the left upper limb

ulnar n.

medial cutaneous n. of forearm

medial cutaneous n. of arm

posterior cutaneous n. of arm

anterior cutaneous n. of arm

anterior view

median n.

radial n.

lateral cutaneous n. of forearm

lower lateral cutaneous n. of arm

upper lateral cutaneous n. of arm

supraclavicular n.

NERVE	ORIGIN	BRANCHES	DISTRIBUTION
cutaneous n. of arm, lower lateral lower lateral brachial cutaneous n. *n. cutaneus brachii lateralis inferior*	radial n.	filaments	skin on lateral aspect of lower part of arm
cutaneous n. of arm, medial medial brachial cutaneous n. *n. cutaneus brachii medialis*	medial cord of brachial plexus	filaments	skin on medial side of arm down to olecranon
cutaneous n. of arm, posterior posterior brachial cutaneous n. *n. cutaneus brachii posterior*	radial n.	filaments	skin on posterior aspect of arm nearly as far as olecranon
cutaneous n. of arm, upper lateral upper lateral brachial cutaneous n. *n. cutaneus brachii lateralis superior*	axillary n.	filaments	skin on lateral aspect of upper part of arm
cutaneous n. of calf, lateral *n. cutaneus surae lateralis*	common peroneal n.	sural, filaments	skin of lateral and posterior aspects of leg (calf)
cutaneous n. of calf, medial *n. cutaneus surae medialis*	tibial n.	sural, filaments	skin of medial and posterior aspects of leg (calf)
cutaneous n. of foot, intermediate dorsal *n. cutaneus dorsalis intermedius pedis*	superficial peroneal n.	dorsal digital (two)	skin of lateral side of ankle and dorsum of foot, and adjacent sides of third, fourth, and fifth toes
cutaneous n. of foot, lateral dorsal *n. cutaneus dorsalis lateralis pedis*	continuation of sural n.	filaments	skin of dorsolateral part of foot
cutaneous n. of foot, medial dorsal *n. cutaneus dorsalis medialis pedis*	superficial peroneal n.	medial dorsal digital, lateral dorsal digital, filaments	skin of medial side of ankle, foot and great toe, skin of adjacent sides of second and third toes
cutaneous n. of forearm, lateral lateral antebrachial cutaneous n. *n. cutaneus antebrachii lateralis*	musculocutaneous n.	anterior, posterior, filaments	skin over radial side of forearm
cutaneous n. of forearm, medial medial antebrachial cutaneous n. *n. cutaneus antebrachii medialis*	medial cord of brachial plexus	filaments, anterior, ulnar	skin over biceps muscle and of ulnar side of forearm
cutaneous n. of forearm, posterior posterior antebrachial cutaneous n. *n. cutaneus antebrachii posterior*	radial n.	proximal, distal, filaments	skin on posterior part of lower half of arm and of forearm
cutaneous n. of thigh, lateral external cutaneous n. *n. cutaneus femoris lateralis*	second and third lumbar n.'s	anterior, posterior, filaments	skin of lateral and anterior part of thigh
cutaneous n. of thigh, posterior small sciatic n. *n. cutaneus femoris posterior*	first, second, and third sacral n.'s	gluteal, perineal, femoral, sural	skin of lower gluteal region, external genitalia, perineum, and posterior aspect of thigh and leg (calf)

nerve ■ nerve

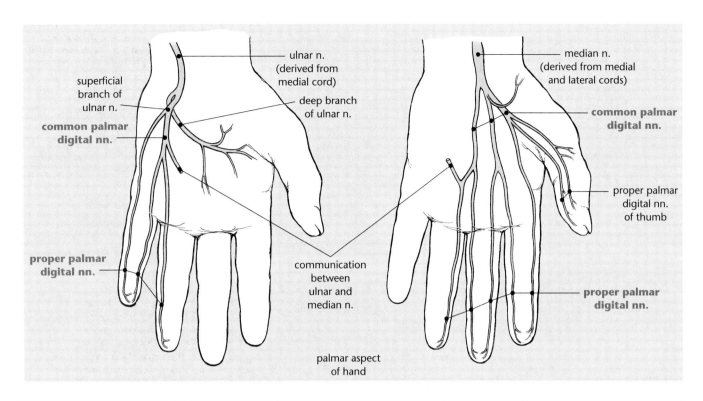

Labels on diagram:

Left hand (palmar aspect):
- superficial branch of ulnar n.
- common palmar digital nn.
- proper palmar digital nn.
- ulnar n. (derived from medial cord)
- deep branch of ulnar n.
- communication between ulnar and median n.
- palmar aspect of hand

Right hand (palmar aspect):
- median n. (derived from medial and lateral cords)
- common palmar digital nn.
- proper palmar digital nn. of thumb
- proper palmar digital nn.

NERVE	ORIGIN	BRANCHES	DISTRIBUTION
dental n.'s	see alveolar nerves		
digital n.'s, common palmar *nn. digitales palmares communes*	median n. ulnar n.	proper palmar digitals	skin of palmar surface and sides of digits I–IV, first two lumbrical muscles
digital n.'s, proper palmar digital collaterals *nn. digitales palmares proprii*	common palmar digital n.'s	proper palmar digitals	skin on adjacent sides of digits; first two lumbrical muscles
digital n.'s of foot, dorsal *nn. digitales dorsales pedis*	intermediate dorsal cutaneous n. of foot	filaments	skin on adjacent sides of third, fourth, and fifth toes
digital n.'s of lateral plantar n., common plantar *nn. digitales plantares communes nervi plantaris lateralis*	superficial branch of lateral plantar n.	proper plantar digitals (medial and lateral)	adjacent sides of fourth and fifth toes; short flexor muscle of little toe
digital n.'s of lateral plantar n., proper plantar *nn. digitales plantares proprii nervi plantaris lateralis*	common plantar digital nerves of lateral plantar n.	filaments	plantar aspect of lateral toes, adjacent sides of fourth and fifth toes
digital n.'s of lateral side of great toe and medial side of second toe *nn. digitales dorsales hallucis lateralis et digiti secundi medialis*	deep peroneal n.	filaments	adjacent sides of great and second toes
digital n.'s of medial plantar n., common plantar *nn. digitales plantares communes nervi plantaris medialis*	medial plantar n.	proper plantar digitals, muscular	plantar aspect of medial toes
digital n.'s of medial plantar n., proper plantar *nn. digitales plantares proprii nervi plantaris medialis*	common plantar digital n.'s	filaments	adjacent sides of first, second, third, and fourth toes
digital n.'s of radial n., dorsal *nn. digitales dorsales nervi radialis*	superficial branch of radial n.	filaments	skin of dorsum of lateral fingers
digital n.'s of ulnar n., common palmar *nn. digitales palmares communes nervi ulnaris*	superficial branch of palmar branch of ulnar n.	proper palmar digitals	skin of palmar surface and adjacent sides of fourth and fifth fingers
digital n.'s of ulnar n., dorsal *nn. digitales dorsales nervi ulnaris*	dorsal branch of ulnar n.	filaments	skin on adjoining sides of third to fifth fingers
digital n.'s of ulnar n., proper palmar *nn. digitales palmares proprii nervi ulnaris*	common palmar digital nerves of ulnar n.	filaments	adjacent sides of fourth and fifth fingers and medial side of fifth finger

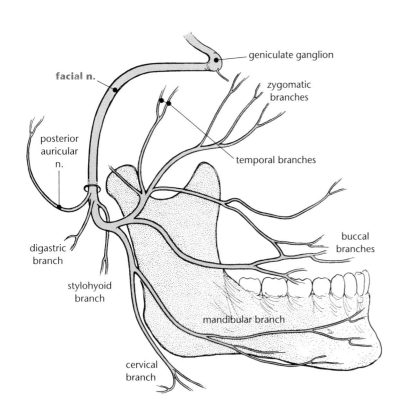

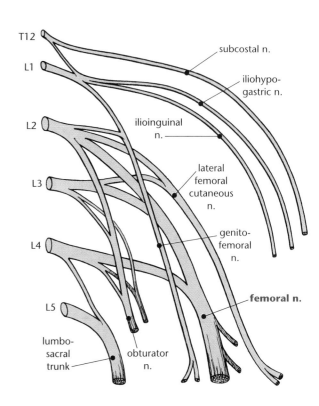

NERVE	ORIGIN	BRANCHES	DISTRIBUTION
dorsal n. of clitoris *n. dorsalis clitoridis*	pudendal n.	filaments	urethra and clitoris
dorsal n. of penis *n. dorsalis penis*	pudendal n.	filaments	urethra and penis
dorsal scapular n.	see scapular n., dorsal		
eighth cranial n.	see vestibulocochlear n.		
eleventh cranial n.	see accessory n.		
ethmoid n., anterior *n. ethmoidalis anterior*	continuation of nasociliary n.	internal, external, lateral, and medial nasal	mucous membrane of nasal cavity
ethmoid n., posterior *n. ethmoidalis posterior*	nasociliary n.	filaments	mucous membrane of posterior ethmoidal and sphenoidal sinuses
facial n. seventh cranial n. *n. facialis*	lower border of pons	petrosal, to tympanic plexus, stapedial, chorda tympani, muscular, auricular, temporal, zygomatic, buccal, mandibular, cervical	*motor part:* muscles of facial expression, scalp, external ear, buccinator, platysma, stapedius, stylohyoid, and posterior belly of digastric; *sensory part:* anterior two-thirds of tongue, parts of external acoustic meatus, soft palate, and adjacent pharynx; *parasympathetic part:* secretomotor fibers of submandibular, sublingual, lacrimal, nasal, and palatine glands
femoral n. anterior crural n. *n. femoralis*	second, third, and fourth lumbar n.'s	articular, muscular, saphenous, anterior cutaneous	skin of anterior and medial side of leg, hip and knee joint, quadriceps muscle of thigh, pectineal, sartorius, and iliac muscles
fifth cranial n.	see trigeminal n.		
first cranial n.	see olfactory n.		
fourth cranial n.	see trochlear n.		
frontal n. *n. frontalis*	ophthalmic n.	supraorbital, supratrochlear, frontal sinus	conjunctiva, skin of upper eyelid and forehead, corrugator and frontal muscles, scalp, frontal sinus

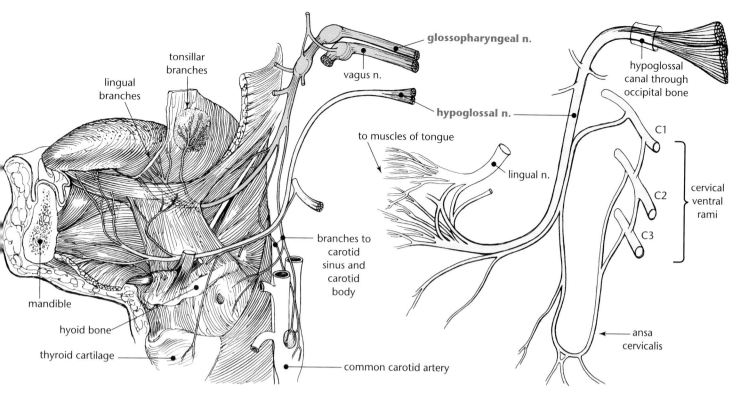

NERVE	ORIGIN	BRANCHES	DISTRIBUTION
n. of geniohyoid *n. geniohyoideus*	first cervical n.	filaments	geniohyoid muscle
genitofemoral n. genitocrural n. *n. genitofemoralis*	first and second lumbar n.'s	genital, femoral	cremaster muscle, skin of scrotum or labium major and adjacent thigh, proximal part of anterior surface of thigh
glossopalatine n.		see intermediate n.	
glossopharyngeal n. ninth cranial n. *n. glossopharyngeus*	upper part of medulla oblongata	tympanic, carotid sinus, pharyngeal, stylopharyngeal, tonsillar, lingual	tongue and pharynx, fauces, palatine tonsil, blood pressure receptor of carotid sinus, stylopharyngeus muscle
gluteal n., inferior *n. gluteus inferior*	fifth lumbar nerve and first and second sacral n.'s	filaments	gluteus maximus muscle
gluteal n. superior *n. gluteus superior*	fourth and fifth lumbar n.'s and first sacral n.	superior, inferior, filaments	gluteus minimus and medius muscles, tensor muscle of fascia lata
hemorrhoidal n.		see rectal n.	
hypogastric n. *n. hypogastricus*	a single large nerve (or several parallel bundles) which interconnects the superior hypogastric plexus with the inferior hypogastric plexus		
hypoglossal n. twelfth cranial n. *n. hypoglossus*	series of rootlets between pyramid and olive of medulla oblongata	meningeal, descending hypoglossal, muscular, lingual	intrinsic and extrinsic muscles of tongue; dura mater
hypoglossal n., small		see lingual n.	
iliohypogastric n. *n. iliohypogastricus*	first lumbar n.	anterior cutaneous, muscular, lateral cutaneous	abdominal muscles, skin of lower part of abdomen and gluteal region
ilioinguinal n. *n. lioinguinalis*	first lumbar n.	anterior scrotal (male), anterior labial (female), muscular, filaments	muscles of abdominal wall, skin of proximal and medial part of thigh, root of penis (male), mons pubis and labium major (female)
infraoccipital n.		see suboccipital n.	
infraorbital n. *n. infraorbitalis*	continuation of maxillary n. after entering orbit through inferior orbital fissure	inferior palpebral, external nasal, superior labial; posterior, middle, and anterior superior alveolar	upper teeth, skin of face, mucous membrane of mouth and floor of nasal cavity
infratrochlear n. *n. infratrochlearis*	nasociliary n.	palpebral	skin of eyelids and side of nose, conjunctiva, lacrimal sac and duct

nerve ■ nerve

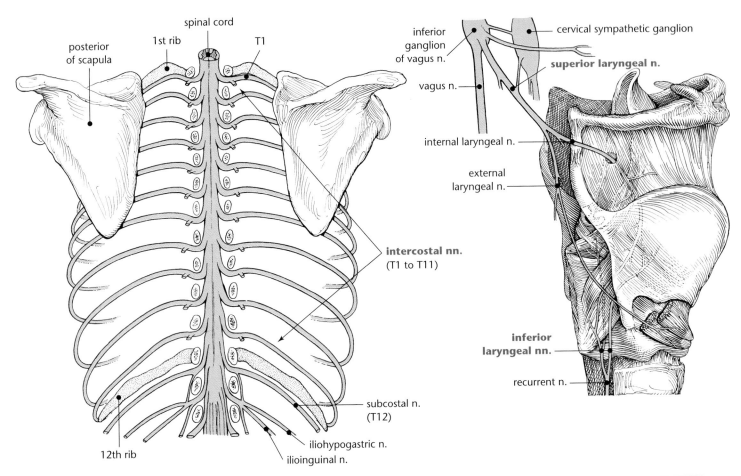

NERVE	ORIGIN	BRANCHES	DISTRIBUTION
intercostal n.'s (ventral rami of upper 11 thoracic nerves between ribs) *nn. intercostales*	thoracic segments of spinal cord	lateral cutaneous, anterior cutaneous, collateral	first two nerves supply fibers to upper limb and thoracic wall; next four supply thoracic wall; lower five supply thoracic and abdominal walls
intercostobrachial n. *n. intercostobrachialis*	second and frequently third intercostal n.	filaments	skin of medial and posterior part of upper arm; axilla
intermediate n. glossopalatine n. n. of Wrisberg *n. intermedius*	brainstem at inferior border of pons	greater petrosal, chorda tympani	taste buds of anterior two-thirds of tongue, glands of soft palate and nose, submandibular and sublingual glands, skin of external acoustic meatus and mastoid process
interosseous n. of forearm, anterior *n. interosseus antebrachii anterior*	median n.	muscular, filaments	most of the deep anterior muscles of forearm
interosseous n. of forearm, posterior *n. interosseus antebrachii posterior*	deep branch of radial n.	muscular, articular	wrist and intercarpal joints, deep extensor muscles of forearm, long abductor and extensor muscles of thumb
interosseous n. of leg *n. interosseus cruris*	tibial n.	filaments	ankle joints, tibia and fibula articulations
jugular n. *n. jugularis*	superior cervical ganglion	filaments	to glossopharyngeal and vagus n.'s
labial n.'s, anterior *nn. labiales anteriores*	ilioinguinal n.	filaments	skin of anterior labial area of female genitalia
labial n.'s, posterior *nn. labiales posteriores*	perineal n.	filaments	skin of posterior part of labium majus and vestibule of vagina
lacrimal n. *n. lacrimals*	ophthalmic n.	superior palpebral, glandular, filaments	lacrimal gland and adjacent conjunctiva, skin of upper eyelid
laryngeal n., inferior *n. laryngeus inferior*	recurrent laryngeal n.	filaments	all intrinsic muscles of larynx except cricothyroid muscle

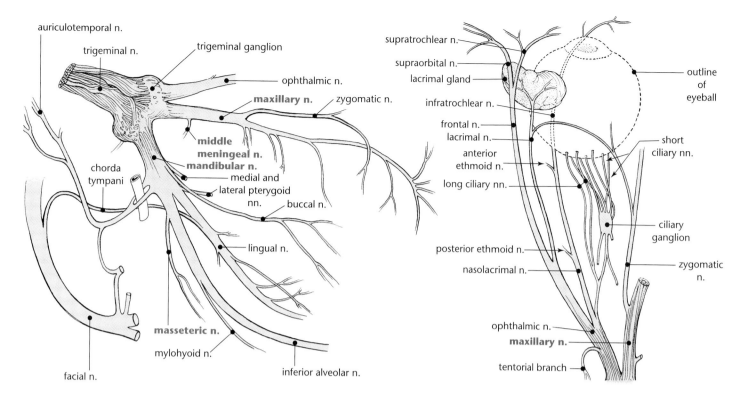

auriculotemporal n.
trigeminal n.
trigeminal ganglion
ophthalmic n.
maxillary n.
zygomatic n.
middle meningeal n.
mandibular n.
chorda tympani
medial and lateral pterygoid nn.
buccal n.
lingual n.
masseteric n.
mylohyoid n.
facial n.
inferior alveolar n.

supratrochlear n.
supraorbital n.
lacrimal gland
infratrochlear n.
frontal n.
lacrimal n.
anterior ethmoid n.
long ciliary nn.
outline of eyeball
short ciliary nn.
ciliary ganglion
posterior ethmoid n.
nasolacrimal n.
zygomatic n.
ophthalmic n.
maxillary n.
tentorial branch

NERVE	ORIGIN	BRANCHES	DISTRIBUTION
laryngeal n., superior *n. laryngeus superior*	vagus n. near the inferior ganglion	external, internal	mucous membrane of larynx and epiglottis; inferior pharyngeal and cricothyroid muscles
laryngeal recurrent n.	see recurrent nerve		
lingual n. small hypoglossal n. *n. lingualis*	mandibular division of trigeminal n.	sublingual, lingual, branches communicating with hypoglossal n., chorda tympani, and submandibular ganglion	mucous membranes of anterior two-thirds of tongue, floor of mouth, gums, and sublingual glands
lumbar n.'s (five pairs of spinal nerves) *nn. lumbales*	lumbar segments of spinal cord	ventral, dorsal	lumbar and sacral plexuses, deep muscles and skin of lower back
mandibular n. inferior maxillary n. *n. mandibularis*	trigeminal ganglion	masseteric, medial pterygoid, lateral pterygoid, deep temporal, buccal, auriculotemporal, lingual, inferior alveolar, meningeal	muscles of mastication, tensor tympani, tensor of palatal velum, anterior belly of digastric, and mylohyoid muscles, mandible, lower teeth and gums, anterior two-thirds of tongue, cheek, lower face, meninges, temporomandibular joint, skin of temporal region, external ear
masseteric n. *n. massetericus*	mandibular n.	filaments	masseter muscle, temporomandibular joint
maxillary n. superior maxillary n. *n. maxillaris*	trigeminal ganglion	middle meningeal, zygomatic, pterygopalatine, infraorbital, superior alveolar, inferior palpebral, external nasal, superior labial	skin of middle part of face, nose, lower eyelid, and upper lip; upper teeth and gums, tonsil and roof of mouth, soft palate, maxillary sinus, mucous membrane of nasopharynx
median n. *n. medianus*	by two roots from medial and lateral cords of brachial plexus	muscular, articular, anterior interosseous, common palmar digitals, proper digital	most of flexor muscles of forearm, short muscles of thumb, lateral lumbricals, skin of hand, hand joints, elbow joint, pulp under nails
meningeal n. *n. meningeus*	vagus	filaments	meninges
meningeal n., middle *n. meningeus medius*	maxillary n.	filaments	meninges, especially dura mater

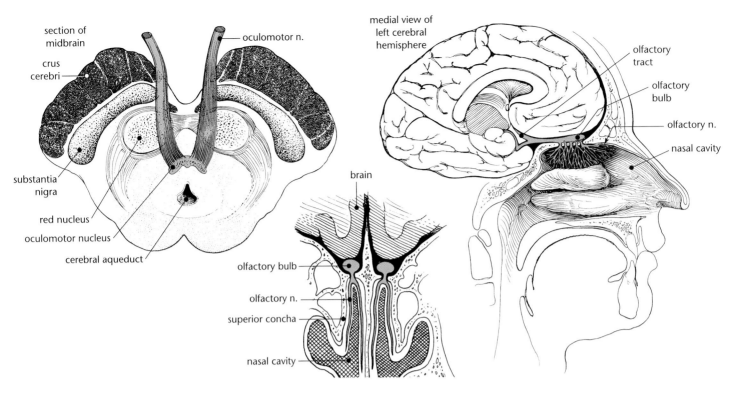

section of midbrain

crus cerebri

substantia nigra

red nucleus

oculomotor nucleus

cerebral aqueduct

oculomotor n.

medial view of left cerebral hemisphere

olfactory tract

olfactory bulb

olfactory n.

nasal cavity

brain

olfactory bulb

olfactory n.

superior concha

nasal cavity

NERVE	ORIGIN	BRANCHES	DISTRIBUTION
mental n. *n. mentalis*	inferior alveolar n.	filaments	skin of chin, mucous membrane of lower lip
musculocutaneous n. *n. musculocutaneus*	lateral cord of brachial plexus	muscular, articular filament, humeral filament, lateral cutaneous n. of forearm	coracobrachialis, brachialis and biceps muscles; skin of lateral side of forearm
musculospiral n.	*see radial n.*		
mylohyoid n. *n. mylohyoideus*	inferior alveolar n. just before it enters mandibular foramen	filaments	mylohyoid and anterior belly of digastric muscles
nasal n.'s, external *nn. nasales externi*	anterior ethmoid n.	filaments	skin on side of nose
nasociliary n. nasal n. *n. nasociliaris*	ophthalmic n.	long ciliary, anterior ethmoidal, posterior ethmoidal, infratrochlear, communication with ciliary ganglion	mucous membranes of nasal cavity, anterior ethmoidal and frontal sinuses; iris, cornea, conjunctiva, lacrimal sac, skin of eyelids and side of nose
nasopalatine n. Scarpa's n. *n. nasopalatinus*	pterygopalatine ganglion and maxillary n.	filaments	mucous membrane of hard palate and nasal septum
ninth cranial n.	*see glossopharyngeal n.*		
obturator n. *n. obturatorius*	second, third, and fourth lumbar n.'s	anterior, posterior, filaments	hip and knee joints, skin of medial side of thigh, gracilis muscle, great, long, and short adductor muscles
obturator n., accessory *n. obturatorius accessorius*	third and fourth lumbar n.'s	muscular, articular	pectineal muscle, hip joint
n. of obturator, internal *n. obturatorius internus*	fifth lumbar and first and second sacral n.'s	muscular, filaments	internal obturator and superior gemelius muscles
occipital n., larger (greater) *n. occipitalis major*	median branch of dorsal division of second cervical n.	muscular, filaments, medial, lateral, auricular	scalp of top and back of head; semispinal muscle of head
occipital n., smaller (lesser) *n. occipitalis minor*	second sacral n.	auricular, filaments	skin of side of head and behind ear
occipital n., third least occipital n. *n. occipitalis tertius*	cutaneous part of third cervical n.	medial, lateral	skin of lower part of back of head
oculomotor n. third cranial n. *n. oculomotorius*	midbrain at medial side of cerebral peduncle	superior, inferior	levator muscle of upper eyelid, most intrinsic and extrinsic muscles of eye

nerve ■ nerve

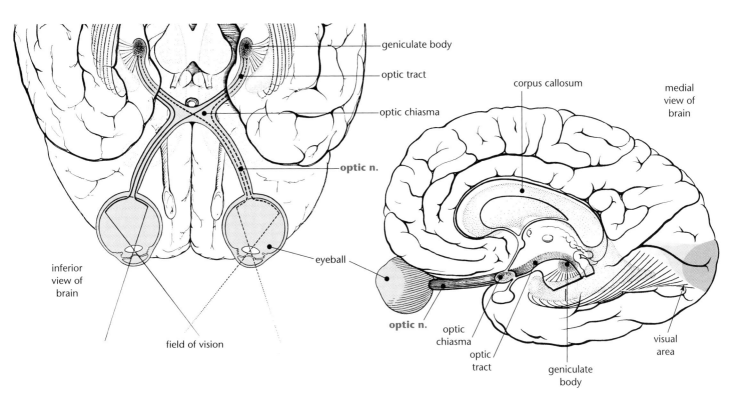

inferior view of brain

geniculate body

optic tract

optic chiasma

optic n.

eyeball

field of vision

corpus callosum

medial view of brain

optic n. optic chiasma

optic tract

geniculate body

visual area

NERVE	ORIGIN	BRANCHES	DISTRIBUTION
olfactory n.'s first cranial n.'s *nn. olfactorii*	olfactory portion of nasal mucosa	filaments	olfactory bulb
ophthalmic n. *n. ophthalmicus*	trigeminal ganglion	tentorial, lacrimal, frontal, nasociliary	dura mater, eyeball, conjunctiva, lacrimal gland, mucous membrane of nose and paranasal sinuses, skin of the forehead, eyelids, and nose
optic n. second cranial n. n. of sight *n. opticus*	ganglionic layer of retina	filaments	optic chiasma
palatine n., large anterior palatine n. *n. palatinus anterior*	pterygopalatine ganglion	posterior inferior nasal, lesser palatine	gums, mucous membrane of hard and soft palates
palatine n.'s, small *nn. palatini medius et posterior*	pterygopalatine ganglion	filaments	soft palate, uvula, palatine tonsil
palpebral n., inferior *n. palpebralis inferior*	infraorbital n.	filaments	lower eyelid
palpebral n., superior *n. palpebralis superior*	lacrimal n.	filaments	upper eyelid
pectoral n., lateral *n. pectoralis lateralis*	lateral cord of brachial plexus	filaments	greater pectoral muscle
pectoral n., medial *n. pectoralis medialis*	medial cord of brachial plexus	filaments	smaller pectoral muscle and caudal part of greater pectoral muscle
perineal n. *n. perinei*	pudendal n.	muscular, posterior scrotal (male), n. to urethral bulb, labial (female)	urogenital diaphragm, skin of external genitalia, perineal muscles, mucous membrane of urethra
peroneal n., common external popliteal n. peroneal n. *n. peroneus communis*	sciatic n.	articular (three), lateral cutaneous n. of calf, deep peroneal, superficial peroneal	knee joint, skin of posterior and lateral surfaces of leg, short head of biceps muscle of thigh, leg muscles
peroneal n., deep anterior tibial n. *n. peroneus profundus*	common peroneal n.	muscular, articular, lateral terminal, medial terminal, dorsal digital	anterior tibial, long extensor of great toe, long extensor of toes, short extensor of toes, third peroneal, ankle joint, tarsal and tarsophalangeal joints of second, third, and fourth toes

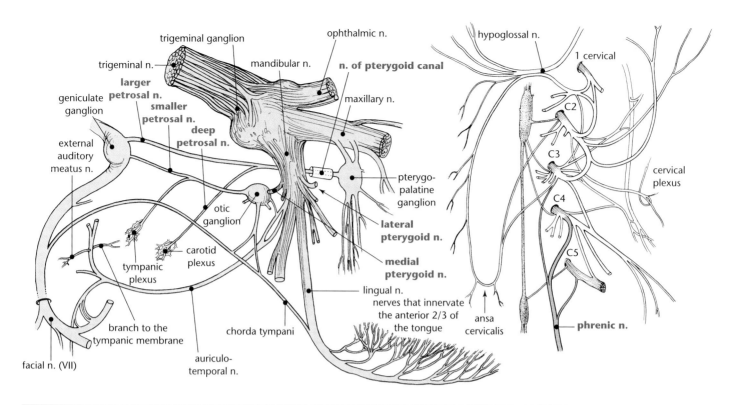

NERVE	ORIGIN	BRANCHES	DISTRIBUTION
peroneal n., superficial musculocutaneous n. *n. peroneus superficialis*	common peroneal n.	muscular, cutaneous filaments, medial dorsal cutaneous, intermediate dorsal cutaneous	long and short peroneal muscles, skin of lower part of leg, skin of medial side of foot, ankle, and side of great toe, skin of adjacent sides of second, third, fourth, and fifth toes
petrosal n., deep *n. petrosus profundus*	internal carotid plexus	joins larger petrosal n. to form n. of the pterygoid canal	glands and blood vessels of the pharynx, nasal cavity, lacrimal gland, and palate
petrosal n., larger (greater) greater superficial petrosal n. *n. petrosus major*	geniculate ganglion of facial n.	joins deep petrosal n. to form n. of pterygoid canal	mucous membrane and glands of palate, nose, lacrimal gland, and nasopharynx
petrosal n., smaller (lesser) lesser superficial petrosal n. *n. petrosus minor*	tympanic plexus	ganglionic, filaments	otic ganglion, parotid gland
phrenic n. internal respiratory n. of Bell *n. phrenicus*	third, fourth, and fifth cervical n.'s	pericardial, phrenicoabdominal	diaphragm, pericardium, mediastinal pleura, sympathetic plexus
phrenic n.'s, accessory *nn. phrenici accessorii*	inconstant branch from fifth cervical n. which arises with subclavian n.	joins phrenic n.	diaphragm
n. of piriform *n. piriformis*	first and second sacral n.'s	filaments	piriform muscle
plantar n., lateral external plantar n. *n. plantaris lateralis*	tibial n.	muscular, superficial, deep	skin of fifth and lateral half of fourth toes, deep muscles of foot
plantar n., medial internal plantar n. *n. plantaris medialis*	tibial n.	common plantar digital, common digitals (three), plantar cutaneous, muscular, articular	skin of sole of foot, skin of adjacent sides of great, second, third, and fourth toes, joints of tarsus and metatarsus, short flexor muscle of great toe, lumbrical muscles of foot
pterygoid canal, n. of Vidian n. *n. canalis pterygoidei*	formed by union of larger petrosal and deep petrosal n.'s	filaments	glands of nose, palate, and pharynx, pterygopalatine ganglion
pterygoid n., lateral *n. pterygoideus lateralis*	mandibular n.	none	deep surface of lateral pterygoid muscle
pterygoid n., medial *n. pterygoideus medialis*	mandibular n.	tensor veli palatini, tensor tympani, filaments	tensor veli palatini, tensor tympani and medial pterygoid muscles

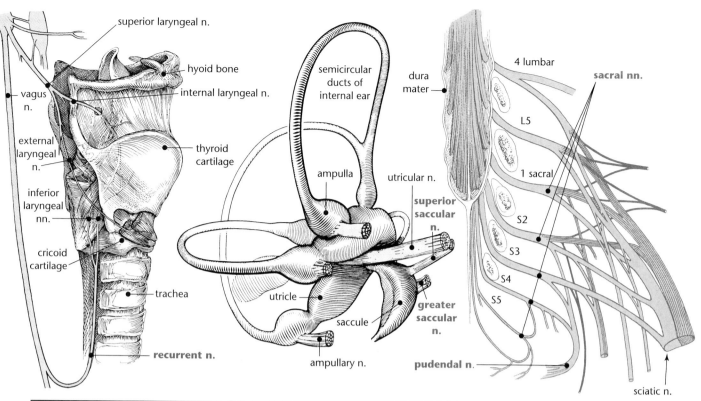

superior laryngeal n.

hyoid bone

internal laryngeal n.

vagus n.

external laryngeal n.

inferior laryngeal nn.

thyroid cartilage

cricoid cartilage

trachea

recurrent n.

semicircular ducts of internal ear

ampulla

utricle

saccule

ampullary n.

utricular n.

superior saccular n.

greater saccular n.

dura mater

4 lumbar

L5

1 sacral

S2

S3

S4

S5

sacral nn.

pudendal n.

sciatic n.

NERVE	ORIGIN	BRANCHES	DISTRIBUTION
pterygopalatine n.'s sphenopalatine n.'s *nn. pterygopalatini* *nn. ganglionares*	maxillary n.	orbital, greater palatine, posterior superior nasal, pharyngeal	mucous membranes of posterior ethmoidal and sphenoidal sinuses, nasal part of pharynx, and hard palate; periosteum of orbit, gums, nasal septum
pudendal n. internal pudic n. *n. pudendus*	second, third, and fourth sacral n.'s	inferior rectal, perineal, dorsal n. of penis (male) or dorsal n. of clitoris (female)	urogenital diaphragm, skin around anus, skin of scrotum or labium major, external sphincter of anus, erectile tissue, muscles of perineum
n. of quadrate muscle of thigh *n. quadratus femoris*	fourth and fifth lumbar and first sacral n.'s	filaments	quadrate muscle of thigh and inferior gemellus muscle
radial n. musculospiral n. *n. radialis*	posterior cord of brachial plexus	muscular, articular, superficial, deep, cutaneous	extensor muscles of arm and forearm, and skin on back of arm, forearm, and hand
rectal n., inferior inferior hemorrhoidal n. *n. rectalis inferior*	pudendal n.	filaments	external sphincter of anus, skin around anus, lining of anal canal
rectal n., middle *n. rectalis medius*	hypogastric plexus	filaments	rectum
rectal n., superior *n. rectalis superior*	inferior mesenteric plexus	filaments	rectum
recurrent n. recurrent laryngeal n. inferior laryngeal n. *n. recurrens*	vagus n.	pharyngeal, inferior laryngeal, tracheal, esophageal, cardiac	all muscles of larynx except cricothyroid; cardiac plexus, trachea, esophagus
saccular n., greater *n. saccularis major*	vestibular ganglion	filaments	larger of two nerves that innervate saccule of internal ear
saccular n., superior *n. saccularis superior*	vestibular ganglion	filaments	smaller of two nerves that innervate saccule of internal ear
sacral n.'s (five pairs of spinal nerves) *nn. sacrales*	sacral segments of spinal cord	dorsal, ventral, pelvic splanchnic	deep muscles and skin of lower back, pelvic viscera, sacral plexus, coccygeal plexus
sacral plexus *plexus sacralis*	fourth and fifth lumbar and first, second, and third sacral n.'s	internal obturator, superior and inferior gluteals, posterior femoral cutaneous, quadrate muscle of thigh, piriform, sciatic, pudendal	muscle and skin of perineum and lower limb; hip joint, buttock

N

nerve ■ nerve

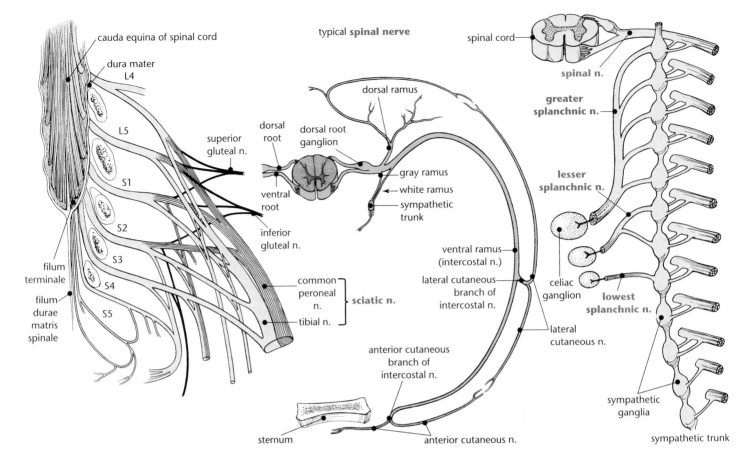

NERVE	ORIGIN	BRANCHES	DISTRIBUTION
saphenous n. *n. saphenus*	femoral n.	infrapatellar, medial crural cutaneous, filaments	skin of medial side of leg and foot, knee joint, patellar plexus
scapular n., dorsal posterior scapular n. *n. dorsalis scapulae*	fifth cervical n. near intervertebral foramen	filaments	greater and smaller rhomboid muscle, levator muscle of scapula
sciatic n. (largest nerve in body) great sciatic n. *n. ischiadicus*	fourth and fifth lumbar and first, second, and third sacral n.'s	articular, muscular, tibial, common peroneal	skin of foot and most of leg, muscles of leg and foot, all joints of lower limb
sciatic n., small	see cutaneous nerve of thigh, posterior		
scrotal n.'s, anterior *nn. scrotales anteriores*	ilioinguinal n.	filaments	skin of anterior scrotal area and root of penis
scrotal n.'s, posterior *nn. scrotales posteriores*	perineal n.	filaments	skin of posterior scrotal area
second cranial n.	see optic n.		
seventh cranial n.	see facial n.		
sixth cranial n.	see abducent n.		
spermatic n., external *n. genitalis externi*	genitofemoral	filaments	skin of scrotum and around inguinal ring area
sphenopalatine n.	see pterygopalatine nerve		
spinal n.'s *nn. spinales*	31 pairs of nerves arising from the spinal cord within the vertebral canal, including 8 cervical, 12 thoracic, 5 lumbar, 5 sacral, and 1 coccygeal		
splanchnic n., greater *n. splanchnicus major*	5th (or 6th) to 9th (or 10th) thoracic sympathetic ganglia	filaments	celiac ganglion, thoracic aorta, adrenal gland, aorti-corenal ganglion
splanchnic n., lesser *n. splanchnicus minor*	9th and 10th thoracic sympathetic ganglia	renal, filaments	aorticorenal ganglion
splanchnic n., lowest least splanchnic n. *n. splanchnicus imus*	last thoracic sympathetic ganglion or lesser splanchnic n.	filaments	renal plexus
splanchnic n.'s, lumbar (two to four in number) *nn. splanchnici lumbales*	lumbar sympathetic trunk at level of first, second, and third lumbar vertebrae	filaments	renal intermesenteric, and hypogastric plexuses

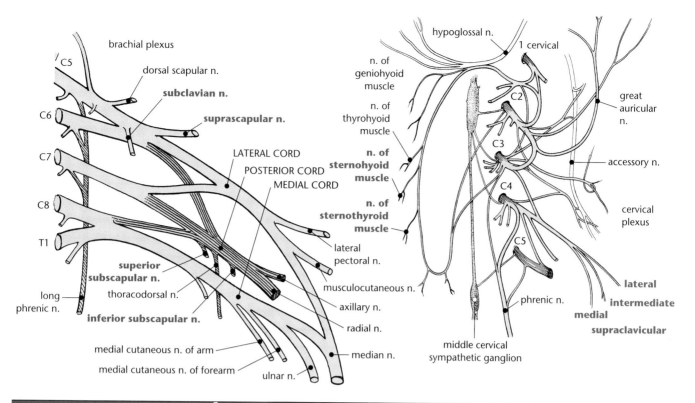

NERVE	ORIGIN	BRANCHES	DISTRIBUTION
splanchnic n.'s, sacral *nn. splanchnici sacrales*	sacral sympathetic ganglion	filaments	inferior hypogastric plexus
splanchnic n.'s, pelvic erigentes n.'s *nn. splanchnici pelvini*	second to fourth sacral nerves	filaments	inferior hypogastric plexus, descending and sigmoid colon, pelvic viscera
n. of stapedius *n. stapedius*	facial n.	filaments	stapedius muscle
n. of sternohyoid *n. sternohyoideus*	convexity of ansa cervicalis	filaments	sternohyoid muscle
n. of sternothyroid *n. sternothyroideus*	convexity of ansa cervicalis	filaments	sternothyroid muscle
subclavian n. *n. subclavius*	superior trunk of brachial plexus	articular, filaments	subclavius muscle, sternoclavicular joint
subcostal n. *n. subcostalis*	12th thoracic n.	anterior cutaneous, lateral cutaneous	skin of lower abdominal wall and gluteal region; some abdominal muscles
sublingual n. *n. sublingualis*	lingual n.	filaments	sublingual gland and mucous membrane of floor of mouth
suboccipital n. infraoccipital n. *n. suboccipitalis*	first cervical n.	filaments	deep muscles of back of neck
subscapular n.'s (usually two in number) *nn. subscapulares*	posterior cord of brachial plexus	superior, inferior	subscapular and teres major muscles
supraclavicular n.'s, intermediate middle supraclavicular n.'s *nn. supraclaviculares intermedii*	common trunk formed by third and fourth cervical nerves	filaments	skin over pectoral and deltoid muscles
supraclavicular n.'s, lateral posterior supraclavicular n.'s super-acromial n.'s *nn. supraclaviculares laterales*	common trunk formed by third and fourth cervical nerves	filaments	skin of upper and dorsal parts of shoulder
supraclavicular n.'s, medial anterior supraclavicular n.'s *nn. supraclaviculares mediales*	common trunk formed by third and fourth cervical nerves	filaments	skin of medial infraclavicular region as far as the midline, sternoclavicular joint
supraorbital n. *n. supraorbitalis*	frontal n.	medial, lateral, filaments	skin of upper eyelid and forehead, mucosa of frontal sinus, scalp
suprascapular n. *n. suprascapularis*	superior trunk of brachial plexus	supraspinous, infraspinous, articular, filaments	supraspinous and infraspinous muscles, shoulder joint

N

nerve ■ nerve

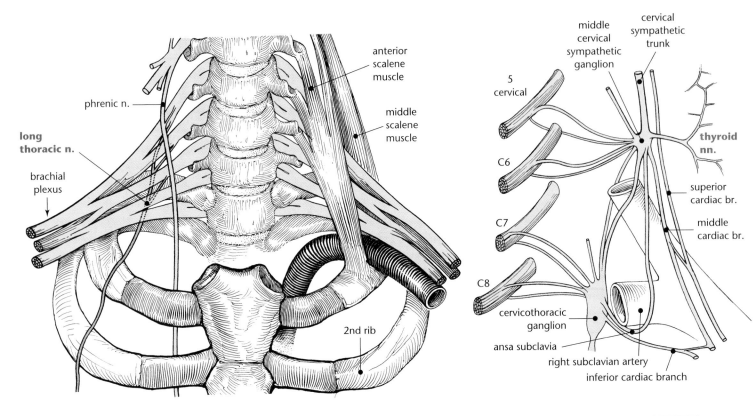

Labels on illustration (left):
phrenic n.
anterior scalene muscle
middle scalene muscle
long thoracic n.
brachial plexus
2nd rib

Labels on illustration (right):
middle cervical sympathetic ganglion
cervical sympathetic trunk
5 cervical
C6
C7
C8
thyroid nn.
superior cardiac br.
middle cardiac br.
cervicothoracic ganglion
ansa subclavia
right subclavian artery
inferior cardiac branch

NERVE	ORIGIN	BRANCHES	DISTRIBUTION
supratrochlear n. *n. supratrochlearis*	frontal n.	filaments, ascending, descending	conjunctiva, skin of upper eyelid and forehead
sural n. short saphenous n. *n. suralis*	medial and lateral cutaneous nerves of calf	lateral dorsal cutaneous, lateral calcaneal	skin of back of leg and lateral side of foot
temporal n.'s, deep (usually two in number) *nn. temporales profundi*	mandibular division of trigeminal n.	filaments	temporal muscle
n. to tensor tympani *n. tensoris tympani*	medial pterygoid n.	filaments	tensor muscle of tympanum
n. to tensor veli palatini *n. tensoris veli palatini*	medial pterygoid n.	filaments	tensor muscle of palatine velum
tenth cranial n.	*see vagus n.*		
tentorial n. *n. tentorii*	ophthalmic n.	filaments	tentorium cerebelli
terminal n. *n. terminalis*	cerebral hemispheres near olfactory trigone	filaments	dura mater, mucous membrane of nasal septum
third cranial n.	*see oculomotor n.*		
thoracic n.'s (12 pairs of spinal nerves) *nn. thoracici*	thoracic segments of spinal cord	dorsal, ventral	thoracic and abdominal walls (parietes) and skin of the buttock
thoracic n., long n. of serratus anterior *n. thoracicus longus*	fifth, sixth, and seventh cervical n.'s	filaments	all digitations of serratus anterior muscle
thoracoabdominal intercostal n.'s *nn. thoracoabdominales intercostales*	ventral primary divisions of 7th to 11th thoracic n.'s beyond the intercostal spaces	filaments	anterior abdominal wall
thoracodorsal n. long subscapular n. n. of latissimus dorsi *n. thoracodorsalis*	posterior cord of brachial plexus	filaments	latissimus dorsi muscle
n. of thyrohyoid *n. thyrohoideus*	first cervical n. traveling with hypoglossal n.	filaments	thyrohyoid muscle
thyroid n.'s *nn. thyroideus*	middle cervical ganglion	filaments	thyroid gland, parathyroid glands
tibial n. internal popliteal n. *n. tibialis*	sciatic n.	articular, medial calcaneal, medial sural cutaneous, medial and lateral plantar	knee and ankle joints, muscles of posterior leg, plantar muscles of foot

N

nerve ■ nerve

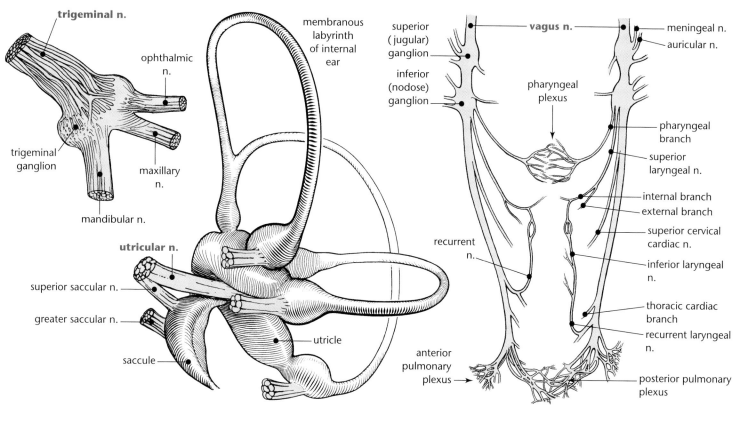

trigeminal n.

ophthalmic n.

trigeminal ganglion

maxillary n.

mandibular n.

membranous labyrinth of internal ear

superior (jugular) ganglion

inferior (nodose) ganglion

pharyngeal plexus

vagus n.

meningeal n.

auricular n.

pharyngeal branch

superior laryngeal n.

internal branch

external branch

superior cervical cardiac n.

inferior laryngeal n.

thoracic cardiac branch

recurrent laryngeal n.

posterior pulmonary plexus

recurrent n.

anterior pulmonary plexus

utricular n.

superior saccular n.

greater saccular n.

saccule

utricle

NERVE	ORIGIN	BRANCHES	DISTRIBUTION
tibial n., anterior	see peroneal nerve, deep		
transverse cervical n. cervical cutaneous n. *n. transversus colli*	second and third cervical n.'s	ascending, descending	skin over anterior and lateral parts of neck
trigeminal n. (largest of the cranial nerves) fifth n. trifacial n. *n. trigeminus*	brainstem at inferior surface of pons	two roots (motor and sensory) expand into trigeminal ganglion near apex of petrous portion of temporal bone, from which ophthalmic, maxillary, and mandibular n.'s arise	skin of face, muscles of mastication, teeth, mouth, and nasal cavity, scalp
trochlear n. (smallest of the cranial nerves) fourth cranial n. *n. trochlearis*	midbrain immediately posterior to the inferior colliculus	filaments	superior oblique muscle of eyeball
twelfth cranial n.	see hypoglossal nerve		
tympanic n. n. of Jacobson *n. tympanicus*	glossopharyngeal n.	lesser petrosal, contributes to formation of tympanic plexus	middle ear chamber, tympanic membrane, mastoid air cells, auditory tube, parotid gland
ulnar n. cubital n. *n. ulnaris*	medial cord of brachial plexus	articular, muscular, dorsal, palmar (superficial and deep)	intrinsic muscles of hand, elbow, wrist and hand joints, skin of medial side of hand
utricular n. *n. utricularis*	utriculoampullar n.	filaments	utricle of the internal ear
utriculoampullar n. *n. utriculoampullaris*	a division of the vestibular portion of the vestibulocochlear n.; it innervates the macula of the utricle and saccule as well as the ampullae of the anterior and lateral semicircular ducts		
vaginal n.'s *nn. vaginales*	uterovaginal plexus	filaments	vagina
vagus n. tenth cranial n. pneumogastric n. *n. vagus*	side of medulla oblongata between the olive and the inferior cerebellar peduncle	meningeal, auricular, pharyngeal, superior laryngeal, superior and inferior cardiac, anterior and posterior bronchial, recurrent, esophageal, gastric, hepatic, celiac	dura mater, skin of posterior surface of external ear, voluntary muscles of larynx and pharynx, heart, nonstriated muscles and glands of esophagus, stomach, trachea, bronchi, biliary tract, and intestines, mucous membranes of pharynx, larynx, bronchi, lungs, digestive tract, and kidney

nerve ■ nerve

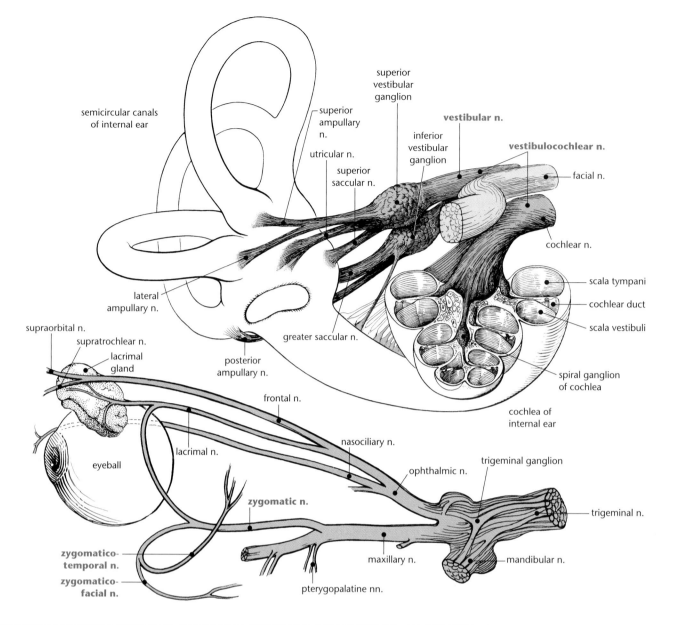

NERVE	ORIGIN	BRANCHES	DISTRIBUTION
vertebral n. *n. vertebralis*	cervicothoracic (stellate) ganglion	meningeal, filaments	meninges, joins cervical nerves, vertebral artery
vestibular n. n. of equilibration *n. vestibularis*	vestibulocochlear n.	utricular, saccular, ampullar	through vestibular ganglion (ganglion of Scarpa) to maculae of utricle and saccule, and to ampullae of semicircular ducts)
vestibulocochlear n. eighth cranial n. auditory n. acoustic n. otic n. *n. vestibulocochlearis*	brainstem between pons and medulla oblongata formed by union of vestibular and cochlear n.'s	vestibular (medial), cochlear (lateral)	receptor organs in membranous labyrinth of inner ear
Vidian n.	see pterygoid canal, n. of		
vomernasal n. *n. vomernasalis*	present in the nasal septum of the fetus but disappears before birth		
zygomatic n. orbital n. temporomalar n. *n. zygomaticus*	maxillary n.	zygomaticotemporal, zygomaticofacial	skin of temple, skin on prominence of cheek (zygomatic arch)
zygomaticofacial n. *n. zygomaticofacialis*	zygomatic n.	filaments	skin over prominence of cheek (zygomatic arch)
zygomaticotemporal n. *n. zygomaticotemporalis*	zygomatic n.	filaments	skin on side of forehead (temple)

nerve ■ nerve

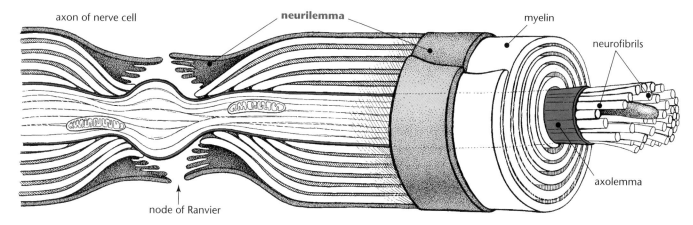

axon of nerve cell   neurilemma   myelin   neurofibrils

node of Ranvier   axolemma

nervous (ner′vus) **1.** Relating to nerves. **2.** Excitable.

nervous breakdown (ner′vus brāk′down) Popular nonspecific term; a euphemism for mental disorder.

nervousness (ner′vus-nes) Undue excitability and irritability.

nervus (ner′vus), pl. ner′vi Latin for nerve.

nesslerize (nes′ler-īz) To treat a blood or urine specimen with Nessler's reagent.

nest (nest) A collection of similar entities (e.g., cells).

    cell n.'s Small collection of cells different from those of surrounding tissue.

net (net) Network.

network (net′werk) **1.** Any structure resembling a net, composed of interlocking filaments. Also called meshwork. **2.** The significant people in a person's immediate surroundings, especially as they relate to the person's illness.

    Purkinje's n. Network of specialized muscle fibers just beneath the inner layer of the ventricular wall of the heart.

network health plan Health plan that partially or wholly restricts coverage to the service of network providers, i.e., health care given by a specified group of physicians, hospitals, and other health care providers agreeing to cooperate with certain criteria (e.g., with some form of cost containment and fee schedules). Network plans include health maintenance organization (HMO), point of service (POS) plan, and preferred provider organization (PPO).

neural (nu′ral) **1.** Relating to the nervous system. **2.** Relating to the dorsal region of the embryo.

neuralgia (nu-ral′je-ah) Severe pain along the course of a nerve. Also called neurodynia.

    Morton's n. See Morton's neuroma, under neuroma.

    occipital n. Piercing pain on one side of the back of the head, caused by entrapment of the greater occipital nerve as it exits from the skull.

    trigeminal n. Condition usually affecting people over 50 years of age, marked by bursts of brief piercing pain in areas of the face supplied by the trigeminal (5th cranial) nerve (i.e., the cheek, chin, lips, or gums on one side of the face); usually induced by touching trigger points on the face. Also called tic douloureux.

neuralgic (nu-ral′jik) Relating to neuralgia.

neuranagenesis (nu-ran-ah-jen′ĕ-sis) Regeneration of an injured nerve.

neurapraxia (nu-rah-prak′se-ah) Loss of impulse conduction due to injury to a nerve, resulting in temporary paralysis.

neurasthenia (nu-ras-the′ne-ah) An outdated term denoting a condition marked by fatigability, irritability, and poor concentration; originally considered a result of exhaustion of the nervous system, now recognized as a form of anxiety neurosis or depression.

    traumatic n. See posttraumatic syndrome, under syndrome.

neuraxis (nu-rak′sis) The central nervous system.

neurectomy (nu-rek′to-me) Surgical removal of a nerve segment.

neurectopia, neurectopy (nu-rek-to′pe-ah, nu-rek′to-pe) Abnormal location of a nerve.

neurergic (nu-rer′jik) Relating to the action of nerves.

neurilemma (nu-rī-lem′mah) The thin cytoplasmic membrane of a Schwann cell enwrapping the axons of myelinated nerve fibers or the axons of certain unmyelinated nerve fibers. Also called sheath of Schwann; neurilemmal sheath; neurolemma.

neurilemoma (nu-rī-le-mo′mah) See schwannoma.

    acoustic n. See vestibular schwannoma, under schwannoma.

neurinoma (nu-rī-no′mah) See schwannoma.

    acoustic n. See vestibular schwannoma, under schwannoma.

neuritis (nu-ri′tis) Inflammation or degeneration of a nerve.

    optic n. General term denoting inflammation, degeneration, or demyelinization of the optic nerve caused by any of various diseases, and having loss of vision as a chief symptom.

        retrobulbar n. A form of optic neuritis involving the posterior portion of the optic nerve and showing no abnormalities of the optic disk.

    toxic n. Neuritis caused by a chemical toxin, as in arsenic or lead poisoning.

    traumatic n. Neuritis occurring after an injury.

neuroanastomosis (nu-ro-ah-nas-to-mo′sis) Surgical union of nerves.

neuroanatomy (nu-ro-ah-nat′o-me) The branch of anatomy concerned with the study of the nervous system.

neuroblast (nu′ro-blast) An embryonic nerve cell.

neuroblastoma (nu-ro-blas-to′mah) A malignant tumor composed of embryonic neural crest cells occurring in young children and infants, including newborns; most commonly seen in the medulla of the adrenal gland but occurring also in other tissues derived from neural crest cells. Also called sympathoblastoma.

neurocardiac (nu-ro-kar′de-ak) **1.** Relating to the nerve supply of the heart. **2.** Relating to cardiac neurosis.

neurocele (nu′ro-sēl) The ventricles within the brain and the central canal within the spinal cord.

neurochemistry (nu-ro-kem′is-tre) The study of chemical activity of nervous tissue.

neurochoroiditis (nu-ro-ko-roi-di′tis) Inflammation of the optic nerve and the middle coat (choroid) of the eyeball.

neurocladism (nu-rok′lah-dizm) Regeneration of a cut nerve by outgrowths of axons sprouting across the gap from the proximal to the distant stump. Also called axonal regeneration.

neurocranium (nu-ro-kra′ne-um) The portion of skull containing the brain.

neurocytoma (nu-ro-si-to′mah) See ganglioneuroma.

neurodermatitis (nu-ro-der-mah-ti′tis) A localized itchy skin inflammation of nervous or psychological origin.

neurodynamic (nu-ro-di-nam′ik) Relating to nervous energy.

neurodynia (nu-ro-din′e-ah) See neuralgia.

neuroectoderm (nu-ro-ek′to-derm) In embryology, the part of the ectoderm giving rise to the neural tube.

neuroendocrine (nu-ro-en′do-krin) Denoting a relationship between the nervous system and the endocrine glands.

neuroendocrinology (nu-ro-en-do-krī-nol′o-je) The study of functional interactions between the nervous system and endocrine glands.

neuroepithelium (nu-ro-ep-ĭ-the′le-um) Specialized epithelial cells that respond to external stimuli (e.g., hair cells of the inner ear).

gelatinous layer with crystals of statoconia

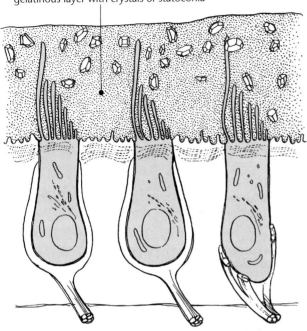

neuroepithelium (hair cells of the utricular macula of the inner ear)

neurofibril (nu-ro-fi′bril) A nerve fibril; one of numerous delicate filaments running parallel with the axon and dendrite but interlacing in the cell body.

neurofibroma (nu-ro-fi-bro′mah) A nonmalignant tumor originating in the connective tissue of nerves, forming a spindle-shaped enlargement of the affected nerve; it occurs most frequently in the skin.

neurofibromatosis (nu-ro-fi-bro-mah-to′sis) Genetic disorder transmitted as a dominant inheritance, characterized by formation of multiple nerve tumors (neurofibromas).

  n. I A type characterized by multiple soft tumors involving nerves of skin and internal organs, light brown (café au lait) spots on the skin, and pigmented (Lisch) nodules in the iris; may be associated

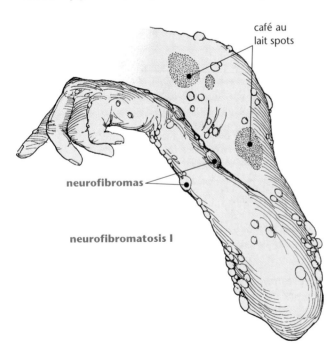

café au lait spots

neurofibromas

neurofibromatosis I

with bone cysts and mental impairment. The defective gene is on chromosome 17. Also called Recklinghausen's disease; von Recklinghausen's disease.

  n. II A central, acoustic form marked by tumors in both vestibulocochlear (8th cranial) nerves. The defective gene is on chromosome 22.

neurogenesis (nu-ro-jen′ĕ-sis) The formation of nerve tissue.

neurogenic (nu-ro-jen′ik) **1.** Originating in, derived from, or caused by the nervous system. **2.** Giving rise to nerve tissue.

neurogenous (nu-roj′ĕ-nus) See neurogenic (1).

neuroglia (nu-rog′le-ah) The nonneuronal tissue of the brain and spinal cord that performs supportive and other ancillary functions; composed of various types of cells collectively called neuroglial cells or glial cells. Also called glia.

neuroglial, neurogliar (nu-rog′le-al, nu-rog′le-ar) Relating to neuroglia.

neurogliomatosis (nu-ro-gli-o-mah-to′sis) See gliomatosis.

neurohistology (nu-ro-his-tol′o-je) Microscopic study of the nervous system.

neurohormone (nu′ro-hor-mōn) A hormone whose secretion is controlled by the nervous system.

neurohumor (nu-ro-hu′mor) An active chemical substance that effects the passage of nerve impulses from one cell to another.

neurohypophyseal (nu-ro-hi-po-fiz′e-al) Relating to the neurohypophysis. Also written neurohypophysial.

neurohypophysis (nu-ro-hi-pof′ĭ-sis) The posterior lobe of the pituitary (hypophysis). Also called neural lobe of pituitary. See also hypophysis.

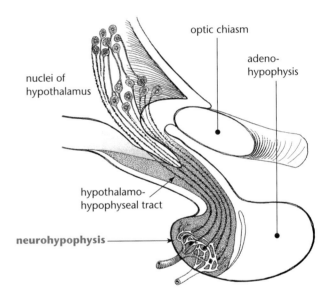

optic chiasm

adeno-hypophysis

nuclei of hypothalamus

hypothalamo-hypophyseal tract

neurohypophysis

neuroid (nu′roid) Resembling a nerve.

neurokeratin (nu-ro-ker′ah-tin) **1.** A proteinaceous and lipid network in the myelin sheath of axons. **2.** The pseudokeratin present in brain tissue.

neurolemma (nu-ro-lem′ah) See neurilemma.

neuroleptic (nu-ro-lep′tik) Any major tranquilizer that acts on the nervous system and has therapeutic effects on psychoses and other types of psychiatric disorders. Also called antipsychotic.

neurologic (nu-ro-loj′ik) Relating to the nervous system.

neurologist (nu-rol′o-jist) A specialist in neurology.

neurology (nu-rol′o-je) The branch of medicine concerned with the nervous system and its diseases.

neurolymph (nu′ro-limf) See cerebrospinal fluid, under fluid.

neurolysin (nu-rol′ĭ-sin) See neurotoxin.

neurolysis (nu-rol′ĭ-sis) **1.** Destruction of nerve tissue. **2.** Operative removal of adhesions from a nerve.

neuroma (nu-ro′mah) General term for any tumor derived from nerve tissue.

N

acoustic n. See vestibular schwannoma, under schwannoma.

amputation n. A mass (often painful) of tangled, intertwined nerve fibers formed at the severed ends of a nerve, formed when the presence of scar tissue prevents regeneration of the nerve. Also called traumatic neuroma.

interdigital nerve n. See Morton's neuroma.

Morton's n. Fibrosis of the sheath covering an interdigital plantar nerve, usually between the second and third toes, forming a painful tumorlike mass; caused by compression of the nerve at the metatarsophalangeal joint. Also called interdigital nerve neuroma; Morton's neuralgia.

traumatic n. See amputation neuroma.

neuromalacia (nu-ro-mah-la′she-ah) Abnormal softening of nerve tissue.

neuromuscular (nu-ro-mus′ku-lar) Relating to nerve and muscle.

neuromyasthenia (nu-ro-mi-as-the′ne-ah) Muscular weakness, especially one of emotional origin.

epidemic n. An epidemic disorder of unknown cause affecting adults almost exclusively; characterized by stiffness of the neck and back, headache, diarrhea, and localized muscular weakness. Also called benign myalgic encephalomyelitis; Iceland disease.

neuromyelitis (nu-ro-mi-ĕ-li′tis) Inflammation of the spinal cord and one or more peripheral nerves. Also called myeloneuritis.

n. optica An uncommon condition of sudden onset, characterized by inflammation of the optic nerves and, frequently, blindness; cause is unknown but considered by many to be a form of multiple sclerosis. Also called Devic's disease.

neuromyopathy (nu-ro-mi-op′ah-the) A muscular disorder due to disease of the nerve supplying the muscle.

neuromyositis (nu-ro-mi-o-si′tis) Inflammation of a nerve and the muscle it supplies.

neuron (nu′ron) A nerve cell; the basic functional and anatomic unit of the nervous system, concerned with conduction of impulses; it is structurally the most complex cell in the body; composed of a cell body, numerous relatively short branched dendrites, and usually one long slender axon. Also called nerve cell.

bipolar n. A neuron that has two separate axons, each extending from opposite ends of the cell body; seen in the retina, olfactory mucosa, inner ear, and taste buds.

Golgi type I n. A relatively large pyramidal neuron with a long axon connecting different parts of the nervous system by leaving the gray matter of the central nervous system and terminating in the periphery.

Golgi type II n. A relatively small stellate neuron with a short axon that terminates close to the cell body; in some cases the axon is absent.

internuncial n. A neuron connecting two other neurons. Also called interneuron.

multipolar n. A neuron with several extensions of the cell body, making up most of the cells of the central nervous system.

pseudounipolar n. See unipolar neuron.

unipolar n. A neuron that has only one axon extending from its cell body, giving rise to both dendritic and axonal branches (e.g., dorsal root ganglion cells). Sometimes called pseudounipolar neuron.

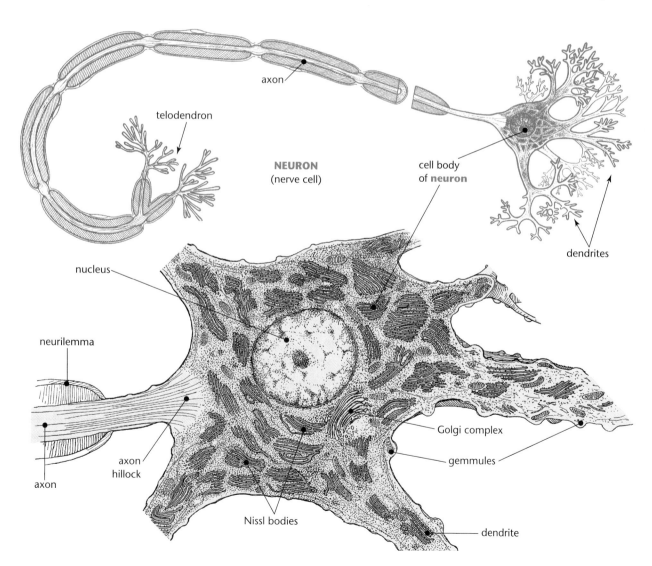

axon

telodendron

NEURON
(nerve cell)

cell body
of **neuron**

dendrites

nucleus

neurilemma

axon
hillock

axon

Nissl bodies

Golgi complex

gemmules

dendrite

neuronal (nu'ro-nal) Relating to a nerve cell (neuron).

neuronitis (nu-ro-ni'tis) Inflammation of nerve cells, especially those in the roots of spinal nerves.

neuronixis (nu-ron-ik'sis) See acupuncture.

neuronophage (nu-ron'o-fāj) A white blood cell that engulfs and digests elements of injured or diseased nerve cells.

neuronophagia (nu-ron-o-fa'je-ah) Ingestion of nerve cell debris by white blood cells.

neuro-ophthalmology (nu'ro of-thal-mol'o-je) The study of the nervous system directly related to the eye. Also written neurophthalmology.

neuropapillitis (nu-ro-pap-ĭ-li'tis) See papillitis (1).

neuroparalysis (nu-ro-pah-ral'ĭ-sis) Paralysis due to disease of the nerve supplying the affected part.

neuropathic (nu-ro-path'ik) Relating to disease of the nervous system.

neuropathogenesis (nu-ro-path-o-jen'ĕ-sis) The origin of diseases affecting the nervous system.

neuropathology (nu-ro-pah-thol'o-je) The study of diseases of the nervous system.

neuropathy (nu-rop'ah-the) Any disease of the nerves, including cerebral (central) and spinal (peripheral).

> **brachial plexus n.** Condition marked by pain around a shoulder followed by weakness of the arm muscles innervated by nerves of the brachial plexus. Spontaneous recovery occurs. The cause is unknown. Also called neuralgic amyotrophy; shoulder-hand syndrome.

> **diabetic n.** A complication of long-standing diabetes mellitus; may include bilateral involvement of peripheral sensory nerves (affecting especially the lower extremities), causing numbness, abnormal sensations, and deep-seated pain; may also include the autonomic nerves supplying the bowel and bladder, which may cause esophageal dysfunction, constipation or diarrhea, incontinence, and, in men, erectile impotence; seen most frequently in older patients.

> **entrapment n.** Any of a group of inflammatory nerve conditions (e.g., carpal tunnel syndrome) caused by traumatic pressure exerted upon the nerve by neighboring structures.

> **familial amyloid n.** Disturbance of nerve function caused by a mutant serum protein (transthyretin) deposited as amyloid in nerve tissue; occurs in a variety of genetic diseases of autosomal dominant inheritance.

> **segmental n.** Loss of myelin in scattered areas of peripheral nerves; seen in various conditions, including lead and arsenic poisoning.

neuropeptide (nu-ro-pep'tid) Any of various substances (e.g., endorphin, vasopressin) present in neural tissue, especially the brain.

neuropharmacology (nu-ro-fahr-mah-kol'o-je) The study of drugs that affect the nervous system.

neurophthalmology (nu-rof-thal-mol'o-je) See neuro-ophthalmology.

neurophysin (nu-ro-fi'sin) Any of a group of soluble proteins produced in the hypothalamus at the base of the brain; they serve as carriers of the hormones vasopressin and oxytocin to the posterior lobe of the pituitary.

neurophysiology (nu-ro-fiz-e-ol'o-je) Study of the normal vital processes of the nervous system.

neuropil, neuropile (nu'ro-pil) A dense network of interwoven axons, dendrites, and neuroglial cells generally constituting the bulk of the gray matter of the central nervous system.

neuroplasm (nu'ro-plazm) The cytoplasm of a nerve cell.

neuroplasticity (nu-ro-plas-tis'ĭ-te) The ability of the brain to change in response to environmental influences (e.g., in the mechanism of posttraumatic stress disorder). See also kindling.

neuroplasty (nu'ro-plas-te) Reparative surgery of a nerve or nerves.

neuropodium (nu-ro-po'de-um), pl. neuropo'dia See axon terminal, under terminal.

neuropsychiatrist (nu-ro-si-ki'ah-trist) A physician who specializes in neuropsychiatry.

neuropsychiatry (nu-ro-si-ki'ah-tre) The study of both organic and functional diseases of the nervous system.

neuropsychologist (nu-ro-si-kol'o-jist) One who specializes in the measurement and evaluation of deficits in psychologic functioning due to organic brain dysfunction.

neuropsychology (nu-ro-si-kol'o-je) The study of the relationship between the mind and the nervous system.

neuropsychopathy (nu-ro-si-kop'ah-the) Functional disease of the nervous system accompanied by mental symptoms.

neuroradiology (nu-ro-ra-de-ol'o-je) The making of x-ray pictures of the central nervous system.

neuroretinitis (nu-ro-ret-ĭ-ni'tis) Inflammation of the head of the optic nerve and surrounding retina.

neurorrhaphy (nu-ror'ah-fe) Suturing together the ends of a cut nerve.

neurosarcocleisis (nu-ro-sar-ko-kli'sis) Removal of bone from a canal surrounding a nerve; a procedure performed for the relief of neuralgia.

neuroscience (nu-ro-si'ens) Any of the scientific disciplines concerned with different aspects of the nervous system (e.g., embryology, physiology, biochemistry, pathology).

neurosecretion (nu-ro-se-kre'shun) Any of several substances secreted by nerve cells that enter the bloodstream and act as hormones.

neurosis (nu-ro'sis), pl. neuro'ses Emotional maladjustment in which symptoms are experienced by the individual as distressing and unacceptable but in which anxiety is experienced on attempting to confront these symptoms; reality testing is grossly intact and behavior does not violate societal norms; the pattern is relatively enduring but amenable to psychotherapeutic intervention. Neuroses are presently classified by their predominant symptoms as various disorders: these disorders are distinguished from psychoses (in which reality testing is impaired) and personality disorders (in which the person's patterns of behavior impair functioning but are not experienced as ego-alien). Formerly called psychoneurosis.

> **battle n.** See war neurosis.

> **cardiac n.** Anxiety resulting from an exaggerated concern with the state of one's heart in the absence of heart disease. Also called cardioneurosis.

> **hysterical n.** See conversion disorder, under disorder.

> **military n.** See war neurosis.

> **posttraumatic n.** See posttraumatic stress disorder, under disorder.

> **war n.** Any mental disorder induced by conditions of warfare. Also called battle neurosis; military neurosis.

neurosplanchnic (nu-ro-splangk'nik) Relating to the sympathetic and parasympathetic nervous systems (which together form the autonomic nervous system).

neurosurgeon (nu-ro-sur'jun) A specialist in surgery of the nervous system.

neurosurgery (nu-ro-sur'jer-e) A surgical specialty concerned with the treatment of conditions and diseases of the brain, spinal cord, and nerves.

neurosyphilis (nu-ro-sif'ĭ-lis) The third stage of syphilis; it affects the central and peripheral nervous systems (e.g., chronic meningitis, tabes dorsalis).

neurotic (nu-rot'ik) Relating to neurosis. Also called psychoneurotic.

neurotization (nu-rot-ĭ-za'shun) Regeneration of a nerve.

neurotomy (nu-rot'o-me) Surgical division of a nerve.

> **retrogasserian n.** See trigeminal rhizotomy, under rhizotomy.

neurotonic (nu-ro-ton'ik) 1. Having a stimulating effect on the function of an impaired nerve. 2. An agent having such an effect.

neurotoxic (nu-ro-tok'sik) Destructive or harmful to nerve tissue.

neurotoxicity (nu-ro-tok-sis'ĭ-te) The property of having a deleterious effect upon the nervous system.

neurotoxicology (nu-ro-tok-sĭ-kol'o-je) The study of poisonous substances with regard to their mode of action and harmful effects on the nervous system.

N

neurotoxin (nu-ro-tok′sin) Any substance that destroys or injures nerve tissue or interferes with its normal functioning; included are: naturally occurring toxins, chemicals and therapeutic agents, organophosphate insecticides, metals, and noxious gases. Also called neurolysin.

neurotransmitter (nu-ro-trans-mit′er) A substance (e.g., acetylcholine, catecholamines, monamines) that facilitates the transmission of impulses from one nerve cell to another, or between nerve cells and receptors of effector cells, at specialized regions (synaptic gaps) located at the end of the nerve cell.

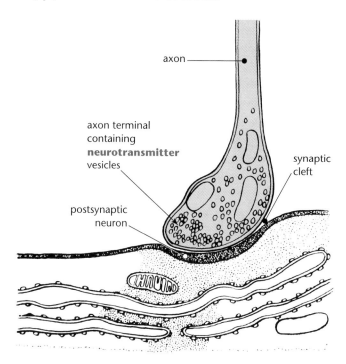

neurotropic (nu-ro-trop′ik) Having an affinity for nerve tissue; applied to certain microorganisms and histologic dyes.

neurulation (nu-roo-la′shun) In embryology, the formation and closure of the neural plate in the early embryo, from which the brain and spinal cord eventually develop.

neutralization (nu-tral-ĭ-za′shun) 1. The chemical reaction between an acid and a base that yields a salt and water. 2. The act of rendering ineffective.

neutralize (nu′tral-ĭz) 1. To render ineffective (e.g., counteracting the effect of a poison). 2. To make neutral.

neutral red (nu′tral red) A dye used as an indicator with pH range of 6.8 to 8.

neutrino (nu-tre′no) A subatomic particle, that has zero rest mass and no charge.

neutro-, neutr- Combining forms meaning neutral.

neutrocytopenia (nu-tro-si-to-pe′ne-ah) See neutropenia.

neutron (nu′tron) (n) An uncharged subatomic particle, slightly heavier than a proton, present in the nuclei of atoms.

neutropenia (nu-tro-pe′ne-ah) An abnormally reduced number of neutrophils in the blood. Also called neutrocytopenia.

neutrophil (nu′tro-fil) A mature white blood cell having a nucleus of three to five lobes joined by thin strands of chromatin; the most numerous of the white blood cell population (50–75% in normal individuals); its primary function is the ingestion and digestion of particulate matter, especially highly virulent bacteria; after it migrates from the bloodstream to a site of infection, it may be called a microphage. Also called polymorphonuclear leukocyte; polymorph; PMN.

neutrophilia (nu-tro-fil′e-ah) Increased number of neutrophils in the blood. Also called neutrophilic leukocytosis.

nevi (ne′vi) Plural of nevus.

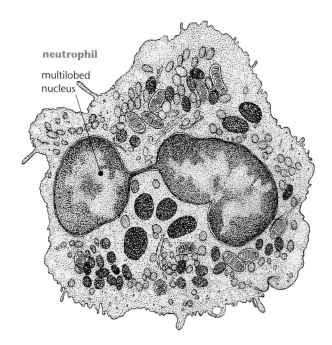

neutrophil
multilobed nucleus

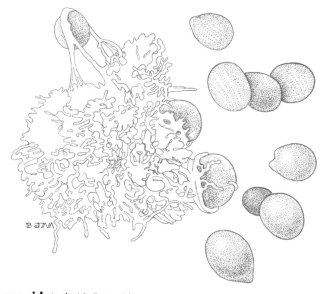

neutrophil
phagocytizing *Candida albicans*

nevoid (ne′void) Resembling a nevus.

nevoxanthoendothelioma (ne′vo-zan′tho-en′do-the′le-o′mah) See juvenile xanthogranuloma, under xanthogranuloma.

nevus (ne′vus), pl. ne′vi A benign lesion of the skin present at birth; may be flat or elevated, smooth or warty, pigmented or nonpigmented.

   n. araneus See spider telangiectasia, under telangiectasia.

   blue n. A uniform, circumscribed, deep blue coloration composed of heavily pigmented melanocytic cells in the deep layer (dermis) of the skin.

   common acquired n. A small (usually less than 1 cm), well-demarcated, tan to brown lesion that is not present at birth but appears later in childhood or adult life.

   compound n. Nevus in which clusters of melanocytic cells are located in both the superficial and deep layers of the skin (epidermis and dermis).

   compound n. of Spitz A rapidly growing nevus but with no malignant potential; occurs primarily in children. Also called Spitz nevus.

   congenital nevocellular n. A relatively large pigmented lesion, often covered with hairs; the melanocytic cells are located in the deepest layers of skin, involving also the subcutaneous fat, often associated with nerves; occasionally may develop malignant potential.

dysplastic n. See atypical mole, under mole.

n. flammeus A purplish red, vascular birthmark that is level with the skin surface and usually tends to be permanent. Also called port-wine stain; port-wine mark; port-wine hemangioma.

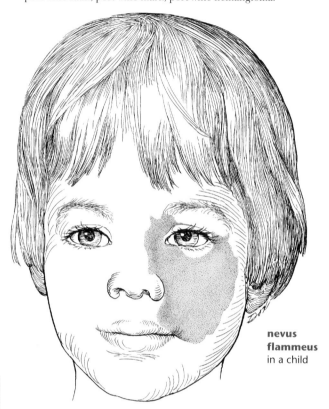

**nevus
flammeus**
in a child

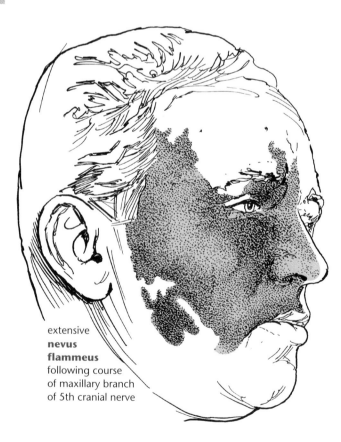

extensive
**nevus
flammeus**
following course
of maxillary branch
of 5th cranial nerve

halo n. A pigmented, frequently depressed nevus surrounded by a depigmented zone, often with associated inflammation.

intradermal n. Nevus in which the nests of melanocytic cells are located within the deep layer (dermis) of the skin.

junctional n. Nevus in which well-defined clusters of melanocytic cells are located along the junction between the deep and superficial layers of the skin (i.e., between the dermis and epidermis).

melanocytic n. See nevocellular nevus.

nevocellular n. Any of various circumscribed pigmented nevi composed of pigment-producing cells (melanocytes), present at birth or acquired in childhood, and varying from smooth to rough and from nonpalpable to nodular. Also called pigmented nevus; melanocytic nevus; commonly called mole.

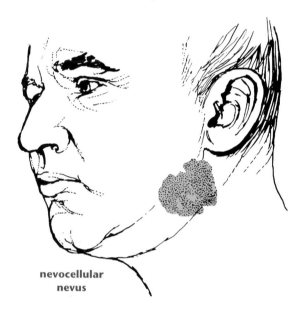

**nevocellular
nevus**

pigmented n. See nevocellular nevus.

spider n. See spider telangiectasia, under telangiectasia.

Spitz n. See compound nevus of Spitz.

systematized n. A widely distributed congenital nevus exhibiting a pattern.

n. vasculosus, n. vascularis See strawberry hemangioma, under hemangioma.

newborn (nu′born) A recently born baby; a neonate.

newton (nu′ton) (N) A unit of force equal to the force required to accelerate a mass of 1 kilogram 1 meter per second squared.

niacin (ni′ah-sin) Official designation for nicotinic acid in its role as a vitamin. See also nicotinic acid.

nib (nib) The working tip of a dental condenser corresponding to the blade of a cutting instrument.

niche (nich) **1.** A small recess. **2.** An eroded area, especially in the wall of an organ, usually detected by radiography with the use of a radiopaque substance.

nickel (nik′el) Metallic element; symbol Ni, atomic number 28, atomic weight 58.71.

nicking (nik′ing) A localized constriction or indentation.

A-V n., arteriovenous n. A depression on a retinal vein at the point where it is crossed by an artery; usually caused by arteriolar sclerosis.

nicotinamide (nik-o-tin′ah-mīd) A water-soluble B-complex vitamin used in the treatment of pellagra. Also called nicotinic acid amide.

nicotinamide adenine dinucleotide (nik-o-tin′ah-mīd ad′ĕ-nēn di-nu′kle-o-tīd) (NAD) One of the coenzymes of the vitamin niacin; it acts as an oxidation-reduction catalyst in association with any of a number of proteins.

nicotinamide adenine dinucleotide phosphate (nik-o-tin′ah-mīd ad′ĕ-nēn di-nu′kle-o-tīd fos′fāt) (NADP) A coenzyme that

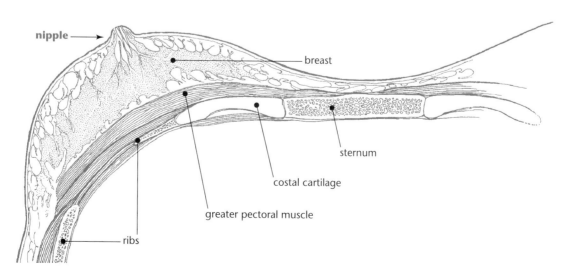

amalgam plugger

nib   nib

participates in biological oxidation reactions; it is structurally and functionally similar to NAD.

nicotine (nik′o-tēn) An alkaloid present in tobacco *(Nicotiana tabacum);* small doses stimulate and large doses depress autonomic ganglia.

nicotinic (nik-o-tin′ik) **1.** Relating to nicotine. **2.** Resembling nicotine; denoting the action certain substances exert on the nervous system.

nicotinic acid (nik-o-tin′ik as′id) A white crystalline compound, part of the vitamin B complex; important for the prevention and treatment of pellagra. Used in larger dosage as a treatment for hyperlipidemia. See also niacin.

nicotinic acid amide (nik-o-tin′ik as′id am′īd) See nicotinamide.

nicotinomimetic (nik-o-tin′o-mī-met′ik) Simulating the action of nicotine.

nicotinyl titrate (nik-o-tin′il ti′trāt) Compound that has a dilating action on peripheral blood vessels; used in the treatment of certain peripheral vascular disorders (e.g., Raynaud's disease).

nictitate (nik′tī-tāt) To wink.

nictitation (nik-tī-ta′shun) Winking.

nidal (ni′dal) Relating to a nidus.

nidation (ni-da′shun) Implantation of the early embryo (the fluid-filled blastocyst) in the inner lining of the uterus (endometrium); occurs approximately five days after fertilization of the ovum.

nidus (ni′dus) **1.** A focus or point of origin (e.g., of an infection). **2.** A nucleus in the central nervous system from which a nerve originates.

    n. avis A depression in the cerebellum, between the central lobe and the uvula, that accommodates the cerebellar tonsil.

nifedipine (ni-fed′ĭ-pēn) A calcium channel-blocking drug used in the treatment of angina pectoris and hypertension. Possible adverse effects include swelling, headache, and dizziness.

nightmare (nit′mār) A dream accompanied by intense anxiety, fear, oppression, and helplessness.

night terror (nīt ter′er) Sleep disorder of children in which the child abruptly awakens agitated and screaming, does not recognize familiar faces, and usually cannot be comforted; gradually the child falls back to sleep and has no recollection of the event the following day.

nihilism (ni′hil-izm) In psychiatry, a delusion of nonexistence; it may be total (including the patient and the world as a whole) or selective (referring to a part of the patient or his or her environment).

    therapeutic n. A disbelief in the value of any type of therapy.

ninhydrin (nin-hi′drin) Triketohydrindene hydrate; a reagent used in analytical determination of amino acids and related substances.

niobium (ni-o′be-um) Metallic element; symbol Nb, atomic number 41, atomic weight 92.91.

nipple (nip′l) The pigmented protrusion at the apex of the breast, surrounded by the areola. Also called mammary papilla.

nit (nit) The egg of a louse.

niter (ni′ter) See potassium nitrate.

nitrate (ni′trāt) A salt of nitric acid.

nitric (ni′trik) Relating to nitrogen.

nitric acid (ni′trik as′id) A colorless or yellowish corrosive liquid obtained commercially by catalytic oxidation of ammonia. Industrial uses include: the production of fertilizers (as ammonium nitrate), manufacture of explosives, as a caustic in photoengraving, in metal etching, and in cleaning of brass and copper; occupational exposure can occur by contact or by inhalation of vapors, producing such symptoms as irritation of skin, mucous membranes, eyes, and respiratory tract.

nitric oxide (ni′trik ok′sīd) A gas by-product of high-temperature combustion; it is a potent vasodilator.

nitridation (ni-trī-da′shun) Formation of nitrides through combination with nitrogen.

nitride (ni′trīd) A compound containing nitrogen and one other element, usually a more electropositive one.

nitrification (ni-trī-fī-ka′shun) **1.** The conversion of nitrogenous matter into nitrates by the action of bacteria. **2.** The treatment of a material with nitrogen or nitrogen compounds.

nitrile (ni′tril) A compound containing trivalent nitrogen attached to one carbon atom.

nitrite (ni′trīt) Any salt of nitrous acid; some (e.g., sodium nitrite) are added to certain foods as preservatives.

nitrofuran (ni-tro-fu′ran) Any of a group of compounds effective against a wide range of bacteria.

nitrofurantoin (ni-tro-fu-ran′to-in) An antibacterial compound used in the treatment of urinary tract infections.

nitrofurazone (ni-tro-fu′rah-zōn) A topical antibacterial compound.

nitrogen (ni′tro-jen) A colorless, odorless, gaseous element forming about 47% of the atmosphere by weight; symbol N, atomic number 7, atomic weight 14.

    blood urea n. (BUN) The nitrogen contained in the urea of the blood. The normal level is 10 to 20 mg per 100 ml.

    nonprotein n. (NPN) The nitrogen content of the blood exclusive of the protein bodies. A rarely used, outmoded term.

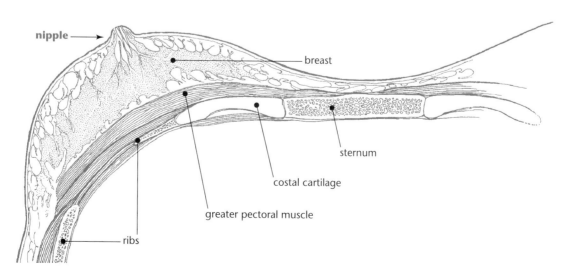

nipple

breast

sternum

costal cartilage

greater pectoral muscle

ribs

N

urea n. The portion of nitrogen derived from the urea content of a biologic sample such as urine or blood.

nitrogenous (ni-troj′ĕ-nus) Containing nitrogen.

nitroglycerin (ni-tro-glis′er-in) A thick explosive liquid used in the production of dynamite; in medicine, the solid form is used as a vasodilator in the treatment of angina pectoris. Also called trinitroglycerin.

nitrosamine (ni-trōs′ah-mēn) Any of several compounds formed by the combination of nitrates with amines; they can be synthesized in the intestinal tract from ingested nitrites and have been implicated as a cause of stomach cancer; some are carcinogenic in laboratory animals.

nitrous (ni′trus) Denoting a compound of nitrogen containing the smallest possible number of oxygen atoms.

nitrous oxide (ni′trus ok′sīd) A colorless gas of sweet taste used as a mild anesthetic. Popularly called laughing gas.

nobelium (no-be′le-um) A radioactive element; symbol No, atomic number 102, atomic weight 253.

Nocardia (no-kar′de-ah) A genus of funguslike soil-dwelling bacteria (family Nocardiaceae); the organisms are delicate, branching, often beaded, intertwining filaments that break into rod-shaped or coccoid forms; some species cause disease in humans (e.g., *Nocardia asteroides*, a cause of nocardiosis, and *Nocardia madurae*, a cause of mycetoma).

nocardiosis (no-kar-de-o′sis) Infection with the soil bacteria *Nocardia asteroides*, acquired through inhalation or by local contamination of an injury and causing pneumonia or multiple abscesses in the brain; persons most at risk are agricultural workers and patients debilitated by chronic illness.

noci- Combining form meaning hurt; pain; injury.

nociceptive (no-se-sep′tiv) Capable of receiving pain sensations.

nociceptor (no-se-sep′tor) A receptor of pain stimuli.

nociperception (no-se-per-sep′shun) Perception of painful stimuli.

noctambulism (nok-tam′bu-lizm) See somnambulism.

nocte maneque (nok′te mah-nek′ĕ) (noct. maneq.) Latin for at night and in the morning.

nocturia (nok-tu′re-ah) Urination during the night.

nodal (no′dal) Relating to a node.

node (nōd) **1.** A circumscribed mass of differentiated tissue. **2.** A swelling or protuberance, either normal or abnormal.

    atrioventricular n. A small, roughly oval node made of interwoven modified cardiac muscle fibers and situated in the right atrial wall of the heart near the orifice of the coronary sinus, just dorsal to the basal attachment of the tricuspid (right atrioventricular) valve. From the atrium it transmits the cardiac impulse, through the Purkinje fibers, to the ventricular walls. It is slightly smaller than the sinoatrial node. Also called A-V node.

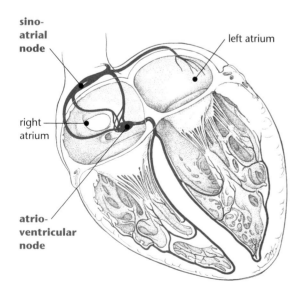

A-V n. See atrioventricular node.

    Bouchard's n. A small, hard node located in the proximal interphalangeal joint of a finger; seen in individuals with osteoarthritis. COMPARE Heberden's node.

    Cloquet's n. The highest of the deep inguinal lymph nodes, located on the lateral part of the femoral ring of the lower abdomen; when greatly enlarged, it could be mistaken for a femoral hernia.

    Delphian n. A midline node encased in fascia and positioned on the isthmus of the thyroid gland. Also called prelaryngeal node.

    gouty n. A concretion of sodium biurate generally occurring in the vicinity of joints in certain individuals afflicted with gouty inflammation.

    Heberden's n. A pea-sized swelling located in the distal interphalangeal joint of a finger; seen in individuals with osteoarthritis. COMPARE Bouchard's node.

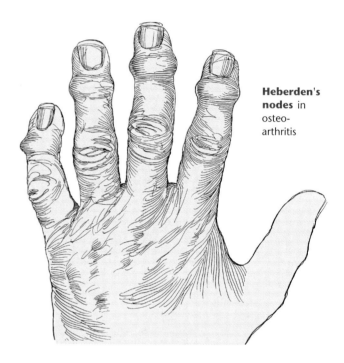

Heberden's nodes in osteoarthritis

    lymph n. A small encapsulated collection of lymphoid tissue; generally oval or kidney-shaped, 2 to 20 mm in diameter; situated interposed in the course of a lymphatic vessel, so that lymph passes through it on its way to the circulating blood; its functions are the production of lymphocytes and the removal of foreign matter from the lymph. A node may be enlarged because of a local infection, a systemic disorder, or a metastatic malignancy. Lymph nodes are most numerous in the chest, posterior abdominal wall, pelvis, neck, and proximal ends of the limbs.

    Osler's n. A small, tender, and discolored node, about the size of a pea, occurring most commonly on the pads of fingers, toes, palms, or soles in patients afflicted with infective endocarditis.

    prelaryngeal n. See Delphian node.

    n. of Ranvier The node of a myelinated axon of nerve cells (neurons) at the junction between two adjacent Schwann cells or oligodendrocytes; it occurs at regular intervals of roughly 1 mm (more precisely, the actual distance varies directly with the diameter of the axon from about 200 to 1,500 μm); the depression created by the gap in the myelin at the site of the node is filled with an acidic mucosubstance.

    S-A n. See sinoatrial node.

    sentinel n. See signal node.

    signal n. An enlarged, palpable, supraclavicular lymph node, especially on the left side, that is sometimes noted as the first presumptive sign of a malignant abdominal neoplasm. Also called sentinel node; Virchow's node.

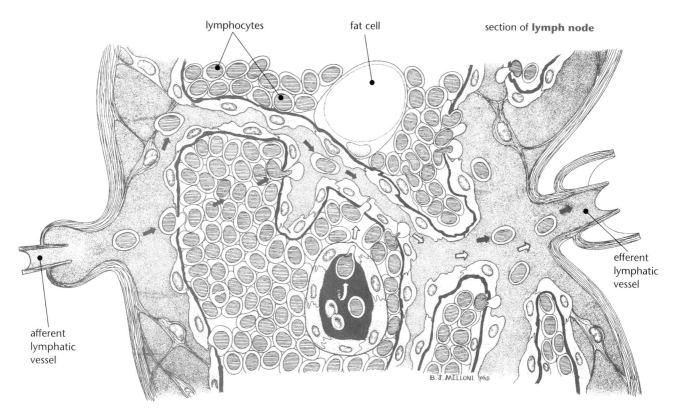

lymphocytes

fat cell

section of **lymph node**

efferent lymphatic vessel

afferent lymphatic vessel

B.J. MELLONI PhD

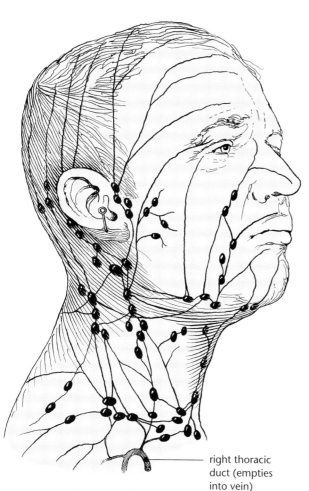

lymph nodes of the head and neck

right thoracic duct (empties into vein)

singer's n. See singer's nodule, under nodule.

sinoatrial n. An elongated elliptical node made of interwoven modified cardiac muscle fibers, situated in the wall of the right atrium near the entrance of the superior vena cava; it receives fibers from both the sympathetic and parasympathetic nervous systems and is responsible for initiating each heartbeat; often referred to as the pacemaker of the heart. It is slightly larger than the atrioventricular node. Also called S-A node; sinuatrial node; sinus node.

sinuatrial n. See sinoatrial node.

sinus n. See sinoatrial node.

syphilitic n. A localized swelling of bone resulting from syphilitic periostitis.

teacher's n. See singer's nodule, under nodule.

Virchow's n. See signal node.

nodose (no'dōs) Having nodes.

nodosity (no-dos'ĭ-te) **1.** A knotlike projection or swelling. **2.** The condition of having nodes.

nodular (nod'u-lar) **1.** Having nodules. **2.** Relating to a nodule.

nodulation (nod-u-la'shun) The condition of having nodules.

nodule (nod'ūl) A small node or closely packed aggregation of cells appearing distinct from surrounding tissue.

aggregated lymphatic n.'s Large groups of densely packed lymphocytes, present in the submucosa of the small bowel, chiefly in the ileum and distal jejunum.

Aschoff n.'s See Aschoff bodies, under body.

bronchial lymphatic n.'s Small lymph nodes on the larger branches of the bronchi, in the substance of the lungs.

cold n. Any nodule in the thyroid gland that fails to take up an administered dose of radioactive iodine as well as the rest of the gland.

gastric lymphatic n. A single mass of lymphoid tissue in the mucous lining of the stomach.

hot n. A nodule in the thyroid gland containing a higher concentration of an administered dose of radioactive iodine than the rest of the gland; generally considered to be benign.

juxta-articular n. An inflammatory nodule situated near a joint.

Lisch n. A minute, abnormal, pigmented mass (iris hamartoma) formed in the iris of persons afflicted with neurofibromatosis I.

nodose ■ nodule

lymphatic n.'s of vermiform appendix Masses of lymphoid tissue in the submucous layer of the vermiform appendix.

rheumatoid n.'s Subcutaneous nodules about 1 to 2 cm in diameter occurring in pressure-point areas, most commonly the elbow, in patients with severe rheumatoid arthritis.

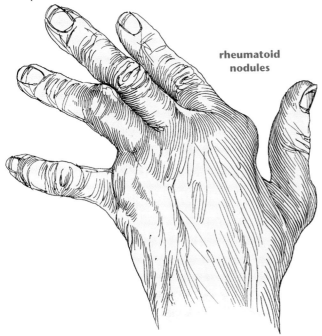

rheumatoid nodules

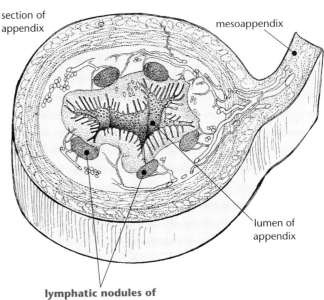

section of appendix

mesoappendix

lumen of appendix

lymphatic nodules of vermiform appendix

singer's n. A small, whitish beadlike nodule on the vocal fold, caused by chronic overuse or abuse of the vocal mechanism, as in prolonged singing, especially of high notes. Also called singer's node; teacher's node.

nodulus (nod'u-lus), pl. nod'uli Latin for nodule.

Noguchia (no-goo'che-ah) A genus of gram-negative motile bacteria (family Brucellaceae).

noma (no'mah) A rapidly destructive gangrenous disease of the mouth, affecting poorly nourished children and debilitated adults. Also called gangrenous stomatitis.

Nomina Anatomica (no'mĭ-nah an-ah-tom'ĭ-kah) (NA) A system of anatomic terminology prepared by the International Congress of Anatomists.

nomogram, nomograph (nom'o-gram, nom'o-graf) A graph showing three graduated lines of different variables arranged in such a way that a straight line connecting two known values on two of the lines intersects the unknown value on the third line; used in estimating the surface area of the body, the two known values being the person's height and weight.

nomotopic (no-mo-top'ik) Located in the normal or usual place.

nonchromogens (non-kro'mo-jens) See group III mycobacteria, under mycobacteria.

non compos (non kom'pos) An individual who is non compos mentis.

non compos mentis (non kom'pos men'tis) Latin for not of sound mind (i.e., afflicted with some form of mental defect), and hence not legally responsible.

nondisease (non-dĭ-zēz') A disease suspected but not confirmed by further appropriate examinations.

nondisjunction (non-dis-junk'shun) Failure of paired chromosomes to separate during cell division (meiosis or mitosis), so that both chromosomes are received by one daughter cell and none by the other, resulting in certain abnormal genetic conditions (e.g., Down's syndrome).

nonelectrolyte (non-e-lek'tro-lit) A substance that, when in solution, does not conduct an electric current.

noninvasive (non-in-va'siv) Not penetrating into; applied especially to diagnostic procedures that do not involve using instruments that penetrate the skin.

nonintervention (non-in-ter-ven'shun) See passive euthanasia, under euthanasia.

non-nucleated (non-nu'kle-āt-ed) Without a nucleus.

nonocclusion (non-ŏ-kloo'zhun) Condition in which a tooth of one jaw fails to make contact with its opposite of the other jaw.

nonparous (non-par'us) See nulliparous.

nonpenetrance (non-pen'ĕ-trans) Lack of clinical expression of a genetic trait even though the genetic elements that usually produce the trait are present.

nonprocedurist (non-pro-se'jur-ist) A specialist in a cognitive-oriented medical specialty such as rheumatology, geriatrics, internal medicine, and infectious diseases, as opposed to procedure-oriented specialties (e.g., surgery, dermatology, cardiology, and gastroenterology).

nomogram for estimating surface area of the body from height and weight (Dubois' formula)

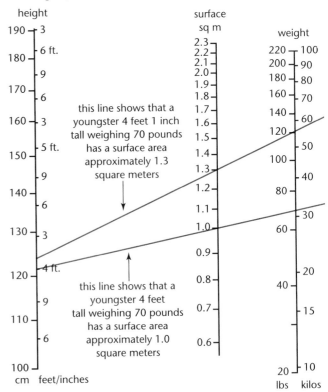

height

surface sq m

weight

this line shows that a youngster 4 feet 1 inch tall weighing 70 pounds has a surface area approximately 1.3 square meters

this line shows that a youngster 4 feet tall weighing 70 pounds has a surface area approximately 1.0 square meters

cm   feet/inches

lbs   kilos

nonproprietary (non-pro-pri′ĕ-ta-re) See nonproprietary name, under name.

nonself (non-self′) In immunology, foreign to the self; applied to molecules that are not normal constituents of the body of a given individual and are recognized as such by the individual's immune system, thereby tending to form antibodies against them.

nonunion (non-ūn′yun) Complication of a bone fracture in which healing stops short of firm union.

nonviable (non-vi′ah-bl) Not capable of living independently; applied especially to a premature infant or a fetus.

noradrenaline (nor-ah-dren′ah-lin) See norepinephrine.

norepinephrine (nor-ep-ĭ-nef′rin) (NE) Hormone secreted by the medulla of the adrenal (suprarenal) gland and by the postganglionic endings of autonomic sympathetic nerves; it is a neurotransmitter, mediating impulses of the sympathetic nervous system; it stimulates constriction of practically all blood vessels in the body. Also called noradrenaline.

    n. bitartrate The medicinal form of norepinephrine.

norethindrone (nor-eth′in-drōn) A progesterone compound used in conjunction with an estrogen in oral contraceptives and in hormone replacement therapy; used alone in the treatment of endometriosis or in absent menstrual periods (amenorrhea).

norgestrel (nor-jes′trel) A synthetic progesterone used in some oral contraceptive preparations.

norm (norm) An ideal standard or pattern regarded as typical for a particular group.

norma (nor′mah) An outline of a body part; applied especially to the skull.

    n. anterior See norma facialis.

    n. basilaris Outline of the skull viewed from below. Also called norma ventralis; norma inferior.

    n. facialis Outline of the skull viewed from the front. Also called norma anterior; norma frontalis.

    n. frontalis See norma facialis.

    n. inferior See norma basilaris.

    n. lateralis Outline of the skull viewed from the side; the profile of the skull. Also called norma temporalis.

    n. occipitalis Outline of the skull viewed from behind. Also called norma posterior.

    n. posterior See norma occipitalis.

    n. sagittalis Outline of any sagittal section through the skull.

    n. superior See norma verticalis.

    n. temporalis See norma lateralis.

    n. ventralis See norma basilaris.

    n. verticalis Outline of the skull viewed from above. Also called norma superior.

normal (nor′mal) **1.** Conformed to an established norm, standard, or pattern. **2.** In bacteriology, denoting an animal or serum that has not been experimentally exposed to or treated with any microorganism; nonimmune.

normalization (nor-mal-ĭ-za′shun) The process of making normal.

normetanephrine (nor-met-ah-nef′rin) A product of the biological breakdown (catabolism) of norepinephrine excreted in the urine.

normoblast (nor′mo-blast) Any immature nucleated red blood cell, a precursor of the erythrocyte (mature non-nucleated red blood cell). The four basic developmental stages of normoblast maturation include the pronormoblast and the basophilic, polychromatophilic, and orthochromatic normoblasts.

    acidophilic n. See orthochromatic normoblast.

    basophilic n. The second stage in the development of the normoblast, following the pronormoblast. Also called basophilic erythroblast; early erythroblast.

    orthochromatic n. The last stage in the development of the normoblast in which 80% of the hemoglobin is synthesized. Also called orthochromatic erythroblast; acidophilic erythroblast; eosinophilic erythroblast; late erythroblast; oxyphilic erythroblast; acidophilic normoblast.

    polychromatic n. The third stage in the development of the normoblast. Also called polychromatic erythroblast; intermediate erythroblast.

normocephalic (nor-mo-se-fal′ik) See mesocephalic.

normochromia (nor-mo-kro′me-ah) Normal or usual color of red blood cells.

normochromic (nor-mo-kro′mik) Relating to normochromia.

normocyte (nor′mo-sit) A red blood cell of usual or normal size.

normoglycemia (nor-mo-gli-se′me-ah) See euglycemia.

normoglycemic (nor-mo-gli-se′mik) See euglycemic.

normokalemia (nor-mo-kah-le′me-ah) The condition of having potassium concentration in the blood within the normal range.

normotensive (nor-mo-ten′siv) Characterized by a normal arterial blood pressure.

normothermia (nor-mo-ther′me-ah) **1.** A body temperature within the normal range. **2.** Environmental temperature that does not affect the activity of body cells.

normotonic (nor-mo-ton′ik) Having normal muscular tone. Also called eutonic.

normotopia (nor-mo-to′pe-ah) The state of being in the normal or usual position.

normovolemia (nor-mo-vo-le′me-ah) The condition of having a normal blood volume.

nortriptyline (nor-trip′tĭ-lēn) Antidepressant compound with sedative properties.

nose (nōz) External organ of the sense of smell and the beginning of the air passages into the lungs.

    saddle n. A nose characterized by a markedly depressed bridge. Seen in congenital syphilis or as a result of trauma.

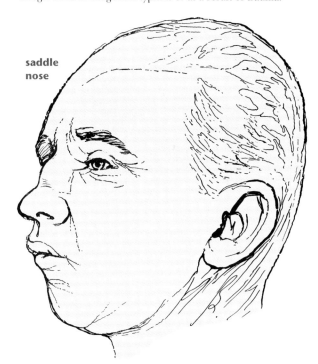

saddle nose

nosebleed (nōz′blēd) Popular name for epistaxis. Also called rhinorrhagia.

nosepiece (nōz′pēs) A microscope attachment for holding two or more interchangeable objectives.

noso- Combining form meaning disease.

nosocomial (nos-o-ko′me-al) **1.** Relating to a hospital. **2.** Originating in a hospital; applied to a newly acquired disease.

nosogenesis, nosogeny (nos-o-jen′ĕ-sis, no-soj′ĕ-ne) Obsolete terms. See pathogenesis.

nosogenic (nos-o-jen′ik) Pathogenic.

nosographer (no-sog′rah-fer) One who writes about diseases.

nosography (no-sog′rah-fe) The systematic written description of diseases.

nosology (no-sol'o-je) **1.** The science concerned with the classification of diseases. Also called nosotaxy. **2.** A classification of diseases.

nosomania (nos-o-ma'ne-ah) An unfounded, abnormal conviction that one is afflicted with a disease.

nosomycosis (nos-o-mi-ko'sis) Any disease caused by a fungus.

nosophilia (nos-o-fil'e-ah) An abnormal desire to be sick.

nosophobia (nos-o-fo'be-ah) Abnormal fear of disease. Also called pathophobia.

nosopoietic (nos-o-poi-et'ik) Pathogenic.

nosotaxy (nos'o-tak-se) See nosology (1).

nosotoxin (nos-o-tok'sin) Any toxin associated with disease.

nostril (nos'tril) One of the two external openings of the nose. Also called naris.

nostrum (nos'trum) A quack medicine.

notal (no'tal) Relating to the back.

notch (noch) **1.** An indentation or depression, usually on a bone, but occasionally applied to an organ. **2.** A deflection on a graphic curve or wave.

    acetabular n. A notch or gap on the inferior margin of the acetabulum of the hipbone; it is bridged by the transverse acetabular ligament.

    aortic n. The small downward deflection in the normal arterial pulse tracing (sphygmogram); it is synchronous with the closure of the aortic valve and immediately precedes the dicrotic wave; used as a marker to signify the end of the ejection period of blood from the ventricles (systole).

    cardiac n. of left lung A notch on the anterior border of the superior lobe of the left lung at the level of the fourth costal cartilage; it accommodates the pericardium enveloping the heart.

    cardiac n. of stomach A notch at the junction of the esophagus and the fundus of the stomach.

    clavicular n. of sternum The indentation on each side of the upper angle of the breastbone (sternum), presenting an oval facet for articulation with the sternal end of the collarbone (clavicle).

    costal n. of sternum One of the seven indentations or facets on each lateral border of the sternum, for articulation with a costal cartilage.

    fibular n. A smooth concavity on the medial side of the lower end of the tibia articulating with the fibula.

    frontal n. A small notch on the orbital margin of the frontal bone, just medial to the supraorbital notch; it transmits the supratrochlear nerve and vessels.

    Hutchinson's crescentic n. The somewhat semilunar notch on the incisal edge of upper central incisors in Hutchinson's teeth of congenital syphilis; seen also occasionally on other anterior teeth.

    interclavicular n. See suprasternal notch.

    intercondylar n. A nonarticulating depression between the condyles at the posterior surface of the distal femur; it provides attachment to the cruciate ligaments. Also called intercondylar fossa.

    jugular n. *(a)* See suprasternal notch. *(b)* The notch of the occipital bone forming the posterior boundary of the jugular foramen.

    lacrimal n. See lacrimal fossa, under fossa.

    mandibular n. The deep semilunar notch on the upper margin of the ramus of the lower jaw (mandible), between the condyle and coronoid process.

    mastoid n. A deep indentation on the inner surface of the mastoid process of the temporal bone of the skull; it provides attachment to the posterior belly of the digastric muscle.

    nasal n. The large notch on the margin of the maxilla that forms the lateral and lower boundary of the bony opening of the anterior nasal cavity. Also called nasal notch of maxilla.

    nasal n. of maxilla See nasal notch.

    pancreatic n. A deep indentation at the junction of the uncinate process and the neck of the pancreas, through which pass the superior mesenteric vessels.

    radial n. The concavity on the upper end of the lateral surface of the coronoid process of the ulna that articulates with the head of the radius.

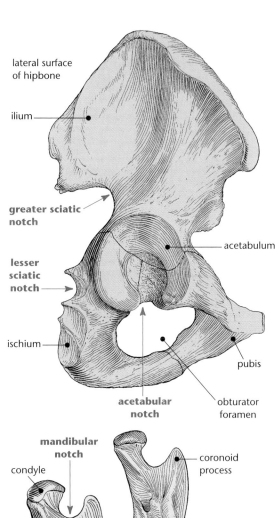

lateral surface of hipbone

ilium

greater sciatic notch

acetabulum

lesser sciatic notch

ischium

pubis

acetabular notch

obturator foramen

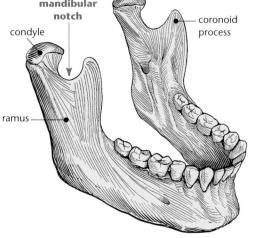

mandibular notch

condyle

coronoid process

ramus

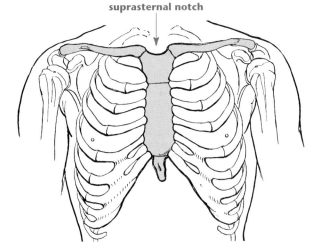

suprasternal notch

scapular n. A semicircular notch on the upper border of the shoulder blade (scapula), at the base of the coracoid process; it is converted into a foramen by the suprascapular ligament, through which passes the suprascapular nerve.

sciatic n.'s Indentations on the posterior border of the hipbone: *Greater sciatic n.*, the deep indentation on the posterior border of the hipbone at the junction of the ilium and ischium, between the posterior inferior iliac spine and the ischial spine; it is converted into the greater sciatic foramen by the sacrospinous and sacrotuberous ligaments. *Lesser sciatic n.*, the notch on the posterior border of the ischium between the ischial spine and the tuberosity; it is converted into the lesser sciatic foramen by the sacrospinous and sacrotuberous ligaments.

sternal n. See suprasternal notch.

supraorbital n. A notch or groove (occasionally a foramen) in the superior margin of the orbit, through which pass the supraorbital nerve and vessels.

suprasternal n. The broad indentation on the upper border of the breastbone (sternum), between the sternal heads of the two sternocleidomastoid muscles. Also called jugular notch; sternal notch; interclavicular notch.

tentorial n. A triangular gap in the dura mater separating the cerebellum from the posterior part of the cerebrum, through which the brainstem extends from the posterior cranial fossa at the base of the skull to the middle cranial fossa.

thyroid n. A deep notch in the middle of the upper part of the thyroid cartilage, partially separating the fused anterior borders of the laminae.

trochlear n. A large semilunar notch on the anterior surface of the proximal end of the ulna, between the olecranon and coronoid processes; it articulates with the trochlea of the humerus at the elbow joint.

ulnar n. A smooth concavity on the medial side of the lower end of the radius that articulates with the head of the ulna.

vertebral n. One of two deep-pocketed indentations (superior and inferior) above and below the border of the pedicle of a vertebra on each side; the notches of two adjacent vertebrae form an intervertebral foramen, which transmits the spinal nerve and vessels.

notochord (no′to-kord) A supporting rod of cells in the embryo of all chordates; in vertebrates, it is replaced partly or wholly by the skull and vertebral column.

noxa (nok′sah), pl. nox′ae Anything that is harmful or injurious to health.

noxious (nok′shus) Harmful or injurious to health.

nucha (nu′kah) See nape.

nuchal (nu′kal) Relating to the back of the neck.

nuclear (nu′kle-ar) Relating to a nucleus.

nuclease (nu′kle-ās) An enzyme that promotes the breakdown of nucleic acid (e.g., DNA and RNA) into nucleotides.

nucleated (nu′kle-āt-ed) Having a nucleus.

nuclei (nu′kle-i) Plural of nucleus.

nucleic acid (nu-kle′ik as′id) Any of a family of macromolecules, either DNA or various types of RNA, present in all living organisms and consisting mainly of a sugar moiety (pentose or deoxypentose), nitrogenous bases (purines and pyrimidines), and phosphoric acid.

nucleo-, nucl- Combining forms meaning nucleus.

nucleocapsid (nu-kle-o-kap′sid) The protein capsule of a virus together with its enclosed nucleic acid; it is the structural unit of a virus and may constitute the whole of a simple virus or part of a complex one.

nucleolonema (nu-kle-o-lo-ne′mah) A coarse branching strand forming a network within the nucleolus of a cell; contains genes involved in transcription of ribosomal RNA.

nucleolus (nu-kle′o-lus), pl. nucle′oli A spherical organelle within the nucleus of a cell; it is an active center of RNA and protein synthesis, as well as an important center for the formation of ribosomes.

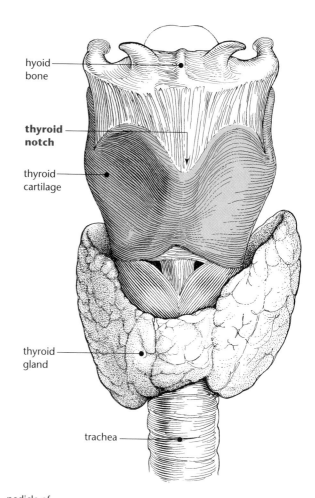

hyoid bone

thyroid notch

thyroid cartilage

thyroid gland

trachea

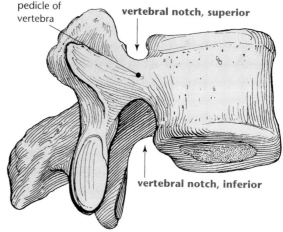

pedicle of vertebra

vertebral notch, superior

vertebral notch, inferior

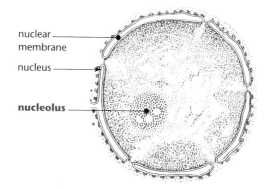

nuclear membrane

nucleus

nucleolus

chromatin n. See karyosome.

false n. See karyosome.

nucleon (nu′kle-on) One of the constituent particles of an atomic nucleus (i.e., a proton or a neutron).

nucleoplasm (nu′kle-o-plazm) The protoplasm of a cell nucleus.

nucleorrhexis (nu-kle-o-rek′sis) The breaking up of a cell nucleus.

nucleosidase (nu-kle-o-si′dās) Enzyme that promotes the splitting of a nucleoside into sugar and a purine or pyrimidine base.

nucleoside (nu′kle-o-sid) Compound composed of a purine or pyrimidine base attached to a sugar (pentose, ribose, or deoxyribose).

nucleotidase (nu-kle-o-ti′dās) Enzyme that promotes the splitting of a nucleotide into nucleosides and phosphoric acid.

nucleotide (nu′kle-o-tīd) One of the compounds into which nucleic acid splits on hydrolysis.

nucleotoxin (nu-kle-o-tok′sin) A toxin affecting the cell nucleus.

nucleus (nu′kle-us) pl. nu′clei **1.** The complex, usually spherical protoplasmic body near the center of the cell that is an essential organelle controlling the activities of the cell, including metabolism, growth, and reproduction; it contains the chromosomes and is surrounded by a pore-studded nuclear membrane, through which substances can pass to and from the surrounding cytoplasm. **2.** A localized mass of gray matter composed of cell bodies of excitable nerve cells (neurons) within the brain and spinal cord, where nerve fibers interconnect. **3.** The heavy, central, positively charged portion of the atom (composed of protons and neutrons); it constitutes the mass of

the atom, about which the electrons revolve in orbit. **4.** A central core, mass, or focal point of a structure.

ambiguus n. A motor nucleus composed of large multipolar cells that send fibers into the glossopharyngeal, vagus, and accessory nerves to supply the pharynx and larynx.

basal nuclei Subcortical nuclear masses of gray matter located in the white matter of each cerebral hemisphere; they serve as important links along various motor pathways of the central nervous system; they include the caudate, lentiform, and amygdaloid nuclei and the claustrum. Also called basal ganglia.

caudate n. A long horseshoe-shaped mass of gray matter closely adjacent to the wall of the lateral ventricle throughout its entirety and composed of three portions designated head, body, and tail; the tail merges with the amygdaloid body in the temporal lobe of the cerebrum.

cochlear n. The nucleus located on the surface of the inferior cerebellar peduncle at the junction of the medulla oblongata and the pons; it receives incoming fibers from the bipolar cells in the spiral ganglion of the cochlea of the inner ear.

dorsal motor n. of vagus nerve A nucleus situated in the floor of the fourth ventricle that sends fibers through the medulla oblongata to the vagus and spinal accessory nerves, which end in vagal sympathetic plexuses in the chest and abdomen.

n. of hypoglossal nerve A cranial nerve nucleus with fibers directed to the lower border of the pyramid to supply the tongue.

hypothalamic nuclei Nuclear aggregations in the hypothala-

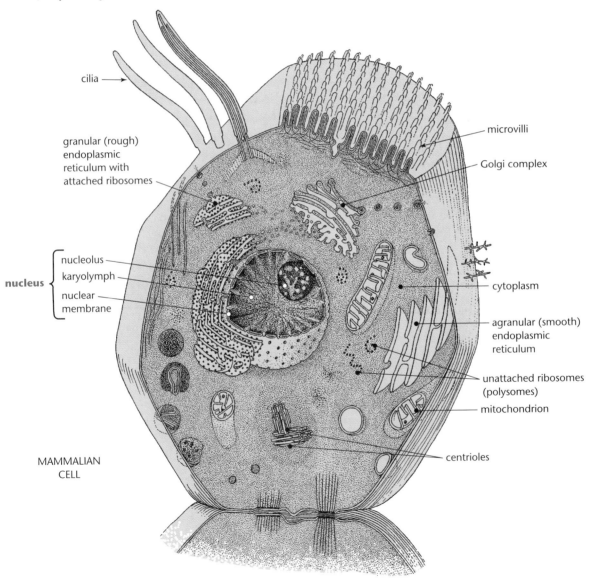

cilia

granular (rough) endoplasmic reticulum with attached ribosomes

nucleus {
nucleolus
karyolymph
nuclear membrane

MAMMALIAN CELL

microvilli

Golgi complex

cytoplasm

agranular (smooth) endoplasmic reticulum

unattached ribosomes (polysomes)

mitochondrion

centrioles

nucleon ■ nucleus

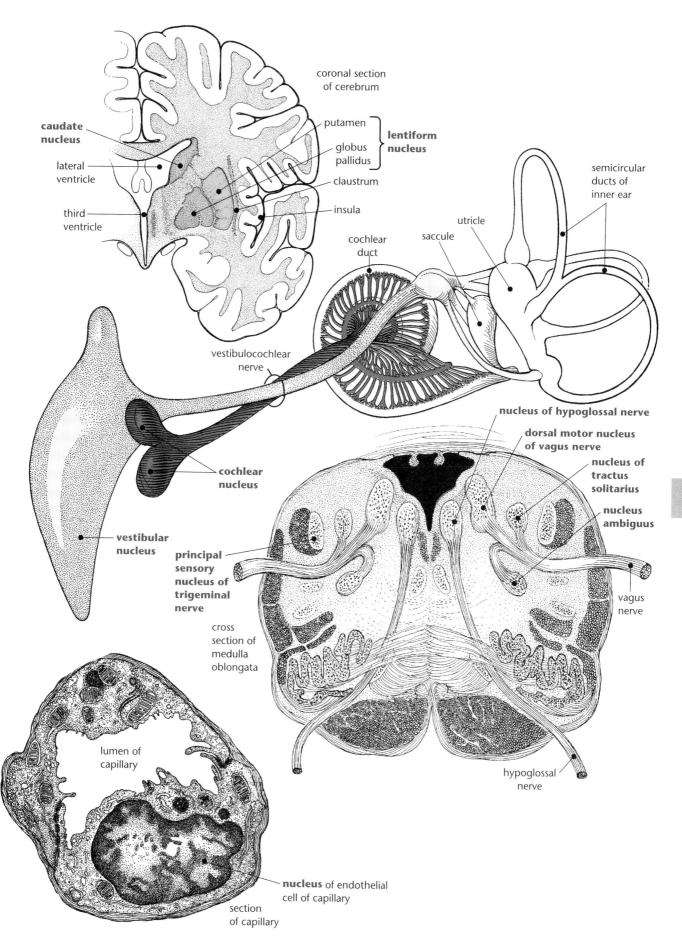

coronal section
of cerebrum

**caudate
nucleus**

putamen

globus
pallidus

**lentiform
nucleus**

lateral
ventricle

claustrum

third
ventricle

insula

semicircular
ducts of
inner ear

utricle

saccule

cochlear
duct

vestibulocochlear
nerve

nucleus of hypoglossal nerve

**dorsal motor nucleus
of vagus nerve**

**nucleus of
tractus
solitarius**

**nucleus
ambiguus**

**cochlear
nucleus**

**vestibular
nucleus**

**principal
sensory
nucleus of
trigeminal
nerve**

vagus
nerve

cross
section of
medulla
oblongata

hypoglossal
nerve

lumen of
capillary

nucleus of endothelial
cell of capillary

section
of capillary

N

nucleus ■ nucleus

mus of the brain, divided according to connectivity and histochemical studies into preoptic, supraoptic, ventromedial, infundibular (arcuate), lateral tuberal, mamillary, lateral hypothalamic, posterior, paraventricular, and dorsomedial nuclei.

inferior colliculus n. An ovoid cellular mass surrounded by a thin cortex that serves as a relay in transmitting auditory impulses to thalamic levels and is involved in acoustic reflexes.

lenticular n. See lentiform nucleus.

lentiform n. A mass of gray matter the size and shape of a Brazil nut, deeply buried in the white matter of the cerebral hemisphere; a vertical plate of white matter divides the nucleus into a large lateral portion (putamen) and a smaller medial portion (globus pallidus); laterally it is covered by a thin external capsule and medially it is separated from the thalamus and caudate nucleus by the internal capsule. Also called lenticular nucleus.

motor n. of facial nerve A nucleus that gives rise to fibers that innervate the voluntary facial muscles.

motor n. of trigeminal nerve A nucleus from which fibers run laterally with the mandibular nerve to innervate the muscles of mastication.

oculomotor n. An elongated nucleus located in front of the cerebral aqueduct that contains a number of cell groups that are correlated with the motor distribution of the oculomotor nerve.

principal sensory n. of trigeminal nerve A cranial sensory nerve nucleus that receives fibers which mediate pain and temperature for the head and face.

n. pulposus A mass of fibers forming the inner core of an intervertebral disk, enclosed in many layers of fibrous tissue (annulus fibrosus); it is viscous at birth, becoming fibrocartilaginous with age. Major strains can cause displacement (herniation) of the nucleus

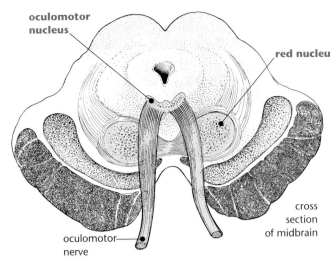

cross section of midbrain

pulposus through the annulus fibrosus, most commonly in the lumbar region, often in a posterolateral direction.

red n. A large oval nucleus situated in the midbrain; it receives fibers mainly from the deep cerebellar nuclei and the cerebral cortex.

superior colliculus n. A laminated nucleus forming the top half of the tectum (roof of the midbrain) that serves as a primary relay in transmitting visual impulses.

thalamic nuclei Nuclear aggregations in the thalamus of the brain that are connected by well-defined fiber bundles with the main subcortical parts of the nervous system; also have reciprocal connections with many parts of the cerebral cortex.

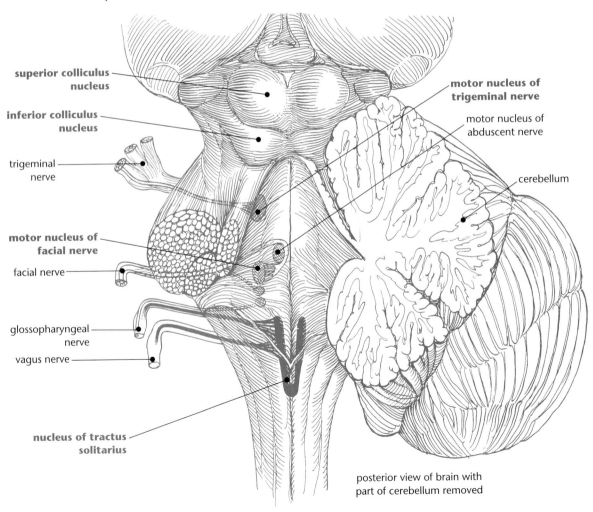

posterior view of brain with part of cerebellum removed

n. of tractus solitarius The nucleus of the solitary tract that receives visceral afferent fibers from the facial, glossopharyngeal, and vagus nerves; it is a slender nucleus extending the length of the medulla oblongata.

vagal nuclei Nuclei in the medulla oblongata that are connected to the vagus nerve; they include the dorsal nucleus, the ambiguus nucleus, the nucleus of tractus solitarius, and the principal sensory nucleus of trigeminal nerve.

vestibular n. A nucleus located in the floor of the fourth ventricle that receives fibers from the bipolar ganglion cells of the vestibular nerve of the inner ear.

nulligravida (nul-ĭ-grav′ĭ-dah) A woman who has never been pregnant.

nullipara (nu-lip′ah-rah) A woman who has not delivered an offspring weighing 500 grams or more, or of a gestation length of 20 weeks or longer.

nulliparity (nul-ĭ-par′ĭ-te) Condition of not having borne children.

nulliparous (nuh-lip′ah-rus) Never having borne children. Also called nonparous.

numb (num) The state of being without sensation.

number (num′ber) (No) A symbol expressing a specified quantity or a definite value in a fixed order derived by counting.

accession n. A number sequentially assigned to each order as it is entered into medical records.

atomic n. (Z) The number in the periodic system of elements that represents the number of protons in an atomic nucleus (the positive charge on the nucleus), and in a neutral atom, the number of electrons outside the atomic nucleus. See periodic table, under table.

Avogadro's n. The number of molecules or particles in 1 gram mole of any compound; it equals 6.022×10^{23}.

Brinell hardness n. (BHN) A number expressing the hardness of a dental material, derived by measuring the diameter of a dent made by pressing a standard carbide ball into the surface of a material under a specified load.

electronic n. The number of electrons present in the outermost orbit of an element.

Knoop hardness n. (KHN) A number representing the hardness of a material (e.g., tooth structure and dental materials), determined by the degree of penetration by a diamond indenting tool.

mass n. (A) The nearest integer to the number expressing the sum of protons and neutrons in the atomic nucleus of an isotope; indicated as a prefix superscript (e.g., ^{16}O).

numbness (num′nes) Insensitivity in a part of the body.

nummiform (num′ĭ-form) See nummular (1).

nummular (num′u-lar) 1. Discoid; shaped like a coin; applied especially to a dermatitis. Also called nummiform. 2. Arranged like a stack of coins.

nummulation (num-u-la′shun) Formation of disk-shaped masses.

nurse (ners) 1. A person trained to care for the sick, disabled, or enfeebled. 2. To breast-feed. 3. To care for or tend one unable to provide for his own needs.

Group	I	II												III	IV	V	VI	VII	O

METALS NONMETALS

Period																			
1	H 1																		He 2
2	Li 3	Be 4												B 5	C 6	N 7	O 8	F 9	Ne 10
3	Na 11	Mg 12				atomic numbers								Al 13	Si 14	P 15	S 16	Cl 17	Ar 18
4	K 19	Ca 20	Sc 21	Ti 22	V 23	Cr 24	Mn 25	Fe 26	Co 27	Ni 28	Cu 29	Zn 30		Ga 31	Ge 32	As 33	Se 34	Br 35	Kr 36
5	Rb 37	Sr 38	Y 39	Zr 40	Nb 41	Mo 42	Tc 43	Ru 44	Rh 45	Pd 46	Ag 47	Cd 48		In 49	Sn 50	Sb 51	Te 52	I 53	Xe 54
6	Cs 55	Ba 56	* 57-71	Hf 72	Ta 73	W 74	Re 75	Os 76	Ir 77	Pt 78	Au 79	Hg 80		Ti 81	Pb 82	Bi 83	Po 84	At 85	Rn 86
7	Fr 87	Ra 88	** 89-103	Rf 104	Ha 105														
*	lanthanid elements (rare earth)	La 57	Ce 58	Pr 59	Nd 60	Pm 61	Sm 62	Eu 63	Gd 64	Tb 65	Dy 66	Ho 67	Er 68	Tm 69	Yb 70	Lu 71			
**	actinide elements	Ac 89	Th 90	Pa 91	U 92	Np 93	Pu 94	Am 95	Cm 96	Bk 97	Cf 98	Es 99	Fm 100	Md 101	No 102	Lw 103			

nulligravida ■ **nurse**

N

certified n. (CN) A registered nurse who has met the criteria for certification established by the American Nurses Association.

charge n. A nurse in charge of supervising the nursing staff of a hospital unit. Also called head nurse.

clinical n. specialist A nurse with an advanced degree and training in a particular specialized area of nursing.

community health n. See public health nurse.

graduate n. A nurse who is a graduate of a school of nursing, generally applied to one who has not been licensed or registered to practice.

head n. See charge nurse.

licensed practical n. (LPN) A licensed nurse who has had one year of vocational training and is required by state law to work under the supervision of a registered nurse or a physician. Also called licensed vocational nurse (LVN).

licensed vocational n. (LVN) See licensed practical nurse.

occupational health n. A nurse who has been trained in occupational health to promote and maintain health in the workplace and to provide treatment for injury or disease when necessary; usually has more autonomy than a hospital-based nurse; functions do not include prescribing drugs or performing surgical procedures.

office n. A registered nurse employed in a physician's office either to perform or to assist in performing certain procedures.

operating room n. A member of the operating room nursing staff who provides assistance in the operating room.

practical n. A nurse who has had practical experience in nursing care; distinguished from licensed practical nurse.

private duty n., private n. A nurse who is not a member of a hospital staff but is privately employed to provide nursing care to a patient in a hospital or elsewhere.

public health n. A registered nurse employed by a public health agency to provide educational and preventive programs or treatment and diagnostic services to the community, usually working under the supervision of a public health official. Also called community health nurse.

registered n. (RN) A graduate nurse registered and licensed to practice by a state board authority.

scrub n. A nurse who dons sterile gown and gloves to assist the surgeon at the operating table.

visiting n. A nurse who provides nursing care to patients in their homes.

wet n. A woman who breast-feeds another woman's infant.

nurse anesthetist (ners ah-nes′thĕ-tist) A registered nurse who has completed postgraduate training in the administration of anesthesia.

nurse-midwife (ners mid′wīf) A registered nurse formally educated to provide care to pregnant women, including delivery and related health services.

nurse practitioner (ners prak-tish′un-er) A registered nurse who has advanced skills in assessing health or illness status through history taking and physical examination and who is specially trained in designing and implementing a nursing care plan.

nursing (ners′ing) 1. Activities that constitute the duties of a nurse. 2. Breast-feeding.

nursing home (ners′ing hōm) A residential health care institution for providing nursing care and limited medical care (usually long-term) for persons who do not require hospitalization.

nutrient (nu′tre-ent) A nourishing constituent of food.

nutrition (nu-trish′un) 1. The process through which a living organism takes in and assimilates food for growth and replacement of tissues. 2. The study of foods in relation to the requirements of living organisms.

enteral n. Introduction of nutrients via a tube inserted directly into the stomach or duodenum.

total parenteral n. (TPN) Intravenous infusion of nutrients in place of oral intake. Also called total parenteral alimentation.

nyctalopia (nik-tah-lo′pe-ah) Difficulty seeing in reduced illumination. Also called night blindness; day sight.

nycto-, nyct- Combining forms meaning night; nocturnal.

nyctophobia (nik-to-fo′be-ah) Abnormally exaggerated, unreasonable fear of darkness.

nymph (nimf) The wingless, immature stage in the development of certain insects immediately after hatching.

nympha (nim′fah), pl. nym′phae See labia minora, under labium.

nympho-, nymph- Combining forms meaning the labia minora.

nympholabia (nim-fo-la′be-ah) Relating to the labia minora and labia majora.

nymphomania (nim-fo-ma′ne-ah) A female psychosexual disorder characterized by excessive and insatiable sexual desire.

nymphomaniac (nim-fo-ma′ne-ak) A woman affected with nyphomania.

nymphoncus (nim-fong′kus) Abnormal enlargement or swelling of the labia minora.

nymphotomy (nim-fot′o-me) A surgical cut into a minor lip (labium minora) of the vulva.

nystagmic (nis-tag′mik) Relating to jerky twitching of the eyeball.

nystagmograph (nis-tag′mo-graf) Apparatus for recording graphically the movements of the eyeball in nystagmus.

nystagmography (nis-tag-mog′rah-fe) The act of recording nystagmic movements of the eyes with a nystagmograph.

nystagmoid (nis-tag′moid) Resembling nystagmus.

nystagmus (nis-tag′mus) Involuntary movements of the eyeballs in either a rotary, horizontal, or vertical direction; most commonly it is a rhythmic jerking with a fast and slow component, and is described by the direction of the quick component.

nystatin (nis′tah-tin) Antifungal drug used in the treatment of candidiasis.

nyxis (nik′sis) A puncture.

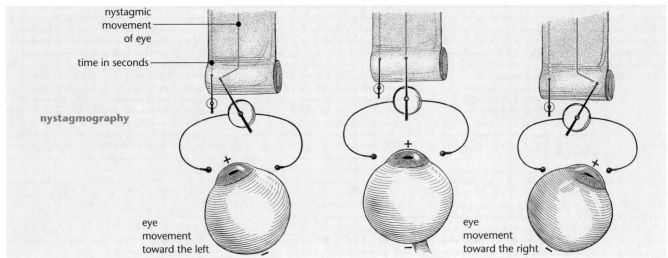

O

obdormition (ob-dor-mish′un) Numbness of a body part caused by pressure on the sensory nerve innervating it.

obelion (o-be′le-on) A point on the skull where the sagittal suture is crossed by a line connecting the two parietal foramina; a craniometric point.

obesity (o-bēs′ĭ-te) Excessive accumulation of fat in the body.

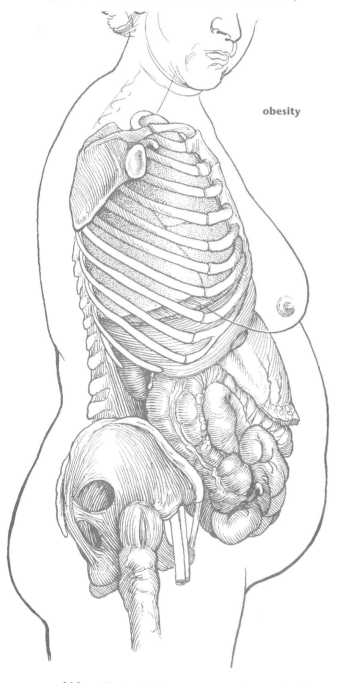

obesity

morbid o. Obesity that is so severe as to threaten health and limit activity.

object (ob-jekt′) **1.** Anything perceptible through any of the senses. **2.** A person or thing arousing any type of emotion in an observer.

sex o. A person or thing that arouses sexual feelings in another.

test o. Device for determining the magnifying power of a microscope.

objective (ob-jek′tiv) The lens or arrangement of lenses in an optical system (e.g., microscope) that receives light from the field of view and forms the first image; so named because it is nearest the object.

immersion o. A high-power objective designed to be used with oil or other liquid instead of air between its front lens and cover glass.

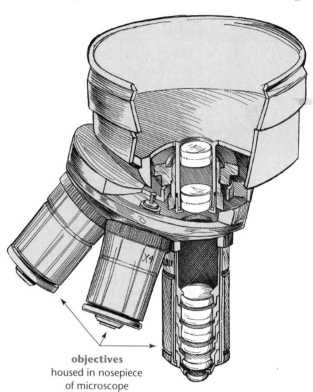

objectives
housed in nosepiece
of microscope

obligate (ob′lĭ-gāt) Capable of surviving in only one environment; applied to certain parasites. COMPARE facultative.

oblique (ŏ-blēk′) Having a slanting direction; deviating from the vertical or horizontal.

obliquity (ob-lik′wĭ-te) See synclitism.

obliquus (ob-li′kwus) Latin for oblique.

oblongata (ob-long-gah′tă) Elongated.

obsession (ob-sesh′un) A persistently recurring and unwanted idea that cannot be eliminated.

obsessive-compulsive (ob-ses′iv kom-pul′siv) Having an obsessive-compulsive disorder. See also obsessive-compulsive disorder, under disorder.

obstetric, obstetrical (ob-stet′rik, ob-stet′re-kal) Relating to obstetrics.

obstetrician (ob-stĕ-trish′un) A physician who is a specialist in obstetrics.

obstetrics (ob-stet′riks) (OB) The branch of medicine concerned principally with the management of pregnancy, labor, and the phenomena following childbirth to complete involution of the uterus.

obstipation (ob-stĭ-pa′shun) Persistent constipation that does not respond to treatment.

obstruent (ob′stroo-ent) 1. Causing obstruction. 2. An agent having such an effect.

obtund (ob-tund′) To diminish pain or the perception of touch.

obtundent (ob-tun′dent) An agent that diminishes perception of touch or pain.

obturation (ob-tu-ra′shun) An obstruction or occlusion; a stoppage.

obturator (ob′too-ra-tor) 1. In anatomy, any structure that closes an opening. 2. A prosthetic device for closing a defect in the hard palate. 3. An instrument used for closing the opening of a hollow tube (cannula) during its insertion into the body.

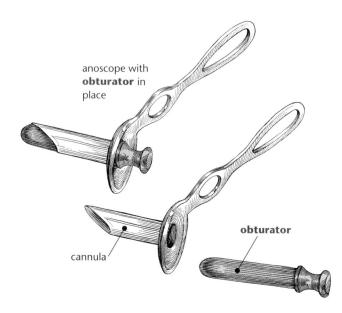

anoscope with **obturator** in place

cannula

obturator

obtusion (ob-too′zhun) Dulling of normal sensibility.

occipital (ok-sip′ĭ-tal) Relating to the back of the head. See table of bones.

occipitalization (ok-sip-ĭ-tal-ĭ-za′shun) Fusion of the first cervical vertebra and the occipital bone of the skull.

occipitoatloid (ok-sip-ĭ-to-at′loid) Relating to the occipital bone and the first cervical vertebra.

occipitobregmatic (ok-sip-ĭ-to-breg-mat′ik) Relating to the occiput and the bregma (a craniometric point); applied to a measurement of the skull.

occipitomental (ok-sip-ĭ-to-men′tal) Relating to the back of the head and the chin.

occipitoparietal (ok-sip-ĭ-to-pah-ri′e-tal) Relating to the occipital and parietal bones of the skull.

occipitotemporal (ok-sip-ĭ-to-tem′po-ral) Relating to the occipital and temporal bones of the skull.

occiput (ok′sĭ-put) The lower back of the head.

occlude (ŏ-klōōd′) 1. To close or obstruct. 2. In dentistry, to bring together the upper and lower teeth.

occluder (ŏ-klōōd′er) In dentistry, a name given to a type of articulator.

occlusal (ŏ-klōō′zal) 1. Relating to a closure. 2. Relating to the chewing surfaces of teeth.

occlusion (o-klōō′zhun) 1. The process of closing. 2. The state of being closed. 3. The contact of upper and lower teeth in any functional relation. 4. In chemistry, the absorption of a gas by a metal.

    abnormal o. See malocclusion.

    afunctional o. Any type of malocclusion that prevents proper chewing.

    centric o. Occlusion in which the upper and lower teeth are together in a normal, relaxed manner, with the upper and lower jaws in centric relation.

    coronary o. Impedance of blood circulation of the heart wall, usually caused by thrombosis.

    eccentric o. Any occlusion of the teeth other than centric occlusion.

    hepatic vein o. Blockage of the hepatic veins usually by tumor infiltration or by thrombosis, causing liver enlargement, portal hypertension, and ascites. Also called Budd-Chiari syndrome; Chiari syndrome.

    lingual o. See linguoclusion.

    pathogenic o. An abnormal occlusal relationship of the teeth capable of incurring damage to supporting tissues.

    protrusive o. Protrusion of the lower jaw from centric position.

occlusive (ŏ-klōō′siv) Closing; causing obstruction.

occlusometer (ok-loo-som′ĕ-ter) See gnathodynamometer.

occult (ŏ-kult′) Hidden (e.g., a concealed internal hemorrhage).

Occupational Safety and Health Administration (OSHA) The primary regulatory agency of the federal government that determines which of the standards proposed by the National Institute for Occupational Safety and Health (NIOSH) will be adapted and enforced. Its standards become law and its officers can inspect the workplace at any time to determine the status of health and safety and to cite employers for noncompliance with the law.

ochrodermia (o-kro-der′me-ah) Yellowish discoloration of the skin.

ochronosis (o-kro-no′sis) Deposition of homogentisic acid in connective tissue and cartilage causing a characteristic blue-black pigmentation of the ears, nose, and cheeks; observed in certain metabolic disorders (e.g., alkaptonuria); has also been reported to occur on exposure to certain chemicals (e.g., phenol and benzene derivatives).

ocrylate (ok′rĭ-lāt) A tissue adhesive used in surgery.

octa-, octi-, octo- Combining forms meaning eight.

octamethyl pyrophosphoramide (ok-tah-meth′il pir-o-fos-for′ah-mid) (OMPA) A systemic insecticide for plants.

octan (ok′tan) Occurring every eighth day; applied to certain recurring fevers.

octapeptide (ok-tah-pep′tid) A peptide composed of eight amino acid residues (e.g., the hormones oxytocin and vasopressin).

octavalent (ok-tah-va′lent) Having the combining power of eight hydrogen atoms.

ocular (ok′u-lar) 1. Relating to the eye. 2. The eyepiece of a microscope.

ocularist (ok′u-lar-ist) One who designs, constructs, and fits artificial eyes.

oculi (ok′u-li) Plural of oculus.

oculist (ok′u-list) Obsolete term for ophthalmologist.

oculo-, ocul- Combining forms meaning eye.

oculocerebrorenal (ok′u-lo-ser′ĕ-bro-re′nal) Relating to the eyes, brain, and kidneys.

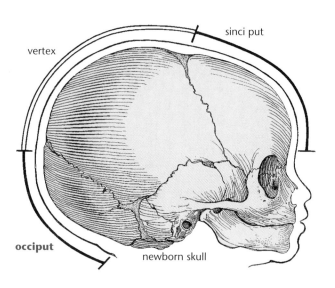

vertex

sinci put

occiput

newborn skull

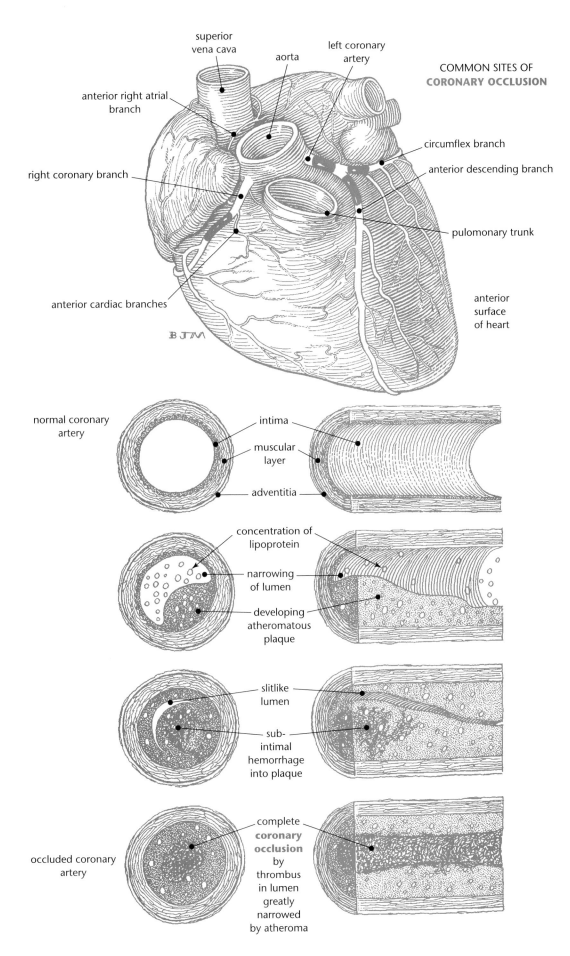

superior
vena cava

aorta

left coronary
artery

COMMON SITES OF
CORONARY OCCLUSION

anterior right atrial
branch

circumflex branch

anterior descending branch

right coronary branch

pulomonary trunk

anterior cardiac branches

anterior
surface
of heart

BJM

normal coronary
artery

intima

muscular
layer

adventitia

concentration of
lipoprotein

narrowing
of lumen

developing
atheromatous
plaque

slitlike
lumen

sub-
intimal
hemorrhage
into plaque

occluded coronary
artery

complete
**coronary
occlusion**
by
thrombus
in lumen
greatly
narrowed
by atheroma

O

oculocutaneous (ok-u-lo-ku-ta′ne-us) Relating to the eyes and the skin.

oculography (ok-u-log′ra-fe) The graphic recording of eye positions and movements.

oculogyria (ok-u-lo-ji′re-ah) Rotation of the eyes.

oculogyric (ok-u-lo-ji′rik) Relating to rotation of the eyeballs.

oculomotor (ok-u-lo-mo′tor) Relating to movements of the eyeballs. See also table of nerves.

oculomycosis (ok-u-lo-mi-ko′sis) See ophthalmomycosis.

oculonasal (ok-u-lo-na′zal) Relating to the eyes and nose.

oculopathy (ok-u-lop′ah-the) See ophthalmopathy.

oculus (ok′u-lus) (O), pl. oc′uli Latin for eye.
    o. dexter (OD) Right eye.
    o. sinister (OS) Left eye.
    o. uterque (OU) The two eyes.

odditis (od-di′tis) Inflammation of the junction between the duodenum and common bile duct.

odontectomy (o-don-tek′to-me) Extraction of a tooth by first removing the bone around its roots.

odontalgia (o-don-tal′je-ah) Toothache.

odontic (o-don′tik) Dental.

odontoblast (o-don′to-blast) A specialized cell that takes part in the formation of dentin in teeth; odontoblasts are present in the papilla of a developing tooth, line the pulp cavity, and may form secondary dentin throughout life.

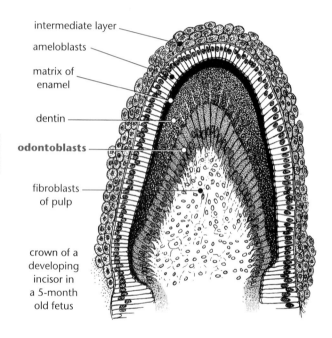

intermediate layer
ameloblasts
matrix of enamel
dentin
odontoblasts
fibroblasts of pulp
crown of a developing incisor in a 5-month old fetus

odontoblastoma (o-don-to-blas-to′mah) A tumor composed chiefly of odontoblasts.

odontoclast (o-don′to-klast) A multinucleated cell believed to be involved in the absorption of the roots of primary teeth.

odontodynia (o-don-to-din′e-ah) Toothache.

odontodysplasia (o-don-to-dis-pla′ze-ah) A developmental defect of tooth formation, resulting in an abnormally shaped, partly erupted tooth with thin, poorly calcified enamel and dentin; the abnormally large pulp chamber occupies most of the tooth; may affect one tooth or include adjacent teeth of primary or secondary dentition; anterior maxillary teeth are most commonly involved. Cause is unknown. Also called odontogenesis imperfecta.

odontogenesis (o-don-to-jen′ĕ-sis) Formation and development of teeth. Also called odontogeny.
    o. imperfecta See odontodysplasia.

odontogeny (o-don-toj′ĕ-ne) See odontogenesis.

odontoid (o-don′toid) Tooth-shaped (e.g., the odontoid process of the second cervical vertebra).

odontology (o-don-tol′o-je) See dentistry.
    forensic o. See forensic dentistry, under dentistry.

odontolysis (o-don-tol′ĭ-sis) Erosion of teeth.

odontoma (o-don-to′mah) An abnormal mass that may or may not resemble a tooth, composed of all tissues involved in tooth formation; the most common clinical manifestation is impacted teeth with retention of primary teeth.

odontopathy (o-don-top′ah-the) Any disease of the teeth.

odontoprisis (o-don-to-pri′sis) See bruxism.

odontorrhagia (o-don-to-ra′je-ah) Profuse bleeding from the tooth socket after a tooth extraction.

odontoscope (o-don′to-skōp) An apparatus for projecting an enlarged image of the oral cavity onto a screen.

odontotomy (o-don-tot′o-me) Cutting into a tooth.

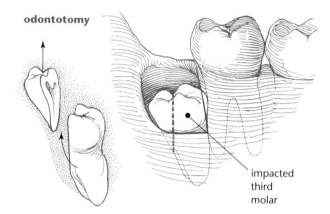

odontotomy

impacted third molar

odor (o′dor) Any emanation perceived by the sense of smell.

odoriferous (o-dor-if′er-us) Giving off an odor.

odorimeter (o-dor-im′ĕ-ter) Instrument for determining the intensity of odors.

odorimetry (o-dor-im′ĕ-tre) Measurement of the relative intensity of odors.

odynacusis (o-din-ah-ku′sis) Hypersensitivity of the organ of hearing (spiral organ of Corti) so that noises cause undue discomfort.

odyno-, odyn- Combining forms meaning pain.

odynometer (o-din-om′ĕ-ter) See algesimeter.

odynophagia (od-ĭ-no-fa′je-ah) Pain on swallowing.

oersted (er′sted) (H) Unit of magnetic field intensity.

Oesophagostomum (e-sof-ah-gos′to-mum) A genus of parasitic roundworms; the larvae of some species infest the walls of human intestines, forming nodules and sometimes causing dysentery-like symptoms; the adults inhabit the intestinal lumen.

oestrid (est′rid) Any of various two-winged botflies; the larval forms are parasitic in animals and humans.

Oestrus (es′trus) Genus of tissue-invading botflies.

official (ŏ-fish′al) In pharmacology, authorized by, or listed in, the U.S. Pharmacopeia or the National Formulary.

officinal (ŏ-fis′ĭ-nal) Kept in stock; available without special preparation; applied to pharmaceuticals.

ohm (ōm) (Ω) Unit of electrical resistance equal to that of any conductor allowing 1 ampere of current to pass from 1 volt across its terminals.

-oid Suffix meaning resemblance (e.g., ameboid).

oil (oil) Any of several substances that are viscous, flammable, unctuous, and not miscible with water but soluble in several organic solvents; classified according to their origin as animal, mineral, or vegetable oils.
    castor o. Oil obtained from the seeds of a plant (*Ricinus communis*); used as a laxative and externally as an emollient for skin disorders.

cod liver o. Oil obtained from fresh livers of codfish; a rich source of vitamins A and D.

mineral o. Liquid petrolatum, a mixture of liquid hydrocarbons obtained from petroleum; used as a vehicle for drugs and as a laxative. Also called white mineral oil; liquid paraffin.

pine o. Volatile oil (crude turpentine) produced by the destructive distillation of pine wood; used as a deodorant and disinfectant.

red o. See oleic acid.

o. of vitriol See sulfuric acid.

wheat germ o. Oil obtained from the embryo of the wheat kernel; a rich source of vitamin E.

white mineral o. See mineral oil.

o. of wintergreen See methyl salicylate, under methyl.

ointment (oint′ment) Any of various semisolid preparations used as a vehicle for external medication, as an emollient, or as a cosmetic.

oleate (o′le-āt) **1.** A salt of oleic acid. **2.** A pharmaceutical preparation containing an alcohol or metallic base and oleic acid.

olecranon (o-lek′rah-non) The prominent bony process of the ulna forming the tip of the elbow. Popularly called point of the elbow; tip of the elbow.

oleic (o-le′ik) Relating to oil.

oleic acid (o-le′ik as′id) An unsaturated fatty acid with a lardlike scent; a constituent of most of the common fats and oils; used in the preparation of lotions and as a pharmaceutical solvent. Also called red oil.

oleo- Combining form meaning oil.

oleometer (o-le-om′ĕ-ter) Instrument for measuring the specific gravity of oils.

oleoresin (o-le-o-rez′in) **1.** A natural compound containing oil and resin, present in some plants (e.g., pines). **2.** An extract of a drug.

oleotherapy (o-le-o-ther′ah-pe) Treatment of disease with oil, especially through injection.

oleovitamin (o-le-o-vi′tah-min) Preparation containing an edible oil and one or more vitamins.

olfactie, olfacty (ol-fak′te) An arbitrary unit of olfactory acuity; expressed as the distance (in centimeters) at which a test odor is just perceived by the person tested.

olfaction (ol-fak′shun) **1.** The sense of smell. **2.** The act of smelling.

olfactology (ol-fak-tol′o-je) The study of the sense of smell.

olfactometer (ol-fak-tom′ĕ-ter) A device for testing the sense of smell.

olfactometry (ol-fak-tom′ĕ-tre) The process of assessing the degree of acuity of olfactory perception.

olfactory (ol-fak′to-re) Relating to the sense of smell. Also called osmatic. See also the table of nerves.

oligemia (ol-ī-ge′me-ah) Deficient or reduced amount of blood in the body (e.g., due to hemorrhage).

oligemic (ol-ī-ge′mik) Relating to oligemia (e.g., oligemic shock).

olighidria (ol-ig-hid′re-ah) Scanty or diminished sweating.

oligo- olig- Combining forms meaning small; few.

oligoamnios (ol-ī-go-am′ne-os) See oligohydramnios.

oligocholia (ol-ī-go-ko′le-ah) Abnormally low secretion of bile.

oligochylia (ol-ī-go-ki′le-ah) Deficiency of chyle.

oligochymia (ol-ī-go-ki′me-ah) A lack of chyme.

oligodactyly, oligodactilia (ol-ī-go-dak′tī-le, ol-ī-go-dak-til′e-ah) Congenital absence of one or more fingers or toes.

oligodendria (ol-ī-go-den′dre-ah) See oligodendroglia.

oligodendrocyte (ol-ī-go-den′dro-sīt) One of the cells constituting the oligodendroglia.

oligodendroglia (ol-ī-go-den-drog′le-ah) The non-nervous supportive tissue surrounding nerve cells and fibers of the brain and spinal cord; composed of small angular cells (oligodendrocytes),

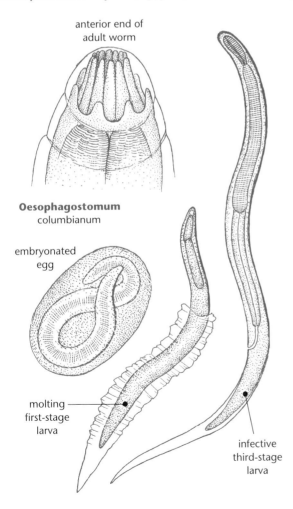

anterior end of adult worm

Oesophagostomum columbianum

embryonated egg

molting first-stage larva

infective third-stage larva

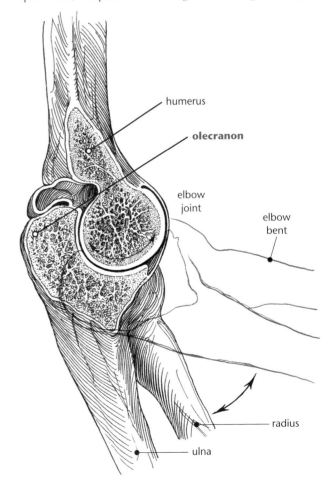

humerus

olecranon

elbow joint

elbow bent

radius

ulna

whose sheetlike processes are wrapped around individual axons, forming the myelin sheaths of the central nervous system. Also called oligodendria.

oligodendroglioma (ol-ī-go-den-dro-gli-o′mah) A relatively slow-growing solid tumor made up of oligodendroglia, most commonly occurring in the cerebral hemispheres of middle-aged people of both sexes.

oligodipsia (ol-ī-go-dip′se-ah) Abnormally diminished thirst.

oligodontia (ol-ī-go-don′she-ah) See hypodontia.

oligodynamic (ol-ī-go-di-nam′ik) Effective in minute quantities.

oligohydramnios (ol-ī-go-hi-dram′ne-os) Severe deficiency of amniotic fluid surrounding the fetus in the uterus during pregnancy; may be due to premature rupture of the membranes, obstruction of the fetal urinary tract, severe intrauterine growth retardation, or death of the fetus. Also called oligoamnios.

oligomenorrhea (ol-ī-go-men-o-re′ah) Reduction in the frequency of menstrual periods (i.e., occurring at intervals exceeding 35 days).

oligoria (ol-ī-gor′e-ah) Abnormal indifference toward or dislike of people.

oligospermia (ol-ī-go-sper′me-ah) Deficiency in the number of spermatozoa per unit volume of semen.

oligotrichosis (ol-ī-go-tri-ko′sis) See hypotrichosis.

oliguria (ol-ī-gu′re-ah) Abnormally low excretion of urine; arbitrarily defined as less than 400 ml of urine per day for an adult of average size.

olive (ol′iv) A smooth prominent oval mass on each side of the medulla oblongata.

olivopontocerebellar (ol′ī-vo-pon′to-ser-ĕ-bel′ar) Relating to a portion of the brain that includes the inferior olivary nucleus, the ventral portion of the pons, and the cerebellar cortex; applied especially to atrophy or degenerative diseases of that area.

-oma Suffix meaning tumor; neoplasm (e.g., hemangioma).

omental (o-men′tal) Relating to the omentum. Also called epiploic.

omentitis (o-men-ti′tis) Nonspecific inflammation of the omentum, often following torsion of the omentum and causing vague abdominal pain. Also called epiploitis.

omentectomy (o-men-tek′to-me) Surgical removal of the omentum, or a portion of it.

omentofixation (o-men-to-fik-sa′shun) See omentopexy.

omentopexy (o-men′to-pek-se) Suturing of the omentum to the abdominal wall. Also called omentofixation; epiplopexy.

omentorrhaphy (o-men-tor′ah-fe) Suturing of the omentum.

omentum (o-men′tum) A fold of peritoneum in the abdominal cavity that connects various organs with each other or with the abdominal wall.

    greater o. A prominent double fold of peritoneum resembling an apron and usually containing large deposits of fat; it descends a variable distance from the greater curvature of the stomach to the front of the small intestine, where it turns upon itself (thereby making four layers) and ascends to the top of the transverse colon.

    lesser o. The fold of peritoneum extending from the liver to the lesser curvature of the stomach and the beginning of the duodenum.

omni hora (om′nĭ o′ra) (omn. hor.) Latin for every hour.

omnivorous (om-niv′o-rus) Living on both animal and plant food.

omo- Combining form meaning shoulder.

omoclavicular (o-mo-klah-vik′u-lar) Relating to the shoulder and collarbone (clavicle).

omohyoid (o-mo-hi′oid) See table of muscles.

omphalectomy (om-fah-lek′to-me) Surgical removal of the navel (umbilicus).

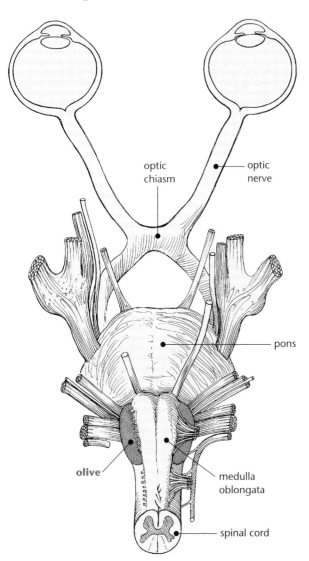

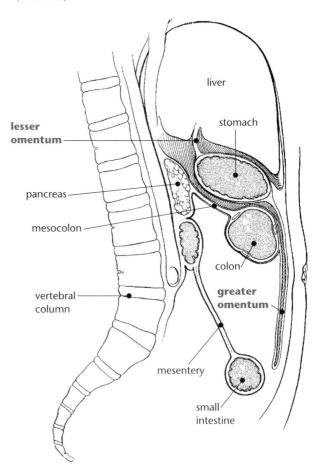

omphalic (om-fal'ik) Umbilical.

omphalitis (om-fah-li'tis) Inflammation of the navel.

omphalo-, omphal- Combining forms meaning the navel (umbilicus).

omphalocele (om'fah-lo-sēl) Protrusion of abdominal contents into the base of the umbilical cord; a membranous sac covers the abdominal contents and the cord structures pass individually over the sac, coming together at its apex to form a normal-looking umbilical cord. Also called exomphalos. COMPARE gastroschisis.

omphalomesenteric (om-fah-lo-mes-en-ter'ik) Relating to the navel and the fold of connective tissue attaching the small intestine to the back of the abdominal wall.

omphalophlebitis (om-fah-lo-flĕ-bi'tis) Inflammation of the umbilical veins.

omphalorrhagia (om-fah-lo-ra'je-ah) Bleeding from the navel.

omphalorrhea (om-fah-lo-re'ah) A discharge from the navel.

omphalotomy (om-fah-lot'o-me) The cutting of the umbilical cord at birth.

onanism (o'nah-nizm) See coitus interruptus, under coitus.

oncho-, onco- Combining forms meaning tumor; bulk; mass; hook; hooklike.

Onchocerca (ong-ko-ser'kah) A genus of parasitic worms of the family Onchoceridae (which includes *Wuchereria* and *Loa*); the worms inhabit connective tissues of humans and animals, usually coiled and entangled within firm nodules; two species, *Onchocerca caecutiens* and *Onchocerca volvulus*, can penetrate the skin.

onchocerciasis (on-ko-ser-ki'ah-sis) Condition caused by infection with threadlike parasites of the genus *Onchocerca*, especially *Onchocerca volvulus*, transmitted by the bite of infected black flies of the genus *Simulium*. The parasites burrow under the skin and live coiled within fibrous cysts encased in subcutaneous nodules, causing painful swellings; adults may grow as long as 2 feet and live 10 to 15 years in a human host, producing millions of offspring (microfilariae), which move freely out of the nodule and migrate through the body under the skin, causing intense itching. See also ocular onchocerciasis. Also called coastal erysipelas; blinding disease; volvulosis.

    ocular o. Ocular complications of chronic onchocerciasis, resulting in a slow deterioration of eyesight that can lead to total blindness. The *Onchocerca volvulus* microfilariae congregate in the eyes, causing inflammation of the cornea, iris, and conjunctiva, and neovascularization of the cornea. Also called river blindness; Robles' disease.

oncocyte (on'ko-sīt) A granular, acidophilic tumor cell.

oncocytoma (ong-ko-si-to'mah) An uncommon, usually dark brown glandular tumor that may reach a large size without becoming cancerous; usually seen in the kidney but also may occur in salivary glands. Also called oxyphil adenoma.

oncogene (ong'ko-jēn) Any gene (viral or cellular) implicated in tumor formation.

    retroviral o. A fully tumorigenic version of a cellular proto-oncogene.

oncogenesis (ong-ko-jen'ĕ-sis) The origin of a neoplasm; may be a chemical, genetic, hormonal, viral, or radiation influence.

oncogenic, oncogenous (ong-ko-jen'ik, ong-koj'ĕ-nus) Causing formation of tumors.

oncolipid (ong-ko-lip'id) A structurally altered fat from a protein molecule found in the blood of many cancer patients.

oncologist (ong-kol'o-jist) A specialist in oncology.

oncology (ong-kol'o-je) The study of the causes, characteristics, diagnosis, and treatment of cancer.

oncolysis (ong-kol'ĭ-sis) Destruction or reduction of any abnormal mass or tumor.

oncornavirus (on-kor'nah-vi'rus) See oncovirus.

oncosis (ong-ko'sis) Condition characterized by the presence of tumors.

oncosphere (ong'ko-sfēr) See hexacanth.

oncotherapy (ong-ko-ther'ah-pe) Treatment of tumors.

oncotic (ong-kot'ik) Relating to any swelling.

oncotropic (ong-ko-trop'ik) Having an affinity for tumor cells.

Oncovirinae (ong-ko-vir'ī-ne) A subfamily of tumor viruses (family Retroviridae) that, on the basis of morphology and antigenicity, are grouped into types A, B, C, and D; associated with malignant diseases.

oncovirus (ong-ko-vi'rus) Any virus of the subfamily Oncovirinae. Also called oncornavirus. See also oncogenic virus, under virus.

oneiric (o-ni'rik) 1. Relating to dreams. 2. Relating to oneirism.

oneirism (o-ni'rizm) An abnormal dreamlike state occurring while the person is awake.

oneiro- Combining form meaning dream.

oneirology (o-ni-rol'o-je) The study of dreams.

onlay (on'la) 1. A graft applied on the surface of a structure (e.g., of a bone). 2. An extended metal restoration attached to the occlusal surface of a posterior tooth or to the lingual surface of an anterior tooth.

onset (on'set) The start or the beginning of a process (e.g., of manifestations of a disease).

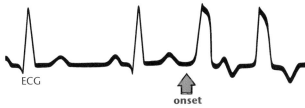

ECG

onset
of ventricular tachycardia

ontogenesis (on-to-jen'ĕ-sis) See ontogeny.

ontogeny (on-toj'ĕ-ne) The biologic development of the individual. Also called ontogenesis.

onychatrophia, onychatrophy (o-nik-ah-tro'fe-ah, on-ik-at'ro-fe) Atrophy or underdevelopment of the nails; may be congenital or acquired.

onychauxis (on-ĭ-kawk'sis) Marked thickening of the nails.

onychectomy (on-ĭ-kek'to-me) Surgical removal of a nail.

onychia (o-nik'e-ah) Inflammation of the matrix of a nail.

onycho-, onych- Combining forms meaning nail.

onychocryptosis (on-ĭ-ko-krip-to'sis) See ingrown nail, under nail.

onychodystrophy (on-ĭ-ko-dis'tro-fe) Deformity of nails.

onychogryposis, onychogryphosis (on-ĭ-ko-grī-po'sis, on-ĭ-ko-grī-fo'sis) Massive clawlike overgrowth, curvature, and thickening of a fingernail or toenail.

onychoid (on'ĭ-koid) Resembling a fingernail.

onycholysis (on-ĭ-kol'ĭ-sis) Detachment of a nail from its nail bed, occasionally with shedding of the nail.

onychomalacia (on-ĭ-ko-mah-la'she-ah) Abnormal softening of the nails.

onychomycosis (on-ĭ-ko-mi-ko'sis) See tinea unguium, under tinea.

onychopathy (on-ĭ-kop'ah-the) Any disease of the nails. Also called onychosis.

onychophagy, onychopaghia (on-ĭ-kof'ah-je, on-ĭ-ko-fa'je-ah) Nailbiting.

onychorrhexis (on-ĭ-ko-rek'sis) Abnormal brittleness and splitting of the nails.

onychosis (on-ĭ-ko'sis) See onychopathy.

onychotillomania (on-ĭ-ko-til-o-ma'ne-ah) Compulsive habit of picking on the cuticles or at the nails.

onychotomy (on-ĭ-kot'o-me) A surgical cut into a fingernail or toenail.

onychotrophy (on-ĭ-kot'ro-fe) Nutrition of the nails.

onyx (on'iks) 1. Greek for fingernail or toenail. 2. Collection of pus behind the cornea resembling a fingernail; a variety of hypopyon.

onyxis (o-nik'sis) Ingrown nail.

oo- Combining form meaning egg; ovum.

oocyesis (o'o-si-e'sis) See ovarian pregnancy, under pregnancy.

oocyte (o'o-sīt) See ovum.

O

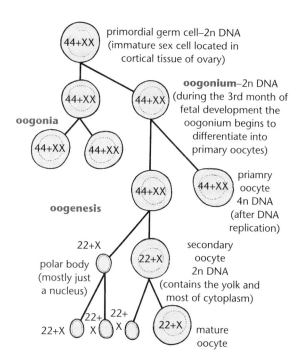

primordial germ cell–2n DNA (immature sex cell located in cortical tissue of ovary)

44+XX

oogonia

44+XX   44+XX

oogonium–2n DNA (during the 3rd month of fetal development the oogonium begins to differentiate into primary oocytes)

44+XX   44+XX

oogenesis

44+XX   44+XX   priamry oocyte 4n DNA (after DNA replication)

22+X   polar body (mostly just a nucleus)

22+X   secondary oocyte 2n DNA (contains the yolk and most of cytoplasm)

22+X   22+X   22+X   22+X   mature oocyte

oogenesis (o'o-jen'ĕ-sis) Formation of an ovum. Also called ovigenesis.

oogenetic (o'o-jĕ-net'ik) Relating to oogenesis.

oogenic, oogenous (o'o-jen'ik, o'o-jen'us) Producing ova.

oogonium (o'o-go'ne-um), pl. oogo'nia One of the cells forming most of the ovarian tissue and serving as a source of oocytes.

ookinesia (o'o-kĭ-ne'ze-ah) The natural movements of the ovum during maturation and fertilization.

oolemma (o'o-lem'ah) The cell membrane of the ovum.

oophoralgia (o'of-or-al'je-ah) See ovarialgia.

oophorectomy (o'of-o-rek'to-me) Removal of one or both ovaries. Also called ovariectomy.

oophoritis (o-of-o-ri'tis) Inflammation of one or both ovaries; may occur secondary to another infection (e.g., mumps). Also called ovaritis.

oophoro-, oophor- Combining forms meaning ovary.

oophorocystectomy (o-of-o-ro-sis-tek'to-me) Surgical removal of an ovarian cyst.

oophorocystosis (o-of-o-ro-sis-to'sis) The presence of cysts in an ovary.

oophoroma (o-of-o-ro'mah) An ovarian tumor. Also called ovarioncus.

oophoron (o-of'o-ron) Greek for ovum; egg.

oophoropathy (o-of-o-rop'ah-the) Any disease of the ovaries. Also called ovariopathy.

oophorosalpingectomy (o-of'o-ro-sal'pin-jek'to-me) Surgical removal of an ovary and its corresponding fallopian (uterine) tube. Also called ovariosalpingectomy.

oophorosalpingitis (o-of'o-ro-sal'pin-ji'tis) Inflammation of an ovary or ovaries and corresponding fallopian (uterine) tube. Also called ovariosalpingitis.

oophorotomy (o-of-o-rot'o-me) A surgical cut into an ovary. Also called ovariotomy.

ooplasm (o'o-plazm) The cytoplasm of an ovum.

opacification (o-pas-ĭ-fĭ-ka'shun) The formation of opacities or the process of losing transparency, as of the lens of the eye.

opacity (o-pas'ĭ-te) 1. The condition resulting from having lost transparency. 2. An area of a structure (e.g., the cornea) that has lost its transparent state.

opaque (o-pāk') Impenetrable by light rays.

open (o'pen) Exposed to the air, affording unobstructed entrance; applied to a wound.

operable (op'er-ah-bl) Subject to treatment by surgical means with a reasonable expectation of cure or relief.

operate (op'er-āt) To perform a surgical procedure.

operation (op-er-a'shun) Any surgical procedure for remedying an injury, deformity, ailment, or dysfunction.

Abbe's o. A procedure for correcting a defect on a lip by transferring a full-thickness flap from the other lip, using an arterial pedicle to ensure survival of the graft.

Billroth's o.'s Procedures for removal of part of the stomach: *Billroth I*, removal of the pylorus followed by end-to-end anastomosis of the stomach and duodenum. *Billroth II*, removal of the pylorus and most of the lesser curvature of the stomach and closure of the cut ends of the stomach and duodenum, followed by a posterior anastomosis of the stomach and jejunum; a rarely used procedure.

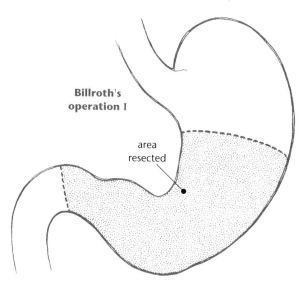

Billroth's operation I

area resected

Blalock-Hanlon o. The creation of a large interatrial opening to allow mixing of oxygenated blood; a palliative measure for abnormality of the heart in which the aorta originates from the right ventricle (instead of the left) and the pulmonary trunk originates from the left ventricle (instead of the right).

Blalock-Taussig o. The anastomosing of the brachiocephalic trunk, or a subclavian or carotid artery, to the pulmonary artery to direct blood from the systemic circulation to the lungs, in cases of congenital pulmonary stenosis with septal defect.

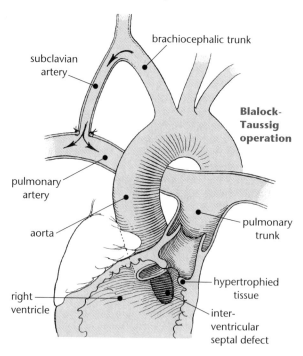

brachiocephalic trunk

subclavian artery

Blalock-Taussig operation

pulmonary artery

aorta

pulmonary trunk

right ventricle

hypertrophied tissue

inter-ventricular septal defect

oogenesis ■ operation

bloodless o. An operation performed with little or no blood loss.

Bricker's o. Diversion of urine disposal from the bladder by connecting the ureter to a pouch of isolated ileum opening onto the abdominal wall.

Caldwell-Luc o. Removal of the contents of a maxillary sinus through an opening on its facial wall above the root of a bicuspid tooth.

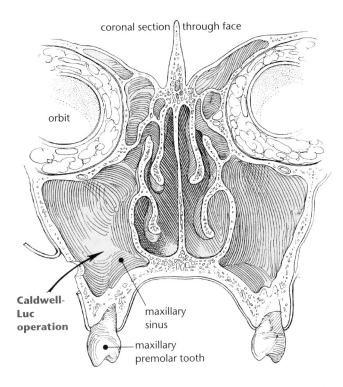

coronal section through face

orbit

Caldwell-Luc operation

maxillary sinus

maxillary premolar tooth

debulking o. Removal of a portion of a cancerous tumor that cannot be removed completely.

fenestration o. A rarely performed operation for the treatment of conduction-type deafness (e.g., otosclerosis); an opening is created between the middle ear chamber and the lateral semicircular canal as an alternate sound access, bypassing the ankylosed stapes at the oval window (fenestra vestibuli).

flap o. *(a)* Any procedure involving partial detachment of tissue. *(b)* In dental surgery, partial detachment of soft tissue from underlying bone to gain access to the area.

Fredet-Ramstedt o. See pyloromyotomy.

Gillies' o. Reduction of fractures of the zygoma and zygomatic arch through an incision above the hairline.

Gritti's o. See Gritti-Stokes amputation, under amputation.

Halsted's o. *(a)* See radical mastectomy, under mastectomy. *(b)* Operation for the repair of a direct inguinal hernia.

Hofmeister's o. Reestablishment of intestinal continuity after partial removal of the stomach by closure of the lesser curvature side of the stomach and the duodenal stump, followed by anastomosis of the greater curvature side of the stomach and jejunum.

Huggins' o. Removal of testes for cancer of the prostate.

Irving's o. A method of female sterilization consisting of: a double ligation of the fallopian (uterine) tubes with nonabsorbable sutures; division of the tubes between the sutures; freeing the stumps from their peritoneal attachments; and either burying both distal and proximal stumps between the two layers of the broad ligament, or burying only the distal stumps and suturing the proximal stump under the serous covering of the uterus, just anterior to the round ligament. Also called Irving's procedure; Irving's technique.

Kazanjian's o. A surgical procedure for extending the vestibular sulcus of edentulous ridges to increase their height and to improve denture retention.

Lisfranc's o. See Lisfranc's amputation, under amputation.

Madlener's o. Procedure for female sterilization consisting of: lifting the middle third of each of the fallopian (uterine) tubes to create a loop, grasping and crushing the base of the loop with a clamp, ligating the crushed region of the loop with a nonabsorbable suture, and covering the ligature site with the round ligament to prevent adhesion formation. Also called Madlener's procedure; Madlener's technique.

Manchester o. High amputation of the uterine cervix and suturing together of the broad ligament bases in front of the shortened cervix; devised to relieve first- and second-degree prolapse of the uterus.

Marshall-Marchetti-Krantz o. An operation for correction of stress incontinence; the tissues on either side of the urethra are sutured together anteriorly, then to the posterior side of the pubis and to the rectus muscle.

Naffziger's o. Removal of the lateral and superior orbital walls for severe malignant exophthalmos.

Pomeroy's o. A method of female sterilization by partial resection of the fallopian (uterine) tubes; consists of: lifting the middle third of each tube to create a loop, ligating the loop at its base, resecting the ligated loop, and covering the wound surface with the round ligament to prevent adhesion formation. Also called Pomeroy's procedure; Pomeroy's technique.

Pott's o. Side-to-side connection between the aorta and the pulmonary artery; a palliative measure for tetralogy of Fallot.

radical o. A thorough procedure aimed at complete elimination of a disease or correction of a defect.

Roux-en-Y o. Procedure in which the jejunum is cut about 15 cm below its origin, the distal cut end is sutured to the stomach, and the proximal cut end is sutured to the side of the jejunum farther down.

stapes mobilization o. Freeing of stapes from overgrowth of bone to restore hearing in individuals with otosclerosis.

Syme's o. See Syme's amputation, under amputation.

Whipple's o. Removal of carcinoma of the head of the pancreas.

operative (op′er-ah-tiv) 1. Relating to a surgical procedure. 2. Active.

operculum (o-per′ku-lum), pl. oper′cula 1. Any anatomic structure resembling a lid or cover, such as the brain tissue covering the insula (island of Reil). 2. The mucus plug sealing the opening of the cervix during pregnancy. 3. The tissue covering (partly or completely) an unerupted tooth. 4. The attached portion of a retinal detachment.

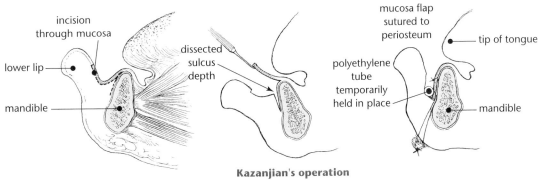

incision through mucosa

lower lip

mandible

dissected sulcus depth

mucosa flap sutured to periosteum

tip of tongue

polyethylene tube temporarily held in place

mandible

Kazanjian's operation

O

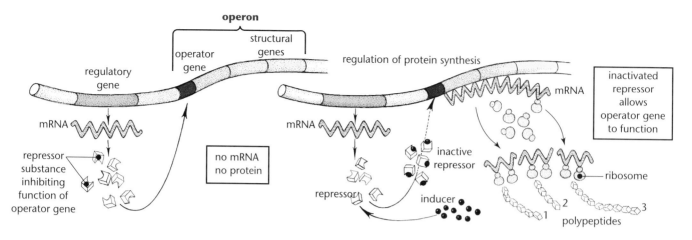

regulation of protein synthesis

operon

operator gene | structural genes

regulatory gene

mRNA

repressor substance inhibiting function of operator gene

no mRNA no protein

mRNA

repressor

inducer

inactive repressor

inactivated repressor allows operator gene to function

ribosome

polypeptides

operon (op′er-on) A cluster of two or more structural genes and an operator gene on a chromosome; it is the functional unit of DNA, governing production of the enzymes of a metabolic pathway.

ophiasis (o-fi′ah-sis) Loss of hair occurring in bands that partly or completely encircle the head.

ophidiasis (o-fĭ-di′ah-sis) Poisoning by the venom of a snake. Also called ophidism.

ophidic (o-fid′ik) Relating to snakes.

ophidiophobia (o-fid-e-o-fo′be-ah) An abnormally exaggerated fear of snakes.

ophidism (o′fĭ-dizm) See ophidosis.

ophryosis (of-re-o′sis) Spasmodic twitching in the area of an eyebrow.

ophthalmalgia (of-thal-mal′je-ah) Pain in the eyeball.

ophthalmia (of-thal′me-ah) Inflammation of the eye.

    gonorrheal o. Acute purulent conjunctivitis caused by gonorrheal infection.

    metastatic o. See sympathetic ophthalmia.

    migratory o. See sympathetic ophthalmia.

    o. neonatorum Acute purulent conjunctivitis of the newborn infant; may be due to infection acquired from its mother during passage through the birth canal (e.g., gonorrheal or chlamydial infection) or may be caused by a staphylococcal or a pseudomonal microorganism, usually acquired as a nosocomial infection in the hospital nursery. Also called neonatal conjunctivitis.

    sympathetic o. Inflammation of the uveal tract of one eye followed by an identical inflammation of the other eye, leading to bilateral blindness; may occur 10 days to several years after a perforating injury in the area of the ciliary body or retention of a foreign body in the same area. Also called sympathetic uveitis; metastatic ophthalmia; migratory ophthalmia; transferred ophthalmia.

    transferred o. See sympathetic ophthalmia.

ophthalmic (of-thal′mik) Relating to the eye.

ophthalmo-, ophthalm- Combining forms meaning eye.

ophthalmodiaphanoscope (of-thal′mo-di-ah-fan′o-skōp) Instrument using transillumination for inspection of the interior of the eye (ocular fundus).

ophthalmodynamometer (of-thal′mo-di-nah-mom′ĕ-ter) Instrument for estimating the blood pressure of the retinal vessels.

ophthalmodynamometry (of-thal′mo-di-nah-mom′ĕ-tre) Measurement of blood pressure in the retinal circulation (within the eye) by means of the ophthalmodynamometer; used to determine the presence of an occluding or constricting lesion in the carotid artery system.

ophthalmograph (of-thal′mo-graf) Instrument for recording eye movements during reading.

ophthalmologist (of-thal-mol′o-jist) A physician who specializes in ophthalmology. Formerly called oculist.

ophthalmology (of-thal-mol′o-je) The medical and surgical specialty concerned with the structure and function of the eye, and the diagnosis and treatment of its diseases and defects.

ophthalmomalacia (of-thal-mo-mah-la′she-ah) Abnormally low pressure within the eyeball, causing a softening.

ophthalmometer (of-thal-mom′ĕ-ter) See keratometer.

ophthalmometry (of-thal-mom′ĕ-tre) See keratometry.

ophthalmomycosis (of-thal-mo-mi-ko′sis) Any fungal disease of the eye or its appendages. Also called oculomycosis.

ophthalmomyiasis (of-thal-mo-mi-i′ah-sis) Infestation of the eye with larvae of certain types of flies.

ophthalmopathy (of-thal-mop′ah-the) Any disease of the eyes. Also called oculopathy.

ophthalmoplegia (of-thal-mo-ple′je-ah) Partial or total paralysis of one or more muscles of the eyes; may be caused by a condition affecting the muscles themselves or the nerves innervating the muscles, or by a lesion in the brain.

    chronic progressive external o. A rare condition of all three nerves supplying the external eye muscles (3rd, 4th, and 6th cranial nerves), characterized by a slowly progressive inability to move the eyes; may start at any age and advance over a 5- to 15-year period to complete paralysis of the eye muscles; may be associated with muscular dystrophy.

    exophthalmic o. Ophthalmoplegia due to thickening of the muscles accompanied by white blood cell infiltration; degeneration of some muscle fibers may also occur; thought to be caused by an autoimmune reaction.

    external o. General term describing an inability to move the eyes normally as a result of a lesion in the brain involving nuclei of the oculomotor, trochlear, or abducent (3rd, 4th, or 6th cranial) nerves.

    migrainous o. A transient unilateral paralysis of the oculomotor (3rd cranial) nerve, occurring in conjunction with an attack of migraine, resulting in a lateral deviation of the affected eye and drooping (ptosis) of the eyelid.

ophthalmoplegic (of-thal-mo-ple′jik) Relating to ophthalmoplegia.

ophthalmoscope (of-thal′mo-skōp) An instrument equipped with a special illumination system for inspecting the interior of the eyeball, especially the retina and associated structures.

ophthalmoscopy (of-thal-mos′ko-pe) Examination of the interior of the eye with the aid of an ophthalmoscope.

ophthalmotrope (of-thal′mo-trōp) A teaching model of the two eyes designed to demonstrate the action of the extrinsic eye muscles.

-opia Suffix meaning vision (e.g., myopia).

opiate (o′pe-āt) Any preparation derived from opium.

opioid (o′pe-oid) Any natural or synthetic compound with a pharmacologic activity similar to that of morphine.

opisthion (o-pis′the-on) The middle point on the posterior margin of the foramen magnum, the large opening at the base of the skull.

opistho- Combining form meaning backward; posterior.

opisthocheilia (o-pis-tho-ki′le-ah) Receding lips.

opisthorchiasis (o-pis-thor-ki′ah-sis) Infection with lancet-shaped liver flukes of the genus *Opisthorchis* (especially *Opisthorchis viverrini*), acquired by ingestion of raw or undercooked infected fish.

opisthotonos (o-pis-thot′o-nos) A muscle spasm causing rigidity of the neck and back and arching of the back; seen in acute cases of tetanus or meningitis.

opium (o′pe-um) Drug prepared from the dried gummy juice of unripe pods of a poppy, *Papaver somniferum;* used as an analgesic.

opponens (o-po′nenz) Opposing; descriptive term applied to several muscles of the hand or foot whose function is to pull the digit across the palm or sole.

opportunistic (op-or-tu-nis′tik) **1.** Denoting a disease that occurs in people whose immune system is impaired by other infections or by ongoing drug therapy (e.g. chemotherapy). **2.** Denoting the organisms causing such a disease, and which do not cause disease (or cause only mild infections) in healthy people.

opsin (op′sin) The protein component of the retinal pigment rhodopsin.

opsoclonus (op-so-klo′nus) An abnormal condition characterized by rapid, multidirectional, nonrhythmic movement of the eyes. Popularly called dancing eyes.

opsonic (op-son′ik) Relating to opsonins.

opsonin (op′so-nin) A substance capable of binding to bacteria or other cells and rendering them susceptible to destruction by phagocytosis; may be antibody or fragments of complement components.

opsonization (op′so-ni-za′shun) The process by which antigens (i.e., bacteria and other cells), are modified, usually by antibody and/or complement, to make them more readily engulfed and destroyed (phagocytized) by white blood cells.

opsonocytophagic (op′so-no-si′to-faj′ik) Relating to the increased phagocytic activity of white blood cells in blood containing specific opsonin.

optesthesia (op-tes-the′ze-ah) Ability to perceive a light stimulus.

optic (op′tik) Relating to the eye.

optical (op′tĭ-kal) Relating to vision.

optician (op-tish′an) **1.** A person who makes or sells lenses, eyeglasses, or other optical instruments. **2.** A person who adjusts eyeglasses after a prescription is furnished by an ophthalmologist or optometrist.

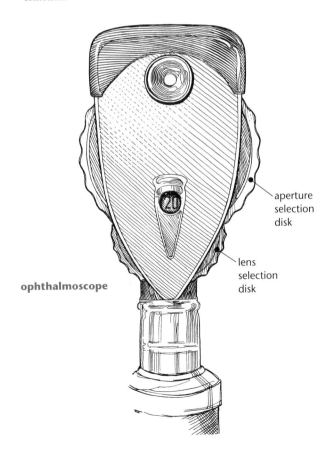

aperture selection disk

lens selection disk

ophthalmoscope

opticociliary (op-tī-ko-sil′e-a-re) Relating to the optic and ciliary nerve.

optics (op′tiks) The science concerned with the study of light and vision.

optimum (op′tĭ-mum) Denoting the most favorable conditions.

opto- Combining form meaning sight; vision.

optometer (op-tom′ĕ-ter) Any of various devices for measuring the refractive power of the eyes.

optometrist (op-tom′ĕ-trist) A person trained to examine the eyes to assess visual acuity and to prescribe, supply, and adjust eyeglasses or contact lenses.

optometry (op-tom′ĕ-tre) The testing and measuring of visual acuity and treatment of visual defects by means of eyeglasses or contact lenses.

optomyometer (op-to-mi-om′ĕ-ter) Device for determining the relative strength of the extrinsic eye muscles.

ora (o′rah), pl. o′rae Border.

    o. serrata The serrated margin of the retina, within the anterior portion of the eyeball.

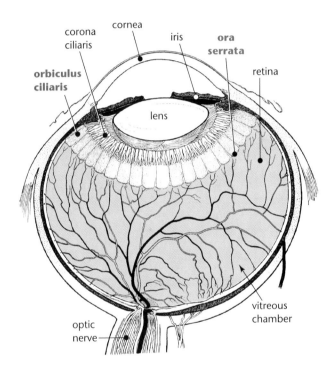

corona ciliaris   cornea   iris   **ora serrata**

orbiculus ciliaris   retina

lens

optic nerve

vitreous chamber

orad (o′rad) Toward the mouth.

oral (o′ral) Relating to the mouth.

orality (or-al′ĭ-te) In psychoanalysis, relating to the oral or earliest stage of sexual development.

orbicular (or-bik′u-lar) Circular.

orbiculus ciliaris (or-bik′u-lus sil-e-a′ris) The dark zone within the eye, along the circumference of the ora serrata.

orbit (or′bit) One of two slightly conical cavities in the skull containing the eyeball and associated structures; formed by portions of seven bones: frontal, maxillary, zygomatic, lacrimal, ethmoid, palatine, and sphenoid. Popularly called eye socket.

orbital (or′bĭ-tal) Relating to the orbit.

orbitography (or-bĭ-tog′rah-fe) The making of x-ray films of the orbit after infusion of a radiopaque substance; a diagnostic technique employed when a blow-out fracture is suspected.

orbitometer (or-bĭ-tom′ĕ-ter) Instrument for measuring the degree of resistance offered by the eyeball when pressed into the socket.

orbitotomy (or-bĭ-tot′o-me) A surgical cut into the orbit.

orcein (or-se′in) A purple dye used in the study of cells (cytology).

orchialgia (or-ke-al′je-ah) Pain in a testicle. Also called testalgia; orchiodynia.

orchichorea (or-ke-ko-re′ah) Involuntary twitching of the testicles.

orchidectomy (or-kĭ-dek′to-me) See orchiectomy.

orchido-, orchio-, orchi- Combining forms meaning testis.

orchidometer (or-kĭ-dom′ĕ-ter) A device for measuring the size of a testicle.

 Prader o. A string of plastic testicle-shaped beads, used for estimating testicular development.

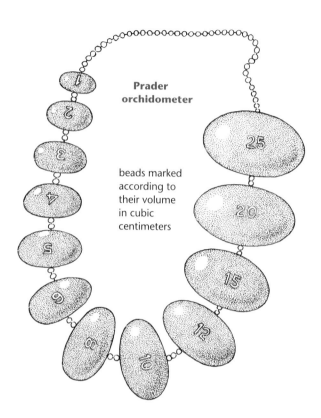

Prader orchidometer

beads marked according to their volume in cubic centimeters

orchidorrhaphy (or-kĭ-dor′ah-fe) See orchiopexy.

orchiectomy (or-ke-ek′to-me) Surgical removal of one or both testes; performed for the treatment of testicular cancer or gangrene, or to reduce production of the hormone testosterone as part of the therapy for cancer of the prostate. Also called testectomy; orchidectomy; (popularly) castration.

orchiepididymitis (or-ke-ep-ĭ-did-ĭ-mi′tis) Inflammation of a testis and epididymis.

orchiocele (or′ke-o-sēl) A swelling or hernial protrusion of the testis.

orchiodynia (or-ke-o-din′e-ah) See orchialgia.

orchioncus (or-ke-ong′kus) A tumor of the testis.

orchiopathy (or-ke-op′ah-the) Any disease of the testis.

orchiopexy (or-ke-o-pek′se) Mobilization of an undescended testis and its suturing onto the scrotum; a procedure usually performed before the age of five years. Also called orchidorrhaphy; orchiorrhaphy.

orchioplasty (or′ke-o-plas-te) Reparative surgery of the testis.

orchiorrhaphy (or-ke-or′ah-fe) See orchiopexy.

orchiotomy (or-ke-ot′o-me) A surgical cut into a testis.

orchis (or′kis) Greek for testis.

orchitis (or-ki′tis) Inflammation of the testes; may occur as a result of mumps. Also called testitis.

order (or′der) **1.** In biological classification, the category just below the class and above the family. **2.** A directive, advisory instruction, or prescription for a specific course of action (e.g., preoperative or postoperative orders).

 do-not-resuscitate o. (DNR) See no-code order.

 no-code o. A direction by the attending physician that cardiopulmonary resuscitation should not be initiated if the patient experiences cardiac or respiratory failure. Also called do-not-resuscitate order.

orderly (or′der-le) An attendant performing a range of services in a hospital ward whose responsibilities do not require professional training.

ordinate (or′dĭ-nāt) The vertical coordinate that, together with a horizontal one (abscissa), forms a frame of reference for plotting data.

orexigenic (o-rek-sĭ-jen′ik) Stimulating the appetite.

orf (orf) A viral disease of sheep and goats occasionally transmitted to humans, especially butchers and veterinarians, causing large inflamed papules that often bleed and ulcerate. Also called contagious ecthyma.

organ (or′gan) A distinct structural unit of the body that performs specific functions.

 acoustic o. See spiral organ of Corti.

 cell o. See organelle.

 o. of Corti See spiral organ of Corti.

 cutaneous sense o.'s The various specialized nerve endings in the skin that detect mechanical, thermal, or painful stimuli applied to the body surface. They include the pacinian corpuscles (respond rapidly to changing mechanical stimulation); free nerve endings (respond to strong mechanical, thermal, and painful stimuli); Merkel's disks (respond to maintained deformation of the skin surface and play a role in the sensing of both touch and pressure); Meissner's corpuscles (receptors subserving the sense of touch); Krause's end-bulbs (respond to thermal stimuli); and corpuscles of Ruffini (sense steady pressure).

 digestive o.'s Organs concerned with the ingestion, mastication, transportation, digestion, and absorption of food products, and the elimination of the unabsorbed residues. Also called digestive apparatus; digestive system.

 end o. (*a*) One of a number of various large, encapsulated terminations of a sensory nerve fiber (e.g., Golgi-Mazzoni corpuscle), as found in muscle tissue, skin, mucous membrane, or glands. (*b*) The site of ultimate damage due to a disease process (e.g., kidney damage secondary to hypertension).

 genital o.'s of the female See reproductive organs of the female.

 genital o.'s of the male See reproductive organs of the male.

 Golgi tendon o. (GTO) Special neurotendinous endings enclosed in a delicate capsule that ramify chiefly about bundles of collagen fibers of tendons near the junction with muscles. The endings are highly activated by passive stretch of the tendon or by active contraction of the muscle. Also called tendon spindle; Golgi corpuscle; neurotendinous organ.

 gustatory o. The organ concerned with the perception of taste, composed of taste buds (gustatory caliculi) in the epithelium covering the tongue, the undersurface of the soft palate, the posterior surface of the epiglottis, and the back wall of the oral part of the pharynx (oropharynx). The greatest concentration of taste buds is on the sides of the vallate papillae at the base of the tongue and also on the foliate papillae found on the sides and tip of the tongue. The number of taste buds decreases with age.

 o. of hearing The organ that is concerned with the collection, conduction, modification, amplification, and parametric analysis of sound waveforms that impinge on the head, leading to the transmission of nerve signals (impulses) to the brain for interpretation as sound.

 neurotendinous o. See Golgi tendon organ.

 reproductive o.'s of the female The various organs in the female concerned with reproduction, consisting of the ovaries, fallopian (uterine) tubes, uterus, vagina, clitoris, labia majora and minora, the bulb of the vestibule, the greater vestibular glands, the vestibule, and the mons pubis. Also called genital organs of the female.

 reproductive o.'s of the male The various organs of the male concerned with reproduction, consisting of the penis, scrotum, testes, epididymides, deferent ducts, ejaculatory ducts, seminal vesicles,

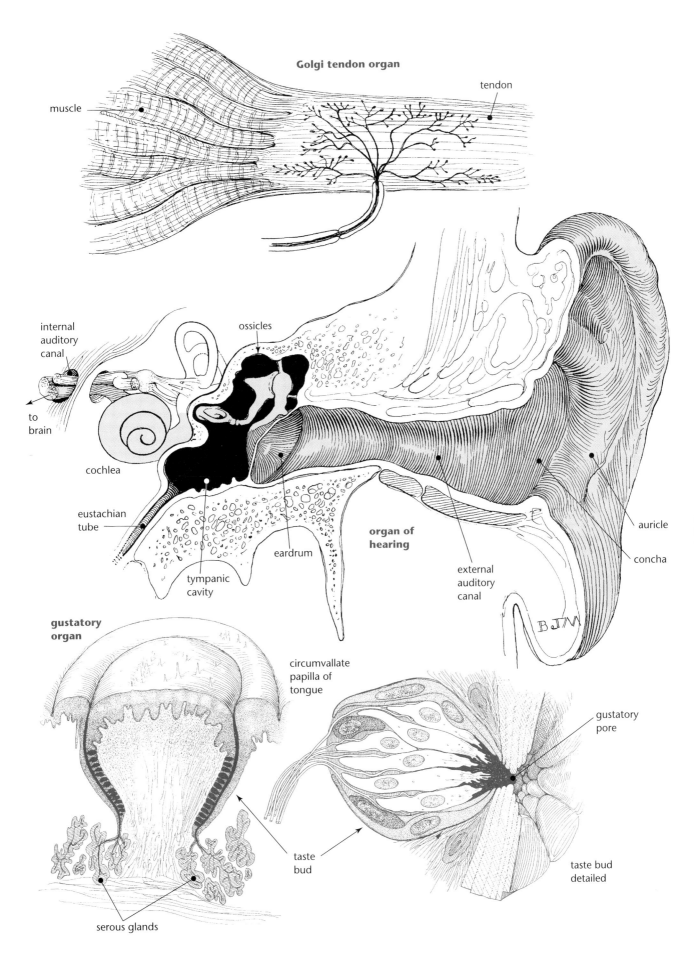

Golgi tendon organ

muscle

tendon

internal
auditory
canal

ossicles

to
brain

cochlea

eustachian
tube

organ of
hearing

eardrum

tympanic
cavity

external
auditory
canal

auricle

concha

O

**gustatory
organ**

circumvallate
papilla of
tongue

gustatory
pore

taste
bud

taste bud
detailed

serous glands

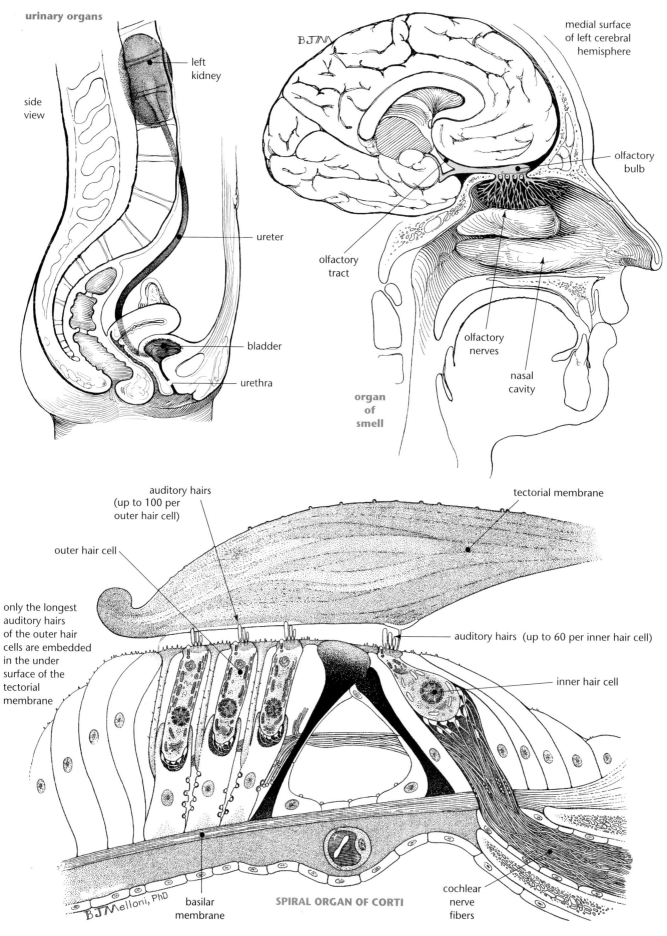

urinary organs

left
kidney

side
view

ureter

bladder

urethra

medial surface
of left cerebral
hemisphere

BJ/M

olfactory
bulb

olfactory
tract

olfactory
nerves

nasal
cavity

organ
of
smell

auditory hairs
(up to 100 per
outer hair cell)

tectorial membrane

outer hair cell

only the longest
auditory hairs
of the outer hair
cells are embedded
in the under
surface of the
tectorial
membrane

auditory hairs (up to 60 per inner hair cell)

inner hair cell

BJMelloni, PhD

basilar
membrane

SPIRAL ORGAN OF CORTI

cochlear
nerve
fibers

O

organ ■ organ

urethra, prostate, and the bulbourethral gland. Also called genital organs of the male.

sense o. Any organ of special sense, which after receiving stimuli gives rise to sensation (e.g., the eye and the accessory structures associated with it). There are three basic types: neuroepithelial (e.g., olfactory), epithelial (e.g., gustatory), and neuronal (e.g., cutaneous sensors).

o. of sight See organ of vision.

o. of smell The nose, nasal cavity, olfactory epithelium and its nervous connections to the brain for interpretation of odors.

spiral o. of Corti The sensory receptor for hearing, contained in the cochlea of the inner ear; it transforms the sound vibrations into electrical signals, which are then transmitted to the brain for interpretation as sound. Also called organ of Corti; acoustic organ.

target o. An organ that is influenced or stimulated by a hormone, as the adrenal (suprarenal) gland by the pituitary hormone corticotropin (ACTH).

urinary o.'s The organs involved with the production and excretion of urine; composed of the kidneys, ureters, urinary bladder, and urethra.

vestibular o. The portion of the membranous labyrinth of the inner ear that has specialized mechanoreceptors; it includes the two small sacs (utricle and saccule), which occupy the vestibule of the inner ear, and the three semicircular ducts, which are enclosed within the semicircular canals. Both the utricle and saccule contain a mechanoreceptor called the macula, which specifically responds to linear acceleration (e.g., the pull of gravity); within the swelling (ampulla) of each of the three semicircular ducts, there is a mechanoreceptor, called the crista, which responds to angular acceleration. Also called vestibular system.

vestibulocochlear o.'s The organs outside the central nervous system (CNS) that serve the function of balance and orientation (equilibrium) and hearing; composed of the outer, middle, and inner ear.

vestigial o. An organ that once was functional but which is now considered rudimentary; its development has been arrested in the course of evolution.

o. of vision The organ conducting visual stimuli to and from the central nervous system that result in sight; it consists of the eyeball, including its fibrous, vascular, and internal coats, optic nerve, and the lens, as well as the accessory structures of the eye. Also called visual organ; organ of sight.

visual o. See organ of vision.

o.'s of Zuckerkandl Small aggregates of chromaffin tissue located along the abdominal aorta at the level of the inferior mesenteric artery; they help to control respiration by monitoring the blood gases. Also called corpora para-aortica; para-aortic bodies.

Organ Procurement Organization (OPO) An organization that is licensed and authorized to perform or coordinate the retrieving, preserving, and transporting of donated organs, and that maintains a system of locating prospective recipients for available organs.

organelle (or-gah-nel′) Any intracellular structural subunit of the cytoplasm characterized by its specific enzymatic content, ultrastructure, and function (the cell organelles are closely integrated with, and vital for, the metabolic processes of the cell); present in all eukaryotic cells, these subcellular units include the nucleus, ribosomes, endoplasmic reticulum, Golgi apparatus, annulate lamellae, lysosomes, centrioles, microtubules, and filaments. Other structures in the cytoplasm not considered organelles are known as inclusion bodies (e.g., pigment granules, stored lipids and glycogen, secretory granules and crystals). Also called cell organ.

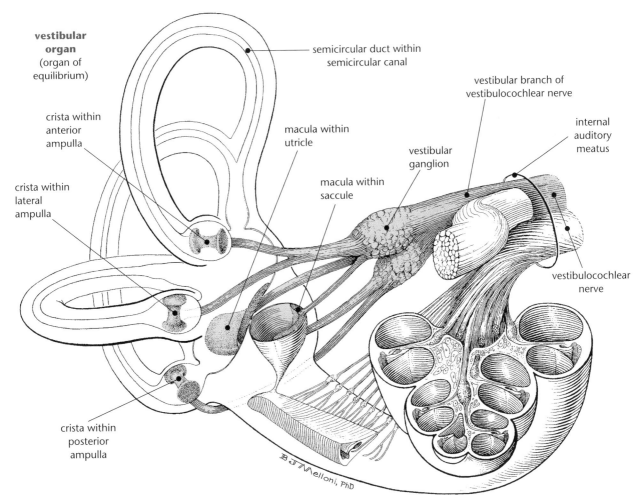

vestibular organ (organ of equilibrium)

semicircular duct within semicircular canal

crista within anterior ampulla

crista within lateral ampulla

macula within utricle

macula within saccule

vestibular ganglion

vestibular branch of vestibulocochlear nerve

internal auditory meatus

vestibulocochlear nerve

crista within posterior ampulla

BJMelloni, PhD

organ ■ organelle

organic (or-gan'ik) **1.** Relating to a body organ. **2.** Derived from or related to plants or animals. **3.** Organized; structural.

organism (or'gah-nizm) Any plant or animal.

   pleuropneumonia-like o.'s (PPLO) A group of bacteria of the order Mycoplasmatales. See also *Mycoplasma.*

organization (or-gah-ni-za'shun) **1.** A group of distinct but dependent parts with varied functions that contribute to the whole. **2.** Process through which tissues are formed into organs. **3.** The replacement of a blood clot or dead tissue by collagen or scar tissue.

organogenesis (or-gah-no-jen'ĕ-sis) In embryology, the formation of organs.

organoid (or'gah-noid) **1.** Resembling an organ. **2.** Composed of the cellular elements of an organ; applied to a tumor.

organoleptic (or-gah-no-lep'tik) **1.** Stimulation of a sense organ. **2.** Capable of receiving a sensory stimulus.

organomegaly (or-gah-no-meg'ah-le) See visceromegaly.

organomercurial (or-gah-no-mer-ku're-al) Denoting an organic compound of mercury; some compounds of this type have diuretic properties.

organophosphates (or-gah-no-fos'fāts) A group of compounds (e.g., malathion, parathion) widely used in agriculture as insecticides; human toxic exposure produces irreversible inhibition of the action of acetylcholinesterase, an enzyme that facilitates transmission of neuromuscular impulses; toxic manifestations include abdominal cramps, diarrhea, salivation, sweating, and constriction of the bronchi.

organotropism (or-gah-not'ro-pizm) A particular predilection for organs or tissues; applied to certain microorganisms and chemicals.

orgasm (or'gazm) The culmination of sexual intercourse or stimulation of the sex organs, accompanied in the male by ejaculation of semen and in the female by involuntary contractions of the vagina.

orientation (o-re-en-ta'shun) **1.** Awareness of oneself in reference to time, space, and other individuals. **2.** The act of finding one's bearings.

orifice (or'ĭ-fis) Any entrance or outlet of a body cavity; an opening of a canal.

   abdominal o. of uterine tube The opening at the lateral, fimbriated end of each fallopian (uterine) tube; through it, the ovum expelled by the ovary enters the tube on its way to the cavity of the uterus.

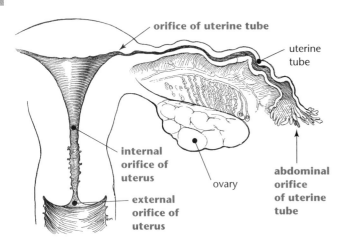

   anal o. See anus.

   external o. of female urethra The slitlike orifice with prominent margins directly in front of the opening of the vagina and behind the clitoris. Also called external meatus of female urethra.

   external o. of male urethra The narrowed part of the urethra at the end of the penis. Also called external meatus of male urethra.

   external o. of uterus The opening between the canal of the cervix and the cavity of the vagina, bounded by the anterior and posterior lips; it is small and round before giving birth and becomes a transverse slit after parturition. Also called external os of uterus; os uteri externum; popularly called mouth of the uterus.

   internal o. of urethra The crescentic opening at the apex of the bladder, leading to the urethra. Also called internal meatus of urethra.

   internal o. of uterus The opening between the cavity of the body of the uterus and the canal of the cervix. Also called internal os of uterus; os uteri internum.

   o. of maxillary sinus See maxillary hiatus, under hiatus.

   oral o. The opening of the mouth. Also called rima oris.

   pharyngeal o. of auditory tube The opening of the auditory tube in the lateral wall of the nasopharynx. Also called pharyngeal orifice of eustachian tube.

   pharyngeal o. of eustachian tube See pharyngeal orifice of auditory tube.

   tympanic o. of auditory tube The opening of the auditory tube in the upper part of the anterior wall of the middle ear chamber. Also called tympanic orifice of eustachian tube; tympanic opening of auditory tube.

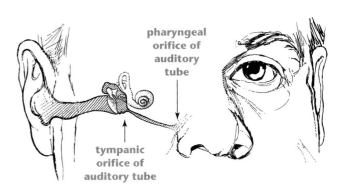

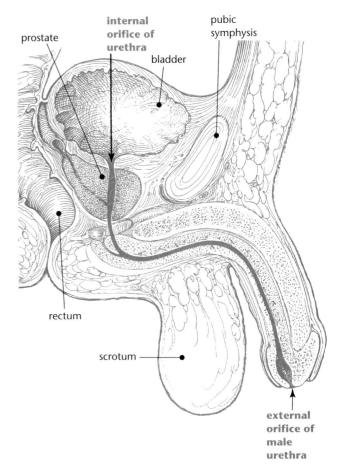

tympanic o. of eustachian tube See tympanic orifice of auditory tube.

o. of ureter The slitlike termination of a ureter through the bladder wall at the posterolateral angle of the trigone.

o. of uterine tube The minute opening of a fallopian (uterine) tube into the superior angle of the cavity of the uterus on either side.

o. of vagina The external opening of the vagina, located just behind the external urethral orifice.

origin (or′ĭ-jin) **1.** The site of attachment of a muscle to a bone that is less movable than another bone to which it is inserted. **2.** The starting point of a nerve.

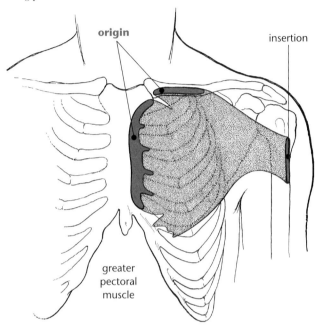

greater
pectoral
muscle

ornithine (or′nĭ-thin) An amino acid that is an important intermediate in the biosynthesis of urea.

Ornithodoros (or-nĭ-thod′o-ros) A genus of ticks (family Argasidae) that includes vectors of relapsing fevers.

Ornithonyssus sylviarum (or-nĭ-tho-nis′us sil-ve-a′rum) A mite that is a parasite on many domestic and wild fowl and the cause of an itchy skin eruption in humans. Also called northern fowl mite.

ornithosis (or-nĭ-tho′sis) Infection with *Chlamydia psittaci*, characterized by influenza-like symptoms or pneumonia; acquired by inhalation of dust-borne contaminated nasal secretions, or excreta from infected domestic birds (e.g., parrots, pigeons, parakeets). Occupational exposure usually occurs in pet shop workers, zoo attendants, and poultry workers.

oro- Combining form meaning mouth.

orolingual (o-ro-ling′gwal) Relating to the mouth and tongue.

oronasal (o-ro-na′zal) Relating to the mouth and nose.

oropharynx (o-ro-far′inks) The central portion of the pharynx directly behind the oral cavity, extending from the inferior border of the soft palate to the lingual surface of the epiglottis; it contains the palatine tonsils and the posterior faucial pillars.

orotic acid (ŏ-rot′ik as′id) An important intermediate in the production of pyrimidine nucleotides.

orphan (or′fan) See orphan product, under product.

orthesis (or-the′sis) See orthosis.

orthetics (or-thet′iks) See orthotics.

ortho-, orth- Combining forms meaning straight; upright; normal; standard; corrective.

orthobiosis (or-tho-bi-o′sis) Living in a manner that promotes health (physical and mental).

orthocephalic (or-tho-sĕ-fal′ik) Having a head of appropriate proportions to the height of the individual; usually with a vertical index in the 70–75 range.

orthochromatic (or-tho-kro-mat′ik) Staining the color of the dye used; denoting certain cells.

orthodigits (or-tho-dij′its) The correction of deformed fingers or toes.

orthodontics (or-tho-don′tiks) Dental specialty concerned with correction and prevention of irregularities of the teeth.

orthodontist (or-tho-don′tist) A specialist in orthodontics.

orthodromic (or-tho-drom′ik) The conduction of nerve impulses along the normal path or direction.

orthogenics (or-tho-jen′iks) The study and treatment of mental or physical defects that obstruct usual development.

orthognathic, orthognathous (or-thog-na′thik, or-thog′nahthus) Having the proper relations of the jaws.

orthograde (or′tho-grād) The erect posture of humans; opposed to pronograde.

orthometer (or-thom′ě-ter) Device for measuring the degree of protrusion of the eyeballs.

Orthomyxoviridae (or-tho-mik-so-vir′ĭ-de) A family of single-stranded RNA viruses that includes the influenzaviruses.

orthopaedics (or-tho-pe′diks) See orthopedics.

orthopedic (or-tho-pe′dik) Relating to orthopedics.

orthopedics (or-tho-pe′diks) The surgically oriented medical specialty concerned with the preservation and restoration of functions of the skeletal system and associated structures. Also spelled orthopaedics.

orthopedist (or-tho-pe′dist) A physician who specializes in orthopedics.

orthopercussion (or-tho-per-kush′un) Percussion in which the middle finger of one hand is flexed at right angle and its tip is placed on the chest wall; the flexed finger is then struck upon the knuckle with a finger of the opposite hand.

orthophoria (or-tho-fo′re-ah) The normal condition of the two eyes in which they are free from a tendency to deviate when they cease fixing the gaze upon an object and integrating the images of the two eyes into one; a rarely seen state. Usually a small degree of deviation is considered "normal."

orthopnea (or-thop-ne′ah) Breathing difficulty except in an upright position.

orthopneic (or-thop-ne′ik) Relating to orthopnea.

orthopod (or′tho-pod) Slang for orthopedist.

Orthopoxvirus (or-tho-poks′vi-rus) Genus of the poxviruses (family Poxviridae) that includes those causing smallpox, ectromelia, and vaccinia (cowpox).

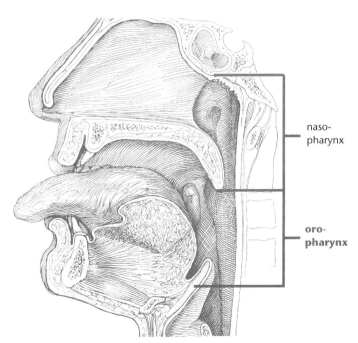

naso-
pharynx

oro-
pharynx

orthopsychiatry (or-tho-si-ki′ah-tre) The promotion of healthy emotional development by the study and treatment of human behavior.

orthoptics (or-thop′tiks) A method of therapy aimed at achieving coordinate function of the two eyes through a set of exercises; used particularly in treating the muscular imbalance of strabismus.

orthoptist (or-thop′tist) A person who treats those affected with ocular muscle imbalance and faulty visual habits by means of specially designed eye exercises.

orthoscope (or′tho-skōp) Instrument for examining the eye; by placing a layer of water in contact with the eye, it eliminates the refractive power of the cornea.

orthoscopic (or-tho-skop′ik) **1.** Relating to the orthoscope. **2.** Having normal vision.

orthoscopy (or-thos′ko-pe) **1.** Examination of the eye with an orthoscope. **2.** The distortion-free state of an optical system.

orthosis (or-tho′sis), pl. ortho′ses An orthopedic appliance; any mechanical device worn on the body to apply the necessary force to a part; used in the treatment of a physical impairment caused either by a congenital defect (e.g., clubfoot, spina bifida, malformation of long bones); by disease (e.g., muscular dystrophy, poliomyelitis, multiple sclerosis); or by trauma (e.g., fractures, spinal cord injuries, tendon tears). Orthoses are generally classified according to the region of the body involved, e.g., ankle-foot orthosis (AFO), knee-ankle-foot orthosis (KAFO), elbow orthosis (EO), wrist orthosis (WO), cervical orthosis (CO), sacroiliac orthosis (SIO). Also called orthotic; orthesis. COMPARE prosthesis.

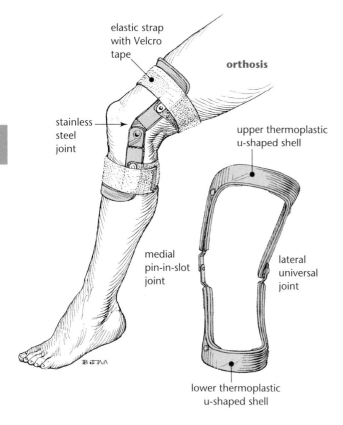

elastic strap with Velcro tape

orthosis

stainless steel joint

upper thermoplastic u-shaped shell

medial pin-in-slot joint

lateral universal joint

lower thermoplastic u-shaped shell

orthostatic (or-tho-stat′ik) Relating to the upright position.

orthothanasia (or-tho-tha-na′ze-ah) Natural death.

orthotic (or-thot′ik) **1.** Occurring in the normal position. **2.** See orthosis.

orthotics (or-thot′iks) The making and fitting of orthopedic appliances. Also called orthetics. See also orthosis.

orthotist (or′tho-tist) One who makes and fits orthopedic appliances.

orthotonos, orthotonus (or-thot′o-nos, or-thot′o-nus) Tetanic spasm in which the head, body, and limbs are held in a rigid straight position.

orthotopic (or-tho-top′ik) Occurring or present in the normal position.

orthotropic (or-tho-trop′ik) Growing along a vertical axis.

orthovoltage (or-tho-vol′tij) A medium electromotive force, from 200 to 400 kilovolts; used in radiation therapy.

os (os), pl. o′ra Latin for mouth; orifice.

os (os), pl. os′sa Latin for bone.

oscheal (os′ke-al) See scrotal.

oscheo-, osche- Combining forms meaning scrotum.

oscheoplasty (os′ke-o-plas-te) See scrotoplasty.

oscillation (os-ĭ-la′shun) Any to-and-fro movement.

oscillogram (o-sil′o-gram) A graphic record traced by an oscillograph.

oscillograph (o-sil′o-graf) An apparatus for graphically recording the oscillations of an electric current.

oscillometer (os-ĭ-lom′ĕ-ter) Apparatus used in measuring variations in blood pressure.

oscillopsia (os-ĭ-lop′se-ah) A state in which observed objects seem to oscillate.

oscilloscope (ŏ-sil′o-skōp) An electronic instrument that temporarily displays a fluctuating electrical quantity on the fluorescent screen of a cathode-ray tube.

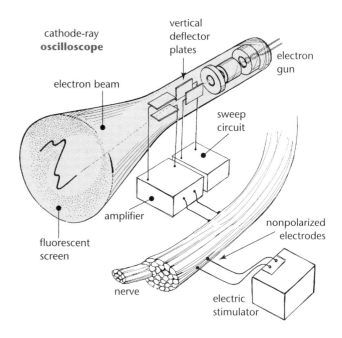

cathode-ray **oscilloscope**

vertical deflector plates

electron gun

electron beam

sweep circuit

fluorescent screen

amplifier

nonpolarized electrodes

nerve

electric stimulator

oscitate (os′ĭ-tāt) To yawn.

osculum (os′ku-lum), pl. os′cula A tiny opening.

-ose Combining form meaning a sugar (e.g., sucrose).

-osis Suffix meaning a physiologic process (e.g., mitosis); a pathologic condition (e.g., sclerosis).

osmatic (oz-mat′ik) See olfactory.

osmidrosis (oz-mĭ-dro′sis) See bromidrosis.

osmiophilic (oz-me-o-fil′ik) Readily stained with osmic dyes; applied to histologic cells and tissues.

osmium (oz′me-um) Metallic element; symbol Os, atomic number 76, atomic weight 190.2.

osmo- Combining form meaning odor.

osmoceptor (oz′mo-sep-tor) See osmoreceptor.

osmolality (oz-mo-lal′ĭ-te) The osmotic concentration of a solution, expressed as osmoles of dissolved substance per kilogram of water (solvent).

osmolar (oz-mo′lar) See osmotic.

osmolarity (oz-mo-lar′ĭ-te) The osmotic concentration of a solution expressed as osmoles of the dissolved substance per liter of solution.

osmole (oz′mōl) (Osm) Molecular weight of a solute, in grams, divided by the number of particles that one molecule provides when it enters solution.

osmometer (oz-mom′ĕ-ter) Instrument for measuring the osmolal concentration of a liquid (e.g., urine).

osmometry (oz-mom′ĕ-tre) The measure of the concentration of solute per kilogram of water (solvent).

osmophilic (oz-mo-fil′ik) Thriving in a solution of high osmotic pressure.

osmophore (oz′mo-fōr) A group of atoms whose presence in a compound causes the characteristic odor of the compound.

osmoreceptor (oz-mo-re-sep′tor) A specialized sensory nerve ending in the brain that responds to changes in osmotic pressure of the blood. Also called osmoceptor.

osmoregulatory (oz-mo-reg′u-lah-to-re) Influencing osmosis.

osmosis (oz-mo′sis) The passage of liquid from a concentrated solution to a diluted one through a semipermeable membrane separating them.

osmotic (oz-mot′ik) Relating to osmosis. Also called osmolar.

osseo- Combining form meaning bone.

osseocartilaginous (os-e-o-kar-tĭ-laj′ĭ-nus) Composed of both bone and cartilage.

osseointegration (os-e-o-in-te-gra′shun) The growing of bone onto an implanted metal device, such as one that serves as a base for a tooth implant.

osseous (os′e-us) Bony.

ossi- Combining form meaning bone.

ossicle (os′sĭ-kl) A tiny bone, especially of the middle ear.

    auditory o.'s The three tiny bones in the middle ear chamber (malleus, incus, stapes), secured to the chamber wall by ligaments; together they form a bony chain across the chamber, from the eardrum (tympanic membrane) to the oval window (adjoining the inner ear). Sound waves striking the eardrum cause the ossicles to vibrate; these vibrations are transmitted to the inner ear, where they are converted to impulses, which are interpreted by the brain as sound. Also called ear ossicles; ear bones.

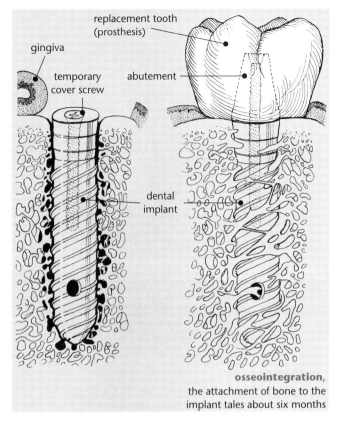

osseointegration, the attachment of bone to the implant tales about six months

    ear o.'s See auditory ossicles.

ossicular (os-sik′u-lar) Relating to an ossicle.

ossiculectomy (os-ĭ-ku-lek′to-me) Surgical removal of one or more ossicles of the middle ear.

ossiculotomy (os-ĭ-ku-lot′o-me) A surgical cut into one of the ossicles of the middle ear or of adhesions impeding their movements.

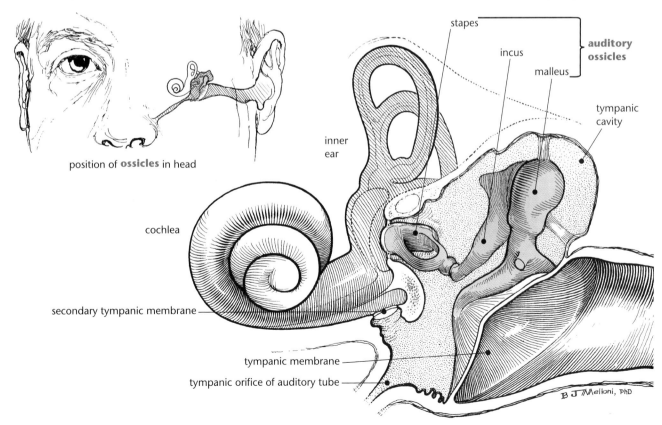

position of **ossicles** in head

ossification (os-ī-fi-ka′shun) **1.** Replacement of cartilage by bone. **2.** Formation of bone.

ossification

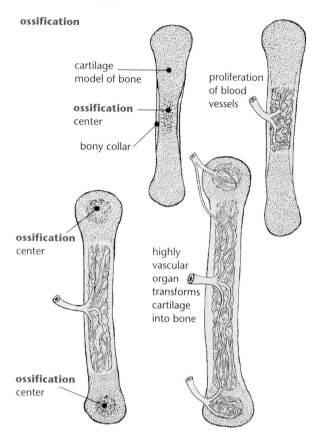

cartilage model of bone

ossification center

bony collar

proliferation of blood vessels

ossification center

highly vascular organ transforms cartilage into bone

ossification center

ossify (os′ĭ-fi) To change into bone.

ostealgia, ostalgia (os-te-al′je-ah, os-tal′je-ah) Pain in a bone. Also called osteodynia.

ostectomy (os-tek′to-me) Surgical removal of bone.

osteitis (os-te-i′tis) Inflammation of bone.

   o. deformans See Paget's disease, under disease.

   o. fibrosa cystica Condition characterized by softening and resorption of bone with formation of cysts within the bone marrow and replacement by fibrous tissue; caused by excessive hormone secretion by the parathyroid glands (hyperparathyroidism). Also called Recklinghausen's disease of bone.

   o. pubis (a) Sclerotic changes of the pubic symphysis. (b) Inflammation of the pubic symphysis occurring secondary to other conditions of the region (e.g., rheumatic changes, pregnancy, surgical procedures).

osteo- Combining form meaning bone.

osteoarthritis (os-te-o-ar-thri′tis) (OA) The most common form of arthritis, characterized by progressive deterioration and loss of articular cartilage, thickening of underlying bone with formation of spurs near the joint margins, and stiffness of affected joints; may occur at an early age secondary to traumatic, congenital, or systemic disorders. Also called degenerative joint disease (DJD); degeneratibe arthritis; hypertrophic arthritis.

osteoarthropathy (os-te-o-ar-throp′ah-the) Disorder involving bones and joints.

   hypertrophic o. Condition marked by periosteal formation of new bone (especially in the distal ends of long bones of the extremities), painful arthritis of adjacent joints, and clubbing of the fingers; it may or may not be secondary to an underlying condition; it most commonly occurs in association with disease of the lungs, especially tumors; also seen in association with heart disease, ulcerative colitis, regional enteritis, and liver disorders.

osteoblast (os′te-o-blast) A bone-forming cell, responsible for the formation of bone matrix.

osteoblastoma (os-te-o-blas-to′mah) A painful noncancerous tumor derived from primitive bone tissue, occurring most frequently on the spine of young individuals. Also called giant osteoid osteoma.

osteochondral (os-te-o-kon′dral) Relating to a bone and its cartilage.

osteochondritis (os-te-o-kon-dri′tis) Inflammation of both bone and its cartilage.

   o. dissecans The gradual separation of a fragment of cartilage and underlying bone within a joint, most frequently the knee; tends to occur in adolescence; cause is unknown although several possible causes have been suggested, including disruption of blood supply to the bone by injury to a blood vessel.

osteochondrodysplasia (os-te-o-kon-dro-dis-pla′ze-ah) Abnormal development of both cartilage and bone.

osteochondrodystrophy (os-te-o-kon-dro-dis′tro-fe) See chondro-osteodystrophy.

osteochondroma (os-te-o-kon-dro′mah) A benign, mushroom-shaped outgrowth of bone capped by growing cartilage; occurs most frequently as a lateral protrusion near the end of a long bone, with its medullary cavity continuous with the underlying marrow cavity; usually affects individuals aged 10 to 20; often discovered as a chance x-ray finding.

osteochondromatosis (os-te-o-kon-dro-mah-to′sis) See hereditary multiple exostosis, under exostosis.

osteochondrosarcoma (os-te-o-kon-dro-sar-ko′mah) A cancerous tumor of cartilage usually arising from a benign bone tumor.

osteochondrosis (os-te-o-kon-dro′sis) Any disorder affecting the ossification centers in the bones of children; characterized by degeneration or death of tissues in the absence of infection.

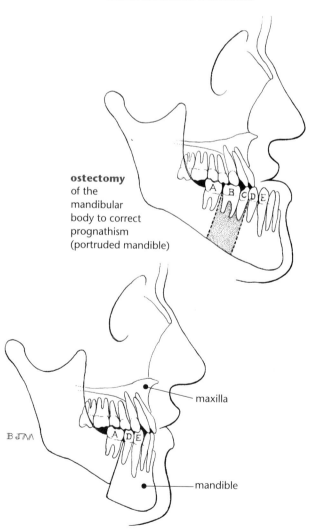

ostectomy of the mandibular body to correct prognathism (portruded mandible)

maxilla

mandible

ossification ■ **osteochondrosis**

osteoclasis, osteoclasia (os-te-ok′lah-sis, os-te-o-kla′ze-ah) Surgical or manual fracture or refracture of a deformed bone for the purpose of resetting of the bone in a more appropriate position. Also called diaclasis.

osteoclast (os′te-o-klast) A large multinucleated cell formed in bone marrow; it functions in the absorption of bone tissue.

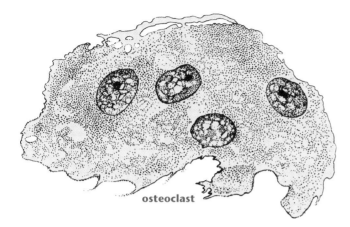

osteoclast

osteoclastoma (os-te-o-klas-to′mah) See giant cell tumor of bone, under tumor.

osteocranium (os-te-o-kra′ne-um) The skull of the fetus after ossification has begun.

osteocystoma (os-te-o-sis-to′mah) See solitary bone cyst, under cyst.

osteocyte (os′te-o-sīt) One of numerous bone cells arising from osteoblasts; it plays a role in maintaining the constituents of bone matrix at normal levels.

osteodentin (os-te-o-den′tin) A hard substance, intermediate between bone and dentin, that partially fills the pulp cavity of elderly people.

osteodermia (os-te-o-der′me-ah) The presence of bony deposits on the skin.

osteodesmosis (os-te-o-des-mo′sis) The abnormal transformation of tendons into bone.

osteodynia (os-te-o-din′e-ah) See ostealgia.

osteodystrophy (os-te-o-dis′tro-fe) Defective bone formation.

    renal o. Generalized bone changes occurring in patients with chronic renal failure; characterized by osteitis fibrosa cystica, osteomalacia, and areas of osteosclerosis.

osteofibroma (os-te-o-fi-bro′mah) A benign growth composed chiefly of bone and fibrous connective tissue.

osteogen (os′te-o-jen) The inner layer of the bone-covering membrane (periosteum) from which new bone is formed.

osteogenesis (os-te-o-jen′ĕ-sis) The formation of bone.

    o. imperfecta (OI) A group of closely related genetic disorders caused by defective bone formation; a common characteristic is bone fragility and susceptibility to fractures; features may also include (depending on degree of genetic defect) deformity of long bones, laxness of ligaments, blueness of scleras, and deafness due to otosclerosis. A rare autosomal recessive variant causes multiple fractures beginning at birth; death occurs in the first year of life. Also called brittle bones disease; brittle bones.

osteogenic, osteogenetic (os-te-o-jen′ik, os-te-o-jĕ-net′ik) Relating to bone formation; derived from bone.

osteoid (os′te-oid) 1. Resembling bone. 2. The soft organic part of intercellular bone matrix that precedes mineralization.

osteology (os-te-ol′o-je) The study of the structure of bones.

osteolysis (os-te-ol′ĭ-sis) Destruction or dissolution of bone tissue.

osteoma (os-te-o′mah) A benign tumor composed of bone tissue, usually protruding from a bone surface; most commonly seen on the facial bones.

    dental o. Osteoma projecting from the root of a tooth.

    giant osteoid o. See osteoblastoma.

osteoid o. A painful growth usually about 1 cm in diameter, most commonly occurring near the ends of long bones of the extremities of children and young adults.

osteomalacia (os-te-o-mah-la′she-ah) Disease of adults similar to childhood rickets, characterized by softening of the bones due to faulty calcification; characterized by increased amounts of bone matrix (osteoid), which either fails to calcify or does so slowly; may be due to vitamin D deficiency or to phosphate depletion.

osteomere (os′te-o-mēr) One of a series of bony structures (e.g., a vertebra).

osteometry (os-te-om′ĕ-tre) The branch of anthropology concerned with the relative size of human bones.

osteomyelitis (os′te-o-mi-ĕ-li′tis) Inflammation of the bone marrow caused by bacteria, such as staphylococci, that gain entry through a wound or injury. Also called bone abscess.

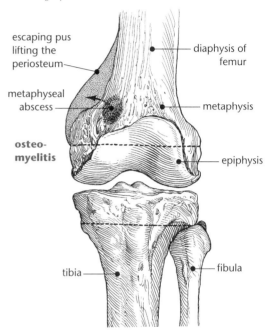

escaping pus lifting the periosteum

diaphysis of femur

metaphyseal abscess

metaphysis

osteo-myelitis

epiphysis

tibia

fibula

osteomyelodysplasia (os-te-o-mi-ĕ-lo-dis-pla′se-ah) Disease characterized by enlargement of bone marrow cavities, thinning of bony tissues, and associated deficiency of white blood cells and fever.

osteon (os′te-on) The basic unit of compact bone, composed of a central canal (conveying blood vessels and nerve endings) and several layers of bony tissue around the canal. Also called haversian system.

osteonecrosis (os-te-o-ne-kro′sis) Death of bone tissue.

osteopath (os′te-o-path) See osteopathic physician, under physician.

osteopathology (os-te-o-pah-thol′o-je) The study of bone diseases.

osteopathy (os′te-op′ah-the) A system of medical practice that, in addition to conventional diagnostic and therapeutic measures, employs manipulative procedures to correct faulty physical structure and maintain normal body mechanics and function. It is based on the concept that all body systems operate in unison and, when in correct alignment, are capable of acting against disease and other toxic conditions. Also called osteopathic medicine.

osteopenia (os-te-o-pe′nĭ-ah) Reduced bone mass or density; may or may not be due to deficient bone formation.

osteoperiostitis (os-te-o-per-ĭ-os-ti′tis) Inflammation of a bone and its covering membrane (periosteum).

osteopetrosis (os′te-o-pe-tro′sis) A rare inherited disease characterized by overgrowth and brittleness of the dense outer (cortical) layer of bones, with reduction in bone marrow, causing frequent fractures and anemia. The ribs, pelvis, and vertebrae are mostly affected. Also called marble bones; marble bones disease; Albers-Schönberg disease.

O

osteophlebitis (os-te-o-fle-bi′tis) Inflammation of the veins of a bone.

osteophony (os-te-of′o-ne) See bone conduction, under conduction.

osteophyte (os′te-o-fīt) A bony outgrowth.

osteoplasty (os′te-o-plas-te) **1.** Bone grafting. **2.** Reparative operation upon a bone (e.g., reshaping of alveolar bone in periodontal surgery).

osteoporosis (os-te-o-po-ro′sis) Disease that appears to be the result of increased resorption of bone and slowing of bone formation, seen most frequently in the elderly of both sexes, especially postmenopausal women; symptoms include bone pain, reduced height, deformity, and susceptibility to fractures; may be associated with other disorders (e.g., osteomalacia, multiple myeloma, hypopituitarism) or may be caused by certain drug therapies.

> **posttraumatic o.** See Sudeck's atrophy, under atrophy.

osteoporosis

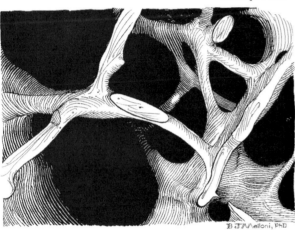

normal bone density

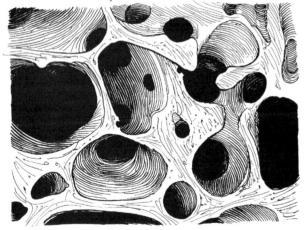

osteoradionecrosis (os-te-o-ra′de-o-ne-kro′sis) Death and degeneration of bones caused by radiation exposure.

osteorrhaphy (os-te-or′ah-fe) Wiring of a broken bone. Also called osteosuture.

osteosarcoma (os-te-o-sar-ko′mah) The most common form of bone cancer, derived from bone-forming cells and occurring usually during active bone growth (under the age of 20 years).

osteosclerosis (os-te-o-skle-ro′sis) Abnormally increased density of bone.

> **o. congenita** See achondroplasia.

osteosuture (os′te-o-su-tūr) See osteorrhaphy.

osteosynthesis (os-te-o-sin′thĕ-sis) Fastening the fractured ends of a bone.

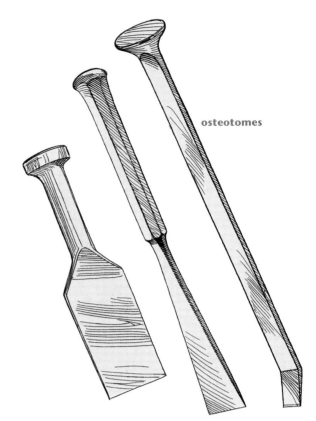

osteotomes

osteotome (os′te-o-t⁻om) A chisellike instrument for cutting bone.

osteotomy (os-te-ot′o-me) Surgical cutting into or through a bone.

> **C-o.** Procedure for correcting a retruded mandible by advancing the anterior portion of a bilateral C-shaped sectioning of the mandible through the rami.

> **vertical o.** Procedure for correcting a protruded mandible by sectioning of the mandibular rami, from the mandibular notch to the angle of the mandible, to facilitate posterior repositioning of the mandibular bodies.

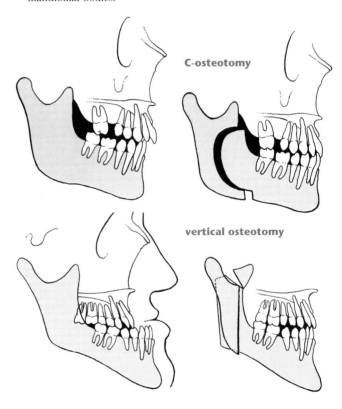

C-osteotomy

vertical osteotomy

ostia (os'te-ah) Plural of ostium.

ostial (os'te-al) Relating to a small orifice or opening.

ostium (os'te-um), pl. os'tia A small opening into a hollow structure.

    o. primum See interatrial foramen primum, under foramen.

    o. secundum See interatrial foramen secundum, under foramen.

ostomy (os'to-me) An artificial opening created surgically.

ot- Combining form meaning ear.

otalgia (o-tal'je-ah) See earache.

otalgic (o-tal'jik) Relating to earache.

othemorrhagia (¯ot-hem-o-ra'je-ah) Bleeding from the ear.

otic (o'tik) Relating to the ear.

otitic (o-tit'ik) Relating to inflammation of the ear.

otitis (o-ti'tis) Inflammation of the ear.

    chronic suppurative o. media Inflammation of the middle ear accompanied by a thick mucopurulent discharge; may be associated with hearing loss, and may progress to involve the bone.

    o. externa Otitis of the external ear canal, caused by any of a variety of skin infections.

    o. interna See labyrinthitis.

    o. media Otitis (acute or chronic) usually due to infection spreading from the upper respiratory tract through the eustachian (auditory) tube.

    secretory o. media See serous otitis media.

    serous o. media Inflammation of the mucosa of the middle ear marked by accumulation of fluid that causes conduction hearing loss. The fluid may be thin, mucoid, or mucopurulent, and usually collects because of eustachian (auditory) tube obstruction, which commonly follows otitis media and upper respiratory infection. Also called secretory otitis media.

oto- Combining form meaning ear.

otoantritis (o-to-an-tri'tis) Inflammation of the air cells of the mastoid process, usually occurring as a complication of chronic suppurative otitis media.

otocephaly (o-to-sef'ah-le) Developmental defect characterized by extreme smallness of the chin and approximation of the ears toward the front of the neck.

otocleisis (o-to-kli'sis) 1. Abnormal closure of the eustachian (auditory) tube. 2. Any obstruction of the external auditory canal.

otoconia (o-to-ko'ne-ah) See statoconia.

otocranium (o-to-kra'ne-um) The portion of the temporal bone containing the middle and inner ear.

otodynia (o-to-din'e-ah) Earache.

otoencephalitis (o-to-en-sef-ah-li'tis) Inflammation of the brain caused by spread of infection from the middle ear.

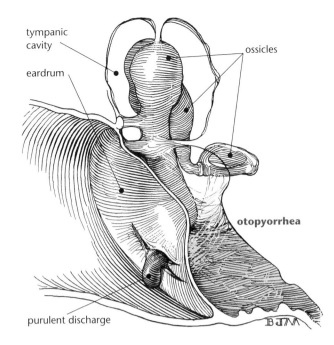

tympanic cavity
ossicles
eardrum
otopyorrhea
purulent discharge

otoganglion (o-to-gang'gle-on) See otic ganglion, under ganglion.

otolaryngologist (o-to-lar-in-gol'o-jist) A specialist in otolaryngology.

otolaryngology (o-to-lar-in-gol'o-je) The branch of medicine concerned with the study of the ear and upper respiratory tract and the diagnosis and treatment of their diseases.

otoliths (o'to-liths) See statoconia.

otologic (o-to-loj'ik) Relating to otology.

otologist (o-tol'o-jist) A specialist in otology.

otology (o-tol'o-je) The branch of medicine concerned with the diagnosis and treatment of diseases of the ear.

otomycosis (o-to-mi-ko'sis) Fungal infection of the external auditory canal.

otoneuralgia (o-to-nu-ral'je-ah) Neuralgic earache.

otopathy (o-top'ah-the) Any disease of the ear.

otoplasty (o'to-plas-te) Any reparative operation on the auricle of the ear, most commonly performed on protruding ears.

otopyorrhea (o-to-pi-o-re'ah) Purulent discharge through a ruptured eardrum (tympanic membrane).

O

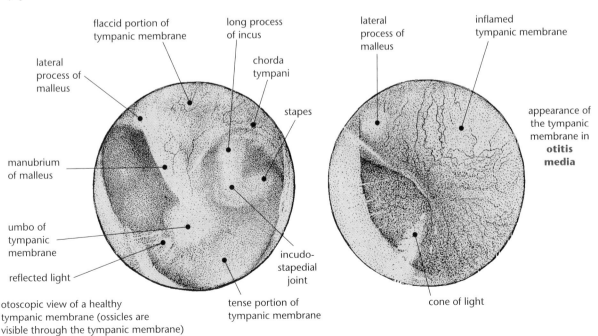

flaccid portion of tympanic membrane
long process of incus
lateral process of malleus
chorda tympani
stapes
manubrium of malleus
umbo of tympanic membrane
reflected light
incudo-stapedial joint
tense portion of tympanic membrane
otoscopic view of a healthy tympanic membrane (ossicles are visible through the tympanic membrane)

lateral process of malleus
inflamed tympanic membrane
appearance of the tympanic membrane in **otitis media**
cone of light

otorhinolaryngology (o-to-ri-no-lar-in-gol′o-je) The branch of medicine dealing with diseases of the ear, nose, and larynx.

otorhinology (o-to-ri-nol′o-je) The study of the ear and the nose.

otorrhagia (o-to-ra′je-ah) Bleeding from the ear.

otorrhea (o-to-re′ah) Abnormal discharge from the ear.

    cerebrospinal fluid (CSF) o. Leakage of cerebrospinal fluid through the ear, usually resulting from a fracture of the base of the skull and a tear of the membranes (meninges) covering the brain; rarely, it may be caused by injury to the membranes during the course of ear surgery.

otosclerosis (o-to-skle-ro′sis) Immobilization of the stapes by an overgrowth of spongy bone along the medial wall of the middle ear; it interferes with conduction of sound waves, leading to hearing impairment.

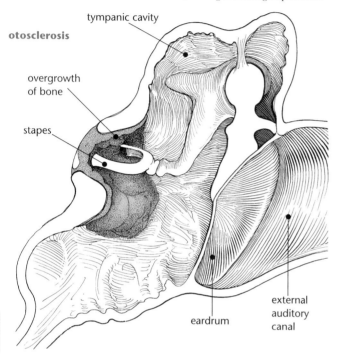

otosclerosis

tympanic cavity

overgrowth of bone

stapes

eardrum

external auditory canal

otoscope (o′to-skōp) Instrument for inspecting the external ear canal and the eardrum (tympanic membrane); it contains magnifying lenses, a light, and a funnel-shaped tip.

    pneumatic o. An otoscope that permits observation of the degree of flaccidity of the eardrum by using alternate positive and negative pressure.

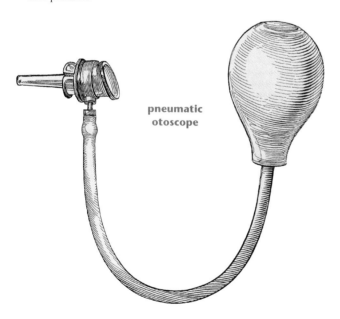

pneumatic otoscope

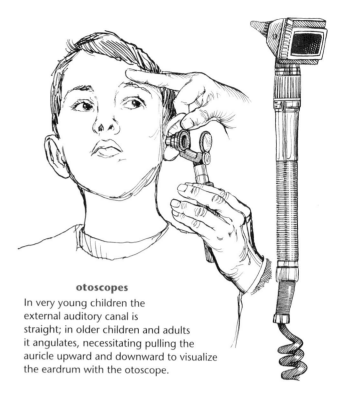

otoscopes

In very young children the external auditory canal is straight; in older children and adults it angulates, necessitating pulling the auricle upward and downward to visualize the eardrum with the otoscope.

otoscopy (o-tos′ko-pe) Examination of the eardrum (tympanic membrane) with an otoscope.

otosteal (o-tos′te-al) Relating to the ear ossicles.

ototomy (o-tot′o-me) **1.** Dissection of the ear. **2.** See myringotomy.

ototoxic (o-to-tok′sik) Having a harmful effect either on the hearing or on the equilibrium component of the ear; said especially of certain drugs that cause hearing loss.

ototoxicity (o-to-toks-is′ĭ-te) The quality of being ototoxic.

ouabain (wah-ba′in) A rapidly acting cardiac glycoside from the seeds of *Strophanthus gratus* or from the wood of *Acocanthera ouabaio*; a constituent of African arrow poison.

ounce (owns) (oz.) **1.** An avoirdupois unit of weight equal to one-sixteenth of a pound. **2.** An apothecaries' unit of weight equal to one–twelfth of a pound.

    fluid o. (fl.oz.) An apothecaries' unit of fluid measure, the equivalent of 29.57 milliliters.

-ous Suffix meaning having (e.g., cancerous).

outbreak (owt′brāk) The sudden occurrence of a disease in several members of a community; the disease may or may not spread sufficiently to become an epidemic.

outlet (owt′let) In anatomy, an opening or passageway that permits an outward movement.

    pelvic o. The lower aperture of the pelvis, bounded by the pubic arch, the ischial tuberosities, the sacrotuberous ligaments, and the tip of the coccyx.

    thoracic o. The outlet of the chest cavity bounded in back by the 12th throacic vertebra, at the sides by the 12th and 11th ribs, and in front by the cartilages of the 10th, 9th, 8th, and 7th ribs; it is closed by the diaphragm. Also called inferior thoracic aperture.

outpatient (owt′pa-shent) A patient treated in a hospital or clinic without being hospitalized.

output (owt′poot) **1.** The quantity of a substance produced by or eliminated from the body in a given time span. **2.** The measure of performance by an organ or organ system. **3.** An immediate quantity or result of professional or institutional health care activities (e.g., outpatient visits, patient hospital days, laboratory tests).

    cardiac o. The quantity of blood pumped by the heart per unit time (usually per minute).

    minute o. The quantity of blood pumped by the heart during one minute, normally 4 to 5 liters at rest in an average-sized person.

stroke o. The quantity of blood ejected with a single heartbeat.

urinary o. The amount of urine excreted by the kidneys per unit time.

ova (o'vah) Plural of ovum.

oval (o'val) **1.** Relating to an ovum. **2.** Egg-shaped.

ovalbumin (o-val-bu'min) The chief protein of egg whites.

ovalocyte (o'vah-lo-sīt) See elliptocyte.

ovalocytosis (o-val-o-si-to'sis) See elliptocytosis.

ovarialgia, ovaralgia (o-va-re-al'je-ah, o-var-al'je-ah) Pain in an ovary. Also called oophoralgia.

ovarian (o-va're-an) Relating to the ovaries.

ovariectomy (o-va-re-ek'to-me) See oophorectomy.

ovario-, ovari- Combining forms meaning ovary.

ovariocentesis (o-va-re-o-sen-te'sis) Puncture of an ovarian cyst.

ovariocyesis (o-va-re-o-si-e'sis) Ovarian pregnancy.

ovariohysterectomy (o-va-re-o-his-ter-ek'to-me) Removal of the ovaries and uterus.

ovariolysis (o-va-re-ol'ī-sis) The cutting away of adhesions that prevent the normal mobility of the ovary; a procedure used in the treatment of certain cases of female infertility.

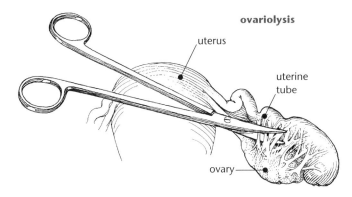

ovariolysis

uterus

uterine tube

ovary

ovarioncus (o-va-re-ong'kus) See oophoroma.

ovariopathy (o-va-re-op'ah-the) See oophoropathy.

ovariorrhexis (o-va-re-o-rek'sis) Rupture of an ovary.

ovariosalpingectomy (o-va-re-o-sal-pin-jek'to-me) See oophorosalpingectomy.

ovariosalpingitis (o-va-re-o-sal-pin-ji'tis) See oophorosalpingitis.

ovariotomy (o-va-re-ot'o-me) See oophorotomy.

ovaritis (o-vah-ri'tis) See oophoritis.

ovarium (o-va're-um) Latin for ovary.

ovary (o'vah-re) One of the paired sexual glands in which ova are formed; situated on either side of the uterus, near the free end of the fallopian (uterine) tube; it produces the female hormones estrogen and progesterone; the female gonad.

large white o. See polycystic ovary.

polycystic o. A diseased, usually enlarged ovary containing multiple cysts and covered with a thick, pearly white capsule; seen in such conditions as Stein-Leventhal syndrome, abnormal bleeding, and virilism; it is associated with infertility. Popularly called large white ovary.

third o. An accessory ovary.

overbite (o'ver-bīt) See vertical overlap, under overlap.

overclosure (o-ver-klo'zhur) Condition in which the mandible rises too far before the teeth make contact; may be due to a changed tooth shape (through grinding), drifting of teeth, or loss of teeth, resulting in a shortened face length.

overcompensation (o-ver-kom-pen-sa'shun) A type of behavior in which an overwhelming feeling of inadequacy inspires exaggerated correction (e.g., overaggressiveness).

overdetermination (o-ver-de-ter-mǐ-na'shun) The multiple causation of a single event, behavior, or emotional symptom.

overdose (o'ver-dōs) **1.** An excessive dose. **2.** (O.D.) To poison with an excessive dose.

overextension (o-ver-eks-ten'shun) See hyperextension.

overhang (o'ver-hang) The portion of a dental filling in excess of, and extending over, the normal tooth contour.

overhydration (o-ver-hi-dra'shun) See hyperhydration.

overjet, overjut (o'ver-jet, o'ver-jut) See horizontal overlap, under overlap.

overlap (o'ver-lap) A projection of one tissue or structure over another.

horizontal o. Excessive projection of the upper anterior and/or posterior teeth beyond their antagonists of the lower jaw in a horizontal direction. Also called overjet; overjut; popularly called buck teeth.

vertical o. The overlapping of the lower incisors by the upper incisors when the posterior teeth are in normal contact. Also called overbite.

overlay (o'ver-la) Any condition that is superimposed on an existing one.

emotional o. An emotional disturbance occurring with, or resulting from, an organic disease.

overriding (o-ver-rīd'ing) The sliding of one fragment of a fractured bone alongside the other.

overt (o-ver't) Evident; demonstrable; not hidden.

over-the-counter (OTC) Denoting medications that are considered safe for use without medical supervision (i.e., nonprescription drugs).

overventilation (o-ver-ven-tǐ-la'shun) See hyperventilation.

ovi- Combining form meaning egg.

ovicidal (o-vǐ-si'dal) Causing destruction of the ovum.

oviduct (o'vǐ-dukt) See uterine tube, under tube.

oviferous (o-vif'er-us) Conveying or containing eggs.

ovigenesis (o-vǐ-jen'ě-sis) See oogenesis.

ovine (o'vīn) Relating to sheep.

oviparous (o-vip'ah-rus) Egg-laying (e.g., fish, birds, reptiles, insects).

ovo- Combining form meaning egg.

ovomucoid (o-vo-mu'koid) The mucoprotein of egg whites.

ovotestis (o-vo-tes'tis) An abnormal gonad in which both testicular and ovarian tissues are present.

ovoviviparous (o-vo-vi-vip'ah-rus) Bearing young that develop from eggs retained within the maternal body (e.g., certain fish and reptiles).

ovulation (o-vu-la'shun) The discharge of an ovum from the mature (vesicular) follicle of an ovary.

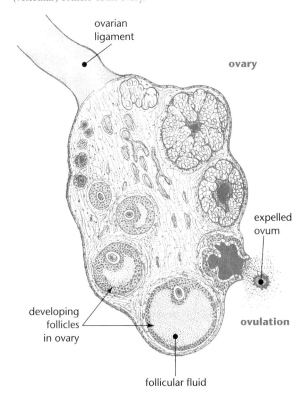

ovarian ligament

ovary

expelled ovum

ovulation

developing follicles in ovary

follicular fluid

ovule (o'vūl) 1. The ovum in the ovarian follicle. 2. Any small egg-shaped structure.

ovulocyclic (o-vu-lo-sik'lik) Associated with, or occurring within, the ovulatory cycle.

ovum (o'vum) pl. o'va The female reproductive cell that, when fused with the male cell (spermatozoon), forms the zygote. Also called egg; oocyte.

oxacillin sodium (oks-ah-sil'in so'de-um) A semisynthetic antibiotic used in the treatment of infections with gram-positive organisms, especially staphylococci, that have become resistant to penicillin due to production of a penicillinase.

oxalate (ok'sah-lāt) A salt of oxalic acid.

oxalic acid (ok-sal'ik as'id) Compound found in many plants and formed in the body by oxidation of glyoxylate; present in excessive amounts in the urine of persons afflicted with primary hyperoxaluria and may lead to formation of kidney stones.

oxaloacetic acid (ok-sah-lo-ah-se'tik as'id) An intermediate in the tricarboxylic acid cycle.

oxalosis (ok-sah-lo'sis) Accumulation of calcium oxalate crystals in the kidneys, bones, arteries, and heart muscle; a feature of primary hyperoxaluria, usually leading to death by kidney failure.

oxalosuccinic acid (ok-sah-lo-suk-sin'ik as'id) An intermediate in the tricarboxylic acid cycle.

oxaluria (ok-sah-lu're-ah) The presence of excessive calcium oxalate in the urine.

oxandrolone (ok-san'dro-lōn) An anabolic steroid sometimes prescribed after a major illness to help increase weight.

oxazepam (oks-az'ĕ-pam) A benzodiazepine tranquilizer used in the treatment of anxiety and insomnia; may cause dependence.

oxidase (ok'sĭ-dās) Any of a group of enzymes that promote oxidation by the addition of oxygen or by the removal of hydrogen or electrons.

oxidation (ok-sĭ-da'shun) Chemical combination with oxygen.

oxidation-reduction (ok-sĭ-da'shun re-duk'shun) Any chemical reaction in which electrons are transferred from one atom or molecule to another. Frequently called redox.

oxidize (ok'sĭ-dīz) To combine or to cause combination with oxygen.

oxidoreductase (ok-sĭ-do-re-duk'tās) Any enzyme promoting an oxidation-reduction reaction.

oximeter (ok-sim'ĕ-ter) Instrument used to photoelectrically measure the degree of oxygen saturation in a sample of blood.

pulse o. A monitor used in anesthetized patients, without pricking their skin, to measure oxygen saturation in the blood (i.e., the percentage of red blood cells that have oxygen attached to them). The monitor provides a continuous record of the oxygen level in the blood and sounds an alarm if the level falls too low.

oxy- Combining form meaning oxygen; pointed; sharp.

oxycephalic (ok-se-sĕ-fal'ik) Relating to oxycephaly. Also called acrocephalic.

oxycephaly (ok-se-sef'ah-le) A skull enlarged in a vertical direction, with a peaked or cone shape; caused by early closure of the lambdoid and coronal sutures of the skull. Also called acrocephaly; popularly called tower skull.

oxychromatic (ok-se-kro-mat'ik) See acidophilic (1).

oxychromatin (ok-se-kro'mah-tin) Chromatin that is readily stained with acid dyes.

oxygen (ok'sĭ-jen) An odorless and colorless gas, essential to animal and plant life; symbol O, atomic number 8, atomic weight 16. It constitutes about one-fifth of the earth's atmosphere.

oxygenase (ok'sĭ-jĕ-nās) Any enzyme promoting the incorporation of both atoms of the oxygen molecule into a single substrate.

oxygenate (ok'sĭ-jĕn-āt) To supply oxygen.

oxygenation (ok-sĭ-jĕ-na'shun) 1. The combination of oxygen with the blood pigment hemoglobin. 2. The supplying of oxygen (e.g., to a tissue or to a person).

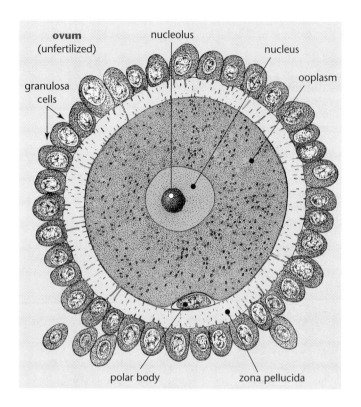

ovum (unfertilized) — nucleolus — nucleus — ooplasm — granulosa cells — polar body — zona pellucida

apneic o. See diffusion respiration, under respiration.

oxygenator (ok-sĭ-jĕ-na'tor) Device for the mechanical oxygenation of venous blood.

oxygenize (ok-sĭ-je'nīz) To oxidize.

oxyhemoglobin (ok-se-he-mo-glo'bin) (HbO₂) Hemoglobin combined with oxygen; present in arterial blood. Also called oxygenated hemoglobin.

oxyphil (ok'se-fil) See eosinophilic leukocyte, under leukocyte.

oxyphonia (ok-se-fo'ne-ah) Abnormal shrillness of the voice.

oxypurine (ok-se-pu'rin) An oxygen-containing purine (e.g., uric acid and xanthine).

oxytocia (ok-se-to'se-ah) Rapid childbirth.

oxytocic (ok-se-to'sik) 1. Relating to a rapid childbirth. 2. Hastening the childbirth process by stimulating uterine contraction.

oxytocin (ok-se-to'sin) (OXT) Hormone produced in the hypothalamus (at the base of the brain) and stored in the posterior lobe of the pituitary; it stimulates smooth muscle contraction; causes strong contraction of the pregnant uterus and ejection of milk from the breast (distinguished from prolactin, a hormone that stimulates milk production).

oxyuriasis (ok-se-u-ri'ah-sis) Infestation with pinworms.

oxyuricide (ok-se-u'rī-sid) An agent that kills pinworms.

oxyurid (ok-se-u'rid) Pinworm.

ozena (o-ze'nah) See atrophic rhinitis, under rhinitis.

ozone (o'zon) (O₃) A poisonous gas, formed naturally from an electric discharge through oxygen or by exposure of oxygen to ultraviolet rays; occurs as a product of photochemical oxidation of automobile exhaust. It is made commercially by passing oxygen over aluminum plates that have been charged with 10,000 volts. Exposure causes nose and eye irritation, cough, chest tightness, and shortness of breath.

ozonometer (o-zo-nom'ĕ-ter) Apparatus for estimating the amount of ozone in the atmosphere by using a series of test papers.

P

pacemaker (pās′māk-er) **1.** A specialized tissue (e.g., sinoatrial node in the heart) or a device that establishes and maintains the rate of a rhythmic activity. **2.** Any device that performs such function. **3.** Any substance that sets the pace for a series of chain reactions.

   artificial cardiac p. An electronic device designed to stimulate contraction of the heart muscle and to maintain a regular heartbeat by electrical impulses; used when impairment of impulse initiation or conduction between atria and ventricles (A-V block) produces severe symptoms.

   demand p. An artificial cardiac pacemaker that automatically discharges impulses only when the heart rate slows or when a heartbeat is missed; a return of the normal heart rate stops the activity of the demand pacemaker.

   ectopic p. Any pacemaker of the heart other than the sinus node.

   external p. An artificial cardiac pacemaker that has an impulse generator designed to be worn outside the body (e.g., on a belt) while the stimulating electrodes are placed within the heart or on its surface.

   fixed-rate p. An artificial cardiac pacemaker that discharges impulses at a steady rate.

   implanted p., internal p. An artificial cardiac pacemaker that has an impulse generator designed to be placed beneath the skin, either on the chest just below the collarbone (clavicle) or on the abdomen.

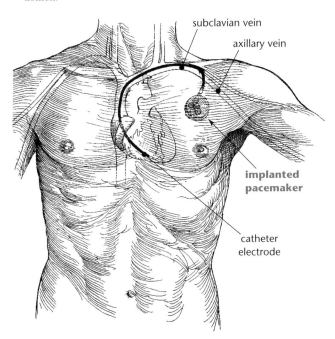

subclavian vein
axillary vein
implanted pacemaker
catheter electrode

   shifting p. See wandering pacemaker.
   wandering p. A disturbance of the heartbeat in which its origin changes from the normal to an abnormal location, or from one abnormal location to another. Also called shifting pacemaker.
pachy- Prefix meaning thick.
pachyblepharon (pak-e-blef′ah-ron) A thickening of the border of an eyelid.
pachycephaly (pak-e-sef′ah-le) Abnormal thickening of the skull.

pachycholia (pak-e-ko′le-ah) Abnormal viscous condition of the bile.
pachychromatic (pak-e-kro-mat′ik) Denoting a nucleus that has a coarse chromatin network.
pachydactyly (pak-e-dak′tĭ-le) Abnormal enlargement of fingers or toes.
pachyderma (pak-e-der′mah) Abnormal thickness or coarseness of the skin. Also called pachydermatosis.
   p. laryngis A form of chronic laryngitis characterized by thickening of the laryngeal lining, especially of the vocal folds; usually caused by chronic irritation.
pachydermatosis (pak-e-der-mah-to′sis) See pachyderma.
pachydermatous (pak-e-der′mah-tus) Relating to pachyderma.
pachydermoperiostosis (pak-e-der′mo-per-e-os-to′sis) An inherited condition characterized by thickening and oiliness of the skin, coarse facial features, deep furrows of the forehead and scalp, and enlargement of hands with clubbing of fingers.
pachygyria (pak-e-ji′re-ah) Unusually large convolutions of the brain.
pachyleptomeningitis (pak-e-lep-to-men-in-ji′tis) Inflammation of the membranes (meninges) covering the brain and spinal cord.
pachylosis (pak-e-lo′sis) A rough and dry condition of the skin, especially of the lower part of the legs.
pachymeningitis (pak-e-men-in-ji′tis) Thickening and inflammation of the dura mater.
pachymeningopathy (pak-e-men-in-gop′ah-te) Any disease of the dura mater.
pachymeter (pah-kim′ĕ-ter) Instrument for measuring thin plates, membranes, or any other thin structure.
pachyonychia (pak-e-o-nik′e-ah) Abnormal thickening of the nails.
   p. congenita Inherited condition, present from birth, in which fingernails and toenails are thick and deformed; may be accompanied by abnormalities of mucous membranes and skin.
pachyperiostitis (pak-e-per-e-os-ti′tis) Inflammatory thickening of periosteum, the membrane that envelops bones.
pachyperitonitis (pak-e-per-e-to-ni′tis) Inflammatory thickening of the peritoneum, the membrane lining the abdominopelvic cavity.
pachysalpingitis (pak-e-sal-pin-ji′tis) Inflammatory swelling and thickening of the fallopian (uterine) tubes.
pachysomia (pak-e-so′me-ah) Abnormal thickening of soft tissue.
pachytene (pak′e-tēn) The stage of cell division (meiosis) in which each chromosome separates into its two components (chromatids), so that each pair of homologous chromosomes becomes one unit composed of four intertwined chromatids.
pack (pak) **1.** To wrap the body or a part with sheets, blankets, or other material for therapeutic purposes. **2.** To fill a cavity or orifice (e.g., to control bleeding). **3.** Any material so used.
   cold p. A sheet, blanket, or towel wrung out of cold water, or a pliable container filled with a cold-retaining substance for wrapping the body or a limb.
   dry p. Dry warmed blankets for wrapping the body to induce profuse sweating.
   hot p. Cloth wrung out of hot water, or a pliable container filled with a heat-retaining substance for wrapping the body or a limb.
   wet p. Wet blankets or sheets, hot or cold, for wrapping the body or a limb.
packer (pak′er) An instrument for introducing an absorbent material into a body cavity or orifice.

P

packing (pak'ing) **1.** The application of a pack. **2.** The material used to fill a wound or cavity.

paclitaxel (pak-li-taks'el) An anticancer drug for treating ovarian cancer that has progressed in spite of standard treatment (refractory ovarian cancer); its mechanism of action appears to be cytotoxicity through inhibition of cell division. Trade name: Taxol.

pad (pad) **1.** A soft material used as a cushion to protect a vulnerable surface or to hold a dressing in place. **2.** A collection of soft tissue serving as a cushion between structures or to fill a space.

    abdominal p. An absorbent pad used in surgical procedures.

    buccal fat p. An encapsulated mass of fat in the cheek, superficial to the buccinator muscle. It is traversed by the parotid duct.

    fat p. A collection of adipose tissue filling a space.

    infrapatellar fat p. A large pad of fat situated below the kneecap (patella); it separates the patellar ligament and part of the kneecap from the enveloping (synovial) membrane of the knee joint.

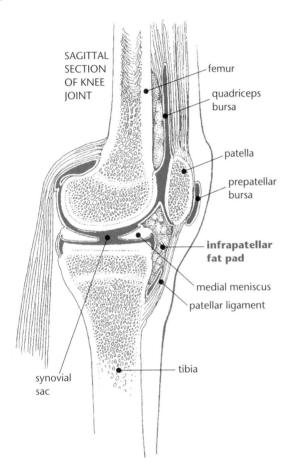

SAGITTAL SECTION OF KNEE JOINT

femur
quadriceps bursa
patella
prepatellar bursa
infrapatellar fat pad
medial meniscus
patellar ligament
tibia
synovial sac

    metatarsal p. Any of various pads designed to be worn inside a shoe, under the metatarsal bones, to lessen the pressure on the weight-bearing areas of the foot.

    Passavant's p. See Passavant's ridge, under ridge.

    sucking p., suctorial p. The prominent buccal fat pad of an infant, believed to help prevent the cheeks from being sucked in while the baby nurses.

pagophagia (pa-go-fa'je-ah) The consumption of large quantities of ice; sometimes associated with iron deficiency.

-pagus Combining form meaning a union (e.g., craniopagus).

pain (pān) A physical or mental sensation of distress or suffering.

    bearing-down p. Pain due to uterine contraction during the second stage of labor.

    false p.'s Pains caused by uterine contractions during pregnancy, frequently mistaken for true labor pains.

    girdle p. Pain felt around the trunk usually accompanying disorders of the spinal cord.

    growing p.'s Leg pains experienced by children, usually at night, resembling rheumatic symptoms but having no discernible cause or significance.

    intermenstrual p. Pelvic pain occurring midway between two menstruations. Also called midpain.

    intractable p. Pain that is not relieved by analgesic medications.

    labor p. Pain caused by the rhythmic contraction of the pregnant uterus at the onset of childbirth; characteristically it increases in frequency, duration, and severity as the moment of birth approaches.

    low back p. Pain arising from any of several structures in the lumbar spine (including ligaments interconnecting the vertebrae, facet joints between vertebrae, vertebral periosteum, muscles and fascia surrounding the vertebrae, blood vessels, spinal nerve roots); causes include: injuries to muscles and ligaments, degenerative changes in the intervertebral disks and facet joints, herniated disk with irritation of adjacent nerve roots, narrowing of spinal canal and outlets for nerve roots, severe spinal anomalies (e.g., scoliosis), underlying systemic disease (e.g., spinal cancer and infections), diseases of organs unrelated to the spine.

    phantom-limb p. Pain felt as though arising from a limb that has been amputated.

    referred p. Pain felt in an area of the body that is not the site of origin of the pain, e.g., pain in the left arm due to heart disease (angina pectoris). Also called synalgia.

    sympathetically maintained p. (SMP) Pain that begins with an injury (e.g., shoulder dislocation, sprained wrist), grows in severity out of proportion to the injury, and recurs intermittently for months or years after the injury heals, usually brought back by anything that stimulates the sympathetic nervous system, such as stress or change in room temperature; caused by malfunctioning of certain nerve cells (nociceptors).

paint (pānt) A liquid medication applied to the skin with a brush.

pair (pār) Two similar things regarded together as a functional or structural unit.

    base p. Either of the two pairs of purine-pyrimidine bases that make up the DNA molecule; they are joined by hydrogen bonds.

palatal (pal'ah-tal) Relating to the palate.

palate (pal'at) The partition between the nasal and oral cavities. Also called palatum; popularly called roof of the mouth.

    cleft p. Congenital fissure of the palate that, when extending through the dental arch, is often associated with a cleft lip.

    hard p. The anterior, bony part of the palate.

    soft p. The posterior, soft, muscular part of the palate; it extends posteriorly from the posterior margin of the hard palate. Also called velum palatinum.

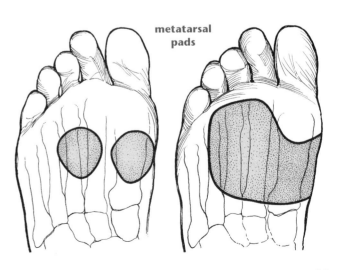

metatarsal pads

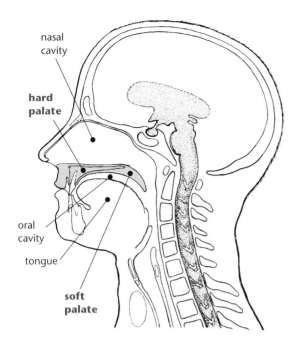

cleft palate (partial)

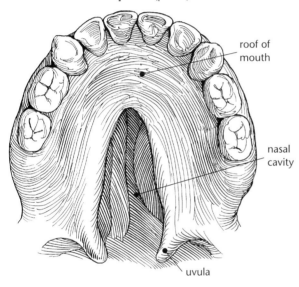

cleft palate (complete)

palatiform (pah-lat'ĭ-form) Resembling the palate.
palatine (pal'ah-tēn) Relating to the palate.
palato- Combining form meaning palate.
palatoglossal (pal-ah-to-glos'al) Relating to the palate and tongue.
palatograph (pal'ah-to-graf) Device for measuring movements of the soft palate during speech and respiration.
palatopharyngeal (pal-ah-to-fah-rin'je-al) Relating to the palate and the pharynx.
palatopharyngoplasty (pal'ah-to-fah-ring'go-plas'te) Shortening of the soft palate by removal of redundant tissue; used to treat severe snoring and sleep apnea.
palatoplasty (pal'ah-to-plas-te) Surgical reconstruction of a cleft palate.
palatoplegia (pal'ah-to-ple'je-ah) Paralysis of the muscles of the soft palate.
palatoschisis (pal-ah-tos'kĭ-sis) Cleft palate.
paleo-, pale- Combining forms meaning old.
palindrome (pal'in-drōm) A sequence in the DNA molecule that reads the same in both directions (i.e., backward and forward).
palindromia (pal-in-dro'me-ah) Recurrence of a disease.
palindromic (pal-in-dro'mik) Recurring.
palingenesis (pal-in-jen'ĕ-sis) The appearance of characteristics in recent descendants that were present in remote ancestors but missing in intervening generations.
palinphrasia (pal-in-fra'ze-ah) Abnormal speech consisting of unnecessary repetition of words and phrases.
palladium (pah-la'de-um) Metallic element; symbol Pd, atomic number 46, atomic weight 106.4.
pallesthesia (pal-es-the'ze-ah) The perception of vibrations, especially those transmitted through bone. Also called vibratory sensibility.
palliate (pal'e-āt) To reduce the severity of.
palliation (pah-le-a'shun) Relief; mitigation.
palliative (pal'e-ah-tiv) **1.** Serving to alleviate symptoms or affording temporary relief without curing the disease. **2.** A medication or treatment producing such an effect.
pallidectomy (pal-ĭ-dek'to-me) Removal or destruction of the globus pallidus in the brain.
pallidotomy (pal-ĭ-dot'o-me) Partial destruction of the globus pallidus in the brain as a measure to reduce involuntary movements.

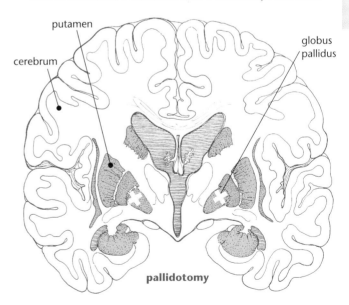

pallidotomy

pallium (pal'e-um) The cerebral cortex and subadjacent white matter.
pallor (pal'or) Lack of color.
palm (palm) The anterior, flat side of the hand, exclusive of digits.
    granular p. Descriptive term for the presence of multiple minute keratoses on the palms caused by chronic arsenic poisoning. See also arsenic poisoning, under poisoning.

palmar (pal′mar) Relating to the palm of the hand.

palmitic acid (pal-mit′ĭk as′id) A saturated fatty acid present in a variety of fats and oils. Also called hexadecanoic acid.

palpable (pal′pah-bl) Perceptible through touch.

palpate (pal′pāt) To examine by gentle pressure with the palm of the hand or the fingers.

palpation (pal-pā′shun) Examination by feeling and pressing with the hand or fingers over an organ or part of the body as an aid to diagnosis.

palpebra (pal-pe′brah), pl. palpe′brae Latin for eyelid.

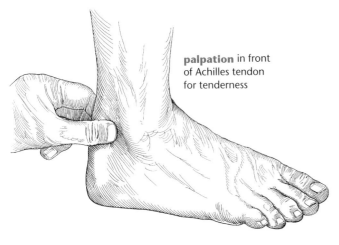

palpation in front of Achilles tendon for tenderness

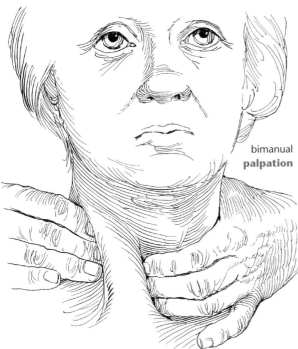

bimanual **palpation**

palpebral (pal-pe′bral) Relating to the eyelids.

palpitation (pal-pĭ-ta′shun) Forceful or rapid heartbeat, perceptible to the person.

palsy (pawl′ze) Paralysis.

    Bell's p. Sudden unilateral paralysis of the face sometimes preceded by pain behind the ear; complete recovery usually occurs within several weeks or months; believed to be caused by damage to the facial (7th cranial) nerve. Also called facial palsy; facioplegia.

    cerebral p. Any impairment of neurologic functions, generally characterized by obvious motor deficits.

    Erb's p. Paralysis of the upper musculature of an infant's arm (deltoid, biceps, anterior brachial, and long supinator muscles);

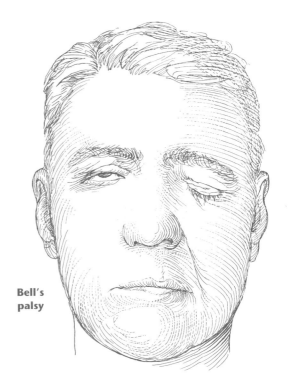

Bell's palsy

caused by injury to the brachial plexus, or to the roots of the fifth and sixth cervical nerves during birth; usually associated with difficult breech delivery or forceps delivery (especially in brow and face presentations). Also called Duchenne-Erb paralysis.

    facial p. See Bell's palsy.

    lead p. Paralysis of the extensor muscles of the wrist, associated with lead poisoning. Also called lead paralysis.

    nursemaid's p. Injury to the lower portion of the brachial plexus and resulting paralysis of a child's arm, caused by jerking or swinging the child by one arm.

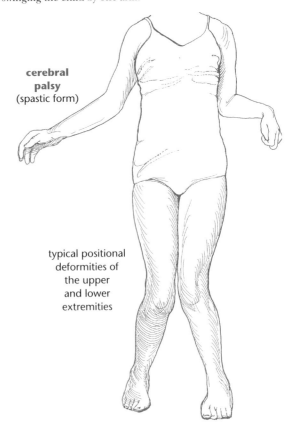

cerebral palsy (spastic form)

typical positional deformities of the upper and lower extremities

palmar ■ palsy

shaking p., trembling p. See parkinsonism.

pan- Prefix meaning all.

panacea (pan-ah-se'ah) A remedy that supposedly cures all diseases; a cure-all.

panagglutinin (pan-ah-gloo'tĭ-nin) An agglutinin that causes aggregation of red blood cells of all members of one species.

panangiitis (pan-an-je-i'tis) Inflammation of all layers of the wall of a blood vessel.

panarthritis (pan-ar-thri'tis) Inflammation of all structures forming a joint or of numerous joints.

panatrophy (pan-at'ro-fe) Generalized shrinkage of the body.

pancarditis (pan-kar-di'tis) Diffuse inflammation of all layers of heart muscle (pericardium, myocardium, endocardium).

pancolectomy (pan-ko-lek'to-me) Removal of the colon.

pancreas (pan'kre-as) An elongated gland situated transversely behind the stomach, between the duodenum and the spleen; it secretes digestive proteins (enzymes) into the duodenum through pancreatic ducts and hormones (which regulate blood sugar levels) directly into the bloodstream.

pancreatectomy (pan-kre-ah-tek'to-me) Removal of all or a portion of the pancreas.

pancreatic (pan-kre-at'ik) Relating to the pancreas.

pancreatico-, pancreato-, pancreat- Combining forms meaning pancreas.

pancreaticoduodenostomy (pan-kre-at'ĭ-ko-du-o-de-nos'to-me) Surgical procedure for creating an opening between the pancreatic duct and the duodenum.

pancreaticojejunostomy (pan-kre-at'ĭ-ko-je-ju-nos'to-me) Surgical anastomosis of the main pancreatic duct with the jejunum.

pancreatin (pan'kre-ah-tin) Substance obtained from the pancreas of pigs; used as a supplement to treat insufficiency of digestives enzymes (i.e., proteins that stimulate digestion of food).

pancreatitis (pan-kre-ah-ti'tis) Inflammation of the pancreas.

pancreatoduodenectomy (pan-kre-at-to-du'o-de-nek'to-me) Removal of the head of the pancreas, encircling duodenum, and distal part of common bile duct.

pancreatogenous, pancreatogenic (pan-kre-ah-toj'ĕ-nus, pan-kre-ah-to-jen'ik) Arising or formed in the pancreas.

pancreatography (pan-kre-ah-tog'rah-fe) The making of an x-ray image of the pancreas or its ducts after infusing a radiopaque substance in the pancreatic duct; a test for pancreatic cancer.

pancreatolith (pan-kre-at'o-lith) A stone formed in the pancreas.

pancreatolithectomy (pan-kre-ah-to-lĭ-thek'to-me) Removal of a stone from the pancreatic duct.

pancreatolithiasis (pan-kre-at'o-lĭ-thi'ah-sis) The presence of stones in the pancreatic duct.

pancreatolithotomy (pan-kre-ah-to-lĭ-thot'o-me) Incision of the pancreas to remove stones.

pancreatotomy (pan-kre-ah-tot'o-me) Incision into the pancreas.

pancreatropic (pan-kre-ah-trop'ik) Having an effect on the pancreas.

pancrelipase (pan-kre-li'pās) A preparation of enzymes obtained from the pancreas of pigs that stimulates chemical reactions in the human pancreas; used to facilitate digestion of food when there is a deficiency of pancreatic enzymes.

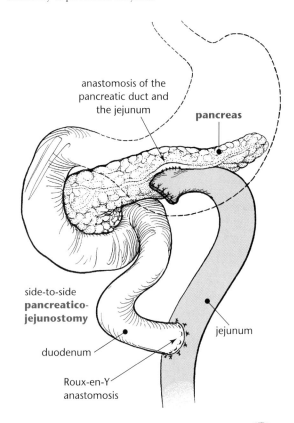

anastomosis of the pancreatic duct and the jejunum

pancreas

side-to-side **pancreaticojejunostomy**

duodenum

jejunum

Roux-en-Y anastomosis

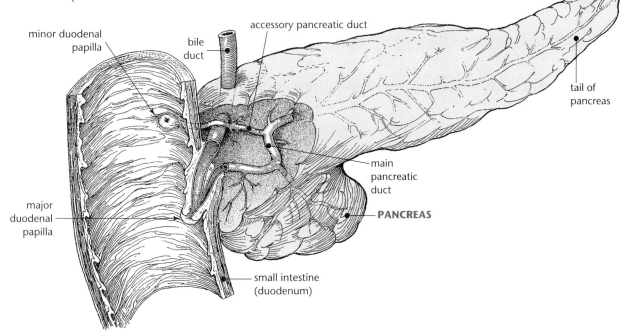

minor duodenal papilla

bile duct

accessory pancreatic duct

tail of pancreas

main pancreatic duct

PANCREAS

major duodenal papilla

small intestine (duodenum)

P

pancreoprivic (pan-kre-o-priv′ik) Lacking a pancreas.

pancreozymin (pan-kre-o-zi′min) See cholecystokinin.

pancytopenia (pan-si-to-pe′ne-ah) Abnormal reduction of all cellular elements of the blood.

pandemic (pan-dem′ik) A disease occurring over a wide geographical area and affecting a large proportion of the population; a widespread epidemic.

panencephalitis (pan-en-sef-ah-li′tis) Generalized inflammation of the brain.

panendoscope (pan-en′do-scōp) A tubular instrument equipped with an optic system that permits a wide-angle visualization of the interior of the bladder and urethra.

pang (pang) A sudden, shooting pain.

    breast p. See angina pectoris.

panhypopituitarism (pan-hi′po-pī-tu′ĭ-tar-izm) Absence or deficiency of all the hormones produced by the anterior portion (adenohypophysis) of the pituitary (hypophysis). Also called Simmonds' disease.

panic (pan′ik) Extreme and unjustified fear or anxiety.

    homosexual p. Acute anxiety caused by unresolved conflict involving homosexuality.

panniculectomy (pah-nik-u-lek′to-me) Surgical removal of large hanging folds of abdominal skin and fat resulting from extreme weight loss in a previously obese individual. It is more extensive than abdominoplasty.

panniculi (pah-nik′u-li) Plural of panniculus.

panniculitis (pah-nik-u-li′tis) Inflammation of subcutaneous fat.

    relapsing febrile nodular p. Recurrent fever with formation of red plaques or nodules in the skin. Also called Weber-Christian disease.

panniculus (pah-nik′u-lus), pl. pannic′uli A layer of tissue.

    p. adiposus Subcutaneous layer composed of connective tissue and fat.

pannus (pan′us) **1.** Infiltration of the cornea by a network of blood vessels, causing an opaque condition of the cornea and reduced vision; a common complication of trachoma. **2.** An abnormal mass of inflamed tissue lining the cavity of an affected joint in rheumatoid arthritis.

panophthalmitis (pan-of-thal-mi′tis) Inflammation of all structures of the eyeball; usually caused by pyogenic bacteria (e.g., staphylococci) gaining entry through a penetrating injury to the eye or, less often, from cellulitis of the eye socket (orbit) or, via the bloodstream, from an infection elsewhere in the body.

pansinusitis (pan-si-nu-si′tis) Inflammation of all the sinuses around the nose.

panto-, pant- Prefixes meaning all.

pantothenic acid (pan-to-the′nik as′id) Component of the vitamin B complex.

papain (pah-pa′in) A proteolytic enzyme obtained from papaya latex; it promotes the breakdown of proteins and peptides; used medicinally as a protein digestant and to promote healing of surface wounds.

Papanicolaou smear (pap-ah-nik′o-lou smēr) See pap test, under test.

papaverine (pah-pav′er-in) A nonnarcotic derivative of opium used as a smooth muscle relaxant to treat reduced blood supply of the extremities (peripheral vascular disease) and impotence.

paper (pa′per) A thin sheet of fibrous material used for filtering or testing.

    articulating p. See occluding paper.

    equilibration p. See occluding paper.

    occluding p. Paper coated with colored ink, placed between opposing teeth to register points of contact. Also called articulating paper; equilibration paper.

papilla (pah-pil′ah), pl. papil′lae A small projection from the surface of any tissue.

    interdental p. The part of the gum (gingiva) between adjoining teeth. Also called gingival septum.

    mammary p. See nipple.

papillary (pap′ĭ-ler-e) Relating to a papilla.

papillectomy (pap-ĭ-lek′to-me) Surgical removal of a papilla.

papilledema (pap-il-ĕ-de′mah) A noninflammatory swelling of the optic disk resulting from obstruction of venous blood flow; caused by increased pressure within the brain (e.g., by a brain tumor). Also called choked disk.

papilliferous (pap-ĭ-lif′er-us) Containing papillae.

P

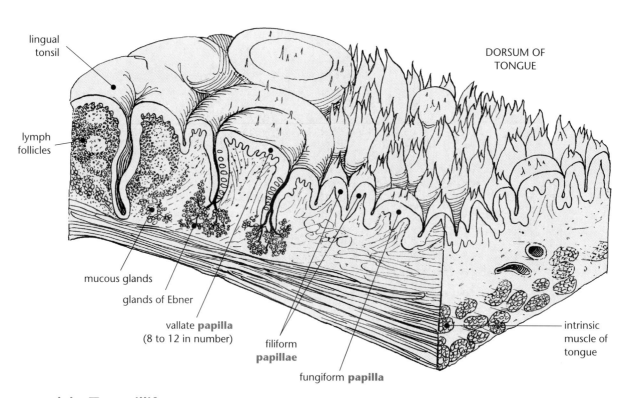

lingual tonsil

lymph follicles

DORSUM OF TONGUE

mucous glands

glands of Ebner

vallate **papilla** (8 to 12 in number)

filiform **papillae**

fungiform **papilla**

intrinsic muscle of tongue

pancreoprivic ■ papilliferous

papilliform (pah-pil'ĭ-form) Shaped like a papilla or small nipple.

papillitis (pap-ĭ-li'tis) **1.** Inflammation of the optic disk. Also called neuropapillitis. **2.** Inflammation of a papilla of the kidney (renal papilla).

　necrotizing p. See renal papillary necrosis, under necrosis.

papilloma (pap-ĭ-lo'mah) A noncancerous tumor arising from the outer layer (epithelium) of skin and mucous membranes, characterized by fingerlike projections from the surface. Also called papillary tumor; villoma.

　choroid plexus p. Papilloma arising in the ventricles of the brain; most commonly seen in children in association with hydrocephalus.

　ductal p. of breast Papilloma arising from the inner lining of a lactiferous duct near the nipple, usually causing a bloody nipple discharge. Also called intraductal papilloma of breast.

　intraductal p. of breast See ductal papilloma of breast.

　p. venereum See condyloma acuminatum.

papillomatosis (pap'ĭ-lo-mah-to'sis) The presence of numerous papillomas.

papillomatous (pap-ĭ-lo'mah-tus) Relating to papilloma.

Papillomavirus (pap-ĭ-lo-mah-vi'rus) A genus of DNA viruses (family Papovaviridae) that cause papillomas and warts.

papillomavirus (pap-ĭ-lo-mah-vi'rus) Any virus of the *Papilloma* genus.

　human p. A species with several serotypes. Types 1 and 2 cause common and plantar warts; types 6, 11, 16, 18, and 31 cause genital disease.

papilloretinitis (pah-pil-o-ret-ĭ-ni'tis) Inflammation of the optic disk and surrounding retinal tissue. Also called retinopapillitis.

papovavirus (pap-o-vah-vi'rus) Any virus of the family Papovaviridae; many of them cause cancer.

papular (pap'u-lar) Relating to papules.

papulation (pap-u-la'shun) Development or formation of papules.

papule (pap'ūl) A superficial, solid elevation on the skin less than 1 cm in diameter; can arise from the superficial or deep layers of the skin (epidermis or dermis), or from a combination of the two.

　moist p. See condyloma latum.

papulopustular (pap-u-lo-pus'tu-lar) Marked by the presence of small solid elevations (papules), some of which contain pus (pustules).

papulosis (pap-u-lo'sis) The presence of numerous papules.

papulosquamous (pap-u-lo-skwa'mus) Denoting a skin condition marked by small solid elevations (papules) and dry scales.

papulovesicular (pap-u-lo-vĕ-sik'u-lar) Denoting the presence of small solid elevations (papules) and small blisters.

para- Prefix meaning beside; beyond; resembling; secondary; diverging from the normal.

para (par'ah) Denoting a woman's past pregnancies that have reached the period of viability, regardless of whether the infant is dead or alive at the time of delivery; used in conjunction with numerals to designate the number of pregnancies (e.g., para I, para II). The term refers to pregnancies, not fetuses; thus a woman who has given birth to twins at the end of her first pregnancy is still para I.

para-aminobenzoic acid (par'ah ah-me-no-ben-zo'ik as'id) (PABA) *p*-aminobenzoic acid; an essential growth factor for bacteria; therefore, it nullifies the bacteriostatic effects of the sulfonamide drugs. Used in the treatment of some collagen diseases. Although a factor of the vitamin B complex, it is not an essential nutrient for humans.

para-aminohippuric acid (par'ah ah-me-no-hip-pūr'ik as'id) (PAH) *p*-aminohippuric acid; a substance used in kidney function tests to determine the amount of plasma flowing through the kidneys.

para-aminosalicylic acid (par'ah ah-me-no-sal-ĭ-sil'ik as'id) (PAS, PASA) *p*-aminosalicylic acid; an antibacterial drug used with other drugs to treat tuberculosis. Adverse effects include skin rash, hemolytic anemia, and inflammation of the optic nerve.

parablepsia (par-ah-blep'se-ah) False vision (e.g., in hallucinations).

paracentesis (par-ah-sen-te'sis) Aspiration of fluid from a body cavity through a fine needle or any other hollow instrument; tapping. When not further modified the term usually refers to removal of fluid from the abdominal cavity (peritoneocentesis); paracentesis from the chest cavity is termed thoracentesis.

paracentral (par-ah-sen'tral) Off center or situated near a central structure.

paracetamol (par-as-et-am'ol) See acetaminophen.

parachordal (par-ah-kor'dal) Situated near the notochord of the embryo.

paracoccidioidomycosis (par-ah-kok-sid'e-oi-do-mi-ko'sis) Infectious disease caused by the fungus *Paracoccidioides brasiliensis;* it enters the body through the respiratory route, resulting in suppurative lesions in the lungs, which disseminate to the skin, lymph nodes, and other internal organs. Also called South American blastomycosis.

P

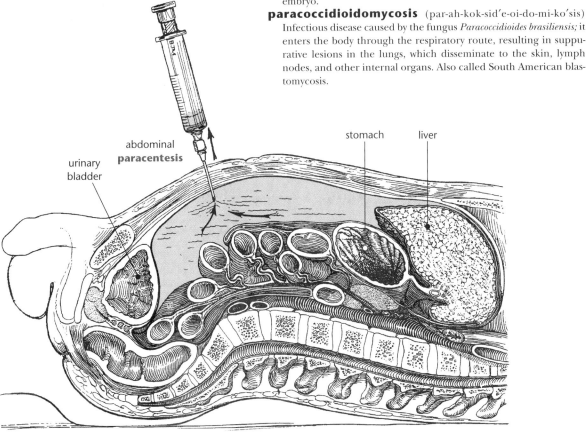

urinary bladder

abdominal **paracentesis**

stomach　liver

paracrine (par′ah-krin) Denoting the release of substances, such as hormones, by endocrine cells that act directly on adjacent cells.

paracusis, paracusia (par-ah-ku′sis, par-ah-ku′se-ah) Any disturbance of hearing.

paracystic (par-ah-sis′tik) Situated near the bladder. Also called paravesical.

paradental (par-ah-den′tal) See periodontal.

paradidymis (par-ah-did′ĭ-mis) A small mass of convoluted tubules sometimes present at the end of the spermatic cord, near the head of the epididymis; a remnant of the embryonic mesonephros.

paradipsia (par-ah-dip′se-ah) Consumption of fluids greatly in excess of needs.

paraffin (par′ah-fin) **1.** A widely used chemically inert, translucent substance derived from petroleum. Also called paraffin wax. **2.** A hydrocarbon of the methane series. Also called paraffin hydrocarbon.

> **liquid p.** See mineral oil, under oil.

> **yellow soft p.** See petrolatum.

paraganglia (par-ah-gang′gle-ah), sin. paragan′glion Small aggregations of tissue whose secretory cells manufacture and store catecholamines (e.g., epinephrine and norepinephrine); found near the sympathetic ganglia and along the aorta and its major branches; their function varies with their location.

paraganglioma (par-ah-gang-gle-o′mah) A highly vascular tumor derived from tissues of a paraganglion; common sites include the carotid body in the neck and the jugular glomus just below the middle ear. The tumor bleeds profusely when handled, which makes its removal difficult.

paraganglion (par-ah-gang′gle-on) Singular of paraganglia.

parageusia (par-ah-gu′se-ah) A distortion of the sense of taste.

paragonimiasis (par-ah-gon-ĭ-mi′ah-sis) Infection with lung flukes of the genus *Paragonimus.*

Paragonimus (par-ah-gon′ĭ-mus) Genus of flukes parasitic in the lungs of humans and many other mammals.

parahepatic (par-ah-hĕ-pat′ik) Near the liver.

parakeratosis (par-ah-ker-ah-to′sis) Abnormal retention of cell nuclei in the superficial layer (stratum corneum) of the epidermis, as seen in psoriasis and exfoliative dermatitis.

parakinesia (par-ah-kĭ-ne′se-ah) Any abnormal motor function.

paralalia (par-ah-la′le-ah) Any speech disorder.

paraldehyde (par-al′dĕ-hīd) An unpleasant-smelling sedative and hypnotic that has been used to treat alcohol withdrawal symptoms.

parallax (par′ah-laks) An apparent displacement of an object when the observer changes position.

paralysis (pah-ral′ĭ-sis), pl. paral′yses Loss of muscular function resulting from disease or injury in the motor pathways of the nervous system or from lesions in the muscles themselves.

> **acute ascending p.** Paralysis of sudden onset and rapid course beginning in the lower extremities and progressing to the upper body; it may end in death. Also called Landry's paralysis.

> **p. agitans** See Parkinson's disease, under disease.

> **ascending p.** Paralysis that progresses upward from the feet or from the periphery to a nerve center.

> **Brown-Séquard p.** See Brown-Séquard syndrome, under syndrome.

> **crutch p.** Paralysis of the arm muscles due to compression of a nerve at the armpit (axilla) by a crutch.

> **Duchenne's p.** See Duchenne's muscular dystrophy, under dystrophy.

> **Duchenne-Erb p.** See Erb's palsy, under palsy.

> **hyperkalemic periodic p.** Inherited disorder characterized by frequent mild attacks of paralysis associated with a rise of serum potassium levels; attacks may last from a few minutes to a few hours. Onset occurs in infancy.

> **hypokalemic periodic p.** Inherited disorder characterized by attacks of paralysis associated with a fall of serum potassium levels; may be precipitated by consumption of a high-carbohydrate meal or alcohol, or by exposure to cold temperatures; attacks may

last from hours to days. Onset occurs between ages of 7 and 21 years.

> **Klumpke's p.** Traction injury of the lower portion of the brachial plexus, characterized by paralysis of the small muscles of the hand (causing clawhand); most commonly seen in newborns, usually caused by manipulation during delivery.

> **Landry's p.** See acute ascending paralysis.

> **lead p.** See lead palsy, under palsy.

> **periodic p.** Recurrent episodes of muscular weakness or paralysis of short duration, occurring in otherwise healthy people.

> **postepileptic p.** See Todd's paralysis.

> **progressive bulbar p.** Progressive degeneration of motor nerves innervating muscles of the lips, tongue, palate, larynx, and pharynx; it results in paralysis and atrophy of the muscles; chewing, swallowing, and talking become increasingly difficult; cause is unknown.

> **tick p.** A rapidly spreading paralysis, beginning in the extremities and progressing to the throat and face; caused by a toxin secreted by certain ticks of the genus *Dermacentor.* Removal of the tick is curative.

> **Todd's p.** Transient paralysis sometimes following a convulsive epileptic attack and lasting from several minutes to several hours. Also called postepileptic paralysis.

> **vasomotor p.** See vasoparalysis.

> **wasting p.** See progressive muscular atrophy, under atrophy.

paralytic (par-ah-lit′ik) Relating to paralysis.

paramedian (par-ah-me′de-an) Near the midline.

paramedic (par-ah-med′ik) A person trained and certified to provide emergency medical treatment.

paramedical (par-ah-med′ĭ-kal) **1.** Ancillary to the science and practice of medicine. **2.** Relating to a paramedic.

paramenia (par-ah-me′ne-ah) Abnormal menstruation.

parametria (par-ah-me′tre-ah) Plural of parametrium.

parametric (par-ah-met′rik) Situated near the uterus.

parametritis (par-ah-mĕ-tri′tis) Inflammation of the parametrium.

parametrium (par-ah-me′tre-um), pl. parame′tria Connective tissue separating the front of the uterine cervix from the bladder; it extends also to both sides of the cervix (between the two layers of the broad ligament), where it contains uterine blood vessels.

paramyotonia (par-ah-mi-o-to′ne-ah) Disorder marked by spastic tonicity of muscles.

Paramyxovirus (par-ah-mik-so-vi′rus) Genus of spherical viruses containing a single RNA strand; includes the mumps and parainfluenza viruses.

paranasal (par-ah-na′zal) Adjacent to the nose.

paranoia (par-ah-noi′ah) Mental condition characterized by the gradual development of an intricate delusionary system of thinking based on misinterpretation of chance remarks or events; the individual has an otherwise intact personality. Distinguished from paranoid disorders and schizophrenia, paranoid type. See also paranoid disorder, under disorder; schizophrenia, paranoid type, under schizophrenia.

paranoiac (par-ah-noi′ak) A person afflicted with paranoia.

paranoid (par′ah-noid) **1.** Relating to paranoia. **2.** Popular term for an overly suspicious and hypersensitive person.

paranuclear (par-ah-nu′kle-ar) Situated near a nucleus.

paranucleus (par-ah-nu′kle-us) A small mass sometimes observed near a cell nucleus.

paraparesis (par-ah-par-ĕ′sis) Partial paralysis or weakness of the legs.

paraperitoneal (par-ah-per-ĭ-to-ne′al) Adjacent to the peritoneum.

paraphasia (par-ah-fa′ze-ah) Disorder of speech in which a person comprehends spoken or written words and speaks fluently but omits parts of words, substitutes incorrect sounds in the word, or uses words incorrectly. A form of aphasia.

paraphilia (par-ah-fil′e-ah) General term for a group of psychosexual disorders characterized by recurrent and persistent sexual urges and sexually arousing fantasies of an unusual nature; may involve the use of a nonhuman object, a child, a nonconsenting partner, or the real

P

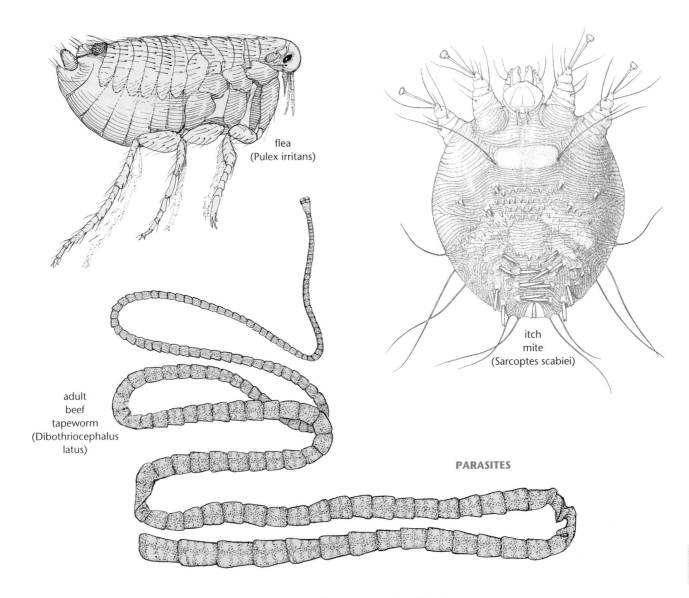

flea
(Pulex irritans)

itch
mite
(Sarcoptes scabiei)

adult
beef
tapeworm
(Dibothriocephalus
latus)

PARASITES

or simulated suffering or humiliation of oneself or one's partner. See also psychosexual disorders, under disorder.

paraphimosis (par-ah-fi-mo′sis) Abnormal swelling of the head (glans) of the penis caused by forcible retraction of an abnormally tight foreskin (prepuce), which cannot be returned to its normal position.

   p. palpebrae Spastic eversion of the eyelids.

paraplegia (par-ah-ple′je-ah) Paralysis of both legs and, sometimes, the lower trunk.

parapraxia (par-ah-prak′se-ah) See parapraxis.

parapraxis (par-ah-prak′sis) The unintentional verbal expressions, actions, or lapses of memory attributed by Freud to be symptomatic of unconscious motives (e.g., slips of the tongue). Also called parapraxia.

paraproteinemia (par-ah-pro-tēn-e′me-ah) Presence of increased amounts of monoclonal immunoglobulin in the blood plasma, usually associated with tumors of B lymphocytes or plasma cells.

parapsychology (par-ah-si-kol′o-je) The study of extrasensory phenomena.

paraquat (par′a-kwat) A toxic weed killer; contact with skin, eyes, and respiratory tract causes acute effects, including irritation and fissuring of skin, cracking and discoloration of fingernails, conjunctivitis, sore throat, and coughing; ingestion of paraquat causes delayed liver, kidney, and lung damage.

parasalpingitis (par-ah-sal-pin-ji′tis) Inflammation of tissues surrounding the fallopian (uterine) tubes.

parasite (par′ah-sīt) An organism that lives in or on another and depends on it for its sustenance.

   facultative p. Parasite capable of leading either an independent or a parasitic existence.

   obligate p. Parasite that takes up permanent residence in, and is completely dependent on, its host.

   pathogenic p. Parasite causing injury to its host by its mechanical and toxic activities.

parasitic (par-ah-sit′ik) Relating to a parasite.

parasiticide (par-ah-sit′ĭ-sid) 1. Destructive to parasites. 2. An agent that has such properties.

parasitism (par′ah-si-tizm) The type of existence between a parasite and its host.

parasitize (par′ah-sī-tīz) To invade and live as a parasite.

parasitology (par-ah-si-tol′o-je) The science dealing with parasites and their relationship to their hosts.

   medical p. The branch of medical sciences dealing with animal parasites living in and on the body of humans and with aspects of the host-parasite relationship having medical significance.

parasitosis (par-ah-si-to′sis) Infestation with parasites.

parasomnia (par-ah-som′ne-ah) Abnormal condition associated with sleep; includes nightmares, night terrors, sleepwalking, sleep paralysis, sleep bruxism, and bed-wetting.

paraspadias (par-ah-spa′de-as) Developmental defect of the penis in which the urethral opening is on the side of the normal location.

parasympathetic (par-ah-sim-pah-thet′ik) Relating to a part of the nervous system not under voluntary control.

parasympatholytic (par-ah-sim-pah-tho-lit′ik) Denoting an agent that interferes with the action of parasympathetic nerves.

parasympathomimetic (par-ah-sim-pah-tho-mĭ-met′ik) Denoting drugs that produce effects similar to those of parasympathetic nerves.

parathion (par-ah-thi′on) Poisonous compound used as an agricultural insecticide; it inhibits the action of the enzyme cholinesterase.

parathormone (par-ah-thor′mōn) See parathyroid hormone, under hormone.

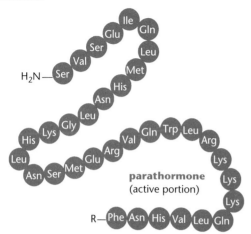

parathormone
(active portion)

parathyroid (par-ah-thi′roid) **1.** Situated near the thyroid gland. **2.** A parathyroid gland; see under gland.

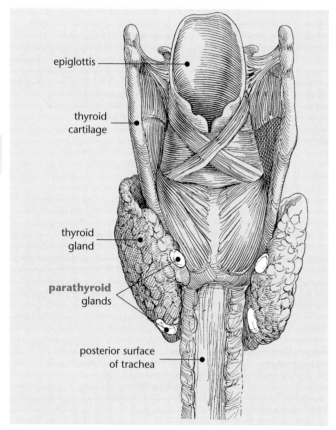

epiglottis

thyroid cartilage

thyroid gland

parathyroid glands

posterior surface of trachea

parathyroidectomy (par-ah-thi-roi-dek′to-me) Removal of the parathyroid glands.

parathyrotropic (par-ah-thi-ro-trop′ik) Acting upon the parathyroid glands.

paratrichosis (par-ah-tri-ko′sis) Any disorder affecting the growth of hair.

paraumbilical (par-ah-um-bil′ĭ-kal) Adjacent to the navel (umbilicus).

paraungual (par-ah-ung′gwal) Adjacent to a fingernail or toenail.

paravaginal (par-ah-vaj′ĭ-nal) Adjacent to the vagina.

paravalvular (par-ah-val′vu-lar) Near a valve.

paravertebral (par-ah-ver-te′bral) Adjacent to the spine (vertebral column).

paravesical (par-ah-ves′ĭ-kal) See paracystic.

parectasis, parectasia (par-ek′tah-sis, par-ek-ta′se-ah) Excessive distention or stretching.

paregoric (par-ĕ-gor′ik) A liquid preparation containing a form of opium that inhibits peristalsis, the propulsive movements of the intestines; used in the treatment of diarrhea.

parenchyma (pah-reng′kĭ-mah) The characteristic functional tissue of an organ; distinguished from connective tissue.

parenchymal (pah-reng′kĭ-mal) Relating to parenchyma.

parenteral (pah-ren′ter-al) Taken into the body through a route other than the gastrointestinal tract (e.g., by subcutaneous, intramuscular, or intravenous injection).

paresis (pah-re′sis, par′ĕ-sis) Mild paralysis; weakness of muscles.

paresthesia (par-es-the′ze-ah) Abnormal tactile sensations occurring spontaneously without a sensory stimulus; often described as burning, tingling, creeping, or pricking.

paretic (pah-ret′ik) Relating to paresis.

paries (pa′re-ez), pl. pari′etes The wall of a cavity or hollow organ.

parietal (pah-ri′ĕ-tal) Relating to the wall of a cavity or hollow organ.

parieto-occipital (pah-ri′ĕ-to ok-sip′ĭ-tal) Relating to the parietal and occipital bones of the skull or to the lobes of the cerebrum.

parity (par′ĭ-te) The state of having borne children.

parkinsonism (par′kin-sun-izm) A disturbance of motor function marked by a stooped posture, rigidity, a typical pill-rolling tremor, and a gait characterized by progressively shortened, accelerated steps (festinating gait); seen in conditions that damage the dopaminergic nerve cells of the substantia nigra (in the brain), principally idiopathic Parkinson's disease; also in carbon monoxide poisoning, heavy metal toxicity, and sometimes after use of neurologic drugs, especially the phenothiazines. Also called shaking palsy; trembling palsy.

paronychia (par-o-nik′e-ah) Inflammation of the tissues around the nails, usually after an injury, caused by infection with *Staphylococcus aureus* (acute infection) or species of *Candida* (chronic infection).

parosmia (par-oz′me-ah) An abnormality of the sense of smell.

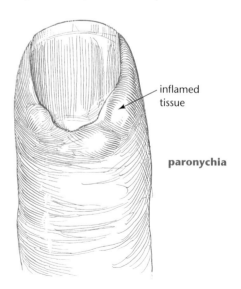

inflamed tissue

paronychia

parotid (pah-rot′id) Situated near the ear, such as the parotid gland.

parotidectomy (pah-rot-ĭ-dek′to-me) Removal of the parotid gland.

parotitis (par-o-ti′tis) Inflammation of a parotid gland.

P

epidemic p. See mumps.

suppurative p. Unilateral parotitis caused by bacterial infection, usually due to *Staphylococcus aureus;* symptoms include pain and swelling, fever, chills, and pus formation; seen in elderly, chronically ill patients with dry mouth.

parous (par'us) Having borne one or more children.

parovarian (par-o-va're-an) Situated next to an ovary.

paroxysm (par'ok-sizm) 1. A sudden recurrence or intensification of symptoms. 2. A convulsion.

paroxysmal (par-ok-siz'mal) Relating to paroxysms.

pars (parz), pl. par'tes Latin for part; a particular portion of a structure, surface, or organ.

 p. flaccida The upper, flaccid portion of the eardrum (tympanic membrane).

 p. tensa The lower, taut portion of the eardrum (tympanic membrane).

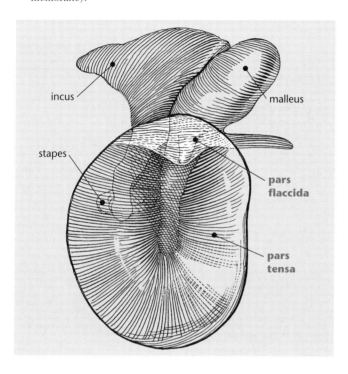

incus

stapes

malleus

pars flaccida

pars tensa

part (part) A portion.

 abdominal p. of esophagus The portion of the esophagus between the diaphragm and the stomach.

 abdominal p. of ureter The portion of the ureter extending from the kidney to the brim of the pelvis; situated behind the peritoneum; it is approximately 14 cm long, the same length as the pelvic part of the ureter.

 alveolar p. of mandible The upper part of the body of the mandible containing sockets for the roots of the lower teeth.

 alveolar p. of maxilla The lower part of the maxilla containing sockets for the roots of the upper teeth.

 ascending p. of duodenum See fourth part of duodenum.

 bony p. of nasal septum The nasal septum composed of the perpendicular plate of the ethmoid bone and the vomer.

 cardiac p. of stomach The part of the stomach that includes and immediately follows the gastric (cardiac) opening of the esophagus.

 cartilaginous p. of nasal septum The flattened cartilaginous plate of the lower anterior nasal septum; it is quadrilateral in shape; attached posteriorly to the perpendicular plate of ethmoid bone and the vomer.

 cervical p. of esophagus The part of the esophagus in the neck extending from the downward continuation of the pharynx (at the lower border of the cricoid cartilage) to the level of the first ribs.

 descending p. of duodenum See second part of duodenum.

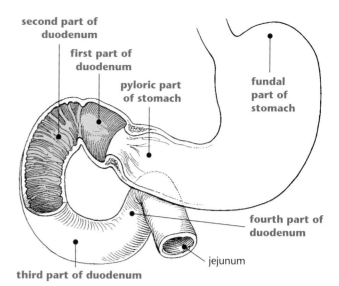

second part of duodenum

first part of duodenum

pyloric part of stomach

fundal part of stomach

fourth part of duodenum

jejunum

third part of duodenum

 first p. of duodenum The shortest part of the duodenum adjacent to the pylorus of the stomach; it contains the duodenal ampulla and forms the superior flexure of the duodenum.

 flaccid p. of eardrum See pars flaccida, under pars.

 fourth p. of duodenum The ascending terminal part of the duodenum extending from the third part of the duodenum to the beginning of the jejunum at the duodenojejunal flexure. Also called ascending part of duodenum.

 fundal p. of stomach The part of the stomach to the left and above the cardiac orifice.

 horizontal p. of duodenum See third part of duodenum.

 membranous p. of male urethra The shortest and narrowest part of the male urethra, extending through the urogenital diaphragm, from the apex of the prostate to the bulb of the penis.

 membranous p. of nasal septum The thickened skin and subcutaneous tissue of the nasal septum at the apex of the nose, immediately under the cartilaginous part of the septum.

 pelvic p. of ureter The part of the ureter that extends from the brim of the pelvis to the urinary bladder; it is approximately the same length as the abdominal part.

 presenting p. In obstetrics, the portion of the fetus closest to the birth canal and which is felt through the cervix on vaginal examination; the presenting part signifies the position of the fetus in the uterus during labor.

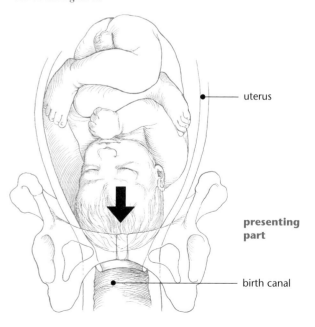

uterus

presenting part

birth canal

prostatic p. of male urethra The portion of the male urethra within the prostate gland; it is the widest and most dilatable part of the urethra.

pyloric p. of stomach The distal part of the stomach consisting of the pyloric antrum, pyloric canal, and pyloric valve (sphincter); the notch on the lesser curvature of the stomach marks the boundary between the pyloric part and body of the stomach.

second p. of duodenum The descending part of the duodenum extending from the superior flexure to the inferior flexure; it receives secretions from the bile and pancreatic ducts. Also called descending part of duodenum.

spongy p. of male urethra The portion of the urethra within the corpus spongiosum of the penis; it extends from the end of the membranous urethra to the end of the penis; it has two dilatations, one near the membranous urethra (intrabulbar fossa), the other near its external urethral orifice (navicular fossa); the external opening is the narrowest part of the urethra.

tense p. of eardrum See pars tensa, under pars.

third p. of duodenum The horizontal part of the duodenum extending from the inferior duodenal flexure to the ascending fourth part of the duodenum. Also called horizontal part of duodenum.

particle (par′tĕ-kl) A minute portion of matter.

alpha p. A positively charged particle ejected from the nucleus of a radioactive atom; an ionized atom of helium, it consists of two neutrons and two protons.

beta p. An electron, either positively charged (positron) or negatively charged (negatron), emitted from an atomic nucleus during beta decay of a radionuclide.

Dane p. The complete virion of the hepatitis B virus, composed of an outer layer containing surface antigen and surrounding a DNA central core.

particulate (par-tik′u-lāt) Composed of tiny particles.

parturient (par-tu′re-ent) Relating to childbirth.

parturifacient (par-tu-re-fa′shent) Inducing labor.

parturition (par-tu-rish′un) Childbirth.

parulis (pah-roo′lis) See gingival abscess, under abscess.

parvicellular (par-vĭ-sel′u-lar) Composed of small cells.

Parvovirus (par-vo-vi′rus) A genus of infectious viruses (family Parvoviridae).

P. B19 Small DNA virus that causes erythema infectiosum.

pascal (pas′kal) The SI unit of pressure; the force of 1 newton per square meter.

pastille, pastil (pas-tēl′, pas′til) A lozenge made with a gelatin base.

past-pointing (past′ point′ing) A patient's inability to place a finger on a designated site, overshooting its target, when certain neurologic tests are performed. An indication of cerebellar dysfunction.

patch (pach) 1. A flat circumscribed area, more than 1 cm in diameter, differing in color or structure from its surroundings. 2. A small piece of material placed on the skin.

clonidine transdermal p. A multilayered skin patch that provides continuous delivery of clonidine (antihypertensive agent) for seven days; most frequent adverse effects include dry mouth, drowsiness, localized skin reactions, and sedation. Trade name: Catapres-TTS.

cotton-wool p.'s White or gray fluffy areas of coagulated exudates formed on the retina; seen in a variety of conditions (e.g., severe high blood pressure, immune suppression, diabetic retinopathy). Also called cotton-wool spots; cotton-wool exudates.

estradiol p. See estradiol transdermal patch.

estradiol transdermal p. A skin patch that provides exogenous estrogen (17β-estradiol) through a rate-limiting membrane continuously upon application to intact skin; it provides systemic estrogen replacement to alleviate symptoms of estradiol deficiency in menopausal women (e.g., postmenopausal osteoporosis). Also called estradiol patch; estradiol transdermal system. Trade name: Estraderm.

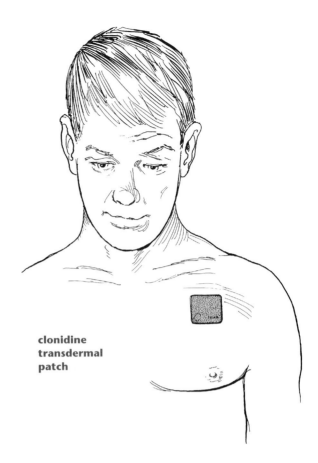

clonidine transdermal patch

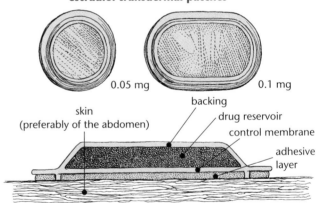

estradiol transdermal patches

0.05 mg   0.1 mg

skin (preferably of the abdomen)

backing
drug reservoir
control membrane
adhesive layer

fentanyl p. See fentanyl transdermal patch.

fentanyl transdermal p. A patch for the transdermal delivery of fentanyl, a powerful parenteral opiate; used for sedation or analgesia; the drug is released slowly, peaking 12 to 24 hours after application of the patch, and is sustained for 72 hours, after which a new patch can be applied on a different location. Also called fentanyl patch.

herald p. A single, sharply defined, large scaling plaque on the skin marking the onset of pityriasis rosea and preceding the generalized skin eruption by several days.

MacCallum's p.'s Irregular thickenings in the inner layer (endocardium) of the heart wall, especially of the left atrium, due to accumulation of inflammatory nodules (Aschoff bodies); over time, they progress to fibrosis, causing plaquelike scarring of the endocardium; seen in rheumatic heart disease (RHD). Also called MacCallum's plaques.

mucous p. The superficial grayish patch in the oral mucosa occurring in secondary syphilis.

nicotine p. See nicotine transdermal patch.

nicotine transdermal p. A patch containing a predetermined dosage of nicotine, designed to be worn on the upper arm for systemic delivery of the chemical through the skin; used as part of a comprehensive behavioral program for smoking cessation. Adverse reactions may include redness, itching, and burning sensation of the skin; effects on the fetus and nursing infants are unknown. Also called nicotine patch. Trade name: Habitrol; Nicotrol; Nicoderm.

nitroglycerine p. See nitroglycerine transdermal patch.

nitroglycerine transdermal p. A skin patch that provides steady delivery of nitroglycerin for a full 24 hours as a treatment for angina pectoris; side effects include transient headaches and orthostatic hypotension. Also called nitroglycerin patch.

Peyer's p.'s Small, whitish aggregates of lymphoid tissue in the wall of the small intestine.

salicylic acid p. See salicylic acid transdermal patch.

salicylic acid transdermal p. A skin patch that provides salicylic acid for the treatment of warts on the sole of the foot (verruca plantaris); placed on the sole of the foot each night before retiring, it provides constant and controlled release of salicylic acid over an eight-hour period. Also called salicylic acid patch. Trade name: Trans-Plantar.

scopolamine p. See scopolamine transdermal patch.

scopolamine transdermal p. A skin patch that provides scopolamine to help prevent the nausea and vomiting of motion sickness for up to three days. The adhesive patch (disk) is placed behind the ear several hours before one travels. Adverse effects may include drowsiness, dryness of mouth, or temporary blurring of vision. Also called scopolamine patch. Trade name: Transderm Scop.

smoker's p. See leukoplakia.

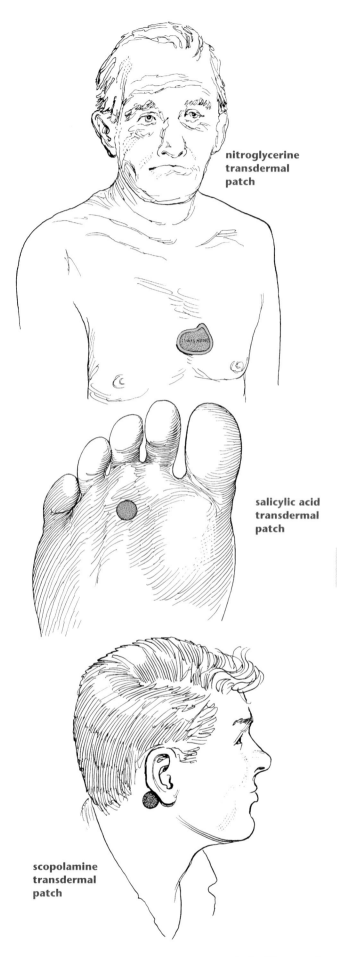

nitroglycerine transdermal patch

salicylic acid transdermal patch

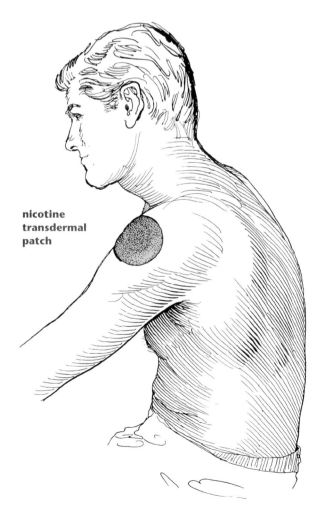

nicotine transdermal patch

scopolamine transdermal patch

P

patch ■ patch

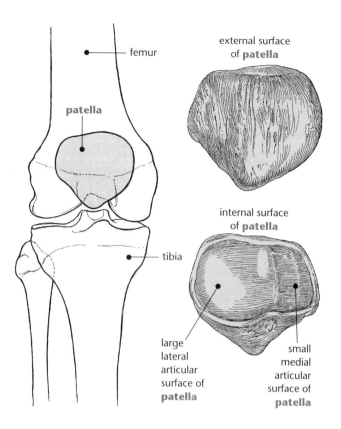

femur

patella

tibia

external surface of **patella**

internal surface of **patella**

large lateral articular surface of **patella**

small medial articular surface of **patella**

patella (pah-tel′ah) A flat, triangular sesamoid bone situated at the front of the knee joint, in the combined tendons of the extensor muscles of the leg. Commonly called kneecap.

patellectomy (pat-ĕ-lek′to-me) Removal of the kneecap (patella).

patency (pa′ten-se) The state of being patent.

patent (pa′tent) 1. Open; unobstructed. 2. Apparent.

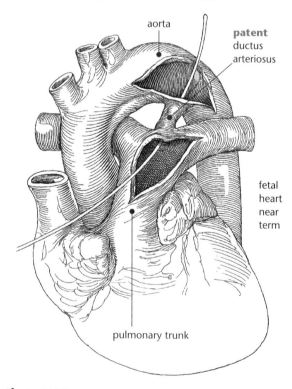

aorta

patent ductus arteriosus

fetal heart near term

pulmonary trunk

path (path) The route taken by a nerve impulse.

pathfinder (path′find-er) A thin cylindrical instrument (bougie) for locating strictures in tubular structures.

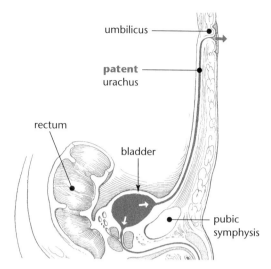

umbilicus

patent urachus

rectum

bladder

pubic symphysis

patho-, -pathy, path- Combining forms meaning disease.

pathogen (path′o-jen) A disease-causing microorganism.

pathogenesis (path-o-jen′ĕ-sis) The abnormal biochemical and pathophysiologic mechanisms that lead to disease. Formerly called nosogenesis.

pathogenic (path-o-jen′ik) Causing disease.

pathogenicity (path-o-jĕ-nis′ĭ-te) The capacity to produce disease.

pathognomonic (path-og-no-mon′ik) An abnormality specifically characteristic of one disease and no other. Also called diagnostic.

pathologic (path-o-loj′ik) Relating to disease.

pathologist (pah-thol′o-jist) A specialist in pathology.

    forensic p. A pathologist who performs postmortem examinations (autopsies) to be reported in a legal setting.

pathology (pah-thol′o-je) 1. In its broadest sense: the logical and scientific basis of medicine; i.e., the study of disease processes, their causes, and their effects (structural and functional) at all levels from molecular change to abnormalities visible to the naked eye; it includes postmortem examinations (autopies) and interpretation of biopsies. In a narrower sense: the medical specialty concerned with the performance of laboratory procedures and interpretation of results. 2. A disease or disorder.

    clinical p. The subspecialty of pathology concerned with identifying substances or microorganisms in body fluids, utilizing the methods and procedures of chemistry, microbiology, immunology, and other related sciences. Results of these procedures, used in conjunction with other evaluations of the patient, facilitate diagnosis of specific diseases.

    experimental p. A subspecialty of pathology concerned with basic scientific research into disease processes, especially at the cellular level, in the laboratory.

    forensic p. The application of the principles and practice of pathology to legal problems (i.e., to determine the cause of death of individuals who die suddenly or under unusual, unexplained, or violent circumstances). Basically, the investigation helps to answer seven questions: *Who* is the deceased? *Where* did the injuries and ensuing death occur? *When* did the death and injuries occur? *What* injuries are present? *Which* injuries are significant? *How* were injuries inflicted? *What* actually caused the death?

    speech p. The study of voice, speech, and language disorders, with special emphasis on rehabilitation of patients with such disorders.

    surgical p. A subspecialty of pathology concerned with microscopic examination of tissue sections removed from living patients for the diagnosis and subsequent care of those patients.

pathophobia (path-o-fo′be-ah) See nosophobia.

pathophysiology (path-o-fiz-e-ol′o-je) The study of disordered body functions, as distinguished from structural defects. Also called pathologic physiology; physiopathology.

pathway (path′wa) 1. The linked nerve fibers providing a structural course for nerve impulses. 2. A sequence of chemical reactions by which one substance is converted into another.

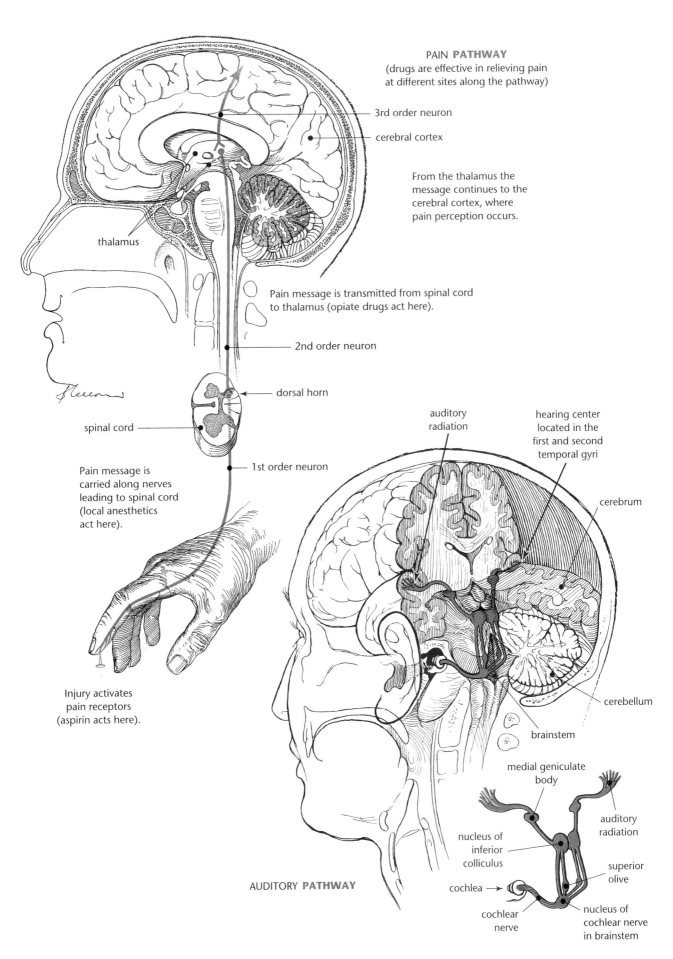

PAIN PATHWAY
(drugs are effective in relieving pain
at different sites along the pathway)

3rd order neuron

cerebral cortex

From the thalamus the
message continues to the
cerebral cortex, where
pain perception occurs.

thalamus

Pain message is transmitted from spinal cord
to thalamus (opiate drugs act here).

2nd order neuron

dorsal horn

spinal cord

Pain message is
carried along nerves
leading to spinal cord
(local anesthetics
act here).

1st order neuron

Injury activates
pain receptors
(aspirin acts here).

auditory
radiation

hearing center
located in the
first and second
temporal gyri

cerebrum

cerebellum

brainstem

medial geniculate
body

auditory
radiation

nucleus of
inferior
colliculus

superior
olive

cochlea

nucleus of
cochlear nerve
in brainstem

cochlear
nerve

AUDITORY PATHWAY

P

patient (pa'shent) (pt) A person receiving medical care.

emergency p. In emergency medicine, a patient whose condition potentially threatens life or function (e.g., cardiac arrest, severe head injuries, body temperature greater than 105° F).

nonurgent p. In emergency medicine, one whose disorder is minor and does not require the resources of an emergency service (e.g., minor headache, minor fracture, or one who is dead on arrival).

urgent p. In emergency medicine, one whose condition is acute but not severe; requires medical attention within a few hours, but is in danger if not treated.

patten (pat'n) A metal support fitted into one shoe to equalize the length of both legs.

pattern (pat'ern) A characteristic arrangement or design.

dicing p.'s See dicing lacerations, under laceration.

wax p. A wax model of lost tooth structure from which a mold is made for casting a tooth restoration.

DNA probe **patterns**

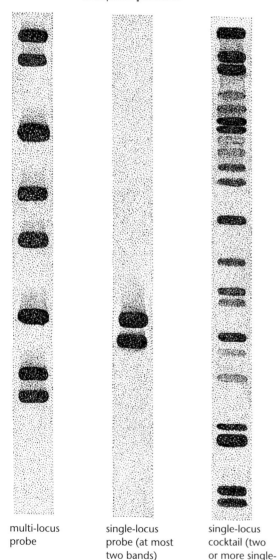

multi-locus probe

single-locus probe (at most two bands)

single-locus cocktail (two or more single-locus probes)

patulous (pat'u-lus) Widely open.

pause (pawz) A temporary stop.

compensatory p. In cardiology, a pause following a premature ectopic ventricular beat; its duration compensates for the short interval preceding the heartbeat, so that the total heart rate is unchanged.

sinus p. In cardiology, a spontaneous interruption in the regular sinus rhythm of the heart; thought to be caused by a high degree of S-A block.

pavementing (pāv'ment-ing) Increased adhesion of white blood cells to the inner lining of blood vessels occurring in acute inflammation.

pearl (perl) 1. A small spherical hard mass. 2. A rounded firm mass of mucus, seen in sputum of patients undergoing an attack of asthma.

enamel p. See enameloma.

Epstein's p.'s Minute, yellowish, keratin-containing cysts normally found on the hard and soft palate of newborns; they resolve spontaneously.

gouty p. Sodium urate concretion formed on the ear cartilage of people with gout.

peau d'orange (po' do-rahnj') An abnormal dimpled condition of the skin, which resembles the skin of an orange; seen in some forms of breast cancer.

pecten (pek'ten) 1. Any structure resembling a comb. 2. The middle third of the anal canal.

p. pubis See pectineal line, under line.

pectinate (pek'tī-nāt) Resembling a comb.

pectineal (pek-tin'e-al) Relating to the pubic bone or to any comb-like structure.

pectoral (pek'to-ral) Relating to the chest.

pectoralgia (pek-to-ral'je-ah) Pain in the chest.

pectoriloquy (pek-to-ril'o-kwe) Transmission of the voice through the chest wall, audible through a stethoscope; most commonly occurs when the underlying lung tissue is consolidated, as in pneumonia.

pectus (pek'tus), pl. pec'tora The anterior wall of the chest cavity.

p. carinatum Protrusion of the breastbone (sternum) with flattening of the rib cage on either side, giving the chest the appearance of the keel of a boat. Also called pigeon breast; keel breast; keel chest.

p. excavatum Backward displacement of the breastbone (sternum), especially its lower portion, which creates a depression of the chest. Also called funnel chest; funnel breast; foveated chest.

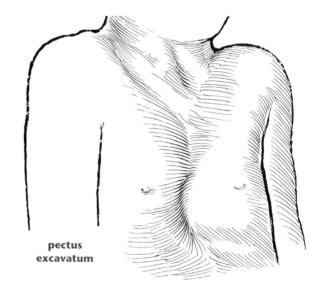

pectus excavatum

pedal (ped'al) Relating to the foot.

pedi-, ped- Combining forms meaning child; feet.

pediatric (pe-de-at'rik) Relating to pediatrics.

pediatrician (pe-de-ah-trish'un) A physician who specializes in pediatrics.

pediatrics (pe-de-at'riks) (Ped) The branch of medicine concerned with the growth, development, and diseases of children.

pedicle (ped'ĭ-kl) 1. A stalklike structure attaching a tumor to normal tissue. 2. A tubular skin graft left temporarily attached to the donor site, through which the graft receives its blood supply. 3. An anatomic structure resembling a short stem.

P

p. of vertebral arch One of two bars of bone extending backward from the bodies of each vertebra; they are parts of the vertebral arch surrounding the spinal cord.

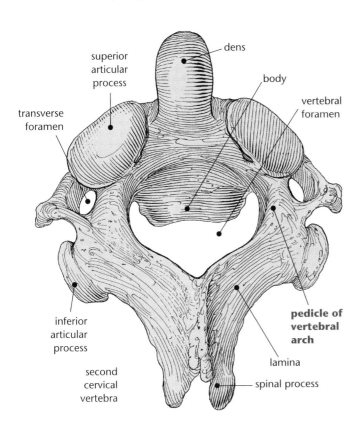

superior articular process
dens
body
vertebral foramen
transverse foramen
inferior articular process
pedicle of vertebral arch
second cervical vertebra
lamina
spinal process

restiform body. *Middle cerebellar p.,* a very thick bundle of nerve fibers that interconnect the cerebellum with the dorsolateral region of the pons. *Superior cerebellar p.,* a large flattened bundle of largely efferent nerve fibers that interconnect the cerebellar hemisphere with the midbrain and thalamus.

cerebral p. The cerebral hemisphere stalk composed of large masses of nerve fibers, located at the upper border of the pons, in front of the cerebral aqueduct.

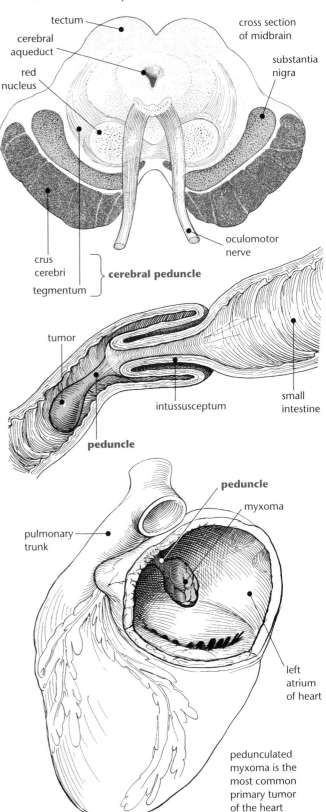

tectum
cerebral aqueduct
red nucleus
cross section of midbrain
substantia nigra
oculomotor nerve
crus cerebri
tegmentum
cerebral peduncle

tumor
intussusceptum
small intestine
peduncle

pulmonary trunk
peduncle
myxoma
left atrium of heart

pedunculated myxoma is the most common primary tumor of the heart

pedicular (pe-dik′u-lar) Relating to lice.

pediculate (pe-dik′u-lāt) Having a pedicle.

pediculicide (pe-dik′u-li-sīd) Any agent destructive to lice.

pediculosis (pe-dik-u-lo′sis) Itchy eruption of the skin caused by infestation with head, body, or crab lice. Also called phthiriviasis.

pediculous (pe-dik′u-lus) Infested with lice.

pedigree (ped′ĭ-gre) **1.** In genetics, a graphic representation of a family's ancestral history. **2.** In medical genetics, a diagrammatic representation of a family history, indicating family members affected with the disease of concern and their relationship to the affected member (proband) who first drew attention to the family for study of the trait.

pedo- Combining form meaning child; feet.

pedodontics (pe-do-don′tiks) The branch of dentistry concerned with the care and treatment of children's teeth and associated structures. Also called pediatric dentistry.

pedodontist (pe-do-don′tist) A specialist in pedodontics.

pedophilia (pe-do-fil′e-ah) Engaging in sexual fantasies and activities with children as a repeatedly preferred or exclusive method by an adult. It includes any form of heterosexual or homosexual activity.

pedophilic (pe-do-fil′ik) Relating to pedophilia.

pedorthics (pe-dor′thiks) The field of prescription footwear.

pedorthist (pe-dor′thist) A shoefitter trained to fill a physician's shoe prescription.

peduncle (pĕ-dung′kl) **1.** A large stalklike mass of nerve fibers connecting structures within the central nervous system. **2.** The narrow part of a structure serving as support or attachment; a stem.

cerebellar p.'s Three pairs of thick bundles of nerve fibers interconnecting each side of the cerebellum with the brainstem (medulla oblongata, pons, and midbrain): *Inferior cerebellar p.,* a thick bundle of largely afferent nerve fibers of the medulla oblongata that interconnect the cerebellum with the medulla oblongata. Also called

p. of flocculus A narrow band of white fibers that emerges from the detached portion of the cerebellum (flocculus) and lies just below the vestibulocochlear (8th cranial) nerve as it enters the brainstem on either side; it interconnects the flocculus with the nodule of the cerebellum.

p. of mamillary body A bundle of nerve fibers passing from the midbrain tegmentum to the mamillary body of the hypothalamus.

p. of pineal body The bilaminar stalk of the pineal body composed of superior and inferior layers (laminae), separated by the pineal recess of the third ventricle of the brain.

p.'s of thalamus Well-defined fanlike bundles of nerve fibers interconnecting the thalamus with the cerebral cortex; subdivided into: *Anterior p. of thalamus,* bundles interconnecting the thalamus with the cerebral cortex of the frontal lobe. *Inferior p. of thalamus,* the smallest bundles interconnecting the thalamus and medial geniculate body with the cerebral cortex of the temporal lobe. *Posterior p. of thalamus,* bundles interconnecting the thalamus and lateral geniculate body with the posterior parietal and occipital lobes. *Superior p. of thalamus,* bundles interconnecting the thalamus with the cerebral cortex of the precentral and postcentral gyri and the immediately adjacent areas of the frontal and parietal lobes.

peduncular (pĕ-dung′ku-lar) Relating to a peduncle.

pedunculated (pĕ-dung′ku-lāt-ed) Having a peduncle.

pedunculotomy (pĕ-dung-ku-lot′o-me) Surgical incision into a cerebral peduncle.

pellagra (pĕ-la′grah) Nutritional disorder caused by niacin deficiency characterized by skin lesions, diarrhea, and mental disorders or abnormalities (e.g., delusions and impaired thinking).

pellagroid (pĕ-lag′roid) Resembling pellagra.

pellagrous (pe-lag′rus) Relating to pellagra.

pellet (pel′et) **1.** A small, sterile pill composed of material (usually a hormone) that is implanted under the skin for slow, prolonged release. **2.** The mass of solid or particulate material remaining at the bottom of the tube after centrifugation of a suspension; specifically, any of several small masses of material containing spermatozoa, which remain at the bottom of the centrifugation tube after a semen specimen has been centrifuged (a stage in the preparation of a semen specimen prior to *in vitro* fertilization).

pellicle (pel′ĭ-kl) **1.** A thin membrane. **2.** A skinlike film on the surface of a liquid.

pelvi-, pelvo- Combining forms meaning the pelvis.

pelvic (pel′vik) Relating to the pelvis.

pelvicephalometry (pel-ve-sef-ah-lom′ĕ-tre) Comparative measurement of the maternal pelvis and fetal head.

pelvimeter (pel-vim′ĕ-ter) A caliper-type instrument for measuring the diameters of the pelvis.

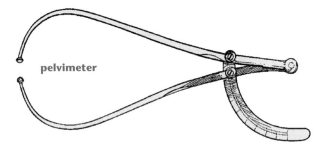

pelvimeter

pelvimetry (pel-vim′ĕ-tre) Measurement of diameters of the female pelvis in pregnancy to determine whether the woman is likely to develop difficult labor due to disproportion between the fetal head and maternal pelvis.

combined p. Pelvimetry made both within the body with the examiner's hand and outside the body with instruments.

radiologic p. See x-ray pelvimetry.

x-ray p. A precise method of assessing the diameters of the vault, midpelvis, and pelvic outlet; performed only if the potential benefit exceeds the risk of radiation injury to the fetus; usually postponed until near term. Also called radiologic pelvimetry.

pelvis (pel′vis), pl. pel′vises, pel′ves **1.** The basin-shaped skeletal structure at the lower end of the trunk, composed of the two hipbones and the sacrum and coccyx; it supports the spinal column and rests on the lower limbs. **2.** A funnel-like dilatation.

achondroplastic p. A broad, flattened pelvis, as seen in achondroplastic dwarfs.

android p. A female pelvis with a wedge-shaped inlet and a narrow anterior segment, characteristics of a typical male pelvis. Also called funnel-shaped pelvis; brachypellic pelvis.

anthropoid p. A pelvis with a long, narrow, oval inlet; its anteroposterior diameter exceeds its transverse diameter. Also called pithecoid pelvis; dolichopellic pelvis.

brachypellic p. See android pelvis.

contracted p. One in which an important diameter of the pelvis is shorter than normal.

cordate p. A pelvis with an inlet that is somewhat heart-shaped; caused by thrusting forward of the sacrum.

dolichopellic p. See anthropoid pelvis.

false p. See major pelvis.

funnel-shaped p. See android pelvis.

greater p. See major pelvis.

gynecoid p. A pelvis with an inlet that has a well-rounded oval shape; it represents the average or normal female pelvis. Also called mesatipellic pelvis.

p. of kidney See renal pelvis.

kyphotic p. A pelvis that, due to kyphoscoliosis, is contracted transversely and appears funnel-shaped with a marked inclination.

lesser p. See minor pelvis.

lordotic p. A pelvis that is deformed by an anterior curvature in the lumbar region of the vertebral column.

major p. The false pelvis; the portion of the pelvis above the oblique plane of the pelvic brim; its cavity is part of the abdomen. Also called false pelvis; greater pelvis.

mesatipellic p. See gynecoid pelvis.

minor p. The true pelvis; a narrowed continuation of the major pelvis; it is short, wide, and curved, and is positioned below and behind the pelvic brim. Also called true pelvis; lesser pelvis.

p. obtecta A pelvis associated with severe kyphosis, in which the vertebral column extends horizontally across the pelvic inlet.

pithecoid p. See anthropoid pelvis.

platypellic p. See platypelloid pelvis.

platypelloid p. An exceedingly flat, uncommon pelvis; one in which the transverse diameter of the pelvic inlet is far greater than the anteroposterior diameter. Also called platypellic pelvis.

renal p. The funnel-shaped dilatation formed by the junction of the calices of the kidney through which urine passes into the ureter. Also called pelvis of kidney; pelvis of ureter.

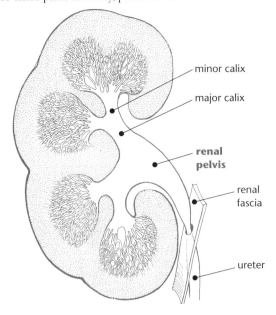

minor calix
major calix
renal pelvis
renal fascia
ureter

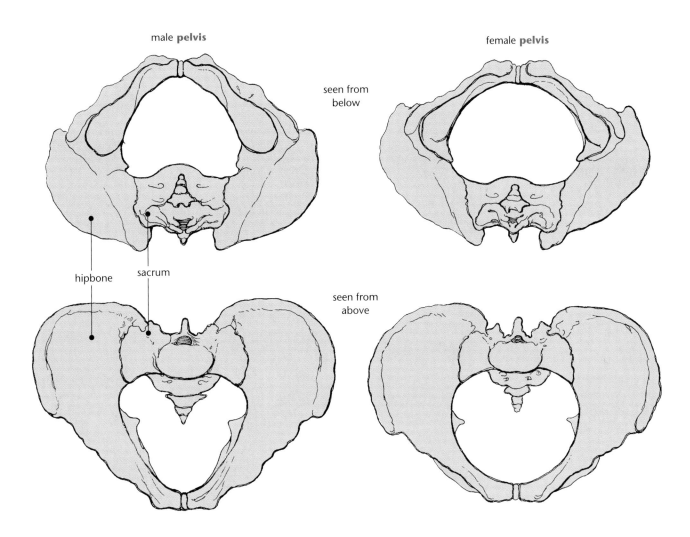

male **pelvis**

seen from
below

female **pelvis**

hipbone   sacrum

seen from
above

scoliotic p. An obliquely deformed pelvis, seen in association with scoliosis.

spondylolisthetic p. A pelvis tilted so posteriorly that the body of the fifth lumbar vertebra is situated on a plane in front of the body of the sacrum.

stove-in p. One in which, as a result of a severe compression injury, part of the pelvis is driven into the pelvic cavity.

true p. See minor pelvis.

p. of ureter See renal pelvis.

pelvisacral (pel-vĭ-sa′kral) Relating to the pelvis and sacrum.

pelviscope (pel′vĭ-skōp) Instrument provided with a light source for inspecting the interior of the pelvis.

pelvospondylitis ossificans (pel-vo-spon-dĭ-li′tis ŏ-sif′ĭ-kanz) The presence of bony deposits between the sacrum and lumbar vertebrae.

pemphigoid (pem′fĭ-goid) Resembling pemphigus

bullous p. An autoimmune skin disease typically affecting elderly people, caused by circulating antibodies depositing along the deepest layer (basement membrane) of the skin; marked by large blisters (up to 4–8 cm in diameter) on the inner thighs, forearms, and lower abdomen.

pemphigus (pem′fĭ-gus) **1.** A group of autoimmune skin diseases typically affecting people 40 to 60 years of age; characterized by blister formation due to the presence of circulating antibody reacting against certain tissue components of the skin. **2.** Pemphigus vulgaris.

p. erythematosus A localized mild form of pemphigus foliaceus typically affecting the sides of the face. Also called Senear-Usher syndrome.

p. foliaceus A mild form affecting primarily the face, scalp, and upper trunk; marked by formation of extremely superficial blis-

ters that typically leave only slight redness and crusting after rupturing.

p. vegetans A rare form characterized by development of large, moist, rough plaques studded with pustules over erupted blisters.

p. vulgaris A chronic, severe, potentially fatal disease, marked by formation of large, flaccid, superficial blisters in the oral mucosa, scalp, face, trunk, and pressure points; the easily ruptured blisters leave shallow, crusted erosions.

penectomy (pe-nek′to-me) Removal of the penis. Also called phallectomy.

penetrance (pen′ĕ-trans) In genetics, the frequency with which a heritable trait is manifested in persons known to carry the gene for the trait.

penetrometer (pen-ĕ-trom′ĕ-ter) A device for measuring the penetrating power of x rays.

-penia Combining form meaning deficiency (e.g., eosinopenia).

penicillamine (pen-ĭ-sil-ah′mēn) A chelating agent used in treating lead poisoning and hepatolenticular degeneration (Wilson's disease).

penicillate (pen-ĭ-sil′lāt) Resembling a tuft or brushlike structure (penicillus).

penicillin (pen-ĭ-sil′in) Any of a family of antibiotic compounds; derived from the fungus *Penicillum notatum* (natural penicillin) or produced synthetically. Penicillin suppresses synthesis of bacterial cell walls, which results in eventual death of the cell when the penicillin-poisoned bacterium outgrows its cell wall.

penicillinase (pen-ĭ-sil′ĭ-nās) Enzyme produced by certain bacteria (e.g., some strains of staphylococcus) that renders penicillin inactive.

penicillus (pen-ĭ-sil′us), pl. penicil′li A small brushlike structure; a tuft.

penile (pe'nĭl) Relating to the penis.

penis (pe'nis) The male organ of copulation and urination; composed of three columns of erectile tissue, two (corpora cavernosa) lying side by side in front of a third (corpus spongiosum), which contains the urethra and forms the head (glans) at the end.

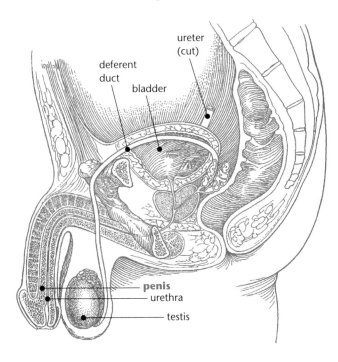

deferent duct
ureter (cut)
bladder
penis
urethra
testis

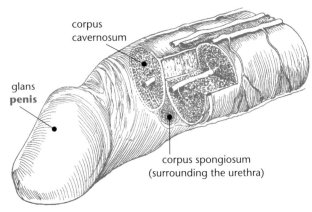

corpus cavernosum
glans **penis**
corpus spongiosum (surrounding the urethra)

pennate (pen'āt) Resembling a feather. Also called penniform.

penniform (pen'ĭ-form) See pennate.

pentamidine isethionate (pen-tam'ĭ-dēn i-sĕ-thi'o-nāt) Drug used in the treatment of African sleeping sickness (trypanosomiasis), leishmaniasis, and pneumonia caused by *Pneumocystis carinii*.

pentazocine (pen-taz'o-sēn) A narcotic painkiller with addiction potential.

pentobarbital (pen-to-bar'bĭ-tal) A sedative drug sometimes used to treat insomnia.

pentose (pen'tōs) Any sugar containing five carbon atoms in a molecule.

pentosuria (pen-to-su're-ah) The presence of pentose in the urine.

pepsin (pep'sin) A digestive enzyme of gastric juice that breaks down protein into polypeptides.

pepsinogen (pep-sin'o-jen) A precursor of pepsin produced and secreted by the stomach lining, converted into pepsin by the action of digestive hydrochloric acid.

pepsinogenous (pep-sin-o'jen-us) Relating to pepsin.

pepsinuria (pep-sĭ-nu're-ah) The presence of pepsin in the urine.

peptic (pep'tik) 1. Relating to digestion. 2. Relating to pepsin.

peptidase (pep'tĭ-dās) Enzyme that promotes the breakdown of peptide bonds in a protein molecule.

peptide (pep'tīd) One of various compounds consisting of two or more amino acid residues.

peptolysis (pep-tol'ĭ-sis) The splitting of peptone molecules.

peptone (pep'tōn) Any of various protein derivatives resulting from the action of enzymes on proteins.

Peptostreptococcus (pep-to-strep-to-kok'us) A genus of gram-positive bacteria found normally in the respiratory, intestinal, and female genital tracts; also found in certain pus-forming infections.

per- Prefix meaning through; largest amount.

per anum (per a'num) Latin for through the anus.

perception (per-sep'shun) The mental process of becoming aware of something through the senses.

percuss (per-kus') To perform percussion.

percussion (per-kush'un) The act of delivering light, quick taps on selected areas of the body for diagnostic or therapeutic purposes.

   auscultatory p. Simultaneous auscultation and percussion (e.g., of the chest) to listen to sounds produced by percussion.

   bimanual p. The tapping of a finger (placed in contact with the body) with a finger of the other hand.

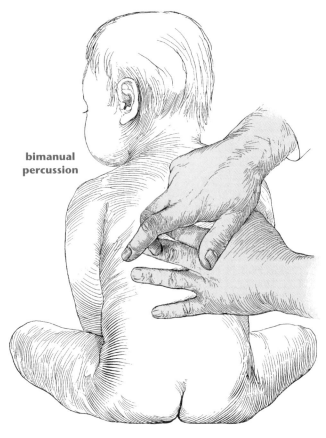

bimanual percussion

percussor (per-kus'or) See plessor.

percutaneous (per-ku-ta'ne-us) Effected or performed through the skin.

perfectionism (per-fek'shun-izm) A tendency to set extremely high standards of performance for oneself.

perflation (per-fla'shun) The forceful blowing of air into a cavity or passage to expel contained matter.

perforans (per'fo-ranz) Term applied to structures that pass through other structures (e.g., certain blood vessels and nerves).

perforation (per-fo-ra'shun) 1. A hole made in a tissue or organ by disease or injury (e.g., of the tympanic membrane by sharp objects or by middle ear infection and of the stomach by a peptic ulcer). 2. The act of piercing.

   cervical p. Perforation of the uterine cervix, which may be caused by the downward displacement or partial expulsion of an IUD (intrauterine device); by wires or knitting needles while performing an illegal abortion; or during therapeutic procedures, such as cervical dilation, sounding of the uterus, cervical conization, or insertion of an intracavitary radium applicator (e.g., a colpostat or tandem).

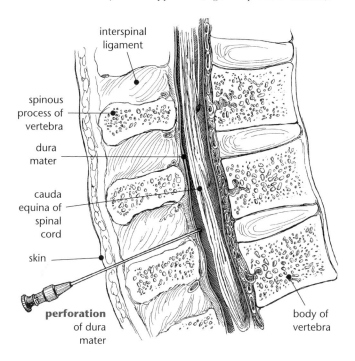

interspinal ligament

spinous process of vertebra

dura mater

cauda equina of spinal cord

skin

perforation of dura mater

body of vertebra

perfusate (per-fu′zāt) A fluid that has been passed through or over an organ or through a membrane.

perfusion (per-fu′shun) The passing of a fluid through an organ or tissue by way of the blood vessels.

peri- Prefix meaning around; about.

periadenitis (per-e-ad-ě-ni′tis) Inflammation of tissues surrounding a gland.

perianal (per-e-a′nal) Situated around the anus. Also called circumanal.

periangiitis, periangitis (per-e-an-je-i′tis, per-e-an-ji′tis) Inflammation of tissues surrounding blood vessels or lymphatic vessels.

periaortic (per-e-a-or′tik) Around the aorta.

periaortitis (per-e-a-or-ti′tis) Inflammation of tissues around the aorta.

periapical (per-e-ap′ĭ-kal) Around a dental root, including the alveolar bone.

periappendicitis (per-e-ah-pen-dī-si′tis) Inflammation of tissues around the vermiform appendix.

periarterial (per-e-ar-te′re-al) Around an artery.

periarteritis (per-e-ar-te-ri′tis) Inflammation of the outermost coat (adventitia) of an artery.

    p. nodosa See polyarteritis nodosa, under polyarteritis.

periarthritis (per-e-ar-thri′tis) Inflammation of tissues surrounding a joint.

peribronchial (per-ĭ-brong′ke-al) Surrounding an air passage (bronchus) in the lung.

peribuccal (per-ĭ-buk′al) Surrounding the cheek.

peribulbar (per-ĭ-bul′bar) Surrounding the eyeball.

peribursal (per-ĭ-ber′sal) Surrounding a bursa.

pericardectomy (per-ĭ-kar-dek′to-me) See pericardiectomy.

pericardiac (per-ĭ-kar′de-ak) See pericardial.

pericardial (per-ĭ-kar′de-al) Relating to the sac enveloping the heart (pericardium); around the heart. Also called pericardiac.

pericardicentesis (per-ĭ-kar-de-sen-te′sis) See pericardiocentesis.

pericardiectomy (per-ĭ-kar-de-ek′to-me) Surgical removal of a portion of the pericardium, the membranous sac that envelops the heart. Also called pericardectomy.

pericardiocentesis (per-ĭ-kar-de-o-sen-te′sis) Needle aspiration of

fluid accumulated within the pericardium, the membranous sac enveloping the heart; performed for therapeutic and diagnostic purposes. Also spelled pericardicentesis.

pericardiophrenic (per-ĭ-kar-de-o-fren′ik) Relating to the diaphragm and the membranous sac that envelops the heart.

pericardiorrhaphy (per-ĭ-kar-de-or′ah-fe) Suturing of the membranous sac that envelops the heart.

pericardiotomy (per-ĭ-kar-de-ot′o-me) A surgical cut into the membranous sac that envelops the heart. Also called pericardotomy.

pericarditis (per-ĭ-kar-di′tis) Inflammation of the pericardium, usually occurring secondary to other disorders of adjacent structures.

    acute p. Pericarditis characterized by chest pain, sometimes resembling a heart attack (myocardial infarction) but relieved by leaning forward; palpitations and fever may also occur; causes include infection (especially viral), chronic kidney failure, and connective tissue diseases.

    chronic adhesive p. Fibrous bands between the two layers of pericardium, between pericardium and heart, or between pericardium and adjacent structures; formed during healing of previous pericarditis.

    chronic constrictive p. A rare form in which the pericardium becomes thick, dense, and fibrous, limiting heart muscle function; results from healing and scar formation of previous pericarditis.

electrocardiogram in **pericarditis**

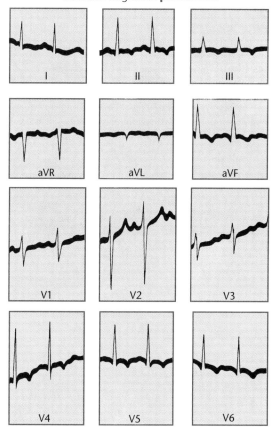

I

II

III

aVR

aVL

aVF

V1

V2

V3

V4

V5

V6

pericardium (per-ĭ-kar′de-um) The double-layered sac, separated by a film of fluid, enveloping the heart and roots of the great vessels (aorta and pulmonary trunk); consists of an outer fibrous layer (fibrous pericardium) and an inner membranous layer (serous pericardium). Also called heart sac.

pericardotomy (per-ĭ-kar-dot′o-me) See pericardiotomy.

pericecal (per-ĭ-se′kal) Surrounding the cecum.

pericellular (per-ĭ-sel′u-lar) Surrounding a cell.

pericholangitis (per-ĭ-ko-lan-ji′tis) Inflammation of tissues around the bile ducts; frequently seen in association with inflammatory bowel disease.

perichondral, perichondrial (per-ĭ-kon′dral, per-ĭ-kon′dre-al) Relating to the perichondrium.

perichondritis (per-ĭ-kon-dri′tis) Inflammation of cartilage.

    peristernal p. See Tietze's syndrome, under syndrome.

perichondrium (per-ĭ-kon′dre-um) The fibrous membrane covering all cartilage except at joint endings; composed of an outer connective tissue layer and an inner one that is responsible for producing new cartilage.

pericolpitis (per-ĭ-kol-pi′tis) See perivaginitis.

pericoronal (per-ĭ-kō-ro′-nal) Surrounding the crown of a tooth.

pericoronitis (per-ĭ-kor-o-ni′tis) Inflammation of the gums around an incompletely erupted tooth.

pericranial (per-ĭ-kra′ne-al) Relating to the membrane adherent to the outer surface of the skull.

pericystic (per-ĭ-sis′tik) Surrounding the bladder, the gallbladder, or a cyst.

pericyte (per′ĭ-sīt) One of the contractile cells in the connective tissue layer around capillaries.

peridental (per-ĭ-den′tal) See periodontal.

peridesmic (per-ĭ-dez′mik) Surrounding a ligament. Also called periligamentous.

peridesmitis (per-ĭ-dez-mi′tis) Inflammation of the peridesmium.

peridesmium (per-ĭ-dez′me-um) The connective tissue covering ligaments.

perienteritis (per-e-en-ter-i′tis) Inflammation of the peritoneal (serous) covering of the intestines. Also called seroenteritis.

periesophageal (per-e-ĕ-sof′ah-je-al) Surrounding the esophagus.

periesophagitis (per-e-ĕ-sof-ah-ji′tis) Inflammation of tissues surrounding the esophagus.

periganglionic (per-ĭ-gang-gle-on′ik) Surrounding a ganglion.

perigastric (per-ĭ-gas′trik) Surrounding the stomach.

perihepatic (per-ĭ-hĕ-pat′ik) Surrounding the liver.

perihepatitis (per-ĭ-hep-ah-ti′tis) Inflammation of the covering membrane of the liver and surrounding structures; may be caused by infection or trauma.

perikaryon (per-ĭ-kar′e-on) The cytoplasm around the nucleus of a nerve cell.

periligamentous (per-ĭ-lig-ah-men′tus) See peridesmic.

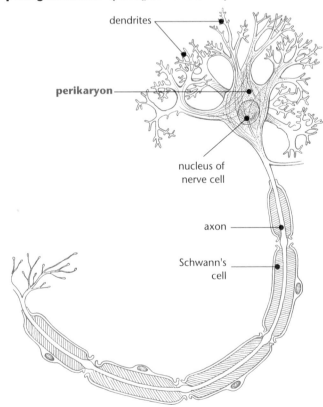

perilymph (per′ĭ-limf) The fluid in the bony labyrinth of the inner ear, surrounding the membranous labyrinth.

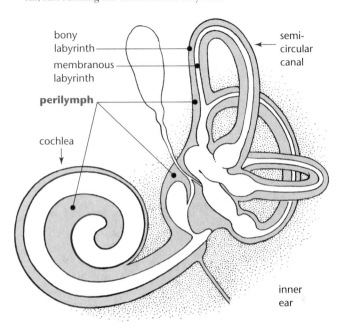

perilymphatic (per-ĭ-lim-fat′ik) **1.** Relating to the perilymph. **2.** Surrounding a lymphatic vessel.

perimeter (pĕ-rim′ĕ-ter) Instrument for measuring the field of vision.

perimetric (per-ĭ-met′rik) **1.** Relating to a perimeter or to measurement of the visual field. **2.** Surrounding the uterus.

perimetritis (per-ĭ-mĕ-tri′tis) Inflammation of the perimetrium.

perimetrium (per-ĭ-me′tre-um) The outer, serous layer of the uterine wall.

perimetry (pĕ-rim′ĕ-tre) Measurement of the visual field, usually performed to diagnose lesions of the visual pathways.

perimysial (per-ĭ-mis′e-al) Relating to the perimysium.

perimysium (per-ĭ-mis′e-um) Connective tissue separating adjacent bundles of skeletal muscle fibers.

perinatal (per-ĭ-na′tal) Relating to the period of time preceding and following birth, from completion of 20 weeks of gestation through the first 28 days after birth.

perinate (per′ĭ-nāt) An infant one week before birth to one week after birth.

perinatology (per-ĭ-na-tol′o-je) The branch of obstetrics and pediatrics concerned with the study and treatment of mother and infant in the last stages of pregnancy and early days after birth. Also called perinatal medicine.

perineal (per-ĭ-ne′al) Relating to the perineum.

perineo- Combining form meaning perineum.

perineoplasty (per-ĭ-ne′o-plas-te) Reparative surgery of the perineum (e.g., to correct a relaxed condition of the musculature).

perineorrhaphy (per-ĭ-ne-or′ah-fe) Suturing of the perineum to repair lacerations or other injuries.

perineotomy (per-ĭ-ne-ot′o-me) See episiotomy.

perinephric (per-ĭ-nef′rik) Around a kidney. Also called perirenal.

perinephrium (per-ĭ-nef′re-um) The connective tissue and fat surrounding the kidney.

perineum (per-ĭ-ne′um) The diamond-shaped area between the thighs extending from the tailbone (coccyx) to the pubis, just below the pelvic floor; the area between the vulva and the anus in the female and the scrotum and the anus in the male.

perineural (per-ĭ-nu′ral) Surrounding a nerve.

perineuritis (per-ĭ-nu-ri′tis) Inflammation of the perineurium.

perineurium (per-ĭ-nu′re-um) A sheath of connective tissue enveloping and supporting a bundle of nerve fibers in a peripheral nerve. Also called lamellar sheath.

perinuclear (per-ĭ-nu′kle-ar) Surrounding a cell nucleus.

period (pe′re-od) **1.** A portion of time. **2.** Popular name for an occurrence of menstruation; menses.

    fertile p. The time in the midportion of the menstrual cycle when ovulation takes place and conception is most likely to occur; usually 10 to 18 days after the first day of the last menstruation.

    gestational p. The duration of pregnancy, i.e., the time between fertilization of the ovum and birth of the fetus. In humans, the average length of the gestational period is 266 days; clinically, it is commonly divided into three parts (trimesters), each lasting about three calendar months.

days	weeks	calendar months	lunar months
266	38	8¾	9½

INCUBATION PERIODS OF VARIOUS DISEASES

DISEASE	INCUBATION PERIOD	RASH
gastroenteritis	6–24 hours	—
diphtheria	2–5 days	—
scarlet fever	1–5 days	1st day
measles	10–15 days	4th day
rubella	14–21 days	1st day
chickenpox	14–21 days	1st day
mumps	7–26 days	—
smallpox	7–16 days	3rd day
whooping cough	2–21 days	—
poliomyelitis	7–21 days	—
virus influenza	1–4 days	—
gonorrhea	1–8 days	—
typhus	8–16 days	5th day
yellow fever	3–6 days	—
viral hepatits A	15–35 days	—
viral hepatitis non A, non B	25–160 days	—
viral hepatitis B	30–180 days	—
brucellosis	7–14 days	—
typhoid fever	3–38 days	—
syphilis	1–6 weeks	—

incubation p. The time between infection with a disease-causing microorganism and the appearance of the first symptoms of the disease. Also called incubative stage; latent period.

    latent p. *(a)* An apparently inactive period; e.g., the time elapsed between exposure to an injurious agent (radiation, poison) and manifestation of effects, or between the application of a stimulus and a response to the stimulus. Also called latent stage. *(b)* See incubation period.

    missed p. Failure of menstruation to occur in any given month.

    puerperal p. The period beginning just after childbirth and the return of the uterus to its original state; usually lasting about six weeks.

    safe p. Time in the menstrual cycle when conception is least likely to occur; usually lasting from about 10 days before to 10 days after the first day of menstruation. Variability in ovulation time from month to month makes this an unreliable contraceptive method.

    vulnerable p. The brief period after contraction of the heart ventricle when a stimulus applied to it is likely to precipitate rapid, quivering contractions (fibrillation) of the heart.

periodic (pe-re-od′ik) Recurring at regular intervals (e.g., the paroxysms and fever of malaria).

periodical (pe-re-od′ik-al) A journal published at regular intervals.

periodicity (pe-re-o-dis′ĭ-te) Recurrence at regular time intervals.

periodontal (per-e-o-don′tal) Around a tooth. Also called peridental.

periodontics (per-e-o-don′tiks) The branch of dentistry concerned with the gums and the bone supporting the teeth and with the treatment and prevention of disease affecting these tissues.

periodontist (per-e-o-don′tist) A specialist in periodontics.

periodontitis (per-e-o-don-ti′tis) Inflammation of the tissues surrounding and supporting the teeth. Also called pyorrhea.

    juvenile p. A rare form of periodontitis affecting adolescents, marked by degeneration of bone, formation of deep pockets, and premature tooth loss. Also called periodontosis.

periodontium (per-e-o-don′she-um) Tissues that surround the teeth, including alveolar bone, cementum, gingiva, and periodontal membrane.

periodontosis (per-e-o-don-to′sis) See juvenile periodontitis, under periodontitis.

perioral (per-e-o′ral) Around the mouth.

periorbita (per-e-or′bĭ-tah) The periosteum lining the eye socket (orbit).

periorbital (per-e-or′bĭ-tal) Around the eye socket (orbit).

periorchitis (per-e-or-ki′tis) Inflammation of the serous pouch containing the testis.

periosteal (per-e-os′te-al) Relating to the periosteum.

periosteo- Combining form meaning periosteum.

periosteomyelitis (per-e-os-te-o-mi-ĕ-li′tis) Inflammation of a bone, including its periosteum and marrow.

periosteotomy (per-e-os-te-ot′o-me) A surgical cut into the periosteum. Also called periostotomy.

periosteum (per-e-os′te-um) The fibrous membrane covering all bones except at points of articulation.

periostitis (per-e-os-ti′tis) Inflammation of periosteum.

periostotomy (per-e-os-tot′o-me) See periosteotomy.

peripapillary (per-ĭ-pap′ĭ-ler-e) Surrounding the optic disk.

peripheral (pĕ-rif′er-al) Relating to the outer surface of the body; located away from the center.

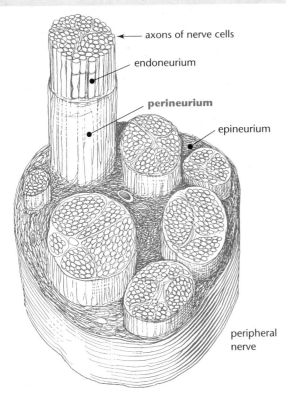

axons of nerve cells

endoneurium

perineurium

epineurium

peripheral nerve

P

periproctitis (per-ĭ-prok-ti′tis) Inflammation of tissues adjacent to the rectum and anus.

perirectal (per-ĭ-rek′tal) Around the rectum.

perirenal (per-ĭ-re′nal) See perinephric.

perisplenitis (per-ĭ-splĕ-ni′tis) Inflammation of the membrane covering the spleen and of adjacent structures.

peristalsis (per-ĭ-stal′sis) The successive waves of contractions passing along a tubular structure (e.g., intestinal tract, ureters), serving to move onward contents of the structure.

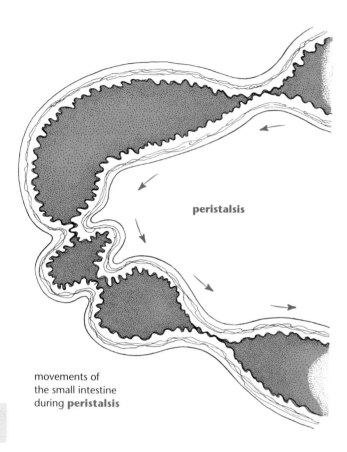

movements of
the small intestine
during **peristalsis**

P

     reversed p., retrograde p. Peristaltic contractions in an opposite direction from the normal, propelling the contents backward.

peristaltic (per-ĭ-stal′tik) Relating to peristalsis.

peristole (per-is′to-le) Tonic contraction of the stomach wall about its contents; distinguished from its peristaltic contractions.

perisynovial (per-ĭ-sĭ-no′ve-al) Around the lining (synovial membrane) of a joint cavity.

peritectomy (per-ĭ-tek′to-me) Removal of a small portion of conjunctiva near the cornea. Also called peritomy.

peritendinitis (per-ĭ-ten-dĭ-ni′tis) Inflammation of the sheath of fibrous tissue covering a tendon. Also called peritenontitis.

peritenontitis (per-ĭ-ten-on-ti′tis) See peritendinitis.

perithelioma (per-ĭ-the-le-o′mah) See hemangiopericytoma.

perithelium (per-ĭ-the′le-um) Thin layer of connective tissue surrounding small blood vessels.

peritomy (pĕ-rit′o-me) See peritectomy.

peritoneal (per-ĭ-to-ne′al) Relating to the peritoneum.

peritoneo- Combining form meaning peritoneum.

peritoneocentesis (per-ĭ-to-ne-o-sen-te′sis) Aspiration of fluid from the abdominal cavity with a fine needle or any other hollow instrument. Also called abdominocentesis; paracentesis.

peritoneoclysis (per-ĭ-to-ne-o-kli′sis) Irrigation of the peritoneal cavity.

peritoneoscope (per-ĭ-to-ne′o-skōp) See laparoscope.

peritoneoscopy (per-ĭ-to-ne-os′ko-pe) See laparoscopy.

peritoneotomy (per-ĭ-to-ne-ot′o-me) See laparotomy.

peritoneum (per-ĭ-to-ne′um) The serous membrane lining the abdominal and pelvic cavities and covering most of the organs contained within. Also called abdominal membrane.

    parietal p. The peritoneum lining the wall of the abdominal and pelvic cavities.

    visceral p. The peritoneum adhering to the surface of abdominal and pelvic organs.

peritonitis (per-ĭ-to-ni′tis) Inflammation of the peritoneum, marked by pain, fever, constipation, and vomiting; may be caused by bacterial infection (e.g., from a ruptured appendix, perforated ulcer, acute inflammation of uterine tubes); by chemical irritation (e.g., escaped bile, leakage of pancreatic enzymes); or by surgically introduced infective material.

    bile p. Peritonitis caused by escape of bile into the peritoneal cavity. Also called choleperitonitis.

peritonsillar (per-ĭ-ton′sĭ-lar) Surrounding a tonsil.

peritracheal (per-ĭ-tra′ke-al) Surrounding the windpipe (trachea).

peritrichous (pĕ-rit′rĭ-kus) Having fine surface projections, such as cilia or flagella; applied to cells, especially bacterial cells.

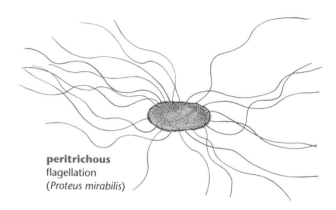

peritrichous
flagellation
(*Proteus mirabilis*)

periumbilical (per-e-um-bil′ĭ-kal) Surrounding the navel (umbilicus).

periungual (per-e-ung′gwal) Surrounding a nail.

periureteral, periureteric (per-ĭ-u-re′ter-al, per-e-u-re-ter′ik) Around the ureter.

periureteritis (per-e-u-re-tĕ-ri′tis) Inflammation of tissues that surround the ureters.

periurethritis (per-e-u-re-thri′tis) Inflammation of tissues about the urethra.

perivaginal (per-ĭ-vaj′ĭ-nal) Near the vagina.

perivaginitis (per-ĭ-vaj-ĭ-ni′tis) Inflammation of tissues adjacent to the vagina. Also called pericolpitis.

perivascular (per-ĭ-vas′ku-lar) Surrounding a blood vessel or lymphatic vessel.

perlèche (per-lesh′) Inflammation with cracks and erosion at the corners of the mouth; may be caused by a primary or a superimposed infection with any of various microorganisms, including *Candida albicans* and streptococci.

permanent (per′-mah-nent) Medically, a term used to imply irreversibility of a condition; a prognosis established with a high degree of clinical certainty, based on probabilities rather than absolutes (e.g., a permanent vegetative state).

permeability (per-me-ah-bil′ĭ-te) The state of being permeable.

permeable (per′me-ah-bl) Allowing passage, as of fluids through a membrane. Also called pervious.

permeant (per′me-ant) Able to pass, as through a membrane.

permease (per′me-ās) A protein in cell membrane that facilitates the passage of substances through the membrane.

pernicious (per-nish′us) Tending to cause death.

pernio (per′ne-o) See chilblain.

pero- Combining form meaning malformed.

peromelia (per-o-me′le-ah) Congenital malformation of the limbs.

peroneal (per-o-ne′al) **1.** Relating to the lateral side of the leg. **2.** Fibular.

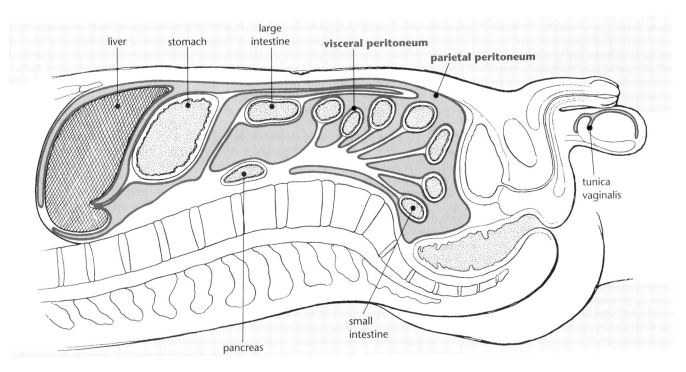

liver stomach large intestine visceral peritoneum parietal peritoneum tunica vaginalis small intestine pancreas

peroral (per-o′ral) Via the mouth.

per os (per os) (p.o.) Latin for by mouth.

peroxidase (pe-rok′sĭ-dās) An enzyme that stimulates oxidation of a wide variety of substances using hydrogen peroxide as oxidant.

peroxisome (pĕ-roks′ĭ-sōm) A membrane-bound vesicle found in the cytoplasm of most cells, but especially concentrated in liver cells. Deficiency is associated with severe diseases of metabolism, many of which are fatal. Also called microbody.

peroxyacetyl nitrate (per-ok-se-ah-se′til ni′trāt) Any of a group of compounds causing eye irritation and respiratory distress; a major air pollutant present in smog.

per rectum (per rek′tum) Via the rectum.

PERRLA Acronym for Pupils Equal, Round, Reactive to Light and Accommodation. A normal finding in neurologic examination.

perseveration (per-sev-er-a′shun) 1. The abnormal repetition of a single response to a variety of questions, or the continuation of an activity no longer appropriate or relevant. 2. The duration of a mental image.

persistent (per-sĭs′tent) Medically, a term used to denote a condition of past and continuing disability with an uncertain future (e.g., a persistent vegetative state).

person (per′son) An individual human being.

  p. of short stature See dwarf.

personality (per-sŭ-nal′ĭ-te) Deeply ingrained patterns of thinking, perceiving, and behavior-response that characterize an individual's lifestyle.

  p. disorders See personality disorders, under disorder.

  psycopathic p. See antisocial personality disorder, under disorder.

  p. traits See personality traits, under trait.

person-years (per′son yirs) In epidemiological studies, a method of measuring incidence (e.g., of a disease) over extended and variable time periods; equal to the sum of the number of years that each person in the study population has been exposed to, or afflicted with, the disease of interest.

perspiration (per-spĭ-ra′shun) 1. The process of sweating. 2. Sweat.

per tubam (per tu′bam) Latin for through a tube.

pertussis (per-tus′is) Acute respiratory tract infection of infants and young children; characterized by inflammation of the air passages (trachea and bronchial tree), causing a paroxysmal cough that ends in a prolonged, high-pitched, crowing sound (the whoop). Commonly called whooping cough.

perversion (per-ver′shun) Deviation from what is considered normal.

pervert (per′vert) One who indulges in perversion.

pervious (per′ve-us) Permeable.

pes (pes) 1. Latin for foot. 2. Any footlike structure.

  p. anserinus (a) See parotid plexus, under plexus. (b) The combined insertions of the tendons of three muscles (sartorius, gracilis, and semitendinous) at the medial border of the tibial tuberosity.

  p. calcaneus See talipes calcaneus, under talipes.

  p. cavus See clawfoot.

  p. equinus See talipes equinus, under talipes.

  p. planovalgus See talipes planovalgus, under talipes.

  p. planus See flatfoot.

  p. pronatus See talipes valgus, under talipes.

  p. valgus See talipes valgus, under talipes.

  p. varus See talipes varus, under talipes.

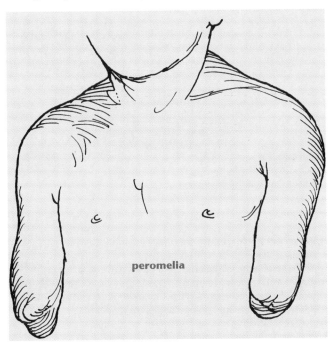

peromelia

P

pessary (pes'ah-re) A device, generally made of rubber or plastic, placed in the vagina (usually as a temporary measure) principally to support the uterus when it deviates from its normal position, to support the cervical stump after a hysterectomy, or to reduce vaginal herniations (cystocele and rectocele). The use of pessaries is usually indicated when treating poor-risk patients or those who refuse surgical measures; generally contraindicated in acute genital tract infections and in adherent retroposition of the uterus.

diaphragmatic p. See contraceptive diaphragm, under diaphragm.

Hodge's p. An elongated, curved, ovoid pessary; one end is placed behind the symphysis, the other in the posterior-superior end (fornix) of the vagina; used to hold a retroverted uterus in place after it has been manually brought into its normal forward position.

inflatable p., doughnut p. A ring-shaped pessary made of soft rubber that, once in place, is inflated with air.

Menge's p. A pessary shaped like a collar button that provides a ringlike platform for the cervix; it is stabilized by a stem that rests upon the perineum; used to correct marked prolapse when the perineum is reasonably adequate.

ring p. A ring placed around the cervix; when in place, it elevates the cervix and distends the vaginal wall, thus reducing a cystocele and a rectocele.

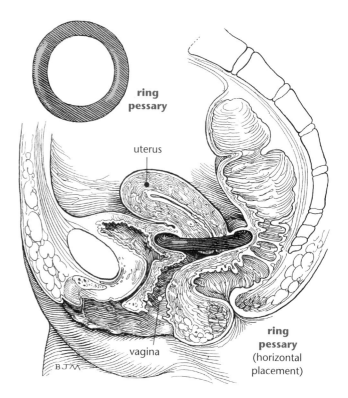

ring pessary

ring pessary (horizontal placement)

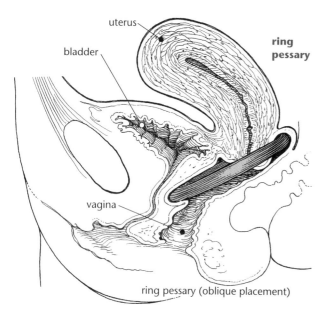

ring pessary (oblique placement)

pesticide (pes'ti-sīd) Any substance or mixture of substances intended for preventing, killing, repelling, or controlling insects, rodents, fungi, nematodes, weeds, or any other form of life declared to be a pest. Pesticides include those substances intended for use as plant regulators, defoliants, or desiccants.

nonpersistent p. A pesticide that is biodegradable within a few weeks.

persistent p. A pesticide that remains in the environment for relatively long periods of time, depending on such factors as the type of soil and its moisture content, temperature, and pH, and the extent of cultivation.

pestilence (pes'ti-lens) Any epidemic of a contagious or infectious disease.

peta- (P) Combining form meaning one quadrillion (10^{15}); used in the SI and metric systems.

-petal Combining form meaning movement toward (e.g., centripetal).

petechia (pĕ-te'ke-ah), pl. pete'chiae Tiny purplish red spots on the skin resulting from subcutaneous bleeding.

petechial (pĕ-te'ke-al) Relating to petechia.

petiolus epiglottidis (pĕ-te'o-lus ep-ĭ-glot'tĭ-dis) Epiglottic peti-

ole; the lower tapered end of the epiglottic cartilage at the front of the larynx, connected by the thyroepiglottic ligament to the back of the thyroid cartilage.

petit mal (pĕ-te' mahl) See absence.

petri dish (pe'tre dish) A shallow circular container, made of thin glass or clear plastic, with a loosely fitting cover; used primarily to cultivate microorganisms in the laboratory.

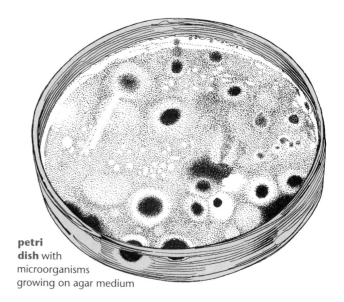

petri dish with microorganisms growing on agar medium

petrifaction (pet-rĭ-fak'shun) The conversion of organic matter into stone.

pétrissage (pa-trĭ-sahzh') Kneading (manipulation) of the muscles in massage.

petro- Combining form meaning stone.

petrolatum (pet-ro-la'tum) A purified, semisolid mixture of hydrocarbons obtained from petroleum; used as a lubricant and in the preparation of ointments. Also called petroleum jelly; yellow soft paraffin.

hydrophilic p. A mixture of stearyl alcohol, cholesterol, white wax, and white petrolatum.

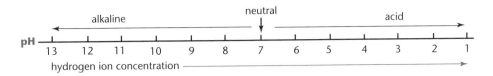

		pH of some fluids			
gastric juice	1.6	urine	5–8	blood plasma	7.4
lemon juice	2.3	saliva	6.5	interstitial fluid	7.4
tomato juice	4.3	cow's milk	6.6	pancreatic juice	7.9

liquid p. See mineral oil, under oil.

petrosal (pě-tro′sal) Relating to the petrous part of the temporal bone.

petrositis (pet-ro-si′tis) Inflammation of the petrous part of the temporal bone.

petrous (pet′rus) **1.** Hard. **2.** Petrosal.

-pexy Suffix meaning fixation (e.g., omentopexy).

peyote (pa-o′te) Common name for the cactus *Lophophora williamsii;* it has a carrot-shaped root and a mushroom-shaped head; it has hallucinatory properties.

pH An expression of the degree of acidity or alkalinity of a solution. The pH is the negative logarithm of the hydrogen ion concentration (e.g., a solution with a hydrogen ion concentration of 1×10^{-3} would have a pH of 3.0). A pH of 7.0 is considered neutral; a lower pH is acid, and a higher pH alkaline. The normal pH value of blood is about 7.4.

phacoanaphylaxis (fak-o-an-ah-fi-lak′sis) Intraocular inflammation due to hypersensitivity to protein of the lens of the eye, induced by escape of lens material; may occur after cataract extraction.

phacocele (fak′o-sēl) Protrusion of the eye lens through the sclera.

phacocyst (fak′o-sist) The capsule of the eye lens.

phacocystectomy (fak-o-sis-tek′to-me) Removal of the lens capsule, completely or partially.

phacoemulsification (fak-o-e-mul-sĭ-fĭ-ka′shun) Cataract removal by emulsifying the diseased lens with low-frequency ultrasonic vibrations, followed by aspiration with a needle.

phacoerysis (fak-o-er-e′sis) Extraction of a cataract with a suction-cup instrument.

phacofragmentation (fak-o-frag-men-ta′shun) Cataract extraction by breaking up and irrigating the diseased eye lens.

phacoid (fak′oid) Lentil-shaped.

phacolysis (fah-kol′ĭ-sis) Liquefaction of the eye lens, as may occur in glaucoma.

phacomalacia (fak-o-mah-la′she-ah) Softening of the eye lens.

phacomatosis (fak-o-mah-to′sis), pl. phacomato′ses Any of a group of disorders characterized by slowly progressive lesions (hamartomas) of the brain, spinal cord, and skin. Major examples include von Hippel–Lindau syndrome, von Recklinghausen's neurofibromatosis (neurofibromatosis I), Sturge-Weber disease, and tuberous sclerosis. Also spelled phakomatosi.

phacoscope (fak′o-skōp) Instrument for observing accommodative changes of the eye lens.

phage (fāj) See bacteriophage.

-phagia, -phage, -phagy Combining forms meaning eating (e.g., hyperphagia, macrophage, cytophagy).

phago- Combining form meaning eating.

phagocyte (fag′o-sīt) A white blood cell (neutrophil or macrophage) capable of surrounding, engulfing, and digesting microorganisms, foreign particles, and cellular debris. Also called scavenger cell.

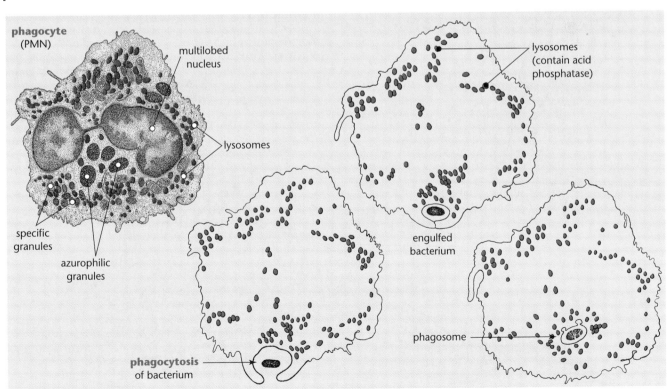

alveolar p. See alveolar macrophage, under macrophage.

phagocytic (fag-o-sit'ik) Relating to phagocytes or their function (phagocytosis).

phagocytin (fag-o-si'tin) A substance found in certain white blood cells (neutrophils) that destroys bacteria.

phagocytize (fag'o-sīt-īz) See phagocytose.

phagocytolysis (fag-o-si-tol'ĭ-sis) Destruction of phagocytes.

phagocytose (fag-o-si'tōs) To engulf and digest; the function of phagocytes. Also called phagocytize.

phagocytosis (fag-o-si-to'sis) The engulfment and digestion of microorganisms, other cells or cell fragments, and foreign particles by certain white blood cells (neutrophils and macrophages).

phakomatosis (fak-o-mah-to'sis) See phacomatosis.

phalangeal (fah-lan'je-al) Relating to a bone of fingers or toes.

phalangectomy (fal-an-jek'to-me) Surgical removal of a bone from a finger or toe.

phalanx (fa'lanks), pl. phalan'ges Any bone of a finger or toe.

phallectomy (fal-ek'to-me) See penectomy.

phallic (fal'ik) Relating to the penis.

phallo-, phall- Combining forms meaning penis.

phallocampsis (fal-o-kamp'sis) Curvature of the erect penis.

phallodynia (fal-o-din'e-ah) Pain in the penis.

phalloplasty (fal'o-plas-te) A reparative surgical procedure on the penis.

phallus (fal'us), pl. phall'i, phall'uses The penis.

phanero- Combining form meaning visible; apparent.

phanerosis (fan-er-o'sis) The process of becoming visible; said chiefly of fatty substances in the tissues that become visible fat droplets.

phantasm (fan'tazm) A hallucination or imaginary image, usually recognized as such by the person who sees it.

phantom (fan'tom) 1. A transparent teaching model of a body part (e.g., one of the female pelvis to demonstrate childbirth). 2. Denoting a sensation felt, which has no physical origin (e.g., pain seemingly originating from an amputated limb).

pharmaceutic (fahr-mah-su'tik) Relating to pharmacy.

pharmaceutical (fahr-mah-su'tĭ-kal) 1. Relating to pharmaceutics. 2. Relating to medicinal drugs. 3. A medicinal drug.

pharmaceutics (fahr-mah-su'tiks) The branch of science concerned with preparation and dosage of medicinal products.

pharmacist (fahr'mah-sist) One who is trained and licensed to prepare and dispense medicinal drugs and who is knowledgeable about their properties.

pharmaco- Combining form meaning drug.

pharmacodiagnosis (fahr-mah-ko-di-ag-no'sis) The use of drugs for diagnostic purposes.

pharmacodynamic (fahr-mah-ko-di-nam'ik) Relating to the action of drugs.

pharmacodynamics (fahr-mah-ko-di-nam'iks) The study of the effects of drugs on the body and the mechanism by which they act.

pharmacoepidemiology (fahr-mah-ko-ep'ĭ-de-me-ol'o-je) The application of the principles of epidemiology to the study and determination of the effects of drugs in large populations.

pharmacogenetics (fahr-mah-ko-jĕ-net'iks) The study of the genetic basis for differences in response to drugs.

pharmacognosist (fahr-mah-kog'no-sist) One who is skilled in pharmacognosy.

pharmacognosy (fahr-mah-kog'no-se) The study of medicinal chemicals in their natural, crude state.

pharmacography (fahr-mah-kog'rah-fe) A treatise on drugs.

pharmacokinetics (fahr'mah-ko-kī-net'iks) The processing of

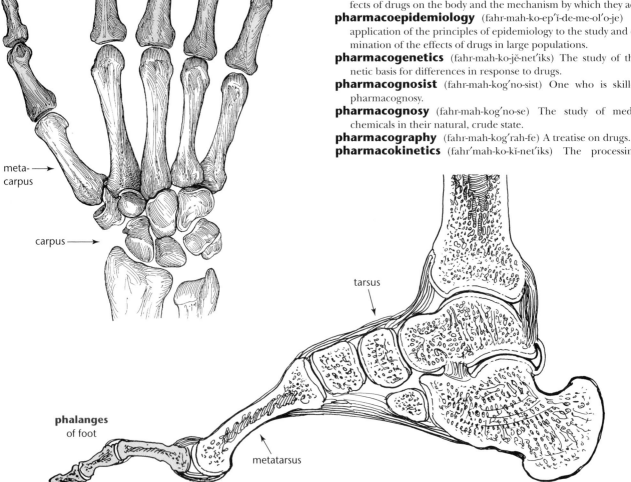

phalanges
of hand

meta-carpus

carpus

phalanges
of foot

metatarsus

tarsus

P

drugs within the body, including their absorption, distribution, metabolism, and excretion.

pharmacologist (fahr-mah-kol′o-jist) A specialist in pharmacology.

pharmacology (fahr-mah-kol′o-je) The science concerned with the study of all aspects of drugs, their interactions and their effects on living organisms.

   clinical p. The branch of pharmacology concerned with therapeutic drugs and their effects on humans.

pharmacopeia (fahr-mah-ko-pe′ah) (P) A book, especially an official publication, that lists all medicinal drugs, their preparation, use, and dosage, and tests for identifying individual drugs and for determining their purity; designated by abbreviations referring to the country of origin (e.g., USP, the United States Pharmacopeia; BP, the British Pharmacopoeia).

pharmacophobia (fahr-mah-ko-fo′be-ah) Irrational fear of taking medicine.

pharmacy (fahr′mah-se) **1.** The science and practice of preparing and dispensing medicinal drugs. **2.** A drugstore or the department of a medical facility responsible for providing medications.

pharyngalgia (far-in-gal′je-ah) Pain in the pharynx. Also called pharyngodynia.

pharyngeal (fah-rin′je-al) Relating to the pharynx.

pharyngectomy (far-in-jek′to-me) Removal of a portion of the pharynx.

pharyngitis (far-in-ji′tis) Inflammation of tissues lining the pharynx.

   acute streptococcal p. Abrupt sore throat, headache, fever, malaise, and enlarged lymph nodes at the neck; children may additionally experience nausea, vomiting, and abdominal pain; caused by species of *Streptococcus,* especially group A, occasionally group C or G; may lead to scarlet fever. Commonly called strep throat.

   gonococcal p. Sexually transmitted infection of the pharynx; may be cause of sore throat, discomfort in swallowing, and, rarely, a mucopurulent discharge with swelling of the uvula; caused by *Neisseria gonorrhoeae* acquired through orogenital contact with a gonorrhea-infected individual. Also called pharyngeal gonorrhea.

pharyngo-, pharyng- Combining forms meaning pharynx.

pharyngocele (fah-ring′go-sēl) An abnormal outpouching in the pharynx.

pharyngodynia (fah-ring-go-din′e-ah) Pharyngalgia.

pharyngoesophageal (fah-ring′go-ĕ-sof′ah-je-al) Relating to the pharynx and esophagus.

pharyngoglossal (fah-ring-go-glos′al) Relating to the pharynx and tongue.

pharyngolaryngeal (fah-ring′go-lah-rin′je-al) Relating to the pharynx and larynx.

pharyngolaryngitis (fah-ring-go-lar-in-ji′tis) Inflammation of the pharynx and the larynx.

pharyngomycosis (fah-ring-go-mi-ko′sis) Fungal infection of the pharynx.

pharyngopalatine (fah-ring-go-pal′ah-tin) Relating to the pharynx and the palate.

pharyngoplasty (fah-ring′go-plas-te) Any reparative operation of the pharynx.

pharyngoplegia (fah-ring-go-ple′je-ah) Paralysis of the muscles of the pharynx.

pharyngorhinoscopy (fah-ring-go-ri-nos′kŏ-pe) Inspection of the back of the nasal cavity; may be done with a mirrored device.

pharyngoscleroma (fah-ring-go-skle-ro′mah) Abnormal hard area on the lining (mucous membrane) of the pharynx.

pharyngoscope (fah-ring′go-skōp) Instrument for inspecting the pharynx.

pharyngoscopy (far-ing-gos′kŏ-pe) Inspection of the pharynx with an instrument (pharyngoscope).

pharyngospasm (fah-ring′go-spazm) Involuntary contractions of the pharyngeal musculature.

pharyngostenosis (fah-ring-go-stĕ-no′sis) Abnormal narrowing of the pharynx.

pharyngotomy (fah-ing-got′ŏ-me) Surgical cutting upon the pharynx.

pharyngotonsillitis (fah-ring-go-ton-si-li′tis) Inflammation of the pharynx and tonsils, causing redness, swelling, and pain (sore throat); may be due to viral or bacterial infections.

pharyngoxerosis (fah-ring-go-ze-ro′sis) Dryness of tissues lining the pharynx.

pharynx (far′inks) The musculomembranous tubular cavity, lined with mucous membrane, extending from the back of the nasal and oral cavities to the beginning of the trachea and esophagus.

phase (fāz) **1.** A relatively distinct part of a process or cycle. **2.** A portion of matter present in a nonhomogeneous system (e.g., an ingredient of an emulsion) that is physically and mechanically separable.

P

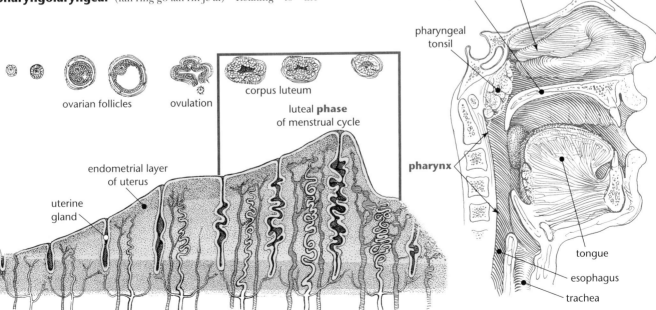

ovarian follicles ovulation corpus luteum

luteal **phase** of menstrual cycle

endometrial layer of uterus

uterine gland

palate nasal cavity

pharyngeal tonsil

pharynx

tongue

esophagus

trachea

pharmacologist ■ phase

phenacetin (fĕ-nas′ĕ-tin) Drug used for the relief of pain and fever. Formerly called acetophenetidin.

phenanthrene (fe-nan′thrēn) Compound derived from coal tar and a major component of steroids; some phenanthrene derivatives are carcinogenic.

phencyclidine (fen-si′klī-dēn) (PCP) Hallucinogenic drug that can produce profound psychological disturbances; toxicity includes necrosis of muscle and liver and severe hypertension. Commonly called angel dust.

pheno-, phen- Combining forms meaning a compound derived from benzene; a showing; an appearance.

phenobarbital (fe-no-bar′bī-tal) A barbiturate drug formerly used extensively as a sedative and hypnotic, currently used mainly as an anticonvulsant agent.

phenocopy (fe-no-kop′e) A condition that is due to environmental factors but resembles one that is of genetic causes.

phenol (fe′nol) An antiseptic and disinfectant compound that may cause local burns and may be absorbed through the skin or lungs, causing such symptoms as headache, dizziness, salivation, nausea, and vomiting. Also called carbolic acid.

phenolphthalein (fe-nol-thal′e-in) Compound used as a pH indicator and laxative.

phenolsulfonphthalein (fe′nol-sul-fōn-thal′e-in) (PSP) Compound used as a pH indicator in culture media and formerly as a test for kidney function.

phenomenon (fĕ-nom′ĕ-non) Any occurrence or manifestation.

   Bell's p. A unilateral upward and outward rolling of the eyeball on attempting to close the eyelids; seen in Bell's palsy.

   dawn p. The abrupt increase of blood sugar (glucose) levels between 5:00 and 9:00 A.M., occurring in diabetic persons receiving insulin therapy.

   declamping p. Shock occurring upon removal of clamps from a large artery during a surgical operation.

   dèjá vu p. The feeling that an experience, occurring for the first time, has been experienced before.

   Doppler p. See Doppler effect, under effect.

   escape p. Failure of the pupil of one eye to remain constricted when both eyes are alternately stimulated with light; seen in optic neuritis.

   Hill's p. See Hill's sign, under sign.

   Raynaud's p. A secondary manifestation of any of several diseases characterized by numbness, and by blanching (sometimes followed by a bluish discoloration) of the hands and feet in response to cold temperatures; when not due to a primary disorder but appearing as an isolated phenomenon it is termed Raynaud's disease.

   R-on-T p. In electrocardiography, a premature ventricular complex of the electrocardiogram (ECG) interrupting the T wave of the preceding heartbeat, associated with an increased risk of disordered contractions of the ventricles.

   Wenckebach p. An increasing lengthening of the atrioventricular (A-V) conduction time (P-R interval) in successive cycles of the heart rhythm until a beat is skipped.

phenothiazine (fe-no-thi′ah-zēn) A compound from which a large number of antipsychotic drugs are synthetically derived. Some of these drugs also have antiemetic properties. A prototype is chlorpromazine (Thorazine®). Also called dibenzothiazine.

phenotype (fe′no-tīp) The entire observable characteristics of an individual, resulting from interactions of the environment and the individual's genetic makeup (genotype).

phenotypic (fe-no-tip′ik) Relating to a phenotype.

phenoxybenzamine hydrochloride (fĕ-nok-se-ben′zah-mēn hi-dro-klo′rīd) An alpha-adrenergic blocking agent; it selectively blocks the response of smooth muscle (including arteriolar walls) and endocrine glands to the action of the hormone epinephrine.

phentolamine hydrochloride (fen-tol′ah-mēn hi-dro-klo′rīd) An alpha-adrenergic blocking agent; it has been used in the diagnosis of pheochromocytoma.

phenylalanine (fen-il-al′ah-nīn) (Phe) An amino acid, component

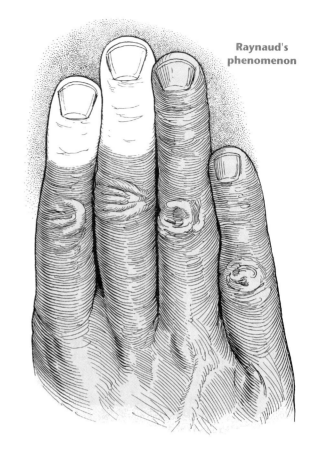

Raynaud's phenomenon

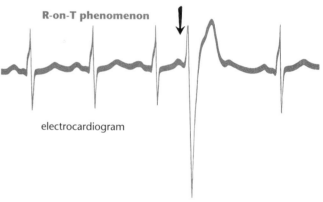

R-on-T phenomenon

electrocardiogram

of many proteins. See also phenylketonuria.

phenylephrine hydrochloride (fen-il-ef′rin hi-dro-klo′rīd) A vasoconstrictor of sustained action; used topically as a nasal decongestant and to dilate the pupil of the eye.

phenylethylene (fen-il-eth′ĭ-lēn) See styrene.

phenylketonuria (fen-il-ke-to-nu′re-ah) (PKU) Inherited disorder characterized by inability to convert the dietary amino acid phenylalanine to tyrosine; the resultant accumulation of phenylalanine and its metabolites causes neurologic abnormalities and mental retardation.

phenylpropanolamine (fen′il-pro-pah-nol′am-in) A sympathomimetic drug taken orally for its nasal decongestant effect in the treatment of hay fever, sinusitis, and the common cold; it is sometimes promoted as an appetite depressant for weight control. High doses may cause nausea, anxiety, and a rise in blood pressure.

phenylthiourea (fen-il-thi′o-u-re′ah) A compound used in genetic linkage studies; the compound tastes bitter to those individuals who carry the trait as a dominant inheritance, but is tasteless to the rest of the population.

P

pheo- Combining form meaning brown or dusky.

pheochrome (fe'o-krōm) Staining a brownish yellow with chromium salts; said of certain embryonic cells.

pheochromoblast (fe-o-kro'mo-blast) An embryonic cell that is the precursor of a pheochromocyte.

pheochromocyte (fe-o-kro'mo-sit) A chromaffin cell forming the medulla of the adrenal (suprarenal) gland, sympathetic paraganglia, and a pheochromocytoma.

pheochromocytoma (fe-o-kro-mo-si-to'mah) A tumor arising within the medulla of an adrenal (suprarenal) gland or sympathetic paraganglia characterized by production of catecholamines (norepinephrine and epinephrine); manifested by hypertension that may be episodic and severe, rapid heartbeat, palpitations, flushing or pallor, and weight loss.

pheresis (fĕ-re'sis) Any procedure (e.g., plasmapheresis) involving the removal of blood from a donor, separation and retention of a portion (e.g., cells, plasma), and retransfusion of the remainder into the donor.

pheronome (fer'o-nōm) A substance secreted by an organism that influences the behavior of other organisms of the same species (e.g., a chemical that by its scent arouses sexual activity).

-philia, -phil Combining forms meaning an affinity or craving for (e.g., eosinophilia, neutrophil).

philtrum (fil'trum) The groove on the upper lip, just below the nose.

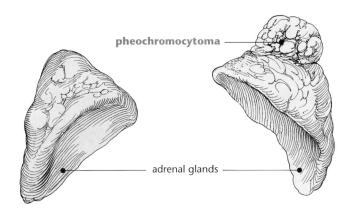

pheochromocytoma

adrenal glands

superficial p. Inflammation of one of the veins near the skin; marked by a red, tender, and swollen area along the path of the vein, which may feel like a rope beneath the skin.

phlebo-, phleb- Combining forms meaning vein.

phleboclysis (flĕ-bok'lĭ-sis) Injection of a fluid into a vein. Also called venoclysis.

phlebogram (fleb'o-gram) A graphic record of the venous pulse; usually the jugular pulse.

phlebograph (flĕb'o-graf) An instrument used in making a phlebogram.

phlebography (fle-bog'rah-fe) The recording of a venous pulse.

phlebolith (fleb'o-lith) A concretion in a vein, considered to be a calcification of an old thrombus; a vein stone.

phlebologist (flĕ-bol'o-jist) A physician who has special interest in treating diseases of the veins.

phlebology (flĕ-bol'o-je)) The study of diseases of the veins.

phleboplasty (fleb'o-plas-te) A reparative operation on a vein.

phleborrhagia (fleb-o-ra'je-ah) Bleeding from a vein.

phleborrhaphy (flĕ-bor'ah-fe) Suturing of a vein.

phleborrhexis (fleb-o-rek'sis) Rupture of a vein.

phlebosclerosis (fleb-o-sklĕ-ro'sis) Fibrous hardening of the venous walls, especially the inner layer.

phlebostasis (flĕ-bos'tah-sis) Slow circulation through the veins due either to pathologic venous distention or to application of a tourniquet. Also called venostasis.

P

philtrum

phimosis (fi-mo'sis) An abnormally small opening of the foreskin (prepuce), limiting the ability to fully retract the foreskin behind the glans; it may be a developmental defect or the consequence of inflammation.

phlebalgia (flĕ-bal'je-ah) Pain originating in a vein, usually due to varicosities.

phlebarteriectasia (fleb-ar-te-re-ek-ta'ze-ah) Dilatation of veins and arteries; vasodilation.

phlebectasia (fleb-ek-ta'ze-ah) Dilatation of the veins.

phlebectomy (fle-bek'to-me) Removal of a vein, or a section of a vein (e.g., in the treatment of varicosities). Also called venectomy.

phlebemphraxis (fleb-em-frak'sis) A venous thrombosis.

phlebitis (flĕ-bi'tis) Inflammation of a vein.

deep p. See deep thrombophlebitis, under thrombophlebitis.

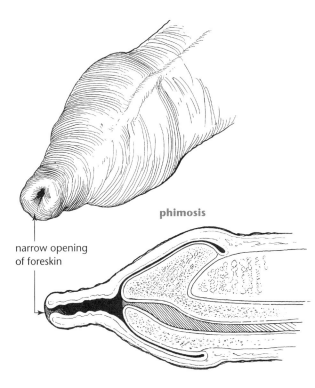

phimosis

narrow opening of foreskin

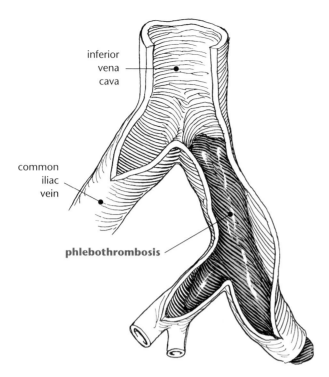

inferior
vena
cava

common
iliac
vein

phlebothrombosis

phlebothrombosis (fleb-o-throm-bo′sis) Blood clotting within a vein, without apparent antecedent inflammation, frequently occurring in varicose veins of the legs. Predisposing factors (in the absence of varicosities) include congestive heart failure, postoperative periods, prolonged immobilization, pregnancy, and local infection.

Phlebotomus (flĕ-bot′o-mus) A genus of bloodsucking sandflies (family Psychodidae).

    P. papatasii A vector of the virus causing sandfly fever (phlebotomus fever) and of the protozoan agents causing cutaneous leishmaniasis.

phlebotomy (flĕ-bot′o-me) Removal of blood from a vein with a needle or cannula (e.g., in the treatment of polycythemia vera). Also called venesection; venotomy.

phlegm (flem) Thick mucus secreted by the mucous lining of the respiratory tract.

phlegmasia (fleg-ma′ze-ah) Obsolete term for inflammation.

    p. alba dolens See puerperal thrombophlebitis, under thrombophlebitis.

phlegmatic (fleg-mat′ik) Unemotional; apathetic.

phlyctena (flik-te′nah), pl. phlycte′nae Seldom-used term for a small burn blister.

phlyctenule (flik′ten-ūl) A minute red ulcerating nodule usually occurring on the transparent covering of the eyeball (conjunctiva) and the cornea.

phobia (fo′be-ah) Any abnormal, irrational fear that results in an avoidance of the feared object, activity, or situation. Also called morbid fear.

    simple p. Persistent irrational fear of specific objects, such as fear of closed spaces (claustrophobia) and heights (acrophobia).

    social p. Persistent irrational fear of any situation where there is risk of scrutiny by others, embarrassment, or humiliation. See also agoraphobia; phobic disorders, under disorder.

phobic (fo′bik) Relating to a phobia.

phocomelia, phocomely (fo-ko-me′le-ah, fo-kom′e-le) Defective development of the limbs, especially the arms; hands may be directly attached to the shoulders.

phonal (fo′nal) Relating to sounds.

phonasthenia (fo-nas-the′ne-ah) Difficult or abnormal production of the voice.

phonation (fo-na′shun) The utterance of vocal sounds in human communication.

phonatory (fo′nah-to-re) Relating to phonation.

phonautograph (fōn-aw′to-graf) Device used to make visible records of vibrations made by sounds.

phoneme (fo′nēm) The smallest sound unit of speech.

phonemic (fo-ne′mik) Relating to phoneme.

phonetic (fo-net′ik) Relating to speech sounds.

phonetics (fo-net′iks) The study of all aspects of speech sounds. Also called phonology.

phoniatrics (fo-ne-at′riks) The study and treatment of speech defects.

phonic (fon′ik) Relating to sound or to the voice.

phonism (fo′nizm) See auditory synesthesia, under synesthesia.

phono-, phon- Combining forms meaning sound or voice.

phonoangiography (fo-no-an-je-og′rah-fe) The recording and analysis of the sound made by blood passing through an artery; useful in determining the degree of narrowing of the vessel's lumen by atherosclerosis.

phonocardiogram (fo-no-kar′de-o-gram) (PCG) A graphic record of sounds produced by the action of the heart.

phonocardiograph (fo-no-kar′de-o-graf) The instrument used to make graphic records of heart sounds.

phonocardiography (fo-no-kar-de-og′rah-fe) The recording of sounds made by the action of the heart.

phonocatheter (fo-no-kath′ĕ-ter) A catheter with a microphone at its tip designed to record heart sounds from within the heart and great vessels.

phonogram (fo′no-gram) A curve representing the duration and intensity of a sound.

phonology (fŏ-nol′ŏ-je) See phonetics.

phonopathy (fo-no′pah-the) Any disorder of the speech apparatus.

phonophoresis (fo-no-fo-re′sis) Use of ultrasound to increase the absorption of drugs through the skin.

phonophotography (fo-no-fo-tog′rah-fe) The photographic recording of vibration curves caused by sound.

phonopsia (fo-nop′se-ah) Subjective visual sensation (e.g., a color) elicited by particular sounds.

phonoreceptor (fo-no-re-sep′tor) A receptor of sound.

phonosurgery (fo-no-sur′jer-e) Any surgical procedure performed on the voice apparatus, especially the vocal folds, to preserve, restore, or enhance the voice.

phorbol (for′bol) The parent alcohol of cancer-producing compounds present in croton oil (from seeds of the plant *Croton tiglium*).

-phore Combining form meaning a carrier or bearer (e.g., chromophore).

phoresis (for-e′sis) See electrophoresis.

phoria (for′e-ah) A tendency of the two eyes to deviate. The direction of the deviation is usually indicated by an appropriate prefix (e.g., exophoria, esophoria, hypophoria, hyperphoria).

phoro-, phor- Combining forms meaning a carrier or bearer.

phorometer (fo-rom′ĕ-ter) An ophthalmologic instrument with rotating disks housing cyclindrical lenses, pinhole disks, occluders, filters and prisms; used for measuring extraocular muscle balance and refractive error.

phosgene (fos′jēn) A highly poisonous gas. Also called carbonyl chloride.

phosphagenic (fos-fah-jen′ik) Phosphate-producing.

phosphatase (fos′fah-tās) Any of a group of enzymes that promote the breakdown of phosphoric esters, releasing inorganic phosphate.

    acid p. A phosphatase that is most effective in an acid milieu (pH 5.4); present in relatively high concentrations in the prostate; may be present in high levels in the blood of patients with prostatic cancer.

    alkaline p. A phosphatase most effective in an alkaline milieu (pH 8.6); present in bone, blood, kidneys, and other tissues. Elevated levels in the blood may indicate obstruction of bile ducts or neoplastic activity of liver or bone.

phosphates (fos′fāts) Salts of phosphoric acid, present in the body in combination with calcium or sodium; they help store and utilize body energy and help regulate calcium levels, carbohydrate and lipid metabolism, and acid-base balance; they are essential to bone and tooth formation.

P

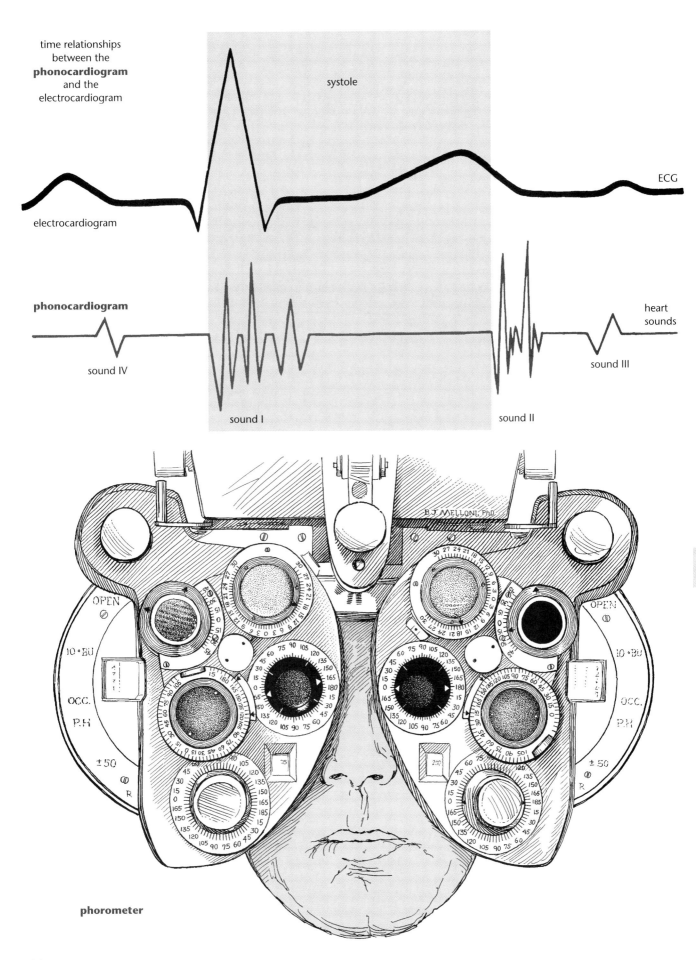

time relationships
between the
phonocardiogram
and the
electrocardiogram

systole

ECG

electrocardiogram

phonocardiogram

heart
sounds

sound IV

sound III

sound I

sound II

B.J. MELLONI, PhD.

OPEN

10 • BU

OCC.

P.H

± 50

R

OPEN

10 • BU

OCC.

P.H

± 50

R

phorometer

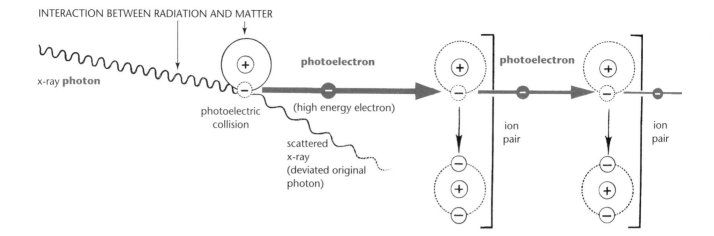

INTERACTION BETWEEN RADIATION AND MATTER

phosphated (fos'fāt-ed) Containing phosphates.

phosphatic (fos-fat'ik) Relating to phosphate.

phosphaturia (fos-fah-tu're-ah) Abnormally high levels of phosphates in the urine.

phosphene (fos'fēn) Visual sensations elicited by mechanical or electrical stimulation of the eyeball.

phosphine (fos'fēn) A poisonous war gas with a disagreeable (garlic-like) odor; also used as the active ingredient in rodenticides.

phosphite (fos'fīt) Any salt of phosphorous acid.

phosphocreatine (fos-fo-kre'ah-tin) A compound of creatine with phosphoric acid; a source of high energy for muscle contraction. Also called creatine phosphate.

phosphoenolpyruvic acid (fos-fo-e'nol-pi-roo'vik as'id) An intermediate in the conversion of glucose to pyruvic acid.

phosphofructokinase (fos-fo-fruk-to-ki'nās) An essential enzyme in the cycle of glucose metabolism; it promotes the formation of fructose 1,6-bisphosphate from fructose 6-phosphate and adenosine triphosphate (ATP).

phospholipase (fos-fo-lip'ās) An enzyme that promotes the breakdown of a phospholipid.

phospholipid (fos-fo-lip'id) Any of several waxy compounds containing phosphoric acid and constituting a major component of cell membranes.

phosphoprotein (fos-fo-pro'tēn) A protein containing phosphoric groups.

phosphor-, phospho-, phos- Combining forms meaning phosphorus.

phosphor (fos'for) A substance that glows when exposed to electromagnetic or radioactive energy; used to detect radioactivity.

phosphorated (fos'fo-rāt-ed) Combined with phosphorus.

phosphorescence (fos-fo-res'ens) 1. The afterglow of a substance without a temperature rise following exposure to light, heat, or electric current. Distinguished from fluorescence. 2. The faint glow of phosphorus in the presence of air, due to slow oxidation.

phosphoribosyltransferase (fos-fo-ri-bo-sil-trans'fer-ās) Any of a group of enzymes important in the biosynthesis of nucleotides.

phosphoric acid (fos-for'ik as'id) A strong acid used in dentistry (in the preparation of cement liquids) and in other industries (e.g., in the production of fertilizers).

phosphorism (fos'fo-rizm) Chronic phosphorus poisoning.

phosphorized (fos'fo-rīzd) Phosphorated.

phosphorolysis (fos-fo-rol'ĭ-sis) A reaction, similar to hydrolysis, in which components of phosphoric acid (rather than of water) are added in the course of splitting a chemical bond.

phosphorous (fos'fo-rus) Containing phosphorus.

phosphorus (fos'fo-rus) A nonmetallic element; symbol P, atomic number 15, atomic weight 30.974. It occurs in nature always in combined form, as inorganic phosphates in minerals and water, and as organic phosphates in all living cells. It is an essential element for energy in many biologic processes.

phosphorus 32 (^{32}P) Radioactive phosphorus isotope used in the treatment of skin conditions, such as eczema, and certain diseases of the blood-forming (hematopoietic) system.

phosphotungstic acid (fos-fo-tung'stik as'id) An acid that precipitates proteins and many organic bases; used in electron microscopy for shadowing certain tissue components.

phosvitin (fos-vi'tin) A protein constituent of egg yolk that has anticoagulant properties.

phot (fōt) A unit of illumination equal to 1 lumen per square centimeter of surface.

photalgia (fo-tal'je-ah) Pain in the eyes caused by light. Also called photodynia.

photesthesia (fo-tes-the'se-ah) Ability to perceive light.

photic (fo'tik) Relating to light.

photism (fo'tizm) Visual perception elicited by stimulation of a sense organ other than the eyes.

photo-, phot- Combining forms meaning light.

photoactinic (fo-to-ak-tin'ik) Relating to radiation that produces both luminous and chemical effects.

photoallergy (fo-to-al'er-je) See photosensitization.

photobiology (fo-to-bi-ol'o-je) The study of the effects of light on living organisms.

photobiotic (fo-to-bi-ot'ik) Living and thriving in light only.

photoceptor (fo-to-sep'tor) See photoreceptor.

photochemistry (fo-to-kem'is-tre) The branch of chemistry dealing with chemical changes brought about by light.

photochemotherapy (fo-to-ke'mo-ther'ah-pe) See photoradiation.

photochromogens (fo-to-kro'mo-jens) See group I mycobacteria, under mycobacteria.

photocoagulation (fo-to-ko-ag-u-la'shun) The use of an intense beam of light (carbon arc or laser), focused to a fine point, to destroy tissue or to create adhesive scars; used especially in intraocular surgery to bond a detached retina, to seal leaking blood vessels, or to reduce abnormal blood vessel growth.

photocoagulator (fo-to-ko-ag-u-la'tor) A device used in photocoagulation.

　laser p. A laser device used to stop minute spots of bleeding. See also laser.

photodermatitis (fo-to-der-mah-ti'tis) Development of skin lesions caused by exposure to ultraviolet rays; may be due to extreme sensitivity, or to photosensitizing factors (e.g., certain drugs or diseases).

photodynamic (fo-to-di-nam'ik) Relating to the energy produced by light.

photodynia (fo-to-din'e-ah) See photalgia.

photoelectric (fo-te-e-lek'trik) Producing electricity by the absorption of light.

photoelectrometer (fo-to-e-lek-trom'ĕ-ter) A device used in measuring the concentration of substances in solution by means of a photoelectric cell.

photoelectron (fo-to-el-ek′tron) An electron that has been set free (ejected from its orbit) by collision with a high energy photon.

photoemulsification (fo-to-e-mul-sĭ-fĭ-ka′shun) Cataract removal by fragmenting the opaque lens of the eye with sound vibrations (ultrasonic energy) and simultaneously irrigating and aspirating the lens material.

photogenic, photogenous (fo-to-jen′ik, fo-toj′e-nus) 1. Induced or produced by light (photogenic epilepsy). 2. Producing light.

photokeratoconjunctivitis (fo-to-ker′ah-to-kon-junk-tĭ-vi′tis) Damage and inflammation of the cornea and conjunctiva, caused by unprotected exposure to ultraviolet radiation as that produced by the welder's arc; may be caused by direct observation of the ultraviolet rays or indirect exposure by simply being near; symptoms are mild at first (up to eight hours), after which they become severe. Also called welder's flash.

photolysis (fo-tol′ĭ-sis) Chemical decomposition of a compound by the action of light.

photolyte (fo′to-lit) A product of photolysis.

photomacrography (fo-to-mah-krog′rah-fe) The photographing of small specimens at low magnification by using a macro lens instead of a microscope.

photometer (fo-tom′ĕ-ter) Instrument used in measuring the intensity of light.

photomicrograph (fo-to-mi′kro-graf) Photograph of a specimen as viewed through the microscope.

photon (fo′ton) A unit or quantum of electromagnetic energy.

photoperceptive (fo-to-per-sep′tiv) Capable of perceiving light.

photoperiodism (fo-to-pe′re-od-izm) The physiologic, biomedical, and behavioral changes occurring in living organisms in response to the regular variations of light and darkness (e.g., the seasons or night and day).

photophobia (fo-to-fo′be-ah) Abnormal visual sensitivity to light.

photophobic (fo-to-fo′bik) Relating to photophobia.

photophthalmia (fo-tof-thal′me-ah) Inflammation of superficial structures of the eyeball caused by exposure to intense light.

photopsia (fo-top′se-ah) Subjective sensation of flashing lights or sparks occurring in certain conditions of the vitreous body and the visual pathways.

photopsin (fo-top′sin) The protein component of the pigment in the cone cells of the retina.

photoradiation (fo-to-ra-de-a′shun) Intravenous injection of a photosensitive dye, which is selectively retained by cancerous tissue, followed by exposure to laser light of appropriate wavelength to produce a photochemical reaction with the dye and consequent destruction of the cancerous tissue. Also called photodynamic therapy; photoradiation therapy; photochemotherapy.

photoreactivation (fo-to-re-ak-tĭ-va′shun) Activation of a process that was previously stopped, accomplished by exposure to light.

photoreceptive (fo-to-re-sep′tiv) Sensitive to light.

photoreceptor (fo-to-re-sep′tor) A specialized cell that is sensitive to light (e.g., the rod and cone cells in the retina). Also called photoceptor.

photoretinitis (fo-to-ret-ĭ-ni′tis) See photoretinopathy.

photoretinopathy (fo-to-ret-ĭ-nop′ah-the) Thermal damage to the retina caused by exposure to intense light. Also called photoretinitis.

photoscan (fo′to-skan) A photograph of the distribution and concentration of an internally administered substance, obtained by photographing the image produced by x ray of a radiopaque substance or by emission of a radionuclide.

photosensitization (fo-to-sen-sĭ-tĭ-za′shun) The process by which the skin's sensitivity to light is heightened, usually by ingestion of certain drugs, plants, or other substances. Also called photoallergy.

photostable (fo-to-sta′bl) Unchanged by light.

phototaxis (fo-to-tak′sis) Movement of an organism toward a light source.

phototherapy (fo-to-ther′ah-pe) Treatment of disease (e.g., psoriasis, certain tumors, jaundice of the newborn) by exposure to light, either sunlight, ultraviolet light, blue light, or lasers.

photothermal (fo-to-ther′mal) Relating to heat created by radiant energy.

phototoxic (fo-to-tok′sik) Denoting certain chemicals that increase the skin's sensitivity to light (such as tetracycline and certain perfumes containing bergamot oil), causing skin reactions limited to sun-exposed areas.

phototoxicity (fo-to-tok-sis′ĭ-te) The property of rendering tissues abnormally sensitive to light.

phren (fren) 1. Greek for diaphragm. 2. The mind.

phrenectomy (fren-ek′to-me) See phrenicectomy.

phrenemphraxis (fren-em-frak′sis) See phreniclasia.

-phrenia Combining form meaning a condition of the mind (e.g., schizophrenia); the diaphragm.

phrenic (fren′ik) 1. Relating to the diaphragm. 2. Relating to the mind.

phrenicectomy (fren-ĭ-sek′to-me) Removal of a portion of the phrenic nerve. Also called phrenectomy.

phreniclasia (fren-ĭ-kla′ze-ah) The operation of crushing a small section of the phrenic nerve.

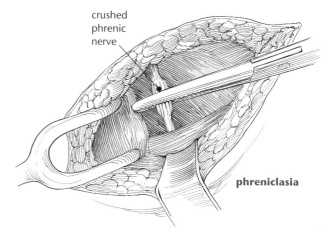

crushed phrenic nerve

phreniclasia

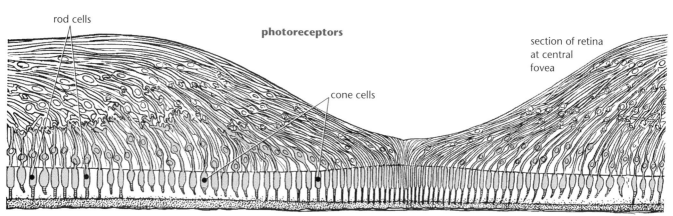

rod cells

photoreceptors

cone cells

section of retina at central fovea

phrenicotomy (fren-ĭ-kot′o-me) Division of the phrenic nerve.

phreno-, phren- Combining forms meaning mind; diaphragm; the phrenic nerve.

phrenocolic (fren-o-kol′ik) Relating to the diaphragm and colon.

phrenogastric (fren-o-gas′trik) Relating to the diaphragm and the stomach.

phrenohepatic (fren-o-hĕ-pat′ik) Relating to the diaphragm and the liver.

phrenoplegia (fren-o-ple′je-ah) Paralysis of the diaphragm.

phrenosin (fren′o-sin) A substance (cerebroside) present in the white matter of the brain. Also called cerebron.

phrenospasm (fren′o-spazm) Spasm of the diaphragm.

phrenotropic (fren-o-trop′ik) Affecting the mind or the brain.

phrynoderma (frin-o-der′mah) A dry eruption of the skin considered a manifestation of vitamin A deficiency.

phthiriasis (thir-i′ah-sis) See pediculosis.

phthisis (ti′sis) Obsolete term for tuberculosis and a wasting away of tissues.

    p. bulbi Collapse and shrinking of the eyeball associated with an untreated bacterial infection of all structures of the eye.

phyco- Combining form meaning seaweed.

phycomycosis (fi-ko-mi-ko′sis) Infection caused by fungi, usually of the *Mucor* genus; characterized by an acute nasal inflammation with extensive tissue necrosis, which spreads to the rest of the respiratory tract and other organs; usually occurs in debilitated patients, such as those undergoing immunosuppressive therapy or those in a diabetic ketoacidotic coma. Also called mucormycosis; zygomycosis.

phylaxis (fi-lak′sis) Protection against infection.

phyllo- Combining form meaning leaf.

phyma (fi′mah) A small skin nodule.

physiatrics (fiz-e-at′riks) See physical medicine and rehabilitation, under medicine.

physiatrist (fiz-e-ah′trist) A physician who specializes in physical medicine and rehabilitation.

physic (fiz′ik) A medicinal drug.

physical (fiz′e-kal) 1. Relating to the body, as opposed to the mind. 2. Popular name for a physical examination.

physician (fi-zish′un) A doctor of medicine; a person trained and licensed to treat the ill and injured.

    admitting p. The physician responsible for admission of a patient to a hospital or other inpatient health institution.

    attending p. The physician responsible for the care provided a patient in a hospital or other health program; usually on the staff of a hospital and often supervising the house staff, fellows, and students. Commonly called attending.

    family p. A specialist in family practice (i.e., a physician who provides comprehensive health care for the whole family). To qualify for board certification by the American Academy of Family Physicians, the physician generally must complete a three-year residency in family practice. COMPARE general practitioner, under practitioner.

    forensic p. See medical examiner, under examiner.

    osteopathic p. A practitioner of osteopathy; an osteopath.

physician assistant (fi-zish′un ah-sis′tant) A person who has been trained in primary care medicine and who is certified and licensed to practice under the supervision of a licensed physician.

Physician Data Query (PDQ) A computer database developed by the National Cancer Institute (NCI); it provides quick access to: state-of-the-art treatment information for both patients and health professionals, information about research studies (clinical trials) that are open to patients, and names of organizations and physicians involved in treating people with cancer.

physicochemical (fiz-ĭ-ko-kem′ĭ-kal) Relating to physical chemistry.

physics (fiz′iks) The study of matter and energy and their interactions.

physio-, physi- Combining forms meaning natural function; the body.

physiogenic (fiz-e-o-jen′ik) Caused by physical activity.

physiologic (fiz-e-o-loj′ik) 1. Relating to physiology. 2. Relating to the normal biologic processes of an organism.

physiologist (fiz-e-ol′o-jist) A specialist in physiology.

physiology (fiz-e-ol′o-je) The study of the normal functions of living organisms.

    pathologic p. See pathophysiology.

physiopathology (fiz-e-o-pah-thol′o-je) See pathophysiology.

physiotherapeutic (fiz-e-o-ther-ah-pu′tik) Relating to physical therapy.

physiotherapist (fiz-e-o-ther′ah-pist) A physical therapist.

physiotherapy (fiz-e-o-ther′ah-pe) See physical therapy, under therapy.

physique (fi-zēk′) The biotype; the physical structure of the body.

physo- Combining form meaning the presence of gas; a tendency to swell.

physostigmine (fiz-o-stig′mēn) An alkaloid extracted from the Calabar bean that inhibits the action of cholinesterase and prevents destruction of the neurotransmitter acetylcholine. Used experimentally to enhance the action of acetylcholine. Also called eserine.

    p. salicylate Compound used as an eyedrop to reduce intraocular pressure in the anterior chamber of the eye in treating glaucoma.

phytin (fi′tin) A salt of phytic acid used as a dietary supplement to provide calcium and phosphorus.

phyto-, phyt- Combining forms meaning plants.

phytobezoar (fi-to-be′zōr) A food ball; a concretion in the stomach composed of vegetable matter.

phytohemagglutinin (fi-to-hem-ah-gloo′tĭ-nin) (PHA) A protein of plant origin that clumps (i.e., agglutinates) red blood cells; used chiefly in studies of immune mechanisms and in cell culture.

phytoid (fi′toid) Resembling a plant.

phytol (fi′tol) An unsaturated alcohol derived from chlorophyll; a constituent of vitamin E.

phytophotodermatitis (fi-to-fo-to-der-mah-ti′tis) A skin lesion resembling a sunburn caused by exposure to sunlight after brushing against plants that contain photosensitizing substances (fucocoumarins or psoralens), such as citrus plants, celery, carrots, and dill.

phytotoxic (fi-to-tok′sik) Having a deleterious effect on plants.

phytotoxin (fi-to-tok′sin) A poisonous substance of plant origin.

pia (pe′ah) See pia mater.

pia-arachnoid (pe′ah ah-rak′noid) See leptomeninges.

pial (pe′al) Relating to the pia mater.

pia mater (pe′ah mah′ter) The delicate, innermost of the three membranes enveloping the brain and spinal cord. Frequently simply called pia.

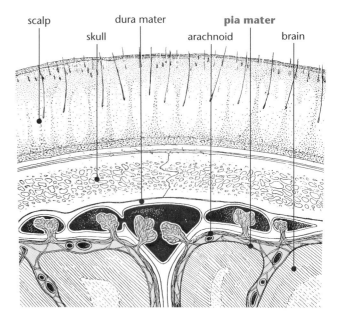

pian (pe-ahn') See yaws.

piarachnoid (pe-ah-rak'noid) See leptomeninges.

pica (pi'kah) A craving for, and the eating of, materials that are not fit for food (e.g., ice, clay, paint); often associated with anemia.

pickling (pik'ling) In dentistry, the process of removing impurities from metallic surfaces by immersion in an acid solution.

pico- (p) Combining form used with SI units meaning one-trillionth (10^{-12}).

picoampere (pi-ko-am'pēr) Unit of electric current equal to one-trillionth (10^{-12}) of an ampere.

picocurie (pi-ko-ku're) Unit of radioactivity equal to one-trillionth (10^{-12}) of a curie.

picogram (pi'ko-gram) Unit of mass or weight equal to one-trillionth (10^{-12}) of a gram. Formerly called micromicrogram.

picometer (pi-kom'e-ter) Unit of length equal to one-trillionth (10^{-12}) of a meter. Formerly called micromicron.

picornavirus (pi-kor-nah-vi'rus) Any RNA infectious virus of the family Picornaviridae, including those that cause poliomyelitis, meningitis, and myocarditis.

picric acid (pik'rik as'id) Compound used as a dye and preservative of histologic samples; it has antiseptic and astringent properties. Also called trinitrophenol.

picrotoxin (pik-ro-tok'sin) The bitter substance obtained from the fruit of *Anamirta cocculus;* formerly used as an antidote for central nervous system depressants, such as barbiturates.

piebaldism (pi'bawld-izm) Patches of depigmentation, especially of the scalp and hair (white forelock); not only the condition but also the exact pattern of pigment loss is passed from generation to generation. It is occasionally seen in certain hereditary syndromes (e.g., Waardenburg's syndrome).

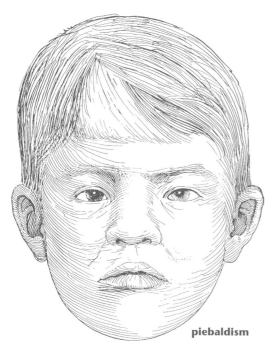

piebaldism

piedra (pe-a'drah) Superficial fungal infection of the hair shaft, characterized by formation of numerous minute nodules along the shaft.

    black p. Infection occurring mainly on hairs of the scalp; caused by *Piedraia hortae.*

    white p. A form occurring on hairs of the scalp, beard, mustache, and genital areas; caused by *Trichosporon beigelii.*

piesesthesia (pi-e-zes-the'ze-ah) The sensation of pressure.

pigment (pig'ment) Any coloring matter.

    bile p. One of several substances derived from catabolism of a blood pigment, giving bile its characteristic color (e.g., bilirubin and biliverdin).

    blood p. See hemoglobin.

    melanotic p. See melanin.

    visual p. The light-sensitive pigment in the rod and cone cells of the retina; it initiates vision by absorbing light.

pigmentation (pig-men-ta'shun) Any normal or abnormal coloration by deposition of pigment.

    arsenic p. A spotty coloration of the skin occurring in chronic arsenic poisoning.

pigmentum nigrum (pig-men'tum ni'grum) The dark coloration of the choroid layer of the eye.

pilar, pilary (pi'lar, pil'a-re) Relating to hair.

pile (pil) A hemorrhoid.

    sentinel p. A thickening or tag of mucous membrane, resembling a hemorrhoid, located at the end of an anal fissure.

piles (pīlz) See hemorrhoids.

pileous (pi'le-us) Hairy.

pileus (pi'le-us) A caul.

pili (pi'li) Plural of pilus.

pill (pil) A small mass of solid medication intended to be swallowed whole. Reference to "the pill" indicates an oral contraceptive.

    birth-control p. See oral contraceptive, under contraceptive.

    bread p. A placebo made of bread.

    morning-after p. See postcoital contraception, under contraception.

    pep p. Common name for a pill containing an amphetamine or other stimulants of the central nervous system.

pillar (pil'ar) Any structure resembling an architectural column in shape or function.

    anterior p. of fauces See palatoglossal arch, under arch.

    posterior p. of fauces See palatopharyngeal arch, under arch.

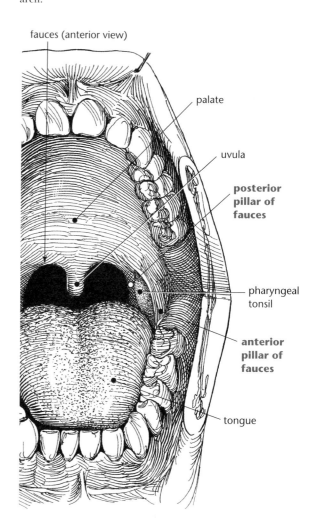

fauces (anterior view)

palate

uvula

posterior pillar of fauces

pharyngeal tonsil

anterior pillar of fauces

tongue

P

pill-rolling (pil′rōl-ing) Involuntary motion or tremor, often seen in Parkinson's disease, in which the tips of opposing thumb and index finger are rubbed against each other in a circular motion.

pilo- Combining form meaning hair.

pilobezoar (pi-lo-be′zōr) See trichobezoar.

pilocarpine (pi-lo-kar′pēn) An alkaloid obtained from shrubs of the genus *Pilocarpus;* it increases salivary secretion and sweating and reduces intraocular pressure.

pilocystic (pi-lo-sis′tik) Cystlike and containing hair, such as certain tumors.

piloerection (pi-lo-e-rek′shun) Erection of hair.

piloid (pi′loid) Resembling hair.

pilomatrixoma (pi-lo-ma-trik-so′mah) A benign tumor of the skin arising from the hair matrix and containing cells like those of skin cancer (basal cell carcinoma); occurs all over the body, mainly in children. Also called Malherbe's calcifying epithelioma.

pilonidal (pi-lo-ni′dal) Having hair as a main feature, such as certain cysts.

pilose (pi′lōs) Hairy.

pilosebaceous (pi-lo-sĕ-ba′shus) Relating to a hair follicle and a sebaceous gland as a unit.

pilosis (pi-lo′sis) See hirsutism.

pilus (pi′lus), pl. pi′li **1.** One of the fine hairs covering the body except the palms and soles. **2.** A fine strawlike appendage of some bacteria that serves to anchor the bacterial cell.

    p. cuniculatus See burrowing hair, under hair.

    p. incarnatus See ingrown hair, under hair.

pimelo- Combining form meaning fat.

pimple (pim′pl) Popular name for a papule or small pustule.

pin (pin) **1.** A short, straight, cylindrical piece of metal, used for fixation of a fractured bone. **2.** A metal peg used to anchor a filling or crown to a prepared tooth cavity. **3.** A small metal dowel or tube.

    p. cutter An instrument for severing metal pins.

    friction-retained p. A retention pin secured in the dentine of a prepared tooth cavity by forceful insertion into a space of lesser diameter than the pin.

    retention p.'s Small pegs extending from a metal casting into a tooth's prepared cavity in dentin; used for retaining and stabilizing a dental restoration.

    self-threading p. A friction-retained pin that is threaded at one end for improved retention in tooth tissue.

    sprue p. A short metal pin used to attach a dental wax pattern of a dental restoration to a crucible former; it provides the entrance through the investment, permitting the molten metal to flow into the interior of the mold. Also called sprue former.

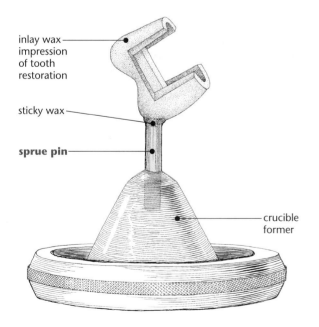

inlay wax impression of tooth restoration

sticky wax

sprue pin

crucible former

Steinmann p. A rigid metal pin used transcutaneously for the internal fixation of fractured long bones (e.g., the femur) and subsequent stabilization by traction; standard sizes are generally 5 to 9 inches in length and from 5/64 to 3/16 inches in diameter.

pincement (pans-maw′) In massage, a gentle pinching manipulation of the skin.

pineal (pin′e-al) **1.** Relating to the pineal body. **2.** Shaped like a pine cone. Also called piniform.

pinealectomy (pin-e-al-ek′to-me) Removal of the pineal body.

pinealoblastoma (pin-e-ah-lo-blas-to′mah) See pineoblastoma.

pinealocyte (pin-e′ah-lo-sīt) One of the chief cells forming the substance of the pineal body.

pinealocytoma (pin-e-ah-lo-si-to′mah) See pineocytoma.

pinealoma (pin-e-ah-lo′mah) See pineoblastoma and pineocytoma.

pineoblastoma (pin-e-o-blas-to′mah) A malignant tumor of the pineal body composed of primitive neuroectodermal cells and resembling a tumor of the cerebellum (cerebellar medulloblastoma); it may invade adjacent structures or spread to distant areas via the cerebrospinal fluid; it occurs predominantly in children. Also called pinealoblastoma.

pineocytoma (pin-e-o-si-to′mah) A benign or low-grade malignant tumor of the pineal body, composed of the typical mature cells of that structure; most commonly seen in adults. Also called pinealocytoma.

pinguecula (ping-gwek′u-lah) A yellowish nodule near the cornea, more commonly on the nasal side, composed of hyaline and yellow elastic tissue; it rarely increases in size; seen predominantly in elderly people. COMPARE pterygium.

piniform (pin′ĭ-form) See pineal (2).

pinkeye (pink′i) See acute contagious conjunctivitis, under conjunctivitis.

pink puffer (pink puf′er) See pink puffer, under puffer.

pinledge (pin′lej) In dentistry, a flat structure prepared within a tooth into which holes are drilled to accommodate the pins of a restoration.

pinna (pin′nah), pl. pin′nae See auricle.

pinocyte (pin′o-sīt, pi′no-sīt) A cell that engulfs liquids in a manner similar to the way a phagocyte engulfs solid particles.

pinocytic (pin-o-sit′ik) Relating to pinocytosis or to a pinocyte.

pinocytosis (pin-o-si-to′sis, pi-no-si-to′sis) A method of active transport across the cell membrane; the cell surface membrane forms minute invaginations, which enclose surrounding fluid and then pinch off to form fluid-filled vesicles (pinosomes) within the cell.

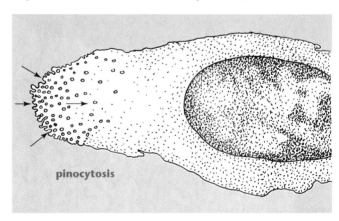

pinocytosis

pinosome (pin′o-sōm) A fluid-filled vesicle within a cell formed during pinocytosis.

pinta (pēn′tah) An infectious disease of the skin caused by a spirochete microorganism *(Treponema carateum),* believed to be transmitted by direct person-to-person contact; characterized by patches of marked changes in skin color; most commonly seen in 10- to 20-year-olds.

pinworm (pin′werm) A nematode worm of the genus *Oxyuris* occurring worldwide as an intestinal parasite of animals and humans. Also called seatworm; threadworm.

piperacillin sodium (pi-per′ah-sil-in so′de-um) A semisynthetic, broad-spectrum antibiotic agent.

piperazine (pi-per′ah-zēn) A compound used against pinworm and roundworm infections.

pipette, pipet (pi-pet′) A tube, opened at both ends, and often calibrated; used in the laboratory to transfer measured amounts of fluid.

piriform (pir′ĭ-form) Pear-shaped.

piroxicam (pēr-ok′sĭ-kam) A nonsteroidal anti-inflammatory agent; it also has pain-relieving and fever-reducing properties.

pisiform (pis′ĭ-form) Pea-shaped.

pit (pit) Any normal or abnormal surface indentation.

    anal p. See proctodeum.

    gastric p.'s See gastric foveolae, under foveola.

    nail p.'s Minute indentations on fingernails associated with psoriasis.

    p. of stomach The upper middle area of the abdomen below the end of the breastbone (sternum); the epigastric region.

pitch (pich) **1.** A dark viscous substance formed as a residue in the distillation of organic matter, especially tar. **2.** A property of sound that is dependent on the number of sound wave vibrations per second. Commonly called tone.

pitchblende (pich′blend) A brown-to-black mineral containing uranium oxide and products of radioactive breakdown; it is the chief source of uranium and radium.

pituicyte (pĭ-tu′ĭ-sit) The main cell type composing the posterior lobe of the pituitary (hypophysis).

pituitary (pĭ-tu′ĭ-tār-e) **1.** Relating to the hypophysis. Also called hypophyseal. **2.** See hypophysis.

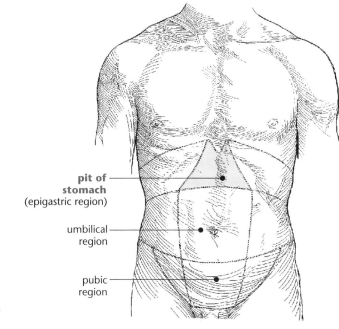

pit of stomach (epigastric region)

umbilical region

pubic region

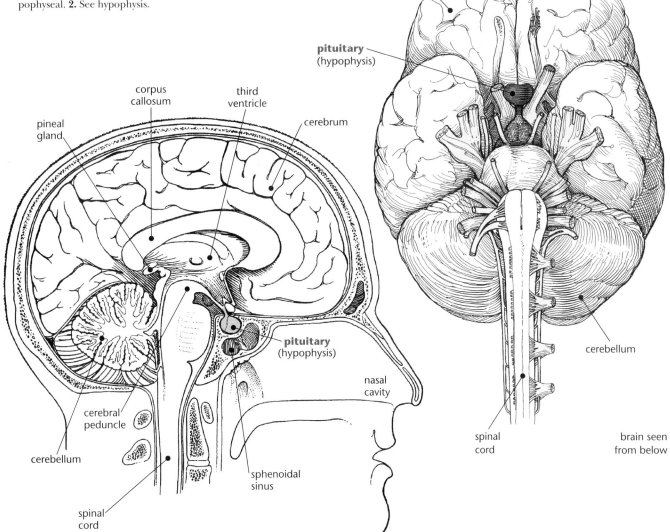

pineal gland

corpus callosum

third ventricle

cerebrum

pituitary (hypophysis)

cerebral peduncle

cerebellum

sphenoidal sinus

nasal cavity

spinal cord

cerebrum

pituitary (hypophysis)

cerebellum

spinal cord

brain seen from below

P

pityriasis (pit-ĭ-ri´ah-sis) A scaly desquamation of the skin.

    p. rosea A self-limited condition characterized by eruption of a sharply defined plaque (herald patch) followed by a generalized skin rash consisting of scaly salmon-pink papules, which last one to two months before disappearing spontaneously; usually occurs in adults 20 to 30 years of age; cause is unknown.

pityroid (pit´ĭ-roid) Flaky, scaly.

placebo (plah-se´bo) An inert substance used in controlled studies to test the efficacy of another substance or to examine the nonspecific response to treatment of any sort. From the Latin "I will please."

placenta (plah-sen´tah) The disk-shaped organ through which the fetus derives its nourishment (via the umbilical cord); it is attached on one side to the interior wall of the uterus and on the other it is connected to the fetus by means of the umbilical cord; at term it weighs 400 to 600 grams and measures 15 to 20 cm in diameter and 2 to 4 cm in thickness.

    accessory p. See succenturiate placenta.

    p. accreta An abnormally adherent placenta; i.e., one that adheres to the uterine wall directly, due to absence of the normally intervening layer of tissue (decidua basalis); classified by degree of adherence into: *placenta accreta vera* (superficial adherence), *placenta increta* (invasion of uterine wall), and *placenta percreta* (penetration of full thickness of uterine wall). It is associated with postpartum hemorrhage, which may become massive, leading to hypotension. Predisposing factors include previous cesarean section, placenta previa, previous uterine curettage, more than six deliveries (grand multiparity), and treatment for Asherman's syndrome.

    battledore p. A placenta that has the umbilical cord attached to its margin.

    bilobate p. A placenta divided into two lobes connected by major blood vessels. An uncommon variety.

    circummarginate p. See circumvallate placenta.

    circumvallate p. A placenta with a central depression on its

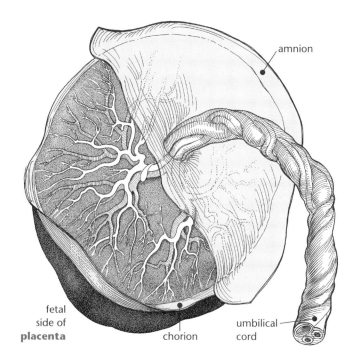

fetal side of **placenta**

amnion

chorion

umbilical cord

circumvallate placenta

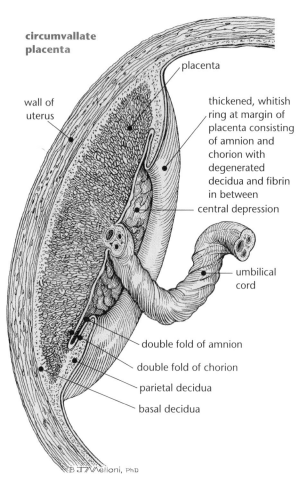

wall of uterus

placenta

thickened, whitish ring at margin of placenta consisting of amnion and chorion with degenerated decidua and fibrin in between

central depression

umbilical cord

double fold of amnion

double fold of chorion

parietal decidua

basal decidua

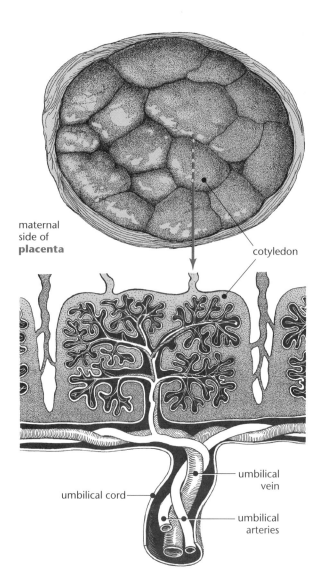

maternal side of **placenta**

cotyledon

umbilical cord

umbilical vein

umbilical arteries

fetal surface surrounded by a dense peripheral ring of a doubled layer of membranes; associated with increased rates of slight to moderate second-trimester bleeding, early delivery, and perinatal death of infant. Also called circummarginate placenta.

fundal p. A placenta implanted in the fundus of the uterus, the usual site.

p. membranacea A thin membranous placenta occupying a larger than normal area; it occasionally causes severe hemorrhage during the third stage of labor since it does not readily separate from the uterine wall.

p. previa A placenta implanted in the lower segment of the uterus within the area of effacement and dilatation of the cervix (over or near the internal opening of the cervix), thus obstructing the descent of the fetus; it causes spotting during first and second trimesters and sudden painless, profuse bleeding in the third trimester. Incidence increases with advancing age, multiparity, and scarring from previous cesarean section. Also called placental presentation.

retained p. Incomplete separation of placental tissue after childbirth; it remains within the uterus, usually causing postpartum hemorrhage; frequently occurs in placenta acreta, in manual removal of the placenta, and in unrecognized succenturiate placenta.

succenturiate p. One or more small portions of placental tissue implanted separately from the main organ but connected to it by blood vessels; may remain attached to the uterus after expulsion of the placenta and cause postpartum hemorrhage.

placental (plah-sen′tal) Relating to the placenta.

placentation (plas-en-ta′shun) The development of the placenta.

placentitis (plas-en-ti′tis) Inflammation of the placenta, usually caused by a bacterial infection ascending from the birth canal.

placentography (plas-en-tog′rah-fe) X-ray visualization of the placenta after injection of a radiopaque substance.

placentotherapy (plas-en-to-ther′ah-pe) The therapeutic use of extracts prepared from placental tissue.

plagio- Combining form meaning oblique.

plagiocephaly (pla-je-o-sef′ah-le) A deformity of the skull in which one side is more developed anteriorly and the other side posteriorly. Usually the skull becomes gradually symmetrical after nine months to two years of age.

plague (plāg) **1.** Any widespread disease associated with a high mortality rate. **2.** Acute infectious disease caused by *Yersinia pestis,* trans-

mitted to humans by fleas that have bitten infected rodents (may be bubonic, pneumonic, septicemic, or ambulant plague).

planchet (plan′chet) A flat metal container on which a radioactive sample is placed while testing its radioactivity.

plane (plān) **1.** A flat or level surface. **2.** An imaginary surface formed by extension through two points or an axis. **3.** A particular level, as a stage in surgical anesthesia.

auriculoinfraorbital p. See Frankfort plane.

coronal p. A vertical plane at right angles to the median plane, dividing the head into anterior and posterior portions; named after the cranial suture of that name. Used interchangeably with frontal plane.

coronal
plane

Frankfort p., Frankfort horizontal p. A craniometric plane of the head represented on an x-ray profile by drawing a line passing through the highest point on the margin of the acoustic meatus and the lowest point on the margin of the orbit. Also called auriculoinfraorbital plane.

frontal p. A vertical plane passing at right angles to the median plane, dividing the body into anterior and posterior halves. COMPARE coronal plane.

horizontal p. The plane extending across the long axis of the body separating an upper part from the lower part. Also called transverse plane.

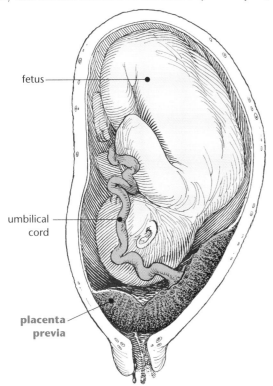

fetus

umbilical
cord

placenta
previa

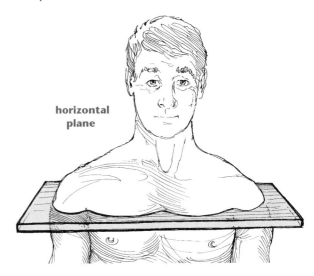

horizontal
plane

placental ■ plane

intercristal p. The horizontal plane passing through the highest points of the iliac crests; it usually lies at the level of the fourth lumbar vertebra.

interspinous p. A horizontal plane transecting the body at the level of the anterior superior iliac spine of the hipbone.

intertubercular p. See transtubercular plane.

lateral rectus sagittal p. The vertical plane passing to the lateral side of the straight muscle of abdomen (rectus abdominis).

median p. A plane that divides the body vertically into right and left halves. Also called midsagittal plane.

midclavicular p. The vertical plane passing through the middle of the clavicle.

midinguinal p. The vertical plane passing through the middle of the inguinal ligament of the hipbone.

midsagittal p. See median plane.

p. of occlusion The horizontal plane formed by the occlusal surfaces of the contacting teeth when the jaws are closed.

parasagittal p. Any vertical plane parallel to the sagittal plane.

pelvic p. of greatest dimension The roomiest portion of the pelvic cavity extending from the middle of the posterior surface of the pubic symphysis anteriorly to the junction of the second and third sacral vertebrae posteriorly; in the average pregnant woman, the anteroposterior diameter is approximately 12.75 cm and its transverse diameter is around 12.5 cm.

pelvic p. of inlet The rounded or oval opening of the true (minor) pelvis, bounded anteriorly by the upper border of the pubis, laterally by the iliopectineal line, and posteriorly by the sacral promontory. Also called superior aperture of minor pelvis; superior pelvic strait.

pelvic p. of least dimension The midpelvis plane, extending from the lower margin of the pubic symphysis through the ischial spines to the apex of the sacrum; in the average pregnant women, the anteroposterior diameter measures approximately 11.5 cm and its

transverse diameter is around 10 cm. Also called pelvic plane of midpelvis.

pelvic p. of midpelvis See pelvic plane of least dimension.

pelvic p. of outlet The plane across the lower opening of the true (minor) pelvis, bounded anteriorly by the pubic symphysis and the sides of the pubic arch, laterally by the ischial tuberosities, and posteriorly by the tip of the coccyx. Also called inferior aperture of minor pelvis; inferior pelvic strait.

principal p. The plane containing the central ray of a radiation beam, used for diagnosis and treatment.

p.'s of reference Planes that serve as a guide for the location of specific organs or sites (e.g., the intersection of the transpyloric plane with the right midinguinal plane marks the usual site of the gallbladder's fundus).

sagittal p. A vertical plane extending in an anteroposterior direction. Named after the suture of the cranium of that name.

subcostal p. A horizontal plane passing through the lowest point of the costal margin on each side, usually at the inferior border of the 10th costal cartilage, which is generally at the level of the body of the third lumbar vertebra.

transpyloric p. The horizontal plane passing through the pylorus part of the stomach, which is generally halfway between the suprasternal notch and the pubic symphysis; it passes through the tip of the ninth costal cartilage, the fundus of the gallbladder, the neck of the pancreas, and the body of the first lumbar vertebra.

transtubercular p. The horizontal plane at the level of the tubercles of the iliac crest of the hipbone; usually the same level as the lower part of the fifth lumbar vertebra. Also called intertubercular plane.

transverse p. See horizontal plane.

umbilical p. The horizontal plane passing through the navel (umbilicus).

planigraphy (plah-nig′rah-fe) See tomography.

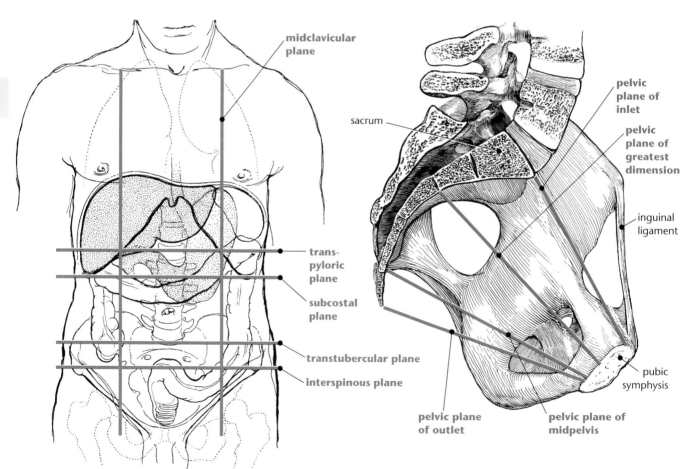

midclavicular plane

sacrum

pelvic plane of inlet

pelvic plane of greatest dimension

inguinal ligament

trans-pyloric plane

subcostal plane

transtubercular plane

interspinous plane

pubic symphysis

pelvic plane of outlet

pelvic plane of midpelvis

P

plane ▪ planigraphy

planing (pla'ning) **1.** The process of making smooth. **2.** See dermabrasion.

    root p. In periodontal therapy, the smoothing of the surfaces of tooth roots after debris has been removed.

plano-, plani-, plan- Combining forms meaning flat.

planoconcave (pla-no-kon'kāv) Flat on one side, concave on the other; applied to a lens of that shape.

planoconvex (pla-no-kon'veks) Flat on one side, convex on the other; applied to a lens of that shape.

planta pedis (plan'tah pe'dis) Latin for the sole of the foot.

plantalgia (plan-tal'je-ah) Pain in the sole of the foot.

plantar (plan'tar) Relating to the sole of the foot.

planuria (pla-nu're-ah) Discharge of urine through an abnormal opening.

plaque (plak) Any elevated lesion or patch.

    argyrophil p. See senile plaque.

    atheromatous p. A yellow-white fibrofatty lesion on the inner layer (intima) of arterial walls protruding into the vessel lumen; formed most predominantly at points of branching of major arteries, such as the aorta; also occurs commonly in the coronary, carotid, vertebrobasilar, renal, and iliofemoral arteries; composed of a semisolid lipid material, cholesterol crystals, and a variety of cells and connective tissue.

    complicated p. An atheromatous plaque that has become calcified and fissured or ulcerated, leading to thrombosis, hemorrhage, and other complications.

    dental p. A variable material bound to the surface of teeth, restorations, or oral appliances, resulting from colonization of several strains of bacteria. It contributes to tooth decay and periodontal disease.

    MacCallum's p.'s See MacCallum's patches, under patch.

    neuritic p. See senile plaque.

    senile p. A cluster of degenerated cellular processes around a central mass of abnormal extracellular material (amyloid); found extensively in the cerebral cortex of individuals with Alzheimer's disease. Also called argyrophil plaque; neuritic plaque.

-plasia Suffix meaning formation (e.g., hyperplasia).

-plasm Combining form meaning a constituent of the cell substance (e.g., cytoplasm).

plasma (plaz'mah) **1.** The fluid component of blood in which its formed elements are suspended; distinguished from serum. **2.** The fluid component of lymph.

    antihemophilic human p. Normal human plasma that has had its original antihemolytic properties preserved; used in temporary arrest of bleeding in hemophilic patients.

    fresh frozen p. (FFP) Plasma that has been frozen within six hours of withdrawal from donor.

plasmablast (plaz'mah-blast) An immature plasma cell.

plasmacyte (plaz'mah-sit) See plasma cell, under cell.

plasmacytoma (plaz-mah-si-to'mah) A malignant plasma cell tumor within bone marrow; it may also occur in other parts of the body.

    multiple p. See multiple myeloma, under myeloma.

plasmacytosis (plaz-mah-si-to'sis) An abnormal increase of plasmacytes in the tissues.

plasma expander (plaz'mah eks-pan'der) See plasma substitute, under substitute.

plasmalemma (plaz-mah-lem'ah) Cell membrane; see under membrane.

plasmalogen (plaz-mal'o-jen) A compound (glycerophospholipid) found in high proportions in lipid from the nervous system.

plasmapheresis (plaz-mah-fĕ-re'sis) Removal of plasma from withdrawn blood and reinfusion of the blood's formed elements suspended in a sterile plasma substitute (e.g., saline).

plasmid (plaz'mid) An extrachromosomal, self-replicating genetic element in bacteria that is not essential for bacterial growth but valuable in other circumstances, such as drug resistance and toxin production.

plasmin (plaz'min) An enzyme that is essential in blood clot dissolution (fibrinolysis).

plasminogen (plaz-min'o-jen) A globulin present in tissues, body fluids, circulating blood, and in blood clots.

Plasmodium (plaz-mo'de-um) A genus of protozoans parasitic in red blood cells of vertebrates; transmitted to humans by the bite of female anopheline mosquitoes, causing malaria. See also malaria.

    P. falciparum The most malignant species infecting humans, causing falciparum (malignant tertian) malaria with a high rate of morbidity and mortality; it is prevalent in tropical and subtropical regions.

    P. malariae The species causing quartan malaria, primarily in subtropical and temperate regions.

    P. vivax The species causing vivax (benign tertian) malaria, found in almost every region where malaria is endemic.

plasmodium (plaz-mo'de-um) pl., plasmo'dia **1.** A malarial parasite. **2.** A mass of protoplasm containing several nuclei.

plasmolysis (plaz-mol'ĭ-sis) A dissolution of cellular protoplasm.

plasmorrhexis (plaz-mo-rek'sis) The bursting of a cell due to increased internal pressure.

plastic (plas'tik) **1.** Capable of being molded or reshaped. **2.** A material produced by polymerization or by chemical treatment that can be molded, cast, or laminated into a variety of articles, films, or filaments. **3.** Serving to reshape (e.g., certain surgical procedures).

plasticity (plas-tis'ĭ-te) The property of being plastic.

plasticizer (plas-tĭ-si'zer) Any of a class of compounds added to plastic materials to increase flexibility, softness, and processibility. Some, such as di(2-ethylhexyl)phthalate, have been shown to have toxic effects on the liver (seen in workers in the plastics industry) and to cause cancer in laboratory animals; others, such as, polyvinyl chloride (PVC), are suspected of causing cancers in humans.

-plasty Suffix meaning molding or shaping (e.g., rhinoplasty).

plate (plāt) **1.** In anatomy, any flattened, relatively thin structure. **2.** In dentistry, an artificial denture, especially the portion to which artificial teeth (pontics) are anchored. **3.** In microbiology, a glass culture receptacle, such as the petri dish. **4.** A smooth, flat metal device of uniform thickness, used for approximating fractured bones. **5.** A thin perforated structure for covering defects sustained during injury or surgery.

    bone p. A flattened metal bar, with perforations for the insertion of bone screws, for immobilization of fractured bone segments.

    chorionic p. The portion of the chorion that is attached to the uterus at an early stage in the formation of the placenta; it gives rise to the chorionic villi.

    cribriform p. of ethmoid bone A perforated strip of a horizontal bony plate that forms a large part of the roof of the nasal cavity; it lodges the olfactory bulbs and provides the numerous perforations that transmit filaments of the olfactory nerve from the bulbs in the calvaria to the olfactory epithelium lining the medial and lateral walls of the roof of the nasal cavity. The midline of the upper surface of the plate bears a slender elevation, the crista galli. Also called cribriform lamina of ethmoid bone.

    epiphyseal p. The plate or disk of specialized hyaline cartilage interposed between the shaft (diaphysis) and the extremity (epiphysis) of a developing long bone; by its growth, the bone lengthens as it grows to maturity. Also called growth plate; epiphyseal cartilage; epiphyseal disk.

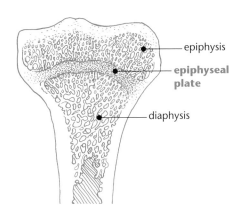

growth p. See epiphysial plate.

Ishihara p.'s A series of plates designed as tests for color blindness; they consist of numbers made of primary-colored dots printed on a background of many dots of various sizes and colors; individuals who are color-blind are unable to see the numbers.

medullary p. See neural plate.

motor p. The motor end-plate between the expanded terminal of the motor axon and the striated muscle fiber it innervates, forming the neuromuscular junction.

neural p. The middle ectodermal thickening in the embryo from which the neural tube develops; the anlage of the brain and spinal cord (central nervous system). Also called medullary plate.

obstetrical measuring p. A calibrated plate for calculating the digital measurements of the true conjugate (anteroposterior diameter of the pelvic inlet), without a pelvimeter.

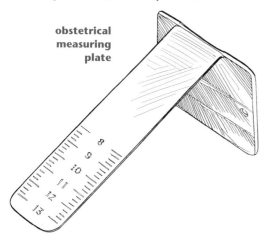

obstetrical
measuring
plate

occlusal plane p. In dentistry, a metal plate used to establish the occlusal plane of the teeth.

pterygoid p.'s A short, broad lateral plate and a long, narrow medial plate that project inferiorly from the sphenoid bone; the pterygoid fossa lies between them.

skull p. A thin perforated plate, generally round or oval, that is screwed to the cranium to replace missing bone fragments.

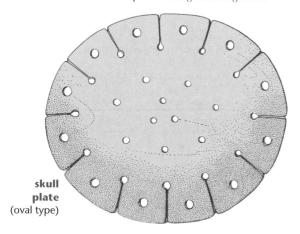

skull
plate
(oval type)

plateau (plah-to') A level segment of an elevation in a graphic record (e.g., of a curve).

ventricular p. A plateau of the intraventricular curve of blood pressure representing the period of sustained contraction of the ventricle.

platelet (plāt'let) A disk-shaped, colorless structure without a nucleus, derived from a megakaryocyte, normally present in large numbers in the blood of all mammals; it is smaller than a red blood cell and has a life span of about eight days; it plays an important role in blood clotting. The normal level in human blood is 150,000 to 300,000 per mm^3.

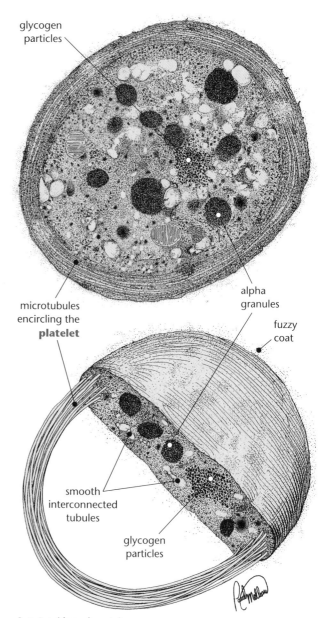

glycogen
particles

microtubules
encircling the
platelet

alpha
granules

fuzzy
coat

smooth
interconnected
tubules

glycogen
particles

platelet (thrombocyte)

plateletpheresis (plāt-let-fĕ-re'sis) Removal of platelets from the drawn blood of a donor and return of remaining blood; used as a therapeutic measure in some patients with thrombocytosis.

plating (plāt'ing) 1. The streaking or application of a sample, thought to contain bacteria, on a nutrient medium in a petri dish. 2. The fastening of a fractured bone to a metal plate to hold the bone fragments in proper alignment.

platinum (plat'ĭ-num) Metallic element; symbol Pt, atomic number 78, atomic weight 195.09.

platy- Combining form meaning flat.

platybasia (plat-e-ba'se-ah) Developmental defect in which the base of the skull is flattened and protrudes inward, especially around the foramen magnum.

platycephaly (plat-e-sef'ah-le) Abnormal flatness of the head, with a breadth-height index of less than 70.

platyhelminth (plat-e-hel'minth) Any flatworm, such as a tapeworm or a fluke.

platyhieric (plat-e-hi-er'ik) Having an abnormally flat sacrum.

platypellic, platypelloid (plat-e-pel'ik, plat-e-pel'oid) Having a wide and flattened pelvis.

plateau ■ **platypellic, platypelloid**

platyrrhine (plat′e-rīn) Having a broad nose.

platysma (plah-tiz′mah) See table of muscles.

platyspondylia (plat-e-spon-dil′e-ah) Abnormal flatness of the bodies of vertebrae.

pledget (plej′et) A small pad, usually of cotton or gauze, used during surgical operations to control bleeding or to buttress sutures.

-plegia Combining form meaning paralysis (e.g., paraplegia).

pleiotropic (pli-o-trop′ik) Characterized by pleiotropy.

pleiotropism (pli-ot′ro-pizm) See pleiotropy.

pleiotropy (pli-ot′ro-pe) In genetics, the multiple end effects of a single mutant gene, or a gene pair, on several organ systems and functions. Also called pleiotropism.

pleo- Combining form meaning more.

pleocytosis (ple-o-si-to′sis) The presence of more than the normal number of cells; originally the term was applied to an increased number of lymphocytes in the spinal fluid (e.g., in syphilis of the central nervous system).

pleomastia (ple-o-mas′te-ah) See polymastia.

pleomorphic (ple-o-mor′fik) Occurring in more than one structural form.

pleomorphism (ple-o-mor′fizm) In cytology, the presence of various abnormal cell sizes, shapes, and nuclear appearances in a cell population.

pleoptics (ple-op′tiks) Any orthoptic technique of treating dimness of vision (amblyopia).

plesio- Combining form meaning similarity.

plessor (ples′or) A small, rubber-headed hammer used in percussion. Also called plexor; percussor.

plethora (pleth′o-rah) 1. An overabundance. 2. A deep, rosy red complexion.

plethoric (pleth-or′ik) Relating to plethora.

plethysmograph (ple-thiz′mo-graf) Instrument for measuring variation in size of an organ or body part.

plethysmography (pleth-iz-mog′rah-fe) The process of measuring and recording variations in the size of a part produced by changes in the circulation of blood within it.

plethysmometer (pleth-iz-mom′ĕ-ter) Instrument for measuring the degree of fullness of a hollow structure, usually a blood vessel.

pleura (ploor′ah) The double-layered serous membrane enveloping the lungs and lining the interior walls of the chest cavity.

   diaphragmatic p. The portion of parietal pleura covering the part of the diaphragm below each lung.

   parietal p. The layer of the pleura that lines the walls of the thoracic cavity.

   pericardiac p. The layer of the pleura covering the pericardium, the membranous sac enveloping the heart.

   visceral p. The layer of the pleura that invests the lungs; it also lines their fissures, thereby separating the different lobes.

pleuralgia (ploor-al′je-ah) Pain in the pleura.

pleurapophysis (ploor-ah-pof′ĭ-sis) See cervical rib, under rib.

pleurisy (ploor′ĭ-se) See pleuritis.

   benign dry p. See epidemic pleurodynia, under pleurodynia.

pleuritis (ploo-ri′tis) Inflammation of the pleura, causing chest pain that is often worsened by deep breathing or coughing; it usually occurs in association with, or as a result of, other conditions. Also called pleurisy.

   hemorrhagic p. Pleuritis marked by a bloody secretion caused by bleeding disorders, tumors, or rickettsial infections.

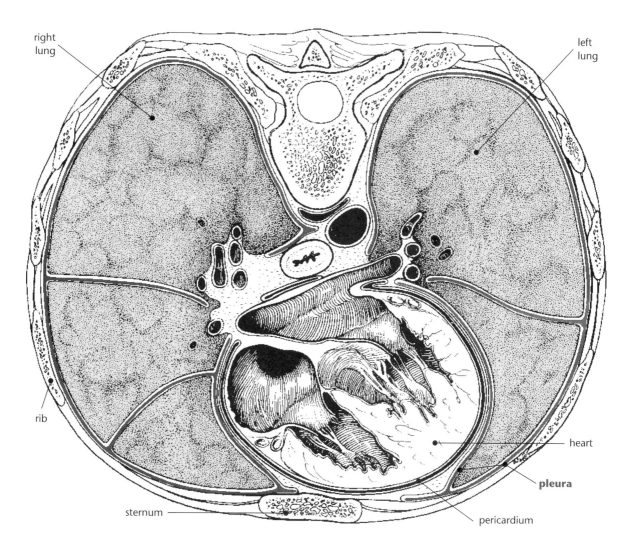

P

serofibrinous p. Pleuritis marked by a fibrinous secretion and accumulation of fluid, caused by an inflammatory process in the lung (e.g., pneumonia, tuberculosis, and abscesses) or by systemic diseases (e.g., rheumatoid arthritis, uremia).

suppurative p. Pleuritis marked by accumulation of pus in the pleural cavity, which may become chronic, leading to fibrinous adhesions and hindrance of lung expansion; caused by infection within the pleural space. Also called empyema.

pleuro-, pleur- Combining forms meaning the pleura; a side; rib.

pleurocentesis (ploor-o-sen-te'sis) See thoracentesis.

pleurodynia (ploor-o-din'e-ah) Pain in the intercostal muscles, usually affecting only one side of the chest.

epidemic p. Viral inflammation of intercostal muscles caused by the Coxsackie B virus; chest pain is aggravated by deep breathing and movement. Chest x-ray films appear normal. Also called devil's grip; benign dry pleurisy; Bornholm disease.

pleurogenic (ploor-o-jen'ik) Originating in the pleura.

pleurolith (ploor'o-lith) A calcification in the pleural cavity, usually formed in the diaphragmatic area; may occur upon prolonged asbestos exposure.

pleuropericarditis (ploor-o-per-ĭ-kar-di'tis) Inflammation of the membranes covering the lungs and the heart (pleura and pericardium).

pleuropulmonary (ploor-o-pul'mo-ner-e) Relating to the pleura and the lungs.

pleurotomy (ploor-ot'o-me) Incision into the pleural cavity.

plexal (plek'sal) Relating to a plexus.

plexectomy (plek-sek'to-me) Removal of a plexus.

plexiform (plek'sĭ-form) Resembling or forming a network of nerves, veins, or lymphatics.

plexor (plek'sor) See plessor.

plexus (plek'sus), pl. plex'uses An interwoven network of nerves, veins, arteries, or lymphatic vessels.

abdominal aortic p. A network of autonomic nerves in front of and alongside the abdominal aorta between the origins of the superior and inferior mesenteric arteries; the plexus is formed by branches from the celiac plexus and the first and second lumbar splanchnic nerves; it sends an extension below the level of the bifurcation of the aorta, where it is known as the superior hypogastric plexus.

anococcygeal p. See coccygeal plexus.

anterior coronary p. of heart See right coronary plexus of heart.

Auerbach's p. See myenteric plexus.

autonomic p.'s Plexuses composed of sympathetic and parasympathetic nerves and ganglia in combination with visceral afferent fibers; located in the thorax (cardiac plexus), abdomen (celiac plexus), and pelvis (hypogastric plexus); from the plexuses, branches are distributed to the viscera.

axillary lymphatic p. A plexus of lymphatic channels in the armpit (axilla) that drain into axillary nodes.

brachial p. A plexus composed of the ventral primary divisions of the fifth to eighth cervical nerves and 1st thoracic nerve, with possible contributions from the fourth cervical and second thoracic nerves. The various nerves unite to form three trunks: upper trunk of the plexus (formed by the fifth and sixth cervical nerves), lower trunk of the plexus (formed by the eighth cervical and first thoracic nerves), middle trunk of the plexus (formed by the seventh cervical nerve alone). Each trunk splits into anterior and posterior divisions: the anterior divisions of the upper and middle trunks unite to form a lateral cord; the anterior division of the lower trunk, after receiving some nerve fibers from the seventh cervical nerve, forms the medial cord; the posterior divisions of all three trunks unite to form the posterior cord. Most of the branches of the brachial plexus originate from the cords in the armpit (axilla) and supply the muscles and skin of the entire upper limb.

cardiac p. A large autonomic nerve plexus situated near the arch of the aorta, behind the bifurcation of the pulmonary trunk and in front of the right pulmonary artery; composed of deep and super-

ficial parts and formed by branches of the vagus (10th cranial) nerve and sympathetic trunk.

carotid p.'s Plexuses of autonomic nerve fibers associated with the carotid artery: *Common carotid p.*, a plexus around the common carotid artery that consists of postganglionic fibers contributed by the middle cervical ganglion. *External carotid p.*, a plexus around the external carotid artery that consists mostly of postganglionic fibers from the superior cervical ganglion; it sends branches to the skin and blood vessels of the scalp and face, the carotid sinus, and the submandibular gland. *Internal carotid p.*, a plexus around the internal carotid artery that consists mostly of postganglionic fibers from the superior cervical ganglion; it sends branches to several cranial nerves (oculomotor [3rd], trochlear [4th], trigeminal [5th], abducent [6th], and glossopharyngeal [9th]); it also sends filaments to the pituitary (hypophysis) and a large branch (deep petrosal nerve) to the sphenopalatine ganglion.

cavernous p. of clitoris An autonomic nerve plexus of the clitoris, derived from the vesical plexus and located in the cavernous tissue at the root of the clitoris.

cavernous p. of nose A network of veins forming a cavernous plexus beneath the mucous membrane of the nasal cavity, seen especially over the lower part of the septum and over the middle and inferior conchae.

cavernous p. of penis An autonomic nerve plexus of the penis, derived from the vesical plexus and located in the cavernous tissue at the root of the penis.

celiac p. A large dense plexus of sympathetic nerves and ganglionic masses, including the paired celiac ganglia, located in the peritoneal cavity, posterior to the stomach, at the level of the 12th thoracic vertebra; it surrounds the origins of the celiac, renal, and superior mesenteric arteries; the plexus and ganglia are supplemented by the greater and lesser splanchnic nerves, in addition to nerve filaments from the vagus (10th cranial) and phrenic nerves; it supplies nerves to the abdominal viscera and to all the adjacent blood vessels. Also called solar plexus.

cervical p. A nerve plexus in the neck, composed of anterior primary divisions of the upper four cervical nerves; it sends numerous cutaneous, muscular, and communicating branches to the muscles and skin of the neck and also to the diaphragm.

choroid p. A network of fringelike folds of the pia mater fused with the epithelial lining (ependyma) of the third and fourth and lateral ventricles of the brain and containing numerous blood vessels and nerves; branches of the internal carotid and posterior cerebral arteries supply the plexuses of the third and lateral ventricles; the posterior cerebellar arteries supply the plexus in the fourth ventricle. The choroid plexus regulates the intraventricular pressure by secretion and absorption of cerebrospinal fluid.

coccygeal p. A small plexus formed by the anterior branches of the fifth sacral and coccygeal nerves, supplemented by some fibers from the anterior branch of the fourth sacral nerve; it forms a small trunk that pierces the coccygeal muscle to enter the pelvis; anococcygeal nerves arise from the plexus to innervate the skin around the coccyx. Also called anococcygeal plexus.

p. of deferent duct A plexus of autonomic nerve fibers that innervate the deferent duct and seminal vesicles in males; considered a subdivision of the inferior hypogastric plexus. Also called plexus of vas deferens.

gastric p. A nerve plexus of the stomach formed by branches of the vagus (10th cranial) nerve in association with a portion of the celiac plexus, with distributions to the lesser and greater curvatures of the stomach.

hypogastric p.'s Plexuses of autonomic nerve fibers located in the pelvis just below the bifurcation of the aorta: *Inferior hypogastric p.'s*, two networks of nerves located in front of the lower sacrum, composed of the right and left hypogastric nerves, pelvic splanchnic nerves, and pelvic parasympathetic nerves; branches of the right and left inferior hypogastric plexuses innervate pelvic organs and blood vessels. *Superior hypogastric p.*, a network of nerves located between the bifurcation of the aorta and the promontory of the sacrum (usually to the left side of the median plane), where it receives contributions from the third and fourth lumbar splanchnic nerves before dividing into the right and left hypogastric nerves, which descend to the inferior hypogastric plexuses, as well as contribute to the testicular or ovarian plexus; branches innervate the pelvic organs and blood vessels.

inferior mesenteric p. An extension of the aortic plexus that surrounds the inferior mesenteric artery; it receives contributions from the second and third lumbar splanchnic nerves; branches from the inferior mesenteric plexus innervate the colon.

inguinal lymphatic p. A plexus of lymphatic channels in the iliopectineal fossa, distributed along the femoral artery and vein.

intercavernous p. A plexus of veins connecting the two cavernous sinuses across the midline at the base of the skull, in front of, and behind, the stalk of the pituitary (hypophysis).

intestinal lymphatic p. A network of efferent lymphatic channels in the intestine; it receives numerous blind lacteal vessels from each villus of the intestine and is joined by vessels from the solitary lymphatic follicles before exiting the intestinal wall to join larger vessels on the way to lymph nodes.

Jacobson's p. See tympanic plexus.

left coronary p. of heart Autonomic nerve fibers derived

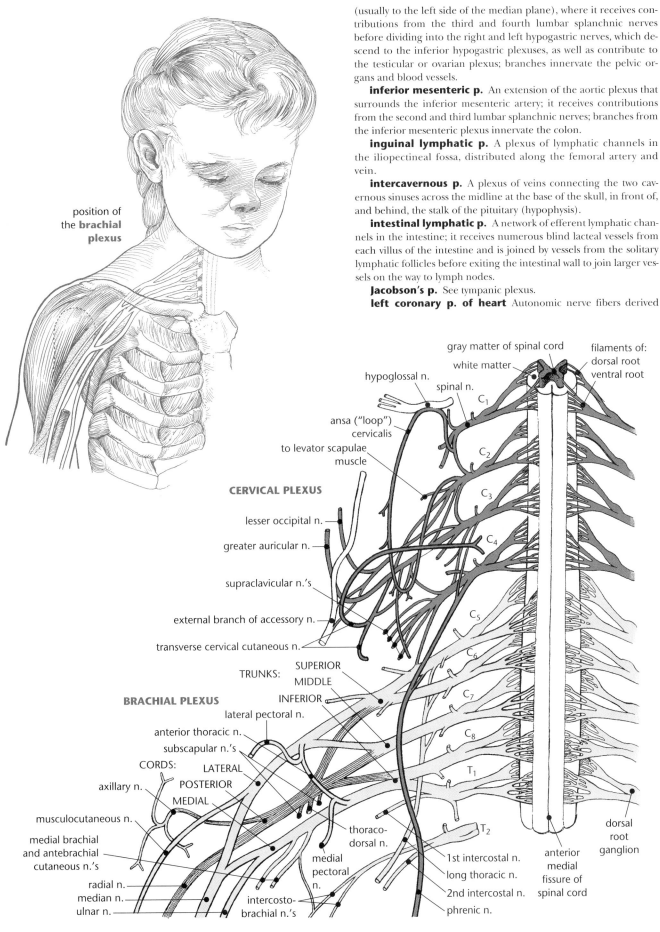

position of the **brachial plexus**

gray matter of spinal cord
white matter
filaments of:
dorsal root
ventral root
hypoglossal n.
spinal n.
C1
ansa ("loop") cervicalis
C2
to levator scapulae muscle
C3
CERVICAL PLEXUS
C4
lesser occipital n.
greater auricular n.
C5
supraclavicular n.'s
C6
external branch of accessory n.
transverse cervical cutaneous n.
C7
TRUNKS:
SUPERIOR
MIDDLE
C8
BRACHIAL PLEXUS
INFERIOR
lateral pectoral n.
T1
anterior thoracic n.
subscapular n.'s
CORDS:
LATERAL
POSTERIOR
axillary n.
MEDIAL
T2
musculocutaneous n.
thoraco-dorsal n.
dorsal root ganglion
medial brachial and antebrachial cutaneous n.'s
medial pectoral n.
1st intercostal n.
anterior medial fissure of spinal cord
radial n.
long thoracic n.
median n.
ulnar n.
intercosto-brachial n.'s
2nd intercostal n.
phrenic n.

chiefly from filaments of the deep part of the cardiac plexus (left half); it accompanies the left coronary artery and distributes branches to the left atrium and left ventricle of the heart. Also called posterior coronary plexus of heart.

lumbar p. A plexus of nerves, located in front of the transverse processes of the lumbar vertebrae; it is composed of the anterior primary divisions of the first three lumbar nerves, the larger portion of the fourth lumbar nerve, and a branch from the last thoracic nerve.

lumbosacral p. The combined lumbar and sacral plexuses.

lymphatic p. Any plexus of interconnecting lymph channels that absorb colloidal material and transport it to larger vessels for drainage into lymph nodes.

mammary arterial p. An extensive network of anastomosing branches of the lateral and internal thoracic arteries, and intercostal arteries; they form a circular plexus around the areola, and a deeper plexus in the region of the acinar structures of the female breast.

mammary lymphatic p. A rich network of lymph vessels divided into two planes, a superficial (subareolar) plexus and the deep (fascial) plexus; both originate in the interlobular spaces and in the wall of the lactiferous ducts, collecting lymph from the central parts of the gland, the skin, areola, and nipple; most of the superficial plexus drains laterally to the axillary lymph nodes; most of the deep fascial plexus drains medially to the internal mammary and mediastinal lymph nodes.

mammary venous p. A circular venous plexus around the base of the nipple and areola that radiates throughout the female breast, draining mostly toward the armpit (axilla) to the axillary vein by way of the lateral thoracic vein; also drained by the internal thoracic vein, which empties into the brachiocephalic vein.

Meissner's p. See submucosal plexus.

myenteric p. A network of autonomic nerve fibers interspersed with ganglia, situated between the circular and longitudinal muscular coats of the esophagus, stomach, and intestines. Also called Auerbach's plexus.

ovarian p. A network of autonomic nerve fibers distributed to the ovaries and fallopian (uterine) tubes; formed by branches from the renal and aortic plexuses and reinforced below by branches from the superior and inferior hypogastric plexuses.

pampiniform p. In the male, a venous plexus, the chief constituent of the spermatic cord, that drains the testis amd epididymis and empties into the testicular vein. In the female, a venous plexus in the broad ligament that drains the ovary and fallopian (uterine) tube and empties into the ovarian vein; it communicates with the uterine plexus; during pregnancy both the pampiniform and uterine plexuses enlarge.

parotid p. A plexus of nerves formed by the terminal branches of the facial (7th cranial) nerve, passing through the parotid gland; it innervates the muscles of facial expression.

pharyngeal p. A plexus of nerves in the wall of the pharynx, composed of pharyngeal branches of the vagus (10th cranial) and glossopharyngeal (9th cranial) nerves, and sympathetic fibers from the superior cervical ganglion; it innervates the pharynx and the soft palate.

posterior coronary p. of heart See left coronary plexus of heart.

prostatic p. Autonomic nerve plexus adjacent to the prostate, an extension of the inferior hypogastric plexus; it innervates the prostate, seminal vesicles, urethra, and erectile tissue of the penis (corpora cavernosa and corpus spongiosum).

prostatic venous p. In the male, a rich network of veins between the pubic symphysis and the front of the prostate; it drains into the vesical and internal iliac veins.

pterygoid venous p. A large venous plexus in the infratemporal fossa of the head, receiving veins from the cavernous sinus, nose, jaws, orbits, and pharyngeal plexus; it drains into the facial vein and retromandibular vein.

pudendal p. Plexus located in the posterior pelvis and formed

by the anterior primary divisions of the second and third sacral nerves and the entire fourth sacral nerve; it supplies the pelvic viscera and the external genitalia. Considered by some to be part of the sacral plexus.

pulmonary p. A plexus of autonomic and visceral afferent fibers, situated in front of and behind the roots of the lungs; formed by bronchial branches of the vagus (10th cranial) nerve and the 2nd to 5th thoracic sympathetic nerves.

rectal venous p. A network of veins surrounding the rectum; in the male it communicates with the vesical plexus, and in the female with the vaginal and uterine plexuses; it consists of two divisions: *Internal rectal venous p.*, situated beneath the epithelium of the rectum and anal canal, it drains chiefly into the superior rectal vein. *External rectal venous p.*, situated outside the muscular coats of the rectum, it drains into the superior, middle, and inferior rectal veins.

right coronary p. of heart Autonomic nerve fibers derived from the superficial part of the cardiac plexus and partly from the deep part of the cardiac plexus (right side); it accompanies the right coronary artery, and distributes branches to the right atrium and right ventricle. Also called anterior coronary plexus of heart.

sacral p. A plexus of nerve fibers located in the posterior wall of the pelvis, formed by the anterior primary divisions of the fourth lumbar to the third sacral nerves; it supplies the buttocks, perineum, lower extremities, and pelvic viscera; it gives rise to the sciatic nerve.

solar p. See celiac plexus.

spermatic p. See testicular plexus.

subcapillary p. A plexus of arterial anastomoses beneath the dermal layer of the skin, from which it gives off capillary tufts into the papillae of the dermis.

submucosal p. A plexus of autonomic nerve fibers that ramifies in the submucosal coat of the gut; it also has ganglia from which nerve fibers pass to the muscles and mucous membrane. Also called Meissner's plexus.

superior mesenteric p. An extension of the lower part of the celiac plexus that surrounds the superior mesenteric artery; it receives a contribution from the right vagus (10th cranial) nerve; branches from the plexus innervate the pancreas, jejunum, ileum, and parts of the colon.

testicular p. A network of autonomic nerve fibers distributed to the testis, epididymis, and deferent duct; formed by branches from the renal and aortic plexuses and reinforced by branches from the superior and inferior hypogastric plexuses. Also called spermatic plexus.

thoracic aortic p. An autonomic nerve plexus around the thoracic aorta, formed by nerve fibers from the sympathetic trunk and vagus (10th cranial) nerves; its branches pass through the diaphragm, becoming continuous with the abdominal aortic plexus and the celiac plexus.

thyroid venous p. A venous plexus on the surface of the thyroid gland, which gives rise to the superior, middle, and inferior thyroid veins.

tympanic p. A plexus of sensory and autonomic nerve fibers on the promontory of the middle ear chamber formed by branches from the glossopharyngeal (9th cranial) and superior and inferior caroticotympanic nerves; it supplies the mucous membrane of the middle ear chamber, mastoid air cells, and the eustachian (auditory) tube. Formerly called Jacobson's plexus.

uterine venous p. A venous plexus on both sides of the uterus within the broad ligament, closely associated with the vaginal and ovarian plexuses; drained by the uterine veins into the internal iliac vein.

vaginal venous p. A venous plexus around the vagina that is closely associated with the uterine, vesical, and rectal venous plexuses; drained by vaginal veins into the internal iliac vein.

p. of vas deferens See plexus of deferent duct.

vertebral venous p.'s Four venous plexuses along the vertebral column: *External vertebral venous p.*, situated outside the length of

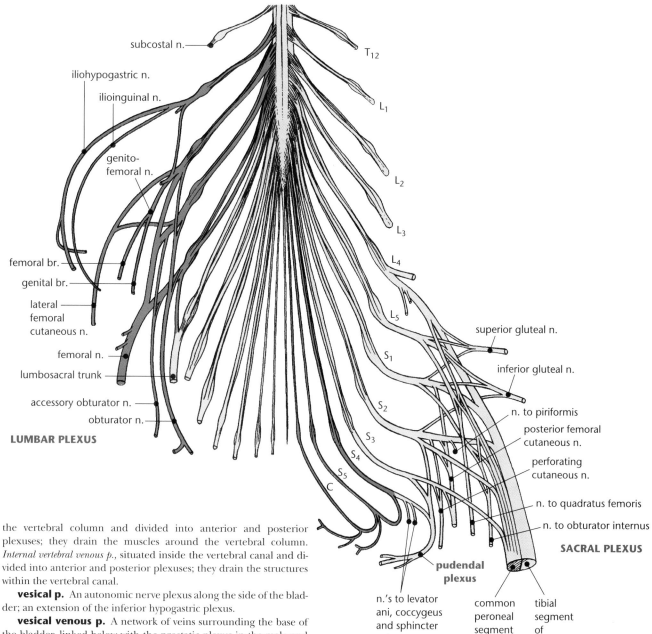

subcostal n.

iliohypogastric n.

ilioinguinal n.

genito-
femoral n.

femoral br.

genital br.

lateral
femoral
cutaneous n.

femoral n.

lumbosacral trunk

accessory obturator n.

obturator n.

LUMBAR PLEXUS

T₁₂

L₁

L₂

L₃

L₄

L₅

S₁

S₂

S₃

S₄

S₅

C

superior gluteal n.

inferior gluteal n.

n. to piriformis

posterior femoral
cutaneous n.

perforating
cutaneous n.

n. to quadratus femoris

n. to obturator internus

SACRAL PLEXUS

**pudendal
plexus**

n.'s to levator
ani, coccygeus
and sphincter
ani externus
muscles

common
peroneal
segment
of
sciatic n.

tibial
segment
of
sciatic n.

P

the vertebral column and divided into anterior and posterior plexuses; they drain the muscles around the vertebral column. *Internal vertebral venous p.*, situated inside the vertebral canal and divided into anterior and posterior plexuses; they drain the structures within the vertebral canal.

vesical p. An autonomic nerve plexus along the side of the bladder; an extension of the inferior hypogastric plexus.

vesical venous p. A network of veins surrounding the base of the bladder, linked below with the prostatic plexus in the male and with the vaginal plexus in the female; it is drained by vesical veins into the internal iliac vein.

plica (pli′kah) pl. pli′cae **1.** A fold, as of skin or membrane. **2.** A matted state of hair, resulting from filth and parasites.

plicae aryepiglottica See aryepiglottic folds, under fold.

plicae cilares See ciliary folds, under fold.

plicae circulares See circular folds, under fold.

p. fimbriata The purplish fringed fold of mucous membrane reflected from the tongue to the floor of the mouth, running adjacent on each side of the frenulum. Also called fimbriated fold of tongue.

p. lacrimalis See lacrimal fold, under fold.

p. palpebronasalis See epicanthus.

p. semilunaris conjunctiva See semilunar fold of conjunctiva, under fold.

p. triangularis of tonsil In fetal life, a free fold of mucous membrane that covers the anteroinferior part of the palatine tonsil. After birth, the fold houses lymphoid tissue and becomes part of the tonsil. In adults it is rarely present. Also called triangular fold of tonsil.

plicae vestibulares See vestibular folds, under fold.

plicae vocales See vocal folds, under fold.

plicate (pli′kāt) Folded; arranged in folds.

plication (pli-ka′shun) The folding and suturing of a muscle or of the wall of a hollow organ to reduce its size.

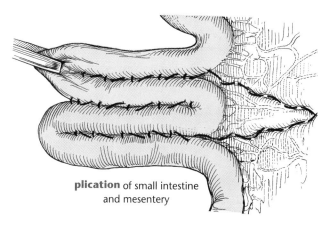

plication of small intestine
and mesentery

plicotomy (pli-kot'o-me) Surgical division of the posterior fold of the eardrum (tympanic membrane).

pliers (pli'erz) Any of several tools having a pair of pivoted jaws, used in dentistry and orthopedic surgery for bending and cutting metal or holding small objects.

ploidy (ploi'de) The number of chromosome sets present in a cell.

plug (plug) Anything that stops up an orifice or passage.

  cervical p. See mucous plug.

  epithelial p. The aggregation of epithelial cells that temporarily blocks the nostrils of the fetus.

  mucous p. A plug of accumulated mucous secretions formed in the cervical canal during pregnancy. Also called cervical plug.

plugger (plug'er) A dental instrument for packing filling material into a tooth cavity or a root canal.

plumbic (plum'bik) Relating to lead.

plumbism (plum'bizm) See lead poisoning, under poisoning.

plumose (plu'mos) Feathery.

pluri- Combining form meaning several.

pluricausal (ploor-ĭ-kaw'zal) Resulting from two or more causes.

pluriglandular (ploor-ĭ-glan'du-lar) Denoting several glands. Also called multiglandular; polyglandular.

pluripotent (ploo-rip'o-tent) **1.** Denoting embryonic cells that can mature into any of several cell types. **2.** Capable of influencing more than one organ.

plutonium (ploo-to'ne-um) A radioactive element; symbol Pu, atomic number 94, atomic weight 242.

P-mitrale (mi-tra'le) A pattern in the electrocardiogram (ECG) occurring in mitral valve disease; it consists of wide, notched P waves in leads I and II, with flat, inverted P waves in III.

pneumarthrosis (nu-mar-thro'sis) The presence of air in a joint.

pneumatic (nu-mat'ik) **1.** Relating to air or gas. **2.** Relating to breathing.

pneumatization (nu-mah-tĭ-za'shun) The development of air spaces in tissues, especially bone tissue.

pneumato-, pneumat-, pneuma- Combining forms meaning air; gas; breathing, respiration.

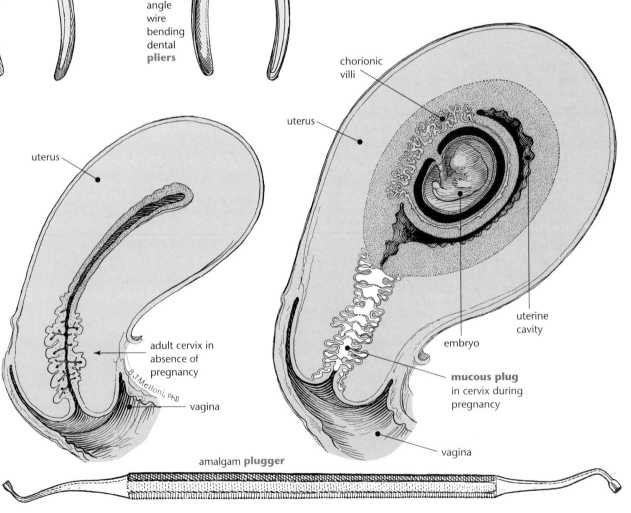

flat nose dental **pliers**

clasp adjusting dental **pliers** (three prongs)

angle wire bending dental **pliers**

B.J.Melloni, PhD

uterus

adult cervix in absence of pregnancy

vagina

chorionic villi

uterus

uterine cavity

embryo

mucous plug in cervix during pregnancy

vagina

amalgam **plugger**

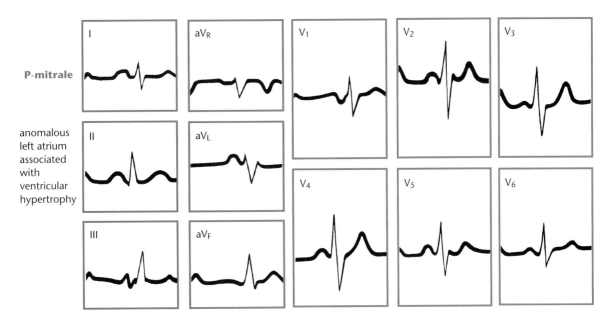

P-mitrale

anomalous left atrium associated with ventricular hypertrophy

I aV_R V_1 V_2 V_3
II aV_L V_4 V_5 V_6
III aV_F

pneumatocele (nu-mat′o-sēl) **1.** A gas-containing cyst in the lung. **2.** An air-containing hernia in the scrotum. **3.** A collection of air within the skull, resulting from a skull fracture. Also called pneumocele.

pneumatorrhachis (nu-mah-tor′ah-kis) See pneumorrhachis.

pneumatosis (nu-mah-to′sis) The abnormal presence of air or gas in any body tissue.

    p. intestinalis Gas within the bowel wall, appearing in the x-ray image as a string of submucosal bubbles; caused by bacterial invasion of the bowel wall; most commonly seen in newborn infants with necrotizing enterocolitis.

pneumaturia (nu-mah-tu′re-ah) Passage of gas with the urine due to entrance of air into the bladder through an abnormal opening.

pneumectomy (nu-mek′to-me) See pneumonectomy.

pneumo- Combining form meaning air; gas; the lungs; breathing.

pneumoarthrography (nu-mo-ar-throg′rah-fe) The making of x-ray images of a joint after injection of air or gas into the joint cavity.

pneumocele (nu′mo-sēl) See pneumatocele.

pneumocephalus (nu-mo-sef′ah-lus) The presence of air within the skull.

pneumocholecystitis (nu-mo-ko-le-sis-ti′tis) Inflammation and gaseous distention of the gallbladder due to the presence of gas-producing microorganisms.

pneumococcemia (nu-mo-kok-se′me-ah) The presence of pneumococci (*Streptococcus pneumoniae*) in the blood.

pneumococci (nu-mo-kok′si) Plural of pneumococcus.

pneumococcus (nu-mo-kok′us) Former name for an organism of the species *Streptococcus pneumoniae*.

pneumoconiosis (nu-mo-ko-ne-o′sis), pl. pneumoconio′ses Lung disease secondary to inhalation of various organic and inorganic particles (coal, silica, asbestos) usually occurring at the workplace.

    coal miner's p. (CMP) A disease of lung tissue caused by inhalation of coal (carbon) dust or smoke; seen most commonly in coal miners but occurring also in urban dwellers. Also called anthracosis; black lung disease.

Pneumocystis carinii (nu-mo-sis′tis kar-in′e) A parasitic protozoan (common in nature) causing pneumocystis carinii pneumonia in debilitated humans, especially infants and those patients whose immune systems are compromised. It has little or no virulence for people with normal immune function.

pneumocystosis (nu-mo-sis-to′sis) See pneumocystis carinii pneumonia, under pneumonia.

pneumocyte (nu′mo-sīt) Any of the cells lining the air sacs (alveoli) of the lungs. Also called pneumonocyte.

    granular p. Type II pneumocyte.

    type I p. One of the thin squamous cells lining the interior of the alveoli of the lungs. Also called alveolar cell; squamous alveolar cell; type I cell.

P

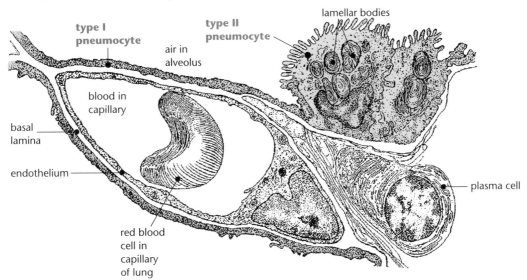

type I pneumocyte · air in alveolus · type II pneumocyte · lamellar bodies · blood in capillary · basal lamina · endothelium · plasma cell · red blood cell in capillary of lung

type II p. One of the cuboidal cells of the alveolar surface that secrete pulmonary surfactant. Also called granular pneumocyte; great alveolar cell; septal cell; type II cell.

pneumodynamics (nu-mo-di-nam′iks) The dynamics of breathing.

pneumoencephalography (nu-mo-en-sef-ah-log′rah-fe) The making of x-ray images of the subarachnoid spaces and ventricles of the brain after injecting a gas via a spinal lumbar puncture.

pneumogram (nu′mo-gram) **1.** The graphic record of respiratory movements made with a pneumograph. **2.** An x-ray image made in pneumoencephalography.

pneumograph (nu′mo-graf) Any instrument for recording respiratory movements.

pneumography (nu-mog′rah-fe) Roentgenography of any body cavity after injection of air. Also called pneumoroentgenography.

pneumohemopericardium (nu-mo-he-mo-per-i-kar′de-um) See hemopneumopericardium.

pneumohemothorax (nu-mo-he-mo-tho′raks) See hemopneumothorax.

pneumohydrometra (nu-mo-hi-dro-me′trah) Accumulation of gas and fluid in the uterine cavity.

pneumohydrothorax (nu-mo-hi-dro-tho′raks) See hydropneumothorax.

pneumolith (nu′mo-lith) A calcification in a lung.

pneumomediastinum (nu′mo-me-de-as-ti′num) (PM) Accumulation of air in the central chest cavity (mediastinum).

    diagnostic p. Deliberate introduction of air or any other gas into the mediastinum as an aid to examination and diagnosis.

pneumonectomy (nu-mo-nek′to-me) Removal of a lung or a part of it. Also called pneumectomy; pulmonectomy.

pneumonia (nu-mo′ne-ah) Inflammation of the lung tissue (parenchyma), usually involving the air sacs (alveoli) and areas of tissue consolidation; caused by a variety of microorganisms, chemicals, and other toxic materials.

    acute necrotizing p. A severe pneumonia of sudden onset characterized by extensive necrosis of lung tissue and bleeding into the lung air sacs (alveoli), often with a rapid progression to death.

    aspiration p. Pneumonia caused by inhalation of foreign material (e.g., food particles, vomited debris, throat secretions).

    bacterial p. Any pneumonia caused by bacteria (e.g., *Streptococcus pneumoniae, Haemophilus influenzae, Staphylococcus aureus*).

    bronchial p. See bronchopneumonia.

    chemical p. Pneumonia resulting from inhalation of toxic gases (e.g., war gases, chlorine).

    chlamydial p. Pneumonia caused by *Chlamydia trachomatis*, seen in infants during the first 3 to 11 weeks of life; usually acquired during vaginal delivery through an infected maternal cervix.

    contusion p., traumatic p. Seldom-used terms denoting a pneumonia developed after a severe blow to the chest or a puncture wound to the lung.

    desquamative interstitial p. (DIP) Pneumonia marked by proliferation of the cells lining the pulmonary air sacs (alveoli) and desquamation into the alveolar lumen.

    double p. Lobar pneumonia in both lungs.

    Eaton agent p. See mycoplasmal pneumonia.

    eosinophilic p. Disorder characterized by excessive eosinophils in peripheral blood, infiltration of eosinophils in the lung air spaces, and focal consolidation of lung tissue. Cause is unknown. Also called idiopathic chronic eosinophilic pneumonia.

    Friedländer's p. A severe form of lobar pneumonia caused by *Klebsiella pneumoniae* (Friedländer's bacillus); characterized by much swelling of the affected pulmonary lobe.

    hypostatic p. Pneumonia occurring in the aged and in debilitated bedridden patients who lie in the same position for extended periods of time. Pneumonia arises from areas of the lung that are dependent and poorly ventilated.

    idiopathic chronic eosinophilic p. See eosinophilic pneumonia.

    lipid p., lipoid p. Pneumonia accompanied by fibrotic changes

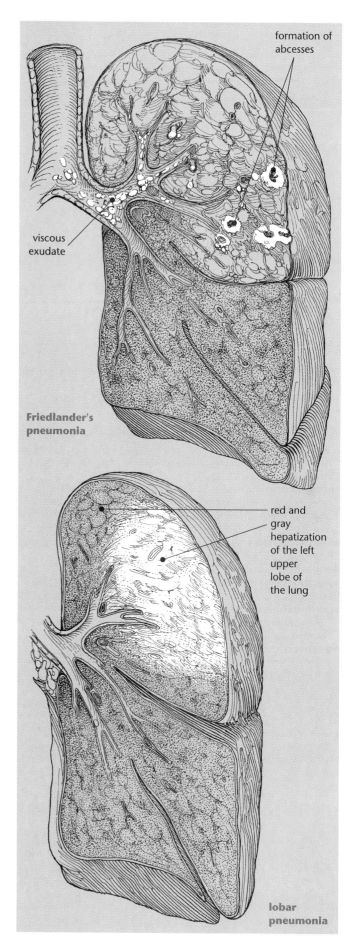

formation of abcesses

viscous exudate

Friedlander's pneumonia

red and gray hepatization of the left upper lobe of the lung

lobar pneumonia

pneumodynamics ■ pneumonia

in the lungs, caused by inhalation of oily or fatty substances (e.g., liquid petroleum).

lobar p. Pneumonia of sudden (acute) onset, usually involving a single lobe of the lungs, which is sharply demarcated from the non-involved lobes; caused by a variety of bacteria, especially *Streptococcus pneumoniae.*

mycoplasmal p. The most common form of pneumonia affecting school-age children and young adults; it is generally a mild illness caused by the bacterium *Mycoplasma pneumoniae,* beginning insidiously after a three-week incubation period; it does not result in consolidation of lung tissue, which is typical of bacterial pneumonias (hence the synonym "atypical" pneumonia). Distinguished from viral pneumonia by the presence of cold agglutinin. Also called primary atypical pneumonia; Eaton agent pneumonia.

pneumococcal p. Lobar pneumonia caused by *Streptococcus pneumoniae.*

pneumocystis carinii p. An opportunistic pneumonia occurring predominantly in individuals with impaired immunity, such as premature or malnourished infants, children with primary immunodeficiency diseases, patients undergoing chemotherapy for cancer or organ transplantation, and patients in the last stage of an HIV infection (AIDS); caused by *Pneumocystis carinii,* through airborne transmission. The organism multiplies in the pulmonary air sacs (alveoli), which become filled with a pink frothy mass. Also called pneumocystosis.

primary atypical p. See mycoplasmal pneumonia.

staphylococcal p. Bacterial pneumonia caused by *Staphylococcus aureus;* it frequently occurs as a complication of viral influenza.

viral p. Pneumonia caused by any of a variety of viruses; may be complicated by a secondary bacterial infection.

pneumonic (nu-mon′ik) **1.** Relating to the lungs. **2.** Relating to pneumonia.

pneumonitis (nu-mo-ni′tis) Inflammation of the lungs.

chemical p. Pneumonitis caused by aspiration of chemical substances, such as aspiration of meconium by a fetus or newborn infant.

hypersensitivity p. An immunologically mediated condition affecting only susceptible individuals and resulting from repeated inhalation of organic dusts over an extended period; symptoms include cough, fever, labored breathing (dyspnea), and progressive patterns of lung dysfunction. Early cessation of exposure to the offending agent prevents progression to irreversible lung fibrosis. The many common terms for the condition reflect the various causative agents, especially in occupational settings. Also called farmer's lung (spores of thermophilic actinomycetes in moldy hay), bird-breeder's and bird-fancier's lung (proteins in bird feathers and droppings), detergent worker's lung (*Bacillus subtilis* enzymes), bagassosis (fungus-infected sugar cane residue), cheese-washer's lung (moldy cheese rind), humidifier fever (bacteria-contaminated furnace or air-conditioning humidifier systems).

lymphocytic interstitial p. (LIP) Extensive infiltration of lung tissue with lymphocytes and plasma cells frequently associated with malignant lymphoma; may be diffuse or involve a circumscribed area. Also called pseudolymphoma.

pneumonocyte (nu-mon′o-sit) See pneumocyte.

pneumonotomy (nu-mo-not′o-me) Incision into a lung. Also called pneumotomy.

pneumoparotitis (nu-mo-pah-ro-ti′tis) A transient swelling of the parotid gland area occurring occasionally in children as a result of blowing up balloons or playing a musical wind instrument; caused by the force of increased intraoral pressure.

pneumopericardium (nu-mo-per-ĭ-kar′de-um) Accumulation of air around the heart, within its enveloping membrane (pericardium); it appears in x-ray films as a halo around the heart.

pneumoperitoneum (nu-mo-per-ĭ-to-ne′um) Abnormal collection of air in the peritoneal cavity; may be due to a pulmonary air leak or to perforation or rupture of an abdominal hollow organ; may occur as part of a disease process or as accidental puncture during certain procedures.

artificial p. Deliberate introduction of air into the peritoneal cavity as a therapeutic measure.

pneumoperitonitis (nu-mo-per-ĭ-to-ni′tis) Inflammation of the peritoneum with collection of gas in the peritoneal cavity.

pneumopyothorax (nu-mo-pi-o-tho′raks) See pyopneumothorax.

pneumoroentgenography (nu-mo-rent-gen-og′rah-fe) See pneumography.

pneumorrhachis (nu-mo-ra′kis) Abnormal presence of air in the spinal canal. Also called pneumatorrhachis.

pneumothorax (nu-mo-tho′raks) Accumulation of air between the two layers of the pleura (pleural space); may be due to trauma (e.g., air leakage from an accidental puncture of a lung or a penetrating wound of the chest wall), or may result from spontaneous rupture of a bulla on the lung surface. In newborn infants it occurs chiefly after meconium aspiration or positive pressure resuscitation, or as a complication of artificial ventilation.

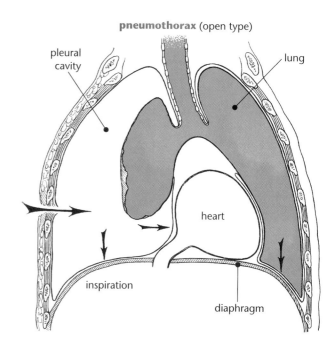

pneumothorax (open type)

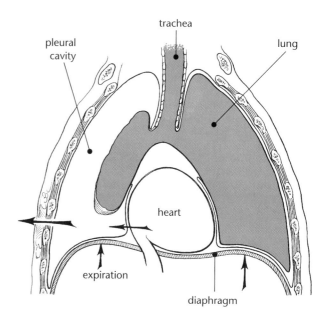

P

pneumonic ■ pneumothorax

tension p. A life-threatening condition occurring when lungs and heart are compressed by the accumulated air in the pleural space.

pneumotomy (nu-mot′o-me) See pneumonotomy.

Pneumovirus (nu-mo-vi′rus) A genus of viruses that includes the respiratory syncytial virus.

pock (pok) The pustule of an eruptive disease, especially smallpox.

pocket (pok′et) In dentistry, a pathologically enlarged space between a tooth and the inflamed gum.

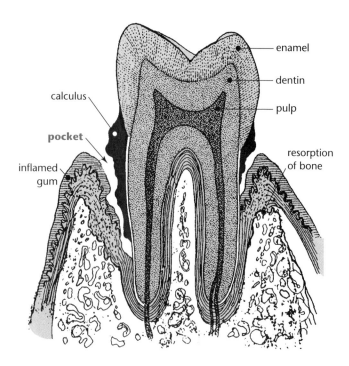

enamel
dentin
calculus
pulp
pocket
resorption of bone
inflamed gum

pockmark (pok′mark) A scar left on the skin after healing of a pustule, especially of smallpox.

podagra (po-dag′rah) Gouty pain in the great toe.

podagral, podagric (pod′ah-gral, po-dag′rik) Relating to podagra.

podalgia (po-dal′je-ah) Pain in the foot.

podalic (po-dal′ik) Relating to the foot.

podarthritis (pod-ar-thri′tis) Inflammation of any of the joints in the feet.

podiatrist (po-di′ah-trist) A practitioner of podiatry. Also called chiropodist.

podiatry (po-di′ah-tre) The medical field concerned with the diagnosis and treatment of foot diseases, injuries, and deformities. Treatment may include prescription of drugs and corrective devices and surgery. Also called podiatric medicine; chiropody.

poditis (po-di′tis) Any inflammation of the foot.

podo-, pod- Combining forms meaning foot.

podobromidrosis (pod-o-brom-i-dro′sis) Sweating of the feet with a strong disagreeable odor.

podocyte (pod′o-sit) Glomerular epithelial cell.

pododynamometer (pod-o-di-nah-mom′ĕ-ter) Device for measuring the strength of foot and leg muscles.

podophyllin (pod-o-fil′in) Caustic resin extracted from the roots of the May apple (*Podophyllum peltatum*), irritating to skin and mucous membranes; it has been used as a paint to treat genital warts, skin tumors, and senile keratoses, and as a purgative taken internally; it may cause central nervous system damage and teratogenesis.

podophyllotoxin (pod-o-fil-o-tok′sin) The main active constituent of podophyllin. It has cathartic and antineoplastic properties.

pogonion (po-go′ne-on) The most anterior midpoint of the lower jaw; a craniometric point. Also called mental point.

-poiesis Combining form meaning development (e.g., erythropoiesis)

poikilo- Combining form meaning varied.

poikilocyte (poi′ki-lo-sit) A red blood cell (erythrocyte) of abnormal irregular shape.

poikilocythemia (poi-kil-o-si-the′me-ah) See poikilocytosis.

poikilocytosis (poi-ki-lo-si-to′sis) The presence of poikilocytes in the blood. Also called poikilocythemia.

poikiloderma (poi-ki-lo-der′mah) An atrophic condition of the skin with patches of either too much or too little pigmentation, and clusters of dilated capillaries.

point (point) 1. A minute spot or area. 2. The sharp or tapered end of an instrument. 3. A specific position, condition, or degree. 4. A minute orifice; punctum.

p. of abscess The part of an abscess where the pus comes closest to the surface and its rupture seems about to occur.

alveolar p. See prosthion.

boiling p. (b.p.) The temperature at which a liquid boils; the vapor pressure of the liquid equals the ambient atmospheric pressure; at sea level, water boils at 100°C (212°F).

cold rigor p. The level of cold temperature at which the activity of a cell ceases and passes into a hibernating state.

contact p. The small area of the interproximal surface of a tooth that is in direct contact with an adjacent tooth. Also called contact area.

craniometric p.'s Fixed standard points on the skull used as landmarks and for measuring the skull. They have special applications in forensic medicine, orthodontics, and plastic surgery.

critical p. (a) The temperature at which it is not possible to liquefy a gas, regardless of the pressure applied. Also called critical state. (b) The highest temperature in which a liquid can exist before turning into gas.

cutoff p. In test interpretation, the value used to separate positive from negative results; a designated limit.

deaf p.'s Points near the ear where a vibrating tuning fork touching them cannot be heard by the person being examined.

Desjardins' p. A point on the surface of the abdomen overlying the head of the pancreas, located 6 to 8 cm from the navel (umbilicus) on a straight line from the navel to the right axilla.

dew p. Temperature at which the moisture of the air condenses (produces saturation and forms dew).

end p. In volumetric analysis of a solution, the point at which a reaction is completed.

p. of fixation The retinal point on which an image is directed and fixed; normally the fovea of the eye.

focal p. (a) The point at which light rays meet when deflected by refraction or reflection. (b) The point of convergence of sound waves.

freezing p. The temperature at which a liquid changes to a solid state; for pure water it is 0°C (32°F).

fusion p. See melting point.

heat rigor p. The temperature at which cell death occurs, usually due to coagulation of cell protoplasm.

isoelectric p. The pH at which an amphoteric electrolyte, such as an amino acid or protein, is electrically neutral owing to equality of ionization; above or below this pH, it acts as an acid or base, respectively.

p. of maximum impulse The point on the chest wall where the beat of the left ventricle of the heart is felt most intensely; normally felt in the left fifth intercostal space, at the midclavicular line.

McBurney's p. The surface marking on the abdominal wall used to determine the location of the appendix; the point is on the lateral third of the line between the right anterior superior iliac spine and the navel (umbilicus); it is especially tender in acute appendicitis.

melting p. (m.p.) The temperature at which a solid changes into a liquid state. Also called fusion point.

mental p. See pogonion.

midclavicular p. The midpoint of the collarbone (clavicle).

P

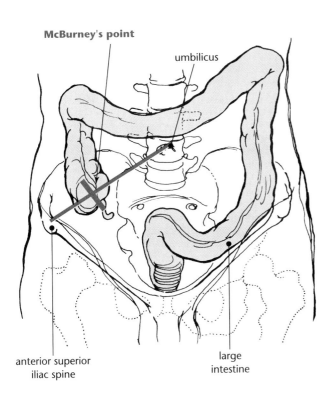

McBurney's point

umbilicus

large
intestine

anterior superior
iliac spine

midinguinal p. The point on the inguinal ligament halfway between the pubic symphysis and the anterior superior iliac spine.

nasal p. See nasion.

neutral p. The point in which a solution is neither acid nor alkaline; represented by the symbol pH 7 (above 7 alkalinity increases, below 7 acidity increases).

occipital p. The most posterior point of the occipital bone, situated in the median plane at the tip of the external occipital protuberance. The plane formed by a line between the occipital point and the glabella represents the maximum anteroposterior length of the skull.

p. of ossification The point or center in a cartilage where the earliest bone formation (ossification) occurs.

pressure p. (a) A point on the body at which pressure can be exerted to control hemorrhage from an arterial injury. (b) A point on the skin that is extremely sensitive to pressure.

pressure-arresting p. The point or area of the skin at which exerted pressure elicits relief of spasm of underlying muscles.

pulse p.'s Sites on the body where the rhythmic expansion of an artery can be readily felt with the finger.

retromandibular tender p. A point behind the earlobe, just in front of the mastoid process; pressure applied on it elicits sharp pain in patients with meningitis.

silver p. A solid cone of silver used to fill the root canal of a nonviable tooth.

sylvian p. See pterion.

thermal death p. The temperature required to kill microorganisms with heat in a standard aqueous culture when exposed for 10 minutes.

trigger p. A circumscribed area of the body that, when touched or pressed, elicits a specific sensation, such as pain or discomfort.

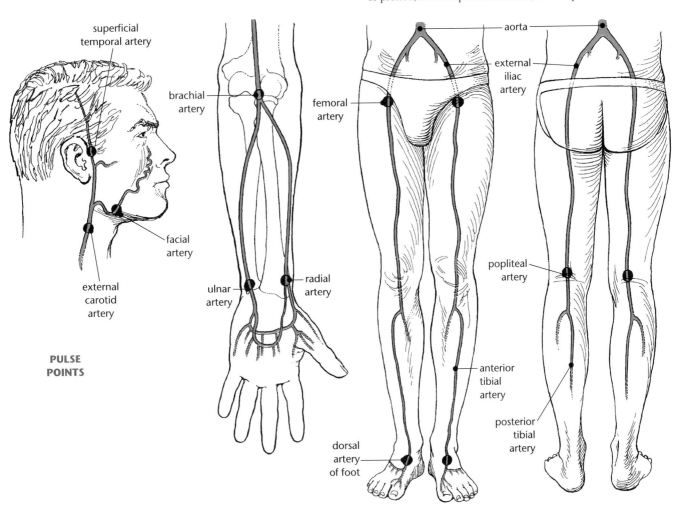

superficial
temporal artery

brachial
artery

femoral
artery

aorta

external
iliac
artery

facial
artery

radial
artery

ulnar
artery

external
carotid
artery

PULSE POINTS

popliteal
artery

anterior
tibial
artery

posterior
tibial
artery

dorsal
artery
of foot

point ■ point

Voillemier's p. The point 6.5 cm below the midpoint of the interspinous plane (the plane connecting the anterior superior iliac spines of the hipbones) where the bladder may be approached for puncture, especially in obese patients.

point-of-service (POS) plan A health care plan that offers enrollees coverage for non-network care, but provides more extensive coverage for network care coordinated by a designated primary care physician. Enrollees can make the choice of network or non-network care at the time they need the service. Those who decide to go outside the plan (non-network) pay more out-of-pocket.

poison (poi′zn) Any substance that is injurious to health or that causes death. Also called toxic substance.

poisoning (poi′zuh-ning) The condition produced by a poison; may be from medicinal substances or domestic chemicals, or from a wide range of substances used in agriculture and industry.

acetylsalicylic acid p. See aspirin poisoning.

arsenic p. Acute or chronic poisoning from ingestion or inhalation of arsenic-containing compounds; skin absorption is limited; sources of exposure include insecticides, rodenticides, fungicides, wood preservatives, and the smelting and galvanizing processes. In the body, arsenic is taken up readily by red blood cells and deposited in the liver, kidney, muscle, bone, skin, nails, and hair. Symptoms of chronic poisoning include skin changes, transverse white bands on fingernails (Mees' lines), laryngitis, and peripheral nerve disease; headache and confusion may occur in both acute and chronic poisoning. In pregnancy, it crosses the placenta, causing fetal malformation and low birth weight. Acute symptoms occur most often in suicide and homicide cases; they include burning throat sensation, abdominal pain, garlic breath, and blood-tinged diarrhea.

aspirin p. Adverse effects of aspirin intake, usually occurring from accidental ingestion (by children) or from overzealous self-treatment; may cause ringing of the ears (tinnitus), rapid pulse, and severe headache. High doses taken during pregnancy may cause increased risk of hemorrhage and prolonged labor, especially if taken during the last trimester. Also called acetylsalicylic acid poisoning.

blood p. Popular name for septicemia.

cadmium p. Acute or chronic poisoning from exposure to cadmium compounds or fumes; occupational exposure occurs in the smelting, mining, and ceramics industries and in the manufacture of batteries, paints, and plastics; nonoccupational exposure occurs primarily through storage of food in improperly glazed ceramic ware, and through water and soil contamination. Acute symptoms include fever, chills, difficult breathing (dyspnea), intestinal disturbances, brown urine, and kidney failure; severe intoxication may cause lung damage (due to pneumonitis and pulmonary edema), respiratory failure, and death. Chronic symptoms include kidney malfunctioning, bone pain and fractures, and emphysema.

carbon monoxide p. Poisoning by inhalation of carbon monoxide, which acts as a chemical suffocant (asphyxiant) by displacing oxygen from red blood cells, thus reducing the amount of oxygen delivered to body tissues by the blood. Initial symptoms include dizziness, headache, nausea, and fainting, leading (in prolonged exposure) to stupor, coma, convulsions, and death. Those who survive a prolonged exposure may suffer brain damage and, often, a lengthy or even permanent personality change. Occupational exposure usually occurs where combustion engines are in use. Existence of chronic carbon monoxide poisoning is currently disputed.

carbon tetrachloride p. Necrosis of liver and kidney tissues caused by inhaling or drinking carbon tetrachloride.

cyanide p. Poisoning caused by inhalation or ingestion of cyanide compounds, which combine with iron-containing enzymes in the body and block energy-releasing metabolism; chemical suffocation (asphyxiation) results. Early effects include vertigo, burning sensation of the mouth and throat, difficult swallowing (dysphagia), and an almond-odor breath; death may occur in minutes.

food p. Acute gastrointestinal illness or neurological condition resulting from ingestion of foods that have become contaminated with microorganisms or harmful chemicals, or may themselves be poisonous.

lead p. Poisoning caused by ingestion or inhalation of lead or its many compounds. Sources of environmental exposure include household dust, drinking water, paint chips and soil (eaten usually by children), and improperly fired ceramics that release lead into food and beverages. Occupational exposure occurs chiefly in mining and in the manufacture of lead batteries, paints, and pigments; painters may be exposed, especially in fine-spray painting operations and torch burning to remove lead-based paint; workers in munitions plants and in rifle ranges (especially indoors) may be exposed to lead dust. Less conventional sources include lead-containing cosmetics and bullets retained in the body. Lead poisoning often occurs as a chronic condition punctuated by acute recurrent episodes. In pregnancy, lead crosses the placenta; maternal exposure prior to or during pregnancy can produce fetal toxicity. Acute symptoms in young children include uncoordinated gait, slurred speech, seizures, and coma, usually preceded by weeks of irritability and sluggishness; a chronic state may lead to mental retardation. In adults, the occurrence of gastrointestinal symptoms may suggest appendicitis or gallbladder colic; chronic symptoms include abdominal cramps, constipation, lethargy, memory loss, wrist drop, and a blue-gray discoloration (lead line) on the gums. Also called plumbism; saturnism.

mercury p. Poisoning from ingesting or inhaling mercury compounds or vapor, most commonly resulting from industrial exposure. Dentists and dental technicians are also at risk of exposure through improper handling and storage of mercury compounds. In pregnancy, mercury crosses the placenta; absorbed mercury compounds are secreted in breast milk. Acute symptoms of mercury poisoning include inflammation of the airways and lungs or vomiting, abdominal pain, and bloody diarrhea; chronic symptoms include anorexia, tremor, personality disturbances (shyness, anxiety, excitability), excessive salivation, stomatitis, and kidney damage. Also called hydrargyrism; hydrargyria.

Salmonella food p. Inflammation of the gastrointestinal tract caused by ingestion of food contaminated with any of several strains of *Salmonella* bacteria; symptoms (within 8 to 12 hours) include abdominal pain, diarrhea, vomiting, and fever.

Staphylococcus food p. A self-limited food poisoning caused by an intestinal toxin (enterotoxin) produced by strains of the bacterium *Staphylococcus aureus;* symptoms appear a few hours after ingestion of contaminated food and include nausea, vomiting, abdominal cramps, and diarrhea.

water p. See water intoxication, under intoxication.

poison ivy, poison oak, poison sumac (poi′zn i′ve, ōk, soo′mak) 1. Shrubs of the genus *Rhus* with foliage that contains an irritating substance (urushiol). 2. Skin eruption and inflammation caused by contact with such plants.

polar (po′lar) Relating to a pole.

polarity (po-lar′ĭ-te) 1. The condition of having two opposite poles. 2. Having two opposite characteristics.

polarization (po-lar-ĭ-za′shun) In physiology, development of ions of opposite charges in two points of living tissue, such as on both sides of a cell membrane.

polarize (po′lar-iz) To induce polarization.

polarography (po-lar-og′rah-fe) In chemical microanalysis, the recording of the relationship between an increasing current flowing through a solution being analyzed and the increasing voltage used to produce the current.

pole (pōl) 1. Either end of an axis. 2. Either of two poles with opposite physical properties.

animal p. The site of an early ovum, near its nucleus, where the polar bodies are formed in succession and where segmentation begins. Also called germinal pole.

germinal p. See animal pole.

polio- Combining form meaning the gray matter of the brain and spinal cord.

P

poison ivy

poison oak

poison sumac

polio (po′le-o) Colloquial term for poliomyelitis.

poliodystrophy (po-le-o-dis′tro-fe) A wasting (atrophy) of the gray substance of the central nervous system (CNS).

polioencephalitis (po-le-o-en-sef-ah-li′tis) Inflammation of the gray substance of the brain.

poliomyelitis (po-le-o-mi-e-li′tis) An infectious disease most commonly affecting children; caused by the poliovirus (genus *Enterovirus*), which attacks the anterior columns of the spinal cord; initial symptoms are fever, muscle pain, sore throat, and headache lasting from two to six days; after several symptom-free days, headache recurs, accompanied by fever, nausea, stiff neck, and spinal rigidity. The disease may be mild and resolve completely, or may be severe and may progress to loss of reflexes and paralysis; involvement of the medulla oblongata causes impairment of swallowing and cardiopulmonary functions, usually with a fatal outcome. Also called polio.

poliomyelopathy (po-le-o-mi-ĕ-lop′ah-the) Any disease of the gray substance of the spinal cord.

poliovirus (po-le-o-vi′rus) The virus causing poliomyelitis in humans; it belongs to the genus *Enterovirus;* serologic types 1, 2, 3, and 4 have been recognized.

pollen (pol′en) The microspores of seed plants that cause hay fever.

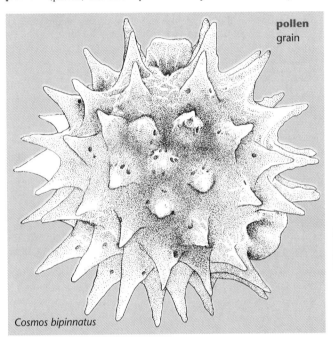

pollen grain

Cosmos bipinnatus

pollinosis, pollenosis (pol-ĭ-no′sis, pol-ĕ-no′sis) Hay fever produced by certain pollens.

pollutant (pŏ-lu′tant) Any agent that contaminates (e.g., chemicals, microorganisms, radioactivity, noise).

pollution (pŏ-lu′shun) The act of making impure.

polonium (po-lo′ne-um) Radioactive element; symbol Po, atomic number 84, atomic weight 210.

poly- Combining form meaning many.

poly (pol′e) Colloquial term for polymorphonuclear leukocyte.

polyacid (pol-e-as′id) An acid that yields more than one hydrogen ion per molecule.

polyadenitis (pol-e-ad-ĕ-ni′tis) Inflammation of several lymph nodes.

polyarteritis (pol-e-ar-tĕ-ri′tis) Inflammation of several arteries.

    p. nodosa (PAN) A systemic disease marked by degenerating (necrotizing) inflammation of small to medium-sized arteries, occurring anywhere throughout the body except in the lungs; it affects mostly young adults, especially males, and is frequently associated with hepatitis B antigens; symptoms depend on the organs involved; generally, they include fever, malaise, and weight loss. Also called periarteritis nodosa.

polyarthritis (pol-e-ar-thri′tis) Inflammation affecting several joints, as seen in rheumatic fever.

polybasic (pol-e-ba′sik) Having several replaceable hydrogen atoms.

polychondritis (pol-e-kon-dri′tis) Inflammation involving several cartilages.

polychromasia (pol-e-kro-ma′ze-ah) See polychromatophilia.

polychromatic (pol-e-kro-mat′ik) Multicolored.

polychromatophil (pol-e-kro-mat′o-fil) Any cell, especially red blood cells that stain readily with different dyes or tints.

polychromatophilia (pol-e-kro-mah-to-fil′e-ah) **1.** Tendency to stain with basic and acidic dyes. **2.** The presence of an excessive number of cells that stain with different dyes (basic, acidic, and neutral). Also called polychromasia.

polyclinic (pol-e-klin′ik) A clinic, dispensary, or hospital that treats any disease or injury.

polyclonal (pol-e-klon′al) Denoting the products of a number of different cell types.

polycystic (pol-e-sis′tik) Containing several cysts.

polycythemia (pol-e-si-the′me-ah) Condition in which there is an increased concentration of red blood cells in the blood. Also called erythrocythemia; erythrocytosis.

   absolute p. The result of an increase in red blood cell numbers; it may be: *Primary absolute p.,* due to intrinsic abnormality of the immature red blood cell (myeloid stem cell), as occurs in polycythemia vera; or *Secondary absolute p.,* due to a response to other conditions (e.g., lung disease, cyanotic heart disease, renal cell carcinoma, hepatocellular carcinoma).

   primary p. See polycythemia vera.

   relative p. Increased red blood cell count due to a reduction in plasma volume (without an increase in red blood cell mass), as seen in dehydration.

   p. rubra vera See polycythemia vera.

   p. vera A disease of unknown cause characterized by proliferation of all the cellular elements of bone marrow and an absolute increase in red blood cell mass; it appears insidiously in people 40 to 60 years of age. Also called polycythemia rubra vera; primary polycythemia; erythremia.

polydactylia (pol-e-dak-til′e-ah) See polydactyly.

polydactylism (pol-e-dak′til-izm) See polydactyly.

polydactyly (pol-e-dak′ti-le) The presence of more than the normal number of digits on the hand or foot. Also called polydactylia; polydactylism.

polydipsia (pol-e-dip′se-ah) Excessive thirst. Polydipsia and polyurea are often presenting symptoms of diabetes mellitus and may also be seen in diabetes insipidus.

   psychogenic p. Compulsive drinking of fluids (up to 6 liters per day), often seen in emotionally disturbed individuals; unlike the thirst of diabetes insipidus, patients are not awakened at night by their thirst. Also called compulsive water drinking.

polydysplasia (pol-e-dis-pla′ze-ah) Abnormal development of several tissues or organs.

polygene (pol′e-jēn) Any one of a group of genes determining a recognizable characteristic (phenotype), although the effect of each gene is not discernible.

polygenic (pol-e-jen′ik) Resulting from the action of many genes whose individual effects are not discernible.

polyglandular (pol-e-glan′du-lar) See pluriglandular.

polygraph (pol′e-graf) An instrument that simultaneously records changes in several physiologic processes (e.g., blood pressure, respiratory movements, and galvanic skin resistance); sometimes used to detect emotional reactions, as in lie detection.

polyhedral (pol-e-he′dral) Having many sides.

polyhydramnios (pol-e-hi-dram′ne-os) An excessive amount of amniotic fluid. Also called hydramnios; hydramnion.

polyhypermenorrhea (pol-e-hi-per-men-o-re′ah) Frequent and excessive menstruation.

polyleptic (pol-e-lep′tik) Occurring in many relapsing episodes.

polylogia (pol-e-lo′je-ah) Continuous talking, which is often incoherent, as seen in certain mental disorders.

polymastia (pol-e-mas′te-ah) The presence of more than two breasts in the human. Also called multimammae; pleomastia.

polymer (pol′ĭ-mer) A complex substance made up of a chain of repeated simple molecules.

polymerase (pol-im′er-ās) An enzyme that promotes polymerization.

polymerization (pol-ĭ-mer-ĭ-za′shun) The chemical joining of several monomers to form a polymer.

polymicrolipomatosis (pol-e-mi-kro-lip′o-mah-to′sis) Condition marked by the presence of several small nodular masses of lipid (lipomas) in the subcutaneous tissues.

polymorph (pol′e-morf) Colloquial term for polymorphonuclear leukocyte.

polymorphic (pol-e-mor′fik) Occurring in many forms. Also called multiform.

polymorphism (pol-e-mor′fizm) **1.** Occurring in various forms either during development of individuals or as adults within a single species. **2.** The presence of two or more recognizable characteristics (phenotypes) within a species.

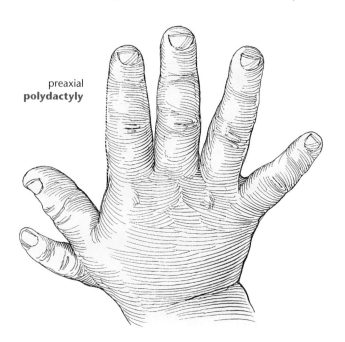

preaxial **polydactyly**

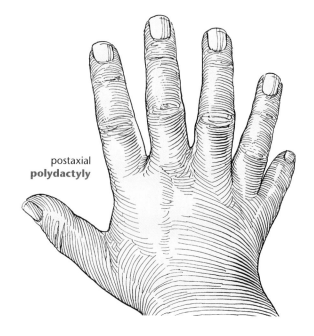

postaxial **polydactyly**

polyarthritis ■ **polymorphism**

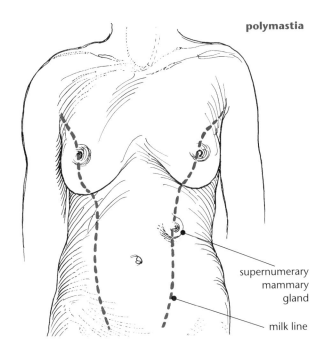

polymastia

supernumerary
mammary
gland

milk line

hyperplastic p. A benign, sessile polyp, usually no larger than 5 mm in diameter, lying on top of a mucosal fold of the large intestine, and producing no symptoms.

inflammatory p. See pseudopolyp.

juvenile p. A large (up to 2 cm in diameter), pedunculated, benign polyp in the rectum, which may cause painless bleeding after defecation; composed of dilated mucosal glands; it occurs in children and young adults, especially children under five years of age. Also called retention polyp.

laryngeal p. A polyp projecting from a vocal fold, causing hoarseness of the voice.

nasal p. A focal inflammatory swelling of the lining of the nasal cavity or sinuses.

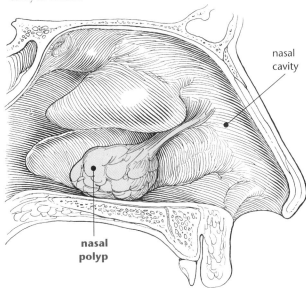

nasal
cavity

nasal
polyp

neoplastic p. A polyp composed of cells that develop the capacity for uncontrolled proliferation, which results in a cancerous process.

pedunculated p. Polyp attached to the tissue of origin by a slender stalk.

polymorphonuclear (pol-e-mor-fo-nu′kle-ar) Having a nucleus so deeply lobulated that it appears as several nuclei.

polymyalgia (pol-e-mi-al′je-ah) Pain in several muscles.

p. rheumatica An illness occurring in older people, more frequently in men than in women, characterized by muscle aches, sometimes fever, and a high erythrocyte sedimentation rate; often associated with temporal arteritis (TA).

polymyositis (pol-e-mi-o-si′tis) An inflammatory disorder (believed to be autoimmune) characterized primarily by skeletal muscle pain and tenderness; it may also affect the skin and connective tissue; the muscles most often affected are those of the pelvic and shoulder girdles and pharynx; often associated with occult malignant tumors; when skin changes are prominent, the disorder is called dermatomyositis.

polymyxin (pol-e-mik′sin) Any of a group of antibiotic substances derived from the soil bacterium *Bacillus polymyxa*.

polyneuritis (pol-e-nu-ri′tis) Inflammation of several peripheral nerves.

idiopathic p. See Guillain-Barré syndrome, under syndrome.

polyneuropathy (pol-e-nu-rop′ah-the) Any disease of peripheral nerves, occurring as a result of other disorders.

polynuclear (pol-e-nu′kle-ar) See multinuclear.

polyopia, polyopsia (pol-e-o′pe-ah, pol-e-op′se-ah) The condition of seeing one object as several objects.

polyorchidism (pol-e-or′ki-dizm) The presence of more than two testes.

polyostotic (pol-e-os-tot′ik) Involving several bones.

polyovular (pol-e-ov′u-lar) Relating to more than one ovum.

polyp (pol′ip) A space-occupying tumor arising from the mucous membrane of a hollow structure (e.g., bladder, colon, nose) and protruding into the lumen; it can be benign or malignant.

adenomatous p. A benign polyp composed of glandular tissue; may be pedunculated or sessile.

cervical p. A relatively common benign polyp frequently arising from the cervical canal and protruding into the vaginal space; most commonly seen in women over the age of 20 years. It may cause intermenstrual or postintercourse bleeding. Also called endocervical polyp.

endocervical p. See cervical polyp.

endometrial p. A pedunculated or sessile polyp arising from the lining of the uterine cavity, with a potential for undergoing a cancerous change, most commonly occurring during the perimenopausal period; it is a frequent cause of postmenopausal bleeding.

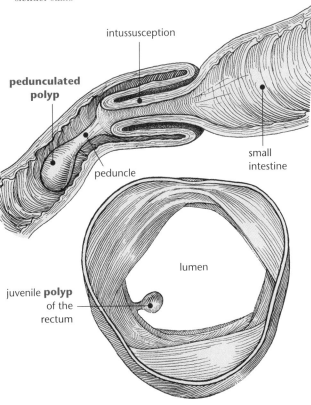

intussusception

pedunculated polyp

peduncle

small intestine

lumen

juvenile **polyp** of the rectum

polymorphonuclear ■ polyp

retention p. See juvenile polyp.

sessile p. Polyp attached to the tissue of origin by a broad base.

polypectomy (pol-i-pek′to-me) Removal of a polyp.

polypeptide (pol-e-pep′tid) A compound composed of two or more amino acids joined by peptide linkage.

polyphagia (pol-e-fa′je-ah) Pathologic overeating.

polypharmacy (pol-e-fahr′mah-se) The practice of prescribing several different drugs to one patient at the same time.

polyplast (pol′e-plast) Derived from many sources.

polyplastic (pol-e-plas′tik) Capable of assuming many forms.

polyplegia (pol-e-ple′je-ah) Paralysis of several muscles.

polyploidy (pol′e-ploi-de) An abnormal increase in the number of chromosomes by exact multiples of the number of chromosomes present in normal diploid cells. Also called tetraploid.

polypoid (pol′e-poid) Resembling a polyp.

polyposis (pol-e-po′sis) The presence of several polyps.

familial p. coli (FPC) Disease occurring in an autosomal inheritance with defect on chromosome 5; characterized by the presence of numerous polyps (500 to over 2000) in the colon, causing intestinal bleeding and a 100% chance of developing cancer of the colon and rectum by age 40; they develop early in life but are usually detected in the second and third decades.

juvenile p. See juvenile polyposis syndrome, under syndrome.

polypotome (po-lip′o-tōm) A cutting instrument for removing polyps.

polypous (pol′e-pus) Resembling or characterized by the presence of polyps.

polyradiculitis (pol-e-rah-dik-u-li′tis) Inflammation of several nerve roots.

polysaccharide (pol-e-sak′ah-rīd) A carbohydrate made up of a large number of saccharide units (e.g., starch and glycogen).

polyserositis (pol-e-se-ro-si′tis) Inflammation of serous membranes. Also called multiple serositis.

polysomnogram (pol-e-som′no-gram) The graphic record obtained in polysomnography.

polysomnography (pol-e-som-nog′rah-fe) The monitoring of physiologic activity during sleep; frequently employed to monitor newborn infants whose breathing stops for a few seconds (apnea) to determine the type of apnea and to relate it to the sleep stage in which it occurs.

polyspermia (pol-e-sper′me-ah) Excessive secretion of semen.

polyspermy (pol-e-sper′me) The entry of more than one sperm into the ovum during fertilization.

polythelia (pol-e-the′le-ah) The presence of more than two nipples. Also called hyperthelia.

polytrichia (pol-e-trik′e-ah) The presence of excessive hair.

polyunsaturated (pol-e-un-sach′e-ra-ted) Containing two or more double bonds between carbon molecules; applied especially to essential fatty acids.

polyuria (pol-e-u′re-ah) The excessive and frequent passage of urine.

polyvinyl chloride (pol-e-vi′nil klo′rīd) (PVC) A plastic material with many industrial applications (e.g., production of plastic piping, floor coverings, home furnishings, toys, records, film, bottles); long-term exposure can result in cirrhosis or liver cancer.

pompholyx (pom′fo-liks) See dyshidrosis.

pons (ponz) 1. The portion of the brainstem situated between the cerebral peduncle above and the medulla oblongata below. 2. Any bridgelike structure.

pontic (pon′tik) An artificial tooth that is part of a bridge or partial denture and substitutes for a missing natural tooth.

pontine, pontile (pon′tīn, pon′tīl) Relating to a pons.

pool (po͞ol) 1. An accumulation, as of blood. 2. Combined resources.

gene p. The total collection of genes available for inheritance among members of a given population who are capable of sexual reproduction.

vaginal p. The secretions accumulated in the upper posterior area of the vagina, used as a specimen for hormonal evaluation and cancer detection.

poples (pop′lez) The back of the knee.

popliteal (pop-lit′e-al) Relating to the back of the knee.

population (pop-u-la′shun) 1. All inhabitants of a given area considered together. 2. In statistical sampling, the aggregate of units from which a sample may be drawn (e.g., persons, microorganisms, cells, institutions, records, events).

monoclonal cell p. A group of cells derived from a single cell type or clone.

polyclonal cell p. Several groups of cells usually in tissue culture, each group derived from a common ancestor by cell division (mitosis).

porcelain (por′se-lin) In dentistry, a powder composed of clay, quartz, and flux used in the manufacture of artificial teeth, jacket crowns, and dentures.

porcine (por′sin) Relating to or derived from pigs.

pore (pōr) A minute opening.

gustatory p. The surface opening of a taste bud.

slit p.'s The narrow gaps between the interdigitating footlike processes of glomerular cells (podocytes) in the kidney, important in the filtration function.

sweat p. The surface opening of a sweat gland.

sweat pores on fingerprint

porencephalia (po-ren-sĕ-fa′le-ah) See porencephaly.

porencephaly (po-ren-sef′ah-le) Congenital malformation of the brain characterized by cystic outpouching of the ventricles, especially the lateral ventricles. Also called porencephalia.

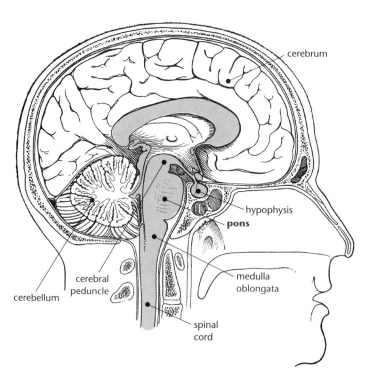

cerebrum

hypophysis

pons

medulla oblongata

spinal cord

cerebral peduncle

cerebellum

poro-, por- Combining forms meaning an opening; a passing through; callus; induration.

porokeratosis (po-ro-ker-ah-to′sis) A rare skin disease characterized by formation of circular depressions with central atrophy and indurated borders.

porphobilinogen (por-fo-bi-lin′o-jen) (PBG) Organic compound excreted in large quantities in the urine of persons with acute or congenital porphyria.

porphyria (por-fe′re-ah) Any of a group of disorders characterized by disturbance of blood pigment (heme) metabolism due to deficiency of various enzymes in the body; each causes a distinct pattern of overproduction, accumulation, and excretion of intermediates (porphyrins) of heme production.

 congenital erythropoietic p. (CEP) Rare genetic disorder transmitted as an autosomal recessive trait involving tissues in the bone marrow; it causes chronic sensitivity to sunlight, hemolytic anemia, and enlargement of the spleen. Death may occur in childhood.

 p. cutanea tarda (PCT) The most common form of porphyria, characterized by blistering of sun-exposed areas of skin, slow healing of wounds, and pink-to-brown discoloration of the skin; sometimes precipitated by liver disease, including alcoholic liver disease.

 intermittent acute p. (IAP) Disorder inherited as an autosomal dominant trait; symptoms usually appear in early adulthood; characterized by attacks of colicky abdominal pain, vomiting, constipation, port wine–colored urine, and neurologic and psychiatric disturbances; attacks may last from days to months and may be induced by certain drugs (e.g., barbiturates, oral contraceptives, alcohol).

 toxic p.'s A group of acquired porphyrias caused by a number of industrial and environmental toxins, which generally cause liver injury and deranged heme synthesis in the liver; toxic substances include certain ingredients of fungicides, herbicides, commercial disinfectants, plastics, and paints.

 variegate p. (VP) A form similar to intermittent acute porphyria but with blistering of sun-exposed skin.

porphyrin (por′fĭ-rin) Any of a group of red-orange fluorescent compounds that are produced in the body during heme biosynthesis; they are present in all cellular protoplasm, take part in energy storage and utilization, and are excreted in the urine in small amounts.

porphyrinuria (por-fĭ-rĭ-nu′re-ah) Excessive amounts of porphyrin in the urine, reflecting impaired heme biosynthesis.

porrigo (po-ri′go) Obsolete term for any scalp disease.

porta (por′tah), pl. por′tae The point at which vessels, nerves, and excretory ducts enter or leave an organ.

 p. hepatis The fissure on the undersurface of the liver providing passage for the hepatic ducts, hepatic artery, and portal vein.

portal (por′tal) Relating to porta, especially the porta hepatis.

portio (por′she-o), pl. portio′nes Latin for port.

portogram (por′to-gram) An x-ray image of the portal vein.

portography (por-tog′rah-fe) Radiographic study of the portal circulation after injection of a radiopaque substance either directly into the portal vein or through the splenic artery or superior mesenteric artery during a surgical operation.

portosystemic (por-to-sis-tem′ik) Relating to the portal vein (of the liver) and the veins of the general systemic circulation.

porus (po′rus), pl. po′ri Latin for pore; a tiny orifice.

position (po-zish′un) **1.** The placement of the body in a particular way to facilitate specific diagnostic or therapeutic procedures. **2.** The arrangement of bodily parts. **3.** In obstetrics, the relationship of a designated point on the presenting part of the fetus to a designated point in the maternal pelvis. **4.** The place occupied. **5.** The place or location of an object in relation to other objects.

 anatomic p. Position in which the human body is erect with the feet together and the arms and hands turned forward.

 centric p. The position of the lower jaw (mandible) in its most retruded relation to the upper jaw (maxilla); the condyles are in the

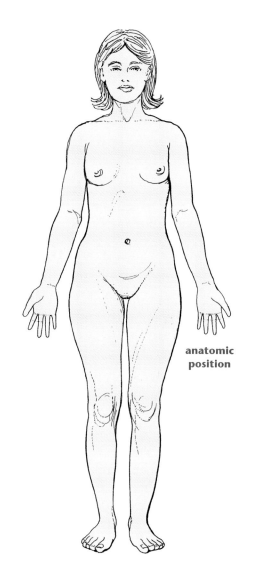

anatomic
position

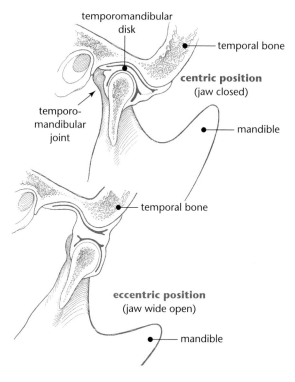

temporomandibular
disk

temporal bone

centric position
(jaw closed)

mandible

temporomandibular
joint

temporal bone

eccentric position
(jaw wide open)

mandible

poro-, por- ■ **position**

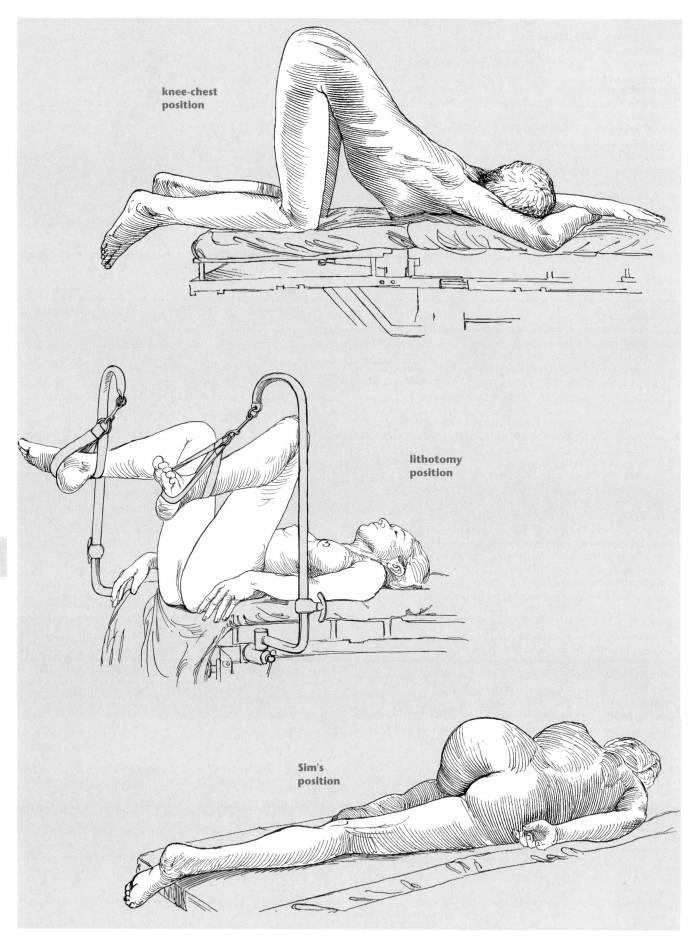

knee-chest
position

lithotomy
position

Sim's
position

most posterior unstrained position in the mandibular fossa, the position in which the jaws are normally closed.

dorsosacral p. See lithotomy position.

eccentric p. Any position of the lower jaw (mandible) other than the centric position (e.g., when the mandibular condyles are in a forward position).

Fowler's p. An inclined position of the body in which the head, shoulders, and knees are raised approximately 18 inches.

genupectoral p. See knee-chest position.

high pelvic p. See Trendelenburg's position.

jackknife p. A urologic position in which the individual is on his back with shoulders elevated, legs flexed, and thighs at right angles to the abdomen; used to facilitate urethral instrumentation.

knee-chest p. A prone position in which the patient rests on the knees and chest with arms crossed and forearms supporting the head; assumed for rectal examination. Also called genupectoral position.

kneeling-squatting p. A squatting position with the body erect and the thighs pressed against the abdomen; assumed in digital palpation of high rectal examination.

lateral recumbent p. See Sims' position.

lithotomy p. A supine position with the patient's buttocks at the end of the examining or operating table, the hips and knees fully flexed, the thighs abducted and externally rotated. Also called dorsosacral position.

obstetric p. See Sims' position.

occlusal p. The relation of the lower jaw (mandible) to the upper jaw (maxilla) when the jaws are closed and the teeth are in maximum contact.

orthopnea p. A sitting position with the patient leaning forward slightly with hands or elbows propped on the arms of a chair or on an overbed table; assumed for relief of shortness of breath when lying down (orthopnea).

prone p. Lying facedown.

recovery p. Position in which an unconscious but breathing person is placed, when no neck injury is suspected; the victim's body is placed on its side, without twisting; the arm under the body is flexed with the hand placed under the chin; the other arm is extended toward the back; and the upper, free leg is partially flexed.

semiprone p. See Sims' position.

Sims' p. Position in which the patient lies on the left side with the right thigh acutely flexed and the left thigh slightly flexed; the left arm is behind the body; used to facilitate vaginal and rectal examinations, curettement of uterus, intrauterine irrigation after labor, tamponade of vagina, etc. Also called semiprone position; lateral recumbent position; obstetrical position.

supine p. Lying on the back with the face up.

Trendelenburg's p. Position in which the patient is supine on an operating table, inclined at various angles (usually from 30° to 45°); the head is lower and the knees are higher than the rest of the body; the table is angulated at the knees, permitting the legs and feet to hang over it. Also called high pelvic position.

positioner (po-zish′un-er) In orthodontics, a removable appliance, consisting of a thin resilient material, fitted over the whole dental arch for effecting minor tooth movement and/or stabilization at the end of an orthodontic treatment.

positive (poz′ĭ-tiv) 1. Having a value opposite another (negative) value. 2. Indicating the presence of a condition (especially one being tested) or the occurrence of a response.

false-p. See false-positive.

positron (poz′ĭ-tron) A subatomic particle having the same mass as the electron and an equal but opposite (positive) charge.

post- Prefix meaning situated behind; subsequent to.

postabortal (pōst-ah-bor′tal) Relating to the period following an abortion.

postbrachial (pōst-bra′ke-al) Relating to the posterior part of the upper arm.

postcibal (pōst-si′bal) After eating.

post cibum (pōst si′bum) (p.c.) Latin for after meals.

postclavicular (pōst-klah-vik′u-lar) Posterior to the collarbone (clavicle).

postcoital (pōst-ko′ĭ-tal) Relating to postcoitus.

post coitum (pōst koi′tum) Latin for after sexual intercourse (coitus).

postcoitus (pōst-ko′ĭ-tus) The period immediately following sexual intercourse (coitus).

postductal (pōst-duk′tal) Relating to the part of the aorta just distal to the ductus/ligamentum arteriosus.

postencephalitic (pōst-en-sef-ah-lit′ik) Occurring after encephalitis.

posterior (pos-tēr′e-or) 1. Situated behind a structure. 2. Relating to the back or dorsal aspect of the body or part.

postero- Combining form meaning back, posterior.

posteroanterior (pos-ter-o-an-tēr′e-or) From the back to the front.

posterolateral (pos-ter-o-lat′er-al) Behind and to one side.

posteromedial (pos-ter-o-me′de-al) Behind and toward the middle.

posteromedian (pos-ter-o-me′de-an) A central position of the back of the body or a part.

postfebrile (pōst-fe′bril) After a fever.

postganglionic (pōst-gang-gle-on′ik) Situated behind or distal to a ganglion.

posthioplasty (pos′the-o-plas-te) Reparative operation upon the foreskin (prepuce).

posthitis (pos-thi′tis) Inflammation of the foreskin (prepuce).

postictal (pōst-ik′tal) Following a seizure.

postmature (pōst-mah-tŭr′) Denoting a fetus that remains in the uterus beyond 42 weeks of gestation.

postmenopausal (pōst-men-o-paw′zal) Occurring after menopause.

postmortem (pōst-mor′tem) Relating to or occurring after death. See also postmortem examination, under examination.

postnasal (pōst-na′zal) Relating to the area behind the nose.

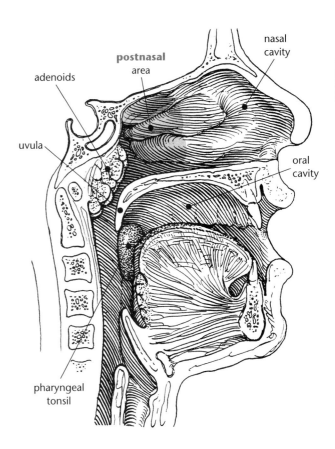

postnatal (pōst-na′tal) Occurring after birth.

postnecrotic (pōst-nĕ-krot′ik) Occurring subsequent to tissue death (necrosis).

postoperative (pōst-op′er-ah-tiv) Occurring after a surgical operation.

postpartum (pōst-par′tum) Relating to the period after childbirth.

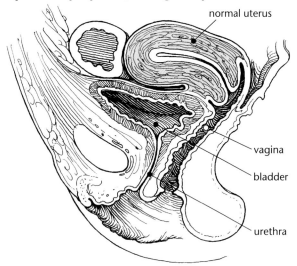

normal uterus

vagina

bladder

urethra

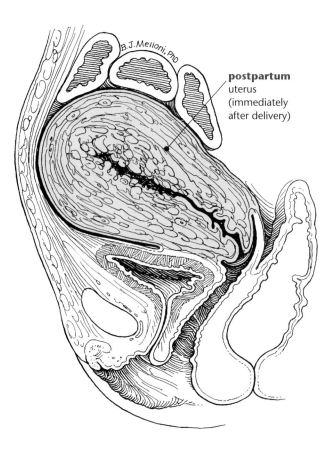

B.J.Melloni, PhD

postpartum
uterus
(immediately
after delivery)

postprandial (pōst-pran′de-al) Following a meal.

postpubertal (pōst-pu′ber-tal) Relating to the period immediately after puberty.

postrenal (pōst-re′nal) Located below the level of the kidney.

postsynaptic (pōst-sī-nap′tik) **1.** Occurring just after the crossing of a synapse (applied to transmission of a nerve impulse). **2.** Situated distal to a synapse.

posttraumatic (pōst-traw-mat′ik) Occurring after or as a result of an injury.

postulate (pos′tu-lāt) An unproven assertion.

  Koch's p.'s The four conditions that must be present to establish the causative relationship between an organism and a specific disease: the organism must be present in all cases of the disease, the organism must be isolated and grown in pure culture, the pure culture must produce the disease when introduced into a susceptible animal, and the organism must be retrieved from the infected animal and grown again in pure culture. Also called Koch's laws.

posture (pos′chur) The physical disposition of the body as a whole.

  decorticate p. Persistent flexion of the arm and extension of the leg on the opposite side of a lesion involving the outer layer of the spinal cord (i.e., the corticospinal tracts).

postvaccinal (pōst-vak′sī-nal) After vaccination.

potable (po′tah-bl) Fit to drink.

potamophobia (pot-ah-mo-fo′be-ah) Irrational fear aroused by the sight of rivers or flowing water.

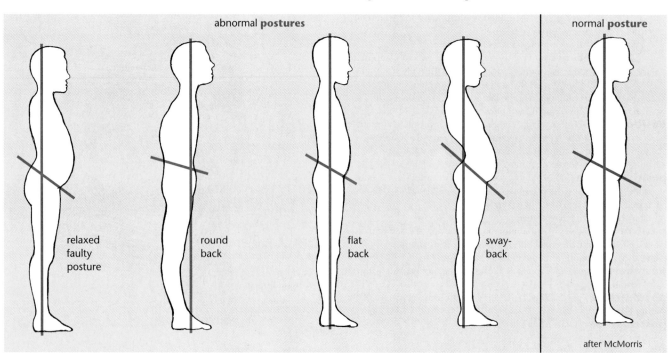

abnormal **postures**

normal **posture**

relaxed faulty posture

round back

flat back

sway-back

after McMorris

postnatal ■ **potamophobia**

P

potassium (po-tas′e-um) Metallic element; symbol K, atomic number 19, atomic weight 39.10. It plays an important role in muscle contraction, conduction of nerve impulses, cell membrane function, and enzyme action. Normal potassium concentration of extracellular fluid is between 3.5 and 5 mEq/liter; normal potassium concentration of intracellular fluid is about 150 mEq/liter.

p. chloride Colorless crystals or powder used to treat potassium deficiency.

p. cyanide A commonly used fumigant.

p. iodide An expectorant and an antifungal agent.

p. nitrate Compound with diuretic properties. Also called niter; saltpeter.

p. permanganate A dark purple crystalline compound with antiseptic, astringent, and deodorizing properties; used in the treatment of certain skin inflammations.

potassium 42 (po-tas′e-um) (^{42}K) An artificial potassium isotope used as a tracer in studies of potassium distribution in body fluid compartments.

potency (po′ten-se) **1.** The quality of having strength or great control. **2.** A capacity for growth. **3.** A comparative expression of drug activity; determined by the dose required to produce a particular effect of given intensity, relative to a standard of reference. It varies inversely with the magnitude of the dose required to produce the effect.

sexual p. The ability of a male to perform sexually; often used to mean the ability to have and maintain adequate erection of the penis during sexual intercourse.

potent (po′tent) **1.** Strong. **2.** Capable of producing a chemical or physiologic effect of strong intensity. **3.** Possessing sexual potency.

potential (po-ten′shal) **1.** Existing in a state with a strong possibility for changing or developing. **2.** The force necessary to drive a unit charge from one point to another in an electrical field; voltage.

action p. The electric current developed in a nerve, muscle, or other excitable tissue during its activity.

demarcation p. The voltage difference between intact nerve or muscle fibers and the injured ends of the same fibers. Also called injury potential.

evoked p. See evoked response, under response.

excitatory postsynaptic p. (EPSP) The change in electrical potential occurring in the membrane of a postsynaptic nerve cell when an impulse that has an excitatory influence arrives at the synapse.

inhibitory postsynaptic p. (IPSP) The change in electrical potential occurring in the membrane of a postsynaptic nerve cell when an impulse that has an inhibitory influence arrives at the synapse.

injury p. See demarcation potential.

membrane p. The voltage difference between the two sides of a cell membrane; in the resting stage, the outside is positive and the inside negative.

visual evoked p. The voltage fluctuations, recorded with an electroencephalograph from the scalp overlying the back of the head, resulting from retinal stimulation by a flashing light.

potentiometer (po-ten-she-om′ĕ-ter) A voltage-measuring instrument.

potion (po′shun) A large dose of a liquid medication.

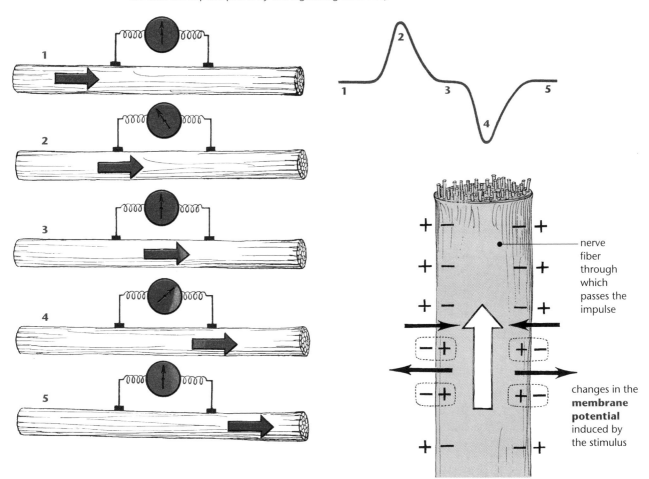

record of the extracellular **action potential** of a nerve fiber (each number of the wave curve represents the membrane potential at the time the impulse passes by the registering electrode)

nerve fiber through which passes the impulse

changes in the **membrane potential** induced by the stimulus

P

pouch (powch) A small sac or pocket-like space, especially occurring as an outgrowth of a larger structure; an anatomic receptacle that resembles a bag.

abdominovesical p. The peritoneal pouch between the distended bladder and the anterior abdominal wall.

craniobuccal p. See Rathke's pouch.

Douglas' p. See rectouterine pouch.

Hartmann's p. An abnormal dilatation of the neck of the gallbladder; regarded by some to be a constant feature of the normal gallbladder.

Heidenhain p. A small pouch, surgically separated from the body of the stomach, with the vagal nerve supply interrupted, which drains to the outside through an opening in the abdominal wall; used in the experimental study of stomach secretions. COMPARE Pavlov pouch.

p. of Luschka In embryology, an angled recess of the endoderm at the roof of the primitive pharynx, which forms the pharyngeal bursa.

Morison's p. See hepatorenal recess, under recess.

neurobuccal p. See Rathke's pouch.

Pavlov p. A small pouch, surgically separated from the body of the stomach by a mucosal septum but with the vagal nerve supply left intact, which drains to the outside through an opening in the abdominal wall; used in the experimental study of stomach secretions. COMPARE Heidenhain pouch.

pharyngeal p.'s A series of four or five paired pouches on the lateral wall of the embryonic pharynx; each pouch is in close relationship to an aortic arch and is situated opposite a branchial cleft.

Rathke's p. In embryology, the outpocketing of the embryonic mouth (stomodeum) formed when the embryo is about three weeks old and subsequently forming the anterior lobe of the pituitary (hypophysis). Also called craniobuccal pouch; neurobuccal pouch.

rectouterine p. The pouchlike space between the posterior wall of the uterus and the anterior wall of the rectum. Also called Douglas' pouch; Douglas' space; rectouterine space.

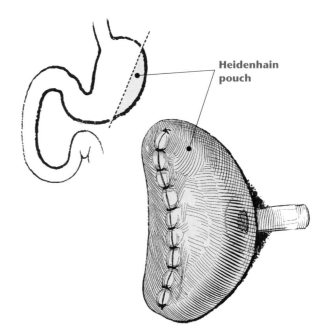

Heidenhain pouch

rectovesical p. The peritoneal pouch between the rectum and the bladder in the male; the opening is directed upward.

superficial inguinal p. An interval or pouch of loose alveolar tissue between the external oblique and the deep layer of superficial fascia overlying the inguinal canal. In very young boys, the testis can often be retracted out of the scrotum into this space.

suprapatellar synovial p. See suprapatellar bursa, under bursa.

uterovesical p. The peritoneal pouch between the uterus and the bladder, bounded laterally by the round ligaments of the uterus.

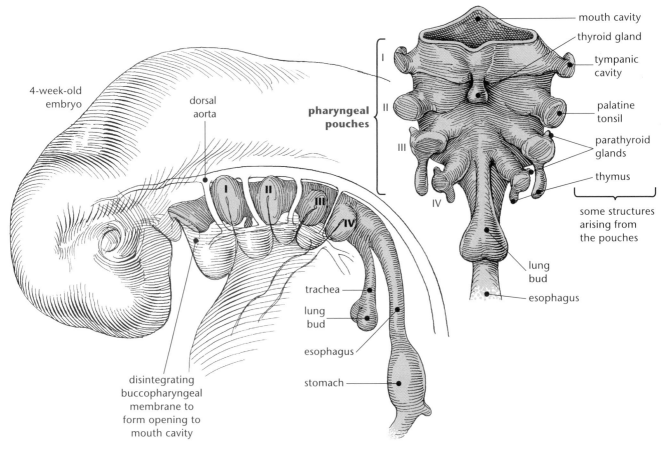

P

pouch ■ pouch

vaginal p. See female condom, under condom.

poultice (pōl′tis) A hot, moist mush of bread meal, linseed, or any other cohesive matter, applied to the skin between two pieces of cloth to soothe, relax, or stimulate an aching or inflamed part of the body.

power (pow′er) In optics, the degree of magnification of a lens.

back vertex p. A standard for measurement of ophthalmic lenses.

resolving p. The ability to discern detail visually.

pox (poks) 1. Any eruptive disease. Term is usually combined with a descriptive addition (e.g., smallpox, chickenpox). 2. An eruption. 3. Obsolete term for syphilis.

Poxviridae (poks-vir′ĭ-de) A family of large, double-stranded DNA viruses.

poxvirus (poks-vi′rus) Any virus of the family Poxviridae.

P-pulmonale (pul-mo-nah′le) The pattern of the electrocardiogram characteristic of cor pulmonale; marked by a tall peaked P wave, usually seen in leads II, III, and AVF.

P-pulmonale

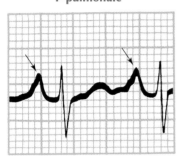
lead II

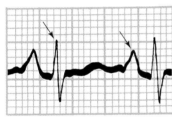
lead III

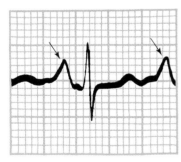
lead aVF

practice (prak′tis) 1. The exercise of one's profession or occupation. 2. Collective term for the patients of a physician.

corporate p. The employment of a physician by an enterprise controlled by nonmedical individuals that sells the physician's services for profit. Distinguished from physician employment by hospitals, health maintenance organizations (HMOs), and similar health care providers.

extramural p. The practice of medical school faculties or full-time hospital staff beyond the confines of their respective institutions.

family p. The practice of a physician who is a specialist in family medicine. Distinguished from general practice.

general p. The practice of a physician, or another health care professional, who is not a specialist in any particular field of medicine. Distinguished from family practice.

group p. A formal association of health care professionals, usually representing several specialties, providing services and sharing all expenses and resources (physical space, equipment, personnel, medical records); income from the practice is pooled and distributed to all members of the group according to an agreed-upon arrangement.

individual p. See solo practice.

private p. Delivery of health care independent of any external policy or managerial control; may be solo or group practice.

solo p. Health care delivery by a self-employed practitioner, not associated with any other individual.

practice patterns (prak′tis pat′erns) Patterns of a physician's practice related to diagnosis and treatment, especially as influenced by cost of the service requested and provided.

practitioner (prak-tish′un-er) A person who practices a profession.

general p. (GP) A physician who, after receiving an MD degree at a medical school, has trained at a hospital for at least one year but has not specialized in any particular field and usually provides primary care for the whole family. COMPARE family physician, under physician.

nurse p. See nurse practitioner after nurse.

pragmatagnosia (prag-mat-ag-no′ze-ah) Loss of the ability to recognize objects.

pramoxine hydrochloride (pram-ok′sēn hi-dro-klo′rīd) Local anesthetic applied to the skin.

prandial (pran′de-al) Relating to a meal.

praseodymium (pra-ze-o-dim′e-um) Rare-earth element; symbol Pr, atomic number 59, atomic weight 140.907.

praxiology (prak-se-ol′o-je) The study of behavior as opposed to thought.

pre- Prefix meaning before in time or in space.

preagonal (pre-ag′o-nal) Just before death.

prealbumin (pre-al-bu′min) A protein component of plasma.

thyroxine-binding p. One of the three carrier proteins of plasma.

preanal (pre-a′nal) In front of the anus.

preanesthetic (pre-an-es-thet′ik) Prior to induction of anesthesia.

preaortic (pre-a-or′tik) In front of the aorta.

preauricular (pre-aw-rik′u-lar) In front of the auricle of the ear.

precancer (pre-kan′ser) A lesion that is known to have the potential to become a cancer.

precancerous (pre-kan′ser-us) Denoting a lesion that precedes, develops into, or has a high risk of becoming a cancer. Also called premalignant.

precipitant (pre-sip′ĭ-tant) Anything that causes a substance in solution to separate as solid particles.

precipitate (pre-sip′ĭ-tāt) 1. To cause a substance in solution to separate as a solid. 2. The solid deposit thus formed. 3. Occurring abnormally fast (e.g., a precipitate labor).

keratic p.'s Nodular clumps of inflammatory cells in the back of the cornea.

precipitation (pre-sip-ĭ-ta′shun) 1. The act of forming a precipitate. 2. Clumping of proteins in serum in response to the action of a specific precipitin.

precipitin (pre-sip′ĭ-tin) An antibody that causes its specific soluble antigen to separate from solution and form solid clumps.

preclinical (pre-klin′ĭ-kal) 1. Before the onset of disease; applied to the stage of a disease before signs and symptoms can be recognized and diagnosed. 2. Occurring before clinical work; applied to the stage of medical education before direct involvement with patients.

precocious (pre-ko′shus) 1. Occurring or developing earlier than usual or normal. 2. Exhibiting such characteristics.

precocity (pre-kos′ĭ-te) Exceptionally early development of physical, mental, or sexual characteristics.

precognition (pre-kog-nish′un) Extrasensory perception or knowledge of an event not yet experienced.

preconscious (pre-kon′shus) In psychoanalysis, thoughts and ideas that are not in immediate awareness but can be recalled at will.

preconvulsive (pre-kon-vul′siv) Preceding a convulsion.

precordial (pre-kor′de-al) Relating to the area of the chest wall over the heart.

P

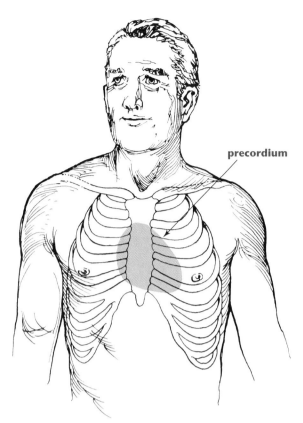

precordium

precordium (pre-kor′de-um) The area of the chest wall that corresponds to the location of the heart.

precostal (pre-kos′tal) In front of the ribs.

precuneus (pre-ku′ne-us) A wedge-shaped convolution of the cortex on the medial surface of each cerebral hemisphere, between the cuneus and the paracentral lobule.

precursor (pre′kur-sor) Anything in the course of a process that precedes, or develops into, a specified product (e.g., an undifferentiated cell or a substance in the earliest stage of a metabolic process).

prediabetes (pre-di-ah-be′tēz) An early stage in the course of diabetes before there is recognizable impairment of carbohydrate metabolism.

predigestion (pre-di-jes′chun) The artificial initiation of digesting food elements before they are used therapeutically as food.

predispose (pre-dis-pōz′) To render vulnerable.

predisposition (pre-dis-po-zish′un) The condition of being susceptible to a disease.

prednisolone (pred-nis′o-lōn) A synthetic glucocorticoid derived from cortisol; it has anti-inflammatory properties.

prednisone (pred′nĭ-sōn) A synthetic glucocorticoid with anti-inflammatory properties; used as a cortisone substitute as it causes less water retention.

predormitum (pre-dor′mĭ-tum) The state of waning consciousness preceding sleep.

predormital (pre-dor′mĭ-tal) Occurring just before sleep.

preductal (pre-duk′tal) Relating to the part of the aorta just proximal to the ligamentum arteriosum (remains of ductus arteriosus).

preeclampsia (pre-e-klamp′se-ah) Disorder occurring in the last trimester of pregnancy characterized by hypertension, edema, and proteinuria; seen most commonly in first pregnancies. Also called toxemia of pregnancy.

preemie (pre′me) See premature infant, under infant.

pre-enzyme (pre-en′zīm) See proenzyme.

preexcitation (pre-ek-si-ta′shun) Premature activation of the ventricular heart muscle due to accelerated conduction in which an impulse bypasses the normal atrioventricular (A-V) conduction pathway; it is an intrinsic feature of the Wolff-Parkinson-White syndrome.

Preferred Provider Organization (PPO) A health plan that offers enrollees access to a panel of health care providers (practitioners and institutions) that have agreed to price discounts and that agree to abide by various kinds of utilization management requirements. See also Health Maintenance Organization (HMO); Point-of-Service (POS) plan.

prefrontal (pre-fron′tal) Relating to the anterior portion of the frontal lobe of the brain.

preganglionic (pre-gang-gle-on′ik) Situated before or proximal to a ganglion.

pregnancy (preg′nan-se) Condition of the female from the time of conception to delivery of the embryo or fetus. A full-term pregnancy usually last 40 weeks. Also called gestation.

   abdominal p. Implantation of a fertilized ovum on a surface within the abdominal cavity, usually resulting from rupture of an early tubal pregnancy.

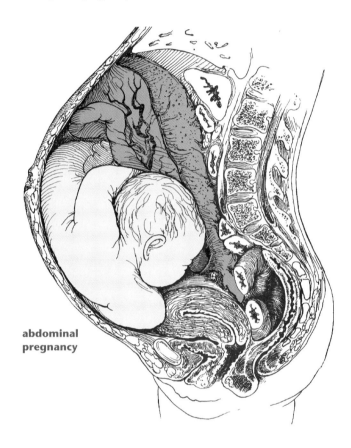

abdominal pregnancy

   adolescent p. Pregnancy in girls under 19 years of age.

   cervical p. Implantation of a fertilized ovum in the lining of the cervical canal; a rare form of ectopic pregnancy.

   cornual p. Pregnancy occurring in women with a double uterus; the fertilized ovum implants within a (usually rudimentary) horn of the uterus.

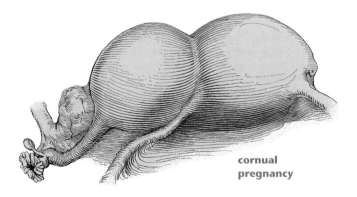

cornual pregnancy

precordium ■ pregnancy

P

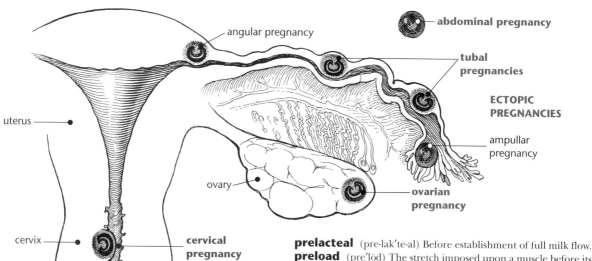

angular pregnancy
abdominal pregnancy
tubal pregnancies
ECTOPIC PREGNANCIES
ampullar pregnancy
uterus
ovarian pregnancy
ovary
cervix
cervical pregnancy
vagina

ectopic p. Implantation of the fertilized ovum outside of the uterine cavity. Also called extrauterine pregnancy; metacyesis; eccyesis.

  extrauterine p. See ectopic pregnancy.
  fallopian p. See tubal pregnancy.
  false p. See pseudocyesis.
  high-risk p. Pregnancy in which the mother, fetus, or newborn is or will be at increased risk of having a disease or of dying before or after delivery; contributing factors include poor nutrition, absence of prenatal care, genetic disorders, unwanted pregnancy; appearance of abruptio placentae or preeclampsia-eclampsia also places the pregnancy at high risk.
  interstitial p. See intramural pregnancy.
  intramural p. Ectopic pregnancy that occurs within the uterine portion of the fallopian (uterine) tube. Also called interstitial pregnancy.
  molar p. See hydatidiform mole, under mole.
  multiple p. Pregnancy with two or more fetuses.
  ovarian p. Ectopic pregnancy occurring within an ovary. Also called oocyesis.
  spurious p. See pseudocyesis.
  tubal p. Ectopic pregnancy occurring within a fallopian (uterine) tube. Also called fallopian pregnancy; salpingocyesis.
pregnane (preg′nān) A saturated steroid hydrocarbon, precursor of the female hormone progesterone and of several hormones of the adrenal cortex.
pregnanediol (preg-nān-di′ol) The chief metabolic end product of the female hormone progesterone; its concentration in the urine indicates corpus luteum function.
pregnanetriol (preg-nān-tri′ol) A precursor in the biosynthesis of the hormone hydrocortisone.
pregnanolone (preg-na′no-lōn) A pregnane found in the urine of pregnant women; it has sedative, anesthetic, and hypnotic properties.
pregnant (preg′nant) Carrying a developing offspring within the body. Also called gravid.
pregnene (preg′nēn) An unsaturated steroid derivative of pregnane.
prehensile (pre-hen′sil) Adapted for grasping.
prehormone (pre-hor′mōn) A glandular secretion that is inactive but capable of being converted into an active hormone.
preictal (pre-ik′tal) Occurring before the onset of a convulsion or stroke.

prelacteal (pre-lak′te-al) Before establishment of full milk flow.
preload (pre′lōd) The stretch imposed upon a muscle before its contraction; in terms of the left ventricle of the heart, it refers to the degree of cardiac return or filling.
premalignant (pre-mah-lig′nant) Precancerous.
premature (pre-mah-tūr′) Occurring before expected, usual, or normal time.
prematurity (pre-mah-tur′ĭ-te) The state of being premature.
premed (pre′med) Popular term for a college student who is preparing for a medical education.
premedicate (pre-med′ĭ-kāt) To administer premedication.
premedication (pre-med-ĭ-ka′shun) A drug or drugs administered prior to induction of anesthesia to allay apprehension and produce sedation, or to prevent or minimize anticipated or possible adverse reactions (e.g., a corticosteroid may be administered prior to the administration of an organic iodine contrast material when there is increased likelihood of an allergic reaction to the contrast substance).
premelanosome (pre-mel′ah-no-sōm) The precursor of a melanin-containing cell (melanosome).
premenarche (pre-mĕ-nar′ke) The period before menstruation is established; before the menarche.
premenstrual (pre-men′stroo-al) Relating to the time of month prior to the onset of the menstrual flow.
premolar (pre-mo′lar) Anterior to a molar tooth; applied to a premolar (bicuspid) tooth.

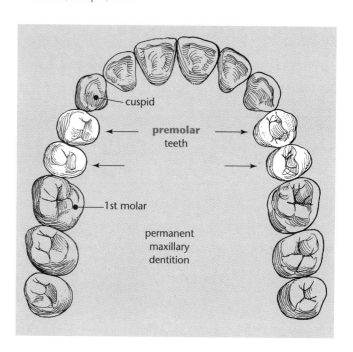

cuspid
premolar teeth
1st molar
permanent maxillary dentition

pregnane ■ premolar

premorbid (pre-mor′bid) Occurring before the appearance of signs and symptoms of a disease.

premunition (pre-mu-nish′un) Relative immunity to a microorganism established after an acute infection becomes chronic; it lasts as long as the infecting organism is in the body.

prenaris (pre-na′ris), pl. prena′res Nostril.

prenatal (pre-na′tal) Before birth. Also called antenatal.

preoperative (pre-op′er-a-tiv) Relating to the period before a surgical operation.

preparation (prep-ah-ra′shun) **1.** Readiness. **2.** In dentistry, reduction of a natural tooth substance prior to inserting a prosthesis (e.g., a crown). **3.** Something that has been made ready for use (e.g., a pharmaceutical agent).

    cavity p. Removal of caries from a tooth and establishment of a cavity that is appropriate to receive and retain a restoration.

    spermicidal p. Any of various vaginal creams, gels, suppositories, and foams that kill sperm; it also acts as a mechanical barrier to the entry of sperm into the cervical canal.

prepatellar (pre-pah-tel′ar) In front of the kneecap (patella).

preprandial (pre-pran′de-al) Occurring before a meal.

prepuce (pre′pūs) **1.** The fold of thin skin overlapping the head of the penis (glans penis) for a variable distance; it is the tissue removed at circumcision. Also called foreskin. **2.** A fold of thin skin overlapping the end of the clitoris (glans clitoris) between the anterior ends of the minor lips (labia minora).

    redundant p. An excessive amount of preputial skin, often difficult to retract over the glans.

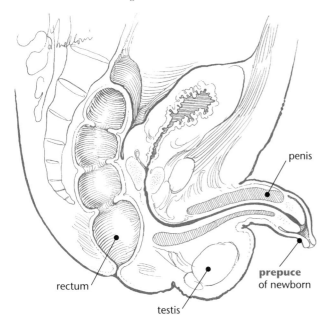

rectum

penis

prepuce of newborn

testis

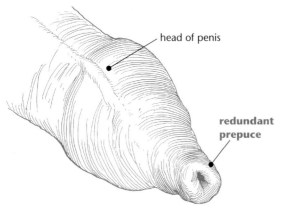

head of penis

redundant prepuce

preputiotomy (pre-pu-she-ot′o-me) Surgical incision of the foreskin (prepuce) of the penis, usually performed to relieve tightness (phimosis).

prepyloric (pre-pi-lor′ik) Relating to the area of the stomach closest to the duodenum, adjacent to the pylorus.

prerenal (pre-re′nal) Situated in front of the kidney or occurring before the kidney.

presbycusis (pres-bĕ-ku′sis) Progressive loss of sound discrimination, especially of the higher frequencies, associated with advancing age.

presbyo-, presby- Combining forms meaning old age.

presbyopia (pres-be-o′pe-ah) (Pr) Increasing loss of visual acuity due to diminished accommodation power of the lens associated with advancing age. Also called old sight.

prescribe (pre-skrīb′) To recommend a remedy for use in the treatment of any disorder.

prescription (pre-skrip′shun) A written instruction by a licensed health practitioner for the preparation and provision of any remedy (e.g., medication, eyeglasses).

    shotgun p. Prescription with several ingredients included in the hope that one or more of them might be effective.

presenility (pre-sĕ-nil′ĭ-te) Premature old age.

present (pre-zent′) **1.** To appear first; applied to the part of the fetus felt by the examining finger during labor. **2.** To become evident; applied to a disease as first noticed by the patient. **3.** To appear for examination or therapy; applied to a patient.

presentation (pre-zen-ta′shun) The position of the fetus in the uterus in relation to the birth canal at the time of labor. Also called fetal presentation.

    breech p. Presentation of the fetal pelvis, named according to three basic forms: *Complete breech p.,* when both thighs are flexed on the abdomen and both legs are flexed at the knee. *Footling breech p.,* when one (single footling breech) or both (double footling breech) legs are extended below the level of the buttocks. *Frank breech p.,* when the legs of the fetus are fully extended over the anterior surface of its body.

    bregma p. A transient cephalic presentation in which the large fontanel of the fetal head is the presenting part and the head is partly extended. Also called sinciput presentation.

    brow p. A transient cephalic presentation in which the brow is the presenting part and the head is partly flexed.

    cephalic p. Presentation in which the fetal head is the presenting part; may be called bregma, brow, face, or vertex presentation, depending on the region of the head that is the presenting part. Also called head presentation.

    compound p. Presentation in which there is a prolapse of an extremity alongside the presenting part into the birth canal.

    p. of the cord See funic presentation.

    face p. A cephalic presentation in which the whole face is the presenting part and the head is sharply extended at the neck.

    footling p. See breech presentation.

    funic p. Presentation in which the umbilical cord prolapses below the level of the presenting part before rupture of the membranes occurs and loops of the cord are palpated through the membranes on pelvic examination. The condition is associated with high fetal mortality and maternal complications. See also prolapse of umbilical cord, under prolapse.

    head p. See cephalic presentation.

    placental p. See placenta previa, under placenta.

    shoulder p. Presentation in which the long axis of the fetus lies transversely with the maternal long axis and one shoulder is the presenting part.

    sinciput p. See bregma presentation.

    vertex p. A cephalic presentation in which the occipital region of the head (the vertex) is the presenting part; the infant's head is sharply flexed, with the chin in contact with the chest.

presomite (pre-so′mīt) Denoting the embryonic stage before the development of somites.

presphygmic (pre-sfig′mik) Preceding a pulse beat; applied to a brief pause following the filling of the heart ventricles with blood before their contraction forces the semilunar valves to open.

pressor (pres'or) Causing constriction of blood vessels and a rise in blood pressure.

pressoreceptor (pres-o-re-sep'tor) See baroreceptor.

pressure (presh'ur) A force exerted against resistance.

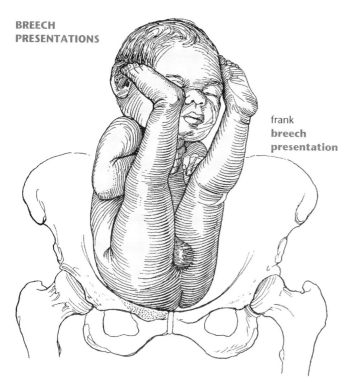

BREECH PRESENTATIONS

frank **breech presentation**

complete **breech presentation**

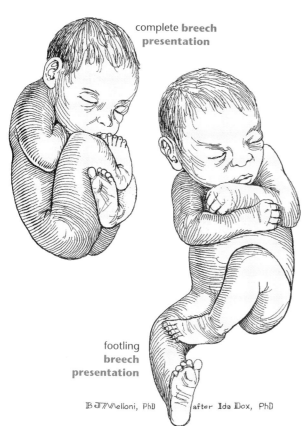

footling **breech presentation**

B.J.Melloni, PhD   after Ida Dox, PhD

alveolar p. The pressure within the terminal air sacs (alveoli) of the lungs.

amniotic p. The pressure within the membranes enveloping the fetus (amniotic sac) secondary to a uterine contraction.

arterial p. Blood pressure within the systemic arteries.

atmospheric p. See barometric pressure.

back p. Pressure exerted upstream in the circulatory system by obstruction to blood flow.

barometric p. (BP) The absolute pressure of the ambient atmosphere. Also called atmospheric pressure.

biting p. See occlusal pressure.

blood p. (BP) Pressure exerted by circulating blood on the arterial walls; it depends on the contraction of the left ventricle, the resistance of the small arteries (arterioles) and capillaries, the elasticity of the arterial walls, and the volume and viscosity of the blood.

central venous p. (CVP) Pressure of blood in the superior or inferior vena cava.

cerebrospinal p. The pressure of the cerebrospinal fluid; normal value, as measured by lumbar puncture with the person lying on one side is 100 to 150 mm of water.

continuous positive airway p. (CPAP) Respiratory therapy in which pressure within the lung airways is maintained above atmospheric pressure throughout the respiratory cycle, preventing collapse of the airway.

diastolic p. The force exerted on the blood vessels when the heart rests; specifically the minimal pressure during any given ventricular cycle.

effective osmotic p. The portion of the total osmotic pressure of a solution controlling the tendency of its solvent to pass through a semipermeable membrane.

expiratory p. The pressure of gas in a patient's airway during exhalation (e.g., when receiving artificial ventilation).

hydrostatic p. In a closed fluid system, the pressure exerted at any level by the weight of the fluid above.

intracranial p. (ICP) Pressure within the skull.

intraocular p. (IOP) Pressure of the fluid within the eye, increased in such conditions as glaucoma. Also called intraocular tension; ocular tension.

intratympanic p. The air pressure within the middle ear chamber (tympanic cavity); normally it is close to that of the ambient atmosphere.

maximum safety p. In anesthesiology, the upper limit of positive pressure permitted in an anesthesia-breathing apparatus, or other related devices; exceeding the limit is considered hazardous to the patient.

mean airway p. (MAP) In respiratory therapy, the average proximal pressure applied to the airway throughout the entire respiratory cycle.

minimum safety p. In anesthesiology, the lower limit of positive pressure permitted in an anesthesia-breathing apparatus, or other related devices; pressure below the limit is considered ineffective.

negative p. Pressure that is less than that of the ambient atmosphere.

negative end-expiratory p. (NEEP) The negative pressure in the lung airways at the end of expiration, as in artificial ventilation.

occlusal p. Any force exerted upon opposing teeth, as when chewing or biting.

oncotic p. Osmotic pressure exerted by colloids in solution.

osmotic p. The pressure that must be exerted to overcome the pressure that substances in solution exert against a barrier (such as a semipermeable membrane) to pull solvent into the solution through the barrier.

partial p. The pressure exerted by a single component of a mixture of several gases.

pleural p. The pressure in the pleural space (between the parietal and visceral layers).

P

pressor ■ pressure

positive end-expiratory p. (PEEP) Technique used in respiratory therapy in which the amount of gases remaining in the lungs is increased by maintaining pressure within the airways.

pulmonary p. Pressure in the pulmonary artery.

pulmonary capillary wedge p. Pressure obtained by wedging the tip of a catheter in a small pulmonary artery; blocking flow provides an indirect measure of the pressure in the left atrium of the heart.

pulp p. Pressure within the pulp cavity of a tooth; it is related to extracellular fluid.

pulse p. Variation in blood pressure in an artery; the difference between systolic (maximal) and diastolic (minimal) blood pressures.

p. of speech Increasingly rapid, and usually loud, speech that is difficult or impossible to interrupt; the individual may talk without any social stimulation and may continue to talk when no one is listening; seen most frequently in manic episodes of manic-depressive disorders; also seen in some organic mental disorders and, occasionally, in acute reactions to stress.

systolic p. The pressure exerted on the blood vessels when the heart contracts; specifically, the maximal pressure reached during any given ventricular cycle.

transmural p. The pressure within a hollow organ relative to the pressure outside its walls.

transpulmonary p. (P_{tp}) The approximate difference between the respired air at the mouth and the pressure around the lungs within the pleural space (pleural pressure).

vapor p. Pressure exerted by molecules of a vapor in equilibrium with its liquid or solid phase.

zero end-expiratory p. (ZEEP) Airway pressure that equals ambient pressure at the end of expiration.

presynaptic (pre-sĭ-nap′tik) 1. Occurring before a synapse is crossed. 2. Situated proximal to a synapse.

presystole (pre-sis′to-le) Immediately preceding a systole.

presystolic (pre-sis-tol′ik) Relating to the interval before a systole.

pretibial (pre-tib′e-al) Relating to the front of the leg.

prevalence (prev′ah-lens) In epidemiology, the number of cases of a disease or other condition in a given population at a designated time.

lifetime p. The total number of persons known to have had the disease under study for at least part of their lives.

period p. The total number of persons known to have had the disease under study at any time during a specified period of time.

point p. The number of persons having a disease under study at a specified point in time.

preventive (pre-ven′tiv) Acting to avert the occurrence of something.

prevertebral (pre-ver′tĕ-bral) In front of a vertebra or of the spine (vertebral column).

prevesical (pre-ves′ĭ-kal) In front of the bladder.

previus (pre′vi-us) Latin for in the way.

priapism (pri′ah-pizm) A condition characterized by continuous erection of the penis without sexual desire; may be associated with certain diseases (e.g., pelvic infections, sickle-cell disease, pelvic tumors), trauma of the penis or spinal cord, or the use of certain medications.

prilocaine hydrochloride (pril′o-kān hi-dro-klo′rĭd) A local anesthetic similar to lidocaine; used for peridural, caudal, and peripheral nerve block anesthesia.

primacy (pri′ma-se) The state of being first or foremost.

primaquine phosphate (prim′ah-kwin fos′fāt) An antimalarial drug.

primary (pri′mar-e) 1. Occurring first; original, not secondary; applied to a disease that has originated in the affected organ or tissue. 2. First or foremost in importance.

prime (prīm) In immunotherapy, to administer an initial sensitization to a substance (an antigen) against which the body would mobilize an immune defense.

primidone (prim′ĭ-dōn) A drug with anticonvulsant properties, usually prescribed in conjunction with another anticonvulsive drug. Adverse effects include clumsiness, drowsiness, and dizziness.

primigravida (pri-mĭ-grav′ĭ-dah) A woman who has been pregnant only once. Also called gravida I.

primipara (pri-mip′ah-rah) A woman who has completed one pregnancy in which the fetus reached the stage of viability, regardless of whether it was a single or multiple birth, or whether the fetus was live or stillborn. Also called para I.

primiparous (pri-mip′ah-rus) Denoting a primipara.

primordium (pri-mor′de-um) A group of cells in an early embryo indicating the first trace of a developing organ or structure of the body; usually denoting a theoretical stage later than anlage.

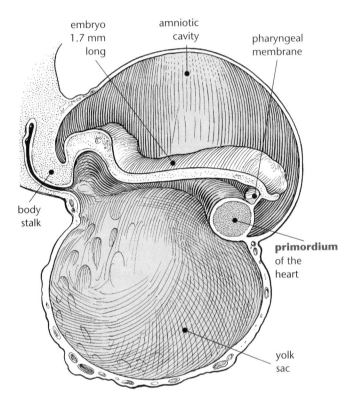

embryo 1.7 mm long — amniotic cavity — pharyngeal membrane — body stalk — primordium of the heart — yolk sac

principle (prin′sĭ-pl) 1. A fundamental tenet or concept. 2. A drug constituent that confers the chief pharmaceutical properties to the drug.

active p. The constituent of a drug to which the drug's physiologic effects are due.

antianemic p. A substance, found mainly in the liver, that stimulates remission of symptoms in pernicious anemia.

Fick p. Principle used in measurement of cardiac output and blood flow to some organs; calculated by dividing oxygen consumption by the arteriovenous difference in blood oxygen concentration.

hematinic p. Vitamin B_{12}.

pain p. An unconscious tendency to strive for pain and death.

pain-pleasure p. In psychoanalytical theory, the concept that humans instinctively avoid pain and discomfort and seek gratification and pleasure. Also called pleasure principle.

pleasure p. See pain-pleasure principle.

reality p. In psychoanalytical theory, the concept that the pain-pleasure principle is normally modified in personality development by the inescapable demands of the external world (e.g., postponement of gratification to a more appropriate time).

repetition-compulsion p. The concept that humans have a need to recreate and dramatize an earlier (usually painful) experience.

prion (pri′on) The smallest known infectious particle; a viruslike entity with at least one protein but no demonstrable nucleic acid (DNA or RNA); it is resistant to inactivation by most commonly used procedures.

prism (priz′m) A transparent body, usually made of optical glass or crystalline material, with at least two polished plane faces inclined toward each other from which light is reflected or through which light is refracted.

P

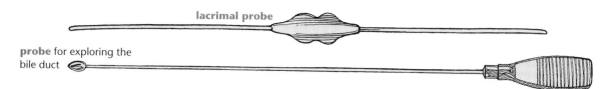

lacrimal probe

probe for exploring the bile duct

privacy (pri'vah-se) **1.** Confidentiality. **2.** In psychiatry and clinical psychology, respect for the nature of the therapist-patient relationship.

pro- Prefix meaning before; forward; precursor of.

proarrhythmia (pro-ah-rith'me-ah) Drug-induced worsening of irregular heartbeat (arrhythmia).

probacteriophage (pro-bak-te're-o-fāj) See prophage.

proband (pro'band) In genetics, the first member of a family in whom a trait is observed, which leads to observation of other family members to study the characteristics of the trait. Also called propositus; index case. COMPARE consultant.

probang (pro'bang) A slender flexible rod with a tuft or ball of a soft material at the tip; used to apply medication or remove material from the esophagus or the larynx.

probe (prōb) **1.** A slender flexible rod with a blunt tip for exploring a wound or a body cavity. **2.** In genetics, a reagent capable of recognizing the clone of concern in a complex mixture of many DNA or RNA sequences. **3.** To explore.

   electric p. One used during a surgical procedure to locate a foreign particle.

   lacrimal p. A probe for passing through the tear drainage channels to remove an obstruction.

   periodontal p. A calibrated probe to measure the depth of pathologic pockets around a tooth.

probenecid (pro-ben'ĕ-sid) A drug that enhances excretion of uric acid by inhibiting its reabsorption by the kidney tubules; it also slows excretion of such antibiotics as penicillin.

probiosis (pro-bi-o'sis) See symbiosis (1).

problem (prob'lem) **1.** Any situation that presents difficulty, conflict, or uncertainty. **2.** In the mental health professions, a term sometimes preferred to the term mental disorder; often used to denote a person whose behavior deviates from the norm (e.g., problem child).

proboscis (pro-bos'is) **1.** A severe developmental malformation of the nasal structures. **2.** A tubular feeding structure of certain animals (e.g., mosquitoes, leeches).

procainamide hydrochloride (pro-kān'ah-mīd hi-dro-klo'rīd) A drug that depresses the irritability of heart muscle; used in the treatment of cardiac arrhythmias.

procaine hydrochloride (pro'kān hi-dro-klo'rīd) Anesthetic drug used for infiltration and spinal anesthesia.

procarbazine hydrochloride (pro-kar'bah-zēn hi-dro-klo'rīd) An anticancer drug.

procarcinogen (pro-kar-sin'o-jen) A substance, usually a chemical, that produces cancer only after it is converted into a metabolically active compound within the body.

procaryote (pro-kar'e-ōt) See prokaryote.

procedure (pro-se'jur) A series of steps undertaken to accomplish something; may be for diagnostic, therapeutic, or surgical purposes.

   Irving's p. See Irving's operation, under operation.

   loop electrosurgical excision p. (LEEP) A method of removing tissue for biopsy (e.g., from the uterine cervix) using an electrosurgical unit that supplies low levels of electrical current for cutting or coagulation with a thin (0.2-mm) stainless steel wire.

   Madlener's p. See Madlener's operation, under operation.

   Pomeroy's p. See Pomeroy's operation, under operation.

   swim-up p. In *in vitro* fertilization (IVF), a method of preparing semen specimens aimed at obtaining high-quality spermatozoa; the specimen is centrifuged several times to concentrate the spermatozoa in pellets of solid material at the bottom of the centrifuge tubes; a special fluid is poured on top, followed by incubation at body temperature for 30 to 60 minutes. The most motile spermatozoa swim out of the solid mass into the fluid, leaving the less active ones at the bottom of the tube.

procedurist (pro-se'jur-ist) A physician who specializes in a procedure-oriented branch of medicine (e.g., surgery, interventional radiology or cardiology, endoscopic gastroenterology) as opposed to a cognitive-oriented specialty (e.g., psychiatry, internal medicine, rheumatology).

procercoid (pro-ser'koid) The larval stage of certain tapeworms.

process (pros'es) **1.** A marked prominence extending from an anatomic structure, usually a bony extension for the attachment of muscles and ligaments. **2.** A series of actions that achieve a specific result. **3.** A course of events.

   acromial p. See acromion.

   articular p. of sacrum One of two rounded processes projecting upwardly from the top surface of the sacrum, bearing the hyaline-coated concave joint surface for articulation with the inferior articular facet of the fifth lumbar vertebra.

P

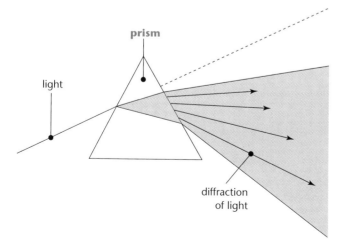

prism

light

diffraction of light

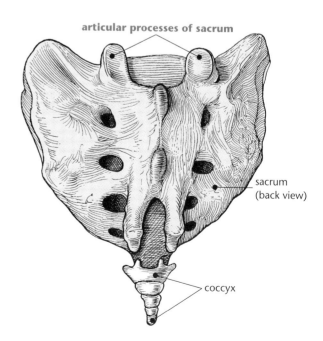

articular processes of sacrum

sacrum (back view)

coccyx

articular p. of vertebra One of the small projections on the upper and lower surfaces of the vertebra, on either side: *Inferior articular p. of vertebra,* one of a pair of downward projections from the lamina of a vertebra, bearing the hyaline-coated facet for articulation with the vertebra below. *Superior articular p. of vertebra,* one of a pair of upward projections from the junction of the pedicle and lamina, bearing the hyaline-coated facet for articulation with the vertebra above.

ciliary p.'s Radiating pigmented ridges (from 70 to 80 in number) on the inner ringlike surface of the ciliary body; formed by the inward folding of the various layers of the choroid; they provide attachment for the suspensory ligament of the lens of the eye.

clinoid p. One of three pairs of extensions from the sphenoid bone of the skull: *Anterior clinoid p.,* one of a pair of tips directed medially, from the posterior border of the lesser wing of the sphenoid bone; it provides attachment for the anterior end of the free border of the tentorium cerebelli. *Middle alinoid p.* A small projection on each side of the hypophyseal fossa, between the anterior and posterior clinoid processes. *Posterior clinoid p.,* one of a pair of processes situated at the anterosuperior border of the dorsum sellae in back of the hypophyseal fossa; it provides attachment for the fixed margin of the tentorium cerebelli.

condylar p. of mandible The projection from the upper part of the posterior margin of the ramus of the lower jaw; composed of a constricted, slightly flattened neck and an expanded head bearing a knuckle-shaped condyle. The process can be felt in front of the tragus of the ear.

coracoid p. A thick, strong, curved bony process arising from the superior border of the shoulder blade (scapula), partly overhanging the glenoid fossa; it provides attachment for the short head of the biceps muscle of arm, the coracobrachial muscle, and the smaller pectoral muscle (pectoralis minor muscle); it also provides attachment for the conoid and coracoacromial ligaments. The process can be felt below the lateral third of the collarbone (clavicle).

coronoid p. of mandible The flattened triangular process at the upper anterior part of the ramus of the lower jaw; it provides attachment for most of the fibers of the temporal muscle.

coronoid p. of ulna A wide bracketlike projection from the front of the proximal end of the ulna at the elbow joint, just below the olecranon; it forms the lower boundary of the trochlear notch.

frontal p. of maxilla The process of the maxilla extending upward to articulate with the frontal, nasal, and lacrimal bones; it forms the medial boundary of the orbit.

P

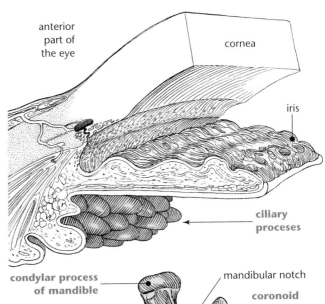

anterior part of the eye

cornea

iris

ciliary processes

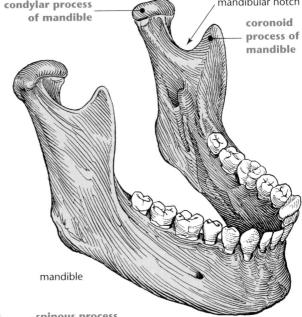

condylar process of mandible

mandibular notch

coronoid process of mandible

mandible

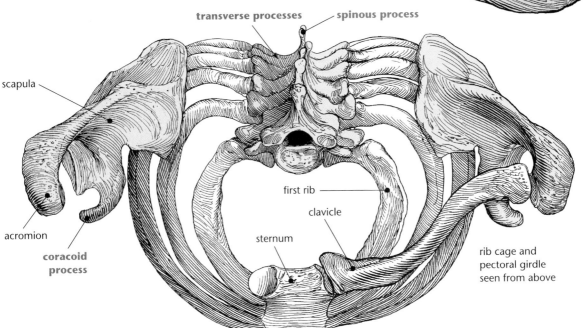

transverse processes

spinous process

scapula

first rib

clavicle

sternum

acromion

coracoid process

rib cage and pectoral girdle seen from above

frontal p. of zygomatic bone The process of the zygomatic bone extending upward to articulate with the frontal bone and behind with the greater wing of the sphenoid bone; it forms the lateral boundary of the orbit.

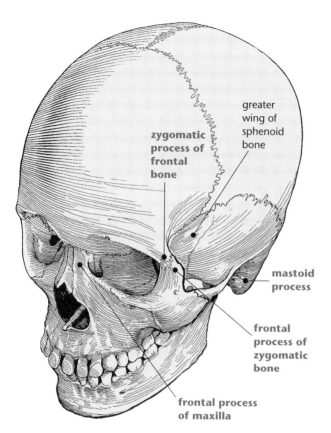

zygomatic process of frontal bone

greater wing of sphenoid bone

mastoid process

frontal process of zygomatic bone

frontal process of maxilla

p.'s of incus Processes projecting from the incus, the middle auditory ossicle: *Long p. of incus,* a slender process projecting downward from the body of the incus; its lower end bends and terminates in a bulbous form (the lenticular process) for articulation with the head of the stapes, the smallest auditory ossicle. *Short p. of incus,* a conical process that projects posteriorly from the body of the incus; it is attached to the wall of the middle ear chamber by small ligaments.

lenticular p. of incus The rounded projection extending at a right angle from the long process of the incus of the middle ear chamber; it articulates with the head of the stapes.

p.'s of malleus Processes projecting from the malleus, the largest auditory ossicle: *Anterior p. of malleus,* a slender bony spicule directed anteriorly from just below the neck of the malleus toward the petrotympanic fissure, where it is connected by small ligaments. *Lateral p. of malleus,* a blunt lateral process that projects from the root of the handle (manubrium) of the malleus, attaching to the upper part of the eardrum (tympanic membrane), thereby dividing the eardrum into a small flaccid part (pars flaccida) above and a larger taut part (pars tensa) below.

mamillary p. of vertebra A small, rough elevation on the superior articular process of the lumbar vertebra for muscle attachment.

mastoid p. A downward conical projection of the mastoid part of the temporal bone of the skull; situated behind the ear with its apex on a level with the middle of the ear lobe; it contains the mastoid air cells, and its lateral surface provides attachment for the sternocleidomastoid muscle and the splenius and longissimus muscles of the head.

odontoid p. of axis A toothlike process, or dens, of the second cervical vertebra that protrudes sharply upward from the vertebral body to articulate with the first cervical vertebra; in the adult, it is about 1.5 cm in length.

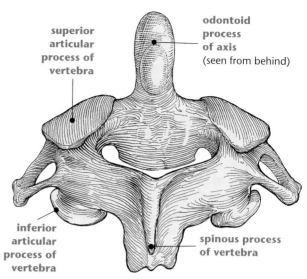

superior articular process of vertebra

odontoid process of axis (seen from behind)

inferior articular process of vertebra

spinous process of vertebra

primary p. In psychoanalysis, a type of thinking characterized by immediate gratification, the lack of any sense of time, and the use of allusion, analogy, and symbolic representation. Also called nonlogical thinking. COMPARE secondary process.

pterygoid p. A long bony mass extending downward from the base of the skull, at the junction of the body of the sphenoid bone and the greater wing, on either side; it consists of parallel medial and lateral plates, the upper anterior parts of which are fused together, while the posterior parts diverge to form the pterygoid fossa.

secondary p. In psychoanalysis, a type of thinking controlled by the laws that govern conscious (or preconscious) mental activity; marked by logical thinking, and by the tendency to delay gratification. COMPARE primary process.

spinous p. of vertebra The elongated process that projects backward from the junction of the laminae of the vertebral arch; it provides attachment for ligaments and muscles of the back. See also vertebral spine, under spine.

styloid p. of fibula A process extending upward on the posterolateral surface of the upper end of the fibular head; it provides attachment for the arcuate popliteal ligament of the knee joint and for the tendon of the biceps muscle of thigh (biceps femoris muscle). Also called apex of head of fibula.

styloid p. of radius A downward-directed blunt conical process on the lateral surface of the lower end of the radius; can be felt through the skin when the overlying tendons are relaxed.

styloid p. of temporal bone A slender, tapering process of variable length, extending downward and slightly forward from the base of the skull; it provides attachment for the stylopharyngeus, styloglossus, and stylohyoid muscles and for the stylomandibular and stylohyoid ligaments.

P

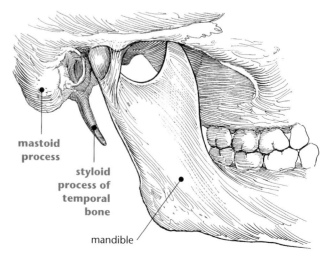

mastoid process

styloid process of temporal bone

mandible

styloid p. of ulna A short, rounded, nonarticular process at the lower end of the posteromedial surface of the ulna; its tip can be felt through the skin on the posteromedial aspect of the wrist.

temporal p. of zygomatic bone The posterior prolongation of the zygomatic bone that articulates with the zygomatic process of the temporal bone to form the zygomatic arch.

transverse p.'s Lateral projections present on each side of the vertebra; in the thorax, they articulate with the ribs.

trochlear p. of calcaneus A small ridgelike projection from the lateral side of the heel bone (calcaneus) that separates the tendons of the long and short peroneal muscles; located approximately 1 inch below the lateral malleolus.

uncinate p. of pancreas The inferior extension of the head of the pancreas, projecting like a hook to the left and behind the superior mesenteric vessels.

xiphoid p. The small, flat, pointed process connected to the lower end of the body of the breastbone (sternum); it is cartilaginous in youth and ossifies with passing age; it provides attachment for the thoracic and abdominal muscles; so called because of its sword shape. Also called xiphoid cartilage.

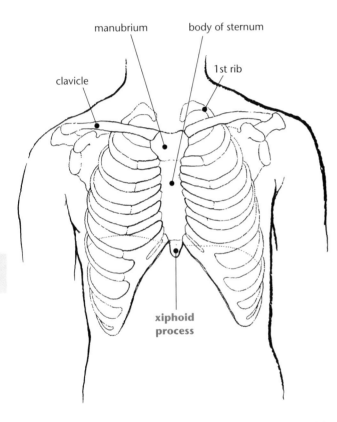

manubrium · body of sternum · clavicle · 1st rib · xiphoid process

zygomatic p. of frontal bone The thick prolongation of the supraorbital margin of the frontal bone that articulates with the frontal process of the zygomatic bone to form the lateral margin of the orbit.

zygomatic p. of maxilla The broad, rough, pyramidal projection from the anterior surface of the maxilla that articulates with the zygomatic bone.

zygomatic p. of temporal bone The narrow prolongation of the temporal bone projecting anteriorly to articulate with the temporal process of the zygomatic bone to form the zygomatic arch.

prochlorperazine (pro-klōr-per'ah-zēn) Compound used as a tranquilizer to relieve the symptoms of certain psychiatric disorders and, in small doses, to arrest nausea and vomiting.

prochondral (pro-kon'dral) Relating to the embryonic stage prior to formation of cartilage.

procidentia (pro-si-den'she-ah) Complete prolapse of an organ.

procollagen (pro-kol'ah-jen) A soluble precursor of collagen.

proconvertin (pro-kon-ver'tin) See factor VII, under factor.

procreate (pro-kre-at') To produce offspring.

proctalgia (prok-tal'je-ah) Pain in the rectum and in or around the anus. Also called proctodynia; rectalgia.

p. fugax Spasm and pain in the anus lasting only a few minutes; cause is unknown. Also called anorectal spasm.

proctatresia (prok-tah-tre'ze-ah) See imperforate anus, under anus.

proctectasia (prok-tek-ta'ze-ah) Dilatation of the anus or rectum.

proctectomy (prok-tek'to-me) Removal of the rectum.

proctencleisis, proctenclisis (prok-ten-kli'sis) See proctostenosis.

proctitis (prok-ti'tis) Inflammation of the mucous membrane of the rectum, usually caused by rectal gonorrhea, chlamydia infection, candidiasis, or syphilis. Symptoms include passage of blood, mucus, or pus with the stools; painful ineffectual straining to defecate (tenesmus); and pain in the anus and rectum.

procto-, proct- Combining forms meaning anus; rectum.

proctocele (prok'to-sēl) See rectocele.

proctoclysis (prok-tok'lĭ-sis) The slow, continuous infusion of saline solution into the rectum and sigmoid colon. Also called rectoclysis.

proctocolitis (prok-to-ko-li'tis) See coloproctitis.

proctocolectomy (prok-to-ko-lek'to-me) Removal of the rectum and part of, or the entire, colon and connection of the end of the remaining intestine to the abdominal wall, with a permanent opening (ostomy) through the wall.

restorative p. Proctocolectomy with formation of an ileoanal reservoir (pouch) instead of an ostomy, thus allowing transanal defecation; performed on patients with such intestinal diseases as ulcerative colitis.

proctocolonoscopy (prok-to-ko-lon-os'ko-pe) Examination of the colon and rectum.

proctocolpoplasty (prok-to-kol'po-plas-te) Surgical closure of an abnormal channel (fistula) between the rectum and vagina.

proctocystocele (prok-to-sis'to-sēl) Bulging of the bladder into the rectum.

proctocystotomy (prok-to-sis-tot'o-me) Incision into the bladder through the rectum.

proctodeum (prok-to-de'um) An ectodermal depression of the embryo at the point where the anal orifice will eventually develop. Also called anal pit.

proctodynia (prok-to-din'e-ah) See proctalgia.

proctologic (prok-to-loj'ik) Relating to proctology.

proctologist (prok-tol'o-jist) A specialist in proctology.

proctology (prok-tol'o-je) The study and treatment of diseases and injuries of the rectum and anus.

proctoparalysis (prok-to-pah-ral'ĭ-sis) Paralysis of the muscles of the anus resulting in fecal incontinence; may be caused by injury or disease.

proctoperineoplasty (prok-to-per-ĭ-ne'o-plas-te) Plastic surgery of the anus and surrounding tissues (perineum). Also called rectoperineorrhaphy.

proctopexy (prok'to-pek-se) The suturing of a prolapsed rectum to another structure into a more normal position. Also called rectopexy.

proctoplasty (prok'to-plas-te) Reparative surgery upon the anus or rectum. Also called rectoplasty.

proctoplegia (prok-to-ple'je-ah) Paralysis of the anus and rectum.

proctoptosia, proctoptosis (prok-top-to'ze-ah, prok-top-to'sis) Prolapse of the rectum and anus.

proctorrhagia (prok-to-ra'je-ah) Passage of a bloody discharge from the rectum.

proctorrhaphy (prok-tor'ah-fe) Reparative suturing of a lacerated rectum or anus. Also called rectorrhaphy.

proctorrhea (prok-to-re'ah) Mucous discharge from the rectum.

proctoscope (prok'to-skōp) An instrument used for inspection of the rectal mucosa. Also called rectoscope.

proctoscopy (prok-tos'ko-pe) Examination of the rectal mucosa

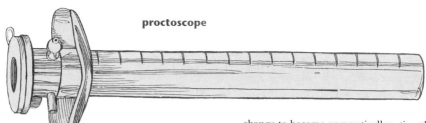

proctoscope

with a proctoscope. It is used to locate, identify, and photograph tissue changes; to obtain biopsy material and perform other surgical procedures; and for introducing medication. Also called rectoscopy.

proctosigmoidectomy (prok-to-sig-moi-dek′to-me) Removal of the rectum and sigmoid colon.

proctosigmoiditis (prok-to-sig-moi-di′tis) Inflammation of the rectum and sigmoid colon.

proctosigmoidoscopy (prok-to-sig-moi-dos′ko-pe) Examination of the sigmoid colon, rectum, and anal canal with a sigmoidoscope; if a flexible instrument is used, the descending colon may also be examined; usually indicated when there have been changes in bowel habits, lower abdominal and perineal pain, prolapse of the rectum on defecation, itchiness (pruritis), or the passage of blood, mucus, or pus in the stool; also performed routinely as a screening technique to detect cancer.

proctospasm (prok′to-spazm) Spasmodic contraction of the anus and rectum.

proctostat (prok′to-stat) A radium-containing tube inserted in the rectum (through the anus) for the treatment of rectal cancer.

proctostenosis (prok-to-stĕ-no′sis) Abnormal narrowing of the anus or rectum. Also called rectostenosis; proctencleisis; proctenclisis.

proctostomy (prok-tos′to-me) The surgical formation of a permanent opening into the rectum.

proctotomy (prok-tot′o-me) A surgical cut into the anus or rectum.

proctovalvotomy (prok-to-val-vot′o-me) A surgical cut into a rectal valve.

procumbent (pro-kum′bent) Lying facedown; prone.

prodromal (pro-dro′mal) Relating to a prodrome.

prodrome (pro′drōm) An early symptom.

prodrug (pro′drug) A medication that must undergo chemical conversion by metabolic processes in the body before becoming a pharmacologically active drug.

product (prod′ukt) Any substance resulting from a natural process, or that is manufactured synthetically.

    cleavage p. A substance produced by the splitting of large, complex molecules into simpler ones.

    drug p. A finished dosage form (e.g., tablet, capsule, or solution) that contains a drug substance, generally (not necessarily) in association with other (single or multiple) ingredients.

    fibrin/fibrinogen p. Any of several small peptides formed in the breakdown of the proteins fibrin and fibrinogen. Also called fibrin-split product; split product.

    fibrin-split p. See fibrin/fibrinogen product.

    gene p. A protein that was formed through gene management (i.e., encoded by a gene).

    orphan p. Drugs, biologicals (e.g., sera, vaccines, antitoxins), tests, or medical devices that, although proven useful, are not manufactured because they are not considered commercially profitable, usually because of very limited application. Also called orphan drug; orphan.

    split p. See fibrin/fibrinogen product.

productive (pro-duk′tiv) Bringing forth (e.g., a cough that brings forth mucus).

proencephalon (pro-en-sef′ah-lon) See prosencephalon.

proenzyme (pro-en′zim) An inactive protein that requires some change to become enzymatically active; the precursor of an enzyme. Also called zymogen; pre-enzyme.

proerythroblast (pro-ĕ-rith′ro-blast) See pronormoblast.

proerythrocyte (pro-ĕ-rith′ro-sit) An immature red blood cell (erythrocyte); unlike an erythrocyte, it has a nucleus.

profile (pro′fil) 1. A summary. 2. A simple outline. 3. A collection of medical data.

    biophysical p. (BPP) In obstetrics, assessment of fetal well-being that takes into consideration fetal body movements and their relationship to fetal heart rate (FHR), position of arms and legs (normally flexed), and amount of fluid in the amniotic sac; data are obtained with ultrasound scanning and external monitoring.

    health p. In occupational medicine, a set of data relating to a person's psychologic, physical, and physiologic attributes that is used as an indicator of fitness for work (includes the person's general condition, vision, hearing, intelligence, and behavior).

profiling (pro-fil′ing) See DNA typing, under typing.

profunda (pro-fun′da) Latin (feminine) for deep; applied to certain anatomic structures (e.g., an artery).

profundus (pro-fun′dus) Latin (masculine) for deep; applied to certain anatomic structures (e.g., a nerve).

progeria (pro-je′re-ah) A rare condition affecting adults and children in which persons undergo accelerated aging, independent of disease processes or environmental factors.

progestational (pro-jes-ta′shun-al) 1. Conducive to conception. 2. Having effects similar to those of progesterone; applied to certain pharmaceutical preparations.

progesterone (pro-jes′tĕ-ron) Steroid hormone, produced in the ovary by the corpus luteum, necessary for establishment and maintenance of pregnancy; it stimulates changes in the uterine wall in preparation for implantation of the fertilized ovum. Luteal-phase deficiency of progesterone is implicated in some cases of infertility.

progestin (pro-jes′tin) 1. A hormone of the corpus luteum that acts on the uterine lining (endometrium). 2. General term for a synthetic drug providing such action.

progestogen (pro-jes′to-jen) An agent that produces biologic effects similar to those of progesterone.

proglossis (pro-glos′is) The tip of the tongue.

prognathic (prog-na′thik) See prognathous.

prognathism (prog′nah-thizm) Abnormal forward projection of one or both jaws.

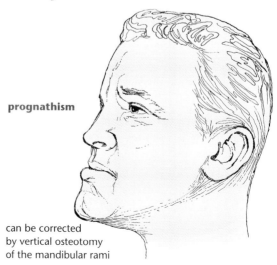

prognathism

can be corrected
by vertical osteotomy
of the mandibular rami

P

prognathous (prog-na'thus) Characterized by prognathism. Also called prognathic.

prognose (prog-nōs') See prognosticate.

prognosis (prog-no'sis) The probable outcome of a disease; the prospects of recovery.

prognosticate (prog-nos'tĭ-kāt) To predict the probable cause and eventual outcome of a disease. Also called prognose.

program (pro'gram) A plan of procedure or action taken toward a desired goal.

  health care quality assurance p. A program designed to ensure the quality of patient care in a health care facility. It may include such activities as review of patient charts (for verification of diagnosis and assessment of conformation to standards of treatment); tabulation of operative morbidity and mortality; implementation of steps to correct deficiencies (if any); and follow-up of corrective steps (if necessary).

progranulocyte (pro-gran'u-lo-sit) See promyelocyte.

progression (pro-gresh'un) 1. An advancement (e.g., of a disease). 2. The forward movement of spermatozoa.

progressive (pro-gres'iv) Denoting increasing involvement or severity of a disease.

prohormone (pro-hor'mōn) A precursor of a hormone.

proinsulin (pro-in'su-lin) The precursor of insulin; a single-chain molecule in the beta cell of the pancreas; it is formed in the endoplasmic reticulum of the cell and transferred to the Golgi apparatus, where its connecting peptide (C peptide) is removed by an enzyme, resulting in the formation of insulin.

projection (pro-jek'shun) 1. A prominence; a part that juts out. 2. The referring of sensations from the sense organs to the source of the stimulus. 3. The connection between the sense organs and the cerebral cortex. 4. An unconscious psychological defense mechanism in which ideas, affects, or traits that are unacceptable to the self are attributed to another person. 5. The application of x rays to a bodily part in a particular direction as it relates to the x-ray tube, e.g., anteroposterior (AP), posteroanterior (PA), right anterior oblique (RAO), right posterior oblique (RPO), left anterior oblique (LAO), left posterior oblique (LPO). Also called view.

  Caldwell p. Radiographic projection obtained by placing the face against the cassette and the x-ray tube 15° caudad in a posteroanterior plane; permits unobstructed viewing of orbital structures and paranasal sinuses.

  erroneous p. See false projection.

  false p. The misjudging of an object's spatial position, due to palsy or underaction of an ocular muscle. Also called erroneous projection.

  geniculostriate p. See optic radiation, under radiation.

  Towne p. Radiographic projection obtained with the patient supine and the back of the head against the cassette and the x-ray tube 30° caudad in an anteroposterior plane; permits viewing of occipital bone, foramen magnum, dorsum sellae, petrous bones, and condyles of mandible.

  Waters p. A radiographic projection of the skull in a posteroanterior plane; permits viewing of facial bones and maxillary sinuses.

prokaryote (pro-kar'e-ōt) Any simple unicellular organism that lacks a nuclear membrane and other cellular elements. Also spelled procaryote.

prolactin (pro-lak'tin) (PRL) A hormone produced in the anterior lobe of the pituitary (adenohypophysis) that stimulates milk secretion.

prolactinoma (pro-lak-tĭ-no'mah) A prolactin-producing adenoma of the anterior lobe of the pituitary (adenohypophysis).

prolapse (pro-laps') The downward displacement of a body part or organ.

  mitral valve p. Posterior displacement of the posterior (occasionally the anterior) leaflet of the mitral valve, occurring in middle or late systole, and often producing a click that may be followed by a late systolic murmur; may cause backflow (regurgitation) of blood through the valve; found with increased incidence in Marfan's syndrome and atrial septal defect. Associated with an increased frequency of arrhythmias. See also Barlow syndrome.

  rectal p. Protrusion of the inner lining of the rectum through the anus; may involve the full thickness of the rectum (a rare condition).

  p. of umbilical cord Descent of the umbilical cord toward the cervix during childbirth; it may lie next to the presenting part (occult cord prolapse) or below the presenting part (overt cord prolapse). See also funic presentation, under presentation.

  p. of uterus Descent of the uterus into the vagina due to stretching and laxity of its supporting structures. Commonly called falling of the womb.

proliferation (pro-lif-ĕ-ra'shun) Increase in numbers (e.g., of cells).

  atypical melanotic p. See melanoma *in situ*, under melanoma.

  pagetoid melanotic p. See melanoma *in situ*, under melanoma.

prolific (pro-lif'ik) Producing many children.

proline (pro'lin) (Pro) An amino acid present in collagen.

promazine hydrochloride (pro'mah-zēn hi-dro-klo'rīd) An antipsychotic drug that acts as a tranquilizer and relieves nausea and vomiting (e.g., after anesthesia). Possible adverse effects include abnormal movements of the face and limbs, dry mouth, and blurred vision.

promegaloblast (pro-meg'ah-lo-blast) A large immature red blood cell; it has a nucleus and represents the earliest stage in the maturation of the megaloblast.

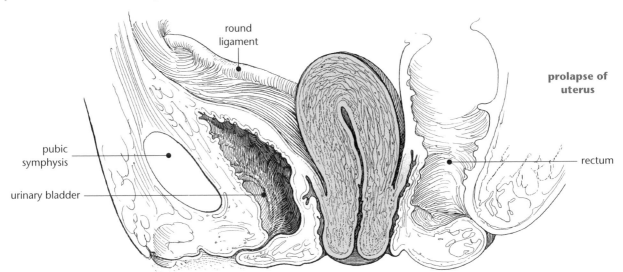

round ligament

pubic symphysis

urinary bladder

prolapse of uterus

rectum

prometaphase (pro-met'ah-fāz) A stage in cell division (mitosis) during which the nuclear membrane disintegrates and the centrioles migrate to the cell poles.

promethazine hydrochloride (pro-meth'ah-zēn hi-dro-klo'rīd) An antihistamine drug that relieves itchy skin conditions caused by allergies; it also relieves nausea and vomiting (e.g., in motion sickness and Ménière's disease). Adverse effects include drowsiness, blurred vision, and dry mouth.

promethium (pro-me'the-um) Radioactive rare-earth element; symbol Pm, atomic number 61.

prominence (prom'ĭ-nens) A projection or elevation.

    canine p. See canine eminence, under eminence.

    laryngeal p. See Adam's apple.

    p. of malleus A small projection on the upper inner surface of the eardrum (tympanic membrane), seen on otoscopic examination, and produced by the underlying lateral process of the first ear ossicle (malleus); it separates the small flaccid part of the eardrum from the larger tense portion.

promontory (prom'on-to-re) A projecting part.

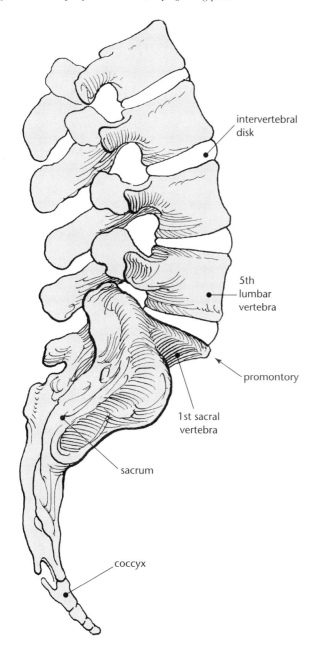

intervertebral disk

5th lumbar vertebra

promontory

1st sacral vertebra

sacrum

coccyx

promoter (pro-mo'ter) **1.** In neoplasia, a chemical substance that has no cancer-causing activity but is capable of enhancing development of a cancerous tumor in a tissue previously exposed to a carcinogen. **2.** In genetics, the area on DNA in which RNA polymerase binds and initiates synthesis of messenger RNA (mRNA), and thereby transcription of genetic code information.

promotion (pro-mo'shun) In chemical carcinogenesis, the stage in the process of cancerous tumor development in which one or more chemicals known as promoters (e.g., drugs, hormones, phorbol compounds) act upon previously initiated cells (i.e., cells that have been exposed to, and permanently changed by, another chemical); the promoters, by themselves, cannot cause tumor formation and their effect is reversible. See also initiation.

promyelocyte (pro-mi'ĕ-lo-sīt) Cell representing a stage in the development of a granular leukocyte, between myeloblast and myelocyte; it contains large granules and, often, nucleoli. Also called progranulocyte.

pronate (pro'nāt) To assume, or to be placed in, a face-down position.

pronation (pro-na'shun) **1.** Rotation of the forearm so that the palm of the hand faces downward or backward. **2.** An act of lying in a face-down position.

pronator (pro-na'tor) Any muscle involved in turning a part into the prone position.

prone (prōn) Lying with the face downward.

pronephros (pro-nef'ros) In embryology, the earliest kidney tissue, consisting of a series of rudimentary tubules.

pronometer (pro-nom'ĕ-ter) See goniometer.

pronormoblast (pro-nor'mo-blast) A cell representing the earliest stage in the development of the normoblast. Also called proerythroblast.

pronucleus (pro-nu'kle-us) One of two nuclei (haploid nuclei) undergoing fusion, as of an egg and sperm at the time of fertilization.

pro-otic (pro ot'ik) In front of the ear.

propagate (prop'ah-gāt) **1.** To reproduce. **2.** To move along; applied to a nerve impulse that moves along a nerve fiber.

propantheline (pro-pan'thĕ-lēn) A drug with antispasmodic properties, effective in such conditions as irritable bowel syndrome. Possible adverse effects include dry mouth, inability to empty the bladder, and constipation.

proparacaine hydrochloride (pro-par'ah-kān hi-dro-klo'rīd) A local anesthetic derived from aminobenzoic acid, used topically on the eye.

properdin (pro'per-din) A natural protein in human blood serum; it is a component of the alternative complement pathway and acts in conjunction with complement and magnesium ions; it plays a role in providing immunity from infectious diseases.

properitoneal (pro-per-ĭ-to-ne'al) In front of the peritoneum.

prophage (pro'fāj) A bacteriophage incorporated into the entire genetic composition of a bacterial cell and replicating along with the bacterial genes. It does not destroy the bacterial cell. Also called probacteriophage.

prophase (pro'fāz) The first stage of cell division (mitosis or meiosis) in which the chromosomes become visible, the nucleus begins to lose its identity, and the centrioles migrate to opposite poles of the cell.

prophylactic (pro-fĭ-lak'tik) **1.** Tending to prevent disease; applied to procedures, drugs, or equipment. **2.** Popular name for a condom.

prophylaxis (pro-fĭ-lak'sis) **1.** Measures taken to prevent disease. **2.** In dentistry, cleaning of the teeth.

propositus (pro-poz'ĭ-tus) See proband.

propoxyphene hydrochloride (pro-pok'se-fēn hi-dro-chlo'rīd) A mild analgesic structurally related to methadone.

propranolol hydrochloride (pro-pran'o-lōl hi-dro-chlo'rīd) An adrenergic beta-receptor blocking drug that reduces the rate and contractile force of the heart, causing a fall in cardiac output and cardiac work. Uses include treatment of high blood pressure, irregular heart rhythms, and prevention of migraine headache.

P

proprietary (pro-pri′ĕ-tă-re) **1.** Privately owned (e.g., a hospital). **2.** Protected by private ownership, which conveys the exclusive right to manufacture and sale (e.g., a drug or a chemical).

p. name See trade name, under name.

proprioceptor (pro-pre-o-sep′tor) A sensory nerve ending, mainly located within muscles and tendons, that collects information relating to sensations of the body's movements and position.

muscle p. See muscle spindle, under spindle.

proptometer (prop-tom′ĕ-ter) See exophthalmometer.

proptosis (prop-to′sis) Protrusion of any organ (e.g., eyeball).

propulsion (pro-pul′shun) Displacement of the center of gravity, resulting in a tendency to lean or fall forward when walking; seen in Parkinson's disease.

propyl alcohol (pro′pil al′ko-hol) Toxic substance widely used as a solvent.

propylthiouracil (pro-pil-thi-o-u′rah-sil) (PTU) A drug that inhibits production of thyroid hormones; used in the treatment of hyperthyroidism.

pro re nata (pro re na′tah) (p.r.n.) Latin for when necessary.

prosector (pro-sek′tor) One who prepares dissections for anatomic demonstrations.

prosectorium (pro-sek-to′re-um) A dissecting room; an anatomy laboratory.

prosencephalon (pros-en-sef′ah-lon) The portion of the embryonic brain developed from the most anterior part of the neural tube; later it forms the telencephalon and the diencephalon. Also called forebrain; proencephalon.

prosodemic (pros-o-dem′ik) Denoting a disease that is transmitted directly from one individual to another.

prosopagnosia (pros-o-pag-no′se-ah) A form of visual agnosia in which a person has lost the ability to recognize familiar faces.

prostacyclin (pros-tah-si′klin) A prostaglandin produced by endothelial cells of the cardiovascular system; it inhibits platelet aggregation and helps maintain the integrity of the endothelial cells. Also called prostaglandin I_2.

prostaglandin (pros-tah-glan′din) (PG) Any of a group of hormone-like lipid-soluble compounds derived from long-chain polyunsaturated fatty acids and occurring in nearly all body tissues and fluids; they have a multitude of physiologic actions (e.g., suppression of stomach secretion, dilatation of peripheral blood vessels, increase of blood flow in kidney, dilatation of bronchial tubes); their production is inhibited by nonsteroidal anti-inflammatory drugs (e.g., aspirin).

p. I_2 See prostacyclin.

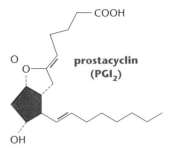

prostacyclin (PGI₂)

prostatalgia (pros-tah-tal′je-ah) Pain in the prostate.

prostate (pros′tāt) A chestnut-shaped structure surrounding the male urethra immediately below the bladder; composed of glandular and fibromuscular tissues; it secretes a milky fluid that is discharged through ducts into the urethra at the time of ejaculation.

prostatectomy (pros-tah-tek′to-me) Removal of a portion of the prostate or the entire prostate.

open p. Prostatectomy performed either through the abdomen (suprapubic) or through the perineum (perineal).

perineal p. Removal of the prostate through an incision in the perineum, between the testicles and the anal orifice; a seldom-used (almost abandoned) approach for a benign enlargement of the prostate.

suprapubic p. Prostatectomy performed through an incision just above the pubic bone; the approach is usually used when the prostate size is over 6 cm, or when additional procedures (e.g., on the bladder) are necessary.

transurethral p. The most commonly used method of removing obstructive prostatic tissue in the treatment of noncancerous enlargement of the prostate (benign prostatic hypertrophy, BPH); performed with a viewing instrument equipped with a cutting tip (resectoscope) introduced through the urethra. Also called transurethral resection of prostate (TURP).

transurethral ultrasound-guide laser-induced p. (TULIP) A method of removing obstructive prostatic tissue in the treatment of enlargement of the prostate (benign prostatic hypertrophy, BPH); a laser-equipped instrument is introduced through the urethra to a point close to the prostate; then the laser beam is used under guidance of ultrasound imaging to destroy the desired portion of the prostate. See also transurethral prostatectomy.

prostatic (pros-tat′ik) Relating to the prostate.

prostatism (pros′tah-tizm) Any condition caused by hypertrophy or any other condition of the prostate; usually refers to obstructive disease of the urinary tract due to prostatic hypertrophy.

prostatitis (pros-tah-ti′tis) Inflammation of the prostate.

acute bacterial p. Prostatitis caused mainly by gram-negative bacteria (e.g., *Escherichia coli, Staphylococcus aureus, Pseudomonas*), which may reach the prostate directly from the urethra or bladder or may be carried from distant sites by lymph and blood (e.g., following surgical manipulation of the lower urinary tract); manifestations include pain around the sacral and pelvic floor areas, fever, chills, painful urination and ejaculation, and a boggish, markedly tender prostate.

chronic abacterial p. The most common form of prostatitis typically affecting sexually active males; manifestations are those of chronic bacterial prostatitis but without a history of recurrent urinary infections.

chronic bacterial p. Prostatitis frequently associated with recurrent urinary tract infections; may be asymptomatic or associated with low back pain and painful urination.

prostato- Combining form meaning prostate.

prostatocystitis (pros-ta-to-sis-ti′tis) Inflammation of prostate and bladder.

prostatocystotomy (pros-ta-to-sis-tot′o-me) A surgical cut through the prostate and the bladder.

prostaglandin A₁ COOH

prostaglandin D₂ COOH

prostaglandin E₂ COOH

prostatolith (pros-tat′o-lith) A stone in the prostate.

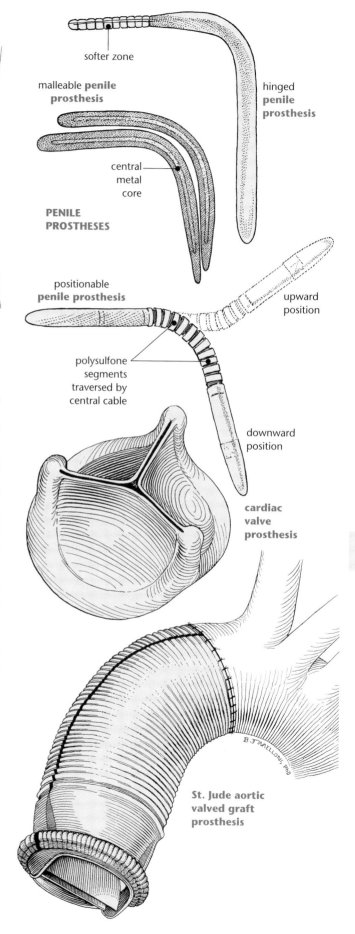

urinary bladder

hypertrophic prostate

pubic symphysis

urethra

prostatoliths
(between the hypertrophic prostate and its capsule)

softer zone

malleable **penile prosthesis**

hinged **penile prosthesis**

central metal core

PENILE PROSTHESES

positionable **penile prosthesis**

upward position

polysulfone segments traversed by central cable

downward position

cardiac valve prosthesis

St. Jude aortic valved graft prosthesis

prostatolithotomy (pros-tat-o-lī-thot′o-me) Incision of the prostate for removal of a stone.

prostatorrhea (pros-tah-to-re′ah) Abnormal discharge from the prostate.

prostatotomy (pros-tah-tot′o-me) A surgical cut into the prostate.

prostatovesiculectomy (pros-tah-to-ve-sik′u-lek′to-me) Surgical removal of the prostate and the seminal vesicles.

prostatovesiculitis (pros-tah-to-vĕ-sik′u-li′tis) Inflammation of the prostate and seminal vesicles.

prosthesis (pros-the′sis), pl. prosthe′ses An artificial replacement for a missing or dysfunctional body part, fabricated and fitted to meet the individual requirement of the intended user. COMPARE orthosis.

   cardiac valve p., heart valve p. Any of various devices designed for implantation within the heart as a substitute for a diseased valve. They may be mechanical devices or pretreated animal valves (bioprosthetic valves). For various types see under valve.

   dental p. A replacement for one or more missing teeth or their supporting structures.

   ocular p. An artificial eye or implant that substitutes for an enucleated eyeball; generally a glass or plastic curved disk featuring a painted iris and pupil that is inserted beneath the eyelids. Also called artificial eye.

   penile p. A device implanted within a penis to permit adequate rigidity for coitus; currently available models include a semirigid rod and a two-cylinder inflatable device. Also called penile implant.

   St. Jude aortic valved graft p. An artificial substitute for the ascending aorta and aortic valve consisting of a St. Jude heart valve sewn into a graft of woven polyester fiber. Its average burst strength is greater than 8000 mmHg. Produced by St. Jude Medical, Inc.

prosthetic (pros-thet′ik) **1.** Relating to prosthetics. **2.** Relating to an artificial part of the body.

prosthetics (pros-thet′iks) The making and fitting of an artificial part of the body.

   dental p. See prosthodontics.

prosthetist (pros′thĕ-tist) A person who constructs and fits prostheses.

prosthion (pros′the-on) A craniometric point at the midpoint of the alveolar rim of the maxilla; it is the most anterior projection, between the two central incisors. Also called alveolar point.

P

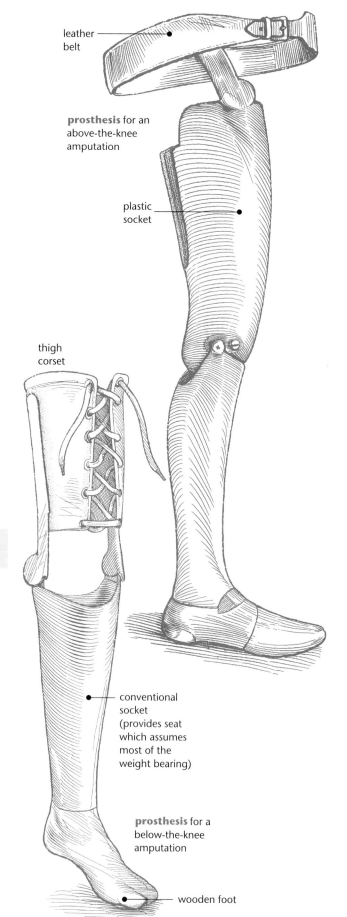

leather belt

prosthesis for an above-the-knee amputation

plastic socket

thigh corset

conventional socket (provides seat which assumes most of the weight bearing)

prosthesis for a below-the-knee amputation

wooden foot

prosthodontics (pros-tho-don'tiks) The branch of dentistry that deals with the restoration and maintenance of oral function by providing suitable substitutes for missing teeth and adjacent structures. Also called dental prosthesis.

prosthodontist (pros-tho-don'tist) A specialist in prosthodontics.

prosthokeratoplasty (pros-tho-ker'ah-to-plas-te) Replacement of diseased corneal tissue by a transparent prosthesis.

prostration (pros-tra'shun) A state of physical collapse.

protactinium (pro-tak-tin'e-um) A radioactive element: symbol Pa, atomic number 91, atomic weight 231.

protamine (pro'tah-min) Any of several simple proteins rich in arginine that neutralize the anticoagulant action of heparin; occurs in fish sperm.

    p. sulfate A heparin antagonist used in certain bleeding disorders caused by excessive amounts of heparin in the blood.

protanopia (pro-tah-no'pe-ah) Inability to differentiate red, orange, yellow, and green.

protean (pro'te-an) Capable of assuming different forms or shapes.

protease (pro'te-ās) Any enzyme that acts to divide the peptide bonds of proteins and peptides; a proteolytic enzyme.

protein (pro'tēn) Any of a group of complex nitrogenous substances that contain amino acids as their fundamental structural units, are present in cells of all plants and animals, and function in all aspects of chemical and physical activity of the cells.

    Alzheimer's disease associated p. (ADAP) A protein found in the brain and spinal fluid of people afflicted with Alzheimer's disease.

    Bence Jones p. An abnormal immunoglobulin found in the urine of some patients with multiple myeloma and other plasma cell tumors. Also called Bence Jones albumin.

    p. C A protein constituent of blood plasma that prevents coagulation of blood. Deficiency of protein C causes recurrent thrombophlebitis.

    catabolite gene activator p. A positive regulatory protein activated by cyclic AMP.

    conjugated p. Compound formed by the combination of a protein with a nonprotein group.

    C-reactive p. (CRP) An abnormal protein present in the blood serum of persons with rheumatic fever (acute stage) and other inflammatory diseases.

    denatured p. A protein that has been changed, with loss of characteristic properties.

    foreign p. Protein different from those normally found in the body fluids or tissues of an organism.

    immune p. Antibody.

    native p. Protein in its natural configuration.

    plasma p. Any protein normally present in blood plasma.

    pregnancy p.'s Proteins produced by the body of pregnant women or by the placenta; may be present only during pregnancy (pregnancy-specific) or also may be found in persons undergoing estrogen therapy or taking oral contraceptives or those with certain malignancies.

    proto-oncogene p. A product of oncogene that normally has no cancer-causing or transforming properties, but is involved in the regulation or differentiation of cell growth.

    receptor p. An intracellular protein having a specific affinity for a substance (e.g., a hormone) that stimulates the cell to activity.

    p. S A vitamin K–dependent protein of blood plasma needed as a cofactor for the antithrombotic functions of protein C.

    simple p. A protein that, upon hydrolysis, yields only amino acids.

proteinaceous (pro-tēn-a'shus) Relating to, or of the nature of, protein.

proteinase (pro'tēn-ās) Any enzyme that promotes the splitting of the peptide bonds of protein molecules.

protein hydrolysate (pro'tēn hi-drol'ĭ-zāt) A sterile solution of amino acids and peptides; given (orally) to infants allergic to milk and (intravenously) to severely ill patients and to those who have undergone surgery of the gastrointestinal tract.

proteinosis (pro-tēn-o′sis) Condition marked by deposits of abnormal proteins in the tissues.

  pulmonary alveolar p. Disease characterized by filling of the lung air sacs (alveoli) with a homogeneous lipid-rich material, causing breathing difficulty, cough, and the presence of a gelatinous material in the sputum; chest x rays show consolidation of the lungs. Cause is unknown; may occur after exposure to irritating dusts and chemicals and in persons with suppressed immunity. Disease is progressive and fatal in some patients; others recover spontaneously.

proteinuria (pro-tēn-u′re-ah) Excretion of protein in the urine in amounts greater than the normal daily levels; an average-size healthy person normally excretes up to 150 mg of protein per day.

  gestational p. Proteinuria occurring during pregnancy in the absence of disease.

  orthostatic p., postural p. The occurrence of proteinuria when the patient is erect and its disappearance when the patient lies down. Also called orthostatic albuminuria.

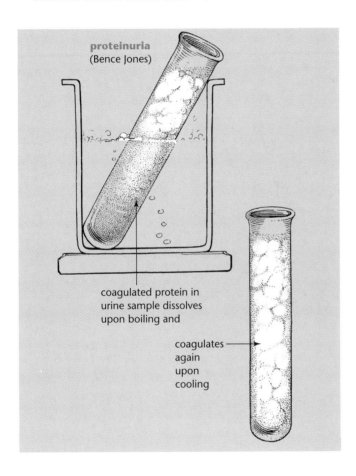

proteinuria
(Bence Jones)

coagulated protein in urine sample dissolves upon boiling and

coagulates again upon cooling

proteo-, prot- Combining forms meaning protein.

proteolipids (pro-te-o-lip′ids) A class of protein-lipid combinations found in abundance in brain tissue; also present in a wide variety of animal and plant tissues. Unlike lipoproteins, they are insoluble in water.

proteolysis (pro-te-ol′ĭ-sis) The breaking down of protein molecules into simpler ones by the action of an enzyme, as in digestion.

proteolytic (pro-te-o-lit′ik) Causing proteolysis.

proteometabolism (pro-te-o-mĕ-tab′o-lism) See protein metabolism, under metabolism.

proteose (pro′te-ōs) One of the intermediate products of protein digestion, between a protein and a peptone.

Proteus (pro′te-us) A genus of aerobic, gram-negative, disease-causing bacteria.

  P. mirabilis A species frequently found in abscesses and commonly associated with genitourinary tract infection.

  P. morganii A common inhabitant of the gastrointestinal tract; found in both normal and diarrheal stools.

  P. vulgaris Species found in putrefying tissues and abscesses; certain strains are agglutinated by typhus serum (Weil-Felix reaction) and therefore are used in diagnosing typhus. It is associated with cystitis and pyelonephritis.

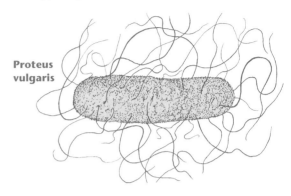

Proteus
vulgaris

prothrombin (pro-throm′bin) A plasma protein that is converted into the enzyme thrombin during the second phase of blood clotting. Formerly called thrombinogen. Also called factor II.

protium (pro′te-um) See hydrogen 1.

proto-, prot- Combining forms meaning first; earliest; primitive; principal.

protocol (pro′to-kol) A detailed description (e.g., of an autopsy) or plan of action (e.g., of an experiment).

  clinical p. A detailed plan for the performance or study of a medical problem and/or treatment.

  rape p. The organized, structured steps followed during a medical examination of a rape victim for the dual purpose of obtaining evidence for a criminal investigation and treating the patient. It includes: a detailed history of the assault; a gynecological history of the victim to assess risks of impregnation and transmission of disease; a history of the victim's activities in the interval between the assault and the examination (e.g., eating, drinking, bathing, douching, urinating, defecating), which may affect findings of the examination; an inspection of the whole body, especially the perineum and vulva, to document location and extent of external injuries; photographing the injuries, or noting them in a diagram; a vaginal and cervical examination with a speculum; collection of specimens from both outside and within the body for laboratory examination; and a detailed description of the findings.

protodiastolic (pro-to-di-ah-stol′ik) Relating to the period immediately following the second heart sound.

proton (pro′ton) (p) A nuclear particle (in the case of the hydrogen atom, the whole nucleus) with a single positive charge numerically equal to that of an electron.

P

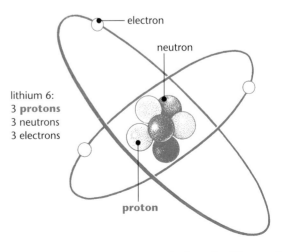

electron

neutron

lithium 6:
3 **protons**
3 neutrons
3 electrons

proton

proteinosis ■ proton

proto-oncogene (pro′to ong′ko-jēn) A cellular gene normally concerned with cell division; may be transformed into a tumor-forming gene (oncogene) if rearranged, mutated, or picked up by a retrovirus.

protoplasm (pro′to-plasm) The essential substance of all living cells.

protoplast (pro′to-plast) A spherical, osmotically fragile bacterial cell from which the rigid cell wall has been removed.

protoporphyria (pro-to-por-fir′e-ah) Increased level of protoporphyrin.

protoporphyrin type III (pro-to-por′fī-rin tip) An important porphyrin that, linked with iron, forms the heme of hemoglobin.

prototype (pro′to-tīp) 1. The ancestral species from which subsequent species evolve or to which they conform. 2. Something that serves as a model.

Protozoa (pro-to-zo′ah) A subkingdom of the animal kingdom that includes all unicellular organisms; most are free-living, some form aggregates.

protozoa (pro-to-zo′ah) Plural of protozoon.

protozoal (pro-to-zo′al) See protozoan (2).

protozoan (pro-to-zo′an) 1. Any of a large group of animals consisting of a single functional cell (e.g., *Entamoeba histolytica*, *Trichomonas vaginalis*, *Pneumocystis carinii*). Also called protozoon. 2. Relating to any unicellular animal. Also called protozoal.

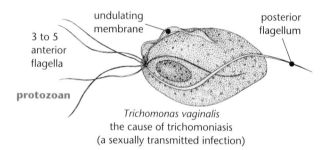

3 to 5 anterior flagella

undulating membrane

posterior flagellum

protozoan

Trichomonas vaginalis
the cause of trichomoniasis
(a sexually transmitted infection)

protozoiasis (pro-to-zo-i′ah-sis) Any disease caused by protozoa.

protozoicide (pro-to-zo′i-sīd) An agent that kills protozoa.

protozoology (pro-to-zo-ol′o-je) The study of protozoa.

protozoon (pro-to-zo′on), pl. protozo′a See protozoan (1).

protozoophage (pro-to-zo′o-fāj) A cell that ingests protozoa.

protraction (pro-trak′shun) The act of drawing forward a part of the body, such as the shoulder or lower jaw.

protractor (pro-trak′tor) 1. An instrument used to extract a foreign object (e.g., a bullet) from a deep wound. 2. A muscle that extends a limb; an extensor muscle.

protrusion (pro-troo′zhun) In dentistry, a forward, or a laterally forward, position of the lower jaw (mandible).

protuberance (pro-tu′ber-ans) A prominence or bulge, usually rounded or blunt.

    p. of chin See mental protuberance.

    external occipital p. A prominence on the back of the skull, at the middle of the outer surface of the occipital bone, midway between the foramen magnum and the summit of the bone, to which the nuchal ligament is attached.

    frontal p. See frontal eminence, under eminence.

    internal occipital p. A prominence at the midpoint of the inner surface of the occipital bone next to the confluence of the sinuses; it divides the bone into four fossae.

    laryngeal p. See Adam's apple.

    mental p. The prominence of the chin formed at the midline of the lower border of the body of the mandible. Also called protuberance of chin.

    parietal p. See parietal eminence, under eminence.

    tubal p. The cartilaginous projection of the posterior lip of the pharyngeal opening of the eustachian (auditory) tube, to which the salpingopharyngeal muscle is attached.

Providencia (prŏ-vĭ-den′se-ah) Genus of gram-negative bacteria that have been found in human feces and urine. Some species are associated with diarrhea and urinary tract infections.

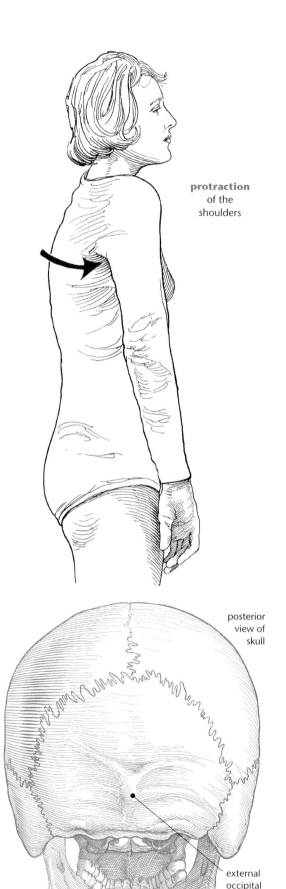

protraction
of the
shoulders

posterior
view of
skull

external
occipital
protuberance

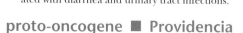

proto-oncogene ■ Providencia

provider In medical insurance, any organization or person that is licensed or certified to give health care services.

provirus (pro-vi′rus) The DNA sequences of a virus that are integrated into the DNA of the host cell and transmitted from one cell generation to the next without destroying the host cell. Proviruses are often associated with cell transformation into cancerous cells and are a key feature of retrovirus biology.

provitamin (pro-vi′tah-min) A substance that can be converted into a vitamin.

proximal (prok′sĭ-mal) **1.** Nearest the center, midline, or point of origin. **2.** In dental anatomy, applied to the surface of a tooth that is nearest an adjacent tooth, on either side.

proximate (prok′sĭ-māt) Nearest; in immediate relation to something else. In medical malpractice, applied to the negligent act that caused the injury of concern.

proximo- Combining form meaning proximal.

proximoataxia (prok-sĭ-mo-ah-tak′se-ah) Lack of muscular coordination of the proximal parts of the limbs.

pruriginous (proo-rij′ĭ-nus) Of the nature of prurigo.

prurigo (proo-ri′go) An itchy skin rash.

pruritic (proo-rit′ik) Relating to pruritus; itchy.

pruritus (proo-ri′tus) Persistent and severe itching of clinically normal skin; may be due to a systemic disease (e.g., chronic kidney failure, thyroid dysfunction, Hodgkin's disease, drug abuse).

> **p. aestivalis** Summer itch; itching of the skin that recurs whenever the weather is hot; may be associated with prickly heat.

> **p. ani** Itching of the skin around the anus.

> **p. scroti** Itching of the scrotum and neighboring skin.

> **p. senilis** Generalized pruritis occurring in old age, possibly from dryness of the skin due to atrophic and degenerative changes.

> **p. vulvae** Itching of the external female genitalia (vulva).

prussiate (prus′e-āt) Cyanide.

psammo- Combining form meaning sand.

psammoma (sam-o′mah) Outmoded term for any tumor that contains psammoma bodies.

pseudankylosis (su-dang-kĭ-lo′sis) See fibrous ankylosis, under ankylosis.

pseudarthrosis (su-dar-thro′sis) An abnormal joint formed on the shaft of a long bone, at the site of an ununited fracture. Also called pseudoarthrosis; false joint; neoarthrosis.

pseudesthesia (su-des-the′ze-ah) A subjective sensation without an external stimulus (e.g., one felt from an amputated limb). Also called pseudoesthesia.

pseudo- Combining form meaning false.

pseudoallele (su-do-ah-lēl′) One of two genes that occupy closely linked sites (loci) on a chromosome but, under certain conditions, appear to occupy the same site.

pseudoaneurysm (su-do-an′u-rizm) Dilatation of an arterial segment resembling an aneurysm.

pseudoarthrosis (su-do-ar-thro′sis) See pseudarthrosis.

pseudocoarctation (su-do-ko-ark-ta′shun) A tortuous condition of the aorta, at the level of insertion of the ligamentum arteriosum, without occlusion of the vessel.

pseudocoma (su-do-ko′mah) See locked-in syndrome, under syndrome.

pseudocroup (su-do-krōōp′) See laryngismus stridulus, under laryngismus.

pseudocryptorchism (su-do-krip-tor′kizm) Condition in which the testes occasionally move high into the inguinal canal.

pseudocyesis (su-do-si-e′sis) Development of pregnancy symptoms in a nonpregnant woman (e.g., menstrual abnormalities, abdominal enlargement, and breast changes). Also called false pregnancy; spurious pregnancy; pseudopregnancy.

pseudocyst (su′do-sist) **1.** An abnormal fluid-filled cavity that does not have an epithelial lining. **2.** A cluster of 50 or more *Toxoplasma* parasites filling the host cell, found especially in the brain.

> **pancreatic p.** A collection of fluid containing a high concentration of enzymes that arise from the pancreas; usually occurs within or adjacent to the pancreas; may occur as a complication of severe acute

inflammation of the pancreas, removal of the spleen, or trauma (in which case symptoms do not appear until several weeks after the injury).

pseudodementia (su-do-de-men′she-ah) A reversible condition secondary to disorders such as depression that resembles, and is often confused with, true dementia.

pseudodiabetes (su-do-di-ah-be′tēz) High levels of glucose in the blood occurring as a transient state in the newborn and, occasionally, in a young child with an infection.

pseudoesthesia (su-do-es-the′ze-ah) See pseudesthesia.

pseudofracture (su-do-frak′tūr) An x-ray image of periosteal thickening and new bone formation in an area of injury, and which gives the appearance of an incomplete fracture.

pseudoganglion (su-do-gang′gle-on) A thickened area in a nerve trunk resembling a ganglion.

pseudogout (su′do-gowt) Disease characterized by deposition of calcium pyrophosphate crystals in joint tissues, most frequently affecting the knee; causes goutlike attacks of pain, swelling, stiffness, and local warmth; may be hereditary or associated with metabolic disorders; also associated with trauma or surgery. Also called calcium pyrophosphate deposition disease (CPDD).

pseudohemoptysis (su-do-he-mop′tĭ-sis) Spitting of bloody material that does not originate from the lungs or bronchi.

pseudohermaphroditism (su-do-her-maf′ro-dit-izm) Condition in which a person has internal sex organs that are distinctly of one sex but has superficial characteristics that are either ambiguous or of the opposite sex. Erroneously called hermaphroditism.

pseudohernia (su-do-her′ne-ah) A swelling resembling a hernia, usually due to inflammation of an inguinal gland or scrotal tissue.

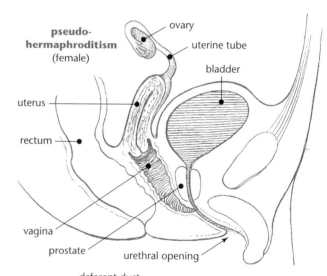

pseudo-hermaphroditism (female)
ovary
uterine tube
bladder
uterus
rectum
vagina
prostate
urethral opening

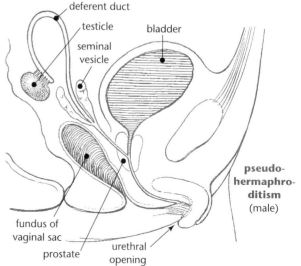

deferent duct
testicle
bladder
seminal vesicle
pseudo-hermaphro-ditism (male)
fundus of vaginal sac
prostate
urethral opening

P

pseudohypoparathyroidism (su-do-hi-po-par-ah-thi′roi-dizm) (PHP) Disorder inherited as an X-linked autosomal trait; it has the clinical and chemical features of hypoparathyroidism but with normal or elevated levels of parathyroid hormone (PTH); defect is primarily unresponsiveness to PTH; affected persons usually have short stature, round face, short metacarpal and metatarsal bones, and diminished intelligence.

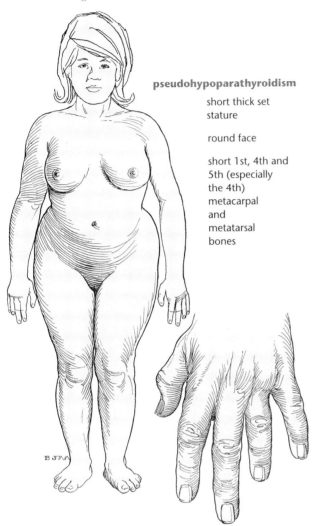

pseudohypoparathyroidism

short thick set stature

round face

short 1st, 4th and 5th (especially the 4th) metacarpal and metatarsal bones

pseudologia fantastica (su-do-lo′je-ah fan–tas′tik-ah) Thinking that is characterized by extensive fantasy construction, often based on a few facts, seen particularly in acting-out types of disorders; it is rapidly abandoned by the person when confronted with contradictory evidence.

pseudolymphoma (su-do-lim-fo′mah) See lymphocytic interstitial pneumonitis.

pseudomelena (su-do-mĕ-le′nah) The passage of dark feces, suggesting internal bleeding or caused by ingestion of iron, bismuth, beets, blueberries, licorice, charcoal, etc.

pseudomembrane (su-do-mem′brān) See false membrane, under membrane.

Pseudomonas (su-do-mo′nas) A genus of widely distributed gram-negative motile bacteria; some species cause disease in humans.

    P. aeruginosa A species found in human feces and skin; it is a frequent contaminant in hospitals, causing opportunistic infections of the lungs, urinary tract, and subarachnoid space through the use of contaminated respirators and instruments.

    P. pseudomallei A species causing melioidosis.

pseudomyopia (su-do-mi-o′pe-ah) Eye condition characterized by spasm of the ciliary muscle, which produces the same focusing defect as myopia.

pseudomyxoma (su-do-mik-so′mah) A gelatinous tumor resembling a myxoma.

    p. peritonei Extensive accumulation of tenacious, semisolid mucin in the abdominal cavity caused by spread of a cancerous tumor (cystadenocarcinoma) of the ovary or appendix that secretes large amounts of mucin.

pseudoneoplasm (su-do-ne′o-plazm) See pseudotumor.

pseudopapilledema (su-do-pap-ĭ-lĕ-de′mah) Eye condition in which the margins of the optic disk have a diffused, blurred appearance, suggesting papilledema, but without its essential feature (intracranial pressure).

pseudoparalysis (su-do-pah-ral′ĭ-sis) Apparent loss of voluntary movement.

pseudoparaplegia (su-do-par-ah-ple′je-ah) Apparent loss of voluntary movement of the legs.

pseudopodium (su-do-po′de-um), pl. pseudopo′dia A temporary cytoplasmic protrusion used by a cell for locomotion and ingestion.

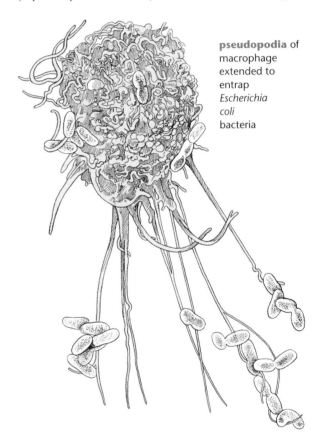

pseudopodia of macrophage extended to entrap *Escherichia coli* bacteria

pseudopolyp (su-do-pol′ip) A mass protruding from a mucous membrane, especially of the colon, composed of inflammatory tissue; usually seen in chronic ulcerative colitis; it has no malignant potential. Also called inflammatory polyp.

pseudopregnancy (su-do-preg′nan-se) See pseudocyesis.

pseudo-pseudohypoparathyroidism (su′do su-do-hi-po-par-ah-thi′roid-izm) (PPHP) Condition that has the external characteristics of pseudohypoparathyroidism (short stature, round face, short hands and feet) but lacks the chemical features.

pseudopterygium (su-do-ter-ij′e-um) Superficial adhesion of the conjunctiva as a result of injury. Also called scar pterygium.

pseudoptosis (su-do-to′sis) Apparent inability to elevate the upper eyelid, occurring when the eyelid lacks support (e.g., with a shrunken or absent eye or an inadequate prosthesis).

pseudosarcoma (su-do-sar-ko′mah) A malignant tumor histologically resembling a sarcoma.

pseudosmallpox (su-do-smawl′poks) See alastrim.

pseudosmia (su-doz′me-ah) Sensation of an odor that is not present.

pseudotubercle (su-do-tu'ber-kl) A nodule resembling a tuberculous granuloma but not caused by the tubercle bacillus.

pseudotumor (su-do-tu'mor) The appearance of symptoms and signs that indicate the presence of a tumor in the absence of one, and subsequent spontaneous recovery. Also called pseudoneoplasm.

    p. cerebri Increased intracranial pressure suggesting the presence of a tumor but due to other causes (e.g., an adverse reaction to a drug).

    orbital p. An uncommon inflammatory reaction of the eye socket (orbit), usually unilateral, that causes restriction of eye movement, protrusion of the eyeball, inflammation of the eyelids and, frequently, pain. Cause is unknown.

pseudoxanthoma elasticum (su-do-zan-tho'mah e-las'tĭ-kum) (PXE) An abnormality of connective tissue inherited as a recessive trait, characterized by formation of flat white or yellow patches (principally on the neck, axillae, and the extremities); ocular angioid streaks; and weakening of arterial walls, which leads to vessel rupture and internal hemorrhage.

Psilocybe mexicana (si-lo-si'be mek'sĭ-kan-ah) A species of mushrooms containing the hallucinogenic substance psilocybin. Commonly called Mexican magic mushroom.

psilocybin (si-lo-si'bin) A hallucinogenic substance obtained from *Psilocybe mexicana*.

psilosis (si-lo'sis) Loss of hair.

psittacosis (sit-ah-ko'sis) Pneumonitis caused by respiratory transmission of *Chlamydia psittaci* from birds, especially parrots and parakeets, by inhalation of dust from infected bird droppings. Most cases occur among pet store workers.

psoas (so'as) See table of muscles.

psoralen (sor'ah-len) Drug used in the treatment of certain skin disorders (e.g., vitiligo and psoriasis); it enhances the action of light on the skin.

psoriasiform (so-re-as'ĭ-form) Resembling psoriasis.

psoriasis (so-ri'ah-sis) A chronic, recurrent skin disorder; characteristic lesion is a well-defined reddish plaque covered with silvery scales, occurring mostly on the knees, elbows, trunk, and sometimes scalp. May be associated with nail changes (onycholysis) and sometimes with severe arthritis.

psoriatic (so-re-at'ik) Relating to psoriasis.

psoric (so'rik) Relating to scabies.

psyche (si'ke) The mind.

psychedelic (si-kĕ-del'ik) Any of several drugs that induce hallucinations, distorted perceptions, and, sometimes, states resembling psychosis; usually refers to self-administered drugs.

psychiatric (si-ke-at'rik) Relating to psychiatry.

psychiatrist (si-ki'ah-trist) A physician who specializes in psychiatry.

psychiatry (si-ki'ah-tre) The branch of medicine concerned with the origin, diagnosis, treatment, and prevention of mental disorders.

    community p. The practical application of social psychiatry.

    existential p. See existential psychotherapy.

    forensic p. The branch of psychiatry concerned with the relationship between the law and disorders manifesting themselves in behaviors that adversely affect society; it is important in such matters as determining competence in contract actions, responsibility for torts and crimes, competence to testify, ability to give informed consent to treatment, and particularly competence to stand trial.

    industrial p. See occupational psychiatry.

    occupational p. The field of psychiatry concerned with the relationship of mental and emotional disorders to the work environment. Also called industrial psychiatry.

    social p. The field of psychiatry concerned with the cultural and sociologic factors that cause, intensify, or prolong mental disorders. Social psychiatry constitutes the body of knowledge upon which the practice of community psychiatry is based.

psychic (si'kik) 1. Relating to the mind. 2. A person who supposedly has extraordinary mental or spiritual abilities (e.g., extrasensory perception).

psycho-, psych- Combining forms meaning the mind.

psychoactive (si-ko-ak'tiv) Exerting effects on the mind; applied to certain drugs.

psychoanalysis (si-ko-ah-nal'i-sis) A theory of mental functioning and human psychosocial development, a method of research, and a psychotherapeutic method that uses dream interpretation, free association, and analysis of the resistances and transference manifestations in order to bring into consciousness repressed feelings and experiences, thus enabling the patient to work through emotional problems. Also called psychoanalytical therapy; frequently called analysis.

psychoanalyst (si-ko-an'ah-list) psychotherapist trained in the techniques of psychoanalytic therapy. Also called analyst.

psychobiology (si-ko-bi-ol'o-je) 1. The branch of biology dealing with the interrelationship of the brain and the mental processes. 2. The school of thought (associated mainly with Adolf Meyer in the early part of the twentieth century) that focuses on the individual as a biologic unit in relation to the environment. Also called objective psychobiology.

    objective p. See psychobiology (2).

psychodiagnosis (si-ko-di-ag-no'sis) The use of psychological tests and interviews to determine the extent and nature of a person's psychopathology, his characteristic defense style, and the strengths and weaknesses of his ego.

psychodrama (si-ko-dram'ah) A method of group psychotherapy that involves a structured, directed, and dramatized acting out of the patient's emotional problems.

psychodynamics (si-ko-di-nam'iks) The science of human behavior and its unconscious motivation.

psychogenesis (si-ko-jen'ĕ-sis) Origination or causation by mental or psychic factors rather than organic (somatic) ones.

psychogenic, psychogenetic (si-ko-jen'ik, si-ko-je-net'ik) Due to mental or emotional factors rather than detectable organic (somatic) causes.

psychokinesis (si-ko-ki-ne'sis) (PK) In parapsychology, the alleged movement of an inanimate object through concentrated directed thought.

psychologic, psychological (si-ko-loj'ik, si-ko-loj'e-kal) Relating to mental processes, emotions, and behavior.

psychologist (si-kol'o-jist) One who is trained to perform psychological evaluation, therapy, or research on mental functioning.

    clinical p. One who holds a doctoral degree from an accredited program that provides appropriate clinical psychology training and is licensed or certified at the independent practice level by the state in which the individual practices. Most states offer only a generic psychologist license, while some have a specific clinical psychologist license.

psychology (si-kol'o-je) The science concerned with the processes of the mind, especially as they are manifested in behavior.

    clinical p. The branch of psychology concerned with the study, assessment, treatment, and prevention of emotional or behavioral disorders, including those of children (clinical child psychology).

    community p. The practical application of social psychology.

    counseling p. The branch of psychology that focuses on healthy adaptation to life situations, generally using brief therapy and educative methods to help people achieve healthier adjustments.

    existential p. See existential psychotherapy.

    forensic p. The branch of psychology concerned with the relationship between the law and disorders manifesting themselves in behaviors that adversely affect society; it is important in such matters as determining competence in contract actions, responsibility for torts and crimes, competence to testify, ability to give informed consent to treatment, and particularly competence to stand trial.

    industrial p. See occupational psychology.

    medical p. The branch of psychology concerned with the collaboration between physicians and psychologists in the management of certain medical problems.

    occupational p. The utilization of methods, principles, and theories of psychology for solution of problems arising in industrial settings (e.g., procedures used in worker selection and training, issues of communication and morale, and conditions to maximize comfort and productivity). Also called industrial psychology.

social p. The field of psychology concerned with the cultural and sociologic factors that cause, intensify, or prolong mental disorders. Social psychology constitutes the body of knowledge upon which the practice of community psychology is based.

psychometry (si-kom′ĕ-tre) The measuring of mental efficiency, function, and potential.

psychomotor (si-ko-mo′tor) Relating to the mental origin of muscular activity (e.g., compulsive movements).

psychoneuroimmunology (si-ko-nu′ro-im-u-nol′o-je) The study of the relationship between the brain, the immune system, and the mind.

psychoneurosis (si-ko-nu-ro′sis) See neurosis.

psychoneurotic (si-ko-nu-rot′ik) See neurotic.

psychopath (si′ko-path) Term applied to a person who manifests the characteristics of antisocial personality.

psychopathology (si-ko-pah-thol′o-je) 1. The study of mental disorders. 2. The manifestations of mental disorders.

psychopathy (si-kop′ah-the) See antisocial personality disorder, under disorder.

psychopharmaceuticals (si-ko-fahr-mah-su′tĭ-kals) A class of drugs used in the treatment of emotional disorders.

psychopharmacologist (si-ko-fahr-mah-kol′o-jist) A psychiatrist who treats mental disorders with drugs (e.g., antipsychotic or antidepressant drugs).

psychopharmacology (si-ko-fahr-mah-kol′o-je) The study of the action of drugs on the mind and emotions.

psychophysical (si-ko-fiz′e-kal) Relating to the mental perception or response invoked by a physical stimulus.

psychophysiologic (si-ko-fiz-e-o-loj′ik) 1. Relating to psychophysiology. 2. See psychosomatic.

psychophysiology (si-ko-fiz-e-ol′o-je) The study of interactions between psychologic and physiologic processes.

psychosensory (si-ko-sen′so-re) Relating to the perception and interpretation of sensory stimuli.

psychosexual (si-ko-seks′u-al) Relating to the emotional factors of sex.

psychosis (si-ko′sis), pl. psycho′ses A severe mental disorder of organic and/or emotional origin in which the ability to think, communicate, respond emotionally, and interpret reality is impaired to such a degree that all aspects of a person's life are affected, rendering that individual unable to meet the ordinary demands of life; frequently, the person also has regressive behavior, hallucinations, and delusions. Gross impairment of reality testing is central to distinguishing psychosis from other mental disorders.

alcoholic p. Mental disorders caused by alcoholism.

Korsakoff's p. See Korsakoff's syndrome, under syndrome.

manic-depressive p. See bipolar disorder, under disorder.

paranoid p. See schizophrenia, paranoid type, under schizophrenia.

prison p. See Ganser syndrome, under syndrome.

reactive p. A brief (less than two weeks) psychotic reaction following a psychosocial stressor, with an eventual return to the premorbid level of functioning.

schizoaffective p. A psychotic mental disorder in which affective symptoms are prominent, particularly in the early stages, but where schizophrenic symptoms are also prominent.

schizophreniform p. A mental disorder sharing essential features of schizophrenia but with a duration less than six months (but more than two weeks) and having a better prognosis; frequently characterized by emotional turmoil, fear, confusion, and vivid hallucinations. See also schizophrenia.

psychosocial (si-ko-so′shal) Involving psychologic and social elements.

psychosomatic (si-ko-so-mat′ik) Relating to the interaction of the mind and the body (soma); refers commonly to physical symptoms

that have at least partially an emotional cause. Also called psychophysiologic.

psychosomimetic (si-ko-so-mī-met′ik) See psychotomimetic.

psychostimulant (si-ko-stim′u-lant) An agent that has mood-elevating properties.

psychosurgery (si-ko-ser′jer-e) The surgical removal or destruction of brain tissue or the severance of fibers connecting one part of the brain with another for the treatment of severe mental disorders or to relieve intractable pain.

psychotherapeutic (si-ko-ther-ah-pu′tik) Relating to psychotherapy.

psychotherapist (si-ko-ther′ah-pist) A person, usually a psychiatrist, a psychologist, or a psychiatric social worker, trained in psychotherapy.

psychotherapy (si-ko-ther′ah-pe) Treatment of behavioral, emotional, and mental disorders or distress conducted by a variety of psychological methods involving communication between a trained therapist and an individual, couple, family, or group. See under therapy for definitions of various psychotherapeutic approaches.

existential p. Psychotherapy, based on existential philosophy, that primarily emphasizes present feelings and spontaneous interactions rather than rational thinking. Also called existential psychiatry.

psychotic (si-kot′ik) 1. Characterized by gross impairment of reality testing. 2. A person afflicted with psychosis.

psychotogen (si-kot′o-jen) Any drug that produces symptoms of psychosis.

psychotomimetic (si-kot-o-mī-met′ik) Denoting the effect of certain drugs (e.g., LSD), which simulate psychotic states. Also called psychosomimetic.

psychotropic (si-ko-trop′ik) Affecting the mind; applied to certain drugs used in treating mental disorders.

psychro- Combining form meaning cold temperature.

psychrophilic (si-kro-fil′ik) Thriving in cold temperature; applied to certain bacteria.

psychrophobia (si-kro-fo′be-ah) 1. Extreme sensitivity to cold. 2. Abnormal fear of cold temperatures.

psyllium (sil′e-um) 1. A plant of the genus *Plantago*. 2. The seeds of *Plantago psyllium,* which, when moist, swell and become gelatinous; useful in treating simple constipation.

ptarmic (tar′mik) Causing sneezing.

pterion (te′re-on) A craniometric point on either side of the skull at the junction of four bones: frontal, sphenoid, parietal, and temporal. Also called sylvian point.

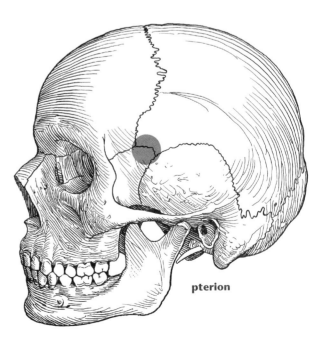

pterion

ptero-, pter- Combining forms meaning wing; feather.

pteroylglutamic acid (ter-o-il-tri-gloo-tam′ik as′id) See folic acid.

pterygium (tĕ-rij′e-um) A slowly advancing, triangular growth on the transparent covering of the eyeball (bulbar conjunctiva), usually extending from the inner corner (medial canthus) of the eye to the border of the cornea or beyond; believed to be caused by ultraviolet radiation; seen in farmers, sheepherders, skiers, and surfers. COMPARE pinguecula.

    scar p. See pseudopterygium.

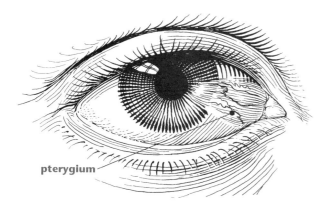

pterygium

pterygoid (ter′ĭ-goid) Resembling the shape of a wing.

pterygopalatine (ter-ĭ-go-pal′ah-tin) Relating to the pterygoid process of the sphenoid bone and the hard palate.

pthiriasis (thi-ri′a-sis) Infestation with pubic lice (*Phthirus pubis*).

ptilosis (ti-lo′sis) Falling out of eyelashes.

ptomaine (to′mān) Vague term for any poisonous substance.

ptosed (tōst) Prolapsed.

-ptosis Suffix denoting a downward displacement (e.g., blepharoptosis).

ptosis (to′sis) **1.** Prolapse of an organ. **2.** Drooping of an upper eyelid when the eye is open.

ptosis
of left upper
eyelid

ptotic (tot′ik) Relating to prolapse.

ptyalin (ti′ah-lin) A digestive enzyme present in saliva, secreted by the salivary glands. Also called salivary alpha-amylase.

ptyalo-, ptyal- Combining forms meaning saliva.

ptyalolith (ti′ah-lo-lith) See sialolith.

ptyalolithiasis (ti-ah-lo-lĭ-thi′ah-sis) See sialolithiasis.

ptyalolithotomy (ti-ah-lo-lĭ-thot′o-me) See sialolithotomy.

pubarche (pu-bar′ke) The beginning of puberty, especially of the growth of pubic hair.

pubertal, puberal (pu′ber-tal, pu′ber-al) Relating to the onset of puberty.

pubertas (pu-ber′tas) Latin for puberty.

    p. precox See precocious puberty, under puberty.

puberty (pu′ber-te) The period during which secondary sexual characteristics develop and reproductive function is attained; menstruation in girls begins. Onset of puberty varies with health, genetic, and socioeconomic factors. Usually, in girls the period extends between the ages of 8 and 16 years, in boys between 10 and 17 years.

    precocious p. Development of secondary sexual characteristics occurring at an abnormally early age, usually before the age of 8 years in girls and 9 years in boys; may be caused by a variety of pathologic processes, including brain lesions, and disorders involving the adrenal (suprarenal) glands, testes, and ovaries. Also called pubertas precox.

pubescence (pu-bes′ens) The beginning of sexual maturity.

pubescent (pu-bes′ent) One who is reaching the age of sexual maturity.

pubic (pu′bik) Relating to the pubic bone or area.

pubis (pu′bis) **1.** The pubic bone. **2.** The region over the pubic bone. **3.** The hair of the pubic region.

pubomadesis (pu-bo-ma-de′sis) Loss or absence of pubic hair.

pubovesical (pu-bo-ves′ĭ-kal) Relating to the pubic bone and the bladder.

pudendal (pu-den′dal) Relating to the genitals.

pudendum (pu-den′dum), pl. puden′da The external genitals, especially the female genitals; the vulva.

puerpera (pu-er′per-ah) A woman who has just given birth.

puerperal (pu-er′per-al) Relating to the puerperium.

puerperium (pu-er-pe′re-um) The postpartum period, from the end of labor to the return of the uterus to normal size, usually from 3 to 6 weeks.

puffer (puf′er) One who exhales forcibly.

    pink p. Informal term for describing a patient afflicted with the lung disease emphysema. The patient is able to maintain an adequate supply of oxygen in the bloodstream (hence the pink complexion) by constantly taking forceful short breaths (puffing). COMPARE blue bloater.

pulicide, pulicicide (pu′li-sīd, pu-lis′ĭ-sīd) An agent that kills fleas.

pulmo (pul′mo), pl. pulmo′nes Latin for lung.

pulmonary (pul′mo-ner-e) Relating to the lungs. Also called pulmonic.

pulmonectomy (pul-mo-nek′to-me) See pneumonectomy.

P

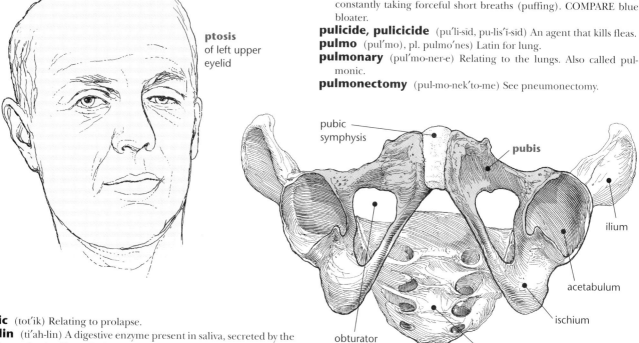

pubic
symphysis

pubis

ilium

acetabulum

ischium

obturator
foramen

sacrum

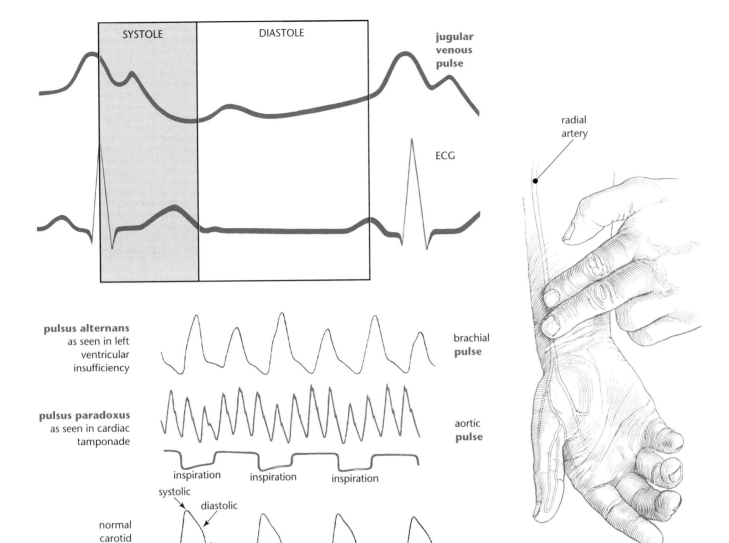

SYSTOLE

DIASTOLE

jugular
venous
pulse

ECG

radial
artery

pulsus alternans
as seen in left
ventricular
insufficiency

brachial
pulse

pulsus paradoxus
as seen in cardiac
tamponade

aortic
pulse

inspiration   inspiration   inspiration

systolic

diastolic

normal
carotid
pulse

dicrotic
notch

left ventricular
ejection time

common site
for **pulse**
taking

---

pulmonic (pul-mon'ik) See pulmonary.

pulmono-, pulmo- Combining forms meaning lung.

pulmonologist (pul-mo-nol'o-jist) A physician who specializes in diseases of the lungs.

pulmotor (pul'mo-tor) Apparatus for inducing artificial respiration.

pulp (pulp) A soft, moist tissue.

   dental p. The connective tissue, blood vessels, and nerves contained within the pulp cavity of a tooth.

pulpal (pul'pal) Relating to pulp.

pulpectomy (pul-pek'to-me) Complete removal of pulp tissue from a tooth.

pulpefaction (pul-pĕ-fak'shun) Reducing to a pulpy state.

pulpitis (pul-pi'tis) Inflammation of the dental pulp.

pulpless (pulp'les) Denoting nonvital or dead tooth; one that has a nonfunctioning or dead pulp.

pulpotomy (pul-pot'o-me) Partial removal of the pulp from a tooth, usually the coronal portion.

pulpy (pul'pe) A soft and moist condition.

pulsate (pul'sāt) To expand and contract rhythmically, such as the heart; to throb.

pulsatile (pul'sah-tīl) Pulsating; throbbing.

pulsation (pul-sa'shun) 1. A single throb or beat. 2. The act of pulsating.

   jugular vein p. See jugular venous pulse, under pulse.

pulse (puls) (p) The rhythmic increase in pressure within a blood vessel caused by the increased volume of blood forced through the vessel with each contraction of the heart.

   alternating p. See pulsus alternans.

   anacrotic p., anadicrotic p. A pulse (usually palpable in the carotid arteries) in which the ascending limb of the pulse tracing shows a secondary notch.

   bigeminal p. A pulse in which two beats occur in rapid succession followed by a pause. Also called coupled pulse.

   capillary p. Rhythmic blanching and reddening of capillary areas (e.g., under the nails); seen in aortic regurgitation. Also called Quincke's pulse; Quincke's sign.

   Corrigan's p. Pulse characterized by an abrupt rise and rapid collapse, seen in aortic regurgitation. Also called water-hammer pulse.

   coupled p. See bigeminal pulse.

   jugular venous p. (JVP), jugular p. The pulsation occurring

---

pulmonic ■ pulse

in a jugular vein. Also called jugular venous pulsation.

paradoxical p. See pulsus paradoxus.

plateau p. A pulse with a slowly rising pressure and sustained peak.

Quincke's p. See capillary pulse.

thready p. A small-volume pulse that is difficult to perceive.

trigeminal p. Pulse occurring in groups of three.

venous p. Pulse occurring in the veins.

water-hammer p. See Corrigan's pulse.

pulseless (puls'lis) Having no pulse.

pulsus (pul'sus) Latin for pulse.

p. alternans A pulse characterized by weak and strong beats; seen in severe left ventricle dysfunction. Also called alternating pulse.

p. bisferiens A pulse with two peaks, the second stronger than the first; seen in aortic regurgitation and hypertrophic cardiomyopathy.

p. paradoxus A pulse that diminishes during inspiration; seen in pericardial effusion and constriction (tamponade) and in obstructive lung disease. Also called paradoxical pulse.

p. parvus A weak pulse due to decreased stroke volume; seen in left ventricular failure and in aortic or mitral stenosis.

p. tardus A pulse that is slow to rise; seen in aortic stenosis.

pultaceous (pul-ta'shus) Macerated.

pulvinar (pul-vi'nar) The expanded posteromedial portion of the thalamus in the brain.

pumice (pum'is) A porous volcanic substance used in dentistry (in powder form) to polish teeth and dentures.

pump (pump) An apparatus for drawing a liquid or gas through tubes from and to any part.

blood p. In cardiac surgery, a pump that drives blood through the tubing of extracorporeal circulation devices; especially designed not to damage the formed elements of the blood.

breast p. A suction pump (manual or electric) for removing milk from a lactating breast.

calcium p. In physiological chemistry, the mechanism of active transport by which calcium is moved across a cell membrane against a concentration gradient; the cell's adenosine triphosphate (ATP) provides the energy required to drive the transport.

Carrel-Lindbergh p. A perfusion pump by means of which an organ taken out of the body may be kept viable; often combined with an oxygenating device and used in such operations as bypass surgery. Also called Lindbergh pump. See also pump-oxygenator.

coronary-sucker p. A pump for aspirating the small quantity of blood that enters the heart while the heart-lung machine is used during open-heart surgery.

counterpulsation p. See intra-aortic balloon pump.

dental suction p. A suction pump used for removing saliva from the mouth during dental procedures. Also called saliva pump; saliva ejector.

electrolyte p. A process that derives its energy from the metabolic activities of the cell and which can cause a solute to move from an area of relatively low to one of higher chemical potential (e.g., a sodium pump located in renal tubular cells).

infusion p. A device for injecting a controlled amount of fluid (e.g., insulin) during a set interval of time.

insulin p. A light-weight, battery-powered, external device used in the management of diabetes mellitus; it is designed to slowly and continuously infuse insulin in specific programmed doses (usually small) throughout the day, thereby simulating the action of the pancreas; the syringe included in the pump can store enough insulin to last several days; the needle is inserted through the skin of the abdomen or thigh and held in place with tape.

intra-aortic balloon p. A pump connected to a balloon that is introduced into the descending aorta to produce counterpulsation. The balloon inflates during diastole and deflates during systole, thereby increasing blood flow to coronary and peripheral vessels and diminishing impedance to left ventricular ejection. Also called counterpulsation pump.

Lindbergh p. See Carrel-Lindbergh pump.

muscle p. The contracting calf muscle act as a pump to propel peripheral venous blood up from the lower extremity toward the heart.

saliva p. See dental suction pump.

sodium p. See electrolyte pump.

stomach p. A suction pump with a flexible tube for removing the contents of the stomach in an emergency, as in a case of poisoning.

pump-oxygenator (pump' ok-si-jĕ-na'tor) An apparatus that facilitates open–heart surgery by temporarily substituting for the heart (pump) and lungs (oxygenator) in extracorporeal circulation of blood.

punch (punch) A surgical instrument for cutting out a piece of tissue (e.g., for biopsy) or for drawing out a foreign body from a tissue.

punchdrunk (punch'drunk) See punchdrunk syndrome, under syndrome.

punctate (punk'tāt) Having minute dots.

punctiform (punk'tī-form) Of the size and shape of a minute point; applied chiefly to describe minute bacterial colonies.

punctum (punk'tum), pl. punc'ta Latin for a point or spot.

lacrimal p. The external opening of a lacrimal canaliculus, at the medial margin of each eyelid near the bridge of the nose.

puncture (pungk'chur) 1. To pierce with a pointed instrument. 2. A minute hole made with a needle.

lumbar p. Procedure in which a hollow needle is inserted into the subarachnoid space of the lower spinal canal (between two lumbar vertebrae) to withdraw cerebrospinal fluid for diagnostic purposes, or to inject an anesthetic. Also called spinal puncture; spinal tap; rachicentesis; rachiocentesis.

spinal p. See lumbar puncture.

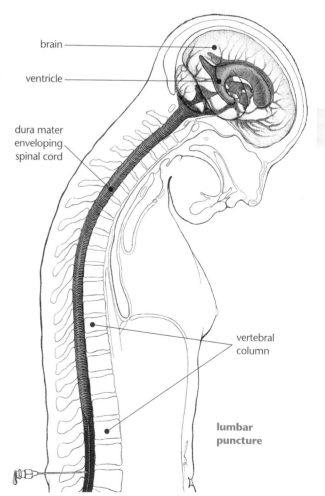

brain

ventricle

dura mater enveloping spinal cord

vertebral column

lumbar puncture

P

pupil (pu′pil) (p) The central opening within the iris through which light enters the eye. Its function is similar to that of the lens aperture of a camera.

Argyll Robertson (AR) p. A small pupil that is less than 3 mm in diameter (miotic) and does not contract in response to light stimulation but constricts normally in response to convergence accommodation; seen in certain conditions involving the cerebral cortex (e.g., neurosyphilis).

fixed p. A pupil that is unresponsive to all stimuli.

tonic p. A larger-than-normal pupil that contracts slowly, or not completely, in response to light stimulation; associated with loss of tendon reflexes due to degeneration of postganglionic nerve fibers, which supply the sphincter muscle of the iris. Seen in Adie's syndrome.

pupillary (pu′pĭ-ler-e) Relating to a pupil.

pupillo- Combining form meaning pupil.

pupillography (pu-pĭl-log′ra-fe) The recording of the pupil's reaction to light.

pupillometer (pu-pĭl-lom′ĕ-ter) Instrument for measuring the pupil of the eye.

pupillometry (pu-pĭl-lom′ĕ-tre) Measuring of the pupil of the eye.

pupillomotor (pu-pĭl-lo-mo′tor) Relating to the motor nerve fibers that supply the iris, thereby affecting the size of the pupil.

pupilloplegia (pu-pĭl-lo-ple′je-ah) Slow or absent response of the pupil to a light.

pupillostatometer (pu-pĭl-lo-stah-tom′ĕ-ter) Device for measuring the distance between the two pupils.

pure (pūr) 1. Unadulterated. 2. Free from harmful contamination.

purgation (pur-ga′shun) Vigorous evacuation of intestinal contents by a cathartic agent. Also called catharsis.

purgative (pur′gah-tiv) 1. Causing vigorous intestinal evacuation. 2. An agent having such an effect.

purging (purj′ing) The act or process of evacuating or cleansing.

bone marrow p. Elimination of subpopulations of cells (usually residual tumor cells) from bone marrow after it has been removed for transplantation; used in both autologous and allogeneic bone marrow transplantation.

purine (pu′rin) The parent substance of a group of organic compounds (e.g., adenine and guanine) known as purine bases or purines.

purpura (pur′pu-rah) The occurrence of spontaneous bleeding into the skin, resulting in multiple pigmented patches of varying sizes; may also occur in mucous membranes and in the serous lining of intestinal organs.

allergic p. See Henoch-Schönlein purpura.

anaphylactoid p. See Henoch-Schönlein purpura.

annular telengiectatic p. Purpura of unknown cause characterized by the appearance of circular lesions, usually in the legs, that have a yellowish necrosed center. Also called Majocchi's disease.

Henoch-Schönlein p. Purpura seen principally in children, caused by a systemic hypersensitivity reaction of unknown cause associated with gastrointestinal symptoms, joint pains, and acute glomerulonephritis; the appearance of cutaneous lesions is preceded by a pinprick itchy sensation. Also called anaphylactoid purpura; allergic purpura; Schönlein's disease; rheumatic purpura.

idiopathic thrombocytopenic p. (ITP) Purpura associated with immune destruction of blood platelets. It occurs in two forms: *Acute idiopathic thrombocytopenic p.*, a self-limited disorder seen mainly in children after a viral infection (e.g., rubella, infectious mononucleosis). *Chronic idiopathic thrombocytopenic p.*, a long-standing disorder with multiple relapses and remissions seen in adults, mostly women of childbearing age. Also called thrombocytopenic purpura.

rheumatic p. See Henoch-Schönlein purpura.

thrombocytopenic p. See idiopathic thrombocytopenic purpura.

thrombotic thrombocytopenic p. (TTP) A rare and severe disorder characterized by formation of minute platelet and fibrin clots in the arterioles and capillaries of many organs; manifestations, in addition to purpura, include a low platelet count (thrombocytopenia), hemolytic anemia, signs of central nervous system involvement, and kidney dysfunction.

purpuric (pur-pu′rik) Relating to purpura.

purpuriferous (pur-pu-rif′er-us) Forming a purple pigment.

purr (pur) A low murmur.

purulence (pu′roo-lens) The condition of containing or producing pus.

purulent (pu′roo-lent) Producing, consisting of, or containing pus.

pus (pus) A yellowish liquid or semisolid substance, product of inflammation, composed of dead white blood cells (leukocytes) and other cellular debri in a thin liquid (liquor puris).

cheesy p. The thick pus of a tuberculous abscess.

pustular (pus′tu-lar) Related to pustules.

pustulation (pus-tu-la′shun) The formation of pustules.

pustule (pus′tūl) A small localized accumulation of pus in the skin.

malignant p. See cutaneous anthrax, under anthrax.

pustuliform (pus′tu-lĭ-form) Resembling pustules.

pustulosis (pus-tu-lo′sis) A pustular eruption.

palmoplantar p. See bacterid.

putamen (pu-ta′men) The dark outer portion of the lentiform nucleus in the brain, medial to the insular cortex.

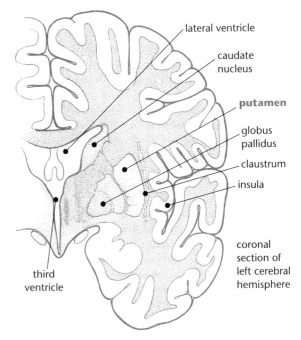

lateral ventricle
caudate nucleus
putamen
globus pallidus
claustrum
insula
third ventricle
coronal section of left cerebral hemisphere

putrefaction (pu-trĕ-fak′shun) Decomposition or breakdown of organic matter by the action of bacteria.

putrefactive (pu-trĕ-fak′tiv) Causing decay.

putrefy (pu′trĕ-fi) 1. To decompose. 2. To cause decomposition.

putrescence (pu-tres′ens) Rottenness.

putrid (pu′trid) Decayed.

PUVA Acronym for psoralen and ultraviolet A; a form of photochemotherapy for the treatment of psoriasis, consisting of oral administration of psoralen followed by exposure to long-wavelength ultraviolet light.

pyarthrosis (pi-ar-thro′sis) The presence of pus in a joint cavity.

pyelectasis (pi-ĕ-lek′tah-sis) Dilatation of the kidney pelvis.

pyelitis (pi-ĕ-li′tis) Outmoded term for pyelonephritis.

pyelo-, pyel- Combining forms meaning the pelvis of the kidney.

pyelocaliectasis (pi-ĕ-lo-kal-e-ek′tah-sis) See caliectasis.

pyelocaliceal (pi-ĕ-lo-kal-ĭ-se′al) See pyelocalyceal.

pyelocalyceal (pi-ĕ-lo-kal-ĭ-se′al) Relating to the kidney pelvis and calices. Also spelled pyelocaliceal.

pyelocystitis (pi-ĕ-lo-sis-ti′tis) Inflammation of the bladder and kidney pelvis.

pyelogram (pi′ĕ-lo-gram) An x-ray image of the kidney pelvis and ureter.

pyelography (pi-ĕ-log'rah-fe) The making of x-ray images of the kidney pelvis and ureter. Also called ureteropyelography.

pyelolithotomy (pi-ĕ-lo-lĭ-thot'o-me) Surgical removal of a stone from the kidney pelvis.

pyelonephritis (pi-ĕ-lo-nĕ-fri'tis) Inflammation of the kidney, especially of the kidney pelvis and calyces. Formerly called pyelitis.

    acute p. A bacterial infection of the kidney usually ascending from the lower urinary tract.

    chronic p. Disorder thought to be caused by inflammatory scarring and contraction of kidney tissues from previous bacterial infections.

    xanthogranulomatous p. A form of chronic pyelonephritis, usually unilateral and associated with prolonged obstruction with kidney stones in the calyces; the kidney is greatly enlarged with a mass that is often indistinguishable from tumor; seen most often in middle-aged diabetic women.

pyeloplasty (pi'ĕ-lo-plas'te) Plastic repair of the kidney pelvis usually to improve drainage or to reduce its size.

pyeloplication (pi-ĕ-lo-pli-ka'shun) An outmoded surgical procedure in which the wall of the kidney pelvis is tucked in with sutures; used to reduce the size of an abnormally dilated kidney pelvis.

pyeloscopy (pi-ĕ-los'ko-pe) Fluoroscopic examination of the kidney pelvis after introduction of a radiopaque solution through the ureter or intravenously.

pyelostomy (pi-ĕ-los'to-me) Surgical formation of an opening into the kidney pelvis.

pyelotomy (pi-ĕ-lot'o-me) A surgical cut into the kidney pelvis.

pyeloureteral (pi-ĕ-lo-u-re'ter-al) Relating to the kidney pelvis and the ureter.

pyeloureterectasis (pi-ĕ-lo-u-re-ter-ek'tah-sis) Dilatation of the kidney pelvis and the ureter, usually caused by hydronephrosis.

pyemesis (pi-em'ĕ-sis) Vomiting pus-containing matter.

pyemia (pi-e'me-ah) A general secondary infection with multiple abscesses in several areas of the body.

pyemic (pi-e'mik) Relating to pyemia.

Pyemotes tritici (pi-ĕ-mo'tez trī-ti'ki) A soft-bodied mite that is a common parasite of insect larvae in stored grain; it is a frequent cause of an itchy skin rash in humans. Also called hay itch mite; grain itch mite.

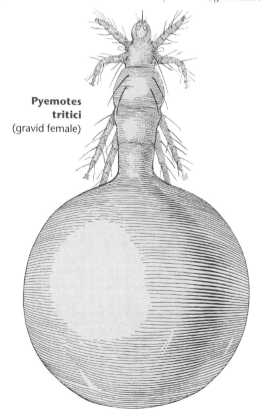

Pyemotes tritici
(gravid female)

pyencephalus (pi-en-sef'ah-lus) See pyocephalus.

pyesis (pi-e'sis) Suppuration.

pygo-, pyg- Combining forms meaning buttocks.

pyknic (pik'nik) Having a short body with ample body cavities.

pykno-, pyk- Combining forms meaning dense; compact.

pyknomorphous (pik-no-mor'fus) Characterized by having the stainable elements densely packed; applied to certain cells.

pyknosis (pik-no'sis) Condensation and shrinking of a cell nucleus (e.g., in normal maturation of the red blood cell and in any cell necrosis).

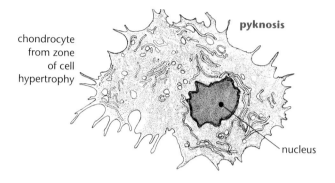

pyknosis

chondrocyte from zone of cell hypertrophy

nucleus

pyla (pi'la) The opening between the third ventricle of the brain and the cerebral aqueduct.

pylemphraxis (pi-lem-frak'sis) Obstruction of the portal vein.

pylephlebectasis (pi-le-fle-bek'tah-sis) Dilatation of the portal vein.

pylephlebitis (pi-le-fle-bi'tis) Inflammation of the portal vein or its branches.

pylethrombophlebitis (pi-le-throm-bo-fle-bi'tis) Inflammation of the portal vein with blood clot (thrombus) formation.

pylethrombosis (pi-le-throm-bo'sis) Formation of blood clots (thrombi) in the portal vein or its branches.

pylic (pi'lik) Relating to the portal vein.

pylon (pi'lon) A temporary artificial leg.

pyloralgia (pi-lo-ral'je-ah) Pain in the pyloric region of the stomach, adjacent to the duodenum.

pylorectomy (pi-lo-rek'to-me) Removal of the pylorus.

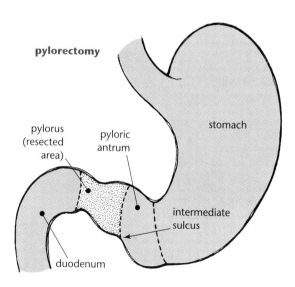

pylorectomy

pylorus (resected area)

pyloric antrum

stomach

intermediate sulcus

duodenum

pyloric (pi-lor'ik) Relating to the pylorus.

pyloristenosis (pi-lor-e-stĕ-no'sis) See pyloric stenosis, under stenosis.

pyloritis (pi-lo-ri'tis) Inflammation of mucous membrane over the lower outlet (pylorus) of the stomach.

pyloro-, pylor- Combining forms meaning pylorus.

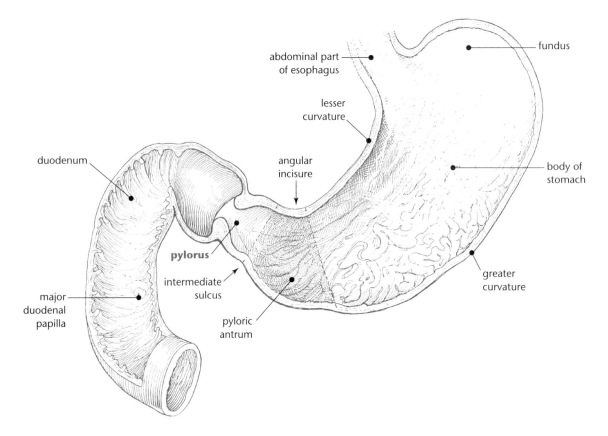

abdominal part of esophagus

fundus

lesser curvature

angular incisure

body of stomach

duodenum

pylorus

intermediate sulcus

greater curvature

major duodenal papilla

pyloric antrum

pylorogastrectomy (pi-lo-ro-gas-trek′to-me) Removal of the lower portion of the stomach, including the pylorus.

pyloromyotomy (pi-lo-ro-mi-ot′o-me) A surgical muscle-splitting incision of the pylorus (up to the mucosal layer) for the relief of hypertrophic pyloric stenosis, a condition occasionally seen in newborn infants. Also called Fredet-Ramstedt operation.

pyloroplasty (pi-lo′ro-plas-te) Plastic operation of the lower stomach outlet (pylorus), especially one to widen a constricted pyloric canal by means of a longitudinal incision through the pylorus and transverse closure; performed when the constriction is caused by a peptic ulcer.

pylorospasm (pi-lo′ro-spazm) Spastic contraction of the lower stomach outlet (pylorus).

pylorotomy (pi-lo-rot′o-me) A surgical cut into the pyloric wall.

pylorus (pi-lo′rus) The narrow terminal portion of the stomach marking the boundary between the stomach and the duodenum and the canal within it.

pyo- Combining form meaning pus.

pyocele (pi′o-sēl) Distention of a body cavity due to accumulation of pus.

pyocephalus (pi-o-sef′ah-lus) The presence of a purulent fluid within the skull. Also called pyencephalus.

pyochezia (pi-o-ke′ze-ah) Discharge of pus with the stools.

pyococcus (pi-o-kok′us) A pus-producing bacterium.

pyocolpos (pi-o-kol′pos) Accumulation of pus in the vagina.

pyocyanic (pi-o-si-an′ik) Relating to blue pus, or to *Pseudomonas aeruginosa*, the bacterium that produces it.

pyocyst (pi′o-sist) A pus-containing cyst.

pyoderma (pi-o-der′mah) Any pus-producing skin disease.

    p. gangrenosum A poorly understood immunologic disease process resulting in chronic ulcerations, most often seen on the legs; it is associated with a variety of systemic diseases (e.g., ulcerative colitis, rheumatoid arthritis).

pyogen (pi′o-jen) Any pus-producing agent.

pyogenesis (pi-o-jen′ĕ-sis) The formation of pus. Also called pyopoiesis.

pyogenic (pi-o-jen′ik) Relating to pus formation.

pyohemothorax (pi-o-he-mo-tho′raks) Presence of pus and blood between the two layers of membrane (pleura) covering the lungs.

pyoid (pi′oid) Resembling pus.

pyolabyrinthitis (pi-o-lab-ĭ-rin-thi′tis) Suppurative inflammation of the labyrinth of the inner ear.

pyometra (pi-o-me′trah) Accumulation of pus in the uterus.

pyometritis (pi-o-mĕ-tri′tis) Inflammation of the wall of the uterus with accumulation of pus in the uterine cavity.

pyomyositis (pi-o-mi-o-si′tis) The presence of single or multiple deep-seated abscesses in voluntary muscles; caused most commonly by *Staphylococcus aureus*.

pyonephrolithiasis (pi-o-nef-ro-li-thi′ah-sis) The presence of pus and stones in the kidney.

pyonephrosis (pi-o-nĕ-fro′sis) The presence of pus in the calices and pelvis of the kidney; usually seen in association with obstruction of outflow from the pelvis.

pyo-ovarium (pi′o o-va′re-um) An ovarian abscess.

pyopericarditis (pi-o-per-ĭ-kar-di′tis) Suppurative inflammation of the pericardium, the membranous sac enveloping the heart.

pyopericardium (pi-o-per-ĭ-kar′de-um) Accumulation of pus in the pericardium, the membranous sac enveloping the heart.

pyoperitonitis (pi-o-per-ĭ-to-ni′tis) Suppurative inflammation of the peritoneum, the membranous lining of the abdominopelvic cavity.

pyophthalmia, pyophthalmitis (pi-of-thal′me-ah, pi-of-thal-mi′tis) Suppurative inflammation of the eye, especially of the mucous membrane lining the inner aspect of the eyelids.

pyophysometra (pi-o-fi-so-me′trah) The presence of pus and gas in the uterine cavity.

pyopneumocholecystitis (pi-o-nu′mo-ko′le-sis-ti′tis) Suppurative inflammation of the gallbladder and distention with gas caused by gas-producing bacteria or by the entry of gas from the intestine through the biliary tree.

pyopneumopericardium (pi-o-nu′mo-per′ĭ-kar′de-um) The presence of pus and gas in the membranous sac (pericardium) surrounding the heart.

pyopneumothorax (pi-o-nu′mo-tho′raks) The presence of pus

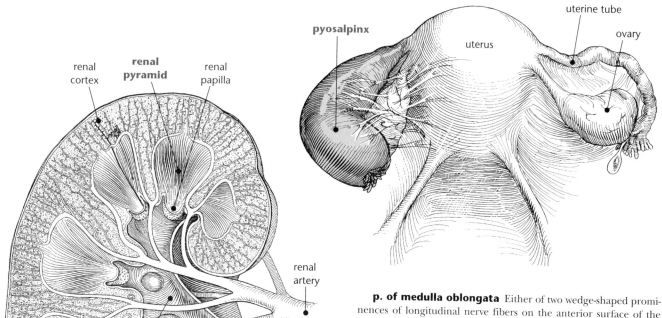

renal cortex

renal pyramid

renal papilla

renal artery

pelvis of kidney

ureter

minor calix

major calix

section of kidney

pyosalpinx

uterus

uterine tube

ovary

and gas between the two layers of pleura, the membrane covering the lungs. Also called pneumopyothorax.

pyopoiesis (pi-o-poi-e′sis) See pyogenesis.

pyopoietic (pi-o-poi-et′ik) Pus-producing.

pyoptysis (pi-op′tĭ-sis) Spitting of purulent material.

pyorrhea (pi-o-re′ah) **1.** A pus-containing discharge. **2.** Popular name for periodontitis.

pyosalpingitis (pi-o-sal-pin-ji′tis) Suppurative inflammation of a fallopian (uterine) tube.

pyosalpingo-oophoritis (pi-o-sal-ping′go o-of-o-ri′tis) Suppurative inflammation of a fallopian (uterine) tube and the adjacent ovary.

pyosalpinx (pi-o-sal′pinks) Accumulation of pus in a fallopian (uterine) tube.

pyosis (pi-o′sis) Suppuration.

pyostatic (pi-o-stat′ik) Denoting any agent that stops pus formation.

pyoureter (pi-o-u-re′ter) Distention of a ureter with pus.

pyramid (pir′ah-mid) Any of numerous anatomic structures that are somewhat pyramidal or conical.

   cerebellar p. The central portion of the inferior vermis of the cerebellum between the uvula and the tuber vermis, and separated from them by the prepyramidal and postpyramidal fissures. Also called pyramid of vermis.

   p. of kidney See renal pyramid.

   p. of light See cone of light, under cone.

   malpighian p. See renal pyramid.

   p. of medulla oblongata Either of two wedge-shaped prominences of longitudinal nerve fibers on the anterior surface of the medulla oblongata on either side of the anterior median fissure; composed of motor fibers from the cerebral cortex to the medulla oblongata and spinal cord.

   olfactory p. See olfactory trigone, under trigone.

   renal p. One of a number of striated pyramidal masses that form the medulla of the kidney, containing part of the secreting and collecting tubules; its apex projects into the minor calix. Also called malpighian pyramid; pyramid of kidney.

   p. of thyroid gland See pyramidal lobe of thyroid gland, under lobe.

   p. of tympanum See pyramidal eminence, under eminence.

   p. of vermis See cerebellar pyramid.

pyramidal (pĭ-ram′ĭ-dal) Denoting an anatomic structure that resembles a pyramid.

pyrantel pamoate (pĭ-ran′tel pam′o-āt) Drug used to eliminate intestinal worms.

pyrazinamide (pi-rah-zin′ah-mīd) Drug used (in combination with others) to treat tuberculosis. Possible adverse effects include liver damage.

pyrectic (pi-rek′tik) Relating to or causing fever.

pyreto- Combining form meaning fever.

pyretogenesis (pi-rĕ-to-jen′ĕ-sis) The causation of fever.

pyretogenetic (pi-rĕ-to-jĕ-net′ik) See pyrogenic.

pyretotherapy (pi-rĕ-to-ther′ah-pe) See fever therapy, under therapy.

pyrexia (pi-rek′se-ah) Fever.

pyrexial (pi-rek′se-al) Relating to fever.

pyridine (pir′ĭ-dēn) A volatile liquid used as a solvent, as a denaturant of alcohol, and in analytical chemistry.

pyridostigmine bromide (pĭr-ĭ-do-stig′mēn bro′mīd) A compound used in the treatment of myasthenia gravis.

pyridoxal phosphate (pĭr-ĭ-dok′sal fos′fāt) A vitamin derivative that is a coenzyme in amino acid metabolism.

pyridoxine (pĭr-ĭ-dok′sēn) One of the active forms of vitamin B_6. Deficiency occurs in alcoholism, in pregnancy, and when taking certain drugs (e.g., oral contraceptives).

pyrimethamine (pĭr-ĭ-meth′ah-mēn) An antimalarial compound.

pyrimidine (pi-rim′ĭ-dēn) The essential substance of several organic bases, some of which are components of nucleic acid.

pyro- Combining form meaning heat; produced by heat.

pyrogallol (pi-ro-gal′ol) Compound used in the treatment of certain skin disorders.

pyrogen (pi′ro-jen) A chemical substance that acts on the temperature-regulating mechanism of the body and produces fever.

pyrogenic (pi-ro-jen′ik) Causing fever. Also called pyretogenic; pyretogenetic.

P

pyrolysis (pi-rol′ĭ-sis) Chemical change induced by heat.

pyromania (pi-ro-ma′ne-ah) A compulsion to set fires.

pyrometer (pi-rom′ĕ-ter) An instrument for measuring extremely high temperatures.

pyronin (pi′ro-nin) A fluorescent red dye used in histologic stains.

pyrophobia (pi-ro-fo′be-ah) Abnormal fear of fires.

pyrophosphatase (pi-ro-fos′fah-tās) Any enzyme that splits pyrophosphates.

pyrophosphate (pi-ro-fos′fāt) (PP) A salt of pyrophosphoric acid.

pyrosis (pi-ro′sis) See heartburn.

pyrotherapy (pi-ro-ther′ah-pe) See fever therapy, under therapy.

pyrotic (pi-rot′ik) **1.** Relating to heartburn. **2.** Caustic.

pyrrole (pĭr′ol) A toxic compound that is the parent of many biologically important substances (e.g., bile, porphyrins, chlorophyll).

pyruvate (pi′roo-vāt) A salt of pyruvic acid.

pyruvate kinase (pi′roo-vāt ki′nās) (PK) An enzyme that promotes the transfer of phosphoenolpyruvate to ADP, yielding ATP and pyruvate. Deficiency of pyruvate kinase in red blood cells is the cause of a hemolytic anemia inherited as an autosomal trait.

pyruvic acid (pi-roo′vik as′id) A compound that is an intermediate product of carbohydrate metabolism.

pyrvinium pamoate (pir-vin′e-um pam′o-āt) Compound used in treating pinworm infections.

pyuria (pi-u′re-ah) The presence of pus in the urine.

Q

quack (kwak) One who fraudulently claims to have medical or dental capability to diagnose and treat disease and who generally makes extravagant claims as to the effects achieved by his worthless treatments; a charlatan.

quackery (kwak′er-e) The practice of a quack.

quadrant (kwod′rant) (Q) **1.** One quarter of a circle. **2.** In anatomy, one of the four areas into which certain roughly circular parts of the body are divided for descriptive purposes (e.g., the eardrum, fundus of the eye, abdomen, breast).

quadrantanopia (kwod-rant-ah-no′pe-ah) Blindness in approximately one quarter of the visual field.

quadrantectomy (kwod-ran-tek′to-me) Removal of one quarter of an organ, especially a breast, as a treatment for a tumor.

quadrate (kwod′rāt) Square; four-sided.

quadri- Combining form meaning four.

quadribasic (kwod-rī-ba′sik) Denoting an acid that has four replaceable hydrogen atoms.

quadriceps (kwod′rī-seps) Having four heads; applied to certain muscles, especially the quadriceps femoris, the large muscle of the anterior thigh.

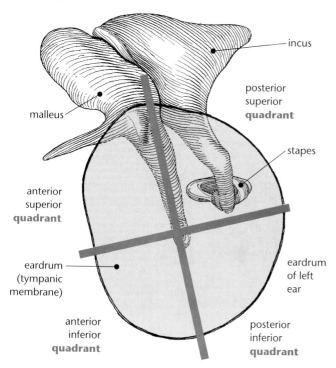

incus

posterior superior **quadrant**

malleus

stapes

anterior superior **quadrant**

eardrum (tympanic membrane)

eardrum of left ear

anterior inferior **quadrant**

posterior inferior **quadrant**

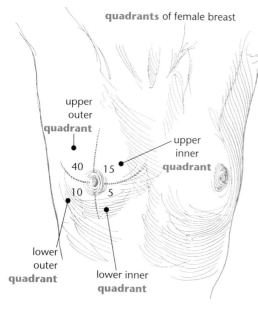

quadrants of female breast

upper outer **quadrant**

upper inner **quadrant**

40   15

10   5

The numbers represent the relative percentage frequency of cancer in various quadrants. The remaining 30% occur under the nipple-areola region.

lower outer **quadrant**

lower inner **quadrant**

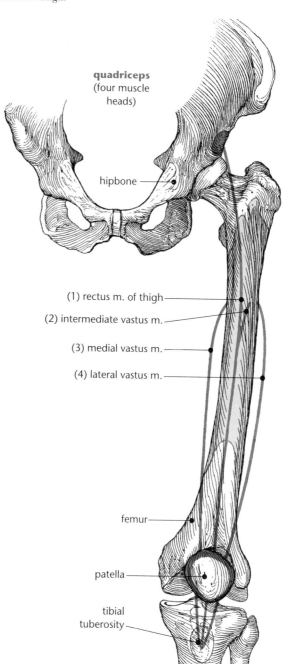

quadriceps (four muscle heads)

hipbone

(1) rectus m. of thigh

(2) intermediate vastus m.

(3) medial vastus m.

(4) lateral vastus m.

femur

patella

tibial tuberosity

Q

quadrigeminal (kwod-rī-jem′ī-nal) Occurring in groups of four; having four parts.

quadriplegia (kwod-rī-ple′je-ah) Paralysis of all four limbs. Also called tetraplegia.

quadriplegic (kwod-rī-ple′jik) One whose four limbs are paralyzed.

quadrivalent (kwod-rī-va′lent) Having the combining capacity of four hydrogen atoms. Also called tetravalent.

quadruplet (kwod′rup-let) One of four offspring born at one birth.

quanta (kwon′tah) Plural of quantum.

quantitative (kwon′tī-ta-tiv) Expressible as a quantity; involving the constituent parts of a compound.

quantum (kwon′tum), pl. quan′ta 1. A unit of radiant energy. 2. A specified amount.

quantum libet (kwon′tum li′bet) (q.l.) Latin for as much as desired.

quantum sufficit (kwon′tum suf′fī-sit) (q.s.) Latin for sufficient amount.

quaque die (kwah′kwe de′a) (q.d.) Latin for every day.

quaque hora (kwah′kwe o′rah) (q.h.) Latin for every hour.

quaque quarta hora (kwah′kwe kwar′tah o′rah) (q.q.h.) Latin for every four hours.

quarantine (kwar′an-tēn) 1. Restriction of freedom of movement of persons or animals that have been exposed to a communicable disease; originally the length of time was 40 days. 2. Isolation of a person afflicted with a communicable disease.

quart (kwort) (qt) 1. A measure of fluid capacity equal to one fourth of a gallon (0.946 liter). 2. A unit of volume in dry measure equal to 1.101 liters.

quartan (kwor′tan) Recurring every four days (e.g., a malarial fever).

quartz (kworts) A form of silica used in dentistry as one of three main ingredients of dental porcelain.

quasidominance (kwa-zī-dom′ī-nans) Direct transmission, from generation to generation, of a recessive trait occurring in inbreeding populations; it results from the mating of a homozygous affected person with a heterozygous carrier of the same recessive gene; the pedigree pattern superficially resembles that of a dominant trait, hence the name.

quater in die (kwah′ter in de′a) (q.i.d.) Latin for four times a day.

quaternary (kwah′ter-ner-e) 1. The member of a series that is fourth in order. 2. In chemistry, a compound containing four different elements.

quenching (kwench′ing) 1. The extinguishing or suppressing of an energy emission (e.g., heat, electrical discharge). 2. In liquid scintillation counting, the lowering of the amount of energy recorded from the sample container.

quick (kwik) A body part that is sensitive or painful to the touch.

quickening (kwik′en-ing) A slight abdominal sensation first felt by a pregnant woman about the fourth or fifth month of pregnancy, caused by the movement of the fetus within the uterus.

quicksilver (kwik′sil-ver) See mercury.

quinacrine (kwin′ah-krin) A bright yellow compound originally used to treat malaria; now used against infections with the protozoon *Giardia lamblia* (giardiasis). Possible adverse effects include nausea, vomiting, and yellow discoloration of the skin; prolonged use may cause blood disorders (e.g., aplastic anemia).

quinidine (kwin′ī-din) An alkaloid from cinchona bark, used in the management of irregular heartbeats (cardiac arrhythmia).

quinine (kwi′nīn) A bitter alkaloid from cinchona bark used in the treatment of malaria.

quininism (kwin′ī-nizm) See cinchonism.

quinolones (kwin′o-lōns) A class of broad-spectrum antibiotics used to treat a variety of bacterial infections.

quinquina (kin-ke′nah) The bark of the cinchona tree from which quinine is extracted.

quinsy (kwin′ze) See peritonsillar abscess, under abscess.

quintuplet (kwin-tup′let) One of five offspring born at one birth.

quotidian (kwo-tid′e-an) Recurring every day (e.g., a fever).

quotient (kwo′shent) A number of times a quantity is contained in another.

   blood q. See color index, under index.

   intelligence q. (IQ) The ratio of a person's attained score on a standardized test of intelligence to the expected mean score for his age, multiplied by 100.

   respiratory q. (RQ) The ratio between the volume of carbon dioxide expired and the volume of oxygen consumed; it varies with the diet, but normally is about 0.82.

R

rabid (rab'id) Relating to rabies.

rabies (ra'bēz) An acute infection of the nervous system with the rabies virus (genus *Lyssavirus*), transmitted through saliva of an infected animal; incubation period varies from 10 days to several months; the virus travels along nerve pathways to the brain, where it causes inflammation; it is invariably fatal in humans unless preventive treatment is instituted. Also called hydrophobia.

racemic (ra-se'mik) Composed of clustered parts (e.g., glands).

racemose (ras'e-mōs) Resembling a bunch of grapes.

rachial (ra'ke-al) Spinal.

rachicentesis (ra-ke-sen-te'sis) See lumbar puncture, under puncture.

rachidian (ra-kid'e-an) Spinal.

rachio-, rachi- Combining forms meaning spine.

rachiocampsis (ra-ke-o-kamp'sis) Any spinal curvature.

rachiocentesis (ra-ke-o-sen-te'sis) See lumbar puncture, under puncture.

rachiopathy (ra-ke-op'ah-the) See spondylopathy.

rachiotome (ra'ke-o-tōm) A surgical bone-cutting instrument used in operations of the vertebral column. Also called rachitome.

rachiotome

rachiotomy (ra-ke-ot'o-me) See laminectomy.

rachischisis (ră-kis'kĭ-sis) See spondyloschisis.

rachitic (ră-kit'ik) Relating to rickets.

rachitogenic (rah-kit-o-jen'ik) Causing rickets.

rachitome (rak'i-tōm) See rachiotome.

rachitomy (rah-kit'o-me) See laminectomy.

rad (rad) An acronym for Radiation Absorbed Dose, a unit of radiation exposure representing the absorbed dose; 1 rad represents absorption of 100 ergs of energy per gram of tissue.

radarkymography (ra-dar-ki-mog'rah-fe) The process of videotaping the heart motions during fluoroscopy with the aid of an image intensifier.

radectomy (ra-dek'to-me) Removal of the root of a tooth, or a portion of it.

radial (ra'de-al) 1. Relating to a bone in the forearm (radius) or to any radius. 2. Diverging in several directions from a central point.

radiant (ra'de-ant) 1. Emitting heat or light rays. 2. A central point from which rays diverge. 3. Emitted as radiation.

radiate (ra'de-āt) 1. To emit radiation. 2. To diverge in many directions from a center.

radiation (ra-de-a'shun) 1. The high-speed emission and projection of energy (waves or particles). 2. A bundle of white fibers interconnecting different parts of the brain.

    background r. Radiation from sources other than the source of interest; may arise from cosmic rays, the natural radioactivity in the environment (e.g., the earth or building materials), inadequately shielded storage areas, spilled radioactive compounds, x-ray machines, etc.

    Cerenkov r. Light produced when high-energy particles travel through a clear liquid at a velocity greater than the speed of light in that liquid.

    corpuscular r. Radiation consisting of a stream of subatomic particles that have a specific mass (e.g., protons, electrons, neutrons, and alpha or beta particles). COMPARE electromagnetic radiation.

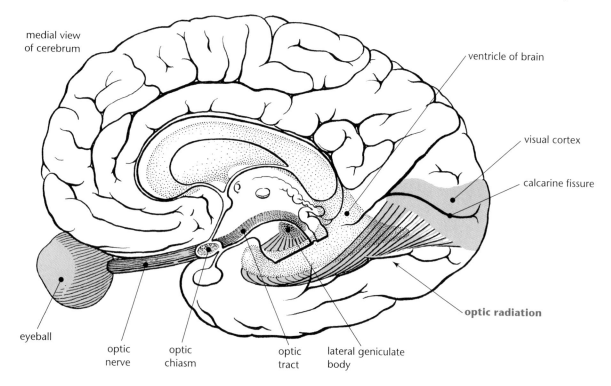

medial view of cerebrum

ventricle of brain

visual cortex

calcarine fissure

optic radiation

eyeball

optic nerve

optic chiasm

optic tract

lateral geniculate body

electromagnetic r. Forms of energy that have no mass and travel in waves at the speed of light; they differ in wavelengths, frequency, and photon energy (e.g., x rays, gamma rays, radio and infrared waves, visible light, and ultraviolet and cosmic radiation). COMPARE corpuscular radiation.

external r. In radiation therapy, the use of a machine, located outside the body, to aim high-energy rays at a cancerous growth.

hyperfractionated r. Radiation treatment in which the total dose of radiation is divided into smaller doses and given more than once a day.

intraoperative r. A type of external radiation in which a large dose of radiation is applied to the tumor bed and surrounding tissues at the time of surgery.

ionizing r. Electromagnetic radiation (e.g., x rays, gamma rays) or corpuscular radiation (e.g., protons, electrons) capable of producing electrically charged atoms (ions) in its passage through matter.

optic r. A band of white fibers in each hemisphere of the brain, passing from the lateral geniculate body of the thalamus out to the superficial layer (cortex) of the medial surface of the occipital lobe, at the back of the head. It constitutes the final relay of the visual impulse. Also called geniculostriate projection; geniculocalcarine tract.

scattered r. Radiation that has changed direction as a result of its collision with matter.

radical (rad′ĭ-kal) **1.** Descriptive term applied to a form of treatment characterized by extreme, extensive, or innovative measures (e.g., a surgical procedure for eradicating a cancerous tumor). Opposite of conservative. **2.** In chemistry, a group of atoms that can pass unchanged from one compound to another, forming one of the basic parts of the molecule.

radicle (rad′ĭ-kl) A minute structure resembling a rootlet.

radicotomy (rad-ĭ-kot′o-me) See rhizotomy.

radiculalgia (rah-dik-u-lal′je-ah) Neuralgia of the sensory root of a spinal nerve (near the spinal cord), usually caused by an irritation.

radicular (rah-dik′u-lar) Relating to the root of an anatomic structure (e.g., of a tooth or a nerve).

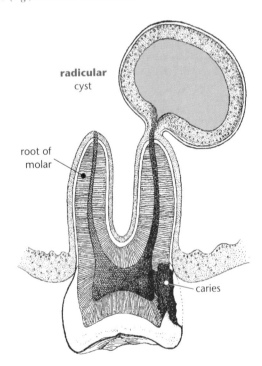

radicular cyst

root of molar

caries

radiculectomy (rah-dik-u-lek′to-me) See rhizotomy.

radiculitis (rah-dik-u-li′tis) Inflammation of a nerve root within the dura mater.

radiculomeningomyelitis (rah-dik-u-lo-mĕ-ning-go-mi-ĕ-li′tis) See rhizomeningomyelitis.

radiculomyelopathy (rah-dik-u-lo-mi-ĕ-lop′ah-the) See myeloradiculopathy.

radiculoneuropathy (rah-dik-u-lo-nu-rop′ah-the) Disease of the spinal nerves and their roots (near the spinal cord).

radiculopathy (rah-dik-u-lop′ah-the) Disease of the spinal nerve roots (near the spinal cord).

radioactive (ra-de-o-ak′tiv) Relating to radioactivity.

radioactivity (ra-de-o-ak-tiv′ĭ-te) The emission of rays or subatomic particles, either due to unstable atomic nuclei or as a result of nuclear reaction.

radiobiology (ra-de-o-bi-ol′o-je) The branch of science concerned with the effects of radiation on living tissues and with the use of radioactive isotopes.

radiocalcium (ra-de-o-kal′se-um) A radioisotope of calcium (e.g., calcium 45), usually employed in bone tumor localization and bone metabolism studies.

radiocarbon (ra-de-o-kar′bon) A radioisotope of carbon (e.g., carbon 14) used as a tracer in metabolic studies.

radiocarpal (ra-de-o-kar′pal) Relating to the radius and the wrist bones (carpus), especially the joint between the lower end of the radius and the proximal row of wrist bones.

radiochemistry (ra-de-o-kem′is-tre) The study of chemical reactions of radioactive elements.

radiocinematography (ra-de-o-sin-ĕ-mah-tog′rah-fe) The technique of making motion pictures of the passage of a radiopaque substance through the internal organs as seen on x-ray examination.

radiocurable (ra-de-o-kūr′ah-bl) Susceptible to cure by irradiation.

radiodense (ra′de-o-dens) See radiopaque.

radiodensity (ra-de-o-den′sĭ-te) See radiopacity.

radiodermatitis (ra-de-o-der-mah-ti′tis) Inflammation of the skin caused by excessive exposure to x or gamma rays; may occur in association with ionizing radiation therapy; the skin may become dry, itchy, smooth, shiny, and discolored, with brittle and striated nails.

radioelectrocardiogram (ra-de-o-e-lek-tro-kar′de-o-gram) An electrocardiogram recorded from a small transmitter carried by the patient.

radioelement (ra-de-o-el′ĕ-ment) Any radioactive chemical element.

radioepidermitis (ra-de-o-ep-ĭ-der-mi′tis) Damage to the superficial layer of the skin by exposure to ionizing radiation.

radiofrequency (ra-de-o-fre′kwen-se) A frequency of electromagnetic radiation in the range between audio frequencies and infrared frequencies.

radiogenesis (ra-de-o-jen′ĕ-sis) The production of radioactivity.

radiogenic (ra-de-o-jen′ik) **1.** Producing rays. **2.** Producing radioactivity.

radiogram (ra′de-o-gram) See roentgenogram.

radiograph (ra′de-o-graf) The processed photographic film produced in radiography.

bite-wing r. X-ray film adapted to show the crowns and cervical third of the roots of both upper and lower teeth and dental arches.

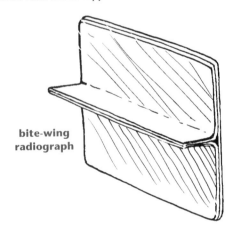

bite-wing radiograph

R

panoramic r. A radiograph showing all the teeth in one film as if the curved dental arches had been straightened into one flat plane.

radiography (ra-de-og′rah-fe) The making of an image of an internal part by transmitting x rays through the body into a sensitized film. Also called roentgenography.

radiohumeral (ra-de-o-hu′mer-al) Relating to two bones, the radius (in the forearm) and the humerus (in the arm).

radioimmunoassay (ra-de-o-im′u-no-as′a) (RIA) Any of a variety of sensitive laboratory techniques for measuring the concentration of antibody, using radioactive reagents.

radioimmunodiffusion (ra-de-o-im′u-no-dif-fu′zhun) Immunodiffusion using radioactive antigen or antibody.

radioimmunoelectrophoresis (ra-de-o-im′u-no-e-lek′tro-fo-re′sis) Immunoelectrophoresis using radioactive antigen or antibody.

radioiodinated (ra-de-o-i′o-din-a-ted) Treated with radioactive isotope of iodine.

radioiron (ra-de-o-i′ern A radioactive isotope of iron.

radioisotope (ra-de-o-i′so-tōp) Any isotope of an element that is naturally or artificially radioactive.

radiologist (ra-de-ol′o-jist) A physician with special training in radiology, in reading diagnostic x-ray pictures and performing specialized x-ray procedures.

radiology (ra-de-ol′o-je) The science concerned with radiant energy (x rays and radioactive isotopes) and its diagnostic and therapeutic use.

radiolucency (ra-de-o-loo′sen-se) The state of being moderately permeable to x rays or other forms of radiation (e.g., the soft body tissues); recorded in x-ray pictures as areas of different shades of gray.

radiolucent (ra-de-o-loo′sent) Allowing a moderate passage of radiant energy.

radiometer (ra-de-om′ĕ-ter) A device for detecting and measuring radiant energy.

radiomimetic (ra-de-o-mi-met′ik) Denoting a chemical substance that has a destructive effect on tissues similar to that of high-energy radiation (e.g., sulfur mustards, nitrogen mustards).

radionecrosis (ra-de-o-ne-kro′sis) Destruction of tissues by radiation.

radioneuritis (ra-de-o-nu-ri′tis) Inflammation of nerve tissue caused by overexposure to x rays or any other type of radiation.

radionuclide (ra-de-o-nu′klīd) A nuclide that disintegrates with emission of radiant energy; a radioactive nuclide.

radiopacity (ra-de-o-pas′ĭ-te) The state of being impenetrable by x rays or any other form of radiation. Also called radiodensity.

radiopaque (ra-de-o-pāk′) Impenetrable by x rays or any other form of radiation. Also called radiodense.

radiopathology (ra-de-o-pah-thol′o-je) The study and treatment of conditions caused by exposure to radiation.

radiopelvimetry (ra-de-o-pel-vim′ĕ-tre) An x-ray technique for determining the size and shape of the pelvis.

radiopharmaceutical (ra-de-o-fahr′mah-su′tĭ-kal) A radioactive pharmaceutical preparation used for diagnostic or therapeutic purposes.

radioreaction (ra-de-o-re-ak′shun) A reaction to radiation, especially of the skin.

radioreceptor (ra-de-o-re-sep′tor) A receptor on a cell surface capable of responding to stimulation by radiant energy (e.g., light, heat).

radioresistance (ra-de-o-re-zis′tans) The relative resistance of cells or tissues to the destructive effects of a usual dose of irradiation.

radioscopy (ra-de-os′ko-pe) See fluoroscopy.

radiosensitivity (ra-de-o-sen-sĭ-tiv′ĭ-te) The relative susceptibility of biologic tissues or substances to the action of radiation.

radiotherapist (ra-de-o-ther′ah-pist) A physician who specializes in radiation therapy.

radiotherapy (ra-de-o-ther′ah-pe) See radiation therapy, under therapy.

radiothermy (ra-de-o-ther′me) Therapeutic use of heat originating from radiant sources.

radiotoxemia (ra-de-o-tok-se′me-ah) See radiation sickness, under sickness.

radiotransparent (ra-de-o-trans-par′ent) Allowing the passage of radiant energy.

radioulnar (ra-de-o-ul′nar) Relating to the two bones of the forearm, the radius and ulna.

radium (ra′de-um) A radioactive metallic element that emits alpha, beta, and gamma radiation and a radioactive gas called radon; it has a half-life of 1,590 years; symbol Ra, atomic number 88, atomic weight 226.05; in medicine, it is used in the treatment of some malignancies.

radius (ra′de-us) 1. The shorter of the two bones of the forearm, situated on the side of the thumb. See table of bones. 2. A straight line extending from the center to the periphery of a circle.

radix (ra′diks), pl. rad′ices Latin for root; applied to the beginning or primary portion of a structure (e.g., of a spinal nerve as it emerges from the spinal cord). See also root.

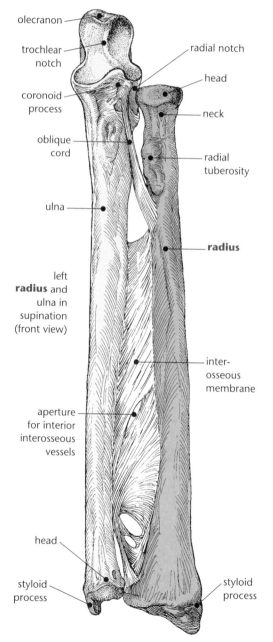

olecranon
trochlear notch
coronoid process
oblique cord
ulna
left **radius** and ulna in supination (front view)
aperture for interior interosseous vessels
head
styloid process

radial notch
head
neck
radial tuberosity
radius
interosseous membrane
styloid process

The stippled portions on the map are areas of the United States and parts of Canada where naturally-occurring soil deposits are found, which can give rise to higher-than-normal levels of **radon**

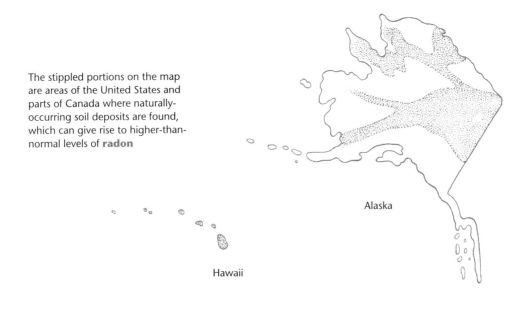

Alaska

Hawaii

common
ragweed

radon (ra'don) A colorless radioactive gas with a half-life of about four days, resulting from the natural radioactive decay of radium; symbol Rn, atomic number 86, atomic weight 222. It constitutes a risk factor for lung cancer, especially when aggravated by cigarette smoke.

raffinose (raf'ĭ-nōs) A sugar present in cottonseed meal and sugar beets, composed of D-galactose, D-glucose, and D-fructose.

rage (rāj) Intense, violent anger.

ragweed (rag'wēd) A weed of the genus *Ambrosia;* the abundant pollen of some species is a hazard to many hay fever sufferers.

rale (rahl) Abnormal sound heard on auscultation of the chest, originating in the airways of the lungs. Rales usually indicate a disease of small bronchi or lungs, as opposed to rhonchi, which originate from larger bronchi.

    atelectatic r. A crackling sound associated with collapse of a part of the lung (atelectasis); may disappear upon deep breathing or coughing; often noted postoperatively.

    crepitant r. A fine sound resembling that made by the rubbing of hair between fingers, produced by a thin secretion in the smallest air passages (bronchioles) in the lungs.

dry r. A whistling or squeaking sound produced by the presence of thick, sticky secretions in the bronchial tubes or by spastic constriction of the tubes, as heard in bronchitis and asthma.

moist r. A rale produced by accumulation of relatively liquid secretions in the airways, as occurs in saccular dilatations of the bronchi (bronchiectasis), especially in the lower portions of the lungs.

rami (ra'mi) Plural of ramus.

ramose, ramous (ra'mos, ra'mus) Branching.

ramulus (ram'u-lus) A minute terminal branch.

ramus (ra'mus), pl. ra'mi Latin for branch; applied to certain anatomic structures (arteries and nerves), especially the first two branches (dorsal and ventral) given off by a spinal nerve as it emerges from the vertebral column, or the bundles of nerve fibers connecting two nerves or a nerve to a ganglion (communicating branches).

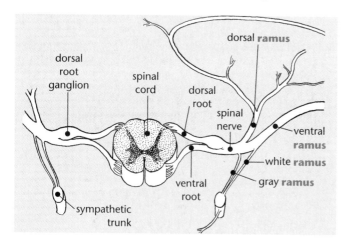

ranine (ra'nin) Relating to the undersurface of the tongue.

ranula (ran'u-lah) A cystic tumor occurring in the floor of the mouth under the tongue. Also called sublingual cyst.

ranular (ran'u-lar) Relating to a ranula.

rape (rāp) An illegal, nonconsensual act of sexual penetration of any body orifice, usually carried out by force or other forms of duress, including intimidation, deceit, impairment of the victim's senses (by any means), or any other method used to overcome the physical and psychological resistance of the victim. Physical damage inflicted upon the female victim may include bruising of the vaginal walls or cervix, swelling of the labia, and tearing of the anus and the area between the anus and genitals (perineum). Psychological damage (posttraumatic stress disorder) usually has an acute phase lasting from a few days to a few weeks, characterized by fear and anger manifested in various ways, depending on the person's usual coping reactions. Symptoms range from talkativeness, crying, trembling, and shock to apparent indifference and acquiescence or even inappropriate smiling. The long-term psychological effects of rape may include flashbacks, nightmares, depression, anxiety, and aversion to sex. The medical examination of a rape victim should follow an established rape protocol. In essence, it encompasses a complete history (e.g., of the assault, of the victim's previous gynecologic status, and of her activities subsequent to the assault); a thorough physical examination for signs of trauma (e.g., bruises, abrasions, bite marks, rope burns, lacerations); and (for laboratory analysis) a collection of specimens from the surface of the body (e.g., fingernail scrapings, hairs, blood, or seminal stains) from the vagina, cervix, and (when indicated) the anus and throat. Formerly rape was considered an offense committed by men against women; many jurisdictions have amended their laws to remove the gender identification and include homosexual offenses; others include rape in marriage (spousal rape) and other sexual offenses, such as incest. Also called aggravated sexual assault; criminal sexual conduct; sexual assault; sexual battery. See also rape protocol, under protocol.

statutory r. The act of sexual penetration usually by an adult with a minor. May also include two minors if the age difference between the two is significant. The legal theory upon which this crime is based is that a minor is unable to give consent to intercourse. Therefore, consent of the minor is no defense.

raphe (ra'fe) A ridge or line marking the union of two similar structures.

r. of medulla oblongata The line between the right and left halves of the medulla oblongata.

pterygomandibular r. A narrow tendinous band extending from the pterygoid hamulus of the skull to the inner surface of the lower jaw at the level of the third molar; it provides attachment anteriorly for the buccinator muscle (of the cheek) and posteriorly for the superior constrictor muscle of the pharynx.

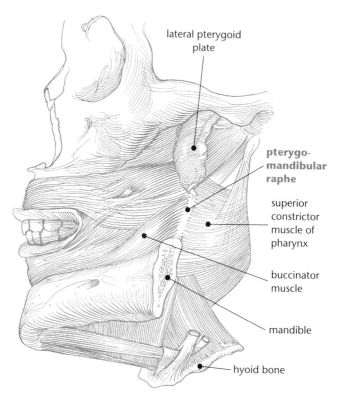

scrotal r. A line extending from the anus to the base of the penis; over the scrotum, it marks the position of the septum that divides the scrotum into two compartments.

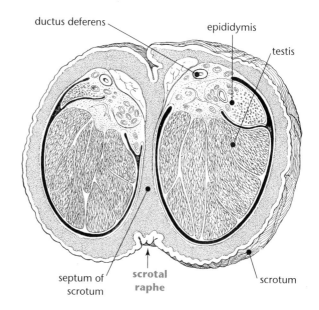

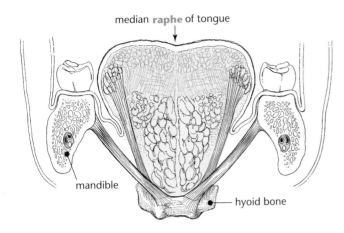

median **raphe** of tongue

mandible

hyoid bone

rarefaction (rār-ĕ-fak′shun) The process of becoming less dense.
rarefy (rār′ĕ-fi) To make less dense or less compact.
rasceta (ră-se′ta) The transverse cutaneous lines on the anterior (palmar) surface of the wrist.
rash (rash) Any eruption on the skin.
    heat r. See prickly heat, under heat.
    nettle r. See urticaria.
raspatory (ras′pah-to-re) Surgical instrument used especially for scraping or smoothing the surface of a bone.
rat (rat) Any of various rodents of the genus *Rattus;* many are vectors of disease-causing organisms.
    albino r.'s White rats used extensively in laboratory experiments.
    inbred r.'s Genetically identical rats developed usually from brother and sister matings that have occurred for 20 or more generations.
    inbred BB r.'s A strain that is used as a model for spontaneous diabetes mellitus.
    nude r.'s A mutant strain of rats that are devoid of hair and a thymus and have diminished or absent T cell function.
    Sprague-Dawley r.'s Genetically similar, inbred strain of white rats used widely in experimental work; developed at the Sprague-Dawley Company.
    transgenic r.'s Laboratory rats genetically engineered to study the effect of changing (adding, deleting, altering) a particular gene; often done to develop disease models that mimic human diseases.
    Wistar r.'s White rats used in experimental biology and medicine; developed at the Wistar Institute.
rate (rāt) Strictly, a measured quantity, or a counted value, per unit time in which there is a distinct relationship between the two (i.e., between the quantity or value and the unit of time). The term is often used less strictly in epidemiologic and demographic studies to express values or quantities that are dimensionless in time.
    basal metabolic r. See basal metabolism, under metabolism.
    birth r. The number of births in a given population per year or any other unit of time.
    death r. See mortality rate.
    erythrocyte sedimentation r. (ESR) The rate (in millimeters per hour) of settling of red blood cells when anticoagulated blood is allowed to stand under standard conditions in a vertical glass column.

Used mainly as an index of inflammation. Also called sedimentation rate.
    fetal heart r. (FHR) The number of fetal heart beats per minute, normally ranging from 120 to 160.
    glomerular filtration r. (GFR) The volume of plasma filtered through the capillary membranes of the filtering unit (glomerulus) of the kidney in one minute.
    growth r. The growth increase (absolute or relative) expressed in units of time.
    infant mortality r. The relation of the number of deaths in the first year of life to the total number of live births in the same population during the same period of time.
    morbidity r. The number of persons with a particular disease in a specified time per given unit of the total population.
    mortality r. The ratio between the number of registered deaths in a specified area and the total population during a given period, usually one year. Also called death rate.
    neonatal mortality r. The number of deaths in infants under 28 days of age in a given year per 1000 live births of that year.
    perinatal mortality r. The number of deaths in infants less than 7 days of age plus the number of fetal deaths after 28 weeks of gestation in a year per 1000 live births of that year.
    pulse r. The number of beats per minute of a peripheral arterial pulse.
    respiratory r., r. of respiration The rate of breathing; the number of inspirations per minute.
    sedimentation r. See erythrocyte sedimentation rate.
ratio (ra′she-o) A proportion.
    accommodative convergence–accommodation r. (AC/A) The ratio of the amount of convergence per the amount of accommodation required to fix both eyes on an object.
    albumin-globulin r. (A/G r) The ratio of albumin to globulin in plasma or (in kidney disease) in urine.
    body-weight r. Body weight (in grams) per height (in centimeters).
    cardiothoracic r. The ratio of the transverse diameter of the heart to the internal diameter of the thoracic cage at its widest point.
    extraction r. (E) The fraction of a substance removed from the blood by an organ, such as the kidney.
    international normalization r. (INR) A system that standardizes prothrombin time (PT) testing by correcting the ratio: patient's PT value divided by the normal PT value, by means of a factor based on the thromboplastin used in the assay; used to make monitoring of warfarin therapy more effective.
    lecithin-sphingomyelin r. (L/S r) The ratio of lecithin to sphingomyelin in amniotic fluid; employed in determining the maturity of the fetal lungs and thus predicting respiratory problems.
    mendelian r. The ratio in which the offspring, or later generations, show characteristics of their parents in accordance with genetic principles.
    nucleocytoplasmic r. The ratio of the volumes of nucleus and cytoplasm within a cell; it is constant for a given cell type, usually increased in malignant tumors.
    therapeutic r. The ratio of the maximally tolerated dose of a drug to the minimal effective dose; the higher the ratio, the safer the drug.

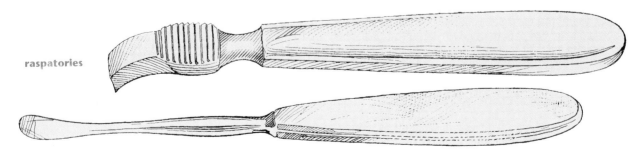

raspatories

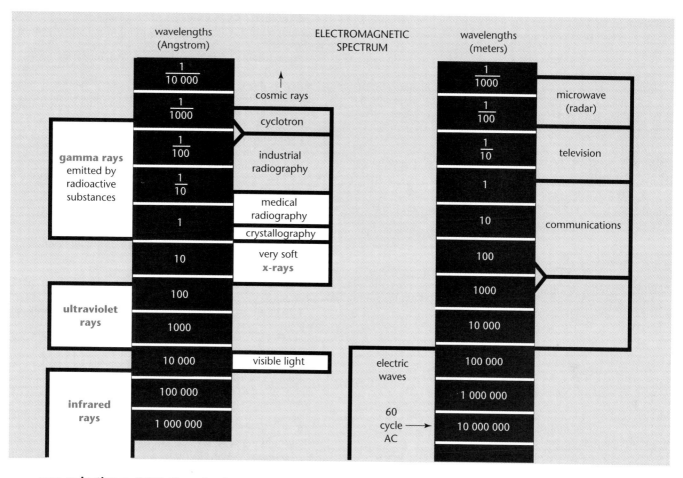

wavelengths (Angstrom)	ELECTROMAGNETIC SPECTRUM		wavelengths (meters)	
$\frac{1}{10\,000}$		↑ cosmic rays	$\frac{1}{1000}$	
$\frac{1}{1000}$		cyclotron	$\frac{1}{100}$	microwave (radar)
$\frac{1}{100}$	gamma rays emitted by radioactive substances	industrial radiography	$\frac{1}{10}$	television
$\frac{1}{10}$		medical radiography	1	
1		crystallography	10	communications
10		very soft x-rays	100	
100	ultraviolet rays		1000	
1000			10 000	
10 000		visible light	100 000	
100 000	infrared rays		1 000 000	
1 000 000			10 000 000	60 cycle AC → / electric waves

urea reduction r. (URR) The ratio of urea concentration in blood, measured as urea in frozen blood urea nitrogen (BUN) before and after hemodialysis.

rational (rash′un-al) 1. In possession of reasoning abilities. 2. Based on reason.

rationalization (rash-un-al-ī-za′shun) A plausible explanation provided as a way of justifying an act that is prompted by factors other than reason.

rauwolfia serpentina (raw-wool′fe-ah ser-pen-ti′nah) The dried root of the tropical shrub *Rauwolfia serpentina;* a source of drugs (e.g., reserpine) with tranquilizing and antihypertensive properties.

ray (rā) 1. A straight beam of electromagnetic radiation (e.g., heat, light). 2. A linear anatomic structure.

actinic r. A ray at the violet and ultraviolet end of the spectrum, capable of producing chemical changes.

alpha (α) r. A ray composed of a stream of high-velocity, positively charged particles (alpha particles) ejected from radioactive substances.

beta (β) r. A ray composed of negatively charged particles (beta particles), especially electrons, ejected from radioactive substances, with a velocity greater than that of the alpha particles; beta rays have a greater penetrance power than alpha rays.

gamma (γ) r. A stream of photons emitted spontaneously by the nucleus of an atom during the radioactive decay process; analogous to the x ray but of shorter wavelength.

grenz r. A very soft ray, with a wavelength between that of the x ray and the ultraviolet ray in the electromagnetic spectrum.

hard r. X ray of short wavelength and high penetrability; produced by a high-voltage tube.

incident r. A ray of radiant energy striking a surface.

infrared r. An electromagnetic ray with a wavelength longer than that of the red end of the spectrum.

medullary r.'s A series of pale radiations in the kidney, extending outward from each pyramid toward and into the kidney cortex;

they consist of the straight tubules (ascending and descending limbs) of the loops of Henle and collecting ducts.

reflected r. A ray of radiant energy bouncing back after striking a nonabsorbent surface.

roentgen r. See x ray.

soft r. A ray of long wavelength and slight penetrability.

ultraviolet r. An electromagnetic, invisible ray, with wavelength beyond the violet end of the spectrum.

x r., roentgen r. An electromagnetic ray with a very short wavelength, generated at the point of impact of a stream of high-speed cathode electrons on a target of an x-ray tube.

rayage (ra′ej) The radiation dosage used in radiation therapy.

re- Prefix meaning backward; again.

reabsorption (re-ab-sorp′shun) 1. The process of absorbing again. 2. The state of being reabsorbed.

tubular r. Selective reabsorption of extracellular fluid by the kidney tubules; it helps restore essential components to the body.

reactant (re-ak′tant) Any substance taking part in a chemical reaction.

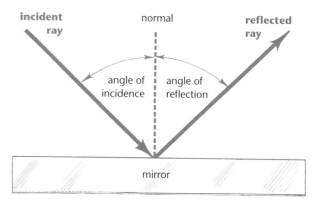

reaction (re-ak'shun) 1. Any response to a stimulus. 2. The observable color change in, or produced by, indicators or reagents in chemical analysis.

  adverse r. An undesirable and sometimes life-threatening reaction to a therapeutic drug; may be caused by a variety of factors, including patient's errors in taking prescribed drugs, administration of a drug along with another that has synergistic action, immunologic mechanisms, and a genetically determined abnormal response (drug idiosyncrasy).

COMMON MANIFESTATIONS OF ADVERSE REACTIONS TO SOME DRUGS

MANIFESTATIONS		DRUGS
dermatologic	urticaria (hives)	penicillin aspirin barbiturates sulfonamides
	exfoliative dermatitis (loss of superficial skin layers)	penicillin barbiturates
respiratory	apnea (difficulty in breathing)	local anesthetics
	inflammation of mucous membranes of nose	reserpine
	pulmonary infection	antineoplastic-immuno-suppressive drugs
cardiovascular	hypotension (fall in blood pressure)	imipramine amitriptyline
	arrhythmia (abnormal rhythm of heart beat)	thyroid hormone sympathomimetic amines
gastrointestinal	swollen or hairy tongue	tetracycline
	discoloration of dental enamel	tetracycline (in children)
	peptic ulceration hemorrhage	aspirin

  alarm r. (AR) The body's response to a sudden exposure to a violent or stressful stimulus.

  allergic r. A reaction stimulated by exposure to a substance (allergen) to which the individual has become sensitized.

  anamnestic r. See secondary response, under response.

  antigen-antibody r. The specific binding of an antibody with the same type of antigen that triggered the formation of the antibody.

  arousal r. A change in the brain wave pattern of a person when suddenly awakened.

  Bence Jones r. Coagulation of Bence-Jones protein when a urine sample from a patient with Bence-Jones proteinuria is heated, followed by its redissolving on boiling, and coagulation again when cooling.

  biuret r. See biuret test, under test.

  Casoni's r. See Casoni intradermal test, under test.

  cell-mediated r. Delayed allergic reaction involving T lymphocytes.

  chain r. A series of chemical reactions, each one initiated by the preceding one.

  complement-fixation r. See complement fixation, under fixation.

  consensual r. Constriction of the pupils of both eyes when a light is flashed into one eye only. Also called consensual response.

  conversion r. See conversion disorder, under disorder.

  cross r. Reaction occurring between an antibody and an antigen of a type different from, but related to, the one that triggered the production of the antibody.

  cytotoxic r. Reaction resulting in destruction or damage of cells.

  delayed r. See delayed-type hypersensitivity, under hypersensitivity.

  dissociative r. A reaction characterized by dissociated behavior (e.g., amnesia, sleepwalking).

  first-order r. Reaction in which the rate is proportional to the concentration of the substance undergoing chemical change. COMPARE zero-order reaction.

  Herxheimer's r. See Jarisch-Herxheimer reaction.

  hyperkinetic r. of childhood See attention-deficit hyperactivity disorder, under disorder.

  id r. An allergic reaction to a cutaneous fungal infection occurring at some distance from it; especially an eruption of vesicles filled with sterile fluid on the hands during an acute fungal infection on the feet or scalp.

  immune r. See immune response, under response.

  Jarisch-Herxheimer r. An inflammatory condition sometimes occurring two to eight hours after instituting antibiotic therapy for syphilis; characterized by chills, fever, headache, muscle pain, and mild low blood pressure; believed to be an allergic reaction to the rapid release of treponemal antigen. Also called Herxheimer's reaction.

  leukemoid r. Condition marked by an increase of white blood cells; similar to, but not associated with, leukemia; seen in certain infectious diseases and some malignant tumors.

  Moloney r. See Moloney test, under test.

  Neufeld r. See capsular swelling, under swelling.

  Pándy's r. The change occurring in a mixture of cerebrospinal fluid (CSF) and a test solution, indicating the abnormal presence of protein in the CSF; the change may range from a slight turbidity to a milky appearance, depending on the amount of protein present. Also called Pándy's test.

  periodic acid–Schiff r. See periodic acid–Schiff stain, under stain.

  polymerase chain r. (PCR) A method of amplifying a short stretch of DNA; applications include genetic testing, detection of difficult-to-isolate pathogens, mutation analysis, DNA sequencing, diagnosis of disease, and analyzing evolutionary relationships.

  quellung r. See capsular swelling, under swelling.

  Wassermann r. (WR) See Wassermann test, under test.

  zero-order r. A reaction that, regardless of the concentration of the reactants, procedes at a definite rate. COMPARE first-order reaction.

reactivate (re-ak'tī-vāt) To restore activity.
reactivity (re-ak-tiv'ĭ-te) The ability to react.
reagent (re-a'jent) Any substance, added to a solution, that participates in a chemical reaction, especially one employed in chemical analysis for the detection of biologic constituents.
reagin (re'ah-jin) 1. Antibody involved in immediate hypersensitivity reactions; the human IgE antibody. 2. Obsolete term for antibodies detected by the Wassermann test for syphilis.
reaginic (re-ah-jin'ik) Relating to a reagin.

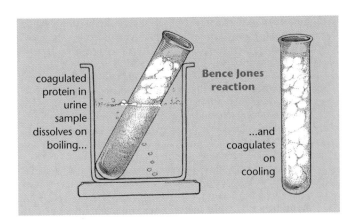

coagulated protein in urine sample dissolves on boiling...

Bence Jones reaction

...and coagulates on cooling

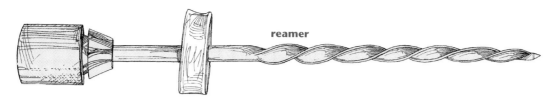

reamer

reality (re-al′ĭ-te) The sum of all things that have an objective existence.

reality testing (re-al′ĭ-te test′ing) The ability to evaluate the outside world and to adequately comprehend one's relationship to it; gross impairment in reality testing is the defining symptom of psychosis.

reamer (re′mer) Dental instrument for enlarging a root canal.

rebase (re-bās′) To replace or alter the base of a denture without changing the occlusal relations of upper and lower teeth.

recall (re′kol) The process of summoning back a memory into consciousness; to remember; often used to describe the recollection of events in the immediate past.

recanalization (re-kan-al-ĭ-za′shun) The gradual establishment of a channel through a blood clot (thrombus) occluding a blood vessel, and restoration of some degree of blood flow; results from the healing of the thrombus.

receiver (re-sēv′er) In chemistry, a container attached to a condenser for the collection of distillation products.

receptaculum (re-sep-tak′u-lum) A pouchlike anatomic structure.

   r. chyli See cisterna chyli, under cisterna.

receptor (re-sep′tor) 1. A molecule on the surface of a cell membrane that binds selectively to a specific substance (protein or peptide), producing a biologic effect that is specific to that binding. 2. The small structure in which a sensory nerve fiber terminates; a sensory end-organ.

   adrenergic r.'s A class of receptors in effector tissues innervated by adrenergic postganglionic fibers of the sympathetic nervous system.

   alpha-adrenergic r.'s, α-adrenergic r.'s A subclass of adrenergic receptors that respond to stimulation by norepinephrine and are blocked by such compounds as phenoxybenzamine and phentolamine; they mediate such actions as constriction of blood vessels and dilatation of the pupils.

   beta-adrenergic r.'s, β-adrenergic r.'s A subclass of adrenergic receptors that are stimulated by epinephrine and respond to such blocking agents as propranolol; there are two kinds: beta$_1$, responsible for acceleration of the heartbeat and lipolysis, and beta$_2$, responsible for dilatation of bronchi and blood vessels.

   opiate r.'s Receptors in specific tissues of the brain that have the capacity to combine with morphine and endorphins.

   stretch r. A receptor (e.g., one in a muscle or a tendon) whose function is to detect elongation.

recess (re′ses) A small shallow cavity or indentation; a depression.

   costodiaphragmatic r. The extension of the pleural cavity between the diaphragm and the rib cage; it is about 5 cm in length.

   epitympanic r. The portion of the middle ear chamber situated above the level of the eardrum (tympanic membrane); it contains the head of the malleus and body of the incus.

   hepatorenal r. A recess of the peritoneal cavity, behind and below the right lobe of the liver and in front of the upper right kidney and right adrenal (suprarenal) gland; it extends down to the transverse mesocolon. Also called Morison's pouch.

   infundibular r. The funnel-shaped recess from the anterior part of the third ventricle down into the base of the infundibulum of the pituitary (hypophysis).

   lateral r. of fourth ventricle The narrow recess on both sides of the fourth ventricle of the brain, which opens by way of the lateral apertures into the subarachnoid space.

   optic r. The anterior prolongation of the third ventricle above the optic chiasm.

   piriform r. An elongated recess in the laryngopharynx on each side of the opening of the larynx.

   subpopliteal r. The extension of the knee joint cavity between the lateral condyle of the femur and the popliteal muscle. Also called bursa of popliteal tendon.

recession (re-sesh′un) The process of withdrawing.

   gingival r. Loss or atrophy of the gums with resulting added exposure of tooth surface.

   tendon r. Surgical procedure for correction of strabismus in which one of the exterior muscles of the eye is cut at its attachment to the eyeball and reattached 4 to 5 mm behind the original site.

recessive (re-ses′iv) 1. Receding. 2. In genetics, denoting a characteristic that is apparent only when genes for it are inherited from both parents.

recessus (re-ses′sus) Latin for recess.

recidivation (re-sid-ĭ-va′shun) Reappearance of a disease, symptom, or pattern of behavior.

recidivism (re-sid′ĭ-vizm) A tendency to return to a previous mode of behavior, especially criminal or delinquent habits.

recidivist (re-sid′ĭ-vist) A person who tends to relapse to a former pattern of criminal behavior after rehabilitation.

recipe (res′ĭ-pe) (R$_x$) 1. Latin for take; used as a heading (superscription) of a physician's prescription. 2. The prescription itself.

recipiomotor (re-sip-e-o-mo′tor) Denoting the recipient of a motor stimulus.

recombinant (re-kom′bĭ-nant) An organism, chromosome, or DNA that has resulted from the introduction of genetic material from an outside source.

recombination (re-kom-bĭ-na′shun) In genetics, the formation of a gene combination in an offspring that is different from the arrangement of those genes in either parent, caused by breakage and exchange of genes (crossing over) between homologous chromosomes during a stage in cell division (meiosis).

reconstitution (re-kon-stĭ-tu′shun) Restoration to original form.

record (rek′ord) A collection of related data.

   dental r. Record containing the data collected during a dental examination; used for diagnosis or treatment planning.

   dental identification r. A standard chart containing characteristic dental features of an unidentified or unrecognizable dead body; it includes notations regarding extracted or unerupted teeth, restorations or prostheses, and malposition of any tooth abnormality; used to confirm or exclude an identity by comparing it with dental records of persons reported missing.

   hospital r. *(a)* A confidential medical record that includes a wide variety of medical and administrative documents reflecting the care provided to the patient, including observations of nursing and medical staff about the patient's progress and response to therapy; may also include a transfer note, if the patient is transferred to another health care institution; an autopsy report, if the patient dies and a post-mortem examination is performed; and records of release against medical advice, when applicable. The record belongs to the hospital but the patient may have access to it. *(b)* A compilation of data relating to hospital activities or programs. It excludes patients' medical records.

   interocclusal r. A record of the positional interrelations of upper and lower teeth.

   maxillomandibular r. A record of the positional interrelations of the upper and lower jaws (maxilla and mandible).

   medical r. A confidential record that documents a patient's medical history and history of medical care, including illness, diagnoses, treatment, and results of treatment. It serves as a basis for the planning and continuity of the patient's care; it provides a means of communication among physicians and other professionals

R

involved in the therapy; it serves as a basis for review, study, and evaluation of the patient's condition; it furnishes documentary evidence of the patient's care; it serves to protect the legal interests of the patient, hospital, and responsible practitioner; and it provides data for use in research and education.

physician's private-office r. The confidential medical record of a private patient; it includes treatment rendered in the physician's office and may include records received from outside sources or facilities (e.g., laboratories, hospitals). The record belongs to the private physician but the patient may have access to it.

problem-oriented medical r. (POMR) See problem-oriented record.

problem-oriented r. (POR) A medical record organized around each of the patient's identified medical problems. A common format for an entry uses the SOAP (Subjective, Objective, Assessment, and Plan) approach. Also called problem-oriented medical record.

recording (re-kord'ing) Preserving in writing, or any other permanent form, the results of a study.

recovery (re-kov'er-e) **1.** Restoration of health after an illness. **2.** The act or process of retrieving.

ultrasonic egg r. The process of obtaining an egg from the ovary by means of an ultrasonically guided needle biopsy; used in *in vitro* fertilization.

recrement (rek'rĕ-ment) A bodily secretion that is reabsorbed by the body.

recrudescence (re-kroo-des'ens) Return of symptoms and signs of a disease process after a short dormant or inactive period.

recruitment (re-krōōt'ment) **1.** In hearing testing, the disproportionate and abnormally rapid increase in loudness experienced by a patient when a sound stimulus is gradually increased. **2.** A gradual increase in response to a stimulus that has a constant intensity but prolonged duration.

rectal (rek'tal) Relating to the rectum.

rectalgia (rek-tal'je-ah) See proctalgia.

rectify (rek'tĭ-fi) **1.** To purify a liquid through redistillation. **2.** To transform an alternating current into a direct one.

rectitis (rek-ti'tis) See proctitis.

recto- Combining form meaning the rectum.

rectoabdominal (rek-to-ab-dom'ĭ-nal) Relating to the rectum and the abdomen.

rectocele (rek'to-sĕl) Prolapse of the rectum into the pelvic floor (perineum). Also called proctoc

rectoclysis (rek-tok'lĭ-sis) See pr

rectocolitis (rek-to-ko-li'tis) See

rectoperineorrhaphy (rek-to-per-ĭ-ne-or'ah-te) See proctoperineoplasty.

rectopexy (rek'to-pek-se) See proctopexy.

rectoplasty (rek'to-plas-te) See proctoplasty.

rectorrhaphy (rek-tor'ah-fe) See proctorrhaphy.

rectoscope (rek'to-skōp) See proctoscope.

rectoscopy (rek-tos'ko-pe) See proctoscopy.

rectosigmoid (rek-to-sig'moid) The rectum and the sigmoid colon considered together, especially the region of the junction of these two portions of the bowel.

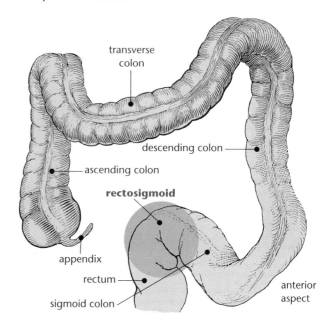

rectostenosis (rek-to-stĕ-no'sis) See proctostenosis.

rectourethral (rek-to-u-re'thral) Relating to the rectum and the urethra.

rectouterine (rek-to-u'ter-in) Relating to the rectum and uterus.

rectovaginal (rek-to-vaj'ĭ-nal) Relating to the rectum and the vagina.

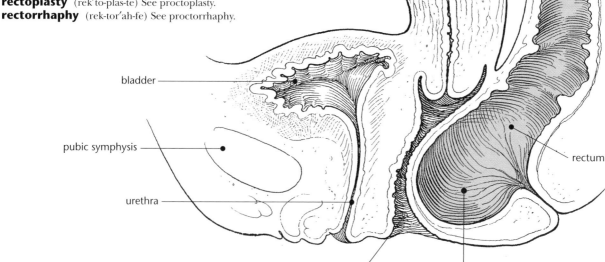

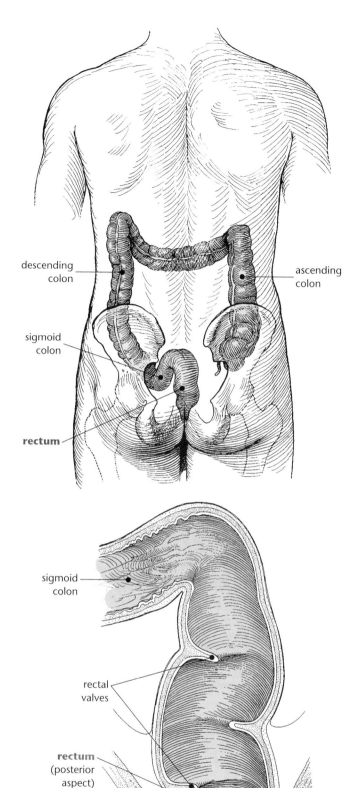

descending colon

ascending colon

sigmoid colon

rectum

sigmoid colon

rectal valves

rectum (posterior aspect)

rectal column

anorectal line

anal sphincter muscle

anus

rectovesical (rek-to-ves′ĭ-kal) Relating to the rectum and the bladder.

rectum (rek′tum) The lowest portion of the intestinal tract, extending from the sigmoid colon (at the level of the sacrum) to the anal canal; in the adult, it is about 12 cm long.

rectus (rek′tus) Latin for straight; applied to certain muscles.

recumbent (re-kum′bent) Lying down; reclining.

recuperate (re-ku′per-āt) To recover; to regain health.

recurrence (re-kur′ens) 1. A return of symptoms occurring as a natural course of certain diseases. 2. A return of a morbid process after a period of abatement.

recurrent (re-kur′ent) Returning after a period of abatement.

recurvation (re-kur-va′shun) A backward curvature.

Red Cross 1. A red Greek cross on a white background; an international emblem to identify those caring for the sick and injured in times of war and natural disasters. 2. The emblem of the American Red Cross Society.

redox (red′oks) In chemistry, a combined shortened version of the term reduction-oxidation.

reduce (re-dūs′) 1. To return a part to its original or normal anatomic position (e.g., the ends of a fractured bone, a hernia). 2. In chemistry, to submit to reduction.

reducible (re-du′sĭ-bl) Capable of being reduced.

reductant (re-duk′tant) In chemistry, the donor of electrons in an oxidation-reduction reaction.

reductase (re-duk′tās) In chemistry, the reducing enzyme in an oxidation-reduction reaction.

reduction (re-duk′shun) 1. The act of correction or repositioning (e.g., of a hernia, a fracture, or a dislocation). Also called repositioning. 2. In chemistry, the removal of oxygen from a substance or the addition of hydrogen; the opposite of oxidation.

reduplication (re-du-plĭ-ka′shun) A doubling.

reduviid (re-du′vĭ-id) Any predatory insect (e.g., assassin bug) of the family Reduviidae; some are vectors of disease-causing microorganisms.

reefing (rēf′ing) The act of folding, such as the surgical folding and suturing of a tissue to reduce its size.

reentry (re-en′tre) The return of an impulse to an area of heart muscle that it has recently stimulated (e.g., in reciprocal heart rhythms).

refine (re-fīn′) To purify.

reflect (re-flekt′) 1. To bend back from a surface (e.g., light rays). 2. To move or turn aside (e.g., to expose an underlying structure). 3. To meditate or think back.

reflection (re-flek′shun) 1. The return of light from an optical surface into the same medium from which it came. 2. A bending back.

reflector (re-flek′tor) Any surface that reflects heat, light, or sound waves.

reflex (re′fleks) 1. An involuntary and immediate response to a stimulus. 2. Turned backward.

　　abdominal r. Contraction of the abdominal wall musculature elicited by light stroking of the overlying skin.

　　accommodation r. The increase in convexity of the lens of the eye when the eyes are directed from a distant to a near object, in order to bring the image into focus; effected by contraction of the ciliary muscle and relaxation of the suspensory ligament of the lens.

　　Achilles r. Contraction of the calf muscles with resulting plantar flexion of the foot, elicited by a sharp tap on the Achilles (calcaneal) tendon. Also called Achilles tendon reflex; ankle reflex; ankle jerk; calcaneal tendon reflex.

　　Achilles tendon r. See Achilles reflex.

　　acquired r. See conditioned reflex.

　　anal r. Contraction of the anal sphincter muscle upon irritation of the perianal area, or upon insertion of the finger into the rectum.

　　ankle r. See Achilles reflex.

　　attitudinal r. See statotonic reflex.

　　Babinski r. See extensor plantar reflex.

R

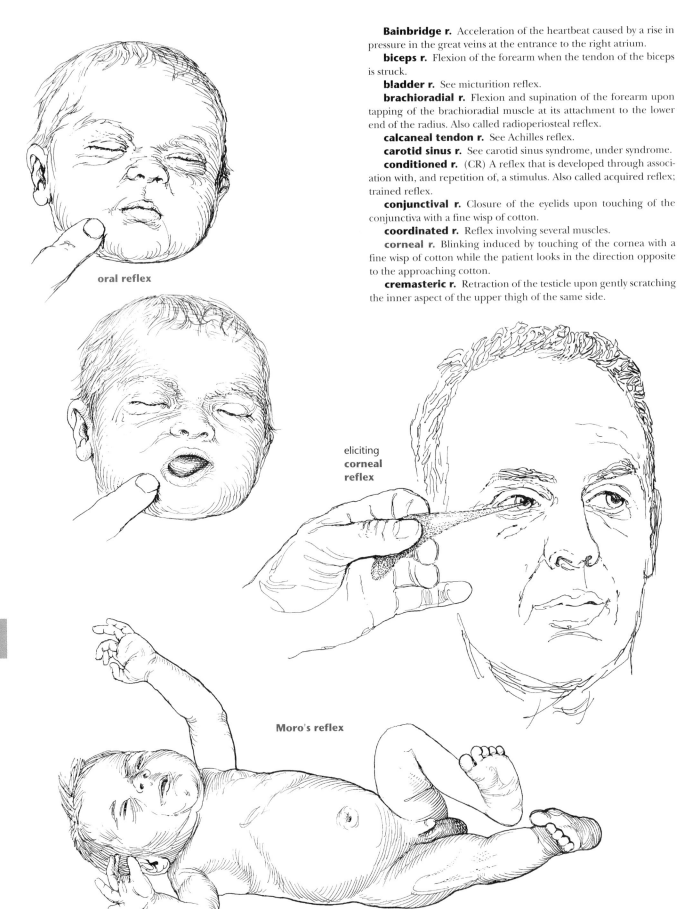

Bainbridge r. Acceleration of the heartbeat caused by a rise in pressure in the great veins at the entrance to the right atrium.

biceps r. Flexion of the forearm when the tendon of the biceps is struck.

bladder r. See micturition reflex.

brachioradial r. Flexion and supination of the forearm upon tapping of the brachioradial muscle at its attachment to the lower end of the radius. Also called radioperiosteal reflex.

calcaneal tendon r. See Achilles reflex.

carotid sinus r. See carotid sinus syndrome, under syndrome.

conditioned r. (CR) A reflex that is developed through association with, and repetition of, a stimulus. Also called acquired reflex; trained reflex.

conjunctival r. Closure of the eyelids upon touching of the conjunctiva with a fine wisp of cotton.

coordinated r. Reflex involving several muscles.

corneal r. Blinking induced by touching of the cornea with a fine wisp of cotton while the patient looks in the direction opposite to the approaching cotton.

cremasteric r. Retraction of the testicle upon gently scratching the inner aspect of the upper thigh of the same side.

oral reflex

eliciting **corneal reflex**

Moro's reflex

reflex ■ reflex

crossed r. A muscular contraction on one side of the body elicited by a sharp tap on the opposite side. Also called crossed jerk.

crossed adductor r. Inward rotation of the leg upon tapping of the sole.

crossed extension r. Response elicited from a newborn infant indicating integrity of the spinal cord; placing the child in the supine position, the examiner extends and presses down on one of the child's legs and stimulates the sole of the foot; this causes the free leg to flex, adduct, and then extend.

crossed knee r. Contraction of the anterior muscles of the thigh in response to a sharp tap on the patellar ligament of the opposite knee. Also called crossed knee jerk.

deep r. Any of a group of reflexes characterized by a sudden brief stretching and then immediate contraction of a muscle, elicited by a sharp tap on the muscle or its tendon. Also called myotatic reflex; deep tendon reflex; tendon reflex; stretch reflex.

deep tendon r. See deep reflex.

elbow r. See triceps reflex.

extensor plantar r. Abnormal reflex characterized by extension of the big toe with fanning of the small toes upon scratching the sole of the foot. Also called Babinski reflex; Babinski sign. COMPARE plantar reflex.

fundus r. The red glow seen in the pupil during inspection of the interior of the eyeball, produced by reflection of light from the choroid.

gag r. Retching elicited by touching the back of the throat (pharynx). Also called pharyngeal reflex.

gastrocolic r. The wavelike contraction of the colon, propelling its contents onward, initiated by introduction of food into the empty stomach.

Gordon r. Abnormal reflex characterized by extension of the big toe elicited by firm squeezing of the calf muscles.

grasp r. The immediate grasping of an object placed in the hand; occurs normally only in infants.

Hering-Breuer r. A mechanism through which breathing is regulated by limiting the duration of inspiration and expiration; it involves the vagus nerves and sensory receptors in the lungs and airways, which are activated by inflation and deflation of the lungs.

Hoffmann's r. See Hoffmann's sign (b), under sign.

knee r. See patellar reflex.

knee-jerk r. See patellar reflex.

light r. Constriction of the pupil upon stimulation of the retina with light.

micturition r. Any of the reflexes controlling effortless urination and the subconscious ability to retain urine within the bladder. Also called bladder reflex; urinary reflex; vesical reflex.

milk-ejection r. Release of milk from the breast upon stimulation of the nipple.

Moro's r., Moro's embrace r. A normal reflex of newborns in response to loud noises or sudden changes in position; characterized by tensing of muscles, a wide embracing motion of the arms, and extension of the thighs, legs, and fingers, except the thumb and index finger, which remain in a "C" position. Also called startle reflex.

myotatic r. See deep reflex.

Oppenheim's r. Abnormal reflex characterized by extension of the toes elicited by pressing down firmly on the shin from the knee to the ankle.

oral r. Normal reflex elicited when the corner of the mouth of a newborn infant is touched; the bottom lip lowers on the same side and the tongue moves forward and toward the examiner's finger.

orbicularis pupillary r. Contraction of the pupil while trying to close the eyelids, which are forcibly held open. Also called Westphal's pupillary reflex.

palm-chin r. See palmomental reflex.

palmomental r. Twitching of one side of the chin upon scratching of the palm of the hand of the same side. Also called palm-chin reflex.

patellar r. Extension of the leg upon tapping of the patellar tendon while the leg hangs loosely at right angles to the thigh. Also

called knee jerk; knee-jerk reflex; knee reflex; patellar tendon reflex; quadriceps reflex.

patellar tendon r. See patellar reflex.

pharyngeal r. See gag reflex.

pilomotor r. Formation of goose flesh on lightly touching the skin, or on exposure to cold or emotional stimuli.

plantar r. Flexion of the toes upon scratching of the sole of the foot; a normal response. Also called sole reflex. COMPARE extensor plantar reflex.

primitive r. Any of the reflexes occurring naturally in the newborn; an indication of normal neuromuscular development; it occurs in the adult only in certain degenerative disorders.

proprioceptive r. Any of various reflexes brought about by stimulation of sensory nerve endings (proprioceptors), which respond to stimuli relating to movements and position of the body.

pupillary r. Any change in the size of the pupils, especially in response to a light stimulus.

pupillary-skin r. Dilatation of the pupil upon scratching of the neck.

quadriceps r. See patellar reflex.

radial r. Flexion of the forearm upon tapping of the lower end of the radius.

radioperiosteal r. See brachioradial reflex.

rectal r. Desire to defecate stimulated by accumulation of feces in the rectum.

rooting r. A normal reflex elicited from a newborn infant, characterized by turning of the head in the direction of a light touch on the cheek, and pursing of the lips in preparation for sucking.

sole r. See plantar reflex.

startle r. See Moro's reflex.

statotonic r. Any of several reflexes stimulated by a change in position of the body in space. Also called attitudinal reflex.

stretch r. See myotatic reflex.

superficial r. Any reflex elicited by stimulation of the skin and mucous membranes.

tendon r. See deep reflex.

trained r. See conditioned reflex.

triceps r. A sudden extension of the forearm on tapping of the triceps tendon at the elbow while the forearm hangs loosely at a right angle to the arm. Also called elbow reflex; elbow jerk.

urinary r. See micturition reflex.

vagovagal r. A cardiac reflex elicited by irritation of the respiratory tract.

vesical r. See micturition reflex.

Westphal's pupillary r. See orbicularis pupillary reflex.

reflexograph (re-flek′so-graf) An apparatus for recording a reflex graphically.

reflux (re′fluks) A backward flow.

hepatojugular r. Distention of the jugular veins (in the neck) induced by pressing firmly upon the liver; indicative of congestive heart failure.

vesicoureteral r. Abnormal flow of urine from the bladder back into a ureter during urination.

refract (re-frakt′) **1.** To change the direction of a propagating wave (e.g., of light). **2.** To measure the refractive and muscular state of the eyes.

refraction (re-frak′shun) (R) **1.** The measurement and/or correction of refractive errors of the eye. **2.** The deflection of a ray of light as a result of passing obliquely from one medium to another of different optical density.

double r. The splitting of light in two slightly different directions to form two light rays. Also called birefringence.

refractive (re-frak′tiv) Relating to refraction.

refractometer (re-frak-tom′ĕ-ter) An instrument for measuring the refractive error of the eyes.

refractoriness (re-frak′tor-e-nes) The inability of nerve cells to respond to a second stimulus delivered immediately after the first stimulus.

refractory (re-frak'to-re) Unresponsive to treatment; applied to a disease or condition.

refracture (re-frak'chur) The breaking again of a bone that was improperly set.

refusal (re-fu'zal) The act of withholding permission, acceptance, or compliance.

    r. to treat. Refusal of a health professional to initiate or continue treatment of a person or a group of people.

    treatment r. Refusal of a person to accept treatment (medical or psychiatric), or his unwillingness to comply with the physician's instructions or prescribed regimens. If the person is legally incompetent, or a minor, the concept may include a third party authorized to make decisions on his behalf.

refusion (re-fu'shun) Return of blood to the circulation after temporary removal from the same individual.

regeneration (re-jen-er-a'shun) Replacement of lost or injured cells by the same type of cell.

    axonal r. See neurocladism.

regimen (rej'ĭ-men) A systematic procedure or regulation of an activity (e.g., exercise, diet) designed to achieve certain ends, usually hygienic or therapeutic in nature.

regio (re'je-o), pl. regio'nes Latin for region.

region (re'jun) **1.** An arbitrary division or continuous area on the surface of the body, with more or less definite boundaries. **2.** A bodily part with a special nervous or vascular supply. **3.** A portion of an organ having a special function, as the olfactory region of the nasal cavity.

    abdominal r.'s The nine regions into which the abdomen is divided by imaginary planes, namely the right and left hypochondriac, epigastric, right and left lumbar, umbilical, right and left inguinal, and pubic.

    anal r. The posterior triangular region of the perineal region that contains the anus and surrounding skin.

    buccal r. The region of the face on either side below the cheek (zygomatic) bone.

    cubital r. A region around the elbow: *Anterior cubital r.,* the front part of the elbow; *Posterior cubital r.,* the back part of the elbow.

    femoral r. The region of the thigh.

    frontal r. The region of the forehead, overlying the frontal bone of the skull.

    gluteal r. The region of the buttock, overlying the gluteal muscles.

    I r. In immunology, the portion of the major histocompatibility complex containing genes that control immune responses.

    infraclavicular r. The region of the chest, just below the collarbone (clavicle).

    infrared r. The region of the electromagnetic radiation spectrum, between those of visible red light and those of microwaves, covering a wavelength range of approximately 100 nm to 1 mm.

    motor r. See motor area, under area.

    nuchal r. The region of the back of the neck.

    occipital r. The part of the scalp in back of the head overlying the occipital bone.

    olfactory r. The thickened part of the mucous membrane at the upper part of the nasal cavity, containing nerve cells whose axons form the fine filaments of the olfactory (1st cranial) nerve.

    patellar r. The part of the leg in front of the knee.

    perineal r. The region overlying the pelvic outlet; it is divided into two triangles by a transverse line connecting the ischial tuberosities: a triangle of the anal region posteriorly and a triangle of the urogenital region (perineum) anteriorly.

    popliteal r. The region in back of the knee.

    precordial r. The region of the anterior chest wall overlying the heart.

    pubic r. The lowest midabdominal region, between the inguinal regions.

    rolandic r. See motor area, under area.

    sacral r. The region of the lower back overlying the sacrum.

    sacrococcygeal r. The region of the lower back overlying the sacrum and coccyx.

    sensory r. See sensory area, under area.

    r.'s of spinal cord The five divisions of the spinal cord, namely cervical, thoracic, lumbar, sacral, and coccygeal.

    supraclavicular r. The hollow above the collarbone (clavicle), on each side.

    suprasternal r. The hollow in the midline of the front of the neck, just above the suprasternal notch.

    umbilical r. The central part of the abdomen surrounding the navel (umbilicus); situated above the transtubercular plane and below the transpyloric plane.

    urogenital r. The triangular part of the external genitalia, comprising the anterior part of the perineal region.

    vestibular r. The region of the vestibule of the nose; the lowest and movable part of the nose; the site of most nosebleeds.

    zygomatic r. The part of the face on either side, over the cheek (zygomatic) bone.

registration (rej-is-tra'shun) In dentistry, a record of jaw relations.

regression (re-gresh'un) **1.** A relapse. **2.** An unconscious psychological defense mechanism in which there is a partial or symbolic return to an earlier pattern of behavior or level of adaptation.

regulation (reg-u-la'shun) **1.** A rule designed to control details or procedure according to a standard. **2.** The act or process of regulating. **3.** The condition of being regulated.

    gene r. A process controlling the formation or suppression of gene products (proteins).

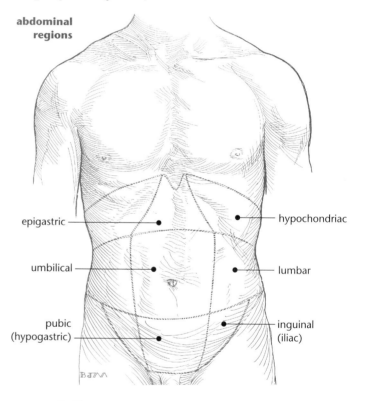

abdominal regions

epigastric — hypochondriac — umbilical — lumbar — pubic (hypogastric) — inguinal (iliac)

regurgitation (re-gur-jĭ-ta'shun) **1.** The bringing up of stomach contents in the absence of nausea and muscular contraction of the abdominal diaphragm. **2.** A backward flow of blood through an incompetent valve of the heart.

    aortic r. Regurgitation of blood through an incompetent aortic valve into the left ventricle during ventricular diastole.

    mitral r. The back flow of blood from the left ventricle to the left atrium due to a malfunctioning mitral valve (left atrioventricular valve).

rehabilitation (re-hah-bil-ĭ-ta'shun) **1.** The process of restoring an impaired function to a normal or near-normal state following illness, injury, or drug or alcohol dependence. **2.** In worker's compensation, a coordinated effort to restore a disabled worker to a reasonable level of economic self-sufficiency. It may include surgical treatment or physical and occupational therapy. See also disability.

alaryngeal voice r. Procedures used to restore voice after surgical removal of the larynx (laryngectomy). They range from instruction by a speech therapist to surgical insertion of a prosthesis.

mouth r. Restoration of the form and function of tooth structure.

vocational r. Rehabilitation encompassing either formal, modified, or alternative occupational retraining. It is preferably instituted as soon as a worker is physically able to participate in a suitable program.

reimplantation (re-im-plan-ta′shun) See replantation.

reinfection (re-in-fek′shun) A second infection by the same agent following recovery or during the course of the primary infection.

reinforcement (re-in-fors′ment) 1. Added force or strength, such as the increased reflex response when the person performs some mental or physical work while the reflex is being elicited. 2. A structural addition to strengthen a denture. 3. The strengthening of a response either by reward or by avoidance of punishment.

reinnervation (re-in-er-va′shun) The restoration of a damaged nerve either by grafting of a live nerve or by spontaneous regrowth of nerve fibers.

reintegration (re-in-te-gra′shun) The resumption of normal functioning after a mental disorder.

rejection (re-jek′shun) An immune response against transplanted tissue that is antigenically incompatible with the host's body, leading to failure of function of the grafted tissue.

relapse (re-laps′) The return of a disease after apparent recovery or improvement.

relation (re-la′shun) The position of one object when considered in association with another.

centric jaw r. The most posterior position of the lower jaw (mandible) from which lateral jaw movements can be made at any given degree of jaw separation.

eccentric jaw r. Any deviation from the centric jaw relation.

rest jaw r. The relation of the lower jaw (mandible) to the upper jaw (maxilla) when the person is resting in an upright position and the jaws are not in contact.

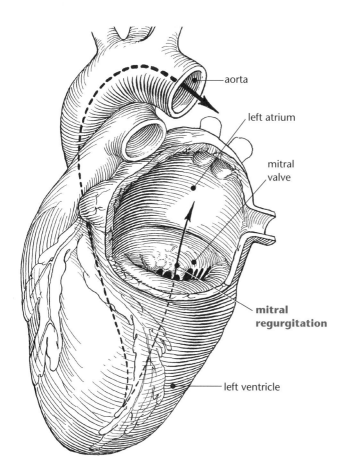

relationship (re-la′shun-ship) An association; a kinship.

object r. The emotional bonds existing between two people or groups.

sadomasochistic r. A complementary relationship, usually sexual, in which one partner enjoys suffering while the other enjoys inflicting pain or humiliation.

relaxant (re-lak′sant) 1. A drug or treatment that produces relaxation by relieving muscular or nervous tension. 2. Tending to reduce tension.

relaxation (re-lak-sa′shun) 1. Loosening. 2. The lengthening of muscle fibers.

relaxin (re-lak′sin) An ovarian hormone, produced by the corpus luteum, that relaxes the pubic symphysis and other pelvic joints and softens and dilates the uterine cervix during childbirth.

relief (re-lēf′) 1. Easing of discomfort; lessening of mental or physical distress. 2. In dentistry, removal of undue pressure from a spot under a denture base.

relieve (re-lēv′) 1. To bring about a reduction (e.g., of pain, stress, anxiety). 2. Colloquially, to eliminate body wastes.

reline (re-lin′) To resurface the underside of a denture with new base material in order to make it fit better.

rem (rem) Roentgen-equivalent-man. A unit of radiation dose equal to the amount of absorbed ionizing radiation that is required to produce a biologic effect equivalent to the absorption of one roentgen of x or gamma rays.

remediable (re-me′de-a-bl) Capable of being cured.

remedial (re-me′de-al) Capable of correcting a deficiency.

remedy (rem′ĕ-de) 1. A drug or a treatment that cures or palliates disease. 2. To effect a cure.

remineralization (re-min-er-al-ĭ-za′shun) Restoration of mineral elements to the body, especially of calcium salts to bone.

remission (re-mish′un) Abatement of the symptoms of a disease.

remit (re-mit′) To undergo or bring about remission; to diminish.

remittent (re-mit′ent) Characterized by alternating periods of abatement and returning of symptoms.

renal (re′nal) Relating to the kidneys. Also called nephric.

reniform (ren′ĭ-form) Kidney-shaped.

renin (re′nin) An enzyme formed in the kidneys and released into the bloodstream; it has an important role in the formation of angiotensin (a potent pressor substance) and thereby in the regulation of blood pressure, and possibly in cardiovascular disorders.

reno-, reni- Combining forms meaning kidney.

renogram (re′no-gram) A graphic record produced by the continuous recording of radioactivity of the kidney after injection of a radioactive substance; an aid in the clinical evaluation of kidney function.

renography (re-nog′rah-fe) The making of x-ray pictures of the kidneys.

renomegaly (re-no-meg′ah-le) Abnormal enlargement of the kidney.

renoprival (re-no-pri′val) Resulting from total absence of kidney function.

renotrophic (re-no-trof′ik) Affecting kidney growth. Also called nephrotropic.

renotrophin (re-no-tro′fin) Any agent affecting kidney growth.

renovascular (re-no-vas′ku-lar) Relating to the blood vessels of the kidneys.

reovirus (re-o-vi′rus) Any of a group of double-stranded RNA viruses (genus *Reovirus*), associated with sporadic upper respiratory infections, skin eruptions, and certain types of pneumonia and encephalitis.

repair (re-pār′) 1. Restoration of damaged tissue by surgical intervention. 2. In wound healing, replacement of dead or damaged tissue by collagen (scar tissue).

repellent (re-pel′ent) 1. Capable of causing or arousing aversion. 2. Any agent that has such properties, especially one that repels insects.

repetatur (re-pe-ta′tūr) (rep.) Latin for let it be renewed.

R

REPLANTATION OF A SEVERED FINGER

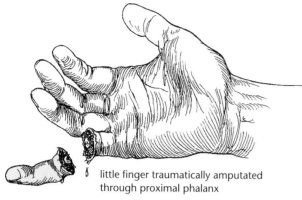

little finger traumatically amputated through proximal phalanx

nonviable tissue is removed (debridement), bone ends trimmed

zigzag incision made on palmar surface, longitudinal incision on dorsal surface

flaps reflected, structures to be joined identified

approximator

needle

suture

adventitia

artery

under dissecting microscope, blood vessels and nerves are positioned in an approximator and connected by sutures

IB JTMELLONI, PhD

proximal phalanx

bone fixed with Kirschner wire inserted diagonally, skin sutured

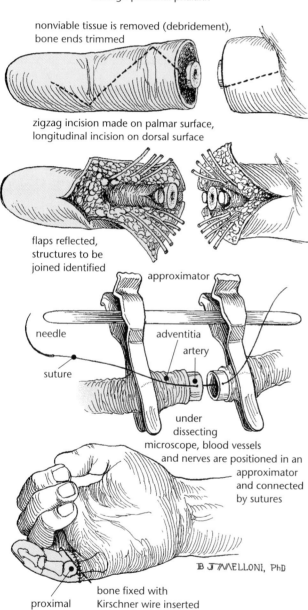

replantation (re-plan-ta'shun) Reattachment of a body part that has been accidentally severed or amputated, frequently performed under the magnification of a surgical microscope. Also called reimplantation.

replication (rep-li-ka'shun) The process of duplicating something (e.g., the repeated formation of the same molecule, as of DNA).

repolarization (re-po-lar-ĭ-za'shun) The return of membrane potential of a cell, immediately following depolarization, with restoration of positive charges on the outer and negative charges on the inner surface of the cell membrane.

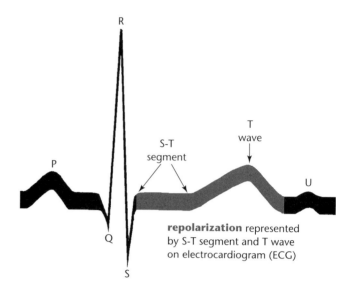

repolarization represented by S-T segment and T wave on electrocardiogram (ECG)

report (re-port') A detailed account of the results of a study or investigation.

   operative procedure r. A report that includes the preoperative diagnosis, procedure performed, postoperative diagnosis, specimens obtained, and the names of the surgical team providing intraoperative care.

   pathology r. The end product of a pathologic procedure indicating the result of the procedure; it may be a number (as in chemical tests), the name of a disease-causing microorganism, or a diagnosis (such as cancer) based on the microscopic characteristics of a tissue section.

reporter (re-por'ter) One who notifies or makes something known to the proper authorities.

   mandated r. A person who by virtue of employment in the health care field is designated by state statutes as legally responsible for reporting a variety of medical conditions to the proper authorities. The requirements may range from reporting sexually transmitted diseases and abuse of minors or vulnerable adults to reporting rabies cases or gunshot wounds. Failure to report by those mandated to do so may have minor criminal ramifications. Also called mandatory reporter.

   mandatory r. See mandated reporter.

repositioning (re-po-zish'un-ing) See reduction (1).

repositor (re-poz'ĭ-tor) Instrument for replacing a prolapsed or dislocated organ, especially the uterus.

repression (re-presh'un) An unconscious psychological defense mechanism in which unacceptable ideas, impulses, and/or affects are forced into the unconscious and kept out of conscious awareness.

reproduction (re-pro-duk'shun) 1. The process of producing offspring. 2. The process of bringing to mind again a past experience (e.g., a memory).

   asexual r. Reproduction without the union of male and female sex cells.

   sexual r. Reproduction by the union of male and female sex cells.

   somatic r. Reproduction by splitting or budding of cells other than sex cells.

repulsion (re-pul'shun) 1. The act of turning away or causing aversion. 2. Extreme dislike.

research (re'surch, re-surch') Investigation or experimentation.

resect (re-sekt') To remove surgically.

replantation ■ resect

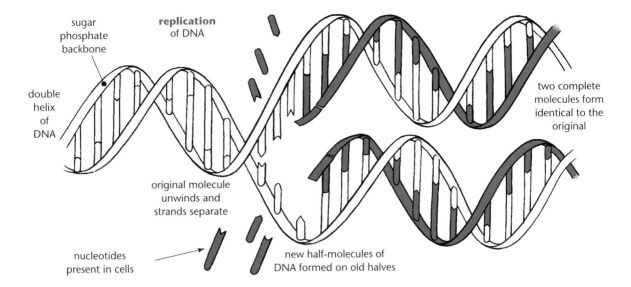

sugar phosphate backbone

replication of DNA

double helix of DNA

two complete molecules form identical to the original

original molecule unwinds and strands separate

nucleotides present in cells

new half-molecules of DNA formed on old halves

resectable (re-sek′tah-bl) Capable of being surgically removed.

resection (re-sek′shun) Surgical removal of tissue or body parts.

    gastric r. See gastrectomy.

    transurethral r. of prostate (TURP) See transurethral prostatectomy, under prostatectomy.

resectoscope (re-sek′to-skōp) A special viewing instrument adapted for removal of tissue, especially obstructive prostatic tissue through the urethra.

reserpine (res′er-pēn) An alkaloid obtained from the roots of *Rauwolfia* plants; used in the treatment of high blood pressure (hypertension) and as a tranquilizer.

reserve (re-zerv′) Something stored and available for future use.

    cardiac r. The potential of the heart to increase its performance when required by extraordinary circumstances.

reset (re-set′) To set again (e.g., a broken bone).

resident (rez′ĭ-dent) An individual who is in graduate training to qualify as a specialist in a field of medicine or dentistry.

residual (re-zid′u-al) Relating to a quantity remaining or left behind at the end of a process.

residue (rez′ĭ-du) The remaining material after removal of substances by a physical or chemical process.

residuum (re-zid′u-um), pl. resid′ua A residue.

resilience (re-zil′e-ens) Elasticity.

resin (rez′in) **1.** Any of several natural substances that range from transparent to yellow or brown, are flammable, soluble in natural solvents (ethanol, ether), and do not conduct electricity. Some are used in the pharmaceutical industry. **2.** Any of various synthetic products used chiefly in the manufacture of plastics and dental prostheses.

    acrylic r. General term applied to a thermoplastic resinous material derived from acrylic acid esters; it is the main ingredient of many plastics used in dentistry.

    amino r. Any thermoset material (liquid, air-dried solid, or powder) derived from the reaction of formaldehyde with an amino group (e.g., urea, melamine); used in industry as adhesives and bonding agents in plywood and particle boards, as crease resistants in textiles, and as surface hardening agents in laminates. Products formed from the thermal decomposition of amino resins include carbon monoxide, formaldehyde, ammonia, and cyanide. Symptoms caused by amino resin exposure include irritation of respiratory tract and mucous membranes and contact dermatitis.

    epoxy r. Any thermoset resin formed by the reaction of epichlorohydrin and bisphenol; used as protective coatings and laminates for woods, metals, and other plastics; as adhesives; and as embedding medium for electron microscopy. Exposure to epoxy resins may cause allergic dermatitis or asthma.

    ion-exchange r. An insoluble, porous solid material of high molecular weight containing an active electrolyte; it contains either acidic groups (cation-active) or basic groups (anion-active); one type is used to lower the potassium content of the body in the treatment of hyperkalemia.

resinous (rez′ĭ-nus) Relating to resin.

res ipsa loquitur (rās ip′sah lok′we-tur) Latin for the thing speaks for itself; a doctrine of law applied to cases in which the defendant had exclusive control of the circumstances that caused the harm and where the harm ordinarily could not have occurred without negligent conduct (e.g., in a medical malpractice claim, when a surgical sponge is retained in the patient's abdomen following surgery).

resistance (re-zis′tans) **1.** Any force that retards motion. **2.** (R) Opposition to the flow of an electric current. **3.** In psychiatry, a person's psychologic defense against recalling unpleasant experiences.

    drug r. A state of diminished responsiveness to drugs that ordinarily inhibit cell growth or cause cell death.

    expiratory r. Resistance in the air passages to the passage of air out of the lungs.

    insulin r. Inability of tissues to respond to the action of insulin; may be caused by defective, or reduced number of, insulin receptors in target cells and occur in association with obesity, or may occur following insulin therapy due to development of antibodies against the bovine or porcine insulin preparations.

    peripheral r. See total peripheral resistance.

    total peripheral r. (TPR) The sum of resistance to the flow of blood through the blood vessels. Also called peripheral resistance.

resolution (rez-o-lu′shun) The process by which a tissue returns to its normal state after an acute inflammatory condition.

resolve (re-zolv′) To return to normal after an inflammation.

resolvent (re-zol′vent) **1.** Causing or capable of causing resolution. **2.** Any substance having such properties.

resonance (rez′o-nans) A particular sound heard on percussion.

    amphoric r. A percussion sound resembling that produced by blowing over the mouth of an empty bottle.

    nuclear magnetic r. (NMR) A phenomenon exhibited by certain atomic nuclei when placed in a strong magnetic field; each nucleus will gyrate around the axis of the magnetic field, the frequency of the gyration being specific for each nucleus; used in spectroscopic studies of covalent bonds; the technique is clinically applied in diagnostic imaging. See also magnetic resonance imaging (MRI), under imaging.

    tympanic r. See tympany.

    vesicular r. Sound heard on percussion of normal lungs.

R

vocal r. (VR) The sound of the voice as heard on auscultation of the chest.

resonator (rez'o-na-ter) An apparatus that creates an electric current of very high potential and small volume.

resorb (re-zorb', re-sorb') To absorb again; the process of resorption.

resorcinol (rĕ-zor'sĭ-nol) A keratolytic compound used in the treatment of acne by producing a mild irritation and peeling.

resorption (re-sorp'shun) **1.** The body's assimilation of excreted material. **2.** Dissolution of soft or bony tissue (e.g., of the gums or bones surrounding the teeth); may be normal or pathologic.

  embryo r. Resorption of a dead embryo occurring at any time before organs are formed.

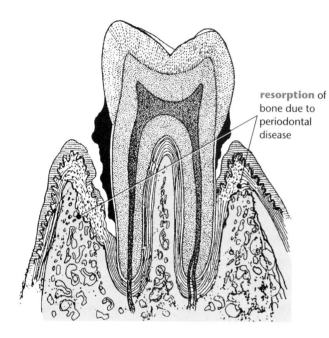

resorption of bone due to periodontal disease

respirable (rĕ-spir'ah-bl) Fit for breathing.

respiration (res-pĭ-ra'shun) (R) **1.** The processes (physical and chemical) through which an organism acquires oxygen and releases carbon dioxide. **2.** The act of breathing.

  abdominal r. Breathing carried out mainly by the action of the abdominal muscles.

  aerobic r. Process of breathing in the presence of air.

  anaerobic r. Respiration carried out by chemical reactions in which free oxygen takes no part.

  artificial r. See artificial ventilation, under ventilation.

  assisted r. See assisted ventilation, under ventilation.

  ataxic r. A gasping, irregular (in rate and depth) breathing; observed in people with lesions in the medulla oblongata. Also called Biot's breathing; Biot's respiration.

  Biot's r. See ataxic respiration.

  Cheyne-Stokes r. A rhythmic increase and decrease in the depth of respiration due to dysfunction in both hemispheres of the brain; commonly seen in metabolic encephalopathies. Also called Cheyne-Stokes breathing; periodic breathing.

  controlled r. See controlled ventilation, under ventilation.

  diffusion r. Introduction of air into the lungs by means of an intratracheal catheter. Also called apneic oxygenation.

  external r. The interchange of gases in the lungs.

  forced r. Voluntary increase in the rate and depth of breathing.

  internal r. See tissue respiration.

  Kussmaul r. Breathing marked by deep sighing, characteristic of diabetic acidosis.

  mouth-to-mouth r. See mouth-to-mouth resuscitation, under resuscitation.

  positive pressure r. See continuous positive pressure ventila-

tion (CPPV) and intermittent positive pressure ventilation (IPPV), under ventilation.

  tissue r. The exchange of gases between tissue cells and blood. Also called internal respiration.

respirator (res'pĭ-ra-tor) An apparatus for administering artificial ventilation.

  Drinker r. An airtight metal tank designed to enclose the body (except the head) and provide artificial respiration by exerting intermittent negative air pressure on the chest. Also called iron lung; tank respirator; tank ventilator.

  pressure-controlled r. A respirator that supplies a predetermined pressure of gases during inhalation.

  tank r. See Drinker respirator.

  volume-controlled r. A respirator that supplies a predetermined volume of gases during inhalation.

respiratory (res'pĭ-rah-to-re) Relating to breathing.

respire (re-spir') To breathe.

respirometer (res-pĭ-rom'ĕ-ter) See spirometer.

response (re-spons') A reaction to a specific stimulus.

  consensual r. See consensual reaction, under reaction.

  evoked r. A change in the electrical activity of the nervous system produced by an incoming sensory stimulus. Also called evoked potential.

  galvanic skin r. (GSR) Changes in the skin associated with sympathetic nerve discharges brought about by a stimulus.

  idiosyncratic r. A genetically determined abnormal response to a given drug. It may be an extreme sensitivity to low doses or extreme insensitivity to high doses; or it may be qualitatively different from the usual effects observed in the majority of people. Distinguished from sensitivity.

  immune r. A specific response resulting in immunity; it includes an initial (afferent) phase during which responsive cells are primed by antigen (immunogen), a central response during which antibodies (immunoglobulins) are formed, and an efferent response in which immunity is carried out by antibodies. Also called immune reaction; immunoreaction.

  primary r. The immune response resulting from an initial encounter with a particular antigen; it may be cellular or humoral.

  secondary r. The immune response that follows a second or subsequent encounter with a particular antigen; characterized by an increased and more rapid production of antibodies. Also called anamnestic reaction.

  triple r. The threefold response of the skin to injury; a red line, a flare around the red line, and a wheal around the flare.

rest (rest) **1.** In dentistry, supportive extension from a partial denture. **2.** A portion of displaced embryonic tissue, usually found in the adult along the route of embryonic migration of structures.

  adrenal r. An accessory adrenal (suprarenal) gland.

  pancreatic r.'s The presence of normal pancreatic tissue in the small intestine, usually producing 1- to 2-cm elevations in the intestinal lumen that may be mistaken for tumors.

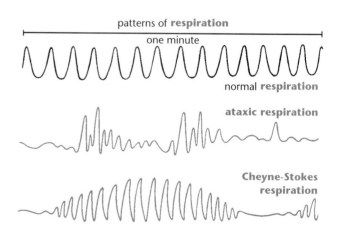

patterns of **respiration**

one minute

normal **respiration**

ataxic **respiration**

Cheyne-Stokes respiration

restenosis (re-stĕ-no′sis) The recurrence of an abnormal constriction after corrective surgery (e.g., of a heart valve), or after balloon dilatation (angioplasty) of a blood vessel.

restiform (res′tĭ-form) Shaped like a rope; applied to certain anatomic structures (e.g., the inferior peduncle connecting the cerebellum to the medulla oblongata).

restitution (res-tĭ-tu′shun) In obstetrics, the return of the rotated infant head to its natural alignment with the shoulders after the head's complete emergence from the maternal vulva.

restoration (res-to-ra′shun) In dentistry, a filling or a prosthetic device that replaces lost tooth structure or oral tissues and restores function.

restorative (re-stōr′ah-tiv) Tending to renew health.

restraint (re-strānt′) **1.** Any device for controlling or preventing the free movement of an excited or violent patient who may cause harm to himself or to others. **2.** Any device (excluding splints and casts) used to stabilize or prevent motion of the body or a body part.

resuscitate (re-sus′ĭ-tat) To restore from a state of apparent or potential death.

resuscitation (re-sus-ĭ-ta′shun) An act of resuscitating, or the state of being resuscitated.
   cardiopulmonary r. (CPR) An emergency procedure involving three basic rescue steps (the ABCs of CPR: airway, breathing, circulation); conducted in ABC order to open and maintain the airway, to restore breathing, and to restore the circulation; each step begins with an assessment stage to determine unresponsivness, breathlessness, and pulselessness, respectively; the specific techniques vary slightly, depending on the particular situation (e.g., whether the victim is an adult, a child, a neonate, a pregnant woman, or an obese person; has a foreign-body airway obstruction; is conscious or unconscious; or whether there is more than one rescuer).

   mouth-to-mouth r. See mouth-to-mouth breathing, under breathing.

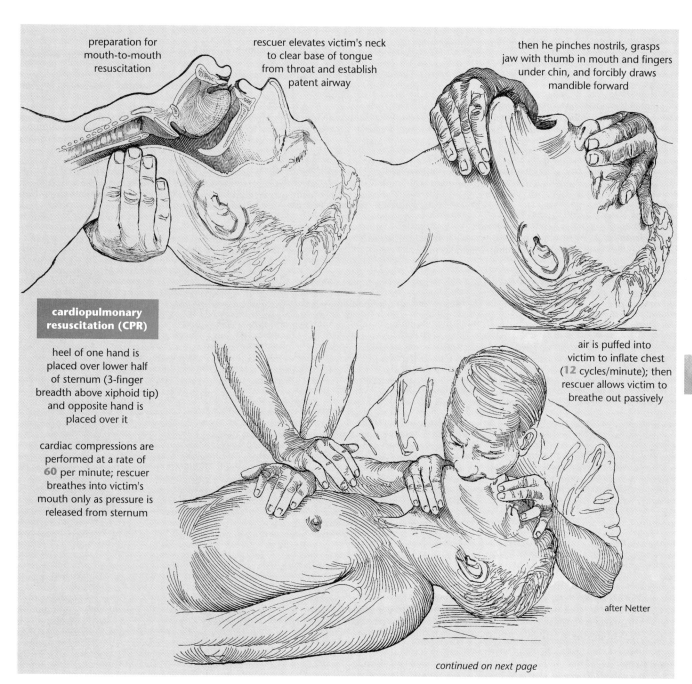

preparation for mouth-to-mouth resuscitation

rescuer elevates victim's neck to clear base of tongue from throat and establish patent airway

then he pinches nostrils, grasps jaw with thumb in mouth and fingers under chin, and forcibly draws mandible forward

cardiopulmonary resuscitation (CPR)

heel of one hand is placed over lower half of sternum (3-finger breadth above xiphoid tip) and opposite hand is placed over it

cardiac compressions are performed at a rate of **60** per minute; rescuer breathes into victim's mouth only as pressure is released from sternum

air is puffed into victim to inflate chest (**12** cycles/minute); then rescuer allows victim to breathe out passively

after Netter

continued on next page

R

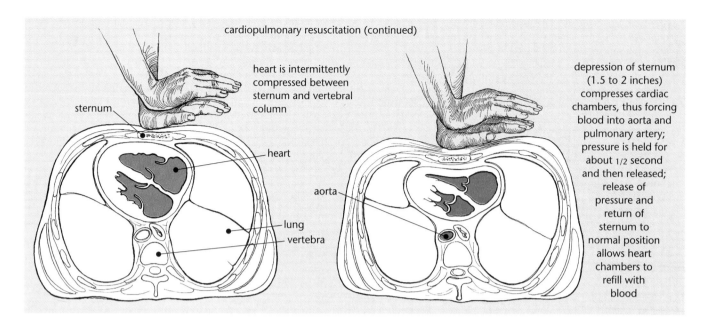

heart is intermittently compressed between sternum and vertebral column

sternum

heart

aorta

lung
vertebra

depression of sternum (1.5 to 2 inches) compresses cardiac chambers, thus forcing blood into aorta and pulmonary artery; pressure is held for about 1/2 second and then released; release of pressure and return of sternum to normal position allows heart chambers to refill with blood

resuscitator (re-sus'ĭ-ta-tor) An apparatus used in artificial ventilation; it forces gas, usually oxygen, into the lungs to initiate breathing.

retainer (re-tān'er) **1.** Device for maintaining teeth in proper alignment after orthodontic treatment. **2.** The part of a dental bridge that attaches the prosthesis to the supporting natural tooth. **3.** Any device (e.g., a clasp) used for the stabilization of a prosthesis.

    continuous bar r. A metal bar placed in contact with the lingual surfaces of teeth to aid in stabilizing the teeth or in retaining a partial denture.

    direct r. A clasp or attachment placed on a supporting natural tooth for maintaining a removable appliance in position.

    indirect r. An attachment of a removable dental bridge that assists the direct retainers in preventing displacement of free-end denture bases.

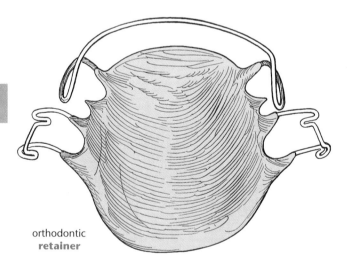

orthodontic **retainer**

retardate (re-tar'dāt) A mentally retarded person.

retardation (re-tar-da'shun) Delayed or diminished development.

    mental r. Subnormal intellectual functioning originating during the individual's developmental period, often associated with impairment of adjustment (social and learning) or maturation, or both; an IQ score of 69 or below on a standardized intelligence test. Also called mental deficiency.

    psychomotor r. A slowing down of physical and emotional reactions; seen in certain forms of severe depression.

retching (rech'ing) The labored rhythmic breathing that usually precedes vomiting without expulsion of stomach contents.

rete (re'te), pl. re'tia A network (e.g., of fine nerve fibers or minute blood vessels).

retention (re-ten'shun) **1.** The holding back of body wastes that are normally discharged. **2.** The ability to remember. **3.** The maintaining of teeth in the position to which they have been moved by orthodontic means.

reticular (rĕ-tik'u-lar) Relating to a reticulum or fine network.

reticulocyte (rĕ-tik'u-lo-sīt) The youngest red blood cell, appearing in circulating blood soon after its release from bone marrow; it constitutes 1% of the red blood cell population.

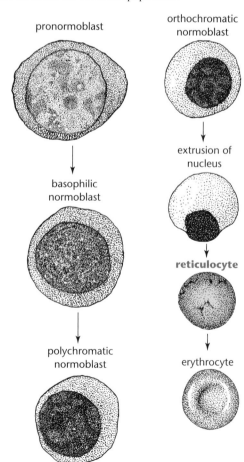

pronormoblast

orthochromatic normoblast

basophilic normoblast

extrusion of nucleus

polychromatic normoblast

reticulocyte

erythrocyte

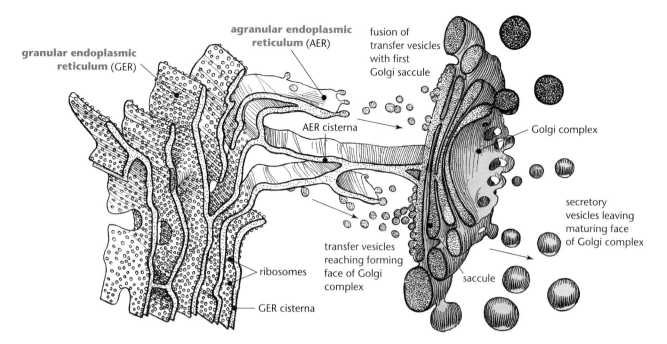

granular endoplasmic reticulum (GER)

agranular endoplasmic reticulum (AER)

fusion of transfer vesicles with first Golgi saccule

AER cisterna

Golgi complex

secretory vesicles leaving maturing face of Golgi complex

transfer vesicles reaching forming face of Golgi complex

saccule

ribosomes

GER cisterna

reticulocytopenia (rĕ-tik-u-lo-si-to-pe′ne-ah) Reduction of reticulocytes in the blood.

reticulocytosis (rĕ-tik-u-lo-si-to′sis) Abnormally high numbers of reticulocytes in the blood.

reticuloendothelial (rĕ-tik-u-lo-en-do-the′le-al) Relating to tissues that have both reticular and endothelial properties.

reticuloendothelioma (rĕ-tik-u-lo-en-do-the-le-o′mah) A localized tumor (e.g., a malignant lymphoma) derived from reticuloendothelial tissues.

reticuloendotheliosis (rĕ-tik-u-lo-en-do-the-le-o′sis) Abnormal conditions, especially proliferation, of cells in the macrophage (reticuloendothelial) system (e.g., in such structures as the spleen and liver).

reticuloendothelium (rĕ-tik-u-lo-en-do-the′le-um) The widely dispersed and morphologically varied cells concerned with phagocytosis, which constitute the macrophage (reticuloendothelial) system.

reticulosis (rĕ-tik-u-lo′sis) A short version of the term reticuloendotheliosis.

reticulum (rĕ-tik′u-lum) A fine network, especially one formed of protoplasmic material within the cell.

agranular endoplasmic r. (AER) An endoplasmic reticulum that is free of ribosomal granules. Also called smooth endoplasmic reticulum (SER).

endoplasmic r. (ER) An extensive network of folded membranes and interconnected tubules within the cytoplasm of a cell; depending on the cell type in which it is located, it can play a role in detoxification of certain drugs, lipid and cholesterol metabolism, production of steroid hormones, and other biological processes.

granular endoplasmic r. (GER) An endoplasmic reticulum with numerous ribosomal granules on its surface. Also called rough endoplasmic reticulum (RER); ergastoplasm.

rough endoplasmic r. (RER) See granular endoplasmic reticulum.

smooth endoplasmic r. (SER) See agranular endoplasmic reticulum.

retiform (re′tĭ-form, ret′ĭ-form) Resembling a fine net.

retina (ret′ĭ-nah) The innermost of the three coats forming the wall of the eyeball; it is composed of an outer pigmented portion and an inner portion (retina proper) composed of light-sensitive nerve elements; the inner portion contains seven microscopic layers, named

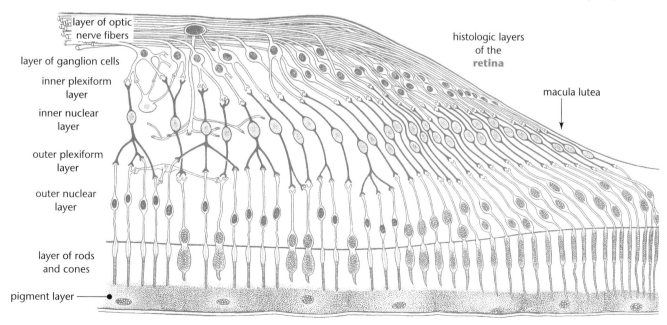

layer of optic nerve fibers

layer of ganglion cells

inner plexiform layer

inner nuclear layer

outer plexiform layer

outer nuclear layer

layer of rods and cones

pigment layer

histologic layers of the **retina**

macula lutea

from within outward as follows: nerve fiber layer, ganglionic layer, inner plexiform layer, inner nuclear layer, outer plexiform layer, outer nuclear layer, and layer of rods and cones.

retinaculum (ret-ĭ-nak′u-lum), pl. retinac′ula A fascial band that retains a structure in place.

   extensor r. of ankle Strong fascial band overlying the ankle joint: *Inferior extensor r. of ankle,* a retinaculum of deep fascia shaped like the letter Y, with the stem extending from the lateral wall of the upper part of the heel bone (calcaneus), passing medially as two segments; the upper segment attaches to the medial malleolus of the tibia and the lower segment descends to the plantar aponeurosis; the retinaculum overrides the tendons of the extensor muscles (anterior tibial muscle, long extensor muscle of big toe, long extensor muscle of toes, and third peroneal muscle) and helps to keep them in their proper place. *Superior extensor r. of ankle,* a thickening of deep fascia anchored to the lower part of the tibia and fibula of the leg; it extends from the anterior border of the tibia transversely to the anterior border of the fibula and overrides the tendons of the extensor muscles (anterior tibial muscle, long extensor muscle of big toe, long extensor muscle of toes, and third peroneal muscle).

   extensor r. of hand See extensor retinaculum of wrist.

   extensor r. of wrist A strong band extending obliquely across the back of the wrist; it retains in position the extensor tendons of the fingers. Also called extensor retinaculum of hand.

   fibular patellar r. See patellar retinaculum, lateral.

   flexor r. of ankle A thickened band of fascia in back of the ankle joint passing from the bottom of the medial malleolus of the tibia, to the medial side of the heel bone (calcaneus) as well as to the plantar aponeurosis; it overrides the tendons of various muscles (posterior tibial muscle, long flexor muscle of toes, long flexor muscle of big toe) as they make their way to the sole of the foot.

   flexor r. of hand See flexor retinaculum of wrist.

   flexor r. of wrist A strong, transverse fibrous band (about 2.5 by 3 cm) that spans the hollow area of the front of the wrist bones (carpus) creating the carpal tunnel, which conveys the median nerve and the flexor tendons of the fingers; a superficial slip projects from it to cross the ulnar vessels and nerve before blending with the rest of the retinaculum. Also called flexor retinaculum of hand.

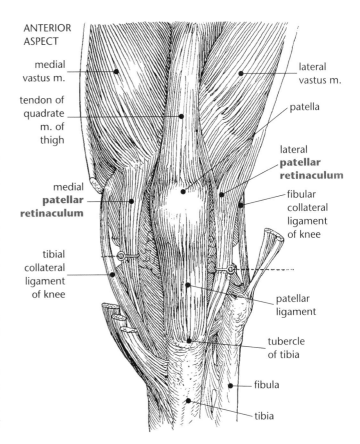

patellar r. Fibrous bands superficial to the knee joint capsule: *Lateral patellar r.,* a downward tendinous expansion of the lateral vastus muscle blending with the knee joint capsule and extending to the margin of the kneecap (patella), patellar ligament, and condyle of the tibia; it is strengthened by the overlying iliotibial tract. Also called fibular patellar retinaculum. *Medial patellar r.,* a downward tendinous expansion of the medial vastus muscle blending with the knee joint capsule and extending to the margin of the kneecap (patella), patellar ligament, and condyle of the tibia. Also called tibial patellar retinaculum.

   peroneal r. Fibrous slings that hold the peroneal tendons in place as they curve around the lateral side of the ankle: *Inferior peroneal r.,* a band that extends from the stem of the Y-shaped inferior extensor retinaculum to the lateral side of the heel bone (calcaneus). *Superior peroneal r.,* A band that extends from the lower part of the lateral malleolus of the fibula to the lateral side of the calcaneus.

   tibial patellar r. See patellar retinaculum, medial.

retinal (ret′ĭ-nal) **1.** Relating to the retina. **2.** See retinaldehyde.

retinaldehyde (ret-ĭ-nal′dĕ-hīd) The organic compound, aldehyde, present in the visual pigments of the retina. Also called retinal.

retinitis (ret-ĭ-ni′tis) Inflammation of the innermost layer of the eyeball (retina).

   r. pigmentosa (RP) Hereditary eye condition transmitted as an autosomal dominant inheritance; characterized by degeneration and atrophy of the retina, usually with migration of pigment into the inner (nervous) layers of the retina, causing progressive reduction of peripheral vision; its first symptom, night blindness, usually occurs in children and adolescents.

   solar r. Injury to the macular area of the retina by ultraviolet radiation, frequently affecting people after a solar eclipse as a result of direct observation of the sun without proper filters. Also called eclipse retinopathy.

retino-, retin- Combining forms meaning the retina.

retinoblastoma (ret-ĭ-no-blas-to′mah) A congenital malignant tumor of the retina, composed of embryonic retinal cells, usually

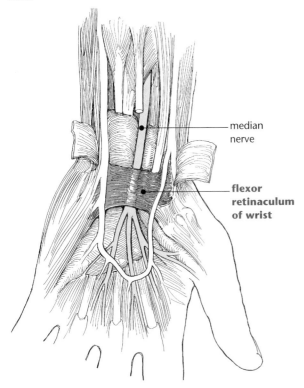

observed before the age of four; may occur as multiple tumors, affecting both eyes, or singly in one eye only.

retinochoroiditis (ret-ĭ-no-ko-roi-di'tis) See chorioretinitis.

retinoic acid (ret-ĭn-o'ik as'id) Compound used topically in the treatment of acne. Also called vitamin A₁ acid.

retinoid (ret'ĭ-noid) **1.** Resembling a resin. **2.** Resembling the retina.

retinoids (ret'ĭ-noidz) Compounds derived from retinoic acid; used to treat severe acne and psoriasis.

retinol (ret'ĭ-nol) A 20-carbon alcohol. Also called vitamin A₁.

retinopapillitis (ret-ĭ-no-pap-ĭ-li'tis) See papilloretinitis.

retinopathy (ret-ĭ-nop'ah-the) Any degenerative noninflammatory disease of the retina.

　　arteriosclerotic r. Changes within the eye associated with arteriosclerosis and benign hypertension; blood vessels show variations in caliber, increased tortuosity, and compression of veins at arteriovenous crossings.

　　diabetic r. Disease of the retinal blood vessels occurring as a complication of diabetes mellitus of long duration; usually includes a nonproliferative phase marked by hemorrhage from minute capillaries, waxy deposits, soft cottonlike deposits, and microaneurysms, and a proliferative phase that includes development of new blood vessels, which frequently encroach on the vitreous body with associated retinal detachment. The condition may lead to severe visual disability.

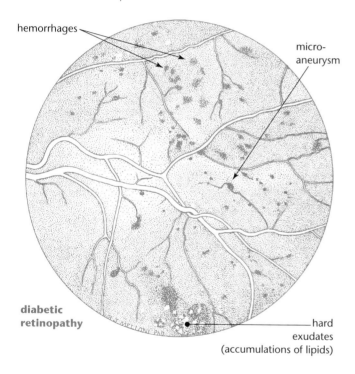

hemorrhages

micro-aneurysm

diabetic retinopathy

hard exudates (accumulations of lipids)

　　eclipse r. See solar retinitis, under retinitis.

　　hypertensive r. Disease of retinal blood vessels occurring as a complication of high blood pressure (hypertension); the initial change is narrowing of the arterioles caused by spasm; in later stages, hemorrhages and exudates are observed; papilledema may occur in extreme cases (e.g., in hypertensive encephalopathy).

　　r. of prematurity (ROP) Eye condition sometimes occurring in premature infants, characterized by constriction and obliteration of the capillary bed of the retina followed by formation of new blood vessels extending into the vitreous, retinal hemorrhages, fibrosis, and eventual retinal detachment; associated with exposure to elevated concentrations of oxygen; in most cases the process is reversed before fibrosis occurs. Formerly called retrolental fibroplasia.

retinopiesis (ret-ĭ-no-pī-e'sis) Reattachment of a detached retina by applying pressure with a gas or fluid.

retinoschisis (ret-ĭ-nos'kī-sis) An eye condition characterized by the splitting of the retina into two layers, producing a cystic bulge that may be mistaken for retinal detachment; elderly people are usually affected; vision is not usually diminished.

retinoscope (ret'ĭ-no-skōp) An optical instrument for determining the refractive state of the eye.

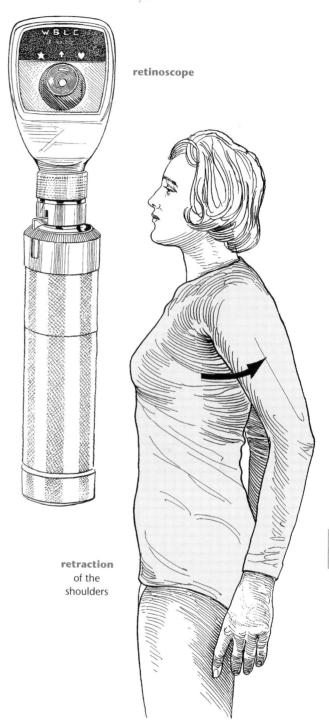

retinoscope

retraction of the shoulders

retinoscopy (ret-ĭ-nos'ko-pe) Examination of the eye with a retinoscope.

retort (re-tort') A closed, long-necked laboratory vessel resembling a flask; used in distillation.

retract (re-trakt') To shrink or pull back.

retractile (re-trak'til) Capable of being pulled back.

retraction (re-trak'shun) Shrinking or drawing back.

　　gingival r. Retraction of the gums away from the teeth due to inflammation.

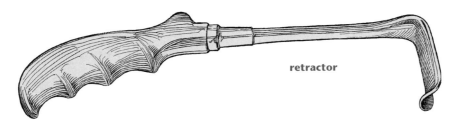

retractor

retractor (re-trak′tor) Surgical instrument for drawing apart the edges of a wound.

retrad (re′trad) Directed posteriorly; toward the back.

retrenchment (re-trench′ment) The surgical removal of excessive or redundant tissue.

retrieval (re-tre′val) The third and final stage in the memory process whereby stored information is brought back into consciousness.

retro- Combining form meaning backward.

retrobulbar (re-tro-bul′bar) **1.** Situated behind the eyeball. **2.** Situated behind the medulla oblongata, at the base of the skull.

retrocecal (re-tro-se′kal) Behind the first portion of the large intestine (cecum), in the lower right side of the abdomen.

retrocervical (re-tro-ser′ve-kal) Behind the uterine cervix.

retrocolic (re-tro-kol′ik) Behind the colon.

retroconduction (re-tro-kon-duk′shun) See retrograde conduction, under conduction.

retrodisplacement (re-tro-dis-plās′ment) Any backward displacement of an organ.

retroflexion (re-tro-flek′shun) Backward bending of an organ.

   r. of uterus Extreme backward bending or angulation of the body of the uterus while the cervix remains in its normal position. COMPARE retroversion of uterus.

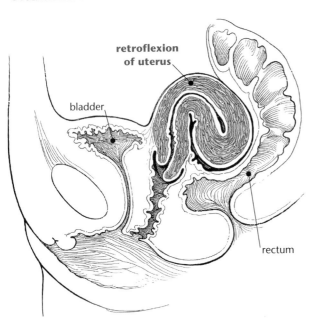

retrognathism (re-tro-nath′ism) Condition in which the lower jaw is displaced backward, without reduction of its size.

retrograde (re′tro-grād) Moving or flowing in a backward direction.

retrogression (re-tro-gresh′un) **1.** A return to an earlier state. **2.** Degeneration; applied especially to tissues.

retrolental (re-tro-len′tal) Behind the lens of the eye.

retromammary (re-tro-mam′er-e) Behind the mammary glands.

retromandibular (re-tro-man-dib′u-lar) Behind the lower jaw.

retroperitoneal (re-tro-per-ĭ-to-ne′al) **1.** Relating to the retroperitoneum. **2.** Situated posterior to the membrane (peritoneum) lining the back of the abdominal cavity.

retroperitoneum (re-tro-per-ĭ-to-ne′um) The space in the poste-

rior body wall behind the abdominal cavity; it contains the pancreas, kidneys, adrenal (suprarenal) glands, and portions of the small and large intestines.

retroperitonitis (re-tro-per-ĭ-to-ni′tis) Inflammation of tissues behind the peritoneum.

   idiopathic fibrous r. See sclerosing retroperitonitis.

   sclerosing r. An inflammatory fibrous overgrowth of retroperitoneal tissues beginning in the area of the sacral promontory; may encircle the lower abdominal aorta or extend laterally, encroaching on and obstructing the ureters; cause is unknown; may be a reaction to certain drugs (e.g., methysergide). Also called retroperitoneal fibromatosis; idiopathic fibrous retroperitonitis; retroperitoneal fibrosis; idiopathic retroperitoneal fibrosis.

retropharyngeal (re-tro-fah-rin′je-al) Behind the pharynx.

retroplasia (re-tro-pla′se-ah) The state of decreased activity in a tissue, below the normal range.

retroposition (re-tro-po-zish′un) Any type of backward displacement of an organ, especially the uterus.

   adherent r. of uterus A fixed retroposition of the uterus caused by adhesions; seen in a variety of pelvic inflammatory conditions (e.g., sexually transmitted infections, endometriosis, pyosalpinx, hydrosalpinx).

retropulsion (re-tro-pul′shun) An involuntary walking or falling backward.

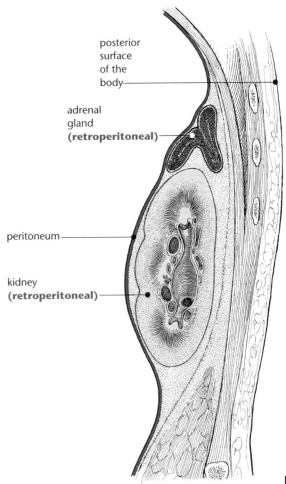

retrospondylolisthesis (re-tro-spon-dĭ-lo-lis-the′sis) Posterior displacement of a vertebra.

retrosternal (re-tro-ster′nal) Behind the breastbone (sternum).

retrouterine (re-tro-u′ter-in) Behind the uterus.

retroversion (re-tro-ver′zhun) Backward tilting of an organ in its entirety.

    r. of uterus Backward inclination of the entire uterus (including the cervix) toward the hollow of the sacrum. COMPARE retroflexion of uterus.

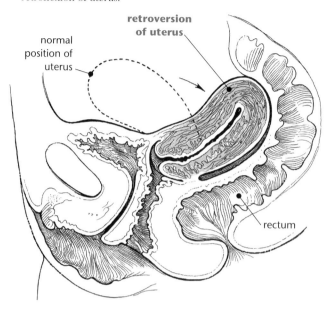

retroverted (ret-ro-vert′ed) Inclined backward.

Retroviridae (re-tro-vir′ĭ-de) A family of viruses, 100 nm in diameter, that have RNA-dependent polymerases; it includes the tumor viruses.

retrovirus (re-tro-vi′rus) Any virus of the family Retroviridae. Retroviruses are named for their ability to convert RNA into DNA and thus use genetic material of the cells they infect to make the proteins they need to survive, causing several diseases in the process. Retroviruses include the cancer-causing virus HTLV (human T cell leukemia/lymphoma virus) and HIV (human immunodeficiency virus), which causes AIDS (acquired immune deficiency syndrome); these viruses have a tropism for T4 (helper) lymphocytes and contain a Mg^{++} dependent reverse transcriptase.

retrusion (re-troo′zhun) Backward displacement of the lower jaw (mandible).

reunient (re-yu′ne-ent) Connecting; applied to a duct (ductus reuniens) that connects the saccule to the cochlear duct in the inner ear.

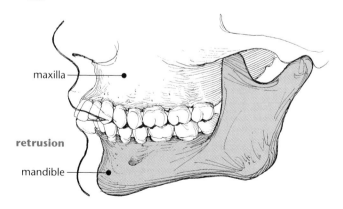

revascularization (re-vas-ku-lar-ĭ-za′shun) The reestablishment of blood supply to a body part by surgical grafting of blood vessels or by the natural development of collateral channels.

reversal (re-ver′sal) A turning in the opposite direction.

    sex r. The apparent change to the opposite sex, as occurs in certain pseudohermaphroditic individuals.

reversible (re-ver′sĭ-bl) Capable of reversal.

reversion (re-ver′zhun) **1.** The appearance in an individual of an ancestral characteristic that has been absent for several generations. **2.** The restoration in a mutant gene of its ability to produce a functional protein.

revivification (re-viv-ĭ-fĭ-ka′shun) See débridement.

Rhabditis (rab-di′tis) A genus of small roundworms; some are parasitic in humans.

rhabdoid (rab′doid) Rod-shaped.

rhabdomyolysis (rab-do-mi-ol′ĭ-sis) An acute disease, characterized by disintegration of skeletal muscle and urine excretion of the muscle pigment myoglobulin; the most common cause is a crush injury. The myoglobin release may result in severe kidney damage (acute tubular necrosis).

rhabdomyoma (rab-do-mi-o′mah) A benign tumor occurring most commonly in the hearts of children.

rhabdomyosarcoma (rab-do-mi-o-sar-ko′mah) A malignant soft-tissue tumor occurring most commonly in children under 10 years of age, especially in the neck, head, and genitourinary tract.

Rhabdoviridae (rab-do-vir′ĭ-de) A family of RNA viruses replicating in the cytoplasm of cells. It includes the rabies virus.

rhagades (rag′ah-dēz) Cracks and fissures of the skin, especially around body openings, occurring in such conditions as congenital syphilis and vitamin deficiencies.

rhagadiform (ra-gad′ĭ-form) Fissurelike.

rhenium (re′ne-um) A silver-white metallic element; symbol Re, atomic number 75, atomic weight 186.2.

rheo- Combining form meaning flow; current.

rheobase (re′o-bās) The minimal strength of an electric current that is capable of stimulating excitable tissue if allowed to flow through it for an adequate time.

rheoencephalography (re-o-en-sef-ah-log′rah-fe) The measurement of blood flow through the brain.

rheology (re-ol′o-je) The study of the deformation and flow of semisolids and liquids (e.g., of blood flow through the heart and blood vessels).

rheometer (re-om′ĕ-ter) **1.** A device for measuring the velocity of viscous liquids such as blood. **2.** A galvanometer.

rheometry (re-om′ĕ-tre) Measurement of a flow or current.

rheotaxis (re-o-tak′sis) The movement of microorganisms in fluids in response to the direction of the fluid's flow.

rhesus monkey (re′sus mung′ke) Generic name for a light brown monkey, *Macaca mulatta*, of India and China; used in medical research.

rheum (room) Any abnormal watery discharge from the nose or eyes.

rheumatic (roo-mat′ik) Relating to rheumatism.

rheumatid (roo′mah-tid) A skin eruption sometimes accompanying disorders of the musculoskeletal system.

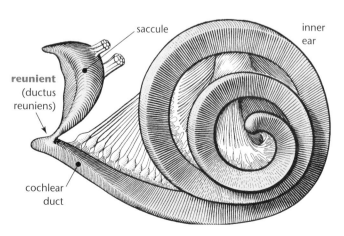

R

rheumatism (roo'mah-tizm) General term applied to any of various disorders that cause pain in the muscles, joints, and fibrous tissues, including minor aches as well as diseases such as osteoarthritis and rheumatoid arthritis.

rheumatoid (roo'mah-toid) Associated with rheumatoid arthritis.

rheumatologist (roo-mah-tol'o-jist) A physician who specializes in treating rheumatic conditions.

rheumatology (roo-mah-tol'o-je) The study and treatment of rheumatic conditions.

rhexis (rek'sis) A rupture (e.g., of an organ or a blood vessel).

rhinal (ri'nal) See nasal.

rhinalgia (ri-nal'je-ah) Pain in the nose.

rhinedema (ri-nĕ-de'mah) Swelling of the inner lining (mucous membrane) of the nose.

rhinencephalon (ri-nen-sef'ah-lon) The region of the brain directly related to the sense of smell; it includes the olfactory bulb, peduncle, and tubercle, and the piriform cortex.

rhineurynter (rin-u-rin'ter) An inflatable bag introduced in the nasal cavity and inflated to arrest a profuse nosebleed.

rhinion (rin'e-on) The lowest end of the union of the two nasal bones; a craniometric point.

rhinitis (ri-ni'tis) Inflammation of the lining membrane of the nasal cavity accompanied by excessive mucus discharge.

    acute r. Infection of the upper respiratory tract; may be caused by a variety of viruses, most commonly by the rhinovirus, influenza virus, myxovirus, paramyxovirus, and adenovirus; characterized by acute inflammation of the nasal mucosa with a copious watery discharge, and sometimes sore throat, fever, and muscle ache. Also called coryza.

    allergic r. Rhinitis usually limited to the nose, ears, and eyes, occasionally producing skin eruptions; may be seasonal, associated with pollens (e.g., hay fever, rose fever), or perennial, associated with a variety of allergens and occurring in variable-length episodes (e.g., in the workplace).

    atrophic r. Chronic rhinitis characterized by thinning of the lining membrane of the nasal cavity, with crust formation and an offensive odor. Also called ozena.

    chronic r. A persistent rhinitis of long duration.

    hypertrophic r. Chronic rhinitis characterized by thickening of mucous membrane, usually with chronically congested veins.

    r. medicomentosa Rhinitis caused by improper use or abuse of topical medicines (e.g., nose drops).

    vasomotor r. Rhinitis occurring without infection; caused by hyperactivity of parasympathetic control of nasal blood vessels and glands.

rhino-, rhin- Combining forms relating to the nose.

rhinoantritis (ri-no-an-tri'tis) Inflammation of the mucous membrane of the nasal cavity and maxillary sinuses.

rhinocanthectomy (ri-no-kan-thek'to-me) Surgical removal of the angle of the eyelids near the bridge of the nose (the inner canthus).

rhinocheiloplasty, rhinochiloplasty (ri-no-ki'lo-plas-te) Reparative surgery of the nose and lip.

rhinocleisis (ri-no-kli'sis) Obstruction of the nasal passages.

rhinodacryolith (ri-no-dak're-o-lith) A stony concretion in the nasolacrimal duct.

rhinogenous (ri-noj'ĕ-nus) Originating in the nose.

rhinokyphosis (rino-ki-fo'sis) The occurrence of an abnormal hump on the nasal ridge.

rhinolalia (ri-no-la'le-ah) Nasal speech resulting from a defect in the nasal passages.

rhinolith (ri'no-lith) An aggregation of stony material (calculus), formed around a foreign body in the nasal cavity; usually seen in children.

rhinolithiasis (ri-no-li-thi'ah-sis) The presence of calculi in the nose.

rhinology (ri-nol'o-je) The study of the nose and its diseases.

rhinomanometer (ri-no-mah-nom'ĕ-ter) Instrument for determining the degree of nasal obstruction.

rhinomycosis (ri-no-mi-ko'sis) Fungal infection of the nasal passages.

rhinopathy (ri-nop'ah-the) Any disease of the nose.

rhinopharyngitis (ri-no-far-in-ji'tis) Inflammation of the nasal passages and the back of the nose.

    r. mutilans See gangosa.

rhinopharynx (ri-no-far'inks) See nasopharynx.

rhinophyma (ri-no-fi'mah) Massive enlargement of the nose usually associated with rosacea, characterized by coarsened, purplish skin, thickened with nodules and pitted scars.

rhinoplasty (ri'no-plas-te) **1.** Plastic surgery of the nose, performed to change its shape or size. **2.** Reconstructive surgery of the nose, frequently with tissue grafts.

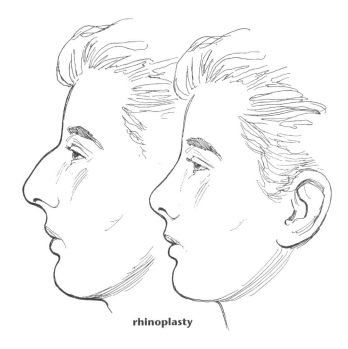

rhinoplasty

rhinorrhagia (ri-no-ra'je-ah) See nosebleed.

rhinorrhea (ri-no-re'ah) Nasal discharge.

    cerebrospinal fluid (CSF) r. Leakage of cerebrospinal fluid through the nose resulting from a fracture of the base of the skull and a tear of the membranes (meninges) covering the brain.

rhinosalpingitis (ri-no-sal-pin-ji'tis) Inflammation of the lining membranes of the nasal cavity and eustachian (auditory) tube or tubes.

rhinoscleroma (ri-no-skle-ro'mah) Chronic disease involving the nostrils, upper lip, nasal cavity, and upper respiratory tract; characterized by formation of hard nodules, sometimes leading to deformity; caused by the bacterium *Klebsiella rhinoscleromatis*.

rhinoscope (ri'no-skōp) Instrument for visual examination of the nasal cavity; a nasal speculum. Also called nasoscope.

rhinoscopy (ri-nos'ko-pe) Inspection of the nasal cavity.

    median r. Inspection of the nasal cavity and the openings of the ethmoid and sphenoid sinuses with a long-handled nasal speculum (nasopharyngoscope).

rhinostenosis (ri-no-stĕ-no'sis) Abnormal narrowing of the nasal passages resulting in nasal obstruction.

rhinotomy (ri-not'o-me) Any surgical cut upon the nose.

Rhinovirus (ri-no-vi'rus) Genus of RNA viruses (family Picornaviridae) that includes those causing the common cold in humans and foot-and-mouth disease in cattle; over 100 antigenic types have been identified.

rhinovirus (ri-no-vi'rus) Any member of the genus *Rhinovirus*.

Rhipicephalus (ri-pĭ-sef'ah-lus) Genus of hard ticks (family Ixodidae) that includes about 50 species; some are vectors of diseases in humans and domestic animals.

R

R. sanguineus The brown dog tick; the principal vector of Rocky Mountain spotted fever in Mexico.

rhizo- Combining form meaning root.

rhizoid (ri'zoid) Rootlike.

rhizomeningomyelitis (ri-zo-mĕ-nin'go-mi-ĕ-li'tis) Inflammation of spinal nerve roots along with the adjacent spinal cord and its covering membranes (meninges). Also called radiculomeningomyelitis.

rhizotomy (ri-zot'o-me) Division or interruption of a nerve root. Also called root section; radicotomy; radiculectomy.

    anterior r. The surgical interruption of anterior (motor) spinal nerve roots; formerly performed to treat essential hypertension.

    posterior r. The surgical interruption of posterior (sensory) spinal nerve roots; usually performed to relieve intractable pain.

    trigeminal r. Surgical interruption of the preganglionic root of the trigeminal (5th cranial) nerve for the relief of spasmodic facial neuralgia (tic douloureux). Also called retrogasserian neurotomy; trigeminal root section.

rhodium (ro'de-um) Metallic element; symbol Rh, atomic number 45, atomic weight 102.91.

rhodo-, rhod- Combining forms meaning a red color.

Rhodococcus equi (ro-do-kok'us ek'wi) A species of *Rhodococcus* bacteria (order Actinomycetales), found in soil and the intestinal tracts of horses, cows, sheep, and pigs; responsible for respiratory infections in humans whose immune systems are compromised by immunosuppressive drug therapy or by AIDS.

rhodopsin (ro-dop'sin) A purplish red, light-sensitive pigment present in the membrane of the outer segments of rod cells in the retina; composed of a vitamin A derivative (11-*cis* retinal) and a protein group (opsin); it undergoes a series of complex reactions in response to visible light, resulting in the transmission of nerve impulses to the brain; thus, it makes possible the transformation of light energy into visual perception. Also called visual purple.

rhombocele (rom'bo-sēl) The natural terminal expansion of the spinal canal, located within the lumbar portion of the spinal cord.

rhonchal, rhonchial (rong'kal, rong'ke-al) Relating to a rhonchus.

rhonchus (rong'kus) A loud rale or snoring sound produced in the bronchi or trachea due to partial obstruction or narrowing of these airways.

Rhus (rus) Genus of shrubs and vines (family Anacardiaceae) that grow abundantly in the United States and southern Canada; the sap of some species contains a potent irritant (urushiol); included in these species are: *Rhus radicans* (poison ivy), *Rhus toxicodendron* (Atlantic States poison oak), *Rhus diversiloba* (Pacific States poison oak), and *Rhus vernix* (poison sumac; swamp sumac); they produce a severe vesicular rash on contact.

rhythm (rith'm) The pattern of recurrence of a biologic cycle (e.g., the heartbeat).

    agonal r. A heart rhythm often occurring in dying patients, seen in the electrocardiogram (ECG) as wide, distorted ventricular complexes.

    alpha r. See alpha wave, under wave.

    beta r. See beta wave, under wave.

    bigeminal r. Heart rhythm in which every beat is followed by a weak premature beat and then a pause, so that the beats appear coupled. Also called coupling.

    cantering r. See gallop.

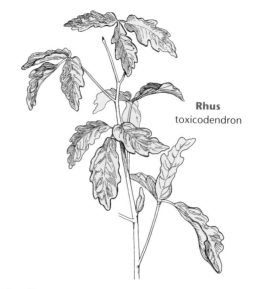

Rhus
toxicodendron

    circadian r. See circadian.

    circus r. See circus movement, under movement.

    coronary sinus r. Heart rhythm thought to originate in the coronary sinus, appearing in the electrocardiogram (ECG) with inverted P waves in inferior leads with a normal P-R interval.

    delta w. See delta wave, under wave.

    ectopic r. Heart rhythm originating from a focus other than the sinus node.

    gallop r. See gallop.

    idionodal r. A slow independent heart rhythm arising in the atrioventricular (A-V) junction and controlling only the ventricles.

    idioventricular r. A slow independent heart rhythm arising in an ectopic center in the ventricles and controlling only the ventricles.

    infradian r. See infradian.

    quadruple r. A quadruple cadence of the heart sounds not heard in normal hearts.

    reciprocal r. Phenomenon in which the impulse arises in the A-V junction of the heart and travels both downward to the ventricles and upward to the atria, but, before reaching the atria, it is reflected and descends to reactivate the ventricles.

    reciprocating r. A rhythm in which the impulse circulates around the A-V junction of the heart and gives off two daughter impulses, one to the atria and one to the ventricles.

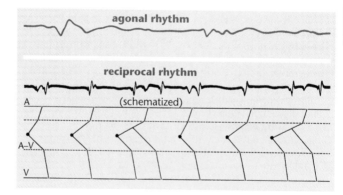

agonal rhythm

reciprocal rhythm

A   (schematized)

A–V

V

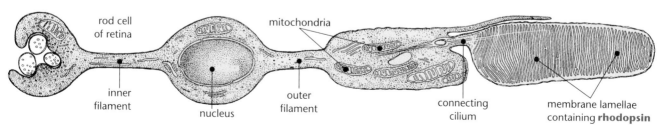

rod cell of retina

mitochondria

inner filament

nucleus

outer filament

connecting cilium

membrane lamellae containing **rhodopsin**

R

sinus r. The normal heart rhythm originating in the sinus node.

theta r. See theta wave, under wave.

trigeminal r. Rhythm in which the heartbeats occur in groups of three; either two premature beats follow each a normal beat, or two normal beats are followed by a premature beat. Also called trigeminy.

triple r. A triple cadence of the heart sounds, generally caused by the presence of a third (diastolic) or fourth (presystolic) heart sound in addition to the usual first and second heart sounds.

ultradian r. See ultradian.

rhytidectomy (rit-ĭ-dek′to-me) Surgical elimination of wrinkles and sagging skin in the facial area, especially along the cheeks, jawline, and neck; usually involves removing excess skin and, often, fat. Also called face-lift; rhytidoplasty.

rhytidoplasty (rit′ĭ-do-plas-te) See rhytidectomy.

rhytidosis (rit-ĭ-do′sis) 1. Premature wrinkling of the face. 2. Wrinkling of the cornea.

rib (rib) One of a series of long, thin, rather elastic curved bones that articulates posteriorly with a thoracic vertebra and extends anteriorly to join the costal cartilage in forming the major part of the thoracic cage; normally there are 12 ribs on each side.

cervical r. An abnormal extra rib connected to the seventh cervical vertebra, with an anterior end that may be free or joined to the first rib or costal cartilage, or rarely, if ever, to the sternum; it may interfere with the innervation and vascularization to the arm by compressing the brachial plexus and the axillary artery. Also called pleurapophysis.

false r. One of the five lower pairs of ribs that does not articulate through its costal cartilage directly with the sternum. Also called vertebrochondral rib; spurious rib.

floating r. One of the two lower pairs of false ribs that is free at the anterior end. Also called vertebral rib.

slipping r. Recurrent dislocation of a rib's costal cartilage.

spurious r. See false rib.

sternal r. See true rib.

true r. One of the seven pairs of upper ribs that is connected anteriorly, through the costal cartilage, to the lateral surface of the sternum. Also called vertebrosternal rib; sternal rib.

vertebral r. See floating rib.

vertebrochondral r. See false rib.

vertebrosternal r. See true rib.

ribavirin (ri-bah-vi′rin) A synthetic drug with antiviral activity against DNA and RNA viruses, including the respiratory syncytial virus (RSV).

riboflavin (ri-bo-fla′vin) A yellow, water-soluble component of the vitamin B complex; present in milk, egg yolk, and fresh meat, and also produced synthetically. Formerly called vitamin B₂.

ribonuclease (ri-bo-nu′kle-ās) (RNase) Enzyme responsible for the breakdown of ribonucleic acid.

ribonucleic acid (ri-bo-nu-kle′ik as′id) (RNA) Any of a family of polynucleotides, components of all living cells (especially cytoplasm and nucleolus); characterized by their constituent sugar (d-ribose) and single-stranded molecules.

messenger RNA (mRNA) An RNA fraction with a base ratio that corresponds to the DNA of the same organism; it carries genetic code information from DNA to the sites in the cell where proteins are manufactured. Also called template RNA.

ribosomal RNA (rRNA) The RNA of ribosomes; it is the most abundant type of RNA found in the cell.

soluble RNA (sRNA) See transfer RNA.

template RNA See messenger RNA.

transfer RNA (tRNA) The smallest biologically active nucleic acid known, present in cells in at least 20 varieties; it transfers an amino acid to a growing polypeptide chain. Also called soluble RNA.

ribonucleoprotein (ri-bo-nu-kle-o-pro′tēn) (RNP) A complex macromolecule containing RNA (ribonucleic acid) and protein.

ribose (ri′bōs) (Rib) A five-carbon sugar present in RNA (ribonucleic acid).

ribosome (ri′bo-sōm) One of the minute granules present in the cytoplasm of cells, either free or attached to the cell's endoplasmic reticulum; it ranges in size from 100 to 150 ;aN in diameter, contains a high concentration of RNA, and plays an important role in protein synthesis.

ribosuria (ri-bo-su′re-ah) Excessive excretion of ribose in the urine; seen in muscular dystrophy.

riboviruses (ri-bo-vi′rus-es) See RNA viruses, under virus.

rib-spreader (rib spred′er) Surgical instrument for separating the ribs during operations within the chest.

RICE Acronym for Rest Ice Compression Elevation; denoting the initial care of an ankle injury.

ricin (ri′sin) A highly poisonous protein present in the castor oil bean; used as a biochemical reagent.

rickets (rik′ets) Disease of infants and young children caused by vitamin D deficiency, resulting in defective bone growth.

renal r. A form of rickets occurring in children as a result of chronic kidney disease.

vitamin D–resistant r. A severe form of rickets that is not relieved by administration of vitamin D; caused by a congenital defect of the kidneys; seen most frequently in males.

Rickettsia (rĭ-ket′se-ah) A genus of gram-negative bacteria, transmitted to humans through bites of infected fleas, ticks, mites, and lice.

R. akari Species causing rickettsialpox; transmitted to humans by the mouse-infecting mite *Liponyssoides sanguineus*.

R. prowazekii Species causing epidemic typhus and Brill-Zinsser disease (the carrier or latent type of typhus); transmitted by body lice.

R. rickettsii Species causing Rocky Mountain spotted fever; transmitted by ixodid ticks, especially *Dermacentor andersoni* and *Dermacentor variabilis*.

R. tsutsugamushi Species causing scrub typhus (tsutsugamushi disease); transmitted by mites.

R. typhi Species causing endemic flea-borne typhus (murine typhus); transmitted by the rat flea.

rickettsial (rĭ-ket′se-al) Relating to *Rickettsia* bacteria.

rickettsialpox (rĭ-ket′se-al-poks) An acute mite-borne illness of several days' duration; characterized by an initial skin lesion, followed about a week later by a rash, fever, backache, and headache; caused by *Rickettsia akari*.

rickettsiosis (rĭ-ket-se-o′sis) Any disease caused by a bacteria of the genus *Rickettsia* (e.g., Rocky Mountain spotted fever, typhus, rickettsialpox, Q fever).

ridge (rij) A linear elevation (e.g., on a bone or a tooth).

alveolar r. The bony ridge of the jaw containing sockets (alveoli) in which the roots of teeth fit.

dental r. Any linear elevation on the surface of a tooth, forming the border of a cusp or the margin of a crown.

lateral supracondylar r. A curved ridge on the lateral surface of the humerus (near the elbow) to which two of the dorsal muscles of the forearm attach.

oblique r. A variable ridge running across the chewing surface of an upper molar.

palatine r. One of four or six transverse ridges on the anterior region of the hard palate.

Passavant's r. The prominence formed in the posterior wall of the pharynx by the contraction of the superior constrictor muscle during the act of swallowing. Also called Passavant's bar; Passavant's cushion; Passavant's pad.

supraorbital r. The curved elevation of the frontal bone forming the upper border of the eye socket.

rifampin (rif′am-pin) A semisynthetic antibiotic drug used in the treatment of tuberculosis and other bacterial infections. Possible adverse reactions include taste disturbance, hyperbilirubinemia, hemolytic anemia, and liver damage.

right to treatment The right of a person to receive medical treatment when placed in or committed to a treatment institution.

rigidity (rĭ-jid′ĭ-te) 1. Abnormal stiffness. 2. In psychiatry, a person's excessive resistance to change.

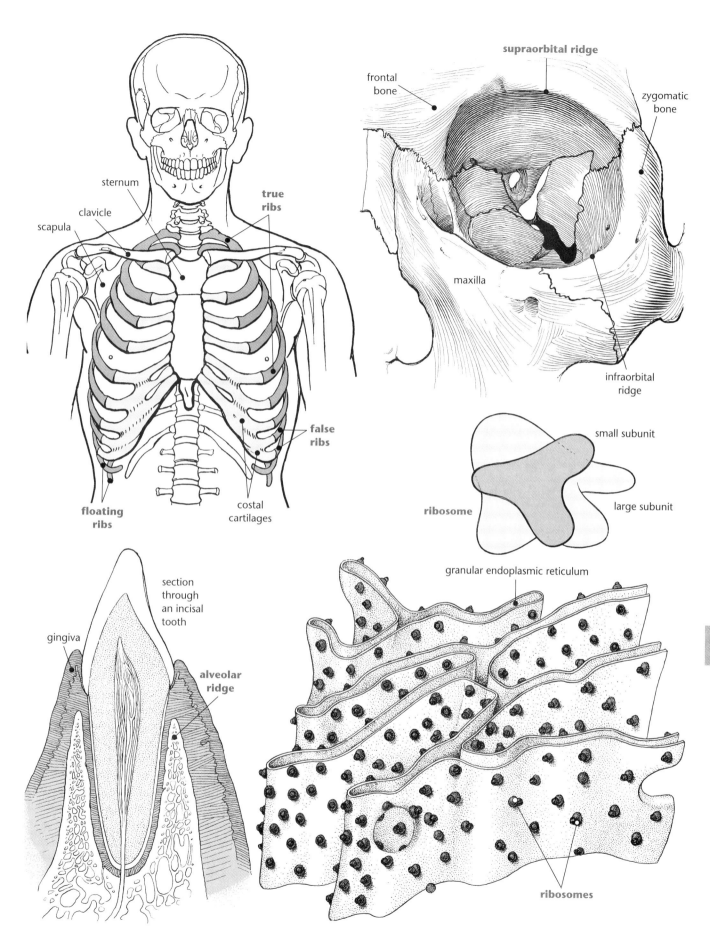

sternum

clavicle

scapula

true ribs

false ribs

floating ribs

costal cartilages

frontal bone

supraorbital ridge

zygomatic bone

maxilla

infraorbital ridge

small subunit

large subunit

ribosome

section through an incisal tooth

gingiva

alveolar ridge

granular endoplasmic reticulum

ribosomes

R

R29

anatomic r. Rigidity of the uterine cervix in labor occurring without pathologic infiltration; the cervix does not dilate beyond a certain point.

cadaveric r. See rigor mortis, under rigor.

clasp-knife r. See clasp-knife spasticity, under spasticity.

cogwheel r. Rigidity of a muscle that, when passively stretched, gives way to a series of small jerks; seen in parkinsonism.

decerebrate r. *(a)* Rigid extension of the extremities of an experimental animal following division of the brainstem above the pons, at the level of the red nucleus. *(b)* In humans, rigidity caused by an extensive, usually bilateral lesion above the brainstem, which results in separation of the vestibular nuclei from brainstem control; characterized by extension of all extremities, or of one arm and leg on the same side of a unilateral lesion, and backward bending of the spine.

lead-pipe r. A diffuse tonic contraction of muscles seen in Parkinson's disease.

mydriatic r. A tonic, usually dilated pupil that responds very slowly, if at all, to light and accommodation.

pathologic r. Rigidity of the uterine cervix in labor, caused by fibrosis, cancer, or other diseases.

postmortem r. See rigor mortis, under rigor.

rigor (rig'or) **1.** A chill and shivering occurring in association with fever of infectious origin. **2.** A stiffening of muscles.

calcium r. Arrest of cardiac function when the heart is in full contraction as a result of calcium poisoning.

instantaneous r. mortis Immediate stiffening of muscles, as when gripping objects with the fingers, occurring at the moment of a sudden violent death. This phenomenon has medicolegal importance since the body retains the position it was in at the moment of death and this positioning persists until full rigor mortis sets in. Also called cadaveric spasm.

r. mortis The stiffening of muscles in dead bodies; it occurs as a result of protein changes in muscle tissue caused by the activity of substances that take part in metabolism (metabolites). Onset of rigor mortis is extremely variable depending on conditions just before death, such as the amount of muscular exertion, ambient temperature, a debilitated state (e.g., from a long-term illness), and the age of the individual. Generally, rigor mortis is detectable 2 to 4 hours after death, reaches completion after 6 to 12 hours, and disappears after 24 to 28 hours. The short muscles (e.g., in eyelids and jaws) stiffen before the long muscle groups. However, muscles strongly exerted immediately before death may develop rigor mortis first regardless of the length, a finding of potential significance in forensic medicine. Also called postmortem rigidity; cadaveric rigidity.

myocardial r. mortis See ischemic contracture of left ventricle, under contracture.

rim (rim) An outer edge, margin, or border.

r. of abrasion See abrasion collar, under collar.

bite r. See occlusion rim.

occlusion r. A wax surface built on a denture base for recording maxillomandibular relations and for arranging teeth. Also called bite rim; record rim.

record r. See occlusion rim.

rima (ri'mah), pl. ri'mae A cleft, fissure, slit, or elongated opening.

r. glottidis See fissure of glottis, under fissure.

r. oris See oral orifice, under orifice.

r. palpebrarum See palpebral fissure, under fissure.

r. pudendi See vulvar cleft, under cleft.

r. vestibuli See fissure of false glottis, under fissure.

ring (ring) **1.** In anatomy, a circular band of tissue surrounding an opening. **2.** In chemistry, an arrangement of atoms graphically representable as a circle. **3.** Any circular device.

abdominal r. See deep inguinal ring.

anterior limiting r. of eye A ridgelike ring composed of collagenous fibers marking the peripheral edge of Descemet's membrane and the anterior border of the trabecular meshwork, as seen by gonioscopy. Also called Schwalbe's ring; Schwalbe's annular line.

common tendinous r. See common annular tendon, under tendon.

contact r. In forensic pathology, a bruising or abrasion surrounding a funnel-shaped wound on the skin caused by a zero-range gunshot; the ring represents the impression or "fingerprint" of the firearm's muzzle.

deep inguinal r. The oval orifice in the transverse fascia of the external oblique muscle marking the deep opening of the inguinal canal. Also called abdominal ring; internal inguinal ring; annulus inguinalis profundus.

external inguinal r. See superficial inguinal ring.

Fallope r. A bandlike ring used to occlude the fallopian (uterine) tubes; a laparoscopic method of tubal sterilization to prevent pregnancy.

femoral r. The abdominal or superior oval opening of the conical femoral canal underlying the inguinal ligament at the groin; it is bounded posteriorly by the pectineus muscle, medially by the lacunar ligament, and laterally by the femoral vein. It is normally filled with extraperitoneal fatty and lymphoid tissues and is a potential site of hernia.

internal inguinal r. See deep inguinal ring.

Kayser-Fleischer r. A greenish brown ring formed around the cornea, resulting from deposition of copper in the posterior limiting (Descemet's) membrane of the eye; seen in Wilson's disease.

lower esophageal r. An abnormal circular narrowing at the junction of the esophagus and the stomach; may be asymptomatic or may cause severe difficulty in swallowing; the cause is unknown but is often associated with a hiatal hernia. Also called Schatzki's ring.

lymphoid r. The masses of lymphoid tissue situated around the entrance to the pharynx. They include the palatine, pharyngeal, and lingual tonsils and the small lymph follicles on the superior oropharyngeal wall. Also called Waldeyer's throat ring; tonsillar ring.

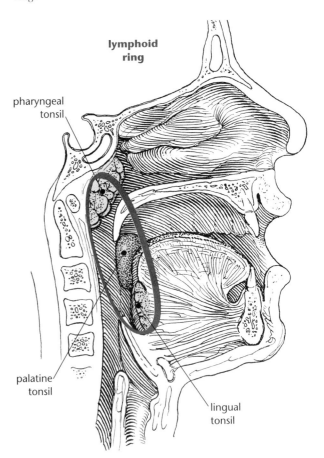

lymphoid ring

pharyngeal tonsil

palatine tonsil

lingual tonsil

Schatzki's r. See lower esophageal ring.

Schwalbe's r. See anterior limiting ring of eye.

subcutaneous inguinal r. See superficial inguinal ring.

superficial inguinal r. The orifice in the aponeurosis of the external oblique muscle forming the external opening of the inguinal canal. Also called external inguinal ring; subcutaneous inguinal ring; annulus inguinalis superficialis.

tonsillar r. See lymphoid ring.

tracheal r.'s See tracheal cartilages, under cartilage.

umbilical r. The opening in the abdominal connective tissue (linea alba) of the fetus through which pass the umbilical arteries and vein.

upper esophageal r.'s See esophageal webs, under web.

Waldeyer's throat r. See lymphoid ring.

ringworm (ring'wurm) See tinea.

r. of foot See tinea pedis, under tinea.

r. of scalp See tinea capitis, under tinea.

r. of smooth skin See tinea corporis, under tinea.

risk (risk) **1.** The probability of suffering harm or a loss. **2.** In toxicology, the probability that a substance will inflict injury under specified conditions of use. **3.** In health insurance, the chance of health care expenses arising from illness or injury.

assumption of r. In negligence law, especially in reference to medical malpractice, the doctrine that a person who consents to a treatment, procedure, or omission of either, with the knowledge that injury may reasonably result, relinquishes the future complaint that injury was caused by negligence on the part of the practitioner. In medical professional liability, assumption of risk provides a valid defense from suit only when medical treatment was administered with proper care. See also negligence.

attributable r. (AR) In epidemiology, the numerical difference between the incidence rate of a disease among people exposed to a risk factor and the incidence rate of the disease among unexposed people.

population attributable r. (PAR) In epidemiology, the proportion of all instances of a disease in the population that can be attributed to the exposure being studied.

recurrence r. The probability that a genetic disorder that has occurred in a family will recur in another member in the same or in future generations of the same family.

relative r. (RR) In epidemiology, the ratio of the incidence rate of a disease among people exposed to a particular risk factor to the incidence of the disease among people unexposed to the risk factor.

risk pooling See risk sharing.

risk pools In health care, legislatively created programs that group together individuals who cannot get health insurance in the private sector. Funding for the pool is subsidized through assessments on insurers or through government revenues. Maximum rates are tied to the rest of the market.

risk sharing The degree to which individuals collectively bear the cost of protecting against loss, rather than individually bear the cost based on their past or expected future expenses. Also called risk pooling; risk spreading.

risk spreading See risk sharing.

risus sardonicus (ri'sus sar-don'i-kus) A grinlike facial expression caused by spasm of facial muscles, as seen in tetanus. Also called sardonic grin.

ritodrine (rit'o-drēn) A drug administered to suppress premature labor by relaxing the musculature of the uterus. Common adverse effects include increased maternal heart rate and, frequently, tremor, nausea, vomiting, and headache.

ritual (rich'u-al) Any psychomotor behavior or activity performed compulsively and repeatedly to relieve or forestall anxiety; commonly observed in obsessive—compulsive neurosis.

riziform (riz'i-form) Resembling grains of rice.

roborant (rob'o-rant) **1.** Tending to strengthen. **2.** Any agent that has such property.

Rochalimaea quintana (ro-kah-li-me'ah kwin-ta'nah) A species of

Rochalimaea bacteria closely resembling *Rickettsia*; it causes trench fever in humans.

rod (rod) **1.** Any cylindrical structure or formation. **2.** One of the cells forming, with the cones, the layer of rods and cones of the retina.

rodenticide (ro-den'tī-sid) Any substance lethal to rodents.

roentgen (rent'gen) (R, r) A unit of radiation exposure equal to 2.58 $\times 10^{-4}$ coulomb per kilogram.

roentgen-equivalent-man (rent'gen e-kwiv'ah-lent man) See rem.

roentgeno- Combining form meaning x rays.

roentgenkymography (rent-gen-ki-mog'rah-fe) Apparatus for recording the movements of the heart and great vessels on a single x-ray film.

roentgenogram (rent-gen'o-gram) A processed photographic film on which an image is produced by x rays striking a sensitized film after their passage through a portion of the body. Also called radiogram; x-ray picture; commonly called x-ray.

cephalographic r. X-ray picture of the skull, including the lower jaw, for purpose of taking measurements.

roentgenography (rent-gen-og'rah-fe) Radiography.

body-section r. See tomography.

mucosal relief r. X-ray picture of the lining of the rectum, made after a barium enema has been evacuated and the rectum has been distended with air; the small amount of barium remaining on the intestinal wall reveals fine details. Also called air contrast study.

sectional r. See tomography

spot-film r. The making of several localized x ray pictures during a fluoroscopic examination.

roentgenologist (rent-gĕ-nol'o-jist) A physician who specializes in the diagnostic and therapeutic use of x rays.

roentgenology (rent-gĕ-nol'o-je) The study of x rays as applied to diagnosis and treatment of disease.

roentgenometry (rent-gĕ-nom'ĕ-tre) **1.** Measurement of the therapeutic dosage of x rays. **2.** Measurement of the penetrating power of x rays.

roentgenoscopy (rent-gĕ-nos'ko-pe) See fluoroscopy.

role (rōl) **1.** The pattern of social behavior that a person develops, influenced by what others expect or demand of him. **2.** A part played by a person in relation to a group.

role-playing (rōl pla'ing) A method of treating emotional conflicts by having the subject assume various roles.

roller (rōl'er) See roller bandage, under bandage.

rongeur (raw-zhur') A strong forceps with sharp curved and often cup-shaped blades, used to gouge or nip away fragments of bone. Also called rongeur forceps.

rongeur

roof (roof) Any structure functioning as the cover of a cavity.

r. of fourth ventricle The upper portion of the fourth ventricle of the brain.

r. of mouth See palate.

r. of skull See calvaria.

room (rōōm) A limited area enclosed by walls in a building.

anechoic r. A room that is devoid of echo; used in acoustic testing.

birthing r. A hospital room in which women undergo both labor and delivery; it is provided with infant warmers and resuscitation equipment. See also birth center, under center.

delivery r. A hospital room to which women in labor are taken for delivery.

emergency r. (ER) An area in a hospital where immediate attention is given by trained personnel to people brought in with sudden and unexpected medical problems, such as acute illness, trauma, etc.

first recovery r. See recovery room (a).

labor r. (LBR) A hospital room in which women in labor are monitored prior to delivery. Also called predelivery room.

operating r. (OR) An area in a hospital that is equipped for performing surgical procedures.

postanesthesia r. See recovery room (a).

predelivery r. See labor room.

recovery r. (RR) (a) A hospital room (usually adjoining an operating or delivery room) that is provided with equipment and personnel for continuous monitoring of postoperative patients immediately following anesthesia, and where special attention is focused on airway management and control of pain, nausea, and vomiting. Also called postanesthesia room; first recovery room. (b) A hospital room where postoperative patients are briefly placed after release from the postanesthesia room, prior to discharge from the hospital. Also called secondary recovery room.

secondary recovery r. See recovery room (b).

rooming-in (room′ing in) The practice of allowing a newborn baby to stay in the mother's hospital room, in a crib, rather than in the nursery, during the hospital stay.

root (root) 1. The embedded part of a structure, as of a tooth, hair, or nail. 2. The origin of a structure (e.g., the proximal end of a nerve surrounded by bone). 3. The underground part of a plant.

anatomic r. The root of a tooth extending from the cervical line to its apical extremity and contained in the bony socket of the jaw; the part of a tooth covered by cementum.

anterior r.'s See ventral roots.

r. of aorta The origin of the ascending aorta from the left ventricle of the heart.

belladonna r. The root of the plant *Atropa belladonna,* the source of various alkaloids, including atropine.

r.'s of brachial plexus The five roots forming the brachial plexus of the arm, consisting of the anterior (ventral) rami of the fifth, sixth, seventh, and eighth cervical nerves and the greater part of the first thoracic nerve; they fuse with one another to form three trunks.

clinical r. The portion of the tooth below the gingival crest, which is not visible in the mouth.

r. of clitoris The proximal part of the clitoris, consisting of two diverging corpora cavernosa that lie deeply in close apposition with the periosteum of the ischiopubic rami.

dandelion r. The root of the plant *Taraxacum officinale,* the source of various alkaloids, including choline, inulin, and pectin.

dorsal r.'s The nerve roots of each spinal nerve that carry sensory impulses from bodily structures to the back of the spinal cord; they are attached along the dorsal lateral sulcus, on either side of the spinal cord, by six to eight rootlets; each bears a spinal ganglion. Also called sensory roots; posterior roots.

r. of hair The proximal part of hair embedded in the deep bulbous portion of the hair follicle lying in the dermis, the deep layer of the skin.

licorice r. See glycyrrhiza.

lingual r. The back part of the tongue, behind the V-shaped furrow (terminal sulcus of tongue).

r. of lung The attachment of either lung, consisting of a pedicle formed by structures entering and leaving the lung at the hilus, including the pulmonary artery, bronchus, superior and inferior pulmonary veins, and lymph nodes.

motor r.'s See ventral roots.

r. of nail The proximal end of the nail, underlying a fold of skin (cuticle).

r. of nose The upper part of the nose adjoining the forehead, between the two orbits.

r. of penis The proximal part of the penis, consisting of two diverging crura of the corpora cavernosa and the bulb, which are attached to the ischiopubic ramus and the perineal membrane, respectively.

posterior r.'s See dorsal roots.

sensory r.'s See dorsal roots.

r. of tooth The part of the tooth below the neck which is normally embedded in the alveolar process and covered with cementum.

MANDIBULAR TEETH	LENGTH OF ROOT OF TOOTH	LENGTH OF CROWN OF TOOTH
central incisor	12.5 mm	9.0 mm
lateral incisor	13.0 mm	9.5 mm
cuspid	13.0 mm	11.0 mm
first bicuspid	14.0 mm	8.5 mm
second bicuspid	14.5 mm	8.5 mm
first molar	14.0 mm	8.0 mm
second molar	13.0 mm	7.5 mm
third molar	11.5 mm	7.0 mm
MAXILLARY TEETH		
central incisor	13.0 mm	10.5 mm
lateral incisor	12.0 mm	9.5 mm
cuspid	17.0 mm	11.0 mm
first bicuspid	14.0 mm	8.5 mm
second bicuspid	14.0 mm	8.5 mm
first molar	12.5 mm	7.5 mm
second molar	11.5 mm	7.0 mm
third molar	10.5 mm	6.5 mm

ventral r.'s The nerve roots that carry impulses from the anterior part of the spinal cord out to muscles and other bodily structures; they emerge from the ventral lateral sulcus, on either side of the spinal cord, in two or three irregular rows of rootlets. Also called anterior roots; motor roots.

rosacea (ro-za′she-ah) A chronic skin disease of unknown cause, most commonly affecting middle-aged people, especially women; characterized by a reddish, acnelike eruption and dilation of capillaries, usually on the nose and cheeks. Sometimes called acne rosacea.

rosary (ro′zah-re) An arrangement resembling a string of beads.

rachitic r. A row of nodular enlargements of the junctions between the ribs and their cartilages, sometimes seen in rachitic children. Also called beading of the ribs.

roseola (ro-ze′o-lah) A reddish rash.

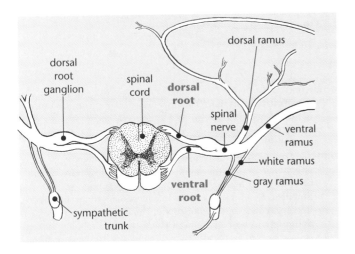

dorsal ramus

dorsal root ganglion

spinal cord

dorsal root

spinal nerve

ventral ramus

white ramus

gray ramus

ventral root

sympathetic trunk

r. infantum See exanthem subitum, under exanthem.

rosin (roz′in) The solid resin of *Pinus palustris;* used in the preparation of plasters and ointments.

rostellum (ros-tel′um) The anterior, hook-bearing portion of a tapeworm.

rostrad (ros′trad) Directed toward the front end of an organism.

rostral (ros′tral) Relating to a rostrum.

rostrum (ros′trum) Any beaklike anatomic structure.

rot (rot) 1. To decay; to decompose. 2. The process of decomposition.

rotameter (ro-tam′ĕ-ter) A tubular device for measuring the flow of gases or liquids, especially the flow rate of gases during administration of anesthesia.

rotation (ro-ta′shun) 1. Movement around an internal axis (e.g., of the eyeball). 2. In obstetrics, the turning of the fetal head or presenting part during birth, whereby it is accommodated to the birth canal.

rotator (ro′ta-tor) Any muscle that rotates a body part.

Rotavirus (ro′tah-vi-rus) Genus of wheel-shaped RNA viruses (family Rotaviridae) including the human gastroenteritis virus; the most important cause of severe dehydrating diarrhea, vomiting, and low-grade fever in children under three years of age.

rotenone (ro′tĕ-nōn) A component of certain roots, especially derris root, used as an insecticide in the treatment of scabies and in veterinary medicine.

rototome (ro′to-tōm) A rotating surgical instrument used for cutting in arthroscopic surgery.

roughage (ruf′ij) Indigestible material in the diet (coarse vegetable fibers and cellulose) that stimulates the propulsive movements (peristalsis) of the bowel.

roundworm (rownd′wurm) Any worm of the phylum Nematoda (e.g., pinworms, hookworms, whipworms).

rubella (roo-bel′ah) Contagious viral disease, usually mild and of short duration, but capable of causing fetal abnormalities from maternal infection during the first three months of pregnancy; characterized by malaise, headache, fever, enlarged lymph nodes (especially behind the ears), and a maculopapular rash. Also called German measles.

rubeola (roo-be-o′lah) See measles.

rubeosis (roo-be-o′sis) Redness.

r. iridis Formation of new intertwining, minute blood vessels on the anterior surface of the iris; may cause secondary glaucoma when extending into the anterior chamber angle of the eye; seen in severe cases of diabetes mellitus; occasionally seen in other conditions.

rubescent (roo-bes′ent) Reddening.

rubidium (roo-bid′e-um) Chemical element; symbol Rb, atomic number 37, atomic weight 85.47.

Rubivirus (roo-bī-vi′rus) A genus of viruses (family Togaviridae) that, unlike other members of the Togaviridae family, are not transmitted by arthropods; humans are the only vertebrate host; includes the rubella (German measles) virus.

rubor (roo′bor) Latin for redness.

rudiment (roo′dī-ment) An incompletely developed body structure.

rudimentary (roo-dī-men′tah-re) Incompletely developed.

ruga (roo′gah), pl. ru′gae A fold or wrinkle.

gastric r. One of many folds in the stomach lining.

r. palatina One of several transverse ridges on the anterior part of the hard palate.

vaginal rugae The transverse folds in the lining of the vagina. Also called vaginal folds.

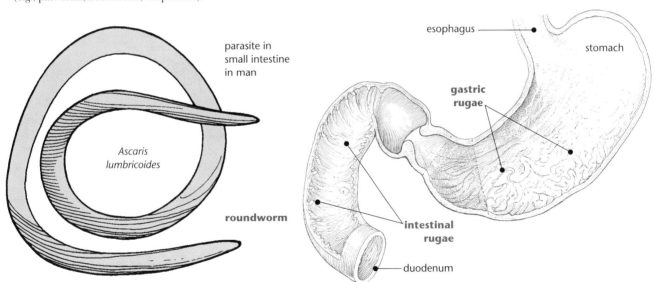

parasite in small intestine in man

Ascaris lumbricoides

roundworm

esophagus

stomach

gastric rugae

intestinal rugae

duodenum

-rrhage Combining form meaning excessive discharge (e.g., hemorrhage).

-rrhaphy Combining form meaning suture (e.g., herniorrhaphy).

-rrhea Combining form meaning a flow (e.g., diarrhea).

rub (rŭb) 1. The act of moving one surface against another with pressure. 2. The sound produced by such an act.

friction r. See friction sound, under sound.

pericardial r. A scraping sound produced by the rubbing together of the two inflamed layers of the pericardial sac enveloping the heart.

pleuritic r. A grating sound produced by the rubbing together of the two inflamed pleural layers around the lungs during breathing.

rubedo (roo-be′do) Temporary redness of the skin.

rubefacient (roo-bĕ-fa′shent) Causing redness and irritation of the skin.

rugal (roo′gal) Creased; corrugated.

rugitus (roo′ji-tus) Intestinal rumbling.

rugose (roo′gōs) Marked by folds or ridges.

rugosity (roo-gos′ĭ-te) 1. The state of having folds. 2. A fold or ruga.

rule (rool) A guide.

American Law Institute r. A 1962 American rule stating, "a person is not responsible for criminal conduct if at the time of such conduct as a result of mental disease or defect he lacks substantial capacity either to appreciate the wrongfulness of his conduct or to conform his conduct to the requirements of law."

delivery date r. See Nägele's rule.

M'Naghten r., McNaughton r. A British test of criminal responsibility stating, "it must be shown that, at the time of committing the act, the accused was acting under such defect of reason from a diseased mind as not to know the nature and quality of the act or if he knew this, that he did not know that what he was doing was wrong."

Nägele's r. Estimation of the day of childbirth by counting back three months from the first day of the last menstrual period and adding seven days. Also called delivery date rule.

r. of nine A method of rapidly determining the amount of fluid replacement required by an adult burn victim by assessing the extent of burns on the skin surface; the head and arms each represent 9% of the skin surface, the anterior or posterior surface of the legs represent 9% each, the anterior and posterior truncal skin represent 18% each, and the inguinal area 1%.

rumination (roo-mī-na′shun) **1.** The bringing up (regurgitation), rechewing, and reswallowing of food from the stomach. **2.** The recurring of the same thought. **3.** Disorder of infants occurring after a period of normal development and functioning; characterized by repeated regurgitation of food, weight loss, and failure to thrive.

Young's rule

$$\text{dose for child} = \text{adult dose} \div \frac{\text{age} + 12}{\text{age of child (in years)}}$$

Clark's rule

$$\text{dose for child} = \text{adult dose} \times \frac{\text{weight of child (in pounds)}}{150 \text{ pounds}}$$

Fried's rule

$$\text{dose for infant} = \text{adult dose} \times \frac{\text{age (in months)}}{150}$$

Nägele's rule

estimated day of birth (of the following year)

		May							June			
	1	2	3	4	5						1	2
6	7	8	9	10	11	12	3	4	5	6	7	8	9
13	14	15	16	17	18	19	10	11	12	13	14	15	16
20	21	22	23	24	25	26	17	18	19	20	21	22	23
27	28	29	30	31			24	25	26	27	28	29	30
		July							August			
1	2	3	4	5	6	7			1	2	3	4
8	9	10	11	12	13	14	5	6	7	8	9	10	11
15	16	17	18	19	20	21	12	13	14	15	16	17	18
22	23	24	25	26	27	28	19	20	21	22	23	24	25
29	30	31					26	27	28	29	30	31

day of last menstrual period

rump (rump) Buttocks or gluteal region.

rupture (rup′chur) **1.** Popular term for a hernia. **2.** A tearing or bursting of an organ or body part.

r. of uterus Rupture of the uterine wall; it may occur during childbirth under certain predisposing conditions, such as the presence of fibroids, an abnormally adherent placenta (placenta increta or percreta), scarring from a previous cesarean section, prolonged labor due to malposition of the fetus (e.g., breech presentation), misuse of forceps, or extensive use of uterine stimulants (e.g., oxytocin, prostaglandins, ergot infusions). Predisposing factors not associated with labor include choriocarcinoma, uterine cancer, and invasive hydatidiform mole.

ruthenium (roo-the′ne-um) Metallic element; symbol Ru, atomic number 44, atomic weight 101.1.

rutherford (ruth′er-ford) Unit of radioactivity, equal to the amount of radioactive material undergoing 1 million disintegrations per second.

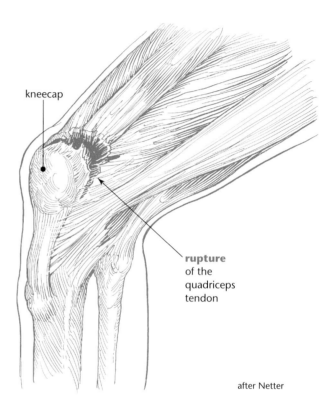

kneecap

rupture of the quadriceps tendon

after Netter

S

sabulous (sab'u-lus) Like sand; gritty.

sac (sak) A pouchlike anatomic structure.

abdominal s. The part of the embryonic sac that develops into the peritoneal cavity of the abdomen.

air s. See pulmonary alveolus, under alveolus.

aneurysmal s. A localized dilatation of a diseased wall of an artery, forming the chamber of a saccular aneurysm.

dental s. See tooth follicle, under follicle.

dural s. The continuation of the loose sheath of the spinal dura mater below the terminal part of the spinal cord; it surrounds the cauda equina and filum terminale and ends at the lower border of the second sacral vertebra.

endolymphatic s. The blind extremity of the endolymphatic duct of the inner ear, situated under the dura mater on the back surface of the petrous part of the temporal bone.

greater s. of peritoneum The main part of the peritoneal cavity, between the parietal and visceral layers of the peritoneum; it extends across the whole breadth of the abdomen, and from the diaphragm to the pelvis. Also called greater peritoneal cavity.

heart s. See pericardium.

hernial s. The lining of a hernia (e.g., the pouch of peritoneum that lines an umbilical hernia).

lacrimal s. An expanded sac at the upper blind end of the nasolacrimal duct; it is about 12 mm in length, lodged in the lacrimal fossa, and receives tear fluid from two lacrimal canaliculi on its lateral surface. Also called tear sac.

lesser s. of peritoneum The smaller part of the peritoneal cavity; a diverticulum of the greater sac of peritoneum, situated behind the lesser omentum; it extends upward as far as the diaphragm, and downward between the layers of the greater omentum, to its opening through the epiploic foramen where it communicates with the greater sac of peritoneum. Also called omental bursa; omental sac; lesser peritoneal cavity.

lymphatic s. See cisterna chyli, under cisterna.

omental s. See lesser sac of peritoneum.

synovial s. A closed pouch of synovial membrane extending beyond the normal confines of the joint; it contains a thick, viscous, lubricating fluid (similar to the white of an egg) that facilitates movement of the joint.

tear s. See lacrimal sac.

vitelline s. See yolk sac.

yolk s. The highly vascular umbilical vesicle enveloping the nutritive yolk of an embryo; it is attached to the embryo's midgut. Also called vitelline sac.

saccades (sah-kāds') Sudden jerky movements of the eye, occurring when the gaze shifts from one point to another.

saccadic (sah-kad'ik) Relating to saccades.

saccate (sak'āt) Like a sac; pouched.

saccaric (sah-kar'ik) Relating to sugar.

saccharide (sak'ah-rīd) Any of several carbohydrates, including the sugars.

sacchariferous (sak'ah-rif'er-us) Containing or producing sugar.

saccarimeter (sak'ah-rim'ĕ-ter) A device for measuring the amount of sugar in a solution.

saccharin (sak'ah-rin) Compound used as a sugar substitute.

saccharine (sak'ah-rīn) Sweet; sugary.

saccharo-, sacchari- Combining forms meaning sugar.

saccharometabolism (sak'ah-ro-mĕ-tab'o-lizm) Utilization of sugar by the body.

saccharose (sak'ah-rōs) See sucrose.

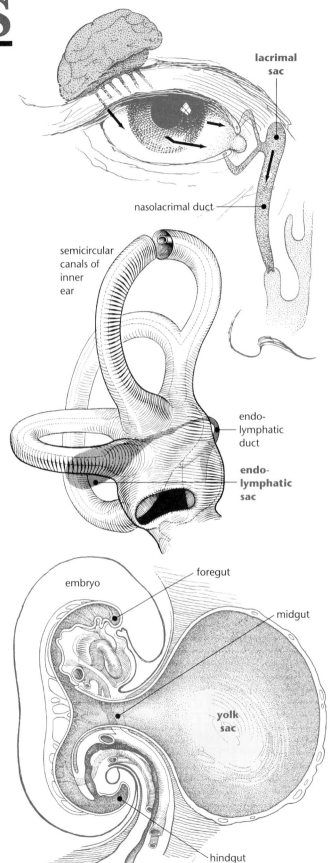

S

sabulous ■ saccharose

saccharum (sak'ah-rum) Latin for sucrose.

sacciform, saccular (sak'sĭ-form, sak'u-lar) Bag-shaped.

sacculated (sak'u-lāt-ed) Formed of or divided into several pouches.

sacculation (sak-u-la'shun) 1. The process of sac formation. 2. The presence of sacs.

saccule, sacculus (sak'ūl, sak'u-lus) 1. A small sac. 2. The smaller of the two membranous sacs within the vestibule of the inner ear; it communicates directly with the basal end of the cochlear duct by a short tube, the ductus reuniens, and indirectly with the utricle by a Y-shaped tube (combined endolymphatic and utriculosaccular ducts); it possesses an oval thickening on its anterior wall called macula of the saccule, which specifically responds to linear acceleration, such as the pull of gravity; it receives a distribution of the saccular fibers of the vestibulocochlear (8th cranial) nerve.

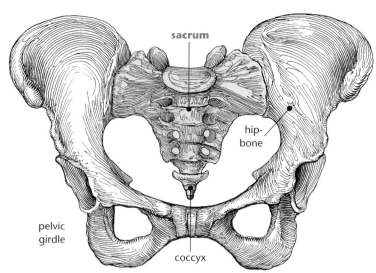

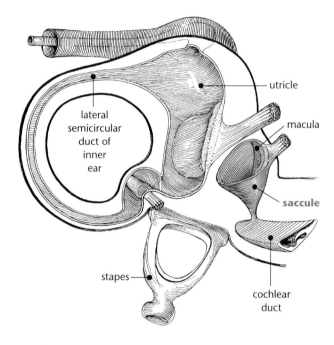

sacculi (sak'u-li) Plural of saccule.

sacculiform (sak'u-lĭ-form) Shaped like a saccule.

sacculocochlear (sak-u-lo-kok'le-ar) Relating to the saccule and the cochlea (in the inner ear).

saccus (sak'kus), pl. sac'ci Latin for sac.

sacrad (sa'krad) Toward the sacrum.

sacral (sa'kral) Relating to the sacrum.

sacralgia (sa-kral'je-ah) Pain in the area of the sacrum. Also called sacrodynia.

sacralization (sa-kral-ĭ-za'shun) Abnormal fusion of the lowest (fifth) lumbar vertebra to the sacrum, present at birth, due to excessive length of the transverse processes of the lumbar vertebra.

sacrectomy (sa-krek'to-me) Surgical removal of a portion of the sacrum.

sacro-, sacr- Combining forms meaning sacrum.

sacrococcygeal (sa-kro-kok-sij'e-al) Relating to the sacrum and the coccyx.

sacrodynia (sa-kro-din'e-ah) See sacralgia.

sacroiliac (sa-kro-il'e-ak) Relating to the sacrum and ilium.

sacroiliitis (sa-kro-il-e-i'tis) Inflammation of the joint between the sacrum and the back of the hipbone (ilium) on either side; chief symptom is pain in the lower back, buttocks, groin, and back of thigh.

sacrosciatic (sa-kro-si-at'ik) Relating to the sacrum and the ischium.

sacrospinal (sa-kro-spi'nal) Relating to the sacrum and the rest of the vertebral column above it.

sacrovertebral (sa-kro-vėr-te'-bral) Relating to the sacrum and vertebrae above it.

sacrum (sa'krum) A slightly curved, triangular bone composed of five fused vertebrae, forming the back of the pelvis; it articulates on each side with the corresponding ilium and with the last lumbar vertebra above, and the coccyx below.

    assimilation s. A condition in which the last lumbar vertebra is fused to the sacrum or the last sacral vertebra is fused to the first coccygeal body.

    tilted s. A forward displacement of the sacrum resulting from separation of the sacroiliac joints.

saddle (sad'l) See denture base, under base.

sadism (sād'izm) The derivation of pleasure from inflicting physical or psychological pain or abuse on others.

    sexual s. A psychosexual disorder in which the infliction of physical or psychological pain on another person is the only or the preferred means of producing sexual excitement.

sadist (sād'ist) A person who practices sadism.

sadomasochism (sād-o-mas'o-kizm) A condition of a high degree of destructive energy in which submissive (masochistic) and aggressive (sadistic) attitudes coexist in an individual's social and/or sexual relationships.

safranin O (saf'rah-nin) A red dye used in biologic stains.

safranophilic (saf'rah-no-fil'ik) Having an affinity for safranin; applied to cells that stain readily with that dye.

sagittal (saj'ĭ-tal) In an anteroposterior direction (i.e., occurring or situated in the median plane of the body or in a plane parallel to it).

salicylamide (sal-ĭ-sil-am'ĭd) A compound that has analgesic properties similar to aspirin.

salicylate (sah-lis'ĭ-lāt) A salt of salicylic acid.

salicylic acid (sal-ĭ-sil'ik as'id) Compound used in the topical treatment of corns and warts.

salicylism (sal'ĭ-sil-izm) Poisoning by the salicylate.

salient (sa'le-ent) 1. A protrusion. 2. Protruding.

salify (sal'ĭ-fi) To convert into a salt.

salimeter (sah-lim'ĕ-ter) Instrument for determining the concentration of saline solutions.

saline (sa'lēn) 1. Relating to or containing salt. 2. See saline solution, under solution.

saliva (sah-li'vah) The mixture of secretions produced by the salivary glands (parotid, sublingual, and submaxillary) and the mucous glands of the oral cavity; it contain the enzyme pytalin, which partially digests carbohydrates.

salivant (sal'ĭ-vant) 1. Increasing the flow of saliva. 2. Any agent producing such an effect.

salivary (sal'ĭ-ver-e) Relating to saliva.

    s. alpha-amylase See ptyalin.

salivate (sal'ĭ-vāt) To secrete saliva.

salivation (sal-ĭ-va'shun) The secretion of saliva.

Salmonella (sal-mo-nel'ah) Genus of gram-negative bacteria; some species cause acute human diseases.

S. arizonae Species found in lizards, snakes, and some warm-blooded animals; has been implicated in causing infections of the intestines, bones, and joints in humans.

S. enteritidis (SE) A widely distributed species that has caused outbreaks of gastroenteritis; found in wild and domestic animals and transmitted to humans by eating undercooked or raw eggs and eggshells from infected chickens.

S. paratyphi Species causing enteric fever in humans.

S. typhi Species causing typhoid fever. Formerly called *Salmonella typhosa.*

S. typhimurium Widely distributed species causing food poisoning in humans.

S. typhosa Former name for *Salmonella typhi.*

salmonellosis (sal-mo-nel-lo'sis) Infection with bacteria of the genus *Salmonella.*

salpingectomy (sal-pin-jek'to-me) Removal of a fallopian (uterine) tube. Also called tubectomy.

salpingemphraxis (sal-pin-jem-frak'sis) Obstruction of a eustachian (auditory) tube or a fallopian (uterine) tube.

salpinges (sal-pin'jez) Plural of salpinx.

salpingian (sal-pin'je-an) Relating to a eustachian (auditory) tube or to a fallopian (uterine) tube.

salpingitis (sal-pin-ji'tis) Inflammation of a fallopian (uterine) tube.

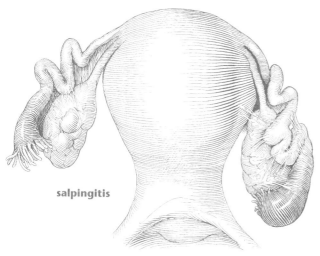

salpingitis

salpingo-, salping- Combining forms meaning tube.

salpingocele (sal-ping'go-sēl) Hernial protrusion of a fallopian (uterine) tube.

salpingocyesis (sal-ping'go-si-e'sis) See tubal pregnancy, under pregnancy.

salpingography (sal-ping-gog'rah-fe) X-ray examination of a fallopian (uterine) tube after infusion of a radiopaque substance through the cervix; usually performed to diagnose tubal occlusion.

salpingolysis (sal-ping-gol'i-sis) The release of adhesions from a fallopian (uterine) tube.

salpingoneostomy (sal-ping-go-ne-os'to-me) See salpingostomy.

salpingo-oophorectomy (sal-ping'go-of-o-rek'to-me) Surgical removal of a fallopian (uterine) tube and its corresponding ovary. Also called tubo-ovariectomy; salpingo-ovariectomy.

salpingo-oophoritis (sal-ping'go-of-o-ri'tis) Inflammation of a fallopian (uterine) tube and its ovary. Also called tubo-ovaritis.

salpingo-ovariectomy (sal-ping'go o-va-re-ek'to-me) See salpingo-oophorectomy.

salpingoperitonitis (sal-ping'go-per-i-to-ni'tis) Inflammation of a fallopian (uterine) tube and adjacent lining membrane (peritoneum) of the pelvic cavity.

salpingopharyngeal (sal-ping'go-fah-rin'je-al) Relating to the eustachian (auditory) tube and the pharynx.

salpingoplasty (sal-ping'go-plas-te) Reparative surgery of a fallopian (uterine) tube. Also called tuboplasty.

salpingorrhaphy (sal-ping-gor'ah-fe) Stitching of a fallopian (uterine) tube.

salpingostomy (sal-ping-gos'to-me) The surgical creation of a new opening in a fallopian (uterine) tube whose fringed end is totally occluded. Also called salpingoneostomy.

salpingotomy (sal-ping-got'o-me) A surgical cut into a fallopian (uterine) tube.

salpinx (sal'pinks), pl. salpin'ges Latin for tube.

salt (sawlt) 1. Compound produced by the reaction of an acid and a base in which all or part of the hydrogen ions of the acid are replaced by one or more radicals of the base. 2. Table salt (sodium chloride).

effervescent s. A mixture of sodium sulfate with sodium bicarbonate and citric or tartaric acid; carbonic acid gas is released when water is added to the mixture.

Epson s. Magnesium sulfate.

smelling s.'s Preparation of ammonium carbonate with any of several aromatic oils, sniffed as a restorative.

saltation (sal-ta'shun) 1. A leaping movement (as seen in certain neurologic disorders). 2. Proceeding by skipping or jumping rather than by a smooth transmission (as the conduction of a nerve impulse that jumps from one node to the next).

salting out (sawl'ting owt) Technique for separating proteins from a solution by adding a salt such as sodium chloride (table salt).

saltpeter (sawlt-pe'ter) See potassium nitrate, under potassium.

salubrius (sah-lu'bre-us) Conducive to health; healthful.

saluresis (sal-u-re'sis) Excretion of sodium in the urine.

saluretic (sal-u-ret'ik) Increasing or facilitating the urinary excretion of sodium.

salutary (sal'u-ta-re) Promoting health.

salvarsan (sal'var-san) See arsphenamine.

salve (sav) Ointment.

samarium (sah-ma're-um) Metallic element; symbol Sm, atomic number 62, atomic weight 150.35.

sample (sam'pl) 1. In biostatistics, the portion of the population selected for study. 2. A specimen.

random s. Sample made in such a way that each member of the population from which the sample is derived has an equal chance (probability) of being selected.

sampling (sam'pling) The acquisition and examination of a sample.

chorionic villus s. (CVS) Sampling of placental tissue (chorionic villi) for genetic analysis to detect chromosomal defects in the developing fetus; cells of the villi are identical to those of the fetus. Tissue may be obtained through the cervix or through an abdominal puncture with a needle and syringe under the guidance of ultrasound visualization. The sampling is performed at an earlier stage of pregnancy (at 8–12 weeks) than amniocentesis but the risks of complications are greater; spontaneous and septic abortions have been reported.

percutaneous umbilical blood s. (PUBS) Sampling of fetal blood to detect the presence of infectious microorganisms, such as those causing toxoplasmosis (*Toxoplasma gondii*), for which maternal blood has tested positive. Fetal blood is obtained from the umbilical cord by abdominal puncture with a needle and syringe under the guidance of ultrasound imaging.

sanative, sanatory (san'ah-tiv, san'ah-to-re) Curative.

sanatorium (san-ah-to're-um) An institution for the treatment of patients afflicted with long-term illnesses (e.g., tuberculosis, mental disorders). COMPARE sanitarium.

sand (sand) Fine, gritty particles.

brain s. See brain sand granules, under granule.

sandfly (sand'fli) A tiny, long-legged fly (genus *Phlebotomus* or *Lutzomyia*); vector of cutaneous leishmaniasis and phlebotomus fever.

sane (sān) Relating to sanity.

sanguiferous (sang-gwif'er-us) Conveying blood.

sanguineous (sang-gwin'e-us) Relating to blood.

sanguino, sangui- Combining forms meaning blood.

sanguinolent (sang-gwin'o-lent) Blood-tinged.

sanguinopurulent (sang-gwi-no-pu'ru-lent) Containing blood and pus.

sanguis (sang′gwis) Latin for blood.

sanguivorous (sang-gwiv′o-rus) Bloodsucking; applied to certain animals.

sanies (sa′ne-ēz) A watery discharge containing blood and pus.

saniopurulent (sa-ne-o-pu′roo-lent) Denoting a blood-tinged discharge mixed with pus.

sanioserous (sa-ne-o-se′rous) Denoting blood-tinged serum.

sanitarium (san-ĭ-ta′re-um) A health resort. COMPARE sanatorium.

sanitary (san′ĭ-ter-e) **1.** Relating to the preservation of health or hygiene. **2.** Free from filth; applied to the environment.

sanity (san′ĭ-te) Soundness of mind.

santonin (san′to-nin) The bitter principle of the flower heads of the plant *Artemisia cina;* has been used to effect expulsion of roundworms.

saphenectomy (saf-ĕ-nek′to-me) Surgical removal of a saphenous vein, a superficial vein of the leg.

saphenous (sah-fe′nus) **1.** Denoting either of two large superficial veins of the leg that carry blood from the toes upward. **2.** Denoting various structures in the leg that are associated with the saphenous veins.

sapid (sap′id) Affecting the organs of taste.

sapon- Combining form denoting soap.

saponaceous (sa-po-na′shus) Resembling soap; soapy.

saponatus (sa-po-na′tus) Mixed with soap.

saponify (sah-pon′ĭ-fi) To convert fat into soap.

saponin (sap′o-nin) A water-soluble plant glycoside with detergent action capable of destroying cells (e.g., blood cells).

sapphism (saf′izm) Lesbianism.

sapro- Combining form meaning putrefying; decayed.

saprogen (sap′ro-jen) Any organism capable of decaying organic matter.

saprogenic (sap-ro-jen′ik) Causing decay.

saprophilous (sah-prof′ĭ-lus) Thriving on decaying organic matter.

saprophyte (sap′ro-fit) An organism that thrives on dead organic matter. Also called necroparasite.

saprophytic (sap-ro-fit′ik) Living in dead organic matter.

saprozoic (sap-ro-zo′ik) Relating to an animal (e.g., a protozoan) that thrives on dead organic tissue.

sarco- Combining form meaning flesh.

sarcoid (sar′koid) Resembling flesh.

    Boeck;s s. See sarcoidosis.

sarcoidosis (sar-koi-do′sis) Systemic granulomatous disease of unknown cause, characterized primarily by the formation of multiple benign nodules affecting any tissue of the body, especially the lungs, and derangement of normal tissue architecture. May be associated with hypercalcemia, erythema nodosum, and anergy. Also called Boeck's sarcoid.

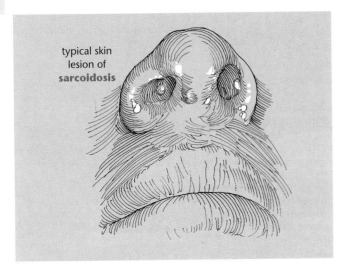

typical skin
lesion of
sarcoidosis

sarcolemma (sar-ko-lem′ah) The delicate plasma membrane covering every striated muscle fiber.

sarcoma (sar-ko′mah) Cancerous tumor composed of connective tissue.

    Ewing's s. An uncommon malignant tumor of any bone, affecting predominantly long tubular and pelvic bones; occurs in children and young adults. Also called Ewing's tumor.

    Kaposi's s. (KS) Malignant tumor of the skin occurring in multiple sites, especially the lower legs, and spreading to mucous membranes, lymph nodes, and internal organs; initial lesions are small red papules that enlarge to form purple to brown plaques and nodules; usually a slowly progressive disease, its course is much more aggressive when occurring as an opportunistic disease in AIDS patients.

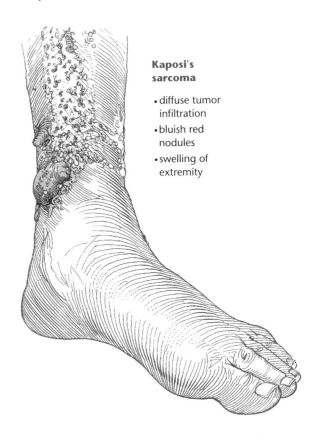

**Kaposi's
sarcoma**

• diffuse tumor
infiltration

• bluish red
nodules

• swelling of
extremity

    synovial s. A highly malignant tumor arising from synovial epithelial cells; seen most commonly around joints rather than within (e.g., in relation to bursae and tendon sheaths); seen also around the pharynx and in the abdominal wall. They average a five-year survival rate after optimal treatment. Also called malignant synovioma.

sarcomatoid (sar-ko′mah-toid) Resembling a sarcoma.

sarcomatous (sar-ko′mah-tus) Relating to sarcoma.

sarcomere (sar′ko-mēr) One of a series of repeated segments of a muscle fibril comprising the fundamental units of muscle contraction; it extends between two Z lines and is composed of overlapping thick and thin myofilaments.

sarcoplasm (sar′ko-plazm) The cytoplasmic substance in a muscle fiber in which the muscle fibrils are embedded.

sarcopoietic (sar-ko-poi-et′ik) Forming muscle.

Sarcoptes scabiei (sar-kop′tēz ska′be-i) The itch mite that causes scabies in humans.

sarcosome (sar′ko-sōm) A mitochondrion of a muscle fiber.

sarcostosis (sar-kos-to′sis) Ossification of muscle tissue.

sarcotubules (sar-ko-tu′būlz) The membranous tubules surrounding each fibril of striated muscle.

sardonic grin (sar-don′ik grin) See risus sardonicus, under risus.

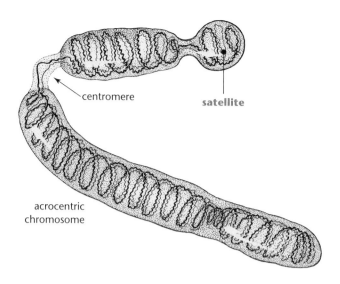

centromere

satellite

acrocentric
chromosome

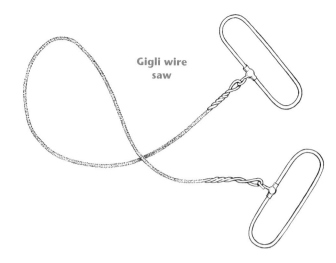

**Gigli wire
saw**

satellite (sat′ĕ-lit) Any structure, lesion, mass, or radiologic density associated with another, usually larger, entity.

    chromosome s. In genetics, a small, round chromatin mass attached by a stalk to the main body of a chromosome, usually associated with the short arm of an acrocentric chromosome.

satellitosis (sat-ĕ-li-to′sis) A phenomenon occurring in tissues of the central nervous system in which certain cells (oligodendroglia), normally found as satellites around nerve cells, increase in number and accumulate about a damaged nerve cell.

saturated (sach′ĕ-rāt-ed) **1.** Unable to hold in solution any more of a specified substance (solute). **2.** Neutral (i.e., having all chemical affinities satisfied).

saturnine (sat′ur-nin) Relating to lead.

saturnism (sat′ur-nizm) See lead poisoning, under poisoning.

satyriasis (sat-ī-ri′ah-sis) Insatiable sexual desire or behavior in the male; the counterpart of nymphomania in the female.

saucerization (saw-ser-ī-za′shun) **1.** A flat, disk-shaped defect formed along the shaft of a long bone; it contains microscopic calcifications and is considered typical of a fibrosarcoma with bone involvement. **2.** Excavation of tissue to form a shallow depression, intended to facilitate drainage from infected areas.

sauriasis (saw-ri′ah-sis) See ichthyosis.

saw (saw) Instrument with a serrated edge for cutting bone.

    Gigli wire s. A wire with saw teeth.

scab (skab) **1.** A crust formed on the surface of a superficial wound. **2.** To develop a scab.

scabicide (ska′bĭ-sīd) Destructive to itch mites.

scabies (ska′bēz) Skin disorder caused by the mite *Sarcoptes scabiei*; the female mite excavates tunnels in the superficial layer of the skin and deposits eggs and excreta, causing intense itching and swelling along the tracks; common sites include the area between fingers, the wrist, and the scrotal folds in men.

scabrites (ska-bri′tez) Roughness of the skin.

scala (ska′lah), pl. sca′lae An anatomic structure resembling a winding staircase; applied especially to some passages of the cochlea (in the inner ear).

    s. media See cochlear duct, under duct.

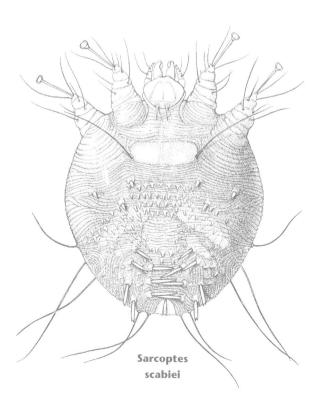

**Sarcoptes
scabiei**

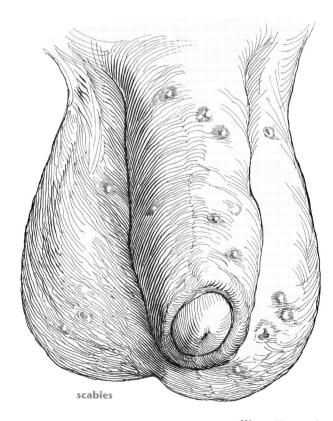

scabies

S

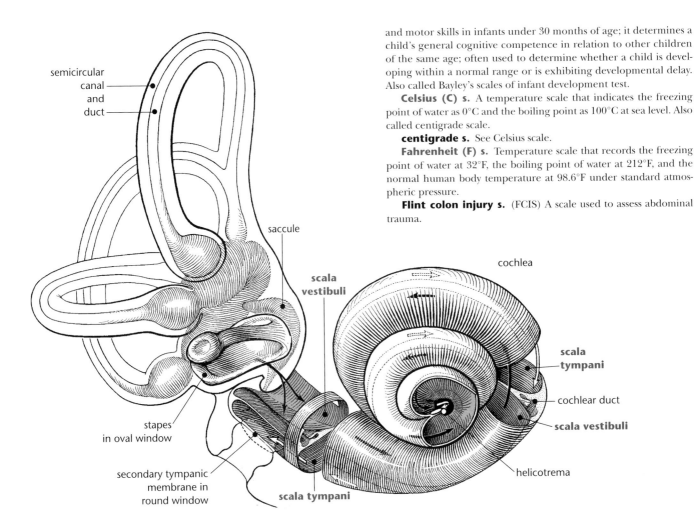

semicircular
canal
and
duct

saccule

scala
vestibuli

stapes
in oval window

secondary tympanic
membrane in
round window

scala tympani

cochlea

scala
tympani

cochlear duct

scala vestibuli

helicotrema

and motor skills in infants under 30 months of age; it determines a child's general cognitive competence in relation to other children of the same age; often used to determine whether a child is developing within a normal range or is exhibiting developmental delay. Also called Bayley's scales of infant development test.

Celsius (C) s. A temperature scale that indicates the freezing point of water as 0°C and the boiling point as 100°C at sea level. Also called centigrade scale.

centigrade s. See Celsius scale.

Fahrenheit (F) s. Temperature scale that records the freezing point of water at 32°F, the boiling point of water at 212°F, and the normal human body temperature at 98.6°F under standard atmospheric pressure.

Flint colon injury s. (FCIS) A scale used to assess abdominal trauma.

s. tympani The perilymph-filled canal, about 36 mm in length, within the cochlea; it is continuous with the scala vestibuli through the helicotrema, a small opening at the apex of the cochlea; it spirals about 2 3/4 turns and increases gradually in diameter from the apex to the base; it ends blindly near the round window (fenestra cochleae), where it is separated from the middle ear chamber by the secondary tympanic membrane. Also called tympanic canal of cochlea.

s. vestibuli The perilymph-filled canal, about 36 mm in length, within the cochlea; it is continuous with the scala tympani through the helicotrema, a small opening at the apex of the cochlea; it spirals about 2 3/4 turns and diminishes gradually in diameter from the base to the apex. The canal begins near the inside of the oval window (fenestra vestibuli), where it is separated from the middle ear chamber by the base or footplate of the smallest ear ossicle (stapes), which occludes the window. Also called vestibular canal of cochlea.

scald (skawld) **1.** To injure with hot liquid or vapor. **2.** The lesion caused in such a manner. **3.** See scall.

scale (skāl) **1.** A flaky accumulation of epithelium that is partly adherent to the skin. **2.** To shed such material. **3.** In dentistry, to remove tartar from the teeth. **4.** A set of graduations (as on an instrument) serving as a standard for measuring. **5.** In psychology, a standardized series of questions and/or tasks to which score values have been assigned for measuring personality or behavioral characteristics.

adaptive behavior s. A behavioral scale for assessing the levels of skills a retarded person has for interacting with the environment.

Bayley s.'s of infant development A principal diagnostic intelligence test that assesses the development of mental processes

Glasgow coma s. A numerical scale for assessing levels of consciousness (e.g., following a head injury), based on precise clinical criteria (i.e., the patient's ability to respond to three tests of neurologic function: eye opening, with a score ranging from 0 to 4; best motor response, with a 0 to 5 range, and best verbal response, with a 0 to 5 range). The sum of the scores provides the level of consciousness.

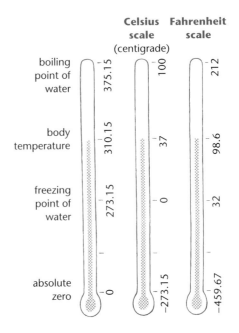

	Celsius scale (centigrade)	Fahrenheit scale
boiling point of water	375.15	100	212
body temperature	310.15	37	98.6
freezing point of water	273.15	0	32
absolute zero	0	−273.15	−459.67

scald ■ scale

global assessment s. (GAS) A scale that records the overall psychosocial functioning of a patient during a specified time period on a continuum from psychological or psychiatric sickness to health.

Kelvin (K) s. Temperature scale measured in degrees Celsius with its zero point at absolute zero (−273.l6°C). Also simply called Kelvin.

Shipley Hartford s. A scale indicative of the assessment of a patient's overall level of intellectual function.

Wechsler Intelligence S. for Children (Revised) A widely used intelligence test designed for children aged 5 to 15, in which they assemble three-dimensional objects, arrange group of pictures so they have a meaning, and repeat a list of numbers, among other tasks. Also called Wechsler Intelligence Test for Children (Revised).

Wechsler Preschool and Primary S. of Intelligence A widely used individual intelligence test designed for children of ages from about 4 1/2 to 6 years, in which verbal and performance competency is assessed. Verbal questions relate to vocabulary, arithmetic, comprehension, sentences, and general information; performance tasks involve adding a missing part to a picture, copying geometric designs, and working through a maze. Scores are not designated numerically, but simply as average, bright average, superior, etc. Also called Wechsler Preschool and Primary Test of Intelligence.

scalene (ska′lēn) Having sides of unequal length; applied to certain muscles. See table of muscles.

scalenectomy (ska-lĕ-nek′to-me) Removal of a scalene muscle, or a portion of it.

scaler (ska′ler) **1.** Instrument designed for removing deposits, especially tartar, from the teeth. **2.** Instrument for counting electrical impulses.

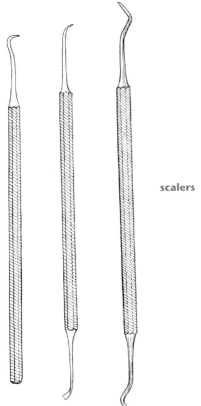

scalers

scaling (skāl′ing) Removal of tartar from the surface of teeth and the area under gum margins with special instruments (scalers).

scall (skawl) Any crusted eruption, especially of the scalp.

scalp (skalp) The skin and subcutaneous tissues covering the cranium.

scalpel (skal′pel) A surgical knife, usually with a disposable blade.

scalpriform (skal′prĭ-form) Shaped like a chisel.

scaly (ska′le) Having scales; flaky.

scan (skan) **1.** To survey by a continuous sweep of a sensing device. **2.** A graphic record of an area or volume so obtained (e.g., of the distribution of a radioactive element within an organ). The term is an abbreviated form of the word *scintiscan* and is often preceded by the structure examined (e.g., brain scan, bone scan), the device or technology used (e.g., CAT scan, radionuclide scan), or the technique used (e.g., perfusion scan, ventilation scan). See also tomography.

thyroid **scan**

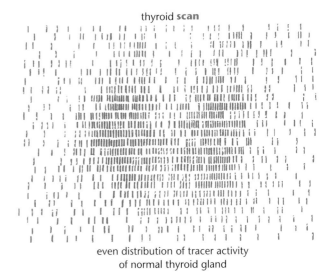

even distribution of tracer activity
of normal thyroid gland

scandium (skan′de-um) Metallic element; symbol Sc, atomic number 2l, atomic weight 44.96.

scanner (skan′er) A sensing device or instrument that scans a region point by point in a continuous, systematic manner.

scanning (skan′ning) The act of surveying an area or region by a continuous sweep of a sensing device. The term is usually preceded by the technology or sensing device used (e.g., PET scanning). See also tomography.

scapha (ska′fah) See scaphoid fossa, under fossa.

scaphocephalic (skaf-o-sĕ-fal′ik) Characterized by scaphocephaly.

scaphocephalism (skaf-o-sef′ah-lizm) See scaphocephaly.

scaphocephaly (skaf-o-sef′ah-le) A deformity in which the skull is abnormally long and narrow with a keel-like ridge along the sagittal suture and an increased anteroposterior diameter, due to a premature closure of the sagittal suture. Also called scaphocephalism.

scaphoid (skaf′oid) Boat-shaped; hollowed.

scapula (skap′u-lah) pl. scap′ulas, scap′ulae Either of two large, flat, triangular bones overlying the upper portion of the ribs, and forming the back of the shoulder; it articulates laterally with the humerus and medially with the clavicle. Also called shoulder blade.

S

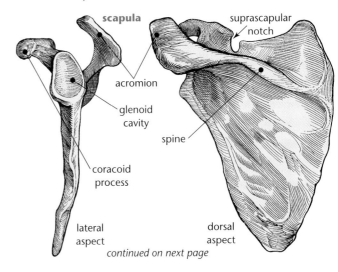

scapula

suprascapular notch

acromion

glenoid cavity

spine

coracoid process

lateral aspect

dorsal aspect

continued on next page

scalene ■ scapula

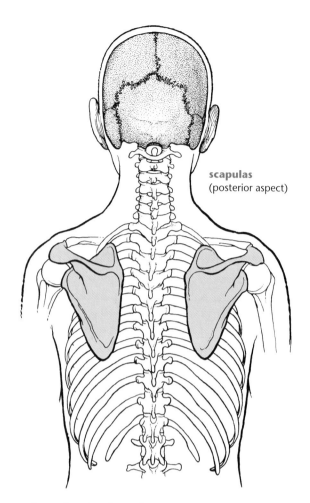

scapulas
(posterior aspect)

alar s. See winged scapula.

Graves' s. See scaphoid scapula.

scaphoid s. A scapula in which the vertebral (medial) border is slightly concave. Also called Graves' scapula.

winged s. A scapula having a prominent vertebral (medial) border that stands out from the thorax; generally caused by paralysis of the anterior serratus muscle. Also called alar scapula.

scapular (skap'u-lar) Relating to the shoulder blade (scapula).

scapuloclavicular (skap-u-lo-klah-vik'u-lar) Relating to the shoulder blade (scapula) and the collarbone (clavicle), two of the three bones forming the shoulder joint.

scapulohumeral (skap-u-lo-hu'mer-al) Relating to the shoulder blade (scapula) and the humerus, two of the three bones forming the shoulder joint.

scar (skahr) A mass of fibrous protein (collagen) that is the end result of repair of an injury.

hesitation s.'s Scars formed on the anterior aspect of the neck or the flexor side of the wrist resulting from self-inflicted superficial cuts made in a suicide attempt. Also called hesitation marks.

scarification (skar-ĭ-fĭ-ka'shun) Superficial scratching of the skin, as when vaccinating.

scarifier, scarificator (skar-ĭ-fi'er, skar'ĭ-fĭ-ka-tor) Instrument with many sharp points for making multiple scratches or punctures on the skin, as for vaccination.

scarlatina (skahr-lah-te'nah) See scarlet fever, under fever.

scarlatiniform (skahr-lah-tin'ĭ-form) Resembling scarlet fever; applied to a skin rash.

scato- Combining form meaning feces.

scatology (skah-tol'o-je) The scientific study and analysis of feces for diagnostic and physiologic purposes.

scatoma (skah-to'mah) Inspissated fecal material in the intestine that feels like a tumor on palpation.

scatophagy (skah-tof'ah-je) The eating of feces.

scatoscopy (skah-tos'ko-pe) Examination of feces for diagnostic purposes.

scattering (skat'er-ing) The deflection in various directions of a beam of subatomic particles or incident radiation by a target material (e.g., dispersal of electrons by the specimen in an electron microscope).

schema (ske'mah) An arrangement.

schindylesis (skin-dĭ-le'sis) A fibrous joint in which the sharp edge of one bone fits into a groove of the other (e.g., the articulation between the vomer and the rostrum of the sphenoid bone in the skull).

schisto- Combining form meaning groove; cleft.

schistocelia (skis-to-se'le-ah) Congenital groove in the abdominal wall.

schistocyte (skis'to-sīt) A fragment of a red blood cell occurring in various sizes and shapes; may be formed as the cell passes through a damaged small blood vessel. Also called schizocyte; helmet cell.

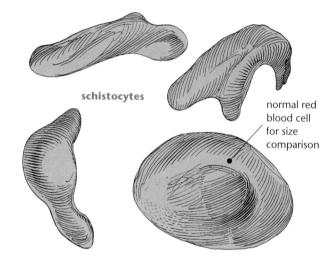

schistocytes

normal red blood cell for size comparison

schistocytosis (skis-to-si-to'sis) The presence of many fragmented red blood cells (schistocytes) in the blood.

schistoglossia (skis-to-glos'e-ah) A congenital fissure on the tongue.

Schistosoma (skis-to-so'mah) A genus of blood flukes; some species are human parasites, causing debilitating illnesses; they penetrate the skin of persons who come in contact with infested waters.

S. haematobium Species whose invertebrate host is a snail of the genera *Bulinus* and *Physopsis;* adult worms live exclusively in humans, within the veins of the bladder, causing symptoms of the urinary tract and, to a lesser degree, of the intestines.

S. japonicum Species whose invertebrate host is a snail of the genus *Oncomelania;* the adult worm infests rodents, domestic animals, and humans; in humans, it lives within the venules of the small intestine and, because of the large number of eggs it deposits, causes the most serious of blood fluke diseases, with intestinal, liver, and lung symptoms.

S. mansoni Species whose invertebrate host is a snail of the genus *Biomphalaria;* in humans, it lives within veins of the large intestine, causing a disease similar to that caused by *Schistosoma japonicum* but milder.

schistosome (skis'to-sōm) Any fluke of the genus *Schistosoma.*

schistosomiasis (skis-to-so-mi'ah-sis) Infestation with blood flukes (schistosomes); involves chiefly the intestines, liver, or bladder.

schizo-, schiz- Combining forms meaning split.

schizocyte (skiz'o-sīt) See schistocyte.

schizoid (skiz'oid) See schizoid personality disorder, under disorder.

schizophasia (skiz-o-fa'ze-ah) The disordered speech of a person afflicted with schizophrenia.

schizophrenia (skiz-o-fre'ne-ah) A group of severe emotional disorders characterized by psychotic features during the active phase; deterioration from a previous level of social, occupational, and self-care functioning; onset before age 45; a duration of at least six

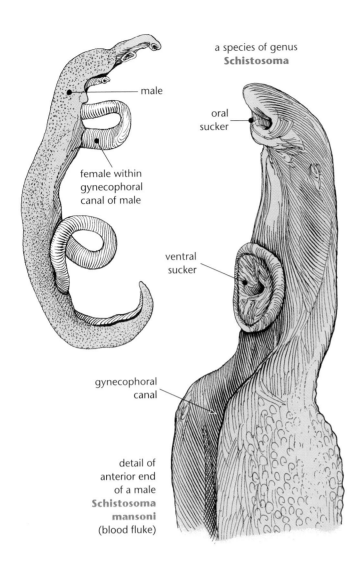

a species of genus
Schistosoma

male

oral
sucker

female within
gynecophoral
canal of male

ventral
sucker

gynecophoral
canal

detail of
anterior end
of a male
**Schistosoma
mansoni**
(blood fluke)

months with a strong likelihood of recurrence; and the presence of multiple symptoms such as delusions, loosening of associations, hallucinations, blunted or inappropriate affect, disturbed sense of self, disturbance in motivation and/or goal-directed activity, and withdrawal from social relationships.

s., catatonic type Schizophrenia in which the essential feature is a marked psychomotor disturbance (see catatonia), either excitement, stupor, or rapid swings between these.

s., disorganized type Schizophrenia in which the essential features are incoherence and flat, silly, or incongruous affect usually associated with extreme social impairment. Also called hebephrenia.

s., paranoid type Schizophrenia in which the essential features are prominent persecutory or grandiose delusions or hallucinations, or delusional jealousy; may often include argumentative or aggressive behavior. Also called paranoid psychosis.

s., residual type A clinical picture without prominent psychotic symptoms where there has been at least one previous schizophrenic episode and where there is continuing evidence of the illness (i.e., it is not in remission).

schizophrenic (skiz-o-fren′ik) Relating to schizophrenia.
schizotrichia (skiz-o-trik′e-ah) A splitting of the hairs at the ends.
schwannoma (shwa-no′mă) A slowly growing, typically single noncancerous tumor originating from Schwann cells; commonly occurs in relation to sensory cranial nerves and the sensory root of spinal nerves.

acoustic nerve s. See vestibular schwannoma.

vestibular s. Schwannoma typically involving the vestibular (rather than the acoustic) division of the vestibulocochlear (8th cranial) nerve of one ear; rate of growth varies, some may not grow for many years, others may grow rapidly and compress vital structures (e.g., brainstem and other cranial nerves); symptoms include progressive sensory hearing loss, ringing in the ear, vertigo, and poor balance. Also called acoustic neuroma; acoustic neurinoma; acoustic neurilemoma; acoustic nerve schwannoma.

sciage (se-azh′) The back-and-forth sawing movement of the hand used in massage.
sciatic (si-at′ik) Relating to the hip or to the ischium.

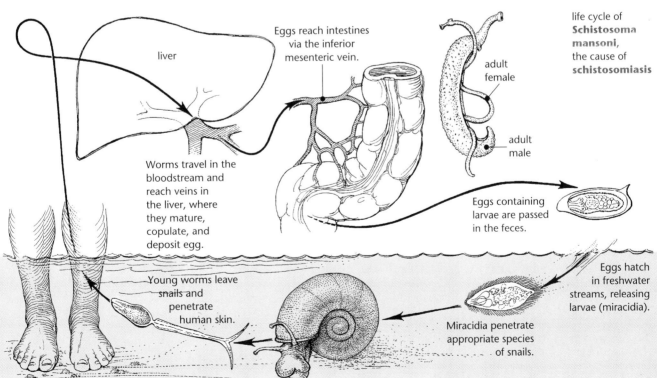

life cycle of
**Schistosoma
mansoni**,
the cause of
schistosomiasis

liver

Eggs reach intestines
via the inferior
mesenteric vein.

adult
female

adult
male

Worms travel in the
bloodstream and
reach veins in
the liver, where
they mature,
copulate, and
deposit egg.

Eggs containing
larvae are passed
in the feces.

Young worms leave
snails and
penetrate
human skin.

Eggs hatch
in freshwater
streams, releasing
larvae (miracidia).

Miracidia penetrate
appropriate species
of snails.

S

schizophrenic ■ sciatic

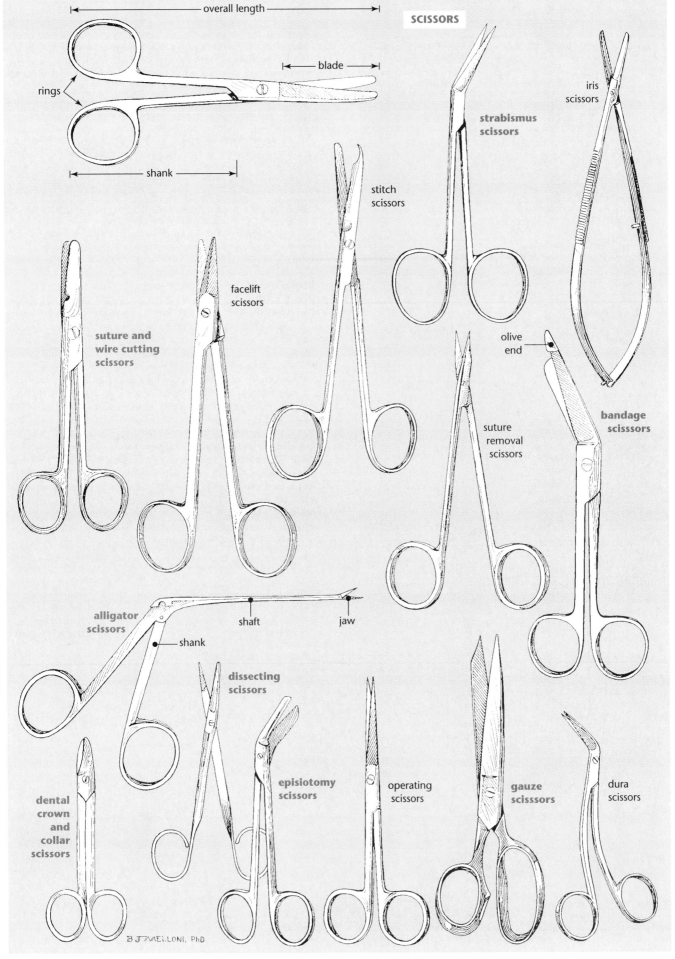

overall length

blade

rings

shank

strabismus
scissors

iris
scissors

stitch
scissors

facelift
scissors

suture and
wire cutting
scissors

olive
end

bandage
scisssors

suture
removal
scissors

alligator
scissors

shaft

jaw

shank

dissecting
scissors

dental
crown
and
collar
scissors

episiotomy
scissors

operating
scissors

gauze
scisssors

dura
scissors

B.J. MELLONI, PhD

S

sciatica (si-at′ĭ-kah) Any condition that is characterized by pain along the sciatic nerve (i.e., along the buttock and down the back of the leg); usually a neuritis and generally caused by mechanical compression or irritation of the fifth lumbar spinal root.

science (si′ens) The body of knowledge relating to facts and natural phenomena accumulated by systematic observation, identification, experimentation, description, and theoretical explanation.

    forensic s. Any of the various sciences (e.g., chemistry, toxicology, psychiatry, entomology) whose principles and theories can be applied to the purposes of law enforcement and administration of justice. See also criminalistics.

scinticisternography (sin′tĭ-cis-tern-og′rah-fe) A test for diagnosing hydrocephalus and for studying the flow of cerebrospinal fluid; conducted by injecting a radioactive substance into the subarachnoid space, then recording its concentration with a scintiscanner.

scintigraphy (sin-tig′rah-fe) Injection of a radioactive substance and determination of its distribution in the tissues with the aid of a scintiscanner.

scintillation (sin-tĭ-la′shun) A tiny flash of light, especially one produced by a chemical crystal by absorption of an ionizing photon. The flash of light seen on a fluorescent screen results from the spontaneous emission of charged alpha particles across the sensitized surface.

scintillator (sin′tĭ-la-ter) A substance that emits light when hit by a subatomic particle, x radiation, or gamma radiation.

scintiphotography (sin-tĭ-fo-tog′rah-fe) The recording on photographic film of the distribution of an internally administered radioactive substance.

scintiscan (sin′tĭ-skan) A graphic pattern recorded on paper of pulses derived from, and revealing the concentration of, a radioactive isotope in an organ or tissue. Also called gammagram.

scintiscanner (sin-tĭ-skan′er) A directional scintillation counter used for diagnostic purposes after injection of a radiation-emitting substance into an organ or tissue; it automatically scans the specific region of the body to produce an image of the amounts of the radioactive substance concentrated at each point of the organ or tissue.

scirrhous (skir′us) Hard; hardened.

scissors (siz′erz) A double-bladed cutting instrument.

    alligator s. Scissors with a small jaw at the end of a shaft; the shaft is usually 3.1 inches (80 mm) in length with projecting blades that usually range from 4 to 8 mm in length. The shank comes off the shaft and terminates in finger rings; used in microsurgery.

    bandage s. Strong scissors with angled blades used for cutting bandages; the end of one blade usually has a soft knob (olive).

    crown and bridge s. See dental crown and collar scissors.

    dental crown and collar s. Strong-bladed scissors used to shape a metal collar around a tooth during the preparation of a dental crown. Also called crown and bridge scissors.

    dissecting s. Delicate scissors, usually with semisharp tips, designed for blunt dissection and cutting of soft tissue; used when delicacy and precision are required, as in blepharoplasty, tip rhinoplasty, hand surgery, or excision of small skin lesions.

    episiotomy s. Scissors with angular blades and blunt points for incising the perineum and vagina (episiotomy) to prevent traumatic tearing during childbirth.

    gauze s. Large, strong-bladed scissors for cutting gauze, bandages, and surgical sponges.

    stitch s. Delicate scissors with a notch near the end of one blade, designed to keep stitches from slipping while being cut.

    strabismus s. Delicate scissors with angular sharp, pointed blades, used in ocular surgery to correct the abnormal deviation of an eye (strabismus).

    suture and wire cutting s. Scissors with a notch on one of the blades to facilitate the cutting of wire; also used for cutting sutures.

sclera (skler′ă) The opaque, fibrous, protective coat of the eye; it covers five-sixths of the eyeball surface (the rest being occupied by the transparent cornea). Commonly called white of the eye.

    blue s. A bluish appearance of the sclera due to structural changes of its collagen fibers, which allow the underlying uveal pigment to become visible; sometimes seen in healthy newborn infants; occurring usually in such pathologic conditions as osteogenesis imperfecta, pseudoxanthoma elasticum, and Marfan's syndrome, or with prolonged use of corticosteroids.

scleradenitis (skler-ad-ĕ-ni′tis) Inflammatory hardening of a gland.

scleral (skler′al) Relating to the sclera.

sclerectasia (skler-ek-ta′ze-ah) Bulging of the sclera.

sclerectomy (skler-ek′to-me) Removal of a portion of the anterior sclera (e.g., for the treatment of glaucoma).

scleredema (skler-ĕ-de′mah) Induration and swelling of the skin and subcutaneous tissues.

sclerema (skler-e′mah) A hardened state of a tissue.

    s. monatorum Diffused hardening of the skin, usually seen in undernourished or premature infants.

scleritis (skler-i′tis) Inflammation of the sclera; frequently associated with systemic disease and causing pain, tenderness, redness, photophobia, and increased tearing.

    annular s. A ring-shaped inflammation around the edges of the cornea.

    anterior s. Scleritis of the exposed, visible portion of the sclera.

    brawny s. Annular scleritis with thickening of episcleral tissues adjoining the cornea.

    necrotizing s. A severe form of scleritis characterized by an acute painful area of localized congestion and degeneration of scleral tissues; occurs on the anterior portion of the sclera.

    posterior s. An uncommon form of scleritis involving the sclera at the back of the eyeball near the optic nerve; usually associated with severe rheumatoid arthritis; symptoms include severe pain, a decrease in visual acuity, double vision, and decreased eye movement.

sclero-, scler- Combining forms meaning hard.

sclerochoroidal (skler-ŏ-ko-roi′dal) Relating to the sclera and choroid, the outer and middle layers of the eyeball.

scleroconjunctival (skler-ŏ-kon-junk-ti′val) Relating to the sclera and the conjunctiva.

sclerocornea (skler-ŏ-kor′ne-ah) The sclera and cornea considered as a unit.

sclerodactyly (skler-ŏ-dak′tĭ-le) Scleroderma localized in the fingers or toes.

scleroderma (skler-ŏ-der′mah) See progressive systemic sclerosis, under sclerosis.

    localized s. See morphea.

sclerodermatitis (skler-ŏ-der-mah-ti′tis) Thickening and inflammation of the skin.

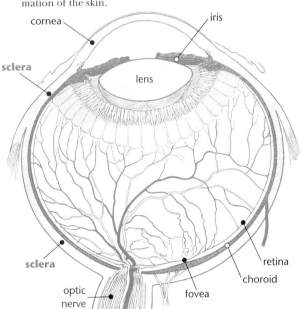

S

sclerogenous, sclerogenic (skler-oj′ĕ-nus, skler-ŏ-jen′ik) Producing induration of tissue.

scleroiritis (skler-ŏ-i-ri′tis) Inflammation of the sclera and iris.

scleroma (skler-ŏ′mah) A circumscribed area of granulation or hard tissue in the skin or mucous membrane, especially of the nose.

scleromalacia (skler-ŏ′mah-la′she-ah) A thinning of the sclera.

    necrotizing s. Extreme thinning and degeneration of scleral tissue without evidence of inflammation, usually associated with severe forms of rheumatoid arthritis. Also called scleromalacia perforans.

    s. perforans. See necrotizing scleromalacia.

scleronychia (skler-ŏ-nik′e-ah) Excessively thickened and hardened condition of the nails.

sclero-oophoritis (skler′ŏ- o-of-o-ri′tis) Inflammation and hardening of the ovary.

sclerophthalmia (skler-of-thal′me-ah) An uncommon congenital condition of the eye in which the opacity of the sclera extends over the cornea, leaving only a small central transparent area.

scleroplasty (skler-ŏ-plas′te) Any reparative surgery of the sclera.

sclerosant (skler-o′sant) A chemical irritant that, when injected into a vein, produces induration and obliteration of the vessel's lumen; used in the treatment of varicose veins.

sclerose (sklĕ-rōz′) To harden; to become sclerotic.

sclerosed (sklĕ-rōzed′) Indurated.

sclerosing (sklĕ-rōs′ing) Tending to undergo sclerosis; applied to certain disorders that are characterized by sclerosis.

sclerosis (sklĕ-ro′sis) Hardening of tissues due to proliferation of connective tissue; frequently originates in chronic inflammation.

    Alzheimer's s. Hyaline degeneration of the small arteries in the brain. Also present to a lesser degree in normal older persons.

    amyotrophic lateral s. (ALS) Disease of motor neurons characterized by degeneration of the lateral motor tracts of the spinal cord, causing progressive atrophy of muscles and exaggerated reflexes. Commonly called Lou Gehrig's disease.

    arterial s. See arteriosclerosis.

    arteriolar s. See arteriolosclerosis.

    endocardial s. See endocardial fibroelastosis, under fibroelastosis.

    Mönckenberg's s. See Mönckenberg's arteriosclerosis, under arteriosclerosis.

    multiple s. (MS) Disease of the brain and spinal cord affecting primarily young adults; characterized by loss of the fatty sheath (myelin) that surrounds nerve fibers, causing multiple patches of scarred (sclerosed) nervous fibers throughout the central nervous system; symptoms vary with distribution of the sclerotic patches, but the most frequently seen are weakness, incoordination, coarse tremors, scanning (halting, monosyllabic) speech, and involuntary oscillation of the eyeballs (nystagmus); symptoms occur with characteristic exacerbations and remissions.

    progressive systemic s. (PSS) Systemic disease that most commonly affects the skin (where it may remain for years) but that eventually may expand to the gastrointestinal tract, kidneys, heart, and lungs; characterized initially by pain in the hands and feet upon exposure to cold (Raynaud's phenomenon) and thickening and tightness of the skin (especially of the face and hands), followed by joint pain, difficulty swallowing, intestinal pain or malabsorption, fibrosis of lung tissue, arrhythmias, and malignant hypertension resulting in kidney failure. Also called scleroderma.

    tuberous s. Rare disorder inherited as an autosomal dominant trait; major features include mental retardation, convulsions, and small skin nodules composed of fibroelastic and blood vessel proliferation; the brain contains hard benign tumors, which sometimes obstruct circulation of cerebrospinal fluid. Also called epiloia; Bourneville's disease.

sclerostomy (skler-os′to-me) Surgical formation of an external opening on the sclera (e.g., for the treatment of glaucoma).

sclerotherapy (skler-ŏ-ther′ah-pe) Injection of an irritating chemical into a vein to produce scarring of the tissue and obliteration of the vein's lumen; a method of treating varicose veins. Also called sclerosing therapy.

sclerotic (skler-ot′ik) Relating to sclerosis.

sclerotome (skler′ŏ-tōm) **1.** In embryology, the group of cells that differentiate into cartilage and eventually form the vertebrae. **2.** Surgical knife used for cutting into the sclera.

sclerotomy (skler-ot′o-me) A surgical cut into the sclera.

sclerous (skler′us) Hardened.

scolex (sko′leks), pl. sco′leces The head of a tapeworm by means of which it attaches to the lining of the small intestine.

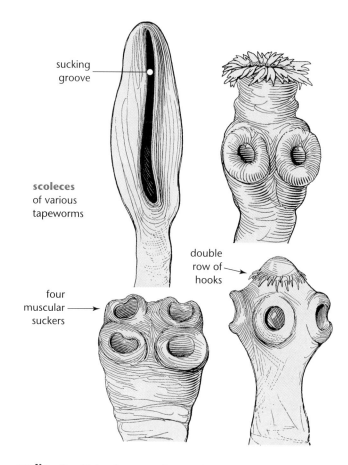

sucking groove

scoleces of various tapeworms

four muscular suckers

double row of hooks

scolio- Combining form meaning crooked.

scoliometer (sko-le-om′ĕ-ter) Device for measuring curves, especially those of the spinal column as in scoliosis. Also called scoliosometer.

scoliosis (sko-le-o′sis) An abnormal, lateral curvature of the spine.

    idiopathic s. Scoliosis of unknown cause.

    myopathic s. Scoliosis due to weakness of spinal muscles.

    neuromuscular s. Scoliosis caused by any of various diseases affecting the motor nerve cells.

    osteopathic s. Scoliosis caused by disease of the vertebrae (e.g., tuberculosis, osteomalacia, tumors, rickets).

    static s. Scoliosis caused by unequal length of the legs.

scoliosometer (sko-le-o-som′ĕ-ter) See scoliometer.

scoliotic (sko-le-ot′ik) Relating to scoliosis.

-scope Combining form meaning instrument for viewing (e.g., endoscope).

scopolamine (sko-pol′ah-mēn) Drug (belladonna alkaloid) with sedative properties used to prevent motion sickness; formerly used extensively in obstetrics; combined with morphine, it produces "twilight sleep." Adverse effects may include dry mouth and blurred vision; in toxic doses, it can cause excitation, hallucinations, delirium, and other peculiar mental effects. See also scopolamine transdermal patch, under patch.

-scopy Combining form meaning observation, especially with a specially designed instrument (e.g., proctoscopy).

scorbutic (skōr-bu′tik) Relating to scurvy.

S

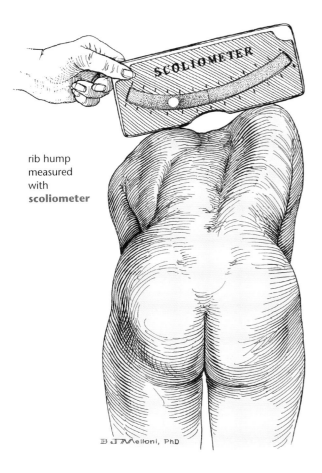

rib hump measured with **scoliometer**

B. J. Melloni, PhD

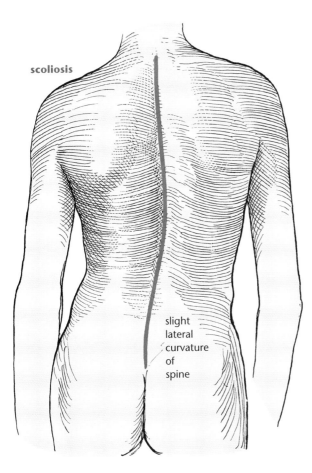

scoliosis

slight lateral curvature of spine

scorbutus (skōr-bu′tus) See scurvy.

score (skōr) An evaluative record, usually expressed numerically.

   Apgar s. A numerical expression of the condition of a newborn infant on a scale of 0 to 10. Numerical values are assigned to the status of skin color, heart rate, respiratory effort, muscle tone, and reflex irritability; scores usually are recorded at one and five minutes after delivery and become a permanent part of the child's health record.

> **Apgar score** determined by asssessing the condition of a newborn baby by noting five features listed on the Apgar chart. Each feature is scored from 0 to 2; most infants score from 7 to 9 and require little assistance. Infants scoring 4 or less require immediate assistance with their breathing.

Skin Color of Baby

– pale skin color 0
– body pink, extremities bluish 1
– overall pink 2

Heart Rate

– absent 0
– less than 100 beats/min 1
– more than 100 beats/min 2

Respiratory Effort

– absent 0
– irregular breathing; weak cry 1
– regular breathing; strong cry 2

Muscle Tone

– limp 0
– flexing some limbs 1
– limbs well flexed; active 2

Reflex Irritability
(response to a catheter in the nostril)

– lack of response 0
– grimace 1
– cry 2

   Gleason's s. See Gleason's grading system, under system.

scoto- Combining form meaning dark.

scotochromogens (sko-to-kro′mo-jens) See group II mycobacteria, under mycobacteria.

scotoma (sko-to′mah) **1.** An area of lost vision, partial or complete. **2.** In psychiatry, an absence of awareness of, or inability to grasp, a mental problem.

scotomatous (sko-tom′ah-tus) Relating to a scotoma.

scotometer (sko-tom′ĕ-ter) Instrument for plotting and measuring an isolated area of absent or reduced vision (scotoma) in the visual field.

scotopia (sko-to′pe-ah) See scotopic vision, under vision.

screen (skrēn) **1.** A structure with a flat surface, such as one against which images are projected, or one used in fluoroscopy. **2.** A substance used as protection against a deleterious influence (e.g., ultraviolet rays). **3.** To conduct a screening.

   fluorescent s. A screen coated with a material (e.g., calcium tungstate) that produces light when exposed to x rays.

   tangent s. A screen, usually black, for plotting the visual field in the clinical testing of vision.

screening (skrēn′ing) The process of examining large groups of people for a given disease or trait.

   genetic s. Any method of identifying individuals in a given population at high risk of having, or transmitting, a specific genetic disorder; used in genetic research or in medical genetic services and public health.

S

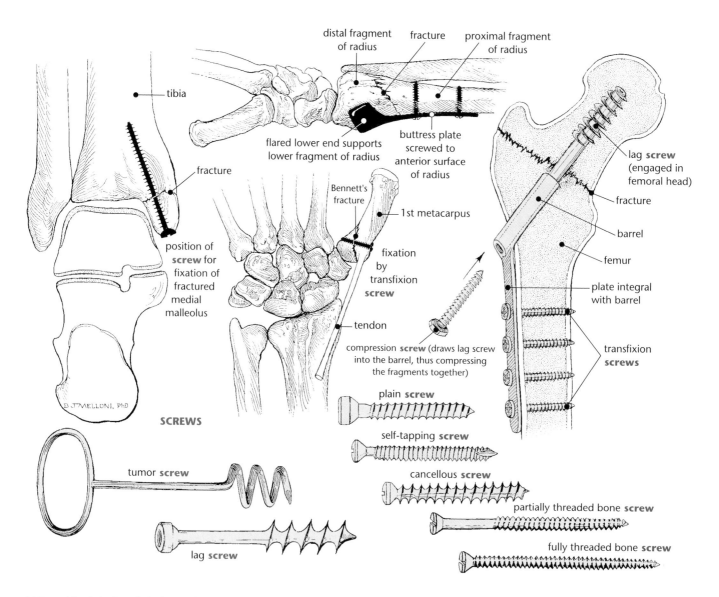

tibia

distal fragment of radius

fracture

proximal fragment of radius

fracture

flared lower end supports lower fragment of radius

buttress plate screwed to anterior surface of radius

lag **screw** (engaged in femoral head)

fracture

barrel

femur

plate integral with barrel

position of **screw** for fixation of fractured medial malleolus

Bennett's fracture

1st metacarpus

fixation by transfixion **screw**

tendon

compression **screw** (draws lag screw into the barrel, thus compressing the fragments together)

transfixion **screws**

D. J. MELLONI, PhD

SCREWS

plain **screw**

self-tapping **screw**

cancellous **screw**

partially threaded bone **screw**

tumor **screw**

lag **screw**

fully threaded bone **screw**

screw (skru) A threaded pin used in several surgical procedures (e.g., in dentistry and in orthopedic surgery).

scrobiculate (skro-bik′u-lāt) Having minute depressions or pits.

scrobiculus (skro-bik′u-lus) A minute depression.

scrofuloderma (skrof-u-lo-der′mah) Skin involvement over a tuberculous lymph node, usually occurring in the neck; caused by *Mycobacterium tuberculosis.*

scrotal (skro′tal) Relating to the scrotum. Also called oscheal.

scrotectomy (skro-tek′to-me) Surgical removal of a portion of the scrotum.

scrotitis (skro-ti′tis) Inflammation of the scrotum.

scrotocele (skro′to-sēl) See scrotal hernia, under hernia.

scrotoplasty (skro′to-plas-te) Operative repair of the scrotum. Also called oscheoplasty.

scrotum (skro′tum) A two-layered fibromuscular sac containing both testes and their accessory organs, including the lower part of the spermatic cord; it is suspended externally from the body at the root of the penis and is divided into right and left halves by a median septum.

scruple (scroo′pl) A unit of apothecary weight equal to 20 grains or one-third of a dram.

scurvy (skur′ve) Disease resulting from vitamin C deficiency in the diet; characterized by swollen and bleeding gums, subcutaneous bleeding, and extreme weakness. Also called scorbutus.

scute (skūt) A thin scalelike plate.

　　tympanic s. The thin bony plate separating the upper part of

the middle ear from the mastoid air cells.

scutiform (sku′tĭ-form) Shaped like a shield.

scybalous (sib′ah-lus) Of the nature of a scybalum.

scybalum (sib′ah-lum), pl. scyb′ala An abnormally hard mass of feces in the intestine.

seal (sēl) 1. To close tightly. 2. Something that produces an airtight closure.

sealant (se′lant) Any material used to prevent seepage of air or moisture.

　　fissure s. Any material used to seal pits and crevices on the surface of teeth to prevent caries.

seasickness (se′sik-nes) Nausea, sweating, and vomiting induced by the motion of a vessel on water.

seatworm (sēt′wurm) See pinworm.

sebaceous (se-ba′shus) Oily; relating to the fatty material (sebum) secreted by certain glands. Also spelled sebaceus.

sebaceus (se-ba′shus) See sebaceous.

sebo-, sebi-, seb- Combining forms meaning sebum.

seborrhea (seb-o-re′ah) Overactivity of the sebaceous glands, causing an oily appearance of the skin.

seborrheic (seb-o-re′ik) Relating to seborrhea.

sebum (se′bum) The secretion of a sebaceous gland.

secobarbitol (se-ko-bar′bĭ-tal) A short-acting, fast-onset sedative and hypnotic. Trade name: Seconal.

secondaries (sek′un-der-es) Colloquial term for the lesions occurring in secondary syphilis.

S

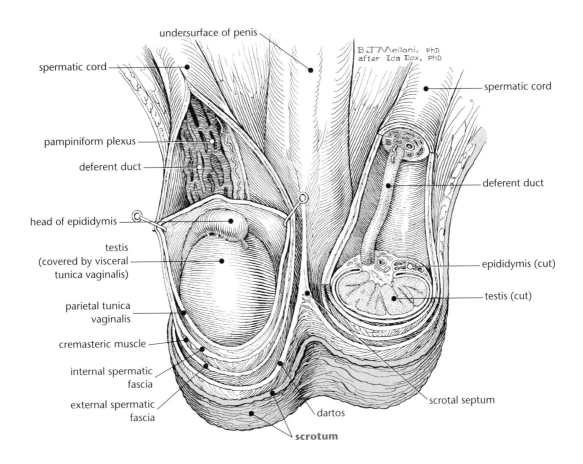

undersurface of penis

spermatic cord

B.J.Melloni, PhD
after Ida Dox, PhD

spermatic cord

pampiniform plexus

deferent duct

deferent duct

head of epididymis

epididymis (cut)

testis
(covered by visceral
tunica vaginalis)

testis (cut)

parietal tunica
vaginalis

cremasteric muscle

internal spermatic
fascia

external spermatic
fascia

scrotal septum

dartos

scrotum

secondary (sek'un-der-e) **1.** Dependent on the occurrence of another event (e.g., a disease or injury); applied to a complication. **2.** Second in importance or in the order in which it occurs (e.g., a stage of a disease).

secreta (se-kre'tah) Secretions.

secretagogue (se-kret'ah-gog) Any agent that stimulates a secretion. Also called secretogogue.

secrete (se-kret') To elaborate and release; applied to the activity of glands.

secretin (se-kre'tin) Intestinal hormone released principally by glands in the lining of the duodenum during digestion; it stimulates secretion of water and bicarbonate by the pancreas.

secretion (se-kre'shun) **1.** The process by which a gland elaborates and releases a specific product. **2.** The substance so produced.

secretogogue (se-kre'to-gog) See secretagogue.

secretomotor (se-kre-to-mo'tor) Denoting nerves that stimulate glandular secretion.

secretor (se-kre'tor) A person who secretes water-soluble forms of the ABO blood group antigens in the saliva and other body fluids; an autosomal dominant trait.

secretory (se'kre-to-re) Relating to secretion.

sectile (sek'til) Capable of being cut or sectioned.

section (sek'shun) **1.** The act of cutting. **2.** One of several component segments of a structure. **3.** A thin slice of tissue suitable for examination under the microscope. **4.** A cut surface.

   abdominal s. See laparotomy.

   anteroposterior s. See sagittal section.

   C s. See cesarean section.

   cervical cesarean s. A cesarean section in which the uterus is entered by a transverse or vertical incision through the lower uterine segment, either transperitoneally or extraperitoneally. Also called low cesarean section.

   cesarean s. An incision through the abdominal and uterine walls for extraction of the fetus; it may be vertical or horizontal. Also called abdominal delivery; commonly called C section.

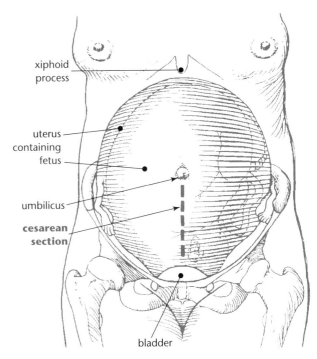

xiphoid
process

uterus
containing
fetus

umbilicus

**cesarean
section**

bladder

   classic cesarean s. A cesarean section in which the upper segment (fundus) of the uterus is vertically incised. Also called corporeal cesarean section.

   coronal s. A vertical cut in a plane parallel to the coronal suture of the skull, at right angles to the sagittal section; it divides the body or structure into a ventral (anterior) and dorsal (posterior) part. Also called frontal section.

   corporeal cesarean s. See classic cesarean section.

S

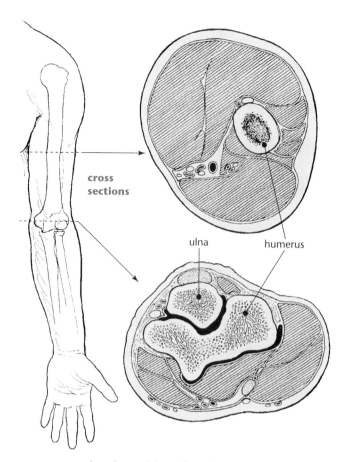

cross sections

ulna   humerus

cross s. A section at right angles to the long axis.

extraperitoneal cesarean s. A cesarean section made in the lower segment of the uterus, after displacing the peritoneum upward and the bladder downward.

frontal s. See coronal section.

frozen s. A section cut by a microtome from tissue preserved by freezing; often used for microscopic diagnosis.

histologic s. See section (3).

horizontal s. See transverse section.

low cesarean s. See cervical cesarean section.

microscopic s. See section (3).

paraffin s. A histologic section cut with a microtome from tissue embedded in paraffin wax.

postmortem s. An emergency cesarean section made in an attempt to save the baby following the death of the mother.

root s. See rhizotomy.

sagittal s. A cut in the anteroposterior (sagittal) plane that divides the body or a structure in approximately equal right and left halves. Also called anteroposterior section.

serial s. One of a number of consecutive histologic sections of a structure (e.g., spinal cord) made for microscopic examination.

transperitoneal cesarean s. Cesarean section of the uterus performed with a surgical incision through the uterovesical fold of peritoneum.

transverse s. A section at right angles to the long axis of a structure or body. Also called a horizontal section.

trigeminal root s. See trigeminal rhizotomy, under rhizotomy.

ultrathin s. An extremely thin section of tissue cut by an ultramicrotome, usually with a diamond or glass cutting knife; made for examination under an electron microscope (EM).

secundigravida (se-kun-di-grav′idah) A woman who has been pregnant twice.

secundines (se-kun′dinz) The placenta, umbilical cord, and membranes expelled from the uterus after delivery of the child. Also called afterbirth.

secundipara (se-kun-dip′ah-rah) A woman who has given birth twice. Also called para-II; formerly called bipara.

sedate (se-dāt′) To administer a sedative drug.

sedation (se-da′shun) Reduction of anxiety or stress by the administration of a sedative drug.

sedative (sed′ah-tiv) A drug that produces calmness by mildly and nonselectively depressing the central nervous system (CNS). COMPARE hypnotic.

sediment (sed′i-ment) A deposit of material settled at the bottom of a liquid.

sedimentation (sed-i-men-ta′shun) The formation of a sediment.

sedimentator (sed-i-men-ta′tor) A centrifuge.

seed (sēd) In bacteriology, to introduce a microorganism into a culture medium.

segment (seg′ment) 1. One of the portions into which a structure can be separated by arbitrarily demarcated boundaries. 2. A naturally differentiated subdivision of an organism (e.g., a metamere).

   anonymous DNA s. A piece of DNA of unknown gene content that has been localized to a chromosome.

segmentation (seg-men-ta′shun) 1. Differentiation into similar parts. 2. Cleavage, as of the fertilized ovum.

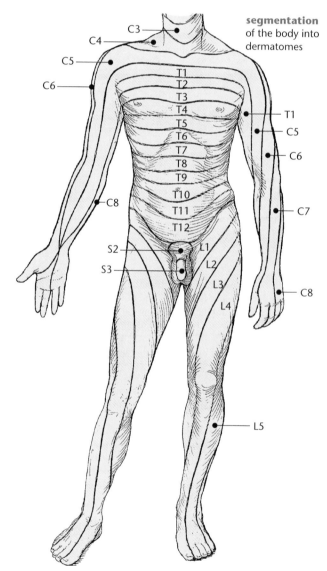

segmentation of the body into dermatomes

segregation (seg-re-ga′shun) In genetics, the separation of two allelic genes (in homologous chromosomes) during meiosis so that each passes to a different sex cell (ovum or sperm).

seizure (se'zhur) **1.** An attack; a sudden onset of a disease or symptom. **2.** An abrupt and temporary change in the electrical activity of the superficial layer of the brain (the cerebral cortex); manifested clinically by a change in consciousness or by a sensory, motor, or behavioral symptom. Specific features of a seizure depend on whether most or only part of the cerebral cortex is involved from the start, on the primary functions of the areas where the seizure starts, and on the subsequent spread of the abnormal electrical discharge within the brain.

    absence s. See absence.

    generalized-onset s. Seizure arising from simultaneous involvement of all or large parts of both cerebral hemispheres from the start.

    partial s., focal s. Seizure arising in an area of one cerebral hemisphere; may be: *Simple partial s.,* in which consciousness is preserved; or *Complex partial s.,* with impairment or cloudiness of consciousness.

selection (sĕ-lek'shun) In population genetics, the biologic process through which some individuals survive while others do not, with the result that the frequency of particular genes in the population is altered.

    artificial s. The purposeful interference with natural selection in order to produce animals and plants with a desired trait.

    natural s. The process tending to cause the survival and reproduction of those individuals best able to adapt to their environment.

    sexual s. A form of natural selection through which male and female members of a species are attracted by certain traits, thus ensuring the perpetuation of those traits by their transmission to subsequent generations.

selectivity (sĕ-lek-tiv'ĭ-te) In pharmacology, a measure of the tendency of one drug to produce several effects; the relationship between the desired and undesired effects of the drug.

selenium (sĕ-le'ne-um) Metalloid element; symbol Se, atomic number 34, atomic weight 78.96. Selenium is a trace element that helps preserve elasticity of body tissues. Its compounds are widely used commercially; medicinally, in dandruff shampoos and topical antifungal lotions; also included in pesticides and in the manufacture of rubber, plastics, electronics, glass, and ceramics. Occupational exposure to airborne fumes and dust may cause acute symptoms (e.g., respiratory tract irritation, skin burns) and chronic effects (e.g., fatigue, nausea, garlic odor in breath and sweat, loss of hair and nails, conjunctivitis).

self (self) **1.** The sum of a person's individuality, sometimes used as equivalent to personality although the term more correctly refers to the totality of body and mental processes. **2.** An individual's awareness of his own being. **3.** In immunology, denoting those cell components (antigens) that are normal constituents of the body of an individual and against which immunologic responses are normally suppressed.

self-care (self kār) The performance of activities or tasks relating to one's health traditionally performed by professional health care providers. Such activities may be based on instructions from professionals.

self-commitment (self ko-mit'ment) Voluntary confinement to a mental hospital.

self-insurance (self in-shur'ans) Medical insurance in which an employer or organization assumes complete responsibility for its employees' medical care expenses with funding derived through internal resources rather than through transfer of risk to an insurer.

self-limited (self lim'it-ed) Denoting a disease that tends to run a definite course in a specific length of time, limited by its own characteristics rather than by external factors.

self-referral (self re-fur'al) The practice of sending patients to clinics, treatment centers, and laboratories in which the referring physician has a financial investment.

self-tolerance (self tol'er-ans) See self tolerance, under tolerance.

sella (sel'ah) See sella turcica.

sella turcica (sel'ah tur'sĭ-kah) A depression with two prominences (anterior and posterior) on the upper surface of the sphenoid bone at the base of the skull, resembling a Turkish saddle; it houses the pituitary (hypophysis). Frequently called sella.

sellar (sel'ar) Relating to the sella turcica.

semen (se'men) The thick whitish ejaculation of the male reproductive organs, composed chiefly of spermatozoa, a fructose-rich fluid from the seminal vesicles, and secretions from the prostate. Also called seminal fluid.

semenuria (se-mĕ-nu're-ah) Excretion of semen in the urine. Also called seminuria; spermaturia.

semi- Prefix meaning half; partly.

semicoma (sem-e-ko'mah) A mild degree of coma; one in which the unconscious person is able to respond to certain stimuli (e.g., can push away the hand of the examiner when pinched).

semicomatose (sem-e-ko'mah-tōs) Being in a state of semicoma.

semiconscious (sem-e-kon'shus) Partly conscious.

semiflexion (sem-e-flek'shun) The position of a limb midway between extension and flexion.

semilunar (sem-e-lu'nar) Shaped like a half-moon.

semimembranous (sem-e-mem'brah-nus) Consisting partly of membrane or connective tissue.

seminal (sem'ĭ-nal) Relating to the semen.

semination (sem-ĭ-na'shun) See insemination.

seminiferous (se-mĭ-nif'er-us) Conveying semen.

seminoma (se-mĭ-no'mah) A cancerous tumor of the testis composed of large germ cells; peak incidence occurs in the fourth decade of life.

seminormal (sem-e-nor'mal) (0.5N, N/2) Denoting a solution containing one-half the standard (normal) strength.

seminuria (se-mĭ-nu're-ah) See semenuria.

semiology (se-me-ol'o-je) Former name for symptomatology.

semipenniform (sem-e-pen'ĭ-form) Shaped like a feather on one side only; applied to certain muscles.

semipermeable (sem-e-per'me-ah-bl) Permitting selective passage, as of molecules; applied to certain membranes.

semiprone (sem-e-prōn') Lying in a position in which the body, or part of the body, approaches the prone or face-down position.

semirecumbent (sem-e-re-kum'bent) Being in a reclined position, between sitting up and lying down.

semis (se'mis) Latin for one half.

semisulcus (sem-e-sul'kus) A slight groove on the edge of a structure (e.g., a bone) that, when united with a similar groove of an adjoining structure, forms a complete sulcus.

semisupine (sem-e-su'pin) Lying in a position in which the body, or part of the body, approaches the supine or face-up position.

semisynthetic (sem-e-sin-thet'ik) Made from a chemical process in which a naturally occurring substance was used as a starting material.

semitendinous (sem-e-ten'dĭ-nus) Partly tendinous; applied to certain muscles.

senescence (se-nes'ens) The natural process of growing old.

senescent (se-nes'ent) Characterized by senescence; one who is growing old.

senile (se'nĭl) **1.** Characteristic of old age; resulting from old age. **2.** Exhibiting mental deterioration with old age.

senility (sĕ-nil'ĭ-te) Old age with the implication of associated pathologic changes or degeneration.

senna (sen'ah) Preparation made from various plants of the genus *Cassia,* which have laxative properties.

senopia (se-no'pe-ah) See second sight, under sight.

sensate (sen'sat) **1.** To perceive through a sense, especially the sense of touch. **2.** One who is so able; referring to a patient who regains sensation after a nerve loss.

sensation (sen-sa'shun) The perception of a stimulus acting on a sense organ.

sense (sens) The faculty of being able to perceive any stimulus.

sensibility (sen-sĭ-bil'ĭ-te) The ability to perceive sensations.

    vibratory s. See pallesthesia.

sensible (sen'sĭ-bl) **1.** Perceptible to the sense organs. **2.** Able to feel.

S

sensimeter (sen-sim′ĕ-ter) Instrument for determining the levels of cutaneous sensation, as in anesthetized areas.

sensitive (sen′sĭ-tiv) **1.** Responsive to external stimulation, often implying the state of being easily irritated or altered by the action of a given stimulus. **2.** Susceptible, as to the action of a drug. **3.** In immunology, the increased capacity to respond specifically to an antigen.

sensitivity (sen-sĭ-tiv′ĭ-te) **1.** The state of being sensitive; often implying a keen perception of, or responsiveness to, a stimulus. **2.** Applied to a screening test: the proportion of persons who truly have a disease in a screened population, and who are identified as such by the screening test.

sensitization (sen-sĭ-tĭ-za′shun) In immunology, the process by which an immune response is activated on first exposure to an antigen, with the result of preparing the body's immune system for a stronger response upon a subsequent exposure to the same antigen (as in a hypersensitivity reaction). Distinguished from immunization.

sensitize (sen′sĭ-tīz) **1.** To render sensitive. **2.** To induce sensitization.

sensitizer (sen′sĭ-ti-zer) Any substance capable of inducing sensitivity.

sensomotor (sen-so-mo′tor) See sensorimotor.

sensor (sen′sor) Any device designed to respond to a physical stimulus (e.g., temperature, light, motion), generating electrical signals for measurement or control.

sensorimotor (sen-so-re-mo′tor) Both sensory and motor; applied to certain nerves and areas of the cerebral cortex. Also called sensomotor.

sensorium (sen-so′re-um) **1.** A sense organ. **2.** In psychiatry, the state of mental clarity at a given time; consciousness.

sensory (sen′so-re) Relating to sensation.

sentiment (sen′tĭ-ment) An attitude, thought, or judgment based on feeling instead of reason.

separation (sep-ah-ra′shun) The act of dividing, detaching, or keeping apart.

  epiphyseal s. See epiphyseal fracture, under fracture.

separator (sep′ah-ra-tor) **1.** Instrument for temporarily forcing apart two teeth in order to gain access to adjacent surfaces. **2.** A substance applied to a surface to prevent other material from adhering to that surface.

sepsis (sep′sis) The systemic response to infection, characterized by (but not limited to) two or more of the following features: elevation of body temperature, heart rate, respiratory rate, and white blood cell count.

septa (sep′tah) Plural of septum.

septal (sep′tal) Relating to a septum or partition.

septate (sep′tāt) Divided into compartments by a septum.

septectomy (sep-tek′to-me) Surgical removal of a septum, especially the partial removal of the nasal septum.

septic (sep′tik) Relating to sepsis.

septicemia (sep-tĭ-se′me-ah) Generalized infection caused by microorganisms or their toxins and spread throughout the body via the bloodstream. Also called hematosepsis; popularly called blood poisoning.

septicemic (sep-tĭ-se′mik) Relating to septicemia.

septivalent (sep-tĭ-va′lent) Having the combining power (valency) of seven.

septo-, sept- Combining forms meaning septum.

septomarginal (sep-to-mar′ji-nal) Relating to the margin of a partition or septum.

septonasal (sep-to-na′zal) Relating to the nasal septum.

septoplasty (sep-to-plas′te) Reparative operation upon a septum, especially the nasal septum (e.g., to correct a deviation or to repair a perforation).

septorhinoplasty (sep-to-ri′no-plas-te) Surgical alteration of the nasal structures involving the septum and external features of the nose.

septotomy (sep-tot′o-me) A surgical cut into a septum.

septulum (sep′tu-lum), pl. sep′tula Latin for a minute partition or septum.

septum (sep′tum), pl. sep′ta A thin wall or partition between two cavities or masses of soft tissue.

  alveolar s. See interalveolar septum.

  atrial s. See interatrial septum.

  femoral s. The delicate layer of connective tissue that closes the femoral ring (anulus femoralis) at the base of the femoral canal; it is perforated by lymphatic vessels.

  gingival s. See interdental papilla, under papilla.

  interalveolar s. The thin alveolar bone that separates the tooth sockets. Also called alveolar septum.

  interatrial s. The partition between the right and left atria of the heart. Also called atrial septum.

  intermuscular s. A fascial sheet that separates adjacent muscles of the limbs or groups of muscles.

  interventricular s. The musculomembranous partition dividing the right and left ventricles of the heart. Also called ventricular septum.

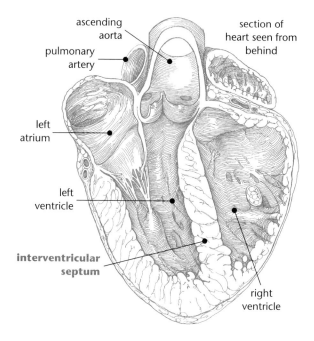

  nasal s. The thin median wall dividing the nasal cavity into right and left halves; composed posteriorly of bone (vomer, perpendicular plate of ethmoid, nasal crests of the maxilla, and palatine bones) and anteriorly of cartilage (septal cartilage).

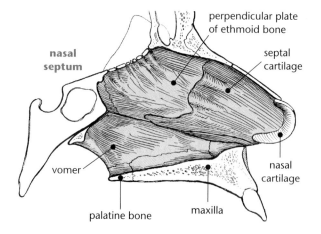

  s. pellucidum A median partition between the right and left lateral ventricles of the brain.

placental septa Incomplete partitions that divide the maternal surface of the placenta into 15 to 20 compartments (cotyledons).

primary atrial s. See septum primum.

s. primum The first atrial septum to appear in the embryonic heart; the sickle-shaped partition that initiates the division of the originally single atrium of the embryonic heart into right and left chambers (atria). Also called primary atrial septum.

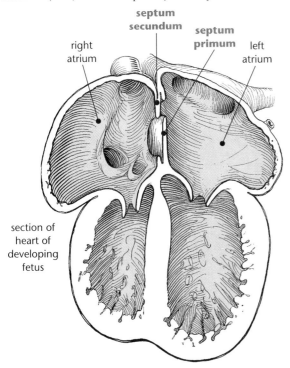

right atrium

septum secundum

septum primum

left atrium

section of heart of developing fetus

rectovaginal s. In the female, the thin layer of fascia separating the vagina from the anterior wall of the rectum. The equivalent in the male is the rectovesical septum.

rectovesical s. In the male, the thin layer of fascia separating the prostate and bladder from the anterior wall of the rectum. The equivalent in the female is the rectovaginal septum.

s. of scrotum A fibromuscular partition in the median plane, dividing the scrotum into two completely separate sacs, each containing a testis and accessory organs.

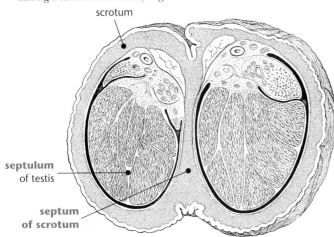

scrotum

septulum of testis

septum of scrotum

secondary atrial s. See septum secundum.

s. secundum The second atrial partition to appear in the embryonic heart; the sickle-shaped muscular partition appearing on the roof of the right atrium, adjacent to the septum primum; it remains open (forming the foramen ovale) until after birth, when pulmonary respiration begins and pressures within the two atria become equalized. Also called secondary atrial septum.

s. of tongue A median fibrous partition that extends throughout the length of the tongue, but fails to reach the dorsal surface; it unites the two halves of the tongue, connects the root of the tongue to the hyoid bone, and gives attachment to the transverse muscle of tongue, vertical muscle of tongue, superior longitudinal muscle of tongue, and to the genioglossus muscle.

ventricular s. See interventricular septum.

sequela (se-kwe′lah), pl. seque′lae **1.** A condition following and caused by another disease. **2.** The consequences of abusive acts, such as physical and/or psychological damage, and the perpetuation of abusive behavior across generations.

sequence (se′kwens) A series of items or events, one following another.

dysmorphic s. A "cascading" pattern of multiple, secondary developmental anomalies caused by a single event, e.g., loss of amniotic fluid (the primary event) can cause compression of the fetus, with the characteristic facial features, underdevelopment of the lungs, and defects of the extremities. Distinguished from syndrome, in which the anomalies occur independently rather than sequentially, although originating from a single cause.

sequester (se-kwes′ter) To detach or isolate abnormally (e.g., mass of tissue).

sequestration (se-kwes-tra′shun) The formation of a sequestrum.

bronchopulmonary s. Congenital anomaly characterized by the presence of an independent mass of lung tissue, with its own air passage (bronchus) and its own blood supply from a branch of the thoracic aorta.

sequestrectomy (se-kwes-trek′to-me) Removal of a sequestrum.

sequestrum (se-kwes′trum) A mass of dead tissue, especially of bone, that has become separated from, or is abnormally attached to, the surrounding healthy tissue.

sera (se′rah) Plural of serum.

series (sēr′ēz) Any group of events, chemical compounds, or objects sharing some characteristic.

aromatic s. Compounds derived from benzene.

erythrocytic s. The group of cells in various stages of development in the bone marrow that ultimately form the mature red blood cells.

fatty s. The series of saturated open-chain hydrocarbons, denoted by the suffix -ane (methane, propane, ethane). Also called methane series; paraffin series.

granulocytic s. The group of cells in various stages of development in the bone marrow that ultimately form the mature white blood cells designated granulocytes.

homologous s. A succession of compounds, each one differing from the preceding one by having one more atomic group such as CH_2.

lymphocytic s. The group of cells in different stages of development leading to the formation of mature lymphocytes.

methane s. See fatty series.

paraffin s. See fatty series.

serine (ser′ēn) A nonessential amino acid; one of the breakdown products of protein.

seriograph (ser′e-o-graf) Instrument for taking a series of radiographic exposures; used in radiography of the blood vessels in the brain.

seriscission (ser-i-sizh′un) Surgical procedure in which soft tissues are divided by means of a tightly encircling silk suture (e.g., in dividing the pedicle of a tumor).

sero- Combining form meaning serum.

seroconversion (se-ro-kon-ver′shun) Production of specific antibodies in response to infection or immunization.

serocystic (se-ro-sis′tik) Composed of serum-filled cysts.

serodiagnosis (se-ro-di-ag-no′sis) Diagnostic procedures involving serologic reactions, which serve to identify microorganisms or to demonstrate the presence of antibodies in the serum.

seroentertis (se-ro-en-tĕ-ri′tis) See perienteritis.

serofibrinous (se-ro-fib′rin-us) Containing serum and fibrin; applied to certain exudates.

serologic (se-ro-loj'ik) Relating to serology.

serology (se-rol'o-je) The branch of science concerned with the study of serum, especially with respect to immunity.

    forensic s. The application of the principles and practices of serology to problems of law enforcement and administration of justice; it is concerned mainly with analysis of blood, saliva, and semen.

seroma (sēr-o'mah) A tumorlike swelling caused by collection of serum in the tissues, usually in a wound site.

seromembranous (se-ro-mem'brah-nus) Relating to a serous membrane.

seromucous (se-ro-mu'kus) Composed of serum and mucus.

seronegative (se-ro-neg'ah-tiv) Lacking antibodies or any other specific immunologic marker for the microorganism of concern.

seropositive (se-ro-poz'i-tiv) Containing antibodies or any other specific immunologic marker for the microorganism under consideration, indicating a previous exposure or an ongoing infection.

seropurulent (se-ro-pu'roo-lent) Containing serum and pus; applied to a discharge.

seropus (se-ro-pus') Serum mixed with pus.

serosa (se-ro'sah) The membrane lining the walls of the body cavities (pleural, pericardial, and peritoneal) and covering the surface of the organs within. Also called serous membrane.

serosanguineous (se-ro-sang-gwin'e-us) Containing serum and blood; applied to a discharge.

seroserous (se-ro-se'rus) Relating to two or more serous membranes.

serositis (se-ro-si'tis) Inflammation of a serous membrane.

    adhesive s. Serositis causing mobile organs to stick together.

    multiple s. See polyserositis.

serosynovitis (se-ro-sin-o-vi'tis) Inflammation of the lining membrane of a joint cavity with effusion of serum into the cavity.

serotonin (ser-o-to'nin) A substance present in various body tissues, especially in the gastrointestinal lining, in small amounts in blood platelets, and in the brain; it stimulates smooth muscle contraction, constricts blood vessels, and inhibits stomach secretions. It has also been found in carcinoid tumors. Also called 5-hydroxytryptamine (5-HT).

serotype (se'ro-tip) See serovar.

serous (se'rus) Relating to serum.

serovaccination (se-ro-vak-sĭ-na'shun) The combined injection of serum to produce passive immunity and vaccination to produce active immunity.

serovar (se'ro-var) A subgroup within a bacterial species distinguishable from other subgroups of the same species on the basis of antigenic characteristics. Also called subtype; serotype.

serpiginous (ser-pij'i-nus) Having a wavy margin and expanding as if by creeping; applied to an ulcer that heals at one margin while expanding on the opposite side.

serpigo (ser-pi'go) 1. Ringworm. 2. Herpes. 3. Any creeping eruption.

serrate, serrated (ser'at, ser'āt-ed) Notched.

Serratia (sĕ-ra'she-ah) A genus of motile, gram-negative bacteria (family Enterobacteriaceae); present in the natural environment (soil, water, and plant surfaces).

    S. marcescens Species causing hospital-acquired (nosocomial) infections, especially in patients with impaired immunity; it produces a characteristic red pigment that is sometimes mistaken for blood.

serration (sĕ-ra'shun) 1. The state of being notched. 2. A saw-toothed edge.

serrefine (ser-e-fēn') A fine, spring forceps used in surgical operations for clamping blood vessels or for approximating the edges of a wound.

serrefine

serrulate, serrulated (ser'u-lāt, ser'u-lāt-ed) Having fine notches.

serum (se'rum), pl. se'rums, se'ra 1. The clear fluid moistening serous membranes. 2. A loosely used term denoting serum that contains antitoxins, used for therapeutic and diagnostic purposes. 3. Blood serum.

    anticomplementary s. Serum that destroys complement.

    antilymphocyte s. (ALS) Serum administered to inhibit rejection of grafts and organ transplants.

    antitoxic s. Serum containing antibodies to the toxin of a disease-causing microorganism.

    blood s. The clear, fluid portion of blood that is left after fibrinogen (a protein) and the cellular elements of blood are removed by coagulation; distinguished from plasma, the cell-free liquid portion of uncoagulated blood.

    convalescent s. Serum obtained from a person recently recovered from an infectious disease; administered by injection to other individuals to provide passive immunity against the disease.

    polyvalent s. Serum containing antibodies against more than one strain of a microorganism.

    truth s. A name for certain chemicals (e.g., sodium amobarbital and sodium thiopental) administered intravenously to facilitate questioning of a person who is unwilling or unable to answers queries; the term is a misnomer, since the person's revelations elicited under the influence of the drug are not necessarily factually true.

serumal (se-roo'mal) Relating to serum.

service (ser'vis) 1. In health care, an activity conducted for a particular group of people with the intent of improving health, providing treatment for, or preventing disease or injury. 2. The medical staff in a hospital or clinic devoted to a specialty.

    extended care s.'s Services provided in a skilled nursing facility for a limited period of time after release from a hospital stay.

    hospital ancillary s.'s Services other than room, board, medical, and nursing services provided to patients during a hospital stay; they include laboratory, pharmacy, radiology, and physical therapy services.

    occupational health s.'s Health services for a working population, usually provided by the employer at the place of work.

    social s.'s Services usually provided by social workers aiming to help and support a patient in dealing with social and related problems (e.g., in applying for medical expense reimbursement, or in overcoming destructive or difficult home situations).

servomechanism (ser-vo-mek'ah-nizm) 1. An automatic control device used to maintain the operation of a mechanical system. 2. A self-regulatory biologic process.

sesamoid (ses'ah-moid) 1. Resembling a sesame seed; nodular. 2. Denoting a small, ovoid bone that is embedded within a tendon or a capsule of a joint to facilitate sliding over a hard structure, such as bone; it is found mainly within the tendons of the extremities; the kneecap (patella) is the largest such bone in the body.

sesqui- Combining form meaning one and a half.

sessile (ses'il) Attached by a broad base rather than a pedicle; applied to certain polyps and tumors.

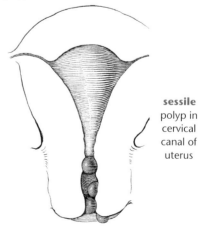

sessile
polyp in
cervical
canal of
uterus

S

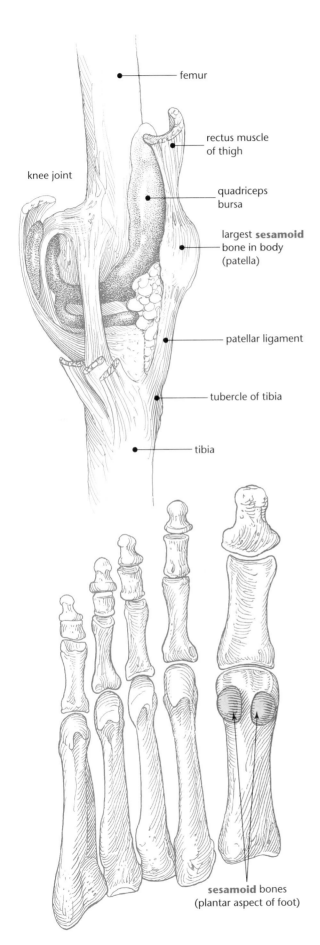

femur

rectus muscle
of thigh

knee joint

quadriceps
bursa

largest **sesamoid**
bone in body
(patella)

patellar ligament

tubercle of tibia

tibia

sesamoid bones
(plantar aspect of foot)

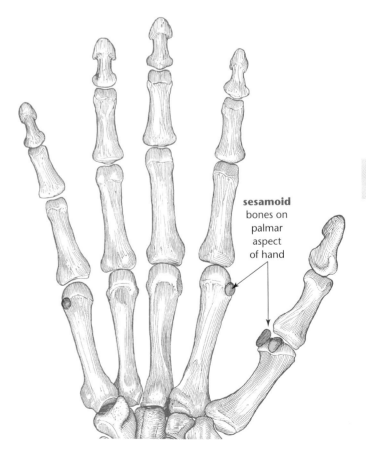

sesamoid
bones on
palmar
aspect
of hand

set (set) **1.** To align in a way that will restore function; applied to a fractured bone. **2.** Hardened (e.g., a plastic material). **3.** In psychology, readiness to respond in a predetermined way when confronted with a particular problem or situation.

seta (se'tah), pl. se'tae A short, bristlelike structure.

setaceous (se-ta'shus) Resembling a bristle.

setiferous (se-tif'er-us) Covered with bristles.

seton (se'ton) A guide wire or similar object used to create a passage through the tissues or to introduce an instrument of a larger caliber.

setting (set'ing) Hardening, as of amalgam or plaster of Paris.

setup (set'up) An arrangement of artificial teeth on a trial denture base, preliminary to construction of a dental appliance.

sex (seks) The classification of organisms as male or female according to their reproductive characteristics.

sexdigitate (seks-dij'ĭ-tāt) Having six digits in a hand or foot.

sex-influenced (seks in'floo-enst) The expression of autosomal traits predominantly in one sex, either male or female.

sexivalent (sek-siv'ah-lent) Having the combining power (valence) of six hydrogen atoms.

sex-limited (seks lim'it-ed) The expression of autosomal traits in one sex only, male or female; a sex-influence in the extreme.

sex-linked (seks' linkt) Carried in a sex (X or Y) chromosome; applied to a gene.

sexology (seks-ol'o-je) The study of the sexes and their relationship.

sextan (seks'tan) Recurring every sixth day; applied to a malarial fever.

sexual (seks'u-al) **1.** Relating to sex. **2.** Evoking sexual desire.

sexuality (seks-u-al'ĭ-te) The state of having sexual characteristics, experiences, and behaviors.

 infantile s. In psychoanalysis, the capacity of the infant and child to have experiences of a sexual nature.

shadow-casting (shad'o kast'ing) A technique for increasing the visibility of ultramicroscopic specimens by coating them with a film of chromium, carbon, or platinum.

shaft (shaft) An elongated or rodlike structure.

shakes (shāks) Colloquial term for severe chills (e.g., those of malarial fever) or a tremor (e.g., one associated with alcohol withdrawal).

shame (shām) An affect that results from not living up to one's expectations of oneself or from the revelation of shortcomings, impulses, thoughts, or feelings unacceptable to the self; loss of self-respect or the respect of others.

shank (shangk) The anterior part of the human leg, from the knee to the ankle.

sheath (shēth) An enveloping structure, usually composed of connective tissue that encloses an organ or part.

   axillary s. A tubular extension of the prevertebral fascia of the neck that encloses the large vessels and nerves of the arm (axillary artery and vein and brachial plexus); located between the collarbone (clavicle) and the first rib.

   carotid s. A tubular sheath derived from the deep fascia of the neck that encloses and binds together the common and internal carotid arteries, internal jugular vein, vagus nerve, and the superior root of the ansa cervicalis; it extends from the base of the skull to the first rib and breastbone (sternum).

   contraceptive s. See condom.

   crural s. See femoral sheath.

   endoneurial s. See endoneurium.

   s. of eyeball See fascial sheath of eyeball.

   fascial s. of eyeball A sheath enclosing the posterior five-sixths of the eyeball, adherent anteriorly to the conjunctiva at the sclerocorneal junction; it intervenes between the eyeball and the orbital fat. Also called capsule of Tenon; bulbar fascia; sheath of eyeball.

   fascial s. of prostate A sheath containing anteriorly the veins of the prostatic venous plexus, encasing the prostate and its capsule; the posterior wall is composed of the rectovesical fascia and is avascular.

   femoral s. A downward funnel-shaped sheath, about 1.25 cm in length, located behind and just below the inguinal ligament of the groin, and derived from the intra-abdominal fascia; it is divided into three compartments: the lateral compartment contains the femoral artery, the middle one contains the femoral vein, the medial one (femoral canal) contains lymphatic vessels and a lymph node. Also called crural sheath.

   fibrous s. A sheath of connective tissue.

   Henle's s. See endoneurium.

   lamellar s. See perineurium.

   medullary s. See myelin sheath.

   meningeal s.'s of optic nerve See sheaths of optic nerve.

   mitochondrial s. A sheath of mitochondria in the middle portion of a spermatozoon arranged in a helical manner (10 to 15 spiral turns) around the axoneme and outer dense fibers.

   myelin s. A flaplike extension of the Schwann cell cytoplasm that spirals around the axon of a nerve cell (neuron) until it is transformed into compacted layers of cell membrane. The inside of the compacted spiral layers of the mylein sheath has a delicate zone of Schwann cell cytoplasm, while the outside of the spiral layers contains the major portion of the cytoplasm and the nucleus of the Schwann cell. Also called medullary sheath.

   neurilemmal s. See neurilemma.

   s.'s of optic nerve The three sheaths (dura, arachnoid, and pia) surrounding the optic nerve and prolonged as far as the back of the eyeball; it is an extension of the meninges of the brain. Also called meningeal sheaths of optic nerve.

   periarteriolar lymphatic s. (PALS) The accumulations of lymphoid tissue constituting the white pulp of the spleen, consisting of lymphocytes and antigen-presenting cells.

   s. of Retzius See endoneurium.

   root s. of hair The downgrowth of surface epithelium encircling the hair root.

   s. of Schwann See neurilemma.

   synovial s. A thin, double-layered sheath commonly found around tendons (tendon synovial sheath), where it lies in contact with bone; it passes under a ligamentous band, or through a fascial

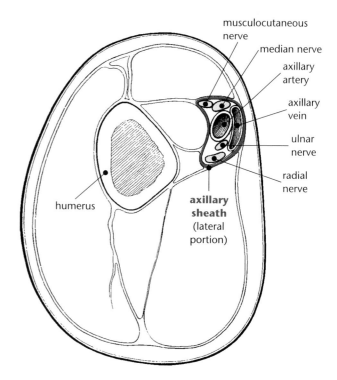

sling or osseofibrous tunnel. The intervening space of the sheath contains a capillary mucuslike film of synovial fluid to facilitate the gliding of the tendon.

sheet (shēt) 1. A large, usually rectangular piece of material used as bedding. 2. A flat, thin anatomic structure or tissue.

   draw s. See drawsheet.

shelf (shelf) Any shelflike structure in the body.

   Blumer's s. See rectal shelf.

   rectal s. A shelflike mass in the rectum resulting from infiltration by a tumor or inflammation. Also called Blumer's shelf.

shield (shēld) 1. Any protective device or substance that serves as a barrier or screen. 2. To afford protection (e.g., from radiation).

   breast s. A rubber cap or dome for protecting inflamed or irritated nipples from contact with clothing.

   embryonic s. The disk in the blastoderm from which the embryo proper develops.

   lead s. In radiology, a lead screen for protecting patients or personnel from radiation.

   nipple s. A round plate with a short central projecting tube fitted with a rubber nipple; used to protect the irritated nipples of a nursing woman; the pressure from the infant's mouth is attenuated by the resistance of the rubber nipple.

shift (shift) A change.

   axis s. See axis deviation, under deviation.

   Doppler s. A change in the frequency of an electromagnetic radiation due to the motion of atoms and molecules.

   s. to the left An increase in the percentage of immature neutrophils in the blood.

   permanent threshold s. (PTS) Irreversible hearing loss resulting from long-term exposure to excessive noise or to ototoxic medication.

   temporary threshold s. (TTS) Deterioration of hearing immediately after exposure to loud noise or to an ototoxic medication followed by complete or almost complete recovery with the passage of time.

   threshold s. A deviation from a person's previous audiogram measured in decibels indicating the degree of hearing loss.

Shigella (shĭ-gel'ah) A genus of gram-negative bacteria (family Enterobacteriaceae) divided into four major groups (A, B, C, D) and subdivided serologically into different types; its organisms are the principal cause of dysentery.

S

shakes ■ Shigella

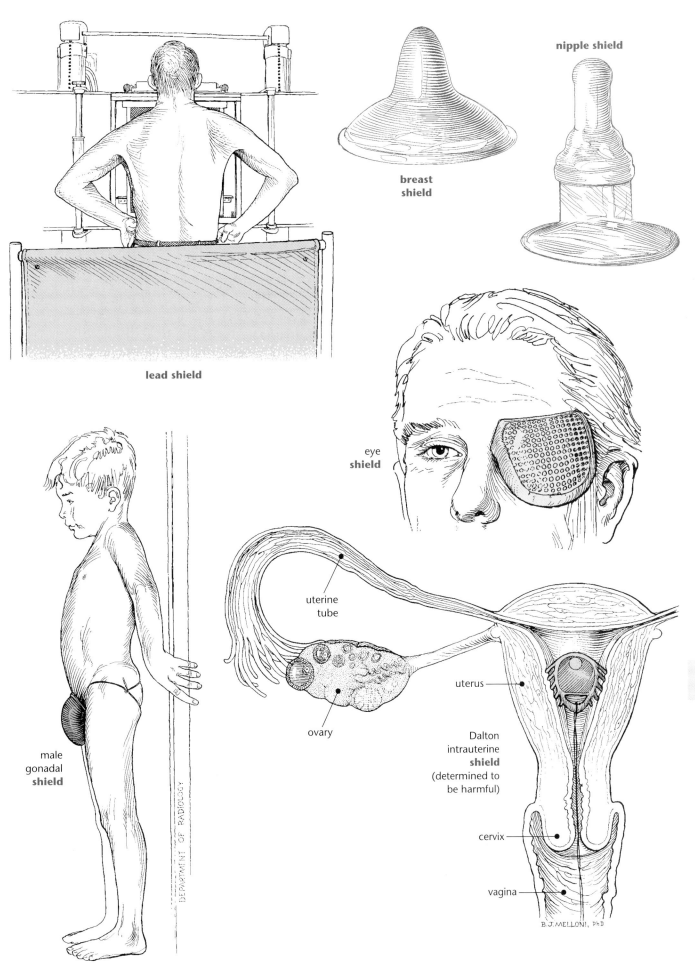

lead shield

breast shield

nipple shield

eye **shield**

male gonadal **shield**

uterine tube

ovary

uterus

Dalton intrauterine **shield** (determined to be harmful)

cervix

vagina

DEPARTMENT OF RADIOLOGY

B.J.MELLONI, PhD

S

S. dysenteriae Group A species, a particularly virulent species causing dysentery in humans; found in the feces of infected people or convalescent carriers.

S. flexneri Group B species, one of the most common causes of dysentery epidemics and sometimes of infantile gastroenteritis.

S. sonnei Group D species, a cause of mild dysentery and summer diarrhea in children.

shigellosis (shĭ-gel-lo'sis) Acute infection of the bowel with bacteria of the genus *Shigella*, causing dysentery, often in epidemic patterns.

shin (shin) The anterior portion of the leg, below the knee.

saber s. An anteriorly bowed tibia; a characteristic bone complication of syphilis.

shinbone (shin'bōn) The tibia. See table of bones.

shingles (shing'glz) See herpes zoster, under herpes.

shin splints (shin' splints) Pain and occasional inflammation of the lower leg, along the front and medial portion of the shinbone (tibia), most often caused by overexercise.

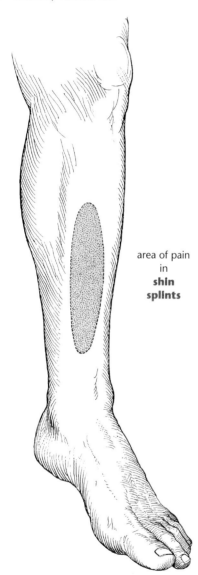

area of pain
in
**shin
splints**

shistocyte (shis'to-sīt) An irregular, contracted, somewhat triangular red blood cell; seen in microangiopathic anemia. Also called helmet cell.

shiver (shiv'er) To shudder, as from a fever-induced chill.

shock (shok) A severe physiologic reaction to bodily trauma; clinical manifestations include pale clammy skin, weak rapid pulse, lowered blood pressure, and sometimes unconsciousness.

anaphylactic s. A severe, often fatal, reaction occurring upon a second exposure to an antigen against which the body has previously formed antibodies.

cardiogenic s. Shock resulting from severe sudden reduction of cardiac output, as occurs in a heart attack (myocardial infarction).

counter s. See countershock.

deferred s., delayed s. Shock occurring several hours after an injury.

electric s. The effects of the passage of an electric current through the body (e.g., pain, muscle contraction).

endotoxin s., endotoxic s. Septic shock caused by the toxins produced and released by microorganisms.

histamine s. Shock resulting from injection of histamine.

hypovolemic s. Shock resulting from a critical reduction in plasma or blood volume, as occurs in hemorrhage or in fluid loss (e.g., in large surface burns).

insulin s. Shock caused by a sudden reduction of blood sugar, as occurs in an overdose of insulin.

irreversible s. Shock that does not respond to any therapeutic effort, occurring when circulatory and metabolic deficits are not corrected; it leads to coma and death.

primary s. Shock directly related to, and immediately following, a severe injury, mainly due to anxiety or pain.

septic s. Shock resulting from bacterial infection, especially with gram-negative bacilli, in which there is heavy bacteremia or release of bacterial toxins into the blood.

spinal s. Transient diminution of spinal reflexes after injury to the spinal cord; manifested in muscles innervated by nerves below the level of the injury.

shortsightedness (short-sīt'ed-nes) See myopia.

shot (shot) Popular name for injection of medication or immunizing agent.

booster s. A booster dose administered by injection.

shoulder (shōl'der) The region of the body where the arm and trunk meet.

shoulder blade (shōl'der blād) See scapula.

show (sho) In obstetrics, a sign of impending labor, indicated by a vaginal discharge of blood-stained mucus; it represents the expulsed mucus plug that filled the cervical canal during pregnancy.

shudder (shŭd'er) A brief tremor.

carotid s. Irregularities at the height of the carotid pulse tracing, as seen in aortic stenosis.

shunt (shunt) **1.** An abnormal communication between two natural channels; it may be congenital (e.g., between heart chambers, between chambers and blood vessels, or between blood vessels), or it may be an anastomosis surgically created to bypass an obstruction (e.g., to divert blood, cerebrospinal fluid, urine, or intestinal contents from one site to another). **2.** To bypass or divert; to provide with a shunt surgically.

arteriovenous s. A synthetic external or subcutaneous tube inserted into a vein and an artery, bypassing the capillary network, to provide repeated vascular access in renal dialysis or in chemotherapy; vessels most commonly used are the radial artery and cephalic vein in the forearm.

Denver s. A variation of the LeVeen shunt equipped with an implanted, valved chamber that is manually compressible to maintain patency.

left-to-right s. A diversion of blood through abnormal channels either from the left to the right side of the heart through an opening between the atria or the ventricles (septal defects), or from the systemic to the pulmonary circulations through a channel between the aorta and the pulmonary trunk (patent ductus arteriosus).

LeVeen s. A device for transporting accumulated fluid from the abdominal cavity to the venous circulation; a plastic tube equipped with a valve is inserted into the peritoneal cavity, tunneled under the skin, and connected to a large vein in the neck.

peritoneovenous s. Any device (e.g., LeVeen and Denver

S

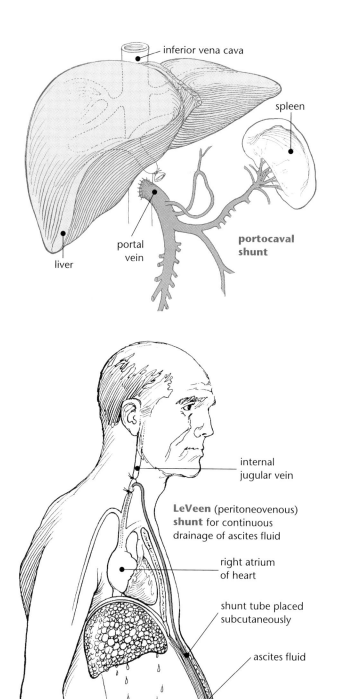

inferior vena cava

spleen

liver

portal vein

portocaval shunt

internal jugular vein

LeVeen (peritoneovenous) **shunt** for continuous drainage of ascites fluid

right atrium of heart

shunt tube placed subcutaneously

ascites fluid

one-way valve system activated by a pressure gradient; it prevents reflux of blood

perforated tube in peritoneal cavity

shunts) for transporting fluid from the peritoneal cavity to the venous circulation, as in the management of ascites.

   portacaval s. A surgical communication established between the portal vein and the inferior vena cava.

   portasystemic s. Any surgical communication established between the portal vein or its tributaries and those of the inferior vena cava.

   reversed s. See right-to-left shunt.

   right-to-left s. The passage of unoxygenated venous blood from the right side of the heart directly into the arterial circulation without passing through the lungs. Also called reversed shunt.

   splenorenal s. A surgical connection between the splenic vein and the left renal vein.

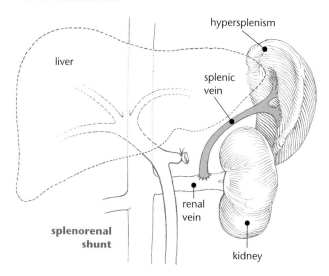

liver

hypersplenism

splenic vein

renal vein

splenorenal shunt

kidney

shunting (shun'ting) The surgical establishment of a shunt.
sialaden (si-al'ah-den) A salivary gland.
sialadenitis (si-al-ad-ĕ-ni'tis) Inflammation of a salivary gland. Also called sialoadenitis.

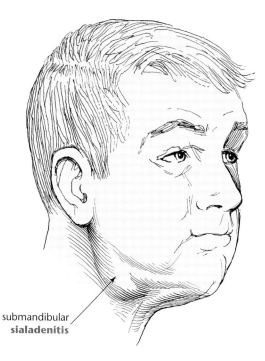

submandibular **sialadenitis**

sialagogue (si-al'ah-gog) Any agent that stimulates the production of saliva. Also called sialogogue.
sialaporia (si-al-ah-po're-ah) Deficient flow of saliva.
sialectasis (si-al-ek-ta'sis) Dilatation of a salivary duct.

S

sialic (si-al'ik) Salivary.

sialic acids (si-al'ik as'ids) A group of naturally occurring derivatives of a 9-carbon, 3-deoxy-5-amino sugar acid; present in bacteria and in animal tissue as components of lipids, polysaccharides, and mucoproteins.

sialism (si'al-izm) See sialorrhea.

sialo-, sial- Combining forms meaning saliva.

sialoadenectomy (si-ah-lo-ad-ĕ-nek'to-me) Removal of a salivary gland.

sialoadenitis (si-ah-lo-ad-ĕ-ni'tis) See sialadenitis.

sialoadenotomy (si-ah-lo-ad-ĕ-not'o-me) An incision into a salivary gland.

sialoangiectasis (si-ah-lo-an-je-ek'tah-sis) 1. Dilatation of a salivary gland and its ducts with stagnated saliva due to obstruction usually by a stony concretion or a stricture. 2. Dilatation of a salivary duct with an instrument such as a bougie.

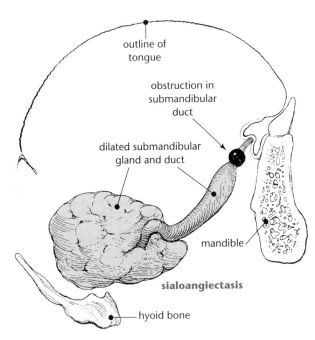

sialoangiectasis

sialoangiitis, sialodochitis (si-ah-lo-an-je-i'tis, si-ah-lo-do-ki'tis) Inflammation of a salivary duct.

sialodochoplasty (si-ah-lo-do'ko-plas-te) Surgical repair of a salivary duct.

sialogenous (si-ah-loj'ĕ-nus) Producing saliva.

sialogogue (si-al'o-gog) See sialagogue.

sialogram (si-al'o-gram) An x-ray image of a salivary gland and its ducts.

sialography (si-ah-log'rah-fe) The process of making x-ray pictures of a salivary gland and its duct system after instillation of a radiopaque substance.

sialolith (si-al'o-lith) A salivary stone (calculus). Also called ptyalolith.

sialolithiasis (si-ah-lo-lĭ-thi'ah-sis) The presence of a stone (calculus) in a salivary gland or duct. Also called ptyalolithiasis.

sialolithotomy (si-ah-lo-lĭ-thot'o-me) A surgical cut into a salivary gland or duct for the removal of a stone (calculus). Also called ptyalolithotomy.

sialorrhea (si-ah-lo-re'ah) Excessive salivary flow. Also called sialism; sialosis.

sialoschesis (si-ah-los'kĕ-sis) Scant salivary secretion.

sialosis (si-ah-lo'sis) See sialorrhea.

sialostenosis (si-ah-lo-stĕ-no'sis) Stricture of a salivary duct.

sialosyrinx (si-ah-lo-si'rinks) 1. A pathologic opening into a salivary gland through the oral mucosa or the skin. 2. A syringe or tube for draining a salivary duct.

sib, sibling (sib, sib'ling) A brother or a sister; a member of a sibship, having the same parents.

sibilant (sib'ĭ-lant) Of a whistling character.

sibilus (sib'ĭ-lus) A hissing or whistling sound heard on auscultation.

sibling (sib'ling) See sib.

sibship (sib'ship) A group of brothers and/or sisters having the same parents.

siccant (sik'ant) Producing drying effects.

siccolabile (sik-o-la'bil) Subject to change or destruction by drying.

siccostabile (sik-o-sta'bil) Remaining unchanged when subjected to drying.

siccus (sik'us) Latin for dry.

sick (sik) 1. Afflicted with a disease. 2. Nauseated.

sickle (sik'kl) To undergo sickling; applied to red blood cells.

sicklemia (sik-le'me-ah) See sickle-cell disease.

sickling (sik'ling) The formation of sickle- or crescent-shaped red blood cells.

sickness (sik'nes) 1. A state of ill health. 2. A disease.

    African sleeping s. See African trypanosomiasis, under trypanosomiasis.

    air s. Motion sickness occurring during air travel.

    altitude s. Condition experienced by some unacclimatized people within a few hours of being in high-altitude regions; symptoms include giddiness, headache, difficult rapid breathing on exertion, insomnia, and nausea. High-altitude pulmonary edema and cerebral edema are later-appearing and more severe forms of altitude sickness. Also called mountain sickness.

    car s. Motion sickness caused by the motion of any land vehicle (automobile, train, bus, etc.).

    decompression s. Disorder occurring in divers, underwater workers, or test pilots; the high pressure causes gases to dissolve in the blood and body tissues; when the person returns too suddenly to normal pressure, the dissolved gases return to their original gaseous form and are trapped as bubbles within blood vessels (air embolism) and tissues; the type and severity of symptoms depend

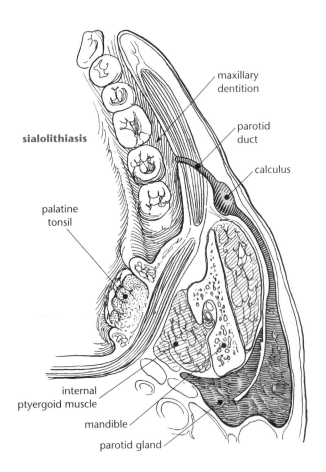

sialolithiasis

on the age, weight, and physical condition of the person; on the degree of physical exertion; on the depth or altitude before decompression; and on the rate and duration of decompression; they usually include acute pain in the large joints, causing the person to assume a stooped posture (the "bends"), bluish red mottling and etching of the skin ("diver's lice"), respiratory distress (the "chokes"), and vertigo. Later complications include aseptic necrosis of bone (osteonecrosis), often occurring 6 to 60 months after decompression, causing permanent impairment if joints are involved. Also called caisson disease; decompression disease.

falling s. See generalized tonic-clonic epilepsy, under epilepsy.

morning s. Nausea and/or vomiting sometimes occurring during pregnancy.

motion s. A group of symptoms, such as pallor, sweating, nausea, vomiting, and frequently incapacitation induced by motion; caused by stimulation of the semicircular canals in the inner ear and/or certain psychic factors.

mountain s. See altitude sickness.

radiation s. Illness resulting from excessive exposure to ionizing radiation; symptoms of massive exposure usually occur in four stages: nausea, vomiting, and sometimes diarrhea and weakness; then follows a period of relative well-being; then fever, loss of appetite, nausea, abdominal distention, bloody diarrhea, and hair loss (death usually occurs at this stage); those who survive experience temporary sterility and eventually develop cataracts. Also called radiotoxemia.

sea s. See seasickness.

serum s. An immune complex reaction following injection of an exogenous serum, characterized by fever, skin eruption, generalized swelling, and painful joints.

sleeping s. See trypanosomiasis.

sidero- Combining form meaning iron.

sideroblast (sid′er-o-blast) An immature red blood cell (erythroblast) containing granules of iron.

siderocyte (sid′er-o-sīt) A mature red blood cell (erythrocyte) containing granules of iron.

sideroderma (sid-er-o-der′mah) Brownish discoloration of the skin, especially of the legs, due to accumulation of iron-containing pigment (hemosiderin).

siderofibrosis (sid-er-o-fi-bro′sis) Abnormal formation of fibrous tissue associated with multiple small deposits of iron.

sideropenia (sid-er-o-pe′ne-ah) Iron deficiency, especially in the blood and bone marrow.

sideropenic (sid-er-o-pe′nik) Relating to iron deficiency.

siderophil (sid′er-o-fil) Any cell or tissue that absorbs iron.

siderophilin (si-der-of′i-lin) See transferrin.

siderosis (sid-er-o′sis) Condition caused by deposition of iron dust or particles in the tissues; may cause degenerative tissue changes (e.g., within the eyeball).

pulmonary s. A benign inflammation of the lungs with a brick red discoloration of lung tissue associated with inhalation of very fine particles of iron or its compounds.

sigh (si) **1.** A deep audible inspiration and expiration made involuntarily under the influence of emotion or an anesthetic. **2.** To make such a sound.

sight (sīt) Vision; the ability to see.

day s. See nyctalopia.

far s. See hyperopia.

near s. See myopia.

night s. See hemeralopia.

old s. See presbyopia.

second s. The spontaneous improvement of near vision to the extent that the person may no longer require eyeglasses for reading, due to the greater convexity of the lens of the eye occurring in the incipient stage of cataract formation. Also called senopia; gerontopia.

short s. See myopia.

sigmatism (sig′mah-tizm) Lisping; inability to pronounce the *s* and *sh* sounds correctly.

sigmoid (sig′moid) Having the shape of the letter S; applied to the distal portion of the colon (adjoining the rectum).

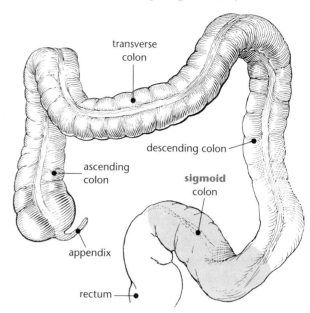

sigmoidectomy (sig-moi-dek′to-me) Removal of part of the sigmoid colon; removal of the sigmoid flexure.

sigmoidopexy (sig-moi′do-pek-se) Suturing of the sigmoid colon to the abdominal wall or other structure, as in the correction of a prolapsed rectum.

sigmoidoscope (sig-moi′do-skōp) Instrument for inspecting the interior of the sigmoid colon. Sometimes called sigmoscope.

sigmoidoscopy (sig-moi-dos′ko-pe) Visual examination of the interior of the sigmoid colon with a sigmoidoscope.

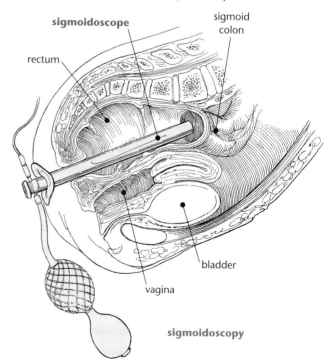

sigmoidoscopy

sigmoidotomy (sig-moi-dot′o-me) Surgical cut into the sigmoid colon.

sigmoscope (sig′mo-skōp) See sigmoidoscope.

sign (sīn) Any objective evidence indicative of disease that is perceptible to the examiner. Some signs are deliberately elicited by means of tests for diagnostic purposes.

accessory s. Any sign that usually, but not always, accompanies a disease.

Allis' s. Relaxation of the normally taut connective tissue at the hip between the iliac crest and the greater trochanter of the femur; occurs in fracture of the neck of the femur.

Babinski's s. *(a)* See extensor plantar reflex, under reflex. *(b)* See pronation sign. *(c)* Reduced contraction of the platysma muscle (at the neck) during movements of the jaw and face; occurs on the affected side in hemiplegia.

Bárány's s. A characteristic movement of the eyes (nystagmus) is normally elicited by irrigating the external ear canal with either cold or warm water; a reduced or absent nystagmus is a sign of inner ear disease.

Battle's s. A purplish discoloration behind the ear, seen in fracture of the base of the skull.

Bielschowsky's s. A sign of paralysis of a superior oblique muscle (of the eye); the affected eye turns upward when the head is tilted.

Broadbent's s. A pulsation observed in the left posterior axillary line of the thorax, occurring synchronously with cardiac systole; indication of adherent pericardium.

Brudzinski's s.'s Signs seen in meningitis: *(a)* flexion of both legs upon abrupt neck flexion of the supine patient; *(b)* flexion of one thigh at the hip causes a similar movement of the other thigh; *(c)* when one leg is flexed and the other extended, lowering the flexed leg causes flexion of the extended one.

Calkin's s. In obstetrics, the change in shape of the uterus at delivery, from discoid to ovoid, indicating separation of the placenta.

Cantelli's s. See doll's eye sign.

Chaddock's s.'s Signs usually indicating lesions in the pyramidal tract (of the brain): *(a)* toe sign, extension of the big toe upon stroking the lateral malleolus and the lateral dorsum of the foot; *(b)* wrist sign, flexion of the wrist with fanning of the fingers upon stroking the wrist on the side of the little finger.

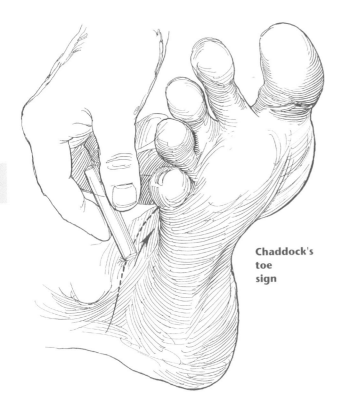

Chaddock's toe sign

Chadwick's s. Bluish discoloration of the vagina and cervix due to congestion of blood vessels; a sign of early pregnancy. Also called Jacquemier's sign.

Chvostek's s. A unilateral spastic contraction of facial muscles elicited by a slight tap over the facial nerve, just in front of the ear, indicative of a low serum calcium concentration.

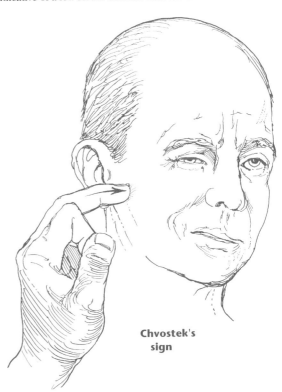

Chvostek's sign

clenched fist s. Pressing a clenched fist against the chest; the gesture of a person with angina pectoris, which indicates the constricting nature of the pain.

Coopernail's s. Bluish coloration of the perineum and scrotum or labia, occurring in fracture of the pelvis.

Courvoisier's s. See Courvoisier's law, under law.

Cruveilhier-Baumgarten s. The occurrence of varicose paraumbilical veins (caput medusae) around the navel associated with a hum heard over that area caused by reverse blood flow from the liver into the abdominal wall; seen in cirrhosis of the liver with portal hypertension.

Cullen's s. Bluish coloration of the skin around the navel, seen in intraperitoneal hemorrhage.

Dalrymple's s. Retraction of the upper eyelid, causing abnormal wideness of the distance between upper and lower lids; seen in Graves' disease.

doll's eye s. Phenomenon occurring in healthy newborn infants; when the head is turned to one side, the eyes tend not to move with it. Also called Cantelli's sign.

drawer s. A sign of ruptured cruciate ligaments at the knee, elicited while the patient lies on his back, knee flexed at 90°; the examiner grasps the upper part of the patient's leg with both hands and pulls the head of the tibia; a forward movement indicates rupture of the anterior cruciate ligament; if the tibia can be pushed under the femoral condyle, the posterior cruciate ligament is ruptured. Also called Rocher's sign.

Ewart's s. An area of dullness over the base of the left lung, at the lower angle of the shoulder blade (scapula), due to compression from a large pericardial effusion. Also called Pins' sign.

Goodell's s. Bluish coloration and softening of the cervix due to increased vascularity during early pregnancy; may be detected as early as the fourth week of pregnancy.

Graefe's s., von Graefe's s. A lag of the upper eyelid when the eyeball moves downward; seen in Graves' disease. Also called lid lag.

Grey Turner's s. Areas of discoloration about the navel and the loins; seen in acute hemorrhagic pancreatitis.

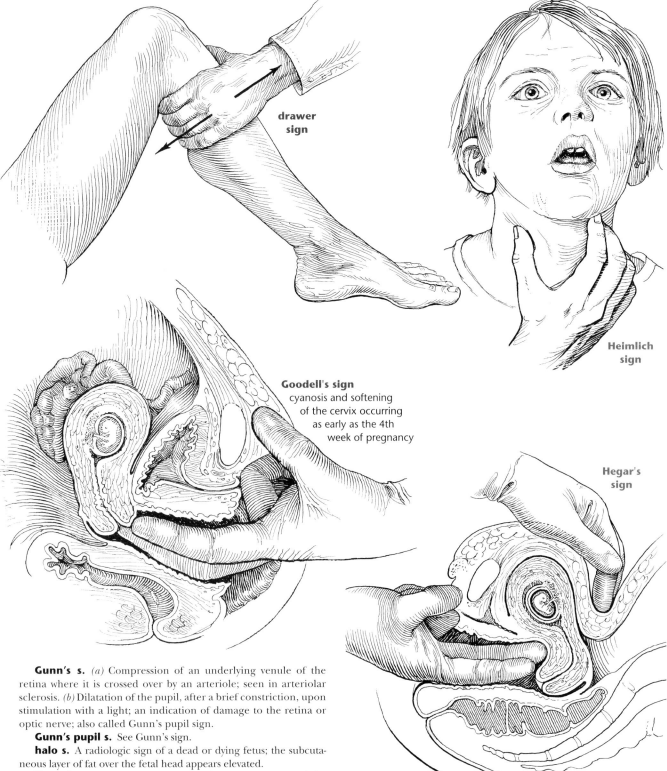

drawer sign

Heimlich sign

Goodell's sign
cyanosis and softening of the cervix occurring as early as the 4th week of pregnancy

Hegar's sign

B JM

S

Gunn's s. (a) Compression of an underlying venule of the retina where it is crossed over by an arteriole; seen in arteriolar sclerosis. (b) Dilatation of the pupil, after a brief constriction, upon stimulation with a light; an indication of damage to the retina or optic nerve; also called Gunn's pupil sign.

Gunn's pupil s. See Gunn's sign.

halo s. A radiologic sign of a dead or dying fetus; the subcutaneous layer of fat over the fetal head appears elevated.

Hegar's s. Increased softening of the lower portion of the uterus (isthmus), occurring in early pregnancy (six to eight weeks), and ascertained through vaginal palpation; one of the most reliable signs of early pregnancy.

Heimlich s. The characteristic sudden gesture of distress of a person with an obstruction of the airway (e.g., with a piece of food or small object or toy); the person brings a hand to his throat with the thumb and index finger spread apart, forming a V.

Hill's s. Greater systolic blood pressure in the legs than in the arms, indicative of aortic insufficiency. Also called Hill's phenomenon.

Hoffmann's s. (a) In tetany, increased excitability of sensory nerves (e.g., mechanical stimulation of the trigeminal nerve causes

pain). (b) A prompt adduction of the thumb and flexion of the index finger elicited by flicking the nail of the patient's middle finger; when occurring unilaterally, it is commonly associated with injury to the pyramidal tract (in the brain). Also called Hoffmann's reflex.

Homan's s. Pain in the calf and back of the knee when the ankle is abruptly dorsiflexed, while the knee is in flexion, suggesting deep-vein thrombosis in the calf.

Hoover's s. (a) Sign sometimes seen in hemiplegia; if the person is asked, when lying on his back, to press down the affected leg, the opposite leg shows an involuntary lifting movement; this phenomenon does not occur in hysterical paralysis and malingering. *(b)* Movement of the rib margins toward the midline when breathing in; occurs bilaterally in emphysema and unilaterally in such conditions as pleural effusion and pneumothorax.

Jacquemier's s. See Chadwick's sign.

Jellinek's s. Brownish pigmentation of the eyelids, seen in people afflicted with Graves' disease.

Kehr's s. Severe referred pain and hyperesthesia at the tip of the left shoulder as seen in some cases of rupture of the spleen.

Kernig's s. Inability to extend the knee from the flexed-thigh position; seen in various cases of meningitis.

Lasègue's s. Pain along the course of the sciatic nerve when the patient, lying on his back, flexes the thigh on the abdomen and then extends the leg at the knee; it indicates disease of the sciatic nerve.

McMurrays s. A painful click produced by rotatory manipulation of the knee joint, caused by a torn meniscus.

Möbius s. Convergence impairment of the eyes occurring in Graves' disease.

mogul s. In radiology, a sharply demarcated protuberance seen in a chest x-ray image, usually indicating an abnormal condition of the heart.

Musset's s. Rhythmic nodding of the head seen in persons affected with incompetence of the aortic valve.

Nikolsky's s. Condition of the skin occurring in pemphigus vulgaris; the superficial layer of apparently normal skin is easily rubbed off with slight friction.

Phalen's s. See Phalen's test, under test.

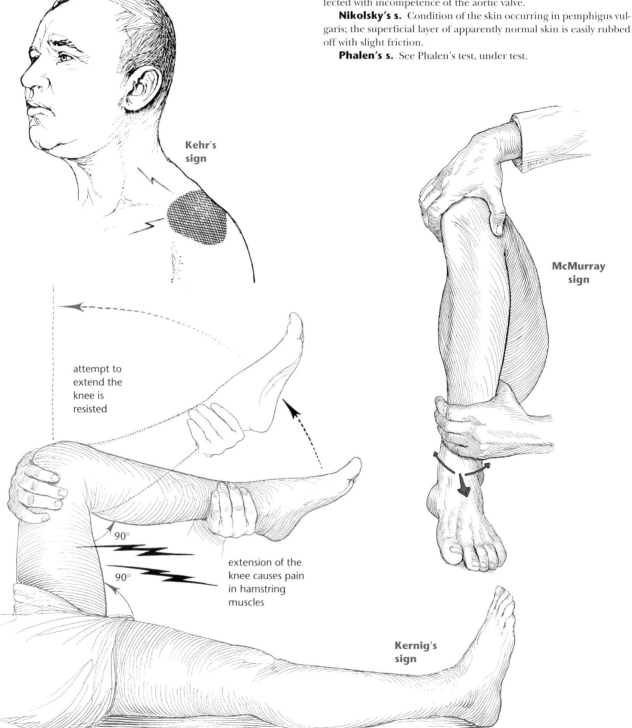

Kehr's sign

attempt to extend the knee is resisted

90°

90°

extension of the knee causes pain in hamstring muscles

McMurray sign

Kernig's sign

sign ∎ sign

S

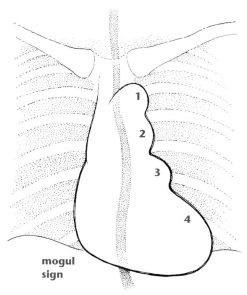

mogul sign

1- aortic arch
2- pulmonary trunk
3- **mogul sign** (abnormal protuberance caused by a herniated or enlarged left atrial appendage, as seen in rheumatic heart disease, left atrial tumor, tetrology of Fallot or in cardiomyopathy)
4- cardiac apex

Pins' s. See Ewart's sign.

Prehn's s. A sign of acute inflammation of the epididymis (epididymitis); rapid unilateral scrotal enlargement with marked tenderness extending to the spermatic cord in the groin, relieved by scrotal elevation.

pronation s. In hemiplegia, when the paralized arm is placed in supination, it spontaneously turns to a pronated position. Also called Babinski's sign.

Quincke's s. See capillary pulse, under pulse.

Rocher's s. See drawer sign.

Romberg's s. See Romberg's test, under test.

Rosenbach's s. (a) Fine tremor of gently closed eyelids, occurring in exophthalmic goiter. (b) Loss of abdominal reflexes in cases of acute inflammation of the abdominal organs.

Spalding's s. Overlapping of the fetal skull bones observed in x-ray pictures, indicating fetal death.

Stellwag's s. Retraction of the upper eyelids associated with occasional incomplete blinking, seen in Graves' disease.

Terry-Thomas s. An increased gap between the scaphoid and lunate bones of the wrist observed in a frontal x-ray image of the wrist; it indicates subluxation of the scaphoid bone, with backward rotation of the proximal pole of the bone and forward rotation of the distal pole.

Tinel's s. A sign of regeneration of an injured peripheral nerve (e.g., in carpal tunnel syndrome); elicited when the nerve is tapped sharply, then a tingling or "pins-and-needles" sensation is felt beyond the site of injury.

Trendelenburg's s. A sign of congenital dislocation of the hip or of weakness of hip abductor muscles; it is elicited when the person stands on the leg of the affected side; then the hip of the opposite, normal, side will not rise as it normally should.

Trousseau's s. Muscular spasm of the hand elicited by compression of the upper arm (e.g., with a blood pressure cuff); a sign of latent tetany.

vital s.'s (VS) Breathing, heartbeat, sustained blood pressure, and temperature; the signs of life.

von Graefe's s. See Graefe's sign.

Winterbottom's s. Swelling of the posterior cervical lymph nodes, indicative of early stages of African sleeping sickness (trypanosomiasis).

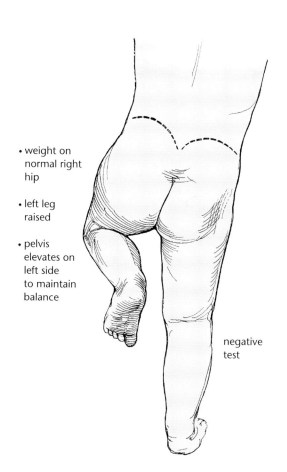

• weight on normal right hip

• left leg raised

• pelvis elevates on left side to maintain balance

negative test

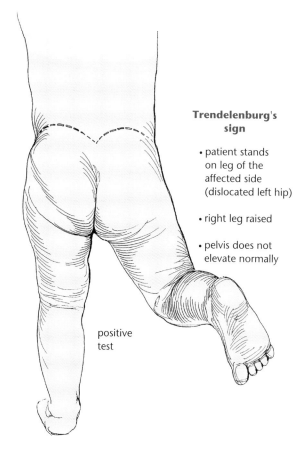

Trendelenburg's sign

• patient stands on leg of the affected side (dislocated left hip)

• right leg raised

• pelvis does not elevate normally

positive test

S

wrist s. A considerable overlap of thumb and middle finger as they encircle the opposite wrist; one of the features of Marfan's syndrome.

signature (sig′nah-chur) (sig.) The part of a pharmaceutical prescription containing instructions to the patient.

significant (sig-nif′ĭ-kant) In statistics, denoting the probability that a given finding is not likely to have occurred by chance.

silent (si′lent) Without detectable signs or symptoms; applied to a disease or pathologic process.

silica (sil′ĭ-kah) Crystalline compound; the principal component of sand; one of the three major ingredients of dental porcelain.

siliceous (sī-lish′us) Containing silica. Also spelled silicious.

silicic (si-lis′ik) Relating to silica.

silicious (sī-lish′us) See siliceous.

silicon (sil′ĭ-kon) Nonmetallic element; symbol Si, atomic number 14, atomic weight 28.09.

silicone (sil′ĭ-kōn) Any of a group of semiorganic polymers that are characterized by physiochemical inertness and a high degree of water repellence and lubricity; used widely in the manufacture of artificial replacement of body parts, protective coatings, and adhesives.

silicosis (sil-ĭ-ko′sis) Condition characterized by persistent inflammation and nodular fibrosis of lung tissue, leading to airflow obstruction and restriction of lung function; caused by inhalation of silica particles (crystalline quartz); sources of exposure include the mining, stonecutting, blasting, quarrying, glass-blowing, and ceramics industries; occurs in three clinical forms (acute, accelerated, and chronic) depending primarily on the intensity of the exposure. Silicosis renders patients susceptible to pulmonary tuberculosis.

silicotuberculosis (sil-ĭ-ko-tu-ber-ku-lo′sis) Silicosis associated with tuberculosis.

silk (sĭlk) The fine lustrous material produced by the mulberry silkworm to make its cocoon.

surgical s. Silk thread used as a permanent suture material in surgical operations.

silver (sil′ver) A malleable, ductile metallic element; symbol Ag, atomic number 47, atomic weight 107.87.

s. nitrate Caustic substance with antiseptic properties, used in dressings for burns and wounds.

simulation (sim-u-la′shun) **1.** A close imitation such as the apparent mimicking of the symptoms of one disease by those of another. **2.** A feigning or pretending, such as malingering.

simulator (sim-u-la′tor) Any device designed to produce effects approximating actual conditions; used for teaching, training, and experimental purposes.

Simulium (si-mu′le-um) A genus of biting black gnats (family Simuliidae); it includes species that are important vectors of disease (e.g., of onchocerciasis).

S

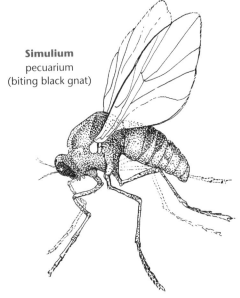

Simulium
pecuarium
(biting black gnat)

sincipital (sin-sip′ĭ-tal) Relating to the forehead and upper part of the head.

sinciput (sin′sĭ-put) The upper frontal surface of the head.

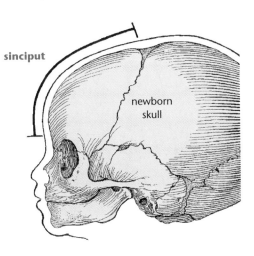

sinciput

newborn
skull

sinew (sin′u) A tendon.

singultation (sing-gul-ta′shun) Hiccuping.

singultous (sing-gul′tus) Relating to hiccups.

singultus (sing-gul′tus) A hiccup.

sinister (sin-is′ter) Latin for left.

sinistrad (sin-is′trad) Toward the left.

sinistral (sin′is-tral) **1.** Relating to the left side. **2.** Left-handed.

sinistrality (sin-is-tral′ĭ-te) Left-handedness.

sinistro- Combining form meaning left.

sinistrocardia (sin-is-tro-kar′de-ah) Displacement of the heart toward the left, beyond its normal position.

sinistrocerebral (sin-is-tro-ser′ĕ-bral) Relating to the left hemisphere of the brain.

sinistrocular (sin-is-trok′u-lar) Relating to a dominant left eye.

sinistropedal (sin-is-trop′ĕ-dal) Denoting a preferential use of the left foot.

sinoatrial (si-no-a′tre-al) Relating to the sinus venosus and the right atrium of the heart (e.g., the sinoatrial node).

sinus (si′nus) **1.** Any cavity within a bone normally filled with air. **2.** A wide channel normally conveying body fluids (i.e., blood, lymph, or aqueous humor). **3.** Abnormal channel or tract (e.g., one leading from an abscess, permitting escape of pus).

anal s. One of several small recesses, between folds of mucous membrane, in the posterior upper end of the anal canal. Also called anal crypt.

aortic s. Any of the three slight dilatations of the aorta between each semilunar valve and the aortic wall.

carotid s. A dilatation of the internal carotid artery situated near the branching off of this vessel from the common carotid artery. The sinus wall is sensitive to pressure, enabling it to bring about modifications in arterial blood pressure. Also called carotid bulb.

cerebral s.'s See sinuses of dura mater.

coronary s. The venous channel on the posterior portion of the atrioventricular groove of the heart; it receives blood from most of the coronary veins and empties into the right atrium.

dermal s. An abnormal skin-lined tract, most commonly leading from the body surface into the spinal canal.

s.'s of dura mater Venous channels that drain blood from the brain and its surrounding bone (cranium); they lie between the two layers of the outer sheath of the brain (dura mater). Also called cerebral sinuses.

ethmoidal s. One of the honeycomb-like air spaces situated in the ethmoid bone, medial to the orbit, and draining into the upper part of the nasal cavity on either side; grouped into anterior, middle, and posterior divisions.

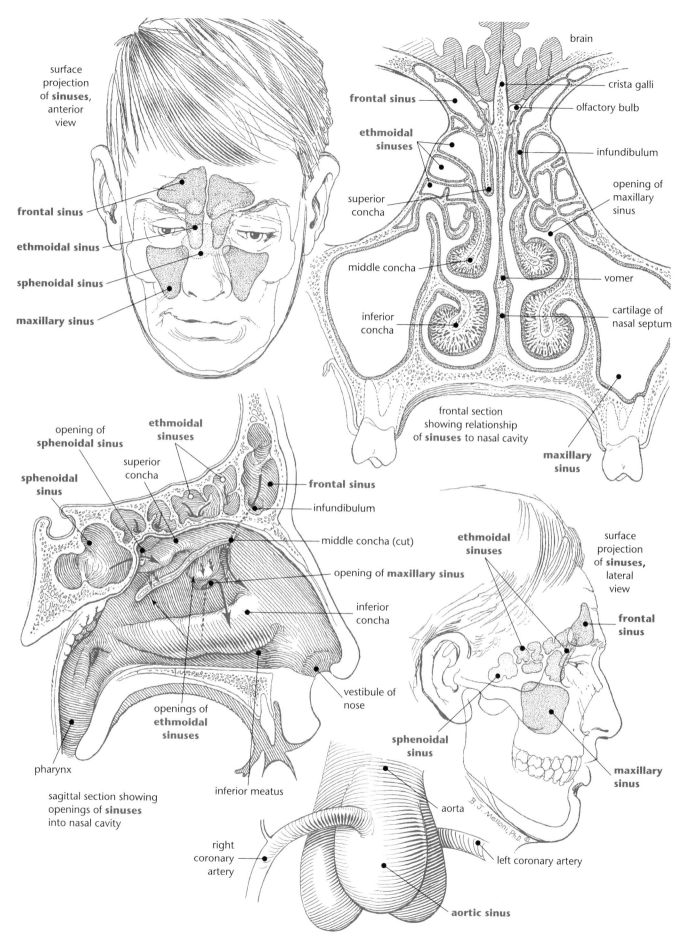

surface projection of **sinuses**, anterior view

frontal sinus

ethmoidal sinus

sphenoidal sinus

maxillary sinus

brain

crista galli

frontal sinus

olfactory bulb

ethmoidal sinuses

infundibulum

superior concha

opening of maxillary sinus

middle concha

vomer

inferior concha

cartilage of nasal septum

frontal section showing relationship of **sinuses** to nasal cavity

maxillary sinus

opening of **sphenoidal sinus**

ethmoidal sinuses

sphenoidal sinus

superior concha

frontal sinus

infundibulum

middle concha (cut)

opening of **maxillary sinus**

inferior concha

vestibule of nose

openings of **ethmoidal sinuses**

pharynx

inferior meatus

sagittal section showing openings of **sinuses** into nasal cavity

surface projection of **sinuses**, lateral view

ethmoidal sinuses

frontal sinus

sphenoidal sinus

maxillary sinus

B. J. Melloni, Ph.D. ©

aorta

right coronary artery

left coronary artery

aortic sinus

S33

sinus ■ sinus

S

frontal s. One of the two air spaces in the frontal bone, just above the eyebrows, that opens into the upper part of the nasal cavity on either side.

lactiferous s. The normal enlargement of a milk (lactiferous) duct within the breast, just before it enters the nipple. It serves as a reservoir of milk.

maxillary s. One of two large air cavities within the upper jaw (maxilla), under the cheekbone, on either side of the nasal cavity, into which it opens. Also called maxillary antrum.

nasal s.'s See paranasal sinuses.

paranasal s.'s The air chambers (frontal, maxillary, ethmoidal, sphenoidal) situated within the bones of the face; they surround, and open into, the nasal cavity and are lined with mucous membrane that is continuous with that of the nasal cavity. Also called nasal sinuses.

pilonidal s. An abnormal pit or tract containing hairs, usually occurring in the upper part of the cleft between the buttocks. Also called pilonidal fistula.

scleral venous s. A ringlike channel or sinus in the eye at the junction of the cornea and sclera; it drains the excess aqueous humor of the anterior chamber of the eye into the anterior ciliary veins. Also called Schlemm's canal; venous sinus of sclera.

sphenoidal s. One of a paired collection of irregular air spaces situated within the sphenoid bone, behind and above the nasal cavity, and separated from its fellow by a thin bony plate at the midline. It opens into the upper part of the nasal cavity.

tarsal s. A sinus or groove situated between the ankle bone (talus) and heel bone (calcaneus); it contains the interosseous talocalcaneal ligament. Also called tarsal canal.

tonsillar s. See tonsillar fossa, under fossa.

s. venosus A collecting reservoir for the principal veins of the embryonic heart; it is attached to the back wall of the primitive atrium and receives blood primarily from the umbilical and vitelline veins.

venous s. of sclera See scleral venous sinus.

sinusitis (si-nŭ-si'tis) Inflammation of the mucous membrane of a sinus, especially of a paranasal sinus.

sinusoid (si'nŭ-soid) **1.** Resembling a sinus. **2.** One of several thin-walled irregular channels for the passage of blood within certain organs (e.g., the spleen, liver, bone marrow).

site (sit) A location.

active s. The area of an enzyme molecule that binds a substrate (substance that undergoes chemical change), initiating a reaction.

allosteric s. The region of an enzyme molecule at which binds an effector (substance that either inhibits or accelerates the enzymatic action without undergoing chemical change).

immunologically privileged s. See privileged site.

privileged s. An area of the body (e.g., brain, cornea) lacking lymphatic drainage and in which a tissue graft (antigen) can be placed without inciting an immune response. Also called immunologically privileged site.

receptor s. A point on a cell surface where viruses, hormones, or other molecules attach.

sitosterol (si-tos'ter-ol) Any of several widely distributed plant sterols, or a mixture of such sterols.

situs (si'tus) Latin for location.

s. inversus Congenital anomaly in which internal organs are located on the side of the body opposite the normal.

skatole (skat'ōl) A compound formed in the intestine as a result of decomposition of protein; found in the feces.

skein (skān) A length of coiled thread; applied to the coiled threads of chromatin seen in the prophase stage of cell division (mitosis).

skeletal (skel'ĕ-tal) Relating to the skeleton.

skeleton (skel'ĕ-ton) **1.** The internal framework of vertebrates composed of bones and cartilages, serving to support the soft tissues. **2.** The bones of the body considered as a whole.

appendicular s. The bones of the limbs and of the shoulder and pelvic girdles.

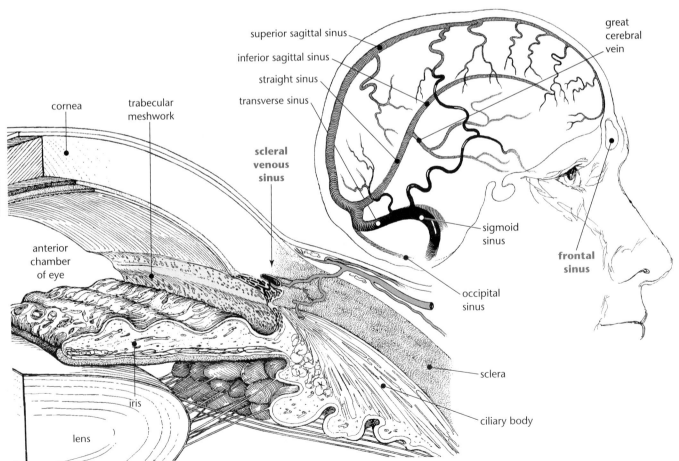

S

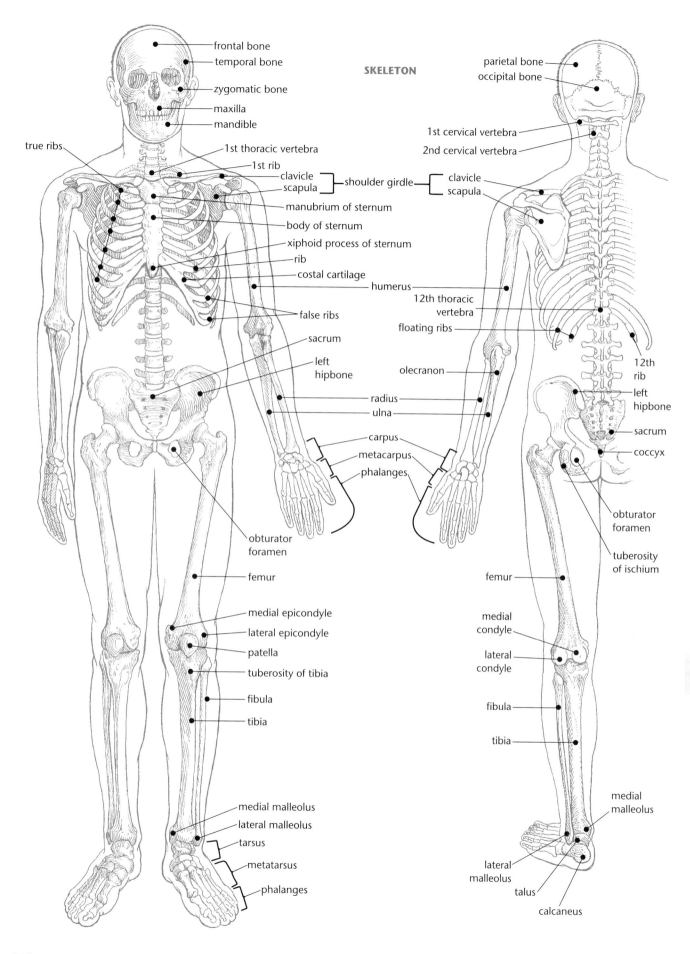

frontal bone
temporal bone
zygomatic bone
maxilla
mandible

parietal bone
occipital bone

true ribs
1st thoracic vertebra
1st rib
clavicle
scapula
manubrium of sternum
body of sternum
xiphoid process of sternum
rib
costal cartilage
false ribs
sacrum
left hipbone

1st cervical vertebra
2nd cervical vertebra
clavicle
scapula

humerus
12th thoracic vertebra
floating ribs

shoulder girdle

olecranon
radius
ulna
carpus
metacarpus
phalanges
obturator foramen
femur
medial epicondyle
lateral epicondyle
patella
tuberosity of tibia
fibula
tibia
medial malleolus
lateral malleolus
tarsus
metatarsus
phalanges

12th rib
left hipbone
sacrum
coccyx
obturator foramen
tuberosity of ischium
femur
medial condyle
lateral condyle
fibula
tibia
medial malleolus
lateral malleolus
talus
calcaneus

S

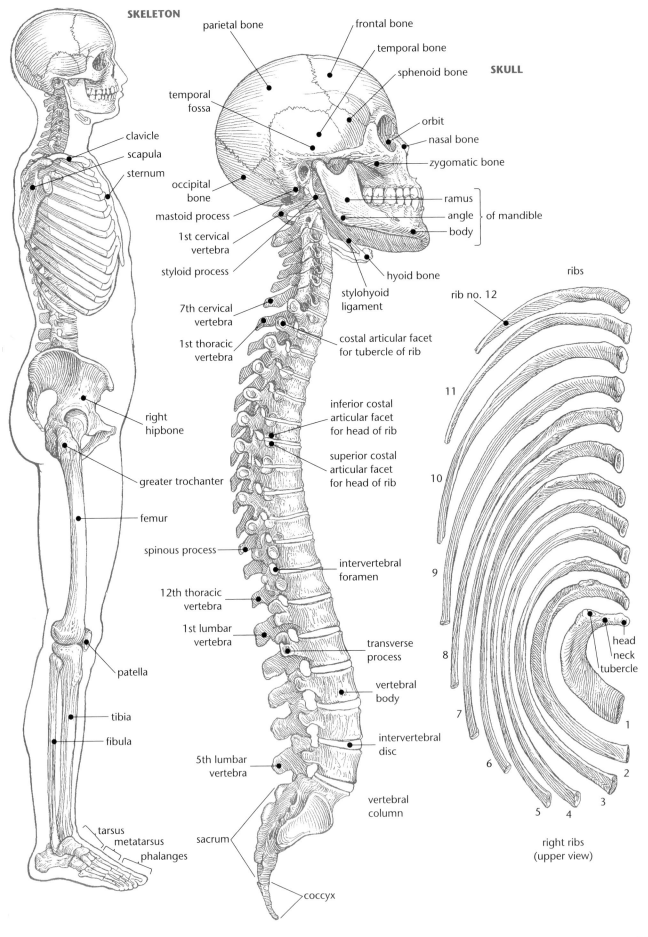

SKELETON

SKULL

parietal bone

frontal bone

temporal bone

sphenoid bone

temporal fossa

orbit

nasal bone

zygomatic bone

clavicle

scapula

sternum

occipital bone

mastoid process

1st cervical vertebra

styloid process

ramus
angle   } of mandible
body

hyoid bone

stylohyoid ligament

7th cervical vertebra

1st thoracic vertebra

costal articular facet for tubercle of rib

right hipbone

inferior costal articular facet for head of rib

superior costal articular facet for head of rib

greater trochanter

femur

spinous process

intervertebral foramen

12th thoracic vertebra

1st lumbar vertebra

transverse process

patella

vertebral body

tibia

fibula

intervertebral disc

5th lumbar vertebra

vertebral column

tarsus
metatarsus
phalanges

sacrum

coccyx

ribs

rib no. 12

11

10

9

8

7

6

5   4

3

2

1

head
neck
tubercle

right ribs (upper view)

S

skeleton ■ skeleton

S36

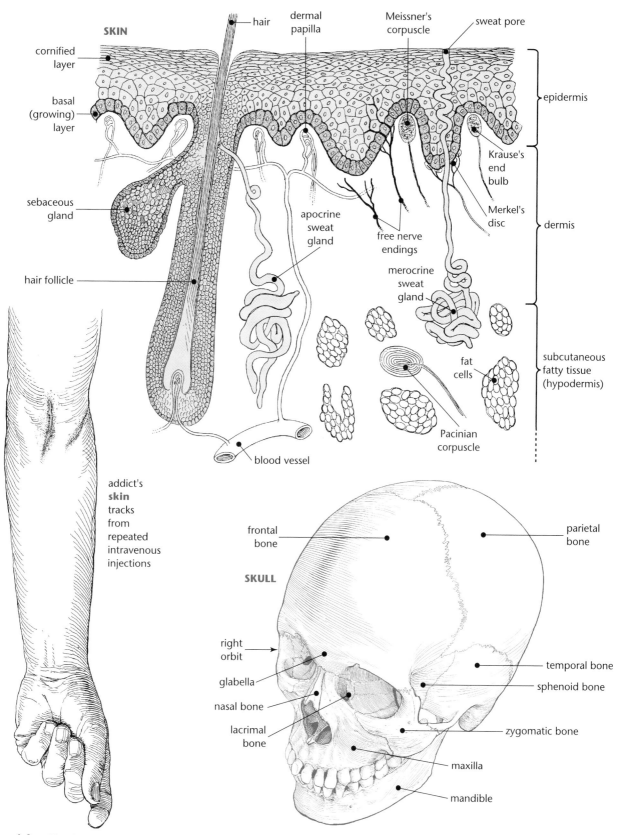

SKIN

cornified layer

basal (growing) layer

sebaceous gland

hair follicle

hair

dermal papilla

Meissner's corpuscle

sweat pore

epidermis

Krause's end bulb

Merkel's disc

dermis

apocrine sweat gland

free nerve endings

merocrine sweat gland

subcutaneous fatty tissue (hypodermis)

fat cells

Pacinian corpuscle

blood vessel

addict's **skin** tracks from repeated intravenous injections

SKULL

frontal bone

parietal bone

right orbit

glabella

nasal bone

lacrimal bone

temporal bone

sphenoid bone

zygomatic bone

maxilla

mandible

S

axial s. The skull and vertebral column.

skeneitis, skenitis (ske-ni′tis) Inflammation of the paraurethral glands (in the female urethra).

skin (skin) The covering of the body, composed of a thin outer layer (epidermis) and a thicker, deeper layer (dermis).

    alligator s. See ichthyosis.

    fish s. See ichthyosis.

piebald s. See vitiligo.

skin popping (skin pop′ing) Slang expression denoting the illegal intradermal injection of a narcotic drug.

skin writing (skin rīt′ing) See dermatographism.

skull (skul) The bony framework of the head; includes the bones encasing the brain and the bones of the face. Also called cranium.

    tower s. See oxycephaly.

skullcap (skul'kap) See calvaria.

sleep (slēp) The natural, periodic recurrence of a state of rest in which consciousness is temporarily interrupted.

non–rapid eye movement (NREM) s. The dreamless period of sleep during which breathing is slow and deep, heart rate and blood pressure are low and regular, and brain waves in the electroencephalogram (EEG) are slow and of high voltage. Also called NREM sleep; non-REM sleep.

non-REM s. See non–rapid eye movement sleep.

NREM s. See non–rapid eye movement sleep.

paroxysmal s. See narcolepsy.

rapid eye movement (REM) s. A stage of sleep during which both eyes move rapidly in unison under the closed eyelids, the brain waves in the electroencephalogram (EEG) are fast and of low voltage, heart rate and respiration are irregular, and there is a higher threshold of arousal; it is the stage of sleep during which dreaming is thought to occur. Also called REM sleep.

REM s. See rapid eye movement sleep.

twilight s. State in which memory of pain is abolished, induced by injection of a mixture of morphine and scopolamine; formerly used in childbirth.

sleeplessness (slēp'lis-nes) Insomnia.

sleeptalking (slēp-tok'ing) See somniloquism.

sleepwalking (slēp-wok'ing) See somnambulism.

slide (slīd) Glass plate for mounting specimens for inspection under the microscope.

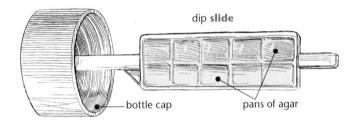

dip **slide**

bottle cap

pans of agar

sling (sling) A device suspended from the neck for immobilizing and supporting an injured arm or hand; usually made of a triangular bandage, but may also consist of other suitable band or material.

sling

slit (slit) A narrow opening or cleft.

vulvar s. The cleft between the major lips (labia majora) of the vulva.

slitlamp (slit'lamp) See biomicroscope.

slough (sluf) Dead tissue separated, or in the process of separating, from its living base.

sludge (sluj) A thick sediment.

sludging (sluj'ing) A phenomenon occurring in acute inflammation in which red blood cells form heavy aggregates (rouleaux) within the blood vessels, thus decreasing the rate of blood flow.

smallpox (smawl'poks) Severe contagious disease with incubation period of 14 to 17 days; at the onset symptoms include headache, fever, and abdominal and muscular pain; after 3 to 4 days, these symptoms lessen and the eruptive stage begins, with painful ulcers in the oral mucosa and papules developing into blisters throughout the body; remains infectious until scabs fall off (in about 3 weeks), leaving permanent markings on the skin (pock marks). Also called variola.

smear (smēr) A specimen spread thinly on a glass slide for examination under the microscope; it may or may not be fixed and stained prior to examination.

buccal s. A smear obtained by lightly scraping the inside of the cheek. Used to obtain cells for examination of chromosomes.

cervical s. General term for specimens obtained from the uterine cervix or cervical canal, as for the detection of infection, cancer, or infertility, or for hormonal evaluation.

cytologic s. A thin layer of cells spread on a glass slide, then fixed and stained for examination under a microscope. Also called cytosmear.

FGT cytologic s. Female genital tract cytologic smear; any cytologic smear obtained from the female genital tract.

Pap s., Papanicolaou s. A smear containing cells from the vaginal wall and the uterine cervix. See also Bethesda System of Classification, under system.

VCE s. A cytologic smear obtained from the vagina, cervix, and cervical canal (endocervix), spread separately on one slide in that order, and fixed; used for identification of the sites of disease.

smegma (smeg'mah) Cheesy material composed of desquamated epidermal cells and sebaceous secretions that tends to accumulate beneath the foreskin (prepuce) as a result of poor hygiene.

smell (smel) To perceive a scent by means of the olfactory apparatus.

smog (smog) Air pollution resulting from the combustion of various materials with production of noxious by-products.

smoke (smōk) A suspension of particulate matter in the atmosphere resulting from combustion.

mainstream s. Smoke produced and inhaled by a person smoking cigarettes or any other tobacco product, creating a health hazard for the smoker.

passive s. See secondhand smoke.

secondhand s. Smoke released to the environment by a smoker of cigarettes or any other tobacco product; it creates a health hazard for nonsmokers, especially perinatal and postnatal infants, pregnant women, debilitated persons (especially those with respiratory diseases), and the elderly. Also called passive smoke; sidestream smoke.

sidestream s. See secondhand smoke.

snap (snap) A sharp sound; applied to heart sounds.

opening s. A high-pitched sound heard during diastole, caused by opening of an abnormal mitral valve of the heart in mitral stenosis.

snare (snār) An instrument with a wire loop for removing a polyp or tumor by tightening the loop around its base.

sneeze (snēz) The forceful expulsion of air through the nose and mouth.

snore (snōr) A raspy sound occurring as air is inhaled during sleep; produced by vibration of the soft palate and uvula, usually due to partial obstruction to the airflow; causes include inflammation of upper respiratory tract, deformities of involved structures, nasal injuries or polyps, and, among children, enlargement of the tonsils

S

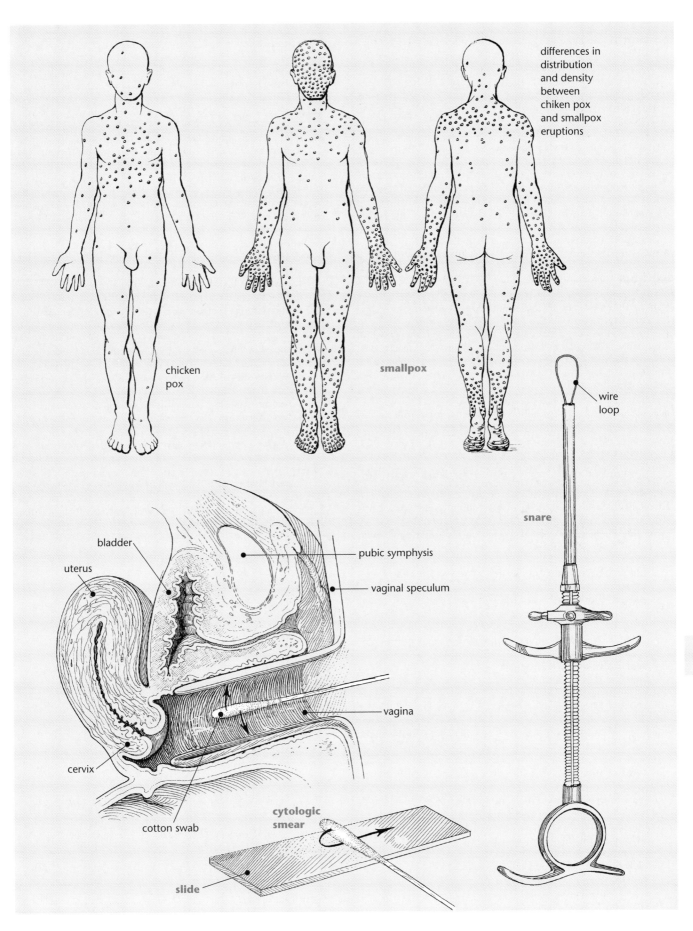

differences in distribution and density between chiken pox and smallpox eruptions

chicken pox

smallpox

wire loop

snare

bladder

uterus

pubic symphysis

vaginal speculum

vagina

cervix

cotton swab

cytologic smear

slide

S

S39

and adenoids; may be caused also by relaxation of the musculature by sedation (e.g., by medication or alcohol intake).

snorting (snort'ing) Slang expression for the act of inhaling an illegal drug, such as cocaine or heroin.

snuff (snuf) Any powder, especially pulverized tobacco, that is taken in through the nostrils.

snuffles (snuf'flz) Noisy breathing caused by obstructed nasal passages; when occurring in newborn infants, it is usually caused by congenital syphilis.

SOAP Acronym for Subjective, Objective, Assessment, and Plan; a common format used for recording daily progress notes in a problem-oriented medical record of a patient. *S* indicates the physician's overall subjective view of the patient; *O* includes data that are objectively gathered, such as vital signs, pertinent physical examination, and laboratory and other test results; *A* refers to assessment or evaluation of the above data; *P* designates the treatment plan, including medication changes, new laboratory orders, or any new orders. See also problem-oriented record, under record.

soap (sōp) The salt of a fatty acid with potassium or sodium; a cleansing agent.

soapstone (sōp'ston) See talc.

sociology (so-se-ol'o-je) The science concerned with group relationships, patterns of collective behavior, and social organizations.

　medical s. *(a)* The study of the social determinants and effects of health and disease. *(b)* The study of the social structure of medical institutions or professions.

sociomedical (so-se-o-med'i-kal) Relating to the interrelations of the practice of medicine and social welfare.

sociopath (so'se-o-path) Former designation for a person afflicted with an antisocial personality disorder.

socket (sok'et) A cavity or hollow into which a compatible or corresponding part fits, such as the socket of the eye, tooth, joint, or stump.

　adjustable s. A socket on a prosthesis that can be adjusted to comfortably accommodate physical changes in an amputated stump.

　dry s. A condition sometimes occurring after extraction of a tooth in which the blood clot in the socket disintegrates, leading to a dry appearance of the exposed bone socket, followed by secondary infection; it is more prevalent after traumatic extractions and is often accompanied by severe pain.

　eye s. See orbit.

　hip s. See acetabulum.

　infected alveolar s. See alveolitis.

　partial contact s. A socket on a prosthesis designed not to make full contact with the amputated stump.

　plug fit s. A snug-fitting socket for above-knee prosthesis in which the body weight is supported entirely by the upper region of the thigh.

　septic alveolar s. See alveolitis.

　suction s. A socket for above-knee prosthesis that provides suction to maintain suspension.

　tooth s. The elongated cavity in the alveolar bone of the jaw in which the root of a tooth is embedded; it can vary in size, shape, and depth according to the tooth it accommodates. In the adult, there are 16 sockets in the lower jaw (mandible) and 16 sockets in the upper jaw (maxilla).

　total contact s. A socket for above-knee prosthesis that provides complete contact with the amputated stump, resulting in greater sensory awareness to facilitate movement.

soda (so'dah) General term commonly used to designate sodium bicarbonate, sodium carbonate, and sodium hydroxide.

　baking s. See sodium bicarbonate.

　benzoate of s. See sodium benzoate.

　bicarbonate s. See sodium bicarbonate.

　caustic s. See sodium hydroxide.

　sal s. See sodium carbonate.

　washing s. See sodium carbonate.

sodium (so'de-um) A soft metallic element; symbol Na, atomic number 11, atomic weight 22.99.

　s. benzoate A crystalline powder used as a food preservative and in the manufacture of pharmaceuticals. Also called benzoate of soda.

　s. bicarbonate A crystalline compound with a slight alkaline taste, used as a gastric antacid. Also called baking soda; bicarbonate of soda.

　s. bisulfite Water-soluble powder used as a preservative, disinfectant, and as an antioxidant in many pharmaceutical preparations.

　s. borate A crystalline compound used as a retardant in dental casting products and in the manufacture of pharmaceuticals and detergents. Also called borax.

　s. carbonate *(a)* A powdery compound used as a reagent and in water treatment. *(b)* Any of several hydrated forms (e.g., washing soda, sal soda).

　s. chloride Water-soluble crystalline compound used medicinally in solution. Also called table salt; common salt.

　s. citrate Water-soluble granular powder used as a blood anticoagulant.

　s. cyanide A highly poisonous compound, used as a test reagent for the function of chemoreceptors and in many industrial processes.

　s. diatrizoate A radiopaque, water-soluble powder, and organic compound of iodine used in excretory radiography of the urinary tract.

　s. fluoride Compound used in the prevention of dental caries, in drinking water, and as a topical application on the teeth.

　s. hydroxide An alkaline, water-soluble compound used in the chemical and pharmaceutical industries. Also called caustic soda.

　s. iodide Crystalline powder used as an iodine supplement.

　s. levothyroxine The sodium salt of the natural isomer of thyroxin, used in thyroid replacement therapy.

　s. nitrite Compound used in meat curing and preserving, as a reagent in analytical chemistry, and as an antidote for cyanide poisoning.

　s. perborate Compound used in solution as a mouthwash and in powder form in toothpaste.

　s. phosphate Crystalline, water-soluble sodium salt of phosphoric acid, used as a laxative.

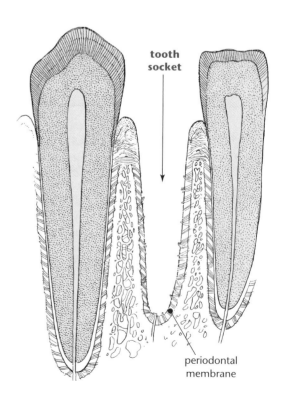

tooth socket

periodontal membrane

S

s. salicylate Compound used as an anti-inflammatory, analgesic, and to reduce fever.

s. tetradecyl sulfate A waxy compound used as a sclerosing agent in sclerotherapy (e.g., in the treatment of varicose veins).

s. thiosulfate A crystalline compound used as an antidote in cyanide poisoning and to prevent ringworm infections.

sodoku (so'do-koo) See rat-bite fever, under fever.

sodomy (sod'o-me) Sexual practice in which the penis is introduced into the anus or mouth of another person, male or female.

sol (sol) A colloidal solution that is capable of setting into a gel.

solar (so'lar) Resembling the stylized representation of the sun and its rays; applied to a plexus (solar plexus) that has radiating nerve fibers.

sole (sōl) The bottom (plantar surface) of the foot.

solid (sol'id) Of a definite shape; not liquid or gaseous.

solubility (sol-u-bil'i-te) Capacity for being dissolved.

soluble (sol'u-bl) Capable of being dissolved.

solute (sol'yūt) The substance dissolved in a solution.

solution (so-lu'shun) 1. A mixture of a gaseous, liquid, or solid substance (solute) with a liquid or noncrystalline solid (solvent), and from which the dissolved substance can be recovered. 2. The process of making such a mixture.

Benedict's s. A water solution of sodium carbonate, sodium sulfate, and copper sulfate; used in urinalysis to detect the presence of reducing substances in the urine.

Burow's s. A water solution of aluminum subacetate and glacial acetic acid; used as an antiseptic and astringent.

Dakin's s. A solution of sodium hypochlorite buffered with sodium bicarbonate; used as an antiseptic.

hyperbaric s. A solution having a higher specific gravity than a standard of reference (e.g., in spinal anesthesia, one with a specific gravity higher than that of cerebrospinal fluid).

hypertonic s. A solution having higher osmotic pressure than a standard of reference (e.g., a solution of sodium chloride that has a higher osmotic pressure than blood plasma); often denotes a solution that, when surrounding a cell, causes water to leave the cell through the semipermeable cell membrane.

hypobaric s. A solution having a lower specific gravity than a standard of reference (e.g., in spinal anesthesia, one with a specific gravity lower than that of cerebrospinal fluid).

hypotonic s. A solution having a lower osmotic pressure than a standard of reference (e.g., sodium chloride solution that has a lower osmotic pressure than that of blood plasma); often denotes a solution that, when surrounding a cell, causes water to enter the cell through the semipermeable cell membrane.

iodine s. A solution containing approximately 2% iodine and 2 ½% sodium chloride in water; generally applied to superficial lacerations to prevent bacterial infections.

Locke's s. An aqueous solution of sodium, calcium, and potassium chlorides with sodium bicarbonate and glucose; used for irrigation of tissues during laboratory experiments.

Locke-Ringer s. An aqueous solution of sodium, calcium, potassium, and magnesium chlorides with sodium bicarbonate and glucose; used as a test solution in physiologic and pharmacologic experiments.

Lugol's iodine s. A deep brown solution containing iodine, potassium iodide, and water; used as a therapeutic source of iodine, as a fixative of histologic stains, and as a testing solution for cancer of the cervix and vaginal mucosa. Also called strong iodine solution.

normal s. (N) A solution containing 1 gram equivalent weight of the dissolved substance in each liter of solution.

Ringer's s. A solution containing sodium, potassium, and calcium chlorides in recently boiled distilled water; it resembles blood serum in its salt components; used topically for burns and wounds. Also called Ringer's mixture.

saline s. A solution of any salt, especially of table salt (sodium chloride), in purified water. Commonly called saline.

saturated s. (sat. sol., sat. soln.) A solution containing the maximum amount of solute that a given amount of solvent can dissolve.

sclerosing s. A solution of an irritating substance that causes scarring of tissues; used in sclerotherapy (e.g., to obliterate a varicose vein).

standard s. A solution of known concentration, used as a basis of comparison.

strong iodine s. See Lugol's iodine solution.

supersaturated s. A solution containing a greater amount of the solute than a given amount of solvent would dissolve at ordinary temperatures.

test s. Any standard solution of a specified substance used in chemical analysis or testing.

Tyrode's s. A modified Locke's solution; it contains sodium, potassium, calcium, and magnesium chlorides with sodium biphosphate, sodium bicarbonate, glucose, and water; used to irrigate the abdominal cavity and in laboratory work.

volumetric s. (VS) A standard solution containing a specified quantity of a substance dissolved in 1 liter of water.

solvate (sol'vāt) Compound formed by the loose and reversible combination of the dissolving substance (solvent) and the substance dissolved (solute).

solve (solv) Latin for dissolve.

solvent (sol'vent) A substance, usually liquid, that causes another substance to pass into solution.

SELECTED SOLVENTS

NAME	MOLECULAR WEIGHT	MELTING POINT °C	BOILING POINT °C
water	18.02	0.0	100.0
methanol	32.04	-97.7	64.7
acetaldehyde	44.05	-123.0	20.4
ethanol	46.07	-114.1	78.3
acetone	58.05	-94.7	56.3
acetic acid	60.05	16.7	117.9
cyclopentane	70.13	-93.8	49.3
benzene	78.12	5.5	80.1
hexane	86.17	-95.3	68.7
pyruvic acid	88.06	13.6	165.0
toluene	92.14	-94.9	110.6
phenol	94.12	40.9	181.8
caprylic acid	144.22	16.5	239.9
engenol	164.20	9.2	255.0
oleic acid	282.47	13.4	360.0

soma (so'mah) 1. The body, distinguished from the mind. 2. All the body's tissues, except its germ cells.

somatesthesia (so-mat-es-the'ze-ah) Body awareness. Also called somesthesia.

somatesthetic (so-mat-es-thet'ik) Relating to somatesthesia.

somatic (so-mat'ik) 1. Relating to the body as distinct from the mind. 2. Relating to the wall of the body cavities rather than the organs; parietal rather than visceral.

somatization (so-mah-ti-za'shun) The unconscious conversion of anxiety into physical symptoms.

somato- Combining form meaning body.

somatoform (so-mat'o-form) Having features of organic disease; applied to certain psychogenic symptoms.

somatogenic (so-mah-to-jen'ik) Of bodily origin; originating in the body cells as opposed to the psyche.

S

somatology (so-mah-tol′o-je) The study of the human body in relation to form and function.

somatomammotropin (so-mah-to-mam-o-tro′pin) See human placental lactogen, under lactogen.

   human chorionic s. See human placental lactogen, under lactogen.

somatomedin (so-mah-to-me′din) An insulin-like polypeptide produced in the liver and probably other organs (e.g., the kidney); released into the blood in response to growth hormone stimulation, it mediates some of the hormone's actions, especially on cartilage, and promotes synthesis of protein, DNA, and RNA.

somatometry (so-mah-tom′ĕ-tre) Measurement of the body.

somatoplasm (so-mat′o-plazm) The totality of protoplasm of all cells (except germ cells) of the body.

somatopsychic (so-mah-to-si′kik) Denoting the effects of the body on the mind, such as mental symptoms produced by a physical illness.

somatopsychosis (so-mah-to-si-ko′sis) An emotional disorder associated with physical disease.

somatosexual (so-mah-to-seks′u-al) Relating to the physical sexual (as opposed to psychosexual) characteristics of an individual, usually referring to physical manifestations of sexual development.

somatostatin (so-mah-to-stat′in) Peptide hormone found in the central nervous system, stomach, small intestine, and islets of Langerhans (in the pancreas); it inhibits release of growth hormone, insulin, and glucagon. Also called somatotropin release-inhibiting factor.

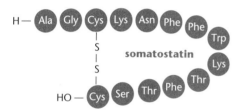

somatostatinoma (so-mah-to-stat′ĭ-no′mah) A somatostatin-secreting tumor of the pancreas associated with diabetes and steatorrhea.

somatotherapy (so-mah-to-ther′ah-pe) Treatment of physical (as opposed to psychiatric) illness.

somatotropic, somatotrophic (so-mah-to-trop′ik, so-mah-to-trōf′ik) Stimulating physical growth.

somatotropin (so-mah-to-tro′pin) See growth hormone, under hormone.

   recombinant bovine s. (rBST) A synthetic version of the naturally occurring pituitary hormone in cows, given to dairy cows to increase milk production. It differs structurally from the human hormone and is considered biologically inactive in humans. Also called bovine growth hormone.

somatotype (so-mat′o-tip) Body type; the physical characteristics of the body.

somatrem (so′mah-trem) A preparation of human growth hormone (hGH), used to treat short stature in children caused by hormone deficiency.

somesthesia (so-mes-the′ze-ah) See somatesthesia.

somite (so′mit) In embryology, one of paired, segmented blocks of epithelioid cells on either side of the neural tube of the embryo; they give rise to connective tissue, bone, muscle, and skin; the size of the embryo may be expressed in terms of the number of somites.

somnambulism (som-nam′bu-lizm) Walking while asleep without any recollection upon awakening. Also called sleepwalking; noctambulism.

somnambulist (som-nam′bu-list) A sleepwalker.

somniloquism, somniloquence (som-nil′o-kwizm, som-nil′o-kwens) Talking while asleep or in a condition resembling sleep. Also called sleeptalking.

somnolence, somnolency (som′no-lens, som′no-len-se) Drowsiness.

somnolent (som′no-lent) Drowsy.

sone (sōn) A unit of loudness; the intensity of a pure tone of 1000 cycles per second at 40 decibels above a person's threshold of audibility.

sonic (son′ik) Relating to sound.

sonicate (son′ĭ-kāt) To expose to high-frequency sound in order to break up a suspension of cells.

sonogram (so′nŏ-gram) See ultrasonogram.

sonograph (so′nŏ-graf) See ultrasonograph.

sonography (so-nog′rah-fe) See ultrasonography.

sonolucent (so-no-loo′sent) See anechoic.

sopor (so′por) Unusually deep sleep.

soporific (so-po-rif′ik) Inducing sleep.

soporous (so′por-us) Relating to an unusually deep sleep.

sorbefacient (sor-bĕ-fa′shent) Facilitating absorption.

sorbic acid (sor′bik as′id) Compound that inhibits the growth of yeasts and molds on food; used as a preservative.

sorbitol (sor′bĭ-tol) A sweet crystalline substance occurring in the berries of the mountain ash tree and made synthetically; used in the preparation of ascorbic acid and, medicinally, to promote bowel movements.

sordes (sor′dēz) A dark crust formed on the lips and gums of debilitated patients with prolonged low-grade fever.

sore (sōr) **1.** Common term for any open skin lesion. **2.** Aching.

   bed s. See decubitus ulcer, under ulcer.

   canker s. See aphthous ulcer, under ulcer.

   cold s. See herpes febrilis, under herpes.

   hard s. See chancre.

   oriental s. See cutaneous leishmaniasis, under leishmaniasis.

   pressure s. See decubitus ulcer, under ulcer.

   soft s. See chancroid.

souffle (soo′fl) A sound, heard on auscultation, that has a soft blowing quality.

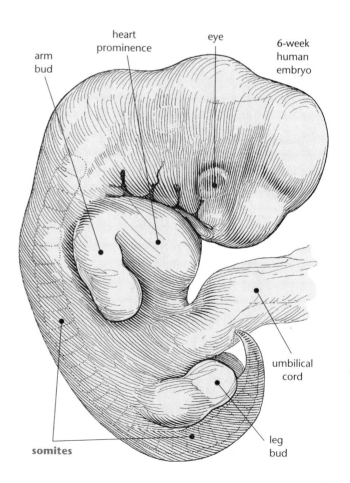

S

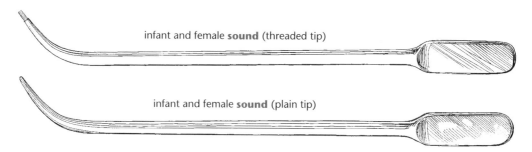

infant and female **sound** (threaded tip)

infant and female **sound** (plain tip)

fetal s. A blowing, whistling sound synchronous with the fetal heartbeat, caused by blood flowing through the umbilical vessels when the cord is subject to torsion, tension, or pressure. Also called umbilical souffle.

mammary s. A blowing sound heard at the medial border of a breast during late pregnancy and lactation; attributed to a change of dynamics in blood flow through the internal thoracic (mammary) artery.

placental s. See uterine souffle.

umbilical s. See fetal souffle.

uterine s. A sound heard over the uterus in late pregnancy, synchronous with the maternal heartbeat; caused by the blood flow through engorged uterine blood vessels; also may be heard in nonpregnant women with large myomatous tumors of the uterus or enlarged ovaries. Also called placental souffle.

sound (sownd) **1.** The sensation perceived by the organ of hearing. **2.** A cylindrical, usually curved, instrument for exploring body cavities or for enlarging tubular structures. **3.** Healthy.

cannon s. See bruit de canon, under bruit.

closing-valve s.'s The sounds of the normal heartbeat made by the closing of two sets of heart valves (atrioventricular and semilunar), heard on auscultation of the heart and likened to the sound "lub-dub." See also heart sounds.

friction s. A grating sound heard on auscultation, caused by the rubbing of two inflamed, roughened surfaces. Also called friction rub.

heart s.'s Sounds heard over the area of the heart: first sound (S1), the normal sound (likened to the sound "lub") made by simultaneous closing of the atrioventricular valves (tricuspid and mitral) located between the atria and ventricles; second sound (S2), the normal sound (likened to the sound "dub") made by simultaneous closing of the semilunar valves (pulmonic and aortic) located between the ventricles and the large blood vessels; third sound (S3), sound heard during the rapid filling of the ventricles, a normal sound in young persons but generally an abnormality in older persons; fourth sound (S4), sound coinciding with contraction of the atria, rarely heard in normal hearts.

soya (soi′ah) The seed of the soybean plant.

soybean (soi′bēn) A climbing plant of Asia *Glycine soya* or *Glycine hispida;* its seeds are rich in protein and low in starch content; used as a substitute milk for people allergic to cow's milk.

space (spās) Any bodily area or volume between specified boundaries; a delimited three-dimensional area.

alveolar dead s. See dead space.

anatomic dead s. See dead space.

antecubital s. See cubital fossa, under fossa.

Bowman's s. See urinary space of glomerular capsule.

corneal s.'s The interlamellar spaces of the cornea, between approximately 240 flattened superimposed lamellae of the corneal stroma (substantia propria); they contain a small amount of ground substance, in which are found fibroblasts.

dead s. *(a)* A space or cavity inadvertently left after improper or incomplete closure of surgical or injury wounds. *(b)* The portion of the respiratory tract from the nostrils to the terminal bronchioles, where no gaseous exchange of oxygen and carbon dioxide can take place. Also called anatomic dead space; alveolar dead space.

Douglas' s. See rectouterine pouch, under pouch.

epidural s. The space between the dura mater of the spinal cord and the periosteum of the vertebral canal (foramen); it contains loose areolar and fibrous tissue, as well as a plexus of veins.

episcleral s. The space between the sclera and the fascial sheath of the eyeball.

epitympanic s. The upper portion of the middle ear chamber above the level of the upper part of the eardrum (tympanic membrane); it contains the head of the malleus and the body of the incus, two of the three middle ear ossicles.

s.'s of Fontana Irregular spaces in the anterior chamber of the eye, at the junction of the iris and cornea (iridocorneal angle); it consists of trabecular tissue that permits aqueous humor of the anterior chamber to drain out of the eyeball by way of the venous sinus of the sclera.

freeway s. See interocclusal distance, under distance.

glomerular s. See urinary space of glomerular capsule.

hypothenar s. See palmar space.

S

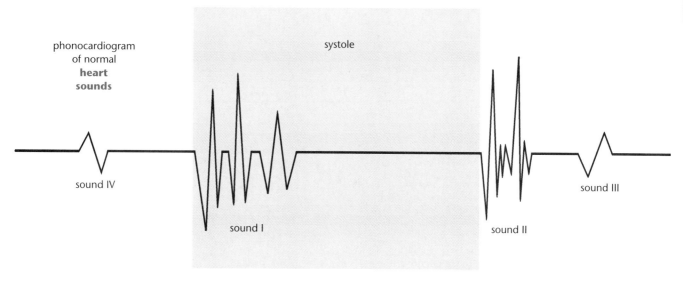

phonocardiogram of normal **heart sounds**

systole

sound IV

sound I

sound II

sound III

intercostal s. (ICS) The intervening space between adjoining ribs; the breadth is greater on the ventral surface and also between the upper ribs, in contrast to the lower ones.

interproximal s. The space between the proximal surfaces of adjacent teeth in the dental arch.

interradicular s. The space between the roots of a multirooted tooth, occupied by bony septum and the periodontal membrane.

intervillous s. The cavernous space in the placenta in which maternal blood bathes the placental villi, thus allowing exchange of materials between the fetal and maternal circulations; it is bounded by the chorionic membrane on the fetal side and by the decidua basalis on the maternal side.

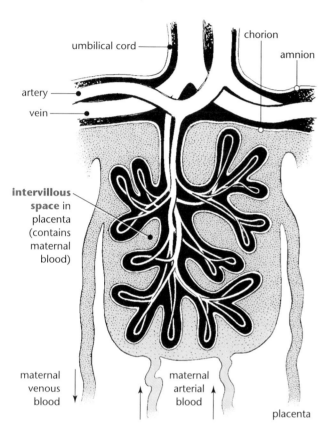

joint s. The space in a joint between two articulating surfaces.

lumbar s.'s *Superior lumbar s.,* see Grynfeltt-Lesshaft triangle, under triangle. *Inferior lumbar s.,* see lumbar triangle, under triangle.

marrow s. See medullary space.

s. medicine See space medicine, under medicine.

medullary s. The marrow-containing central cavity in spongy (cancellous) bone. Also called marrow space.

palmar s. A large fascial space in the hand between the thenar and hypothenar eminences, divided by a fibrous septum into the middle palmar space (toward the little finger) and the thenar space (toward the thumb). Also called hypothenar space.

pharyngeal s. The space within the pharynx (i.e., within the nasopharynx, oropharynx, and laryngopharynx).

pleural s. The potential space between the visceral and parietal pleura comprising the closed sac enveloping each lung.

postnasal s. See nasopharynx.

rectouterine s. See rectouterine pouch, under pouch.

retroperitoneal s. The space between the posterior parietal peritoneum and the muscles and bones of the posterior abdominal wall; it is occupied by the kidneys, adrenal glands, pancreas, ureters, duodenum, and ascending and descending colon, as well as by nerves and vessels.

retropubic s. The extraperitoneal space containing loose connective tissue separating the lower part of the bladder from the pos-

terosuperior part of the pubis, below the level where the peritoneum reflecting off the anterior abdominal wall joins the top part of the bladder. Also called Retzius' space.

Retzius' s. See retropubic space.

subarachnoid s. The space containing cerebrospinal fluid (CSF) between the arachnoid membrane and the underlying pia mater that closely follows the contours of the brain and spinal cord; it contains a delicate meshwork of fibrous trabeculae extending from the arachnoid to the pia mater and appears throughout the entire subarachnoid space except below the level of the second sacral vertebra.

subdural s. The very narrow or potential space between the dura mater and the arachnoid covering the brain and spinal cord; it contains only a small amount of fluid, sufficient to moisten the opposing surfaces of the two membranes (meninges).

subphrenic s. The peritoneal recess between the lower surface of the diaphragm and the upper surface of the organs immediately below it, such as the liver, stomach, and spleen.

thenar s. See palmar space.

Traube's s. A semilunar space on the left side of the chest about 7.6 cm wide, bounded on the right side by the sternum, above by the oblique line from the cartilage of the sixth rib to the ninth rib, and below by the inferior border of the rib cage; the site where sounds made by air in the stomach can be best heard.

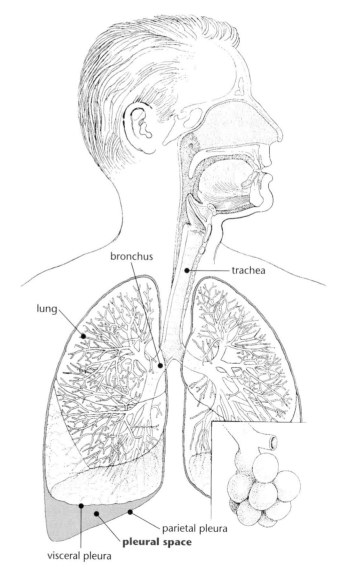

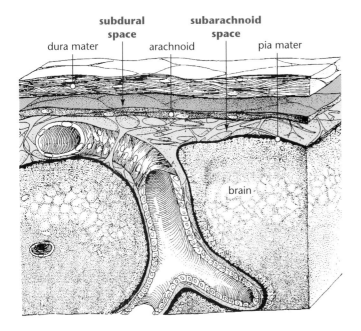

dura mater / subdural space / arachnoid / subarachnoid space / pia mater / brain

urinary s. of Bowman's capsule See urinary space of glomerular capsule.

urinary s. of glomerular capsule A flattened space or sac between the visceral and parietal epithelia of the renal corpuscle; it receives the filtrate (primary urine) of the blood from the glomerular vessels; although the urinary space may be collapsed, it distends in size depending on the secretory activity of the glomerulus; the urinary space of the glomerular capsule is continuous with the lumen of the proximal convoluted tubule of the kidney. Also called glomerular space; Bowman's space; urinary space of Bowman's capsule.

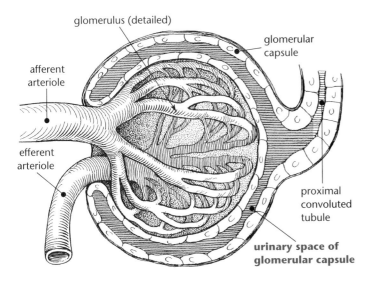

glomerulus (detailed) / glomerular capsule / afferent arteriole / efferent arteriole / proximal convoluted tubule / **urinary space of glomerular capsule**

space maintainer (spās măn-tān′er) A dental appliance, either fixed or removable, used to preserve the space created by the premature loss of a tooth.

space obtainer (spās ob-tān′er) An orthodontic appliance for slowly increasing space between teeth.

spall (spawl) **1.** A splinter; a fragment. **2.** To break up into small pieces.

spallation (spawl-la′shun) **1.** The process of breaking up into small fragments. **2.** A type of nuclear reaction in which nuclei eject a number of protons and alpha particles when struck by high-energy particles.

span (span) A full extent of distance or of time.

attention s. (a) The greatest amount of visually perceived in-

formation that a person can apprehend during a single brief display. (b) Popular term for the length of time a person can continuously concentrate on one subject.

auditory s. The maximum number of words, letters, or digits that a person can repeat after hearing them once; used to test immediate memory.

sparganosis (spar-gah-no′sis) Infection with tapeworm larvae, usually of the genus *Spirometra*.

sparganum (spar-ga′num), pl. sparga′na The intramuscular parasitic larva of tapeworms of the genus *Spirometra*.

spasm (spazm) An involuntary, abrupt contraction of a muscle or of a group of muscles.

anorectal s. See proctalgia fugax, under proctalgia.

bronchial s. See bronchospasm.

cadaveric s. See instantaneous rigor mortis, under rigor.

carpopedal s. Spasm of the hands and feet, characteristic of tetany and calcium deficiency.

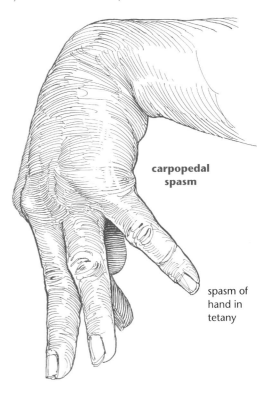

carpopedal spasm

spasm of hand in tetany

clonic s. A spasm characterized by alternate rigidity and relaxation of muscles.

diffused esophageal s. Condition in which muscles of the esophagus go into spontaneous nonpropulsive, painful contractions, usually induced by swallowing, or may be accompanied by difficult swallowing. The severe chest pain is felt behind the breastbone (sternum) and may be mistaken for a heart condition.

fatigue s. See occupational cramp, under cramp.

functional s. See occupational cramp, under cramp.

hemifacial s. Sudden synchronous contractions of muscles innervated by the facial nerve, affecting only one side of the face; contractions may subside immediately or last for several seconds and may occur several times a day; usually caused by mechanical irritation of the facial nerve.

intention s. Spasm precipitated by a voluntary movement.

nictating s. Involuntary winking.

occupational s. See occupational cramp, under cramp.

professional s. See occupational cramp, under cramp.

tailor's s. See tailor's cramp, under cramp.

tonic s. Spasm in which the muscular contraction is persistent.

vasomotor s. Spasm of small arteries.

writer's s. See writer's cramp, under cramp.

S

spasmodic (spaz-mod′ik) Relating to spasm.

spasmogenic (spaz-mo-jen′ik) Causing spasms.

spasmolysis (spaz-mol′ĭ-sis) The relief or elimination of spasm.

spasmolytic (spaz-mo-lit′ik) Reducing or eliminating spasm; applied to a drug that has such property. Also called antispasmodic.

spastic (spas′tik) Relating to spasm.

spasticity (spas-tis′ĭ-te) A state of increased tone or rigidity of a muscle or group of muscles.

  clasp-knife s. Rigidity of the extensor muscles of a joint induced by passive flexion of the joint which suddenly gives way on exertion of further pressure, allowing the joint to be easily flexed; the rigidity represents an exaggeration of the stretch reflex. Also called clasp-knife rigidity; clasp-knife effect.

spatula (spach′ŭ-lah) **1.** A thin, blunt blade-shaped device for mixing or spreading pharmaceutical or dental materials. **2.** A device for scraping tissue for biopsy.

  Ayre wooden s. Device for obtaining biopsy cells and/or secretions from a surface, such as the uterine cervix.

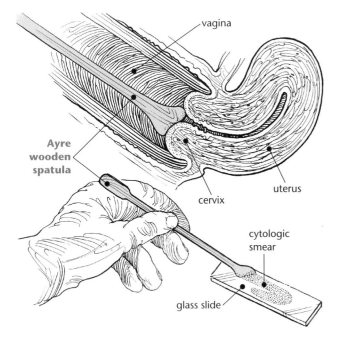

vagina

Ayre
wooden
spatula

uterus

cervix

cytologic
smear

glass slide

  Roux s. A tiny steel spatula for transferring bits of infected material to a culture tube.

spatulate (spach′ŭ-lāt) **1.** Shaped like a spatula. **2.** To mix substances by compression with a spatula.

spatulation (spach-ŭ-la′shun) The blending of two or more substances into a homogeneous mass by firmly turning and scraping them together with a spatula on a flat surface.

specialist (spesh′al-ist) One whose training, practice, and/or research is devoted to a particular branch of knowledge. In the usual medical context, a physician who has received advanced training, and is board-eligible or board-certified in a recognized field of medicine.

specialize (spesh′ă-līz) To channel one's training or practice to a particular branch of a field of study or profession.

species (spe′shēz) A taxonomic classification of organisms that bear a close resemblance to one another and that are capable of interbreeding; it ranks after a genus and before a variety (the individual).

species-specific (spe′shēz spĕ-sif′ik) Affecting a particular species in a characteristic way.

specific (spĕ-sif′ik) **1.** Relating to a species. **2.** Relating to a single disease. **3.** A remedy intended for a particular disease. **4.** In immunology, a special affinity, such as that of an antibody for the corresponding antigen.

specificity (spes-ĭ-fis′ĭ-te) **1.** The state of being specific, having a

fixed affinity, as the antigen-antibody relation. **2.** Applied to a screening test: the proportion of persons who are truly free of a disease in a screened population, and who are identified as such by the test.

specimen (spes′ĭ-men) A small sample (e.g., tissue, blood, urine) obtained for analysis or diagnosis.

  primary s. In laboratory medicine, any specimen, aseptically collected, from a which disease-causing agent could be isolated.

spectacles (spek′tah-klz) Eyeglasses.

  Frenzel s. Plano spectacles with built-in illumination and 20-diopter lenses for the pupose of dazzling the eyes and preventing their fixation on an external object; used in a darkened room to observe and record nystagmus.

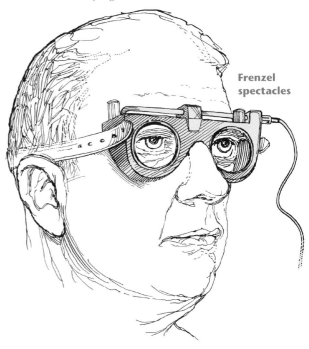

Frenzel
spectacles

  Masselon's s. Spectacles with a small attachment to keep the upper eyelid open above the pupil in cases of paralytic ptosis.

  stenopeic s. (*a*) Spectacles having, in place of lenses, opaque disks with slits in the center to allow the passage of only a minimum amount of light; used as a protection against snowblindness. (*b*) Opaque disks with multiple central perforations; designed for aiding vision in incipient cataract and in discrete corneal opacities.

spectinomycin (spek-tĭ-no-mi′sin) An antibacterial agent used in the treatment of gonorrhea in a person allergic to penicillin. Adverse effects may include nausea and fever.

spectrochemistry (spek-tro-kem′is-tre) Analysis of chemical substances by their ability to absorb or emit light.

spectrocolorimeter (spek-tro-kul-or-im′ĕ-ter) Instrument for detecting color blindness for one color, using a light source from a selected wavelength.

spectrogram (spek′tro-gram) A photograph or graphic pattern representing a spectrum.

spectrograph (spek′tro-graf) Instrument designed for photographic recording of a spectrum, as from electromagnetic waves.

spectrometer (spek-trom′ĕ-ter) Instrument designed to break up light from a source into its constituent wavelengths and to indicate wavelength on its calibrated scale.

spectrometry (spek-trom′ĕ-tre) The measurement of the wavelengths of rays of the spectrum by means of the spectrometer.

spectrophotofluorimetry (spek-tro-fo-to-floo-o-rim′ĕ-tre) The photometric measurement and analysis of the intensity and quality of fluorescence.

spectrophotometer (spek-tro-fo-tom′ĕ-ter) An optical instrument for measuring the intensity of light of a particular wavelength (ultraviolet, visible, or infrared) absorbed by a colored sample solution; it provides a measure of the amount of material absorbing light in the solution. See also enzyme-linked immunosorbent assay (ELISA), under assay.

infrared s. In industrial hygiene, an instrument that can be used for measuring concentrations of gases and vapors in the workplace.

spectrophotometry (spek-tro-fo-tom′ĕ-tre) Analysis using a spectrophotometer.

spectropolarimeter (spek-tro-po-lar-im′ĕ-ter) Instrument for measuring optical rotation of different wavelengths of light passing through a solution or translucent solid.

spectroscope (spek′tro-skōp) Any optical instrument for dispersing light and observing the resulting spectrum.

spectroscopy (spek-tros′ko-pe) The experimental study of optical spectra.

spectrum (spek′trum), pl. spec′tra, spec′trums **1.** An orderly distribution of colors displayed when white light is dispersed by passing through a prism or a diffraction grating. **2.** A range of activity of pathogenic microorganisms affected by an antibiotic or antibacterial agent.

antibiotic s. See spectrum (2).

speculum (spek′u-lum), pl. specula Instrument for dilating and holding open the orifice of a body cavity or canal to facilitate inspection of its interior.

anoscope s. A speculum used to inspect the anal canal.

Brinckerhoff rectal s. A conical tube with a closed extremity and a sliding lateral panel which provides an opening for the examination of the walls of the rectum.

Castroviejo eye s. A speculum measuring 3½ inches long designed to keep the eyelids apart during ocular surgery.

duck-bill s. See Graves vaginal speculum.

ear s. (a) A speculum attached to an otoscope for the examination of the external auditory canal and the eardrum. (b) A two-bladed speculum that dilates the external auditory canal when the handles are approximated; it facilitates the visualization of the eardrum.

Graves vaginal s. A two-valved vaginal speculum; available in small, medium, and large sizes. Also called duck-bill speculum.

illuminated nasal s. A nasal speculum with a source of light to illuminate the nasal cavity.

laryngeal s. A speculum that is passed through the mouth to expose the larynx and surrounding structures.

Pedersen's s. A duck-bill speculum with narrow, flat blades, used to inspect the vagina and cervix of a patient with a small introitus.

Sawyer rectal s. A retractor-like speculum for exposing the interior of the rectum.

Sims s. A double-ended vaginal speculum.

Sims rectal s. A speculum with fenestrated blades for examining the rectum.

Sisson-Cottler nasal s. A speculum used to dilate the nostrils (nares) or the nasal cavity; the blades are separated when the handles are approximated.

weighted vaginal s. A single-blade retractor-like vaginal speculum with a weighted element that frees both hands of the examiner or surgeon; frequently used on obese patients and patients that have borne many children.

speech (spēch) The production of articulate sounds to express thoughts.

alaryngeal s. Any pneumatic or electronic method of speech production, enabling a person without a larynx or with a nonfunctioning larynx to speak.

esophageal s. A form of alaryngeal speech in which speech sounds are produced by the controlled release of a column of air in the esophagus; used by individuals without a larynx, or with a nonfunctioning larynx.

explosive s. Speech characterized by a variable volume, some syllables being uttered with greater force than intended; associated with lesions in the cerebellum.

scanning s. Slow, hesitant speech with undue pauses between syllables; seen in cerebellar dysfunction and the late stages of multiple sclerosis.

staccato s. Jerky, abrupt speech associated with cerebellar dysfunction.

telegraphic s. Sparse speech consisting mainly of nouns, important adjectives, and transitive verbs, omitting articles, prepositions, and conjunctions; seen in certain types of aphasia.

speed (spēd) Slang name for methamphetamine hydrochloride.

sperm (sperm) See spermatozoon.

spermatic (sper-mat′ik) Relating to sperm.

spermatid (sper′mah-tid) One of the four cells resulting from the division of the spermatocyte; it develops into the spermatozoon without further division.

spermatoblast (sper′mah-to-blast) See spermatogonium.

spermatocele (sper′mah-to-sēl) A painless, small cystic mass, usually less than 1 cm in diameter, containing sperm in a milky fluid; located within a sperm-transporting tubule, just above and posterior to (but separate from) the testis; caused by obstruction of the tubule. Also called spermatocyst.

spermatocide (sper′mah-to-sīd) See spermicide.

spermatocyst (sper′mah-to-sist) See spermatocele.

spermatocyte (sper′mah-to-sit) One of the spherical cells housed in the wall of a seminiferous tubule of the testis; it represents an early stage in the development of a spermatozoon.

primary s. A large cell in the outer wall of the seminiferous tubule resulting from the mitotic division of a type B spermatogonium (stem cell); it contains the full diploid number of chromosomes (46).

secondary s. A cell resulting from the meiotic division of the primary spermatocyte; it contains the haploid number of chromosomes (23) and represents the first reduction division, followed by the second reduction division (by mitosis), which results in two spermatids.

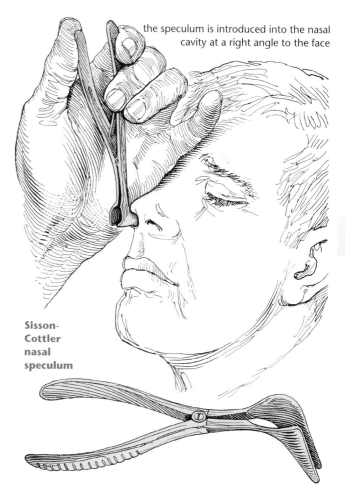

the speculum is introduced into the nasal cavity at a right angle to the face

Sisson-Cottler nasal speculum

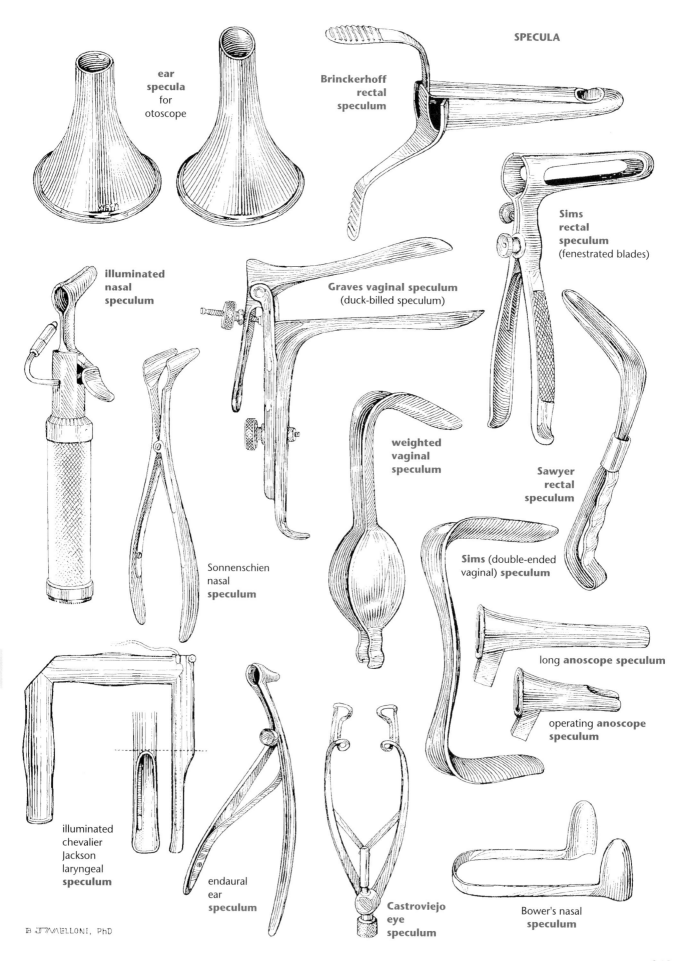

SPECULA

ear specula for otoscope

Brinckerhoff rectal speculum

Sims rectal speculum (fenestrated blades)

illuminated nasal speculum

Graves vaginal speculum (duck-billed speculum)

Sonnenschien nasal **speculum**

weighted vaginal speculum

Sawyer rectal speculum

Sims (double-ended vaginal) **speculum**

long **anoscope speculum**

operating **anoscope speculum**

illuminated chevalier Jackson laryngeal **speculum**

endaural ear speculum

Castroviejo eye speculum

Bower's nasal speculum

B. J. MELLONI, PhD

S48

spermatocytogenesis (sper-mah-to-si′to-jen′ĕ-sis) The mitotic proliferation of the undifferentiated germ cell (spermatogonium) and development of first spermatocytes, then spermatids; first stage in the process of sperm differentiation in the testis.

spermatogenesis (sper-mah-to-jen′ĕ-sis) The whole process of formation of spermatozoa, including spermatocytogenesis and spermiogenesis, carried out in the seminiferous tubules of the testis.

spermatogenetic (sper-mah-to-je-net′ik) See spermatogenic.

spermatogenic (sper-mah-to-jen′ik) Sperm-producing. Also called spermatogenetic.

spermatogonium (sper-mah-to-go′ne-um), pl. spermatogo′nia An undifferentiated young cell located in the seminiferous tubules of the testis; it either gives rise to new spermatogonia (type A) or differentiates to a more developed primary spermatocyte (type B), which eventually becomes a spermatozoon. Also called spermatoblast.

spermatoid (sper′mah-toid) Resembling spermatozoa.

spermatolysin (sper-mah-tol′ĭ-sin) A specific antibody to spermatozoa formed in the female following exposure to spermatozoa.

spermatolysis (sper-mah-tol′ĭ-sis) Destruction and dissolution of spermatozoa.

spermatolytic (sper-mah-to-lit′ik) Destructive to spermatozoa.

spermatorrhea (sper-mah-to-re′ah) Abnormal involuntary discharge of semen without orgasm.

spermatotoxin (sper-mah-to-tok′sin) A cytotoxic antibody that kills spermatozoa. Also called spermotoxin.

spermatozoa (sper-mah-to-zo′ah) Plural of spermatozoon.

spermatozoon (sper-mah-to-zo′on), pl. spermatozo′a The mature male sex cell produced in the testes; in humans, it consists of an ovoid head (4–6 μm long) containing the nucleus, a short neck (0.3 μm), a middle section (4 μm) containing mitochondria, and a long motile tail (40–50 μm) containing circular fibers and by means of which the cell moves freely; a spermatozoon is capable of moving through the female reproductive tract, after ejaculation during sexual intercourse, to fertilize the female sex cell (ovum). Also called sperm; sperm cell.

spermaturia (sper-mah-tu′re-ah) See semenuria.

spermicide (sper′mĭ-sīd) Any agent that kills spermatozoa. Also called spermatocide.

spermiogenesis (sper-me-o-jen′ĕ-sis) Process by which the immature round cell (spermatid) transforms morphologically and biochemically into the elongated testicular spermatozoon; second stage in the formation of spermatozoa.

spermolith (sper′mo-lith) A stone in the deferent (spermatic) duct.

spermotoxin (sper-mo-tok′sin) See spermatotoxin.

sphacelate (sfas′ĕ-lāt) To develop gangrene.

sphaceloderma (sfas-ĕ-lo-der′mah) A gangrenous condition of the skin.

sphacelous (sfas′ĕ-lus) Necrotic; gangrenous.

sphenion (sfe′ne-on) A craniometric point located at the tip of the sphenoid angle of the parietal bone.

spheno- Combining form meaning shaped like a wedge.

sphenoid (sfe′noid) Wedge-shaped; applied to a large wedge-shaped bone at the base of the skull. See table of bones.

sphenoidal (sfe-noi′dal) Relating to the sphenoid bone.

sphenoiditis (sfe-noi-di′tis) Inflammation of the mucous lining of the sphenoid sinus.

sphenoidostomy (sfe-noi-dos′to-me) Surgical enlargement of the opening of the sphenoid sinus.

sphenoidotomy (sfe-noi-dot′o-me) Incision into the sphenoid sinus.

sphenopalatine (sfe-no-pal′ah-tin) Relating to the sphenoid and palatine bones.

sphenoparietal (sfe-no-pah-ri′ĕ-tal) Relating to the sphenoid and parietal bones.

sphenopetrosal (sfe-no-pe-tro′sal) Relating to the sphenoid bone and the petrous portion of the temporal bone.

sphenorbital (sfe-nor′bĭ-tal) Relating to the sphenoid bone and the orbit, or the portion of the sphenoid bone forming part of the orbit.

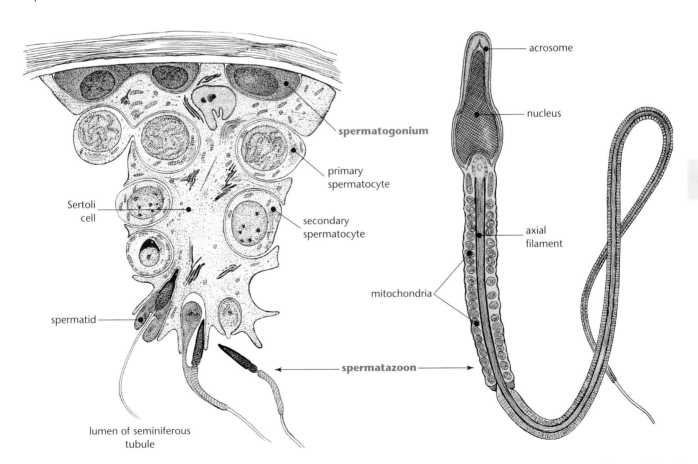

spermatogonium

primary spermatocyte

Sertoli cell

secondary spermatocyte

spermatid

acrosome

nucleus

axial filament

mitochondria

spermatazoon

lumen of seminiferous tubule

S

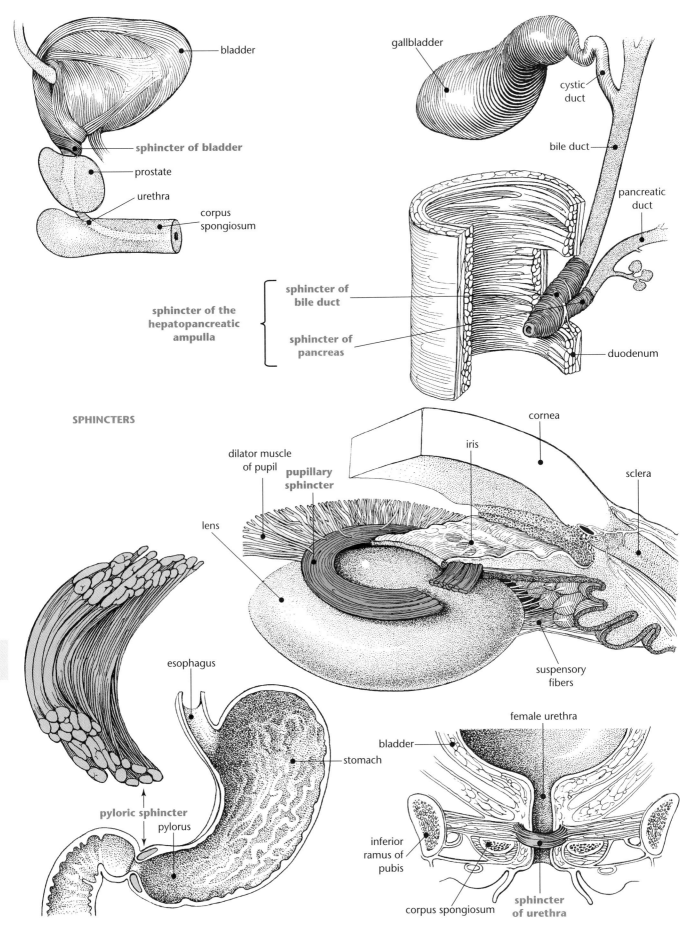

bladder

sphincter of bladder

prostate

urethra

corpus
spongiosum

gallbladder

cystic
duct

bile duct

pancreatic
duct

sphincter of
bile duct

sphincter of the
hepatopancreatic
ampulla

sphincter of
pancreas

duodenum

SPHINCTERS

cornea

dilator muscle
of pupil

iris

pupillary
sphincter

sclera

lens

suspensory
fibers

esophagus

stomach

female urethra

bladder

pyloric sphincter

pylorus

inferior
ramus of
pubis

corpus spongiosum

sphincter of urethra

S

S50

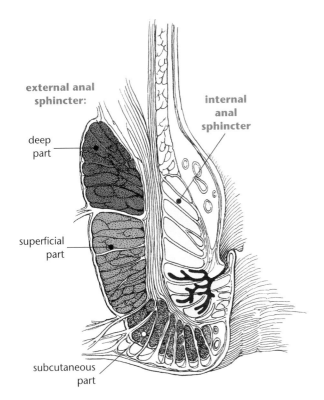

external anal sphincter:

deep part

superficial part

subcutaneous part

internal anal sphincter

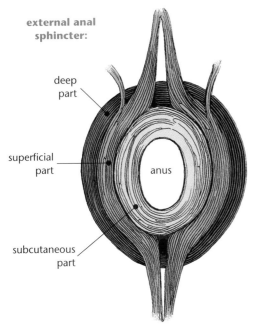

external anal sphincter:

deep part

superficial part

anus

subcutaneous part

sphenosquamosal (sfe-no-skwa-mo′sal) Relating to the sphenoid bone and the squamous portion of the temporal bone. Also called squamosphenoid.

spherocyte (sfe′ro-sīt) A small, abnormal red blood cell, appearing spherical (rather than biconcave), with a diameter of less than 6 μm in diameter (normal size is 7.2–8.6 μm); it has a greater than normal density of hemoglobin; found in the blood of patients with hereditary spherocytosis and certain other hemolytic anemias.

spherocytosis (sfe-ro-si-to′sis) The presence of spherocytes in the blood.

hereditary s. (HS) Congenital disorder, with autosomal dominant inheritance, characterized by a defect in the red blood cell membrane that renders the cell spherical, fragile, and susceptible to spontaneous destruction; characteristic manifestations include anemia and jaundice.

spherule (sfer′ūl) **1.** A small sphere. **2.** A minute, thick-walled structure containing many fungal spores; characteristic of the parasitic stage of *Coccidioides immitis*.

sphincter (sfingk′ter) **1.** Any circular muscle that normally maintains constriction of a natural body opening and that is capable of relaxing in order to permit passage of substances through the opening. **2.** A portion of a tubular structure that functions as a sphincter.

　s. of bile duct A sphincter of smooth muscle around the lower part of the common bile duct within the wall of the duodenum, from the duodenal entrance to its junction with the pancreatic duct; it regulates bile flow and, retrogressively, the filing of the gallbladder. Also called sphincter choledochus.

　s. of bladder A thickening of the middle circular layer of the muscular fibers of the bladder surrounding the internal urethral opening at the neck of the bladder; it is composed of nonstriated (smooth) muscle and is not under voluntary control. Along with the sphincter of the urethra, it controls the outflow of urine from the bladder. Also called sphincter vesicae; vesicular sphincter.

　s. choledochus See sphincter of bile duct.

　external anal s. A flat band of muscular fibers, elliptical in shape, encircling the anal opening; consists of three parts: subcutaneous, superficial, and deep; it closes the anal canal and anus.

　s. of the hepatopancreatic ampulla The sphincter of smooth circular muscle fibers around the terminal part of the main pancreatic duct and common bile duct, including the duodenal ampulla (papilla of Vater); it constricts both the lower part of the common bile duct and the main pancreatic duct so that reflux cannot occur. Also called sphincter of Oddi.

　ileocecal s. See ileocecal valve, under valve.

　internal anal s. A muscular ring formed of the thickened inner circular coat at the caudal end of the bowel, surrounding about 2.5 cm of the anal canal; it is in contact with, but separate from, the external anal sphincter; it closes the anal canal and anus.

　lower esophageal s. (LES) A high-pressure zone in the distal portion of the esophagus where resting pressure is usually higher than pressure in the fundus of the stomach; cannot be identified anatomically but its pressure can be determined; normally it straddles the diaphragm extending 1 to 3 cm below to 1 to 2 cm above the diaphragmatic hiatus; it acts as a barrier preventing the reflux of gastric contents.

　s. of Oddi See sphincter of hepatopancreatic ampulla.

　s. of pancreas A sphincter of smooth circular muscle fibers around the terminal (intraduodenal) part of the main pancreatic duct where it joins the common bile duct before entering into the duodenum; it constricts the terminal part of the main pancreatic duct. Also called sphincter of pancreatic duct.

　s. of pancreatic duct See sphincter of pancreas.

　s. of pupil See pupillary sphincter.

　pupillary s. A circular, flattened band of muscle slightly less than 1 mm in width, in the pupillary margin of the iris; it regulates the size of the pupil. Also called sphincter of pupil.

　pyloric s. A muscular ring formed by a thickening of the circular layer of the stomach at the pyloric orifice; it acts as a valve to close the pyloric lumen.

　s. of urethra A flat striated muscle that closely surrounds the membranous portion of the urethra in the male and the terminal part of the urethra in the female; along with the vesicular sphincter, it controls the outflow of urine from the urinary bladder by compressing the urethra; it is under voluntary control after early infancy. Also called sphincter urethrae.

　s. urethrae See sphincter of urethra.

　s. vesicae See sphincter of bladder.

　vesicular s. See sphincter of bladder.

sphincteral (sfingk′ter-al) Relating to a sphincter muscle.

sphincteralgia (sfingk-ter-al′je-ah) Pain in a sphincter muscle, especially of the anus.

sphincteritis (sfingk-ter-i′tis) Inflammation of a sphincter muscle, especially of the hepatopancreatic duct.

S

sphincterotomy (sfingk-ter-ot'o-me) Surgical division of a sphincter muscle, usually performed for the relief of persistent spasm.

sphingolipid (sfing-go-lip'id) A group of lipids found primarily in tissues of the central nervous system (e.g., ceramide, cerebroside, ganglioside, sphingomyelin).

sphingolipidosis (sfing-go-lip-ĭ-do'sis) General designation for a group of disorders characterized by abnormal metabolism of sphingolipids.

    cerebral s. Any of a group of inherited diseases associated with a disturbance of metabolism and increased storage of lipids in the brain; characterized by progressive loss of vision leading to complete blindness (usually within two years), severe mental deterioration, convulsions, and paralysis; includes: infantile type (Tay-Sachs disease), early juvenile type (Jansky-Bielschowsky or Bielschowsky's disease), late juvenile type (Spielmeyer-Vogt or Batten-Mayou disease), and adult type (Kufs' disease).

sphingomyelin (sfing-go-mi'ĕ-lin) Any of a group of phospholipids present in large quantities in brain and nerve tissue.

sphingosine (sfing'go-sin) A complex amino alcohol, constituent of cerebrosides.

sphygmic (sfig'mik) Relating to the pulse.

sphygmo-, sphygm- Combining forms meaning pulse.

sphygmogram (sfig'mo-gram) A graphic curve representing the arterial pulse, made with a sphygmograph.

sphygmograph (sfig'mo-graf) Instrument for making a graphic record (tracing) of the arterial pulse.

sphygmography (sfig-mog'rah-fe) The process of making pulse tracings with a sphygmograph.

sphygmoid (sfig'moid) Resembling the pulse.

sphygmomanometer (sfig-mo-mah-nom'ĕ-ter) Instrument for measuring the arterial blood pressure.

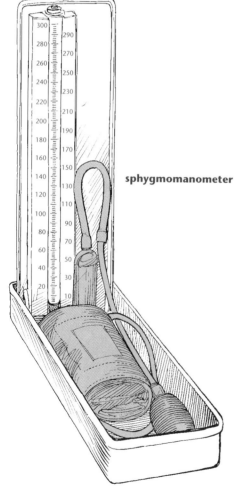

sphygmomanometer

sphygmometer (sfig-mom'ĕ-ter) Sphygmomanometer.

sphygmopalpation (sfig-mo-pal-pa'shun) Palpation of the pulse; "taking" the pulse.

sphygmophone (sfig'mo-fōn) Instrument for rendering audible the vibration of each pulse beat.

sphygmoscope (sfig'mo-skōp) Instrument for rendering the pulse beat visible.

spicule (spik'ūl) A small needle-shaped structure.

spider (spi'der) **1.** Any arachnoid with four pairs of legs, a body divided into a cephalothorax and an abdomen, a complex of spinnerets, and a cluster of up to eight eyes. Venomous spiders include the black widow (*Latrodectus mactans*), brown recluse (*Loxosceles reclusa*), Chilean brown (*Loxosceles laeta*), and red-legged widow (*Latrodectus bishopi*). **2.** A spider-shaped pattern.

    arterial s. See spider telangiectasia, under telangiectasia.

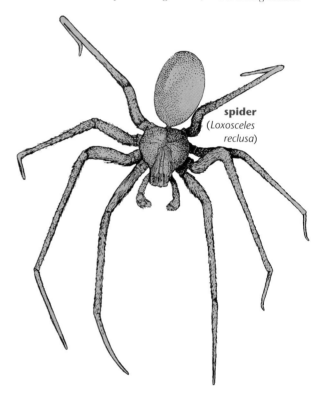

spider
(*Loxosceles reclusa*)

spike (spīk) In electroencephalography, a sharply rising and falling curve caused by a brief electrical cerebral activity.

spiking (spīk'ing) **1.** The sharp alternation between a highest and lowest point (e.g., of temperature, as shown in a fever chart). **2.** The occurrence of sharp rising and falling, or vice versa, of blood glucose levels in a diabetic person.

spillway (spil'wa) The small channels through which food passes from the occlusal surfaces of teeth during chewing.

spin- Combining form meaning spine.

spina (spi'nah) pl. spi'nae **1.** The vertebral column. **2.** Any sharp bony projection.

    s. bifida Congenital defect of the vertebral column in which the posterior portion (vertebral arch) of one or several vertebrae fails to develop; the resulting gap allows spinal membranes and sometimes the spinal cord and nerve roots to protrude. Also called cleft spine.

    s. bifida occulta Spina bifida without protrusion of the spinal cord or its membranes. Also called cryptomerorachischisis.

spinal (spi'nal) **1.** Relating to a spine. **2.** Relating to the vertebral column.

spindle (spin'dl) Any spindle-shaped or fusiform anatomic structure; an elongated form with a thick central portion and tapered extremities.

    achromatic s. See mitotic spindle.

S

central s. The middle mitotic spindle between the centrioles in a dividing cell.

intermediate muscle s. A muscle spindle possessing a single secondary nerve ending as well as the primary nerve ending.

mitotic s. The fusiform figure characteristic of a dividing cell formed by fine, viscous microtubules extending between the two centrioles, along which the migrating chromosomes are distributed. Also called achromatic spindle; nuclear spindle.

muscle s. A specialized sensory organ in voluntary muscle that consists of a small bundle of delicate muscle fibers (intrafusal fibers) invested in a multilaminar fibrous capsule within which the sensory nerve fibers terminate; it is positioned parallel to the extrafusal fibers, varies in length from 0.8 to 5 mm, and has a fusiform appearance. Also called neuromuscular spindle; muscle proprioceptor.

neuromuscular s. See muscle spindle.

nuclear s. See mitotic spindle.

simple muscle s. A muscle spindle that contains only a primary nerve ending.

sleep s. In electroencephalography, rhythmic waveforms of about 15 Hz that are usually seen during early and intermediate quiet sleep (non–rapid eye movement sleep).

tendon s. See Golgi tendon organ, under organ.

spine (spīn) 1. A sharp-pointed projection of bone. 2. The vertebral column; see under column. 3. A short projection.

anterior nasal s. The pointed median projection of bone of the maxilla situated on the lower margin of the bony external nares.

bamboo s. See poker spine.

basal s. See pharyngeal spine.

cervical s. The seven cervical vertebrae considered as a whole.

cleft s. See spina bifida.

dendritic s.'s Small thornlike extensions of the dendritic branches of nerve cells (neurons) that play an important role as a receptive area for afferent stimuli; the number of dendritic spines

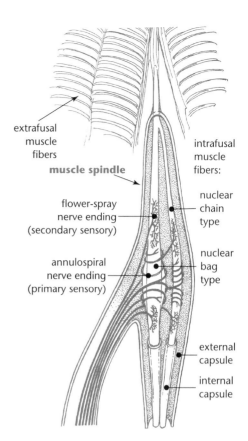

extrafusal muscle fibers

muscle spindle

flower-spray nerve ending (secondary sensory)

annulospiral nerve ending (primary sensory)

intrafusal muscle fibers:

nuclear chain type

nuclear bag type

external capsule

internal capsule

is reflective of the volume of incoming synapses. Also called gemmules.

s. of greater tubercle of humerus A bony projection on the greater tubercle of the humerus, at the shoulder, forming the lateral border of the intertubercular groove. Also called crista tuberculi majoris.

s. of helix The small pointed projection on the anterior border of the auricular cartilage of the ear where the helix bends upward.

s. of smaller tubercle of humerus A bony projection on the smaller (lesser) tubercle of the humerus, at the shoulder, forming the medial border of the intertubercular groove. Also called crista tuberculi minoris.

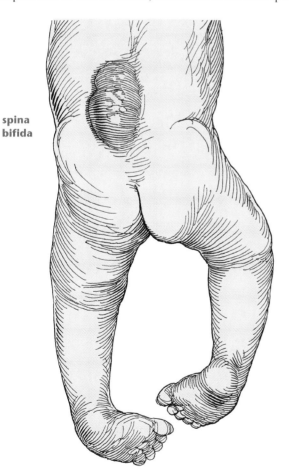

spina bifida

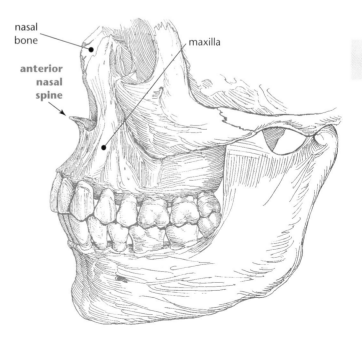

nasal bone

maxilla

anterior nasal spine

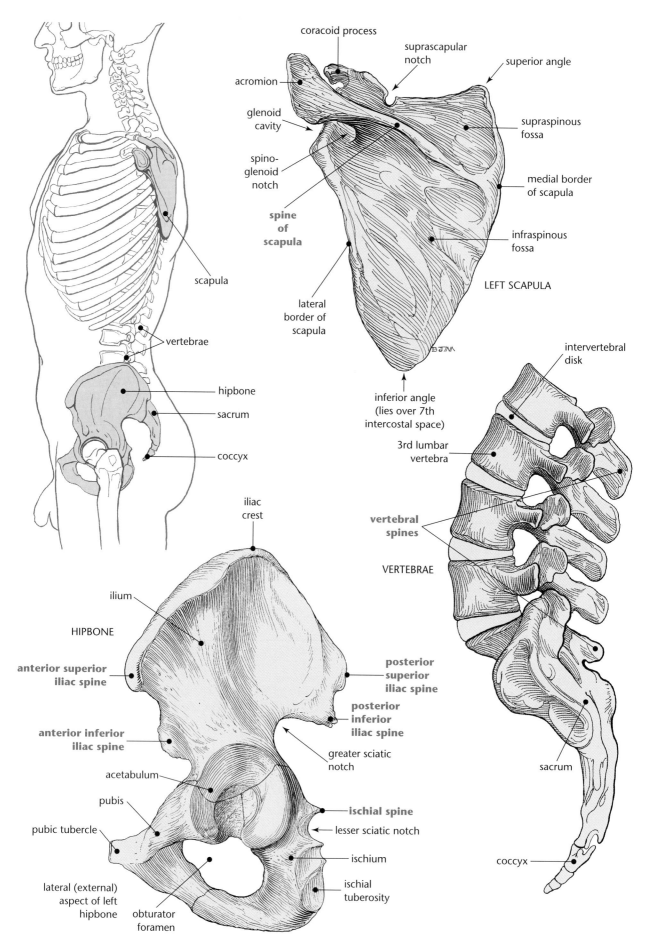

coracoid process

suprascapular notch

superior angle

acromion

glenoid cavity

supraspinous fossa

spino-glenoid notch

medial border of scapula

spine of scapula

infraspinous fossa

LEFT SCAPULA

lateral border of scapula

inferior angle (lies over 7th intercostal space)

scapula

vertebrae

hipbone

sacrum

coccyx

intervertebral disk

3rd lumbar vertebra

vertebral spines

VERTEBRAE

iliac crest

sacrum

coccyx

ilium

HIPBONE

anterior superior iliac spine

posterior superior iliac spine

posterior inferior iliac spine

anterior inferior iliac spine

greater sciatic notch

acetabulum

pubis

ischial spine

pubic tubercle

lesser sciatic notch

ischium

lateral (external) aspect of left hipbone

obturator foramen

ischial tuberosity

S

spine ■ spine

iliac s. Any of the four spines of the ilium (part of the hipbone): *Anterior inferior iliac s.,* the spine (blunt projection) on the front border of the ilium just above the anterior part of the acetabulum; it provides attachment to the rectus muscle of the thigh (rectus femoris muscle) and to the iliofemoral ligament. *Anterior superior iliac s.,* the spine forming the front end of the crest of the ilium; it provides attachment to the lateral end of the inguinal ligament and just below to the sartorius muscle. It lies at the lateral end of the fold of the groin and is easily felt. *Posterior inferior iliac s.,* the spine (wide projection) at the lower end of the posterior border of the ilium, where it makes a sharp bend forward to form the upper border of the greater sciatic notch; it provides attachment to the piriform muscle. *Posterior superior iliac s.,* the spine forming the back end of the crest of the ilium; it provides attachment to the sacrotuberal ligament and the dorsal (posterior) sacroiliac ligament. The spine cannot usually be felt, but its position is indicated by a prominent dimple about 4 cm lateral to the second spinous tubercle of the sacrum.

ischial s. A bony spine situated on the posterior aspect of the ischium (part of the hipbone) near the posteroinferior border of the acetabulum; it provides attachment to the sacrospinal ligament. Also called sciatic spine.

kissing s.'s Abnormal contact between the tips of the spinous processes of adjacent vertebrae (usually between any two lumbar vertebrae or between the fifth lumbar and the first sacral) resulting in midline lower back pain that intensifies on extension of the spine. Also called Baastrup's disease.

lumbar s. The five lumbar vertebrae considered as a whole.

mental s.'s See genial tubercles, under tubercle.

nasal s. of frontal bone A sharp median spine projecting downward from the nasal part of the frontal bone and articulating in front with the upper part of the nasal bone, and behind with the ethmoid bone; it forms part of the roof of the nasal cavity as well as a small part of the nasal septum.

nasal s. of palatine bone See posterior nasal spine.

peroneal s. of calcaneus See peroneal trochlea, under trochlea.

pharyngeal s. A small midline elevation on the inferior surface of the basilar part of the occipital bone, about 1 cm in front of the foramen magnum; it provides attachment to the fibrous raphe of the pharynx. Also called basal spine; pharyngeal tubercle.

poker s. The spine characteristic of ankylosing spondylitis, sometimes called bamboo spine because of its resemblance to a rigid bamboo shoot (lipping of vertebral margins) on x-ray film. Also called rigid spine; bamboo spine.

posterior nasal s. A small, sharp bony spine projecting backward from the median end of the posterior border of the horizontal plate of the palatine bone; it provides attachment to the muscle of the uvula. Also called nasal spine of palatine bone.

pubic s. See pubic tubercle, under tubercle.

rigid s. See poker spine.

s. of scapula The somewhat triangular shelf of bone projecting from the back of the scapula, extending from the vertebral border laterally across to the shoulder joint where it bears the acromion; it is covered by skin and superficial fascia and provides attachment to the supraspinous and infraspinous muscles.

sciatic s. See ischial spine.

s. of Spix See lingula of mandible, under lingula.

thoracic s. The 12 thoracic vertebrae considered as a whole.

tibial s. See intercondylar eminence, under eminence.

vertebral s. The spinous process of vertebrae projecting backward from the vertebral arch (junction of laminae), providing attachment to muscles of the back, which extend and rotate the vertebral column. It can vary in shape, size, and direction from the short, bifid process of some cervical vertebrae to the large, thick quadrangular process seen in lumbar vertebrae. The vertebral spine of the seventh cervical vertebra is very prominent; it is long and ends in a tubercle that is easily palpable at the lower end of the nuchal furrow; the vertebral spine of the first thoracic vertebra is equally prominent, while the typical thoracic vertebral spines are not outstanding and simply slant backward and downward. The first cervical vertebra does not have a vertebral spine.

spinnbarkeit (spin′bahr-kit) A state of stretchability of the cervical mucus which, when spread on a glass slide, dries in a fernlike pattern; indicative of ovulation; it peaks on the 14th day of the menstrual cycle. Also spelled spinnbarkheit.

spinobulbar (spi-no-bul′bar) See bulbospinal.

spinocerebellar (spi-no-ser-e-bel′ar) Relating to the spinal cord and the cerebellum.

spinous (spi′nus) Relating to a spine or spines.

spiradenoma (spi-rad-ĕ-no′mah) A benign overdevelopment of sweat glands.

spiral (spi′ral) Winding around a central axis.

  Curschmann's s.'s Coiled masses of mucus sometimes seen in the sputum of patients with bronchial asthma.

spiro-, spir- Combining forms meaning coiled; breathing.

spirogram (spi′ro-gram) The tracing or curve made by a spirometer.

spirometer (spi-rom′ĕ-ter) Apparatus used in spirometry; it records the rate at which a patient exhales air from the lungs and the total volume of air exhaled. Also called respirometer.

spirometric (spi-ro-met′rik) Relating to spirometry.

spirometry (spi-rom′ĕ-tre) Procedure using a spirometer to help diagnose a lung disorder or to monitor ongoing treatment.

spironolactone (spēr-o-no-lak′tōn) Diuretic drug that blocks the action of the adrenal hormone aldosterone on the kidney tubules, producing sodium loss with potassium retention. Adverse effects may include numbness, weakness, nausea, and vomiting.

spissitude (spis′i-tūd) The state of being thickened by evaporation or absorption of fluid.

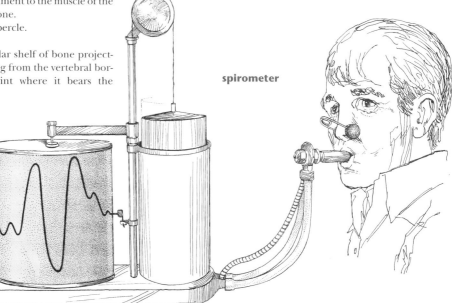

normal
spirogram

spirometer

S

spittle (spit'l) Saliva.

splanchnectopia (splank-nek-to'pe-ah) Malposition of any of the abdominal organs. Also called splanchnodiastasis.

splanchnic (splank'nik) Relating to any organ of the thoracic or abdominal cavities; visceral.

splanchnicectomy (splank-ne-sek'to-me) Surgical removal of a portion of the greater splanchnic nerve.

splanchno-, splanchni-, splanch- Combining forms meaning viscera.

splanchnocele (splank'no-sēl) **1.** Hernia of an abdominal organ. **2.** The embryonic body cavity.

splanchnodiastasis (splank-no-di-as'tah-sis) See splanchnectopia.

splanchnomegaly (splank-no-meg'ah-le) See visceromegaly.

splayfoot (spla'foot) See flatfoot.

spleen (splēn) A large vascular lymphatic organ situated in the upper left area of the abdominal cavity, below the diaphragm; it is the sole lymphatic tissue specialized to filter blood, removing worn out cells from the circulatory system; it stores red blood cells and iron and is a blood-forming organ in the fetus. Also called lien.

    accessory s. A mass of splenic tissue sometimes found attached to the spleen or in one of the peritoneal folds.

    sago s. A spleen containing deposits of an abnormal protein-polysaccharide complex (amyloid), which resembles tapioca granules.

splenectomy (sple-nek'to-me) Surgical removal of the spleen.

spleneolus (sple-ne'o-lus) Accessory spleen.

splenetic (sple-net'ik) **1.** Bad-tempered. **2.** See splenic.

splenic (splen'ik) Relating to the spleen. Also called splenetic.

splenitis (sple-ni'tis) Inflammation of the spleen.

splenium (sple'ne-um) A bandlike structure in the body.

    s. of corpus callosum The thick, posterior portion of the corpus callosum of the brain.

spleno-, splen- Combining forms meaning spleen.

splenocele (sple'no-sēl) **1.** A hernial protrusion of the spleen. **2.** A cystic tumor of the spleen.

splenocolic (sple-no-kol'ik) Relating to the spleen and the colon (e.g., the peritoneal fold connecting the two organs).

splenography (sple-nog'rah-fe) X-ray examination of the spleen following injection of a radiopaque substance.

splenohepatomegaly (sple-no-he-pat'o-meg'ah-le) Abnormal enlargement of both spleen and liver.

splenomalacia (sple-no-mah-la'she-ah) Abnormal softening of the spleen.

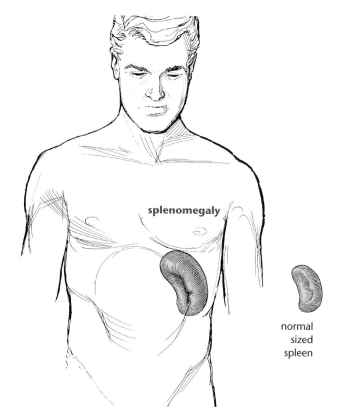

splenomegaly

normal sized spleen

splenomegalia (sple-no-me-ga'le-ah) See splenomegaly.

splenomegaly (sple-no-meg'ah-le) Enlargement of the spleen. Also called splenomegalia; megalosplenia.

    chronic congestive s. Condition usually following hypertension of the portal vein; characterized by enlargement of the spleen, anemia, and, sometimes, gastrointestinal bleeding; occasionally accompanied by deficiency of blood platelets (thrombopenia) and leukocytes (leukopenia). Also called Banti's syndrome.

    tropical s. See visceral leishmaniasis, under leishmaniasis.

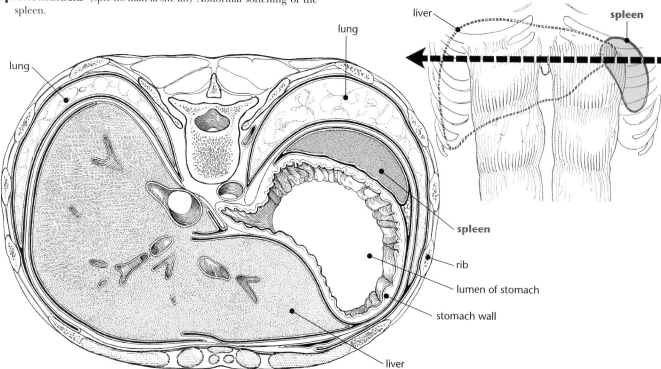

liver — lung

spleen

lung

lung

spleen

rib

lumen of stomach

stomach wall

liver

splenonephric (sple-no-nef′rik) See splenorenal.

splenopancreatic (sple-no-pan-kre-at′ik) Relating to the spleen and the pancreas.

splenopathy (sple-nop′ah-the) Any disease of the spleen.

splenophrenic (splen-o-fren′ik) Relating to the spleen and the diaphragm.

splenoportogram (sple-no-por′to-gram) X-ray picture of the splenic and portal veins after injection of a radiopaque substance into the circulation.

splenoptosis (sple-nop-to′sis) Downward displacement of the spleen.

splenorenal (sple-no-re′nal) Relating to the spleen and the kidney. Also called splenonephric; lienorenal.

splenorrhagia (sple-no-ra′je-ah) Bleeding from a ruptured spleen.

splenosis (sple-no′sis) The presence of multiple small masses of splenic tissue growing in scattered areas on the peritoneal surfaces throughout the abdominal cavity; distinguished from accessory spleens by the absence of elastic or smooth muscle fibers in their covering capsules; may (rarely) stimulate formation of adhesions and intestinal obstruction; generally they are discovered during an abdominal operation for unrelated conditions; caused by dissemination and autotransplantation of splenic tissue following traumatic rupture of the spleen.

splenotomy (sple-not′o-me) Surgical cut into the spleen.

splenotoxin (sple-no-tok′sin) A cytotoxin that has a special affinity for the cells of the spleen.

splint (splint) A device for immobilizing, supporting, and correcting displaced, injured, or deformed structures.

acrylic resin bite-guard s. A removable dental appliance designed to eliminate movement of teeth. Also called occlusal splint.

air s. See inflatable splint.

airplane s. Splint designed to hold the arm in abduction at shoulder level.

Balkan s. See Balkan frame, under frame.

baseball s. A splint applied to the anterior aspect of the forearm and hand; the palm part of the splint holds the hand in a position as if it were holding a baseball.

cast cap s. A one-piece metallic or plastic appliance, cemented over the crowns of teeth to immobilize a fractured jaw.

coaptation s. A splint consisting of two short, rigid boardlike parts for placing on either side of a limb to prevent overriding of a fractured bone; usually held together by an outer dressing or by a longer splint to fix the entire limb.

Cramer's s. See ladder splint.

Denis-Browne s. An attachment to the soles of a pair of shoes with a connecting crossbar for maintaining the lower limbs of an infant in abduction and the desired rotation; used in the correction of clubfoot (talipes equinovarus).

drop-foot s. A short-leg splint consisting of a band for attaching to the calf of the leg and an extension for fitting onto the heel of the shoe; used for holding the foot in a neutral position, preventing its plantar flexion.

dynamic s. Any splint device that allows for or provides movement by transferring motion forces from one body part to another, or by incorporating external forces such as springs, elastic bands, or electricity.

Frejka s. A soft pillow that maintains separation of an infant's thighs to correct congenital dislocation of the hip.

Hodgen s. A device similar to a Thomas splint consisting of only half a ring; used to apply balanced traction in fractures of the middle or lower part of the femur.

inflatable s. A splint consisting of a double-walled plastic jacket with a zipper fastener for placing around an injured limb; the outer wall has a valve to allow inflation of the jacket. Also called air splint.

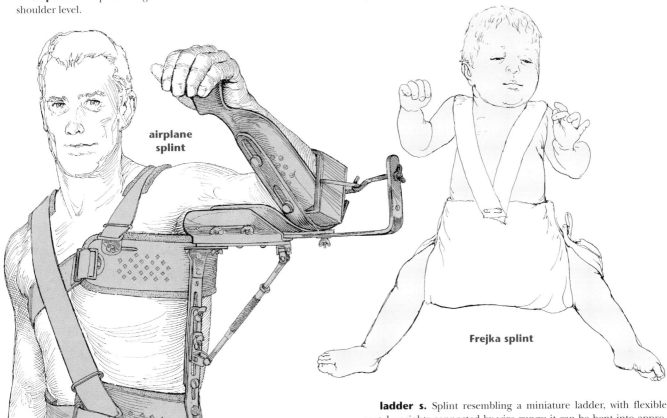

airplane
splint

Frejka splint

ladder s. Splint resembling a miniature ladder, with flexible metal uprights connected by wire rungs; it can be bent into appropriate shape, padded, and bandaged to the injured part. Also called Cramer splint.

long-leg s. Any splint extending from the thigh to the lower calf or to the foot.

occlusal s. See acrylic resin bite-guard splint.

plaster s. A splint made of gauze impregnated with plaster of Paris.

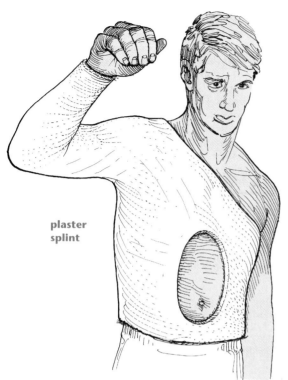

plaster splint

short-leg s. Any splint extending from the upper calf to the foot.

Taylor s. A bracelike steel support for a derangement of the vertebral column; used to prevent flexion of the thoracolumbar spine. Also called Taylor back brace.

Thomas s. Splint consisting of a ring that fits on the upper thigh (near the groin) connected to a continuous bar that has a W shape at the opposite end; used to immobilize the leg.

wrist s. A splint worn on the wrist to alleviate the symptoms of carpal tunnel syndrome.

splinting (splint′ing) 1. Immobilization by means of a splint. 2. Stiffening of a body part to reduce pain caused by motion.

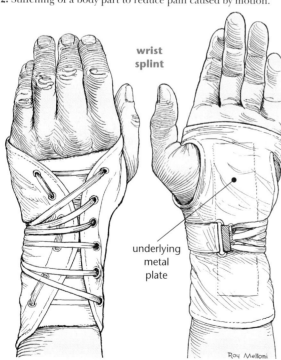

wrist splint

underlying metal plate

Roy Melloni

splitting (split′ing) 1. In chemistry, conversion of a complex substance into two or more simpler substances by the breakup of molecular bonds. 2. In psychoanalytic theory, the dividing of the ego into separate suborganizations (as occurs in the development of multiple personalities). 3. A rather primitive unconscious defense mechanism that protects against the anxiety arising from conflictful, ambivalent feelings toward another; seen, for example, in persons with borderline personality disorder who may see one person as all good and another as all bad.

spodogenous (spo-doj′ĕ-nus) Caused by accumulation of waste matter.

spodography (spo-dog′rah-fe) See microincinerator.

spondylalgia (spon-dĭ-lal′je-ah) Pain in a vertebra or vertebrae.

spondylarthritis (spon-dil-ar-thri′tis) Arthritis of the vertebral column.

spondylitis (spon-dĭ-li′tis) Inflammation of a vertebra or vertebrae.

    ankylosing s. Inflammatory disease of the spinal joints with involvement of the hip and shoulder joints and occasionally peripheral joints; may progress to eventual bony transformation of spinal ligaments, producing a "bamboo spine" appearance of the spine in x-ray pictures; associated with the presence of HLA antigen. Also called Marie-Strümpell disease; rheumatoid spondylitis.

    s. deformans A rigid rounded deformity of the back caused by formation of nodules around the fibrocartilaginous pads between vertebrae (intervertebral disks) and ossification of articulations and ligaments that connect the vertebrae. Also called poker back; Bechterew's disease; Strümpell's disease.

        rheumatoid s. See ankylosing spondylitis.

        tuberculous s. Tuberculosis of the midthoracic spine with anterior erosion of vertebral bodies and abscess formation. Rare in developed countries. Also called Pott's disease.

spondylo-, spondyl- Combining forms meaning a relationship to a vertebra or to the vertebral column.

spondyloarthropathy (spon-dĭ-lo-ar-throp′ah-the) Any disease affecting the joints of the vertebral column.

spondylolisthesis (spon-dĭ-lo-lis′the-sis) Forward slippage of one vertebra over the vertebra below, usually of the fifth lumbar over the sacrum or, less often, of the fourth lumbar over the fifth lumbar; causing low-back pain, limitation of movement, and protrusion of the involved spinous process; generally manifested in late childhood and adolescence. Also called spondyloptosis.

spondylolisthetic (spon-dĭ-lo-lis-thet′ik) Relating to spondylolisthesis.

spondylolysis (spon-dĭ-lol′ĭ-sis) Breaking down or degeneration of a vertebra.

spondylomalacia (spon-dĭ-lo-mah-la′she-ah) Softening of the vertebrae.

spondylopathy (spon-dĭ-lop′ah-the) Any disease of the vertebral column. Also called rachiopathy.

spondyloptosis (spon-dĭ-lop-to′sis) See spondylolisthesis.

spondylopyosis (spon-dĭ-lo-pi-o′sis) Suppurative inflammation of the body of a vertebra.

spondyloschisis (spon-dĭ-los′kĭ-sis) A congenital cleft in the vertebral arch of one or more vertebrae. Also called rachischisis.

spondylosis (spon-dĭ-lo′sis) Abnormal thickening and immobility of a vertebral joint.

sponge (spunj) 1. The fibrous skeleton of some aquatic animals. 2. A piece of cotton, folded gauze, or rolled collagen.

    absorbable gelatin s. A sterile absorbable gelatin-based sponge used to control bleeding.

    contraceptive s. A type of barrier contraceptive consisting of a disposable circular piece of polyurethane foam impregnated with a spermicide (nonoxynol 9), which is released by wetting of the sponge and the action of intercourse; the spermicide is effective for 24 hours.

spongiform (spon′jĭ-form) Like a sponge.

spongioblast (spun′je-o-blast) An embryonic cell of the supportive (non-neuronal) component of tissues in the central nervous system.

S

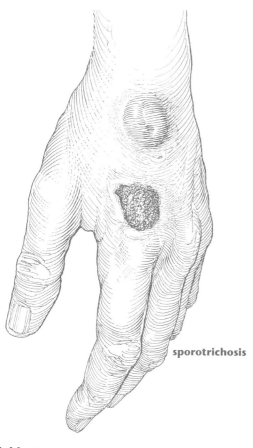

sporotrichosis

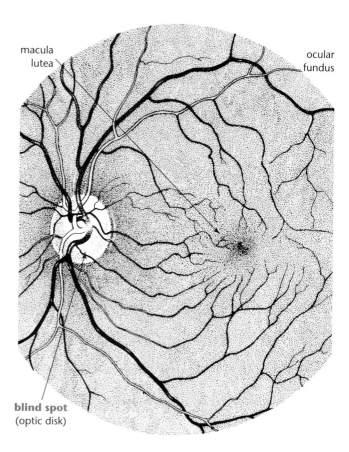

macula lutea

ocular fundus

blind spot
(optic disk)

spongioblastoma (spun-je-o-blas-to'mah) Tumor composed chiefly of spongioblasts.

spongiocyte (spun'je-o-sīt) 1. A cell of the supportive tissue of the central nervous system. 2. One of the cells in the cortex of the adrenal gland containing several vacuoles.

spongiosis (spun-je-o'sis) Swelling of the spongy layer of the skin; seen in eczema.

spongiositis (spun-je-o-si'tis) Inflammation of the corpus spongiosum of the penis.

spontaneous (spon-ta'ne-us) Occurring without apparent cause.

spoon (spoon) Implement consisting of a small shallow bowl on a handle.

   cataract s. A small spoon-shaped instrument for removing a cataractous lens from the eye.

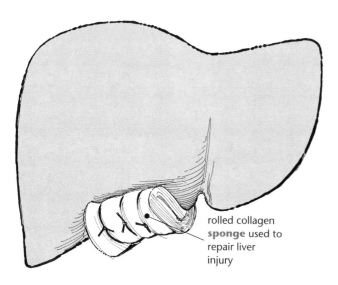

rolled collagen **sponge** used to repair liver injury

   sharp s. A spoon-shaped instrument with sharp edges for removing diseased tissue (e.g., skin granulations and carious bone).

sporadic (spo-rad'ik) 1. Occurring infrequently. 2. Not widespread. 3. In medical genetics, a disease caused by a new mutation.

sporangia (spo-ran'je-ah) Plural of sporangium.

sporangiophore (spo-ran'je-o-fōr) A structure of fungi that contains one or more sporangia.

sporangium (spo-ran'je-um), pl. sporan'gia A capsule within a plant such as a fungus in which spores are produced.

spore (spōr) A minute, thick-walled reproductive unit, usually unicellular, capable of giving rise to a new organism without fusion with another cell.

sporicide (spo'rĭ-sīd) Any substance that destroys spores.

sporo-, spori-, spor- Combining forms meaning seed; spore.

sporogenesis (spor'o-jen'ĕ-sis) See sporogony.

sporogony (spo-rog'ŏ-ne) The production of spores. Also called sporogenesis.

sporont (spo'ront) A sexually mature protozoan parasite.

sporotrichosis (spo-ro-tri-ko'sis) Fungal infection of cutaneous, subcutaneous, and local lymphatic tissues; caused by *Sporothrix schenckii;* usually occurring in florists, gardners, and nursery workers.

sporule (spor'ūl) A minute spore.

spot (spot) 1. A small circumscribed area that differs in color from its surroundings. 2. To discharge a slight amount of blood through the vagina.

   blind s. The blind area in the visual field that corresponds to the optic disk. See also scotoma; optic disk, under disk.

   blue s. *(a)* A bluish mark on the skin caused by the bite of a flea or lice. *(b)* See mongolian spot.

   café au lait s.'s Demarcated brown spots on the skin; characteristic of neurofibromatosis but also seen in individuals not afflicted with this disease.

   cherry-red s. The bright red spot in the macular area of the retina, seen in patients afflicted with Tay-Sachs disease and Niemann-Pick disease. Also called Tay's cherry-red spot.

S

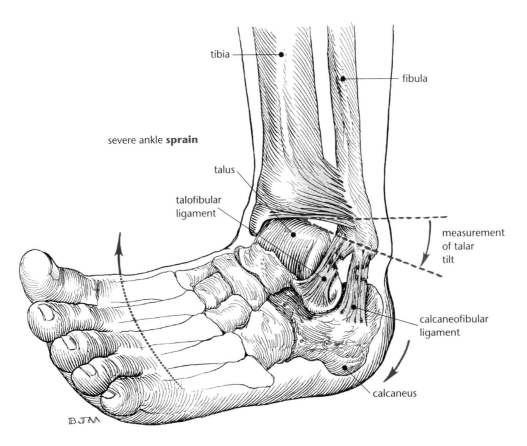

severe ankle **sprain**

- tibia
- fibula
- talus
- talofibular ligament
- measurement of talar tilt
- calcaneofibular ligament
- calcaneus

B.J.M

cotton-wool s.'s See cotton-wool patches, under patch.

Fordyce's s.'s Small, slightly raised yellowish spots on the inner surface of the lips and cheeks, due to the presence of misplaced (ectopic) sebaceous glands within the epithelium. Also called Fordyce's granules; Fordyce's disease.

Koplik's s.'s One of the signs of measles; minute bluish white lesions surrounded by a bright reddish color on the inner lining of the cheeks; they appear about two days prior to eruption of the skin rash.

liver s. See senile lentigo, under lentigo.

mongolian s. A bluish or purplish bruiselike area on the skin; a type of birthmark most commonly occurring on the lower back over the sacrum, but occasionally noted on the shoulders, back, and buttocks; usually fades over the years but traces may persist into adulthood. The lesion may be mistaken for a bruise, causing suspicion of child abuse. Also called blue spot.

rose s.'s Pinkish spots on the abdomen, seen in the early stages of typhoid fever.

Roth's s.'s White spots sometimes observed in the retina of patients with bacterial endocarditis.

shin s.'s Atrophic, brown skin spots on the front of the legs, sometimes seen in diabetes mellitus.

soft s. See fontanel.

Tardieu's s.'s The multiple, small, dark spots (petechiae) that are found in the skin and mucous membranes of the dependent parts of a corpse in livor mortis; they appear as a result of excessive accumulation of blood within capillaries and subsequent rupture of the vessel walls, causing escape of blood into the tissues.

Tay's cherry-red s. See cherry-red spot.

yellow s. See macula lutea.

spotting (spot'ing) Slight unexpected vaginal bleeding; it may be insignificant (e.g., occurring as the fertilized ovum attaches to the uterine wall), or it may indicate an abnormal condition.

sprain (sprān) Injury to the fibrous band (ligament) joining two bones of a joint, usually occurring when the joint is wrenched or twisted beyond its normal range of motion, which tears fibers but leaves the integrity of the ligament intact.

spread (spred) **1.** To disseminate; applied to an infectious disease. **2.** See metastasize.

sprue (sproo) **1.** Failure of the intestines to absorb nutrients; a malabsorptive disorder. **2.** In dentistry, the material used to form the opening through which molten metal or resin is poured into a mold to make a casting.

celiac s. See celiac disease, under disease.

s. former See sprue pin, under pin.

nontropical s. See celiac disease, under disease.

tropical s. Disease occurring in certain tropical areas, characterized by abnormal structure of the small intestine and resulting malabsorption of nutrients; caused by vitamin deficiencies and/or bacterial infection of the intestines. COMPARE celiac disease.

spud (spŭd) Small surgical instrument with a broad triangular blade; used for blunt dissection or for removing foreign bodies from tissues (e.g., the cornea).

spur (sper) An abnormal spinelike projection from a bone or a horny outgrowth from the skin.

calcaneal s. A projection from the plantar surface of the heel bone (calcaneus); often causes pain when walking. Also called heel spur.

heel s. See calcaneal spur.

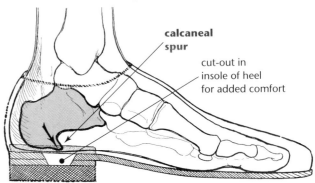

calcaneal spur

cut-out in insole of heel for added comfort

S

sputum (spu'tum) Material coughed up from the air passages.

squama (skwa'mah), pl. squa'mae **1.** A thin plate of bone. **2.** A scalelike structure.

squamomastoid (skwa-mo-mas'toid) Relating to the squamous and mastoid parts of the temporal bone.

squamopetrosal (skwa-mo-pe-tro'sal) Relating to the squamous and petrous parts of the temporal bone.

squamosa (skwa-mo'sah) The platelike portion of the temporal bone.

squamosphenoid (skwa-mo-sfe'noid) See sphenosquamosal.

squamous (skwa'mus) **1.** Scaly. **2.** Resembling scales.

squint (skwint) See strabismus.

    convergent s. See esotropia.

    divergent s. See exotropia.

stability (stah-bil'ĭ-te) The condition of being resistant to change.

    denture s. The quality that renders a denture able to resist displacement by functional forces.

    dimensional s. The resistance by a material to change in size or form.

stabilize (sta'bĭ-līz) **1.** To make or hold steady. **2.** To prevent or limit fluctuations.

stabilizer (sta'bĭ-li-zer) **1.** Any agent or object that provides stability. **2.** Any substance used to maintain the equilibrium or velocity of a chemical reaction.

    endodontic s. A pin implant passed through the apex of a tooth and root canal and into the alveolar bone to immobilize the tooth.

stable (sta'bl) Resisting change; fixed; in a state of equilibrium; neither deteriorating nor improving.

stactometer (stak-tom'ĕ-ter) A device designed for measuring drops.

staff (staf) **1.** The professional personnel of an institution such as a hospital. **2.** See director (2).

    attending s. Physicians who are members of a hospital staff and regularly see their patients at the hospital; may also supervise members of the house staff, fellows, and medical students.

    consulting s. Specialists in a particular medical field, affiliated with a hospital, who serve in an advisory role to the attending physician.

    house s. Physicians (house officers) in specialty training who care for the patients under the supervision and responsibility of the attending staff.

staff of Aesculapius (staf of es-ku-la'pe-us) A rod encircled by a single snake (without wings); symbol of the medical profession and emblem of the American Medical Association, the Royal Army Medical Corps, and the Royal Canadian Army Medical Corps.

stage (stāj) **1.** A phase in any process, such as the course of a disease, the life cycle of an organism, a physiologic development, or a procedure. **2.** The platform of a microscope on which the slide with the specimen is placed for viewing.

    exoerythrocytic s. Stage in the life cycle of the malarial parasite (plasmodium) within the substance of the host's liver, before invading the red blood cells (erythrocytes).

    incubative s. See incubation period, under period.

    s.'s of labor. See labor.

    latent s. See latent period, under period.

    prodromal s. The early stage of a disease, following the incubation period, in which some clinical manifestations appear but before the characteristic symptoms and signs of the disease are noted.

    resting s. The apparently quiescent period in the life of a cell when no mitotic changes occur. More properly called interphase.

stagger (stag'er) To walk unsteadily.

staging (sta'jing) A clinical method of providing an estimate of the gravity of a cancerous tumor, based on the size of the primary tumor and the extent of local and distant spread. Also called tumor staging.

    TNM (tumor-node-metastasis) **s.** An international system for staging tumors, used as a basis for treating cancer; it measures three basic parameters: T for the size and local invasion of the primary tumor, N for the number of involved lymph nodes, M for the presence of metastasis; each letter is followed by a number, from 0 through 4, to indicate the extent of involvement. Lowercase letters are sometimes added as a means of providing additional information: aTNM (autopsy staging), cTNM (clinical-diagnostic staging), pTNM (postsurgical pathologic staging), rTNM (retreatment staging), sTNM (surgical-evaluation staging).

    tumor s. See staging.

stagnation (stag-na'shun) The slowing or stopping of a flow, as of blood or any other body fluid.

stain (stān) **1.** Any dye used to render cells or tissues visible for microscopic study. **2.** To impart color to cells or tissues for microscopic examination. **3.** A superficial discoloration, as of the skin.

    acid s. A salt whose acid radical combines with the basic (alkaline) components of cells; it stains mainly the protoplasm.

    basic s. A salt whose basic (alkaline) radical combines with the acidic components of cells; it stains mainly the nuclei.

    contrast s. See counterstain.

    differential s. A dye that stains tissues nonselectively but can be extracted with a solvent at different rates to facilitate differentiation of elements in a specimen.

    Giemsa s. A stain composed of azure II eosin, azure II, and glycerin dissolved in methanol; used for staining blood cells, Negri bodies, certain protozoan parasites, and for chromosomes to demonstrate characteristic banding patterns.

    Gram's s., Gram's method Method used to classify bacteria based on the ability of the organism to retain a basic dye (crystal violet); those retaining the violet stain are gram-positive and those that do not retain it are gram-negative.

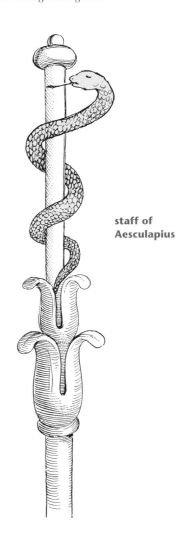

**staff of
Aesculapius**

S

hematoxylin-eosin s., H-E s. A mixture of hematoxylin, eosin, and water; it stains cytoplasm pink and nuclei blue; used widely for routine examination of tissues.

Mallory's trichrome s. A trichrome stain especially suitable for studying connective tissue fibers.

metachromatic s. A dye (e.g., methylene blue, azure A, thionin) that stains varied cell elements in colors that are different than the dye itself.

Nissl's s. See Nissl's method, under method.

Papanicolaou's s. Stain applied to smears of body secretions to detect the presence of cancer; consists generally of aqueous hematoxylin with several counterstaining dyes in ethyl alcohol.

periodic acid–Schiff s., PAS s. A tissue stain for demonstrating glycogen basement membranes and neutral mucopolysaccharides; periodic acid is used to oxidize the aldehyde groups of carbohydrates, which in turn convert colorless Schiff reagent to magenta. Also called periodic acid-Schiff reaction.

port wine s. See nevus flammeus, under nevus.

supravital s. A relatively nontoxic dye (e.g., neutral red) used to study living cells.

vital s. A dye introduced into a living organism.

Weigert's s. for myelin A histologic technique using ferric chloride and hematoxylin; intact myelin stains deep blue, degenerated myelin light yellow.

Wright's s. A mixture of both acid and basic dyes (eosin and methylene blue) commonly used for demonstrating blood cells and malarial parasites.

Ziehl-Neelsen s. Stain used for identifying the tubercle bacillus and other bacterial cells.

staining (stān'ing) **1.** The coloration of microscopic specimens with a dye to improve their visibility. **2.** In dentistry, alteration of the color of teeth.

stalagmometer (stal-ag-mom'ĕ-ter) Device for obtaining and measuring drops from a liquid at definite intervals for the purpose of calculating the surface tension of the liquid.

stalk (stawk) An elongated connection resembling a stem.

allantoic s. A narrow connection between the urogenital sinus of the embryo and the allantoic sac.

body s. A precursor of the umbilical cord, composed of a mesenchymal mass of tissue connecting the ventral portion of the tail end of the embryo to the inner face of the chorionic vesicle.

hypophysial s. See infundibulum of hypophysis, under infundibulum.

infundibular s. See infundibulum of hypophysis, under infundibulum.

optic s. A slender structure in the early embryo connecting the optic vesicle to the forebrain; it develops into the optic nerve.

pineal s. The slender structure attaching the pineal body to the roof of the third ventricle of the brain.

pituitary s. See infundibulum of hypophysis, under infundibulum.

yolk s. The stalk connecting the yolk sac to the ventral aspect of a young embryo.

stammering (stam'er-ing) A faltering way of speaking, characterized by involuntary pauses and repetitions of syllables; distinguished from stuttering.

standard (stan'dard) A unit or specification established as a measure or model for comparison, uniformity, or control.

s. of care A description of the conduct expected of an individual in a given situation regarding the care of a patient.

hazard communication s. A standard of information issued by the Occupational Safety and Health Administration (OSHA). Its goal is to reduce the incidence of chemical-source illness and injuries in the workplace by establishing uniform requirements for evaluating the hazards of all chemicals produced, imported, or used in the U.S. workplace and for transmitting this information to involved employers and exposed employees.

minimum s. A standard of medical care based on modes of treatment used by a medical specialty group in good standing.

standardization (stan-dard-ĭ-za'shun) **1.** The formulation of standards. **2.** The act of bringing something (e.g., a pharmaceutical preparation; a procedure) into conformity with a standard.

stannic (stan'ik) Containing tin with a valence of four.

stannous (stan'us) Containing tin with a valence of two.

stannum (stan'um) Latin for tin.

stapedectomy (sta-pĕ-dek'to-me) Surgical removal of the smallest ear ossicle (stapes) from the middle ear chamber.

stapedial (stah-pe'de-al) Relating to the smallest ossicle (stapes) of the middle ear chamber.

stapediotenotomy (stah-pe-de-o-tĕ-not'o-me) Surgical division of the tendon of the stapedius muscle in the middle ear chamber.

stapediovestibular (stah-pe-de-o-ves-tib'u-lar) Relating to both the stapes of the middle ear chamber and the vestibule of the inner ear.

stapedius (stah-pe'de-us) See table of muscles.

stapes (sta'pēz) The smallest and innermost of the three movable ossicles of the middle ear; it articulates by its head with the incus (middle ossicle), and its base (footplate) is inserted and attached to the margin of the oval window (fenestra vestibuli); the smallest bone in the body, it resembles a stirrup and is sometimes called by that name. See also table of bones.

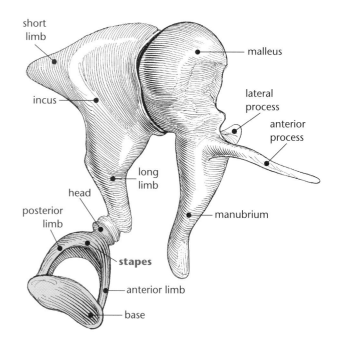

staphylectomy (staf-il-lek'tome) See uvulectomy.

staphyline (staf'ĭ-lin) See botryoid.

staphylion (stah-fil'e-on) A craniometric landmark; the midpoint of the posterior edge of the hard palate.

staphylo- Combining form meaning grapelike; the uvula.

staphylococcal (staf-ĭ-lo-kok'al) Relating to staphylococci.

staphylococcemia (staf-ĭ-lo-kok-se'me-ah) The presence of staphylococci in the blood.

staphylococci (staf-ĭ-lo-kok'si) Plural of staphylococcus.

Staphylococcus (staf-ĭ-lo-kok'us) Genus of gram-positive, nonmotile bacteria (family Micrococcaceae) that tend to aggregate in grapelike clusters.

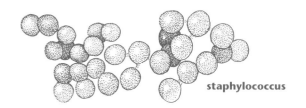

staphylococcus

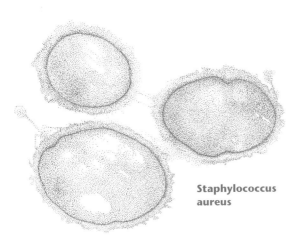

Staphylococcus aureus

S. aureus A species often carried in the nasal cavity; it is the causative agent of boils, carbuncles, abscesses, and other pus-forming infections.

S. epidermidis A variety normally present on the skin, causing minor infections in skin wounds (e.g., stitch abscesses).

staphylococcus (staf-ĭ-lo-kok'us), pl. staphylococ'ci Any microorganism of the genus *Staphylococcus*.

staphyloderma (staf-ĭ-lo-der'mah) Any pus-forming skin disorder caused by staphylococci.

staphylolysin (staf-ĭ-lol'ĭ-sin) **1.** A substance produced by a staphylococcus that causes destruction of red blood cells and liberation of the blood pigment hemoglobin. **2.** An antibody that causes dissolution of staphylococci.

staphyloma (staf-ĭ-lo'mah) A localized bulge of the cornea or sclera usually lined with uveal tissue.

staphyloplasty (staf'ĭ-lo-plas-te) Surgical repair of the uvula and (often) the soft palate.

staphyloptosis (staf-ĭ-lop-to'sis) See uvuloptosis.

stapling (sta'pling) The act of closing surgical wounds with specially designed staples.

gastric s. See vertical banded gastroplasty, under gastroplasty.

stomach s. See vertical banded gastroplasty, under gastroplasty.

starch (starch) **1.** A carbohydrate converted into dextrin and glucose by the action of amylase enzyme in saliva and pancreatic juice. **2.** A substance composed of granules separated from the mature grain of Indian corn (*Zea mays*); used in pharmaceuticals and as a dusting powder.

starch eating (starch ēt'ing) See amylophagia.

stasis (sta'sis) Reduction or stoppage of a flow (e.g., of blood or lymph).

venous s. Impairment or cessation of blood flow in a vein. Also called hypostatic congestion.

state (stāt) A condition.

appallic s. Former term for persistent vegetative state.

carrier s. The condition of harboring disease-causing microorganisms without being affected by them.

central excitatory s. A condition of hyperexcitability of nerve cells produced by the storing of subthreshold stimuli in a reflex center of the spinal cord.

convulsive s. See status epilepticus.

de-efferented s. See locked-in syndrome, under syndrome.

dreamy s. A prolonged state of detachment or semiconscious condition associated with epilepsy.

permanent vegetative s. A persistent vegatative state that has been diagnosed irreversible with a high degree of clinical certainty, based on probabilities (not absolutes). COMPARE persistent vegetative state.

persistent vegetative s. (PVS) A clinical condition of complete unawareness of the self and the environment, accompanied by sleep-wake cycles with either complete or partial preservation of hypothalamic and brainstem autonomic functions; the patient does not require respiratory or circulatory assistance but requires nutritional support (parenteral or via a nasogastric tube); may move the limbs or the trunk in a meaningless way, and may occasionally shed tears; the condition is usually caused by trauma or insufficient supply of oxygen to the brain and lasts more than a few weeks (at least one month); can also result from the progression of degenerative or metabolic neurologic diseases, or from developmental malformations of the nervous system. PVS can be diagnosed according to the following criteria: no evidence of awareness of self or environment and inability to interact with others; no evidence of sustained, purposeful, or voluntary behavioral responses to external stimuli (visual, auditory, tactile, or noxious); no evidence of language comprehension or expression; intermittent wakefulness manifested by the presence of sleep-wake cycles; sufficient hypothalamic and brainstem autonomic functions to allow survival with medical and nursing care; bladder and bowel incontinence; and variably preserved cranial-nerve reflexes and spinal reflexes. Distinguished from locked-in syndrome) in which part of the brainstem is damaged but the cortex is intact); PET scan shows cortical glucose metabolism to be very low in PVS but only slightly less than normal in locked-in syndrome. Formerly called appallic state; appallic syndrome. COMPARE permanent vegetative state. See also locked-in syndrome, under syndrome.

refractory s. Reduced excitability of a nerve following a re-

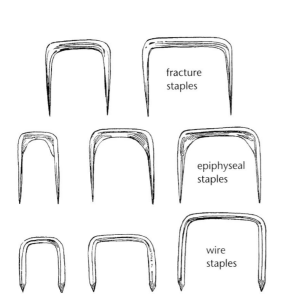

fracture staples

epiphyseal staples

wire staples

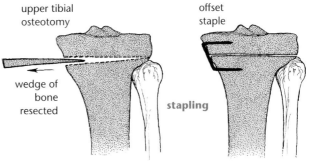

upper tibial osteotomy

offset staple

wedge of bone resected

stapling

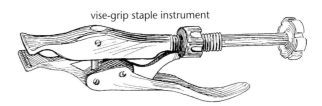

vise-grip staple instrument

S

sponse to previous stimulation.

steady s. Any condition that remains constant because opposing forces or processes cancel each other's effects.

twilight s. Condition of impaired consciousness in which a person may perform complex acts and have no recollection afterward.

vegetative s. A condition in which self-awareness and all evidence of learned behavior has been lost. See also permanent vegetative state; persistent vegetative state.

state-mandated benefits laws State laws requiring insurance contractors to provide coverage for certain health services (e.g., *in vitro* fertilization), or for services provided by certain health care providers (e.g., audiologists). Self-insured employers or organizations are exempt. See also self-insurance.

statim (sta′tim) (stat) Latin for at once; immediately.

statistics (stah-tis′tiks) **1.** The science that deals with variation in data by means of collection, classification, and analysis in such a manner as to obtain reliable results. **2.** An aggregate of organized numerical data.

medical s. The branch of statistics concerned with quantitative information relating to the incidence, prevalence, course, and management of disease.

vital s. Tabulated information concerning human births, health, diseases, and deaths based on nationally recorded data.

statoconia (stat-o-ko′ne-ah) Granular particles of calcium carbonate and protein that are normally embedded in the gelatinous membrane of the macula within the utricle and saccule of the inner ear. Also called otoconia; otoliths.

stature (stat′ūr) The natural height of a person.

status (sta′tus) State; condition.

s. asthmaticus Asthma attack in which the airway obstruction persists for several days or weeks.

s. epilepticus Prolonged or repetitive epileptic seizures without recovery between individual seizures; condition may occur with grand mal, absence, or partial seizures. Also called convulsive state.

steal (stēl) Reduction of blood supply to a tissue due to an arterial obstruction, which causes a reverse rerouting of blood flow.

subclavian s. See subclavian steal syndrome, under syndrome.

stearic acid (ste-ah′rik as′id) A fatty acid resulting from the breakdown of fats; used in pharmaceutical preparations.

stearo- Combining form meaning fat.

steato- Combining form meaning fat.

steatocystoma (ste-ah-to-sis-to′mah) A sebaceous cyst.

steatolysis (ste-ah-tol′ĭ-sis) The breakdown of fat molecules in the process of digestion.

steatonecrosis (ste′ah-to-ně-kro′sis) See fat necrosis, under necrosis.

steatopygia, steatopyga (ste-ah-to-pij′e-ah, ste-ah-to-pij′ah) Excessive accumulation of fat in the buttocks.

steatorrhea (ste-ah-to-re′ah) The presence of excessive amounts of fat in the feces, as seen in malabsorption syndromes.

steatosis (ste-ah-to′sis) Accumulation of fat in the tissues.

hepatic s. See fatty liver, under liver.

stegnosis (steg-no′sis) A constriction.

steinstrasse (stīn-straz′er) The x-ray appearance of stone fragments filling a portion of the ureter after a large kidney stone has been broken up by extracorporeal lithotripsy. The term means street of stone in German.

stellate (stel′āt) Shaped like a star.

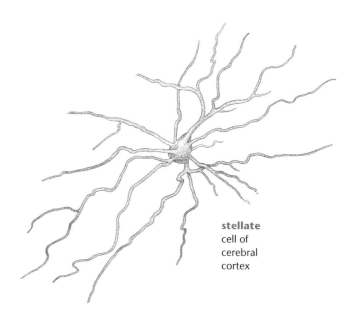

stellate cell of cerebral cortex

stellectomy (stel-lek′to-me) Removal of the stellate ganglion (at the base of the neck); usually performed for the relief of pain that does not respond to analgesic treatment. Also called stellate ganglionectomy.

stenion (sten′e-on) One of two craniometric points located in the temporal areas of the skull, at each end of the shortest transverse diameter.

steno- Combining form meaning narrowness.

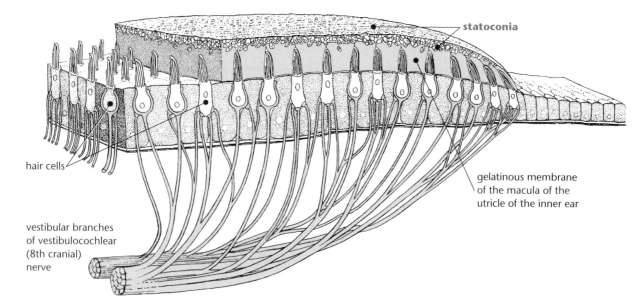

statoconia

hair cells

gelatinous membrane of the macula of the utricle of the inner ear

vestibular branches of vestibulocochlear (8th cranial) nerve

state-mandated benefits laws ■ **steno-**

stenochoria (sten-o-ko're-ah) Abnormal constriction of a duct, canal, or opening.

stenopeic, stenopaic (sten-o-pe'ik, sten-o-pa'ik) Having a narrow opening.

stenosed (stĕ-nōzd') Abnormally constricted.

stenosis (stĕ-no'sis), pl. steno'ses Abnormal constriction or narrowness of a channel or an opening.

    aortic s. (AS) Narrowing of the opening between the aorta and the left ventricle of the heart; may be congenital or acquired.

    calcific aortic valve s. Aortic stenosis caused by accumulation of calcified masses in the aortic valve; an age-related (usually mild) degenerative condition occurring in the sixth to seventh decade.

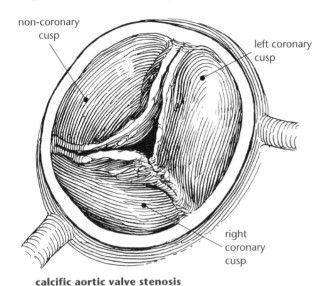

calcific aortic valve stenosis

    congenital hypertrophic pyloric s. See hypertrophic pyloric stenosis.

    congenital pyloric s. See hypertrophic pyloric stenosis.

    hypertrophic pyloric s. Condition seen in newborn infants, marked by an increase in the size of the circular and longitudinal muscles of the pylorus at the lower end of the stomach, causing a narrowing of the orifice leading to the small intestine; symptoms begin in the third to fifth weeks of life; they include vomiting, weight loss, hunger, and infrequent small stools. Also called congenital pyloric stenosis; congenital hypertrophic pyloric stenosis; infantile hypertrophic pyloric stenosis.

    idiopathic hypertrophic subaortic s. (IHSS) Disease of the heart muscle marked by disproportionate thickening of the interventricular septum and left ventricular wall, sometimes causing obstruction to the left outflow tract. Cause is unknown. Also called muscular subaortic stenosis; asymmetric septal hypertrophy (ASH).

    infantile hypertrophic pyloric s. See hypertrophic pyloric stenosis.

    infundibular s. Obstruction of the outflow tract of the right ventricle of the heart, usually caused by either or both of two conditions: a fibrous ring just below the pulmonic valve, or hypertrophy of heart muscle surrounding the infundibulum.

    mitral s. Narrowing of the mitral valve opening (between the left atrium and left ventricle of the heart).

    muscular subaortic s. See idiopathic hypertrophic subaortic stenosis.

    pulmonary s. Narrowing of the opening between the pulmonary trunk and the right ventricle of the heart.

    pyloric s. An abnormal narrowing of the lower outlet (pylorus) of the stomach, which prevents food from passing into the small intestine; may be caused by scarring of the mucosal lining from peptic ulcers and chronic gastritis. May be simulated by cancerous tumors. Also called pyloristenosis.

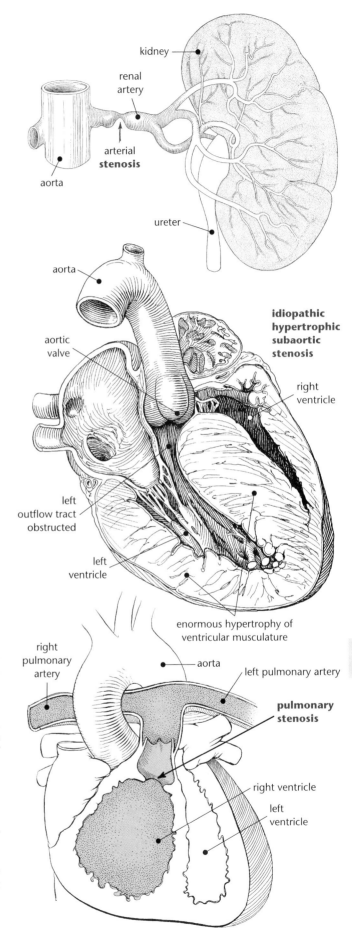

subaortic s., subvalvular s. Obstruction of the outflow tract of the left ventricle of the heart, caused by a fibrous band or by hypertrophy of the muscular septum just below the aortic valve.

tricuspid s. Narrowing of the tricuspid valve opening (between the right atrium and right ventricle of the heart).

stenostenosis (sten-o-stĕ-no′sis) Constriction of the parotid duct.

stenostomia (sten-o-sto′me-ah) Abnormal narrowness of the mouth.

stenothermal (sten-o-ther′mal) Capable of withstanding only slight changes in temperature.

stenothorax (sten-o-tho′raks) Abnormal narrowness of the chest or thoracic cavity.

stenotic (stĕ-not′ik) Affected with stenosis; narrowed abnormally.

stent (stent) A device used for support of a tubular structure during a surgical procedure (e.g., anastomosis), or a body orifice or cavity during skin grafting. Also used in a blood vessel or ureter after correction of a blockage.

urethral s. Device for keeping open the urethral channel (urethra) when compressed by an enlarged prostate.

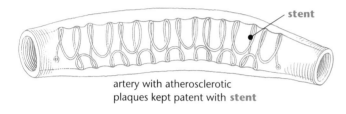

artery with atherosclerotic plaques kept patent with **stent**

stenting (stent′ing) The introduction of a stent into a body structure.

stephanion (stĕ-fa′ne-on) A craniometric point at the intersection of the coronal suture and the inferior temporal line.

steppage (step′aj) See steppage gait, under gait.

sterco- Combining form meaning feces.

stercobilin (ster-ko-bi′lin) One of the main pigments of feces, derived from bile.

stercolith (ster′ko-lith) See fecalith.

stercoraceous (ster-ko-ra′shus) Containing or composed of feces.

stero- Combining form meaning firm; solid; three-dimensional.

stereoanesthesia (ste-re-o-an-es-the′ze-ah) See astereognosis.

stereoarthrolysis (ste-re-o-ar-throl′ĭ-sis) Surgical formation of a movable joint.

stereocampimeter (ste-re-o-kam-pim′ĕ-ter) A binocular apparatus for examining the central visual field of each eye separately while both eyes fixate similar targets.

stereochemistry (ste-re-o-kem′is-tre) The branch of chemistry concerned with the spatial arrangement of atoms in a compound.

stereocilia (ste-re-o-sil′e-ah) Plural of stereocilium.

stereocilium (ste-re-o-sil′e-um) A tuft of long, nonmotile, hairlike outgrowths from the free surface of an epithelial cell; seen in the epididymis of the male reproductive system.

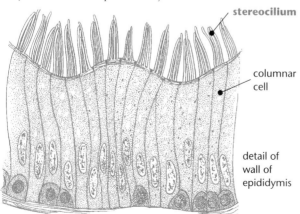

stereocilium

columnar cell

detail of wall of epididymis

stereocinefluorography (ste-re-o-sin′ĕ-floo-or-og′rah-fe) Three-dimensional motion picture photography of x-ray images obtained by stereoscopic fluoroscopy.

stereognosis (ste-re-og-no′sis) The faculty of being able to sense the three-dimensional form of something touched.

stereopsis (ste-re-op′sis) The perception of depth occurring in normal binocular vision. Also called stereoscopic vision.

stereospecific (ster-e-o-spĭ-sif′ik) Denoting enzymes or synthetic organic reactions that act only with a given molecule or with a limited class of molecules.

stereotaxic (ste-re-o-tak′sik) Relating to stereotaxy.

stereotaxis (ste-re-o-tak′sis) 1. The localization of three-dimensional arrangements (as of body structures) by means of coordinate landmarks. 2. The movement of an organism as a whole toward or away from a rigid surface with which it comes in contact.

stereotaxy (ste-re-o-tak′se) A technique for introducing an electrode or a probe into a specific area of the brain by means of a three-dimensional coordinate system attached to the skull; used to destroy minute fiber tracts or nuclear masses deep within the brain. Also called sterotaxic surgery; stereotactic surgery.

stereotropism (ste-re-ot′ro-pizm) The movement of parts of an organism toward or away from a rigid surface with which it comes in contact.

stereotypy (ste′re-o-ti-pe) The incessant, mechanical repetition of certain movements or speech; commonly seen in schizophrenia.

oral s. See verbigeration.

steric (ste′rik) Relating to stereochemistry.

sterile (ster′il) 1. Incapable of reproducing. 2. Free from living disease-causing microorganisms. Also called aseptic.

sterility (stĕ-ril′ĭ-te) 1. Inability to produce offspring. In males, lack of sperm production; in females, inability to conceive. Sterility may or may not be reversible. COMPARE infertility. 2. The state of being free from living microorganisms.

sterilization (ster-ĭ-lĭ-za′shun) 1. Destruction or elimination of living microorganisms by physical methods, chemical agents, or filtration. 2. A treatment that deprives living organisms of the ability to reproduce.

female s. See tubal sterilization.

male s. See vasectomy.

tubal s. Sterilization of the female by any of several surgical techniques performed on the fallopian (uterine) tubes; may be a simple tying (ligation) of the tubes, constriction of a small loop of the tubes with a tight band, insertion of a plastic or metal clip on each tube to obstruct the lumen, electrocoagulation of tubal tissues to seal the lumen, or cutting away a section of the tubes or their fimbriated ends. Also called female sterilization. See also fimbriation; tubal ligation, under ligation; Irving's operation, Madlener's operation, and Pomeroy's operation, under operation.

sterilizer (ster′ĭ-liz-er) An apparatus for rendering anything germ-free.

sternad (ster′nad) Toward or in the direction of the breastbone (sternum).

sternal (ster′nal) Relating to the breastbone (sternum).

sternalgia (ster-nal′je-ah) Pain in the sternal area. Also called sternodynia.

sterno-, stern- Combining forms meaning sternum.

sternoclavicular (ster-no-klah-vik′u-lar) Relating to the breastbone (sternum) and the collarbone (clavicle). Also called sternocleidal.

sternocleidal (ster-no-kli′dal) See sternoclavicular.

sternocleidomastoid (ster-no-kli′do-mas′toid) Relating to the sternum, clavicle, and mastoid process; applied to the neck muscle that has its origin and insertion on these bones.

sternocostal (ster-no-kos′tal) Relating to the breastbone (sternum) and the ribs.

sternodynia (ster-no-din′e-ah) See sternalgia.

sternoschisis (ster-nos′kĭ-sis) Congenital cleft of the sternum; may involve the upper or lower portions or the entire bone.

sternotomy (ster-not′o-me) A surgical cut into or through the sternum.

S

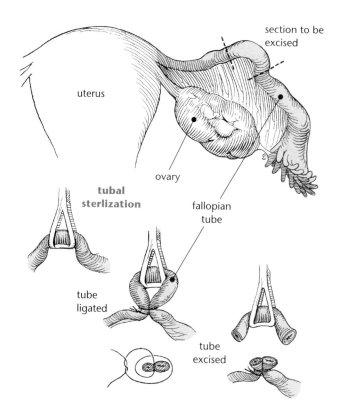

section to be excised

uterus

ovary

tubal sterlization

fallopian tube

tube ligated

tube excised

sternum (ster′num) A long, flat bone forming the middle part of the anterior wall of the thoracic cage; composed of three parts: manubrium, body, and xiphoid process; it articulates with the collarbones (clavicles) and cartilages of the first seven pairs of ribs.

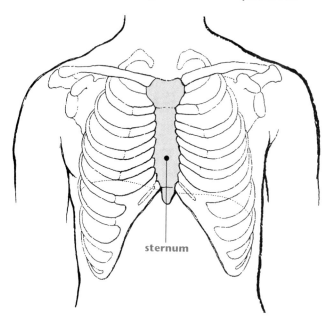

sternum

sternutatory (ster-nu′tah-tor-e) Causing sneezing.

steroid (ste′roid) One of a large family of chemical substances that includes the adrenocortical hormones, the male and female sex hormones, and the D vitamins.

　　anabolic s. Any of a group of drugs with protein-building properties that are synthetic derivatives of the male hormone testosterone; they help to strengthen bones and to accelerate muscle recovery after injury caused by strenous exercise. Anabolic steroids have been abused by athletes, resulting in severe depression upon withdrawal; other adverse effects of abuse include acne, baldness, liver and adrenal gland damage, infertility and impotence in men,

and virilization in women; if taken in childhood, they may stunt growth.

steroidogenesis (ste-roi-do-jen′ĕ-sis) The natural production of steroids.

sterol (ste′rol) One of a group of simple steroids, present in all animal and plant tissue except bacteria; the best-known member of the group is cholesterol.

stertor (ster′tor) A snoring sound produced in breathing.

stertorous (ster′to-rus) Characterized by snoring.

stethalgia (steth-al′je-ah) Pain in the chest.

stetho-, steth- Combining forms meaning chest.

stethograph (steth′o-graf) An apparatus for recording the breathing movements of the chest.

stethoscope (steth′o-skōp) Instrument for listening to sounds occurring within the body, especially respiratory and vascular sounds.

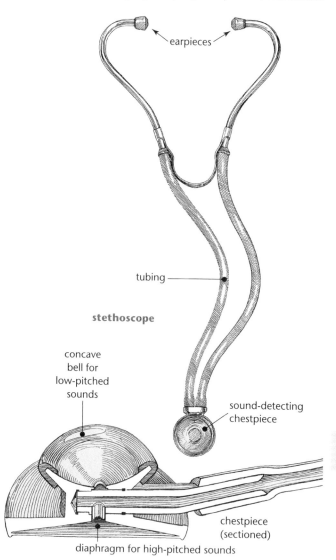

earpieces

tubing

stethoscope

concave bell for low-pitched sounds

sound-detecting chestpiece

chestpiece (sectioned)

diaphragm for high-pitched sounds

stibialism (stib′e-al-izm) Poisoning with antimony.

stigma (stig′mah), pl. stig′mata, stig′mas Any visible evidence characteristic of a disease (e.g., a spot, rash, sign, symptom).

　　personal stigmata In forensic medicine, anything on an unidentified corpse that serves to establish its identity; may be congenital defects (e.g., talipes, cleft lip); scars (e.g., from surgery, burns, old injuries); old amputations and fractures; artificial eye; moles; etc.

stigmata (stig′mah-tah) Alternate plural of stigma.

stilbestrol (stil-bes′trol) See diethylstilbestrol.

stillbirth (stil′berth) Death of the fetus while in the uterus.

S

stillborn (stil′born) Born dead.

stilus (sti′lus) Stylus.

stimulant (stim′u-lant) **1.** Causing acceleration of organic activity. **2.** Any agent that produces such an effect.

  general central nervous system s. Any agent capable of increasing excitability of the central nervous system (CNS) on a continuum as a function of dosage, from mild excitability to severe convulsions (e.g., caffeine, amphetamines, cocaine, strychnine).

  local s. A stimulant that affects only a restricted part of the body.

stimulation (stim-u-la′shun) **1.** The act of exciting the body or any of its parts to increased functional activity. **2.** The state of being stimulated.

  epidermal s. See transcutaneous electrical nerve stimulation.

  percutaneous s. See transcutaneous electrical nerve stimulation.

  photic s. In electroencephalography, the use of a flickering light in an attempt to evoke latent or subclinical abnormalities (e.g., epilepsy).

  transcutaneous electrical nerve s. (TENS) A method of treatment for the relief of persistent pain that has not responded to drug therapy; minute electrical impulses are applied to nerve endings lying within the skin by means of electrodes on, or surgically implanted into, the skin. Also called epidermal stimulation; percutaneous stimulation.

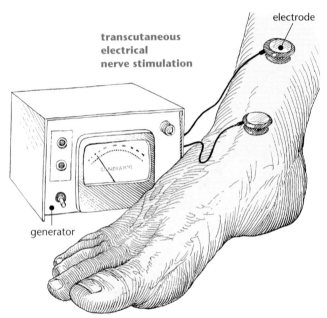

transcutaneous electrical nerve stimulation

electrode

generator

stimulator (stim-u-la′tor) **1.** See stimulant. **2.** Any device for delivering low-voltage electrical stimuli to any part of the body.

  long-acting thyroid s. (LATS) A substance found in the blood of most patients with Graves′ disease; it mimics the stimulating action of the hormone thyrotropin but its effect on the thyroid gland is more prolonged.

stimulus (stim′u-lus), pl. stim′uli **1.** A stimulant. **2.** Anything that is capable of eliciting a physiologic or psychologic response.

  conditioned s. (CS) A stimulus that originally does not evoke a particular response but acquires this capacity after repeated pairing with another stimulus that is naturally capable of eliciting the response.

  unconditioned s. (UCS) A stimulus that normally elicits a particular response.

sting (sting) **1.** A sharp brief pain produced by pricking of the skin (e.g., by certain species of arthropods, fish, or plants). **2.** The organ or part of an animal or plant that inflicts such pain.

stirrup (stir′up) See stapes.

stitch (stich) **1.** A suture used to close a wound. **2.** A sudden brief, sharp pain.

stoichiometry (stoi-ke-om′ĕ-tre) The study of the combining proportions (by weight and volume) of elements participating in a chemical reaction.

stoma (sto′mah) **1.** Any small opening. **2.** An artificial opening made between two body cavities or channels or between any body cavity or tube and the exterior.

stomach (stum′uk) The saclike portion of the digestive tract, between the esophagus and small intestine, where ingested food is acted on by the enzymes and hydrochloric acid of gastric juice before it is released into the duodenum by peristalsis; the stomach is entirely covered by peritoneum and, in the adult, it generally has a capacity of about 1 liter.

  hourglass s. A stomach with an abnormal constriction at the midpoint.

  leather-bottle s. See linitis plastica, under linitis.

  sclerotic s. See linitis plastica, under linitis.

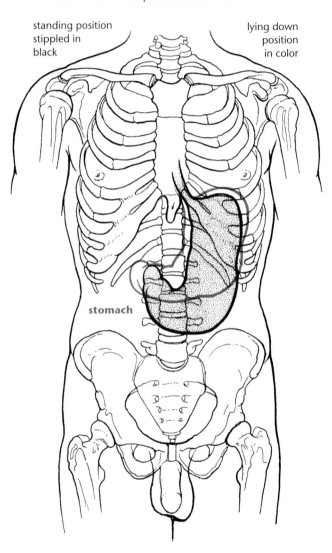

standing position stippled in black

lying down position in color

stomach

stomachache (stum′uk-āk) Popular term for abdominal pain; pain often originates from sites other than the stomach.

stomachal (stum′ah-kal) Relating to the stomach.

stomal (sto′mal) Relating to a stoma.

stomata (sto′mah-tah) Alternate plural of stoma.

stomatal (sto′mah-tal) Relating to a stoma.

stomatalgia (sto-mah-tal′je-ah) Pain in the mouth. Also called stomatodynia.

stomatic (sto-mat′ik) Relating to the mouth; oral.

stomatitis (sto-mah-ti′tis) Inflammation of the mucous lining of the mouth.

S

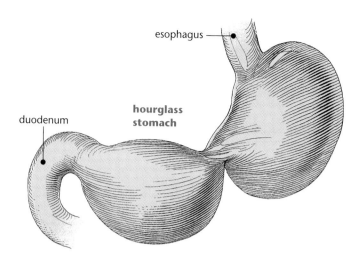

esophagus

hourglass
stomach

duodenum

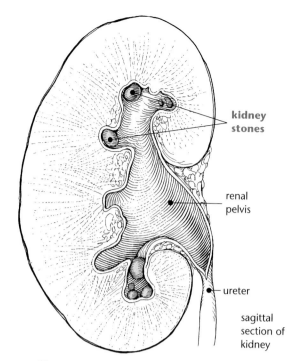

kidney
stones

renal
pelvis

ureter

sagittal
section of
kidney

angular s. Superficial fissuring and inflammation of the angles of the mouth; may be due to a variety of conditions (e.g., riboflavin deficiency and monilial infections).

gangrenous s. See noma.

recurrent aphthous s. A recurrent condition characterized by the appearance of small, single or multiple shallow ulcers (aphthous ulcers) on the mucous lining of the mouth. Cause is unknown, but factors such as immunologic abnormalities and nutritional deficiencies (e.g., of iron, vitamin B_{12}, or folic acid) have been proposed as the underlying cause. A variety of situations have been identified as factors precipitating an outbreak of ulcers, including: local trauma, psychic stress, local allergic reactions, and endocrine activity (e.g., related to the menstrual cycle). Also called canker; canker sore; ulcerative stomatitis. See also aphthous ulcer, under ulcer.

ulcerative s. See recurrent aphthous stomatitis.

stomato-, stom- Combining forms meaning mouth.

stomatodynia (sto-mah-to-din'e-ah) See stomatalgia.

stomatology (sto-mah-tol'o-je) The study of the structures and functions of the mouth in health and disease.

stomatomalacia (sto-mah-to-mah-la'she-ah) Abnormal softening of any structure in the mouth.

stomatomycosis (sto-mah-to-mi-ko'sis) Any fungal disease of the mouth.

stomatopathy (sto-mah-top'ah-the) Any disease of structures within the oral cavity.

stomatorrhagia (sto-mah-to-ra'je-ah) Bleeding from any structure in the mouth.

stomodeum (sto-mo-de'um) A depression between the maxillary and mandibular processes of the embryo that later develops into the oral cavity.

-stomy Combining form meaning artificial or surgical opening (e.g., colostomy).

stone (stōn) An abnormal concretion in the body, usually in the lumen of ducts or hollow organs, formed by accumulation of mineral salts. Also called calculus.

articular s. Concretion formed within a joint.

biliary s. See gallstone.

calcium s. A calcium-containing stone usually occurring as calcium oxalate or calcium phosphate; in the urinary tract, it is often associated with such disorders as hypercalciuria, sarcoidosis, hyperparathyroidism, and renal tubular acidosis.

chalk s. See tophus.

cystine s. Renal stone usually occurring in people with the inherited metabolic disorder cystinuria.

gallbladder s. See gallstone.

infection s. See struvite stone.

kidney s. Stone formed in the kidney, ranging in size from a tiny particle to a large concretion filling the renal pelvis; usually composed of calcium oxalate, calcium phosphate, and uric acid. Also called renal stone; renal calculus; nephrolith.

mulberry s. Concretion resembling a mulberry, composed chiefly of calcium oxalate and formed in the bladder.

pulp s. A collection of calcified material in the pulp chamber of a tooth, or a projection into the chamber from the cavity wall. Also called endolith; denticle.

renal s. See kidney stone.

salivary s. A concretion in a salivary gland or duct.

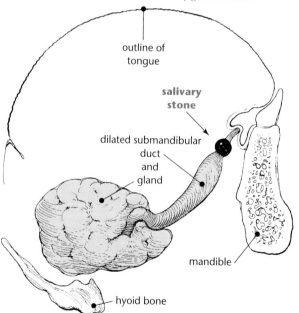

outline of
tongue

salivary
stone

dilated submandibular
duct
and
gland

mandible

hyoid bone

staghorn s. A large renal stone with many branches filling the pelvis and calices of the kidney.

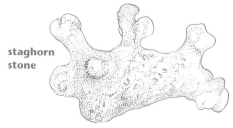

staghorn
stone

S

struvite s. Renal stone associated with chronic infections of the urinary tract with urea-splitting bacteria that convert urea to ammonia (e.g., species of the genera *Pseudomonas*, *Klebsiella*, and *Staphylococcus*). Also called infection stone; triple phosphate stone.

    tear s. See dacryolith.

    triple phosphate s. See struvite stone.

    ureteral s. A urinary stone lodged in the ureter, often in either of three areas where the diameter of the ureter is smallest: at the junction of the renal pelvis and ureter, at the point where the ureter crosses over the iliac vessels, or at the junction of the ureter and bladder.

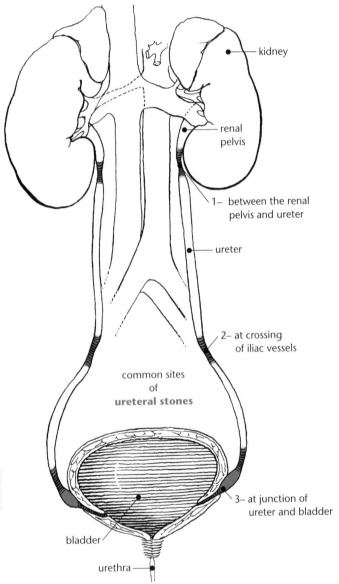

kidney

renal pelvis

1– between the renal pelvis and ureter

ureter

2– at crossing of iliac vessels

common sites of **ureteral stones**

3– at junction of ureter and bladder

bladder

urethra

    uric acid s. A urinary tract stone composed chiefly of uric acid, sometimes associated with certain metabolic abnormalities (e.g., primary gout and Lesch-Nyhan syndrome), chronic diarrhea, and excessive excretion of uric acid (hyperuricosuria).

    urinary s. Concretion formed anywhere within the urinary tract (kidney, ureter, bladder, urethra); frequently causing obstruction, bleeding, and pain. Also called urinary calculus; urolith.

    vesical s. Concretion formed or retained in the bladder. Also called cystolith; vesical calculus.

stool (stūl) A bowel movement; feces.

    tarry s. A stool of very dark, tarlike color; may be caused by bleeding within the stomach or upper intestinal tract or by certain substances (e.g., iron).

storage (stor'ij) The second stage in the memory process (following encoding and preceding retrieval) in which modified (encoded) sensory stimuli are mentally retained.

storm (storm) A sudden increase in the severity of an illness.

    thyroid s. See thyrotoxic crisis, under crisis.

strabismal, strabismic (strah-biz'mal, strah-biz'mik) Relating to strabismus.

strabismus (strah-biz'mus) Eye disorder marked by inability of one eye to focus with the other. Also called heterotropia; squint.

    convergent s. See esotropia.

    divergent s. See exotropia.

strain (strān) **1.** Tearing of a muscle or its tendon caused by extreme pulling, pushing, or overstretching of the muscle or tendon insertion, as in lifting a heavy weight or bearing an external force (usually a traction force). **2.** To produce such an injury. **3.** In bacteriology, a group of microorganisms originating from a common ancestor and retaining the characteristics of the ancestor.

strait (strāt) A narrow passage or space.

    inferior pelvic s. See pelvic plane of outlet, under plane.

    superior pelvic s. See pelvic plane of inlet, under plane.

straitjacket, straightjacket (strāt'jak-et) A garment with long sleeves that can secure the arms tightly against the body; used to restrain a violent patient.

stramonium (strah-mo'ne-um) The dried leaves of jimsonweed (*Datura stramonium*), formerly used in the treatment of asthma.

strangle (strang'gl) To suffocate by compressing the trachea so as to prevent breathing; to choke.

strangulation (strang-gu-la'shun) **1.** The act of terminating normal breathing by constriction of air passages. **2.** Constriction that cuts off blood supply to a part, particularly to a loop of intestine.

strangury (strang'gu-re) Slow, difficult, and painful emptying of the urinary bladder.

strap (strap) **1.** A strip of adhesive plaster. **2.** To bind with strips of adhesive plaster.

stratified (strat'ĭ-fĭd) Arranged in layers.

stratum (stra'tum), pl. stra'ta Latin for layer, especially of differentiated tissue comprising one of several associated layers. See layer.

    s. corneum See cornified layer of skin, under layer.

    s. lucidum See clear layer of skin, under layer.

    s. opticum See nerve fiber layer of retina, under layer.

    s. spinosum See prickle-cell layer of skin, under layer.

streak (strēk) **1.** A line or stripe. **2.** Inoculation of bacteria on a culture medium by a loop.

    angioid s.'s Brownish red lines seen within the eye radiating from the optic disk and resembling blood vessels; caused by breaks in the lamina vitrea of the choroid due to degeneration of elastic tissues; may occur in association with such conditions as pseudoxanthoma elasticum and sickle-cell anemia. Also called Knapp's streaks.

    Knapp's s.'s See angioid streaks.

    primitive s. In embryology, a midline groove on the caudal end of the embryonic disk; it is clearly visible in a 15- to 16-day embryo and provides the earliest evidence of the cephalocaudal axis.

streaking (strēk'ing) **1.** The act of inoculating bacteria on a culture medium. **2.** Appearance of a colored line (e.g., in cellulitis).

strephosymbolia (stref-o-sim-bo'le-ah) A perception disorder, seen most commonly in children, in which certain letters or words are seen reversed, as if in a mirror.

Streptobacillus (strep-to-bah-sil'us) A genus of gram-negative rod-shaped bacteria (family Bacteriodaceae) that inhabit the nasopharynx of wild and laboratory rats and mice; a species (*Streptobacillus moniliformis*) is the causative agent of a type of rat-bite fever in humans.

Streptobacillus moniliformis (strep-to-bah-sil'us mon-il-ĭ-for'mis) A species of anaerobic bacteria (genus *Streptobacillus*) commonly found in the nasopharynx of rats; the cause of rat-bite fever in humans.

streptococcal (strep-to-kok'al) Relating to streptococcus.

streptococcemia (strep-to-kok-se'me-ah) The presence of streptococci in the blood.

S

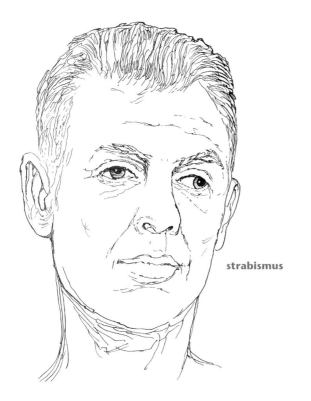

strabismus

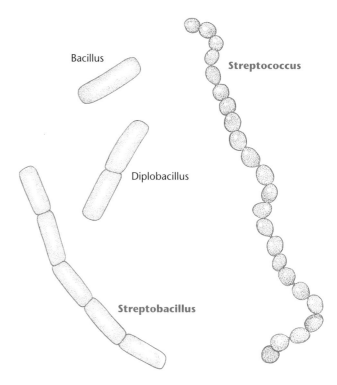

Bacillus

Streptococcus

Diplobacillus

Streptobacillus

streptococci (strep-to-kok′si) Plural of streptococcus.
streptococcosis (strep-to-kou-ko′sis) A streptococcal infection.
Streptococcus (strep-to-kok′us) A genus of gram-positive round or ovoid bacteria occurring in pairs or in chains held together by incomplete wall separation; some species occur harmlessly in the mouth, throat, or intestinal tract of humans, others can cause disease. They are classified according to their hemolytic activity on blood agar into alpha, beta, or gamma streptococci and according to their antigenic composition into groups A through O.

S. faecalis Former name for *Enterococcus faecalis*.
S. faecium Former name for *Enterococcus faecium*.
S. fecalis Species found in the intestinal tract; a cause of subacute bacterial endocarditis.
S. mutans A species associated with dental plaques and caries.
S. pneumoniae A species that is the most common cause of lobar pneumonia, frequently causing meningitis, sinusitis, middle ear infections, and other infections; over 80 types are known. Formerly called *Diplococcus pneumoniae*.

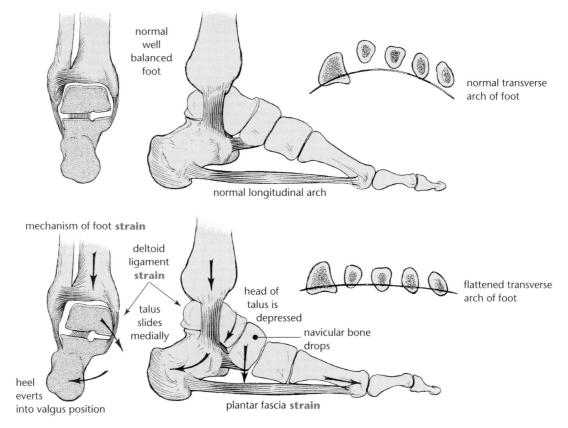

normal
well
balanced
foot

normal transverse
arch of foot

normal longitudinal arch

mechanism of foot **strain**

deltoid
ligament
strain

talus
slides
medially

head of
talus is
depressed

navicular bone
drops

flattened transverse
arch of foot

heel
everts
into valgus position

plantar fascia **strain**

S

S. pyogenes A species causing a variety of pus-forming infections, such as erysipelas, septic sore throat, and scarlet fever; it has been isolated from skin lesions, blood, inflammatory exudates, and the upper respiratory tract of humans.

S. salivarius Species found in saliva and the intestinal tract; generally nonpathogenic but has been implicated in contributing to the formation of dental caries.

streptococcus (strep-to-kok'us), pl. streptococ'ci Any member of the genus *Streptococcus.*

streptodermatitis (strep-to-der-mah-ti'tis) Skin disease caused by streptococci.

streptodornase (strep-to-dor'nās) (SD) Enzyme produced by hemolytic streptococci, capable of dissolving thick, purulent exudates. Also called dornase.

streptokinase (strep-to-ki'nās) (SK) Enzyme released by hemolytic streptococci, capable of dissolving fibrin; used to dissolve blood clots and fibrinous adhesions. Possible adverse effects include severe spontaneous bleeding, fever, chills, wheezing, and rash.

streptolysin (strep-tol'ĭ-sin) A substance produced by streptococci that destroys red blood cells.

Streptomyces (strep-to-mi'sēz) A genus of gram-positive soil bacteria (family Streptomycetaceae); some are parasitic on plants or animals; many are the source of antibiotics.

streptomycete (strep-to-mi'sēt) Any member of the genus *Streptomyces.*

streptomycin (strep'to-mi-sin) An antibiotic obtained from *Streptomyces griseus,* formerly used to treat a variety of infections, especially tuberculosis; excessive dosage may damage the vestibulocochlear (8th cranial) nerve, disturbing balance and causing ringing in the ears and hearing impairment.

stress (stres) **1.** Any physical or psychological condition that tends to disrupt the normal functions of the body or mind. **2.** In dentistry, pressure exerted against the teeth and their attachments during mastication. **3.** In orthopedic context, the force applied to a structure and the intensity of that force per unit area.

compressile s. A force directed against a structure.

shear s. A force occurring parallel to the surface of a structure.

tensile s. A force pulling away (distracting) a structure.

stress-breaker (stres' brāk-er) In dental prosthesis, an attachment in a partial denture that relieves the anchoring teeth of all or part of the pressure during mastication.

stretcher (strech'er) A conveyance for transporting the sick or injured.

stria (stri'ah), pl. stri'ae A thin stripe or line on a tissue, especially one of several that are more or less parallel.

striae atrophicae A series of glistening white streaks in the skin of the abdomen, buttocks, thighs, and breasts caused by overstretching and weakening of elastic tissues; associated with pregnancy, obesity, rapid growth during puberty, and Cushing's syndrome. Also called stretch marks; lineae albicantes; gravidic lines; lineae gravidarum.

striatal (stri-a'tal) Relating to the corpus striatum in the brain.

striate, striated (stri'āt, stri'āt-ed) Having striae; striped.

striation (stri-a'shun) **1.** A stria. **2.** The condition of being marked by stria.

stricture (strik'chur) An abnormal narrowing of a tubular structure.

stridor (stri'dor) A shrill respiratory sound, such as one often heard in acute laryngeal obstruction.

stridulous (strid'u-lus) Having a harsh or shrill sound.

strip (strip) **1.** To remove or express fluid from a tubular structure by gently running a finger along the structure; to milk. **2.** To surgically remove one tissue from another, such as a varicose vein from a leg. **3.** Any narrow piece.

abrasive s. A piece of linen coated with an abrasive material on one side; used to shape and polish proximal surfaces of artificial teeth.

lightening s. A piece of metal coated with an abrasive material on one side; used to remove rough or improper points of contact between artificial teeth.

stripe (strīp) A streak.

Mees' s.'s See Mees' lines, under line.

stripper (strip'er) Instrument for the removal of a diseased vein (usually a varicose vein); generally consists of a cable with a cup (olive) at one end and a guide tip at the other.

strobila (stro-bi'lah), pl. strobi'lae The linear arrangement of segments forming the body of a tapeworm.

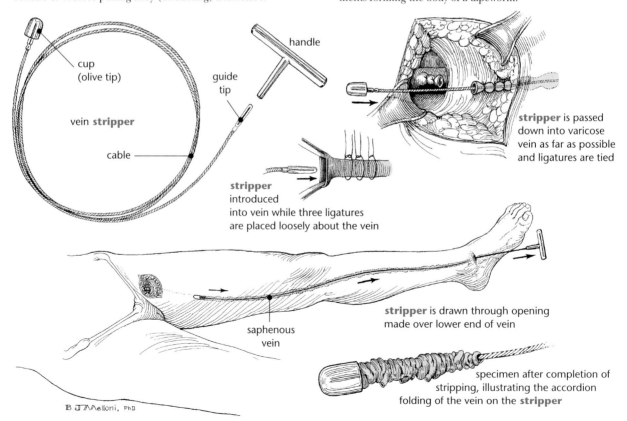

cup (olive tip)

guide tip

handle

vein **stripper**

cable

stripper is passed down into varicose vein as far as possible and ligatures are tied

stripper introduced into vein while three ligatures are placed loosely about the vein

stripper is drawn through opening made over lower end of vein

saphenous vein

specimen after completion of stripping, illustrating the accordion folding of the vein on the **stripper**

B J Melloni, PhD

streptococcus ■ strobila

strobiloid (stro′bĭ-loid) Resembling the segmented body of a tapeworm.

stroboscope (stro′bo-skōp) Instrument for observing moving objects by making them appear stationary through intermittently interrupted illumination.

stroke (strōk) **1.** Imprecise term commonly applied to an abrupt onset of a variety of symptoms and focal neurologic deficits resulting from damage to a portion of the brain; caused by interruption of its blood supply or by leakage of blood from a ruptured blood vessel. Also called vascular accident; cerebral vascular accident; cerebrovascular accident. **2.** A pulsation.

    heart s. The impact of the tip of the heart against the chest wall.

    heat s. See heatstroke.

    sun s. See sunstroke.

stroma (stro′mah) The framework of an organ, usually composed of connective tissue, which serves to support the functional elements, the cells.

stromal, stromic (stro′mal, stro′mik) Relating to stroma.

stromatogenous (stro-mah-toj′ĕ-nus) Originating in the connective tissue of an organ.

Strongyloides (stron-jĭ-loi′dēz) A genus of threadworms that are parasitic in the small intestine of higher vertebrates, especially mammals.

strongyloidiasis, strongyloidosis (stron-jĭ-loi-di′ah-sis, stron-jĭ-loi-do′sis) Infection with the threadlike worm *Strongyloides stercoralis;* the worms enter the body through the skin or mucous membrane of the mouth, travel to the lungs (where they may cause pneumonia), and eventually reach the intestines, where the female lays her eggs. Pneumonia occurs most frequently in those individuals whose immune systems are compromised.

strontium (stron′she-um) Metallic element; symbol Sr, atomic number 38, atomic weight 87.62.

strontium 90 (⁹⁰Sr) A radioactive isotope that emits a high-energy beta particle and has a half-life of 28 years; it is present in radioactive fallout and is incorporated into bone tissue upon absorption.

Strophanthus (stro-fan′thus) A genus of African vines (family Apocynaceae) containing several poisonous species.

structure (struk′chur) The configuration of the component parts of an entity.

    denture-supporting s.'s The structures in the mouth (e.g., teeth or ridges) that serve as the foundation for partial or complete dentures.

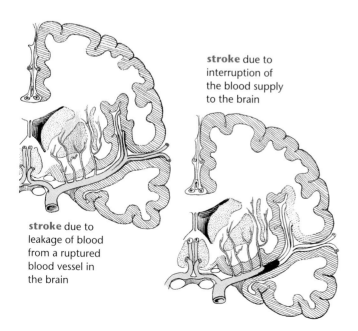

stroke due to interruption of the blood supply to the brain

stroke due to leakage of blood from a ruptured blood vessel in the brain

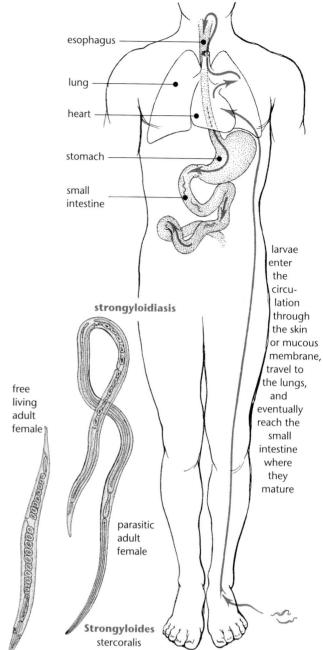

esophagus

lung

heart

stomach

small intestine

larvae enter the circulation through the skin or mucous membrane, travel to the lungs, and eventually reach the small intestine where they mature

strongyloidiasis

free living adult female

parasitic adult female

Strongyloides stercoralis

    fine s. See ultrastructure.

    submicroscopic s. See ultrastructure.

struma (stroo′mah) Goiter.

    Hashimoto's s. See Hashimoto's thyroiditis, under thyroiditis.

    s. lymphomatosa See Hashimoto's thyroiditis, under thyroiditis.

    Riedel's s. See Riedel's thyroiditis, under thyroiditis.

strumiform (stroo′mĭ-form) Resembling a goiter.

strumitis (stroo-mi′tis) See thyroiditis.

strychnine (strik′nīn) A bitter, highly poisonous alkaloid used to kill rats; formerly used as a central nervous system stimulant; may be ingested by humans with suicidal or homicidal intent.

study (stud′e) The pursuit and acquisition of information.

    air contrast s. See mucosal relief roentgenography, under roentgenography.

    blind s. See blind trial, under trial.

    case comparison s. See case control study.

    case-control s. Epidemiological study that begins with identification of persons with the disease of interest, and a comparison

S

(control) group of people without the disease; the relationship of a particular attribute (e.g., age, sex, race) to the disease is examined by comparing the frequency with which the attribute appears in both groups. Also called case comparison study; case history study; case referent study.

    case history s. See case-control study.

    case referent s. See case-control study.

    cohort s. An epidemiological study of a defined population with a statistical factor in common (e.g., smokers, recipients of a medication) that is supposed to influence the occurrence of a disease or other outcome; the study is conducted over a prolonged period (e.g., a year). Also called longitudinal study.

    double-blind s. See double-blind trial, under trial.

    longitudinal s. See cohort study.

stump (stump) **1.** The remaining portion of an amputated limb. **2.** The pedicle of a tumor remaining after the tumor has been removed.

stun (stun) **1.** To render senseless by a blow or other violent force. **2.** In cardiac muscle, to impair function markedly, but temporarily, as a result of an ischemic episode.

stupe (stūp) A dampened, medicated, hot compress applied locally as a counterirritant.

stupefacient (stu-pĕ-fa′shent) **1.** Causing stupor. **2.** Any agent that produces stupor.

stupor (stu′por) A state of semiconsciousness in which vigorous stimuli are needed to evoke a response.

stuporous (stu′por-us) In a semiconscious state.

stuttering (stut′er-ing) Speech disorder most often characterized by spasmodic hesitation and staccato repetition of the first sounds of a phrase; may be accompanied by grimacing in its most severe form.

St. Vitus' dance (sānt vi′tus dans) See Sydenham's chorea, under chorea.

sty (sti), pl. sties See external hordeolum, under hordeolum.

stylet (sti′let) A thin wire inserted into the lumen of a flexible catheter to increase its rigidity, thus facilitating the passage of the catheter.

styliform (sti′lĭ-form) See styloid.

stylo- Combining form meaning styloid.

styloglossus (sti-lo-glos′us) Relating to the styloid process of the temporal bone of the skull and the tongue; applied to certain structures (e.g., a muscle).

styloid (sti′loid) Shaped like a peg; applied to certain bony processes. Also called styliform.

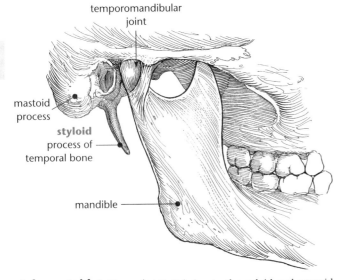

stylomastoid (sti-lo-mas′toid) Relating to the styloid and mastoid processes of the temporal bone.

stylosteophyte (sti-los′te-o-fit) A peg-shaped outgrowth from a bone.

stylus (sti′lus) **1.** A pencillike device for applying medicines or caustics topically. **2.** A needlelike device for tracing a graphic recording on paper (e.g., in an electrocardiogram).

stype (stīp) A tampon.

stypsis (stip′sis) Astringency.

styptic (stip′tik) **1.** Tending to contract tissue; astringent. **2.** An agent having such property.

styrene (sti′rēn) A colorless, volatile liquid at room temperature from which many consumer products are made (e.g., insulation, packaging, drain pipes, tires, hoses, storage tanks). Occupational exposure may occur through direct contact and, chiefly, via inhalation; may produce acute effects (irritation of eyes, respiratory tract, and skin) or chronic effects (headache, weakness, fatigue, dizziness, memory loss). Also called phenylethylene; vinylbenzene.

subacromial (sub-ah-kro′me-al) Situated beneath the large process (acromium) of the shoulder blade (scapula).

subacute (sub-ah-kūt′) A state between acute and chronic (e.g., the intensity of a disease or the toxicity of a chemical).

subalimentation (sub-al-ĭ-men-ta′shun) Insufficient nourishment. Also called hypoalimentation.

subarachnoid (sub-ah-rak′noid) Beneath the delicate, cobweblike membrane (arachnoid) of the brain or spinal cord.

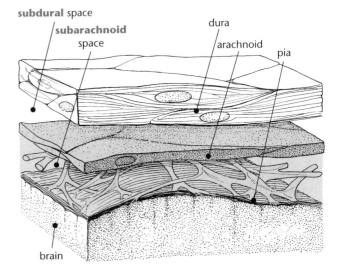

subarcuate (sub-ar′ku-āt) Slightly bowed.

subareolar (sub-ah-re′o-lar) Beneath an areola, especially of the breast.

subatomic (sub-ah-tom′ik) Relating to the components of the atom.

subaural (sub-aw′ral) Below the ear.

subauricular (sub-aw-rik′u-lar) Below an auricle, especially of the ear.

subcallosal (sub-kah-lo′sal) Below the corpus callosum of the brain.

subcapsular (sub-kap′su-lar) Beneath a capsule (e.g., of the lens of the eye).

subcarbonate (sub-kar′bo-nāt) Any basic carbonate (e.g., bismuth subcarbonate); a complex of a base and its carbonate.

subcartilaginous (sub-kar-tĭ-laj′ĭ-nus) **1.** Beneath a cartilage. **2.** Partly cartilaginous.

subcecal (sub-se′kal) Below the pouchlike portion of the large intestine (cecum).

subchondral (sub-kon′dral) Beneath or just under the cartilages of the ribs.

subclavian (sub-kla′ve-an) Beneath the collarbone (clavicle).

subclavicular (sub-klah-vik′u-lar) Beneath the collarbone (clavicle).

subclinical (sub-klin′ĭ-kal) Without manifestation of symptoms; applied to a disorder that produces no symptoms because it is very mild or because it is at an early phase of its course.

subconjunctival (sub-kon-junk-ti′val) Beneath the transparent membrane covering the eye and inner aspect of the eyelids.

subconscious (sub-kon′shus) Not fully conscious.

subcortex (sub-kor′teks) The portion of an organ just below or interior to the external portion, especially beneath the cerebral cortex.

subcostal (sub-kos′tal) Beneath the ribs.

subcranial (sub-kra′ne-al) Below the skull.

subcutaneous (sub-ku-ta′ne-us) (s.c., SQ) Beneath the skin. Also called hypodermic; subdermic.

subcuticular (sub-ku-tik′u-lar) See subepidermal.

subcutis (sub-ku′tis) The loose connective tissue just beneath the skin. Also called tela subcutanea.

subdermic (sub-der′mik) Subcutaneous.

subdiaphragmatic (sub-di-ah-frag-mat′ik) Below the diaphragm. Also called subphrenic.

subdural (sub-du′ral) Beneath or internal to the dura mater (i.e., the outer, fibrous covering of the brain and spinal cord).

subendocardial (sub-en-do-kar′de-al) Beneath the membrane enclosing the heart.

subependymal (sub-ep-en′dĭ-mal) Beneath the membrane lining the central canal of the spinal cord and ventricles of the brain.

subepidermal, subepidermic (sub-ep-ĭ-der′mal, sub-ep-ĭ-der′mik) Beneath the epidermis. Also called subcuticular.

subfalcial, subfalcine (sub-fal′shal, sub-fal′sēn) Beneath the falx cerebri (e.g., a herniation of brain tissue).

subfascial (sub-fash′e-al) Beneath any fascia.

subfertility (sub-fer-til′ĭ-te) Less than normal ability to reproduce.

subgingival (sub-jin′jĭ-val) At a level below the gingival margin.

subglottic (sub-glot′ik) Inferior to the opening between the vocal folds in the larynx. Also called infraglottic.

subhepatic (sub-hĕ-pat′ik) Below the liver.

subintimal (sub-in′tĭ-mal) Beneath the inner layer of an arterial wall.

subinvolution (sub-in-vo-lu′shun) Failure of an organ to return completely to its normal size, as when the uterus remains abnormally large after childbirth.

subjacent (sub-ja′sent) Immediately below or beneath.

subject (sub′jekt) A person or animal that is the object of an experiment or treatment.

subjective (sub-jek′tiv) Perceived by a person (e.g., a patient), not by an observer or examiner.

sublation (sub-la′shun) Detachment of a body part.

sublethal (sub-le′thal) Slightly less than lethal.

sublimate (sub′lĭ-māt) **1.** To convert a solid into a gas and back into a solid without passing through the liquid state. **2.** A substance that has been subjected to sublimation. **3.** To unconsciously divert drives or impulses that are consciously unacceptable into personally and socially acceptable channels.

sublimation (sub-lĭ-ma′shun) The process of sublimating.

subliminal (sub-lim′ĭ-nal) Below the level of sensory perception.

sublimis (sub-lĭ′mis) Latin for superficial.

sublingual (sub-ling′gwal) Beneath the tongue.

subluxation (sub-luk-sa′shun) Partial dislocation of a body part.

submandibular (sub-man-dib′u-lar) Beneath the lower jaw (mandible).

submaxillary (sub-mak′sĭ-ler-e) Beneath the upper jaw (maxilla).

submental (sub-men′tal) Under the chin.

submicroscopic (sub-mi-kro-skop′ik) Too small to be seen through an ordinary light microscope.

submucosa (sub-mu-ko′sah) The layer of tissue located beneath a mucous membrane.

subnasion (sub-na′ze-on) The point at the junction of the nasal septum and the upper lip.

subnormal (sub-nor′mal) Below a standard or a level usually observed.

suboccipital (sub-ok-sip′ĭ-tal) Below the occipital bone or the back of the head (occiput).

suborbital (sub-or′bĭ-tal) See infraorbital.

suboxide (sub-ok′sĭd) An oxide of an element (e.g., carbon suboxide) that contains the smallest proportion of oxygen.

subphrenic (sub-fren′ik) See subdiaphragmatic.

subscapular (sub-skap′u-lar) Beneath or below the shoulder blade (scapula).

subscleral (sub-skle′ral) Beneath the white portion of the eye.

subscription (sub-skrip′shun) The part of a pharmaceutical prescription that contains instructions to the pharmacist.

subserous (sub-se′rus) Beneath a serous membrane.

substage (sub′stāj) The attachment to a microscope, beneath the stage, by means of which accessory parts (mirror, diaphragm, or condensor) are held in place.

substance (sub′stans) Matter; material of a specified constitution.

   ad s. A substance that facilitates transmission of a nerve impulse across a synapse.

     alpha s. See reticular substance.

     black s. See substantia nigra, under substantia.

     compact s. of bone See compact bone, under bone.

     controlled drug s. Any of the drugs with potential for abuse or substances with potential for addiction; regulated under the Controlled Substances Act.

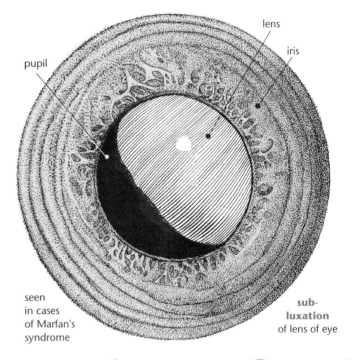

pupil

lens

iris

seen in cases of Marfan's syndrome

sub-luxation of lens of eye

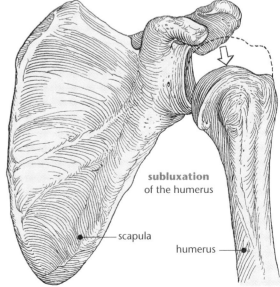

subluxation of the humerus

scapula

humerus

cortical s. of bone See compact bone, under bone.

gap s. An acidic mucosubstance that fills the depression (narrowing of axon) at each neuronal node of Ranvier; it forms a reservoir of ions in the conduction of nerve impulses.

gray s. See gray matter, under matter.

ground s. An amorphous viscous gel that, along with fibers (collagen, reticulum, and elastin), make up the extracellular matrix of connective tissue; it is the nonfibrous element of matrix in which cells and other components are embedded. Also called interstitial substance.

interstitial s. See ground substance.

s. P A polypeptide found in the brain (concentrated in the substantia nigra) and elsewhere; a potent vasoactive substance and a sensory transmitter that mediates pain, touch, and temperature perceptions; may also serve as a neurohormone.

pressor s. A substance that increases blood pressure.

proper s. of cornea See substantia propria corneae, under substantia.

radiopaque s. See contrast medium, under medium.

reticular s. *(a)* The mass of filaments seen in immature red blood cells. Also called alpha substance. *(b)* See reticular formation, under formation.

Rolando's s. See substantia gelatinosa of Rolando, under substantia.

slow-reacting s. (SRS) Substance (possibly a leukotriene) released in anaphylactic shock, formed through the interaction of antigen with sensitized cells; produces a slow, prolonged contraction of smooth muscle.

specific capsular s. A polysaccharide present in the capsule of many bacteria, believed to have a role in the transport of nutrients and protection against noxious agents. Also called specific soluble substance.

specific soluble s. (SSS) See specific capsular substance.

spongy s. of bone See spongy bone, under bone.

toxic s. See poison.

transmitter s. See neurotransmitter.

white s. See white matter, under matter.

substantia (sub-stan′she-ah) Latin for substance.

s. alba See white matter, under matter.

s. gelatinosa of Rolando The mass of translucent gelatinous tissue, containing small nerve cells, on the posterior gray column of the spinal cord; it appears in cross section as a crescentic cap over the horn. Also called Rolando's substance.

s. grisea See gray matter, under matter.

s. nigra A layer of gray substance in the cerebral peduncles containing deeply pigmented nerve cells; it extends from the upper border of the pons into the subthalamic region; on cross section it appears crescentic. Also called black substance.

s. propria corneae The largest layer of the cornea, between the anterior limiting membrane (Bowman's membrane) and the posterior limiting membrane (Descemet's membrane); it is fibrous, compact, unyielding, and transparent. Also called proper substance of cornea.

substernal (sub-ster′nal) Beneath the breastbone.

substitute (sub′stĭ-tūt) Something that can take the place of another; a replacement.

plasma s. Any sterile solution administered intravenously to replace fluid volume; usually a saline solution, frequently with dextrans or serum albumins; used to treat such conditions as dehydration, hemorrhage, and shock. Also called plasma expander.

salt s. Any low-sodium food additive (e.g., potassium chloride) used as a dietary alternative to table salt.

substitution (sub-stĭ-tu′shun) 1. The replacing of one thing or person for another. 2. Defense mechanism in which a person unconsciously replaces an unacceptable feeling or emotion for one that is acceptable.

generic s. The act of dispensing a different brand or an unbranded drug product for the drug product prescribed (i.e., dispensing one that is chemically the exact drug entity in the same dosage form, but distributed by a different company (e.g., unbranded ampicillin for Polycillin®).

pharmaceutical s. The act of dispensing a pharmaceutical alternative for the drug product prescribed (i.e., dispensing one that contains the identical therapeutic moiety and strength but not the same salt, ester, or dosage form as the one prescribed; e.g., ampicillin suspension for ampicillin capsules).

therapeutic s. The act of dispensing a therapeutic alternative for the drug product prescribed (i.e., dispensing one that contains different therapeutic moieties but that belongs to the same pharmacologic and/or therapeutic class as the one prescribed; e.g., chlorothiazide for hydrochlorothiazide, or prednisone for prednisolone).

substrate (sub′strāt) Any substance upon which an enzyme or ferment acts.

renin s. See angiotensinogen.

substratum (sub-stra′tum) Any layer of tissue located beneath another.

substructure (sub′struk-chur) Any structure that is partly or entirely beneath the surface.

implant denture s. A metal framework embedded beneath soft tissues, in contact with bone, for supporting and stabilizing the superstructural portion of an implant denture.

subthalamic (sub-thah-lam′ik) Relating to the structures located beneath the thalamus in the brain.

subthalamus (sub-thal′ah-mus) The portion of the brain situated between the thalamus dorsally and the cerebral peduncle ventrally.

subtype (sub-tīp′) See serovar.

subungual (sub-ung′gwal) Beneath a fingernail or toenail.

suburethral (sub-u-re′thral) Beneath the urethra.

subvitrinal (sub-vit′rĭ-nal) Beneath the vitreous body in the eye.

subvolution (sub-vo-lu′shun) The operative technique of inverting a tissue flap to prevent the formation of adhesions.

succagogue (suk′ah-gog) 1. Stimulating glandular secretion. 2. Any agent producing such an effect.

succedaneum (suk-sĕ-da′ne-um) A material or drug that can replace another of similar properties.

succenturiate (suk-sen-tu′re-āt) Serving as a substitute.

succinic acid (suk-sin′ik as′id) An intermediate in the metabolism of tricarboxylic acid.

succinylcholine (suk-sĭ-nil-ko′lēn) A compound with muscle-relaxing properties, used as an adjunct during anesthesia.

succorrhea (suk-o-re′ah) An excessive flow of a digestive fluid, such as saliva or gastric juice.

succussion (sŭ-kush′un) The act of shaking the body as a diagnostic procedure; a splashing sound is produced by the presence of fluid or gas in a body cavity.

sucrase (su′krās) An enzyme that promotes the breakdown of sucrose.

sucrose (su′krōs) A disaccharide made up of glucose and fructose obtained chiefly from sugar cane and sugar beet; used as a sweetener and preservative. Also called cane sugar; saccharose.

suction (suk′shun) The act of aspirating or sucking.

suctorial (suk-to′re-al) Relating to suction.

sudamen (su-da′men), pl. sudam′ina A tiny cyst on the skin formed by retention of sweat.

sudation (su-da′shun) Sweating.

sudomotor (su-do-mo′tor) Stimulating sweat glands.

sudor (su′dor) Latin for sweat.

sudoral (su′dor-al) Relating to sweat.

sudoresis (su-do-re′sis) Profuse sweating.

sudoriferous (su-do-rif′er-us) Conveying sweat.

sudorific (su-do-rif′ik) Causing the production of sweat.

sudoriparous (su-do-rip′ah-rus) Producing sweat.

suffocate (suf′o-kāt) To cut off the supply of air; to choke.

suffusion (sŭ-fu′zhun) 1. The act of pouring a fluid over a surface. 2. The condition of being permeated with a fluid.

sugar (shoog′ar) A type of sweet carbohydrate.

blood s. See glucose.

brain s. See galactose.

cane s. See sucrose.

fruit s. See fructose.

invert s. A mixture of equal parts of glucose and fructose, used in solution as a parenteral nutrient.

malt s. See maltose.

milk s. See lactose.

suicide (soo′ĭ-sīd) **1.** Self-murder; violent death produced by an act of the dead person, committed with the intent to kill himself or herself. **2.** A person who has committed such an act.

suicidology (soo-ĭ-si-dol′o-je) The study of suicide, its causes and control.

suit (sūt) An outer garment.

antiblackout s. See anti-G suit.

anti-G s. A garment designed for pilots to help them withstand the effects of high acceleration; during positive G maneuvers, bladders in the suit expand, applying external pressure on the abdomen and lower limbs, thereby preventing the pooling of blood in those areas. Also called antiblackout suit.

sulcal (sul′kal) Relating to a sulcus.

sulcate (sul′kāt) Grooved; furrowed.

sulci (sul′si) Plural of sulcus.

sulculus (sul′ku-lus) A small groove.

sulcus (sul′kus), pl. sul′ci A groove, furrow, or depression.

alveololabial s. The oral sulcus between the lips and the jaws. Also called gingivolabial sulcus.

alveololingual s. The oral sulcus on the floor of the mouth, on each side of the frenulum, between the lower jaw (mandible) and the tongue. Also called gingivolingual sulcus.

arterial sulci Grooves on the internal surface of the skull that house the meningeal arteries and their branches. Also called arterial grooves.

s. of calcaneus The broad, deep, transverse groove on the top surface of the heel bone (calcaneus), located between the medial and posterior articular facets; in association with a corresponding groove on the ankle bone (talus), it forms the tarsal sinus, which contains the interosseous talocalcaneal ligament.

calcarine s. A sulcus on the medial surface of the occipital lobe of the cerebral hemisphere, separating the cuneus gyrus above from the lingual gyrus below. The primary visual cortex is located in both walls of the sulcus and adjacent parts of the occipital pole. Also called calcarine fissure.

callosal s. See sulcus of corpus callosum.

carotid s. of sphenoid bone See carotid groove of sphenoid bone, under groove.

carpal s. The broad, deep concavity on the front (volar surface) of the wrist (carpus) formed by the arching carpal bones; it transmits the flexor tendons and the median nerve to the palm of the hand.

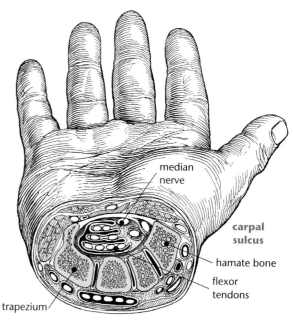

median nerve

carpal sulcus

hamate bone

flexor tendons

trapezium

central s. See cerebral central sulcus.

cerebellar horizontal s. See cerebellar horizontal fissure, under fissure.

cerebral central s. A deep oblique sulcus on the lateral suface of each cerebral hemisphere between the frontal and parietal lobes. Also called cerebral central fissure; fissure of Rolando; rolandic sulcus; central sulcus.

cerebral lateral s. A deep cleft on the inferior and lateral surfaces of the cerebral hemisphere separating the temporal lobe below from the frontal and parietal lobes above; it divides into three branches: anterior horizontal branch (**2.5** cm long), anterior as-

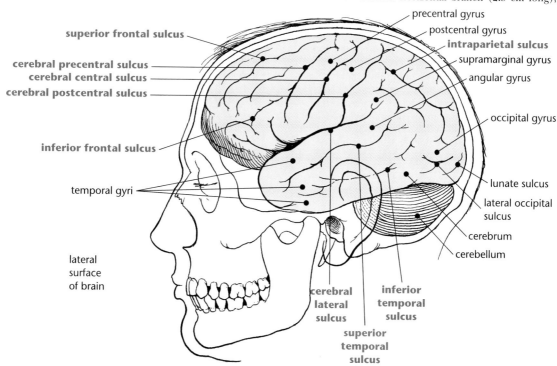

superior frontal sulcus

cerebral precentral sulcus

cerebral central sulcus

cerebral postcentral sulcus

inferior frontal sulcus

temporal gyri

lateral surface of brain

precentral gyrus

postcentral gyrus

intraparietal sulcus

supramarginal gyrus

angular gyrus

occipital gyrus

lunate sulcus

lateral occipital sulcus

cerebrum

cerebellum

cerebral lateral sulcus

inferior temporal sulcus

superior temporal sulcus

S

cending branch (2.5 cm long), and posterior branch (7.5 cm long). Also called sylvian sulcus; fissure of Sylvius; lateral cerebral fissure.

cerebral sulci The grooves that separate the convolutions (gyri) on the surface of the cerebral cortex. Also called cerebral fissures.

cingulate s. A sulcus on the medial surface of each cerebral hemisphere, extending from the front of the corpus callosum and curving around to a point just behind the central sulcus; it separates the cingulate gyrus below from the medial frontal gyrus and the paracentral lobule above.

collateral s. A long, deep sagittal sulcus on the inferior surface of each temporal lobe of the cerebral hemisphere; it separates the medial occipitotemporal gyrus laterally from the parahippocampal gyrus medially, along with its anterior extension (uncus) and its posterior extension (lingual gyrus).

coronary s. A sulcus encircling the outside surface of the heart between the atria and ventricles, and lodging the coronary arterial and venous blood vessels. Also called atrioventricular groove.

s. of corpus callosum A fissure seen on the medial surface of the cerebral hemisphere between the convex surface of the corpus callosum and the overlying cingulate gyrus. Also called callosal sulcus.

costal s. See costal groove, under groove.

dorsal lateral s. of spinal cord A shallow longitudinal sulcus on either side of the dorsal median sulcus of the spinal cord; it marks the line of entrance of the posterior (dorsal) nerve roots.

dorsal median s. of spinal cord A shallow sulcus in the median line of the posterior (dorsal) surface of the spinal cord.

frontal sulci Two oblique sulci on the lateral surface of the frontal lobe of the cerebrum: *Inferior frontal s.*, the lower of the two frontal sulci; it separates the inferior frontal gyrus from the middle frontal gyrus, and extends from the precentral sulcus in a forward and downward direction, *Superior frontal s.*, the upper and longer of the two frontal sulci; it separates the middle frontal gyrus from the superior frontal gyrus.

gingival s. The shallow space or groove between a tooth and the free gingiva.

gingivolabial s. See alveololabial sulcus.

gingivolingual s. See alveololingual sulcus.

gluteal s. See gluteal fold, under fold.

intertubercular s. of humerus The longitudinal groove on the front of the upper humerus between the greater and lesser tubercles, which accommodates the tendon of the long head of the biceps muscle of arm (biceps brachii muscle). Also called bicipital groove of humerus.

interventricular s. See interventricular groove, under groove.

intraparietal s. A horizontal sulcus dividing the posterior part of the parietal lobe of the cerebrum into upper and lower lobules; it stems off the postcentral sulcus and passes posteriorly on the upper lateral surface of the cerebral cortex.

malleolar s. A broad vertical groove on the posterior surface of the medial malleolus of the lower tibia; it accommodates the tendons of the posterior tibial muscle and the long flexor muscle of the toes (flexor digitorum longus muscle). Also called malleolar groove.

median s. of tongue A slight, median, longitudinal depression running forward on the dorsal surface of the tongue from the foramen cecum; it divides the tongue into symmetrical halves.

mentolabial s. The variable inward contour or groove between the lower lip and the chin. Also called mentolabial furrow.

mylohyoid s. of mandible A groove on the medial surface of the ramus of the lower jaw (mandible), extending anteroinferiorly from the mandibular foramen; it transmits the mylohyoid nerve and blood vessels. Also called mylohyoid groove.

s. of nail The cutaneous groove formed by the infolding of skin in which the proximal and lateral borders of the nail are embedded. Also called nail groove.

nasolabial s. The depression extending downward and laterally from the side of the nose to the angle of the mouth; the junction

between the cheek and the lips. Also called nasolabial groove.

nymphocaruncular s. A crescentic groove, between the labium minor and the hymen encircling the vaginal orifice, into which the duct of the greater vestibular (Bartholin's) gland opens; more specifically, it refers to the groove between the labium minor and the small elevations of mucous membrane representing the remains of the hymen.

occlusal s. A sulcus on the occlusal surface of a tooth.

olfactory s. of frontal lobe An anteroposterior sulcus on the inferior surface of the frontal lobe, which accommodates the olfactory lobe and olfactory tract.

paracolic sulci See paracolic grooves, under groove.

parietooccipital s. A deep oblique sulcus on the medial surface of the occipital region of each cerebral hemisphere, extending obliquely from the anterior part of the calcarine sulcus; it separates the occipital lobe from the parietal lobe. Also called parietooccipital fissure.

postcentral s. A somewhat vertical sulcus on the lateral surface of the parietal lobe of the cerebrum, posterior and parallel to the central sulcus; it separates the postcentral gyrus from the rest of the parietal lobe.

posterior lateral s. of spinal cord A shallow groove on each side of the posterior aspect of the spinal cord from where the dorsal spinal roots enter the cord to convey afferent impulses from somatic, visceral, and vascular sources.

posterior median s. of spinal cord A shallow groove in the midline of the posterior aspect of the spinal cord from which a median septum extends forward approximately 5 mm in the adult; along with the anterior median fissure, it divides the spinal cord into symmetrical halves. Also called posterior median fissure of spinal cord.

precentral s. A somewhat vertical sulcus, occasionally interrupted, on the lateral surface of the frontal lobe of the cerebrum, anterior and parallel to the central sulcus; it separates the precentral gyrus from the rest of the frontal lobe.

s. of pterygoid hamulus A smooth groove on the lateral surface of the pterygoid hamulus of the sphenoid bone of the skull; it forms a pulley for movements of the tendon of the tensor muscle of the soft palate (tensor veli palatini muscle).

pulmonary s. of thorax The broad, deep vertical groove lying on either side of the vertebral column in the thorax, resulting from the posterior curvature of the ribs; it accommodates the posterior, bulky part of the lung.

rolandic s. See cerebral central sulcus.

scleral s. A shallow circular groove on the outer surface of the eyeball, indicating the union of the sclera and the cornea; the slight groove is the result of the greater convexity of the cornea meeting with the lesser convexity of the sclera. Also called scleral furrow.

s. of sigmoid sinus See groove of sigmoid sinus, under groove.

s. of spinal nerves A groove on the upper surface of the transverse processes of the third through the sixth cervical vertebrae, accommodating the emerging anterior rami of the spinal nerves.

s. of subclavian artery See groove of subclavian artery, under groove.

s. of subclavian vein See groove of subclavian vein, under groove.

s. of superior sagittal sinus See groove of superior sagittal sinus, under groove.

sylvian s. See cerebral lateral sulcus.

s. of talus The broad, deep, transverse groove on the bottom of the ankle bone (talus), located between the medial and posterior articular facets; in association with a corresponding groove on the heel bone (calcaneus), it forms the tarsal sinus, which contains the interosseous talocalcaneal ligament.

temporal sulci Grooves on the temporal lobe of the cerebrum: *Inferior temporal s.*, the somewhat horizontal groove that separates the

S

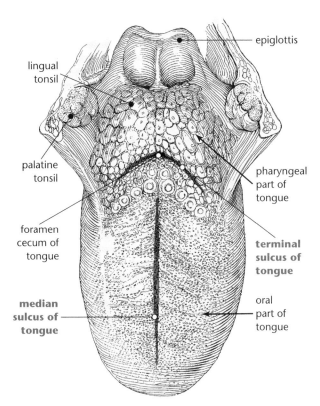

epiglottis

lingual tonsil

palatine tonsil

foramen cecum of tongue

median sulcus of tongue

pharyngeal part of tongue

terminal sulcus of tongue

oral part of tongue

middle gyrus from the inferior gyrus on the lateral surface of the temporal lobe, *Superior temporal s.*, the somewhat horizontal groove that separates the superior gyrus from the middle gyrus on the lateral surface of the temporal lobe.

    s. of tendon of long flexor muscle of big toe See groove of tendon of long flexor muscle of big toe, under groove.

    terminal s. of tongue A shallow V-shaped groove on the tongue running laterally and forward from the foramen cecum; it marks the separation between the oral part of the tongue (anterior two-thirds) and the pharyngeal part of the tongue (posterior third).

    s. of transverse sinus See groove of transverse sinus, under groove.

    s. of ulnar nerve See groove of ulnar nerve, under groove.

    ventral lateral s. of spinal cord An indistinct sulcus on either side of the ventral median fissure of the spinal cord, marking the line of exit of the anterior (ventral) nerve roots.

sulfa (sul′fah) Denoting the sulfa drugs chemically similar to sulfonamide.

sulfacetamide sodium (sul-fah-set′ah-mīd so′de-um) A sulfonamide (sulfa drug), used topically in the treatment of eye infections, especially bacterial conjunctivitis.

sulfasalazine (sul-fah-sal′ah-zēn) A sulfonamide (sulfa drug) with a marked affinity for connective tissue, used primarily as an oral medication in the treatment of ulcerative colitis; possible adverse effects are usually dose-related and include nausea, headache, and (rarely) hemolytic anemia.

sulfate (sul′fāt) A salt of sulfuric acid.

sulfide (sul′fīd) A compound of bivalent sulfur with a metal.

sulfite (sul′fīt) A salt of sulfurous acid.

sulfobromophthalein sodium (sul-fo-bro-mo-thal′e-in so′de-um) A crystalline water-soluble powder formerly used in testing liver function. Trade name: Bromsulphalein (BSP).

sulfonamides (sul-fon′ah-mīds) A group of synthetic antibacterial compounds effective against a wide range of gram-positive and gram-negative organisms; currently used only in specific circumstances. Commonly called sulfa drugs.

sulfonylureas (sul-fo-nil-u-re′ahs) A group of compounds, chemically related to the sulfonamides, that have hypoglycemic properties; many are used in the management of non-insulin-dependent diabetes mellitus (NIDDM).

sulfosalicylic acid (sul-fo-sal-ī-sil′ik as′id) A water-soluble solid used as a test for albumin and ferric ion.

sulfur (sul′fur) A nonmetallic element; symbol S, atomic number 16, atomic weight 32.06; used in fumigants, fungicides, and in the preparation of some pharmaceuticals.

sulfur 35 (sul′fur) (^{35}S) A radioactive sulfur isotope, used as a tracer in studying the metabolism of proteins.

sulfuric acid (sul-fūr′ik as′id) An oily, corrosive liquid. Also called oil of vitriol.

sumac (su′mak) See *Rhus.*

    swamp s. See *Rhus.*

summary (sum′ah-re) A brief restatement or recapitulation.

    discharge s. A document prepared by the attending physician upon release of a hospitalized patient; it summarizes the admitting diagnosis, therapy received in the hospital, discharge diagnosis, prognosis, and plan of action after release.

summation (sum-ma′shun) **1.** A totality, such as the total effect of several stimuli applied to a nerve or a muscle. **2.** In pharmacology, the property exhibited by two drugs when they evoke the same overt response (regardless of their mechanism of action) and this combined effect is the algebraic sum of their individual effects (e.g., when small doses of codeine and aspirin are concurrently taken for the relief of pain). COMPARE synergism.

sunburn (sun′bern) An inflammation or blistering of the skin caused by excessive exposure to ultraviolet rays of the sun.

sunstroke (sun′strōk) A state of extreme prostration and collapse caused by prolonged exposure to intense sunlight and heat.

super- Prefix meaning above; over; superior; excessive.

superacidity (su-per-ah-sid′ĭ-te) An excess of acid, especially increased acidity of the gastric juice.

superacute (su-per-ah-kūt′) Extremely acute (e.g., a disease marked by extremely rapid onset and severe symptoms).

superalimentation (su-per-al-ĭ-men-ta′shun) Administration of nutrients in excess of the patient's requirements as a therapy for certain wasting disorders.

superciliary (su-per-sil′e-a-re) Relating to the area of the eyebrow.

supercilium (su-per-sil′e-um) Eyebrow.

superego (su-per-e′go) In psychoanalytic theory, the part of the psychic apparatus that judges the individual against standards adopted early in life mainly through identification with significant persons, especially parents; the conscience.

superexcitation (su-per-ek-si-ta′shun) Excessive stimulation.

superfatted (su-per-fat′ed) Containing additional fat; applied to soaps.

superficial (su-per-fish′al) Near the surface.

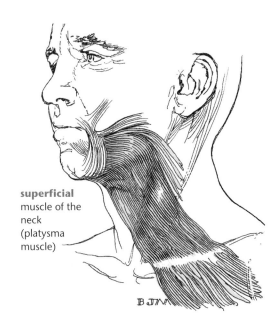

superficial muscle of the neck (platysma muscle)

B JM

superinfection (su-per-in-fek'shun) A second infection occurring during the course of another infection; may be caused by a resistant strain of the microorganism causing the first infection, by a different infectious organism, or by one of the many organisms that are normally present in the body without causing disease.

superior (su-pe're-or) Above; higher; (upright posture in humans) near the top of the head.

supernatant (su-per-na'tant) Floating on a surface; applied to a fluid remaining above a precipitate or a fluid layer of greater density.

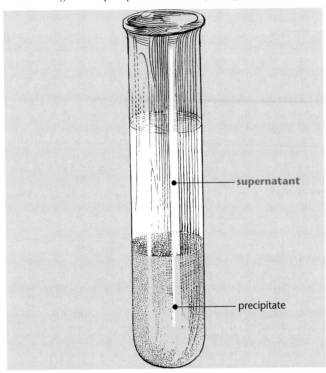

supernumerary (su-per-nu'mer-ar-e) Exceeding the usual or normal number.

supersaturate (su-per-sat'u-rāt) To add a substance beyond saturation.

superscription (su-per-skrip'shun) The symbol in a pharmaceutical prescription.

supersonic (su-per-son'ik) **1.** Relating to speed greater than the speed of sound. **2.** Relating to sound vibrations of high frequencies, above the level of audibility by the human ear.

superstructure (su-per-struk'chur) Any structure above a surface.
 implant denture s. A dental prosthesis that is supported by a structure implanted beneath the oral soft tissues.

supervoltage (su-per-vol'tij) In radiation therapy, a voltage over 1 million volts.

supination (su-pǐ-na'shun) **1.** The act of lying on the back. **2.** Rotation of the arm so that the palm of the hand faces forward or upward.

supinator (su-pǐ-na'tor) A muscle that supinates the forearm.

supine (su'pīn) Lying on the back.

support (sup-port') **1.** The sustaining of continued function. **2.** A device for stabilizing or holding a body part in position.
 advanced life s. (ALS) Emergency care that includes basic life support plus some or all of the following (depending on need): the use of special devices, equipment, and techniques for establishing and maintaining effective breathing and circulation; electrocardiographic monitoring and the recognition of arrhythmia; establishment and maintenance of an intravenous access; therapies for emergency treatment of patients with cardiac or respiratory arrest, or with suspected acute myocardial infarction; and treatment of patients with shock.
 basic life s. (BLS) The essentials of emergency care that include (depending on need): cardiopulmonary resuscitation (CPR), control of bleeding, and stabilization of injuries.

suppository (su-poz'ǐ-to-re) A solid medication designed for introduction into and dissolving within a body cavity other than the mouth, most commonly the rectum.

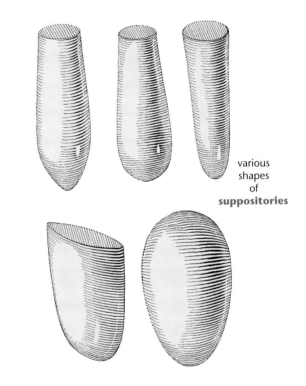

various shapes of **suppositories**

suppression (sŭ-presh'un) **1.** The deliberate exclusion from awareness of painful memories or feelings; distinguished from repression, which is an unconscious process. **2.** The cessation of a secretion; distinguished from retention, in which secretion occurs without discharge from the body.

suppuration (sup-u-ra'shun) The production and discharge of pus.

suppurative (sup'u-ra-tiv) Producing pus.

supra- Prefix meaning above.

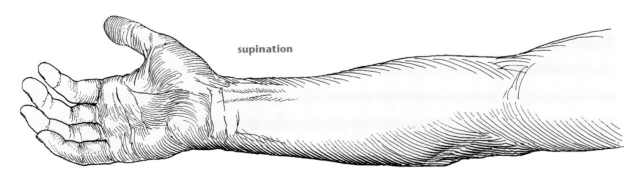

supination

supra-anal (su′prah a′nal) Above the anus.

suprabuccal (su-prah-buk′al) Above the cheek.

supracallosal (su-prah-kah-lo′sal) Above the corpus callosum in the brain.

suprachoroid (su-prah-kor′oid) The outer portion of the vascular layer (choroid) of the eye; composed chiefly of pigmented loose connective tissue.

supraclavicular (su-prah-klah-vik′u-lar) Above the collarbone (clavicle).

supracondylar (su-prah-kon′dī-lar) Above a condyle.

supracostal (su-prah-kos′tal) Above the ribs.

supradiaphragmatic (su-prah-di-ah-frag-mat′ik) Above the diaphragm.

supraduction (su-prah-duk′shun) The upward movement of one eye.

suprahepatic (su-prah-he-pat′ik) Above the liver.

suprahyoid (su-prah-hi′oid) Above the hyoid bone.

suprainguinal (su-prah-in′gwĭ-nal) Above the groin.

supraliminal (su-prah-lim′ĭ-nal) Above the level of sensory perception.

supralumbar (su-prah-lum′bar) Above the lumbar area.

supramandibular (su-prah-man-dib′u-lar) Above the lower jaw (mandible).

supramaxillary (su-prah-mak′sĭ-ler-e) Above the upper jaw (maxilla).

supramental (su-prah-men′tal) Above the chin.

supranuclear (su-prah-nu′kle-ar) In neurology, above the level of a nucleus; applied to certain pathways and lesions of the central nervous system.

supraorbital (su-prah-or′bĭ-tal) Above the eye socket (orbit).

suprapubic (su-prah-pu′bik) Above the pubic arch.

suprarenal (su-prah-re′nal) Above or over the kidney.

suprascapular (su-prah-skap′u-lar) Above or in the upper part of the shoulder blade (scapula).

suprasellar (su-prah-sel′ar) Above the sella turcica in the brain.

supraspinal (su-prah-spi′nal) Above or over a spine or spinal column.

supraspinous (su-prah-spi′nus) Above a spine, especially the vertebrae.

suprasternal (su-prah-ster′nal) Above the breastbone (sternum).

supratympanic (su-prah-tim-pan′ik) Above the middle ear chamber.

supraventricular (su-prah-ven-trik′u-lar) Above a ventricle, especially of the heart.

supraversion (su-prah-ver′zhun) 1. The voluntary upward movement of both eyes. 2. Malocclusion in which the teeth extend well beyond the occlusal line; a deep overbite.

sura (su′rah) Latin for the calf of the leg.

sural (su′ral) Relating to the calf of the leg.

surface (sur′fis) 1. The outer boundary or outermost aspect of an object. 2. The surface of a structure that faces in a specific direction. 3. The uppermost part of a fluid substance.

    articular s. The surface of an articulating joint.

    articular s. of acetabulum The horseshoe-shaped articular portion of the acetabulum that articulates with the head of the femur in the hip joint.

    buccal s. (a) The surface of premolars and molars facing the cheek. (b) The mucosa of the cheek. (c) The side of a denture facing the cheek.

    distal s. (a) The surface of a structure that is farther from the point of reference. (b) The proximal or contact surface of a tooth facing away from the midline of the dental arch.

    facial s. See vestibular surface.

    labial s. (a) The surface of incisors and cuspids facing the lip. (b) The inner surface of the lip.

    lateral s. (a) The surface facing the direction of the side of the body. (b) The contact surface of the incisor or cuspid tooth facing away from the midline of the dental arch.

    lingual s. (a) The surface of a tooth facing the tongue. (b) The convex surface of the tongue. (c) The side of a denture facing the tongue.

    medial s. The surface of a structure that is closer to the point of reference. Also called mesial surface.

    mesial s. (a) See medial surface. (b) The proximal or contact surface of the incisor or cuspid tooth facing the midline of the dental arch.

    occlusal s. The grinding surface of a posterior tooth that comes in contact with one in the opposing jaw during occlusion; the working part of a tooth during mastication.

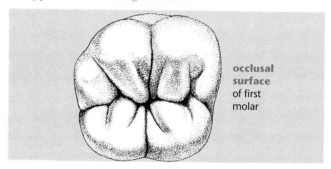

occlusal surface of first molar

    patellar articulating s. The upper posterior surface of the kneecap (patella), divided by a vertical median ridge into two smooth surfaces that articulate with both condyles of the femur.

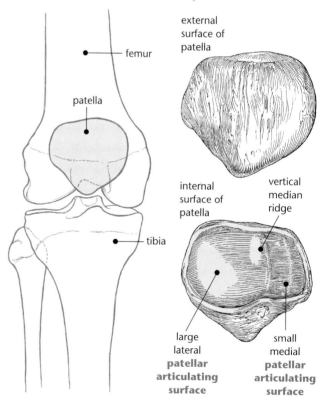

    proximal s. (a) The surface that is nearer to a point of reference. (b) The surface of a tooth facing an adjacent tooth in the same dental arch.

    respiratory s. The surface of the alveolocapillary (respiratory) membrane within the alveoli of the lung, through which there is an exchange of gases.

    tentorial s. The surface of the cerebrum that overlies the tentorium of the cerebellum (tentorium cerebelli).

    tooth s.'s The five surfaces of a tooth: occlusal (O), buccal (B), lingual (L), distal (D), and mesial (M).

    vestibular s. The surface of a tooth facing outwardly toward the vestibule of the mouth, comprising the labial, buccal, or combined labiobuccal surface. Also called facial surface.

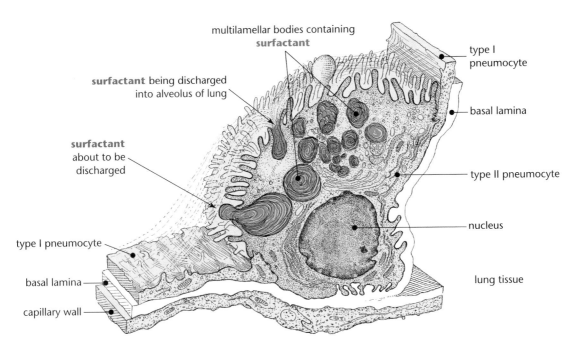

multilamellar bodies containing **surfactant**

type I pneumocyte

surfactant being discharged into alveolus of lung

basal lamina

surfactant about to be discharged

type II pneumocyte

nucleus

type I pneumocyte

basal lamina

capillary wall

lung tissue

surface-active (sur′fis ak′tiv) Having the capacity to alter the surface of a liquid, usually by reducing the surface tension.

surfactant (sur-fak′tant) A surface-active lipoprotein that normally decreases the surface tension of fluids within the lung's air sacs (alveoli); thus it permits lung tissues to expand during inspiration and prevents alveoli from collapsing and sticking together after each breath; in the fetus, it is produced after the 35th week of gestation.

surgeon (sur′jun) A physician who specializes in surgery.

    attending s. A member of the attending staff of a surgical department.

    dental s. A dentist.

    house s. A resident training in surgery in a hospital who acts under the orders of the attending surgeon.

surgeon general (sur′jun jen′er-al) The chief medical officer in the United States Army, Navy, Air Force, or Public Health Service.

surgery (sur′jer-e) Medical specialty concerned with the treatment of disease, injury, or deformity by means of manual and instrumental procedures.

aesthetic eyelid s. See blepharoplasty.

aesthetic s. See cosmetic surgery.

ambulatory s. Operative procedures performed on an outpatient basis; may be performed in a physician's office, a surgical center, or a hospital. Also called outpatient surgery.

cardiovascular s. Surgery performed on the heart and/or blood vessels.

cosmetic s. Plastic surgery in which the principal objective is to improve the appearance of the person (e.g., by removing skin blemishes or wrinkles, changing the shape of the nose, removing "bags" from under the eyes). Also called aesthetic surgery. See also blepharoplasty; rhinoplasty; rhytidectomy.

cutaneous s. Any surgical procedure on the skin, including diagnostic skin biopsies, elective cosmetic removal of benign lesions, and removal of skin cancers.

elective s. Surgery of a nonemergency nature; although recommended, it can be scheduled in advance without affecting the health of the patient or the expected result of the procedure.

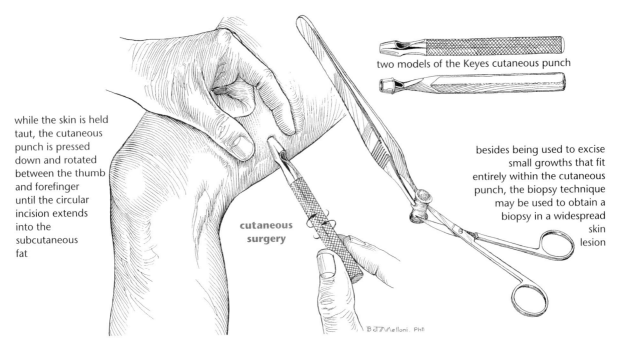

while the skin is held taut, the cutaneous punch is pressed down and rotated between the thumb and forefinger until the circular incision extends into the subcutaneous fat

cutaneous surgery

two models of the Keyes cutaneous punch

besides being used to excise small growths that fit entirely within the cutaneous punch, the biopsy technique may be used to obtain a biopsy in a widespread skin lesion

exploratory s. Any operation performed to determine the extent of a disease or to establish a diagnosis.

laser s. The use of laser beams (e.g., carbon dioxide, argon, excimer) for thermal cutting, vaporizing, coagulation, or destruction of tissues.

Mohs' s. A microscopically controlled surgical technique for removing broad-based but shallow skin tumors (especially basal and squamous cell carcinoma); it is a form of cancer chemosurgery in which the surface of the tumor plus a 3- to 5-mm margin is fixed (coagulated) with dichloracetic acid, overlaid with zinc chloride paste, and covered with a dressing; after 24 to 48 hours, sections of the tissue are examined at the border of the lesion and the procedure continues until tumor-free margins are obtained. The procedure is designed to accomplish complete removal of the tumor with the least possible disfigurement; usually applied to lesions of the face and other exposed areas. Also called microscopically controlled excision; Mohs' technique.

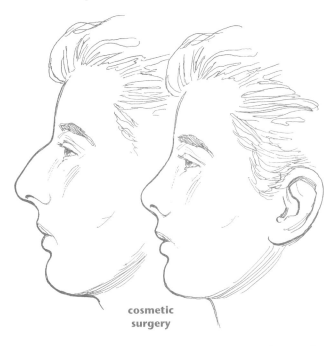

cosmetic
surgery

open-heart s. Procedure performed within the heart and requiring the use of extracorporeal circulation.

oral s. The dental specialty concerned with diagnosis and surgical treatment of diseases, deformities, and injuries of the oral and maxillofacial regions.

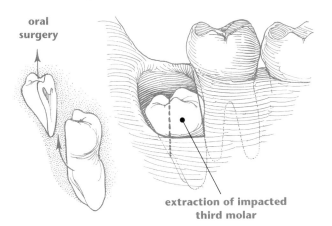

oral
surgery

**extraction of impacted
third molar**

orthopedic s. The branch of surgery concerned with the treatment of injuries and deformities of bones and chronic joint diseases.

outpatient s. See ambulatory surgery.

plastic s. Surgical procedures for the repair of physical deformities or for the restoration, reconstruction, or replacement of tissues and structures damaged or lost through injury or disease.

preprosthetic oral s. Any surgical procedure performed on or around a dental arch so that a denture can rest on a firm base, free from bony protrusions, interfering muscle attachments, or growths.

reconstructive s. Plastic surgery for restoring the form and/or function of a body part.

stereotactic s. See stereotaxy.

stereotaxic s. See stereotaxy.

thoracic s. Any operative procedure performed upon the chest or its contents.

transsexual s. A series of major operations on the urogenital tract designed to change a person's anatomical gender. Procedures may include some or all of the following: *Male-to-female change*, breast implantation, removal of penile erectile tissue, repositioning of urethra, creation of a vaginal pouch, removal of testes, and creation of

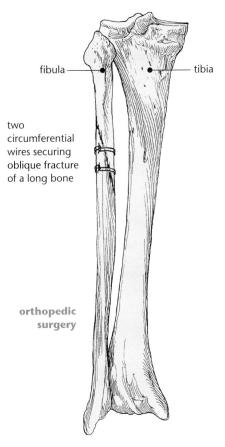

fibula — — tibia

two
circumferential
wires securing
oblique fracture
of a long bone

orthopedic
surgery

labia. *Female-to-male change*, removal of breasts, uterus, and ovaries; formation of a penile graft; and reconstruction of a new urethra.

surrogate (sur'o-gāt) **1.** A person who substitutes for another. **2.** In psychiatry, refers to a person who replaces a parent in the feelings of the patient.

mother s. One who replaces an individual's mother in his emotional feelings.

survey (sur-vā') **1.** To form a comprehensive view of a situation. **2.** An estimate; a determination.

skeletal s. A series of x-ray images made in cases of suspected physical abuse to differentiate old from new bone fractures.

surveying (sur-vā'ing) In dentistry, assessment of the relative position of teeth and related structures before designing a removable partial denture, the objective being to select a path of insertion and removal of the denture that will encounter the least interference.

suspension (sus-pen'shun) **1.** A pharmaceutical preparation of fine particles dispersed in a liquid. **2.** The hanging of a body part from a support for traction of the part.

surrogate ■ suspension

suspensory (sus-pen′so-re) Supporting; suspensory; applied to any structure (e.g., ligament) serving to keep an organ in place, or any device designed to support a dependent body part (e.g., the scrotum).

sustentacular (sus-ten-tak′u-lar) Supporting.

sustentaculum (sus-ten-tak′u-lum) A supporting structure.

   s. tali A shelflike process projecting medially from the anterior end of the heel bone (calcaneus); it serves to support the head of the ankle bone (talus).

susurrus (su-sur′us) Latin for murmur.

sutura (su-tu′rah) Latin for suture.

suture (su′chur) **1.** Stitch or stitches used in surgery to unite two surfaces. **2.** To apply a surgical stitch. **3.** The material used in closing a wound with stitches. **4.** An immovable fibrous joint uniting the bones of the cranium.

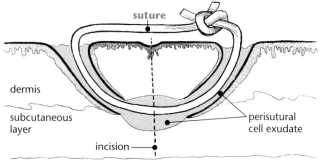

absorbable surgical s. A sterile strand obtained from tissues of healthy animals (e.g., catgut) that is capable of being gradually absorbed by living tissue; it may be treated to alter its absorbability, may be impregnated with antimicrobial substances, and may be treated with coloring material.

apposition s. A stitch or a number of stitches for securing two tissue edges in exact anatomic approximation. Also called coaptation suture.

atraumatic s. A suture made with a thread that is fused onto the end of a small eyeless needle to facilitate passage through tissue with minimal trauma.

Bell s. A suture in which the needle is inserted from within the wound outwardly, alternating on the two edges of the wound in a locking pattern.

blanket s. A continuous self-locking stitch that is passed beneath the loops of the preceding stitches; commonly used to approximate the skin of a wound and in intestinal surgery. Also called lock-stitch suture.

bolster s. A type of retention suture with the free ends tied over a small, tight roll of gauze or rubber tubing; used to lessen the pressure on the skin and reduce the stress on the primary suture line.

buried s. A deeply positioned suture that is concealed by the skin edges of the wound.

button s. One in which the ends of the strand are passed through the eyes of a buttonlike disk and then tied; it prevents the stitch from cutting through the skin.

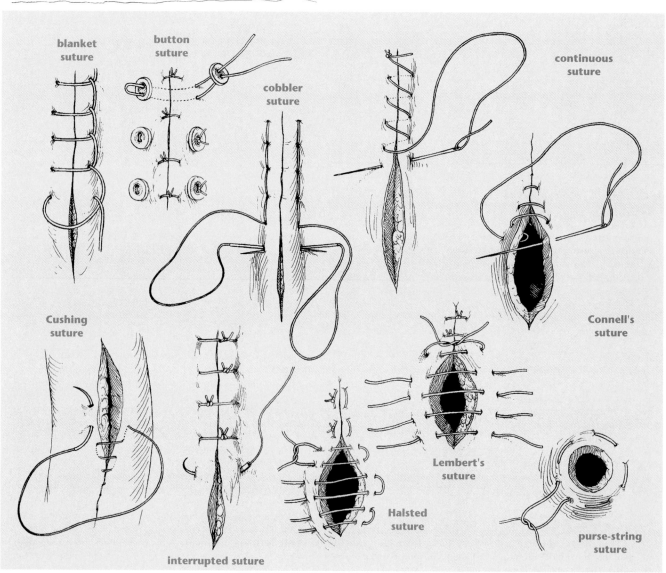

catgut s. See catgut.

chain s. A continuous suture resembling a common sewing machine stitch, in which each loop of thread is connected to the next adjacent loop. Also called chain-stitch suture.

chain-stitch s. See chain suture.

coaptation s. See apposition suture.

cobbler s. A suture made with a needle at each end of the strand; commonly used in vascular surgery. Also called doubly armed suture.

Connell's s. An inverted continuous suture, parallel to the edge of a surgical wound, that passes through all layers of the structure to be closed, such as the incised bowel; commonly used for inverting the gastric and intestinal walls in intestinal anastomoses.

continuous s. A suture running the length of the wound with only two anchoring knots, at the beginning and at the end; commonly used for closing long wounds. Also called uninterrupted suture; continuous running suture; running suture.

continuous running s. See continuous suture.

coronal s. The line of junction on top of the skull, between the posterior border of the frontal bone and the anterior borders of the two parietal bones.

cranial s. A type of immovable fibrous articulation between two bones of the cranium.

cruciform s. A suture of the hard (bony) palate formed by the intermaxillary and interpalatine sutures in the median plane, crossed by the palatomaxillary suture in the coronal plane.

Cushing s. A continuous inverting suture passed through the seromuscular layers of the gastrointestinal tract.

Czerny's s. A suture used for intestinal anastomosis in which the thread is passed only through the seromuscular layer; the needle is inserted through the serosa and passed out of the muscularis, and then reinserted in the muscularis of the opposite side, before emerging from the serosa.

Czerny-Lembert s. An intestinal anastomosis suture applied in two layers; the inner stitch is a Czerny's suture and the outer stitch is a Lembert suture.

denticulate s. An articulation between two bones in which the bone margins are small toothlike projections that often widen toward the free ends; it provides a highly effective interlocking mechanism.

doubly armed s. See cobbler suture.

ethmoid maxillary s. The line of junction in the inferomedial part of the eye socket (orbit), between the lower margin of orbital plate of the ethmoid bone and the orbital margin of the maxilla.

everting s. A surgical suture that turns the approximated edges of a wound outward.

false s. Articulation between contiguous complementary bone surfaces without interlocking or fibrous union. Also called plane suture; flat suture.

figure-of-eight s. A surgical suture passed deeply through each side of the wound and then crossed over and passed through the superficial layers on the opposite side, assuming the contours of the figure 8.

flat s. See false suture.

frontal s. The suture between the two halves of the developing frontal bone, commonly seen in newborns and infants prior to complete ossification into one bone; ossification usually is active from the second year of life to about the eighth year, when the process is completed.

frontolacrimal s. The line of junction between the orbital part of the frontal bone and the uppermost border of the lacrimal bone.

frontomaxillary s. The suture between the frontal bone and the frontal process of the maxilla.

frontonasal s. The line of junction on the front of the skull between the frontal bone and the uppermost border of the nasal bones. Also called nasofrontal suture.

frontosphenoid s. See sphenofrontal suture.

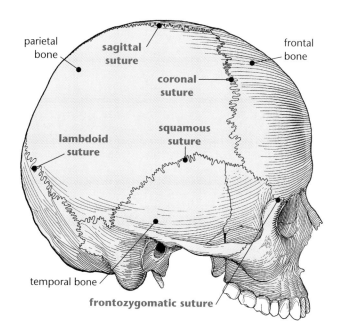

frontozygomatic s. The line of junction on the lateral border of the orbit, between the zygomatic process of the frontal bone and the frontal process of the zygomatic bone. Also called zygomaticofrontal suture.

guy s. A strong surgical suture that divides the wound into small subsections, thereby supporting the closure of the wound while additional sutures are inserted. Also called stay suture.

Halsted s. Interrupted inverted stitch parallel to the surgical wound on one side, with both free ends piercing through to the opposite side, where they are drawn and tied.

hemostatic s. A suture used primarily to control the oozing of blood from a cut surface.

horizontal mattress s. A surgical suture made parallel to both edges of the wound, with deep back-and-forth crossings into the tissue from one side to the other; as used to secure the repositioned areola during breast augmentation surgery.

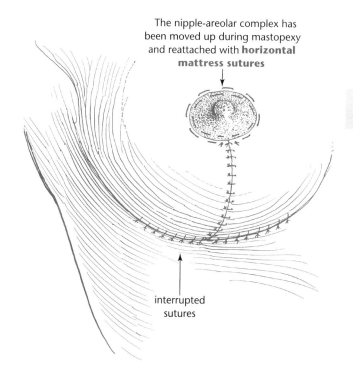

The nipple-areolar complex has been moved up during mastopexy and reattached with **horizontal mattress sutures**

interrupted sutures

imbricating s. A suture passed through the mucosal edge of a surgical wound, then through the underlying fascia, across to the other side, and out to the surface through the mucosal edge of the contralateral side; when the suture is drawn tight, the underlying wound is infolded and the mucosal edges are approximated. Used in such operations as the repair of excessive vaginal looseness or rectoceles.

intermaxillary s. The suture between the apposing maxillae, located on the median plane at the anterior part of the hard palate (on the roof of the mouth); it is continuous posteriorly with the interpalatine suture and forms the anterior part of the cruciform suture.

internasal s. The line of junction between the medial margins of the two nasal bones.

interpalatine s. The suture between the apposing horizontal plates of the two palatine bones, located on the median plane at the posterior part of the hard palate (on the roof of the mouth); it is continuous anteriorly with the intermaxillary suture and forms the posterior part of the cruciform suture. Also called middle palatine suture.

interrupted s. One of several single stitches placed in a row across two sides of a wound and tied; each stitch is made with a separate strand; commonly used in surgery (e.g., in closure of joint capsules).

intradermic s. A suture inserted into the deepest part of the skin (dermis), parallel with the edges of the wound; commonly used in plastic surgery.

inverting s. A stitch that turns inward (invaginates) the apposing surfaces of a wound; commonly used in intestinal anastomoses to facilitate a realignment of the serous surfaces of the two segments.

lacrimomaxillary s. The line of junction on the medial wall of the eye socket (orbit), between the lacrimal bone and the maxilla.

lambdoid s. The line of junction at the back of the skull, between the occipital and parietal bones; it resembles the Greek letter lambda (λ). Also called parietooccipital suture.

Lembert s. An inverting suture, either continuous or interrupted, commonly used to join together two segments of intestine without entering the lumen of the gut.

lock-stitch s. See blanket suture.

long cut s. A suture that is cut a great distance from the surgical knot, for easy retrieval postoperatively.

mattress s. See horizontal mattress suture; vertical mattress suture.

middle palatine s. See interpalatine suture.

nasofrontal s. See frontonasal suture.

nasomaxillary s. The line of junction between the lateral border of the nasal bone and the anterior border of the frontal process of the maxilla.

nonabsorbable surgical s. Any permanent suture that is not absorbed by the action of living tissues; made of a variety of materials (e.g., silk, cotton, alloy steel wire, and synthetic fibers) and in various diameters and tensile strengths.

occipitomastoid s. The line of junction on the posterolateral surface of the skull, between the occipital bone and the posterior margin of the temporal bone; it is a continuation of the lambdoid suture.

palatomaxillary s. The suture between the maxillary bone and the palatine bone; it forms the coronal part of the cruciform suture.

Paré's s. A surgical suture that entails the adhering of strips of cloth to the wound margins to facilitate apposition of the skin, followed by stitching of the cloth in place of the skin.

parietomastoid s. The line of junction on the lateral surface of the skull, between the posterior inferior angle of the parietal bone and the mastoid bone; it is a continuation of the lambdoid suture.

parietooccipital s. See lambdoid suture.

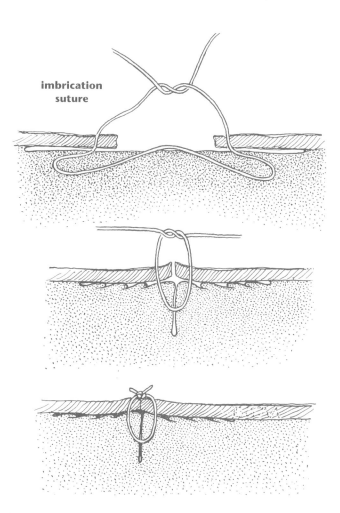

imbrication suture

plane s. See false suture.

purse-string s. A continuous, circular inverting suture, placed around a circular surgical opening that is to be inverted, such as the opening left after removal of the appendix.

radial hemostatic s. A suture used to control oozing of blood, especially after the removal of a cone of tissue from the cervix that is larger than 3 cm in diameter; it is placed circumferentially about the cervix and the cone site.

relaxation s. A stitch that can be loosened, if needed, to relieve tissue tension on the wound.

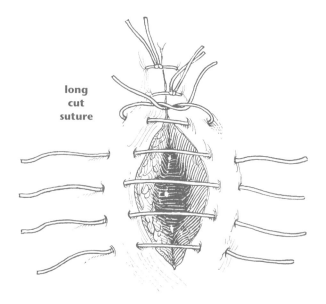

long cut suture

retention s. A reinforcing suture generally used for closing large abdominal wounds, using silk or steel strands and encompassing large amounts of tissue in each stitch; used to relieve undue stress on the primary suture line, thereby preventing postoperative wound disruption. Also called tension suture.

running s. See continuous suture.

sagittal s. The median suture between the upper serrated margins of the two parietal bones located at the top of the skull.

serrate s. A suture in which the bone margins are highly complex and irregular, with spikes and recesses intimately interdigitated.

sphenofrontal s. A suture in the internal surface of the base of the skull, between the posterior border of the orbital part of the frontal bone and the sphenoid bone on either side of the skull. Also called frontosphenoid suture.

sphenoparietal s. The suture in the temporal fossa (at the pterion, an important craniometric point), between the upper tip of the greater wing of the sphenoid bone and the anterior part of the lower border of the parietal bone.

sphenosquamosal s. The suture between the posterior margin of the greater wing of the sphenoid bone and the anterior margin of the squamous part of the temporal bone.

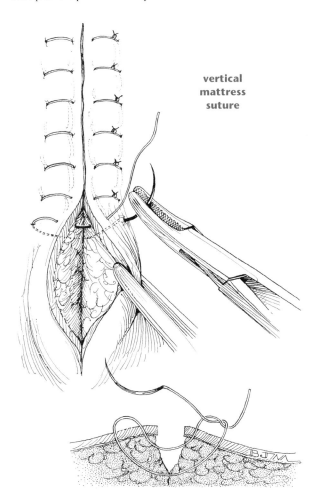

vertical mattress suture

sphenozygomatic s. A suture between the anterior border of the greater wing of the sphenoid bone and the orbital surface of the zygomatic bone. Also called zygomaticosphenoid suture.

squamosoparietal s. The suture on the side of the skull, between the squamous part of the temporal bone and the parietal bone.

squamous s. A type of suture in which one bone margin overlaps its apposing bone margin, as the suture between the temporal and parietal bones.

stay s. See guy suture.

subcuticular s. Continuous surgical stitches placed in the tissues immediately under the skin (subcuticular), parallel to the edge of the wound, without penetrating the skin; a method of skin closure.

temporozygomatic s. See zygomaticotemporal suture.

tension s. See retention suture.

uninterrupted s. See continuous suture.

vertical mattress s. A surgical suture made at right angles to both edges of the wound; the needle is passed through the wound twice, first shallowly, close to the edges of the wound, then more deeply, further from the edges, with back and forth crossings into the tissue from one side to the other.

vomero-ethmoidal s. The suture of the thin bony nasal septum between the vomer and the overriding perpendicular plate of the ethmoid bone. The vomer forms the lower and posterior part of the nasal septum, while the perpendicular plate of the ethmoid bone forms the upper and anterior part of the septum and is continuous above with the cribriform plate. When the nasal septum is deviated, the defect usually occurs at the line of the vomero-ethmoidal suture.

zygomaticofrontal s. See frontozygomatic suture.

zygomaticomaxillary s. A suture between the maxillary border of the zygomatic bone and the zygomatic process (upper oblique surface) of the maxilla.

zygomaticosphenoid s. See sphenozygomatic suture.

zygomaticotemporal s. A suture between the zygomatic process of the temporal bone and the temporal process of the zygomatic bone; easily palpable where the cheek and temple meet each other. Also called temporozygomatic suture.

swab (swahb) A small ball of cotton or other absorbent material at one end of a stick or wire; used to apply medication, collect a specimen for microscopic study, or cleanse a surface.

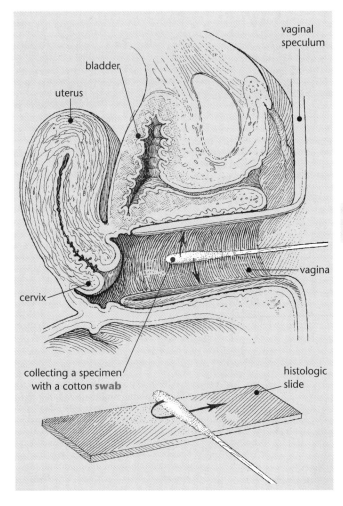

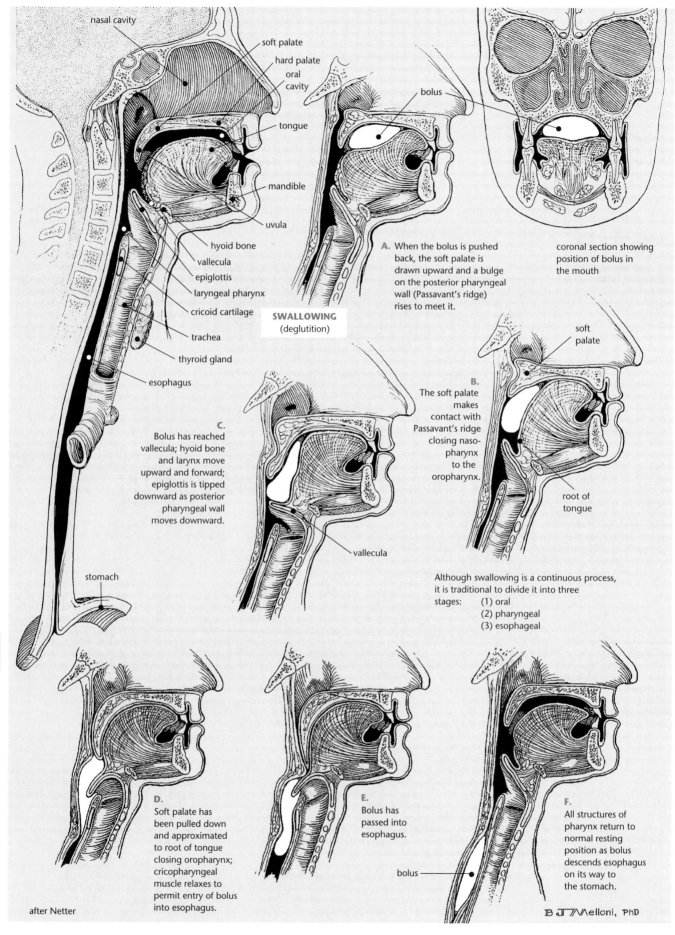

nasal cavity

soft palate
hard palate
oral cavity

bolus

tongue

mandible

uvula

hyoid bone

vallecula

epiglottis

laryngeal pharynx

cricoid cartilage

trachea

thyroid gland

esophagus

coronal section showing position of bolus in the mouth

A. When the bolus is pushed back, the soft palate is drawn upward and a bulge on the posterior pharyngeal wall (Passavant's ridge) rises to meet it.

SWALLOWING
(deglutition)

B. The soft palate makes contact with Passavant's ridge closing naso-pharynx to the oropharynx.

soft palate

root of tongue

C. Bolus has reached vallecula; hyoid bone and larynx move upward and forward; epiglottis is tipped downward as posterior pharyngeal wall moves downward.

vallecula

stomach

Although swallowing is a continuous process, it is traditional to divide it into three stages: (1) oral
(2) pharyngeal
(3) esophageal

D. Soft palate has been pulled down and approximated to root of tongue closing oropharynx; cricopharyngeal muscle relaxes to permit entry of bolus into esophagus.

after Netter

E. Bolus has passed into esophagus.

F. All structures of pharynx return to normal resting position as bolus descends esophagus on its way to the stomach.

bolus

B.J.Melloni, PhD

S

swallowing (swahl′o-ing) The act of moving materials from the mouth to the stomach via the esophagus. Also called deglutition.

swayback (swa′bak) See lordosis.

sweat (swet) 1. Perspiration. 2. To perspire.

swelling (swel′ing) 1. An enlargement that may be inflammatory or noninflammatory; like fever, it is not a disease in itself but a sign of an underlying disorder. 2. In embryology, an elevation or protuberance indicating an early stage of development of certain structures.

    capsular s. The swelling of the capsules of pneumococci when the organisms are exposed to pneumococcal antibodies. Also called Neufeld reaction; quellung reaction.

sycoma (si-ko′mah) A pendulous growth.

sycosiform (si-ko′sĭ-form) Resembling sycosis.

sycosis (si-ko′sis) Inflammatory condition of the hair follicles, especially of the beard, forming pustules and crusting on the skin.

symbiont, symbiot (sim′bi-ont, sim′bi-ōt) One of two organisms associated with another in a symbiotic relationship.

symbiosis (sim-bi-o′sis) 1. The living together in intimate association of two dissimilar organisms. 2. The mutually reinforcing dependency between two people, a normal relationship between a mother and her infant.

symblepharon (sim-blef′ah-ron) Adhesion of the eyelid to the eyeball, usually resulting from trauma.

symblepharopterygium (sim-blef′ah-ro-ter-ij′e-um) Adhesion of the eyelid to the eyeball by a band of scar tissue resembling a pterygium.

symbol (sim′bul) 1. A written mark, sign, or character adopted by convention to represent a substance, quantity, relation, unit of measurement, mathematical constant, etc. 2. An object that represents something else.

CHEMICAL SYMBOLS

Sb	antimony	N	nitrogen
As	arsenic	Os	osmium
Ba	barium	O	oxygen
Bi	bismuth	Pb	palladium
Br	bromine	P	phosphorus
Cd	cadmium	Pt	platinum
Ca	calcium	Pu	plutonium
C	carbon	K	potassium
Cl	chlorine	Ra	radium
Cr	chromium	Rn	radon
Co	cobalt	Se	selenium
Cu	copper	Si	silicone
F	fluorine	Ag	silver
Au	gold	Na	sodium
He	helium	Sr	strontium
H	hydrogen	S	sulfur
I	iodine	Sn	tin
Fe	iron	W	tungsten
Pb	lead	U	Uranium
Mg	magnesium	Xe	xenon
Mn	manganese	Y	yttrium
Hg	mercury	Zn	zinc

symbolization (sim-bol-ĭ-za′shun) An unconscious mental process whereby one object or idea comes to stand for another through some characteristic that both have in common.

symmetry (sim′ĕ-tre) An exact correspondence of parts on opposite sides of a plane or around an axis.

sympathectomy (sim-pah-thek′to-me) Surgical removal of a segment of a sympathetic nerve and/or ganglia.

    chemical s. Interruption of a sympathetic nervous pathway by means of chemical substances (e.g., guanethidine), which selectively act on adrenergic nerves.

sympathetic (sim-pah-thet′ik) 1. Relating to the thoracolumbar portion of the autonomic nervous system. 2. Relating to sympathy.

sympathicotripsy (sim-path-ĭ-ko-trip′se) Therapeutic crushing of a ganglion of the sympathetic nervous system.

sympathicotropic (sim-path-ĭ-ko-trōp′ik) Having an affinity for or affecting the sympathetic nervous system.

sympatho-, sympath- Combining forms meaning the sympathetic portion of the autonomic nervous system.

sympathoadrenal (sim-path-o-ah-dre′nal) Relating to the sympathetic nervous system and the medulla of the adrenal gland (especially its hormones epinephrine and norepinephrine).

sympathoblast (sim-path′o-blast) In embryology, one of the undifferentiated cells that migrate from the neural crest and give rise to sympathetic ganglion cells and the medulla of the adrenal gland.

sympathoblastoma (sim-pah-tho-blas-to′mah) See neuroblastoma.

sympatholytic (sim-pah-tho-lit′ik) Inhibiting the activity of the sympathetic nervous system. Also called sympathoparalytic.

sympathomimetic (sim-pah-tho-mi-met′ik) Producing effects similar to those of the sympathetic nervous system.

sympathoparalytic (sim-pah-tho-par-ah-lit′ik) See sympatholytic.

sympathy (sim′pah-the) 1. The physiologic or pathologic interrelationship between parts of the body. 2. The capacity for understanding the feelings, or for sharing the concerns, of another person.

symphysial, symphyseal (sim-fiz′e-al) Relating to the symphysis.

Symbols Used in Genetics

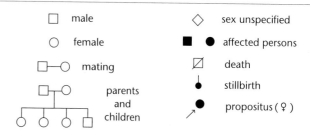

- male
- female
- mating
- parents and children
- sex unspecified
- affected persons
- death
- stillbirth
- propositus (♀)

emergency medical identification (**symbol** designates special medical problem of bearer)

radiation hazard **symbol**

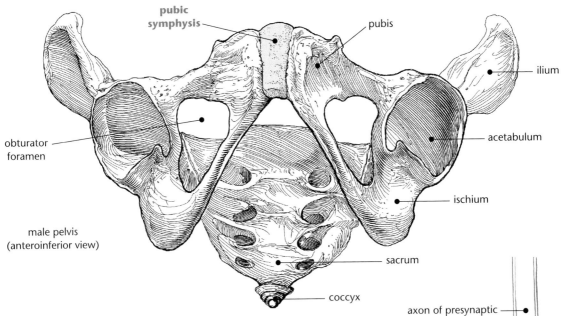

pubic symphysis

pubis

ilium

obturator foramen

acetabulum

ischium

male pelvis (anteroinferior view)

sacrum

coccyx

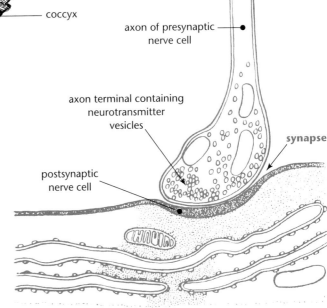

axon of presynaptic nerve cell

axon terminal containing neurotransmitter vesicles

synapse

postsynaptic nerve cell

symphysis (sim′fĭ-sis), pl. sym′physes **1.** A type of articulation in which two opposing surfaces of bones are covered with a thin layer of hyaline cartilage and united by fibrocartilage. **2.** In pathology, the abnormal fusion of two surfaces.

 pubic s. The symphysis between the pubic bones where they meet at the median plane of the pelvis; the bones are connected by an interpubic disk of fibrocartilage, and by the superior pubic ligament above and the arcuate pubic ligament below.

symport (sim′port) The simultaneous transport of two different compounds across a cell membrane in the same direction by the same carrier mechanism.

symptom (simp′tum) Any manifestation of an abnormal physical or mental state that is experienced and detectable by the patient.

 cardinal s. A symptom that is of primary diagnostic significance.

 Duroziez's s. See Duroziez's murmur, under murmur.

 withdrawal s. Any of a group of physiologic and psychic disturbances that follow the abrupt cessation of use of a psychoactive substance taken for a prolonged period of time; the substances include alcohol, amphetamines, cocaine, anxiolytics, opioids, sedatives, hypnotics, and nicotine. Also called withdrawal syndrome.

symptomatic (simp-to-mat′ik) Relating to a symptom.

symptomatology (simp-tom-ah-tol′o-je) **1.** The group of symptoms of a disease. **2.** The study of the symptoms of diseases, their causes, and the information they furnish. Formerly called semiology.

syn- Prefix meaning together; joined; with.

synalgia (sin-al′je-ah) See referred pain, under pain.

synapse (sin′aps) **1.** The gap (10–50 nm wide) a nerve impulse must pass through to be transmitted from one nerve cell to another, or from one nerve cell to a muscle or gland cell. Transmission is accomplished by release of a special substance (neurotransmitter) from the presynaptic nerve cell into the gap. **2.** To form a synapse.

 axodendritic s. The junction of the axon of a nerve cell with a dendrite of another nerve cell.

 axosomatic s. The junction of the axon of a nerve cell with the cell body of another.

synapsis (sĭ-nap′sis) Process occurring in the prophase stage of meiosis in which homologous chromosomes pair off and unite.

synaptic (sĭ-nap′tik) Relating to synapsis.

synarthrosis (sin-ar-thro′sis), pl. synarthro′ses See fibrous joint, under joint.

syncanthus (sin-kan′thus) Abnormal adhesions between the eyeball and the eye socket (orbit).

synchondrosis (sin-kon-dro′sis), pl. synchondro′ses The union of two bones by cartilage; usually the cartilage is replaced by bone (e.g., the junction between skull bones of the newborn infant).

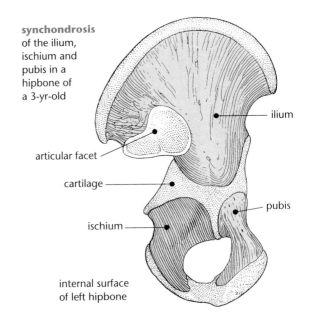

synchondrosis of the ilium, ischium and pubis in a hipbone of a 3-yr-old

ilium

articular facet

cartilage

pubis

ischium

internal surface of left hipbone

symphysis ■ synchondrosis

S

synchronia (sin-kro′ne-ah) **1.** See synchronism. **2.** The formation and development of tissues at the usual time.

synchronism (sin′kro-nizm) The simultaneous occurrence of two or more events. Also called synchronia.

synchrotron (sin′kro-tron) A machine for generating high-speed electrons or protons around a fixed circular path by a radio-frequency potential.

synchysis (sin′kĭ-sis) Condition of the eye in which the vitreous body (within the eyeball) becomes liquefied.

　s. scintillans Condition marked by the presence of numerous glistening white cholesterol crystals that tend to settle in the lowest part of a liquefied vitreous when the eyes are motionless; they spring up and float around in great showers when the eyes are moved. The person is unaware of the condition; it is observed only by the examiner; no correlation with high blood cholesterol levels has been established, and the person's vision is unaffected.

synclitism (sin′klit-izm) In obstetrics, the attitude of the fetal head in relation to the maternal pelvis as it descends into the pelvis; the head enters the pelvis with its sagittal suture line in the transverse plane of the maternal pelvis, midway between the pubis and the sacrum. Also called obliquity.

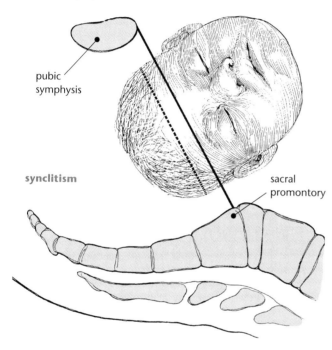

pubic symphysis

synclitism

sacral promontory

syncopal (sin′ko-pal) Relating to fainting.

syncope (sin′ko-pe) A brief loss of consciousness; a faint; sudden loss of consciousness lasting seconds or, at most, minutes, and from which a person awakens alert and aware of surroundings; the underlying mechanism is a temporary reduction of blood flow to the brain; most common cause is a drop in blood pressure for any of various reasons.

syncytiotrophoblast (sin-sit-e-o-trof′o-blast) In embryology, the peripheral part of the trophoblast; it penetrates maternal tissues to attach the blastocyst to the uterus and eventually enters into the formation of the placenta. Also called syntrophoblast.

syncytium (sin-sish′e-um) A mass of multinucleated protoplasm, seemingly formed from the union of several cells.

syndactyly, syndactylism (sin-dak′tĭ-le, sin-dak′tĭ-lizm) Partial or total fusion of two or more fingers or toes. Also called zygodactyly.

syndesmectomy (sin-des-mek′to-me) Removal of a section of a ligament.

syndesmitis (sin-des-mi′tis) Inflammation of a ligament.

syndesmo- Combining form meaning ligament.

syndesmopexy (sin-des′mo-pek′se) Reattachment of a ligament.

syndesmoplasty (sin-des′mo-plas-te) Reparative surgery of a ligament.

syndesmorrhaphy (sin-des-mor′ah-fe) The suturing of a ligament.

syndesmosis (sin-des-mo′sis), pl. syndesmo′ses A type of fibrous articulation in which the fibrous tissue between the bones forms a membrane or ligament, as the articulation between the tibia and fibula or the union of the footplate (base) of the stapes to the oval window (fenestra of vestibule) of the inner ear.

syndesmotomy (sin-des-mot′o-me) Surgical division of a ligament.

syndrome (sin′drōm) A set of signs and/or symptoms that occur together with reasonable consistency.

　abdominal muscle deficiency s. See prune-belly syndrome.

　acquired immune deficiency s. See AIDS.

　acute organic brain s. Any sudden, often reversible, impairment of brain function secondary to systemic metabolic disorders or to drug ingestion, usually associated with delirium.

　acute radiation s. A syndrome caused by brief but heavy exposure of all or part of the body to ionizing radiation; severity of illness depends on dosage, body distribution, and duration of exposure. Clinical manifestations occur in four stages: prodromal, latent, overt, and recovery. Most affected are reproductive, gastrointestinal, and blood-forming tissues.

　Adams-Stokes s. See Stokes-Adams syndrome.

　adiposogenital s. See adiposogenital dystrophy, under dystrophy.

　adult respiratory distress s. (ARDS) A life-threatening condition occurring shortly after trauma, usually within 24 to 48 hours; characterized by accumulation of fluid in the lungs, acute respiratory failure, and shock; may be precipitated by a variety of factors, including direct chest injury, near drowning, aspiration of stomach contents, inhalation of toxic gases, cardiopulmonary bypass, and similar trauma. Also called posttraumatic pulmonary insufficiency; shock lung; wet lung; pump lung.

　afferent loop s. Chronic partial obstruction of the duodenum and jejunum occurring after a surgical connection of the jejunum to the stomach (gastrojejunostomy) and causing pain and distention of the intestinal loop after eating.

　air-leak s.'s A group of conditions having as the underlying cause an overdistention of air sacs (alveoli) or terminal airways (bronchioles) in the lungs, leading to disruption of airway integrity, and resulting in escape of air into surrounding tissues; included are: pneumothorax, pneumomediastinum, pulmonary interstitial emphysema (PIE), and pneumopericardium.

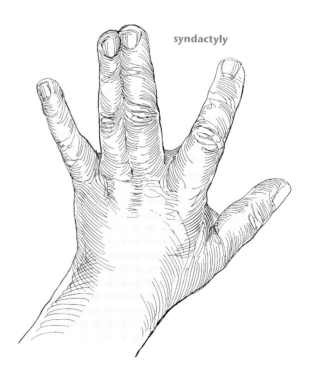

syndactyly

S

synchronia ■ syndrome

Albright's s. Bone disorder affecting children; characterized by fibrous dysplasia with cystic transformation involving several bones of the skeleton, accompanied by pigmented spots on the skin and sexual precocity (especially in females).

alcohol withdrawal s. Symptom complex occurring when alcohol is withdrawn from a person who is physically and psychologically dependent on alcohol; characterized by hand tremors, weakness, nausea, hyperactivity of the autonomic nervous system, and anxiety or depression. If prolonged, it may progress to hallucinations. See also delirium tremens.

Aldrich's s. See Wiskott-Aldrich syndrome.

Alport's s. Condition inherited as an autosomal dominant trait consisting of glomerular and interstitial inflammation of the kidney associated with deafness; although males and females are affected with nearly equal frequency, the males are usually affected to a greater extent.

angio-osteohypertrophy s. Condition affecting one extremity characterized by overdevelopment (hypertrophy) of bone and adjacent soft tissues, and a large nevus flammeus usually overlying the defect. Also called Klippel-Trenaunay syndrome.

anterior scalene s. See scalenus anterior syndrome.

anterior tibial compartment s. Inflammation and necrosis of the leg muscles within the anterior fascial compartment resulting from blood vessel insufficiency, secondary to specific vessel disease or injury or to segmental spasm of the anterior tibial artery.

anticardiolipin s. See antiphospholipid antibody syndrome.

antiphospholipid s. See antiphospholipid antibody syndrome.

antiphospholipid antibody s. (APS) The presence of antiphospholipid antibody or lupus anticoagulant antibody in the circulating blood associated with any or all of the following: recurrent arterial and venous blood clot occlusions (thromboses), recurrent miscarriages, and abnormally low number of platelets in the circulating blood (thrombocytopenia). Also called anticardiolipin syndrome; antiphospholipid syndrome; lupus anticoagulant syndrome.

anxiety s. See generalized anxiety disorder, under disorder.

aortic arch s. Occlusion of one or more of the large arteries branching off the aortic arch (i.e., the brachiocephalic trunk, left common carotid artery, and left subclavian artery), leading to diminished or absent pulse in the neck and arms; caused by plaque formation and inflammation of the vessels, with secondary blood clots (thrombosis). Also called Martorell's syndrome.

appallic s. See persistent vegetative state, under state.

s. of approximate answers See Ganser syndrome.

Asherman's s. See posttraumatic uterine adhesions, under adhesion.

Asperger's s. A type of character disorder in which autistic thinking predominates; the person can function in the normal world but lacks normal human understanding, sensitivity, and intuition.

bacterial overgrowth s. Condition of the jejunum marked by the presence of an abnormally large number of aerobic and anaerobic bacteria similar to those that normally inhabit the colon, accompanied by pathologic changes in the bowel wall; most frequently seen in conditions obstructing the jejunal lumen.

Banti's s. See chronic congestive splenomegaly, under splenomegaly.

Barlow s. A systolic click or a late systolic murmur, or both, heard on auscultation of the heart due to prolapse of the mitral (atrioventricular) valve into the left atrium of the heart (floppy valve syndrome).

Barrett's s. See Barrett's esophagus, under esophagus.

Bartter's s. Disorder inherited as an autosomal recessive trait with symptoms and signs usually beginning in childhood; characterized by juxtaglomerular cell hyperplasia, secondary hyperaldosteronism, hypokalemic alkalosis, and a marked increase in prostaglandin production in the absence of high blood pressure.

battered child s. Multiple physical and psychologic injuries inflicted upon a child by an older individual, usually an adult and often a parent; injuries include bruises, burns, and fractures (especially of ribs and long bones); often older, partially healed fractures are discovered incidental to examination and x-raying; syndrome includes emotional scars left by the betrayal and rejection that characterize such abuse; the syndrome thus may include such symptoms in the child as depression, withdrawal, phobic anxiety, or poorly controlled aggression and deliquency. Without intervention this pattern tends to repeat across generations. See also child abuse, under abuse.

battered woman s. A condition of fear of serious bodily harm or danger of death, isolation, guilt, emotional dependency, learned helplessness, and hypersuggestibility occurring in a woman as cumulative effects of long-term, constant, and severe physical and psychologic abuse by her partner, companion, or spouse. The syndrome may apply to men as well as women.

Behçet's s. See Behçet's disease, under disease.

Bernheim's s. Right heart failure manifested by distended veins in the neck, edema, and enlarged liver, occurring without pulmonary congestion in persons with an enlarged left ventricle of the heart from any cause.

binge-and-purge s. See bulemia.

blind loop s. Retention of bowel contents in a pouch or "dead-end" loop of the intestine (either present at birth or created in certain surgical procedures); the bowel contents stagnate; bacteria multiply and spread to other intestinal regions, where they interfere with absorption of fat and vitamin B_{12}, causing diarrhea with pale yellow bulky feces (steatorrhea), fatigue, and weight loss.

Boerhaave's s. Spontaneous rupture of the lower esophagus.

Briquet's s. See somatization disorder, under disorder.

Brock's s. See middle lobe syndrome.

Brown-Séquard s. Symptom complex due to damage to one side of the spinal cord (e.g., by a tumor or trauma), marked by paralysis and loss of discriminatory sensation on the side of the lesion and loss of pain and temperature sensation on the opposite side. Also called Brown-Séquard paralysis.

Budd-Chiari s. See hepatic vein occlusion, under occlusion.

Burnett's s. See milk-alkali syndrome.

Caffey's s. See infantile cortical hyperostosis, under hyperostosis.

Caplan's s. Multiple large nodules consisting of collections of inflammatory cells surrounding blood vessels, usually occurring in the lungs of coal miners afflicted with pneumoconiosis and rheumatoid arthritis.

carcinoid s. A group of symptoms associated with carcinoid tumors that have spread from the intestinal tract to the liver; major features include skin flushing, watery diarrhea, lesions in the lining of the right atrium of the heart and over the tricuspid (right atrioventricular) valve, and episodes of asthmalike wheezing; caused by tumor secretion of biologically active substances (e.g., histamine, prostaglandins, bradykinin, and, especially, serotonin).

carotid sinus s. A fall of blood pressure and slow pulse with fainting and, occasionally, convulsions caused by overstimulation of the carotid sinus. Also called carotid sinus reflex.

carpal tunnel s. A complex of symptoms caused by abnormal pressure upon the median nerve as it passes between the transverse carpal ligament and the wrist bones (carpus), causing numbness of the first three digits, pain in the wrist and the palm, and eventual atrophy of the thenar muscles (between the thumb and the wrist). Symptoms may result from an injury (e.g., direct blow to the dorsiflexed wrist or a Colles' fracture), from repetitive wrist and finger movements (e.g., in typing), or may appear during pregnancy. Seen more often in hypothyroidism.

cat-cry s. See cri du chat syndrome.

cauda equina s. A dull pain and lack of sensation (anesthesia) in the buttocks, genitals, and posterolateral area of the thighs with impairment of bladder and sexual functions; usually caused by injury to the roots of lumbosacral and coccygeal nerves, as seen in vertebral fractures.

cavernous sinus s. Any symptom complex that includes multiple nerve paralysis of the third, fourth, and fifth cranial nerves

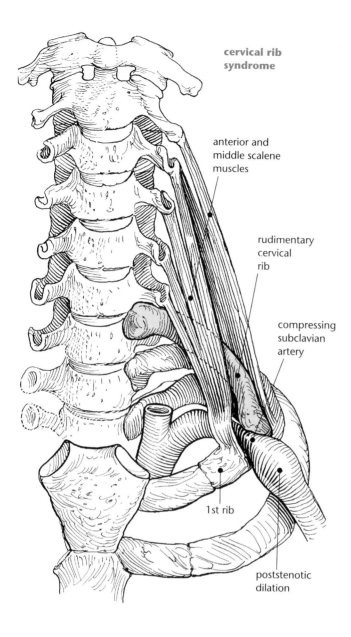

cervical rib syndrome

anterior and middle scalene muscles

rudimentary cervical rib

compressing subclavian artery

1st rib

poststenotic dilation

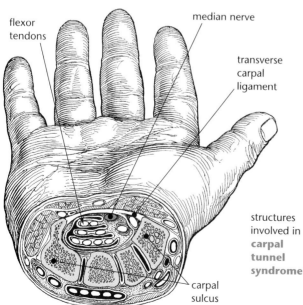

flexor tendons

median nerve

transverse carpal ligament

structures involved in **carpal tunnel syndrome**

carpal sulcus

usually due to nerve damage from a lesion of the cavernous sinus within the skull; e.g., blood clot formation in the cavernous sinus (thrombosis) resulting from direct spread of a facial infection along the venous channels draining the face. Also called Foix's syndrome.

cerebrohepatorenal s. See Zellweger's syndrome.

cervical compression s. See cervical disk syndrome.

cervical disk s. Pain, numbness, and muscular spasm of the neck, radiating to the shoulder, caused by compression and irritation of the cervical nerve roots by a protruding intervertebral disk. Also called cervical compression syndrome.

cervical fusion s. See Klippel-Feil syndrome.

cervical rib s. Pain and tingling along the forearm and hand caused by pressure upon the brachial plexus and subclavian artery by a rudimentary cervical rib, fibrous band, first thoracic rib, or a tight scalene muscle.

Chédiak-Higashi s. (CHS) An inherited white blood cell defect found in infants and young children. It is characterized by massive cytoplasmic inclusions in the leukocytes; decreased pigmentation of skin, eyes, and hair; recurrent infections; and early death.

Chiari's s. See hepatic vein occlusion, under occlusion.

Chiari-Frommel s. Prolonged milk secretion, amenorrhea, and atrophy of the uterus after childbirth; generally associated with a benign tumor of the anterior lobe of the pituitary (hypophysis).

Chinese restaurant s. Syndrome occurring in people who are unusually sensitive to monosodium glutamate; mainly characterized by feelings of tightness of facial muscles, chest pains, and a burning sensation in various parts of the body; symptoms occur about 30 minutes after eating food heavily seasoned with monosodium glutamate (such as is served in some Chinese restaurants).

Churg-Strauss s. Inflammation of blood vessels of various organ systems (especially the lungs and spleen), formation of intra- and extravascular granulomas, eosinophilia, and severe asthma. Also called allergic granulomatosis; allergic granulomatous angiitis.

closed building s. A set of symptoms of unknown cause occurring among occupants of usually new buildings with centrally controlled ventilation systems that depend on a significant proportion of recirculated air. Symptoms typically occur shortly after entering the building and are relieved soon after leaving; they include headache, eye irritation, difficulty in wearing contact lenses, nasal and sinus congestion, throat irritation, chest tightness or burning, nausea, and dizziness. Also called tight building syndrome; sick building syndrome.

compartment s. Injury occurring during exercise due to expansion and compression of a muscle group within its confined fascial space.

Conn's s. See primary aldosteronism, under aldosteronism.

costoclavicular s. Disorder of blood vessels of the arms resulting from neuromuscular compression between the collarbone (clavicle) and the first rib.

CREST s. A variant of progressive systemic sclerosis, characterized by deposition of calcium salts in the skin and subcutaneous tissues, numbness and pallor of the fingers and toes, dysfunction of the esophagus, stiffness of the skin of fingers with atrophy of fingertips, and dilatation of capillaries.

cri du chat s. Congenital disorder marked by severe mental retardation, a typical mewing catlike cry in infancy, and anomalies of the heart; caused by a chromosomal defect in which chromosome 5 lacks the short arm. Also called cat-cry syndrome.

Crigler-Najjar s. An inherited disorder that may be: *type I*, a rare severe form, usually fatal soon after birth, associated with total absence of the bilirubin enzyme glucuronyltransferase; or *type II*, a mild form in which the enzyme deficiency is partial and life expectancy of the person is normal. Also called Crigler-Najjar disease.

crocodile tears s. Secretion of tears while eating, occurring during partial recovery from facial paralysis on the same side as an injury to the facial nerve.

crush s. A shocklike state following a severe crushing injury that damages soft tissue; the protein pigment myoglobin is released into

S

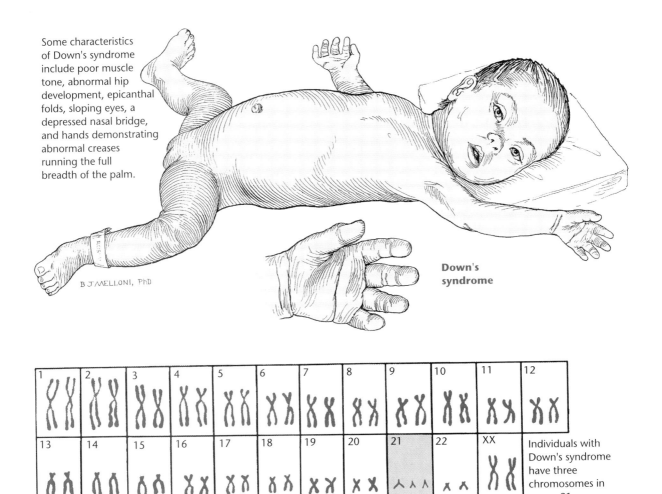

Some characteristics of Down's syndrome include poor muscle tone, abnormal hip development, epicanthal folds, sloping eyes, a depressed nasal bridge, and hands demonstrating abnormal creases running the full breadth of the palm.

B J MELLONI, PhD

Down's syndrome

Individuals with Down's syndrome have three chromosomes in group 21.

the bloodstream from the damaged muscles, causing decreased urine output, necrosis of kidney tubules, and kidney failure. Also called compression syndrome.

Cruveilhier-Baumgarten s. Cirrhosis of the liver with portal hypertension, associated with congenital patency of umbilical or paraumbilical veins. See also Cruveilhier-Baumgarten sign, under sign.

Cushing's s. The group of symptoms and physical characteristics of Cushing's disease, including a round face, central obesity, prominent fat pad on the upper back ("buffalo hump"), reddish complexion, abdominal striations, high blood pressure (hypertension), and impaired carbohydrate tolerance; may be caused by long-term corticosteroid therapy, abnormalities of the pituitary or adrenal glands, or ACTH-secreting nonpituitary tumors.

DAM-N s. See familial atypical mole and melanoma syndrome.

Dandy-Walker s. Congenital hydrocephalus in infants due to obstruction to the flow of cerebrospinal fluid at the median aperture of the fourth ventricle and the lateral apertures of the fourth ventricle.

dead fetus s. See retained dead fetus syndrome.

De Toni-Fanconi s. Multiple defects of renal tubular function manifested by aminoaciduria, phosphaturia, glycosuria, a variable degree of renal tubular acidosis, and abnormal softening of bone tissue.

dialysis disequilibrium s. Symptoms occurring occasionally with early hemodialysis treatments, including nausea, vomiting, high blood pressure, and central nervous system disturbance (e.g., convulsions); related to rapid urea depletion and movement of water into cells.

DiGeorge's s. A multiorgan congenital disorder resulting from damage to the third and fourth pharyngeal pouches during early embryonic development (before the eighth week of pregnancy); char-

acterized by a reduced development or total absence of the thymus and parathyroid glands, frequently accompanied by anomalies of other structures that are formed at the same embryonic age, including defects of the heart and great vessels, stricture (atresia) of the esophagus, widely separated eyes, and low-set ears. Also called thymic hypoplasia syndrome.

Di Guglielmo's s. See erythremic myelosis, under myelosis.

Down's s. The occurrence of various degrees of mental retardation and characteristic physical features such as flattened skull, slanting eyes, thickened tongue, broad hands and feet, and other anomalies; caused by the abnormal presence of three chromosomes (trisomy) instead of the normal two for the pair designated number 21. Also called trisomy 21 syndrome; mongolism (outmoded).

Dressler's s. See postmyocardial infarction syndrome.

dry eye s. See keratoconjunctivitis sicca, under keratoconjunctivitis.

Dubin-Johnson s. Autosomal recessive defect in the excretory function of the liver resulting in recurrent mild jaundice, the presence of large amounts of bilirubin in the blood and, frequently, a dark pigment in the liver cells; the exact nature of the pigment is unknown. Also called chronic idiopathic jaundice.

dumping s. Symptoms occurring within 30 minutes after the end of a meal including palpitations, sweating, weakness, nausea, belching, diarrhea, and pain in the upper abdomen; the degree of severity varies widely; usually caused by excessively rapid emptying of the stomach after removal of a part of the stomach that includes the pylorus. Also called postgastrectomy syndrome.

dysplastic nevus s. See familial atypical mole and melanoma syndrome.

Eaton-Lambert s. See Lambert-Eaton syndrome.

S

ectopic ACTH s. Secretion of adrenocorticotropic hormone (ACTH) or, less often, corticotropin-releasing factor (CRF) by nonendocrine malignant tumors, including bronchogenic carcinoma, malignant thymoma, and pancreatic islet cell tumor; associated with bilateral adrenal hyperplasia. Also called ectopic Cushing's syndrome.

ectopic Cushing's s. See ectopic ACTH syndrome.

Edward's s. See trisomy 18 syndrome.

Ehlers-Danlos s. A group of several disorders, occurring as either autosomal dominant or recessive inheritance and resulting from some defect in the quality or quantity of collagen; marked by hyperelasticity of the skin, fragility of cutaneous blood vessels, overmobility of joints (which are also prone to dislocation), formation of pigmented nodules (raisin tumors) at the site of a skin injury; and by internal complications (including rupture of the colon and large arteries, diaphragmatic hernia, and retinal detachment).

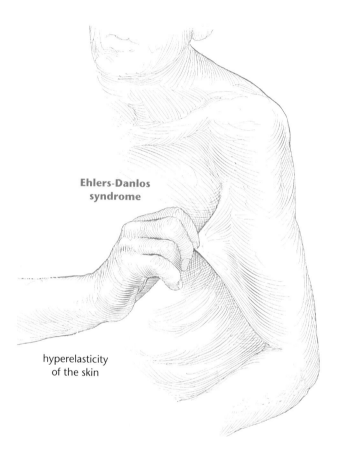

Ehlers-Danlos syndrome

hyperelasticity of the skin

Eisenmenger's s. Strictly defined, the occurrence of a ventricular septal defect, overriding aorta, right ventricular hypertrophy, and a dilated pulmonary artery. Because these terms have been frequently used to describe cases with right and left shunt without all the above components, they are not regarded as useful by cardiologists.

Ellis–van Creveld s. See chondroectodermal dysplasia, under dysplasia.

failure-to-thrive s. A clinical syndrome most often seen in children under one year of age; characterized by deficient height, weight, and motor coordination (significantly below the average rates of normal children). There may be an organic cause (e.g., heart, kidney, or intestinal disease; inborn errors of metabolism; or brain damage); or it may be due to a deficient interaction between primary caretaker and child, resulting in physical and emotional neglect of the child. Sometimes the syndrome has both organic and nonorganic origins.

familial atypical mole and melanoma (DAM-N) s. Inherited condition characterized by occurrence of melanoma in one or more first- or second-degree relatives; presence of numerous (50+) moles, some of which are atypical (tending to occur on both sun-exposed and nonexposed areas) and often variable in size; and moles that demonstrate certain distinct histologic features. Affected persons have an increased risk of developing melanoma. Also called dysplastic nevus syndrome. See also atypical mole, under mole.

Fanconi's s. A functional disturbance of the proximal kidney tubules resulting in glucosuria, generalized aminoaciduria, phosphaturia, and renal tubular acidosis; it may occur as a recessive hereditary disease (e.g., cystinosis), or as a consequence of numerous causes including drugs, heavy metals, or such disease processes as amyloidosis.

Felty's s. Rheumatoid arthritis, deficient number of white blood cells, and enlargement of the spleen.

fetal alcohol s. A syndrome that includes growth retardation, abnormally small head (microcephaly), characteristic facial features, mental retardation, and heart and kidney abnormalities; affects infants born to mothers who ingest excessive quantities of alcohol during early pregnancy.

fetal cocaine s. Characteristic small size for gestational age, hyperirritability, anomalies of the genitourinary tract (e.g., hypospadias, hydronephrosis), prune belly, and abnormally small head, occurring in infants born to cocaine abusers.

fetal hydantoin s. Broad low nasal bridge, epicanthal folds, prominent ears, mental and growth deficiency, with a high incidence of absent fifth finger or toenail resulting from maternal ingestion of hydantoin analogs.

Fitz-Hugh-Curtis s. Inflammation of the peritoneum and tissues surrounding the liver in women with gonorrhea of the pelvic organs, resulting from spread of the infection.

floppy valve s. Prolapse of the mitral (left atrioventricular) valve into the left ventricle during systole; a feature of the Barlow syndrome; associated with enhanced tendency for cardiac arrhythmia, chest wall discomfort, and increased susceptibility to mitral valvular infection. Also called mitral valve prolapse syndrome.

Foix's s. See cavernous sinus syndrome.

Forbes-Albright s. Combination of secretion of milk and absence of menstruation, unassociated with recent pregnancy or acromegaly; caused by a pituitary tumor that stimulates overproduction of the hormone prolactin.

Foster Kennedy's s. The association of unilateral loss of the sense of smell and atrophy of the optic disk of the same side with swelling of the optic disk of the opposite side; caused by a tumor (meningioma) at the base of the frontal lobe. Also called Kennedy's syndrome.

fragile X s. Inherited defect of the chromosome X causing mental retardation, large testicles, and big ears and chin in males, and mild mental retardation in females.

Franceschetti's s. See mandibulofacial dysostosis, under dysostosis.

Friderichsen's s. See Waterhouse-Friderichsen syndrome.

Friderichsen-Waterhouse s. See Waterhouse-Friderichsen syndrome.

Fröhlich's s. See adiposogenital dystrophy, under dystrophy.

Froin's s. The changes in the cerebrospinal fluid caused by obstruction of the fluid's circulation by a tumor or inflammatory condition; namely, a yellow coloration of the normally clear fluid, increased protein content, and rapid coagulation.

Gaisböck's s. High blood pressure and polycythemia but without enlargement of the spleen; the polycythemia is relative, with normal red blood cell mass but decreased plasma volume; cause is unknown.

Ganser s. A factitious disorder consisting of bizarre behaviors and nonsensical inappropriate responses often observed among prisoners who, it is hypothesized, might expect more leniency if they are seen as mentally ill or defective. Also called nonsense syndrome; syndrome of approximate answers; prison psychosis.

Gardner's s. An autosomal dominant inheritance characterized by a combination of numerous polyps (over 500) in the colon, multiple bone tumors (e.g., in the lower jaw), and cutaneous cysts; cancer of the colon usually develops by age 40; prophylactic removal of the colon is usually advised.

Gianotti-Crosti s. Cutaneous manifestation of hepatitis B virus infection occurring in young children; characterized by widespread eruption of papules, especially on the arms and sides of the face, associated with mild fever and malaise; it generally disappears without treatment within 30 to 60 days. Also called papular acrodermatitis of childhood.

Gilbert's s. Disorder transmitted as an autosomal dominant inheritance, which affects the way the liver processes the bile pigment bilirubin; characterized by transient episodes of mild jaundice due to elevated amounts of unprocessed bilirubin in the blood; usually there are no other symptoms; there is no evidence of liver damage, breakdown of red blood cells, or bile flow obstruction. Also called familial nonhemolytic jaundice; Gilbert's disease; benign familial icterus.

Gilles de la Tourette's s. Condition that begins in childhood with repetitive grimaces and tics involving primarily the head and neck, sometimes the arms, legs, and trunk; progresses to the involuntary making of noises (e.g., grunts and barks), and episodes of using foul language (coprolalia). Most commonly seen in males. Also called Tourette's syndrome; Tourette's disease; Gilles de la Tourette's disease.

Gjessing's s. Recurrent episodes of catatonic stupor or excitement associated with nitrogen retention due to impaired protein metabolism.

Goodpasture's s. Glomerulonephritis associated with diffuse pulmonary hemorrhage; caused by an antigen directed against the basement membranes of capillaries in the filtration units of the kidneys and the air sacs in the lungs.

Grönblad-Strandberg s. Degeneration of elastic tissue involving the retina, gastrointestinal tract, and especially the skin.

Guillain-Barré s. (GBS) Disorder of motor nerves occurring after a viral infection, trauma, or surgery; characterized by inflammatory changes of peripheral nerves (near the spinal cord), causing bilateral weakness progressing rapidly to paralysis; patients usually recover completely if respiratory and vasomotor failure do not occur; thought to be an autoimmune reaction. Also called idiopathic polyneuritis.

Gunn's s. See jaw-winking syndrome.

Hamman-Rich s. Progressive fibrosis of lung tissue leading to pulmonary insufficiency, right-sided heart failure, and death; the cause is unknown.

hemolytic-uremic s. (HUS) Hemolytic anemia with abnormally shaped red blood cells and acute renal failure occurring most commonly in young children, usually preceded by a minor respiratory or gastrointestinal infection; also seen in adults, especially in women after childbirth.

hepatorenal s. Kidney failure occurring in severe liver damage or in patients undergoing surgery of the biliary tract; characterized by reduced urine excretion, marked sodium retention, and a rise in blood urea nitrogen usually out of proportion to the increase in serum creatinine.

Horner's s. Drooping of the upper eyelid of one eye, sinking of the eyeball within the orbit, swelling of the lower eyelid, decreased sweating on the opposite side, and warmth of the face; may be caused by lesions involving the sympathetic pathway in the brainstem or by tumors in the neck (parotid gland or carotid body), upper chest, lymph nodes, or cavernous sinus.

Houssay s. Abatement of diabetes mellitus resulting from surgical removal of, or a destructive lesion in, the pituitary (hypophysis).

Hunter's s. Inherited metabolic disorder in which there is a deficiency of the enzyme L-iduronosulfate with excessive excretion of the mucopolysaccharide heparan sulfate in the urine; occurs in a wide range of severity; clinical features include progressive deafness and degeneration of the retina; severe cases include mild retardation, enlargement of the liver and spleen, stiff joints, and heart valve involvement; an X-linked recessive inheritance. Also called type II mucopolysaccharidosis.

Hurler's s. An inherited metabolic disorder in which there is a deficiency of the enzyme alpha-L-iduronidase and excessive excretion of the mucopolysaccharide heparan sulfate; clinical features include severe skeletal deformities, joint stiffness, progressive mental retardation, coronary artery lesions, heart valve lesions, enlargement of liver, and clouding of the cornea. It is an autosomal recessive inheritance with onset at 6 to 8 months of age and a life expectancy of 6 to 10 years. Also called type I mucopolysaccharidosis; lipochondrodystrophy.

hyperabduction s. Pain and numbness of the arm and hand due to prolonged abduction of the arm, which compresses the axillary blood vessels and nerves; may occur during sleep (as a temporary condition) or as an occupational disorder.

hypereosinophilic s. A persistent presence of an abnormally high number of eosinophils in peripheral blood, leading to infiltration of bone marrow, heart, and other organs, associated with a variety of other symptoms, such as night sweats, loss of appetite, weight loss, cough, and skin lesions.

hyperkinetic s. Excessive energy and motility, emotional instability, and short attention span; may be seen in children with attention deficit disorder, brain injury, or certain types of epilepsy.

hyperventilation s. A syndrome that is almost always a manifestation of acute anxiety and is characterized by difficult, deep, and rapid breathing accompanied by weakness and fatigue, pain or tightness of the chest, palpitations, and a feeling of suffocation; lightheadedness is commonly present, and tingling of the hands may occur as a result of marked decrease of carbon dioxide in the blood produced by the excessive breathing; it may last half an hour or longer and may recur a few times a day; the attacks may be partly controlled by breath-holding or by breathing into a paper bag.

hyperviscosity s. Visual impairment, neurologic problems, spontaneous bleeding, sluggish blood flow, and organ congestion consequent to increased blood viscosity; seen in Waldenström's macroglobulinemia.

hypoplastic left heart s. (HLHS) Underdevelopment of the left atrium and ventricle of the heart with closure or stricture of the aortic and/or mitral (left atrioventricular) valve and underdevelopment of the aorta.

immotile-cilia s. Syndrome of autosomal recessive inheritance characterized by chronic sinus and lung infections, reduced fertility in women and sterility in men; due to impairment of the propelling function of ciliated structures.

immune deficiency s., immunologic deficiency s. A group of symptoms indicating impairment of one or more of the major functions of the immune system; may be primary, which is usually hereditary and evident between six months to two years of age, or secondary, which is the result of altered immune function by a variety of factors (e.g., infection, chemotherapy, irradiation, immunosuppression, autoimmunity).

s. of inappropriate secretion of antidiuretic hormone (SIADH) Persistently high levels of antidiuretic hormone (ADH), with expansion of the extracellular fluid compartment, abnormal resorption of water, and low levels of sodium in plasma; causes include pulmonary tuberculosis, pneumonia, lung cancer, meningitis, and cerebral infarcts.

inguinal s. Painful inflammation of the lymph nodes in the groin and around the rectum occurring one to three weeks after exposure to the sexually transmitted disease lymphogranuloma venereum; subsequently nodes become matted and fistulas develop.

irritable bowel s. Disorder characterized by chronic abdominal pain, gas, diarrhea or constipation (sometimes alternating), passage of mucus, and absence of detectable organic disease. Also called mucous colitis; spastic colon; irritable colon.

jaw-winking s. Involuntary unilateral lowering of the upper eyelid, occurring while chewing; the person appears to be winking. Also called Gunn's syndrome.

S

juvenile polyposis s. Inherited condition affecting children and young adults, characterized by the presence of numerous benign tumors composed of cystically enlarged mucous glands (retention polyps) throughout the small and large intestines, especially the colon; causes intestinal bleeding, abdominal pain, and diarrhea. The polyps are not associated with increased risk of cancer. Also called juvenile polyposis.

Kallmann's s. Inherited deficiency of the gonadotropins follicle-stimulating hormone (FSH) and leuteinizing hormone (LH) absent sense of smell (in some individuals), midline skeletal defects, and underdeveloped testes. Also called hypogonadotropic hypogonadism.

Kartagener's s. Displacement of the viscera to the opposite side of the body (situs inversus) associated with dilatation of the bronchi (bronchiectasis) and chronic sinusitis. Also called Kartagener's triad.

Kennedy's s. See Foster Kennedy's syndrome.

Kleine-Levin s. Intermittent episodes of prolonged sleep (up to 18 hours), abnormally large consumption of food, hypersexuality, and disturbed behavior during the attacks; occurs in adolescence, most commonly affecting males; may be precipitated by an acute illness or stress.

Klinefelter's s. Syndrome occurring in males only, characterized by underdeveloped testes containing sclerosed tubules, infertility due to lack of sperm production, enlarged breasts, eunuchoid body, and failure of secondary male characteristics to develop; associated with the presence of one or more extra X chromosomes and at least one Y chromosome. Also called XXY syndrome; seminiferous tubule dysgenesis.

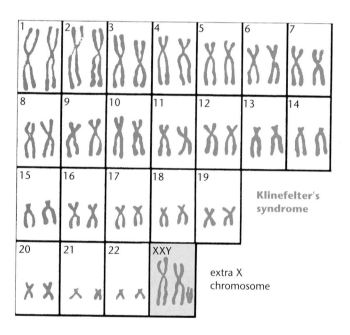

Klinefelter's syndrome

extra X chromosome

Klippel-Feil s. A developmental defect marked chiefly by fusion of two or more vertebrae of the neck (cervical vertebrae), which results in a short, thick neck with limited movements. Also called cervical fusion syndrome.

Klippel-Trenaunay s. See angio-osteohypertrophy syndrome.

Korsakoff's s. Severe impairment of memory, especially of recent events, with confabulation, associated with chronic alcoholism. Also called Korsakoff's psychosis.

Lambert-Eaton s. Syndrome almost always associated with cancer, particularly small cell carcinoma of the lung; characterized by progressive muscle weakness (similar to that of myasthenia gravis) with early involvement of ocular muscles; results from abnormality in the release of the neurotransmitter acetylcholine by nerve endings;

diagnosed by electromyography. Also called Eaton-Lambert syndrome.

lateral medullary s. See posterior inferior cerebellar artery syndrome.

Laurence-Biedl s. See Laurence-Moon-Biedl syndrome.

Laurence-Moon-Bardet-Biedl s. See Laurence-Moon-Biedl syndrome.

Laurence-Moon-Biedl s. A recessive hereditary syndrome characterized by some or all of the following: mental retardation, obesity, more than 10 fingers or toes, underdeveloped gonads, and visual disturbance. Also called Laurence-Biedl syndrome; Laurence-Moon-Bardet-Biedl syndrome.

Leriche's s. See aortoiliac occlusive disease, under disease.

Lesch-Nyhan s. Disorder of purine metabolism and excess uric acid; clinical features include severe mental retardation and compulsive, self-mutilating behavior; death usually occurs during childhood due to kidney failure; an X-linked recessive inheritance.

locked-in s. Syndrome characterized by a reduced motor response to stimuli while receptivity of stimuli remains intact; the patient is fully conscious, can breathe, and can open the eyes and look upward or downward but cannot speak, swallow, move his limbs, or look sideways; caused most often by a blood clot in the basilar artery (between the cerebral hemispheres) with resulting infarct damaging part of the brainstem (at the base of the pons) and interrupting the descending motor pathways; the cortex remains intact, thus ascending pathways are spared; distinguished from persistent vegetative state (PVS); PET scan shows cortical glucose metabolism to be only slightly less than normal in locked-in syndrome but very low in PVS. Commonly called de-efferented state; pseudocoma. See also persistent vegetative state, under state.

Löffler's s. See simple pulmonary eosinophilia, under eosinophilia.

Lowe's s. See oculocerebrorenal syndrome.

lupus anticoagulant s. See antiphospholipid antibody syndrome.

Lutembacher's s. Congenital heart abnormality consisting of atrial septal defect (ASD), constriction of the mitral (left atrioventricular) valve, and enlargement of the right atrium.

mad hatter s. Personality changes occurring as part of the symptom complex of mercury poisoning, an occupational condition that may develop after many years of inhalation of inorganic mercury vapors (especially in low levels); symptoms include anxiety, emotional instability, irritability, eccentricity, and reclusiveness; has occurred among workers in the felt hat industry (from which the expression "mad as a hatter" originated).

Maffucci's s. The combined presence of multiple benign cartilage tumors within bones and extensive birthmarks (hemangiomas) in subcutaneous tissues and the oral cavity; deformities of the hands and feet are usually evident.

malabsorption s. A condition marked by weakness, weight loss, pallor, protuberant abdomen, bleeding tendency, and other signs and symptoms caused by any disease that impairs absorption of nutrients; commonly involves inability to absorb fats associated with bulky, foul-smelling stools.

Mallory-Weiss s. Irregular linear tears at the junction of the esophagus and stomach associated with vomiting of blood, usually following severe retching and vomiting, or bouts of coughing; bleeding may be profuse; frequently seen in alcoholics.

Marchiafava-Micheli s. See paroxysmal nocturnal hemoglobinuria.

Marfan's s. Genetic disorder of connective tissue affecting primarily the skeletal, ocular, and cardiovascular systems; characterized by any number of the following features: tall stature with disproportionately long extremities, laxity of joint ligaments, long slender fingers and toes, dislocation of the lenses of the eyes, mitral valve prolapse, and dissecting aneurysm of the aorta; caused by a defective gene, located on chromosome 15, which is responsible for the production of the protein fibrillin; transmitted as an autosomal dominant inheritance. See illustration on following page.

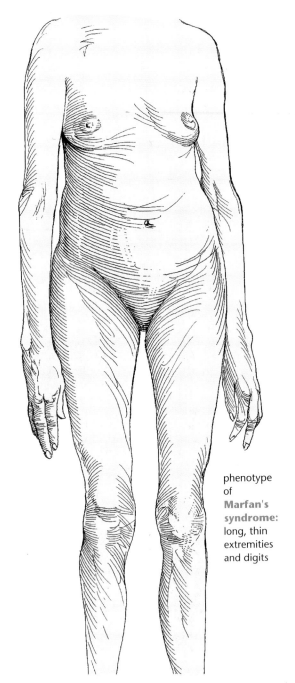

phenotype
of
**Marfan's
syndrome:**
long, thin
extremities
and digits

Ménière's s. See Ménière's disease, under disease.

middle lobe s. A form of chronic atelectasis marked by collapse of the middle lobe in the right lung resulting from compression of the right middle airway (bronchus); caused by tumor, inflamed lymph nodes, or other conditions; symptoms include chronic cough, wheezing, recurrent respiratory infections, and chest pains. Also called Brock's syndrome.

Mikulicz's s. Painless enlargement of the lacrimal and salivary glands of one or both sides associated with dryness of the mouth and reduced secretion of tears; may be caused by immune-mediated destruction of the glands or by complications of sarcoidosis, leukemia, or lymphoma.

milk-alkali s. Abnormally high level of calcium in the blood (hypercalcemia) accompanied by reduced blood acidity (alkalosis); symptoms include weakness, muscle pains, irritability, and apathy; it is reversible in its early stages but, if undetected, may lead to kidney failure; caused by prolonged intake of absorbable calcium-containing antacid drugs and milk as treatment for peptic ulcer. The chronic form is called Burnett's syndrome.

Milkman's s. Osteoporosis causing multiple fractures, usually in postmenopausal women.

Millard-Gubler s. Paralysis of facial muscles on one side and paralysis of the opposite arm and leg caused by a unilateral lesion of the pons (in the brainstem).

mitral valve prolapse s. See floppy valve syndrome.

Möbius s. Congenital bilateral paralysis of facial muscles sometimes associated with musculoskeletal anomalies and neurologic disorders. Also called congenital facial diplegia.

Morgagni-Adams-Stokes s. See Stokes-Adams syndrome.

Morquio's s. A variant of mucopolysaccharidosis, with autosomal recessive inheritance, characterized by severe skeletal defects (dwarfism, deformed hands and chest, flat vertebrae, osteoporosis), and cloudiness of the cornea, with excretion of keratan sulfate in the urine. Also called type IV mucopolysaccharidosis.

mucocutaneous lymph node s. Acute illness affecting mostly infants and young children, characterized by prolonged fever that is unresponsive to antibiotics, conjunctivitis, redness of the oral cavity and lips, inflammation of lymph nodes of the neck, rash on the trunk and extremities, and redness of the hands and feet with peeling of the toes and fingers. Cause is unknown. Also called Kawasaki's disease.

multiple organ dysfunction s. (MODS) The presence of altered organ dysfunction in an acutely ill patient, such that homeostasis cannot be maintained without intervention. It may be primary, characterized by organ dysfunction occurring early and as a direct result of a well-defined insult; or secondary, occurring as a consequence of a response to a variety of severe clinical conditions.

Munchausen s. A factitious disorder characterized by a continual fabrication of a wide variety of physical symptoms, self-defined or self-induced in order to be admitted into a hospital or gain medical attention.

Munchausen-by-proxy s. Condition of a parent or caretaker of a child (usually the mother) who frequently and persistently reports illnesses in the child that are factitious, or even induced by the adult, to obtain medical attention.

myeloproliferative s.'s See myeloproliferative diseases, under disease.

myofascial s. A painful condition of muscle that can be elicited by pressure on one or more discrete hypersensitive areas termed trigger points; these trigger points produce pain in the area of the patient's symptoms, which may occur anywhere in the body; a typical example is the temporomandibular joint (TMJ).

nail-patella s. Hereditary underdevelopment of both kneecaps (patellae), deformity and dislocation of the head of the radius (at the elbow), and dystrophy of fingernails; transmitted as an autosomal dominant inheritance.

Nelson's s. Increased skin pigmentation, and aggressive growth of an ACTH-secreting pituitary adenoma, occurring after surgical removal of the adrenal (suprarenal) glands.

S

Maroteaux-Lamy s. An error in metabolism of mucopolysaccharide resulting in dwarfism, chest deformities, stiff joints, corneal clouding, short hands and fingers, and excessive excretion of a mucopolysaccharide (dermatan sulfate) in the urine. Also called type VI mucopolysaccharoidosis.

Martorell's s. See aortic arch syndrome.

meconium aspiration s. In neonatology, air obstruction and an intense inflammatory reaction resulting in severe respiratory distress of the newborn; caused by fetal aspiration of meconium-stained amniotic fluid during intrauterine life or during the birth process.

meconium plug s. Total obstruction of the lower intestinal tract (rectosigmoid) with meconium in a newborn infant, associated with abdominal distention.

Meigs' s. The presence of a benign ovarian tumor (fibroma) associated with accumulation of fluid in the abdominal cavity (ascites) and around a lung (pleural effusion).

melanoma s. See atypical mole, under mole.

Ménétrièr's s. See Ménétrièr's disease, under disease.

nephrotic s. (NS) A clinical symptom complex caused by a variety of kidney diseases in adults and children; characterized by generalized swelling with sodium and water retention, low plasma albumin concentration, and severe proteinuria; it occurs in minimal change disease, membranous glomerulonephritis, and varieties of chronic proliferative glomerulonephritis. It also may be secondary to lupus erythematosus, diabetes mellitus, or amyloid; or to infections or allergies (e.g., to drugs or insect bites). Also called nephrosis.

neuroleptic malignant s. High fever, muscle rigidity, and coma; a rare, life-threatening reaction to neuroleptic drugs.

nonsense s. See Ganser syndrome.

Noonan's s. Low-set ears and a downward slant of the eyes at the outer (temporal) angles associated with valvular pulmonic stenosis.

oculocerebrorenal s. An X-linked recessive inheritance characterized by congenital cataracts and glaucoma, mental retardation, and dysfunction of the kidney tubules leading to proteinuria, glycosuria, aminoaciduria, and inability to concentrate and acidify the urine. Also called Lowe's syndrome.

organic brain s. (OBS), **organic mental s.** (OMS) A syndrome whose essential feature is psychologic or behavioral abnormality associated with transient or permanent dysfunction of the brain; if the specific organic etiology is known, then the diagnosis would be a specific organic mental disorder. See also organic mental disorder, under disorder.

Osgood-Schlatter s. See traumatic tibial epiphysitis, under epiphysitis.

osteomyelofibrotic s. See myelofibrosis.

Pancoast's s. A symptom complex consisting of unilateral weakness and wasting of small muscles of the hand, numbness of the medial side of the arm (brachial plexus involvement), constriction of the pupil, and paralysis of the eyelid (Horner's syndrome due to sympathetic nerve involvement); caused by a cancerous tumor at the apex of the lung.

paraneoplastic s. Any group of symptoms in a cancer patient directly attributed to the physical presence of the cancerous tumor or its spread to other areas of the body.

Patau's s. See trisomy 13 syndrome.

Pendred's s. Inherited condition characterized by congenital nerve deafness and goiter, with or without hypothyroidism. Also called familial goiter with deaf-mutism.

Peutz-Jeghers s. A familial condition characterized by the presence of numerous polyps throughout the gastrointestinal tract, with greater concentration in the jejunum, and dark spots on the lips, oral mucosa, and fingers. There is a slightly increased risk of developing cancer of the colon.

pickwickian s. Extreme (morbid) obesity associated with res-

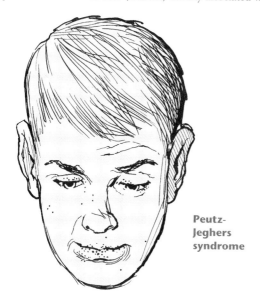

Peutz-Jeghers syndrome

piratory insufficiency and breathlessness, carbon dioxide retention, and daytime sleepiness.

Pierre Robin s. A developmental anomaly characterized by an abnormally small lower jaw (mandible), cleft palate, and a backward displacement of the tongue, which may produce airway obstruction in the newborn. Also called Robin's syndrome.

Plummer-Vinson s. Syndrome usually seen in middle-aged women with iron deficiency anemia, characterized by difficult swallowing (dysphagia), dry mouth, and lesions in the mucous membranes of the mouth, pharynx, and esophagus. Also called sideropenic dysphagia.

POEMS s. A chronic, progressive multisystem condition of obscure origin, characterized by polyneuropathy, organomegaly, endocrinopathy, monoclonal gammopathy, and skin changes.

polycystic ovary s. Disorder affecting young women characterized by bilaterally enlarged ovaries that are studded with multiple cysts in the outer region and covered by a thickened membrane (capsule); associated with scanty or absent menstruation, infertility due to failure to produce ova, and virilism. Also called Stein-Leventhal syndrome.

polyposis s. Any of a variety of syndromes, often hereditary,

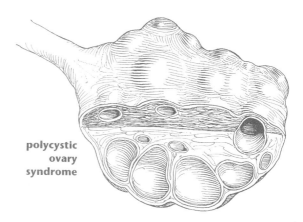

polycystic ovary syndrome

marked by the presence of several tumors (pedunculated or sessile) arising from the mucous membrane of the digestive tract, either in one segment (especially the colon) or in several segments.

polysplenia s. Developmental defect in which the infant is born with multiple right-sided spleens, a midline liver, absent inferior vena cava, and heart malformations.

postcardiotomy s. See postpericardiotomy syndrome.

postcholecystectomy s. A group of symptoms suggestive of biliary disease (e.g., pain in the upper right abdomen, indigestion, food intolerance) that persist after removal of the gallbladder (cholecystectomy).

postcommissurotomy s. A sudden onset of fever, chest pain, and inflammation of the membranes covering the heart and lungs (pericardium and pleura), occurring within a few weeks after an operation on the heart valves, especially for the correction of mitral stenosis.

postconcussion s. See posttraumatic syndrome.

posterior inferior cerebellar artery s. A group of symptoms occurring when the posterior inferior cerebellar artery is occluded; they include muscular weakness and insensitivity to pain and temperature of the face, soft palate, pharynx, and larynx on the same side of the occlusion, associated with insensitivity to pain and temperature on the trunk and extremities on the side opposite the occlusion. Also called lateral medullary syndrome; Wallenberg's syndrome.

postgastrectomy s. See dumping syndrome.

postmyocardial infarction s. Symptom complex occurring a week or more after a myocardial infarction; consists of fever and inflammation of the pericardial membrane (enveloping the heart), often accompanied by inflammation of the pleural membrane (enveloping the lungs). Also called Dressler's syndrome.

S

postpericardiotomy s. A complication of open-heart surgery that occurs one to two or more weeks after the operation; it appears to be a delayed autoimmune reaction; characterized by fever, chest pain, inflammation of the membranes enveloping the heart and lungs (pericardium and pleura), and a raised erythrocyte sedimentation rate. Also called postcardiotomy syndrome.

postphlebitis s. Syndrome developed as a complication of deep venous thrombosis of the legs; characterized by subcutaneous swelling of the lower leg and ankle, brownish pigmentation of the ankle, and pain; it progresses to fibrosis of subcutaneous tissues due to long-standing edema and ulceration.

postpolio s. See postpoliomyelitis syndrome.

postpoliomyelitis s. Neuromuscular symptoms developing years after recovery from poliomyelitis; primarily characterized by slowly progressive muscle weakness usually involving muscles that previously were clinically unaffected by the acute disease; may also involve previously affected muscles. Symptoms may vary from simple deterioration of function with joint pains, fatigue, and subsequent recovery, to atypical forms of spinal muscular dystrophy. Popularly called postpolio syndrome.

posttraumatic s. A group of symptoms following head injury (with or without concussion) and persisting from weeks to a year or longer; they include: persistent headache, irritability, giddiness, fatigue, difficulty in concentration, disturbance of sleep, anxiety, and depression. Also called postconcussion syndrome; traumatic neurasthenia; posttraumatic nervous instability.

posttraumatic stress s. See posttraumatic stress disorder (PTSD), under disorder.

Prader-Willi s. Congenital muscular laxity, underactivity of testes or ovaries (hypogonadism), obesity, and mild mental retardation. Cause is unknown.

preexcitation s. See Wolff-Parkinson-White syndrome.

preinfarction s. The sudden onset or worsening of angina pectoris which may herald impending myocardial infarction.

premenstrual s. (PMS) The occurrence of all or some of the following symptoms during the week preceding onset of the menstrual flow: lumbar and low abdominal pain, irritability, headache, tenderness of breasts, pelvic congestion, fluid retention, and weight gain. Also called premenstrual tension.

prisoner of war s., POW s. Apathy, withdrawal, and even death occurring as a reaction to capture and imprisonment.

prune-belly s. Congenital abnormality affecting males almost exclusively; marked by absence of the abdominal wall musculature associated with urinary tract abnormalities and undescended testicles (cryptorchidism). Also called abdominal muscle deficiency syndrome.

pseudothrombophlebitis s. Condition resembling venous thrombosis of the leg; caused by rupture of a synovial (Baker's) cyst at the knee, with escape of synovial fluid and accumulation in the calf.

punchdrunk s. Condition seen in boxers and alcoholics supposedly caused by repeated brain concussions or brief loss of consciousness; characterized by slurred speech, hand tremors, impaired concentration, and slowed thought processes.

reflex sympathetic dystrophy s. Pain and tenderness associated with skin atrophy, blood vessel disturbance, and demineralization of bones, usually occurring in a hand or foot following local trauma (e.g., sprain or fracture), stroke, or peripheral nerve injury.

Refsum's s. A rare recessive hereditary condition marked by cerebellar ataxia, chronic polyneuritis, pigmentary degeneration of the retina, and night blindness; death is commonly due to degenerative heart disease at an early age.

Reifenstein's s. A familial form of male pseudohermaphrodism associated with hypospadias, small testes and sterility, absence of beard, short stature, and often enlarged breasts.

Reiter's s. (RS) Urethritis, conjunctivitis, arthritis, and sometimes mucocutaneous lesions; recurrences or chronicity occurs in more than one-half of patients. Cause is unknown; usually develops after nonspecific urethritis or bacillary dysentery.

Rendu-Osler-Weber s. See hereditary hemorrhagic telangiectasia, under telangiectasia.

respiratory distress s. (RDS) of the newborn Acute difficult breathing and bluish coloration of the skin most commonly occurring as a complication of premature birth; also seen in infants born to diabetic mothers and in those delivered by cesarean section; caused by deficient fetal production of surfactant, a substance that prevents the air sacs (alveoli) in the infant's lungs from collapsing and sticking together. An adequate level of surfactant is normally reached after the 35th week of gestation. Also called hyaline membrane disease of newborn.

restless legs s. Abnormal sensations of creepiness and twitchiness deep in the legs, which provoke continuous leg movements; they usually occur in the elderly upon lying down. Cause is unknown.

retained dead fetus s. Symptom complex occurring when a dead fetus remains in the uterus; may include disseminated intravascular coagulation (DIC) and, after five weeks, abnormally low level of fibrinogen in the circulating blood; may cause excessive bleeding during delivery. Also called dead fetus syndrome.

Rett's s. Progressive hereditary syndrome affecting girls and becoming obvious by 12 to 18 months of age; characterized by regression of learned skills (e.g., walking, talking), repetitive writhing of the hands and limbs, autism, and, often, inappropriate outbursts of laughter or crying.

Reye's s. An acute, frequently fatal, postviral illness mainly affecting children, often associated with aspirin intake; characterized by edema of the brain, hepatitis, and fatty accumulation in several organs; usually starts as a mild illness with respiratory and gastrointestinal symptoms of a few days' duration; complete recovery may occur then, or there may be progression to rapid brain swelling and liver enlargement, convulsions, coma, and death.

Riley-Day s. See familial dysautonomia, under dysautonomia.

Robin's s. See Pierre Robin syndrome.

Rothmund's s., Rothmund-Thomson s. A syndrome transmitted as an autosomal recessive inheritance; characterized by juvenile cataracts, saddle nose, premature graying and loss of hair, and wasting of muscles.

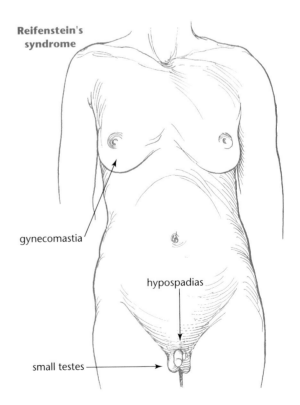

Reifenstein's syndrome

gynecomastia

hypospadias

small testes

Rotor's s. Inherited syndrome occurring in children, characterized by conjugated hyperbilirubinemia and jaundice, without pigmentation of the liver; transmitted as an autosomal recessive inheritance.

Sanfilippo's s. A form of mucopolysaccharidosis characterized by severe mental retardation and excretion of heparan sulfate in the urine; skeleton is usually normal but may exhibit slight dwarfism; an autosomal recessive inheritance. Also called type III mucopolysaccharidosis.

scalded skin s. (SSS) See staphylococcal scalded skin syndrome.

scalenus anterior s. Pain in the shoulder, often radiating along the arm and back of the neck, due to compression of nerves and the subclavian artery against the first thoracic rib and a hypertonic anterior scalene muscle. Also called anterior scalene syndrome.

Scheie' s. Inherited metabolic disorder in which there is a deficiency of the enzyme alpha-L-iduronidase and excessive excretion of the mucopolysaccharide heparan sulfate; clinical features include aortic valve lesions, clouding of the cornea, finger stiffness, and short stature. It is a variant of Hurler's syndrome with onset after five years of age; an autosomal recessive inheritance. Also called type IS mucopolysaccharidosis.

Schmidt's s. (a) The association of primary hypothyroidism and adrenocortical insufficiency; organ-specific antibodies against the adrenal and thyroid glands may be present; diabetes mellitus may also be present. (b) Unilateral paralysis of vocal folds, palate, and the trapezius and sternocleidomastoid muscles.

Senear-Usher s. See pemphigus erythematosus, under pemphigus.

Sézary s. A form of cutaneous T cell lymphoma characterized by a generalized redness and scaliness of the skin and the presence of atypical T lymphocytes ("Sézary" cells) in the blood circulation.

shaken baby s. (SBS) Syndrome observed in infants usually under one year of age, most commonly under six months, who have been victims of a severe, forceful shaking; characterized by retinal hemorrhage and hemorrhage within the skull (subdural and/or subarachnoid hemorrhages); may cause brain injury, sometimes with a fatal outcome; symptoms may include drowsiness, lethargy, and seizures or unexplained vomiting.

Sheehan's s. Syndrome usually caused by lack of blood supply to the anterior lobe of the pituitary (adenohypophysis); it is typically associated with hemorrhage and shock during childbirth (postpartum necrosis of the pituitary); common symptoms include atrophy of sex organs, inability to lactate, hair loss, cold intolerance, and wrinkling of skin. The syndrome may also occur in males and nonpregnant females in association with sickle-cell anemia, trauma, and disseminated intravascular coagulation (DIC).

short-bowel s. Condition developed after surgical removal of an extensive portion of the small intestine; characterized by difficult to treat (intractable) diarrhea with impaired absorption of fats and other nutrients. Also called short-bowel disease.

shoulder-hand s. See brachial plexus neuropathy, under neuropathy.

Shy-Drager s. Condition charaterized by dizziness and fainting when arising (postural hypotension), tremors, muscular wasting, atrophy of the iris, ocular palsies and, in the later stages, incontinence; caused by degeneration of the central nervous system.

sicca s. See Sjögren's syndrome.

sick building s. See closed building syndrome.

sick sinus s. (SSS) Syndrome caused by failure of the sinus node in the heart to maintain normal rhythm of the heart's activity, characterized by bradycardia interspersed with multiple and recurrent ectopic beats and atrial or nodal tachycardia.

Sipple's s. See familial endocrine adenomatosis, type II.

Sjögren's s. Immunologic disorder marked by progressive destruction of lacrimal and salivary glands; characterized by dry eyes (keratoconjunctivitis sicca) and dry mouth (xerostomia); may occur in association with other diseases, such as rheumatoid arthritis, systemic lupus erythematosus (SLE), or scleroderma; usually seen in women 40 to 60 years of age. Also called sicca syndrome.

splenic flexure s. Painful discomfort in the upper left area of the abdomen; may radiate to the area over the heart and to the left shoulder; believed to be caused by distention or spasmodic contraction of the colon.

staphylococcal scalded skin s. (SSSS) Skin condition affecting infants characterized by rapid blistering and peeling of large areas of the skin (resembling a second-degree burn) with little or no inflammation; the denuded areas are bright red; caused by an exotoxin elaborated by *Staphylococcus aureus* resulting from an upper respiratory infection. Also called Ritter's disease; Lyell's disease; scalded skin syndrome.

Stein-Leventhal s. See polycystic ovary syndrome.

steroid withdrawal s. A symptom complex occurring when a long-term course of steroid therapy is stopped or markedly reduced; includes weakness, nausea, fever, malaise, and low blood pressure (hypotension).

Stevens-Johnson s. A severe form of erythema multiforme typically occurring in children; characterized by erosion, crusting, and bleeding of lips, oral mucous membrane, anal and genital areas, and the transparent covering of the eye (conjunctiva). Also called erythema multiforme bullosum.

stiff-man s. Disorder of unknown cause characterized by muscular rigidity and spasm, initially, progressing to ultimate generalized rigidity of the extremities, trunk, and neck; associated with severe muscle pain, difficult swallowing, and weight loss.

Stokes-Adams s. Condition marked by recurrent, brief loss of consciousness, with or without convulsions, caused by heart block (i.e., interruption of the impulse's passage through the specialized conducting system of the heart). Also called Adams-Stokes disease; Adams-Stokes syndrome; Morgagni-Adams-Stokes syndrome.

Sturge-Weber s. Syndrome consisting of a large, unilateral, purple birthmark (nevus flammeus) on the face; venous malformations in the cerebral membranes; and glaucoma in late childhood; often associated with intracranial calcifications, neurologic deficits on the opposite side of the lesion, mental retardation, and seizures. Also called Sturge-Weber disease.

subclavian steal s. Reduced blood supply of the brain stem caused by obstruction of the subclavian artery close to the origin of the vertebral artery (at the base of the neck); blood flow through the vertebral artery is consequently reversed and diverted downward from the brainstem to the arm; thus the subclavian artery "steals" blood from the brain.

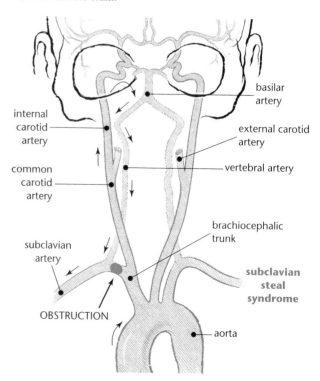

internal carotid artery

common carotid artery

subclavian artery

OBSTRUCTION

basilar artery

external carotid artery

vertebral artery

brachiocephalic trunk

subclavian steal syndrome

aorta

S

sudden infant death s. (SIDS) A poorly understood disorder characterized by sudden and unexpected death of an apparently well infant that remains unexplained even after an adequate postmortem examination. Most deaths occur in infants ranging in age from a few weeks to six months, with a peak incidence at two months of age. Also called crib death.

superior cerebellar artery s. Symptom complex occurring in occlusion of a superior cerebellar artery; consists of loss of pain and temperature sensations on the side of the face and body opposite to that of the occlusion, with incoordination while trying to execute skilled movements.

superior vena cava s. Swelling of the face, neck, and/or upper arms; engorgement of veins in the neck and upper thorax; headache; and visual disturbances; most commonly caused by lung cancer or a lymphoma invading the middle compartment (mediastinum) of the chest cavity.

supraspinatus s. Severe pain in the shoulder experienced upon abduction of the arm; caused by compression of an injured tendon of the supraspinatus muscle against the large process (acromion) of the shoulder blade.

systemic inflammatory response s. (SIRS) Condition characterized by two or more clinical signs of systemic inflammation, the presence of a disorder known to cause endothelial inflammation, and absence of any other known cause for such abnormalities; the clinical signs also constitute evidence of sepsis in patients with a known infection.

Takayasu's s. See Takayasu's disease, under disease.

Taussig-Bing s. Developmental malformation of the heart in which the aorta arises from the right ventricle instead of the left and the pulmonary artery arises from both ventricles, in front of the aorta; a hole in the muscular wall dividing the two ventricles (ventricular septal defect) is also present.

testicular feminization s. Male pseudohermaphroditism due to decreased end-organ response to androgen; characterized by a female external appearance with female external genitalia but with a short vaginal pouch and no uterus; in spite of the female appearance, the individual is genetically a male, with testes either in the abdomen or the inguinal canals, or within the major lips of the vulva; transmitted as an X-linked recessive inheritance.

thalamic s. Syndrome usually occurring during recovery from a lesion in the thalamus (lateral to the third ventricle of the brain), resulting from an arterial occlusion; characterized by loss of sensation in parts of the body on the opposite side of the lesion, followed by a severe burning pain.

thoracic outlet s. Abnormal sensations of fingers (e.g., numbness, burning, pins and needles) attributed to compression of one or more nerve trunks of the brachial plexus, at the base of the neck. Similar symptoms also may be caused by cervical disk or carpal tunnel syndromes.

thrombocytopenia–absent radius (TAR) s. Developmental bone defect of the arm in which the radius is absent, associated with deficiency of platelets in the blood (thrombocytopenia); frequently associated with heart defects, such as the presence of a hole in the wall dividing the atria (atrial defect) and/or tetralogy of Fallot.

thymic hypoplasia s. See DiGeorge's syndrome.

Tietze's s. Pain and tenderness near the breastbone (sternum), at the junction of ribs and their cartilages. The pain may be mistaken for coronary artery disease. Also called peristernal perichondritis.

tight building s. See closed building syndrome.

TORCH s. Chronic nonbacterial infections occurring in the perinatal period (i.e., shortly before, during, or shortly after birth) and causing similar clinical and laboratory findings. The term is an acronym for Toxoplasma, Other infections (e.g., syphilis, hepatitis B, coxsackievirus, Epstein-Barr virus, varicella-zoster, and human parvovirus), Rubella, Cytomegalovirus infection, and herpes simplex.

Tourette's s. See Gilles de la Tourette's syndrome.

toxic shock s. (TSS) Sudden onset of high fever, muscle ache, vomiting, diarrhea, and a rash on the palms and soles, followed by low body temperature, low blood pressure, and shock; multiple organ dysfunction is common and may include kidneys, liver, mucous membranes, and central nervous system; caused by infection with toxin-producing strains of *Staphylococcus aureus* or *Streptococcus pyogenes* (e.g., in the vagina in association with prolonged tampon use, contraceptive cap, diaphragm, or sponge; in surgical wounds, typically after second day of surgery; and in focal tissue infections).

Treacher Collins s. See mandibulofacial dysostosis, under dysostosis.

triple-X s. See triple-X chromosomal aberration, under aberration.

trisomy 8 s. Mental retardation, short stature, congenital heart disease, and urinary tract anomalies; caused by the presence of an extra chromosome in the number 8 pair.

trisomy 9 s. Mental retardation, congenital heart disease, and urinary tract anomalies; caused by the presence of an extra chromosome in the number 9 pair.

trisomy 13 s. Uncommon syndrome characterized by cleft lip and palate; extra fingers or toes; abnormalities of the heart, abdominal organs, and genitalia, and defects of the central nervous system associated with mental retardation; caused by the presence of chromosome 13 in triplicate rather than the normal duplicate. Most affected infants die soon after birth. Also called Patau's syndrome.

trisomy 18 s. Uncommon syndrome marked by mental retardation, skull deformities, abnormally small chin, low-set ears, webbed neck, deafness, heart defects, and Meckel's diverticulum; caused by the presence of chromosome 18 in triplicate rather than the normal duplicate. Few children survive beyond the first year. Also called Edward's syndrome.

trisomy 21 s. See Down's syndrome.

trisomy 22 s. Mental and growth retardation; abnormally small head (microcephaly) and jaws (micrognathia), congenital heart disease, cleft palate, and deformed thumbs and lower extremities; caused by the presence of an extra chromosome in the number 22 pair.

Trousseau's s. See migratory thrombophlebitis, under thrombophlebitis.

Turcot s. The combined occurrence of polyps in the colon and malignant tumors in the brain.

Turner's s. Anomaly affecting females in which there are only 45 chromosomes instead of the normal 46, the missing chromosome being one of the X chromosomes; main features include rudimentary or absent ovaries, infantile genitalia, webbed neck, and short stature.

twin-twin transfusion s. Syndrome diagnosed in identical (monozygotic) twins when there is a hemoglobin difference greater than 5 g/dL between the twins; it occurs when the fetuses share a single (monochorionic) placenta and there is a blood vessel communication between the two umbilical circulations, with a deep artery-to-vein flow from one twin to the other without a compensatory return flow. The donor twin tends to be pale, anemic, dehydrated, of low birth weight and decreased blood volume; it may die of heart failure. The recipient twin frequently has an abnormally large number of red blood cells, a high birth weight, increased organ mass, and an enlarged heart; although ruddy and apparently healthy, it may die of heart failure within 24 hours. Also called third circulation.

Usher's s. Nerve deafness and retinitis pigmentosa occurring as an autosomal recessive inheritance.

von Hippel–Lindau s. See von Hippel–Lindau disease, under disease.

Waardenburg's s. Syndrome of autosomal dominant inheritance, characterized by anomalies of certain skeletal structures of the face, congenital deafness, and disorders of pigmentation (of hair, skin, and eyes). The cause may be defective development of the neural crest. Several clinical types are known.

Waldenström's s. See Waldenström's macroglobulinemia, under macroglobulinemia.

Wallenberg's s. See posterior inferior cerebellar artery syndrome.

Waterhouse-Friderichsen s. Acute hemorrhagic necrosis of

S

syndrome ■ syndrome   S102 the adrenal (suprarenal) glands, occurring secondary to bacteremia, especially meningococcemia; characterized by hemorrhage of both adrenal glands, extensive purpuric rash, shock, and circulatory collapse; may have a fatal outcome. Also called Friderichsen-Waterhouse syndrome; Friderichsen's syndrome.

Wermer's s. See familial endocrine adenomatosis, type I, under adenomatosis.

Wernicke-Korsakoff s. Disorder of the central nervous system caused by abusive intake of alcohol and nutritional depletion, especially of thiamin; primary features include sudden weakness and paralysis of eye muscles, double vision, and inability to stand or walk unaided, followed by derangement of mental functions (e.g., confusion, apathy, loss of retentive memory, and confabulation); it may terminate in death.

Wiskott-Aldrich s. (WAS) A syndrome consisting of eczema, low platelet count (thrombocytopenia), and increased susceptibility to infections due to a defect in cellular immunity; bloody diarrhea is a common feature; an X-linked recessive inheritance of males affecting primarily infants and young children. Also called Aldrich syndrome.

withdrawal s. See withdrawal symptom, under symptom.

Wolff-Parkinson-White (WPW) s. Congenital heart condition that has as its main feature an abnormal conduction of the nerve impulse in the heart; conduction occurs through an accessory pathway between atria and ventricles, bypassing the normal atrioventricular (A-V) path; manifested by irregular heartbeats and distorted patterns of the electrocardiogram (i.e., a shortened P-R interval and a prolonged QRS complex).

Wolff-Parkinson-White syndrome

XXY s. See Klinefelter's syndrome.

XYY s. The presence of an extra Y chromosome in males. Controversial evidence has associated the chromosomal anomaly with aggressiveness and antisocial behavior. Initial studies suggested that the proportion of men with the XYY anomaly was higher in the population of maximum-security prisons than in the general population, leading to the conclusion that the chromosomal abnormality produced antisocial behavior. These findings have not been confirmed.

Zellweger's s. Autosomal recessive inheritance affecting newborn infants, causing death within the first few months; characterized by craniofacial malformations, profound neurologic dysfunction, hearing impairment, and abnormality of liver and kidney; caused by absence of peroxisomes, the cellular organelles important in peroxide metabolism. Also called cerebrohepatorenal syndrome.

Zieve's s. Jaundice, hyperlipemia, and hemolytic anemia, associated with cirrhosis and fatty liver.

Zollinger-Ellison s., Z-E s. The presence of gastrin-producing tumor in the pancreas, a high concentration of hydrochloric acid in the stomach, and refractory ulcers in the esophagus and upper intestinal tract; symptoms include malabsorption, diarrhea, pain, and nausea. The syndrome is often associated with other endocrine abnormalities, especially hyperparathyroidism.

syndromic (sin-drom'ik) Relating to a syndrome.

synechia (sĭ-nek'e-ah), pl. synech'iae An adhesion, especially of the iris to the cornea (anterior synechiae) or to the lens of the eye (posterior synechiae).

synechotomy (sin-ĕ-kot'o-me) Surgical division of the adhesions in synechia.

synechtenterotomy (sin-ek-ten-ter-ot'o-me) Surgical division of intestinal adhesions.

syneresis (sĭ-ner'ĕ-sis) 1. The contraction of gels occurring on prolonged standing, causing the solid components to become more concentrated and the fluid component to be squeezed out and to form droplets on the surface (e.g., the shrinkage of blood clots). 2. A degenerative eye condition most commonly seen in people over 60 years of age; characterized by the formation of fluid-filled cavities in the vitreous body (within the eyeball); young people afflicted with myopia may also be affected.

synergism, synergy (sin'er-jizm, sin'er-je) 1. Cooperation in action (e.g., that of two muscles) so that the combined effect of participating elements is greater than that of each element acting alone. 2. In pharmacology, a term usually reserved for the effect produced by two drugs acting at different sites, with one drug (the synergist) increasing the effect of the second drug either by changing its biotransformation, distribution, or excretion; thus the intensity of the effect may be increased or the duration of action prolonged. COMPARE summation.

synergist (sin'er-jist) Any structure or chemical that aids or increases the action or effect of another.

synergy (sin'er-je) See synergism.

synesthesia (sin-es-the'ze-ah) Disorder of sensory perception in which a stimulus, in addition to the normal sensation, produces another unrelated sensation.

auditory s. Synesthesia in which the secondary sensation is that of a sound. Also called phonism.

synesthesialgia (sin-es-the'ze-al'je-ah) Disorder in which a stimulus, in addition to the normal sensation, produces pain somewhere else in the body.

syngamy (sing'gah-me) The union of the nuclei of a spermatozoon and an ovum during fertilization, resulting in a single zygote nucleus.

syngeneic (sin-jĕ-ne'ik) See isogeneic.

syngenesiotransplantation (sin-jĕ-ne-ze-o-trans'plan-ta'shun) Transplantation of tissues involving two closely related individuals (e.g., mother and child; brother and sister).

syngenesis (sin-jen'ĕ-sis) Sexual reproduction.

syngraft (sin'graft) See isograft.

synkaryon (sin-kar'e-on) The single nucleus resulting from the fusion of the nuclei of two cells (spermatozoon and ovum) during fertilization.

synkinesis (sin-ki-ne'sis) Involuntary movement of one part of the body when another part is voluntarily moved.

synoptophore (sin-op'to-fōr) A stereoscopic device used to aid strabismus-afflicted individuals in learning to use the two eyes together (binocular function).

synorchidism, synorchism (sin-or'kĭ-dizm, sin'or-kizm) Congenital fusion of the testes.

synostosis (sin-os-to'sis) Abnormal fusion of the bones forming a joint by proliferation of bony tissue. Also called true ankylosis; bony ankylosis.

synovectomy (sin-o-vek'to-me) Surgical removal of synovial membrane, especially one lining a joint cavity.

synovia (sĭ-no've-ah) The clear, thick lubricating fluid in a joint, bursa, or tendon sheath that is lined by synovial membrane; it is secreted by the membrane.

synovial (sĭ-no've-al) Relating to synovia.

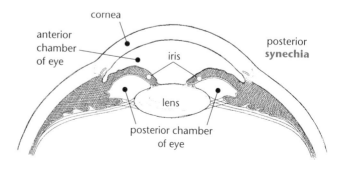

DISEASE	APPEARANCE	MUCIN CLOT VISCOSITY	LEUKOCYTES PER ML (% polymorphonuclear leukocytes)	OTHER FEATURES
normal	clear, straw-colored	good	<200 (<25%)	sugar is 90% of serum level
GROUP I NONINFLAMMATORY				
osteoarthritis	clear, straw-colored	good	100–1,000 (<25%)	
traumatic arthritis	clear to bloody	good	1,000 (<25%)	red blood cells may be present
GROUP II INFLAMMATORY—IMMUNOLOGICAL				
systemic lupus erythematosus	clear to slightly cloudy	good to fair	2,000–5,000 (10–15%)	low complement + LE prep
rheumatoid arthritis	cloudy, light yellow	poor	8,000–20,000 (60–75%)	low complement, slightly low sugar
Reiter's syndrome	cloudy	poor	10,000–40,000 (60–90%)	high complement
GROUP III INFLAMMATORY—CRYSTALLINE				
gout	cloudy	poor	10,000–20,000 (60–95%)	sodium urate crystals (negatively birefringent)
pseudogout	cloudy	fair to poor	5,000–40,000 (60–95%)	calcium pyro-phosphate crystals (weakly positive birefringent)
GROUP IV INFLAMMATORY—INFECTIONS				
acute bacterial arthritis	cloudy, gray	poor	50,000+ (98%)	low sugar (less than 2/3 plasma level)
tuberculosis arthritis	cloudy, yellow or gray	poor	25,000 (50–90%)	low sugar (less than 1/2 plasma level)

S

synovianalysis (sĭ-no-ve-ah-nal'ĭ-sis) The microscopic examination, crystal identification, and cell count of synovial fluid (synovia) extracted from a joint. Five categories can be distinguished: normal, noninflammatory, inflammatory-immunologic, inflammatory-crystalline, and inflammatory-infectious.

synovioma (sĭ-no-ve-o'mah) A benign tumor of synovial origin.
   malignant s. See synovial sarcoma, under sarcoma.

synovitis (sin-o-vi'tis) Inflammation of the membrane lining a joint.
   pigmented villonodular s. Diffuse inflammation and nodular thickening of the synovial membrane of a joint, usually of the knee, often with orange-brown outgrowths containing hemosiderin pigment; it has a tendency to recur after surgical excision due to incomplete removal, causing destruction of underlying bone and joint disability. Cause is unknown.
   traumatic s. See traumatic tenosynovitis, under tenosynovitis.

syntenic (sin-ten'ik) Relating to synteny.

synteny (sin'tĕ-ne) In genetics, the presence of two or more gene loci on the same chromosome, regardless of linkage.

synthermal (sin-ther'mal) Of the same temperature.

synthesis (sin'thĕ-sis), pl. syn'theses **1.** The combining of separate elements to form a coherent whole. **2.** The process of forming a compound by combining simpler compounds or substances.

synthesize (sin-the-sīz') To put together or make something by synthesis.

synthetase (sin'thĕ-tās) A common (trivial) name for ligase.

synthetic (sin-thet'ik) Produced by synthesis.

syntonic (sin'ton-ik) In balance.

syntrophism (sin'trŏf-izm) Enhanced growth of a strain of bacteria resulting from the products produced by another strain growing in the same medium.

syntrophoblast (sin-trof'o-blast) See syncytiotrophoblast.

syphilid (sif'ĭ-lid) Any of the infectious skin lesions of secondary syphilis; they may last weeks or months after onset and are rarely itchy although they resemble a variety of highly itchy skin rashes; some occur on the trunk and extremities and resemble the lesions of measles, others are brown macules and papules on the palms and soles, others resemble psoriasis around the hairline, others are pus-filled blisters at the nasolabial fold and the mouth.

syphilis (sif'ĭ-lis) An infectious disease caused by *Treponema pallidum*, transmitted through sexual contact or any other primary contact;

synovianalysis ■ syphilis

first symptoms develop after an incubation period of 12 to 30 days. The microorganisms can cross the placenta and infect the fetus.

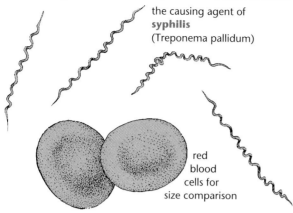

the causing agent of
syphilis
(Treponema pallidum)

red blood cells for size comparison

congenital s. Syphilis present at birth.

primary s. The first stage of the disease, characterized by the appearance of a small ulcer that develops into a chancre and heals 6 to 12 weeks later; it occurs either on the genitals or oral cavity, or near the anus.

secondary s. The second stage of syphilis, beginning after healing of the initial chancre and lasting indefinitely; marked by variable infectious skin lesions, mucous patches, fever, and other constitutional symptoms.

tertiary s. The final, noninfectious stage of the disease, beginning after a lapse of several months or years; may take one or more of three forms: widespread development of masses of granulomatous tissue (gummas); involvement of the cardiovascular system (e.g., aneurysm in the ascending aorta and aortic valve incompetence); or involvement of the central nervous system.

syphilitic (sif-ĭ-lit′ik) Relating to syphilis.

syphilo-, syphil- Combining forms meaning syphilis.

syphiloid (sif′ĭ-loid) Resembling syphilis.

syphilologist (sif-ĭ-lol′o-jist) A specialist in syphilis, its diagnosis, treatment, and epidemiologic control.

syphiloma (sif-ĭ-lo′mah) A gumma.

syringadenoma (sĭ-ring-ad-ĕ-no′mah) A benign tumor of a sweat gland. Also called syringoadenoma.

syringadenosus (sĭ-ring-ad-ĕ-no′sus) Relating to a sweat gland.

syringe (sĭ-rinj′) A device used for injecting or withdrawing fluids.

aural s. See ear syringe.

disposable s. A syringe with an attached needle, designed to be discarded after use (e.g., insulin syringe).

ear s. A large–capacity syringe for irrigation and aspiration; primarily used for washing ear wax (cerumen) from the external auditory canal. Also called aural syringe.

fountain s. An apparatus consisting of a reservoir for holding water or special solutions and a tube with a nozzle at the end; it injects the liquid by the action of gravity; used for enemas and vaginal irrigations (douches).

hypodermic s. A syringe for introducing fluids through a needle into subcutaneous tissues.

lacrimal s. A small syringe for washing out the lacrimal passages. Also called probe syringe.

Luer-Lok s. A sturdy glass syringe with a metal locking device for securing a needle firmly in place.

Pitkin s. A control type of self-filling syringe that permits injection of large amounts of solution.

probe s. See lacrimal syringe.

tuberculin s. A narrow, small-capacity calibrated syringe, used to administer small doses of tuberculin.

water s. A dental apparatus that projects a jet of water; used to wash debris in preparing a tooth for restoration.

syringitis (sir-in-ji′tis) Inflammation of a tubular structure of the body (e.g., of a uterine tube).

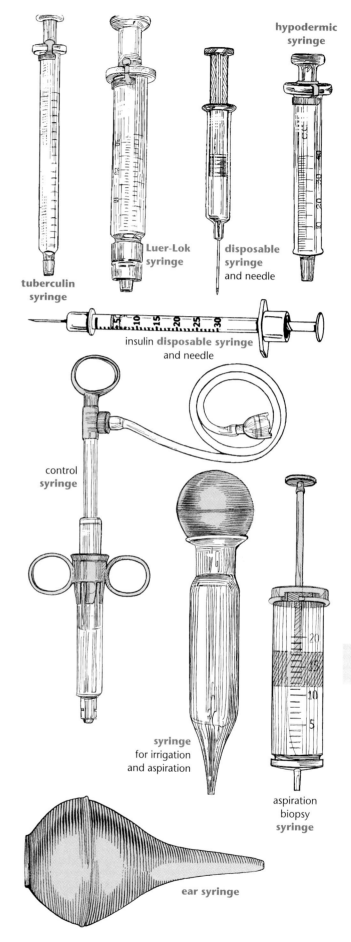

hypodermic syringe

Luer-Lok syringe

disposable syringe and needle

tuberculin syringe

insulin **disposable syringe** and needle

control syringe

syringe for irrigation and aspiration

aspiration biopsy syringe

ear syringe

S

syringo- syring- Combining forms meaning tube; fistula.

syringoadenoma (sĭ-ring-go-ad-ĕ-no′mah) See syringadenoma.

syringobulbia (sĭ-ring-go-bul′be-ah) The occurrence of abnormal fluid-filled cavities in the brainstem.

syringocystoma (sĭ-ring-go-sis-to′mah) A cystic growth in a hair follicle.

syringoma (sir-ing-go′mah) A tiny benign tumor of sweat glands, usually multiple, occurring most frequently about the lower eyelids and cheeks.

syringomyelia (sĭ-ring-go-mi-e′le-ah) The presence of a central fluid-filled cavity in the spinal cord in the neck, possibly resulting from obstruction to the free flow of cerebrospinal fluid within the spinal canal; causes sensory loss of pain and temperature; may cause wasting of hand muscles, spastic paraplegia, and nystagmus.

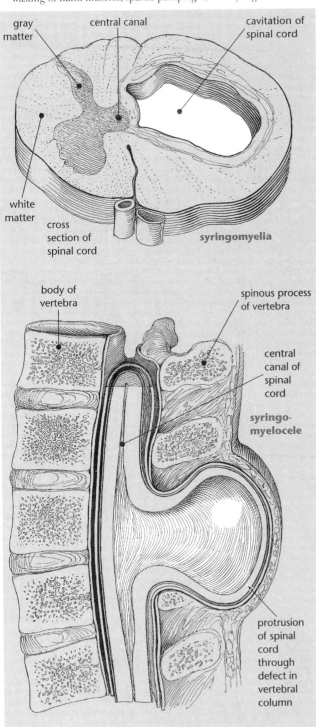

gray matter
central canal
cavitation of spinal cord
white matter
cross section of spinal cord
syringomyelia

body of vertebra
spinous process of vertebra
central canal of spinal cord
syringo-myelocele
protrusion of spinal cord through defect in vertebral column

syringomyelocele (sĭ-ring-go-mi′ĕ-lo-sēl) Protrusion of a portion of spinal cord with a greatly enlarged, fluid-filled central canal through an abnormal gap in the vertebrae.

syringotomy (sir-in-got′o-me) See fistulotomy.

syrinx (sir′inks) A tubular cavity.

syrup (sir′up) In pharmacy, a solution of sugar in water used as a vehicle for active ingredients of drugs.

syssarcosis (sis-sar-ko′sis) A muscular articulation; the union of bones by muscle (e.g., the connection between the hyoid bone and the lower jaw).

system (sis′tem) **1.** A functionally related group of parts or organs (e.g., a group of organs united in a common function, as the digestive system). **2.** An organized set of interrelated ideas, procedures, techniques, etc. **3.** A method of arrangement or classification. **4.** A school or method of instruction and practice in medicine based on a specific set of principles.

APUD s. See APUD.

arousal s. See reticular activating system.

autonomic nervous s. (ANS) The division of the nervous system that innervates the striated muscles of the heart and the smooth muscles and glands of the body; composed of two complementary parts, the sympathetic nervous system and the parasympathetic nervous system, which differ in structure and function.

Bethesda s. of classification A system of classification used in cytopathology reports for describing results of the cytologic examination of a cervical/vaginal specimen (Pap smear). It is basically composed of three categories: *Specimen adequacy* (e.g., satisfactory; satisfactory but limited by . . . ; unsatisfactory); *General categorization* (e.g., within normal limits; benign cellular changes; epithelial cell abnormality); and *Descriptive diagnosis* (e.g., low–grade squamous intraepithelial lesion [mild dysplasia]; high-grade squamous intraepithelial lesion [severe dysplasia]; cancer [adenocarcinoma; squamous cell carcinoma]).

blood-vascular s. The extensive pathways by which blood is circulated through the body, including the arteries, arterioles, capillaries, venules, and veins. Also called vascular system.

cardiovascular s. (CVS) The heart and blood vessels through which blood is pumped and circulated in the body.

centimeter-gram-second (CGS, cgs) s. A system of metric units in which the basic units of length, mass, and time are the centimeter, gram, and second.

central nervous s. (CNS) The portion of the vertebrate nervous system consisting of the brain (encephalon) and spinal cord (medulla spinalis).

clinical laboratory information s. Information system, usually computer–assisted, designed for planning, organizing, directing, and controlling administrative and clinical activities associated with the provision and utilization of clinical laboratory services.

clinical pharmacy information s. Information system, usually computer–assisted, designed for planning, organizing, directing, and controlling administrative activities associated with the provision and utilization of clinical pharmacy services.

closed urinary drainage s. An indwelling urinary drainage system designed to reduce or eliminate the possibility of contamination and infection of the urinary tract; consists of an apparatus packed under sterile conditions that includes catheter, lubricant, gloves, drainage tube, and collection reservoir.

conducting s. of heart The tracts and network of various cell types (nodal, transitional, and Purkinje myocytes) that are responsible for the conduction of impulses through the heart; they cause the heart to beat about 60 to 100 cycles per minute, maintaining perfusion of blood through the pulmonary and systemic tissues.

digestive s. The alimentary canal from the mouth to the anus and the associated glands; the organs associated with the ingestion, digestion, and absorption of food, and with the elimination of those constituents that are unabsorbed. Also called digestive apparatus; digestive organs.

Duke's staging s. See Duke's classification, under classification.

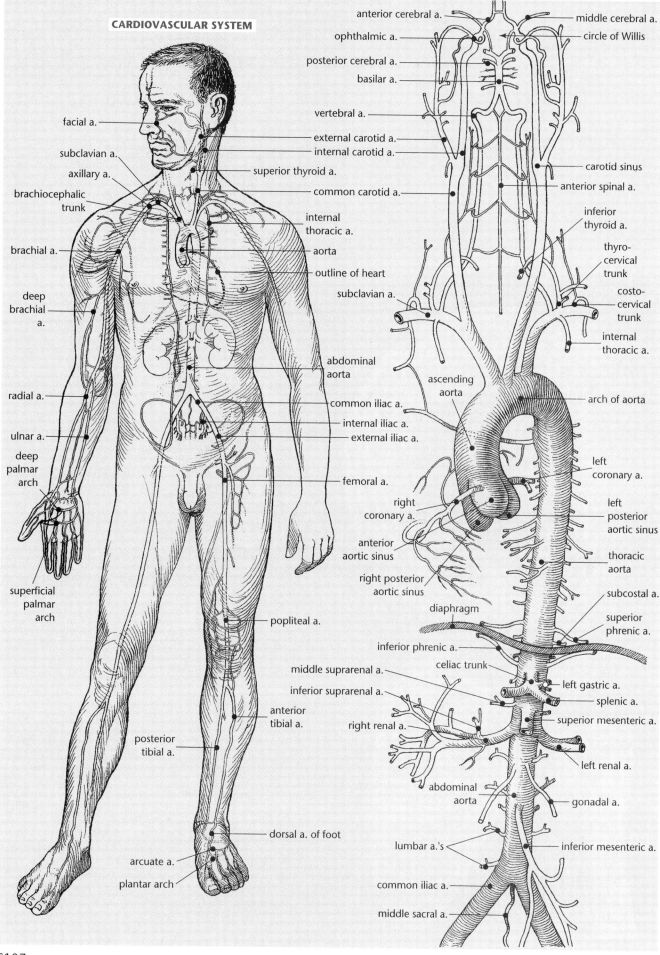

CARDIOVASCULAR SYSTEM

facial a.

subclavian a.

axillary a.

brachiocephalic trunk

brachial a.

deep brachial a.

radial a.

ulnar a.

deep palmar arch

superficial palmar arch

posterior tibial a.

anterior cerebral a.

ophthalmic a.

posterior cerebral a.

basilar a.

vertebral a.

external carotid a.

internal carotid a.

superior thyroid a.

common carotid a.

internal thoracic a.

aorta

outline of heart

subclavian a.

abdominal aorta

common iliac a.

internal iliac a.

external iliac a.

femoral a.

popliteal a.

anterior tibial a.

dorsal a. of foot

arcuate a.

plantar arch

middle cerebral a.

circle of Willis

carotid sinus

anterior spinal a.

inferior thyroid a.

thyro-cervical trunk

costo-cervical trunk

internal thoracic a.

ascending aorta

arch of aorta

left coronary a.

right coronary a.

left posterior aortic sinus

anterior aortic sinus

thoracic aorta

right posterior aortic sinus

subcostal a.

diaphragm

superior phrenic a.

inferior phrenic a.

celiac trunk

middle suprarenal a.

left gastric a.

inferior suprarenal a.

splenic a.

right renal a.

superior mesenteric a.

left renal a.

abdominal aorta

gonadal a.

lumbar a.'s

inferior mesenteric a.

common iliac a.

middle sacral a.

S

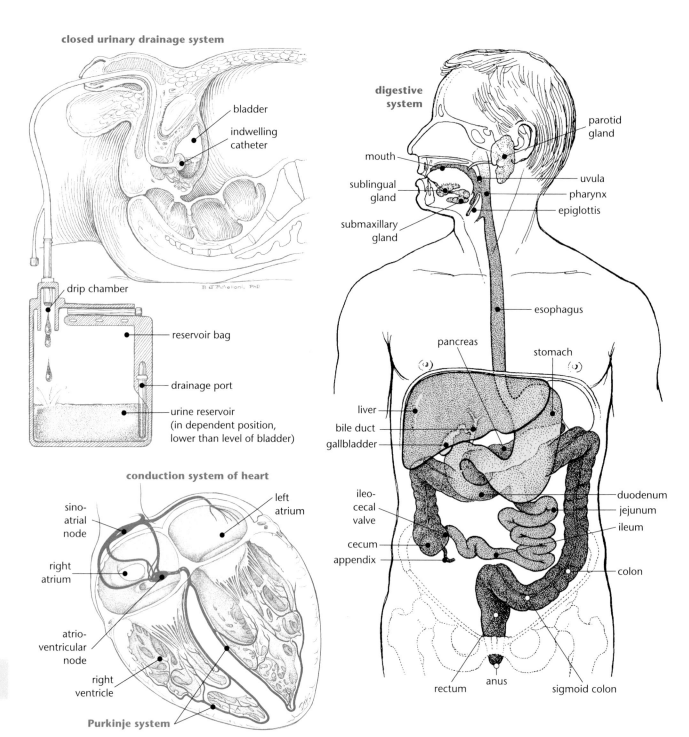

closed urinary drainage system

bladder

indwelling catheter

drip chamber

reservoir bag

drainage port

urine reservoir
(in dependent position,
lower than level of bladder)

B. J. Melloni, PhD

digestive system

parotid gland

mouth

sublingual gland

submaxillary gland

uvula

pharynx

epiglottis

esophagus

pancreas

stomach

liver

bile duct

gallbladder

ileo-cecal valve

cecum

appendix

duodenum

jejunum

ileum

colon

rectum

anus

sigmoid colon

conduction system of heart

left atrium

sino-atrial node

right atrium

atrio-ventricular node

right ventricle

Purkinje system

---

endocrine s. The system composed of glands of internal secretion; namely, discrete ductless glands, which produce secretions (hormones) that are transported in the blood to distant effector cells to influence body functions. The endocrine system includes the pituitary (hypophysis), adrenal, thyroid, and parathyroid glands; pineal body; pancreatic islets; the interstitial cells of the testis; the interstitial, follicular, and luteal cells of the ovary; the placenta; and certain specialized cells of the thymus, kidney, and lungs.

estradiol transdermal s. See estradiol transdermal patch, under patch.

extrapyramidal s. A functional system of tracts in the brain that controls and coordinates motor activities, especially postural, static, and supportive.

genital s. See reproductive system.

genitourinary s. The reproductive organs and the organs for the secretion and passage of urine. Also called urogenital system.

Gleason's grading s. A widely used histologic system of grading cancer of the prostate; in this system, two numbers are assigned to each area of prostatic cancer, based on a major and minor pattern of tissue differentiation in the area; numbers 2–4 indicate a well differentiated cancer; 5–7, a moderately differentiated cancer; and 8–10, a poorly differentiated cancer. The Gleason's grading system provides a correlation between the histologic appearance and the prognosis of the tumor (most well-differentiated cancers have a good prognosis).

haversian s. See osteon.

hematopoietic s. The blood-producing tissues concerned with the formation of blood and its cellular constituents.

heterogeneous s. A combination of matter containing two or more distinct and separable components (e.g., a suspension or an emulsion).

INTERNATIONAL SYSTEM OF UNITS (SI)

PREFIXES AND THEIR SYMBLS USED TO DESIGNATE DECIMAL MULTIPES AND SUBMULTIPLES

Quantity	Name	Symbol
Si base units:		
length	meter	m
mass	kilogram	kg
time	second	s
elctric current	ampere	A
thermodynamic temperature	kelvin	K
amount of substance	mole	mol
luminous intensity	candela	cd
Si supplementary units:		
plane angle	radian	rad
solid angle	steradian	sr

Prefix	Symbol	Factor
tera	T	$10^{12} =$
giga	G	$10^9 = 1\ 000\ 000\ 000$
mega	M	$10^6 = 1\ 000\ 000$
kilo	k	$10^3 = 1\ 000$
hecto	h	$10^2 = 100$
deka	da	$10^1 = 10$
deci	d	$10^{-1} = 0.1$
centi	c	$10^{-2} = 0.01$
milli	m	$10^{-3} = 0.001$
micro	μ	$10^{-6} = 0.000\ 001$
nano	n	$10^{-9} = 0.000\ 000\ 001$
pico	p	$10^{-12} = 0.000\ 000\ 000\ 001$
femto	f	$10^{-15} = 0.000\ 000\ 000\ 000\ 001$
atto	a	$10^{-18} = 0.000\ 000\ 000\ 000\ 000\ 001$

EXAMPLES OF SI DERIVED UNITS EXPRESSED IN TERMS OF BASE UNITS

Quantity	Si unit	Unit Symbol
area	square meter	m^2
volume	cubic meter	m^3
speed, velocity	meter per second	m/s
acceleration	meter per second squared	m/s^2
wave number	1 per meter	m^{-1}
density, mass density	kilogram per cubic meter	kg/m^3
current density	ampere per square meter	A/m^2
magnetic field strength	ampere per meter	A/m
concentration (of amount of substance)	mole per cubic meter	$mol/^3$
specific volume	cubic meter per kilogram	m^3/kg
luminance	candela per square meter	cd/m^2

SI DERIVED UNITS WITH SPECIAL NAMES

Quantity	Name	Symbol	Expression in terms of other units
frequency	hertz	Hz	s^{-1}
force	newton	N	kg·m/s2
pressure, stress	pascal	Pa	N/m^2
energy, work, quantity of heat	joule	J	N·m
power, radiant flux	watt	W	J/s
quantity of electricity, electric charge	coulomb	C	A·s
electric potential, potential difference, electromotive force	volt	V	W/A
capacitance	farad	F	C/V
electric resistance	ohm	ω	V/A
conductance	siemens	S	A/V
magnetic flux	weber	Wb	V·
magnetic flux density	tesla	T	Wb/m^2
inductance	henry	H	Wb/A
luminous flux	lumen	lm	cd·sr
illuminance	lux	lx	lm/m^2
activity (of a radionuclide)	becquerel	Bq	s^{-1}
absorbed dose	gray	Gy	J/kg

RECOMMENDED UNITS

Quantity	Symbol	Dimension	Unit	Unit symbol	Recommended sub-units	Not recommended units
Length	I	L	meter	m	mm, μm, m	cm, μ, u, mμ, mu, A
Area	A	L^2	square meter	m^2	mm^2, μm^2	cm^2, μ^2
Volume	V	L^3	cubic meter / liter	m^3 / l	dm^3, cm^3, mm^3, μm^3 / ml, μl, nl, pl, fl	cc, ccm, μ^3, u^3 / L, λ, ul, $\mu\mu$l, uul
Mass	m	M	kilogram	kg	g, mg, μg, ng, pg	Kg, gr, γ, ug, mμg, mug, $\gamma\gamma$, $\mu\mu$g, uug
Number	N	I	one	1	10^9, 10^6, 10^3, 10^{-3}	all other factors
Amount of substance	n	N	mol	mol	mmol, μmol, nmol	M, eq, val, g-mol, mM, meq, mval, μM μeq, μval, nM, neq, nval
Mass concentration		$K^{-3}m$	kilogram per liter	kg/l	g/l, mg/l, μg/l, ng/l	g/ml, %, g%, % (w/v), g/100 ml, g/dl, ‰, ‰, ‰(w/x), mg%, mg% (w/v), mg/100 ml, mg/dl, ppm, ppm (w/v), μg%, μg% (W/v), μg/100 ml, μ/dl, gl%, ppb, ppb (w/v), $\mu\mu$g/ml, uug/ml
Substance concentration	c	$L^{-3} N$	mol per liter	mol/l	mmol/l, lgmmol/l, nmol/l	M, eq/l, val/l, N, n, mM, meq/l, mval/l, μM, uM, μeq/l, nM, neq/l
Molality	m	$M^{-1} N$	mol per kilogram	mol/kg	mmol/kg, μmol/kg	m, mmol/g, μmol/mg, mm, μm, mm

S

immune s. A complex system of cells (T lymphocytes) and protein molecules (major histocompatibility complex) acting together to protect the body from harmful organisms and substances; it normally distinguishes between foreign (nonself) proteins and the body's own (self) proteins.

information s. Any of several sets of files, procedures, and equipment for the storage, manipulation, and retrieval of information or data.

International S. of Units A system of units for the basic quantities of length, mass, time, electric current, temperature, luminous intensity, and amount of substance; the corresponding units are: meter, kilogram, second, ampere, Kelvin, candela, and mole. It is abbreviated SI in all languages (from Système International d'Unités).

limbic s. Term loosely applied to the part of the brain that controls autonomic functions, along with some aspects of emotion and behavior; some of the structures include the hippocampus, dentate gyrus, parahippocampal gyrus, amygdaloid body, cingulate gyrus, medial part of the thalamus, olfactory nerves, bulbs, tracts, and gyri, and at the center of the limbic system, the hypothalamus.

lymphatic s. A closed system consisting of lymphoid tissue, lymph nodes, and lymphatic vessels; it forms an alternative route for the absorption of lymph and its return to the blood via the thoracic duct and right lymphatic duct.

lymphoid s. Specialized lymphoid tissues and organs considered collectively; they have in common the ability to produce substances, such as antibodies, that can inactivate foreign matter; it includes the thymus, bone marrow, lymph nodes, spleen, and gut-associated lymphoid tissue; it operates in close association with the macrophage system.

macrophage s. The phagocytic cells present in the bone marrow, spleen, and liver, where they free the blood or lymph of foreign matter; it includes all major phagocytic cell types, except the polymorphonuclear leukocytes. Also called mononuclear phagocyte system. Formerly called the reticuloendothelial system.

meter-kilogram-second (MKS, mks) s. An absolute system of units; the system upon which the International System of Units (SI) is based.

metric s. A decimal system of measures and weights based upon the meter and the gram, respectively.

mononuclear phagocyte s. See macrophage system.

muscular s. The muscles of the body considered collectively.

musculoskeletal s. All the muscles and bones of the body and their connecting structures considered collectively.

nervous s. The nervous tissues of the body; includes the brain and spinal cord (central nervous system), the cranial and spinal nerves (peripheral nervous system), and the sympathetic and parasympathetic nerves (autonomic nervous system); it is the most complex system of the body; it directs the adjustments and reactions of the body to internal and environmental conditions.

neuroendocrine s. See APUD.

neuromuscular s. The nerves and the muscles they innervate.

parasympathetic nervous s. The smaller of the two divisions of the autonomic nervous system (ANS) that emerges from certain cranial and sacral spinal nerves (craniosacral outflow); some of the structures innervated include: the ciliary muscles of the eye, the sphincter muscle of the pupil, salivary glands, heart, stomach, small intestine, cecum, appendix, colon, rectum, bladder, erectile tissue of penis/clitoris, testes, ovaries, fallopian (uterine) tubes, and the uterus. Physiologically, parasympathetic action is usually localized (e.g., an increase in the glandular and peristaltic activities of the intestine).

peripheral nervous s. (PNS) The nervous system that connects the central nervous system (CNS) to the rest of the body; composed of the 12 pairs of cranial nerves arising from the brain, the 31 pairs of spinal nerves arising from the spinal cord, and the sympathetic trunks and their ganglia and branches.

portal s. A blood vessel that divides into capillaries at either end, such as the portal vein (connecting the capillaries from the intestines with the capillaries in the substance of the liver) or the portal system of the pituitary (connecting the capillaries from the hypothalamus with the capillaries of the anterior lobe of the pituitary).

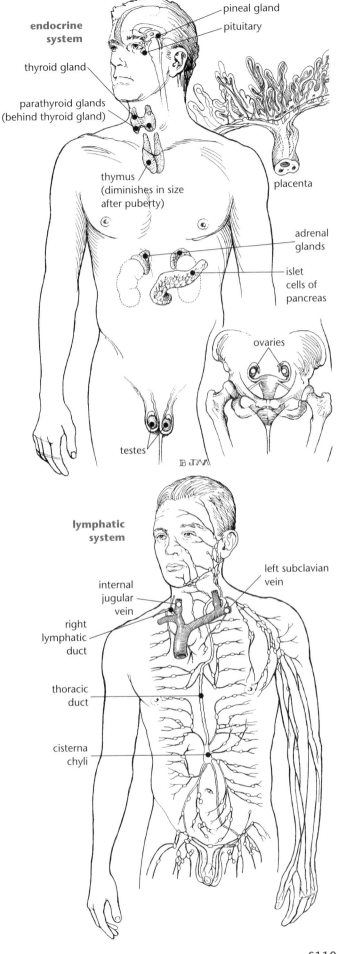

endocrine system

pineal gland

pituitary

thyroid gland

parathyroid glands (behind thyroid gland)

thymus (diminishes in size after puberty)

placenta

adrenal glands

islet cells of pancreas

ovaries

testes

lymphatic system

internal jugular vein

left subclavian vein

right lymphatic duct

thoracic duct

cisterna chyli

S110

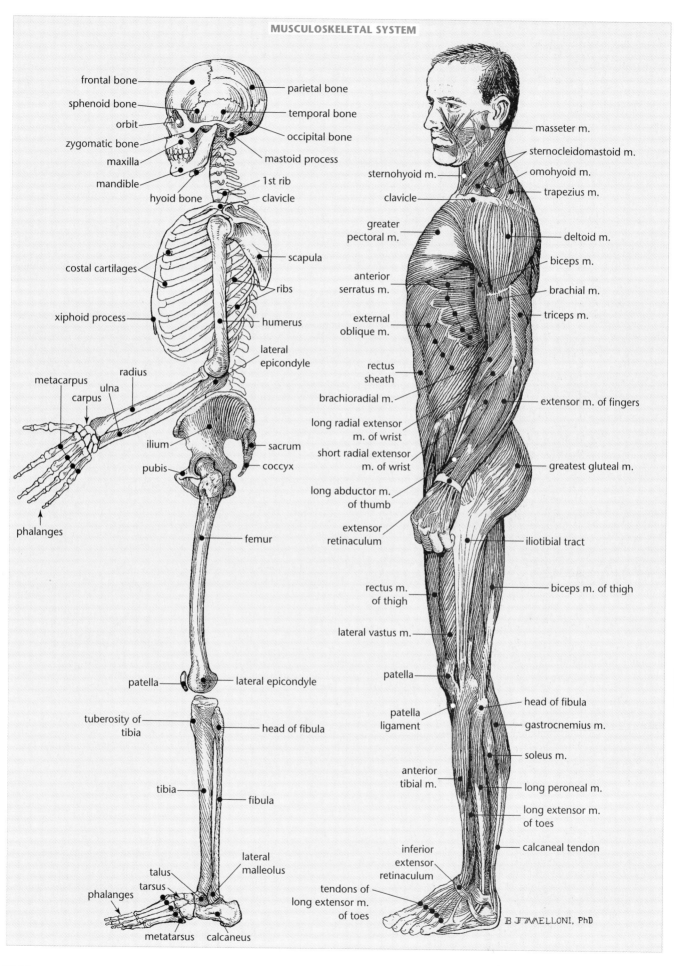

frontal bone

parietal bone

sphenoid bone

temporal bone

orbit

occipital bone

zygomatic bone

mastoid process

maxilla

mandible

1st rib

hyoid bone

clavicle

costal cartilages

scapula

ribs

xiphoid process

humerus

lateral
epicondyle

radius

metacarpus

ulna

carpus

ilium

sacrum

pubis

coccyx

phalanges

femur

patella

lateral epicondyle

tuberosity of
tibia

head of fibula

tibia

fibula

lateral
malleolus

talus

tarsus

phalanges

tendons of
long extensor m.
of toes

metatarsus   calcaneus

masseter m.

sternocleidomastoid m.

sternohyoid m.

omohyoid m.

trapezius m.

clavicle

greater
pectoral m.

deltoid m.

biceps m.

anterior
serratus m.

brachial m.

triceps m.

external
oblique m.

rectus
sheath

brachioradial m.

extensor m. of fingers

long radial extensor
m. of wrist

short radial extensor
m. of wrist

greatest gluteal m.

long abductor m.
of thumb

extensor
retinaculum

iliotibial tract

rectus m.
of thigh

biceps m. of thigh

lateral vastus m.

patella

patella
ligament

head of fibula

gastrocnemius m.

soleus m.

anterior
tibial m.

long peroneal m.

long extensor m.
of toes

calcaneal tendon

inferior
extensor
retinaculum

B. J. MELLONI, PhD

S

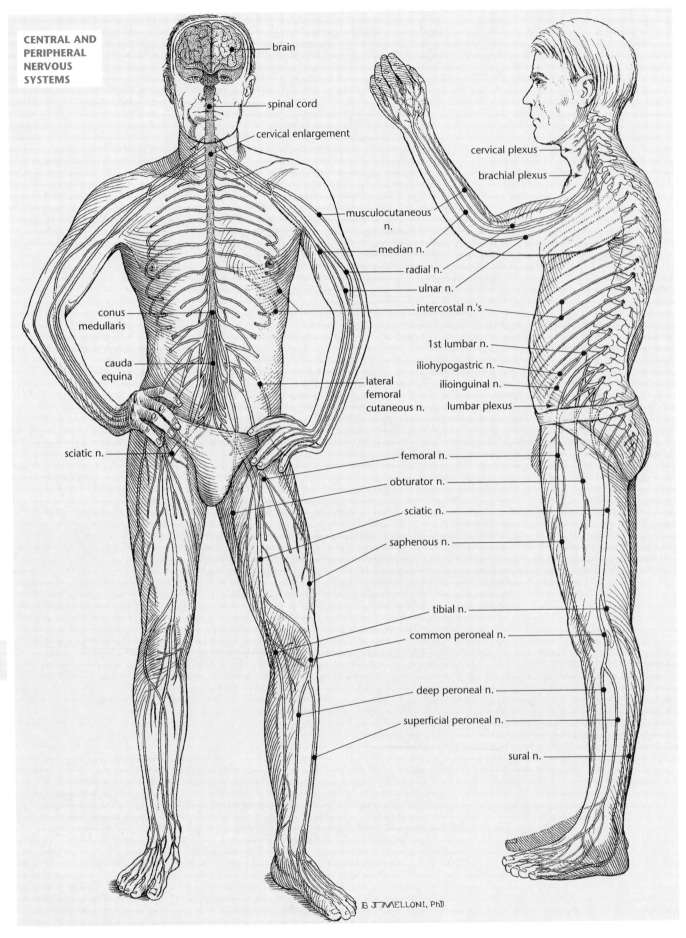

brain

spinal cord

cervical enlargement

cervical plexus

brachial plexus

musculocutaneous n.

median n.

radial n.

ulnar n.

intercostal n.'s

1st lumbar n.

iliohypogastric n.

ilioinguinal n.

lumbar plexus

conus medullaris

cauda equina

lateral femoral cutaneous n.

sciatic n.

femoral n.

obturator n.

sciatic n.

saphenous n.

tibial n.

common peroneal n.

deep peroneal n.

superficial peroneal n.

sural n.

B. J. MELLONI, PhD

S

system ■ system

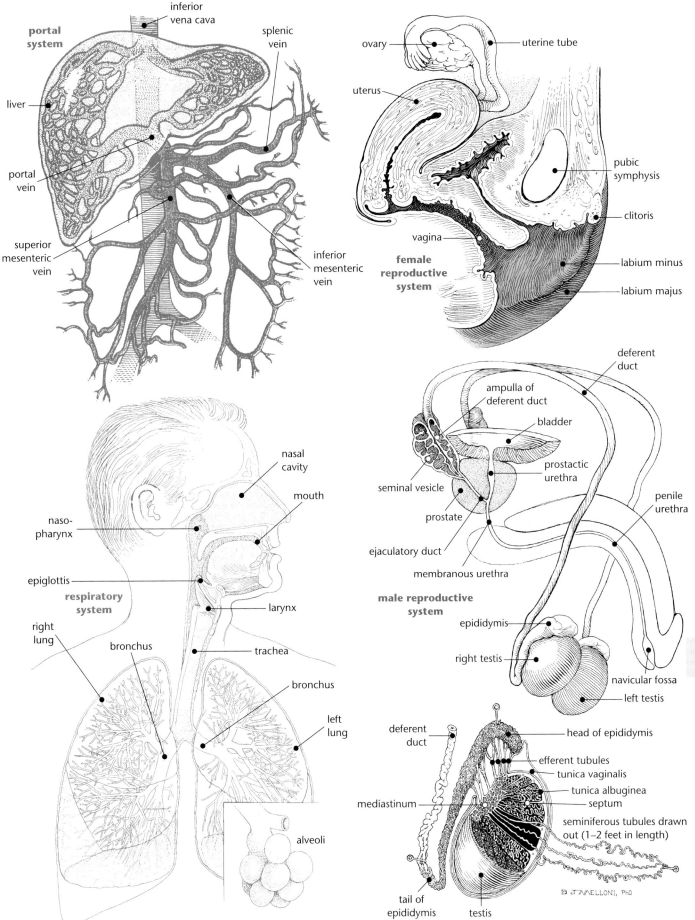

portal system

inferior vena cava

splenic vein

liver

portal vein

superior mesenteric vein

inferior mesenteric vein

ovary

uterine tube

uterus

pubic symphysis

clitoris

vagina

female reproductive system

labium minus

labium majus

deferent duct

ampulla of deferent duct

bladder

seminal vesicle

prostactic urethra

prostate

penile urethra

ejaculatory duct

membranous urethra

epididymis

right testis

navicular fossa

left testis

nasal cavity

mouth

naso-pharynx

epiglottis

respiratory system

larynx

right lung

bronchus

trachea

bronchus

left lung

male reproductive system

deferent duct

head of epididymis

efferent tubules

tunica vaginalis

tunica albuginea

mediastinum

septum

seminiferous tubules drawn out (1–2 feet in length)

tail of epididymis

testis

alveoli

B J MELLONI, PhD

S

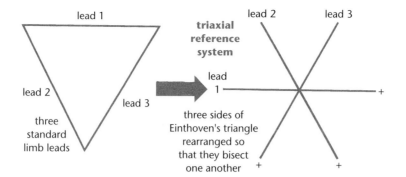

Purkinje s. The specialized system of modified muscle fibers in the heart concerned with conduction of impulses.

renin-angiotensin s. A biochemical feedback system important in the regulation of blood pressure, fluid volume, and sodium balance.

reproductive s. The organs and structures associated with reproduction and with the procreative act. Also called genital system. *Female reproductive s.*, the genital organs in the female, consisting of the ovaries, fallopian (uterine) tubes, uterus, vagina, and external genitalia. *Male reproductive s.*, the genital organs in the male, consisting of the testes, excretory ducts, seminal vesicles, prostate, and penis.

respiratory s. The air passages (nasal cavities, pharynx, larynx, trachea, bronchi), lungs, and the muscles of respiration, by means of which pulmonary ventilation and gas exchange between ambient air and the blood are consummated.

reticular activating s. (RAS) A portion of the central cephalic brainstem and its cranial extensions to the cerebral cortex that control wakefulness, arousal from sleep, and focusing of attention. Also called arousal system.

reticuloendothelial s. Former name of the macrophage system.

sympathetic nervous s. The larger of the two divisions of the autonomic nervous system (ANS), confined to the thoracolumbar region; some of the structures innervated include: all sweat glands of the skin, erector muscles of the hairs, muscular walls of blood vessels, heart, lungs, and abdominopelvic viscera. Physiologically, sympathetic action is systemic (e.g., general constriction of cutaneous arteries, with consequent increase in the blood supply to the heart, muscles, and brain).

T s. A system of transverse intracellular tubular invaginations of the sarcolemma at the level of the Z lines of skeletal and cardiac muscle fibers; it serves as a pathway for the dispersal of electrical excita-

tion and relaxation of myofibrils. Also called transverse tubules; T tubules; triad system.

triad s. See T system.

triaxial reference s. In electrocardiography, the graphic figure resulting from rearranging the sides of the Einthoven triangle (which represent the three standard limb leads) so that they bisect one another.

urogenital s. See genitourinary system.

vascular s. See blood-vascular system.

vestibular s. See vestibular organ, under organ.

systematic (sis-tĕ-mat′ik) Relating to a system.

systematization (sis-tem-ah-tī-za′shun) The process of arranging according to a system or in an orderly sequence.

Système International d'Unités See International System of Units, under system.

systemic (sis-tem′ik) Affecting the entire body.

systole (sis′to-le) The period of contraction of the heart muscle.

atrial s. Contraction of the atria giving impetus to the blood flow from the atria into the ventricles; it lasts about 0.1 seconds.

ventricular s. Contraction of the ventricles immediately following atrial systole; it has two phases: the period of isometric contraction during which the ventricular pressure firmly closes the atrioventricular valves, and the period of ejection during which ventricular pressure overcomes the diastolic pressure of the aorta and pulmonary trunk, causing the aortic and pulmonic valves to open with ejection of blood from the ventricles into the vessels; the ejection period lasts about 0.3 seconds in a person with a heart rate of 70 beats per minute.

systolic (sis-tol′ik) Relating to systole.

systremma (sis-trem′ah) A muscular cramp, especially of the leg muscles (chiefly of the bellies of the gastrocnemius and soleus muscles); the contracted muscles form a hard bulge.

S

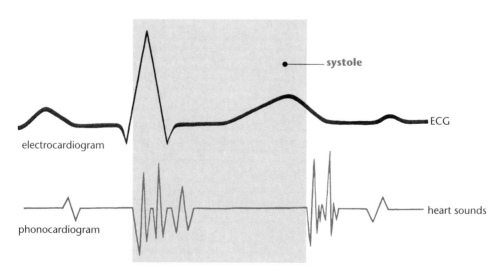

T

periodic table

METALS   NONMETALS

Group	I	II												III	IV	V	VI	VII	O
Period 1	H 1																		He 2
2	Li 3	Be 4												B 5	C 6	N 7	O 8	F 9	Ne 10
3	Na 11	Mg 12												Al 13	Si 14	P 15	S 16	Cl 17	Ar 18
4	K 19	Ca 20	Sc 21	Ti 22	V 23	Cr 24	Mn 25	Fe 26	Co 27	Ni 28	Cu 29	Zn 30		Ga 31	Ge 32	As 33	Se 34	Br 35	Kr 36
5	Rb 37	Sr 38	Y 39	Zr 40	Nb 41	Mo 42	Tc 43	Ru 44	Rh 45	Pd 46	Ag 47	Cd 48		In 49	Sn 50	Sb 51	Te 52	I 53	Xe 54
6	Cs 55	Ba 56	* 57-71	Hf 72	Ta 73	W 74	Re 75	Os 76	Ir 77	Pt 78	Au 79	Hg 80		Ti 81	Pb 82	Bi 83	Po 84	At 85	Rn 86
7	Fr 87	Ra 88	** 89-103	Rf 104	Ha 105														

*	lanthanide elements (rare earth)	La 57	Ce 58	Pr 59	Nd 60	Pm 61	Sm 62	Eu 63	Gd 64	Tb 65	Dy 66	Ho 67	Er 68	Tm 69	Yb 70	Lu 71
**	actinide elements	Ac 89	Th 90	Pa 91	U 92	Np 93	Pu 94	Am 95	Cm 96	Bk 97	Cf 98	Es 99	Fm 100	Md 101	No 102	Lw 103

Tabanus (tah-ba′nus) Genus of biting flies commonly called horse-flies or gadflies; some species transmit blood-borne parasites.

tabes (ta′bēz) Progressive wasting away.

    t. dorsalis Manifestations of the tertiary stage of syphilis (neurosyphilis) resulting from damage to the sensory nerve roots and the posterior column of the spinal cord; characterized by loss of muscular coordination, shooting pains in the extremities, Charcot joints, incontinence, and impotence. Also called locomotor ataxia.

tabescent (tah-bes′ent) Wasting away progressively.

tabetic (tah-bet′ik) Relating to tabes.

tabetiform (tah-bet′ĭ-form) Resembling tabes dorsalis.

table (ta′bl) **1.** An orderly arrangement of data. **2.** A flat layer, as of the inner and outer plates forming the bones of the skull. **3.** An article of furniture.

    Aub-Dubois t. Table of normal metabolic rates for all age-groups, expressed in calories per square meter of body surface per hour.

    examining t. Table on which a person sits or lies during a medical examination.

    operating t. Table on which a person is placed during a surgical procedure.

    periodic t. An arrangement of chemical elements placed according to their atomic number; it demonstrates recurrence of similar properties after certain periodic intervals.

    Reuss' color t. Any of several diagrams containing colored letters superimposed on colored backgrounds used for testing color blindness.

    tilt t. Table equipped with a rotating top that can be brought up to a vertical position; used in physical therapy treatments.

tablespoon (ta′bl-spoon) (tbs, tbsp) Spoon used as a measure in the dosage of liquid medicines; equivalent to 15 milliliters, 4 liquid drams, or 3 teaspoons.

tablet (tab′let) A compressed solid dosage of a medicinal substance.

    buccal t. Tablet placed between the cheek and the gum, where it dissolves quickly; the medication is absorbed through the oral mucosa.

enteric coated t. Tablet intended to be dissolved in the intestines rather than in the stomach; it is coated with material that does not disintegrate in stomach fluids.

hypodermic t. Water-soluble tablet, intended to be dissolved in the barrel of a hypodermic syringe prior to injection.

sublingual t. Tablet to be held under the tongue for direct absorption of the medication through the oral mucosa.

taboparesis (ta-bo-pah-re'sis) Condition marked by a combination of tabes dorsalis and a generalized weakness; often seen in tertiary syphilis (neurosyphilis).

tabular (tab'u-lar) **1.** Arranged as a table. **2.** Having a flat surface.

tache (tahsh) A flat spot on the skin or mucous membrane.

t. noire (a) A black spot resembling a cigarette burn at the site of a tick bite. (b) In forensic medicine, a postmortem ocular change occurring in a dry environment, characterized by the development of a blackish brown discoloration in the exposed areas of the partly open eyes of a corpse; this phenomenon may be mistakenly interpreted as bruising.

tachistesthesia (tah-kis-tes-the'ze-ah) Perception of a flicker of light.

tachistoscope (tah-kis'to-skōp) Device that flashes a test pattern briefly; used to measure the speed of conscious visual perception.

tachogram (tak'o-gram) Graphic record made by tachography.

tachography (tah-kog'rah-fe) The process of recording speed or rate (e.g., the rate of arterial blood flow).

tachometer (ta-kom'e-ter) Instrument used in tachography.

tachy- Combining form meaning speed.

tachyarrhythmia (tak-e-ah-rith'me-ah) Any disturbance of the heart rhythm in which the heart rate exceeds 100 beats per minute.

tachycardia (tak-e-kar'de-ah) An abnormally fast heartbeat; usually applied to one over 100 beats per minute. Also called tachyrhythmia; tachysystole.

atrial t. Tachycardia originating in the atrial walls.

fetal t. Tachycardia of the fetus in which the heart rate is 160 beats per minute or more (normal rate is 120–160 beats/minute); causes may include maternal or fetal infection, fetal oxygen deficiency (hypoxia), or maternal use of certain drugs.

paroxysmal t. Abrupt and recurrent attacks of tachycardia; they may arise from the atria, ventricles, or atrioventricular junctional tissue.

tachycardiac (tak-e-kar'de-ak) Relating to an excessively rapid heartbeat.

tachycrotic (tak-e-krot'ik) Relating to a rapid pulse.

tachykinin (tak-e-ki'nin) One of a group of structurally related peptides involved in blood vessel dilatation, smooth muscle contraction, stimulation of saliva secretion, and neurotransmission of painful stimuli.

tachylalia (tak-e-la'le-ah) See tachylogia.

tachylogia (tak-e-lo'je-ah) Rapid speech. Also called tachylalia; tachyphrasia.

tachyphrasia (tak-e-fra'ze-ah) See tachylogia.

tachyphylaxis (tak-e-fi-lak'sis) **1.** The acute development of tolerance to the rapid, repeated administration of a drug. **2.** A decreased responsiveness to additional dosing (not immunologic).

tachypnea (tak-ip-ne'ah) Abnormally rapid, shallow breathing.

transient t. of newborn Benign condition of near-term or term babies who have respiratory distress shortly after delivery; usually lasts three to five days; thought to be caused by delayed resorption of fetal lung fluid. Popularly called wet lung.

tachyrhythmia (tak-e-rith'me-ah) See tachycardia.

tachysterol (tak-is'te-rol) An irradiation product of ergosterol.

tachysystole (tak-e-sis'to-le) See tachycardia.

tactile (tak'til) Relating to the sense of touch.

taction (tak'shun) **1.** Touching; a touch. **2.** The sense of touch.

tactometer (tak-tom'ĕ-ter) See esthesiometer.

tactor (tak'tor) A tactile (sensory) end-organ.

tactual (tak'tu-al) Relating to the sense of touch.

Taenia (te'ne-ah) Genus of large tapeworms.

T. saginata The common beef tapeworm transmitted to

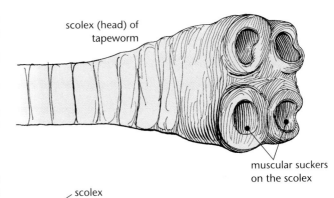

scolex (head) of tapeworm

muscular suckers on the scolex

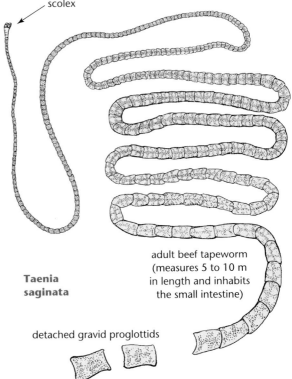

scolex

Taenia saginata

adult beef tapeworm (measures 5 to 10 m in length and inhabits the small intestine)

detached gravid proglottids

proglottid (mature segment)

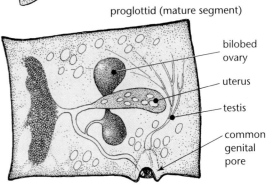

bilobed ovary

uterus

testis

common genital pore

humans by eating undercooked infected beef.

T. solium The pork tapeworm transmitted to humans by eating undercooked infected pork.

taenia (te'ne-ah) See tenia.

taeniasis (te-ni'ah-sis) Infection with tapeworms of the genus *Taenia*.

tag (tag) **1.** A small outgrowth. **2.** To introduce or add an easily identifiable substance (e.g., a radioactive isotope) as a marker or label. **3.** The material so introduced or added.

anal skin t. A polyplike projection in the anus.

skin t. A soft, flesh-colored or deeply pigmented appendage of skin, usually occurring on the neck. Also called acrochordon.

T

tagging (tag'ing) The process of using chemical or radioactive substances as a label or marker for diagnostic or experimental purposes. Also called labeling.

take (tāk) Denoting a successful establishment of a graft or showing signs of an effective vaccination.

talalgia (tal-al'je-ah) Pain in the heel.

talar (ta'lar) Relating to the ankle bone (talus).

talc, talcum (tălk, tal'kum) A soft, fine-grained hydrous magnesium silicate used in cosmetic and pharmaceutical preparations. Also called soapstone.

talcosis (tal-ko'sis) Lung disease resulting from inhalation of talc, usually in association with other minerals (e.g., asbestos and silica); it occurs in workers exposed to such materials.

taliped, talipedic (tal'ĭ-ped, tal-ĭ-pe'dik) Clubfooted.

talipes (tal'ĭ-pēz) General term that denotes a deformity involving the talus (ankle bone) and the foot, which results in an abnormal shape and position.

  t. arcuatus See talipes cavus.

  t. calcaneovalgus A relatively common congenital disorder in which the ankle joint is dorsiflexed and the foot is everted; believed to be caused by the position of the fetus in the uterus; the opposite of clubfoot (talipes equinovarus).

  t. calcaneovarus A deformity of the ankle and foot with combined features of talipes calcaneus and talipes varus.

  t. calcaneus Foot deformity characterized by an elevated forefoot and a depressed heel, placing the weight of the body on the heel; generally the result of calf muscle paralysis. Also called pes calcaneus.

  t. cavus An exaggerated longitudinal arch of the foot due to

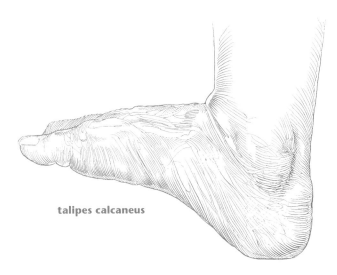

talipes calcaneus

contraction of the plantar fascia; may also be caused by a deformed bony arch. Also called talipes arcuatus; cavus.

  t. equinovalgus Foot deformity in which the characteristics of talipes equinus and talipes valgus are present, with weight borne on the metatarsophalangeal joints; the heel is elevated and turned outward from the body's midline.

  t. equinovarus Congenital deformity of the foot in which only the outer portion of the foot touches the ground; with the ankle plantar flexed, the foot is inverted, and the anterior half of the foot is directed toward the middle. Also called clubfoot.

  t. equinus A deformity characterized by fixed plantar extension of the foot, causing the weight of the body to rest on the ball of the foot or the metatarsophalangeal joints; the ankle joint is plantar flexed. Also called tip foot; pes equinus.

  t. planovalgus A deformity of the foot in which the characteristics of both talipes planus (flatfoot) and talipes valgus are present, with body weight distributed along the medial edge of the everted foot; the heel is turned outward and the foot's outer border is more elevated than the inner border; it may be congenital (permanent) or caused by reflex spasm of the muscles controlling the foot. Also called pes planovalgus.

  t. planus See flatfoot.

  t. valgus Outward turning of the foot, causing only the inner side of the sole to touch the ground; accompanied by flattening of the longitudinal arch. Also called pes valgus; pes pronatus.

  t. varus Deformity considered to be an incomplete form of clubfoot (talipes equinovarus); characterized by a turning inward of the foot, causing only the outer part of the sole to touch the ground; accompanied by increased height of the longitudinal arch. Also called crossfoot; pes varus.

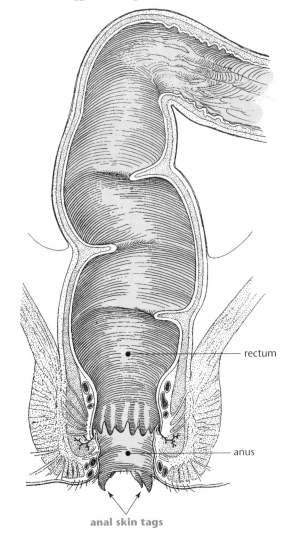

rectum

anus

anal skin tags

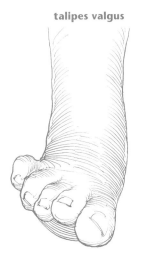

talipes valgus

talipes varus

T

talo- Combining form meaning the ankle bone (talus).

talocalcaneal, talocalcanean (ta-lo-kal-ka'ne-al, ta-lo-kal-ka'ne-an) Relating to the ankle bone and the heel bone (talus and calcaneus).

talocrural (ta-lo-kroo'ral) Relating to the ankle joint.

talofibular (ta-lo-fib'u-lar) Relating to the ankle bone and the thin bone in the leg, the fibula.

talonavicular (ta-lo-nah-vik'u-lar) Relating to the ankle bone (talus) and the navicular bone (in the foot).

taloscaphoid (ta-lo-skaf'oid) Talonavicular.

talotibial (ta-lo-tib'e-al) Relating to the ankle bone (talus) and the shinbone (tibia).

talus (ta'lus) The large bone at the ankle articulating with the two leg bones (tibia and fibula) to form the ankle joint. Popularly called ankle bone; formerly called astragalus. See also table of bones.

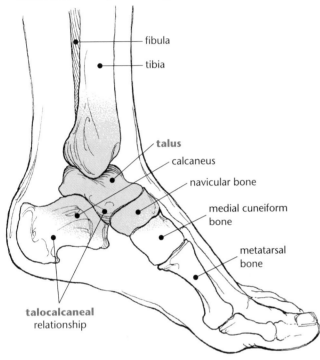

tambour (tam-boor') A drum-shaped apparatus for recording arterial pulsations.

tamoxifen (tah-moks'ĭ-fen) An antiestrogen agent administered orally for the palliative treatment of breast cancer.

tampon (tam'pon) A plug or ball of any absorbent material placed in a canal or cavity to absorb secretions or to control bleeding.

tamponade (tam-pon-ād') Application of external pressure (e.g., to stop a bleeding).

   cardiac t. Restriction of the heart's capacity to fill with blood due to compression by accumulation of fluid in the heart's enveloping sac (pericardium).

tamponing, tamponment (tam'pon-ing, tam-pon'ment) The placing of a tampon.

tandem (tan'dem) **1.** An intracavitary applicator containing radioactive material used in local irradiation (e.g., of a gynecological cancer). **2.** Denoting an arrangement of two or more objects placed one behind the other.

tangle (tang'gl) A twisted, interwoven mass of fibers.

   neurofibrillary t. Bundles of fibrils in the cytoplasm of nerve cells that displace and encircle the nuclei; found in the brain in various conditions, including Alzheimer's disease and postencephalitic Parkinson's disease.

tannate (tan'āt) A salt of tannic acid.

tannic acid (tan'ik as'id) Substance present in the bark and fruit of various plants and in tea leaves; used as an astringent; formerly used in the treatment of diarrhea; it can cause liver damage. Also called tannin.

tannin (tan'in) See tannic acid.

tantalum (tan'tah-lum) A metalic element; symbol Ta, atomic number 73, atomic weight 180.95; used in surgical appliances and prostheses (e.g., skull plate, wire mesh in the abdominal wall). Inhalation of industrial tantalum dust can cause acute and chronic injury to the airways and lung tissues.

tantrum (tan'trum) Unprovoked outburst of bad temper or unreasonable anger; it may be accompanied by violent acts or gestures.

tap (tap) **1.** To deliver a quick, gentle blow or blows (e.g., when eliciting a tendon reflex). **2.** To strike lightly but sharply and audibly. **3.** To withdraw fluid from a body cavity.

   spinal t. See lumbar puncture, under puncture.

tapetum (tah-pe'tum) **1.** In the brain, the portions of the corpus callosum that border the posterior horns (laterally) of the lateral ventricles. **2.** In the eye, the outer and posterior part of the vascular coat (choroid) of the eyeball.

tapeworm (tāp'werm) A ribbon-shaped worm (class Cestoda) that infects human or animal intestines; its body consists of a head (scolex) with hooks or sucking structures by which it attaches to the intestinal wall of its host, and a series of four to several thousand segments (proglottids) containing reproductive organs.

   beef t. See *Taenia saginata*, under *Taenia*.

   dwarf mouse t. See *Hymenolepis nana*, under *Hymenolepis*.

   fish t. See *Diphyllobothrium latum*, under *Diphyllobothrium*.

   mouse t. See *Hymenolepis nana*, under *Hymenolepis*.

   pork t. See *Taenia solium*, under *Taenia*.

tapinocephalic (tap-ĭ-no-se-fal'ik) Relating to a flattened skull.

tapinocephaly (tap-ĭ-no-sef'ah-le) Deformity in which the skull is abnormally flat.

tapotement (tah-pōt-maw') Tapping with the side of the hand; a hand movement used in massage.

TAR Acronym for Thrombocytopenia and Absent Radius. See under syndrome.

tar (tahr) Any dark, semisolid, organic fluid, especially coal tar.

   coal t. A by-product of the destructive distillation of bituminous coal; used topically in the treatment of chronic skin disorders such as psoriasis.

   pine t. A by-product of the destructive distillation of pine wood; used topically in the treatment of such skin disorders as eczema.

tarantula (tah-ran'tu-lah) Any large hairy spider capable of inflicting a painful but not significantly poisonous bite.

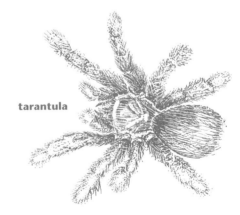

tarantula

   American t. *Eurypelma hentzii*, a large, greatly feared, although harmless spider; it causes a pinprick bite similar to a bee sting.

tardive (tahr'div) Late; applied to the characteristic lesion of a disease, or symptoms that are late in appearing.

target (tahr'get) The object toward which an activity is directed (e.g., the object upon which the eye is fixed in vision training or testing).

tarry (tar'e) Tarlike. See also tarry stool, under stool.

tarsadenitis (tahr-sad-ĕ-ni'tis) Inflammation of the borders of the eyelids, including the sebaceous (tarsal) glands.

tarsal (tahr'sal) **1.** Relating to the bones forming the posterior portion of the foot (the tarsus). **2.** Relating to the borders of an eyelid.

tarsalgia (tahr-sal'je-ah) Pain in the posterior portion of the foot (the tarsus).

tarsectomy (tahr-sek'to-me) **1.** Removal of bones from the posterior portion of the foot (the tarsus). **2.** Removal of the margin of an eyelid, or part of it.

tarsitis (tahr-si'tis) **1.** Inflammation of the margin of an eyelid. **2.** Inflammation of the bones or joints of the posterior part of the foot (the tarsus).

tarso-, tars- Combining forms meaning tarsus.

tarsoclasis, tarsoclasia (tahr-sok'lah-sis, tahr-so-kla'ze-ah) Operative fracture of the tarsus as part of a reparative procedure.

tarsomalacia (tahr-so-mah-la'she-ah) Softening of the tarsal cartilage of an eyelid.

tarsometatarsal (tahr-so-met-ah-tahr'sal) Relating to the tarsus and metatarsus.

tarsophyma (tahr-so-fi'mah) A tumor on the margin of an eyelid.

tarsorrhaphy (tahr-sor'ah-fe) Suturing of the upper and lower eyelids; may be done partially to reduce the length of the palpebral fissure or to protect the cornea in certain conditions.

tarsotomy (tahr-sot'o-me) Surgical cut of an eyelid.

tarsus (tahr'sus) **1.** The skeleton of the posterior part of the foot between the leg and the metatarsus; it consists of seven bones. **2.** The fibrous tissue that strengthens the edge of the eyelid.

tartar (tahr'tahr) See dental calculus, under calculus.

taste (tāst) **1.** The special sense that distinguishes different sensations evoked by substances in contact with the taste buds. **2.** To perceive such sensations.

tattoo (tah-tu') The intentional or accidental introduction of pigment into the tissues through punctures.

  amalgam t. In dentistry, a symptomatic blue-black spot most commonly seen on the gums (gingiva) or adjacent areas, caused by introduction of silver amalgam material into the mucous membrane either by inadvertent laceration during removal of old fillings, by fragmentation of amalgam and deposition into the tooth socket during tooth extraction, or by deposition of amalgam fragments into the surgical wound during root canal therapy.

tau (tou) (T,τ) A protein that plays an important role in the transport of nutrients within nerve cells (neurons). Abnormal function of tau protein may be involved in the genesis of Alzheimer's disease.

taurine (taw'rin) Water-soluble crystals produced by the decomposition of taurocholic acid.

taurocholate (taw-ro-ko'lāt) A salt of taurocholic acid.

taurocholic acid (taw-ro-ko'lik as'id) A constituent of bile.

taurodontism (taw-ro-don'tizm) Abnormal development of the molars marked by enlargement of crown and pulp cavity with short roots; affects primarily permanent teeth (secondary dentition).

taxis (tak'sis) **1.** Movement or growth of organisms in response to a physical stimulus (e.g., light, heat, electricity), either toward or away from the stimulus. **2.** Correction by applying gentle pressure (e.g., to a dislocation or a hernia).

Taxol (tak'sol) Trade name for a preparation of paclitaxel.

taxon (tak'son), pl. tax'a One of the categories in a systematic classification (e.g., species, genus, family).

taxonomy (tak-son'o-me) The classification of organisms into categories (taxa) and the assignment of scientific names that reflect their relationships.

team (tēm) A group of people working as a collaborative unit.

  multidisciplinary t. A group of professional individuals representing a variety of health disciplines who coordinate their efforts to diagnose and treat problems, especially cases of child abuse and neglect.

tear (tēr) **1.** Fluid secreted by the lacrimal glands, which keeps the eye surface moist. **2.** The act of secreting tears.

  artificial t.'s Liquid preparations to supplement deficient secretion of tears (e.g., in keratoconjunctivitis sicca).

  crocodile t.'s See crocodile tears syndrome, under syndrome.

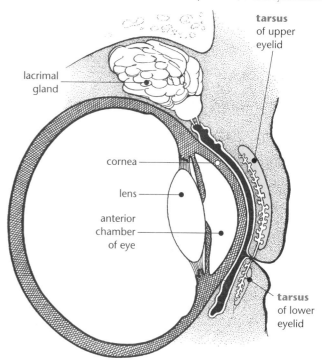

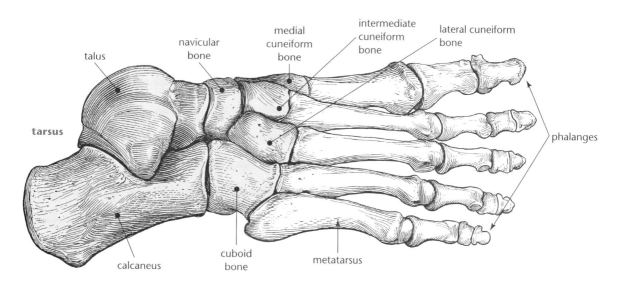

tear (tār) 1. To rip or pull apart. 2. A rip or break of continuity of a structure.

    bowstring t. A longitudinal split of a meniscus, a semilunar cartilage within the knee joint; the anterior and posterior portions of the cartilage remain attached to the joint capsule while the free inner border becomes displaced across the joint like a bowstring. Also called bucket-handle tear.

    bucket-handle t. See bowstring tear.

    meningeal t. A tear of the membranes (meninges) covering the brain and spinal cord, usually occurring with a fracture of the base of the skull, manifested clinically as a discharge of cerebrospinal fluid (CSF) through the nose or ears.

    retinal t. Tear of the retina typically characterized by the presence of retinal tissue or "lid" (operculum) over the tear; caused by mechanical force, usually by vitreous traction or trauma.

tease (tēz) To separate tissues gently with a fine instrument such as a needle.

teaspoon (te'spoon) (tsp) Small spoon used as a measure in the dosage of liquid medicines; equivalent to 5 milliliters or 1 dram.

teat (tēt) A nipple or breast.

technetium (tek-ne'she-um) Artificial radioactive element; symbol Tc, atomic number 43, atomic weight 99. It has specialized industrial applications.

technetium 99m (^{99m}Tc) Radioisotope of technetium with a physical half-life of 6 hours; it is suitable for many clinical and research purposes as a radiotracer for scanning many organs because of its readily detected 140 keV gamma rays and relatively short half-life. However, radioactivity has been reported to remain in the milk of lactating women from 15 hours to 3 days.

technical (tek'nĭ-kal) Relating to a technique.

technician (tek-nish'an) A person who has been trained in the performance of special technical procedures.

    dental laboratory t. Person trained in the making of dental appliances (e.g., dentures, orthodontic appliances, restorations, crown and bridge work).

    x-ray t. Person trained to make x-ray films of body parts.

technique (tek-nēk') A systematic method of accomplishing a skillful task, especially a surgical operation, a scientific experiment, laboratory testing, and the operation of diagnostic and therapeutic devices.

    fluorescent antibody t. Either of two techniques (direct and indirect) that use antibody treated with a fluorescent dye to detect the presence of antigen in tissue sections; useful for detecting *Streptococcus pneumoniae*, group B streptococci, respiratory syncytial virus, and other infectious microorganisms. Also called direct fluorescent antibody test.

    flush t. Technique for determining the systolic blood pressure of infants, whereby the hand or foot is blanched by manual squeezing or application of an elastic bandage before applying the pressure cuff on the extremity; the flush of the extremity is observed as the cuff pressure is slowly reduced; used for detecting coarctation of the aorta when applied simultaneously to upper and lower extremities.

    hydro-flow t. In dentistry, a method of cavity preparation in which the tooth being prepared is kept under a stream of water.

    Irving's t. See Irving's operation, under operation.

    Madlener's t. See Madlener's operation, under operation.

    McDonald's t. In obstetrics, measurement of the uterus by placing a centimeter tape on the abdomen and following the curvature of the abdominal surface from the pubic bone margin to the top of the uterine mass; useful for detecting fetal growth retardation, especially in the third trimester. Also called McDonald's maneuver.

    Mohs' t. See Mohs' surgery, under surgery.

    Pomeroy's t. See Pomeroy's operation, under operation.

technologist (tek-nol'o-jist) A technician.

    medical t. A laboratory worker who is a graduate of a four-year college with special training in the performance of various procedures in clinical pathology.

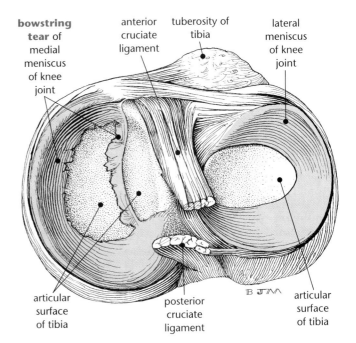

bowstring tear of medial meniscus of knee joint — anterior cruciate ligament — tuberosity of tibia — lateral meniscus of knee joint — articular surface of tibia — posterior cruciate ligament — articular surface of tibia

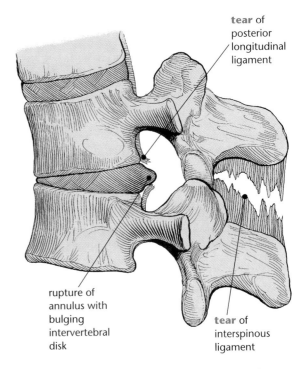

tear of posterior longitudinal ligament — rupture of annulus with bulging intervertebral disk — tear of interspinous ligament

    radiation t. See radiation therapist, under therapist.

technology (tek-nol'o-je) The application of scientific knowledge to the practical purposes of any field, including methods, techniques, and instrumentation.

    dental t. The field of dentistry concerned with the design and construction of dental appliances.

    medical t. Application of technology to the field of medicine, including a variety of diagnostic procedures and therapeutic and surgical methods and techniques.

    pharmaceutical t. Application of technology to pharmacy, pharmacology, and the pharmaceutical industry; it includes methods, techniques, and instrumentation in the preparation, dispensing, packaging, and storing of all preparations used for diagnosis and treatment.

tectiform (tek'tĭ-form) Shaped like a roof.

tectorial (tek-to're-al) Relating to an overlying or rooflike structure.

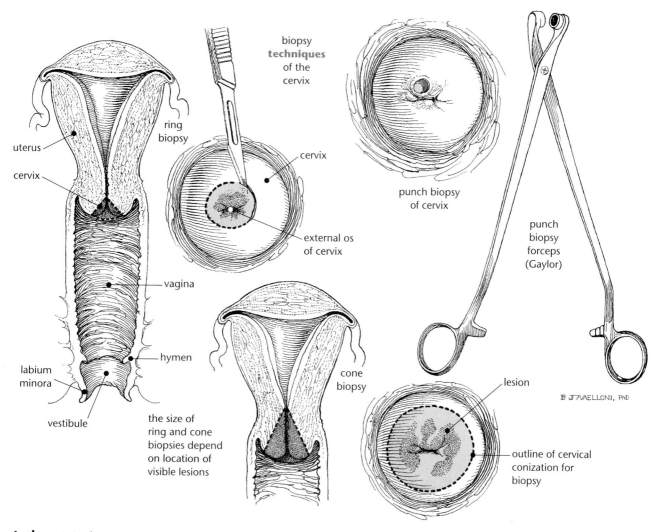

biopsy **techniques** of the cervix

uterus

cervix

vagina

hymen

labium minora

vestibule

ring biopsy

cervix

external os of cervix

cone biopsy

the size of ring and cone biopsies depend on location of visible lesions

punch biopsy of cervix

punch biopsy forceps (Gaylor)

lesion

outline of cervical conization for biopsy

B J VAELLONI, PhD

tectorium (tek-to′re-um) Any overlying structure.

tectum (tek′tum) Any rooflike structure, especially the roof plate of the midbrain.

teething (tēth′ing) Eruption of teeth in a baby.

tegmen (teg′men) Rooflike structure that covers a part.

   t. tympani The roof of the middle ear chamber.

   t. ventriculi quarti The roof of the fourth ventricle of the brain.

tegmentum (teg-men′tum) The larger dorsal portion of the brainstem.

tegument (teg′u-ment) See integument.

tela (te′lah) pl. te′lae A delicate weblike membrane.

   t. subcutanea See subcutis.

telalgia (tel-al′je-ah) Referred pain.

telangiectasia (tel-an′je-ek-ta′ze-ah) Abnormal dilatation of groups of tiny blood vessels in skin or mucous membranes.

hereditary hemorrhagic t. Uncommon inherited disorder characterized by multiple small (less than 5 mm) dilatations on skin and mucous membranes, especially of the face, nose, and gastrointestinal tract, causing bleeding; it worsens with advancing age; an autosomal dominant inheritance. Also called Osler-Weber-Rendu disease; Osler's disease; Rendu-Osler-Weber syndrome.

   spider t. A group of tiny focal dilated arterioles (often pulsating) arranged in a radial pattern around a central core, occurring

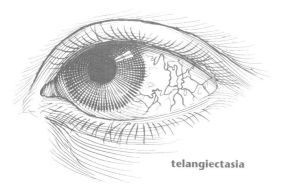

telangiectasia

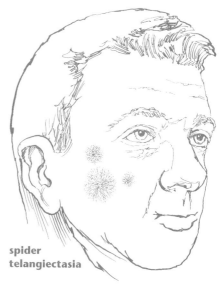

spider telangiectasia

T

typically above the waist. A small number of spider telangiectasias frequently is associated with hyperestrogenic states (e.g., pregnancy and estrogen therapy); they are also seen normally in children. A large number usually indicates an underlying systemic disease (e.g., cirrhosis of the liver). Also called arterial spider; spider nevus; nevus araneus.

telangiectatic (tel-an-je-ek-tat′ik) Relating to telangiectasia.

telangioma (tel-an-je-o′mah) Tumor made up of dilated capillaries or arterioles.

tele-, telo- Combining forms meaning at a distance; end.

telecardiogram (tel-ĕ-kar′de-o-gram) See telelectrocardiogram.

telecardiophone (tel-ĕ-kar′de-o-fōn) Instrument for relaying heart sounds to listeners at a distance from the patient.

telediagnosis (tel-ĕ-di-ag-no′sis) Diagnosis by means of electronic devices that relay data from a patient located at a distance from a receiving station where the physician evaluates the data received.

telelectrocardiogram (tel-ĕ-lek-tro-kar′de-o-gram) Electrocardiogram recorded at some site distant from the patient. Also called telecardiogram.

telemetry (tĕ-lem′e-tre) The science and technology of remote sensing for monitoring living systems with radio transmitters placed in or on animal or human subjects.

 cardiac t. Transmission of electrical signals from the heart to a receiving location where the electrocardiogram is displayed for monitoring.

telepathy (tĕ-lep′ah-te) Communication of thought and feelings from one person to another without the aid of physical means; generally not accepted as a scientifically valid phenomenon since the means of thought transference is unknown.

telereceptor (tel-ĕ-re-sep′tor) An organ (e.g., the eye) that perceives sense stimulation from a distance.

teletherapy (tel-ĕ-ther′ah-pe) Treatment in which the radiation source is at a distance from the body, using such equipment as a cobalt machine or a linear accelerator.

tellurium (tĕ-lu′re-um) Semimetallic element; symbol Te, atomic number 52, atomic weight 127.6. It has many industrial uses, especially in the rubber and electronics industries. Symptoms of acute and chronic occupational exposure to tellurium and its compounds include respiratory irritation, garlicky breath odor, metallic taste, fatigue, drowsiness, dryness of mouth and skin, and skin discoloration.

telomere (tel′o-mēr) One of the two ends of a chromosome.

telophase (tel′o-fāz) The last stage of cell division by mitosis.

temperament (tem′per-ah-ment) The unique predispositions of an individual that influence his or her way of thinking, behaving, and reacting.

temperature (tem′per-ah-tūr) (t) 1. Heat intensity as measured in any of several arbitrary scales. 2. Popular term for fever.

 absolute t. (T) Temperature measured on an absolute scale.

 critical t. Temperature above which a gas cannot be reduced to a liquid.

 maximum t. Temperature above which bacteria will not grow.

 neonate t. The range of normal temperatures in a term newborn infant. Skin temperature: 96.9 to 97.7°F (36.0–36.5°C); core temperature: 97.7 to 99.5°F (36.5–37.5°C).

 normal body t. The average oral temperature in healthy human adults (40 years or younger): 98.2°F (36.8°C), with upper limits ranging between an early morning temperature of 98.9°F (37.2°C) and an evening temperature of 99.9°F (37.7°C); other variables include exercise, eating and drinking, age, and, in women, the time of the menstrual cycle.

template (tem′plāt) 1. In dentistry, a curved or flat plate used as a guide in the setting of artificial teeth. 2. In genetics, the macromolecular mold for the synthesis of complementary macromolecules, as in replication of DNA and the transcription of DNA to RNA.

temple (tem′pl) The lateral area of the head on either side of the forehead above the zygomatic arch.

tempolabile (tem-po-la′bil) Changed or destroyed with the passage of time; applied to a serum.

temporal (tem′po-ral) 1. Relating to the side of the head or temple (e.g., bones of the skull, lobes of the brain). 2. Not permanent.

temporo- Combining form meaning the temple.

temporomandibular (tem′po-ro-man-dib′u-lar) Relating to the temporal bone and lower jaw (mandible) (e.g., a joint connecting the mandible to the skull).

temporo-occipital (tem′po-ro oks-ip′ĭ-tal) Relating to the temporal and occipital bones of the skull.

temporoparietal (tem′po-ro-pah-ri′ĕ-tal) Relating to the temporal and the parietal bones, at the sides and upper part of the head.

tempostabile, tempostable (tem-po-sta′bil, tem-po-sta′bl) Not subject to change by the passage of time; applied to certain chemicals.

tenacious (tĕ-na′shus) Sticky.

tenacity (tĕ-nas′ĭ-te) The condition of being sticky.

tenaculum (tĕ-nak′u-lum) A hooked surgical clamp designed to hold structures such as blood vessels without undue pressure.

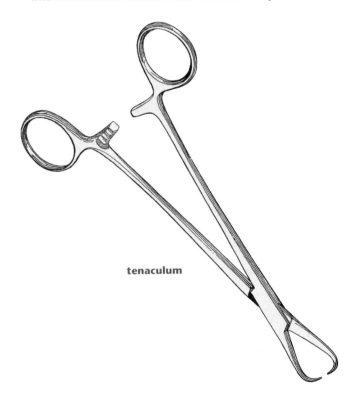

tenaculum

tenalgia (te-nal′je-ah) Pain in a tendon. Also called tenontodynia; tenodynia.

tender (ten′der) Painful or highly sensitive on pressure.

tenderness (ten′der-nes) Abnormal sensitivity to pressure or contact, usually a sign of inflammation.

 rebound t. Pain felt when pressure is released suddenly; in the abdomen it is typical of peritonitis.

tendinitis (ten-dī-ni′tis) See tendonitis.

tendinoplasty (ten′dī-no-plas′te) See tenoplasty.

tendinous (ten′dī-nus) Relating to a tendon.

tendo- Combining form meaning tendon.

tendo Achillis (ten′do ah-kil′ez) See calcaneal tendon, under tendon.

NORMAL RECTAL BODY TEMPERATURES

SPECIES	°F (±1°F)	°C(±0.5°C)
mouse	97	36
man	98.6	37.0
cat	101.5	38.5
dog	102	39
chicken	106.2	41.5

T

tendo calcaneus (ten'do kal-ka'ne-us) See calcaneal tendon, under tendon.

tendolysis (ten-dol'ĭ-sis) Operation to free a tendon from adhesions by cutting them away from the tendon surface. Also called tenolysis.

tendon (ten'dun) Fibrous band attaching a muscle to a bone.

   Achilles t. See calcaneal tendon.

   calcaneal t. The common tendon attaching the gastrocnemius and soleus muscles of the calf to the heel bone (calcaneus). Also called Achilles tendon; tendo calcaneus; tendo Achillis; heel tendon.

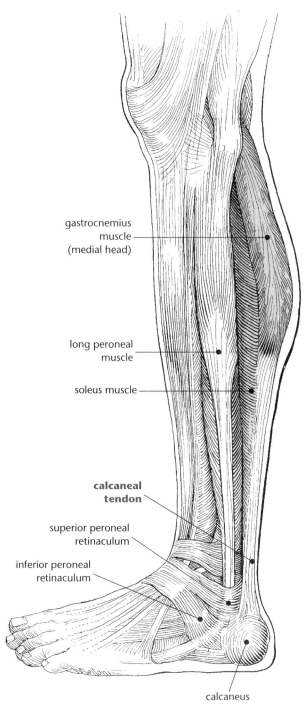

gastrocnemius muscle (medial head)

long peroneal muscle

soleus muscle

calcaneal tendon

superior peroneal retinaculum

inferior peroneal retinaculum

calcaneus

   common annular t. A fibrous ring situated within the back of the eye socket (orbit) and attached to the superior, inferior, and medial margins of the optic canal; it serves as origin for the four rectus muscles of the eye. Also called anulus tendineus communis; common tendinous ring; ligament of Zinn.

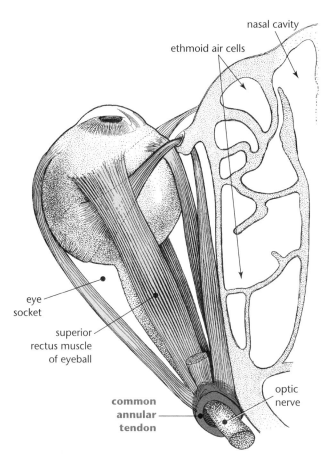

nasal cavity

ethmoid air cells

eye socket

superior rectus muscle of eyeball

common annular tendon

optic nerve

   conjoined t. The fused tendons of two abdominal muscles: the transverse muscle of abdomen (transversus abdominis) and the internal oblique muscle of abdomen (obliquus internus abdominis); it inserts onto the crest of the pubic bone and the pectineal line. Also called inguinal falx; conjoint tendon.

   conjoint t. See conjoined tendon.

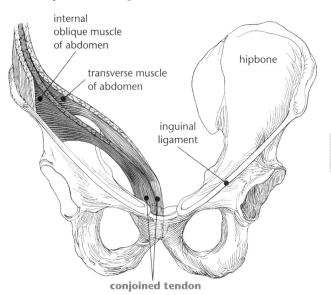

internal oblique muscle of abdomen

transverse muscle of abdomen

hipbone

inguinal ligament

conjoined tendon

   hamstring t. One of the strong tendons at the back of the knee, on either side of the popliteal fossa, that attach the back muscles of the thigh to bones of the leg: *lateral hamstring t.*, a tendon attaching the biceps muscle of thigh (biceps femoris) to the fibula; and *medial hamstring t.*, tendon attaching the semitendinous (semitendinosus) and the semimembranous (semimembranosus) muscles to the tibia.

T

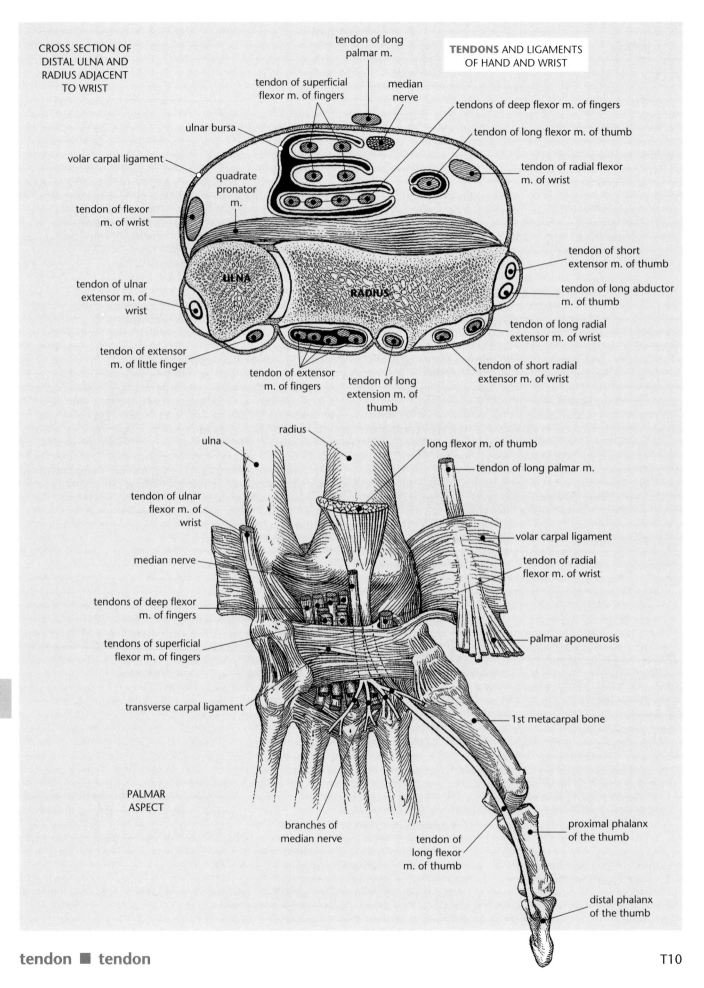

CROSS SECTION OF
DISTAL ULNA AND
RADIUS ADJACENT
TO WRIST

TENDONS AND LIGAMENTS
OF HAND AND WRIST

tendon of long
palmar m.

tendon of superficial
flexor m. of fingers

median
nerve

tendons of deep flexor m. of fingers

tendon of long flexor m. of thumb

ulnar bursa

volar carpal ligament

quadrate
pronator
m.

tendon of radial flexor
m. of wrist

tendon of flexor
m. of wrist

ULNA

RADIUS

tendon of short
extensor m. of thumb

tendon of ulnar
extensor m. of
wrist

tendon of long abductor
m. of thumb

tendon of long radial
extensor m. of wrist

tendon of extensor
m. of little finger

tendon of extensor
m. of fingers

tendon of long
extension m. of
thumb

tendon of short radial
extensor m. of wrist

radius

ulna

long flexor m. of thumb

tendon of long palmar m.

tendon of ulnar
flexor m. of
wrist

volar carpal ligament

median nerve

tendon of radial
flexor m. of wrist

tendons of deep flexor
m. of fingers

tendons of superficial
flexor m. of fingers

palmar aponeurosis

transverse carpal ligament

1st metacarpal bone

PALMAR
ASPECT

branches of
median nerve

tendon of
long flexor
m. of thumb

proximal phalanx
of the thumb

distal phalanx
of the thumb

T

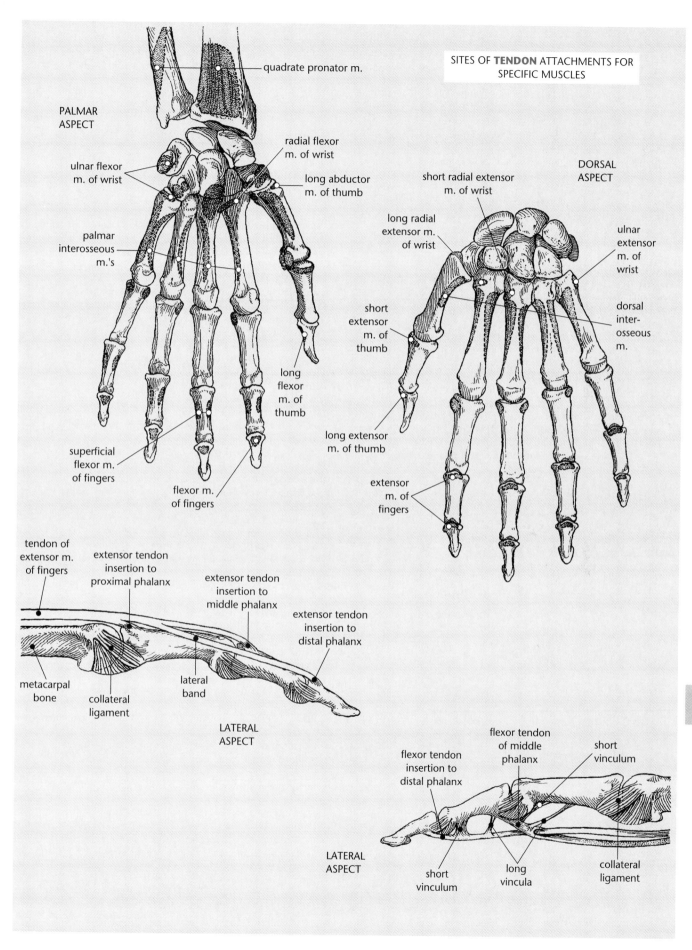

SITES OF **TENDON** ATTACHMENTS FOR SPECIFIC MUSCLES

quadrate pronator m.

PALMAR ASPECT

ulnar flexor m. of wrist

radial flexor m. of wrist

long abductor m. of thumb

palmar interosseous m.'s

superficial flexor m. of fingers

flexor m. of fingers

long flexor m. of thumb

DORSAL ASPECT

short radial extensor m. of wrist

long radial extensor m. of wrist

ulnar extensor m. of wrist

short extensor m. of thumb

dorsal interosseous m.

long extensor m. of thumb

extensor m. of fingers

tendon of extensor m. of fingers

extensor tendon insertion to proximal phalanx

extensor tendon insertion to middle phalanx

extensor tendon insertion to distal phalanx

metacarpal bone

collateral ligament

lateral band

LATERAL ASPECT

flexor tendon of middle phalanx

short vinculum

flexor tendon insertion to distal phalanx

short vinculum

long vincula

collateral ligament

LATERAL ASPECT

heel t. See calcaneal tendon.

tendonitis (ten-do-ni'tis) Inflammation of a tendon, the fibrous tissue attaching muscle to bone or to another muscle, most frequently caused by repeated or severe trauma, strain, or excessive unaccustomed exercise; or it may result from inflammatory lesions (e.g., rheumatoid arthritis); usually accompanied by inflammation of the membrane enveloping the tendon. Also called tendinitis; tenonitis. See also tenosynovitis.

    calcific t. Tendonitis resulting from deposition of calcium salts in a tendon, causing pain that may be sudden and severe.

    suppurative t. Tendonitis with pus formation frequently occurring in the fingers, causing swelling and tenderness, with flexion of the digit and pain on extension.

tendoplasty (ten'do-plas-te) See tenoplasty.

tendotomy (ten-dot'o-me) See tenotomy.

tendosynovitis (ten-do-sin-o-vi'tis) See tenosynovitis.

tendovaginal (ten-do-vaj'ĭ-nal) Relating to a tendon and its covering sheath.

tendovaginitis (ten-do-vaj-i-ni'tis) See tenosynovitis.

tenectomy (te-nek'to-me) Removal of a portion of a tendon.

tenesmic (te-nez'mik) Relating to tenesmus.

tenesmus (te-nez'mus) A painful, ineffectual straining to defecate or urinate.

tenia, taenia (te'ne-ah), pl. te'niae, tae'niae **1.** Any narrow bandlike anatomic structure. **2.** Any flatworm of the genus *Taenia*. **3.** The line of attachment of a choroid plexus.

    t. coli Any of three conspicuous bands formed by the longitudinal fibers of the muscular layer of the colon extending from the cecum to the rectum, where the fibers disperse; the bands are about 3/8 inch broad, somewhat equidistant from each other, and because they are invariably shorter than the other coats of the colon, cause sacculations of the intervening wall of the colon. The bands increase in thickness as they progress distally; they consist of the tenia libera, tenia mesocolica, and tenia omentalis.

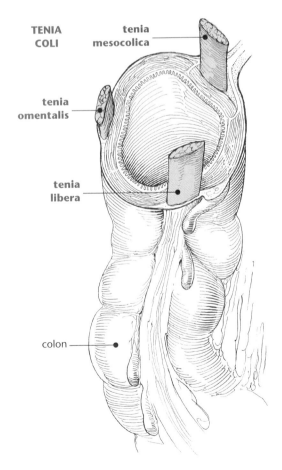

TENIA COLI

tenia mesocolica

tenia omentalis

tenia libera

colon

t. libera One of the teniae coli positioned anteriorly along the entire colon, except for the transverse segment, where it is placed inferiorly; it lies almost midway between the tenia mesocolica and tenia omentalis. Also called free band of colon; anterior band of colon.

    t. mesocolica One of the teniae coli positioned on the posteromedial surface of the entire colon, except for the transverse segment, where it is placed posteriorly; it lies along the attachment of the mesocolon to the colon. Also called mesocolic band.

    t. omentalis One of the teniae coli positioned on the posterolateral surface of the entire colon, except for the transverse segment, where it is placed anterosuperiorly; it lies along the site of attachment of the posterior layers of the greater omentum. Also called omental band.

    t. thalami The tenia, or line of attachment, of the choroid plexus that runs along the dorsomedial border of the thalamus; the lateral ventricles lie above it and the third ventricle lies below it. Also called tenia of thalamus; tenia of third ventricle.

    t. of thalamus See tenia thalami.

    t. of third ventricle See tenia thalami.

teniacide (te'ne-ah-sīd) An agent that kills tapeworms.

teniafuge (te'ne-ah-fūj) An agent causing expulsion of tapeworms.

tenial (te'ne-al) **1.** Relating to tapeworms. **2.** Relating to a ribbonlike band of tissue (tenia).

teniasis (te-ni'ah-sis) Infestation with tapeworms.

tenioid (te'ne-oid) Resembling a tapeworm.

tenodesis (ten-od'ĕ-sis) The anchoring of a tendon by suturing.

tenodynia (ten-o-din'e-ah) See tenalgia.

tenolysis (te-nol'ĭ-sis) See tendolysis.

tenonectomy (ten-o-nek'to-me) Procedure for shortening a tendon by removing a segment and joining the two remaining ends.

tenonitis (ten-o-ni'tis) See tendonitis.

tenonto-, tenon-, teno- Combining forms meaning tendon.

tenontodynia (ten-on-to-din'e-ah) See tenalgia.

tenontoplasty (ten-on'to-plas-te) See tenoplasty.

tenophyte (ten'o-fīt) A growth of cartilaginous or bony tissue on a tendon.

tenoplasty (ten'o-plas-te) Reparative surgery of a tendon. Also called tendonoplasty; tendoplasty; tenontoplasty.

tenorrhaphy (ten-or'ah-fe) Suturing of a divided tendon, the junction made by end-to-end stitching or by weaving one tendon segment with the other, using nylon or wire stitches.

tenosynovectomy (ten-o-sin-o-vek'to-me) Surgical removal of the sheath enveloping a tendon.

tenosynovitis (ten-o-sin-o-vi'tis) Inflammation of the inner lining of a tendon sheath and enclosed tendon; may be associated with systemic disorders (e.g., rheumatoid arthritis, gout, amyloidosis), with elevated blood cholesterol levels, with gonococcal infection (in females), or may be caused by mechanical strain; although simultaneously involving the enclosed tendon, the sheath lining is the site of maximum inflammation. Also called tendosynovitis; tendovaginitis. See also tendonitis.

    t. crepitans Tenosynovitis that produces a crackling sound upon movement of the affected tendon.

    nodular t. A sharply localized tenosynovitis involving usually peripheral joints, considered by some authorities to be a benign tumor, rather than an inflammatory condition, with a tendency to recur after surgical removal. Also called giant cell tumor of tendon sheath.

    stenosing t. Tenosynovitis occurring when there is a disproportion between the diameter of a tendon and the space or tunnel in which the tendon glides, causing scarring of the tendon sheath and a flexion contraction (e.g., of a finger).

    suppurative t. Tenosynovitis caused by direct invasion by pus-forming bacteria; organisms may gain entry into the tendon sheath cavity through a wound (e.g., when a surgeon accidentally punctures the tendon sheath while suturing adjacent structures).

    traumatic t. Accumulation of synovial fluid and fibrin in a tendon sheath cavity, which may progress to adhesion formation;

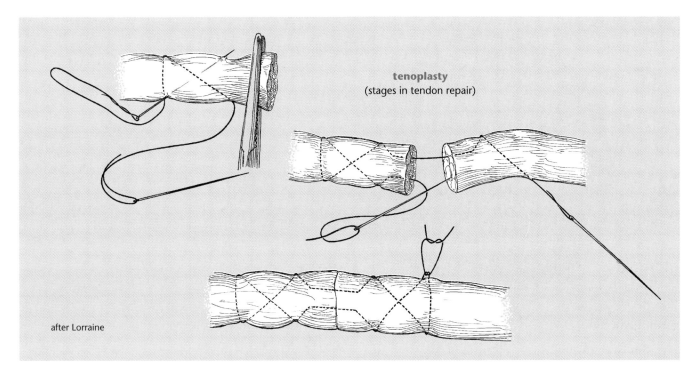

tenoplasty
(stages in tendon repair)

after Lorraine

most often occurs as an occupational condition (e.g., in the arms of laborers and the wrists of stenographers). Also called traumatic synovitis.

tenotomy (ten-ot'o-me) The cutting of a tendon as a corrective measure in certain conditions. Also called tendotomy.

tenovaginitis (ten-o-vaj-ĭ-ni'tis) See tenosynovitis.

tension (ten'shun) (T) **1.** The act of stretching. **2.** The state of being taut; tautness. **3.** A force tending to produce expansion (e.g., of a liquid or gas) when a confining force is removed. **4.** Emotional strain.

   arterial t. The pressure on the wall of an artery produced by the blood current at the peak of a pulse wave.

   interfacial surface t. The resistance to separation posed by a film separating two surfaces, such as that of a film of saliva separating a denture base and the oral tissues.

   intraocular t. See intraocular pressure, under pressure.

   ocular t. (Tn) See intraocular pressure, under pressure.

   premenstrual t. See premenstrual syndrome, under syndrome.

   surface t. Force tending to pull together molecules on the surface of a liquid.

tensor (ten'sor) Tending to make a part tense or firm; applied to muscles (e.g., the tensor tympani muscle that renders the eardrum taut).

tent (tent) **1.** A covering of plastic or canvas placed over a patient's bed for inhalation of oxygen (oxygen tent) or steam (steam tent). **2.** An expandable, cylindrical plug for keeping an orifice open.

   laminaria t. A sterile tent made of dried stems of the seaweed *Laminaria digitata,* measuring 1 to 2 mm in diameter and 5 to 7 mm in length, with a cord attached to one end to facilitate removal. The tent is inserted in the cervical canal and left in place 6 to l2 hours for gradual, atraumatic expansion of the cervix; employed as a preoperative procedure in first-trimester abortion by suction aspiration or D & C, or during second-trimester abortion as a supplement to other procedures; also used to soften and dilate an "unripe" cervix in preparation for induction of labor at or near term. See also *Laminaria digitata.*

   plastic face t. Tent placed over the patient's face to facilitate administration of gaseous medications.

tentorial (ten-to're-al) Relating to the tentorium of the cerebellum.

tentorium cerebelli (ten-to're-um ser-e-bel'li) The tentorium of the cerebellum; a fold of dura mater separating the cerebellum from the occipital lobes of the cerebrum.

tephromalacia (tef-ro-mah-la'she-ah) Abnormal softening of the gray substance of the brain and spinal cord.

ter- Combining form meaning three times.

terato- Combining form meaning developmental malformation.

teratocarcinoma (ter'ah-to-kar-sĭ-no'mah) A highly malignant tumor found most frequently in the testis, composed of several types of cells and ranging in appearance from a hemorrhagic mass to a small lesion with a fibrous scar.

teratogen (ter'ah-to-jen) Any environmental agent, microorganism, or drug that causes physical defects in the developing embryo or fetus.

teratogenesis (ter'ah-to-jen'ĕ-sis) The origin of fetal malformations.

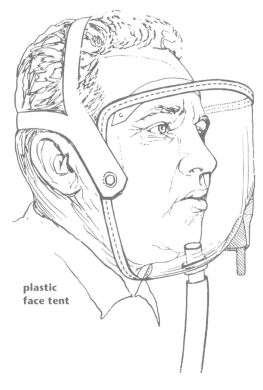

plastic
face tent

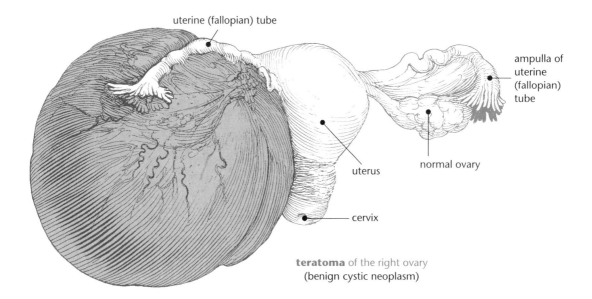

uterine (fallopian) tube

ampulla of uterine (fallopian) tube

normal ovary

uterus

cervix

teratoma of the right ovary
(benign cystic neoplasm)

teratogenic (ter-ah-to-jen′ik) Causing birth defects in the developing embryo.

teratoid (ter′ah-toid) Resembling a malformed fetus.

teratology (ter-ah-tol′o-je) The subspecialty of developmental anatomy concerned with abnormal development in all its aspects.

teratoma (ter-ah-to′mah) Any of a group of tumors containing a variety of tissues (e.g., hair, bone, teeth, skin) that are normally found in different parts of the body; occurs most commonly in the ovary, testis, and along the midline of the chest between the lungs; some are benign, others malignant; may occur at any age.

  benign cystic t. See dermoid cyst, under cyst.

  mature benign t. See dermoid cyst, under cyst.

teratomatous (ter-ah-to′mah-tus) Of the nature of teratomas.

teratophobia (ter-ah-to-fo′be-ah) Abnormally exaggerated fear of giving birth to a malformed baby.

terbium (ter′be-um) Metallic element; symbol Tb, atomic number 65, atomic weight 158.924.

terbutaline (ter-bu′tah-lēn) Drug used primarily as a bronchodilator in the treatment of asthma and emphysema. Adverse effects include tremors, nausea, restlessness, and, rarely, palpitations.

teres (te′rēz) Round and elongated; applied to ligaments and muscles.

terfenadine (ter-fen′ah-dēn) An antihistamine drug useful in the treatment of hay fever (seasonal allergic rhinitis), asthma, allergic conjunctivitis, and chronic hives of unknown cause. It causes less drowsiness than most antihistamines; possible adverse effects include nausea, loss of appetite, and skin rash.

term (term) A definite time period; applied to a newborn infant at the end of a normal-length pregnancy.

terminal (ter′mĭ-nal) 1. Relating to an end. 2. Relating to or forming an extremity or end of any body part.

  axon t. The knoblike terminal expansion of an axonal branch at the site of a synapse; it is in apposition either to other nerve cells (forming interneuronal zones), to muscles (forming neuromuscular junctions), or to glands (forming neuroglandular junctions). Also called bouton terminaux; terminal bouton; terminal button; endfoot; neuropodium.

terra (ter′ah) Latin for earth.

  t. alba See kaolin.

tertian (ter′shun) Recurring every third day, such as certain malarial fevers.

tesla (T) (tes′lah) The unit of magnetic flux density in the International System of Units, equal to 1 weber per square meter.

test (test) 1. An examination. 2. A means of determining the presence, quality, constitution, or concentration of a substance. 3. To perform such a function. 4. A systematic procedure to assess the function of specific parts of the body. 5. A substance used in a test.

  achievement t. A standardized educational test that measures the degree of knowledge or skills acquired after instruction in specific subjects, as opposed to an intelligence test. Widely used achievement tests include the Stanford Achievement Test and the Wide Range Achievement Test, Revised.

  acidified serum lysis t. A test to establish the diagnosis of paroxysmal nocturnal hemoglobinuria (PNH) by determining the susceptibility of red blood cells (erythrocytes) to lyse when incubated with the patient's acidified fresh serum; normally red blood cells do not undergo hemolysis; when hemolysis occurs, it indicates PNH. Also called Ham's test.

  acid perfusion t. See esophageal acid infusion test.

  acid phosphatase t. A test to detect cancer of the prostate gland by determining the level of serum acid phosphatase, the group of phosphatase enzymes that appear primarily in the prostate gland and semen; a markedly increased acid phosphatase level indicates that a tumor has metastasized beyond the prostatic capsule (the more widespread the tumor, the greater the probability of higher levels being evident); moderately increased levels could indicate prostatic infarction, Paget's disease, or Gaucher's disease.

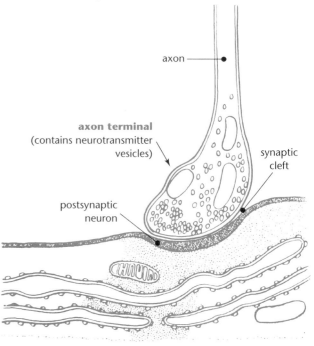

axon

axon terminal
(contains neurotransmitter vesicles)

synaptic cleft

postsynaptic neuron

T

acid phosphatase t. for semen A forensic medical test for semen from a rape victim's vaginal aspirate or lavage, determined by acid phosphatase activity (semen has a very high concentration of acid phosphatase compared with other body fluids); a high level of acid phosphatase is a positive sign of semen, even though sperm may not be demonstrated.

acid reflux t. A test to evaluate competency of the lower esophageal sphincter by detecting the amount of backward flow of acid (reflux) from the stomach to the esophagus; performed by monitoring the pH in the distal esophagus with an electrode attached to a manometric catheter; the pH of the esophagus is normally above 5.0; a sharp increase in backflow may acidify the pH to as low as 1.5. Repeated reflux causes inflammation, resulting in heartburn (pyrosis). Also called esophageal acidity test.

acoustic reflex t. A test that measures the normal bilateral contraction of the stapedius muscles and tensor tympani muscles in response to loud acoustic stimuli (from 70 dB to 100 dB above hearing threshold). The contracted stapedius muscle normally draws the innermost ossicle, the stapes, outward and upward, and the contracted tensor tympani muscle normally draws the eardrum slightly inward; these movements reduce the transmission of vibrations from the eardrum to the inner ear. Absence of a response may indicate lesions of the vestibulocochlear (8th cranial) nerve or brainstem, sensorineural hearing loss, or fixation of the stapes; used to differentiate between conductive and sensorineural deafness and to diagnose vestibular schwannoma.

ACTH t. See ACTH stimulation test.

ACTH stimulation t. A test for adrenal cortex function, specifically a measurement of cortisol production following administration of adrenocorticotropic hormone (ACTH); it normally evokes a pronounced rise in plasma cortisol levels; a noticeably limited increase or absence of any increase of the level of plasma cortisol indicates Addison's disease. Also called ACTH test.

activated partial thromboplastin time (APTT) t. A test for evaluating the clotting factors of the intrinsic pathways by measuring the time required for formation of a fibrin clot; normally a fibrin clot forms 25 to 35 seconds after the addition of reagent; prolonged bleeding time indicates deficiency of certain clotting factors, the presence of heparin, or the presence of antibodies to specific clotting factors. The test reflects platelet response to injury.

adhesion t. See erythrocyte adhesion test.

Adson's t. A test for the detection of thoracic outlet syndrome; the patient is seated with hands resting on thighs, chin held high, head turned to the side to be examined; if on deep inspiration the radial pulse diminishes or diappears on the affected side, the test is positive. Also called Adson's maneuver.

agglutination inhibition t. for pregnancy See immunologic pregnancy test.

Albini's E t. A test for visual acuity utilizing the E test chart for three- or four-year-old children or illiterates by asking them to indicate in which direction the legs of the "E" are pointing to; the visual acuity chart comprises a bold letter E of various sizes and in various directions. Also called illiterate E test; E-type eye chart test.

alkali denaturation t. A test to determine the concentration of fetal hemoglobin (HgF) in a blood sample; the test is predicated on the fact that hemoglobins, with the exception of HgF, are denatured and precipitated by alkali to alkaline hematin; HgF is alkali-resistant.

alpha-fetoprotein t. A simple blood test to assess the fetus for down's syndrome and certain brain and spinal malformations. Unlike amniocentesis and chorionic villus sampling (CVS), the test does not increase the risk of miscarriage.

alternate cover t. A test for ocular alignment assumed by the eyes during binocular fixation on a small object; while the patient is observing the object, an occluder is alternately placed in front of each eye for a few seconds without permitting interim binocular viewing; if the eye moves when it is uncovered, a phoria or strabismus is present. The condition can be neutralized with a corrective prism. Also called cover text; see also unilateral cover test.

amebocyte lysate t. See limulus lysate test.

Ames t. A widely used screening test for detecting carcinogenicity; a mutant strain of the bacteria *Salmonella typhinium*, which does not have the capacity to synthesize histidine, is inoculated into a histidine-deficient medium containing the test substance; if the substance produces mutations that develop the capacity to synthesize histidine, the substance is a mutagen and considered carcinogenic.

Amsler t. A test for detecting and measuring defects in the central visual field demonstrated onto an Amsler chart.

ANA t. See antinuclear antibody test.

antibiotic sensitivity t. A test of various antimicrobial agents to determine the most effective in combating a specific bacterial infection; disks impregnated with different drugs are placed on a growing bacterial culture in a petri dish in which agar is used as the solidifying agent; the drug on the disk with the least growth around it is deemed the drug of choice. Also called antimicrobial susceptibility test.

antibody screening t. See indirect Coombs' test.

antimicrobial susceptibility t. See antibiotic sensitivity test.

antinuclear antibody (ANA) t. A test that measures the relative concentration of antinuclear antibodies in a serum sample by identifying circulating antibodies using the indirect Coombs' test (antibody screening test). The test is normal for antinuclear antibodies at a titer of 1:32 or below. Slightly elevated titers may be indicative of viral disease, autoimmune disease, collagen vascular disease, or chronic liver disease. High antinuclear antibody titers indicate systemic lupus erythematosus (SLE). Used in screening for SLE and to monitor the effectiveness of immunosuppressive therapy for SLE.

antistreptolysin-O t. See streptococcal antibody test.

t. anxiety t. A self-reporting test consisting of items concerning fear and worry about taking tests and physiological activity, such as heart rate, sweating, etc., before, during, and after tests.

aptitude t. A general test that measures a person's skills, interests, talents, and abilities to undertake study or training in a given field; designed to anticipate a person's probable level of success in various types of learning, before any instruction or training takes place; useful in vocational counseling.

ASLO t. See streptococcal antibody test.

ASO t. See streptococcal antibody test.

association t. A test based on association reaction; a method of examining the content of the mind, whereby the subject is required to respond as quickly as possible to a given stimulus word with the first word (reactive word) that comes to mind; the reaction time and the nature of the reactive words are noted; used as a diagnostic aid in psychology and psychiatry. Also called word association test.

autohemolysis t. A test to assess certain hemolytic states by quantifying spontaneous hemolysis when sterile defibrinated blood is incubated at 37°C for 24 to 48 hours; the integrity of the cell membrane of normal red blood cells slowly breaks down, causing release of hemoglobin; cells with metabolic defects undergo spontaneous hemolysis to a far greater extent.

Bagolini striated glass t. A test to assess the state of binocularity (retinal correspondence) of the eyes, using a Bagolini striated glass mounted in front of each eye, with the striations oriented 90° apart, while the subject views a test target and light source; the number of streaks perceived or the relative positions of streaks to each other indicate the state of retinal correspondence.

band t. See lupus band test.

Bárány's caloric t. A clinical test for vestibular function of the ear performed by irrigating the external auditory canal with either hot or cold water; this normally stimulates the vestibular apparatus, causing involuntary, rapid, rhythmic movement of the eyeball (nystagmus) and incoordination of voluntary movements (past-pointing); in vestibular dysfunction, the response is noticeably diminished or completely lacking. Also called nystagmus test.

Bayley Scales of Infant Development T. See Bayley Scales of Infant Development, under scale.

Bender gestalt t. A diagnostic assessment test of visual motor function in which the subject is asked to copy nine standard geometric designs on blank paper. The drawings are scored by test professionals (usually clinical psychologists) based on proficiency of shape, pattern, and orientation; its chief application is to determine learning disabilities, general developmental delay, or organic brain dysfunction in both children and adults and the level of development of visual motor function in children; secondarily used to assess personality variables. Also called Bender visual-motor gestalt test.

Bender visual-motor gestalt t. See Bender gestalt test.

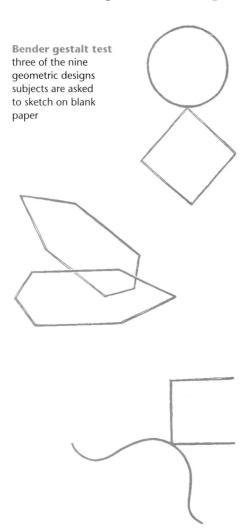

Bender gestalt test
three of the nine geometric designs subjects are asked to sketch on blank paper

benzidine t. A chemical test to detect the presence of occult blood in urine or feces; a benzidine agent (benzidine, glacial acetic acid, and hydrogen peroxide) is added to the specimen; a blue color develops in the presence of blood.

Bernstein t. See esophageal acid infusion test.

Binet t. See Stanford-Binet Intelligence Test.

biuret t. A chemical test used to determine the presence of biuret (a derivative of urea) or two or more peptide bonds in body fluids; the alkaline solution of the sample is mixed with alkaline copper sulfate; a positive test is indicated when a reddish purple color appears. Also called biuret reaction.

blind t. A method of evaluation that uses an independent observer to record the results of tests or procedures without knowing the contents of the samples or the results that are anticipated or might be expected.

bromsulphalein t. A test for liver (hepatic) function and biliary excretory capacity in which the dye bromsulphalein (a hepatic function determinant) is injected intravenously into the patient;

after 45 minutes, a sample of venous blood is analyzed for the dye; a measurement of less than 5% of the dye remaining in the circulation after 45 minutes is considered normal; if there is a larger amount remaining, it may be due to decreased blood flow through the liver, biliary obstruction, or damage to liver cells. Also called BSP test.

BSP t. See bromsulphalein test.

bubble stability t. See foam stability test.

CAGE t. A screening test for alcoholism. Patients are asked if they ever cut down on drinking; feel annoyed by criticisms about drinking; have guilty feelings about drinking; have an eye opener in the morning.

14^C-aminopyrine breath test A test of aminopyrine absorption and its metabolism in the liver, by measuring the amount of radioactive carbon exhaled following an oral dose of 14^C-labeled aminopyrine.

capillary fragility t. A tourniquet test to determine the weakness of the capillary walls and to identify platelet deficiency; a circle 2.5 cm in diameter is drawn on the inner aspect of the forearm 4 cm below the elbow crease, and a blood pressure cuff is inflated above the elbow to the mean arterial pressure for 10 minutes; the minute hemorrhagic spots (cutaneous petechiae) that appear within the circle are counted; up to 10 cutaneous petechiae are considered normal, anything over 20 is not normal and usually occurs in conditions related to bleeding defects, such as thrombocytopenia, thromboasthenia, vitamin C deficiency (scurvy), and purpura senilis; anything between 10 and 20 is marginal. Also called Rumpel-Leede test; capillary resistance test; tourniquet test.

capillary resistance t. See capillary fragility test.

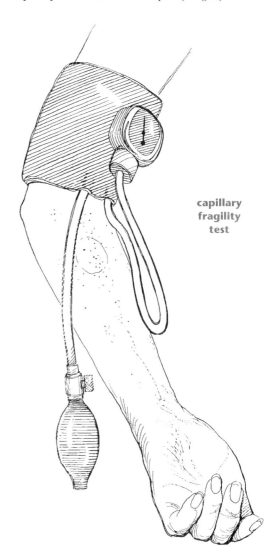

capillary fragility test

carbohydrate utilization t. A biochemical test used in the identification of clinically important fungi or bacteria, based on the ability of the organism to ferment carbohydrate in the presence of an indicator.

Casoni intradermal t. A test to diagnose hydatid disease, in which hydatid fluid is injected into the skin; an immediate or delayed development of a wheal-and-flare skin reaction denotes hydatid infection. Also called Casoni skin test; echinococcus skin test.

Casoni skin t. See Casoni intradermal test.

cholesterol t. See total cholesterol test.

chorionic villus sampling (CVS) t. A test for prenatal diagnosis that allows the detection of fetal defects as early as the eighth week of pregnancy; a sample of placental tissue (chorionic villi) is obtained either through the uterine cervix or through an abdominal puncture with a needle and syringe under the guidance of ultrasound visualization; the chromosomes of the chorionic cells are then analyzed.

clomiphene t. A test for the diagnosis of subnormal secretion of sex hormones by measuring the pituitary gonadotropin reserve following the administration of the gonad-stimulating nonsteroid compound clomiphene.

coccidioidin t. A skin test to determine current or past infection with the fungus *Coccidioides immitis,* by intracutaneous injection of antigens prepared from the fungus; delayed hypersensitivity indicates a positive reaction.

complement fixation t. A widely used test to detect the presence of antibodies and antigens in serum; based on the fact that antibodies, when combined with their specific antigens, are able to fix or remove complement (a system of at least 20 serum proteins designed to destroy foreign cells and to help remove foreign matter), thus making it undetectable in a subsequent test.

contact t's. See patch tests.

contraction stress t. (CST) In obstetrics, a test for assessing a fetus at risk for compromised placental respiratory function (uteroplacental insufficiency). A monitoring device is placed on the maternal abdomen to continuously monitor the fetal heart rate and uterine contractions. Normally, the fetal heart rate increases in response to a contraction; no decelerations occur during the contraction. For the test, contractions are induced (e.g., by intravenous infusion of dilute oxytocin) until three (no more than five) contractions occur, each lasting at least 40 to 60 seconds, for a period of 10 minutes; uterine stimulation is then discontinued but monitoring of the fetal heart rate is continued until uterine contractions have subsided. Test results are interpreted as follows: *Negative (normal),* no late decelerations occur; baseline fetal heart rate is normal. *Postive (abnormal),* late decelerations occur with each three contractions in a 10-minute period, indicating that uteroplacental insufficiency is probably present; may result in a poor fetal outcome. *Equivocal (suspicious),* intermittent, late decelerations occur with the uterine contractions; additional testing is performed, usually within 24 hours. When oxytocin is used to evoke the uterine contractions, the test is called oxytocin challenge test (OCT).

copper sulfate t. An expeditious test to find the specific gravity of blood that serves as an indirect measure of hematocrit, for use in determining blood donor acceptability. An adequate level of hematocrit in adult females for blood donation is 12.5 g/dL, which corresponds to a specific gravity of 1.053; in adult males a hematocrit of 13.5 g/dL is adequate for blood donation, and it corresponds to a specific gravity of 1.055.

cover t. See alternate cover test; see also unilateral cover test.

cover-uncover t. See unilateral cover test.

creatinine t. A blood test to assess glomular filtration function of the kidney and to screen for kidney damage; kidney impairment causes the elevation of creatinine (a nonprotein end product of creatine metabolism); its level in the blood is directly related to the glomerular filtration rate; normal levels in adult males range from 0.7 to 1.4 mg/dL; in adult females, from 0.6 to 1.0 mg/dL. Elevated levels are generally indicative of diminished function of the kidney. See also creatinine.

cutaneous t. See skin test.

cyanide-nitroprusside t. A qualitative test for the diagnosis of abnormal excretion of cystine (cystinuria) or homocystine (homocystinuria) in the urine or in kidney stones; the test is positive when the urine specimen turns to a purplish red color after sequential exposure to sodium cyanide and nitroprusside.

cytotoxicity t. One used in testing for compatibility for organ transplant, by detecting a complement-requiring reaction between cytotoxic antibodies and cell-surface antigens; living cells are mixed with serum and complement; if antibody to a cell-bound antigen is present, cell death will occur in the presence of complement. Also called cytoxicity test.

cytoxicity t. See cytotoxicity test.

Denver Development Screening T., Revised A commonly used screening test for preschool children that assesses general development.

dexamethasone suppression t. A test for the diagnosis of Cushing's syndrome; the administration of 1 mg of dexamethasone suppresses cortisol secretion to low levels in normal persons but not in those with Cushing's syndrome. Sometimes used to test for organic depression.

differential renal function t. See differential ureteral catheterization test.

differential ureteral catherization t. A test to determine the functional capacity of the left kidney as compared to the right one; ureteral catheters are carefully positioned during cystoscopy into the ureter or pelvis of the kidney bilaterally, and separate measurements are made of urine flow, endogenous creatinine, insulin, para-aminohippuric (PAH) acid, or various urinary solutes from each side. Also called differential renal function test.

dinitrophenylhydrazine t. A screening test for the diagnosis of maple syrup urine disease; an acidic solution of 2,4-dinitrophenyl-hydrazine is added to a subject's urine specimen; if a whitish precipitate forms in the presence of ketoacids, the subject has the disease.

direct antiglobulin t. See direct Coombs' test.

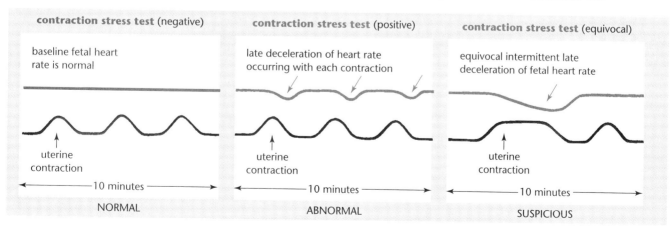

contraction stress test (negative)

baseline fetal heart rate is normal

uterine contraction

← 10 minutes →

NORMAL

contraction stress test (positive)

late deceleration of heart rate occurring with each contraction

uterine contraction

← 10 minutes →

ABNORMAL

contraction stress test (equivocal)

equivocal intermittent late deceleration of fetal heart rate

uterine contraction

← 10 minutes →

SUSPICIOUS

T

test ■ test

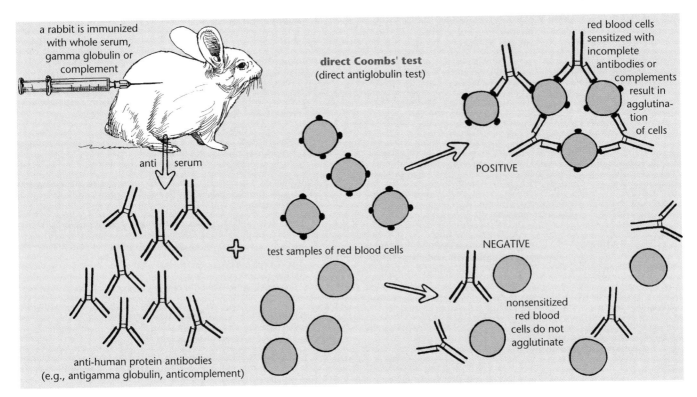

a rabbit is immunized with whole serum, gamma globulin or complement

anti serum

anti-human protein antibodies (e.g., antigamma globulin, anticomplement)

test samples of red blood cells

direct Coombs' test (direct antiglobulin test)

red blood cells sensitized with incomplete antibodies or complements result in agglutination of cells

POSITIVE

NEGATIVE

nonsensitized red blood cells do not agglutinate

direct Coombs' t. A test used to diagnose hemolytic disease in the newborn (HDN) and other types of acquired hemolytic anemias, by detecting antibodies (immunoglobulins) on the surface of circulating red blood cells (RBCs) that occur when the cells become sensitized to an antigen, such as the Rh factor; a sample of the patient's RBCs is washed with saline and mixed with Coombs' antihuman globulin, then centrifuged; clumping (agglutination) results if immunoglobulins or complement is present (positive test). Called a direct test because it requires only one step—the addition of Coombs' serum to washed RBCs. Also called direct antiglobulin test.

direct fluorescent antibody t. See fluorescent antibody technique, under technique.

do-it-yourself diagnostic t. A health test usually performed at home, using a test kit sold over the counter at drugstores, including home pregnancy test, blood-glucose monitoring test, ovulation test, impotence test, urinary tract infection test, hidden (occult) fecal blood test, and test for degenerative vision problems, such as glaucoma and macular degeneration.

double-blind t. A test in which neither the person giving the test nor the subject receiving it knows whether the drug used is active or inert.

double diffusion t. in two dimensions See Ouchterlony test.

draw-a-person t. (a) A psychological test to determine a child's level of intellectual development based upon the complexity of the subject's "best" drawing of a human figure. Also called Goodenough test. (b) A projective personality test requiring a subject to draw a human figure; the drawing reflects the subject's character traits and significant conflicts when assessed against standards that correlate features of the drawing with diagnostic categories. Also called Machover test.

drawer t. A test to assess the state of the cruciate ligaments of the knee; with the knee bent at a 90° angle, if the tibia can be drawn forward on the lower femur, it indicates laxity or tear of the anterior cruciate ligament; if it can be drawn backward, it indicates laxity or tear of the posterior cruciate ligament.

Dugas' t. A test of an injured shoulder to distinguish a dislocation from a fracture; if the elbow of the affected side cannot be brought to touch the chest while the hand is placed on the opposite shoulder, a dislocation of the shoulder is often present.

echinococcus skin t. See Casoni intradermal test.

effort tolerance t. See exercise test.

erythrocyte adherence t. An immune adherence procedure designed to detect the presence of complement-binding antibodies against cell-surface antigens, shown by the immune adhesion phenomenon, that is, adherence of red blood cells (erythrocytes) to the target cells. Also called adhesion test; red cell adhesion test.

erythrocyte fragility t. A test that measures the degree of resistance of red blood cells (erythrocytes) to detruction (hemolysis) in various concentrations of saline solutions; normal erythrocytes show signs of initial hemolysis at concentrations of 0.45 to 0.40% and complete hemolysis at 0.35 to 0.30%. The test is usually performed to confirm the diagnosis of hereditary spherocytosis, by showing a markedly increased level of erythrocyte fragility; increased levels may also be indicative of severe burns, chemical poisoning, and hemolytic disease of the newborn; reduced levels may be indicative of thalassemia, obstructive jaundice, or sickle-cell anemia. Also called fragility test; osmotic fragility test.

erythrocyte sedimentation rate (ESR) t. A test to monitor inflammatory or malignant disease or to detect occult diseases (e.g., tuberculosis) by measuring the time required for red blood cells (erythrocytes) in a whole blood sample to settle to the bottom of a test tube; normal ESRs range up to 20 mm/hour.

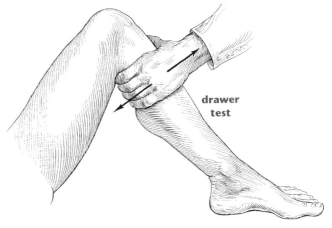

drawer test

test ■ test

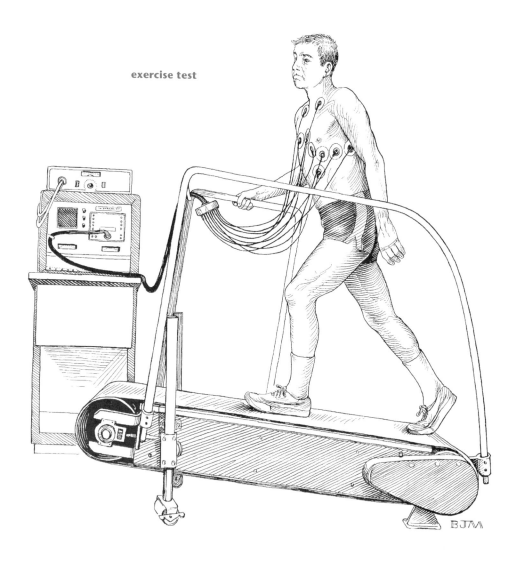

exercise test

esophageal acid infusion t. Test to establish that a pain under the breastbone (sternum) is due to reflux esophagitis; a weak hydrochloric acid solution is instilled into the lower esophagus at a rate of 120 drops per minute; the pain that it causes disappears when the acid solution is replaced by saline solution. Also called Bernstein test; acid perfusion test.

esophageal acidity t. See acid reflux test.

E-type eye chart t. See Albini's E test.

exercise t. A test to assess cardiovascular function through the use of exercise on a treadmill or pedaling a stationary bicycle (bicycle ergometer) while under continuous electrocardiographic monitoring; useful in detecting coronary artery disease. Also called stress test; exercise tolerance test; effort tolerance test.

exercise tolerance t. See exercise test.

FANA t. See fluorescent antinuclear antibody test.

fern t. A test to determine the presence or absence of ovulation or the time of ovulation; a qualitative test of estrogenic activity; cervical mucus is spread on a histologic slide; upon drying, a fern-frond pattern is indicative of the presence of estrogen without the influence of progesterone; the extent of ferning is reflected in the level of estrogen, being especially elevated at the time of ovulation; a non-frond pattern is indicative of the absence of ovulation.

ferric chloride t. A test for the diagnosis of phenylketonuria, which is indicated when a sample of urine turns blue-green with the addition of ferric chloride.

ferritin t. A test to screen for iron deficiency (low iron storage) and iron overload by determining the ferritin level (iron-storage protein level) by radioimmunoassay; the level is directly related to the amount of iron stored in the body; the serum ferritin ranges from 20 to 300 ng/ml in normal men, and from 20 to 140 ng/ml in normal women; increased levels may indicate iron overload, infection, or inflammation; decreased levels may indicate chronic iron deficiency. See also ferritin.

finger-to-finger t. A clinical test for coordinated movements of the arms in which the subject is told, with arms extended, to approximate the tips of both index fingers; tremors and inability to comply, with eyes opened or closed, are indicative of an impairment.

finger-nose t. A clinical test to assess the ability to coordinate voluntary movement of the arm; with arm extended to one side of the body, the person, first with the eyes open, then with them closed, is asked to slowly touch the end of his or her nose with the tip of an extended index finger.

Fishberg concentration t. An assessment of kidney function by testing kidney water conservation; the subject drinks 200 ml of fluid with dinner, and overnight is deprived of additional fluid; urine specimens are collected upon awakening and again one and two hours later, and specific gravity is measured; if less than 1.024, there is a high probability of impairment of kidney function, or deficiency of antidiuretic hormone.

fluorescein instillation t. A test to determine the patency of the nasolacrimal drainage system (from the eye to the nasal cavity); a dilute solution of fluorescein (orange-red crystalline compound) is instilled in the conjunctival sac, behind the eyelid; if the passage is not obstructed the fluorescein appears in the nasal cavity (at the inferior nasal meatus).

fluorescent antinuclear antibody t. A test for identifying

T

T19

test ■ test

antibodies in serum by the use of fluorescence-labeled antiglobulin serum; useful in the diagnosis of collagen-vascular diseases, such as lupus erythematosus and mixed connective tissue disease. Also called FANA test.

fluorescent treponemal antibody absorption t. A confirmatory test for syphilis; the patient's serum (after removal of nonspecific antibodies) is incubated with a slide preparation of a special spirochete strain of *Treponema pallidum* (as antigen); specific antibodies attaching to the treponemal organisms are demonstrated with fluorescence-labeled antihuman globulin serum; positive tests are seen in 80 to 90% of cases of primary syphilis, and practically all cases of secondary and late syphilis; minimally reactive tests may be indicative of systemic lupus erythematosus, pregnancy, or genital herpes; normal findings show no fluorescence. *Treponema pallidum* does not cause detectable immunologic changes in the blood for 14 to 21 days after initial infection. The test is also used to screen for suspected false-positive results of Venereal Disease Research Laboratory (VDRL) tests. Also called FTA-ABS test; FTA test.

foam stability t. An amniotic fluid test to detect risk of respiratory distress syndrome (RDS) in the fetus; amniotic fluid from mature fetal lungs contains an essential surface-active substance (surfactant); when the amniotic fluid is placed in a test tube, along with saline and ethanol, and shaken vigorously for 15 seconds before being placed upright for 15 minutes, the surfactant causes a ring of bubbles to occur on the surface of the solution, indicating pulmonary maturity; if the bubbles fail to appear or are poorly formed, the test is negative and indicates varying degrees of high risk of respiratory distress syndrome. Also called shake test; bubble stability test.

forensic t. Any test that provides information for legal proceedings or argumentation.

fragility t. See erythrocyte fragility test.

FTA t. See fluorescent treponemal antibody absorption test.

FTA-ABS t. See fluorescent treponemal antibody absorption test.

genetic screening t. A test performed on subsets of a population at high risk of transmitting a specific genetic disorder or having a specific disorder; used to identify individuals at risk of developing or passing on inherited illnesses, such as cystic fibrosis; carriers of cystic fibrosis can now be identified by new genetic tests.

glucose oxidase t. A specific test to detect the presence of glucose in urine (glycosuria), in which a commercial reagent test strip (Clinistix, Diastix, or Tes Tape) is dipped into a urine specimen for a specific length of time, then removed; the color the test strip acquired from being in the urine is then compared with the reference color chart (blocks) on the label of the strip container to determine a reading of the glucose level. Normally, no glucose is in the urine; the presence of glucose usually indicates diabetes mellitus, but may also occur in other situations. Also called glucose oxidase paper strip test.

glucose oxidase paper strip t. See glucose oxidase test.

glucose tolerance t. See oral glucose tolerance test and intravenous glucose tolerance test.

glycosylated hemoglobin t. A diagnostic test to monitor the treatment of diabetes mellitus; it measures the amount of detectable glucose that becomes bonded with the hemoglobin A (HgbA) of the red blood cells (glycosylated hemoglobin). The test reflects the average blood glucose level during the preceding two to three months and therefore is a measure of the long-term effectiveness of the diabetes therapy. Normal levels are usually from 5.5 to 7% (percentage of the total hemoglobin); the level increases markedly in patients with uncontrolled or poorly controlled diabetes mellitus.

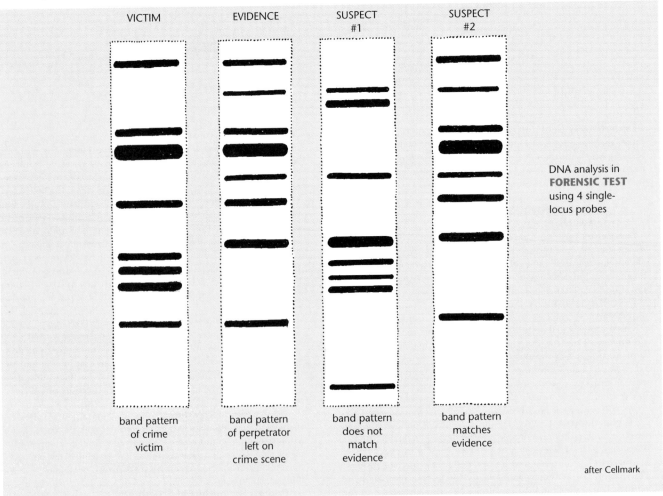

VICTIM — band pattern of crime victim

EVIDENCE — band pattern of perpetrator left on crime scene

SUSPECT #1 — band pattern does not match evidence

SUSPECT #2 — band pattern matches evidence

DNA analysis in **FORENSIC TEST** using 4 single-locus probes

after Cellmark

Goodenough t. See draw-a-person test *(a).*

group t. A test, usually to assess aptitude or intelligence, designed to be administered to a number of persons at one time, in contrast to an individually administered test. Examples include the Scholastic Achievement Test and the Stanford-Binet Intelligence Test.

guaiac t. A chemical test for detection of occult blood; specimen is mixed with glacial acetic acid and gum guaiac solution; blood is present if a blue tint appears upon the addition of hydrogen peroxide.

Gunderson Lyme disease t. A blood test that confirms a diagnosis of Lyme disease by detecting a bacteria-killing antibody in the blood of Lyme victims; it avoids the false-positive problem of other Lyme disease tests.

Guthrie screening t. A test to screen infants for phenylketonuria (PKU) by detecting elevated serum levels of the amino acid phenylalanine; it detects the abnormal phenylalanine levels through growth of *Bacillus subtilis,* an organism that requires phenylalanine to survive. Also called phenylalanine screening test.

HAI t. See rubella HI test.

Ham's t. See acidified serum lysis test.

heat coagulation t. A qualitative test to estimate the amount of protein in urine, by heating the urine specimen and observing the amount of turbidity produced, which serves as a guide for estimating the degree of proteinuria present.

heel-knee t. A test to assess the coordinated movements of the lower extremities; the subject, while lying on his back (supine), is instructed to touch the knee of one leg with the heel of the other, followed by moving the heel slowly down the front of the shinbone (tibia) to the foot; the subject is then asked to repeat the motion with the other leg. Also called heel-shin test.

heel-shin t. See heel-knee test.

Hemoccult t. A proprietary name for a qualitative test to detect blood that is not readily apparent (occult), based upon observing the peroxidase activity of hemoglobin; available as a home kit for the detection of fecal occult blood.

histamine t. *(a)* A test to determine the capacity of the stomach to secrete acid; after aspirating the contents of the stomach and making a basal measurement of the gastric juice, a dose of histamine is injected subcutaneously to stimulate acid production; the gastric contents are then collected in 15-minute aliquots for one hour and analyzed for volume, pH, and tritratable acidity. *(b)* A provocative test for pheochromocytoma; histamine phosphate is administered intravenously; normally there is a prompt, slight decrease in blood pressure, but if a lesion is present in the medulla of the adrenal gland or in the sympathetic paraganglia, a marked rise in blood pressure occurs immediately after the fall. Also called histamine stimulation test.

histamine stimulation t. See histamine test.

HIV infection t.'s Tests for detecting HIV infection; there are three types: Detection of the virus by culturing it, detection of antigens elaborated by the virus and present in the blood, and detection of HIV-specific antibodies that are produced by the infected person's immune system. Two common testing programs, ELISA (enzyme-linked immunosorbent assay) and Western blot analysis, are of the third type. In ELISA, the presence of antibodies in a blood sample is indicated by a reaction-dependent color, its intensity measured by spectrophotometry. In current practice, all blood donors are ELISA-tested; if the test is negative the unit of blood is acceptable; if there is a positive reaction, two further ELISA tests are performed on the same unit; if both are negative, the unit is acceptable; if either is positive, the unit is classified as "repeatably reactive" and is destroyed. Unlike ELISA, the Western blot analysis gives information about particular antibodies among the several that HIV antigens may elicit; it uses electrophoresis and is thus more expensive and demanding of expertise than the ELISA; and it is less likely to give a false-positive or false-negative result. If the specimen is Western-blot positive, the donor is regarded as infected with HIV. False-negatives cannot be totally eliminated because some sera contain too little anti-HIV antibody to be detected (e.g., sera from individuals who have been infected very recently, typically during the first six weeks of infection, or from individuals who form antibody very slowly). Other approaches to testing for HIV infection include fluorescent antibody (FA) techniques for detecting infected T4 lymphocytes and techniques for detecting viral proteins, based either on antigen capture or on reverse transcriptase (RT) activation and synthesis of HIV DNA. See also enzyme-linked immunosorbent assay (ELISA), under assay; Western blot analysis, under analysis.

human chorionic gonadotropin pregnancy t. See immunologic pregnancy test.

t. for hydrocephalus See scinticisternography.

17-hydroxycorticosteroid (17-OHCS) t. A test to assess adrenocortical function by measuring urine levels of 17-OHCS with column chromatography and spectrophotofluorometry using the Porter-Silber reagent; normal urine 17-OHCS values range from 4.5 to 13 mg/24 hours in males, and from 2.5 to l0 mg/24 hours in females; increased levels of urine 17-OHCS are primarily indicative of pituitary tumor, cancer of the adrenal gland, or Cushing's syndrome; decreased levels of urine 17-OHCS are indicative of hypothyroidism or Addison's disease. Also called 17-OHCS test.

hyperemia t. See Moschcowitz test.

illiterate E t. See Albini's test.

immunologic pregnancy t. A test for detection and confirmation of pregnancy by measuring human chorionic gonadotropin (hCG); a common test measures hCG in urine by hemagglutination inhibition, based on antigen-antibody reaction (measurable hCG is not normally found in the urine of nonpregnant women); the test utilizes latex particles coated with hCG as antigen; if the latex particles do not clump, the test results are positive, and the woman is pregnant. Radioimmunoassay and radioreceptor assays may also be used on blood or urine samples. Also called agglutination inhibition test for pregnancy; human chorionic gonadotropin pregnancy test; pregnancy test.

impedance audiometry t. A hearing test that has three parts: tympanometry and measurements of acoustic reflex and reflex decay; it objectively measures acoustic reflex and provides data on sensorineural function.

indirect antiglobulin t. See indirect Coombs' test.

indirect Coombs' t. A test to detect unexpected circulating antibodies to red blood cell (RBC) antigens in the recipient's or donor's serum before transfusion; used in crossmatching of blood and transfusion reaction studies; the patient's serum is incubated with a suspension of donor RBCs; after a washing with saline, antiglobulin (Coombs') serum is added; if no clumping (agglutination) appears, the patient's serum contains no antibodies; agglutination indicates that the cells had been coated or sensitized by antibodies present in the patient's serum; such a reaction demonstrates donor and recipient incompatibility. Also called antibody screening test; indirect antiglobulin test.

inoculation t. A diagnostic test to determine acute anterior polio (poliomyelitis); a patient thought to have polio, prior to evident symptoms, provides a cerebrospinal fluid specimen that is injected into a monkey; if the monkey is afflicted with paralysis within 7 days, acute anterior polio is confirmed in the patient.

intelligence t. Any test that attempts to rate a person's general cognitive competence in relation to that of other people; it generally assesses general knowledge, reasoning, judgment, and organization of analytical skills.

intradermal tuberculin t. See Mantoux test.

intravenous glucose tolerance t. A glucose tolerance test for patients with gastrointestinal abnormalities, such as malabsorption; a rapid infusion of glucose is followed by serial plasma glucose measurements to determine the disappearance rate of glucose per minute; it reflects the patient's ability to dispose of a glucose load.

Ishihara's t. A test for the detection and classification of color blindness, based on the ability to perceive figures (patterns) in a series of multicolored plates in which the numbers or letters are

T

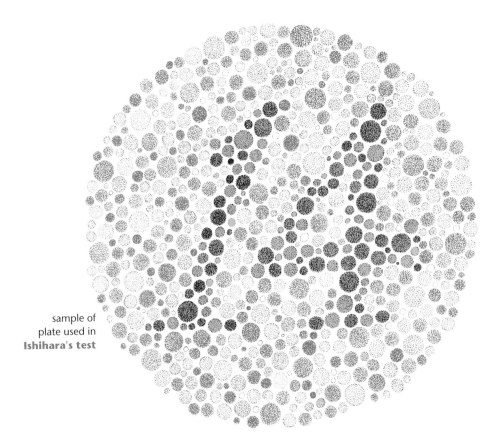

sample of
plate used in
Ishihara's test

printed in primary colors (in dots) surrounded by a multitude of other dots in varied colors. Subjects who are color-blind are not able to distinguish the figures.

¹³¹I uptake t. A test of thyroid function; ¹³¹I-iodide is administered orally; starting 24 hours later the amount of uptake by the thyroid gland is measured at specific intervals and compared against normal values. A greater than normal uptake is indicative of hyperthyroidism; a lower than normal uptake indicates hypothyroidism but may also occur when the subject has received unlabeled iodine. Also called radioactive iodine uptake test; RAI test.

jerk t. See pivot shift test.

Kaufman assessment battery t. for children An individually administered test that assesses intelligence and achievement; designed for young children; often used as a diagnostic test for children who may have learning problems.

Kolmer's t.'s (a) A complement-fixation test for certain bacterial diseases. (b) A rarely used modified Wassermann test for syphilis that employs complement fixation rather than flocculation as the indicator reaction.

Korotkoff's t. A test to assess the integrity of collateral circulation involving an aneurysm; with the artery above the aneurysm compressed, the collateral circulation is deemed good if the blood pressure of the distal or peripheral circulation remains fairly strong.

Kveim t. A test to detect sarcoidosis; Kveim antigen (derived from spleens of individuals with sarcoidosis) is injected intradermally; any nodule developing at the site of inoculation within 1-1/2 months is biopsied and considered positive if it shows evidence of sarcoid tissue (epithelioid cell granulomas). Also called Kveim-Siltzbach test; Nickerson-Kveim test.

Kveim-Siltzbach t. See Kveim test.

Lachman t. A test to determine the integrity of the anterior cruciate ligament of the knee joint; with the patient on his or her back, the knee is flexed 20° to 30°; the tibia is then pulled forward and the amount of anterior movement is estimated and compared with that of the normal limb; the point (end point) at which the forward displacement stops is noted. A distinct end point suggests that the anterior cruciate ligament is intact; a soft, indistinct end point indicates that the anterior cruciate ligament is ruptured (positive test).

latex t. See latex agglutination test.

latex agglutination t. A passive agglutination test in which minute spherical particles of latex in suspension are used as passive carriers of absorbed antigens; the particles agglutinate in the presence of antibody specific for the absorbed antigen (e.g., when rheumatoid factor is present in the serum, clumping of the latex particles occurs); frequently used as a test for rheumatoid arthritis, and for the detection of urine human chorionic gonadotropin (hCG) in testing for pregnancy. Also called latex fixation test; latex particle agglutination test; latex test.

latex fixation t. See latex agglutination test.

latex particle agglutination t. See latex agglutination test.

LE cell t. A laboratory test for the diagnosis of systemic lupus erythematosus (SLE); *in vitro* incubation of blood from patients with the disease causes the formation of characteristic LE cells; polymorphonuclear leukocytes (PMNs) engulf (phagocytose) nuclear material from damaged white blood cells, forming the LE cells. This test has been supplanted by the antinuclear antibody test for the diagnosis of SLE.

lepromin t. A test to determine the body's capacity to develop a defense against leprosy by observing skin reactions to an intradermal injection of lepromin (a sterilized extract of leprosy bacilli); persons with cellular immunity to the leprosy bacilli, as well as those with tuberculoid leprosy, develop an inflammatory papule; persons with lepromatous leprosy do not exhibit a reaction. Also called Mitsuda test.

leukocyte bactericidal assay t. An *in vitro* procedure for evaluating the ability (phagocytic capacity) of circulating leukocytes to destroy a culture of live bacteria; deficiencies are attributable to malignancies, systemic illnesses, and certain drug therapies.

Liebermann-Burchard t. A colorimetric test for cholesterol;

T

the specimen is dissolved in chloroform and then mixed with concentrated sulfuric acid and acetic anhydride; the presence of cholesterol is confirmed by the appearance of a violet color that soon changes to green.

limulus t. See limulus lysate test.

limulus lysate t. An *in vitro* test for the detection of gram-negative bacteria; a lysate prepared from the blood cells (amebocytes) of the horseshoe crab (*Limulus polyphemus*) is exposed to a sample of a patient's blood; gram-negative endotoxin induces coagulation of the lysate; toxins from gram-positive bacteria do not coagulate the lysate. Also called amebocyte lysate test; lumulus test.

lupus band t. An immunofluorescence test to determine the existence and prevalence of immunoglobulin (IgG) and complement (C3) deposits at the dermal-epidermal junction of skin specimens from patients with systemic lupus erythematosus (SLE) and discoid lupus erythematosus (DLE); 80% of patients with lupus erythematosus have bands of immunoglobulins in sun-exposed skin, while just 50% of those patients have bands in non-sun-exposed skin. Bands can be seen in a number of other conditions, including contact dermatitis, autoimmune thyroiditis, rheumatoid arthritis, scleroderma, dermatomyositis, acne rosacea, and lepromatous leprosy. Also called band test.

Machover t. See draw-a-person test (*b*).

Mantoux t. A standard type of tuberculin test in which graduated doses of a derivative of tuberculin, such as purified protein derivative (PPD), serves as an antigen (allergen) when injected intradermally using a needle and syringe; considered positive if redness (erythema) and induration of 10-mm diameter occur. Also called intradermal tuberculin test.

Master's two-step exercise t. An electrocardiographic test for coronary insufficiency in which the subject repeatedly ascends and descends two steps, each 9 inches high, for 1-1/2 minutes, repeated again 2 and 6 minutes later; a depression of the RS-T segment of the electrocardiogram (ECG) suggests coronary insufficiency. This test has been replaced by the treadmill stress test.

McCarthy screening t. A developmental screening test designed for children in the early school grades; it assesses motor skills and cognitive development by employing a variety of puzzles and gamelike tasks.

McMurray's t. A test for tears of the posterior aspect of the meniscus in the knee joint. With the patient's knee fully flexed, the examiner palpates the knee with one hand and rotates the foot with the other (a lateral rotation for the medial meniscus, a medial rotation for the lateral meniscus); a palpable painful click indicates a tear (positive test).

MIF t. See migration inhibitory factor test.

migration inhibition t. See migration inhibitory factor test.

migration inhibitory factor (MIF) t. An *in vitro* test for the evaluation of cell-mediated immunity by determining the production of MIF by lymphocytes in response to specific antigens. MIF production does not exist in certain immunodeficiency disorders, such as Hodgkin's disease. Also called MIF test; migration inhibition test.

Mills' t. A test to confirm tennis elbow; with the patient's wrist and fingers fully bent (flexed) and the forearm in a prone position, pain is felt upon extension of the elbow.

Minnesota Multiphasic Personality Inventory (MMPI) t. A widely used psychological test in the form of a questionnaire designed for individuals 16 years of age and over; composed of 500 true-false items that cover facets of personality, including those related to mental disorders; answers are scored by codes, standardized on different diagnostic groups and personality types, and the results are graphed on a personality profile sheet.

Mitsuda t. See lepromin test.

mixed lymphocyte culture t. Test to determine an individual's ability to accept a tissue transplant; lymphocytes from donor and recipient are mixed in culture, whereupon the degree of incompatibility is measured by estimating the number of cells that have undergone transformation and mitosis, or by the amount of absorption of radioactive isotope-labeled thymidine. Also called MLC test.

MLC t. See mixed lymphocyte culture test.

Moloney t. A test for delayed sensitivity to diphtheria toxoid; a small amount of diluted toxoid is administered intradermally; the appearance of a red induration of more than 12 mm in diameter, within 12 to 24 hours, is a positive reaction. Also called Moloney reaction.

Monospot t. See spot test for infectious mononucleosis.

Moschcowitz t. A diagnostic test for arteriosclerosis; a lower limb is made somewhat bloodless with an Esmarch tourniquet bandage; after five minutes, the bandage is removed; normally the color returns to the limb in a few seconds, but in a limb with arteriosclerosis, the color return is markedly slower. Also called hyperemia test.

mucin clot t. A test that assesses synovial fluid, by adding a sample of the fluid to a solution of acetic acid; it should form a good clot; if the formation of the clot is poor, it is indicative of an inflammatory condition (e.g., rheumatoid or septic arthritis). Also called Ropes test.

NBT t. See nitroblue tetrazolium test.

Nickerson-Kveim t. See Kveim test.

nitroblue tetrazolium (NBT) t. Test of neutrophil (polymorphonuclear leukocyte) capacity to destroy (phagocytize) bacteria; incubating NBT with normally active neutrophils causes clumping of reduced NBT, known as formazan pigment; absence of clumping of NBT indicates neutrophil defects, as in chronic granulomatous disease. Also called NBT test.

nitroprusside t. A test for cystinuria; sodium cyanide is first added to the urine specimen, followed by a solution of sodium

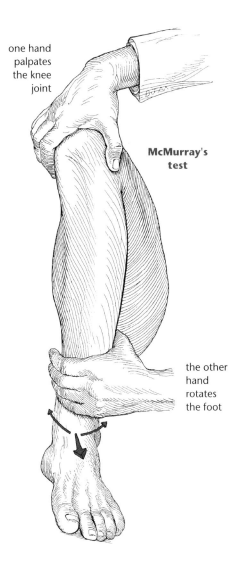

one hand palpates the knee joint

McMurray's test

the other hand rotates the foot

test ■ test

nitroprusside; a red-purple color develops if the cyanide reduces any cystine present in the urine to cysteine.

nonstress t. (NST) In obstetrics, a test for detecting fetal hypoxia; fetal movements are recorded and fetal heart rate changes are monitored by applying a recording system to the maternal abdomen (i.e., by external monitoring). Normally, an increase of the fetal heart rate occurs in response to spontaneous fetal activity; decreased movements usually occur during fetal sleep; they can also occur with such situations as maternal intake of alcohol or drugs or chronic smoking. Test results are interpreted as follows: *Reactive,* at least four fetal movements occur in a 20-minute period and the heart rate accelerates by at least 15 beats per minute during fetal movements; indicates well-being of the fetus. *Nonreactive,* no fetal movement occurs in a 20-minute period, or no heart rate acceleration occurs with fetal movement; usually indicates fetal compromise and frequently is associated with a poor outcome; an oxytocin challenge test (OCT) is usually performed. Deep fetal sleep that lasts up to 45 minutes (resulting in absent fetal movement) may give a false nonreactive result. *Uncertain reactivity,* fewer than four fetal movements ocur in a 20-minute period, or the heart rate accelerates less than 15 beats per minute with fetal movements; additional testing is usually performed.

nonverbal intelligence t. See performance test.

Norland-Cameron single-photon absorptiometry t. See single-photon absorptiometry test.

nystagmus t. See Bárány's caloric test.

17-OHCS t. See 17-hydroxycorticosteroid test.

one-stage prothrombin time t. See prothrombin test.

oral glucose tolerance t. Test measuring the ability of an individual to absorb and metabolize an oral glucose load; used for assessing the presence of diabetes mellitus or reactive hypoglycemia. A minimum of 150 to 200 grams per day of carbohydrate should be included in the diet for three days prior to the test; the subject should refrain from eating anything after midnight preceding the test day; adults ingest 75 grams of glucose in 300 ml of water; children are given 1.75 grams of glucose per kilogram of ideal body weight; blood samples are taken at 0, 30, 60, 90, and 120 minutes after the ingestion of the glucose; the test is normal if the 2-hour value is below 140 mg/dL and the level in none of the samples exceeds 200 mg/dL; a 2-hour value of greater than 200 mg/dL in addition to one other value greater than 200 mg/dL is diagnostic of diabetes mellitus. A fasting plasma glucose above 140 mg/dL on more than one occasion also establishes the diagnosis of diabetes mellitus; infection, severe emotional stress, diuretics, oral contraceptives, glucocorticoids, excess thyroxine, and some psychotropic drugs may cause false-positive results. For diagnosis of reactive hypoglycemia, additional blood samples are obtained at intervals up to 5 hours after ingestion of the glucose.

osmotic fragility t. See erythrocyte fragility test.

Ouchterlony t. A double diffusion test in two dimensions to determine antigenic relationships; antigen and antiserum solutions are placed in separate shallow receptacles (troughs) cut into a flat agar plate that allows radial diffusion of both reactants toward each other; the bands of precipitate forming where the reactants meet (precipitin line) reflect the relative proportion of the reactants. Also called double diffusion test in two dimensions; Ouchterlony technique.

overnight polysomnogram t. A test using a polysomnograph to monitor a patient's sleep through the night in order to diagnose sleep apnea or nocturnal myoclonus. Also called sleep test; sleep apnea test.

oxytocin challenge t. (OCT) See contraction stress test (CST).

Pándy's t. See Pándy's reaction, under reaction.

Pap t. See Papanicolaou test.

Papanicolaou t. A microscopic examination of cells shed or scraped from the female genital tract for evidence of abnormal cells; used especially for early detection of cancer of the cervix. The same test may also be used to examine the respiratory, urinary, and gastrointestinal tracts; and to detect intracellular inclusions indicative of herpesvirus infection. Also called Pap test; Pap smear; Pap smear test; Papanicolaou examination; Papanicolaou smear.

Pap smear t. See Papanicolaou test.

patch t.'s Skin tests to determine which substances cause allergic reactions; filter paper or gauze saturated with a suspected allergen is placed on the skin (usually on the forearm) under a small patch; two days later the patch is removed; a positive reaction is indicated by swelling or redness (erythema) at the site, identifying the substance that caused the allergic contact dermatitis. Also called contact tests.

Patrick's t. A test to assess the possible presence of sacroiliac disorder; with the subject supine, the thigh and knee are flexed and

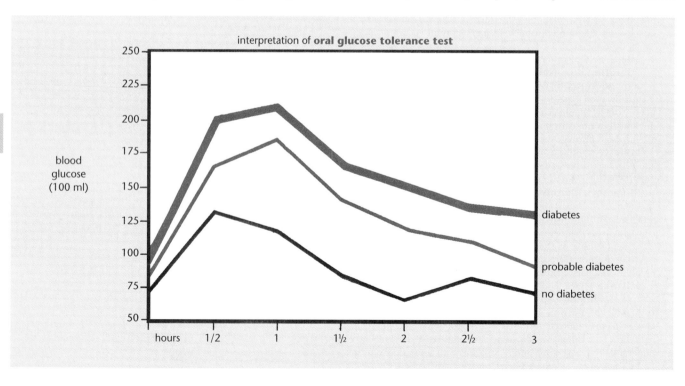

interpretation of **oral glucose tolerance test**

the external malleolus is positioned over the kneecap (patella) of the opposite leg; the knee is then depressed; normally there is no discomfort associated with the procedure; however, if the procedure elicits discomfort, it is indicative of sacroiliac disorder, such as arthritis of the hip.

performance t. A test that minimizes the use of language in assessing intelligence; it relies on the subject to carry out specific actions (e.g., manipulation of objects or copying an intricate network of hedged pathways), thereby examining abilities to deal with objects and their relationships rather than the meanings of language. Also called nonverbal intelligence test.

personality t.'s A general term for psychological tests designed to evaluate the characteristics of a person's self, emotions, and behavior. Also called projection tests.

Phalen's t. A test for determining median nerve compression in the carpal tunnel of the wrist; the wrist is placed in an acute flexed position; if there is median nerve compression, paresthesias of the thumb and adjacent two fingers usually occur after several seconds; normal individuals may develop paresthesias after a few minutes of sustained acute wrist flexion. Also called Phalen's sign.

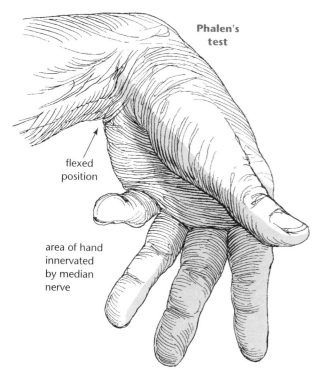

Phalen's test

flexed position

area of hand innervated by median nerve

phentolamine t. Test for pheochromocytoma in patients with established hypertension; intravenous administration of 5 mg of phentolamine (an alpha-adrenergic blocking agent) produces a sustained fall in diastolic blood pressure only in the presence of pheochromocytoma.

phenylalanine screening t. See Guthrie screening test.

pivot shift t. A test to confirm the anterolateral instability of the knee, due to a deficiency of the anterior cruciate ligament; the deficiency is evident (positive test) if, when the knee is fully extended, there is an immediate subluxation of the lateral tibial condyle upon the distal end of the femur. Also called jerk test.

platelet aggregation t. A blood test to assess the ability of platelets to adhere to each other (aggregate) to form a blood clot to prevent bleeding after vascular injury; a standard concentration of platelets is exposed to substances such as epinephrine, adenosine diphosphate (ADP), collagen, or serotonin that normally cause platelets to aggregate; normal platelet aggregation usually occurs in three to five minutes; reduced platelet aggregation may be indicative of Von Willebrand's disease as well as other disorders, including polycythemia vera; it may also be the result of taking certain drugs,

such as aspirin, indomethacin, or other nonsteroidal anti-inflammatory drugs.

porphobilinogen t. See Watson-Schwartz test.

postcoital t. General term for any examination and testing performed after sexual intercourse (coitus) to determine the cause of infertility.

PPD t. See tuberculin test.

precipitation t. See precipitin test.

precipitin t. Any serologic test in which a positive result is indicated by the formation of a precipitate (precipitin reaction), such as an insoluble complex formed when the soluble form of antigen combines with the soluble antibody in the presence of an electrolyte. Also called precipitation test.

pregnancy t. See immunologic pregnancy test.

preimplantation t. A woman's unfertilized eggs (ova) are removed and fertilized in a petri dish; some cells are later removed from each embryo and tested for genetic defects; only those embryos found to be disease-free are transferred to the uterus for implantation.

projection t.'s See personality tests.

prostate-specific antigen t. Blood test for detection of cancer of the prostate; it measures serum concentrations of a protein (antigen) produced exclusively by prostate epithelial cells; levels of up to 4 micrograms/liter are generally considered normal; higher levels are seen when the gland is enlarged or in the presence of cancer. Also called PSA test.

prothrombin t. A test that determines the amount of prothrombin present in blood, based on the clotting time of oxalated blood plasma in the presence of extrinsic thromboplastin (rabbit brain extract) and calcium; normal prothrombin time (PT) ranges from 9.5 to 11.8 seconds; prolonged PT is commonly associated with abnormal bleeding and is indicative of deficiencies in fibrinogen, prothrombin, or factors V, VII, or X; it may also indicate ongoing oral anticoagulant therapy. The test serves as a useful guide to monitor the response to oral anticoagulant therapy. Also called Quick's test; one-stage prothrombin time test.

provocative t. Any test or procedure intentionally performed to elicit an abnormal event, such as giving histamine to a patient with suspected pheochromocytoma when blood pressure is normal, to provoke release of catecholamines.

PSA t. See prostate-specific antigen test.

psychological t. Any test designed to assess a person's development, achievement, intelligence, aptitude, personality, and behavior and mental processes.

psychomotor t. A test to assess the speed and accuracy in carrying out simple sensorimotor responses, such as copying designs, placing building blocks, or manipulating controls.

pulp t. A diagnostic test to determine the vitality of the pulp in a tooth by assessing its sensitivity to various thermal (hot or cold) or electrical stimulations; the sensitivity of the pulp reflects its health. Also called vitality test.

Queckenstedt's t. A test to assess a blockage of the vertebral canal; when the jugular vein in the neck of a healthy individual is compressed on either side, there is a rapid rise in the pressure of the cerebrospinal fluid (CSF), and an equally rapid return to normal when pressure is released from the neck; when there is an obstruction in the spinal (vertebral) canal (usually in the subarachnoid channel), compression of the jugular vein causes little or no increase of CSF pressure below the site of obstruction. Also called Queckenstedt-Stookey test.

Queckenstedt-Stookey t. See Queckenstedt's test.

Quick's t. See prothrombin test.

Quinlan's t. A test to confirm the presence of bile; a 3-mm layer of liquid specimen is examined through a spectroscope (which disperses light into its spectrum, magnifies it, and displays it for analysis); if bile is present in the specimen, some of the violet color of the spectrum will be absorbed, forming absorption lines in the violet.

radioactive iodine (RAI) uptake t. See ^{131}I uptake test.

T

test ■ **test**

radioallergosorbent t. (RAST) A radioimmunoassay test to measure serum levels of immunoglobulin E (IgE) antibody directed against a specific antigen; used to identify specific allergens that cause asthma, hay fever, drug reactions, or rashes; the allergen extract is bound to a solid matrix (immunosorbent) and reacted with radiolabeled antibody against human IgE antibody; uptake of the labeled antibody is in proportion to the level of specific serum IgE antibodies to the allergen; elevated serum IgE is indicative of hypersensitivity to the specific allergen used. RAST is an alternative to skin tests to determine sensitivity to suspected allergens.

RAI t. See ^{131}I uptake test.

rapid plasma reagin t.'s A group of commonly performed screening tests for syphilis using unheated serum with a standard cardiolipin antigen containing choline chloride and small charcoal particles; normal serum shows no flocculation. Also called RPR test.

red cell adherence t. See erythrocyte adhesion test.

reflex decay t. A test to differentiate between a lesion in the cochlea and one of the vestibulocochlear (8th cranial) nerves. An acoustic reflex is elicited by introducing a sustained 10-dB tone above reflex threshold for 10 seconds. Normally the reflex persists for the entire 10 seconds; in patients with vestibular schwannoma of the cochlear nerve, the reflex diminishes by half during the first 5 seconds.

resorcinol t. A test to identify fructose in urine (fructosuria); to a fresh urine specimen is added an equal volume of hydrochloric acid (HCl) containing resorcinol; the appearance of a burgundy-red precipitate, after boiling for 10 seconds, is indicative of fructose. Also called resorcinol-hydrochloric acid test; Selivanoff's test.

resorcinol-hydrochloric acid t. See resorcinol test.

ring t. (a) See ring precipitin test. (b) A test of antibiotic activity.

ring precipitin t. An immunoprecipitin test in which an antigen solution is layered over an antibody solution (in a concentration gradient) in a glass tube; as diffusion occurs, a precipitin ring forms at the interface where the antibody ratio is optimal.

Rinne t. A standard tuning fork hearing test; the handle of a vibrating tuning fork is first placed firmly against the mastoid process to assess the conduction of sound by bone; then the vibrating tines are placed beside and parallel to the ear to test air conduction. If the sound is perceived as louder when the vibrating tines are held beside the ear, hearing is normal or sensorineural loss is present. If the sound is louder when the handle of the vibrating tuning fork is against the mastoid process, the patient has a conduction hearing loss. A patient with fluid in the middle ear (serous otitis media) perceives the sound as louder when the vibrating tines are placed against the bone than when they are next to the ear.

Romberg's t. A test of balance used in differentiating between cerebellar ataxia (cerebellar disease) and peripheral ataxia (afferent neuron disease). The patient is told to stand with feet together and eyes open; in the presence of afferent neuron limb disease, the patient can adjust for the loss of sensory input by using visual orientation to maintain desired position; when told to close his eyes, the

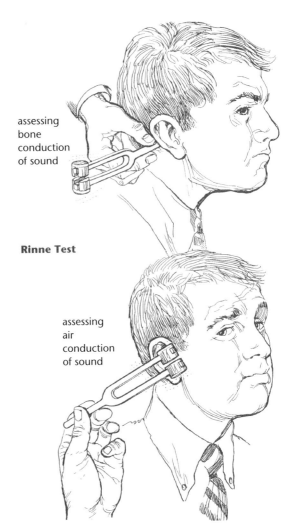

assessing bone conduction of sound

Rinne Test

assessing air conduction of sound

patient will sway with a tendency to fall. Cerebellar lesions show the same degree of unsteadiness regardless of whether the eyes are opened or closed. Also called Romberg's sign; station test.

Ropes t. See mucin clot test.

Rorschach t. Projective psychological test for evaluating the subject's thought processes, defensive structure, affective integration, and intrapsychic conflicts through a complex analysis of the individual's associations to a series of ten bisymmetric inkblot patterns.

Rosenbach-Gmelin t. A test to determine the presence of bile pigment in the urine; the urine specimen is passed through the same filter paper several times; the filter paper is then dried; a drop of nitric acid with a trace of nitrous acid is applied on the inside of the

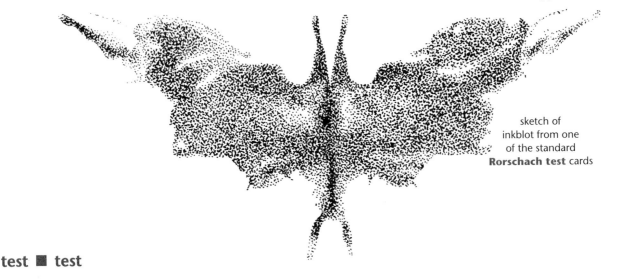

sketch of inkblot from one of the standard **Rorschach test** cards

paper; if bile is present, a yellowish spot will appear, surrounded by rings of red, violet, blue, and green.

RPR t. See rapid plasma reagin test.

rubella HI t. A hemagglutination inhibition (HI) test for German measles (rubella), to determine whether a patient has immune antibodies to rubella or stands at risk for infection; the test is performed routinely during the prenatal examination of pregnant women. Also called HAI test.

Rubin's t. See tubal insufflation test.

Rumpel-Leede t. See capillary fragility test.

Sabin-Feldman dye t. A serologic test for the diagnosis of toxoplasmosis, based on the failure of living toxoplasmas *(Toxoplasma gondii)* to stain with alkaline methylene blue in the presence of specific antibody and complement-like factor.

Schellong t. A test to assess the function of the circulatory system; while the subject stands for 15 minutes, his blood pressure is recorded continuously; a decrease in systolic pressure of 20 mm Hg or more during this time frame is indicative of poor circulatory function.

Schick t. An assessment test to determine susceptibility or immunity to diphtheria (a highly contagious bacterial infection); 0.1 ml of purified diphtheria toxin dissolved in buffered human serum albumin is administered intradermally on one forearm (test site), and the identical quantity of the same, but heat-inactivated, diphtheria toxoid is administered into the other forearm (control site); patients immune to diphtheria will show no reaction at either site; patients susceptible to diphtheria exhibit inflammation and induration at the test site of injection within 24 hours and peak reaction within 7 days, while the control site shows no reaction. Also called Schick method.

Schiller's t. A test performed when cancer of the cervix or vaginal mucosa is suspected. The suspect area is painted with Lugol's iodine solution; a normal cervix stains dark brown; any portion of the epithelium that does not accept the dye indicates either scar tissue or a neoplasm.

Schilling t. A test to determine the ability to absorb ingested vitamin B_{12}; inability to absorb vitamin B_{12} is a cause of pernicious anemia. Cyanocobalamin is tagged with a radioisotope of cobalt (^{57}Co) and administered orally; the amount of radioactivity excreted in the urine over the next 24 hours is indicative of the amount of vitamin B_{12} absorbed by the body; absorption is considered good if 7% or more of the oral dose is excreted in the urine.

Schirmer's t. A test of tear production (lacrimal secretion) in which a narrow strip of filter paper is hooked over the lower eyelid, with the free end of the paper hanging down to the cheek; wetting is measured by the extent of moisture on the paper when left in position for five minutes.

Schober t. A test that measures the diversion between two marks on the skin of the back during forward flexion; it is commonly used for quantifying reduced flexion (reduced spinal mobility).

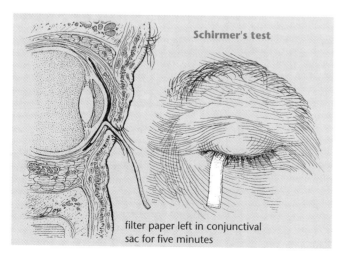

Schirmer's test

filter paper left in conjunctival sac for five minutes

Scholastic Achievement T. See group test.

scratch t. A skin test in which antigen is brought in contact with a superficial scratch in the skin. See skin test.

screening t. *(a)* A test applied to a group of apparently healthy people to separate some members of the group on the basis of established criteria. *(b)* A testing procedure designed to separate chemicals according to an established characteristic, such as carcinogenicity.

Seashore t. A musical aptitude test in which the sense of pitch, rhythm, loudness discrimination, timbre, duration, tonal memory, and other capacities of innate musical ability can be scored. Some of the subsets of the test can be used for auditory functioning assessments.

secretin t. A test for pancreatic exocrine function; the volume and bicarbonate level of duodenal content are determined before and after the intravenous administration of secretin; 2 to 4 ml of pancreatic secretion per kilogram body weight and 90 to 130 mEq/liter of barcarbonate are considered normal; low levels are seen in patients afflicted with chronic pancreatitis, pancreatic carcinoma, or cystic fibrosis.

Selivanoff's t. See resorcinol test.

shake t. See foam stability test.

sickle-cell t. See sickling test.

sickling t. A test to demonstrate the presence of abnormal sickle hemoglobin S (Hb S) in blood; when a blood sample is mixed with an equal amount of 2% sodium metabisulfite (or sodium thiosulfate), red blood cells containing the abnormal Hb S assume a crescentic or elongated shape. Also called sickle-cell test.

single-photon absorptiometry t. A test commonly used to measure mineral content of the long bones; a monoenergetic photon source of iodine 125 is coupled with a sodium iodide scintillation counter; the difference in photon absorption in bone and in soft tissue allows measurement of the mineral content in the extremities; useful in assessing osteoporosis. Also called Norland-Cameron single-photon absorptiometry test.

skin t. Any test in which antigen is applied to the skin or injected intracutaneously in order to assess the body's response; named according to the method of antigen application, as scratch test, patch test, and intradermal test; used to detect sensitivity to various allergens (e.g., pollen), to facilitate diagnoses and differentiate infectious diseases, to evaluate immune responses, to detect sensitivity to disease-causing microorganisms (e.g., tuberculosis), and to assess a patient's response to immunotherapy. Also called cutaneous test.

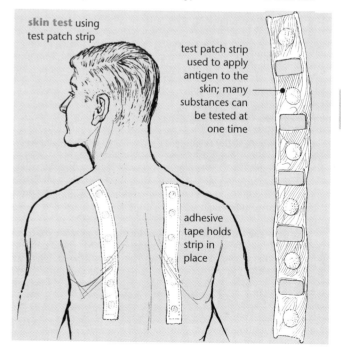

skin test using test patch strip

test patch strip used to apply antigen to the skin; many substances can be tested at one time

adhesive tape holds strip in place

test ■ test

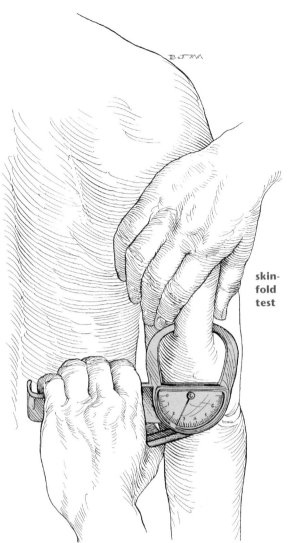

skin-fold test

Stanford Achievement T. See achievement test.

Stanford-Binet Intelligence T. A widely used and highly acclaimed verbal intelligence test with some nonverbal items interspersed throughout the test; designed for people from three years of age and older; organized and available by age levels. The results are designated as a single raw score, which is converted to an intelligence quotient (IQ); IQ scores are generally classified as follows: gifted, 140 and above; very superior, 130 through 139; superior, 120 through 129; above average, 110 through 119; average, 90 through 109; below average, 80 through 89; borderline, 70 through 79; mild mental retardation, 60 through 69; moderate mental retardation, 50 through 59; severe mental retardation, 49 and under. The test is often used to identify children who may benefit from special education. Also called Binet test; Stanford-Binet intelligence scale. See also group test.

station t. See Romberg's test.

streptococcal antibody t. A serologic test performed to confirm an infection with beta-hemolytic streptococci, and to aid in the diagnosis of acute rheumatic fever and acute poststreptococcal glomerulonephritis; measurements are made of the relative serum concentrations of the antibody to streptolysin O, an enzyme produced by group A beta-hemolytic streptococci. Also called antistreptolysin-O test; ASO test; ASLO test.

stress t. See exercise test.

Tensilon t. A diagnostic test for myasthenia gravis (MG); the strength of individual skeletal muscles (e.g., the extraocular muscles) is assessed following intravenous injection of Tensilon (edrophonium chloride, a short-acting anticholinesterase that improves muscle response to nerve impulses); in MG, the muscle strength improves promptly, usually within 30 seconds; individuals without MG usually develop fasciculations.

test anxiety t. A self-reporting test consisting of items concerning fear and worry about taking tests and physiological activity, such as heart rate, sweating, etc., before, during, and after tests.

thematic apperception t. (TAT) A psychological test for exploring some aspects of the subject's personality. The subject is

skin-fold t. Measurement of skin folds with special constant-tension calipers to estimate the degree of obesity.

sleep t., sleep apnea t. See overnight polysomnogram test.

Snellen eye chart t. An eye test employing a chart imprinted in bold typeface comprising rows of letters of various sizes (categorized in fractions, such as 20/50, 20/40, 20/30, 20/20) used in testing distant visual acuity. The chart is read from a standard distance of 20 feet, represented by the upper number of the fraction; the lower number identifies the size letters individuals are able to read from 20 feet. Thus 20/20 vision means the individual can see the letters a normal eye can see at 20 feet; 20/50 vision means the individual being tested can read those letters at 20 feet that a normal eye can read at 50 feet.

speed t. A test to diagnose inflammation of the long head of the biceps muscle of the arm (biceps brachii); with the patient's arm completely extended with palm up, pressure is applied to the palm; if the pressure elicits pain in the shoulder, it most likely results from bicipital tendonitis, since resistance requires biceps contraction. Useful test in differentiating bicipital tendonitis from rotator cuff diseases.

spot t. for infectious mononucleosis A rapid-slide diagnostic test for infectious mononucleosis (IM), relying on the agglutination of horse red blood cells by heterophil infectious mononucleosis antibodies. False-positive tests may be seen in some conditions such as lymphoma, leukemia, or carcinoma of the pancreas. Frequently called Monospot test.

standardized t. A statistically valid test developed through uniform (standard) procedures on a large population, resulting in values constituting a norm to which a subject's test results are compared.

Snellen eye chart test

20/200	E	1
20/100	F P	2
20/70	T O Z	3
20/50	L P E D	4
20/40	P E C F D	5
20/30	E D F C Z P	6
20/25	F E L O P Z D	7
20/20	D E F P O T E C	8
20/15	L E F O D P C T	9

asked to tell stories based on each of a series of standard pictures depicting life situations that are susceptible to multiple interpretation. The test may reveal some psychological preoccupations and conflicts.

three-glass t. Test for determining the site of inflammation of the male urinary tract and associated structures; the patient urinates into three glass containers; the contents of each container reveal the approximate site of infection; the urine in the first container has washings from the anterior urethra, that in the second from the bladder; after prostatic massage, the third has cells from the prostate, seminal vesicles, and posterior urethra.

thyroid suppression t. A thyroid test, currently replaced by the thyrotropin-releasing hormone (TRH) stimulation test.

thyrotropin-releasing hormone (TRH) stimulation t. A test to assess the response of the pituitary (hypophysis) to an intravenous injection of 500 μg of TRH over a period of 15 to 30 seconds. The quantity of TRH injected normally stimulates the pituitary to produce an increase of thyroid-stimulating hormone (TSH) of at least 6 μU/ml within 15 to 30 minutes in adults under 40 years of age. The TSH response is slightly higher in women than in men. The test is most sensitive in the diagnosis of mild hyperthyroidism; it also can distinguish between secondary (pituitary) and tertiary (hypothalamic) hypothyroidism. In patients with primary hypothyroidism, an exaggerated response is noticed; an impaired or absent TSH response in hypothyroid patients indicates hypothalamic-pituitary failure. Useful in the evaluation of Graves' disease and thyrotoxicosis. Also called TRH test.

tilt t. *(a)* A rise in pulse or drop in blood pressure as a patient moves from the supine toward the upright position, indicating a loss of extracellular fluid (e.g., during hemorrhage or dehydration). *(b)* Test to measure predilection for fainting (syncope); excretion of urinary epinephrine and norepinephrine is measured during three consecutive intervals with the patient first in a horizontal and then in a nearly vertical position; a marked increase in the second period indicates a positive test.

tine t. Test performed by pressing antigen-impregnated tines (four tines, each 2 mm in length) into the skin; used for tuberculin testing. See tuberculin test.

tolbutamide t. A provocative test to detect insulin-producing islet-cell tumors of the pancreas. After rapid intravenous administration of 1 gram of tolbutamide, plasma insulin and glucose are measured periodically for up to 6 hours; markedly higher amounts of insulin accompanied by lower glucose levels characterize the pancreatic tumor, insulinoma. Obesity manifests a high insulin response, but is not accompanied by low glucose levels. Also called tolbutamide tolerance test.

tolbutamide tolerance t. See tolbutamide test.

total cholesterol t. A quantitative analysis of serum cholesterol to measure the circulating levels of free cholesterol and cholesterol esters; abnormally high serum cholesterol levels are associated with an increased risk of coronary artery disease; inherited lipid disorders, hypothyroidism, diabetes, and nephrotic syndrome are among the causes; abnormally low serum cholesterol levels are seen in malnutrition. Also called cholesterol test.

tourniquet t. See capillary fragility test.

TPHA t. See Treponema pallidum hemagglutination test.

TPI t. See Treponemal immobilization test.

treadmill stress t. A test to assess cardiovascular function through the use of exercise on a treadmill while under continuous electrocardiographic monitoring; significant depression of the RS-T segment in the electrocardiogram (ECG) is indicative of coronary insufficiency.

Trendelenburg's t. *(a)* A test for hip abnormalities; with the subject standing, weight is borne on the normal side of the hip, the opposite side of the pelvis is elevated to maintain balance (negative test); when weight is borne on the dislocated side, the opposite side of the pelvis does not elevate (positive test), as seen in congenital dislocation of the hip, deformity of the femoral neck, or weakness of the hip abductor muscles. Also called Trendelenburg's sign. *(b)* A test for determining the presence of incompetent valves in the communicating veins between the superficial and deep vessels in patients with varicose veins in the lower extremity. The patient lies

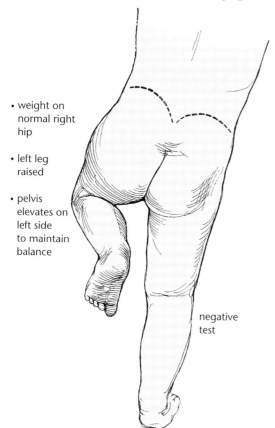

• weight on normal right hip

• left leg raised

• pelvis elevates on left side to maintain balance

negative test

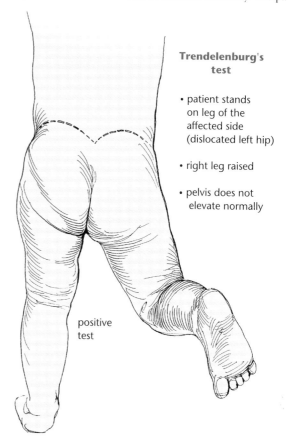

Trendelenburg's test

• patient stands on leg of the affected side (dislocated left hip)

• right leg raised

• pelvis does not elevate normally

positive test

T

test ■ test

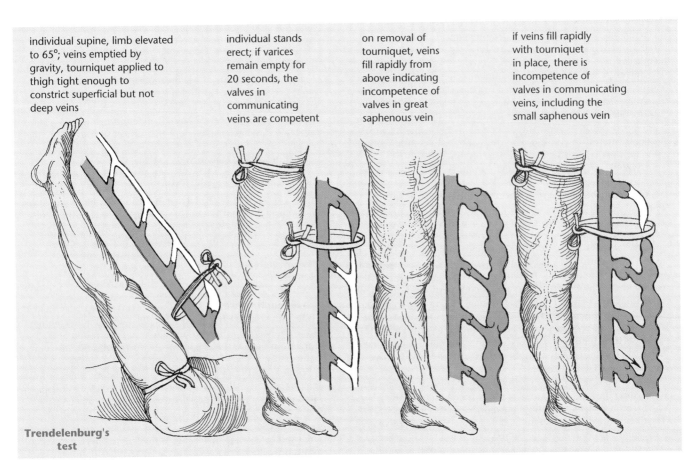

individual supine, limb elevated to 65°; veins emptied by gravity, tourniquet applied to thigh tight enough to constrict superficial but not deep veins

individual stands erect; if varices remain empty for 20 seconds, the valves in communicating veins are competent

on removal of tourniquet, veins fill rapidly from above indicating incompetence of valves in great saphenous vein

if veins fill rapidly with tourniquet in place, there is incompetence of valves in communicating veins, including the small saphenous vein

Trendelenburg's test

on his or her back with the leg elevated 65°; after the blood in the veins empties by gravity, a tourniquet is applied around the thigh tight enough to constrict superficial veins but not the deep veins; patient stands erect; if varices remain empty for 20 seconds, the valves in the communicating veins are competent; on removal of the tourniquet, veins fill rapidly from above, indicating incompetence of valves in the great saphenous vein; if veins fill rapidly with tourniquet in place, there is incompetence of valves in communicating veins, including the small saphenous vein. Also called Brodie-Trendelenburg test.

Treponemal immobilization t. Test for syphilis; serum from a syphilitic patient will (in the presence of complement) immobilize the actively motile *Treponema pallidum* obtained from testes of a syphilitic rabbit. Also called TPI test.

Treponemal pallidum hemagglutination t. A serologic test for syphilis; tanned sheep red blood cells are coated with *Treponema pallidum* antigen and are combined with absorbed test serum; hemagglutination (positive reaction) occurs in the presence of specific anti–*Treponema pallidum* antibodies in the patient's serum. Also called TPHA test.

T₃ resin uptake t. See triiodothyronine (T_3) uptake text.

TRH t. See thyrotropin-releasing hormone stimulation test.

triiodothyronine (T_3) uptake t. Radioimmunoassay to determine the status of thyroid function; an absorbent (usually a resin) is added to a patient's test serum containing radiolabeled T_3; the amount of radioactive T_3 absorbed is indicative of the hormone level in the patient; the test can be altered by changes in the level of thyroxine-binding globulin. Also called T_3 uptake test; T_3 resin uptake test.

tubal insufflation t. A test to determine patency of the fallopian (uterine) tubes by transcervical insufflation of the uterus with carbon dioxide; if the tubes are patent, the escape of gas into the abdominal cavity is heard on auscultation over the lower abdomen; the gas often accumulates under the diaphragm, which can be demonstrated by x-ray film; it may be accompanied by discomfort or pain in the shoulder region. The test is generally administered as part of an evaluation of infertility. Also called Rubin's test.

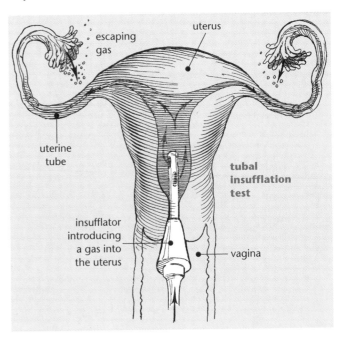

tubal insufflation test

tuberculin t. Any test for tuberculosis in which tuberculin or its purified protein derivative (PPD) is introduced into the skin by means of intradermal injection (Mantoux test), multiple punctures (tine test), or an adhesive patch (patch test). A delayed hypersensitivity reaction, manifested by a palpable and visible area of erythema and induration larger than 5 mm in diameter, within 48 to 72 hours, is indicative of a positive reaction. Also called PPD test.

T₃ uptake t. See triiodothyronine (T₃) uptake test.

Tzanck t. Microscopic examination of fluid from vesicles or blisters to identify characteristic cells of certain vesicular diseases, such as the identification of Tzanck cells (degenerated epithelial cells that have lost connections with contiguous cells in the epidermis) as seen in pemphigus. Also used to identify varicella, herpes simplex, and herpes zoster.

unilateral cover t. A binocular function test for determining the presence of a deviation of the visual axis (phoria), in which one eye is covered and uncovered with an opaque occluder while the subject's attention is directed to a small fixation object at a given test distance; if the eye moves to see the object after removal of the cover, phoria (strabismus) is noted. Also called cover-uncover test.

urine concentration t. A test to assess the tubular function of the kidneys by measuring the relative density or osmolality of urine after a period of restricted fluids and controlled diet; the specific gravity of normal urine should measure 1.020 or more after several hours without fluids.

van den Bergh's t. A test that measures serum levels of the predominant pigment in bile (bilirubin), the major product of hemoglobin catabolism; in adults, normal levels of total serum bilirubin measure 1.1 mg/dL or less, with direct serum bilirubin being less than 0.5 mg/dL; however in normal newborns the levels range from 1 to 12 mg/dL. Increased levels are indicative of disorders that include liver damage, hemolytic anemia, and biliary obstruction; newborns with dangerously high levels of unconjugated bilirubin may require an exchange transfusion or phototherapy.

vanillylmandelic acid (VMA) t. Test for catecholamine-secreting tumors, such as pheochromocytoma; levels of VMA (the major urinary metabolite of norepinephrine and epinephrine) are measured in a 24-hour urine specimen; normal VMA levels range from 0.7 to 6.8 mg/24 hours. Also called VMA test.

VDRL t. A nonspecific serologic test for diagnosing syphilis, using heat-activated serum and cardiolipin-lecithin-cholesterol antigen, as developed by the Venereal Disease Research Laboratory of the U.S. Public Health Service; a positive reaction is determined when flocculation appears in the test.

vitality t. See pulp test.

VMA t. See vanillylmandelic acid test.

Wada t. A test to determine which cerebral hemisphere is dominant for language function; intracarotid injection of amobarbital temporarily abolishes the power of speech (transient aphasia) in the dominant cerebral hemisphere for language function, while it does not interfere with the power of speech in the nondominant cerebral hemisphere.

Waldenström's t. A quantitative analysis urine test for porphyrins (fluorescent compounds produced during heme biosynthesis) that uses Ehrlich's aldehyde reagent to produce a red-orange color; it is diagnostic for congenital or acquired porphyrias (most notably uroporphyrins, coproporphyrins, and their precursor porphyrinogens); normally excreted in urine in small amounts; elevated levels reflect impaired heme biosynthesis, as seen in inherited enzyme deficiencies (congenital porphyria) or in hemolytic anemia or hepatic disease (acquired porphyria).

Wassermann t. The original effective serologic test for the diagnosis of syphilis, dating back to 1906. It was a complement-fixation test between the subject's serum and a known antigen. Also called Wassermann reaction.

Watson-Schwartz t. A test for diagnosing acute intermittent porphyria, based on the formation of red coloration upon addition of Ehrlich's aldehyde reagent to a urine specimen. Also called porphobilinogen test.

Weber t. A standard tuning fork hearing test designed to reveal gross abnormalities in hearing due to disorders of bone or air conduction (it does not measure the degree of hearing loss). A vibrating tuning fork is placed against the center of the patient's forehead. Individuals with normal hearing, or with equal hearing impairment in both ears, perceive the sound equally in both ears. With conduction hearing loss, the sound will appear louder in the ear that is

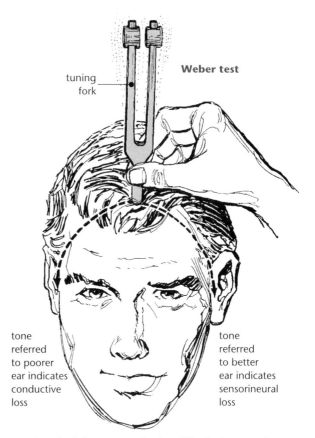

tuning fork

Weber test

tone referred to poorer ear indicates conductive loss

tone referred to better ear indicates sensorineural loss

more impaired (because conduction difficulty improves bone conduction by decreasing ambient noise); tone referred to the better ear indicates sensorineural loss.

Wechsler Intelligence T. for Children, Revised See Wechsler Intelligence Scale for Children, Revised, under scale.

Wechsler Preschool and Primary T. of Intelligence See Wechsler Preschool and Primary Scale of Intelligence, under scale.

Wide Range Achievement T., Revised. See achievement test.

word association t. See association test.

D-xylose absorption t. A test of gastrointestinal absorption; after fasting for eight hours, a patient drinks a 25-gram dose of D-xylose dissolved in 250 ml of water, followed immediately by another 250 ml of water; all urine voided during the following five hours is pooled; since poor renal function may affect the test, blood samples are tested; normally 16 to 33% of the ingested xylose should be excreted over the five-hour period; less than this amount is indicative of intestinal malabsorption. Also called D-xylose tolerance test.

D-xylose tolerance t. See D-xylose absorption test.

testalgia (tes-tal′je-ah) See orchialgia.

testectomy (tes-tek′to-me) See orchiectomy.

testes (tes′tēz) Plural of testis.

testicle (tes′tĭ-kl) See testis.

undescended t. See cryptorchidism.

testicular (tes-tik′u-lar) Relating to the testes.

testis (tes′tis), pl. tes′tes One of two glands that produce spermatozoa and hormones (testosterone and small quantities of estrogenic hormones), normally suspended in the scrotum; the left testis often hangs 1 cm lower than the right one. Also called testicle.

ectopic t. Abnormal condition in which a testis has strayed from its normal path of descent into the scrotum. Most common location is superficial to and over the inguinal canal; other (rare) locations are: just in front of the anus (perineal), over the femoral vessels (femoral or crural), under the skin at the root of the penis (penile), within the pelvic cavity (pelvic), and both testes in the same inguinal canal (transverse). Distinguished from cryptorchidism. Also called ectopia testis.

T

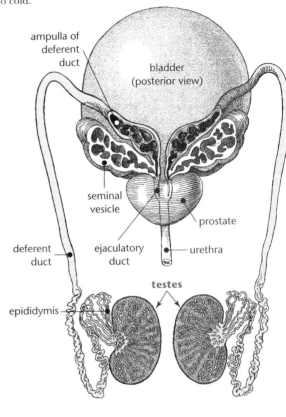

ectopic
testis

penile

superficial
inguinal
(most common)

femoral

ampulla of
deferent
duct

bladder
(posterior view)

seminal
vesicle

prostate

deferent
duct

ejaculatory
duct

urethra

testes

epididymis

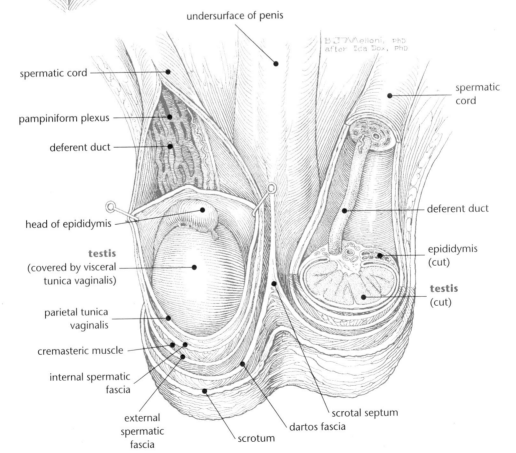

undersurface of penis

B.J.Melloni, PhD
after Ida Dox, PhD

spermatic cord

pampiniform plexus

deferent duct

head of epididymis

testis
(covered by visceral
tunica vaginalis)

parietal tunica
vaginalis

cremasteric muscle

internal spermatic
fascia

external
spermatic
fascia

scrotum

dartos fascia

scrotal septum

testis
(cut)

epididymis
(cut)

deferent duct

spermatic
cord

testis ■ testis

undescended t. See cryptorchidism.

testitis (tes-ti'tis) See orchitis.

testosterone (tes-tos'tĕ-rōn) The most potent of the naturally produced male hormones (androgens), responsible for the development and maintenance of secondary sexual characteristics; produced in the testes by the Leydig's cells under the control of leuteinizing hormone of the pituitary.

test types (test tīps) Printed letters or figures used to test visual acuity.

    Jaeger's t.t. Words and phrases printed in ordinary printer's type of varying sizes.

    Snellen's t.t. (a) Block letters (stymie typeface) of varying sizes printed on a white card. (b) A simplified chart that does not require that the subject understand letters; instead, one must simply indicate which direction the three prongs of the letter E point.

tetanic (tĕ-tan'ik) Relating to tetanus or tetany.

tetaniform (tĕ-tan'ĭ-form) Resembling tetanus.

tetanize (tet'ah-nīz) To produce a sustained muscular contraction by applying numerous stimuli in rapid succession.

tetano-, tetan- Combining forms meaning tetanus; tetany.

tetanode (tet'ah-nōd) An interval between muscle spasms in tetanus.

tetanoid (tet'ah-noid) 1. Resembling tetanus. 2. Resembling tetany.

tetanolysin (tet-ah-nol'ĭ-sin) The blood-destructive component of the tetanus toxin produced by the bacillus *Clostridium tetani.*

tetanospasmin (tet-ah-no-spaz'min) The neurotoxin produced by *Clostridium tetani,* the bacillus causing tetanus; it interferes with neuromuscular transmission by inhibiting the release of acetylcholine from nerve terminals in muscles, producing the characteristic symptoms of tetanus.

tetanotoxin (tet-ah-no-tok'sin) See tetanus toxin, under toxin.

tetanus (tet'ah-nus) An infectious, bacterial disease caused by the toxin of *Clostridium tetani;* initial symptoms include pain and stiffness in jaw, abdomen, and back muscles progressing to rigidity (trismus) and reflex spasm; may follow any penetrating wound.

    generalized t. The most common form of tetanus, involving most of the muscles of the body.

    local t., localized t. A mild form with manifestations restricted to the area surrounding an infected wound; may progress to the generalized form.

    t. neonatorum Tetanus of the newborn due to infection of the umbilical stump.

tetany (tet'ah-ne) Intermittent muscle spasms, usually beginning in the hands and feet; may progress to involve other muscles and to produce convulsions; occurs as a manifestation of a biochemical disturbance in the body, most commonly low levels of ionized calcium (hypocalcemia).

    hyperventilation t. Tetany produced by deep rapid breathing due to reduction of carbon dioxide in the blood.

    latent t. Tetany made apparent only by certain stimulating procedures.

tetra- Prefix meaning four.

tetracaine hydrochloride (tet'rah-kān hi-dro-klo'rīd) A local or spinal anesthetic.

tetrachloride (tet-rah-klo'rīd) Compound containing four atoms of chlorine per molecule.

tetracycline (tet-rah-si'klēn) Any of a group of broad-spectrum antibiotic drugs prescribed to treat a variety of infections; possible side effects include nausea, vomiting, and diarrhea; may discolor developing teeth or worsen the blood level of protein metabolites when kidney function is diminished.

tetrad (tet'rad) A set of related things; tetralogy.

tetradactyl (tet-rah-dak'tĭ-le) Having only four digits in a hand or foot.

tetrahydrocannabinol (tet-rah-hi'dro-kah-nab'ĭ-nol) (THC) The pharmacologically active constituent of marijuana.

tetralogy (tĕ-tral'o-je) A combination of four related entities.

    t. of Fallot Cyanotic congenital heart disease produced by coexistence of the following four abnormalities: narrowed valve of pulmonary artery (pulmonary stenosis), displaced aorta (dextroposition of aorta), hole in the muscular wall separating the ventricles (ventricular septal defect), and thickened wall of the right ventricle (right ventricular hypertrophy).

tetraplegia (tet-rah-ple'je-ah) See quadriplegia.

tetraploid (tet'rah-ploid) Characterized by the abnormal condition of having four haploid sets of chromosomes; applied to a cell, tissue, or organism.

tetravalent (tet-rav'ah-lent) See quadrivalent.

tetrose (tet'rōs) A four-carbon sugar.

textiform (teks'tĭ-form) Weblike.

thalamic (thah-lam'ik) Relating to the thalamus.

thalamo- Combining form meaning thalamus.

thalamocortical (thal-ah-mo-kor'tĭ-kal) Relating to the thalamus and the superficial gray layer (cortex) of the brain; applied to the nerve pathways connecting these structures.

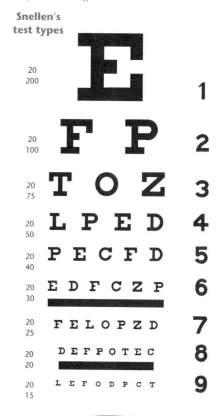

Snellen's test types

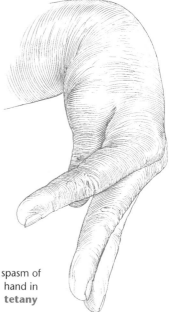

spasm of hand in **tetany**

T

thalamotomy (thal-ah-mot'o-me) Operative destruction of a portion of the thalamus for therapeutic purposes.

thalamus (thal'ah-mus), pl. thal'ami One of two large ovoid masses of nuclei, about 4 cm in length, situated on either side of the third ventricle of the brain; it serves primarily as a relay center for sensory impulses entering the brain. Occasionally, the two thalami are connected by an intermediate tissue, which seemingly has no neurologic function.

thalassemia (thal-ah-se'me-ah) A group of hereditary disorders characterized by deficient or absent production of one of the polypeptide chains in the hemolytic molecule (in the red blood cell).

    alpha-t., α-t. Disorder characterized by reduced formation of alpha-globin chains in erythrocyte precursor cells in bone marrow, caused by deletion of one or more of the four alpha-globin genes normally present in each cell. The number of deletions determines the severity of the disorder; lack of a single gene produces a silent carrier state, which has little or no effect on the blood and is completely asymptomatic; a lack of all four genes is incompatible with life. The condition caused by lack of three alpha-globin genes was formerly called hemoglobin H disease.

    beta-t., β-t. Disorder characterized by a reduced quantity of hemoglobin in red blood cells (erythrocytes) due to diminished formation of the beta-globin chains in hemoglobin; may be beta" thalassemia, beta$^+$ thalassemia, or beta^{++} thalassemia depending on whether the mutant gene directs formation of no beta-globin, a small amount, or a moderate amount of beta-globin, respectively.

    major t. A generally severe form of thalassemia beginning in early childhood, usually the result of inheritance of genes for beta thalassemia from both parents (homozygous state); characterized by severe anemia, bone abnormalities, growth retardation, enlargement of spleen and liver, and jaundice. Death usually occurs before puberty. Also called Cooley's anemia.

    minor t. Mild thalassemia due to inheritance of an alpha or a beta thalassemia gene from only one parent (thalassemia trait); may produce symptoms resembling those of iron deficiency anemia. Also called Cooley's trait.

thalidomide (thah-lid'o-mīd) A sedative-hypnotic drug; it produces fetal deformities of the limbs and other defects when taken by pregnant women.

thallium (thal'e-um) Metalic element; symbol Tl, atomic number 81, atomic weight 204.37.

thallotoxicosis (thal-o-tok-sī-ko'sis) Poisoning from exposure to thallium or its salts; clinical features depend on degree of exposure; they include gastrointestinal inflammation and pain, neurologic disturbances, hair loss of body and scalp, and, in severe cases, hallucinations and coma. Individuals at highest risk of occupational exposure are those engaged in the production of thallium salt derivatives; exposure can also occur in cement production and at smelters, especially in the maintenance and cleaning of ducts and flues.

thanato- Combining form meaning death.

thanatoid (than'ah-toid) 1. Resembling death. 2. Deadly.

thanatology (than-ah-tol'o-je) 1. The study of death and dying. 2. In forensic medicine, the study of all the circumstances under which a death occurred, particularly as they relate to the phenomena produced after death (immediately or otherwise).

thanatophobia (than-ah-to-fo'be-ah) Extreme fear of death.

thanatopsy (than'ah-top-se) Autopsy.

theca (the'kah), pl. the'cae A sheath or capsule enveloping a structure.

    t. folliculi The envelope surrounding the vesicular ovarian follicle, composed of an external, fibrous layer (theca externa) and an internal, vascular, secretory layer (theca interna).

thecitis (the-si'tis) Inflammation of a tendon sheath.

thecoma (the-ko'mah) A firm benign tumor of the ovary, found most commonly in the fifth to seventh decade of life; it has estrogenic activity.

thelarche (the-lar'ke) The beginning of breast development in girls.

theleplasty (the'le-plas-te) See mamillaplasty.

thelium (the'le-um) A nipple or nipplelike structure.

thelo-, thel- Combining forms meaning nipple.

thelorrhagia (the-lo-ra'je-ah) Bleeding from the nipple.

thenar (the'nar) The fleshy mass of the palm at the base of the thumb.

theophylline (the-of'ĭ-lin) An alkaloid occurring naturally in caffeine and in tea leaves; synthetic preparation is used as a bron-

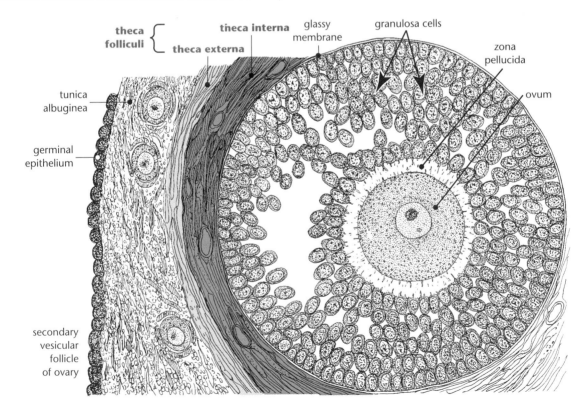

thalamotomy ■ theophylline

T34

chodilator in the treatment of asthma. Adverse reactions may include nausea, vomiting, and seizures.

t. ethylenediamine See aminophylline.

theorem (the'o-rem) A proven proposition.

theory (the'o-re) A hypothetical concept formulated to provide a coherent basis for investigation or to account for observed phenomena.

    clonal selection t. of immunity The fundamental basis of lymphocyte activation in which an antigen selectively stimulates proliferation of only those cells that carry surface antibody receptors that are specific for the particular antigen.

    germ layer t. The concept that there develop in the young embryo three primary layers of cells (ectoderm, mesoderm, endoderm) and that each layer gives rise to specific tissues and organs.

    gestalt t. Theory proposing that mental phenomena are total configurations and cannot be analyzed into their component parts.

    lamarckian t. The concept that acquired characteristics may be transmitted to descendants.

    Planck's t. See quantum theory.

    quantum t. Theory proposing that atoms emit and absorb energy discontinuously, in finite discrete amounts (quanta) in individual acts of emission and absorption, rather than continuously. Also called Planck's theory.

    reentry t. In cardiology, the concept that premature ectopic heartbeats arise because of reentry of the same impulse that initiated the preceding beat.

    van't Hoff's t. The theory that substances in dilute solutions obey the gas laws.

    Young-Helmholtz t. Theory proposing that perception of colors depends on three sets of receptors in the retina: for red, green, and violet.

therapeutic (ther-ah-pu'tik) 1. Relating to the treatment of disease. 2. Curative.

therapeutics (ther-ah-pu'tiks) The treatment of disease.

therapist (ther'ah-pist) A person trained to conduct a specific type of therapy.

    inhalation t. See respiratory therapist.

    radiation t. A specially trained person who runs the equipment for delivery of radiation in diagnostic or therapeutic procedures. Sometimes called radiation technologist.

    respiratory t. One specially trained to provide treatment to persons with disorders of the respiratory tract; training usually includes techniques of inhalation therapy, administration of oxygen, chest percussion, and often determination of blood gases. Also called inhalation therapist.

therapy (ther'ah-pe) Treatment of disease, especially as undertaken in accordance with specific modalities.

    adjuvant t. Treatment used in addition to the primary therapy (e.g., radiation therapy, in addition to surgery).

    allergy injection t. See desensitization.

    anticoagulant t. The use of drugs that prevent or arrest clot formation within blood vessels or the heart.

    behavior modification t. See behavior modification, under modification.

    biological t. Stimulation of the body's immune system as a method of treatment.

    brief t. A form of psychotherapy with a (usually predefined) limited number of sessions, at most 20, using directive and reeducative methods, focused on specific problems or symptoms.

    chelation t. Treatment for heavy metal poisoning by administration of agents that sequester the metal from organs or tissues and bind it firmly within the chemical structure of a new compound, which can be eliminated from the body.

    cognitive t. Psychotherapeutic treatment that aims to alter a patient's distorted thinking process; based on the belief that the way a person perceives and thinks about the world determines his feelings and behavior.

    conventional (standard) insulin t. Treatment of insulin-dependent diabetes mellitus that includes monitoring of blood sugar (glucose) levels once or twice a day, taking one or two daily injections of insulin, exercising daily, close following of meal plans, and visiting healthcare professionals once every three months. COMPARE intensive insulin therapy.

    electroconvulsive t. (ECT) Use of electric current, passed through two electrodes on the head, to induce convulsive seizures; a method of treating certain psychiatric illnesses, especially severe depression. Also called electroshock therapy; shock therapy; shock treatment; electroshock treatment; electroconvulsive treatment.

    electroshock t. (EST) See electroconvulsive therapy.

    extracorporeal shock-wave t. See extracorporeal shock-wave lithotripsy, under lithotripsy.

    fever t. Treatment by artificially elevating body temperature. Also called pyrotherapy; pyretotherapy.

    gene t. Introduction of one or more specific genes into the cells of an organism for correction of a specific defect.

    gestalt t. Psychotherapeutic treatment concerned with developing the human potential through a growth process involving the whole person as he experiences and interacts with the environment.

    hyperbaric oxygen (HBO) t. The use of 100% oxygen in an airtight compression chamber at a greater than normal prevailing pressure; or it may be applied locally to an extremity in cases of crushed or degloving injuries, i.e., when the skin has been stripped from the hands or feet (as seen in industrial roller accidents). Also called hybaroxia.

    inhalation t. Administration of gases, steam, or vaporized medications through inhalation.

    intensive insulin t. Treatment of insulin-dependent diabetes mellitus that includes monitoring of blood sugar (glucose) levels at least four times a day, taking three or more daily injections of insulin, exercising daily, close following of meal plans, and visiting healthcare professionals often; designed to achieve near normal blood sugar levels, thereby avoiding or at least delaying, such long-term complications as blindness, kidney failure, nerve damage, and heart problems. COMPARE conventional (standard) insulin therapy.

    internal radiation t. See brachytherapy.

    interpersonal t. (IPT) Psychotherapeutic treatment that focuses on interpersonal behavior rather than intrapsychic phenomena, aiming to change the way the patient thinks, feels, and acts in current problematic relationships.

    maintenance drug t. In chemotherapy, administration of drugs at a dose level sufficient to forestall aggravation of the condition.

    mechanical t. In orthopedics, the use of adhesive dressings and appliances to assist in both preoperative and postoperative care, or as a means of correcting structural and functional disorders in their early stages and of supporting established deformities and controlling their painful symptoms, especially of the foot.

    megavitamin t. The therapeutic intake of large doses of water-soluble vitamins far in excess of minimal daily requirements.

    microwave t. See microkymatotherapy.

    nicotine replacement t. The use of nicotine gum or a transdermal nicotine patch to alleviate the symptoms of nicotine withdrawal while trying to quit smoking; used in conjunction with a behavioral intervention and training program for smoking cessation.

    occupational t. (OT) (a) The use of craft or work activities as an aid to treatment for the rehabilitation of patients. (b) The field of allied health concerned with that form of adjunct therapy.

    oral rehydration t. (ORT) A mixture of sugar and an electrolyte (e.g., salt) administered orally to young children suffering from diarrhea to alleviate the dehydration caused by the condition.

    oxygen t. Treatment with oxygen inhalation.

    palliative t. A treatment that may relieve symptoms but does not cure the disease.

    parenteral t. Introduction of medication into the body through a route other than the alimentary canal (e.g., into a vein or a muscle).

T

periodontal t. Therapy that aims to restore diseased tissues supporting the teeth to a healthy state, either by removing plaque and calculus (scaling), by smoothing root surfaces after debris has been removed (root planing), or by removing inflamed tissues from pockets around the teeth and tooth roots (curettage).

photodynamic t. See photoradiation.

photoradiation t. See photoradiation.

physical t. (PT) *(a)* The use of physical means (e.g., light, heat, electricity, ultrasound, exercise) to restore function and prevent disability following disease or injury. Also called physiotherapy. *(b)* The health profession devoted to such method of treatment.

play t. A method of psychotherapy for treating emotional disorders of children in which the child's play with toys, pictures, drawings, etc., is used as a communication medium between the child and the therapist.

psychoanalytical t. See psychoanalysis.

psychodynamic t. Psychotherapeutic treatment that focuses on intrapsychic conflict, aiming to help the patient change by gaining insight into both conscious and unconscious factors affecting thoughts, feelings, and behavior.

radiation t. Treatment of disease with high-energy rays or subatomic particles, such as x rays, alpha and beta particles, gamma rays; radioactive materials include cobalt, radium, cesium, and iridium. Also called radiotherapy.

replacement t. Administration of natural body products (e.g., hormones) or synthetic analogs to correct a deficiency.

respiratory t. The care of patients with deficiencies and abnormalities of the cardiopulmonary system, including the use of medical gases, humidification, aerosols, ventilatory supports, bronchopulmonary drainage, and maintenance of natural and artificial airways.

sclerosing t. See sclerotherapy.

shock t. See electroconvulsive therapy.

TIL t. Experimental treatment for certain cancers (e.g., melanoma) in which antigen-specific tumor-infiltrating T lymphocytes (TILs) are isolated from the patient's tissues by a biopsy and reintroduced in combination with interleukin-2.

therm (therm) General term for any of the following units of quantity of heat: a small calorie; a large calorie; 1,000 large calories; 100,000 British thermal units.

thermal (ther′mal) Relating to heat.

thermalgesia (ther-mal-je′ze-ah) Extreme sensitivity to heat.

thermalgia (ther-mal′je-ah) A burning pain.

thermanalgesia (therm-an-al-je′ze-ah) See thermoanesthesia.

thermatology (ther-mah-tol′o-je) The study of heat in relation to treatment of disease.

thermelometer (ther-mel-om′ĕ-ter) An electric thermometer.

thermo-, therm- Combining forms meaning heat.

thermoanesthesia (ther-mo-an-es-the′ze-ah) Loss of the ability to distinguish between heat and cold, or inability to feel temperature changes. Also called thermanalgesia.

thermocautery (ther-mo-kaw′ter-e) Destruction of tissue with a heated wire.

thermochemistry (ther-mo-kem′is-tre) The branch of chemistry dealing with the interrelationship of chemical action and heat.

thermochrose (ther′mo-krōz) The property of heat rays that makes them subject to reflection, refraction, and absorption.

thermocoagulation (ther-mo-ko-ag-u-la′shun) Coagulation of tissue by application of heat.

thermocouple (ther′mo-kup-l) A sensor for slight temperature changes formed by the junction of two dissimilar metal conductors. Also called thermojunction.

thermodiffusion (ther-mo-dĭ-fu′zhun) Diffusion of a gas or a liquid produced by a rise in temperature, which increases molecular motion.

thermodilution (ther-mo-di-lu′shun) Change in temperature of a liquid occurring when it is added to a warmer or colder one; the volume of the latter can be calculated from the degree of change in its temperature. The principle is employed to measure the volume or the rate of flow through a chamber (e.g., ventricular volume, cardiac output, or renal blood flow).

thermodynamics (ther-mo-di-nam′iks) The branch of physics dealing with heat and its conversion to other forms of energy.

thermoesthesia (ther-mo-es-the′ze-ah) Ability to perceive temperature changes.

thermogenesis (ther-mo-jen′ĕ-sis) Heat production, especially by the body.

thermogram (ther′mo-gram) A depiction of a body part, produced by sensing devices, showing variations in surface temperature.

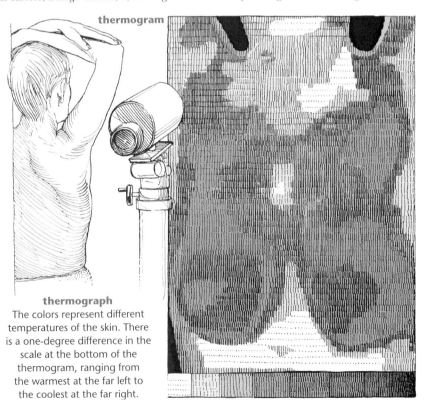

thermogram

thermograph
The colors represent different temperatures of the skin. There is a one-degree difference in the scale at the bottom of the thermogram, ranging from the warmest at the far left to the coolest at the far right.

thermograph (ther'mo-graf) Device used to make a thermogram.

thermography (ther-mog'rah-fe) The technique of recording visually, in the form of an image, temperature patterns on the surface of the skin; used to provide clues to the presence of diseases or abnormalities that alter skin temperature (e.g., circulation problems, inflammation, tumors). Further investigation is usually necessary to confirm a diagnosis.

  infrared t. Thermography conducted with the use of a camera or scanner that picks up heat radiation emitted by the skin.

  liquid crystal t. The use of flexible plates containing temperature-sensitive liquid crystals that, when applied to the skin, change color in response to changes in temperature.

thermohyperesthesia (ther-mo-hi'per-es-the'ze-ah) Extreme sensitivity to temperature fluctuations.

thermohypesthesia (ther-mo-hi'pes-the'ze-ah) Diminished sensitivity to temperature fluctuations. Also called thermohypoesthesia.

thermohypoesthesia (ther-mo-hi'po-es-the'ze-ah) See thermohypesthesia.

thermoinhibitory (ther-mo-in-hib'ĭ-tor-e) Preventing generation of heat.

thermojunction (ther-mo-junk'shun) See thermocouple.

thermolabile (ther-mo-la'bil) Tending to be changed or destroyed by heat.

thermolysis (ther-mol'ĭ-sis) **1.** Chemical decomposition induced by heat. **2.** Loss of body heat.

thermomassage (ther-mo-mah-sahzh') Combination of heat and massage; used in physical therapy.

thermometer (ther-mom'ĕ-ter) Instrument to measure temperature.

  clinical t. A small scaled glass tube containing mercury, used to measure the maximum temperature in the mouth, axilla, or rectum.

  digital t. A version of the clinical thermometer, equipped with a temperature-sensitive, electronic probe connected to a digital readout display.

  surface t. A disposable skin thermometer consisting of a disk that contains heat-sensitive chemicals, which change color at specific temperatures; generally considered less accurate than the clinical or digital thermometers.

  Thermoscan ™ instant t. A battery-operated device placed in the ear canal to measure body temperature in one second; it contains a temperature-sensitive probe, a mode switch to convert ear temperatures to familiar frame references (i.e., infant/toddler, child/adult), and a digital readout display.

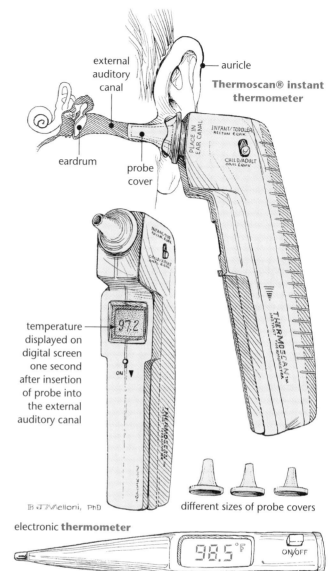

external auditory canal

auricle

Thermoscan® instant thermometer

eardrum

probe cover

temperature displayed on digital screen one second after insertion of probe into the external auditory canal

97.2

B J Melloni, PhD

electronic thermometer

different sizes of probe covers

98.5 °F

ON/OFF

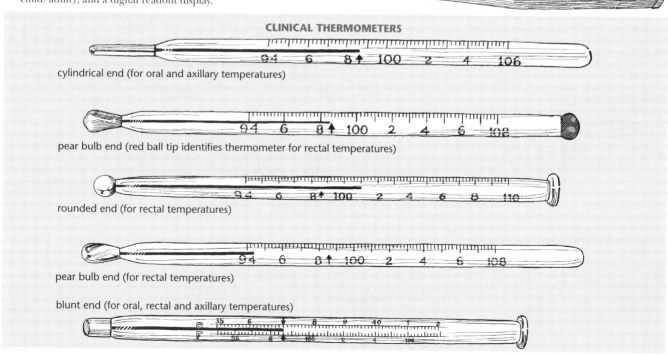

CLINICAL THERMOMETERS

cylindrical end (for oral and axillary temperatures)

pear bulb end (red ball tip identifies thermometer for rectal temperatures)

rounded end (for rectal temperatures)

pear bulb end (for rectal temperatures)

blunt end (for oral, rectal and axillary temperatures)

T

thermometry (ther-mom'ĕ-tre) Measurement of temperature.

thermophile, thermophil (ther'mo-fil, ther'mo-fil) Any organism that grows in high temperatures.

thermophore (ther'mo-fōr) A device for applying heat to the body.

thermoplacentography (ther-mo-plas-en-tog'rah-fe) Thermography of the placenta; i.e., determination of the placental location by recording increased temperature (due to large amounts of blood within the placenta).

thermoplegia (ther-mo-ple'je-ah) See heat stroke.

thermoreceptor (ther-mo-re-sep'tor) A special nerve ending that is sensitive to temperature fluctuations.

thermoregulation (ther-mo-reg-u-la'shun) Regulation of body core temperature, controlled by a special region of the hypothalamus in the brain.

thermoset (ther'mo-set) Any material that hardens when exposed to heat.

thermostable (ther-mo-sta'bl) Not subject to change by moderate heat.

thermotaxis (ther-mo-tak'sis) 1. Movement of an organism toward or away from heat. 2. Adjustment of the body to temperature changes.

thermotherapy (ther-mo-ther'ah-pe) The use of heat as an aid to treatment of disease.

thiabendazole (thi-ah-ben'dah-zol) An anthelmintic drug used to treat a variety of worm infestations, including trichinosis, strongyloidiasis, and toxocariasis. Adverse effects may include dizziness, drowsiness, headache, vomiting, and diarrhea.

thiaminase (thi-am'ĭ-nās) A thiamine-splitting enzyme.

thiamine (thi'ah-min) A vitamin of the B complex, present in yeast, meat, and the bran coat of grains; essential for the chemical breakdown of carbohydrates and in the functioning of nerves, muscles, and heart; severe lack of thiamine causes beriberi. Also called vitamin B_1.

thiamphenicol (thi-am-fen'ĭ-kōl) An antibiotic and immunosuppressive drug.

thiazides (thi'ah-zīds) Shortened name for benzothiadiazides, a class of diuretics used in the treatment of swelling due to water retention (edema) and of high blood pressure (hypertension).

thigh (thi) The portion of the lower limb between the hip and the knee.

    driver's t. Inflammation of the sciatic nerve (at the back of the thigh) due to persistent pressure on the nerve, as in prolonged use of the accelerator pedal in long-distance driving of an automobile.

thighbone (thi'bōn) See femur, in table of bones.

thigmesthesia (thig-mes-the'ze-ah) Sensitiveness to touch.

thimerosal (thi-mer'o-sal) An antiseptic preparation used topically on the skin and mucous membranes and as a preservative in pharmaceuticals. Also called thiomerosal.

thinking (thingk'ing) The mental process of reasoning based on past learning and experience.

    autistic t. Thinking that is subjective, mainly emanating from the unconscious, focused on the self to the exclusion of external reality; characteristic symptom of schizophrenia.

    magical t. The irrational equating of thoughts with actions; that is, believing that one's thoughts alone can cause something to happen, or prevent something from happening.

thiocyclodine (thi-o-si'klo-din) (TCP) A drug that produces altered perceptual states (hallucinations, illusions, euphoria); it has a potential for abuse and overdose.

thioguanine (thi-o-gwah'nēn) Antitumor drug used in the treatment of acute nonlymphocytic leukemia.

thionic (thi-on'ik) Relating to sulfur.

thiopental sodium (thi-o-pen'tal so'de-um) A barbiturate drug widely used as a general anesthetic, capable of producing unconsciousness quite rapidly when introduced intravenously or rectally, but with effects of short duration.

thioridazine (thi-o-rid'ah-zēn) A tranquilizer and antipsychotic drug used in the treatment of such disorders as schizophrenia and mania; it reduces symptoms, rendering the patient amenable to psychotherapy. Adverse effects include abnormal movements, muscle stiffness, dry mouth, and dizziness.

thiotepa (thi-o-te'pah) A highly toxic drug used to ameliorate the symptoms and signs of cancer. Adverse effects include pulmonary fibrosis, bone marrow damage, sterility, and secondary cancers.

thiothixene (thi-o-thiks'ēn) An antipsychotic drug that has been used in the management of depression and schizophrenia. Most frequent adverse effects are fever, fatigue, and drowsiness.

thiouracil (thi-o-u'rah-sil) Compound that retards the production of thyroid hormones.

thioxanthene (thi-o-zan'thēn) Any of a group of antipsychotic drugs that include thiothixene and chlorprothixene, which have been used in the treatment of schizophrenia and depression.

third party payer Any organization, public or private, that either pays or insures health care expenses on behalf of the actual recipients of such care.

thirst (therst) A physiological need to drink water.

    excessive t. See polydipsia.

thoracalgia (tho-rah-kal'je-ah) Chest pain.

thoracectomy (tho-rah-sek'to-me) Removal of part of a rib.

thoracentesis (tho-rah-sen-te'sis) Drainage of fluid from the pleural cavity, usually by needle puncture and aspiration for diagnostic analysis of the fluid. Also called thoracocentesis; pleurocentesis.

thoracic (tho-ras'ik) Relating to the thorax or chest.

thoracico- thoraco- Combining forms meaning the chest (thorax).

thoracicoacromial (tho-ras'i-ko-ah-kro'me-al) See acromiothoracic.

thoracoabdominal (tho'rah-ko-ab-dom'ĭ-nal) Relating to the thorax and abdomen.

thoracoacromial (tho'rah-ko-ah-kro'me-al) See acromiothoracic.

thoracocentesis (tho'rah-ko-sen-te'sis) See thoracentesis.

thoracocyllosis (tho'rah-ko-si-lo'sis) A deformity of the thorax.

thoracolumbar (tho'rah-ko-lum'bar) Relating to the thoracic and lumbar regions of the spine (vertebral column).

thoracomyodynia (tho'rah-ko-mi-o-din'e-ah) Pain in the musculature of the chest wall.

thoracopathy (tho'rah-kop'ah-the) Any disease of the chest (thorax).

thoracoplasty (tho'rah-ko-plas'te) Reparative or reconstructive surgery of the chest wall.

thoracopneumoplasty (tho'rah-ko-nu-mo-plas'te) Reparative surgery of the chest and lung.

thoracoscopy (tho'rah-kos'ko-pe) Examination of the chest cavity with an endoscope.

thoracostomy (tho'rah-kos'to-me) Surgical creation of an opening (stoma) in the chest wall.

thoracotomy (tho'rah-kot'o-me) A surgical cut into the chest wall.

thorax (tho'raks) The part of the body between the neck and the diaphragm; it contains the chief organs of circulatory and respiratory systems.

thorium (tho're-um) Radioactive element; symbol Th, atomic number 90, atomic weight 232.038.

thorn apple (thōrn' ap'l) See jimsonweed.

threadworm (thred'werm) See pinworm.

threonine (thre'o-nin) (Thr) An amino acid present in the protein molecule; it is essential to a mammalian diet.

threshold (thresh'hold) The level of intensity at which a stimulus (mental or physical) just begins to produce a sensation and below which the stimulus cannot be perceived.

    absolute t. The lowest possible level of a stimulus that will produce a sensation or cause a response.

    auditory t. The level at which a sound is just perceptible. Also called hearing threshold.

    t. of consciousness The lowest gradient of sensation that can be perceived.

    hearing t. Auditory threshold.

    renal t. Concentration of a substance in the plasma above

T

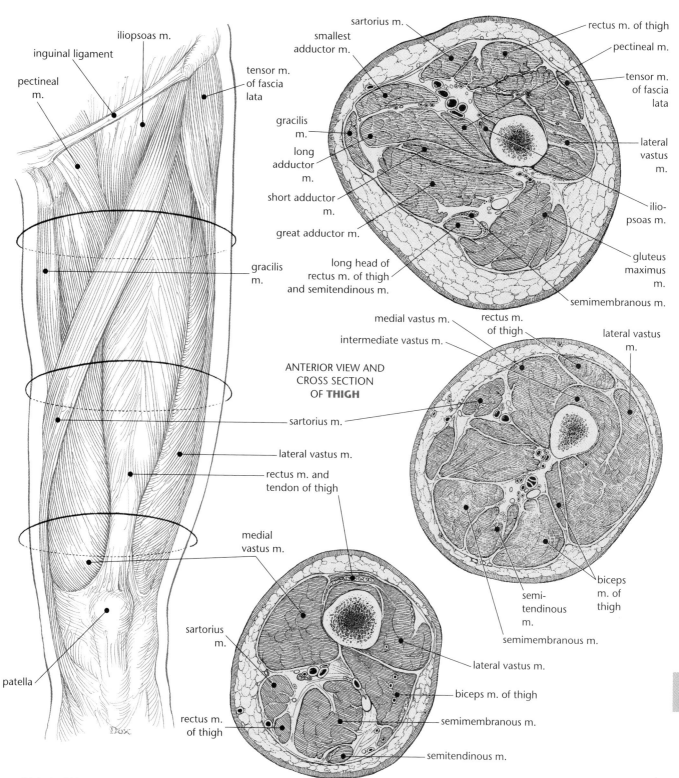

iliopsoas m.
inguinal ligament
pectineal m.
tensor m. of fascia lata
gracilis m.
patella
Dox

sartorius m.
smallest adductor m.
gracilis m.
long adductor m.
short adductor m.
great adductor m.
long head of rectus m. of thigh and semitendinous m.
rectus m. of thigh
pectineal m.
tensor m. of fascia lata
lateral vastus m.
iliopsoas m.
gluteus maximus m.
semimembranous m.

medial vastus m.
intermediate vastus m.
rectus m. of thigh
lateral vastus m.
sartorius m.
lateral vastus m.
rectus m. and tendon of thigh
semitendinous m.
semimembranous m.
biceps m. of thigh

ANTERIOR VIEW AND CROSS SECTION OF **THIGH**

medial vastus m.
sartorius m.
rectus m. of thigh
semitendinous m.
lateral vastus m.
biceps m. of thigh
semimembranous m.

T

which the kidney can no longer reabsorb it and some of it appears in the urine.

thrill (thril) A vibrating sensation felt when the flat of the hand is placed on the chest, associated with a vascular or heart murmur; caused by abnormal blood flow in the heart, usually due to some heart defect or valve disease; also may be felt over a peripheral vessel with a large turbulent flow, as in an arteriovenous fistula.

throat (thrōt) 1. Popular name for the pharynx, extending from the back of the mouth and nose to the esophagus. 2. The front of the neck.

    sore t. Throat condition marked by discomfort or pain on swal-lowing due to inflammation of mucous membranes.

    strep t. Popular name for acute streptococcal pharyngitis; see under pharyngitis.

throb (throb) 1. To pulsate. 2. A pulsating sensation.

throe (thro) A seizure of pain, as experienced in childbirth.

thrombasthenia (throm-bas-the'ne-ah) Abnormality of blood platelets, causing a bleeding disorder characterized by prolonged bleeding time, and absent clot retraction; an autosomal recessive inheritance. Also called Glanzmann's disease.

thrombectomy (throm-bek'to-me) Surgical removal of a blood clot (thrombus) that is partly or completely obstructing a blood vessel.

thrill ■ thrombectomy

thrombi (throm'bi) Plural of thrombus.

thrombin (throm'bin) An enzyme of blood plasma that converts the plasma protein fibrinogen into a network of fine filaments (fibrin), thus causing formation of a blood clot.

thrombinogen (throm-bin'o-jen) See prothrombin.

thrombo-, thromb- Combining forms meaning blood clot.

thromboangiitis (throm'bo-an-je-i'tis) Inflammation of blood vessel walls and clot formation.

    t. obliterans Thromboangiitis of small arteries and veins of the extremities with extension to accompanying nerves; may lead to ulceration or gangrene of digits; seen most commonly in young heavy smokers. Also called Buerger's disease.

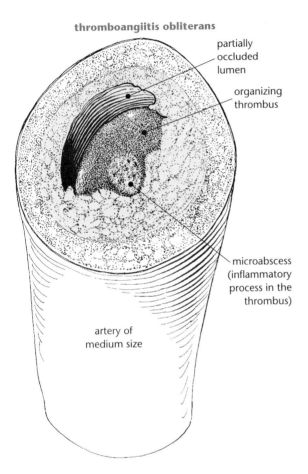

thromboangiitis obliterans

partially occluded lumen

organizing thrombus

microabscess (inflammatory process in the thrombus)

artery of medium size

thrombocytasthenia (throm'bo-si-tas-the'ne-ah) Any of various disorders of blood platelet function characterized by abnormal adhesion and/or aggregation of platelets, which renders them ineffective in blood clotting; some varieties are congenital, others are acquired, especially in uremia.

thrombocyte (throm'bo-sit) A blood platelet.

thrombocythemia (throm'bo-si-the'me-ah) See thrombocytosis.

thrombocytopathy (throm'bo-si-top'ah-the) Any blood-clotting disorder due to dysfunction of blood platelets. Also called thrombopathy.

thrombocytopenia (throm'bo-si-to-pe'ne-ah) Decreased number of platelets in blood (less than 150,000 per μL) Also called thrombopenia.

    isoimmune t. Thrombocytopenia caused by development of antiplatelet antibodies and consequent platelet destruction.

    neonatal t. Thrombocytopenia occurring in a newborn baby; may originate from the mother (e.g., infections, drug therapy, or maternal-fetal platelet incompatibility) or from the infant (e.g., disorders causing platelet destruction or dysfunction).

thrombocytosis (throm-bo-si-to'sis) An abnormally high number of platelets in the blood. Also called thrombocythemia.

thromboembolectomy (throm'bo-em-bo-lek'to-me) Extraction of a blood clot that obstructs blood flow through a vessel.

thromboembolism (throm'bo-em'bo-lizm) The transport of detached fragments of a blood clot (thrombus) in the circulation from its site of formation to another blood vessel, where it becomes impacted, causing obstruction at the site of impaction.

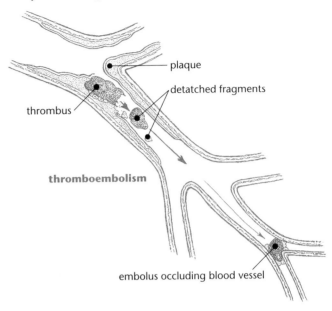

plaque

detached fragments

thrombus

thromboembolism

embolus occluding blood vessel

thromboendarterectomy (throm'bo-end-ar-ter-ek'to-me) Surgical removal of an obstructing blood clot from an artery or vein, together with the corresponding section of inner lining of the vessel.

thrombogenic (throm'bo-jen'ik) Forming blood clots.

thrombolysis (throm-bol'i-sis) Dissolution of blood clots within blood vessels.

thrombopathy (throm-bop'ah-the) See thrombocytopathy.

thrombopenia (throm'bo-pe'ne-ah) See thrombocytopenia.

thrombophlebitis (throm'bo-fle-bi'tis) Inflammation of a vein associated with formation of blood clots (thrombi), causing tenderness, and swelling along the involved vessel; when a superficial vein is involved, there will also be redness of the overlying skin.

    deep t. Thrombophlebitis occurring in a deep vein, especially of the calf and thigh. Also called deep phlebitis.

    migratory t. Inflammation appearing first in one site, then another; associated with cancer, especially of internal organs. Also called Trousseau's syndrome.

    puerperal t. Thrombophlebitis occurring in a vein in the iliofemoral area during late pregnancy and after delivery; characterized by extreme swelling of the leg, severe pain, tenderness and increased temperature; caused by compression of the vein by the pregnant uterus and the hypercoagulability of pregnancy. Also called milk leg; painful white leg; phlegmasia alba dolens.

    septic pelvic t. Clotting in the veins of the pelvis, caused by bacterial invasion of the vessels' walls; may occur after childbirth. Predisposing factors include cesarean section after long labor, premature rupture of membranes, difficult delivery, existing systemic disease, anemia, and malnourishment.

thromboplastin (throm'bo-plas'tin) Protein complex that initiates the clotting of blood. Also called factor III.

thromboplastinogen (throm'bo-plas-tin'o-jen) See factor VIII, under factor.

thrombopoiesis (throm'bo-poi-e'sis) 1. The formation of a blood clot. 2. The formation of blood platelets.

thrombosis (throm-bo'sis) Formation of blood clots (thrombi) within an intact blood vessel.

    cerebral t. Obstruction of a blood vessel in the brain by a thrombus, one of the causes of stroke.

    coronary t. The presence of a thrombus in one of the arteries

T

supplying the heart muscle, causing obstruction and depriving the muscle of oxygen; it is one of the causes of heart attack (myocardial infarction). Popularly called coronary.

    deep venous t. (DVT) Clotting of blood inside deep-seated veins, especially of the legs, often causing pain and tenderness in the thigh or calf; seen most commonly in people immobilized for long periods, those with chronic debilitating diseases, surgical patients, and those with cancer. Condition is a common source of embolism, especially pulmonary embolism.

thrombus (throm'bus), pl. throm'bi A blood clot; a solid or semisolid mass formed inside an intact blood vessel (distinct from one formed to seal a cut or injured vessel); it is composed of the constituents of blood, primarily platelets and fibrin.

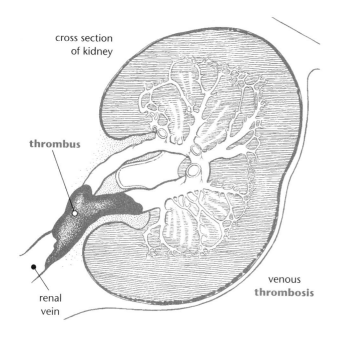

cross section of kidney

thrombus

renal vein

venous thrombosis

throwback (thro'bak) See atavus.

thrush (thrush) Infection of the mouth with the fungus *Candida albicans,* which forms white patches in the mucous membrane; seen most frequently in infants and in patients with suppressed or deficient immune system, especially after a course of antibiotic treatment.

thrust (thrust) To push forth with physical force.

    tongue t. Inappropriate or excessive pressure of the tongue against the anterior teeth while eating, talking or at rest.

thulium (thu'le-um) Metallic element; symbol Tm, atomic number 69, atomic weight 168.934.

thumb (thum) The first digit of the hand.

    gamekeeper's t. Rupture of the ulnar collateral ligament of the metacarpophalangeal joint of the thumb by forcible abduction; if untreated may lead to progressive subluxation.

    tennis t. Inflammation and calcification of the tendon of the long flexor muscle of the thumb due to activities in which the thumb is subject to great pressure and strain (e.g., in tennis playing).

    trigger t. Condition in which the thumb is arrested in a bent position at the beginning of attempted extension and then suddenly released with an audible click; caused by interference with movement of the tendon within its sheath due to inflammation; commonly associated with osteoarthritis.

thumbprinting (thum'print-ing) A sign of submucosal edema of the bowel wall; the colon appears in the x-ray image as having a series of smooth depressions, reminiscent of a thumbprint; seen in such disorders as Crohn's disease and ischemia.

thymectomy (thi-mek'to-me) Removal of the thymus.

-thymia Combining form meaning mind; emotions (e.g., parathymia).

thymic (thi'mik) Relating to the thymus.

thymidine (thi'mi-dēn) (dThd, dT) A condensation product of thymine with deoxyribose; one of the four major nucleosides in DNA.

thymidylic acid (thi-mi-dil'ik as'id) A constituent of DNA.

thymine (thi'min) A component of DNA and thymidylic acid.

thymitis (thi-mi'tis) Inflammation of the thymus.

thymo-, thymi-, thym- Combining forms meaning thymus; the mind.

thymocyte (thi'mo-sīt) A white blood cell that is the precursor of the thymus-derived lymphocyte (T lymphocyte); important in cell-mediated immunity.

thymogenic (thi-mo-jen'ik) Of affective origin.

thymokinetic (thi-mo-ki-net'ik) Stimulating the thymus.

thymoma (thi-mo'mah) Tumor (most commonly benign) located within the upper part of the chest; derived from epithelial cells of the thymus and associated with a variety of diseases, including myasthenia gravis, blood abnormalities, and hypogammaglobulinemia. It may undergo malignant change.

thymopoietin (thi-mo-poi'ě-tin) Immunologically active hormone secreted by epithelial cells of the thymus; it stimulates formation of the white blood cell lymphocyte; it also blocks neuromuscular transmission of nerve impulses.

thymus (thi'mus) A two-lobed lymphoid organ responsible for T cell production and maturation, situated just behind the top of the breastbone (sternum); it grows until puberty and then begins to decrease in size until, in old age, it is replaced by fat and connective tissue, with little thymic tissue left; it is the principal organ involved in development of normal immunologic function in early life and in monitoring the total lymphoid system throughout life.

thyro-, thyr- Combining forms meaning the thyroid gland.

thyroaplasia (thi-ro-ah-pla'ze-ah) Congenital abnormalities associated with faulty thyroid functioning.

thyroarytenoid (thi-ro-ar-ī-te'noid) Relating to both the thyroid and arytenoid cartilages.

thyrocalcitonin (thi-ro-kal-sī-to'nin) See calcitonin.

thyrocricotomy (thi-ro-kri-kot'o-me) Surgical cut through the cricothyroid membrane.

thyroglobulin (thi-ro-glob'u-lin) Protein produced by the thyroid gland whose function is to store the thyroid hormones thyroxine (T_4) and triiodothyronine (T_3), which it releases on hydrolysis.

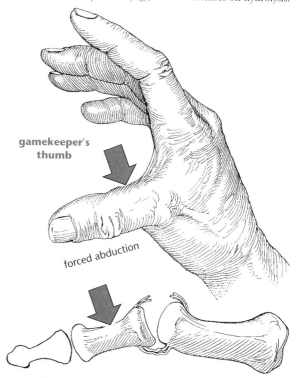

gamekeeper's thumb

forced abduction

thyroglossal (thi-ro-glos′al) Relating to the thyroid cartilage and the tongue.

thyrohyoid (thi-ro-hi′oid) Relating to the thyroid cartilage and the hyoid bone.

thyroid (thi′roid) 1. Resembling a shield. 2. The thyroid gland. 3. Preparation derived from thyroid glands of certain domestic animals; used as replacement therapy in thyroid deficiencies.

thyroidectomy (thi-roi-dek′to-me) Removal of the thyroid gland.

thyroiditis (thi-roi-di′tis) Inflammation of the thyroid gland. Also called strumitis.

> **de Quervain's t.** See subacute granulomatous thyroiditis.
>
> **granulomatous t.** See subacute granulomatous thyroiditis.
>
> **Hashimoto's t.** Autoimmune inflammatory disorder responsible for most cases of primary hypothyroidism; characterized by progressive, painless enlargement of the thyroid gland, which becomes firm and rubbery and then slowly diminishes in size, eventually becoming atrophic and fibrous; seen most commonly in women between 30 and 50 years old. Also called Hashimoto's disease; Hashimoto's struma; struma lymphomatosa.
>
> **infectious t.** A transient inflammation caused by various microorganisms, including *Staphylococcus aureus*, *Salmonella*, streptococci, and fungi.
>
> **Riedel's t.** Uncommon condition in which the thyroid gland is replaced by fibrous tissue, which extends to contiguous neck structures. Also called Reidel's struma.
>
> **subacute granulomatous t.** Thyroiditis of unknown cause, believed to be of viral origin; usually follows a viral infection, especially of the upper respiratory tract; marked by a self-limited enlargement of the thyroid gland, fever, and, occasionally, transient hyperthyroidism; seen most commonly in women between 20 and 50 years old. Also called de Quervain's thyroiditis; granulomatous thyroiditis.
>
> **subacute lymphocytic t.** Thyroiditis of unknown cause marked by lymphoid infiltration of the gland's substance, occurs mostly in women after childbirth.

thyromegaly (thi-ro-meg′ah-le) Enlarged state of the thyroid gland.

thyroparathyroidectomy (thi-ro-par′ah-thi′roi-dek′to-me) Removal of the thyroid and parathyroid glands.

thyropathy (thi-rop′ah-the) Any disease of the thyroid gland.

thyroprival (thi-ro-pri′val) Caused by the surgical removal of the thyroid gland or by the arrest of its function.

thyroprotein (thi-ro-pro′tēn) Preparation made by combining protein (e.g., casein) with iodine; it has a physiologic effect similar to that of the thyroid hormone thyroxine (T_4).

thyrotomy (thi-rot′o-me) 1. Surgical cut into the thyroid cartilage. 2. Operative cutting of the thyroid gland.

thyrotoxicosis (thi-ro-tok′si-ko′sis) Toxic condition reflecting the response of tissues to an excess of thyroid hormone.

thyrotropic (thi-ro-trop′ik) 1. Influencing the thyroid gland. 2. Stimulating the thyroid gland.

thyrotropin (thi-rot′ro-pin) Hormone of the anterior lobe of the pituitary (adenohypophysis) that stimulates the growth and function of the thyroid gland. Also called thyrotrophic hormone; thyrotropic hormone; thyroid-stimulating hormone. Formerly called thyrotropic-releasing factor.

thyroxine (thi-rok′sin) (T_4) Iodine-containing hormone, produced by the thyroid gland; its chief function is to aid in regulating the body's metabolism. Synthetic preparations are used in replacement therapy for deficiency states (e.g., hypothyroidism, cretinism, myxedema).

tibia (tib′e-ah) The larger of the two bones of the leg between the knee and the ankle, medial to the fibula. Popularly called shinbone. See also table of bones.

tibio- Combining form meaning the shinbone (tibia).

tibiocalcaneal (tib′e-o-kal-ka′ne-al) Relating to the shinbone (tibia) and the heel bone (calcaneus).

tibiofemoral (tib′e-o-fem′or-al) Relating to the shinbone (tibia) and the thighbone (femur).

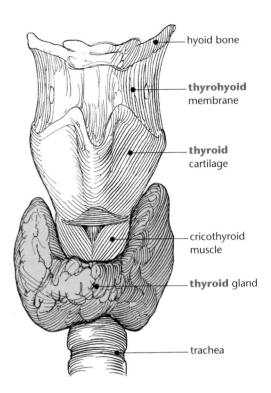

- hyoid bone
- **thyrohyoid** membrane
- **thyroid** cartilage
- cricothyroid muscle
- **thyroid** gland
- trachea

scan from patient with lymphocytic **thyroiditis**

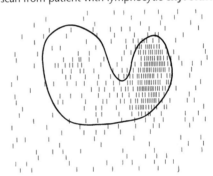

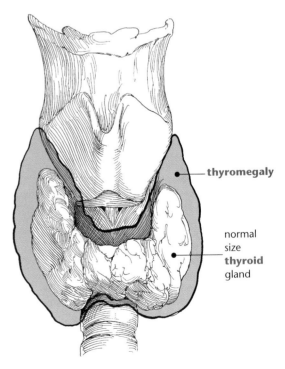

- **thyromegaly**
- normal size **thyroid** gland

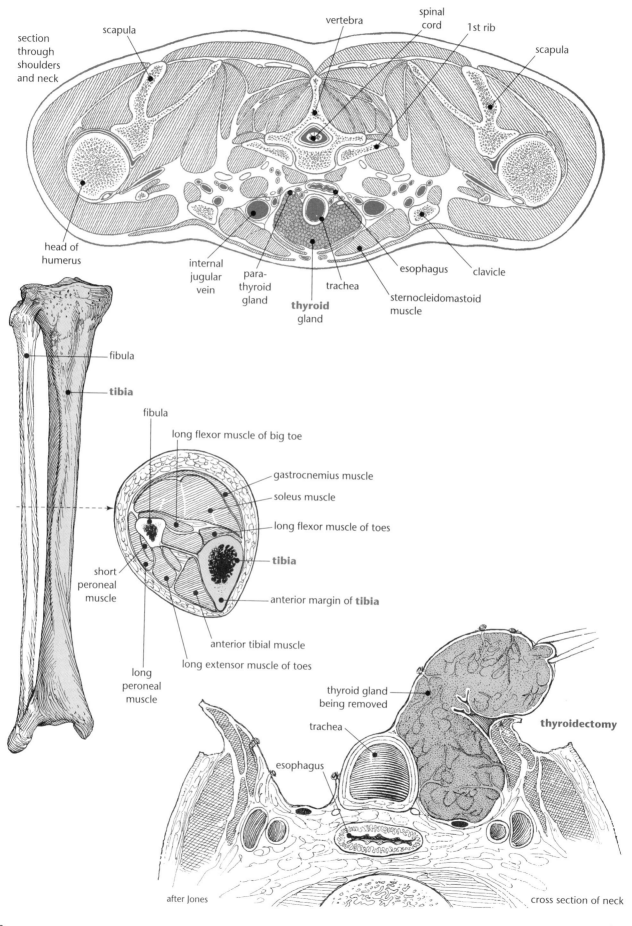

section through shoulders and neck

scapula

spinal cord

vertebra

1st rib

scapula

head of humerus

internal jugular vein

para-thyroid gland

trachea

thyroid gland

esophagus

clavicle

sternocleidomastoid muscle

fibula

tibia

fibula

long flexor muscle of big toe

gastrocnemius muscle

soleus muscle

long flexor muscle of toes

tibia

anterior margin of **tibia**

short peroneal muscle

long peroneal muscle

anterior tibial muscle

long extensor muscle of toes

thyroid gland being removed

trachea

esophagus

thyroidectomy

after Jones

cross section of neck

T

tibiofibular (tib´e-o-fib´u-lar) Relating to the two bones of the leg, the tibia and fibula. Also called tibioperoneal.

tibioperoneal (tib´e-o-per-o-ne´al) See tibiofibular.

tic (tik) Involuntary, brief, and recurrent twitching of a muscle or a group of muscles usually involving the face, neck, or shoulders (e.g., needless blinking and shoulder shrugging).

  t. douloureux See trigeminal neuralgia, under neuralgia.

tick (tik) An eight-legged animal of the families Ixodidae (hard-shell ticks) and Argasidae (soft-shell ticks); some are bloodsucking parasites that carry and transmit disease-causing microorganisms.

  deer t. Either of two species of hard-shelled ticks, *Ixodes dammini* or *Ixodes pacificus,* that transmit Lyme disease.

  dog t. A hard-shelled tick, *Dermacentor variabilis,* vector of Rocky Mountain spotted fever.

  hard t.'s See Ixodidae.

  Rocky Mountain wood t. A hard-shelled tick, *Dermacentor andersoni,* the most important vector of Rocky Mountain spotted fever; also spreads tularemia, Q fever, and Colorado tick fever; it is the cause of tick paralysis.

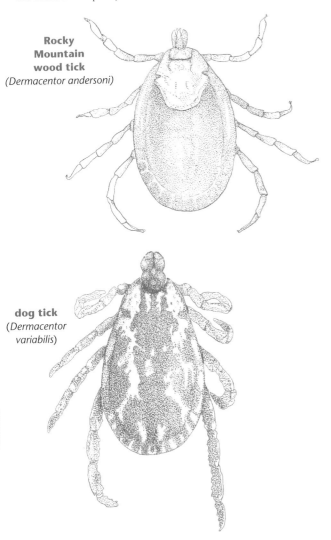

Rocky Mountain wood tick
(*Dermacentor andersoni*)

dog tick
(*Dermacentor variabilis*)

ticlopidine hydrochloride (ti-klo´pi-dēn hi-dro-klo´rīd) A platelet-aggregation inhibitor drug prescribed to reduce the risk of stroke, especially useful for patients who have suffered a stroke-precursor event such as a transient ischemic attack (TIA). Trade name: Ticlid.

tide (tīd) An increase.

  alkaline t. Transient increase in the pH (alkalinity) of the urine following ingestion of food, a consequence of stomach secretion of acids.

time (tīm) The duration of something such as an event or a process.

  bleeding t. The length of time a small puncture made on the skin bleeds, normally from one to three minutes.

  circulation t. The time required for blood to flow once between two designated points in the circulatory system.

  clot retraction t. Time required for a blood clot to become firm and separated from the sides of the tube containing it; about 50% retraction is considered normal.

  clotting t. See coagulation time.

  coagulation t. Time required for blood to clot in a test tube. Also called clotting time.

  doubling t. Time required for a population of cells to double in number.

  prothrombin t. Time required for a clot to form after calcium has been added to plasma in the presence of tissue thromboplastin.

  reaction t. Time passed between application of a stimulus and an observable response.

  recognition t. Time passed between application of a stimulus and sensory recognition of its nature.

  survival t. *(a)* The duration of life after such events as onset of illness, therapeutic intervention, or an experimental procedure. *(b)* The life span of cells.

tin (tin) Metallic element; symbol Sn, atomic number 50, atomic weight 118.69.

tinctorial (tink-to´re-al) Relating to the act of staining.

tincture (tink´tur) (tr.) An alcohol or water-alcohol solution of ingredients of animal, vegetable, or chemical origin.

  alcoholic t. One made with undiluted alcohol.

  hydroalcoholic t. One made with alcohol diluted in varied proportions of water.

tine (tīn) **1.** A device for introducing an antigen into the skin. **2.** One of the two slender arms of a tuning fork.

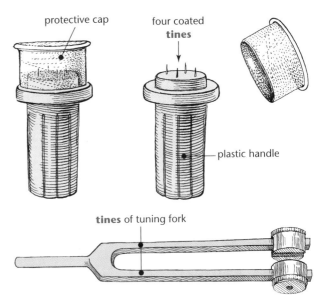

protective cap

four coated **tines**

plastic handle

tines of tuning fork

tinea (tin´e-ah) Fungal infection of the skin, nails, or scalp usually caused by fungi belonging to the genera *Trichophyton, Microsporum,* and *Epidermophyton.* Organisms live on the dead layer of the skin and produce an enzyme that enables them to digest keratin, thus disintegrating hair, nails, and the hardened layers of the skin. Also called ringworm.

  t. barbae Tinea of the beard area characterized by dark red lesions dotted with abscesses around hair follicles; may be acquired from pets or farm animals. Also called barber's itch; folliculitis barbae.

  t. capitis Infection of the scalp and hair causing patches of round, itchy, balding areas; likely sources of infection include hair clippers, theater seats, and domestic animals. Also called tinea of scalp; ringworm of scalp.

T

t. corporis Tinea occurring anywhere on the body; a highly contagious form most commonly seen in children, acquired from pets and from other children; characterized by typical round or oval scaly lesions of advancing vesicles and papules. Also called ringworm of smooth skin.

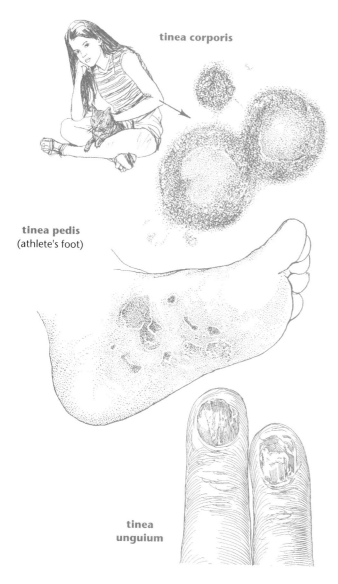

tinea corporis

tinea pedis
(athlete's foot)

tinea
unguium

t. cruris A reddened itchy area spreading from the genitals to the groin, perianal area, and inner thighs. Also called jock itch; tinea of groin; eczema marginatum.

t. of groin See tinea cruris.

t. pedis Tinea of the feet characterized either by dry scaling of the skin or by itchy blistering on the instep of the feet and between the toes. Also called ringworm of foot; commonly called athlete's foot.

t. of scalp See tenia capitis.

t. unguium Tinea of the nails; an infection involving usually one or two nails, especially toenails; degree of nail changes ranges from mild scaling and cracking to splitting and almost complete separation of the nail plate; initial sign is a yellow discoloration and thickening of the nail. Also called onychomycosis.

t. versicolor Patches of dark and light scales on the skin, occurring most commonly on the trunk; light scraping of the skin usually yields a profusion of scales; caused by a yeastlike fungus, *Malassezia furfur.*

tingling (ting´gling) A prickling sensation, as after striking the ulnar nerve at the elbow; the "funny bone" sensation.

tinnitus (tǐ-ni´tus) A ringing, buzzing, hissing, etc., heard in the absence of environmental noise.

TIPS Acronym for Transjugular Intrahepatic Portosystemic Shunts; a procedure for lessening portal hypertension in chronic liver disease. A catheter is passed from the right internal jugular vein through the superior and inferior venae cavae into the right hepatic vein; a needle is then extended from the catheter through the liver to create an opening between the hepatic vein and a branch of the portal vein; the opening is then widened and a stent inserted.

tissue (tish´u) A mass of similar cells and the substance that surrounds them, united to perform a particular function.

adenoid t. Lymphoid tissue situated in the nasal part of the pharynx; when swollen, it may obstruct nasal respiration, resulting in mouth breathing.

adipose t. Connective tissue composed of fat cells clumped together and surrounded by reticular fibers. Also called fatty tissue.

alveolar t. A loose, interlacing connective tissue with sparse collagenous, elastic, and reticular fibers in a protein polysaccharide ground substance; its extensibility permits adjacent structures some mobility.

areolar t. A type of connective tissue composed of loosely woven collagenous bundles and elastic fibers, with comparatively wide interspaces that are filled with a semifluid mucopolysaccharide ground substance containing such cells as fibroblasts and macrophages.

bone t. A hard form of connective tissue that is highly vascular, mineralized, and constantly changing; it consists of cells (osteocytes) embedded in a tough fibrous matrix containing collagen fibers and deposits of mineral salts (calcium phosphate, carbonate, and fluoride); it develops either by transformation of condensed mesenchyme or by replacement of a cartilaginous model. Also called bony tissue; osseous tissue.

bony t. See bone tissue.

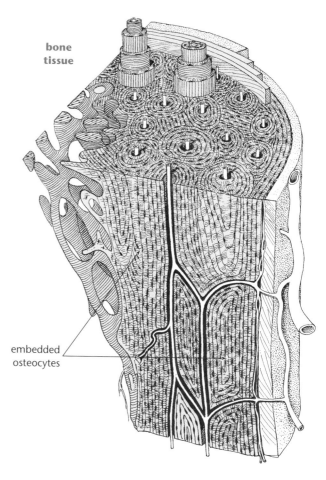

bone
tissue

embedded
osteocytes

T

tingling ■ tissue

cancellous t. The loose, latticelike spongy bone containing numerous marrow cavities; found in the interior of all bones, especially toward the articular ends of long bones.

cavernous t. See erectile tissue.

chondrogenic t. A connective tissue forming the inner layer of the fibrous membrane that covers cartilage (perichondrium), responsible for the production of new cartilage.

connective t. A general term denoting the principal supporting tissue of the body formed by a considerable proportion of fibrous and ground substance with numerous cell types (fibroblasts, macrophages, plasma cells, neutrophils, eosinophils, lymphocytes, fat cells, etc.) as well as supportive proteins, such as collagen and elastin; it supports and connects various structures throughout the body with the exception of the nervous system; bones, cartilage, fascia, ligaments, and tendons, are some examples of connective tissue. Also called interstitial tissue.

elastic t. Connective tissue composed chiefly of yellow elastic fibers, giving the tissue elasticity and a yellowish hue; found in some ligaments (e.g., flaval and nuchal ligaments) and in the walls of large arteries and air passages. Also called fibroelastic tissue.

epithelial t. See epithelium.

erectile t. Tissue containing an abundance of vascular spaces which, when engorged with blood, render the part firm, as in the external genitalia. Also called cavernous tissue.

fatty t. See adipose tissue.

fibroelastic t. See elastic tissue.

fibrous t. A dense form of connective tissue containing bundles of closely packed strands of collagenous fibers with little intercellular matrix; found in tendons, ligaments, aponeuroses, and some membranes such as the dura mater.

granulation t. Newly formed vascular tissue that appears in the early stages of wound healing, composed of different cell types and young sprouting blood vessels.

gut-associated lymphoid t. Various configurations of lymphoid tissue that line the alimentary (digestive) canal; may appear as pinhead-sized solitary nodules, as in the jejunum, or as large aggregate ellipsoid nodules (Peyer's patch), exclusively confined to the ileum, where they are invariably located opposite the attachment of the mesentery.

hemopoietic t. Blood cell–forming tissue; tissue that is actively involved with the development of formed elements of the blood, as in the medulla of long bones.

interstitial t. See connective tissue.

lymphatic t. See lymphoid tissue.

lymphoid t. A lattice of reticular cells and fibers with interspaces containing predominantly masses of developing and mature lymphocytes; might also include some macrophages or other cells, as seen in lymph nodes, adenoids, spleen, tonsils, etc. Also called lymphatic tissue.

lymphoreticular t. Tissue that carries out the functions of immunity through a variety of cell types, each performing a specific function, either by direct cell action or through the elaboration of antibody.

mesenchymal t. See mesenchyme.

mucoid t. A loose form of connective tissue in which the matrix is jellylike due to the presence of mucopolysaccharides, as seen in the umbilical cord (Wharton's jelly). Also called mucous tissue.

mucous t. See mucoid tissue.

muscular t. The substance of a muscle composed of threadlike fibers, either striated (skeletal and cardiac) or nonstriated (smooth), which contract upon stimulation.

myeloid t. The red bone marrow of the ribs, vertebrae and other small bones, which forms both red and white blood cells, consisting of the developmental and adult stages of erythrocytes, granulocytes, and megakaryocytes in a stroma of reticular cells and fibers.

nervous t. Tissue from the central nervous system (CNS) or peripheral nervous system (PNS), consisting of basically two distinct sets of cells: the excitable cells (neurons), which specialize in the reception, conduction, and transmission of neural impulses, and the nonexcitable cells (neuroglia, ependyma, Schwann cells, and associated elements), which serve as the supporting element.

osseous t. See bone tissue.

osteogenic t. A fibrous connective tissue comprising the loose inner layer of the membrane covering the surface of bones (periosteum), containing osteoblasts that engage in the formation of bone tissue.

osteoid t. Bone matrix prior to calcification; uncalcified bone tissue produced by osteoblasts and osteogenic cells, normally found as a thin layer on the advancing surface of developing bone.

reticular t. The most delicate type of connective tissue, composed of a network of fine reticular cells and reticulin fibers arranged in a mesh to facilitate the free movement of cells and fluids; found in

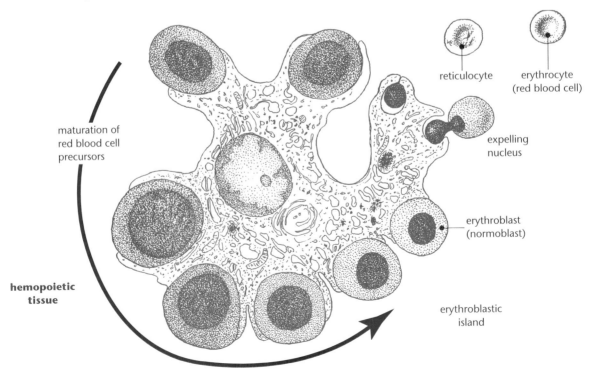

maturation of red blood cell precursors

hemopoietic tissue

reticulocyte

erythrocyte (red blood cell)

expelling nucleus

erythroblast (normoblast)

erythroblastic island

tissue ■ **tissue**

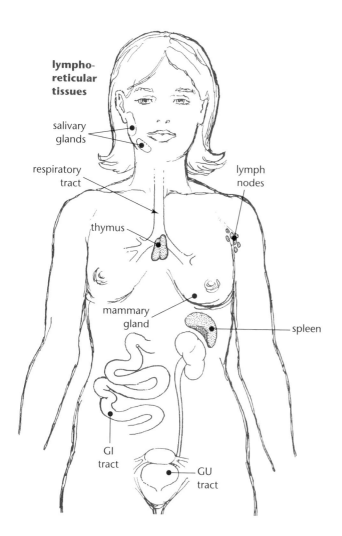

lympho- reticular tissues

salivary glands

respiratory tract

lymph nodes

thymus

mammary gland

spleen

GI tract

GU tract

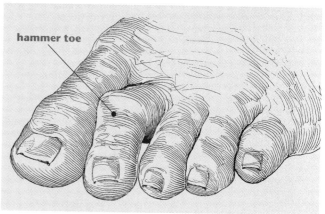

hammer toe

smokeless t. A preparation of powdered tobacco to be inhaled through the nose (snuff) or made into a wad for chewing (chewing tobacco); both practices cause cancer, of the nasal tissues in the first and the oral tissues in the second.

tobramycin (to-brah-mi′sin) Broad-spectrum antibiotic drug of the amino glycoside type produced by *Streptomyces tenebrarius;* active against gram-negative bacteria, especially *Pseudomonas aeruginosa.*

toco- Combining form meaning childbirth.

tocodynamometer (to-ko-di′nah-mom′e-ter) A pressure sensor instrument placed on the abdomen of a women in labor to determine the frequency and duration of uterine contractions. It does not measure accurately the intensity of contractions or the resting tone of the uterus. Also called tocometer.

tocometer (to-kom′ĕ-ter) See tocodynamometer.

tocopherol (to-kof′er-ol) (T) Generic name for vitamin E and its compounds.

toe (to) One of the digits of the feet.

    great t. The hallux.

    hammer t. A deformed second toe (usually associated with hallux valgus) in which the second phalanx is permanently flexed and the first phalanx compensates by hyperextending.

    pigeon t. See intoe.

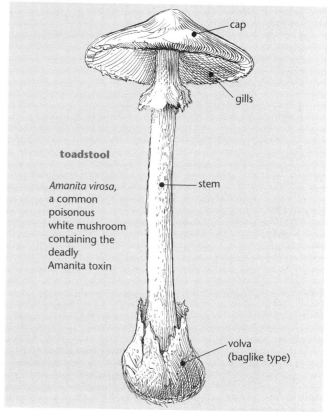

toadstool

Amanita virosa, a common poisonous white mushroom containing the deadly Amanita toxin

cap

gills

stem

volva (baglike type)

many structures, including lymph nodes, bone marrow, and the spleen.

    subcutaneous t. The loose, generally fatty tissue just beneath the skin, attached to the dermis by coarse fibers (retinacula cutis).

    target t. In immunology, the tissue against which antibodies are formed.

titanium (ti-ta′ne-um) Metallic element; symbol Ti, atomic number 22, atomic weight 47.90.

    t. oxide White powder used in creams and powders to relieve itchiness and as protection against the sun's rays.

titer (ti′ter) A measure of the strength of a solution or the degree of dilution of a substance that will still provide a measurable reaction, as in agglutination reactions; used as an index of the degree of immune responsiveness to a particular antigen; obtained to determine whether a person is immune to viruses, bacteria, or bacterial by-products; or whether a person has recently been exposed to a specific infectious microorganism.

titrate (ti′trāt) To analyze the concentration of a solution by titration.

titration (ti-tra′shun) Estimation of the quantity of a substance in solution by adding to the sample a measured amount of standard test solution until a reaction of known proportion is reached. The reaction could be a sudden color change, development of turbidity, or a change in the electrical state of the sample.

TM-mode (TM mōd) See M-mode.

toadstool (tōd′stul) Popular name for an umbrella-shaped poisonous mushroom.

tobacco (to-bak′o) The dried, prepared leaves of the tobacco plant, *Nicotiana tabacum,* containing the alkaloid nicotine; tobacco smoke is a health hazard for smokers and exposed nonsmokers, including the fetus.

T

webbed t.'s Toes joined abnormally by a skin fold.

toenail (to'nāl) The plate on the dorsal surface of the tip of each toe.

ingrown t. Condition in which an edge of the toenail presses against, and is overgrown by, adjacent tissue, frequently producing a purulent infection.

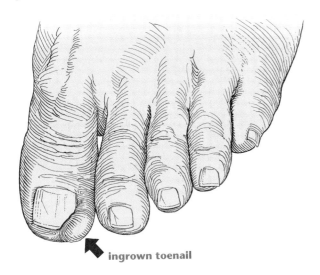

ingrown toenail

Togaviridae (to-gah-vir'ĭ-de) Family of viruses that contain single-stranded RNA and replicate in cytoplasm; it includes the virus causing German measles (rubella).

togavirus (to-gah-vi'rus) Any member of the family Togaviridae.

toilet (toi'let) The cleansing of a patient (e.g., after childbirth), of a wound and surrounding skin, of a tracheostomy tube, etc.

tolbutamide (tol-bu'tah-mĭd) An oral hypoglycemic drug used in the management of non-insulin-dependent diabetes; it stimulates insulin release from the pancreas.

tolerance (tol'er-ans) **1.** The body's ability to endure an insult (e.g., physiologic, chemical, or mechanical) without showing unfavorable effects. **2.** Tendency toward a reduced degree of response to repeated exposure to a stimulus.

acoustic t. The maximum sound pressure level (SPL) a person can endure without harmful effects.

cross t. Resistance to the effects of one drug resulting from an acquired tolerance to another, pharmacologically related, drug.

drug t. See drug tolerance, after drug.

immunologic t. The nonreactivity, or a lessened reactivity, to a particular antigen by an otherwise immunocompetent individual, acquired by previous exposure to that antigen. Also called immunotolerance.

impaired glucose t. See latent diabetes mellitus, under diabetes.

natural t. See self tolerance.

self t. Lack of immune activity against the body's own antigens. Also called natural tolerance.

species t. Unresponsiveness to a drug occurring as a characteristic of a particular species.

vibration t. The maximum vibratory movements that a person can endure without pain.

tolerogen (tol'er-o-jen) A particular antigen toward which the body has acquired immunologic nonreactivity (i.e., a state of tolerance for that particular antigen).

tolerogenic (tol-er-o-jen'ik) Producing immunologic tolerance.

tolnaftate (tol-naf'tāt) Antifungal agent used topically to treat fungal infections of the skin such as ringworm (tinea).

toluene (tol'u-ēn) A volatile liquid used in the extraction of principles from plants and the manufacture of dyes and explosives. Long-term exposure in the workplace may cause dermatitis and neurobehavioral dysfunction. Also called methylbenzene.

-tome Combining form meaning instrument for cutting (e.g., microtome); a section (e.g., dermatome).

tomogram (to'mo-gram) An x-ray image of a section of the body made by tomography.

tomograph (to'mo-graf) An x-ray machine for making sectional images (tomograms) of the body.

tomography (to-mog'rah-fe) Any imaging method that sequentially produces a clear image of one selected plane of internal structures of the body while all background and foreground planes appear blurred; used to detect abnormalities in living tissues. Also called sectional roentgenography; body-section roentgenography; planigraphy; laminagraphy.

computed t. (CT) The combined use of x-ray transmission and a computer to construct cross-sectional (axial) images of a body part. Also called computed axial tomography.

computed axial t. (CAT) See computed tomography.

positron emission t. (PET) A method of visually recording information about a tissue's metabolism by computer construction of three-dimensional images; the procedure involves injecting a radioactive substance that decays by emitting positively charged particles (positrons); these positrons emit gamma rays (photons) when colliding with the negatively charged electrons normally present in the tissues; the path of the photons is then traced by external censors, producing the images. Prior to injecting the positron-emitting substance into the bloodstream, it is combined with (tagged to) another substance, such as glucose, that takes part in metabolic processes. Concentration of the tagged substance in the tissue is directly related to the degree of metabolic activity of the tissue; the variations are recorded in the computer image.

single photon emission computed t. (SPECT) A method of computed tomography using radioactive substances that decay by emitting a single gamma ray (photon) of a given energy. The camera is rotated 180° or 360° degrees around the patient to obtain images at multiple positions; the computer is then used to construct images (sagittal, coronal, and cross-sectional) from the three-dimensional distribution of the radioactive substance in the organ of concern. By using SPECT, it is possible to observe biochemical and physiologic processes and the size and volume of the organ. Also called SPECT imaging.

tomomania (to-mo-ma'ne-ah) **1.** The tendency of certain surgeons to perform operations for minor ailments. **2.** An irrational desire to be operated upon.

-tomy Combining form meaning surgical cutting (e.g., thyroidotomy).

tone (tōn) **1.** The tension of a muscle at rest. **2.** See pitch (2).

tongue (tung) The mobile muscular structure covered with mucous membrane and arising from the floor of the mouth; it serves as the chief organ of taste and aids in chewing, swallowing, and articulation of sound.

bifid t. A tongue with a notch at its tip. Also called cleft tongue.

black t. A tongue with brown or black patches of matted, overdeveloped papillae on its dorsal aspect. The dark pigment is believed to be caused by microorganisms or by antibiotic drugs. Also called hairy tongue; glossotrichia; trichoglossia.

cleft t. See bifid tongue.

coated t. A whitish or yellowish appearance of the dorsal surface of the tongue frequently occurring when chewing is impaired and the person is on a liquid or soft diet; also seen in mouth breathing or in dehydration. Also called furry tongue.

fissured t. A tongue with numerous irregular grooves on its dorsal aspect, frequently seen in children affected with trisomy 21 and in other retarded persons with the habit of chewing on the protruded tongue. Also called scrotal tongue.

furry t. See coated tongue.

geographic t. A tongue with areas denuded of papillae, presenting a smooth surface with patterns that can change from day to day; the condition is painless and benign, may last months or years, and is uncommon after age six; cause is unknown. Also called benign migratory glossitis.

hairy t. See black tongue.

magenta t. A reddish purple tongue seen in riboflavin deficiency.

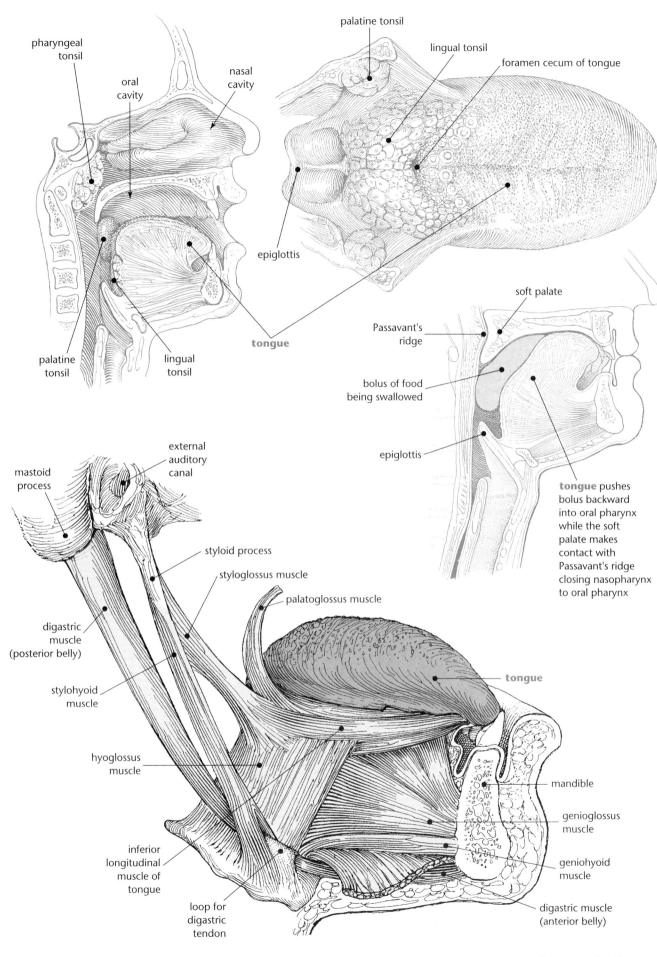

pharyngeal tonsil

oral cavity

nasal cavity

palatine tonsil

palatine tonsil

lingual tonsil

epiglottis

tongue

lingual tonsil

foramen cecum of tongue

soft palate

Passavant's ridge

bolus of food being swallowed

epiglottis

tongue pushes bolus backward into oral pharynx while the soft palate makes contact with Passavant's ridge closing nasopharynx to oral pharynx

mastoid process

external auditory canal

styloid process

styloglossus muscle

palatoglossus muscle

digastric muscle (posterior belly)

stylohyoid muscle

tongue

hyoglossus muscle

mandible

genioglossus muscle

geniohyoid muscle

inferior longitudinal muscle of tongue

loop for digastric tendon

digastric muscle (anterior belly)

T49

tongue ■ tongue

scrotal t. See fissured tongue.

strawberry t. A tongue dotted with enlarged red papillae protruding through a whitish coating; seen in scarlet fever.

tongue-tie An abnormal shortness of the fold of mucous membrane (frenulum) anchoring the tongue to the floor of the mouth. Also called ankyloglossia.

tonic (ton′ik) **1.** Relating to a state of continuous or prolonged muscular contraction. **2.** A remedy that is supposed to restore vigor.

tonicity (to-nis′ĭ-te) **1.** The normal condition of tension, as the slight continuous contraction of skeletal muscle. Also called tonus. **2.** Osmotic pressure of a solution, usually compared with that of plasma.

tono- Combining form meaning tone; tension; pressure.

tonoclonic (ton-o-klon′ik) Marked by prolonged (tonic) contractions alternating with short, rapid (clonic) contractions; applied to muscular spasms.

tonofibril (ton′o-fi-bril) One of numerous fine fibrils found in the cytoplasm of epithelial cells, forming a supporting framework for the cell.

tonofilament (ton-o-fil′ah-ment) A structural cytoplasmic protein, bundles of which form a tonofibril.

tonometer (to-nom′ĕ-ter) An instrument for measuring pressure within the eyeball.

air-puff t. Instrument that, without touching the eye, applies a small jet of air to the cornea; intraocular pressure is determined by the instantaneous computer analysis of the amount of flattening the air produces on the cornea; used for glaucoma screening.

applanation t. Tonometer consisting of a flat disk (applanation head) mounted on a light source that is equipped with a magnifier viewer (slit lamp biomicroscope). The disk is applied to the anesthetized cornea. The force needed to flatten a corneal surface of constant size, indicated on a calibrated knob on the tonometer, is a measure of the pressure within the eye.

Schiøtz t. Tonometer that measures the amount of indentation produced on the cornea by a given weight; used while the patient is in a reclining position. It consists of a curved footplate, which rests on the anesthetized corneal surface, and a weighted plunger that indents the cornea. The amount of corneal indentation, indicated on a scale, is indirectly proportional to the pressure within the eye.

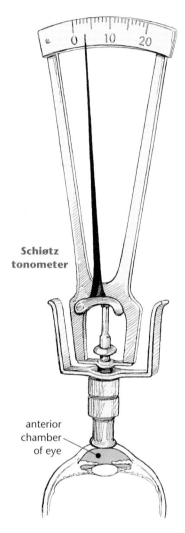

Schiøtz
tonometer

anterior
chamber
of eye

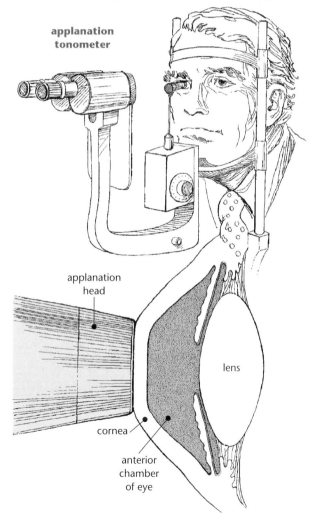

applanation
tonometer

applanation
head

lens

cornea

anterior
chamber
of eye

tonometry (to-nom′ĕ-tre) Measurement of tension or pressure, especially measurement of pressure within the eyeball with a tonometer.

tonsil (ton′sil) **1.** A small aggregation or rounded mass of lymphoid tissue; unless specified, it usually designates the palatine tonsil. **2.** Any anatomic structure resembling a palatine tonsil.

adenoid t. See pharyngeal tonsil.

t. of auditory tube See tubal tonsil.

cerebellar t. A circumscribed portion of the cerebellum in intimate relation with the undersurface of each cerebellar hemisphere; it is connected to the uvular part of the cerebellum by a strip of cortex (furrowed band).

eustachian t. See tubal tonsil.

Gerlach's t. See tubal tonsil.

lingual t. An aggregation of lymphoid nodules in the submucous layer of the posterior one-third or base of the tongue; the underlying nodules exhibit characteristic lingual swellings on the surface.

nasopharyngeal t. See pharyngeal tonsil.

tongue-tie ■ tonsil

palatine t. One of two oval masses of lympoid tissue, situated in the tonsillar fossa on the lateral wall of the oral part of the pharynx (oropharynx), between the pillars of the fauces (palatoglossal and palatopharyngeal arches); the medial surface contains about 15 orifices leading into deep, narrow pits (tonsillar crypts), which penetrate a good portion of the tonsil; it is of variable size and a frequent site of inflammation.

pharyngeal t. A collection of lymphoid tissue on the roof and posterior wall of the nasopharynx; generally prominent in young children, but begins to atrophy by the age of seven or eight years; when infected or enlarged, it is often referred to as adenoids. Also called nasopharyngeal tonsil; adenoid tonsil; third tonsil.

third t. See pharyngeal tonsil.

t. of torus tubarius See tubal tonsil.

tubal t. An aggregation of lymphoid tissue surrounding the pharyngeal orifice of the eustachian (auditory) tube on the lateral wall of the nasopharynx; seen as a lateral extension of the pharyngeal tonsil. Also called eustachian tonsil; tonsil of auditory tube; tonsil of torus tubarius; Gerlach's tonsil.

tonsillar, tonsillary (ton'sĭ-lar, ton'sĭ-la-re) Relating to a tonsil, especially the palatine tonsil.

tonsillectomy (ton-sĭ-lek'to-me) Removal of the tonsils.

tonsillith (ton'sĭ-lith) See tonsillolith.

tonsillitis (ton'si-li'tis) Inflammation of a tonsil or tonsils.

tonsillo- Combining form meaning tonsil.

tonsillolith (ton-sil'o-lith) A stony concretion in a tonsil. Also called tonsillith.

tonsillotome (ton-sil'o-tōm) Instrument for removing a tonsil.

tonsillotomy (ton-sĭ-lot'o-me) Removal of a portion of a palatine tonsil.

tonus (to'nus) See tonicity (1).

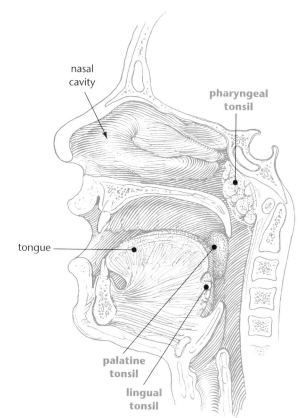

nasal cavity

pharyngeal tonsil

tongue

palatine tonsil

lingual tonsil

INDENTATION **TONOMETRY**

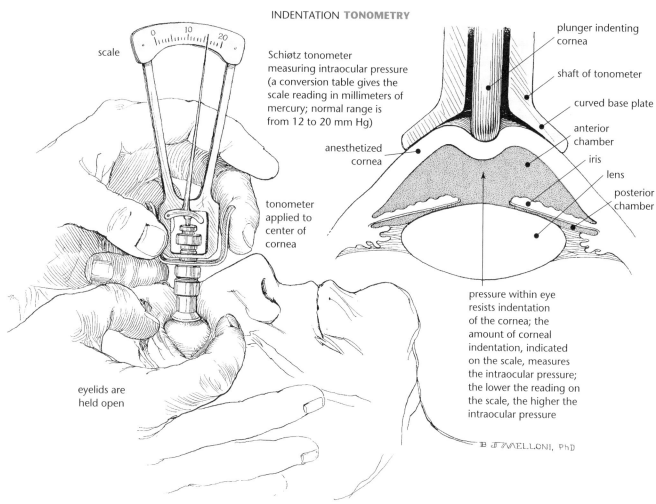

scale

Schiøtz tonometer measuring intraocular pressure (a conversion table gives the scale reading in millimeters of mercury; normal range is from 12 to 20 mm Hg)

tonometer applied to center of cornea

eyelids are held open

plunger indenting cornea

shaft of tonometer

curved base plate

anterior chamber

anesthetized cornea

iris

lens

posterior chamber

pressure within eye resists indentation of the cornea; the amount of corneal indentation, indicated on the scale, measures the intraocular pressure; the lower the reading on the scale, the higher the intraocular pressure

B J MELLONI, PhD

T

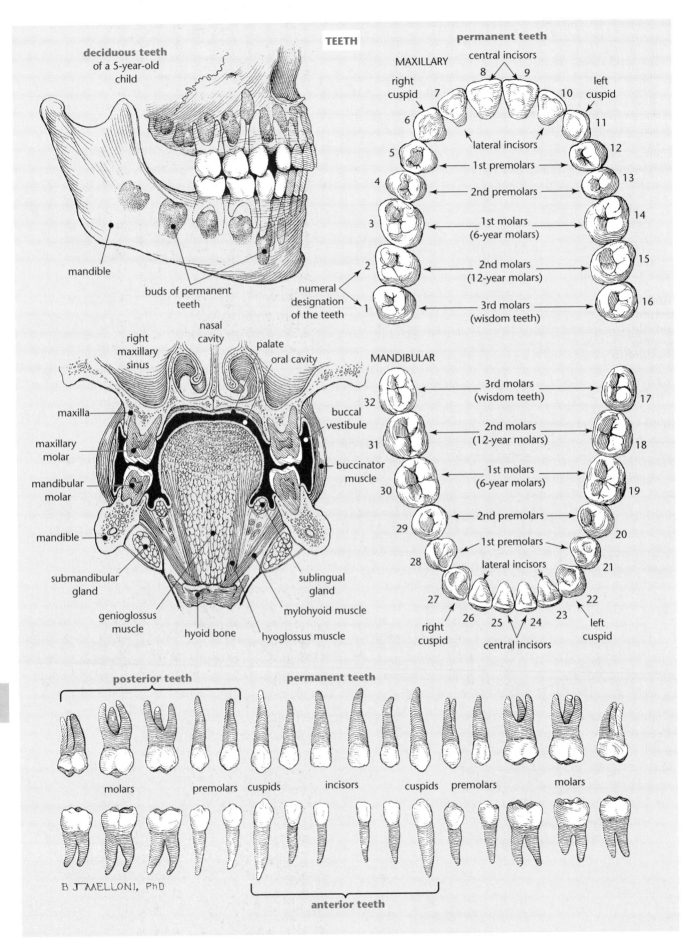

TEETH

deciduous teeth
of a 5-year-old child

mandible

buds of permanent teeth

permanent teeth

MAXILLARY

central incisors

right cuspid

left cuspid

8 9

7 10

6 11

lateral incisors

5 12

4 1st premolars 13

2nd premolars

3 14

1st molars
(6-year molars)

2 15

2nd molars
(12-year molars)

1 16

numeral designation
of the teeth

3rd molars
(wisdom teeth)

right maxillary sinus

nasal cavity

palate

oral cavity

maxilla

maxillary molar

mandibular molar

mandible

submandibular gland

genioglossus muscle

hyoid bone

buccal vestibule

buccinator muscle

sublingual gland

mylohyoid muscle

hyoglossus muscle

MANDIBULAR

3rd molars
(wisdom teeth)

32 17

2nd molars
(12-year molars)

31 18

1st molars
(6-year molars)

30 19

2nd premolars

29 20

1st premolars

28 21

lateral incisors

27 22

26 25 24 23

right cuspid

left cuspid

central incisors

posterior teeth

permanent teeth

molars   premolars cuspids   incisors   cuspids premolars   molars

B.J. MELLONI, PhD

anterior teeth

tooth ■ tooth

T52

tooth (tōōth), pl. **teeth** Any of the bonelike structures suspended within sockets in the upper and lower jaws by a relatively soft periodontal ligament, which allows slight movement; used to seize, hold, and masticate food; also to assist in articulation of sounds; it is the hardest and chemically most stable tissue in the body, composed of hard dentin surrounding a pulp cavity and covered by enamel on the crown and by cement (cementum) on the root. Because of their durability, teeth are of great forensic importance for identification of otherwise unrecognizable bodies, since their pattern can be compared with dental records of missing persons.

abutment t. See abutment.

anchor t. A tooth used to stabilize an orthodontic appliance.

anterior teeth The teeth situated in the front part of the upper and lower jaws, consisting of the central incisors, lateral incisors, and cuspids. Also called labial teeth.

artificial t. Any imitation tooth designed to substitute for a missing natural tooth.

baby teeth See deciduous teeth.

buccal teeth See posterior teeth.

buck teeth See horizontal overlap, under overlap.

canine t. See cuspid.

cutting teeth See central and lateral incisors, under incisor.

dead t. See nonvital tooth.

deciduous teeth The 20 teeth of the first dentition that generally erupt between the 6th and 30th months of life, and after shedding are replaced by permanent teeth; they include four incisors, two cuspids, and four molars in each jaw; the usual times of eruption are: central incisors, 6 to 8 months; lateral incisors, 8 to 10 months; first molars, 12 to 16 months; cuspids, 16 to 20 months; second molars, 20 to 30 months; they calcify partly before birth and partly after birth; their roots are progressively resorbed by osteoclasts prior to their being replaced, and as a result the shed or extracted deciduous teeth seem to have short roots. Also called baby teeth; milk teeth; primary teeth; temporary teeth.

dog t. See cuspid.

eye t. Upper cuspid. See cuspid.

Hutchinson's teeth Malformed, barrel-shaped permanent incisors with underdeveloped enamel and a notched, narrow edge; occasionally the first molars are also affected and appear dome-shaped, with a pitted occlusal surface. Hutchinson's teeth are considered a sign of congenital syphilis. Also called notched teeth; syphilitic teeth; pegged teeth; screwdriver teeth.

impacted t. A tooth that is incapable of erupting completely or even partially, due to its angle of eruption or by being so placed in the jaw as to meet resistance from an adjacent tooth.

labial teeth See anterior teeth.

malacotic teeth Structurally soft teeth that are abnormally susceptible to caries.

mandibular teeth Teeth situated in the lower jaw (mandible).

maxillary teeth Teeth situated in the upper jaw (maxilla).

milk teeth See deciduous teeth.

mottled teeth Teeth characterized by underdevelopment of the enamel and marked by white chalky areas, which in time undergo brown discoloration; usually caused by drinking water containing excessive fluorides during the time of tooth development.

natal t. A deciduous tooth present at birth.

nonvital t. A tooth from which the pulp has been removed or one in which the pulp has died. Also called dead tooth; pulpless tooth.

notched teeth See Hutchinson's teeth.

pegged teeth See Hutchinson's teeth.

permanent teeth The 32 teeth of the second dentition that generally erupt between the ages of 6 and 21 years; they include four incisors, two cuspids, four bicuspids, and six molars in each jaw; the usual times of eruption are: first molars, 6 to 7 years; central incisors, 6 to 8 years; lateral incisors, 7 to 9 years; cuspids, 9 to 12 years; first and second premolars, 10 to 12 years; second molars, 11 to 13 years;

third molars, 17 to 21 years; the cuspid roots are the longest, the first upper molar is the largest tooth, and the lower third molar, which frequently erupts anterosuperiorly, is often impacted against the second molar. Also called succedaneous teeth.

posterior teeth The premolar and molar teeth situated in the back part of the upper and lower jaws. Also called buccal teeth.

premolar teeth The permanent teeth between the cuspid and first molar. See permanent teeth.

primary teeth See deciduous teeth.

protruding teeth Teeth that extend beyond the normal contours of the dental arches, often in an anterior direction.

pulpless t. See nonvital tooth.

sclerotic t. A structurally hard tooth that is resistant to caries.

screwdriver teeth See Hutchinson's teeth.

snaggle t. A tooth out of proper line in relation to the others in the arch.

spaced teeth Teeth that have shifted and lost proximal contact with adjacent teeth.

succedaneous teeth See permanent teeth.

supernumerary t. An accessory natural tooth, in excess of the normal number; most commonly seen in the incisal area.

syphilitic teeth See Hutchinson's teeth.

temporary teeth See deciduous teeth.

tube t. An artificial tooth that can be firmly adhered to a cylindrical pin on a denture base.

unerupted t. (a) A tooth prior to eruption through the gingiva. (b) A tooth that is incapable of erupting through the gingiva.

vital t. A tooth with a living (vital) pulp, in which the nerve and vascular supply are functional.

wisdom t. Third permanent molar; erupts between the ages of 17 and 21 years; so called because it is the last of the permanent teeth to erupt.

toothache (tōōth'āk) Pain in or about a tooth.

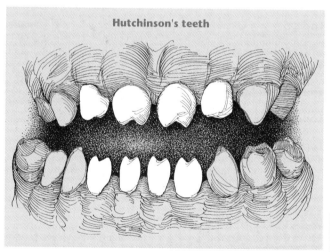

Hutchinson's teeth

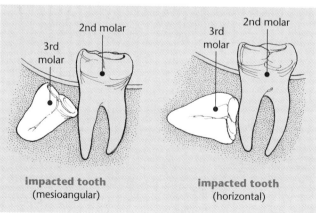

impacted tooth
(mesioangular)

impacted tooth
(horizontal)

topagnosis (top-ag-no′sis) Loss of the ability to identify the exact place where the body is touched in a neurologic test. Also called topoanesthesia.

topalgia (to-pal′je-ah) Localized pain.

topectomy (to-pek′to-me) Removal of one specific portion of the superficial layer (cortex) of the brain; a type of psychosurgery.

topesthesia (top-es-the′ze-ah) Ability to identify which part of the skin is touched in a neurologic test.

tophaceous (to-fa′shus) Gritty, like a tophus.

tophus (to′fus), pl. to′phi The characteristic lesion of gout, an accumulation of urate crystals in tissues; most common sites include the helix of the ear, the knee, and the elbow. Also called chalk stone.

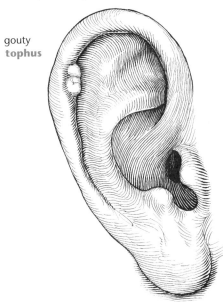

gouty **tophus**

topical (top′e-kal) Relating to a circumscribed area, usually on the skin or mucous membranes; said of medications that are applied to the body's surface.

topo-, top- Combining forms meaning place; region; local.

topoanesthesia (top-o-an-es-the′ze-ah) See topagnosis.

topognosis (top-og-no′sis) Ability to recognize the location of a sensation.

topography (to-pog′rah-fe) Description of a limited region of the body.

toponarcosis (top-o-nar-ko′sis) Anesthesia in a localized area.

TORCH Acronym for Toxoplasmosis, Other infections, Rubella, Cytomegalovirus infection, and Herpes (simplex). See also TORCH syndrome, under syndrome.

toric (to′rik) Relating to a protuberance or swelling.

torpor (tor′por) Sluggishness; slow response to ordinary stimuli.

torque (tork) A twisting force (e.g., one applied to a denture base).

torsade de pointes (tor-sahd′ dě pwahnt) In cardiology, "twisting of the points"; a form of ventricular tachycardia in which the QRS complexes of the electrocardiogram are of changing amplitude and appear to twist around an electrically neutral (isoelectric) point; hence the name.

torsion (tor′shun) A turning or twisting along a long axis.

t. of spermatic cord Twisting of a spermatic cord with resulting obstruction of blood flow, leading to ischemic death of the testis and epididymis often within four to six hours of onset; symptoms range from moderate scrotal swelling and little or no pain to severe pain and swelling, reddening of scrotal skin, lower abdominal pain, nausea, and vomiting; it typically occurs in young males with preexisting structural abnormalities, such as incompletely descended testis, absence of scrotal ligaments and, especially, a large enclosing membrane of the testis (tunica vaginalis) that inserts high on the cord, allowing the testis to rotate within it. The twisting is usually initiated by trauma or any violent movement; preservation of the testis is doubtful if treatment is not instituted within 24 hours. Also called torsion of testis; torsion of testicle.

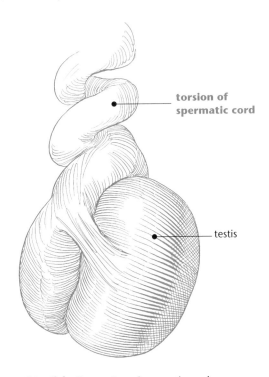

torsion of spermatic cord

testis

t. of testicle See torsion of spermatic cord.

t. of testis See torsion of spermatic cord.

t. of umbilical cord Twisting of the umbilical cord usually occurring counterclockwise and which, if extreme, results in asphyxiation of the fetus.

torso (tor′so) The trunk.

tort (tort) An act that causes harm to another person or his property for which the injured party is seeking monetary compensation from the wrongdoer (tort-feasor).

intentional t. In medical malpractice, a treatment involving bodily contact for which the patient gave neither actual nor implied consent; frequently refers to surgical procedures performed on a body structure for which patient's consent was not previously obtained (e.g., removing both ovaries when consent was obtained

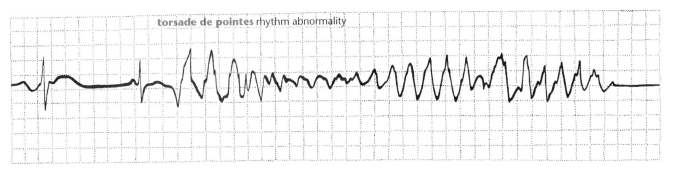

torsade de pointes rhythm abnormality

topagnosis ■ **tort**

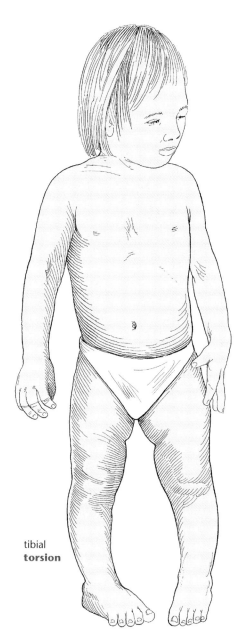

tibial **torsion**

side of the lower jaw between the cuspid and first premolar (bicuspid) teeth. It is asymptomatic but interferes with the fitting of dentures.

    t. palatinus A bony outgrowth in the midline of the hard palate; a common developmental abnormality of the oral cavity that may interfere with the fitting of a denture.

    t. tubarius A normal ridge posterior to the pharyngeal opening of the eustachian (auditory) tube. Also called eustachian cushion.

totipotency (to-te-po′ten-se) The ability of a cell to differentiate into any type of cell of an organism (e.g., the fertilized ovum).

touch (tuch) **1.** The tactile sense. **2.** To examine by feeling with the fingers.

tourniquet (toor′nĭ-ket) Any device or constrictive wide band placed around an arm or leg for temporary compression of blood vessels; used to engorge veins for an intravenous injection or withdrawal of blood and to stop bleeding (a practice currently discouraged because leaving a tourniquet on too long can cause gangrene).

toxemia (tok-se′me-ah) The presence of bacterial poisons (toxins) in the bloodstream.

    t. of pregnancy See preeclampsia.

toxic (tok′sik) **1.** Harmful; poisonous. **2.** Relating to a toxin. **3.** Caused by a toxin.

toxicant (toks′ĭ-kant) **1.** Poisonous. **2.** Any poisonous agent.

    local t. A chemical substance producing effects at the site of first contact with a biologic system, such as caustic or irritant materials.

    systemic t. A substance that usually requires absorption and distribution to produce adverse effects on the body. Some may also produce local effects.

toxicity (tok-sis′ĭ-te) The quality of being poisonous or harmful to plant or animal life; the capacity to produce harmful effects on biologic systems.

    acute t. Toxicity that occurs when exposure to a chemical or drug is sudden and severe and when absorption is rapid.

    cumulative t. Toxicity caused by accumulation of a substance in the body as a result of repeated exposure to even small amounts of the substance over a period of time.

    subacute t. Toxicity resulting from frequent, repeated exposure over a period of several hours or days to a dose of drug that does not produce toxic effects when taken as a single dose.

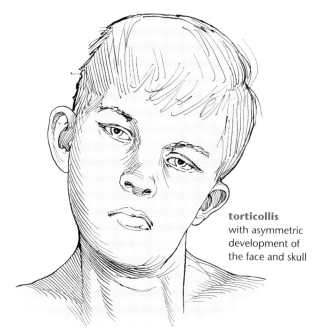

torticollis
with asymmetric
development of
the face and skull

contracture of the left sternocleidomastoid
muscle has caused tilting of the head to the left
and turning of the chin to the right

for only one, or tying fallopian (uterine) tubes in addition to performing the cesarean section for which consent was obtained). See also informed consent, under consent.

    negligent t. In medical malpractice, the most common of medical professional liability actions; basically, it involves a claim that the physician violated a standard of care. See also standard of care; negligence.

torticollis (tor-tĭ-kol′is) A contracted state of the muscles on one side of the neck, causing the head to tilt toward that side and to rotate so that it faces the opposite side. Also called wryneck; stiff neck.

    spasmodic t. See cervical dystonia, under dystonia.

Torulopsis (tor-u-lop′sis) A genus of yeasts; some species are natural inhabitants of the human digestive tract; some species (e.g., *Torulopsis glabrata*) occasionally cause disease.

torulopsosis (tor-u-lop′so-sis) Yeast infection usually involving the respiratory or genitourinary tract; caused by *Torulopsis glabrata;* seen usually as an opportunistic disease in severely debilitated persons, in those undergoing immunosuppressive therapy, or those with immune deficiency (e.g., AIDS).

torulus (tor′u-lus) A small projection.

torus (to′rus) A protuberance or rounded projection.

    t. mandibularis A benign bony projection on the lingual

T

toxico-, toxi- Combining forms meaning poison; toxin.

Toxicodendron (tok-sĭ-ko-den′dron) See *Rhus.*

toxicoderma (tok-sĭ-ko-der′mah) Any skin disease caused by a poison.

toxicodermatitis (tok-sĭ-ko-der-mah-ti′tis) Inflammation of the skin caused by a poison.

toxicodynamics (tok-sĭ-ko-di-nam′iks) The study of the relationship between the dose of a harmful substance entering the body and the measured response. The magnitude of a toxic response is usually related to the concentration of the harmful substance at its site of action in the body.

toxicokinetics (tok-sĭ-ko-kĭ-net′iks) The science that deals with the movement of harmful substances within the body (i.e., their absorption, distribution, metabolism, and excretion) and the relationship between the dose that enters the body and the amount of harmful substance found in the blood, urine, or other biologic specimens.

toxicogenic (tok-sĭ-ko-jen′ik) 1. Producing a poison. 2. Produced by a poison.

toxicoid (tok′sĭ-koid) Producing effects similar to those of a poison.

toxicologic (tok-sĭ-ko-loj′ik) Relating to toxicology.

toxicologist (tok-sĭ-kol′o-jist) A specialist in toxicology.

    clinical t. Toxicologist who treats individuals poisoned by any chemical or drug and who aims to develop new techniques for diagnosing and treating such intoxications.

    descriptive t. One who performs toxicity tests to gather data that can be used to evaluate the risk posed to humans and the environment by exposure to a chemical.

    forensic t. A toxicologist who assists in establishing the cause of death by applying toxicological principles to postmortem investigations.

    mechanistic t. One who attempts to determine the manner in which chemicals exert harmful effects on living organisms; useful in developing tests for predicting risks, in facilitating the search for safer chemicals, and in treating manifestations of toxicity.

    regulatory t. Toxicologist who determines whether a drug or other chemical has a low enough risk to make it available for its intended use.

toxicology (tok-sĭ-kol′o-je) The branch of pharmacology concerned with the adverse effects of drugs, those used in therapy as well as all chemicals that may be responsible for household, environmental, or industrial poisoning.

    clinical t. The study of diseases that are caused by, or are closely associated with, toxic substances.

    forensic t. Application of the fundamental principles and practice of toxicology to problems of law; concerned primarily with identification and quantification of toxic substances found in the tissues or body fluids of persons whose death is thought to be caused by exposure, ingestion, or injection of such substances.

toxin (tok′sin) A poisonous substance elaborated by certain microorganisms, animals (e.g., snakes), and plants (e.g., mushrooms).

    botulinus t. The protein neurotoxin released by *Clostridium botulinum;* of the seven immunologically distinct types that have been identified, only three (A, B, and E) are signifiant causes of botulism.

    extracellular t. See exotoxin.

    intracellular t. See endotoxin.

    tetanus t. A highly poisonous substance produced by the bacterium *Clostridium tetani;* the cause of tetanus; it seems to affect the nervous system by blocking inhibitory impulses at the synaptic sites. May infect newborn infants through the umbilical stump. Also called tetanotoxin.

toxipathy (tok-sip′ah-the) Any disease caused by the action of a poison.

TOXLINE Toxicology information on-line; a computerized system of data that includes bibliographic references covering pharmacologic, biochemical, physiologic, environmental, and toxicologic effects of drugs and other chemicals. It is one of the databases of MEDLARS, based at the National Library of Medicine. See also MEDLARS.

toxo- Combining form meaning poison; toxin.

Toxocara (tok-so-ka′rah) Genus of parasitic roundworms (family Ascaridae); the larvae of some species cause human disease.

toxocariasis (tok-so-kār-i′ah-sis) Infestation with larvae of the dog and cat parasites, *Toxocara canis* and *Toxocara cati;* acquired primarily by children through inadvertent ingestion of eggs passed by contaminated animals in play areas; ingested eggs hatch, penetrate the intestinal wall, and migrate to such organs as the liver, lungs, and heart, where they die, causing a granulomatous inflammatory reaction; symptoms include fever, loss of appetite, inflammation of the liver, and, sometimes, cough and abdominal distention. Also called visceral larva migrans.

toxoid (tok′soid) Toxin treated with chemicals that render it nontoxic but able to induce production of antibodies, therefore, capable of producing active immunity.

toxophore (tok′so-fōr) The group of atoms in a toxin molecule that is responsible for the toxin's poisonous activity.

Toxoplasma gondii (toks-o-plaz′mah gon′de-e) Intracellular protozoon parasite of the genus *Toxoplasma,* which causes toxoplasmosis in humans.

toxoplasmosis (tok-so-plaz-mo′sis) Disease caused by infection with *Toxoplasma gondii;* it may resemble a mild cold or infectious mononucleosis in adults; a disseminated form may lead to inflammation of the liver, lungs, heart muscle, or of the brain and spinal cord and their membranes; another form of the disease involves the eyes; an infected pregnant woman can spread the disease to her unborn child, causing eye or brain damage or even death; most common way of acquiring the disease is by eating raw or undercooked meat from infected animals.

trabecula (trah-bek′u-lah), pl. trabec′ulae A connecting anchoring strand made up of connective tissue, bone, or muscle fibers.

    septomarginal t. A thick band of heart muscle usually extending from the interventricular septum to the base of the anterior papillary muscle in the right ventricle; it provides passage for the right branch of the atrioventricular bundle of nerve fibers from the septum to the opposite wall of the ventricle. It may also help in preventing overdistention of the right ventricle.

    trabeculae carneae cordis Irregular muscular projections from most of the inner surface of the ventricles of the heart.

trabecular (trah-bek′u-lar) Relating to trabeculae.

trabeculation (trah-bek-u-la′shun) The presence of trabeculae.

    vesical t. Extensive trabeculation of the bladder caused by a partial urinary obstruction at the bladder neck; it often occurs in association with an enlarged prostate.

trabeculectomy (trah-bek-u-lek′to-me) Microsurgery of the eye for relieving intraocular pressure caused by open-angle glaucoma; a small portion of the trabecular meshwork and adjacent Schlemm's canal, just beneath the sclera, are removed to enhance drainage of aqueous humor from the anterior chamber.

trace (trās) 1. An extremely small but detectable amount. 2. Inprint or vestige of a past event, phenomenon, or action. 3. In muscle testing, a grade given to a muscle or group of muscles whose contraction is perceptible but not strong enough to move the corresponding joint.

tracer (trās′er) 1. A chemical or radioactive substance that is added to some pharmaceutical or other material under study (the vector) to gain knowledge about the vector's mode of action. Also called label. 2. A device for recording the movements of the lower jaw (mandible).

trachea (tra′ke-ah) A cartilaginous and membranous tube extending from, and continuous with, the lower part of the larynx to the bronchi. Popularly called windpipe.

tracheal (tra′ke-al) Relating to the trachea.

trachealgia (tra-ke-al′je-ah) Pain in the trachea.

tracheitis (tra-ke-i′tis) Inflammation of the mucous lining of the trachea, usually caused by a viral infection and aggravated by inhalation of fumes such as tobacco smoke.

trachelectomy (tra-ke-lek′to-me) See cervicectomy.

trachelism, trachelismus (tra′kĕ-lizm, tra-kĕ-liz′mus) A spasmodic

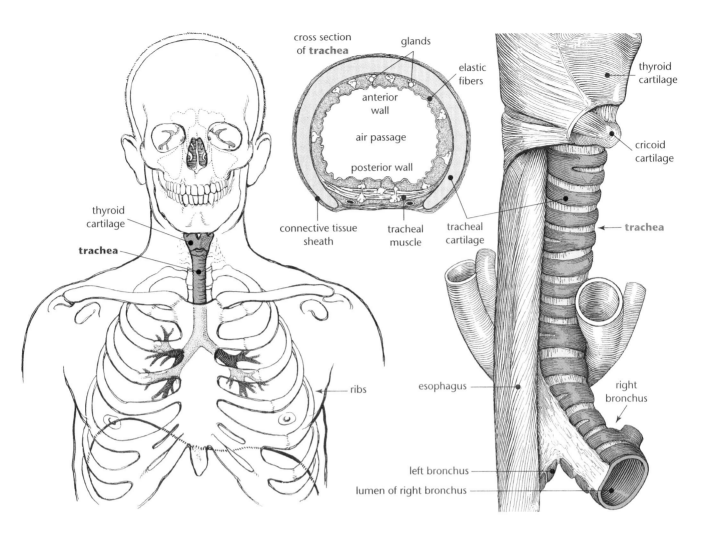

cross section of **trachea**

glands

elastic fibers

anterior wall

air passage

posterior wall

connective tissue sheath

tracheal muscle

tracheal cartilage

thyroid cartilage

trachea

cricoid cartilage

thyroid cartilage

trachea

esophagus

right bronchus

left bronchus

lumen of right bronchus

ribs

backward bending of the neck.

trachelitis (tra-kĕ-li′tis) See cervicitis.

trachelo-, trachel- Combining forms meaning neck.

trachelodynia (tra′kĕ-lo-din′e-ah) See cervicodynia.

trachelorrhaphy (tra′kĕ-lor′ah-fe) Reparative operation on the neck of the uterus (uterine cervix).

tracheo-, trache- Combining forms meaning trachea.

tracheobronchial (tra′ke-o-brong′ke-al) Relating to the trachea and a bronchus or the bronchi.

tracheobronchitis (tra′ke-o-brong-ki′tis) Inflammation of the mucous membrane of the trachea and bronchi.

tracheobroncoscopy (tra′ke-o-brong-kos′ko-pe) Inspection of the interior of the trachea and bronchi with an endoscope.

tracheocele (tra′ke-o-sēl) Outward protrusion of the mucous membrane through an abnormal space in the tracheal wall.

tracheoesophageal (tra′ke-o-e-sof′ah-je-al) Relating to the trachea and esophagus.

tracheolaryngeal (tra′ke-o-lah-rin′je-al) Relating to the trachea and larynx.

tracheomalacia (tra′ke-o-mah-la′she-ah) Softening and degeneration of the connective tissue of the trachea.

tracheomegaly (tra′ke-o-meg′ah-le) Abnormally enlarged tracheal lumen. Cause is unknown.

tracheopathy (tra-ke-op′ah-the) Any disease of the trachea.

tracheophony (tra-ke-of′o-ne) The hollow sound of the voice heard on auscultation over the trachea.

tracheoplasty (tra′ke-o-plas-te) Plastic surgery of the trachea.

tracheorrhea (tra′ke-o-re′ah) Bleeding originating from the mucous membrane of the trachea.

tracheoscopy (tra-ke-os′ko-pe) Direct inspection of the interior of the trachea with a viewing instrument (tracheoscope).

tracheostenosis (tra′ke-o-stĕ-no′sis) Abnormal constriction of the trachea.

tracheostoma (tra-ke-os′to-mah) An artificial opening into the trachea through the neck, made to maintain an adequately patent airway.

tracheostomy (tra-ke-os′to-me) 1. The surgical procedure for making a direct opening into the trachea through the neck and the placing of a tracheostomy tube through the opening; performed for a variety of purposes, e.g., to bypass an obstruction to the upper airway; to alleviate respiratory insufficiency by providing a route for mechanical ventilation; to provide a route for the mechanical aspiration of secretions from the lower airways; or to provide an alternate airway after surgical removal of, or traumatic injury to, the larynx. 2. The artificial opening (stoma) so produced.

tracheotome (tra′ke-o-tōm) A knife for cutting into the trachea through the skin.

tracheotomize (tra-ke-ot′o-miz) To perform a tracheotomy.

tracheotomy (tra-ke-ot′o-me) A surgical cut into the trachea through the neck.

trachoma (trah-ko′mah) Contagious disease of the eye caused by infection with *Chlamydia trachomatis*; marked by inflammation of the anterior surface covering of the eye (conjunctiva) and the cornea, followed by formation of numerous granules, even within the eyelids. It is one of the leading causes of blindness in some parts of the world, especially the Middle East.

trachomatous (trah-ko′mah-tus) Affected with trachoma.

tracing (trās′ing) A line or pattern of lines, made by a pointed instrument on thin paper or plate, representing movement (e.g., of cardiovascular activity or movements of the lower jaw) or pertinent landmarks of skull measurement in an x-ray image of the head.

tracks (traks) Slang expression for linear scars on the skin caused by

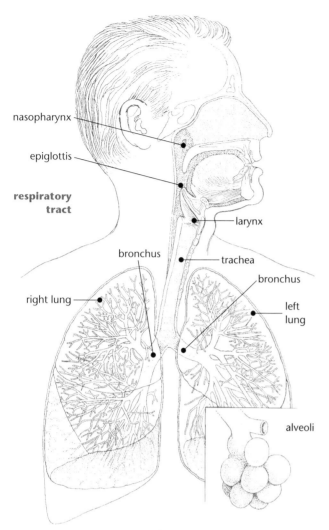

nasopharynx

epiglottis

respiratory tract

larynx

bronchus

trachea

bronchus

right lung

left lung

alveoli

frequent narcotics injections into the veins.

tract (trakt) **1.** A series of structures constituting a body system that performs a specialized function (e.g., the respiratory tract). **2.** A collection of nerve fibers possessing the same origin, termination, and function. **3.** A path.

alimentary t. See digestive tract.

anterior spinocerebellar t. A band of nerve fibers that ascends along the lateral funiculus of the spinal cord to the cerebellum, via the superior cerebellar peduncle. Also called ventral spinocerebellar tract.

anterior spinothalamic t. A band of nerve fibers in the anterolateral funiculus of the spinal cord that crosses over in the anterior white commissure before ascending to the ventral posterolateral nucleus of the thalamus. Also called ventral spinothalamic tract.

ascending t. Any band of nerve fibers conveying impulses rostrally toward the brain, either from lower to higher centers in the central nervous system, or from afferent pathways in the spinal cord.

association t. of cerebrum A bundle of nerve fibers linking different regions of the cortex within the same cerebral hemisphere.

biliary t. The passageway along which the bile flows from the biliary canaliculi in the liver (where it is secreted) to the gallbladder (where it is stored), and finally to the opening of the common bile duct in the duodenum (where it is discharged).

bullet t. The path of tissue injuries left by a bullet proceeding forward through the body from the entrance wound to the exit wound. Bullet tracts are dissected and measured as part of a medicolegal autopsy to obtain relevant information. See also entrance wound; exit wound, under wound.

central t. of cochlear nerve The pathway of fibers in the

brain by which auditory impulses generated by the inner and outer hair cells of the spiral organ of Corti, in the cochlea, reach the cerebral cortex of the first and second temporal gyri; the nerve fibers from the cochlear division of the vestibulocochlear (8th cranial) nerve reach the cochlear nucleus, and from there most of the fibers cross the midline to ascend (contralaterally) to the inferior colliculus; the remaining nerve fibers that do not cross the midline ascend to the inferior colliculus of the same side; the nerve fibers from the inferior colliculi pass to their respective medial geniculate bodies before radiating to the receiving auditory areas of the cerebral cortex. At the auditory cortex the impulses are interpreted as sound.

corticospinal t.'s Pyramidal tracts composed of nerve fibers that originate from the sensorimotor regions of the cerebral cortex, pass through the medullary pyramid, and descend into the spinal cord.

descending t. Any band or pathway of nerve fibers that conveys impulses from the brain downward toward the periphery of the nervous system, or from a higher to lower center in the central nervous system, such as those from the cerebral cortex to the brainstem.

digestive t. The mucous membrane–lined tubular passage of the digestive system, from the mouth to the anus and including the pharynx, esophagus, stomach, and small and large intestines. Also called alimentary tract; alimentary canal.

dorsal spinocerebellar t. See posterior spinocerebellar tract.

gastrointestinal t. The portion of the digestive tract that consists of the stomach and the small and large intestines, including the anus.

geniculocalcarine t. See optic radiation, under radiation.

genitourinary t. See urogenital apparatus, under apparatus.

iliotibial t. A strong, wide, thickened reinforcement of a portion of the fascia lata on the lateral side of the thigh; it extends from the iliac crest of the hipbone to the lateral condyle of the tibia; it receives the greater part of the insertion of the greater gluteal (gluteus maximus) muscle; the tract protects many of the prominent bony points near the knee joint, such as the condyles of the femur and tibia, and the head of the fibula.

intestinal t. The part of the digestive tract between the stomach and anus, namely the small and large intestines.

lateral spinothalamic t. A band of nerve fibers in the anterolateral funiculus of the spinal cord that ascends to the ventral posterolateral nucleus of the thalamus, with some branches going to the reticular formation.

mamillothalamic t. Nerve fibers in the brain connecting the mamillary body to the anterior thalamic nuclear complex.

nerve t. A bundle or group of nerve fibers in the central nervous system (brain and spinal cord).

olfactory t. A band of nerve fibers on the undersurface of the frontal lobe, on either side of the brain, that connects the olfactory bulb to the cerebral hemisphere.

optic t. A flattened band of nerve fibers, on either side, that extends backward from the optic chiasm to the lateral geniculate body (where most of the fibers terminate) and to the superior colliculus of the midbrain, with some reflex fibers passing to the spinal cord.

posterior spinocerebellar t. A tract that lies in the lateral funiculus of the spinal cord and conveys nerve fibers from the thoracic nucleus to the cerebellum, via the inferior cerebellar peduncle. Also called dorsal spinocerebellar tract.

pyramidal t. A term generally used to designate the corticospinal projections arising from the cerebral cortex and descending in the internal capsule, cerebral peduncle, and pons to the medulla oblongata. Strictly, the term refers to nerve fibers that pass through the pyramid.

respiratory t. The conducting airway consisting of the nose, mouth, pharynx, larynx, trachea, bronchi, bronchioles, alveolar ducts, and alveolar sacs; it permits the exchange of gases and the production of speech.

T

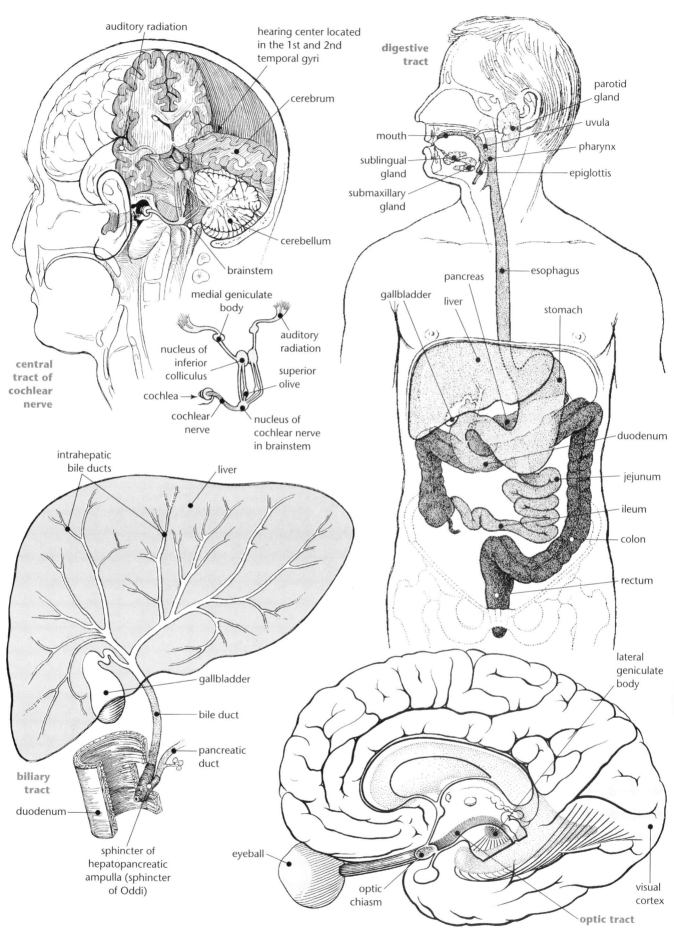

auditory radiation

hearing center located in the 1st and 2nd temporal gyri

cerebrum

cerebellum

brainstem

medial geniculate body

auditory radiation

nucleus of inferior colliculus

superior olive

cochlea

cochlear nerve

nucleus of cochlear nerve in brainstem

central tract of cochlear nerve

intrahepatic bile ducts

liver

gallbladder

bile duct

pancreatic duct

biliary tract

duodenum

sphincter of hepatopancreatic ampulla (sphincter of Oddi)

digestive tract

parotid gland

uvula

mouth

pharynx

sublingual gland

epiglottis

submaxillary gland

pancreas

gallbladder

liver

esophagus

stomach

duodenum

jejunum

ileum

colon

rectum

lateral geniculate body

eyeball

optic chiasm

optic tract

visual cortex

T

rubrospinal t. The band of nerve fibers that originate in the red nucleus, the oval cell mass in the central part of the midbrain tegmentum, then cross over the midline (decussate) and descend the length of the spinal cord.

solitary t. of medulla oblongata A tract that begins in the upper medulla oblongata and extends to the upper cervical segments of the spinal cord; it terminates along the course of the solitary nucleus; formed primarily by visual afferent and taste fibers from the vagus, glossopharyngeal, and facial nerves.

spinal t. Any one of a large number of bundles of ascending or descending nerve fibers of the spinal cord.

spinal t. of trigeminal nerve A descending bundle of nerve fibers of the trigeminal (5th cranial) nerve that extends from the middle of the pons to the uppermost cervical spinal segments, where they terminate in the adjacent spinal trigeminal nucleus; the tract conveys predominantly pain, temperature, and touch impulses from the face.

supraopticohypophyseal t. A bundle of unmyelinated nerve fibers arising from the supraoptic and paraventricular nuclei of the hypothalamus and descending to the posterior lobe of the pituitary (neurohypophysis), where it branches profusely to form the bulk of the lobe; the fibers convey neurosecretory substances.

urinary t. The passageway for the excretion of urine; it extends from the pelvis of the kidney, downward to the ureter, bladder, and urethra, and ends at the external urethral orifice.

urogenital t. See urogenital apparatus, under apparatus.

uveal t. See uvea.

ventral spinocerebellar t. See anterior spinocerebellar tract.

ventral spinothalamic t. See anterior spinothalamic tract.

traction (trak'shun) The procedure of applying tension to a part of the body to correct displacement or misalignment of two structures, especially of bones.

Buck's t. See Buck's extension, under extension.

skeletal t. Traction to realign a fractured bone in which the traction grip is obtained by a pin inserted through the skin into the appropriate part of the bone.

tractor (trak'tor) Instrument used to apply traction.

tractotomy (trak-tot'o-me) Surgical division of a nerve tract, in the brain or spinal cord, usually performed to relieve pain when other palliative measures have failed and when the pain is neuroanatomically localized, so that it can be eradicated without producing major neurologic dysfunction.

spinothalamic t., spinal thalamic t. Division of the spinothalamic tract to eradicate pain distal to the level of the division; may be performed in the spinal cord, medulla oblongata, or brainstem.

trigeminal t. Section of the descending branch of the trigeminal (5th cranial) nerve to relieve facial pain.

tractus (trak'tus) Latin for tract.

tragacanth (trag'ah-kanth) A gummy exudate from plants of the genus *Astragalus*, used as an emulsifier in foods, cosmetics, and pharmaceuticals.

tragal (tra'gal) Relating to the tragus.

tragus (tra'gus) The small projection of cartilage in front of the opening of the external ear.

trait (trāt) **1.** A distinguishing attribute or characteristic. **2.** In genetics, any inherited gene-determined characteristic; applied to a normal variation or to a disease. **3.** A distinctive pattern of behavior.

Cooley's t. See minor thalassemia, under thalassemia.

personality t.'s Prominent, relatively stable aspects of personality; may be adaptive or maladaptive.

trajector (trah-jek'tor) An instrument for locating the path of a bullet in a wound.

trance (trans) A sleeplike state.

tranquilizer (tran-kwī-liz'er) A drug that produces a calming effect.

major t. See antipsychotic agent, under agent.

minor t. See antianxiety agent, under agent.

trans- **1.** Prefix meaning through; across; beyond. **2.** In genetics, the position of two genes on opposite chromosomes of a homologous pair. **3.** In organic chemistry, having certain atoms or groups of radicals on opposite sides of the molecule.

transacetylation (trans-as-ĕ-til-a'shun) Metabolic reaction involving the transfer of an acetyl group.

transaction (trans-ak'shun) Interaction between two or more individuals involving a social stimulus and response.

transaminase (trans-am'ĭ-nās) See aminotransferase.

transamination (trans-am-ĭ-na'shun) The process of amino group transfer.

transantral (trans-an'tral) Through a body cavity, especially a cavity within a bone; applied to a surgical approach.

transaortic (trans-a-or'tik) Across the aorta.

transaxial (trans-ak'se-al) Across an axis; a cross section.

transbronchial (trans-brong'ke-al) Through the bronchi, such as a method of obtaining material for biopsy from within the airways.

transcervical (trans-ser'vĭ-kal) Through the opening of the uterine cervix.

transcondylar (trans-kon'dĭ-lar) Through the condyles of a bone; applied to the level of an amputation.

transcortical (trans-kor'tĭ-kal) Passing through the superficial layer (cortex) of an organ such as the cerebrum, cerebellum, kidney, etc.

transcranial (trans-kra'ne-al) Across the skull; applied to certain imaging techniques (e.g., of circulation of the brain).

transcriptase (trans-krip'tās) Any enzyme that promotes transcription of genetic information. See also transcription.

reverse t. An enzyme found in RNA tumor viruses (retroviruses of the family Retroviridae) that functions in transferring genetic code information back from RNA onto DNA, that is, in reverse order from the usual DNA-to-RNA transcription. Used in genetic engineering.

transcription (trans-krip'shun) The transfer of genetic code information from various parts of the DNA molecule to new strands of messenger RNA (mRNA), which then carry this information from the cell nucleus to the cytoplasm.

transcriptionist (trans-kript'shun-ist) One who writes or types out fully, as from an electronic recording machine.

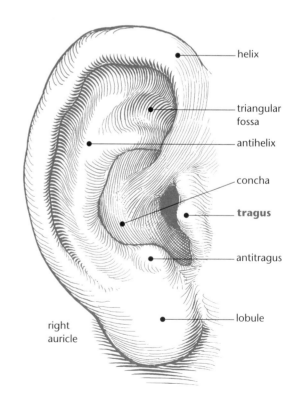

right auricle

helix

triangular fossa

antihelix

concha

tragus

antitragus

lobule

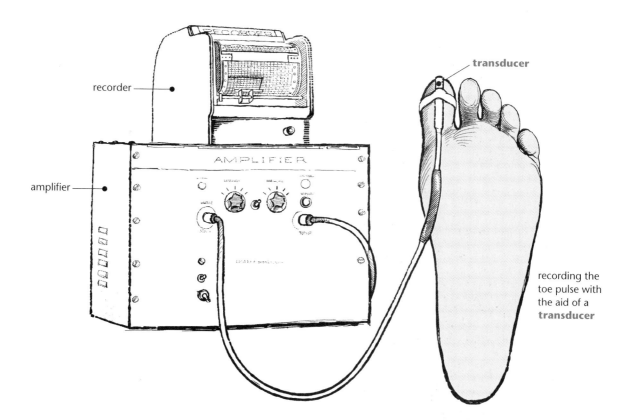

recorder

amplifier

transducer

recording the
toe pulse with
the aid of a
transducer

medical t. Person who makes machine transcription of physician-dictated medical reports relating to a patient's health care. The transcribed reports become part of the patient's permanent medical record.

transcutaneous (trans-ku-ta′ne-us) See transdermal.

transdermal (trans-der′mal) Applied on or entering through the skin, such as an electric nerve stimulation or certain prolonged-release pharmaceuticals (e.g., testosterone patches in replacement therapy). Also called transcutaneous.

Transderm Scōp® (trans′derm skōp) Trade name for the transdermal scopolamine patch; see under patch.

transducer (trans-du′ser) Device that transforms one form of energy to another; a major component of ultrasonic devices.

transduction (trans-duk′shun) **1.** A mechanism of gene transfer in which a virus incorporates host cell DNA into its own DNA, then introduces the host cell DNA into a different host. The technique is commonly used in genetic engineering to manufacture a variety of therapeutic substances (e.g., clotting factors for the treatment of hemophilia). **2.** Conversion of one form of energy to another.

transection (tran-sek′shun) **1.** A cross section. **2.** Cut across.

transesophageal (trans-ĕ-sof-ah-je′al) Through the esophagus (e.g., to place transducers for ultrasonographic imaging of the heart).

transethmoidal (trans-eth-moi′dal) Across or through the ethmoid bone in the skull.

transfection (trans-fek′shun) Uptake of external DNA by a cell that has been made transiently permeable.

transfer (trans′fer) A passage from one place to another.

　　embryo t. Procedure in which an embryo at the blastocyst stage (acquired through *in vitro* or *in vivo* fertilization) is transferred to the recipient's uterus through the vagina. The embryo may also be transferred to the recipient's fallopian (uterine) tubes via an abdominal incision.

　　gamete intrafallopian t. (GIFT) Procedure in which ova and sperm are placed together in the fallopian (uterine) tubes to enhance the possibility of fertilization. The procedure is performed with a laparoscope through the abdominal wall.

　　in vitro fertilization and embryo t. (IVF-ET) Procedure in which ova are taken from the mother, fertilized with the sperm from the father in a petri dish (i.e., *in vitro*), and the resulting embryo is then placed in the mother's uterus.

　　zygote intrafallopian t. (ZIFT) Procedure in which ova are fertilized in a petri dish (i.e., in vitro) and the resulting zygotes are then placed in the fallopian (uterine) tubes.

transferase (trans′fer-ās) Any enzyme promoting the transfer of a chemical group from one molecule to another.

transference (trans-fer′ens) The unconscious shifting to others of feelings and attitudes that were originally experienced in significant early relationships. In psychotherapy, analyzing transference is a tool for understanding how early relationships were experienced. See also countertransference.

transferrin (trans-fer′rin) Iron-binding beta globulin; it facilitates transportation of iron to bone marrow and tissue storage areas. Also called siderophilin.

transfix (trans′fiks) **1.** To pierce through with a pointed instrument. **2.** To immobilize as with terror.

transformation (trans-for-ma′shun) **1.** The conversion of a cell from a normal state to a malignant state due either to infection with a cancer-producing virus or to environmental factors. **2.** In molecular biology, genetic changes incurred by a cell through incorporation of DNA from another species.

　　neoplastic cell t. Abnormal cell changes including escape from control mechanism, increased growth potential, changes in cell surface, biochemical deviations, and other attributes that invest the cell with the potential ability to invade, metastasize, and kill.

transfusion (trans-fu′zhun) Introduction of a fluid (e.g., blood, plasma) into the bloodstream. A blood transfusion is considered an assault if performed against the will of a mentally competent person who is not pregnant, has no children, and refuses transfusion on religious grounds.

　　autologous t., autologous blood t. (ABT) Transfusion of the patient's own predeposited blood or blood components; blood is usually collected at several intervals during the five weeks (approximately) preceding an elective surgical procedure; useful in avoiding hazards of donor blood (e.g., transmission of infections such as AIDS) and for patients with red blood cell antibodies.

T

direct t. Transfusion of blood from one person (donor) to another (recipient) without an intermediate receptacle. Also called immediate transfusion.

exchange t. Removal of blood containing a toxic substance and replacing it with donor blood, as performed in newborn infants with Rh-incompatibility isoimmune hemolytic anemia. Also called substitution transfusion.

immediate t. See direct transfusion.

indirect t. Transfer of blood from a donor into a suitable container and thence to the recipient. Also called mediate transfusion.

intraoperative autologous t. (IAT) Procedure in which blood shed during a surgical operation is collected under sterile conditions, filtered, and reintroduced into the patient's circulation as a packed unit of red blood cells; indicated as an adjunct in the management of major trauma.

intrauterine t. Exchange transfusion of the fetus in the uterus by percutaneous umbilical vein catherization under ultrasound guidance; conducted to maintain an effective red cell mass within the fetal circulation and to maintain the pregnancy.

mediate t. See indirect transfusion.

platelet t. Transfusion of platelet concentrates; a method of treatment to increase the number of platelets in the blood. Platelets from a single donor are used in patients with immunologic liability.

substitution t. See exchange transfusion.

transgenic (trans-jen′ik) In genetic engineering, containing genes inserted from a set of chromosomes of another species.

transgenics (trans-jen′iks) In genetic engineering, the insertion of a selected gene into an organism, compelling it to produce a specified protein; thus a human disease can be replicated in a laboratory animal to study ways of treating the disease.

transhiatal (trans-hi-a′tal) Through a gap or opening that has been either acquired naturally or created surgically.

transient (tran′shent) Short-lived.

transiliac (trans-il′e-ak) From one ilium to the other.

transillumination (trans-ĭ-lu-mĭ-na′shun) Examination of a mass in the abdomen or a swelling in a testicle by passing a light through it.

transischiac (trans-is′ke-ak) From one ischium (of the hipbone) to the other.

translation (trans-la′shun) In molecular biology, the decoding of genetic information contained in the messenger RNA molecule and conversion of this data into a protein that has a particular amino acid sequence, as directed by the mRNA.

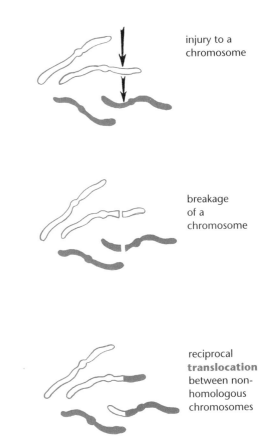

injury to a chromosome

breakage of a chromosome

reciprocal **translocation** between non-homologous chromosomes

translocation (trans-lo-ka′shun) An error occurring during replication of chromosomes whereby a chromosome, or a fragment of it, becomes attached to another chromosome.

translucent (trans-lu′sent) Permitting partial passage of light; partially transparent.

transluminal (trans-lu′mĭ-nal) Through a lumen (e.g., of a blood vessel).

transmembrane (trans-mem′brān) Through a membrane.

transmigration (trans-mi-gra′shun) Movement across a barrier, such as the normal passage of blood cells through capillary walls.

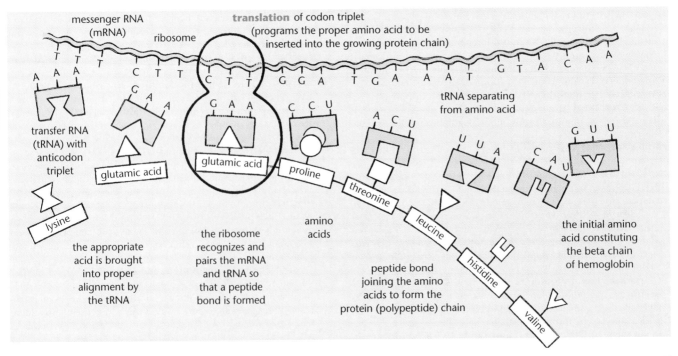

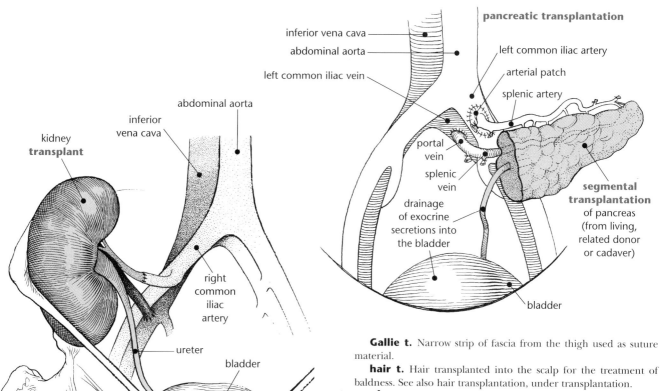

kidney
transplant

inferior
vena cava

abdominal aorta

right
common
iliac
artery

ureter

bladder

kidney
transplantation

pancreatic transplantation

inferior vena cava

abdominal aorta

left common iliac vein

left common iliac artery

arterial patch

splenic artery

portal vein

splenic vein

drainage of exocrine secretions into the bladder

segmental transplantation of pancreas (from living, related donor or cadaver)

bladder

transmissible (trans-mis'ĭ-bl) Capable of being passed from one person to another (e.g., a disease).

transmission (trans-mish'un) **1.** Transfer, as of disease or genetic information, from one individual to another. **2.** Conveyance (e.g., of nerve impulses).

iatrogenic t. Transmission of infectious microorganisms through medical or dental interference (e.g., by contaminated instruments or equipment).

vertical t. Direct, prenatal passage of infective agent or genetic characteristic from mother to child.

transmural (trans-mu'ral) Across the wall of an organ or cyst.

transmutation (trans-mu-ta'shun) A transformation.

transocular (trans-ok'u-lar) Through the eye.

transperitoneal (trans-per-ĭ-to-ne'al) Through the membrane (peritoneum) lining the abdominopelvic cavity.

transpirable (tran-spi'rah-bl) Capable of being passed or given off by transpiration.

transpiration (tran-spi-ra'shun) Diffusion, as of air or water through the skin or through a thin membrane or layer of cells.

pulmonary t. The passage of water from the bloodstream into airways within the lungs.

transpire (tran-spir') To give off moisture through skin or mucous membranes.

transplacental (trans-plah-sen'tal) Through the placenta; applied to the passage of any substance from maternal to fetal circulation.

transplant (trans-plant') **1.** To transfer living tissue from one part of the body to another or from one individual to another. (trans'plant) **2.** The material so transferred.

Gallie t. Narrow strip of fascia from the thigh used as suture material.

hair t. Hair transplanted into the scalp for the treatment of baldness. See also hair transplantation, under transplantation.

transplantar (trans-plan'tar) Extending across the sole of the foot; applied to connective tissue.

transplantation (trans-plan-ta'shun) The transfer of living tissues or organs from one site to another in the same individual, between individuals of the same species, or between individuals of different species.

autologous bone marrow t. (ABMT) Treatment modality for patients with recurrent malignant disease and when an appropriate donor cannot be found; bone marrow tissue is obtained from the patient, is freed of leukemic cells, and is reinfused after the patient has received large levels of chemotherapy and irradiation. The procedure is performed at a time when the patient is in remission.

bone marrow t. Transplantation of bone marrow tissue from the iliac crest of the donor's hipbone; used for blood malignancies, aplastic anemia, or immunodeficiency states.

corneal t. See keratoplasty.

hair t. Any of various cosmetic operations for the treatment of baldness; the most common method is by placing plugs of hair from another part of the body into punched-out areas of the hairless scalp (punch grafting); the procedure is performed gradually over a period of several months to allow healing; generally the transplanted hair does not last indefinitely.

heart t. Replacement of a severely damaged heart with an entire organ from a person who has just been declared brain dead.

heart-lung t. Transplantation of the heart and lungs as one unit; used in primary irreversible disease of those organs.

kidney t. Transplantation of a kidney from a compatible donor to restore function in irreversible kidney failure. Also called renal transplantation.

liver t. Transplantation of a liver in cases of irreversible, progressive liver disease or to correct congenital enzyme deficiencies or inborn error of metabolism. The donor is generally a young trauma victim who has sustained irreversible brain damage but has retained intact circulation.

pancreatic t. Transplantation of an entire pancreas, or of a portion of it, as a treatment modality for insulin-dependent diabetes.

renal t. See kidney transplantation.

segmental t. Transplantation of only a portion of an organ (e.g., of a pancreas or liver).

T

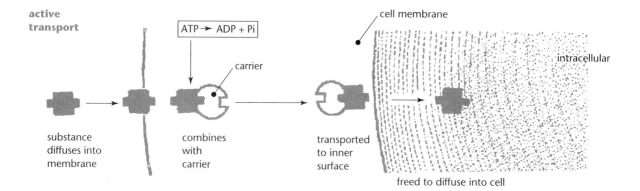

active transport

ATP → ADP + Pi

carrier

cell membrane

intracellular

substance diffuses into membrane

combines with carrier

transported to inner surface

freed to diffuse into cell

tendon t. Insertion of a slip from the tendon of a sound muscle into the tendon of a nonfunctional (paralyzed) muscle.

tooth t. Insertion of a tooth or tooth germ into a dental socket (alveolus).

transpleural (trans-ploor′al) Through the membrane covering the lung (the pleura) or through the pleural cavity.

transport (trans′port) Movement of substances in the body, especially across cell membranes.

active t. Passage of molecules or ions across a cell membrane against a chemical or electrical gradient by an energy-consuming process rather than by passive diffusion.

transposition (trans-po-zish′un) **1.** The surgical movement of tissues or structures from one place to another. **2.** The presence of an organ or structure on the wrong side of the body. **3.** The state of being reversed. **4.** In genetics, the DNA-mediated movement of genetic material from one site to another in the chromosomes.

t. of great vessels, t. of great arteries Developmental defect in which the aorta and pulmonary trunk arise from abnormal, opposite sites in the heart (i.e., the aorta originates from the right ventricle, the pulmonary trunk from the left ventricle). In essence, two independent blood circulations are formed, without exchange of oxygenated and unoxygenated blood; some anatomic communication must exist between the two systems for the infant to survive; this occurs when holes (septal defects) in the walls separating the right and left atria and ventricles are formed during fetal life and when the ductus arteriosus (which normally closes after birth) remains open; symptoms include blueness of the skin and shortness of breath. The transposition occurs most frequently in children of diabetic mothers, especially boys. If not corrected surgically, the infant dies within a year.

transposon (tranz-po′zon) Any DNA sequence that may be transferred from one cell to another, resulting in rearrangement of the recipient cell's DNA.

transrectal (trans-rek′tal) Through the rectum, as in certain procedures (e.g., prostatic biopsy, ultrasonic evaluation of the genitourinary system).

transseptal (trans-sep′tal) Across or through a septum.

transsexual (trans-seks′u-al) **1.** Relating to the surgical or hormonal intervention to alter an individual's external characteristics so that they resemble those of the opposite sex. **2.** Relating to transsexualism.

transsexualism (trans-seks′u-ah-lizm) The overpowering desire to be of the opposite sex; overwhelming feeling of being in the wrong body and desiring corrective surgery, usually from an early age.

transsphenoidal (trans-sfe-noi′dal) Through the sphenoid bone of the skull; applied to an injury or to a surgical approach (e.g., to remove a tumor from the pituitary).

transsynaptic (trans-si-nap′tik) Relating to the transmission of a nerve impulse across a synapse.

transtentorial (trans-ten-to′re-al) Relating to a tentorium (i.e., a partition within the skull made up of dura mater); applied to herniation of brain tissue or to a surgical approach.

transthoracic (trans-tho-ras′ik) Across the chest, or performed through the chest wall.

transudate (trans′u-dāt) A fluid that passes through a membrane (e.g., a capillary wall) as a result of differences in hydrostatic pressure between the two sides of the membrane. It has a protein content significantly lower than that of plasma.

transudation (trans-u-da′shun) The passage of fluid through a membrane.

transureteroureterostomy (trans′u-re′ter-o-u-re′ter-os′to-me) Surgical attachment of a cut ureter to the intact ureter of the opposite side, by direct or elliptical end-to-side technique; employed to divert urine flow.

transurethral (trans-u-re′thral) Through the urethra.

transvaginal (trans-vaj′ĭ-nal) Through the vagina.

transverse (trans-vers′) Crosswise.

transversion (trans-ver′zhun) **1.** Eruption of a tooth in the wrong place or order. **2.** In genetics, mutation in which a purine is substituted for a pyrimidine, or vice versa.

transvestism (trans-ves′tizm) The persistent desire and practice of dressing in clothing of the opposite sex; especially by a male and usually for sexual gratification. Also called cross-dressing.

transvestite (trans-ves′tit) A person who practices transvestism.

trapezius (trah-pe′ze-us) See table of muscles.

trauma (traw′mah) Injury or damage, physical or mental. See also injury.

acoustic t. Hearing loss due to a sudden loud noise or a sudden blow to the head.

cumulative t. Damage to tissues by repetitive minor injuries, which would not otherwise cause significant damage. Also called cumulative injury.

occlusal t. Abnormal stress and resulting pathologic changes on a tooth and surrounding tissues, caused by improper alignment of the teeth.

psychic t. A painful emotional experience.

t. X Colloquialism for the physical signs of child abuse.

traumatic (traw-mat′ik) Relating to trauma or injury.

traumatize (traw′mah-tiz) To injure or wound, physiologically or psychologically.

traumato- Combining form meaning trauma; wound; injury.

traumatologist (traw-mah-tol′o-jist) A specialist in traumatology.

traumatology (traw-mah-tol′o-je) The subspecialty concerned with the care and treatment of acute trauma resulting from accidents (traffic, industrial, or domestic) or from criminal acts (shootings, stabbings, or beatings).

traumatopathy (traw-mah-top′ah-the) Any disease or abnormal condition originating from an injury.

tray (tra) Any shallow receptacle with raised edges (e.g., those on which surgical or dental instruments are placed for ready access).

acrylic resin t. In dentistry, an impression tray made of autopolymerizing acrylic resin.

impression t. In dentistry, a receptacle with a flanged body and a handle for use in carrying impression material to the mouth and holding it in position against the teeth or oral tissues while the material sets.

trazodone (tra′zo-dōn) An antidepressant drug with strong sedative properties; useful in the treatment of depression accompanied by anxiety and insomnia. Possible adverse effects include dizziness, constipation, dry mouth, and, rarely, a painful persistent erection (priapism).

treadmill (tred′mil) A moving belt mechanism of varying speeds (and often an adjustable degree of incline) that permits people to walk or run in a stationary location under controlled conditions; used in studies of physiologic functions, especially cardiac stress testing.

treadmill

treat (trēt) To provide health care.

treatment (trēt′ment) Any course of action or program adopted to restore health, prevent disease, or relieve symptoms.

conservative t. Management of disease with the least aggressive of therapeutic options. Sometimes the term is used to mean medical as opposed to surgical.

electroconvulsive t. (ECT) See electroconvulsive therapy, under therapy.

electroshock t. (EST) See electroconvulsive therapy, under therapy.

futile t. A treatment that has no apparent therapeutic benefit.

maintenance t. Treatment aimed at stabilizing the patient's condition, especially when no cure is available.

medical t. Treatment of disease by means other than surgery.

palliative t. Treatment aimed at mitigating symptoms rather than curing the disease.

preventive t., prophylactic t. Treatment given to prevent a person from acquiring a disease to which he was exposed or is expected to be exposed.

root canal t. Removal of the pulp of a tooth and filling of the root canal.

shock t. See electroconvulsive therapy, under therapy.

treatment port (trēt′ment port) In radiation therapy, the spot on the body at which the radiation beam is directed.

Trematoda (trem-ah-to′dah) A class of flatworms, including flukes, that are parasitic in humans and animals.

trematode (trem′ah-tod) Any flatworm of the class Trematoda; a fluke.

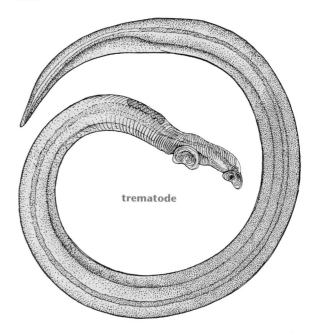

trematode

tremor (trem′or) An involuntary rhythmic contraction and relaxation of opposing muscle groups; causes are varied and include intake of caffeine, amphetamines, and antidepressant drugs.

coarse t. Tremor in which muscle contractions are slow (four to five per second) and of large amplitude.

essential t. A fine tremor, especially of the extremities, occurring during voluntary movement or when limbs are outstretched; tremor disappears when limbs are relaxed; occurs in members of the same family, as an autosomal dominant inheritance. It is not associated with disease. Also called heredofamilial tremor.

fine t. Tremor characterized by rapid muscle vibrations (10–12 per second).

flapping t. See asterixis.

heredofamilial t. See essential tremor.

intention t. Tremor that is induced or intensified by a voluntary movement.

kinetic t. Any tremor occurring during movement of a limb; usually denotes a coarse tremor caused by disease of the middle portion of the cerebellum. In such cases, a coarse side-to-side tremor of the arm may be elicited by having the patient alternately touch his nose and then touch the examiner's finger, which is held at arm's length from the patient; a similar side-to-side tremor may be brought about in the leg by asking the patient to place the heel of one foot on the knee of the other leg and to run the heel down the shin.

mercurial t. A coarse tremor that begins in the hands and usually spreads slowly to the rest of the extremities, facial muscles, and the tongue; it is the characteristic feature of mercury poisoning due to long-standing inhalation of inorganic mercury in the workplace.

pill-rolling t. The rubbing of index finger and thumb together as if rolling a small object, as seen in parkinsonism. Also called coin-counting.

positional t. See static tremor.

postural t. See static tremor.

saturnine t. Tremor sometimes seen in advanced cases of lead poisoning.

senile t. A slight persistent tremor often seen in elderly people; it is unrelated to disease.

static t. A coarse tremor occurring when a person tries to hold the limbs in a certain position (e.g., holding arms extended, parallel to the floor, with palms open); seen in disease of the middle portion of the cerebellum. Also called positional tremor; postural tremor.

vocal t. Quavering of the voice due to involuntary mild approximations and separations of the vocal folds, caused by dysfunction of nerves supplying the folds.

volitional t. Tremor that can be stopped by a strong effort.

tremulous (trem'u-lus) Trembling; quivering.

trepanation (trep-ah-na'shun) See trephination.

trephination (tref-ĭ-na'shun) Removal of a piece of bone from the skull with a trephine. Also called trepanation.

trephine (trĕ-fin') A cyclindrical saw for cutting circular pieces of tissue (e.g., bone, cornea).

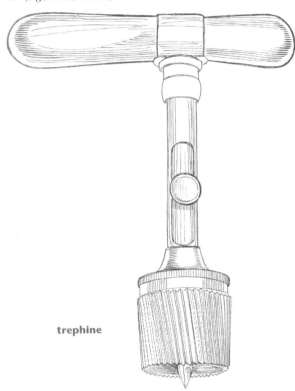

trephine

Treponema (trep-o-ne'mah) A genus of spiral bacteria (family Treponemataceae); several species cause disease in humans.

T. carateum The causative agent of the skin disease pinta.

T. pallidum Species causing human syphilis; it is a highly motile organism that moves by corkscrew rotation and varies in size from 5 to 15 μ in length, with 6 to 15 spirals.

T. pertenue The causative agent of yaws.

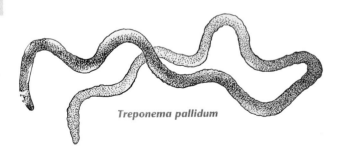

Treponema pallidum

treponeme (trep'o-nem) Any member of the genus *Treponema*.

treponemiasis (trep-o-ne-mi'ah-sis) Infection with a treponeme.

treponemicidal (trep-o-ne-mi-si'dal) Destructive to microorganisms of the genus *Treponema*. Also called antitreponemal.

tretinoin (tret'ĭ-noin) Compound chemically related to vitamin A,

used topically in the treatment of acne; may cause skin irritation and peeling.

triacylglycerol (tri-ā-sil-glis'er-ol) See triglyceride.

triad (tri'ad) A group of closely related signs, symptoms, or anatomic structures.

Charcot's t. *(a)* Fever, abdominal pain in the right upper area, and jaundice; usually seen in inflammation of the bile duct. *(b)* Nystagmus, intention tremor, and a slow, halting speech; seen (rarely) in advanced stages of multiple sclerosis.

hemochromatosis t. Liver enlargement, diabetes mellitus, and bronze pigmentation of skin (bronze diabetes).

hepatic portal t. A triad at the angle of the liver lobule consisting of branches of the portal vein, hepatic artery, and bile duct.

Hutchinson's t. Interstitial inflammation of the cornea, nerve deafness, and notched (Hutchinson) teeth; indicative of congenital syphilis.

Kartagener's t. See Kartagener's syndrome, under syndrome.

Pettit's t. Dilation of the pupils, increased pressure within the eyes, and changes in the retinal vessels due to activity of the autonomic nervous system.

Plummer-Vinson t. Iron deficiency anemia, atrophy of the tongue and stomach lining (mucosa), and formation of smooth mucosal ledges in the upper esophagus (esophageal webs).

Saint's t. Combination of hiatal hernia, diverticulosis, and gallstones.

triaditis (tri-ad-i'tis) Inflammation of the connective tissue around the hepatic portal triad (i.e., branches of the portal vein, hepatic artery, and bile duct).

triage (trē-ahzh') The process of sorting and evaluating multiple casuality victims to assign priorities of medical treatment based on the severity of injuries.

trial (tri'al) An experiment or exploratory activity.

blind t. A trial in which either the experimenter or the subject does not know to which group the subject has been assigned (e.g., whether a patient is in the group receiving a medication or the one receiving a placebo). Also called blind experiment; blind study.

clinical t. Controlled study on human volunteers for the safety, efficacy, or optimal dosage (if appropriate) of a diagnostic, therapeutic, or prophylactic drug, device, or technique; the subjects are selected according to predetermined criteria and observed for predefined evidence of effects, both favorable and unfavorable; in some trials one treatment modality may be compared with another for efficacy and side effects.

double-blind t. A trial in which both investigator and subjects do not know which group of subjects is exposed to the variable (e.g., a drug) being tested. Also called double-blind experiment; double-blind study.

triamcinolone (tri-am-sin'o-lōn) A potent glucocorticoid drug used to treat inflammatory conditions; especially used in topical form.

triamterene (tri-am'ter-ēn) A mild diuretic drug used for treatment of high blood pressure and water retention. In contrast to many diuretics, it blocks loss of potassium from the kidney; commonly used in combination with hydrochlorothiazide.

triangle (tri'ang-gl) A figure or area formed by connecting three points; a three-cornered area.

anal t. A triangular space with the angles placed at both ischial tuberosities and at the tip of the coccyx; the posterior part of the perineum containing the termination of the anal canal (anal orifice).

anterior cervical t. A large triangular area of the anterior neck, bounded on top by the mandible, behind by the anterior margin of the sternocleidomastoid muscle, and in front by the midline of the neck. The triangle is subdivided into the muscular, carotid, submental, and digastric triangles.

t. of bladder See trigone of bladder, under trigone.

Bonwill t. An equilateral triangle with the angles placed at the center of each mandibular condyle and at the mesial contact area of

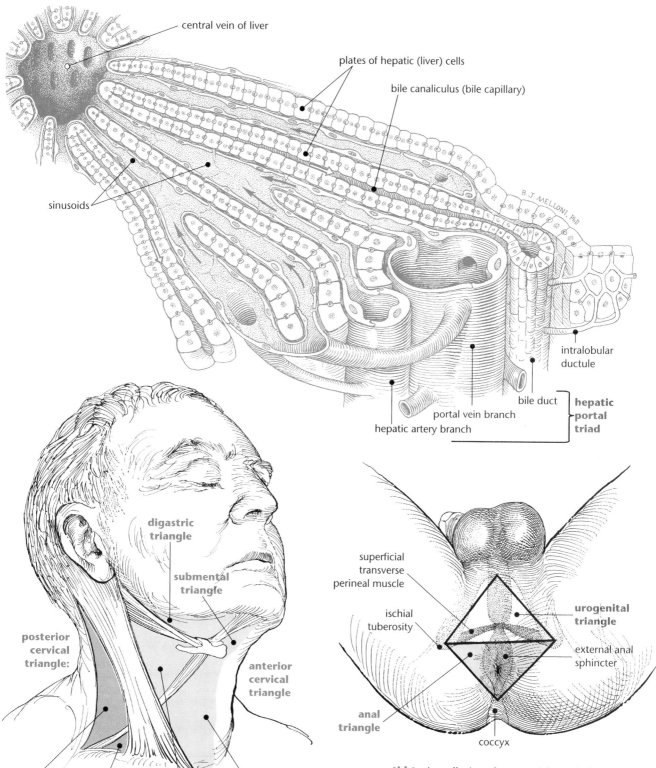

central vein of liver

plates of hepatic (liver) cells

bile canaliculus (bile capillary)

B.J. MELLONI, PhD

sinusoids

intralobular
ductule

bile duct

**hepatic
portal
triad**

portal vein branch

hepatic artery branch

digastric
triangle

submental
triangle

superficial
transverse
perineal muscle

ischial
tuberosity

**urogenital
triangle**

external anal
sphincter

**anal
triangle**

coccyx

posterior
cervical
triangle:

anterior
cervical
triangle

occipital
triangle

supraclavicular
triangle

carotid
triangle

muscular
triangle

the mandibular central incisors; each distance in an adult mandible is about 4 inches in length.

t. of Calot A somewhat triangular area formed by the cystic artery superiorly, the cystic duct inferiorly, and the hepatic duct medially; an area of considerable importance to surgeons due to variations of great significance. Also called cystohepatic triangle; cystic triangle of Calot.

carotid t. A small triangular area of the neck, bounded above by the posterior belly of the digastric muscle, behind by the sternocleidomastoid muscle, and below by the superior belly of the omohyoid muscle; it contains the upper part of the common carotid and its bifurcation into the external and internal carotid arteries. It is best seen when the neck is extended and the head slightly rotated contralaterally.

crural t. The triangular area formed by the inner aspects of the thigh and lower abdominal, inguinal, and genital regions, with the base traversing the navel (umbilicus); the area where the petechial rash of smallpox is initially seen.

cystic t. of Calot See triangle of Calot.

T

cystohepatic t. See triangle of Calot.

digastric t. The triangular area bounded above by the mandible and behind, below, and in front by the posterior and anterior bellies of the digastric muscle; the area contains the submandibular gland. Also called submandibular triangle.

Einthoven's t. A hypothetical equilateral triangle surrounding the heart, formed by lines representing the three standard limb leads of the electrocardiogram (ECG), in which the apices are situated in the two arms and the left leg.

t. of elbow See cubital fossa, under fossa.

femoral t. A triangular area just below the fold of the groin, at the upper and inner part of the thigh; it is bounded above by the inguinal ligament, laterally by the medial border of the sartorius muscle, and medially by the medial border of the long adductor (adductor longus) muscle; the femoral vessels divide the triangle into two parts. Also called Scarpa's triangle; femoral trigone.

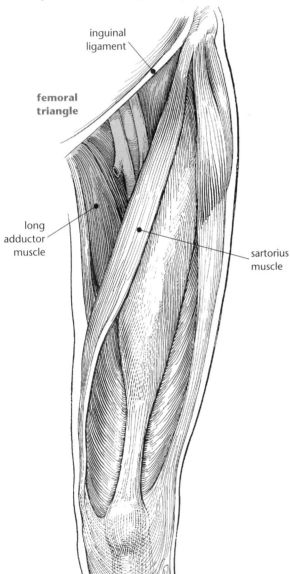

inguinal ligament

femoral triangle

long adductor muscle

sartorius muscle

Grynfeltt's t. See Grynfeltt-Lesshaft triangle.

Grynfeltt-Lesshaft t. A triangular area bounded above by the 12th rib and the serratus posterior inferior muscle, medially by the erector muscle of spine, and inferolaterally by the internal oblique muscle; it is a weak area that offers little resistance to pressure from within, therefore, it is a likely site for protrusion of intra-abdominal structures (lumbar hernia). Also called Grynfeltt's triangle; superior lumbar space.

triangle ■ **triangle**

Hesselbach's t. See inguinal triangle.

inguinal t. A triangular area of the anterior abdominal wall bounded below by the medial half of the inguinal ligament, medially by the lower edge of the straight muscle of abdomen (rectus abdominus), and laterally by a line from the middle of the inguinal ligament to the navel (umbilicus); an important area relating to direct and indirect inguinal hernias. Also called Hesselbach's triangle.

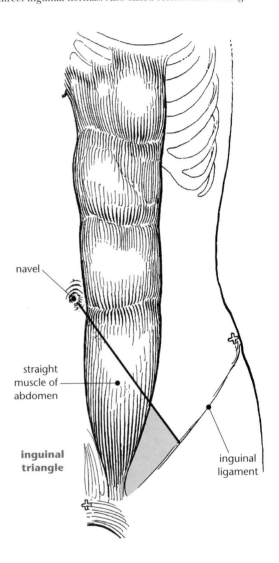

navel

straight muscle of abdomen

inguinal triangle

inguinal ligament

Laimer's t. A triangular area of the upper posterior part of the esophagus, immediately below the cricopharyngeus muscle, in which the posterior wall is variably deficient; it is a likely site for an esophageal diverticulum to occur. Also called V-shaped area of Laimer.

lumbar t. A small triangular area bounded by the edges of the lateral margin of the latissimus dorsi and the medial margin of the external oblique muscles and the crest of the ilium. Also called lumbar triangle of Petit; inferior lumbar space.

lumbar t. of Petit See lumbar triangle.

muscular t. A triangular area limited in front by the midline of the neck, from the hyoid bone to the breastbone (sternum), and in back by the angle formed by the anterior margin of the sternocleidomastoid and the superior belly of the omohyoid muscle; it is the largest subdivision of the anterior cervical triangle.

occipital t. The triangular area of the posterior neck formed by the sternocleidomastoid, trapezius, and omohyoid muscles; the larger division of the posterior cervical triangle.

olfactory t. See olfactory trigone, under trigone.

posterior cervical t. A triangular area of the posterior neck, bounded in front by the posterior margin of the sternocleidomastoid muscle, behind by the anterior margin of the trapezius muscle, below by the collarbone (clavicle). The inferior belly of the omohyoid muscle divides the triangle into an upper occipital triangle and a lower supraclavicular triangle.

    Scarpa's t. See femoral triangle.

    subclavian t. See supraclavicular triangle.

    submandibular t. See digastric triangle.

    submental t. Triangular region bounded laterally by the anterior belly of the digastric muscle, medially by the midline of the neck from the hyoid bone to the chin (mental symphysis), and below by the hyoid bone. Also called suprahyoid triangle.

    supraclavicular t. The small triangular area of the neck, bounded by the sternocleidomastoid muscle, the inferior belly of the omohyoid muscle, and the collarbone (clavicle); the smaller division of the posterior cervical triangle. Also called subclavian triangle.

    suprahyoid t. See submental triangle.

    umbilicomamillary t. A triangular area formed by a line joining the nipples of the breast with its apex at the navel (umbilicus).

    urogenital t. A triangular space with the angles placed at both ischial tuberosities and at the pubic symphysis; it contains the external urogenital organs.

    vesical t. See trigone of bladder, under trigone.

    Ward's t. A triangular area in the neck of the femur near the hip joint, seen on x-ray film and characterized by diminished density in the trabecular pattern; it represents a relatively weak area that is vulnerable to fracture. It is one of the areas commonly assessed by densitometry to estimate the extent of osteoporosis.

triazolam (tri-a′zo-lam) Sedative drug used in the short-term treatment of insomnia.

tribasic (tri-ba′sik) Denoting a molecule with three replaceable hydrogen atoms.

tribe (trīb) See kindred.

triceps (tri′seps) Having three sites of origin (e.g., the triceps muscle). See table of muscles.

trichatrophia (trik-ah-tro′fe-ah) Atrophy of the hair bulbs, causing hair loss.

trichiasis (trī-ki′ah-sis) Inversion of hairs about an orifice, such as eyelashes that turn in against the eyeball and cause irritation of the cornea; frequently seen in trachoma.

trichina (trī-ki′nah) A larval worm of the genus *Trichinella*.

Trichinella spiralis (trik-ĭ-nel′ah spi-ra′lis) Parasitic roundworm (genus *Trichinella*) that causes trichinosis; its larvae are found coiled within cysts in striated muscle of infected mammals, including humans; disease is acquired by eating undercooked infected pork. Also called pork worm; trichina worm.

trichinosis (trik-ĭ-no′sis) Disease caused by the parasite *Trichinella spiralis*, usually through ingestion of infested undercooked meat, especially pork; the parasites become encysted in muscle, causing muscle stiffness and pain, swelling around the eyelids, nausea, diarrhea, fever, and sometimes prostration.

trichloroacetic acid (tri-klor′o-ah-se′tik as′id) A strong acid used in solution to remove warts; widely used as a protein precipitant.

trichloroethane (tri-klor-o-eth′ān) Toxic compound used extensively as industrial solvent; has been used in various home-use products (e.g., spot removers and inhalant decongestant sprays); causes depression of cardiovascular and central nervous systems and liver damage.

trichloroethylene (tri-klo-ro-eth′ĭ-lēn) Toxic hydrocarbon formerly used as an anesthetic in obstetrical practice; it is widely used in industry and has caused acute kidney failure in people who inhale it while using it as a cleaning solvent; mild exposure produces euphoria, which may lead to addiction.

tricho-, trichi- Combining forms meaning hair.

trichobezoar (trik-o-be′zōr) A concretion composed of hairs formed within the stomach or intestines. Also called hairball; pilobezoar.

trichoclasia, trichoclasis (trik-o-kla′se-ah, trik-ok′lah-sis) Brittleness and eventual breakage of hair, as in monilethrix and tricorrhexis nodosa.

trichocryptosis (trik-o-krip-to′sis) Any disease of hair follicles.

trichoepithelioma (trik-o-ep′ĭ-the-le-o′mah) A noncancerous skin tumor originating in hair follicles, usually on the face.

trichoesthesia (trik-o-es-the′ze-ah) **1.** Sensation felt when hair on the skin is touched. **2.** Abnormal sensation of having a hair in the mouth or the eye.

trichogen (trik′o-jen) Anything that stimulates hair growth.

trichoglossia (trik-o-glos′e-ah) See black tongue, under tongue.

trichoid (trik′oid) Resembling hair.

trichology (tri-kol′o-je) The study of hair in all its aspects.

trichomonad (trī-ko-mo′nad) Any member of the genus *Trichomonas*.

Trichomonas (trī-ko-mo′-nas) Genus of parasitic protozoan flagellates (family Trichomonadidae).

    T. vaginalis Species found in the vagina and in the genital tract of men; transmitted through sexual intercourse and frequently causing inflammation, especially in women.

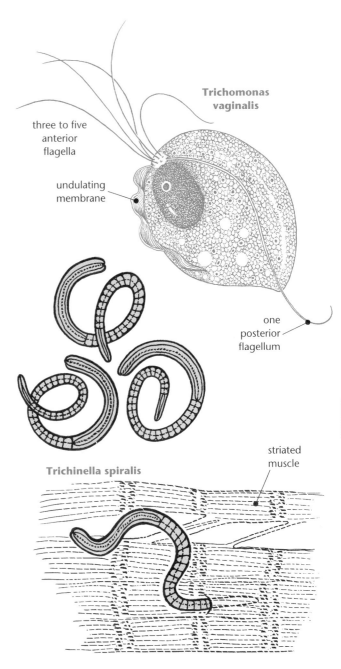

Trichomonas vaginalis

three to five anterior flagella

undulating membrane

one posterior flagellum

striated muscle

Trichinella spiralis

trichomoniasis (trik-o-mo-ni′ah-sis) Infection of the genital tract with *Trichomonas vaginalis* almost always acquired through sexual intercourse; it causes varying degrees of genital irritation and itching and vaginal discharge; infected males are usually asymptomatic, serving mostly as vectors for transmission through sexual intercourse; in pregnant women, the infection may give rise to low birth weight or premature infants.

trichomycosis axillaris (trik-o-mi-ko′sis ak′sĭ-lar-is) Colored bacterial colonies of *Corynebacterium tenius* forming concretions on the shaft of axillary or pubic hairs; color ranges from yellow to red to black. Formerly thought to be a fungal infection. Also called lepothrix.

trichopathy (tri-kop′ah-the) Any disease of the hair.

trichophytobezoar (trik-o-fi-to-be′zōr) A hard ball composed of hair and vegetable fibers sometimes found in the stomach of humans and some domestic animals.

Trichophyton (tri-kof′ĭ-ton) Genus of disease-causing fungi parasitic in the skin, nails, and hair follicles of humans and some animals. They cause ringworm (tinea).

    T. mentagrophytes A species causing itchy infection of scalp and beard hair, skin, and nails; a strain causes athlete's foot; commonly infects pets and farm animals.

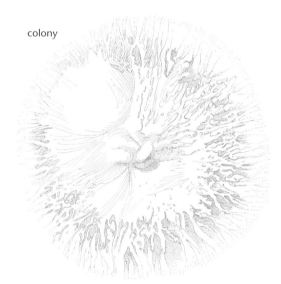

colony

Trichophyton mentagrophytes

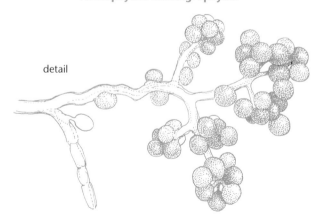

detail

    T. rubrum A species that causes persistent, difficult-to-treat infection of the nails; may spread to the feet and hands and cause fine dry scaling.

    T. schoenleinii A species that causes favus, a severe form of chronic ringworm of the scalp, with destruction of hair follicles and permanent hair loss.

    T. tonsurans Species causing a seborrhea-like ringworm of the scalp; fungus grows within the hair shaft, causing it to break off at the scalp surface, leaving stubble that looks like black dots (black dot fungus).

trichophytosis (trik-o-fi-to′sis) Infection with species of *Trichophyton;* tinea.

trichorrhexis (trik-o-rek′sis) Condition in which hair tends to break off easily.

    t. nodosa Nodular appearance of the hair caused by transverse breakage of the shaft's cortex with subsequent longitudinal splitting into fine strands.

trichosanthin (tri-ko-san′thin) Plant protein, obtained from root tubers of the Chinese cucumber (Trichosantes kirilowii); it has been used in the treatment of trophoblastic tumors and as an agent for inducing second-trimester abortions; a highly purified form (compound Q) has been proposed as antiviral treatment for AIDS.

trichosis (tri-ko′sis) Any disease of the hair.

Trichosporon (tri-kos′po-ron) Genus of imperfect fungi that are normal inhabitants of the respiratory and digestive tracts. Some species may cause disease in debilitated patients.

trichosporosis (trik-o-spo-ro′sis) Any fungal condition caused by species of the genus *Trichosporon.*

trichotillomania (trik-o-til-o-ma′ne-ah) A compulsion to pull, twist, and tug at one's scalp hair.

trichuriasis (trik-u-ri′ah-sis) Intestinal infestation with the whipworm *Trichuris trichiura;* usually asymptomatic, but heavy infections produce severe diarrhea and bleeding.

Trichuris (trik-u′ris) Genus of roundworms of the class Nematoda.

    T. trichiura A minute whiplike worm parasitic in human intestines, transmitted by direct hand-to-mouth contact or by ingestion of contaminated food or water. Also called whipworm.

tricrotic (tri-krot′ik) Having three waves; applied to an arterial pulse tracing.

tricuspid (tri-kus′pid) Having three cusps; applied to a valve in the heart.

triethylene glycol (tri-eth′ĭ-lēn gli′kol) Compound used in the vapor state as an air disinfectant.

triethylenemelamine (tri-eth′ĭ-lēn-mel′ah-mēn) (TEM) Compound formerly used in the treatment of chronic leukemia.

trifluridine (tri-floor′ĭ-den) Antiviral compound used in eyedrops to treat herpes simplex infections of the eye. Adverse effects include dryness or itching of the eyes and swelling of the eyelids.

trifocal (tri-fo′kal) Having three focal lengths.

trifurcation (tri-fur-ka′shun) Branching into three parts.

trigastric (tri-gas′trik) Denoting a muscle with three bellies.

trigeminal (tri-jem′ĭ-nal) **1.** Triple. **2.** Denoting the fifth cranial nerve (trigeminal nerve). See table of nerves.

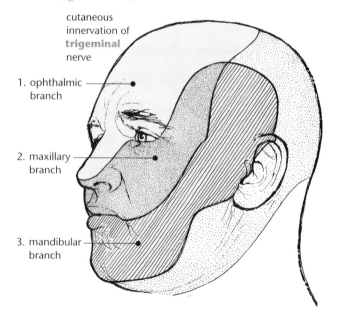

cutaneous innervation of **trigeminal** nerve

1. ophthalmic branch

2. maxillary branch

3. mandibular branch

trigeminy (tri-jem′ĭ-ne) See trigeminal rhythm, under rhythm.

triglyceride (tri-glis′er-id) (TG) The most important of three groups of neutral fats; it serves as the major storage form of fatty acids in the body and is a major constituent of adipose tissue. Also called triacylglycerol.

trigonal (tri′go-nal) 1. Relating to a trigone. 2. Triangular.

trigone (tri′gon) Triangle; a triangular space, eminence, or fossa.

t. of bladder A small, triangular, smooth area at the lower part of the bladder, whose apices are the two slitlike openings of the ureters and the internal orifice of the urethra; in this area the mucosa is closely adherent to the muscular layer of the bladder wall. Also called vesical triangle; vesical trigone; triangle of bladder.

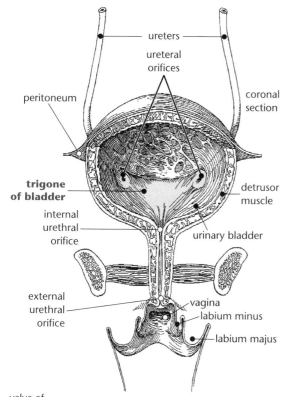

ureters

ureteral orifices

peritoneum

coronal section

trigone of bladder

internal urethral orifice

detrusor muscle

urinary bladder

external urethral orifice

vagina

labium minus

labium majus

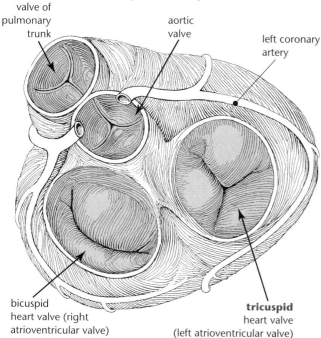

valve of pulmonary trunk

aortic valve

left coronary artery

bicuspid heart valve (right atrioventricular valve)

tricuspid heart valve (left atrioventricular valve)

collateral t. A somewhat triangular eminence in the floor of the lateral ventricle of the brain between the posterior and inferior (descending) horns. Also called trigone of lateral ventricle.

femoral t. See femoral triangle, under triangle.

interpeduncular t. The midline fossa or depression at the base of the brain between the two cerebral peduncles; the site of the interpeduncular cistern. Also called interpeduncular fossa.

t. of lateral ventricle See collateral trigone.

left fibrous t. of heart A somewhat triangular portion of fibrous tissue of the heart, situated between the aortic fibrous ring (aortic fibrous annulus) anteriorly and the front of the left atrioventricular fibrous ring posteriorly; it provides an attachment for part of the anterior leaflet (cusp) of the mitral valve.

olfactory t. The flat grayish triangular eminence at the posterior end of the olfactory tract where it diverges into three roots (medial, intermediate, and lateral olfactory striae); it lies above the optic nerve near the chiasma. Also called olfactory triangle; olfactory pyramid.

right fibrous t. of heart A somewhat triangular portion of fibrous tissue of the heart, situated between the aortic fibrous ring (aortic fibrous annulus) anteriorly and the atrioventricular fibrous rings posteriorly; it provides powerful structural and functional links between the aortic, mitral, and tricuspid orifices. Also called central fibrous body of heart.

vesical t. See trigone of bladder.

trigonitis (trig-o-ni′tis) Inflammation of the lower portion (trigone) of the bladder.

trihydric (tri-hi′drik) Having three replaceable hydrogen atoms.

triiodothyronine (tri-i-o-do-thi′ro-nēn) (TITh, T_3) One of the two principal hormones secreted by the thyroid gland (the other being thyroxine); it aids in regulating the body's metabolism. Also called liothyronine.

reverse t., reverse T_3 (rT_3) A product of the peripheral degradation of thyroxine; present in elevated levels in certain disease states; useful as an aid for diagnosis of fetal and infantile hypothyroidism.

trilaminar (tri-lam′ĭ-nar) Composed of three layers.

trilogy (tril′o-je) A group of three related entities.

t. of Fallot The combined presence of atrial septal defect, pulmonary stenosis, and enlargement of the heart ventricles.

trimellitic anhydride (tri-mel-it′ik an-hi′drīd) (TMA) Compound used in industry as a hardening agent for epoxy resins, as a plasticizer, and in the manufacture of paints. Exposure to TMA fumes and dust in the workplace has been associated with four clinical conditions: an immediate allergic reaction, characterized by inflammation of the nasal passages, conjunctivitis, or asthma; a delayed reaction occurring four to six hours after exposure ("TMA flu"), characterized by cough and occasional wheezing, chills, malaise, and muscle and joint pain; lung disease and anemia occurring after repeated high-dose exposure to volatile fumes as TMA is sprayed on heated metal surfaces; and an irritant respiratory condition characterized by cough and difficult breathing, occurring with the first high-dose exposure to TMA powder and fumes.

trimeprazine (tri-mep′rah-zēn) An antihistamine drug used to relieve itching caused by allergic conditions; also used to sedate children prior to surgery or other procedures.

trimester (tri-mes′ter) A period of three months.

first t. The period of pregnancy from the 1st day of the last menstrual period before conception to the 98th day; the first 14 weeks of gestation.

second t. The period of pregnancy from the 15th to the 28th week of gestation.

third t. The period of pregnancy from the 29th through the 42nd week of gestation.

trimethadione (tri-meth-ah-di′ōn) Drug with anticonvulsant properties; may cause abnormalities or death of the fetus when taken by a pregnant woman; abnormalities include intrauterine growth retardation, impaired hearing, heart defects, and other physical abnormalities.

T

trimethoprim (tri-meth′o-prim) An antibacterial drug used, usually in conjunction with a sulfonamide, in the treatment of urinary tract infection, shigellosis, otitis media, and respiratory tract infections including pneumocystis carinii pneumonia in AIDS patients. Possible adverse effects include rash, nausea, vomiting, sore tongue, and diarrhea.

trimethoxytriptamine (tri-meth-ok-sī-trip′tah-min) A hallucinogenic drug with a potential for overdose.

trimming (trim′ing) Term used to describe a method of "correcting" experimental data by eliminating (trimming) the high and low values in excess of the mean in an experimental "run." The practice is considered a form of scientific misrepresentation.

trimorphous (tri-mor′fus) Occurring in three forms.

trinitroglycerin (tri-ni-tro-glis′er-in) See nitroglycerin.

trinitrophenol (tri-ni-tro-fe′nol) See picric acid.

trinitrotoluene (tri-ni-tro-tol′u-ēn) (TNT) Explosive obtained by nitrating toluene, reported to cause aplastic anemia and liver damage through exposure in occupational settings.

triose (tri′ōs) A sugar with three carbon atoms in a molecule (e.g., glyceraldehyde).

triplet (trip′let) **1.** One of three individuals born at one birth. **2.** In molecular biology, a unit of three successive bases in DNA or RNA that code for a specific amino acid in a protein molecule. **3.** Any group of three objects or items (e.g., three lenses mounted together and used to correct an aberration).

triploblastic (trip-lo-blas′tik) Containing tissue derived from all three embryonic layers (ectoderm, mesoderm, endoderm).

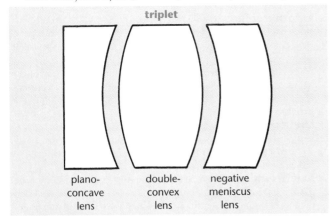

triplet

plano-concave lens   double-convex lens   negative meniscus lens

triploid (trip′loid) Having three sets of chromosomes in its cell nucleus.

triplopia (trip-lo′pe-ah) Visual defect in which one object is seen as three objects.

triradius (tri-ra′de-us) In dermatoglyphics, a point at the base of each finger (seen in fingerprints) in which the dermal ridges course in three directions.

trisaccharide (tri-sak′ah-rid) A carbohydrate (e.g., raffinose) that upon hydrolysis yields three simple sugars.

tris(hydroxymethyl)aminomethane (tris′hi-drok′se-meth′il-am′ī-no-meth′rān) (tris, TRIS) See tromethamine.

trismic (triz′mik) Relating to trismus.

trismus (triz′mus) Sustained involuntary contraction of the jaw muscles, which keeps the mouth tightly closed; usually the first symptom of tetanus. Also called lockjaw.

trisomic (tri-so′mik) Relating to trisomy.

trisomy (tri′so-me) An abnormality in which an additional chromosome is present in the cells (i.e., 47 instead of 46); the extra chromosome is a copy of one of an existing pair, so that one particular chromosome is present in triplicate. The consequences of trisomy can range from early fetal death and spontaneous abortion to numerous abnormalities in the live-born child.

tritium (trit′e-um) See hydrogen 3.

triturable (trich′er-ah-bl) Capable of being triturated.

trituration (trich′ĕ-ra′shun) **1.** The process of reducing a solid to a powder by rubbing. **2.** The mixing of dental alloy and mercury.

trocar (tro′kar) A sharp-pointed rod, used in a tube (cannula) for piercing the wall of a body cavity, after which it is withdrawn, leaving the cannula in place for further purposes (e.g., evacuating fluid from the cavity). Also spelled trochar.

trochanter (tro-kan′ter) One of two prominences (greater and lesser) on the upper end of the femur, near the hip joint.

trochanteric (tro-kan-ter′ik) Relating to a trochanter.

trochar (tro′kar) See trocar.

troche (tro′ke) A small medicated tablet; a lozenge.

trochlea (trok′le-ah) **1.** Any pulley-like structure. **2.** The fibrous loop in the eye socket (orbit) through which passes the tendon of the superior oblique muscle of the eyeball.

    peroneal t. A small elevation on the lateral side of the heel bone (calcaneus), about 2 cm below the lateral malleolus; it separates the tendons of the long peroneal muscle (peroneus longus) from the short peroneal muscle (peroneus brevis). Also called peroneal spine of calcaneus.

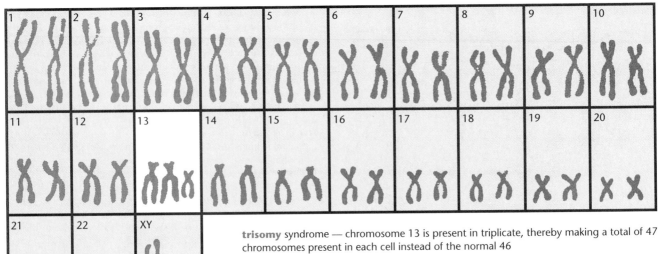

trisomy syndrome — chromosome 13 is present in triplicate, thereby making a total of 47 chromosomes present in each cell instead of the normal 46

karyotype of a male with **trisomy** syndrome

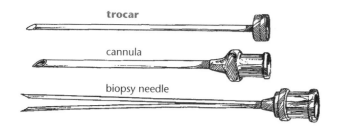

trocar

cannula

biopsy needle

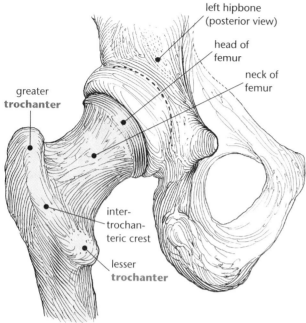

greater **trochanter**

left hipbone (posterior view)

head of femur

neck of femur

inter-trochan-teric crest

lesser **trochanter**

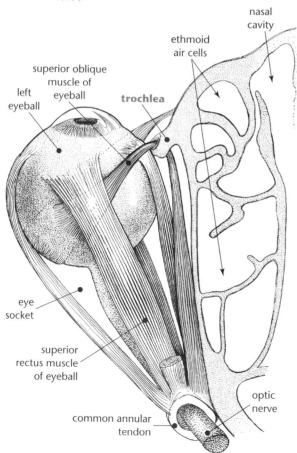

nasal cavity

ethmoid air cells

superior oblique muscle of eyeball

left eyeball

trochlea

eye socket

superior rectus muscle of eyeball

common annular tendon

optic nerve

trochlear (trok'le-ar) **1.** Relating to a trochlea or pulley. **2.** Denoting the trochlear (4th cranial) nerve. See table of nerves.

trochleiform (trok'le-ĭ-form) Pulley-shaped.

trochoid (tro'koid) Permitting rotation, as a pivot; applied to certain articulations.

Trombicula (trom-bik'u-lah) Genus of mites (family Trombiculidae) whose larvae (chiggers or red bugs) can infest humans and transmit rickettsial diseases and scrub typhus (tsutsugamushi disease).

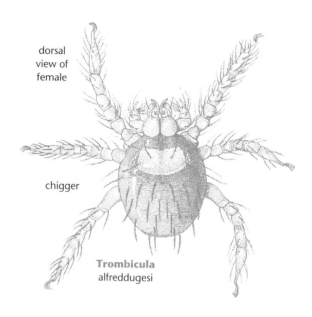

dorsal view of female

chigger

Trombicula alfreddugesi

trombiculiasis (trom-bik-u-li'ah-sis) Infestation with mites of the genus *Trombicula*.

trombiculid (trom-bik'u-lid) Any mite of the family Trombiculidae.

tromethamine (tro-meth'ah-mēn) (THAM) Substance used as a buffer in enzyme reactions. Also called tris(hydroxymethyl)amino-methane.

trophic (trof'ik) Relating to nutrition.

tropho-, troph- Combining forms meaning nutrition.

trophoblast (trof'o-blast) The outer layer of cells forming the wall of the blastocyst; the trophoblast plays an important role in attaching this early embryo to the uterine wall and in the eventual formation of the placenta.

trophoblastoma (trof-o-blas-to'mah) See choriocarcinoma.

trophoneurosis (trof-o-nu-ro'sis) Alteration of any tissue due to interruption of its nerve supply.

trophotropism (trof-o-tro'pizm) Movement of living cells toward nutritive material.

-trophy Combining form meaning growth (e.g., hypertrophy).

tropia (tro'pe-ah) Deviation of the eyes from their normal position.

tropine (tro'pin) Poisonous alkaloid derived from atropine and scopolamine.

tropocollagen (tro-po-kol'ah-jen) The basic molecular unit of collagen fibrils.

tropometer (tro-pom'ĕ-ter) **1.** Device for measuring the degree of rotation of the eyeball. **2.** Device for measuring the torsion of the shaft of a long bone.

tropomyosin B (tro-po-mi'o-sin) Fibrous protein concentrated in the Z line of muscles; it inhibits muscle contraction unless its position is modified by troponin.

troponin (tro'po-nin) One of the protein components of skeletal muscle; it has affinity for calcium and participates in regulating contraction of muscles.

trough (trof) **1.** A narrow, shallow depression. **2.** The minimum serum concentration of a drug (administered at regular intervals); used in monitoring of therapeutic drugs to ascertain that a minimum affective level of the drug is present at all times.

T

truncal (trun′kal) Relating to any trunk.

truncate (trun′kāt) Cut across the main axis.

truncus (trun′kus) Latin for trunk.

t. arteriosus The main arterial trunk of the embryonic heart; it gives rise to the aorta and the pulmonary trunk.

persistent t. arteriosus Congenital cardiovascular defect due to failure of the pulmonary trunk and aorta to separate during embryonic development; it results in a single blood vessel that takes origin astride a ventricular septal defect, receiving blood from both right and left ventricles.

trunk (trungk) **1.** The human body excluding the head and the extremities. Also called torso. **2.** The main part or stem (usually short in length) of a nerve, vessel, or duct before it branches or divides. **3.** The main axis. **4.** A large collection of lymphatic vessels.

atrioventricular t. See atrioventricular bundle, under bundle.

brachial plexus t.'s The three trunks of the brachial plexus. See table of nerves.

brachiocephalic t. The first and largest artery branching off the aortic arch; it divides into the right common carotid and right subclavian arteries; occasionally it also gives off the lowest thyroid artery.

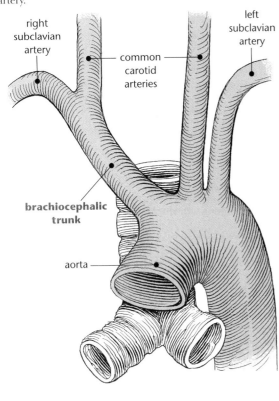

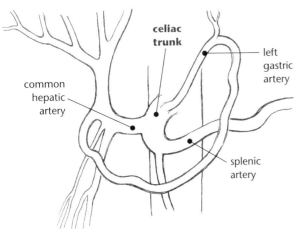

celiac t. A large artery arising from the front of the abdominal aorta just beneath the diaphragm; it divides into the left gastric, common hepatic, and splenic arteries, which supply the esophagus, stomach, duodenum, liver, gallbladder, spleen, and pancreas. Also called celiac axis.

costocervical t. A short arterial trunk that arises from the back of the subclavian artery on each side and, in the vicinity of the neck of the first rib, divides into the deep cervical and highest intercostal branches.

intestinal lymphatic t.'s Large lymphatic vessels that drain lymph from the gastrointestinal tract, pancreas, spleen, and lower portion of the liver; it empties the lymph into the cisterna chyli.

jugular t. A large terminal lymph vessel, on either side of the neck, that drains lymph into the thoracic duct on the left side and into the right lymphatic duct on the right side.

lumbar lymphatic t.'s Two large collecting lymphatic vessels, right and left, that drain lymph upward from the lumbar lymph nodes to the cisterna chyli.

lumbosacral t. A large nerve formed by the union of the lower part of the ventral division of the fourth lumbar nerve and the entire ventral branch of the fifth lumbar nerve; it enters into the formation of the sacral plexus.

lymphatic t.'s Large vessels that convey lymph to the thoracic duct, right lymphatic duct, or to the cisterna chyli.

pulmonary t. A great vessel about 5 cm in length and 3 cm in diameter, that arises from the base of the right ventricle of the heart and divides into right and left pulmonary arteries; it conveys unoxygenated blood from the heart to the lungs.

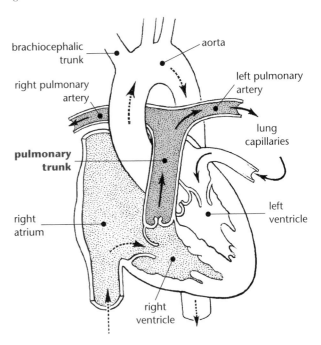

sympathetic t.'s Two long chains of sympathetic ganglia on either side of the vertebral column, extending from the base of the skull to the coccyx; the two chains meet each other in front of the coccyx in an unpaired terminal ganglion (ganglion impar).

thyrocervical t. A short artery that arises from the front of the subclavian artery, on either side, just medial to the anterior scalene muscle; it divides into the inferior thyroid, suprascapular, and transverse cervical arteries.

vagal t. One of the two vagal nerve bundles, anterior and posterior.

trusion (troo′zhun) A displacement (e.g., of a tooth).

truss (trus) Device consisting of a belt and a pad for retaining a hernia in place after it has been pushed back (reduced), or to prevent an enlargement of an irreducible hernia.

Trypanosoma (tri-pan-o-so′mah) Genus of protozoa (family

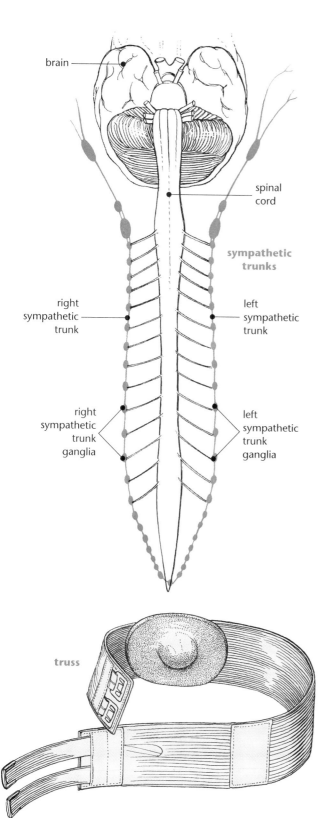

brain

spinal cord

sympathetic trunks

right sympathetic trunk

left sympathetic trunk

right sympathetic trunk ganglia

left sympathetic trunk ganglia

truss

panosomiasis, transmitted by tsetse flies, especially *Glossina morsitans.* Also called *Trypanosoma rhodesiense.*

T. cruzi The species causing American trypanosomiasis (Chagas' disease), transmitted by a variety of insects.

T. gambiense See *Trypanosoma brucei gambiense.*

T. rhodesiense See *Trypanosoma brucei rhodesiense.*

trypanosome (tri-pan'o-sōm) Any member of the genus *Trypanosoma.*

trypanosomiasis (tri-pan-o-so-mi'ah-sis) Any of a group of diseases caused by *Trypanosoma* protozoa.

African t. Disease of the central nervous system occurring in two forms: Gambian, a chronic disease causing sleeping sickness and ending in death in approximately two years; and Rhodesian, an acute febrile form that is usually fatal within one year. Also called African sleeping sickness.

American t. See Chagas' disease, under disease.

trypsin (trip'sin) One of the protein-splitting (proteolytic) enzymes in the pancreatic juice.

trypsinogen (trip-sin'o-jen) Substance secreted by the pancreas and converted to trypsin in the intestine by the action of the enzyme enterokinase.

tryptic (trip'tik) Relating to the proteolytic enzyme trypsin.

tryptophan (trip'to-făn) (Trp) Essential amino acid present in common proteins; it is not manufactured by the body but is a necessary component of human nutrition.

tsetse (tset'se) See *Glossina.*

tubal (too'bal) Relating to a tube.

tube (tūb) **1.** A hollow cylinder designed to function as a passage. **2.** A channel or canal. **3.** A sealed enclosure, either vacuous or containing a gas.

auditory t. A bony and cartilaginous tube connecting the cavity of the middle ear with the nasal part of the pharynx (nasopharynx); responsible for equalizing the air pressure in the middle ear with the atmospheric pressure. Also called eustachian tube; pharyngotympanic tube.

Cantor t. A rubber tube with a mercury-filled bag at the extreme end, used for intestinal intubation; it is usually introduced via the nose and directed into the stomach; with proper positioning of the patient, the weight of the mercury bag helps to lead the tube through the pyloric sphincter and into the small intestine beyond.

cathode ray t. (CRT) A vacuum tube containing a filament that, when low-voltage electric current is passed through it, becomes incandescent and produces a beam of electrons, which is deflected to fall on a fluorescent screen.

Celestin's t. A plastic tube used to keep the esophagus patent in unresectable esophageal cancer, thus permitting ingestion of certain substances.

Chaoul t. A low-voltage x-ray tube used for superficial x-ray therapy; designed so the anode can be placed close to the patient's body, thereby permitting intense but superficial tissue penetration of an x-ray beam.

Coolidge t. A hot-cathode x-ray tube that develops its electrons from a heated filament.

T

Coolidge tube

Dominici t. A tube that allows the passage of only beta and gamma rays; used for the therapeutic application of radium.

drainage t. Tube placed within a wound or cavity to permit the escape of fluids.

empyema t. A rubber tube that is passed through the chest wall for draining pus or purulent matter in thoracic empyema.

Trypanosomatidae) that are parasitic in the blood or lymph of vertebrates.

T. brucei gambiense A subspecies causing Gambian or West African trypanosomiasis (African sleeping sickness), transmitted by tsetse flies, especially *Glossina palpalis.* Also called *Trypanosoma gambiense.*

T. brucei rhodesiense Subspecies causing Rhodesian try-

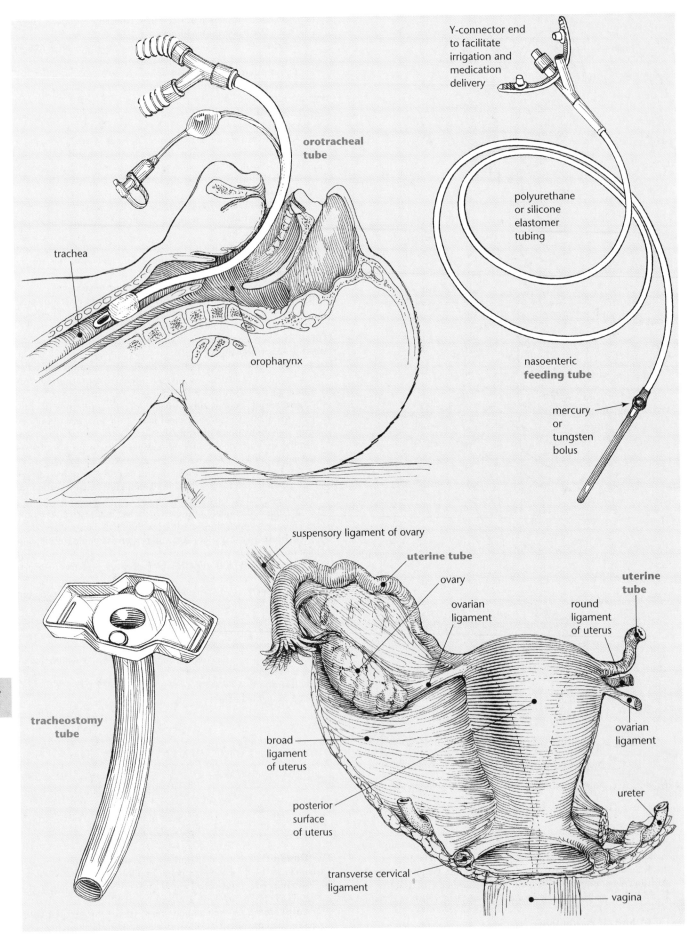

Y-connector end
to facilitate
irrigation and
medication
delivery

orotracheal
tube

trachea

oropharynx

polyurethane
or silicone
elastomer
tubing

nasoenteric
feeding tube

mercury
or
tungsten
bolus

suspensory ligament of ovary

uterine tube

ovary

ovarian
ligament

uterine
tube

round
ligament
of uterus

tracheostomy
tube

broad
ligament
of uterus

ovarian
ligament

posterior
surface
of uterus

ureter

transverse cervical
ligament

vagina

T

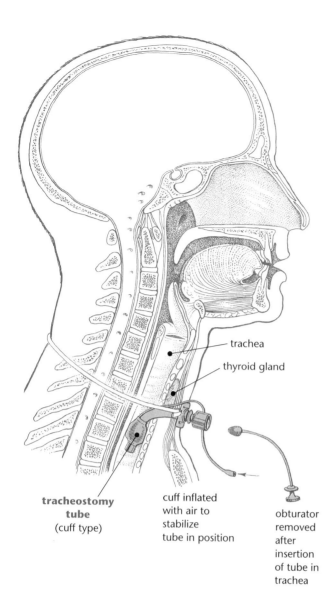

trachea

thyroid gland

tracheostomy tube
(cuff type)

cuff inflated with air to stabilize tube in position

obturator removed after insertion of tube in trachea

endobronchial t. A double-lumen tube with an inflatable cuff at the distal end that can be positioned in the airway so as to restrict ventilation to one lung, permitting deflation of the other lung; used in thoracic surgery.

endotracheal t. A rubber tube inserted in the trachea as an airway in endotracheal intubation. Also called intratracheal tube; tracheal tube.

eustachian t. See auditory tube.

Ewald t. A large-bore flexible tube used for emptying the stomach.

fallopian t. See uterine tube.

feeding t. Any soft flexible tube used to feed a patient by introducing liquid foods of high caloric value into the stomach.

Geiger t., Geiger-Muller t. (GM tube) A gas-filled tube containing a cylindrical cathode and axial wire electrode, used to detect radioactivity; radioactive particles penetrate the tube's shell and produce momentary current pulsations in the gas.

Harris t. A single-lumen tube with a mercury weight, used for intestinal diagnostic studies.

intratracheal t. See endotracheal tube.

Levin t. A flexible tube introduced into the duodenum or stomach, usually through the nose, after an operation; used to facilitate intestinal decompression.

Miller-Abbott t. A double lumen intestinal tube, used for diagnosing and treating obstructions of the small intestine.

nasogastric t. A pliable plastic tube passed through the nose

into the stomach for removal of stomach secretions or the introduction of solutions.

neural t. The epithelial tube of the early embryo formed by the closure of the neural groove; it develops into the brain and spinal cord.

orotracheal t. An endotracheal tube inserted through the mouth into the trachea.

pharyngotympanic t. See auditory tube.

photomultiplier t. Apparatus used to amplify images of low intensity.

pressure-equalizing t. See tympanostomy tube.

Sengstaken-Blakemore t. Device consisting of three tubes, two with an inflatable balloon and the third one attached to a suction apparatus; used to stop bleeding from the esophagus due to esophageal varices. The lowermost balloon is inflated in the stomach to hold the tube in place. The upper balloon is then used to apply pressure against the varices.

stomach t. A flexible 40-cm tube passed into the stomach for introducing nutrient solutions or for washing out the stomach.

T t. A self-retaining drainage tube shaped like the capital letter T; used to relieve pressure within the common bile duct postoperatively.

test t. A clear glass tube opened at one end and rounded and closed at the other end; used in a variety of laboratory procedures.

tracheal t. See endotracheal tube.

tracheostomy t. A metal or glass tube inserted into the trachea through a tracheostomy opening to facilitate breathing. Also called tracheotomy tube.

tracheotomy t. See tracheostomy tube.

tympanostomy t. A tiny tube inserted through an incision in the eardrum (tympanic membrane); the tube acts as an auxiliary eustachian (auditory) tube for aerating the middle ear chamber; used in treating serous otitis media that is unresponsive to antibiotic and decongestant therapy. Also called pressure-equalizing tube.

uterine t. One of two slender tubes, about 10 cm long, on either side of the upper uterus and extending to the area of the ovary; it conveys the egg (ovum) from the ovary to the uterine cavity and is the site where conception normally occurs. Also called fallopian tube; oviduct.

vacuum t. A sealed glass electron tube from which air has been almost completely removed to permit electrons to move with low interactions with any residual gas molecules; supplanted by transistors in some instances.

x-ray t. A vacuum tube used for the production of x-rays; the enclosed electrodes accelerate electrons and direct them to an anode, where their impacts produce high-energy photons (x rays).

tubectomy (too-bek'to-me) See salpingectomy.

tube housing (tūb hou'zing) A lead-shielded container for holding the x-ray tube, transformers, and insulating oils; it provides protection from radiation leakage when the tube is in operation for diagnostic or therapeutic purposes.

tuber (too'ber), pl. tub'era A small prominence.

t. cinereum A small mass of gray matter at the base of the hypothalamus that protrudes into the floor of the third ventricle of the brain.

tubercle (too'ber-kl) 1. A rounded elevation on a structure, such as a bone. 2. The specific grayish lesion of tuberculosis. 3. A nodule on the skin.

adductor t. of femur A small projection on the medial surface of the lower part of the femur, situated on the upper part of the medial condyle, which provides attachment to the tendon of the great adductor (adductor magnus) muscle; it is an important surgical landmark and can be easily palpated.

anterior t. of atlas A median conical protuberance on the front of the anterior arch of the atlas (first cervical vertebra); it provides attachment to the anterior longitudinal ligament.

anterior t. of calcaneus A small rounded tubercle on the bottom of the front part of the heel bone (calcaneus); it marks the distal limit of the attachment of the long plantar ligament.

areolar t. of nipple One of numerous tubercles of the areola surrounding the nipple (papilla) overlying the sebaceous areolar glands; the oily secretion provides a lubricant for the nipple and areola during breast-feeding.

t. of auricle See auricular tubercle.

auricular t. A small elevation on the ear frequently seen on the inner edge of the helix. Also called tubercle of auricle; tubercle of Darwin; darwinian tubercle.

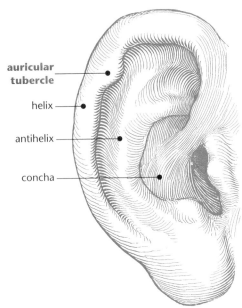

auricular tubercle
helix
antihelix
concha

Carabelli t. See cusp of Carabelli, under cusp.

carotid t. The large anterior tubercle on either side of the sixth cervical vertebra; the common carotid artery lies anteriorly to it and can be compressed against it.

conoid t. A prominent elevation on the bottom surface of the lateral part of the collarbone (clavicle) that gives attachment to the conoid ligament.

corniculate t. The elevation on either side of the larynx produced by the underlying corniculate cartilage of the posterior part of the aryepiglottic fold of mucous membrane.

costal t. See tubercle of rib.

cuneate t. One of two ovoid elevations on the dorsal surface of the medulla oblongata on either side, lateral to the gracile tubercle and overlying the nucleus cuneatus.

t. of Darwin See auricular tubercle.

darwinian t. See auricular tubercle.

genial t.'s Small bony elevations on the lower part of the inner surface of the chin (mental protuberance); they provide attachment for the geniohyoid and genioglossus muscles. Also called mental spines.

Ghon's t. See Ghon's primary lesion, under lesion.

gracile t. One of two elevations on the dorsal surface of the medulla oblongata, on either side of the posterior (dorsal) median sulcus at the lower end of the fourth ventricle, overlying the nucleus gracilis. Also called clava.

greater t. of humerus A large bony prominence on the lateral side of the upper end of the arm bone (humerus), to which the supraspinatus, infraspinatus, and teres minor muscles are attached; it is the most lateral bony prominence of the shoulder region and is responsible for the rounded contour of the shoulder. Also called greater tuberosity of humerus.

t. of iliac crest A prominence on the outer lip of the iliac crest of the hipbone, approximately 2 inches above and behind the anterior superior iliac spine.

infraglenoid t. A roughened prominence just below the glenoid fossa of the scapula; it provides attachment for the tendon of the long head of the triceps muscle of arm (triceps brachii muscle).

intercondylar t. One of two bony tubercles (lateral and medial) of the eminence on the intercondylar area of the uppermost part of the tibia.

labial t. The slight ridgelike elevation at the base of the vertical groove of the upper lip (philtrum) between the skin and mucous membrane of the lip.

lesser t. of humerus A bony prominence on the anterior surface of the humerus just beyond its anatomical neck, near the shoulder joint; it provides attachment for the subscapular muscle; its lateral edge forms the medial border of the intertubercular sulcus. Also called lesser tuberosity of humerus.

nuchal t. The prominent elevation formed by the tip of the spinous process of the seventh cervical vertebra, clearly seen and easily palpated at the lower end of the nuchal furrow at the back of the neck.

pharyngeal t. See pharyngeal spine, under spine.

posterior t. of atlas A median conical protuberance on the back of the posterior arch of the atlas (first cervical vertebra); it represents a rudimentary spinous process and provides attachment to the nuchal ligament.

pubic t. A small tubercle at the lateral end of the pubic crest, on either side, about 3/4 inch from the pubic symphysis; it provides attachment to the tendons of the straight muscle of abdomen (rectus abdominis muscle) and the pyramidal muscle. Also called pubic spine.

t. of radius See radial tuberosity, under tuberosity.

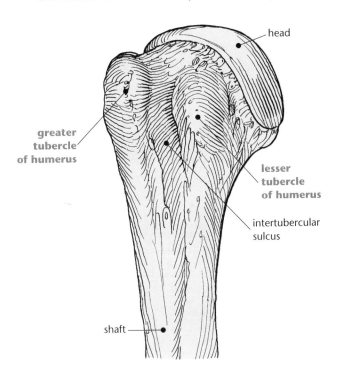

head
greater tubercle of humerus
lesser tubercle of humerus
intertubercular sulcus
shaft

t. of rib A knoblike eminence on the posterior surface of a rib at the junction of its neck and shaft; it articulates with the transverse process of the corresponding thoracic vertebra. Also called costal tubercle.

scalene t. A small area of elevated roughness on the inner border of the upper surface of the first rib, separating the groove for the subclavian artery from the groove for the subclavian vein; it provides attachment to the tendon of the anterior scalene muscle.

t. of sella turcica The slight transverse ridge in front of the pituitary (hypophyseal) fossa at the base of the skull.

supraglenoid t. An elevated roughened area immediately above the glenoid fossa of the scapula; it provides attachment to the tendon of the short head biceps muscle of arm (biceps brachii muscle).

t. of tibia See tibial tuberosity, under tuberosity.

tubercle ■ **tubercle**

T

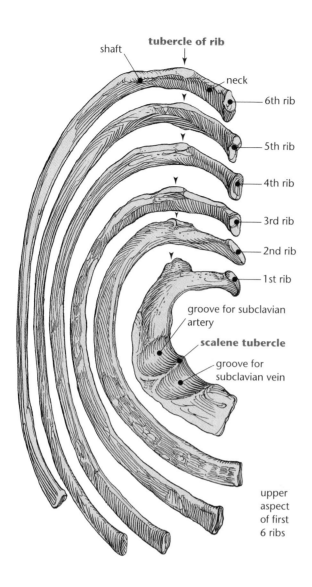

shaft

tubercle of rib

neck

6th rib

5th rib

4th rib

3rd rib

2nd rib

1st rib

groove for subclavian artery

scalene tubercle

groove for subclavian vein

upper aspect of first 6 ribs

tubercular (too-ber′ku-lar) Relating to tubercles. The term is sometimes used incorrectly instead of tuberculous to describe a person afflicted with tuberculosis.

tuberculate, tuberculated (too-ber′ku-lāt, too-ber′ku-lāt-ed) Having tubercles; nodular.

tuberculation (too-ber′ku-la′shun) 1. Formation of nodules. 2. The presence of nodules.

tuberculid (tu-ber′ku-lid) A noninfectious skin eruption due to hypersensitivity to tubercle bacilli; occurs in persons previously exposed to the microorganisms.

    papulonecrotic t. Sterile blisters that undergo central ulceration and scar formation upon healing; usually seen on the ears, legs, and buttocks.

tuberculin (too-ber′ku-lin) Substance made from the tubercle bacillus (*Mycobacterium tuberculosis*), used in the diagnosis of tuberculosis; originally developed by Koch for use in the treatment of tuberculosis.

    purified protein derivative of t. (PPD) An extract from tubercle bacilli prepared in a protein-free liquid medium.

tuberculitis (too-ber-ku-li′tis) Inflammation of any tubercle.

tuberculo- Combining form meaning tubercle; tuberculosis.

tuberculoid (too-ber′ku-loid) 1. Resembling tuberculosis. 2. Resembling a tubercle.

tuberculoma (too-ber-ku-lo′mah) A well-defined tumorlike mass of tuberculous origin, usually seen in the lungs and the brain.

tuberculosis (too-ber-ku-lo′sis) (TB, tb, TBC) A chronic, communicable disease caused by the tubercle bacillus (*Mycobacterium tuberculosis*), which causes a distinctive ulcerating lesion in the tissues affect-

ed; human infections are most commonly caused by *Mycobacterium hominis* and *bovis*, acquired by inhaling airborne droplets of the coughing and sneezing from infected persons and, only rarely, by drinking infected milk; people most at risk are those with debilitating or immunosuppressive conditions, including malnutrition, alcoholism, diabetes, chronic lung disease, extensive corticosteroid use, and AIDS.

    atypical t. A tuberculosis-like disease of the lungs caused by atypical organisms of the genus *Mycobacterium* (either *Mycobacterium avium–intracellulare* or *Mycobacterium kansasii*); occurs primarily in people with an underlying lung disease (e.g., silicosis) or as an opportunistic infection in immunodepressed patients (e.g., AIDS patients).

    cutaneous t. A group of skin disorders caused either by the presence of microorganisms in the subcutaneous tissues or by a hypersensitivity reaction to a previous infection.

    disseminated t. See miliary tuberculosis.

    miliary t. A form in which the bloodstream has carried the organisms to several organs (especially the liver, bone marrow, kidneys, and spleen), causing simultaneous development of numerous, minute foci of infection. Also called disseminated tuberculosis.

    postprimary t. See secondary tuberculosis.

    primary t. The usually asymptomatic phase of a tuberculous infection immediately following invasion of tissues by tubercle bacilli; it occurs in individuals who did not have previous contact with the organism.

    pulmonary t. Tuberculosis of the lungs marked by ulceration and formation of cavities in lung tissues, accompanied by cough and fever; infection may be arrested, leaving scars that contain dormant bacilli, or it may progress and spread to lymph nodes of the neck or throughout the body via the bloodstream.

    reinfection t. See secondary tuberculosis.

    secondary t. An active tuberculosis infection in an individual who has been sensitized by a previous contact with the organism; mostly it is a reactivation of dormant microorganisms from a primary infection; occasionally it represents a new infection. Also called postprimary tuberculosis; reinfection tuberculosis.

tuberculous (too-ber′ku-lus) Afflicted with tuberculosis.

tuberculum (too-ber′ku-lum) Latin for tubercle.

tuberosity (too-bĕ-ros′ĭ-te) A rounded protuberance from the surface of a bone or cartilage.

    calcaneal t. The prominent posterior plantar extremity of the calcaneus that forms the projection of the heel; it bears lateral and medial processes.

    deltoid t. A linear, raised area on the lateral surface of the middle part of the humerus to which the deltoid muscle is attached.

    greater t. of humerus See greater tubercle of humerus, under tubercle.

    ischial t. The enlarged rough lower part of the ischium of the hipbone; divided by a transverse ridge into an upper and lower area; the upper part provides attachment for the hamstring muscles and the inferior gemellus muscle; the lower part (on which the body rests in the sitting position) affords attachment to the great adductor (adductor magnus) muscle and the sacrotuberous ligament.

T

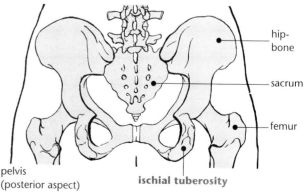

hip-bone

sacrum

femur

pelvis (posterior aspect)

ischial tuberosity

tubercular ■ tuberosity

lesser t. of humerus See lesser tubercle of humerus, under tubercle.

radial t. A broad bony prominence on the medial surface of the radius just below its neck, which affords attachment to the biceps muscle of arm (biceps brachii). Also called tuberosity of radius; tubercle of radius.

t. of radius See radial tuberosity.

t. of tibia See tibial tuberosity.

tibial t. A broad triangular projection on the front of the upper end of the tibia; the upper portion of the tuberosity provides attachment for the ligament of the patella and the lower portion is associated with the infrapatellar bursa. Also called tuberosity of tibia; tubercle of tibia.

tuberous (too′ber-us) Nodular; lumpy.

tubocornual (too-bo-kor′nu-al) Relating to a fallopian (uterine) tube and one of the upper elongated portions (cornua) of the uterus.

tubocurarine chloride (too-bo-ku-rah′rin klo′rĭd) Compound used to produce muscular relaxation during surgical operations.

tubo-ovarian (too′bo o-va′re-an) Relating to a fallopian (uterine) tube and an ovary.

tubo-ovariectomy (too′bo o-va-re-ek′to-me) See salpingo-oophorectomy.

tubo-ovaritis (too′bo o-vah-ri′tis) See salpingo-oophoritis.

tuboperitoneal (too′bo-per-ĭ-to-ne′al) Relating to the fallopian (uterine) tubes and the lining (peritoneum) of the abdominopelvic cavity.

tuboplasty (too′bo-plas-te) See salpingoplasty.

tubule (too′būl) A small tube or canal.

collecting t.'s See collecting ducts, under duct.

connecting t. (CNT) The distal part of the nephron in the cortex of the kidney that connects the distal convoluted tubule to the cortical collecting duct, and is functionally different from both.

dental t.'s The numerous minute channels in the dentin of a tooth, extending radially from the pulp toward the enamel; they contain cytoplasmic processes of a cell body (odontoblast) located within the pulp. Also called dental canaliculi.

distal convoluted t. (DCT) The tortuous segment of the renal tubule leading from the straight distal tubule to the connecting tubule.

distal straight t. (DST) The distal straight segment of the renal tubule connecting the thin ascending part of the intermediate tubule to the distal convoluted tubule. Also called thick ascending limb.

intermediate renal t. (IRT) The entire thin tubule connecting the proximal straight tubule to the distal straight tubule by way of the nephronic loop; composed of ascending and descending thin limbs.

proximal convoluted t. (PCT) The tortuous segment of the renal tubule leading from the glomerular (Bowman's) capsule to the straight proximal tubule.

proximal straight t. (PST) The proximal straight segment of the renal tubule connecting the proximal convoluted tubule to the thin descending part of the intermediate tubule (loop of Henle). Also called thick descending limb.

renal t. The part of the nephron responsible for conveying the glomerular filtrate to the collecting duct leading to the renal pelvis while transforming the filtrate into the final urine product; it consists of the glomerular (Bowman's) capsule, proximal convoluted tubule, proximal straight tubule, intermediate tubule, nephronic (Henle's) loop, distal straight tubule, distal convoluted tubule, and the connecting tubule.

seminiferous t.'s Long, threadlike, convoluted tubules packed in loose connective tissue in each of the approximately 250 lobules of the testis; they are the channels in which the spermatozoa develop and through which they are conveyed to the lumina of rete testis before passing out of the testis to the epididymis.

T t.'s See T system, under system.

transverse t.'s See T system, under system.

tubulization (too-bu-li-za′shun) Protection of an injured or sutured nerve with a cylinder of slowly absorbable material to promote healing of the nerve.

tubulorrhexis (too-bu-lo-rek′sis) Localized disintegration of epithelium and basement membrane of the kidney tubules, characteristic of acute tubular necrosis.

tuft (tuft) A small cluster.

glomerular t. A small cluster of capillaries at the beginning of each renal tubule in the kidney, enclosed in the Bowman's (glomerular) capsule. Formerly called malpighian tuft. See also glomerulus; glomerular capsule.

malpighian t. See glomerular tuft.

tularemia (too-lah-re′me-ah) Infectious disease caused by the bacterium *Francisella tularensis*, characterized by prolonged or recurrent fever and swelling of the lymph nodes; transmitted to humans from

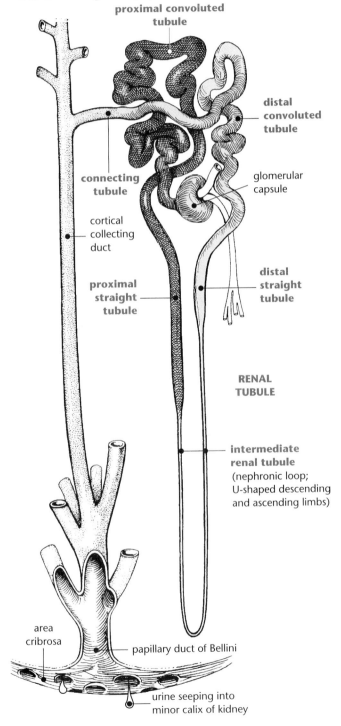

proximal convoluted tubule

distal convoluted tubule

connecting tubule

glomerular capsule

cortical collecting duct

proximal straight tubule

distal straight tubule

RENAL TUBULE

intermediate renal tubule (nephronic loop; U-shaped descending and ascending limbs)

area cribrosa

papillary duct of Bellini

urine seeping into minor calix of kidney

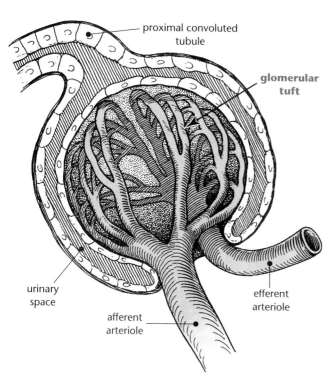

proximal convoluted tubule

glomerular tuft

urinary space

efferent arteriole

afferent arteriole

seminal vesicle

bladder

ampulla of deferent duct

ejaculatory duct

utricle

deferent duct

prostate

urethra

penis

bulbourethral gland

epididymis (reservoir for spermatozoa)

testis

seminiferous tubules coiled in place

infected animals by the bite of insects or by direct contact with infected blood, tissues, or secretions from infected animals; people at risk of occupational exposure include veterinarians, farmers, hunters, and forestry workers. Also called rabbit fever; deer-fly fever.

TULIP Acronym for Transurethral Ultrasound-guide Laser-Induced Prostatectomy. See under prostatectomy.

tumefacient (too-me-fa′shent) Tending to cause swelling.

tumefaction (too-me-fak′shun) The process of swelling.

tumescence (too-mes′ens) The swollen state. Also called turgescence.

tumid (too′mid) Engorged.

tumor (too′mor) An overgrowth of tissue; a neoplasm.

　adenomatoid t. Benign, gray-white nodules of uncertain origin occurring usually in the epididymis and along the spermatic cord in the male and around the fallopian (uterine) tube in the female.

　adipose t. See lipoma.

　anaplastic t. A poorly differentiated tumor containing cells of various shapes and sizes and displaying a total disarray of the normal tissue architecture.

　benign t. A slow-growing tumor that does not spread to other areas of the body, does not infiltrate adjacent structures, and is unlikely to recur once removed.

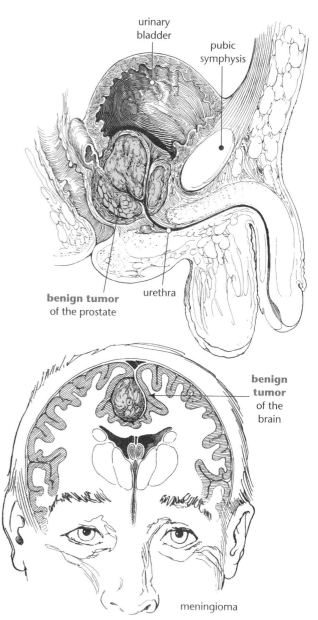

urinary bladder

pubic symphysis

benign tumor of the prostate

urethra

benign tumor of the brain

meningioma

T

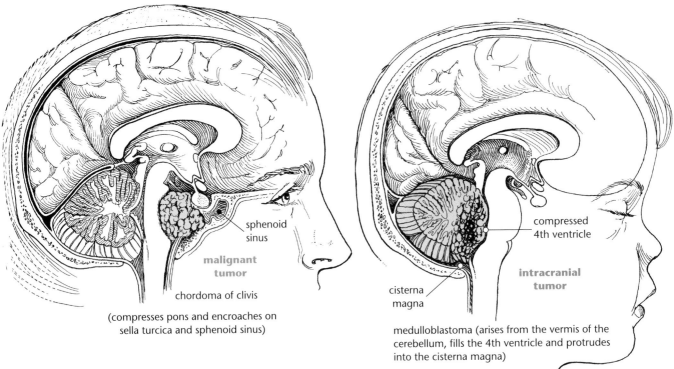

sphenoid
sinus

**malignant
tumor**

chordoma of clivis

(compresses pons and encroaches on
sella turcica and sphenoid sinus)

compressed
4th ventricle

**intracranial
tumor**

cisterna
magna

medulloblastoma (arises from the vermis of the
cerebellum, fills the 4th ventricle and protrudes
into the cisterna magna)

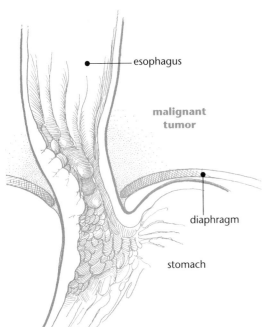

esophagus

**malignant
tumor**

diaphragm

stomach

blood t. A swelling containing blood; term is sometimes used to denote an aneurysm, a hemangioma, or a hematoma.

Brenner's t. A yellowish brown solid tumor of the ovary typically benign but (rarely) may undergo malignant transformation; usually occurs unilaterally in postmenopausal women.

Buschke-Löwenstein t. See giant condyloma, under condyloma.

carcinoid t. A small, usually benign but potentially malignant growth in the lining of the intestinal tract, especially of the appendix; also found in the lung. Also called argentaffinoma; frequently called carcinoid.

carotid body t. See chemodectoma.

desmoid t. See aggressive fibromatosis, under fibromatosis.

embryonal t. General term for any tumor (usually malignant) believed to be derived from embryonic tissues. Also called embryoma.

Ewing's t. See Ewing's sarcoma, under sarcoma.

fibroid t. See leiomyoma.

giant cell t. of bone A soft, reddish brown, benign (but potentially malignant) tumor of long bones with a tendency to recur after removal; composed chiefly of multinucleated giant cells and ovoid or spindle-shaped cells; occurs in both men and women with equal frequency and typically in the 20 to 50 age-group, rarely in younger people. Also called giant cell myeloma; osteoclastoma.

giant cell t. of tendon sheath See nodular tenosynovitis, under tenosynovitis.

glomus t. An extremely painful, small, benign tumor in the skin arising from cells of a temperature receptor (glomus); often seen under fingernails and toenails. Also called glomangioma.

granular cell t. A predominantly benign tumor of uncertain origin; it may occur anywhere in the body, most commonly seen in the tongue and subcutaneous tissue of the trunk (especially the breast) and upper extremities. Formerly called granular cell myoblastoma.

granulosa cell t. An uncommon, benign (potentially malignant) tumor of the ovary that typically secretes estrogens; it may occur in any age-group and is commonly associated with pseudoprecocious puberty. Also called granulosa-theca cell tumor; folliculoma.

granulosa-theca cell t. See granulosa cell tumor.

Grawitz's t. See renal adenocarcinoma, under adenocarcinoma.

heterologous t. Tumor composed of tissue different from the one in which it grows.

homologous t. Tumor made up of the same kind of tissue as the one in which it grows.

intracranial t. A tumor occurring within the skull; when located within the brain, a well-circumscribed tumor may be considered pathologically benign but clinically "malignant" if its location makes removal impossible (e.g., an ependymoma of the floor of the 4th ventricle).

Krukenberg's t. Malignant tumor, usually bilateral, spread from a primary mucin-producing cancer most frequently found in the gastrointestinal tract, especially the stomach.

malignant t. A tumor that spreads from its original location to affect other parts of the body (i.e., forms metastases), may recur after removal, and eventually causes death if not treated early and appropriately. Often called cancer.

melanotic neuroectodermal t. Benign tumor of the anterior portion of the upper jaw (maxilla), usually seen in infants below the age of six months; it causes displacement of tooth buds. Also called melanoameloblastoma.

mixed t. Tumor composed of more than one tissue or cell type.

mixed t. of salivary gland Tumor containing epithelial cells and cells of salivary glands, all arising from epithelial cells of salivary ducts; most frequently seen in the parotid gland. Also called pleomorphic adenoma.

Pancoast's t. A tumor at the thoracic inlet near the apex of the lung causing the Pancoast's syndrome. Also called pulmonary sulcus tumor.

papillary t. See papilloma.

phantom t. A circumscribed accumulation of fluid in the interlobar spaces of the lung and seen in chest x-ray pictures as opacities suggestive of a tumor; associated with congestive heart failure.

pontine angle t. A tumor located in the proximal portion of the vestibulocochlear (8th cranial) nerve.

Pott's puffy t. A localized swelling of the scalp overlying a diseased area of the skull or an extradural abscess.

pulmonary sulcus t. See Pancoast's tumor.

Sertoli's cell t. See androblastoma.

Warthin's t. See adenolymphoma.

Wilms' t. Malignant tumor of the kidney affecting young children, with peak incidence between two and four years of age. Some adult occurrences have been reported. Also called embryoma of kidney; nephroblastoma.

Zollinger-Ellison t. Tumor of the pancreas causing the Zollinger-Ellison syndrome.

tumorigenesis (too-mor-ĭ-jen′ĕ-sis) The formation of new growth.

tumorigenic (too-mor-ĭ-jen′ik) Causing tumors.

tumorous (too′mor-us) Resembling a tumor.

tungsten (tung′sten) (W) Chemical element; atomic number 74, atomic weight 183.85; it has a high melting point; used as the target material of an x-ray tube.

tunic (too′nik) A coat or covering. Also called tunica.

mucous t. See tunica mucosa, under tunica.

nervous t. of eyeball The retina.

tunica (too′nĭ-kah), pl. tu′nicae A coat of condensed connective tissue covering an organ or lining a space. Also called tunic.

t. adventitia The relatively thin fibrous outer layer of a blood vessel containing some muscular and elastic fibers that run predominantly in a longitudinal direction; situated immediately adjacent to the tunica media. Also called tunica externa; tunica fibrosa.

t. albuginea of ovary A delicate collagenous covering of the ovary situated between the outer germinal epithelium and the cortex of the ovary; it increases in density with passing age.

t. albuginea of penis A fibrous envelop consisting of superficial and deep layers that surround the corpora cavernosa and the corpus spongiosum of the penis; the deep fibers envelop each corpus cavernosum separately and form by their junction the septum of the penis; the superficial fibers envelop both corpora cavernosa as a single tube; the corpus spongiosum, which is traversed throughout its entire length by the urethra, is surrounded by a separate fibrous envelop.

t. albuginea of spleen The fibroelastic capsule around the entire spleen.

t. albuginea of testis A thick fibrous capsule encasing the testis (testicular parenchyma), just beneath and closely adherent to the visceral layer of the tunica vaginalis of testis; multiple septa from the capsule divide the interior of the testicle into several hundred pyramid-shaped lobules, each containing one or several tortuous seminiferous tubules.

t. dartos A layer of smooth (nonstriated) muscular tissue underlying the skin of the scrotum; its deeper fibers form a septum that divides the scrotum into two compartments.

t. externa See tunica adventitia.

t. fibrosa See tunica adventitia.

t. interna See tunica intima.

t. intima The inner, serous layer of an artery or vein composed of a single layer of endothelial cells resting on a basal lamina and a layer of connective tissue. Also called tunica interna.

t. media The middle muscular layer of arteries and veins, consisting of smooth muscles and some elastic tissue. The difference between the walls of arteries and veins is seen in this middle layer; veins contain a smaller content of muscle and elastic fibers (related to the lower venous blood pressure); arteries have large bundles of muscles with elastic and collagen fibers.

t. mucosa The mucous coat or membrane of various tubular structures. Also called mucous tunic.

t. mucosa of colon The inner mucous coat of the colon.

t. mucosa of esophagus The inner mucous coat of the esophagus.

t. mucosa of trachea The inner mucous coat of the trachea.

t. mucosa of uterus The endometrium.

t. mucosa of vagina The mucous membrane of the vagina.

t. vaginalis of testis The closed serous pouch investing the front and sides of the testis and epididymis in the scrotum, formed by the lowermost extremity of the peritoneum preceding the descent of the testis from the abdomen into the scrotum; it consists of an outer (parietal) and inner (visceral) layer.

tuning fork (toon′ing fork) A forklike metal instrument with two prongs (tines) that, when struck, produce a sound of fixed pitch; used for testing hearing and vibratory sensation. The higher the frequency (i.e., number of vibrations per second), the higher the pitch (e.g., 256 Hz produces a middle C; 512 Hz produces the same note one octave higher).

turbidimetric (tur-bid-ĭ-met′rik) Relating to the measurement of turbidity of a fluid.

turbidimetry (tur-bĭ-dim′ĕ-tre) Measurement of the degree of cloudiness of a fluid.

turbidity (tur-bid′ĭ-te) Cloudiness caused by the stirring up of sediment or insoluble particles suspended in a fluid.

turbinate (tur′bĭ-nāt) Shaped like a scroll or a cone; applied to a bone. See table of bones.

inferior t. See inferior concha, under concha.

middle t. See middle concha, under concha.

superior t. See superior concha, under concha.

turbinectomy (tur-bĭ-nek′to-me) Removal of a turbinate bone.

turgescence (tur-jes′ens) See tumescence.

turgid (tur′jid) Distended; congested; tumid.

turgor (tur′gor) Fullness.

turista (tu-rēs′tah) Spanish for tourist; used colloquially for traveler's diarrhea. See traveler's diarrhea, under diarrhea.

turn (tern) To move a fetus in the uterus from a malposition to one that will facilitate normal delivery.

TURP Acronym for transurethral resection of the prostate. See transurethral prostatectomy, under prostatectomy.

tussis (tus′is) A cough.

tussive (tus′iv) Relating to a cough.

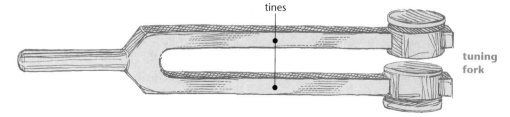

tines

tuning
fork

twin (twin) One of two children born at one birth.

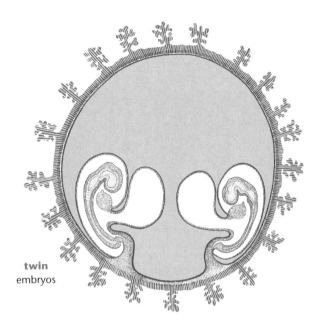

twin
embryos

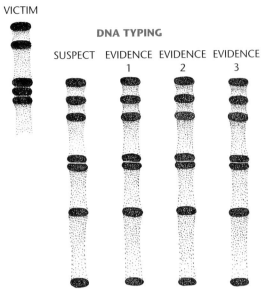

VICTIM

DNA TYPING

SUSPECT   EVIDENCE   EVIDENCE   EVIDENCE
1   2   3

    conjoined t.'s Twins with a varying degree of connection or fusion with each other. Also called Siamese twins.

    dizygotic t.'s See fraternal twins.

    fraternal t.'s Twins developed from two separate eggs fertilized at the same time; they may or may not be of the same sex. Also called dizygotic twins; heterozygous twins.

    heterozygous t.'s See fraternal twins.

    identical t.'s Twins resulting from a single egg that splits at an early stage of development; they are always of the same sex, have the same genetic constitution, and have pronounced resemblance to each other. Also called monozygotic twins; uniovular twins.

    monozygotic t.'s See identical twins.

    Siamese t.'s See conjoined twins.

    uniovular t.'s See identical twins.

    vanishing t. Colloquial term for the spontaneous release of amniotic fluid occurring in the first trimester of pregnancy, with the pregnancy usually continuing normally to term; cause is unknown; believed to be due to a twin pregnancy in which the second fetus and its amniotic sac (membrane) are liquefied by enzymatic action (probably from the second fetus itself) early in the pregnancy, with consequent release of the amniotic fluid.

twinge (twinj) Sudden, short, sharp pain.

twitch (twich) 1. A short, spasmodic contraction of a muscle fiber. 2. To move spasmodically; to jerk.

tyloma (ti-lo'mah) A callosity.

    t. conjunctivae An eye condition marked by a localized cornification of the conjunctiva.

tylosis (ti-lo'sis) Formation of a callosity.

tympanectomy (tim-pah-nek'to-me) Surgical removal of the eardrum (tympanic membrane).

tympanic (tim-pan'ik) 1. Relating to the middle ear chamber. 2. Resonant.

tympanites (tim-pah-ni'tēz) Distention of the abdomen due to accumulation of gas in the intestines or in the abdominal cavity.

tympanitic (tim-pah-nit'ik) 1. Relating to tympanites. 2. Producing a drumlike sound on percussion.

tympano-, tympan- Combining forms meaning the middle ear chamber.

tympanocentesis (tim-pah-no-sen-te'sis) Aspiration of fluid from the middle ear chamber with a needle inserted through the eardrum (tympanic membrane); a diagnostic procedure for persistent middle ear infections (otitis media).

tympanogram (tim-pan'o-gram) A graph made while testing the

degree of conductive hearing impairment by means of impedance audiometry; the deflection pattern on the chart reveals the extent of elasticity of the eardrum and ear ossicles.

tympanomastoiditis (tim-pah-no-mas'toi-di'tis) Inflammation of the middle ear and the air cells in the adjoining mastoid bone.

tympanometry (tim-pah-nom'ĕ-tre) Determination of middle ear damage occurring in conductive deafness; it measures the degree of movement (compliance) of the eardrum as air of varying pressures is pumped into the external ear canal, while a probe at the entrance of the canal emits a continuous sound. The reflections of sound from the eardrum are graphically recorded on a chart (tympanogram).

tympanoplasty (tim-pah-no-plas'te) A general term denoting any of several surgical procedures designed to restore hearing in patients with middle ear (conductive) hearing loss.

tympanosclerosis (tim-pah-no-sklĕ-ro'sis) Scarring of the eardrum (tympanic membrane), causing hearing impairment.

tympanosquamosal (tim-pah-no-skwah-mo'sal) Relating to the tympanic and squamous parts of the temporal bone.

tympanotomy (tim-pah-not'o-me) See myringotomy.

tympanum (tim'pah-num) The tympanic cavity; middle ear chamber.

tympany (tim'pah-ne) A drumlike sound sometimes heard on percussion. Also called tympanic resonance.

type (tīp) A pattern of characteristics common to a number of individuals, chemical substances, diseases, etc.

    blood t. See blood type.

typhoid (ti'foid) 1. Resembling typhus. 2. See typhoid fever, under fever.

typhoidal (ti-foid'al) Relating to typhoid fever.

typhous (ti'fus) Relating to typhus.

typhus (ti'fus) An infectious and contagious disease caused by species of *Rickettsia;* marked by sustained high fever, severe headache, and a characteristic rash. Also called typhus fever.

    endemic t. See murine typhus.

    epidemic t. Typhus caused by *Rickettsia prowazekii,* transmitted by body lice.

    flea-borne t. See murine typhus.

    mite-borne t. See tsutsugamushi disease.

    murine t. Typhus caused by *Rickettsia mooseri* transmitted by the rat flea. Also called endemic or flea-borne typhus.

    recrudescent t. See Brill-Zinsser disease.

    scrub t. See tsutsugamushi disease.

typing (tīp'ing) Determination of the type category to which any entity belongs.

    blood t. See blood grouping.

    DNA t. Test on a nucleated cell (e.g., of semen, blood, hair roots) to detect characteristics in genetic structure that are as unique

1 Sample of nucleated cells is collected, usually from blood, semen, or hair roots.

2 DNA is extracted from the nuclei of the cells.

3 DNA is fragmented at specific sequences by a *restriction enzyme.*

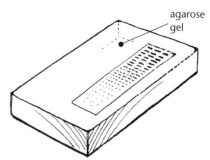

agarose gel

4 Using electrophoresis, the DNA fragments are separated. The fragments migrate by size into invisible bands. Then the double strands of DNA separate into single strands (denaturation).

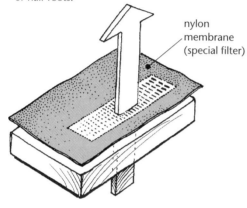

nylon membrane (special filter)

5 To preserve the band pattern, the DNA is transferred to a nylon membrane by a technique called *Southern blotting.*

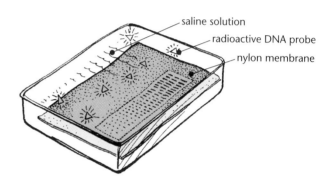

saline solution

radioactive DNA probe

nylon membrane

6 Radioactive DNA probe is added to a saline solution in which the nylon membrane is immersed. The probe binds to specific complementary bands of repetitive DNA sequences on the membrane.

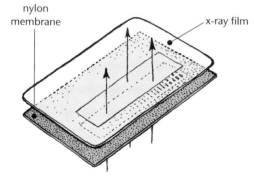

nylon membrane

x-ray film

7 X-ray film is placed on the nylon membrane to detect where the radioactive DNA probe has bound.

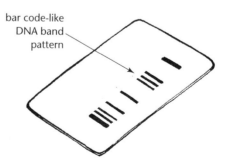

bar code-like DNA band pattern

8 The pattern of DNA bands becomes visible when the x-ray film is developed. Each band occurs where the probe has unerringly located and zipped-up with its correct partner strand (repetitive sequence).

after CELLMARK DIAGNOSTICS

T

typing ■ typing

to an individual as fingerprints. Also called DNA fingerprinting; profiling.

tyramine (ti′rah-mēn) An amine that produces effects similar to those of epinephrine; it is a product of the decarboxylation of the amino acid tyrosine and can have harmful effects on patients undergoing therapy with inhibitors of amine oxidase. It has been used as a provocative agent in the diagnosis of pheochromocytoma.

tyroid (ti′roid) Having the texture of cheese.

tyrosinase (ti-ro′sin-ās) See monophenol monooxygenase.

tyrosine (ti′ro-sēn) (Tyr) Amino acid present in most proteins.

tyrosinemia (ti-ro-sī-ne′me-ah) Disoder characterized by elevated blood concentration of tyrosine, increased urinary excretion of tyrosine and tyrosol compounds, enlargement of the liver and spleen, and defects of renal tubules.

hereditary t. A form occurring as an autosomal recessive inheritance.

t. of newborn A form occurring in newborn infants, especially premature, characterized by failure to thrive, diarrhea, and vomiting; the urine has a characteristic odor of decaying cabbage. The condition usually resolves spontaneously within three months and almost always without aftereffects.

tyrosinosis (ti-ro-sī-no′sis) An uncommon, possibly hereditary, disorder of tyrosine metabolism; characterized by excessive excretion of para-hydroxyphenylpyruvic acid.

U

ulcer (ul′ser) Loss of tissue on the skin or mucous membrane, extending into the subcutaneous or submucosal tissues, frequently accompanied by inflammation.

aphthous u. The characteristic lesion of aphthous stomatitis; a small whitish ulcer surrounded by a reddish border occurring in the oral mucosa; may be minor, occurring as a single ulcer less than 1 cm in diameter, lasting 7 to 14 days, and healing without scarring; or may be major, occurring in clusters larger than 1 cm in diameter, lasting weeks to months, and healing with scarring. See also recurrent aphthous stomatitis, under stomatitis.

Curling's u. Duodenal ulcer occurring in severe burns or bodily injuries. Also called stress ulcer.

Cushing's u. One or multiple small ulcers occurring throughout the stomach and duodenum after severe head trauma.

decubitus u. An ulcer in pressure areas of the body, especially over bony prominences, occurring in bedridden patients who are allowed to lie in the same position for long periods. Also called bedsore; pressure sore.

dendritic u. A superficial ulcer on the cornea that spreads in a branching pattern, caused by infection with the human herpesvirus 1 or 2.

dental u. An ulcer in the oral mucous membrane caused by constant trauma (e.g., friction from a sharp edge on a tooth).

diabetic u. Ulcer associated with diabetes mellitus, occurring most frequently in the lower limbs, especially the toes.

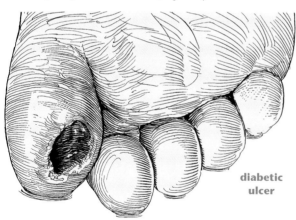

diabetic ulcer

gastric u. Ulcer of the stomach, usually on or near the lesser curvature.

gummatous u. An ulcer on the skin appearing in the late stage of syphilis.

Hunner's u. See interstitial cystitis, under cystitis.

indolent u. An ulcer that does not respond to treatment.

penetrating u. An ulcer that extends into the deep tissues of the organ or structure.

peptic u. Gastrointestinal ulcer, epecially of the stomach or duodenum, caused by the agressive actions of acid-pepsin juices; it develops mainly from a *Helicobacter pylori* infection, also a s a result of treatment with nonsteroidal antiinflammatory drugs, or rarely from excessive acid secretion caused by a gastrinoma.

perforated u. An ulcer of a hollow organ (e.g., stomach) that has eroded through the wall of the organ.

rodent u. See basal cell carcinoma, under carcinoma.

stercoral u. Ulcer of the colon caused by impacted feces.

stomal u. A postoperative ulcer occurring on the jejunal mucous membrane at or near the surgical union of the stomach and jejunum.

stress u. See Curling's ulcer.

trophic u. Ulcer occurring in areas deprived of blood circulation.

tropical u. Ulcer caused by bacterial infection of a minor superficial injury.

varicose u. Ulcer due to and overlying a varicose vein.

venereal u. See chancroid.

ulcerate (ul′sĕ-rāt) To form an ulcer.

ulceration (ul-sĕ-ra′shun) 1. The formation of an ulcer. 2. An ulcer.

ulcerative (ul′ser-a-tiv) 1. Relating to ulcers. 2. Marked by ulceration.

ulcerogenic (ul-ser-o-jen′ik) Causing ulcer formation.

ulcerous (ul′ser-us) Characterized by the presence of ulcers.

ulerythema (u-ler-ĭ-the′mah) Inflammatory process resulting ultimately in atrophy or scarring of tissues.

u. ophryogenes Inflammatory plugging of the eyebrow follicles, leaving scars upon healing.

ulna (ul′nah) The larger of the two bones of the forearm, extending from the elbow to the wrist on the opposite side of the thumb. Popularly called elbow bone. See table of bones.

ulnar (ul′nar) Relating to the ulna.

ulnoradial (ul-no-ra′de-al) Relating to the two bones of the forearm, the ulna and radius.

ultra- Prefix meaning excess; beyond.

ultracentrifuge (ul-trah-sen′trĭ-fūj) A high-speed centrifuge used to separate large molecules.

ultradian (ul-tra′de-an) Relating to biorhythms that occur in cycles more frequent than 24 hours. Also called ultradian rhythm.

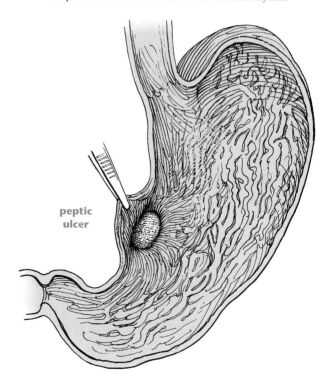

peptic ulcer

ultrafilter (ul-trah-fil′ter) A semipermeable membrane capable of removing all but the smallest particles.

ultrafiltration (ul-trah-fil-tra′shun) Filtration using an ultrafilter.

ultraligation (ul-trah-lī-ga′shun) The tying of a blood vessel beyond the point where a branch is given off.

ultramicroscope (ul-trah-mi′kro-skōp) A darkfield microscope with high-intensity refracted illumination for viewing particles of colloidal size.

ultramicroscopic (ul-trah-mi-kro-skop′ik) Too small to be seen under the ordinary microscope.

ultramicrotome (ul-trah-mi′kro-tōm) Instrument for cutting tissue into very thin sections (0.1 μ or less in thickness) for electron microscopy.

ultrasonic (ul-trah-son′ik) Relating to sound waves above 30,000 cycles per second, not perceptible by the human ear.

ultrasonogram (ul-trah-son′o-gram) A record made by ultrasonography. Also called sonogram; echogram.

ultrasonograph (ul-trah-son′o-graf) The apparatus used in ultrasonography. Also called sonograph; echograph.

ultrasonography (ul-trah-son-og′rah-fe) (US) A diagnostic technique that bounces high-frequency sound waves off tissues within the body and converts the echoes into a pictorial display. The varying densities of tissues reflect sound waves differently. Also called sonography; echography.

   Doppler u. Diagnostic technique to record changes in the frequency of a continuous ultrasound wave, indicative of changes in a moving target (e.g., blood flow in underlying vessels).

   gray-scale u. Amplification and processing of echoes (by a television video-scan converter) into a visual display ranging from white to varying shades of gray, depending on the strength of the echoes.

ultrasonosurgery (ul-trah-son′o-sur′jer-e) The use of high-frequency sound waves (ultrasound) to disrupt tissues, especially of the nervous system.

ultrasound (ul′trah-sownd) Sound waves of a frequency higher than the range audible to the human ear, especially in the 1- to 10-MHz range; the waves are propagated at a speed determined by the physical properties of the medium through which they travel; used in medicine for diagnostic purposes.

ultrastructure (ul′trah-struk′chur) The ultimate structure or organization of protoplasm, as seen with the aid of the electron microscope. Also called fine structure; submicroscopic structure.

ultraviolet (ul-trah-vi′o-let) (UV) Beyond the visible portion of the spectrum; applied to electromagnetic radiation that has a wavelength shorter than that of the violet end of the spectrum but longer than that of x rays.

ululation (u-lu-la′shun) 1. The loud, inarticulate crying of emotionally disturbed persons, especially hysterical ones. 2. Loud lamentation.

umbilical (um-bil′ĭ-kal) Relating to the umbilicus. Also called omphalic.

umbilicated, umbilicate (um-bil′ĭ-kāt-ed, um-bil′ĭ-kāt) Having a central depression; applied to a superficial lesion.

umbilication (um-bil-ĭ-ka′shun) A pit or depression.

umbilicus (um-bil′ĭ-kus, um-bĭ-li′kus) The depressed area on the abdominal wall where the umbilical cord was attached to the fetus. Popularly called navel; belly button.

umbo (um′bo), pl. umbo′nes 1. Projection on a surface. 2. The inner projection of the eardrum (tympanic membrane) into the middle ear chamber made by traction of the malleus, the middle ear ossicle to which the membrane is attached.

un- Prefix meaning not.

uncal (ung′kal) Relating to the uncus (i.e., to the anterior portion of the parahippocampal gyrus of the brain).

unciform (un′sĭ-form) See uncinate.

uncinate (un′sĭ-nāt) 1. Shaped like a hook. Also called unciform. 2. Relating to the uncus (in the brain).

unconscious (un-kon′shus) 1. Inability to respond to sensory stimuli. 2. In psychoanalytic theory, the part of the mind containing feelings,

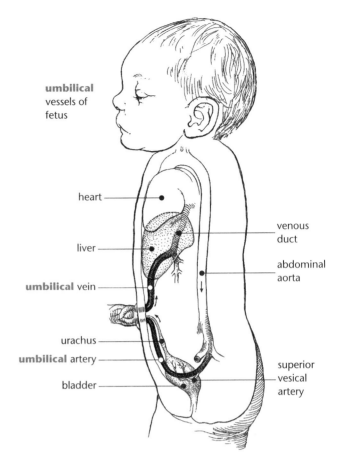

umbilical vessels of fetus

heart —
liver —
umbilical vein —
urachus —
umbilical artery —
bladder —
— venous duct
— abdominal aorta
— superior vesical artery

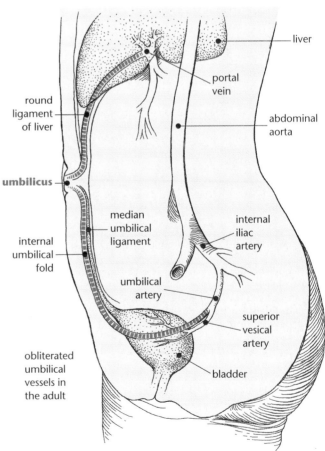

round ligament of liver —
umbilicus —
internal umbilical fold —
median umbilical ligament
umbilical artery
obliterated umbilical vessels in the adult
— liver
— portal vein
— abdominal aorta
— internal iliac artery
— superior vesical artery
— bladder

U

urges, and experiences of which the person is only briefly or never aware.

uncoupler (un-kup′ler) Any substance (e.g., dinitrophenol) that separates two normally concomitant reactions in a metabolic process; one reaction alone may proceed as a result.

uncus (ung′kus) The hook-shaped anterior portion of the parahippocampal gyrus, situated in the medial aspect of the temporal lobe of the brain.

undecylenic acid (un-de-sil-en′ik as′id) An antifungal agent used in pharmaceutical preparations for the treatment of fungal infections of the skin.

underachiever (un-der-ah-chev′er) A person, especially a student, who manifestly performs below his capacity as determined by tests of intelligence, aptitude, or ability.

undercut (un′der-kut) **1.** The portion of a prepared tooth cavity that mechanically locks in the filling. **2.** The portion of a tooth that lies between the gingiva and the crest of contour. **3.** The contour of a dental arch preventing proper insertion of a denture.

undernutrition (un-der-nu-trish′un) Condition resulting from a negative nutritive balance, when metabolic utilization plus excretion of one or more essential nutrients exceeds the supply.

undescended (un-de-send′ed) Not descended to a normal position (e.g., a testis). See also cryptorchidis.

undifferentiated (un-dif-er-en′she-a-ted) Not differentiated; usually applied to cells.

undoing (un-doo̅′ing) An unconscious psychological defense mechanism in which an unacceptable prior action is acted out in reverse, often symbolically or magically; seen especially in obsessive-compulsive disorders.

undulate (un′joo-lāt) **1.** To fluctuate in wavelike patterns (e.g., a fever). **2.** Having a wavy border or appearance (e.g., certain bacterial colonies).

ungual (ung′gwal) Relating to the nails. Also called unguinal.

unguent (ung′gwent) Ointment.

unguentum (ung-gwen′tum (ung.) Latin for ointment.

unguiculate (ung-gwik′u-lāt) Having nails or claws.

unguinal (ung′gwi-nal) See ungual.

unguis (ung′gwis), pl. un′gues Latin for nail (toenail or fingernail).

uni- Prefix meaning one; single.

uniaxial (u-ne-ak′se-al) **1.** Having one axis only. **2.** Developing mainly in one direction.

unicameral (u-nĭ-kam′er-al) See monolocular.

unicellular (u-nĭ-sel′u-lar) Consisting of one cell (e.g., a protozoon).

unicuspid (u-nĭ-kus′pid) Denoting a tooth with one cuspid.

uniform (u′ni-form) Consistent in appearance; without variation in form.

unilaminar (u-nĭ-lam′ĭ-nar) Having only one layer.

unilateral (u-nĭ-lat′er-al) Occurring only on one side.

unilocular (u-nĭ-lok′u-lar) Having only one compartment.

uninuclear, uninucleate (u-ni-nu′kle-ar, u-ni-nu′kle-āt) Having only one nucleus.

uniocular (u-ne-ok′u-lar) Relating to only one eye.

union (ūn′yun) The process of growing or joining together.

   faulty u. Condition in which tissues have united in an improper position.

   fibrous u. Formation of a fibrous callus on a bone at the site of a fracture without development of bone tissue.

   primary u. See healing by first intention, under healing.

   secondary u. See healing by second intention, under healing.

   vicious u. A faulty union that results in deformity.

unipennate (u-nĭ-pen′āt) Feather-shaped on one side only; applied to a muscle that has a tendon on one side. Also called demipenniform.

unipolar (u-nĭ-po′lar) **1.** Having a single pole; applied to a cell. **2.** Located at one pole.

uniport (u′nĭ-port) Transport of one substance across a cell membrane by a protein carrier.

unit (u′nit) (u) An entity regarded as an elementary constituent of a larger whole.

   Angström u. (Å) See angstrom.

   antigen u. The smallest amount of antigen that, in the presence of specific antiserum, will fix one unit of complement so as to prevent hemolysis.

   antitoxin u. The unit for expressing the amount of antitoxin that will neutralize 100 minimal lethal doses of toxin.

   base u. Any one of the fundamental units of a system of measurement, such as those of the International System of Units (SI): the meter (m), kilogram (kg), second (s), ampere (A), kelvin (K), mole (mol), and candela (cd).

   British thermal u. (BTU) The amount of heat required to increase the temperature of 1 pound of water 1°, from 39° to 40° F. Also called unit of heat.

UNITS OF MEASUREMENT AND THEIR ABBREVIATIONS

UNITS OF CONCENTRATION	
molar (mol/liter)	M
parts per million	ppm

UNITS OF LENGTH	
meter	m
micrometer (micron)	μm (μ)
Angstrom (0.1 nm)	A

UNITS OF VOLUME	
milliliter	ml
microliter	μl

UNITS OF MASS	
gram	g
microgram	μg

UNITS OF TIME	
hour	hr
minute	min
second	s, sec

UNITS OF ELECTRICITY	
ampere	amp
milliampere	mA
volt	V
ohm	Ω

UNITS OF ENERGY AND WORK	
joule	J
calorie	cal

UNITS OF TEMPERATURE	
degree centigrade	°
thermodynamic temperature (Kelvin)	K

UNITS OF RADIOACTIVITY	
counts per minute	cpm
curie(s)	Ci

MISCELLANEOUS UNITS	
revolutions per minute	rpm
cycles per second (hertz)	Hz
pascal (newton/meter$_2$)	Pa
lux	lx
candela	cd
lumen	lm

PREFIXES TO NAMES OF UNITS						
exa	10^{18}	F	milli	10^{-3}	m
peta	10^{15}	P	micro	10^{-6}	μ
tera	10^{12}	T	nano	10^{-9}	n
giga	10^{9}	G	pico	10^{-12}	p
mega	10^{6}	M	femto	10^{-15}	f
kilo	10^{3}	k	atto	10^{-18}	a
centi	10^{-2}	c			

U

centimeter-gram-second u. (CGS unit) A metric unit denoting a rate of work.

coronary care u. (CCU) An area in a hospital designed to provide maximal surveillance and optimal therapy for patients suspected of having a heart attack (myocardial infarction) or other acute cardiac disorders requiring continuous monitoring.

critical care u. (CCU) See intensive care unit.

u. of force See dyne.

u. of heat (a) See calorie. (b) See British thermal unit.

hospital u. An area of a hospital designed and organized to provide specialized patient care (e.g., intensive care unit). Hospital units are considered departments.

Hounsfield u. Unit of x-ray attenuation used for CT scans, based on a scale in which air is −1000, water is 0, and bone is +1000.

insulin u. See international insulin unit.

intensive care u. (ICU) A specially equipped area in a hospital operated by trained personnel for the care of critically ill persons requiring immediate and continuous (24-hours-a-day) attention. Distinguished from recovery room. Also called critical care unit.

international u. (IU) The amount of a biologic substance (e.g., vitamin, hormone) that produces a specified effect; established by the World Health Organization (WHO) and accepted worldwide.

international insulin u. The activity contained in 0.045 mg of pure international standard zinc-insulin crystals.

International System of U.'s (SI) See under system.

map u. See centimorgan.

motor u. A motor nerve cell and the muscle fibers it innervates.

u. of oxytocin The oxytocic activity of 0.5 mg of the USP Posterior-pituitary Reference Standard; 1 mg of synthetic oxytocin corresponds to 500 international units of oxytocin activity.

u. of penicillin The penicillin activity of 0.6 μg of penicillin G.

SI u. See International System of units, under system.

Svedberg u. A unit of time and velocity measuring the sedimentation constant of a colloid solution, equal to 10^{-13} seconds.

USP u. A United States Pharmacopeia measure of the potency of any pharmacologic preparation.

u. of vasopressin The pressor activity of 0.5 mg of the USP Posterior-pituitary Reference Standard.

United Network for Organ Sharing (UNOS) An organization established by the National Organ Transplant Act of 1987 for optimizing the use of transplantable organs; it links local procurement centers with a national registry of waiting recipients and establishes mandatory criteria for selection of recipients, based on degree of histocompatibility, time on the waiting list, medical emergency status, and geographic factors.

United States Adopted Name (USAN) Designation for nonproprietary names for new drugs adopted by the USAN Council in cooperation with the manufacturers of the drugs; applicable only to those names adopted since June l961.

United States Adopted Name Council An enterprise assigning nonproprietary names to new drugs; it replaced the older AMA-USP Nomenclature Committee.

United States Pharmacopeia (USP) See pharmacopeia.

univalent (u-nī-va′lent) See monovalent.

unmyelinated (un-mī′ĕ-lĭ-nāt-ed) Devoid of a myelin sheath; applied to certain nerve fibers.

unsaturated (un-sat′u-rāt-ed) **1.** Not saturated; applied to a solution capable of dissolving more solute at a given temperature. **2.** Denoting an organic compound in which double or triple bonds unite two or more atoms. **3.** Denoting a chemical compound that has the potential for adding other atoms or radicals.

unstriated (un-strī′āt-ed) Lacking stripes; applied to smooth muscles.

upper (up′per) Slang expression for an amphetamine or any other substance that acts as a mood elevator.

uptake (up′tāk) The absorption of a substance by any living body tissue.

urachal (u′rah-kal) Relating to the urachus.

urachus (u′rah-kus) A canal present in the fetus between the navel and the apex of the bladder; it obliterates early during intrauterine life, becoming a thick fibrous cord known after birth as the median umbilical ligament. Occasionally the fetal structure remains completely or partly patent, forming a congenital anomaly (either a fistula, a cyst, or a sinus).

patent u. See urachal fistula, under fistula.

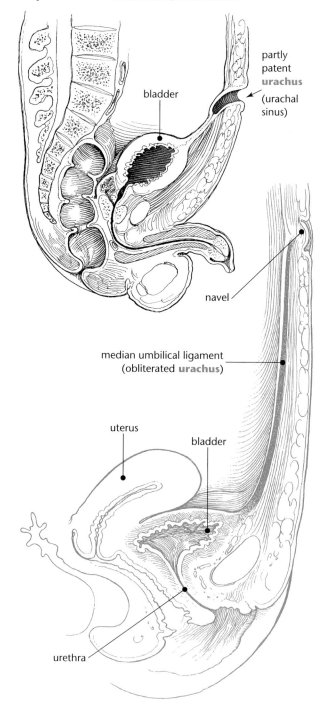

uracil (u′rah-sil) A pyrimidine present in nucleic acid.

uranium (u-ra′ne-um) A radioactive metallic element occurring in several minerals, especially pitchblende; symbol U, atomic number 92, atomic weight 238.03. It has a half-life of 4.5×10^9 years.

uranium 235 (^{235}U) An isotope of uranium with a half-life of 713 million years.

uranium 238 (^{235}U) An isotope of uranium with a half-life of 4.5 billion years.

urano- Combining form meaning hard palate.

uranostaphyloplasty (u-rah-no-staf′ĭ-lo-plas′te) Surgical repair of a defect (usually a cleft) of both the hard and soft palate. Also called uranostaphylorrhaphy.

uranostaphylorrhaphy (u-rah-no-staf′ĭ-lor′ah-fe) See uranostaphyloplasty.

uranostaphyloschisis (u-rah-no-staf′ĭ-los′kĭ-sis) A fissure or cleft of both hard and soft palate.

urate (ūr′āt) A salt of uric acid; commonly present in urinary stones.

urea (u-re′ah) 1. The normal end product of the breakdown (catabolism) of protein, formed in the liver, carried in the bloodstream to the kidneys, and excreted in the urine; normally accounts for approximately half of urinary solids. Formerly called carbamide. 2. Synthetic preparations used in the treatment of several conditions, such as skin diseases and to reduce pressure within the skull or the eye.

ureal (u′re-al) Relating to urea.

urease (u′re-ās) Enzyme that promotes the breakdown of urea into ammonia and carbon dioxide.

urecchysis (u-rek′ĭ-sis) Escape of urine into the tissues, as occurs in rupture of the bladder or ureters by trauma or disease.

uredema (u-rĕ-de′mah) A swollen condition of tissues caused by infiltration of urine escaped from the bladder or ureters.

uredo (u-re′do) 1. See urticaria. 2. A burning or itching sensation in the skin.

urelcosis (u-rel-ko′sis) An ulceration in the urinary tract.

uremia (u-re′me-ah) A toxic condition caused by retention in the blood of waste substances, the products of metabolism that are normally excreted in the urine; symptoms may include lethargy, loss of appetite, vomiting, anemia, blood–clotting disorders, an abnormal mental state, pericarditis, and colitis.

uremic (u-re′mik) Relating to uremia.

uresis (u-re′sis) Urination.

ureter (u-re′ter) A long, slender, muscular tube conveying urine from the pelvis of the kidney into the base of the bladder; in the adult, it measures from 25 to 30 cm in length and is slightly constricted in three places.

ureteral (u-re′ter-al) Relating to the ureter. Also called ureteric.

ureteralgia (u-re-ter-al′je-ah) Pain in a ureter.

ureterectasia (u-re-ter-ek-ta′se-ah) Abnormal dilation of a ureter.

ureterectomy (u-re-ter-ek′to-me) Removal of a ureter or a segment of it.

ureteric (u-rĕ-ter′ik) See ureteral.

uretero- Combining form meaning ureter.

ureterocele (u-re′ter-o-sēl) A saclike dilatation of the lower end of a ureter; may penetrate the bladder wall and protrude into the bladder or, more commonly, may occur in an ectopic ureter that ends at the bladder neck or in the urethra.

ureterocystostomy (u-re-ter-o-sis-tos′to-me) See ureteroneocystostomy.

ureteroenterostomy (u-re-ter-o-en-ter-os′to-me) The surgical procedure of constructing a connection between a ureter and the intestine in order to divert the urine flow.

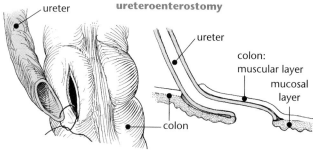

ureteroenterostomy

suturing ureteral transplant

ureterography (u-re-ter-og′rah-fe) The process of making x-ray pictures of the ureter following injection of a radiopaque substance into its lumen.

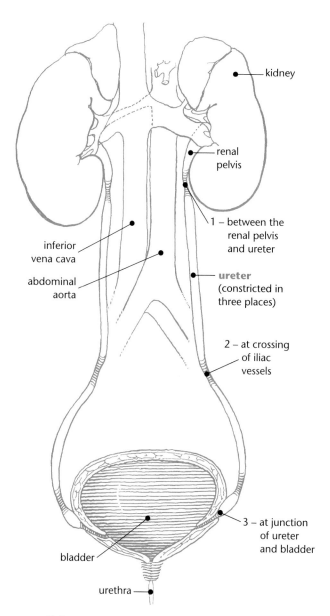

ureterolith (u-re′ter-o-lith) A stone in the ureter.

ureterolithiasis (u-re-ter-o-lĭ-thi′ah-sis) The presence of a stone in a ureter.

ureterolithotomy (u-re-ter-o-lĭ-thot′o-me) Surgical removal of a stone from a ureter.

ureterolysis (u-re-ter-ol′ĭ-sis) 1. Rupture of a ureter by trauma or disease. 2. Surgical freeing of a ureter from entrapment by adhesions or a fibrous plaque.

ureteroneocystostomy (u-re-ter-o-ne-o-sis-tos′to-me) Transplantation of the distal end of a ureter to a site in the bladder other than the normal one. Also called ureterocystostomy.

ureteronephrectomy (u-re-ter-o-nĕ-frek′to-me) Removal of a kidney and its ureter.

ureteropelvic (u-re-ter-o-pel′vik) Relating to a ureter and the adjoining renal pelvis.

ureteropelvicaliceal (u-re-ter-o-pel′ve-kal-ĭ-se′al) Relating to a ureter and the adjoining renal pelvis and calices.

ureteropyelitis (u-re-ter-o-pi-ĕ-li′tis) Inflammation of a ureter extending up to and including the pelvis of the kidney.

ureteropyelography (u-re-ter-o-pi-ĕ-log′rah-fe) See pyelography.

ureteropyeloneostomy (u-re-ter-o-pi′ĕ-lo-ne-os′to-me) Surgical procedure in which a section of a ureter is removed and the remainder is sutured to a new opening made into the kidney pelvis. Also called ureteropyelostomy.

U

ureteropyeloplasty (u-re-ter-o-pi′ĕ-lo-plas-te) Reparative surgery of a ureter and kidney pelvis.

ureteropyelostomy (u-re-ter-o-pi-ĕ-los′to-me) See ureteropyeloneostomy.

ureteropyosis (u-re-ter-o-pi-o′sis) Accumulation of pus in a ureter.

ureterosigmoid (u-re-ter-o-sig′moid) Relating to a ureter and the sigmoid colon.

ureterosigmoidostomy (u-re-ter-o-sig-moi-dos′to-me) Surgical implantation of a ureter into the sigmoid colon.

ureterostenosis (u-re-ter-o-stĕ-no′sis) Abnormal constriction of a ureter.

ureterostomy (u-re-ter-os′to-me) Attachment of the distal end of a divided ureter to the skin of the lower abdomen and creation of an external opening through which urine may be discharged when the bladder has been removed.

ureterotomy (u-re-ter-ot′o-me) Surgical division of a ureter.

ureterotrigonal (u-re-ter-o-tri′go-nal) Relating to the ureters and the triangular smooth area (trigone) at the base of the bladder.

ureteroureterostomy (u-re-ter-o-u-re-ter-os′to-me) Surgical connection of the two ureters or of two sections of a ureter.

ureterovaginal (u-re-ter-o-vaj′ĭ-nal) Relating to a ureter and the vagina.

ureterovesical (u-re-ter-o-ves′ĭ-kal) Relating to a ureter and the bladder.

ureterovesicostomy (u-re-ter-o-ves-ĭ-kos′to-me) Surgical procedure in which a divided ureter is implanted into a new site in the bladder.

urethra (u-re′thrah) The canal conveying urine from the bladder to the exterior of the body.

    anterior u. The portion of the male urethra extending from the bulb to the tip of the glans penis; consists of three parts: bulbous, pendulous, and glandular.

    female u. The channel extending from the neck of the bladder to the urinary opening behind the clitoris.

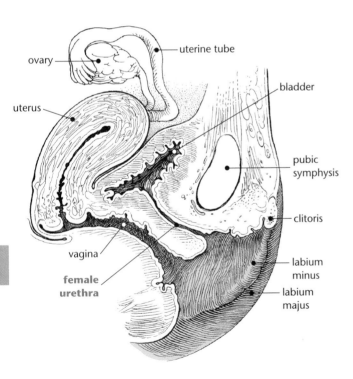

    male u. The channel extending from the neck of the bladder to the opening at the tip of the glans penis; it conveys seminal secretions as well as urine.

    membranous u. See membranous part of male urethra, under part.

    posterior u. The portion of the male urethra extending from the neck of the bladder to the bulb; consists of two parts: prostatic and membranous.

    prostatic u. See prostatic part of male urethra, under part.

    spongy u. See spongy part of male urethra, under part.

urethral (u-re′thral) Relating to the urethra.

urethralgia (u-rĕ-thral′je-ah) Pain in the urethra.

urethratresia (u-re-thrah-tre′ze-ah) Congenital imperforation or occlusion of the urethra.

urethrectomy (u-rĕ-threk′to-me) Removal of the urethra, or a portion of it.

urethrism, urethrismus (u′rĕ-thrizm, u′rĕ-thriz′mus) Irritability or chronic spasm of the urethra, usually associated with inflammation that also may involve the lower portion of the bladder. Also called urethrospasm.

urethritis (u-rĕ-thri′tis) Inflammation of the urethra; most common symptom is a burning sensation when passing urine; usually caused by infections (e.g., by sexually transmitted diseases and catheters left in place to drain the bladder); less frequently may be caused by chemical irritation (e.g., by antiseptics and spermicides).

    chlamydial u. Sexually transmitted disease caused by the bacterium *Chlamydia trachomatis.* See also nongonococcal urethritis.

    gonococcal u. Urethritis caused by gonococci; a form of gonorrhea; appears two to seven days after sexual intercourse with an individual infected with gonorrhea.

    nongonococcal u. (NGU) A sexually transmitted disease caused by a variety of microorganisms, most commonly *Chlamydia trachomatis;* routine bacterial cultures often do not reveal the organisms. In males, the infection usually produces a mild burning sensation on urination and a slight grayish discharge, especially apparent before the first urination of the day; in females, it is usually asymptomatic. A pregnant woman may infect her newborn infant, with serious consequences for the child. Also called nonspecific urethritis.

    nonspecific u. (NSU) See nongonococcal urethritis.

urethro-, urethr- Combining forms meaning urethra.

urethrocele (u-re′thro-sēl) A prolapse or sagging of the posterior wall of the female urethra into the vagina, commonly associated with a cystocele; often associated with (not the cause of) urinary incontinence.

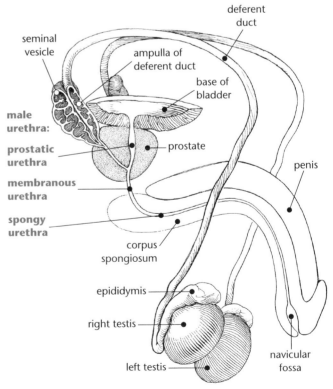

U

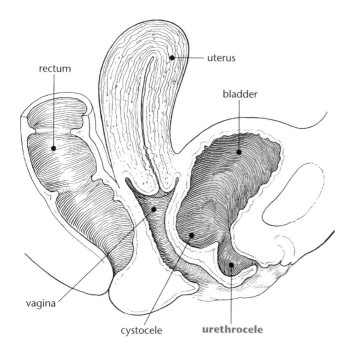

rectum

uterus

bladder

vagina

cystocele

urethrocele

urethrocystitis (u-re-thro-sis-ti′tis) Inflammation of the urethra and bladder.

urethrocystopexy (u-re-thro-sis′to-pek-se) Operation for the relief of stress incontinence in which the junction of the urethra and the bladder is sutured to the back of the pelvic bone.

urethrography (u-rĕ-throg′rah-fe) X-ray examination of the urethra (especially the male urethra) after introduction of a radiopaque substance.

urethrometer (u-rĕ-throm′ĕ-ter) Instrument for measuring the caliber of the urethra.

urethrometry (u-rĕ-throm′ĕ-tre) **1.** Measurement of the intraurethral pressure. **2.** Measurement of the caliber of the urethra.

urethropenile (u-re-thro-pe′nil) Relating to the urethra and penis.

urethrophyma (u-re-thro-fi′mah) Any circumscribed growth of the urethra.

urethroplasty (u-re′thro-plas-te) Surgical repair of an injury or defect of the urethra.

urethroprostatic (u-re-thro-pros-tat′ik) Relating to the urethra and prostate.

urethrorectal (u-re-thro-rek′tal) Relating to the urethra and rectum.

urethrorrhagia (u-re-thro-ra′je-ah) Bleeding from the urethra.

urethrorrhea (u-re-thro-re′ah) Abnormal discharge from the urethra.

urethroscope (u-re′thro-skōp) Instrument for inspecting the interior of the urethra.

urethroscopy (u-rĕ-thros′ko-pe) Visual examination of the urethra with a urethroscope.

urethrospasm (u-re′thro-spazm) See urethrism.

urethrostenosis (u-re-thro-stĕ-no′sis) Abnormal constriction of the urethra.

urethrostomy (u-rĕ-thros′to-me) Surgical construction of an opening into the urethra for temporary or permanent diversion of urine.

urethrotome (u-re′thro-tōm) Instrument for cutting into a urethral stricture.

urethrotomy (u-rĕ-throt′o-me) Surgical cutting into the urethra to relax a constriction or to remove a foreign body.

urethrovaginal (u-re-thro-vaj′ĭ-nal) Relating to the urethra and the vagina.

urethrovesical (u-re-thro-ves′ĭ-kal) Relating to the urethra and bladder.

-uretic Combining form meaning urine (e.g., diuretic).

urgency (ur′jen-se) A strong urge to urinate.

urhidrosis (ur-hid-ro′sis) See uridrosis.

-uria Combining form meaning the presence of a particular substance in the urine (e.g., proteinuria).

uric (u′rik) Relating to urine.

uric acid (ūr′ik as′id) A white crystalline compound that is a normal constituent of urine.

urico-, uric-, uri- Combining forms meaning uric acid.

uricolysis (u-rī-kol′ĭ-sis) The chemical splitting of uric acid molecules.

uricosuria (u-rī-ko-su′re-ah) The presence of excessive amounts of uric acid in the urine.

uricosuric (u-rī-ko-su′rik) An agent that tends to increase the excretion of uric acid in the urine.

uridine (u′rī-dēn) (Urd) A ribonucleoside containing uracil; important in carbohydrate metabolism.

uridrosis (u-rī-dro′sis) The presence of urea or uric acid in a person's sweat, sometimes deposited on the skin as minute crystals. Also spelled urhidrosis.

urinalysis (ur-ī-nal′ĭ-sis) Analysis of urine.

urinary (u′rī-ner-e) Relating to urine.

urinate (ur′ĭ-nāt) To discharge urine; to void; to micturate.

urination, (u-rī-na′shun) The passing of urine. Also called micturition.

urine (u′rin) The fluid excreted by the kidneys, normally stored in the bladder, and discharged through the urethra; composed of approximately 96% water and 4% solid matter (chiefly urea and sodium chloride), including many metabolic wastes.

    residual u. (RU) The urine left in the bladder after urination.

uriniferous (u-rī-nif′er-us) Conveying urine.

urino-, urin- Combining forms meaning urine.

urinogenous (u-rī-noj′ĕ-nus) Producing urine.

urinometer (u-rī-nom′ĕ-ter) A device for determining the specific gravity of urine. Also called urometer; urogravimeter.

uro- Combining form meaning urine.

urobilin (u-ro-bi′lin) Pigment found normally in small amounts in urine; formed by oxidation of urobilinogen.

urobilinemia (u-ro-bil-ĭ-ne′me-ah) The presence of urobilin in the blood.

urobilinogen (u-ro-bī-lin′o-jen) A colorless compound present in large amounts in feces and in small amounts in urine; formed in the intestines by the reduction of the pigment bilirubin; upon oxidation it forms urobilin.

urocele (u′ro-sēl) Distention of the scrotal sac with extravasated urine.

urochrome (u′ro-krōm) A brownish or yellow substance that imparts the characteristic yellowish color to urine.

urocystic (u-ro-sis′tik) Relating to the urinary bladder.

urodilatin (u-ro-di-la′tin) A 32-amino acid polypeptide found in urine, believed to facilitate sodium excretion.

urodynamics (u-ro-di-nam′iks) The study of the activities of the urinary bladder, urethral sphincter muscle, and pelvic musculature by means of various pressure devices.

urodynia (u-ro-din′e-ah) Pain or discomfort experienced during urination.

uroflowmetry (u-ro-flo′mĕ-tre) A urodynamic test for assessing the functional state of the lower urinary tract, especially the urethra; usually performed with the aid of an electronic device.

urogastrone (u-ro-gas′trōn) A polypeptide extractable from urine; when injected into the body, it inhibits stomach secretions.

urogenital (u-ro-jen′ĭ-tal) See genitourinary.

urogram (u′ro-gram) X-ray image of the urinary tract obtained with the use of a radiopaque medium.

urography (u-rog′rah-fe) X-ray examination of any part of the urinary tract.

    retrograde u. Urography following introduction of a radiopaque substance into the bladder or ureters.

U

urogravimeter (u-ro-grah-vim′ĕ-ter) See urinometer.

urokinase (u-ro-ki′nās) A plasminogen activator enzyme present in blood and urine; used by infusion to dissolve blood clots; it converts the globulin plasminogen to plasmin (the enzyme important in blood clot dissolution).

urolith (u′ro-lith) See urinary stone, under stone.

urolithiasis (u-ro-lǐ-thi′ah-sis) The formation of urinary stones and the resulting disease condition.

urolithic (u-ro-lith′ik) Relating to urinary stones.

urologic (u-ro-loj′ik) Relating to urology.

urologist (u-rol′o-jist) A specialist in urology.

urology (u-rol′o-je) The branch of medicine concerned with the study, diagnosis, and treatment (especially by surgical techniques) of diseases of the urinary tract of both male and female, and of the genital organs of the male.

urometer (u-rom′ĕ-ter) See urinometer.

uropathy (u-rop′ah-the), Any disease of the urinary tract.

uroplania (u-ro-pla′ne-ah) Escape of urine into the tissues.

uropoiesis (u-ro-poi-e′sis) The formation of urine.

uroporphyrin (u-ro-por′fĭ-rin) A porphyrin usually found in small amounts in the urine; excretion of an excessive amount may occur in heavy metal poisoning or in cutaneous porphyria (porphyria cutanea tarda) or congenital erythropoietic porphyria.

uroschesis (u-ros′kĕ-sis) Retention or suppression of urine.

urosepsis (u-ro-sep′sis) Sepsis resulting from the absorption and decomposition of extravasated urine in the tissues.

ursodeoxycholic acid (ur-so-de-ok′se-ko′lik as′id) Drug prepared from the bile acid chenodiol; used to dissolve gallstones.

Urtica (ur-ti′kah) A genus of plants (family Urticaceae) that have stinging hairs on their leaves.

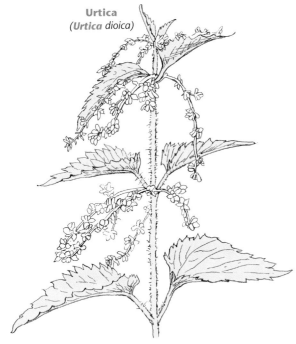

Urtica
(*Urtica* dioica)

urticant (ur′tĭ-kant) **1.** Producing an itching or stinging sensation. **2.** Any agent producing such an effect.

urticaria (ur-tĭ-kā′re-ah) A transitory eruption of itchy wheals, often occurring as a hypersensitivity reaction to foods or drugs, or due to emotional factors. Popularly called hives; nettle rash.

    cholinergic u. Clusters of tiny itchy papules usually brought on by exercise or stress.

    cold-induced u. Wheals formed on exposure to cold temperatures; may be life-threatening under certain conditions (e.g., swimming in cold water).

    giant u. See angioedema.

    u. medicamentosa Urticaria occurring as a reaction to a drug.

    papular u. Clustered reddish papules surrounded by wheals, seen usually on the upper arms, shoulders, and buttocks of infants; they represent a delayed hypersensitivity reaction to insect bites or stings usually from fleas, less commonly from mosquitoes, lice, mites, and scabies.

    u. pigmentosa A type of mastocytosis characterized chiefly by an eruption of yellow-brown macules and papules involving the skin almost exclusively; most commonly seen in children.

urticarial, urticarious (ur-tĭ-ka′re-al, ur-tĭ-ka′re-us) Relating to hives (urticaria).

uterine (u′ter-ĭn) Relating to the uterus.

utero-, uter- Combining forms meaning uterus.

utero-ovarian (u′ter-o o-va′re-an) Relating to the uterus and an ovary.

uteroplasty (u′ter-o-plas-te) Reparative surgery of the uterus.

uterosacral (u-ter-o-sa′kral) Relating to the uterus and the sacrum.

uterotomy (u-ter-ot′o-me) See hysterotomy.

uterotonic (u-ter-o-ton′ik) **1.** Overcoming relaxation of the uterine wall. **2.** Any agent producing such an effect.

uterotubal (u-ter-o-tu′bal) Relating to the uterus and a fallopian (uterine) tube.

uterovaginal (u-ter-o-vaj′ĭ-nal) Relating to the uterus and vagina.

uterovesical (u-ter-o-ves′ĭ-kal) Relating to the uterus and bladder.

uterus (u′ter-us) A hollow muscular organ of the female mammal situated in the pelvis between the bladder and rectum; its function is the nourishment of the developing young prior to birth; the mature human uterus is pear-shaped, thick-walled, and approximately 76 mm long, reaching adult size by the 15th year and diminishing after the menopause; it consists of a main portion (the corpus or body), an upper rounded portion (the fundus) into which opens on either side a fallopian (uterine) tube, and a lower portion (the cervix or neck) opening into the vagina. Popularly called womb.

    anomalous u. A malformed uterus.

    u. bicornis A uterus with a fundus that is indented and the uterine body bifurcated (in varying degrees) forming two distinct horns. Also called bicornuate uterus.

    bicornuate u. See uterus bicornis.

    u. didelphys A uterus separated throughout its length, each side having one fallopian (uterine) tube; may or may not have a double vagina. Also called double uterus.

    double u. See uterus didelphys.

    gravid u. A pregnant uterus.

    inverted u. A uterus that is, in effect, turned inside out, with its fundus prolapsed toward or through the cervix into the vagina; occasionally, the whole uterus protrudes through the vaginal opening; it is almost always due to childbirth, occurring after delivery of the newborn and made worse by excessive pulling of the umbilical cord before the placenta separates. It is usually successfully corrected after delivery is completed.

    pubescent u. An underdeveloped uterus.

    u. septus A uterus in which the uterine cavity is completely divided by a partition (septum).

    u. subseptus A uterus in which the uterine cavity is partly divided by a partition (septum) extending down from the fundus.

utilization The use of health care services and supplies; usually measured in terms of average length of stay in a health institution, number of admissions, and days of care.

utilization management A set of techniques used to contain costs of health care through case-by-case assessment to justify proposed medical services. See also managed care, under care.

utilization review Evaluation of the medical necessity, appropriateness, and efficiency of the delivery of medical services.

utricle (u′tre-kl) **1.** Any small sac. **2.** The larger of the two small membranous sacs within the vestibule of the inner ear; it is irregularly oblong, with a thickening on its lateral wall (macula of the utricle) that specifically responds to linear acceleration, such as the pull of gravity; it receives the semicircular ducts and a distribution of utricular fibers from the vestibulocochlear (8th cranial) nerve.

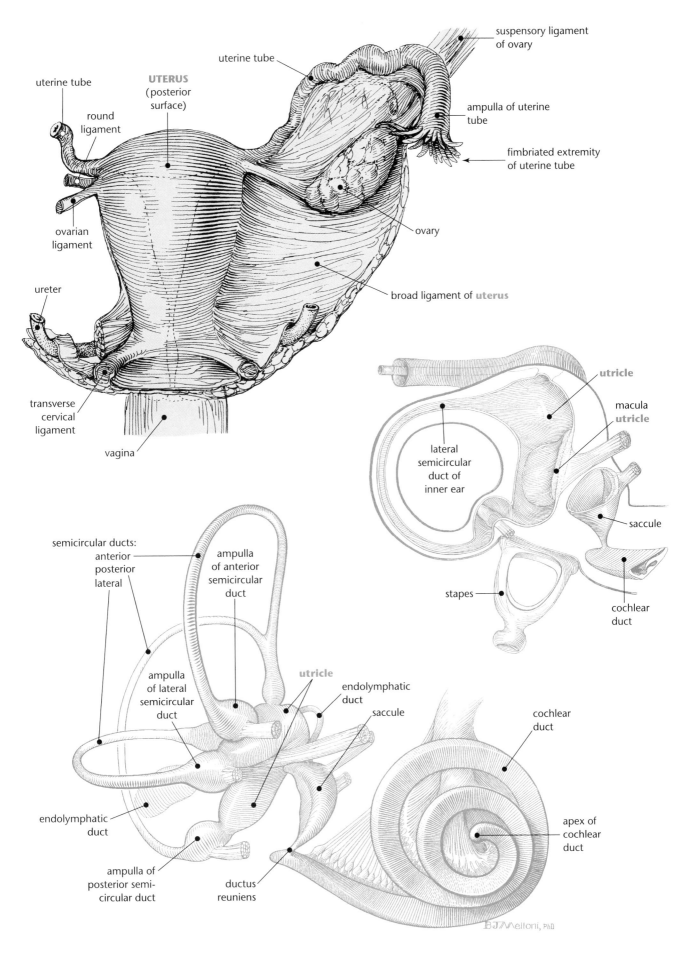

suspensory ligament of ovary

uterine tube

UTERUS (posterior surface)

uterine tube

round ligament

ovarian ligament

ureter

transverse cervical ligament

vagina

ampulla of uterine tube

fimbriated extremity of uterine tube

ovary

broad ligament of **uterus**

utricle

macula utricle

lateral semicircular duct of inner ear

saccule

stapes

cochlear duct

semicircular ducts:
anterior
posterior
lateral

ampulla of anterior semicircular duct

ampulla of lateral semicircular duct

utricle

endolymphatic duct

saccule

cochlear duct

endolymphatic duct

ampulla of posterior semi-circular duct

ductus reuniens

apex of cochlear duct

BJ Melloni, PhD

U

U9

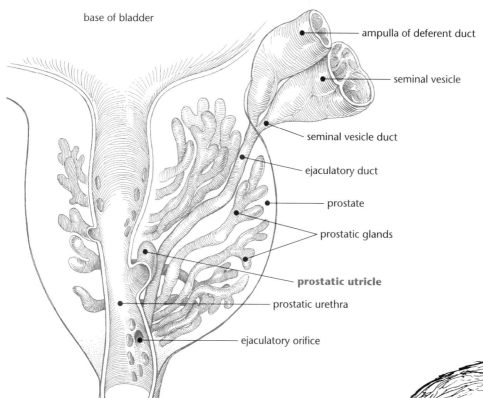

base of bladder
ampulla of deferent duct
seminal vesicle
seminal vesicle duct
ejaculatory duct
prostate
prostatic glands
prostatic utricle
prostatic urethra
ejaculatory orifice

prostatic u. A small, blind, nonfunctioning pouch about 6 mm long that extends backward into the substance of the prostate from its orifice on the crest of the prostatic urethra. The openings of the ejaculatory ducts lie on either side of it.

utricular (u-trik'u-lar) Relating to a utricle.

utriculosaccular (u-trik-u-lo-sak'u-lar) Relating to the utricle and the saccule of the inner ear.

utriculus (u-trik'u-lus) See utricle.

uvea (u've-ah) The middle, pigmented, vascular layer of the eye consisting of the choroid, the ciliary body, and the iris. Also called uveal tract.

uveitic (u-ve-it'ik) Relating to the uveitis.

uveitis (u-ve-i'tis) An eye condition consisting of inflammation of a portion of or the entire uveal tract (i.e., iris, ciliary body, and choroid). Also called choroidocyclitis.

    sympathetic u. See sympathetic ophthalmia, under ophthalmia.

uviform (u'vĭ-form) Resembling grapes.

uvula (u'vu-lah) **1.** Any body structure resembling a small grape. **2.** The palatine uvula.

    palatine u. The conical mass of tissue extending from the free edge of the soft palate, above the back of the tongue. Also called uvula.

    vesical u. A mucosal elevation projecting within the neck of the bladder in males, just behind the opening of the urethra, formed by the underlying medial lobe of the prostate.

uvulectomy (u-vu-lek'to-me) Surgical removal of the uvula. Also called staphylectomy.

uvulitis (u-vu-li'tis) Inflammation of the uvula.

uvuloptosis (u-vu-lop-to'sis) Relaxation and lengthening of the uvula. Also called staphyloptosis.

uvulotomy (u-vu-lot'o-me) Surgical cut into the uvula.

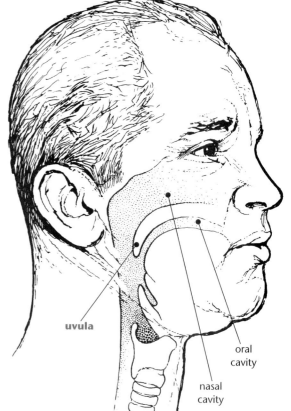

uvula
oral cavity
nasal cavity

U

utricular ■ uvulotomy

V

vaccinate (vak′sĭ-nāt) To inoculate with a vaccine in order to produce active immunity against a given infectious disease.

vaccination (vak-sĭ-na′shun) The act of vaccinating.

vaccinator (vak′sĭ-na-tor) **1.** A person who vaccinates. **2.** Instrument used in vaccination.

vaccine (vak′sēn) A preparation of dead or attenuated live viruses or bacteria for use in the prevention of infectious diseases by inducing active immunity.

  attenuated v. See live vaccine.

  autogenous v. Vaccine made from organisms obtained from the individual to be inoculated.

  bacillus Calmette-Guérin v. See BCG vaccine.

  BCG v. A suspension of an artificially weakened (attenuated), viable strain of *Mycobacterium tuberculosis*, bovine type; inoculated into the skin to provide immunity to tuberculosis. Also called bacillus Calmette-Guérin vaccine; Calmette-Guérin vaccine.

  Calmette-Guérin v. See BCG vaccine.

  cholera v. A sterile suspension of killed strains of *Vibrio cholerae;* given intramuscularly or subcutaneously to provide immunity to cholera.

  diphtheria and tetanus toxoids and pertussis v. A vaccine used for active immunization against diphtheria, tetanus, and whooping cough, administered to children as a basic series; diphtheria and tetanus toxoids are used without pertussis vaccine for a booster dose in adults. Tetanus toxoid is also available alone.

  hepatitis B v. Vaccine containing a formalin-inactivated hepatitis B surface antigen obtained from plasma of human carriers of the virus, or a genetically engineered (recombinant) subunit of the virus.

  human diploid cell v. (HDCV) A vaccine against rabies prepared from rabies virus grown in human diploid cell culture and then inactivated with tri-*n*-butyl phosphate.

  inactivated v. Any vaccine in which the nucleic acid components in the core of the infectious microorganism have been destroyed by chemical or physical means (e.g., formaldehyde or gamma radiation) without affecting the immunogenicity of the outer coat proteins.

  inactivated poliovirus v. (IPV) See poliovirus vaccine

  influenza virus v. A sterile, aqueous suspension of inactivated influenza virus grown in egg allantoic fluid and killed usually with formalin. The vaccine is reformulated annually, based on strains of the virus present in the previous years or anticipated for the upcoming season.

  live v. A vaccine prepared from living microorganisms that have been made to undergo physical changes by submission either to radiation or unfavorable temperatures, or to serial passage in laboratory animals or infected tissue/cell cultures; the result is a living avirulent, mutant strain capable of inducing protective immunity against the original organisms. Live vaccines are contraindicated in febrile or immunosuppressed patients and in pregnant women. Also called attenuated vaccine.

  measles v. Vaccine containing live, attenuated measles viruses, administered subcutaneously.

  mumps v. A suspension of live, attenuated mumps virus, administered subcutaneously.

  oral poliovirus v. See poliovirus vaccine.

  poliovirus v., poliomyelitis v. Vaccine providing immunity against poliomyelitis; available in two forms: *Inactived poliovirus v.* (IPV), an aqueous suspension of formaldehyde-inactivated strains of poliomyelitis virus, administered subcutaneously. Also called Salk vaccine. *Oral poliovirus v.* (OPV), an aqueous suspension of live, attenuated strains of poliomyelitis virus, administered orally. Also called Sabin vaccine.

  rabies v. See human diploid cell vaccine.

  rubella v. A live, attenuated vaccine containing a strain of the virus either alone or combined with measles vaccine (MR) or with measles and mumps vaccines (MMR).

  Sabin v. See poliovirus vaccine, oral.

  Salk v. See poliovirus vaccine, inactivated.

  typhoid v. *(a)* A suspension of chemically-killed or heat-killed *Salmonella typhi*, the organism causing typhoid fever, administered subcutaneously. *(b)* A live attenuated vaccine for oral administration.

  typhus v. A suspension of formaldehyde-inactivated *Rickettsia prowazekii*, the organism causing typhus, administered subcutaneously.

  yellow fever v. Vaccine containing live attenuated yellow fever virus, grown in chick embryos and then freeze-dried, administered subcutaneously as a reconstituted solution.

vaccinia (vak-sin′e-ah) **1.** The cutaneous lesion found at the site of vaccination with smallpox (vaccinia) virus. **2.** See cowpox.

  v. gangrenosa See progressive vaccinia.

  generalized v. Secondary skin lesions occurring after a smallpox vaccination.

  progressive v. A severe, often fatal, complication of smallpox vaccination, characterized by formation of widespread vaccinial lesions following a smallpox vaccination; usually occurs in individuals who fail to produce antibodies. Also called vaccinia gangrenosa.

vaccinial (vak-sin′e-al) Relating to vaccinia.

vacciniform (vak-sin′ĭ-form) Resembling vaccinia.

vaccinogen (vak-sin′o-jen) A source from which vaccine is produced.

vacuolate, vacuolated (vak′u-o-lāt, vak′u-o-lāt-ed) Containing vacuoles.

vacuolation (vak-u-o-la′shun) The formation of vacuoles.

vacuole (vak′u-ōl) A small space or cavity in a cell or a tissue.

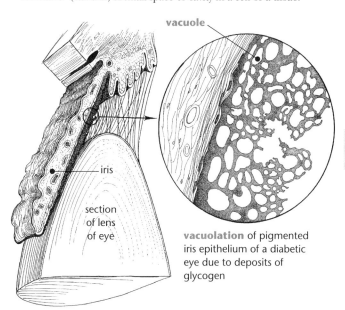

vacuole

iris

section of lens of eye

vacuolation of pigmented iris epithelium of a diabetic eye due to deposits of glycogen

V

secretory v.'s See secretory granules, under granule.

vacuum (vak'u-um) A space devoid of air or any gas.

vagal (va'gal) Relating to the vagus (10th cranial) nerve.

vagectomy (va-jek'to-me) Removal of a segment of the vagus (10th cranial) nerve.

vagina (vah-ji'nah) **1.** The musculomembranous structure of a female extending from the uterine cervix to the vulva. **2.** Any sheathlike structure.

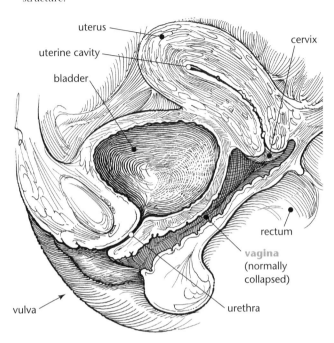

vaginal (vaj'ĭ-nal) **1.** Relating to the vagina. **2.** Relating to any sheath.

vaginalitis (vaj'ĭ-nah-li'tis) Inflammation of the tunica vaginalis testis.

vaginate (vaj'ĭ-nāt) **1.** To form a sheath. **2.** To enclose within a sheath.

vaginectomy (vaj'ĭ-nek'to-me) Partial or total removal of the vagina.

vaginismus (vaj-ĭ-niz'mus) Painful spasmodic contractions of the vaginal wall, which prevent vaginal sexual intercourse. Also called colpospasm.

vaginitis (vaj'ĭ-ni'tis) Inflammation of the vagina.

    emphysematous v. Vaginitis characterized by formation of gas-filled cysts within the upper vaginal tissues.

    Gardnerella vaginalis v. A sexually transmitted bacterial infection caused by *Gardnerella vaginalis;* causes a thin grayish white discharge and frequently coexists with other infections (e.g., candidiasis), which makes its detection difficult.

    senile v. Vaginitis often causing formation of adhesions that obliterate the canal; occurs in elderly women.

vaginocele (vaj'ĭ-no-sēl) See colpocele (1).

vaginodynia (vaj'ĭ-no-din'e-ah) Pain in the vagina. Also called colpodynia.

vaginofixation (vaj'ĭ-no-fiks-a'shun) See vaginopexy.

vaginohysterectomy (vaj'ĭ-no-his-tĕ-rek'to-me) See vaginal hysterectomy, under hysterectomy.

vaginolabial (vaj'ĭ-no-la'be-al) Relating to the vagina and the labia.

vaginomycosis (vaj'ĭ-no-mi-ko'sis) Any fungal infection of the vagina.

vaginopathy (vaj'ĭ-nop'ah-the) Any vaginal disorder.

vaginoperineal (vaj'ĭ-no-per-ĭ-ne'al) Relating to the vagina and perineum.

vaginoperineorrhaphy (vaj'ĭ-no-per-ĭ-ne-or'ah-fe) See colpoperineorrhaphy.

vaginopexy (vaj'ĭ-no-pek-se) Suturing a prolapsed vaginal wall in an elevated normal position. Also called vaginofixation; colporrhaphy.

vaginoplasty (vaj'ĭ-no-plas-te) Reparative surgery of the vagina. Also called colpoplasty.

vaginoscopy (vaj-ĭ-nos'ko-pe) Visual examination of the vagina, usually with the aid of an instrument (vaginoscope).

vaginotomy (vaj-ĭ-not'o-me) See colpotomy.

vaginovesical (vaj-ĭ-no-ves'ĭ-kal) Relating to the vagina and bladder.

vaginovulvar (vaj-ĭ-no-vul'var) See vulvovaginal.

vagitis (vah-ji'tus) Inflammation of the vagus (10th cranial) nerve.

vago- Combining form meaning the vagus (10th cranial) nerve.

vagolysis (va-gol'ĭ-sis) Surgical destruction of a segment of the vagus (10th cranial) nerve (e.g., in the esophageal branch for the relief of spasm at the gastroesophageal junction).

vagolytic (va-go-lit'ik) **1.** Causing destruction of the vagus (10th cranial) nerve. **2.** Any agent causing such an effect.

vagomimetic (va-go-mĭ-met'ik) Initiating the action of the vagus (10th cranial) nerve.

vagotomy (va-got'o-me) Surgical division of the vagus (10th cranial) nerve.

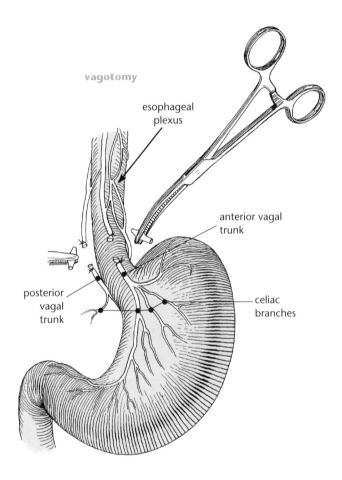

vagotomy

vagotonia (va-go-to'ne-ah) Excessive excitability of the vagus (10th cranial) nerve.

vagus (va'gus) See table of nerves.

valence, valency (va'lens, va'len-se) The combining power of one atom or group of atoms, using the hydrogen atom as the unit of comparison.

valgus (val'gus) Bent outward; away from the middle.

valine (val'in) (Val) An essential amino acid, constituent of many proteins.

vallate (val'āt) Cupped; a depression bounded by a circular elevation.

vallecula (vah-lek'u-lah) In anatomy, a groove or depression.

V

v. cerebelli A deep depression on the inferior surface of the cerebellum, between the two cerebellar hemispheres, in which rests the medulla oblongata.

v. epiglottica A depression between the epiglottis and the root of the tongue on either side of the median glossoepiglottic fold.

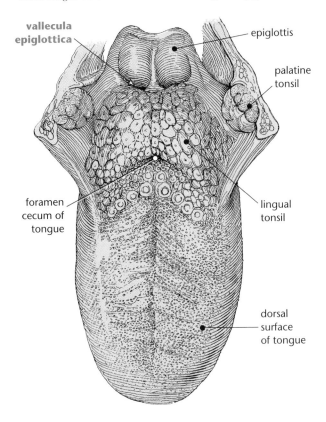

vallecula epiglottica — epiglottis — palatine tonsil — foramen cecum of tongue — lingual tonsil — dorsal surface of tongue

vallum (val'um), pl. val'la Any raised surface surrounded by a circular depression.

value (val'u) A calculated or measured numerical quantity; a number expressing a property.

caloric v. The measured heat generated by a food when metabolized by the body.

globular v. See color index, under index.

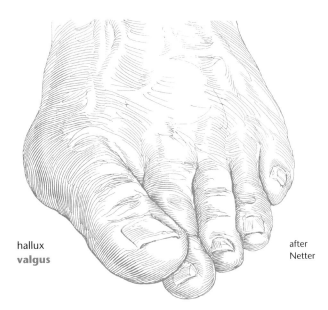

hallux **valgus** — after Netter

threshold limit v. (TLV) In occupational medicine, the maximum concentration of a chemical or physical agent considered a tolerable level in the workplace, as set forth in an annual publication by the American Conference of Governmental Industrial Hygienists. The list of physical agents includes heat, ionizing radiation, lasers, ultraviolet and infrared radiation, microwave radiation, noise and vibration, radio frequency, and visible light. The TLVs are not to be considered "safe levels"; rather, they are intended for use only as guidelines for control of workplace atmospheres by personnel with adequate training and experience in industrial hygiene.

valvate (val'vāt) Containing valves or valvelike components.

valve (valv) A fold of the lining membrane within a tubular structure or hollow organ, so placed as to permit passage of a body fluid in one direction only.

anterior urethral v. A crescentic valve in the male urethra, near the junction of the scrotum and penis.

aortic v. The valve between the left ventricle and the ascending aorta; consists of three cusps designated according to their location in the fetus as posterior, left, and right (in the adult, a more accurate description is anterior, right posterior, and left posterior).

Bianchi's v. See lacrimal fold, under fold.

eustachian v. See inferior vena cava valve.

ileocecal v. A valve between the small and large intestines, at the junction of the ileum and cecum; it regulates the flow of intestinal contents and prevents their backward flow. Also called ileocolic valve.

ileocolic v. See ileocecal valve.

inferior vena cava v. The crescent-shaped fold of cardiac tissue situated at the anterior margin of the opening of the inferior vena cava into the right atrium of the heart. Also called eustachian valve.

Kerckring's v.'s See circular folds, under fold.

left atrioventricular v. The valve composed of two cusps and situated between the left atrium and the left ventricle of the heart. Also called mitral valve.

NORMAL VALUES OF BLOOD PLASMA

BASE	
sodium (Na$^+$)	142 mEq/1
potassium (K$^+$)	4 mEq/1
calcium (Ca^{++})	5 mEq/1
magnesium (Mg^{++})	2 mEq/1
ACID	
HCO$_3$-	27 mEq/1
Cl_	103 mEq/1
HPO$_4$	2 mEq/1
SO$_4$	1 mEq/1
organic acids	4 mEq/1
protein	16 mEq/1

THRESHOLD LIMIT VALUES OF SOME ENVIRONMENTAL CONTAMINANTS

SUBSTANCE	
ammonia	50 ppm
carbon monoxide	50 ppm
carbon dioxide	5000 ppm
hydrogen sulfide	10 ppm
ozone	0.1 ppm
mercury	0.1 mg/m^3
cement dust	30 mppcf

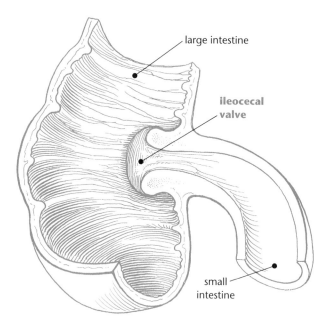

large intestine

ileocecal valve

small intestine

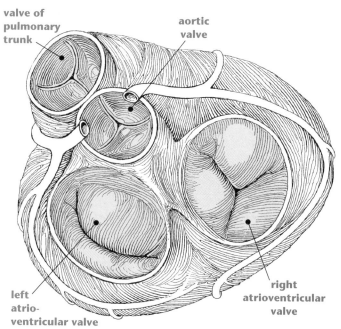

valve of pulmonary trunk

aortic valve

left atrio-ventricular valve

right atrioventricular valve

mitral v. See left atrioventricular valve.
posterior urethral v.'s Abnormal congenital folds of mucous membrane found in the distal prostatic urethra; they constitute the most common obstructive lesions in the urethra of male newborns and infants.
pulmonary v. See valve of pulmonary trunk.

v. of pulmonary trunk Valve situated at the opening of the pulmonary trunk as it leaves the right ventricle; composed of three semilunar cusps designated right, left, and anterior according to their location in the fetus (in the adult, a more accurate description is right anterior, left anterior, and posterior cusps).
rectal v.'s See transverse folds of rectum, under fold.

ST. JUDE MEDICAL® HEART VALVE

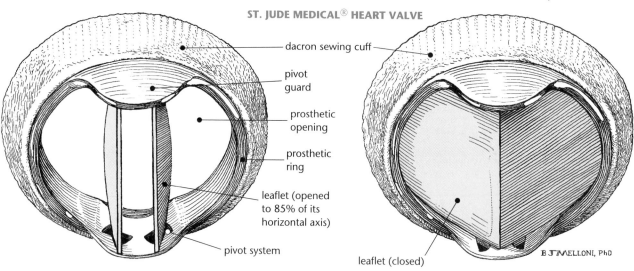

dacron sewing cuff

pivot guard

prosthetic opening

prosthetic ring

leaflet (opened to 85% of its horizontal axis)

pivot system

leaflet (closed)

B.J. MELLONI, PhD

OPEN

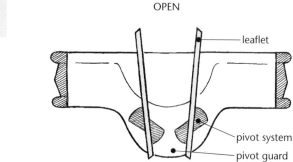

leaflet

pivot system

pivot guard

CLOSED

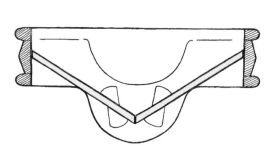

V

right atrioventricular v. The valve between the right atrium and the right ventricle of the heart; composed of three cusps (anterior, posterior, and septal). Also called tricuspid valve.

semilunar v. A valve composed of crescent-shaped cusps.

St. Jude Medical® heart v. An artificial low-profile heart valve designed to replace a diseased aortic or mitral valve. It consists of a ring and bileaflets made of pyrolytic carbon, a pivot area (where the leaflet tabs move as the valve opens to 85° and then closes), and a sewing cuff made of double-velour polyester fiber.

tricuspid v. See right atrioventricular valve.

urethral v.'s See anterior urethral valve; posterior urethral valve.

venous v. One of the small cup-shaped valves found in many veins, preventing a backward flow of blood.

valviform (val′vĭ-form) Shaped like a valve.

valvoplasty (val′vo-plas-te) Surgical reconstruction of a heart valve. Also called valvuloplasty.

valvotomy (val-vot′o-me) A surgical cut into a valve, especially a valve of the heart. Also called valvulotomy.

valvula (val′vu-lah), pl. val′vulae A small valve. Also called valvule.

valvular (val′vu-lar) Relating to a valve.

valvule (val′vul) See valvula.

valvulitis (val-vu-li′tis) Inflammation of a valve, especially a valve of the heart.

valvuloplasty (val′vu-lo-plas-te) See valvoplasty.

valvulotome (val′vu-lo-tōm) Surgical instrument for cutting a valve.

valvulotomy (val-vu-lot′o-me) See valvotomy.

vanadium (vah-na′de-um) Metallic element; symbol V, atomic number 23, atomic weight 50.94. Occupational exposure to dust or fumes of vanadium compounds causes respiratory tract irritation, asthma, and green discoloration of the tongue.

vanillylmandelic acid (vah-nil′il-man-del′ik as′id) (VMA) A compound excreted in the urine that is the major breakdown product of catecholamines (e.g., epinephrine and norepinephrine); normal range of excretion is 2 to 10 mg per day; elevated levels of excretion suggest the presence of (pheochromocytoma).

vapor (va′por) The gaseous state of any substance that is liquid or solid at ordinary temperatures.

vaporize (va′por-īz) To change into a vapor by heating.

vaporizer (va-por-i′zer) An apparatus for reducing liquids to vapors for inhalation.

vapotherapy (va-po-ther′ah-pe) The treatment of any disorder with vapor, steam, or spray.

variable (vār′e-ah-bl) Subject to change; changeable.

variance (vār′e-ans) 1. A difference. 2. The state of being different or variable. 3. A measure of the variation evident in a set of observations.

variant (vār′e-ant) Tending to deviate from a standard.

L-phase v. A strain of bacteria with defective cell walls and with nutritive needs similar to the strain from which it originated; capable of reverting to its original parental form. Also called L-form.

variceal (var-ĭ-se′al) Relating to a varix.

varicella (var-ĭ-sel′ah) See chickenpox.

varicelliform (var-ĭ-sel′ĭ-form) Resembling chickenpox.

varices (var′ĭ-sēz) Plural of varix.

variciform (var-is′ĭ-form) Resembling a varix.

varicocele (var′ĭ-ko-sēl) A mass of dilated, tortuous veins just above and posterior to the testis, sometimes extending up to the groin, with the left side most commonly involved; it results from backflow of blood secondary to incompetent or absent valves in the spermatic veins. It is a frequent finding in infertile men.

varicocelectomy (var-ĭ-ko-sĕ-lek′to-me) Operation for removal of a varicocele.

varicography (var-ĭ-kog′rah-fe) X-ray visualization of varicose veins following introduction of a radiopaque substance into the veins.

varicophlebitis (var-ĭ-ko-fle-bi′tis) Inflammation of varicose veins.

varicose (var′ĭ-kōs) Abnormally dilated and tortuous; applied to lymphatic vessels, arteries, and especially veins.

varicosity (var-ĭ-kos′ĭ-te) 1. The state of being abnormally swollen.

2. A varicose vein.

varicotomy (var-ĭ-kot′o-me) Surgical removal of a varicose vein.

varicula (vah-rik′u-lah) A varicose condition of minute veins, especially of the transparent membrane (conjunctiva) covering the eye.

varicule (var′ĭ-kyool) A small varicose vein.

variola (vah-ri′o-lah) See smallpox.

v. minor See alastrim.

variolar (vah-ri′o-lar) Relating to smallpox.

varioliform (va-re-o′lĭ-form) Resembling smallpox.

varix (vār′iks), pl. var′ices A dilated tortuous vessel, especially a vein.

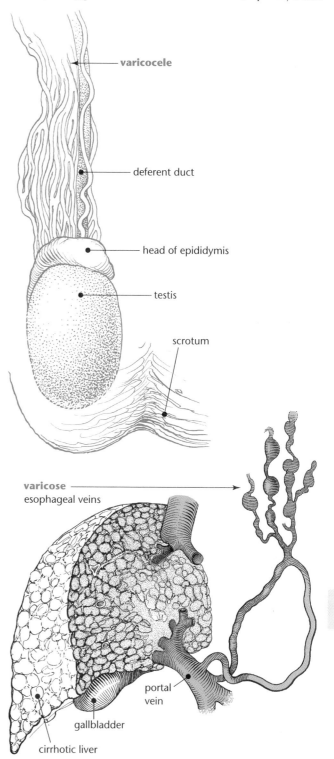

varicocele

deferent duct

head of epididymis

testis

scrotum

varicose esophageal veins

portal vein

gallbladder

cirrhotic liver

aneurysmal v. Varix resulting from a direct communication between a vein and an adjacent artery.

esophageal varices Varicosities of the submucosal veins of the lower esophagus and its junction with the stomach.

varnish (var′nish) A solution of a resin in a suitable solvent and an evaporating binder.

dental v. A solution of natural resins and gums in an organic solvent, applied over the walls and floor of a prepared tooth cavity; it protects the underlying tooth structure against constituents of the filling material and thermal shock.

varus (varus) Bent inward, toward the midline.

vas (vas), pl. **vasa** A channel conveying body fluids such as blood, lymph, chyle, or semen; a vessel.

v. aberrans hepatis Any of numerous blind-ending bile ducts located in the capsule or fibrous appendix of the liver.

v. afferens glomeruli renis See afferent glomerular arteriole, under arteriole.

vasa brevia Short gastric arteries; see table of arteries.

v. deferens See deferent duct, under duct.

v. efferens glomeruli renis See efferent glomerular arteriole, under arteriole.

v. lymphaticum See lymphatic vessel, under vessel.

vasa previa In obstetrics, a state in which the blood vessels of the umbilical cord are situated in front of the presenting part at the time of delivery, due to the abnormal insertion of the umbilical cord early in embryonic life; the umbilical vessels separate and insert onto the fetal membranes (velamentous insertion) instead of on the chorionic plate of the placenta. The condition is associated with a high risk of rupture of the vessels, leading to exsanguination and death of the infant.

vasa recta See arteriolae rectae, under arteriola.

v. vasorum One of many small nutrient blood vessels in the walls of larger arteries and their corresponding veins.

vascular (vas′ku-lar) Relating to vessels.

vascularity (vas-ku-lar′ĭ-te) The state of containing blood vessels.

vascularization (vas-ku-lar-ĭ-za′shun) The formation of new blood vessels in any body part.

vasculature (vas′ku-lah-chūr) The system of blood vessels supplying an organ.

vasculitis (vas-ku-li′tis), pl. **vasculi′tides** Inflammation of, and damage to, one or more blood vessels, usually compromising the vessel lumen; may be due to direct injury (e.g., trauma, toxins, infections) or may occur secondary to a variety of diseases (e.g., serum sickness, systemic lupus erythematosis, syphilis, delayed-type hypersensitivity reactions).

vasculo- Combining form meaning blood vessel.

vasculogenesis (vas-ku-lo-jen′ĕ-sis) The development of the system of blood vessels.

vasectomy (vah-sek′to-me) Removal of a section of both deferent ducts as a method of male sterilization. Also called deferenectomy; male sterilization.

vasiform (vas′ĭ-form) Tubular.

vasitis (vah-si′tis) See deferentitis.

vasoactive (vas-o-ak′tiv) Having an effect on blood vessels.

vasoconstriction (vas-o-kon-strik′shun) Narrowing of the lumen of blood vessels, especially of arterioles.

vasoconstrictor (vas-o-kon-strik′tor) A drug or nerve that causes constriction of blood vessels.

vasodepressor (vas-o-de-pres′sor) 1. Reducing vascular tone, thereby lowering blood pressure. 2. Any agent causing such an effect.

vasodilation (vas-o-di-la′shun) Widening of the lumen of blood vessels, especially of arterioles, leading to increased blood flow to a body part.

vasodilator (vas-o-di-lāt′or) A drug or nerve that causes dilatation of blood vessels.

vasoganglion (vas-o-gang′gle-on) A dense mass of minute blood vessels.

vasogenic (vas-o-jen′ik) Originating from blood vessels.

vasography (vah-sog′rah-fe) 1. X-ray visualization of blood vessels.

2. X-ray examination of the deferent duct.

vasoinhibitor (vas-o-in-hib′ĭ-tor) An agent causing diminished action of vasomotor nerves.

vasoinhibitory (vas-o-in-hib′ĭ-tor-e) Diminishing the action of nerves innervating the musculature of blood vessel walls (vasomotor nerves).

vasoligation (vas-o-li-ga′shun) Surgical ligation of the deferent duct.

vasomotion (vas-o-mo′shun) The dilatation and constriction of blood vessel walls. Also called angiokinesis.

vasomotor (vas-o-mo′tor) Causing dilatation or constriction of blood vessel walls; applied to nerves that produce this effect.

vasoneuropathy (vas-o-nu-rop′ah-the) Any disease affecting blood vessels and nerves.

vasoneurosis (vas-o-nu-ro′sis) See angioneurosis.

vasoparalysis (vas-o-pah-ral′ĭ-sis) Relaxation of blood vessel walls. Also called vasomotor paralysis.

vasopressin (vas-o-pres′in) (VP) See antidiuretic hormone, under hormone.

vasopressor (vas-o-pres′or) 1. Producing constriction of blood vessels and a rise of blood pressure. 2. Any agent causing such an effect.

vasosensory (vas-o-sen′so-re) Denoting the sensory nerves innervating blood vessels.

vasospasm (vas′o-spazm) Spastic contraction of blood vessel walls. Also called angiospasm; angiohypertonia.

vasostimulant (vas-o-stim′u-lant) 1. Exciting dilatation or constriction of blood vessels. 2. Any agent having such property.

vasotomy (vah-sot′o-me) A surgical cut into the deferent duct.

vasotonic (vas-o-ton′ik) 1. Relating to the tone or tension of blood vessel walls. 2. An agent that increases the tone or tension of blood vessels.

vasotrophic (vas-o-trof′ik) Relating to the nutrition of blood vessels or lymphatic vessels.

vasotropic (vas-o-trop′ik) Tending to act upon blood vessels.

vasovagal (vas-o-va′gal) Relating to the action of the vagus (10th cranial) nerve upon blood vessels.

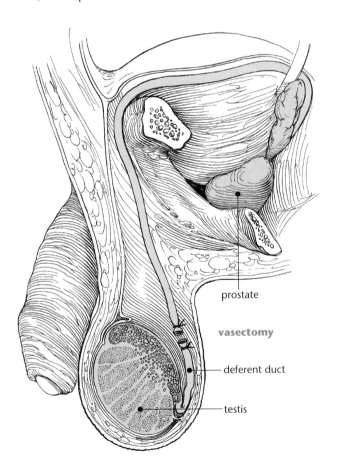

prostate

vasectomy

deferent duct

testis

vasovasostomy (vas-o-vah-sos′to-me) Surgical union of the divided ends of a deferent duct; may be performed to restore fertility in a male upon whom a vasectomy was previously performed.

vasovesiculectomy (vas-o-ve-sik-u-lek′to-me) Removal of a deferent duct and seminal vesicle.

vault (vawlt) Any arched anatomic structure resembling a dome.

vection (vek′shun) Transmission of the causative agents of disease by a vector.

vector (vek′tor) 1. An organism (e.g., tick, rat, dog) that transmits pathologic microorganisms (bacteria and viruses) from one host to another. 2. Anything (e.g., electromotive force, velocity) that has a magnitude and a direction. 3. A DNA molecule into which a gene of interest is cloned and which is capable of replicating itself in a particular host.

    biologic v. A vector (e.g., the *Anopheles* mosquito) in whose body an infective microorganism must develop before becoming infective to its primary host.

    mechanical v. A vector (e.g., the housefly) that simply transports an infective microorganism on its feet or mouth parts from one host to another and is not essential to the life cycle of the parasite.

vectorcardiogram (vek-tor-kar′de-o-gram) (VCG) A record (usually a photograph) of the direction and magnitude of the electromotive force of the heart displayed as a voltage loop.

vectorcardiography (vek-tor-kar-de-og′rah-fe) The recording of the direction and magnitude of the heart's electromotive forces at any point in time; represented by vector loops.

    spatial v. Vectorcardiography in which the voltage loop is projected three-dimensionally on the frontal, horizontal, and sagittal reference planes.

vegetarian (vej-e-tār′e-an) A person who does not eat food derived from animals (e.g., meat, eggs, milk); one whose diet is exclusively of vegetable origin.

vegetations (vej-e-ta′shuns) An abnormal deposit growing on or within tissues; specifically, a growth composed of fibrin and fused blood platelets adherent to a diseased heart valve or within the heart muscle; circulating bacteria or fungi of blood-borne infections tend to plant at these sites.

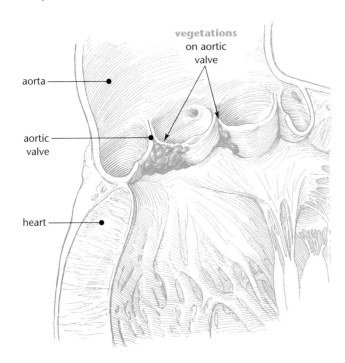

vegetations on aortic valve

aorta — aortic valve — heart

vegetative (vej′e-ta-tiv) Having a role in the processes of nutrition and growth.

vehicle (ve′ĭ-kl) Any (usually) inert substance used as a carrier of the active ingredient of a drug; may be a liquid, grease, or powder in vary-

ing proportions depending on the final consistency required. Also called base.

veil (vāl) Popular name for caul.

vein (vān) (v) 1. A vessel carrying blood toward the heart. For specific veins, see table of veins. 2. A vessel in the heart wall carrying blood to the right atrium.

    cardinal v.'s In embryology, the major vessels draining the cephalic part (anterior cardinal vein) and caudal part (posterior cardinal vein) of the embryo and emptying into the heart via the common cardinal vein.

    emissary v.'s Veins draining the intracranial venous sinuses and transporting the blood to a vessel outside the skull; they serve as drainage channels in case of increased intracranial pressure.

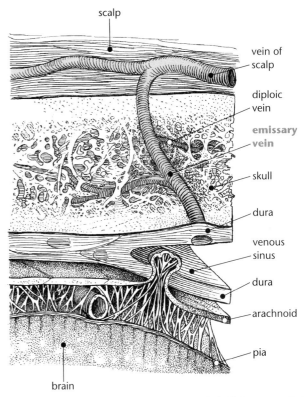

scalp — vein of scalp — diploic vein — emissary vein — skull — dura — venous sinus — dura — arachnoid — pia — brain

    large v. A vein with walls that characteristically have a markedly thin or absent middle layer (tunica media) and a thick outer layer (adventitia) that contains large bundles of longitudinally arranged muscle fibers.

    medium v. A vein with walls that characteristically have a thick middle layer (tunica media) composed of connective tissue with elastic fibers intermingled with circularly arranged muscle fibers; the outer layer (adventitia) contains longitudinally arranged elastic fibers.

    pulmonary v.'s The four veins returning oxygenated blood from the lungs to the left atrium of the heart. See also table of veins.

    sausage-link v.'s Descriptive term for the pattern formed by engorgement of retinal veins with intervals of vessel constriction at arteriovenous crossings; observed in such conditions as Waldenström's macroglobulinemia due to marked increase of plasma viscosity and sluggishness of blood flow.

    small v. A vein that has walls formed from a network of longitudinal elastic fibers arranged in thin, poorly defined layers; some contain a few smooth muscle fibers arranged circularly.

    varicose v.'s Abnormally dilated tortuous veins, resulting from prolonged increased pressure within the vessels; occur most commonly in the superficial veins of the legs; contributing factors include hereditary defects in the venous walls, obesity, compression by tumors, and prolonged dependent position of the legs.

    vitelline v.'s In embryology, veins returning blood from the yolk sac of an early embryo; they form a network around the duodenum and liver and empty directly into the primitive heart.

V

superficial temporal v.

posterior retromandibular v.

anterior jugular v.

internal jugular v.

superior vena cava

hepatic v.'s

supratrochlear v.

supraorbital v.

angular v.

facial v.

ant. retromandibular v.

left brachiocephalic v.

subclavian v.

cephalic v.

axillary v.

basilic v.

brachial v.'s

renal v.

inferior vena cava

intermediate cubital v.

common iliac v.

ulnar v.'s

radial v.'s

femoral v.

great saphenous v.

femoral v.

popliteal v.

small saphenous v.

great saphenous v.

anterior tibial v.

posterior tibial v.'s

venous plexus on dorsum of foot

dorsal venous arch

dorsal v. of foot

B J MELLONI, PhD

inferior sagittal sinus

superior cerebral v.

superior sagittal sinus

angular v.

straight sinus

pterygoid plexus

transverse sinus

superior labial v.

sigmoid sinus

inferior labial v.

occipital v.

facial v.

post. retro-mandibular v.

lingual v.

ant. retro-mandibular v.

superior laryngeal v.

external jugular v.

superior thyroid v.

internal jugular v.

inferior laryngeal v.

inferior thyroid v.

supra-scapular v.

left brachio-cephalic v.

anterior jugular v.

superior vena cava

subclavian v.

vertebral v.

internal jugular v.

ext. jugular v.

subclavian v.

right brachiocephalic v.

superior vena cava

superior intercostal v.

outline of heart

azygous v.

accessory hemiazygous v.

hepatic v.'s

inferior vena cava

hemiazygous v.

lumbar azygous v.'s

subcostal v.

right renal v.

left renal v.

gonadal v.

inferior vena cava

middle sacral v.

common iliac v.

external iliac v.

internal iliac v.

vein ■ vein

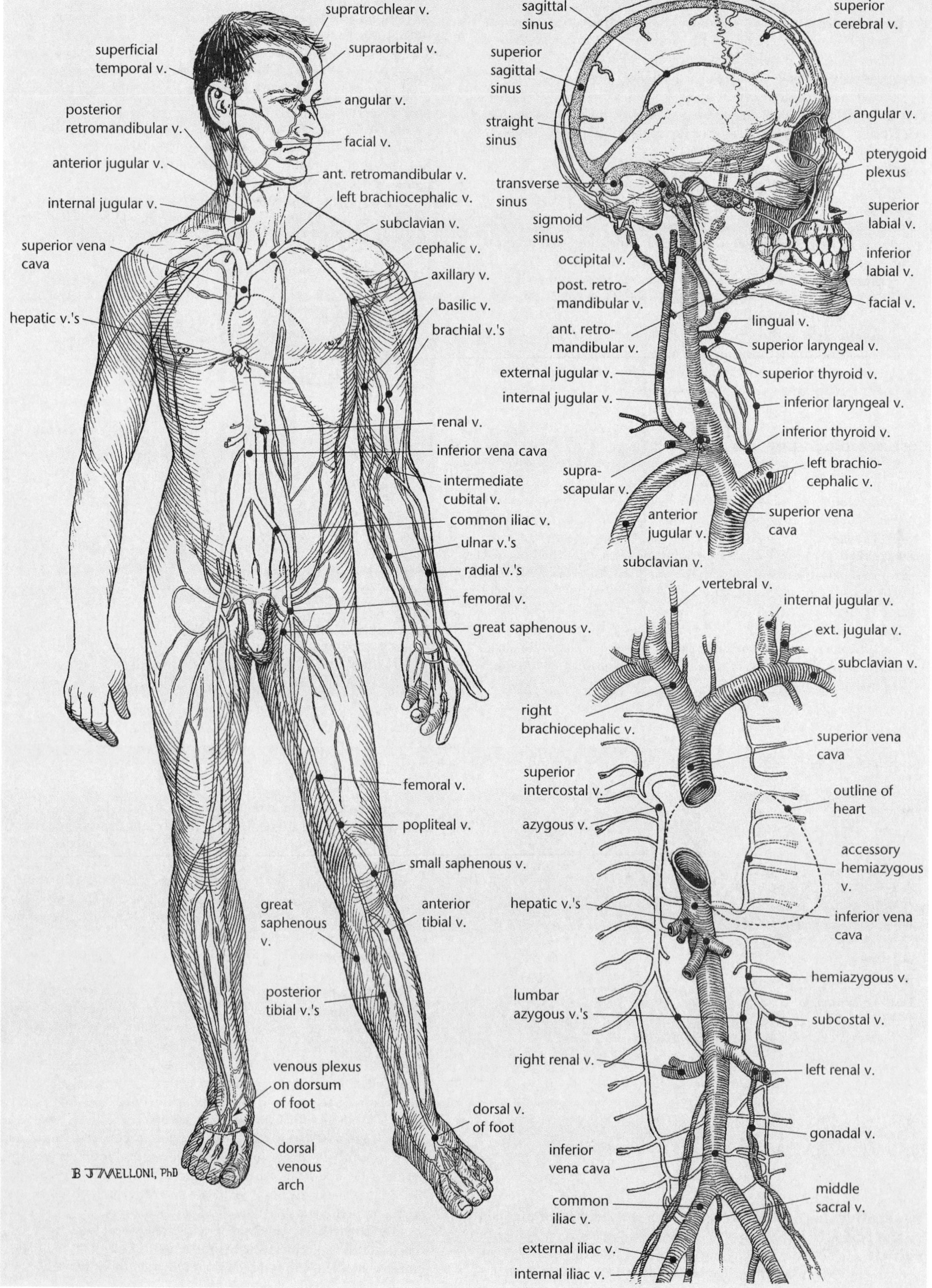

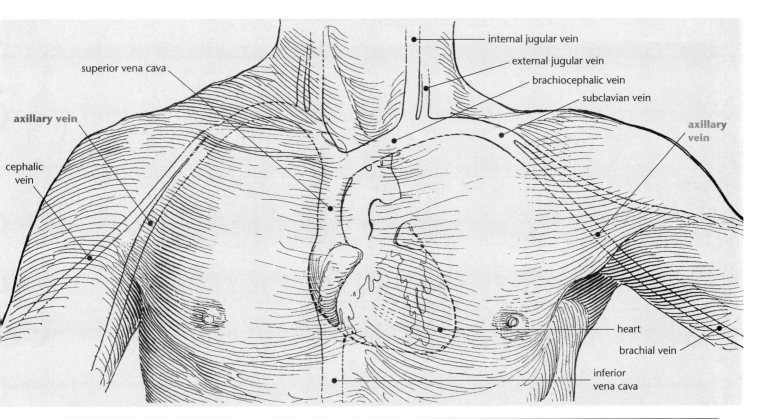

superior vena cava

axillary vein

cephalic vein

internal jugular vein

external jugular vein

brachiocephalic vein

subclavian vein

axillary vein

heart

brachial vein

inferior vena cava

VEINS	LOCATION	DRAINS	EMPTIES INTO
alveolar v., inferior inferior dental v. *v. alveolaris inferior*	from mandibular canal it passes up the ramus of lower jaw	teeth and body of lower jaw; lower lip	pyterygoid plexus, facial v., retromandibular v.
anastomotic v., inferior v. of Labbé *v. anastomotica inferior*	courses over posterior part of temporal lobe of brain	superficial middle cerebral v., temporal lobe	transverse sinus
anastomotic v., superior v. of Trolard *v. anastomotica superior*	from lateral sulcus of brain across parietal lobe	superficial middle cerebral v., parietal lobe	superior sagittal sinus
angular v. *v. angularis*	anterior angle of orbit and root of nose	formed by union of frontal and supraorbital v.'s; receives infraorbital, superior and inferior palpebral and external nasal v.'s	facial v. (behind facial artery) at junction with superior labial v.'s
antebrachial v., median	see median vein of forearm		
appendicular v. *v. appendicularis*	along mesentery of vermiform appendix	appendix	ileocolic v.
v. of aqueduct of vestibule *v. aquaeductus vestibuli*	through aqueduct of vestibule (accompanied by endolymphatic duct)	semicircular ducts of inner ear, utricle, saccule	superior petrosal sinus or inferior petrosal sinus
arcuate v.'s of kidney *vv. arcuatae renis*	in corticomedullary zone of kidney	interlobular v.'s, venulae rectae	interlobar v.
auditory v.'s, internal	see labyrinthine v.'s		
auricular v.'s, anterior *vv. auriculares anteriores*	front part of ear	external ear	superficial temporal v.
auricular v., posterior *v. auricularis posterior*	side of head in back of ear	plexus on side of head, tributaries from back of ear, stylomastoid v.	external jugular v. in union with retromandibular v.
axillary v. *v. axillaris*	upper limb from lower border of teres major muscle to outer border of first rib	junction of basilic and brachial v.'s; cephalic v., deep brachial comitans	subclavian v. (at outer border of first rib)
azygos v. *v. azygos*	from front of first lumbar vertebra it passes to right side of fourth thoracic vertebra where it arches over roots of right lung	ascending lumbar, right subcostal, intercostal, hemiazygos, esophageal, mediastinal, pericardial, and right bronchial v.'s	superior vena cava, near its entrance into pericardium
azygos v., left	see hemiazygos v.		
basal v. *v. basalis*	from anterior perforated substance it passes posteriorly around cerebral peduncle	anterior perforated substance; anterior cerebral v., deep middle cerebral v., inferior striate v.'s	internal cerebral v. in union with great cerebral v. (just under splenium of corpus callosum)

V

VEINS	LOCATION	DRAINS	EMPTIES INTO
basilic v. *v. basilica*	from ulnar part of hand it passes up forearm and continues along medial border of the biceps	dorsal venous network of hand; tributaries from ulnar side of forearm	joins brachial v. to form axillary v.
basivertebral v.'s *vv. basivertebrales*	tortuous channels in substance of vertebral bodies	vertebral bodies	anterior external, and internal vertebral venous plexuses
brachial v.'s *vv. brachiales*	from neck of radius, courses upward to lower border of teres major muscle	radial and ulnar v.'s, superior and inferior ulnar collateral v.'s, deep brachial v.	axillary v. in union with basilic v.
brachiocephalic v.'s innominate v.'s *vv. brachiocephalicae*	root of neck, medial end of clavicle	*right side:* internal jugular, subclavian, internal thoracic, and inferior thyroid v.'s; *left side:* internal jugular, subclavian, and left highest intercostal v.'s	superior vena cava
bronchial v.'s *vv. bronchiales*	near bronchi	larger bronchi and roots of lungs	*right side:* azygos v.; *left side:* left highest intercostal or accessory hemiazygos v.'s
v. of bulb of penis *v. bulbi penis*	penis	expanded posterior part of the corpus spongiosum penis (bulb of penis)	internal pudendal v.
v. of bulb of vestibule *v. bulbi vestibuli*	vestibule	mass of erectile tissue on either side of vagina	internal pudendal v.
cardiac v.'s, anterior (three to four in number) *vv. cordis anteriores*	ventral side of heart	ventral side of right ventricle	right atrium
cardiac v., great left coronary v. *v. cordis magna*	from apex of heart it ascends to front of heart	tributaries from left atrium and both ventricles; left marginal v.	left extremity of coronary sinus
cardiac v., middle *v. cordis media*	ascends up back of heart from apex	tributaries from both ventricles	right extremity of coronary sinus
cardiac v., small right coronary v. *v. cordis parva*	ascends up heart from back of right atrium and ventricle	back of right atrium and ventricle; right marginal v.	right extremity of coronary sinus or right atrium
cardiac v.'s, smallest (many minute veins) v.'s of Thebesius *vv. cordis minimae*	in muscular wall of heart	muscular wall of heart	mostly in atria, some in ventricles
cavernous v.'s of penis *vv. cavernosae penis*	penis	cavernous venous spaces in the erectile tissue of the penis (corpora cavernosae)	deep dorsal v. of penis, prostatic plexus
central v.'s of liver *vv. centrales hepatis*	liver	sinusoids in liver substance	sublobular v.
central v. of retina *v. centralis retinae*	from eyeball it passes out in optic nerve	retinal v.'s	superior ophthalmic v., cavernous sinus
cephalic v. *v. cephalica*	from radial part of hand it passes up forearm to groove along lateral border of biceps muscle of arm and more proximally between deltoid and pectoralis major muscles	radial side of dorsal venous plexus of hand; palmar and dorsal tributaries in forearm; thoracoacromial v.	axillary v. just caudal to clavicle
cephalic v., accessory *v. cephalica accessoria*	radial side of forearm	dorsal venous network of hand	cephalic v. at elbow
cerebellar v.'s, inferior *vv. cerebelli inferiores*	bottom of cerebellum	inferior surface of cerebellum	inferior petrosal sinus, transverse and sigmoid sinuses, straight sinus
cerebellar v.'s, superior *vv. cerebelli superiores*	top of cerebellum (superior vermis)	upper surface of cerebellum	transverse sinus, superior petrosal sinus, great cerebral v. or straight sinus
cerebral v., anterior *v. cerebri anterior*	from upper surface of corpus callosum down through longitudinal fissure, above optic nerve to lateral cerebral sulcus	anterior perforated substance, lamina terminalis, rostrum of corpus callosum, septum pellucidum, striate v.	basal v. in union with deep middle cerebral v.
cerebral v., deep middle deep Sylvian v. *v. cerebri media profunda*	lower part of lateral cerebral sulcus	tributaries from insula, neighboring gyri	basal v. in union with anterior cerebral v.

V

vein ■ vein

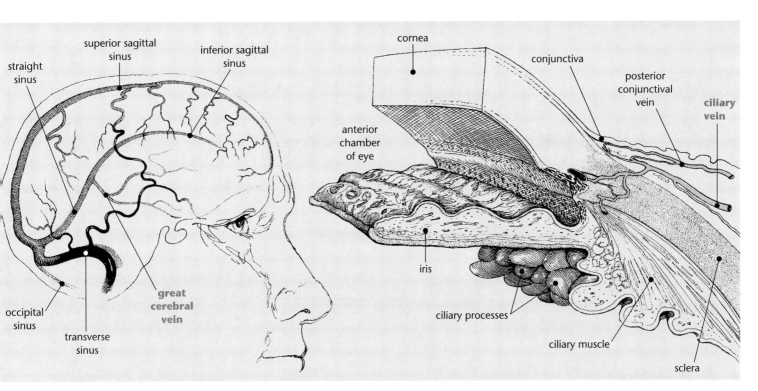

superior sagittal sinus

inferior sagittal sinus

straight sinus

cornea

conjunctiva

posterior conjunctival vein

ciliary vein

anterior chamber of eye

iris

occipital sinus

great cerebral vein

transverse sinus

ciliary processes

ciliary muscle

sclera

VEINS	LOCATION	DRAINS	EMPTIES INTO
cerebral v., great great v. of Galen *v. cerebri magna*	around back part of corpus callosum of brain	internal cerebral v.'s	anterior extremity of straight sinus, in union with inferior sagittal sinus
cerebral v.'s, inferior *vv. cerebri inferiores*	bottom of brain	inferior surface of cerebral hemispheres	*frontal lobe portion:* superior sagittal sinus; *temporal lobe portion:* cavernous, superior petrosal, and transverse sinuses: *occipital lobe portion:* straight sinus
cerebral v.'s, internal (two in number) v.'s of Galen deep cerebral v.'s *vv. cerebri internae*	from interventricular foramen they pass backward between the layers of the tela choroidea of the third ventricle	the deep parts of the cerebral hemispheres; thalamostriate, choroid, and basal v.'s	great cerebral v. in union with basal v.'s
cerebral v., superficial middle superficial Sylvian v. *v. cerebri media superficialis*	lateral surface of brain	lateral surface of cerebral hemispheres, corpus striatum, internal capsule	cavernous and sphenoparietal sinuses
cerebral v.'s, superior (8–12 in number) *vv. cerebri superiores*	sulci between gyri of brain	superior, lateral, and medial surfaces of cerebral hemispheres	superior sagittal sinus
cervical v., deep posterior deep cervical v. posterior vertebral v. *v. cervicalis profunda*	from suboccipital region it follows deep cervical artery down neck to level of first rib	plexus in suboccipital triangle, occipital v., deep muscles of back of neck, plexuses around spinal processes of cervical vertebrae	inferior part of vertebral v. or brachiocephalic v.
cervical v.'s, transverse *vv. transversae colli*	posterior triangle of neck	trapezius muscle and neighboring structures	subclavian v. or external jugular v.
choroid v. *v. choroidea*	lateral ventricle of brain	lateral ventricle, choroid plexus, corpus callosum	internal cerebral v.
ciliary v.'s (anterior and posterior) *vv. ciliares*	from outer surface of choroidal layer of eyeball they pass through sclera	ciliary body, scleral venous sinus, conjunctiva, iris, choroid	ophthalmic v.'s, superior and inferior
cochlear v.'s *v. cochleares*	from lamina spiralis and basilar membrane to base of modiolus	cochlea	labyrinthine v.
colic v, left *v. colica sinistra*	alongside descending colon	descending colon and left colic (splenic) flexure	inferior mesenteric v.
colic v., middle *v. colica media*	just behind transverse colon	transverse colon	superior mesenteric v.
colic v., right *v. colica dextra*	alongside ascending colon	ascending colon and right colic (hepatic) flexure	superior mesenteric v.
conjunctival v.'s *vv. conjunctivales*	eye	bulba conjunctiva	superior ophthalmic v.

V

VEINS	LOCATION	DRAINS	EMPTIES INTO
coronary v. gastric v. *v. gastrica dextra et sinistra*	see gastric vein		
coronary v., left	see cardiac vein, great		
coronary v., right	see cardiac vein, small		
coronary sinus (wide venous channel about 2.25 cm in length) *sinus coronarius*	posterior part of coronary sulcus (covered by muscular fibers from left atrium)	great, small, and middle cardiac v.'s, posterior v. of left ventricle, oblique v. of left atrium	right atrium between opening of inferior vena cava and atrioventricular aperture
cubital v., median *v. mediana cubiti*	passes obliquely across bend of elbow	cephalic v. below elbow	basilic v.
cystic v. *v. cystica*	in liver accompanying cystic duct	gallbladder	right branch of portal v.
digital v.'s, plantar *vv. digitales plantares*	plantar surface of toes	plexuses on the plantar surface of toes	unite to form four plantar metatarsal v.'s
diploic v., anterior temporal *v. diploica temporalis anterior*	middle layer (diploë) of frontal bone and parts of parietal bones of cranium	frontal bone and anterior part of parietal bones	sphenoparietal sinus and deep temporal v.
diploic v., frontal *v. diploica frontalis*	middle layer (diploë) of frontal bone of cranium	frontal bone	supraorbital v. and superior sagittal sinus
diploic v., occipital (largest of the four diploic veins) *v. diploica occipitalis*	middle layer (diploë) of occipital bone of cranium	parietal bone	occipital v. or transverse sinus
diploic v., posterior temporal *v. diploica temporalis posterior*	middle layer (diploë) of parietal bone of cranium	parietal bone	transverse sinus
dorsal v. of clitoris, deep (unpaired) dorsal v. of clitoris *v. dorsalis clitoridis profunda*	dorsal midline of clitoris; it passes under the pubic symphysis	body and glans of clitoris	primarily into the vesical venous plexus, internal pudendal v.
dorsal v.'s of clitoris, superficial *vv. dorsales clitoridis superficiales*	dorsal midline of clitoris	subcutaneous layers of clitoris, prepuce	external pudendal v.'s or femoral v.
dorsal v. of penis, deep (unpaired) dorsal v. of penis *v. dorsalis penis profunda*	dorsal midline of penis; it passes under the pubic symphysis	body and glans of penis	prostatic venous plexus, internal pudendal v.
dorsal v.'s of penis, superficial *vv. dorsales penis superficiales*	dorsal midline of penis	skin and subcutaneous layers of penis, prepuce	external pudendal v.'s or superficial epigastric v.
dorsal v.'s of tongue	see lingual veins, dorsal		
emissary v., condylar *v. emissaria condylaris*	through condylar canal of cranium	area of foramen magnum	deep veins of neck
emissary v.'s, foramen lacerum (two or three in number) *vv. emissariae foraminis lacerum*	through foramen lacerum of cranium	cavernous sinus	pterygoid plexus
emissary v., foramen of Vesalius *v. emissaria foraminis Vesalii*	through foramen of Vesalius (when present)	cavernous sinus	pterygoid plexus
emissary v., mastoid *v. emissaria mastoidea*	through mastoid foramen of cranium	transverse sinus	posterior auricular v. or occipital v.
emissary v., parietal *v. emissaria parietalis*	through parietal foramen of cranium	scalp	superior sagittal sinus
epigastric v., inferior deep epigastric v. *v. epigastrica inferior*	from area of umbilicus it descends to deep inguinal ring area	abdominal wall; *in male:* ductus deferens; *in female:* round ligament	external iliac v. about 1.25 cm proximal to inguinal ligament
epigastric v. superficial *v. epigastrica superficialis*	from umbilicus it runs downward and laterally toward inguinal ligament	cutaneous part of lower and medial part of abdominal wall	great saphenous v. or femoral v.
epigastric v.'s superior *v. epigastricae superiores*	from abdomen they ascend toward diaphragm	rectus muscle of abdomen; xiphoid process, diaphragm	internal thoracic v.'s
episcleral v.'s *vv. episclerales*	in sclera close to corneal margin	angle of eye, sclera, conjunctiva	anterior ciliary veins
esophageal v.'s (several in number) *vv. esophageae*	along the esophagus	esophagus	azygos, hemiazygos, left gastric, and left brachiocephalic v.'s

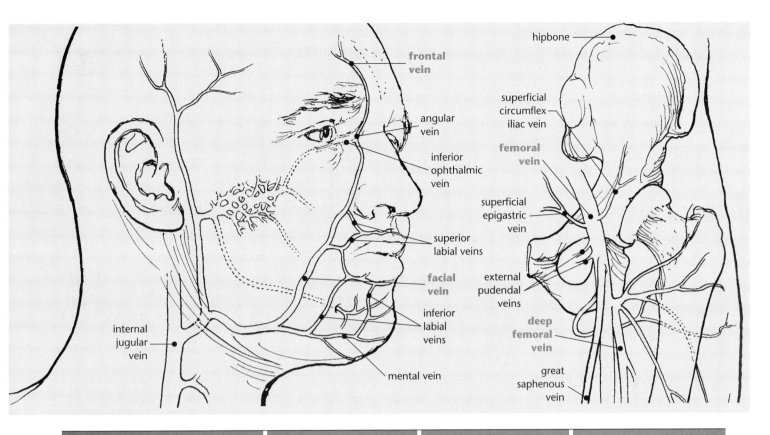

VEINS	LOCATION	DRAINS	EMPTIES INTO
ethmoidal v.'s *vv. ethmoidales*	ethmoidal sinuses	ethmoidal sinuses, frontal sinus, dura mater, walls and septum of nasal cavity	superior ophthalmic v.
facial v. anterior facial v. *v. facialis*	from medial angle of eye across face to neck, crossing lower margin of body of mandible	superficial structures of face; *tributaries include:* frontal, supraorbital, deep facial, superficial temporal, posterior auricular, occipital, and retromandibular v.'s	internal jugular v. or common facial v.
facial v., common	former term for the lower trunk of the facial v. (sometimes joined by retromandibular v.) which empties into the internal jugular v.			
facial v., deep *v. facialis profunda*	face, from infratemporal fossa, courses downward on maxilla just below zygomatic bone	pterygoid plexus; small tributaries from buccinator, zygomatic, and masseter muscles	facial v.
facial v., transverse *v. facialis transversa*	from cheek it passes backward (just below zygomatic arch) to front of ear	muscles and related structures near the zygoma	superficial temporal v.
femoral v. *v. femoralis*	proximal two-thirds of thigh up to inguinal ligament	popliteal v., great saphenous v., deep femoral v., muscular tributaries	external iliac v. at level of inguinal ligament
femoral v., deep profunda femoris v. *v. profunda femoris*	accompanies deep femoral artery	medial and lateral femoral circumflex v.'s; through muscular tributaries it anastomoses with popliteal v. distally and inferior gluteal v. proximally	femoral v.
femoral circumflex v.'s, lateral *vv. circumflexae femoris laterales*	winds around lateral side of upper femur	muscles of thigh, especially posterior muscles; lateral half of hip	femoral v. or deep femoral v.
femoral circumflex v.'s, medial *vv. circumflexae femoris mediales*	winds around medial side of upper femur	muscles of upper thigh, especially posterior muscles; hip joint	femoral v. or deep femoral v.
fibular v.'s	see peroneal v.'s			
frontal v. *v. frontalis*	from forehead to root of nose	plexus of forehead and scalp	facial v.
gastric v. coronary v. *v. gastrica*	from right to left along lesser curvature of stomach down peritoneum of lesser sac (omental bursa)	tributaries from both surfaces of stomach	portal vein
gastric v.'s, short (four or five in number) *vv. gastricae breves*	greater curvature of stomach, between fundus of stomach and spleen	fundus and left part of greater curvature of stomach	splenic v.

V

VEINS	LOCATION	DRAINS	EMPTIES INTO
gastroepiploic v., left *v. gastroepiploica sinistra*	from right to left along upper part of greater curvature of stomach	tributaries from ventral and dorsal surfaces of stomach and greater omentum	splenic v.
gastroepiploic v., right *v. gastroepiploica dextra*	from left to right along lower part of greater curvature of stomach	tributaries from greater omentum and parts of stomach	superior mesenteric v.
gluteal v.'s, inferior sciatic v.'s *vv. gluteae inferiores*	from the proximal part of posterior thigh they enter the pelvis through the greater sciatic foramen	skin and muscles of buttock and back of thigh; medial femoral circumflex and first perforating v.'s	internal iliac v.
gluteal v.'s, superior gluteal v.'s *vv. gluteae superiores*	from buttock through greater sciatic foramen to pelvis	tributaries from buttock, skin over sacrum	internal iliac v.
hemiazygos v. left azygos v. inferior minor azygos v. *v. hemiazygos*	in thorax, it ascends on left side of vertebral column to ninth thoracic vertebra before horizontally crossing over vertebral column to join the azygos v.	left ascending lumbar v.'s, caudal four or five intercostal v.'s, left subcostal v., esophageal and mediastinal v.'s	azygos v.
hemiazygos v., accessory superior minor azygos v. *v. hemiazygos accessoria*	descends on left side of vertebral column in thorax and usually crosses over vertebral column at eighth thoracic vertebra	fourth to seventh posterior intercostal v.'s, mediastinum, bronchus	azygos v. or hemiazygos v.
hemorrhoidal v.'s		see rectal veins	
hepatic v.'s *vv. hepaticae*	posterior surface of right, left, and caudate lobes of liver	substance of liver; central, intralobular, and sublobular v.'s	*upper group:* three large v.'s drain into the inferior vena cava below the diaphragm; *lower group:* several small v.'s drain into the inferior vena cava lower down
hypogastric v.		see iliac vein, internal	
ileocolic v. *v. ileocolica*	right iliac fossa	terminal ileum, appendix, cecum, lower part of ascending colon	superior mesenteric v.
iliac v., common *v. iliaca communis*	from sacroiliac articulation, ascends to fifth lumbar vertebra	internal and external iliac v.'s; iliolumbar and lateral sacral v.'s (in addition, left common iliac v. receives middle sacral v.)	unites with its member of opposite side to form inferior vena cava at level of fifth lumbar vertebra
iliac v., external *v. iliaca externa*	from under inguinal ligament, along brim and lesser pelvis, to sacroiliac articulation	lower limb and lower abdominal wall; inferior epigastric, deep circumflex and pubic v.'s	common iliac v. in union with internal iliac v.
iliac v., internal hypogastric v. *v. iliaca interna*	from greater sciatic foramen it passes upward to brim of pelvis	pelvic viscera, superior gluteal, inferior gluteal, internal pudendal, obturator, lateral sacral, middle sacral, dorsal veins of penis, vesical, uterine, vaginal	common iliac v. in union with external iliac v.
iliac circumflex v., deep *v. circumflexa ilium profunda*	inner aspect of ilium in lower abdomen	venae comitantes of deep iliac circumflex artery, internal oblique, transverse abdominal, iliac, psoas, and sartorius muscles	external iliac v. about 2 cm above inguinal ligament
innominate v.'s		see brachiocephalic veins	
intercostal v.'s, anterior (12 pairs) *vv. intercostales anteriores*	lower border of each rib	ribs, intercostal and pectoral muscles, breast, skin of chest	internal thoracic and musculophrenic v.'s
intercostal v., left highest left superior intercostal v. *v. intercostalis suprema sinistra*	first intercostal space	first left intercostal space	left brachiocephalic v. or vertebral v.
intercostal v., left superior *v. intercostalis superior sinistra*	from the upper left intercostal spaces, courses obliquely to area of left side of aortic arch	left second, third, and fourth intercostal v.'s	left brachiocephalic v. or accessory hemiazygos v.

V

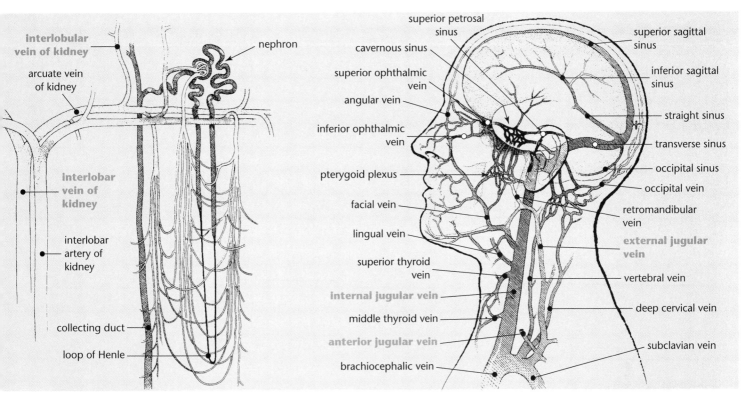

VEINS	LOCATION	DRAINS	EMPTIES INTO
intercostal v., right highest right superior intercostal v. *v. intercostalis suprema dextra*	posterior wall of upper thorax	first right intercostal space	azygos v.
intercostal v.'s, posterior *vv. intercostales posteriores*	one in each intercostal space	skin and muscles of back and spinal tributary from vertebral plexuses	*right side:* azygos v., right highest intercostal v.; *left side:* left brachiocephalic v., hemiazygos v.
intercostal v., right superior *v. intercostalis superior dextra*	posterior mediastinum	right second, third, and fourth intercostal spaces	azygos v.
interlobar v.'s of kidney *vv. interlobares renis*	between pyramids of kidney	arcuate v.'s, venous arcades of kidney	renal v.
interlobular v.'s of kidney *vv. interlobulares renis*	cortex of kidney	cortex of kidney; stellate, capsular, and perforating v.'s	arcuate v.'s of kidney
interlobular v.'s of liver *vv. interlobulares hepatis*	in substance of liver between lobules	central or intralobular and sublobular v.'s	hepatic v.'s
intervertebral v.'s *vv. intervertebrales*	intervertebral foramen	internal and external vertebral plexuses; v.'s from spinal cord	vertebral, intercostal, lumbar, and lateral sacral v.'s
intestinal v.'s (usually 10–15 in number) jejunal and ileal v.'s *vv. intestinales*	run parallel with superior mesenteric artery between layers of mesentery	walls of jejunum and ileum	superior mesenteric v.
jejunal and ileal v.'s	see intestinal veins		
jugular v., anterior (usually two in number) *v. jugularis anterior*	from near hyoid bone it passes down anterior part of neck	laryngeal and thyroid v.'s, neck muscles	external jugular or subclavian v.
jugular v., external *v. jugularis externa*	from substance of parotid gland it runs perpendicularly down neck	deep parts of face, exterior of cranium, retromandibular and posterior auricular v.'s	subclavian v., internal jugular v., or brachiocephalic v.
jugular v., internal *v. jugularis interna*	from jugular fossa it descends side of neck lateral to internal carotid artery, and then lateral to common carotid artery	brain, face, and neck; transverse sinus, inferior petrosal sinus, facial, lingual, pharyngeal, superior and middle thyroid and at times the occipital v.'s	brachiocephalic v., after union with subclavian v.
jugular v., posterior external *v. jugularis externa posteriores*	from occipital region down to middle third of external jugular	skin and superficial muscles of back of head and neck	external jugular v.
labial v.'s, anterior *vv. labiales anteriores*	vulva	anterior portion of labia majora; mons pubis	external pudendal v.

V

vein ■ vein

VEINS	LOCATION	DRAINS	EMPTIES INTO
labial v.'s, inferior *vv. labiales inferiores*	edge of lower lip to angle of mouth	labial glands, mucous membrane and muscles of lower lip	facial v. or submental v.
labial v.'s, posterior *vv. labiales posteriores*	vulva	posterior portion of labia majora; vestibule, labia minora	internal pudendal v.
labial v.'s, superior *vv. labiales superiores*	edge of upper lip between mucous membrane and muscle	upper lip, tributaries from nose, nasal septum	facial v.
labyrinthine v.'s internal auditory v.'s *vv. labyrinthi*	from inner ear through internal acoustic meatus	inner ear (utricle, saccule, semicircular canals, lamina spiralis, basilar membrane)	inferior petrosal sinus or sigmoid sinus
lacrimal v. *v. lacrimalis*	orbit	lacrimal glands, eyelids, conjunctiva	superior ophthalmic v.
laryngeal v., inferior *v. laryngea inferior*	dorsal part of larynx	muscles and mucous membrane of larynx	inferior thyroid v.
laryngeal v., superior *v. laryngea superior*	larynx	glands, mucous membrane, and muscles of larynx	superior thyroid v.
lingual v. *v. lingualis*	tongue	tongue by way of two or three tributaries, sublingual gland, tonsil, gums, epiglottis	internal jugular or lower part of facial v.
deep lingual v. ranine v. *profunda v. linguae*	tongue	tip and deep part of tongue	vena comitans of deep lingual artery
lingual v.'s, dorsal dorsal v.'s of tongue *vv. dorsales linguae*	tongue	posterior part of tongue	lingual v.
lumbar v.'s (usually four in number on each side) *vv. lumbales*	lumbar walls	dorsal tributaries from skin and muscles of loin and by abdominal tributaries from abdominal wall; vertebral plexus	first and second drain into ascending lumbar v.; third and fourth drain into inferior vena cava
lumbar v., ascending *v. lumbalis ascendens*	ventral to transverse process of lumbar vertebrae	sacral and lumbar v.'s	*right side:* azygos v. in union with subcostal v.; *left side:* hemiazygos v. in union with subcostal v.
maxillary v. *v. maxillaris*	short trunk between condyle of mandible and sphenomandibular ligament	pterygoid plexus, ear, sinuses, auditory tube, pterygoid and temporal muscles, temporomandibular joint	retromandibular v. in union with superficial temporal v.
median v. of forearm median antebrachial v. *v. mediana antebrachii*	from base of thumb to middle of palmar forearm	venous plexus on palmar surface of hand	basilic v. and/or cephalic v., or median cubital v.
mediastinal v.'s anterior mediastinal v.'s *vv. mediastinales*	mediastinum	areolar tissue and lymph nodes of anterior mediastinum; pericardium	azygos v., brachiocephalic v., or superior vena cava
meningeal v.'s, anterior *vv. meningeae anteriores*	over small wing of sphenoid bone in endosteal layer of dura mater	dura mater of anterior cranial fossa; cranium	ethmoidal and diploic v.'s, venous sinuses
meningeal v.'s, middle *vv. meningeae mediae*	from endosteal layer of dura mater it leaves cranium via foramen spinosum of sphenoid bone	dura mater, internal surface of cranium, trigeminal ganglion, tensor tympani muscle	pterygoid venous plexus or parietosphenoidal sinus
mesenteric v., inferior *v. mesenterica inferior*	from rectum it ascends under cover of peritoneum to level of pancreas	upper rectum; sigmoid and descending parts of colon	splenic v. or junction of splenic v. and superior mesenteric v.
mesenteric v., superior *v. mesenterica superior*	from right iliac fossa it ascends between two layers of mesentery to the level of pancreas	small intestine, cecum, appendix, and ascending and transverse parts of colon	portal v. in union with splenic v.
metacarpal v.'s, dorsal *vv. metacarpeae dorsales*	on dorsum of hand over distal two-thirds of metacarpus	dorsal metacarpal region	dorsal venous rete of hand
metacarpal v.'s, palmar *vv. metacarpeae palmares*	palmar surface of hand	palmar metacarpal region	deep palmar venous arch
metatarsal v.'s, dorsal dorsal interosseous v.'s of foot *vv. metatarseae dorsales*	run proximally in metatarsal spaces of dorsal surface of foot	dorsal digital v.'s at clefts of toes; metatarsal bones and neighboring muscles	dorsal venous arch of foot
metatarsal v.'s, plantar *vv. metatarseae plantares*	between metatarsal bones of plantar surface of foot	plantar digital v.'s at clefts of toes; metatarsal bones and neighboring muscles	deep plantar venous arch of foot

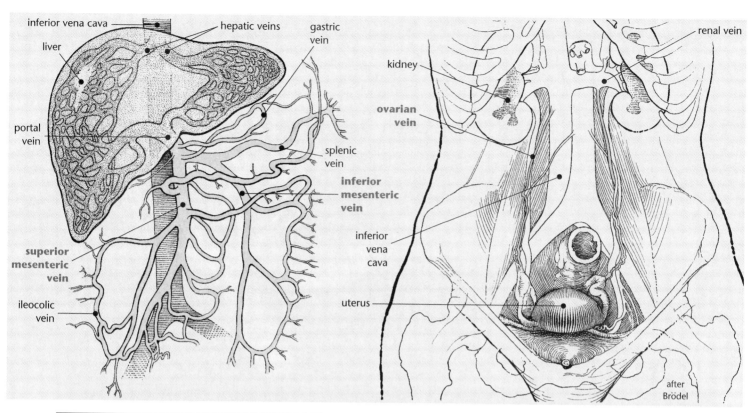

inferior vena cava — hepatic veins — gastric vein

liver

portal vein

splenic vein

inferior mesenteric vein

superior mesenteric vein

ileocolic vein

kidney

ovarian vein

inferior vena cava

uterus

renal vein

after Brödel

VEINS	LOCATION	DRAINS	EMPTIES INTO
musculophrenic v.'s *vv. musculophrenicae*	from diaphragm, along inner surface of costal cage at attachment of diaphragm, to sixth costal cartilage	diaphragm and lower intercostal spaces, abdominal wall	internal thoracic v.
nasal v.'s, external (several in number) *vv. nasales externae*	from nose extending upward	external aspect of nose	angular and facial v.'s
nasofrontal v. *v. nasofrontalis*	anterior medial part of orbit	supraorbital and angular v.'s	superior ophthalmic v.
oblique v. of left atrium *v. obliqua atrii sinistri*	posterior wall of left atrium of heart	heart wall	coronary sinus
obturator v. *v. obturatoria*	from proximal portion of adductor region of thigh to pelvis through obturator foramen	hip joint and regional muscles	internal iliac v., sometimes the inferior epigastric or common iliac v.
occipital v. *v. occipitalis*	from back part of scalp it passes to suboccipital triangle of neck	plexus on posterior part of head; tributaries from posterior auricular and superficial temporal v.'s; parietal emissary, mastoid emissary, and occipital diploic v.'s	deep cervical v. and vertebral v., occasionally the internal jugular v.
ophthalmic v., inferior *v. ophthalmica inferior*	from floor of orbit it passes posteriorly through superior orbital fissure	lower eyelid, lacrimal sac, muscles of eyeball	cavernous sinus or superior ophthalmic v.
ophthalmic v., superior *v. ophthalmica superior*	from inner angle of orbit, through superior orbital fissure into cavernous sinus	eyeball, eye muscles, and eyelid	cavernous sinus
ovarian v.'s *vv. ovaricae*	in broad ligament near ovary and uterine tube	pampiniform plexus of broad ligament, ovary, uterus	*right side:* inferior vena cava; *left side:* left renal v.
palatine v., external *v. palatina externa*	palate region	tonsils and soft palate, pharyngeal wall	pterygoid and tonsillar plexuses; facial v.
palpebral v.'s, inferior *vv. palpebrales inferiores*	from lower eyelid, downward over cheek	lower eyelid, conjunctiva, nasolacrimal duct	facial v. or angular v.
palpebral v.'s, superior *vv. palpebrales superiores*	upper eyelid	upper eyelid, conjunctiva	angular v. or superior ophthalmic v.
pancreatic v.'s *vv. pancreaticae*	at pancreas	tributaries from body and tail of pancreas	splenic v.
pancreaticoduodenal v.'s *vv. pancreaticoduodenales*	head of pancreas and proximal part of duodenum	pancreas and duodenum	upper part of superior mesenteric v., portal v.

V

vein ■ vein

Top left (liver/portal system): liver, inferior vena cava, hepatic veins, splenic vein, inferior mesenteric vein, superior mesenteric vein, ileocolic vein

Top middle (leg veins): external iliac vein, deep femoral vein, femoral vein, popliteal vein, femur, patella, posterior tibial vein

Top right (heart): left pulmonary veins, left atrium, coronary sinus, superior vena cava, right atrium, great cardiac vein, small cardiac vein, inferior vena cava, posterior vein of left ventricle, middle cardiac vein, inferoposterior view of heart

VEINS	LOCATION	DRAINS	EMPTIES INTO
paraumbilical v.'s parumbilical v.'s Sappey's v.'s *vv. paraumbilicales*	from umbilical area they pass along round ligament to liver and medial umbilical ligament to bladder	cutaneous v.'s about the umbilicus	accessory portal v.'s in liver
parotid v.'s *vv. parotideae*	parotid gland	part of parotid gland and overlying skin	facial v. or retromandibular v.
perforating v.'s *vv. perforantes*	perforate great adductor muscle to reach back of thigh	thigh muscles, especially hamstrings	deep femoral v.
pericardiac v.'s (several in number) *vv. pericardiaceae*	membranous capsule of heart (pericardium)	pericardium	brachiocephalic v. superior vena cava, or azygos v.
pericardiacophrenic v.'s superior phrenic v.'s *vv. pericardiacophrenicae*	parallel to phrenic nerve between pleura and pericardium	diaphragm; tributaries from pericardium; pleura	brachiocephalic v., superior vena cava, or internal thoracic v.
peroneal v.'s fibular v.'s *vv. peroneae*	from lateral side of heel up back of leg just below knee	calcaneus, leg muscles, tibiofibular syndesmosis	posterior tibal v. after uniting with popliteal v.
petrosal sinus, inferior *sinus petrosus inferior*	inferior petrosal sulcus	cavernous sinus, internal auditory v.'s, v.'s from medulla oblongata, pons, and inferior surface of cerebellum	bulb of internal jugular v.
petrosal sinus, superior *sinus petrosus superior*	superior petrosal sulcus in head	cavernous sinus	transverse sinus or sigmoid sinus
pharyngeal v.'s (several in number) *vv. pharyngeae*	outer surface of pharynx	posterior meningeal v.'s and v. of the pterygoid canal; pharyngeal plexus	internal jugular v., occasionally the facial v.
phrenic v.'s, inferior *vv. phrenicae inferior*	undersurface of diaphragm	substance of diaphragm	*right side:* inferior vena cava; *left side:* left suprarenal v. (often a second vein on left side enters inferior vena cava)
popliteal v. *v. poplitea*	from lower border of popliteal muscle, through popliteal fossa to adductor hiatus	anterior and posterior tibial v.'s, skin and muscles of thigh and calf	femoral v. at adductor hiatus
portal v. (about 8 cm in length) *v. portae*	in abdomen behind neck of pancreas at level of second lumbar vertebra	superior mesenteric, splenic, gastric, pyloric, cystic, and paraumbilical v.'s	right and left terminal branches in liver
posterior v. of left ventricle *v. posterior ventriculi sinistri*	from apex of heart it travels parallel to posterior interventricular sulcus	diaphragmatic surface of left ventricle	coronary sinus of great cardiac v.
prepyloric v. v. of Mayo *v. prepylorica*	pyloric end of stomach	pylorus	right gastic v.

V

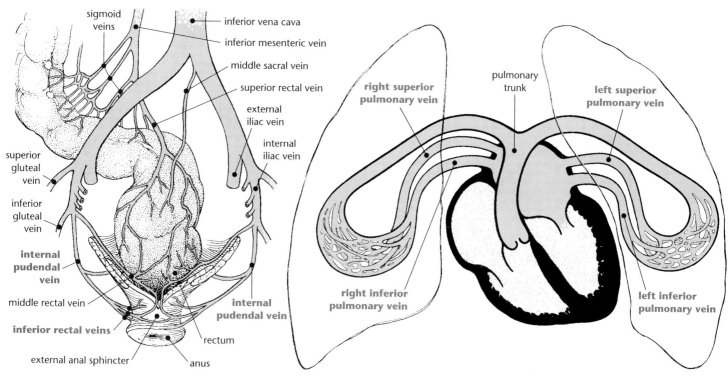

Diagram labels (left illustration):

sigmoid veins
inferior vena cava
inferior mesenteric vein
middle sacral vein
superior rectal vein
external iliac vein
internal iliac vein
superior gluteal vein
inferior gluteal vein
internal pudendal vein
middle rectal vein
internal pudendal vein
inferior rectal veins
external anal sphincter
rectum
anus

Diagram labels (right illustration):

right superior pulmonary vein
pulmonary trunk
left superior pulmonary vein
right inferior pulmonary vein
left inferior pulmonary vein

VEINS	LOCATION	DRAINS	EMPTIES INTO
profunda femoris v.	see femoral vein, deep		
profunda linguae v.	see lingual vein, deep		
v. of pterygoid canal Vidian v. *v. canalis pterygoidel*	from ear and throat through pterygoid canal	sphenoid sinus	pterygoid plexus or cavernous sinus
pterygoid plexus *plexus pterygoldeus*	infratemporal fossa	*tributaries from:* inferior alveolar, middle, meningeal, deep temporal, masseter, buccal, posterior superior alveolar, pharyngeal, descending palatine, infraorbital, pterygoid canal, and sphenopalatine v.'s	maxillary v.
pubic v. *v. pubis*	from dorsum of penis through obturator foramen to pelvis	pubic area	external iliac v.
pudendal v.'s, external external pudic v.'s *vv. pudendae externae*	from lower abdomen and genitalia to upper thigh	skin of lower part of abdomen; *in male:* anterior scrotal and superficial dorsal v.'s of penis; *in female:* anterior labial and superficial dorsal v.'s of clitoris	great saphenous v. or femoral v.
pudendal v.'s, internal internal pudic v.'s *vv. pudendae internae*	from perineum and genitalia to pelvis through greater sciatic foramen	perineum and genitalia	internal iliac v. (distal part)
pulmonary v., left inferior *v. pulmonalis inferior sinistra*	from left lung to heart	left lower lobe	left atrium of heart
pulmonary v., left superior *v. pulmonalis superior sinistra*	from left lung to heart	left upper lobe	left atrium of heart
pulmonary v., right inferior *v. pulmonalis inferior dextra*	from right lung to heart	right lower lobe	left atrium of heart
pulmonary v., right superior *v. pulmonalis superior dextra*	from right lung to heart	right upper and middle lobe	left atrium of heart
pyloric v. *v. pylorus*	along pyloric portion of lesser curvature of stomach	pylorus and lesser omentum	portal v.
radial v.'s *vv. radiales*	from hand, winds around lateral side of carpus up forearm to front of elbow	dorsal metacarpal v.'s, muscles of forearm, wrist, and hand; radius, ulna, elbow joint	brachial v.'s after uniting with ulnar v.'s
ranine v.	see lingual vein, deep		
rectal v.'s inferior inferior hemorrhoidal v.'s *vv. rectales inferiores*	near anal canal and rectum	lower part of external rectal plexus and anal canal	internal pudendal v.

V

VEINS	LOCATION	DRAINS	EMPTIES INTO
rectal v., middle middle hemorrhoidal v. *v. rectalis media*	middle of rectum in lesser pelvis	rectal plexus; tributaries from bladder, prostate gland, and seminal vesicle	internal iliac v. or inferior gluteal v.
rectal v.'s, superior superior hemorrhoidal v.'s *vv. rectales superiores*	upper rectum to brim of pelvis	upper part of rectal plexus	inferior mesenteric v.
renal v.'s *vv. renales*	at right angle to hilum of kidneys	kidneys; testicular, inferior phrenic, and suprarenal v.'s	inferior vena cava (right renal v. opens into inferior vena cava at a slightly lower level than left)
retromandibular v. posterior facial v. *v. retromandibularis*	from substance of parotid gland it passes alongside ramus of lower jaw	superficial temporal, maxillary, and tributaries from parotid gland and masseter muscle	external jugular v. in union with posterior auricular v; facial v.
sacral v.'s, lateral *vv. sacrales laterales*	anterior surface of sacrum	skin and muscles of dorsum of sacrum and coccyx	internal iliac v. or superior gluteal v.'s
sacral v., middle *v. sacralis media*	front of sacrum	region of posterior surface of rectum	left common iliac v.
saphenous v., accessory *v. saphena accessoria*	medial and posterior parts of thigh	inner and posterior parts of superficial thigh	great saphenous v.
saphenous v., great (longest vein in body) long saphenous v. *v. saphena magna*	from medial aspect of foot to 3 cm below inguinal ligament	tributaries from sole of foot; small saphenous v., anterior and posterior tibial v.'s, accessory saphenous v., superficial epigastric v., superficial iliac circumflex v., superficial external pudendal v.	femoral v.
saphenous v., small short saphenous v. *v. saphena parva*	from lateral ankle to middle of back of leg to 5 cm above knee joint	lateral marginal v., deep v.'s of dorsum of foot, large tributaries from back of leg	popliteal v. or great saphenous v.
scrotal v.'s, anterior *vv. scrotales anteriores*	scrotum	front part of scrotum	external pudendal v.
scrotal v.'s, posterior *vv. scrotales posteriores*	scrotum	back part of scrotum	vesical venous plexus or internal pudendal veins
sigmoid v.'s (several in number) *vv. sigmoideae*	lower left side of colon	sigmoid colon and descending colon	inferior mesenteric v.
spinal v.'s *vv. spinales*	in pia mater of spinal cord where it forms a tortuous venous plexus	spinal cord and pia mater	internal vertebral venous plexus
spiral v. of modiolus *v. spiralis modioli*	modiolus of cochlea	cochlea	labyrinthine v.'s
splenic v. lienal v. *v. lienalis*	from hilum of spleen to vicinity of neck of pancreas	short gastric, left gastroepiploic, pancreatic, and inferior mesenteric v.'s	portal v.
stellate v.'s of kidney *vv. stellatae renis*	cortex of kidney near capsule	superficial part of cortex of kidney	interlobular v.'s of kidney
sternocleidomastoid v. sternomastoid v. *v. sternocleidomastoidea*	neck	sternocleidomastoid, omohyoid, sternohyoid, sternothyroid, and platysma muscles, skin of neck	internal jugular v.
striate v.'s, inferior *vv. thalamostriatae inferiores*	corpus striatum	anterior perforated substance of cerebrum	basal v.
stylomastoid v. *v. stylomastoidea*	descends vertically from stylomastoid foramen	mastoid cells, middle ear chamber, semicircular canals	retromandibular v. or posterior auricular v.
subclavian v. *v. subclavia*	from outer border of first rib to sternal end of clavicle	continues from axillary v.; external jugular v., anterior jugular v. (occasionally)	joined by internal jugular to form brachiocephalic v.
subcostal v. *v. subcostalis*	in abdominal wall along caudal border of 12th rib	upper abdominal wall below 12th rib	*right side:* azygos v.; *left side:* hemiazygos v.
subcutaneous v.'s of abdomen *vv. subcutaneae obdominis*	abdominal wall	superficial layers of abdominal wall	thoracoepigastric, superficial epigastric, or deep v.'s of abdominal wall
sublingual v. *v. sublingualis*	below tongue	sublingual gland, mylohyoid and neighboring muscles, mucous membranes of mouth and gums, alveolar process of mandible	lingual v. or facial v.

V

vein ■ vein

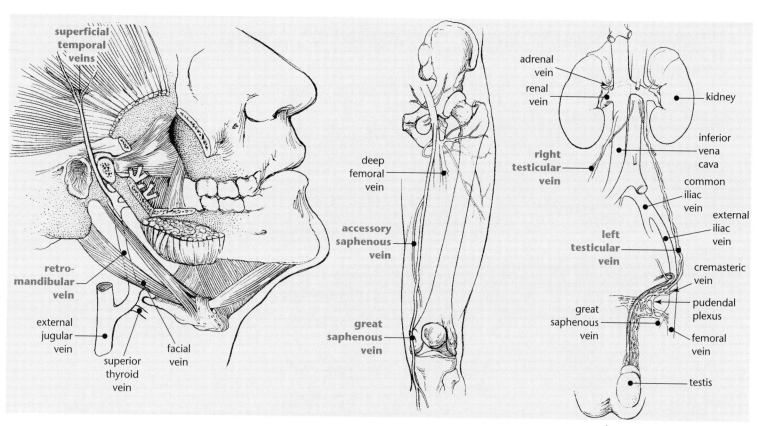

VEINS	LOCATION	DRAINS	EMPTIES INTO
submental v. *v. submentalis*	below margin of mandible	submandibular gland; mylo-hyoid, digastric, and platys-ma muscles	facial v.
supraorbital v. *v. supraorbitalis*	courses medially and down-ward to medial angle of eye	frontal muscle, frontal diploic v., superior rectus and levator palpebral muscles, frontal sinus	angular v. (beginning of facial v.), in union with supra-trochlear v.
suprarenal v., left *v. suprarenalis sinistra*	hilium of left adrenal gland	left adrenal gland	left renal v. or left inferior phrenic v.
suprarenal v., right *v. suprarenalis dextra*	hilium of right adrenal gland	right adrenal gland	inferior vena cava
suprascapular v. transverse scapular v. *v. suprascapularis*	from posterior surface of scapula it passes through scapular notch, runs parallel with clavicle and then crosses over brachial plexus and subclavian artery	acromioclavicular and shoul-der joints, scapula, clavicle, and neighboring muscles and skin	external jugular v. or subcla-vian v.
supratrochlear v.'s (usually two in number) *vv. supratrochleares*	front and top of head; course to medial angle of orbit	venous plexus of forehead, scalp of medial forehead, dorsum of nose	in union with angular v.
temporal v.'s, deep *vv. temorales profundae*	from side of head, course down behind zygomatic arch	deep areas of temporal mus-cle	pterygoid venous plexus
temporal v., middle *v. temporalis media*	from lateral angle of orbit, it passes to side of ear	temporal muscle; zygomati-coorbital v.	retromandibular v. or superficial and deep temporal v.'s
temporal v.'s, superficial *vv. temporales superficiales*	from scalp on side of head down to parotid gland in front of ear	plexus on side of head; transverse facial, anterior auricular, and middle tempo-ral v.'s	retromandibular v. in union with maxillary v.
temporomandibular v.'s *vv. temporomandibulares*	temporomandibular joint (TMJ)	area surrounding temporo-mandibular joint; tympanic v.'s	retromandibular v. or maxil-lary v.
testicular v., left left spermatic v. *v. testicularis sinistra*	from testis it ascends along spermatic cord through deep inguinal canal into abdomen	testis, epididymis, ureter, cremaster muscle	left renal v.
testicular v., right right spermatic v. *v. testicularis dextra*	from testis it ascends along spermatic cord through deep inguinal canal into abdomen	testis, epididymis, ureter, cremaster muscle	inferior vena cava
thalamostriate v. *v. thalamostriata superior*	deep part of brain	corpus striatum, thalamus, and corpus callosum	internal cerebral v.

V

vein ■ vein

VEINS	LOCATION	DRAINS	EMPTIES INTO
thoracic v., internal internal mammary v. *v. thoracica interna*	thorax	superior phrenic, superior epigastric, musculophrenic, perforating, anterior intercostal, sternal, thymic, mediastinal, and pericardiacophrenic v.'s	brachiocephalic v.
thoracic v., lateral long thoracic v. *v. thoracica lateralis*	lateral thoracic wall	lateral thoracic wall; mammary gland; axillary lymph nodes; costoaxillary v.'s	axillary v.
thoracoacromial v.'s acromiothoracic v.'s *vv. thoracoacromiales*	top of shoulder	acromion, coracoid process, sternoclavicular joint, tributaries from deltoid, subclavius, pectoralis major and minor muscles	subclavian v. or axillary v.
thoracoepigastric v. *v. thoracoepigastrica*	anterior and lateral aspect of trunk (in subcutaneous tissue)	skin and subcutaneous tissue of anterolateral aspect of trunk	*superiorly:* lateral thoracic v.; *inferiorly:* superficial epigastric v.
thymic v.'s *vv. thymicae*	thymus gland	substance of thymus gland	left brachiocephalic and thyroid v.'s
thyroid v.'s, inferior (two to four in number) *vv. thyroideae inferiores*	lower neck, anterior to fifth, sixth, and seventh tracheal rings	venous plexus of thyroid gland; esophageal, tracheal, and inferior laryngeal v.'s	brachiocephalic v.'s (occasionally just the left brachiocephalic v.)
thyroid v.'s, middle *vv. thyroideae mediae*	from thyroid gland they pass laterally over common carotid artery	lower part of thyroid gland; tributaries from trachea and larynx	lower part of internal jugular v. just below level of cricoid cartilage
thyroid v.'s, superior *v. thyroideae superiores*	from thyroid gland it passes up toward head	superior part of thyroid gland; superior laryngeal and cricothyroid v.'s	upper part of internal jugular v.
tibial v.'s, anterior *vv. tibiales anteriores*	from foot and ankle joint up front of leg between tibia and fibula about 5 cm below knee joint	venae comitantes of dorsal artery of foot; muscles and bones of anterior leg	popliteal v. in union with posterior tibial v.
tibial v.'s, posterior (usually two in number) *vv. tibiales posteriores*	from sole of foot to tibial side of leg where it ascends obliquely to back of leg just below bend of knee	muscles and bones of posterior leg	popliteal v. in union with anterior tibial v.
tracheal v.'s (several in number) *vv. tracheales*	trachea	substance of trachea	thyroid venous plexus, brachiocephalic v., or superior vena cava
v. of tympanic cavity *v. cavum tympani*	middle ear chamber	middle ear chamber (cavity), tympanic membrane, mastoid cells, auditory tube	pterygoid plexus and superior petrosal sinus
v.'s of tympanic membrane *vv. tympanicae membranae*	tympanic membrane (eardrum)	tympanic membrane	v.'s of middle ear chamber and external ear canal
ulnar v.'s *vv. ulnares*	from hand it runs along medial border of wrist, up forearm to bend of elbow	deep palmar venous arches; superficial v.'s at wrist; palmar and dorsal interosseous v.'s	brachial v.'s in union with radial v.'s
umbilical v. *v. umbilicalis*	accompanying umbilical cord	placenta	fetus
uterine v.'s *vv. uterinae*	sides and superior angles of uterus between two layers of broad ligament	uterine plexus	internal iliac v.
vaginal v.'s *vv. vaginales*	sides of vagina	vaginal plexus	internal iliac v., occasionally uterine v.
vena cava, inferior (largest vein in body) *vena cava inferior*	from level of fifth lumbar vertebra it ascends along vertebral column to right side of heart	both common iliac v.'s; lumbar, renal, testicular (male), ovarian (female), suprarenal, inferior phrenic, and hepatic v.'s	lower part of right atrium of heart
vena cava, superior (second largest vein in body) *vena cava superior*	from close behind sternum to upper portion of right side of heart	cranial half to body via brachiocephalic v.'s	upper part of right atrium
vertebral v. *v. vertebralis*	from suboccipital triangle through transverse foramina of first six cervical vertebrae	suboccipital venous plexus, occipital v., internal and external vertebral venous plexuses, anterior cerebral v., deep cervical v.'s, first intercostal v. (occasionally)	brachiocephalic v.

V

vein ■ vein

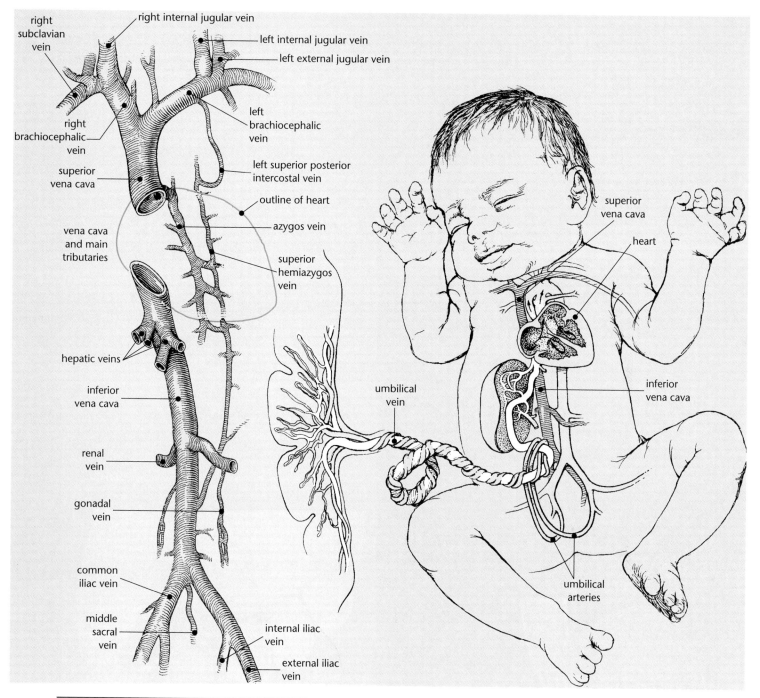

right subclavian vein

right internal jugular vein

left internal jugular vein

left external jugular vein

right brachiocephalic vein

left brachiocephalic vein

superior vena cava

left superior posterior intercostal vein

vena cava and main tributaries

outline of heart

azygos vein

superior hemiazygos vein

hepatic veins

inferior vena cava

renal vein

gonadal vein

common iliac vein

middle sacral vein

internal iliac vein

external iliac vein

superior vena cava

heart

umbilical vein

inferior vena cava

umbilical arteries

VEINS	LOCATION	DRAINS	EMTPIES INTO
vertebral v., accessory *v. vertebralis accessoria*	when present it accompanies vertebral vein and emerges through transverse foramen of seventh cervical vertebra	venous plexus of vertebral artery, suboccipital venous plexus	brachiocephalic v.
vertebral v., anterior ascending cervical v. *v. vertebralis anterior*	from transverse processes of cervical vertebrae it descends between anterior scalene and longus capitis muscles (it accompanies ascending cervical artery)	plexus around transverse processes of cervical vertebrae; muscles of neck	terminal part of vertebral v.
vesical v.'s *vv. vesicales*	back part of bladder	vesical venous plexus	internal iliac v.
vestibular v.'s *vv. vestibulares*	vestibule of inner ear	utricle, saccule, semicircular ducts	labyrinthine v.'s and v.'s of vestibular aqueduct
vorticose v.'s (usually four or five in number) vortex v.'s *vv. vorticosae*	eyeball, midway between cribosa and sclerocorneal junction	choroid layer of eyeball	superior or inferior ophthalmic v.'s

V

vein ■ vein

vela (ve'lah) Plural of velum.

velamentous (vel-ah-men'tus) Resembling a curtain or veil; applied to certain body structures and membranes.

vellus (vel'us) Fine, soft, nonpigmented downy hair that replaces the lanugo hair (primary hair); it begins to appear in the early months of postnatal life. Also called vellus hair; secondary hair.

velopharyngeal (vel-o-fah-rin'je-al) Relating to the soft palate and the back of the nasal and oral cavities (the pharynx).

velum (ve'lum), pl. ve'la **1.** Any structure resembling a curtain. **2.** Any covering membrane.

    inferior medullary v. A thin sheet of white matter forming part of the roof of the fourth ventricle of the brain, posteriorly.

    v. palatinum See soft palate, under palate.

    superior medullary v. A thin layer of white matter between the cerebellar peduncles, forming part of the roof of the fourth ventricle of the brain anteriorly.

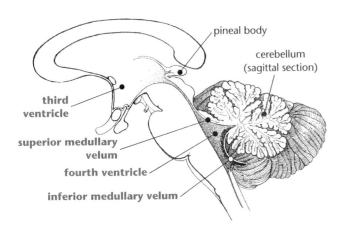

pineal body
cerebellum (sagittal section)
third ventricle
superior medullary velum
fourth ventricle
inferior medullary velum

vena (ve'nah), pl. ve'nae Latin for vein.

    v. cava See table of veins.

    venae comitantes Two or more veins (usually two) accompanying a corresponding artery.

venation (ve-na'shun) The distribution of veins.

venectomy (ve-nek'to-me) See phlebectomy.

veneer (vĕ-nēr') In dentistry, a facing made of resin or porcelain and applied to a crown or pontic for esthetic purposes.

venenation (ven-ĕ-na'shun) Poisoning.

veneniferous (ven-ĕ-nif'er-us) Conveying poison.

venenous (ven'ĕ-nus) Poisonous.

venereal (ve-ne're-al) Relating to or resulting from sexual contact (e.g., a sexually transmitted disease).

venereology (ve-ne-re-ol'o-je) The study of venereal disease.

venesection (ven-ĕ-sek'shun) See phlebotomy.

venipuncture (ven'ĭ-punk-tūr) The puncture of a vein through the skin to collect blood, instill a medication, initiate an infusion of fluid, or inject a diagnostic material.

veno-, veni- Combining forms meaning veins.

venoclysis (ve-nok'lĭ-sis) See phleboclysis.

venogram (ve'no-gram) An x-ray picture of a vein or veins made after intravenous injection of a radiopaque substance.

venography (ve-nog'rah-fe) The making of a venogram.

venom (ven'um) A poisonous animal secretion produced in specialized glands and delivered through any of various specialized structures (e.g., fangs, spines, stingers); effects on humans range from mild skin irritations to severe allergic reactions and death.

venomotor (ve-no-mo'tor) Causing dilatation or constriction of veins.

venopressor (ve-no-pres'or) An agent that causes constriction of veins, thereby increasing venous pressure.

venostasis (ve-no-sta'sis) See phlebostasis.

venotomy (ve-not'o-me) See phlebotomy.

venous (ve'nus) Relating to a vein.

venovenostomy (ve-no-ve-nos'to-me) Surgical union of two veins.

ventilate (ven'tĭ-lāt) To aerate, and thereby oxygenate, the blood in the minute blood vessels of the lungs.

ventilation (ven-tĭ-la'shun) The physiologic process through which air in the lungs is exchanged with atmospheric air.

    alveolar v. The amount of inspired gas per minute entering the tiny air sacs in the lungs.

    artificial v. The maintenance of respiratory movements by manual or mechanical means. Also called artificial respiration.

    assisted v. Respiration in which the patient's own breathing effort initiates the cycle but the volume of air entering the lungs is increased by mechanical means. Also called assisted respiration.

    continuous positive pressure v. (CPPV) Administration of air or a mixture of gases to the lungs under continuously positive pressure applied by a life-supporting machine (ventilator). The pressure in the airways fluctuates to allow air or gases to flow in and out of the lungs. Also called continuous positive pressure breathing; positive pressure respiration.

    controlled v. Artificial ventilation requiring no effort from the patient; each inspiration is initiated by a timing mechanism of the respirator. Also called controlled respiration.

    controlled mechanical v. (CMV) (a) See continuous positive pressure ventilation. (b) See intermittent positive pressure ventilation.

    high-frequency v. A variety of ventilatory methods and devices designed to provide ventilation at rapid rates and low tidal volumes, hence reducing the risk of causing injury by pressure changes (barotrauma).

    intermittent positive pressure v. (IPPV) Administration of air or a mixture of gases to the lungs under intermittent positive pressure applied by a life-supporting machine (ventilator) during each inspiration. Also called intermittent positive pressure breathing; positive pressure respiration.

    maximum voluntary v. The maximum volume of air that a person can voluntarily breathe as deeply and as quickly as possible in a given period of time (e.g., 12 seconds). Also called maximum breathing capacity (MBC).

    mechanical v. Ventilation accomplished by automatically cycling devices.

    negative pressure v. Mechanical assistance in exhaling (expiration) by applying negative pressure, e.g., with an iron lung (Drinker respirator).

ventilator (ven-tĭ-la'tor) Any device used to provide ventilation.

    babybird v. An infant ventilator (one of the earliest) that requires an adjunct monitor and an alarm system.

    tank v. See Drinker respirator, under respirator.

ventrad (ven'trad) Toward the ventral or anterior aspect of the body.

ventral (ven'tral) Relating to the ventral or anterior aspect of the body.

ventricle (ven'trĭ-kl) A cavity, especially within the heart or the brain.

    cerebral v.'s The fluid-filled cavities within the brain (two lateral, the third and the fourth). See also lateral ventricle; third ventricle; fourth ventricle.

    fourth v. A cavity in the brain filled with cerebrospinal fluid (CSF); it lies in front of the cerebellum and behind the pons and upper half of the medulla oblongata; the cavity is continuous with the third ventricle above, by way of the cerebral aqueduct, and directly with the central canal of the spinal cord below; it also communicates with the subarachnoid space through its lateral and median openings (foramina).

    v.'s of the heart The two lower and larger chambers of the heart. See also right ventricle; left ventricle.

    lateral v. The relatively large, irregular cavity located within each hemisphere of the brain and filled with cerebrospinal fluid (CSF); consists of a central part with anterior, posterior, and inferior horns contained within the frontal, occipital, and temporal lobes; it is continuous with the third ventricle below by way of the interventricular foramen; the two lateral ventricles are separated from each other by the septum pellucidum.

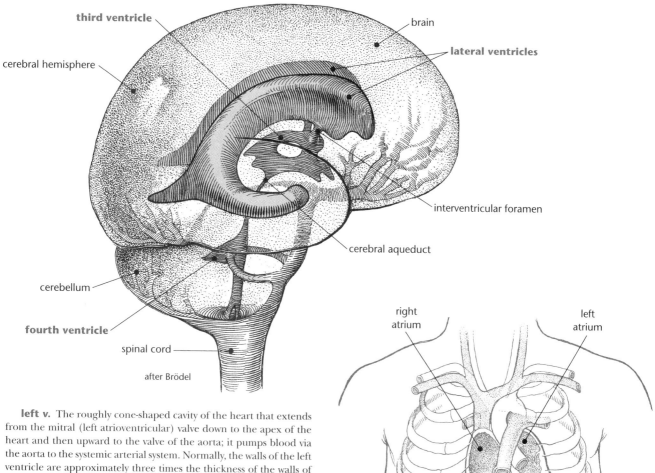

third ventricle

brain

lateral ventricles

cerebral hemisphere

interventricular foramen

cerebral aqueduct

cerebellum

fourth ventricle

spinal cord

after Brödel

right atrium

left atrium

right ventricle

left ventricle

left v. The roughly cone-shaped cavity of the heart that extends from the mitral (left atrioventricular) valve down to the apex of the heart and then upward to the valve of the aorta; it pumps blood via the aorta to the systemic arterial system. Normally, the walls of the left ventricle are approximately three times the thickness of the walls of the right ventricle.

right v. The cavity of the heart into which blood enters via the tricuspid (right atrioventricular) valve and from which blood exits via the valve of the pulmonary trunk; it pumps blood via the pulmonary trunk to the lungs.

third v. A narrow median cleft in the brain between two thalami and hypothalamus; it is filled with cerebrospinal fluid (CSF) and communicates with the two lateral ventricles above, through the interventricular openings (foramina), and with the fourth ventricle below through the narrow cerebral aqueduct.

ventricular (ven-trik′u-lar) Relating to any ventricle.

ventriculitis (ven-trik-u-li′tis) Inflammation of the lining of a cerebral ventricle.

ventriculocisternostomy (ven-trik-u-lo-sis-ter-nos′to-me) Surgical creation of an opening between a cerebral ventricle and the cisterna magna.

ventriculography (ven-trik-u-log′rah-fe) X-ray visualization of the ventricles of the brain following injection of a gas or a radiopaque substance.

ventriculoplasty (ven-trik′u-lo-plas-te) Surgical repair of a defect in a ventricle of the heart.

ventriculopuncture (ven-trik′u-lo-punk′tur) Needle perforation of a cerebral ventricle.

ventriculostomy (ven-trik-u-los′to-me) Surgical creation of an opening into a ventricle of the brain (e.g., in the treatment of hydrocephalus).

ventriculotomy (ven-trik-u-lot′o-me) A surgical cut into a ventricle.

ventriculus (ven-trik′u-lus) Latin for ventricle.

venula (ven′u-lah), pl. ven′ulae Latin for venule.

venulae rectae The numerous ascending venules that drain the medullary pyramids of the kidney and empty into arcuate veins.

venulae stellatae The star-shaped groups of venules in the kidney cortex, near the capsule.

venule (ven′ūl) A minute vein, usually less than 100 μm in diameter.

high endothelial v.'s See postcapillary venules.

postcapillary v.'s Venules located in the cortex of lymph nodes and gut-associated lymphoid tissue; their walls are composed of elongated endothelial cells, which allow passage of lymphocytes from the blood to the lymph. Also called high endothelial venules.

verapamil (ver-ap′ah-mil) A calcium channel-blocking compound used in the treatment of angina pectoris, especially variant angina, and hypertension. Possible adverse effects include headache, dizziness, swollen ankles, and constipation.

verbigeration (ver-bij-er-a′shun) A repetition of words and phrases without a coherent meaning; observed in certain mental disorders. Also called oral stereotypy.

verge (verj) Margin.

anal v. Area between the anal canal and the skin around the anus.

vergence (ver′jens) Movement of the eyes in opposite directions.

vermi- Combining form meaning worm.

V

vermicide (ver′mĭ-sīd) Any agent that kills intestinal worms.

vermicular (ver-mik′u-lar) Relating to worms.

vermiculation (ver-mik-u-la′shun) A movement resembling that of a worm (e.g., a peristalsis).

vermicule (ver′mĭ-kūl) A small wormlike body structure.

vermiculous, vermiculose (ver-mik′u-lus, ver-mik′u-lōs) **1.** Infected with worms. **2.** Wormlike.

vermiform (ver′mĭ-form) Having the shape of a worm (e.g., the vermiform appendix).

vermifuge (ver′mĭ-fūj) Any agent that expels intestinal worms.

vermilionectomy (ver-mil-yon-ek′to-me) Surgical removal of the vermilion border of the lips.

vermin (ver′min) Parasitic animals.

verminous (ver′mĭ-nus) Infested with vermin.

vermis (ver′mis) Latin for worm; applied to anatomic structures that resemble a worm.

  v. cerebelli The narrow median portion of the cerebellum that connects the two cerebellar hemispheres.

vermix (ver′miks) The vermiform appendix. See under appendix.

vernix (ver′niks) Latin for varnish.

  v. caseosa A whitish cheesy substance normally covering the body of a fetus and, in lesser amounts, the body of a newborn infant; consists chiefly of sebaceous secretions and desquamated epithelial cells.

verruca (vĕ-roo′kah), pl. verru′cae A wart.

  v. acuminata See condyloma acuminatum.

  v. palmaris See palmar wart, under wart.

  v. plana See flat wart, under wart.

  v. plantaris See plantar wart, under wart.

  v. vulgaris See common wart, under wart.

verruciform (vĕ-roo′sĭ-form) In the shape of a wart.

verrucose (ver′oo-kōs) See verrucous.

verrucosis (ver-oo-ko′sis) The condition of having multiple warts.

verrucous (ver′oo-kus) Having a wartlike roughness. Also called verrucose.

  v. carcinoma See giant condyloma, under condyloma.

verruga (vĕ-roo′gah) See verruca.

  v. peruana See bartonellosis.

versicolor (ver-sik′o-lor) Turning or changing color.

version (ver′zhun) **1.** In obstetrics, the manual turning of a fetus in the uterus to alter its position to one more favorable for delivery. **2.** The turning of both eyes in the same direction.

  bimanual v., bipolar v. A maneuver for turning the fetus by using two hands; may be external or combined.

  Braxton Hicks v. A seldom-used procedure in which the forefinger and/or middle finger is introduced through the vagina into the uterus to displace the presenting part of the fetus (often the shoulder) while the head is guided toward the birth canal by the operator's external hand.

  cephalic v. Version performed in modern obstetrics only by external manipulations, usually with the aid of ultrasonographic scanning; the procedure is used to turn the fetal presenting part from breech to cephalic presentation. The operator's hands are placed on the patient's abdomen and each pole of the fetus is located by palpation; then gently but firmly the breech is displaced upward and laterally while moving the fetal head downward toward the birth canal (forward somersault).

  combined v. Version in which one hand is introduced into the uterus and the other is placed on the patient's abdomen.

  external v. Version conducted entirely by placing the hands on the patient's abdomen for application of force.

  internal v. Direct turning of the fetus by introducing a hand into the uterus.

  podalic v. Internal version performed only rarely, usually as a lifesaving measure (e.g., for a second twin with fetal distress or for a small dead fetus in a transverse lie); a hand is introduced into the uterus through the fully dilated cervix; the fetus is turned by seizing both feet and drawn through the cervix; a breech extraction is then performed.

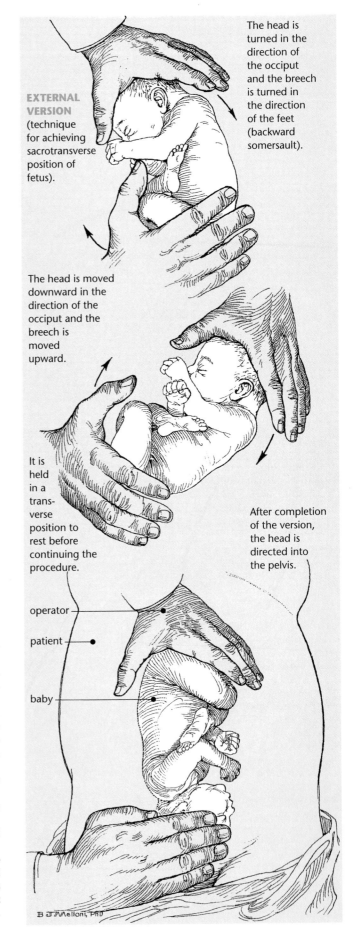

EXTERNAL VERSION (technique for achieving sacrotransverse position of fetus).

The head is turned in the direction of the occiput and the breech is turned in the direction of the feet (backward somersault).

The head is moved downward in the direction of the occiput and the breech is moved upward.

It is held in a transverse position to rest before continuing the procedure.

After completion of the version, the head is directed into the pelvis.

operator

patient

baby

B. J. Melloni, PhD

spontaneous v. Version accomplished by contractions of the uterus alone.

vertebra (ver'tĕ-brah), pl. ver'tebrae One of the 33 bones forming the spinal column; they are divided into 7 cervical, 12 thoracic, 5 lumbar, 5 sacral, and 4 coccygeal vertebrae. See also table of bones.

vertebral (ver'te-bral) Relating to a vertebra.

vertebrate (ver'tĕ-brāt) **1.** Having a vertebral column. **2.** Any animal that has a vertebral column.

vertebrectomy (ver-tĕ-brek'to-me) Surgical removal of a portion of a vertebra.

vertex (ver'teks) **1.** The highest point at the vault of the skull. **2.** In obstetrics, the crown of the fetal head.

vertical (ver'tĭ-kal) **1.** Relating to a vertex. **2.** At right angles to the horizon.

verticil (ver'tĭ-sil) A circular arrangement; a whorl.

verticillate (ver-tis'ĭ-lāt) Forming a whorl; circularly arranged.

vertiginous (ver-tij'ĭ-nus) Associated with or producing vertigo.

vertigo (ver'tĭ-go) An attack characterized by a rapidly spinning or whirling sensation either of oneself or of objects in one's environment,

accompanied when severe by nausea and vomiting. Distinguished from dizziness, which is characterized by a swaying sensation.

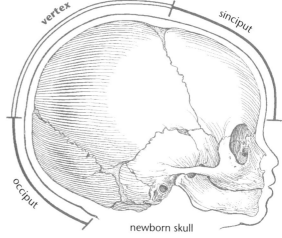

newborn skull

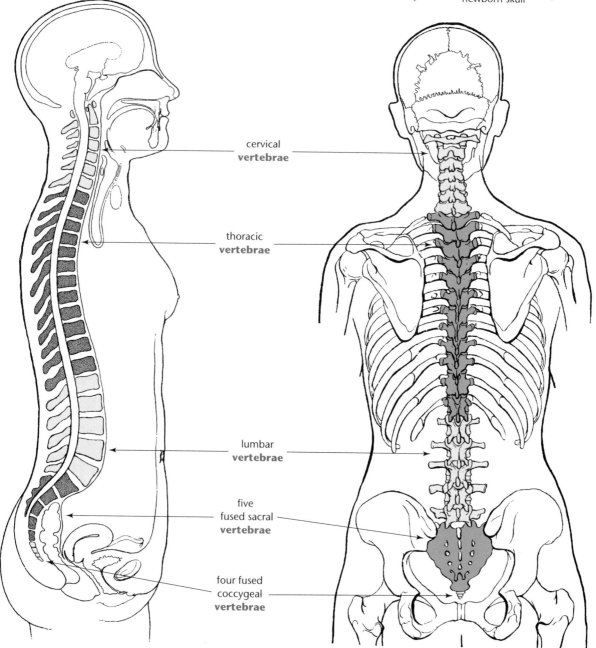

cervical **vertebrae**

thoracic **vertebrae**

lumbar **vertebrae**

five fused sacral **vertebrae**

four fused coccygeal **vertebrae**

V

vertebra ■ vertigo

auditory v. Vertigo occurring in Ménière's disease. See also Ménière's disease, under disease.

aural v. Vertigo caused by disease of the inner ear.

benign positional v. Vertigo characterized by brief attacks (one minute or less) accompanied by nystagmus, precipitated by certain critical positions of the head (e.g., leaning backward, or turning over while lying down).

organic v. Vertigo caused by a lesion in the brain.

verumontanitis (ve-ru-mon-tah-ni'tis) Inflammation of the verumontanum. Also called colliculitis.

verumontanum (ve-ru-mon-ta'num) A small elevation on the posterior wall of the prostatic urethra upon which open the two ejaculatory ducts and the utricle of the prostate. Also called colliculus seminalis.

vesica (vĕ-si'kah) Latin for bladder; blister.

vesical (ves'ĭ-kal) Relating to the bladder, usually the urinary bladder.

vesicant (ves'ĭ-kant) Any agent that produces blisters. Also called epispastic.

vesicate (ves'ĭ-kāt) To blister.

vesication (ves-ĭ-ka'shun) See vesiculation.

vesicle (ves'ĭ-kl) **1.** A small fluid-filled blister on the skin. **2.** Any small saclike structure.

blastodermic v. See blastocyst.

seminal v. One of two saclike glandular structures situated behind the bladder in the male; its secretion is one of the components of semen.

synaptic v.'s The numerous small spherical, intracellular vesicles situated near the presynaptic membrane of a nerve cell; they contain neurotransmitter substance, which, when released into the synaptic gap, mediates the passage of the nerve impulse across the synaptic junction.

vesico-, vesic- Combining forms meaning bladder; vesicle.

vesicobullous (ves-ĭ-ko-bul'us) Having serum-filled blisters.

vesicocele (ves'ĭ-ko-sēl) See cystocele.

vesicoclysis (ves-ĭ-kok'lĭ-sis) Washing out (lavage) of the bladder.

vesicolithiasis (ves-ĭ-ko-lĭ-thi'ah-sis) See cystolithiasis.

vesicolithotomy (ves-ĭ-ko-lĭ-thot'o-me) See cystolithotomy.

vesicoprostatic (ves-ĭ-ko-pros-tat'ik) Relating to the bladder and the prostate.

vesicopubic (ves-ĭ-ko-pu'bic) Relating to the bladder and pubic bone.

vesicorectal (ves-ĭ-ko-rek'tal) Relating to the bladder and the rectum.

vesicostomy (ves-ĭ-kos'to-me) See cystostomy.

vesicotomy (ves-ĭ-kot'o-me) See cystotomy.

vesicoureteral (ves-ĭ-ko-u-re'ter-al) Relating to the bladder and ureters.

vesicourethral (ves-ĭ-ko-u-re'thral) Relating to the bladder and urethra.

vesicouterine (ves-ĭ-ko-u'ter-in) Relating to the bladder and uterus.

vesicouterovaginal (ves-ĭ-ko-u-ter-o-vaj'ĭ-nal) Relating to the bladder, uterus, and vagina.

vesicovaginal (ves-ĭ-ko-vaj'ĭ-nal) Relating to the bladder and vagina.

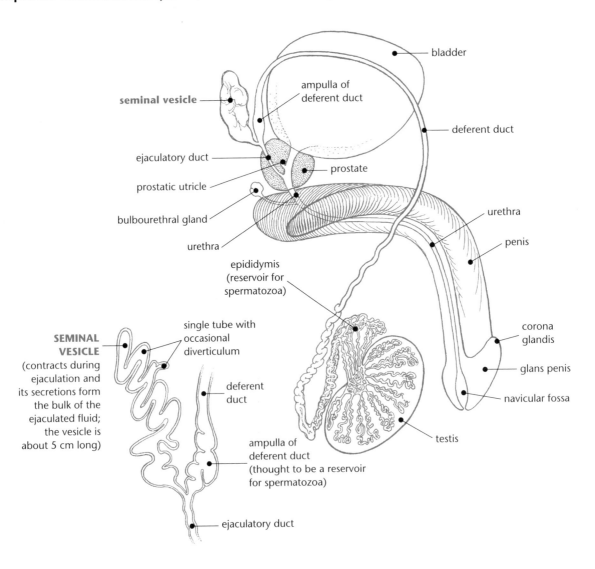

vesicovaginorectal (ves-ĭ-ko-vaj′ĭ-no-rek′tal) Relating to the bladder, vagina, and rectum.

vesicula (vĕ-sik′u-lah), pl. vesic′ulae Latin for vesicle.

vesicular (vĕ-sik′u-lar) 1. Relating to vesicles. 2. Containing vesicles.

vesiculation (vĕ-sik-u-la′shun) 1. The formation of small blisters. Also called vesication. 2. The condition of having numerous small blisters.

vesiculectomy (vĕ-sik-u-lek′to-me) Removal of a seminal vesicle, partly or completely.

vesiculiform (vĕ-sik′u-lĭ-form) Blisterlike.

vesiculitis (vĕ-sik′u-li′tis) Inflammation of a seminal vesicle.

vesiculopapular (vĕ-sik′u-lo-pap′u-lar) Relating to vesicles and papules.

vesiculoprostatitis (vĕ-sik′u-lo-pros-tah-ti′tis) Inflammation of the bladder and prostate.

vesiculopustular (vĕ-sik′u-lo-pus′tu-lar) Relating to vesicles and pustules.

vesiculotomy (vĕ-sik′u-lot′o-me) A surgical cut into a seminal vesicle.

vessel (ves′el) In anatomy, a tubular structure conveying a body fluid.
   lymphatic v., lymph v. A vessel conveying lymph. Also called vas lymphaticum.

vestibular (ves-tib′u-lar) Relating to a vestibule, especially of the inner ear where balance functions are governed.

vestibule (ves′tĭ-būl) A small cavity or chamber at the entrance of a canal.
   aortic v. The small space within the left ventricle of the heart, just below the aortic opening. Also called Sibson's aortic vestibule.
   buccal v. The part of the vestibule of the mouth between the cheeks and the teeth and gums.
   v. of the ear The oval cavity in the bony labyrinth of the inner ear; it communicates with the cochlea anteriorly and the semicircular canals posteriorly.
   labial v. The part of the vestibule of the mouth between the lips and the teeth and gums.
   v. of the mouth The space in the oral cavity between the cheeks and lips and the gums and teeth.
   v. of the nose The space just inside the nostrils.
   Sibson's aortic v. See aortic vestibule.
   v. of vagina The space between the two small lips of the vulva into which open the vagina, urethra, and the ducts of the greater and lesser vestibular glands. Also called vestibule of vulva.
   v. of vulva See vestibule of vagina.

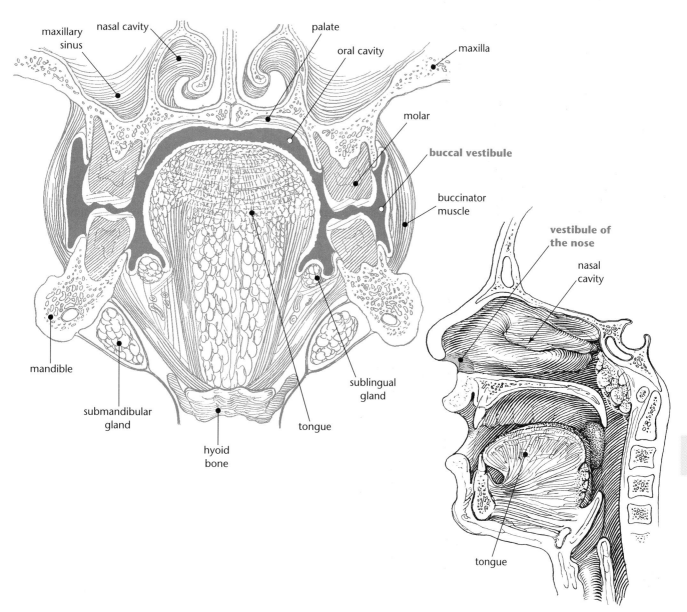

V

vestibulitis (ves-ti-bu-li'tis) Inflammation of a vestibule.

vulvar v. Condition marked by redness and irritation in the vestibule of the vagina, with small red patches in the vulvar region; causes are varied; may arise from abrasions from sexual intercourse, using tampons, bike riding, or wearing tight-fitting pants; may also be caused by recurrent yeast infection or trauma (e.g., from caustic chemicals or laser surgery used to treat vulvar genital warts); often the cause is unknown.

vestibulo- Combining form meaning a vestibule.

vestibuloplasty (ves-tib'u-lo-plas-te) Operative procedure for increasing the height of a dental ridge by deepening the sulcus.

vestibulotomy (ves-tib-u-lot'o-me) Surgical opening into the vestibule of the inner ear.

vestibulourethral (ves-tib'u-lo-u-re'thral) Relating to the vestibule of the vagina and the urethra.

vestibulum (ves-tib'u-lum), pl. vestib'ula Latin for vestibule.

vestige (ves'tij) **1.** A rudimentary structure; usually the remnant of a structure that was functional in, and normally part of, the embryo. **2.** An imperfectly developed organ that has ceased to function.

vestigial (ves-tij'e-al) Relating to vestige.

vestigium (ves-tij'e-um) Latin for vestige.

veterinarian (vet-er-ĭ-nār'e-an) A person trained and licensed to diagnose and treat diseases of both domestic and wild animals.

veterinary (vet'er-ĭ-ner-e) Relating to the diagnosis and treatment of diseases of animals.

via (vi'ah), pl. vi'ae Any passage.

viability (vi-ah-bil'ĭ-te) The condition of being viable.

viable (vi'ah-bl) Capable of living (e.g., a fetus that has developed sufficiently to be able to live outside of the uterus).

vial (vi'al) A small glass container for holding liquid medicines.

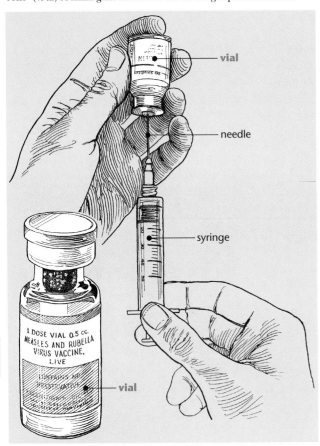

vial
needle
syringe
vial

vibration (vi-bra'shun) **1.** A shaking or trembling motion. **2.** A rapid to-and-fro movement; oscillation.

vibrator (vi'bra-tor) A device that vibrates or causes vibrations.

Vibrio (vib're-o) A genus of motile, gram-negative bacteria (family Spirillaceae) found in salt water and fresh water and in soil; some species cause disease.

V. cholerae A species that causes cholera in humans. Also called Koch's bacillus; *Vibrio comma.*

V. comma See *Vibrio cholerae.*

vibrio (vib're-o) Any bacterium of the genus *Vibrio.*

vibrissa (vi-bris'ah), pl. vibris'sae **1.** One of the hairs just within the nostrils. **2.** One of the stiff tactile hairs or bristles around the muzzle of animals.

vibrotherapeutics (vi-bro-ther-ah-pu'tiks) The therapeutic use of vibrating devices (e.g., in massage).

vicarious (vi-kar'e-us) **1.** Serving as a substitute. **2.** Occurring in a part of the body not normally associated with that particular function.

view (vyoo) See projection *(5).*

vigilambulism (vij-il-am'bu-lizm) A condition, resembling sleepwalking but occurring in the wakeful state, in which the person is unaware of his surroundings.

vigilance (vij'ĭ-lans) A state of watchfulness or alertness.

villi (vil'i) Plural of villus.

villoma (vĭ-lo'mah) See papilloma.

villositis (vil-o-si'tis) Inflammation of the villous portion of the placenta.

villosity (vĭ-los'ĭ-te) The presence of villi.

villous (vil'us) Covered with minute hairlike projections (villi).

villus (vil'us), pl. vil'li A minute, vascular, hairlike projection from the free surface of a membrane.

arachnoid villi See arachnoid granulations, under granulation.

chorionic villi The slender vascular projections of the chorion that enter into the formation of the placenta and through which all substances are exchanged between maternal and fetal circulations.

intestinal villi Villi projecting from the mucous lining of the small intestine, the site of absorption of fluids and nutrients; they are leaf-shaped in the duodenum and finger-shaped, shorter, and sparser in the ileum.

vincristine sulfate (vin-kris'tēn sul'fāt) A salt of an antineoplastic alkaloid obtained from the periwinkle plant *Vinca rosea;* used primarily in the treatment of acute leukemias, lymphomas, and solid tumors in children. Adverse effects include nausea and vomiting, loss of hair, and bone marrow depression.

vinculum (ving'ku-lum), pl. vin'cula A frenulum or restrictive bandlike structure.

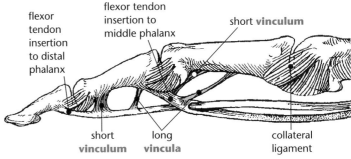

flexor tendon insertion to distal phalanx
flexor tendon insertion to middle phalanx
short **vinculum**
short **vinculum**
long **vincula**
collateral ligament

vinic (vi'nik) Derived from wine.

vinyl (vi'nil) **1.** A hydrocarbon radical derived from ethylene by removal of one hydrogen atom. **2.** A polymer of a vinyl compound or a product (e.g., a textile fiber) derived from one.

v. chloride A colorless, highly flammable gas, used extensively in the plastics industry; long-term exposure has been suspected of causing liver cancer (angiosarcoma).

vinylbenzene (vi'nil-ben'zēn) See styrene.

vinylidene chloride (vi-nil'i-dēn klor'id) A flammable liquid compound used in the manufacture of plastics; it is highly toxic, especially to the kidneys; its toxicity is enhanced by alcohol consumption.

violaceous (vi-o-la'shus) A violet tinge; applied to a discoloration, especially of the skin.

violet (vi'o-let) A hue of the visible spectrum evoked by wavelengths shorter than 450 nm.

V

visual v. See iodopsin.

viper (vi'per) A poisonous snake of the family Viperidae.

viral (vi'ral) Relating to a virus.

viremia (vi-re'me-ah) The presence of viable viruses in the blood.

virgin (vir'jin) **1.** A person who has never had sexual intercourse. **2.** Term used in reference to a part of the body or a pathologic condition that has not been previously treated by a surgical procedure (e.g., virgin lumbar anatomy, virgin disk herniation).

virginity (vir-jin'i-te) The state of not having experienced sexual intercourse.

virile (vir'il) **1.** Relating to male sexual functions. **2.** Having male characteristics.

virilism (vir'i-lizm) The occurrence of secondary male characteristics in the female or prepubescent males, usually caused by excessive amounts of androgenic hormone.

virility (vi-ril'i-te) The state of being virile.

virilization (vir-i-li-za'shun) The abnormal appearance of secondary male characteristics, especially in the female. Also called masculinization.

virion (vi're-on) A structurally complete virus.

viroid (vi'roid) Any of a group of microorganisms comprising the smallest known agents to cause disease in higher plants; they are unencapsulated and composed of single-stranded RNA.

virologist (vi-rol'o-jist) A specialist in virology.

virology (vi-rol'o-je) The study of viruses and the diseases they cause.

viropexis (vi-ro-pek'sis) The engulfing of virus particles by cells.

virucide (vi'ru-sid) Any agent that kills viruses.

virulence (vir'u-lens) The degree to which a microorganism is capable of causing pathologic changes in tissues once it infects the host; the state of being toxic.

viruliferous (vir-u-lif'er-us) Conveying viruses.

viruria (vir-oo're-ah) The presence of viruses in urine.

virus (vi'rus), pl. vi'ruses An infectious parasite thriving and replicating only within living cells; usually composed of a protein shell enclosing a nucleic acid, either DNA or RNA (not both); viruses range in size from 30 to 300 nm, are visible under the electron microscope, and are spherical, polyhedral, or rod-shaped.

    adeno-associated v. (AAV) See *Dependovirus*.

    adeno-pharyngeal-conjunctival v., A-P-C v. See *Dependovirus*.

    adenosatellite v. See *Dependovirus*.

    attenuated v. A virus so modified as to be incapable of producing a disease.

    common cold v. Any virus, especially of the genus *Rhinovirus*, associated with the common cold.

    Coxsackie v. See coxsackievirus.

    dengue v. A virus of the genus *Flavivirus* that causes dengue in humans; transmitted by mosquitoes of the genus *Aedes*.

    DNA v.'s A class of viruses having an inner core of DNA and multiplying chiefly in the nuclei of cells; included are those causing herpes simplex, herpes zoster, chickenpox, smallpox, warts, and certain malignant tumors.

    ECHO v. See echovirus.

    enteric v. See enterovirus.

    epidemic gastroenteritis v. The causative agent of epidemics of nonbacterial diarrhea.

    epidemic keratoconjunctivitis v. A type 8 adenovirus causing epidemic inflammation of the conjunctiva at the border of the cornea (shipyard eye); also associated with swimming pool conjunctivitis.

    Epstein-Barr v. (EBV, EBv.) See human herpesvirus 4, under herpesvirus.

    equine encephalomyelitis v. A virus of the genus *Alphavirus* that causes encephalomyelitis in horses and humans; named after the region where it occurs, as eastern (EEE) virus, Venezuelan (VEE) virus, and western (WEE) virus.

    filtrable v. Old term for virus.

    hepatitis A v. (HAV) A 27-nm RNA virus (genus *Enterovirus*, family Picornaviridae) causing hepatitis A, often as self-limited out-

breaks in day care centers and residential institutions; spread by contaminated food and water. Also called infectious hepatitis virus.

    hepatitis B v. (HBV) A 42-nm DNA virus (family Hepadnoviridae) causing hepatitis B; found in body fluids, including saliva; spreads via transfusion, needle-stick accidents, shared needles, sexual route, or in childbirth. Also called serum hepatitis virus.

    hepatitis C v. (HCV) A 10-kb RNA virus (family Flaviviridae), the cause of hepatitis C; spreads chiefly through transfusion and shared needles. Formerly classified as a non-A, non-B virus.

    hepatitis delta v. (HDV) A 37-nm RNA virus that requires the presence of the HBV (coinfection) to survive; spreads by infected blood or sexual contact. Also called delta agent.

    hepatitis E v. (HEV) A 7.5-kb RNA virus (family Caliciviridae) causing hepatitis E, mainly by contaminated water, via the gastrointestinal tract. Formerly classified as a non-A, non-B virus.

    herpes v. See herpesvirus.

    human immunodeficiency v. (HIV) A virus (subfamily Lentivirinae, family Retroviridae) causing acquired immune deficiency syndrome (AIDS); two types are known (HIV-1, HIV-2); the two types produce identical symptoms, but HIV-2 can linger in the body for up to 20 years (about twice as long as HIV-1) before causing symptoms. Also called human T cell lymphoma/leukemia virus type III.

    human T cell lymphotropic v. (HTLV) A virus (subfamily Oncovirinae, family Retroviridae) causing T cell leukemia or lymphoma; two types are known (HTLV-1, HTLV-2). Also called human T cell lymphoma/leukemia virus.

    infectious hepatitis v. See hepatitis A virus.

    influenza v. A virus belonging to the genus *Influenzavirus* (family Orthomyxoviridae) that causes influenza (flu).

    JC v. A virus of the genus *Polyomavirus* (family Papovaviridae) causing progressive multifocal leukoencephalopathy; named after the patient identified by the initials JC in whom it was discovered.

    lymphocytic choriomeningitis v., LCM v. A virus of the genus *Arenavirus* (family Arenaviridae) causing congenital lymphocytic choriomeningitis in mice; believed to be associated with other inapparent and influenza-like infections.

    measles v. A virus of the genus *Morbillivirus* (family Paramyxoviridae) that causes measles. Also called rubeola virus.

    neurotropic v. Any virus that thrives in nerve tissue.

    oncogenic v. Any of a variety of DNA and RNA viruses that are known to cause cancer in animals and others that have been im-

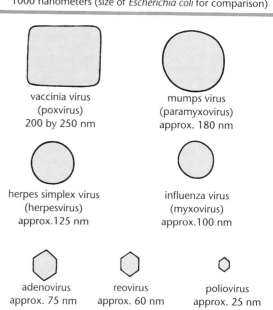

relative sizes of various animal **viruses**
1000 nanometers (size of *Escherichia coli* for comparison)

vaccinia virus
(poxvirus)
200 by 250 nm

mumps virus
(paramyxovirus)
approx. 180 nm

herpes simplex virus
(herpesvirus)
approx.125 nm

influenza virus
(myxovirus)
approx.100 nm

adenovirus
approx. 75 nm

reovirus
approx. 60 nm

poliovirus
approx. 25 nm

plicated in causing cancer in humans, including the human papillomavirus (HPV), Epstein-Barr virus (EBV), hepatitis B virus (HBV), and human T-cell leukemia virus (HTLV). Also called tumor virus.

orphan v. One that has been isolated but not yet identified with any disease.

poliomyelitis v. See poliovirus.

rabies v. A virus of the genus *Lyssavirus* (family Rhabdoviridae) that causes rabies.

respiratory syncytial v., RS v. (RSV) A virus of the genus *Pneumovirus* (family Paramyxoviridae) that causes pneumonia and bronchiolitis in infants; derives its name from its capacity to fuse cells into a multinucleated mass (syncytium).

RNA v.'s A large class of viruses having an inner core of RNA and multiplying chiefly in the cytoplasm of cells; included are those causing poliomyelitis, meningitis, yellow fever, encephalitis, mumps, measles, rabies, German measles, and the common cold. Also called riboviruses.

rubella v. A virus of the genus *Rubivirus* (family Togaviridae) causing German measles (rubella).

rubeola v. See measles virus.

serum hepatitis v. See hepatitis B virus.

slow v. Any virus causing a disease, such as subacute inclusion-body encephalitis, that is characterized by a long unremitting course and, once symptoms appear, a gradual progression.

tumor v. See oncogenic virus.

vaccinia v. The poxvirus used for vaccination against smallpox.

varicella-zoster v., VZ v. See herpesvirus 3, under herpesvirus.

vis (vis), pl. vi'res Latin for force or energy.

viscance (vis'kans) A measure of the dissipation of energy in the flow of body fluids.

viscera (vis'er-ah) Plural of viscus.

viscerad (vis'er-ad) Toward an internal organ, especially in the abdomen.

visceral (vis'er-al) Relating to the internal organs (viscera).

visceral larva migrans (vis'er-al lar'vah mi'grāns) See toxocariasis.

visceroinhibitory (vis'er-o-in-hib'ĭ-tor-e) Diminishing the functional activity of internal organs.

visceromegaly (vis-er-o-meg'ah-le) Abnormal largeness of the abdominal or thoracic organs (viscera). Also called splanchnomegaly; organomegaly.

visceromotor (vis'er-o-mo'tor) Causing functional activity of internal organs.

visceroparietal (vis'er-o-pah-ri'ĕ-tal) Relating to the abdominal organs and the abdominal wall.

visceroptosis, visceroptosia (vis'er-op-to'sis, vis'er-op-to'se-ah) Downward displacement of the abdominal organs.

viscerosensory (vis'er-o-sen'so-re) Relating to the sensory nerve supply to internal organs.

viscerotropic (vis'er-o-trop'ik) Affecting the organs.

viscid (vis'id) Thick and sticky.

viscidity (vĭ-sid'ĭ-te) Stickiness.

viscosimeter (vis-ko-sim'ĕ-ter) Apparatus for measuring the viscosity of a fluid (e.g., of blood).

viscosity (vis-kos'ĭ-te) The resistance that a fluid offers to flow due to molecular cohesion.

viscous (vis'kus) Characterized by a relatively high resistance to flow.

viscus (vis'kus), pl. vis'cera Any organ situated in a body cavity, especially in the abdominal cavity.

visile (viz'īl) Relating to vision; applied to the ability to comprehend or remember most easily what has been seen, as opposed to what has been heard. COMPARE audile.

vision (vizh'un) (V) Sight.

binocular v. Vision in which both eyes contribute to the formation of one fused image.

double v. See diplopia.

night v. See scotopic vision.

peripheral v. Ability to see objects outside of the direct line of vision.

scotopic v. Inability to distinguish colors and small details, while the ability to detect motion and low luminous intensities remains intact. Also called scotopia; twilight vision.

stereoscopic v. See stereopsis.

tubular v. See tunnel vision.

tunnel v. Vision in which the visual field is severely contracted. Also called tubular vision.

twilight v. See scotopic vision.

yellow v. See xanthopsia.

visual (vizh'u-al) Relating to vision.

visualize (vizh'u-al-iz) **1.** To make a mental image. **2.** To view.

visual purple (vizh'u-al pur'pl) See rhodopsin.

visual violet (vizh'u-al vi'o-let) See iodopsin.

visuoauditory (vizh'u-o-aw'dĭ-tor-e) Relating to both vision and hearing.

visuopsychic (vizh'u-o-si'kik) Relating to the visual association areas of the occipital cortex of the brain, concerned with the interpretation or judgment of visual impressions.

visuosensory (vizh'u-o-sen'sor-e) Relating to the perception of a visual stimulus.

visuscope (viz'u-skōp) Instrument designed to identify the fixation characteristics of a partially blind (amblyopic) eye.

vita (vi'tah) Latin for life.

vital (vi'tal) Relating to life.

vitality (vi-tal'ĭ-te) Vigor; energy.

vitalometer (vi-tah-lom'ĕ-ter) An electrical device used in determining the vital condition of a tooth pulp. Also called pulp tester.

vitals (vi'tals) See viscera.

vitamer (vi'tah-mer) Substance performing a vitamin function.

vitamin (vi'tah-min) (V) General term for any of several organic substances essential for normal metabolic processes and which, when absent in the diet, produce deficiency states.

v. A A fat-soluble vitamin necessary for normal bone development and the health of certain specialized epithelial tissues, especially the retina for production of visual purple; present in green and yellow vegetables as a provitamin or precursor, which the body transforms into its active form; occurs in its preformed state in animal products (e.g., liver, eggs, and dairy products).

v. A$_1$ See retinol.

v. A$_1$ acid See retinoic acid.

v. B A member of the vitamin B complex.

v. B complex A group of water-soluble compounds found together in foodstuffs; some are believed to be chiefly concerned with release of energy from food (e.g., nicotinamide, riboflavin, thiamine, and biotin), others with the formation of red blood cells (e.g., vitamin B$_{12}$).

v. B$_1$ See thiamine.

v. B$_2$ Old term for riboflavin.

v. B$_6$ See pyridoxine.

v. B$_{12}$ A protein complex occurring in foods of animal source; lack of vitamin B$_{12}$ causes pernicious anemia. Also called cobalamin.

v. C See ascorbic acid.

v. D A group of fat-soluble sterols that promote retention of calcium and phosphorus, thus aiding in bone formation; lack of vitamin D causes rickets in children and osteomalacia in adults; present in fish liver oils; can be formed in the body upon exposure of the skin to sunlight.

v. D$_2$ Vitamin formed by irradiation of ergosterol; used in the prevention and treatment of vitamin D deficiency. Also called ergocalciferol; calciferol.

v. D$_3$ A sterol of the vitamin D group formed in the skin by the action of ultraviolet rays in sunlight upon the provitamin 7-dehydrocholesterol. Also called cholecalciferol.

v. E A group of naturally occurring fat-soluble substances that have antioxidant properties; in experimental animals, a lack of vita-

VITAMIN	SOURCES	FUNCTIONS	DEFICIENCY
A	green and yellow vegetables, liver, eggs, dairy products	helps maintain normal body growth and health of specialized tissues especially retina	nightblindness, skin lesions, xerophthalmia (keratinization and dryness of tissues of the eye)
B₁ (thiamine)	yeast, meat, bran coat of cereals	involved in carbohydrate metabolism	beriberi
B₂ (riboflavin)	milk, egg yolk, fresh meat	hydrogen transfer from metabolites to blood stream	proliferation of blood vessels around cornea, abnormal reddening of lips, ulceration of corners of mouth, inflammation of tongue
B₆ (pyridoxine)	meat, vegetables	involved in protein metabolism	convulsions, muscular weakness, dermatitis of face
B₁₂	foods of animal source	involved in nucleic acid metabolism	pernicious anemia
C (ascorbic acid)	citrus fruits, green leafy vegetables, new potatoes	development of normal bones, cartilage and collagen	scurvy
D	fish liver oil	essential in formation of bone	rickets in children, osteomalacia in adults
E	green leafy vegetables, wheat germ, rice	antioxidant	impairment of fat absorption
K	fish, cereal	involved in clotting of blood	tendency to hemorrhage

min E may lead to sterilty and muscular degeneration. Also called alpha-tocopherol.

v. K A group of fat-soluble compounds essential for clotting of blood; produced in the body by normal intestinal bacteria.

vitaminic (vi-tah-min'ik) Relating to vitamins.

vitellin (vi-tel'in) The chief protein present in egg yolk.

vitelline (vi-tel'in) Relating to egg yolk.

vitellus (vi-tel'us) The yolk of an egg.

vitiliginous (vit-ĭ-lij'ĭ-nus) Characterized by vitiligo.

vitiligo (vit-ĭ-li'go) , pl. vitilig'ines Condition characterized by the occurrence of sharply demarcated, milky white patches on the skin, usually on the face, neck, hands, and lower abdomen; due to absence of the pigment melanin. Also called acquired leukoderma; piebald skin.

vitrectomy (vĭ-trek'to-me) An intraocular surgical procedure for removing the vitreous body from the eye, along with the vitreal membranes.

vitreoretinopathy (vit-re-o-ret-ĭ-nop'ah-the) Any disease of the eye involving the vitreous body and the retina.

vitreous (vit're-us) Transparent. The term is frequently used to designate the vitreous body. See also vitreous body, under body.

vitrification (vit-ri-fi-ka'shun) Conversion of dental porcelain into a glassy substance by heating.

vitriol (vit're-ol) Any of various sulfates of heavy metals such as blue vitriol (cupric sulfate), green vitriol (ferrous sulfate), white vitriol (zinc sulfate).

vivarium (vī-va're-um) A building or space in which animals are kept for observation or medical research. Commonly called animal house.

vivi- Combining form meaning alive.

vividialysis (viv-ĭ-di-al'ĭ-sis) Dialysis through a living membrane (e.g., in lavage of the peritoneal cavity).

vividiffusion (viv-ĭ-dĭ-fu'zhun) The passage of circulating blood through a membrane and its return to the living body without exposure to air; the principle used in kidney dialysis with the artificial kidney.

vivification (viv-ĭ-fi-ka'shun) See debridement.

viviparous (vi-vip'ah-rus) Giving birth to living offspring that developed entirely within the maternal body. Also called zoogonous.

viviperception (viv-ĭ-per-sep'shun) The study of the vital processes in a living organism.

vivisection (viv-ĭ-sek'shun) The performance of experimental surgery on living animals.

vocal (vo'kal) Relating to the voice.

voice (vois) The sound produced by air passing through the larynx, upper respiratory tract, and oral structures.

v. box See larynx.

void (void) 1. To discharge a body waste, especially urine. 2. Having no legal or binding effect or force.

vola (vo'lah) Latin for the palm of the hand or the sole of the foot.

volar (vo'lar) Relating to the palm of the hand or the sole of the foot.

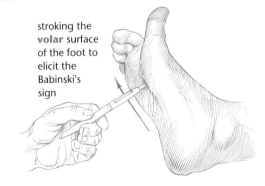

stroking the **volar** surface of the foot to elicit the Babinski's sign

volatile (vol'ah-til) Tending to evaporate rapidly at average temperatures and pressures.

volatilization (vol-ah-til-ĭ-za'shun) Evaporation.

volatilize (vol'ah-tĭ-līz) 1. To evaporate. 2. To cause evaporation.

volley (vol'e) A group of synchronous impulses.

volt (volt) (V, v) A unit of electromotive force, equal to that necessary to produce a current of 1 ampere in a circuit that has a resistance of 1 ohm.

voltage (vōl'tij) Electromotive force expressed in volts.

voltameter (vōl-tam'ē-ter) Instrument for measuring volts and amperes. Also spelled voltammeter.

voltammeter (vōlt-am'me-ter) See voltameter.

V

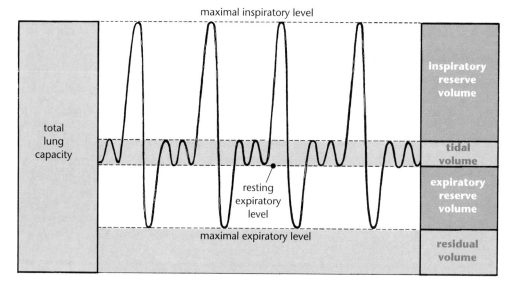

maximal inspiratory level

total lung capacity

inspiratory reserve volume

tidal volume

resting expiratory level

expiratory reserve volume

maximal expiratory level

residual volume

voltampere (vōlt-am′pēr) A unit of electric power, equal to 1 volt times 1 ampere.

voltmeter (vōlt′me-ter) An apparatus for measuring in volts the difference in electrical potential between two points.

volume (vol′ūm) (V, v) A measure of the space occupied by matter in any state or form.

   closing v. (CV) Lung volume at which airways at the bases of the lungs begin to close during expiration and airflow from the lungs is mainly from the upper portions.

   v. of distribution (Vd) *(a)* The volume of body fluid in which a tracer or solute is evenly distributed. *(b)* In toxicology, an estimate of the degree of distribution of a toxic agent in tissues; calculated by dividing the dose of the administered toxic substance by the concentration in the blood.

   end-diastolic v. The amount of blood present in the ventricles of the heart just before contraction of the heart muscle; it is a measure of the filling capacity of the heart between beats.

   end-systolic v. The amount of blood in the ventricles of the heart at the end of a cardiac ejection; it is a measure of the emptying capacity of the heart.

   expiratory reserve v. (ERV) The quantity of air that can be expelled from the lungs after a normal expiration. Formerly called supplemental air; residual air.

   forced expiratory v. (FEV) Maximal volume of air exhaled from the lungs during a particular time interval, starting from maximal inspiration.

   inspiratory reserve v. (IRV) The quantity of air that can be inspired after a normal inspiration. Formerly called complemental air.

   minute v. *(a)* The volume of air expelled from the lungs in 1 minute. *(b)* The volume of blood pumped by the left ventricle of the heart in 1 minute, normally 4 to 5 liters at rest.

   packed cell v. (PCV) The volume of blood cells in a centrifuged blood sample, expressed as a percentage.

   residual v. (RV) The amount of air remaining in the lungs after a maximum expiration. Also called residual air; residual capacity.

   stroke v. The quantity of blood expelled from each ventricle of the heart with each heartbeat.

   tidal v. The amount of air expired or inspired in one breath in normal breathing. Also called tidal air.

volumetric (vol-u-met′rik) Relating to measurement of, or by, volume.

voluntary (vol′un-tār-e) Initiated by one's own free will.

volute (vo′lūt) Rolled up.

volvulosis (vol-vu-lo′sis) See onchocerciasis.

volvulus (vol′vu-lus) Twisting of a segment of intestine, causing obstruction.

vomer (vo′mer) A thin flat bone forming the lower and back portions of the nasal septum. See table of bones.

vomerine (vo′mer-in) Relating to the vomer.

vomica (vom′ĭ-kah) Expectoration of purulent material.

vomit (vom′it) 1. To expel the stomach contents forcibly through the mouth. 2. The material so expelled. Also called vomitus.

vomiting (vom′it-ing) The forceful expulsion of stomach contents through the mouth.

   pernicious v. Persistent, uncontrollable vomiting.

   v. of pregnancy Vomiting occurring during pregnancy, usually at 2 to 12 weeks' gestation, especially in the morning but may occur at any time.

   projectile v. Vomiting with great force, often occurring suddenly, not preceded by nausea.

vomitus (vom′ĭ-tus) Vomited material.

vortex (vor′teks), pl. vor′tices General anatomic term for a whorled or spiral arrangement.

   v. coccygeus The whorl of hairs sometimes present over the tip of the coccyx.

   v. cordis The whorl of muscular fibers at the tip (apex) of the heart.

   v. lentis The star-shaped pattern of light lines visible on the surface of the lens of the eye.

   vortices pilorum The spiral arrangement of hair growth (e.g., on the scalp).

vorticose (vor′tĭ-kōs) Having a whorled appearance (e.g., the veins in the choroid layer of the eye).

vox (voks) Latin for voice.

voyeur (voi-yer′) One who practices voyeurism.

voyeurism (voi′yer-izm) The practice of deriving sexual gratification from watching people who are nude, undressing, or engaging in sexual acts.

vulgaris (vul-ga′ris) Latin for common; of the usual type.

vulva (vul′vah) The external female genitalia; consists of the prominence over the pubic bone (mons pubis), the labia majora, labia minora, clitoris, and the glands opening into the vestibule of the vagina. Also called pudendum.

vulvar, vulval (vul′var, vul′val) Relating to the vulva.

vulvectomy (vul-vek′to-me) Partial or complete removal of the vulva.

vulvitis (vul-vi′tis) Inflammation of the vulva.

   diabetic v. Vulvitis associated with diabetes mellitus; caused by a chronic vulvovaginal infection by the yeastlike fungus *Candida albicans;* it may respond poorly to treatment if the diabetes is not controlled.

   gonorrheal v. Vulvitis caused by infection of the glandular structures of the vulva by the bacterium *Neisseria gonorrhoeae.*

vulvo- Combining form meaning vulva.

vulvocrural (vul-vo-kroo′ral) Relating to the vulva and the thigh.

vulvouterine (vul-vo-u′ter-in) Relating to the vulva and uterus.

vulvovaginal (vul-vo-vaj′ĭ-nal) Relating to the vulva and vagina. Also called vaginovulvar.

vulvovaginitis (vul-vo-vaj-ī-ni′tis) Inflammation of the vulva and vagina.

V

wadding (wahd′ing) A soft layer of fibrous cotton or wool used for surgical dressings.

waist (wāst) The part of the body between the rib cage and the hips.

    w. of the heart The middle part of the heart as seen in an x-ray picture; it contains the pulmonary salient (protuberance).

walk (wok) **1.** To move or advance on foot. **2.** A manner of moving on foot. See also gait.

wall (wawl) In anatomy, a structure serving to enclose, divide, or protect a body cavity or part.

    cavity w. One of the enclosing surfaces bounding a prepared cavity in a tooth.

    enamel w. The enamel part of the wall of a prepared cavity of a tooth.

walleye (wahl′i) See exotropia.

ward (ward) **1.** A large room in a hospital containing several beds for patients. **2.** A section in a hospital for care and treatment of a special group of patients.

warfarin (war′fah-rin) Compound used in the prevention and treatment of abnormal blood clotting. Also used as a rat poison.

wart (wort) A small horny outgrowth on the skin or mucous membrane, usually of viral origin. Also called verruca.

    anorectal w. See condyloma acuminatum.

    common w. A wart with an irregular upper surface, usually ranging in size from 1 mm to 2 cm in diameter; seen most commonly on the back (dorsum) of the hand. Also called verruca vulgaris.

    digitate w. A wart resembling a skin tag, seen most commonly on the neck.

    fig w. See condyloma acuminatum.

    filiform w. A long thin wart usually occurring in multiples; seen most commonly in adult males, in the beard area of the face; also occurring about the nostrils and on the eyelids.

    flat w. A type of wart occurring as clusters of tiny, flat, skin-colored growths, usually on the face of children and young adults; it is difficult to diagnose and treat. Also called verruca plana; plane wart.

    genital w. See condyloma acuminatum.

    moist w. See condyloma acuminatum.

    palmar w. A calluslike wart on the palm of the hand. Also called verruca palmaris.

    plane w. See flat wart.

    plantar w. A flat form of the common wart on the sole of the foot or the toes. Also called verruca plantaris.

    pointed w. See condyloma acuminatum.

    telangiectatic w. See angiokeratoma.

    venereal w. See condyloma acuminatum.

wash (wosh) A solution for irrigating or cleansing a part (e.g., the eye or the mouth).

washing (wosh′ing) The removal of soluble material (e.g., from cells).

    sperm w. An adjunct to intrauterine insemination in which the semen sample is diluted and centrifuged prior to introduction into the uterus.

wasp (wosp) Any stinging insect of the family Vespidae; their venoms include such substances as enzymes, histamine-releasing factors, biogenic amines, and kinins.

waste (wāst) **1.** To cause, or to undergo, a gradual loss of body tissue. **2.** Material excreted by the body as a by-product during or at the end of a process.

wasting (wāst′ing) **1.** The process of losing body tissue and strength. **2.** The process of excreting by-products of the body's biologic processes.

    salt w. An excessive renal excretion of salt.

watchful waiting An option that involves not intervening in a disease process (or changing treatment) but closely monitoring its progress (e.g., a low-grade, low-volume prostatic cancer progressing so slowly that it does not pose an immediate threat to the patient, while standard treatments for the disease may cause adverse effects that diminish the quality of life, notably impotence and urinary incontinence). Also called observation and follow-up.

water (wah′ter) **1.** A clear, colorless liquid that is present in all organic tissues, and is essential for life. **2.** Colloquialism for urine.

    alkaline w. Water containing appreciable amounts of the bicarbonates of calcium, lithium, potassium, or sodium.

    bound w. Water in body tissues held tenaciously by the pull of colloids.

    w. of combustion See water of metabolism.

    distilled w. Water purified by the heat-dependent process of distillation.

    free w. (*a*) Water present in the body unattached to colloids; it can be removed by ultrafiltration. (*b*) The amount of dilute urine formed per minute that can be considered free of dissolved substances (solute), assuming that the remainder of the urine is isotonic.

    hard w. Water containing ions, such as Mg^{++} and Ca^{++}, that form insoluble salts with fatty acids, especially water containing more than 90 parts per million of calcium carbonate; it generally resists the action of soap to form a lather.

    heavy w. Compound in which most of the hydrogen atoms are deuterium (heavy hydrogen); it has higher boiling and freezing points than ordinary water. Also called deuterium oxide.

    w. of injection Distilled water used in the preparation of products for intravenous or intramuscular injection.

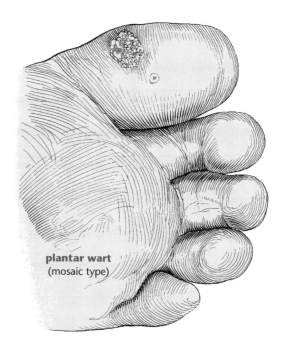

plantar wart
(mosaic type)

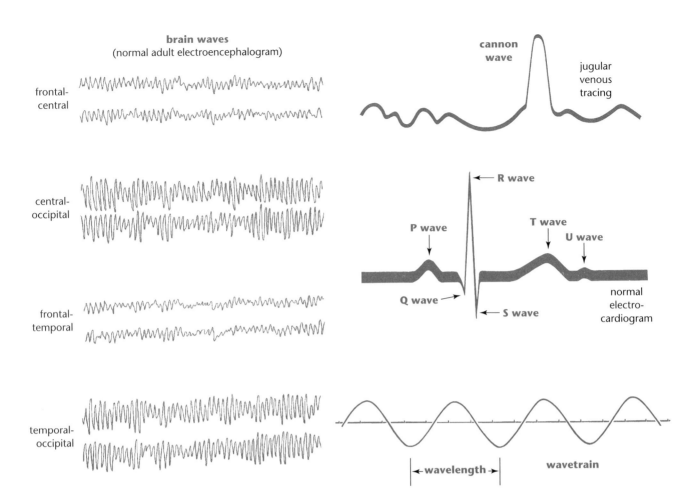

brain waves
(normal adult electroencephalogram)

frontal-central

central-occipital

frontal-temporal

temporal-occipital

cannon wave

jugular venous tracing

R wave

P wave

T wave

U wave

Q wave

S wave

normal electro-cardiogram

←wavelength→

wavetrain

metabolic w. See water of metabolism.

w. of metabolism The water in the body derived from the oxidation of the hydrogen of a food element such as starch, glucose, or fat; the largest amount is produced in the breakdown of fat. Also called water of combustion; metabolic water.

mineral w. Water that has appreciable amounts of mineral salts in solution.

potable w. Drinkable water free from contamination.

saline w. Water containing neutral salts (e.g., chlorides, sulfates, iodides) in appreciable amounts.

soft w. Water containing few or no ions that form insoluble salts with fatty acids, especially water with less than 80 parts per million of calcium carbonate; ordinary soap can lather in it easily.

water-borne (wah'ter born) Spread by contaminated water; applied to certain diseases.

water brash (wah'ter brash') The filling of the mouth with reflux fluid from the esophagus, usually associated with heartburn.

water-on-the-brain Colloquialism for hydrocephalus.

water-on-the-knee Colloquialism for accumulation of fluid within or around the knee joint, usually caused by bursitis.

waters (wah'ters) Colloquial term for amniotic fluid, the fluid in the amniotic sac surrounding the fetus.

watt (wot) (W) The amount of electrical power produced by 1 volt with 1 ampere of current.

wave (wāv) A periodic increase and subsidence, as an oscillation propagated from point to point in a medium, characterized by alternate elevations and depressions.

alpha w. A wave in the electroencephalogram (EEG) with a frequency band from 8 to 13 Hz. Also called alpha rhythm.

arterial w. A wave in the jugular phlebogram due to the vibration produced by the carotid pulse.

beta w. A wave in the electroencephalogram (EEG) with a frequency band of 18 to 30 Hz. Also called beta rhythm.

brain w.'s Electrical potential waves of the brain.

cannon w. A large positive venous pulse wave produced by atrial contraction; it occurs when the right atrium contracts at the same time the tricuspid valve is closed by right ventricular systole, as in complete heart block and ventricular premature beats.

delta w. A wave in the electroencephalogram (EEG) with a frequency band of less than 4 Hz. Also called delta rhythm.

dicrotic w. The second notch in the tracing of the normal arterial pulse.

f w.'s Small irregular waves or oscillations of the atria, characteristically seen in atrial fibrillation.

F w.'s Regular rapid undulating atrial waves seen in atrial flutter; thought to represent the manifestation of atrial depolarization and repolarization occurring in rapid succession from an ectopic focus.

fluid w. A sign of free fluid in the abdominal cavity; percussion on one side of the abdomen transmits a wave that is felt on the opposite side.

microelectric w. See microwave.

P w. The initial deflection of the electrocardiogram (ECG), representing depolarization of the atria; if retrograde or ectopic, it is labeled P′.

pulse w. A wave originated by the impact of ejection of blood from the left ventricle into the full aorta and propagated to the periphery through the column of blood and the arterial walls.

Q w. The initial deflection of the QRS complex when such deflection is downward (negative).

R w. The first upward deflection of the QRS complex in the electrocardiogram (ECG).

random w.'s Brain waves in the electroencephalogram (EEG) produced by irregular changes of electric potential.

retrograde w. A distorted P wave pattern in the electrocardiogram (ECG), inverted in several leads where it should be upright, caused by an ectopic impulse from the ventricle spreading backward into the atria.

S w. A downward (negative) deflection of the QRS complex following an R wave.

    sound w. System of longitudinal pressure waves passing through any medium; may or may not be audible.

    T w. The deflection of the normal electrocardiogram (ECG) which follows the QRS complex; it represents ventricular repolarization.

    theta w. A wave in the electroencephalogram (EEG) with a frequency between 4 and 7 Hz. Also called theta rhythm.

    tidal w. The second and lesser of the two waves forming the main systolic arterial pulse wave.

    U w. A minor deflection of the normal electrocardiogram (ECG), which occasionally occurs in early ventricular diastole following the T wave; especially prominent in persons with electrolyte imbalance.

    ultrasonic w. A high-frequency sound wave, greater than 20,000 Hz; it cannot be heard by humans; used therapeutically and in diagnostic imaging.

wavelength (wāv'length) The distance between the crest of one wave and the same phase of the succeeding one.

wax (waks) A heat-sensitive substance formed by insects, or obtained from plants or petroleum; soluble in most organic solvents, insoluble in water; consists essentially of high-molecular-weight hydrocarbons or esters of fatty acids.

    baseplate w. A hard wax used in dentistry for making baseplates.

    bone w. An antiseptic wax used in bone surgery to stop bleeding by filling bone cavities.

    ear w. See cerumen.

    grave w. See adipocere.

weakness (wēk'nis) A decreased power and endurance of muscle contraction.

wean (wēn) **1.** A gradual substitution (e.g., of solid food for milk or formula in an infant's diet). **2.** Withdrawal (e.g., of a medication or a life-support system).

web (web) A membrane or membranous fold.

    esophageal w.'s Smooth ledges of mucous membrane, 2 to 4 mm thick, that protrude into the lumen of the esophagus above the level of the aortic arch; they progress over the years, causing difficult swallowing (dysphagia), especially of solid food; most commonly seen in women over 40 years of age. Also called upper esophageal rings.

weber (web'er) (Wb) In the International System of Units, the unit of magnetic flux that, linking a circuit of one turn, produces in it an electromotive force of 1 volt when it is reduced to 0 at a uniform rate in 1 second; 1 weber = 1 volt × 1 second.

wedging (wej'ing) The act of forcing or crowding into a limited space.

    anterior w. Collapse of a vertebral body in such a way that the anterior border becomes shorter and bowed in.

weeping (wēp'ing) The oozing of serum (e.g., from a skin eruption).

weight (wāt) The product of the pull of gravity upon a body.

    atomic w. (at wt) The weight of an atom as compared with the weight of an atom of carbon 12, taken as 12.00000.

    molecular w. (mol wt, MW) The sum of the atomic weights of all the atoms making up a molecule.

weight bearing (wāt bār'ing) The state or condition of supporting an applied load, such as bones and joints that support the body's weight, particularly those of the vertebral column, hips, knees, and feet.

weightlessness (wāt'les-nes) The state of experiencing no gravitational pull.

welt (welt) See wheal.

wen (wen) A sebaceous cyst, especially of the scalp.

wheal (hwēl) A transitory ridgelike or round swelling on the skin.

wheel (hwēl) A circular device that revolves around a central axis.

    rag w. An abrasive disk for polishing teeth; made up of cloth impregnated with pumice. Also called cloth disk.

wheeze (hwēz) **1.** To emit a whistling sound while breathing; usually due to constriction of the air passages, especially the bronchioles. **2.** The sound produced.

whiplash (hwip'lash) See whiplash injury, under injury.

whey (hwā) The thin fluid in milk remaining after separation of the casein; it contains water (92%), milk sugar (lactose), and water-soluble vitamins and minerals.

whipworm (hwip'wurm) See *Trichuris trichiura*, under Trichuris.

white of the eye Popular term for the visible part of the sclera.

whitehead (hwīt'hed) Popular term for milium.

whites (hwīts) Popular term for leukorrhea.

whitlow (hwit'lo) See felon.

    herpetic w. A herpesvirus infection of the nail bed characterized by a recurrent cluster of blisters; the virus gains entrance through abrasions on the finger; most commonly acquired by dentists, dental hygienists, and nurses while working on an infected mouth.

    melanomic w. See acral lentiginous melanoma, under melanoma.

    thecal w. Suppurative inflammation of the distal phalanx of a finger, involving the synovial sheath of the flexor tendon.

whoop (hoop) The shrill, noisy, paroxysmal gasp characteristic of whooping cough.

    systolic w. See systolic honk, under honk.

whooping cough (hoop'ing kawf) See pertussis.

whorl (hwerl) Any spiral arrangement, such as any of the circular ridges of a fingerprint, the muscular fibers at the apex of the heart, or the hairs growing in a radial manner on the scalp.

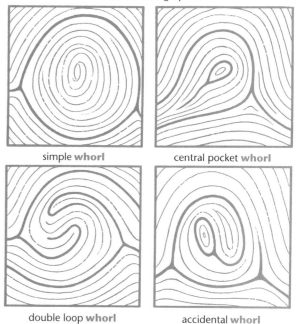

whorls of fingerprint

simple **whorl**   central pocket **whorl**

double loop **whorl**   accidental **whorl**

will (wil) **1.** A legal declaration of a person's wishes concerning disposition of his property after death. **2.** The processes involved in deciding upon a course of action and occurring at a conscious level.

    living w. A written document, signed by an adult of sound mind, instructing physicians about his wishes regarding life-sustaining treatment if in the future the person suffers from a disease or injury from which no recovery can reasonably be expected and during which the individual is not competent to make a decision as to the course of treatment, or can no longer communicate his wishes. Not all states have enacted laws giving effect to living wills, and the terms and provisions of existing laws vary from state to state.

    nuncupative w. An oral statement intended as a last will made by a person in anticipation of death. A nuncupative will may or may not be recognized by the laws of the decedent's state of residence.

windage (win'dej) Injury to internal organs caused by a sudden impact of the pressure of compressed air. Also called wind contusion.

windburn (wind'burn) Irritation of the skin caused by exposure to wind.

window (win'do) **1.** In anatomy, an opening in any partition-like structure or membrane. **2.** In radiology, a clear (radiolucent) area in an x-ray picture. **3.** In pharmacology, a range of drug concentration in the blood. **4.** A time interval (e.g., between ingestion of a poison and the production of irreversible organ damage).

    aortic w. In radiography of the chest, a clear space below the aortic arch and between the bifurcation of the trachea and the left pulmonary artery; visible in the left anterior oblique position.

    cochlear w. See fenestra of cochlea, under fenestra.

    implantation w. The time period during which the uterine wall will allow implantation of the fertilized ovum; its length in humans has been estimated to be between one and four days.

    oval w. See fenestra of vestibule, under fenestra.

    round w. See fenestra of cochlea, under fenestra.

    therapeutic w. The range of a drug's concentration within which a desired effect is most probable to occur. The therapeutic window may vary among individual patients.

    vestibular w. See fenestra of vestibule, under fenestra.

windpipe (wind'pīp) Popular term for the trachea.

wing (wing) Any anatomic structure resembling a wing of a bird.

wire (wīr) **1.** A metallic strand used in surgery and dentistry. **2.** To bind or secure with a wire.

    arch w. An orthodontic wire attached to molar bands positioned around the dental arch; used to provide tooth stabilization and/or maintain controlled pressure for tooth movement.

    Kirschner w. A heavy-gauge steel wire used for applying traction and fixation of a fractured bone.

    ligature w. In orthodontics, a soft slender wire used to tie an arch wire to the band attachment around a tooth.

wiring (wīr'ing) In orthopedics, fixation of the ends of broken bones by means of wire.

withdrawal (with-draw'al) **1.** The act of removing, relinquishing, or discontinuing. **2.** An abnormal detachment or retreat from emotional involvement with people or the environment; seen in its extreme in those afflicted with schizophrenia. **3.** See withdrawal symptoms, under symptoms.

womb (woōm) Popular term for uterus.

    falling of w. See prolapse of uterus, under prolapse.

    neck of w. See uterine cervix, under cervix.

woodchuck (wood'chuk) See marmot.

word salad (werd sal'ad) The mixing of unrelated words and phrases that lack comprehensible meaning, seen in schizophrenia.

working through (werk'ing throo) In psychoanalysis, the active exploration of a problem by patient and therapist until a satisfactory solution is found or until a symptom is traced to its unconscious source; it generally involves bringing into conscious awareness infan-

tile, repressed, unconscious material.

work-up (werk'up) Procedures performed to arrive at a diagnosis.

World Health Organization (WHO) An agency of the United Nations concerned with health on an international level.

worm (wurm) Common name for any of the elongated soft-bodied invertebrates of the phyla Annelida (segmented worms), Nematoda (roundworms), and Platyhelminthes (flatworms).

    eye w. See *Loa loa*.

    pin w. See pinworm.

    pork w. See *Trichinella spiralis*.

    seat w. See pinworm.

    trichina w. See *Trichinella spiralis*.

wound (woōnd) Injury or trauma in any tissue with interruption of the continuity of the tissue.

    aseptic w. (*a*) A wound made under sterile conditions (e.g., a surgical incision). (*b*) A wound that is free of infective microorganisms.

    avulsed w. An open wound, usually caused by a blunt object, in which the full thickness of the skin and underlying tissues are removed.

    blowing w. See sucking wound.

    crease w. See gutter wound.

    defense w.'s Nonlethal wounds on the arms and hands of an assault victim incurred while trying to protect his face or chest from the assailant's weapon.

    entrance w. A wound, typically with inverted edges, made by a projectile discharged from a high-velocity weapon; it varies in shape and size depending on the range and velocity of the projectile and its trajectory angle at the instant of impact, the presence or absence of intervening clothing or other materials or objects, the site of impact on the body (e.g., bony or soft tissue areas), and the shape of the missile itself. Also called entry wound; in-shoot wound. See also abrasion collar, under collar. COMPARE exit wound.

    entry w. See entrance wound.

    exit w. A wound made by a projectile discharged from a high-velocity weapon as it emerges from the body; it has an irregular configuration usually with everted edges and is larger than the entrance wound; the size and eversion of the wound may be lessened when the skin has been supported by outside pressure (e.g., tight clothing or by resting upon a hard surface). Also called out-shoot wound. COMPARE entrance wound.

    glancing w. See gutter wound.

    gunshot w. Wound made by a projectile discharged from a firearm. See also entrance wound; exit wound; bullet tract, under tract.

    gutter w. A tangential wound that produces a furrowlike injury.

    hesitation w.'s Superficial nonlethal cuts, sometimes numerous, running parallel to and on either side of a main, deep, suicidal cut; seen on the neck and/or wrists of a suicide victim; also seen in victims of failed suicide attempts.

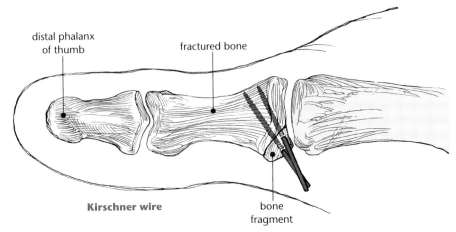

distal phalanx of thumb   fractured bone

Kirschner wire   bone fragment

W

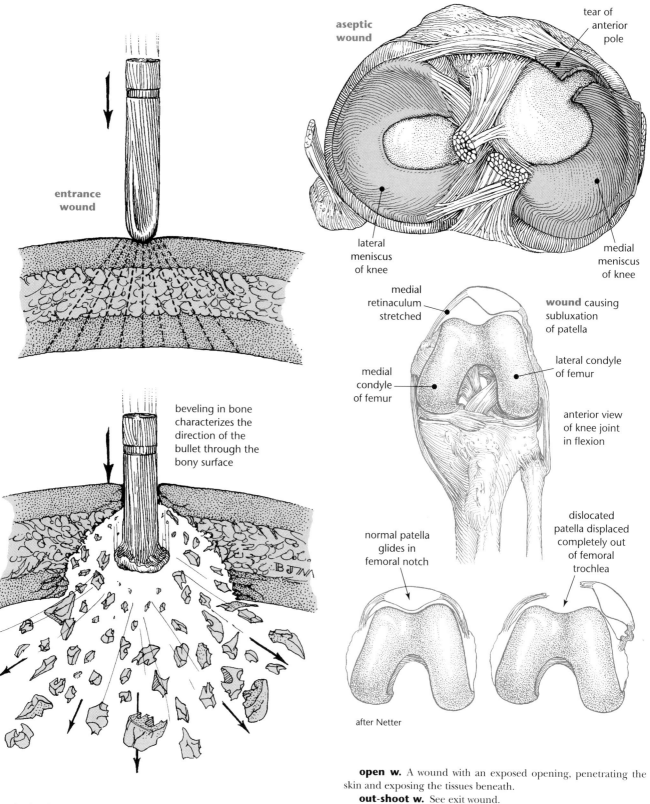

entrance wound

aseptic wound

tear of anterior pole

lateral meniscus of knee

medial meniscus of knee

beveling in bone characterizes the direction of the bullet through the bony surface

medial retinaculum stretched

wound causing subluxation of patella

medial condyle of femur

lateral condyle of femur

anterior view of knee joint in flexion

normal patella glides in femoral notch

dislocated patella displaced completely out of femoral trochlea

after Netter

incised w. A wound with clean, smooth edges, made with a sharp instrument or device.

in-shoot w. See entrance wound.

lacerated w. A wound with jagged edges caused by tearing (e.g., an animal or human bite).

nonpenetrating w. Injury to tissues occurring without disruption of skin continuity, usually caused by the impact of a blunt object.

open w. A wound with an exposed opening, penetrating the skin and exposing the tissues beneath.

out-shoot w. See exit wound.

penetrating w. A wound that interrupts the continuity of the skin.

perforating w. A wound through the wall of a body cavity.

puncture w. A narrow wound made by a spiked instrument or weapon.

septic w. An infected wound.

seton w. A wound that enters and exits on the same side of the injured part, usually made by stabbing.

W

wound ■ wound

stab w. In forensic medicine, an incised wound that has a depth of penetration greater than its surface length. Most stab wounds are homicidal. COMPARE cut.

sucking w. An open penetrating wound through the chest wall, exposing the lung of the same side to atmospheric pressure and causing it to collapse.

wrinkle (ring′kl) A crease or furrow.

wrist (rist) The carpal bones and adjoining structures between the forearm and the hand. See table of bones.

gymnast's w. Prominence of the head of the ulna at the wrist, with pain and limited range of motion and, sometimes, abnormalities of the growth plates of the radius and ulna; caused by repetitive compression of the bones during gymnastic exercises (e.g., handstands).

wristdrop (rist′drop) Paralysis of the extensor muscles of the hand and fingers, usually caused by injury to the radial nerve. Also called drop hand.

wryneck (ri′neck) See torticollis.

Wuchereria (voo-ker-e′re-ah) A genus of parasitic roundworms (family Onchocercidae).

W. bancrofti A parasite of the lymphatic vessels, causing elephantiasis; transmitted by mosquitoes.

wuchereriasis (voo-ker-e-ri′ah-sis) Infection with worms of the genus *Wuchereria*.

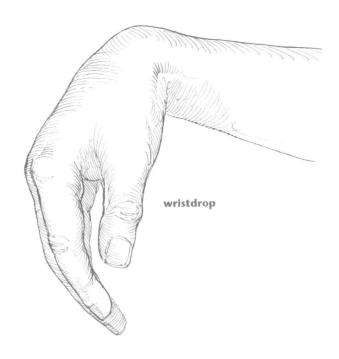

wristdrop

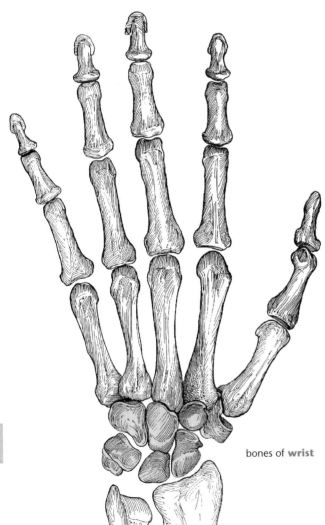

bones of **wrist**

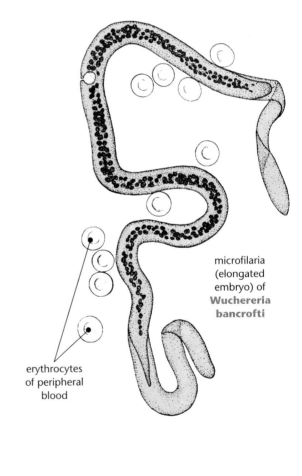

microfilaria (elongated embryo) of **Wuchereria bancrofti**

erythrocytes of peripheral blood

W

wrinkle ■ wuchereriasis

xanthelasma (zan-thel-az′mah) A type of xanthoma occurring as soft yellowish plaques on the eyelids, especially at the medial angle near the bridge of the nose.

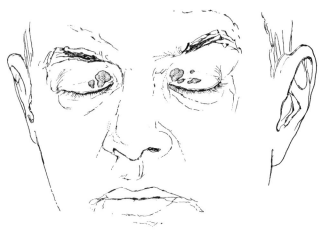

xanthelasma of the eyelids

xanthemia (zan-the′me-ah) See carotenemia.

xanthene (zan′thēn) A crystalline compound that is the basic structure of many dyestuffs.

xanthic (zan′thik) **1.** Yellow. **2.** Relating to xanthine.

xanthine (zan′thēn) A white purine base present in most of the body tissues, converted to uric acid by xanthine oxidase; xanthine derivatives include caffeine and theophylline.

xanthinuria (zan-thin-u′re-ah) Presence of excessive amounts of xanthine in the urine.

xantho-, xanth- Combining forms meaning yellowish.

xanthochromic (zan-tho-kro′mik) Having a yellowish color.

xanthodont (zan′tho-dont) A person who has yellowish teeth.

xanthogranuloma (zan-tho-gran-u-lo′mah) Infiltration of tissue by lipid-laden macrophages.

    juvenile x. A benign condition of infants and children, most commonly seen in infants during the first months of life; characterized by the presence of yellowish nodules on the skin, with an occasional ocular involvement; they regress spontaneously. Also called nevoxanthoendothelioma.

xanthoma (zan-tho′mah) A slightly raised yellow plaque on the skin; may be due to a disorder of fat metabolism or to unknown causes.

    eruptive x. Sudden appearance of groups of xanthomas on the buttocks, posterior thighs, knees, and elbows; associated with changing plasma levels of triglyceride and lipids.

    x. multiplex See xanthomatosis.

    plane x. Yellow bands occurring in skin folds or creases, especially on the palms; occasionally associated with primary cirrhosis of the liver.

    tendinous x. Yellowish nodules occurring over the Achilles tendon (tendo calcaneus) and extensor tendons of the fingers.

    tuberous x. Yellowish nodules of varying size occurring chiefly over joints, especially the knees, elbows, and feet.

xanthomatosis (zan-tho-mah-to′sis) The presence of multiple xanthomas. Also called lipid granulomatosis; lipoid granulomatosis; xanthoma multiplex.

    cerebrotendinous x. Genetic disorder transmitted as an autosomal recessive inheritance; characterized by deposition of cholesterol in tendons, lungs, and the brain, causing pulmonary insufficiency and neurologic dysfunction; it usually develops after puberty.

xanthomatous (zan-tho′mah-tus) Relating to xanthomas.

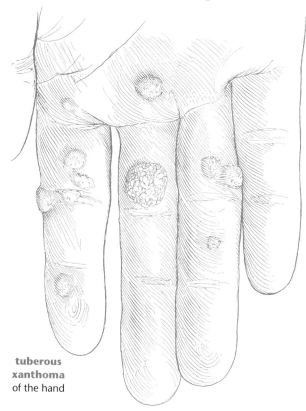

tuberous xanthoma of the hand

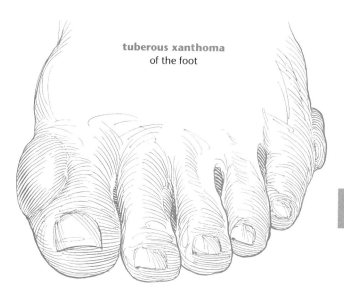

tuberous xanthoma of the foot

xanthophyll (zan'tho-fil) A yellow carotenoid pigment present in plants and egg yolk; seen in human plasma as a result of eating food containing the pigment.

xanthopsia (zan-thop'se-ah) A defective color vision in which everything appears yellow. Also called yellow vision.

xanthosine (zan'tho-sēn) (Xao) A nucleoside formed by the removal of the amino group (deamination) from guanosine.

xanthosis (zan-tho'sis) A yellowish discoloration of the skin, sometimes seen in patients afflicted with cancer.

xanthous, (zan'thus) Yellowish.

xanthurenic acid (zanth-u-ren'ik as'id) A metabolite excreted in large amounts during pregnancy and pyridoxine-deficient states.

xeno-, xen- Combining forms meaning foreign; extraneous.

xenobiotic, (zen-o-bi-ot'ik) Any chemical substance that is not produced by the living organism and is, therefore, foreign to it (e.g., carcinogens, insecticides, drugs, natural compounds).

xenogeneic (zen-o-jen-a'ik) Relating to different species; applied especially to xenografts. Also called heterologous.

xenograft (zen'o-graft) A graft obtained from tissues of another species. Also called xenogeneic graft; heterotransplant.

xenon (ze'non) An odorless gaseous element; symbol Xe, atomic number 54, atomic weight 131.3; present in minute proportions in the atmosphere.

xenon 133 (^{133}Xe) A gamma-emitting radioactive inert gas with a half-life of 5.27 days; used to measure blood flow and regional pulmonary ventilation.

xenophobia (zen-o-fo'be-ah) An irrational fear of strangers or foreigners.

xenophthalmia (zen-of-thal'me-ah) Inflammation of the transparent covering of the eye (conjunctiva) due to injury or the presence of a foreign body.

Xenopsylla (zen-op-sil'ah) A genus of fleas (family Pulicidae); many species are vectors of disease.

    X. cheopis The rat flea; vector of *Pasteurella pestis,* the causative agent of bubonic plague.

xeransis (ze-ran'sis) A drying out of tissues.

xerantic (ze-ran'tik) Causing dryness.

xero- Combining form meaning dry.

xerocheilia (ze-ro-ki'le-ah) Dryness of the lips.

xeroderma (ze-ro-der'mah) Condition characterized by dryness, roughness, and discoloration of the skin.

    x. pigmentosum (XP) An inherited autosomal recessive disease due to a lack of one or more multigene products and chromosome fragility, which renders the body unable to repair sunlight-damaged skin; manifestations range from heightened sensitivity to sunlight to severe sunburn in infancy, abnormal freckling, thinning of the skin, and development of malignant tumors at an early age. Also called atrophoderma pigmentosum.

xerography (ze-rog'rah-fe) See xeroradiography.

xeromenia (ze-ro-me'ne-ah) The occurrence of the usual symptoms of menstruation but without a menstrual blood flow.

xerophthalmia (ze-rof-thal'me-ah) A degenerative condition of the eye characterized by extreme dryness and thickening of the conjunctiva with diminished secretion of tears.

xeroradiography (ze-ro-ra-de-og'rah-fe) A photoelectric method of recording x-ray images using, instead of films, a specially coated metal plate, low-energy photon beams, and dry chemical developers instead of liquids. Also called xerography.

xerosis (ze-ro'sis) Abnormal dryness of mucous membranes and conjunctiva.

xerostomia (ze-ro-sto'me-ah) Abnormal dryness of the mouth; causes are many, ranging from emotional stress to salivary gland disease and intake of certain pharmaceutical preparations. Popularly called dry mouth.

xerotic (ze-rot'ik) Abnormally dry.

xerotocia (ze-ro-to'se-ah) See dry labor, under labor.

xiphisternum (zif-ī-ster'num) The xiphoid process.

xiphocostal (zif-o-kos'tal) Relating to the xiphoid process and the ribs.

xiphodynia (zif-o-din'e-ah) Pain in the area of the xiphoid process.

xiphoid (zif'oid) Shaped like a sword; applied especially to the xiphoid process. See under process.

X-linked (eks'linkt) Determined by a gene located on the X chromosome.

x ray (eks'ra) See under ray.

x-ray The common term for roentgenogram. See under roentgenogram.

xylene (zi'lēn) A flammable hydrocarbon obtained from wood and coal tar; used as a solvent. Also called xylol.

xylo-, xyl- Combining forms meaning wood.

xylol (zi'lol), See xylene.

xylose (zi'lōs) A pentose sugar present in beechwood, straw, and vegetable gums; used in a diagnostic test in suspected cases of malabsorption.

xylulose (zi'lu-lōs) A pentose sugar found in two forms: D-*xylulose,* an intermediate in pentose metabolism; and L-*xylulose,* an abnormal constituent of urine occurring in essential pentosuria.

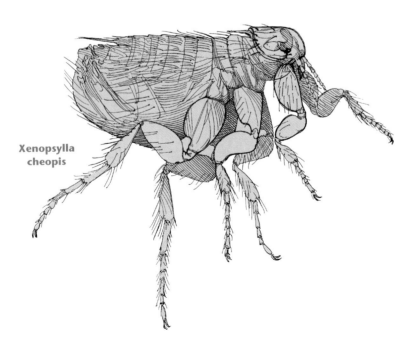

Xenopsylla cheopis

Y

yaw (yaw) One of the skin lesions occurring in yaws.

yawn (yawn) A deep inspiration, usually involuntary, through the open mouth.

yaws (yawz) A bacterial skin infection characterized by eruptions of papules on the face, hands, feet, and around the external genitalia; caused by a spirochete, *Treponema pertenue.* Also called frambesia; pian.

yeast (yēst) **1.** Any of several fungi capable of fermenting carbohydrates. **2.** A commercial preparation, in either dry or moist form, used as a leavening agent or as a dietary supplement.

   brewer's y. A by-product of the brewing of beer, used as a source of protein and vitamin B complex.

yellow jacket (yel'o jak'et) Any of various small, stinging wasps of the family Vespidae, having yellow and black markings; their stings can cause severe and lethal allergic reactions in hypersensitive people.

Yersinia (yer-sin'e-ah) Genus of coccoid, oval, or rod-shaped bacteria (family Enterobacteriaceae).

   Y. enterocolitica Species found in wild and domestic animals; in humans it causes yersiniosis.

   Y. pestis The causative agent of plague in humans, transmitted by fleas from infected rats, squirrels, and prairie dogs.

yersiniosis (yer-sin-e-o'sis) Infection with the bacterium *Yersinia enterocolitica,* characterized by diarrhea, lymph node inflammation, especially in the abdomen, and arthritis.

yogurt (yo'goort) Curdled milk fermented by the combined action of *Lactobacillus acidophilus* and *Streptococcus thermophilus.*

yohimbine (yo-him'bēn) An alkaloid with a structure similar to that of reserpine; it is a relatively selective inhibitor of alpha$_2$-adrenergic receptors.

yolk (yōk) **1.** The nutritive portion of an ovum, especially prominent in the eggs of birds and reptiles. **2.** The fatty substance present in the unprocessed wool of sheep that, when purified, becomes lanolin.

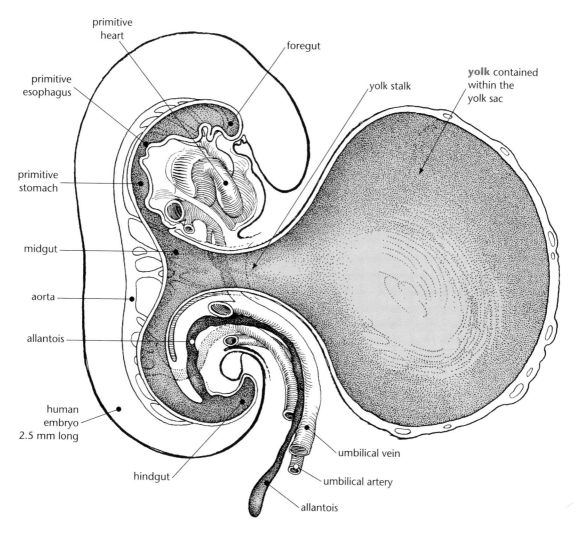

primitive heart

primitive esophagus

primitive stomach

midgut

aorta

allantois

human embryo 2.5 mm long

hindgut

allantois

foregut

yolk stalk

yolk contained within the yolk sac

umbilical vein

umbilical artery

Y

ytterbium (ĭ-ter′be-um) A rare-earth element; symbol Yb, atomic number 70, atomic weight 173.04.

yttrium (ĭ′tre-um) Metallic element; symbol Y, atomic number 39, atomic weight 88.9.

yttrium 90 (^{90}Y) A radioactive isotope of yttrium; has been used in the treatment of breast and prostatic cancer.

Group	I	II												III	IV	V	VI	VII	O

Period

METALS — yttrium — NONMETALS

periodic table

1	H 1																		He 2
2	Li 3	Be 4												B 5	C 6	N 7	O 8	F 9	Ne 10
3	Na 11	Mg 12												Al 13	Si 14	P 15	S 16	Cl 17	Ar 18
4	K 19	Ca 20	Sc 21	Ti 22	V 23	Cr 24	Mn 25	Fe 26	Co 27	Ni 28	Cu 29	Zn 30	Ga 31	Ge 32	As 33	Se 34	Br 35	Kr 36
5	Rb 37	Sr 38	Y 39	Zr 40	Nb 41	Mo 42	Tc 43	Ru 44	Rh 45	Pd 46	Ag 47	Cd 48	In 49	Sn 50	Sb 51	Te 52	I 53	Xe 54
6	Cs 55	Ba 56	* 57-71	Hf 72	Ta 73	W 74	Re 75	Os 76	Ir 77	Pt 78	Au 79	Hg 80	Ti 81	Pb 82	Bi 83	Po 84	At 85	Rn 86
7	Fr 87	Ra 88	** 89-103	Rf 104	Ha 105													

ytterbium ↓

| * | lanthanide elements (rare earth) | La 57 | Ce 58 | Pr 59 | Nd 60 | Pm 61 | Sm 62 | Eu 63 | Gd 64 | Tb 65 | Dy 66 | Ho 67 | Er 68 | Tm 69 | Yb 70 | Lu 71 |
| ** | actinide elements | Ac 89 | Th 90 | Pa 91 | U 92 | Np 93 | Pu 94 | Am 95 | Cm 96 | Bk 97 | Cf 98 | Es 99 | Fm 100 | Md 101 | No 102 | Lw 103 |

Y

Z

zelotypia (ze-lo-tip′e-ah) Extreme, abnormal zeal in advocating any cause.

zeolite (ze′o-līt) A hydrated sodium aluminum silicate occurring naturally; an ion exchanger used for softening of hard water by exchanging its Na^+ for the Ca^{++} of the water. Zeolites have no chemical relationship with synthetic ion exchangers.

zero (ze′ro) 1. The absence of quantity. 2. In thermometry, the point from which the graduation of a thermometer starts. In the centigrade scale, the freezing point of distilled water.

    absolute z. The hypothetical point in a temperature scale at which there is complete absence of heat; in kinetic theory, absence of relative linear molecular motion, postulated as $-273.2°C$.

zidovudine (zi-do′vu-dēn) A drug used in the management of immune deficiency syndrome (AIDS); adverse effects include anemia and gastrointestinal symptoms. Formerly called azidothymidine (AZT).

ZIFT Acronym for Zygote Intrafallopian Transfer. See under transfer.

zinc (zingk) Metallic element; symbol Zn, atomic number 30, atomic weight 65.37.

    z. chloride A water-soluble caustic powder, formerly used to destroy tissue (e.g., in the treatment of skin lesions).

    z. oxide White powder that is a mild astringent and antiseptic; incorporated in dusting powders, ointments, and lotions (the main ingredient of calamine lotion); also used as a replacement for lead carbonate in paints. Also called zinc white.

    z. oxide and eugenol (ZOE) Compound used in dentistry as a base material beneath a tooth restoration, a temporary filling, an impression paste, and root canal filling; also used as a hardening material for demineralized dentin.

    z. permanganate Dark brown, water-soluble crystals; used in solution as an antiseptic and astringent.

    z. peroxide (ZPO) A yellowish powder, insoluble in water; used as a wash (suspended in four parts of water) for oral infections and to disinfect, deodorize, and promote healing of wound infections.

    z. stearate White greasy granules, insoluble in water; used in powder form as an antiseptic and water repellent to protect superficial skin lesions.

    z. sulfate White water-soluble powder, used in solution as an eyewash to treat mild eye irritations, and as a lotion (white lotion) to treat skin conditions (e.g., acne, impetigo, ivy poisoning). Also called white vitriol.

    z. white See zinc oxide.

zinciferous (zing-kif′er-us) Containing zinc.

zirconium (zir-ko′ne-um) Metallic element; symbol Zr, atomic number 40, atomic weight 91.22.

zoacanthosis (zo-ak-an-tho′sis) Any skin eruption or inflammation resulting from the implantation of such foreign materials as animal bristles, hairs, and stingers.

zoanthropic (zo-an-throp′ik) Relating to zoanthropy.

zoanthropy (zo-an′thro-pe) The delusion of being an animal.

zoetic (zo-et′ik) Relating to life; living.

zoic (zo′ik) Relating to animal life.

zona (zo′nah), pl. zo′nae A zone, especially an encircling region distinguished from adjacent parts by some distinctive characteristic.

    z. ciliaris See ciliary zonule, under zonule.

    z. dermatica An area of thick elevated skin surrounding the protrusion of a meningocele.

    z. fasciculata The wide middle region in the cortex of the adrenal gland, between the zona glomerulosa and the zona reticularis; composed of lipid-rich cells arranged in radially directed cords; it is (together with the zona reticularis) the region where adrenal steroids, other than aldosterone, are produced.

    z. glomerulosa The thin outermost layer of the cortex of the adrenal gland, just below the capsule; it is the site of aldosterone production.

    z. hemorrhoidalis The portion of the anal canal containing the rectal venous plexus.

    z. orbicularis The deep, circularly arranged fibers of the articular capsule that encircle the hip joint. Also called orbicular zone of hip joint.

    z. pellucida A gellike glycoprotein layer surrounding a developing ovum in the ovarian follicle; it plays a role in fertilization as it is penetrated by the sperm; it persists while the zygote undergoes cell divisions up to the blastocyst stage, when it degenerates and disappears just prior to implantation into the uterine wall.

    z. reticularis The inner layer of the cortex of the adrenal gland, adjacent to the adrenal medulla; it is (together with the zona fasciculata) the region where adrenal steroids, other than aldosterone, are produced.

zonal (zo′nal) Relating to a zone.

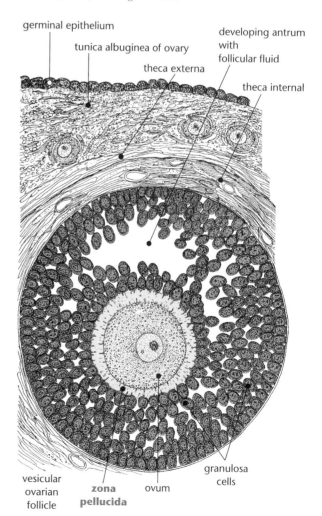

germinal epithelium

tunica albuginea of ovary

theca externa

developing antrum with follicular fluid

theca internal

granulosa cells

vesicular ovarian follicle

zona pellucida

ovum

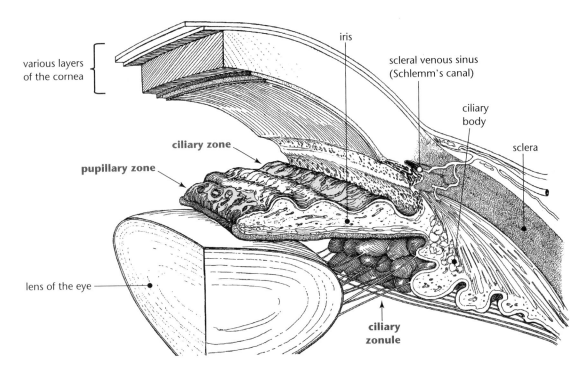

various layers of the cornea

iris

scleral venous sinus (Schlemm's canal)

ciliary body

sclera

ciliary zone

pupillary zone

ciliary zonule

lens of the eye

zone (zōn) (z) Any area or space with differentiating characteristics; a region.

   ciliary z. The circular region at the periphery of the anterior surface of the iris. COMPARE pupillary zone.

   comfort z. An environmental temperature between 28° and 30°C (70°–82°F) in which the naked body heat is maintained in equilibrium, without sweating or shivering.

   z.'s of discontinuity Concentric bands of varying optical density in the lens of the eye.

   erogenous z., erotogenic z. Any area of the body that on appropriate stimulation produces sexual sensations.

   Golgi z. The portion of cytoplasm near the nucleus that is occupied by the Golgi apparatus; in a secretory cell, it is between the nucleus and the luminal side of the cell through which expulsion of the secretion takes place.

   orbicular z. of hip joint See zona orbicularis, under zona.

   pupillary z. The central region of the anterior surface of the iris, surrounding the pupil.

   transitional z. The circular region in the equator of the lens of the eye, adjacent to the lens capsule, where new lens fibers develop from the anterior epithelial cells.

zonesthesia (zo-nes-the′ze-ah) A constricting sensation, as by a band.

zonula (zōn′u-lah) Latin for zonule.

   z. occludens See tight junction, under junction.

zonular (zon′u-lar) Relating to a zonule.

zonule (zōn′ul) A small zone, usually circular.

   ciliary z. The suspensory apparatus of the lens of the eye; consists of fine fibers extending from the ciliary processes to the lens, attached to the lens capsule close to the equator. Also called zonule of Zinn; zona ciliaris.

   z. of Zinn See ciliary zonule.

zonulolysis (zon-u-lol′ĭ-sis) Dissolution of the ciliary zonule with an enzyme (e.g., chymotripsin) to facilitate removal of the lens of the eye in some types of cataract extraction.

zoo-, zo- Combining forms meaning animal.

zooanthroponosis (zo′o-an′thro-po-no′sis) A disease usually occurring in humans that is transmissible to animals.

zoogonous (zo-og′o-nus) See viviparous.

zooid (zo′oid) 1. Resembling an animal. 2. An animal cell capable of independent movement within a living organism (e.g., a sperm).

zoologist (zo-ol′o-jist) A specialist in zoology.

zoology (zo-ol′o-je) The branch of biology concerned with the study of animals.

zoonosis (zo-o-no′sis) Any disease acquired from animals, or shared by humans and other vertebrates.

zoonotic (zo-o-not′ik) Relating to zoonosis.

zooparasite (zo-o-par′ah-sit) A parasite animal organism.

zoopathology (zo-o-pah-thol′o-je) Veterinary pathology; the study of diseases of animals.

zoophilic (zo-o-fil′ik) Denoting a preference for animals; applied to parasites.

zoophobia (zo-o-fo′be-ah) Abnormal fear of animals.

zoophyte (zo′o-fit) An invertebrate animal that superficially resembles a plant (e.g., a sponge).

zootic (zo-ot′ik) Relating to animals.

zootoxin (zo-o-tok′sin) A substance elaborated by certain animals that has poisonous or antigenic properties (e.g., snake venom, secretions of certain insects).

zosteroid (zos′ter-oid) Resembling herpes zoster.

Z-plasty (ze-plas′te) Procedure used in plastic surgery for relaxing tension in a contracted tissue, or to lengthen an area of skin in primary wound closure; useful for revising scars, especially of the face, and for releasing scar contractions across joints (e.g., on fingers or armpits), which may restrict movement; consists of making a Z-shaped incision, creating two V-shaped flaps by separating skin from underlying tissue, and transposing and suturing the flaps.

zwitterion (tsvit′er-i-on) An ion that has both positive and negative charges; a dipolar ion.

zygal (zi′gal) Shaped like a yoke.

zygo-, zyg- Combining forms meaning a joining.

zygodactyly (zi-go-dak′tĭ-le) See syndactyly.

zygoma (zi-go′mah) 1. See zygomatic arch, under arch. 2. Term sometimes applied to the zygomatic bone. See table of bones.

zygomatic (zi-go-mat′ik) Relating to the cheekbone (zygomatic bone).

zygomycosis (zi-go-mi-ko′sis) See phycomycosis.

zygosis (zi-go′sis) The fusion of two unicellular organisms, with exchange of nuclear material.

zygosity (zi-gos′ĭ-te) A state relating to the fertilized egg (zygote); often used as a word termination. Relating to twin pregnancies, development from one zygote (monozygosity) or from two zygotes (dizygosity). Relating to the genetic characteristic, whether they are identical (homozygosity) or different (heterozygosity).

zygote (zi′gōt) The single fertilized cell formed by the fusion of the male and female reproductive cells (gametes).

zygotene (zi'go-tēn) In meiosis, the second stage of prophase in which the homologous chromosomes approach each other and begin to pair.

zymo-, zym- Combining forms meaning fermentation; enzyme.

zymogen (zi'mo-jen) See proenzyme.

zymogenesis (zi-mo-jen'ĕ-sis) The formation of an active enzyme from a proenzyme (inactive precursor).

zymogenic, zymogenous (zi-mo-jen'ik, zi-moj'ĕ-nus) **1.** Relating to a proenzyme or to zymogenesis. **2.** Producing fermentation.

zymogram (zi'mo-gram) A graphic representation of electrophoretically separated enzymes.

zymology (zi-mol'o-je) See enzymology.

zymosan (zi'mo-san) An insoluble anticomplementary factor composed of lipids, polysaccharides, proteins, and ash of variable concentrations; derived from the walls of yeast cells; used in the assay of the protein properdin.

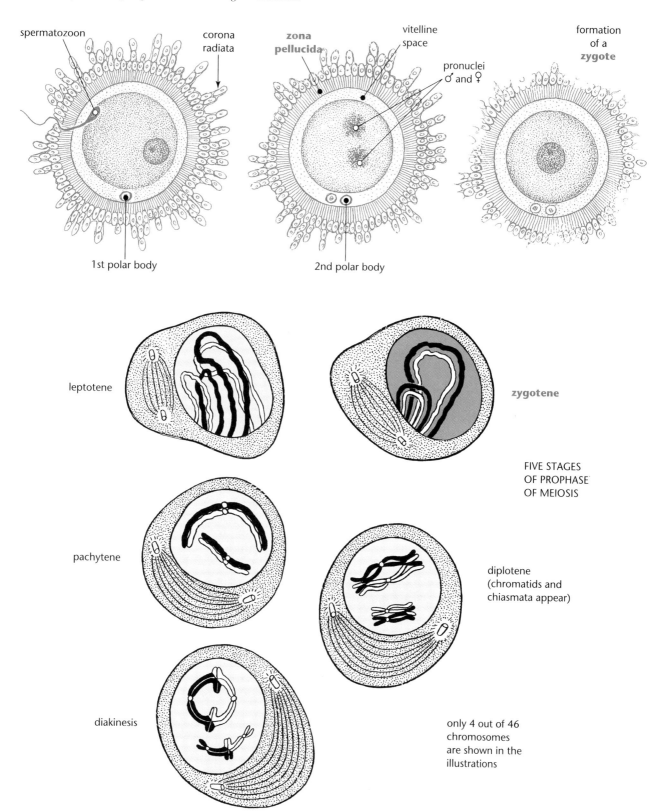

spermatozoon

corona radiata

zona pellucida

vitelline space

pronuclei ♂ and ♀

formation of a zygote

1st polar body

2nd polar body

leptotene

zygotene

FIVE STAGES OF PROPHASE OF MEIOSIS

pachytene

diplotene (chromatids and chiasmata appear)

diakinesis

only 4 out of 46 chromosomes are shown in the illustrations

APPENDIX

Selected Abbreviations
Used in Medicine

A alveolar gas (as a subscript); mass number

A accommodation; admittance; adult; age; angstrom (unit); area; atrium; auricle; blood type A$^+$, A$^-$; dominant allele

A1 aortic first heart sound

A2 aortic second heart sound

a accommodation; recessive allele

a. *ante* [Latin] before; *arteria* [Latin] artery

AA achievement age; Addicts Anonymous; Alcoholic Anonymous; amino acid

A&A awake and aware

aa. *arteriae* [Latin] arteries

AAA abdominal aortic aneurysm; acute anxiety attack

AAAS American Association for the Advancement of Science

AABB American Association of Blood Banks

AAD American Academy of Dermatology

AAF acetylaminofluorene

AAFP American Academy of Family Physicians

AAEM American Academy of Environmental Medicine

AAI American Association of Immunologists

AAL anterior axillary line

AAMRA American Association of Medical Record Administrators

AAN American Academy of Neurology; attending's admission notes

AANS American Academy of Neurological Surgery

AAO American Academy of Ophthalmology; American Academy of Otolaryngology

AAOS American Academy of Orthopaedic Surgeons

AAP American Academy of Pediatrics; American Association of Pathologists

AAPMR American Academy of Physical Medicine and Rehabilitation

AAPS American Association of Plastic Surgeons

AART American Association for Rehabilitation Therapy

AAS aortic arch syndrome

AASD American Academy of Stress Disorders

AAST American Association for the Surgery of Trauma

AATS American Association of Thoracic Surgery

AAV adeno-associated virus

AB abnormal; asthmatic bronchitis; blood type AB+, AB−

A/B acid base (ratio)

Ab abortion; antibody

abbr. abbreviated

ABC airway, breathing, and circulation; antigen binding capacity; aspiration biopsy cytology

abd. abduction; abdomen; abduct

ABE acute bacterial endocarditis

ABFP American Board of Forensic Psychiatry

ABG arterial blood gas

ABMS American Board of Medical Specialties

ABMT autologous bone marrow transplant

abn. abnormal

ABO blood groups A, B, AB, and O

ABOS American Board of Orthopaedic Surgery

ABP arterial blood pressure

ABPA allergic bronchopulmonary aspergillosis

ABR absolute bed rest; auditory brainstem response

ABS admitting blood sugar; at bedside

abs. absent

abs. feb. *absente febre* [Latin] while fever is absent

abstr. abstract

ABT autologous blood transfusion

ABVD adriamycin (doxorubicin), bleomycin, vinblastine, dacarbazine (a chemotherapeutic regimen for treating cancer)

ABX antibiotics

AC acromioclavicular (joint); adrenal cortex; air conduction; alternating current; anticoagulant

Ac actinium

aC arabinosylcytosine

ac acromioclavicular (joint); acute; adrenal cortex; air conduction; alternating current; anchored catheter; anterior chamber (of eye)

a.c. *ante cibum* [Latin] before meals

ACA anterior cerebral artery

AC/A accommodative convergence-accommodation (ratio)

ACBE air contrast barium enema

ACC ambulatory care center; American College of Cardiology

acc. accident; accommodation

ACCP American College of Chest Physicians

ACD acid citrate dextrose

ACDCPR active compression-decompression cardiopulmonary resuscitation

ACE angiotensin converting enzyme; adrenocortical extract

ace. acetone

ACEI angiotensin converting enzyme inhibitor

ACEP American College of Emergency Physicians

ACG American College of Gastroenterology; angiocardiogram; angiocardiography

ac-g accelerator globulin

ACGME Accreditation Council for Graduate Medical Education

ACh acetylcholine

AChE acetylcholinesterase

AChR acetylcholine receptor

ACI after-care instructions

ACIP Advisory Committee on Immunization Practices

ACJ acromioclavicular joint

ACL anterior cruciate ligament

ACLS advanced cardiac life support

ACOG American College of Obstetricians and Gynecologists

ACOM American College of Occupational Medicine

ACP acid phosphatase; acyl-carrier protein; American College of Physicians; aspirin-caffeine-phenacetin

ACPS acrocephalopolysyndactyly

ACR American College of Radiology;

ACRM American Congress of Rehabilitation Medicine

ACS American Cancer Society; American Chemical Society

ACSM American College of Sports Medicine

ACT activated clotting time; alternate cover test

ACTH adrenocorticotropic hormone

ACTH ST adrenocorticotropic horome (ACTH) stimulation test

ACV acyclovir

AD addict; adenoid; adenovirus; Alzheimer's disease; analgesic dose; autosomal dominant

a.d. *alternis diebus* [Latin] every other day; *auris dextra* [Latin] right ear

ADA adenosine deaminase; American Dental Association; American Diabetes Association

ADAP Alzheimer's disease associated protein

AdC adrenal cortex

ADCC antibody-dependent cell-mediated cytotoxicity

ADD attention deficit disorder

add. adduction

addict. addiction

ADDU alcohol and drug dependency unit

ADEM acute disseminating encephalomyelitis

ADH alcohol dehydrogenase; antidiuretic hormone

ADHD attention deficit hyperactivity disorder

ADI acceptable daily intake

ADL activities of daily living

ad. lib. *ad libitum* [Latin] as desired

adm. admission

Ado adenosine

ADODM adult-onset diabetes mellitus

ADP adenosine diphosphate

ADPase adenosine diphosphatase

ADPKD autosomal dominant polycystic kidney disease

ADPL average daily patient load

ADR adverse drug reaction

adr. adrenalin

ADS anonymous donor's sperm

adst. feb. *adstante febre* [Latin] when fever is present

ADT adenosine triphosphate; admission-discharge-transfer; anterior drawer test

ad us. ext. *ad usum externum* [Latin] for external use

ADV adenovirus

AE above elbow (said of amputations and prostheses); adverse event

AEA above elbow amputation

AEC at earliest convenience

AF amniotic fluid; anterior fontanelle; atrial fibrillation; atrial flutter

AFAFP amniotic fluid alpha-fetoprotein

AFB acid-fast bacteria

AFC antibody-forming cells

AFCR American Federation for Clinical Research

AFE amniotic fluid embolism

aff. afferent

AFIP Armed Forces Institute of Pathology

AFL atrial flutter

AFO ankle-foot orthosis

AFP alpha-fetoprotein

AFX atypical fibroxanthoma

AG antigravity; atrial gallop

A/G albumin/globulin ratio

Ag antigen; silver

AGA appropriate for gestational age

AGE angle of greatest extension

AGF angle of greatest flexion

AGG agammaglobulinemia

agit. ante sum. *agita ante sumendum* [Latin] shake before taking

AGL acute granulocytic leukemia

AGN acute glomerulonephritis

A/G r albumin/globulin ratio

agt agent

AH abdominal hysterectomy; arterial hypertension; artificial heart

AHA American Heart Association; American Hospital Association; autoimmune hemolytic anemia

AHC acute hemorrhagic conjunctivitis

AHCPR Agency for Health Care Policy and Research

AHD arteriosclerotic heart disease

AHF acute heart failure; antihemophilic factor

AHFS American Hospital Formulary Service

AHG antihemophilic globulin

AI aortic insufficiency; artificial insemination; artificial intelligence

AID acute infectious disease; anti-inflammatory drug; artificial insemination by donor; automatic implantable defibrillator

AIDS acquired immune deficiency syndrome

AIH artificial insemination-husband (homologous insemination)

AIHA autoimmune hemolytic anemia

AJ ankle jerk

AK above knee (said of amputations or prostheses); actinic keratosis

AKA above knee amputation

a.k.a. also known as

AL acute leukemia

Al aluminum

ALA American Lung Association

Ala alanine

alb. albumin

AlcR alcohol rub

ALD adrenoleukodystrophy; alcoholic liver disease

ALG antilymphocyte globulin

alk. alkaline

ALL acute lymphoblastic leukemia

ALM acral lentiginous melanoma

ALOS average length of stay

ALP alkaline phosphatase; anterior lobe of pituitary

ALS advanced life support; amyotrophic lateral sclerosis; antilymphocyte serum

ALT alanine transaminase; argon laser trabeculoplasty

alt. dieb. *alternis diebus* [Latin] every other day

alt. hor. *alternis horis* [Latin] every other hour

AM amalgam; atrial myxoma

Am americium

AMA against medical advice; American Medical Association; antimitochondrial antibodies

A.M.A.P. as much as possible

amb. ambulatory

AMF Asian, middle-aged female

AMI acute myocardial infarction

AML acute myeloblastic leukemia; anterior mitral leaflet

AMM Asian, middle-aged male

AMP adenosine monophosphate

amp ampule; amputation

AMRA American Medical Record Association

AMRL Aerospace Medical Research Laboratories

AMS auditory memory span

AN anesthesia; aneurysm; anorexia nervosa

ANA acetylneuraminic acid; American Nurses' Association; antinuclear antibody

AND anterior nasal discharge

anes. anesthesia

ANF antinuclear factor

ANG angiogram

ANLL acute non-lymphoblastic leukemia

ANOVA analysis of variance

ANS anterior nasal spine; autonomic nervous system

ANSI American National Standards Institute

ant. anterior

ANUG acute necrotizing ulcerative gingivitis

anx. anxiety

A.O.A.P. as often as possible

AOB alcohol on breath

AOBS acute organic brain syndrome

AOC area of concern

AOD arterial occlusive disease

AODM adult onset diabetes mellitus

AOHS angio-osteohypertrophy syndrome

AOM acute otitis media

AON acute optic neuritis

AOPA American Orthotics and Prosthetics Association

AORN Association of Operating Room Nurses

AOTA American Occupational Therapy Association

AP acid phosphatase; alkaline phosphatase; angina pectoris; antepartum; anterior pituitary; anteroposterior (view); appendix; arterial pressure

A & P auscultation and palpation; auscultation and percussion

a.p. *ante prandium* [Latin] before dinner

APA American Pharmaceutical Association; American Psychiatric Association; antipernicious anemia (factor)

APACHE Acute Physiology and Chronic Health Evaluation System

APB atrial premature beat

APC acetylsalicylic acid, phenacetin, and caffeine; antigen-presenting cells; atrial premature contraction

APD automated peritoneal dialysis

APE acute psychotic episode; anterior pituitary extract

APH antepartum hemorrhage; anterior pituitary hormone

APHA American Public Health Association

APKD adult polycystic kidney disease

APL acute promyelocytic leukemia

APM aspartame

APN acute pyelonephritis

APP amyloid precursor protein

app. apparent; appendix

appr. approximate

appt appointment

appx appendix

appy appendectomy

APSGN acute poststreptococcal glomerulonephritis

APT acid phosphatase test

APTA American Physical Therapy Association

APTS acid phosphatase test for semen

APTT activated partial thromboplastin time

APUD Amine Precursor Uptake and Decarboxylation

APV atrial premature beat

AQ achievement quotient; any quantity

aq aqueous

AR alarm reaction; aortic regurgitation; artificial respiration; attributable risk; autosomal recessive

Ar argon

A & R advised and released

ARA American Rheumatism Association

ARBD alcohol-related birth defects

ARC AIDS-related complex; American Red Cross

ARD acute respiratory disease; acute respiratory distress

ARDS acute respiratory distress syndrome; adult respiratory distress syndrome

ARF acute renal failure; acute respiratory failure; acute rheumatic fever

ARLD alcohol-related liver disease

ARM artificial rupture of membranes

AROM active range of motion

ARP at-risk period

ARPE acute reactive psychotic episode

ARR adverse reaction report

Arry arrhythmia

ART acid reflux test; acoustic reflex test

art. artery

AS anal sphincter; aortic stenosis; arteriosclerosis; artificial sweetner; atherosclerosis

As arsenic; astigmatism

a.s. *auris sinistra* [Latin] left ear

ASA acetylsalicylic acid (aspirin); antisperm antibody

ASAM American Society of Addiction Medicine

ASAP as soon as possible

ASB anesthesia standby

ASCUS Atypical Squamous Cells of Undetermined Significance

ASCVD arteriosclerotic cardiovascular disease

ASD atrial septal defect

ASDA American Sleep Disorder Association

ASDH acute subdural hematoma

ASH asymmetrical septal hypertrophy

ASHD arteriosclerotic heart disease

ASHI Association for the Study of Human Infertility

ASIS anterosuperior iliac spine

ASLHA American Speech-Language-Hearing Association

Asn asparagine

ASO antistreptolysin O; arteriosclerosis obliterans

asst assistant

AST angiotensin sensitivity test; antibiotic sensitivity test; aspartate transaminase

Ast astigmatism

as tol. as tolerated

ASU acute stroke unit

ASV antisnake venom

ASX asymptomatic

AT Achilles tendon; air temperature; antithrombin; atrial tachycardia

At astatine

ATB antibiotic

ATC anterior tibial compartment (syndrome); around the clock

ATFL anterior talofibular ligament

ATG antithymocyte globulin

ATL adult T-cell leukemia

ATN acute tubular necrosis

ATP adenosine triphosphate

ATPase adenosine triphosphatase

atr. atrial; atrophy

ATS antitetanus serum; anxiety tension state

at. wt. atomic weight

a.u. *auris uterque* [Latin] each ear

Au gold

AUA American Urological Association

AV aortic valve; arteriovenous; atrioventricular

A-V arteriovenous; atrioventricular

Av. average

AVD aortic valve disease

AVF arteriovenous fistula

Avg average

AVH acute viral hepatitis

AVM arteriovenous malformation

AVN atrioventricular node; avascular necrosis

AVP arginine vasopressin

AVRT atrioventricular reciprocating tachycardia

AWS alcohol withdrawal syndrome

Ax. axis

AZT zidovudine

B bacillus; base (of prism); blood type B$^+$, B$^-$; bel; bicuspid; boron

b blood (as a subscript); born

b. *bis* [Latin] twice

BA backache; bile acid; blood alcohol; bone age; boric acid: bronchial asthma

BAC blood alcohol concentration

Ba barium

BaEn barium enema

BAER brainstem auditory evoked response

BAF B cell-activating factor

BAL blood alcohol level; British antilewisite (dimercaprol); bronchoalveolar lavage

BALT bronchus-associated lymphoid tissue

BAT blunt abdominal trauma

BAVP balloon aortic valvuloplasty

BB bad breath; bed bath; belly button; blood bank; breast biopsy

BBA born before arrival (of physician or midwife)

BBB blood-brain barrier; bundle-branch block

BBBB bilateral bundle branch block

BBD brittle bone disease

BBT basal body temperature

BC birth control; blood culture; bone conduction; bronchial carcinoma

Bc beryllium

B & C board and care

BCA balloon catheter angioplasty

BCC basal cell cancer; basal call carcinoma
BCD basal cell dysplasia
BCG bacillus Calmette-Guerin (vaccine); ballistocardiograph
BCGF B cell growth factor
BCLSS Basic Cardiac Life Support System
BCP birth control pill
BCS battered child syndrome; Budd-Chiari syndrome
BCT Barany's caloric test
BD behavioral disorder; belladonna; below diaphragm; bile duct; birth defect; Bowen's disease; brain dead
b.d. *bis die* [Latin] twice a day
BDT bronchodilator therapy
BE barium enema; below elbow (said of amputations or prostheses); breast examination
b.e. bacterial endocarditis; barium enema
Be beryllium
BEAM brain electrical activity mapping
BEC bacterial endocarditis
BF black female; bone fragment
BFPR biologic false-positive reaction
BG blood glucose; bone graft
bGH bovine growth hormone
BGT Bender gestalt test
Bi bismuth
BID brought in dead
b.i.d. *bis in die* [Latin] twice a day
BIH benign intracranial hypertension
bil. bilirubin
b.i.n. *bis in nocte* [Latin] twice a night
BJ Bence Jones (protein); biceps jerk
BK below knee (said of amputations or prostheses)
Bk berkelium
bk back
bkf breakfast
bkg background
BKO below-knee orthosis
blad. bladder
BLD black lung disease
Bld blood
Bld Bk blood bank
BLS basic life support; blind loop syndrome
BM basal metabolism; basement membrane; black male; bone marrow; bone mass; bowel movement
BMD bone mineral density
BMF black, middle-aged female
BMI body mass index
bmk birthmark
BMM black, middle-aged male
BMR basal metabolic rate
BMT bone marrow transplant
BNA Basle Nomina Anatomica
BNS benign nephrosclerosis
BO bowel obstruction
BOA born on arrival
BOD biochemical oxygen demand
BOLD blood oxygen level-dependent
BOW bag of waters
BP bathroom privileges; bedpan; birthplace; blood pressure; bypass
b.p. boiling point
BPD bronchopulmonary dysplasia
BPH benign prostatic hyperplasia; benign prostatic hypertrophy
BPIP bactericidal permeability-increasing protein
BPM beats per minute; breaths per minute
BPP biophysical profile
BPS binge-and-purge syndrome
Bq becquerel
B.R. bed rest
Br bromine

BRBPR bright red blood per rectum
BRP bathroom privileges
BS blood sugar; breath sounds; bowel sounds
BSA body surface area; bovine serum albumin
BSE breast self examination
BSER brainstem evoked response
BSL blood sugar level
BSP Bromsulphalein
BSPT Bromsulphalein test
BT bedtime; benzidine test; biuret test; blind test; blood transfusion; body temperature
BTC basal temperature chart
BTL bilateral tubal ligation
BTU British thermal unit
BUN bleeding of unknown origin; blood, urea, nitrogen; bruising of unknown origin
BV blood vessel; blood volume
BVAD biventricular assist device
BW birth weight; body weight
BWS battered woman syndrome
Bx biopsy
C calculus; carbohydrate; carbon; cathode; Celsius; centigrade; cervical (vertebrae); cesarean; complement; concentration; contraction; coulomb; large calorie
c curie; cycle; cylinder; small calorie
c. *cum* [Latin] with
c̄ *cum* [Latin] with
C1 first cervical spinal nerve; first cervical vertebra
C2 second cervical spinal nerve; second cervical vertebra
C3 third cervical spinal nerve; third cervical vertebra
C4 fourth cervical spinal nerve; fourth cervical vertebra
C5 fifth cervical spinal nerve; fifth cervical vertebra
C6 sixth cervical spinal nerve; sixth cervical vertebra
C7 seventh cervical spinal nerve; seventh cervical vertebra
C1Q protein of the complement system
CA cancer; cardiac arrest; chronologic age
Ca calcium; cancer; carotid artery; cathode; cerebral aqueduct; chronological age
ca cancer
ca. *circa* [Latin] about
CABG coronary artery bypass graft
CABS coronary artery bypass surgery
CAD computer-assisted diagnosis; coronary artery disease
CAH chronic active hepatitis; congenital adrenal hyperplasia
CAHD coronary artery heart disease
CAI computer-assisted instruction
Cal large calorie
cal small calorie
calef. *calefac* [Latin] make warm
CALLA common acute lymphoblastic leukemia antigen
cAMP cyclic adenosine monophosphate
CAN cord (umbilical) around neck
CAO chronic airflow obstruction
CAP cancer of prostate; catabolite activator protein
cap. *capiat* [Latin] let him (the patient) take; capacity; capsule
CAPD chronic ambulatory peritoneal dialysis; continuous ambulatory peritoneal dialysis
CAS carotid artery stenosis; cerebral arteriosclerosis
CASA computer-assisted semen analysis
CAT cataract; computerized axial tomography
cath. catheter; catheterize
cath'd catheterized
CATSCAN computer-assisted tomography scanner
Cau. Caucasian
CAVB complete atrioventricular block
CAVS calcified aortic valve stenosis
CAWO closing abductory wedge osteotomy
CB catheterized bladder; cesarean birth; chronic bronchitis; code blue

C & B crown and bridge
Cb columbium
CBC complete blood count
CBD common bile duct; closed bladder drainage
CBE clinical breast examination
CBF cerebral blood flow
CBG capillary blood gases; corticosteroid-binding globulin
CBH cutaneous basophil hypersensitivity
CBR complete bed rest
CBS closed building syndrome
CBT cognitive-behavioral therapy
CC cardiac catheterization; cardiac cycle; cerebral concussion; chief complaint; chronic complainer; creatinine clearance; critical care
cc cubic centimeter
CCA common carotid artery
CCB calcium channel blocker
CCCR closed-chest cardiac resuscitation
CCF congestive cardiac failure
CCG cholecystogram
CCI chronic coronary insufficiency
CCJ costochondral junction
CCK cholecystokinin
CCMS clean-catch midstream [urine specimen]
CCN coronary care nursing
CCPD chronic cyclic peritoneal dialysis
Ccr creatinine clearance
CCRIS Chemical Carcinogenesis Research Information System
CCRU critical care recovery unit
CCS costoclavicular syndrome
CCU cardiac care unit; coronary care unit; critical care unit
CD cadaver donor; cardiac disease; cesarean delivery; cluster designation; cluster determinant; cluster of differentiation (system); communicable disease; consanguineous donor; contact dermatitis; contagious disease; curative dose
c.d. *conjugata diagonalis* [Latin] diagonal conjugate
CD3 antigenic marker on T cell associated with T cell receptor
CD4 antigenic marker of helper/inducer T cells
CD8 antigenic marker of suppressor/cytotoxic T cells
Cd cadmium
cd candela
CDC Centers for Disease Control (and Prevention)
CDCP Centers for Disease Control and Prevention
CDH congenital diaphragmatic hernia; congenital dislocation of the hip; congenitally dysplastic hip
CDMAS computerized database management and analysis systems
cDNA complementary deoxyribonucleic acid
CDP cytidine diphosphate
CDR continuing disability review
CDRH Center for Devices and Radiological Health
CDS cervical disk syndrome
CDT carbon dioxide therapy
CE continuing education; cardiac emergency
Ce cerium
CEA carcinoembryonic antigen
CEN Certified Emergency Nurse
CEP congenital erythropoietic porphyria
CER conditioned emotional response
CE & R central episiotomy and repair
cerv. cervical; cervix
CES cauda equina syndrome
CF cancer-free; cardiac failure; Caucasian female; citrovorum factor; complement fixation; complement-fixing (antibody); counting fingers (used in ophthalmology); coupling factor; cystic fibrosis
Cf californium; *confer* [Latin] compare
CFA colonization factor antigens
CFL calcaneofibular ligament (of the ankle joint)
CFS Chiari-Frommel syndrome
CFT capillary fragility test; complement-fixation test

CFU colony-forming unit
CG cholecystogram; chorionic gonadotropin; chronic glomerulonephritis
cg centigram
CGB chronic gastrointestinal bleeding
CGD chronic granulomatous disease
CGL chronic granulocytic leukemia
cGMP cyclic guanosine monophosphate
CGN chronic glomerulonephritis
CGS centimeter-gram-second
CH child; cholesterol; cluster headache
C-H crown-heel (applied to the length of a fetus)
CHA chronic hemolytic anemia
CHD congenital heart disease; congenital hip dislocation; coronary heart disease
ChE cholinesterase
CHES Certified Health Education Specialist
CHF congestive heart failure
CHN congenital hairy nevus
CHO carbohydrate
chol. cholesterol
chpx chickenpox
chr. chronic
CHS Chediak-Higashi syndrome
CI color index
Ci curie
cib. *cibus* [Latin] food
CIBD chronic inflammatory bowel disease
CIC cardioinhibitory center; clean intermittent catheterization
CID cytomegalovirus inclusion disease
CIDS continuous insulin delivery system
Cig cytoplasmic immunoglobulin
Cin insulin clearance
CIN cervical intraepithelial neoplasia
CIN I cervical intraepithelial neoplasia (with mild dysplasia)
CIN II cervical intraepithelial neoplasia (with moderate dysplasia)
CIN III cervical intraepithelial neoplasia (with severe dysplasia)
CIS carcinoma *in situ*; Cancer Information Service
CIT Casoni intradermal test
CJD Creutzfeldt-Jakob disease
CK creatine kinase; cytokinin
CL corpus luteum; critical list
Cl chlorine
cl centiliter
CLA Certified Laboratory Assistant
clav. clavicle
cldy cloudy
CLL chronic lymphocytic leukemia
CLP cleft lip and palate
CM cardiac monitor; cardiomyopathy; common migraine; continuous murmur
Cm curium
cM centimorgan
cm centimeter
CMA Certified Medical Assistant
CMADL Controlled Medical Assistance Drug List
C-max maximum concentration
CMC carpometacarpal; chronic mucocutaneous candidiasis
CMCC chronic mucocutaneous candidiasis
CME continuing medical education; cystic macular edema
CMF cyclophosphamide, methotrexate, and fluorouracil (anticancer chemotherapeutic combination)
CMI cell-mediated immunity; chronically mentally ill
CMID cytomegalic inclusion disease
c/min cycles per minute
CML cell-mediated lympholysis; chronic myeloid leukemia
cmm cubic millimeter
CMN cystic medial necrosis
CMO calculated mean organism; Chief Medical Officer

CMP cardiomyopathy; cytidine monophosphate
CMPGN chronic membranoproliferative glomerulonephritis
CMR cerebral metabolic rate
CMV controlled mechanical ventilation; cytomegalovirus
CN Certified Nurse; charge nurse; cranial nerve
CNM Certified Nurse-Midwife
CNP continuous negative pressure
CNS central nervous system
CNT cyanide-nitroprusside test
CO carbon monoxide; cardiac output; cervical orthosis
Co cobalt; coenzyme
c/o complains of
CoA coarctation of the aorta; coenzyme A
COAD chronic obstructive airway disease; chronic obstructive arterial disease
CoI coenzyme 1
CoII coenzyme II
COC calcifying odontogenic cyst; cathode opening contraction
coc coccygeal
coch. mag. *chochleare magnum* [Latin] tablespoon
COD cause of death
COLD chronic obstructive lung disease
collat. collateral
comp. complication; compound; compress
C-ONC cellular oncogene
cons. consultation
const. constant
consult. consultant; consultation
cont. containing; content; continue
contin. *continuetur* [Latin] let it be continued
COP colloid osmotic pressure
COPD chronic obstructive pulmonary disease
cor. coronary
CORD chronic obstructive respiratory disease
CP cerebral palsy; chemically pure; chest pain; chronic pain; cleft palate; cor pulmonale; creatine phosphate
C & P cystoscopy and pyelography
CPA chlorpropamide
CPAP continuous positive air pressure; continuous positive airway pressure
CPC clinicopathological conference
CPD comparison point decision; compound
CPDD calcium pyrophosphate disposition disease (pseudogout)
CPE cardiogenic pulmonary edema; chronic pulmonary emphysema
CPGN chronic proliferative glomerulonephritis
CPH Certificate in Public Health; chronic persistent hepatitis
CPID chronic pelvic inflammatory disease
CPK creatine phosphokinase
CPKD childhood polycystic kidney disease
cpl complete
CPM cardiac pacemaker; central pontine myelinolysis; continue present management; continuous passive motion; counts per minute; cycles per minute
cpm counts per minute; cycles per minute
CPN chronic pyelonephritis
CPP cerebral perfusion pressure
CPPB continuous positive pressure breathing
CPPD calcium pyrophosphate dihydrate
CPPV continuous positive pressure ventilation
CPR cardiac pulmonary reserve; cardiopulmonary resuscitation
CPS cumulative probability of success
cps counts per second; cycles per second
CPT carotid pulse tracing; *Current Procedural Terminology*
CPTH chronic post traumatic headache
CPUE chest pain of undetermined etiology
CPX complete physical examination
CR cardiorespiratory; cellular receptor; chest roentgenogram; clinical record; closed reduction (of a fracture); code red; colon resection; complete remission; conditioned reflex; conditioned response; creatinine

C-R crown-rump (applied to length of fetus)
Cr chromium; creatinine
CRC colorectal cancer
CRD chronic renal disease; chronic respiratory disease
CRE cumulative radiation effect
creat. creatine
CREST Calcinosis, Raynaud's phenomenon, Esophageal motility disorders, Sclerodactyly, Telangiectasia
CRF chronic renal failure; corticotropin-releasing factor
CRH corticotropin-releasing hormone
CRL crown-rump length (of fetus)
CRNA Certified Registered Nurse Anesthetist
CRO cathode ray oscilloscope
CRP cAMP receptor protein; C-reactive protein
CRS Chinese restaurant syndrome; colorectal surgery
CRT cardiac resuscitation team; cathode ray tube
CS carcinoid syndrome; cardiogenic shock; carotid sinus; cesarean section; cigarette smoke; cigarette smoker; conditioned stimulus; congenital syphilis
Cs cesium
CSA colony-stimulating activity
CSAA Child Study Association of America
CSAP Center for Substance Abuse Prevention
CSD cat-scratch disease
C section cesarean section
CSF cerebrospinal fluid; colony-stimulating factor
CSII continuous subcutaneous insulin infusion
CSM cerebrospinal meningitis
CSOM chronic serous otitis media
CSP criminal sexual psychopath
C-spine cervical spine
CSR corrected sedimentation rate
CST contraction stress test
CT calcitonin; carotid tracing; carpal tunnel; cerebral thrombosis; clotting time; coagulation time; computed tomography; connective tissue; corneal transplant
ct count
CTB ceased to breathe
CTD connective tissue disease
CTL cytotoxic T lymphocyte; cytotoxic lymphocyte
CTP comprehensive treatment plan
CTR carpal tunnel release
CTS carpal tunnel syndrome
CTT cytotoxicity test
CTZ chemoreceptor trigger zone
CU cause unknown; clinical unit; convalescent unit
Cu copper
cu cubic
CUC chronic ulcerative colitis
CUT carbohydrate utilization test
CV cardiovascular; closing volume (of lung); coefficient of variation
CVA cardiovascular accident; cerebrovascular accident; costovertebral angle
CVC central venous catheter
CVD cardiovascular disease
CVID common variable immunodeficiency
CVM cardiovascular monitor
CVP central venous pressure
CVS cardiovascular system; chorionic villus sampling
CUSA cavitron ultrasonic surgical aspirator
CVST chorionic villus sampling test
CWP childbirth without pain
Cx cervix; convex
CXR chest x-ray
cyc cycle
cyclic AMP cyclic adenosine monophosphate
cyclic GMP cyclic guanosine monophosphate
Cyd cytidine
cyl cylinder

CYS cystoscopy
Cys cysteine
Cyt cytosine
D day; deceased; deciduous (teeth); deuterium; diagnosis; diopter; donor; dorsal; dose; drug; duration
d day; deceased; density; deuteron; died
D/3 distal third
DA delayed action; dental assistant; developmental age; disability assistance; drug addict; ductus arteriosus
dA deoxyadenosine
DAD dispense as directed
DAF delayed auditory feedback.
DAI diffuse axonal injury
DALA delta-aminolevulinic acid
DAT delayed action tablet
DB date of birth; disability
Db diabetic
dB decibel
db decibel
dbl double
DBS Denis Browne splint
DBT double-blind test
DBW desirable body weight
DC dendritic cells; diagonal conjugate; diagnostic center; direct current; discharge; discontinue; Doctor of Chiropractic
D & C dilatation and curettage
DC & B dilatation, curettage, and biopsy
DCCT Diabetes Control and Complications Trial
DCB dichlorobenzedine
DCIS ductal carcinoma *in situ*
DCPN direction changing positional nystagmus
DCT direct Coombs' test; distal convoluted tubule
DD dangerous drug; degenerative disease; differential diagnosis
d.d. *detur ad,* [Latin] let it be given to
D & D diarrhea and dehydration
DDAVP deamino D-arginine vasopressin (desmopressin acetate)
DDS dialysis disequilibrium syndrome; Doctor of Dental Surgery
DDST Denver Development Screening Test
DDT dichlorodiphenyltrichloroethane
DDx differential diagnosis
DE dermoepidermal
D & E dilatation and evacuation
DEA Drug Enforcement Administration
def. defecation
dehyd. dehydration
DEF decayed, extracted, filled (teeth)
DEN dienestrol
depr. depressed
DES diethylstilbestrol
DESI direct egg sperm injection
DET diethyltryptamine
detox. detoxify
d. et s. *detur et signetur* [Latin] let it be given and labelled
DF decayed and filled (permanent teeth); dysgonic fermenter
df decayed and filled (deciduous teeth)
DFA direct fluorescent antibody
DFS dead fetus syndrome
DFU dead fetus *in utero*
DGI disseminated gonococcal infection
DH delayed hypersensitivity; dental hygienist; dermatitis herpetiformis; diaphragmatic hernia; drug hypersensitivity
DHEA dehydroepiandrosterone
DHEAS dehydroepiandrosterone sulfate
DHHS Department of Health and Human Services
DHS duration of hospital stay
DHT dihydrotestosterone
DI diabetes insipidus
DIA Drug Information Association
diag. diagnosis

diam. diameter
diaph. diaphragm
dias. diastolic
DIB disability insurance benefits
DIC disseminated intravascular coagulation
DIE died in emergency room
dieb. alt. *diebus alternis* [Latin] every other day
diff. differential; difference
digit I big toe; first digit; thumb
digit II index finger; second digit; second toe
digit III middle finger; third digit; third toe
digit IV fourth digit; fourth toe; ring finger
digit V fifth digit; little finger; little toe
dil. dilute
dilat. dilatation; dilated
dim. *dimidus* [Latin] one-half
DIP desquamative interstitial pneumonia; distal interphalangeal (joint)
diph. diphtheria
DIPJ distal interphalangeal joint
dis. disability; disease; dislocation
disc. discontinue
disch. discharge
DISH Diffuse Idiopathic Skeletal Hyperostosis
DISI dorsiflexed intercalated segment instability
disl. dislocation
disp. dispensary; dispense
distal/3 distal third
DIT diiodotyrosine
DJD degenerative joint disease
DKA diabetic ketoacidosis
DKB deep knee bends
DL danger list; diffuse lymphoma; disabled list
dl deciliter
DLE dialyzable leukocyte extract; discoid lupus erythematosus; disseminated lupus erythematosus
DLMP date of last menstrual period
DM diabetes mellitus; diabetic mother; distolic murmur; dopamine
dM decimorgan
DMD Duchenne's muscular dystrophy
DMF decayed, missing, and filled (permanent teeth)
dmf decayed, missing, and filled (deciduous teeth)
DMOOC diabetes mellitus out of control
DMSA dimercaptosuccinic acid
DMSO dimethyl sulfoxide
DMT dimethyltryptamine
DNA does not apply; deoxyribonucleic acid
DNase deoxyribonuclease
DNC did not come
DND died a natural death
DNI do not intubate
DNR do not report; do not resuscitate (order)
DNS deviated nasal septum
DO Doctor of Osteopathy
DOA date of admission; dead on arrival
DOB date of birth
DOC deoxycholate; deoxychorticosterone
DOD date of death
DOE date of examination; dyspnea on exertion
DOI date of injury
DOM dominance
DOOR Deafness, Onycho-Osteodystrophy, (mental) Retardation
DOPA dopamine
DORx date of treatment
DOS date of surgery
DOT died on (operating room) table
DP diastolic pressure; displaced person; distal phalanx; Doctor of Pharmacy; donor's plasma
DPA dual-photon absorptiometry
DPM discontinue previous medication

DPN diphosphopyridine nucleotide
DPT diphtheria-pertussis-tetanus (vaccine)
DR delivery room; diabetic retinopathy
dr dram
DRE digital rectal examination
DRG diagnosis-related group
DS decompression sickness; discharge summary; donor's serum; double strength; Down's syndrome; dry socket
DSA digital subtraction angiography
DSBL disabled
DSc Doctor of Science
DSD dry sterile dressing
DSM *Diagnostic and Statistical Manual (of Mental Disorders)*
DSMO dimethyl sulfoxide
DST distal straight tubule; donor-specific (blood) transfusion
DT delirium tremens; diphtheria and tetanus (vaccine); duration of tetany
DTH delayed-type hypersensitivity
DTP diphtheria, tetanus, pertussis (vaccine); distal tingling on percussion
DTR deep tendon reflex
DU decubitus ulcer; diagnosis undetermined; duodenal ulcer
DUCT differential ureteral catherization test
DUI driving under the influence
dur. dolor. *durante dolore* [Latin] while the pain lasts
D & V diarrhea and vomiting
DVM Doctor of Veterinary Medicine
DVT deep vein thrombosis
DW distilled water
D/W dextrose in water
Dx diagnosis
Dxd discontinued
Dy dysprosium
DZ disease; dizygotic (twins); dizziness
E edema; electrode potential; enema; enzyme; epinephrine; erythrocyte; esophagus; eye
e electron
EA early antigens; erythrocyte amboceptor
ea each
EAA essential amino acid
EAC erythrocyte amboceptor complement; external auditory canal
ead. *eadem* [Latin] the same
EAE experimental allergic encephalitis
EAHF eczema-asthma-hay fever
EAM external auditory meatus
EB elementary body; epidermolysis bullosa; Epstein-Barr (virus)
EBBA Eye Bank Association of America
EBD exploration of bile duct
EBF erythroblastosis fetalis
EBL estimated blood loss
EBM expressed breast milk
EBT early bedtime
EBV Epstein-Barr virus
EC entering complaint; eyes closed
ECC emergency cardiac care
ECCE extracapsular cataract extraction
ECF eosinophil chemotactic factor; extended care facility; extracellular fluid
ECG echocardiogram; electrocardiogram; electrocardiograph; electrocardiography
ECH extended care hospital
ECHO echocardiogram; echoencephalogram; Enteric Cytopathogenic Human Orphan (virus)
ECM extracellular matrix
ECMO extracorporeal membrane oxygenation
E. coli *Escherichia coli*
ECS electrocerebral silence; electroconvulsive shock
ECT electroconvulsive therapy; electroconvulsive treatment; enteric-coated tablet
ECW extracellular water

ED effective dose; electrodialysis; epidural; evidence of disease
EDC estimated date of confinement
EDD effective drug duration; expected date of delivery
EDR effective direct radiation
EDRF endothelium-derived relaxing factor
EDS Ehlers-Danlos syndrome
EDTA ethylenediaminetetra-acetic acid
EDU eating disorder unit
EEE eastern equine encephalitis; eastern equine encephalomyelitis
EEG electroencephalogram; electroencephalograph; electroencephalography
EENT eye, ear, nose, and throat
EF emotional factor; endurance factor
EFA enhancing factor of allergy; essential fatty acid
EFE endocardial fibroelastosis
EFM electronic fetal monitoring
EFT erythrocyte fragility test
EGF epidermal growth factor
EGOT erythrocyte glutamic oxaloacetic transaminase
EH enlarged heart; essential hypertension
EHB elevate head of bed
EHBF estimated hepatic blood flow
EHBP essential high blood pressure
EHO extrahepatic obstruction
EHP extrahigh potency
EI enzyme inhibitor
EIA electroimmunoassay; enzyme immunoassay; exercise-induced asthma
EIB exercise-induced bronchospasm
EJ elbow jerk
EKG electrocardiogram; electrocardiograph; electrocardiography
EKY electrokymogram
EL exercise limit
elev. elevated
ELISA enzyme-linked immunosorbent assay
elix. elixir
ELOS estimated length of stay
ELP electrophoresis
ELSS Emergency Life Support System
EM electron micrograph; electron microscope; electron microscopy; emergency medicine; emotionally disturbed; external monitor
EMB endometrial biopsy
EMC emergency medical care; endometrial curettage
EMF electromotive force; erythrocyte maturation factor
EMG electromyogram; electromyography
EMI Emergency Medical Information
EMIT enzyme-multiplied immunoassay technique
e.m.p. *ex modo prescripto* [Latin] in the manner prescribed
EMS early morning specimen; emergency medical service
EMSS emergency medical service system
EMT emergency medical technician
EMU electromagnetic unit
En. enema
ENA extractable nuclear antigen
ENBS early neurobehavioral score
ENDO endoscopy
ENG electronystagmogram
ENT ear, nose, and throat
enz enzyme
EO elbow orthosis
eod every other day
EOG electro-oculogram; electro-olfactogram
EOM extraocular movement; extraocular muscle
EP ectopic pregnancy; electrophoresis; emergency procedure; erythropoietin
EPA Environmental Protection Agency
EPI epinephrine; evoked potential index
epis. episiotomy
epith. epithelium
EPM electronic pacemaker

EPO eosinophil peroxidase

EPS exophthalmos-producing substance

EPSP excitatory postsynaptic potential

Eq equivalent

ER emergency room; endoplasmic reticulum; estrogen receptor; evoked response

Er erbium

ERA evoked response audiometry

ERBF effective renal blood flow

ERCP endoscopic retrograde cholangiopancreatography

ERE external rotation in extension

ERF external rotation in flexion

ERG electroretinogram

ERP early receptor potential; emergency room physician

ERPF effective renal plasma flow

ERT estrogen replacement therapy

ERV expiratory reserve volume

ES extrasystole

Es einsteinium

ESEP extreme somatosensory evoked potential

ESF erythropoiesis-stimulating factor (erythropoietin)

ESIN elastic stable intramedullary nailing

ESKD end-stage kidney disease

ESP eosinophil stimulator promoter; extrasensory perception

ESR electron spin resonance; erythrocyte sedimentation rate

ESRD end stage renal disease

ESRD-DM end stage renal disease - diabetes mellitus

ESRF end stage renal failure

ESRT erythrocyte sedimentation rate test

EST electroshock therapy; electroshock treatment

Est estrogen

ESV end-systolic volume

ESWL extracorporeal shock wave lithotripsy

ET embryo transfer; endotracheal; endotracheal tube; etiology; eustachian tube; exercise test; exercise treadmill; expiratory time

ETC estimated time of conception

EtO ethylene oxide

ETS environmental tobacco smoke

ETT endotracheal tube; exercise tolerance test

EU excretory urography

Eu europium

EUS external urethral sphincter

eV electron-volt

ev electron-volt

eval. evaluate

Ex excision

ex. example

exam. examination

exer. exercise

exog. exogenous

EXP exploration

exp. experiment; expired

expir. expiration; expiratory

ext. external; extraction

extens. extension; extensor

extr. extremity

exx examples

Ez eczema

F factor; Fahrenheit; failure; family; farad; fasting; fat; feces; female; fertility; fetal; finger; flow; fluorine; foramen; force; formula; fracture; visual field

F₁ first filial generation

F₂ second filial generation

f fluid; focal length; frequency;

FA false aneurysm; far advanced; fatty acid; femoral artery; fetal age; first aid; fluorescent antibody; folic acid

FAAT fluorescent antinuclear antibody test

Fab antigen-binding fragment

FABER flexion in abduction and external rotation

FACOSH Federal Advisory Committee on Occupational Safety and Health

FACS fluorescence-activated cell sorter

FAD familial Alzheimer's disease; flavin adenine dinucleotide

FADIR flexion in adduction and internal rotation

FAE fetal alcohol effects

FAM-M familial atypical mole and melanoma (syndrome)

FANA fluorescent antinuclear antibody

FAS fetal alcohol syndrome

FB feedback; foreign body

FBN Federal Bureau of Narcotics

FBP femoral blood pressure

FBS fasting blood sugar; fetal blood sample

Fc crystallizable fragment (of immunoglobulin); footcandle

Fcath Foley catheter

FCC follicular center cell

FCD fibrocystic disease

FCI flow cytometric immunophenotyping

FCIS Flint Colon Injury Scale

FCM flow cytometry

FCR fractional catabolic rate

FCS fetal cocaine syndrome

FCT ferric chloride test

FD fatal dose; forceps delivery

FDA Food and Drug Administration

FDIU fetal death *in utero*

FDLMP first day of last menstrual period

FDP fibrin degradation product; fibrinogen degradation product

FDS for duration of stay

Fe iron

FEB free erythrocyte protoporphyrin

feb. dur. *febre durante* [Latin] while the fever lasts

FECG fetal electrocardiogram

FEF forced expiratory flow

FES functional electrical stimulation

FET forced expiratory time

FEV forced expiratory volume

FEV1 forced expiratory volume in one second

FF fat free; filtration fraction; flat feet; force fluids

FFA free fatty acids

FFC fixed flexion contracture

FFI free from infection

FFP fresh frozen plasma

FG fibrinogen

FGF fibroblast growth factor

FGT female genital tract

FH family history

FHCM familial hypertrophic cardiomyopathy

FHH fetal heart heard

FHNH fetal heart not heard

FHR fetal heart rate

FHT fetal heart tone

FHx family history

FICU fetal intensive care unit

FIGLU formiminoglutamic acid

fist. fistula

FIUO for internal use only

fl. fluid

fld field; fluid

fld rest. fluid restriction

flex. flexion

flex. sig. flexible sigmoidoscopy

flu influenza

fluoro. fluoroscopy

FM face mask; fetal monitor; fetal movements; forensic medicine

Fm fermium

FMC fetal movement count

FMD foot-and-mouth disease

FMF familial Mediterranean fever; fetal movement felt

FMG foreign medical graduate
FMP first menstrual period
FMX full mouth x-ray
FN false-negative
FNA fine needle aspiration
FNAB fine-needle aspiration biopsy
FOB fecal occult blood; fiberoptic bronchoscopy
FOD free of disease
FOOB fell out of bed
FP false-positive; family physician; family planning; food poisoning; frozen plasma
fp freezing point
FPC familial polyposis coli
fps foot-pound-second (system of units)
fPt fasting patient
F & R force and rhythm (of pulse)
FR flocculation reaction
Fr francium
fract. fracture
fract. dos. *fracta dosi* [Latin] in divided doses
FRC functional residual capacity
FRJM full range of joint movement
Fru fructose
FSGN focal sclerosing glomerulonephritis; focal segmental glomerulosclerosis
FSH follicle-stimulating hormone
FSH-LH follicle-stimulating hormone-luteinizing hormone
FSH-RF follicle-stimulating hormone-releasing factor
FSH-RH follicle stimulating hormone-releasing hormone
FSP fibrin split product
FST foam stability test
FT family therapy; full term
FTA fluorescent titer antibody
FTAAT fluorescent treponemal antibody absorption test
FTG full thickness graft
FTND full term normal delivery
FTR for the record
FTS-ABS fluorescent treponema antibody-absorption (test)
FTT failure to thrive
FTTS failure to thrive syndrome
FU follow up
FUDR floxuridine; fluorodeoxyuridine
FUE fever of undetermined etiology
FUO fever of undetermined origin; fever of unknown origin
FVC forced vital capacity
FVS floppy valve syndrome
FWB full weight-bearing
Fx fracture
Fx-dis fracture-dislocation
FXS fragile X syndrome
G gas; gauge; gauss; glucose; glycine; glycogen; gram; guanosine
g gender; gram; gravitational constant; gravity; group
GA gastric analysis; general anesthesia; gestational age
Ga gallium
GABA gamma-aminobutyric acid
GALT gut-associated lymphoid tissue
gang. ganglion
gast. fl. gastric fluid
GB gallbladder
GBM glomerular basement membrane
GBG glycine-rich beta-glycoprotein
GC gas chromatography; geriatric care; gonococcus; gonorrheal cervicitis
GC/MS gas chromatography/mass spectrometery
GCS Glasgow Coma Scale
GCT giant cell tumor
G & D growth and development
Gd gadolinium
GDB guide dog for the blind

GDD guide dog for the deaf
GDM gestational diabetes mellitus
GDS gradual dosage schedule
GE gastroenterology; gel electrophoresis
Ge germanium
GEF glycosylation-enhancing factor
GEJ gastroesophageal junction
GEN gender; generic; genetics; genital
gen'l general
GEPH gestational edema with proteinuria and hypertension
GER gastroesophageal reflux; geriatrics
GERD gastroesophageal reflux disease
GF gastric fluid; germ-free; growth factor
GFR glomerular filtration rate
GGG glycine-rich gammaglycoprotein
GH growth hormone; general hospital
GHD growth hormone deficiency
GH-RF growth hormone-releasing factor
GH-RH growth hormone-releasing hormone
GHT glycosylated hemoglobin test
GI gastrointestinal; gingival index
GIF glycosylation inhibition factor
GIFT gamete intrafallopian transfer
GIP gastric inhibitory polypeptide
GIS gas in stomach; gastrointestinal series
GIT gastrointestinal tract
GJ gap junction; gastrojejunostomy
GL gastric lavage
gl. gland
g/l grams per liter
GLA Giardia Lamblia antigen
GLC gas-liquid chromatography
glc glaucoma
Glm glutamine
Glu glucose; glutamic acid
Gly glycine
gm gram
GMP guanosine monophosphate (guanylic acid)
GN glomerulonephritis; graduate nurse; gram-negative
Gn gonadotropin
GN-RH gonadotropin-releasing hormone
GNC general nursing care
GOT gamma-glutamyl transferase; glucose oxidase test; glutamic-oxaloacetic transaminase
GP general paresis; general physician; general practitioner; gram-positive
gp glycoprotein
G6PD glucose-6-phosphate dehydrogenase
GPI gingival-periodontal index
GPN graduate practical nurse
GPT glutamic pyruvic transaminase
gr. grain
GRAS Generally Regarded As Safe
grav. gravid
GRF growth hormone-releasing factor
GRIF growth hormone-inhibiting factor
GS general surgery; glomerular sclerosis
GSC gas-solid chromatography
GSD-1 glycogen storage disease, type 1
GSE grip strong and equal
GSH growth-stimulating hormone
GSR galvanic-skin response
GST genetic screening test
GSW gunshot wound
GT glucose tolerance; guaiac test
gt. *gutta* [Latin] a drop
GTD gestational trophoblastic disease
GTT glucose tolerance test
gtt. *guttae* [Latin] drops

GU gastric ulcer; genitourinary
GUS genitourinary system
GV gingivectomy
GVH graft-versus-host (disease or reaction)
GVHD graft-versus-host disease
GVHR graft-versus-host reaction
GXT graded exercise etst
GYN gynecology
5-HIAA 5-hydroxyindoleacetic acid
H hair; head; heart; hemisphere; henry; hernia; heroin; hot; hydrogen; hyperopia; hypodermic
H$^+$ hydrogen ion
h height; horizontal; hour; hundred
h̲ Plank's constant
HA headache; hearing aid; hemolytic anemia; hepatitis A; high anxiety; hospital admission
H/A headache
HAA hepatitis-associated antigen
HAAg hepatitis A antigen
HAC hyperactive child
HAE hereditary angioneurotic edema
HAI hospital-acquired infection
HAL hyperalimentation
halluc. hallucination
HANE hereditary angioneurotic edema
HAP hospital-acquired pneumonia
HAPE high altitude pulmonary edema
HAPS hepatic arterial perfusion scintigraphy
HAQ Headache Assessment Questionnaire; Health Assessment Questionnaire
HARM Hypertension, Anemia, Renal, Malabsorption
HAS hypertensive arteriosclerosis
HASHD hypertensive arteriosclerotic heart disease
HAV hepatitis A virus
HB bundle of His; heart block; hepatitis B; hospital bed
Hb hemoglobin
HbA adult hemoglobin; hemoglobin A
HBAb hepatitis B antibody
HBAg hepatitis B antigen
HbAS heterozygosity for hemoglobin A and hemoglobin S
HBB hospital blood bank
HBc hepatitis B core
HBcAb antibody to hepatitis B core antigen
HBcAg hepatitis B core antigen
HbCO carboxyhemoglobin
HBD has been drinking
HBe hepatitis B e
HbE hemoglobin E
HBeAb antibody to hepatitis B e antigen
HBeAg hepatitis B e antigen
HbF fetal hemoglobin; hemoglobin F
HBGM home blood glucose monitoring
HbH hemoglobin H
HBIG hepatitis B immune globulin
HBO hyperbaric oxygen
HbO$_2$ oxyhemoglobin
HBOT hyperbaric oxygen therapy
HBP high blood pressure
HbS hemoglobin S
HBs hepatitis B surface
HBsAb antibody to the hepatitis B surface antigen
HBsAg hepatitis B surface antigen
HBV hepatitis B virus
HBW high birth weight
HC head circumference; home care; hydrocortisone; hydroxycorticoid
HCAP handicapped
HCC hepatocellular carcinoma
HCD heavy chain disease
HCFA Health Care Financing Administration

hCG human chorionic gonadotropin
HCL hairy-cell leukemia; hard contact lens
HCM health care maintenance; hypertrophic cardiomyopathy
HCO$_3$ bicarbonate
HCP health care provider
hCS human chorionic somatomammotropin
HCT heat coagulation test
Hct hematocrit
HCTU home cervical traction unit
HCV hepatitis C virus
HCVD hypertensive cardiovascular disease
HCW health care worker
HD herniated disk; high dose; Hodgkin's disease; hospital day; Huntington's disease
h.d. *heloma durum* [Latin] hard corn; *hora decubitus,* [Latin] at bedtime
HDCV human diploid-cell vaccine
HDL high-density lipoprotein
HDL-C high-density lipoprotein cholesterol
HDN high-density nebulizer
HDRV human diploid cell rabies vaccine
HDU hemodialysis unit
HDV hepatitis D (Delta) virus
H & E hematoxylin and eosin (stain); heredity and environment
He helium
HEENT head, ears, eyes, nose, and throat
hem. hemorrhage; hemorrhoid
hep heparin; hepatitis
HEV hepatitis E virus; high endothelial venules
HF hay fever; heart failure
Hf hafnium
HFD high forceps delivery
HFHL high-frequency hearing loss
HFMD hand-foot-and-mouth disease
HFPPV high-frequency positive pressure ventilation
Hfr high frequency
HG herpes genitalis
Hg hemoglobin; mercury
Hgb hemoglobin
hG human gonadotropin
hGH human growth hormone
hgt height
HH hard of hearing; hiatal hernia
HHN hand-held nebulizer
HI head injury; health insurance; hemagglutination inhibition
His histidine
histo. histology
HIV human immunodeficiency virus
HIV-1 human immunodeficiency virus type 1
HIV-2 human immunodeficiency virus type 2
HIVD herniated intervertebral disk
HKAFO hip-knee-ankle-foot orthosis
HKO hip-knee orthosis
HL hearing level; hearing loss; Hodgkin's lymphoma
HI latent hyperopia
HLA human leukocyte antigen
HLD herniated lumbar disk
hLH human luteinizing hormone
HLHS hypoplastic left heart syndrome
HM hand movement; heart murmur; human milk; hydatidiform mole
Hm manifest hyperopia
HMD hyaline membrane disease
hMG human menopausal gonadotropin
HMO health maintenance organization
HN head nurse
HNP herniated nucleus pulposus
HNV has not voided
HO hand orthosis; hip orthosis
Ho holmium
HOB head of bed

HOCM hypertrophic obstructive cardiomyopathy
HOH hard of hearing; high oxygen pressure
HOPA hospital-based organ procurement agency
hor. decub. *hora decubitus* [Latin] at bedtime
hor. som. *hora somni* [Latin] at bedtime.
HP handicapped person; hot pack; house physician
Hp *Helicobacter pylori*
H & P history and physical (examination)
HPA human papillomavirus
HPD high protein diet; home peritoneal dialysis
HPI history of present illness
hPL human placental lactogen
HPV human papillomavirus
HPVD hypertensive pulmonary vascular disease
HR heart rate; hemorrhagic retinopathy; hospital record
H & R hysterectomy and radiation
HRCT high-resolution computed tomography
HRF homologous restriction factor
HRIG human rabies immune globulin (vaccine)
HRP horseradish peroxidase
HRT hormone replacement therapy; hyperparathyroidism
HRV human rotavirus
HS half-strength; hazardous substance; heart sounds; hereditary spherocytosis; herpes simplex; house surgeon
h.s. *hora somni* [Latin] at bedtime
HSA human serum albumin
HSAS hypertrophic subaortic stenosis
HSE herpes simplex encephalitis
HSF hepatocyte-stimulating factor; histamine-sensitizing factor
HSV herpes simplex virus
HT hammertoe; Hashimoto's thyroiditis; height; high temperature; hypertension; hypertropia
Ht heart; height; total hyperopia
HTB hot tub bath
HTL hearing threshold level
HTLV-I human T-cell leukemia virus-type I
HTLV-II human T-cell leukemia virus-type II
HTN hypertension
hTSS human toxic shock syndrome
HUGO Human Genome Organization
HUS hemolytic-uremic syndrome
HV has voided; herpes virus; hyperventilation
HVA homovanillic acid
HVD hypertensive vascular disease
HVGR host-versus-graft reaction
HVO hallux valgus orthosis
HWB hot water bottle
Hx history; hospitalization
Hy hyperopia
Hyg. hygiene
hyperal. hyperalimentation
hypno. hypnosis
hypo hypodermic syringe
hyst. hysterectomy
HZ herpes zoster
Hz hertz
I intensity of electric current; intensity of magnetism; internist; iodine
IA image amplification; incurred accidently; infected area
I & A irrigation and aspiration
IABC intra-aortic balloon catheter
IABP intra-aortic balloon pump
IAC internal auditory canal
IAO immediately after onset
IANC International Anatomical Nomenclature Committee
IAP intermittent acute porphyria
IARC International Agency for Research on Cancer
IAS interatrial septum
IASD interatrial septal defect
IAT impedance audiometry test; intraoperative autologous transfusion

IB inclusion body; infectious bronchitis
IBC iron-binding capacity
IBD inflammatory bowel disease
IBI intermittent bladder irrigation
IBS irritable bowel syndrome
IC immediate care; immune complex; indwelling catheter; inspiratory capacity; intensive care; intercarpal; intermitten catheterization; intracranial; irritable colon
i.c. *inter cibos* [Latin] between meals
ICA internal carotid artery; intracranial aneurysm; islet cell antibody
ICAO internal carotid artery occlusion
ICC intensive coronary care
ICCE intracapsular cataract extraction
ICCU intensive coronary care unit
ICD immune complex disease; *International Classification of Diseases;* intrauterine contraceptive device
ICD 9 CM *International Classification of Diseases, Ninth Revision, Clinical Modification*
ICF intermediate care facility; intracellular fluid
ICH intracranial hemorrhage
ICIDH International Classification of Impairments, Disabilities, and Handicaps
ICN intensive care nursery
ICOH International Commission on Occupational Health
ICP intracranial pressure
ICPP intubated continuous positive pressure
ICRP International Commission on Radiological Protection
ICS intercostal space
ICSA islet-cell surface antibody
ICSH interstitial cell-stimulating hormone
ICT indirect Coombs' test; insulin coma therapy; intermittent cervical traction
ICU intensive care unit
ICW intracellular water
ID idiotype; immunodeficiency; infectious disease; infective dose; initial dose; intradermal
I & D incision and drainage; irrigation and drainage
IDA iron deficiency anemia
IDAM infant of drug-abusing mother; infant of drug-addicted mother
IDDM insulin-dependent diabetes mellitus
IDIPF idiopathic diffuse interstitial pulmonary fibrosis
IDK internal derangement of the knee
IDM infant of diabetic mother
IDP intraductal papilloma
IDU idoxuridine; injecting-drug user
IE infective endocarditis
IEL intraepithelial lymphocyte
IEM inborn error of metabolism
IF interferon; interstitial fluid; intrinsic factor
IFA immunofluorescence assay; indirect fluorescent antibody (test)
IFE immunofixation electrophoresis
IFN interferon
Ig immunoglobulin
IgA immunoglobulin A (gamma A globulin)
IgD immunoglobulin D (gamma D globulin)
IGDM infant of gestational diabetic mother
IgE immunoglobulin E (gamma E globulin)
IGF insulin-like growth factor
IgG immunoglobulin G (gamma G globulin)
IgM immunoglobulin M (gamma M globulin)
IGT impaired glucose tolerance
IGTT intravenous glucose tolerance test
IH immediate hypersensitivity; inguinal hernia
IHB incomplete heart block
IHD ischemic heart disease
IHSS idiopathic hypertrophic subaortic stenosis
IHW inner heel wedge
IICU infant intensive care unit
IL interleukin

IL 1 interleukin 1
IL 2 interleukin 2
IL 3 interleukin 3
ILD inflammatory lung disease; interstitial lung disease
Ile isoleucine
IM infectious mononucleosis; intramuscular
im intramuscular
IMB intermenstrual bleeding
ImD$_{50}$ median immunizing dose
imp. impression (tentaive diagnosis)
IMR individual medical record; infant mortality rate
IMV intermittent mandatory ventilation
IN internist; interstitial nephritis
In indium
INC incontinence
incr. increased; increasing
in d. *in dies* [Latin] daily
IndMed *Index Medicus*
INF infant; interferon; intravenous nutritional feeding
inf. infection; inferior
INFH ischemic necrosis of femoral head
inj. injection
Ino inosine
inoc. inoculation
inop. inoperable
IN-PT inpatient
INR international normalized ratio
Ins. insulin; insurance
inspr. inspiration; inspiratory
insuff. insufflation
INT intermittent; internal; internist
int. cib. *inter cibos* [Latin] between meals
int. noct. *inter noctem* [Latin] during the night
int. obst. intestinal obstruction
I & O intake and output
IODAM infant of drug-addicted mother
IODM infant of diabetic mother
IOF intraocular fluid
IOP intraocular pressure
IOPA independent organ procurement agency
IOV initial office visit
IP incubation period; inpatient; interphalangeal (joint); intraperitoneal
IPA invasive pulmonary aspergillosis
IPCD infantile polycystic disease
IPD inflammatory pelvic disease; intermittent peritoneal dialysis
IPJ interphalangeal joint
IPP inflatable penile prosthesis; intermittent positive pressure
IPPA inspection, palpation, percussion, and auscultation
IPPB intermittent positive pressure breathing
IPPV intermittent positive pressure ventilation
IPS initial prognostic score
IPSID immunoproliferative small intestinal disease
IPSP inhibitory postsynaptic potential
IPT immunologic pregnancy test
IPV inactivated poliovirus vaccine
IQ intelligence quotient
i.q. *idem quod* [Latin] the same as
IR immune response; infrared; insulin reaction; insulin resistance; insulin resistant
Ir iridium
IRC inspiratory reserve capacity
IRDS infant respiratory distress syndrome
IRE internal rotation in extension
IRF internal rotation in flexion
IRIC International Research Information Center
IRMA immunoradiometric assay
IRT intermediate renal tubule
IRV inspiratory reserve volume

IS immunosuppressive; inguinal syndrome; intercostal space
ISD iron-storage disease
ISF interstitial fluid
ISG immune serum globulin
ISO International Standards Organization
i.s.q. *in status quo* [Latin] unchanged
IT immunity test; inhalation therapy; inspiratory time; intensive therapy
ITP idiopathic thrombocytopenic purpura
ITT internal tibial torsion
IU immunizing unit; International Units; intrauterine
IUCD intrauterine contraceptive device
IUD intrauterine (contraceptive) device
IUGR intrauterine growth retardation
IUI intrauterine insemination
IV interventricular; intravenous
iv intravenous
i.v. *in vitro* [Latin] within glass; *in vivo* [Latin] within a living body
IVC inferior vena cava; inspiratory vital capacity
IVD intervertebral disk
IVDA intravenous drug abuse; intravenous drug abuser
IVF *in vitro* fertilization
IVF-ET *in vitro* fertilization and embryo transfer
IVH intraventricular hemorrhage
IVIg intravenous immunoglobulin
IVP intravenous pyelogram; intravenous pyelography; increased vascular permeability
IVT intravenous transfusion
IVU intravenous urography
J joint; joule; journal; juice; juvenile
JA juvenile atrophy
JAMA *Journal of the American Medical Association*
JAMG juvenile autoimmune myasthenia gravis
jaund. jaundice
jc juice
JCA juvenile chronic arthritis
JCAH Joint Commission on Accreditation of Hospitals
JCAHO Joint Commission on Accreditation of Healthcare Organizations
JCMHC Joint Commission on Mental Health of Children
JCML juvenile chronic myelocytic leukemia
jct junction
JCV JC virus
JD juvenile delinquent; juvenile diabetes
JDC Joslin Diabetes Center
JDF Juvenile Diabetes Foundation
JDM juvenile-onset diabetes mellitus
jej. jejunum
JGA juxtaglomerular apparatus
JGC juxtaglomerular complex
j-g complex juxtaglomerular complex
JLP juvenile laryngeal papilloma
JND just noticeable difference
jnt joint
JOD juvenile-onset diabetes
JODM juvenile-onset diabetes mellitus
Jour. journal
JP juvenile periodontitis
JPB junctional premature beat
JPS juvenile polyposis syndrome
JRA juvenile rheumatoid arthritis
J seg joining segment (of DNA encoding immunoglobulins)
JT joint
junct. junction
JV jugular vein
JVD jugular venous distention
JVP jugular venous pressure; jugular venous pulse
JXG juvenile xanthogranuloma
K constant; kidney; kilogram; potassium
k constant; Kelvin; reaction rate
KA ketoacidosis

KAFO knee-ankle-foot orthosis
KAO knee-ankle orthosis
KB ketone bodies
kb kilobase
KC keratoconus; Kupffer cells
kc kilocycle
K cell killer cell
KCS keratoconjunctivitis sicca
KD knee disarticulation
KDA known drug allergies
keV kiloelectron-volt
Kg kilogauss; kilogram
KJ knee jerk
km kilometer
Kn knee
KNO keep needle open
KO keep open; knee orthosis
KOH potassium hydroxide
KP keratic precipitates
Kr krypton
KS Kaposi's sarcoma; ketosteroid
17-KS 17-ketosteroids
KS/OI Kaposi's sarcoma and opportunistic infections
KT kidney transplant
KTU kidney transplant unit
KUB kidney, ureter, and bladder
KUF kidney ultrafiltration rate
kv kilovolt
kw kilowatt
L inductance; *Lactobacillus;* lambert; lethal; lidocaine; light; liter; lumbar vertebra; lumen; lung; lymphocyte; lysosome
l left; length; lethal; long
l. ligament
L1 first lumbar spinal nerve; first lumbar vertebra
L2 second lumbar spinal nerve; second lumbar vertebra
L3 third lumbar spinal nerve; third lumbar vertebra
L4 fourth lumbar spinal nerve; fourth lumbar vertebra
L5 fifth lumbar spinal nerve; fifth lumbar vertebra
LA left arm; left atrium; left auricle; local anesthesia; long acting; low anxiety
L & A light and accommodation (reaction of the pupil); living and active
La labial; lanthanum
lab laboratory
LAC laceration; long-arm cast
LAD left anterior descending (coronary artery); left axis deviation; leukocyte adhesion deficiency
LADCA left anterior descending coronary artery
LAE left atrial enlargement
LAF leukocyte-activating factor
LAG lymphangiogram
LAH left atrial hypertrophy
LAK lymphokine-activated killer (cells)
LAL left axillary line
LAM late ambulatory monitoring; left atrial myxoma
lam laminectomy; laminogram
LAMB Lentigines, Atrial myxoma, Mucocutaneous myxomas, and Blue nevi
lami laminotomy
LANC long-arm navicular cast
LAO left anterior oblique (view)
LAP laparotomy; left arterial pressure; left atrial pressure; leucine aminopeptidase; leukocyte alkaline phosphatase
LAPSE long-term ambulatory physiologic surveillance
laryn. laryngitis
LAS laxative abuse syndrome; long-arm splint; lower abdominal surgery
LASER Light Amplification by Stimulated Emission of Radiation
LASH left anterosuperior hemiblock

L-ASP L-asparaginase
lat. latent; lateral; latex
lat. men. lateral meniscectomy
LATS long-acting thyroid stimulator
LAV lymphadenopathy-associated virus
lax. laxative
LB large bowel; left breast; left buttock; live birth
LBAT leukocyte bactericidal assay test
LBB left breast biopsy
LBBB left bundle branch block
LBH length, breadth, and height
LBM lean body mass
LBO large bowel obstruction
LBP low back pain; low blood pressure
LBW low birth weight
LBWI low birth weight infant
LC lethal concentration; life care; living child; living children; low calorie
LCA left coronary artery; left carotid artery
LCCA left circumflex coronary artery; left common carotid artery
LCCS low cervical cesarean section
LCD liquid crystal display
LCIS lobular carcinoma *in situ*
LCL lateral capsular ligament; lymphocytic leukemia
LCLC large cell lung carcinoma
LCM lymphocytic choriomeningitis
LCMV lymphocytic choriomeningitis virus
LCR late cutaneous reaction
LCS low continuous suction
LCSW licensed clinical social worker
LD learning disability; lethal dose; levodopa; living donor; loading dose; low dosage; Lyme disease
L & D labor and delivery
LDH lactate dehydrogenase
LDL low-density lipoprotein; loudness discomfort level
LDL-C low-density lipoprotein cholesterol
L-dopa levodopa
LDR labor, delivery, and recovery (room)
LE left eye; lower extremity; lupus erythematosus
LE cell lupus erythematosus cell
LEEP loop electrosurgical excision procedure
leio. leiomyoma
LEL lowest effect level
LE prep lupus erythematosus preparation
LES Lambert-Eaton syndrome; local excitatory state; lower esophageal sphincter
Leu leucine
leuk. leukemia
LF low forceps; low frequency
LFA left femoral artery; left frontoanterior (fetal position); low friction arthroplasty; lymphocyte functional antigen
LFD lactose-free diet; low fat diet
LFH left femoral hernia
LFP left frontoposterior (fetal position)
LFT left frontotransverse (fetal position)
LG laryngectomy
lg large
LGA large for gestational age
LGL large granular lymphocyte
lgth length
LGV lymphogranuloma venereum
LH left hand; luteinizing hormone
LHC left hypochondrium
LHF left heart failure; luteinizing hormone-releasing factor
LHON Leber's hereditary optic neuropathy
LH-RF luteinizing hormone-releasing factor
LH-RH luteinizing hormone-releasing hormone
Li lithium
LIB left in bottle
LIC left iliac crest

LICA left internal carotid artery
LICM left intercostal margin
LICS left intercostal space
LIF left iliac fossa; leukocyte inhibiting factor
lig. *ligamentum* [Latin] ligament
ligg ligature
LIH left inguinal hernia
LIP lymphocytic interstitial pneumonia
liq. liquid
LIS locked-in syndrome
litho lithotripsy
LK left kidney
LL large lymphocyte; left leg; left lung; long leg (brace); lower lip; lymphoblastic lymphoma
LLC long-leg cast
LLD leg length discrepancy
LLE left lower extremity
LLL left long leg (brace); left lower limb; left lower lobe (of lung)
LLQ left lower quadrant (of abdomen)
LLS long-leg splint
LLWC long-leg walking cast
LM legal medicine; licentiate in midwifery; light microscopy
LMA left mentoanterior (fetal position)
LMBS Laurence-Moon-Biedl syndrome
LMCA left main coronary artery
LMD local medical doctor
LME left mediolateral episiotomy
LMI leukocyte migration inhibition
L/min liters per minute
LMM lentigo maligna melanoma
LMN lower motor neuron
LMP last menstrual period; left mentoposterior (fetal position); lumbar puncture
LMT left mentotransverse (fetal position)
LN lymph node
LNB lymph node biopsy
LNMP last normal menstrual period
LOA left occipito-anterior (fetal position)
LOC laxative of choice; level of care; level of consciousness; loss of consciousness
loc. dol. *loco dolenti* [Latin] to the painful spot
LOI level of injury
LOM left otitis media; limitation of movement
LoNa low sodium
LOP left occipitoposterior (fetal position)
LOPS length of patient stay
LOS length of stay
LOT left occipitotransverse (fetal position)
lot. *lotio* [Latin] lotion
LP lichen planus; light perception; lipoprotein; lumbar puncture
Lp(a) lipoprotein (a)
LPN Licensed Practical Nurse
L proj. light projection
LPS last Papanicolaou smear; lipopolysaccharide
LPT Licensed Physical Therapist
LPV left pulmonary vein; lymphotropic papovavirus
lq liquid
LR labor room; light reaction
Lr lawrencium
LRA left renal artery
LRD living renal donor
LRH luteinizing hormone-releasing hormone
LRI lower respiratory infection
LRR labor room
LRV left renal vein
LS lichen sclerosis; lumbosacral
LSA left sacroanterior (fetal position)
LSCS lower segment cesarean section
LSCV left subclavian vein

LSD life-sustaining device; lysergic acid diethylamide
LSH lutein-stimulating hormone;
LSK liver, spleen, and kidneys
LSL left short leg (brace)
LSO lumbosacral orthosis
L/S ratio lecithin/sphingomyelin ratio
LSV left subclavian vein
LT left; leukotriene; long term; low temperature; lymphotoxin
lt left
LTC long-term care
LTCS low transverse cesarean section
LTG long-term goal
LTM long-term memory
Lu lutetium
LUE left upper extremity
LUL left upper limb; left upper lobe (of lung)
lum lumbar
LUQ left upper quadrant (of abdomen)
LV left ventricle; leukemia virus; live vaccine; lung volume
Lv leave
LVA left ventricular aneurysm
LVD left ventricular dysfunction
LVE left ventricular enlargement
LVET left ventricular ejection time
LVF left ventricular failure
LVH left ventricular hypertrophy
LVI left ventricular insufficiency
LVM left ventricular mass
LVN Licensed Vocational Nurse
LVSP left ventricular systolic pressure
LW lacerating wound
LX local irradiation
lym lymphocyte
Lys lysine
M echomotion; male; malignant; married; masculine; mass; massage; maximum; median; medical; memory; meter; minimum; mol; molar; morgan; mother; murmur; muscle; myopia
m meter; molar; motile; murmur
m. *misce* [Latin] mix; *musculus* [Latin] muscle
M/3 middle third
MA medical assistant; medical audit; medical authorization; menstrual age; mental age; milliampere; moderately advanced
Ma male
mA milliampere
ma milliampere
MAA macroaggregated albumin
Mab monoclonal antibody
MABP mean arterial blood pressure
MAC maximum allowable concentration (of hazardous substance); maximum allowable cost (of program); membrane-attack complex; minimum alveolar (anesthetic) concentration; *Mycobacterium avium* complex
Mac-1 macrophage-1 glycoprotein
MAD mind-altering drug
MAF macrophage-activating factor
MAIDS Murine Acquired Immune Deficiency Syndrome.
MAL midaxillary line
malig. malignant
MALT mucosa-associated lymphoid tissue
mammo. mammogram
mand. mandible
manip. manipulation
man. pr. *mane primo* [Latin] early in the morning
MAO maximal acid output; monoamine oxidase
MAOI monoamine oxidase inhibitor
MAP mean airway pressure; mean arterial pressure; muscle action potential
MAS meconium aspiration syndrome; milk-alkali syndrome
mas. masculine

MASER Microwave Amplification by Stimulated Emission of Radiation
MAST medical antishock trousers
mast. mastoid
MAT multifocal atrial tachycardia
max maxillary; maximum
m.b. *misce bene* [Latin] mix well
Mb myoglobin
MBC maximum breathing capacity
MBD minimal brain damage; minimal brain dysfunction
MBL menstrual blood loss
MBM mother's breast milk
MBP myelin basic protein; mean blood pressure
MBPS Munchausen-by-proxy syndrome
MC mast cell; maximum concentration; metacarpal; miscarriage
M & C morphine and cocaine
mCi millicurie
MCA middle carotid artery; middle cerebral artery; multiple congenital abnormalities
McB pt McBurney's point
MCC midstream clean-catch (urine sample)
MCD minimal change disease
mcg microgram
MCH mean corpuscular hemoglobin
MCHC mean corpuscular hemoglobin concentration
MCL maximum contamination level; midclavicular line
MCP membrane cofactor protein; metacarpophalangeal (joint)
M-CSF monocyte-macrophage colony-stimulating factor
MCT mean circulating time; medium-chain triglycerides; mucin clot test
MCTD mixed connective tissue disease
MCU maximum care unit
MCV mean corpuscular volume
MD manic-depressive; mean deviation; medical doctor; medium dosage; mental deficiency; muscular dystrophy
Md mendelevium
MDD male development disorder; major depressive disorder; mean daily dose
MDF myocardial depressant factor
MDI manic depressive illness; multiple daily injections
MDMA 3, 4-methylenedioxymethamphetamine
mdn median
MDR multidrug resistance
MDRI multidrug-resistant infection
MDY month, date, and year
ME macular edema; medial episiotomy; mediastinal emphysema; medical examiner; middle ear
Me methyl
meas. measure
mec. meconium
MED medicine; medium; minimal effective dose
med. medial; medicine
MEDLARS MEDical Literature Analysis and Retrieval System
MEDLINE MEDlars on-LINE
med.men. medial meniscectomy
MEE middle ear effusion
MEN multiple endocrine neoplasia
mEq milliequivalent
meq milliequivalent
MESA microsurgical epididymal sperm aspiration
MET metastasis
Met methionine
m. et n. *mane et nocte* [Latin] morning and night
m. et sig. *misce et signa* [Latin] mix and label
MeV megavolt; megavoltage; million electron volts
MF mitogenic factor; mycosis fungoides
M&F male and female; mother and father
MFD mid-forceps delivery; minimum fatal dose
MFW multiple fragment wounds
MG mammary gland; myasthenia gravis
Mg magnesium

mg milligram
MGUS Monoclonal Gammopathy of Undetermined Significance
MH medical history; menstrual history; mental health
MHA major histocompatibility antigen
MHC major histocompatibility complex; mental health clinic
MHD minimum hemolytic dilution; minimum hemolytic dose
NHL non-Hodgkin's lymphoma
MHW medial heel wedge
M Hx medical history
MHz megahertz
MI maturation index; mitral insufficiency; myocardial infarction
MIC minimal inhibitory concentration
MICU medical intensive care unit
MID minimal infecting dose; minimal inhibiting dose; multi-infarct dementia
mid/3 middle third
min minimal; minor; minute
MIO minimal identifiable odor
MIP minimal invasive procedure
MIRS medical improvement review standard
misc. miscarriage; miscellaneous
mIU milli-International Unit
mks meter-kilogram-second (system)
ML malignant lymphoma
ml milliliter
mL milliliter
MLA Medical Library Association
MLC mixed leukocyte culture
MLCT mixed lymphocyte culture test
MLD minimal lethal dose
MLE midline episiotomy
MLNS mucocutaneous lymph node syndrome
MLR mixed leukocyte reaction; mixed leukocyte response; mixed lymphocyte reaction; mixed lymphocyte response
MLS mean life span; middle lobe syndrome
MLT medical laboratory technologist
MM medial malleolus; mucous membrane
mM millimole
mm millimeter; mucous membrane
mm. *musculi* [Latin] muscles
MMEF maximal midexpiratory flow
MMFR maximal midexpiratory flow rate
mmHg millimeters of mercury
MMI macrophage migration inhibition
mmol millimole
MMPI Minnesota Multiphasic Personality Inventory (test)
mmpp millimeters partial pressure
MMR measles, mumps, rubella (vaccine)
MMT manual muscle testing
MMWR *Morbidity and Mortality Weekly Report*
MN mononuclear
mn midnight
mng morning
MND motor neuron disease
Mn manganese
MNJ myoneural junction
MNM motile (sperm) with normal morphology
MO Medical Officer; medulla oblongata; mineral oil
Mo molybdenum
mo. month
MOA mechanism of action
MOAb monoclonal antibody
MOD mesio-occlusodistal
mod moderate
MODS multiple organ dysfunction syndrome
MODY maturity-onset diabetes of youth
MOF multiple organ failure
mol mole; molecule
mol wt molecular weight

MOM milk of magnesia
MONAb monoclonal antibody
monos monocytes
MOPD multiple oocytes per disk
MOR morphine; morphology
mor. dict. *moro dicto* [Latin] as directed
mOsm milliosmole
MOTT mycobacterium other than tubercle bacilli
MP mean pressure; menstrual period; metacarpophalangeal (joint); middle phalanx; multiparous
mp melting point
MPB male pattern baldness
MPD maximal permissible dose; multiple personality disorder
MPE malignant pericardial effusion
MPL maximum permissible level
MPS meconium plug syndrome; mononuclear phagocyte system; mucopolysaccharide; mucopolysaccharidosis
MPV mean platelet volume
MR may repeat; medical record; medical resident; mental retardation; mitral regurgitation; Moro's reflex
mR milliroentgen
MRD minimal reactive dose
MRI magnetic resonance imaging
MPJ metaphalangeal joint
mRNA messenger ribonucleic acid
MRSA methicillin-resistant *Staphylococcus aureus*
MRSE methicillin-resistant *Staphylococcus epidermis*
MS mitral stenosis; morphine sulfate; multiple sclerosis; musculoskeletal
Ms murmurs
ms millisecond
MSAFP maternal serum alfa-fetoprotein
msec millisecond
MSG monosodium glutamate
MSH medical self-help; melanocyte-stimulating hormone
MSL midsternal line
MSN mildly subnormal
MST McCarthy screening test; mean survival time
MSUD maple syrup urine disease
MT mammary tumor; medical technologist; medical transcriptionist; muscles and tendons
MT bar metatarsal bar
MTD maximal tolerated dose
MTDDA Minnesota Test for Differential Diagnosis of Aphasia
mtDNA mitochondrial deoxyribonucleic acid (DNA)
MTF modulation transfer function
MTJ midtarsal joint
MTP metatarsophalangeal (joint)
MTV metatarsus varus
mu million units; mouse unit
MUC maximum urinary concentration
MUDDLES miosis, urination, diarrhea, defecation, lacrimation, excitation, and salivation
multip multiparous
musc. muscle; muscular
MV mitral valve
mV millivolt
MVC maximum vital capacity
MVI multiple vitamin infusion
MVP mitral valve prolapse
MVS mitral valve stenosis
MVV maximal voluntary ventilation
MW molecular weight
MWD microwave diathermy
My myopia
N nasal; negative; nerve; nitrogen; normal (solution); normal concentration; number
n nasal; neutron; refractive index
n. *nervus* [Latin] nerve

NA Narcotics Anonymous; *Nomina Anatomica;* not admitted; nuclear antigen; nurse anesthetist
Na sodium
NAA no apparent abnormalities
NABS normoactive bowel sounds
NAD nicotinamide adenine dinucleotide; no apparent distress; no appreciable disease; nothing abnormal detected
NADP nicotinamide adenine dinucleotide phosphate
NAME National Association of Medical Examiners; Nevi, Atrial myxoma, Myxoid neurofibroma, and Ephilides
NANA *N*-acetylneuraminic acid
NANB non-A, non-B (hepatitis)
NAPA *N*-actylprocainamide
NAPAP National Acid Precipitation Assessment Program
Narc narcotic
Narco narcolepsy
NAS National Academy of Science; no added salt
NB needle biopsy; newborn
Nb niobium
NBM no bowel movement; nothing by mouth
NBN newborn nursery
NBS National Bureau of Standards
NBT nitroblue tetrazolium
NBTT nitroblue tetrazolium test
NBTE nonbacterial thrombotic endocarditis
NBW normal birth weight
NC no change; no charge; no complaints; non-compliance; not completed; nurse counseling
NCI National Cancer Institute
NCT nerve conduction time
NCV nerve conduction velocity
ND natural death; neonatal death; neoplastic disease; new drug; no disease; normal delivery; nose drops; not diagnosed; notifiable disease
Nd neodymium
NE nerve ending; neurologic examination; no effect; norepinephrine
Ne neon
NEC necrotizing enterocolitis
NED no evidence of disease; no expiration date
neg negative
NEFA nonesterified fatty acids
NEJM *New England Journal of Medicine*
NEO neonatology
NER no evidence of recurrence
NF *National Formulary;* neurofibromatosis; not found
NFAR no further action required
NFTD normal full-term delivery
NG nitroglycerin
ng nanogram; nasogastric
NGU nongonococcal urethritis
NH nursing home
NHC National Health Council
NHL non-Hodgkin's lymphoma
NHLI National Heart and Lung Institute
NI neonatal isoerythrolysis; no improvement
Ni nickel
NIAID National Institute of Allergy and Infectious Diseases
NIAMD National Institute of Arthritis and Metabolic Diseases
NICC neonatal intensive care center
NICHHD National Institute of Child Health and Human Development
NICU neonatal intensive care unit
NIDA National Institute on Drug Abuse
NIDDM non-insulin dependent diabetes mellitus
NIDR National Institute of Dental Research
NIEHS National Institute of Environmental Health Sciences
NIGMS National Institute of General Medical Sciences
NIH National Institutes of Health
NIHL noise-induced hearing loss
NIL nothing in light microscopy (disease)
NIMH National Institute of Mental Health

NINDB National Institute of Neurological Diseases and Blindness
NIOSH National Institute for Occupational Safety and Health
NK natural killer (cells); no ketones
NKA no known allergies
NKDA no known drug allergies
NL normal limits
NLMC nocturnal leg muscle cramp
NM neuromuscular; nodular melanoma
nm nanometer
NMJ neuromuscular junction
NMP normal menstrual period
NMR nuclear magnetic resonance
NMS neuroleptic malignant syndrome
NMSC nonmelanoma skin cancer
NMT no more than
NN nurse's notes
nn. *nervi* [Latin] nerves
NNACS neonatal neurologic and adaptive capacity score
NND *New and Nonofficial Drugs*
No nobelium; number
noct. maneq. *nocte maneque* [Latin] at night and in the morning
non rep. *non repetatur* [Latin] no refill
NOR noradrenaline
NP nasopharynx; no pain; not pregnant; nurse practitioner
Np neptunium
NPC nasal point of conversion; no previous complaint
NPCC National Poison Control Center
NPH neutral protamine Hagedorn (insulin); no previous history; normal-pressure hydrocephalus
NPhx nasopharynx
NPN nonprotein nitrogen
n.p.o. *nulla per os* [Latin] nothing by mouth
NPT nocturnal penile tumescent
NR normal range; not recorded
NREM non-rapid eye movement (sleep)
nRNA nuclear ribonucleic acid
NRT nicotine replacement therapy
NS nephrosclerosis; nephrotic syndrome; nonsymptomatic; normal saline; no sample; no specimen; not significant
NSA no significant abnormality
nsa no salt added
NSAIA nonsteroidal anti-inflammatory analgesic
NSAID nonsteroidal anti-inflammatory drug
NSC no significant change
NSD no significant defect
NSR normal sinus rhythm
NST nonstress test
NSU nonspecific urethritis
NT nasotracheal; nephrostomy tube; neurotransmitter; not tested
NTD neural tube defect
NTE not to exceed
NTG nitroglycerin
NTMI nontransmural myocardial infarction
NTP normal temperature and pressure
NTT nasotracheal tube
NUG necrotizing ulcerative gingivitis
NV neurovascular; next visit; nonvenereal
N&V nausea and vomiting
NVD nausea, vomiting, and diarrhea; neck vein distention
nWA normal when awake
NWB non-weight-bearing
NYD not yet diagnosed
O opium; oxygen
o oral
o. *oculus* [Latin] eye
ō none
O3 ozone
OA ocular albinism; old age; osteoarthritis

O & A observation and assessment
OAD obstructive airway disease
OAS opiate abstinence syndrome
OAWO opening abductory wedge osteotomy
OB obstetrics; occult bleeding
OBD organic brain disease
OB/GYN obstetrics and gynecology
obl. oblique
OBN occult blood negative
OBP occult blood positive
OBS organic brain syndrome
obs. observation
OC office call; on call; only child; oral contraceptive
OCA oculocutaneous albinism
OCCC oocyte-cumulus-corona complex
OCCM open chest cardiac massage
OCD obsessive-compulsive disorder; osteochondritis dissecans
OCT oxytocin challenge test
OD Doctor of Optometry; on duty; overdose
o.d. *omni die* [Latin] every day; *oculus dexter* [Latin] right eye
ODA overall disease assessment; right occipitoanterior (fetal position)
ODP right occipitoposterior (fetal position)
ODT right occipitotransverse (fetal position)
OE on examination
OGTT oral glucose tolerance test
OFA oncofetal antigen
OFC occipital frontal circumference
o.h. *omni hora* [Latin] every hour
OHA oral hyperglycemia agent
17-OHCS 17-hydroxycorticosteroid
OHS open heart surgery
OI opportunistic infection; ostegenesis imperfecta
OLD occupational lung disease
olf. olfactory
OLP left occipitoposterior (fetal position)
OLT left occipitotransverse (fetal position)
OM osteomalacia; osteomyelitis; otitis media
omn. bih. *omni bihors* [Latin] every two hours
omn. hor. *omni hora* [Latin] every hour
omn. man. *omni mane* [Latin] every morning
omn. quar. hor. *omni quadrante hora* [Latin] every quarter of an hour
OMS osteomalacia senile
ON overnight
ONCO oncology
ONTR order not to resuscitate
OOB out of bed
OOC out of control
OPD outpatient department
OPO organ procurement organization
OOR out of room
OP operative procedure; osteoporosis
OPD outpatient department
OPt outpatient
OPTN Organ Procurement and Transportation Network
OPV oral poliovirus vaccine
OR open reduction (of a fracture); operating room
ORIF open reduction/internal fixation
ORN operating room nurse
Orn ornithine
ORT operating room technician; oral rehydration therapy
Ortho orthopedics
OS opening snap; oral surgery; orthopedic surgery; osteogenic sarcoma; osteosclerosis
Os osmium
o.s. *oculus sinister* [Latin] left eye
OSHA Occupational Safety and Health Administration
Osm osmole

OT occupational therapy; oral temperature; oxytocin

OTC over the counter (drugs)

o.u. *oculus uterque* [Latin] each eye

OV office visit; ovary; ovum

Ov ovary; ovum

OVD occlusal vertical dimension

OW open wedge

OXT oxytocin

oz ounce

P pain; part; passive; peripheral; phosphate; phosphorus; pint; placebo; plasma; positive; pressure; progesterone; protein; pulse; pupil

P$_{alv}$ alveolar pressure

P$_{ao}$ pressure at airway opening

P$_{bs}$ pressure at external surface of chest

P$_{pl}$ pleural pressure

^{32}**P** phosphorus-32

p page; papilla; pint; pulse; pupil; short arm of chromosome

P1 first parental generation

P$_1$ first pulmonic heart sound

P$_2$ second pulmonic heart sound

P/3 proximal third

PA paralysis agitans; pernicious anemia; physician assistant; posteroanterior; prior to admission; prolonged action; psycoanalyst; pulmonary artery

P-A posteroanterior

P & A percussion and auscultation

pA picoampere

PABA para-aminobenzoic acid

PAC premature atrial contraction

PAD peripheral arterial disease

p. ae. *partes aequales* [Latin] in equal parts

PAF platelet-activating factor; platelet-aggregating factor

PAH para-aminohippuric (acid); pulmonary artery hypertension; pulmonary artery hypotension

PAHO Pan American Health Organization

PAL posterior axillary line

Palp. palpable; palpate; palpated

PALS periarteriolar lymphatic sheath

PAN polyarteritis nodosa

PAOD peripheral arterial occlusive disease

PAP Papanicolaou (test); peroxidase antiperoxidase (complex); prostatic acid phosphatase

Pap smear Papanicolaou smear

Pap test Papanicolaou test

P & PD percussion and postural drainage

PAR population attributable risk; postanesthesia room; pulmonary arteriolar resistance

paracent. paracentesis

part. aeq. *partes aequales* [Latin] in equal parts

PARR postanesthetic recovery room

PAS para-aminosalicylic (acid); periodic acid-Schiff (stain); pulmonary artery stenosis

PASA para-aminosalicylic acid

PAT paroxysmal atrial tachycardia; platelet aggregation test; preadmission testing

Path pathogenic; pathologic

PATI penetrating abdominal trauma index

PB paraffin bath; phenobarbital; premature birth

Pb lead

PBC primary biliary cirrhosis

PBD proliferative breast disease

PBG porphobilinogen

PBI protein-bound iodine

PBLC premature-birth living child

PBV percutaneous balloon valvuloplasty

PBZ pyribenzamine

PC platelet count; postcoital; premature contraction

p.c. *post cibum* [Latin] after a meal

PCA patient care aide; patient-controlled anesthesia; posterior cerebral artery

PCAN potential child abuse and neglect

PCB polychlorinated biphenyl; postcoital bleeding

PCC pericardiocentesis; Poison Control Center

PCCU postcoronary care unit

PCE physical capacities evaluation

PCG phonocardiogram

pCi picocurie

PCKD polycystic kidney disease

PCL persistent corpus luteum; posterior cruciate ligament

PCLD polycystic liver disease

PCM protein-calorie malnutrition

pCO$_2$ partial pressure of carbon dioxide

PCP phencyclidine pill (phencyclidine hydrochloride); *Pneumocystis carinii* pneumonia; primary care physician; principal care provider

PCR polymerase chain reaction; protein catabolic rate

PCT porphyria cutanea tarda; proximal convoluted tubule

pct percent

PCU pain control unit

PCV packed cell volume

PD patent ductus; periodontal disease; peritoneal dialysis; postnasal drainage; postnasal drip

pd potential difference; prism diopter; pupillary distance

PDA patent ductus arteriosus

PDGF platelet-derived growth factor

PDI periodontal disease index

PDLL poorly differentiated lymphocytic lymphoma

PDN private duty nurse; private duty nursing

PDQ physician data query

PDR *Physicians' Desk Reference;* proliferative diabetic retinopathy

pdr powder

PDS peritoneal dialysis system

PE physical education; physical examination; pleural effusion; probable error; pulmonary edema; pulmonary embolis

PED pre-existing disease

PEEP positive end-expiratory pressure

PEFR peak expiratory flow rate

PEG pneumoencephalogram

PEL permissible exposure limit

PEMF pulsating electromagnetic fields

Per. permission

PERRLA Pupils Equal, Round, and React(ive) to Light and Accommodation

PET positron emission tomography; pre-eclamptic toxemia

PETT positron emission transaxial tomography

PF peak factor; posterior fontanelle; pulmonary fibrosis; push fluids

PFC pelvic flexion contracture; persistent fetal circulation; plaque-forming cell

PFFD proximal femoral focal deficiency

PFO patent foramen ovale

PFT pulmonary function test

PFU plaque-forming unit

PG postgraduate; pregnant; prostaglandin

pg page; picogram

PGH pituitary growth hormone

PGM phosphoglucomutase

PGU postgonococcal urethritis

PGY-1 first year postgraduate training

PGY-2 second year postgraduate training

PGY-3 third year postgraduate training

PGY-4 fourth year postgraduate training

PH past history; personal history; poor health

pH hydrogen-ion concentration

PHA phytohemagglutinin

phal. phalanges; phalanx

PHC posthospital care

PhD Doctor of Philosophy

phono. phonocardiogram
PHP pseudohypoparathyroidism
PHS Public Health Service
PHT pulmonary hypertension
PhysTh physical therapy
PI patient's interests; Periodontal Index; personal injury; physician intervention; poison ivy; pregnancy induced; present illness; pulmonary infarction; pulmonary insufficiency
PICU pediatric intensive care unit
PID pelvic inflammatory disease; prolapsed intervertebral disk
PIE pulmonary interstitial emphysema
PIF prolactin-inhibiting factor
PIH pregnancy-induced hypertension
PIP peak inspiratory pressure; proximal interphalangeal (joint)
PIPJ proximal interphalangeal joint
PIVD protruded intervertebral disk
PJ Peutz-Jeghers (syndrome)
PK pyruvate kinase
PKD polycystic kidney disease
PKU phenylketonuria
PL placebo
Pl. fl. pleural fluid
PLM percent-labeled mitosis
PLN pelvic lymph node
PLT platelet
Plt platelet
plx plexus
PM pacemaker; petit mal; physical medicine; pneumomediastinum; presystolic murmur; preventive medicine; prostatic massage
pm picometer
p.m. *post mortem* [Latin] after death
PMA Pharmaceutical Manufacturers Association
PMB postmenopausal bleeding
PMBV percutaneous mitral balloon valvotomy
PMD progressive muscular dystrophy; private medical doctor
PMF progressive massive fibrosis
PMHx past medical history
PMI past medical illness
PML progressive multifocal leukoencephalopathy
PMN polymorphonuclear neutrophil
PMO postmenopausal osteoporosis
PMP plasma membrane protein
PMR physical medicine and rehabilitation; polymyalgia rheumatica
PM & R physical medicine and rehabilitation
PMRS physical medicine and rehabilitation service
PMS passive maternal smoking; premenstrual syndrome
PMT premenstrual tension
PN peripheral neuropathy; practical nurse; pyelonephritis
Pn pneumonia
PNB prostatic needle biopsy
PNC prenatal care
PND paroxysmal nocturnal dyspnea; postnasal drainage; postnasal drip
PNF proprioceptive neuromuscular facilitation (reaction)
PNH paroxysmal nocturnal hemoglobinuria
PNI peripheral nerve injury
PNP peripheral neuropathy; purine nucleoside phosphorylase
PNPB positive-negative pressure breathing
PNS peripheral nervous system
PNTX pneumothorax
Pnx pneumothorax
PO postoperative
Po polonium
p.o. *per os* [Latin] by mouth; postoperative
POA pancreatic oncofetal antigen
POB place of birth
POC point of care; postoperative care
POD podiatry; postoperative day

POEMS Polyneuropathy, Organomegaly, Endocrinopathy, Monoclonal gammopathy, and Skin changes (syndrome)
POL premature onset of labor
polio poliomyelitis
polys polymorphonuclear neutrophils
POMR problem-oriented medical record
POP plaster of Paris
POR problem-oriented record
POS polycystic ovary syndrome
pos. positive
post. posterior
post op postoperative
post-stim post-stimulation
pot. AGT potential abnormality of glucose tolerance
PP pink puffer; pin prick; postprandial; proximal phalanx; pyrophosphate
PPA phenylpropanolamine
PPBS postprandial blood sugar
PPCA proserum prothrombin conversion accelerator
PPD purified protein derivative (TB skin test); postpartum day
PPH primary pulmonary hypertension
PPHP pseudo-pseudohypoparathyroidism
PPLO pleuropneumonia-like organisms
ppm parts per million
PPMS postpoliomyelitis syndrome
PPO preferred-provider organization
PPPPPP Pain, Pallor, Paresthesia, Pulselessness, Paralysis, Prostration (mnemonic of 6 symptoms of acute arterial occlusion)
ppt precipitate
PR partial remission; peer review; proctologist
Pr presbyopia
p.r. *per rectum* [Latin] through the rectum
PRA plasma renin activity
PRBC packed red blood cells
PRCA pure red cell aplasia
PRE progressive resistive exercise
pre-op preoperative
prep. preparation (for surgery); prepare for
prev. AGT previous abnormality of glucose tolerance
PRF prolactin-releasing factor
primip. primiparous
PRL prolactin
p.r.n. *pro re nata* [Latin] as needed
Pro proline
PROG progesterone
prog. prognosis
PROM premature rupture of membranes
pron. pronator; pronation
prot. protein
pro. time prothrombin time
prox. proximal
prox/3 proximal third
PRP platelet-rich plasma
PRRE Pupils Round, Regular, and Equal
PS paradoxical sleep; physical status; plastic surgery; pulmonary stenosis
P & S pain and suffering
PSA prostate-specific antigen
PSAT prostate-specific antigen test
PSC primary sclerosing cholangitis
PSGN poststreptococcal glomerulonephritis
PSIS posterosuperior iliac spine
PSP phenolsulfonphthalein
PSR Physicians for Social Responsibility
PSRO Professional Standard Review Organization
PSS progressive systemic sclerosis
PT parathyroid; paroxysmal tachycardia; physical therapy; prothrombin time
Pt platinum

pt patient

PTA plasma thromboplastin antecedent; pretreatment anxiety; prior to admission

PTB patellar-tendon-bearing (base or prosthesis); prior to birth

PTC plasma thromboplastin component

PTCA percutaneous transluminal coronary angioplasty

PTD permanent and total disability; prior to discharge

PTH parathyroid hormone; posttransfusion hepatitis

PTP posterior tibial pulse

PTS permanent threshold shift

PTSD posttraumatic stress disorder

PTT partial thromboplastin time; patellar tendon transfer

PTU propylthiouracil

PTX pneumothorax

PU peptic ulcer; pressure ulcer

Pu plutonium

PUBS percutaneous umbilical blood sampling

PUD peptic ulcer disease

PUE pyrexia of unknown etiology

PUL percutaneous ultrasonic lithotripsy

PUO pyrexia of unknown origin

PUPPP Pruritic Urticarial Papules and Plaques of Pregnancy

PUVA psoralen (plus) ultraviolet A

PV peripheral vessels; polycythemia vera; portal vein

p.v. *per vaginam* [Latin] through the vagina

PVC polyvinyl chloride; premature ventricular contraction

PVD peripheral vascular disease; pulmonary vascular disease

PVE prosthetic valvular endocarditis

PVL periventricular leukomalacia

PVS persistent vegetative state

pvt private

PW plantar wart

PWA person with AIDS

PWB partial weight-bearing

PWM pokeweed mitogen

Px physical examination; pneumothorax; prognosis

PXE pseudoxanthoma elasticum

PYLL potential years of life lost

PZI protamine zinc insulin

Q coulomb; electric quantity; quadrant; quantity; question; quotient; volume of blood

q long arm of chromosome

q. *quaque* [Latin] every

QA quality assurance

q.a.m. *quaque ante meridiem* [Latin] every morning

QC quality control

q.d. *quaque die* [Latin] every day

q.d.s. *quater die sumendum* [Latin] to be taken four times daily

QF quick freeze

q.h. *quaque hora* [Latin] every hour

q.2h. *quaque secunda hora* [Latin] every 2 hours

q.3h. *quaque tertia hora* [Latin] every 3 hours

q.h.s. *quaque hora somni* [Latin] at bedtime

q.i.d. *quater in die* [Latin] four times a day

q.l. *quantum libet* [Latin] as much as desired

q.m. *quaque mane* [Latin] every morning

q.n. *quaque nocte* [Latin] every night

q.p. *quantum placeat* [Latin] as much as desired

QPC quality of patient care

q.q.h. *quaque quarta hora* [Latin] every four hours

QR quick recovery

QS quiet sleep

q.s. *quantum sufficit* [Latin] sufficient amount

q. suff. *quantum sufficit* [Latin] sufficient amount

QT quiet

quad. quadriceps; quadriplegic

quant. quantity

quotid. *quotidie* [Latin] daily

q.v. *quo vide* [Latin] which see

R arginine; gas constant; organic radical; race; rate; reaction; rectum; regular; resident; resistance; respiratory rate/min; review; right (eye); roentgen; rough; rub

R$_{aw}$ airway resistance (resistance of tracheobronchial tree to flow of air into lungs)

r oxidation-reduction potential; roentgen

RA radioactive; radium; ragweed antigen; residual air; rheumatoid arthritis; right atrium

Ra radium

RAD right axis deviation

rad radiation absorbed dose

RAE right atrium enlargement

RAI radioactive iodine

RAIU radioactive iodine uptake (test)

RAM random access memory

RANA rheumatoid agglutinin nuclear antigen

RAO right anterior-oblique (view)

RAP recurrent abdominal pain

RAS reticular activating system; rheumatoid arthritis serum

RA slide rheumatoid arthritis slide (test)

RAST radioallergosorbent test

RAU recurrent aphthous ulceration

RAV Rous-associated virus

RB right bronchus; right buttock

Rb rubidium

RBA rescue breathing apparatus

RBB right breast biopsy

RBBB right bundle branch block

RBC red blood cell; red blood count

rbc red blood cell

RBE relative biological effectiveness

RBF renal blood flow

RBN retrobulbar neuritis

RBOW ruptured bag of waters

RBP resting blood pressure

RBS random blood sugar

rBST recombinant bovine somatotropin

RC radial-carpal; red cell; Red Cross; retention catheter; root canal; rotator cuff

RCA right coronary artery

RCC rape crisis center; red cell count; renal cell carcinoma

RCG radiocardiography

R/CS repeat cesarean section

RCT root canal therapy

RCV red cell volume

RD reaction of degeneration; Registered Dietician; renal dialysis; retinal detachment; ruptured disk

RDA recommended daily allowance; recommended dietary allowance

RDFS ratio of decayed and filled surfaces

RDFT ratio of decayed and filled teeth

RDH Registered Dental Hygienist

rDNA recombinant deoxyribonucleic acid

RDS respiratory distress syndrome

RDT regular dialysis treatment

RDVT recurrent deep vein thrombosis

RE rectal examination; regional enteritis; reticuloendothelial; retinol equivalent; retrograde ejaculation; right eye

Re rhenium

REC radioelectrocardiogram

Rec. recommendation

rec'd received

redox reduction oxidation

REG radioencephalogram

REL recommended exposure limit

REM rapid eye movement; reticular erythematous mucinosis

rem roentgen-equivalent-man

REM sleep rapid eye movement sleep

ren. sem. *renovetum semel* [Latin] renewable only once
reovirus respiratory and enteric orphan virus
rep. *repetatur* [Latin] let it be renewed; repetition; report
RER rough endoplasmic reticulum
RES research; reticuloendothelial system
REVL reviewed by laboratory (pathologist)
RF renal failure; respiratory failure; rheumatic fever; rheumatoid factor; riboflavin; risk factor
Rf rutherfordium
RFA right frontoanterior (fetal position)
RFB retained foreign body (in surgery)
RFLP restriction fragment length polymorphism
RFP right frontoposterior (fetal position)
RFT right frontotransverse (fetal position)
RH relative humidity; releasing hormone; right hand
Rh rhodium
RHB raise head of bed
RHC respiration has ceased
RHD rheumatic heart disease
RHF right heart failure
RhIg Rh immunoglobulin
RI radiation intensity; radioisotope; regional ileitis; regular insulin
RIA radioimmune assay; radioimmunoassay
Rib ribose
RICS right intercostal space
RID radial immunodiffusion
RIF right iliac fossa
RIH right inguinal hernia
RIND reversible ischemic neurologic deficit.
RISA radioiodinated serum albumin
RIST radioimmunosorbent test
RIU radioactive iodine uptake
RK radial keratoplasty; right kidney
RL right lung
RLE right lower extremity
RLF retrolental fibroplasia
RLL right lower limb; right lower lobe (of lung)
RLN recurrent laryngeal nerve; regional lymph nodes
RLQ right lower quadrant (of abdomen)
RLS restless legs syndrome
RLX relaxin
RM radical mastectomy; repetition maximum
Rm remission
RMI repetitive motion injury
RML right middle lobe (of lung)
RMP right mentoposterior (fetal position)
RMSF Rocky Mountain spotted fever
RMT right mentotransverse (fetal position)
RN Registered Nurse
Rn radon
RNA ribonucleic acid
RNase ribonuclease
PNL percutaneous nephrolithotomy
RNP ribonucleoprotein
RO reality orientation
R/O rule out
ROM range of motion (of a joint); read only memory; rupture of membranes
ROMI rule out myocardial infarction
ROO register of operations
ROP retinopathy of prematurity
ROS review of (organ) systems
ROT right occipitotransverse (fetal position)
RP radial pulse; Raynaud's phenomenon; relapse prevention; retinitis pigmentosa
RPF relaxed pelvic floor; renal plasma flow (rate)
RPGN rapidly progressive glomerulonephritis
RPh Registered Pharmacist
RPLND retroperitoneal lymph node dissection

RPR rapid plasma reagin; Reiter protein reagin
RPRTs rapid plasma reagin tests
RPT Registered Physical Therapist; ring precipitin test
RQ respiratory quotient
RR recovery room; relative risk; respiratory rate
RR-1 first recovery room
RR-2 second recovery room
RRC Residency Review Committee
RRE round, regular, and equal
rRNA ribosomal ribonucleic acid
RS rectal sinus; rheumatoid spondylitis; right side; Ringer's solution
RSD reflex sympathetic dystrophy (syndrome); relative standard deviation
RSDS reflex sympathetic dystrophy syndrome
RSV respiratory syncytial virus; Rous sarcoma virus
rT3 reverse triiodothyronine
RT radiation therapy; radiologic technician; radiotherapy; recreational therapy; rectal temperature; Registered Technologist; renal transplant; room temperature; rubella titer
RTA renal tubular acidosis
RTC return to clinic; round the clock
RTx radiation therapy
RU radial-ulnar; residual urine; roentgen unit
Ru ruthenium
RUE right upper extremity
RUL right upper limb; right upper lobe (of lung); right upper lung
RUQ right upper quadrant (of abdomen)
RV residual volume; return visit; right ventricle; rubella vaccine; rubella virus
RVAD right ventricular assist device
RVF recto-vaginal fistula
RVH right ventricular hypertrophy
RVT renal vein thrombosis
RVU retroversion of uterus
Rx drug; medication; prescription; recipe
S heart sound; sacral vertebrae (S1 through S5); saline; saturated; section; sedimentation coefficient; selection coefficient; senile; septum; serum; solid; soluble; spherical (lens); spleen; suction; sulfur; Svedberg unit; systolic
s. *semis* [Latin] half; *sinister* [Latin] left
s̄ *sine* [Latin] without
S1 first sacral spinal nerve; first sacral vertebra
S2 second sacral spinal nerve; second sacral vertebra
S3 third sacral spinal nerve; third sacral vertebra
S4 fourth sacral spinal nerve; fourth sacral vertbra
S5 fifth sacral spinal nerve; fifth sacral vertebra
S$_1$ first heart sound
S$_2$ second heart sound
S$_3$ third heart sound
S$_4$ fourth heart sound
SA salicylic acid; salt added; sarcoma; semen analysis; serum albumin; sinoatrial; sinus arrhythmia; surface antigen; sustained action
S-A sinoatrial
SAA severe aplastic anemia
SAB spontaneous abortion
SAC short-arm cast
SACT sinoatrial conduction time
SAD seasonal affective disorder
SADS sudden arrhythmia death syndrome
SAH subarachnoid hemorrhage
sal saliva; salt
SAM self-administered medication
SAN sinoatrial node
SANC short-arm navicular cast
S-A node sinoatrial node
SAP systemic arterial pressure
SART sinoatrial recovery time
SAS scalenus anterior syndrome; short-arm splint; supravalvular aortic stenosis
SAT Scholastic Achievement Test; streptococcal antibody test

sat. saturated
SB shortness of breath; spina bifida; stillbirth; stillborn
Sb antimony; strabismus
SBA standby assistance
SBE subacute bacterial endocarditis
SBIT Stanford-Binet Intelligence Test
SBP subacute bacterial peritonitis
SBR strict bed rest
SBS shaken baby syndrome
SC sclerocorneal; secretory component; self-care; sternoclavicular (joint); subclavian; subcutaneous; sugar coated
Sc scandium
sc subcutaneous
SCA sickle-cell anemia; sudden cardiac arrest
SCAN scintiscan; suspected child abuse or neglect
SCB strictly confined to bed
SCC squamous cell carcinoma; squamous skin cancer
SCD sudden cardiac death
ScD Doctor of Science
SCFE slipped capital femoral epiphysis
SCI spinal cord injury
SCID severe combined immunodeficiency
SCJ sclerocorneal junction
SCOP scopolamine
SCP standard care plan
SCT sickle-cell trait; sugar-coated tablet
SD senile dementia; septal defect; serologically defined; standard deviation; sterile dressing; streptodornase; sudden death
SDA specific dynamic action
SDAT senile dementia, Alzheimer type
SDD sterile dry dressing
SDH subdural hematoma
SDR surgical dressing room
SDS same-day surgery
SE side effect; standard error
Se selenium
sec. second
SEH subependymal hemorrhage
SEM scanning electron microscopy; standard error of the mean; systolic ejection murmur
sem. semen
SEO shoulder-elbow orthosis
SER somatosensory evoked response; smooth endoplasmic reticulum
Ser serine
SF seminal fluid; spinal fusion; symptom-free; synovial fluid
SG skin graft
SGA small for gestational age (infant)
SGOT serum glutamic oxaloacetic transaminase
SGPT serum glutamic pyruvic transaminase
SH short; shoulder; shower; social history
SHCS second hand cigarette smoke
SHM self-help method
SHTS second hand tobacco smoke
SI International System of Units; sacroiliac (joint); self-inflicted injury; stress incontinence
Si silicon
SIA stress-induced anesthesia; sulfite-induced asthma
SIADH syndrome of inappropriate secretion of antidiuretic hormone
sib sibling
SICU surgical intensive care unit
SIDS sudden infant death syndrome
SIG sigmoidoscopy
SIg surface immunoglobulin
sig. *signa* [Latin] let it be labeled (directions)
sigmo sigmoidoscopy
SIJ sacroiliac joint
SIMV spontaneous intermittent mandatory ventilation; synchronized intermittent mandatory ventilation
SIO sacroiliac orthosis

si op. sit *si opus sit* [Latin] if needed
SIRS soluble immune response suppressor; systemic inflammatory response syndrome
SIW self-inflicted wound
SK seborrheic keratosis; streptokinase
SKSD streptokinase-streptodornase
SL sublingual
s.l. *secundum legem* [Latin] according to the law
SLC short-leg cast
SLE systemic lupus erythematosus
SLL small lymphocytic lymphoma
SLN superior laryngeal nerve
SLR straight leg raising
SLS short-leg splint
SM sadomasochism; self-monitoring; simple mastectomy; small; smoker; smooth muscle; synovial membrane; systolic murmur
Sm samarium
SMA sequential multichannel autoanalyzer; smooth-muscle antibody
SMD senile macular degeneration
SMP sympathetically maintained pain
SMR standardized mortality ratio; submucous resection
SMS sperm motility study
Sn tin
SNagg serum normal agglutinator
SNF skilled nursing facility
SNHL sensorineural hearing loss
SO second opinion; sex offender; standing order
SOAP Subjective, Objective, Assessment, Plan
SOB shortness of breath
Sod. sodomy
sol. solution
soln. solution
solv. *solve* [Latin] dissolve
SOM serous otitis media
sono. sonogram
SOP standard operating procedure
S.O.S. *si opus sit* [Latin] if needed
SP sodium pentothal; speech pathology; standard procedure; surgery performed
sp. species; specific
SpA staphylococcal protein A
SPA single-photon absorptiometry; spermatozoa penetration assay; suprapubic aspiration
SPBT suprapubic bladder tap
SPC salicyamide, phenacetin, and caffeine; standard platelet count
SPCA serum prothrombin conversion accelerator
sp. cd spinal cord
SPE serum protein electrophoresis
SPECT Single Photon Emission Computerized Tomography
SPF specific-pathogen free; sun-protection factor
sp. fl. spinal fluid
spg sponge
sp. gr. specific gravity
SPH severely and profoundly handicapped
Sph spherical (lens)
SPL sound pressure level
SPM synchronous pacemaker
SPROM spontaneous premature rupture of membranes
sp. tap spinal tap
sput. sputum
SQ subcutaneous
SR sarcoplasmic reticulum; sedimentation rate; sinus rhythm; stomach rumble; suture removed; systems review
Sr strontium
s-r stimulus-response (psychology)
SRH somatotropin-releasing hormone
SRI severe renal insufficiency
sRNA soluble ribonucleic acid (RNA)
SRS slow-reacting substance

SRS-A slow-reacting substance of anaphylaxis
SRT sedimentation rate test; speech reception threshold; stroke rehabilitation technician
SRU side rails up
SS saline solution; saliva sample; salt substitute; Sezary syndrome; short stay; social service; somatostatin; standard score; statistically significant; sterile solution
S/S signs and symptoms
S & S signs and symptoms
ss. *semis* [Latin] one-half
SSC stainless steel crown
SSc systemic sclerosis
SSD Social Security disability
SSE soap suds enema
SSKI saturated solution of potassium iodide
SSM superficial spreading melanoma
SSPE subacute sclerosing panencephalitis
SSRO sagittal split ramus osteotomy
SSRS Social Security Reporting Service
SSS soluble specific substance; subclavian steal syndrome
SSSS staphylococcal scalded skin syndrome
s.s.v. *sub signo veneni* [Latin] under a poison label
ST scar tissue; sinus tachycardia; smokeless tobacco; speech therapist; stable toxin; survival time
STAG split thickness autogenous graft
staph. *Staphylococcus* (usually implies *Staphylococcus aureus*)
stat. *statim* [Latin] at once; immediately
stats statistics
STB stillborn
ST BY stand by
STD sexually transmitted disease; standard test dose
std standard
STEL short-term exposure limit
STH somatotrophic hormone
STI soft tissue injury
STJ subtalar joint
STM short-term memory
STP supracondylar tibial prosthesis
strep. streptococcic; *Streptococcus*
STS serologic test for syphilis
STSG split-thickness skin graft
STU shock trauma unit
STUMP smooth-muscle tumor of undetermined malignant potential
subcu. subcutaneous (injection)
SUD sudden unexpected death; sudden unexplained death
SUID sudden unexpected infant death; sudden unexplained infant death
sum. *sumantur* [Latin] take
sup. superior
Supp. suppository
surg. surgery
SV severe; snake venom
SVBPG saphenous vein bypass graft
SVC superior vena cava
SVD sudden vaginal delivery
SW social worker; stab wound
SWD shortwave diathermy
SWS slow wave sleep (non-rapid eye movement sleep); Sturge-Weber syndrome
Swt sweat
sympt. symptom
synd. syndrome
syn. fl. synovial fluid
sx surgery
T tablespoon; temperature; tension; term; tesla thoracic; thorax; thyroid; time; tissue; tocopherol; total; toxicity; trace; tritium; type
T absolute temperature
t teaspoon; temperature; tertiary; tocopherol; translocation
T1/2 biologic half-life

T1 first thoracic spinal nerve; first thoracic vertebra
T2 second thoracic spinal nerve; second thoracic vertebra
T3 third thoracic spinal nerve; third thoracic vertebra
T$_3$ triiodothyronine
T4 fourth thoracic spinal nerve; fourth thoracic vertebra
T$_4$ thyroxine
T5 fifth thoracic spinal nerve; fifth thoracic vertebra
T6 sixth thoracic spinal nerve; sixth thoracic vertebra
T7 seventh thoracic spinal nerve; seventh thoracic vertebra
T8 eighth thoracic spinal nerve; eighth thoracic vertebra
T9 ninth thoracic spinal nerve; ninth thoracic vertebra
T10 tenth thoracic spinal nerve; tenth thoracic vertebra
T11 eleventh thoracic spinal nerve; eleventh thoracic vertebra
T12 twelfth thoracic spinal nerve; twelfth thoracic vertebra
TA toothache; toxin-antitoxin; traffic accident; transplantation antigen; tricuspid atresia; truncus arteriosus
T & A tonsillectomy and adenoidectomy
TAA thoracic aortic aneurysm; tumor-associated antigen
tab. tablet
Tac T cell activation receptor
tachy. tachycardia
TAD transient acantholytic dermatosis
TAE total abdominal eventration
TAF tumor-angiogenesis factor
TAH total abdominal hysterectomy
TAO thromboangiitis obliterans
TAP titanium acetabular prosthesis
TAR thrombocytopenia and absent radius (syndrome)
TAT tetanus antitoxin; thematic appreciation test; till all taken; toxin-antitoxin
TATA tumor-associated transplantation antigen
TB tracheobronchitis; tuberculin; tuberculosis
Tb terbium
TBA to be added; to be admitted
TBC tuberculosis
TBG thyroid-binding globulin; thyroxine-binding globulin
TBII thyroid-binding inhibitory immunoglobulin
TBLC term birth, living child
TBM tubular basement membrane
TBP thyroxine-binding protein
TBR total bed rest
TBSA total burn surface area
tbsp tablespoon
TBV total blood volume
TBW total body water
TC thoracic cage; throat culture; tissue culture; total cholesterol; treatment completed
Tc technetium
TCA terminal cancer; transluminal coronary angioplasty; trichloroacetic acid
TCAB triple coronary artery bypass
TCDD tetrachlorodibenzo-p-dioxin
TCGF T cell growth factor
TCI transient cerebral ischemia
TCMI T cell-mediated immunity
TCR T cell receptor
TCT thrombin-clotting time; total cholesterol test
TD tardive dyskinesia; temporary disability; tetanus and diphtheria; thymus-dependent; total disability; traveler's diarrhea; treatment discontinued
Td tetanus and diphtheria toxoids, adult type
TDD telecommunication device for the deaf
TDI toulene diisocyanate; therapeutic donor insemination
TDM therapeutic drug management
tDNA transfer deoxyribonucleic acid (DNA)
t.d.s. *ter die sumendum* [Latin] to be taken three times a day
TdT terminal deoxynucleotidyl transferase
TE tennis elbow; thromboembolism; tooth extracted; total ejaculate (number of sperm); treadmill exercise

Te tellurium; tetanus
TEBG testosterone-estradiol-binding globulin
TEC total eosinophil count
TED threshold erythema dose
TEE transesophageal echocardiography
TEF tracheoesophageal fistula
TEM transmission electron microscope; triethylenemelanine
TEN toxic epidermal necrolysis
TENS transcutaneous electrical nerve stimulation
TEPA triethylenephosphoramide
TEPP tetraethyl pyrophosphate
TESD total end-systolic diameter
TEST tubal embryo stage transfer
TET treadmill exercise test; tubal embryo transfer
TEV talipes equinovarus
TF tetralogy of Fallot; tracheal fistula; transfer factor; tube feeding; tuning fork
TG tendon graft; thyroglobulin; triglyceride
TGC time-varied gain control
TGE transmissible gastroenteritis
TGFA triglyceride fatty acid
TGSI thyroid growth-stimulating immunoglobulin
TGV thoracic gas volume
TH thyroid hormone; total hysterectomy
Th thorium
THA total hip arthroplasty
THAM trishydroxymethylaminomethane
THAN transient hyperammonemia of newborn
THC tetrahydrocannabinol; transhepatic cholangiography
THIO thiopental sodium
thor. thoracic; thorax
THR total hip replacement
Thr threonine
thromb. thrombosis
TI tricuspid insufficiency
Ti titanium
TIA transient ischemic attack
TIBC total iron-binding capacity
TID therapeutic insemination, donor
t.i.d. *ter in die* [Latin] three times a day
TIG tetanus immune globulin
TIH therapeutic insemination, husband
TIL tumor-infiltrating lymphocyte
t.i.n. *ter in nocte* [Latin] three times nightly
tinc. tincture
TIPS Transjugular Intrahepatic Portosystemic Shunts
TIS tumor *in situ*
TIT tubal insufflation test
TITh triiodothyronine
TJR total joint replacement
TK through knee (amputation; prosthesis)
TKA total knee arthroplasty
TKD tokodynamometer
TKG tokodynagraph
TKO technical knock-out (selection)
TKR total knee replacement
TL temporal lobe; thymic lymphocyte; time lapse; total lipids; tubal ligation
Tl thallium
TLC thin-layer chromatography; total lung capacity; total lymphocyte count
TLE thin-layer electrophoresis
TLI total lymphoid irradiation
TLSO thoracolumbosacral orthosis
TLV threshhold limit value
TM transmetatarsal (amputation); tropical medicine; tympanic membrane
Tm thulium; transport maximum; tubular maximum
TMI transmandibular implant

TMJ temporomandibular joint
TMJS temporomandibular joint syndrome
TMST treadmill stress test
TMT tarsometatarsal (joint)
TN trigeminal neuralgia
T & N tar and nicotine
Tn normal intraocular tension
TNDS transdermal nicotine delivery system
TNF tumor necrosis factor
TNI total nodal irradiation
TNM tumor-node-metastasis (staging)
TNS transcutaneous nerve stimulation
TNTC too numerous to count (applied to bacteria in a culture plate or blood cells in a urine specimen)
TO target organ
TOA time of arrival; tubo-ovarian abscess
TOF tetralogy of Fallot
tomo tomogram
TOP termination of pregnancy
TORCH Toxoplasmosis, Other infections, Rubella, Cytomegalovirus infection, and Herpes (simplex)
TORCHS Toxoplasmosis, Other infections, Rubella, Cytomegalovirus infection, Herpes (simplex), and Syphilis
TOS thoracic outlet syndrome
tox toxic
TP terminal phalanx; trigger point; tubal pregnancy
Tp precursor T cells
T & P temperature and pressure
tPA tissue plasminogen activator
TPC thromboplastic plasma component; total patient care
TPE therapeutic plasma exchange
TPH transplacental (fetal) hemorrhage
TPHA *Treponema pallidum* hemagglutination assay
TPI *Treponema pallidum* immobilization (test)
TPM temporary pacemaker
TPN total parenteral nutrition
TPP thiamine pyrophosphate
TPR temperature, pulse, and respiration; testosterone production rate; total peripheral resistance
TQ tourniquet
TR tricuspid regurgitation; tubular reabsorption
tr tincture
TRA thyrotropin receptor antibody
Trach trachea
TRAP tartrate-resistant acid phosphatase
TRBF total renal blood flow
TRF thyrotropin-releasing factor
trf transfer
TRH thyrotropin-releasing hormone
TRHST thyrotropin-releasing hormone stimulation test
TRIC trachoma inclusion cojunctivitis
tRNA transfer ribonucleic acid
Trp tryptophan
trt treatment
TRUS transrectal ultrasonography
TS test solution; thoracic surgery; total solids; toxic substance; transsexual; tricuspid stenosis
Ts suppressor T cells
TSA total shoulder arthroplasty; tumor-specific antigen
TSAS total severity assessment score
TSE testicular self-examination; total skin examination
TSF triceps skinfold
TSH thyroid-stimulating hormone
TSH-RF thyroid-stimulating hormone-releasing factor
TSH-RH thyroid-stimulating hormone-releasing hormone
TSI thyroid-stimulating immunoglobulin
tsp teaspoon
T-spine thoracic spine
TSS toxic shock syndrome

TST treadmill stress test
TSTA tumor-specific transplantation antigen
TT tendon transfer; thrombin time; tilt table; total time
TTD tissue tolerance dose
TTN transient tachypnea of the newborn
TTP thrombotic thrombocytopenic purpura
TTS temporary threshold shift; through the skin; transdermal therapeutic system
TTTS twin-twin transfusion syndrome
TU toxic unit; tuberculin unit
TUBD transurethral balloon dilatation
tub. lig. tubal ligation
TUIP transurethral incision of prostate
TULIP Transurethral Ultrasound-guide Laser-Induced Prostatectomy
TUR transurethral resection
TURP transurethral resection of prostate
TV total volume; transvestite; tricuspid valve
TVC total vital capacity
TVH total vaginal hysterectomy
TW tapwater
TWZ triangular working zone
Tx thromboxane; traction; transplant; treatment
typ. typical
Tyr tyrosine
U unit; upper; uracil; uranium; uridine; urine; urology
u unit
UA uncertain about; unstable angina; uric acid; urinalysis
U/A urinalysis
UAC umbilical artery catheterization
UAO upper airway obstruction
UC ulcerative colitis; unchanged; unsatisfactory condition; urea clearance; urine culture; uterine contraction
UCO urinary catheter out
ucs unconscious
u.d. *ud dictum* [Latin] as directed
UDCA ursodeoxycholic acid
UDE undetermined etiology
UDO undetermined origin
UDP uridine diphosphate
UDPG uridine diphosphate glucose
UF unknown factor
UG urogenital
UGA under general anesthesia
UGI upper gastrointestinal
UI unidentified; urinary incontinence
u.i.d. *uno in die* [Latin] once every day
UM unmarried
umb. umbilical; umbilicus
UMCD uremic medullary cystic disease
UMI unstable myocardial ischemia
UN ulnar nerve; unilateral neglect; urea nitrogen
ung. *unguentum* [Latin] ointment
unk. unknown
UNOS United Network for Organ Sharing
uns. unsatisfactory
UO under observation; urinary output
u/o under observation
UP upright position
UQ upper quadrant
URD upper respiratory disease
Urd uridine
urg. urgent
URI upper respiratory (tract) infection
url unrelated
URR urea reduction ratio
US ultrasonography; ultrasound
USAN United States Adopted Name (Council)
USI urinary stress incontinence
USP *The United States Pharmacopeia*

USPHS United States Public Health Service
UT urinary tract; uterus
UTD up-to-date
ut dict. *ut dictum* [Latin] as directed
UTI urinary tract infection
UTV unable to void
UV ultraviolet
UVA ultraviolet A
UVB ultraviolet B
UVC umbilical vein catherization; ultraviolet C
UVL ultraviolet light
UVR ultraviolet radiation
V vanadium; virus; volt
v valve; ventilation; ventral; ventricular; vision; vitamin; voice; volt; volume; vomiting
v. *vena* [Latin] vein
V max maximum velocity (in an enzymatic reaction)
VA Veterans Administration; visual acuity
vacc. vaccination
VACTERL Vertebral, Anal, Cardiac, Tracheal, Esophageal, Renal, Limb (a pattern of associated congenital anomalies)
VAD ventricular assist device
Vag. vagina
Val valine
var. variety
vas vas deferens
vasc. vascular
VATER Vertebral defects, Anal atresia, Tracheoesophageal fistula, Esophageal atresia, Renal anomalies (a pattern of associated congenital anomalies)
VB vertebral body; viable birth
VBAC vaginal birth after (previous) cesarean section
VBG venous blood gas
VC vasoconstriction; vena cava; visual cortex; vital capacity
VCA viral capsid antigen
VCG vectocardiogram
VCT venous clotting time
VD vasodilator; venereal disease; viral diarrhea; voided
Vd volume of distribution
VDDR vitamin D-dependent rickets
VDG venereal disease - gonorrhea
VDRL Venereal Disease Research Laboratory
VDRR vitamin D-resistant rickets
VDS venereal disease - syphilis
VE vaginal examination; visual efficiency
VEE Venezuelan equine encephalomyelitis
vel. velocity
vent. ventricular
vent. fib. ventricular fibrillation
VEP visually evoked potential
VER visually evoked response
VF ventricular fibrillation; visual field
VFI ventricular flutter
VG vein graft
VGH very good health
VH vaginal hysterectomy; ventricular hypertrophy; viral hepatitis; visually handicapped
VHD valvular heart disease
VHDL very high density lipoprotein
VI vaginal irritation
VIN vulvar intraepithelial neoplasia
VIN I vulvar intraepithelial neoplasia, mild (with mild dysplasia)
VIN II vulvar intraepithelial neoplasia, moderate (with moderate dysplasia)
VIN III vulvar intraepithelial neoplasia, severe (with severe dysplasia)
VIP vasoactive intestinal polypeptide; very important patient; voluntary interruption of pregnancy
VIS vaginal irrigation smear
VISI volar-flexed intercalated segment instability

VLA very late activation (antigen)
VLBW very low birth weight
VLDL very low-density lipoprotein
VLP virus-like particle
VMA vanillylmandelic acid
VMAT vanillylmandelic acid test
VN visiting nurse
VO verbal order
VOD venous occlusive disease
V-ONC viral oncogene
VP variegate porphyria; vasopressin; venipuncture; venous pressure
VPB ventricular premature beat
VPC ventricular premature contractions
VR valve replacement; vascular resistance; vocal resonance
VRE vancomycin resistant enterococci
VRI viral respiratory infection
VS vital sign; volumetric solution; voluntary sterilization
VSD ventricular septal defect; virtual safe dose
VSS vital signs stable
VT venous thrombosis; ventricular tachycardia; vitality test
V tach. ventricular tachycardia
VU very urgent
VV varicose veins; vesicovaginal
vv veins
v/v volume (of solute) per volume (of solvent)
VVF vesico vaginal fistula
VW vessel wall
VZ varicella zoster
VZIG varicella-zoster immune globulin
VZV varicella zoster virus
W tungsten; watt; week; weight; white; widow; widower; width; wife
w week; white; wife; with
WA when awake; while awake
WAS Wiskott-Aldrich syndrome
WB water bottle; weber; whole blood
WBC white blood cell; white blood count
wbc white blood cell
WBCT whole blood clotting time
WBS whole body shower
WC white (blood) cell; whooping cough
WCC white (blood) cell count
WD wallerian degeneration; warm and dry; watery diarrhea; well developed; wet dressing; wrist dislocation
WDHA watery diarrhea, hypokalemia, achlorhydria (syndrome)
WDLL well differentiated lymphocytic lymphoma
WDWN well developed, well nourished
W/E wound of entry (of a bullet)
WEE western equine encephalomyelitis
WEST work evaluation systems technology
WF white female
WFE Williams flexion exercise
wgt weight
WH walking heel (cast); white
wh. ch. wheelchair
WHO World Health Organization; wrist-hand orthosis
whp whirlpool
WIMC walk-in medical center
wk week
WL waiting list; wavelength
WLI whiplash injury
WM white male
WMF white, middle-aged female
WMM white, middle-aged male
WMX whirlpool, massage, and exercise
WN well nourished
WNL within normal limits
WO wrist orthosis; written order
WOP without pain
WPB whirlpool bath

WPW Wolff-Parkinson-White (syndrome)
WR washroom; Wassermann reaction; water retention; wrist
WRE whole ragweed extract
WS withdrawal syndrome
WT Wada test
wt weight
WtB weight bearing
W/U work up
w/v weight (of solute) per volume (of solvent)
WWAC walk with aid of cane
W/X wound of exit (of a bullet)
X crossed with; except; extra; reactance; removal; times
x axis (of cylindric lens); except
x̄ mean value
Xaa unknown amino acid
X & D examination and diagnosis
XCCE extracapsular cataract extraction
Xe xenon
^{133}**Xe** xenon-133
XL extra large; X-linked
XLR X-linked recessive
X match cross match
XMP xanthosine monophosphate
XO extraction of
XP xeroderma pigmentosum
XR roentgen ray; x ray
XRT x-ray technician; x-ray therapy
XS cross section
xs excess
XT exotropia
XU excretory urogram
46XX normal number of female chromosomes
46XY normal number of male chromosomes
Xylo xylocaine
Y yellow; yttrium
y year
Yb ytterbium
YF yellow fever
YJV yellow jacket venom
YOB year of birth
YPLL years of potential life lost
YS yolk sac
YST yeast
Z standard score; zero; zone
z atomic number; standardized device; zone
ZD zero defects
ZDV zidovudine
ZIFT Zygote IntraFallopian (tube) Transfer
ZIG zoster immune globulin
Zn zinc
ZOE zinc oxide and eugenol
ZPO zinc peroxide
ZPG zero population growth
Zr zirconium
ZSR zeta sedimentation ratio

APPENDIX
B

Selected Symbols
Used in Medicine

Å   angstrom (unit)

Ⓐ   axilla

ā   before

c̄   with

✓c̄   check with

✓'d   checked; examined

✓g   checking

✓ing   checking

p̄   after

✓qs   voided sufficient quantity

℞   prescription

s̄   without

✕   magnification

ⓧ   end of anesthesia; end of operation

α   alpha

β   beta

Δ   delta; increment; occipital triangle;
    prism diopeter; temperature

ΔP   change in pressure (ophthalmology)

δ   delta

ε   epsilon

γ   gamma

λ   lambda

μ   micro–; micron

⊙   carrier of sex-linked recessive (gene)

⊕   normal

∅   no

♂   male

♀   female

♀   standing

○—   recumbent

♀   sitting

□   male (in pedigree charts)

○   female (in pedigree charts)

□—○   marriage (in pedigree charts)

□═○   consanguineous marriage (in pedigree charts)

◇   sex unknown (in pedigree charts)

↑   above; elevated; enlarged; improved; increased

↗   increasing

↓   below; decreased; deficiency; deteriorating; diminished

↘   decreasing

>   greater than

≯   not greater than

<   less than

≮   not less than

≃   about; approximately

≐   nearly equal to

≂   approximate

=   equal

≠   unequal

≡   identical

≢   not identical

//   for

⌐ right upper quadrant

∟ right lower quadrant

⌐ left upper quadrant

⌐ left lower quadrant

∝ variant

\# fracture (bone); has been done; has been given; number; pound

\+ acid reaction; diminished (reflexes); mild; one plus (markedly impaired pulse); plus; positive; slight reaction; trace reaction

(+) significant

++ moderate; normally active (reflexes); notable reaction; trace; two plus (moderately impaired pulse)

+++ moderate amount; moderate reaction; moderately hyperactive (reflexes); moderately severe; three plus (slightly impaired pulse)

++++ four plus (normal pulse); markedly hyperactive (reflexes); markedly severe pain with spastic muscles; pronounced reaction; severe

± doubtful; indefinite; more or less

(±) possibly significant

± to + minimal pain

− absent; alkaline reaction; minus; negative

(−) insignificant

⊖ absent; negative

? doubtful; flicker (reflexes); unknown

APPENDIX
C

Reference Values
for Laboratory Tests
of Clinical Importance

The following reference values represent the range of values usually found in healthy individuals. These values may vary somewhat from one laboratory to another, especially if a different method is used for the determination. The interpretation of "normal" or "abnormal" results gen- erally requires additional information, such as knowledge of the individual, the conditions under which the sample was obtained, and concomitant medications.

TEST NAME	REFERENCE RANGE

ACID PHOSPHATASE, TOTAL and PROSTATIC, Enzymatic	Total:
	  Male: 0–5.4 U/L
	  Female:0–5.0 U/L
	Prostatic: 0–1.2 U/L

ACTIVATED PARTIAL THROMBOPLASTIN TIME, PTT	Patient: 20–35 seconds
ADENOVIRUS ANTIBODY, Serum	Negative <1:8
ADRENAL MEDULLARY FUNCTION PROFILE (Catecholamines - VMA), Urine	Catecholamines: 69–515 mcg/24 hrs. VMA: 2.0–10.0 mg/24 hrs.
ADRENOCORTICAL FUNCTION PROFILE (17-Ketosteroids Total, 17-Hydroxycorticosteroids—P.S.)	17-Ketosteroids: Male: 8–20 mg/24 hrs. Female: 4–15 mg/24 hrs. 17-Hydroxycorticosteroids: Male: 3–10 mg/24 hrs. Female: 2–6 mg/24 hrs.
ADRENOCORTICOTROPIC HORMONE (ACTH)	9–52 pg/mL: Intact (whole molecule) ACTH measured.
ALANINE AMINOTRANSFERASE (ALT, SGPT)	<1 yr: 0–63 U/L >1 yr: 0–45 U/L
ALBUMIN, Serum	1–4 days: 2.8–4.9 gm/dL 5d–13 yr: 3.8–5.9 gm/dL 14–17 yr: 3.2–5.0 gm/dL 18–60 yr: 3.5–5.5 gm/dL >60 yr: 3.4–5.3 gm/dL
ALBUMIN, Spinal Fluid	12–27 mg/dL
ALBUMIN, Urine	0.0–2.0 mg/dL 3.9–24.4 mg/24 hrs.
ALCOHOL (Ethanol), Blood	Negative Clinically Toxic:* >200 mg/dL

*local jurisdictions have different levels for DWI

TEST NAME	REFERENCE RANGE
ALDOLASE	Female: (14–79 yrs.) 1.0–9.6 U/L Male: (17–81 yrs.) 2.2–10.4 U/L
ALDOSTERONE, Serum	Based on normal sodium intake. Male: 6–22 ng/dL Female: 5–30 ng/dL Recumbent: 2.0–16.0 ng/dL
ALDOSTERONE, Urine	Normal salt diet: 6–25 mcg/24 hrs. Low salt diet: 17–44 mcg/24 hrs. High salt diet: 0–6 mcg/24 hrs.
ALKALINE PHOSPHATASE	Female: 1–15 yr: 25–490 U/L >15 yr: 25–140 U/L Male: 1–11 yr: 25–490 U/L 12–19 yr: 25–700 U/L >20 yr: 25–140 U/L
ALKALINE PHOSPHATASE, ISOENZYMES, Electrophoresis	Total: 40–120 U/L Intestinal: 0–30 U/L Liver: 26–120 U/L Bone: 0–42 U/L
ALPHA-2-ANTIPLASMIN, Plasma	87–155%
ALPHA-1–ANTITRYPSIN	85–213 mg/dL
ALPHA-1–ANTITRYPSIN PHENOTYPE	Phenotype MM
ALPHA FETOPROTEIN, Amniotic Fluid (Depends on gestational age and maternal age, weight, race, date of LMP, and insulin dependent status.)	See laboratory report

TEST NAME	REFERENCE RANGE	TEST NAME	REFERENCE RANGE
ALPHA FETOPROTEIN NONMATERNAL, Serum	<10 IU/mL	**AMINO ACID SCREEN,** Urine Qualitative	Normal pattern
ALPHA FETOPROTEIN MATERNAL, Serum	See laboratory report	**AMIODARONE (Cordarone) PROFILE**	Therapeutic trough level: Amiodarone: 1.0–2.5 mcg/mL Desethylamiodarone: 0.5–1.4 mcg/mL
ALPHA FETOPROTEIN, Tumor Marker	0–15 ng/mL		
ALPHA FETOPROTEIN-3 SCREEN, Serum (Includes Maternal AFP, Quant HCG, and Free Estriol. This test is a better predictor of Down's risk than AFP alone.)	See laboratory report	**AMITRIPTYLINE** (Elavil) (Includes Nortriptyline metabolite)	Therapeutic Amitriptyline plus Nortriptyline: 120–250 ng/mL Toxic: >500 ng/mL
ALPHA-2-MACROGLOBULIN	120–269 mg/dL Note: Elevated values seen in estrogen therapy, pregnancy, and nephrotic syndrome.	**AMMONIA,** Plasma	17–80 mcg/dL
		AMOBARBITAL, Serum	Therapeutic: 5–8 mcg/mL Toxic: >10 mcg/mL
ALPHA INTERFERON, Serum	<10 U/mL	**AMOEBIC ANTIBODY (ENTAMOEBA HISTOLYTICA ANTIBODY); IgG**	Negative: <40 EU/mL
17-ALPHA HYDROXYPROGESTERONE	Adult Male: 0.4–3.3 ng/mL Adult Female: Follicular: 0.1–1.2 ng/mL Luteal: 0.3–4.8 ng/mL Postmenopausal: 0.1–0.6 ng/mL Prepubertal: <0.6 ng/mL		
		AMOXAPINE (Asendin)	8–Hydroxyamoxapine: 150–400 ng/mL Total: 200–500 ng/mL
ALPHA SUBUNIT (Measures the alpha subunit of LH, FSH, TSH and HCG)	Children: <1.0 ng/mL Male: 1.0 ng/mL Female: Follicular: <1.0 ng/mL Midcycle: <3.6 ng/mL Luteal: <1.0 ng/mL Post-menopausal: <3.6 ng/mL Hypothyroid: <2.5 ng/mL	**AMPHETAMINES SCREEN-EMIT**	Negative Detection limit: 1000 ng/mL
		AMPHETAMINES, Urine-GC/MS	Negative Detection limit: 500 ng/mL
		AMYLASE, Serum	24–97 U/L
		AMYLASE, Urine	1–17 U/hr
		AMYLASE ISOENZYMES	Pancreatic: 0–54 U/L Salivary: 0–62 U/L Total: 24–105 U/L
ALUMINUM, Blood	0–40 mcg/L		
ALUMINUM, Urine	0–31 mcg/L Industrial: up to 220 mcg/L	**ANDROSTENEDIOL,** Serum	Male: 70–190 ng/dL Female: 30–100 ng/dL
AMEBIC ANTIBODY	Negative: <40 EU/mL	**ANDROSTENEDIONE**	Male: 0.3–2.63 ng/mL Female: 0.1–2.99 ng/mL Post menopausal females have normally lower androstenedione values than pre-menopausal females and are reported in the literature to be less than 1 ng/mL
AMIKACIN, Peak and trough	Therapeutic, peak: 20–30 mcg/mL Therapeutic, trough: 1–8 mcg/mL Toxic level, peak: >30 mcg/mL Toxic level, trough: >10 mcg/mL		
		ANGIOTENSIN-1-CONVERTING ENZYME (ACE)	8–52 U/L
		ANTI-BASEMENT MEMBRANE ANTIBODIES	<1:20
AMIKACIN, Peak	Therapeutic: 20–30 mcg/mL Toxic level: >30 mcg/mL	**ANTI-CARDIOLIPIN ANTIBODY-IgG**	<23 GPL
		ANTI-CARDIOLIPIN ANTIBODY-IgA	Not Detected
AMINO ACID FRACTIONATION, Plasma Quantitative	See laboratory report	**ANTI-CARDIOLIPIN ANTIBODY-IgM**	<11 MPL
AMINO ACID FRACTIONATION, Urine, Quantitative	See laboratory report	**ANTI-CARDIOLIPIN ANTIBODY PROFILE** (Includes IgG, IgA, and IgM)	IgG: <23 GPL IgA: Not detected IgM: <11 MPL
AMINO ACID SCREEN, Plasma Qualitative	Normal pattern	**ANTI-CENTROMERE ANTIBODIES**	Negative: <1:40

TEST NAME	REFERENCE RANGE
ANTI-DIURETIC HORMONE (Vasopressin)	1–6 pg/mL
ANTI-DNA ANTIBODY, (Double Strand), IFA, with crithidea luciliae	<1:10
ANTI-EPIDERMAL ANTIBODIES, IFA	<1:20 IFA Titer
ANTI-GLOMERULAR BASEMENT MEMBRANE ANTIBODIES, IFA	<1:10 IFA Titer
ANTI-HYALURONIDASE TITER	<1:256 Titer
ANTI-INTERCELLULAR SUBSTANCE	Negative: <1:40
ANTI-MITOCHONDRIAL ANTIBODIES	<1:20 IFA Titer
ANTI-MYOCARDIAL ANTIBODY	<1:40 IFA Titer
ANTI-NUCLEAR ANTIBODIES Fluorescent Screen (ANA) (Includes pattern and titer if positive.)	Negative: <1:40
ANTI-PARIETAL CELL ANTIBODIES	Negative: <1:20
ANTI-RETICULIN ANTIBODIES	Negative: <1:10
ANTI-SMOOTH MUSCLE ANTIBODIES	<1:20 IFA Titer
ANTI-SPERMATOZOAL ANTIBODY, IFA	See laboratory report
ANTI-STREPTOLYSIN O, Quantitative	Pediatric: <100 IU/mL Young adult: <250 Adult: <200
ANTI-STRIATED MUSCLE ANTIBODY	<1:40 Titer
ANTI-THROMBIN III (AT-III)	76–131%
ANTI-THYROGLOBULIN ANTIBODY (Thyroglobulin Antibody)	0.0–1.0 U/mL
ANTI-THYROID ANTIBODY PROFILE (Anti-Thyroglobulin and Anti-Thyroid Peroxidase Antibodies)	0.0–1.0 U/mL
ANTI-THYROID PEROXIDASE ANTIBODY	0.0–1.0 U/mL
ANTIMONY, Urine	0.0–10 mcg/mL
APOLIPOPROTEIN A-1	Male: 94–178 mg/dL Female: 101–199 mg/dL
APOLIPOPROTEIN B	Male: 63–133 mg/dL Female: 60–126 mg/dL
APOLIPOPROTEIN PANEL (Includes A-1 and B)	See individual values
ARSENIC, Hair or Nails	0–200 mcg/100 grams
ARSENIC, Blood	0.0–20.0 mcg/dL
ARSENIC, Urine	0–100 mcg/L
ASO TITER	See Anti-Streptolysin O

TEST NAME	REFERENCE RANGE
ASPARTATE AMINOTRANSFERASE (AST, SGOT)	<1 yr: 0.120 U/L 1–60 yr: 0–40 U/L >60 yr: 0–50 U/L
ASPERGILLUS ANTIBODY BY CF	CF Negative: <1:8 CF Titer
ATENOLOL (Tenormin), Serum	See laboratory report
ATYPICAL ANTIBODY SCREEN	None Detected
AZT (ZIDOVUDINE), Serum	<1 nmol/L
B	
BARR BODIES, Sex Chromatin	Male: X-Chromatin Negative Female: >10% of cells X-Chromatin positive
BERYLLIUM, Urine	Less than 1.0 mcg/mL
BETA-HCG	See HCG
BETA-2-MICROGLOBULIN, Serum	Under age 60: 0.0–2.4 mg/L Over age 60: 0.0–3.0 mg/L
BETA-2-MICROGLOBULIN, Urine	0.0–0.3 ng/L
BILE ACID (as Cholylglycine)	Fasting: 0–60 mcg/dL Post-prandial values are approximately 3 times the fasting level.
BILIRUBIN, Amniotic Fluid	Liley method: Zone 1: No Hemolytic Process
BILIRUBIN, Total	0–1 day: 1.4–8.7 mg/dL 1–2 day: 3.4–11.5 mg/dL 3–5 day: 1.5–12.0 mg/dL >5 day: 0.1–1.2 mg/dL
BILIRUBIN, Total, Direct and Indirect	Total: See Above Direct 0.0–0.4 mg/dL Indirect: 0.1–1.0 mg/dL
BLEEDING TIME	1–3 minutes
BONE GLA PROTEIN (BGP)	1.6–9.2 ng/mL
BORDETELLA PERTUSSIS ANTIBODY, IgG	See laboratory report
BROMIDES, Serum, Quantitative	0–50 mg/dL
BROMOCRIPTINE, Serum	See laboratory report
BRUCELLA ABORTUS AGGLUTINATION	Compare acute and convalescent sera. A four fold increase in titer indicates recent infection.
BUN	See Urea Nitrogen
BUTABARBITAL, Serum	Therapeutic: 5–8 mcg/mL Toxic: >10 mcg/mL
BUTALBITAL, Serum	Therapeutic: 1–5 mcg/mL
C	
C-PEPTIDE, Serum	1.0–3.0 ng/mL
C-PEPTIDE, Urine	11–53 ng/mg Creatinine
C-REACTIVE PROTEIN, Quantitative	<0.8 mg/dL

TEST NAME	REFERENCE RANGE
C-1 ESTERASE INHIBITOR ACTIVITY	>69% Mean Normal
C-1 ESTERASE INHIBITOR, Quantitative	5.3–34.0 mg/dL
C1Q COMPLEMENT, Quantitative	51–150 units
CADMIUM, Blood	0–10.0 mcg/L
CADMIUM, Urine	0–20 mcg/L
CALCITONIN (Thyrocalcitonin)	0–100 pg/mL
CALCIUM, Ionized and Total	Ionized Calcium: 4.5–5.8 mg/dL Total Calcium: 8.5–10.8 mg/dL
CALCIUM, Total, Serum	0–10d: 7.7–11.0 mg/dL 10d–1y: 9.1–11.6 mg/dL 2–11y: 8.9–11.4 mg/dL 12–60y: 8.5–10.8 mg/dL >60y: 8.9–10.6 mg/dL
CALCIUM, Urine	50–300 mg/24 hrs.
CANCER ANTIGEN 125 (CA 125), Serum	0–35 U/mL Equivocal 35–65 U/mL
CANCER ANTIGEN 15-3 (CA 15-3), Serum	<33 U/mL For investigational use only. The performance characteristics of this test have not been established. This reference range applies to normal non-pregnant adults.
CANCER ANTIGEN 19-9 (CA 19-9), Serum	Normals: <33 U/mL Indicative of pancreatic cancer: >70 U/mL. For investigational use only. The performance characteristics of this test have not been established.
CARBAMAZEPINE (Tegretol)	Therapeutic: 5–12 mcg/mL Toxic >15.0 mcg/mL
CARBON DIOXIDE, Serum	<1yr: 20–32 mEq/L 1–17 yr: 20–32 mEq/L 18–60 yr: 22–32 mEq/L >60 yr: 23–35 mEq/L
CARBON MONOXIDE (Measured as Carboxyhemoglobin)	Non-smokers: 0–4% Smokers: 0–8% Toxic symptoms: >20% Can be fatal: >40%
CARCINOEMBRYONIC ANTIGEN, CEA	Non-smokers: <3.0 ng/mL Smokers: <5.0 ng/mL
CAROTENE	0.6–2.0 mg/dL
CAT SCRATCH FEVER ANTIBODIES	Less than 4-fold increase between acute and convalescent samples.
CATECHOLAMINES, Fractionation, Plasma	Norepinephrine: 90–500 pg/mL Epinephrine: 65–140 pg/mL Dopamine: <40 pg/mL Total Catecholamines: 155–700 pg/mL

TEST NAME	REFERENCE RANGE
CATECHOLAMINES, Fractionation, Urine	Epinephrine: 2–15 ug/24 hrs. Norepinephrine: 2–100 ug/24 hrs. Dopamine: 65–400 ug/24 hrs. Total Catecholamines: 69–515 ug/24 hrs.
CATECHOLAMINES, Total, Plasma	155–700 pg/mL
CATECHOLAMINES, Urine	69–515 mg/24 hrs.
CEA	See Carcinoembryonic Antigen
CELL COUNT AND DIFFERENTIAL, Peritoneal Fluid	WBC: 0–100 cells/cu mm Neutrophils: 0–40%
CELL COUNT AND DIFFERENTIAL, Synovial Fluid	WBC: 0–200 cells/cu mm Lymphocytes: 0–78% Neutrophils: 0–25% Monocytes: 0–71% Synovial cells: 0–12%
CERULOPLASMIN	21–53 mg/dL
CHLAMYDIA TRACHOMATIS, Culture	Negative
CHLAMYDIA TRACHOMATIS, DNA - probe	Negative
CHLAMYDIA - by DFA	See laboratory report
CHLORDANE	None detected Toxic: >2 mcg/mL
CHLORPROMAZINE (Thorazine)	Thorazine: 50–500 ng/mL
CHLORIDE, CSF	118–132 mEq/L
CHLORIDE, Serum	0–30 days: 96–115 mEq/L >30 days: 96–109 mEq/L
CHLORIDE, Urine	110–250 mEq/24 hr.
CHOLESTEROL	Desirable: <200 mg/dL Border: 200–240 mg/dL Elevated: >240 mg/dL
CHOLESTEROL ESTERS	Total Cholesterol: 220 mg/dL Cholesterol Esters: 65–75% of total cholesterol
CHOLINESTERASE, Erythrocyte	5600–10500 U/L
CHOLINESTERASE, Plasma or Serum (Pseudocholinesterase)	4100–9900 U/L
CHOLINESTERASE, Plasma and Erythrocyte	Plasma: 4100–9900 U/L Erythrocyte: 5600–10500 U/L

TEST NAME	REFERENCE RANGE	TEST NAME	REFERENCE RANGE
CHORIONIC GONADOTROPIN, (HCG) Serum, Quantitative	Male: 0–5 mIU/mL Female: Non-pregnant: 0–5 mIU/mL Pregnant: >25 mIU/mL Indeterm: 5–25 mIU/mL Weeks Post Conception mIU/mL 1–2: 5–1000 3–4: 100–1000 5–6: 1500–100000 7–12: 16000–300000 13–26: 24000–55000 27–39: 6000–48000	**COMPLEMENT,** Total (CH50)	189–420 units
		COMPLETE BLOOD COUNT (CBC Without Differential)	See addendum
		COMPOUND "S", Serum (11-Deoxycortisol)	0.0–8.0 ng/mL
		COMPOUND "S", Urine (11-Deoxycortisol)	<1 mg/24 hrs.
		COPPER, Serum	70–150 mcg/dL
		COPPER, Urine	20–50 mcg/24 hrs.
		COPROPORPHYRIN, Urine, Quantitative	60–280 mcg/24 hrs.
CHORIONIC GONADOTROPIN, (HCG), Urine, Quantitative	Male: 0–10 IU/24 hrs. Female Non-pregnant: 0–10 IU/24 hrs. Weeks post conception: 2–3: 30–150 IU/24 hrs. 3–4: 100–1000 IU/24 hrs. Months Post Conception: 1–3: up to 500,000 IU/24 hrs. 3–5: 10,000–25,000 IU/24 hrs. 5–9: 5,000–15,000 IU/24 hrs.	**COPRO- AND UROPORPHYRINS,** Urine, Quantitative	Copro: 60–280 mcg/24 hrs. Uro: 10–50 mcg/24 hrs.
		CORTISOL	Random sample: 5–25 mcg/dL a.m. sample: 5–25 mcg/dL p.m. sample: 2–12 mcg/dL
CITRATE, Urine	Excretion: 0.15–100 gm/24 hrs.	**CORTISOL,** FREE, Urine	20–90 mcg/24 hrs.
CITRIC ACID, Serum	1.3–2.6 mg/dL	**COXIELLA** (Q-Fever), Antibody	IgG: Negative <1:16 Titer Low Positive: 1:16–1:28 Titer High Positive: 1:256 or greater IgM: Negative: <1:10 Titer
CLOMIPRAMINE	Clomipramine: 70–200 ng/mL Desmethylclomipramine: 70–160 ng/mL Total: 100–400 ng/mL		
CLONAZEPAM (Klonopin)	20–75 ng/mL	**COXSACKIE A VIRUS ANTIBODY** (A4, A7, A9, A10, A16, A21)	A4: Negative <1:8 CF Titer A7: Negative <1:8 CF Titer A9: Negative <1:8 CF Titer A10: Negative <1:8 CF Titer A16: Negative <1:8 CF Titer A21: Negative <1:8 CF Titer
CLOTTING TIME, Capillary	2–6 minutes		
CLOTTING TIME, Lee White	6–12 minutes		
COCAINE METABOLITE, Urine - GC/MS	Negative Detection limit: 150 ng/mL	**COXSACKIE B VIRUS ANTIBODY** (B1, B2, B3, B4, B5, B6)	B1: Negative <1:8 Titer B2: Negative <1:8 Titer B3: Negative <1:8 Titer B4: Negative <1:8 Titer B5: Negative <1:8 Titer B6: Negative <1:8 Titer
COCAINE METABOLITE SCREEN-EMIT	Negative Detection limit: 300 ng/mL		
COCCIDIOIDES ANTIBODY SCREEN	CF Negative: <1:2 Titer ID Negative		
COCCIDIOIDES ANTIBODY (CF)	Negative: <1:2 Titer	**CPK**	See Creatine Phosphokinase
COLD AGGLUTININS	Negative	**CPK ISOENZYMES** (Creatine Phosphokinase Isoenzymes)	BB: 0–3% MB: 0–5% MM: 90–100%
COMPLEMENT C'1Q	51–150 units		
COMPLEMENT C'2	51–150 units	**CREATINE,** Serum	Male: 0.2–0.7 mg/dL Female: 0.3–1.0 mg/dL
COMPLEMENT C'3	83–177 mg/dL		
COMPLEMENT C'4	15–45 mg/dL	**CREATINE,** Urine	Male: 0–40 mg/24 hrs. Female: 0–80 mg/24 hrs.
COMPLEMENT C'5	15–22 mg/dL		
COMPLEMENT C'6	3.6–7.5 mg/dL	**CREATINE PHOSPHOKINASE** (CPK)	Male: 20–220 U/L Female: 20–150 U/L
COMPLEMENT C'7	2.5–7.5 mg/dL		
COMPLEMENT C'8	See laboratory report	**CREATINE PHOSPHOKINASE-MB**	See CPK Isoenzyme
COMPLEMENT FACTOR B	See laboratory report		
COMPLEMENT, Total (CH100)	70–150 CH 100 units/mL	**CREATINE,** Amniotic Fluid	Fetal Maturity: >2.0

CREATININE, Serum

<1y: 0.2–0.5 mg/dL
2–12y: 0.3–0.8 mg/dL
13–17y: 0.5–1.2 mg/dL
>17y: 0.6–1.5 mg/dL

CREATININE, Urine

Male: 1.0–1.9 g/24 hrs.
Female: 0.8–1.7 g/24 hrs.

CREATININE CLEARANCE

Male: 97–137 mL/min
Female: 88–128 mL/min

CRP

See C-Reactive Protein

0119-9 **CRYOFIBRINOGEN**

Fibrinogen:
200–400 mg/dL
Precipitate:
None detected

CRYOGLOBULIN SCREEN

Negative

CRYPTOCOCCUS ANTIGEN, Serum

Negative

CYANIDE, Blood

0–30 mcg/dL

CYCLIC AMP, Plasma

6.5–24.0 nmol/L

CYCLIC AMP, Urine (Includes plasma and urine creatinine)

Plasma 1.2–2.1 nmole/100 mL. With normal fasting urine specimens, a mean concentration of 270 nmole/100 mL has been observed. Nephrogenous Cyclic AMP is calculated by correcting for Urine Creatinine, Plasma Creatinine, and Plasma Cyclic AMP. Normal range is 0.3–3.4 nmole/100 mL of glomerular filtrate.

CYCLOSPORINE

100–400ng/mL

CYSTINE, Quantitative

10–100 mg/24 hrs.

CYTOLOGY, Sex Chromatin (Barr Bodies)

Male: Barr body Negative
Female: >10% of cells Barr body positive

D

D-DIMER, Plasma

<0.5 ug/mL

DEHYDROEPI-ANDROSTERONE (DHEA) Serum

Suggested DHEA reference ranges according to age and sex:

Age Group	Females (ng/mL)	Males (ng/mL)
20–29	1.1–7.2	1.0–7.3
30–39	0.55–4.0	0.75–5.1
40–49	0.4–3.6	0.7–4.6
50–59	0.3–2.8	0.55–4.6
60–69	0.1–1.8	0.4–2.1
70–79	0.1–1.5	0.1–1.7

0–2.0 mg/24 hrs.

DEHYDROEPI-ANDROSTERONE (DHEA), Urine

DEHYDROEPI-ANDROSTERONE SULFATE,

Age Group	Females (ug/dL)	Males (ug/dL)
20–29	65–380	280–640
30–39	45–270	120–520
40–49	32–240	95–530
50–59	26–200	70–310
60–69	13–130	42–290
70–79	17–90	28–175
Postmenopausal: 10–190		

DELTA-AMINOLEVULINIC ACID (DALA)

1.3–7.0 mg/24 hrs.

11-DEOXYCORTISOL

See Compound-S

DEPAKENE

See Valproic Acid

DESIPRAMINE

Therapeutic: 150–250 ng/mL

DEXAMETHASONE SUPPRESSION TEST Useful in diagnosing of melancholic depression)

4 p.m.: <5 mcg/dL
11 p.m.: <5 mcg/dL

DEXAMETHAZONE SUPPRESSION TEST, for the diagnosis of Cushing's Syndrome

DIAZEPAM (Valium), and **NORDIAZEPAM,** Serum

0.1–0.4 ug/mL
Toxic: >5.0 ug/mL

DIGITOXIN (Digitalis)

Therapeutic: 9–25 ng/mL for 0.1 mg/day dose.
Toxic: >25 ng/mL

DIGOXIN (Lanoxin)

Therapeutic: 0.5–2.0 ng/mL
Toxic: >2.0 ng/mL

DIHYDROTESTOSTERONE

ng/dL
Female: Follicular 6–200
Luteal 16–40.0
Postmenopausal <5
Prepuberal: <3
Adult Male: 60–300

1,25-DIHYDROXY VITAMIN D

12–40 pg/mL

DIRECT ANTIGLOBULIN TEST

DOPAMINE, Urine

See Catecholamines, Fractionated

DOXEPINE (Sinequan)

Doxepin + Desmethyldoxepin total: 110–250 ng/mL

DRUG ABUSE SCREEN, Serum Includes Amphetamine, Methamphetamine, Cannabinoids, Cocaine, Morphine, Codeine, and PCP

None detected

E

EBV ANTIBODY- Early Antigen (EA)

Negative: <111
Equivocal: 111–119
Positive: >119

EBV ANTIBODY- Nuclear Antigen (NA)-IgG

Negative: <56
Positive: >56

EBV ANTIBODY- Nuclear Antigen (NA)-IgM

Negative: <56
Positive: >56

EBV ANTIBODY- Viral Capsid Antigen (VCA)-IgG

Negative: <101
Equivocal: 101–109
Positive: >109

EBV ANTIBODY- Viral Capsid Antigen (VCA)-IgM

Negative: <90
Equivocal: 91–99
Positive: >99

ECHINOCOCCUS ANTIBODY

Negative: <1:80

ECHO VIRUS ANTIBODY, Serum (Type 30)

Negative: <1:8 Titer

ECHO VIRUS TYPE IV ANTIBODY (CF) Negative: <1:8

ELAVIL See Amitriptyline

ENCAINIDE (Enkade)
Therapeutic:
Encainide: 15–100 ng/mL
Mode: 60–300 ng/mL
Ode: 100–300 ng/mL

ENDOTOXIN LIM. AMEB. EU/mL

EOSINOPHIL COUNT 100–300 cell/cc mm

EOSINOPHIL COUNT, Nasal None seen.

EPINEPHRINE/ NOREPINEPHRINE See Catecholamine Fractionation

EPSTEIN BARR VIRUS ANTIBODY-Viral Capsid Antigen (VCA)-IgM See EBV Antibody-Viral Capsid Antigen (VCA)-IgM

ERA/PRA Estrogen Receptor Assay/Progesterone Receptor Assay Methodology: RIA
Estrogen Receptor:
Negative
<0.3 fm/mg Protein
Progesterone Receptor:
Negative
<0.3 fm/mg Protein

ERA/PRA/DNA Estrogen Receptor Assay/Progesterone Receptor Assay/DNA Methodology: RIA
Report includes:
Estrogen Receptor:
Negative
<3 fmole/mg Protein
Progest. Receptor:
Negative
<3 fmole/mg Protein
DNA Sample Description
DNA Index
% Resting Phase %
% S (Synthesis) %
% G2/M %
DNA Index II
DNA Index III
Interpretation required;
refer to laboratory report.

ERYTHROPOIETIN, Serum 9.1–30.8 mU/mL

ESR - Erythrocyte Sedimentation Rate See Sedimentation Rate

ESTRADIOL, Serum
Male: 0–44 pg/mL
Female:
Early follicular: 10–50 pg/mL
Late follicular: 60–200 pg/mL
Midcycle: 120–375 pg/mL
Luteal: 50–260 pg/mL
Postmenopausal:
0–14 pg/mL

ESTRIOL, Total, Serum
Male (adult): <2 ng/mL
Female (Non-pregnant):
<2 ng/mL
Gestational Range:
26 weeks: 11–127 ng/mL
28 weeks: 22–142 ng/mL
30 weeks: 24–152 ng/mL
32 weeks: 29–151 ng/mL
34 weeks: 42–178 ng/mL
36 weeks: 39–214 ng/mL
38 weeks: 53–284 ng/mL
40 weeks: 72–336 ng/mL

ESTRIOL, Unconjugated, Serum
Gestational Range:
30 weeks: 3–12 ng/mL
31 weeks: 3.5–14.6 ng/mL
32 weeks: 4–16.5 ng/mL
33 weeks: 4–18.5 ng/mL
34 weeks: 4–21 ng/mL
35 weeks: 4–23 ng/mL
36 weeks: 5–26 ng/mL
37 weeks: 6–28 ng/mL
38 weeks: 6–31.5 ng/mL
39 weeks: 7–33 ng/mL
40 weeks: 7.5–36 ng/mL

ESTRIOL, Urine
Gestational Range:
26 weeks: 4–13 mg/24 hrs.
28 weeks: 5–15 mg/24 hrs.
30 weeks: 6–18 mg/24 hrs.
32 weeks: 7–21 mg/24 hrs.
34 weeks: 8–26 mg/24 hrs.
36 weeks: 10–30 mg/24 hrs.
38 weeks: 12–36 mg/24 hrs.
40 weeks: 13–42 mg/24 hrs.

ESTROGENS, Total, Serum
Male:
Prepubertal: <40 pg/mL
Adult: <115 pg/mL
Female:
Follicular: 61–394 pg/mL
Midcycle: 122–437 pg/mL
Luteal: 400–800 pg/mL
Postmenopausal:
<40 pg/mL

ESTROGENS, Total, Urine
ug/24 hr.
Female:
Preovulatory 5–25
Ovulatory 25–100
Luteal 25–105
Postmenopausal 0–20
Male: 4–25

ESTRONE, Serum
pg/mL
Female: Follicular 30–130
Luteal 90–200
Male: 10–80
Prepuberal Children: <10

ETHANOL, Blood See Alcohol, Blood

ETHOSUXIMIDE (Zarontin)
Therapeutic:
40–100 mcg/mL
Toxic: >150 mcg/mL

ETHOTOIN (Peganon) See laboratory report

ETHYLENE GLYCOL
None detected
Toxic: Any amount is significant

ETIOCHOLANOLONE, Urine
Male: <5.0 mg/24 hrs.
Female: <3.5 mg/24 hrs.

F

FACTOR II Coagulation 50–150%

FACTOR V Coagulation 50–150%

FACTOR VII Coagulation 50–150%

FACTOR VIII Coagulation 50–150%

FACTOR IX Coagulation 50–150%

FACTOR X Coagulation 50–150%

TEST NAME	REFERENCE RANGE
FACTOR XI Coagulation	50–150%
FACTOR XII Coagulation	50–150%
FACTOR XIII Coagulation	Clot present after 24 hours.
FAT, Feces, Quantitative	1–7 g fat/24 hrs.
FATTY ACIDS, Unesterified	0.10–0.90 mEq/L
FEBRILE AGGLUTINATION BATTERY (Typhoid O, Typhoid H, Paratyphoid A, Paratyphoid B, Brucella abortus, Proteus OX 2, Proteus OX 19 Proteus OX K)	A four fold or greater rise in titer between acute and convalescent samples indicates recent infection.
FERRITIN	<1m: 25–360 ng/mL 1m: 200–1080 ng/mL 2–5m: 50–360 ng/mL 6m-15y: 7–252 ng/mL Male >15y: 20–450 ng/mL Female 16–45y: 8–200 ng/mL Female >45y: 10–350 ng/mL
FETAL HEMOGLOBIN	0.0–2.0%
FIBRINOGEN	200–400 mg/dL
FLECAINIDE (Tombocor)	Therapeutic: 0.2–1.0 mcg/mL
FLUORIDE, Serum	16–55 mcg/dL
FLUORIDE, Urine	See laboratory report
FLUOXETINE (Prozac), Serum	Therapeutic: Fluoxetine: 100–800 ng/mL Norfluoxetine: 100–600 ng/mL Total: 100–800 ng/mL
FOLATE, RBC	>160 ng/mL
FORMALDEHYDE, Blood	Negative
FORMIC ACID, Blood	0–12 mcg/mL
FREE ANDROGEN Index	Result calculated as the ratio of testosterone (ng/dL) to SHBG (nmole/1). Studies have shown that greater than 90% of normal females have an index of <2.04, and greater than 80% of hirsute patients have an index of >2.04.
FREE RBC PROTOPORPHYRIN (FEP)	Children: <35 mcg/dL Adults: <50 mcg/dL
FREE TESTOSTERONE	See Testosterone-free
FREE THYROXINE by equilibrium dialysis, includes Total T4	Adults: 0.8–2.7 ng/dL
FREE THYROXINE (FREE T-4)	0.8–1.5 ng/mL
FRUCTOSAMINE, Serum	174–286 umol/L
FRUCTOSE, Semen	Positive

TEST NAME	REFERENCE RANGE
FUNGAL ANTIBODY SCREEN (Histoplasma, Blastomyces, Coccidioides and Aspergillus antibodies)	Histoplasma Yeast CF Negative <1.8 CF Titer Histoplasma Mycel CF Negative <1.8 CF Titer Histoplasma AB ID Negative Blastomyces AB CF Negative <1:8 CF Titer Blastomyces AB ID Negative Coccidioides AB CF Negative <1:2 CF Titer Coccidioides AB ID Negative Aspergillus AB CF Negative <1:8 CF Titer Aspergillus AB ID Negative
G	
GALACTOSEMIA SCREEN	Detectable enzyme activity
GAMMA-GLUTAMYL TRANSFERASE (GGT)	Male: 0–85 U/L Female: 0–70 U/L
GASTRIC ACIDITY	Free acidity: 0–40 mEq/L Total acidity: 10–50 mEq/L
GASTRIN, Serum	0–100 pg/mL
GENTAMICIN Peak	Therapeutic peak level: 6–10 mcg/mL
GLUCAGON, Plasma	20–100 pg/mL
GLUCOSE, Fasting	1d: 37–66 mg/dL >1d–12y: 46–88 mg/dL 12–17y: 56–110 mg/dL 18–60y: 65–115 mg/dL 61–69y: 74–126 mg/dL >70y: 77–120 mg/dL
GLUCOSE, 2-hour	70–140 mg/dL diabetic: >140
GLUCOSE, 1-hr (50 gm load) (during pregnancy)	<140 mg/dL indicates a Negative screen
GLUCOSE, Fasting Plasma or Serum	65–115 mg/dL
GLUCOSE, Spinal Fluid (with normal concomitant blood sugar)	45–100 mg/dL
GLUCOSE, Synovial Fluid	65–115 mg/dL
GLUCOSE-6-PHOSPHATE DEHYDROGENASE (G-6-PD), Quantitative	221–570 U/L
GRISEOFULVIN, Serum	Therapeutic: 1.0–3.0 mcg/mL Detection limit: 0.2 mcg/mL
GROWTH HORMONE (HGH) adult	0.0–5.0 ng/mL
H	
HAPTOGLOBIN	27–139 mg/dL

TEST NAME	REFERENCE RANGE	TEST NAME	REFERENCE RANGE
HCG, Serum (Human Chorionic Gonadotropin), Qualitative, Pregnancy Test	Negative	**HERPES SIMPLEX I & II Ab, IgM EIA**	(Type I): Negative <0.91 EIA Index (Type II): Negative: <0.91 EIA Index (Type I): Negative: <1:5 IFA Titer (Type II): Negative <1:5 IFA Titer
HCG, Serum, (Human Chorionic Gonadotropin), Quantitative	Male: 0–5 mIU/mL Female: Non-pregnant: 0–5 mIU/mL Indeterminant: 5–25 mIU/mL Pregnant >25 mIU/mL Weeks post conception: mIU/mL 1–2: 5–1000 3–4: 100–10000 5–6: 1500–100000 7–12: 16000–300000 13–26: 24000–55000 27–39: 6000–48000	**HERPES ZOSTER**	See Varicella Zoster
		HETEROPHILE AGGLUTINATION for Infectious Mononucleosis, includes presumptive, diagnosis, differential, and titer, if indicated.	Horse kidney: Negative Beef cell: Negative Titer: <1:2
		HEXOSAMINIDASE, Serum	Hex Total: 500–1000 nMole/mL/hr. Hex A: 56–77% of total normal
HCG, Urine (Human Chorionic Gonadotropin), Quantitative (TUMOR MARKER)	Male: 0–10 IU/24 hrs Female: Non-pregnant: 0–10 IU/24 hrs Weeks post conception: 2–3: 30–150 IU/24 hrs. 3–4: 100–1000 IU/24 hrs. Months Post Conception: 1–3: Less than 500,000 IU/24 hrs. 3–5: 10,000–25,000 IU/24 hrs. 5–9: 5,000–15,000 IU/24 hrs.	**HEXOSAMINIDASE A and Total,** Leukocyte	Total: 16.4–36.2 u/g Hexosaminidase A: 61–75% of total is normal
		HISTAMINE, Blood	20–200 ng/mL
		HISTAMINE, Urine	<110 ng/mL
		HISTIDINE	1.0–1.0 mg/dL
		HOMOVANILLIC ACID (HVA)	1.6–7.5 mg/24 hrs.
		HUMAN GROWTH HORMONE (HGH), Adult	0.0–5.0 ng/mL
HDL - CHOLESTEROL	Male: 30–75 mg/dL Female: 35–80 mg/dL	**HUMAN PLACENTAL LACTOGEN (HPL)**	Gestational Range: 10–13: 0.0–1.2 14–26: 0.3–7.5 27–28: 1.7–8.4 29–30: 2.5–9.9 31–32: 3.0–10.9 33–34: 3.8–13.0 35–36: 4.2–12.5 37–38: 4.1–13.4 39–40: 3.8–11.8
HEAVY METALS, Blood; Arsenic, Mercury and Lead	Arsenic blood: 0–20.0 mcg/dL Mercury blood: 0–10.0 mcg/dL Lead, blood: 0–40 mcg/dL (Adult) 0–25 mcg/dL (Child)		
HEMATOCRIT	Male: 36–50% Female: 34–44%	**17-HYDROXYCORTICO-STEROIDS** (Porter-Silber Method)	Male: 3–10 mg/24 hrs. Female: 2–6 mg/24 hrs.
HEMOGLOBIN	Male: 12.5–17.0 g/dL Female: 11.5–15.0 g/dL	**5-HYDROXYINDOLEACETIC ACID,** (5–HIAA), Quantitative	2–10 mg/24 hrs.
HEMOGLOBIN A-2 (by anion exchange column)	1.5–3.0% of total hemoglobin	**17-HYDROXY-PREGNENOLONE**	Male: 40–450 ng/dL Female: 20–400 ng/dL Prepubertal: <100 ng/dL
HEMOGLOBIN A1C (by HPLC)	4.3–6.1%		
HEMOGLOBIN ELECTROPHORESIS (Qualitative)	A1 A2	**17-HYDROXY-PROGESTERONE**	Adult Male: 0.4–3.3 ng/mL Adult Female: Follicular: 0.1–1.2 ng/mL Luteal: 0.3–4.8 ng/mL Postmenopausal: 0.1–0.6 ng/mL Prepubertal: <0.6 ng/mL
HEMOGLOBIN ELECTROPHORESIS (Quantitative)	A:1 93.5–97.2% A:2 0.0–3.5% F: 0.0–2.0%		
HEMOGLOBIN, Fetal	0.0–2.0%		
HEMOGLOBIN, Plasma	0–5 mg/dL	**HYDROXYPROLINE,** Free	0.2–1.8 mg/24 hrs.
HEPATITIS B SURFACE ANTIBODY-IMMUNE INDICATOR (Post-vaccination immunity indication)	Immunity indicated by a value >10 mIU/mL	**HYDROXYPROLINE,** Total	20–77 mg/24 hrs.

TEST NAME	REFERENCE RANGE
I	
IMIPRAMINE (Tofranil) Includes Desipramine Metabolites	Therapeutic: Imipramine plus Desipramine 150–250 ng/mL Toxic: >500 ng/mL
IMMUNE COMPLEX DETECTION By C'1Q	0–20 mcg/mL
IMMUNE COMPLEX DETECTION, By RAJI Cell	0–15 mcg eq/mL
IMMUNOGLOBULIN A (IgA)	83–490 mg/dL
IMMUNOGLOBULIN D (IgD)	Caucasian: Male: 0.5–19.7 mg/dL Female: 0.5–19.5 mg/dL African American: Male: 0.6–25.0 mg/dL Female: 0.8–23.1 mg/dL
IMMUNOGLOBULIN E (IgE)	< 1yr: <16 U/mL 1–4yr: <19 U/mL 5–10yr: <32 U/mL 11–15yr: <34 U/mL > 15 yr: <158 U/mL
IMMUNOGLOBULIN G (IgG)	878–1844 mg/dL
IMMUNOGLOBULIN G, Spinal Fluid	0.5–6.1 mg/dL
IMMUNOGLOBULIN M (IgM)	45–385 mg/dL
INFLUENZA VIRUS ANTIBODY, (CF) (A, B)	Type A Negative: <1:8 CF Titer Type B Negative: <1:8 CF Titer
INSULIN	4.0–20.0 uU/mL
INTERLEUKIN-2 RECEPTOR (IL-2R), Plasma	<900 units/mL
IODINE, Total, Serum	4.5–9.0 mcg/dL
IONIZED CALCIUM	See Calcium, Ionized
IRON, Total	<30d: 100–250 mcg/dL 30d–<1y: 40–100 mcg/dL 1–17y: 50–120 mcg/dL >17y:3 5–175 mcg/dL
IRON, AND TOTAL IRON BINDING CAPACITY (Iron and TIBC)	Iron: See above TIBC: <30d: 98–356 mcg/dL >30d: 245–400 mcg/dL
IRON, TOTAL IRON BINDING, CAPACITY, AND % SATURATION	Iron: See above TIBC: See above % Sat: 16–55%
K	
KETOCONAZOLE (Nizoral)	On a single 200 mg/day oral dose: Peak: 1.5–4.5 mcg/mL Trough: <0.05 mcg/mL On 800 mg/day oral dose: Peak: 15 mcg/mL
17–KETOGENIC STEROIDS	Male: 5–23 mg/24 hrs. Female: 3–15 mg/24 hrs.

TEST NAME	REFERENCE RANGE
17-KETOSTEROIDS, Total	Male: 8–20 mg/24 hrs. Female: 6–15 mg/24 hrs.
L	
LACTIC ACID, Blood	3–12 mg/dL
LACTIC DEHYDROGENASE (LDH), Serum	0–4d: 0–979 U/L 5–10d: 0–2526 U/L 11d–<2y: 0–543 U/L 2–11y: 0–373 U/L 12–60y: 0–240 U/L >60y: 0–265 U/L
LACTIC DEHYDROGENASE (LDH), Spinal Fluid	8–40 U/L
LACTIC DEHYDROGENASE ISOENZYMES (Five Fractions), Quantitative	Total: 0–240 U/L LDH-1: 21–37% LDH-2: 30–46% LDH-3: 14–29% LDH-4: 5–11% LDH-5: 2–11%
LEAD, Blood	Children: <10 mcg/dL Adult: 0–40 mcg/dL OSHA limit: <40 mcg/dL
LEAD, Hair	5.0–29.0 mcg/g hair
LEAD, Urine	0–100 mcg/24 hrs.
LEAD, Water	EPA, Limit 50 mcg/L
LECITHIN/SPHINGOMYELIN RATIO with Phosphatidylglycerol (L/S Ratio with PG)	L/S Ratio of less than 2 suggests pulmonary immaturity; ratio of 2–3 probably represents maturity, but a ratio of 3 or greater is more reassuring. If PG is detectable, then pulmonary maturity is probably present. If L/S Ratio is 2 or greater and PG is detectable, then pulmonary maturity is almost assuredly present.
LEGIONELLA PNEUMOPHILIA ANTIBODY	Negative: <1:256 IFA Titer
LEUCINE AMINOPEPTIDASE (LAP), Serum	Male: 1.1–3.4 U/mL Female: 1.2–3.0 U/mL
LEUKOCYTE ALKALINE PHOSPHATASE	37–98
LIPASE, Serum	0–140 U/L
LITHIUM	Therapeutic: 0.5–1.5 mEq/L Toxic: >2.0 mEq/L
LUTEINIZING RELEASING HORMONE	4.0–8.0 pg/mL-TR
LYME DISEASE ANTIBODY TOTAL Polyvalent	Negative: <0.80 Equivocal: 0.80–1.00 Positive: >1.00
LYME DISEASE ANTIBODY-IgG	(IgG-IgM) Negative: <0.80 EIA Index
LYME DISEASE ANTIBODY-IgM	Negative: <0.80 Indeterminate: 0.80–1.00 Positive: >1.0
LYMPHOGRANULOMA VENEREUM (LGV) ANTIBODY IgG	Negative: <1:8 IFA Titer

TEST NAME	REFERENCE RANGE	TEST NAME	REFERENCE RANGE
M		**PENTAZOCINE** (Talwin) (Forensic)	Therapeutic: 0.05–0.20 mcg/mL
MAGNESIUM, Serum	1.6–2.6 mg/dL		
MAGNESIUM, Urine	15–300 mg/24 hrs.	**PENTOBARBITAL** (Nembutal)	Therapeutic: 1–7 mcg/mL Toxic: >10 mcg/mL
MANGANESE, Serum	0.0–1.0 mcg/L		
MANGANESE, Urine	0.0–10.0 mcg/L	**PEPSINOGEN 1**	25–100 ng/mL
MERCURY, Blood	0–10 mcg/dL	**PHENOL,** Urine, Quantitative	Recommended OSHA Range: 0–75 ug/mL
MERCURY, Urine	0–20 mcg/24 hrs.		
METANEPHRINES	Metanephrine: 53–341 mcg/24 hrs. Normetanephrine: 88–444 mcg/24 hrs.	**PHENOBARBITAL,** Serum	Therapeutic: 15–40 mcg/mL Toxic: >40 mcg/mL
		PHENYLALANINE Quantitative for PKU	0–5 mg/dL
METHEMOGLOBIN	0.0–0.8 g/dL 0–3% of total Hgb	**PHOSPHORUS,** Serum	0–9d: 4.2–9.0 mg/dL 10d-24m: 4.2–6.7 mg/dL 2–11y: 4.2–5.5 mg/dL 12–60y: 2.5–4.5 mg/dL Male >60y: 2.1–3.7 mg/dL Female >60y: 2.6–4.1 mg/dL
MICROALBUMIN, Urine	3.0–24.4 mg/24 hrs. 0.0–2.0 mg/dL: Random collection.		
MUMPS ANTIBODY IgG	Negative: <0.80 EIA Index		
MUMPS ANTIBODY IgM	Negative: <1:10 IFA Titer	**PLACENTAL LACTOGEN (HPL)**	Gestation: Range: 10–13 wks: 0–1.2 mcg/mL 14–26 wks: 0.3–7.5 mcg/mL 27–28 wks: 1.7–8.4 mcg/mL 29–30 wks: 2.5–9.9 mcg/mL 31–32 wks: 3.0–10.9 mcg/mL 33–34 wks: 3.8–13.0 mcg/mL 35–36 wks: 4.2–12.5 mcg/mL 37–38 wks: 4.1–13.4 mcg/mL 39–40 wks: 3.8–11.8 mcg/mL
MYCOPLASMA PNEUMONIAE ANTIBODY - IgG	Negative: <1.00 EIA Index		
MYOGLOBIN, Serum	6–85 ng/mL		
MYOGLOBIN, Urine	0–50 ng/mL		
N			
NICKEL, Blood	1.5–4.0 ng/mL		
NICKEL, Urine	2–8 mcg/L	**PLASMINOGEN ACTIVITY**	2.4–3.8 CTA U/mL
NIRVANOL (Phenylethylhydantoin)	Therapeutic: 10–20 mcg/mL	**PLATELET ASSOCIATED IgG**	See laboratory report
		PLATELET COUNT	155–385 thousands/cu mm
NOREPINEPHRINE - EPINEPHRINE (Catecholamine Fractionation)	Epinephrine: 2–15 ug/24 hrs. Norepinephrine: 2–100 ug/24 hrs. Dopamine: 65–400 ug/24 hrs. Catecholamines. Total: 69–515 ug/24 hrs.	**PLATINUM,** Serum	0–25 mcg/dL
		PNEUMOCOCCAL ANTIBODY Includes serotypes 3,7,8, and 14	See laboratory report
		PORPHYRINS, Feces, Quantitative	Coproporphyrin: 200–1200 mcg/24 hr. Uroporphyrin: 10–40 mcg/24 hr Protoporphyrin: Up to 1800 mcg/24 hr.
5′ NUCLEOTIDASE	3–15 U/L		
O			
OSMOLALITY, Serum	270–300 mosm/kg water	**PORPHYRINS,** Urine, Quantitative	Coproporphyrin: 60–280 mcg/24 hrs. Uroporphyrin: 10–50 mcg/24 hrs.
OSMOLALITY, Urine	50–1500 mosm/kg water		
OXALATE, Urine, Quantitative	M: 7–44 mg/24 hrs. F: 4–31 mg/24 hrs.		
P		**POTASSIUM,** Serum	<10d: 3.7–6.1 mEq/L 10d–<1y: 4.1–5.5 mEq/L 1–12y: 3.4–4.9 mEq/L >12y: 3.5–5.3 mEq/L
PARATHYROID HORMONE, MID-MOLECULE (C-terminal) (Includes Calcium)	PTH: 29–85 pmol/L Calcium: 8.5–10.8 mg/dL		
		POTASSIUM, Urine	25–100 mEq/24 hr.
PARATHYROID HORMONE, INTACT (N-terminal) (Includes Calcium)	PTH: 10–65 pg/mL Calcium: 8.5–10.8 mg/dL	**PREALBUMIN,** Serum	17–42 mg/dL
PCB (Polychlorinated Biphenyls)	<30 ng/mL TR		

TEST NAME	REFERENCE RANGE
PREGNANEDIOL	mg/24 hrs. 2 weeks–2 years: 0.02–0.2 2–5 years: <0.5 5–15 years: <1.5 >15 years: <2.0 mg/24 hrs. × 2.97 = umol/24 hrs.
PREGNANETRIOL	CHILD: mg/24 hrs. <2 years: <0.1 3–5 years: <0.3 6–9 years: <0.5 10–15 years: Male 0.1–.07 Female 0.1–1.2 ADULT: Male: 0.6–1.5 Female: Follicular: <1.0 Luteal: 2–7 Postmenopausal: 2.0–1.0 WEEKS OF PREGNANCY: 18: 5–21 20: 6–26 24: 12–32 28: 19–51 32: 22–66 36: 13–77 40: 23–63
PROCAINAMIDE (Pronestyl) **AND N-ACETYLPROCAINAMIDE (NAPA)**	Therapeutic: Procainamide & NAPA: 5–30 mcg/mL Procainamide: 4–8 mcg/mL NAPA: 9–19 mcg/mL Toxic: Procainamide: >12 mcg/mL NAPA: Not available
PROGESTERONE	Male: 0.0–0.6 ng/mL Female: Follicular 0.1–1.5 ng/mL Luteal: 2.8–28 ng/mL Postmenopausal: 0.0–0.7 ng/mL Oral Contraceptive: 0.1–0.3 ng/mL
PROGESTERONE (Gestational)	1st trimester: 9–47 ng/mL 2nd trimester: 17–146 ng/mL 3rd trimester: 55–255 ng/mL
PROINSULIN	Less than 0.5 ng/mL
PROLACTIN	Female: 2.8–29.9 ng/mL Male: 2.1–17.7 ng/mL
PROSTATE SPECIFIC ANTIGEN	<4.0 ng/ml
PROSTATIC ACID PHOSPHATASE - By EIA	0–2.8 ng/mL
PROTEIN C ANTIGENS	Protein C: 70–140%

TEST NAME	REFERENCE RANGE
PROTEIN ELECTROPHORESIS, Serum	Total protein: 6.0–8.5 g/dL Albumin: 3.5–5.5 g/dL Alpha-1–globulin: 0.1–0.3 g/dL Alpha-2–globulin: 0.5–1.0 g/dL Beta-globulin: 0.6–1.0 g/dL Gamma-globulin: 0.5–1.8 g/dL A/G ratio: 1.0–2.4 g/dL
PROTEIN ELECTROPHORESIS, CSF	Total protein: 15–45 mg/dL Prealbumin: 2–7% of total Albumin: 56–76% of total Alpha-1-globulin: 2–7% of total Alpha-2-globulin: 4–12% of total Beta-globulin: 8–18% of total Gamma-globulin: 3–12% of total Oligoclonal Bands: Negative
PROTEIN ELECTROPHORESIS, Urine	Total Protein: 0–150 mg/24 hr Electrophoretic pattern: Normal
PROTEIN S Antigen	Protein S: 70–140%
PROTEIN TOTAL, Serum	1–7d: 4.3–7.2 g/dL 1w-6m: 4.1–7.8 g/dL 7m–12m: 4.8–7.5 g/dL 1–2y: 5.3–7.7 g/dL 3–17y: 5.6–8.2 g/dL 18–60y: 6.0–8.5 g/dL >60y: 5.8–8.3 g/dL
PROTEIN TOTAL, ALBUMIN, GLOBULIN AND A/G RATIO	Total protein: 6.0–8.5 g/dL Albumin: 3.5–5.5 g/dL Globulin: 2.2–4.1 g/dL A/G ratio: 0.9–2.0 g/dL
PROTEIN TOTAL, Fluid (Not Spinal or Synovial)	Not established
PROTEIN TOTAL, Urine Quantitative	0–150 mg/24 hr.
PROTHROMBIN TIME (PT)	Patient: 10.5–14.0 secs. INR: 2.0–3.5
PSITTICOSIS ANTIBODY	Negative: <1.8 Titer
PYRIDOXAL PHOSPHATE (Vitamin B6)	3–18 ng/mL
Q	
Q FEVER (Coxiella) Antibody	IgG: Negative: <1:16 Titer Low Positive: 1:16–1:128 Titer High Positive: 1:256 or greater IgM: Negative <1:10 Titer
QUINIDINE, Quantitative	Therapeutic: 2.0–5.0 mcg/mL Toxic: >6.0 mcg/mL

R

RED BLOOD COUNT (RBC)
Male:
4.1–5.6 million/cu.mm
Female:
3.8–5.1 million/cu.mm

RENIN ACTIVITY - By RIA
Low salt:
2.3–9.6 ng/mL/hr
Normal salt:
0.0–3.5 ng/mL/hr
High salt:
0.0–1.8 ng/mL/hr

REOVIRUS ANTIBODY
Negative: <1.8
A four fold or greater rise in titer between acute and convalescent samples indicates recent infection.

RESPIRATORY SYNCYTIAL VIRUS ANTIBODY
Negative: <1.8 CF Titer

RETICULOCYTE COUNT
0.2–2.5%

REVERSE TRIIODOTHYRONINE (rT$_3$)
100–500 pg/ml

RHEUMATOID FACTOR, Quantitative
0–30 IU/mL

RICKETTSIAL ANTIBODY - IgG
Spotted Fever Group
Negative: <1:64 IFA Titer
Typhus Fever Group
Negative: <1:64 IFA Titer

RICKETTSIA SPOTTED FEVER ANTIBODY PANEL, IgG (Serum)
Includes Rickettsia antibody, and Typhus fever antibody
Negative: <1:64 IFA Titer

RUBELLA ANTIBODY - IgG
Non-immune: <1.0
Immunity: >1.0
Any index greater than 1.0 shows immunity. The higher the index, the larger the amount of antibody present.

RUBELLA ANTIBODY - IgM
Negative: <1.00 EIA Index

RUBEOLA ANTIBODY - IgG
Negative: <0.80 EIA Index

RUBEOLA ANTIBODY - IgM
Negative: <1:10 IFA Titer

S

SALICYLATES, Serum
Therapeutic: 5–25 mg/dL
Toxic: >30 mg/dL

SCHISTOSOMA MANSONI ANTIBODY, Elisa
Negative: <1:128

SEDIMENTATION RATE - WESTERGREN
Male: 0–15 mm/hr
Female: 0–20 mm/hr

SEDIMENTATION RATE - WINTROBE
Male: 0–10 mm/hr
Female: 0–20 mm/hr

SELENIUM, Plasma
55–130 mcg/L

SELENIUM, Urine
0–100 ug/L

SEMEN ANALYSIS, Complete
pH: 7.0–8.4
Volume: >1.5 mL
Total Count: 60–150 million/mL
Motility: >80%
Viscosity: Normal
Abnormal forms: <30%

SEROTONIN (5-Hydroxytryptamine)
50–220 ng/mL

SEROTONIN METABOLITE (5-HIAA), Quantitative
2.5–10 mg/24 hrs.

SEX HORMONE BINDING GLOBULIN
Children (Bone-Age <10 yr.): 44–127 nmol/L
Pregnancy (3rd Trimester): 315–508 nmol/L
Adult Male: 10–73 nmol/L
Adult Female: 16–120 nmol/L

SGOT (AST), Serum
<1 year: 0–120 U/L
1–60 yr: 0–40 U/L
>60 yr: 0–50 U/L

SGOT (AST), CSF
0–19 U/L

SGPT (ALT), Serum
<1 year: 0–63 U/L
>1 year: 0–45 U/L

SILVER, Urine
Therapeutic:
0.4–4.0 mcg/24 hr.

SODIUM, Serum
135–147 mEq/L

SODIUM, Urine
20–260 mEq/24 hr*

SODIUM AND POTASSIUM, Serum
Sodium: 135–147 mEq/L
Potassium: 3.5–5.3 mEq/L

SOMATOMEDIN-C
Vary with age and sex. Refer to table below for specific ranges:

Age Group	Males Mean	Range (U/mL)
0–3 yrs.	0.30	0.08–1.1
3–6 yrs.	0.44	0.12–1.6
6–11 yrs.	0.78	0.22–2.8
11–13 yrs.	1.01	0.28–3.7
13–15 yrs.	2.25	0.90–5.6
15–18 yrs.	1.67	0.91–3.1
18–64 yrs.	0.79	0.34–1.9

Age Group	Females Mean	Range (U/mL)
0–3 yrs.	0.49	0.11–2.2
3–6 yrs.	0.66	0.18–2.4
6–11 yrs.	1.36	0.41–4.5
11–13 yrs.	2.59	0.99–6.8
13–15 yrs.	2.63	1.20–5.9
15–18 yrs.	1.70	0.71–4.1
18–64 yrs.	0.98	0.45–2.2

SPERM ANALYSIS, Routine
Fresh semen sample. Test must be performed within 3 hours of collection.
Volume: >1.5 mL
Total count: 60–150 millions/mL
Motility: >80%
Viscosity: Normal
pH: 7.0–8.4
Abnormal forms: <30%

T

T-3 - By RIA
60–200 ng/dL

T-3 - UPTAKE
25–35%

T-4 - By RIA
4.5–13.0 mcg/dL

*depends on intake

TEST NAME	REFERENCE RANGE
TBG (Thyroxine Binding Globulin) - By RIA	Male: 1–12 mos.: 16–36 mcg/mL 1–10 yrs.: 12–28 mcg/mL >10 yrs.: 12–24 mcg/mL Female: 1–12 mos.: 17–37 mcg/mL 1–10 yrs.: 15–27 mcg/mL >10 yrs.: 14–30 mcg/mL
TEICHOIC ACID Antibody	Not detected.
TERBUTALINE, Serum	Peak level: <9 ng/mL (after 5 mg oral dose)

TESTOSTERONE, Free

Age	Male	Female
20–29	19–41	0.9–3.2
30–39	18–39	0.8–3.0
40–49	16–33	0.6–2.5
50–59	13–31	0.3–2.7
60–69	11–26	0.4–2.2
70–79	9–25	0.2–2.0

TEST NAME	REFERENCE RANGE
TESTOSTERONE, Total	Male: 260–1250 ng/dL Female: 2–94 ng/dL
TESTOSTERONE BINDING GLOBULIN	See Sex Hormone Binding Globulin
THEOPHYLLINE (Aminophylline)	Therapeutic: 10–20 mcg/mL Toxic: >20 mcg/mL
THIAMINE (Vitamin B1)	2.3–4.1 mcg/dL
THYROGLOBULIN	Adults: 2.0–60.0 ng/mL
THYROID RELEASING HORMONE (TRH) Serum	<40 pg/mL
THYROID STIMULATING HORMONE (TSH)	0.4–6.0 mIU/mL
THYROID STIMULATING HORMONE 3RD GENERATION	0.5–4.60 mIU/mL <55 0.5–4.60 >55 0.5–8.9
THYROXINE (T-4), Total	4.5–13.0 mcg/dL
THYROXINE, (T-4) Free	0.7–2.2 ng/dL
TOBRAMYCIN, Peak	Peak level: 4–10 mcg/mL Toxic peak: >10 mcg/mL
TOCAINIDE (Tonocard)	4–10 mcg/mL
TOXOPLASMA ANTIBODY - IgM	Negative: <1:10
TRIGLYCERIDES	30–150 mg/dL
TRIIODOTHYRONINE T-3 - Free	2.8–5.4 pg/mL
TRIIODOTHYRONINE T-3 - Total	60–200 ng/dL
TRYPSIN, Serum	17–65 ng/mL
TRYPTOPHAN	1.4–3.0 mg/dL
TSH (Thyroid Stimulating Hormone)	0.4–6.0 uIU/mL
TSH 3RD GENERATION	0.5–4.6 uIU/mL

TEST NAME	REFERENCE RANGE
TSH RECEPTOR ANTIBODY (TSI)	Absence of Antibody: <10 U/L Negative <10 U/L Equivocal 10–15 U/L Positive >15 U/L TSH Receptor Antibody is measured by competitive binding radioreceptor assay using TSH receptors and I-125 TSH. Serum TSH values greater than 100 IU/mL may interfere with this assay.
TYPHUS FEVER ANTIBODY	Negative: <1:64 IFA Titer
TYROSINE, Plasma	3.2–8.7 mol/dL
U	
UREA NITROGEN, Serum (BUN)	5–25 mg/dL
UREA NITROGEN, Urine	10–15 g/24 hr.
URIC ACID, Serum	0–11y: 1.6–6.5 mg/dL 12–60y: Male: 3.5–9.0 mg/dL Female: 2.2–7.7 mg/dL >60 y: Male: 3.3–9.0 mg/dL Female: 2.8–8.4 mg/dL
URIC ACID, Synovial	2.5–8.0 mg/dL
URIC ACID, Urine	250–750 mg/24 hrs.
URO- AND COPROPORPHYRINS, Urine, (Quantitative)	Copro: 60–280 mcg/24 hrs. Uro: 10–50 mcg/24 hrs.
UROBILINOGEN, Urine (Semiquantitative)	0.05–4.0 EU/24 hrs.
UROPORPHYRINS, Urine (Quantitative)	10–50 mcg/24 hrs.
V	
VALIUM	See Diazepam
VALPROIC ACID (Depakene)	Therapeutic: 50–100 mcg/mL Toxic: >125 mcg/mL
VANCOMYCIN, Peak & Trough	Therapeutic: Trough: 5–10 mcg/mL Peak: 20–30 mcg/mL Toxic: Trough: >15 mcg/mL Peak: >50 mcg/mL
VANILLYLMANDELIC ACID (VMA)	2.0–10.0 mg/24 hr.
VARICELLA-ZOSTER ANTIBODY - IgG	Negative: <0.80 EIA Index
VARICELLA-ZOSTER ANTIBODY - IgM	Negative: <1:10 IFA Titer
VASOACTIVE INTESTINAL POLYPEPTIDE (VIP)	23–63 pg/mL
VISCOSITY, Serum	1.5–2.0 minutes
VITAMIN B12	Normal: 250–1100 pg/mL

TEST NAME	REFERENCE RANGE
VITAMIN B12 BINDING CAPACITY	870–1800 ng/l
VITAMIN D, 1, 25-DIHYDROXY	12–40 pg/mL
VMA (Vanillylmandelic Acid)	2.0–10.0 mg/24 hr.
W	
WHITE BLOOD COUNT	3.7–10.5 thous/cu mm
Z	
ZINC, Plasma	68–136 ug/dL
ZINC, Urine	300–600 ug/24 hr.

COMPLETE BLOOD COUNT	
TEST NAME	**REFERENCE RANGE**
Hematocrit	M: 36–50 F: 34–44%
Hemoglobin	M: 12.5–17.0 F: 11.5–15.0 g/dL
Red Blood Count Mil./CU.MM.	M: 4.1–5.6 F: 3.8–5.1
MCV	80–98 CU. Microns
MCH	27.0–34.0 Micro-Micro.GMS
MCHC	32.0–36.0%
White Blood Count	3.7–10.5 Thous/CU.MM.
Lymphocyte	14–46%
Neutrophil	40–74%
Monocyte	4–13%
Eosinophil	0–7%
Basophil	0–3%
Platelet Count	155–385 Thous/CU.MM.

Index of Illustrations

abdomen, A1
abduction, A1
abortion
    threatened a., A3
abrachia, A3
abrasion collar, C61
abscess
    alveolar a., A3
    apical a., A4
    brain a., A4
    lanced a., L5
    lung a., A4
    metaphyseal a., O21
    pelvic a., A5
    tooth pulp a., A5
    tubo-ovarian a., A5
acantocyte, A6
acarid, A6
accommodation, A7, A8
acetabulum, A8, **B23,** B25, C23, **L27,** L32
achalasia, A9
achondroplasia, A9, H4
acrocephalosyndactyly, A12
acromegaly, A12, H4
acromion, A13, B40, **J3, L28**
acrosomal reaction, F9
acrosome, A13
actin, A13, **A14**
actinomyosin, **A14**
active transport, A14
Adam's apple, A15
adduction, A15
adenine, D42
adenohypophysis, **A16,** N32
adenoids, A16, F6
adenoma
    islet cell a., A16
    parathyroid a., A17
    thyroid a., H43
adenomyosis, A17
adhesions, abdominal, A17
adrenomegaly, A18
adventitia, A19, A53, A80
Aedes aegypti, F11
Aesculapius
    staff of A., S61
afferent lymphatic vessel, N39
agglutination of RBCs, A21
agonist, A21
agranulocytes, A21
albuginea, A22
albumin, B17
alcohol, A23
alcoholic liver disease, D28
allantois, M22, M29, **Y1**
allergen, A24
alopecia areata, A25
Alternaria, A25
alveoloplasty, A26

alveolus, A26, B34, **D47, M2,** S113
amalgamator, A26
amalgam plugger, N37
Amanita muscaria, A27
Amanita phalloides, A27
Amanita virosa, T47
amino acids, A10, A11
amniocentesis, **A28**
amnion, A29, **C44,** C51, D4, M22
amniotic fluid, A28
amniotic membrane perforator, I14
ampule, A29
ampulla
    a. of deferent duct, **D48**
    a. of internal ear, **A30**
    a. of semicircular canal, C6, **E3**
    a. of semicircular duct, C6, **C87, E2,** U9
    a. of uterine tube, U9
amputation (below the knee), A30
anal fistula, F19
anal skin tabs, H17
anaphase, A32
anastomosis
    intestine-to-intestine a., A32
anatomy
    topographical a., A32
Ancylostoma duodenale, A33
anesthesia
    caudal a., **A34**
    spinal a., **A34**
aneurysm
    berry a., A35
    micro-a., M32
    retinal micro-a., M32
    saccular a., A35
angina pectoris, A35
angiography
    percutaneous transluminal a., **A36**
angle
    anterior a. of eye, A37
    inferior a. of scapula, S54
    a. of mandible, **J2,** J8, M7
    sternal a., A37
    superior a. of scapula, S54
annulus fibrosis, A38, D37, **L29**
Anopheles, A38
anorexia nervosa, **A39**
anoscope, A39
ansa cervicalis, A39
antagonist, A21
anteflexion of uterus, A40
antibody
    5 classes of a.'s, **A41**
    complement-fixing a., A41
anus, **A44**
    imperforate a., A44
articular disk, L28
antihelix, A43
antitragus, A43

aorta, A82, C79, A54
    abdominal a., A35, A45, C89
    arch of a., A45, A50
    ascending a., A45, A50, H7
    descending a., A45, A50, H7
    thoracic a., A45, A54, A55, L50
aortic hiatus, H23
aortic incompetence, I12
aponeurosis
    epicranial a., A46
    palmar a., T10
    plantar a., A46
apparatus
    juxtaglomerular a., A47, M3
    lacrimal a., A47
appendicitis, A47
appendix, A47, L49
applanation, A48
approximator
    fallopian a., A48
    microsurgical a., A48, R16
    nerve a., A48
    vasovasostomy a., A48
apron, leaded, A48
aqueduct, cerebral, A49
aqueous humor, H33
arachnodactyly, A49
arachnoid, **A49,** D51, S45
arborization, A49
arch
    a. of aorta, A50, **H7**
    longitudinal a. of foot, A50
    pubic a. (female), A50
    pubic a. (male), A50
    simple a., D14
    tent a. (dermatoglyphics), D14
    vertebral a., A55, A73, A75
    zygomatic a., A50
area
    aortic a., A51
    a. cribrosa (of kidney), D47, L48
    auditory a., A51
    mitral a., A51
    pulmonary a., A51
    tricuspid a., A51
    visual a., A51
areola, G16
arterial circle (circle of Willis), **C48,** A55
arteriogram, A52
arteriography, coronary, A53
arteriole, B8
    afferent a., A47
    efferent a., A47
    maternal a., C51
    retinal a., L10
    spiral a., L9
    straight a., L9
artery
    angular a., A54, A61

diaphysis, P43
diastole, **D23**
    atrial d., C73
    ventricular d., C73
diencephalon, D24, M71
diffraction of light waves, D25
Digitalis purpurea, D25, F40
dilator
    pneumatic d., D26
Diphyllobothrium latum, H32
diplococcus, D26
diploe, D27
disease
    alcoholic liver d., D28
    Blount' s d., D28
    chronic obstructive pulmonary d., D29
    connective tissue d., D29
    Crohn's d., D30
    diverticular d. of colon, D30
    genetic d., D31
    Lyme d., D32
    periodontal d., D33
    polycystic kidney d., D34
    rheumatic heart d., D34
    Roger's d., D34
disk
    articular d., D36, L28
    herniated d., **D37**
    interpubic d., D36, **J5**
    intervertebral d., D37, L29
    optic d., **D37**, E46
    temporomandibular articular d., **D36**
dislocation
    closed d. of carpus at radiocarpal joint, D38
    closed d. of elbow, D38
    d. of lens of eye, D38
    closed d. of lower jaw, D38
    d. of patella, W5
distance
    inner canthal d., D41
    interpupillary d., D41
    nasolabial d., D41
    outer canthal d., D41
distention of ascending colon, D41
diverticulum, D30
    Meckel's d., D42
    urethral d., D42
DNA analysis, **A31**
DNA (model), D42
dorsiflexion, D43
dorsum sellae, B27, F32
double helix (DNA), H9
dowel, D43
drain
    cigarette d., D44
    Jackson-Pratt d., D44
    subdural brain d., D44
drill
    craniotome d., D45
duct
    accessory pancreatic d., **D49**
    alveolar d., A26, D47
    bile d., T59
    cochlear d., D47, **E2, E3,** L2, M3, M39
    common hepatic d., D46, G2
    cortical (straight) collecting d., D47
    cystic d., D46, G2
    deferent d., **D48**, E30, T32, **T81**
    ejaculatory d., **D48**

endolymphatic d., D47, L2
d. of epididymis, C27
intercalated d., G15
intrahepatic bile d.'s, T59
lactiferous d., D49, G16
main pancreatic d., **D49**
membranous semicircular d.'s, **C6**
mesonephric d., M29
metanephric d., M29
nasolacrimal d., D49
pancreatic d., P5, T59
papillary d. of Bellini, **D47,** L48
parotid d., D49
right lymphatic d., D49
semicircular d., D47, L2, M3, U9
seminal vesicle d., **D48,** U10
straight collecting d., L48
sublingual d.'s, D49
submandibular d., D49
thoracic d., **D49**
venous d, U2
ductus arteriosus, D50, P14
ductus reuniens, E2
ductus venosus, C49
duodenum, **D51,** J2, L11
dura mater, A38, D27, **D51,** L20, M24, S45
dysplasia
    chondroectodermal d., D53
    congenital acetabular d., D53

ear
    external e., E1
    middle e., A19, E1, **E4**
    inner (internal) e., E1, **E2, E3, E4,** L2
    e. physiology, E5
eardrum, A19, C5, M5
Echinococcus granulosus, E5
echocardiogram, E5
echocardiography, E6
ectasia
    mammary duct e., E6
ectoderm, E7, L11
ectoparasite, E7
ectopic pregnancies (possible sites), E7
ectropion, E8
edentulous, E8
efferent lymphatic vessels, N39
electrocardiogram (ECG), **E10,** P33
electrocoagulation, E12
electrode
    catheter e., E12
    ECG wrist-clip e., E12
    EEG needle e., E12
    EEG surface e., E12
electroencephalogram (EEG), E13
electromagnetic spectrum, R7
electromyogram (EMG), E13
electron, E13
electro-oculogram (EOG), M43
electrophoresis, paper, E14
electroretinogram (ERG), E14
elevator, E15
embolism (pathogenesis), E15
    e. in cerebral artery, E16
    e. occluding blood vessel, E15
    pulmonary e., E16
embryo, A24, A29, C44, C76, D4, L11, L14
    20-day old e., G31

1.7 mm long e., P72
2.5 mm long e., Y1
e. development, **E17**
4-week old e., E17
5-week old e., E17
6-week old e., E17, S42
7-week old e., E17
8-week old e., E17
9-week old e., E17
twin e.'s, T84
embryoblast, B14
eminence
    frontal e., E18
    hypothenar e., E18
    parietal e., E18
    pyramidal e., C88
    thenar e., E18
emphysema, D29, **E19**
enamel, D11, **E20**
encephalocele, E20
end bulb
    Krause's e.b., E44
ending
    annulospiral nerve e., E21
    flower-spray nerve e., E21
    free nerve e., D16, E44
    synaptic e.'s, E22
endocardium, E22
endoderm, E23, L11
endometriosis, **E23**
    e. interna (adenomyosis), **E23**
endometrium, C93, **D4, E23,** L9, M26
endoneurium, E31, M71
endoplasmic reticulum
    rough (granular) e.r., E27, L54, N44, R29
    smooth (agranular) e.r., E27, L54, N44
endoscope, E24
endoscopy of sigmoid colon, E24
endothelium, B6
enlargement
    cervical e. (of spinal cord), C77
    lumbar e. (of spinal cord), C77
Entamoeba histolytica, E25
enteritis, regional, D30
Enterobius vermicula.is, E25
enteropeptidase, F ΅
enterospasm, E26
enterozoa, **E27**
enzyme
    restriction e., T85
eosinophils, B17, C26, G30
epicanthus, E28
epicondyle
    lateral, C9, E11, E28, L22
    medial, C9, E11, E28, G32, L22
epicranial aponeurosis, A46
epidermis, **E29,** D16
epididymis, A22, A29, **E30,** S15, T81
epiglottis, B20, C35, D7, **E30,** F6, L7, M23
epineurium, E31
epiphyseal line of femur, J4
epiphyseal line of tibia, J4
episiotomy, E32
epispadias, E32
epithelioma, E32
epithelium
    ciliated pseudostratified columnar e., E33
    germinal e., Z1
    simple columnar e., E33

fontanel
anterior f., F30
mastoid f., F30
posterior f., F30
sphenoidal f., F30
foot
ball of f., B3
footplate of stapes vibrating in oval window, E5, F30
foramen
anterior ethmoidal f., F32
anterior sacral foramina, C6
f. cecum of frontal bone, F32
f. cecum of tongue, T49
foramina of cribriform plate, F32
dorsal sacral f., L27
emissary sphenoidal f., F32
greater sciatic f., **F31,** L27
interatrial f. primum, F31
intervertebral f., L29
jugular f., F32
lesser sciatic f., **F31,** L27
f. magnum, B28, C56, F32
mandibular f., M7, J2, **J8**
mastoid f., F32
mental f., B24, J2
obturator f., B23, B25, **J5,** L27, N42
f. ovale, C49, F32
pelvic sacral f., J7
posterior ethmoidal f., F32
f. rotundum, F32
f. spinosum, F32
stylomastoid f., G4
transverse f. of atlas, L20
transverse f. of axis, P17
vertebral f., B21, L20, L26
forceps
alligator f., F35
Allis tissue f., F35
axis-traction f., F35
Babcock tissue f., F35
bayonet f., F35
biopsy f., F35
biopsy f. with needle, G8
bone cutting f., F35
bone holding f., F35
chalazion f., F35
clip-applying f., F35
coagulation f., F34
double-action f., F35
ellipsoid biopsy f., G8
Hegenbarth f., C55
Heifetz f., C55
hemostatic f., F34
Magill f., I29
punch f., F35, T7
Raney f., C55
tenaculum f., F35
thumb f., F34
Wachenfeldt f., C55
Wexler f., C55
Yasargil f., C55
foregut, Y1
foreskin, P31, P70
formula
empirical f., F36
stereochemical f., F36
structural f., F37

fornix
anterior f. of vagina, F37
inferior f. of conjunctiva, F37
posterior f. of vagina, F37
superior f. of conjunctiva, F37
fossa
acetabular f., F37
anterior cranial f., F38
glenoid f., F38, F39
hypophyseal f., B27, C22, F32, F38, L32
iliac f., L27
infraspinous f., S54
intracondylar f., B22
middle cranial f., F38
navicular f., F39
olecranon f., E11, F39, L22
f. ovalis, H7
posterior cranial f., F38
pterygoid f., M7
radial f., E11, L22
supraspinous f., L28, S54
triangular f., A43, C24
vestibular f., I29
fovea centralis (central fovea), **D37,** E46
foxglove, F40
fracture
articular f., F40
avulsion f., F41
blow-out f., F41
f. of cheek bone, F41
closed f., F42
Colles' f., F41
comminuted f., F40, F41, F44
compression f., F42
depressed skull f., F41
displaced transverse f. of patella, F44
fatigue f., F41
intracapsular f., F42
Le Fort I f., F40
Le Fort II f., F40
Le Fort III f., F40
linear f., F41
oblique f., F40
open f., F43
pathologic f., F43
Pott's f., F43
spiral f., F40, F44
stellate f. of skull, F44
supracondylar f., F40
transcervical f., F44
transverse f. of patella, F44
framework, F45
free nerve ending, D16
frenulum
f. of lower lip, F45
f. of tongue, F45
fundus
ocular f., F47, M3
f. of stomach, F47
f. of uterus, F47
funiculus
anterior f., F48
lateral f., F48
posterior f., F48
furrow
gluteal f., F27
lower palpebral f., F48
upper palpebral f., 48

fusion
renal f., F48

gallbladder, C40, C41, **G2**
gallop
atrial g., G2
gallstone, G2
gamma globulin levels, G20
ganglion
cervicothoracic g., G3
dorsal root (spinal) g., N10
g. of facial nerve, G4
middle cervical g., G3
pterygopalatine g., G4
spiral g. of cochlea, D47, M39
superior cervical g., G3
sympathetic g., C77, N10
thoracic ganglia, G3
trigeminal g., G5
vestibular g., G4
gap
intercellular g., C25
gastrectomy and anastomosis with small intestine, G6
gastric lavage, L8
gastric pits, G15
gastroanastomosis, G6
gastroduodenostomy, G7
gastroscope, G8
gauge
Boley g., G8
gemmules, N33
gene
operator g., G9
regulator g., G9
structural g., G9
genu
g. of corpus callosum, G10
g. valgum (knock-knee), G11
g. varum (bowleg), G11
Giardia lamblia, G11
giadiasis, G11
Gigli wire saw, S5
gingiva, C23, R29
attached g., G12
free g., G12
free margin of g., G12
gingivitis, G12
necrotizing ulcerative g., G12
girdle
pelvic g., G13
shoulder g., G13
gland
adrenal g., A18, **G13,** P31
apocrine sweat g., D16, G16, **G17**
bulbourethral g.'s, **G13,** T81
cardiac g.'s, G15
duodenal g.'s, G15
endocrine g.'s, G14
endoexocrine g., **G15**
exocrine g., G15
lacrimal g., B19, C7, L3
mammary g., **G16**
merocrine sweat g., **G17**
mixed salivary g., D9
parathyroid g., A17, G17, P10, T43
parotid g., D49

pineal g., H47
proper gastric g.'s, G15
sebaceous g., D16, G17
secretory g. lobules (of breast), G16
serous g.'s, B37
sublingual g., C22, D49
submandibular g., C22, D49
sudoriferous g., D16
tarsal g. of eyelid, E46, G19
thyroid g., A15, G17, **G18,** N3, N43,
    T42, T43
glans penis, C80
glaucoma
    angle-closure g., G19
glenoidal labrum, L28
glioma, G20
globulins, B17
glomerulus, D47, **G21,** L48, M3
Glossina palpalis, G22
glycocalyx, G23
gnat, G23
    biting black g., S32
gnathion, G25
goiter, G24
    diffuse nontoxic g., G24
    intrathoracic g., G24
Golgi complex (Golgi apparatus), C25,
    L54, M19
gomphosis, G25
goniometer, G25
gonion, G25
gonioscope, G25
gonioscopy, G25
gouge, G26
gout
    tophaceous g. of auricular cartilage, G26
    tophaceous g. of joints, G26
graft
    aortic valved g., G28
    full-thickness skin g., G27
    pinch g., G27
    skin g., G27
    split-thickness skin g., G27
granulation
    arachnoid g.'s, G28
granules
    basophilic g.'s, G28
    beta g., G29
    cortical g., F9
    mast-cell g.'s, G29
granulocytes, G30
gray ramus communicans, N10
groove
    free gingival g., G12
    interventricular g., G31
    g. for middle meningeal vessels, F32
    neural g., G31
    obturator g., L27
    g. for occipital sinus, F32
    g. for sigmoid sinus, F32
    g. of subclavian artery, G32
    g. of subclavian vein, G32
    g. for superior sagittal sinus, F32
    g. for transverse sinus, F32
    g. of ulnar nerve, G32
guanine, D42
guillotine (for rib resection), G33
guinea pig, G33

gyrus
    angular g., G34
    frontal gyri, G34
    occipital gyri, G34
    postcentral g., G34
    precentral g., G34
    supramarginal g., G34
    temporal gyri, G34

hair
    auditory h.'s, H1
    h. follicle, D16
    type I h. cell, H2
    type II h. cell, H2
    vestibular h.'s, H2
half-life, H2
hallux
    h. rigidus, H3
    h. valgus, A77, H3
halter
    orthopedic head h., H3
hamate bone, B21
hand
    spade h., H4
    trident h., A9, H4
handpiece
    high-speed h., H4
haptic, I33
hashish, H5
haustra, H5
head
    h. of femur, **J3**
    h. of radius, E11
headgear, H6
hearing aid, H6
heart, H7, L50
    artificial h., H8
    primitive h., Y1
heel
    Stryker h., H9
    Thomas h., H9
helicotrema, **C59,** E3
helix, A43
hemangioma
    strawberry h., H10
hematoma
    epidural h., H11
    intramural h., H12
    subdural h., H11
hemianopia
    binasal h., H12
    bitemporal h., H12
    congruous h., H12
    crossed h., H12
    incomplete h., H12
hemigastrectomy, H12
hemlock, H13
hemocytoblast, H14
hemodialyzer, **H14**
hemopericardium, H15
hemopoiesis
    h. of erythrocyte, H16
    h. of neutrophilic leukocyte, H16
hemorrhage
    cerebral h., H16
    internal h., H17
    subintimal h., O3

hemorrhoids
    external h., H17
    internal h., H17
hemostasis, H17
hemostat, H17
hepatocytes, H19
hepatomegaly, H19
heredity (colorblindness), H19
hernia
    hiatal h., H20
    indirect inguinal h., H20
    umbilical h., H21
hiatus
    aortic h., H23
    esophageal h., H23
    sacral h., H23
    vena caval h., H23
hilum
    of kidney, H24
    of lymph node, E9, H24
hindgut, M29, Y1
hipbone, B23, B27, B41, **H24, H25,** J7, L27
hippocampus, H25
Histoplasma capsulatum, H26
homocystinuria, D38
homunculus
    motor h., H28
    sensory h., H28
hookworm
    American h., H29
    Ancylostoma duodenale h., H29
    Necator americanus, h. E27, H29
    Old World h., H29
hormone
    parathyroid h., H30
horn
    anterior h. of lateral ventricle, H30
    anterior h. of spinal cord, H30
    greater h. of hyoid bone, H31, L7
    h. of hyoid bone, B23, L7
    inferior h. of lateral ventricle, H30
    lateral h. of spinal cord, H30
    lesser h. of hyoid bone, H31
    posterior h. of lateral ventricle, H30
    posterior h. of spinal cord, H30
hornet, H31
host
    definitive h., H32
    intermediate h., H32
humerus, **B23,** C92, **E11,** S35
humor
    aqueous h., H33
    vitreous h., H33
hyalin, H33
hydrocele, H34
hydrocephalus, H34
hydrometer, H35
hydromyelia, H35
hydronephrosis, H36
hydroureter, H36
hydrosalpinx, H36
hymen, **H37,** L1
    annular h., I29
    cribriform h., H37
    infundibuliform h., H37
    septate h., H37
hyperdistention of colon, H38
hyperelasticity of skin, D31

hyperextension
  h. of arm, H39
  h. of neck, C75, H39, I20
hyperflexion
  h. of neck, I20
  h. of uterus, H39
hyperlipoproteinemia, H40
hyperopia, H41
hyperopia corrected, H41
hyperplasia
  gingival h., H42
  nodular h. of prostate, H42
hyperthyroidism
  primary h., H43
hyperventilation, H44
hyphema, H44
hypochondrium, H45
hypodactylia, H45
hypoesophoria, H45
hypogastrium, H45
hypognathous, H46
hyponychium, H46
hypophysis, B32, C35, **H47,** H48
  anterior lobe of h., H47
  posterior lobe of h., H47
hypospadias
  h. in newborn female, H47
  h. in newborn male, H48
hypothalamus, **H48**
hysterectomy
  abdominal h., total, H50
  supracervical h., H49
  total h., H49

ice
  i. bag, B3
  i. ball, C90
ileocecum, I2
ileum, D51, **J2**
iliac crest, L27
ilium, B23, C23, C86, I2, N42
illusion
  Muller-Lyer i., I3
  Poggendorf's i., I3
  Schroder's i., I3
  Wundt's i., I3
image
  retinal i., I4
  virtual i., I4
immobilization of joint with bandage, I4
immunoglobulins, I5
impaction
  distoangular i., I6
  high-level i., I6
  horizontal i., I6
  low-level i., I6
  mesioangular i., I6
  i. of third molar, I6
  vertical i., I6
impetigo, I7
  i. contagiosa, I7
implant
  breast, I7, M6
  endosseous dental i., I8
  intraocular i. (anterior chamber lens), I9
  intraocular i. (posterior chamber lens),
    I9

implantation
  abdominal i., I9
  ampullar i., I9
  i., of blastocyst in uterus, I9
  ectopic i.'s, I9
  infundibular i., I9
  interstitial i., I9
  isthmic i., I9
  ovarian i., I9
incision
  abdominal i.'s, I10
  Battle's i., I10
  cesarean i.'s, I11
  J uterine i., I11
  low uterine transverse i., I11
  low uterine vertical i., I11
  McBurney's i., I10
  median i., I10
  paramedian i., I10
  pararectus i., I10
  Pfannenstiel's i., I10
  subcostal i., I10
  transverse i., I10
  T uterine i., I11
  vertical uterine i., I11
incisor, D11
incisura
  cardiac i., L11
incompetence
  aortic i., I12
incus, B23, C24, **I12,** M74
index
  cephalic i., I13
inducing labor, I14
infarct
  cerebral i., I15
  i. in liver, I15
infarction
  myocardial i., I15
inferior vena cava, A82
infertility, I17
infiltration of fat into myocardium, I16
infundibulum
  ethmoidal i., I18
  i. of hypophysis, I18
  i. of uterine tube, I18
inhaler
  Duke i., I18
  metered dose i., I18
inion, I19
injection
  intramuscular i., I19
injury
  blunt i., I20
  whiplash i., I20
inlet
  thoracic i., I21
insertion
  i. of biceps muscle of arm, I22
  i. of greater pectoral muscle, O17
inspiration (position of diaphragm), I22
instep, I22
insufficiency
  valvular (aortic) i., I23
  valvular (mitral) i., I23
insufflation
  tubal i., I23
insulin, I24

NPH i., I24
NPH + regular i., I24
regular i., I24
ultralente i., I24
insula, C54
interneuron, I27
interpubic fibrocartilage, L27
interval
  P-R i., I27
  QRS i., I27
  Q-T i., I27
  R-R i., I27
  S-T i., I27
interventricular sulcus
  anterior i. s., H7
  posterior i. s., H7
intervertebral disk, L29
intestine
  large i., C4, C24, **I28**
  small i., A17, C4, **I28,** M27
intraocular
  i. tumor, I29
intrauterine devices
  Copper 7 i.d., D18
  Copper T i.d., D18
  Dalkon Shield i.d., D18
  Lippes Loop i.d., D18
  Progestasert i.d., D18
introducer, I29
introitus
  nonparous i., I29
  parous i., I29
intubation
  endotracheal i., I30
intussusception
  ileocolic i., I31
intussusceptum, I31
intussuscipiens, I31
inversion
  paracentric i., I31
ion pair, P34
iridectomy
  peripheral i., I32
iris, B19, C78, D37, **I33,** L39
  i. bombe, I33
  i. tuck, I33
ischium, **B23,** D36, I34
island
  erythroblastic i., E36
islet of Langerhans, I35
  i.o.L. in diabetes, **D20,** H33
isomers, I35
isthmus
  i. of thyroid gland, I36

jaundice disorders, J1
jaw
  alligator j.'s (biopsy forceps), G8
  lower j., **J2**
  upper j., **J2**
jejunum, D51, **J2**
jimsonweed, J3
joint
  acromioclavicular j., **J3**
  amphiarthrodial j., **J5**
  ball and socket j., **J3**
  bicondylar j., **J4**

calcaneocuboid j., **J5**
carpometacarpal j.'s, **J4**
carpometacarpal j. of thumb, J4
costochondral j.'s, **J5**
cuneonavicular j., J5
distal interphalangeal j., D6
elbow j., **E11,** O5
fibrous j., J5
hinge j., **J4**
intercarpal j.'s, **J4**
interchondral j.'s, J5
intermetacarpal j., J4
intermetatarsal j., J6
intertarsal j.'s, J6
knee j., **J6**
lumbosacral j., J7
manubriosternal j., **D36**
metacarpophalangeal j., **J4**
metatarsophalangeal j., H3, **J6**
pin-in-slot j., O18
proximal interphalangeal j., D6
sacrococcygeal j., **J7**
sacroiliac j., **J7**
sacrolumbar j., L27
sternoclavicular j., J5
subtalar j., **J7**
synovial j., J6
talocalcaneonavicular j., **J7**
talocrural j., **J7**
temporomandibular j., **J8,** S74
universal j., O18
junction
    anorectal j., **J9**
    cementodentinal j., J9
    cementoenamel j., J9
    esophagogastric j., **J9**
    gap j., C25
    ileocecal j., C24
    intercellular j., C25
    intermediate j. (zone of aherence), J10
    tight j., B6, C25, J10

karyotype
    normal female k., **K1**
    normal male k., **K1**
keratitis, herpetic, K2
keratoconus, K2
keratome, K3
keratoplasty
    lamellar k., **K4**
keratoscope, K4
kidney, A18, B14, **K5,** K6
    artificial k., M21
    horseshoe k., **K6**
kinocilium, C28, H2
Kirschner wire, R16, W4
knee joint, L31
    anterior aspect of k.j., L24, L25
    lateral aspect of k.j., L24, L25
    medial aspect of k.j., K7, L24, L25
    sagittal section of k.j., J6, L24
    posterior aspect of k.j., B41, L24, L25
knot
    clove-hitch k., K8
    granny k., K8
    square k., K8
    surgeon's k., K8

labium
    l. anterius, L1
    l. majus, B14, C56, L1
    l. minus, B14, C56, **I29,** L1
    l. posterius, L1
    l. uteri, L1
lancet, L1
labyrinth
    bony l., **E3,** L2
    ethmoid l., L2
    membranous l., **E2, E3,** L2
lacrimal canaliculus, A47
lacrimal caruncle, **C17**
lacrimal gland, A47, L3
lacrimal lake, A47, L3
lamina (of vertebral arch), B26, L26
lancet, L5
larva, F26, H32, L6
laryngeal prominence, L7
laryngitis
    acute l., L6
    membranous l., L6
laryngopharynx, L7
laryngoscope, I29, I30, L7
larynx, A15, C35, L6, L7
lateral lemniscus, L13
lavage
    gastric l., L8
    peritoneal l., L8
leaded apron, A48
leads
    limb l.'s, L12
    precordial l., L12
leiomyoma, L13
lens
    concavoconvex l., L14
    contact l., L14
    convexoconcave l., L14
    double convex l., L14
    l. of eye, B19, **D37,** H33, L14, S50
    intraocular l., I33
    planoconcave l., L14
    planoconvex l., L14
lentigo, senile, L15
Leptospira interrogans, L15
leukemia
    chronic myelocytic l., L16
    hairy-cell l., L17
leukocyte, B17
    agranular l., L17
    basophilic l., L17
    eosinophilic l., L17
    granular l., L17
    neutrophilic l., L17
    nongranular l., L17
    nonsegmented l., H16, L18
    segmented l., H16, L18
leukocytopoiesis, L18
levator, L19
ligament
    acromioclavicular l., L28
    alar l., L20
    annular l. of radius, L22
    anterior atlanto-occipital l., L20
    anterior cruciate l. of knee, L25, L31, M25
    anterior longitudinal l., L20, L26, L27,
        L29, L32, L33
    anterior sacroiliac l., L27
    anterior sternoclavicular l., L28

anterior talofibular l., L21, L36
anterior tibiofibular l., L21
anterior tibiotalar l., L21
apical odontoid l., L20
arcuate pubic l., D36, J5, L27
broad l. of uterus, L30, L34, T76, U9
calcaneofibular l., L21, L36, S60
collateral l. of phalanx, C10
conoid l., L28
coracoacromial l., L28
coracoclavicular l., L28
coracohumeral l., L28
coronary l. of knee, L25
costoclavicular l., L28
costotransverse l., L26
cruciate l. of atlas, L32
cruciform l. of atlas, L20
deep dorsal sacrococcygeal l., L27
deep transverse metacarpal l., L23
deltoid l., L21
dorsal calcaneocuboid l., L21
dorsal calcaneonavicular l., L21
dorsal intercarpal l., L23
dorsal metacarpal l., L23
dorsal radiocarpal l., L23
dorsal sacroiliac l., J7, L27
dorsal tarsometatarsal l., L21
external collateral l. of ankle, L21
fibular collateral l. of knee, L24, L25, L31
flaval l., L26, L29, L32
hamatometacarpal l., L23
hyoepiglottic l., L7, L20, L37
iliofemoral l., L27
iliolumbar l., L27
inferior transverse scapular l., L28
inguinal l., J5, L32
interclavicular l., L28
internal craniocervical l., L20
interosseous sacroiliac l., J7
interosseous talocalcaneal l., L21
interspinal l., L29, L33
intertransverse l., L26
intra-articular l., L26
ischiocapsular l., L27, L32
lacunar l., J5
lateral costotransverse l., L26
lateral palpebral l., L34
lateral sacrococcygeal l., L27
lateral talocalcaneal l., L21
long plantar l., L21, L33
medial palpebral l., L34
medial thyrohyoid l., C79
median cricothyroid l., L37
median umbilical l., U4
meniscofemoral l., L25
nuchal l., L20, L32, L33
ovarian l., C80, L34, T76
patellar l., L24, L25, L31
thyroepiglottic l., L7
tibial collateral l. of knee, L24, L25, L31
palmar l., L23
palmar carpometacarpal l., L23
palmar metacarpal l., L23
palmar radiocarpal l., L23
palmar ulnocarpal l., L23
patellar l., J6, M25, R22
pectineal l., L27
periodontal l., C23, L34

sartorius m., M63
short abductor m. of thumb, M48
short adductor m., M48
short extensor m. of thumb, M52
short flexor m. of big toe, M48
short flexor m. of little finger, M53
short flexor m. of little toe, M53
short peroneal m., M60, T43
short radial extensor m. of wrist, M52
skeletal m.'s, M47
smaller rhomboid m., M62
smaller zygomatic m., M56
soleus m., T9, T43
sphincter m., M47
sphincter m. of bile duct, D46
sphincter m. of pancreas, D46
sphincter m. of pupil, M51
splenius m. of head, M65, M68
splenius m. of neck, M65
stapedius m., C88
sternocleidomastoid m., M65, N3, T43
sternohyoid m., M59, M65, M68
sternothyroid m., M65, **M67**, M68
m.'s of stomach, L11
styloglossus m., T49
stylohyoid m., T49
subclavius m., M65
subcostal m., M55
subscapular m., C92
superficial flexor m. of fingers, M52
superficial transverse perineal m., T67
superior constrictor m. of pharynx,
    M50, R5
superior longitudinal m. of tongue, M68
superior oblique m. of eyeball, **M58**, T73
superior posterior serratus m., M64
superior rectus m. of eyeball, **M58**, T9, T73
supinator m., M49
supraspinous m., C92
suspensory m. of duodenum, H23
temporal m., M66
m. with tendinous intersections, M47
teres major m., B40, **M67**, M68
teres minor m., C92, **M67**
thyroarytenoid m., M67
thyroepiglottic m., M67
thyrohyoid m., M50, M67
tracheal m., C17
transverse arytenoid m., M49
transverse m. of abdomen, T9
transverse m. of thorax (transverse
    thoracic m.), M55, **M68**
transverse m. of tongue, M68
trapezius m., M55, M62, M68
triceps m. of arm, M49, **M68**
twin-bellied m., M47
ulnar flexor m. of wrist, M53
unipennate m., M47
vertical m. of tongue, M68
vocal m., L37
muscular dystrophy
    Duchenne's m.d., D54
mushroom, A27
myelencephalon, M71
myelin, M71, N31
myeloblast, H14, H16, L16, L18
myelocyte, H16, L18
myocardial infarction, I15
myocardium, M73

myofibril, A14
myometrium of uterus, C51, D4
myopia, M73
myringotomy, M74
myxoma, M74

nail, H46, N1
    ingrown n., N1
nasion, N2
nasopharynx, L7, **N2**
nearsightedness, M73
neck
    cross section of n., N3
    n. of mandible, J2
    n. of radius, E11
necrolysis, N4
necrosis
    renal papillary n., N5
needle
    acupuncture n., N5
    aneurysm n., N5
    aspirating n., N5
    biopsy n., C8
    caudal n., N5
    disposable n., N5
    hemorrhoidal n., N5
    hypodermic n., N5
    spinal n., N5
    surgical n., N5
    Wasserman n., N5
needle holder, H27
nematode
    Trichinella spiralis, N6
neonate, N7
nephrolithiasis, N8
nephron, **N8**
nephronic loop, L48
nephrostomy, N9
nephrotuberculosis, N9
nephroureterectomy, N9
nerve
    abducent n. (6th cranial n.), N14
    accessory n. (11th cranial n.), N11, N14
    afferent n., A20
    alveolar n.'s, G5
    ampullary n., C87
    anterior cutaneous n., N26
    anterior ethmoid n., N21
    anterior superior alveolar n.'s, N11
    auricular n., N29
    auriculotemporal n., N12, N21, N24
    autonomic n.'s, N10
    axillary n., N12
    buccal n., N12, N21
    chorda tympani n., G4, **N14**, N21, N24
    cochlear n., H1, L13, M39, N15
    common palmar digital n.'s, N17
    common peroneal n., N26
    cranial n.'s, N14
    deep petrosal n., G4, **N24**
    deep temporal n.'s, N12
    dorsal root of spinal n., N10
    dorsal scapular n., N12
    efferent n., A20
    efferent visceral preganglionic n., E9
    efferent visceral somatic n., E9
    external auditory meatus n., N24
    external carotid n.'s, N13

external laryngeal n., N20
facial n. (7th cranial n.), G4, N14, N15,
    N18, N24, N46
femoral n., N18
free n. ending, D16
frontal n., N21
n. of geniohyoid muscle, N13
genitofemoral n., N18
glossopharyngeal n. (9th cranial n.), G4,
    N13, N14, **N19**, N46
greater saccular n., G4, N15, N29, N30
greater splanchnic n., N26
hypoglossal n. (12th cranial n.), N11,
    N13, **N19**
iliohypogastric n., N18, N20
ilioinguinal n., N18, N20
inferior alveolar n., N11, N21
inferior cervical cardiac n., N13
inferior gluteal n., N26
inferior laryngeal n., N20
inferior subscapular n., N27
infraorbital n., G5, N11
intercostal n.'s, N20
intermediate supraclavicular n., N27
internal carotid n., N13
internal laryngeal n., N20
intratrochlear n., N21
lacrimal n., N21
larger petrosal n., N24
lateral ampullary n., N15, N30
lateral cutaneous n., N26
lateral cutaneous n. of forearm, N16
lateral femoral cutaneous n., N18
lateral pectoral n., N12
lateral supraclavicular n., N27
lesser petrosal n., N14
lesser splanchnic n., N26
lingual n., N11, N14, N19, N21
long ciliary n.'s, N14, N21
long thoracic n., N12, **N28**
lower lateral cutaneous n. of arm, N16
lowest splanchnic n., N26
mandibular n., G5, N11, N12, N14, **N21**,
    N24, N29
masseteric n., N21
maxillary n., **G5**, N11, **N21**, **N24**, N29
medial cutaneous n. of arm, N12, N16
medial cutaneous n. of forearm,
    N12, N16
medial pectoral n., N12
medial pterygoid n., N24
medial supraclavicular n., N27
median n., N12, N17, R22, S22, T10
meningeal n., N29
mental n., N11
middle cervical cardiac n., N13
middle meningeal n., N21
middle superior alveolar n.'s, N11
motor n., N10
musculocutaneous n., N12, S22
mylohyoid n., N11
nasociliary n., N14
nasolacrimal n., N21
obturator n., N18
oculomotor n. (3rd cranial n.), N14,
    N22, N46
olfactory n. (1st cranial n.), N22
n. of omohyoid muscle, N13
ophthalmic n., G5, N21, N24, N29